THE
INTERLINEAR
GREEK-
ENGLISH
NEW
TESTAMENT

COMPANION TEXTS FOR NEW TESTAMENT STUDIES

A Critical Lexicon and Concordance to the English-Greek New Testament (Bullinger)

A Dictionary of New Testament Greek Synonyms (Berry)

A Grammar of Septuagint Greek (Conybeare and Stock)

A Greek-English Lexicon of the New Testament and Other Early Christian Literature (Bauer, Arndt, Gingrich, and Danker)

A Greek Grammar of the New Testament and Other Early Christian Literature (Blass and Debrunner, Funk)

A Linguistic Key to the Greek New Testament (Rienecker, Rogers)

A Reader's Greek-English Lexicon of the New Testament (Kubo)

A Shorter Lexicon of the Greek New Testament (Gingrich)

An Index to Bauer, Arndt, Gingrich, Greek Lexicon — 2nd Edition (Alsop)

Do It Yourself Hebrew and Greek (Goodrick)

Greek-English Lexicon to the New Testament (Greenfield, Green)

Greek-English Lexicon of the New Testament (Thayer)

New Testament Greek Primer (Marshall)

The Analytical Greek Lexicon Revised (Moulton)

The Englishman's Greek Concordance of the New Testament (Wigram)

The Englishman's Greek New Testament (Newberry)

The Greek New Testament Slidaverb Conjugation Chart (Peterson)

The Interlinear Greek-English New Testament (Berry)

The Interlinear Greek-English New Testament (Marshall)

The New International Dictionary of New Testament Theology (Brown)

The NIV Interlinear Greek-English New Testament (Marshall)

The RSV Interlinear Greek-English New Testament (Marshall)

The Zondervan Parallel New Testament in Greek and English (Marshall)

THE
INTERLINEAR GREEK-ENGLISH NEW TESTAMENT

ALFRED MARSHALL

Regency
Reference Library
Zondervan Publishing House
Grand Rapids, Michigan

Book Title: INTERLINEAR GREEK-ENGLISH N.T.

First Zondervan printing 1975
Cloth: ISBN 0-310-20380-5
Vinyl: ISBN 0-310-20550-6
Leather: ISBN 0-310-20540-9

Regency Reference Library is an imprint of Zondervan
Publishing House, 1415 Lake Drive, S.E.,
Grand Rapids, Michigan 49506

Printed in the United States of America

86 87 88 89 90 / 15 14 13 12 11 10

*F*OREWORD

THE REVEREND PREBENDARY J. B. PHILLIPS M.A.

There is undoubtedly a revived interest in the reading of the New Testament today. The sales of modern versions have, I think, surprised everybody while the demand for the Authorized Version continues as before. It seems that a great many people are turning again to these inspired documents to see for themselves the foundations on which the Christian Faith is built. Naturally, to any Christian these are the most important documents in the world. If we believe with our adult minds that we live on a planet visited by God Himself in human form, the record of His life and teaching and that of the movement which He began are of supreme importance to the entire human race. Anything therefore which makes the significance and relevance of the Personal Visit clearer to the reader is to be welcomed with open arms.

As a modern translator I am delighted to see this new Interlinear Greek-English New Testament. By no means everybody knows of the quiet patient work of the textual critics who, with the utmost care and reverence, compare and revise Greek texts so that we may possess Greek as near as possible to the original documents, none of which, alas, survives. In this book we have the Greek text in its most modern revised form; it is the fruit of many years of diligent scholarship and, to my mind, should be accepted with the respect it deserves. A lot has been learned and a good deal of fresh material has been discovered since the Authorized Version was made in 1611 and indeed since the issue of the Revised Version in 1881. Here, interlined with probably the most accurate Greek that we can arrive at, is a literal English version. Dr. Marshall has obviously done this work of putting the nearest English equivalents to the Greek words with great care and skill and his work should prove of the highest value to any student of the New Testament.

It need hardly be said that this giving of verbal equivalents is not a full translation, but it is an essential stage in that process. The art of translation itself is not only the transferring of words from one language to another but also the accurate transmission of thought, feeling, atmosphere and even of style. But no translator can do his work properly without the transitional stage which Dr. Marshall exhibits so brilliantly in this book. Anyone with even a small knowledge of Greek will be able to see how and why the Authorized Version translators did their work as they did, and will also see how and why a modern translator produces a vastly different verbal result. The intelligent reader cannot fail to find this transitional stage, which is here so clearly shown, both fascinating and revealing. And if, with only a small knowledge of Greek, he should try to make his own translation, so much the better! He will at least be saved from over-familiarity with extremely meaningful words and sayings; and the chances are that the Truth will break over him afresh, as it does over any translator, ancient or modern, professional or amateur.

Although I consider that Dr. Marshall has done his work supremely well, it is a good thing to bear in mind that you cannot always either give an English equivalent for a Greek word or expression, or even always render the same Greek word by the same English one. May I take one word, the Greek verb $EKBA\Lambda\Lambda\Omega$ with its basic meaning of "throwing out". Dr. Marshall renders this word variously: it is "pluck out" (Matthew *ch.* 7, *v.* 5), "cast out" (Matthew *ch.* 8, *v.* 12), "put out" (Matthew *ch.* 9, *v.* 25), "expel" (Matthew *ch.* 12, *v.* 24), "puts forth" (Matthew *ch.* 12, *v.* 35), and "take out" (Luke *ch.* 6, *v.* 42)! And of course there are many other cases where absolute consistency is impossible; for words are not static things but expressions of thought which are inevitably modified by their context. But we must not expect impossibilities and I for one am grateful for an alert and intelligent literal translation wedded to the latest and most reliable Greek

Text. I am glad, for example, to see that Dr. Marshall has not missed the peculiar Greek construction in Matthew *ch.* 16, *v.* 19, where Jesus tells Peter that "what he binds on earth" will be "what has been bound" in Heaven. There is a world of difference between guaranteeing celestial endorsement of the Apostle's actions and promising that his actions guided by the Holy Spirit will be in accordance with the Heavenly pattern! Again, since I know there are many who imagine that the Authorized Version is a particularly literal and accurate translation of the Greek, it is refreshing to turn to Matthew *ch.* 27, *v.* 44 and see that not one single word of the expression "cast the same in his teeth" is in fact in the Greek! It is further made clear that the "bottles" of Matthew *ch.* 9, *v.* 17, were in reality wineskins, and that in Jesus' time people did not "sit at meat" so much as recline! (Luke *ch.* 7, *v.* 36), and naturally there are scores of further examples which are both interesting and important.

It would be unwise to omit reading Dr. Marshall's Introduction; for in it he not only explains some peculiarities of Greek construction, of which the ordinary reader may be quite unaware, but also clearly shows the rules he has set for himself in making this literal translation. Moreover, his Notes on Particular Passages are well worth our attention. In all, I have the greatest pleasure in recommending this book. It is timely because of the great contemporary interest in the New Testament. And it is profoundly interesting because we have here, combined in the most intimate fashion, the results of a great deal of textual research and the interpretation of a scholar thoroughly familiar with New Testament Greek.

INTRODUCTION

THE REVEREND ALFRED MARSHALL D.LITT

THE GREEK TEXT

THE text of the Greek New Testament has come down to us in various manuscripts, printing not being invented until the 15th century (Erasmus published his Greek New Testament in 1516). Some of these manuscripts are more important than others (age is not necessarily determinative of importance). The study of the various manuscript copies, and the assessment of their individual value in attempting to reconstruct the original as nearly as possible, constitutes the science of Textual Criticism. For those who wish to study this seriously there are many books available; it is sufficient to say here that, after Erasmus, a great number of scholars have, over a long period, applied themselves to the task of constructing a reliable text out of the mass of various readings which have arisen from copying and making copies from copies of the old manuscripts: such scholars as Mill, Stephens, Griesbach, Lachmann, Tischendorf, Tregelles, Alford, and many more.

The Authorized Version of 1611 follows what is known as the Received Text (Textus Receptus, or T.R.). But this is now generally recognized as unreliable; also, since it was compiled in 1550 by Stephens (or Stephanus) many further manuscripts have come to light.

The Greek text used in this book is that of the 21st edition of Eberhard Nestle's *Novum Testamentum Graece*, based on the study and critical research of generations of scholars, except that the passage John 7. 53, 8. 1-11 is not in that text but is relegated to the foot of the page as a critical note. It is here retained in the text. The critical notes of Nestle's work, which enable students to follow the reasons for variations in the text, have been omitted as being outside the scope of this publication. The student who requires these critical notes is referred to the Greek edition published in this country by the British and Foreign Bible Society and in Germany (Stuttgart) by Privilegierte Württembergische Bibelanstalt, by whose permission this recension is used.

In certain places in the Greek text square brackets are found; these indicate only that, according to Nestle, some editors include and others omit the word or words so enclosed. Translation has been made here in the usual way.

Avoiding interpretation, then, we give some details of how we have proceeded in the matter of a literal translation. These should be studied and understood if proper use is to be made of this attempt to promote an intelligent reading of the Greek New Testament.

THE ENGLISH TRANSLATION

The relationship between the Greek text and the interlinear English is as follows: Greek words not required in the translation into English are (*a*) represented by a short dash, as for example the definite article with proper names. Alternatively (*b*) italic type is used to show that words or even in some cases letters are not really needed for an idiomatic English rendering. 'Man' is sometimes redundant (see Matthew *ch*. 20, *v*. 1 and Acts *ch*. 2, *v*. 22) and so on. On the other hand, words supplied in English for which there is no Greek equivalent are placed in square brackets [. . .]. Naturally, there will be differences of judgment as to this practice in the passages involved.

In the interlinear translation, a comma has in a number of places been introduced after "Behold". The reason for this is as follows: the Greek ἰδού (or other form), properly an imperative of the defective verb ὁράω, is used as an exclamation, as is its English equivalent; that is to say, it is not then an active verb taking a direct object in the accusative case, but is simply exclamatory and is followed by a noun in the nominative, with its predicate or complement understood.

For example, in John *ch.* 1, *v.* 29, there is not a command to behold the Lamb of God, but, as it might be said (and as in fact a preacher was recently heard to say), "Look! [there goes] . . . " The position is different in such passages as Matthew *ch.* 28, *v.* 6 and Romans *ch.* 11, *v.* 22, where there is a command. Strangely enough, the Authorized Version inserts a comma in I. John *ch.* 3, *v.* 1, where it is not required. There is here a command as in the two passages just cited: "See what manner of love . . . ".

The modern form for the third person singular of verbs (present indicative) has been used (loves) in place of the now obsolete -(e)th (loveth); but the older 'ye' has been retained for the nominative ('you' for the oblique cases) of the second person plural pronoun; and 'thou' (thee), not 'you', for the second person singular. It is a loss that in modern English these differences have disappeared; so unaccustomed are we now to them that even the average reader of the Authorized Version misses the point of Luke *ch.* 22, *v.* 31. The loss is even more to be regretted when God is addressed as 'You'.

The subjunctive mood is dying out in English, and no attempt has been made to represent consistently the Greek mood, except by the use of the analytic form "I may . . . ", with its related optative (of which latter there are only 37 examples in the New Testament, 15 of these being the familiar γένοιτο =may it be). But such words as ἵνα and compounds of ἄν *(ὅταν, ἐάν)*, etc., introducing a subjective or hypothetical element into a verbal idea, require to be followed by the subjunctive mood.

The Greek perfect can generally be taken as represented by an English present: a past action continuing in its effect down to the present, in contrast to an action wholly in the past. But in a literal translation the English perfect has been retained. In John *ch.* 11, *v.* 27, the Authorized Version is idiomatically correct but the Revised Version is literally so (πεπίστευκα =I have believed); *cf.* II. Timothy *ch.* 1, *v.* 12, where the Authorized Version adopts the literal equivalent. So, *e.g.*, τετέλεσται =it has been finished =it is finished. In participles, italics show that the auxiliary verbs may be dispensed with in English.

Where some word other than the strictly literal one seems to be needed in the translation, the former is printed in parentheses immediately after the latter; *e.g.*, Matthew *ch.* 10, *v.* 17, "beware from(of) men."

Occasionally it is not feasible to give a literal rendering without undue explanation; some idiomatic word or phrase has to be used. There are only a few of such passages and they are indicated by the mark †.

There are a number of Greek phrases, other than where † is used, which are not to be taken word for word, but as a whole:

ἐπὶ τὸ αὐτό =on the same =together
διὰ τοῦτο =because-of this =therefore
ἵνα μή =in-order-that not =lest
καθ' ὑπερβολήν =by-way-of excess =excessively

In familiar proper names there will appear some inconsistency, a compromise between the actual spellings preferred by Nestle and the Authorized Version; but this is of no great importance.

Εὐαγγελίζω. This and its cognate noun have been anglicized (evangelize, evangel). But while we can 'evangelize' a city, we do not 'evangelize' a person or a subject; so we must speak of 'preaching (good tidings) to' a person or of 'preaching' a subject. We can of course speak of 'evangelizing' absolutely, as in I. Corinthians *ch.* 1, *v.* 17. Ellicott on I. Thessalonians *ch.* 3, *v.* 6 has some useful information for the student.

There are five idiomatic Greek constructions which, being of frequent occurrence, call for explanation.
a. The *genitive absolute*. This is made up of a participle and a noun or pronoun, both in the genitive case and agreeing otherwise as well, but having no grammatical relation to the context. It is used to indicate time during or at which something takes place, or in some circumstances connected therewith. The close of such a Greek phrase is shown by the superior letter [a]; see Luke *ch.* 3, *v.* 1. There are variations of this. In Luke *ch.* 12, *v.* 36, two participles are used with no noun—it has to be supplied from the context.

So also II. Corinthians *ch.* 7, *v.* 15, and see the note on Romans *ch.* 9, *v.* 11 under "Notes on Particular Passages" below.

b. The *accusative* (or other case) *and infinitive*. Here what is in English the subject of the verb (the doer of the action) is put in the accusative (or other) case and the verb itself in the infinitive. A superior letter ᵇ closes such a phrase; see Luke *ch.* 1, *v.* 21.

c. The *dative of possession*. The possessor is put in the dative case. The idea may be grasped by comparing our English way of saying that a thing 'belongs to so-and-so'. The superior letter ᶜ shows this idiom; see Luke *ch.* 1, *v.* 5, 7, 14.

d. The *genitive of purpose* or *result*. The infinitive of a verb is in the genitive case, as shown by the preceding definite article. The article itself can be ignored. Again the appropriate letter ᵈ shows the existence of the idiom; see Matthew *ch.* 2, *v.* 13. The same idea can be shown without any article; see Matthew *ch.* 4, *v.* 1.

e. The *dative of time*. A point of time 'in' or 'at' which a thing happens is thus shown (ἐν may or may not be used). The letter ᵉ shows this; see Luke *ch.* 2, *v.* 43, and *ch.* 18, *v.* 35.

The constructions b and e can sometimes be combined; see Luke *ch.* 1, *v.* 8.

There is no indefinite article in Greek. The use of it in translation is a matter of individual judgment. The numeral 'one' is sometimes found; whether this means that just one, and no more, is to be understood is again open to argument. See Matthew *ch.* 21, *v.* 19 and *ch.* 26, *v.* 69. We have inserted 'a' or 'an' as a matter of course where it seems called for.

The definite article must sometimes be rendered by a pronoun or a possessive adjective. This is particularly so where parts of the body are indicated; *e.g.*, Matthew *ch.* 8, *v.* 3. Sometimes it is used 'pronominally'—that is, it must be rendered 'he' (or otherwise according to the gender) or 'they'; see Mark *ch.* 10, *v.* 4.

The ending of a Greek verb normally indicates the person (1st, 2nd, or 3rd, sing. or pl.). If the pronoun is separately expressed, this can be clearly seen in the interlinear translation.

μέν ... δέ. These two particles, in contrasted clauses, are not translatable literally, unless "indeed ... but" be used, as we have done in some places. But by adopting the phrases "on one hand ... on the other" the contrast is brought out. These particles are, in fact, somewhat elusive as to their force. See John *ch.* 19, *v.* 24 and 32, where μέν has been left untranslated—an example of the difficulty of rendering it satisfactorily in a literal translation.

It has not been considered necessary always to indicate the order of a noun and its adjective; a knowledge of English is sufficient for this. But where there is any risk of ambiguity small superior figures indicate the order in which the words should be read.

A number of Greek particles are said to be 'post-positive'—that is to say, they cannot stand as the first word in a sentence, but are found in the second, third, or even in the fourth place. Such words must of course be taken first in English; but it has not been thought necessary to show this, as the construction is sufficiently obvious. They include γάρ (for), δέ (and, but, now), οὖν (therefore; "therefore" can be post-positive in English), τις (a certain), μέν (indeed), γε (really—generally too subtle to be reproduced in English).

ὅτι as a conjunction, when meaning "that", is used to introduce spoken words as recorded; it is then known as the 'recitative ὅτι'. In English the original present tense of any verb would in such a construction ('indirect speech') be changed to the past: He said that the man was a liar. But Greek retains the original tense as actually used. What the speaker really said was "The man is a liar". The conjunction thus becomes superfluous and the reported words would in modern usage be put within quotation marks, as above. These, however, are not used in this translation. See Matthew *ch.* 21, *v.* 3.

ἵνα is, strictly, a 'telic' particle—*i.e.*, it denotes purpose (τέλος, an end); hence a full translation is "in order that". But inasmuch as in New Testament times there was a tendency to use it where ὅτι would be expected, it sometimes means no more than the conjunction "that"; see Matthew *ch.* 5, *v.* 29. Sometimes, then, where there may be room for difference of opinion as to its precise force, or even where there is none, "*in order* that" will be found in the literal translation.

A peculiarity of Greek construction is that a neuter plural subject may take a singular verb; but this is by no means invariable, and there appears to be no rule to go by. In translating, the position is sometimes shown by the use of an italic letter for the ending of the verb ([they] commit*s*); at other times the alternative is given in parenthesis (is(are)). But there are places where neither course is possible without taking up too much space, and the matter is left to the intelligence of the reader.

Where there is more than one subject of a verb, Greek will often put the verb in the singular to agree with the nearest subject. This is not in accordance with English grammar, which requires a plural verb if there is more than one subject. In Revelation *ch.* 9, *v.* 2, "sun" and "air" call for the plural "were darkened", as in the Authorized Version. But the Greek verb is in the singular. It is sometimes typographically possible to indicate the difference of grammatical usage, but not always.

In Greek, gender belongs to the word and not necessarily to what is indicated by the word; whereas of course in English we keep the ideas of masculine, feminine, and neuter to men, women, and inanimate things respectively. (English, by the way, is the only great modern language to do so.) Allowance must be made for this in translating: sometimes it is possible to transfer the idea from one language to another, but not always. The note to Revelation *ch.* 13, *v.* 1, may be consulted.

The construction of the demonstrative adjectives is peculiar in Greek. The definite article is used as well as the demonstrative adjective in one of two possible positions: either—

οὗτος ὁ οἶκος
this *the* house

or—

ὁ οἶκος οὗτος
the house this

The definite article is of course not wanted in English, and the proper translation of the phrase is obvious—"this house".

ἐκεῖνος (that) similarly. It is sometimes possible typographically to treat the three-word phrase as a whole, with the idiomatic translation underneath.

Similarly, the definite article is used in Greek with a possessive adjective, as in Matthew *ch*. 18, *v*. 20—

εἰς τὸ ἐμὸν ὄνομα

in *the* my name

or, alternatively again, the construction may be, say—

εἰς τὸ ὄνομα τὸ ἐμόν

in *the* name *the* my

This remark applies only to the first and second persons, singular and plural, but not to the third, where the only possible construction in this respect would be "in the name of him/her/them". This has been followed literally, as the reader can always make the needful English construction for himself. Occasionally such a construction as "in the name of me" will be found, meaning the same thing.

The neuter form of an adjective may be used as an adverb. ἀληθῆ in John *ch*. 19, *v*. 35, is the neuter of ἀληθής (true) and must be rendered "truly". So πρῶτον (firstly), though "first" is quite often used in English as an adverb. Conversely, an adverb may be used as an adjective; *e.g.* νῦν, now=present.

ταῦτα=these things (neuter plural) might be rendered by the singular "this", as in the common phrase μετὰ ταῦτα=after this; but this liberty has not been taken in the present literal translation.

The gender of an adjective may demand 'man', 'woman', or 'thing' to be supplied; *e.g.* Matthew *ch*. 9, *v*. 27—"two blind men".

Greek will often use a preposition in a compound verb and then repeat it (or use one similar) before a noun in the same sentence; in such passages the preposition would not be used twice in English. But in such a phrase as εἰσέρχεσθαι εἰς οἶκον we can say 'to enter into a house' (this has a counterpart in French—*entrer dans une maison*). We can indeed say simply 'to enter a house'. Another exception would be ἀπέρχεσθαι ἀπό =to go away from. But διαφέρειν διὰ τοῦ ἱεροῦ = to carry *through* through the temple (see Mark *ch*. 11, *v*. 16).

As the negatives οὐ(κ) (categorical) and μή (hypothetical) are easily recognizable, it has not been thought necessary always to render them separately, but they are included with any verb with which they may be used. But whereas in English the negative follows the verb, in Greek it precedes; see Matthew *ch.* 3, *v.* 11. If such a phrase happens to be broken at the end of a line this course has not been feasible.

The double negative οὐ μή has been consistently rendered "by no means".

Incidentally, though of importance, these two negative particles, or their compounds, when introducing questions, expect different answers. οὐ appeals to the fact, anticipating 'Yes, it is so'; *e.g.* John *ch.* 11, *v.* 9, "Are there not twelve hours of the day?" The answer would be 'Yes, there are'. μή, on the contrary, denies the suggestion and expects the reply 'No, it is not so'; or, if not so explicit as that, doubts whether it is so; *e.g.* John *ch.* 18, *v.* 35. The form of the question in the Authorized Version and the Revised Version indicates that Pilate was asking for information, whereas he was rejecting the idea with scorn and contempt—'I am not a Jew [am I]?' The answer, if any, would be—'No, certainly not.' This distinction is largely overlooked in the English Versions. To assist to the correct nuance of thought, in such places the latter negative in the interlinear translation is italicized, and the reader must read into the original what is intended; the result is sometimes surprising.

An article in *The Bible Translator* for January, 1953, may be consulted.

While on the subject of negatives, Greek favours the use of two such, one strengthening the other. In such sentences the second negative has to be replaced in English by a positive; *e.g.* Matthew *ch.* 22, *v.* 46.

There is the *genitive of quality*, of which there are many examples in the New Testament. If in English we say "a man of courage" or "an act of kindness", this is equivalent to "a courageous man" or "a kind act" respectively. We have translated literally, with an occasional footnote where this construction is not generally recognized. The Authorized Version itself is not consistent—*cf.* Philippians *ch.* 3, *v.* 21, with Colossians *ch.* 1, *v.* 22, where surely the distinction is between "his glorious body" and "his fleshly body".

Necessity or compulsion is most frequently expressed by the use of an impersonal verb (or a verb used impersonally), with the person concerned in the accusative as the object of the verb: δεῖ με=it behoves me=I must.

As 'first' is used as an adverb as well as 'firstly' it has not been thought necessary always to print 'first*ly*'; the matter is of no great importance.

Finally, but certainly not least in importance, there are the Greek participles, to which we now give special attention.

Greek is "a participle-loving language", said the late A. T. Robertson, and it uses this part of speech much more frequently than we do, and in different ways.

To begin with, it is absolutely essential to grasp the distinction between *continuous, momentary*, and *completed* action. The first is commonly, but wrongly, spoken of as a present participle; the second as an aorist (which does not mean "past"); and the third as a perfect. (There is a rare future participle—continuous in the future.) Now—

1. A participle may be used as an adjective qualifying a noun, just as in English; *e.g.* I. Thessalonians *ch.* 1, *v.* 9—"a living God"; Hebrews *ch.* 7, *v.* 8—"dying men". This is so simple as not to need further remark.

2. A participle may be used, again as in English, as a verb to describe some action; *e.g.* Acts *ch.* 9, *v.* 39—"all the widows stood by . . . weeping and showing . . .".

3. A participle may be used, with the definite article, with, say, "one" understood, where we should use a noun or a relative phrase; *e.g.*, frequently, ὁ πιστεύων=the [one] believing=the believer *or* he who believes. Here the participle is continuous; in Luke *ch.* 1, *v.* 45, it is momentary (and, naturally, feminine in gender as referring to Mary's one act of faith at the Annunciation). If two participles are used with but one definite article, as in John *ch.* 5, *v.* 24, the meaning is that one person is doubly

described, not two persons doing two things. This feature has been preserved in our translation.

4. Very frequently indeed, where in English we use two or more finite verbs to describe associated actions, Greek will use participles and only one finite verb for the main action. But here judgment is necessary to distinguish two (or more) simultaneous actions from consecutive ones; and as we have no aorist participle in English the matter is not always free from difficulty. In Acts *ch.* 10, *v.* 34, "Peter opening his mouth said", the two actions were obviously simultaneous! So in Acts *ch.* 1, *v.* 24—"praying they said". But sometimes one action must be completed before another could begin; *e.g.* Luke *ch.* 22, *v.* 17—"having given thanks, he said . . .". Here the act of giving thanks to God would be complete before Jesus addressed His disciples; therefore the aorist participle must be represented in English by the analytic "having given thanks". That this is not unimportant is shown by Matthew *ch.* 26, *v.* 30—"having sung a hymn they went out". To translate the aorist participle here by "singing a hymn" would certainly convey the idea that the singing occurred as they went out. In Acts *ch.* 21, *v.* 14, it is not easy to see how the keeping silence and the saying could be contemporaneous: "Having said, The will of the Lord be done, we kept silence." These few examples should, we think, suffice to show the principles involved.

NOTES ON PARTICULAR PASSAGES

Mark *ch.* 10, *v.* 11.—An article by Dr. Nigel Turner in *The Bible Translator* for October, 1956, gives good reasons for understanding the verse thus, αὐτήν referring to the last woman mentioned (ἄλλην).

Mark *ch.* 14, *v.* 6.—The use of ἐν here is somewhat puzzling. The parallel in Matthew (*ch.* 26, *v.* 10) has εἰς, which would mean 'to', 'toward', or 'for'; and Mark's ἐν must then be taken as equivalent in meaning to εἰς. This may throw light on I John *ch.* 4, *v.* 16.

Luke *ch.* 7, *v.* 14.—ἐγέρθητι. It does not seem right to insist here on the passive voice; compare with *ch.* 8, *v.* 54, and, in another connection, *ch.* 11, *v.* 8. But our Lord "was raised", as are the dead generally (they do not "rise"). See I. Corinthians *ch.* 15, etc.

John *ch.* 8, *v.* 25.—"The answer of Jesus is one of the most disputed passages in the Gospel" (Godet). Nestle punctuates as a question; hence we have given what appears to be a reasonable rendering interrogatively.

Acts *ch.* 7, *v.* 46.—οἴκῳ is a manuscript variant for θεῷ. There is some uncertainty as to how this reading arose; see the Authorized Version. Has Psalm 24, *v.* 6, text and margin, any bearing on the matter?

Acts *ch.* 18, *v.* 10.—λαὸς πολύς must not be understood as meaning "many persons". λαός is the regular word for the chosen people, Israel (almost without exception). Here in Corinth was to be a new community, taking the place of the Jewish population. Translate—"a great people".

Romans *ch.* 1, *v.* 12.—That is, their faith (=confidence) in one another—Paul and his readers. "Mutual" is correct in A.V., but is generally misunderstood as being equivalent to "common", which it is not.

Romans *ch.* 9, *v.* 11.—There is no noun agreeing with the two participles. But it is nevertheless a 'genitive absolute' construction. The Authorized Version supplies the subject.

II. Corinthians *ch.* 11, *v.* 28.—There is another view of Paul's words here. ἐπίστασις occurs in the New Testament only here and in Acts *ch.* 24, *v.* 12. The related noun ἐπιστάτης (one standing over, superintendent, master) is peculiar to Luke (six times in his gospel). Then there is a variant reading in our verse, μου instead of μοι. So the meaning may be—"my daily superintendence *or* attention". This would bring it into line with the remainder of the verse.

Philippians *ch.* 3, *v.* 16.—This is, according to Burton, the only certain use in the New Testament of the 'imperatival infinitive', Romans *ch.* 12, *v.* 15 being a probable example. Moulton thinks it highly probable in Titus *ch.* 2, *v.* 1-10. The epistolary χαίρειν (Acts *ch.* 15, *v.* 23, *ch.* 23, *v.* 26; James *ch.* 1, *v.* 1) is said to be the same in origin, though a verb of bidding may be assumed, as in fact we do find in II. John *vs.* 10, 11. *Cf.* the French warning in railway carriages—*Ne pas se pencher au dehors*. In English we have such a full expression as "You are 'to do' so and so"; see

II. Thessalonians *ch*. 3, *v*. 14. If Nestle's text is accepted here, it is an additional instance to those given under Philippians *ch*. 3, *v*. 16 above, though with a negative as a prohibition. (Textus Receptus, etc., give a plain imperative.) But perhaps we may insert "so as" —"mark this man, so as not to mix with him."

II. Timothy *ch*. 4, *v*. 3.—The construction of the last three words of this verse is difficult. "Having itching ears" may be a workable paraphrase, but it cannot be said to represent literally the actual Greek. There is no word for "having"; and there is nothing corresponding to "itching" as a participial adjective qualifying "ears". τὴν ἀκοήν is accusative singular, the object of a verb—and the only verb is the participle which precedes. This is masculine plural, agreeing with διδασκάλους, and, while this latter is accusative, whereas the participle is nominative, this must be taken as an example of rational rather than grammatical concord. It is the teachers who "tickle" the ears of those concerned.

Hebrews *ch*. 2, *v*. 10.—That is, it is God who perfected Jesus Christ (the author, or captain, of our salvation) by means of sufferings, whose work it is to lead many sons to glory. This is not what the Authorized Version nor the Revised Version says, but it is demanded by the grammar: ἀγαγόντα (leading) agrees with ἀρχηγόν not with αὐτῷ (=God). Besides, there is a parallel between Joshua and Jesus, as both leaders of their peoples. (The Berkeley version adopts this view, though we were not aware of it until our own order of words had been adopted.) In fine, it is the function of a captain to lead, and Jesus is the leader here.

Hebrews *ch*. 9, *vs*. 16-17.—We are aware of the problem in regard to διαθήκη in this passage; but this translation is no place for purporting to settle a question that has divided commentators. It must suffice to say that we have translated the word consistently as 'covenant'; the idea of a legatee receiving something on the death of a testator by reason of the latter's having made a 'testament' or 'will' is, so far as we can see, quite non-biblical. The covenant victim, then, is 'the one making covenant', unless the person establishing the covenant is to be understood as identifying himself with it; and the covenant is in fact ratified over the dead body or bodies. But other views are taken of the matter.

James *ch.* 2, *v.* 1.—There are other instances of such a construction—two genitives in apposition. Colossians *ch.* 1, *v.* 18: the meaning must be 'of the body (,) *of* the Church'—the body is the Church, as verse 24 says. Colossians *ch.* 2, *v.* 2: 'of God, of Christ'. Romans *ch.* 11, *v.* 17: see note at that place. John *ch.* 8, *v.* 44: 'of the father (,) *of* the devil'—their father was the devil.

Revelation *ch.* 16, *v.* 14: 'Almighty' is not an adjective but another noun in apposition.

NOTE on Mat. 16. 3, 27. 65; Luke 12. 56; Acts 21. 37; I. Thes. 4. 4; I. Tim. 3. 5; Jas. 4. 17; II. Pet. 2. 9.

As in French, so in the Greek of the N.T., we have the idea of "to know (how) to do" a thing as being the same as "to be able to do" it. But while *savoir* only is used in this way, not *connaître*, both γινώσκω and οἶδα are found in the N.T. In fact it is the former in Mat. 16. 3 and the latter in the parallel in Luke (12. 56). So, in French, *Savez-vous nager?* = Know you to swim? = Can you swim? In all the above passages this seems to be the meaning. It may be noted that the A.V. so renders the verbs in some passages, in others giving "know how". The James instance may be arguable. Phil. 4. 12 also may be considered, and Mat. 7. 11 = Luke 11. 13.

THE GREEK ALPHABET

A α	Alpha	a	
B β	Beta	b	
Γ γ	Gamma	g	hard, as in be*g*in[1]
Δ δ	Delta	d	
E ε	Epsilon	e	short, as in m*e*t
Z ζ	Zeta	z	
H η	Eta	e	long, as in sc*e*ne
Θ θ	Theta	th	as in *th*in
I ι	Iota	i	
K κ	Kappa	k	
Λ λ	Lambda	l	
M μ	Mu	m	
N ν	Nu	n	
Ξ ξ	Xi	x	
O ο	Omicron	o	short, as in l*o*t
Π π	Pi	p	
P ρ	Rho	r	
Σ σ, *final* ς	Sigma	s[2]	
T τ	Tau	t	
Y υ	Upsilon	u	
Φ φ	Phi	ph	
X χ	Chi	ch	hard, as in lo*ch*
Ψ ψ	Psi	ps	
Ω ω	Omega	o	long, as in thr*o*ne

[1] Except that before κ, χ or another γ it is nasal—ng, as in a*nch*or.
[2] Sharp as in thi*s*, but flat before β or μ, as in a*s*bestos, di*s*mal.

THE NAMES AND ORDER OF THE BOOKS
OF THE NEW TESTAMENT

CHAPTER 1

THE book of the generation of Jesus Christ, the son of David, the son of Abraham.
2 Abraham begat Isaac; and Isaac begat Jacob; and Jacob begat Judas and his brethren;
3 And Judas begat Phares and Zara of Thamar; and Phares begat Esrom; and Esrom begat Aram;
4 And Aram begat Aminadab; and Aminadab begat Naasson; and Naasson begat Salmon;
5 And Salmon begat Booz of Rachab; and Booz begat Obed of Ruth; and Obed begat Jesse;
6 And Jesse begat David the king; and David the king begat Solomon of her *that had been the wife* of Urias;
7 And Solomon begat Roboam; and Roboam begat Abia; and Abia begat Asa;
8 And Asa begat Josaphat; and Josaphat begat Joram; and Joram begat Ozias;
9 And Ozias begat Joatham; and Joatham begat

1 Βίβλος γενέσεως Ἰησοῦ Χριστοῦ
[The] book of [the] generation of Jesus Christ
υἱοῦ Δαυὶδ υἱοῦ Ἀβραάμ.
son of David son of Abraham.
2 Ἀβραὰμ ἐγέννησεν τὸν Ἰσαάκ, Ἰσαὰκ δὲ
Abraham begat — Isaac, and Isaac
ἐγέννησεν τὸν Ἰακώβ, Ἰακὼβ δὲ ἐγέννησεν τὸν
begat — Jacob, and Jacob begat —
Ἰούδαν καὶ τοὺς ἀδελφοὺς αὐτοῦ, 3 Ἰούδας δὲ
Judas and the brothers of him, and Judas
ἐγέννησεν τὸν Φάρες καὶ τὸν Ζάρα ἐκ τῆς
begat — Phares and — Zara out of —
Θαμάρ, Φάρες δὲ ἐγέννησεν τὸν Ἐσρώμ,
Thamar, and Phares begat — Esrom,
Ἐσρὼμ δὲ ἐγέννησεν τὸν Ἀράμ, 4 Ἀρὰμ δὲ
and Esrom begat — Aram, and Aram
ἐγέννησεν τὸν Ἀμιναδάβ, Ἀμιναδὰβ δὲ
begat — Aminadab, and Aminadab
ἐγέννησεν τὸν Ναασσών, Ναασσὼν δὲ ἐγέννησεν
begat — Naasson, and Naasson begat
τὸν Σαλμών, 5 Σαλμὼν δὲ ἐγέννησεν τὸν Βόες
— Salmon, and Salmon begat — Booz
ἐκ τῆς Ῥαχάβ, Βόες δὲ ἐγέννησεν τὸν Ἰωβὴδ
out of — Rachab, and Booz begat — Obed
ἐκ τῆς Ῥούθ, Ἰωβὴδ δὲ ἐγέννησεν τὸν Ἰεσσαί,
out of — Ruth, and Obed begat — Jesse.
6 Ἰεσσαὶ δὲ ἐγέννησεν τὸν Δαυὶδ τὸν βασιλέα.
and Jesse begat — David the king.
Δαυὶδ δὲ ἐγέννησεν τὸν Σολομῶνα ἐκ τῆς
And David begat — Solomon out of the
τοῦ Οὐρίου, 7 Σολομὼν δὲ ἐγέννησεν
[one who had been the wife]–of Uriah, and Solomon begat
τὸν Ῥοβοάμ, Ῥοβοὰμ δὲ ἐγέννησεν τὸν
— Roboam, and Roboam begat —
Ἀβιά, Ἀβιὰ δὲ ἐγέννησεν τὸν Ἀσάφ, 8 Ἀσὰφ
Abia, and Abia begat — Asaph, and Asaph
δὲ ἐγέννησεν τὸν Ἰωσαφάτ, Ἰωσαφὰτ δὲ
begat — Josaphat, and Josaphat
ἐγέννησεν τὸν Ἰωράμ, Ἰωρὰμ δὲ ἐγέννησεν τὸν
begat — Joram, and Joram begat —
Ὀζίαν, 9 Ὀζίας δὲ ἐγέννησεν τὸν Ἰωαθάμ,
Ozias, and Ozias begat — Joatham,
Ἰωαθὰμ δὲ ἐγέννησεν τὸν Ἀχάζ, Ἀχὰζ δὲ
and Joatham begat — Achaz, and Achaz

2   **MATTHEW 1**

Achaz; and Achaz begat Ezekias;

10 And Ezekias begat Manasses; and Manasses begat Amon; and Amon begat Josias;

11 And Josias begat Jechonias and his brethren, about the time they were carried away to Babylon:

12 And after they were brought to Babylon, Jechonias begat Salathiel; and Salathiel begat Zorobabel;

13 And Zorobabel begat Abiud; and Abiud begat Eliakim; and Eliakim begat Azor;

14 And Azor begat Sadoc; and Sadoc begat Achim; and Achim begat Eliud;

15 And Eliud begat Eleazar; and Eleazar begat Matthan; and Matthan begat Jacob;

16 And Jacob begat Joseph the husband of Mary, of whom was born Jesus, who is called Christ.

17 So all the generations from Abraham to David *are* fourteen generations; and from David until the carrying away into Babylon *are* fourteen generations; and from the carrying away into Babylon unto Christ *are* fourteen generations.

18 ¶ Now the birth of Jesus Christ was on this

ἐγέννησεν τὸν Ἐζεκίαν, **10** Ἐζεκίας δὲ
begat   –   Hezekias,   and Hezekias

ἐγέννησεν τὸν Μανασσῆ, Μανασσῆς δὲ ἐγέννησεν
begat   –   Manasses,   and Manasses   begat

τὸν Ἀμώς, Ἀμὼς δὲ ἐγέννησεν τὸν Ἰωσίαν,
 –   Amos,   and Amos   begat   –   Josias,

11 Ἰωσίας δὲ ἐγέννησεν τὸν Ἰεχονίαν καὶ
     and Josias   begat   –   Jechonias   and

τοὺς ἀδελφοὺς αὐτοῦ ἐπὶ τῆς μετοικεσίας
the   brothers   of him   at   the   deportation

Βαβυλῶνος. **12** Μετὰ δὲ τὴν μετοικεσίαν
of Babylon.   And after the   deportation

Βαβυλῶνος Ἰεχονίας ἐγέννησεν τὸν Σαλαθιήλ,
of Babylon Jechonias   begat   –   Salathiel,

Σαλαθιὴλ δὲ ἐγέννησεν τὸν Ζοροβαβέλ,
and Salathiel   begat   –   Zorobabel,

13 Ζοροβαβὲλ δὲ ἐγέννησεν τὸν Ἀβιούδ,
     and Zorobabel   begat   –   Abiud,

Ἀβιοὺδ δὲ ἐγέννησεν τὸν Ἐλιακίμ, Ἐλιακὶμ δὲ
and Abiud   begat   –   Eliakim,   and Eliakim

ἐγέννησεν τὸν Ἀζώρ, **14** Ἀζὼρ δὲ ἐγέννησεν
begat   –   Azor,   and Azor   begat

τὸν Σαδώκ, Σαδὼκ δὲ ἐγέννησεν τὸν Ἀχίμ,
 –   Sadoc,   and Sadoc   begat   –   Achim,

Ἀχὶμ δὲ ἐγέννησεν τὸν Ἐλιούδ, **15** Ἐλιοὺδ δὲ
and Achim   begat   –   Eliud,   and Eliud

ἐγέννησεν τὸν Ἐλεαζάρ, Ἐλεαζὰρ δὲ ἐγέννησεν
begat   –   Eleazar,   and Eleazar   begat

τὸν Ματθάν, Ματθὰν δὲ ἐγέννησεν τὸν Ἰακώβ,
 –   Matthan, and Matthan   begat   –   Jacob,

16 Ἰακὼβ δὲ ἐγέννησεν τὸν Ἰωσὴφ τὸν ἄνδρα
    and Jacob   begat   –   Joseph   the husband

Μαρίας, ἐξ ἧς ἐγεννήθη Ἰησοῦς ὁ λεγόμενος
of Mary, of whom   was born   Jesus the [one] called

Χριστός.
Christ.

17 Πᾶσαι οὖν αἱ γενεαὶ ἀπὸ Ἀβραὰμ
    Therefore all the generations from   Abraham

ἕως Δαυὶδ γενεαὶ δεκατέσσαρες, καὶ ἀπὸ
until David generations   fourteen,   and from

Δαυὶδ ἕως τῆς μετοικεσίας Βαβυλῶνος γενεαὶ
David until the deportation of Babylon generations

δεκατέσσαρες, καὶ ἀπὸ τῆς μετοικεσίας Βαβυ-
fourteen,   and from the   deportation   of Baby-

λῶνος ἕως τοῦ Χριστοῦ γενεαὶ δεκατέσσαρες.
lon until the   Christ generations fourteen.

18 Τοῦ δὲ Ἰησοῦ Χριστοῦ ἡ γένεσις
     – Now ²of Jesus ⁴Christ ¹the ³birth

wise: When as his mother Mary was espoused to Joseph, before they came together, she was found with child of the Holy Ghost.

19 Then Joseph her husband, being a just *man*, and not willing to make her a publick example, was minded to put her away privily.

20 But while he thought on these things, behold, the angel of the Lord appeared unto him in a dream, saying, Joseph, thou son of David, fear not to take unto thee Mary thy wife: for that which is conceived in her is of the Holy Ghost.

21 And she shall bring forth a son, and thou shalt call his name JESUS: for he shall save his people from their sins.

22 Now all this was done, that it might be fulfilled which was spoken of the Lord by the prophet, saying,

23 Behold, a virgin shall be with child, and shall bring forth a son, and they shall call his name Emmanuel, which being interpreted is, God with us.

24 Then Joseph being raised from sleep did as the

οὕτως ἦν. μνηστευθείσης τῆς μητρὸς αὐτοῦ
⁶thus ⁵was. Being betrothed the mother of him
=When his mother Mary was betrothed

Μαρίας τῷ Ἰωσήφ, πρὶν ἢ συνελθεῖν αὐτοὺς
Mary⁴ - to Joseph, before to come together them⁵
=before they came together

εὑρέθη ἐν γαστρὶ ἔχουσα ἐκ πνεύματος
¹she was found ³in ⁴womb ²having of(by)[the] Spirit
= she was pregnant

ἁγίου. 19 Ἰωσὴφ δὲ ὁ ἀνὴρ αὐτῆς,
Holy. Now Joseph the husband of her,

δίκαιος ὢν καὶ μὴ θέλων αὐτὴν δειγμα-
²just ¹being and not wishing her to hold up as an

τίσαι, ἐβουλήθη λάθρα ἀπολῦσαι αὐτήν.
example, resolved secretly to dismiss her.

20 ταῦτα δὲ αὐτοῦ ἐνθυμηθέντος, ἰδοὺ
But these things him thinking on,⁴ behold
=while he thought on these things,

ἄγγελος κυρίου κατ' ὄναρ ἐφάνη
an angel of [the] Lord by a dream appeared

αὐτῷ λέγων· Ἰωσὴφ υἱὸς Δαυίδ, μὴ
to him saying: Joseph son of David, ²not

φοβηθῇς παραλαβεῖν Μαρίαν τὴν
¹fear thou to take Mary the

γυναῖκά σου· τὸ γὰρ ἐν αὐτῇ γεννηθὲν
wife of thee: for the thing in her begotten

ἐκ πνεύματός ἐστιν ἁγίου. 21 τέξεται δὲ
⁴of ⁵[the] Spirit ¹is ⁶Holy. And she will bear

υἱόν, καὶ καλέσεις τὸ ὄνομα αὐτοῦ
a son, and thou shalt call the name of him

Ἰησοῦν· αὐτὸς γὰρ σώσει τὸν λαὸν
Jesus; for he will save the people

αὐτοῦ ἀπὸ τῶν ἁμαρτιῶν αὐτῶν. 22 Τοῦτο δὲ
of him from the sins of them. Now ⁵this

ὅλον γέγονεν ἵνα πληρωθῇ τὸ ῥηθὲν
¹all has occurred in order that might be fulfilled the [thing] spoken

ὑπὸ κυρίου διὰ τοῦ προφήτου λέγοντος·
by [the] Lord through the prophet saying:

23 ἰδοὺ ἡ παρθένος ἐν γαστρὶ ἕξει
Behold the virgin ²in ³womb ¹will have

καὶ τέξεται υἱόν, καὶ καλέσουσιν τὸ
and will bear a son, and they will call the

ὄνομα αὐτοῦ Ἐμμανουήλ, ὃ ἐστιν
name of him Emmanuel, which is

μεθερμηνευόμενον μεθ' ἡμῶν ὁ θεός.
being interpreted with us - God.

24 ἐγερθεὶς δὲ [ὁ] Ἰωσὴφ ἀπὸ τοῦ
Then ²being raised - ¹Joseph from the(his)

ὕπνου ἐποίησεν ὡς προσέταξεν αὐτῷ ὁ
sleep did as bade him the

angel of the Lord had bidden him, and took unto him his wife:

25 And knew her not till she had brought forth her firstborn son: and he called his name JESUS.

ἄγγελος κυρίου, καὶ παρέλαβεν τὴν
angel of [the] Lord, and took the

γυναῖκα αὐτοῦ· 25 καὶ οὐκ ἐγίνωσκεν
wife of him; and knew not

αὐτὴν ἕως [οὗ] ἔτεκεν υἱόν· καὶ ἐκάλεσεν
her until she bore a son; and he called

τὸ ὄνομα αὐτοῦ Ἰησοῦν.
the name of him Jesus.

CHAPTER 2

NOW when Jesus was born in Bethlehem of Judæa in the days of Herod the king, behold, there came wise men from the east to Jerusalem,

2 Saying, Where is he that is born King of the Jews? for we have seen his star in the east, and are come to worship him.

3 When Herod the king had heard *these things*, he was troubled, and all Jerusalem with him.

4 And when he had gathered all the chief priests and scribes of the people together, he demanded of them where Christ should be born.

5 And they said unto him, In Bethlehem of Judæa: for thus it is written by the prophet,

6 And thou Bethlehem, *in* the land of Juda, art not the least among the princes of Juda: for out of thee shall come a Governor, that shall rule my people Israel.

2 Τοῦ δὲ Ἰησοῦ γεννηθέντος ἐν Βηθλέεμ
- Now Jesus having been born* in Bethlehem
=when Jesus was born

τῆς Ἰουδαίας ἐν ἡμέραις Ἡρῴδου τοῦ
- of Judæa in [the] days of Herod the

βασιλέως, ἰδοὺ μάγοι ἀπὸ ἀνατολῶν
king, behold magi from [the] east

παρεγένοντο εἰς Ἱεροσόλυμα 2 λέγοντες·
arrived in Jerusalem saying:

ποῦ ἐστιν ὁ τεχθεὶς βασιλεὺς τῶν
Where is the [one] born king of the

Ἰουδαίων; εἴδομεν γὰρ αὐτοῦ τὸν ἀστέρα
Jews? for we saw of him the star

ἐν τῇ ἀνατολῇ, καὶ ἤλθομεν προσκυνῆσαι
in the east, and came to worship

αὐτῷ. 3 ἀκούσας δὲ ὁ βασιλεὺς Ἡρῴδης
him. Now hearing [this] the king Herod

ἐταράχθη, καὶ πᾶσα Ἱεροσόλυμα μετ᾽
was troubled, and all Jerusalem with

αὐτοῦ, 4 καὶ συναγαγὼν πάντας τοὺς
him, and having assembled all the

ἀρχιερεῖς καὶ γραμματεῖς τοῦ λαοῦ
chief priests and scribes of the people

ἐπυνθάνετο παρ᾽ αὐτῶν ποῦ ὁ χριστὸς
he inquired from them where the Christ

γεννᾶται. 5 οἱ δὲ εἶπαν αὐτῷ· ἐν
is being born. And they told him: In

Βηθλέεμ τῆς Ἰουδαίας· οὕτως γὰρ
Bethlehem - of Judæa; for thus

γέγραπται διὰ τοῦ προφήτου· 6 καὶ
it has been written through the prophet: And

σὺ Βηθλέεμ, γῆ Ἰούδα, οὐδαμῶς ἐλαχίστη
thou Bethlehem, land of Juda, ²not at all ³least

εἶ ἐν τοῖς ἡγεμόσιν Ἰούδα. ἐκ σοῦ γὰρ
¹art among the governors of Juda. For out of thee

ἐξελεύσεται ἡγούμενος, ὅστις ποιμανεῖ
will come forth a governor, who will shepherd

τὸν λαόν μου τὸν Ἰσραήλ.
the people of me - Israel.

7 Then Herod, when he had privily called the wise men, enquired of them diligently what time the star appeared.

8 And he sent them to Bethlehem, and said, Go and search diligently for the young child; and when ye have found *him*, bring me word again, that I may come and worship him also.

9 When they had heard the king, they departed; and, lo, the star, which they saw in the east, went before them, till it came and stood over where the young child was.

10 When they saw the star, they rejoiced with exceeding great joy.

11 ¶ And when they were come into the house, they saw the young child with Mary his mother, and fell down, and worshipped him: and when they had opened their treasures, they presented unto him gifts; gold, and frankincense, and myrrh.

12 And being warned of God in a dream that they should not return to Herod, they departed into their own country another way.

13 ¶ And when they were departed, behold, the angel of the Lord appeareth to Joseph in a dream, saying, Arise, and take the young

7 Τότε	Ἡρώδης	λάθρα	καλέσας	τοὺς
Then	Herod	secretly	calling	the
μάγους	ἠκρίβωσεν	παρ'	αὐτῶν	τὸν
magi	inquired carefully	from	them	the
χρόνον	τοῦ	φαινομένου	ἀστέρος,	8 καὶ
time	of the	appearing	star,	and
πέμψας	αὐτοὺς	εἰς	Βηθλέεμ	εἶπεν·
sending	them	to	Bethlehem	said:
πορευθέντες	ἐξετάσατε	ἀκριβῶς	περὶ	τοῦ
Going	question ye	carefully	concerning	the
παιδίου·	ἐπὰν	δὲ	εὕρητε,	ἀπαγγείλατέ
child;	and when		ye find,	report
μοι,	ὅπως	κἀγὼ	ἐλθὼν	προσκυνήσω αὐτῷ.
to me,	so that	I also	coming	may worship him.

9 οἱ δὲ ἀκούσαντες τοῦ βασιλέως ἐπορεύθησαν·
So they hearing the king went;

καὶ ἰδοὺ ὁ ἀστήρ, ὃν εἶδον ἐν τῇ
and behold the star, which they saw in the

ἀνατολῇ, προῆγεν αὐτοὺς ἕως ἐλθὼν
east, went before them until coming

ἐστάθη ἐπάνω οὗ ἦν τὸ παιδίον. 10 ἰδόντες
it stood over where was the child. [2]seeing

δὲ τὸν ἀστέρα ἐχάρησαν χαρὰν μεγάλην
[1]And the star they rejoiced [with] a joy great

σφόδρα. 11 καὶ ἐλθόντες εἰς τὴν οἰκίαν
exceedingly. And coming into the house

εἶδον τὸ παιδίον μετὰ Μαρίας τῆς μητρὸς
they saw the child with Mary the mother

αὐτοῦ, καὶ πεσόντες προσεκύνησαν αὐτῷ,
of him, and falling they worshipped him,

καὶ ἀνοίξαντες τοὺς θησαυροὺς αὐτῶν
and opening the treasures of them

προσήνεγκαν αὐτῷ δῶρα, χρυσὸν καὶ
they offered to him gifts, gold and

λίβανον καὶ σμύρναν. 12 καὶ χρηματισθέντες
frankincense and myrrh. And having been warned

κατ' ὄναρ μὴ ἀνακάμψαι πρὸς Ἡρώδην,
by a dream not to return to Herod,

δι' ἄλλης ὁδοῦ ἀνεχώρησαν εἰς τὴν
by another way they departed to the

χώραν αὐτῶν.
country of them.

13 Ἀναχωρησάντων δὲ αὐτῶν, ἰδοὺ
Now having departed them,[a] behold
= when they had departed,

ἄγγελος κυρίου φαίνεται κατ' ὄναρ τῷ
an angel of [the] Lord appears by a dream –

Ἰωσὴφ λέγων· ἐγερθεὶς παράλαβε τὸ
to Joseph saying: Rising take thou the

child and his mother, and
flee into Egypt, and be thou
there until I bring thee
word: for Herod will seek
the young child to destroy
him.

14 When he arose, he
took the young child and
his mother by night, and
departed into Egypt:

15 And was there until
the death of Herod: that
it might be fulfilled which
was spoken of the Lord by
the prophet, saying, Out of
Egypt have I called my son.

16 ¶ Then Herod, when
he saw that he was mocked
of the wise men, was ex-
ceeding wroth, and sent
forth, and slew all the
children that were in
Bethlehem, and in all the
coasts thereof, from two
years old and under, ac-
cording to the time which
he had diligently enquired
of the wise men.

17 Then was fulfilled
that which was spoken by
Jeremy the prophet, saying,

18 In Rama was there a
voice heard, lamentation,
and weeping, and great
mourning, Rachel weeping
for her children, and would
not be comforted, because
they are not.

19 ¶ But when Herod
was dead, behold, an angel
of the Lord appeareth in

παιδίον καὶ τὴν μητέρα αὐτοῦ, καὶ φεῦγε
child and the mother of him, and flee

εἰς Αἴγυπτον, καὶ ἴσθι ἐκεῖ ἕως ἂν εἴπω
into Egypt, and be there until I tell

σοι· μέλλει γὰρ Ἡρῴδης ζητεῖν τὸ παιδίον τοῦ
thee; for ²is about ¹Herod to seek the child –

ἀπολέσαι αὐτό. 14 ὁ δὲ ἐγερθεὶς παρέλαβεν
to destroy[d] him. So he rising took

τὸ παιδίον καὶ τὴν μητέρα αὐτοῦ
the child and the mother of him

νυκτὸς καὶ ἀνεχώρησεν εἰς Αἴγυπτον,
of(by) night and departed to Egypt,

15 καὶ ἦν ἐκεῖ ἕως τῆς τελευτῆς Ἡρῴδου·
and was there until the death of Herod;

ἵνα πληρωθῇ τὸ ῥηθὲν ὑπὸ κυρίου
in order that might be fulfilled the [thing] spoken by [the] Lord

διὰ τοῦ προφήτου λέγοντος· ἐξ
through the prophet saying: Out of

Αἰγύπτου ἐκάλεσα τὸν υἱόν μου.
Egypt I called the son of me.

16 Τότε Ἡρῴδης ἰδὼν ὅτι ἐνεπαίχθη
Then Herod seeing that he was mocked

ὑπὸ τῶν μάγων ἐθυμώθη λίαν, καὶ
by the magi was angered exceedingly, and

ἀποστείλας ἀνεῖλεν πάντας τοὺς παῖδας
sending killed all the boy-children

τοὺς ἐν Βηθλέεμ καὶ ἐν πᾶσι τοῖς
– in Bethlehem and in all the

ὁρίοις αὐτῆς ἀπὸ διετοῦς καὶ κατωτέρω,
districts of it from two years and under,

κατὰ τὸν χρόνον ὃν ἠκρίβωσεν παρὰ τῶν
according to the time which he strictly inquired from the

μάγων. 17 τότε ἐπληρώθη τὸ ῥηθὲν διὰ
magi. Then was fulfilled the [thing] spoken through

Ἰερεμίου τοῦ προφήτου λέγοντος· 18 φωνὴ
Jeremiah the prophet saying: A voice

ἐν Ῥαμὰ ἠκούσθη, κλαυθμὸς καὶ ὀδυρμὸς
in Rama was heard, weeping and mourning

πολύς· Ῥαχὴλ κλαίουσα τὰ τέκνα αὐτῆς,
much; Rachel weeping for the children of her,

καὶ οὐκ ἤθελεν παρακληθῆναι, ὅτι
and would not *to* be comforted, because

οὐκ εἰσίν.
they are not.

19 Τελευτήσαντος δὲ τοῦ Ἡρῴδου, ἰδοὺ
But dying – Herod,[a] behold
= Herod having died,

ἄγγελος κυρίου φαίνεται κατ' ὄναρ τῷ
an angel of [the] Lord appears by a dream

a dream to Joseph in Egypt,

20 Saying, Arise, and take the young child and his mother, and go into the land of Israel: for they are dead which sought the young child's life.

21 And he arose, and took the young child and his mother, and came into the land of Israel.

22 But when he heard that Archelaus did reign in Judæa in the room of his father Herod, he was afraid to go thither: notwithstanding, being warned of God in a dream, he turned aside into the parts of Galilee:

23 And he came and dwelt in a city called Nazareth: that it might be fulfilled which was spoken by the prophets, He shall be called a Nazarene.

'Ιωσὴφ   ἐν   Αἰγύπτῳ   20 λέγων·   ἐγερθεὶς
to Joseph   in   Egypt   saying: Rising

παράλαβε   τὸ   παιδίον   καὶ   τὴν   μητέρα
take thou   the   child   and   the   mother

αὐτοῦ,   καὶ   πορεύου   εἰς   γῆν   'Ισραήλ·
of him,   and   go   into [the] land   of Israel;

τεθνήκασιν   γὰρ   οἱ   ζητοῦντες   τὴν   ψυχὴν
for have died   the [ones]   seeking   the   life

τοῦ   παιδίου.   21 ὁ   δὲ   ἐγερθεὶς   παρέλαβεν
of the   child.   So he   rising   took

τὸ   παιδίον   καὶ   τὴν   μητέρα   αὐτοῦ   καὶ
the   child   and   the   mother   of him   and

εἰσῆλθεν   εἰς   γῆν   'Ισραήλ.   22 ἀκούσας   δὲ
entered   into [the] land   of Israel.   But hearing

ὅτι   'Αρχέλαος   βασιλεύει   τῆς   'Ιουδαίας
that   Archelaus   reigns over   -   Judæa

ἀντὶ   τοῦ   πατρὸς   αὐτοῦ   'Ηρώδου   ἐφοβήθη
instead of   the   father   of him   Herod   he feared

ἐκεῖ   ἀπελθεῖν·   χρηματισθεὶς   δὲ   κατ'
there   to go;   and being warned   by

ὄναρ   ἀνεχώρησεν   εἰς   τὰ   μέρη   τῆς
a dream   he departed   into   the   parts   -

Γαλιλαίας,   23 καὶ   ἐλθὼν   κατώκησεν   εἰς
of Galilee,   and   coming   dwelt   in

πόλιν   λεγομένην   Ναζαρέθ·   ὅπως   πληρωθῇ
a city   called   Nazareth;   so that   was fulfilled

τὸ   ῥηθὲν   διὰ   τῶν   προφητῶν   ὅτι
the [thing]   spoken   through   the   prophets[,]   -

Ναζωραῖος   κληθήσεται.
A Nazarene   he shall be called.

CHAPTER 3

IN those days came John the Baptist, preaching in the wilderness of Judæa,

2 And saying, Repent ye: for the kingdom of heaven is at hand.

3 For this is he that was spoken of by the prophet Esaias, saying, The voice of one crying in the wilderness, Prepare ye the way of the Lord, make his paths straight.

3 'Εν   δὲ   ταῖς   ἡμέραις   ἐκείναις   παραγίνεται
Now in   -   days   those   arrives

'Ιωάννης   ὁ   βαπτιστὴς   κηρύσσων   ἐν   τῇ
John   the   Baptist   proclaiming   in   the

ἐρήμῳ   τῆς   'Ιουδαίας,   2 λέγων·   μετανοεῖτε·
wilderness   -   of Judæa,   saying: Repent ye;

ἤγγικεν   γὰρ   ἡ   βασιλεία   τῶν   οὐρανῶν.
for has come near   the   kingdom   of the   heavens.

3 οὗτος   γάρ   ἐστιν   ὁ   ῥηθεὶς   διὰ   'Ησαΐου
For this   is   the [one] spoken [of] through   Isaiah

τοῦ   προφήτου   λέγοντος·   φωνὴ   βοῶντος
the   prophet   saying: A voice   of [one] crying

ἐν   τῇ   ἐρήμῳ·   ἑτοιμάσατε   τὴν   ὁδὸν
in   the   wilderness: Prepare ye   the   way

κυρίου,   εὐθείας   ποιεῖτε   τὰς   τρίβους
of [the] Lord,   straight   make   the   paths

4 And the same John had his raiment of camel's hair, and a leathern girdle about his loins; and his meat was locusts and wild honey.

5 ¶ Then went out to him Jerusalem, and all Judæa, and all the region round about Jordan,

6 And were baptized of him in Jordan, confessing their sins.

7 But when he saw many of the Pharisees and Sadducees come to his baptism, he said unto them, O generation of vipers, who hath warned you to flee from the wrath to come?

8 Bring forth therefore fruits meet for repentance:

9 And think not to say within yourselves, We have Abraham to our father: for I say unto you, that God is able of these stones to raise up children unto Abraham.

10 And now also the ax is laid unto the root of the trees: therefore every tree which bringeth not forth good fruit is hewn down, and cast into the fire.

11 I indeed baptize you with water unto repentance: but he that cometh

αὐτοῦ. 4 Αὐτὸς δὲ ὁ Ἰωάννης εἶχεν
of him. Now ²himself – ¹John had

τὸ ἔνδυμα αὐτοῦ ἀπὸ τριχῶν καμήλου
the raiment of him from hairs of a camel

καὶ ζώνην δερματίνην περὶ τὴν ὀσφὺν
and a girdle leathern round the loin[s]

αὐτοῦ· ἡ δὲ τροφὴ ἦν αὐτοῦ ἀκρίδες
of him; and the food ²was ¹of him locusts

καὶ μέλι ἄγριον. 5 Τότε ἐξεπορεύετο πρὸς
and honey wild. Then went out to

αὐτὸν Ἱεροσόλυμα καὶ πᾶσα ἡ Ἰουδαία
him Jerusalem and all – Judæa

καὶ πᾶσα ἡ περίχωρος τοῦ Ἰορδάνου,
and all the neighbourhood of the Jordan,

6 καὶ ἐβαπτίζοντο ἐν τῷ Ἰορδάνῃ ποταμῷ
and were baptized in the Jordan river

ὑπ᾽ αὐτοῦ ἐξομολογούμενοι τὰς ἁμαρτίας
by him confessing the sins

αὐτῶν. 7 Ἰδὼν δὲ πολλοὺς τῶν
of them. And seeing many of the

Φαρισαίων καὶ Σαδδουκαίων ἐρχομένους
Pharisees and Sadducees coming

ἐπὶ τὸ βάπτισμα εἶπεν αὐτοῖς· γεννήματα
to the baptism he said to them: Offspring

ἐχιδνῶν, τίς ὑπέδειξεν ὑμῖν φυγεῖν ἀπὸ
of vipers, who warned you to flee from

τῆς μελλούσης ὀργῆς; 8 ποιήσατε οὖν
the coming wrath? Produce therefore

καρπὸν ἄξιον τῆς μετανοίας· 9 καὶ
fruit worthy – of repentance; and

μὴ δόξητε λέγειν ἐν ἑαυτοῖς· πατέρα
think not to say among [your]selves: ³[as] father

ἔχομεν τὸν Ἀβραάμ· λέγω γὰρ ὑμῖν ὅτι
¹We have – ²Abraham; for I tell you that

δύναται ὁ θεὸς ἐκ τῶν λίθων τούτων
²is able – ¹God out of – stones these

ἐγεῖραι τέκνα τῷ Ἀβραάμ. 10 ἤδη δὲ
to raise children – to Abraham. And already

ἡ ἀξίνη πρὸς τὴν ῥίζαν τῶν δένδρων
the axe at the root of the trees

κεῖται· πᾶν οὖν δένδρον μὴ ποιοῦν
is laid; therefore every tree not producing

καρπὸν καλὸν ἐκκόπτεται καὶ εἰς πῦρ
fruit good is cut down and into [the] fire

βάλλεται. 11 ἐγὼ μὲν ὑμᾶς βαπτίζω
is cast. I indeed you baptize

ἐν ὕδατι εἰς μετάνοιαν· ὁ δὲ
in water to repentance; but the [one]

after me is mightier than I, whose shoes I am not worthy to bear: he shall baptize you with the Holy Ghost, and *with* fire:

12 Whose fan *is* in his hand, and he will throughly purge his floor, and gather his wheat into the garner; but he will burn up the chaff with unquenchable fire.

13 ¶ Then cometh Jesus from Galilee to Jordan unto John, to be baptized of him.

14 But John forbad him, saying, I have need to be baptized of thee, and comest thou to me?

15 And Jesus answering said unto him, Suffer *it to be so* now: for thus it becometh us to fulfil all righteousness. Then he suffered him.

16 And Jesus, when he was baptized, went up straightway out of the water: and, lo, the heavens were opened unto him, and he saw the Spirit of God descending like a dove, and lighting upon him:

17 And lo a voice from heaven, saying, This is my beloved Son, in whom I am well pleased.

ὀπίσω μου ἐρχόμενος ἰσχυρότερός μού
after me coming ²stronger ²[than] ⁴I

ἐστιν, οὗ οὐκ εἰμὶ ἱκανὸς τὰ ὑποδήματα
¹is, of whom I am not worthy the sandals

βαστάσαι· αὐτὸς ὑμᾶς βαπτίσει ἐν πνεύματι
to bear; he ²you ¹will baptize in [the] Spirit

ἁγίῳ καὶ πυρί· 12 οὗ τὸ πτύον ἐν τῇ
Holy and fire; of whom the fan [is] in the

χειρὶ αὐτοῦ, καὶ διακαθαριεῖ τὴν ἅλωνα
hand of him, and he will thoroughly cleanse the threshing-floor

αὐτοῦ, καὶ συνάξει τὸν σῖτον αὐτοῦ
of him, and will gather the wheat of him

εἰς τὴν ἀποθήκην, τὸ δὲ ἄχυρον κατα-
into the barn, but the chaff he will

καύσει πυρὶ ἀσβέστῳ.
consume with fire unquenchable.

13 Τότε παραγίνεται ὁ Ἰησοῦς ἀπὸ τῆς
Then arrives – Jesus from –

Γαλιλαίας ἐπὶ τὸν Ἰορδάνην πρὸς τὸν
Galilee at the Jordan to –

Ἰωάννην τοῦ βαπτισθῆναι ὑπ' αὐτοῦ.
John – to be baptized[d] by him.

14 ὁ δὲ διεκώλυεν αὐτὸν λέγων· ἐγὼ
But he forbade him saying: I

χρείαν ἔχω ὑπὸ σοῦ βαπτισθῆναι, καὶ σὺ
²need ¹have ⁴by ⁵thee ³to be baptized, and thou

ἔρχῃ πρὸς μέ; 15 ἀποκριθεὶς δὲ ὁ
comest to me? But answering –

Ἰησοῦς εἶπεν αὐτῷ· ἄφες ἄρτι· οὕτως γὰρ
Jesus said to him: Permit now; for thus

πρέπον ἐστὶν ἡμῖν πληρῶσαι πᾶσαν
²fitting ¹it is to us to fulfil all

δικαιοσύνην. τότε ἀφίησιν αὐτόν.
righteousness. Then he permits him.

16 βαπτισθεὶς δὲ ὁ Ἰησοῦς εὐθὺς ἀνέβη
And having been baptized - Jesus immediately went up

ἀπὸ τοῦ ὕδατος· καὶ ἰδοὺ ἠνεῴχθησαν
from the water; and behold ²were opened

οἱ οὐρανοί, καὶ εἶδεν πνεῦμα θεοῦ
¹the ²heavens, and he saw [the] Spirit of God

καταβαῖνον ὡσεὶ περιστεράν, ἐρχόμενον ἐπ'
coming down as a dove, coming upon

αὐτόν· 17 καὶ ἰδοὺ φωνὴ ἐκ τῶν
him; and behold a voice out of the

οὐρανῶν λέγουσα· οὗτός ἐστιν ὁ υἱός
heavens saying: This is the son

μου ὁ ἀγαπητός, ἐν ᾧ εὐδόκησα.
of me the beloved, in whom I was well pleased.

CHAPTER 4

THEN was Jesus led up of the spirit into the wilderness to be tempted of the devil.

2 And when he had fasted forty days and forty nights, he was afterward an hungered.

3 And when the tempter came to him, he said, If thou be the Son of God, command that these stones be made bread.

4 But he answered and said, It is written, Man shall not live by bread alone, but by every word that proceedeth out of the mouth of God.

5 Then the devil taketh him up into the holy city, and setteth him on a pinnacle of the temple,

6 And saith unto him, If thou be the Son of God, cast thyself down: for it is written, He shall give his angels charge concerning thee: and in *their* hands they shall bear thee up, lest at any time thou dash thy foot against a stone.

7 Jesus said unto him, It is written again, Thou shalt not tempt the Lord thy God.

8 Again, the devil taketh him up into an exceeding high mountain, and sheweth him all the kingdoms of the world, and the glory of them;

---

4 Τότε ὁ Ἰησοῦς ἀνήχθη εἰς τὴν
Then - Jesus was led up into the

ἔρημον ὑπὸ τοῦ πνεύματος πειρασθῆναι
wilderness by the Spirit to be tempted

ὑπὸ τοῦ διαβόλου. **2** καὶ νηστεύσας ἡμέρας
by the devil. And having fasted days

τεσσεράκοντα καὶ τεσσεράκοντα νύκτας
forty and forty nights

ὕστερον ἐπείνασεν. **3** καὶ προσελθὼν ὁ
afterward he hungered. And approaching the

πειράζων εἶπεν αὐτῷ· εἰ υἱὸς εἶ τοῦ
tempting [one] said to him: If Son thou art -

θεοῦ, εἰπὲ ἵνα οἱ λίθοι οὗτοι ἄρτοι
of God, say *in order* that - stones these ²loaves

γένωνται. **4** ὁ δὲ ἀποκριθεὶς εἶπεν·
¹may become. But he answering said:

γέγραπται· οὐκ ἐπ' ἄρτῳ μόνῳ ζήσεται
It has been written: Not on bread only shall live

ὁ ἄνθρωπος, ἀλλ' ἐπὶ παντὶ ῥήματι
- man, but on every word

ἐκπορευομένῳ διὰ στόματος θεοῦ. **5** Τότε
proceeding through [the] mouth of God. Then

παραλαμβάνει αὐτὸν ὁ διάβολος εἰς τὴν
takes him the devil into the

ἁγίαν πόλιν, καὶ ἔστησεν αὐτὸν ἐπὶ τὸ
holy city, and stood him on the

πτερύγιον τοῦ ἱεροῦ, **6** καὶ λέγει αὐτῷ·
wing of the temple, and says to him:

εἰ υἱὸς εἶ τοῦ θεοῦ, βάλε σεαυτὸν
If Son thou art - of God, cast thyself

κάτω· γέγραπται γὰρ ὅτι τοῖς ἀγγέλοις
down; for it has been written[,] - To the angels

αὐτοῦ ἐντελεῖται περὶ σοῦ καὶ ἐπὶ χειρῶν
of him he will give command concerning thee and on hands

ἀροῦσίν σε, μήποτε προσκόψῃς πρὸς
they will bear thee, lest thou strike against

λίθον τὸν πόδα σου. **7** ἔφη αὐτῷ ὁ
a stone the foot of thee. Said to him -

Ἰησοῦς· πάλιν γέγραπται· οὐκ ἐκπειράσεις
Jesus: Again it has been written: Not overtempt shalt thou

κύριον τὸν θεόν σου. **8** Πάλιν παρα-
[the] Lord the God of thee. Again

λαμβάνει αὐτὸν ὁ διάβολος εἰς ὄρος
takes him the devil to a mountain

ὑψηλὸν λίαν, καὶ δείκνυσιν αὐτῷ πάσας
high exceedingly, and shows him all

τὰς βασιλείας τοῦ κόσμου καὶ τὴν
the kingdoms of the world and the

9 And saith unto him, All these things will I give thee, if thou wilt fall down and worship me.

10 Then saith Jesus unto him, Get thee hence, Satan: for it is written, Thou shalt worship the Lord thy God, and him only shalt thou serve.

11 Then the devil leaveth him, and, behold, angels came and ministered unto him.

12 ¶ Now when Jesus had heard that John was cast into prison, he departed into Galilee;

13 And leaving Nazareth, he came and dwelt in Capernaum, which is upon the sea coast, in the borders of Zabulon and Nephthalim:

14 That it might be fulfilled which was spoken by Esaias the prophet, saying,

15 The land of Zabulon, and the land of Nephthalim, by the way of the sea, beyond Jordan, Galilee of the Gentiles;

16 The people which sat in darkness saw great light; and to them which sat in the region and shadow of death light is sprung up.

17 From that time Jesus began to preach, and to say, Repent: for the kingdom of heaven is at hand.

δόξαν αὐτῶν, 9 καὶ εἶπεν αὐτῷ· ταῦτά
glory of them, and said to him: These things

σοι πάντα δώσω, ἐὰν πεσὼν προσκυνήσῃς
to thee all I will give, if falling thou wilt worship

μοι. 10 τότε λέγει αὐτῷ ὁ Ἰησοῦς·
me. Then says to him – Jesus:

ὕπαγε, σατανᾶ· γέγραπται γάρ· κύριον
Go, Satan; for it has been written: [The] Lord

τὸν θεόν σου προσκυνήσεις καὶ αὐτῷ
the God of thee thou shalt worship and him

μόνῳ λατρεύσεις. 11 Τότε ἀφίησιν αὐτὸν
only thou shalt serve. Then leaves him

ὁ διάβολος, καὶ ἰδοὺ ἄγγελοι προσῆλθον
the devil, and behold angels approached

καὶ διηκόνουν αὐτῷ.
and ministered to him.

12 Ἀκούσας δὲ ὅτι Ἰωάννης παρεδόθη
Now hearing that John was delivered up

ἀνεχώρησεν εἰς τὴν Γαλιλαίαν. 13 καὶ
he departed to – Galilee. And

καταλιπὼν τὴν Ναζαρὰ ἐλθὼν κατῴκησεν
leaving – Nazareth coming he dwelt

εἰς Καφαρναοὺμ τὴν παραθαλασσίαν ἐν
in Capernaum – beside the sea in [the]

ὁρίοις Ζαβουλὼν καὶ Νεφθαλίμ· 14 ἵνα
districts of Zebulon and Naphthali; in order that

πληρωθῇ τὸ ῥηθὲν διὰ Ἡσαΐου
might be fulfilled the [thing] spoken through Isaiah

τοῦ προφήτου λέγοντος· 15 γῆ Ζαβουλὼν
the prophet saying: Land of Zebulon

καὶ γῆ Νεφθαλίμ, ὁδὸν θαλάσσης,
and land of Naphthali, way of [the] sea,

πέραν τοῦ Ἰορδάνου, Γαλιλαία τῶν ἐθνῶν,
beyond the Jordan, Galilee of the nations,

16 ὁ λαὸς ὁ καθήμενος ἐν σκοτίᾳ φῶς
the people – sitting in darkness ¹light

εἶδεν μέγα, καὶ τοῖς καθημένοις ἐν
¹saw ²a great, and to the [ones] sitting in

χώρᾳ καὶ σκιᾷ θανάτου, φῶς ἀνέτειλεν
a land and shadow of death, light sprang up

αὐτοῖς.
to them.

17 Ἀπὸ τότε ἤρξατο ὁ Ἰησοῦς κηρύσσειν
From then began – Jesus to proclaim

καὶ λέγειν· μετανοεῖτε· ἤγγικεν γὰρ
and to say: Repent ye; for has drawn near

ἡ βασιλεία τῶν οὐρανῶν.
the kingdom of the heavens.

18 ¶ And Jesus, walking by the sea of Galilee, saw two brethren, Simon called Peter, and Andrew his brother, casting a net into the sea: for they were fishers.

19 And he saith unto them, Follow me, and I will make you fishers of men.

20 And they straightway left *their* nets, and followed him.

21 And going on from thence, he saw other two brethren, James *the son* of Zebedee, and John his brother, in a ship with Zebedee their father, mending their nets; and he called them.

22 And they immediately left the ship and their father, and followed him.

23 ¶ And Jesus went about all Galilee, teaching in their synagogues, and preaching the gospel of the kingdom, and healing all manner of sickness and all manner of disease among the people.

24 And his fame went throughout all Syria: and they brought unto him all sick people that were taken with divers diseases and

18 Περιπατῶν δὲ παρὰ τὴν θάλασσαν
And walking beside the sea
τῆς Γαλιλαίας εἶδεν δύο ἀδελφούς, Σίμωνα
- of Galilee he saw two brothers, Simon
τὸν λεγόμενον Πέτρον καὶ Ἀνδρέαν τὸν
- called Peter and Andrew the
ἀδελφὸν αὐτοῦ, βάλλοντας ἀμφίβληστρον εἰς
brother of him, casting a net into
τὴν θάλασσαν· ἦσαν γὰρ ἁλεεῖς. 19 καὶ
the sea; for they were fishers. And
λέγει αὐτοῖς· δεῦτε ὀπίσω μου, καὶ
he says to them: Come after me, and
ποιήσω ὑμᾶς ἁλεεῖς ἀνθρώπων. 20 οἱ
I will make you fishers of men. [2]they
δὲ εὐθέως ἀφέντες τὰ δίκτυα ἠκολούθη-
[1]And immediately leaving the nets fol-
σαν αὐτῷ. 21 Καὶ προβὰς ἐκεῖθεν εἶδεν
lowed him. And going on thence he saw
ἄλλους δύο ἀδελφούς, Ἰάκωβον τὸν τοῦ
other two brothers, James the [son] -
Ζεβεδαίου καὶ Ἰωάννην τὸν ἀδελφὸν
of Zebedee and John the brother
αὐτοῦ, ἐν τῷ πλοίῳ μετὰ Ζεβεδαίου τοῦ
of him, in the boat with Zebedee the
πατρὸς αὐτῶν καταρτίζοντας τὰ δίκτυα
father of them mending the nets
αὐτῶν· καὶ ἐκάλεσεν αὐτούς. 22 οἱ δὲ
of them; and he called them. And they
εὐθέως ἀφέντες τὸ πλοῖον καὶ τὸν
immediately leaving the boat and the
πατέρα αὐτῶν ἠκολούθησαν αὐτῷ.
father of them followed him.
23 Καὶ περιῆγεν ἐν ὅλῃ τῇ Γαλιλαίᾳ,
And he went about in all - Galilee,
διδάσκων ἐν ταῖς συναγωγαῖς αὐτῶν
teaching in the synagogues of them
καὶ κηρύσσων τὸ εὐαγγέλιον τῆς βασιλείας
and proclaiming the gospel of the kingdom
καὶ θεραπεύων πᾶσαν νόσον καὶ πᾶσαν
and healing every disease and every
μαλακίαν ἐν τῷ λαῷ. 24 καὶ ἀπῆλθεν ἡ
illness among the people. And went the
ἀκοὴ αὐτοῦ εἰς ὅλην τὴν Συρίαν· καὶ
report of him into all - Syria; and
προσήνεγκαν αὐτῷ πάντας τοὺς κακῶς
they brought to him all the [ones] [2]ill
=those who were ill
ἔχοντας ποικίλαις νόσοις καὶ βασάνοις
[1]having [2]various [3]diseases [4]and [5]tortures

torments, and those which were possessed with devils, and those which were lunatick, and those that had the palsy; and he healed them.

25 And there followed him great multitudes of people from Galilee, and *from* Decapolis, and *from* Jerusalem, and *from* Judæa, and *from* beyond Jordan.

συνεχομένους, δαιμονιζομένους καὶ σεληνιαζ-
¹suffering from,   demon-possessed   and   luna-

ομένους καὶ παραλυτικούς, καὶ ἐθεράπευσεν
tics   and   paralysed,   and   he healed

αὐτούς. 25 καὶ ἠκολούθησαν αὐτῷ ὄχλοι
them.   And   ³followed   ⁴him   ²crowds

πολλοὶ ἀπὸ τῆς Γαλιλαίας καὶ Δεκαπόλεως
¹many   from –   Galilee   and   Decapolis

καὶ Ἱεροσολύμων καὶ Ἰουδαίας καὶ πέραν
and   Jerusalem   and   Judæa   and   beyond

τοῦ Ἰορδάνου.
the   Jordan.

CHAPTER 5

AND seeing the multitudes, he went up into a mountain: and when he was set, his disciples came unto him:

2 And he opened his mouth, and taught them, saying,

3 Blessed *are* the poor in spirit: for their's is the kingdom of heaven.

4 Blessed *are* they that mourn: for they shall be comforted.

5 Blessed *are* the meek: for they shall inherit the earth.

6 Blessed *are* they which do hunger and thirst after righteousness: for they shall be filled.

7 Blessed *are* the merciful: for they shall obtain mercy.

8 Blessed *are* the pure in heart: for they shall see God.

9 Blessed *are* the peacemakers: for they shall be called the children of God.

10 Blessed *are* they which are persecuted for righteousness' sake: for

5 Ἰδὼν δὲ τοὺς ὄχλους ἀνέβη εἰς
And seeing   the   crowds   he went up   into

τὸ ὄρος· καὶ καθίσαντος αὐτοῦ προσῆλθαν
the mountain;   and   sitting   him*   ⁴approached
=when he sat

αὐτῷ οἱ μαθηταὶ αὐτοῦ· 2 καὶ ἀνοίξας τὸ
⁵to him ¹the ²disciples ³of him;   and   opening   the

στόμα αὐτοῦ ἐδίδασκεν αὐτοὺς λέγων·
mouth   of him   he taught   them   saying:

3 Μακάριοι οἱ πτωχοὶ τῷ πνεύματι,
Blessed [are]   the   poor –   in spirit,

ὅτι αὐτῶν ἐστιν ἡ βασιλεία τῶν οὐρανῶν.
for of them   is   the   kingdom   of the   heavens.

4 μακάριοι οἱ πενθοῦντες, ὅτι αὐτοὶ
Blessed [are]   the   mourning [ones],   for   they

παρακληθήσονται. 5 μακάριοι οἱ πραεῖς,
shall be comforted.   Blessed [are]   the   meek,

ὅτι αὐτοὶ κληρονομήσουσιν τὴν γῆν.
for   they   shall inherit   the   earth.

6 μακάριοι οἱ πεινῶντες καὶ διψῶντες
Blessed [are]   the   hungering   and   thirsting [ones] [after]

τὴν δικαιοσύνην, ὅτι αὐτοὶ χορτασ-
 –   righteousness,   for   they   shall be

θήσονται. 7 μακάριοι οἱ ἐλεήμονες, ὅτι
satisfied.   Blessed [are]   the   merciful,   for

αὐτοὶ ἐλεηθήσονται. 8 μακάριοι οἱ καθαροὶ
they   shall obtain mercy.   Blessed [are]   the   clean

τῇ καρδίᾳ, ὅτι αὐτοὶ τὸν θεὸν ὄψονται.
 –   in heart,   for   they –   ²God   ¹shall see.

9 μακάριοι οἱ εἰρηνοποιοί, ὅτι [αὐτοὶ]
Blessed [are]   the   peacemakers,   for   they

υἱοὶ θεοῦ κληθήσονται. 10 μακάριοι οἱ
sons of God   shall be called.   Blessed [are] the [ones]

δεδιωγμένοι ἕνεκεν δικαιοσύνης, ὅτι αὐτῶν
having been persecuted for the sake of righteousness, for of them

their's is the kingdom of heaven.

11 Blessed are ye, when *men* shall revile you, and persecute *you*, and shall say all manner of evil against you falsely, for my sake.

12 Rejoice, and be exceeding glad: for great *is* your reward in heaven: for so persecuted they the prophets which were before you.

13 ¶ Ye are the salt of the earth: but if the salt have lost his savour, wherewith shall it be salted? it is thenceforth good for nothing, but to be cast out, and to be trodden under foot of men.

14 Ye are the light of the world. A city that is set on an hill cannot be hid.

15 Neither do men light a candle, and put it under a bushel, but on a candlestick; and it giveth light unto all that are in the house.

16 Let your light so shine before men, that they may see your good works, and glorify your Father which is in heaven.

17 ¶ Think not that I am come to destroy the law, or the prophets: I am not come to destroy, but to fulfil.

ἐστιν ἡ βασιλεία τῶν οὐρανῶν. 11 μακάριοί
is the kingdom of the heavens. Blessed

ἐστε ὅταν ὀνειδίσωσιν ὑμᾶς καὶ διώξωσιν
are ye when they reproach you and persecute

καὶ εἴπωσιν πᾶν πονηρὸν καθ᾽ ὑμῶν
and say all evil against you

ψευδόμενοι ἕνεκεν ἐμοῦ. 12 χαίρετε
lying for the sake of me. Rejoice

καὶ ἀγαλλιᾶσθε, ὅτι ὁ μισθὸς ὑμῶν
and be glad, because the reward of you [is]

πολὺς ἐν τοῖς οὐρανοῖς· οὕτως γὰρ
much in the heavens; for thus

ἐδίωξαν τοὺς προφήτας τοὺς πρὸ
they persecuted the prophets – before

ὑμῶν.
you.

13 Ὑμεῖς ἐστε τὸ ἅλας τῆς γῆς· ἐὰν δὲ
Ye are the salt of the earth; but if

τὸ ἅλας μωρανθῇ, ἐν τίνι ἁλισθήσεται;
the salt be tainted, by what shall it be salted?

εἰς οὐδὲν ἰσχύει ἔτι εἰ μὴ βληθὲν ἔξω
for nothing is it strong longer except being cast out

καταπατεῖσθαι ὑπὸ τῶν ἀνθρώπων. 14 Ὑμεῖς
to be trodden down by – men. Ye

ἐστε τὸ φῶς τοῦ κόσμου. οὐ δύναται
are the light of the world. ⁹Not ⁸can

πόλις κρυβῆναι ἐπάνω ὄρους κειμένη·
¹a city ⁷to be hid ³on ⁴a mountain ⁵set;

15 οὐδὲ καίουσιν λύχνον καὶ τιθέασιν
nor do they light a lamp and place

αὐτὸν ὑπὸ τὸν μόδιον, ἀλλ᾽ ἐπὶ τὴν
it under the bushel, but on the

λυχνίαν, καὶ λάμπει πᾶσιν τοῖς ἐν τῇ
lampstand, and it lightens all the [ones] in the

οἰκίᾳ. 16 οὕτως λαμψάτω τὸ φῶς ὑμῶν
house. Thus let shine the light of you

ἔμπροσθεν τῶν ἀνθρώπων, ὅπως ἴδωσιν
before – men, so that they may see

ὑμῶν τὰ καλὰ ἔργα καὶ δοξάσωσιν
of you the good works and may glorify

τὸν πατέρα ὑμῶν τὸν ἐν τοῖς οὐρανοῖς.
the Father of you – in the heavens.

17 Μὴ νομίσητε ὅτι ἦλθον καταλῦσαι
Think not that I came to destroy

τὸν νόμον ἢ τοὺς προφήτας· οὐκ ἦλθον
the law or the prophets; I came not

καταλῦσαι ἀλλὰ πληρῶσαι. 18 ἀμὴν γὰρ
to destroy but to fulfil. For truly

18 For verily I say unto you, Till heaven and earth pass, one jot or one tittle shall in no wise pass from the law, till all be fulfilled.

19 Whosoever therefore shall break one of these least commandments, and shall teach men so, he shall be called the least in the kingdom of heaven: but whosoever shall do and teach *them*, the same shall be called great in the kingdom of heaven.

20 For I say unto you, That except your righteousness shall exceed *the righteousness* of the scribes and Pharisees, ye shall in no case enter into the kingdom of heaven.

21 ¶ Ye have heard that it was said by them of old time, Thou shalt not kill; and whosoever shall kill shall be in danger of the judgment:

22 But I say unto you, That whosoever is angry with his brother without a cause shall be in danger of the judgment: and whosoever shall say to his brother, Raca, shall be in danger of the council: but whosoever shall say, Thou fool, shall be in danger of hell fire.

23 Therefore if thou bring thy gift to the altar, and there rememberest that thy brother hath ought against thee;

λέγω ὑμῖν, ἕως ἂν παρέλθῃ ὁ οὐρανὸς
I say to you, until pass away the heaven

καὶ ἡ γῆ, ἰῶτα ἓν ἢ μία κεραία οὐ
and the earth, iota one or one point by no

μὴ παρέλθῃ ἀπὸ τοῦ νόμου, ἕως ἂν
means shall pass away from the law, until

πάντα γένηται. 19 ὃς ἐὰν οὖν λύσῃ
all things come to pass. ²Whoever ¹therefore breaks

μίαν τῶν ἐντολῶν τούτων τῶν ἐλαχίστων
one - commandments of these the least

καὶ διδάξῃ οὕτως τοὺς ἀνθρώπους, ἐλάχιστος
and teaches thus - men, least

κληθήσεται ἐν τῇ βασιλείᾳ τῶν οὐρανῶν·
he shall be called in the kingdom of the heavens;

ὃς δ' ἂν ποιήσῃ καὶ διδάξῃ, οὗτος
but whoever does and teaches, this [one]

μέγας κληθήσεται ἐν τῇ βασιλεια τῶν
great shall be called in the kingdom of the

οὐρανῶν. 20 λέγω γὰρ ὑμῖν ὅτι ἐὰν μὴ
heavens. For I tell you that except

περισσεύσῃ ὑμῶν ἡ δικαιοσύνη πλεῖον
shall exceed of you the righteousness more [than] [that]

τῶν γραμματέων καὶ Φαρισαίων, οὐ μὴ
of the scribes and Pharisees, by no means

εἰσέλθητε εἰς τὴν βασιλείαν τῶν οὐρανῶν.
shall ye enter into the kingdom of the heavens.

21 Ἠκούσατε ὅτι ἐρρέθη τοῖς ἀρχαίοις·
Ye heard that it was said to the ancients:

οὐ φονεύσεις· ὃς δ' ἂν φονεύσῃ,
Thou shalt not kill; and whoever kills,

ἔνοχος ἔσται τῇ κρίσει. 22 ἐγὼ δὲ
liable shall be to the judgment. But I

λέγω ὑμῖν ὅτι πᾶς ὁ ὀργιζόμενος τῷ
tell you that everyone being angry with the

ἀδελφῷ αὐτοῦ ἔνοχος ἔσται τῇ κρίσει·
brother of him liable shall be to the judgment;

ὃς δ' ἂν εἴπῃ τῷ ἀδελφῷ αὐτοῦ ρ α κ ά ,
and whoever says to the brother of him[,] Raca,

ἔνοχος ἔσται τῷ συνεδρίῳ· ὃς δ' ἂν εἴπῃ
liable shall be to the council; and whoever says[,]

μωρέ, ἔνοχος ἔσται εἰς τὴν γέενναν
Fool, liable shall be to the gehenna

τοῦ πυρός. 23 ἐὰν οὖν προσφέρῃς τὸ
- of fire. Therefore if thou bringest the

δῶρόν σου ἐπὶ τὸ θυσιαστήριον κἀκεῖ
gift of thee to the altar and there

μνησθῇς ὅτι ὁ ἀδελφός σου ἔχει τι
rememberest that the brother of thee has something

24 Leave there thy gift before the altar, and go thy way; first be reconciled to thy brother, and then come and offer thy gift.

25 Agree with thine adversary quickly, whiles thou art in the way with him; lest at any time the adversary deliver thee to the judge, and the judge deliver thee to the officer, and thou be cast into prison.

26 Verily I say unto thee, Thou shalt by no means come out thence, till thou hast paid the uttermost farthing.

27 ¶ Ye have heard that it was said by them of old time, Thou shalt not commit adultery:

28 But I say unto you, That whosoever looketh on a woman to lust after her hath committed adultery with her already in his heart.

29 And if thy right eye offend thee, pluck it out, and cast it from thee : for it is profitable for thee that one of thy members should perish, and not that thy whole body should be cast into hell.

30 And if thy right hand offend thee, cut it off, and cast it from thee: for it is profitable for thee that one of thy members should perish, and not that thy whole body should be cast into hell.

κατὰ σοῦ,   24 ἄφες ἐκεῖ τὸ δῶρόν σου
against thee,   leave there the gift of thee

ἔμπροσθεν τοῦ θυσιαστηρίου, καὶ ὕπαγε
before the altar, and go

πρῶτον διαλλάγηθι τῷ ἀδελφῷ σου, καὶ
first be reconciled to the brother of thee, and

τότε ἐλθὼν πρόσφερε τὸ δῶρόν σου.
then coming offer the gift of thee.

25 ἴσθι εὐνοῶν τῷ ἀντιδίκῳ σου
Be well disposed to the opponent of thee

ταχὺ ἕως ὅτου εἶ μετ᾽ αὐτοῦ ἐν τῇ
quickly while thou art with him in the

ὁδῷ· μήποτέ σε παραδῷ ὁ ἀντίδικος τῷ
way; lest ⁴thee ³deliver ¹the ²opponent to the

κριτῇ καὶ ὁ κριτὴς τῷ ὑπηρέτῃ, καὶ
judge and the judge to the attendant, and

εἰς φυλακὴν βληθήσῃ. 26 ἀμὴν λέγω
into prison thou be cast; truly I say

σοι, οὐ μὴ ἐξέλθῃς ἐκεῖθεν ἕως ἂν
to thee, by no means shalt thou come out thence until

ἀποδῷς τὸν ἔσχατον κοδράντην.
thou repayest the last farthing.

27 Ἠκούσατε ὅτι ἐρρέθη· οὐ μοιχεύσεις.
Ye heard that it was said: Thou shalt not commit adultery.

28 ἐγὼ δὲ λέγω ὑμῖν ὅτι πᾶς ὁ βλέπων
But I tell you that everyone seeing

γυναῖκα πρὸς τὸ ἐπιθυμῆσαι [αὐτὴν]
a woman with a view – to desire her

ἤδη ἐμοίχευσεν αὐτὴν ἐν τῇ καρδίᾳ
already committed adultery with her in the heart

αὐτοῦ. 29 εἰ δὲ ὁ ὀφθαλμός σου ὁ δεξιὸς
of him. So if the ²eye ³of thee – ¹right

σκανδαλίζει σε, ἔξελε αὐτὸν καὶ βάλε
⁴causes ⁵to stumble ⁵thee, pluck out it and cast

ἀπὸ σοῦ· συμφέρει γάρ σοι ἵνα ἀπόληται
from thee; for it is expedient for thee that ¹perish

ἐν τῶν μελῶν σου καὶ μὴ ὅλον τὸ
¹one ²of the ³members ⁴of thee and not all the

σῶμά σου βληθῇ εἰς γέενναν. 30 καὶ
body of thee be cast into gehenna. And

εἰ ἡ δεξιά σου χείρ σκανδαλίζει σε, ἔκκοψον
if the ¹right ⁴of thee ²hand ⁴causes ⁵to stumble ⁵thee, cut out

αὐτὴν καὶ βάλε ἀπὸ σοῦ· συμφέρει γάρ
it and cast from thee; for it is expedient

σοι ἵνα ἀπόληται ἐν τῶν μελῶν σου
for thee that ⁵perish ¹one ²of the ³members ⁴of thee

καὶ μὴ ὅλον τὸ σῶμά σου εἰς γέενναν
and not all the body of thee into gehenna

31 ¶ It hath been said, Whosoever shall put away his wife, let him give her a writing of divorcement:

32 But I say unto you, That whosoever shall put away his wife, saving for the cause of fornication, causeth her to commit adultery: and whosoever shall marry her that is divorced committeth adultery.

33 ¶ Again, ye have heard that it hath been said by them of old time, Thou shalt not forswear thyself, but shalt perform unto the Lord thine oaths:

34 But I say unto you, Swear not at all; neither by heaven; for it is God's throne:

35 Nor by the earth; for it is his footstool: neither by Jerusalem; for it is the city of the great King.

36 Neither shalt thou swear by thy head, because thou canst not make one hair white or black.

37 But let your communication be, Yea, yea; Nay, nay: for whatsoever is more than these cometh of evil.

38 ¶ Ye have heard that it hath been said, An eye for an eye, and a tooth for a tooth:

39 But I say unto you, That ye resist not evil: but whosoever shall smite thee on thy right cheek, turn to him the other also.

ἀπέλθῃ. **31** Ἐρρέθη δέ· ὃς ἂν ἀπολύσῃ
go away.   And it was said: Whoever   dismisses

τὴν γυναῖκα αὐτοῦ, δότω αὐτῇ ἀποστάσιον.
the   wife   of him, let him give   her   a bill of divorce.

32 ἐγὼ δὲ λέγω ὑμῖν ὅτι πᾶς ὁ ἀπολύων
But I   tell   you   that everyone   dismissing

τὴν γυναῖκα αὐτοῦ παρεκτὸς λόγου
the   wife   of him   apart from   a matter

πορνείας ποιεῖ αὐτὴν μοιχευθῆναι,
of fornication   makes   her   *to* commit adultery,

καὶ ὃς ἐὰν ἀπολελυμένην γαμήσῃ,
and   whoever   ²a dismissed [woman]   ¹marries,

μοιχᾶται. **33** Πάλιν ἠκούσατε ὅτι ἐρρέθη
commits adultery.   Again   ye heard   that   it was said

τοῖς ἀρχαίοις· οὐκ ἐπιορκήσεις, ἀποδώσεις
to the   ancients: Thou shalt not perjure,   ²shalt repay

δὲ τῷ κυρίῳ τοὺς ὅρκους σου. **34** ἐγὼ δὲ
¹but to the Lord   the   oaths   of thee.   But I

λέγω ὑμῖν μὴ ὀμόσαι ὅλως· μήτε ἐν τῷ
tell   you   not   to swear   at all;   neither   by   the

οὐρανῷ, ὅτι θρόνος ἐστὶν τοῦ θεοῦ·
heaven,   because [the] throne   it is   –   of God;

35 μήτε ἐν τῇ γῇ, ὅτι ὑποπόδιόν
nor   by   the   earth,   because   footstool

ἐστιν τῶν ποδῶν αὐτοῦ· μήτε εἰς
it is   of the   feet   of him;   nor   by

Ἱεροσόλυμα, ὅτι πόλις ἐστὶν τοῦ μεγάλου
Jerusalem,   because   city   it is   of the   great

βασιλέως· **36** μήτε ἐν τῇ κεφαλῇ σου
King;   nor   by   the   head   of thee

ὀμόσῃς, ὅτι οὐ δύνασαι μίαν τρίχα
swear,   because   thou canst not   one   hair

λευκὴν ποιῆσαι ἢ μέλαιναν. **37** ἔστω
white   *to* make   or   black.   ³let ⁶be

δὲ ὁ λόγος ὑμῶν ναὶ ναί, οὒ οὔ·
¹But ²the   ⁴word   ⁵of you   Yes   yes,   No   no;

τὸ δὲ περισσὸν τούτων ἐκ τοῦ πονηροῦ
for the   excess   of these   of   –   evil

ἐστιν. **38** Ἠκούσατε ὅτι ἐρρέθη· ὀφθαλμὸν
is.   Ye heard   that   it was said: An eye

ἀντὶ ὀφθαλμοῦ καὶ ὀδόντα ἀντὶ ὀδόντος.
instead of an eye   and   a tooth   instead of   a tooth.

39 ἐγὼ δὲ λέγω ὑμῖν μὴ ἀντιστῆναι
But I   tell   you   not   to oppose

τῷ πονηρῷ· ἀλλ' ὅστις σε ῥαπίζει εἰς
–   evil;   but   who   thee   strikes   on

τὴν δεξιὰν σιαγόνα [σου], στρέψον αὐτῷ
the   right   cheek   of thee,   turn   to him

40 And if any man will sue thee at the law, and take away thy coat, let him have *thy* cloke also.

41 And whosoever shall compel thee to go a mile, go with him twain.

42 Give to him that asketh thee, and from him that would borrow of thee turn not thou away.

43 ¶ Ye have heard that it hath been said, Thou shalt love thy neighbour, and hate thine enemy.

44 But I say unto you, Love your enemies, bless them that curse you, do good to them that hate you, and pray for them which despitefully use you, and persecute you;

45 That ye may be the children of your Father which is in heaven: for he maketh his sun to rise on the evil and on the good, and sendeth rain on the just and on the unjust.

46 For if ye love them which love you, what reward have ye? do not even the publicans the same?

47 And if ye salute your brethren only, what do ye more *than others*? do not even the publicans so?

48 Be ye therefore perfect, even as your Father which is in heaven is perfect.

καὶ τὴν ἄλλην· **40** καὶ τῷ θέλοντί
also the other;   and to the [one] wishing

σοι κριθῆναι καὶ τὸν χιτῶνά σου λαβεῖν,
thee to judge and the tunic of thee to take,

ἄφες αὐτῷ καὶ τὸ ἱμάτιον· **41** καὶ
allow him also the [outer] garment;   and

ὅστις σε ἀγγαρεύσει μίλιον ἕν, ὕπαγε
who ²thee ¹shall impress ⁴mile ³one, go

μετ' αὐτοῦ δύο. **42** τῷ αἰτοῦντί
with him two.   To the [one] asking

σε δός, καὶ τὸν θέλοντα ἀπὸ σοῦ
thee give, and the [one] wishing from thee

δανείσασθαι μὴ ἀποστραφῇς. **43** Ἠκούσατε
to borrow turn not away.   Ye heard

ὅτι ἐρρέθη· ἀγαπήσεις τὸν πλησίον σου
that it was said: Thou shalt love the neighbour of thee

καὶ μισήσεις τὸν ἐχθρόν σου. **44** ἐγὼ
and thou shalt hate the enemy of thee.   ¹I

δὲ λέγω ὑμῖν· ἀγαπᾶτε τοὺς ἐχθροὺς
¹But tell you: Love ye the enemies

ὑμῶν καὶ προσεύχεσθε ὑπὲρ τῶν
of you and pray ye for the [ones]

διωκόντων ὑμᾶς· **45** ὅπως γένησθε υἱοὶ
persecuting you;   so that ye may become sons

τοῦ πατρὸς ὑμῶν τοῦ ἐν οὐρανοῖς,
of the Father of you – in heavens,

ὅτι τὸν ἥλιον αὐτοῦ ἀνατέλλει ἐπὶ
because the sun of him he makes to rise on

πονηροὺς καὶ ἀγαθοὺς καὶ βρέχει ἐπὶ
evil men and good and rains on

δικαίους καὶ ἀδίκους. **46** ἐὰν γὰρ
just men and unjust.   For if

ἀγαπήσητε τοὺς ἀγαπῶντας ὑμᾶς, τίνα
ye love the [ones] loving you, what

μισθὸν ἔχετε; οὐχὶ καὶ οἱ τελῶναι τὸ
reward have ye? ²not ³even ⁴the ¹tax-collectors ⁶the

αὐτὸ ποιοῦσιν; **47** καὶ ἐὰν ἀσπάσησθε
⁷same ¹do?   and if ye greet

τοὺς ἀδελφοὺς ὑμῶν μόνον, τί περισσὸν
the brothers of you only, what excess

ποιεῖτε; οὐχὶ καὶ οἱ ἐθνικοὶ τὸ αὐτὸ
do ye? ²not ³even ⁴the ⁵gentiles ⁶the ⁷same

ποιοῦσιν; **48** Ἔσεσθε οὖν ὑμεῖς τέλειοι
¹do?   Be therefore ye perfect

ὡς ὁ πατὴρ ὑμῶν ὁ οὐράνιος τέλειός
as the ²Father ³of you – ¹heavenly perfect

ἐστιν.
is.

CHAPTER 6

TAKE heed that ye do not your alms before men, to be seen of them: otherwise ye have no reward of your Father which is in heaven.

2 Therefore when thou doest *thine* alms, do not sound a trumpet before thee, as the hypocrites do in the synagogues and in the streets, that they may have glory of men. Verily I say unto you, They have their reward.

3 But when thou doest alms, let not thy left hand know what thy right hand doeth:

4 That thine alms may be in secret: and thy Father which seeth in secret himself shall reward thee openly.

5 ¶ And when thou prayest, thou shalt not be as the hypocrites *are:* for they love to pray standing in the synagogues and in the corners of the streets, that they may be seen of men. Verily I say unto you, They have their reward.

6 But thou, when thou prayest, enter into thy closet, and when thou hast shut thy door, pray to thy Father which is in secret;

6 Προσέχετε δὲ τὴν δικαιοσύνην ὑμῶν
And take ye heed the righteousness of you

μὴ ποιεῖν ἔμπροσθεν τῶν ἀνθρώπων πρὸς
not to do in front of — men with a view to

τὸ θεαθῆναι αὐτοῖς· εἰ δὲ μή γε, μισθὸν
— to be seen by them; otherwise, reward

οὐκ ἔχετε παρὰ τῷ πατρὶ ὑμῶν τῷ
ye have not with the Father of you —

ἐν τοῖς οὐρανοῖς. **2** Ὅταν οὖν ποιῇς
in the heavens. [2]When [1]therefore thou doest

ἐλεημοσύνην, μὴ σαλπίσῃς ἔμπροσθέν σου,
alms, sound not a trumpet before thee,

ὥσπερ οἱ ὑποκριταὶ ποιοῦσιν ἐν ταῖς
as the hypocrites do in the

συναγωγαῖς καὶ ἐν ταῖς ῥύμαις, ὅπως
synagogues and in the streets, so that

δοξασθῶσιν ὑπὸ τῶν ἀνθρώπων· ἀμὴν
they may be glorified by — men; truly

λέγω ὑμῖν, ἀπέχουσιν τὸν μισθὸν αὐτῶν.
I tell you, they have the reward of them.

3 σοῦ δὲ ποιοῦντος[a] ἐλεημοσύνην μὴ
But thee doing[a] alms not
= when thou doest

γνώτω ἡ ἀριστερά σου τί ποιεῖ ἡ
let know the left [hand] of thee what does the

δεξιά σου, **4** ὅπως ᾖ σου ἡ ἐλεημοσύνη
right of thee, so that [4]may be [3]of thee [1]the [2]alms

ἐν τῷ κρυπτῷ· καὶ ὁ πατήρ σου
in — secret; and the Father of thee

ὁ βλέπων ἐν τῷ κρυπτῷ ἀποδώσει σοι.
the [one] seeing in — secret will repay thee.

5 Καὶ ὅταν προσεύχησθε, οὐκ ἔσεσθε
And when ye pray, be not ye

ὡς οἱ ὑποκριταί· ὅτι φιλοῦσιν ἐν ταῖς
as the hypocrites; because they love in the

συναγωγαῖς καὶ ἐν ταῖς γωνίαις τῶν
synagogues and in the corners of the

πλατειῶν ἑστῶτες προσεύχεσθαι, ὅπως
open streets standing to pray, so that

φανῶσιν τοῖς ἀνθρώποις· ἀμὴν λέγω
they may appear — to men; truly I tell

ὑμῖν, ἀπέχουσιν τὸν μισθὸν αὐτῶν. **6** σὺ
you, they have the reward of them. [2]thou

δὲ ὅταν προσεύχῃ, εἴσελθε εἰς τὸ ταμιεῖόν
[1]But [3]when [4]prayest, enter into the private room

σου καὶ κλείσας τὴν θύραν σου πρόσευξαι
of thee and having shut the door of thee pray

τῷ πατρί σου τῷ ἐν τῷ κρυπτῷ·
to the Father of thee the [one] in — secret;

and thy Father which seeth in secret shall reward thee openly.

7 But when ye pray, use not vain repetitions, as the heathen *do*: for they think that they shall be heard for their much speaking.

8 Be not ye therefore like unto them: for your Father knoweth what things ye have need of, before ye ask him.

9 After this manner therefore pray ye: Our Father which art in heaven, Hallowed be thy name.

10 Thy kingdom come. Thy will be done in earth, as *it is* in heaven.

11 Give us this day our daily bread.

12 And forgive us our debts, as we forgive our debtors.

13 And lead us not into temptation, but deliver us from evil: For thine is the kingdom, and the power, and the glory, for ever. Amen.

14 For if ye forgive men their trespasses, your heavenly Father will also forgive you:

15 But if ye forgive not men their trespasses, neither will your Father forgive your trespasses.

16¶ Moreover when ye fast, be not, as the hypocrites, of a sad counte-

καὶ   ὁ   πατήρ   σου   ὁ   βλέπων   ἐν   τῷ
and   the   Father   of thee   the [one]   seeing   in   -

κρυπτῷ   ἀποδώσει   σοι.   7 Προσευχόμενοι   δὲ
secret   will repay   thee.   But praying

μὴ   βατταλογήσητε   ὥσπερ   οἱ   ἐθνικοί·
do not utter empty words   as   the   gentiles;

δοκοῦσιν   γὰρ   ὅτι   ἐν   τῇ   πολυλογίᾳ   αὐτῶν
for they think   that   in   the   much speaking   of them

εἰσακουσθήσονται.   8 μὴ   οὖν   ὁμοιωθῆτε
they will be heard.   Not   therefore   be ye like

αὐτοῖς·   οἶδεν   γὰρ   [ὁ   θεὸς]   ὁ   πατὴρ
them;   for [5]knows   -   [1]God   [2]the   [3]Father

ὑμῶν   ὧν   χρείαν   ἔχετε   πρὸ   τοῦ   ὑμᾶς
[4]of you   of what things   [2]need   [1]ye have   before   -   you

αἰτῆσαι   αὐτόν.   9 οὕτως   οὖν   προσεύχεσθε
to ask[b]   him.   [2]Thus   [1]therefore   pray

ὑμεῖς·   Πάτερ   ἡμῶν   ὁ   ἐν   τοῖς   οὐρανοῖς·
ye: Father   of us   the [one]   in   the   heavens:

Ἁγιασθήτω   τὸ   ὄνομά   σου·   10 ἐλθάτω
Let it be hallowed   the   name   of thee;   let it come

ἡ   βασιλεία   σου·   γενηθήτω   τὸ   θέλημά   σου,
the   kingdom   of thee;   let it come about   the   will   of thee,

ὡς   ἐν   οὐρανῷ   καὶ   ἐπὶ   γῆς·.   11 Τὸν
as   in   heaven   also   on   earth;   The

ἄρτον   ἡμῶν   τὸν   ἐπιούσιον   δὸς   ἡμῖν
[2]bread   [3]of us   -   [1]daily   give   to us

σήμερον·   12 καὶ   ἄφες   ἡμῖν   τὰ   ὀφειλή-
to-day;   and   forgive   us   the   debts

ματα   ἡμῶν,   ὡς   καὶ   ἡμεῖς   ἀφήκαμεν
of us,   as   indeed,   we   forgave

τοῖς   ὀφειλέταις   ἡμῶν·   13 καὶ   μὴ   εἰσενέγκῃς
the   debtors   of us;   and   not   bring

ἡμᾶς   εἰς   πειρασμόν,   ἀλλὰ   ῥῦσαι   ἡμᾶς   ἀπὸ
us   into   temptation,   but   rescue   us   from

τοῦ   πονηροῦ.   14 Ἐὰν   γὰρ   ἀφῆτε   τοῖς
evil.   For if   ye forgive   -

ἀνθρώποις   τὰ   παραπτώματα   αὐτῶν,   ἀφήσει
men   the   trespasses   of them,   will forgive

καὶ   ὑμῖν   ὁ   πατὴρ   ὑμῶν   ὁ   οὐράνιος·
also   you   the   [2]Father   [3]of you   -   [1]heavenly;

15 ἐὰν   δὲ   μὴ   ἀφῆτε   τοῖς   ἀνθρώποις,
but if   ye forgive not   -   men,

οὐδὲ   ὁ   πατὴρ   ὑμῶν   ἀφήσει   τὰ   παραπτώ-
neither the   Father   of you   will forgive   the   tres-

ματα   ὑμῶν.   16 Ὅταν   δὲ   νηστεύητε,
passes   of you.   And when   ye fast,

μὴ   γίνεσθε   ὡς   οἱ   ὑποκριταὶ   σκυθρωποί·
be not   as   the   hypocrites   gloomy;

nance: for they disfigure their faces, that they may appear unto men to fast. Verily I say unto you, They have their reward.

17 But thou, when thou fastest, anoint thine head, and wash thy face;

18 That thou appear not unto men to fast, but unto thy Father which is in secret: and thy Father, which seeth in secret, shall reward thee openly.

19 ¶ Lay not up for yourselves treasures upon earth, where moth and rust doth corrupt, and where thieves break through and steal:

20 But lay up for yourselves treasures in heaven, where neither moth nor rust doth corrupt, and where thieves do not break through nor steal:

21 For where your treasure is, there will your heart be also.

22 The light of the body is the eye: if therefore thine eye be single, thy whole body shall be full of light.

23 But if thine eye be evil, thy whole body shall be full of darkness. If therefore the light that is in thee be darkness, how great is that darkness!

ἀφανίζουσιν γὰρ τὰ πρόσωπα αὐτῶν
for they disfigure   the   faces   of them

ὅπως φανῶσιν τοῖς ἀνθρώποις νηστεύοντες·
so that they may appear –   to men   fasting;

ἀμὴν λέγω ὑμῖν, ἀπέχουσιν τὸν μισθὸν
truly   I tell you,   they have   the   reward

αὐτῶν. 17 σὺ δὲ νηστεύων ἄλειψαί σου
of them.   But thou   fasting   anoint   of thee.

τὴν κεφαλὴν καὶ τὸ πρόσωπόν σου νίψαι,
the   head   and the   face   of thee. wash,

18 ὅπως μὴ φανῇς τοῖς ἀνθρώποις νηστεύων
so that thou appearest not –   to men   fasting

ἀλλὰ τῷ πατρί σου τῷ ἐν τῷ κρυφαίῳ·
but   to the Father of thee the [one] in   –   secret;

καὶ ὁ πατήρ σου ὁ βλέπων ἐν τῷ
and the Father of thee the [one] seeing   in   –

κρυφαίῳ ἀποδώσει σοι.
secret   will repay   thee.

19 Μὴ θησαυρίζετε ὑμῖν θησαυροὺς
Do not lay up treasure for you   treasures

ἐπὶ τῆς γῆς, ὅπου σὴς καὶ βρῶσις
on the earth, where moth and   rust

ἀφανίζει, καὶ ὅπου κλέπται διορύσσουσιν
removes,   and where thieves   dig through

καὶ κλέπτουσιν· 20 θησαυρίζετε δὲ ὑμῖν
and   steal;   but lay up treasure for you

θησαυροὺς ἐν οὐρανῷ, ὅπου οὔτε σὴς
treasures   in   heaven,   where neither moth

οὔτε βρῶσις ἀφανίζει, καὶ ὅπου κλέπται
nor   rust   removes,   and where thieves

οὐ διορύσσουσιν οὐδὲ κλέπτουσιν· 21 ὅπου
do not dig through   nor   steal;   ²where

γὰρ ἐστιν ὁ θησαυρός σου, ἐκεῖ
¹for   is   the   treasure   of thee, there

ἔσται καὶ ἡ καρδία σου. 22 Ὁ λύχνος
will be also the heart of thee.   The   lamp

τοῦ σώματός ἐστιν ὁ ὀφθαλμός. ἐὰν οὖν
of the body   is   the   eye.   ²If ¹therefore

ᾖ ὁ ὀφθαλμός σου ἁπλοῦς, ὅλον τὸ σῶμά
⁴be ¹the ²eye ³of thee single,   all the body

σου φωτεινὸν ἔσται· 23 ἐὰν δὲ ὁ
of thee shining   will be;   but if   the

ὀφθαλμός σου πονηρὸς ᾖ, ὅλον τὸ σῶμά
eye   of thee   evil   be,   all the body

σου σκοτεινὸν ἔσται. εἰ οὖν τὸ φῶς
of thee dark   will be.   ²If ¹therefore the light

τὸ ἐν σοὶ σκότος ἐστιν, τὸ σκότος
–   in thee darkness   is,   the darkness

24 No man can serve two masters: for either he will hate the one, and love the other; or else he will hold to the one, and despise the other. Ye cannot serve God and mammon.

25 Therefore I say unto you, Take no thought for your life, what ye shall eat, or what ye shall drink; nor yet for your body, what ye shall put on. Is not the life more than meat, and the body than raiment?

26 Behold the fowls of the air: for they sow not, neither do they reap, nor gather into barns; yet your heavenly Father feedeth them. Are ye not much better than they?

27 Which of you by taking thought can add one cubit unto his stature?

28 And why take ye thought for raiment? Consider the lilies of the field, how they grow; they toil not, neither do they spin:

29 And yet I say unto you, That even Solomon in all his glory was not arrayed like one of these.

30 Wherefore, if God so clothe the grass of the field, which to day is, and to morrow is cast into the oven,

---

πόσον.   **24** Οὐδεὶς δύναται δυσὶ κυρίοις
how great.   No one   can   two   lords

δουλεύειν· ἢ γὰρ τὸν ἕνα μισήσει καὶ
to serve;   for either   the   one   he will hate   and

τὸν ἕτερον ἀγαπήσει, ἢ ἑνὸς ἀνθέξεται
the   other   he will love,   or   one   he will hold to

καὶ τοῦ ἑτέρου καταφρονήσει.   οὐ δύνασθε
and   the   other   he will despise.   Ye cannot

θεῷ δουλεύειν καὶ μαμωνᾷ.   **25** Διὰ
God   to serve   and   mammon.   There-

τοῦτο λέγω ὑμῖν· μὴ μεριμνᾶτε τῇ
fore   I say   to you: Be not anxious   for the

ψυχῇ ὑμῶν τί φάγητε [ἢ τί πίητε],
life   of you[,] what   ye may eat   or what ye may drink,

μηδὲ τῷ σώματι ὑμῶν τί ἐνδύσησθε.
nor   for the   body   of you[,] what ye may put on.

οὐχὶ ἡ ψυχὴ πλεῖόν ἐστιν τῆς τροφῆς καὶ τὸ
²not ²the ⁴life   ⁵more   ¹Is [than] the   food   and   the

σῶμα τοῦ ἐνδύματος;   **26** ἐμβλέψατε εἰς
body [than] the   raiment?   Look ye   at

τὰ πετεινὰ τοῦ οὐρανοῦ, ὅτι οὐ σπείρουσιν
the   birds   of heaven,   that   they sow not

οὐδὲ θερίζουσιν οὐδὲ συνάγουσιν εἰς
nor   reap   nor   gather   into

ἀποθήκας, καὶ ὁ πατὴρ ὑμῶν ὁ οὐράνιος
barns,   and the ²Father   ³of you – ¹heavenly

τρέφει αὐτά· οὐχ ὑμεῖς μᾶλλον διαφέρετε
feeds   them;   do not ye   more   excel

αὐτῶν;   **27** τίς δὲ ἐξ ὑμῶν μεριμνῶν
them?   But who of   you   being anxious

δύναται προσθεῖναι ἐπὶ τὴν ἡλικίαν αὐτοῦ
can   to add   to   the   stature   of him

πῆχυν ἕνα;   **28** καὶ περὶ ἐνδύματος τί
cubit   one?   and concerning   clothing   why

μεριμνᾶτε; καταμάθετε τὰ κρίνα τοῦ ἀγροῦ,
be ye anxious?   consider   the   lilies   of the   field,

πῶς αὐξάνουσιν· οὐ κοπιῶσιν οὐδὲ
how   they grow;   they labour not   nor

νήθουσιν·   **29** λέγω δὲ ὑμῖν ὅτι οὐδὲ Σολομὼν
spin;   but I tell   you   that   not   Solomon

ἐν πάσῃ τῇ δόξῃ αὐτοῦ περιεβάλετο ὡς
in   all   the   glory   of him   was clothed   as

ἓν τούτων.   **30** εἰ δὲ τὸν χόρτον τοῦ
one   of these.   But if   the   grass   of the

ἀγροῦ σήμερον ὄντα καὶ αὔριον εἰς
field   to-day   being   and   to-morrow   into

κλίβανον βαλλόμενον ὁ θεὸς οὕτως
an oven   being thrown   –   God   thus

shall he not much more *clothe* you, O ye of little faith?

31 Therefore take no thought, saying, What shall we eat? or, What shall we drink? or, Wherewithal shall we be clothed?

32 (For after all these things do the Gentiles seek:) for your heavenly Father knoweth that ye have need of all these things.

33 But seek ye first the kingdom of God, and his righteousness; and all these things shall be added unto you.

34 Take therefore no thought for the morrow: for the morrow shall take thought for the things of itself. Sufficient unto the day *is* the evil thereof.

ἀμφιέννυσιν, οὐ πολλῷ μᾶλλον ὑμᾶς,
clothes, not much more you,

ὀλιγόπιστοι; 31 μὴ οὖν μεριμνήσητε
little-faiths? Therefore be ye not anxious

λέγοντες· τί φάγωμεν; ἤ· τί
saying: What may we eat? or: What

πίωμεν; ἤ· τί περιβαλώμεθα; 32 πάντα
may we drink? or: What may we put on? ²all

γὰρ ταῦτα τὰ ἔθνη ἐπιζητοῦσιν· οἶδεν
¹for these things the nations seek after; ⁶knows

γὰρ ὁ πατὴρ ὑμῶν ὁ οὐράνιος ὅτι
¹for ²the ⁴Father ⁵of you – ³heavenly that

χρῄζετε τούτων ἁπάντων. 33 ζητεῖτε δὲ
ye need these things of all. But seek ye

πρῶτον τὴν βασιλείαν καὶ τὴν δικαιοσύνην
first the kingdom and the righteousness

αὐτοῦ, καὶ ταῦτα πάντα προστεθήσεται
of him, and these things all shall be added

ὑμῖν. 34 μὴ οὖν μεριμνήσητε εἰς τὴν
to you. Therefore be ye not anxious for the

αὔριον, ἡ γὰρ αὔριον μεριμνήσει
morrow, for the morrow will be anxious

ἑαυτῆς· ἀρκετὸν τῇ ἡμέρᾳ ἡ κακία αὐτῆς.
of itself; sufficient to the day the evil of it.

CHAPTER 7

JUDGE not, that ye be not judged.

2 For with what judgment ye judge, ye shall be judged: and with what measure ye mete, it shall be measured to you again.

3 And why beholdest thou the mote that is in thy brother's eye, but considerest not the beam that is in thine own eye?

4 Or how wilt thou say to thy brother, Let me pull out the mote out of thine eye; and, behold, a beam *is* in thine own eye?

5 Thou hypocrite, first cast out the beam out of thine own eye; and then

7 Μὴ κρίνετε, ἵνα μὴ κριθῆτε· 2 ἐν ᾧ
Judge not, lest ye be judged; ²with ³what

γὰρ κρίματι κρίνετε κριθήσεσθε, καὶ
¹for judgment ye judge ye shall be judged, and

ἐν ᾧ μέτρῳ μετρεῖτε μετρηθήσεται ὑμῖν.
with what measure ye measure it shall be measured to you.

3 τί δὲ βλέπεις τὸ κάρφος τὸ ἐν
And why seest thou the chip – in

τῷ ὀφθαλμῷ τοῦ ἀδελφοῦ σου, τὴν
the eye of the brother of thee, ²the

δὲ ἐν τῷ σῷ ὀφθαλμῷ δοκὸν οὐ κατα-
¹but ⁴in – ³thine ⁵eye ³beam thou consider-

νοεῖς; 4 ἢ πῶς ἐρεῖς τῷ ἀδελφῷ σου·
est not? or how wilt thou say to the brother of thee:

ἄφες ἐκβάλω τὸ κάρφος ἐκ τοῦ ὀφθαλμοῦ
Allow [that] I may pluck out the chip out of the eye

σου, καὶ ἰδοὺ ἡ δοκὸς ἐν τῷ ὀφθαλμῷ
of thee, and behold the beam in the eye

σου; 5 ὑποκριτά, ἔκβαλε πρῶτον ἐκ τοῦ
of thee? hypocrite, pluck out first out of the

ὀφθαλμοῦ σου τὴν δοκόν, καὶ τότε
eye of thee the beam, and then

shalt thou see clearly to cast out the mote out of thy brother's eye.

6 ¶ Give not that which is holy unto the dogs, neither cast ye your pearls before swine, lest they trample them under their feet, and turn again and rend you.

7 ¶ Ask, and it shall be given you; seek, and ye shall find; knock, and it shall be opened unto you:

8 For every one that asketh receiveth; and he that seeketh findeth; and to him that knocketh it shall be opened.

9 Or what man is there of you, whom if his son ask bread, will he give him a stone?

10 Or if he ask a fish, will he give him a serpent?

11 If ye then, being evil, know how to give good gifts unto your children, how much more shall your Father which is in heaven give good things to them that ask him?

12 Therefore all things whatsoever ye would that men should do to you, do ye even so to them: for this is the law and the prophets.

13 ¶ Enter ye in at the strait gate: for wide is the gate, and broad is the way,

---

διαβλέψεις   ἐκβαλεῖν   τὸ   κάρφος   ἐκ
thou wilt see clearly   to pluck *out*   the   chip   out of

τοῦ   ὀφθαλμοῦ   τοῦ   ἀδελφοῦ   σου.   6 Μὴ
the   eye   of the   brother   of thee.   not

δῶτε   τὸ   ἅγιον   τοῖς   κυσίν,   μηδὲ   βάλητε
Give   the   holy   to the   dogs,   neither   cast

τοὺς   μαργαρίτας   ὑμῶν   ἔμπροσθεν   τῶν
the   pearls   of you   before   the

χοίρων,   μήποτε   καταπατήσουσιν   αὐτοὺς
pigs,   lest   they will trample   them

ἐν   τοῖς   ποσὶν   αὐτῶν   καὶ   στραφέντες
with   the   feet   of them   and   turning

ῥήξωσιν   ὑμᾶς.   7 Αἰτεῖτε,   καὶ   δοθήσεται
may rend   you.   Ask,   and   it shall be given

ὑμῖν·   ζητεῖτε,   καὶ   εὑρήσετε·   κρούετε,
to you;   seek,   and   ye shall find;   knock,

καὶ   ἀνοιγήσεται   ὑμῖν.   8 πᾶς   γὰρ   ὁ   αἰτῶν
and   it shall be opened   to you.   For every   asking [one]

λαμβάνει,   καὶ   ὁ   ζητῶν   εὑρίσκει,   καὶ
receives,   and   the   seeking [one]   finds,   and

τῷ   κρούοντι   ἀνοιγήσεται.   9 ἢ   τίς   ἐστιν
to the knocking [one]   it shall be opened.   Or   [1]what   [3]is there

ἐξ   ὑμῶν   ἄνθρωπος,   ὃν   αἰτήσει   ὁ   υἱὸς
[4]of   [5]you   [2]man,   whom   [4]will ask   [1]the   [2]son

αὐτοῦ   ἄρτον,   μὴ   λίθον   ἐπιδώσει   αὐτῷ;
[3]of him   [6]a loaf,   *not*   a stone   he will give   him?

10 ἢ   καὶ   ἰχθὺν   αἰτήσει,   μὴ   ὄφιν   ἐπιδώσει
or   also   a fish   he will ask,   *not*   a serpent   he will give

αὐτῷ;   11 εἰ   οὖν   ὑμεῖς   πονηροὶ   ὄντες
him?   If   therefore   ye   [2]evil   [1]being

οἴδατε   δόματα   ἀγαθὰ   διδόναι   τοῖς   τέκνοις
know   gifts   good   to give   to the   children

ὑμῶν,   πόσῳ   μᾶλλον   ὁ   πατὴρ   ὑμῶν   ὁ
of you,   how much   more   the   Father   of you   –

ἐν   τοῖς   οὐρανοῖς   δώσει   ἀγαθὰ   τοῖς
in   the   heavens   will give   good things   to the [ones]

αἰτοῦσιν   αὐτόν.   12 Πάντα   οὖν   ὅσα   ἐὰν
asking   him.   All things therefore   as many soever as

θέλητε   ἵνα   ποιῶσιν   ὑμῖν   οἱ   ἄνθρωποι,
ye wish   that   may do   to you   –   men,

οὕτως   καὶ   ὑμεῖς   ποιεῖτε   αὐτοῖς·   οὗτος
thus   also   ye   do   to them;   [2]this

γάρ   ἐστιν   ὁ   νόμος   καὶ   οἱ   προφῆται.
[1]for   is   the   law   and   the   prophets.

13 Εἰσέλθατε   διὰ   τῆς   στενῆς   πύλης·
Enter ye in   through   the   narrow   gate;

ὅτι   πλατεῖα   [ἡ   πύλη]   καὶ   εὐρύχωρος
because   wide   the   gate   and   broad

that leadeth to destruction, and many there be which go in thereat:

14 Because strait *is* the gate, and narrow *is* the way, which leadeth unto life, and few there be that find it.

15 ¶ Beware of false prophets, which come to you in sheep's clothing, but inwardly they are ravening wolves.

16 Ye shall know them by their fruits. Do men gather grapes of thorns, or figs of thistles?

17 Even so every good tree bringeth forth good fruit; but a corrupt tree bringeth forth evil fruit.

18 A good tree cannot bring forth evil fruit, neither *can* a corrupt tree bring forth good fruit.

19 Every tree that bringeth not forth good fruit is hewn down, and cast into the fire.

20 Wherefore by their fruits ye shall know them.

21 ¶ Not every one that saith unto me, Lord, Lord, shall enter into the kingdom of heaven: but he that doeth the will of my Father which is in heaven.

22 Many will say to me in that day, Lord, Lord,

ἡ ὁδὸς ἡ ἀπάγουσα εἰς τὴν ἀπώλειαν,
the way – leading away to – destruction,

καὶ πολλοί εἰσιν οἱ εἰσερχόμενοι δι'
and many are the [ones] going in through

αὐτῆς· 14 ὅτι στενὴ ἡ πύλη καὶ τεθλιμ-
it; because strait the gate and made

μένη ἡ ὁδὸς ἡ ἀπάγουσα εἰς τὴν ζωήν,
narrow the way – leading away to – life,

καὶ ὀλίγοι εἰσὶν οἱ εὑρίσκοντες αὐτήν.
and few are the [ones] finding it.

15 Προσέχετε ἀπὸ τῶν ψευδοπροφητῶν,
Beware from(of) – false prophets,

οἵτινες ἔρχονται πρὸς ὑμᾶς ἐν ἐνδύμασι
who come to you in clothes

προβάτων, ἔσωθεν δέ εἰσιν λύκοι ἅρπαγες.
of sheep, but within are wolves greedy.

16 ἀπὸ τῶν καρπῶν αὐτῶν ἐπιγνώσεσθε
From the fruits of them ye will know

αὐτούς. μήτι συλλέγουσιν ἀπὸ ἀκανθῶν σταφυλὰς
them. They do not gather from thorns grapes

ἢ ἀπὸ τριβόλων σῦκα; 17 οὕτως πᾶν
or from thistles figs? So ¹every

δένδρον ἀγαθὸν καρποὺς καλοὺς ποιεῖ,
²tree ³good ⁴fruits ⁵good ⁶produces,

τὸ δὲ σαπρὸν δένδρον καρποὺς πονηροὺς
but the corrupt tree fruits evil

ποιεῖ. 18 οὐ δύναται δένδρον ἀγαθὸν
produces. ³Cannot ²tree ¹a good

καρποὺς πονηροὺς ἐνεγκεῖν, οὐδὲ δένδρον
⁵fruits ⁶evil ⁴to bear, nor ²tree

σαπρὸν καρποὺς καλοὺς ἐνεγκεῖν. 19 πᾶν
¹a corrupt ⁵fruits ⁴good ³to bear. Every

δένδρον μὴ ποιοῦν καρπὸν καλὸν ἐκκόπτεται
tree not producing fruit good is cut down

καὶ εἰς πῦρ βάλλεται. 20 ἄρα γε ἀπὸ
and into fire is cast. Therefore from

τῶν καρπῶν αὐτῶν ἐπιγνώσεσθε αὐτούς.
the fruits of them ye will know them.

21 Οὐ πᾶς ὁ λέγων μοι κύριε κύριε,
Not everyone saying to me Lord[,] Lord,

εἰσελεύσεται εἰς τὴν βασιλείαν τῶν οὐρανῶν,
will enter into the kingdom of the heavens,

ἀλλ' ὁ ποιῶν τὸ θέλημα τοῦ πατρός
but the [one] doing the will of the Father

μου τοῦ ἐν τοῖς οὐρανοῖς. 22 πολλοὶ
of me – in the heavens. Many

ἐροῦσίν μοι ἐν ἐκείνῃ τῇ ἡμέρᾳ· κύριε
will say to me in that – day: Lord[,]

have we not prophesied in thy name? and in thy name have cast out devils? and in thy name done many wonderful works?

23 And then will I profess unto them, I never knew you: depart from me, ye that work iniquity.

24 ¶ Therefore whosoever heareth these sayings of mine, and doeth them, I will liken him unto a wise man, which built his house upon a rock:

25 And the rain descended, and the floods came, and the winds blew, and beat upon that house; and it fell not: for it was founded upon a rock.

26 And every one that heareth these sayings of mine, and doeth them not, shall be likened unto a foolish man, which built his house upon the sand:

27 And the rain descended, and the floods came, and the winds blew, and beat upon that house; and it fell: and great was the fall of it.

κύριε, οὐ τῷ σῷ ὀνόματι ἐπροφητεύσαμεν,
Lord, not – in thy name we prophesied,

καὶ τῷ σῷ ὀνόματι δαιμόνια ἐξεβάλομεν,
and – in thy name demons we expelled,

καὶ τῷ σῷ ὀνόματι δυνάμεις πολλὰς
and – in thy name mighty works many

ἐποιήσαμεν; 23 καὶ τότε ὁμολογήσω
did? and then I will declare

αὐτοῖς ὅτι οὐδέποτε ἔγνων ὑμᾶς· ἀπο-
to them[,] – Never I knew you; de-

χωρεῖτε ἀπ' ἐμοῦ οἱ ἐργαζόμενοι τὴν
part from me the [ones] working –

ἀνομίαν.
lawlessness.

24 Πᾶς οὖν ὅστις ἀκούει μου τοὺς
Everyone therefore who hears of me –

λόγους τούτους καὶ ποιεῖ αὐτούς,
words these and does them,

ὁμοιωθήσεται ἀνδρὶ φρονίμῳ, ὅστις ᾠκοδό-
shall be likened man to a prudent. who built

μησεν αὐτοῦ τὴν οἰκίαν ἐπὶ τὴν πέτραν.
of him the house on the rock.

25 καὶ κατέβη ἡ βροχὴ καὶ ἦλθον οἱ
And came down the rain and came the

ποταμοὶ καὶ ἔπνευσαν οἱ ἄνεμοι καὶ
rivers and blew the winds and

προσέπεσαν τῇ οἰκίᾳ ἐκείνῃ, καὶ οὐκ
fell against – house that, and not

ἔπεσεν· τεθεμελίωτο γὰρ ἐπὶ τὴν
it fell; for it had been founded on the

πέτραν. 26 καὶ πᾶς ὁ ἀκούων μου
rock. And everyone hearing of me

τοὺς λόγους τούτους καὶ μὴ ποιῶν
– words these and not doing

αὐτοὺς ὁμοιωθήσεται ἀνδρὶ μωρῷ, ὅστις
them shall be likened man to a foolish, who

ᾠκοδόμησεν αὐτοῦ τὴν οἰκίαν ἐπὶ τὴν
built of him the house on the

ἄμμον. 27 καὶ κατέβη ἡ βροχὴ καὶ
sand. And came down the rain and

ἦλθον οἱ ποταμοὶ καὶ ἔπνευσαν οἱ
came the rivers and blew the

ἄνεμοι καὶ προσέκοψαν τῇ οἰκίᾳ ἐκείνῃ,
winds and beat against – house that,

καὶ ἔπεσεν, καὶ ἦν ἡ πτῶσις αὐτῆς
and it fell, and was the fall of it

μεγάλη.
great.

28 ¶ And it came to pass, when Jesus had ended these sayings, the people were astonished at his doctrine:
29 For he taught them as *one* having authority, and not as the scribes.

28 Καὶ ἐγένετο ὅτε ἐτέλεσεν ὁ Ἰησοῦς
And it came to pass when finished – Jesus
τοὺς λόγους τούτους, ἐξεπλήσσοντο οἱ
– words these, were astounded the
ὄχλοι ἐπὶ τῇ διδαχῇ αὐτοῦ· 29 ἦν γὰρ
crowds at the teaching of him; for he was
διδάσκων αὐτοὺς ὡς ἐξουσίαν ἔχων, καὶ
teaching them as authority having, and
οὐχ ὡς οἱ γραμματεῖς αὐτῶν.
not as the scribes of them.

CHAPTER 8

WHEN he was come down from the mountain, great multitudes followed him.
2 And, behold, there came a leper and worshipped him, saying, Lord, if thou wilt, thou canst make me clean.
3 And Jesus put forth *his* hand, and touched him, saying, I will; be thou clean. And immediately his leprosy was cleansed.
4 And Jesus saith unto him, See thou tell no man; but go thy way, shew thyself to the priest, and offer the gift that Moses commanded, for a testimony unto them.
5 ¶ And when Jesus was entered into Capernaum, there came unto him a centurion, beseeching him,
6 And saying, Lord, my servant lieth at home sick of the palsy, grievously tormented.
7 And Jesus saith unto him, I will come and heal him.

8 Καταβάντος δὲ αὐτοῦ ἀπὸ τοῦ ὄρους
And coming down himᵃ from the mountain
=as he came down
ἠκολούθησαν αὐτῷ ὄχλοι πολλοί. 2 καὶ
followed him crowds many. And
ἰδοὺ λεπρὸς προσελθὼν προσεκύνει αὐτῷ
behold a leper approaching worshipped him
λέγων· κύριε, ἐὰν θέλῃς, δύνασαι με
saying: Lord, if thou art willing, thou art able me
καθαρίσαι. 3 καὶ ἐκτείνας τὴν χεῖρα
to cleanse. And stretching out the(his) hand
ἥψατο αὐτοῦ λέγων· θέλω, καθαρίσθητι.
he touched him saying: I am willing, be thou cleansed.
καὶ εὐθέως ἐκαθαρίσθη αὐτοῦ ἡ λέπρα.
And immediately was cleansed of him the leprosy.
4 καὶ λέγει αὐτῷ ὁ Ἰησοῦς· ὅρα μηδενὶ
And says to him – Jesus: See *to* no one
εἴπῃς, ἀλλὰ ὕπαγε σεαυτὸν δεῖξον τῷ
thou tellest, but go thyself show to the
ἱερεῖ καὶ προσένεγκον τὸ δῶρον ὃ
priest and offer the gift which
προσέταξεν Μωϋσῆς, εἰς μαρτύριον αὐτοῖς.
commanded Moses, for a testimony to them.
5 Εἰσελθόντος δὲ αὐτοῦ εἰς Καφαρναοὺμ
And entering himᵃ into Capernaum,
=as he entered
προσῆλθεν αὐτῷ ἑκατόνταρχος παρακαλῶν
approached *to* him a centurion beseeching
αὐτὸν 6 καὶ λέγων· κύριε, ὁ παῖς μου
him and saying: Lord, the boy of me
βέβληται ἐν τῇ οἰκίᾳ παραλυτικός,
has been laid [aside] in the house a paralytic,
δεινῶς βασανιζόμενος. 7 λέγει αὐτῷ·
terribly *being* tortured. He says to him:
ἐγὼ ἐλθὼν θεραπεύσω αὐτόν. 8 ἀποκριθεὶς
I coming will heal him. answering

8 The centurion answered and said, Lord, I am not worthy that thou shouldest come under my roof: but speak the word only, and my servant shall be healed.

9 For I am a man under authority, having soldiers under me: and I say to this *man*, Go, and he goeth; and to another, Come, and he cometh; and to my servant, Do this, and he doeth *it*.

10 When Jesus heard *it*, he marvelled, and said to them that followed, Verily I say unto you, I have not found so great faith, no, not in Israel.

11 And I say unto you, That many shall come from the east and west, and shall sit down with Abraham, and Isaac, and Jacob, in the kingdom of heaven.

12 But the children of the kingdom shall be cast out into outer darkness: there shall be weeping and gnashing of teeth.

13 And Jesus said unto the centurion, Go thy way; and as thou hast believed, *so* be it done unto thee. And his servant was healed in the selfsame hour.

14 ¶ And when Jesus was come into Peter's house, he saw his wife's mother laid, and sick of a fever.

δὲ ὁ ἑκατόνταρχος ἔφη· κύριε, οὐκ εἰμὶ
But the   centurion   said: Lord,   I am not
ἱκανὸς ἵνα μου ὑπὸ τὴν στέγην εἰσέλθῃς·
worthy   that of me   under   the   roof   thou mayest enter;
ἀλλὰ μόνον εἰπὲ λόγῳ, καὶ ἰαθήσεται ὁ παῖς
but   only   say in a word, and   will be healed   the   boy
μου.   9 καὶ γὰρ ἐγὼ ἄνθρωπός εἰμι
of me.   also   For   I   a man   am
ὑπὸ ἐξουσίαν, ἔχων ὑπ' ἐμαυτὸν στρατιώτας,
under   authority, having under   myself   soldiers,
καὶ λέγω τούτῳ· πορεύθητι, καὶ πορεύεται,
and   I say   to this: Go,   and   he goes,
καὶ ἄλλῳ· ἔρχου, καὶ ἔρχεται, καὶ τῷ
and to another: Come,   and   he comes,   and to the
δούλῳ μου· ποίησον τοῦτο, καὶ ποιεῖ.
slave   of me: Do   this,   and   he does [it].
10 ἀκούσας δὲ ὁ Ἰησοῦς ἐθαύμασεν
And hearing   Jesus   marvelled
καὶ εἶπεν τοῖς ἀκολουθοῦσιν· ἀμὴν λέγω
and   said   to the [ones]   following: Truly   I tell
ὑμῖν, παρ' οὐδενὶ τοσαύτην πίστιν ἐν τῷ
you,   from   no one   such   faith   in   –
Ἰσραὴλ εὗρον. 11 λέγω δὲ ὑμῖν ὅτι
Israel   I found.   And I tell   you   that
πολλοὶ ἀπὸ ἀνατολῶν καὶ δυσμῶν ἥξουσιν
many   from   east   and   west   will come
καὶ ἀνακλιθήσονται μετὰ Ἀβραὰμ καὶ
and   will recline   with   Abraham   and
Ἰσαὰκ καὶ Ἰακὼβ ἐν τῇ βασιλείᾳ τῶν
Isaac   and   Jacob   in   the   kingdom   of the
οὐρανῶν· 12 οἱ δὲ υἱοὶ τῆς βασιλείας
heavens;   but the   sons   of the   kingdom
ἐκβληθήσονται εἰς τὸ σκότος τὸ ἐξώτερον·
will be cast out   into   the   darkness   –   outer;
ἐκεῖ ἔσται ὁ κλαυθμὸς καὶ ὁ βρυγμὸς
there   will be   the   weeping   and   the   gnashing
τῶν ὀδόντων. 13 καὶ εἶπεν ὁ Ἰησοῦς τῷ
of the   teeth.   And   said   –   Jesus   to the
ἑκατοντάρχῃ· ὕπαγε, ὡς ἐπίστευσας γενη-
centurion: Go,   as   thou believedst   let it
θήτω σοι. καὶ ἰάθη ὁ παῖς ἐν τῇ
be   to thee.   And   was healed   the   boy   in   –
ὥρα ἐκείνῃ.
hour   that.

14 Καὶ ἐλθὼν ὁ Ἰησοῦς εἰς τὴν οἰκίαν
And   coming   –   Jesus   into   the   house
Πέτρου εἶδεν τὴν πενθερὰν αὐτοῦ βεβλη-
of Peter   he saw   the   mother-in-law   of him   *having been*

15 And he touched her hand, and the fever left her: and she arose, and ministered unto them.

16 ¶ When the even was come, they brought unto him many that were possessed with devils: and he cast out the spirits with *his* word, and healed all that were sick:

17 That it might be fulfilled which was spoken by Esaias the prophet, saying, Himself took our infirmities, and bare *our* sicknesses.

18 ¶ Now when Jesus saw great multitudes about him, he gave commandment to depart unto the other side.

19 And a certain scribe came, and said unto him, Master, I will follow thee whithersoever thou goest.

20 And Jesus saith unto him, The foxes have holes, and the birds of the air *have* nests; but the Son of man hath not where to lay *his* head.

21 And another of his disciples said unto him, Lord, suffer me first to go and bury my father.

22 But Jesus said unto

μένην καὶ πυρέσσουσαν·
laid [aside] and fever-stricken;
τῆς χειρὸς αὐτῆς, καὶ ἀφῆκεν αὐτὴν ὁ
the hand of her, and left her the
πυρετός· καὶ ἠγέρθη, καὶ διηκόνει αὐτῷ.
fever; and she arose, and ministered to him.

15 καὶ ἥψατο
and he touched

16 'Οψίας δὲ γενομένης προσήνεγκαν
And evening coming[a] they brought
= when evening came
αὐτῷ δαιμονιζομένους πολλούς· καὶ ἐξέβαλεν
to him *being* demon-possessed many; and he expelled
τὰ πνεύματα λόγῳ, καὶ πάντας τοὺς
the spirits with a word, and all the [ones]
= those
κακῶς ἔχοντας ἐθεράπευσεν· **17** ὅπως
ill having he healed; so that
who were ill
πληρωθῇ τὸ ῥηθὲν διὰ 'Ησαΐου τοῦ
was fulfilled the [thing] spoken through Isaiah the
προφήτου λέγοντος· αὐτὸς τὰς ἀσθενείας
prophet saying: He the weaknesses
ἡμῶν ἔλαβεν καὶ τὰς νόσους ἐβάστασεν.
of us took and the diseases he bore.

18 'Ιδὼν δὲ ὁ 'Ιησοῦς ὄχλον περὶ
But [2]seeing – [1]Jesus a crowd around
αὐτὸν ἐκέλευσεν ἀπελθεῖν εἰς τὸ πέραν.
him commanded to go away to the other side.

19 Καὶ προσελθὼν εἷς γραμματεὺς εἶπεν
And approaching one scribe said
αὐτῷ· διδάσκαλε, ἀκολουθήσω σοι
to him: Teacher, I will follow thee
ὅπου ἐὰν ἀπέρχῃ. **20** καὶ λέγει αὐτῷ
wherever thou mayest go. And says to him
ὁ 'Ιησοῦς· αἱ ἀλώπεκες φωλεοὺς ἔχουσιν
– Jesus: The foxes holes have
καὶ τὰ πετεινὰ τοῦ οὐρανοῦ κατα-
and the birds of the heaven nests,
σκηνώσεις, ὁ δὲ υἱὸς τοῦ ἀνθρώπου
but the Son of man
οὐκ ἔχει ποῦ τὴν κεφαλὴν κλίνῃ.
has not where the(his) head he may lay.

21 ἕτερος δὲ τῶν μαθητῶν εἶπεν
And another of the disciples said
αὐτῷ· κύριε, ἐπίτρεψόν μοι πρῶτον
to him: Lord, allow me first
ἀπελθεῖν καὶ θάψαι τὸν πατέρα μου.
to go away and bury the father of me.

22 ὁ δὲ 'Ιησοῦς λέγει αὐτῷ· ἀκολούθει
– But Jesus says to him: Follow thou

him, Follow me; and let the dead bury their dead.

23 ¶ And when he was entered into a ship, his disciples followed him.

24 And, behold, there arose a great tempest in the sea, insomuch that the ship was covered with the waves: but he was asleep.

25 And his disciples came to *him*, and awoke him, saying, Lord, save us: we perish.

26 And he saith unto them, Why are ye fearful, O ye of little faith? Then he arose, and rebuked the winds and the sea; and there was a great calm.

27 But the men marvelled, saying, What manner of man is this, that even the winds and the sea obey him!

28 ¶ And when he was come to the other side into the country of the Gergesenes, there met him two possessed with devils, coming out of the tombs, exceeding fierce, so that no man might pass by that way.

29 And, behold, they cried out, saying, What have we to do with thee, Jesus, thou Son of God? art thou come hither to torment us before the time?

μοι, καὶ ἄφες τοὺς νεκροὺς θάψαι τοὺς
me, and leave the dead to bury the

ἑαυτῶν νεκρούς.
of themselves dead.

23 Καὶ ἐμβάντι αὐτῷ εἰς τὸ πλοῖον,
And embarking him[e] in the ship,
=as he embarked

ἠκολούθησαν αὐτῷ οἱ μαθηταὶ αὐτοῦ.
followed him the disciples of him.

24 καὶ ἰδοὺ σεισμὸς μέγας ἐγένετο ἐν
And behold storm a great there was in

τῇ θαλάσσῃ, ὥστε τὸ πλοῖον καλύπτ-
the sea, so as the ship to be en-

εσθαι ὑπὸ τῶν κυμάτων· αὐτὸς δὲ ἐκάθευδεν.
veloped by the waves; but he was sleeping.

25 καὶ προσελθόντες ἤγειραν αὐτὸν λέγοντες·
And approaching they roused him saying:

κύριε, σῶσον, ἀπολλύμεθα. 26 καὶ λέγει
Lord, save, we are perishing. And he says

αὐτοῖς· τί δειλοί ἐστε, ὀλιγόπιστοι;
to them: Why fearful are ye, little-faiths?

τότε ἐγερθεὶς ἐπετίμησεν τοῖς ἀνέμοις καὶ
Then rising he rebuked the winds and

τῇ θαλάσσῃ, καὶ ἐγένετο γαλήνη μεγάλη.
the sea, and there was calm a great.

27 οἱ δὲ ἄνθρωποι ἐθαύμασαν λέγοντες·
And the men marvelled saying:

ποταπός ἐστιν οὗτος, ὅτι καὶ οἱ ἄνεμοι
Of what sort is this [man], that even the winds

καὶ ἡ θάλασσα αὐτῷ ὑπακούουσιν;
and the sea him obey?

28 Καὶ ἐλθόντος αὐτοῦ εἰς τὸ πέραν εἰς
And coming him[a] to the other side into
=when he came

τὴν χώραν τῶν Γαδαρηνῶν ὑπήντησαν
the country of the Gadarenes met

αὐτῷ δύο δαιμονιζόμενοι ἐκ τῶν μνημείων
him two demon-possessed out of the tombs

ἐξερχόμενοι, χαλεποὶ λίαν, ὥστε μὴ
coming out, dangerous exceedingly, so as not

ἰσχύειν τινὰ παρελθεῖν διὰ τῆς ὁδοῦ
to be able anyone[b] to pass through the way

ἐκείνης. 29 καὶ ἰδοὺ ἔκραξαν λέγοντες·
that. And behold they cried out saying:

τί ἡμῖν καὶ σοί, υἱὲ τοῦ θεοῦ; ἦλθες
What to us and to thee, Son – of God? camest thou

ὧδε πρὸ καιροῦ βασανίσαι ἡμᾶς; 30 ἦν
here before [the] time to torture us? there was

30 And there was a good way off from them an herd of many swine feeding.
31 So the devils besought him, saying, If thou cast us out, suffer us to go away into the herd of swine.
32 And he said unto them, Go. And when they were come out, they went into the herd of swine: and, behold, the whole herd of swine ran violently down a steep place into the sea, and perished in the waters.
33 And they that kept them fled, and went their ways into the city, and told every thing, and what was befallen to the possessed of the devils.
34 And, behold, the whole city came out to meet Jesus: and when they saw him, they besought *him* that he would depart out of their coasts.

δὲ	μακρὰν	ἀπ'	αὐτῶν	ἀγέλη	χοίρων
Now	far off	from	them	a herd	pigs
πολλῶν	βοσκομένη.		**31** οἱ	δὲ	δαίμονες
of many	feeding.		And the		demons
παρεκάλουν	αὐτὸν	λέγοντες·	εἰ	ἐκβάλλεις
besought	him	saying:	If	thou expellest
ἡμᾶς,	ἀπόστειλον	ἡμᾶς	εἰς	τὴν	ἀγέλην
us,	send	us	into	the	herd
τῶν	χοίρων.	**32** καὶ	εἶπεν	αὐτοῖς·
of the	pigs.	And	he said	to them:
ὑπάγετε.	οἱ	δὲ	ἐξελθόντες	ἀπῆλθον	εἰς
Go ye.	So the		coming out [ones]	went away	into
τοὺς	χοίρους·	καὶ	ἰδοὺ	ὥρμησεν	πᾶσα	ἡ
the	pigs;	and	behold	rushed	all	the
ἀγέλη	κατὰ	τοῦ	κρημνοῦ	εἰς	τὴν	θάλασσαν,
herd	down	the	precipice	into	the	sea,
καὶ	ἀπέθανον	ἐν	τοῖς	ὕδασιν.	**33** οἱ
and	died	in	the	waters.	the
δὲ	βόσκοντες	ἔφυγον,	καὶ	ἀπελθόντες
But	feeding [ones]	fled,	and	going away
εἰς	τὴν	πόλιν	ἀπήγγειλαν	πάντα	καὶ
into	the	city	reported	all things	and
τὰ	τῶν	δαιμονιζομένων.	**34** καὶ	ἰδοὺ
the [things] of the		demon-possessed [ones].	And	behold
πᾶσα	ἡ	πόλις	ἐξῆλθεν	εἰς	ὑπάντησιν
all	the	city	came out	with a view to	a meeting [with]
τῷ	Ἰησοῦ,	καὶ	ἰδόντες	αὐτὸν	παρεκάλεσαν
-	Jesus,	and	seeing	²him	¹besought
ὅπως	μεταβῇ	ἀπὸ	τῶν	ὁρίων	αὐτῶν.
so that	he might remove	from	the	borders	of them.

CHAPTER 9

A ND he entered into a ship, and passed over, and came into his own city.
2 And, behold, they brought to him a man sick of the palsy, lying on a bed: and Jesus seeing their faith said unto the sick of the palsy; Son, be of good cheer; thy sins be forgiven thee.
3 And, behold, certain of the scribes said within themselves, This *man* blasphemeth.

9 Καὶ	ἐμβὰς	εἰς	πλοῖον	διεπέρασεν,
And	embarking	in	a ship	he crossed over,
καὶ	ἦλθεν	εἰς	τὴν	ἰδίαν	πόλιν.	**2** Καὶ
and	came	into	the(his)	own	city.	And
ἰδοὺ	προσέφερον	αὐτῷ	παραλυτικὸν	ἐπὶ
behold	they brought	to him	a paralytic	on
κλίνης	βεβλημένον.	καὶ	ἰδὼν	ὁ	Ἰησοῦς
a mattress	*having been* laid.	And	²seeing	-	¹Jesus
τὴν	πίστιν	αὐτῶν	εἶπεν	τῷ	παραλυτικῷ
the	faith	of them	said	to the	paralytic:
θάρσει,	τέκνον,	ἀφίενταί	σου	αἱ	ἁμαρτίαι.
Be of good cheer,	child,	are forgiven	of thee	the	sins.
3 καὶ	ἰδού	τινες	τῶν	γραμματέων	εἶπαν
And	behold	some	of the	scribes	said
ἐν	ἑαυτοῖς·	οὗτος	βλασφημεῖ.	**4** καὶ
among	themselves:	This [man]	blasphemes.	And

4 And Jesus knowing their thoughts said, Wherefore think ye evil in your hearts?

5 For whether is easier, to say, *Thy* sins be forgiven thee; or to say, Arise, and walk?

6 But that ye may know that the Son of man hath power on earth to forgive sins, (then saith he to the sick of the palsy,) Arise, take up thy bed, and go unto thine house.

7 And he arose, and departed to his house.

8 But when the multitudes saw *it*, they marvelled, and glorified God, which had given such power unto men.

9 ¶ And as Jesus passed forth from thence, he saw a man, named Matthew, sitting at the receipt of custom: and he saith unto him, Follow me. And he arose, and followed him.

10 ¶ And it came to pass, as Jesus sat at meat in the house, behold, many publicans and sinners came and sat down with him and his disciples.

11 And when the Pharisees saw *it*, they said unto his disciples, Why eateth your Master with publicans and sinners?

εἰδὼς ὁ Ἰησοῦς τὰς ἐνθυμήσεις αὐτῶν
[2]knowing - [1]Jesus the thoughts of them
εἶπεν· ἱνατί ἐνθυμεῖσθε πονηρὰ ἐν ταῖς
said: Why think ye evil things in the
καρδίαις ὑμῶν; 5 τί γάρ ἐστιν εὐκοπώ-
hearts of you? for which is easier,
τερον, εἰπεῖν· ἀφίενταί σου αἱ ἁμαρτίαι, ἢ
to say: [4]are forgiven [3]of thee [1]The [2]sins, or
εἰπεῖν· ἔγειρε καὶ περιπάτει; 6 ἵνα δὲ
to say: Rise and walk? But in order that
εἰδῆτε ὅτι ἐξουσίαν ἔχει ὁ υἱὸς τοῦ
ye may know that authority has the Son -
ἀνθρώπου ἐπὶ τῆς γῆς ἀφιέναι ἁμαρτίας
of man on the earth to forgive sins—
τότε λέγει τῷ παραλυτικῷ· ἔγειρε ἆρόν
then he says to the paralytic: Rise[,] take
σου τὴν κλίνην καὶ ὕπαγε εἰς τὸν οἶκόν
of thee the mattress and go to the house
σου. 7 καὶ ἐγερθεὶς ἀπῆλθεν εἰς τὸν
of thee. And rising he went away to the
οἶκον αὐτοῦ. 8 ἰδόντες δὲ οἱ ὄχλοι
house of him. But seeing the crowds
ἐφοβήθησαν καὶ ἐδόξασαν τὸν θεὸν τὸν
feared and glorified - God the [one]
δόντα ἐξουσίαν τοιαύτην τοῖς ἀνθρώποις.
giving [2]authority [1]such - to men.
9 Καὶ παράγων ὁ Ἰησοῦς ἐκεῖθεν εἶδεν
And [2]passing by - [1]Jesus thence saw
ἄνθρωπον καθήμενον ἐπὶ τὸ τελώνιον,
a man sitting at the custom house,
Μαθθαῖον λεγόμενον, καὶ λέγει αὐτῷ·
Matthew named, and says to him:
ἀκολούθει μοι. καὶ ἀναστὰς ἠκολούθησεν
Follow me. And rising up he followed
αὐτῷ. 10 Καὶ ἐγένετο αὐτοῦ ἀνακει-
him. And it came to pass him reclin-
=as he was reclining
μένου ἐν τῇ οἰκίᾳ, καὶ ἰδοὺ πολλοὶ
ing[a] in the house, and behold many
τελῶναι καὶ ἁμαρτωλοὶ ἐλθόντες συνανέκειντο
tax-collectors and sinners coming reclined at table with
τῷ Ἰησοῦ καὶ τοῖς μαθηταῖς αὐτοῦ.
- Jesus and the disciples of him.
11 καὶ ἰδόντες οἱ Φαρισαῖοι ἔλεγον τοῖς
And [2]seeing [1]the [2]Pharisees said to the
μαθηταῖς αὐτοῦ· διὰ τί μετὰ τῶν τελωλῶν
disciples of him: Why with - tax-collectors
καὶ ἁμαρτωλῶν ἐσθίει ὁ διδάσκαλος ὑμῶν;
and sinners eats the teacher of you?

12 But when Jesus heard *that*, he said unto them, They that be whole need not a physician, but they that are sick.

13 But go ye and learn what *that* meaneth, I will have mercy, and not sacrifice: for I am not come to call the righteous, but sinners to repentance.

14 ¶ Then came to him the disciples of John, saying, Why do we and the Pharisees fast oft, but thy disciples fast not?

15 And Jesus said unto them, Can the children of the bridechamber mourn, as long as the bridegroom is with them? but the days will come, when the bridegroom shall be taken from them, and then shall they fast.

16 No man putteth a piece of new cloth unto an old garment, for that which is put in to fill it up taketh from the garment, and the rent is made worse.

17 Neither do men put new wine into old bottles: else the bottles break, and the wine runneth out, and the bottles perish: but they

12 ὁ δὲ ἀκούσας εἶπεν· οὐ χρείαν
But he hearing said: Not need
ἔχουσιν οἱ ἰσχύοντες ἰατροῦ ἀλλ’ οἱ
have the [ones] being strong of a physician but the [ones]
=those
κακῶς ἔχοντες. 13 πορευθέντες δὲ μάθετε
ill having. But going learn ye
who are ill.
τί ἐστιν· ἔλεος θέλω καὶ οὐ θυσίαν· οὐ
what it is: Mercy I desire and not sacrifice; not
γὰρ ἦλθον καλέσαι δικαίους ἀλλὰ
for I came to call righteous [people] but
ἁμαρτωλούς.
sinners.

14 Τότε προσέρχονται αὐτῷ οἱ μαθηταὶ
Then approach to him the disciples
Ἰωάννου λέγοντες· διὰ τί ἡμεῖς καὶ οἱ
of John saying: Why we and the
Φαρισαῖοι νηστεύομεν, οἱ δὲ μαθηταί
Pharisees fast, but the disciples
σου οὐ νηστεύουσιν; 15 καὶ εἶπεν
of thee fast not? And said
αὐτοῖς ὁ Ἰησοῦς· μὴ δύνανται οἱ
to them - Jesus: not Can the
υἱοὶ τοῦ νυμφῶνος πενθεῖν, ἐφ’ ὅσον
sons of the bridechamber to mourn, so long as
μετ’ αὐτῶν ἐστιν ὁ νυμφίος; ἐλεύσονται
with them is the bridegroom? ²will come
δὲ ἡμέραι ὅταν ἀπαρθῇ ἀπ’ αὐτῶν ὁ
¹but ²days when is taken away from them the
νυμφίος, καὶ τότε νηστεύσουσιν. 16 οὐδεὶς
bridegroom, and then they will fast. no one
δὲ ἐπιβάλλει ἐπίβλημα ῥάκους ἀγνάφου
Now puts on a patch cloth of unfulled
ἐπὶ ἱματίῳ παλαιῷ· αἴρει γὰρ τὸ
on garment an old; for takes away the
πλήρωμα αὐτοῦ ἀπὸ τοῦ ἱματίου, καὶ
fullness of it from the garment, and
χεῖρον σχίσμα γίνεται. 17 οὐδὲ
a worse rent becomes. Neither
βάλλουσιν οἶνον νέον εἰς ἀσκοὺς
do they put wine new into wineskins
παλαιούς· εἰ δὲ μή γε, ῥήγνυνται
old; otherwise, are burst
οἱ ἀσκοί, καὶ ὁ οἶνος ἐκχεῖται καὶ
the wineskins, and the wine is poured out and
οἱ ἀσκοὶ ἀπόλλυνται. ἀλλὰ βάλλουσιν
the wineskins are destroyed. But they put

put new wine into new bottles, and both are preserved.

18 ¶ While he spake these things unto them, behold, there came a certain ruler, and worshipped him, saying, My daughter is even now dead: but come and lay thy hand upon her, and she shall live.

19 And Jesus arose, and followed him, and *so did* his disciples.

20 ¶ And, behold, a woman, which was diseased with an issue of blood twelve years, came behind *him*, and touched the hem of his garment:

21 For she said within herself, If I may but touch his garment, I shall be whole.

22 But Jesus turned him about, and when he saw her, he said, Daughter, be of good comfort; thy faith hath made thee whole. And the woman was made whole from that hour.

23 And when Jesus came into the ruler's house, and saw the minstrels and the people making a noise,

24 He said unto them, Give place: for the maid is not dead, but sleepeth. And they laughed him to scorn.

25 But when the people were put forth, he went in,

οἶνον	νέον	εἰς	ἀσκοὺς	καινούς,	καὶ
wine	new	into	wineskins	fresh,	and

ἀμφότεροι	συντηροῦνται.
both	are preserved.

18 Ταῦτα αὐτοῦ λαλοῦντος αὐτοῖς,
These things   him   speaking[a]   to them,
= As he was speaking these things

ἰδοὺ ἄρχων [εἷς] προσελθὼν προσ-
behold   ruler   one   approaching   wor-

εκύνει αὐτῷ λέγων ὅτι ἡ θυγάτηρ
shipped   him   saying[,]   –   The   daughter

μου ἄρτι ἐτελεύτησεν· ἀλλὰ ἐλθὼν
of me   just now   died;   but   coming

ἐπίθες τὴν χεῖρά σου ἐπ' αὐτήν,
lay *on*   the   hand   of thee   on   her,

καὶ ζήσεται. **19** καὶ ἐγερθεὶς ὁ Ἰησοῦς
and   she will live.   And   rising   –   Jesus

ἠκολούθει αὐτῷ καὶ οἱ μαθηταὶ αὐτοῦ.
followed   him[,]   also   the   disciples   of him.

20 Καὶ ἰδοὺ γυνὴ αἱμορροοῦσα
And   behold   a woman   suffering from a flow of blood

δώδεκα ἔτη προσελθοῦσα ὄπισθεν ἥψατο
twelve   years   approaching   behind   touched

τοῦ κρασπέδου τοῦ ἱματίου αὐτοῦ·
the   fringe   of the   garment   of him;

21 ἔλεγεν γὰρ ἐν ἑαυτῇ· ἐὰν μόνον
for she was saying   in   herself: If   only

ἅψωμαι τοῦ ἱματίου αὐτοῦ, σωθήσομαι.
I may touch   the   garment   of him,   I shall be healed.

22 ὁ δὲ Ἰησοῦς στραφεὶς καὶ ἰδὼν
–   And   Jesus   turning   and   seeing

αὐτὴν εἶπεν· θάρσει, θύγατερ· ἡ
her   said: Be of good cheer,   daughter;   the

πίστις σου σέσωκέν σε. καὶ ἐσώθη
faith   of thee   has healed   thee.   And was healed

ἡ γυνὴ ἀπὸ τῆς ὥρας ἐκείνης. **23** Καὶ
the woman   from   –   hour   that.   And

ἐλθὼν ὁ Ἰησοῦς εἰς τὴν οἰκίαν τοῦ ἄρχοντος
coming   –   Jesus   into   the   house   of the   ruler

καὶ ἰδὼν τοὺς αὐλητὰς καὶ τὸν ὄχλον
and   seeing   the   flute-players   and   the   crowd

θορυβούμενον **24** ἔλεγεν· ἀναχωρεῖτε· οὐ
terrified   he said: Depart ye;   not

γὰρ ἀπέθανεν τὸ κοράσιον ἀλλὰ καθεύδει.
for   died   the   girl   but   sleeps.

καὶ κατεγέλων αὐτοῦ. **25** ὅτε δὲ
And   they ridiculed   him.   But when

ἐξεβλήθη ὁ ὄχλος, εἰσελθὼν ἐκράτησεν
was put out   the   crowd,   entering   he took hold of

and took her by the hand, and the maid arose.

26 And the fame hereof went abroad into all that land.

27 ¶ And when Jesus departed thence, two blind men followed him, crying, and saying, *Thou* son of David, have mercy on us.

28 And when he was come into the house, the blind men came to him: and Jesus saith unto them, Believe ye that I am able to do this? They said unto him, Yea, Lord.

29 Then touched he their eyes, saying, According to your faith be it unto you.

30 And their eyes were opened; and Jesus straitly charged them, saying, See *that* no man know *it*.

31 But they, when they were departed, spread abroad his fame in all that country.

32 ¶ As they went out, behold, they brought to him a dumb man possessed with a devil.

33 And when the devil was cast out, the dumb spake: and the multitudes marvelled, saying, It was never so seen in Israel.

34 But the Pharisees

τῆς	χειρὸς	αὐτῆς,	καὶ	ἠγέρθη	τὸ	κορα-
the	hand	of her,	and	was raised	the	girl.

σιον.	**26** καὶ	ἐξῆλθεν	ἡ	φήμη	αὕτη
	And	went out	–	report	this

εἰς	ὅλην	τὴν	γῆν	ἐκείνην.	**27** Καὶ
into	all	–	land	that.	And

παράγοντι ἐκεῖθεν τῷ 'Ιησοῦ ἠκολούθησαν
passing by thence – Jesus[e] followed
=as Jesus passed by thence

δύο τυφλοὶ κράζοντες καὶ λέγοντες· ἐλέησον
two blind men crying out and saying: Pity

ἡμᾶς, υἱὸς Δαυίδ. **28** ἐλθόντι δὲ εἰς
us, son of David. And coming[e] into
=when he came

τὴν οἰκίαν προσῆλθον αὐτῷ οἱ τυφλοί,
the house approached *to* him the blind men,

καὶ λέγει αὐτοῖς ὁ 'Ιησοῦς· πιστεύετε
and says to them – Jesus: Believe ye

ὅτι δύναμαι τοῦτο ποιῆσαι; λέγουσιν
that I can this *to* do? They say

αὐτῷ· ναί, κύριε. **29** τότε ἥψατο τῶν
to him: Yes, Lord. Then he touched the

ὀφθαλμῶν αὐτῶν λέγων· κατὰ τὴν
eyes of them saying: According to the

πίστιν ὑμῶν γενηθήτω ὑμῖν. **30** καὶ
faith of you let it be to you. And

ἠνεῴχθησαν αὐτῶν οἱ ὀφθαλμοί. καὶ
were opened of them the eyes. And

ἐνεβριμήθη αὐτοῖς ὁ 'Ιησοῦς λέγων·
sternly admonished them – Jesus saying:

ὁρᾶτε μηδεὶς γινωσκέτω. **31** οἱ δὲ
See [a]no one [1]let [a]know. But they

ἐξελθόντες διεφήμισαν αὐτὸν ἐν ὅλῃ
going out spread about him in all

τῇ γῇ ἐκείνῃ. **32** Αὐτῶν δὲ ἐξερχομένων,
– land that. And them going out,[a]
=as they were going out,

ἰδοὺ προσήνεγκαν αὐτῷ κωφὸν δαι-
behold they brought to him a dumb man *being*

μονιζόμενον. **33** καὶ ἐκβληθέντος τοῦ
demon-possessed. And being expelled the
=when the demon was expelled

δαιμονίου ἐλάλησεν ὁ κωφός. καὶ ἐθαύμασαν
demon[a] spoke the dumb man. And marvelled

οἱ ὄχλοι λέγοντες· οὐδέποτε ἐφάνη οὕτως
the crowds saying: Never it appeared thus

ἐν τῷ 'Ισραήλ. **34** οἱ δὲ Φαρισαῖοι
in – Israel. But the Pharisees

said, He casteth out devils through the prince of the devils.

35 ¶ And Jesus went about all the cities and villages, teaching in their synagogues, and preaching the gospel of the kingdom, and healing every sickness and every disease among the people.

36 But when he saw the multitudes, he was moved with compassion on them, because they fainted, and were scattered abroad, as sheep having no shepherd.

37 Then saith he unto his disciples, The harvest truly *is* plenteous, but the labourers *are* few;

38 Pray ye therefore the Lord of the harvest, that he will send forth labourers into his harvest.

CHAPTER 10

A ND when he had called unto *him* his twelve disciples, he gave them power *against* unclean spirits, to cast them out, and to heal all manner of sickness and all manner of disease.

2 Now the names of the twelve apostles are these; The first, Simon, who is called Peter, and Andrew 'his brother; James, *the son*

ἔλεγον·   ἐν   τῷ   ἄρχοντι   τῶν   δαιμονίων
said: By   the   ruler   of the   demons

ἐκβάλλει   τὰ   δαιμόνια.
he expels   the   demons.

35 Καὶ   περιῆγεν   ὁ   Ἰησοῦς   τὰς
And   went about   –   Jesus   the

πόλεις   πάσας   καὶ   τὰς   κώμας,   διδάσκων
cities   all   and   the   villages,   teaching

ἐν   ταῖς   συναγωγαῖς   αὐτῶν   καὶ   κηρύσσων
in   the   synagogues   of them   and   proclaiming

τὸ   εὐαγγέλιον   τῆς   βασιλείας   καὶ   θεραπεύων
the   gospel   of the   kingdom   and   healing

πᾶσαν   νόσον   καὶ   πᾶσαν   μαλακίαν.
every   disease   and   every   illness.

36 Ἰδὼν   δὲ   τοὺς   ὄχλους   ἐσπλαγχνίσθη
And seeing   the   crowds   he was filled with tenderness

περὶ   αὐτῶν,   ὅτι   ἦσαν   ἐσκυλμένοι   καὶ
concerning   them,   because   they were   distressed   and

ἐρριμμένοι   ὡσεὶ   πρόβατα   μὴ   ἔχοντα
prostrate   as   sheep   not   having

ποιμένα.   37 τότε   λέγει   τοῖς   μαθηταῖς
a shepherd.   Then   he says   to the   disciples

αὐτοῦ·   ὁ   μὲν   θερισμὸς   πολύς,   οἱ   δὲ
of him: Indeed the   harvest [is]   much,   but the

ἐργάται   ὀλίγοι·   38 δεήθητε   οὖν   τοῦ   κυρίου
workmen   few;   pray ye   therefore   the   Lord

τοῦ   θερισμοῦ   ὅπως   ἐκβάλῃ
of the   harvest   so that   he may thrust forth

ἐργάτας   εἰς   τὸν   θερισμὸν   αὐτοῦ.   10 Καὶ
workmen   into   the   harvest   of him.   And

προσκαλεσάμενος   τοὺς   δώδεκα   μαθητὰς
calling forward   the   twelve   disciples

αὐτοῦ   ἔδωκεν   αὐτοῖς   ἐξουσίαν   πνευμάτων
of him   he gave   to them   authority   of(over) spirits

ἀκαθάρτων   ὥστε   ἐκβάλλειν   αὐτά,   καὶ
unclean   so as   to expel   them,   and

θεραπεύειν   πᾶσαν   νόσον   καὶ   πᾶσαν   μαλα-
to heal   every   disease   and   every   ill-

κίαν.   2 Τῶν   δὲ   δώδεκα   ἀποστόλων
ness.   Now of the   twelve   apostles

τὰ   ὀνόματά   ἐστιν   ταῦτα·   πρῶτος   Σίμων
the   names   is(are)   these: first   Simon

ὁ   λεγόμενος   Πέτρος   καὶ   Ἀνδρέας   ὁ
the [one]   named   Peter   and   Andrew   the

ἀδελφὸς   αὐτοῦ,   καὶ   Ἰάκωβος   ὁ   τοῦ
brother   of him,   and   James   the [son]   –

of Zebedee, and John his brother;

3 Philip, and Bartholomew; Thomas, and Matthew the publican; James *the son* of Alphæus, and Lebbæus, whose surname was Thaddæus;

4 Simon the Canaanite, and Judas Iscariot, who also betrayed him.

5 These twelve Jesus sent forth, and commanded them, saying, Go not into the way of the Gentiles, and into *any* city of the Samaritans enter ye not:

6 But go rather to the lost sheep of the house of Israel.

7 And as ye go, preach, saying, The kingdom of heaven is at hand.

8 Heal the sick, cleanse the lepers, raise the dead, cast out devils: freely ye have received, freely give.

9 Provide neither gold, nor silver, nor brass in your purses,

10 Nor scrip for *your* journey, neither two coats, neither shoes, nor yet staves: for the workman is worthy of his meat.

11 And into whatsoever city or town ye shall enter, enquire who in it is worthy; and there abide till ye go thence.

Ζεβεδαίου καὶ Ἰωάννης ὁ ἀδελφὸς αὐτοῦ,
of Zebedee and John the brother of him,

3 Φίλιππος καὶ Βαρθολομαῖος, Θωμᾶς
Philip and Bartholomew, Thomas

καὶ Μαθθαῖος ὁ τελώνης, Ἰάκωβος
and Matthew the tax-collector, James

ὁ τοῦ Ἀλφαίου καὶ Θαδδαῖος, 4 Σίμων
the [son] – of Alphæus and Thaddæus, Simon

ὁ Καναναῖος καὶ Ἰούδας ὁ Ἰσκαριώτης
the Cananæan and Judas – Iscariot

ὁ καὶ παραδοὺς αὐτόν. 5 Τούτους
the [one] also betraying him. These

τοὺς δώδεκα ἀπέστειλεν ὁ Ἰησοῦς
– twelve sent forth – Jesus

παραγγείλας αὐτοῖς λέγων·
giving charge to them saying:

Εἰς ὁδὸν ἐθνῶν μὴ ἀπέλθητε, καὶ
Into [the] way of [the] nations go ye not, and

εἰς πόλιν Σαμαριτῶν μὴ εἰσέλθητε·
into a city of Samaritans enter not;

6 πορεύεσθε δὲ μᾶλλον πρὸς τὰ πρόβατα
but go rather unto the sheep

τὰ ἀπολωλότα οἴκου Ἰσραήλ. 7 πορευ-
the lost of [the] house of Israel. And

όμενοι δὲ κηρύσσετε λέγοντες ὅτι ἤγγικεν
going proclaim ye saying[,] – has drawn near

ἡ βασιλεία τῶν οὐρανῶν. 8 ἀσθενοῦντας
The kingdom of the heavens. Ailing [ones]

θεραπεύετε, νεκροὺς ἐγείρετε, λεπροὺς
heal ye, dead [ones] raise, lepers

καθαρίζετε, δαιμόνια ἐκβάλλετε· δωρεὰν
cleanse, demons expel; freely

ἐλάβετε, δωρεὰν δότε. 9 Μὴ κτήσησθε
ye received, freely give. Do not provide

χρυσὸν μηδὲ ἄργυρον μηδὲ χαλκὸν εἰς
gold nor silver nor brass in

τὰς ζώνας ὑμων, 10 μὴ πήραν εἰς ὁδὸν
the girdles of you, not a wallet for [the] way

μηδὲ δύο χιτῶνας μηδὲ ὑποδήματα μηδὲ
nor two tunics nor sandals nor

ῥάβδον· ἄξιος γὰρ ὁ ἐργάτης τῆς
a staff; for worthy [is] the workman of the

τροφῆς αὐτοῦ. 11 εἰς ἢν δ' ἂν πόλιν
food of him. And into whatever city

ἢ κώμην εἰσέλθητε, ἐξετάσατε τίς ἐν
or village ye may enter, inquire who in

αὐτῇ ἄξιός ἐστιν· κἀκεῖ μείνατε ἕως ἂν
it worthy is; and there remain until

12 And when ye come into an house, salute it.

13 And if the house be worthy, let your peace come upon it: but if it be not worthy, let your peace return to you.

14 And whosoever shall not receive you, nor hear your words, when ye depart out of that house or city, shake off the dust of your feet.

15 Verily I say unto you, It shall be more tolerable for the land of Sodom and Gomorrha in the day of judgment, than for that city.

16 ¶ Behold, I send you forth as sheep in the midst of wolves: be ye therefore wise as serpents, and harmless as doves.

17 But beware of men: for they will deliver you up to the councils, and they will scourge you in their synagogues;

18 And ye shall be brought before governors and kings for my sake, for a testimony against them and the Gentiles.

19 But when they deliver you up, take no thought how or what ye shall speak: for it shall be given you in that same hour what ye shall speak.

ἐξέλθητε.   **12** εἰσερχόμενοι δὲ εἰς τὴν
ye may go out.   And entering   into   the

οἰκίαν ἀσπάσασθε αὐτήν· **13** καὶ ἐὰν μὲν
house   greet   it;   and   if indeed

ᾖ ἡ οἰκία ἀξία, ἐλθάτω ἡ εἰρήνη ὑμῶν
be the house worthy, let come the peace of you

ἐπ᾽ αὐτήν· ἐὰν δὲ μὴ ᾖ ἀξία, ἡ εἰρήνη
on   it;   but if it be not worthy, the peace

ὑμῶν πρὸς ὑμᾶς ἐπιστραφήτω.   **14** καὶ
of you unto you   let return.   And

ὃς ἂν μὴ δέξηται ὑμᾶς μηδὲ ἀκούσῃ
whoever   may not receive   you   nor   hear

τοὺς λόγους ὑμῶν, ἐξερχόμενοι ἔξω
the   words   of you,   going out   outside

τῆς οἰκίας ἢ τῆς πόλεως ἐκείνης ἐκτινά-
-   house   or   -   city   that   shake

ξατε τὸν κονιορτὸν τῶν ποδῶν ὑμῶν.
off   the   dust   of the   feet   of you.

15 ἀμὴν λέγω ὑμῖν, ἀνεκτότερον ἔσται
Truly   I tell   you,   more tolerable   it will be [for]

γῇ Σοδόμων καὶ Γομόρρων ἐν ἡμέρᾳ κρίσεως
[the] land of Sodom and   Gomorra in [the] day of judgment

ἢ τῇ πόλει ἐκείνῃ.   **16** Ἰδοὺ ἐγὼ
than [for] -   city   that.   Behold   I

ἀποστέλλω ὑμᾶς ὡς πρόβατα ἐν μέσῳ
send forth   you   as   sheep   in [the] midst

λύκων· γίνεσθε οὖν φρόνιμοι ὡς οἱ
of wolves;   be ye   therefore   prudent   as   -

ὄφεις καὶ ἀκέραιοι ὡς αἱ περιστεραί.
serpents and   harmless   as   -   doves.

17 Προσέχετε δὲ ἀπὸ τῶν ἀνθρώπων·
    And beware   from(of)   -   men;

παραδώσουσιν γὰρ ὑμᾶς εἰς συνέδρια,
for they will deliver up   you   to   councils,

καὶ ἐν ταῖς συναγωγαῖς αὐτῶν μαστιγώ-
and in   the   synagogues   of them   they will

σουσιν ὑμᾶς· **18** καὶ ἐπὶ ἡγεμόνας δὲ καὶ
scourge   you;   and before   leaders   and also

βασιλεῖς ἀχθήσεσθε ἕνεκεν ἐμοῦ, εἰς
kings   ye will be led   for the sake of   me,   for

μαρτύριον αὐτοῖς καὶ τοῖς ἔθνεσιν.
a testimony   to them   and   to the   nations.

19 ὅταν δὲ παραδῶσιν ὑμᾶς, μὴ μεριμνή-
    But when   they deliver up   you,   do not be

σητε πῶς ἢ τί λαλήσητε· δοθήσεται
anxious   how   or   what   ye may say;   [2]it will be given

γὰρ ὑμῖν ἐν ἐκείνῃ τῇ ὥρᾳ τί λαλήσητε·
[1]for   to you   in   that   -   hour   what   ye may say;

20 For it is not ye that speak, but the Spirit of your Father which speaketh in you.

21 And the brother shall deliver up the brother to death, and the father the child: and the children shall rise up against *their* parents, and cause them to be put to death.

22 And ye shall be hated of all *men* for my name's sake: but he that endureth to the end shall be saved.

23 But when they persecute you in this city, flee ye into another: for verily I say unto you, Ye shall not have gone over the cities of Israel, till the Son of man be come.

24 The disciple is not above *his* master, nor the servant above his lord.

25 It is enough for the disciple that he be as his master, and the servant as his lord. If they have called the master of the house Beelzebub, how much more *shall they call* them of his household?

26 Fear them not therefore: for there is nothing covered, that shall not be revealed; and hid, that shall not be known.

27 What I tell you in darkness, *that* speak ye in

20 οὐ γὰρ ὑμεῖς ἐστε οἱ λαλοῦντες,
for not   ye   are the [ones] speaking,
ἀλλὰ τὸ πνεῦμα τοῦ πατρὸς ὑμῶν τὸ
but   the Spirit of the Father of you the [one]
λαλοῦν ἐν ὑμῖν. 21 παραδώσει δὲ
speaking in   you.   And ²will deliver up
ἀδελφὸς ἀδελφὸν εἰς θάνατον καὶ πατὴρ
¹brother brother   to   death   and father
τέκνον, καὶ ἐπαναστήσονται τέκνα ἐπὶ
child,   and   will stand up   children against
γονεῖς καὶ θανατώσουσιν αὐτούς. 22 καὶ
parents and   put to death   them.   And
ἔσεσθε μισούμενοι ὑπὸ πάντων διὰ
ye will be being hated   by   all men on account of
τὸ ὄνομά μου· ὁ δὲ ὑπομείνας εἰς
the name of me; but the [one] enduring   to
τέλος, οὗτος σωθήσεται. 23 ὅταν δὲ
[the] end, this   will be saved.   But when
διώκωσιν ὑμᾶς ἐν τῇ πόλει ταύτῃ,
they persecute you   in - city   this,
φεύγετε εἰς τὴν ἑτέραν· ἀμὴν γὰρ
flee ye   to   - [an]other· for truly
λέγω ὑμῖν, οὐ μὴ τελέσητε τὰς πόλεις
I tell you, by no means ye will complete the cities
[τοῦ] Ἰσραὴλ ἔως ἔλθη ὁ υἱὸς τοῦ ἀν-
 - of Israel until comes the Son -   of
θρώπου. 24 Οὐκ ἔστιν μαθητὴς ὑπὲρ
man.   not   is   A disciple above
τὸν διδάσκαλον οὐδὲ δοῦλος ὑπὲρ τὸν
the   teacher   nor   a slave above the
κύριον αὐτοῦ. 25 ἀρκετὸν τῷ μαθητῇ
lord   of him.   Enough   for the disciple
ἵνα γένηται ὡς ὁ διδάσκαλος αὐτοῦ,
that   he be   as the   teacher   of him,
καὶ ὁ δοῦλος ὡς ὁ κύριος αὐτοῦ. εἰ
and the slave   as the lord of him. If
τὸν οἰκοδεσπότην Βεεζεβούλ ἐπεκάλεσαν,
the   housemaster   Beelzebub   they called,
πόσω μᾶλλον τοὺς οἰκιακοὺς αὐτοῦ.
how much more   the members of [the] household of him.
26 μὴ οὖν φοβηθῆτε αὐτούς· οὐδὲν γάρ
   Therefore fear ye not   them;   for nothing
ἐστιν κεκαλυμμένον ὃ οὐκ ἀποκαλυφ-
is   having been veiled which   will not be un-
θήσεται, καὶ κρυπτὸν ὃ οὐ γνωσθήσεται.
veiled,   and hidden which will not be made known.
27 ὃ λέγω ὑμῖν ἐν τῇ σκοτίᾳ, εἴπατε
What I say to you in the darkness,   say ye

light: and what ye hear in the ear, *that* preach ye upon the housetops.

28 And fear not them which kill the body, but are not able to kill the soul: but rather fear him which is able to destroy both soul and body in hell.

29 Are not two sparrows sold for a farthing? and one of them shall not fall on the ground without your Father.

30 But the very hairs of your head are all numbered.

31 Fear ye not therefore, ye are of more value than many sparrows.

32 Whosoever therefore shall confess me before men, him will I confess also before my Father which is in heaven.

33 But whosoever shall deny me before men, him will I also deny before my Father which is in heaven.

34 Think not that I am come to send peace on earth: I came not to send peace, but a sword.

35 For I am come to set a man at variance against his father, and the daughter against her mother, and the

ἐν τῷ φωτί· καὶ ὃ εἰς τὸ οὖς ἀκούετε,
in the light; and what in the ear ye hear,

κηρύξατε ἐπὶ τῶν δωμάτων. 28 καὶ
proclaim on the housetops. And

μὴ φοβεῖσθε ἀπὸ τῶν ἀποκτεννόντων
do not fear - the [ones] killing

τὸ σῶμα, τὴν δὲ ψυχὴν μὴ δυναμένων
the body, but the soul not being able

ἀποκτεῖναι· φοβεῖσθε δὲ μᾶλλον τὸν
to kill; but fear ye rather the [one]

δυνάμενον καὶ ψυχὴν καὶ σῶμα ἀπολέσαι
being able both soul and body to destroy

ἐν γεέννῃ. 29 οὐχὶ δύο στρουθία ἀσσα-
in gehenna. Not two sparrows of(for) a

ρίου πωλεῖται; καὶ ἓν ἐξ αὐτῶν οὐ
farthing are sold? and one of them not

πεσεῖται ἐπὶ τὴν γῆν ἄνευ τοῦ πατρὸς
will fall on the earth without the Father

ὑμῶν. 30 ὑμῶν δὲ καὶ αἱ τρίχες τῆς
of you. But of you even the hairs of the

κεφαλῆς πᾶσαι ἠριθμημέναι εἰσίν. 31 μὴ
head all having been numbered are. not

οὖν φοβεῖσθε· πολλῶν στρουθίων διαφέρετε
Therefore fear ye; ³many ⁴sparrows ²excel

ὑμεῖς. 32 Πᾶς οὖν ὅστις ὁμολογήσει
¹ye. Everyone therefore who shall confess

ἐν ἐμοὶ ἔμπροσθεν τῶν ἀνθρώπων,
- me before - men,

ὁμολογήσω κἀγὼ ἐν αὐτῷ ἔμπροσθεν
will confess I also - him before

τοῦ πατρός μου τοῦ ἐν τοῖς οὐρανοῖς·
the Father of me - in the heavens;

33 ὅστις δ' ἂν ἀρνήσηται με ἔμπροσθεν
and whoever denies me before

τῶν ἀνθρώπων, ἀρνήσομαι κἀγὼ αὐτὸν
- men, will deny I also him

ἔμπροσθεν τοῦ πατρός μου τοῦ ἐν
before the Father of me - in

τοῖς οὐρανοῖς. 34 Μὴ νομίσητε ὅτι
the heavens. Do not suppose that

ἦλθον βαλεῖν εἰρήνην ἐπὶ τὴν γῆν· οὐκ ἦλθον
I came to bring peace on the earth; I came not

βαλεῖν εἰρήνην ἀλλὰ μάχαιραν. 35 ἦλθον γὰρ
to bring peace but a sword. For I came

διχάσαι ἄνθρωπον κατὰ τοῦ πατρὸς
to make hostile a man against the father

αὐτοῦ καὶ θυγατέρα κατὰ τῆς μητρὸς
of him and a daughter against the mother

daughter in law against her mother in law.

36 And a man's foes *shall be* they of his own household.

37 He that loveth father or mother more than me is not worthy of me: and he that loveth son or daughter more than me is not worthy of me.

38 And he that taketh not his cross, and followeth after me, is not worthy of me.

39 He that findeth his life shall lose it: and he that loseth his life for my sake shall find it.

40 He that receiveth you receiveth me, and he that receiveth me receiveth him that sent me.

41 He that receiveth a prophet in the name of a prophet shall receive a prophet's reward; and he that receiveth a righteous man in the name of a righteous man shall receive a righteous man's reward.

42 And whosoever shall give to drink unto one of these little ones a cup of cold *water* only in the name of a disciple, verily I say unto you, he shall in no wise lose his reward.

αὐτῆς καὶ νύμφην κατὰ τῆς πενθερᾶς
of her and a bride against the mother-in-law

αὐτῆς, 36 καὶ ἐχθροὶ τοῦ ἀνθρώπου οἱ
of her, and [the] enemies – of a man the

οἰκιακοὶ αὐτοῦ. 37 Ὁ φιλῶν πατέρα
members of [the] household of him. The [one] loving father

ἢ μητέρα ὑπὲρ ἐμὲ οὐκ ἔστιν μου ἄξιος·
or mother beyond me is not of me worthy;

καὶ ὁ φιλῶν υἱὸν ἢ θυγατέρα ὑπὲρ
and the [one] loving son or daughter beyond

ἐμὲ οὐκ ἔστιν μου ἄξιος· 38 καὶ ὃς
me is not of me worthy; and [he] who

οὐ λαμβάνει τὸν σταυρὸν αὐτοῦ καὶ
takes not the cross of him and

ἀκολουθεῖ ὀπίσω μου, οὐκ ἔστιν μου
follows after me, is not of me

ἄξιος. 39 ὁ εὑρὼν τὴν ψυχὴν αὐτοῦ
worthy. The [one] finding the life of him

ἀπολέσει αὐτήν, καὶ ὁ ἀπολέσας τὴν
will lose it, and the [one] losing the

ψυχὴν αὐτοῦ ἕνεκεν ἐμοῦ εὑρήσει αὐτήν.
life of him for the sake of me will find it.

40 Ὁ δεχόμενος ὑμᾶς ἐμὲ δέχεται, καὶ
The [one] receiving you me receives, and

ὁ ἐμὲ δεχόμενος δέχεται τὸν
the [one] me receiving receives the [one]

ἀποστείλαντά με. 41 ὁ δεχόμενος προ-
having sent me. The [one] receiving a pro-

φήτην εἰς ὄνομα προφήτου μισθὸν
phet in [the] name of a prophet [the] reward

προφήτου λήμψεται, καὶ ὁ δεχόμενος
of a prophet will receive, and the [one] receiving

δίκαιον εἰς ὄνομα δικαίου μισθὸν
a righteous man in [the] name of a righteous man [the] reward

δικαίου λήμψεται. 42 καὶ ὃς ἐὰν ποτίσῃ
of a righteous man will receive. And whoever gives to drink

ἕνα τῶν μικρῶν τούτων ποτήριον ψυχροῦ
one – of these little [ones] a cup of cold water

μόνον εἰς ὄνομα μαθητοῦ, ἀμὴν λέγω ὑμῖν,
only in [the] name of a disciple, truly I tell you,

οὐ μὴ ἀπολέσῃ τὸν μισθὸν αὐτοῦ.
on no account will he lose the reward of him.

CHAPTER 11

AND it came to pass, when Jesus had made an end of commanding his twelve disciples, he departed thence to teach and to preach in their cities.

2 ¶ Now when John had heard in the prison the works of Christ, he sent two of his disciples,

3 And said unto him, Art thou he that should come, or do we look for another?

4 Jesus answered and said unto them, Go and shew John again those things which ye do hear and see:

5 The blind receive their sight, and the lame walk, the lepers are cleansed, and the deaf hear, the dead are raised up, and the poor have the gospel preached to them.

6 And blessed is *he*, whosoever shall not be offended in me.

7 ¶ And as they departed, Jesus began to say unto the multitudes concerning John, What went ye out into the wilderness to see? A reed shaken with the wind?

8 But what went ye out for to see? A man clothed in soft raiment? behold, they that wear soft *clothing* are in kings' houses.

9 But what went ye out for to see? A prophet? yea,

---

11 Καὶ   ἐγένετο   ὅτε   ἐτέλεσεν   ὁ
And   ᵗit came to pass when   ended   -

'Ιησοῦς   διατάσσων   τοῖς   δώδεκα   μαθηταῖς
Jesus   giving charge   to the   twelve   disciples

αὐτοῦ,   μετέβη   ἐκεῖθεν   τοῦ   διδάσκειν
of him,   he removed   thence   -   to teachᵈ

καὶ   κηρύσσειν   ἐν   ταῖς   πόλεσιν   αὐτῶν.
and   to proclaimᵈ   in   the   cities   of them.

2 Ὁ   δὲ   'Ιωάννης   ἀκούσας   ἐν   τῷ
-   But   John   hearing   in   the

δεσμωτηρίῳ   τὰ   ἔργα   τοῦ   Χριστοῦ,
prison   the   works   -   of Christ,

πέμψας   διὰ   τῶν   μαθητῶν   αὐτοῦ   **3** εἶπεν
sending through the   disciples   of him   said

αὐτῷ·   σὺ   εἶ   ὁ   ἐρχόμενος,   ἢ   ἕτερον
to him: Thou art the   coming [one], or   another

προσδοκῶμεν;   **4** καὶ   ἀποκριθεὶς   ὁ
may we expect?   And   answering   -

'Ιησοῦς   εἶπεν   αὐτοῖς·   πορευθέντες   ἀπαγ-
Jesus   said   to them: Going   report

γείλατε   'Ιωάννῃ   ἃ   ἀκούετε   καὶ   βλέπετε·
ye   to John [the things] which   ye hear   and   see:

5 τυφλοὶ   ἀναβλέπουσιν   καὶ   χωλοὶ
blind men   see again   and   lame men

περιπατοῦσιν,   λεπροὶ   καθαρίζονται   καὶ   κωφοὶ
walk,   lepers   are cleansed   and deaf men

ἀκούουσιν,   καὶ   νεκροὶ   ἐγείρονται   καὶ
hear,   and   dead men   are raised   and

πτωχοὶ   εὐαγγελίζονται·   **6** καὶ   μακάριός
poor men   are evangelized;   and   blessed

ἐστιν   ὃς   ἐὰν   μὴ   σκανδαλισθῇ   ἐν   ἐμοι.
is   whoever   is not offended   in   me.

7 Τούτων   δὲ   πορευομένων   ἤρξατο   ὁ
And these   goingᵃ   began   -
            = as these were going

'Ιησοῦς   λέγειν   τοῖς   ὄχλοις   περὶ   'Ιωάννου·
Jesus   to say   to the   crowds   concerning   John:

τί   ἐξήλθατε   εἰς   τὴν   ἔρημον   θεάσασθαι;
What went ye out   into   the   wilderness   to see?

κάλαμον   ὑπὸ   ἀνέμου   σαλευόμενον;   **8** ἀλλὰ
a reed   by   wind   being shaken?   But

τί   ἐξήλθατε   ἰδεῖν;   ἄνθρωπον   ἐν   μαλακοῖς
what went ye out   to see?   a man   in   soft material

ἠμφιεσμένον;   ἰδοὺ   οἱ   τὰ   μαλακὰ
having been clothed?   Behold[,] the [ones]   -   soft material

φοροῦντες   ἐν   τοῖς   οἴκοις   τῶν   βασιλέων.   **9** ἀλλὰ
wearing [are] in   the   houses   -   of kings.   But

τί   ἐξήλθατε;   προφήτην   ἰδεῖν;   ναὶ   λέγω
why   went ye out?   a prophet   to see?   Yes[,]   I tell

I say unto you, and more than a prophet.

10 For this is *he*, of whom it is written, Behold, I send my messenger before thy face, which shall prepare thy way before thee.

11 Verily I say unto you, Among them that are born of women there hath not risen a greater than John the Baptist: notwithstanding he that is least in the kingdom of heaven is greater than he.

12 And from the days of John the Baptist until now the kingdom of heaven suffereth violence, and the violent take it by force.

13 For all the prophets and the law prophesied until John.

14 And if ye will receive *it*, this is Elias, which was for to come.

15 He that hath ears to hear, let him hear.

16 But whereunto shall I liken this generation? It is like unto children sitting in the markets, and calling unto their fellows,

17 And saying, We have piped unto you, and ye have not danced; we have mourned unto you, and ye have not lamented.

18 For John came neither eating nor drinking, and they say, He hath a devil.

19 The Son of man came eating and drinking, and

ὑμῖν, καὶ περισσότερον προφήτου. 10 οὗτός
you, and more [than] a prophet. This

ἐστιν περὶ οὗ γέγραπται· ἰδοὺ ἐγὼ
is he concerning whom it has been written: Behold[,] I

ἀποστέλλω τὸν ἄγγελόν μου πρὸ προσώπου
send forth the messenger of me before [the] face

σου, ὃς κατασκευάσει τὴν ὁδόν σου
of thee, who will prepare the way of thee

ἔμπροσθέν σου. 11 ἀμὴν λέγω ὑμῖν,
before thee. Truly I tell you,

οὐκ ἐγήγερται ἐν γεννητοῖς γυναικῶν
there has not arisen among [those] born of women

μείζων Ἰωάννου τοῦ βαπτιστοῦ· ὁ δὲ
a greater [than] John the Baptist; but the

μικρότερος ἐν τῇ βασιλείᾳ τῶν οὐρανῶν
lesser in the kingdom of the heavens

μείζων αὐτοῦ ἐστιν. 12 ἀπὸ δὲ τῶν
greater [than] he is. And from the

ἡμερῶν Ἰωάννου τοῦ βαπτιστοῦ ἕως
days of John the Baptist until

ἄρτι ἡ βασιλεία τῶν οὐρανῶν βιάζεται,
now the kingdom of the heavens is forcibly treated,

καὶ βιασταὶ ἁρπάζουσιν αὐτήν. 13 πάντες γὰρ
and forceful men seize it. For all

οἱ προφῆται καὶ ὁ νόμος ἕως
the prophets and the law until

Ἰωάννου ἐπροφήτευσαν· 14 καὶ εἰ θέλετε
John prophesied; and if ye are willing

δέξασθαι, αὐτός ἐστιν Ἠλίας ὁ μέλλων
to receive [it *or* him], he is Elias the [one] about

ἔρχεσθαι. 15 ὁ ἔχων ὦτα ἀκουέτω.
to come. The [one] having ears let him hear.

16 Τίνι δὲ ὁμοιώσω τὴν γενεὰν ταύτην;
But to what shall I liken – generation this?

ὁμοία ἐστὶν παιδίοις καθημένοις ἐν ταῖς
Like it is to children sitting in the

ἀγοραῖς ἃ προσφωνοῦντα τοῖς ἑτέροις
marketplaces who calling to the others

17 λέγουσιν· ηὐλήσαμεν ὑμῖν καὶ οὐκ
say: We piped to you and not

ὠρχήσασθε· ἐθρηνήσαμεν καὶ οὐκ ἐκόψασθε.
ye did dance; we lamented and ye did not mourn.

18 ἦλθεν γὰρ Ἰωάννης μήτε ἐσθίων μήτε
For came John neither eating nor

πίνων, καὶ λέγουσιν· δαιμόνιον ἔχει.
drinking, and they say: a demon He has.

19 ἦλθεν ὁ υἱὸς τοῦ ἀνθρώπου ἐσθίων καὶ
Came the Son – of man eating and

they say, Behold a man gluttonous, and a wine-bibber, a friend of publicans and sinners. But wisdom is justified of her children.

20 ¶ Then began he to upbraid the cities wherein most of his mighty works were done, because they repented not:

21 Woe unto thee, Chorazin! woe unto thee, Bethsaida! for if the mighty works, which were done in you, had been done in Tyre and Sidon, they would have repented long ago in sackcloth and ashes.

22 But I say unto you, It shall be more tolerable for Tyre and Sidon at the day of judgment, than for you.

23 And thou, Capernaum, which art exalted unto heaven, shalt be brought down to hell: for if the mighty works, which have been done in thee, had been done in Sodom, it would have remained until this day.

24 But I say unto you, That it shall be more tolerable for the land of Sodom in the day of judgment, than for thee.

25 ¶ At that time Jesus answered and said, I thank thee, O Father, Lord of heaven and earth, because thou hast hid these things from the wise and prudent,

πίνων, καὶ λέγουσιν· ἰδοὺ ἄνθρωπος
drinking, and they say: Behold[,] a man

φάγος καὶ οἰνοπότης, τελωνῶν φίλος καὶ
gluttonous and a wine-drinker, of tax-collectors a friend and

ἁμαρτωλῶν. καὶ ἐδικαιώθη ἡ σοφία ἀπὸ
of sinners. And was(is) justified - wisdom from(by)

τῶν ἔργων αὐτῆς.
the works of her.

20 Τότε ἤρξατο ὀνειδίζειν τὰς πόλεις
Then he began to reproach the cities

ἐν αἷς ἐγένοντο αἱ πλεῖσται δυνάμεις
in which happened the very many powerful deeds

αὐτοῦ, ὅτι οὐ μετενόησαν· **21** οὐαί σοι,
of him, because they repented not: Woe to thee,

Χοραζίν· οὐαί σοι, Βηθσαϊδά· ὅτι εἰ
Chorazin; woe to thee, Bethsaida; because if

ἐν Τύρῳ καὶ Σιδῶνι ἐγένοντο αἱ δυνάμεις
in Tyre and Sidon happened the powerful deeds

αἱ γενόμεναι ἐν ὑμῖν, πάλαι ἂν
- having happened in you, long ago -

ἐν σάκκῳ καὶ σποδῷ μετενόησαν.
in sackcloth and ashes they would have repented.

22 πλὴν λέγω ὑμῖν, Τύρῳ καὶ Σιδῶνι
However I tell you, For Tyre and for Sidon

ἀνεκτότερον ἔσται ἐν ἡμέρᾳ κρίσεως ἢ
more tolerable it will be in [the] day of judgment than

ὑμῖν. **23** καὶ σύ, Καφαρναούμ, μὴ
for you. And thou, Capernaum, not

ἕως οὐρανοῦ ὑψωθήσῃ; ἕως ᾅδου
as far as heaven wast thou exalted? as far as hades

καταβήσῃ· ὅτι εἰ ἐν Σοδόμοις ἐγενήθησαν
thou shalt descend; because if in Sodom happened

αἱ δυνάμεις αἱ γενόμεναι ἐν σοί,
the powerful deeds - having happened in thee,

ἔμεινεν ἂν μέχρι τῆς σήμερον. **24** πλὴν
it would have remained until - to-day. However

λέγω ὑμῖν ὅτι γῇ Σοδόμων ἀνεκτότερον
I tell you that for [the] land of Sodom more tolerable

ἔσται ἐν ἡμέρᾳ κρίσεως ἢ σοί.
it will be in [the] day of judgment than for thee.

25 Ἐν ἐκείνῳ τῷ καιρῷ ἀποκριθεὶς
At that - time answering

ὁ Ἰησοῦς εἶπεν· ἐξομολογοῦμαί σοι,
- Jesus said: I give thanks to thee,

πάτερ, κύριε τοῦ οὐρανοῦ καὶ τῆς γῆς,
Father, lord of the heaven and of the earth,

ὅτι ἔκρυψας ταῦτα ἀπὸ σοφῶν καὶ συνε-
because thou hiddest these things from wise and intel-

and hast revealed them
unto babes.

26 Even so, Father: for
so it seemed good in thy
sight.

27 All things are delivered unto me of my Father:
and no man knoweth the
Son, but the Father;
neither knoweth any man
the Father, save the Son,
and *he* to whomsoever the
Son will reveal *him*.

28 ¶ Come unto me, all
ye that labour and are
heavy laden, and I will give
you rest.

29 Take my yoke upon
you, and learn of me; for I
am meek and lowly in
heart: and ye shall find
rest unto your souls.

30 For my yoke *is* easy,
and my burden is light.

τῶν,   καὶ   ἀπεκάλυψας   αὐτὰ   νηπίοις·
ligent men,   and   didst reveal   them   to infants;

26 ναί,   ὁ   πατήρ,   ὅτι   οὕτως   εὐδοκία
   yes,   –   Father,   because   thus   good pleasure

ἐγένετο   ἔμπροσθέν   σου.   27 Πάντα   μοι
it was   before   thee.   All things   to me

παρεδόθη   ὑπὸ   τοῦ   πατρός   μου,   καὶ
were delivered   by   the   Father   of me,   and

οὐδεὶς   ἐπιγινώσκει   τὸν   υἱὸν   εἰ   μὴ   ὁ
no one   fully knows   the   Son   except   the

πατήρ,   οὐδὲ   τὸν   πατέρα   τις   ἐπιγινώσκει
Father,   neither   the   Father   anyone   fully knows

εἰ   μὴ   ὁ   υἱὸς   καὶ   ᾧ   ἐὰν   βούληται   ὁ
except   the   Son   and [he] to whom   if   wills   the

υἱὸς   ἀποκαλύψαι.   28 Δεῦτε   πρός   με
Son   to reveal.   Come   unto   me

πάντες   οἱ   κοπιῶντες   καὶ   πεφορτισμένοι,
all   the [ones]   labouring   and   *having been* burdened,

κἀγὼ   ἀναπαύσω   ὑμᾶς.   29 ἄρατε   τὸν
and I   will rest   you.   Take   the

ζυγόν   μου   ἐφ'   ὑμᾶς   καὶ   μάθετε   ἀπ'
yoke   of me   on   you   and   learn   from

ἐμοῦ,   ὅτι   πραΰς   εἰμι   καὶ   ταπεινὸς   τῇ
me,   because   meek   I am   and   lowly   –

καρδίᾳ,   καὶ   εὑρήσετε   ἀνάπαυσιν   ταῖς
in heart,   and   ye will find   rest   to the

ψυχαῖς   ὑμῶν·   30 ὁ   γὰρ   ζυγός   μου
souls   of you;   for the   yoke   of me

χρηστὸς   καὶ   τὸ   φορτίον   μου   ἐλαφρόν
gentle   and   the   burden   of me   light

ἐστιν.
is.

CHAPTER 12

A T that time Jesus
went on the sabbath
day through the corn;
and his disciples were an
hungred, and began to
pluck the ears of corn, and
to eat.

2 But when the Pharisees
saw *it*, they said unto him,
Behold, thy disciples do
that which is not lawful
to do upon the sabbath
day.

12 Ἐν   ἐκείνῳ   τῷ   καιρῷ   ἐπορεύθη   ὁ
   At   that   –   time   went   –

Ἰησοῦς   τοῖς   σάββασιν   διὰ   τῶν   σπορίμων·
Jesus   on the   sabbath   through   the   cornfields;

οἱ   δὲ   μαθηταὶ   αὐτοῦ   ἐπείνασαν,   καὶ
and the   disciples   of him   hungered,   and

ἤρξαντο   τίλλειν   στάχυας   καὶ   ἐσθίειν.
began   to pluck   ears [of corn]   and   to eat.

2 οἱ   δὲ   Φαρισαῖοι   ἰδόντες   εἶπαν   αὐτῷ·
   But the   Pharisees   seeing   said   to him:

ἰδοὺ   οἱ   μαθηταί   σου   ποιοῦσιν   ὃ   οὐκ
Behold[,] the   disciples   of thee   are doing   what   not

ἔξεστιν   ποιεῖν   ἐν   σαββάτῳ.   3 ὁ   δὲ
it is lawful   to do   on   a sabbath.   And he

3 But he said unto them, Have ye not read what David did, when he was an hungred, and they that were with him;

4 How he entered into the house of God, and did eat the shewbread, which was not lawful for him to eat, neither for them which were with him, but only for the priests?

5 Or have ye not read in the law, how that on the sabbath days the priests in the temple profane the sabbath, and are blameless?

6 But I say unto you, That in this place is *one* greater than the temple.

7 But if ye had known what *this* meaneth, I will have mercy, and not sacrifice, ye would not have condemned the guiltless.

8 For the Son of man is Lord even of the sabbath day.

9 ¶ And when he was departed thence, he went into their synagogue:

10 And, behold, there was a man which had *his* hand withered. And they asked him, saying, Is it lawful to heal on the sabbath days? that they might accuse him.

11 And he said unto them, What man shall there be among you, that shall have one sheep, and if it fall into a pit on the sabbath day, will he not lay hold on it, and lift *it* out?

εἶπεν αὐτοῖς· οὐκ ἀνέγνωτε τί ἐποίησεν
said   to them: Did ye not read   what   did

Δαυίδ, ὅτε ἐπείνασεν καὶ οἱ μετ᾽
David,   when   he hungered   and   the [ones]   with

αὐτοῦ; 4 πῶς εἰσῆλθεν εἰς τὸν οἶκον
him?   how   he entered   into   the   house

τοῦ θεοῦ καὶ τοὺς ἄρτους τῆς προ-
–   of God   and   the   loaves   of the   set-

θέσεως ἔφαγον, ὃ οὐκ ἐξὸν ἦν αὐτῷ
ting forth   ate,   which   not   lawful   it was   for him

φαγεῖν οὐδὲ τοῖς μετ᾽ αὐτοῦ, εἰ μὴ
to eat   neither   the [ones]   with   him,   except

τοῖς ἱερεῦσιν μόνοις; 5 ἢ οὐκ ἀνέγνωτε
for the   priests   only?   or   did ye not read

ἐν τῷ νόμῳ ὅτι τοῖς σάββασιν οἱ
in   the   law   that   on the   sabbaths   the

ἱερεῖς ἐν τῷ ἱερῷ τὸ σάββατον βεβηλοῦ-
priests   in   the   temple   the   sabbath   pro-

σιν καὶ ἀναίτιοί εἰσιν; 6 λέγω δὲ
fane   and   guiltless   are?   And I tell

ὑμῖν ὅτι τοῦ ἱεροῦ μεῖζόν ἐστιν ὧδε.
you   that [than]   the temple   a greater [thing] is   here.

7 εἰ δὲ ἐγνώκειτε τί ἐστιν· ἔλεος
But if   ye had known   what   it is: Mercy

θέλω καὶ οὐ θυσίαν, οὐκ ἂν κατε-
I desire   and   not   sacrifice,   ye would not have

δικάσατε τοὺς ἀναιτίους. 8 κύριος γάρ
condemned   the   guiltless.   For Lord

ἐστιν τοῦ σαββάτου ὁ υἱὸς τοῦ ἀνθρώπου.
is   of the   sabbath   the Son   –   of man.

9 Καὶ μεταβὰς ἐκεῖθεν ἦλθεν εἰς τὴν
And   removing   thence   he came   into   the

συναγωγὴν αὐτῶν. 10 καὶ ἰδοὺ ἄνθρωπος
synagogue   of them.   And behold[,]   a man

χεῖρα ἔχων ξηράν· καὶ ἐπηρώτησαν αὐτὸν
²[his] hand   ¹having   ³withered;   and   they questioned   him

λέγοντες· εἰ ἔξεστιν τοῖς σάββασιν
saying: If   it is lawful   on the   sabbaths

θεραπεῦσαι; ἵνα κατηγορήσωσιν αὐτοῦ.
to heal?   in order that   they might accuse   him.

11 ὁ δὲ εἶπεν αὐτοῖς· τίς ἔσται ἐξ
So he   said   to them: ¹What   ²will there be   ⁶of

ὑμῶν ἄνθρωπος ὃς ἕξει πρόβατον ἕν,
⁵you   ⁴man   who   will have   sheep   one,

καὶ ἐὰν ἐμπέσῃ τοῦτο τοῖς σάββασιν
and   if   ²fall *in*   ¹this   on the   sabbaths

εἰς βόθυνον, οὐχὶ κρατήσει αὐτὸ καὶ
into   a ditch,   will he not lay hold of   it   and

12 How much then is a man better than a sheep? Wherefore it is lawful to do well on the sabbath days.

13 Then saith he to the man, Stretch forth thine hand. And he stretched *it* forth; and it was restored whole, like as the other.

14 ¶ Then the Pharisees went out, and held a council against him, how they might destroy him.

15 But when Jesus knew *it*, he withdrew himself from thence: and great multitudes followed him, and he healed them all;

16 And charged them that they should not make him known:

17 That it might be fulfilled which was spoken by Esaias the prophet, saying,

18 Behold my servant, whom I have chosen; my beloved, in whom my soul is well pleased; I will put my spirit upon him, and he shall shew judgment to the Gentiles.

19 He shall not strive, nor cry; neither shall any man hear his voice in the streets.

20 A bruised reed shall he not break, and smoking flax shall he not quench, till he send forth judgment unto victory.

21 And in his name shall the Gentiles trust.

ἐγερεῖ; **12** πόσῳ οὖν διαφέρει ἄνθρωπος
raise? By how much then surpasses a man

προβάτου. ὥστε ἔξεστιν τοῖς σάββασιν
a sheep. So that it is lawful on the sabbaths

καλῶς ποιεῖν. **13** τότε λέγει τῷ ἀνθρώπῳ·
well to do. Then he says to the man:

ἔκτεινόν σου τὴν χεῖρα. καὶ ἐξέτεινεν,
Stretch forth of thee the hand. And he stretched forth,

καὶ ἀπεκατεστάθη ὑγιὴς ὡς ἡ ἄλλη.
and it was restored healthy as the other.

14 ἐξελθόντες δὲ οἱ Φαρισαῖοι συμβούλιον
And going out the Pharisees counsel

ἔλαβον κατ᾽ αὐτοῦ, ὅπως αὐτὸν ἀπολέ-
took against him, so as him they might

σωσιν. **15** Ὁ δὲ Ἰησοῦς γνοὺς ἀνε-
destroy. - But Jesus knowing de-

χώρησεν ἐκεῖθεν. καὶ ἠκολούθησαν αὐτῷ
parted thence. And followed him

πολλοί, καὶ ἐθεράπευσεν αὐτοὺς πάντας,
many, and he healed them all,

16 καὶ ἐπετίμησεν αὐτοῖς ἵνα μὴ φανερὸν
and warned them that ²not ⁴manifest

αὐτὸν ποιήσωσιν· **17** ἵνα πληρωθῇ τὸ
⁵him ¹they ²should ⁴make; that might be fulfilled the [thing]

ῥηθὲν διὰ Ἡσαΐου τοῦ προφήτου
spoken through Isaiah the prophet

λέγοντος· **18** ἰδοὺ ὁ παῖς μου ὃν
saying: Behold[,] the servant of me whom

ᾑρέτισα, ὁ ἀγαπητός μου ὃν εὐδόκησεν
I chose, the beloved of me [with] whom was well pleased

ἡ ψυχή μου· θήσω τὸ πνεῦμα μου ἐπ᾽
the soul of me; I will put the spirit of me on

αὐτόν, καὶ κρίσιν τοῖς ἔθνεσιν ἀπαγγελεῖ.
him, and judgment to the nations he will announce.

19 οὐκ ἐρίσει οὐδὲ κραυγάσει, οὐδὲ
He will not strive nor *will* shout, nor

ἀκούσει τις ἐν ταῖς πλατείαις τὴν
will hear anyone in the streets the

φωνὴν αὐτοῦ. **20** κάλαμον συντετριμμένον
voice of him. A reed *having been* bruised

οὐ κατεάξει καὶ λίνον τυφόμενον οὐ
he will not break and flax smoking not

σβέσει, ἕως ἂν ἐκβάλῃ εἰς νῖκος τὴν
he will quench, until he put forth to victory -

κρίσιν. **21** καὶ τῷ ὀνόματι αὐτοῦ ἔθνη
judgment. And in the name of him nations

ἐλπιοῦσιν.
will hope.

22 ¶ Then was brought unto him one possessed with a devil, blind, and dumb: and he healed him, insomuch that the blind and dumb both spake and saw.

23 And all the people were amazed, and said, Is not this the son of David?

24 But when the Pharisees heard *it*, they said, This *fellow* doth not cast out devils, but by Beelzebub the prince of the devils.

25 And Jesus knew their thoughts, and said unto them, Every kingdom divided against itself is brought to desolation; and every city or house divided against itself shall not stand:

26 And if Satan cast out Satan, he is divided against himself; how shall then his kingdom stand?

27 And if I by Beelzebub cast out devils, by whom do your children cast *them* out? therefore they shall be your judges.

28 But if I cast out devils by the Spirit of God, then the kingdom of God is come unto you.

29 Or else how can one enter into a strong man's house, and spoil his goods,

---

22 Τότε προσηνέχθη   αὐτῷ   δαιμονιζ-
   Then   was brought   to him   a demon-

όμενος   τυφλὸς   καὶ   κωφός·   καὶ   ἐθεράπευσεν
possessed man   blind   and   dumb;   and   he healed

αὐτόν,   ὥστε   τὸν   κωφὸν   λαλεῖν   καὶ
him,   so as   the   dumb   to speak   and

βλέπειν.   23 καὶ   ἐξίσταντο   πάντες   οἱ
to see[b].   And   were astonished   all   the

ὄχλοι   καὶ   ἔλεγον·   μήτι   οὗτός   ἐστιν   ὁ
crowds   and   said: *not*   This   is   the

υἱὸς   Δαυίδ;   24 οἱ   δὲ   Φαρισαῖοι   ἀκού-
son   of David?   But the   Pharisees   hear-

σαντες   εἶπον·   οὗτος   οὐκ   ἐκβάλλει   τὰ
ing   said: This man   does not expel   the

δαιμόνια   εἰ   μὴ   ἐν   τῷ   Βεεζεβοὺλ   ἄρχοντι
demons   except   by   -   Beelzebub   ruler

τῶν   δαιμονίων.   25 εἰδὼς   δὲ   τὰς   ἐνθυμήσεις
of the   demons.   But knowing   the   thoughts

αὐτῶν   εἶπεν   αὐτοῖς·   πᾶσα   βασιλεία
of them   he said   to them: Every   kingdom

μερισθεῖσα   καθ'   ἑαυτῆς   ἐρημοῦται,
divided   against   itself   is brought to desolation,

καὶ   πᾶσα   πόλις   ἢ   οἰκία   μερισθεῖσα   καθ'
and   every   city   or   house   divided   against

ἑαυτῆς   οὐ   σταθήσεται.   26 καὶ   εἰ
itself   will not stand.   And   if

ὁ   σατανᾶς   τὸν   σατανᾶν   ἐκβάλλει,   ἐφ'
-   Satan   the   ²Satan   ¹expels,   against

ἑαυτὸν   ἐμερίσθη·   πῶς   οὖν   σταθή-
himself   he was(is) divided;   how   therefore   will

σεται   ἡ   βασιλεία   αὐτοῦ;   27 καὶ   εἰ
stand   the   kingdom   of him?   And   if

ἐγὼ   ἐν   Βεεζεβοὺλ   ἐκβάλλω   τὰ   δαιμόνια,
I   by   Beelzebub   expel   the   demons,

οἱ   υἱοὶ   ὑμῶν   ἐν   τίνι   ἐκβάλλουσιν;
the   sons   of you   by   what   do they expel?

διὰ   τοῦτο   αὐτοὶ   κριταὶ   ἔσονται   ὑμῶν.
therefore   they   judges   shall be   of you.

28 εἰ   δὲ   ἐν   πνεύματι   θεοῦ   ἐγὼ
   But if   by [the]   Spirit   of God   I

ἐκβάλλω   τὰ   δαιμόνια,   ἄρα   ἔφθασεν
expel   the   demons,   then   came

ἐφ'   ὑμᾶς   ἡ   βασιλεία   τοῦ   θεοῦ.   29 ἢ
upon   you   the   kingdom   -   of God.   Or

πῶς   δύναταί   τις   εἰσελθεῖν   εἰς   τὴν
how   can   anyone   *to* enter   into   the

οἰκίαν   τοῦ   ἰσχυροῦ   καὶ   τὰ   σκεύη   αὐτοῦ
house   of the   strong man   and   the   vessels   of him

except he first bind the
strong man? and then he
will spoil his house.

30 He that is not with
me is against me; and he
that gathereth not with me
scattereth abroad.

31 Wherefore I say unto
you, All manner of sin and
blasphemy shall be for-
given unto men: but the
blasphemy *against* the *Holy*
Ghost shall not be for-
given unto men.

32 And whosoever spea-
keth a word against the
Son of man, it shall be
forgiven him: but whoso-
ever speaketh against the
Holy Ghost, it shall not be
forgiven him, neither in
this world, neither in the
world to come.

33 Either make the tree
good, and his fruit good:
or else make the tree corrupt, and his fruit corrupt;
for the tree is known by *his*
fruit.

34 O generation of
vipers, how can ye, being
evil, speak good things?
for out of the abundance
of the heart the mouth
speaketh.

35 A good man out of
the good treasure of the
heart bringeth forth good
things: and an evil man
out of the evil treasure
bringeth forth evil things.

ἁρπάσαι,	ἐὰν	μὴ	πρῶτον	δήσῃ	τὸν
to seize,	if	not	first	he binds	the

ἰσχυρόν;	καὶ	τότε	τὴν	οἰκίαν	αὐτοῦ
strong man?	and	then	the	house	of him

διαρπάσει.	**30** ὁ	μὴ	ὢν	μετ’	ἐμοῦ
he will plunder.	The [one] not		being	with	me

κατ’	ἐμοῦ	ἐστιν,	καὶ	ὁ	μὴ	συνάγων	μετ’
against	me	is,	and	the [one] not		gathering	with

ἐμοῦ	σκορπίζει.	**31** Διὰ	τοῦτο	λέγω
me	scatters.		Therefore	I tell

ὑμῖν,	πᾶσα	ἁμαρτία	καὶ	βλασφημία
you,	all	sin	and	blasphemy

ἀφεθήσεται	τοῖς	ἀνθρώποις,	ἡ	δὲ	τοῦ
will be forgiven	-	to men,	but the		of the

πνεύματος	βλασφημία	οὐκ	ἀφεθήσεται.
Spirit	blasphemy		will not be forgiven.

32 καὶ	ὃς	ἐὰν	εἴπῃ	λόγον	κατὰ	τοῦ
And	whoever		speaks	a word	against	the

υἱοῦ	τοῦ	ἀνθρώπου,	ἀφεθήσεται	αὐτῷ·
Son	-	of man,	it will be forgiven	*to* him;

ὃς	δ’	ἂν	εἴπῃ	κατὰ	τοῦ	πνεύματος
but whoever			speaks	against	the	Spirit

τοῦ	ἁγίου,	οὐκ	ἀφεθήσεται	αὐτῷ
-	Holy,		it will not be forgiven	*to* him

οὔτε	ἐν	τούτῳ	τῷ	αἰῶνι	οὔτε	ἐν	τῷ
neither	in	this	-	age	nor	in	the [one]

μέλλοντι.	**33** Ἢ	ποιήσατε	τὸ	δένδρον
coming.	Either	make	the	tree

καλὸν	καὶ	τὸν	καρπὸν	αὐτοῦ	καλόν,
good	and	the	fruit	of it	good,

ἢ	ποιήσατε	τὸ	δένδρον	σαπρὸν	καὶ	τὸν
or	make	the	tree	bad	and	the

καρπὸν	αὐτοῦ	σαπρόν·	ἐκ	γὰρ	τοῦ
fruit	of it	bad;	for of (by)		the

καρποῦ	τὸ	δένδρον	γινώσκεται.	**34** γεννή-
fruit	the	tree	is known.	Off-

ματα	ἐχιδνῶν,	πῶς	δύνασθε	ἀγαθὰ	λαλεῖν
spring	of vipers,	how	can ye	good things	*to* speak

πονηροὶ	ὄντες;	ἐκ	γὰρ	τοῦ	περισ-
²evil	¹being?	for out of		the	abund-

σεύματος	τῆς	καρδίας	τὸ	στόμα	λαλεῖ.
ance	of the	heart	the	mouth	speaks.

35 ὁ	ἀγαθὸς	ἄνθρωπος	ἐκ	τοῦ	ἀγαθοῦ
The	good	man	out of	the	good

θησαυροῦ	ἐκβάλλει	ἀγαθά,	καὶ	ὁ	πονηρὸς
treasure	puts forth	good things,	and	the	evil

ἄνθρωπος	ἐκ	τοῦ	πονηροῦ	θησαυροῦ
man	out of	the	evil	treasure

36 But I say unto you, That every idle word that men shall speak, they shall give account thereof in the day of judgment.

37 For by thy words thou shalt be justified, and by thy words thou shalt be condemned.

38 ¶ Then certain of the scribes and of the Pharisees answered, saying, Master, we would see a sign from thee.

39 But he answered and said unto them, An evil and adulterous generation seeketh after a sign; and there shall no sign be given to it, but the sign of the prophet Jonas:

40 For as Jonas was three days and three nights in the whale's belly; so shall the Son of man be three days and three nights in the heart of the earth.

41 The men of Nineveh shall rise in judgment with this generation, and shall condemn it: because they repented at the preaching of Jonas; and, behold, a greater than Jonas *is* here.

42 The queen of the south shall rise up in the judgment with this genera-

ἐκβάλλει πονηρά. **36** λέγω δὲ
puts forth evil things. But I tell

ὑμῖν ὅτι πᾶν ῥῆμα ἀργὸν ὃ λαλήσουσιν
you that every word idle which will speak

οἱ ἄνθρωποι, ἀποδώσουσιν περὶ αὐτοῦ
- men, they will render concerning it

λόγον ἐν ἡμέρᾳ κρίσεως· **37** ἐκ γὰρ
account in [the] day of judgment; for of(by)

τῶν λόγων σου δικαιωθήσῃ, καὶ ἐκ
the words of thee thou wilt be justified, and of(by)

τῶν λόγων σου καταδικασθήσῃ.
the words of thee thou wilt be condemned.

38 Τότε ἀπεκρίθησαν αὐτῷ τινες τῶν
Then answered him some of the

γραμματέων καὶ Φαρισαίων λέγοντες·
scribes and Pharisees saying:

διδάσκαλε, θέλομεν ἀπὸ σοῦ σημεῖον ἰδεῖν.
Teacher, we wish from thee a sign to see.

39 ὁ δὲ ἀποκριθεὶς εἶπεν αὐτοῖς·
But he answering said to them:

γενεὰ πονηρὰ καὶ μοιχαλὶς σημεῖον
generation An evil and adulterous a sign

ἐπιζητεῖ, καὶ σημεῖον οὐ δοθήσεται
seeks, and a sign shall not be given

αὐτῇ εἰ μὴ τὸ σημεῖον Ἰωνᾶ τοῦ
to it except the sign of Jonas the

προφήτου. **40** ὥσπερ γὰρ ἦν Ἰωνᾶς
prophet. For as was Jonas

ἐν τῇ κοιλίᾳ τοῦ κήτους τρεῖς ἡμέρας
in the belly of the sea monster three days

καὶ τρεῖς νύκτας, οὕτως ἔσται ὁ υἱὸς
and three nights, so will be the Son

τοῦ ἀνθρώπου ἐν τῇ καρδίᾳ τῆς γῆς
- of man in the heart of the earth

τρεῖς ἡμέρας καὶ τρεῖς νύκτας. **41** ἄνδρες
three days and three nights. Men

Νινευῖται ἀναστήσονται ἐν τῇ κρίσει
Ninevites will stand up in the judgment

μετὰ τῆς γενεᾶς ταύτης καὶ κατα-
with - generation this and will

κρινοῦσιν αὐτήν· ὅτι μετενόησαν εἰς τὸ
condemn it; because they repented at the

κήρυγμα Ἰωνᾶ, καὶ ἰδοὺ πλεῖον Ἰωνᾶ
proclamation of Jonas, and behold a greater thing [than] Jonas

ὧδε. **42** βασίλισσα νότου ἐγερθήσεται
[is] here. [The] queen of [the] south will be raised

ἐν τῇ κρίσει μετὰ τῆς γενεᾶς ταύτης
in the judgment with - generation this

tion, and shall condemn it: for she came from the uttermost parts of the earth to hear the wisdom of Solomon; and, behold, a greater than Solomon *is* here.

43 When the unclean spirit is gone out of a man, he walketh through dry places, seeking rest, and findeth none.

44 Then he saith, I will return into my house from whence I came out; and when he is come, he findeth *it* empty, swept, and garnished.

45 Then goeth he, and taketh with himself seven other spirits more wicked than himself, and they enter in and dwell there: and the last *state* of that man is worse than the first. Even so shall it be also unto this wicked generation.

46 ¶ While he yet talked to the people, behold, *his* mother and his brethren stood without, desiring to speak with him.

47 Then one said unto him, Behold, thy mother and thy brethren stand without, desiring to speak with thee.

48 But he answered and said unto him that told him, Who is my mother? and who are my brethren?

καὶ κατακρινεῖ αὐτήν· ὅτι ἦλθεν ἐκ
and will condemn it; because she came out of

τῶν περάτων τῆς γῆς ἀκοῦσαι τὴν σοφίαν
the limits of the earth to hear the wisdom

Σολομῶνος, καὶ ἰδοὺ πλεῖον Σολομῶνος
of Solomon, and behold a greater thing [than] Solomon

ὧδε. 43 Ὅταν δὲ τὸ ἀκάθαρτον πνεῦμα
[is] here. Now when the unclean spirit

ἐξέλθῃ ἀπὸ τοῦ ἀνθρώπου, διέρχεται δι'
goes out from – a man, he goes through

ἀνύδρων τόπων ζητοῦν ἀνάπαυσιν, καὶ
dry places seeking rest, and

οὐχ εὑρίσκει. 44 τότε λέγει· εἰς τὸν
finds not. Then he says: Into the

οἶκόν μου ἐπιστρέψω ὅθεν ἐξῆλθον·
house of me I will return whence I came out;

καὶ ἐλθὸν εὑρίσκει σχολάζοντα [καὶ]
and coming he finds [it] standing empty and

σεσαρωμένον καὶ κεκοσμημένον. 45 τότε
having been swept and *having been* furnished. Then

πορεύεται καὶ παραλαμβάνει μεθ' ἑαυτοῦ
he goes and takes with him*self*

ἑπτὰ ἕτερα πνεύματα πονηρότερα ἑαυτοῦ,
seven other spirits more evil [than] himself,

καὶ εἰσελθόντα κατοικεῖ ἐκεῖ· καὶ
and entering dwells there; and

γίνεται τὰ ἔσχατα τοῦ ἀνθρώπου ἐκείνου
becom*es* the last things – man of that

χείρονα τῶν πρώτων. οὕτως ἔσται
worse [than] the first. Thus it will be

καὶ τῇ γενεᾷ ταύτῃ τῇ πονηρᾷ.
also – ²generation ¹to this – ²evil.

46 Ἔτι αὐτοῦ λαλοῦντος τοῖς ὄχλοις,
Yet him speaking² to the crowds,
=While he was still speaking

ἰδοὺ ἡ μήτηρ καὶ οἱ ἀδελφοὶ αὐτοῦ
behold the mother and the brothers of him

εἱστήκεισαν ἔξω ζητοῦντες αὐτῷ λαλῆσαι.
stood outside seeking to him to speak.

47 [εἶπεν δέ τις αὐτῷ· ἰδοὺ ἡ μήτηρ
And said someone to him: Behold[,] the mother

σου καὶ οἱ ἀδελφοί σου ἔξω ἑστήκασιν
of thee and the brothers of thee outside are standing

ζητοῦντές σοι λαλῆσαι.] 48 ὁ δὲ
seeking to thee to speak.] And he

ἀποκριθεὶς εἶπεν τῷ λέγοντι αὐτῷ· τίς
answering said to the [one] saying to him: Who

ἐστιν ἡ μήτηρ μου, καὶ τίνες εἰσὶν οἱ
is the mother of me, and who are the

49 And he stretched forth his hand toward his disciples, and said, Behold my mother and my brethren!

50 For whosoever shall do the will of my Father which is in heaven, the same is my brother, and sister, and mother.

ἀδελφοί μου;
brothers of me?

χεῖρα [αὐτοῦ]
hand of him

εἶπεν·
he said:

μου.
of me.

τοῦ πατρός
of the Father

μου ἀδελφὸς
of me brother

49 καὶ ἐκτείνας τὴν
And stretching forth the

ἐπὶ τοὺς μαθητὰς αὐτοῦ
on the disciples of him

ἰδοὺ ἡ μήτηρ μου καὶ οἱ ἀδελφοί
Behold[,] the mother of me and the brothers

50 ὅστις γὰρ ἂν ποιήσῃ τὸ θέλημα
For whoever does the will

μου τοῦ ἐν οὐρανοῖς, αὐτός
of me – in heavens, he

καὶ ἀδελφὴ καὶ μήτηρ ἐστίν.
and sister and mother is.

CHAPTER 13

THE same day went Jesus out of the house, and sat by the sea side.

2 And great multitudes were gathered together unto him, so that he went into a ship, and sat; and the whole multitude stood on the shore.

3 And he spake many things unto them in parables, saying, Behold, a sower went forth to sow;

4 And when he sowed, some *seeds* fell by the way-side, and the fowls came and devoured them up:

5 Some fell upon stony places, where they had not much earth: and forthwith they sprung up, because they had no deepness of earth:

6 And when the sun was up, they were scorched;

13 Ἐν τῇ ἡμέρᾳ ἐκείνῃ ἐξελθὼν ὁ
On – day that ²going out of –

Ἰησοῦς τῆς οἰκίας ἐκάθητο παρὰ τὴν
¹Jesus of the house sat beside the

θάλασσαν· **2** καὶ συνήχθησαν πρὸς αὐτὸν
sea; and were assembled to him

ὄχλοι πολλοί, ὥστε αὐτὸν εἰς πλοῖον
crowds many, so as him in a ship
=so that embarking in a ship he sat,

ἐμβάντα καθῆσθαι, καὶ πᾶς ὁ ὄχλος
embarking to sit[b], and all the crowd

ἐπὶ τὸν αἰγιαλὸν εἱστήκει. **3** καὶ ἐλάλησεν
on the beach stood. And he spoke

αὐτοῖς πολλὰ ἐν παραβολαῖς λέγων·
to them many things in parables saying:

Ἰδοὺ ἐξῆλθεν ὁ σπείρων τοῦ σπείρειν.
Behold went out the [one] sowing – to sow[d].

4 καὶ ἐν τῷ σπείρειν αὐτὸν ἃ μὲν
And in the to sow him[e] some indeed
=as he sowed

ἔπεσεν παρὰ τὴν ὁδόν, καὶ ἐλθόντα τὰ
fell beside the way, and coming the

πετεινὰ κατέφαγεν αὐ ά. **5** ἄλλα δὲ
birds devoured them. But others

ἔπεσεν ἐπὶ τὰ πετρώδη ὅπου οὐκ
fell on the rocky places where not

εἶχεν γῆν πολλήν, καὶ εὐθέως ἐξανέτειλεν
it had earth much, and immediately it sprang up

διὰ τὸ μὴ ἔχειν βάθος γῆς· **6** ἡλίου
on account of the not to have depth of earth; [the] sun
=because it had not

δὲ ἀνατείλαντος ἐκαυματίσθη, καὶ διὰ
But having risen[a] it was scorched, and on account of
=when the sun rose   =because

and because they had no root, they withered away.

7 And some fell among thorns; and the thorns sprung up, and choked them:

8 But other fell into good ground, and brought forth fruit, some an hundredfold, some sixtyfold, some thirtyfold.

9 Who hath ears to hear, let him hear.

10 ¶ And the disciples came, and said unto him, Why speakest thou unto them in parables?

11 He answered and said unto them, Because it is given unto you to know the mysteries of the kingdom of heaven, but to them it is not given.

12 For whosoever hath, to him shall be given, and he shall have more abundance: but whosoever hath not, from him shall be taken away even that he hath.

13 Therefore speak I to them in parables: because they seeing see not; and hearing they hear not, neither do they understand.

14 And in them is fulfilled the prophecy of Esaias, which saith, By hearing ye shall hear, and shall not understand; and seeing ye shall see, and shall not perceive:

15 For this people's heart is waxed gross, and *their* ears are dull of hear-

τὸ μὴ ἔχειν ῥίζαν ἐξηράνθη. 7 ἄλλα δὲ
the not to have root it was dried up. But others
it had not

ἔπεσεν ἐπὶ τὰς ἀκάνθας, καὶ ἀνέβησαν
fell on the thorns, and came up

αἱ ἄκανθαι καὶ ἀπέπνιξαν αὐτά. 8 ἄλλα δὲ
the thorns and choked them. And others

ἔπεσεν ἐπὶ τὴν γῆν τὴν καλὴν καὶ
fell on the earth - good and

ἐδίδου καρπόν, ὃ μὲν ἑκατόν, ὃ δὲ
gave fruit, the one a hundred, the other

ἐξήκοντα, ὃ δὲ τριάκοντα. 9 ὁ ἔχων
sixty, the other thirty. The [one] having

ὦτα ἀκουέτω. 10 Καὶ προσελθόντες οἱ
ears let him hear. And approaching the

μαθηταὶ εἶπαν αὐτῷ· διὰ τί ἐν παρα-
disciples said to him: Why in par-

βολαῖς λαλεῖς αὐτοῖς; 11 ὁ δὲ
ables speakest thou to them? And he

ἀποκριθεὶς εἶπεν· ὅτι ὑμῖν δέδοται
answering said: Because to you it has been given

γνῶναι τὰ μυστήρια τῆς βασιλείας τῶν
to know the mysteries of the kingdom of the

οὐρανῶν, ἐκείνοις δὲ οὐ δέδοται. 12 ὅστις
heavens, but to those it has not been given. [he] who

γὰρ ἔχει, δοθήσεται αὐτῷ καὶ περισ-
For has, it will be given to him and he will

σευθήσεται· ὅστις δὲ οὐκ ἔχει, καὶ
have abundance; but [he] who has not, even

ὃ ἔχει ἀρθήσεται ἀπ' αὐτοῦ. 13 διὰ
what he has will be taken from him. There-

τοῦτο ἐν παραβολαῖς αὐτοῖς λαλῶ, ὅτι
fore in parables to them I speak, because

βλέποντες οὐ βλέπουσιν καὶ ἀκούοντες
seeing they see not and hearing

οὐκ ἀκούουσιν οὐδὲ συνιοῦσιν. 14 καὶ
they hear not neither understand. And

ἀναπληροῦται αὐτοῖς ἡ προφητεία Ἡσαΐου
is fulfilled in them the prophecy of Isaiah

ἡ λέγουσα· ἀκοῇ ἀκούσετε καὶ οὐ μὴ
- saying: In hearing ye will hear and by no means

συνῆτε, καὶ βλέποντες βλέψετε
understand, and seeing ye will see

καὶ οὐ μὴ ἴδητε. 15 ἐπαχύνθη γὰρ
and by no means perceive. For waxed gross

ἡ καρδία τοῦ λαοῦ τούτου, καὶ τοῖς
the heart - people of this, and with the

ing, and their eyes they have closed; lest at any time they should see with *their* eyes, and hear with *their* ears, and should understand with *their* heart, and should be converted, and I should heal them.

16 But blessed *are* your eyes, for they see: and your ears, for they hear.

17 For verily I say unto you, That many prophets and righteous *men* have desired to see *those things* which ye see, and have not seen *them;* and to hear *those things* which ye hear, and have not heard *them*.

18¶ Hear ye therefore the parable of the sower.

19 When any one heareth the word of the kingdom, and understandeth *it* not, then cometh the wicked *one,* and catcheth away that which was sown in his heart. This is he which received seed by the way side.

20 But he that received the seed into stony places, the same is he that heareth the word, and anon with joy receiveth it;

21 Yet hath he not root in himself, but dureth for a while: for when tribulation or persecution ariseth because of the word, by and by he is offended.

ὦσὶν βαρέως ἤκουσαν, καὶ τοὺς ὀφθαλμοὺς
ears   heavily   they heard,   and   the   eyes

αὐτῶν ἐκάμμυσαν· μήποτε ἴδωσιν τοῖς
of them   they closed;   lest   they see   with the

ὀφθαλμοῖς καὶ τοῖς ὦσὶν ἀκούσωσιν
eyes   and   with the   ears   hear

καὶ τῇ καρδίᾳ συνῶσιν καὶ ἐπιστρέψωσιν,
and   with the   heart   understand   and   turn back,

καὶ ἰάσομαι αὐτούς.   16 ὑμῶν δὲ μακάριοι
and   I will heal   them.   But of you   blessed

οἱ ὀφθαλμοὶ ὅτι βλέπουσιν, καὶ τὰ
the   eyes   because   they see,   and   the

ὦτα [ὑμῶν] ὅτι ἀκούουσιν.   17 ἀμὴν
ears   of you   because   they hear.   truly

γὰρ λέγω ὑμῖν ὅτι πολλοὶ προφῆται καὶ
For   I say   to you   that   many   prophets   and

δίκαιοι ἐπεθύμησαν ἰδεῖν ἃ
righteous men   desired   to see   [the things] which

βλέπετε καὶ οὐκ εἶδαν, καὶ ἀκοῦσαι
ye see   and   did not see,   and   to hear

ἃ ἀκούετε καὶ οὐκ ἤκουσαν.
[the things] which   ye hear   and   did not hear.

18 Ὑμεῖς οὖν ἀκούσατε τὴν παραβολὴν
²Ye   ²therefore   ¹hear   the   parable

τοῦ σπείραντος.   19 Παντὸς ἀκούοντος
of the   sowing [one].   Everyone   hearingᵃ
                                   = When anyone hears

τὸν λόγον τῆς βασιλείας καὶ μὴ συνιέντος
the   word   of the   kingdom   and   not understandingᵃ
                                = does not understand

ἔρχεται ὁ πονηρὸς καὶ ἁρπάζει τὸ
comes   the   evil one   and   seizes the [thing]

ἐσπαρμένον ἐν τῇ καρδίᾳ αὐτοῦ· οὗτός
having been sown   in   the   heart   of him;   this

ἐστιν ὁ παρὰ τὴν ὁδὸν σπαρείς. 20 ὁ
is   the [word]   by   the   way   sown.   the [word]

δὲ ἐπὶ τὰ πετρώδη σπαρείς, οὗτός ἐστιν
And   on   the   rocky places   sown,   this   is

ὁ τὸν λόγον ἀκούων καὶ εὐθὺς μετὰ
the [one]   ²the   ²word   ¹hearing   and   immediately with

χαρᾶς λαμβάνων αὐτόν· 21 οὐκ ἔχει δὲ
joy   receiving   it;   but he has not

ῥίζαν ἐν ἑαυτῷ ἀλλὰ πρόσκαιρός ἐστιν,
root   in   himself   but   short-lived   is,

γενομένης δὲ θλίψεως ἢ διωγμοῦ
and occurring   tribulation   or   persecutionᵃ
               = when tribulation or persecution occurs

διὰ τὸν λόγον εὐθὺς σκανδαλίζεται.
on account of the   word   immediately   he is offended.

22 He also that received seed among the thorns is he that heareth the word; and the care of this world, and the deceitfulness of riches, choke the word, and he becometh unfruitful.

23 But he that received seed into the good ground is he that heareth the word, and understandeth *it;* which also beareth fruit, and bringeth forth, some an hundredfold, some sixty, some thirty.

24 ¶ Another parable put he forth unto them, saying, The kingdom of heaven is likened unto a man which sowed good seed in his field:

25 But while men slept, his enemy came and sowed tares among the wheat, and went his way.

26 But when the blade was sprung up, and brought forth fruit, then appeared the tares also.

27 So the servants of the householder came and said unto him, Sir, didst not thou sow good seed in thy field? from whence then hath it tares?

28 He said unto them, An enemy hath done this.

---

22 ὁ δὲ εἰς τὰς ἀκάνθας σπαρείς, οὗτός
But the [word] in the thorns sown, this

ἐστιν ὁ τὸν λόγον ἀκούων, καὶ ἡ
is the [one] ²the ²word ¹hearing, and the

μέριμνα τοῦ αἰῶνος καὶ ἡ ἀπάτη
anxiety of the age and the deceit

τοῦ πλούτου συμπνίγει τὸν λόγον, καὶ
– of riches chokes the word, and

ἄκαρπος γίνεται. **23** ὁ δὲ ἐπὶ τὴν
unfruitful it becomes. And the [word] on the

καλὴν γῆν σπαρείς, οὗτός ἐστιν ὁ
good earth sown, this is the [one]

τὸν λόγον ἀκούων καὶ συνιείς, ὃς
²the ²word ¹hearing ²and ³understanding, who

δὴ καρποφορεῖ καὶ ποιεῖ ὃ μὲν ἑκατόν,
indeed bears fruit and produces one indeed a hundred,

ὃ δὲ ἑξήκοντα, ὃ δὲ τριάκοντα.
the other sixty, the other thirty.

24 Ἄλλην παραβολὴν παρέθηκεν αὐτοῖς
Another parable he set before them

λέγων· ὡμοιώθη ἡ βασιλεία τῶν
saying: was(is) likened The kingdom of the

οὐρανῶν ἀνθρώπῳ σπείραντι καλὸν σπέρμα
heavens to a man sowing good seed

ἐν τῷ ἀγρῷ αὐτοῦ. **25** ἐν δὲ τῷ
in the field of him. But in the
                                                        = while men slept

καθεύδειν τοὺς ἀνθρώπους ἦλθεν αὐτοῦ
to sleep – men^e came of him

ὁ ἐχθρὸς καὶ ἐπέσπειρεν ζιζάνια ἀνὰ μέσον
the enemy and oversowed tares in between

τοῦ σίτου καὶ ἀπῆλθεν. **26** ὅτε δὲ
the wheat and went away. But when

ἐβλάστησεν ὁ χόρτος καὶ καρπὸν
sprouted the grass and fruit

ἐποίησεν, τότε ἐφάνη καὶ τὰ ζιζάνια.
produced, then appeared also the tares.

27 προσελθόντες δὲ οἱ δοῦλοι τοῦ οἰκο-
So approaching the slaves of the house-

δεσπότου εἶπον αὐτῷ· κύριε, οὐχὶ καλὸν
master said to him: Lord, not good

σπέρμα ἔσπειρας ἐν τῷ σῷ ἀγρῷ;
seed sowedst thou in – thy field?

πόθεν οὖν ἔχει ζιζάνια; **28** ὁ δὲ ἔφη
whence then has it tares? And he said

αὐτοῖς· ἐχθρὸς ἄνθρωπος τοῦτο ἐποίησεν.
to them: An enemy *man* this did.

The servants said unto him, Wilt thou then that we go and gather them up?

29 But he said, Nay; lest while ye gather up the tares, ye root up also the wheat with them.

30 Let both grow together until the harvest: and in the time of harvest I will say to the reapers, Gather ye together first the tares, and bind them in bundles to burn them: but gather the wheat into my barn.

31 ¶ Another parable put he forth unto them, saying, The kingdom of heaven is like to a grain of mustard seed, which a man took, and sowed in his field:

32 Which indeed is the least of all seeds: but when it is grown, it is the greatest among herbs, and becometh a tree, so that the birds of the air come and lodge in the branches thereof.

33 ¶ Another parable spake he unto them; The kingdom of heaven is like unto leaven, which a woman took, and hid in three measures of meal, till the whole was leavened.

οἱ δὲ δοῦλοι αὐτῷ λέγουσιν· θέλεις
So the slaves to him say: Willest thou

οὖν ἀπελθόντες συλλέξωμεν αὐτά; 29 ὁ
then going away we may collect them? he

δέ φησιν· οὔ, μήποτε συλλέγοντες τὰ
But says: No, lest collecting the

ζιζάνια ἐκριζώσητε ἅμα αὐτοῖς τὸν
tares ye should root up together with them the

σῖτον. 30 ἄφετε συναυξάνεσθαι ἀμφότερα
wheat. Leave to grow together both

ἕως τοῦ θερισμοῦ· καὶ ἐν καιρῷ τοῦ
until the harvest; and in time of the

θερισμοῦ ἐρῶ τοῖς θερισταῖς· συλλέξατε
harvest I will say to the reapers: Collect ye

πρῶτον τὰ ζιζάνια καὶ δήσατε αὐτὰ
first the tares and bind them

εἰς δέσμας πρὸς τὸ κατακαῦσαι αὐτά,
in bundles - - to burn them,

τὸν δὲ σῖτον συναγάγετε εἰς τὴν ἀποθήκην
but the wheat gather ye into the barn

μου. 31 Ἄλλην παραβολὴν παρέθηκεν
of me. Another parable he set before

αὐτοῖς λέγων· ὁμοία ἐστὶν ἡ βασιλεία
them saying: Like is the kingdom

τῶν οὐρανῶν κόκκῳ σινάπεως, ὃν
of the heavens to a grain of mustard, which

λαβὼν ἄνθρωπος ἔσπειρεν ἐν τῷ ἀγρῷ
²taking ¹a man sowed in the field

αὐτοῦ· 32 ὃ μικρότερον μέν ἐστιν
of him; which less indeed is

πάντων τῶν σπερμάτων, ὅταν δὲ
[than] all the seeds, but when

αὐξηθῇ, μεῖζον τῶν λαχάνων ἐστὶν
it grows, greater [than] the herbs it is

καὶ γίνεται δένδρον, ὥστε ἐλθεῖν τὰ
and becomes a tree, so as to come the

πετεινὰ τοῦ οὐρανοῦ καὶ κατασκηνοῦν
birds of the heaven and dwell

ἐν τοῖς κλάδοις αὐτοῦ. 33 Ἄλλην
in the branches of it. Another

παραβολὴν ἐλάλησεν αὐτοῖς· ὁμοία
parable he spoke to them: Like

ἐστὶν ἡ βασιλεία τῶν οὐρανῶν ζύμῃ,
is the kingdom of the heavens to leaven,

ἣν λαβοῦσα γυνὴ ἐνέκρυψεν εἰς ἀλεύρου
which ²taking ¹a woman hid in ³of meal

σάτα τρία, ἕως οὗ ἐζυμώθη ὅλον.
²measures ¹three, until was leavened [the] whole.

34 All these things spake Jesus unto the multitude in parables; and without a parable spake he not unto them:

35 That it might be fulfilled which was spoken by the prophet, saying, I will open my mouth in parables; I will utter things which have been kept secret from the foundation of the world.

36 ¶ Then Jesus sent the multitude away, and went into the house: and his disciples came unto him, saying, Declare unto us the parable of the tares of the field.

37 He answered and said unto them, He that soweth the good seed is the Son of man;

38 The field is the world; the good seed are the children of the kingdom; but the tares are the children of the wicked *one;*

39 The enemy that sowed them is the devil; the harvest is the end of the world; and the reapers are the angels.

40 As therefore the tares are gathered and burned in the fire; so shall it be in the end of this world.

41 The Son of man shall send forth his angels, and they shall gather out of

---

34 Ταῦτα πάντα ἐλάλησεν ὁ Ἰησοῦς ἐν
These things all spoke – Jesus in

παραβολαῖς τοῖς ὄχλοις, καὶ χωρὶς παραβολῆς
parables to the crowds, and without a parable

οὐδὲν ἐλάλει αὐτοῖς· 35 ὅπως πληρωθῇ
nothing he spoke to them; so that was fulfilled

τὸ ῥηθὲν διὰ τοῦ προφήτου λέγοντος·
the [thing] spoken through the prophet saying:

ἀνοίξω ἐν παραβολαῖς τὸ στόμα μου,
I will open in parables the mouth of me,

ἐρεύξομαι κεκρυμμένα ἀπὸ καταβολῆς.
I will utter things having been hidden from [the] foundation.

36 Τότε ἀφεὶς τοὺς ὄχλους ἦλθεν
Then sending away the crowds he came

εἰς τὴν οἰκίαν. Καὶ προσῆλθον αὐτῷ
into the house. And approached to him

οἱ μαθηταὶ αὐτοῦ λέγοντες· διασάφησον
the disciples of him saying: Explain thou

ἡμῖν τὴν παραβολὴν τῶν ζιζανίων τοῦ
to us the parable of the tares of the

ἀγροῦ. 37 ὁ δὲ ἀποκριθεὶς εἶπεν· ὁ
field. And he answering said: The [one]

σπείρων τὸ καλὸν σπέρμα ἐστὶν ὁ
sowing the good seed is the

υἱὸς τοῦ ἀνθρώπου· 38 ὁ δὲ ἀγρός
Son – of man; and the field

ἐστιν ὁ κόσμος· τὸ δὲ καλὸν σπέρμα,
is the world; and the good seed,

οὗτοί εἰσιν οἱ υἱοὶ τῆς βασιλείας· τὰ δὲ
these are the sons of the kingdom; and the

ζιζάνιά εἰσιν οἱ υἱοὶ τοῦ πονηροῦ, 39 ὁ
tares are the sons of the evil [one], the

δὲ ἐχθρὸς ὁ σπείρας αὐτά ἐστιν ὁ
and enemy the [one] sowing them is the

διάβολος· ὁ δὲ θερισμὸς συντέλεια
devil; and the harvest [the] completion

αἰῶνός ἐστιν, οἱ δὲ θερισταὶ ἄγγελοί
of [the] age is, and the reapers angels

εἰσιν. 40 ὥσπερ οὖν συλλέγεται τὰ
are. As therefore are collected the

ζιζάνια καὶ πυρὶ κατακαίεται, οὕτως
tares and with fire are consumed, thus

ἔσται ἐν τῇ συντελείᾳ τοῦ αἰῶνος·
it will be at the completion of the age;

41 ἀποστελεῖ ὁ υἱὸς τοῦ ἀνθρώπου
will send forth the Son – of man

τοὺς ἀγγέλους αὐτοῦ, καὶ συλλέξουσιν
the angels of him, and they will collect

his kingdom all things that offend, and them which do iniquity;

42 And shall cast them into a furnace of fire: there shall be wailing and gnashing of teeth.

43 Then shall the righteous shine forth as the sun in the kingdom of their Father. Who hath ears to hear, let him hear.

44 ¶ Again, the kingdom of heaven is like unto treasure hid in a field; the which when a man hath found, he hideth, and for joy thereof goeth and selleth all that he hath, and buyeth that field.

45 ¶ Again, the kingdom of heaven is like unto a merchant man, seeking goodly pearls:

46 Who, when he had found one pearl of great price, went and sold all that he had, and bought it.

47 ¶ Again, the kingdom of heaven is like unto a net, that was cast into the sea, and gathered of every kind:

48 Which, when it was full, they drew to shore, and sat down, and gathered the good into vessels, but cast the bad away.

ἐκ τῆς βασιλείας αὐτοῦ πάντα
out of the kingdom of him all

τὰ σκάνδαλα καὶ τοὺς ποιοῦντας
the things leading to sin and the [ones] doing

τὴν ἀνομίαν, 42 καὶ βαλοῦσιν αὐτοὺς εἰς
– lawlessness, and will cast them into

τὴν κάμινον τοῦ πυρός· ἐκεῖ ἔσται ὁ
the furnace – of fire; there will be the

κλαυθμὸς καὶ ὁ βρυγμὸς τῶν ὀδόντων.
wailing and the gnashing of the teeth.

43 τότε οἱ δίκαιοι ἐκλάμψουσιν ὡς ὁ
Then the righteous will shine forth as the

ἥλιος ἐν τῇ βασιλείᾳ τοῦ πατρὸς
sun in the kingdom of the Father

αὐτῶν. ὁ ἔχων ὦτα ἀκουέτω.
of them. The [one] having ears let him hear.

44 Ὁμοία ἐστὶν ἡ βασιλεία τῶν
Like is the kingdom of the

οὐρανῶν θησαυρῷ κεκρυμμένῳ ἐν τῷ
heavens to treasure *having been* hidden in the

ἀγρῷ, ὃν εὑρὼν ἄνθρωπος ἔκρυψεν, καὶ
field, which ²finding ¹a man hid, and

ἀπὸ τῆς χαρᾶς αὐτοῦ ὑπάγει καὶ πωλεῖ
from the joy of him goes and sells

ὅσα ἔχει καὶ ἀγοράζει τὸν ἀγρὸν
what things he has and buys – field

ἐκεῖνον. 45 Πάλιν ὁμοία ἐστὶν ἡ
that. Again like is the

βασιλεία τῶν οὐρανῶν ἐμπόρῳ ζητοῦντι
kingdom of the heavens to a merchant seeking

καλοὺς μαργαρίτας· 46 εὑρὼν δὲ ἕνα πολύτιμον
beautiful pearls; and finding one valuable

μαργαρίτην ἀπελθὼν πέπρακεν πάντα
pearl going away sold all things

ὅσα εἶχεν καὶ ἠγόρασεν αὐτόν.
what he had and bought it.

47 Πάλιν ὁμοία ἐστὶν ἡ βασιλεία τῶν
Again like is the kingdom of the

οὐρανῶν σαγήνῃ βληθείσῃ εἰς τὴν θάλασσαν
heavens to a net cast into the sea

καὶ ἐκ παντὸς γένους συναγαγούσῃ·
and of every kind gathering;

48 ἣν ὅτε ἐπληρώθη ἀναβιβάσαντες ἐπὶ
which when it was filled bringing up onto

τὸν αἰγιαλὸν καὶ καθίσαντες συνέλεξαν
the shore and sitting collected

τὰ καλὰ εἰς ἄγγη, τὰ δὲ σαπρὰ ἔξω
the good into vessels, but the bad out

49 So shall it be at the end of the world: the angels shall come forth, and sever the wicked from among the just,

50 And shall cast them into the furnace of fire: there shall be wailing and gnashing of teeth.

51 Jesus saith unto them, Have ye understood all these things? They say unto him, Yea, Lord.

52 Then said he unto them, Therefore every scribe *which is* instructed unto the kingdom of heaven is like unto a man *that is* an householder, which bringeth forth out of his treasure *things* new and old.

53 ¶ And it came to pass, *that* when Jesus had finished these parables, he departed thence.

54 And when he was come into his own country, he taught them in their synagogue, insomuch that they were astonished, and said, Whence hath this *man* this wisdom, and *these* mighty works?

55 Is not this the carpenter's son? is not his mother called Mary? and his brethren, James, and Joses, and Simon, and Judas?

56 And his sisters, are

ἔβαλον. **49** οὕτως ἔσται ἐν τῇ συντελείᾳ
cast.   Thus it will be at the completion
τοῦ αἰῶνος· ἐξελεύσονται οἱ ἄγγελοι καὶ
of the age: will go forth   the angels   and
ἀφοριοῦσιν τοὺς πονηροὺς ἐκ μέσου
will separate the   evil men from [the] midst
τῶν δικαίων, **50** καὶ βαλοῦσιν αὐτοὺς
of the righteous,   and   will cast   them
εἰς τὴν κάμινον τοῦ πυρός· ἐκεῖ
into the furnace   -   of fire;   there
ἔσται ὁ κλαυθμὸς καὶ ὁ βρυγμὸς τῶν
will be the wailing   and the gnashing of the
ὀδόντων. **51** Συνήκατε ταῦτα πάντα;
teeth.   Did ye understand ²these things ¹all?
λέγουσιν αὐτῷ· ναί. **52** ὁ δὲ εἶπεν
They say to him: Yes.   So he said
αὐτοῖς· διὰ τοῦτο πᾶς γραμματεὺς
to them: Therefore   every   scribe
μαθητευθεὶς τῇ βασιλείᾳ τῶν οὐρανῶν
made a disciple to the kingdom of the heavens
ὅμοιός ἐστιν ἀνθρώπῳ οἰκοδεσπότῃ,
like   is   to a man   a housemaster,
ὅστις ἐκβάλλει ἐκ τοῦ θησαυροῦ
who   puts forth out of the   treasure
αὐτοῦ καινὰ καὶ παλαιά.
of him new and old things.

53 Καὶ ἐγένετο ὅτε ἐτέλεσεν ὁ
And it came to pass when ended   -
Ἰησοῦς τὰς παραβολὰς ταύτας, μετῆρεν
Jesus   -   parables these, he removed
ἐκεῖθεν. **54** καὶ ἐλθὼν εἰς τὴν πατρίδα
thence.   And coming into the native town
αὐτοῦ ἐδίδασκεν αὐτοὺς ἐν τῇ συνα-
of him he taught   them in the syna-
γωγῇ αὐτῶν, ὥστε ἐκπλήσσεσθαι αὐτοὺς
gogue of them, so as to be astounded them
                = so that they were astounded
καὶ λέγειν· πόθεν τούτῳ ἡ σοφία αὕτη
and to sayᵇ: Whence to this man - wisdom this
and said:
καὶ αἱ δυνάμεις; **55** οὐχ οὗτός ἐστιν
and the powerful deeds?   not this man is
ὁ τοῦ τέκτονος υἱός; οὐχ ἡ μήτηρ
the of the carpenter son? not the mother
αὐτοῦ λέγεται Μαριὰμ καὶ οἱ ἀδελφοὶ
of him called   Mary   and the brothers
αὐτοῦ Ἰάκωβος καὶ Ἰωσὴφ καὶ Σίμων
of him James   and Joseph and Simon
καὶ Ἰούδας; **56** καὶ αἱ ἀδελφαὶ αὐτοῦ
and Judas?   and the sisters of him

they not all with us? Whence then hath this *man* all these things?

57 And they were offended in him. But Jesus said unto them, A prophet is not without honour, save in his own country, and in his own house.

58 And he did not many mighty works there because of their unbelief.

οὐχὶ πᾶσαι πρὸς ἡμᾶς εἰσιν; πόθεν
not all with us are? Whence
οὖν τούτῳ ταῦτα πάντα; 57 καὶ
then to this man these things all? And
ἐσκανδαλίζοντο ἐν αὐτῷ. ὁ δὲ Ἰησοῦς
they were offended in him. – But Jesus
εἶπεν αὐτοῖς· οὐκ ἔστιν προφήτης
said to them: ²not ²is ¹A prophet
ἄτιμος εἰ μὴ ἐν τῇ πατρίδι καὶ
unhonoured except in the(his) native town and
ἐν τῇ οἰκίᾳ αὐτοῦ. 58 καὶ οὐκ ἐποίησεν ἐκεῖ
in the house of him. And not he did there
δυνάμεις πολλὰς διὰ τὴν ἀπιστίαν αὐτῶν.
powerful deeds many because of the unbelief of them.

CHAPTER 14

A T that time Herod the tetrarch heard of the fame of Jesus,

2 And said unto his servants, This is John the Baptist; he is risen from the dead; and therefore mighty works do shew forth themselves in him.

3 ¶ For Herod had laid hold on John, and bound him, and put *him* in prison for Herodias' sake, his brother Philip's wife.

4 For John said unto him, It is not lawful for thee to have her.

5 And when he would have put him to death, he feared the multitude, because they counted him as a prophet.

6 But when Herod's birthday was kept, the daughter of Herodias danced before them, and pleased Herod.

14 Ἐν ἐκείνῳ τῷ καιρῷ ἤκουσεν
At that – time heard
Ἡρῴδης ὁ τετραάρχης τὴν ἀκοὴν Ἰησοῦ,
Herod the tetrarch the report of Jesus,
2 καὶ εἶπεν τοῖς παισὶν αὐτοῦ· οὗτός
and said to the servants of him: This
ἐστιν Ἰωάννης ὁ βαπτιστής· αὐτός
is John the Baptist; he
ἠγέρθη ἀπὸ τῶν νεκρῶν, καὶ διὰ τοῦτο
was raised from the dead, and therefore
αἱ δυνάμεις ἐνεργοῦσιν ἐν αὐτῷ.
the powerful deeds operate in him.
3 Ὁ γὰρ Ἡρῴδης κρατήσας τὸν Ἰωάννην
– For Herod seizing the John
ἔδησεν καὶ ἐν φυλακῇ ἀπέθετο διὰ
bound and in prison put away on account of
Ἡρῳδιάδα τὴν γυναῖκα Φιλίππου τοῦ
Herodias the wife of Philip the
ἀδελφοῦ αὐτοῦ· 4 ἔλεγεν γὰρ ὁ Ἰωάννης
brother of him; for said – John
αὐτῷ· οὐκ ἔξεστίν σοι ἔχειν αὐτήν.
to him: It is not lawful for thee to have her.
5 καὶ θέλων αὐτὸν ἀποκτεῖναι ἐφοβήθη
And wishing him to kill he feared
τὸν ὄχλον, ὅτι ὡς προφήτην αὐτὸν
the crowd, because as a prophet him
εἶχον. 6 γενεσίοις δὲ γενομένοις τοῦ
they had. Now on the birthday occurring° –
Ἡρῴδου ὠρχήσατο ἡ θυγάτηρ τῆς
of Herod danced the daughter –
Ἡρῳδιάδος ἐν τῷ μέσῳ καὶ ἤρεσεν
of Herodias in the midst and pleased

7 Whereupon he promised with an oath to give her whatsoever she would ask.

8 And she, being before instructed of her mother, said, Give me here John Baptist's head in a charger.

9 And the king was sorry: nevertheless for the oath's sake, and them which sat with him at meat, he commanded *it* to be given *her*.

10 And he sent, and beheaded John in the prison.

11 And his head was brought in a charger, and given to the damsel: and she brought *it* to her mother.

12 And his disciples came, and took up the body, and buried it, and went and told Jesus.

13 ¶ When Jesus heard *of it*, he departed thence by ship into a desert place apart: and when the people had heard *thereof*, they followed him on foot out of the cities.

14 And Jesus went forth and saw a great multitude, and was moved with compassion toward them, and he healed their sick.

15 ¶ And when it was evening, his disciples came to him, saying, This is a desert place, and the time

---

τῷ   'Ηρῴδη,   7 ὅθεν   μεθ'   ὅρκου   ὡμολόγησεν
-   Herod,   whence   with   an oath   he promised

αὐτῇ   δοῦναι   ὃ   ἐὰν   αἰτήσηται.   8 ἡ   δὲ
²her   ¹to give   whatever   she might ask.   So she

προβιβασθεῖσα   ὑπὸ   τῆς   μητρὸς   αὐτῆς·
being instructed   by   the   mother   of her:

δός   μοι,   φησίν,   ὧδε   ἐπὶ   πίνακι   τὴν
Give   me,   she says,   here   on   a platter   the

κεφαλὴν   'Ιωάννου   τοῦ   βαπτιστοῦ.   9 καὶ
head   of John   the   Baptist.   And

λυπηθεὶς   ὁ   βασιλεὺς   διὰ   τοὺς
being grieved   the   king   on account of   the

ὅρκους   καὶ   τοὺς   συνανακειμένους
oaths   and   the [ones] reclining at table with [him]

ἐκέλευσεν   δοθῆναι,   10 καὶ   πέμψας
he commanded   to be given,   and   sending

ἀπεκεφάλισεν   'Ιωάννην   ἐν   τῇ   φυλακῇ.
beheaded   John   in   the   prison.

11 καὶ   ἠνέχθη   ἡ   κεφαλὴ   αὐτοῦ   ἐπὶ
And   was brought   the   head   of him   on

πίνακι   καὶ   ἐδόθη   τῷ   κορασίῳ,   καὶ
a platter   and   was given   to the   maid,   and

ἤνεγκεν   τῇ   μητρὶ   αὐτῆς.   12 καὶ
she brought [it]   to the   mother   of her.   And

προσελθόντες   οἱ   μαθηταὶ   αὐτοῦ   ἦραν   τὸ
⁴approaching   ¹the   ²disciples   ³of him   took   the

πτῶμα   καὶ   ἔθαψαν   αὐτόν,   καὶ   ἐλθόντες
corpse   and   buried   him,   and   coming

ἀπήγγειλαν   τῷ   'Ιησοῦ.   13 'Ακούσας   δὲ
reported   -   to Jesus.   And ²hearing

ὁ   'Ιησοῦς   ἀνεχώρησεν   ἐκεῖθεν   ἐν
-   ¹Jesus   departed   thence   in

πλοίῳ   εἰς   ἔρημον   τόπον   κατ'   ἰδίαν·
a ship   to   a desert   place   privately;

καὶ   ἀκούσαντες   οἱ   ὄχλοι   ἠκολούθησαν
and   ²hearing   ¹the   ²crowds   followed

αὐτῷ   πεζῇ   ἀπὸ   τῶν   πόλεων.   14 Καὶ
him   afoot   from   the   cities.   And

ἐξελθὼν   εἶδεν   πολὺν   ὄχλον,   καὶ
going forth   he saw   a much   crowd,   and

ἐσπλαγχνίσθη   ἐπ'   αὐτοῖς   καὶ
was filled with tenderness   over   them   and

ἐθεράπευσεν   τοὺς   ἀρρώστους   αὐτῶν.
healed   the   sick   of them.

15 ὀψίας   δὲ   γενομένης   προσῆλθον   αὐτῷ
Now evening   coming onª   approached   *to* him
= when evening came on

οἱ   μαθηταὶ   λέγοντες·   ἔρημός   ἐστιν   ὁ
the   disciples   saying: Desert   is   the

is now past; send the multitude away, that they may go into the villages, and buy themselves victuals.

16 But Jesus said unto them, They need not depart; give ye them to eat.

17 And they say unto him, We have here but five loaves, and two fishes.

18 He said, Bring them hither to me.

19 And he commanded the multitude to sit down on the grass, and took the five loaves, and the two fishes, and looking up to heaven, he blessed, and brake, and gave the loaves to *his* disciples, and the disciples to the multitude.

20 And they did all eat, and were filled: and they took up of the fragments that remained twelve baskets full.

21 And they that had eaten were about five thousand men, beside women and children.

22 ¶ And straightway Jesus constrained his disciples to get into a ship, and to go before him unto the other side, while he sent the multitudes away.

23 And when he had sent the multitudes away, he went up into a mountain

τόπος	καὶ	ἡ	ὥρα	ἤδη	παρῆλθεν·
place	and	the	hour	already	passed;

ἀπόλυσον	οὖν	τοὺς	ὄχλους,	ἵνα	ἀπελθόντες
dismiss	therefore	the	crowds,	that	going away

εἰς	τὰς	κώμας	ἀγοράσωσιν	ἑαυτοῖς
into	the	villages	they may buy	for themselves

βρώματα.	**16** ὁ	δὲ	Ἰησοῦς	εἶπεν	αὐτοῖς·
foods.	– But		Jesus	said	to them:

οὐ	χρείαν	ἔχουσιν	ἀπελθεῖν·	δότε
Not	need	they have	to go away;	give

αὐτοῖς	ὑμεῖς	φαγεῖν.	**17** οἱ	δὲ	λέγουσιν
them	ye	to eat.	But they		say

αὐτῷ·	οὐκ	ἔχομεν	ὧδε	εἰ	μὴ	πέντε
to him:	We have not		here	except		five

ἄρτους	καὶ	δύο	ἰχθύας.	**18** ὁ	δὲ	εἶπεν·
loaves	and	two	fishes.	And he		said:

φέρετέ	μοι	ὧδε	αὐτούς.	**19** καὶ	κελεύσας
Bring	to me	here	them.	And	having commanded

τοὺς	ὄχλους	ἀνακλιθῆναι	ἐπὶ	τοῦ	χόρτου,
the	crowds	to recline	on	the	grass,

λαβὼν	τοὺς	πέντε	ἄρτους	καὶ	τοὺς	δύο
taking	the	five	loaves	and	the	two

ἰχθύας,	ἀναβλέψας	εἰς	τὸν	οὐρανὸν
fishes,	looking up	to	–	heaven

εὐλόγησεν,	καὶ	κλάσας	ἔδωκεν	τοῖς
he blessed,	and	breaking	gave	to the

μαθηταῖς	τοὺς	ἄρτους,	οἱ	δὲ	μαθηταὶ
disciples	the	loaves,	and the		disciples

τοῖς	ὄχλοις.	**20** καὶ	ἔφαγον	πάντες	καὶ
to the	crowds.	And	ate	all	and

ἐχορτάσθησαν·	καὶ	ἦραν	τὸ	περισσεῦον
were satisfied;	and	they took	the	excess

τῶν	κλασμάτων,	δώδεκα	κοφίνους	πλήρεις.
of the	fragments,	twelve	baskets	full.

21 οἱ	δὲ	ἐσθίοντες	ἦσαν	ἄνδρες	ὡσεὶ
And the [ones]		eating	were	men	about

πεντακισχίλιοι	χωρὶς	γυναικῶν	καὶ
five thousand	apart from	women	and

παιδίων.	**22** Καὶ	[εὐθέως]	ἠνάγκασεν
children.	And	immediately	he constrained

τοὺς	μαθητὰς	ἐμβῆναι	εἰς	τὸ	πλοῖον
the	disciples	to embark	in	the	ship

καὶ	προάγειν	αὐτὸν	εἰς	τὸ	πέραν,
and	to go before	him	to	the	other side,

ἕως	οὗ	ἀπολύσῃ	τοὺς	ὄχλους.	**23** Καὶ
until	he should dismiss	the	crowds.	And

ἀπολύσας	τοὺς	ὄχλους	ἀνέβη	εἰς	τὸ
having dismissed	the	crowds	he went up	into	the

apart to pray: and when the evening was come, he was there alone.

24 But the ship was now in the midst of the sea, tossed with waves: for the wind was contrary.

25 And in the fourth watch of the night Jesus went unto them, walking on the sea.

26 And when the disciples saw him walking on the sea, they were troubled, saying, It is a spirit; and they cried out for fear.

27 But straightway Jesus spake unto them, saying, Be of good cheer; it is I; be not afraid.

28 And Peter answered him and said, Lord, if it be thou, bid me come unto thee on the water.

29 And he said, Come. And when Peter was come down out of the ship, he walked on the water, to go to Jesus.

30 But when he saw the wind boisterous, he was afraid; and beginning to sink, he cried, saying, Lord, save me.

31 And immediately Jesus stretched forth *his* hand, and caught him, and said unto him, O thou of

ὄρος κατ' ἰδίαν προσεύξασθαι. ὀψίας
mountain privately to pray. evening
=And when

δὲ γενομένης μόνος ἦν ἐκεῖ. **24** τὸ δὲ
And coming onᵃ alone he was there. But the
evening came on

πλοῖον ἤδη σταδίους πολλοὺς ἀπὸ τῆς
ship now furlongs many from the

γῆς ἀπεῖχεν, βασανιζόμενον ὑπὸ τῶν
land was away, being distressed by the

κυμάτων, ἦν γὰρ ἐναντίος ὁ ἄνεμος.
waves, ⁴was ¹for ⁵contrary ²the ³wind.

25 τετάρτῃ δὲ φυλακῇ τῆς νυκτὸς
Now in [the] fourth watch of the night

ἦλθεν πρὸς αὐτοὺς περιπατῶν ἐπὶ τὴν
he came toward them walking on the

θάλασσαν. **26** οἱ δὲ μαθηταὶ ἰδόντες
sea. And the disciples seeing

αὐτὸν ἐπὶ τῆς θαλάσσης περιπατοῦντα
him on the sea walking

ἐταράχθησαν λέγοντες ὅτι φάντασμά
were troubled saying[,] – A phantasm

ἐστιν, καὶ ἀπὸ τοῦ φόβου ἔκραξαν.
it is, and from – fear they cried out.

27 εὐθὺς δὲ ἐλάλησεν [ὁ Ἰησοῦς]
But immediately spoke – Jesus

αὐτοῖς λέγων· θαρσεῖτε, ἐγώ εἰμι·
to them saying: Be of good cheer, I am;

μὴ φοβεῖσθε. **28** ἀποκριθεὶς δὲ αὐτῷ ὁ
do not fear. And answering him –

Πέτρος εἶπεν· κύριε, εἰ σὺ εἶ, κέλευσόν
Peter said: Lord, if thou art, command

με ἐλθεῖν πρὸς σὲ ἐπὶ τὰ ὕδατα. **29** ὁ
me to come to thee on the waters. he

δὲ εἶπεν· ἐλθέ. καὶ καταβὰς ἀπὸ τοῦ
And said: Come. And going down from the

πλοίου Πέτρος περιπάτησεν ἐπὶ τὰ ὕδατα
ship Peter walked on the waters

καὶ ἦλθεν πρὸς τὸν Ἰησοῦν. **30** βλέπων δὲ
and came toward – Jesus. But seeing

τὸν ἄνεμον ἐφοβήθη, καὶ ἀρξάμενος
the wind he was afraid, and beginning

καταποντίζεσθαι ἔκραξεν λέγων·
to sink he cried out saying:

κύριε, σῶσόν με. **31** εὐθέως δὲ ὁ
Lord, save me. And immediately –

Ἰησοῦς ἐκτείνας τὴν χεῖρα ἐπελάβετο
Jesus stretching out the(his) hand took hold

αὐτοῦ, καὶ λέγει αὐτῷ· ὀλιγόπιστε,
of him, and says to him: Little-faith,

little faith, wherefore didst thou doubt?

32 And when they were come into the ship, the wind ceased.

33 Then they that were in the ship came and worshipped him, saying, Of a truth thou art the Son of God.

34 ¶ And when they were gone over, they came into the land of Gennesaret.

35 And when the men of that place had knowledge of him, they sent out into all that country round about, and brought unto him all that were diseased;

36 And besought him that they might only touch the hem of his garment: and as many as touched were made perfectly whole.

εἰς τί ἐδίστασας;
why didst thou doubt?

32 καὶ ἀναβάντων
And going up
=as they went up

αὐτῶν εἰς τὸ πλοῖον ἐκόπασεν ὁ ἄνεμος.
them into the ship ceased the wind.

33 οἱ δὲ ἐν τῷ πλοίῳ προσεκύνησαν αὐτῷ
And the [ones] in the ship worshipped him

λέγοντες· ἀληθῶς θεοῦ υἱὸς εἶ. **34** Καὶ
saying: Truly of God Son thou art. And

διαπεράσαντες ἦλθον ἐπὶ τὴν γῆν εἰς
crossing over they came onto the land to

Γεννησαρέτ. **35** καὶ ἐπιγνόντες αὐτὸν
Gennesaret. And recognizing him

οἱ ἄνδρες τοῦ τόπου ἐκείνου ἀπέστειλαν
the men - place of that sent

εἰς ὅλην τὴν περίχωρον ἐκείνην, καὶ
into all - neighbourhood that, and

προσήνεγκαν αὐτῷ πάντας τοὺς κακῶς
brought to him all the [ones] ill
=those who were ill,

ἔχοντας, **36** καὶ παρεκάλουν αὐτὸν ἵνα
having, and besought him that

μόνον ἅψωνται τοῦ κρασπέδου τοῦ
only they might touch the fringe of the

ἱματίου αὐτοῦ· καὶ ὅσοι ἥψαντο διεσώθησαν.
garment of him; and as many as touched were completely
healed.

CHAPTER 15

THEN came to Jesus scribes and Pharisees, which were of Jerusalem, saying,

2 Why do thy disciples transgress the tradition of the elders? for they wash not their hands when they eat bread.

3 But he answered and said unto them, Why do ye also transgress the commandment of God by your tradition?

4 For God commanded, saying, Honour thy father and mother: and, He that

15 Τότε προσέρχονται τῷ Ἰησοῦ
Then approach - to Jesus

ἀπὸ Ἱεροσολύμων Φαρισαῖοι καὶ γραμματεῖς
from Jerusalem Pharisees and scribes

λέγοντες· **2** διὰ τί οἱ μαθηταί σου
saying: Why the disciples of thee

παραβαίνουσιν τὴν παράδοσιν τῶν
transgress the tradition of the

πρεσβυτέρων; οὐ γὰρ νίπτονται τὰς χεῖρας
elders? for not they wash the(ir) hands

ὅταν ἄρτον ἐσθίωσιν. **3** ὁ δὲ ἀπο-
whenever bread they eat. And he answer-

κριθεὶς εἶπεν αὐτοῖς· διὰ τί καὶ ὑμεῖς
ing said to them: Why indeed ye

παραβαίνετε τὴν ἐντολὴν τοῦ θεοῦ
transgress the commandment - of God

διὰ τὴν παράδοσιν ὑμῶν; **4** ὁ γὰρ
on account of the tradition of you? - For

θεὸς εἶπεν· τίμα τὸν πατέρα καὶ τὴν
God said: Honour the father and the

μητέρα, καί· ὁ κακολογῶν πατέρα
mother, and: The [one] speaking evil of father

curseth father or mother,
let him die the death.

5 But ye say, Whoso-
ever shall say to *his* father
or *his* mother, *It is* a gift, by
whatsoever thou mightest
be profited by me;

6 And honour not his
father or his mother, *he
shall be free.* Thus have
ye made the command-
ment of God of none effect
by your tradition.

7 *Ye* hypocrites, well did
Esaias prophesy of you,
saying,

8 This people draweth
nigh unto me with their
mouth, and honoureth me
with *their* lips; but their
heart is far from me.

9 But in vain they do
worship me, teaching *for*
doctrines the command-
ments of men.

10 ¶ And he called the
multitude, and said unto
them, Hear, and under-
stand:

11 Not that which goeth
into the mouth defileth
a man; but that which
cometh out of the mouth,
this defileth a man.

12 Then came his dis-
ciples, and said unto him,
Knowest thou that the
Pharisees were offended,
after they heard this saying?

13 But he answered and
said, Every plant, which
my heavenly Father hath
not planted, shall be rooted
up.

14 Let them alone: they
be blind leaders of the

ἢ   μητέρα   θανάτῳ   τελευτάτω.   5 ὑμεῖς   δὲ
or   mother   by death   let him die.   But ye

λέγετε·   ὃς   ἂν   εἴπῃ   τῷ   πατρὶ   ἢ
say: Whoever   says   to the(his)   father   or

τῇ   μητρί·   δῶρον   ὃ   ἐὰν   ἐξ   ἐμοῦ
to the(his) mother: A gift   whatever   by   me

ὠφεληθῇς,   6 οὐ   μὴ   τιμήσει   τὸν
thou mightest be owed,   by no means   shall he honour   the

πατέρα   αὐτοῦ   ἢ   τὴν   μητέρα   αὐτοῦ·
father   of him   or   the   mother   of him;

καὶ   ἠκυρώσατε   τὸν   λόγον   τοῦ   θεοῦ
and   ye annulled   the   word   –   of God

διὰ   τὴν   παράδοσιν   ὑμῶν.   7 ὑποκρι-
on account of   the   tradition   of you.   Hypocrites,

ταί,   καλῶς   ἐπροφήτευσεν   περὶ   ὑμῶν
well   prophesied   concerning   you

Ἡσαΐας   λέγων·   8 ὁ   λαὸς   οὗτος   τοῖς
Isaiah   saying: This people   with the

χείλεσίν   με   τιμᾷ,   ἡ   δὲ   καρδία   αὐτῶν
lips   me   honours,   but the   heart   of them

πόρρω   ἀπέχει   ἀπ᾿   ἐμοῦ·   9 μάτην   δὲ
far   is away   from   me;   and vainly

σέβονται   με,   διδάσκοντες   διδασκαλίας
they worship   me,   teaching   teachings

ἐντάλματα   ἀνθρώπων.   10 Καὶ   προσκαλε-
ordinances   of men.   And   calling

σάμενος   τὸν   ὄχλον   εἶπεν   αὐτοῖς·
forward   the   crowd   he said   to them:

ἀκούετε   καὶ   συνίετε·   11 οὐ   τὸ   εἰσερχ-
Hear ye   and   understand: Not the [thing] enter-

όμενον   εἰς   τὸ   στόμα   κοινοῖ   τὸν   ἄνθρωπον,
ing   into   the   mouth   defiles   the   man,

ἀλλὰ   τὸ   ἐκπορευόμενον   ἐκ   τοῦ   στόματος,
but   the [thing]   coming forth   out of   the   mouth,

τοῦτο   κοινοῖ   τὸν   ἄνθρωπον.   12 Τότε
this   defiles   the   man.   Then

προσελθόντες   οἱ   μαθηταὶ   λέγουσιν   αὐτῷ·
approaching   the   disciples   say   to him:

οἶδας   ὅτι   οἱ   Φαρισαῖοι   ἀκούσαντες   τὸν
Dost thou know that the   Pharisees   hearing   the

λόγον   ἐσκανδαλίσθησαν;   13 ὁ   δὲ   ἀπο-
saying   were offended?   And he   answer-

κριθεὶς   εἶπεν·   πᾶσα   φυτεία   ἣν   οὐκ
ing   said: Every   plant   which   not

ἐφύτευσεν   ὁ   πατήρ   μου   ὁ   οὐράνιος   ἐκριζω-
planted   the   Father   of me   –   heavenly   shall be

θήσεται.   14 ἄφετε   αὐτούς·   τυφλοί   εἰσιν
uprooted.   Leave   them;   blind   they are

blind. And if the blind lead the blind, both shall all into the ditch.

15 Then answered Peter and said unto him, Declare unto us this parable.

16 And Jesus said, Are ye also yet without understanding?

17 Do not ye yet understand, that whatsoever entereth in at the mouth goeth into the belly, and is cast out into the draught?

18 But those things which proceed out of the mouth come forth from the heart: and they defile the man.

19 For out of the heart proceed evil thoughts, murders, adulteries, fornications, thefts, false witness, blasphemies:

20 These are *the things* which defile a man: but to eat with unwashen hands defileth not a man.

21 ¶ Then Jesus went thence, and departed into the coasts of Tyre and Sidon.

22 And, behold, a woman of Canaan came out of the same coasts, and cried unto him, saying, Have mercy on me, O Lord, *thou* son of David; my daughter is grievously vexed with a devil.

23 But he answered her not a word. And his dis-

ὁδηγοὶ τυφλῶν· τυφλὸς δὲ τυφλὸν
leaders of blind; ³a blind man ¹and ²a blind man

ἐὰν ὁδηγῇ, ἀμφότεροι εἰς βόθυνον πεσοῦνται.
²if ⁴leads, both into a ditch will fall.

15 Ἀποκριθεὶς δὲ ὁ Πέτρος εἶπεν αὐτῷ·
And answering – Peter said to him:

φράσον ἡμῖν τὴν παραβολήν. 16 ὁ δὲ
Explain to us the parable. So he

εἶπεν· ἀκμὴν καὶ ὑμεῖς ἀσύνετοί
said: Thus also ye unintelligent

ἐστε; 17 οὐ νοεῖτε ὅτι πᾶν τὸ
are? Do ye not understand that everything

εἰσπορευόμενον εἰς τὸ στόμα εἰς τὴν
entering into the mouth into the

κοιλίαν χωρεῖ καὶ εἰς ἀφεδρῶνα ἐκβάλλεται;
stomach goes and into a drain is cast out?

18 τὰ δὲ ἐκπορευόμενα ἐκ τοῦ
but the things coming forth out of the

στόματος ἐκ τῆς καρδίας ἐξέρχεται,
mouth out of the heart comes forth,

κἀκεῖνα κοινοῖ τὸν ἄνθρωπον. 19 ἐκ
and those defiles the man. out of

γὰρ τῆς καρδίας ἐξέρχονται διαλογισμοὶ
For the heart come forth thoughts

πονηροί, φόνοι, μοιχεῖαι, πορνεῖαι, κλοπαί,
evil, murders, adulteries, fornications, thefts,

ψευδομαρτυρίαι, βλασφημίαι. 20 ταῦτά
false witnessings, blasphemies. These things

ἐστιν τὰ κοινοῦντα τὸν ἄνθρωπον·
is(are) the [ones] defiling the man;

τὸ δὲ ἀνίπτοις χερσὶν φαγεῖν οὐ
– but with unwashed hands to eat not

κοινοῖ τὸν ἄνθρωπον.
defiles the man.

21 Καὶ ἐξελθὼν ἐκεῖθεν ὁ Ἰησοῦς
And going forth thence – Jesus

ἀνεχώρησεν εἰς τὰ μέρη Τύρου καὶ
departed into the parts of Tyre and

Σιδῶνος. 22 καὶ ἰδοὺ γυνὴ Χαναναία
Sidon. And behold woman a Canaanite

ἀπὸ τῶν ὁρίων ἐκείνων ἐξελθοῦσα
from – borders those coming forth

ἔκραζεν λέγουσα· ἐλέησόν με, κύριε
cried out saying: Pity me, Lord[,]

υἱὸς Δαυίδ· ἡ θυγάτηρ μου κακῶς
son of David; the daughter of me badly

δαιμονίζεται. 23 ὁ δὲ οὐκ ἀπεκρίθη
is demon-possessed. But he answered not

ciples came and besought him, saying, Send her away; for she crieth after us.

24 But he answered and said, I am not sent but unto the lost sheep of the house of Israel.

25 Then came she and worshipped him, saying, Lord, help me.

26 But he answered and said, It is not meet to take the children's bread, and to cast *it* to dogs.

27 And she said, Truth, Lord: yet the dogs eat of the crumbs which fall from their masters' table.

28 Then Jesus answered and said unto her, O woman, great *is* thy faith: be it unto thee even as thou wilt. And her daughter was made whole from that very hour.

29 ¶ And Jesus departed from thence, and came nigh unto the sea of Galilee; and went up into a mountain, and sat down there.

30 And great multitudes came unto him, having with them *those that were* lame, blind, dumb, maimed, and many others, and cast them down at Jesus' feet; and he healed them:

αὐτῇ λόγον. καὶ προσελθόντες οἱ μαθηταὶ
her a word. And approaching the disciples

αὐτοῦ ἠρώτων αὐτὸν λέγοντες· ἀπόλυσον
of him besought him saying: Dismiss

αὐτήν, ὅτι κράζει ὄπισθεν ἡμῶν. 24 ὁ
her, because she is crying out behind us. he

δὲ ἀποκριθεὶς εἶπεν· οὐκ ἀπεστάλην
But answering said: I was not sent

εἰ μὴ εἰς τὰ πρόβατα τὰ ἀπολωλότα
except to the sheep - lost

οἴκου Ἰσραήλ. 25 ἡ δὲ ἐλθοῦσα
of [the] house of Israel. But she coming

προσεκύνει αὐτῷ λέγουσα· κύριε, βοήθει
worshipped him saying: Lord, help

μοι. 26 ὁ δὲ ἀποκριθεὶς εἶπεν· οὐκ
me. But he answering said: not

ἔστιν καλὸν λαβεῖν τὸν ἄρτον τῶν τέκνων
It is good to take the bread of the children

καὶ βαλεῖν τοῖς κυναρίοις. 27 ἡ δὲ
and to throw to the dogs. And she

εἶπεν· ναί, κύριε· καὶ γὰρ τὰ κυνάρια
said: Yes, Lord; but even the dogs

ἐσθίει ἀπὸ τῶν ψιχίων τῶν πιπτόντων
eats from the crumbs - falling

ἀπὸ τῆς τραπέζης τῶν κυρίων αὐτῶν.
from the table of the masters of them.

28 τότε ἀποκριθεὶς ὁ Ἰησοῦς εἶπεν αὐτῇ·
Then answering - Jesus said to her:

ὦ γύναι, μεγάλη σου ἡ πίστις· γενηθήτω
O woman, great of thee the faith; let it be

σοι ὡς θέλεις. καὶ ἰάθη ἡ
to thee as thou desirest. And was healed the

θυγάτηρ αὐτῆς ἀπὸ τῆς ὥρας ἐκείνης.
daughter of her from - hour that.

29 Καὶ μεταβὰς ἐκεῖθεν ὁ Ἰησοῦς
And removing thence - Jesus

ἦλθεν παρὰ τὴν θάλασσαν τῆς Γαλιλαίας,
came by the sea of Galilee,

καὶ ἀναβὰς εἰς τὸ ὄρος ἐκάθητο ἐκεῖ.
and going up into the mountain he sat there.

30 καὶ προσῆλθον αὐτῷ ὄχλοι πολλοὶ ἔχοντες
And approached *to* him crowds many having

μεθ' ἑαυτῶν χωλούς, κυλλούς, τυφλούς,
with themselves lame, maimed, blind,

κωφούς, καὶ ἑτέρους πολλούς, καὶ ἔρριψαν
dumb, and others many, and cast

αὐτοὺς παρὰ τοὺς πόδας αὐτοῦ· καὶ
them at the feet of him; and

31 Insomuch that the multitude wondered, when they saw the dumb to speak, the maimed to be whole, the lame to walk, and the blind to see: and they glorified the God of Israel.

32 ¶ Then Jesus called his disciples *unto him*, and said, I have compassion on the multitude, because they continue with me now three days, and have nothing to eat: and I will not send them away fasting, lest they faint in the way.

33 And his disciples say unto him, Whence should we have so much bread in the wilderness, as to fill so great a multitude?

34 And Jesus saith unto them, How many loaves have ye? And they said, Seven, and a few little fishes.

35 And he commanded the multitude to sit down on the ground.

36 And he took the seven loaves and the fishes, and gave thanks, and brake *them*, and gave to his disciples, and the disciples to the multitude.

37 And they did all eat, and were filled: and they took up of the broken *meat* that was left seven baskets full.

38 And they that did eat were four thousand

ἐθεράπευσεν αὐτούς·
he healed   them;

31 ὥστε τὸν ὄχλον
so as   the   crowd
=so that the crowd marvelled

θαυμάσαι βλέποντας κωφοὺς λαλοῦντας,
to marvel[b]   seeing   dumb men   speaking,

κυλλοὺς ὑγιεῖς καὶ χωλοὺς περιπατοῦντας
maimed   whole   and   lame   walking

καὶ τυφλοὺς βλέποντας· καὶ ἐδόξασαν
and   blind   seeing;   and   they glorified

τὸν θεὸν Ἰσραήλ. **32** Ὁ δὲ Ἰησοῦς
the   God   of Israel.   – And   Jesus

προσκαλεσάμενος τοὺς μαθητὰς αὐτοῦ
calling forward   the   disciples   of him

εἶπεν· σπλαγχνίζομαι ἐπὶ τὸν ὄχλον,
said: I am filled with tenderness   over   the   crowd,

ὅτι ἤδη ἡμέραι τρεῖς προσμένουσίν
because now   days   three   they remain

μοι καὶ οὐκ ἔχουσιν τί φάγωσιν·
with me and   have not   anything they may eat;

καὶ ἀπολῦσαι αὐτοὺς νήστεις οὐ θέλω,
and   to dismiss   them   without food I am not willing,

μήποτε ἐκλυθῶσιν ἐν τῇ ὁδῷ. **33** καὶ
lest   they fail   in   the   way.   And

λέγουσιν αὐτῷ οἱ μαθηταί· πόθεν
say   to him   the   disciples: Whence

ἡμῖν ἐν ἐρημίᾳ ἄρτοι τοσοῦτοι ὥστε
to us   in   a desert   loaves   so many   so as

χορτάσαι ὄχλον τοσοῦτον; **34** καὶ λέγει
to satisfy   a crowd   so great?   And   says

αὐτοῖς ὁ Ἰησοῦς· πόσους ἄρτους ἔχετε;
to them   – Jesus: How many   loaves   have ye?

οἱ δὲ εἶπαν· ἑπτά, καὶ ὀλίγα ἰχθύδια.
And they   said: Seven,   and   a few   fishes.

35 καὶ παραγγείλας τῷ ὄχλῳ ἀναπεσεῖν
And   having enjoined   the   crowd   to recline

ἐπὶ τὴν γῆν **36** ἔλαβεν τοὺς ἑπτὰ
on   the   ground   he took   the   seven

ἄρτους καὶ τοὺς ἰχθύας καὶ εὐχαριστήσας
loaves   and   the   fishes   and   giving thanks

ἔκλασεν καὶ ἐδίδου τοῖς μαθηταῖς, οἱ δὲ
he broke   and   gave   to the   disciples,   and the

μαθηταὶ τοῖς ὄχλοις. **37** καὶ ἔφαγον πάντες
disciples   to the crowds.   And   ate   all

καὶ ἐχορτάσθησαν, καὶ τὸ περισσεῦον τῶν
and   were satisfied,   and   the   excess   of the

κλασμάτων ἦραν, ἑπτὰ σπυρίδας πλήρεις.
fragments   they took,   seven   baskets   full.

38 οἱ δὲ ἐσθίοντες ἦσαν τετρακισχίλιοι
And the [ones]   eating   were   four thousand

men, beside women and children.

39 And he sent away the multitude, and took ship, and came into the coasts of Magdala.

ἄνδρες   χωρὶς   γυναικῶν   καὶ   παιδίων.
men   apart from   women   and   children.

39 Καὶ   ἀπολύσας   τοὺς   ὄχλους   ἐνέβη   εἰς
And   having dismissed   the   crowds   he embarked   in

τὸ   πλοῖον,   καὶ   ἦλθεν   εἰς   τὰ   ὅρια   Μαγαδάν.
the   ship,   and   came   into   the   borders   of Magadan.

CHAPTER 16

THE Pharisees also with the Sadducees came, and tempting desired him that he would shew them a sign from heaven.

2 He answered and said unto them, When it is evening, ye say, *It will be* fair weather: for the sky is red.

3 And in the morning, *It will be* foul weather to day: for the sky is red and lowring. O *ye* hypocrites, ye can discern the face of the sky; but can ye not *discern* the signs of the times?

4 A wicked and adulterous generation seeketh after a sign; and there shall no sign be given unto it, but the sign of the prophet Jonas. And he left them, and departed.

5 ¶ And when his disciples were come to the other side, they had forgotten to take bread.

6 Then Jesus said unto them, Take heed and beware of the leaven of the Pharisees and of the Sadducees.

7 And they reasoned among themselves, saying, *It is* because we have taken no bread.

8 *Which* when Jesus perceived, he said unto them,

16 Καὶ   προσελθόντες   οἱ   Φαρισαῖοι   καὶ
And   approaching   the   Pharisees   and

Σαδδουκαῖοι   πειράζοντες   ἐπηρώτησαν   αὐτὸν
Sadducees   tempting   asked   him

σημεῖον   ἐκ   τοῦ   οὐρανοῦ   ἐπιδεῖξαι
a sign   out of the   heaven   to show

αὐτοῖς.   2 ὁ   δὲ   ἀποκριθεὶς   εἶπεν   αὐτοῖς·
to them.   But he   answering   said   to them:

[ὀψίας   γενομένης   λέγετε·   εὐδία,
Evening   coming on[a] ye say: Fair weather,
= When evening comes on

πυρράζει   γὰρ   ὁ   οὐρανός·   3 καὶ   πρωΐ·
for is red   the   heaven(sky);   and in the morning:

σήμερον   χειμών,   πυρράζει   γὰρ   στυγνάζων
To-day   stormy weather,   for is red   being overcast

ὁ   οὐρανός.   τὸ   μὲν   πρόσωπον   τοῦ
the   heaven(sky).   The   -   face   of the

οὐρανοῦ   γινώσκετε   διακρίνειν,   τὰ   δὲ
heaven(sky)   ye know*   to discern,   but the

σημεῖα   τῶν   καιρῶν   οὐ   δύνασθε;]   4 γενεὰ
signs   of the   times   can ye not?   A generation

πονηρὰ   καὶ   μοιχαλὶς   σημεῖον   ἐπιζητεῖ,
evil   and   adulterous   a sign   seeks,

καὶ   σημεῖον   οὐ   δοθήσεται   αὐτῇ   εἰ   μὴ
and   a sign   shall not be given   to it   except

τὸ   σημεῖον   Ἰωνᾶ.   καὶ   καταλιπὼν   αὐτοὺς
the   sign   of Jonah.   And   leaving   them

ἀπῆλθεν.   5 Καὶ   ἐλθόντες   οἱ   μαθηταὶ   εἰς
he went away.   And   coming   the   disciples   to

τὸ   πέραν   ἐπελάθοντο   ἄρτους   λαβεῖν.
the   other side   they forgot   loaves   to take.

ὁ   δὲ   Ἰησοῦς   εἶπεν   αὐτοῖς·   6 ὁρᾶτε   καὶ
-    And   Jesus   said   to them: Beware   and

προσέχετε   ἀπὸ   τῆς   ζύμης   τῶν   Φαρισαίων
take heed   from   the   leaven   of the   Pharisees

καὶ   Σαδδουκαίων.   7 οἱ   δὲ   διελογίζοντο
and   Sadducees.   But they   reasoned

ἐν   ἑαυτοῖς   λέγοντες   ὅτι   ἄρτους   οὐκ
among themselves   saying[:]   -   Loaves   not

ἐλάβομεν.   8 γνοὺς   δὲ   ὁ   Ἰησοῦς   εἶπεν·
we took.   But knowing   -   Jesus   said:

* See note on page xviii. Note the use in the next line of δύνασθε.

O ye of little faith, why reason ye among yourselves, because ye have brought no bread?

9 Do ye not yet understand, neither remember the five loaves of the five thousand, and how many baskets ye took up?

10 Neither the seven loaves of the four thousand, and how many baskets ye took up?

11 How is it that ye do not understand that I spake *it* not to you concerning bread, that ye should beware of the leaven of the Pharisees and of the Sadducees?

12 Then understood they how that he bade *them* not beware of the leaven of bread, but of the doctrine of the Pharisees and of the Sadducees.

13 ¶ When Jesus came into the coasts of Cæsarea Philippi, he asked his disciples, saying, Whom do men say that I the Son of man am?

14 And they said, Some *say that thou art* John the Baptist: some, Elias; and others, Jeremias, or one of the prophets.

15 He saith unto them, But whom say ye that I am?

16 And Simon Peter answered and said, Thou art the Christ, the Son of the living God.

17 And Jesus answered

τί διαλογίζεσθε ἐν ἑαυτοῖς, ὀλιγόπιστοι,
Why reason ye among yourselves, little-faiths,

ὅτι ἄρτους οὐκ ἔχετε; 9 οὔπω νοεῖτε,
because loaves ye have not? Do ye not yet understand,

οὐδὲ μνημονεύετε τοὺς πέντε ἄρτους τῶν
neither remember ye the five loaves of the

πεντακισχιλίων καὶ πόσους κοφίνους
five thousand and how many baskets

ἐλάβετε; 10 οὐδὲ τοὺς ἑπτὰ ἄρτους τῶν
ye took? Neither the seven loaves of the

τετρακισχιλίων καὶ πόσας σπυρίδας
four thousand and how many baskets

ἐλάβετε; 11 πῶς οὐ νοεῖτε ὅτι οὐ
ye took? How do ye not understand that not

περὶ ἄρτων εἶπον ὑμῖν; προσέχετε δὲ ἀπὸ
concerning loaves I said to you? But take heed from

τῆς ζύμης τῶν Φαρισαίων καὶ Σαδ-
the leaven of the Pharisees and Sad-

δουκαίων. 12 τότε συνῆκαν ὅτι οὐκ
ducees. Then they understood that not

εἶπεν προσέχειν ἀπὸ τῆς ζύμης [τῶν
he said to take heed from the leaven of the

ἄρτων], ἀλλὰ ἀπὸ τῆς διδαχῆς τῶν
loaves, but from the teaching of the

Φαρισαίων καὶ Σαδδουκαίων.
Pharisees and Sadducees.

13 Ἐλθὼν δὲ ὁ Ἰησοῦς εἰς τὰ μέρη
And coming - Jesus into the parts

Καισαρείας τῆς Φιλίππου ἠρώτα τοὺς
of Cæsarea - of Philip he questioned the

μαθητὰς αὐτοῦ λέγων· τίνα λέγουσιν οἱ
disciples of him saying: Whom say the

ἄνθρωποι εἶναι τὸν υἱὸν τοῦ ἀνθρώπου;
men to be the Son - of man?

14 οἱ δὲ εἶπαν· οἱ μὲν Ἰωάννην τὸν
And they said: Some indeed John the

βαπτιστήν, ἄλλοι δὲ Ἠλίαν, ἕτεροι δὲ
Baptist, and others Elias, and others

Ἱερεμίαν ἢ ἕνα τῶν προφητῶν. 15 λέγει
Jeremias or one of the prophets. He says

αὐτοῖς· ὑμεῖς δὲ τίνα με λέγετε εἶναι;
to them: But ³ye ¹whom ⁴me ²say to be?

16 ἀποκριθεὶς δὲ Σίμων Πέτρος εἶπεν·
And answering Simon Peter said:

17 σὺ εἶ ὁ χριστὸς ὁ υἱὸς τοῦ θεοῦ
Thou art the Christ the Son - of God

τοῦ ζῶντος. ἀποκριθεὶς δὲ ὁ Ἰησοῦς
of the living. And answering - Jesus

and said unto him, Blessed art thou, Simon Bar-jona: for flesh and blood hath not revealed *it* unto thee, but my Father which is in heaven.

18 And I say also unto thee, That thou art Peter, and upon this rock I will build my church; and the gates of hell shall not prevail against it.

19 And I will give unto thee the keys of the kingdom of heaven: and whatsoever thou shalt bind on earth shall be bound in heaven: and whatsoever thou shalt loose on earth shall be loosed in heaven.

20 Then charged he his disciples that they should tell no man that he was Jesus the Christ.

21 ¶ From that time forth began Jesus to shew unto his disciples, how that he must go unto Jerusalem, and suffer many things of the elders and chief priests and scribes, and be killed, and be raised again the third day.

22 Then Peter took him, and began to rebuke him, saying, Be it far from thee, Lord: this shall not be unto thee.

23 But he turned, and

εἶπεν	αὐτῷ·	μακάριος	εἶ,	Σίμων
said	to him:	Blessed	art thou,	Simon

Βαριωνᾶ,	ὅτι	σὰρξ	καὶ	αἷμα	οὐκ	ἀπεκά-
Barjonas,	because	flesh	and	blood		did not

λυψέν σοι ἀλλ' ὁ πατήρ μου - ἐν
reveal to thee but the Father of me - in

τοῖς οὐρανοῖς. 18 κἀγὼ δέ σοι λέγω
the heavens. And I also to thee say[,]

ὅτι σὺ εἶ Πέτρος, καὶ ἐπὶ ταύτῃ τῇ
- Thou art Peter, and on this -

πέτρᾳ οἰκοδομήσω μου τὴν ἐκκλησίαν,
rock I will build of me the church,

καὶ πύλαι ᾅδου οὐ κατισχύσουσιν
and [the] gates of hades will not prevail against

αὐτῆς. 19 δώσω σοι τὰς κλεῖδας τῆς
it. I will give thee the keys of the

βασιλείας τῶν οὐρανῶν, καὶ ὃ ἐὰν
kingdom of the heavens, and whatever

δήσῃς ἐπὶ τῆς γῆς ἔσται δεδεμένον ἐν τοῖς
thou bindest on the earth shall be *having been* bound in the

οὐρανοῖς, καὶ ὃ ἐὰν λύσῃς ἐπὶ τῆς
heavens, and whatever thou loosest on the

γῆς ἔσται λελυμένον ἐν τοῖς οὐρανοῖς.
earth shall be *having been* loosed in the heavens.

20 τότε ἐπετίμησεν τοῖς μαθηταῖς ἵνα
Then he warned the disciples that

μηδενὶ εἴπωσιν ὅτι αὐτός ἐστιν ὁ
to no one they should tell that he is the

χριστός.
Christ.

21 Ἀπὸ τότε ἤρξατο Ἰησοῦς Χριστὸς
From then began Jesus Christ

δεικνύειν τοῖς μαθηταῖς αὐτοῦ ὅτι δεῖ
to show to the disciples of him that it behoves

αὐτὸν εἰς Ἱεροσόλυμα ἀπελθεῖν καὶ
him to Jerusalem to go and

πολλὰ παθεῖν ἀπὸ τῶν πρεσβυτέρων καὶ
many things to suffer from the elders and

ἀρχιερέων καὶ γραμματέων καὶ ἀποκτανθῆναι
chief priests and scribes and to be killed

καὶ τῇ τρίτῃ ἡμέρᾳ ἐγερθῆναι. 22 καὶ
and on the third day to be raised. And

προσλαβόμενος αὐτὸν ὁ Πέτρος ἤρξατο
taking him - Peter began

ἐπιτιμᾶν αὐτῷ λέγων· ἵλεώς σοι,
to rebuke him saying: Propitious to thee,
= May God help thee,

κύριε· οὐ μὴ ἔσται σοι τοῦτο. 23 ὁ δὲ
Lord: by no means shall be to thee this. But he

said unto Peter, Get thee behind me, Satan: thou art an offence unto me: for thou savourest not the things that be of God, but those that be of men.

24 Then said Jesus unto his disciples, If any *man* will come after me, let him deny himself, and take up his cross, and follow me.

25 For whosoever will save his life shall lose it: and whosoever will lose his life for my sake shall find it.

26 For what is a man profited, if he shall gain the whole world, and lose his own soul? or what shall a man give in exchange for his soul?

27 For the Son of man shall come in the glory of his Father with his angels; and then he shall reward every man according to his works.

28 Verily I say unto you, There be some standing here, which shall not taste of death, till they see the Son of man coming in his kingdom.

στραφεὶς εἶπεν τῷ Πέτρῳ· ὕπαγε ὀπίσω
turning said to Peter: Go behind

μου, σατανᾶ· σκάνδαλον εἶ ἐμοῦ,
me, Satan; an offence thou art of me,

ὅτι οὐ φρονεῖς τὰ τοῦ θεοῦ
because thou thinkest not the things — of God

ἀλλὰ τὰ τῶν ἀνθρώπων. 24 Τότε ὁ
but the things — of men. Then —

Ἰησοῦς εἶπεν τοῖς μαθηταῖς αὐτοῦ· εἴ
Jesus said to the disciples of him: If

τις θέλει ὀπίσω μου ἐλθεῖν, ἀπαρνησάσθω
anyone wishes after me to come, let him deny

ἑαυτὸν καὶ ἀράτω τὸν σταυρὸν αὐτοῦ,
himself and let him take the cross of him,

καὶ ἀκολουθείτω μοι. 25 ὃς γὰρ ἐὰν
and let him follow me. For whoever

θέλῃ τὴν ψυχὴν αὐτοῦ σῶσαι, ἀπολέσει
wishes the life of him to save, he will lose

αὐτήν· ὃς δ' ἂν ἀπολέσῃ τὴν ψυχὴν
it; and whoever loses the life

αὐτοῦ ἕνεκεν ἐμοῦ, εὑρήσει αὐτήν. 26 τί
of him for the sake of me, he will find it. what

γὰρ ὠφεληθήσεται ἄνθρωπος, ἐὰν τὸν
For will be benefited a man, if the

κόσμον ὅλον κερδήσῃ, τὴν δὲ ψυχὴν
world whole he should gain, but the soul

αὐτοῦ ζημιωθῇ; ἢ τί δώσει ἄνθρωπος
of him loses? or what will give a man

ἀντάλλαγμα τῆς ψυχῆς αὐτοῦ; 27 μέλλει
an exchange of the soul of him? is about

γὰρ ὁ υἱὸς τοῦ ἀνθρώπου ἔρχεσθαι ἐν τῇ
For the Son — of man to come in the

δόξῃ τοῦ πατρὸς αὐτοῦ μετὰ τῶν ἀγγέλων
glory of the Father of him with the angels

αὐτοῦ, καὶ τότε ἀποδώσει ἑκάστῳ
of him, and then he will reward *to* each man

κατὰ τὴν πρᾶξιν αὐτοῦ. 28 ἀμὴν λέγω
according to the conduct of him. Truly I say

ὑμῖν ὅτι εἰσίν τινες τῶν ὧδε ἑστώτων
to you[,] — There are some of the [ones] here standing

οἵτινες οὐ μὴ γεύσωνται θανάτου ἕως ἂν
who by no means may taste of death until

ἴδωσιν τὸν υἱὸν τοῦ ἀνθρώπου ἐρχόμενον
they see the Son — of man coming

ἐν τῇ βασιλείᾳ αὐτοῦ.
in the kingdom of him.

CHAPTER 17

A ND after six days
Jesus taketh Peter,
James, and John his
brother, and bringeth them
up into an high mountain
apart,

2 And was transfigured
before them: and his face
did shine as the sun, and
his raiment was white as
the light.

3 And, behold, there
appeared unto them Moses
and Elias talking with
him.

4 Then answered Peter,
and said unto Jesus, Lord,
it is good for us to be here:
if thou wilt, let us make
here three tabernacles; one
for thee, and one for Moses,
and one for Elias.

5 While he yet spake,
behold, a bright cloud
overshadowed them: and
behold a voice out of the
cloud, which said, This is
my beloved Son, in whom
I am well pleased; hear ye
him.

6 And when the disciples
heard it, they fell on their
face, and were sore afraid.

7 And Jesus came and
touched them, and said,
Arise, and be not afraid.

8 And when they had
lifted up their eyes, they
saw no man save Jesus only.

---

17 Καὶ   μεθ'   ἡμέρας   ἓξ   παραλαμβάνει   ὁ
And   after   days   six   takes   -

'Ιησοῦς   τὸν   Πέτρον   καὶ   'Ιάκωβον   καὶ
Jesus   -   Peter   and   James   and

'Ιωάννην   τὸν   ἀδελφὸν   αὐτοῦ,   καὶ   ἀναφέρει
John   the   brother   of him,   and   leads up

αὐτοὺς   εἰς   ὄρος   ὑψηλὸν   κατ'   ἰδίαν.   **2** καὶ
them   to   mountain   a high   privately.   And

μετεμορφώθη   ἔμπροσθεν   αὐτῶν,   καὶ
he was transfigured   before   them,   and

ἔλαμψεν   τὸ   πρόσωπον   αὐτοῦ   ὡς   ὁ   ἥλιος,
shone   the   face   of him   as   the   sun,

τὰ   δὲ   ἱμάτια   αὐτοῦ   ἐγένετο   λευκὰ   ὡς
and the   garments   of him   became   white   as

τὸ   φῶς.   **3** καὶ   ἰδοὺ   ὤφθη   αὐτοῖς   Μωϋσῆς
the   light.   And behold   was seen   by them   Moses

καὶ   'Ηλίας   συλλαλοῦντες   μετ'   αὐτοῦ.
and   Elias   conversing   with   him.

4 ἀποκριθεὶς   δὲ   ὁ   Πέτρος   εἶπεν   τῷ
And answering   -   Peter   said   -

'Ιησοῦ·   κύριε,   καλόν   ἐστιν   ἡμᾶς   ὧδε
to Jesus: Lord,   good   it is   us   here

εἶναι·   εἰ   θέλεις,   ποιήσω   ὧδε   τρεῖς
to be;   if   thou willest,   I will make   here   three

σκηνάς,   σοὶ   μίαν   καὶ   Μωϋσεῖ
tents,   for thee   one   and   for Moses

μίαν   καὶ   'Ηλίᾳ   μίαν.   **5** ἔτι   αὐτοῦ
one   and   for Elias   one.   Yet   him
=While he was yet

λαλοῦντος,   ἰδοὺ   νεφέλη   φωτεινὴ   ἐπεσκίασεν
speaking[a],   behold   cloud   a bright   overshadowed
speaking,

αὐτούς,   καὶ   ἰδοὺ   φωνὴ   ἐκ   τῆς   νεφέλης
them,   and   behold   a voice   out of   the   cloud

λέγουσα·   οὗτός   ἐστιν   ὁ   υἱός   μου   ὁ
saying: This   is   the   son   of me   the

ἀγαπητός,   ἐν   ᾧ   εὐδόκησα·   ἀκούετε
beloved,   in whom   I was well pleased;   hear ye

αὐτοῦ.   **6** καὶ   ἀκούσαντες   οἱ   μαθηταὶ
him.   And   hearing   the   disciples

ἔπεσαν   ἐπὶ   πρόσωπον   αὐτῶν   καὶ
fell   on   [the] face[s]   of them   and

ἐφοβήθησαν   σφόδρα.   **7** καὶ   προσῆλθεν   ὁ
feared   exceedingly.   And   approached   -

'Ιησοῦς   καὶ   ἁψάμενος   αὐτῶν   εἶπεν·
Jesus   and   touching   them   said:

ἐγέρθητε   καὶ   μὴ   φοβεῖσθε.   **8** ἐπάραντες   δὲ
Rise   and   do not fear.   And lifting up

τοὺς   ὀφθαλμοὺς   αὐτῶν   οὐδένα   εἶδον   εἰ
the   eyes   of them   no one   they saw   ex-

9¶ And as they came down from the mountain, Jesus charged them, saying, Tell the vision to no man, until the Son of man be risen again from the dead.

10 And his disciples asked him, saying, Why then say the scribes that Elias must first come?

11 And Jesus answered and said unto them, Elias truly shall first come, and restore all things.

12 But I say unto you, That Elias is come already, and they knew him not, but have done unto him whatsoever they listed. Likewise shall also the Son of man suffer of them.

13 Then the disciples understood that he spake unto them of John the Baptist.

14¶ And when they were come to the multitude, there came to him a *certain* man, kneeling down to him, and saying,

15 Lord, have mercy on my son: for he is lunatick, and sore vexed: for ofttimes he falleth into the fire, and oft into the water.

16 And I brought him to thy disciples, and they could not cure him.

μὴ αὐτὸν Ἰησοῦν μόνον. **9** Καὶ κατα-
cept himself Jesus only. And com-
=as

βαινόντων αὐτῶν ἐκ τοῦ ὄρους ἐνετείλατο
ing down them out of the mountain enjoined
they were coming down

αὐτοῖς ὁ Ἰησοῦς λέγων· μηδενὶ εἴπητε
them - Jesus saying: To no one tell

τὸ ὅραμα ἕως οὗ ὁ υἱὸς τοῦ ἀνθρώπου
the vision until the Son - of man

ἐκ νεκρῶν ἐγερθῇ. **10** Καὶ ἐπηρώτησαν
out of dead be raised. And questioned

αὐτὸν οἱ μαθηταὶ λέγοντες· τί οὖν
him the disciples saying: Why then

οἱ γραμματεῖς λέγουσιν ὅτι Ἡλίαν δεῖ
the scribes say that ²Elias ¹it behoves

ἐλθεῖν πρῶτον; **11** ὁ δὲ ἀποκριθεὶς εἶπεν·
to come first? And he answering said:

Ἡλίας μὲν ἔρχεται καὶ ἀποκαταστήσει
Elias indeed is coming and will restore

πάντα· **12** λέγω δὲ ὑμῖν ὅτι Ἡλίας
all things; but I tell you that Elias

ἤδη ἦλθεν, καὶ οὐκ ἐπέγνωσαν
already came, and they did not recognize

αὐτόν, ἀλλ᾽ ἐποίησαν ἐν αὐτῷ ὅσα
him, but did by him whatever things

ἠθέλησαν· οὕτως καὶ ὁ υἱὸς τοῦ ἀνθρώπου
they wished; thus also the Son - of man

μέλλει πάσχειν ὑπ᾽ αὐτῶν. **13** τότε
is about to suffer by them. Then

συνῆκαν οἱ μαθηταὶ ὅτι περὶ
understood the disciples that concerning

Ἰωάννου τοῦ βαπτιστοῦ εἶπεν αὐτοῖς.
John the Baptist he spoke to them.

14 Καὶ ἐλθόντων πρὸς τὸν ὄχλον προσ-
And [they] coming to the crowd ap-

ῆλθεν αὐτῷ ἄνθρωπος γονυπετῶν αὐτὸν
proached *to* him a man falling on knees to him

15 καὶ λέγων· κύριε, ἐλέησόν μου τὸν
and saying: Lord, pity of me the

υἱόν, ὅτι σεληνιάζεται καὶ κακῶς ἔχει·
son, because he is moonstruck and ill has;
=is ill;

πολλάκις γὰρ πίπτει εἰς τὸ πῦρ καὶ
for often he falls into the fire and

πολλάκις εἰς τὸ ὕδωρ. **16** καὶ προσήνεγκα
often into the water. And I brought

αὐτὸν τοῖς μαθηταῖς σου, καὶ οὐκ
him to the disciples of thee, and not

ἠδυνήθησαν αὐτὸν θεραπεῦσαι. **17** ἀπο-
they were able him to heal. an-

17 Then Jesus answered and said, O faithless and perverse generation, how long shall I be with you? how long shall I suffer you? bring him hither to me.

18 And Jesus rebuked the devil; and he departed out of him: and the child was cured from that very hour.

19 Then came the disciples to Jesus apart, and said, Why could not we cast him out?

20 And Jesus said unto them, Because of your unbelief: for verily I say unto you, If ye have faith as a grain of mustard seed, ye shall say unto this mountain, Remove hence to yonder place; and it shall remove; and nothing shall be impossible unto you.

21 Howbeit this kind goeth not out but by prayer and fasting.

22 ¶ And while they abode in Galilee, Jesus said unto them, The Son of man shall be betrayed into the hands of men:

23 And they shall kill him, and the third day he shall be raised again. And they were exceeding sorry.

24 ¶ And when they were come to Capernaum, they that received tribute *money*

κριθεὶς δὲ ὁ Ἰησοῦς εἶπεν· ὦ γενεὰ
swering And – Jesus said: O generation
ἄπιστος καὶ διεστραμμένη, ἕως πότε
unbelieving and *having been* perverted, until when
μεθ' ὑμῶν ἔσομαι; ἕως πότε
with you shall I be? until when
ἀνέξομαι ὑμῶν; φέρετέ μοι αὐτὸν
shall I endure you? bring to me him
ὧδε. 18 καὶ ἐπετίμησεν αὐτῷ ὁ Ἰησοῦς,
here. And rebuked it – Jesus,
καὶ ἐξῆλθεν ἀπ' αὐτοῦ τὸ δαιμόνιον,
and came out from him the demon,
καὶ ἐθεραπεύθη ὁ παῖς ἀπὸ τῆς ὥρας
and was healed the boy from – hour
ἐκείνης. 19 Τότε προσελθόντες οἱ μαθηταὶ
that. Then ³approaching ¹the ²disciples
τῷ Ἰησοῦ κατ' ἰδίαν εἶπον· διὰ
– to Jesus privately said: Why
τί ἡμεῖς οὐκ ἠδυνήθημεν ἐκβαλεῖν αὐτό;
we were not able to expel it?
20 ὁ δὲ λέγει αὐτοῖς· διὰ τὴν ὀλιγο-
And he says to them: Because of the little
πιστίαν ὑμῶν· ἀμὴν γὰρ λέγω ὑμῖν, ἐὰν
faith of you; for truly I say to you, if
ἔχητε πίστιν ὡς κόκκον σινάπεως,
ye have faith as a grain of mustard,
ἐρεῖτε τῷ ὄρει τούτῳ· μετάβα
ye will say – mountain to this: Remove
ἔνθεν ἐκεῖ, καὶ μεταβήσεται, καὶ οὐδὲν
hence there, and it will be removed, and nothing
ἀδυνατήσει ὑμῖν. ‡
will be impossible to you.
22 Συστρεφομένων δὲ αὐτῶν ἐν τῇ
And strolling them* in –
= as they were strolling
Γαλιλαίᾳ εἶπεν αὐτοῖς ὁ Ἰησοῦς· μέλλει
Galilee said to them – Jesus: is about
ὁ υἱὸς τοῦ ἀνθρώπου παραδίδοσθαι εἰς
The Son – of man to be delivered into
χεῖρας ἀνθρώπων, 23 καὶ ἀποκτενοῦσιν
[the] hands of men, and they will kill
αὐτόν, καὶ τῇ τρίτῃ ἡμέρᾳ ἐγερθήσεται.
him, and on the third day he will be raised.
καὶ ἐλυπήθησαν σφόδρα.
And they were grieved exceedingly.
24 Ἐλθόντων δὲ αὐτῶν εἰς Καφαρναοὺμ
And coming them* to Capernaum
= when they came
προσῆλθον οἱ τὰ δίδραχμα λαμβάνοντες
approached the [ones] the didrachmæ receiving

‡ Verse 21 omitted by Nestle; *cf.* R.V. marg., etc.

came to Peter, and said,
Doth not your master pay
tribute?

25 He saith, Yes. And
when he was come into
the house, Jesus prevented
him, saying, What thinkest
thou, Simon? of whom do
the kings of the earth take
custom or tribute? of their
own children, or of strangers?

26 Peter saith unto him,
Of strangers. Jesus saith
unto him, Then are the
children free.

27 Notwithstanding, lest
we should offend them, go
thou to the sea, and cast
an hook, and take up the
fish that first cometh up;
and when thou hast opened
his mouth, thou shalt find
a piece of money: that
take, and give unto them
for me and thee.

τῷ　Πέτρῳ　καὶ　εἶπαν·　ὁ　διδάσκαλος
－　Peter　and　said:　The　teacher
ὑμῶν　οὐ　τελεῖ　δίδραχμα;　λέγει·　ναί.
of you　not　pays　drachmae?　He says:　Yes.
25 καὶ　ἐλθόντα　εἰς　τὴν　οἰκίαν　προ-
And　⁴coming　⁵into　⁶the　⁷house　²pre-
έφθασεν　αὐτὸν　ὁ　Ἰησοῦς　λέγων·　τί　σοι
ceded　³him　－　¹Jesus　saying:　What to thee
δοκεῖ,　Σίμων;　οἱ　βασιλεῖς　τῆς　γῆς
seems it,　Simon?　the　kings　of the　earth
ἀπὸ　τίνων　λαμβάνουσιν　τέλη　ἢ　κῆνσον;
from　whom　do they take　toll　or　poll-tax?
ἀπὸ　τῶν　υἱῶν　αὐτῶν　ἢ　ἀπὸ　τῶν　ἀλλοτρίων;
from　the　sons　of them　or　from　－　strangers?
26 εἰπόντος　δέ·　ἀπὸ　τῶν　ἀλλο-
and [he] sayingᵃ:　From　－　strangers,
　　=when he said:
τρίων,　ἔφη　αὐτῷ　ὁ　Ἰησοῦς·　ἄρα　γε
said　to him　－　Jesus:　Then
ἐλεύθεροί　εἰσιν　οἱ　υἱοί.　**27** ἵνα　δὲ　μὴ
free　are　the　sons.　But lest
σκανδαλίσωμεν　αὐτούς,　πορευθεὶς　εἰς
we should offend　them,　going　to
θάλασσαν　βάλε　ἄγκιστρον　καὶ　τὸν
[the] sea　cast　a hook　and　the
ἀναβάντα　πρῶτον　ἰχθὺν　ἆρον,　καὶ　ἀνοίξας
²coming up　³first　¹fish　take,　and　opening
τὸ　στόμα　αὐτοῦ　εὑρήσεις　στατῆρα·
the　mouth　of it　thou wilt find　a stater;
ἐκεῖνον　λαβὼν　δὸς　αὐτοῖς　ἀντὶ　ἐμοῦ　καὶ
that　taking　give　them　for　me　and
σοῦ.
thee.

CHAPTER 18

A T the same time came
the disciples unto
Jesus, saying, Who is the
greatest in the kingdom of
heaven?

2 And Jesus called a
little child unto him, and set
him in the midst of them,

3 And said, Verily I say
unto you, Except ye be
converted, and become as
little children, ye shall not

18 Ἐν　ἐκείνῃ　τῇ　ὥρᾳ　προσῆλθον　οἱ
In　that　－　hour　approached　the
μαθηταὶ　τῷ　Ἰησοῦ　λέγοντες·　τίς　ἄρα
disciples　－ to Jesus　saying:　Who　then
μείζων　ἐστὶν　ἐν　τῇ　βασιλείᾳ　τῶν　οὐρανῶν;
greater　is　in the　kingdom　of the　heavens?
2 καὶ　προσκαλεσάμενος　παιδίον　ἔστησεν
And　calling forward　a child　he set
αὐτὸ　ἐν　μέσῳ　αὐτῶν　**3** καὶ　εἶπεν·　ἀμὴν
him　in [the] midst　of them　and　said:　Truly
λέγω　ὑμῖν,　ἐὰν　μὴ　στραφῆτε　καὶ
I say　to you,　except　ye turn　and
γένησθε　ὡς　τὰ　παιδία,　οὐ　μὴ
become　as　－　children,　by no means

enter into the kingdom of heaven.

4 Whosoever therefore shall humble himself as this little child, the same is greatest in the kingdom of heaven.

5 And whoso shall receive one such little child in my name receiveth me.

6 But whoso shall offend one of these little ones which believe in me, it were better for him that a millstone were hanged about his neck, and *that* he were drowned in the depth of the sea.

7 ¶ Woe unto the world because of offences! for it must needs be that offences come; but woe to that man by whom the offence cometh!

8 Wherefore if thy hand or thy foot offend thee, cut them off, and cast *them* from thee: it is better for thee to enter into life halt or maimed, rather than having two hands or two feet to be cast into everlasting fire.

9 And if thine eye offend thee, pluck it out, and cast *it* from thee: it is better for thee to enter into life with one eye, rather than having two eyes to be cast into hell fire.

εἰσέλθητε εἰς τὴν βασιλείαν τῶν
may ye enter into the kingdom of the

οὐρανῶν. 4 ὅστις οὖν ταπεινώσει ἑαυτὸν
heavens. ²[he] who ¹Therefore will humble himself

ὡς τὸ παιδίον τοῦτο, οὗτός ἐστιν ὁ
as - child this, this [one] is the

μείζων ἐν τῇ βασιλείᾳ τῶν οὐρανῶν.
greater in the kingdom of the heavens.

5 καὶ ὃς ἐὰν δέξηται ἓν παιδίον
And whoever receives one child

τοιοῦτο ἐπὶ τῷ ὀνόματί μου, ἐμὲ δέχεται·
such on(in) the name of me, me receives;

6 ὃς δ' ἂν σκανδαλίσῃ ἕνα τῶν
and whoever offends one

μικρῶν τούτων τῶν πιστευόντων εἰς ἐμέ,
little [ones] of these - believing in me,

συμφέρει αὐτῷ ἵνα κρεμασθῇ μύλος
it is expedient for him that be hanged an upper

ὀνικὸς περὶ τὸν τράχηλον αὐτοῦ καὶ
millstone round the neck of him and

καταποντισθῇ ἐν τῷ πελάγει τῆς θαλάσσης.
he be drowned in the depth of the sea.

7 Οὐαὶ τῷ κόσμῳ ἀπὸ τῶν σκανδάλων·
Woe to the world from - offences;

ἀνάγκη γὰρ ἐλθεῖν τὰ σκάνδαλα, πλὴν
for [it is] a necessity to come - offences, but

οὐαὶ τῷ ἀνθρώπῳ δι' οὗ τὸ σκάνδαλον
woe to the man through whom the offence

ἔρχεται. 8 Εἰ δὲ ἡ χείρ σου ἢ ὁ
comes. Now if the hand of thee or the

πούς σου σκανδαλίζει σε, ἔκκοψον αὐτὸν
foot of thee offends thee, cut off it

καὶ βάλε ἀπὸ σοῦ· καλόν σοί ἐστιν
and cast from thee; good for thee it is

εἰσελθεῖν εἰς τὴν ζωὴν κυλλὸν ἢ χωλόν,
to enter into - life maimed or lame,

ἢ δύο χεῖρας ἢ δύο πόδας ἔχοντα βληθῆναι
than two hands or two feet having to be cast

εἰς τὸ πῦρ τὸ αἰώνιον. 9 καὶ εἰ ὁ
into the fire the - eternal. And if the

ὀφθαλμός σου σκανδαλίζει σε, ἔξελε αὐτὸν
eye of thee offends thee, pluck out it

καὶ βάλε ἀπὸ σοῦ· καλόν σοί ἐστιν
and cast from thee; good for thee it is

μονόφθαλμον εἰς τὴν ζωὴν εἰσελθεῖν, ἢ
one-eyed into *the* life to enter, than

δύο ὀφθαλμοὺς ἔχοντα βληθῆναι εἰς
two eyes having to be cast into

10 ¶ Take heed that ye despise not one of these little ones; for I say unto you, That in heaven their angels do always behold the face of my Father which is in heaven.

11 For the Son of man is come to save that which was lost.

12 How think ye? if a man have an hundred sheep, and one of them be gone astray, doth he not leave the ninety and nine, and goeth into the mountains, and seeketh that which is gone astray?

13 And if so be that he find it, verily I say unto you, he rejoiceth more of that *sheep*, than of the ninety and nine which went not astray.

14 Even so it is not the will of your Father which is in heaven, that one of these little ones should perish.

15 ¶ Moreover if thy brother shall trespass against thee, go and tell him his fault between thee and him alone: if he shall hear thee, thou hast gained thy brother.

16 But if he will not hear *thee*, *then* take with thee one or two more, that in the mouth of two or three witnesses every word may be established.

17 And if he shall neglect to hear them, tell *it* unto the church: but if he

τὴν γέενναν τοῦ πυρός. **10** Ὁρᾶτε μὴ
the gehenna — of fire.   See [that] not

καταφρονήσητε ἑνὸς τῶν μικρῶν τούτων·
ye despise   one   —   little [ones]   of these;

λέγω γὰρ ὑμῖν ὅτι οἱ ἄγγελοι αὐτῶν
for I tell   you   that   the   angels   of them

ἐν οὐρανοῖς διὰ παντὸς βλέπουσι τὸ
in   heavens   always   see   the

πρόσωπον τοῦ πατρός μου τοῦ ἐν οὐρανοῖς.‡
face   of the   Father   of me   —   in   heavens.

12 Τί ὑμῖν δοκεῖ; ἐὰν γένηταί τινι
What   to you   seems it?   if   there be   to any
                             =any man has

ἀνθρώπῳ ἑκατὸν πρόβατα καὶ πλανηθῇ
manᵉ   a hundred   sheep   and   wanders

ἐν ἐξ αὐτῶν, οὐχὶ ἀφήσει τὰ ἐνενήκοντα
one of   them,   will he not leave   the   ninety-

ἐννέα ἐπὶ τὰ ὄρη καὶ πορευθεὶς ζητεῖ τὸ
nine   on   the   mountains   and   going   seeks   the

πλανώμενον; **13** καὶ ἐὰν γένηται
wandering [one]?   And   if   he happens

εὑρεῖν αὐτό, ἀμὴν λέγω ὑμῖν ὅτι
to find   it,   truly   I say   to you   that

χαίρει ἐπ' αὐτῷ μᾶλλον ἢ ἐπὶ τοῖς
he rejoices   over   it   more   than over   the

ἐνενήκοντα ἐννέα τοῖς μὴ πεπλανημένοις.
ninety-nine   —   not   having wandered.

14 οὕτως οὐκ ἔστιν θέλημα ἔμπροσθεν
So   it is not   [the] will   before

τοῦ πατρὸς ὑμῶν τοῦ ἐν οὐρανοῖς ἵνα
the   Father   of you   —   in   heavens   that

ἀπόληται ἐν τῶν μικρῶν τούτων.
should perish   one   —   little [ones]   of these.

15 Ἐὰν δὲ ἁμαρτήσῃ ὁ ἀδελφός σου,
Now if   sins   the   brother   of thee,

ὕπαγε ἔλεγξον αὐτὸν μεταξὺ σοῦ καὶ
go   reprove   him   between   thee   and

αὐτοῦ μόνου. ἐάν σου ἀκούσῃ, ἐκέρδησας
him   alone.   If   thee   he hears,   thou gainedst

τὸν ἀδελφόν σου· **16** ἐὰν δὲ μὴ
the   brother   of thee;   but if   not

ἀκούσῃ, παράλαβε μετὰ σοῦ ἔτι ἕνα ἢ
he hears,   take   with   thee   more   one   or

δύο, ἵνα ἐπὶ στόματος δύο μαρτύρων
two,   that   on(by)   [the] mouth   of two   witnesses

ἢ τριῶν σταθῇ πᾶν ῥῆμα· **17** ἐὰν δὲ
or   three   may be established   every   word;   but if

παρακούσῃ αὐτῶν, εἰπὸν τῇ ἐκκλησίᾳ·
he refuses to hear   them,   tell   *to* the   church;

‡ Ver. 11 omitted by Nestle; *cf.* R.V. marg.

neglect to hear the church, let him be unto thee as an heathen man and a publican.

18 Verily I say unto you, Whatsoever ye shall bind on earth shall be bound in heaven: and whatsoever ye shall loose on earth shall be loosed in heaven.

19 Again I say unto you, That if two of you shall agree on earth as touching any thing that they shall ask, it shall be done for them of my Father which is in heaven.

20 For where two or three are gathered together in my name, there am I in the midst of them.

21 ¶ Then came Peter to him, and said, Lord, how oft shall my brother sin against me, and I forgive him? till seven times?

22 Jesus saith unto him, I say not unto thee, Until seven times: but, Until seventy times seven.

23 ¶ Therefore is the kingdom of heaven likened unto a certain king, which would take account of his servants.

24 And when he had begun to reckon, one was brought unto him, which

ἐὰν δὲ καὶ τῆς ἐκκλησίας παρακούσῃ,
and if even the church he refuses to hear,

ἔστω σοι ὥσπερ ὁ ἐθνικὸς καὶ
let him be to thee as the gentile and

ὁ τελώνης. 18 Ἀμὴν λέγω ὑμῖν,
the tax-collector. Truly I say to you,

ὅσα ἐὰν δήσητε ἐπὶ τῆς γῆς ἔσται
whatever things ye bind on the earth shall be

δεδεμένα ἐν οὐρανῷ, καὶ ὅσα ἐὰν
having been bound in heaven, and whatever things

λύσητε ἐπὶ τῆς γῆς ἔσται λελυμένα
ye loose on the earth shall be having been loosed

ἐν οὐρανῷ. 19 Πάλιν [ἀμὴν] λέγω
in heaven. Again truly I say

ὑμῖν ὅτι ἐὰν δύο συμφωνήσωσιν ἐξ
to you that if two agree of

ὑμῶν ἐπὶ τῆς γῆς περὶ παντὸς πράγ-
you on the earth concerning every

ματος οὗ ἐὰν αἰτήσωνται, γενήσεται
thing whatever they ask, it shall be

αὐτοῖς παρὰ τοῦ πατρός μου τοῦ ἐν
to them from the Father of me – in

οὐρανοῖς. 20 οὐ γάρ εἰσιν δύο ἢ τρεῖς
heavens. For where are two or three

συνηγμένοι εἰς τὸ ἐμὸν ὄνομα, ἐκεῖ εἰμι
having been assembled in – my name, there I am

ἐν μέσῳ αὐτῶν.
in [the] midst of them.

21 Τότε προσελθὼν ὁ Πέτρος εἶπεν
Then approaching – Peter said

αὐτῷ· κύριε, ποσάκις ἁμαρτήσει εἰς
to him: Lord, how often will sin against

ἐμὲ ὁ ἀδελφός μου καὶ ἀφήσω αὐτῷ;
me the brother of me and I will forgive him?

ἕως ἑπτάκις; 22 λέγει αὐτῷ ὁ Ἰησοῦς·
until seven times? says to him – Jesus:

οὐ λέγω σοι ἕως ἑπτάκις, ἀλλὰ
I tell not to thee until seven times, but

ἕως ἑβδομηκοντάκις ἑπτά. 23 Διὰ τοῦτο
until seventy times seven. Therefore

ὡμοιώθη ἡ βασιλεία τῶν οὐρανῶν
was(is) likened the kingdom of the heavens

ἀνθρώπῳ βασιλεῖ, ὃς ἠθέλησεν συνᾶραι
to a man a king, who wished to take

λόγον μετὰ τῶν δούλων αὐτοῦ. 24 ἀρξα-
account with the slaves of him. And

μένου δὲ αὐτοῦ συναίρειν, προσήχθη
beginning him* to take, *was brought forward
=as he began

owed him ten thousand talents.

25 But forasmuch as he had not to pay, his lord commanded him to be sold, and his wife, and children, and all that he had, and payment to be made.

26 The servant therefore fell down, and worshipped him, saying, Lord, have patience with me, and I will pay thee all.

27 Then the lord of that servant was moved with compassion, and loosed him, and forgave him the debt.

28 But the same servant went out, and found one of his fellowservants, which owed him an hundred pence: and he laid hands on him, and took *him* by the throat, saying, Pay me that thou owest.

29 And his fellowservant fell down at his feet, and besought him, saying, Have patience with me, and I will pay thee all.

30 And he would not: but went and cast him into prison, till he should pay the debt.

31 So when his fellowservants saw what was done, they were very sorry, and came and told unto their lord all that was done.

32 Then his lord, after that he had called him,

εἰς   αὐτῷ   ὀφειλέτης   μυρίων   ταλάντων.
¹one   ⁶to him   ²debtor   ³of ten thousand ⁴talents.

25 μὴ   ἔχοντος   δὲ   αὐτοῦ   ἀποδοῦναι, ἐκέλευσεν
And not having   him*   to repay,   commanded
=as he had not

αὐτὸν   ὁ   κύριος   πραθῆναι   καὶ   τὴν
him   the   lord   to be sold   and   the(his)

γυναῖκα   καὶ   τὰ   τέκνα   καὶ   πάντα   ὅσα
wife   and   –   children and   all things whatever

ἔχει,   καὶ   ἀποδοθῆναι.   26 πεσὼν   οὖν   ὁ
he has, and   to be repaid.   Falling therefore the

δοῦλος   προσεκύνει   αὐτῷ   λέγων·   μακρο-
slave   did obeisance   to him   saying: Defer

θύμησον   ἐπ᾽ ἐμοί,   καὶ   πάντα   ἀποδώσω
anger   over me,   and   all things I will repay

σοι.   27 σπλαγχνισθεὶς   δὲ   ὁ   κύριος   τοῦ
thee.   And filled with tenderness   the   lord   –

δούλου   ἐκείνου   ἀπέλυσεν   αὐτόν,   καὶ   τὸ
slave /   of that   released   him,   and   the

δάνειον   ἀφῆκεν   αὐτῷ.   28 ἐξελθὼν   δὲ
loan   forgave   him.   But going out

ὁ   δοῦλος   ἐκεῖνος   εὗρεν   ἕνα   τῶν
–   slave   that   found   one   of the

συνδούλων   αὐτοῦ,   ὃς   ὤφειλεν   αὐτὸν   ἑκατὸν
fellow-slaves of him,   who   owed   him   a hundred

δηνάρια,   καὶ   κρατήσας   αὐτὸν   ἔπνιγεν
denarii,   and   seizing   him   throttled

λέγων·   ἀπόδος   εἴ   τι   ὀφείλεις.
saying: Repay   if   something thou owest.

29 πεσὼν   οὖν   ὁ   σύνδουλος   αὐτοῦ   παρε-
Falling therefore the   fellow-slave   of him   be-

κάλει   αὐτὸν   λέγων·   μακροθύμησον   ἐπ᾽
sought   him   saying: Defer anger   over

ἐμοί,   καὶ   ἀποδώσω   σοι.   30 ὁ   δὲ   οὐκ
me,   and   I will repay   thee.   But he   not

ἤθελεν,   ἀλλὰ   ἀπελθὼν   ἔβαλεν   αὐτὸν   εἰς
wished,   but   going away   threw   him   into

φυλακὴν   ἕως   ἀποδῷ   τὸ   ὀφειλόμενον.
prison   until he should repay the thing owing.

31 ἰδόντες   οὖν   οἱ   σύνδουλοι   αὐτοῦ   τὰ
Seeing   therefore the   fellow-slaves   of him   the things

γενόμενα   ἐλυπήθησαν   σφόδρα,   καὶ
having taken place they were grieved   exceedingly,   and

ἐλθόντες   διεσάφησαν   τῷ   κυρίῳ   ἑαυτῶν
coming   explained   to the   lord   of themselves

πάντα   τὰ   γενόμενα.   32 τότε   προσ-
all   the things having taken place.   Then   ¹call-

καλεσάμενος   αὐτὸν   ὁ   κύριος   αὐτοῦ   λέγει
ing ²forward   ³him   the   lord   of him   says

said unto him, O thou wicked servant, I forgave thee all that debt, because thou desiredst me:

33 Shouldest not thou also have had compassion on thy fellowservant, even as I had pity on thee?

34 And his lord was wroth, and delivered him to the tormentors, till he should pay all that was due unto him.

35 So likewise shall my heavenly Father do also unto you, if ye from your hearts forgive not every one his brother their trespasses.

αὐτῷ· δοῦλε πονηρέ, πᾶσαν τὴν ὀφειλὴν
to him: ²Slave ¹wicked, all – debt

ἐκείνην ἀφῆκά σοι, ἐπεὶ παρεκάλεσάς με·
that I forgave thee, since thou besoughtest me;

33 οὐκ ἔδει καὶ σὲ ἐλεῆσαι τὸν
did it not behove also thee to pity the

σύνδουλόν σου, ὡς κἀγὼ σὲ ἠλέησα;
fellow-slave of thee, as I also thee pitied?

34 καὶ ὀργισθεὶς ὁ κύριος αὐτοῦ
And being angry the lord of him

παρέδωκεν αὐτὸν τοῖς βασανισταῖς ἕως οὗ
delivered him to the tormentors until

ἀποδῷ πᾶν τὸ ὀφειλόμενον αὐτῷ.
he should repay all the thing owing to him.

35 Οὕτως καὶ ὁ πατήρ μου ὁ οὐράνιος
Thus also the Father of me – heavenly

ποιήσει ὑμῖν, ἐὰν μὴ ἀφῆτε ἕκαστος
will do to you, unless ye forgive each one

τῷ ἀδελφῷ αὐτοῦ ἀπὸ τῶν καρδιῶν
the brother of him from the hearts

ὑμῶν.
of you.

CHAPTER 19

AND it came to pass, *that* when Jesus had finished these sayings, he departed from Galilee, and came into the coasts of Judæa beyond Jordan;

2 And great multitudes followed him; and he healed them there.

3 ¶ The Pharisees also came unto him, tempting him, and saying unto him, Is it lawful for a man to put away his wife for every cause?

4 And he answered and said unto them, Have ye not read, that he which made *them* at the beginning made them male and female,

19 Καὶ ἐγένετο ὅτε ἐτέλεσεν ὁ
And it came to pass when ended –

Ἰησοῦς τοὺς λόγους τούτους, μετῆρεν
Jesus – words these, he removed

ἀπὸ τῆς Γαλιλαίας καὶ ἦλθεν εἰς τὰ
from the Galilee and came into the

ὅρια τῆς Ἰουδαίας πέραν τοῦ Ἰορδάνου.
borders – of Judæa across the Jordan.

2 καὶ ἠκολούθησαν αὐτῷ ὄχλοι πολλοί,
And followed him crowds many,

καὶ ἐθεράπευσεν αὐτοὺς ἐκεῖ.
and he healed them there.

3 Καὶ προσῆλθον αὐτῷ Φαρισαῖοι
And approached to him Pharisees

πειράζοντες αὐτὸν καὶ λέγοντες· εἰ ἔξεστιν
tempting him and saying: If it is lawful

ἀπολῦσαι τὴν γυναῖκα αὐτοῦ κατὰ πᾶσαν
to dismiss the wife of him for every

αἰτίαν; 4 ὁ δὲ ἀποκριθεὶς εἶπεν· οὐκ
cause? And he answering said: not

ἀνέγνωτε ὅτι ὁ κτίσας ἀπ᾽
Did ye read that the [one] creating from

ἀρχῆς ἄρσεν καὶ θῆλυ ἐποίησεν αὐτούς;
[the] beginning male and female made them?

5 And said, For this cause shall a man leave father and mother, and shall cleave to his wife: and they twain shall be one flesh?

6 Wherefore they are no more twain, but one flesh. What therefore God hath joined together, let not man put asunder.

7 They say unto him, Why did Moses then command to give a writing of divorcement, and to put her away?

8 He saith unto them, Moses because of the hardness of your hearts suffered you to put away your wives: but from the beginning it was not so.

9 And I say unto you, Whosoever shall put away his wife, except it be for fornication, and shall marry another, committeth adultery: and whoso marrieth her which is put away doth commit adultery.

10 ¶ His disciples say unto him, If the case of the man be so with his wife, it is not good to marry.

11 But he said unto them, All men cannot receive this saying, save they to whom it is given.

12 For there are some eunuchs, which were so born from their mother's womb: and there are some eunuchs, which were made eunuchs of men: and there be eunuchs, which have

5 καὶ εἶπεν· ἕνεκα τούτου καταλείψει
And he said: For the sake of this shall leave

ἄνθρωπος τὸν πατέρα καὶ τὴν μητέρα
a man the(his) father and the(his) mother

καὶ κολληθήσεται τῇ γυναικὶ αὐτοῦ,
and shall cleave to the wife of him,

καὶ ἔσονται οἱ δύο εἰς σάρκα μίαν·
and ²shall be ¹the ³two ⁴in ⁶flesh ⁵one;

6 ὥστε οὐκέτι εἰσὶν δύο ἀλλὰ σὰρξ μία.
so as no longer are they two but flesh one.

ὃ οὖν ὁ θεὸς συνέζευξεν, ἄνθρωπος
What therefore - God yoked together, a man

μὴ χωριζέτω. 7 λέγουσιν αὐτῷ· τί οὖν
let not separate. They say to him: Why then

Μωϋσῆς ἐνετείλατο δοῦναι βιβλίον ἀπο-
²Moses ¹did ³enjoin to give a document of

στασίου καὶ ἀπολῦσαι; 8 λέγει αὐτοῖς·
divorce and to dismiss? He says to them:

ὅτι Μωϋσῆς πρὸς τὴν σκληροκαρδίαν
- Moses in view of the obduracy

ὑμῶν ἐπέτρεψεν ὑμῖν ἀπολῦσαι τὰς
of you allowed you to dismiss the

γυναῖκας ὑμῶν· ἀπ' ἀρχῆς δὲ οὐ
wives of you; but from [the] beginning not

γέγονεν οὕτως. 9 λέγω δὲ ὑμῖν ὅτι
it has been so. But I say to you that

ὃς ἂν ἀπολύσῃ τὴν γυναῖκα αὐτοῦ
whoever dismisses the wife of him

μὴ ἐπὶ πορνείᾳ καὶ γαμήσῃ ἄλλην,
not of(for) fornication and marries another,

μοιχᾶται. 10 λέγουσιν αὐτῷ οἱ μαθηταί·
commits adultery. Say to him the disciples:

εἰ οὕτως ἐστὶν ἡ αἰτία τοῦ ἀνθρώπου
If so is the cause of the man

μετὰ τῆς γυναικός, οὐ συμφέρει γαμῆσαι.
with the wife, it is not expedient to marry.

11 ὁ δὲ εἶπεν αὐτοῖς· οὐ πάντες χωροῦσιν
And he said to them: Not all men grasp

τὸν λόγον τοῦτον, ἀλλ' οἷς δέδοται.
- saying this, but [those] to whom it has been given.

12 εἰσὶν γὰρ εὐνοῦχοι οἵτινες ἐκ κοιλίας
For there are eunuchs who from [the] womb

μητρὸς ἐγεννήθησαν οὕτως, καὶ εἰσὶν
of a mother were born so, and there are

εὐνοῦχοι οἵτινες εὐνουχίσθησαν ὑπὸ τῶν
eunuchs who were made eunuchs by the

ἀνθρώπων, καὶ εἰσὶν εὐνοῦχοι οἵτινες
men, and there are eunuchs who

made themselves eunuchs for the kingdom of heaven's sake. He that is able to receive *it*, let him receive *it*.

13 ¶ Then were there brought unto him little children, that he should put *his* hands on them, and pray: and the disciples rebuked them.

14 But Jesus said, Suffer little children, and forbid them not, to come unto me: for of such is the kingdom of heaven.

15 And he laid *his* hands on them, and departed thence.

16 ¶ And, behold, one came and said unto him, Good Master, what good thing shall I do, that I may have eternal life?

17 And he said unto him, Why callest thou me good? *there is* none good but one, *that is*, God: but if thou wilt enter into life, keep the commandments.

18 He saith unto him, Which? Jesus said, Thou shalt do no murder, Thou shalt not commit adultery, Thou shalt not steal, Thou shalt not bear false witness,

19 Honour thy father and *thy* mother: and, Thou shalt love thy neighbour as thyself.

20 The young man saith unto him, All these things have I kept from my youth up: what lack I yet?

εὐνούχισαν   ἑαυτοὺς   διὰ   τὴν
made eunuchs   themselves   on account of   the
βασιλείαν   τῶν   οὐρανῶν.   ὁ   δυνάμενος
kingdom   of the   heavens.   The [one]   *being* able
χωρεῖν   χωρείτω.
to grasp [it]   let him grasp.

13 Τότε   προσηνέχθησαν   αὐτῷ   παιδία,
Then   were brought   to him   children,
ἵνα   τὰς   χεῖρας   ἐπιθῇ   αὐτοῖς   καὶ
that   the(his)   hands   he should put on   them   and
προσεύξηται·   οἱ   δὲ   μαθηταὶ   ἐπετίμησαν
pray;   but the   disciples   rebuked
αὐτοῖς.   14 ὁ   δὲ   Ἰησοῦς   εἶπεν·   ἄφετε
them.   – But   Jesus   said: Permit
τὰ   παιδία   καὶ   μὴ   κωλύετε   αὐτὰ   ἐλθεῖν
the   children   and   do not prevent   them   to come
πρός   με·   τῶν   γὰρ   τοιούτων   ἐστὶν   ἡ
unto   me;   –   for   of such   is   the
βασιλεία   τῶν   οὐρανῶν.   15 καὶ   ἐπιθεὶς
kingdom   of the   heavens.   And   putting on
τὰς   χεῖρας   αὐτοῖς   ἐπορεύθη   ἐκεῖθεν.
the(his)   hands   *on* them   he went   thence.

16 Καὶ   ἰδοὺ   εἷς   προσελθὼν   αὐτῷ   εἶπεν·
And   behold   one   approaching   *to* him   said:
διδάσκαλε,   τί   ἀγαθὸν   ποιήσω   ἵνα
Teacher,   what   good thing   may I do   that
σχῶ   ζωὴν   αἰώνιον;   ὁ   δὲ   εἶπεν   αὐτῷ·
I may have   life   eternal?   And he   said   to him:
17 τί   με   ἐρωτᾷς   περὶ   τοῦ   ἀγαθοῦ;
Why   me questionest thou concerning   the   good?
εἷς   ἐστιν   ὁ   ἀγαθός·   εἰ   δὲ   θέλεις   εἰς
one   is   the   good;   but if   thou wishest   into
τὴν   ζωὴν   εἰσελθεῖν,   τήρει   τὰς   ἐντολάς.
–   life   to enter,   keep   the commandments.
18 λέγει   αὐτῷ·   ποίας;   ὁ   δὲ   Ἰησοῦς
He says   to him: Which?   –   And   Jesus
ἔφη·   τὸ   οὐ   φονεύσεις,   οὐ   μοιχεύσεις,
said: –   Thou shalt not kill,   Thou shalt not commit adultery,
οὐ   κλέψεις,   οὐ   ψευδομαρτυρήσεις,
Thou shalt not steal,   Thou shalt not bear false witness,
19 τίμα   τὸν   πατέρα   καὶ   τὴν   μητέρα,
Honour   the(thy)   father   and   the(thy)   mother,
καὶ   ἀγαπήσεις   τὸν   πλησίον   σου   ὡς
and   Thou shalt love   the   neighbour   of thee   as
σεαυτόν.   20 λέγει   αὐτῷ   ὁ   νεανίσκος·
thyself.   Says   to him   the   young man:
ταῦτα   πάντα   ἐφύλαξα·   τί   ἔτι   ὑστερῶ;
²These things   ¹all   I kept;   what   yet   do I lack?

21 Jesus said unto him, If thou wilt be perfect, go *and* sell that thou hast, and give to the poor, and thou shalt have treasure in heaven: and come *and* follow me.

22 But when the young man heard that saying, he went away sorrowful: for he had great possessions.

23 ¶ Then said Jesus unto his disciples, Verily I say unto you, That a rich man shall hardly enter into the kingdom of heaven.

24 And again I say unto you, It is easier for a camel to go through the eye of a needle, than for a rich man to enter into the kingdom of God.

25 When his disciples heard *it*, they were exceedingly amazed, saying, Who then can be saved?

26 But Jesus beheld *them*, and said unto them, With men this is impossible; but with God all things are possible.

27 ¶ Then answered Peter and said unto him, Behold, we have forsaken all, and followed thee; what shall we have therefore?

28 And Jesus said unto them, Verily I say unto you, That ye which have followed me, in the regen-

---

21 ἔφη αὐτῷ ὁ Ἰησοῦς· εἰ θέλεις τέλειος
Said to him – Jesus: If thou wishest perfect

εἶναι, ὕπαγε πώλησόν σου τὰ ὑπάρχοντα
to be, go sell of thee the belongings

καὶ δὸς πτωχοῖς, καὶ ἔξεις
and give to [the] poor, and thou shalt have

θησαυρὸν ἐν οὐρανοῖς, καὶ δεῦρο ἀκολούθει
treasure in heavens, and come follow

μοι. 22 ἀκούσας δὲ ὁ νεανίσκος τὸν
me. But hearing the young man –

λόγον [τοῦτον] ἀπῆλθεν λυπούμενος·
word this went away grieving;

ἦν γὰρ ἔχων κτήματα πολλά. 23 Ὁ
for he was having possessions many. –

δὲ Ἰησοῦς εἶπεν τοῖς μαθηταῖς αὐτοῦ·
So Jesus said to the disciples of him:

ἀμὴν λέγω ὑμῖν ὅτι πλούσιος δυσκόλως
Truly I tell you that a rich man hardly

εἰσελεύσεται εἰς τὴν βασιλείαν τῶν
will enter into the kingdom of the

οὐρανῶν. 24 πάλιν δὲ λέγω ὑμῖν,
heavens. And again I tell you,

εὐκοπώτερόν ἐστιν κάμηλον διὰ τρήματος
easier it is a camel through [the] eye

ῥαφίδος εἰσελθεῖν ἢ πλούσιον εἰς τὴν
of a needle to enter than a rich man into the

βασιλείαν τοῦ θεοῦ. 25 ἀκούσαντες δὲ
kingdom – of God. And hearing

οἱ μαθηταὶ ἐξεπλήσσοντο σφόδρα
the disciples were astounded exceedingly

λέγοντες· τίς ἄρα δύναται σωθῆναι;
saying: Who then can *to* be saved?

26 ἐμβλέψας δὲ ὁ Ἰησοῦς εἶπεν
And looking upon – Jesus said

αὐτοῖς· παρὰ ἀνθρώποις τοῦτο ἀδύνατόν
to them: With men this impossible

ἐστιν, παρὰ δὲ θεῷ πάντα δυνατά.
is, but with God all things [are] possible.

27 Τότε ἀποκριθεὶς ὁ Πέτρος εἶπεν αὐτῷ·
Then answering – Peter said to him:

ἰδοὺ ἡμεῖς ἀφήκαμεν πάντα καὶ
Behold we left all things and

ἠκολουθήσαμέν σοι· τί ἄρα ἔσται
followed thee; what then shall be
= shall we have?

ἡμῖν; 28 ὁ δὲ Ἰησοῦς εἶπεν αὐτοῖς·
to usᵉ? – And Jesus said to them:

ἀμὴν λέγω ὑμῖν ὅτι ὑμεῖς οἱ ἀκολουθή-
Truly I tell you that ye the [ones] having

eration when the Son of
man shall sit in the throne
of his glory, ye also shall
sit upon twelve thrones,
judging the twelve tribes
of Israel.

29 And every one that
hath forsaken houses, or
brethren, or sisters, or
father, or mother, or wife,
or children, or lands, for
my name's sake, shall re-
ceive an hundredfold, and
shall inherit everlasting
life.

30 But many *that are*
first shall be last; and the
last *shall be* first.

σαντές   μοι,   ἐν   τῇ   παλιγγενεσίᾳ,   ὅταν
followed   me,   in   the   regeneration,   when

καθίσῃ   ὁ   υἱὸς   τοῦ   ἀνθρώπου   ἐπὶ   θρόνου
sits   the   Son   -   of man   on [the] throne

δόξης   αὐτοῦ,   καθήσεσθε   καὶ   αὐτοὶ   ἐπὶ
of glory   of him,   ye will sit   also   [your]selves   on

δώδεκα   θρόνους   κρίνοντες   τὰς   δώδεκα
twelve   thrones   judging   the   twelve

φυλὰς   τοῦ   Ἰσραήλ.   29 καὶ   πᾶς   ὅστις
tribes   -   of Israel.   And   everyone   who

ἀφῆκεν   οἰκίας   ἢ   ἀδελφοὺς   ἢ   ἀδελφὰς   ἢ
left   houses   or   brothers   or   sisters   or

πατέρα   ἢ   μητέρα   ἢ   τέκνα   ἢ   ἀγροὺς
father   or   mother   or   children   or   fields

ἕνεκεν   τοῦ   ἐμοῦ   ὀνόματος,   πολλαπλα-
for the sake of   -   my   name,   mani-

σίονα   λήμψεται   καὶ   ζωὴν   αἰώνιον
fold   will receive   and   life   eternal

κληρονομήσει.   30 Πολλοὶ   δὲ   ἔσονται   πρῶτοι
will inherit.   But many   [1]will be   [1]first

ἔσχατοι   καὶ   ἔσχατοι   πρῶτοι.
[2]last   and   last   first.

CHAPTER 20

FOR the kingdom of
heaven is like unto a
man *that is* an householder,
which went out early in the
morning to hire labourers
into his vineyard.

2 And when he had
agreed with the labourers
for a penny a day, he sent
them into his vineyard.

3 And he went out about
the third hour, and saw
others standing idle in the
marketplace.

4 And said unto them;
Go ye also into the vine-
yard, and whatsoever is
right I will give you. And
they went their way.

5 Again he went out

20 Ὁμοία   γάρ   ἐστιν   ἡ   βασιλεία   τῶν
For like   is   the   kingdom   of the

οὐρανῶν   ἀνθρώπῳ   οἰκοδεσπότῃ,   ὅστις
heavens   to *a man*   a housemaster,   who

ἐξῆλθεν   ἅμα   πρωῒ   μισθώσασθαι
went out   early in the morning   to hire

ἐργάτας   εἰς   τὸν   ἀμπελῶνα   αὐτοῦ.   2 συμ-
workmen   in   the   vineyard   of him.   And

φωνήσας   δὲ   μετὰ   τῶν   ἐργατῶν   ἐκ   δηναρίου
agreeing   with   the   workmen   out of(for)   a denarius

τὴν   ἡμέραν   ἀπέστειλεν   αὐτοὺς   εἰς   τὸν
the   day   he sent   them   into   the

ἀμπελῶνα   αὐτοῦ.   3 καὶ   ἐξελθὼν   περὶ
vineyard   of him.   And   going out   about

τρίτην   ὥραν   εἶδεν   ἄλλους   ἑστῶτας
[the] third   hour   he saw   others   standing

ἐν   τῇ   ἀγορᾷ   ἀργούς,   4 καὶ   ἐκείνοις
in   the   marketplace   idle,   and   to those

εἶπεν·   ὑπάγετε   καὶ   ὑμεῖς   εἰς   τὸν
said: Go   also   ye   into   the

ἀμπελῶνα,   καὶ   ὃ   ἐὰν   ᾖ   δίκαιον   δώσω
vineyard,   and   whatever may be   just   I will give

ὑμῖν.   οἱ   δὲ   ἀπῆλθον.   5 πάλιν   [δὲ]
you.   And they   went.   And again

about the sixth and ninth hour, and did likewise.

6 And about the eleventh hour he went out, and found others standing idle, and saith unto them, Why stand ye here all the day idle?

7 They say unto him, Because no man hath hired us. He saith unto them, Go ye also into the vineyard; and whatsoever is right, *that* shall ye receive.

8 So when even was come, the lord of the vineyard saith unto his steward, Call the labourers, and give them *their* hire, beginning from the last unto the first.

9 And when they came that *were hired* about the eleventh hour, they received every man a penny.

10 But when the first came, they supposed that they should have received more; and they likewise received every man a penny.

11 And when they had received *it*, they murmured against the goodman of the house,

12 Saying, These last have wrought *but* one hour, and thou hast made them equal unto us, which have borne the burden and heat of the day.

13 But he answered one of them, and said, Friend, I do thee no wrong: didst not thou agree with me for a penny?

14 Take *that* thine is,

ἐξελθὼν περὶ ἕκτην καὶ ἐνάτην ὥραν
going out   about [the] sixth   and [the] ninth   hour

ἐποίησεν ὡσαύτως.   6 περὶ δὲ τὴν
he did   similarly.   And about   the

ἐνδεκάτην ἐξελθὼν εὗρεν ἄλλους ἑστῶτας,
eleventh   going out   he found   others   standing,

καὶ λέγει αὐτοῖς· τί ὧδε ἑστήκατε
and   says   to them: Why   here   stand ye

ὅλην τὴν ἡμέραν ἀργοί;   7 λέγουσιν αὐτῷ·
all   the   day   idle?   They say   to him:

ὅτι οὐδεὶς ἡμᾶς ἐμισθώσατο. λέγει αὐτοῖς·
Because no one   us   hired.   He says   to them:

ὑπάγετε καὶ ὑμεῖς εἰς τὸν ἀμπελῶνα.
Go   also   ye   into   the   vineyard.

8 ὀψίας δὲ γενομένης λέγει ὁ κύριος
And evening   having come*   says   the   lord
= when evening had come

τοῦ ἀμπελῶνος τῷ ἐπιτρόπῳ αὐτοῦ·
of the   vineyard   to the   steward   of him:

κάλεσον τοὺς ἐργάτας καὶ ἀπόδος τὸν
Call   the   workmen   and   pay   the

μισθόν, ἀρξάμενος ἀπὸ τῶν ἐσχάτων
wage,   beginning   from   the   last ones

ἕως τῶν πρώτων.   9 ἐλθόντες δὲ οἱ
until   the   first.   And coming   the [ones]

περὶ τὴν ἐνδεκάτην ὥραν ἔλαβον ἀνὰ
about   the   eleventh   hour   received   each

δηνάριον.   10 καὶ ἐλθόντες οἱ πρῶτοι
a denarius.   And   coming   the   first

ἐνόμισαν ὅτι πλεῖον λήμψονται· καὶ
supposed   that   more   they will receive;   and

ἔλαβον τὸ ἀνὰ δηνάριον καὶ αὐτοί.
they received the   ²each   ¹denarius   also [them]selves.

11 λαβόντες δὲ ἐγόγγυζον κατὰ τοῦ
And receiving   they grumbled   against   the

οἰκοδεσπότου λέγοντες· 12 οὗτοι οἱ ἔσχατοι
housemaster   saying: These   –   last

μίαν ὥραν ἐποίησαν, καὶ ἴσους αὐτοὺς
one   hour   wrought,   and   equal   them

ἡμῖν ἐποίησας τοῖς βαστάσασι τὸ
to us   thou madest   the [ones]   having borne   the

βάρος τῆς ἡμέρας καὶ τὸν καύσωνα.
burden   of the   day   and   the   heat.

13 ὁ δὲ ἀποκριθεὶς ἑνὶ αὐτῶν εἶπεν·
But he   answering   one   of them   said:

ἑταῖρε, οὐκ ἀδικῶ σε· οὐχὶ
Comrade,   I do not injure   thee;   not

δηναρίου συνεφώνησάς μοι; 14 ἆρον
of(for) a denarius   thou didst agree with   me?   take

and go thy way: I will give unto this last, even as unto thee.

15 Is it not lawful for me to do what I will with mine own? Is thine eye evil, because I am good?

16 So the last shall be first, and the first last: for many be called, but few chosen.

17 ¶ And Jesus going up to Jerusalem took the twelve disciples apart in the way, and said unto them,

18 Behold, we go up to Jerusalem; and the Son of man shall be betrayed unto the chief priests and unto the scribes, and they shall condemn him to death,

19 And shall deliver him to the Gentiles to mock, and to scourge, and to crucify *him:* and the third day he shall rise again.

20 ¶ Then came to him the mother of Zebedee's children with her sons, worshipping *him*, and desiring a certain thing of him.

21 And he said unto her, What wilt thou? She saith unto him, Grant that these my two sons may sit, the one on thy right hand, and

τὸ   σὸν   καὶ   ὕπαγε·   θέλω   δὲ
the   thine   and   go;   but I wish
— that which is thine

τούτῳ   τῷ   ἐσχάτῳ   δοῦναι   ὡς   καὶ
to this   –   last man   to give   as   also

σοί·   15 οὐκ   ἔξεστίν   μοι   ὃ   θέλω
to thee;   is it not lawful   to me   what   I wish

ποιῆσαι   ἐν   τοῖς   ἐμοῖς;   ἢ   ὁ
to do   among   the   my things?   or   the

ὀφθαλμός   σου   πονηρός   ἐστιν   ὅτι   ἐγὼ
eye   of thee   evil   is   because   I

ἀγαθός   εἰμι;   16 Οὕτως   ἔσονται   οἱ   ἔσχατοι
good   am?   Thus   will be   the   last [ones]

πρῶτοι   καὶ   οἱ   πρῶτοι   ἔσχατοι.
first   and   the   first   last.

17 Μέλλων   δὲ   ἀναβαίνειν   Ἰησοῦς   εἰς
And being about   to go up   Jesus   to

Ἰεροσόλυμα   παρέλαβεν   τοὺς   δώδεκα   κατ'
Jerusalem   he took   the   twelve   private-

ἰδίαν,   καὶ   ἐν   τῇ   ὁδῷ   εἶπεν   αὐτοῖς·
ly,   and   in   the   way   said   to them:

18 ἰδοὺ   ἀναβαίνομεν   εἰς   Ἰεροσόλυμα,   καὶ
Behold   we are going up   to   Jerusalem,   and

ὁ   υἱὸς   τοῦ   ἀνθρώπου   παραδοθήσεται   τοῖς
the Son   –   of man   will be delivered   to the

ἀρχιερεῦσιν   καὶ   γραμματεῦσιν,   καὶ   κατα-
chief priests   and   scribes,   and   they will

κρινοῦσιν   αὐτὸν   εἰς   θάνατον,   19 καὶ
condemn   him   to   death,   and

παραδώσουσιν   αὐτὸν   τοῖς   ἔθνεσιν   εἰς
they will deliver   him   to the   nations   for

τὸ   ἐμπαῖξαι   καὶ   μαστιγῶσαι   καὶ
–   to mock   and   to scourge   and

σταυρῶσαι,   καὶ   τῇ   τρίτῃ   ἡμέρᾳ   ἐγερθή-
to crucify,   and   on the   third   day   he will be

σεται.
raised.

20 Τότε   προσῆλθεν   αὐτῷ   ἡ   μήτηρ   τῶν
Then   approached   to him   the   mother   of the

υἱῶν   Ζεβεδαίου   μετὰ   τῶν   υἱῶν   αὐτῆς
sons   of Zebedee   with   the   sons   of her

προσκυνοῦσα   καὶ   αἰτοῦσά   τι   ἀπ'   αὐτοῦ.
doing obeisance   and   asking   something from   him.

21 ὁ   δὲ   εἶπεν   αὐτῇ·   τί   θέλεις;   λέγει
And he   said   to her: What wishest thou?   She says

αὐτῷ·   εἰπὲ   ἵνα   καθίσωσιν   οὗτοι   οἱ
to him: Say   that   may sit   these   the

δύο   υἱοί   μου   εἷς   ἐκ   δεξιῶν   καὶ   εἷς
two   sons   of me   one   on [the] right   and   one

the other on the left, in thy kingdom.

22 But Jesus answered and said, Ye know not what ye ask. Are ye able to drink of the cup that I shall drink of, and to be baptized with the baptism that I am baptized with? They say unto him, We are able.

23 And he saith unto them, Ye shall drink indeed of my cup, and be baptized with the baptism that I am baptized with: but to sit on my right hand, and on my left, is not mine to give, but *it shall be given to them* for whom it is prepared of my Father.

24 And when the ten heard *it,* they were moved with indignation against the two brethren.

25 But Jesus called them *unto him,* and said, Ye know that the princes of the Gentiles exercise dominion over them, and they that are great exercise authority upon them.

26 But it shall not be so among you: but whosoever will be great among you, let him be your minister;

27 And whosoever will be chief among you, let him be your servant:

28 Even as the Son of man came not to be ministered unto, but to minister, and to give his life a ransom for many.

29 ¶ And as they departed from Jericho, a

ἐξ	εὐωνύμων	σου	ἐν τῇ	βασιλείᾳ
on [the] left		of thee	in the	kingdom

σου.   **22** ἀποκριθεὶς   δὲ   ὁ   Ἰησοῦς
of thee.   And answering   -   Jesus

εἶπεν·   οὐκ   οἴδατε   τί   αἰτεῖσθε.
said: Ye know not   what   ye ask.

δύνασθε   πιεῖν   τὸ   ποτήριον   ὃ   ἐγὼ
Can ye   *to* drink   the   cup   which   I

μέλλω   πίνειν;   λέγουσιν   αὐτῷ·   δυνάμεθα.
am about   to drink?   They say   to him: We can.

23 λέγει   αὐτοῖς·   τὸ μὲν   ποτήριόν   μου
He says   to them: Indeed the   cup   of me

πίεσθε,   τὸ δὲ   καθίσαι   ἐκ   δεξιῶν
ye shall drink,   -   but   to sit   on [the] right

μου   καὶ   ἐξ   εὐωνύμων   οὐκ   ἔστιν
of me   and   on [the] left   is not

ἐμὸν   τοῦτο   δοῦναι,   ἀλλ'   οἷς   ἡτοί-
mine   this   to give,   but   to whom   it has

μασται   ὑπὸ   τοῦ   πατρός   μου.   **24** καὶ
been prepared by   the   Father   of me.   And

ἀκούσαντες   οἱ   δέκα   ἠγανάκτησαν   περὶ
hearing   the   ten   were incensed   about

τῶν   δύο   ἀδελφῶν.   **25** ὁ δὲ   Ἰησοῦς
the   two   brothers.   - So   Jesus

προσκαλεσάμενος   αὐτοῖς   εἶπεν·   οἴδατε
calling forward   them   said: Ye know

ὅτι   οἱ   ἄρχοντες   τῶν   ἐθνῶν   κατακυριεύουσιν
that the   rulers   of the   nations   lord it over

αὐτῶν   καὶ   οἱ   μεγάλοι   κατεξουσιάζουσιν
them   and   the   great ones   have authority over

αὐτῶν.   **26** οὐχ   οὕτως   ἐστὶν   ἐν   ὑμῖν·
them.   Not   thus   is it   among   you;

ἀλλ'   ὃς   ἐὰν   θέλῃ   ἐν   ὑμῖν   μέγας   γενέσθαι,
but   whoever   wishes   among you   great   to become,

ἔσται   ὑμῶν   διάκονος,   **27** καὶ   ὃς   ἂν
will be   of you   servant,   and   whoever

θέλῃ   ἐν   ὑμῖν   εἶναι   πρῶτος,   ἔσται   ὑμῶν
wishes among   you   to be   first,   he shall be   of you

δοῦλος·   **28** ὥσπερ   ὁ   υἱὸς   τοῦ   ἀνθρώπου
slave;   as   the   Son   -   of man

οὐκ   ἦλθεν   διακονηθῆναι,   ἀλλὰ   διακο-
came not   to be served,   but   to

νῆσαι   καὶ   δοῦναι   τὴν   ψυχὴν   αὐτοῦ
serve   and   to give   the   life   of him

λύτρον   ἀντὶ   πολλῶν.
a ransom   instead of   many.

29 Καὶ   ἐκπορευομένων   αὐτῶν   ἀπὸ   Ἰεριχὼ
And   going out   them*   from   Jericho
= as they were going out

great multitude followed him.

30 And, behold, two blind men sitting by the way side, when they heard that Jesus passed by, cried out, saying, Have mercy on us, O Lord, *thou* son of David.

31 And the multitude rebuked them, because they should hold their peace: but they cried the more, saying, Have mercy on us, O Lord, *thou* son of David.

32 And Jesus stood still, and called them, and said, What will ye that I shall do unto you?

33 They say unto him, Lord, that our eyes may be opened.

34 So Jesus had compassion *on them*, and touched their eyes: and immediately their eyes received sight, and they followed him.

ἠκολούθησεν αὐτῷ ὄχλος πολύς. 30 καὶ
followed   him   crowd   a much.   And
ἰδοὺ   δύο   τυφλοὶ   καθήμενοι παρὰ τὴν
behold two blind men sitting   beside the
ὁδόν,   ἀκούσαντες ὅτι Ἰησοῦς παράγει,
way,   hearing   that Jesus   is passing by,
ἔκραξαν λέγοντες· κύριε, ἐλέησον ἡμᾶς,
cried out saying: Lord,   pity   us,
υἱὸς Δαυίδ. 31 ὁ δὲ ὄχλος ἐπετίμησεν
son of David.   But the crowd   rebuked
αὐτοῖς ἵνα σιωπήσωσιν· οἱ δὲ μεῖζον
them that they should be silent; but they more
ἔκραξαν λέγοντες· κύριε, ἐλέησον ἡμᾶς,
cried out saying: Lord,   pity   us,
υἱὸς Δαυίδ. 32 καὶ στὰς ὁ Ἰησοῦς
son of David.   And standing -   Jesus
ἐφώνησεν αὐτοὺς καὶ εἶπεν· τί θέλετε
called   them   and said: What wish ye
ποιήσω ὑμῖν; 33 λέγουσιν αὐτῷ· κύριε,
I may do to you?   They say   to him: Lord,
ἵνα   ἀνοιγῶσιν οἱ ὀφθαλμοὶ ἡμῶν.
that   may be opened the   eyes   of us.
34 σπλαγχνισθεὶς δὲ ὁ Ἰησοῦς ἥψατο
And being filled with tenderness - Jesus   touched
τῶν ὀμμάτων αὐτῶν, καὶ εὐθέως ἀνέβλεψαν
the   eyes   of them, and immediately they saw again
καὶ ἠκολούθησαν αὐτῷ.
and   followed   him.

CHAPTER 21

AND when they drew nigh unto Jerusalem, and were come to Bethphage, unto the mount of Olives, then sent Jesus two disciples,

2 Saying unto them, Go into the village over against you, and straightway ye shall find an ass tied, and a colt with her: loose *them*, and bring *them* unto me.

3 And if any *man* say ought unto you, ye shall say, The Lord hath need of them; and straight-

21 Καὶ ὅτε ἤγγισαν εἰς Ἰεροσόλυμα
   And when they drew near to   Jerusalem
καὶ ἦλθον εἰς Βηθφαγὴ εἰς τὸ ὄρος τῶν
and came   to Bethphage to the mount of the
ἐλαιῶν, τότε Ἰησοῦς ἀπέστειλεν δύο
olives,   then Jesus   sent   two
μαθητὰς 2 λέγων αὐτοῖς· πορεύεσθε εἰς
disciples   telling   them: Go ye   into
τὴν κώμην τὴν κατέναντι ὑμῶν, καὶ εὐθὺς
the village   -   opposite   you,   and at once
εὑρήσετε ὄνον δεδεμένην καὶ πῶλον μετ’
ye will find an ass *having been* tied and a colt with
αὐτῆς· λύσαντες ἀγάγετέ μοι. 3 καὶ ἐάν
her/it; loosening   bring   to me.   And   if
τις   ὑμῖν εἴπῃ τι, ἐρεῖτε ὅτι ὁ
anyone to you says anything, ye shall say[,] - The
κύριος αὐτῶν χρείαν ἔχει· εὐθὺς δὲ
Lord   of them need   has; and immediately

way he will send them.
4 All this was done, that it might be fulfilled which was spoken by the prophet, saying,
5 Tell ye the daughter of Sion, Behold, thy King cometh unto thee, meek, and sitting upon an ass, and a colt the foal of an ass.
6 And the disciples went, and did as Jesus commanded them,
7 And brought the ass, and the colt, and put on them their clothes, and they set *him* thereon.
8 And a very great multitude spread their garments in the way; others cut down branches from the trees, and strawed *them* in the way.
9 And the multitudes that went before, and that followed, cried, saying, Hosanna to the son of David: Blessed *is* he that cometh in the name of the Lord; Hosanna in the highest.
10 ¶ And when he was come into Jerusalem, all the city was moved, saying, Who is this?
11 And the multitude said, This is Jesus the prophet of Nazareth of Galilee.
12 ¶ And Jesus went into the temple of God, and

ἀποστελεῖ αὐτούς. 4 Τοῦτο δὲ γέγονεν
he will send them. Now this has happened
ἵνα πληρωθῇ τὸ ῥηθὲν διὰ τοῦ
that might be fulfilled the thing spoken through the
προφήτου λέγοντος· 5 εἴπατε τῇ θυγατρὶ
prophet saying: Tell ye the daughter
Σιών· ἰδοὺ ὁ βασιλεύς σου ἔρχεταί σοι
of Zion: Behold[,] the king of thee comes to thee
πραῢς καὶ ἐπιβεβηκὼς ἐπὶ ὄνον καὶ ἐπὶ
meek and having mounted on an ass and on
πῶλον υἱὸν ὑποζυγίου. 6 πορευθέντες δὲ
a colt son(foal) of an ass. And going
οἱ μαθηταὶ καὶ ποιήσαντες καθὼς συνέταξεν
the disciples and doing as directed
αὐτοῖς ὁ Ἰησοῦς 7 ἤγαγον τὴν ὄνον καὶ
them – Jesus they brought the ass and
τὸν πῶλον, καὶ ἐπέθηκαν ἐπ’ αὐτῶν
the colt, and put *on* on them
τὰ ἱμάτια, καὶ ἐπεκάθισεν ἐπάνω αὐτῶν.
the(ir) garments, and he sat *on* on them.
8 ὁ δὲ πλεῖστος ὄχλος ἔστρωσαν ἑαυτῶν
And the very large crowd strewed of them*selves*
τὰ ἱμάτια ἐν τῇ ὁδῷ, ἄλλοι δὲ ἔκοπτον
the garments in the way, and others cut
κλάδους ἀπὸ τῶν δένδρων καὶ ἐστρών-
branches from the trees and strewed
νυον ἐν τῇ ὁδῷ. 9 οἱ δὲ ὄχλοι
in the way. And the crowds the[ones]
προάγοντες αὐτὸν καὶ οἱ ἀκολουθοῦντες
going before him and the[ones] following
ἔκραζον λέγοντες· ὡσαννὰ τῷ υἱῷ Δαυίδ·
cried out saying: Hosanna to the son of David;
εὐλογημένος ὁ ἐρχόμενος ἐν ὀνόματι
blessed the [one] coming in [the] name
κυρίου· ὡσαννὰ ἐν τοῖς ὑψίστοις. 10 καὶ
of [the] Lord; hosanna in the highest [places]. And
εἰσελθόντος αὐτοῦ εἰς Ἱεροσόλυμα ἐσείσθη
entering him* into Jerusalem was shaken
=as he entered
πᾶσα ἡ πόλις λέγουσα· τίς ἐστιν οὗτος;
all the city saying: Who is this?
11 οἱ δὲ ὄχλοι ἔλεγον· οὗτός ἐστιν ὁ
And the crowds said: This is the
προφήτης Ἰησοῦς ὁ ἀπὸ Ναζαρὲθ τῆς
prophet Jesus the [one] from Nazareth –
Γαλιλαίας.
of Galilee.
12 Καὶ εἰσῆλθεν Ἰησοῦς εἰς τὸ ἱερὸν
And entered Jesus into the temple

cast out all them that sold and bought in the temple, and overthrew the tables of the moneychangers, and the seats of them that sold doves,

13 And said unto them, It is written, My house shall be called the house of prayer; but ye have made it a den of thieves.

14 And the blind and the lame came to him in the temple; and he healed them.

15 And when the chief priests and scribes saw the wonderful things that he did, and the children crying in the temple, and saying, Hosanna to the son of David; they were sore displeased,

16 And said unto him, Hearest thou what these say? And Jesus saith unto them, Yea; have ye never read, Out of the mouth of babes and sucklings thou hast perfected praise?

17 And he left them, and went out of the city into Bethany; and he lodged there.

18 ¶ Now in the morning as he returned into the city, he hungered.

19 And when he saw a fig tree in the way, he came to it, and found nothing thereon, but leaves only, and said unto it, Let no fruit grow on thee henceforward for ever. And

καὶ ἐξέβαλεν πάντας τοὺς πωλοῦντας καὶ
and cast out all the [ones] selling and
ἀγοράζοντας ἐν τῷ ἱερῷ, καὶ τὰς τραπέζας
buying in the temple, and the tables
τῶν κολλυβιστῶν κατέστρεψεν καὶ τὰς
of the money-changers he overturned and the
καθέδρας τῶν πωλούντων τὰς περιστεράς,
seats of the [ones] selling the doves,
13 καὶ λέγει αὐτοῖς· γέγραπται· ὁ οἶκός
and says to them: It has been written: The house
μου οἶκος προσευχῆς κληθήσεται, ὑμεῖς
of me a house of prayer shall be called, ²ye
δὲ αὐτὸν ποιεῖτε σπήλαιον λῃστῶν. 14 Καὶ
¹but ⁴it ³are making a den of robbers. And
προσῆλθον αὐτῷ τυφλοὶ καὶ χωλοὶ ἐν τῷ
approached to him blind and lame [ones] in the
ἱερῷ, καὶ ἐθεράπευσεν αὐτούς. 15 ἰδόντες
temple, and he healed them. ⁷seeing
δὲ οἱ ἀρχιερεῖς καὶ οἱ γραμματεῖς τὰ
¹But ²the ³chief priests ⁴and ⁵the ⁶scribes the
θαυμάσια ἃ ἐποίησεν καὶ τοὺς παῖδας
marvels which he did and the children
τοὺς κράζοντας ἐν τῷ ἱερῷ καὶ λέγοντας·
– crying out in the temple and saying:
ὡσαννὰ τῷ υἱῷ Δαυίδ, ἠγανάκτησαν, 16 καὶ
Hosanna to the son of David, they were incensed, and
εἶπαν αὐτῷ· ἀκούεις τί οὗτοι λέγουσιν;
said to him: Hearest thou what these are saying?
ὁ δὲ Ἰησοῦς λέγει αὐτοῖς· ναί· οὐδέποτε
– And Jesus says to them: Yes; never
ἀνέγνωτε ὅτι ἐκ στόματος νηπίων καὶ
did ye read[,] – Out of [the] mouth of infants and
θηλαζόντων κατηρτίσω αἶνον; 17 Καὶ
sucking [ones] thou didst prepare praise? And
καταλιπὼν αὐτοὺς ἐξῆλθεν ἔξω τῆς
leaving them he went forth outside the
πόλεως εἰς Βηθανίαν, καὶ ηὐλίσθη ἐκεῖ.
city to Bethany, and lodged there.
18 Πρωὶ δὲ ἐπαναγαγὼν εἰς τὴν πόλιν
Now early going up to the city
ἐπείνασεν. 19 καὶ ἰδὼν συκῆν μίαν ἐπὶ τῆς
he hungered. And seeing fig-tree one on the
ὁδοῦ ἦλθεν ἐπ᾽ αὐτήν, καὶ οὐδὲν εὗρεν
way he went up(to) it, and nothing found
ἐν αὐτῇ εἰ μὴ φύλλα μόνον, καὶ λέγει
in it except leaves only, and says
αὐτῇ· οὐ μηκέτι ἐκ σοῦ καρπὸς γένηται
to it: Never of thee fruit may be

presently the fig tree
withered away.

20 And when the disciples saw *it*, they marvelled, saying, How soon is the fig tree withered away!

21 Jesus answered and said unto them, Verily I say unto you, If ye have faith, and doubt not, ye shall not only do this *which is done* to the fig tree, but also if ye shall say unto this mountain, Be thou removed, and be thou cast into the sea; it shall be done.

22 And all things, whatsoever ye shall ask in prayer, believing, ye shall receive.

23 ¶ And when he was come into the temple, the chief priests and the elders of the people came unto him as he was teaching, and said, By what authority doest thou these things? and who gave thee this authority?

24 And Jesus answered and said unto them, I also will ask you one thing, which if ye tell me, I in like wise will tell you by what authority I do these things.

25 The baptism of John, whence was it? from heaven, or of men? And they reasoned with themselves, saying, If we shall say, From heaven; he will say unto us, Why did ye not then believe him?

εἰς τὸν αἰῶνα. καὶ ἐξηράνθη παραχρῆμα
to the age. And was dried up instantly

ἡ συκῆ. 20 καὶ ἰδόντες οἱ μαθηταὶ
the fig-tree. And seeing the disciples

ἐθαύμασαν λέγοντες· πῶς παραχρῆμα
marvelled saying: How instantly

ἐξηράνθη ἡ συκῆ; 21 ἀποκριθεὶς δὲ ὁ
was withered the fig-tree? And answering

'Ιησοῦς εἶπεν αὐτοῖς· ἀμὴν λέγω ὑμῖν,
Jesus said to them: Truly I say to you,

ἐὰν ἔχητε πίστιν καὶ μὴ διακριθῆτε,
If ye have faith and do not doubt,

οὐ μόνον τὸ τῆς συκῆς ποιήσετε, ἀλλὰ
not only the* of the fig-tree ye will do, but

κἂν τῷ ὄρει τούτῳ εἴπητε· ἄρθητι
also if – mountain to this ye say: Be thou taken

καὶ βλήθητι εἰς τὴν θάλασσαν, γενήσεται·
and cast into the sea, it shall be;

22 καὶ πάντα ὅσα ἂν αἰτήσητε ἐν τῇ
and all things whatever ye may ask in

προσευχῇ πιστεύοντες λήμψεσθε.
prayer believing ye shall receive.

23 Καὶ ἐλθόντος αὐτοῦ εἰς τὸ ἱερὸν
And coming him* into the temple
=as he came

προσῆλθον αὐτῷ διδάσκοντι οἱ ἀρχιερεῖς
approached *to* him teaching* the chief priests
=while he taught

καὶ οἱ πρεσβύτεροι τοῦ λαοῦ λέγοντες·
and the elders of the people saying:

ἐν ποίᾳ ἐξουσίᾳ ταῦτα ποιεῖς; καὶ
By what authority these things doest thou? and

τίς σοι ἔδωκεν τὴν ἐξουσίαν ταύτην;
who thee gave – authority this?

24 ἀποκριθεὶς δὲ ὁ 'Ιησοῦς εἶπεν αὐτοῖς·
And answering – Jesus said to them:

ἐρωτήσω ὑμᾶς κἀγὼ λόγον ἕνα, ὃν
will question you I also word one, which

ἐὰν εἴπητέ μοι, κἀγὼ ὑμῖν ἐρῶ ἐν ποίᾳ
if ye tell me, I also you will tell by what

ἐξουσίᾳ ταῦτα ποιῶ· 25 τὸ βάπτισμα
authority these things I do: The baptism

τὸ 'Ιωάννου πόθεν ἦν; ἐξ οὐρανοῦ ἢ
– of John whence was it? from heaven or

ἐξ ἀνθρώπων; οἱ δὲ διελογίζοντο ἐν
from men? And they reasoned among

ἑαυτοῖς λέγοντες· ἐὰν εἴπωμεν· ἐξ οὐρανοῦ,
themselves saying: If we say: From heaven,

ἐρεῖ ἡμῖν· διὰ τί οὖν οὐκ ἐπιστεύσατε
he will say to us: Why then believed ye not

* Some such word as 'sign' must be supplied.

26 But if we shall say,
Of men; we fear the people;
for all hold John as a
prophet.
27 And they answered
Jesus, and said, We cannot
tell. And he said unto
them, Neither tell I you
by what authority I do
these things.
28 ¶ But what think ye?
A *certain* man had two
sons; and he came to the
first, and said, Son, go
work to day in my vine-
yard.
29 He answered and
said, I will not: but afterward he repented, and
went.
30 And he came to the
second, and said likewise.
And he answered and said,
I *go*, sir: and went not.
31 Whether of them
twain did the will of *his*
father? They say unto him,
The first. Jesus saith unto
them, Verily I say unto
you, That the publicans and
the harlots go into the
kingdom of God before
you.
32 For John came unto
you in the way of right-
eousness, and ye believed
him not: but the publicans
and the harlots believed
him: and ye, when ye had
seen *it*, repented not afterward, that ye might believe
him.
33 ¶ Hear another para-
ble: There was a certain

αὐτῷ;   26 ἐὰν δὲ   εἴπωμεν·   ἐξ ἀνθρώπων,
him?   But if   we say: From   men,
φοβούμεθα   τὸν   ὄχλον·   πάντες   γὰρ   ὡς
we fear   the   crowd: for all   as
προφήτην   ἔχουσιν   τὸν 'Ιωάννην.   27 καὶ
a prophet   have   –   John.   And
ἀποκριθέντες   τῷ   'Ιησοῦ   εἶπαν·   οὐκ
answering   –   Jesus   they said: We do
οἴδαμεν.   ἔφη   αὐτοῖς   καὶ   αὐτός·   οὐδὲ
not know.   said   to them   also   He: Neither
ἐγὼ   λέγω   ὑμῖν   ἐν   ποίᾳ   ἐξουσίᾳ   ταῦτα
I   tell   you   by   what   authority   these things
ποιῶ.   28 Τί   δὲ   ὑμῖν   δοκεῖ;   ἄνθρωπος
I do.   But what   to you   seems it?   A man
εἶχεν   τέκνα   δύο·   προσελθὼν   τῷ   πρώτῳ
had   children   two;   approaching   *to* the   first
εἶπεν·   τέκνον,   ὕπαγε   σήμερον   ἐργάζου   ἐν
he said: Child,   go   to-day   work   in
τῷ   ἀμπελῶνι.   29 ὁ   δὲ   ἀποκριθεὶς   εἶπεν·
the   vineyard.   But he   answering   said:
ἐγὼ   κύριε,   καὶ   οὐκ   ἀπῆλθεν.   30 προσ-
I [go],   lord,   and   went not.   And
ελθὼν   δὲ   τῷ   δευτέρῳ   εἶπεν   ὡσαύτως.
approaching   *to* the   second   he said   similarly.
ὁ   δὲ   ἀποκριθεὶς   εἶπεν·   οὐ   θέλω,   ὕστερον
And he   answering   said: I will not,   later
μεταμεληθεὶς   ἀπῆλθεν.   31 τίς   ἐκ   τῶν   δύο
repenting   he went.   Which of   the   two
ἐποίησεν   τὸ   θέλημα   τοῦ   πατρός;   λέγουσιν·
did   the   will   of the   father?   They say:
ὁ   ὕστερος.   λέγει   αὐτοῖς   ὁ   'Ιησοῦς·   ἀμὴν
The latter.   Says   to them   –   Jesus: Truly
λέγω   ὑμῖν   ὅτι   οἱ   τελῶναι   καὶ   αἱ   πόρναι
I tell   you[,]   –   The tax-collectors   and   the   harlots
προάγουσιν   ὑμᾶς   εἰς   τὴν   βασιλείαν   τοῦ
are going before   you   into   the   kingdom   –
θεοῦ.   32 ἦλθεν   γὰρ   'Ιωάννης   πρὸς   ὑμᾶς
of God.   For came   John   to   you
ἐν   ὁδῷ   δικαιοσύνης,   καὶ   οὐκ   ἐπιστεύσατε
in   a way   of righteousness,   and   ye believed not
αὐτῷ·   οἱ   δὲ   τελῶναι   καὶ   αἱ   πόρναι
him;   but the   tax-collectors   and   the   harlots
ἐπίστευσαν   αὐτῷ·   ὑμεῖς   δὲ   ἰδόντες   οὐδὲ
believed   him;   but ye   seeing   not
μετεμελήθητε   ὕστερον   τοῦ   πιστεῦσαι   αὐτῷ.
repented   later   –   to believe[d]   him.
                                         =so as to believe
33 "Αλλην   παραβολὴν   ἀκούσατε.   "Ανθρωπος
Another   parable   hear ye.   A man

householder, which planted a vineyard, and hedged it round about, and digged a winepress in it, and built a tower, and let it out to husbandmen, and went into a far country:

34 And when the time of the fruit drew near, he sent his servants to the husbandmen, that they might receive the fruits of it.

35 And the husbandmen took his servants, and beat one, and killed another, and stoned another.

36 Again, he sent other servants more than the first: and they did unto them likewise.

37 But last of all he sent unto them his son, saying, They will reverence my son.

38 But when the husbandmen saw the son, they said among themselves, This is the heir; come, let us kill him, and let us seize on his inheritance.

39 And they caught him, and cast *him* out of the vineyard, and slew *him*.

40 When the lord therefore of the vineyard cometh, what will he do unto those husbandmen?

41 They say unto him, He will miserably destroy those wicked men, and will let out *his* vineyard unto other husbandmen,

ἦν οἰκοδεσπότης ὅστις ἐφύτευσεν ἀμπελῶνα,
there was a housemaster who planted a vineyard,

καὶ φραγμὸν αὐτῷ περιέθηκεν καὶ ὤρυξεν
and ²a hedge ³it ¹put round and dug

ἐν αὐτῷ ληνὸν καὶ ᾠκοδόμησεν πύργον,
in it a winepress and built a tower,

καὶ ἐξέδοτο αὐτὸν γεωργοῖς, καὶ ἀπεδή-
and let it to husbandmen, and departed.

μησεν. 34 ὅτε δὲ ἤγγισεν ὁ καιρὸς τῶν
And when drew near the time of the

καρπῶν, ἀπέστειλεν τοὺς δούλους αὐτοῦ
fruits, he sent the slaves of him

πρὸς τοὺς γεωργοὺς λαβεῖν τοὺς καρποὺς
to the husbandmen to receive the fruits

αὐτοῦ. 35 καὶ λαβόντες οἱ γεωργοὶ
of it. And ²taking ¹the ²husbandmen

τοὺς δούλους αὐτοῦ ὃν μὲν ἔδειραν, ὃν
the slaves of him this one they flogged, that

δὲ ἀπέκτειναν, ὃν δὲ ἐλιθοβόλησαν. 36 πάλιν
one they killed, another they stoned. Again

ἀπέστειλεν ἄλλους δούλους πλείονας τῶν
he sent other slaves more [than] the

πρώτων, καὶ ἐποίησαν αὐτοῖς ὡσαύτως.
first [ones], and they did to them similarly.

37 ὕστερον δὲ ἀπέστειλεν πρὸς αὐτοὺς
But later he sent to them

τὸν υἱὸν αὐτοῦ λέγων· ἐντραπήσονται
the son of him saying: They will reverence

τὸν υἱόν μου. 38 οἱ δὲ γεωργοὶ ἰδόντες
the son of me. But the husbandmen seeing

τὸν υἱὸν εἶπον ἐν ἑαυτοῖς· οὗτός ἐστιν
the son said among themselves: This is

ὁ κληρονόμος· δεῦτε ἀποκτείνωμεν αὐτὸν
the heir; come[,] let us kill him

καὶ σχῶμεν τὴν κληρονομίαν αὐτοῦ·
and let us possess the inheritance of him;

39 καὶ λαβόντες αὐτὸν ἐξέβαλον ἔξω τοῦ
and taking ²him ¹they cast *out* outside the

ἀμπελῶνος καὶ ἀπέκτειναν. 40 ὅταν οὖν
vineyard and killed. When therefore

ἔλθῃ ὁ κύριος τοῦ ἀμπελῶνος, τί ποιήσει
comes the lord of the vineyard, what will he do

τοῖς γεωργοῖς ἐκείνοις; 41 λέγουσιν αὐτῷ·
- husbandmen to those? They say to him:

κακοὺς κακῶς ἀπολέσει αὐτούς, καὶ τὸν
Bad men badly he will destroy them, and the

ἀμπελῶνα ἐκδώσεται ἄλλοις γεωργοῖς,
vineyard he will give out to other husbandmen,

which shall render him the fruits in their seasons.

42 Jesus saith unto them, Did ye never read in the scriptures, The stone which the builders rejected, the same is become the head of the corner: this is the Lord's doing, and it is marvellous in our eyes?

43 Therefore say I unto you, The kingdom of God shall be taken from you, and given to a nation bringing forth the fruits thereof.

44 And whosoever shall fall on this stone shall be broken: but on whomsoever it shall fall, it will grind him to powder.

45 And when the chief priests and Pharisees had heard his parables, they perceived that he spake of them.

46 But when they sought to lay hands on him, they feared the multitude, because they took him for a prophet.

οἵτινες ἀποδώσουσιν αὐτῷ τοὺς καρποὺς
who will render to him the fruits

ἐν τοῖς καιροῖς αὐτῶν. 42 λέγει αὐτοῖς ὁ
in the seasons of them. Says to them -

Ἰησοῦς· οὐδέποτε ἀνέγνωτε ἐν ταῖς
Jesus: Did ye never read in the

γραφαῖς· λίθον ὃν ἀπεδοκίμασαν οἱ
scriptures: A stone which rejected the

οἰκοδομοῦντες, οὗτος ἐγενήθη εἰς κεφαλὴν
building [ones], this became - head

γωνίας· παρὰ κυρίου ἐγένετο αὕτη, καὶ
of [the] corner; from [the] Lord became this, and

ἔστιν θαυμαστὴ ἐν ὀφθαλμοῖς ἡμῶν; 43 διὰ
it is marvellous in [the] eyes of us? There-

τοῦτο λέγω ὑμῖν ὅτι ἀρθήσεται ἀφ' ὑμῶν
fore I tell you[,] - will be taken from you

ἡ βασιλεία τοῦ θεοῦ καὶ δοθήσεται
The kingdom - of God and will be given

ἔθνει ποιοῦντι τοὺς καρποὺς αὐτῆς.
to a nation producing the fruits of it.

44 [καὶ ὁ πεσὼν ἐπὶ τὸν λίθον τοῦτον
And the [one] falling on - stone this

συνθλασθήσεται· ἐφ' ὃν δ' ἂν πέσῃ,
will be broken in pieces; but on whomever it falls,

λικμήσει αὐτόν.] 45 Καὶ ἀκούσαντες οἱ
it will crush to powder him. And hearing the

ἀρχιερεῖς καὶ οἱ Φαρισαῖοι τὰς παραβολὰς
chief priests and the Pharisees the parables

αὐτοῦ ἔγνωσαν ὅτι περὶ αὐτῶν λέγει·
of him they knew that concerning them he tells;

46 καὶ ζητοῦντες αὐτὸν κρατῆσαι ἐφοβήθησαν
and seeking him to seize they feared

τοὺς ὄχλους, ἐπεὶ εἰς προφήτην αὐτὸν εἶχον.
the crowds, since for a prophet him they had.

CHAPTER 22

AND Jesus answered and spake unto them again by parables, and said,

2 The kingdom of heaven is like unto a certain king, which made a marriage for his son,

3 And sent forth his servants to call them that were bidden to the

22 Καὶ ἀποκριθεὶς ὁ Ἰησοῦς πάλιν
And answering - Jesus again

εἶπεν ἐν παραβολαῖς αὐτοῖς λέγων·
spoke in parables to them saying:

2 ὡμοιώθη ἡ βασιλεία τῶν οὐρανῶν
Was(is) likened the kingdom of the heavens

ἀνθρώπῳ βασιλεῖ, ὅστις ἐποίησεν γάμους
to a man a king, who made a wedding feast

τῷ υἱῷ αὐτοῦ. 3 καὶ ἀπέστειλεν τοὺς
for the son of him. And he sent the

δούλους αὐτοῦ καλέσαι τοὺς κεκλημένους
slaves of him to call the [ones] *having been* invited

wedding: and they would not come.

4 Again, he sent forth other servants, saying, Tell them which are bidden, Behold, I have prepared my dinner: my oxen and *my* fatlings *are* killed, and all things *are* ready: come unto the marriage.

5 But they made light of *it*, and went their ways, one to his farm, another to his merchandise:

6 And the remnant took his servants, and entreated *them* spitefully, and slew *them*.

7 But when the king heard *thereof*, he was wroth: and he sent forth his armies, and destroyed those murderers, and burned up their city.

8 Then saith he to his servants, The wedding is ready, but they which were bidden were not worthy.

9 Go ye therefore into the highways, and as many as ye shall find, bid to the marriage.

10 So those servants went out into the highways, and gathered together all as many as they found, both bad and good: and the wedding was furnished with guests.

11 And when the king came in to see the guests,

εἰς τοὺς γάμους, καὶ οὐκ ἤθελον ἐλθεῖν.
to the feast, and they wished not to come.

4 πάλιν ἀπέστειλεν ἄλλους δούλους λέγων·
Again he sent other slaves saying:

εἴπατε τοῖς κεκλημένοις· ἰδοὺ τὸ
Tell the [ones] *having been* invited: Behold[,] the

ἄριστόν μου ἡτοίμακα, οἱ ταῦροί μου
supper of me I have prepared, the oxen of me

καὶ τὰ σιτιστὰ τεθυμένα, καὶ πάντα
and the fatted beasts having been killed, and all things

ἕτοιμα· δεῦτε εἰς τοὺς γάμους. 5 οἱ δὲ
[are] ready; come to the feast. But they

ἀμελήσαντες ἀπῆλθον, ὃς μὲν εἰς τὸν
not caring went off, one to the(his)

ἴδιον ἀγρόν, ὃς δὲ ἐπὶ τὴν ἐμπορίαν
own field, another on the trading

αὐτοῦ· 6 οἱ δὲ λοιποὶ κρατήσαντες
of him; and the rest seizing

τοὺς δούλους αὐτοῦ ὕβρισαν καὶ ἀπέκτειναν.
the slaves of him insulted and killed.

7 ὁ δὲ βασιλεὺς ὠργίσθη, καὶ πέμψας
So the king became angry, and sending

τὰ στρατεύματα αὐτοῦ ἀπώλεσεν τοὺς
the armies of him destroyed -

φονεῖς ἐκείνους καὶ τὴν πόλιν αὐτῶν
murderers those and the city of them

ἐνέπρησεν. 8 τότε λέγει τοῖς δούλοις
burned. Then he says to the slaves

αὐτοῦ· ὁ μὲν γάμος ἕτοιμός ἐστιν, οἱ δὲ
of him: Indeed the feast ready is, but the [ones]

κεκλημένοι οὐκ ἦσαν ἄξιοι· 9 πορεύεσθε
having been invited were not worthy; go ye

οὖν ἐπὶ τὰς διεξόδους τῶν ὁδῶν, καὶ
therefore onto the partings of the ways, and

ὅσους ἐὰν εὕρητε καλέσατε εἰς τοὺς
as many as ye find call to the

γάμους. 10 καὶ ἐξελθόντες οἱ δοῦλοι
feast. And going forth - slaves

ἐκεῖνοι εἰς τὰς ὁδοὺς συνήγαγον πάντας
those into the ways assembled all

οὓς εὗρον, πονηρούς τε καὶ ἀγαθούς·
whom they found, both bad and good;

καὶ ἐπλήσθη ὁ νυμφὼν ἀνακειμένων.
and was filled the wedding chamber of(with) reclining [ones].

11 εἰσελθὼν δὲ ὁ βασιλεὺς θεάσασθαι
But entering the king to behold

τοὺς ἀνακειμένους εἶδεν ἐκεῖ
the reclining [ones] he saw there

he saw there a man which had not on a wedding garment:

12 And he saith unto him, Friend, how camest thou in hither not having a wedding garment? And he was speechless.

13 Then said the king to the servants, Bind him hand and foot, and take him away, and cast *him* into outer darkness; there shall be weeping and gnashing of teeth.

14 For many are called, but few *are* chosen.

15 ¶ Then went the Pharisees, and took counsel how they might entangle him in *his* talk.

16 And they sent out unto him their disciples with the Herodians, saying, Master, we know that thou art true, and teachest the way of God in truth, neither carest thou for any *man:* for thou regardest not the person of men.

17 Tell us therefore, What thinkest thou? Is it lawful to give tribute unto Cæsar, or not?

18 But Jesus perceived their wickedness, and said, Why tempt ye me, *ye* hypocrites?

19 Shew me the tribute

ἄνθρωπον οὐκ ἐνδεδυμένον ἔνδυμα γάμου·
a man not *having been* dressed[in] a dress of wedding;

12 καὶ λέγει αὐτῷ· ἑταῖρε, πῶς
and he says to him: Comrade, how

εἰσῆλθες ὧδε μὴ ἔχων ἔνδυμα γάμου;
enteredst thou here not having a dress of wedding?

ὁ δὲ ἐφιμώθη. 13 τότε ὁ βασιλεὺς
And he was silenced. Then the king

εἶπεν τοῖς διακόνοις· δήσαντες αὐτοῦ
said to the servants: Binding of him

πόδας καὶ χεῖρας ἐκβάλετε αὐτὸν
feet and hands throw out him

εἰς τὸ σκότος τὸ ἐξώτερον· ἐκεῖ ἔσται
into the darkness - outer: there will be

ὁ κλαυθμὸς καὶ ὁ βρυγμὸς τῶν
the wailing and the gnashing of the

ὀδόντων. 14 Πολλοὶ γάρ εἰσιν κλητοί,
teeth. For many are called,

ὀλίγοι δὲ ἐκλεκτοί.
but few chosen.

15 Τότε πορευθέντες οἱ Φαρισαῖοι συμ-
Then going the Pharisees coun-

βούλιον ἔλαβον ὅπως αὐτὸν παγιδεύσωσιν
sel took so as him they might ensnare

ἐν λόγῳ. 16 καὶ ἀποστέλλουσιν αὐτῷ
in a word. And they send to him

τοὺς μαθητὰς αὐτῶν μετὰ τῶν Ἡρῳ-
the disciples of them with the Hero-

διανῶν λέγοντας· διδάσκαλε, οἴδαμεν
dians saying: Teacher, we know

ὅτι ἀληθὴς εἶ καὶ τὴν ὁδὸν τοῦ
that truthful thou art and the way -

θεοῦ ἐν ἀληθείᾳ διδάσκεις, καὶ οὐ
of God in truth thou teachest, and not

μέλει σοι περὶ οὐδενός, οὐ γὰρ
it concerns *to* thee about no one(anyone), ²not ¹for

βλέπεις εἰς πρόσωπον ἀνθρώπων·
²thou lookest to face of men;

17 εἰπὸν οὖν ἡμῖν, τί σοι δοκεῖ;
tell therefore us, what to thee seems it?

ἔξεστιν δοῦναι κῆνσον Καίσαρι ἢ οὔ;
is it lawful to give tribute to Cæsar or no?

18 γνοὺς δὲ ὁ Ἰησοῦς τὴν πονηρίαν
But knowing - Jesus the wickedness

αὐτῶν εἶπεν· τί με πειράζετε, ὑποκριταί;
of them said: Why me tempt ye, hypocrites?

19 ἐπιδείξατέ μοι τὸ νόμισμα τοῦ κήνσου.
Show me the money of the tribute.

money. And they brought
unto him a penny.

20 And he saith unto
them, Whose *is* this image
and superscription?

21 They say unto him,
Cæsar's. Then saith he
unto them, Render there-
fore unto Cæsar the things
which are Cæsar's; and
unto God the things that
are God's.

22 When they had heard
these words, they marvelled,
and left him, and went
their way.

23 ¶ The same day came
to him the Sadducees,
which say that there is no
resurrection, and asked
him,

24 Saying, Master,
Moses said, If a man die,
having no children, his
brother shall marry his
wife, and raise up seed
unto his brother.

25 Now there were with
us seven brethren: and the
first, when he had married
a wife, deceased, and, having no issue, left his wife
unto his brother:

26 Likewise the second
also, and the third, unto
the seventh.

27 And last of all the
woman died also.

28 Therefore in the re-
surrection whose wife shall
she be of the seven? for they
all had her.

29 Jesus answered and
said unto them, Ye do err,

οἱ	δὲ	προσήνεγκαν	αὐτῷ	δηνάριον.	20 καὶ
And they		brought	to him	a denarius.	And

λέγει	αὐτοῖς·	τίνος	ἡ	εἰκὼν	αὕτη
he says	to them:	Of whom	–	image	this

καὶ	ἡ	ἐπιγραφή;	21 λέγουσιν·	Καίσαρος.
and	–	superscription?	They say:	Of Cæsar.

τότε	λέγει	αὐτοῖς·	ἀπόδοτε	οὖν	τὰ
Then	he says	to them:	Render	then	the things

Καίσαρος	Καίσαρι	καὶ	τὰ	τοῦ	θεοῦ
of Cæsar	to Cæsar	and	the things	–	of God

τῷ	θεῷ.	22 καὶ	ἀκούσαντες	ἐθαύμασαν,
–	to God.	And	hearing	they marvelled,

καὶ	ἀφέντες	αὐτὸν	ἀπῆλθαν.
and	leaving	him	went away.

23 Ἐν	ἐκείνῃ	τῇ	ἡμέρᾳ	προσῆλθον
On	that	–	day	approached

αὐτῷ	Σαδδουκαῖοι,	λέγοντες	μὴ	εἶναι
to him	Sadducees,	saying	not	to be

ἀνάστασιν,	καὶ	ἐπηρώτησαν	αὐτὸν
a resurrection,	and	questioned	him

24 λέγοντες·	διδάσκαλε,	Μωϋσῆς	εἶπεν·
saying:	Teacher,	Moses	said:

ἐάν	τις	ἀποθάνῃ	μὴ	ἔχων	τέκνα,
If	any man	dies	not	having	children,

ἐπιγαμβρεύσει	ὁ	ἀδελφὸς	αὐτοῦ	τὴν
shall take to wife after	the	brother	of him	the

γυναῖκα	αὐτοῦ	καὶ	ἀναστήσει	σπέρμα
wife	of him	and	shall raise up	seed

τῷ	ἀδελφῷ	αὐτοῦ.	25 ἦσαν	δὲ	παρ'
to the	brother	of him.	Now there were		with

ἡμῖν	ἑπτὰ	ἀδελφοί·	καὶ	ὁ	πρῶτος
us	seven	brothers;	and	the	first

γήμας	ἐτελεύτησεν,	καὶ	μὴ	ἔχων
having married	died,	and	not	having

σπέρμα	ἀφῆκεν	τὴν	γυναῖκα	αὐτοῦ	τῷ
seed	left	the	wife	of him	to the

ἀδελφῷ	αὐτοῦ·	26 ὁμοίως	καὶ	ὁ	δεύτερος
brother	of him;	likewise	also	the	second

καὶ	ὁ	τρίτος,	ἕως	τῶν	ἑπτά.	27 ὕστερον
and	the	third,	until	the	seven.	last

δὲ	πάντων	ἀπέθανεν	ἡ	γυνή.	28 ἐν	τῇ
And	of all	died	the	woman.	In	the

ἀναστάσει	οὖν	τίνος	τῶν	ἑπτὰ	ἔσται
resurrection	then	of which	of the	seven	will she be

γυνή;	πάντες	γὰρ	ἔσχον	αὐτήν.	29 ἀπο-
wife?	for all		had	her.	an-

κριθεὶς	δὲ	ὁ	Ἰησοῦς	εἶπεν	αὐτοῖς·
swering	And	–	Jesus	said	to them:

not knowing the scriptures, nor the power of God.

30 For in the resurrection they neither marry, nor are given in marriage, but are as the angels of God in heaven.

31 But as touching the resurrection of the dead, have ye not read that which was spoken unto you by God, saying,

32 I am the God of Abraham, and the God of Isaac, and the God of Jacob? God is not the God of the dead, but of the living.

33 And when the multitude heard *this*, they were astonished at his doctrine.

34 ¶ But when the Pharisees had heard that he had put the Sadducees to silence, they were gathered together.

35 Then one of them, *which was* a lawyer, asked *him a question*, tempting him, and saying,

36 Master, which *is* the great commandment in the law?

37 Jesus said unto him, Thou shalt love the Lord thy God with all thy heart, and with all thy soul, and with all thy mind.

38 This is the first and great commandment.

39 And the second *is* like unto it, Thou shalt love thy neighbour as thyself.

40 On these two commandments hang all the law and the prophets.

πλανᾶσθε μὴ εἰδότες τὰς γραφὰς μηδὲ
Ye err   not knowing the scriptures nor

τὴν δύναμιν τοῦ θεοῦ. 30 ἐν γὰρ τῇ
the power   –   of God.   For in   the

ἀναστάσει οὔτε γαμοῦσιν οὔτε γαμίζονται,
resurrection neither they marry nor are given in marriage,

ἀλλ' ὡς ἄγγελοι ἐν τῷ οὐρανῷ εἰσιν.
but   as   angels   in *the* heaven   are.

31 περὶ δὲ τῆς ἀναστάσεως τῶν νεκρῶν
But concerning the   resurrection   of the   dead

οὐκ ἀνέγνωτε τὸ ῥηθὲν ὑμῖν ὑπὸ
did ye not read the thing said   to you   by

τοῦ θεοῦ λέγοντος· 32 ἐγώ εἰμι ὁ θεὸς
–   God saying: I   am   the God

Ἀβραὰμ καὶ ὁ θεὸς Ἰσαὰκ καὶ ὁ θεὸς
of Abraham and the God of Isaac and the God

Ἰακώβ; οὐκ ἔστιν [ὁ] θεὸς νεκρῶν
of Jacob? He is not   the God of dead men

ἀλλὰ ζώντων. 33 καὶ ἀκούσαντες οἱ ὄχλοι
but of living [ones]. And   hearing   the crowds

ἐξεπλήσσοντο ἐπὶ τῇ διδαχῇ αὐτοῦ.
were astounded over(at) the teaching   of him.

34 Οἱ δὲ Φαρισαῖοι ἀκούσαντες ὅτι
But the   Pharisees   hearing   that

ἐφίμωσεν τοὺς Σαδδουκαίους, συνήχθησαν
he silenced the   Sadducees,   were assembled

ἐπὶ τὸ αὐτό, 35 καὶ ἐπηρώτησεν εἷς
together,   and ⁶questioned   ¹one

ἐξ αὐτῶν νομικὸς πειράζων αὐτόν· 36 δι-
²of ³them ⁴a lawyer ⁵tempting him: Teach-

δάσκαλε, ποία ἐντολὴ μεγάλη ἐν τῷ
er,   what commandment [is] great in the

νόμῳ; 37 ὁ δὲ ἔφη αὐτῷ· ἀγαπήσεις
law?   And he said to him: Thou shalt love

κύριον τὸν θεόν σου ἐν ὅλῃ τῇ καρδίᾳ
[the] Lord the God of thee with all the   heart

σου καὶ ἐν ὅλῃ τῇ ψυχῇ σου καὶ ἐν
of thee and with all the soul of thee and with

ὅλῃ τῇ διανοίᾳ σου. 38 αὕτη ἐστὶν ἡ
all the understanding of thee. This   is   the

μεγάλη καὶ πρώτη ἐντολή. 39 δευτέρα
great   and   first commandment. [The] second

ὁμοία αὐτῇ· ἀγαπήσεις τὸν πλησίον σου
[is] like to it: Thou shalt love the neighbour of thee

ὡς σεαυτόν. 40 ἐν ταύταις ταῖς δυσὶν ἐντολαῖς
as thyself.   In(on) these   –   two commandments

ὅλος ὁ νόμος κρέμαται καὶ οἱ προφῆται.
all   the law   hangs   and the prophets.

41 ¶ While the Pharisees were gathered together, Jesus asked them,

41 Συνηγμένων δὲ τῶν Φαρισαίων
And having assembled the Pharisees[a]
= when the Pharisees were assembled

42 Saying, What think ye of Christ? whose son is he? They say unto him, *The son* of David.

ἐπηρώτησεν αὐτοὺς ὁ ᾽Ιησοῦς **42** λέγων· τι
questioned them - Jesus saying: What
ὑμῖν δοκεῖ περὶ τοῦ χριστοῦ; τίνος
to you seems it concerning the Christ? of whom
υἱός ἐστιν; λέγουσιν αὐτῷ· τοῦ Δαυίδ.
son is he? They say to him: - Of David.

43 He saith unto them, How then doth David in spirit call him Lord, saying,

43 λέγει αὐτοῖς· πῶς οὖν Δαυὶδ ἐν
He says to them: How then David in
πνεύματι καλεῖ αὐτὸν κύριον λέγων·
spirit calls him Lord saying:

44 The LORD said unto my Lord, Sit thou on my right hand, till I make thine enemies thy footstool?

44 εἶπεν κύριος τῷ κυρίῳ μου·
Said [the] LORD to the Lord of me:
κάθου ἐκ δεξιῶν μου ἕως ἂν θῶ τοὺς
Sit on [the] right of me until I put the
ἐχθρούς σου ὑποκάτω τῶν ποδῶν σου;
enemies of thee underneath the feet of thee?

45 If David then call him Lord, how is he his son?

45 εἰ οὖν Δαυὶδ καλεῖ αὐτὸν κύριον, πῶς
If then David calls him Lord, how

46 And no man was able to answer him a word, neither durst any *man* from that day forth ask him any more *questions*.

υἱὸς αὐτοῦ ἐστιν; **46** καὶ οὐδεὶς ἐδύνατο
son of him is he? And no one was able
ἀποκριθῆναι αὐτῷ λόγον οὐδὲ ἐτόλμησέν
to answer him a word nor dared
τις ἀπ᾽ ἐκείνης τῆς ἡμέρας ἐπερωτῆσαι
anyone from that - day *to* question
αὐτὸν οὐκέτι.
him no (any) more.

CHAPTER 23

THEN spake Jesus to the multitude, and to his disciples,

23 Τότε ὁ ᾽Ιησοῦς ἐλάλησεν τοῖς ὄχλοις
Then - Jesus spoke to the crowds
καὶ τοῖς μαθηταῖς αὐτοῦ **2** λέγων· ἐπὶ
and to the disciples of him saying: On

2 Saying, The scribes and the Pharisees sit in Moses' seat:

τῆς Μωϋσέως καθέδρας ἐκάθισαν οἱ
the of Moses seat sat the
γραμματεῖς καὶ οἱ Φαρισαῖοι. **3** πάντα
scribes and the Pharisees. All things

3 All therefore whatsoever they bid you observe, *that* observe and do; but do not ye after their works: for they say, and do not.

οὖν ὅσα ἐὰν εἴπωσιν ὑμῖν ποιήσατε
therefore whatever they may tell you do ye
καὶ τηρεῖτε, κατὰ δὲ τὰ ἔργα αὐτῶν
and keep, but according to the works of them
μὴ ποιεῖτε· λέγουσιν γὰρ καὶ οὐ ποιοῦσιν.
do ye not; for they say and do not.

4 For they bind heavy burdens and grievous to be borne, and lay *them* on men's shoulders; but they

4 δεσμεύουσιν δὲ φορτία βαρέα καὶ
And they bind burdens heavy and
ἐπιτιθέασιν ἐπὶ τοὺς ὤμους τῶν ἀνθρώπων,
put *on* on the shoulders - of men,

themselves will not move them with one of their fingers.

5 But all their works they do for to be seen of men: they make broad their phylacteries, and enlarge the borders of their garments,

6 And love the uppermost rooms at feasts, and the chief seats in the synagogues,

7 And greetings in the markets, and to be called of men, Rabbi, Rabbi.

8 But be not ye called Rabbi: for one is your Master, *even* Christ; and all ye are brethren.

9 And call no *man* your father upon the earth: for one is your Father, which is in heaven.

10 Neither be ye called masters: for one is your Master, *even* Christ.

11 But he that is greatest among you shall be your servant.

12 And whosoever shall exalt himself shall be abased; and he that shall humble himself shall be exalted.

13 ¶ But woe unto you, scribes and Pharisees, hypocrites! for ye shut up the kingdom of heaven against men: for ye neither go in *yourselves*, neither suffer ye

αὐτοὶ δὲ τῷ δακτύλῳ αὐτῶν οὐ
but they   with the   finger   of them   not

θέλουσιν κινῆσαι αὐτά. 5 πάντα δὲ
are willing   to move   them.   But all

τὰ ἔργα αὐτῶν ποιοῦσιν πρὸς τὸ θεαθῆναι
the works   of them   they do   for   -   to be seen

τοῖς ἀνθρώποις· πλατύνουσιν γὰρ τὰ
-   by men;   for they broaden   the

φυλακτήρια αὐτῶν καὶ μεγαλύνουσιν τὰ
phylacteries   of them   and   enlarge   the

κράσπεδα, 6 φιλοῦσιν δὲ τὴν πρωτο-
fringes,   and they like   the   chief

κλισίαν ἐν τοῖς δείπνοις καὶ τὰς πρωτο-
place   in   the   suppers   and   the   chief

καθεδρίας ἐν ταῖς συναγωγαῖς 7 καὶ τοὺς
seats   in   the   synagogues .   and   the

ἀσπασμοὺς ἐν ταῖς ἀγοραῖς καὶ
greetings   in   the   marketplaces   and

καλεῖσθαι ὑπὸ τῶν ἀνθρώπων ῥαββί.
to be called   by   -   men   rabbi.

8 ὑμεῖς δὲ μὴ κληθῆτε ῥαββί· εἷς γὰρ
But ye   be not called   rabbi;   for one

ἔστιν ὑμῶν ὁ διδάσκαλος, πάντες δὲ ὑμεῖς
is   of you the   teacher,   and all   ye

ἀδελφοί ἐστε. 9 καὶ πατέρα μὴ καλέσητε
brothers   are.   And   father   call ye not

ὑμῶν ἐπὶ τῆς γῆς· εἷς γάρ ἐστιν
of you   on   the   earth;   for one   is

ὑμῶν ὁ πατὴρ ὁ οὐράνιος. 10 μηδὲ
of you   the   Father   -   heavenly.   Neither

κληθῆτε καθηγηταί, ὅτι καθηγητὴς
be ye called   leaders,   because   leader

ὑμῶν ἐστιν εἷς ὁ Χριστός. 11 ὁ δὲ
of you   is   one   the   Christ.   And the

μείζων ὑμῶν ἔσται ὑμῶν διάκονος.
greater   of you   shall be   of you   servant.

12 Ὅστις δὲ ὑψώσει ἑαυτὸν ταπεινωθήσεται,
And [he] who   will exalt   himself   shall be humbled,

καὶ ὅστις ταπεινώσει ἑαυτὸν ὑψωθήσεται.
and   [he] who   will humble   himself   shall be exalted.

13 Οὐαὶ δὲ ὑμῖν, γραμματεῖς καὶ Φαρισαῖοι
But woe   to you,   scribes   and   Pharisees

ὑποκριταί, ὅτι κλείετε τὴν βασιλείαν
hypocrites,   because   ye shut   the   kingdom

τῶν οὐρανῶν ἔμπροσθεν τῶν ἀνθρώπων·
of the   heavens   before   -   men;

ὑμεῖς γὰρ οὐκ εἰσέρχεσθε, οὐδὲ τοὺς
for ye   do not enter,   nor the [ones]

them that are entering to go in.

14 Woe unto you, scribes and Pharisees, hypocrites! for ye devour widows' houses, and for a pretence make long prayer: therefore ye shall receive the greater damnation.

15 Woe unto you, scribes and Pharisees, hypocrites! for ye compass sea and land to make one proselyte, and when he is made, ye make him twofold more the child of hell than yourselves.

16 Woe unto you, ye blind guides, which say, Whosoever shall swear by the temple, it is nothing; but whosoever shall swear by the gold of the temple, he is a debtor!

17 Ye fools and blind: for whether is greater, the gold, or the temple that sanctifieth the gold?

18 And, Whosoever shall swear by the altar, it is nothing; but whosoever sweareth by the gift that is upon it, he is guilty.

19 Ye fools and blind: for whether is greater, the gift, or the altar that sanctifieth the gift?

20 Whoso therefore shall swear by the altar, sweareth by it, and by all things thereon.

21 And whoso shall swear by the temple, sweareth by it, and by him that dwelleth therein.

22 And he that shall swear by heaven, sweareth by the throne of God, and by him that sitteth thereon.

23 Woe unto you, scribes and Pharisees, hypocrites! for ye pay tithe

---

εἰσερχομένους ἀφίετε εἰσελθεῖν.‡ 15 Οὐαὶ
entering   do ye allow to enter. Woe

ὑμῖν, γραμματεῖς καὶ Φαρισαῖοι ὑποκριταί,
to you, scribes and Pharisees hypocrites,

ὅτι περιάγετε τὴν θάλασσαν καὶ τὴν
because ye go about the sea and the

ξηρὰν ποιῆσαι ἕνα προσήλυτον, καὶ ὅταν
dry [land] to make one proselyte, and when

γένηται, ποιεῖτε αὐτὸν υἱὸν γεέννης διπλό-
he becomes, ye make him a son of gehenna twofold

τερον ὑμῶν. 16 Οὐαὶ ὑμῖν, ὁδηγοὶ τυφλοὶ
more [than] you. Woe to you, leaders blind

οἱ λέγοντες· ὃς ἂν ὁμόσῃ ἐν τῷ ναῷ,
the [ones] saying: Whoever swears by the shrine,

οὐδέν ἐστιν· ὃς δ' ἂν ὁμόσῃ ἐν τῷ χρυσῷ
nothing it is; but whoever swears by the gold

τοῦ ναοῦ, ὀφείλει. 17 μωροὶ καὶ τυφλοί,
of the shrine, he owes. Fools and blind,

τίς γὰρ μείζων ἐστιν, ὁ χρυσὸς ἢ ὁ ναὸς
for which greater is, the gold or the shrine

ὁ ἁγιάσας τὸν χρυσόν; 18 καί· ὃς ἂν
- sanctifying the gold? And: whoever

ὁμόσῃ ἐν τῷ θυσιαστηρίῳ, οὐδέν ἐστιν·
swears by the altar, nothing it is;

ὃς δ' ἂν ὁμόσῃ ἐν τῷ δώρῳ τῷ ἐπάνω
but whoever swears by the gift the upon

αὐτοῦ, ὀφείλει. 19 τυφλοί, τί γὰρ μεῖζον,
it, he owes. Blind, for which [is] greater,

τὸ δῶρον ἢ τὸ θυσιαστήριον τὸ
the gift or the altar -

ἁγιάζον τὸ δῶρον; 20 ὁ οὖν ὁμόσας
sanctifying the gift? Therefore the [one] swearing

ἐν τῷ θυσιαστηρίῳ ὁμνύει ἐν αὐτῷ καὶ
by the altar swears by it and

ἐν πᾶσι τοῖς ἐπάνω αὐτοῦ· 21 καὶ ὁ
by all the things upon it; and the [one]

ὁμόσας ἐν τῷ ναῷ ὁμνύει ἐν αὐτῷ
swearing by the shrine swears by it

καὶ ἐν τῷ κατοικοῦντι αὐτόν· 22 καὶ
and by the [one] inhabiting it; and

ὁ ὁμόσας ἐν τῷ οὐρανῷ ὁμνύει ἐν τῷ
the [one] swearing by the heaven swears by the

θρόνῳ τοῦ θεοῦ καὶ ἐν τῷ καθημένῳ
throne - of God and by the [one] sitting

ἐπάνω αὐτοῦ. 23 Οὐαὶ ὑμῖν, γραμματεῖς
upon it. Woe to you, scribes

καὶ Φαρισαῖοι ὑποκριταί, ὅτι ἀποδεκατοῦτε
and Pharisees hypocrites, because ye tithe

---

‡ Ver. 14 omitted by Nestle; cf. R.V. marg., etc.

of mint and anise and cummin, and have omitted the weightier *matters* of the law, judgment, mercy, and faith: these ought ye to have done, and not to leave the other undone.

24 *Ye* blind guides, which strain at a gnat, and swallow a camel.

25 Woe unto you, scribes and Pharisees, hypocrites! for ye make clean the outside of the cup and of the platter, but within they are full of extortion and excess.

26 *Thou* blind Pharisee, cleanse first that *which is* within the cup and platter, that the outside of them may be clean also.

27 Woe unto you, scribes and Pharisees, hypocrites! for ye are like unto whited sepulchres, which indeed appear beautiful outward, but are within full of dead *men's* bones, and of all uncleanness.

28 Even so ye also outwardly appear righteous unto men, but within ye are full of hypocrisy and iniquity.

29 Woe unto you, scribes and Pharisees, hypocrites! because ye build the tombs of the prophets, and garnish the sepulchres of the righteous,

τὸ ἡδύοσμον καὶ τὸ ἄνηθον καὶ τὸ
the mint and the dill and the

κύμινον, καὶ ἀφήκατε τὰ βαρύτερα
cummin, and ye [have] left the heavier things

τοῦ νόμου, τὴν κρίσιν καὶ τὸ ἔλεος
of the law, — judgment and — mercy

καὶ τὴν πίστιν· ταῦτα δὲ ἔδει ποιῆσαι
and — faith; but these things it behoved to do

κἀκεῖνα μὴ ἀφεῖναι. 24 ὁδηγοὶ τυφλοί,
and those not to leave. Leaders blind,

οἱ διϋλίζοντες τὸν κώνωπα, τὴν δὲ
the [ones] straining the gnat, but ²the

κάμηλον καταπίνοντες. 25 Οὐαὶ ὑμῖν,
²camel ¹swallowing. Woe to you,

γραμματεῖς καὶ Φαρισαῖοι ὑποκριταί, ὅτι
scribes and Pharisees hypocrites, because

καθαρίζετε τὸ ἔξωθεν τοῦ ποτηρίου καὶ
ye cleanse the outside of the cup and

τῆς παροψίδος, ἔσωθεν δὲ γέμουσιν ἐξ
the dish, but within they are full of

ἁρπαγῆς καὶ ἀκρασίας. 26 Φαρισαῖε τυφλέ,
robbery and intemperance. Pharisee blind,

καθάρισον πρῶτον τὸ ἐντὸς τοῦ ποτηρίου
cleanse thou first the inside of the cup

ἵνα γένηται καὶ τὸ ἐκτὸς αὐτοῦ καθαρόν.
that may be also the outside of it clean.

27 Οὐαὶ ὑμῖν, γραμματεῖς καὶ Φαρισαῖοι
Woe to you, scribes and Pharisees

ὑποκριταί, ὅτι παρομοιάζετε τάφοις κεκονια-
hypocrites, because ye resemble graves having been

μένοις, οἵτινες ἔξωθεν μὲν φαίνονται
whitewashed, who(which) outwardly indeed appear

ὡραῖοι, ἔσωθεν δὲ γέμουσιν ὀστέων
beautiful, but within they are full of bones

νεκρῶν καὶ πάσης ἀκαθαρσίας. 28 οὕτως
of dead men and of all uncleanness. Thus

καὶ ὑμεῖς ἔξωθεν μὲν φαίνεσθε τοῖς
also ye outwardly indeed appear —

ἀνθρώποις δίκαιοι, ἔσωθεν δέ ἐστε μεστοὶ
to men righteous, but within ye are full

ὑποκρίσεως καὶ ἀνομίας. 29 Οὐαὶ ὑμῖν,
of hypocrisy and of lawlessness. Woe to you

γραμματεῖς καὶ Φαρισαῖοι ὑποκριταί,
scribes and Pharisees hypocrites,

ὅτι οἰκοδομεῖτε τοὺς τάφους τῶν προφητῶν
because ye build the graves of the prophets

καὶ κοσμεῖτε τὰ μνημεῖα τῶν δικαίων,
and adorn the monuments of the righteous,

30 And say, I₁ we had been in the days of our fathers, we would not have been partakers with them in the blood of the prophets.

31 Wherefore ye be witnesses unto yourselves, that ye are the children of them which killed the prophets.

32 Fill ye up then the measure of your fathers.

33 *Ye* serpents, *ye* generation of vipers, how can ye escape the damnation of hell?

34 Wherefore, behold, I send unto you prophets, and wise men, and scribes: and *some* of them ye shall kill and crucify; and *some* of them shall ye scourge in your synagogues, and persecute *them* from city to city:

35 That upon you may come all the righteous blood shed upon the earth, from the blood of righteous Abel unto the blood of Zacharias son of Barachias, whom ye slew between the temple and the altar.

36 Verily I say unto you, All these things shall come upon this generation.

37 O Jerusalem, Jerusalem, *thou* that killest the prophets, and stonest them which are sent unto thee, how often would I have gathered thy children together, even as a hen gathereth her chickens under

30 καὶ λέγετε· εἰ ἤμεθα ἐν ταῖς ἡμέραις
and say: If we were in the days

τῶν πατέρων ἡμῶν, οὐκ ἂν ἤμεθα
of the fathers of us, we would not have been

αὐτῶν κοινωνοὶ ἐν τῷ αἵματι τῶν προ-
of them partakers in the blood of the pro-

φητῶν. **31** ὥστε μαρτυρεῖτε ἑαυτοῖς ὅτι
phets. So ye witness to [your]selves that

υἱοί ἐστε τῶν φονευσάντων τοὺς προφήτας.
sons ye are of the [ones] having killed the prophets.

32 καὶ ὑμεῖς πληρώσατε τὸ μέτρον τῶν
And ²ye ¹fulfil the measure of the

πατέρων ὑμῶν. **33** ὄφεις, γεννήματα ἐχιδνῶν,
fathers of you. Serpents, offspring of vipers,

πῶς φύγητε ἀπὸ τῆς κρίσεως τῆς γεέννης;
how escape ye from the judgment – of gehenna?

34 διὰ τοῦτο ἰδοὺ ἐγὼ ἀποστέλλω πρὸς
Therefore behold I send to

ὑμᾶς προφήτας καὶ σοφοὺς καὶ γραμ-
you prophets and wise men and scribes;

ματεῖς· ἐξ αὐτῶν ἀποκτενεῖτε καὶ
of them ye will kill and

σταυρώσετε, καὶ ἐξ αὐτῶν μαστιγώσετε
will crucify, and of them ye will scourge

ἐν ταῖς συναγωγαῖς ὑμῶν καὶ διώξετε
in the synagogues of you and will persecute

ἀπὸ πόλεως εἰς πόλιν· **35** ὅπως ἔλθη
from city to city; so comes

ἐφ᾽ ὑμᾶς πᾶν αἷμα δίκαιον ἐκχυννόμενον
on you all blood righteous being shed

ἐπὶ τῆς γῆς ἀπὸ τοῦ αἵματος Ἄβελ τοῦ
on the earth from the blood of Abel the

δικαίου ἕως τοῦ αἵματος Ζαχαρίου υἱοῦ
righteous until the blood of Zacharias son

Βαραχίου, ὃν ἐφονεύσατε μεταξὺ τοῦ ναοῦ
Barachias, whom ye murdered between the shrine

καὶ τοῦ θυσιαστηρίου. **36** ἀμὴν λέγω
and the altar. Truly I tell

ὑμῖν, ἥξει ταῦτα πάντα ἐπὶ τὴν
you, will come all these things on –

γενεὰν ταύτην. **37** Ἰερουσαλὴμ Ἰερουσαλήμ,
generation this. Jerusalem Jerusalem,

ἡ ἀποκτείνουσα τοὺς προφήτας καὶ
the [one] killing the prophets and

λιθοβολοῦσα τοὺς ἀπεσταλμένους πρὸς αὐτήν,
stoning the [ones] sent to her,

ποσάκις ἠθέλησα ἐπισυναγαγεῖν τὰ τέκνα
how often I wished to gather the children

her wings, and ye would not!

38 Behold, your house is left unto you desolate.

39 For I say unto you, Ye shall not see me henceforth, till ye shall say, Blessed *is* he that cometh in the name of the Lord.

σου, ὃν τρόπον ὄρνις ἐπισυνάγει τὰ
of thee, as a bird gathers the

νοσσία [αὐτῆς] ὑπὸ τὰς πτέρυγας, καὶ
young of her under the(her) wings, and

οὐκ ἠθελήσατε. 38 ἰδοὺ ἀφίεται ὑμῖν ὁ
ye wished not. Behold is left to you the

οἶκος ὑμῶν. 39 λέγω γὰρ ὑμῖν, οὐ μὴ
house of you. For I tell you, by no means

με ἴδητε ἀπ’ ἄρτι ἕως ἂν εἴπητε·
me ye see from now until ye say:

εὐλογημένος ὁ ἐρχόμενος ἐν ὀνόματι
Blessed the [one] coming in [the] name

κυρίου.
of [the] Lord.

CHAPTER 24

AND Jesus went out, and departed from the temple: and his disciples came to *him* for to shew him the buildings of temple.

2 And Jesus said unto them, See ye not all these things? verily I say unto you, There shall not be left here one stone upon another, that shall not be thrown down.

3 ¶ And as he sat upon the mount of Olives, the disciples came unto him privately, saying, Tell us, when shall these things be? and what *shall be* the sign of thy coming, and of the end of the world?

4 And Jesus answered and said unto them, Take heed that no man deceive you.

5 For many shall come in my name, saying, I am Christ; and shall deceive many.

24 Καὶ ἐξελθὼν ὁ Ἰησοῦς ἀπὸ τοῦ
And going forth Jesus from the

ἱεροῦ ἐπορεύετο, καὶ προσῆλθον οἱ μαθηταὶ
temple went, and ⁴approached ¹the ²disciples

αὐτοῦ ἐπιδεῖξαι αὐτῷ τὰς οἰκοδομὰς
³of him to show him the buildings

τοῦ ἱεροῦ. 2 ὁ δὲ ἀποκριθεὶς εἶπεν
of the temple. And he answering said

αὐτοῖς· οὐ βλέπετε ταῦτα πάντα; ἀμὴν
to them: See ye not all these things? Truly

λέγω ὑμῖν, οὐ μὴ ἀφεθῇ ὧδε λίθος ἐπὶ
I tell you, by no means will be left here stone on

λίθον ὃς οὐ καταλυθήσεται. 3 Καθημένου
stone which shall not be overthrown. sitting

δὲ αὐτοῦ ἐπὶ τοῦ ὄρους τῶν ἐλαιῶν
and himᵃ on the mount of the olives
=And as he sat

προσῆλθον αὐτῷ οἱ μαθηταὶ κατ’ ἰδίαν
approached *to* him the disciples privately

λέγοντες· εἰπὲ ἡμῖν, πότε ταῦτα ἔσται,
saying: Tell us, when these things will be,

καὶ τί τὸ σημεῖον τῆς σῆς παρουσίας
and what the sign – of thy presence

καὶ συντελείας τοῦ αἰῶνος; 4 καὶ ἀπο-
and of [the] completion of the age? And answer-

κριθεὶς ὁ Ἰησοῦς εἶπεν αὐτοῖς· βλέπετε
ing – Jesus said to them: See ye

μή τις ὑμᾶς πλανήσῃ. 5 πολλοὶ γὰρ
not(lest) anyone ²you ¹cause ²to err. For many

ἐλεύσονται ἐπὶ τῷ ὀνόματί μου λέγοντες·
will come on(in) the name of me saying:

ἐγώ εἰμι ὁ χριστός, καὶ πολλοὺς πλανή-
I am the Christ, and ²many ¹will cause

6 And ye shall hear of
wars and rumours of wars:
see that ye be not troubled:
for all *these things* must
come to pass, but the end
is not yet.

7 For nation shall rise
against nation, and king-
dom against kingdom: and
there shall be famines, and
pestilences, and earth-
quakes, in divers places.

8 All these *are* the beginning of sorrows.

9 Then shall they deliver
you up to be afflicted, and
shall kill you: and ye shall
be hated of all nations for
my name's sake.

10 And then shall many
be offended, and shall betray one another, and shall
hate one another.

11 And many false pro-
phets shall rise, and shall
deceive many.

12 And because iniquity
shall abound, the love of
many shall wax cold.

13 But he that shall en-
dure unto the end, the same
shall be saved.

14 And this gospel of the
kingdom shall be preached
in all the world for a witness
unto all nations; and then
shall the end come.

15 When ye therefore
shall see the abomination
of desolation, spoken of by

σουσιν.   **6** μελλήσετε   δὲ   ἀκούειν   πολέ-
³to err.   But ye will be about   to hear   [of]

μους   καὶ   ἀκοὰς   πολέμων·   ὁρᾶτε   μὴ
wars   and   rumours   of wars;   see   not

θροεῖθε·   δεῖ   γὰρ   γενέσθαι,   ἀλλ'
ye are disturbed;   for it behoves   to happen,   but

οὔπω   ἐστὶν   τὸ   τέλος.   **7** ἐγερθήσεται   γὰρ
not yet   is   the   end.   For will be raised

ἔθνος   ἐπὶ   ἔθνος   καὶ   βασιλεία   ἐπὶ   βασιλείαν,
nation   against   nation   and   kingdom   against   kingdom,

καὶ   ἔσονται   λιμοὶ   καὶ   σεισμοὶ
and   there will be   famines   and   earthquakes

κατὰ   τόπους·   **8** πάντα   δὲ   ταῦτα   ἀρχὴ
throughout places;   but all these things [are] beginning

ὠδίνων.   **9** τότε   παραδώσουσιν   ὑμᾶς
of birth-pangs.   Then   they will deliver   you

εἰς   θλῖψιν   καὶ   ἀποκτενοῦσιν   ὑμᾶς,
to   affliction   and   will kill   you,

καὶ   ἔσεσθε   μισούμενοι   ὑπὸ   πάντων
and   ye will be   *being* hated   by   all

τῶν   ἐθνῶν   διὰ   τὸ   ὄνομά   μου.
the   nations   because of   the   name   of me.

10 καὶ   τότε   σκανδαλισθήσονται   πολλοὶ   καὶ
   And   then   will be offended   many   and

ἀλλήλους   παραδώσουσιν   καὶ   μισήσουσιν
one another   will deliver   and   they will hate

ἀλλήλους·   **11** καὶ   πολλοὶ   ψευδοπροφῆται
one another;   and   many   false prophets

ἐγερθήσονται   καὶ   πλανήσουσιν   πολλούς·
will be raised   and   will cause to err   many;

12 καὶ   διὰ   τὸ   πληθυνθῆναι   τὴν
   and   because of   –   to be increased   *the*

ἀνομίαν   ψυγήσεται   ἡ   ἀγάπη   τῶν
lawlessness   will grow cold   the   love   of the

πολλῶν.   **13** ὁ   δὲ   ὑπομείνας   εἰς   τέλος,
many.   But the [one]   enduring   to   [the] end,

οὗτος   σωθήσεται.   **14** καὶ   κηρυχθήσεται
this   will be saved.   And   will be proclaimed

τοῦτο   τὸ   εὐαγγέλιον   τῆς   βασιλείας
this   –   gospel   of the   kingdom

ἐν   ὅλῃ   τῇ   οἰκουμένῃ   εἰς   μαρτύριον
in   all   the   inhabited earth   for   a testimony

πᾶσιν   τοῖς   ἔθνεσιν,   καὶ   τότε   ἥξει   τὸ
to all   the   nations,   and   then   will come   the

τέλος.   **15** Ὅταν   οὖν   ἴδητε   τὸ
end.   When   therefore   ye see   the

βδέλυγμα   τῆς   ἐρημώσεως   τὸ   ῥηθὲν   διὰ
abomination   –   of desolation   –   spoken   through

Daniel the prophet, stand in the holy place, (whoso readeth, let him understand:)

16 Then let them which be in Judæa flee into the mountains:

17 Let him which is on the housetop not come down to take any thing out of his house:

18 Neither let him which is in the field return back to take his clothes.

19 And woe unto them that are with child, and to them that give suck in those days!

20 But pray ye that your flight be not in the winter, neither on the sabbath day:

21 For then shall be great tribulation, such as was not since the beginning of the world to this time, no, nor ever shall be.

22 And except those days should be shortened, there should no flesh be saved: but for the elect's sake those days shall be shortened.

23 Then if any man shall say unto you, Lo, here is Christ, or there; believe it not.

24 For there shall arise false Christs, and false prophets, and shall shew great signs and wonders; insomuch that, if it were possible, they shall deceive the very elect.

25 Behold, I have told you before.

26 Wherefore if they shall say unto you, Behold,

Δανιὴλ τοῦ προφήτου ἑστὸς ἐν τόπῳ
Daniel   the   prophet   stand   in   place

ἁγίῳ, ὁ ἀναγινώσκων νοείτω,
holy,   the [one]   reading   let him understand,

16 τότε οἱ ἐν τῇ Ἰουδαίᾳ φευγέτωσαν
then   the [ones] in   –   Judæa   let them flee

εἰς τὰ ὄρη, 17 ὁ ἐπὶ τοῦ δώματος μὴ
to   the mountains, the [one] on   the   housetop   let him

καταβάτω ἆραι τὰ ἐκ τῆς οἰκίας αὐτοῦ,
not come down to take the things out of the   house   of him,

18 καὶ ὁ ἐν τῷ ἀγρῷ μὴ ἐπιστρεψάτω
and the [one] in   the   field   let him not turn back

ὀπίσω ἆραι τὸ ἱμάτιον αὐτοῦ. 19 οὐαὶ
behind to take   the   garment   of him.   woe

δὲ ταῖς ἐν γαστρὶ ἐχούσαις καὶ ταῖς
And to the women in   womb   having   and to the [ones]
        = the pregnant women

θηλαζούσαις ἐν ἐκείναις ταῖς ἡμέραις.
giving suck   in   those   –   days.

20 προσεύχεσθε δὲ ἵνα μὴ γένηται ἡ
And pray ye   lest   happen   the

φυγὴ ὑμῶν χειμῶνος μηδὲ σαββάτῳ·
flight of you   of(in) winter   nor   on a sabbath;

21 ἔσται γὰρ τότε θλῖψις μεγάλη, οἵα οὐ
for will be   then   affliction   great,   such as not

γέγονεν ἀπ᾽ ἀρχῆς κόσμου ἕως
has happened from [the] beginning of [the] world   until

τοῦ νῦν οὐδ᾽ οὐ μὴ γένηται. 22 καὶ
–   now   neither   by no means   may happen.   And

εἰ μὴ ἐκολοβώθησαν αἱ ἡμέραι ἐκεῖναι,
except   were cut short   the   days   those,

οὐκ ἂν ἐσώθη πᾶσα σάρξ· διὰ δὲ τοὺς
not   –   was saved   all   flesh; but on account of   the
=no flesh would be saved;

ἐκλεκτοὺς κολοβωθήσονται αἱ ἡμέραι ἐκεῖναι.
chosen   will be cut short   the   days   those.

23 τότε ἐάν τις ὑμῖν εἴπῃ· ἰδοὺ ὧδε
Then   if   anyone to you   says: Behold   here

ὁ χριστός, ἤ· ὧδε, μὴ πιστεύσητε·
the   Christ,   or: Here,   do not believe;

24 ἐγερθήσονται γὰρ ψευδόχριστοι καὶ
for will be raised   false Christs   and

ψευδοπροφῆται, καὶ δώσουσιν σημεῖα μεγάλα
false prophets,   and they will give   signs   great

καὶ τέρατα, ὥστε πλανῆσαι, εἰ δυνατόν,
and   marvels,   so as   to cause to err,   if   possible,

καὶ τοὺς ἐκλεκτούς. 25 ἰδοὺ προείρηκα
even   the   chosen.   Behold I have before told

ὑμῖν. 26 ἐὰν οὖν εἴπωσιν ὑμῖν· ἰδοὺ
you.   If   therefore   they say   to you: Behold

he is in the desert; go not forth: behold, *he is* in the secret chambers; believe *it* not.

27 For as the lightning cometh out of the east, and shineth even unto the west; so shall also the coming of the Son of man be.

28 For wheresoever the carcase is, there will the eagles be gathered together.

29 ¶ Immediately after the tribulation of those days shall the sun be darkened, and the moon shall not give her light, and the stars shall fall from heaven, and the powers of the heavens shall be shaken:

30 And then shall appear the sign of the Son of man in heaven: and then shall all the tribes of the earth mourn, and they shall see the Son of man coming in the clouds of heaven with power and great glory.

31 And he shall send his angels with a great sound of a trumpet, and they shall gather together his elect from the four winds, from one end of heaven to the other.

32 ¶ Now learn a parable of the fig tree; When his

ἐν   τῇ   ἐρήμῳ   ἐστίν,   μὴ   ἐξέλθητε·   ἰδοὺ
in   the   desert   he is,   go not ye forth;   Behold

ἐν   τοῖς   ταμιείοις,   μὴ   πιστεύσητε·
in   the   private rooms,   do not ye believe;

27 ὥσπερ   γὰρ   ἡ   ἀστραπὴ   ἐξέρχεται   ἀπὸ
for as   the   lightning   comes forth   from

ἀνατολῶν   καὶ   φαίνεται   ἕως   δυσμῶν,
[the] east   and   shines   unto   [the] west,

οὕτως   ἔσται   ἡ   παρουσία   τοῦ   υἱοῦ
so   will be   the   presence   of the   Son

τοῦ   ἀνθρώπου·   28 ὅπου   ἐὰν   ᾖ   τὸ
-   of man;   wherever   may be   the

πτῶμα,   ἐκεῖ   συναχθήσονται   οἱ   ἀετοί.
carcase,   there   will be assembled   the   eagles.

29 Εὐθέως   δὲ   μετὰ   τὴν   θλῖψιν   τῶν
And immediately   after   the   affliction

ἡμερῶν   ἐκείνων   ὁ   ἥλιος   σκοτισθήσεται,
days   of those   the   sun   will be darkened,

καὶ   ἡ   σελήνη   οὐ   δώσει   τὸ   φέγγος
and   the   moon   will not give   the   light

αὐτῆς,   καὶ   οἱ   ἀστέρες   πεσοῦνται   ἀπὸ   τοῦ
of her,   and   the   stars   will fall   from   -

οὐρανοῦ,   καὶ   αἱ   δυνάμεις   τῶν   οὐρανῶν
heaven,   and   the   powers   of the   heavens

σαλευθήσονται.   30 καὶ   τότε   φανήσεται
will be shaken.   And   then   will appear

τὸ   σημεῖον   τοῦ   υἱοῦ   τοῦ   ἀνθρώπου   ἐν
the   sign   of the   Son   -   of man   in

οὐρανῷ,   καὶ   τότε   κόψονται   πᾶσαι   αἱ
heaven,   and   then   will bewail   all   the

φυλαὶ   τῆς   γῆς   καὶ   ὄψονται   τὸν   υἱὸν
tribes   of the   land   and   they will see   the   Son

τοῦ   ἀνθρώπου   ἐρχόμενον   ἐπὶ   τῶν
-   of man   coming   on   the

νεφελῶν   τοῦ   οὐρανοῦ   μετὰ   δυνάμεως   καὶ
clouds   -   of heaven   with   power   and

δόξης   πολλῆς·   31 καὶ   ἀποστελεῖ   τοὺς
glory   much;   and   he will send   the

ἀγγέλους   αὐτοῦ   μετὰ   σάλπιγγος   μεγάλης,
angels   of him   with   trumpet   a great,

καὶ   ἐπισυνάξουσιν   τοὺς   ἐκλεκτοὺς   αὐτοῦ
and   they will assemble   the   chosen   of him

ἐκ   τῶν   τεσσάρων   ἀνέμων   ἀπ᾽   ἄκρων
out of   the   four   winds   from [the]   extremities

οὐρανῶν   ἕως   [τῶν]   ἄκρων   αὐτῶν.   32 Ἀπὸ
of [the] heavens   unto   the   extremities   of them.   from

δὲ   τῆς   συκῆς   μάθετε   τὴν   παραβολήν·
Now   the   fig-tree   learn ye   the   parable:

branch is yet tender, and putteth forth leaves, ye know that summer *is* nigh:

33 So likewise ye, when ye shall see all these things, know that it is near, *even* at the doors.

34 Verily I say unto you, This generation shall not pass, till all these things be fulfilled.

35 Heaven and earth shall pass away, but my words shall not pass away.

36 ¶ But of that day and hour knoweth no *man*, no, not the angels of heaven, but my Father only.

37 But as the days of Noe *were*, so shall also the coming of the Son of man be.

38 For as in the days that were before the flood they were eating and drinking, marrying and giving in marriage, until the day that Noe entered into the ark,

39 And knew not until the flood came, and took them all away; so shall also the coming of the Son of man be.

40 Then shall two be in the field; the one shall be taken, and the other left.

41 Two *women shall be* grinding at the mill; the

ὅταν ἤδη ὁ κλάδος αὐτῆς γένηται ἁπαλὸς
When now the branch of it becomes tender

καὶ τὰ φύλλα ἐκφύῃ, γινώσκετε ὅτι
and the leaves it puts forth, ye know that

ἐγγὺς τὸ θέρος· 33 οὕτως καὶ ὑμεῖς
near [is] the summer; so also ye

ὅταν ἴδητε πάντα ταῦτα, γινώσκετε ὅτι
when ye see all these things, know that

ἐγγύς ἐστιν ἐπὶ θύραις. 34 ἀμὴν λέγω
near it is on(at) [the] doors. Truly I tell

ὑμῖν ὅτι οὐ μὴ παρέλθῃ ἡ γενεὰ
you that by no means passes away - generation

αὕτη ἕως ἂν πάντα ταῦτα γένηται.
this until all these things happens.

35 ὁ οὐρανὸς καὶ ἡ γῆ παρελεύσεται, οἱ
The heaven and the earth will pass away, ²the

δὲ λόγοι μου οὐ μὴ παρέλθωσιν. 36 Περὶ
¹but words of me by no means may pass away. concerning

δὲ τῆς ἡμέρας ἐκείνης καὶ ὥρας οὐδεὶς
But - day that and hour no one

οἶδεν, οὐδὲ οἱ ἄγγελοι τῶν οὐρανῶν
knows, neither the angels of the heavens

οὐδὲ ὁ υἱός, εἰ μὴ ὁ πατὴρ μόνος.
nor the Son, except the Father only.

37 ὥσπερ γὰρ αἱ ἡμέραι τοῦ Νῶε, οὕτως
For as the days - of Noah, so

ἔσται ἡ παρουσία τοῦ υἱοῦ τοῦ ἀνθρώπου.
will be the presence of the Son - of man.

38 ὡς γὰρ ἦσαν ἐν ταῖς ἡμέραις
For as they were in - days

[ἐκείναις] ταῖς πρὸ τοῦ κατακλυσμοῦ
those the [ones] before the flood

τρώγοντες καὶ πίνοντες, γαμοῦντες καὶ
eating and drinking, marrying and

γαμίζοντες, ἄχρι ἧς ἡμέρας εἰσῆλθεν
being given in marriage, until which day entered

Νῶε εἰς τὴν κιβωτόν, 39 καὶ οὐκ ἔγνωσαν
Noah into the ark, and knew not

ἕως ἦλθεν ὁ κατακλυσμὸς καὶ ἦρεν
until came the flood and took

ἅπαντας, οὕτως ἔσται καὶ ἡ παρουσία
all, so will be also the presence

τοῦ υἱοῦ τοῦ ἀνθρώπου 40 τότε ἔσονται
of the Son - of man. Then will be

δύο ἐν τῷ ἀγρῷ, εἷς παραλαμβάνεται
two men in the field, one is taken

καὶ εἷς ἀφίεται· 41 δύο ἀλήθουσαι
and one is left; two women grinding

one shall be taken, and the other left.

42 ¶ Watch therefore: for ye know not what hour your Lord doth come.

43 But know this, that if the goodman of the house had known in what watch the thief would come, he would have watched, and would not have suffered his house to be broken up.

44 Therefore be ye also ready: for in such an hour as ye think not the Son of man cometh.

45 Who then is a faithful and wise servant, whom his lord hath made ruler over his household, to give them meat in due season?

46 Blessed *is* that servant, whom his lord when he cometh shall find so doing.

47 Verily I say unto you, That he shall make him ruler over all his goods.

48 But and if that evil servant shall say in his heart, My lord delayeth his coming;

49 And shall begin to smite *his* fellowservants, and to eat and drink with the drunken;

50 The lord of that servant shall come in a day when he looketh not for *him*, and in an hour that he is not aware of,

ἐν τῷ μύλῳ, μία παραλαμβάνεται καὶ
in(at) the ~ mill, one is taken and

μία ἀφίεται. 42 γρηγορεῖτε οὖν, ὅτι
one is left. Watch ye therefore, because

οὐκ οἴδατε ποίᾳ ἡμέρᾳ ὁ κύριος
ye know not on what day the lord

ὑμῶν ἔρχεται. 43 Ἐκεῖνο δὲ γινώσκετε
of you is coming. And that know ye

ὅτι εἰ ᾔδει ὁ οἰκοδεσπότης ποίᾳ
that if knew the housemaster in what

φυλακῇ ὁ κλέπτης ἔρχεται, ἐγρηγόρησεν
watch the thief is coming, he would have

ἂν καὶ οὐκ ἂν εἴασεν διορυχθῆναι
watched and would not have allowed to be dug through

τὴν οἰκίαν αὐτοῦ. 44 διὰ τοῦτο καὶ
the house of him. Therefore also

ὑμεῖς γίνεσθε ἕτοιμοι, ὅτι ᾗ οὐ δοκεῖτε
ye be ready, because ¹in which ²ye think not

ὥρᾳ ὁ υἱὸς τοῦ ἀνθρώπου ἔρχεται. 45 Τίς
²hour the Son - of man comes. Who

ἄρα ἐστὶν ὁ πιστὸς δοῦλος καὶ φρόνιμος
then is the faithful slave and prudent

ὃν κατέστησεν ὁ κύριος ἐπὶ τῆς οἰκετείας
whom appointed the lord over the household

αὐτοῦ τοῦ δοῦναι αὐτοῖς τὴν τροφὴν ἐν
of him - to give^d to them the food in

καιρῷ; 46 μακάριος ὁ δοῦλος ἐκεῖνος ὃν
season? blessed [is] - slave that whom

ἐλθὼν ὁ κύριος αὐτοῦ εὑρήσει οὕτως
coming the lord of him will find so

ποιοῦντα· 47 ἀμὴν λέγω ὑμῖν ὅτι ἐπὶ
doing; truly I tell you that over

πᾶσιν τοῖς ὑπάρχουσιν αὐτοῦ καταστήσει
all the goods of him he will appoint

αὐτόν. 48 ἐὰν δὲ εἴπῃ ὁ κακὸς δοῦλος
him. But if says - wicked slave

ἐκεῖνος ἐν τῇ καρδίᾳ αὐτοῦ· χρονίζει
that in the heart of him: Delays

μου ὁ κύριος, 49 καὶ ἄρξηται τύπτειν
of me the lord, and begins to strike

τοὺς συνδούλους αὐτοῦ, ἐσθίῃ δὲ καὶ
the fellow-slaves of him, and eats and

πίνῃ μετὰ τῶν μεθυόντων, 50 ἥξει ὁ
drinks with the [ones] being drunk, will come the

κύριος τοῦ δούλου ἐκείνου ἐν ἡμέρᾳ ᾗ
lord - slave of that on a day on which

οὐ προσδοκᾷ καὶ ἐν ὥρᾳ ᾗ οὐ
he does not expect and in an hour in which not

51 And shall cut him asunder, and appoint *him* his portion with the hypocrites: there shall be weeping and gnashing of teeth.

γινώσκει,   51 καὶ   διχοτομήσει   αὐτόν,
he knows,   and   will cut asunder   him,

καὶ   τὸ   μέρος   αὐτοῦ   μετὰ   τῶν
and   the   portion   of him   with   the

ὑποκριτῶν   θήσει·   ἐκεῖ   ἔσται   ὁ
hypocrites   will place;   there   will be   the

κλαυθμὸς   καὶ   ὁ   βρυγμὸς   τῶν   ὀδόντων.
wailing   and   the   gnashing   of the   teeth.

CHAPTER 25

THEN shall the kingdom of heaven be likened unto ten virgins, which took their lamps, and went forth to meet the bridegroom.

2 And five of them were wise, and five *were* foolish.

3 They that *were* foolish took their lamps, and took no oil with them:

4 But the wise took oil in their vessels with their lamps.

5 While the bridegroom tarried, they all slumbered and slept.

6 And at midnight there was a cry made, Behold, the bridegroom cometh; go ye out to meet him.

7 Then all those virgins arose, and trimmed their lamps.

8 And the foolish said unto the wise, Give us of your oil; for our lamps are gone out.

9 But the wise answered,

25 Τότε   ὁμοιωθήσεται   ἡ   βασιλεία
Then   shall be likened   the   kingdom

τῶν   οὐρανῶν   δέκα   παρθένοις,   αἵτινες
of the   heavens   to ten   virgins,   who

λαβοῦσαι   τὰς   λαμπάδας   ἑαυτῶν   ἐξῆλθον
taking   the   lamps   of them*   went forth

εἰς   ὑπάντησιν   τοῦ   νυμφίου.   2 πέντε   δὲ
to   a meeting   of the bridegroom.   Now five

ἐξ   αὐτῶν   ἦσαν   μωραὶ   καὶ   πέντε   φρόνιμοι.
of   them   were   foolish   and   five   prudent.

3 αἱ   γὰρ   μωραὶ   λαβοῦσαι   τὰς   λαμπάδας
For the   foolish [ones]   taking   the   lamps

οὐκ   ἔλαβον   μεθ'   ἑαυτῶν   ἔλαιον.
did not take   with   them   oil.

4 αἱ   δὲ   φρόνιμοι   ἔλαβον   ἔλαιον   ἐν
But the   prudent [ones]   took   oil   in

τοῖς   ἀγγείοις   μετὰ   τῶν   λαμπάδων   ἑαυτῶν.
the   vessels   with   the   lamps   of them.

5 χρονίζοντος   δὲ   τοῦ   νυμφίου   ἐνύσταξαν
But delaying   the   bridegroom°   slumbered
=while the bridegroom delayed

πᾶσαι   καὶ   ἐκάθευδον.   6 μέσης   δὲ
all   and   slept.   And of(in) [the] middle

νυκτὸς   κραυγὴ   γέγονεν·   ἰδοὺ   ὁ
of [the] night   a cry   there has been: Behold[,]   the

νυμφίος,   ἐξέρχεσθε   εἰς   ἀπάντησιν.   7 τότε
bridegroom,   go ye forth   to   a meeting.   Then

ἠγέρθησαν   πᾶσαι   αἱ   παρθένοι   ἐκεῖναι
were raised   all   –   virgins   those

καὶ   ἐκόσμησαν   τὰς   λαμπάδας   ἑαυτῶν.
and   trimmed   the   lamps   of them.

8 αἱ   δὲ   μωραὶ   ταῖς   φρονίμοις   εἶπαν·
So the   foolish [ones]   to the   prudent   said:

δότε   ἡμῖν   ἐκ   τοῦ   ἐλαίου   ὑμῶν,   ὅτι
Give   us   of   the   oil   of you, because

αἱ   λαμπάδες   ἡμῶν   σβέννυνται.   9 ἀπεκρί-
the   lamps   of us   are being quenched.   But

*Here, and in the three following occurrences, as elsewhere, the strict meaning is emphatic or reflexive—'of themselves'; but this cannot be insisted on.

saying, *Not so;* lest there be not enough for us and you: but go ye rather to them that sell, and buy for yourselves.

10 And while they went to buy, the bridegroom came; and they that were ready went in with him to the marriage: and the door was shut.

11 Afterward came also the other virgins, saying, Lord, Lord, open to us.

12 But he answered and said, Verily I say unto you, I know you not.

13 Watch therefore, for ye know neither the day nor the hour wherein the Son of man cometh.

14 ¶ For *the kingdom of heaven is* as a man travelling into a far country, *who* called his own servants, and delivered unto them his goods.

15 And unto one he gave five talents, to another two, and to another one; to every man according to his several ability; and straightway took his journey.

16 Then he that had received the five talents went and traded with the same, and made *them* other five talents.

17 And likewise he that *had received* two, he also gained other two.

18 But he that had received one went and digged

θησαν δὲ αἱ φρόνιμοι λέγουσαι· μήποτε
answered ⁻ the prudent saying: Lest

οὐ μὴ ἀρκέσῃ ἡμῖν καὶ ὑμῖν·
by no means it suffices to us and to you;

πορεύεσθε μᾶλλον πρὸς τοὺς πωλοῦντας
go ye rather to the [ones] selling

καὶ ἀγοράσατε ἑαυταῖς. 10 ἀπερχομένων
and buy for [your]selves. And going
= as they

δὲ αὐτῶν ἀγοράσαι ἦλθεν ὁ νυμφίος,
away them* to buy came the bridegroom,
were going away

καὶ αἱ ἕτοιμοι εἰσῆλθον μετ' αὐτοῦ
and the ready [ones] went in with him

εἰς τοὺς γάμους, καὶ ἐκλείσθη ἡ
to the wedding festivities, and was shut the

θύρα. 11 ὕστερον δὲ ἔρχονται καὶ αἱ
door. Then later come also the

λοιπαὶ παρθένοι λέγουσαι· κύριε κύριε,
remaining virgins saying: Lord[,] Lord,

ἄνοιξον ἡμῖν. 12 ὁ δὲ ἀποκριθεὶς εἶπεν·
open to us. But he answering said:

ἀμὴν λέγω ὑμῖν, οὐκ οἶδα ὑμᾶς.
Truly I say to you, I know not you.

13 Γρηγορεῖτε οὖν, ὅτι οὐκ οἴδατε
Watch ye therefore, because ye know not

τὴν ἡμέραν οὐδὲ τὴν ὥραν. 14 Ὥσπερ
the day nor the hour. as

γὰρ ἄνθρωπος ἀποδημῶν ἐκάλεσεν
For a man going from home called

τοὺς ἰδίους δούλους καὶ παρέδωκεν αὐτοῖς
the(his) own slaves and delivered to them

τὰ ὑπάρχοντα αὐτοῦ, 15 καὶ ᾧ μὲν ἔδωκεν
the goods of him, and to one he gave

πέντε τάλαντα, ᾧ δὲ δύο, ᾧ δὲ
five talents, to another two, to another

ἕν, ἑκάστῳ κατὰ τὴν ἰδίαν δύναμιν,
one, to each according to the(his) own ability,

καὶ ἀπεδήμησεν. 16 εὐθέως πορευθεὶς
and went from home. Immediately going

ὁ τὰ πέντε τάλαντα λαβὼν ἠργάσατο
the [one] the five talents receiving traded

ἐν αὐτοῖς καὶ ἐκέρδησεν ἄλλα
in them and gained other

πέντε· 17 ὡσαύτως ὁ τὰ δύο ἐκέρδησεν
five; similarly the [one] the two gained
[receiving]

ἄλλα δύο. 18 ὁ δὲ τὸ ἓν λαβὼν
other two. But the [one] the one receiving

in the earth, and hid his lord's money.

19 After a long time the lord of those servants cometh, and reckoneth with them.

20 And so he that had received five talents came and brought other five talents, saying, Lord, thou deliveredst unto me five talents: behold, I have gained beside them five talents more.

21 His lord said unto him, Well done, *thou* good and faithful servant: thou hast been faithful over a few things, I will make thee ruler over many things: enter thou into the joy of thy lord.

22 He also that had received two talents came and said, Lord, thou deliveredst unto me two talents: behold, I have gained two other talents beside them.

23 His lord said unto him, Well done, good and faithful servant; thou hast been faithful over a few things, I will make thee ruler over many things: enter thou into the joy of thy lord.

24 Then he which had received the one talent came and said, Lord, I knew thee that thou art an hard man, reaping where

ἀπελθὼν　ὤρυξεν　γῆν　καὶ　ἔκρυψεν
going away　dug　earth　and　hid

τὸ　ἀργύριον　τοῦ　κυρίου　αὐτοῦ.
the　silver　of the　lord　of him.

19 μετὰ　δὲ　πολὺν　χρόνον　ἔρχεται　ὁ
Then after　much　time　comes　the

κύριος　τῶν　δούλων　ἐκείνων　καὶ　συναίρει
lord　–　slaves　of those　and　takes

λόγον　μετ'　αὐτῶν.　**20** καὶ　προσελθὼν
account　with　them.　And　approaching

ὁ　τὰ　πέντε　τάλαντα　λαβὼν　προσ-
the [one] the　five　talents　receiving　brought

ήνεγκεν　ἄλλα　πέντε　τάλαντα　λέγων·　κύριε,
other　five　talents　saying:　Lord,

πέντε　τάλαντά　μοι　παρέδωκας·　ἴδε　ἄλλα
five　talents　to me　thou deliveredst;　behold　other

πέντε　τάλαντα　ἐκέρδησα.　**21** ἔφη　αὐτῷ
five　talents　I gained.　Said　to him

ὁ　κύριος　αὐτοῦ·　εὖ,　δοῦλε　ἀγαθὲ　καὶ
the　lord　of him:　Well,　slave　good　and

πιστέ,　ἐπὶ　ὀλίγα　ἦς　πιστός,
faithful,　over　a few things　thou wast　faithful,

ἐπὶ　πολλῶν　σε　καταστήσω·　εἴσελθε
over　many　thee　I will set;　enter thou

εἰς　τὴν　χαρὰν　τοῦ　κυρίου　σου.　**22** προσ-
into　the　joy　of the　lord　of thee.　Ap-

ελθὼν　καὶ　ὁ　τὰ　δύο　τάλαντα
proaching　also　the [one]　the　two　talents
　　　　[having received]

εἶπεν·　κύριε,　δύο　τάλαντά　μοι
said:　Lord,　two　talents　to me

παρέδωκας·　ἴδε　ἄλλα　δύο　τάλαντα
thou deliveredst;　behold　other　two　talents

ἐκέρδησα.　**23** ἔφη　αὐτῷ　ὁ　κύριος　αὐτοῦ·
I gained.　Said　to him　the　lord　of him:

εὖ,　δοῦλε　ἀγαθὲ　καὶ　πιστέ,　ἐπὶ
Well,　slave　good　and　faithful,　over

ὀλίγα　ἦς　πιστός,　ἐπὶ　πολλῶν
a few things　thou wast　faithful,　over　many

σε　καταστήσω·　εἴσελθε　εἰς　τὴν
thee　I will set;　enter thou　into　the

χαρὰν　τοῦ　κυρίου　σου.　**24** προσ-
joy　of the　lord　of thee.　ap-

ελθὼν　δὲ　καὶ　ὁ　τὸ　ἓν　τάλαντον
proaching　And　also　the [one]　the　one　talent

εἰληφὼς　εἶπεν·　κύριε,　ἔγνων　σε
having received　said:　Lord,　I knew　thee

ὅτι　σκληρὸς　εἶ　ἄνθρωπος,　θερίζων
that　²a hard　¹thou art　³man,　reaping

thou hast not sown, and
gathering where thou hast
not strawed:

25 And I was afraid, and
went and hid thy talent in
the earth: lo, *there* thou
hast *that is* thine.

26 His lord answered
and said unto him, *Thou*
wicked and slothful ser-
vant, thou knewest that I
reap where I sowed not,
and gather where I have
not strawed:

27 Thou oughtest there-
fore to have put my money
to the exchangers, and *then*
at my coming I should have
received mine own with
usury.

28 Take therefore the
talent from him, and give *it*
unto him which hath ten
talents.

29 For unto every one
that hath shall be given,
and he shall have abun-
dance: but from him that
hath not shall be taken
away even that which he
hath.

30 And cast ye the un-
profitable servant into
outer darkness: there shall
be weeping and gnashing
of teeth.

31 ¶ When the Son of
man shall come in his
glory, and all the holy
angels with him, then shall
he sit upon the throne of
his glory:

32 And before him shall
be gathered all nations:

ὅπου   οὐκ   ἔσπειρας,   καὶ   συνάγων
where   Thou didst not sow,   and   gathering

ὅθεν   οὐ   διεσκόρπισας·   **25** καὶ   φοβηθεὶς
whence   thou didst not scatter;   and   fearing

ἀπελθὼν   ἔκρυψα   τὸ   τάλαντόν   σου
going away   I hid   the   talent   of thee

ἐν   τῇ   γῇ·   ἴδε   ἔχεις   τὸ   σόν.
in   the   earth; behold thou hast the   thine.

26 ἀποκριθεὶς   δὲ   ὁ   κύριος   αὐτοῦ   εἶπεν
And answering   the   lord   of him   said

αὐτῷ·   πονηρὲ   δοῦλε   καὶ   ὀκνηρέ,
to him: Evil   slave   and   slothful,

ᾔδεις   ὅτι   θερίζω   ὅπου   οὐκ   ἔσπειρα,
thou knewest that   I reap   where   I sowed not,

καὶ   συνάγω   ὅθεν   οὐ   διεσκόρπισα;
and   I gather   whence   I did not scatter?

27 ἔδει   σε   οὖν   βαλεῖν   τὰ   ἀργύριά
it behoved   thee   therefore   to put   the   silver pieces

μου   τοῖς   τραπεζίταις,   καὶ   ἐλθὼν   ἐγὼ
of me   to the   bankers,   and   coming   I

ἐκομισάμην   ἂν   τὸ   ἐμὸν   σὺν   τόκῳ.
would have received   the   mine   with   interest.

28 ἄρατε   οὖν   ἀπ’   αὐτοῦ   τὸ   τάλαντον
Take   therefore   from   him   the   talent

καὶ   δότε   τῷ   ἔχοντι   τὰ   δέκα   τάλαντα·
and   give   to the [one] having   the   ten   talents;

29 τῷ   γὰρ   ἔχοντι   παντὶ   δοθήσεται   καὶ
for to   having   everyone   will be given   and

περισσευθήσεται·   τοῦ   δὲ   μὴ   ἔχοντος
he will have abundance;   but from the [one]   not   having

καὶ   ὃ   ἔχει   ἀρθήσεται   ἀπ’   αὐτοῦ.
even   what   he has   will be taken   from   him.

30 καὶ   τὸν   ἀχρεῖον   δοῦλον   ἐκβάλετε   εἰς
And   the   useless   slave   cast ye out   into

τὸ   σκότος   τὸ   ἐξώτερον·   ἐκεῖ   ἔσται   ὁ
the   darkness   -   outer;   there   will be   the

κλαυθμὸς   καὶ   ὁ   βρυγμὸς   τῶν   ὀδόντων
wailing   and   the   gnashing   of the   teeth.

31 Ὅταν   δὲ   ἔλθῃ   ὁ   υἱὸς   τοῦ   ἀνθρώπου
And when   comes   the   Son   -   of man

ἐν   τῇ   δόξῃ   αὐτοῦ   καὶ   πάντες   οἱ   ἄγγελοι
in   the   glory   of him   and   all   the   angels

μετ’   αὐτοῦ,   τότε   καθίσει   ἐπὶ   θρόνου
with   him,   then   he will sit   on   a throne

δόξης   αὐτοῦ·   **32** καὶ   συναχθήσονται
of glory   of him;   and   will be assembled

ἔμπροσθεν   αὐτοῦ   πάντα   τὰ   ἔθνη,   καὶ
before   him   all   the   nations,   and

and he shall separate them one from another, as a shepherd divideth *his* sheep from the goats:

33 And he shall set the sheep on his right hand, but the goats on the left.

34 Then shall the King say unto them on his right hand, Come, ye blessed of my Father, inherit the kingdom prepared for you from the foundation of the world:

35 For I was an hungred, and ye gave me meat: I was thirsty, and ye gave me drink: I was a stranger, and ye took me in:

36 Naked, and ye clothed me: I was sick, and ye visited me: I was in prison, and ye came unto me.

37 Then shall the righteous answer him, saying, Lord, when saw we thee an hungred, and fed *thee*? or thirsty, and gave *thee* drink?

38 When saw we thee a stranger, and took *thee* in? or naked, and clothed *thee*?

39 Or when saw we thee sick, or in prison, and came unto thee?

40 And the King shall answer and say unto them, Verily I say unto you, Inasmuch as ye have done *it* unto one of the least of

ἀφορίσει αὐτοὺς ἀπ᾽ ἀλλήλων, ὥσπερ
he will separate them from one another, as

ὁ ποιμὴν ἀφορίζει τὰ πρόβατα ἀπὸ
the shepherd separates the sheep from

τῶν ἐρίφων, 33 καὶ στήσει τὰ μὲν
the goats, and will set the –

πρόβατα ἐκ δεξιῶν αὐτοῦ, τὰ δὲ ἐρίφια
sheep on [the] right of him, but the goats

ἐξ εὐωνύμων. 34 τότε ἐρεῖ ὁ
on [the] left. Then will say the

βασιλεὺς τοῖς ἐκ δεξιῶν αὐτοῦ·
king to the [ones] on [the] right of him:

δεῦτε οἱ εὐλογημένοι τοῦ πατρός μου,
Come the [ones] blessed of the Father of me,

κληρονομήσατε τὴν ἡτοιμασμένην ὑμῖν
inherit ye the ²having been prepared ³for you

βασιλείαν ἀπὸ καταβολῆς κόσμου.
¹kingdom from [the] foundation of [the] world.

35 ἐπείνασα γὰρ καὶ ἐδώκατέ μοι
For I hungered and ye gave me

φαγεῖν, ἐδίψησα καὶ ἐποτίσατέ με,
to eat, I thirsted and ye gave ²drink ¹me,

ξένος ἤμην καὶ συνηγάγετέ με,
a stranger I was and ye entertained me,

36 γυμνὸς καὶ περιεβάλετέ με, ἠσθένησα
naked and ye clothed me, I ailed

καὶ ἐπεσκέψασθέ με, ἐν φυλακῇ ἤμην
and ye visited me, in prison I was

καὶ ἤλθατε πρός με. 37 τότε ἀποκριθή-
and ye came to me. Then will

σονται αὐτῷ οἱ δίκαιοι λέγοντες· κύριε,
answer him the righteous saying: Lord,

πότε σε εἴδομεν πεινῶντα καὶ ἐθρέψαμεν,
when thee saw we hungering and fed,

ἢ διψῶντα καὶ ἐποτίσαμεν; 38 πότε δέ
or thirsting and gave drink? and when

σε εἴδομεν ξένον καὶ συνηγάγομεν,
thee saw we a stranger and entertained,

ἢ γυμνὸν καὶ περιεβάλομεν; 39 πότε δέ
or naked and clothed? and when

σε εἴδομεν ἀσθενοῦντα ἢ ἐν φυλακῇ καὶ
thee saw we ailing or in prison and

ἤλθομεν πρός σέ; 40 καὶ ἀποκριθεὶς ὁ
came to thee? And answering the

βασιλεὺς ἐρεῖ αὐτοῖς· ἀμὴν λέγω
king will say to them: Truly I tell

ὑμῖν, ἐφ᾽ ὅσον ἐποιήσατε ἑνὶ τούτων
you, inasmuch as ye did to one of these

these my brethren, ye
have done it unto me.

41 Then shall he say also
unto them on the left hand,
Depart from me, ye cursed,
into everlasting fire, prepared for the devil and his
angels:

42 For I was an hun-
gred, and ye gave me no
meat: I was thirsty, and ye
gave me no drink:

43 I was a stranger, and
ye took me not in: naked,
and ye clothed me not:
sick, and in prison, and ye
visited me not.

44 Then shall they also
answer him, saying, Lord,
when saw we thee an
hungred, or athirst, or a
stranger, or naked, or sick,
or in prison, and did not
minister unto thee?

45 Then shall he answer
them, saying, Verily I say
unto you, Inasmuch as ye
did it not to one of the least
of these, ye did it not to me.

46 And these shall go
away into everlasting
punishment: but the righteous into life eternal.

τῶν   ἀδελφῶν   μου   τῶν   ἐλαχίστων,   ἐμοὶ
  –   brothers   of me   the   least,   to me

ἐποιήσατε.   **41** τότε   ἐρεῖ   καὶ   τοῖς   ἐξ
ye did.   Then   he will say also to the [ones] on

εὐωνύμων·   πορεύεσθε   ἀπ'   ἐμοῦ   κατ-
[the] left: Go   from   me   having been

ηραμένοι   εἰς   τὸ   πῦρ   τὸ   αἰώνιον
cursed [ones]   into   the   fire   –   eternal

τὸ   ἡτοιμασμένον   τῷ   διαβόλῳ   καὶ   τοῖς
 – having been prepared for the devil   and   the

ἀγγέλοις   αὐτοῦ.   **42** ἐπείνασα   γὰρ   καὶ
angels   of him.   For I hungered and

οὐκ   ἐδώκατέ   μοι   φαγεῖν,   ἐδίψησα
ye gave not   me   to eat,   I thirsted

καὶ   οὐκ   ἐποτίσατέ   με,   **43** ξένος
and   ye ¹gave ²not ⁴drink   ²me,   a stranger

ἤμην   καὶ   οὐ   συνηγάγετέ   με,   γυμνὸς
I was and   ye entertained not   me,   naked

καὶ   οὐ   περιεβάλετέ   με,   ἀσθενὴς   καὶ   ἐν
and   ye clothed not   me,   ill   and   in

φυλακῇ   καὶ   οὐκ   ἐπεσκέψασθέ   με.   **44** τότε
prison   and   ye visited not   me.   Then

ἀποκριθήσονται   καὶ   αὐτοὶ   λέγοντες·   κύριε,
will answer   also   they   saying: Lord,

πότε   σε   εἴδομεν   πεινῶντα   ἢ   διψῶντα   ἢ
when thee saw we   hungering or thirsting or

ξένον   ἢ   γυμνὸν   ἢ   ἀσθενῆ   ἢ   ἐν   φυλακῇ
a stranger or naked or   ill   or in   prison

καὶ   οὐ   διηκονήσαμέν   σοι;   **45** τότε
and   did not minister to thee?   Then

ἀποκριθήσεται   αὐτοῖς   λέγων·   ἀμὴν   λέγω
he will answer   them   saying: Truly   I tell

ὑμῖν,   ἐφ'   ὅσον   οὐκ   ἐποιήσατε   ἑνὶ
you,   inasmuch as   ye did not   to one

τούτων   τῶν   ἐλαχίστων,   οὐδὲ   ἐμοὶ
of these   –   least [ones],   neither   to me

ἐποιήσατε.   **46** καὶ   ἀπελεύσονται   οὗτοι   εἰς
ye did.   And   will go away   these   into

κόλασιν   αἰώνιον,   οἱ   δὲ   δίκαιοι   εἰς
punishment eternal,   but the   righteous   into

ζωὴν   αἰώνιον.
life   eternal.

CHAPTER 26

AND it came to pass, when Jesus had finished all these sayings, he said unto his disciples,

2 Ye know that after two days is *the feast of* the passover, and the Son of man is betrayed to be crucified.

3 ¶ Then assembled together the chief priests, and the scribes, and the elders of the people, unto the palace of the high priest, who was called Caiaphas,

4 And consulted that they might take Jesus by subtilty, and kill *him*.

5 But they said, Not on the feast *day*, lest there be an uproar among the people.

6 ¶ Now when Jesus was in Bethany, in the house of Simon the leper,

7 There came unto him a woman having an alabaster box of very precious ointment, and poured it on his head, as he sat *at meat*.

8 But when his disciples saw *it*, they had indignation, saying, To what purpose *is* this waste?

9 For this ointment might have been sold for much, and given to the poor.

10 When Jesus understood *it*, he said unto them, Why trouble ye the woman? for she hath wrought a good work upon me.

---

26 Καὶ ἐγένετο ὅτε ἐτέλεσεν ὁ
And   it came to pass when ended   -

'Ιησοῦς πάντας τοὺς λόγους τούτους,
Jesus   all   words   these,

εἶπεν τοῖς μαθηταῖς αὐτοῦ· 2 οἴδατε
he said to the disciples of him: Ye know

ὅτι μετὰ δύο ἡμέρας τὸ πάσχα γίνεται,
that after two days the passover occurs,

καὶ ὁ υἱὸς τοῦ ἀνθρώπου παραδίδοται εἰς
and the Son - of man is delivered -

τὸ σταυρωθῆναι. 3 Τότε συνήχθησαν οἱ
- to be crucified. Then were assembled the

ἀρχιερεῖς καὶ οἱ πρεσβύτεροι τοῦ λαοῦ
chief priests and the elders of the people

εἰς τὴν αὐλὴν τοῦ ἀρχιερέως τοῦ
in the court of the high priest -

λεγομένου Καϊαφᾶ, 4 καὶ συνεβουλεύ-
named   Caiaphas, and con-

σαντο ἵνα τὸν 'Ιησοῦν δόλῳ κρατή-
sulted that - Jesus by guile they might

σωσιν καὶ ἀποκτείνωσιν· 5 ἔλεγον δέ·
seize and might kill; but they said:

μὴ ἐν τῇ ἑορτῇ, ἵνα μὴ θόρυβος
Not at the feast, lest a disturbance

γένηται ἐν τῷ λαῷ.
occurs among the people.

6 Τοῦ δὲ 'Ιησοῦ γενομένου ἐν Βηθανίᾳ
- And Jesus being[a] in Bethany
              = when Jesus was

ἐν οἰκίᾳ Σίμωνος τοῦ λεπροῦ,
in [the] house of Simon the leper,

7 προσῆλθεν αὐτῷ γυνὴ ἔχουσα ἀλάβαστρον
approached *to* him a woman having an alabaster phial

μύρου βαρυτίμου καὶ κατέχεεν ἐπὶ
of ointment very expensive and poured [it] on

τῆς κεφαλῆς αὐτοῦ ἀνακειμένου. 8 ἰδόντες
the head of him reclining. And see-

δὲ οἱ μαθηταὶ ἠγανάκτησαν λέγοντες·
ing the disciples were angry saying:

εἰς τί ἡ ἀπώλεια αὕτη; 9 ἐδύνατο γὰρ
To what - waste this? for could

τοῦτο πραθῆναι πολλοῦ καὶ δοθῆναι
this *to* be sold of(for) much and *to* be given

πτωχοῖς. 10 γνοὺς δὲ ὁ 'Ιησοῦς εἶπεν
to poor. And knowing - Jesus said

αὐτοῖς· τί κόπους παρέχετε τῇ γυναικί;
to them: Why trouble ye the woman?

ἔργον γὰρ καλὸν ἠργάσατο εἰς ἐμέ·
for work a good she wrought to me;

11 For ye have the poor always with you; but me ye have not always.

12 For in that she hath poured this ointment on my body, she did it for my burial.

13 Verily I say unto you, Wheresoever this gospel shall be preached in the whole world, there shall also this, that this woman hath done, be told for a memorial of her.

14 ¶ Then one of the twelve, called Judas Iscariot, went unto the chief priests,

15 And said unto them, What will ye give me, and I will deliver him unto you? And they covenanted with him for thirty pieces of silver.

16 And from that time he sought opportunity to betray him.

17 ¶ Now the first day of the feast of unleavened bread the disciples came to Jesus, saying unto him, Where wilt thou that we prepare for thee to eat the passover?

18 And he said, Go into the city to such a man, and say unto him, The Master saith, My time is at hand; I will keep the passover at thy house with my disciples.

19 And the disciples did

---

11 πάντοτε γὰρ τοὺς πτωχοὺς ἔχετε μεθ'
for always the poor ye have with

ἑαυτῶν, ἐμὲ δὲ οὐ πάντοτε ἔχετε·
yourselves, but me not always ye have;

12 βαλοῦσα γὰρ αὕτη τὸ μύρον τοῦτο
for ²putting ¹this woman – ⁴ointment ³this

ἐπὶ τοῦ σώματός μου πρὸς τὸ ἐνταφιάσαι
on the body of me for – to bury

με ἐποίησεν. 13 ἀμὴν λέγω ὑμῖν, ὅπου
me she did. Truly I tell you, wher-

ἐὰν κηρυχθῇ τὸ εὐαγγέλιον τοῦτο ἐν
ever is proclaimed – gospel this in

ὅλῳ τῷ κόσμῳ, λαληθήσεται καὶ ὃ
all the world, will be spoken also what

ἐποίησεν αὕτη εἰς μνημόσυνον αὐτῆς.
did this woman for a memorial of her.

14 Τότε πορευθεὶς εἰς τῶν δώδεκα, ὁ
Then going one of the twelve, the [one]

λεγόμενος Ἰούδας Ἰσκαριώτης, πρὸς
named Judas Iscariot, to

τοὺς ἀρχιερεῖς 15 εἶπεν· τί θέλετέ μοι
the chief priests he said: What are ye willing me

δοῦναι, κἀγὼ ὑμῖν παραδώσω αὐτόν;
to give, and I to you will deliver him?

οἱ δὲ ἔστησαν αὐτῷ τριάκοντα ἀργύρια.
And they weighed him thirty pieces of silver.

16 καὶ ἀπὸ τότε ἐζήτει εὐκαιρίαν ἵνα
And from then he sought opportunity that

αὐτὸν παραδῷ.
him he might deliver.

17 Τῇ δὲ πρώτῃ τῶν ἀζύμων
Now on the first [day] – of unleavened bread

προσῆλθον οἱ μαθηταὶ τῷ Ἰησοῦ
approached the disciples – to Jesus

λέγοντες· ποῦ θέλεις ἑτοιμάσωμέν
saying: Where willest thou we may prepare

σοι φαγεῖν τὸ πάσχα; 18 ὁ δὲ
for thee to eat the passover? So he

εἶπεν· ὑπάγετε εἰς τὴν πόλιν πρὸς
said: Go ye into the city to

τὸν δεῖνα καὶ εἴπατε αὐτῷ· ὁ
such a one and say to him: The

διδάσκαλος λέγει· ὁ καιρός μου
teacher says: The time of me

ἐγγύς ἐστιν· πρὸς σὲ ποιῶ τὸ πάσχα
near is; with thee I make the passover

μετὰ τῶν μαθητῶν μου. 19 καὶ ἐποίησαν
with the disciples of me. And did

as Jesus had appointed them; and they made ready the passover.

20 ¶ Now when the even was come, he sat down with the twelve.

21 And as they did eat, he said, Verily I say unto you, that one of you shall betray me.

22 And they were exceeding sorrowful, and began every one of them to say unto him, Lord, is it I?

23 And he answered and said, He that dippeth *his* hand with me in the dish, the same shall betray me.

24 The Son of man goeth as it is written of him: but woe unto that man by whom the Son of man is betrayed! it had been good for that man if he had not been born.

25 Then Judas, which betrayed him, answered and said, Master, is it I? He said unto him, Thou hast said.

26 ¶ And as they were eating, Jesus took bread, and blessed *it*, and brake *it*, and gave *it* to the disciples, and said, Take, eat; this is my body.

27 And he took the cup, and gave thanks, and gave

οἱ   μαθηταὶ   ὡς   συνέταξεν   αὐτοῖς   ὁ
the   disciples   as   enjoined   them   -

᾽Ιησοῦς,   καὶ   ἡτοίμασαν   τὸ   πάσχα.   20 ᾽Οψίας
Jesus,   and   prepared   the   passover.   evening

δὲ   γενομένης   ἀνέκειτο   μετὰ   τῶν   δώδεκα
And   coming*   he reclined   with   the   twelve
= when evening came

[μαθητῶν].   21 καὶ   ἐσθιόντων   αὐτῶν   εἶπεν·
disciples.   And   eating*   he said:
= as they were eating

ἀμὴν   λέγω   ὑμῖν   ὅτι   εἷς   ἐξ   ὑμῶν   παρα-
Truly   I tell   you   that   one   of   you   will

δώσει   με.   22 καὶ   λυπούμενοι   σφόδρα
betray   me.   And   grieving   exceedingly

ἤρξαντο   λέγειν   αὐτῷ   εἷς   ἕκαστος·
they began   to say   to him   ²one   ¹each:

μήτι   ἐγώ   εἰμι,   κύριε;   23 ὁ   δὲ   ἀποκριθεὶς
Not   I   am,   Lord?   And he   answering
= It is not I,

εἶπεν·   ὁ   ἐμβάψας   μετ᾽   ἐμοῦ   τὴν
said: The [one]   dipping   with   me   the(his)

χεῖρα   ἐν   τῷ   τρυβλίῳ,   οὗτός   με   παρα-
hand   in   the   dish,   this man   me   will

δώσει.   24 ὁ   μὲν   υἱὸς   τοῦ   ἀνθρώπου
betray.   Indeed the   Son   -   of man

ὑπάγει   καθὼς   γέγραπται   περὶ   αὐτοῦ,
goes   as   it has been written   concerning   him,

οὐαὶ   δὲ   τῷ   ἀνθρώπῳ   ἐκείνῳ   δι᾽
but woe   -   man   to that   through

οὗ   ὁ   υἱὸς   τοῦ   ἀνθρώπου   παραδίδοται·
whom the   Son   -   of man   is betrayed;

καλὸν   ἦν   αὐτῷ   εἰ   οὐκ   ἐγεννήθη
good   were it   for him   if   was not born

ὁ   ἄνθρωπος   ἐκεῖνος.   25 ἀποκριθεὶς   δὲ
-   man   that.   And answering

᾽Ιούδας   ὁ   παραδιδοὺς   αὐτὸν   εἶπεν·
Judas   the [one]   betraying   him   said:

μήτι   ἐγώ   εἰμι,   ῥαββί;   λέγει   αὐτῷ·
Not   I   am,   rabbi?   He says   to him:
= It is not I,

σὺ   εἶπας.   26 ᾽Εσθιόντων   δὲ   αὐτῶν
Thou   saidst.   And eating   them*
= as they were eating

λαβὼν   ὁ   ᾽Ιησοῦς   ἄρτον   καὶ   εὐλογήσας
taking   -   Jesus   a loaf   and   blessing

ἔκλασεν   καὶ   δοὺς   τοῖς   μαθηταῖς   εἶπεν·
he broke   and   giving   to the   disciples   said:

λάβετε   φάγετε·   τοῦτό   ἐστιν   τὸ   σῶμά
Take ye[,]   eat ye: this   is   the   body

μου.   27 καὶ   λαβὼν   ποτήριον   καὶ   εὐχαρι-
of me.   And   taking   a cup   and   giving

it to them, saying, Drink ye all of it;

28 For this is my blood of the new testament, which is shed for many for the remission of sins.

29 But I say unto you, I will not drink henceforth of this fruit of the vine, until that day when I drink it new with you in my Father's kingdom.

30 ¶ And when they had sung an hymn, they went out into the mount of Olives.

31 Then saith Jesus unto them, All ye shall be offended because of me this night: for it is written, I will smite the shepherd, and the sheep of the flock shall be scattered abroad.

32 But after I am risen again, I will go before you into Galilee.

33 Peter answered and said unto him, Though all *men* shall be offended because of thee, *yet* will I never be offended.

34 Jesus said unto him, Verily I say unto thee, That this night, before the cock crow, thou shalt deny me thrice.

35 Peter said unto him, Though I should die with thee, yet will I not deny

---

στήσας ἔδωκεν αὐτοῖς λέγων· πίετε ἐξ
thanks he gave to them saying: Drink ye of

αὐτοῦ πάντες· 28 τοῦτο γάρ ἐστιν τὸ
it all; for this is the

αἷμά μου τῆς διαθήκης τὸ περὶ πολλῶν
blood of me of the covenant the [blood] concerning many

ἐκχυννόμενον εἰς ἄφεσιν ἁμαρτιῶν. 29 λέγω
being shed for forgiveness of sins. I tell

δὲ ὑμῖν, οὐ μὴ πίω ἀπ' ἄρτι ἐκ
And you, by no means will I drink from now of

τούτου τοῦ γενήματος τῆς ἀμπέλου ἕως
this - fruit of the vine until

τῆς ἡμέρας ἐκείνης ὅταν αὐτὸ πίνω μεθ'
- day that when it I drink with

ὑμῶν καινὸν ἐν τῇ βασιλείᾳ τοῦ πατρός
you new in the kingdom of the Father

μου.
of me.

30 Καὶ ὑμνήσαντες ἐξῆλθον εἰς τὸ
And having sung a hymn they went forth to the

ὄρος τῶν ἐλαιῶν. 31 Τότε λέγει αὐτοῖς ὁ
mount of the olives. Then says to them -

Ἰησοῦς· πάντες ὑμεῖς σκανδαλισθήσεσθε
Jesus: All ye will be offended

ἐν ἐμοὶ ἐν τῇ νυκτὶ ταύτῃ· γέγραπται
in me in the to-night; it has been written

γάρ· πατάξω τὸν ποιμένα, καὶ δια-
for: I will strike the shepherd, and will

σκορπισθήσονται τὰ πρόβατα τῆς ποίμνης·
be scattered the sheep of the flock;

32 μετὰ δὲ τὸ ἐγερθῆναί με προάξω
but after the to be raised me[b] I will go before
              =I am raised

ὑμᾶς εἰς τὴν Γαλιλαίαν. 33 ἀποκριθεὶς
you to - Galilee. answering

δὲ ὁ Πέτρος εἶπεν αὐτῷ· εἰ πάντες
And - Peter said to him: If all men

σκανδαλισθήσονται ἐν σοί, ἐγὼ οὐδέποτε
shall be offended in thee, I never

σκανδαλισθήσομαι. 34 ἔφη αὐτῷ ὁ Ἰησοῦς·
will be offended. Said to him - Jesus:

ἀμὴν λέγω σοι ὅτι ἐν ταύτῃ τῇ νυκτὶ
Truly I tell thee that to-night

πρὶν ἀλέκτορα φωνῆσαι τρὶς ἀπαρνήσῃ
before a cock to crow[b] three times thou wilt deny

με. 35 λέγει αὐτῷ ὁ Πέτρος· κἂν
me. Says to him — Peter: Even if

δέῃ με σὺν σοὶ ἀποθανεῖν, οὐ μή σε
it behoves me with thee to die, by no means thee
=I must die with thee,

thee. Likewise also said all the disciples.

36 ¶ Then cometh Jesus with them unto a place called Gethsemane, and saith unto the disciples, Sit ye here, while I go and pray yonder.

37 And he took with him Peter and the two sons of Zebedee, and began to be sorrowful and very heavy.

38 Then saith he unto them, My soul is exceeding sorrowful, even unto death: tarry ye here, and watch with me.

39 And he went a little farther, and fell on his face, and prayed, saying, O my Father, if it be possible, let this cup pass from me: nevertheless not as I will, but as thou *wilt*.

40 And he cometh unto the disciples, and findeth them asleep, and saith unto Peter, What, could ye not watch with me one hour?

41 Watch and pray, that ye enter not into temptation: the spirit indeed *is* willing, but the flesh *is* weak.

42 He went away again the second time, and prayed, saying, O my

ἀπαρνήσομαι.   ὁμοίως   καὶ   πάντες   οἱ
I will deny.   Likewise   also   all   the

μαθηταὶ   εἶπαν.
disciples   said.

36 Τότε   ἔρχεται   μετ᾽   αὐτῶν   ὁ   Ἰησοῦς
Then   comes   with   them   -   Jesus

εἰς   χωρίον   λεγόμενον   Γεθσημανί,   καὶ   λέγει
to a piece of land   called   Gethsemane,   and   says

τοῖς   μαθηταῖς·   καθίσατε   αὐτοῦ   ἕως   οὗ
to the   disciples: Sit ye   here   until

ἀπελθὼν   ἐκεῖ   προσεύξωμαι.   37 καὶ   παρα-
going away   there   I may pray.   And   tak-

λαβὼν   τὸν   Πέτρον   καὶ   τοὺς   δύο   υἱοὺς
ing   -   Peter   and   the   two   sons

Ζεβεδαίου   ἤρξατο   λυπεῖσθαι   καὶ   ἀδημονεῖν.
of Zebedee   he began   to grieve   and to be distressed.

38 τότε   λέγει   αὐτοῖς·   περίλυπός   ἐστιν
Then   he says   to them: Deeply grieved   is

ἡ   ψυχή   μου   ἕως   θανάτου·   μείνατε
the   soul   of me   unto   death;   remain ye

ὧδε   καὶ   γρηγορεῖτε   μετ᾽   ἐμοῦ.   39 καὶ
here   and   watch ye   with   me.   And

προελθὼν   μικρὸν   ἔπεσεν   ἐπὶ   πρόσωπον
going forward   a little   he fell   on   [the] face

αὐτοῦ   προσευχόμενος   καὶ   λέγων·   πάτερ
of him   praying   and   saying: Father

μου,   εἰ   δυνατόν   ἐστιν,   παρελθάτω   ἀπ᾽
of me,   if   possible   it is,   let pass   from

ἐμοῦ   τὸ   ποτήριον   τοῦτο·   πλὴν   οὐχ
me   the   cup   this;   yet   not

ὡς   ἐγὼ   θέλω   ἀλλ᾽   ὡς   σύ.   40 καὶ
as   I   will   but   as   thou.   And

ἔρχεται   πρὸς   τοὺς   μαθητὰς   καὶ   εὑρίσκει
he comes   to   the   disciples   and   finds

αὐτοὺς   καθεύδοντας,   καὶ   λέγει   τῷ   Πέτρῳ·
them   sleeping,   and   says   -   to Peter:

οὕτως   οὐκ   ἰσχύσατε   μίαν   ὥραν
So   were ye not able   one   hour

γρηγορῆσαι   μετ᾽   ἐμοῦ;   41 γρηγορεῖτε   καὶ
to watch   with   me?   Watch ye   and

προσεύχεσθε,   ἵνα   μὴ   εἰσέλθητε   εἰς
pray,   lest   ye enter   into

πειρασμόν·   τὸ   μὲν   πνεῦμα   πρόθυμον,
temptation;   indeed the   spirit   [is] eager,

ἡ   δὲ   σὰρξ   ἀσθενής.   42 πάλιν   ἐκ
but the   flesh   weak.   Again   -

δευτέρου   ἀπελθὼν   προσηύξατο   λέγων·
second [time]   going away   he prayed   saying:

Father, if this cup may not pass away from me, except I drink it, thy will be done.

43 And he came and found them asleep again: for their eyes were heavy.

44 And he left them, and went away again, and prayed the third time, saying the same words.

45 Then cometh he to his disciples, and saith unto them, Sleep on now, and take your rest: behold, the hour is at hand, and the Son of man is betrayed into the hands of sinners.

46 Rise, let us be going: behold, he is at hand that doth betray me.

47 ¶ And while he yet spake, lo, Judas, one of the twelve, came, and with him a great multitude with swords and staves, from the chief priests and elders of the people.

48 Now he that betrayed him gave them a sign, saying, Whomsoever I shall kiss, that same is he: hold him fast.

49 And forthwith he came to Jesus, and said, Hail, master; and kissed him.

50 And Jesus said unto him, Friend, wherefore art thou come? Then came

---

πάτερ μου, εἰ οὐ δύναται τοῦτο παρελθεῖν
Father of me, if cannot this to pass away

ἐὰν μὴ αὐτὸ πίω, γενηθήτω τὸ θέλημά
except it I drink, let be done the will

σου. **43** καὶ ἐλθὼν πάλιν εὗρεν αὐτοὺς
of thee. And coming again he found them

καθεύδοντας, ἦσαν γὰρ αὐτῶν οἱ ὀφθαλμοὶ
sleeping, for were of them the eyes

βεβαρημένοι. **44** καὶ ἀφεὶς αὐτοὺς πάλιν
having been burdened. And leaving them again

ἀπελθὼν προσηύξατο ἐκ τρίτου, τὸν
going away he prayed a third [time], the

αὐτὸν λόγον εἰπὼν πάλιν. **45** τότε ἔρχεται
same word saying again. Then he comes

πρὸς τοὺς μαθητὰς καὶ λέγει αὐτοῖς·
to the disciples and says to them:

καθεύδετε λοιπὸν καὶ ἀναπαύεσθε·
Sleep ye now and rest;

ἰδοὺ ἤγγικεν ἡ ὥρα καὶ ὁ υἱὸς τοῦ
behold has drawn near the hour and the Son

ἀνθρώπου παραδίδοται εἰς χεῖρας
of man is betrayed into [the] hands

ἁμαρτωλῶν. **46** ἐγείρεσθε, ἄγωμεν· ἰδοὺ
of sinners. Rise ye, let us be going; behold

ἤγγικεν ὁ παραδιδούς με.
has drawn near the [one] betraying me.

47 Καὶ ἔτι αὐτοῦ λαλοῦντος, ἰδοὺ
And still him speaking,[a] behold
= while he was still speaking,

Ἰούδας εἷς τῶν δώδεκα ἦλθεν, καὶ μετ᾽
Judas one of the twelve came, and with

αὐτοῦ ὄχλος πολὺς μετὰ μαχαιρῶν καὶ
him crowd a much with swords and

ξύλων ἀπὸ τῶν ἀρχιερέων καὶ πρεσβυτέρων
clubs from the chief priests and elders

τοῦ λαοῦ. **48** ὁ δὲ παραδιδοὺς αὐτὸν ἔδωκεν
of the people. Now the [one] betraying him gave

αὐτοῖς σημεῖον λέγων· ὃν ἂν φιλήσω
them a sign saying: Whomever I may kiss

αὐτός ἐστιν· κρατήσατε αὐτόν. **49** καὶ
he it is; seize ye him. And

εὐθέως προσελθὼν τῷ Ἰησοῦ εἶπεν· χαῖρε,
immediately approaching – to Jesus he said: Hail,

ῥαββί, καὶ κατεφίλησεν αὐτόν. **50** ὁ
rabbi, and affectionately kissed him. -

δὲ Ἰησοῦς εἶπεν αὐτῷ· ἑταῖρε,
But Jesus said to him: Comrade, [do that]

ἐφ᾽ ὃ πάρει. τότε προσελθόντες ἐπέβαλον
on what thou art here. Then approaching they laid *on*

they, and laid hands on Jesus, and took him.

τὰς χεῖρας ἐπὶ τὸν Ἰησοῦν καὶ ἐκράτησαν
the(ir) hands on - Jesus and seized

51 And, behold, one of them which were with Jesus stretched out *his* hand, and drew his sword, and struck a servant of the high priest's, and smote off his ear.

αὐτόν. **51** καὶ ἰδοὺ εἷς τῶν μετὰ
him. And behold one of the [ones] with

Ἰησοῦ ἐκτείνας τὴν χεῖρα ἀπέσπασεν
Jesus stretching out the(his) hand drew

τὴν μάχαιραν αὐτοῦ, καὶ πατάξας τὸν
the sword of him, and striking the

52 Then said Jesus unto him, Put up again thy sword into his place: for all they that take the sword shall perish with the sword.

δοῦλος τοῦ ἀρχιερέως ἀφεῖλεν αὐτοῦ τὸ
slave of the high priest cut off of him the

ὠτίον. **52** τότε λέγει αὐτῷ ὁ Ἰησοῦς·
ear. Then says to him - Jesus:

ἀπόστρεψον τὴν μάχαιράν σου εἰς τὸν
Put back the sword of thee into the

τόπον αὐτῆς· πάντες γὰρ οἱ λαβόντες
place of it; for all the [ones] taking

53 Thinkest thou that I cannot now pray to my Father, and he shall presently give me more than twelve legions of angels?

μάχαιραν ἐν μαχαίρῃ ἀπολοῦνται. **53** ἢ
a sword by a sword will perish. Or

δοκεῖς ὅτι οὐ δύναμαι παρακαλέσαι
thinkest thou that I cannot *to ask*

54 But how then shall the scriptures be fulfilled, that thus it must be?

τὸν πατέρα μου, καὶ παραστήσει μοι
the Father of me, and he will provide me

ἄρτι πλείω δώδεκα λεγιῶνας ἀγγέλων;
now more [than] twelve legions of angels?

55 In that same hour said Jesus to the multitudes, Are ye come out as against a thief with swords and staves for to take me? I sat daily with you teaching in the temple, and ye laid no hold on me.

54 πῶς οὖν πληρωθῶσιν αἱ γραφαὶ ὅτι
how then may be fulfilled the scriptures that

οὕτως δεῖ γενέσθαι; **55** Ἐν ἐκείνῃ τῇ ὥρᾳ
thus it must be? In that - hour

εἶπεν ὁ Ἰησοῦς τοῖς ὄχλοις· ὡς ἐπὶ
said - Jesus to the crowds: As against

λῃστὴν ἐξήλθατε μετὰ μαχαιρῶν καὶ
a robber came ye forth with swords and

56 But all this was done, that the scriptures of the prophets might be fulfilled. Then all the disciples forsook him, and fled.

ξύλων συλλαβεῖν με; καθ' ἡμέραν ἐν
clubs to take me? daily in

τῷ ἱερῷ ἐκαθεζόμην διδάσκων, καὶ οὐκ
the temple I sat teaching, and not

ἐκρατήσατέ με. **56** τοῦτο δὲ ὅλον
ye seized me. But this all

57 ¶ And they that had laid hold on Jesus led *him* away to Caiaphas the high priest, where the scribes

γέγονεν ἵνα πληρωθῶσιν αἱ γραφαὶ
has come to pass that may be fulfilled the scriptures

τῶν προφητῶν. Τότε οἱ μαθηταὶ πάντες
of the prophets. Then the disciples all

ἀφέντες αὐτὸν ἔφυγον.
leaving him fled.

57 Οἱ δὲ κρατήσαντες τὸν Ἰησοῦν
But the [ones] having seized - Jesus

ἀπήγαγον πρὸς Καϊαφᾶν τὸν ἀρχιερέα,
led [him] away to Caiaphas the high priest,

and the elders were assembled.

58 But Peter followed him afar off unto the high priest's palace, and went in, and sat with the servants, to see the end.

59 Now the chief priests, and elders, and all the council, sought false witness against Jesus, to put him to death;

60 But found none: yea, though many false witnesses came, *yet* found they none. At the last came two false witnesses,

61 And said, This *fellow* said, I am able to destroy the temple of God, and to build it in three days.

62 And the high priest arose, and said unto him, Answerest thou nothing? what *is it which* these witness against thee?

63 But Jesus held his peace. And the high priest answered and said unto him, I adjure thee by the living God, that thou tell us whether thou be the Christ, the Son of God.

64 Jesus saith unto him, Thou hast said: nevertheless I say unto you, Hereafter shall ye see the Son of man sitting on the right hand of power, and coming in the clouds of heaven.

ὅπου οἱ γραμματεῖς καὶ οἱ πρεσβύτεροι
where the scribes and the elders
συνήχθησαν. **58** ὁ δὲ Πέτρος ἠκολούθει
were assembled. – And Peter followed
αὐτῷ [ἀπὸ] μακρόθεν ἕως τῆς αὐλῆς
him from afar up to the court
τοῦ ἀρχιερέως, καὶ εἰσελθὼν ἔσω ἐκάθητο
of the high priest, and entering within sat
μετὰ τῶν ὑπηρετῶν ἰδεῖν τὸ τέλος.
with the attendants to see the end.
59 Οἱ δὲ ἀρχιερεῖς καὶ τὸ συνέδριον
And the chief priests and the council
ὅλον ἐζήτουν ψευδομαρτυρίαν κατὰ τοῦ
whole sought false witness against –
Ἰησου ὅπως αὐτὸν θανατώσωσιν, **60** καὶ
Jesus so as him they might put to death, and
οὐχ εὗρον πολλῶν προσελθόντων
did not find[,] many approaching
=when many false witnesses approached.
ψευδομαρτύρων. ὕστερον δὲ προσελθόντες
false witnesses[a]. But later approaching
δύο **61** εἶπαν· οὗτος ἔφη· δύναμαι κατα-
two said: This man said: I can to de-
λῦσαι τὸν ναὸν τοῦ θεοῦ καὶ διὰ τριῶν
stroy the shrine – of God and through(after) three
ἡμερῶν οἰκοδομῆσαι. **62** καὶ ἀναστὰς
days to build. And standing up
ὁ ἀρχιερεὺς εἶπεν αὐτῷ· οὐδὲν
the high priest said to him: Nothing
ἀποκρίνῃ, τί οὗτοί σου κατα-
answerest thou, what these men thee give
μαρτυροῦσιν; **63** ὁ δὲ Ἰησοῦς ἐσιώπα.
evidence against? – But Jesus remained silent.
καὶ ὁ ἀρχιερεὺς εἶπεν αὐτῷ· ἐξορκίζω
And the high priest said to him: I adjure
σε κατὰ τοῦ θεοῦ τοῦ ζῶντος ἵνα ἡμῖν
thee by – God the living that us
εἴπῃς εἰ σὺ εἶ ὁ χριστὸς ὁ υἱὸς τοῦ
thou tell if thou art the Christ the Son –
θεοῦ. **64** λέγει αὐτῷ ὁ Ἰησοῦς· σὺ εἶπας·
of God. Says to him – Jesus: Thou saidst;
πλὴν λέγω ὑμῖν, ἀπ' ἄρτι ὄψεσθε τὸν
yet I tell you, from now ye will see the
υἱὸν τοῦ ἀνθρώπου καθήμενον ἐκ
Son – of man sitting on [the]
δεξιῶν τῆς δυνάμεως καὶ ἐρχόμενον
right [hand] of the power and coming
ἐπὶ τῶν νεφελῶν τοῦ οὐρανοῦ. **65** τότε
on the clouds – of heaven. Then

65 Then the high priest rent his clothes, saying, He hath spoken blasphemy; what further need have we of witnesses ? behold, now ye have heard his blasphemy.

66 What think ye ? They answered and said, He is guilty of death.

67 Then did they spit in his face, and buffeted him; and others smote *him* with the palms of their hands,

68 Saying, Prophesy unto us, thou Christ, Who is he that smote thee?

69 ¶ Now Peter sat without in the palace: and a damsel came unto him, saying, Thou also wast with Jesus of Galilee.

70 But he denied before *them* all, saying, I know not what thou sayest.

71 And when he was gone out into the porch, another *maid* saw him, and said unto them that were there, This *fellow* was also with Jesus of Nazareth.

72 And again he denied with an oath, I do not know the man.

73 And after a while came unto *him* they that stood by, and said to Peter, Surely thou also art *one* of them; for thy speech bewrayeth thee.

74 Then began he to curse and to swear, *saying,*

ὁ   ἀρχιερεὺς   διέρρηξεν   τὰ   ἱμάτια   αὐτοῦ
the   high priest   rent   the   garments   of him

λέγων·   ἐβλασφήμησεν·   τί   ἔτι   χρείαν   ἔχομεν
saying: He blasphemed;   what   yet   need   have we

μαρτύρων;   ἴδε   νῦν   ἠκούσατε   τὴν   βλασφη-
of witnesses?   behold   now   ye heard   the   blas-

μίαν·   66 τί   ὑμῖν   δοκεῖ;   οἱ   δὲ   ἀπο-
phemy;   what to you   seems it?   And they   answer-

κριθέντες   εἶπαν·   ἔνοχος   θανάτου   ἐστίν.
ing   said: Liable   of(to) death   he is.

67 Τότε   ἐνέπτυσαν   εἰς   τὸ   πρόσωπον   αὐτοῦ
Then   they spat   in   the   face   of him

καὶ   ἐκολάφισαν   αὐτόν,   οἱ   δὲ
and   violently maltreated   him,   and they

ἐρράπισαν   68 λέγοντες·   προφήτευσον   ἡμῖν,
slapped [him]   saying: Prophesy thou   to us,

χριστέ,   τίς   ἐστιν   ὁ   παίσας   σε;
Christ,   who   is it   the [one] having struck   thee?

69 Ὁ   δὲ   Πέτρος   ἐκάθητο   ἔξω   ἐν
—   And   Peter   sat   outside   in

τῇ   αὐλῇ·   καὶ   προσῆλθεν   αὐτῷ   μία
the   court;   and   approached   *to* him   one

παιδίσκη   λέγουσα·   καὶ   σὺ   ἦσθα   μετὰ
maidservant   saying: Also   thou   wast   with

Ἰησοῦ   τοῦ   Γαλιλαίου.   70 ὁ   δὲ   ἠρνήσατο
Jesus   the   Galilæan.   But he   denied

ἔμπροσθεν   πάντων   λέγων·   οὐκ   οἶδα
before   all   saying: I know not

τί   λέγεις.   71 ἐξελθόντα   δὲ   εἰς   τὸν
what thou sayest.   And ⁴going out   ⁵into   ⁶the

πυλῶνα   εἶδεν   αὐτὸν   ἄλλη   καὶ   λέγει
⁷porch   ²saw   ³him   ¹another   and   says

τοῖς   ἐκεῖ·   οὗτος   ἦν   μετὰ   Ἰησοῦ   τοῦ
to the [ones] there: This man   was   with   Jesus   the

Ναζωραίου.   72 καὶ   πάλιν   ἠρνήσατο
Nazarene.   And   again   he denied

μετὰ   ὅρκου   ὅτι   οὐκ   οἶδα   τὸν   ἄνθρωπον.
with   an oath[,]   –   I know not   the   man.

73 μετὰ   μικρὸν   δὲ   προσελθόντες   οἱ
And after a little   approaching the [ones]

ἑστῶτες   εἶπον   τῷ   Πέτρῳ·   ἀληθῶς   καὶ
standing   said   –   to Peter: Truly   also

σὺ   ἐξ   αὐτῶν   εἶ,   καὶ   γὰρ   ἡ   λαλιά   σου
thou   of   them   art,   for indeed   the   speech   of thee

δῆλόν   σε   ποιεῖ.   74 τότε   ἤρξατο   καταθε-
manifest thee   makes.   Then   he began   to

ματίζειν   καὶ   ὀμνύειν   ὅτι   οὐκ   οἶδα   τὸν
curse   and   to swear[,]   –   I know not   the

I know not the man. And immediately the cock crew.

75 And Peter remembered the word of Jesus, which said unto him, Before the cock crow, thou shalt deny me thrice. And he went out, and wept bitterly.

ἄνθρωπον.   καὶ   εὐθὺς   ἀλέκτωρ   ἐφώνησεν
man.   And immediately   a cock   crowed.

75 καὶ   ἐμνήσθη   ὁ   Πέτρος   τοῦ   ῥήματος
And   remembered   –   Peter   the   word

Ἰησοῦ   εἰρηκότος   ὅτι   πρὶν   ἀλέκτορα
of Jesus   having said[,]   –   Before   a cock

φωνῆσαι   τρὶς   ἀπαρνήσῃ   με·   καὶ
to crow[b]   three times   thou wilt deny   me;   and

ἐξελθὼν   ἔξω   ἔκλαυσεν   πικρῶς.
going forth   outside   he wept   bitterly.

CHAPTER 27

WHEN the morning was come, all the chief priests and elders of the people took counsel against Jesus to put him to death:

2 And when they had bound him, they led *him* away, and delivered him to Pontius Pilate the governor.

3 ¶ Then Judas, which had betrayed him, when he saw that he was condemned, repented himself, and brought again the thirty pieces of silver to the chief priests and elders,

4 Saying, I have sinned in that I have betrayed the innocent blood. And they said, What *is that* to us? see thou *to that.*

5 And he cast down the pieces of silver in the temple, and departed, and went and hanged himself.

6 And the chief priests took the silver pieces, and said, It is not lawful for to put them into the treasury, because it is the price of blood.

7 And they took counsel, and bought with them

27 Πρωΐας   δὲ   γενομένης   συμβούλιον
And early morning   coming[a]   counsel
= when early morning came

ἔλαβον   πάντες   οἱ   ἀρχιερεῖς   καὶ   οἱ
took   all   the   chief priests   and   the

πρεσβύτεροι   τοῦ   λαοῦ   κατὰ   τοῦ
elders   of the   people   against   –

Ἰησοῦ   ὥστε   θανατῶσαι   αὐτόν·   **2** καὶ
Jesus   so as   to put to death   him;   and

δήσαντες   αὐτὸν   ἀπήγαγον   καὶ   παρ-
having bound   him   they led away   and   de-

έδωκαν   Πιλάτῳ   τῷ   ἡγεμόνι.   **3** Τότε
livered   to Pilate   the   governor.   Then

ἰδὼν   Ἰούδας   ὁ   παραδοὺς   αὐτὸν
²seeing   ¹Judas   ³the [one]   ³having betrayed   ⁴him

ὅτι   κατεκρίθη,   μεταμεληθεὶς   ἔστρεψεν   τὰ
that   he was condemned,   repenting   returned   the

τριάκοντα   ἀργύρια   τοῖς   ἀρχιερεῦσιν
thirty   pieces of silver   to the   chief priests

καὶ   πρεσβυτέροις   **4** λέγων·   ἥμαρτον
and   elders   saying: I sinned

παραδοὺς   αἷμα   ἀθῷον.   οἱ   δὲ   εἶπαν·
betraying   blood   innocent.   But they   said:

τί   πρὸς   ἡμᾶς;   σὺ   ὄψῃ.   **5** καὶ   ῥίψας
What   to   us?   thou shalt see [to it].   And   tossing

τὰ   ἀργύρια   εἰς   τὸν   ναὸν   ἀν-
the   pieces of silver   into   the   shrine   he

εχώρησεν,   καὶ   ἀπελθὼν   ἀπήγξατο.   **6** οἱ
departed,   and   going away   hanged himself.   the

δὲ   ἀρχιερεῖς   λαβόντες   τὰ   ἀργύρια   εἶπαν·
But   chief priests   taking   the   pieces of silver   said:

οὐκ   ἔξεστιν   βαλεῖν   αὐτὰ   εἰς   τὸν
It is not lawful   to put   them   into   the

κορβανᾶν,   ἐπεὶ   τιμὴ   αἵματός   ἐστιν.
treasury,   since   price   of blood   it is.

7 συμβούλιον   δὲ   λαβόντες   ἠγόρασαν   ἐξ
So counsel   taking   they bought   of(with)

the potter's field, to bury strangers in.

8 Wherefore that field was called, The field of blood, unto this day.

9 Then was fulfilled that which was spoken by Jeremy the prophet, saying, And they took the thirty pieces of silver, the price of him that was valued, whom they of the children of Israel did value;

10 And gave them for the potter's field, as the Lord appointed me.

11 ¶ And Jesus stood before the governor: and the governor asked him, saying, Art thou the King of the Jews? And Jesus said unto him, Thou sayest.

12 And when he was accused of the chief priests and elders, he answered nothing.

13 Then said Pilate unto him, Hearest thou not how many things they witness against thee?

14 And he answered him to never a word, insomuch that the governor marvelled greatly.

15 ¶ Now at that feast the governor was wont to release unto the people a prisoner, whom they would.

16 And they had then a notable prisoner, called Barabbas.

αὐτῶν τὸν ἀγρὸν τοῦ κεραμέως εἰς ταφὴν
them the field of the potter for burial

τοῖς ξένοις. 8 διὸ ἐκλήθη ὁ ἀγρὸς
for the strangers. Wherefore was called - field

ἐκεῖνος ἀγρὸς αἵματος ἕως τῆς σήμερον.
that Field of blood until - to-day.

9 τότε ἐπληρώθη τὸ ῥηθὲν διὰ
Then was fulfilled the [thing] spoken through

Ἰερεμίου τοῦ προφήτου λέγοντος· καὶ
Jeremiah the prophet saying: And

ἔλαβον τὰ τριάκοντα ἀργύρια, τὴν
they took the thirty pieces of silver, the

τιμὴν τοῦ τετιμημένου ὃν ἐτιμήσαντο
price of the [one] having been priced whom they priced

ἀπὸ υἱῶν Ἰσραήλ, 10 καὶ ἔδωκαν
from [the] sons of Israel, and gave

αὐτὰ εἰς τὸν ἀγρὸν τοῦ κεραμέως, καθὰ
them for the field of the potter, as

συνέταξέν μοι κύριος. 11 Ὁ δὲ
directed me [the] Lord. - And

Ἰησοῦς ἐστάθη ἔμπροσθεν τοῦ ἡγεμόνος·
Jesus stood before the governor;

καὶ ἐπηρώτησεν αὐτὸν ὁ ἡγεμὼν λέγων·
and questioned him the governor saying:

σὺ εἶ ὁ βασιλεὺς τῶν Ἰουδαίων; ὁ δὲ
Thou art the king of the Jews? - And

Ἰησοῦς ἔφη· σὺ λέγεις. 12 καὶ ἐν
Jesus said: Thou sayest. And in

τῷ κατηγορεῖσθαι αὐτὸν ὑπὸ τῶν
the to be accused himᵉ by the
=as he was accused

ἀρχιερέων καὶ πρεσβυτέρων οὐδὲν
chief priests and elders nothing

ἀπεκρίνατο. 13 τότε λέγει αὐτῷ ὁ Πιλᾶτος·
he answered. Then says to him - Pilate:

οὐκ ἀκούεις πόσα σου κατα-
Hearest thou not what things ᵃthee ¹they

μαρτυροῦσιν; 14 καὶ οὐκ ἀπεκρίθη αὐτῷ
ᵃgive evidence against? And he answered not him

πρὸς οὐδὲ ἓν ῥῆμα, ὥστε θαυμάζειν
to not one word, so as to marvel
=so that the governor marvelled

τὸν ἡγεμόνα λίαν. 15 Κατὰ δὲ ἑορτὴν
the governorᵇ exceedingly. Now at a feast

εἰώθει ὁ ἡγεμὼν ἀπολύειν ἕνα τῷ ὄχλῳ
was accustomed the governor to release ³one ¹to the ²crowd

δέσμιον ὃν ἤθελον. 16 εἶχον δὲ τότε
⁴prisoner whom they wished. And they had then

δέσμιον ἐπίσημον λεγόμενον Βαραββᾶν
prisoner a notable named Barabbas.

17 Therefore when they were gathered together, Pilate said unto them, Whom will ye that I release unto you? Barabbas, or Jesus which is called Christ?

18 For he knew that for envy they had delivered him.

19 ¶ When he was set down on the judgment seat, his wife sent unto him, saying, Have thou nothing to do with that just man: for I have suffered many things this day in a dream because of him.

20 But the chief priests and elders persuaded the multitude that they should ask Barabbas, and destroy Jesus.

21 The governor answered and said unto them, Whether of the twain will ye that I release unto you? They said, Barabbas.

22 Pilate saith unto them, What shall I do then with Jesus which is called Christ? *They* all say unto him, Let him be crucified.

23 And the governor said, Why, what evil hath he done? But they cried out the more, saying, Let him be crucified.

24 When Pilate saw that he could prevail nothing, but *that* rather a tumult was made, he took water, and washed *his* hands before the multitude, saying,

---

17 συνηγμένων οὖν αὐτῶν εἶπεν αὐτοῖς
Therefore having assembled them[a] said to them
= when they were assembled

ὁ Πιλᾶτος· τίνα θέλετε ἀπολύσω
Pilate: Whom do ye wish I may release

ὑμῖν, [τὸν] Βαραββᾶν ἢ Ἰησοῦν τὸν
to you, – Barabbas or Jesus –

λεγόμενον χριστόν; **18** ἤδει γὰρ ὅτι
called Christ? for he knew that

διὰ φθόνον παρέδωκαν αὐτόν. **19** Καθη-
because of envy they delivered him. sit-

μένου δὲ αὐτοῦ ἐπὶ τοῦ βήματος
ting Now him[a] on the tribunal
= Now as he sat

ἀπέστειλεν πρὸς αὐτὸν ἡ γυνὴ αὐτοῦ
sent to him the wife of him

λέγουσα· μηδὲν σοὶ καὶ τῷ δικαίῳ
saying: Nothing to thee and – just man

ἐκείνῳ· πολλὰ γὰρ ἔπαθον σήμερον κατ᾽
to that; for many things I suffered to-day by

ὄναρ δι᾽ αὐτόν. **20** Οἱ δὲ ἀρχιερεῖς
a dream because of him. But the chief priests

καὶ οἱ πρεσβύτεροι ἔπεισαν τοὺς
and the elders persuaded the

ὄχλους ἵνα αἰτήσωνται τὸν Βαραββᾶν,
crowds that they should ask – Barabbas,

τὸν δὲ Ἰησοῦν ἀπολέσωσιν. **21** ἀπο-
– and Jesus should destroy. So

κριθεὶς δὲ ὁ ἡγεμὼν εἶπεν αὐτοῖς·
answering the governor said to them:

τίνα θέλετε ἀπὸ τῶν δύο ἀπολύσω
Which do ye wish from the two I may release

ὑμῖν; οἱ δὲ εἶπαν· τὸν Βαραββᾶν.
to you? And they said: – Barabbas.

22 λέγει αὐτοῖς ὁ Πιλᾶτος· τί οὖν
Says to them – Pilate: What then

ποιήσω Ἰησοῦν τὸν λεγόμενον χριστόν;
may I do [to] Jesus – called Christ?

λέγουσιν πάντες· σταυρωθήτω. **23** ὁ δὲ
They say all: Let him be crucified. But he

ἔφη· τί γὰρ κακὸν ἐποίησεν; οἱ δὲ
said: Why what evil did he? But they

περισσῶς ἔκραζον λέγοντες· σταυρω-
more cried out saying: Let him be

θήτω. **24** ἰδὼν δὲ ὁ Πιλᾶτος ὅτι οὐδὲν
crucified. And seeing – Pilate that nothing

ὠφελεῖ ἀλλὰ μᾶλλον θόρυβος γίνεται,
is gained but rather an uproar occurs,

λαβὼν ὕδωρ ἀπενίψατο τὰς χεῖρας
taking water he washed the(his) hands

I am innocent of the blood of this just person: see ye *to it.*

25 Then answered all the people, and said, His blood *be* on us, and on our children.

26 Then released he Barabbas unto them: and when he had scourged Jesus, he delivered *him* to be crucified.

27 ¶ Then the soldiers of the governor took Jesus into the common hall, and gathered unto him the whole band *of soldiers.*

28 And they stripped him, and put on him a scarlet robe.

29 ¶ And when they had platted a crown of thorns, they put *it* upon his head, and a reed in his right hand: and they bowed the knee before him, and mocked him, saying, Hail, King of the Jews!

30 And they spit upon him, and took the reed, and smote him on the head.

31 And after that they had mocked him, they took the robe off from him, and put his own raiment on him, and led him away to crucify *him.*

32 And as they came out, they found a man of Cyrene, Simon by name:

κατέναντι τοῦ ὄχλου λέγων· ἀθῷός
in front of the crowd saying: Innocent

εἰμι ἀπὸ τοῦ αἵματος τούτου· ὑμεῖς
I am from the blood of this man; ye

ὄψεσθε. 25 καὶ ἀποκριθεὶς πᾶς ὁ λαὸς
will see [to it]. And answering all the people

εἶπεν· τὸ αἷμα αὐτοῦ ἐφ' ἡμᾶς καὶ
said: The blood of him on us and

ἐπὶ τὰ τέκνα ἡμῶν. 26 τότε ἀπέλυσεν
on the children of us. Then he released

αὐτοῖς τὸν Βαραββᾶν, τὸν δὲ Ἰησοῦν
to them — Barabbas, — but Jesus

φραγελλώσας παρέδωκεν ἵνα σταυρωθῇ.
having scourged he delivered that he might be crucified.

27 Τότε οἱ στρατιῶται τοῦ ἡγεμόνος
Then the soldiers of the governor

παραλαβόντες τὸν Ἰησοῦν εἰς τὸ πραιτώ-
having taken — Jesus into the præ-

ριον συνήγαγον ἐπ' αὐτὸν ὅλην τὴν
torium assembled against him all the

σπεῖραν. 28 καὶ ἐκδύσαντες αὐτὸν χλαμύδα
band. And stripping him cloak

κοκκίνην περιέθηκαν αὐτῷ, 29 καὶ
a purple they placed round him, and

πλέξαντες στέφανον ἐξ ἀκανθῶν ἐπέθηκαν
having plaited a crown of thorns they placed [it] on

ἐπὶ τῆς κεφαλῆς αὐτοῦ καὶ κάλαμον
on the head of him and a reed

ἐν τῇ δεξιᾷ αὐτοῦ, καὶ γονυπετή-
in the right [hand] of him, and bowing

σαντες ἔμπροσθεν αὐτοῦ ἐνέπαιξαν αὐτῷ
the knee in front of him mocked at him

λέγοντες· χαῖρε, βασιλεῦ τῶν Ἰουδαίων,
saying: Hail, king of the Jews,

30 καὶ ἐμπτύσαντες εἰς αὐτὸν ἔλαβον
and spitting at him took

τὸν κάλαμον καὶ ἔτυπτον εἰς τὴν κεφαλὴν
the reed and struck at the head

αὐτοῦ. 31 καὶ ὅτε ἐνέπαιξαν αὐτῷ,
of him. And when they mocked at him,

ἐξέδυσαν αὐτὸν τὴν χλαμύδα καὶ ἐνέδυσαν
they took off him the cloak and put on

αὐτὸν τὰ ἱμάτια αὐτοῦ, καὶ ἀπήγαγον
him the garments of him, and led away

αὐτὸν εἰς τὸ σταυρῶσαι. 32 Ἐξερχόμενοι
him — to crucify. going forth

δὲ εὗρον ἄνθρωπον Κυρηναῖον, ὀνό-
And they found *a man* a Cyrenian, by

him they compelled to bear his cross.

33 And when they were come unto a place called Golgotha, that is to say, a place of a skull,

34 They gave him vinegar to drink mingled with gall: and when he had tasted *thereof*, he would not drink.

35 And they crucified him, and parted his garments, casting lots: that it might be fulfilled which was spoken by the prophet, They parted my garments among them, and upon my vesture did they cast lots.

36 And sitting down they watched him there;

37 And set up over his head his accusation written, THIS IS JESUS THE KING OF THE JEWS.

38 Then were there two thieves crucified with him, one on the right hand, and another on the left.

39 ¶ And they that passed by reviled him, wagging their heads,

40 And saying, Thou that destroyest the temple, and buildest *it* in three days, save thyself. If thou be the Son of God, come down from the cross.

41 Likewise also the chief priests mocking *him*, with the scribes and elders, said,

42 He saved others; himself he cannot save. If

ματι	Σίμωνα·	τοῦτον	ἠγγάρευσαν	ἵνα
name	Simon;	this man	they impressed	that

ἄρῃ   τὸν   σταυρὸν   αὐτοῦ.   33 Καὶ
he should bear the   cross   of him.   And

ἐλθόντες   εἰς   τόπον   λεγόμενον   Γολγοθά,
coming   to   a place   called   Golgotha,

ὅ   ἐστιν   κρανίου   τόπος   λεγόμενος,
which   is   ³of a skull   ²A place   ¹called,

34 ἔδωκαν   αὐτῷ   πιεῖν   οἶνον   μετὰ
they gave   him   to drink   wine   with

χολῆς   μεμιγμένον·   καὶ   γευσάμενος   οὐκ
gall   *having been* mixed;   and   tasting   not

ἠθέλησεν   πιεῖν.   35 σταυρώσαντες   δὲ
he would   *to* drink.   And having crucified

αὐτὸν   διεμερίσαντο   τὰ   ἱμάτια   αὐτοῦ
him   they divided   the   garments   of him

βάλλοντες   κλῆρον,   36 καὶ   καθήμενοι   ἐτήρουν
casting   a lot,   and   sitting   they guarded

αὐτὸν   ἐκεῖ.   37 καὶ   ἐπέθηκαν   ἐπάνω
him   there.   And   they placed *on*   above

τῆς   κεφαλῆς   αὐτοῦ   τὴν   αἰτίαν   αὐτοῦ
the   head   of him   the   charge   of him

γεγραμμένην·   *OYTOΣ   EΣTIN   IHΣOYΣ*
having been written: THIS   IS   JESUS

O BAΣIΛEYΣ TΩN IOYΔAIΩN.   38 Τότε
THE   KING   OF THE   JEWS.   Then

σταυροῦνται   σὺν   αὐτῷ   δύο   λῃσταί,
are crucified   with   him   two   robbers,

εἷς   ἐκ   δεξιῶν   καὶ   εἷς   ἐξ   εὐωνύμων.
one   on [the] right   and   one   on [the] left.

39 Οἱ   δὲ   παραπορευόμενοι   ἐβλασφήμουν
And the [ones]   passing by   blasphemed

αὐτὸν   κινοῦντες   τὰς   κεφαλὰς   αὐτῶν
him   wagging   the   heads   of them

40 καὶ   λέγοντες·   ὁ   καταλύων   τὸν   ναὸν
and   saying: The [one] destroying   the   shrine

καὶ   ἐν   τρισὶν   ἡμέραις   οἰκοδομῶν,
and   in   three   days   building [it],

σῶσον   σεαυτόν,   εἰ   υἱὸς   εἶ   τοῦ   θεοῦ,
save   thyself,   if   Son   thou art   -   of God,

καὶ   κατάβηθι   ἀπὸ   τοῦ   σταυροῦ.   41 ὁμοίως
and   come down   from   the   cross.   Likewise

[καὶ]   οἱ   ἀρχιερεῖς   ἐμπαίζοντες   μετὰ
also   the   chief priests   mocking   with

τῶν   γραμματέων   καὶ   πρεσβυτέρων   ἔλεγον·
the   scribes   and   elders   said:

42 ἄλλους   ἔσωσεν,   ἑαυτὸν   οὐ   δύναται
Others   he saved,   himself   he cannot

he be the King of Israel, let him now come down from the cross, and we will believe him.

43 He trusted in God; let him deliver him now, if he will have him: for he said, I am the Son of God.

44 The thieves also, which were crucified with him, cast the same in his teeth.

45 ¶ Now from the sixth hour there was darkness over all the land unto the ninth hour.

46 And about the ninth hour Jesus cried with a loud voice, saying, Eli, Eli, lama sabachthani? that is to say, My God, my God, why hast thou forsaken me?

47 Some of them that stood there, when they heard that, said, This man calleth for Elias.

48 And straightway one of them ran, and took a spunge, and filled it with vinegar, and put it on a reed, and gave him to drink.

49 The rest said, Let be, let us see whether Elias will come to save him.

50 ¶ Jesus, when he had cried again with a loud voice, yielded up the ghost.

51 And, behold, the veil of the temple was rent in twain from the top to the bottom; and the earth did

σῶσαι·　βασιλεὺς　'Ισραὴλ　ἐστιν,
to save;　King　of Israel　he is,

καταβάτω　νῦν　ἀπὸ　τοῦ　σταυροῦ　καὶ
let him come down　now　from　the　cross　and

πιστεύσομεν　ἐπ'　αὐτόν.　43 πέποιθεν
we will believe　on　him.　He has trusted

ἐπὶ　τὸν　θεόν,　ῥυσάσθω　νῦν　εἰ　θέλει
on　-　God,　let him rescue　now　if　he wants

αὐτόν·　εἶπεν　γὰρ　ὅτι　θεοῦ　εἰμι　υἱός.
him;　for he said[,]　-　of God　I am　Son.

44 τὸ δ'　αὐτὸ　καὶ　οἱ　λῃσταὶ　οἱ　συσταυρω-
And the　same　also　the　robbers　-　crucified

θέντες　σὺν　αὐτῷ　ὠνείδιζον　αὐτόν.　45 'Απὸ
with　with　him　reproached　him.　from

δὲ　ἕκτης　ὥρας　σκότος　ἐγένετο　ἐπὶ
Now [the] sixth　hour　darkness　occurred　over

πᾶσαν　τὴν　γῆν　ἕως　ὥρας　ἐνάτης.
all　the　land　until　hour　[the] ninth.

46 περὶ　δὲ　τὴν　ἐνάτην　ὥραν　ἀνεβόησεν　ὁ
And about　the　ninth　hour　cried out

'Ιησοῦς　φωνῇ　μεγάλῃ　λέγων·　ἠλὶ　ἠλὶ
Jesus　voice　with a great　saying:　Eli　Eli

λεμὰ　σαβαχθάνι;　τοῦτ'　ἔστιν·　θεέ　μου,
lema　sabachthani?　this　is:　God of me[,]

θεέ　μου,　ἱνατί　με　ἐγκατέλιπες;　47 τινὲς
God　of me,　why　me　didst thou forsake?　some

δὲ　τῶν　ἐκεῖ　ἑστηκότων　ἀκούσαντες
And　of the [ones]　there　standing　hearing

ἔλεγον　ὅτι　'Ηλίαν　φωνεῖ　οὗτος.
said[,]　-　³Elias　²calls　¹this man.

48 καὶ　εὐθέως　δραμὼν　εἷς　ἐξ　αὐτῶν　καὶ
And　immediately　running　one　of　them　and

λαβὼν　σπόγγον　πλήσας　τε　ὄξους　καὶ
taking　a sponge　and filling　of(with) vinegar　and

περιθεὶς　καλάμῳ　ἐπότιζεν　αὐτόν.
putting [it] round　a reed　gave to drink　him.

49 οἱ　δὲ　λοιποὶ　εἶπαν·　ἄφες　ἴδωμεν
But the　rest　said:　Leave[,]　let us see

εἰ　ἔρχεται　'Ηλίας　σώσων　αὐτόν.　50 ὁ
if　comes　Elias　saving　him.　-

δὲ　'Ιησοῦς　πάλιν　κράξας　φωνῇ
And　Jesus　again　crying out　voice

μεγάλῃ　ἀφῆκεν　τὸ　πνεῦμα.　51 Καὶ
with a great　released　the(his)　spirit.　And

ἰδοὺ　τὸ　καταπέτασμα　τοῦ　ναοῦ　ἐσχίσθη
behold　the　veil　of the shrine　was rent

[ἀπ']　ἄνωθεν　ἕως　κάτω　εἰς　δύο,　καὶ　ἡ
from　above　to　below　in　two,　and the

quake, and the rocks rent;

52 And the graves were opened; and many bodies of the saints which slept arose,

53 And came out of the graves after his resurrection, and went into the holy city, and appeared unto many.

54 Now when the centurion, and they that were with him, watching Jesus, saw the earthquake, and those things that were done, they feared greatly, saying, Truly this was the Son of God.

55 And many women were there beholding afar off, which followed Jesus from Galilee, ministering unto him:

56 Among which was Mary Magdalene, and Mary the mother of James and Joses, and the mother of Zebedee's children.

57 ¶ When the even was come, there came a rich man of Arimathæa, named Joseph, who also himself was Jesus' disciple:

58 He went to Pilate, and begged the body of Jesus. Then Pilate commanded the body to be delivered.

59 And when Joseph had taken the body, he

γῆ	ἐσείσθη,	καὶ	αἱ πέτραι ἐσχίσ-
earth	was shaken,	and	the rocks were

θησαν,	52 καὶ	τὰ	μνημεῖα ἀνεῴχθησαν
rent,	and	the	tombs were opened

καὶ	πολλὰ	σώματα	τῶν κεκοιμημένων
and	many	bodies	of the having fallen asleep

ἁγίων	ἠγέρθησαν·	53 καὶ	ἐξελθόντες
saints	were raised;	and	coming forth

ἐκ	τῶν	μνημείων	μετὰ τὴν	ἔγερσιν
out of	the	tombs	after the	rising

αὐτοῦ	εἰσῆλθον	εἰς τὴν	ἁγίαν πόλιν	καὶ
of him	entered	into the	holy city	and

ἐνεφανίσθησαν	πολλοῖς.	54 Ὁ δὲ ἑκατόν-
appeared	to many.	And the centu-

ταρχος	καὶ οἱ μετ'	αὐτοῦ	τηροῦντες
rion	and the [ones] with	him	guarding

τὸν	Ἰησοῦν	ἰδόντες	τὸν σεισμὸν καὶ
–	Jesus	seeing	the earthquake and

τὰ	γινόμενα	ἐφοβήθησαν	σφόδρα,
the things	happening	feared	exceedingly,

λέγοντες·	ἀληθῶς	θεοῦ	υἱὸς ἦν οὗτος.
saying:	Truly	⁴of God	³Son ²was ¹this man.

55 Ἦσαν	δὲ	ἐκεῖ	γυναῖκες πολλαὶ
Now there were		there	women many

ἀπὸ	μακρόθεν	θεωροῦσαι,	αἵτινες ἠκολού-
from	afar	beholding,	who followed

θησαν	τῷ	Ἰησοῦ ἀπὸ	τῆς Γαλιλαίας
	–	Jesus from	the Galilee

διακονοῦσαι	αὐτῷ·	56 ἐν	αἷς ἦν
ministering	to him;	among	whom was

Μαρία	ἡ	Μαγδαληνή,	καὶ Μαρία ἡ
Mary	the	Magdalene,	and Mary the

τοῦ	Ἰακώβου	καὶ Ἰωσὴφ	μήτηρ, καὶ ἡ
–	of James	and of Joseph	mother, and the

μήτηρ	τῶν υἱῶν	Ζεβεδαίου.
mother	of the sons	of Zebedee.

57 Ὀψίας	δὲ	γενομένης ἦλθεν ἄνθρωπος
Now evening		having come* came man
		=when evening had come

πλούσιος	ἀπὸ Ἀριμαθαίας,	τοὔνομα Ἰωσήφ,
a rich	from Arimathæa,	the name Joseph,

ὃς	καὶ αὐτὸς	ἐμαθητεύθη	τῷ Ἰησοῦ·
who	also himself	was discipled	– to Jesus;

58 οὗτος	προσελθὼν	τῷ Πιλάτῳ	ᾐτήσατο
this man	approaching	– to Pilate	asked

τὸ	σῶμα	τοῦ Ἰησοῦ.	τότε ὁ Πιλᾶτος
the	body	– of Jesus.	Then – Pilate

ἐκέλευσεν	ἀποδοθῆναι.	59 καὶ	λαβὼν
commanded [it]	to be given [him].	And	taking

wrapped it in a clean linen cloth,

60 And laid it in his own new tomb, which he had hewn out in the rock: and he rolled a great stone to the door of the sepulchre, and departed.

61 And there was Mary Magdalene, and the other Mary, sitting over against the sepulchre.

62 ¶ Now the next day, that followed the day of the preparation, the chief priests and Pharisees came together unto Pilate,

63 Saying, Sir, we remember that that deceiver said, while he was yet alive, After three days I will rise again.

64 Command therefore that the sepulchre be made sure until the third day, lest his disciples come by night, and steal him away, and say unto the people, He is risen from the dead: so the last error shall be worse than the first.

65 Pilate said unto them, Ye have a watch: go your way, make it as sure as ye can.

66 So they went, and made the sepulchre sure, sealing the stone, and setting a watch.

τὸ σῶμα ὁ Ἰωσὴφ ἐνετύλιξεν αὐτὸ [ἐν]
the body – Joseph wrapped it in

σινδόνι καθαρᾷ, 60 καὶ ἔθηκεν αὐτὸ ἐν
sheet a clean, and placed it in

τῷ καινῷ αὐτοῦ μνημείῳ ὃ ἐλατό-
the new of him tomb which he

μησεν ἐν τῇ πέτρα, καὶ προσκυλίσας
hewed in the rock, and having rolled to

λίθον μέγαν τῇ θύρᾳ τοῦ μνημείου
stone a great to the door of the tomb

ἀπῆλθεν. 61 *Ἦν δὲ ἐκεῖ Μαριὰμ
went away. And there was there Mary

ἡ Μαγδαληνὴ καὶ ἡ ἄλλη Μαρία,
the Magdalene and the other Mary,

καθήμεναι ἀπέναντι τοῦ τάφου. 62 Τῇ
sitting opposite the grave. on the

δὲ ἐπαύριον, ἥτις ἐστὶν μετὰ τὴν παρα-
And morrow, which is after the prepara-

σκευήν, συνήχθησαν οἱ ἀρχιερεῖς
tion, were assembled the chief priests

καὶ οἱ Φαρισαῖοι πρὸς Πιλᾶτον 63 λέ-
and the Pharisees to Pilate say-

γοντες· κύριε, ἐμνήσθημεν ὅτι ἐκεῖνος
ing: Sir, we remembered that that

ὁ πλάνος εἶπεν ἔτι ζῶν· μετὰ τρεῖς
– deceiver said yet living: After three

ἡμέρας ἐγείρομαι. 64 κέλευσον οὖν
days I am raised. Command therefore

ἀσφαλισθῆναι τὸν τάφον ἕως τῆς
to be made fast the grave until the

τρίτης ἡμέρας, μήποτε ἐλθόντες οἱ μαθηταὶ
third day, lest coming the disciples

κλέψωσιν αὐτὸν καὶ εἴπωσιν τῷ λαῷ·
may steal him and may say to the people:

ἠγέρθη ἀπὸ τῶν νεκρῶν, καὶ ἔσται
He was raised from the dead, and will be

ἡ ἐσχάτη πλάνη χείρων τῆς πρώτης.
the last deceit worse [than] the first.

65 ἔφη αὐτοῖς ὁ Πιλᾶτος· ἔχετε κου-
Said to them – Pilate: Ye have a

στωδίαν· ὑπάγετε ἀσφαλίσασθε ὡς οἴδατε.
guard; go ye make fast as ye know*.

66 οἱ δὲ πορευθέντες ἠσφαλίσαντο τὸν
And they going made fast the

τάφον σφραγίσαντες τὸν λίθον μετὰ τῆς
grave sealing the stone with the

κουστωδίας.
guard.

* can. See note on page xviii.

CHAPTER 28

IN the end of the sab-
bath, as it began to
dawn toward the first *day*
of the week, came Mary
Magdalene and the other
Mary to see the sepulchre.

2 And, behold, there
was a great earthquake:
for the angel of the Lord
descended from heaven,
and came and rolled back
the stone from the door,
and sat upon it.

3 His countenance was
like lightning, and his
raiment white as snow:

4 And for fear of him
the keepers did shake, and
became as dead *men.*

5 And the angel an-
swered and said unto the
women, Fear not ye: for I
know that ye seek Jesus,
which was crucified.

6 He is not here: for he
is risen, as he said. Come,
see the place where the
Lord lay.

7 And go quickly, and
tell his disciples that he is
risen from the dead; and,
behold, he goeth before
you into Galilee; there
shall ye see him: lo, I have
told you.

8 And they departed
quickly from the sepulchre
with fear and great joy: and
did run to bring his dis-
ciples word.

9 ¶ And as they went to
tell his disciples, behold,

28 Ὀψὲ   δὲ   σαββάτων,   τῇ   ἐπιφωσκούσῃ
But late   of [the] sabbaths, at the   drawing on

εἰς   μίαν   σαββάτων,   ἦλθεν   Μαριὰμ   ἡ
toward one   of [the] sabbaths, came   Mary   the
= the first day of the week,

Μαγδαληνὴ   καὶ   ἡ   ἄλλη   Μαρία   θεωρῆσαι
Magdalene   and the other   Mary   to view

τὸν   τάφον.   2 καὶ   ἰδοὺ   σεισμὸς   ἐγένετο
the   grave.   And   behold earthquake occurred

μέγας·   ἄγγελος   γὰρ   κυρίου   καταβὰς
a great;   for an angel   of [the] Lord   descending

ἐξ   οὐρανοῦ   καὶ   προσελθὼν   ἀπεκύλισεν
out of heaven   and   approaching   rolled away

τὸν   λίθον   καὶ   ἐκάθητο   ἐπάνω   αὐτοῦ.
the   stone   and   sat   upon   it.

3 ἦν   δὲ   ἡ   εἰδέα   αὐτοῦ   ὡς   ἀστραπή,
And was   the appearance of him   as   lightning,

καὶ   τὸ   ἔνδυμα   αὐτοῦ   λευκὸν   ὡς   χιών.
and the   dress   of him   white   as   snow.

4 ἀπὸ   δὲ   τοῦ   φόβου   αὐτοῦ   ἐσείσθησαν
And from   the   fear   of him   were shaken

οἱ   τηροῦντες   καὶ   ἐγενήθησαν   ὡς
the [ones] guarding   and   they became   as

νεκροί.   5 ἀποκριθεὶς   δὲ   ὁ   ἄγγελος
dead.   And answering   the   angel

εἶπεν   ταῖς   γυναιξίν·   μὴ   φοβεῖσθε   ὑμεῖς·
said   to the   women: Fear not   ye;

οἶδα   γὰρ   ὅτι   Ἰησοῦν   τὸν   ἐσταυρω-
for I know   that   Jesus   the [one] *having been*

μένον   ζητεῖτε·   6 οὐκ   ἔστιν   ὧδε·
crucified   ye seek;   he is not   here;

ἠγέρθη   γὰρ   καθὼς   εἶπεν·   δεῦτε   ἴδετε   τὸν
for he was raised as   he said;   come   see ye   the

τόπον   ὅπου   ἔκειτο.   7 καὶ   ταχὺ   πορευθεῖσαι
place   where   he lay.   And   quickly   going

εἴπατε   τοῖς   μαθηταῖς   αὐτοῦ   ὅτι   ἠγέρθη
tell   the   disciples   of him   that he was raised

ἀπὸ   τῶν   νεκρῶν,   καὶ   ἰδοὺ   προάγει   ὑμᾶς
from   the   dead,   and   behold he goes before you

εἰς   τὴν   Γαλιλαίαν,   ἐκεῖ   αὐτὸν   ὄψεσθε.
to   -   Galilee,   there   him   ye will see.

ἰδοὺ   εἶπον   ὑμῖν.   8 καὶ   ἀπελθοῦσαι   ταχὺ
Behold I told   you.   And   going away   quickly

ἀπὸ   τοῦ   μνημείου   μετὰ   φόβου   καὶ   χαρᾶς
from   the   tomb   with   fear   and   joy

μεγάλης   ἔδραμον   ἀπαγγεῖλαι   τοῖς
great   they ran   to announce   to the

μαθηταῖς   αὐτοῦ.   9 καὶ   ἰδοὺ   Ἰησοῦς
disciples   of him.   And   behold   Jesus

Jesus met them, saying, All hail. And they came and held him by the feet, and worshipped him.

10 Then said Jesus unto them, Be not afraid: go tell my brethren that they go into Galilee, and there shall they see me.

11 ¶ Now when they were going, behold, some of the watch came into the city, and shewed unto the chief priests all the things that were done.

12 And when they were assembled with the elders, and had taken counsel, they gave large money unto the soldiers,

13 Saying, Say ye, His disciples came by night, and stole him *away* while we slept.

14 And if this come to the governor's ears, we will persuade him, and secure you.

15 So they took the money, and did as they were taught: and this saying is commonly reported among the Jews until this day.

16 ¶ Then the eleven disciples went away into Galilee, into a mountain where Jesus had appointed them.

17 And when they saw

ὑπήντησεν αὐταῖς λέγων· χαίρετε. αἱ δὲ
met   them   saying: Hail.   And they

προσελθοῦσαι ἐκράτησαν αὐτοῦ τοὺς πόδας
approaching   held   of him   the   feet

καὶ προσεκύνησαν αὐτῷ. 10 τότε λέγει
and   worshipped   him.   Then says

αὐταῖς ὁ Ἰησοῦς· μὴ φοβεῖσθε· ὑπάγετε
to them - Jesus: Fear ye not; go ye

ἀπαγγείλατε τοῖς ἀδελφοῖς μου ἵνα
announce   to the brothers   of me that

ἀπέλθωσιν εἰς τὴν Γαλιλαίαν, κἀκεῖ
they may go away into -   Galilee,   and there

με ὄψονται. 11 Πορευομένων δὲ αὐτῶν
me they will see.   And going   them ª
                     =as they were going

ἰδού τινες τῆς κουστωδίας ἐλθόντες εἰς
behold some of the guard   coming   into

τὴν πόλιν ἀπήγγειλαν τοῖς ἀρχιερεῦσιν
the city   announced   to the chief priests

ἅπαντα τὰ γενόμενα. 12 καὶ συν-
all the things   having happened.   And   being

ἀχθέντες μετὰ τῶν πρεσβυτέρων συμβούλιόν
assembled with the   elders   ²counsel

τε λαβόντες ἀργύρια ἱκανὰ ἔδωκαν τοῖς
¹and ²taking   silver   enough gave   to the

στρατιώταις, 13 λέγοντες· εἴπατε ὅτι οἱ
soldiers,   saying: Say ye that the

μαθηταὶ αὐτοῦ νυκτὸς ἐλθόντες ἔκλεψαν
disciples of him of(by) night coming stole

αὐτὸν ἡμῶν κοιμωμένων. 14 καὶ ἐὰν
him   we   sleeping.ª   And if
              =while we slept.

ἀκουσθῇ τοῦτο ἐπὶ τοῦ ἡγεμόνος,
be heard   this before the   governor,

ἡμεῖς πείσομεν καὶ ὑμᾶς ἀμερίμνους
we   will persuade and   you   free from anxiety

ποιήσομεν. 15 οἱ δὲ λαβόντες ἀργύρια
we will make.   And they   taking   silver

ἐποίησαν ὡς ἐδιδάχθησαν. Καὶ διεφη-
did   as   they were taught. And was spread

μίσθη ὁ λόγος οὗτος παρὰ Ἰουδαίοις
about   - saying this   by   Jews

μέχρι τῆς σήμερον [ἡμέρας]. 16 Οἱ δὲ
until   the to-day.   So the

ἔνδεκα μαθηταὶ ἐπορεύθησαν εἰς τὴν
eleven disciples   went   to   -

Γαλιλαίαν, εἰς τὸ ὄρος οὗ ἐτάξατο
Galilee,   to the mountain where appointed

αὐτοῖς ὁ Ἰησοῦς, 17 καὶ ἰδόντες αὐτὸν
them   - Jesus,   and seeing   him

him, they worshipped him: but some doubted.

18 And Jesus came and spake unto them, saying, All power is given unto me in heaven and in earth.

19 Go ye therefore, and teach all nations, baptizing them in the name of the Father, and of the Son, and of the Holy Ghost:

20 Teaching them to observe all things whatsoever I have commanded you: and, lo, I am with you alway, *even* unto the end of the world. Amen.

προσεκύνησαν, οἱ δὲ ἐδίστασαν. 18 καὶ
they worshipped, but some doubted. And

προσελθὼν ὁ Ἰησοῦς ἐλάλησεν αὐτοῖς
approaching – Jesus talked with them

λέγων· ἐδόθη μοι πᾶσα ἐξουσία ἐν
saying: was given to me All authority in

οὐρανῷ καὶ ἐπὶ [τῆς] γῆς. 19 πορευθέντες
heaven and on the earth. Going

οὖν μαθητεύσατε πάντα τὰ ἔθνη, βαπτίζ-
therefore disciple ye all the nations, baptiz-

οντες αὐτοὺς εἰς τὸ ὄνομα τοῦ πατρὸς
ing them in the name of the Father

καὶ τοῦ υἱοῦ καὶ τοῦ ἁγίου πνεύματος,
and of the Son and of the Holy Spirit,

20 διδάσκοντες αὐτοὺς τηρεῖν πάντα
teaching them to observe all things

ὅσα ἐνετειλάμην ὑμῖν· καὶ ἰδοὺ ἐγὼ
whatever I gave command to you; and behold I

μεθ' ὑμῶν εἰμι πάσας τὰς ἡμέρας ἕως
with you am all the days until

τῆς συντελείας τοῦ αἰῶνος.
the completion of the age.

KATA MAPKON
According to Mark

CHAPTER 1

THE beginning of the gospel of Jesus Christ, the Son of God;

2 As it is written in the prophets, Behold, I send my messenger before thy face, which shall prepare thy way before thee.

3 The voice of one crying in the wilderness, Prepare ye the way of the Lord, make his paths straight.

4 John did baptize in the wilderness, and preach the baptism of repentance for the remission of sins.

5 And there went out unto him all the land of Judæa, and they of Jerusalem, and were all baptized of him in the river of Jordan, confessing their sins.

6 And John was clothed with camel's hair, and with a girdle of a skin about his loins; and he did eat locusts and wild honey;

7 And preached, saying, There cometh one mightier than I after me, the latchet of whose shoes I am not worthy to stoop down and unloose.

8 I indeed have baptized you with water: but he shall baptize you with the Holy Ghost.

9 ¶ And it came to pass in those days, that Jesus came from Nazareth of

1 Ἀρχὴ τοῦ εὐαγγελίου Ἰησοῦ Χριστοῦ.
[The] beginning of the   gospel   of Jesus   Christ.

2 Καθὼς γέγραπται ἐν τῷ Ἡσαΐᾳ τῷ
As   it has been written in   –   Isaiah   the

προφήτῃ· ἰδοὺ ἀποστέλλω τὸν ἄγγελόν μου
prophet: Behold[,]   I send   the   messenger of me

πρὸ προσώπου σου, ὃς κατασκευάσει τὴν ὁδόν
before [the] face   of thee, who   will prepare   the   way

σου· 3 φωνὴ βοῶντος ἐν τῇ ἐρήμῳ· ἑτοιμάσατε
of thee; a voice of [one] crying in the   desert: Prepare ye

τὴν ὁδὸν κυρίου, εὐθείας ποιεῖτε τὰς τρίβους
the   way of [the] Lord, straight   make   the   paths

αὐτοῦ, 4 ἐγένετο Ἰωάννης ὁ βαπτίζων ἐν τῇ
of him,   came   John   the [one] baptizing in   the

ἐρήμῳ κηρύσσων βάπτισμα μετανοίας εἰς
desert   proclaiming   a baptism   of repentance   for

ἄφεσιν ἁμαρτιῶν. 5 καὶ ἐξεπορεύετο πρὸς
forgiveness   of sins.   And   went out   to

αὐτὸν πᾶσα ἡ Ἰουδαία χώρα καὶ οἱ Ἱεροσο-
him   all   the   Judæan   country and the   Jerusa-

λυμῖται πάντες, καὶ ἐβαπτίζοντο ὑπ' αὐτοῦ
lemites   all,   and   were baptized   by   him

ἐν τῷ Ἰορδάνῃ ποταμῷ ἐξομολογούμενοι τὰς
in the   Jordan   river   confessing   the

ἁμαρτίας αὐτῶν. 6 καὶ ἦν ὁ Ἰωάννης
sins   of them.   And was   –   John

ἐνδεδυμένος τρίχας καμήλου καὶ ζώνην
having been clothed [in] hairs of a camel   and   girdle

δερματίνην περὶ τὴν ὀσφὺν αὐτοῦ, καὶ ἔσθων
a leathern   round the   loin[s] of him,   and   eating

ἀκρίδας καὶ μέλι ἄγριον. 7 καὶ ἐκήρυσσεν
locusts   and   honey   wild.   And   he proclaimed

λέγων· ἔρχεται ὁ ἰσχυρότερός μου ὀπίσω
saying: Comes the [one] stronger   of me   after
=than I

[μου], οὗ οὐκ εἰμὶ ἱκανὸς κύψας λῦσαι
me, of whom I am not   competent stooping to loosen

τὸν ἱμάντα τῶν ὑποδημάτων αὐτοῦ. 8 ἐγὼ
the   thong   of the   sandals   of him.   I

ἐβάπτισα ὑμᾶς ὕδατι, αὐτὸς δὲ βαπτίσει ὑμᾶς
baptized   you in water,   but he   will baptize   you

πνεύματι ἁγίῳ.
Spirit   in [the] Holy.

9 Καὶ ἐγένετο ἐν ἐκείναις ταῖς ἡμέραις
And it came to pass in   those   –   days

ἦλθεν Ἰησοῦς ἀπὸ Ναζαρὲθ τῆς Γαλιλαίας
came   Jesus   from   Nazareth   –   of Galilee

Galilee, and was baptized of John in Jordan.

10 And straightway coming up out of the water, he saw the heavens opened, and the Spirit like a dove descending upon him:

11 And there came a voice from heaven, *saying*, Thou art my beloved Son, in whom I am well pleased.

12 ¶ And immediately the spirit driveth him into the wilderness.

13 And he was there in the wilderness forty days, tempted of Satan; and was with the wild beasts; and the angels ministered unto him.

14 ¶ Now after that John was put in prison, Jesus came into Galilee, preaching the gospel of the kingdom of God,

15 And saying, The time is fulfilled, and the kingdom of God is at hand: repent ye, and believe the gospel.

16 ¶ Now as he walked by the sea of Galilee, he saw Simon and Andrew his brother casting a net into the sea: for they were fishers.

17 And Jesus said unto them, Come ye after me, and I will make you to become fishers of men.

18 And straightway they

καὶ ἐβαπτίσθη εἰς τὸν Ἰορδάνην ὑπὸ
and was baptized in the Jordan by

Ἰωάννου. 10 καὶ εὐθὺς ἀναβαίνων ἐκ τοῦ
John. And immediately going up out of the

ὕδατος εἶδεν σχιζομένους τοὺς οὐρανοὺς
water he saw being rent the heavens

καὶ τὸ πνεῦμα ὡς περιστερὰν καταβαῖνον
and the Spirit as a dove coming down

εἰς αὐτόν· 11 καὶ φωνὴ [ἐγένετο] ἐκ τῶν
to him; and a voice there was out of the

οὐρανῶν· σὺ εἶ ὁ υἱός μου ὁ ἀγαπητός,
heavens: Thou art the Son of me the beloved,

ἐν σοὶ εὐδόκησα. 12 Καὶ εὐθὺς τὸ
in thee I was well pleased. And immediately the

πνεῦμα αὐτὸν ἐκβάλλει εἰς τὴν ἔρημον.
Spirit him thrusts forth into the desert.

13 καὶ ἦν ἐν τῇ ἐρήμῳ τεσσεράκοντα
And he was in the desert forty

ἡμέρας πειραζόμενος ὑπὸ τοῦ σατανᾶ, καὶ
days being tempted by – Satan, and

ἦν μετὰ τῶν θηρίων, καὶ οἱ ἄγγελοι
was with the wild beasts, and the angels

διηκόνουν αὐτῷ.
ministered to him.

14 Καὶ μετὰ τὸ παραδοθῆναι τὸν
And after the to be delivered –
= after John was delivered

Ἰωάννην ἦλθεν ὁ Ἰησοῦς εἰς τὴν Γαλιλαίαν
John[b] came – Jesus into – Galilee

κηρύσσων τὸ εὐαγγέλιον τοῦ θεοῦ 15 [καὶ
proclaiming the gospel – of God and

λέγων], ὅτι πεπλήρωται ὁ καιρὸς καὶ
saying, – Has been fulfilled the time and

ἤγγικεν ἡ βασιλεία τοῦ θεοῦ· μετανοεῖτε
has drawn near the kingdom – of God; repent ye

καὶ πιστεύετε ἐν τῷ εὐαγγελίῳ. 16 Καὶ
and believe in the gospel. And

παράγων παρὰ τὴν θάλασσαν τῆς Γαλιλαίας
passing along beside the sea – of Galilee

εἶδεν Σίμωνα καὶ Ἀνδρέαν τὸν ἀδελφὸν
he saw Simon and Andrew the brother

Σίμωνος ἀμφιβάλλοντας ἐν τῇ θαλάσσῃ·
of Simon casting [a net] in the sea;

ἦσαν γὰρ ἁλεεῖς. 17 καὶ εἶπεν αὐτοῖς
for they were fishers. And said to them

ὁ Ἰησοῦς· δεῦτε ὀπίσω μου, καὶ ποιήσω
– Jesus: Come after me, and I will make

ὑμᾶς γενέσθαι ἁλεεῖς ἀνθρώπων. 18 καὶ
you to become fishers of men. And

forsook their nets, and
followed him.

19 And when he had
gone a little farther thence,
he saw James the *son* of
Zebedee, and John his
brother, who also were
in the ship mending their
nets.

20 And straightway he
called them: and they left
their father Zebedee in the
ship with the hired servants,
and went after him.

21 And they went into
Capernaum; and straight-
way on the sabbath day he
entered into the synagogue,
and taught.

22 And they were aston-
ished at his doctrine: for
he taught them as one that
had authority, and not as
the scribes.

23 And there was in
their synagogue a man
with an unclean spirit; and
he cried out,

24 Saying, Let *us* alone;
what have we to do with
thee, thou Jesus of Naza-
reth? art thou come to
destroy us? I know thee
who thou art, the Holy
One of God.

25 And Jesus rebuked
him, saying, Hold thy
peace, and come out of
him.

26 And when the un-
clean spirit had torn him,
and cried with a loud voice,
he came out of him.

27 And they were all
amazed, insomuch that

εὐθὺς   ἀφέντες   τὰ   δίκτυα   ἠκολούθησαν
immediately leaving   the   nets   they followed

αὐτῷ.   19 Καὶ   προβὰς   ὀλίγον   εἶδεν
him.   And   going forward   a little   he saw

’Ιάκωβον   τὸν   τοῦ   Ζεβεδαίου   καὶ   ’Ιωάννην
James   the [son]   –   of Zebedee   and   John

τὸν   ἀδελφὸν   αὐτοῦ   καὶ   αὐτοὺς   ἐν   τῷ
the   brother   of him   even   them   in   the

πλοίῳ   καταρτίζοντας   τὰ   δίκτυα.   20 καὶ
ship   mending   the   nets.   And

εὐθὺς   ἐκάλεσεν   αὐτούς·   καὶ   ἀφέντες   τὸν
immediately he called   them;   and   leaving   the

πατέρα   αὐτῶν   Ζεβεδαῖον   ἐν   τῷ   πλοίῳ
father   of them   Zebedee   in   the   ship

μετὰ   τῶν   μισθωτῶν   ἀπῆλθον   ὀπίσω   αὐτοῦ.
with   the   hired servants   they went   after   him.

21 Καὶ   εἰσπορεύονται   εἰς   Καφαρναούμ·
And   they enter   into   Capernaum;

καὶ   εὐθὺς   τοῖς   σάββασιν   εἰσελθὼν
and   immediately on the   sabbaths   entering

εἰς   τὴν   συναγωγὴν   ἐδίδασκεν.   22 καὶ
into   the   synagogue   he taught.   And

ἐξεπλήσσοντο   ἐπὶ   τῇ   διδαχῇ   αὐτοῦ·   ἦν
they were astounded on(at) the   teaching   of him;   ²he was

γὰρ   διδάσκων   αὐτοὺς   ὡς   ἐξουσίαν   ἔχων,
¹for   teaching   them   as   authority   having,

καὶ   οὐχ   ὡς   οἱ   γραμματεῖς.   23 Καὶ   εὐθὺς
and   not   as   the   scribes.   And   immediately

ἦν   ἐν   τῇ   συναγωγῇ   αὐτῶν   ἄνθρωπος
there was in the   synagogue   of them   a man

ἐν   πνεύματι   ἀκαθάρτῳ,   καὶ   ἀνέκραξεν
in   spirit   an unclean,   and   he cried out

24 λέγων·   τί   ἡμῖν   καὶ   σοί,   ’Ιησοῦ
saying: What   to us   and   to thee,   Jesus

Ναζαρηνέ;   ἦλθες   ἀπολέσαι   ἡμᾶς;   οἶδά
Nazarene?   camest thou   to destroy   us?   I know

σε   τίς   εἶ,   ὁ   ἅγιος   τοῦ   θεοῦ.   25 καὶ
thee   who thou art, the   holy [one]   –   of God.   And

ἐπετίμησεν   αὐτῷ   ὁ   ’Ιησοῦς   [λέγων]·
rebuked   him   –   Jesus   saying:

φιμώθητι   καὶ   ἔξελθε   [ἐξ   αὐτοῦ].   26 καὶ
Be quiet   and   come *out* out of   him.   And

σπαράξαν   αὐτὸν   τὸ   πνεῦμα   τὸ   ἀκάθαρτον
throwing   him   the   spirit   –   unclean

καὶ   φωνῆσαν   φωνῇ   μεγάλῃ   ἐξῆλθεν   ἐξ
and   shouting   voice   with a great   he came *out* out of

αὐτοῦ.   27 καὶ   ἐθαμβήθησαν   ἅπαντες,   ὥστε
him.   And   were astounded   all,   so as
                                                         = so that

they questioned among themselves, saying, What thing is this? what new doctrine is this? for with authority commandeth he even the unclean spirits, and they do obey him.

28 And immediately his fame spread abroad throughout all the region round about Galilee.

29 ¶ And forthwith, when they were come out of the synagogue, they entered into the house of Simon and Andrew, with James and John.

30 But Simon's wife's mother lay sick of a fever, and anon they tell him of her.

31 And he came and took her by the hand, and lifted her up; and immediately the fever left her, and she ministered unto them.

32 ¶ And at even, when the sun did set, they brought unto him all that were diseased, and them that were possessed with devils.

33 And all the city was gathered together at the door.

34 And he healed many that were sick of divers diseases, and cast out many devils; and suffered not the devils to speak, because they knew him.

35 ¶ And in the morning, rising up a great while before day, he went out,

---

συζητεῖν αὐτοὺς λέγοντας· τί ἐστιν τοῦτο;
to debate them[b] saying: What is this?
they debated

διδαχὴ καινὴ κατ' ἐξουσίαν· καὶ τοῖς
teaching a new by authority; and the

πνεύμασι τοῖς ἀκαθάρτοις ἐπιτάσσει, καὶ
spirits - unclean he commands, and

ὑπακούουσιν αὐτῷ. 28 καὶ ἐξῆλθεν ἡ
they obey him. And went forth the

ἀκοὴ αὐτοῦ εὐθὺς πανταχοῦ εἰς ὅλην
report of him immediately everywhere into all

τὴν περίχωρον τῆς Γαλιλαίας. 29 Καὶ
the neighbourhood - of Galilee. And

εὐθὺς ἐκ τῆς συναγωγῆς ἐξελθόντες ἦλθον
immediately out of the synagogue going forth they came

εἰς τὴν οἰκίαν Σίμωνος καὶ Ἀνδρέου
into the house of Simon and Andrew

μετὰ Ἰακώβου καὶ Ἰωάννου. 30 ἡ δὲ
with James and John. Now the

πενθερὰ Σίμωνος κατέκειτο πυρέσσουσα,
mother-in-law of Simon was laid [aside] fever-stricken,

καὶ εὐθὺς λέγουσιν αὐτῷ περὶ αὐτῆς.
and immediately they tell him about her.

31 καὶ προσελθὼν ἤγειρεν αὐτὴν κρατήσας
And approaching he raised her holding

τῆς χειρός· καὶ ἀφῆκεν αὐτὴν ὁ πυρετός,
the(her) hand; and left her the fever,

καὶ διηκόνει αὐτοῖς. 32 Ὀψίας δὲ γενο-
and she served them. And evening com-
= when evening

μένης, ὅτε ἔδυσεν ὁ ἥλιος, ἔφερον πρὸς
ing,[a] when set the sun, they brought to
came,

αὐτὸν πάντας τοὺς κακῶς ἔχοντας καὶ
him all the [ones] ill having and
= those who were ill

τοὺς δαιμονιζομένους· 33 καὶ ἦν ὅλη ἡ
the being demon-possessed; and was all the

πόλις ἐπισυνηγμένη πρὸς τὴν θύραν.
city having been assembled at the door.

34 καὶ ἐθεράπευσεν πολλοὺς κακῶς ἔχοντας
And he healed many ill having
= who were ill

ποικίλαις νόσοις, καὶ δαιμόνια πολλὰ
with various diseases, and demons many

ἐξέβαλεν, καὶ οὐκ ἤφιεν λαλεῖν τὰ δαιμόνια,
he expelled, and did not allow to speak the demons,

ὅτι ᾔδεισαν αὐτόν. 35 Καὶ πρωῒ ἔννυχα
because they knew him. And [3]early [4]in the night

λίαν ἀναστὰς ἐξῆλθεν καὶ ἀπῆλθεν εἰς
[a]very [1]rising up he went out and went away to

and departed into a solitary place, and there prayed.

36 And Simon and they that were with him followed after him.

37 And when they had found him, they said unto him, All *men* seek for thee.

38 And he said unto them, Let us go into the next towns, that I may preach there also: for therefore came I forth.

39 And he preached in their synagogues throughout all Galilee, and cast out devils.

40 ¶ And there came a leper to him, beseeching him, and kneeling down to him, and saying unto him, If thou wilt, thou canst make me clean.

41 And Jesus, moved with compassion, put forth *his* hand, and touched him, and saith unto him, I will; be thou clean.

42 And as soon as he had spoken, immediately the leprosy departed from him, and he was cleansed.

43 And he straitly charged him, and forthwith sent him away;

44 And saith unto him, See thou say nothing to any man: but go thy way, shew thyself to the priest, and offer for thy cleansing those things which Moses commanded, for a testimony unto them.

45 But he went out, and began to publish *it* much, and to blaze abroad the matter, insomuch that

---

ἔρημον τόπον, κἀκεῖ προσηύχετο. **36** καὶ
a desert place, and there prayed. And

κατεδίωξεν αὐτὸν Σίμων καὶ οἱ μετ'
hunted down him Simon and the [ones] with

αὐτοῦ, καὶ εὗρον αὐτὸν καὶ λέγουσιν
him, and found him and say

αὐτῷ **37** ὅτι πάντες ζητοῦσίν σε. **38** καὶ
to him[,] – All are seeking thee. And

λέγει αὐτοῖς· ἄγωμεν ἀλλαχοῦ εἰς τὰς
he says to them: Let us go elsewhere into the

ἐχομένας κωμοπόλεις, ἵνα καὶ ἐκεῖ
neighbouring towns, that also there

κηρύξω· εἰς τοῦτο γὰρ ἐξῆλθον. **39** καὶ
I may proclaim; for for this [purpose] I came forth. And

ἦλθεν κηρύσσων εἰς τὰς συναγωγὰς αὐτῶν
he came proclaiming in the synagogues of them

εἰς ὅλην τὴν Γαλιλαίαν καὶ τὰ δαιμόνια
in all – Galilee and the demons

ἐκβάλλων.
expelling.

40 Καὶ ἔρχεται πρὸς αὐτὸν λεπρὸς
And comes to him a leper

παρακαλῶν αὐτὸν καὶ γονυπετῶν λέγων
beseeching him and falling on [his] knees saying

αὐτῷ ὅτι ἐὰν θέλῃς δύνασαί με καθαρίσαι.
to him[,] – If thou art willing thou art able me to cleanse.

41 καὶ σπλαγχνισθεὶς ἐκτείνας τὴν
And being filled with tenderness stretching forth the(his)

χεῖρα αὐτοῦ ἥψατο καὶ λέγει αὐτῷ· θέλω,
hand ¹him ¹he touched and says to him: I am willing,

καθαρίσθητι. **42** καὶ εὐθὺς ἀπῆλθεν ἀπ'
be thou cleansed. And immediately departed from

αὐτοῦ ἡ λέπρα, καὶ ἐκαθαρίσθη. **43** καὶ
him the leprosy, and he was cleansed. And

ἐμβριμησάμενος αὐτῷ εὐθὺς ἐξέβαλεν αὐτόν,
sternly admonishing him immediately he put out him,

44 καὶ λέγει αὐτῷ· ὅρα μηδενὶ μηδὲν
and says to him: See no one no(any)thing

εἴπῃς, ἀλλὰ ὕπαγε σεαυτὸν δεῖξον τῷ
thou tellest, but go thyself show to the

ἱερεῖ καὶ προσένεγκε περὶ τοῦ καθαρισμοῦ σου
priest and offer concerning the cleansing of thee

ἃ προσέταξεν Μωϋσῆς, εἰς μαρτύριον
[the things] which commanded Moses, for a testimony

αὐτοῖς. **45** ὁ δὲ ἐξελθὼν ἤρξατο κηρύσσειν
to them. But he going out began to proclaim

πολλὰ καὶ διαφημίζειν τὸν λόγον, ὥστε
many things and to spread about the matter, so as
= so that

Jesus could no more openly enter into the city, but was without in desert places: and they came to him from every quarter.

μηκέτι   αὐτὸν   δύνασθαι   φανερῶς   εἰς   πόλιν
no longer   him   to be able[b]   openly   into   a city
he was no longer able

εἰσελθεῖν,   ἀλλ'   ἔξω   ἐπ'   ἐρήμοις   τόποις
to enter,   but   outside   on(in)   desert   places

ἦν·   καὶ   ἤρχοντο   πρὸς   αὐτὸν   πάντοθεν.
he was;   and   they came   to   him   from all directions.

CHAPTER 2

AND again he entered into Capernaum after *some* days; and it was noised that he was in the house.

2 And straightway many were gathered together, insomuch that there was no room to receive *them*, no, not so much as about the door: and he preached the word unto them.

3 And they come unto him, bringing one sick of the palsy, which was borne of four.

4 And when they could not come nigh unto him for the press, they uncovered the roof where he was: and when they had broken *it* up, they let down the bed wherein the sick of the palsy lay.

5 When Jesus saw their faith, he said unto the sick of the palsy, Son, thy sins be forgiven thee.

6 But there were certain of the scribes sitting there, and reasoning in their hearts,

7 Why doth this *man* thus speak blasphemies? who can forgive sins but God only?

8 And immediately when Jesus perceived in his spirit that they so reasoned within themselves, he said

2 Καὶ   εἰσελθὼν   πάλιν   εἰς   Καφαρναοὺμ
And   entering   again   into   Capernaum

δι'   ἡμερῶν   ἠκούσθη   ὅτι   ἐν   οἴκῳ   ἐστίν.
through days   it was heard   that   at home   he is(was).
= after [some] days

2 καὶ   συνήχθησαν   πολλοί,   ὥστε   μηκέτι
And   were assembled   many,   so as   no longer

χωρεῖν   μηδὲ   τὰ   πρὸς   τὴν   θύραν,   καὶ
to have room   not   –   at   the   door,   and

ἐλάλει   αὐτοῖς   τὸν   λόγον.   3 καὶ   ἔρχονται
he spoke   to them   the   word.   And   they come

φέροντες   πρὸς   αὐτὸν   παραλυτικὸν   αἰρόμενον
carrying   to   him   a paralytic   being borne

ὑπὸ   τεσσάρων.   4 καὶ   μὴ   δυνάμενοι
by   four [men].   And   not   being able

προσενέγκαι   αὐτῷ   διὰ   τὸν   ὄχλον
to bring   to him   because of   the   crowd

ἀπεστέγασαν   τὴν   στέγην   ὅπου   ἦν,   καὶ
they unroofed   the   roof   where   he was,   and

ἐξορύξαντες   χαλῶσι   τὸν   κράβατον   ὅπου   ὁ
having opened up   they lower   the   mattress   where   the

παραλυτικὸς   κατέκειτο.   5 καὶ   ἰδὼν   ὁ
paralytic   was lying.   And   seeing   –

Ἰησοῦς   τὴν   πίστιν   αὐτῶν   λέγει   τῷ
Jesus   the   faith   of them   he says   to the

παραλυτικῷ·   τέκνον,   ἀφίενταί   σου   αἱ
paralytic: Child,   are forgiven   of thee   the

ἁμαρτίαι.   6 ἦσαν   δέ   τινες   τῶν   γραμματέων
sins.   Now there were   some   of the   scribes

ἐκεῖ   καθήμενοι   καὶ   διαλογιζόμενοι   ἐν   ταῖς
there   sitting   and   reasoning   in the

καρδίαις   αὐτῶν·   7 τί   οὗτος   οὕτως   λαλεῖ;
hearts   of them·   Why this man   thus   speaks?

βλασφημεῖ·   τίς   δύναται   ἀφιέναι   ἁμαρτίας
he blasphemes;   who   can   *to* forgive   sins

εἰ   μὴ   εἷς   ὁ   θεός;   8 καὶ   εὐθὺς   ἐπιγνοὺς
except   one[,]   –   God?   And immediately   knowing

ὁ   Ἰησοῦς   τῷ   πνεύματι   αὐτοῦ   ὅτι   οὕτως
–   Jesus   in the   spirit   of him   that   thus

διαλογίζονται   ἐν   ἑαυτοῖς,   λέγει   αὐτοῖς·
they reason   among   themselves,   he says   to them:

unto them, Why reason ye
these things in your hearts?

9 Whether is it easier to
say to the sick of the palsy,
Thy sins be forgiven thee;
or to say, Arise, and take
up thy bed, and walk ?

10 But that ye may
know that the Son of man
hath power on earth to
forgive sins, (he saith to
the sick of the palsy,)

11 I say unto thee,
Arise, and take up thy bed.
and go thy way into thine
house.

12 And immediately he
arose, took up the bed, and
went forth before them all;
insomuch that they were
all amazed, and glorified
God, saying, We never saw
it on this fashion.

13 ¶ And he went forth
again by the sea side; and
all the multitude resorted
unto him, and he taught
them.

14 And as he passed by,
he saw Levi the *son* of
Alphæus sitting at the
receipt of custom, and said
unto him, Follow me.
And he arose and followed
him.

15 And it came to pass,
that, as Jesus sat at meat
in his house, many pub-
licans and sinners sat also
together with Jesus and

τί ταῦτα διαλογίζεσθε ἐν ταῖς καρδίαις
Why these things reason ye in the hearts

ὑμῶν; 9 τί ἐστιν εὐκοπώτερον, εἰπεῖν
of you? What is easier, to say

τῷ παραλυτικῷ· ἀφίενταί σου αἱ ἁμαρτίαι,
to the paralytic: are forgiven of thee the sins,

ἢ εἰπεῖν· ἔγειρε καὶ ἆρον τὸν κράβατόν
or to say: Rise and take the mattress

σου καὶ περιπάτει; 10 ἵνα δὲ εἰδῆτε
of thee and walk? But that ye may know

ὅτι ἐξουσίαν ἔχει ὁ υἱὸς τοῦ ἀνθρώπου
that authority has the Son - of man

ἀφιέναι ἁμαρτίας ἐπὶ τῆς γῆς,—λέγει τῷ
to forgive sins on the earth,—he says to the

παραλυτικῷ· 11 σοὶ λέγω, ἔγειρε ἆρον
paralytic: To thee I say, rise[,] take

τὸν κράβατόν σου καὶ ὕπαγε εἰς τὸν
the mattress of thee and go to the

οἶκόν σου. 12 καὶ ἠγέρθη καὶ εὐθὺς
house of thee. And he arose and immediately

ἄρας τὸν κράβατον ἐξῆλθεν ἔμπροσθεν
taking the mattress he went forth before

πάντων, ὥστε ἐξίστασθαι πάντας καὶ
all, so as to be astonished all and
       = so that they were all astonished and glorified

δοξάζειν τὸν θεὸν λέγοντας ὅτι οὕτως
to glorify[b] - God saying[,] - Thus

οὐδέποτε εἴδαμεν.
never we saw.

13 Καὶ ἐξῆλθεν πάλιν παρὰ τὴν θάλασσαν·
And he went forth again by the sea;

καὶ πᾶς ὁ ὄχλος ἤρχετο πρὸς αὐτόν,
and all the crowd came to him,

καὶ ἐδίδασκεν αὐτούς. 14 Καὶ παράγων
and he taught them. And passing along

εἶδεν Λευὶν τὸν τοῦ Ἀλφαίου καθήμενον
he saw Levi the [son] - Alphæus sitting

ἐπὶ τὸ τελώνιον, καὶ λέγει αὐτῷ· ἀκολούθει
on(in or at) the custom house, and says to him: Follow

μοι. καὶ ἀναστὰς ἠκολούθησεν αὐτῷ.
me. And rising up he followed him.

15 Καὶ γίνεται κατακεῖσθαι αὐτὸν ἐν τῇ
And it comes to pass to recline him[b] in the
       = he reclines

οἰκίᾳ αὐτοῦ, καὶ πολλοὶ τελῶναι καὶ
house of him, and many tax-collectors and

ἁμαρτωλοὶ συνανέκειντο τῷ Ἰησοῦ καὶ
sinners reclined with - Jesus and

his disciples: for there were many, and they followed him.

16 And when the scribes and Pharisees saw him eat with publicans and sinners, they said unto his disciples, How is it that he eateth and drinketh with publicans and sinners?

17 When Jesus heard *it*, he saith unto them, They that are whole have no need of the physician, but they that are sick: I came not to call the righteous, but sinners to repentance.

18 ¶ And the disciples of John and of the Pharisees used to fast: and they come and say unto him, Why do the disciples of John and of the Pharisees fast, but thy disciples fast not?

19 And Jesus said unto them, Can the children of the bridechamber fast, while the bridegroom is with them? as long as they have the bridegroom with them, they cannot fast.

20 But the days will come, when the bridegroom shall be taken away from them, and then shall they fast in those days.

21 No man also seweth a piece of new cloth on an old garment: else the new

τοῖς μαθηταῖς αὐτοῦ· ἦσαν γὰρ πολλοί,
the disciples of him; for there were many,

καὶ ἠκολούθουν αὐτῷ. 16 καὶ οἱ γραμματεῖς
and they followed him. And the scribes

τῶν Φαρισαίων ἰδόντες ὅτι ἐσθίει
of the Pharisees seeing that he eats(ate)

μετὰ τῶν ἁμαρτωλῶν καὶ τελωνῶν ἔλεγον
with – sinners and tax-collectors said

τοῖς μαθηταῖς αὐτοῦ· ὅτι μετὰ τῶν
to the disciples of him: – With –

τελωνῶν καὶ ἁμαρτωλῶν ἐσθίει; 17 καὶ
tax-collectors and sinners does he eat? And

ἀκούσας ὁ Ἰησοῦς λέγει αὐτοῖς [ὅτι] οὐ
hearing Jesus says to them[,] Not

χρείαν ἔχουσιν οἱ ἰσχύοντες ἰατροῦ ἀλλ'
need have the [ones] being strong of a physician but

οἱ κακῶς ἔχοντες· οὐκ ἦλθον καλέσαι
the [ones] ill having; I came not to call
= those who are ill;

δικαίους ἀλλὰ ἁμαρτωλούς. 18 Καὶ ἦσαν
righteous men but sinners. And ⁷were

οἱ μαθηταὶ Ἰωάννου καὶ οἱ Φαρισαῖοι
¹the ²disciples ³of John ⁴and ⁵the ⁶Pharisees

νηστεύοντες. καὶ ἔρχονται καὶ λέγουσιν
⁸fasting. And they come and say

αὐτῷ· διὰ τί οἱ μαθηταὶ Ἰωάννου καὶ
to him: Why the disciples of John and

οἱ μαθηταὶ τῶν Φαρισαίων νηστεύουσιν,
the disciples of the Pharisees fast,

οἱ δὲ σοὶ μαθηταὶ οὐ νηστεύουσιν; 19 καὶ
– but thy disciples do not fast? And

εἶπεν αὐτοῖς ὁ Ἰησοῦς· μὴ δύνανται οἱ
said to them – Jesus: *not* can the

υἱοὶ τοῦ νυμφῶνος, ἐν ᾧ ὁ νυμφίος
sons of the bridechamber, while† the bridegroom

μετ' αὐτῶν ἐστιν, νηστεύειν; ὅσον χρόνον
with them is, *to* fast? what time

ἔχουσιν τὸν νυμφίον μετ' αὐτῶν, οὐ
they have the bridegroom with them, not

δύνανται νηστεύειν. 20 ἐλεύσονται δὲ ἡμέραι
they can *to* fast. But will come days

ὅταν ἀπαρθῇ ἀπ' αὐτῶν ὁ νυμφίος, καὶ
when taken away from them the bridegroom, and

τότε νηστεύσουσιν ἐν ἐκείνῃ τῇ ἡμέρᾳ.
then they will fast in that day.

21 Οὐδεὶς ἐπίβλημα ῥάκους ἀγνάφου ἐπιράπτει
No one a patch cloth of unfulled sews

ἐπὶ ἱμάτιον παλαιόν· εἰ δὲ μή, αἴρει
on garment an old; otherwise, ⁹takes

piece that filled it up taketh away from the old, and the rent is made worse.

22 And no man putteth new wine into old bottles: else the new wine doth burst the bottles, and the wine is spilled, and the bottles will be marred: but new wine must be put into new bottles.

23 ¶ And it came to pass, that he went through the corn fields on the sabbath day; and his disciples began, as they went, to pluck the ears of corn.

24 And the Pharisees said unto him, Behold, why do they on the sabbath day that which is not lawful ?

25 And he said unto them, Have ye never read what David did, when he had need, and was an hungred, he, and they that were with him ?

26 How he went into the house of God in the days of Abiathar the high priest, and did eat the shewbread, which is not lawful to eat but for the priests, and gave also to them which were with him?

27 And he said unto them, The sabbath was made for man, and not man for the sabbath:

28 Therefore the Son of man is Lord also of the sabbath.

τὸ πλήρωμα ἀπ᾽ αὐτοῦ τὸ καινὸν τοῦ
⁴the ⁵fulness ⁶from ⁹itself ¹the ²new ⁷the
παλαιοῦ, καὶ χεῖρον σχίσμα γίνεται. 22 καὶ
⁸old, and a worse rent occurs. And
οὐδεὶς βάλλει οἶνον νέον εἰς ἀσκοὺς παλαιούς·
no one puts wine new into wineskins old;
εἰ δὲ μή, ῥήξει ὁ οἶνος τοὺς ἀσκούς,
otherwise, ²will burst ¹the ²wine the wineskins,
καὶ ὁ οἶνος ἀπόλλυται καὶ οἱ ἀσκοί.
and the wine perishes and the wineskins.
[ἀλλὰ οἶνον νέον εἰς ἀσκοὺς καινούς.]
But wine new into wineskins fresh.

23 Καὶ ἐγένετο αὐτὸν ἐν τοῖς σάββασιν
And it came to pass him on the sabbaths
= as he passed on the sabbath
παραπορεύεσθαι διὰ τῶν σπορίμων, καὶ
to passᵇ through the cornfields, and
οἱ μαθηταὶ αὐτοῦ ἤρξαντο ὁδὸν ποιεῖν
the disciples of him began way to make
τίλλοντες τοὺς στάχυας. 24 καὶ οἱ Φαρισαῖοι
plucking the ears of corn. And the Pharisees
ἔλεγον αὐτῷ· ἴδε τί ποιοῦσιν τοῖς σάββασιν
said to him: Behold[,] why do on the sabbaths
ὃ οὐκ ἔξεστιν; 25 καὶ λέγει αὐτοῖς·
what is not lawful ? And he says to them:
οὐδέποτε ἀνέγνωτε τί ἐποίησεν Δαυίδ,
never read ye what did David,
ὅτε χρείαν ἔσχεν καὶ ἐπείνασεν αὐτὸς
when need he had and hungered he
καὶ οἱ μετ᾽ αὐτοῦ; 26 [πῶς] εἰσῆλθεν
and the [ones] with him ? how he entered
εἰς τὸν οἶκον τοῦ θεοῦ ἐπὶ Ἀβιαθὰρ
into the house - of God on(in the days of) Abiathar
ἀρχιερέως καὶ τοὺς ἄρτους τῆς προθέσεως
high priest and the loaves of the setting forth
ἔφαγεν, οὓς οὐκ ἔξεστιν φαγεῖν εἰ μὴ
ate, which it is not lawful to eat except
τοὺς ἱερεῖς, καὶ ἔδωκεν καὶ τοῖς σὺν
the priests, and gave also to the [ones] with
αὐτῷ οὖσιν; 27 καὶ ἔλεγεν αὐτοῖς·
him being ? And he said to them:
τὸ σάββατον διὰ τὸν ἄνθρωπον ἐγένετο,
The sabbath on account of - man was,
καὶ οὐχ ὁ ἄνθρωπος διὰ τὸ σάββατον·
and not - man on account of the sabbath;
28 ὥστε κύριός ἐστιν ὁ υἱὸς τοῦ ἀνθρώπου
so as Lord is the Son - of man
καὶ τοῦ σαββάτου.
also of the sabbath.

CHAPTER 3

AND he entered again into the synagogue; and there was a man there which had a withered hand.

2 And they watched him, whether he would heal him on the sabbath day; that they might accuse him.

3 And he saith unto the man which had the withered hand, Stand forth.

4 And he saith unto them, Is it lawful to do good on the sabbath days, or to do evil? to save life, or to kill? But they held their peace.

5 And when he had looked round about on them with anger, being grieved for the hardness of their hearts, he saith unto the man, Stretch forth thine hand. And he stretched *it* out: and his hand was restored whole as the other.

6 And the Pharisees went forth, and straightway took counsel with the Herodians against him, how they might destroy him.

7 ¶ But Jesus withdrew himself with his disciples to the sea: and a great multitude from Galilee followed him, and from Judæa,

8 And from Jerusalem, and from Idumæa, and *from* beyond Jordan; and they about Tyre and Sidon, a great multitude, when they had heard what great things he did, came unto him.

---

3 Καὶ εἰσῆλθεν πάλιν εἰς συναγωγήν.
And he entered again into a synagogue.

καὶ ἦν ἐκεῖ ἄνθρωπος ἐξηραμμένην ἔχων
And there was there a man *having been* withered ¹having

τὴν χεῖρα· 2 καὶ παρετήρουν αὐτὸν εἰ
²the ³hand; and they watched carefully him if

τοῖς σάββασιν θεραπεύσει αὐτόν, ἵνα
on the sabbaths he will heal him, that

κατηγορήσωσιν αὐτοῦ. 3 καὶ λέγει τῷ
they might accuse him. And he says to the

ἀνθρώπῳ τῷ τὴν χεῖρα ἔχοντι ξηράν·
man – the hand having dry:

ἔγειρε εἰς τὸ μέσον. 4 καὶ λέγει αὐτοῖς·
Rise into the midst. And he says to them:

ἔξεστιν τοῖς σάββασιν ἀγαθὸν ποιῆσαι
Lawful on the sabbaths good to do

ἢ κακοποιῆσαι, ψυχὴν σῶσαι ἢ ἀποκτεῖναι;
or to do evil, life to save or to kill?

οἱ δὲ ἐσιώπων. 5 καὶ περιβλεψάμενος
But they were silent. And looking round

αὐτοὺς μετ' ὀργῆς, συλλυπούμενος ἐπὶ
[on] them with anger, being greatly grieved on(at)

τῇ πωρώσει τῆς καρδίας αὐτῶν, λέγει
the hardness of the heart of them, he says

τῷ ἀνθρώπῳ· ἔκτεινον τὴν χεῖρα. καὶ
to the man: Stretch forth the hand. And

ἐξέτεινεν, καὶ ἀπεκατεστάθη ἡ χεὶρ αὐτοῦ.
he stretched forth, and was restored the hand of him.

6 καὶ ἐξελθόντες οἱ Φαρισαῖοι εὐθὺς μετὰ
And going forth the Pharisees immediately with

τῶν Ἡρῳδιανῶν συμβούλιον ἐδίδουν κατ'
the Herodians counsel gave against

αὐτοῦ, ὅπως αὐτὸν ἀπολέσωσιν.
him, that him they might destroy.

7 Καὶ ὁ Ἰησοῦς μετὰ τῶν μαθητῶν
And – Jesus with the disciples

αὐτοῦ ἀνεχώρησεν πρὸς τὴν θάλασσαν·
of him departed to the sea;

καὶ πολὺ πλῆθος ἀπὸ τῆς Γαλιλαίας
and a much(great) multitude from – Galilee

ἠκολούθησεν· καὶ ἀπὸ τῆς Ἰουδαίας 8 καὶ
followed; and from – Judæa and

ἀπὸ Ἱεροσολύμων καὶ ἀπὸ τῆς Ἰδουμαίας
from Jerusalem and from – Idumæa

καὶ πέραν τοῦ Ἰορδάνου καὶ περὶ Τύρον
and beyond the Jordan and round Tyre

καὶ Σιδῶνα, πλῆθος πολύ, ἀκούοντες ὅσα
and Sidon, multitude a much(great), hearing what things

9 And he spake to his disciples, that a small ship should wait on him because of the multitude, lest they should throng him.

10 For he had healed many; insomuch that they pressed upon him for to touch him, as many as had plagues.

11 And unclean spirits, when they saw him, fell down before him, and cried, saying, Thou art the Son of God.

12 And he straitly charged them that they should not make him known.

13 ¶ And he goeth up into a mountain, and calleth *unto him* whom he would: and they came unto him.

14 And he ordained twelve, that they should be with him, and that he might send them forth to preach,

15 And to have power to heal sicknesses, and to cast out devils:

16 And Simon he surnamed Peter;

17 And James the *son* of Zebedee, and John the brother of James; and he surnamed them Boanerges, which is, The sons of thunder:

18 And Andrew, and Philip, and Bartholomew, and Matthew, and Thomas, and James the *son* of Alphæus, and Thaddæus,

ποιεῖ, ἦλθον πρὸς αὐτόν. **9** καὶ εἶπεν
he does, came to him. And he told

τοῖς μαθηταῖς αὐτοῦ ἵνα πλοιάριον προσκαρτέρῃ
the disciples of him that a boat should remain near

αὐτῷ διὰ τὸν ὄχλον, ἵνα μὴ θλίβωσιν
him because of the crowd, lest they should press upon

αὐτόν· **10** πολλοὺς γὰρ ἐθεράπευσεν, ὥστε
him; for many he healed, so as

ἐπιπίπτειν αὐτῷ ἵνα αὐτοῦ ἅψωνται
to fall upon him that him they might touch

ὅσοι εἶχον μάστιγας. **11** καὶ τὰ πνεύματα
as many as had plagues. And the spirits

τὰ ἀκάθαρτα, ὅταν αὐτὸν ἐθεώρουν, προσέπιπτον
- unclean, when him they saw, fell before

αὐτῷ καὶ ἔκραζον λέγοντα ὅτι σὺ εἶ ὁ
him and cried out saying[,] - Thou art the

υἱὸς τοῦ θεοῦ. **12** καὶ πολλὰ ἐπετίμα
Son - of God. And much he warned

αὐτοῖς ἵνα μὴ αὐτὸν φανερὸν ποιήσωσιν.
them that not him manifest they should make.

13 Καὶ ἀναβαίνει εἰς τὸ ὄρος, καὶ
And he goes up into the mountain, and

προσκαλεῖται οὓς ἤθελεν αὐτός, καὶ
calls to [him] [those] whom wished he, and

ἀπῆλθον πρὸς αὐτόν. **14** καὶ ἐποίησεν δώδεκα
they went to him. And he made' twelve

ἵνα ὦσιν μετ' αὐτοῦ, καὶ ἵνα ἀποστέλλῃ
that they might be with him, and that he might send

αὐτοὺς κηρύσσειν **15** καὶ ἔχειν ἐξουσίαν
them to proclaim and to have authority

ἐκβάλλειν τὰ δαιμόνια· **16** καὶ ἐποίησεν
to expel the demons ; and he made

τοὺς δώδεκα, καὶ ἐπέθηκεν ὄνομα τῷ
the twelve, and he added a name -

Σίμωνι Πέτρον· **17** καὶ Ἰάκωβον τὸν τοῦ
to Simon[,] Peter; and James the [son] -

Ζεβεδαίου καὶ Ἰωάννην τὸν ἀδελφὸν τοῦ
of Zebedee and John the brother -

Ἰακώβου, καὶ ἐπέθηκεν αὐτοῖς ὄνομα
of James, and he added to them a name[,]

Βοανηργές, ὅ ἐστιν υἱοὶ βροντῆς· **18** καὶ
Boanerges, which is sons of thunder; and

Ἀνδρέαν καὶ Φίλιππον καὶ Βαρθολομαῖον
Andrew and Philip and Bartholomew

καὶ Μαθθαῖον καὶ Θωμᾶν καὶ Ἰάκωβον
and Matthew and Thomas and James

τὸν τοῦ Ἀλφαίου καὶ Θαδδαῖον καὶ
the [son] - of Alphæus and Thaddæus and

and Simon the Canaanite,
19 And Judas Iscariot,
which also betrayed him:
and they went into an
house.

20 ¶ And the multitude
cometh together again, so
that they could not so
much as eat bread.

21 And when his friends
heard *of it*, they went out
to lay hold on him: for they
said, He is beside himself.

22 ¶ And the scribes
which came down from
Jerusalem said, He hath
Beelzebub, and by the
prince of the devils casteth
he out devils.

23 And he called them
unto him, and said unto
them in parables, How can
Satan cast out Satan?

24 And if a kingdom be
divided against itself, that
kingdom cannot stand.

25 And if a house be
divided against itself, that
house cannot stand.

26 And if Satan rise up
against himself, and be
divided, he cannot stand,
but hath an end.

27 No man can enter
into a strong man's house,
and spoil his goods, except
he will first bind the strong
man; and then he will spoil
his house.

28 Verily I say unto you,
All sins shall be forgiven

Σίμωνα   τὸν   Καναναῖον   **19** καὶ   Ἰούδαν
Simon   the   Cananæan   and   Judas

Ἰσκαριώθ,   ὃς   καὶ   παρέδωκεν   αὐτόν.
Iscariot,   who   indeed   betrayed   him.

20 Καὶ   ἔρχεται   εἰς   οἶκον·   καὶ   συνέρχεται
      And   he comes into   a house;   and   comes together

πάλιν   [ὁ]   ὄχλος,   ὥστε   μὴ   δύνασθαι
again   the   crowd,   so as   not   to be able
                                   = so that they were not able

αὐτοὺς   μηδὲ   ἄρτον   φαγεῖν.   **21** καὶ   ἀκούσαντες
them[b]   *not*   bread   to eat.   And   hearing

οἱ   παρ’   αὐτοῦ   ἐξῆλθον   κρατῆσαι   αὐτόν·
the[ones] with   him   went forth   to seize   him;
= his relations

ἔλεγον   γὰρ   ὅτι   ἐξέστη.   **22** καὶ   οἱ
for they said[,]   – He is beside himself.   And   the

γραμματεῖς   οἱ   ἀπὸ   Ἱεροσολύμων   καταβάντες
scribes   –   from   Jerusalem   coming down

ἔλεγον   ὅτι   Βεεζεβοὺλ   ἔχει,   καὶ   ὅτι   ἐν
said[,]   –   Beelzebub   he has, and[,]   By

τῷ   ἄρχοντι   τῶν   δαιμονίων   ἐκβάλλει   τὰ
the   ruler   of the   demons   he expels   the

δαιμόνια.   **23** καὶ   προσκαλεσάμενος   αὐτοὺς
demons.   And   calling to [him]   them

ἐν   παραβολαῖς   ἔλεγεν   αὐτοῖς·   πῶς   δύναται
in   parables   he said   to them: How   can

σατανᾶς   σατανᾶν   ἐκβάλλειν;   **24** καὶ   ἐὰν
Satan   [1]Satan   [1]to expel ?   and   if

βασιλεία   ἐφ’   ἑαυτὴν   μερισθῇ,   οὐ   δύναται
a kingdom   against   itself   be divided,   cannot

σταθῆναι   ἡ   βασιλεία   ἐκείνη·   **25** καὶ   ἐὰν
stand   –   kingdom   that;   and   if

οἰκία   ἐφ’   ἑαυτὴν   μερισθῇ,   οὐ   δυνήσεται
a house   against   itself   be divided,   will not be able

ἡ   οἰκία   ἐκείνη   στῆναι.   **26** καὶ   εἰ   ὁ
–   house   that   to stand.   And   if   –

σατανᾶς   ἀνέστη   ἐφ’   ἑαυτὸν   καὶ   ἐμερίσθη,
Satan   stood up   against   himself   and   was divided,

οὐ   δύναται   στῆναι   ἀλλὰ   τέλος   ἔχει.
he cannot   *to* stand   but   an end   has.

27 ἀλλ’   οὐ   δύναται   οὐδεὶς   εἰς   τὴν   οἰκίαν
     But   cannot   no(any)one   into   the   house

τοῦ   ἰσχυροῦ   εἰσελθὼν   τὰ   σκεύη   αὐτοῦ
of the   strong man   entering   the   goods   of him

διαρπάσαι,   ἐὰν   μὴ   πρῶτον   τὸν   ἰσχυρὸν
to plunder,   unless   first   the   strong man

δήσῃ,   καὶ   τότε   τὴν   οἰκίαν   αὐτοῦ   διαρπάσει.
he bind, and   then   the   house   of him   he will plunder.

28 Ἀμὴν   λέγω   ὑμῖν   ὅτι   πάντα   ἀφεθήσεται
     Truly   I tell   you   that   all   will be forgiven

unto the sons of men, and blasphemies wherewith soever they shall blaspheme:

29 But he that shall blaspheme against the Holy Ghost hath never forgiveness, but is in danger of eternal damnation:

30 Because they said, He hath an unclean spirit.

31 ¶ There came then his brethren and his mother, and, standing without, sent unto him, calling him.

32 And the multitude sat about him, and they said unto him, Behold, thy mother and thy brethren without seek for thee.

33 And he answered them, saying, Who is my mother, or my brethren?

34 And he looked round about on them which sat about him, and said, Behold my mother and my brethren!

35 For whosoever shall do the will of God, the same is my brother, and my sister, and mother.

τοῖς   υἱοῖς   τῶν   ἀνθρώπων   τὰ   ἁμαρτήματα
to the   sons   –   of men   the   sins

καὶ   αἱ   βλασφημίαι,   ὅσα   ἐὰν   βλασφημήσωσιν·
and   the   blasphemies,   whatever   they may blaspheme;

29 ὃς   δ'   ἂν   βλασφημήσῃ   εἰς   τὸ   πνεῦμα
but whoever   blasphemes   against   the   Spirit

τὸ   ἅγιον,   οὐκ   ἔχει   ἄφεσιν   εἰς   τὸν   αἰῶνα,
–   Holy,   has not   forgiveness   unto   the   age,

ἀλλὰ   ἔνοχός   ἐστιν   αἰωνίου   ἁμαρτήματος.
but   liable   is   of an eternal   sin.

30 ὅτι   ἔλεγον·   πνεῦμα   ἀκάθαρτον   ἔχει.
Because   they said: spirit   an unclean   he has.

31 Καὶ   ἔρχονται   ἡ   μήτηρ   αὐτοῦ   καὶ   οἱ
And   come   the   mother   of him   and   the

ἀδελφοὶ   αὐτοῦ,   καὶ   ἔξω   στήκοντες   ἀπέστειλαν
brothers   of him,   and outside   standing   sent

πρὸς   αὐτὸν   καλοῦντες   αὐτόν.   32 καὶ
to   him   calling   him.   And

ἐκάθητο   περὶ   αὐτὸν   ὄχλος,   καὶ   λέγουσιν
sat   round   him   a crowd,   and   they say

αὐτῷ·   ἰδοὺ   ἡ   μήτηρ   σου   καὶ   οἱ   ἀδελφοί
to him: Behold[,] the   mother   of thee   and   the   brothers

σου   καὶ   αἱ   ἀδελφαί   σου   ἔξω   ζητοῦσίν   σε.
of thee   and   the   sisters   of thee outside   seek   thee.

33 καὶ   ἀποκριθεὶς   αὐτοῖς   λέγει·   τίς   ἐστιν
And   answering   them   he says: Who   is

ἡ   μήτηρ   μου   καὶ   οἱ   ἀδελφοί;   34 καὶ
the   mother   of me   and   the   brothers?   And

περιβλεψάμενος   τοὺς   περὶ   αὐτὸν   κύκλῳ
looking round   [at] the [ones] round   him   in a circle

καθημένους   λέγει·   ἴδε   ἡ   μήτηρ   μου
sitting   he says: Behold[,] the   mother   of me

καὶ   οἱ   ἀδελφοί   μου.   35 ὃς   ἂν   ποιήσῃ   τὸ
and   the   brothers of me.   Whoever   does   the

θέλημα   τοῦ   θεοῦ,   οὗτος   ἀδελφός   μου
will   –   of God,   this one   brother   of me

καὶ   ἀδελφὴ   καὶ   μήτηρ   ἐστίν.
and   sister   and   mother   is.

CHAPTER 4

AND he began again to teach by the sea side: and there was gathered unto him a great multitude, so that he entered into a ship, and sat in the sea; and the

4 Καὶ   πάλιν   ἤρξατο   διδάσκειν   παρὰ   τὴν
And   again   he began   to teach   by   the

θάλασσαν·   καὶ   συνάγεται   πρὸς   αὐτὸν   ὄχλος
sea;   and   is assembled   to   him   crowd

πλεῖστος,   ὥστε   αὐτὸν   εἰς   πλοῖον   ἐμβάντα
a very large,   so as   him   in   a ship   embarking
= so that embarking in a ship he sat

καθῆσθαι   ἐν   τῇ   θαλάσσῃ,   καὶ   πᾶς   ὁ
to sit[b]   in   the   sea,   and   all   the

whole multitude was by the sea on the land.

2 And he taught them many things by parables, and said unto them in his doctrine,

3 Hearken; Behold, there went out a sower to sow:

4 And it came to pass, as he sowed, some fell by the way side, and the fowls of the air came and devoured it up.

5 And some fell on stony ground, where it had not much earth; and immediately it sprang up, because it had no depth of earth:

6 But when the sun was up, it was scorched; and because it had no root, it withered away.

7 And some fell among thorns, and the thorns grew up, and choked it, and it yielded no fruit.

8 And other fell on good ground, and did yield fruit that sprang up and increased; and brought forth, some thirty, and some sixty, and some an hundred.

9 And he said unto them, He that hath ears to hear, let him hear.

10 ¶ And when he was alone, they that were about him with the twelve asked of him the parable.

11 And he said unto them, Unto you it is given to know the mystery of the

ὄχλος πρὸς τὴν θάλασσαν ἐπὶ τῆς γῆς
crowd toward the sea on the land

ἦσαν. 2 καὶ ἐδίδασκεν αὐτοὺς ἐν παραβολαῖς
were. And he taught them in parables

πολλά, καὶ ἔλεγεν αὐτοῖς ἐν τῇ διδαχῇ
many things, and said to them in the teaching

αὐτοῦ· 3 ἀκούετε. ἰδοὺ ἐξῆλθεν ὁ σπείρων
of him: Hear ye. Behold[,] went out the [one] sowing

σπεῖραι. 4 καὶ ἐγένετο ἐν τῷ σπείρειν
to sow. And it came to pass in the to sow[e]
= as he sowed

ὃ μὲν ἔπεσεν παρὰ τὴν ὁδόν, καὶ ἦλθεν
some fell by the way, and came

τὰ πετεινὰ καὶ κατέφαγεν αὐτό. 5 καὶ
the birds and devoured it. And

ἄλλο ἔπεσεν ἐπὶ τὸ πετρῶδες ὅπου οὐκ
other fell on the rocky place where not

εἶχεν γῆν πολλήν, καὶ εὐθὺς ἐξανέτειλεν
it had earth much, and immediately it sprang up

διὰ τὸ μὴ ἔχειν βάθος γῆς·
on account of the not to have depth of earth·
= because it had no depth of earth;

6 καὶ ὅτε ἀνέτειλεν ὁ ἥλιος ἐκαυματίσθη, καὶ
and when rose the sun it was scorched, and

διὰ τὸ μὴ ἔχειν ῥίζαν ἐξηράνθη. 7 καὶ
on account of the not to have root it was withered. And
= because it had no root

ἄλλο ἔπεσεν εἰς τὰς ἀκάνθας, καὶ ἀνέβησαν
other fell among the thorns, and came up

αἱ ἄκανθαι καὶ συνέπνιξαν αὐτό, καὶ
the thorns and choked it, and

καρπὸν οὐκ ἔδωκεν. 8 καὶ ἄλλα ἔπεσεν
fruit it gave not. And others fell

εἰς τὴν γῆν τὴν καλὴν καὶ ἐδίδου καρπὸν
into the earth – good and gave fruit

ἀναβαίνοντα καὶ αὐξανόμενα καὶ ἔφερεν
coming up and growing and bore

εἰς τριάκοντα καὶ ἐν ἑξήκοντα καὶ ἐν
in thirty and in sixty and in

ἑκατόν. 9 καὶ ἔλεγεν· ὃς ἔχει ὦτα
a hundred. And he said: Who has ears

ἀκούειν ἀκουέτω. 10 Καὶ ὅτε ἐγένετο
to hear let him hear. And when he was

κατὰ μόνας, ἠρώτων αὐτὸν οἱ περὶ
alone,† asked him the [ones] round

αὐτὸν σὺν τοῖς δώδεκα τὰς παραβολάς.
him with the twelve the parables.

11 καὶ ἔλεγεν αὐτοῖς· ὑμῖν τὸ μυστήριον
And he said to them: To you the mystery

kingdom of God: but unto them that are without, all *these* things are done in parables:

12 That seeing they may see, and not perceive; and hearing they may hear, and not understand; lest at any time they should be converted, and *their* sins should be forgiven them.

13 And he said unto them, Know ye not this parable? and how then will ye know all parables?

14 ¶ The sower soweth the word.

15 And these are they by the way side, where the word is sown; but when they have heard, Satan cometh immediately, and taketh away the word that was sown in their hearts.

16 And these are they likewise which are sown on stony ground; who, when they have heard the word, immediately receive it with gladness;

17 And have no root in themselves, and so endure but for a time: afterward, when affliction or persecution ariseth for the word's sake, immediately they are offended.

18 And these are they which are sown among thorns; such as hear the word,

19 And the cares of this world, and the deceitfulness of riches, and the lusts of other things entering in,

δέδοται τῆς βασιλείας τοῦ θεοῦ· ἐκείνοις δὲ
has been given of the   kingdom   – of God;   but to those

τοῖς ἔξω ἐν παραβολαῖς τὰ πάντα
the [ones] outside in   parables   – all things

γίνεται, 12 ἵνα βλέποντες βλέπωσιν καὶ
is(are),   that   seeing   they may see   and

μὴ ἴδωσιν, καὶ ἀκούοντες ἀκούωσιν καὶ
not   perceive,   and   hearing   they may hear   and

μὴ συνιῶσιν, μήποτε ἐπιστρέψωσιν καὶ
not   understand,   lest   they should turn   and

ἀφεθῇ αὐτοῖς. 13 καὶ λέγει αὐτοῖς·
it should be forgiven them.   And   he says   to them:

οὐκ οἴδατε τὴν παραβολὴν ταύτην, καὶ πῶς
Know ye not   –   parable   this,   and how

πάσας τὰς παραβολὰς γνώσεσθε; 14 ὁ
all   the   parables   will ye know?   The [one]

σπείρων τὸν λόγον σπείρει. 15 οὗτοι δέ εἰσιν
sowing ²the ³word ¹sows.   And these   are

οἱ παρὰ τὴν ὁδόν, ὅπου σπείρεται ὁ
the [ones] by   the   way,   where   is sown   the

λόγος, καὶ ὅταν ἀκούσωσιν, εὐθὺς ἔρχεται
word,   and   when   they hear,   immediately comes

ὁ σατανᾶς καὶ αἴρει τὸν λόγον τὸν
–   Satan   and   takes   the   word   –

ἐσπαρμένον εἰς αὐτούς. 16 καὶ οὗτοί εἰσιν
having been sown in   them.   And   these   are

ὁμοίως οἱ ἐπὶ τὰ πετρώδη σπειρόμενοι,
likewise the [ones] on   the   rocky places   being sown,

οἳ ὅταν ἀκούσωσιν τὸν λόγον εὐθὺς
who when   they hear   the   word immediately

μετὰ χαρᾶς λαμβάνουσιν αὐτόν, 17 καὶ
with   joy   receive   it,   and

οὐκ ἔχουσιν ῥίζαν ἐν ἑαυτοῖς ἀλλὰ
have not   root   in   themselves   but

πρόσκαιροί εἰσιν, εἶτα γενομένης θλίψεως
shortlived   are,   then   happening   affliction
= when affliction or persecution happens

ἢ διωγμοῦ διὰ τὸν λόγον εὐθὺς
or   persecution² on account of the   word immediately

σκανδαλίζονται. 18 καὶ ἄλλοι εἰσὶν οἱ εἰς
they are offended.   And   others   are the [ones] among

τὰς ἀκάνθας σπειρόμενοι· οὗτοί εἰσιν οἱ
the   thorns   being sown;   these   are the [ones]

τὸν λόγον ἀκούσαντες, 19 καὶ αἱ μέριμναι
the   word   hearing,   and the   cares

τοῦ αἰῶνος καὶ ἡ ἀπάτη τοῦ πλούτου
of the   age   and   the deceitfulness   – of riches

καὶ αἱ περὶ τὰ λοιπὰ ἐπιθυμίαι
and   ¹the   ²about   ⁴the   ⁵other things   ³desires

choke the word, and it becometh unfruitful.

20 And these are they which are sown on good ground; such as hear the word, and receive *it*, and bring forth fruit, some thirtyfold, some sixty, and some an hundred.

21 ¶ And he said unto them, Is a candle brought to be put under a bushel, or under a bed ? and not to be set on a candlestick ?

22 For there is nothing hid, which shall not be manifested; neither was any thing kept secret, but that it should come abroad.

23 If any man have ears to hear, let him hear.

24 And he said unto them, Take heed what ye hear: with what measure ye mete, it shall be measured to you: and unto you that hear shall more be given.

25 For he that hath, to him shall be given: and he that hath not, from him shall be taken even that which he hath.

26 ¶ And he said, So is the kingdom of God, as if a man should cast seed into the ground;

27 And should sleep, and rise night and day, and the seed should spring and grow up, he knoweth not how.

28 For the earth bringeth forth fruit of herself;

εἰσπορευόμεναι συμπνίγουσιν τὸν λόγον, καὶ
coming in   choke   the   word,   and

ἄκαρπος γίνεται.   **20** καὶ ἐκεῖνοί εἰσιν
unfruitful   it becomes.   **And**   those   are

οἱ ἐπὶ τὴν γῆν τὴν καλὴν σπαρέντες,
the [ones] on   the   earth   –   good   sown,

οἵτινες ἀκούουσιν τὸν λόγον καὶ παραδέχονται
who   hear   the   word   and   welcome [it]

καὶ καρποφοροῦσιν ἐν τριάκοντα καὶ ἐν
and   bear fruit   in   thirty   and   in

ἑξήκοντα καὶ ἐν ἑκατόν.   **21** Καὶ ἔλεγεν
sixty   and   in   a hundred.   **And**   he said

αὐτοῖς ὅτι μήτι ἔρχεται ὁ λύχνος ἵνα
to them[,]   –   not   Comes   the   lamp   that

ὑπὸ τὸν μόδιον τεθῇ ἢ ὑπὸ τὴν
under   the   bushel   it may be placed   or   under   the

κλίνην; οὐχ ἵνα ἐπὶ τὴν λυχνίαν
couch ?   not   that   on   the   lampstand

τεθῇ;   **22** οὐ γάρ ἐστίν τι κρυπτόν,
it may be placed ?   **For** there is not   anything   hidden,

ἐὰν μὴ ἵνα φανερωθῇ· οὐδὲ ἐγένετο
except   that it may be manifested;   nor   became

ἀπόκρυφον, ἀλλ' ἵνα ἔλθῃ εἰς φανερόν.
covered,   but   that it may come into [the] open.

23 εἴ τις ἔχει ὦτα ἀκούειν ἀκουέτω.
If anyone has   ears   to hear   let him hear.

24 Καὶ ἔλεγεν αὐτοῖς· βλέπετε τί
And   he said   to them: Take heed   what

ἀκούετε. ἐν ᾧ μέτρῳ μετρεῖτε
ye hear.   With   what   measure   ye measure

μετρηθήσεται ὑμῖν, καὶ προστεθήσεται ὑμῖν.
it will be measured   to you,   and   it will be added   to you.

25 ὃς γὰρ ἔχει, δοθήσεται αὐτῷ· καὶ ὃς
For [he] who   has,   it will be given   to him;   and   who

οὐκ ἔχει, καὶ ὃ ἔχει ἀρθήσεται ἀπ'
has not,   even   what he has   will be taken   from

αὐτοῦ. **26** Καὶ ἔλεγεν· οὕτως ἐστὶν ἡ
him.   **And**   he said: Thus   is   the

βασιλεία τοῦ θεοῦ, ὡς ἄνθρωπος βάλῃ
kingdom   –   of God,   as   a man   might cast

τὸν σπόρον ἐπὶ τῆς γῆς, **27** καὶ καθεύδῃ
the   seed   on   the   earth,   and   might sleep

καὶ ἐγείρηται νύκτα καὶ ἡμέραν, καὶ ὁ
and   rise   night   and   day,   and the

σπόρος βλαστᾷ καὶ μηκύνηται ὡς οὐκ
seed   sprouts   and   lengthens   as   not

οἶδεν αὐτός. **28** αὐτομάτη ἡ γῆ καρποφορεῖ,
knows   he.   **Of its own accord** the earth   bears fruit,

first the blade, then the ear,
after that the full corn in
the ear.

29 But when the fruit is
brought forth, immediately
he putteth in the sickle,
because the harvest is come.

30 ¶ And he said, Where-
unto shall we liken the
kingdom of God ? or with
what comparison shall we
compare it ?

31 *It is* like a grain of
mustard seed, which, when
it is sown in the earth, is
less than all the seeds that
be in the earth:

32 But when it is sown,
it groweth up, and be-
cometh greater than all
herbs, and shooteth out
great branches; so that the
fowls of the air may lodge
under the shadow of it.

33 And with many such
parables spake he the word
unto them, as they were
able to hear *it.*

34 But without a parable
spake he not unto them:
and when they were alone,
he expounded all things to
his disciples.

35 ¶ And the same day,
when the even was come,
he saith unto them, Let us
pass over unto the other
side.

36 And when they had
sent away the multitude,
they took him even as he
was in the ship. And there
were also with him other
little ships.

37 And there arose a
great storm of wind, and

πρῶτον χόρτον, εἶτεν στάχυν, εἶτεν πλήρης
first   grass,   then   an ear,   then   full

σῖτος ἐν τῷ στάχυϊ. 29 ὅταν δὲ παραδοῖ
corn in the ear.   But when   permits

ὁ καρπός, εὐθὺς ἀποστέλλει τὸ δρέπανον,
the fruit, immediately he sends(puts) forth the sickle,

ὅτι παρέστηκεν ὁ θερισμός. 30 Καὶ ἔλεγεν·
because has come the   harvest.   And he said:

πῶς ὁμοιώσωμεν τὴν βασιλείαν τοῦ θεοῦ,
How   may we liken   the   kingdom   –   of God,

ἢ ἐν τίνι αὐτὴν παραβολῇ θῶμεν; 31 ὡς
or by [1]what [4]it [2]parable [3]may we place ?   As

κόκκῳ σινάπεως, ὃς ὅταν σπαρῇ ἐπὶ τῆς
a grain of mustard, which when it is sown on the

γῆς, μικρότερον ὂν πάντων τῶν σπερμάτων
earth, smaller being [than] all   the   seeds

τῶν ἐπὶ τῆς γῆς, 32 καὶ ὅταν σπαρῇ,
–   on the earth,   and when it is sown,

ἀναβαίνει καὶ γίνεται μεῖζον πάντων τῶν
comes up   and becomes greater [than] all the

λαχάνων, καὶ ποιεῖ κλάδους μεγάλους,
herbs,   and makes branches   great,

ὥστε δύνασθαι ὑπὸ τὴν σκιὰν αὐτοῦ τὰ
so as to be able under the shade   of it the
= so that the birds of heaven are able to dwell under its shade.

πετεινὰ τοῦ οὐρανοῦ κατασκηνοῦν. 33 Καὶ
birds   –   of heaven   to dwell.[b]   And

τοιαύταις παραβολαῖς πολλαῖς ἐλάλει αὐτοῖς
[2]such   [3]parables   [1]in many he spoke to them

τὸν λόγον, καθὼς ἠδύναντο ἀκούειν·
the word,   as   they were able to hear;

34 χωρὶς δὲ παραβολῆς οὐκ ἐλάλει αὐτοῖς,
and without a parable   he spoke not to them,

κατ᾽ ἰδίαν δὲ τοῖς ἰδίοις μαθηταῖς ἐπέλυεν
but privately to the(his) own disciples he explained

πάντα.
all things.

35 Καὶ λέγει αὐτοῖς ἐν ἐκείνῃ τῇ
And he says to them on   that   –

ἡμέρα ὀψίας γενομένης· διέλθωμεν εἰς τὸ
day evening having come[a]: Let us pass over to the
= when evening had come:

πέραν. 36 καὶ ἀφέντες τὸν ὄχλον
other side.   And leaving   the crowd

παραλαμβάνουσιν αὐτὸν ὡς ἦν ἐν τῷ
they take   him   as he was in the

πλοίῳ, καὶ ἄλλα πλοῖα ἦν μετ᾽ αὐτοῦ.
ship,   and other ships were with him.

37 καὶ γίνεται λαῖλαψ μεγάλη ἀνέμου,
And occurs storm   a great   of wind,

the waves beat into the ship, so that it was now full.

38 And he was in the hinder part of the ship, asleep on a pillow: and they awake him, and say unto him, Master, carest thou not that we perish?

39 And he arose, and rebuked the wind, and said unto the sea, Peace, be still. And the wind ceased, and there was a great calm.

40 And he said unto them, Why are ye so fearful? how is it that ye have no faith?

41 And they feared exceedingly, and said one to another, What manner of man is this, that even the wind and the sea obey him?

καὶ τὰ κύματα ἐπέβαλλεν εἰς τὸ πλοῖον,
and the waves struck into the ship,

ὥστε ἤδη γεμίζεσθαι τὸ πλοῖον. **38** καὶ
so as now to be filled the ship.[b] And

αὐτὸς ἦν ἐν τῇ πρύμνῃ ἐπὶ τὸ
he was in the stern on the

προσκεφάλαιον καθεύδων. καὶ ἐγείρουσιν
pillow sleeping. And they rouse

αὐτὸν καὶ λέγουσιν αὐτῷ· διδάσκαλε, οὐ μέλει
him and say to him: Teacher, matters it not

σοι ὅτι ἀπολλύμεθα; **39** καὶ διεγερθεὶς
to thee that we are perishing? And being roused

ἐπετίμησεν τῷ ἀνέμῳ καὶ εἶπεν τῇ
he rebuked the wind and said to the

θαλάσσῃ· σιώπα, πεφίμωσο. καὶ ἐκόπασεν
sea: Be quiet, be muzzled. And dropped

ὁ ἄνεμος, καὶ ἐγένετο γαλήνη μεγάλη.
the wind, and there was calm a great.

40 καὶ εἶπεν αὐτοῖς· τί δειλοί ἐστε
And he said to them: Why fearful are ye

οὕτως; πῶς οὐκ ἔχετε πίστιν; **41** καὶ
thus? how have ye not faith? And

ἐφοβήθησαν φόβον μέγαν, καὶ ἔλεγον πρὸς
they feared fear a great, and said to

ἀλλήλους· τίς ἄρα οὗτός ἐστιν, ὅτι καὶ
one another: Who then this man is, that both

ὁ ἄνεμος καὶ ἡ θάλασσα ὑπακούει αὐτῷ;
the wind and the sea obeys him?

CHAPTER 5

A ND they came over unto the other side of the sea, into the country of the Gadarenes.

2 And when he was come out of the ship, immediately there met him out of the tombs a man with an unclean spirit,

3 Who had *his* dwelling among the tombs; and no man could bind him, no, not with chains:

4 Because that he had been often bound with fetters and chains, and the

5 Καὶ ἦλθον εἰς τὸ πέραν τῆς θαλάσσης
And they came to the other side of the sea

εἰς τὴν χώραν τῶν Γερασηνῶν. **2** καὶ
into the country of the Gerasenes. And

ἐξελθόντος αὐτοῦ ἐκ τοῦ πλοίου, [εὐθὺς]
coming out him[a] out of the ship, immediately
= as he came *out*

ὑπήντησεν αὐτῷ ἐκ τῶν μνημείων ἄνθρωπος
met him out of the tombs a man

ἐν πνεύματι ἀκαθάρτῳ, **3** ὃς τὴν κατοίκησιν
in(with) spirit an unclean, who the(his) dwelling

εἶχεν ἐν τοῖς μνήμασιν, καὶ οὐδὲ ἁλύσει
had among the tombs, and not with a chain
= no one any more

οὐκέτι οὐδεὶς ἐδύνατο αὐτὸν δῆσαι, **4** διὰ
no longer no one was able him to bind, on account of
was able to bind him with a chain, = because

τὸ αὐτὸν πολλάκις πέδαις καὶ ἁλύσεσιν
the him often with fetters and chains
he had often been bound with fetters and chains, and . . .

chains had been plucked asunder by him, and the fetters broken in pieces: neither could any *man* tame him.

5 And always, night and day, he was in the mountains, and in the tombs, crying, and cutting himself with stones.

6 But when he saw Jesus afar off, he ran and worshipped him,

7 And cried with a loud voice, and said, What have I to do with thee, Jesus, *thou* Son of the most high God? I adjure thee by God, that thou torment me not.

8 For he said unto him, Come out of the man, *thou* unclean spirit.

9 And he asked him, What *is* thy name? And he answered, saying, My name *is* Legion: for we are many.

10 And he besought him much that he would not send them away out of the country.

11 Now there was there nigh unto the mountains a great herd of swine feeding.

12 And all the devils besought him, saying, Send us into the swine, that we may enter into them.

13 And forthwith Jesus gave them leave. And the unclean spirits went out, and entered into the swine: and the herd ran violently down a steep place into the

δεδέσθαι,   καὶ   διεσπάσθαι ὑπ’ αὐτοῦ τὰς
to have been bound, and   to be burst   by   him   the

ἀλύσεις καὶ   τὰς   πέδας   συντετρῖφθαι, καὶ
chains   and   the   fetters   to have been broken, and

οὐδεὶς   ἴσχυεν   αὐτὸν   δαμάσαι·   5 καὶ
no one   was able   him   to subdue;   and

διὰ παντὸς νυκτὸς καὶ ἡμέρας ἐν τοῖς μνήμασιν
always of(by) night and   day   among the   tombs

καὶ   ἐν   τοῖς   ὄρεσιν   ἦν   κράζων   καὶ
and   in   the   mountains   he was   crying out   and

κατακόπτων   ἑαυτὸν   λίθοις.   6 καὶ   ἰδὼν
cutting   himself   with stones.   And   seeing

τὸν ᾽Ιησοῦν ἀπὸ μακρόθεν ἔδραμεν καὶ
-     Jesus   from   afar   he ran   and

προσεκύνησεν αὐτόν, 7 καὶ κράξας φωνῇ
worshipped   him,   and   crying out   with a voice

μεγάλῃ   λέγει·   τί   ἐμοὶ   καὶ   σοί, ᾽Ιησοῦ
great(loud) he says: What to me   and   to thee,   Jesus

υἱὲ   τοῦ   θεοῦ   τοῦ   ὑψίστου;   ὁρκίζω   σε
Son   -   of God   the   most high? I adjure   thee

τὸν   θεόν,   μή   με   βασανίσῃς.   8 ἔλεγεν
-     by God,   not   me   thou mayest torment.   he said

γὰρ αὐτῷ· ἔξελθε τὸ πνεῦμα τὸ ἀκάθαρτον
For to him: Come out the spirit   -   unclean

ἐκ τοῦ ἀνθρώπου. 9 καὶ ἐπηρώτα αὐτόν·
out of the   man.   And he questioned   him:

τί ὄνομά σοι; καὶ λέγει αὐτῷ· λεγιὼν
What name to thee?⁰ And he says to him: Legion
= What name hast thou ?   = My

ὄνομά μοι, ὅτι πολλοί ἐσμεν.   10 καὶ
name   to me,⁰ because many   we are.   And
name is Legion,

παρεκάλει αὐτὸν πολλὰ ἵνα μὴ αὐτὰ
he besought   him   much   that not   them

ἀποστείλῃ ἔξω τῆς χώρας.   11 ἦν   δὲ
he would send outside the country.   Now there was

ἐκεῖ πρὸς τῷ ὄρει ἀγέλη χοίρων μεγάλη
there near   the mountain herd   of pigs   a great

βοσκομένη·   12 καὶ   παρεκάλεσαν   αὐτὸν
feeding;   and   they besought   him

λέγοντες· πέμψον ἡμᾶς εἰς τοὺς χοίρους,
saying: Send   us   into   the   pigs,

ἵνα εἰς αὐτοὺς εἰσέλθωμεν.   13 καὶ ἐπέτρεψεν
that into them   we may enter.   And he allowed

αὐτοῖς. καὶ ἐξελθόντα τὰ πνεύματα τὰ
them.   And coming out   the   spirits   -

ἀκάθαρτα εἰσῆλθον εἰς τοὺς χοίρους, καὶ
unclean   entered   into   the   pigs,   and

ὥρμησεν ἡ ἀγέλη κατὰ τοῦ κρημνοῦ εἰς
rushed   the   herd   down   the   precipice   into

sea, (they were about two thousand;) and were choked in the sea.

14 And they that fed the swine fled, and told *it* in the city, and in the country. And they went out to see what it was that was done.

15 And they come to Jesus, and see him that was possessed with the devil, and had the legion, sitting, and clothed, and in his right mind: and they were afraid.

16 And they that saw *it* told them how it befell to him that was possessed with the devil, and *also* concerning the swine.

17 And they began to pray him to depart out of their coasts.

18 And when he was come into the ship, he that had been possessed with the devil prayed him that he might be with him.

19 Howbeit Jesus suffered him not, but saith unto him, Go home to thy friends, and tell them how great things the Lord hath done for thee, and hath had compassion on thee.

20 And he departed, and began to publish in Decapolis how great things Jesus had done for him: and all *men* did marvel.

21 ¶ And when Jesus was passed over again by ship unto the other side, much people gathered unto

---

τὴν θάλασσαν, ὡς δισχίλιοι, καὶ ἐπνίγοντο
the   sea,   about two thousand, and were choked

ἐν τῇ θαλάσσῃ. 14 καὶ οἱ βόσκοντες
in the   sea.   And the [ones] feeding

αὐτοὺς ἔφυγον καὶ ἀπήγγειλαν εἰς τὴν
them   fled   and   reported   in   the

πόλιν καὶ εἰς τοὺς ἀγρούς· καὶ ἦλθον
city   and in   the   fields;   and they came

ἰδεῖν τί ἐστιν τὸ γεγονός. 15 καὶ
to see what is the thing having happened.   And

ἔρχονται πρὸς τὸν Ἰησοῦν, καὶ θεωροῦσιν τὸν
they come to   -   Jesus,   and   see   the

δαιμονιζόμενον καθήμενον ἱματισμένον καὶ
demon-possessed man sitting   *having been* clothed and

σωφρονοῦντα, τὸν ἐσχηκότα τὸν λεγιῶνα,
being in his senses, the man having had the legion,

καὶ ἐφοβήθησαν. 16 καὶ διηγήσαντο αὐτοῖς οἱ
and they were afraid.   And   related   to them the [ones]

ἰδόντες πῶς ἐγένετο τῷ δαιμονιζομένῳ
seeing   how   it happened   to the demon-possessed man

καὶ περὶ τῶν χοίρων. 17 καὶ ἤρξαντο
and about the   pigs.   And they began

παρακαλεῖν αὐτὸν ἀπελθεῖν ἀπὸ τῶν ὁρίων
to beseech   him   to depart   from   the   territory

αὐτῶν. 18 καὶ ἐμβαίνοντος αὐτοῦ εἰς τὸ
of them.   And   embarking   him[a]   in   the
     = as he embarked

πλοῖον παρεκάλει αὐτὸν ὁ δαιμονισθεὶς
ship   besought   him the [one] demon-possessed

ἵνα μετ' αὐτοῦ ᾖ. 19 καὶ οὐκ ἀφῆκεν
that with   him he might be.   And   he permitted not

αὐτόν, ἀλλὰ λέγει αὐτῷ· ὕπαγε εἰς τὸν
him,   but   says   to him: Go   to   the

οἶκόν σου πρὸς τοὺς σούς, καὶ ἀπάγγειλον
house of thee to   the   thine,   and   report
     = thy people,

αὐτοῖς ὅσα ὁ κύριός σοι πεποίηκεν καὶ
to them what things the Lord to thee has done   and

ἠλέησέν σε. 20 καὶ ἀπῆλθεν καὶ ἤρξατο
pitied   thee.   And   he departed   and   began

κηρύσσειν ἐν τῇ Δεκαπόλει ὅσα ἐποίησεν
to proclaim   in   -   Decapolis what things   did

αὐτῷ ὁ Ἰησοῦς, καὶ πάντες ἐθαύμαζον.
to him   -   Jesus,   and   all men   marvelled.

21 Καὶ διαπεράσαντος τοῦ Ἰησοῦ ἐν τῷ
And   crossing over   -   Jesus[a]   in   the
     = when Jesus had crossed over

πλοίῳ πάλιν εἰς τὸ πέραν συνήχθη ὄχλος
ship   again to   the   other side was assembled   crowd

him: and he was nigh unto the sea.

22 And, behold, there cometh one of the rulers of the synagogue, Jairus by name; and when he saw him, he fell at his feet,

23 And besought him greatly, saying, My little daughter lieth at the point of death: *I pray thee*, come and lay thy hands on her, that she may be healed; and she shall live.

24 And *Jesus* went with him; and much people followed him, and thronged him.

25 ¶ And a certain woman, which had an issue of blood twelve years,

26 And had suffered many things of many physicians, and had spent all that she had, and was nothing bettered, but rather grew worse,

27 When she had heard of Jesus, came in the press behind, and touched his garment.

28 For she said, If I may touch but his clothes, I shall be whole.

29 And straightway the fountain of her blood was dried up; and she felt in *her* body that she was healed of that plague.

30 And Jesus, immediately knowing in himself that virtue had gone out of him, turned him about in the press, and said, Who touched my clothes?

31 And his disciples said unto him, Thou seest the

πολὺς ἐπ᾽ αὐτόν, καὶ ἦν παρὰ τὴν θάλασσαν.
a much(great) to him, and he was by the sea.

22 Καὶ ἔρχεται εἷς τῶν ἀρχισυναγώγων,
And comes one of the synagogue chiefs,

ὀνόματι Ἰάϊρος, καὶ ἰδὼν αὐτὸν πίπτει
by name Jairus, and seeing him falls

πρὸς τοὺς πόδας αὐτοῦ, 23 καὶ παρακαλεῖ
at the feet of him, and beseeches

αὐτὸν πολλὰ λέγων ὅτι τὸ θυγάτριόν μου
him much saying[,] – The daughter of me

ἐσχάτως ἔχει, ἵνα ἐλθὼν ἐπιθῇς
is at the point of death,† that coming thou mayest lay *on*

τὰς χεῖρας αὐτῇ, ἵνα σωθῇ καὶ ζήσῃ.
the(thy) hands on her, that she may be healed and may live.

24 καὶ ἀπῆλθεν μετ᾽ αὐτοῦ. καὶ ἠκολούθει αὐτῷ
And he went with him. And followed him

ὄχλος πολύς, καὶ συνέθλιβον αὐτόν. 25 Καὶ
crowd a much(great), and pressed upon him. And

γυνὴ οὖσα ἐν ῥύσει αἵματος δώδεκα
a woman being in a flow of blood twelve
= having

ἔτη, 26 καὶ πολλὰ παθοῦσα ὑπὸ πολλῶν
years, and many things suffering by many

ἰατρῶν καὶ δαπανήσασα τὰ παρ᾽ αὐτῆς
physicians and having spent *the* with her

πάντα, καὶ μηδὲν ὠφεληθεῖσα ἀλλὰ μᾶλλον
all things, and nothing having been profited but rather

εἰς τὸ χεῖρον ἐλθοῦσα, 27 ἀκούσασα τὰ
to the worse having come, hearing the things

περὶ τοῦ Ἰησοῦ, ἐλθοῦσα ἐν τῷ ὄχλῳ
about – Jesus, coming in the crowd

ὄπισθεν ἥψατο τοῦ ἱματίου αὐτοῦ· 28 ἔλεγεν
behind touched the garment of him; she said[,]

γὰρ ὅτι ἐὰν ἅψωμαι κἂν τῶν ἱματίων
for – If I may touch even the garments

αὐτοῦ, σωθήσομαι. 29 καὶ εὐθὺς ἐξηράνθη
of him, I shall be healed. And immediately was dried up

ἡ πηγὴ τοῦ αἵματος αὐτῆς, καὶ ἔγνω
the fountain of the blood of her, and she knew

τῷ σώματι ὅτι ἴαται ἀπὸ τῆς
in the(her) body that she is(was) cured from the

μάστιγος. 30 καὶ εὐθὺς ὁ Ἰησοῦς ἐπιγνοὺς ἐν
plague. And immediately – Jesus knowing in

ἑαυτῷ τὴν ἐξ αὐτοῦ δύναμιν ἐξελθοῦσαν,
himself ¹the ⁴out of ⁵him ²power ³going forth,

ἐπιστραφεὶς ἐν τῷ ὄχλῳ ἔλεγεν· τίς μου ἥψατο τῶν
turning in the crowd said: Who of me touched the

ἱματίων; 31 καὶ ἔλεγον αὐτῷ οἱ μαθηταὶ
garments? And said to him the disciples

multitude thronging thee, and sayest thou, Who touched me?

32 And he looked round about to see her that had done this thing.

33 But the woman fearing and trembling, knowing what was done in her, came and fell down before him, and told him all the truth.

34 And he said unto her, Daughter, thy faith hath made thee whole; go in peace, and be whole of thy plague.

35 ¶ While he yet spake, there came from the ruler of the synagogue's *house certain* which said, Thy daughter is dead: why troublest thou the Master any further?

36 As soon as Jesus heard the word that was spoken, he saith unto the ruler of the synagogue, Be not afraid, only believe.

37 And he suffered no man to follow him, save Peter, and James, and John the brother of James.

38 And he cometh to the house of the ruler of the synagogue, and seeth the tumult, and them that wept and wailed greatly.

39 And when he was come in, he saith unto them, Why make ye this ado, and weep? the damsel is not dead, but sleepeth.

40 And they laughed him to scorn. But when he had put them all out,

---

αὐτοῦ· βλέπεις τὸν ὄχλον συνθλίβοντά σε,
of him: Thou seest the crowd pressing upon thee,

καὶ λέγεις· τίς μου ἥψατο; 32 καὶ
and thou sayest: Who me touched? And

περιεβλέπετο ἰδεῖν τὴν τοῦτο ποιήσασαν.
he looked round to see the [one] this having done.

33 ἡ δὲ γυνὴ φοβηθεῖσα καὶ τρέμουσα,
And the woman fearing and trembling,

εἰδυῖα ὃ γέγονεν αὐτῇ, ἦλθεν καὶ προσέ-
knowing what has happened to her, came and fell

πεσεν αὐτῷ καὶ εἶπεν αὐτῷ πᾶσαν τὴν ἀλήθειαν.
before him and told him all the truth.

34 ὁ δὲ εἶπεν αὐτῇ· θυγάτηρ, ἡ πίστις
And he said to her: Daughter, the faith

σου σέσωκέν σε· ὕπαγε εἰς εἰρήνην, καὶ
of thee has healed thee; go in peace, and

ἴσθι ὑγιὴς ἀπὸ τῆς μάστιγός σου. 35 Ἔτι
be whole from the plague of thee. Still = While

αὐτοῦ λαλοῦντος ἔρχονται ἀπὸ τοῦ
him speaking[a] they come from the
he was still speaking

ἀρχισυναγώγου λέγοντες ὅτι ἡ θυγάτηρ
synagogue chief saying[.] – The daughter

σου ἀπέθανεν· τί ἔτι σκύλλεις τὸν διδάσκαλον;
of thee died; why still troublest thou the teacher?

36 ὁ δὲ Ἰησοῦς παρακούσας τὸν λόγον
– But Jesus overhearing the word

λαλούμενον λέγει τῷ ἀρχισυναγώγῳ· μὴ
being spoken says to the synagogue chief: not

φοβοῦ, μόνον πίστευε. 37 καὶ οὐκ ἀφῆκεν
Fear, only believe. And he allowed not

οὐδένα μετ' αὐτοῦ συνακολουθῆσαι εἰ μὴ
no(any)one with him to accompany except

τὸν Πέτρον καὶ Ἰάκωβον καὶ Ἰωάννην
– Peter and James and John

τὸν ἀδελφὸν Ἰακώβου. 38 καὶ ἔρχονται
the brother of James. And they come

εἰς τὸν οἶκον τοῦ ἀρχισυναγώγου, καὶ
into the house of the synagogue chief, and

θεωρεῖ θόρυβον, καὶ κλαίοντάς καὶ
he sees an uproar, and [men] weeping and

ἀλαλάζοντας πολλά, 39 καὶ εἰσελθὼν λέγει
crying aloud much, and entering he says

αὐτοῖς· τί θορυβεῖσθε καὶ κλαίετε; τὸ
to them: Why make ye an uproar and weep? the

παιδίον οὐκ ἀπέθανεν ἀλλὰ καθεύδει.
child did not die but sleeps.

40 καὶ κατεγέλων αὐτοῦ. αὐτὸς δὲ ἐκβαλὼν
And they ridiculed him. But he putting out

he taketh the father and
the mother of the damsel,
and them that were with
him, and entereth in where
the damsel was lying.

41 And he took the
damsel by the hand, and
said unto her, Talitha
cumi; which is, being
interpreted, Damsel, I say
unto thee, arise.

42 And straightway the
damsel arose, and walked;
for she was *of the age* of
twelve years. And they
were astonished with a
great astonishment.

43 And he charged them
straitly that no man should
know it; and commanded
that something should be
given her to eat.

πάντας   παραλαμβάνει   τὸν   πατέρα   τοῦ
all   takes   the   father   of the

παιδίου   καὶ   τὴν   μητέρα   καὶ   τοὺς   μετ'
child   and   the   mother   and the [ones] with

αὐτοῦ,   καὶ   εἰσπορεύεται   ὅπου   ἦν   τὸ
him,   and   goes in   where was the

παιδίον.   **41** καὶ   κρατήσας   τῆς   χειρὸς
child.   And   taking hold   of the hand

τοῦ   παιδίου   λέγει   αὐτῇ·   ταλιθὰ   κούμ,   ὅ
of the child   he says to her: Talitha   koum, which

ἐστιν   μεθερμηνευόμενον·   τὸ   κοράσιον,   σοὶ
is   being interpreted: –   Maid,   to thee

λέγω,   ἔγειρε.   **42** καὶ   εὐθὺς   ἀνέστη   τὸ
I say,   arise.   And   immediately rose up the

κοράσιον   καὶ   περιεπάτει·   ἦν   γὰρ
maid   and   walked;   for she was

ἐτῶν   δώδεκα.   καὶ   ἐξέστησαν   εὐθὺς
[of the age] twelve.   And they were astonished immediately
of years   =immediately they were exceedingly astonished.

ἐκστάσει   μεγάλῃ.   **43** καὶ   διεστείλατο
astonishment with a great.   And   he ordered

αὐτοῖς   πολλὰ   ἵνα   μηδεὶς   γνοῖ   τοῦτο,   καὶ
them   much   that   no one should know this,   and

εἶπεν   δοθῆναι   αὐτῇ   φαγεῖν.
told   to be given   to her   to eat.
=[them] to give her [something] to eat.

CHAPTER 6

A ND he went out from
thence, and came in-
to his own country; and
his disciples follow him.

2 And when the sabbath
day was come, he began to
teach in the synagogue:
and many hearing *him* were
astonished, saying, From
whence hath this *man* these
things ? and what wisdom
is this which is given unto
him, that even such mighty
works are wrought by his
hands ?

3 Is not this the car-
penter, the son of Mary,
the brother of James, and

6 Καὶ   ἐξῆλθεν   ἐκεῖθεν,   καὶ   ἔρχεται   εἰς
And   he went forth thence,   and   comes   into

τὴν   πατρίδα   αὐτοῦ,   καὶ   ἀκολουθοῦσιν
the   native place .of him,   and   follow

αὐτῷ   οἱ   μαθηταὶ   αὐτοῦ.   **2** καὶ   γενομένου
him   the   disciples   of him.   And   coming
                                            = when

σαββάτου   ἤρξατο   διδάσκειν   ἐν   τῇ   συναγωγῇ·
a sabbath[a] he began   to teach   in   the   synagogue;
a sabbath came

καὶ   οἱ   πολλοὶ   ἀκούοντες   ἐξεπλήσσοντο
and   the   many   hearing   were astonished

λέγοντες·   πόθεν   τούτῳ   ταῦτα,   καὶ   τίς   ἡ
saying: Whence to this man these things, and what the

σοφία   ἡ   δοθεῖσα   τούτῳ;   καὶ   αἱ   δυνάμεις
wisdom   –   given   to this(him) ? And *the* powerful deeds

τοιαῦται   διὰ   τῶν   χειρῶν   αὐτοῦ   γινόμεναι;
such   through the   hands   of him   coming about?

3 οὐχ   οὗτός   ἐστιν   ὁ   τέκτων,   ὁ   υἱὸς
³Not ²this man   ¹is   the   carpenter,   the   son

τῆς   Μαρίας   καὶ   ἀδελφὸς   Ἰακώβου   καὶ
–   of Mary   and   brother   of James   and

Joses, and of Juda, and Simon ? and are not his sisters here with us ? And they were offended at him.

4 But Jesus said unto them, A prophet is not without honour, but in his own country, and among his own kin, and in his own house.

5 And he could there do no mighty work, save that he laid his hands upon a few sick folk, and healed *them.*

6 And he marvelled because of their unbelief. And he went round about the villages, teaching.

7 ¶ And he called *unto him* the twelve, and began to send them forth by two and two; and gave them power over unclean spirits;

8 And commanded them that they should take nothing for *their* journey, save a staff only; no scrip, no bread, no money in *their* purse:

9 But *be* shod with sandals; and not put on two coats.

10 And he said unto them, In what place soever ye enter into an house, there abide till ye depart from that place.

11 And whosoever shall not receive you, nor hear you, when ye depart thence,

Ἰωσῆτος καὶ Ἰούδα καὶ Σίμωνος; καὶ
Joses and Judas and Simon? and

οὐκ εἰσὶν αἱ ἀδελφαὶ αὐτοῦ ὧδε πρὸς
²not ¹are the sisters of him here with

ἡμᾶς; καὶ ἐσκανδαλίζοντο ἐν αὐτῷ. 4 καὶ
us? And they were offended in(at) him. And

ἔλεγεν αὐτοῖς ὁ Ἰησοῦς ὅτι οὐκ ἔστιν
said to them – Jesus[,] – ᶜnot ²is

προφήτης ἄτιμος εἰ μὴ ἐν τῇ πατρίδι
¹A prophet unhonoured except in the native place

αὐτοῦ καὶ ἐν τοῖς συγγενεῦσιν αὐτοῦ
of him and among the relatives of him

καὶ ἐν τῇ οἰκίᾳ αὐτοῦ. 5 καὶ οὐκ
and in the house of him. And not

ἐδύνατο ἐκεῖ ποιῆσαι οὐδεμίαν δύναμιν,
he could there to do no(any) powerful deed,

εἰ μὴ ὀλίγοις ἀρρώστοις ἐπιθεὶς τὰς
except on a few sick [ones] laying on the(his)

χεῖρας ἐθεράπευσεν. 6 καὶ ἐθαύμασεν διὰ
hands he healed. And he marvelled because of

τὴν ἀπιστίαν αὐτῶν.
the unbelief of them.

Καὶ περιῆγεν τὰς κώμας κύκλῳ
And he went round the villages in circuit

διδάσκων. 7 Καὶ προσκαλεῖται τοὺς δώδεκα,
teaching. And he calls to [him] the twelve,

καὶ ἤρξατο αὐτοὺς ἀποστέλλειν δύο δύο,
and began them to send forth two [by] two,

καὶ ἐδίδου αὐτοῖς ἐξουσίαν τῶν πνευμάτων
and gave them authority the spirits

τῶν ἀκαθάρτων, 8 καὶ παρήγγειλεν αὐτοῖς
– of(over) unclean, and charged them

ἵνα μηδὲν αἴρωσιν εἰς ὁδὸν εἰ μὴ ῥάβδον
that nothing they should take in [the] way except a staff

μόνον, μὴ ἄρτον, μὴ πήραν, μὴ εἰς τὴν
only, not bread, not a wallet, not in the

ζώνην χαλκόν, 9 ἀλλὰ ὑποδεδεμένους·σανδάλια,
girdle copper [money], but having had tied on sandals,

καὶ μὴ ἐνδύσησθε δύο χιτῶνας. 10 καὶ
and do not put on two tunics. And

ἔλεγεν αὐτοῖς· ὅπου ἐὰν εἰσέλθητε εἰς
he said to them: Wherever ye enter into

οἰκίαν, ἐκεῖ μένετε ἕως ἂν ἐξέλθητε
a house, there remain until ye go out

ἐκεῖθεν. 11 καὶ ὃς ἂν τόπος μὴ δέξηται
thence. And whatever place receives not

ὑμᾶς μηδὲ ἀκούσωσιν ὑμῶν, ἐκπορευόμενοι
you nor they hear you, going out

shake off the dust under your feet for a testimony against them. Verily I say unto you, It shall be more tolerable for Sodom and Gomorrha in the day of judgment, than for that city.

12 And they went out, and preached that men should repent.

13 And they cast out many devils, and anointed with oil many that were sick, and healed *them*.

14 ¶ And king Herod heard *of him;* (for his name was spread abroad:) and he said, That John the Baptist was risen from the dead, and therefore mighty works do shew forth themselves in him.

15 Others said, That it is Elias. And others said, That it is a prophet, or as one of the prophets.

16 But when Herod heard *thereof*, he said, It is John, whom I beheaded: he is risen from the dead.

17 For Herod himself had sent forth and laid hold upon John, and bound him in prison for Herodias' sake, his brother Philip's wife: for he had married her.

18 For John had said unto Herod, It is not lawful for thee to have thy brother's wife.

19 Therefore Herodias had a quarrel against him, and would have killed him; but she could not:

20 For Herod feared John, knowing that he was

ἐκεῖθεν ἐκτινάξατε τὸν χοῦν τὸν ὑποκάτω
thence   shake off   the   dust   –   under

τῶν ποδῶν ὑμῶν εἰς μαρτύριον αὐτοῖς.
the feet of you for a testimony to them.

12 Καὶ ἐξελθόντες ἐκήρυξαν ἵνα μετανοῶσιν,
And going forth they proclaimed that men should repent,

13 καὶ δαιμόνια πολλὰ ἐξέβαλλον, καὶ
and demons many they expelled, and

ἤλειφον ἐλαίῳ πολλοὺς ἀρρώστους καὶ
anointed with oil many sick [ones] and

ἐθεράπευον.
healed.

14 Καὶ ἤκουσεν ὁ βασιλεὺς Ἡρώδης,
And heard the king Herod,

φανερὸν γὰρ ἐγένετο τὸ ὄνομα αὐτοῦ, καὶ
for manifest became the name of him, and

ἔλεγον ὅτι Ἰωάννης ὁ βαπτίζων ἐγήγερται
they said[,] – John the baptizing [one] has been raised

ἐκ νεκρῶν, καὶ διὰ τοῦτο ἐνεργοῦσιν αἱ
from [the] dead, and therefore operate the

δυνάμεις ἐν αὐτῷ. 15 ἄλλοι δὲ ἔλεγον
powerful deeds in him. But others said[,]

ὅτι Ἡλίας ἐστίν· ἄλλοι δὲ ἔλεγον ὅτι
– Elias it/he is; and [yet] others said[,] –

προφήτης ὡς εἷς τῶν προφητῶν. 16 ἀκούσας δὲ
A prophet as one of the prophets. But hearing

ὁ Ἡρώδης ἔλεγεν· ὃν ἐγὼ ἀπεκεφάλισα
– Herod said: ³whom ³I ⁴beheaded

Ἰωάννην, οὗτος ἠγέρθη. 17 Αὐτὸς γὰρ ὁ
¹John, this was raised. For ²himself –

Ἡρώδης ἀποστείλας ἐκράτησεν τὸν Ἰωάννην
¹Herod sending seized – John

καὶ ἔδησεν αὐτὸν ἐν φυλακῇ διὰ Ἡρωδιάδα
and bound him in prison because of Herodias

τὴν γυναῖκα Φιλίππου τοῦ ἀδελφοῦ αὐτοῦ,
the wife of Philip the brother of him,

ὅτι αὐτὴν ἐγάμησεν· 18 ἔλεγεν γὰρ ὁ
because her he married; for said –

Ἰωάννης τῷ Ἡρώδῃ ὅτι οὐκ ἔξεστίν
John – to Herod[,] – It is not lawful

σοι ἔχειν τὴν γυναῖκα τοῦ ἀδελφοῦ σου.
for thee to have the wife of the brother of thee.

19 ἡ δὲ Ἡρωδιὰς ἐνεῖχεν αὐτῷ καὶ
– Now Herodias had a grudge against him and

ἤθελεν αὐτὸν ἀποκτεῖναι, καὶ οὐκ ἠδύνατο·
wished ²him ¹to kill, and could not;

20 ὁ γὰρ Ἡρώδης ἐφοβεῖτο τὸν Ἰωάννην,
– for Herod feared – John,

162   MARK 6

a just man and an holy, and observed him; and when he heard him, he did many things, and heard him gladly.

21 And when a convenient day was come, that Herod on his birthday made a supper to his lords, high captains, and chief *estates* of Galilee;

22 And when the daughter of the said Herodias came in, and danced, and pleased Herod and them that sat with him, the king said unto the damsel, Ask of me whatsoever thou wilt, and I will give *it* thee.

23 And he sware unto her, Whatsoever thou shalt ask of me, I will give *it* thee, unto the half of my kingdom.

24 And she went forth, and said unto her mother, What shall I ask? And she said, The head of John the Baptist.

25 And she came in straightway with haste unto the king, and asked, saying, I will that thou give me by and by in a charger the head of John the Baptist.

26 And the king was exceeding sorry; *yet* for his oath's sake, and for their sakes which sat with him, he would not reject her.

εἰδὼς αὐτὸν ἄνδρα δίκαιον καὶ ἅγιον, καὶ
knowing him a man just and holy, and

συνετήρει αὐτόν, καὶ ἀκούσας αὐτοῦ πολλὰ
kept safe him, and hearing him much
  = was

ἠπόρει, καὶ ἡδέως αὐτοῦ ἤκουεν. 21 καὶ
was in difficulties, and gladly him heard. And
in great difficulties,

γενομένης ἡμέρας εὐκαίρου ὅτε Ἡρώδης
coming day a suitable[a] when Herod
= when a suitable day came

τοῖς γενεσίοις αὐτοῦ δεῖπνον ἐποίησεν τοῖς
on the birthday festivities of him a supper made for the

μεγιστᾶσιν αὐτοῦ καὶ τοῖς χιλιάρχοις καὶ
courtiers of him and the chiliarchs and

τοῖς πρώτοις τῆς Γαλιλαίας, 22 καὶ
the chief men - of Galilee, and

εἰσελθούσης τῆς θυγατρὸς αὐτῆς τῆς
entering the daughter [a]of herself -
= when the daughter of Herodias herself entered and danced,

Ἡρωδιάδος καὶ ὀρχησαμένης, ἤρεσεν τῷ
[a]of Herodias and dancing,[a] she pleased -

Ἡρώδῃ καὶ τοῖς συνανακειμένοις. ὁ δὲ
Herod and the [ones] reclining with [him]. And the

βασιλεὺς εἶπεν τῷ κορασίῳ· αἴτησόν με
king said to the girl: Ask me

ὃ ἐὰν θέλῃς, καὶ δώσω σοι· 23 καὶ
whatever thou wishest, and I will give thee; and

ὤμοσεν αὐτῇ ὅτι ὃ ἐὰν αἰτήσῃς δώσω
he swore to her[,] - Whatever thou askest I will give

σοι ἕως ἡμίσους τῆς βασιλείας μου.
thee up to half of the kingdom of me.

24 καὶ ἐξελθοῦσα εἶπεν τῇ μητρὶ αὐτῆς·
And going out she said to the mother of her:

τί αἰτήσωμαι; ἡ δὲ εἶπεν· τὴν κεφαλὴν
What may I ask? And she said: The head

Ἰωάννου τοῦ βαπτίζοντος. 25 καὶ
of John the [one] baptizing. And

εἰσελθοῦσα εὐθὺς μετὰ σπουδῆς πρὸς τὸν
entering immediately with haste to the

βασιλέα ᾐτήσατο λέγουσα· θέλω ἵνα ἐξαυτῆς
king she asked saying: I wish that at once

δῷς μοι ἐπὶ πίνακι τὴν κεφαλὴν Ἰωάννου
thou mayest give me on a dish the head of John

τοῦ βαπτιστοῦ. 26 καὶ περίλυπος γενόμενος
the Baptist. And deeply grieved becoming

ὁ βασιλεὺς διὰ τοὺς ὅρκους καὶ τοὺς
the king because of the oaths and the [ones]

ἀνακειμένους οὐκ ἠθέλησεν ἀθετῆσαι αὐτήν.
reclining did not wish to reject her.

27 And immediately the king sent an executioner, and commanded his head to be brought: and he went and beheaded him in the prison,

28 And brought his head in a charger, and gave it to the damsel: and the damsel gave it to her mother.

29 And when his disciples heard *of it*, they came and took up his corpse, and laid it in a tomb.

30 ¶ And the apostles gathered themselves together unto Jesus, and told him all things, both what they had done, and what they had taught.

31 And he said unto them, Come ye yourselves apart into a desert place, and rest a while: for there were many coming and going, and they had no leisure so much as to eat.

32 And they departed into a desert place by ship privately.

33 And the people saw them departing, and many knew him, and ran afoot thither out of all cities, and outwent them, and came together unto him.

34 And Jesus, when he came out, saw much people, and was moved with compassion toward them, because they were as sheep not having a shepherd: and he began to

27 καὶ εὐθὺς ἀποστείλας ὁ βασιλεὺς
And immediately ⁸sending ⁴the ⁸king

σπεκουλάτορα ἐπέταξεν ἐνέγκαι τὴν κεφαλὴν
an executioner gave order to bring the head

αὐτοῦ. καὶ ἀπελθὼν ἀπεκεφάλισεν αὐτὸν
of him. And going he beheaded him

ἐν τῇ φυλακῇ, 28 καὶ ἤνεγκεν τὴν κεφαλὴν
in the prison, and brought the head

αὐτοῦ ἐπὶ πίνακι καὶ ἔδωκεν αὐτὴν τῷ
of him on a dish and gave it to the

κορασίῳ, καὶ τὸ κοράσιον ἔδωκεν αὐτὴν
girl, and the girl gave it

τῇ μητρὶ αὐτῆς. 29 καὶ ἀκούσαντες οἱ
to the mother of her. And hearing the

μαθηταὶ αὐτοῦ ἦλθαν καὶ ἦραν τὸ πτῶμα
disciples of him went and took the corpse

αὐτοῦ καὶ ἔθηκαν αὐτὸ ἐν μνημείῳ.
of him and put it in a tomb.

30 Καὶ συνάγονται οἱ ἀπόστολοι πρὸς
And assemble the apostles to

τὸν Ἰησοῦν, καὶ ἀπήγγειλαν αὐτῷ πάντα
– Jesus, and reported to him all things

ὅσα ἐποίησαν καὶ ὅσα ἐδίδαξαν. 31 καὶ
which they did and which they taught. And

λέγει αὐτοῖς· δεῦτε ὑμεῖς αὐτοὶ κατ᾽
he says to them: Come ye [your]selves pri-

ἰδίαν εἰς ἔρημον τόπον καὶ ἀναπαύσασθε ὀλίγον.
vately to a desert place and rest a little.

ἦσαν γὰρ οἱ ἐρχόμενοι καὶ οἱ
For ²were ³the [ones] ⁴coming ⁵and ⁶the [ones]

ὑπάγοντες πολλοί, καὶ οὐδὲ φαγεῖν
⁷going ¹many, and not to eat

εὐκαίρουν. 32 καὶ ἀπῆλθον ἐν τῷ πλοίῳ
they had opportunity. And they went away in the ship

εἰς ἔρημον τόπον κατ᾽ ἰδίαν. 33 καὶ
to a desert place privately. And

εἶδον αὐτοὺς ὑπάγοντας καὶ ἐπέγνωσαν
²saw ³them ⁴going ⁵and ⁶knew

πολλοί, καὶ πεζῇ ἀπὸ πασῶν τῶν πόλεων
¹many, and on foot from all the cities

συνέδραμον ἐκεῖ καὶ προῆλθον αὐτούς.
ran together there and came before them.

34 Καὶ ἐξελθὼν εἶδεν πολὺν ὄχλον, καὶ
And going forth he saw a much(great) crowd, and

ἐσπλαγχνίσθη ἐπ᾽ αὐτοὺς ὅτι ἦσαν ὡς
had compassion on them because they were as

πρόβατα μὴ ἔχοντα ποιμένα, καὶ ἤρξατο
sheep not having a shepherd, and he began

teach them many things.

35 And when the day was now far spent, his disciples came unto him, and said, This is a desert place, and now the time *is* far passed:

36 Send them away, that they may go into the country round about, and into the villages, and buy themselves bread: for they have nothing to eat.

37 He answered and said unto them, Give ye them to eat. And they say unto him, Shall we go and buy two hundred pennyworth of bread, and give them to eat?

38 He saith unto them, How many loaves have ye? go and see. And when they knew, they say, Five, and two fishes.

39 And he commanded them to make all sit down by companies upon the green grass.

40 And they sat down in ranks, by hundreds, and by fifties.

41 And when he had taken the five loaves and the two fishes, he looked up to heaven, and blessed, and brake the loaves, and gave *them* to his disciples to set before them; and the two fishes divided he among them all.

διδάσκειν αὐτοὺς πολλά. **35** Καὶ ἤδη ὥρας
to teach　them　many things.　　And　now an hour
　　　　　　　　　　　　　　　　　　= it being

πολλῆς γενομένης προσελθόντες αὐτῷ οἱ
much　coming[a]　approaching　to him　the
late

μαθηταὶ αὐτοῦ ἔλεγον ὅτι ἔρημός ἐστιν
disciples　of him　said[,]　–　Desert　is

ὁ τόπος καὶ ἤδη ὥρα πολλή· **36** ἀπόλυσον
the place　and　now　hour　a much;　dismiss
　　　　　　　　　　　= it is late;

αὐτούς, ἵνα ἀπελθόντες εἰς τοὺς κύκλῳ
them,　that　going away　to　the round about

ἀγροὺς καὶ κώμας ἀγοράσωσιν ἑαυτοῖς τί
fields　and　villages　they may buy　for themselves　what

φάγωσιν. **37** ὁ δὲ ἀποκριθεὶς εἶπεν αὐτοῖς·
they may eat.　But he　answering　said　to them:

δότε αὐτοῖς ὑμεῖς φαγεῖν. καὶ λέγουσιν
Give　them　ye　to eat.　And　they say

αὐτῷ· ἀπελθόντες ἀγοράσωμεν δηναρίων
to him:　Going away　may we buy　[3]of(for) [4]denarii

διακοσίων ἄρτους, καὶ δώσομεν αὐτοῖς
[2]two hundred　[1]loaves,　and　shall we give　them

φαγεῖν; **38** ὁ δὲ λέγει αὐτοῖς· πόσους
to eat?　And he　says　to them:　How many

ἔχετε ἄρτους; ὑπάγετε ἴδετε. καὶ γνόντες
have ye　loaves?　Go　see.　And　knowing

λέγουσιν· πέντε, καὶ δύο ἰχθύας. **39** καὶ
they say:　Five,　and　two　fishes.　And

ἐπέταξεν αὐτοῖς ἀνακλιθῆναι πάντας συμπόσια
he instructed　them　to recline　all　companies

συμπόσια ἐπὶ τῷ χλωρῷ χόρτῳ. **40** καὶ
companies　on　the　green　grass.　And

ἀνέπεσαν πρασιαὶ πρασιαὶ κατὰ ἑκατὸν
they reclined　groups　groups　by　a hundred

καὶ κατὰ πεντήκοντα. **41** καὶ λαβὼν τοὺς
and　by　fifty.　And　taking　the

πέντε ἄρτους καὶ τοὺς δύο ἰχθύας,
five　loaves　and　the　two　fishes,

ἀναβλέψας εἰς τὸν οὐρανὸν εὐλόγησεν καὶ
looking up　to　–　heaven　he blessed　and

κατέκλασεν τοὺς ἄρτους καὶ ἐδίδου τοῖς
broke　the　loaves　and　gave　to the

μαθηταῖς ἵνα παρατιθῶσιν αὐτοῖς, καὶ
disciples　that they might set before　them,　and

τοὺς δύο ἰχθύας ἐμέρισεν πᾶσιν. **42** καὶ
the　two　fishes　he divided　to all.　And

42 And they did all eat, and were filled.

43 And they took up twelve baskets full of the fragments, and of the fishes.

44 And they that did eat of the loaves were about five thousand men.

45 ¶ And straightway he constrained his disciples to get into the ship, and to go to the other side before unto Bethsaida, while he sent away the people.

46 And when he had sent them away, he departed into a mountain to pray.

47 And when even was come, the ship was in the midst of the sea, and he alone on the land.

48 And he saw them toiling in rowing; for the wind was contrary unto them: and about the fourth watch of the night he cometh unto them, walking upon the sea, and would have passed by them.

49 But when they saw him walking upon the sea, they supposed it had been a spirit, and cried out:

50 For they all saw him, and were troubled. And immediately he talked with them, and saith unto them, Be of good cheer: it is I; be not afraid.

51 And he went up unto them into the ship; and the wind ceased: and they were sore amazed in themselves beyond measure, and wondered.

ἔφαγον πάντες καὶ ἐχορτάσθησαν, **43** καὶ
they ate all and were satisfied, and

ἦραν κλάσματα δώδεκα κοφίνων πληρώματα
they took fragments twelve ²of baskets ¹fullnesses

καὶ ἀπὸ τῶν ἰχθύων **44** καὶ ἦσαν οἱ
and from the fishes. And were the

φαγόντες τοὺς ἄρτους πεντακισχίλιοι ἄνδρες.
[ones] eating the loaves five thousand males.

45 Καὶ εὐθὺς ἠνάγκασεν τοὺς μαθητὰς
And immediately he constrained the disciples

αὐτοῦ ἐμβῆναι εἰς τὸ πλοῖον καὶ προάγειν
of him to embark in the ship and to go before

εἰς τὸ πέραν πρὸς Βηθσαϊδάν, ἕως αὐτὸς
to the other side to Bethsaida, until he

ἀπολύει τὸν ὄχλον. **46** καὶ ἀποταξάμενος
dismisses the crowd. And having said farewell

αὐτοῖς ἀπῆλθεν εἰς τὸ ὄρος προσεύξασθαι.
to them he went away to the mountain to pray.

47 καὶ ὀψίας γενομένης ἦν τὸ πλοῖον ἐν
And evening coming onᵃ was the ship in
= when evening came on

μέσῳ τῆς θαλάσσης, καὶ αὐτὸς μόνος ἐπὶ
[the] midst of the sea, and he alone on

τῆς γῆς. **48** καὶ ἰδὼν αὐτοὺς βασανιζομένους
the land. And seeing them being distressed

ἐν τῷ ἐλαύνειν, ἦν γὰρ ὁ ἄνεμος ἐναντίος
in the to row, ⁴was ¹for ²the ³wind contrary

αὐτοῖς, περὶ τετάρτην φυλακὴν τῆς νυκτὸς
to them, about [the] fourth watch of the night

ἔρχεται πρὸς αὐτοὺς περιπατῶν ἐπὶ τῆς
he comes toward them walking on the

θαλάσσης· καὶ ἤθελεν παρελθεῖν αὐτούς.
sea; and wished to go by them.

49 οἱ δὲ ἰδόντες αὐτὸν ἐπὶ τῆς θαλάσσης
But they seeing him on the sea

περιπατοῦντα ἔδοξαν ὅτι φάντασμά ἐστιν,
walking thought that a phantasm it is(was),

καὶ ἀνέκραξαν· **50** πάντες γὰρ αὐτὸν εἶδαν
and cried out; for all him saw

καὶ ἐταράχθησαν. ὁ δὲ εὐθὺς ἐλάλησεν
and were troubled. But he immediately talked

μετ᾽ αὐτῶν, καὶ λέγει αὐτοῖς· θαρσεῖτε,
with them, and says to them: Be of good cheer,

ἐγώ εἰμι· μὴ φοβεῖσθε. **51** καὶ ἀνέβη
I am; be ye not afraid. And he went up

πρὸς αὐτοὺς εἰς τὸ πλοῖον, καὶ ἐκόπασεν
to them into the ship, and ceased

ὁ ἄνεμος· καὶ λίαν ἐκ περισσοῦ ἐν ἑαυτοῖς
the wind; and very much exceedingly in themselves

52 For they considered not *the miracle* of the loaves: for their heart was hardened.

53 And when they had passed over, they came into the land of Gennesaret, and drew to the shore.

54 And when they were come out of the ship, straightway they knew him,

55 And ran through that whole region round about, and began to carry about in beds those that were sick, where they heard he was.

56 And whithersoever he entered, into villages, or cities, or country, they laid the sick in the streets, and besought him that they might touch if it were but the border of his garment: and as many as touched him were made whole.

ἐξίσταντο·	**52** οὐ	γὰρ	συνῆκαν	ἐπὶ
they were astonished ;	for they did not understand	concerning

τοῖς ἄρτοις, ἀλλ᾽ ἦν αὐτῶν ἡ καρδία
the loaves, but was of them the heart

πεπωρωμένη. **53** Καὶ διαπεράσαντες ἐπὶ
having been hardened. And crossing over ²onto

τὴν γῆν ἦλθον εἰς Γεννησαρὲτ καὶ
³the ⁴land ¹they came to Gennesaret and

προσωρμίσθησαν. **54** καὶ ἐξελθόντων αὐτῶν
anchored. And coming *out* them
= as they came

ἐκ τοῦ πλοίου εὐθὺς ἐπιγνόντες αὐτὸν
out of the ship immediately knowing him

55 περιέδραμον ὅλην τὴν χώραν ἐκείνην
they ran round all – country that

καὶ ἤρξαντο ἐπὶ τοῖς κραβάτοις τοὺς
and began on the pallets the [ones]
= those

κακῶς ἔχοντας περιφέρειν, ὅπου ἤκουον
ill having to carry round, where they heard
who were ill

ὅτι ἐστίν. **56** καὶ ὅπου ἂν εἰσεπορεύετο
that he is(was). And wherever he entered

εἰς κώμας ἢ εἰς πόλεις ἢ εἰς ἀγρούς,
into villages or into cities or into country,

ἐν ταῖς ἀγοραῖς ἐτίθεσαν τοὺς ἀσθενοῦντας,
in the marketplaces they put the ailing [ones],

καὶ παρεκάλουν αὐτὸν ἵνα κἂν τοῦ
and besought him that if even the

κρασπέδου τοῦ ἱματίου αὐτοῦ ἅψωνται·
fringe of the garment of him they might touch;

καὶ ὅσοι ἂν ἥψαντο αὐτοῦ ἐσώζοντο.
and as many as touched him were healed.

CHAPTER 7

THEN came together unto him the Pharisees, and certain of the scribes, which came from Jerusalem.

2 And when they saw some of his disciples eat bread with defiled, that is to say, with unwashen, hands, they found fault.

3 For the Pharisees, and all the Jews, except they wash *their* hands oft, eat

7 Καὶ συνάγονται πρὸς αὐτὸν οἱ Φαρισαῖοι
And assemble to him the Pharisees

καὶ τινες τῶν γραμματέων ἐλθόντες ἀπὸ
and some of the scribes coming from

Ἱεροσολύμων. **2** καὶ ἰδόντες τινὰς τῶν
Jerusalem. And seeing some of the

μαθητῶν αὐτοῦ ὅτι κοιναῖς χερσίν, τοῦτ᾽
disciples of him that with unclean hands, this

ἔστιν ἀνίπτοις, ἐσθίουσιν τοὺς ἄρτους,
is unwashed, they eat bread,

3 — οἱ γὰρ Φαρισαῖοι καὶ πάντες οἱ
— for the Pharisees and all the

Ἰουδαῖοι ἐὰν μὴ πυγμῇ νίψωνται τὰς
Jews unless with [the] fist they wash the
= ? carefully

not, holding the tradition of the elders.

4 And *when they come* from the market, except they wash, they eat not. And many other things there be, which they have received to hold, *as* the washing of cups, and pots, brasen vessels, and of tables.

5 Then the Pharisees and scribes asked him, Why walk not thy disciples according to the tradition of the elders, but eat bread with unwashen hands ?

6 He answered and said unto them, Well hath Esaias prophesied of you hypocrites, as it is written, This people honoureth me with *their* lips, but their heart is far from me.

7 Howbeit in vain do they worship me, teaching *for* doctrines the commandments of men.

8 For laying aside the commandment of God, ye hold the tradition of men, *as* the washing of pots and cups: and many other such like things ye do.

9 And he said unto them, Full well ye reject the commandment of God, that ye may keep your own tradition.

10 For Moses said, Honour thy father and thy mother; and, Whoso curseth father or mother, let him die the death:

11 But ye say, If a man shall say to his father or

χεῖρας οὐκ ἐσθίουσιν, κρατοῦντες τὴν
hands   eat not,   holding   the

παράδοσιν τῶν πρεσβυτέρων, 4 καὶ ἀπ'
tradition of the   elders,   and from

ἀγορᾶς ἐὰν μὴ ῥαντίσωνται οὐκ ἐσθίουσιν, καὶ
marketplaces unless they sprinkle they eat not, and

ἄλλα πολλά ἐστιν ἃ παρέλαβον κρατεῖν,
other things many there are which they received to hold,

βαπτισμοὺς ποτηρίων καὶ ξεστῶν καὶ
washings   of cups   and of utensils and

χαλκίων, — 5 καὶ ἐπερωτῶσιν αὐτὸν οἱ
of bronze vessels, — and questioned   him the

Φαρισαῖοι καὶ οἱ γραμματεῖς· διὰ τί
Pharisees and the   scribes: Why

οὐ περιπατοῦσιν οἱ μαθηταί σου κατὰ τὴν
walk not   the disciples of thee according to the

παράδοσιν τῶν πρεσβυτέρων, ἀλλὰ κοιναῖς
tradition of the   elders,   but with unclean

χερσὶν ἐσθίουσιν τὸν ἄρτον; 6 ὁ δὲ εἶπεν
hands   eat   -   bread ? And he said

αὐτοῖς· καλῶς ἐπροφήτευσεν Ἡσαίας περὶ
to them: Well prophesied   Esaias concerning

ὑμῶν τῶν ὑποκριτῶν, ὡς γέγραπται ὅτι
you   the hypocrites, as it has been written[:] –

οὗτος ὁ λαὸς τοῖς χείλεσίν με τιμᾷ,
This - people with the lips   me honours,

ἡ δὲ καρδία αὐτῶν πόρρω ἀπέχει ἀπ'
but the heart of them [2]far [1]is [2]away from

ἐμοῦ· 7 μάτην δὲ σέβονταί με, διδάσκοντες
me;   and in vain they worship me,   teaching

διδασκαλίας ἐντάλματα ἀνθρώπων. 8 ἀφέντες
teachings [which are] commands of men.   Leaving

τὴν ἐντολὴν τοῦ θεοῦ κρατεῖτε τὴν
the commandment - of God ye hold   the

παράδοσιν τῶν ἀνθρώπων. 9 καὶ ἔλεγεν
tradition   - of men.   And he said

αὐτοῖς· καλῶς ἀθετεῖτε τὴν ἐντολὴν τοῦ
to them: Well ye set aside the commandment -

θεοῦ, ἵνα τὴν παράδοσιν ὑμῶν τηρήσητε.
of God, that the tradition of you ye may keep.

10 Μωϋσῆς γὰρ εἶπεν· τίμα τὸν πατέρα σου
For Moses   said: Honour, the father of thee

καὶ τὴν μητέρα σου, καὶ· ὁ κακολογῶν
and the mother of thee, and: The [one] speaking evil of

πατέρα ἢ μητέρα θανάτῳ τελευτάτω. 11 ὑμεῖς
father or mother by death let him end(die).   ye

δὲ λέγετε· ἐὰν εἴπῃ ἄνθρωπος τῷ πατρὶ
But say: If says a man   to the(his) father

mother, *It is* Corban, that is to say, a gift, by whatsoever thou mightest be profited by me; *he shall be free.*

12 And ye suffer him no more to do ought for his father or his mother;

13 Making the word of God of none effect through your tradition, which ye have delivered: and many such like things do ye.

14 ¶ And when he had called all the people *unto him*, he said unto them, Hearken unto me every one *of you*, and understand:

15 There is nothing from without a man, that entering into him can defile him: but the things which come out of him, those are they that defile the man.

16 If any man have ears to hear, let him hear.

17 And when he was entered into the house from the people, his disciples asked him concerning the parable.

18 And he saith unto them, Are ye so without understanding also? Do ye not perceive, that whatsoever thing from without entereth into the man, *it* cannot defile him;

19 Because it entereth not into his heart, but into the belly, and goeth out into the draught, purging all meats?

20 And he said, That which cometh out of the man, that defileth the man.

21 For from within, out

ἢ   τῇ   μητρί·   κορβᾶν,   ὅ   ἐστιν   δῶρον,
or to the   mother: Korban,   which   is   a gift,

ὃ   ἐὰν   ἐξ   ἐμοῦ   ὠφεληθῇς,   12 οὐκέτι   ἀφίετε
whatever by   me   thou mightest profit,   no longer   ye allow

αὐτὸν   οὐδὲν   ποιῆσαι   τῷ   πατρὶ   ἢ   τῇ
him   no(any)thing   to do   for the   father   or   the

μητρί,   13 ἀκυροῦντες   τὸν   λόγον   τοῦ   θεοῦ
mother,   annulling   the   word   –   of God

τῇ   παραδόσει   ὑμῶν   ᾗ   παρεδώκατε·   καὶ
by the   tradition   of you   which   ye received;   and

παρόμοια   τοιαῦτα   πολλὰ   ποιεῖτε.   14 Καὶ
³similar things   ²such   ¹many   ye do.   And

προσκαλεσάμενος   πάλιν   τὸν   ὄχλον   ἔλεγεν
calling to [him]   again   the   crowd   he said

αὐτοῖς·   ἀκούσατέ   μου   πάντες   καὶ   σύνετε.
to them: Hear ye   me   all   and understand.

15 οὐδέν   ἐστιν   ἔξωθεν   τοῦ   ἀνθρώπου
Nothing   there is   from without   –   a man

εἰσπορευόμενον   εἰς   αὐτὸν   ὃ   δύναται   κοινῶσαι
entering   into   him which   can   *to* defile

αὐτόν·   ἀλλὰ   τὰ   ἐκ   τοῦ   ἀνθρώπου   ἐκπο-
him;   but the things out of –   a man   coming

ρευόμενά   ἐστιν   τὰ   κοινοῦντα   τὸν   ἄνθρωπον. ‡
forth   are the [ones]   defiling   –   a man.

17 Καὶ   ὅτε   εἰσῆλθεν   εἰς   οἶκον   ἀπὸ   τοῦ
And   when   he entered   into   a house   from   the

ὄχλου,   ἐπηρώτων   αὐτὸν   οἱ   μαθηταὶ   αὐτοῦ
crowd,   questioned   him   the   disciples   of him

τὴν   παραβολήν.   18 καὶ   λέγει   αὐτοῖς·
the   parable.   And   he says   to them:

οὕτως   καὶ   ὑμεῖς   ἀσύνετοί   ἐστε;   οὐ
Thus   also   ye   undiscerning   are?   do ye not

νοεῖτε   ὅτι   πᾶν   τὸ   ἔξωθεν   εἰσπορευόμενον
understand that   everything   from without   entering

εἰς   τὸν   ἄνθρωπον   οὐ   δύναται   αὐτὸν
into   –   a man   cannot   him

κοινῶσαι,   19 ὅτι   οὐκ   εἰσπορεύεται   αὐτοῦ
to defile,   because   it enters not   of him

εἰς   τὴν   καρδίαν   ἀλλ'   εἰς   τὴν   κοιλίαν,
into   the   heart   but   into   the   belly,

καὶ   εἰς   τὸν   ἀφεδρῶνα   ἐκπορεύεται,   καθα-
and   into   the   drain   goes out,   purg-

ρίζων   πάντα   τὰ   βρώματα;   20 ἔλεγεν   δὲ
ing   all   –   foods?   And he said[,]

ὅτι   τὸ   ἐκ   τοῦ   ἀνθρώπου   ἐκπορευόμενον,
–   The thing out of –   a man   coming forth,

ἐκεῖνο   κοινοῖ   τὸν   ἄνθρωπον.   21 ἔσωθεν
that   defiles   –   a man.   from within

‡Verse 16 omitted by Nestle; *cf.* R.V. marg., etc.

of the heart of men, proceed evil thoughts, adulteries, fornications, murders,

22 Thefts, covetousness, wickedness, deceit, lasciviousness, an evil eye, blasphemy, pride, foolishness:

23 All these evil things come from within, and defile the man.

24 ¶ And from thence he arose, and went into the borders of Tyre and Sidon, and entered into an house, and would have no man know *it:* but he could not be hid.

25 For a *certain* woman, whose young daughter had an unclean spirit, heard of him, and came and fell at his feet:

26 The woman was a Greek, a Syrophenician by nation; and she besought him that he would cast forth the devil out of her daughter.

27 But Jesus said unto her, Let the children first be filled: for it is not meet to take the children's bread, and to cast *it* unto the dogs.

28 And she answered and said unto him, Yes, Lord: yet the dogs under the table eat of the children's crumbs.

29 And he said unto her, For this saying go thy way;

γὰρ ἐκ τῆς καρδίας τῶν ἀνθρώπων
For out of the heart - of men
οἱ διαλογισμοὶ οἱ κακοὶ ἐκπορεύονται,
- thoughts - evil come forth,
πορνεῖαι, κλοπαί, φόνοι, 22 μοιχεῖαι,
fornications, thefts, murders, adulteries,
πλεονεξίαι, πονηρίαι, δόλος, ἀσέλγεια, ὀφθαλμὸς
greedinesses, iniquities, deceit, lewdness, eye
πονηρός, βλασφημία, ὑπερηφανία, ἀφροσύνη·
an evil, blasphemy, arrogance, foolishness;
23 πάντα ταῦτα τὰ πονηρὰ ἔσωθεν ἐκπορεύεται
all these - evil things from within comes forth
καὶ κοινοῖ τὸν ἄνθρωπον.
and defile - a man.

24 Ἐκεῖθεν δὲ ἀναστὰς ἀπῆλθεν εἰς τὰ ὅρια
And thence rising up he went away into the district
Τύρου. Καὶ εἰσελθὼν εἰς οἰκίαν οὐδένα ἤθελεν
of Tyre. And entering into a house no one he wished
γνῶναι, καὶ οὐκ ἠδυνάσθη λαθεῖν· 25 ἀλλ'
to know, and could not to be hidden; but
εὐθὺς ἀκούσασα γυνὴ περὶ αὐτοῦ, ἧς
immediately ²hearing ¹a woman about him, of whom
= whose
εἶχεν τὸ θυγάτριον αὐτῆς πνεῦμα ἀκάθαρτον,
had the daughter of her spirit an unclean,
daughter had
ἐλθοῦσα προσέπεσεν πρὸς τοὺς πόδας αὐτοῦ·
coming fell at the feet of him;
26 ἡ δὲ γυνὴ ἦν Ἑλληνίς, Συροφοινίκισσα
and the woman was a Greek, a Syrophenician
τῷ γένει· καὶ ἠρώτα αὐτὸν ἵνα τὸ
- by race; and she asked him that the
δαιμόνιον ἐκβάλῃ ἐκ τῆς θυγατρὸς αὐτῆς.
demon he would expel out of the daughter of her.
27 καὶ ἔλεγεν αὐτῇ· ἄφες πρῶτον
And he said to her: Permit first
χορτασθῆναι τὰ τέκνα· οὐ γάρ ἐστιν καλὸν
to be satisfied the children; for it is not good
λαβεῖν τὸν ἄρτον τῶν τέκνων καὶ τοῖς
to take the bread of the children and to the
κυναρίοις βαλεῖν. 28 ἡ δὲ ἀπεκρίθη καὶ
dogs to throw [it]. And she answered and
λέγει αὐτῷ· ναί, κύριε· καὶ τὰ κυνάρια
says to him: Yes, Lord; and yet the dogs
ὑποκάτω τῆς τραπέζης ἐσθίουσιν ἀπὸ τῶν
under the table eat from the
ψιχίων τῶν παιδίων. 29 καὶ εἶπεν αὐτῇ·
crumbs of the children. And he said to her:
διὰ τοῦτον τὸν λόγον ὕπαγε, ἐξελήλυθεν
Because of this - word go, has gone forth

the devil is gone out of thy daughter.

30 And when she was come to her house, she found the devil gone out, and her daughter laid upon the bed.

31 ¶ And again, departing from the coasts of Tyre and Sidon, he came unto the sea of Galilee, through the midst of the coasts of Decapolis.

32 And they bring unto him one that was deaf, and had an impediment in his speech; and they beseech him to put his hand upon him.

33 And he took him aside from the multitude, and put his fingers into his ears, and he spit, and touched his tongue;

34 And looking up to heaven, he sighed, and saith unto him, Ephphatha, that is, Be opened.

35 And straightway his ears were opened, and the string of his tongue was loosed, and he spake plain.

36 And he charged them that they should tell no man: but the more he charged them, so much the more a great deal they published it;

37 And were beyond measure astonished, saying, He hath done all things well: he maketh both the deaf to hear, and the dumb to speak.

ἐκ τῆς θυγατρός σου τὸ δαιμόνιον. **30** καὶ
out of the daughter of thee the demon. And

ἀπελθοῦσα εἰς τὸν οἶκον αὐτῆς εὗρεν τὸ
going away to the house of her she found the

παιδίον βεβλημένον ἐπὶ τὴν κλίνην καὶ τὸ
child having been laid on the couch and the

δαιμόνιον ἐξεληλυθός. **31** Καὶ πάλιν ἐξελθὼν
demon having gone forth. And again going forth

ἐκ τῶν ὁρίων Τύρου ἦλθεν διὰ Σιδῶνος
out of the district of Tyre he came through Sidon

εἰς τὴν θάλασσαν τῆς Γαλιλαίας ἀνὰ
to the sea – of Galilee in the

μέσον τῶν ὁρίων Δεκαπόλεως. **32** Καὶ
midst of the district of Decapolis. And

φέρουσιν αὐτῷ κωφὸν καὶ μογιλάλον, καὶ
they bring to him a man deaf and speaking with difficulty, and

παρακαλοῦσιν αὐτὸν ἵνα ἐπιθῇ αὐτῷ τὴν
they beseech him that he would put on on him the(his)

χεῖρα. **33** καὶ ἀπολαβόμενος αὐτὸν ἀπὸ
hand. And taking away him from

τοῦ ὄχλου κατ᾽ ἰδίαν ἔβαλεν τοὺς δακτύλους
the crowd privately he put the fingers

αὐτοῦ εἰς τὰ ὦτα αὐτοῦ καὶ πτύσας
of him into the ears of him and spitting

ἥψατο τῆς γλώσσης αὐτοῦ, **34** καὶ
he touched the tongue of him, and

ἀναβλέψας εἰς τὸν οὐρανὸν ἐστέναξεν,
looking up to – heaven he groaned,

καὶ λέγει αὐτῷ· ἐφφαθά, ὅ ἐστιν διανοίχθητι.
and says to him: Ephphatha, which is Be thou opened.

35 καὶ ἠνοίγησαν αὐτοῦ αἱ ἀκοαί, καὶ
And were opened of him the ears, and

εὐθὺς ἐλύθη ὁ δεσμὸς τῆς γλώσσης αὐτοῦ,
immediately was loosened the bond of the tongue of him,

καὶ ἐλάλει ὀρθῶς. **36** καὶ διεστείλατο
and he spoke correctly. And he ordered

αὐτοῖς ἵνα μηδενὶ λέγωσιν· ὅσον δὲ
them that no one they should tell; but as much as

αὐτοῖς διεστέλλετο, αὐτοὶ μᾶλλον περισσότερον
them he ordered, they more exceedingly

ἐκήρυσσον. **37** καὶ ὑπερπερισσῶς ἐξεπλήσσοντο
proclaimed. And most exceedingly they were astounded

λέγοντες· καλῶς πάντα πεποίηκεν, καὶ
saying: Well all things he has done, both

τοὺς κωφοὺς ποιεῖ ἀκούειν καὶ ἀλάλους
the deaf he makes to hear and dumb

λαλεῖν.
to speak.

CHAPTER 8

IN those days the multitude being very great, and having nothing to eat, Jesus called his disciples *unto him*, and saith unto them,

2 I have compassion on the multitude, because they have now been with me three days, and have nothing to eat:

3 And if I send them away fasting to their own houses, they will faint by the way: for divers of them came from far.

4 And his disciples answered him, From whence can a man satisfy these *men* with bread here in the wilderness?

5 And he asked them, How many loaves have ye? And they said, Seven.

6 And he commanded the people to sit down on the ground: and he took the seven loaves, and gave thanks, and brake, and gave to his disciples to set before *them;* and they did set *them* before the people.

7 And they had a few small fishes: and he blessed, and commanded to set them also before *them.*

8 So they did eat, and were filled: and they took up of the broken *meat* that was left seven baskets.

9 And they that had eaten were about four thousand: and he sent them away.

10 ¶ And straightway he entered into a ship with his disciples, and came into

---

8 Ἐν ἐκείναις ταῖς ἡμέραις πάλιν πολλοῦ
In those – days again a much(great)
= there being

ὄχλου ὄντος καὶ μὴ ἐχόντων τί φάγωσιν,
crowd being[s] and not having[e] anything they might eat,
a great crowd

προσκαλεσάμενος τοὺς μαθητὰς λέγει αὐτοῖς·
calling to [him] the disciples he says to them:

2 σπλαγχνίζομαι ἐπὶ τὸν ὄχλον, ὅτι ἤδη
I have compassion on the crowd, because now

ἡμέραι τρεῖς προσμένουσίν μοι καὶ οὐκ
days three they remain with me and not

ἔχουσιν τί φάγωσιν· 3 καὶ ἐὰν ἀπολύσω
they have anything they may eat; and if I dismiss

αὐτοὺς νήστεις εἰς οἶκον αὐτῶν, ἐκλυθήσονται
them fasting to house of them, they will faint

ἐν τῇ ὁδῷ· καί τινες αὐτῶν ἀπὸ μακρόθεν
in the way; and some of them from afar

εἰσίν. 4 καὶ ἀπεκρίθησαν αὐτῷ οἱ μαθηταὶ
are. And answered him the disciples

αὐτοῦ ὅτι πόθεν τούτους δυνήσεταί τις
of him[.] [1]Whence [6]these people [5]will [6]be able [5]anyone

ὧδε χορτάσαι ἄρτων ἐπ᾽ ἐρημίας; 5 καὶ
[8]here [5]to satisfy [7]of(with) loaves [9]on(in) [10]a desert? And

ἠρώτα αὐτούς· πόσους ἔχετε ἄρτους;
he asked them: How many have ye loaves?

οἱ δὲ εἶπαν· ἑπτά. 6 καὶ παραγγέλλει τῷ
And they said: Seven. And he commands the

ὄχλῳ ἀναπεσεῖν ἐπὶ τῆς γῆς· καὶ λαβὼν
crowd to recline on the ground; and taking

τοὺς ἑπτὰ ἄρτους εὐχαριστήσας ἔκλασεν
the seven loaves giving thanks he broke

καὶ ἐδίδου τοῖς μαθηταῖς αὐτοῦ ἵνα
and gave to the disciples of him that

παρατιθῶσιν, καὶ παρέθηκαν τῷ ὄχλῳ.
they might serve, and they served the crowd.

7 καὶ εἶχον ἰχθύδια ὀλίγα· καὶ εὐλογήσας
And they had fishes a few; and blessing

αὐτὰ εἶπεν καὶ ταῦτα παρατιθέναι. 8 καὶ
them he told also these to be served. And

ἔφαγον καὶ ἐχορτάσθησαν, καὶ ἦραν
they ate and were satisfied, and took

περισσεύματα κλασμάτων, ἑπτὰ σπυρίδας.
excesses of fragments, seven baskets.

9 ἦσαν δὲ ὡς τετρακισχίλιοι. καὶ ἀπέλυσεν
Now they were about four thousand. And he dismissed

αὐτούς. 10 Καὶ εὐθὺς ἐμβὰς εἰς τὸ
them. And immediately embarking in the

πλοῖον μετὰ τῶν μαθητῶν αὐτοῦ
ship with the disciples of him

the parts of Dalmanutha.

11 And the Pharisees came forth, and began to question with him, seeking of him a sign from heaven, tempting him.

12 And he sighed deeply in his spirit, and saith, Why doth this generation seek after a sign ? verily I say unto you, There shall no sign be given unto this generation.

13 And he left them, and entering into the ship again departed to the other side.

14 ¶ Now *the disciples* had forgotten to take bread, neither had they in the ship with them more than one loaf.

15 And he charged them, saying, Take heed, beware of the leaven of the Pharisees, and *of* the leaven of Herod.

16 And they reasoned among themselves, saying, *It is* because we have no bread.

17 And when Jesus knew *it*, he saith unto them, Why reason ye, because ye have no bread ? perceive ye not yet, neither understand ? have ye your heart yet hardened ?

18 Having eyes, see ye not ? and having ears, hear ye not ? and do ye not remember ?

19 When I brake the five loaves among five thousand, how many baskets full of fragments took

ἦλθεν εἰς τὰ μέρη Δαλμανουθά.
he came into the region of Dalmanutha.

11 Καὶ ἐξῆλθον οἱ Φαρισαῖοι καὶ ἤρξαντο
And came forth the Pharisees and began

συζητεῖν αὐτῷ, ζητοῦντες παρ' αὐτοῦ
to debate with him, seeking from him

σημεῖον ἀπὸ τοῦ οὐρανοῦ, πειράζοντες
a sign from – heaven, tempting

αὐτόν. **12** καὶ ἀναστενάξας τῷ πνεύματι
him. And groaning in the spirit

αὐτοῦ λέγει· τί ἡ γενεὰ αὕτη ζητεῖ
of him he says: Why – ²generation ³this ¹does ⁴seek

σημεῖον; ἀμὴν λέγω ὑμῖν, εἰ δοθήσεται
a sign ? Truly I tell you, if will be given

τῇ γενεᾷ ταύτῃ σημεῖον. **13** καὶ ἀφεὶς
– generation to this a sign. And leaving

αὐτοὺς πάλιν ἐμβὰς ἀπῆλθεν εἰς τὸ
them again embarking he went away to the

πέραν. **14** Καὶ ἐπελάθοντο λαβεῖν ἄρτους,
other side. And they forgot to take loaves,

καὶ εἰ μὴ ἕνα ἄρτον οὐκ εἶχον μεθ'
and except one loaf they had not with

ἑαυτῶν ἐν τῷ πλοίῳ. **15** καὶ διεστέλλετο
themselves in the ship. And he charged

αὐτοῖς λέγων· ὁρᾶτε, βλέπετε ἀπὸ τῆς
them saying : See, look ye from the
=Beware of

ζύμης τῶν Φαρισαίων καὶ τῆς ζύμης
leaven of the Pharisees and of the leaven

Ἡρῴδου. **16** καὶ διελογίζοντο πρὸς ἀλλήλους
of Herod. And they reasoned with one another

ὅτι ἄρτους οὐκ ἔχουσιν. **17** καὶ γνοὺς
because loaves they have(had) not. And knowing

λέγει αὐτοῖς· τί διαλογίζεσθε ὅτι ἄρτους
he says to them: Why reason ye because loaves

οὐκ ἔχετε; οὔπω νοεῖτε οὐδὲ συνίετε;
ye have not ? not yet understand ye nor realize ?

πεπωρωμένην ἔχετε τὴν καρδίαν ὑμῶν;
having been hardened have ye the heart of you ?

18 ὀφθαλμοὺς ἔχοντες οὐ βλέπετε, καὶ
eyes having see ye not, and

ὦτα ἔχοντες οὐκ ἀκούετε; καὶ
ears having hear ye not ? and

οὐ μνημονεύετε, **19** ὅτε τοὺς πέντε ἄρτους
do ye not remember, when the five loaves

ἔκλασα εἰς τοὺς πεντακισχιλίους, πόσους
I broke to the five thousand, how many

κοφίνους κλασμάτων πλήρεις ἤρατε; λέγουσιν
baskets of fragments full ye took ? They say

ye up? They say unto him, Twelve.

20 And when the seven among four thousand, how many baskets full of fragments took ye up? And they said, Seven.

21 And he said unto them, How is it that ye do not understand?

22 ¶ And he cometh to Bethsaida; and they bring a blind man unto him, and besought him to touch him.

23 And he took the blind man by the hand, and led him out of the town; and when he had spit on his eyes, and put his hands upon him, he asked him if he saw ought.

24 And he looked up, and said, I see men as trees, walking.

25 After that he put *his* hands again upon his eyes, and made him look up: and he was restored, and saw every man clearly.

26 And he sent him away to his house, saying, Neither go into the town, nor tell *it* to any in the town.

27 ¶ And Jesus went out, and his disciples, into the towns of Cæsarea Philippi: and by the way he asked his disciples, saying unto them, Whom do men say that I am?

28 And they answered, John the Baptist: but some

αὐτῷ· δώδεκα. **20** ὅτε τοὺς ἑπτὰ εἰς
to him: Twelve. When the seven to

τοὺς τετρακισχιλίους, πόσων σπυρίδων
the four thousand, ²of how many ³baskets

πληρώματα κλασμάτων ἤρατε; καὶ λέγουσιν·
¹fullnesses ⁴of fragments ye took? And they say:

ἑπτά. **21** καὶ ἔλεγεν αὐτοῖς· οὔπω συνίετε;
Seven. And he said to them: Not yet do ye realize?

22 Καὶ ἔρχονται εἰς Βηθσαϊδάν. Καὶ
And they come to Bethsaida. And

φέρουσιν αὐτῷ τυφλόν, καὶ παρακαλοῦσιν
they bring to him a blind man, and beseech

αὐτὸν ἵνα αὐτοῦ ἄψηται. **23** καὶ ἐπιλαβόμενος
him that him he would touch. And laying hold of

τῆς χειρὸς τοῦ τυφλοῦ ἐξήνεγκεν αὐτὸν
the hand of the blind man he led forth him

ἔξω τῆς κώμης, καὶ πτύσας εἰς τὰ
outside the village, and spitting in the

ὄμματα αὐτοῦ, ἐπιθεὶς τὰς χεῖρας αὐτῷ,
eyes of him, putting *on* the hands on him,

ἐπηρώτα αὐτόν· εἴ τι βλέπεις; **24** καὶ
questioned him: If anything thou seest? And

ἀναβλέψας ἔλεγεν· βλέπω τοὺς ἀνθρώπους,
looking up he said: I see – men,

ὅτι ὡς δένδρα ὁρῶ περιπατοῦντας.
that as trees I behold walking.

25 εἶτα πάλιν ἐπέθηκεν τὰς χεῖρας ἐπὶ
Then again he put *on* the hands on

τοὺς ὀφθαλμοὺς αὐτοῦ, καὶ διέβλεψεν καὶ
the eyes of him, and he looked steadily and

ἀπεκατέστη, καὶ ἐνέβλεπεν τηλαυγῶς ἅπαντα.
was restored, and saw clearly all things.

26 καὶ ἀπέστειλεν αὐτὸν εἰς οἶκον αὐτοῦ
And he sent him to house of him

λέγων· μηδὲ εἰς τὴν κώμην εἰσέλθῃς.
saying: Not into the village thou mayest enter.

27 Καὶ ἐξῆλθεν ὁ Ἰησοῦς καὶ οἱ μαθηταὶ
And went forth – Jesus and the disciples

αὐτοῦ εἰς τὰς κώμας Καισαρείας τῆς
of him to the villages of Cæsarea –

Φιλίππου· καὶ ἐν τῇ ὁδῷ ἐπηρώτα τοὺς
of Philip; and in the way he questioned the

μαθητὰς αὐτοῦ λέγων αὐτοῖς· τίνα με
disciples of him saying to them: Whom me

λέγουσιν οἱ ἄνθρωποι εἶναι; **28** οἱ δὲ
say – men to be? And they

εἶπαν αὐτῷ λέγοντες ὅτι Ἰωάννην τὸν
told him saying[,] – John the

say, Elias; and others, One of the prophets.

29 And he saith unto them, But whom say ye that I am? And Peter answereth and saith unto him, Thou art the Christ.

30 And he charged them that they should tell no man of him.

31 ¶ And he began to teach them, that the Son of man must suffer many things, and be rejected of the elders, and of the chief priests, and scribes, and be killed, and after three days rise again.

32 And he spake that saying openly. And Peter took him, and began to rebuke him.

33 But when he had turned about and looked on his disciples, he rebuked Peter, saying, Get thee behind me, Satan: for thou savourest not the things that be of God, but the things that be of men.

34 ¶ And when he had called the people unto him with his disciples also, he said unto them, Whosoever will come after me, let him deny himself, and take up his cross, and follow me.

35 For whosoever will save his life shall lose it; but whosoever shall lose

βαπτιστήν, καὶ ἄλλοι Ἠλίαν, ἄλλοι δὲ
Baptist, ▪ and others Elias, but others[,]

ὅτι εἷς τῶν προφητῶν. 29 καὶ αὐτὸς
- one of the prophets. And he

ἐπηρώτα αὐτούς· ὑμεῖς δὲ τίνα με λέγετε
questioned them: But ye whom me say ye

εἶναι; ἀποκριθεὶς ὁ Πέτρος λέγει αὐτῷ·
to be? Answering - Peter says to him:

σὺ εἶ ὁ χριστός. 30 καὶ ἐπετίμησεν
Thou art the Christ. And he warned

αὐτοῖς ἵνα μηδενὶ λέγωσιν περὶ αὐτοῦ.
them that no one they might tell about him.

31 Καὶ ἤρξατο διδάσκειν αὐτοὺς ὅτι δεῖ
And he began to teach them that it behoves

τὸν υἱὸν τοῦ ἀνθρώπου πολλὰ παθεῖν,
the Son - of man many things to suffer,

καὶ ἀποδοκιμασθῆναι ὑπὸ τῶν πρεσβυτέρων
and to be rejected by the elders

καὶ τῶν ἀρχιερέων καὶ τῶν γραμματέων
and the chief priests and the scribes

καὶ ἀποκτανθῆναι καὶ μετὰ τρεῖς ἡμέρας
and to be killed and after three days

ἀναστῆναι· 32 καὶ παρρησίᾳ τὸν λόγον
to rise again; and openly the word

ἐλάλει. καὶ προσλαβόμενος ὁ Πέτρος
he spoke. And ²taking ⁴aside - ¹Peter

αὐτὸν ἤρξατο ἐπιτιμᾶν αὐτῷ. 33 ὁ δὲ
³him began to rebuke him. But he

ἐπιστραφεὶς καὶ ἰδὼν τοὺς μαθητὰς αὐτοῦ
turning round and seeing the disciples of him

ἐπετίμησεν Πέτρῳ καὶ λέγει· ὕπαγε ὀπίσω
rebuked Peter and says: Go behind

μου, σατανᾶ, ὅτι οὐ φρονεῖς τὰ τοῦ
me, Satan, because thou mindest not the things -

θεοῦ ἀλλὰ τὰ τῶν ἀνθρώπων. 34 Καὶ
of God but the things - of men. And

προσκαλεσάμενος τὸν ὄχλον σὺν τοῖς μαθηταῖς
calling to [him] the crowd with the disciples

αὐτοῦ εἶπεν αὐτοῖς· εἴ τις θέλει ὀπίσω
of him he said to them: If anyone wishes after

μου ἐλθεῖν, ἀπαρνησάσθω ἑαυτὸν καὶ ἀράτω
me to come, let him deny himself and take

τὸν σταυρὸν αὐτοῦ, καὶ ἀκολουθείτω μοι.
the cross of him, and let him follow me.

35 ὃς γὰρ ἐὰν θέλῃ τὴν ψυχὴν αὐτοῦ σῶ-
For whoever wishes the life of him to

σαι, ἀπολέσει αὐτήν· ὃς δ' ἂν ἀπολέσει
save, will lose it; but whoever will lose

his life for my sake and the gospel's, the same shall save it.

36 For what shall it profit a man, if he shall gain the whole world, and lose his own soul?

37 Or what shall a man give in exchange for his soul?

38 Whosoever therefore shall be ashamed of me and of my words in this adulterous and sinful generation; of him also shall the Son of man be ashamed, when he cometh in the glory of his Father with the holy angels.

τὴν ψυχὴν αὐτοῦ ἕνεκεν ἐμοῦ καὶ τοῦ
the   life   of him for the sake of   me   and   the
εὐαγγελίου, σώσει αὐτήν. 36 τί γὰρ ὠφελεῖ
gospel,   will save   it.   For what   profits
ἄνθρωπον κερδῆσαι τὸν κόσμον ὅλον καὶ
a man   to gain   the   world   whole   and
ζημιωθῆναι τὴν ψυχὴν αὐτοῦ; 37 τί γὰρ
to be fined   the   soul   of him?   For what
δοῖ ἄνθρωπος ἀντάλλαγμα τῆς ψυχῆς αὐτοῦ;
might give a man   an exchange   of the   soul   of him?
38 ὃς γὰρ ἐὰν ἐπαισχυνθῇ με καὶ
For whoever   is ashamed of   me   and
τοὺς ἐμοὺς λόγους ἐν τῇ γενεᾷ ταύτῃ
-   my   words   in   -   generation   this
τῇ μοιχαλίδι καὶ ἁμαρτωλῷ, καὶ ὁ
-   adulterous   and   sinful,   also   the
υἱὸς τοῦ ἀνθρώπου ἐπαισχυνθήσεται αὐτόν,
Son   -   of man   will be ashamed of   him,
ὅταν ἔλθῃ ἐν τῇ δόξῃ τοῦ πατρὸς
when   he comes   in   the   glory   of the   Father
αὐτοῦ μετὰ τῶν ἀγγέλων τῶν ἁγίων.
of him   with   the   angels   -   holy.

CHAPTER 9

AND he said unto them, Verily I say unto you, That there be some of them that stand here, which shall not taste of death, till they have seen the kingdom of God come with power.

2 ¶ And after six days Jesus taketh *with him* Peter, and James, and John, and leadeth them up into an high mountain apart by themselves: and he was transfigured before them.

3 And his raiment became shining, exceeding white as snow; so as no fuller on earth can white them.

9 καὶ ἔλεγεν αὐτοῖς· ἀμὴν λέγω ὑμῖν
And   he said   to them: Truly   I tell   you
ὅτι εἰσίν τινες ὧδε τῶν ἑστηκότων
that   there are   some   here   of the [ones]   standing
οἵτινες οὐ μὴ γεύσωνται θανάτου ἕως ἂν
who   by no means   may taste   of death   until
ἴδωσιν τὴν βασιλείαν τοῦ θεοῦ ἐληλυθυῖαν
they see   the   kingdom   -   of God   having come
ἐν δυνάμει.
in   power.

2 Καὶ μετὰ ἡμέρας ἓξ παραλαμβάνει
And   after   days   six   takes
ὁ Ἰησοῦς τὸν Πέτρον καὶ τὸν Ἰάκωβον
-   Jesus   -   Peter   and   -   James
καὶ Ἰωάννην, καὶ ἀναφέρει αὐτοὺς εἰς
and   John,   and   leads up   them   into
ὄρος ὑψηλὸν κατ' ἰδίαν μόνους. καὶ
mountain   a high   privately   alone.   And
μετεμορφώθη ἔμπροσθεν αὐτῶν, 3 καὶ τὰ
he was transfigured   before   them,   and   the
ἱμάτια αὐτοῦ ἐγένετο στίλβοντα λευκὰ λίαν,
garments   of him   became   gleaming   white exceedingly,
οἷα γναφεὺς ἐπὶ τῆς γῆς οὐ δύναται
such as   fuller   on   the   earth   cannot

4 And there appeared unto them Elias with Moses: and they were talking with Jesus.

5 And Peter answered and said to Jesus, Master, it is good for us to be here: and let us make three tabernacles; one for thee, and one for Moses, and one for Elias.

6 For he wist not what to say; for they were sore afraid.

7 And there was a cloud that overshadowed them: and a voice came out of the cloud, saying, This is my beloved Son: hear him.

8 And suddenly, when they had looked round about, they saw no man any more, save Jesus only with themselves.

9 And as they came down from the mountain, he charged them that they should tell no man what things they had seen, till the Son of man were risen from the dead.

10 And they kept that saying with themselves, questioning one with another what the rising from the dead should mean.

11 ¶ And they asked him, saying, Why say the scribes that Elias must first come?

12 And he answered and told them, Elias verily cometh first, and restoreth all things; and how it is written of the Son of man, that he must suffer many

---

οὕτως λευκᾶναι. 4 καὶ ὤφθη αὐτοῖς Ἠλίας
so   to whiten.   And appeared to them Elias

σὺν Μωϋσεῖ, καὶ ἦσαν συλλαλοῦντες τῷ
with Moses, and they were conversing with

Ἰησοῦ. 5 καὶ ἀποκριθεὶς ὁ Πέτρος λέγει
Jesus.   And answering   –   Peter says

τῷ Ἰησοῦ· ῥαββί, καλόν ἐστιν ἡμᾶς ὧδε
– to Jesus: Rabbi, good it is us here

εἶναι, καὶ ποιήσωμεν τρεῖς σκηνάς, σοὶ
to be, and let us make three tents, for thee

μίαν καὶ Μωϋσεῖ μίαν καὶ Ἠλίᾳ μίαν.
one and for Moses one and for Elias one.

6 οὐ γὰρ ᾔδει τί ἀποκριθῇ· ἔκφοβοι γὰρ
For he knew not what he answered; for exceedingly afraid

ἐγένοντο. 7 καὶ ἐγένετο νεφέλη ἐπισκιάζουσα
they became.   And there came a cloud overshadowing

αὐτοῖς, καὶ ἐγένετο φωνὴ ἐκ τῆς νεφέλης·
them, and there came a voice out of the cloud:

οὗτός ἐστιν ὁ υἱός μου ὁ ἀγαπητός,
This is the Son of me the beloved,

ἀκούετε αὐτοῦ. 8 καὶ ἐξάπινα περιβλεψάμενοι
hear ye him.   And suddenly looking round

οὐκέτι οὐδένα εἶδον εἰ μὴ τὸν Ἰησοῦν
no longer no(any)one they saw except – Jesus

μόνον μεθ' ἑαυτῶν. 9 Καὶ καταβαινόντων
only with themselves.   And coming down
                    = as they came down

αὐτῶν ἐκ τοῦ ὄρους διεστείλατο αὐτοῖς
thema out of the mountain he ordered them

ἵνα μηδενὶ ἃ εἶδον διηγήσωνται,
that to no one [the] things which they saw they should relate,

εἰ μὴ ὅταν ὁ υἱὸς τοῦ ἀνθρώπου ἐκ νεκρῶν
except when the Son – of man out of [the] dead

ἀναστῇ. 10 καὶ τὸν λόγον ἐκράτησαν πρὸς
should rise.   And the word they held to

ἑαυτοὺς συζητοῦντες τί ἐστιν τὸ ἐκ
themselves debating what is the "out of

νεκρῶν ἀναστῆναι. 11 Καὶ ἐπηρώτων αὐτὸν
[the] dead to rise."   And they questioned him

λέγοντες· ὅτι λέγουσιν οἱ γραμματεῖς ὅτι
saying: Why say the scribes that

Ἠλίαν δεῖ ἐλθεῖν πρῶτον; 12 ὁ δὲ ἔφη
Elias it behoves to come first?   And he said

αὐτοῖς· Ἠλίας μὲν ἐλθὼν πρῶτον
to them: Elias indeed coming first

ἀποκαθιστάνει πάντα· καὶ πῶς γέγραπται
will restore all things; and how has it been written

ἐπὶ τὸν υἱὸν τοῦ ἀνθρώπου, ἵνα πολλὰ
on(concerning) the Son – of man, that many things

things, and be set at nought.

13 But I say unto you, That Elias is indeed come, and they have done unto him whatsoever they listed, as it is written of him.

14 ¶ And when he came to *his* disciples, he saw a great multitude about them, and the scribes questioning with them.

15 And straightway all the people, when they beheld him, were greatly amazed, and running to *him* saluted him.

16 And he asked the scribes, What question ye with them?

17 And one of the multitude answered and said, Master, I have brought unto thee my son, which hath a dumb spirit;

18 And wheresoever he taketh him, he teareth him: and he foameth, and gnasheth with his teeth, and pineth away: and I spake to thy disciples that they should cast him out; and they could not.

19 He answereth him, and saith, O faithless generation, how long shall I be with you? how long shall I suffer you? bring him unto me.

20 And they brought him unto him: and when he saw him, straightway the spirit tare him; and he fell on the ground, and wallowed foaming.

πάθη καὶ ἐξουδενηθῇ; 13 ἀλλὰ λέγω ὑμῖν
he should suffer and be set at naught? But I tell you

ὅτι καὶ 'Ηλίας ἐλήλυθεν, καὶ ἐποίησαν
that indeed Elias has come, and they did

αὐτῷ ὅσα ἤθελον, καθὼς γέγραπται
to him what they wished, as it has been written

ἐπ' αὐτόν.
on(concerning) him.

14 Καὶ ἐλθόντες πρὸς τοὺς μαθητὰς
And coming to the disciples

εἶδον ὄχλον πολὺν περὶ αὐτοὺς καὶ
they saw crowd a much(great) around them and

γραμματεῖς συζητοῦντας πρὸς αὐτούς.
scribes debating with them.

15 καὶ εὐθὺς πᾶς ὁ ὄχλος ἰδόντες αὐτὸν
And immediately all the crowd seeing him

ἐξεθαμβήθησαν, καὶ προστρέχοντες ἠσπάζοντο
were greatly astonished, and running up to greeted

αὐτόν. 16 καὶ ἐπηρώτησεν αὐτούς· τί
him. And he questioned them: What

συζητεῖτε πρὸς αὐτούς; 17 καὶ ἀπεκρίθη
are ye debating with them? And answered

αὐτῷ εἷς ἐκ τοῦ ὄχλου· διδάσκαλε,
him one of the crowd: Teacher,

ἤνεγκα τὸν υἱόν μου πρὸς σέ, ἔχοντα
I brought the son of me to thee, having

πνεῦμα ἄλαλον· 18 καὶ ὅπου ἐὰν αὐτὸν
spirit a dumb; and wherever him

καταλάβῃ, ῥήσσει αὐτόν, καὶ ἀφρίζει καὶ
it seizes, it tears him, and he foams and

τρίζει τοὺς ὀδόντας καὶ ξηραίνεται· καὶ
grinds the(his) teeth and he wastes away; and

εἶπα τοῖς μαθηταῖς σου ἵνα αὐτὸ
I told the disciples of thee that it

ἐκβάλωσιν, καὶ οὐκ ἴσχυσαν. 19 ὁ δὲ
they might expel, and they were not able. And he

ἀποκριθεὶς αὐτοῖς λέγει· ὦ γενεὰ ἄπιστος,
answering them says: O generation unbelieving,

ἕως πότε πρὸς ὑμᾶς ἔσομαι; ἕως πότε
until when with you shall I be? how long
= how long

ἀνέξομαι ὑμῶν; φέρετε αὐτὸν πρός με.
shall I endure you? bring him to me.

20 καὶ ἤνεγκαν αὐτὸν πρὸς αὐτόν. καὶ
And they brought him to him. And

ἰδὼν αὐτὸν τὸ πνεῦμα εὐθὺς συνεσπάραξεν
seeing him the spirit immediately violently threw

αὐτόν, καὶ πεσὼν ἐπὶ τῆς γῆς ἐκυλίετο
him, and falling on the earth he wallowed

21 And he asked his father, How long is it ago since this came unto him? And he said, Of a child.

22 And ofttimes it hath cast him into the fire, and into the waters, to destroy him: but if thou canst do any thing, have compassion on us, and help us.

23 Jesus said unto him, If thou canst believe, all things *are* possible to him that believeth.

24 And straightway the father of the child cried out, and said with tears, Lord, I believe; help thou mine unbelief.

25 When Jesus saw that the people came running together, he rebuked the foul spirit, saying unto him, *Thou* dumb and deaf spirit, I charge thee, come out of him, and enter no more into him.

26 And *the spirit* cried, and rent him sore, and came out of him: and he was as one dead; insomuch that many said, He is dead.

27 But Jesus took him by the hand, and lifted him up; and he arose.

28 And when he was come into the house, his disciples asked him privately, Why could not we cast him out?

29 And he said unto them, This kind can come

ἀφρίζων. **21** καὶ ἐπηρώτησεν τὸν πατέρα
foaming.　　　And　he questioned　the　father

αὐτοῦ· πόσος χρόνος ἐστὶν ὡς τοῦτο
of him:　What　time　is it　while　this

γέγονεν αὐτῷ; ὁ δὲ εἶπεν· ἐκ παιδιόθεν·
has happened to him? And he said:　From childhood;

22 καὶ πολλάκις καὶ εἰς πῦρ αὐτὸν
and　often　both　into　fire　him

ἔβαλεν καὶ εἰς ὕδατα ἵνα ἀπολέσῃ αὐτόν· ἀλλ᾽
it threw and into waters that it may destroy him;　but

εἴ τι δύνῃ, βοήθησον ἡμῖν σπλαγχνισθεὶς
if anything thou canst,　help　us　having compassion

ἐφ᾽ ἡμᾶς. **23** ὁ δὲ Ἰησοῦς εἶπεν αὐτῷ· τὸ εἰ
on us.　- And Jesus　said to him: The "if

δύνῃ, πάντα δυνατὰ τῷ πιστεύοντι.
thou canst," all things　possible to the [one]　believing.

24 εὐθὺς κράξας ὁ πατὴρ τοῦ παιδίου
Immediately crying out the　father　of the　child

ἔλεγεν· πιστεύω· βοήθει μου τῇ ἀπιστίᾳ.
said:　I believe;　help thou of me the　unbelief.

25 ἰδὼν δὲ ὁ Ἰησοῦς ὅτι ἐπισυντρέχει
And ²seeing - ¹Jesus　that is(was) running together

ὄχλος, ἐπετίμησεν τῷ πνεύματι τῷ ἀκαθάρτῳ
a crowd,　rebuked　the　spirit　-　unclean

λέγων αὐτῷ· τὸ ἄλαλον καὶ κωφὸν
saying　to it:　-　Dumb　and　deaf

πνεῦμα, ἐγὼ ἐπιτάσσω σοι, ἔξελθε ἐξ
spirit,　I　command　thee,　come forth out of

αὐτοῦ καὶ μηκέτι εἰσέλθῃς εἰς αὐτόν.
him　and　no more mayest thou enter into　him.

26 καὶ κράξας καὶ πολλὰ σπαράξας
And　crying out　and　much convulsing [him]

ἐξῆλθεν· καὶ ἐγένετο ὡσεὶ νεκρός, ὥστε
it came out; and he became as　dead,　so as

τοὺς πολλοὺς λέγειν ὅτι ἀπέθανεν. **27** ὁ
-　many　to say[b]　that　he died.　　The
= many said

δὲ Ἰησοῦς κρατήσας τῆς χειρὸς αὐτοῦ
But Jesus taking hold of the　hand　of him

ἤγειρεν αὐτόν, καὶ ἀνέστη. **28** καὶ
raised　him,　and　he stood up.　　And

εἰσελθόντος αὐτοῦ εἰς οἶκον οἱ μαθηταὶ
entering　him[a] into a house the　disciples
= when he entered

αὐτοῦ κατ᾽ ἰδίαν ἐπηρώτων αὐτόν· ὅτι
of him　privately　questioned　him:　Why

ἡμεῖς οὐκ ἠδυνήθημεν ἐκβαλεῖν αὐτό;
we　were not able　to expel　it?

29 καὶ εἶπεν αὐτοῖς· τοῦτο τὸ γένος ἐν
And　he told　them:　This　-　kind　by

forth by nothing, but by prayer and fasting.

30 ¶ And they departed thence, and passed through Galilee; and he would not that any man should know it.

31 For he taught his disciples, and said unto them, The Son of man is delivered into the hands of men, and they shall kill him; and after that he is killed, he shall rise the third day.

32 But they understood not that saying, and were afraid to ask him.

33 ¶ And he came to Capernaum: and being in the house he asked them, What was it that ye disputed among yourselves by the way?

34 But they held their peace: for by the way they had disputed among themselves, who *should be* the greatest.

35 And he sat down, and called the twelve, and saith unto them, If any man desire to be first, *the same* shall be last of all, and servant of all.

36 And he took a child, and set him in the midst of them: and when he had taken him in his arms, he said unto them,

37 Whosoever shall receive one of such children in my name, receiveth me: and whosoever shall receive me, receiveth not me, but him that sent me.

38 ¶ And John answered

οὐδενὶ δύναται ἐξελθεῖν εἰ μὴ ἐν προσευχῇ.
nothing   can   to come out   except   by   prayer.

30 Κἀκεῖθεν ἐξελθόντες παρεπορεύοντο διὰ
And thence   going forth   they passed   through

τῆς Γαλιλαίας, καὶ οὐκ ἤθελεν ἵνα
-   Galilee,   and   he wished not   that

τις γνοῖ· **31** ἐδίδασκεν γὰρ τοὺς μαθητὰς
anyone should know;   for he was teaching   the disciples

αὐτοῦ, καὶ ἔλεγεν αὐτοῖς ὅτι ὁ υἱὸς τοῦ
of him,   and   told   them[,]   -   The Son   -

ἀνθρώπου παραδίδοται εἰς χεῖρας ἀνθρώπων,
of man   is betrayed   into [the] hands   of men,

καὶ ἀποκτενοῦσιν αὐτόν, καὶ ἀποκτανθεὶς
and   they will kill   him,   and   being killed

μετὰ τρεῖς ἡμέρας ἀναστήσεται. **32** οἱ
after   three   days   he will rise up.   they

δὲ ἠγνόουν τὸ ῥῆμα, καὶ ἐφοβοῦντο
But did not know   the   word,   and   feared

αὐτὸν ἐπερωτῆσαι.
him   to question.

33 Καὶ ἦλθον εἰς Καφαρναούμ. Καὶ
And   they came   to   Capernaum.   And

ἐν τῇ οἰκίᾳ γενόμενος ἐπηρώτα αὐτούς·
in   the   house   being   he questioned   them:

τί ἐν τῇ ὁδῷ διελογίζεσθε; **34** οἱ δὲ
What in   the   way   were ye debating?   And they

ἐσιώπων· πρὸς ἀλλήλους γὰρ διελέχθησαν
were silent;   ³with   ²one another   ¹for   they debated

ἐν τῇ ὁδῷ τίς μείζων. **35** καὶ καθίσας
in   the   way   who [was] greater.   And   sitting

ἐφώνησεν τοὺς δώδεκα καὶ λέγει αὐτοῖς·
he called   the   twelve   and   says   to them:

εἴ τις θέλει πρῶτος εἶναι, ἔσται πάντων
If anyone   wishes   first   to be,   he shall be   of all

ἔσχατος καὶ πάντων διάκονος. **36** καὶ
last   and   of all   servant.   And

λαβὼν παιδίον ἔστησεν αὐτὸ ἐν μέσῳ
taking   a child   he set   it(him)   in [the] midst

αὐτῶν, καὶ ἐναγκαλισάμενος αὐτὸ εἶπεν
of them,   and   folding in [his] arms   it   he said

αὐτοῖς· **37** ὃς ἂν ἓν τῶν τοιούτων παιδίων
to them: Whoever   one   -   of such   children

δέξηται ἐπὶ τῷ ὀνόματί μου, ἐμὲ δέχεται·
receives   on(in) the   name   of me,   me   receives;

καὶ ὃς ἂν ἐμὲ δέχηται, οὐχ ἐμὲ δέχεται
and   whoever   me   receives,   not   me   receives

ἀλλὰ τὸν ἀποστείλαντά με. **38** Ἔφη αὐτῷ
but   the [one]   having sent   me.   Said   to him

him, saying, Master, we saw one casting out devils in thy name, and he followeth not us: and we forbad him, because he followeth not us.

39 But Jesus said, Forbid him not: for there is no man which shall do a miracle in my name, that can lightly speak evil of me.

40 For he that is not against us is on our part.

41 For whosoever shall give you a cup of water to drink in my name, because ye belong to Christ, verily I say unto you, he shall not lose his reward.

42 And whosoever shall offend one of *these* little ones that believe in me, it is better for him that a millstone were hanged about his neck, and he were cast into the sea.

43 And if thy hand offend thee, cut it off: it is better for thee to enter into life maimed, than having two hands to go into hell, into the fire that never shall be quenched:

44 Where their worm dieth not, and the fire is not quenched.

45 And if thy foot offend thee, cut it off: it is better for thee to enter halt into life, than having two feet to be cast into

ὁ Ἰωάννης· διδάσκαλε, εἴδομέν τινα ἐν
\- John   Teacher,   we saw someone in

τῷ ὀνόματί σου ἐκβάλλοντα δαιμόνια, ὃς
the   name   of thee   expelling   demons,   who

οὐκ ἀκολουθεῖ ἡμῖν, καὶ ἐκωλύομεν αὐτόν,
does not follow   us,   and   we forbade   him,

ὅτι οὐκ ἠκολούθει ἡμῖν. 39 ὁ δὲ Ἰησοῦς
because he was not following   us.   - But   Jesus

εἶπεν· μὴ κωλύετε αὐτόν· οὐδεὶς γὰρ
said: Do not forbid   him: for no one

ἐστιν ὃς ποιήσει δύναμιν ἐπὶ τῷ ὀνόματί
there is who shall do   a mighty work on(in) the   name

μου καὶ δυνήσεται ταχὺ κακολογῆσαί με·
of me and   will be able   quickly   to speak evil of   me;

40 ὃς γὰρ οὐκ ἔστιν καθ᾽ ἡμῶν, ὑπὲρ
   for who   is not   against   us,   for

ἡμῶν ἐστιν. 41 Ὃς γὰρ ἂν ποτίσῃ
us   is.   For whoever   [1]gives [3]drink

ὑμᾶς ποτήριον ὕδατος ἐν ὀνόματι, ὅτι
[2]you   a cup   of water   in   [the] name, because

Χριστοῦ ἐστε, ἀμὴν λέγω ὑμῖν ὅτι
of Christ   ye are,   truly   I tell   you   that

οὐ μὴ ἀπολέσῃ τὸν μισθὸν αὐτοῦ. 42 Καὶ
by no means he will lose   the   reward   of him.   And

ὃς ἂν σκανδαλίσῃ ἕνα τῶν μικρῶν τούτων
whoever   offends   one   - [3]little [ones] [1]of these

τῶν πιστευόντων, καλόν ἐστιν αὐτῷ μᾶλλον
   [2]believing,   good   is it   for him   rather

εἰ περίκειται μύλος ὀνικὸς περὶ τὸν
if   be laid *round*   a [heavy] millstone   round   the

τράχηλον αὐτοῦ καὶ βέβληται εἰς τὴν
neck   of him   and   he be thrown   into   the

θάλασσαν. 43 Καὶ ἐὰν σκανδαλίσῃ σε ἡ
sea.   And   if   offends   thee the

χείρ σου, ἀπόκοψον αὐτήν· καλόν ἐστίν
hand of thee,   cut off   it;   good   is it

σε κυλλὸν εἰσελθεῖν εἰς τὴν ζωήν, ἢ τὰς
thee maimed   to enter   into   -   life,   than the

δύο χεῖρας ἔχοντα ἀπελθεῖν εἰς τὴν
two   hands   having   to go away   into   -

γέενναν, εἰς τὸ πῦρ τὸ ἄσβεστον.‡ 45 καὶ
gehenna,   into   the   fire   *the* unquenchable.   And

ἐὰν ὁ πούς σου σκανδαλίζῃ σε, ἀπόκοψον
if   the   foot   of thee   offends   thee,   cut off

αὐτόν· καλόν ἐστίν σε εἰσελθεῖν εἰς τὴν
it;   good   is it   thee   to enter   into   -

ζωὴν χωλόν, ἢ τοὺς δύο πόδας ἔχοντα
life   lame,   than the   two   feet   having

‡ Verse 44 omitted by Nestle; *cf.* R.V. marg., etc.

hell, into the fire that never shall be quenched:

46 Where their worm dieth not, and the fire is not quenched.

47 And if thine eye offend thee, pluck it out: it is better for thee to enter into the kingdom of God with one eye, than having two eyes to be cast into hell fire:

48 Where their worm dieth not, and the fire is not quenched.

49 For every one shall be salted with fire, and every sacrifice shall be salted with salt.

50 Salt *is* good: but if the salt have lost his saltness, wherewith will ye season it? Have salt in yourselves, and have peace one with another.

βληθῆναι εἰς τὴν γέενναν.‡ 47 καὶ ἐὰν ὁ
to be cast into   –   gehenna.   And if the

ὀφθαλμός σου σκανδαλίζῃ σε, ἔκβαλε αὐτόν·
eye   of thee   offends   thee, cast out it;

καλόν σέ ἐστιν μονόφθαλμον εἰσελθεῖν εἰς
good thee is it   one-eyed   to enter into

τὴν βασιλείαν τοῦ θεοῦ, ἢ δύο ὀφθαλμοὺς
the   kingdom   –   of God, than two   eyes

ἔχοντα βληθῆναι εἰς τὴν γέενναν, 48 ὅπου
having   to be cast into   –   gehenna,   where

ὁ σκώληξ αὐτῶν οὐ τελευτᾷ καὶ τὸ
the   worm   of them   dies not   and the

πῦρ οὐ σβέννυται. 49 Πᾶς γὰρ πυρὶ
fire   is not quenched.   For everyone with fire

ἁλισθήσεται. 50 καλὸν τὸ ἅλας· ἐὰν δὲ
shall be salted.   Good [is]   –   salt;   but if

τὸ ἅλας ἄναλον γένηται, ἐν τίνι αὐτὸ
–   salt   saltless   becomes,   by   what   it

ἀρτύσετε; ἔχετε ἐν ἑαυτοῖς ἅλα καὶ
will ye season?   Have   in   yourselves   salt   and

εἰρηνεύετε ἐν ἀλλήλοις.
be at peace   among   one another.

CHAPTER 10

A ND he arose from thence, and cometh into the coasts of Judæa by the farther side of Jordan: and the people resort unto him again; and, as he was wont, he taught them again.

2 ¶ And the Pharisees came to him, and asked him, Is it lawful for a man to put away *his* wife? tempting him.

3 And he answered and said unto them, What did Moses command you?

4 And they said, Moses suffered to write a bill of divorcement, and to put *her* away.

5 And Jesus answered and said unto them, For the hardness of your heart he wrote you this precept.

10 Καὶ ἐκεῖθεν ἀναστὰς ἔρχεται εἰς τὰ
And thence rising up he comes into the

ὅρια τῆς Ἰουδαίας καὶ πέραν τοῦ
territory – of Judæa   and   beyond the

Ἰορδάνου, καὶ συμπορεύονται πάλιν ὄχλοι
Jordan,   and   ²go with   ¹again ²crowds

πρὸς αὐτόν, καὶ ὡς εἰώθει πάλιν ἐδίδασκεν
⁴with ⁵him, and as he was wont again he taught

αὐτούς. 2 Καὶ προσελθόντες Φαρισαῖοι
them.   And ³approaching ¹Pharisees

ἐπηρώτων αὐτὸν εἰ ἔξεστιν ἀνδρὶ γυναῖκα
questioned him if it is(was) lawful for a man a wife

ἀπολῦσαι, πειράζοντες αὐτόν. 3 ὁ δὲ
to dismiss,   testing   him.   And he

ἀποκριθεὶς εἶπεν αὐτοῖς· 4 τί ὑμῖν ἐνετείλατο
answering said to them: What you ordered

Μωϋσῆς; οἱ δὲ εἶπαν· ἐπέτρεψεν Μωϋσῆς
Moses? And they said: permitted Moses

βιβλίον ἀποστασίου γράψαι καὶ ἀπολῦσαι.
a roll of divorce to write and to dismiss.

5 ὁ δὲ Ἰησοῦς εἶπεν αὐτοῖς· πρὸς τὴν
– And Jesus said to them: For the

σκληροκαρδίαν ὑμῶν ἔγραψεν ὑμῖν τὴν
hardheartedness of you he wrote to you –

‡ Verse 46 omitted by Nestle; *cf.* R.V. **marg.**, etc.

6 But from the beginning of the creation God made them male and female.

7 For this cause shall a man leave his father and mother, and cleave to his wife;

8 And they twain shall be one flesh: so then they are no more twain, but one flesh.

9 What therefore God hath joined together, let not man put asunder.

10 And in the house his disciples asked him again of the same *matter*.

11 And he saith unto them, Whosoever shall put away his wife, and marry another, committeth adultery against her.

12 And if a woman shall put away her husband, and be married to another, she committeth adultery.

13 ¶ And they brought young children to him, that he should touch them: and *his* disciples rebuked those that brought *them*.

14 But when Jesus saw *it*, he was much displeased, and said unto them, Suffer the little children to come unto me, and forbid them not: for of such is the kingdom of God.

15 Verily I say unto you, Whosoever shall not receive the kingdom of God as a little child, he shall not enter therein.

16 And he took them up in his arms, put *his* hands upon them, and blessed them.

ἐντολὴν ταύτην. 6 ἀπὸ δὲ ἀρχῆς κτίσεως
this commandment.   But from [the] beginning of creation

ἄρσεν καὶ θῆλυ ἐποίησεν αὐτούς· 7 ἕνεκεν
male and female he made them; for the sake of

τούτου καταλείψει ἄνθρωπος τὸν πατέρα
this shall leave a man the father

αὐτοῦ καὶ τὴν μητέρα, 8 καὶ ἔσονται
of him and the mother, and shall be

οἱ δύο εἰς σάρκα μίαν· ὥστε οὐκέτι
the two – flesh one; so as no longer

εἰσὶν δύο ἀλλὰ μία σάρξ. 9 ὃ οὖν ὁ
are they two but one flesh. What then –

θεὸς συνέζευξεν, ἄνθρωπος μὴ χωριζέτω.
God yoked together, ²man ¹not ¹let ⁴separate.

10 καὶ εἰς τὴν οἰκίαν πάλιν οἱ μαθηταὶ
And in the house again the disciples

περὶ τούτου ἐπηρώτων αὐτόν. 11 καὶ
about this questioned him. And

λέγει αὐτοῖς· ὃς ἂν ἀπολύσῃ τὴν γυναῖκα
he says to them: Whoever dismisses the wife

αὐτοῦ καὶ γαμήσῃ ἄλλην, μοιχᾶται ἐπ᾽
of him and marries another, commits adultery with

αὐτήν· 12 καὶ ἐὰν αὐτὴ ἀπολύσασα τὸν
her; and if she having dismissed the

ἄνδρα αὐτῆς γαμήσῃ ἄλλον, μοιχᾶται.
husband of her marries another, she commits adultery.

13 Καὶ προσέφερον αὐτῷ παιδία ἵνα
And they brought to him children that

αὐτῶν ἅψηται· οἱ δὲ μαθηταὶ ἐπετίμησαν
them he might touch; but the disciples rebuked

αὐτοῖς. 14 ἰδὼν δὲ ὁ Ἰησοῦς ἠγανάκτησεν
them. But ²seeing – ¹Jesus was angry

καὶ εἶπεν αὐτοῖς· ἄφετε τὰ παιδία
and said to them: Allow the children

ἔρχεσθαι πρός με, μὴ κωλύετε αὐτά·
to come to me, do not prevent them;

τῶν γὰρ τοιούτων ἐστὶν ἡ βασιλεία τοῦ
– for of such is the kingdom –

θεοῦ. 15 ἀμὴν λέγω ὑμῖν, ὃς ἂν
of God. Truly I tell you, whoever

μὴ δέξηται τὴν βασιλείαν τοῦ θεοῦ ὡς
receives not the kingdom – of God as

παιδίον, οὐ μὴ εἰσέλθῃ εἰς αὐτήν. 16 καὶ
a child, by no means may enter into it. And

ἐναγκαλισάμενος αὐτὰ κατευλόγει τιθεὶς τὰς
folding in [his] arms them he blesses putting the(his)

χεῖρας ἐπ᾽ αὐτά.
hands on them.

17 ¶ And when he was gone forth into the way, there came one running, and kneeled to him, and asked him, Good Master, what shall I do that I may inherit eternal life ?

18 And Jesus said unto him, Why callest thou me good ? *there is* none good but one, *that is*, God.

19 Thou knowest the commandments, Do not commit adultery, Do not kill, Do not steal, Do not bear false witness, Defraud not, Honour thy father and mother.

20 And he answered and said unto him, Master, all these have I observed from my youth.

21 Then Jesus beholding him loved him, and said unto him, One thing thou lackest: go thy way, sell whatsoever thou hast, and give to the poor, and thou shalt have treasure in heaven: and come, take up the cross, and follow me.

22 And he was sad at that saying, and went away grieved: for he had great possessions.

23 ¶ And Jesus looked round about, and saith unto his disciples, How hardly shall they that have riches enter into the kingdom of God!

24 And the disciples were astonished at his words. But Jesus answereth again, and saith unto them,

17 Καὶ ἐκπορευομένου αὐτοῦ εἰς ὁδὸν
And   going forth   him[a]   into [the] way
= as he went forth

προσδραμὼν εἷς καὶ γονυπετήσας αὐτὸν
running to   one   and   kneeling to   him

ἐπηρώτα αὐτόν· διδάσκαλε ἀγαθέ, τί ποιήσω
questioned   him: Teacher   good,   what   may I do

ἵνα ζωὴν αἰώνιον κληρονομήσω; 18 ὁ δὲ
that   life   eternal   I may inherit ?   – And

Ἰησοῦς εἶπεν αὐτῷ· τί με λέγεις ἀγαθόν;
Jesus   said   to him: Why   me callest thou   good ?

οὐδεὶς ἀγαθὸς εἰ μὴ εἷς ὁ θεός. 19 τὰς ἐντολὰς
no one   good   except one – God.   The commandments

οἶδας· μὴ φονεύσῃς, μὴ μοιχεύσῃς,
thou knowest: Do not kill,   Do not commit adultery,

μὴ κλέψῃς, μὴ ψευδομαρτυρήσῃς, μὴ
Do not steal,   Do not bear false witness,   Do

ἀποστερήσῃς, τίμα τὸν πατέρα σου καὶ
not defraud,   Honour   the   father   of thee   and

τὴν μητέρα. 20 ὁ δὲ ἔφη αὐτῷ· διδάσκαλε,
the   mother.   And he said   to him: Teacher,

ταῦτα πάντα ἐφυλαξάμην ἐκ νεότητός μου.
all these things   I observed   from   youth   of me.

21 ὁ δὲ Ἰησοῦς ἐμβλέψας αὐτῷ ἠγάπησεν
– But   Jesus   looking at   him   loved

αὐτὸν καὶ εἶπεν αὐτῷ· ἓν σε ὑστερεῖ·
him   and   said   to him: One thing thee   is wanting:

ὕπαγε, ὅσα ἔχεις πώλησον καὶ δὸς [τοῖς]
go,   what things thou hast   sell   and give to the

πτωχοῖς, καὶ ἕξεις θησαυρὸν ἐν οὐρανῷ,
poor,   and thou wilt have   treasure   in   heaven,

καὶ δεῦρο ἀκολούθει μοι. 22 ὁ δὲ στυγνάσας
and come   follow   me.   But he   being sad

ἐπὶ τῷ λόγῳ ἀπῆλθεν λυπούμενος, ἦν
at   the   word   went away   grieving,   [b]he was

γὰρ ἔχων κτήματα πολλά. 23 Καὶ
[1]for   having   possessions   many.   And

περιβλεψάμενος ὁ Ἰησοῦς λέγει τοῖς
looking round   –   Jesus   says   to the

μαθηταῖς αὐτοῦ· πῶς δυσκόλως οἱ τὰ
disciples   of him: How   hardly   the [ones] the

χρήματα ἔχοντες εἰς τὴν βασιλείαν τοῦ
riches   having   into   the   kingdom   –

θεοῦ εἰσελεύσονται. 24 οἱ δὲ μαθηταὶ
of God   shall enter.   And the   disciples

ἐθαμβοῦντο ἐπὶ τοῖς λόγοις αὐτοῦ. ὁ δὲ
were amazed   at   the   words   of him.   – And

Ἰησοῦς πάλιν ἀποκριθεὶς λέγει αὐτοῖς·
Jesus   again   answering   says   to them:

Children, how hard is it for them that trust in riches to enter into the kingdom of God!

25 It is easier for a camel to go through the eye of a needle, than for a rich man to enter into the kingdom of God.

26 And they were astonished out of measure, saying among themselves, Who then can be saved?

27 And Jesus looking upon them saith, With men *it is* impossible, but not with God: for with God all things are possible.

28 ¶ Then Peter began to say unto him, Lo, we have left all, and have followed thee.

29 And Jesus answered and said, Verily I say unto you, There is no man that hath left house, or brethren, or sisters, or father, or mother, or wife, or children, or lands, for my sake, and the gospel's,

30 But he shall receive an hundredfold now in this time, houses, and brethren, and sisters, and mothers, and children, and lands, with persecutions; and in the world to come eternal life.

31 But many *that are* first shall be last; and the last first.

32 ¶ And they were in the way going up to

τέκνα, πῶς δύσκολόν ἐστιν εἰς τὴν
Children, how hard it is into the

βασιλείαν τοῦ θεοῦ εἰσελθεῖν· 25 εὐκοπώτερόν
kingdom – of God to enter; easier

ἐστιν κάμηλον διὰ τῆς τρυμαλιᾶς τῆς
it is a camel through the eye –

ῥαφίδος διελθεῖν ἢ πλούσιον εἰς τὴν
of a needle to go *through* than a rich man into the

βασιλείαν τοῦ θεοῦ εἰσελθεῖν. 26 οἱ δὲ
kingdom – of God to enter. But they

περισσῶς ἐξεπλήσσοντο λέγοντες πρὸς
exceedingly were astonished saying to

ἑαυτούς· καὶ τίς δύναται σωθῆναι;
themselves: And who can to be saved?

27 ἐμβλέψας αὐτοῖς ὁ Ἰησοῦς λέγει· παρὰ
Looking at them – Jesus says: With

ἀνθρώποις ἀδύνατον, ἀλλ' οὐ παρὰ θεῷ·
men [it is] impossible, but not with God;

πάντα γὰρ δυνατὰ παρὰ τῷ θεῷ. 28 Ἤρξατο
for all things [are] possible with – God. Began

λέγειν ὁ Πέτρος αὐτῷ· ἰδοὺ ἡμεῖς ἀφήκαμεν
to say – Peter to him: Behold [,] we left

πάντα καὶ ἠκολουθήκαμέν σοι. 29 ἔφη ὁ
all things and have followed thee. Said –

Ἰησοῦς· ἀμὴν λέγω ὑμῖν, οὐδείς ἐστιν
Jesus: Truly I tell you, no one there is

ὃς ἀφῆκεν οἰκίαν ἢ ἀδελφοὺς ἢ ἀδελφὰς
who left house or brothers or sisters

ἢ μητέρα ἢ πατέρα ἢ τέκνα ἢ ἀγροὺς
or mother or father or children or fields

ἕνεκεν ἐμοῦ καὶ ἕνεκεν τοῦ εὐαγγελίου,
for the sake of me and for the sake of the gospel,

30 ἐὰν μὴ λάβῃ ἑκατονταπλασίονα νῦν
but he receives a hundredfold now

ἐν τῷ καιρῷ τούτῳ οἰκίας καὶ ἀδελφοὺς
in – time this houses and brothers

καὶ ἀδελφὰς καὶ μητέρας καὶ τέκνα καὶ
and sisters and mothers and children and

ἀγροὺς μετὰ διωγμῶν, καὶ ἐν τῷ αἰῶνι
fields with persecutions, and in the age

τῷ ἐρχομένῳ ζωὴν αἰώνιον. 31 πολλοὶ δὲ
– coming life eternal. And [1]many

ἔσονται πρῶτοι ἔσχατοι καὶ οἱ ἔσχατοι
[3]will be [2]first [4]last and the last

πρῶτοι.
first.

32 Ἦσαν δὲ ἐν τῇ ὁδῷ ἀναβαίνοντες
Now they were in the way going up

Jerusalem; and Jesus went before them: and they were amazed; and as they followed, they were afraid. And he took again the twelve, and began to tell them what things should happen unto him,

33 *Saying*, Behold, we go up to Jerusalem; and the Son of man shall be delivered unto the chief priests, and unto the scribes; and they shall condemn him to death, and shall deliver him to the Gentiles:

34 And they shall mock him, and shall scourge him, and shall spit upon him, and shall kill him: and the third day he shall rise again.

35 ¶ And James and John, the sons of Zebedee, come unto him, saying, Master, we would that thou shouldest do for us whatsoever we shall desire.

36 And he said unto them, What would ye that I should do for you?

37 They said unto him, Grant unto us that we may sit, one on thy right hand, and the other on thy left hand, in thy glory.

38 But Jesus said unto them, Ye know not what ye ask: can ye drink of the cup that I drink of? and be baptized with the

---

εἰς Ἱεροσόλυμα, καὶ ἦν προάγων αὐτοὺς
to   Jerusalem,   and   was   going before   them

ὁ Ἰησοῦς, καὶ ἐθαμβοῦντο, οἱ δὲ
–   Jesus,   and   they were astonished,   and the

ἀκολουθοῦντες ἐφοβοῦντο. καὶ παραλαβὼν
[ones] following   were afraid.   And   taking

πάλιν τοὺς δώδεκα ἤρξατο αὐτοῖς λέγειν
again   the   twelve   he began   them   to tell

τὰ μέλλοντα αὐτῷ συμβαίνειν, 33 ὅτι ἰδοὺ
the things   about   to him   to happen,   – Behold

ἀναβαίνομεν εἰς Ἱεροσόλυμα, καὶ ὁ υἱὸς
we are going up   to   Jerusalem,   and   the   Son

τοῦ ἀνθρώπου παραδοθήσεται τοῖς
–   of man   will be betrayed   to the

ἀρχιερεῦσιν καὶ τοῖς γραμματεῦσιν, καὶ
chief priests   and   to the   scribes,   and

κατακρινοῦσιν αὐτὸν θανάτῳ καὶ παραδώσουσιν
they will condemn   him   to death   and   will deliver

αὐτὸν τοῖς ἔθνεσιν 34 καὶ ἐμπαίξουσιν
him   to the   nations   and   they will mock

αὐτῷ καὶ ἐμπτύσουσιν αὐτῷ καὶ μαστι-
him   and   will spit at   him   and   will

γώσουσιν αὐτὸν καὶ ἀποκτενοῦσιν, καὶ
scourge   him   and   will kill,   and

μετὰ τρεῖς ἡμέρας ἀναστήσεται.
after   three   days   he will rise again.

35 Καὶ προσπορεύονται αὐτῷ Ἰάκωβος
And   approach   *to* him   James

καὶ Ἰωάννης οἱ [δύο] υἱοὶ Ζεβεδαίου
and   John   the   two   sons   of Zebedee

λέγοντες αὐτῷ· διδάσκαλε, θέλομεν ἵνα ὃ ἐὰν
saying   to him: Teacher,   we wish   that   whatever

αἰτήσωμέν σε ποιήσῃς ἡμῖν. 36 ὁ
we may ask   thee   thou mayest do   for us.   he

δὲ εἶπεν αὐτοῖς· τί θέλετέ με ποιήσω
And   said   to them: What   wish ye   me   I may do

ὑμῖν; 37 οἱ δὲ εἶπαν αὐτῷ· δὸς ἡμῖν
for you?   And they   said   to him: Give   us

ἵνα εἷς σου ἐκ δεξιῶν καὶ εἷς ἐξ
that   one   of thee   out of(on)   [the] right   and   one   on
       = on thy right

ἀριστερῶν καθίσωμεν ἐν τῇ δόξῃ σου.
[thy] left   we may sit   in   the   glory   of thee.

38 ὁ δὲ Ἰησοῦς εἶπεν αὐτοῖς· οὐκ οἴδατε
–   And   Jesus   said   to them: Ye know not

τί αἰτεῖσθε. δύνασθε πιεῖν τὸ ποτήριον
what   ye ask.   Can ye   *to* drink   the   cup

ὃ ἐγὼ πίνω, ἢ τὸ βάπτισμα ὃ ἐγὼ
which   I   drink,   or   the   baptism   which   I

baptism that I am baptized with ?

39 And they said unto him, We can. And Jesus said unto them, Ye shall indeed drink of the cup that I drink of; and with the baptism that I am baptized withal shall ye be baptized:

40 But to sit on my right hand and on my left hand is not mine to give; but *it shall be given to them* for whom it is prepared.

41 And when the ten heard *it*, they began to be much displeased with James and John.

42 But Jesus called them *to him*, and saith unto them, Ye know that they which are accounted to rule over the Gentiles exercise lordship over them; and their great ones exercise authority upon them.

43 But so shall it not be among you: but whosoever will be great among you, shall be your minister:

44 And whosoever of you will be the chiefest, shall be servant of all.

45 For even the Son of man came not to be ministered unto, but to minister, and to give his life a ransom for many.

46 ¶ And they came to Jericho: and as he went out of Jericho with his disciples and a great number of people, blind

βαπτίζομαι βαπτισθῆναι; **39** οἱ δὲ εἶπαν
am baptized *to* be baptized [with] ? And they said

αὐτῷ· δυνάμεθα. ὁ δὲ Ἰησοῦς εἶπεν
to him: We can. – And Jesus said

αὐτοῖς· τὸ ποτήριον ὃ ἐγὼ πίνω πίεσθε,
to them: The cup which I drink shall ye drink,

καὶ τὸ βάπτισμα ὃ ἐγὼ βαπτίζομαι
and the baptism which I am baptized [with]

βαπτισθήσεσθε· **40** τὸ δὲ καθίσαι ἐκ δεξιῶν
ye shall be baptized; – but to sit on right

μου ἢ ἐξ εὐωνύμων οὐκ ἔστιν ἐμὸν
of me or on [my] left is not mine

δοῦναι, ἀλλ᾽ οἷς ἡτοίμασται. **41** Καὶ
to give, but for whom it has been prepared. And

ἀκούσαντες οἱ δέκα ἤρξαντο ἀγανακτεῖν
[3]hearing [1]the [2]ten began to be incensed

περὶ Ἰακώβου καὶ Ἰωάννου. **42** καὶ
about James and John. And

προσκαλεσάμενος αὐτοὺς ὁ Ἰησοῦς λέγει
[1]calling [3]to [4][him] [2]them – Jesus says

αὐτοῖς· οἴδατε ὅτι οἱ δοκοῦντες ἄρχειν
to them: Ye know that the [ones] thinking to rule

τῶν ἐθνῶν κατακυριεύουσιν αὐτῶν καὶ
the nations lord it over them and

οἱ μεγάλοι αὐτῶν κατεξουσιάζουσιν αὐτῶν.
the great [ones] of them exercise authority over them.

43 οὐχ οὕτως δέ ἐστιν ἐν ὑμῖν· ἀλλ᾽
[2]not [3]so [1]But is it among you; but

ὃς ἂν θέλῃ μέγας γενέσθαι ἐν ὑμῖν,
whoever wishes great to become among you,

ἔσται ὑμῶν διάκονος, **44** καὶ ὃς ἂν
shall be of you servant, and whoever

θέλῃ ἐν ὑμῖν εἶναι πρῶτος, ἔσται πάντων
wishes among you to be first, shall be of all

δοῦλος· **45** καὶ γὰρ ὁ υἱὸς τοῦ ἀνθρώπου
slave; for even the Son – of man

οὐκ ἦλθεν διακονηθῆναι ἀλλὰ διακονῆσαι
did not come to be served but to serve

καὶ δοῦναι τὴν ψυχὴν αὐτοῦ λύτρον ἀντὶ
and to give the life of him a ransom instead of

πολλῶν.
many.

46 Καὶ ἔρχονται εἰς Ἰεριχώ. Καὶ
And they come to Jericho. And

ἐκπορευομένου αὐτοῦ ἀπὸ Ἰεριχὼ καὶ τῶν
going out him[a] from Jericho and the
= as he was going out

μαθητῶν αὐτοῦ καὶ ὄχλου ἱκανοῦ ὁ υἱὸς
disciples[a] of him and crowd a considerable[a] the son

Bartimæus, the son of Timæus, sat by the highway side begging.

47 And when he heard that it was Jesus of Nazareth, he began to cry out, and say, Jesus, *thou* son of David, have mercy on me.

48 And many charged him that he should hold his peace: but he cried the more a great deal, *Thou* son of David, have mercy on me.

49 And Jesus stood still, and commanded him to be called. And they call the blind man, saying unto him, Be of good comfort, rise; he calleth thee.

50 And he, casting away his garment, rose, and came to Jesus.

51 And Jesus answered and said unto him, What wilt thou that I should do unto thee? The blind man said unto him, Lord, that I might receive my sight.

52 And Jesus said unto him, Go thy way; thy faith hath made thee whole. And immediately he received his sight, and followed Jesus in the way.

Τιμαίου Βαρτιμαῖος, τυφλὸς προσαίτης,
of Timæus   Bartimæus,   a blind   beggar,

ἐκάθητο παρὰ τὴν ὁδόν. 47 καὶ ἀκούσας
sat   by   the   way.   And   hearing

ὅτι Ἰησοῦς ὁ Ναζαρηνός ἐστιν ἤρξατο
that   Jesus   the   Nazarene   it is(was)   he began

κράζειν καὶ λέγειν· υἱὲ Δαυὶδ Ἰησοῦ,
to cry out   and   to say: Son   of David   Jesus,

ἐλέησόν με. 48 καὶ ἐπετίμων αὐτῷ πολλοὶ
pity   me.   And   rebuked   him   many

ἵνα σιωπήσῃ· ὁ δὲ πολλῷ μᾶλλον ἔκραζεν·
that he should be quiet. But he   much   more   cried out:

υἱὲ Δαυίδ, ἐλέησόν με. 49 καὶ στὰς
Son   of David,   pity   me.   And   standing

ὁ Ἰησοῦς εἶπεν· φωνήσατε αὐτόν. καὶ
-   Jesus   said: Call   him.   And

φωνοῦσιν τὸν τυφλὸν λέγοντες αὐτῷ·
they call   the   blind man   saying   to him:

θάρσει, ἔγειρε, φωνεῖ σε. 50 ὁ δὲ
Be of good courage,   rise,   he calls   thee.   So he

ἀποβαλὼν τὸ ἱμάτιον αὐτοῦ ἀναπηδήσας ἦλθεν
throwing away   the   garment   of him   leaping up   came

πρὸς τὸν Ἰησοῦν. 51 καὶ ἀποκριθεὶς αὐτῷ ὁ
to   -   Jesus.   And   answering   him -

Ἰησοῦς εἶπεν· τί σοι θέλεις ποιήσω;
Jesus   said: What for thee wishest thou   I may do?

ὁ δὲ τυφλὸς εἶπεν αὐτῷ· ῥαββουνί, ἵνα
And the   blind man   said   to him: Rabboni,   that

ἀναβλέψω. 52 καὶ ὁ Ἰησοῦς εἶπεν αὐτῷ·
I may see again.   And   -   Jesus   said   to him:

ὕπαγε, ἡ πίστις σου σέσωκέν σε. καὶ
Go,   the   faith   of thee   has healed   thee.   And

εὐθὺς ἀνέβλεψεν, καὶ ἠκολούθει αὐτῷ ἐν
immediately he saw again,   and   followed   him   in

τῇ ὁδῷ.
the   way.

CHAPTER 11

AND when they came nigh to Jerusalem, unto Bethphage and Bethany, at the mount of Olives, he sendeth forth two of his disciples,

2 And saith unto them, Go your way into the village over against you:

11 Καὶ ὅτε ἐγγίζουσιν εἰς Ἰεροσόλυμα
And   when   they draw near   to   Jerusalem

εἰς Βηθφαγὴ καὶ Βηθανίαν πρὸς τὸ
to   Bethphage   and   Bethany   at   the

ὄρος τῶν ἐλαιῶν, ἀποστέλλει δύο τῶν
mount   of the   olives,   he sends   two   of the

μαθητῶν αὐτοῦ 2 καὶ λέγει αὐτοῖς· ὑπάγετε
disciples   of him   and   tells   them: Go ye

εἰς τὴν κώμην τὴν κατέναντι ὑμῶν, καὶ
into   the   village   -   opposite   you,   and

and as soon as ye be entered into it, ye shall find a colt tied, whereon never man sat; loose him, and bring *him*.

3 And if any man say unto you, Why do ye this ? say ye that the Lord hath need of him; and straightway he will ;end him hither.

4 And they went their way, and found the colt tied by the door without in a place where two ways met; and they loose him.

5 And certain of them that stood there said unto them, What do ye, loosing the colt ?

6 And they said unto them even as Jesus had commanded: and they let them go.

7 And they brought the colt to Jesus, and cast their garments on him; and he sat upon him.

8 And many spread their garments in the way: and others cut down branches off the trees, and strawed *them* in the way.

9 And they that went before, and they that followed, cried, saying, Hosanna; Blessed *is* he that cometh in the name of the Lord:

10 Blessed *be* the kingdom of our father David, that cometh in the name of the Lord: Hosanna in the highest.

11 And Jesus entered into Jerusalem, and into the temple: and when he had looked round about

---

εὐθὺς   εἰσπορευόμενοι   εἰς   αὐτὴν   εὑρήσετε
immediately   entering   into   it   ye will find

πῶλον   δεδεμένον   ἐφ᾽   ὃν   οὐδεὶς   οὔπω
a colt   *having been* tied   on   which   [1]no one   [2]not yet

ἀνθρώπων   ἐκάθισεν·   λύσατε   αὐτὸν   καὶ
[2]of men   [4]sat;   loosen   it   and

φέρετε.   3 καὶ   ἐάν   τις   ὑμῖν   εἴπῃ·   τί
bring.   And   if   anyone   to you   says: Why

ποιεῖτε   τοῦτο;   εἴπατε·   ὁ   κύριος   αὐτοῦ
do ye   this ?   say: The   Lord   of it

χρείαν   ἔχει,   καὶ   εὐθὺς   αὐτὸν   ἀποστέλλει
need   has,   and   immediately   it   he sends

πάλιν   ὧδε.   4 καὶ   ἀπῆλθον   καὶ   εὗρον
again   here.   And   they went   and   found

πῶλον   δεδεμένον   πρὸς   θύραν   ἔξω   ἐπὶ
a colt   *having been* tied   at   a door   outside   on

τοῦ   ἀμφόδου,   καὶ   λύουσιν   αὐτόν.   5 καὶ
the   open street,   and   they loosen   it.   And

τινες   τῶν   ἐκεῖ   ἑστηκότων   ἔλεγον   αὐτοῖς·
some   of the [ones] there   standing   said   to them:

τί   ποιεῖτε   λύοντες   τὸν   πῶλον;   6 οἱ   δὲ
What   do ye   loosening   the   colt ?   And they

εἶπαν   αὐτοῖς   καθὼς   εἶπεν   ὁ   Ἰησοῦς·
said   to them   as   said   –   Jesus;

καὶ   ἀφῆκαν   αὐτούς.   7 καὶ   φέρουσιν   τὸν
and   they let go   them.   And   they bring   the

πῶλον   πρὸς   τὸν   Ἰησοῦν,   καὶ   ἐπιβάλλουσιν
colt   to   –   Jesus,   and   they throw on

αὐτῷ   τὰ   ἱμάτια   αὐτῶν,   καὶ   ἐκάθισεν
it   the   garments   of them,   and   he sat

ἐπ᾽ αὐτόν.   8 καὶ   πολλοὶ   τὰ   ἱμάτια   αὐτῶν
on   it.   And   many   the   garments   of them

ἔστρωσαν   εἰς   τὴν   ὁδόν,   ἄλλοι   δὲ   στιβάδας,
strewed   in   the   way,   and others wisps of twigs,

κόψαντες   ἐκ   τῶν   ἀγρῶν.   9 καὶ   οἱ
cutting   out of   the   fields.   And the [ones]

προάγοντες   καὶ   οἱ   ἀκολουθοῦντες   ἔκραζον·
going before   and the [ones]   following   cried out:

ὡσαννά·   εὐλογημένος   ὁ   ἐρχόμενος   ἐν
Hosanna;   blessed   the [one]   coming   in

ὀνόματι   κυρίου·   10 εὐλογημένη   ἡ   ἐρχομένη
[the] name   of [the] Lord;   blessed   the   coming

βασιλεία   τοῦ   πατρὸς   ἡμῶν   Δαυίδ·   ὡσαννὰ
kingdom   of the   father   of us   David;   Hosanna

ἐν   τοῖς   ὑψίστοις.   11 Καὶ   εἰσῆλθεν   εἰς
in   the   highest [places].   And   he entered   into

Ἱεροσόλυμα   εἰς   τὸ   ἱερόν·   καὶ   περιβλεψάμενος
Jerusalem   into   the   temple;   and   looking round at

upon all things, and now the eventide was come, he went out unto Bethany with the twelve.

12 ¶ And on the morrow, when they were come from Bethany, he was hungry:

13 And seeing a fig tree afar off having leaves, he came, if haply he might find any thing thereon: and when he came to it, he found nothing but leaves; for the time of figs was not yet.

14 And Jesus answered and said unto it, No man eat fruit of thee hereafter for ever. And his disciples heard it.

15 ¶ And they come to Jerusalem: and Jesus went into the temple, and began to cast out them that sold and bought in the temple, and overthrew the tables of the moneychangers, and the seats of them that sold doves;

16 And would not suffer that any man should carry any vessel through the temple.

17 And he taught, saying unto them, Is it not written, My house shall be called of all nations the house of prayer? but ye have made it a den of thieves.

18 And the scribes and chief priests heard it, and sought how they might destroy him: for they

πάντα, ὀψὲ ἤδη οὔσης τῆς ὥρας, ἐξῆλθεν
all things, ⁶late ⁴now ³being ¹the ²hour,ᵃ he went forth

εἰς Βηθανίαν μετὰ τῶν δώδεκα.
to Bethany with the twelve.

12 Καὶ τῇ ἐπαύριον ἐξελθόντων αὐτῶν
And on the morrow going forth themᵃ
= as they went forth

ἀπὸ Βηθανίας ἐπείνασεν. 13 καὶ ἰδὼν
from Bethany he hungered. And seeing

συκῆν ἀπὸ μακρόθεν ἔχουσαν φύλλα ἦλθεν
a fig-tree from afar having leaves he came

εἰ ἄρα τι εὑρήσει ἐν αὐτῇ, καὶ ἐλθὼν
if perhaps something he will find in it, and coming

ἐπ᾽ αὐτὴν οὐδὲν εὗρεν εἰ μὴ φύλλα·
upon it nothing he found except leaves;

ὁ γὰρ καιρὸς οὐκ ἦν σύκων. 14 καὶ
for the time was not of figs. And

ἀποκριθεὶς εἶπεν αὐτῇ· μηκέτι εἰς τὸν
answering he said to it: No more to the

αἰῶνα ἐκ σοῦ μηδεὶς καρπὸν φάγοι.
age of thee no one fruit may eat.
= May no one eat fruit of thee for ever.

καὶ ἤκουον οἱ μαθηταὶ αὐτοῦ. 15 Καὶ
And ⁴heard ¹the ²disciples ³of him. And

ἔρχονται εἰς Ἱεροσόλυμα. Καὶ εἰσελθὼν
they come to Jerusalem. And entering

εἰς τὸ ἱερὸν ἤρξατο ἐκβάλλειν τοὺς
into the temple he began to cast out the [ones]

πωλοῦντας καὶ τοὺς ἀγοράζοντας ἐν τῷ
selling and the [ones] buying in the

ἱερῷ, καὶ τὰς τραπέζας τῶν κολλυβιστῶν
temple, and the tables of the moneychangers

καὶ τὰς καθέδρας τῶν πωλούντων τὰς
and the seats of the [ones] selling the

περιστερὰς κατέστρεψεν, 16 καὶ οὐκ ἤφιεν
doves he overturned, and did not permit

ἵνα τις διενέγκῃ σκεῦος διὰ τοῦ
that anyone should carry through a vessel through the

ἱεροῦ, 17 καὶ ἐδίδασκεν καὶ ἔλεγεν αὐτοῖς· οὐ
temple, and taught and said to them: Not

γέγραπται ὅτι ὁ οἶκός μου οἶκος προσευχῆς
has it been written that the house of me a house of prayer

κληθήσεται πᾶσιν τοῖς ἔθνεσιν; ὑμεῖς δὲ
shall be called for all the nations? but ye

πεποιήκατε αὐτὸν σπήλαιον λῃστῶν. 18 καὶ
have made it a den of robbers. And

ἤκουσαν οἱ ἀρχιερεῖς καὶ οἱ γραμματεῖς,
⁶heard ¹the ²chief priests ³and ⁴the ⁵scribes,

καὶ ἐζήτουν πῶς αὐτὸν ἀπολέσωσιν·
and they sought how him they might destroy;

feared him, because all the
people was astonished at
his doctrine.

19 And when even was
come, he went out of the
city.

20 ¶ And in the morning,
as they passed by, they saw
the fig tree dried up from
the roots.

21 And Peter calling to
remembrance saith unto
him, Master, behold, the
fig tree which thou cursedst
is withered away.

22 And Jesus answering
saith unto them, Have faith
in God.

23 For verily I say unto
you, That whosoever shall
say unto this mountain,
Be thou removed, and be
thou cast into the sea; and
shall not doubt in his heart,
but shall believe that those
things which he saith shall
come to pass; he shall have
whatsoever he saith.

24 Therefore I say unto
you, What things soever
ye desire, when ye pray,
believe that ye receive
them, and ye shall have
them.

25 And when ye stand
praying, forgive, if ye have
ought against any: that
your Father also which
is in heaven may forgive
you your trespasses.

26 But if ye do not
forgive, neither will your
Father which is in heaven
forgive your trespasses.

27 ¶ And they come
again to Jerusalem: and
as he was walking in the
temple, there come to him
the chief priests, and the
scribes, and the elders,

ἐφοβοῦντο γὰρ αὐτόν, πᾶς γὰρ ὁ ὄχλος
for they feared   him,   for all   the   crowd

ἐξεπλήσσετο ἐπὶ τῇ διδαχῇ αὐτοῦ. 19 Καὶ
was astounded   at   the   teaching   of him.   And

ὅταν ὀψὲ ἐγένετο, ἐξεπορεύοντο ἔξω τῆς
when late   it became,   they went forth   outside   the

πόλεως. 20 Καὶ παραπορευόμενοι πρωὶ
city.   And   passing along   early

εἶδον τὴν συκῆν ἐξηραμμένην ἐκ ῥιζῶν.
they saw   the   fig-tree   *having been* withered   from [the] roots.

21 καὶ ἀναμνησθεὶς ὁ Πέτρος λέγει αὐτῷ·
And   ²remembering   ¹Peter   says   to him:

ῥαββί, ἴδε ἡ συκῆ ἣν κατηράσω
Rabbi,   behold[,]   the   fig-tree   which   thou cursedst

ἐξήρανται. 22 καὶ ἀποκριθεὶς ὁ Ἰησοῦς λέγει
has been withered.   And   answering   –   Jesus   says

αὐτοῖς· ἔχετε πίστιν θεοῦ. 23 ἀμὴν λέγω ὑμῖν
to them: Have [the] faith   of God.   Truly   I tell   you

ὅτι ὃς ἂν εἴπῃ τῷ ὄρει τούτῳ· ἄρθητι
that   whoever   says   –   mountain to this: Be thou taken

καὶ βλήθητι εἰς τὴν θάλασσαν, καὶ μὴ
and   be thou cast   into   the   sea,   and   not

διακριθῇ ἐν τῇ καρδίᾳ αὐτοῦ ἀλλὰ πιστεύῃ
doubts   in   the   heart   of him   but   believes

ὅτι ὃ λαλεῖ γίνεται, ἔσται αὐτῷ. 24 διὰ
that what he says happens,   it will be   to him.ᶜ   There-
= he will have it.

τοῦτο λέγω ὑμῖν, πάντα ὅσα προσεύχεσθε
fore   I tell   you,   all things   which   ye pray

καὶ αἰτεῖσθε, πιστεύετε ὅτι ἐλάβετε, καὶ
and   ask,   believe   that   ye received,   and

ἔσται ὑμῖν. 25 καὶ ὅταν στήκετε
it will be   to you.ᵉ   And   when   ye stand
= ye will have it.

προσευχόμενοι, ἀφίετε εἴ τι ἔχετε κατά
praying,   forgive   if anything ye have against

τινος, ἵνα καὶ ὁ πατὴρ ὑμῶν ὁ ἐν τοῖς
anyone,   that   also the   Father   of you –   in   the

οὐρανοῖς ἀφῇ ὑμῖν τὰ παραπτώματα ὑμῶν.‡
heavens   may forgive   you the   trespasses   of you.

27 Καὶ ἔρχονται πάλιν εἰς Ἱεροσόλυμα.
And   they come   again   to   Jerusalem.

καὶ ἐν τῷ ἱερῷ περιπατοῦντος αὐτοῦ
And   in   the   temple   walking   himᵃ
=as he walked

ἔρχονται πρὸς αὐτὸν οἱ ἀρχιερεῖς καὶ οἱ
come   to   him   the   chief priests   and the

γραμματεῖς καὶ οἱ πρεσβύτεροι, 28 καὶ
scribes   and   the   elders,   and

‡ Verse 26 omitted by Nestle; *cf.* R.V. marg., etc.

28 And say unto him, By what authority doest thou these things ? and who gave thee this authority to do these things ?

29 And Jesus answered and said unto them, I will also ask of you one question, and answer me, and I will tell you by what authority I do these things.

30 The baptism of John, was it from heaven, or of men ? answer me.

31 And they reasoned with themselves, saying, If we shall say, From heaven; he will say, Why then did ye not believe him ?

32 But if we shall say, Of men; they feared the people: for all men counted John, that he was a prophet indeed.

33 And they answered and said unto Jesus, We cannot tell. And Jesus answering saith unto them, Neither do I tell you by what authority I do these things.

CHAPTER 12

AND he began to speak unto them by parables. A certain man planted a vineyard, and set an hedge about it, and digged a place for the winefat, and built a tower, and let it out to husbandmen, and went into a far country.

2 And at the season he sent to the husbandmen a servant, that he might receive from the husbandmen of the fruit of the vineyard.

ἔλεγον αὐτῷ· ἐν ποίᾳ ἐξουσίᾳ ταῦτα
said   to him: By   what authority these things
ποιεῖς; ἢ τίς σοι ἔδωκεν τὴν ἐξουσίαν
doest thou? or who thee gave   -   authority
ταύτην ἵνα ταῦτα ποιῇς; 29 ὁ δὲ Ἰησοῦς
this that these things thou mayest do? - And Jesus
εἶπεν αὐτοῖς· ἐπερωτήσω ὑμᾶς ἕνα λόγον,
said to them: I will question you one word,
καὶ ἀποκρίθητέ μοι, καὶ ἐρῶ ὑμῖν ἐν
and answer ye me, and I will tell you by
ποίᾳ ἐξουσίᾳ ταῦτα ποιῶ. 30 τὸ βάπτισμα
what authority these things I do. The baptism
τὸ Ἰωάννου ἐξ οὐρανοῦ ἦν ἢ ἐξ ἀνθρώπων;
- of John of heaven was it or of men ?
ἀποκρίθητέ μοι. 31 καὶ διελογίζοντο πρὸς
answer ye me. And they debated with
ἑαυτοὺς λέγοντες· ἐὰν εἴπωμεν· ἐξ οὐρανοῦ,
themselves saying: If we say: Of heaven,
ἐρεῖ διὰ τί οὖν οὐκ ἐπιστεύσατε αὐτῷ;
he will say: Why then did ye not believe him ?
32 ἀλλὰ εἴπωμεν· ἐξ ἀνθρώπων;—ἐφοβοῦντο
But may we say: Of men ? — they feared
τὸν ὄχλον· ἅπαντες γὰρ εἶχον τὸν Ἰωάννην
the crowd; for all men held - John
ὄντως ὅτι προφήτης ἦν. 33 καὶ
³really ¹that ²a prophet ³he was. And
ἀποκριθέντες τῷ Ἰησοῦ λέγουσιν· οὐκ
answering - Jesus they say: not
οἴδαμεν. καὶ ὁ Ἰησοῦς λέγει αὐτοῖς·
We know. And - Jesus says to them:
οὐδὲ ἐγὼ λέγω ὑμῖν ἐν ποίᾳ ἐξουσίᾳ
Neither I tell you by what authority
ταῦτα ποιῶ. 12 Καὶ ἤρξατο αὐτοῖς ἐν
these things I do. And he began to them in
παραβολαῖς λαλεῖν. ἀμπελῶνα ἄνθρωπος
parables to speak. ³a vineyard ¹A man
ἐφύτευσεν, καὶ περιέθηκεν φραγμὸν καὶ ὤρυξεν
²planted, and put round [it] a hedge and dug
ὑπολήνιον καὶ ᾠκοδόμησεν πύργον, καὶ
a winepress and built a tower, and
ἐξέδοτο αὐτὸν γεωργοῖς, καὶ ἀπεδήμησεν.
let out it to husbandmen, and went away.
2 καὶ ἀπέστειλεν πρὸς τοὺς γεωργοὺς τῷ
And he sent to the husbandmen at the
καιρῷ δοῦλον, ἵνα παρὰ τῶν γεωργῶν
time a slave, that from the husbandmen
λάβῃ ἀπὸ τῶν καρπῶν τοῦ ἀμπελῶνος·
he might from(of) the fruits of the vineyard;
receive

3 And they caught *him*, and beat him, and sent *him* away empty.

4 And again he sent unto them another servant; and at him they cast stones, and wounded *him* in the head, and sent *him* away shamefully handled.

5 And again he sent another; and him they killed, and many others; beating some, and killing some.

6 Having yet therefore one son, his wellbeloved, he sent him also last unto them, saying, They will reverence my son.

7 But those husbandmen said among themselves, This is the heir; come, let us kill him, and the inheritance shall be our's.

8 And they took him, and killed *him*, and cast *him* out of the vineyard.

9 What shall therefore the lord of the vineyard do? he will come and destroy the husbandmen, and will give the vineyard unto others.

10 And have ye not read this scripture; The stone which the builders rejected is become the head of the corner:

11 This was the Lord's doing, and it is marvellous in our eyes?

12 And they sought to lay hold on him, but feared the people: for they knew that he had spoken the parable against them: and

3 καὶ λαβόντες αὐτὸν ἔδειραν καὶ ἀπέστειλαν
And taking him they beat and sent away

κενόν. 4 καὶ πάλιν ἀπέστειλεν πρὸς αὐτοὺς
empty. And again he sent to them

ἄλλον δοῦλον· κἀκεῖνον ἐκεφαλαίωσαν καὶ
another slave; and that one they wounded in the head and

ἠτίμασαν. 5 καὶ ἄλλον ἀπέστειλεν· κἀκεῖνον
insulted. And another he sent; and that one

ἀπέκτειναν, καὶ πολλοὺς ἄλλους, οὓς μὲν
they killed, and many others, ²some

δέροντες, οὓς δὲ ἀποκτέννοντες. 6 ἔτι ἕνα
¹beating, ²others ¹killing. Still one

εἶχεν, υἱὸν ἀγαπητόν· ἀπέστειλεν αὐτὸν
he had, a son beloved; he sent him

ἔσχατον πρὸς αὐτοὺς λέγων ὅτι ἐντραπήσονται
last to them saying[,] – They will reverence

τὸν υἱόν μου. 7 ἐκεῖνοι δὲ οἱ γεωργοὶ
the son of me. But those – husbandmen

πρὸς ἑαυτοὺς εἶπαν ὅτι οὗτός ἐστιν ὁ
to themselves said[,] – This is the

κληρονόμος· δεῦτε ἀποκτείνωμεν αὐτόν, καὶ
heir; come[,] let us kill him, and

ἡμῶν ἔσται ἡ κληρονομία. 8 καὶ λαβόντες
of us will be the inheritance. And taking

ἀπέκτειναν αὐτόν, καὶ ἐξέβαλον αὐτὸν
they killed him, and cast out him

ἔξω τοῦ ἀμπελῶνος. 9 τί ποιήσει ὁ
outside the vineyard. What will do the

κύριος τοῦ ἀμπελῶνος; ἐλεύσεται καὶ
lord of the vineyard? he will come and

ἀπολέσει τοὺς γεωργούς, καὶ δώσει τὸν
will destroy the husbandmen, and will give the

ἀμπελῶνα ἄλλοις. 10 οὐδὲ τὴν γραφὴν
vineyard to others. ²not – ⁴scripture

ταύτην ἀνέγνωτε· λίθον ὃν ἀπεδοκίμασαν
³this ¹Read ye: A stone which ³rejected

οἱ οἰκοδομοῦντες, οὗτος ἐγενήθη εἰς κεφαλὴν
¹the [ones] ²building, this became for head

γωνίας· 11 παρὰ κυρίου ἐγένετο αὕτη,
of corner; from [the] Lord was this,

καὶ ἔστιν θαυμαστὴ ἐν ὀφθαλμοῖς ἡμῶν;
and it is marvellous in eyes of us?

12 Καὶ ἐζήτουν αὐτὸν κρατῆσαι, καὶ
And they sought him to seize, and

ἐφοβήθησαν τὸν ὄχλον· ἔγνωσαν γὰρ
feared the crowd; for they knew

ὅτι πρὸς αὐτοὺς τὴν παραβολὴν
that to them the parable

they left him, and went
their way.

13 ¶ And they send unto
him certain of the Pharisees
and of the Herodians, to
catch him in *his* words.

14 And when they were
come, they say unto him,
Master, we know that thou
art true, and carest for no
man: for thou regardest
not the person of men, but
teachest the way of God in
truth: Is it lawful to give
tribute to Cæsar, or not?

15 Shall we give, or
shall we not give? But
he, knowing their hypo-
crisy, said unto them, Why
tempt ye me? bring me a
penny, that I may see *it*.

16 And they brought *it*.
And he saith unto them,
Whose *is* this image and
superscription? And they
said unto him, Cæsar's.

17 And Jesus answering
said unto them, Render to
Cæsar the things that are
Cæsar's, and to God the
things that are God's.
And they marvelled at him.

18 ¶ Then come unto
him the Sadducees, which
say there is no resurrection;
and they asked him, saying,

19 Master, Moses wrote
unto us, If a man's brother
die, and leave *his* wife
behind him, and leave no
children, that his brother

εἶπεν. καὶ ἀφέντες αὐτὸν ἀπῆλθον.
he told. And leaving him they went away.

13 Καὶ ἀποστέλλουσιν πρὸς αὐτόν τινας τῶν
And they send to him some of the

Φαρισαίων καὶ τῶν Ἡρῳδιανῶν ἵνα αὐτὸν
Pharisees and of the Herodians that him

ἀγρεύσωσιν λόγῳ. 14 καὶ ἐλθόντες
they might catch in a word. And coming

λέγουσιν αὐτῷ· διδάσκαλε, οἴδαμεν ὅτι
they say to him: Teacher, we know that

ἀληθὴς εἶ καὶ οὐ μέλει σοι περὶ
true thou art and it matters not to thee about

οὐδενός· οὐ γὰρ βλέπεις εἰς πρόσωπον
no(any)one; for thou lookest not at [the] face

ἀνθρώπων, ἀλλ’ ἐπ’ ἀληθείας τὴν ὁδὸν
of men, but on(in) truth the way

τοῦ θεοῦ διδάσκεις· ἔξεστιν δοῦναι κῆνσον
- of God teachest; is it lawful to give tribute

Καίσαρι ἢ οὔ; δῶμεν ἢ μὴ δῶμεν;
to Cæsar or no? may we give or may we not give?

15 ὁ δὲ εἰδὼς αὐτῶν τὴν ὑπόκρισιν εἶπεν
But he knowing of them the hypocrisy said

αὐτοῖς· τί με πειράζετε; φέρετέ μοι
to them: Why me tempt ye? bring me

δηνάριον ἵνα ἴδω. 16 οἱ δὲ ἤνεγκαν. καὶ
a denarius that I may see. And they brought. And

λέγει αὐτοῖς· τίνος ἡ εἰκὼν αὕτη καὶ ἡ
he says to them: Of whom - image this and the

ἐπιγραφή; οἱ δὲ εἶπαν αὐτῷ· Καίσαρος.
superscription? And they tell him: Of Cæsar.

17 ὁ δὲ Ἰησοῦς εἶπεν αὐτοῖς· τὰ Καίσαρος
- So Jesus said to them: The things of Cæsar

ἀπόδοτε Καίσαρι καὶ τὰ τοῦ θεοῦ τῷ
render to Cæsar and the things - of God -

θεῷ. καὶ ἐξεθαύμαζον ἐπ’ αὐτῷ.
to God. And they marvelled at him.

18 Καὶ ἔρχονται Σαδδουκαῖοι πρὸς αὐτόν,
And come Sadducees to him,

οἵτινες λέγουσιν ἀνάστασιν μὴ εἶναι, καὶ
who say resurrection not to be, and
= that there is no resurrection,

ἐπηρώτων αὐτὸν λέγοντες· 19 διδάσκαλε,
questioned him saying: Teacher,

Μωϋσῆς ἔγραψεν ἡμῖν ὅτι ἐάν τινος
Moses wrote to us that if of anyone

ἀδελφὸς ἀποθάνῃ καὶ καταλίπῃ γυναῖκα
a brother should die and leave behind a wife

καὶ μὴ ἀφῇ τέκνον, ἵνα λάβῃ ὁ ἀδελφὸς
and leave not a child, - ⁴may take ¹the ³brother

should take his wife, and raise up seed unto his brother.

20 Now there were seven brethren: and the first took a wife, and dying left no seed.

21 And the second took her, and died, neither left he any seed: and the third likewise.

22 And the seven had her, and left no seed: last of all the woman died also.

23 In the resurrection therefore, when they shall rise, whose wife shall she be of them ? for the seven had her to wife.

24 And Jesus answering said unto them, Do ye not therefore err, because ye know not the scriptures, neither the power of God ?

25 For when they shall rise from the dead, they neither marry, nor are given in marriage; but are as the angels which are in heaven.

26 And as touching the dead, that they rise: have ye not read in the book of Moses, how in the bush God spake unto him, saying, I *am* the God of Abraham, and the God of Isaac, and the God of Jacob ?

27 He is not the God of the dead, but the God of the living: ye therefore do greatly err.

28 ¶ And one of the scribes came, and having heard them reasoning together, and perceiving that

αὐτοῦ τὴν γυναῖκα καὶ ἐξαναστήσῃ σπέρμα
³of him　the　wife　and　may raise up　seed

τῷ ἀδελφῷ αὐτοῦ. 20 ἑπτὰ ἀδελφοὶ ἦσαν·
to the brother　of him.　　Seven　brothers there were;

καὶ ὁ πρῶτος ἔλαβεν γυναῖκα, καὶ
and　the　first　took　a wife,　and

ἀποθνῆσκων οὐκ ἀφῆκεν σπέρμα· 21 καὶ
dying　left not　seed;　and

ὁ δεύτερος ἔλαβεν αὐτήν, καὶ ἀπέθανεν μὴ
the second　took　her,　and　died　not

καταλιπὼν σπέρμα· καὶ ὁ τρίτος ὡσαύτως·
leaving behind　seed;　and the　third　similarly;

22 καὶ οἱ ἑπτὰ οὐκ ἀφῆκαν σπέρμα.
and　the seven　left not　seed.

ἔσχατον πάντων καὶ ἡ γυνὴ ἀπέθανεν.
Last　of all　also　the　wife　died.

23 ἐν τῇ ἀναστάσει, ὅταν ἀναστῶσιν,
In　the　resurrection,　when　they rise again,

τίνος αὐτῶν ἔσται γυνή; οἱ γὰρ ἑπτὰ
of which　of them　will she be　wife ?　for　the　seven

ἔσχον αὐτὴν γυναῖκα. 24 ἔφη αὐτοῖς ὁ
had　her　[as] wife.　Said　to them　–

Ἰησοῦς· οὐ διὰ τοῦτο πλανᾶσθε μὴ
Jesus:　³not　⁴therefore　¹Do ²ye ⁵err　not

εἰδότες τὰς γραφὰς μηδὲ τὴν δύναμιν
knowing　the　scriptures　nor　the　power

τοῦ θεοῦ; 25 ὅταν γὰρ ἐκ νεκρῶν
–　of God ?　for when　out of　[the] dead

ἀναστῶσιν, οὔτε γαμοῦσιν οὔτε γαμίζονται,
they rise again,　they neither marry　nor　are given in marriage,

ἀλλ' εἰσὶν ὡς ἄγγελοι ἐν τοῖς οὐρανοῖς.
but　are　as　angels　in　the　heavens.

26 περὶ δὲ τῶν νεκρῶν ὅτι ἐγείρονται,
But concerning　the　dead　that　they are raised,

οὐκ ἀνέγνωτε ἐν τῇ βίβλῳ Μωϋσέως ἐπὶ
did ye not read　in　the　roll　of Moses　at

τοῦ βάτου πῶς εἶπεν αὐτῷ ὁ θεὸς λέγων·
the　bush　how　said　to him　–　God　saying:

ἐγὼ ὁ θεὸς Ἀβραὰμ καὶ θεὸς Ἰσαὰκ
I [am] the　God　of Abraham　and　God　of Isaac

καὶ θεὸς Ἰακώβ; 27 οὐκ ἔστιν θεὸς
and　God　of Jacob ?　he is not　God

νεκρῶν ἀλλὰ ζώντων. πολὺ πλανᾶσθε.
of dead [persons]　but　of living [ones].　Much　ye err.

28 Καὶ προσελθὼν εἷς τῶν γραμματέων,
And　⁴approaching　¹one ²of the　³scribes,

ἀκούσας αὐτῶν συζητούντων, εἰδὼς ὅτι
hearing　them　debating,　knowing　that

he had answered them well, asked him, Which is the first commandment of all ?
29 And Jesus answered him, The first of all the commandments *is*, Hear, O Israel; The Lord our God is one Lord:
30 And thou shalt love the Lord thy God with all thy heart, and with all thy soul, and with all thy mind, and with all thy strength: this *is* the first commandment.
31 And the second *is* like, *namely* this, Thou shalt love thy neighbour as thyself. There is none other commandment greater than these.
32 And the scribe said unto him, Well, Master, thou hast said the truth: for there is one God; and there is none other but he:
33 And to love him with all the heart, and with all the understanding, and with all the soul, and with all the strength, and to love *his* neighbour as himself, is more than all whole burnt offerings and sacrifices.
34 And when Jesus saw that he answered discreetly, he said unto him, Thou art not far from the kingdom of God. And no man after that durst ask him *any question*.
35 ¶ And Jesus answered

καλῶς ἀπεκρίθη αὐτοῖς, ἐπηρώτησεν αὐτόν·
well he answered them, questioned him:

ποία ἐστὶν ἐντολὴ πρώτη πάντων;
What is [the] commandment first of all ?

29 ἀπεκρίθη ὁ Ἰησοῦς ὅτι πρώτη ἐστίν·
Answered – Jesus[,] – [The] first is:

ἄκουε, Ἰσραήλ, κύριος ὁ θεὸς ἡμῶν κύριος
Hear, Israel, Lord the God of us Lord
= The Lord our God is one Lord,

εἷς ἐστιν, 30 καὶ ἀγαπήσεις κύριον τὸν
one is, and thou shalt love Lord the

θεόν σου ἐξ ὅλης τῆς καρδίας σου καὶ
God of thee from(with) all the heart of thee and

ἐξ ὅλης τῆς ψυχῆς σου καὶ ἐξ ὅλης
with all the soul of thee and with all

τῆς διανοίας σου καὶ ἐξ ὅλης τῆς ἰσχύος
the mind of thee and with all the strength

σου. 31 δευτέρα αὕτη· ἀγαπήσεις τὸν
of thee. [The] second [is] this: Thou shalt love the

πλησίον σου ὡς σεαυτόν. μείζων τούτων
neighbour of thee as thyself. Greater [than] these

ἄλλη ἐντολὴ οὐκ ἔστιν. 32 καὶ εἶπεν
other commandment there is not. And said

αὐτῷ ὁ γραμματεύς· καλῶς, διδάσκαλε, ἐπ᾽
to him the scribe: Well, teacher, on(in)

ἀληθείας εἶπες ὅτι εἷς ἐστιν καὶ οὐκ
truth thou sayest that one there is and not

ἔστιν ἄλλος πλὴν αὐτοῦ· 33 καὶ τὸ
there is another besides him; and –

ἀγαπᾶν αὐτὸν ἐξ ὅλης τῆς καρδίας καὶ ἐξ
to love him with all the heart and with

ὅλης τῆς συνέσεως καὶ ἐξ ὅλης τῆς
all the understanding and with all the

ἰσχύος, καὶ τὸ ἀγαπᾶν τὸν πλησίον ὡς
strength, and – to love the(one's) neighbour as

ἑαυτὸν περισσότερόν ἐστιν πάντων τῶν
himself more is [than] all the

ὁλοκαυτωμάτων καὶ θυσιῶν. 34 καὶ ὁ
burnt offerings and sacrifices. And –

Ἰησοῦς, ἰδὼν αὐτὸν ὅτι νουνεχῶς ἀπεκρίθη,
Jesus, seeing him that sensibly he answered,

εἶπεν αὐτῷ· οὐ μακρὰν εἶ ἀπὸ τῆς
said to him: Not far thou art from the

βασιλείας τοῦ θεοῦ. καὶ οὐδεὶς οὐκέτι
kingdom – of God. And no one no(any) more

ἐτόλμα αὐτὸν ἐπερωτῆσαι.
dared him to question.

35 Καὶ ἀποκριθεὶς ὁ Ἰησοῦς ἔλεγεν
And answering – Jesus said

and said, while he taught in the temple, How say the scribes that Christ is the son of David ?

36 For David himself said by the Holy Ghost, The LORD said to my Lord, Sit thou on my right hand, till I make thine enemies thy footstool.

37 David therefore himself calleth him Lord; and whence is he *then* his son ? And the common people heard him gladly.

38 ¶ And he said unto them in his doctrine, Beware of the scribes, which love to go in long clothing, and *love* salutations in the marketplaces,

39 And the chief seats in the synagogues, and the uppermost rooms at feasts:

40 Which devour widows' houses, and for a pretence make long prayers: these shall receive greater damnation.

41 ¶ And Jesus sat over against the treasury, and beheld how the people cast money into the treasury: and many that were rich cast in much.

42 And there came a certain poor widow, and she threw in two mites, which make a farthing.

43 And he called *unto him* his disciples, and saith

διδάσκων ἐν τῷ ἱερῷ· πῶς λέγουσιν οἱ
teaching in the temple: How say the

γραμματεῖς ὅτι ὁ χριστὸς υἱός Δαυὶδ
scribes that the Christ son of David

ἐστιν; 36 αὐτὸς Δαυὶδ εἶπεν ἐν τῷ πνεύματι
is? himself David said by the Spirit

τῷ ἁγίῳ· εἶπεν κύριος τῷ κυρίῳ μου·
- Holy: said [the] LORD to the Lord of me:

κάθου ἐκ δεξιῶν μου ἕως ἂν θῶ τοὺς
Sit at [the] right [hand] of me until I put the

ἐχθρούς σου ὑποκάτω τῶν ποδῶν σου.
enemies of thee under the feet of thee.

37 αὐτὸς Δαυὶδ λέγει αὐτὸν κύριον, καὶ
himself David says(calls) him Lord, and

πόθεν αὐτοῦ ἐστιν υἱός;
whence of him is he son ?

Καὶ ὁ πολὺς ὄχλος ἤκουεν αὐτοῦ
And the much crowd heard him

ἡδέως. 38 Καὶ ἐν τῇ διδαχῇ αὐτοῦ
gladly. And in the teaching of him

ἔλεγεν· βλέπετε ἀπὸ τῶν γραμματέων
he said: Beware from(of) the scribes

τῶν θελόντων ἐν στολαῖς περιπατεῖν καὶ
the [ones] wishing in robes to walk about and

ἀσπασμοὺς ἐν ταῖς ἀγοραῖς 39 καὶ
greetings in the marketplaces and

πρωτοκαθεδρίας ἐν ταῖς συναγωγαῖς καὶ
chief seats in the synagogues and

πρωτοκλισίας ἐν τοῖς δείπνοις· 40 οἱ
chief places in the dinners; the [ones]

κατέσθοντες τὰς οἰκίας τῶν χηρῶν καὶ
devouring the houses of the widows and

προφάσει μακρὰ προσευχόμενοι, οὗτοι
under pretence long praying, these

λήμψονται περισσότερον κρίμα. 41 Καὶ
will receive greater condemnation. And

καθίσας κατέναντι τοῦ γαζοφυλακείου ἐθεώρει
sitting opposite the treasury he beheld

πῶς ὁ ὄχλος βάλλει χαλκὸν εἰς τὸ
how the crowd puts copper money into the

γαζοφυλακεῖον· καὶ πολλοὶ πλούσιοι ἔβαλλον
treasury; and many rich men put

πολλά· 42 καὶ ἐλθοῦσα μία χήρα πτωχὴ
much; and coming one widow poor

ἔβαλεν λεπτὰ δύο, ὅ ἐστιν κοδράντης.
put lepta two, which is a quadrans.

43 καὶ προσκαλεσάμενος τοὺς μαθητὰς αὐτοῦ
And calling to [him] the disciples of him

unto them, Verily I say
unto you, That this poor
widow hath cast more in,
than all they which have
cast into the treasury;

44 For all *they* did cast
in of their abundance; but
she of her want did cast in
all that she had, *even* all
her living.

εἶπεν   αὐτοῖς·   ἀμὴν   λέγω   ὑμῖν   ὅτι
he said   to them: Truly   I tell   you   that
ἡ   χήρα   αὕτη   ἡ   πτωχὴ   πλεῖον   πάντων
-   ³widow   ¹this   -   ²poor   ⁵more [than]   ⁶all
ἔβαλεν   τῶν   βαλλόντων   εἰς   τὸ   γαζοφυλακεῖον·
⁴put   the [ones] putting   into the   treasury;
44 πάντες   γὰρ   ἐκ   τοῦ   περισσεύοντος   αὐτοῖς
for all   out of the   abounding   to them°
= their abundance
ἔβαλον,   αὕτη   δὲ   ἐκ   τῆς   ὑστερήσεως   αὐτῆς
put,   but this woman   out of the   want   of her
πάντα   ὅσα   εἶχεν   ἔβαλεν,   ὅλον   τὸν   βίον
²all things   ³how many   ⁴she had   ¹put,   all   the   living
αὐτῆς.
of her.

CHAPTER 13

A ND as he went out of
the temple, one of
his disciples saith unto him,
Master, see what manner
of stones and what build-
ings *are here!*

2 And Jesus answering
said unto him, Seest thou
these great buildings? there
shall not be left one stone
upon another, that shall
not be thrown down.

3 And as he sat upon
the mount of Olives over
against the temple, Peter
and James and John and
Andrew asked him pri-
vately,

4 Tell us, when shall
these things be? and what
shall be the sign when all
these things shall be fulfilled?

5 And Jesus answering
them began to say, Take
heed lest any *man* deceive
you:

6 For many shall come
in my name, saying, I am

13 Καὶ   ἐκπορευομένου   αὐτοῦ   ἐκ   τοῦ
And   going forth   himª   out of   the
= as he went forth
ἱεροῦ   λέγει   αὐτῷ   εἷς   τῶν   μαθητῶν   αὐτοῦ·
temple   says   to him   one   of the   disciples   of him:
διδάσκαλε,   ἴδε   ποταποὶ   λίθοι   καὶ   ποταπαὶ
Teacher,   behold[,]   what great   stones   and   what great
οἰκοδομαί.   2 καὶ   ὁ   Ἰησοῦς   εἶπεν   αὐτῷ·
buildings.   And   -   Jesus   said   to him:
βλέπεις   ταύτας   τὰς   μεγάλας   οἰκοδομάς;
Seest thou   these   -   great   buildings?
οὐ   μὴ   ἀφεθῇ   λίθος   ἐπὶ   λίθον   ὃς   οὐ
by no means   be left   stone   on   stone   which by no
= there shall by no means be left stone on stone which will not
μὴ   καταλυθῇ.   3 Καὶ   καθημένου   αὐτοῦ
means be overthrown.   And   sitting   himª
be overthrown.   = as he sat
εἰς   τὸ   ὄρος   τῶν   ἐλαιῶν   κατέναντι   τοῦ
in(on)   the   mount   of the   olives   opposite   the
ἱεροῦ,   ἐπηρώτα   αὐτὸν   κατ᾽   ἰδίαν   Πέτρος
temple,   questioned   him   privately   Peter
καὶ   Ἰάκωβος   καὶ   Ἰωάννης   καὶ   Ἀνδρέας·
and   James   and   John   and   Andrew:
4 εἰπὸν   ἡμῖν,   πότε   ταῦτα   ἔσται,   καὶ   τί
Tell   us,   when   these things will be,   and   what
τὸ   σημεῖον   ὅταν   μέλλῃ   ταῦτα   συντελεῖσθαι
the   sign   when   ³are about   ²these things   ⁴to be completed
πάντα;   5 ὁ   δὲ   Ἰησοῦς   ἤρξατο   λέγειν
¹all?   -   And   Jesus   began   to say
αὐτοῖς·   βλέπετε   μή   τις   ὑμᾶς   πλανήσῃ.
to them: See   lest   anyone   you   lead astray.
6 πολλοὶ   ἐλεύσονται   ἐπὶ   τῷ   ὀνόματί   μου
Many   will come   on(in)   the   name   of me

Christ; and shall deceive many.

7 And when ye shall hear of wars and rumours of wars, be ye not troubled: for *such things* must needs be; but the end *shall* not *be* yet.

8 For nation shall rise against nation, and kingdom against kingdom: and there shall be earthquakes in divers places, and there shall be famines and troubles: these *are* the beginnings of sorrows.

9 ¶ But take heed to yourselves: for they shall deliver you up to councils; and in the synagogues ye shall be beaten: and ye shall be brought before rulers and kings for my sake, for a testimony against them.

10 And the gospel must first be published among all nations.

11 But when they shall lead *you*, and deliver you up, take no thought beforehand what ye shall speak, neither do ye premeditate: but whatsoever shall be given you in that hour, that speak ye: for it is not ye that speak, but the Holy Ghost.

12 Now the brother shall betray the brother to death, and the father the son; and children shall rise up against *their* parents, and shall cause them to be put to death.

13 And ye shall be hated of all *men* for my name's sake: but he that shall endure unto the end, the same shall be saved.

14 ¶ But when ye shall see the abomination of

λέγοντες ὅτι ἐγώ εἰμι, καὶ πολλοὺς
saying[,]   -   I   am,   and   many

πλανήσουσιν. **7** ὅταν δὲ ἀκούσητε πολέμους
they will lead astray.   But when   ye hear   [of] wars

καὶ ἀκοὰς πολέμων, μὴ θροεῖσθε· δεῖ
and   rumours   of wars,   be not disturbed;   it behoves

γενέσθαι, ἀλλ' οὔπω τὸ τέλος. **8** ἐγερθήσεται
to happen,   but   not yet   the   end.   will be raised

γὰρ ἔθνος ἐπ' ἔθνος καὶ βασιλεία ἐπὶ
For   nation   against   nation   and   kingdom   against

βασιλείαν. ἔσονται σεισμοὶ κατὰ τόπους,
kingdom.   There will be earthquakes   in places,

ἔσονται λιμοί· ἀρχὴ ὠδίνων ταῦτα.
there will be famines;   beginning of birth-pangs   these things [are].

9 Βλέπετε δὲ ὑμεῖς ἑαυτούς· παραδώσουσιν
But see;   ye   yourselves;   they will deliver

ὑμᾶς εἰς συνέδρια καὶ εἰς συναγωγὰς
you   to   councils   and   in   synagogues

δαρήσεσθε καὶ ἐπὶ ἡγεμόνων καὶ βασιλέων
ye will be beaten   and   before   rulers   and   kings

σταθήσεσθε ἕνεκεν ἐμοῦ, εἰς μαρτύριον
ye will stand   for the sake of me,   for   a testimony

αὐτοῖς. **10** καὶ εἰς πάντα τὰ ἔθνη πρῶτον
to them.   And   to   all   the nations   first

δεῖ κηρυχθῆναι τὸ εὐαγγέλιον. **11** καὶ ὅταν
it behoves to be proclaimed the   gospel.   And when
= the gospel must be proclaimed.

ἄγωσιν ὑμᾶς παραδιδόντες, μὴ προμεριμνᾶτε
they lead   ycu   delivering,   be not anxious beforehand

τί λαλήσητε, ἀλλ' ὃ ἐὰν δοθῇ ὑμῖν ἐν
what ye speak,   but   whatever is given   you   in

ἐκείνῃ τῇ ὥρᾳ, τοῦτο λαλεῖτε· οὐ γάρ
that   hour.   this   speak ye;   for not

ἐστε ὑμεῖς οἱ λαλοῦντες ἀλλὰ τὸ πνεῦμα
are   ye   the [ones] speaking   but   the   Spirit

τὸ ἅγιον. **12** καὶ παραδώσει ἀδελφὸς
-   Holy.   And   ²will deliver   ¹a brother

ἀδελφὸν εἰς θάνατον καὶ πατὴρ τέκνον, καὶ
a brother   to   death   and   a father   a child,   and

ἐπαναστήσονται τέκνα ἐπὶ γονεῖς καὶ
²will rise *against*   ¹children   against   parents   and

θανατώσουσιν αὐτούς· **13** καὶ ἔσεσθε
will put to death   them;   and   ye will be

μισούμενοι ὑπὸ πάντων διὰ τὸ ὄνομά
being hated   by   all men   on account of the   name

μου· ὁ δὲ ὑπομείνας εἰς τέλος, οὗτος
of me;   but the [one]   enduring   to [the] end,   this

σωθήσεται. **14** Ὅταν δὲ ἴδητε τὸ βδέλυγμα
will be saved.   But when   ye see   the   abomination

desolation, spoken of by Daniel the prophet, standing where it ought not, (let him that readeth understand,) then let them that be in Judæa flee to the mountains:

15 And let him that is on the housetop not go down into the house, neither enter *therein*, to take any thing out of his house:

16 And let him that is in the field not turn back again for to take up his garment.

17 But woe to them that are with child, and to them that give suck in those days!

18 And pray ye that your flight be not in the winter.

19 For *in* those days shall be affliction, such as was not from the beginning of the creation which God created unto this time, neither shall be.

20 And except that the Lord had shortened those days, no flesh should be saved: but for the elect's sake, whom he hath chosen, he hath shortened the days.

21 And then if any man shall say to you, Lo, here *is* Christ; or, lo, *he is* there; believe *him* not:

22 For false Christs and false prophets shall rise, and shall shew signs and wonders, to seduce, if *it were* possible, even the elect.

23 But take ye heed: behold, I have foretold you all things.

24 ¶ But in those days,

τῆς ἐρημώσεως ἑστηκότα ὅπου οὐ δεῖ, ὁ
\- of desolation　stand　where it behoves not, the

ἀναγινώσκων νοείτω, τότε οἱ ἐν τῇ
[one] reading　let him understand,　then　the [ones]　in　-

Ἰουδαίᾳ φευγέτωσαν εἰς τὰ ὄρη, 15 ὁ ἐπὶ
Judæa　let them flee　to　the mountains, the [one]　on

τοῦ δώματος μὴ καταβάτω μηδὲ εἰσελθάτω
the　roof　let him not come down　nor　let him enter

τι ἆραι ἐκ τῆς οἰκίας αὐτοῦ, 16 καὶ ὁ
anything to take out of the　house　of him,　and the [one]

εἰς τὸν ἀγρὸν μὴ ἐπιστρεψάτω εἰς τὰ
in　the　field　let him not return　to the things

ὀπίσω ἆραι τὸ ἱμάτιον αὐτοῦ. 17 οὐαὶ
behind　to take　the　garment　of him.　woe

δὲ ταῖς ἐν γαστρὶ ἐχούσαις καὶ ταῖς
But to the women　pregnant†　and　to the

θηλαζούσαις ἐν ἐκείναις ταῖς ἡμέραις.
[ones] giving suck　in　those　days.

18 προσεύχεσθε δὲ ἵνα μὴ γένηται χειμῶνος·
But pray ye　that it may not happen of(in) winter;

19 ἔσονται γὰρ αἱ ἡμέραι ἐκεῖναι θλῖψις, οἵα
for ³will be　-　³days　¹those ⁴affliction, of such a kind

οὐ γέγονεν τοιαύτη ἀπ᾿ ἀρχῆς κτίσεως
²has not happened ¹as　from [the] beginning of [the] creation

ἣν ἔκτισεν ὁ θεὸς ἕως τοῦ νῦν καὶ οὐ
which created　- God　until　-　now　and by

μὴ γένηται. 20 καὶ εἰ μὴ ἐκολόβωσεν
no means may be.　And　unless　³shortened

κύριος τὰς ἡμέρας, οὐκ ἂν ἐσώθη πᾶσα
¹[the] Lord the　days,　would not be saved　all
　　　　　　　　　= no flesh would be saved;

σάρξ· ἀλλὰ διὰ τοὺς ἐκλεκτοὺς οὓς
flesh;　but on account of the　chosen　whom

ἐξελέξατο ἐκολόβωσεν τὰς ἡμέρας. 21 καὶ
he chose　he shortened　the　days.　And

τότε ἐάν τις ὑμῖν εἴπῃ· ἴδε ὧδε ὁ
then　if anyone ²you ¹tells: Behold here [is] the

χριστός, ἴδε ἐκεῖ, μὴ πιστεύετε· 22 ἐγερθή-
Christ, behold there,　believe ye not;　⁵will be

σονται δὲ ψευδόχριστοι καὶ ψευδοπροφῆται
raised　¹and ²false Christs ³and　⁴false prophets

καὶ ποιήσουσιν σημεῖα καὶ τέρατα πρὸς
and　they will do　signs　and　wonders　for

τὸ ἀποπλανᾶν, εἰ δυνατόν, τοὺς ἐκλεκτούς.
\- to lead astray, if　possible,　the　chosen.

23 ὑμεῖς δὲ βλέπετε· προείρηκα ὑμῖν πάντα.
But ²ye　¹see;　¹I have told ⁴before ²you ³all things.

24 Ἀλλὰ ἐν ἐκείναις ταῖς ἡμέραις μετὰ
But　in　those　-　days　after

after that tribulation, the sun shall be darkened, and the moon shall not give her light,

25 And the stars of heaven shall fall, and the powers that are in heaven shall be shaken.

26 And then shall they see the Son of man coming in the clouds with great power and glory.

27 And then shall he send his angels, and shall gather together his elect from the four winds, from the uttermost part of the earth to the uttermost part of heaven.

28 Now learn a parable of the fig tree; When her branch is yet tender, and putteth forth leaves, ye know that summer is near:

29 So ye in like manner, when ye shall see these things come to pass, know that it is nigh, *even* at the doors.

30 Verily I say unto you, that this generation shall not pass, till all these things be done.

31 Heaven and earth shall pass away: but my words shall not pass away.

32 ¶ But of that day and *that* hour knoweth no man, no, not the angels which are in heaven, neither the Son, but the Father.

33 Take ye heed, watch

τὴν θλῖψιν ἐκείνην ὁ ἥλιος σκοτισθήσεται,
the affliction that the sun will be darkened,

καὶ ἡ σελήνη οὐ δώσει τὸ φέγγος αὐτῆς,
and the moon will not give the light of her,

25 καὶ οἱ ἀστέρες ἔσονται ἐκ τοῦ οὐρανοῦ
and the stars [1]will be [2]out of - [4]heaven

πίπτοντες, καὶ αἱ δυνάμεις αἱ ἐν τοῖς
[3]falling, and the powers in the

οὐρανοῖς σαλευθήσονται. 26 καὶ τότε ὄψονται
heavens will be shaken. And then they will see

τὸν υἱὸν τοῦ ἀνθρώπου ἐρχόμενον ἐν
the Son - of man coming in

νεφέλαις μετὰ δυνάμεως πολλῆς καὶ δόξης.
clouds with power much and glory.

27 καὶ τότε ἀποστελεῖ τοὺς ἀγγέλους καὶ
And then he will send the angels and

ἐπισυνάξει τοὺς ἐκλεκτοὺς [αὐτοῦ] ἐκ τῶν
they will assemble the chosen of him out of the

τεσσάρων ἀνέμων ἀπ' ἄκρου γῆς ἕως
four winds from [the] extremity of earth to

ἄκρου οὐρανοῦ. 28 Ἀπὸ δὲ τῆς συκῆς
[the] extremity of heaven. Now from the fig-tree

μάθετε τὴν παραβολήν· ὅταν ἤδη ὁ
learn the parable; when now the

κλάδος αὐτῆς ἀπαλὸς γένηται καὶ ἐκφύῃ
branch of it tender becomes and puts forth

τὰ φύλλα, γινώσκετε ὅτι ἐγγὺς τὸ θέρος
the leaves, ye know that near the summer

ἐστίν· 29 οὕτως καὶ ὑμεῖς, ὅταν ἴδητε
is; so also ye, when ye see

ταῦτα γινόμενα, γινώσκετε ὅτι ἐγγύς ἐστιν
these things happening, know that near he/it is

ἐπὶ θύραις. 30 ἀμὴν λέγω ὑμῖν ὅτι οὐ
at [the] doors. Truly I tell you that by no

μὴ παρέλθῃ ἡ γενεὰ αὕτη μέχρις οὗ
means passes - generation this until

ταῦτα πάντα γένηται. 31 ὁ οὐρανὸς καὶ
these things all happen. The heaven and

ἡ γῆ παρελεύσονται, οἱ δὲ λόγοι μου
the earth will pass away, but the words of me

οὐ παρελεύσονται. 32 Περὶ δὲ τῆς ἡμέρας
will not pass away. But concerning - day

ἐκείνης ἢ τῆς ὥρας οὐδεὶς οἶδεν, οὐδὲ
that or - hour no one knows, not

οἱ ἄγγελοι ἐν οὐρανῷ οὐδὲ ὁ υἱός, εἰ
the angels in heaven neither the Son, ex-

μὴ ὁ πατήρ. 33 Βλέπετε, ἀγρυπνεῖτε·
cept the Father. Look, be wakeful;

and pray: for ye know not
when the time is.

34 *For the Son of man is*
as a man taking a far
journey, who left his house,
and gave authority to his
servants, and to every man
his work, and commanded
the porter to watch.

35 Watch ye therefore:
for ye know not when the
master of the house com-
eth, at even, or at midnight,
or at the cockcrowing, or
in the morning:

36 Lest coming suddenly
he find you sleeping.

37 And what I say unto
you I say unto all, Watch.

οὐκ οἴδατε γὰρ πότε ὁ καιρός ἐστιν.
for ye know not   when   the   time   is.

34 ὡς ἄνθρωπος ἀπόδημος ἀφεὶς τὴν οἰκίαν
As   a man   away from home leaving the house
αὐτοῦ καὶ δοὺς τοῖς δούλοις αὐτοῦ τὴν
of him and giving to the slaves   of him   –
ἐξουσίαν, ἑκάστῳ τὸ ἔργον αὐτοῦ, καὶ
authority, to each the   work   of him, and
τῷ θυρωρῷ ἐνετείλατο ἵνα γρηγορῇ.
the doorkeeper he commanded that he should watch.

35 γρηγορεῖτε οὖν· οὐκ οἴδατε γὰρ πότε
Watch ye therefore;   for ye know not   when
ὁ κύριος τῆς οἰκίας ἔρχεται, ἢ ὀψὲ ἢ
the lord of the house comes, either late or
μεσονύκτιον ἢ ἀλεκτοροφωνίας ἢ πρωΐ·
at midnight or at cock-crowing or early;

36 μὴ ἐλθὼν ἐξαίφνης εὕρῃ ὑμᾶς καθεύδ-
lest coming suddenly he find you   sleep-
οντας. 37 ὃ δὲ ὑμῖν λέγω, πᾶσιν λέγω,
ing.   And what to you I say,   to all I say,
γρηγορεῖτε.
watch ye.

CHAPTER 14

AFTER two days was
the feast of the pass-
over, and of unleavened
bread: and the chief priests
and the scribes sought how
they might take him by
craft, and put *him* to death.

2 But they said, Not on
the feast *day*, lest there be
an uproar of the people.

3 ¶ And being in Bethany
in the house of Simon the
leper, as he sat at meat,
there came a woman
having an alabaster box of
ointment of spikenard very
precious; and she brake
the box, and poured *it* on
his head.

14 Ἦν δὲ τὸ πάσχα καὶ τὰ ἄζυμα
Now it was the Passover and [the feast of] the
unleavened bread†
μετὰ δύο ἡμέρας. καὶ ἐζήτουν οἱ ἀρχιερεῖς
after two   days.   And sought the chief priests
καὶ οἱ γραμματεῖς πῶς αὐτὸν ἐν δόλῳ
and the scribes   how ²him ³by ⁴guile
κρατήσαντες ἀποκτείνωσιν. 2 ἔλεγον γάρ·
¹seizing   they might kill.   For they said :
μὴ ἐν τῇ ἑορτῇ, μήποτε ἔσται θόρυβος
Not at the feast,   lest there will be a disturbance
τοῦ λαοῦ.
of the people.

3 Καὶ ὄντος αὐτοῦ ἐν Βηθανίᾳ ἐν τῇ
And   being himᵃ in Bethany   in the
      = when he was
οἰκίᾳ Σίμωνος τοῦ λεπροῦ, κατακειμένου
house of Simon the leper,   reclining
                               = as he reclined
αὐτοῦ ἦλθεν γυνὴ ἔχουσα ἀλάβαστρον
himᵃ   came a woman having an alabaster phial
μύρου νάρδου πιστικῆς πολυτελοῦς·
of ointment ³nard   ¹of pure   ²costly;
συντρίψασα τὴν ἀλάβαστρον κατέχεεν αὐτοῦ
breaking   the alabaster phial she poured over of him

4 And there were some that had indignation within themselves, and said, Why was this waste of the ointment made?

5 For it might have been sold for more than three hundred pence, and have been given to the poor. And they murmured against her.

6 And Jesus said, Let her alone; why trouble ye her? she hath wrought a good work on me.

7 For ye have the poor with you always, and whensoever ye will ye may do them good: but me ye have not always.

8 She hath done what she could: she is come aforehand to anoint my body to the burying.

9 Verily I say unto you, Wheresoever this gospel shall be preached throughout the whole world, *this* also that she hath done shall be spoken of for a memorial of her.

10 ¶ And Judas Iscariot, one of the twelve, went unto the chief priests, to betray him unto them.

11 And when they heard *it*, they were glad, and promised to give him money. And he sought how he might conveniently betray him.

12 ¶ And the first day of unleavened bread, when they killed the passover, his disciples said unto him,

τῆς κεφαλῆς. 4 ἦσαν δέ τινες ἀγανακτοῦντες
the   head.   Now there were some   being angry

πρὸς ἑαυτούς· εἰς τί ἡ ἀπώλεια αὕτη
with   themselves: Why   –   waste   this

τοῦ μύρου γέγονεν; 5 ἠδύνατο γὰρ τοῦτο
of the ointment has occurred?   for ³could   ¹this

τὸ μύρον πραθῆναι ἐπάνω δηναρίων
–   ²ointment   *to* be sold   [for] over   denarii

τριακοσίων καὶ δοθῆναι τοῖς πτωχοῖς·
three hundred   and   *to* be given   to the   poor;

καὶ ἐνεβριμῶντο αὐτῇ. 6 ὁ δὲ Ἰησοῦς
and they were indignant with her.   –   But   Jesus

εἶπεν· ἄφετε αὐτήν· τί αὐτῇ κόπους
said: Leave   her;   why ³to her ²troubles

παρέχετε; καλὸν ἔργον ἠργάσατο ἐν ἐμοί.
¹cause ye?   a good   work   she wrought   in   me.

7 πάντοτε γὰρ τοὺς πτωχοὺς ἔχετε μεθ᾽
   For always   the   poor   ye have   with

ἑαυτῶν, καὶ ὅταν θέλητε δύνασθε αὐτοῖς
yourselves,   and   whenever ye wish   ye can   to them

εὖ ποιῆσαι, ἐμὲ δὲ οὐ πάντοτε ἔχετε.
well *to* do,   but me   not   always   ye have.

8 ὃ ἔσχεν ἐποίησεν· προέλαβεν μυρίσαι τὸ
  What she had   she did;   she was beforehand to anoint   the

σῶμά μου εἰς τὸν ἐνταφιασμόν. 9 ἀμὴν
body   of me   for   the   burial.   truly

δὲ λέγω ὑμῖν, ὅπου ἐὰν κηρυχθῇ τὸ
And   I tell   you,   wherever   is proclaimed   the

εὐαγγέλιον εἰς ὅλον τὸν κόσμον, καὶ ὃ
gospel   in   all   the   world,   also what

ἐποίησεν αὕτη λαληθήσεται εἰς μνημόσυνον
did   this woman will be spoken   for   a memorial

αὐτῆς. 10 Καὶ Ἰούδας Ἰσκαριώθ, ὁ εἷς
of her.   And   Judas   Iscariot,   the one

τῶν δώδεκα, ἀπῆλθεν πρὸς τοὺς ἀρχιερεῖς
of the twelve,   went   to   the   chief priests

ἵνα αὐτὸν παραδοῖ αὐτοῖς. 11 οἱ δὲ
that   him   he might betray to them.   And they

ἀκούσαντες ἐχάρησαν καὶ ἐπηγγείλαντο αὐτῷ
hearing   rejoiced   and   promised   him

ἀργύριον δοῦναι. καὶ ἐζήτει πῶς αὐτὸν
silver   to give.   And   he sought   how   him

εὐκαίρως παραδοῖ.
opportunely he might betray.

12 Καὶ τῇ πρώτῃ ἡμέρᾳ τῶν ἀζύμων,
   And   on the   first   day   of unleavened bread,†

ὅτε τὸ πάσχα ἔθυον, λέγουσιν αὐτῷ οἱ
when the   passover they sacrificed,   say   to him   the

Where wilt thou that we go and prepare that thou mayest eat the passover?

13 And he sendeth forth two of his disciples, and saith unto them, Go ye into the city, and there shall meet you a man bearing a pitcher of water: follow him.

14 And wheresoever he shall go in, say ye to the goodman of the house, The Master saith, Where is the guestchamber, where I shall eat the passover with my disciples?

15 And he will shew you a large upper room furnished *and* prepared: there make ready for us.

16 And his disciples went forth, and came into the city, and found as he had said unto them: and they made ready the passover.

17 And in the evening he cometh with the twelve.

18 And as they sat and did eat, Jesus said, Verily I say unto you, One of you which eateth with me shall betray me.

19 And they began to be sorrowful, and to say unto him one by one, Is it I? and another *said*, Is it I?

20 And he answered and said unto them, *It is* one of the twelve, that dippeth with me in the dish.

21 The Son of man indeed goeth, as it is written of him: but woe

μαθηταὶ αὐτοῦ· ποῦ θέλεις ἀπελθόντες
disciples of him: Where wishest thou , going
ἐτοιμάσωμεν ἵνα φάγῃς τὸ πάσχα; 13 καὶ
we may prepare that thou eatest the passover? And
ἀποστέλλει δύο τῶν μαθητῶν αὐτοῦ καὶ
he sends two of the disciples of him and
λέγει αὐτοῖς· ὑπάγετε εἰς τὴν πόλιν, καὶ
tells them: Go ye into the city, and
ἀπαντήσει ὑμῖν ἄνθρωπος κεράμιον ὕδατος
will meet you a man a pitcher of water
βαστάζων· ἀκολουθήσατε αὐτῷ, 14 καὶ ὅπου
carrying; follow him, and wher-
ἐὰν εἰσέλθῃ εἴπατε τῷ οἰκοδεσπότῃ ὅτι ὁ
ever he enters tell the housemaster[,] – The
διδάσκαλος λέγει· ποῦ ἐστιν τὸ κατάλυμά
teacher says: Where is the guest room
μου, ὅπου τὸ πάσχα μετὰ τῶν μαθητῶν
of me, where the passover with the disciples
μου φάγω; 15 καὶ αὐτὸς ὑμῖν δείξει
of me I may eat? And he you will show
ἀνάγαιον μέγα ἐστρωμένον ἕτοιμον· καὶ
upper room a large *having been* spread ready; and
ἐκεῖ ἑτοιμάσατε ἡμῖν. 16 καὶ ἐξῆλθον οἱ
there prepare ye for us. And went forth the
μαθηταὶ καὶ ἦλθον εἰς τὴν πόλιν καὶ
disciples and came into the city and
εὗρον καθὼς εἶπεν αὐτοῖς, καὶ ἡτοίμασαν
found as he told them, and they prepared
τὸ πάσχα. 17 Καὶ ὀψίας γενομένης ἔρχεται
the passover. And evening coming[a] he comes
= when evening came
μετὰ τῶν δώδεκα. 18 καὶ ἀνακειμένων
with the twelve. And reclining
= as they reclined and ate
αὐτῶν καὶ ἐσθιόντων ὁ Ἰησοῦς εἶπεν·
them and eating[a] – Jesus said:
ἀμὴν λέγω ὑμῖν ὅτι εἷς ἐξ ὑμῶν παραδώσει
Truly I tell you that one of you will betray
με, ὁ ἐσθίων μετ’ ἐμοῦ. 19 ἤρξαντο
me, the [one] eating with me. They began
λυπεῖσθαι καὶ λέγειν αὐτῷ εἷς κατὰ εἷς·
to grieve and to say to him one by one:
μήτι ἐγώ; 20 ὁ δὲ εἶπεν αὐτοῖς· εἷς τῶν
Not I? And he said to them: One of the
δώδεκα, ὁ ἐμβαπτόμενος μετ’ ἐμοῦ εἰς
twelve, the [one] dipping with me in
τὸ [ἓν] τρύβλιον. 21 ὅτι ὁ μὲν υἱὸς τοῦ
the one dish. Because indeed the Son –
ἀνθρώπου ὑπάγει καθὼς γέγραπται περὶ
of man is going as it has been written concerning

to that man by whom the
Son of man is betrayed!
good were it for that man
if he had never been born.

22 ¶ And as they did
eat, Jesus took bread, and
blessed, and brake *it*, and
gave to them, and said,
Take, eat: this is my body.

23 And he took the cup,
and when he had given
thanks, he gave *it* to them:
and they all drank of it.

24 And he said unto
them, This is my blood of
the new testament, which
is shed for many.

25 Verily I say unto you,
I will drink no more of the
fruit of the vine, until that
day that I drink it new in
the kingdom of God.

26 ¶ And when they had
sung an hymn, they went
out into the mount of
Olives.

27 And Jesus saith unto
them, All ye shall be
offended because of me
this night: for it is written,
I will smite the shepherd,
and the sheep shall be
scattered.

28 But after that I am
risen, I will go before you
into Galilee.

29 But Peter said unto
him, Although all shall be
offended, yet *will* not I.

30 And Jesus saith unto

αὐτοῦ· οὐαὶ δε τῷ ἀνθρώπῳ ἐκείνῳ δι’
him;   but woe -   man   to that through

οὗ ὁ υἱὸς τοῦ ἀνθρώπου παραδίδοται·
whom the Son   -   of man   is betrayed;

καλὸν αὐτῷ εἰ οὐκ ἐγεννήθη ὁ ἄνθρωπος
good for him if   was not born   -   man

ἐκεῖνος. 22 Καὶ ἐσθιόντων αὐτῶν λαβὼν
that.   And eating   them[a] taking
          = as they were eating

ἄρτον εὐλογήσας ἔκλασεν καὶ ἔδωκεν αὐτοῖς
a loaf blessing   he broke and gave to them

καὶ εἶπεν· λάβετε· τοῦτό ἐστιν τὸ σῶμά
and said: Take ye; this is   the body

μου. 23 καὶ λαβὼν ποτήριον εὐχαριστήσας
of me.   And taking   a cup   giving thanks

ἔδωκεν αὐτοῖς, καὶ ἔπιον ἐξ αὐτοῦ πάντες.
he gave to them, and drank of it   all.

24 καὶ εἶπεν αὐτοῖς· τοῦτό ἐστιν τὸ αἷμά
And he said to them: This is   the blood

μου τῆς διαθήκης τὸ ἐκχυννόμενον ὑπὲρ
of me of the covenant   -   being shed   for

πολλῶν. 25 ἀμὴν λέγω ὑμῖν ὅτι οὐκέτι
many.   Truly I tell you[,] -   No more

οὐ μὴ πίω ἐκ τοῦ γενήματος τῆς ἀμπέλου
by no(any) will I drink of the fruit   of the vine
means

ἕως τῆς ἡμέρας ἐκείνης ὅταν αὐτὸ πίνω
until   -   day   that   when it   I drink

καινὸν ἐν τῇ βασιλείᾳ τοῦ θεοῦ.
new   in the kingdom   - of God.

26 Καὶ ὑμνήσαντες ἐξῆλθον εἰς τὸ
And having sung a hymn they went forth to the

ὄρος τῶν ἐλαιῶν. 27 Καὶ λέγει αὐτοῖς ὁ
mount of the olives.   And says to them

Ἰησοῦς ὅτι πάντες σκανδαλισθήσεσθε, ὅτι
Jesus[,] -   [3]All [1]ye [2]will [4]be offended, because

γέγραπται· πατάξω τὸν ποιμένα, καὶ τὰ
it has been written: I will strike the shepherd, and the

πρόβατα διασκορπισθήσονται. 28 ἀλλὰ μετὰ
sheep   will be scattered.   But   after

τὸ ἐγερθῆναί με προάξω ὑμᾶς εἰς τὴν
the to be raised me[b] I will go before you to   -
= I am raised

Γαλιλαίαν. 29 ὁ δὲ Πέτρος ἔφη αὐτῷ·
Galilee.   - And Peter   said to him:

εἰ καὶ πάντες σκανδαλισθήσονται, ἀλλ’
If even all men   shall be offended,   yet

οὐκ ἐγώ. 30 καὶ λέγει αὐτῷ ὁ Ἰησοῦς·
not I.   And says to him - Jesus:

him, Verily I say unto thee, That this day, *even* in this night, before the cock crow twice, thou shalt deny me thrice.

31 But he spake the more vehemently, If I should die with thee, I will not deny thee in any wise. Likewise also said they all.

32 ¶ And they came to a place which was named Gethsemane: and he saith to his disciples, Sit ye here, while I shall pray.

33 And he taketh with him Peter and James and John, and began to be sore amazed, and to be very heavy;

34 And saith unto them, My soul is exceeding sorrowful unto death: tarry ye here, and watch.

35 And he went forward a little, and fell on the ground, and prayed that, if it were possible, the hour might pass from him.

36 And he said, Abba, Father, all things *are* possible unto thee; take away this cup from me: nevertheless not what I will, but what thou wilt.

37 And he cometh, and findeth them sleeping, and saith unto Peter, Simon, sleepest thou? couldest not thou watch one hour?

38 Watch ye and pray,

ἀμὴν λέγω σοι ὅτι σὺ σήμερον ταύτῃ τῇ
Truly I tell thee[,] – Thou to-day in this –
νυκτὶ πρὶν ἢ δὶς ἀλέκτορα φωνῆσαι τρίς
night before twice a cock to sound[b] thrice
με ἀπαρνήσῃ. 31 ὁ δὲ ἐκπερισσῶς ἐλάλει·
me thou wilt deny. But he more exceedingly said:
ἐὰν δέῃ με συναποθανεῖν σοι, οὐ μή
If it should behove me *to* die with thee, by no means
= I must
σε ἀπαρνήσομαι. ὡσαύτως [δὲ] καὶ πάντες
thee will I deny. And similarly also all
ἔλεγον.
said.

32 Καὶ ἔρχονται εἰς χωρίον οὗ τὸ
And they come to a piece of land of which the
ὄνομα Γεθσημανί, καὶ λέγει τοῖς μαθηταῖς
name [was] Gethsemane, and he says to the disciples
αὐτοῦ· καθίσατε ὧδε ἕως προσεύξωμαι.
of him: Sit ye here while I pray.
33 καὶ παραλαμβάνει τὸν Πέτρον καὶ τὸν
And he takes – Peter and –
Ἰάκωβον καὶ τὸν Ἰωάννην μετ᾽ αὐτοῦ,
James and – John with him,
καὶ ἤρξατο ἐκθαμβεῖσθαι καὶ ἀδημονεῖν,
and began to be greatly astonished and to be distressed,
34 καὶ λέγει αὐτοῖς· περίλυπός ἐστιν ἡ
and says to them: Deeply grieved is the
ψυχή μου ἕως θανάτου· μείνατε ὧδε καὶ
soul of me unto death; remain ye here and
γρηγορεῖτε. 35 καὶ προελθὼν μικρὸν ἔπιπτεν
watch. And going forward a little he fell
ἐπὶ τῆς γῆς, καὶ προσηύχετο ἵνα εἰ
on the ground, and prayed that if
δυνατόν ἐστιν παρέλθῃ ἀπ᾽ αὐτοῦ ἡ ὥρα,
possible it is might pass away from him the hour,
36 καὶ ἔλεγεν· ἀββὰ ὁ πατήρ, πάντα
and said: Abba – Father, all things
δυνατά σοι· παρένεγκε τὸ ποτήριον τοῦτο
[are] possible to thee; remove – cup this
ἀπ᾽ ἐμοῦ· ἀλλ᾽ οὐ τί ἐγὼ θέλω ἀλλὰ
from me; but not what I wish but
τί σύ. 37 καὶ ἔρχεται καὶ εὑρίσκει
what thou. And he comes and finds
αὐτοὺς καθεύδοντας, καὶ λέγει τῷ Πέτρῳ·
them sleeping, and says – to Peter:
Σίμων, καθεύδεις; οὐκ ἴσχυσας μίαν ὥραν
Simon, sleepest thou? couldest thou not one hour
γρηγορῆσαι; 38 γρηγορεῖτε καὶ προσεύχεσθε,
to watch? Watch ye and pray,

lest ye enter into temptation. The spirit truly *is* ready, but the flesh *is* weak.

39 And again he went away, and prayed, and spake the same words.

40 And when he returned, he found them asleep again, (for their eyes were heavy,) neither wist they what to answer him.

41 And he cometh the third time, and saith unto them, Sleep on now, and take *your* rest: it is enough, the hour is come; behold, the Son of man is betrayed into the hands of sinners.

42 Rise up, let us go; lo, he that betrayeth me is at hand.

43 ¶ And immediately, while he yet spake, cometh Judas, one of the twelve, and with him a great multitude with swords and staves, from the chief priests and the scribes and the elders.

44 And he that betrayed him had given them a token, saying, Whomsoever I shall kiss, that same is he; take him, and lead *him* away safely.

45 And as soon as he was come, he goeth straightway to him, and saith, Master, master; and kissed him.

46 And they laid their hands on him, and took him.

47 And one of them

ἵνα μὴ ἔλθητε εἰς πειρασμόν· τὸ μὲν
lest ye come into temptation; indeed the

πνεῦμα πρόθυμον, ἡ δὲ σὰρξ ἀσθενής.
spirit [is] eager, but the flesh weak.

39 καὶ πάλιν ἀπελθὼν προσηύξατο τὸν
And again going away he prayed ²the

αὐτὸν λόγον εἰπών. 40 καὶ πάλιν ἐλθὼν
³same ⁴word ¹saying. And again coming

εὗρεν αὐτοὺς καθεύδοντας, ἦσαν γὰρ αὐτῶν
he found them sleeping, for were of them

οἱ ὀφθαλμοὶ καταβαρυνόμενοι, καὶ οὐκ
the eyes becoming heavy, and not

ᾔδεισαν τί ἀποκριθῶσιν αὐτῷ. 41 καὶ
they knew what they might answer him. And

ἔρχεται τὸ τρίτον καὶ λέγει αὐτοῖς·
he comes the third [time] and says to them:

καθεύδετε τὸ λοιπὸν καὶ ἀναπαύεσθε·
Sleep ye now† and rest;

ἀπέχει· ἦλθεν ἡ ὥρα, ἰδοὺ παραδίδοται ὁ
it is enough; came the hour, behold is betrayed the

υἱὸς τοῦ ἀνθρώπου εἰς τὰς χεῖρας τῶν
Son – man into the hands –

ἁμαρτωλῶν. 42 ἐγείρεσθε, ἄγωμεν· ἰδοὺ ὁ
of sinners. Rise ye, let us go; behold the

παραδιδούς με ἤγγικεν. 43 Καὶ εὐθὺς ἔτι
[one] betraying me has drawn near. And immediately yet

αὐτοῦ λαλοῦντος παραγίνεται [ὁ] Ἰούδας
him speaking⁸ arrives – Judas
= while he was still speaking

εἷς τῶν δώδεκα, καὶ μετ' αὐτοῦ ὄχλος
one of the twelve, and with him a crowd

μετὰ μαχαιρῶν καὶ ξύλων παρὰ τῶν
with swords and clubs from the

ἀρχιερέων καὶ τῶν γραμματέων καὶ τῶν
chief priests and the scribes and the

πρεσβυτέρων. 44 δεδώκει δὲ ὁ παραδιδοὺς
elders. ¹Now ⁴had given ²the [one] ³betraying

αὐτὸν σύσσημον αὐτοῖς λέγων· ὃν ἂν
⁴him ⁷a signal ⁶them saying: Whomever

φιλήσω αὐτός ἐστιν· κρατήσατε αὐτὸν καὶ
I may kiss he is; seize ye him and

ἀπάγετε ἀσφαλῶς. 45 καὶ ἐλθὼν εὐθὺς
lead away securely. And coming immediately

προσελθὼν αὐτῷ λέγει· ῥαββί, καὶ
approaching to him he says: Rabbi, and

κατεφίλησεν αὐτόν· 46 οἱ δὲ ἐπέβαλαν τὰς
fervently kissed him; and they ¹laid ⁴on ²the(their)

χεῖρας αὐτῷ καὶ ἐκράτησαν αὐτόν. 47 εἷς
³hands him and seized him. ⁶one

that stood by drew a sword, and smote a servant of the high priest, and cut off his ear.

48 And Jesus answered and said unto them, Are ye come out, as against a thief, with swords and *with* staves to take me ?

49 I was daily with you in the temple teaching, and ye took me not: but the scriptures must be fulfilled.

50 And they all forsook him, and fled.

51 And there followed him a certain young man, having a linen cloth cast about *his* naked *body;* and the young men laid hold on him:

52 And he left the linen cloth, and fled from them naked.

53 ¶ And they led Jesus away to the high priest: and with him were assembled all the chief priests and the elders and the scribes.

54 And Peter followed him afar off, even into the palace of the high priest: and he sat with the servants, and warmed himself at the fire.

55 And the chief priests and all the council sought for witness against Jesus to put him to death; and found none.

56 For many bare false

δέ   τις   τῶν   παρεστηκότων   σπασάμενος
¹But ²a certain of the [ones] standing by   drawing

τὴν   μάχαιραν   ἔπαισεν   τὸν   δοῦλον   τοῦ   ἀρχιερέως
the   sword   struck   the   slave   of the   high priest

καὶ   ἀφεῖλεν   αὐτοῦ   τὸ   ὠτάριον.   48 καὶ
and   cut off   of him   the   ear.   And

ἀποκριθεὶς   ὁ   Ἰησοῦς   εἶπεν   αὐτοῖς·   ὡς
answering   –   Jesus   said   to them: As

ἐπὶ   λῃστὴν   ἐξήλθατε   μετὰ   μαχαιρῶν   καὶ
against   a robber   came ye forth   with   swords   and

ξύλων   συλλαβεῖν   με;   49 καθ'   ἡμέραν   ἤμην
clubs   to arrest   me?   Daily   I was

πρὸς   ὑμᾶς   ἐν   τῷ   ἱερῷ   διδάσκων,   καὶ   οὐκ
with   you   in   the   temple   teaching,   and   not

ἐκρατήσατέ   με·   ἀλλ'   ἵνα   πληρωθῶσιν   αἱ
ye did seize   me;   but   that   may be fulfilled   the

γραφαί.   50 καὶ   ἀφέντες   αὐτὸν   ἔφυγον
scriptures.   And   leaving   him   they fled

πάντες.   51 Καὶ   νεανίσκος   τις   συνηκολούθει
all.   And   a certain young man   accompanied

αὐτῷ   περιβεβλημένος   σινδόνα   ἐπὶ   γυμνοῦ,
him   having been clothed [in] a nightgowh   over   [his] naked [body],

καὶ   κρατοῦσιν   αὐτόν·   52 ὁ   δὲ   καταλιπὼν
and   they seize   him;   and he   leaving

τὴν   σινδόνα   γυμνὸς   ἔφυγεν.
the   nightgown   naked   fled.

53 Καὶ   ἀπήγαγον   τὸν   Ἰησοῦν   πρὸς   τὸν
And   they led away   –   Jesus   to   the

ἀρχιερέα,   καὶ   συνέρχονται   πάντες   οἱ
high priest,   and   come together   all   the

ἀρχιερεῖς   καὶ   οἱ   πρεσβύτεροι   καὶ   οἱ
chief priests   and   the   elders   and   the

γραμματεῖς.   54 καὶ   ὁ   Πέτρος   ἀπὸ   μακρόθεν
scribes.   And   –   Peter   from   afar

ἠκολούθησεν   αὐτῷ   ἕως   ἔσω   εἰς   τὴν   αὐλὴν
followed   him   until   within   in   the   court

τοῦ   ἀρχιερέως,   καὶ   ἦν   συγκαθήμενος   μετὰ
of the   high priest,   and   was   sitting   with   with

τῶν   ὑπηρετῶν   καὶ   θερμαινόμενος   πρὸς   τὸ
the   attendants   and   warming himself   by   the

φῶς.   55 Οἱ   δὲ   ἀρχιερεῖς   καὶ   ὅλον   τὸ
bright fire.   Now the   chief priests   and   all   the

συνέδριον   ἐζήτουν   κατὰ   τοῦ   Ἰησοῦ
council   sought   against   –   Jesus

μαρτυρίαν   εἰς   τὸ   θανατῶσαι   αὐτόν,   καὶ
witness   for   the   to put to death   him,   and
= so as

οὐχ   ηὕρισκον·   56 πολλοὶ   γὰρ   ἐψευδομαρτύρουν
found not;   for many   falsely witnessed

witness against him, but
their witness agreed not
together.

57 And there arose cer-
tain, and bare false wit-
ness against him, saying,

58 We heard him say, I
will destroy this temple
that is made with hands,
and within three days I will
build another made with-
out hands.

59 But neither so did
their witness agree to-
gether.

60 And the high priest
stood up in the midst, and
asked Jesus, saying,
Answerest thou nothing?
what is it which these
witness against thee?

61 But he held his peace,
and answered nothing.
Again the high priest asked
him, and said unto him,
Art thou the Christ, the
Son of the Blessed?

62 And Jesus said, I am:
and ye shall see the Son of
man sitting on the right
hand of power, and coming
in the clouds of heaven.

63 Then the high priest
rent his clothes, and saith,
What need we any further
witnesses?

64 Ye have heard the
blasphemy: what think ye?
And they all condemned
him to be guilty of death.

65 And some began to
spit on him, and to cover
his face, and to buffet him,

κατ'   αὐτοῦ,   καὶ   ἴσαι   αἱ   μαρτυρίαι   οὐκ
against   him,   and ⁵identical ¹the ²testimonies ⁴not

ἦσαν.   **57** καί τινες ἀναστάντες ἐψευδομαρτύρουν
³were.   And some standing up   falsely witnessed

κατ'   αὐτοῦ λέγοντες **58** ὅτι ἡμεῖς ἠκούσαμεν
against   him   saying[,]   -   We   heard

αὐτοῦ   λέγοντος   ὅτι   ἐγὼ   καταλύσω   τὸν
him   saying[,]   -   I   will overthrow -

ναὸν   τοῦτον   τὸν   χειροποίητον   καὶ   διὰ
²shrine ¹this   -   ²handmade   and through(after)

τριῶν   ἡμερῶν   ἄλλον   ἀχειροποίητον   οἰκο-
three   days   another   not handmade   I will

δομήσω.   **59** καὶ   οὐδὲ   οὕτως   ἴση   ἦν   ἡ
build.   And   not   so   identical was the

μαρτυρία   αὐτῶν.   **60** καὶ   ἀναστὰς   ὁ
witness   of them.   And   standing up   the

ἀρχιερεὺς   εἰς   μέσον   ἐπηρώτησεν   τὸν   Ἰησοῦν
high priest   in [the] midst   questioned   -   Jesus

λέγων· οὐκ ἀποκρίνῃ   οὐδὲν   τί   οὗτοί   σου
saying: Answerest thou not no(any)thing what these men ²thee

καταμαρτυροῦσιν;   **61** ὁ   δὲ   ἐσιώπα   καὶ
¹testify against?   But he   was silent and

οὐκ   ἀπεκρίνατο   οὐδέν.   πάλιν   ὁ   ἀρχιερεὺς
answered not   no(any)thing. Again the high priest

ἐπηρώτα   αὐτὸν   καὶ   λέγει   αὐτῷ·   σὺ   εἶ   ὁ
questioned   him   and   says   to him: Thou art the

χριστὸς   ὁ   υἱὸς   τοῦ   εὐλογητοῦ;   **62** ὁ   δὲ
Christ   the Son   of the Blessed [one]?   -   And

Ἰησοῦς   εἶπεν·   ἐγώ   εἰμι,   καὶ   ὄψεσθε
Jesus   said: I   am,   and   ye will see

τὸν υἱὸν τοῦ ἀνθρώπου   ἐκ   δεξιῶν   καθήμενον
the Son   -   of man   ²at [the] right [hand] ¹sitting

τῆς   δυνάμεως   καὶ   ἐρχόμενον   μετὰ   τῶν
of the   Power   and   coming   with   the

νεφελῶν   τοῦ   οὐρανοῦ.   **63** ὁ   δὲ   ἀρχιερεὺς
clouds   -   of heaven.   And the   high priest

διαρήξας   τοὺς   χιτῶνας   αὐτοῦ   λέγει·   τί
rending   the   tunics   of him   says: What

ἔτι   χρείαν   ἔχομεν   μαρτύρων;   **64** ἠκούσατε
more   need   have we   of witnesses?   ye heard

τῆς   βλασφημίας·   τί   ὑμῖν   φαίνεται;   οἱ   δὲ
the   blasphemy;   what to you appears it? And they

πάντες   κατέκριναν   αὐτὸν   ἔνοχον   εἶναι
all   condemned   him   liable   to be

θανάτου.   **65** Καὶ   ἤρξαντό   τινες   ἐμπτύειν
of(to) death.   And   began   some   to spit at

αὐτῷ   καὶ   περικαλύπτειν   αὐτοῦ   τὸ   πρόσωπον
him   and   to cover   of him   the   face

and to say unto him,
Prophesy: and the servants
did strike him with the
palms of their hands.

66 ¶ And as Peter was
beneath in the palace,
there cometh one of the
maids of the high priest:

67 And when she saw
Peter warming himself,
she looked upon him, and
said, And thou also wast
with Jesus of Nazareth.

68 But he denied, say-
ing, I know not, neither
understand I what thou
sayest. And he went out
into the porch; and the
cock crew.

69 And a maid saw him
again, and began to say to
them that stood by, This
is *one* of them.

70 And he denied it
again. And a little after,
they that stood by said
again to Peter, Surely thou
art *one* of them: for thou
art a Galilæan, and thy
speech agreeth *thereto*.

71 But he began to
curse and to swear, *saying*,
I know not this man of
whom ye speak.

72 And the second time
the cock crew. And Peter
called to mind the word
that Jesus said unto him,
Before the cock crow twice,
thou shalt deny me thrice.
And when he thought
thereon, he wept.

καὶ κολαφίζειν αὐτὸν καὶ λέγειν αὐτῷ·
and to maltreat him and to say to him:

προφήτευσον, καὶ οἱ ὑπηρέται ῥαπίσμασιν
Prophesy, and the attendants with slaps

αὐτὸν ἔλαβον. 66 Καὶ ὄντος τοῦ Πέτρου
[3]him [1]took. And being Peter[a]
= as Peter was

κάτω ἐν τῇ αὐλῇ ἔρχεται μία τῶν
below in the court comes one of the

παιδισκῶν τοῦ ἀρχιερέως, 67 καὶ ἰδοῦσα
maidservants of the high priest, and seeing

τὸν Πέτρον θερμαινόμενον ἐμβλέψασα αὐτῷ
– Peter warming himself looking at him

λέγει· καὶ σὺ μετὰ τοῦ Ναζαρηνοῦ ἦσθα
says: And [1]thou [3]with [4]the [5]Nazarene [2]wast

τοῦ Ἰησοῦ. 68 ὁ δὲ ἠρνήσατο λέγων· οὔτε
– [6]Jesus. But he denied saying: [1]neither

οἶδα οὔτε ἐπίσταμαι σὺ τί λέγεις. καὶ
[1] [3]know [4]nor [5]understand [7]thou [6]what [8]sayest. And

ἐξῆλθεν ἔξω εἰς τὸ προαύλιον· 69 καὶ ἡ
he went forth outside into the forecourt; and the

παιδίσκη ἰδοῦσα αὐτὸν ἤρξατο πάλιν λέγειν
maidservant seeing him began again to say

τοῖς παρεστῶσιν ὅτι οὗτος ἐξ αὐτῶν ἐστιν.
to the [ones] standing by[,] – This man of them is.

70 ὁ δὲ πάλιν ἠρνεῖτο. καὶ μετὰ μικρὸν
But he again denied. And after a little

πάλιν οἱ παρεστῶτες ἔλεγον τῷ Πέτρῳ·
again the [ones] standing by said – to Peter:

ἀληθῶς ἐξ αὐτῶν εἶ· καὶ γὰρ Γαλιλαῖος
Truly of them thou art; [2]indeed [1]for [4]a Galilæan

εἶ. 71 ὁ δὲ ἤρξατο ἀναθεματίζειν καὶ
[3]thou art. And he began to curse and

ὀμνύναι ὅτι οὐκ οἶδα τὸν ἄνθρωπον
to swear[,] that I know not – man

τοῦτον ὃν λέγετε. 72 καὶ εὐθὺς ἐκ
this whom ye say. And immediately a

δευτέρου ἀλέκτωρ ἐφώνησεν. καὶ ἀνεμνήσθη
second time a cock crew. And remembered

ὁ Πέτρος τὸ ῥῆμα ὡς εἶπεν αὐτῷ ὁ
– Peter the word as said to him –

Ἰησοῦς ὅτι πρὶν ἀλέκτορα δὶς φωνῆσαι
Jesus[,] – Before a cock twice *to* crow[b]

τρίς με ἀπαρνήσῃ· καὶ ἐπιβαλὼν ἔκλαιεν.
thrice me thou wilt deny; and thinking thereon he wept.

CHAPTER 15

AND straightway in the morning the chief priests held a consultation with the elders and scribes and the whole council, and bound Jesus, and carried *him* away, and delivered *him* to Pilate.

2 And Pilate asked him, Art thou the King of the Jews ? And he answering said unto him, Thou sayest *it*.

3 And the chief priests accused him of many things: but he answered nothing.

4 And Pilate asked him again, saying, Answerest thou nothing ? behold how many things they witness against thee.

5 But Jesus yet answered nothing; so that Pilate marvelled.

6 ¶ Now at *that* feast he released unto them one prisoner, whomsoever they desired.

7 And there was *one* named Barabbas, *which* lay bound with them that had made insurrection with him, who had committed murder in the insurrection.

8 And the multitude crying aloud began to desire *him to do* as he had ever done unto them.

9 But Pilate answered them, saying, Will ye that I release unto you the King of the Jews ?

10 For he knew that the chief priests had delivered him for envy.

11 But the chief priests moved the people, that he should rather release Barabbas unto them.

---

15 Καὶ εὐθὺς πρωῒ συμβούλιον ἑτοιμάσαντες
And immediately early   [a] council   [1] preparing

οἱ ἀρχιερεῖς μετὰ τῶν πρεσβυτέρων καὶ
the chief priests with the elders and

γραμματέων καὶ ὅλον τὸ συνέδριον, δήσαντες
scribes   and all the   council,   having bound

τὸν Ἰησοῦν ἀπήνεγκαν καὶ παρέδωκαν
 –   Jesus led [him] away and   delivered [him]

Πιλάτῳ.   **2** καὶ ἐπηρώτησεν αὐτὸν ὁ
to Pilate.   And questioned   him   –

Πιλᾶτος· σὺ εἶ ὁ βασιλεὺς τῶν Ἰουδαίων;
Pilate: Thou art the king of the Jews ?

ὁ δὲ ἀποκριθεὶς αὐτῷ λέγει· σὺ λέγεις.
And he answering him says: Thou sayest.

3 καὶ κατηγόρουν αὐτοῦ οἱ ἀρχιερεῖς πολλά.
And   accused   him the chief priests many things.

4 ὁ δὲ Πιλᾶτος πάλιν ἐπηρώτα αὐτόν [λέγων]·
 – But Pilate again questioned him   saying:

οὐκ ἀποκρίνῃ οὐδέν; ἴδε πόσα
Answerest thou not no(any)thing ? Behold how many things

σου κατηγοροῦσιν. **5** ὁ δὲ Ἰησοῦς οὐκ-
thee they accuse.   – But Jesus no(any)

έτι οὐδὲν ἀπεκρίθη, ὥστε θαυμάζειν
more nothing answered,   so as to marvel
                                     = so that Pilate marvelled.

τὸν Πιλᾶτον. **6** Κατὰ δὲ ἑορτὴν ἀπέλυεν
 –   Pilate[b].   Now at a feast he released

αὐτοῖς ἕνα δέσμιον ὃν παρῃτοῦντο. **7** ἦν δὲ
to them one prisoner whom they begged. Now there was

ὁ λεγόμενος Βαραββᾶς μετὰ τῶν
the [one] named Barabbas with the

στασιαστῶν δεδεμένος, οἵτινες ἐν τῇ στάσει
rebels having been bound, who[*] in the rebellion

φόνον πεποιήκεισαν. **8** καὶ ἀναβὰς ὁ ὄχλος
murder had done.   And going up the crowd

ἤρξατο αἰτεῖσθαι καθὼς ἐποίει αὐτοῖς.
began   to ask   as he used to do for them.

9 ὁ δὲ Πιλᾶτος ἀπεκρίθη αὐτοῖς λέγων·
 – But Pilate answered them saying:

θέλετε ἀπολύσω ὑμῖν τὸν βασιλέα τῶν
Do ye wish I may release to you the king of the

Ἰουδαίων; **10** ἐγίνωσκεν γὰρ ὅτι διὰ φθόνον
Jews ?   For he knew that on account of envy

παραδεδώκεισαν αὐτὸν οἱ ἀρχιερεῖς. **11** οἱ
had delivered him the chief priests.   the

δὲ ἀρχιερεῖς ἀνέσεισαν τὸν ὄχλον ἵνα
But chief priests stirred up the crowd that

μᾶλλον τὸν Βαραββᾶν ἀπολύσῃ αὐτοῖς.
rather   –   Barabbas he should release to them.

*Note the plural.

12 And Pilate answered and said again unto them, What will ye then that I shall do *unto him* whom ye call the King of the Jews?

13 And they cried out again, Crucify him.

14 Then Pilate said unto them, Why, what evil hath he done? And they cried out the more exceedingly, Crucify him.

15 And *so* Pilate, willing to content the people, released Barabbas unto them, and delivered Jesus, when he had scourged *him*, to be crucified.

16 ¶ And the soldiers led him away into the hall, called Prætorium; and they call together the whole band.

17 And they clothed him with purple, and platted a crown of thorns, and put it about his *head*,

18 And began to salute him, Hail, King of the Jews!

19 And they smote him on the head with a reed, and did spit upon him, and bowing *their* knees worshipped him.

20 And when they had mocked him, they took off the purple from him, and put his own clothes on him, and led him out to crucify him.

21 And they compel one Simon a Cyrenian, who passed by, coming out of

12 ὁ δὲ Πιλᾶτος πάλιν ἀποκριθεὶς ἔλεγεν
\- So Pilate again answering said

αὐτοῖς· τί οὖν ποιήσω [ὃν] λέγετε τὸν
to them: What then may I do [to him] whom ye call the

βασιλέα τῶν Ἰουδαίων; 13 οἱ δὲ πάλιν
king of the Jews? And they again

ἔκραξαν· σταύρωσον αὐτόν. 14 ὁ δὲ
cried out: Crucify him. \- But

Πιλᾶτος ἔλεγεν αὐτοῖς· τί γὰρ ἐποίησεν
Pilate said to them: Indeed what ²did he

κακόν; οἱ δὲ περισσῶς ἔκραξαν· σταύρωσον
¹evil? and they more cried out: Crucify

αὐτόν. 15 ὁ δὲ Πιλᾶτος βουλόμενος τῷ
him. \- And Pilate resolving the

ὄχλῳ τὸ ἱκανὸν ποιῆσαι ἀπέλυσεν αὐτοῖς
crowd to satisfy† released to them

τὸν Βαραββᾶν, καὶ παρέδωκεν τὸν Ἰησοῦν
\- Barabbas, and delivered \- Jesus

φραγελλώσας ἵνα σταυρωθῇ.
having scourged [him] that he might be crucified.

16 Οἱ δὲ στρατιῶται ἀπήγαγον αὐτὸν
Then the soldiers led away him

ἔσω τῆς αὐλῆς, ὅ ἐστιν πραιτώριον, καὶ
inside the court, which is prætorium, and

συγκαλοῦσιν ὅλην τὴν σπεῖραν. 17 καὶ
they call together all the cohort. And

ἐνδιδύσκουσιν αὐτὸν πορφύραν καὶ περιτιθέασιν
they put on him a purple [robe] and place round

αὐτῷ πλέξαντες ἀκάνθινον στέφανον· 18 καὶ
him plaiting a thorny crown; and

ἤρξαντο ἀσπάζεσθαι αὐτόν· χαῖρε, βασιλεῦ
they began to salute him: Hail, king

τῶν Ἰουδαίων· 19 καὶ ἔτυπτον αὐτοῦ τὴν
of the Jews; and they struck of him the

κεφαλὴν καλάμῳ καὶ ἐνέπτυον αὐτῷ, καὶ
head with a reed and spat at him, and

τιθέντες τὰ γόνατα προσεκύνουν αὐτῷ.
placing(bending) the(their) knees worshipped him.

20 καὶ ὅτε ἐνέπαιξαν αὐτῷ, ἐξέδυσαν
And when they mocked him, they took off

αὐτὸν τὴν πορφύραν καὶ ἐνέδυσαν αὐτὸν
him the purple [robe] and put on him

τὰ ἱμάτια αὐτοῦ. Καὶ ἐξάγουσιν αὐτὸν
the garments of him. And they lead forth him

ἵνα σταυρώσωσιν αὐτόν. 21 καὶ ἀγγαρεύουσιν
that they might crucify him. And they impress

παράγοντά τινα Σίμωνα Κυρηναῖον ἐρχόμενον
passing by a certain Simon a Cyrenian coming

the country, the father of Alexander and Rufus, to bear his cross.

22 And they bring him unto the place Golgotha, which is, being interpreted, The place of a skull.

23 And they gave him to drink wine mingled with myrrh: but he received *it* not.

24 And when they had crucified him, they parted his garments, casting lots upon them, what every man should take.

25 And it was the third hour, and they crucified him.

26 And the superscription of his accusation was written over, THE KING OF THE JEWS.

27 And with him they crucify two thieves; the one on his right hand, and the other on his left.

28 And the scripture was fulfilled, which saith, And he was numbered with the transgressors.

29 ¶ And they that passed by railed on him, wagging their heads, and saying, Ah, thou that destroyest the temple, and buildest *it* in three days,

30 Save thyself, and come down from the cross.

31 Likewise also the chief priests mocking said among themselves with the scribes, He saved others; himself he cannot save.

32 Let Christ the King of Israel descend now from the cross, that we may see and believe. And they that

ἀπ' ἀγροῦ, τὸν πατέρα 'Αλεξάνδρου καὶ
from [the] country, the father of Alexander and

'Ρούφου, ἵνα ἄρῃ τὸν σταυρὸν αὐτοῦ.
of Rufus, that he might bear the cross of him.

22 καὶ φέρουσιν αὐτὸν ἐπὶ τὸν Γολγοθᾶν
And they bring him to the Golgotha

τόπον, ὅ ἐστιν μεθερμηνευόμενος κρανίου
place, which is being interpreted of a skull

τόπος. 23 καὶ ἐδίδουν αὐτῷ ἐσμυρνισμένον
place. And they gave him ¹having been spiced
with myrrh

οἶνον· ὃς δὲ οὐκ ἔλαβεν. 24 καὶ σταυροῦσιν
¹wine; but who(he) received not. And they crucify

αὐτόν, καὶ διαμερίζονται τὰ ἱμάτια αὐτοῦ,
him, and divide the garments of him,

βάλλοντες κλῆρον ἐπ' αὐτὰ τίς τί ἄρῃ.
casting a lot on them ²one ¹what might take.

25 ἦν δὲ ὥρα τρίτη καὶ ἐσταύρωσαν
Now it was hour third and they crucified

αὐτόν. 26 καὶ ἦν ἡ ἐπιγραφὴ τῆς αἰτίας
him. And was the superscription of the accusation

αὐτοῦ *having been* written over· Ο ΒΑΣΙΛΕΥΣ ΤΩΝ
of him THE KING OF THE

ΙΟΥΔΑΙΩΝ. 27 Καὶ σὺν αὐτῷ σταυροῦσιν
JEWS. And with him they crucify

δύο λῃστάς, ἕνα ἐκ δεξιῶν καὶ ἕνα ἐξ
two robbers, one on [the] right and one on

εὐωνύμων αὐτοῦ. ‡ 29 Καὶ οἱ παραπορευόμενοι
[the] left of him. And the [ones] passing by

ἐβλασφήμουν αὐτὸν κινοῦντες τὰς κεφαλὰς
blasphemed him wagging the heads

αὐτῶν καὶ λέγοντες· οὐὰ ὁ καταλύων
of them and saying: Ah the [one] overthrowing

τὸν ναὸν καὶ οἰκοδομῶν [ἐν] τρισὶν
the shrine and building in three

ἡμέραις, 30 σῶσον σεαυτὸν καταβὰς ἀπὸ
days, save thyself coming down from

τοῦ σταυροῦ. 31 ὁμοίως καὶ οἱ ἀρχιερεῖς
the cross. Likewise also the chief priests

ἐμπαίζοντες πρὸς ἀλλήλους μετὰ τῶν
mocking to one another with the

γραμματέων ἔλεγον· ἄλλους ἔσωσεν, ἑαυτὸν
scribes said: Others he saved, himself

οὐ δύναται σῶσαι· 32 ὁ χριστὸς ὁ βασιλεὺς
he cannot *to* save; the Christ the king

'Ισραὴλ καταβάτω νῦν ἀπὸ τοῦ σταυροῦ,
of Israel let come down now from the cross,

ἵνα ἴδωμεν καὶ πιστεύσωμεν. καὶ οἱ
that we may see and believe. And the

‡ Verse 28 omitted by Nestle; *cf.* R.V. marg., etc.

were crucified with him
reviled him.

33 ¶ And when the sixth
hour was come, there was
darkness over the whole
land until the ninth hour.

34 And at the ninth
hour Jesus cried with a
loud voice, saying, Eloi,
Eloi, lama sabachthani?
which is, being interpreted,
My God, my God, why
hast thou forsaken me?

35 And some of them
that stood by, when they
heard it, said, Behold, he
calleth Elias.

36 And one ran and
filled a spunge full of
vinegar, and put it on a
reed, and gave him to
drink, saying, Let alone;
let us see whether Elias
will come to take him
down.

37 And Jesus cried with
a loud voice, and gave up
the ghost.

38 And the veil of the
temple was rent in twain
from the top to the
bottom.

39 ¶ And when the cen-
turion, which stood over
against him, saw that he so
cried out, and gave up the
ghost, he said, Truly this
man was the Son of God.

40 There were also
women looking on afar off:
among whom was Mary
Magdalene, and Mary the
mother of James the less
and of Joses, and Salome;

41 (Who also, when he
was in Galilee, followed
him, and ministered unto

συνεσταυρωμένοι σὺν αὐτῷ ὠνείδιζον αὐτόν.
[ones] crucified *with* with him reproached him.

33 Καὶ γενομένης ὥρας ἕκτης σκότος
And becoming hour sixth* darkness
= when it was the sixth hour

ἐγένετο ἐφ᾽ ὅλην τὴν γῆν ἕως ὥρας
came over all the land until [the] hour

ἐνάτης. 34 καὶ τῇ ἐνάτῃ ὥρᾳ ἐβόησεν ὁ
ninth. And at the ninth hour cried -

Ἰησοῦς φωνῇ μεγάλῃ· ἐλωὶ ἐλωὶ λαμὰ
Jesus with a voice great(loud): Eloi[,] Eloi[,] lama

σαβαχθάνι; ὅ ἐστιν μεθερμηνευόμενον· ὁ
sabachthani? which is being interpreted: The

θεός μου ὁ θεός μου, εἰς τί ἐγκατέλιπές
God of me[,] the God of me, why didst thou forsake

με; 35 καί τινες τῶν παρεστηκότων
me? And some of the [ones] standing by

ἀκούσαντες ἔλεγον· ἴδε Ἠλίαν φωνεῖ.
hearing said: Behold Elias he calls.

36 δραμὼν δέ τις γεμίσας σπόγγον ὄξους
And running one having filled a sponge of(with) vinegar

περιθεὶς καλάμῳ ἐπότιζεν αὐτόν, λέγων·
placing it round a reed ¹gave ²to drink ³him, saying:

ἄφετε ἴδωμεν εἰ ἔρχεται Ἠλίας καθελεῖν
Leave[,] let us see if comes Elias ¹to take ³down

αὐτόν. 37 ὁ δὲ Ἰησοῦς ἀφεὶς φωνὴν
²him. - But Jesus letting go voice

μεγάλην ἐξέπνευσεν. 38 Καὶ τὸ καταπέτασμα
a great(loud) expired. And the veil

τοῦ ναοῦ ἐσχίσθη εἰς δύο ἀπ᾽ ἄνωθεν
of the shrine was rent in two from top

ἕως κάτω. 39 Ἰδὼν δὲ ὁ κεντυρίων ὁ
to bottom. And ⁶seeing ¹the ²centurion -

παρεστηκὼς ἐξ ἐναντίας αὐτοῦ ὅτι οὕτως
³standing by ⁴opposite ⁵him that thus

ἐξέπνευσεν, εἶπεν· ἀληθῶς οὗτος ὁ ἄνθρωπος
he expired, said: Truly this - man

υἱὸς θεοῦ ἦν. 40 Ἦσαν δὲ καὶ γυναῖκες
son of God was. Now there were also women

ἀπὸ μακρόθεν θεωροῦσαι, ἐν αἷς καὶ
from afar beholding, among whom both

Μαρία ἡ Μαγδαληνὴ καὶ Μαρία ἡ
Mary the Magdalene and Mary ¹the

Ἰακώβου τοῦ μικροῦ καὶ Ἰωσῆτος μήτηρ
³of James ⁴the ⁵little ⁶and ⁷of Joses ²mother

καὶ Σαλώμη, 41 αἳ ὅτε ἦν ἐν τῇ Γαλιλαίᾳ
and Salome, who when he was in - Galilee

ἠκολούθουν αὐτῷ καὶ διηκόνουν αὐτῷ, καὶ
followed him and served him, and

him;) and many other women which came up with him unto Jerusalem.

42 ¶ And now when the even was come, because it was the preparation, that is, the day before the sabbath,

43 Joseph of Arimathæa, an honourable counsellor, which also waited for the kingdom of God, came, and went in boldly unto Pilate, and craved the body of Jesus.

44 And Pilate marvelled if he were already dead: and calling *unto him* the centurion, he asked him whether he had been any while dead.

45 And when he knew *it* of the centurion, he gave the body to Joseph.

46 And he bought fine linen, and took him down, and wrapped him in the linen, and laid him in a sepulchre which was hewn out of a rock, and rolled a stone unto the door of the sepulchre.

47 And Mary Magdalene and Mary *the mother* of Joses beheld where he was laid.

ἄλλαι πολλαὶ αἱ συναναβᾶσαι αὐτῷ εἰς
others many – having come up with him to
Ἱεροσόλυμα.
Jerusalem.

42 Καὶ ἤδη ὀψίας γενομένης, ἐπεὶ ἦν
And now evening coming,ᵃ since it was
= when it was evening,
παρασκευή, ὅ ἐστιν προσάββατον, 43 ἐλθὼν
[the] preparation, which is the day before the sabbath, coming
Ἰωσὴφ ὁ ἀπὸ Ἀριμαθαίας, εὐσχήμων
Joseph the [one] from Arimathæa, an honourable
βουλευτής, ὃς καὶ αὐτὸς ἦν προσδεχόμενος
councillor, who also [him]self was expecting
τὴν βασιλείαν τοῦ θεοῦ, τολμήσας εἰσῆλθεν
the kingdom – of God, taking courage went in
πρὸς τὸν Πιλᾶτον καὶ ἠτήσατο τὸ σῶμα
to – Pilate and asked the body
τοῦ Ἰησοῦ. 44 ὁ δὲ Πιλᾶτος ἐθαύμασεν
– of Jesus. – And Pilate marvelled
εἰ ἤδη τέθνηκεν, καὶ προσκαλεσάμενος τὸν
if already he has died, and calling to [him] the
κεντυρίωνα ἐπηρώτησεν αὐτὸν εἰ πάλαι
centurion questioned him if long ago
ἀπέθανεν· 45 καὶ γνοὺς ἀπὸ τοῦ κεντυρίωνος
he died; and knowing from the centurion
ἐδωρήσατο τὸ πτῶμα τῷ Ἰωσήφ. 46 καὶ
he granted the corpse – to Joseph. And
ἀγοράσας σινδόνα καθελὼν αὐτὸν ἐνείλησεν
having bought a piece of taking down him he wrapped
unused linen
τῇ σινδόνι καὶ κατέθηκεν αὐτὸν ἐν μνήματι
with the linen and deposited him in a tomb
ὃ ἦν λελατομημένον ἐκ πέτρας, καὶ
which was *having been* hewn out of rock, and
προσεκύλισεν λίθον ἐπὶ τὴν θύραν τοῦ
rolled a stone against the door of the
μνημείου. 47 ἡ δὲ Μαρία ἡ Μαγδαληνὴ
tomb. – And Mary the Magdalene
καὶ Μαρία ἡ Ἰωσῆτος ἐθεώρουν ποῦ
and Mary the [mother] of Joses beheld where
τέθειται.
he has been laid.

CHAPTER 16

A ND when the sabbath was past, Mary Magdalene, and Mary the

16 Καὶ διαγενομένου τοῦ σαββάτου [ἡ]
And passing the sabbathᵃ –
= when the sabbath was past
Μαρία ἡ Μαγδαληνὴ καὶ Μαρία ἡ [τοῦ]
Mary the Magdalene and Mary the [mother] –

mother of James, and Salome, had bought sweet spices, that they might come and anoint him.

2 And very early in the morning the first *day* of the week, they came unto the sepulchre at the rising of the sun.

3 And they said among themselves, Who shall roll us away the stone from the door of the sepulchre?

4 And when they looked, they saw that the stone was rolled away: for it was very great.

5 And entering into the sepulchre, they saw a young man sitting on the right side, clothed in a long white garment; and they were affrighted.

6 And he saith unto them, Be not affrighted: Ye seek Jesus of Nazareth, which was crucified: he is risen; he is not here: behold the place where they laid him.

7 But go your way, tell his disciples and Peter that he goeth before you into Galilee: there shall ye see him, as he said unto you.

8 And they went out quickly, and fled from the sepulchre; for they trembled and were amazed: neither said they any thing to any *man;* for they were afraid.

9 ¶ Now when *Jesus* was risen early the first *day* of the week, he appeared first to Mary Magdalene, out of whom he had cast seven devils.

10 *And* she went and

Ἰακώβου καὶ Σαλώμη ἠγόρασαν ἀρώματα
of James   and   Salome   bought   spices

ἵνα ἐλθοῦσαι ἀλείψωσιν αὐτόν. 2 καὶ λίαν
that coming they might anoint him.   And very

πρωῒ [τῇ] μιᾷ τῶν σαββάτων ἔρχονται
early on the first day of the week†   they come

ἐπὶ τὸ μνῆμα, ἀνατείλαντος τοῦ ἡλίου.
upon the   tomb,   rising   the   sun.ᵃ
                                           = as the sun rose.

3 καὶ ἔλεγον πρὸς ἑαυτάς· τίς ἀποκυλίσει
  And they said to themselves: Who will roll away

ἡμῖν τὸν λίθον ἐκ τῆς θύρας τοῦ μνημείου;
for us the stone out of the door   of   the tomb?

4 καὶ ἀναβλέψασαι θεωροῦσιν ὅτι ἀνακεκύλισται
  And looking up   they behold that has been rolled back

ὁ λίθος· ἦν γὰρ μέγας σφόδρα.   5 καὶ
the stone: for it was great exceedingly.   And

εἰσελθοῦσαι εἰς τὸ μνημεῖον εἶδον νεανίσκον
entering   into the   tomb   they saw a young man

καθήμενον ἐν τοῖς δεξιοῖς περιβεβλημένον
sitting   on   the   right   having been clothed

στολὴν λευκήν, καὶ ἐξεθαμβήθησαν. 6 ὁ δὲ
robe   [in] a white, and they were greatly astonished. But he

λέγει αὐταῖς· μὴ ἐκθαμβεῖσθε· Ἰησοῦν
says   to them: Be not greatly astonished;   Jesus

ζητεῖτε τὸν Ναζαρηνὸν τὸν ἐσταυρωμένον·
ye seek   the   Nazarene   -   having been crucified;

ἠγέρθη, οὐκ ἔστιν ὧδε· ἴδε ὁ τόπος
he was raised, he is not here; behold[,] the place

ὅπου ἔθηκαν αὐτόν. 7 ἀλλὰ ὑπάγετε εἴπατε
where they put him.   But   go ye   tell

τοῖς μαθηταῖς αὐτοῦ καὶ τῷ Πέτρῳ ὅτι
the   disciples   of him and -   Peter   that

προάγει ὑμᾶς εἰς τὴν Γαλιλαίαν· ἐκεῖ
he goes before you to   -   Galilee;   there

αὐτὸν ὄψεσθε, καθὼς εἶπεν ὑμῖν. 8 καὶ
him   ye will see, as   he told you.   And

ἐξελθοῦσαι ἔφυγον ἀπὸ τοῦ μνημείου, εἶχεν
going forth   they fled from the   tomb,   ⁵had

γὰρ αὐτὰς τρόμος καὶ ἔκστασις· καὶ
¹for ⁶them ²trembling ³and ⁴bewilderment; and

οὐδενὶ οὐδὲν εἶπαν· ἐφοβοῦντο γάρ.
no one no(r.ny)thing they told; for they were afraid.

9 Ἀναστὰς δὲ πρωῒ πρώτῃ σαββάτου
  And rising   early on the first day of the week†

ἐφάνη πρῶτον Μαρίᾳ τῇ Μαγδαληνῇ, παρ'
he appeared first   to Mary the   Magdalene,   from

ἧς ἐκβεβλήκει ἑπτὰ δαιμόνια. 10 ἐκείνη
whom he had expelled seven   demons.   That [one]
                                                = She

told them that had been with him, as they mourned and wept.

11 And they, when they had heard that he was alive, and had been seen of her, believed not.

12 ¶ After that he appeared in another form unto two of them, as they walked, and went into the country.

13 And they went and told *it* unto the residue: neither believed they them.

14 ¶ Afterward he appeared unto the eleven as they sat at meat, and upbraided them with their unbelief and hardness of heart, because they believed not them which had seen him after he was risen.

15 And he said unto them, Go ye into all the world, and preach the gospel to every creature.

16 He that believeth and is baptized shall be saved; but he that believeth not shall be damned.

17 And these signs shall follow them that believe; In my name shall they cast out devils; they shall speak with new tongues;

18 They shall take up serpents; and if they drink any deadly thing, it shall not hurt them; they shall lay hands on the sick, and they shall recover.

19 ¶ So then after the Lord had spoken unto

πορευθεῖσα　ἀπήγγειλεν　τοῖς　μετ᾽　αὐτοῦ
going　　　　reported　　to the [ones]　with　him
　　　　　　　　　　　　= those who had been with him

γενομένοις　πενθοῦσι καὶ κλαίουσιν·　11 κἀκεῖνοι
having been　mourning　and　weeping;　　　and those

ἀκούσαντες　ὅτι ζῇ καὶ ἐθεάθη ὑπ᾽ αὐτῆς
hearing　　　that he lives and was seen by　her

ἠπίστησαν.　12 Μετὰ δὲ ταῦτα δυσὶν ἐξ
disbelieved.　And after　these things to two　of

αὐτῶν　περιπατοῦσιν ἐφανερώθη ἐν ἑτέρᾳ
them　　walking　　　he was manifested in a different

μορφῇ πορευομένοις εἰς ἀγρόν·　13 κἀκεῖνοι
form　going　　　into [the] country;　and those

ἀπελθόντες ἀπήγγειλαν τοῖς λοιποῖς· οὐδὲ
going　　　reported　　　to the　rest;　neither

ἐκείνοις ἐπίστευσαν.　14 Ὕστερον [δὲ]
those　they believed.　　　And later

ἀνακειμένοις αὐτοῖς τοῖς ἕνδεκα ἐφανερώθη,
to the reclining　them　the　eleven he was manifested,
= to the eleven as they reclined

καὶ ὠνείδισεν τὴν ἀπιστίαν αὐτῶν καὶ
and　reproached　the　disbelief　of them　and

σκληροκαρδίαν ὅτι τοῖς θεασαμένοις αὐτὸν
hardness of heart because the [ones] beholding　him

ἐγηγερμένον οὐκ ἐπίστευσαν.　15 καὶ εἶπεν
having been raised they did not believe.　And　he said

αὐτοῖς· πορευθέντες εἰς τὸν κόσμον ἅπαντα
to them:　Going　　into ²the ³world　　¹all

κηρύξατε τὸ εὐαγγέλιον πάσῃ τῇ κτίσει.
proclaim ye the　gospel　to all the　creation.

16 ὁ πιστεύσας καὶ βαπτισθεὶς σωθήσεται,
The [one] believing　and being baptized will be saved,

ὁ δὲ ἀπιστήσας κατακριθήσεται.　17 σημεῖα
but the [one] disbelieving　will be condemned.　²signs

δὲ τοῖς πιστεύσασιν ταῦτα παρακολουθήσει·
¹And ⁴the [ones]　believing　⁶these　　⁵will follow:

ἐν τῷ ὀνόματί μου δαιμόνια ἐκβαλοῦσιν,
in　the　name　of me demons　they will expel,

γλώσσαις λαλήσουσιν καιναῖς,　18 ὄφεις
²tongues　¹they will speak ¹with new,　serpents

ἀροῦσιν κἂν θανάσιμόν τι πίωσιν
they will take and if　²deadly　²anything ¹they drink

οὐ μὴ αὐτοὺς βλάψῃ, ἐπὶ ἀρρώστους χεῖρας
by no means them it will hurt, on　sick [ones]　hands

ἐπιθήσουσιν καὶ καλῶς ἕξουσιν.　19 Ὁ μὲν
they will place on and　well they will have.　¹The ⁴there-
　　　　　　　　　　= they will recover.

οὖν κύριος [Ἰησοῦς] μετὰ τὸ λαλῆσαι
fore　²Lord　　³Jesus　after　the　to speak
　　　　　　　　　　　　= speaking

them, he was received up into heaven, and sat on the right hand of God.

20 And they went forth, and preached every where, the Lord working with *them*, and confirming the word with signs following. Amen.

αὐτοῖς ἀνελήμφθη εἰς τὸν οὐρανὸν καὶ
to them   was taken up   into   –   heaven   and

ἐκάθισεν ἐκ δεξιῶν τοῦ θεοῦ. **20** ἐκεῖνοι
sat   at [the] right [hand] –   of God.   those

δὲ ἐξελθόντες ἐκήρυξαν πανταχοῦ, τοῦ
But   going forth   proclaimed   everywhere,   the

κυρίου συνεργοῦντος καὶ τὸν λόγον
Lord   working with   and   the   word
= while the Lord worked with [them] and confirmed the word

βεβαιοῦντος διὰ τῶν ἐπακολουθούντων
confirming[a]   through   the   accompanying

σημείων.
signs.

CHAPTER 1

FORASMUCH as many
have taken in hand to
set forth in order a declaration of those things which
are most surely believed
among us,

2 Even as they delivered
them unto us, which from
the beginning were eye-
witnesses, and ministers of
the word;

3 It seemed good to me
also, having had perfect
understanding of all things
from the very first, to
write unto thee in order,
most excellent Theophilus,

4 That thou mightest
know the certainty of those
things, wherein thou hast
been instructed.

5 ¶ THERE was in the
days of Herod,
the king of Judæa, a
certain priest named Zacharias, of the course of
Abia : and his wife *was* of
the daughters of Aaron,
and her name *was* Elisa-
beth.

6 And they were both
righteous before God,
walking in all the com-
mandments and ordinances
of the Lord blameless.

7 And they had no
child, because that Elisabeth was barren, and they
both were *now* well stricken
in years.

8 And it came to pass,
that while he executed the
priest's office before God

1 Ἐπειδήπερ πολλοὶ ἐπεχείρησαν ἀνατάξασθαι
Since   many   took in hand   to draw up

διήγησιν   περὶ   τῶν   πεπληροφορημένων
a narrative concerning [1]the   [2]having been fully carried out

ἐν   ἡμῖν   πραγμάτων, **2** καθὼς   παρέδοσαν   ἡμῖν
[4]among [5]us   [2]matters,   as   delivered   to us

οἱ   ἀπ'   ἀρχῆς   αὐτόπται   καὶ   ὑπηρέται
the [ones] from [the] beginning eyewitnesses and   attendants

γενόμενοι   τοῦ   λόγου,   **3** ἔδοξε   κἀμοὶ
becoming   of the   Word,   it seemed good to me also

παρηκολουθηκότι   ἄνωθεν   πᾶσιν   ἀκριβῶς
having investigated from their source all things accurately

καθεξῆς   σοι   γράψαι,   κράτιστε   Θεόφιλε,
[3]in order [2]to thee [1]to write, most excellent Theophilus,

4 ἵνα   ἐπιγνῷς   περὶ   ὧν
that   thou mightest know   [4]concerning [5]which

κατηχήθης   λόγων   τὴν   ἀσφάλειαν.
[6]thou wast instructed [3]of [the] things [1]the [2]reliability.

5 Ἐγένετο   ἐν   ταῖς   ἡμέραις
There was   in   the   days

Ἡρῴδου   βασιλέως   τῆς   Ἰουδαίας   ἱερεύς
of Herod   king   –   of Judæa   [2]priest

τις   ὀνόματι   Ζαχαρίας   ἐξ   ἐφημερίας   Ἀβιά,
[1]a certain by name Zacharias of [the] course   of Abia,

καὶ   γυνὴ   αὐτῷ   ἐκ   τῶν   θυγατέρων   Ἀαρών,
and   wife   to him [c] of   the   daughters   of Aaron,
      =his wife

καὶ   τὸ   ὄνομα   αὐτῆς   Ἐλισάβετ.   **6** ἦσαν   δὲ
and the   name   of her   Elisabeth.   And they were

δίκαιοι   ἀμφότεροι   ἐναντίον   τοῦ   θεοῦ,
righteous   both   before   –   God,

πορευόμενοι   ἐν   πάσαις   ταῖς   ἐντολαῖς   καὶ
going   in   all   the   commandments and

δικαιώμασιν   τοῦ   κυρίου   ἄμεμπτοι.   **7** καὶ
ordinances   of the   Lord   blameless.   And

οὐκ   ἦν   αὐτοῖς   τέκνον,   καθότι   ἦν   ἡ
there was not to them a child,[c] because [2]was –
=they had no child,

Ἐλισάβετ   στεῖρα,   καὶ   ἀμφότεροι   προβεβηκότες
[1]Elisabeth barren, and   both   *having* advanced

ἐν   ταῖς   ἡμέραις   αὐτῶν   ἦσαν.   **8** Ἐγένετο
in   the   days   of them were.   it came to pass

δὲ   ἐν   τῷ   ἱερατεύειν   αὐτὸν   ἐν   τῇ   τάξει
Now in the   to serve as priest him[be] in the   order
=while he served as priest

in the order of his course,

9 According to the custom of the priest's office, his lot was to burn incense when he went into the temple of the Lord.

10 And the whole multitude of the people were praying without at the time of incense.

11 And there appeared unto him an angel of the Lord standing on the right side of the altar of incense.

12 And when Zacharias saw *him*, he was troubled, and fear fell upon him.

13 But the angel said unto him, Fear not, Zacharias : for thy prayer is heard; and thy wife Elisabeth shall bear thee a son, and thou shalt call his name John.

14 And thou shalt have joy and gladness; and many shall rejoice at his birth.

15 For he shall be great in the sight of the Lord, and shall drink neither wine nor strong drink; and he shall be filled with the Holy Ghost, even from his mother's womb.

16 And many of the children of Israel shall he turn to the Lord their God.

17 And he shall go before him in the spirit and power of Elias, to turn the hearts of the fathers to the children, and the disobedient to the wisdom of

τῆς ἐφημερίας αὐτοῦ ἔναντι τοῦ θεοῦ,
of the　course　of him　before　–　God,

9 κατὰ τὸ ἔθος τῆς ἱερατείας ἔλαχε τοῦ
according to the custom of the priesthood his lot was –

θυμιᾶσαι εἰσελθὼν εἰς τὸν ναὸν τοῦ κυρίου,
to burn incense[d] entering into the shrine of the Lord,

10 καὶ πᾶν τὸ πλῆθος ἦν τοῦ λαοῦ
and all ¹the ²multitude ⁴was ³of the ⁴people

προσευχόμενον ἔξω τῇ ὥρᾳ τοῦ θυμιάματος.
praying　outside at the hour　–　of incense.

11 ὤφθη δὲ αὐτῷ ἄγγελος κυρίου ἑστὼς
And there appeared to him an angel of [the] Lord standing

ἐκ δεξιῶν τοῦ θυσιαστηρίου τοῦ θυμιάματος.
on [the] right of the　altar　–　of incense.

12 καὶ ἐταράχθη Ζαχαρίας ἰδών, καὶ φόβος
And was troubled Zacharias seeing, and fear

ἐπέπεσεν ἐπ᾽ αὐτόν. 13 εἶπεν δὲ πρὸς
fell *on* upon him.　But said　to

αὐτὸν ὁ ἄγγελος· μὴ φοβοῦ, Ζαχαρία,
him the angel:　Fear not,　Zacharias,

διότι εἰσηκούσθη ἡ δέησίς σου, καὶ ἡ
because was heard the request of thee, and the

γυνή σου Ἐλισάβετ γεννήσει υἱόν σοι,
wife of thee Elisabeth will bear a son to thee,

καὶ καλέσεις τὸ ὄνομα αὐτοῦ Ἰωάννην·
and thou shalt call the name of him John;

14 καὶ ἔσται χαρά σοι καὶ ἀγαλλίασις,
and there shall be joy to thee and gladness,[e]
=thou shalt have joy and gladness,

καὶ πολλοὶ ἐπὶ τῇ γενέσει αὐτοῦ χαρή-
and many over the birth of him will

σονται. 15 ἔσται γὰρ μέγας ἐνώπιον
rejoice.　For he will be　great　in the eyes of

κυρίου, καὶ οἶνον καὶ σίκερα οὐ μὴ
[the] Lord, and wine and strong drink by no means

πίῃ, καὶ πνεύματος ἁγίου πλησθήσεται
may he drink, and of(with) Spirit [the] Holy he will be filled

ἔτι ἐκ κοιλίας μητρὸς αὐτοῦ, 16 καὶ
even from [the] womb of [the] mother of him, and

πολλοὺς τῶν υἱῶν Ἰσραὴλ ἐπιστρέψει ἐπὶ κύριον
many of the sons of Israel he will turn to [the] Lord

τὸν θεὸν αὐτῶν· 17 καὶ αὐτὸς προελεύσεται
the God of them; and he will go *before*

ἐνώπιον αὐτοῦ ἐν πνεύματι καὶ δυνάμει
before him in [the] spirit and power

Ἠλίου, ἐπιστρέψαι καρδίας πατέρων ἐπὶ
of Elias, to turn [the] hearts of fathers to

τέκνα καὶ ἀπειθεῖς ἐν φρονήσει
children and disobedient [ones] to [the] understanding

the just; to make ready a people prepared for the Lord.

18 And Zacharias said unto the angel, Whereby shall I know this? for I am an old man, and my wife well stricken in years.

19 And the angel answering said unto him, I am Gabriel, that stand in the presence of God; and am sent to speak unto thee, and to shew thee these glad tidings.

20 And, behold, thou shalt be dumb, and not able to speak, until the day that these things shall be performed, because thou believest not my words, which shall be fulfilled in their season.

21 And the people waited for Zacharias, and marvelled that he tarried so long in the temple.

22 And when he came out, he could not speak unto them : and they perceived that he had seen a vision in the temple : for he beckoned unto them, and remained speechless.

23 And it came to pass, that, as soon as the days of his ministration were accomplished, he departed to his own house.

24 And after those days his wife Elisabeth conceived, and hid herself five months, saying,

δικαίων, ἑτοιμάσαι κυρίῳ λαὸν κατεσκευασ-
of [the] just, to prepare for [the] Lord a people *having been*

μένον. 18 καὶ εἶπεν Ζαχαρίας πρὸς τὸν ἄγγελον·
prepared. And said Zacharias to the angel :

κατὰ τί γνώσομαι τοῦτο; ἐγὼ γάρ εἰμι
By what shall I know this? for I am

πρεσβύτης καὶ ἡ γυνή μου προβεβηκυῖα
old and the wife of me *having* advanced

ἐν ταῖς ἡμέραις αὐτῆς. 19 καὶ ἀποκριθεὶς
in the days of her. And answering

ὁ ἄγγελος εἶπεν αὐτῷ· ἐγώ εἰμι Γαβριὴλ
the angel said to him : I am Gabriel

ὁ παρεστηκὼς ἐνώπιον τοῦ θεοῦ, καὶ
the [one] standing before – God, and

ἀπεστάλην λαλῆσαι πρὸς σὲ καὶ εὐαγ-
I was sent to speak to thee and to

γελίσασθαί σοι ταῦτα· 20 καὶ ἰδοὺ
announce to thee these things; and behold

ἔσῃ σιωπῶν καὶ μὴ δυνάμενος λαλῆσαι
thou shalt be being silent and not being able to speak

ἄχρι ἧς ἡμέρας γένηται ταῦτα, ἀνθ’ ὧν οὐκ
until which day happen*s* these things, because not
=the day when these things happen,

ἐπίστευσας τοῖς λόγοις μου, οἵτινες πληρω-
thou believedst the words of me, which will be

θήσονται εἰς τὸν καιρὸν αὐτῶν. 21 καὶ ἦν
fulfilled in the time of them. And was

ὁ λαὸς προσδοκῶν τὸν Ζαχαρίαν, καὶ
the people expecting – Zacharias, and

ἐθαύμαζον ἐν τῷ χρονίζειν ἐν τῷ ναῷ
they marvelled in(at) the to delay in the shrine
=when he delayed in the shrine.

αὐτόν. 22 ἐξελθὼν δὲ οὐκ ἐδύνατο λαλῆσαι
him.^be And going out he was not able to speak

αὐτοῖς καὶ ἐπέγνωσαν ὅτι ὀπτασίαν ἑώρακεν
to them, and they knew that a vision he has(had) seen

ἐν τῷ ναῷ· καὶ αὐτὸς ἦν διανεύων
in the shrine; and he was beckoning

αὐτοῖς, καὶ διέμενεν κωφός. 23 καὶ
to them, and remained dumb. And

ἐγένετο ὡς ἐπλήσθησαν αἱ ἡμέραι τῆς
it came to pass when were fulfilled the days of the

λειτουργίας αὐτοῦ, ἀπῆλθεν εἰς τὸν οἶκον
service of him, he went away to the house

αὐτοῦ. 24 Μετὰ δὲ ταύτας τὰς ἡμέρας
of him. And after these – days

συνέλαβεν Ἐλισάβετ ἡ γυνὴ αὐτοῦ, καὶ
conceived Elisabeth the wife of him, and

περιέκρυβεν ἑαυτὴν μῆνας πέντε, λέγουσα
hid herself months five, saying[,]

25 Thus hath the Lord dealt with me in the days wherein he looked on *me*, to take away my reproach among men.

26 ¶ And in the sixth month the angel Gabriel was sent from God unto a city of Galilee, named Nazareth,

27 To a virgin espoused to a man whose name was Joseph, of the house of David; and the virgin's name *was* Mary.

28 And the angel came in unto her, and said, Hail, *thou that art* highly favoured, the Lord *is* with thee : blessed *art* thou among women.

29 And when she saw *him*, she was troubled at his saying, and cast in her mind what manner of salutation this should be.

30 And the angel said unto her, Fear not, Mary : for thou hast found favour with God.

31 And, behold, thou shalt conceive in thy womb, and bring forth a son, and shalt call his name JESUS.

32 He shall be great, and shall be called the Son of the Highest : and the Lord God shall give unto him the throne of his father David :

33 And he shall reign over the house of Jacob for ever; and of his kingdom there shall be no end.

34 Then said Mary unto the angel, How shall this

25 ὅτι   οὕτως   μοι   πεποίηκεν   κύριος   ἐν
 –   Thus   to me   has done   [the] Lord   in

ἡμέραις   αἷς   ἐπεῖδεν   ἀφελεῖν   ὄνειδός
 days   in which   he looked upon   to take away   reproach

μου   ἐν   ἀνθρώποις.
of me   among   men.

26 Ἐν   δὲ   τῷ   μηνὶ   τῷ   ἕκτῳ   ἀπεστάλη
 Now in   –   the   month   –   sixth   was sent

ὁ   ἄγγελος   Γαβριὴλ   ἀπὸ   τοῦ   θεοῦ   εἰς
the   angel   Gabriel   from   –   God   to

πόλιν   τῆς   Γαλιλαίας   ᾗ   ὄνομα   Ναζαρέθ,
a city   –   of Galilee   to which nameᵉ   Nazareth,
 = the name of which [was]

27 πρὸς   παρθένον   ἐμνηστευμένην   ἀνδρὶ   ᾧ   ὄνομα
 to   a virgin   *having been*   to a man   to whom
 betrothed   nameᵉ

Ἰωσήφ,   ἐξ   οἴκου   Δαυίδ,   καὶ   τὸ   ὄνομα
Joseph,   of [the] house   of David,   and   the   name

τῆς   παρθένου   Μαριάμ.   28 καὶ   εἰσελθὼν
of the   virgin   [was] Mary.   And   entering

πρὸς   αὐτὴν   εἶπεν·   χαῖρε,   κεχαριτωμένη,   ὁ
 to   her   he said : Hail,   *having been* favoured [one],   the

κύριος   μετὰ   σοῦ.   29 ἡ   δὲ   ἐπὶ   τῷ   λόγῳ
Lord [is]   with   thee.   And she   at   the   saying

διεταράχθη,   καὶ   διελογίζετο   ποταπὸς   εἴη
was greatly disturbed,   and   considered   of what sort   ²might be

ὁ   ἀσπασμὸς   οὗτος.   30 καὶ   εἶπεν   ὁ   ἄγγελος
 –   ²greeting   ¹this.   And   said   the   angel

αὐτῇ·   μὴ   φοβοῦ,   Μαριάμ·   εὗρες   γὰρ
to her :   Fear not,   Mary :   for thou didst find

χάριν   παρὰ   τῷ   θεῷ.   31 καὶ   ἰδοὺ   συλλήμψῃ
favour with   –   God.   And behold   thou wilt conceive

ἐν   γαστρὶ   καὶ   τέξῃ   υἱόν,   καὶ   καλέσεις   τὸ
in   womb   and   bear   a son,   and   thou shalt call the

ὄνομα   αὐτοῦ   Ἰησοῦν.   32 οὗτος   ἔσται   μέγας
name   of him   Jesus.   This   will be   great

καὶ   υἱὸς   ὑψίστου   κληθήσεται,   καὶ   δώσει
and   Son   of [the] Most High   will be called,   and   will give

αὐτῷ   κύριος   ὁ   θεὸς   τὸν   θρόνον   Δαυὶδ
him   [the] Lord   –   God   the   throne   of David

τοῦ   πατρὸς   αὐτοῦ,   33 καὶ   βασιλεύσει   ἐπὶ
the   father   of him,   and   he will reign   over

τὸν   οἶκον   Ἰακὼβ   εἰς   τοὺς   αἰῶνας,   καὶ
the   house   of Jacob   unto   the   ages,   and
 = for ever,

τῆς   βασιλείας   αὐτοῦ   οὐκ   ἔσται   τέλος.
of the   kingdom   of him   there will not be   an end.

34 εἶπεν   δὲ   Μαριὰμ   πρὸς   τὸν   ἄγγελον·
 And said   Mary   to   the   angel :

be, seeing I know not a man?

35 And the angel answered and said unto her, The Holy Ghost shall come upon thee, and the power of the Highest shall overshadow thee : therefore also that holy thing which shall be born of thee shall be called the Son of God.

36 And, behold, thy cousin Elisabeth, she hath also conceived a son in her old age : and this is the sixth month with her, who was called barren.

37 For with God nothing shall be impossible.

38 And Mary said, Behold the handmaid of the Lord; be it unto me according to thy word. And the angel departed from her.

39 ¶ And Mary arose in those days, and went into the hill country with haste, into a city of Juda;

40 And entered into the house of Zacharias, and saluted Elisabeth.

41 And it came to pass, that, when Elisabeth heard the salutation of Mary, the babe leaped in her womb; and Elisabeth was filled with the Holy Ghost :

42 And she spake out with a loud voice, and said, Blessed art thou among women, and blessed is the fruit of thy womb.

43 And whence is this to

πῶς ἔσται τοῦτο, ἐπεὶ ἄνδρα οὐ γινώσκω;
How will be this, since a man I know not?

35 καὶ ἀποκριθεὶς ὁ ἄγγελος εἶπεν αὐτῇ·
And answering the angel said to her :

πνεῦμα ἅγιον ἐπελεύσεται ἐπὶ σέ, καὶ
[The] ²Spirit ¹Holy will come upon upon thee, and

δύναμις ὑψίστου ἐπισκιάσει σοι· διὸ
[the] power of [the] Most High will overshadow thee; wherefore

καὶ τὸ γεννώμενον ἅγιον κληθήσεται υἱὸς θεοῦ.
also the thing being born holy will be called[,] Son of God.

36 καὶ ἰδοὺ Ἐλισάβετ ἡ συγγενίς σου καὶ
And behold Elisabeth the relative of thee also

αὐτὴ συνείληφεν υἱὸν ἐν γήρει αὐτῆς, καὶ
she conceived a son in old age of her, and

οὗτος μὴν ἕκτος ἐστὶν αὐτῇ τῇ καλουμένῃ
this month sixth is with her the [one] being called

στείρᾳ· 37 ὅτι οὐκ ἀδυνατήσει παρὰ τοῦ
barren; because will not be impossible with –

θεοῦ πᾶν ῥῆμα. 38 εἶπεν δὲ Μαριάμ· ἰδοὺ ἡ
God every word. And said Mary: Behold[,] the

δούλη κυρίου· γένοιτό μοι κατὰ
handmaid of [the] Lord; may it be to me according to

τὸ ῥῆμά σου. καὶ ἀπῆλθεν ἀπ' αὐτῆς
the word of thee. And went away from her

ὁ ἄγγελος. 39 Ἀναστᾶσα δὲ Μαριὰμ ἐν
the angel. And rising up Mary in

ταῖς ἡμέραις ταύταις ἐπορεύθη εἰς τὴν
– days these she went to the

ὀρεινὴν μετὰ σπουδῆς εἰς πόλιν Ἰούδα,
mountain country with haste to a city of Juda,

40 καὶ εἰσῆλθεν εἰς τὸν οἶκον Ζαχαρίου
and entered into the house of Zacharias

καὶ ἠσπάσατο τὴν Ἐλισάβετ. 41 καὶ
and greeted – Elisabeth. And

ἐγένετο ὡς ἤκουσεν τὸν ἀσπασμὸν τῆς
it came to pass when ²heard ³the ⁴greeting

Μαρίας ἡ Ἐλισάβετ, ἐσκίρτησεν τὸ βρέφος
⁵of Mary – ¹Elisabeth, leaped the babe

ἐν τῇ κοιλίᾳ αὐτῆς, καὶ ἐπλήσθη πνεύματος
in the womb of her, and ²was filled ³of(with) ⁶Spirit

ἁγίου ἡ Ἐλισάβετ, 42 καὶ ἀνεφώνησεν
⁴[the] Holy – ¹Elisabeth, and she called out

κραυγῇ μεγάλῃ καὶ εἶπεν· εὐλογημένη
cry with a great and said : Blessed [art]

σὺ ἐν γυναιξίν, καὶ εὐλογημένος ὁ καρπὸς
thou among women, and blessed [is] the fruit

τῆς κοιλίας σου. 43 καὶ πόθεν μοι τοῦτο
of the womb of thee. And whence to me this

me, that the mother of my Lord should come to me?

44 For, lo, as soon as the voice of thy salutation sounded in mine ears, the babe leaped in my womb for joy.

45 And blessed *is* she that believed : for there shall be a performance of those things which were told her from the Lord.

46 ¶ And Mary said, My soul doth magnify the Lord,

47 And my spirit hath rejoiced in God my Saviour.

48 For he hath regarded the low estate of his handmaiden : for, behold, from henceforth all generations shall call me blessed.

49 For he that is mighty hath done to me great things; and holy *is* his name.

50 And his mercy *is* on them that fear him from generation to generation.

51 He hath shewed strength with his arm; he hath scattered the proud in the imagination of their hearts.

52 He hath put down the mighty from *their* seats, and exalted them of low degree.

53 He hath filled the hungry with good things; and the rich he hath sent empty away.

54 He hath holpen his servant Israel, in remembrance of *his* mercy;

55 As he spake to our fathers, to Abraham,

ἵνα ἔλθῃ ἡ μήτηρ τοῦ κυρίου μου πρὸς
that comes the mother of the Lord of me to

ἐμέ; 44 ἰδοὺ γὰρ ὡς ἐγένετο ἡ φωνὴ τοῦ
me? For behold when came the sound of the

ἀσπασμοῦ σου εἰς τὰ ὦτά μου, ἐσκίρτησεν
greeting of thee in the ears of me, leaped

ἐν ἀγαλλιάσει τὸ βρέφος ἐν τῇ κοιλίᾳ
in gladness the babe in the womb

μου. 45 καὶ μακαρία ἡ πιστεύσασα ὅτι
of me. And blessed the [one] believing because

ἔσται τελείωσις τοῖς λελαλημένοις αὐτῇ
there shall be a completion to the things *having been* to her
spoken

παρὰ κυρίου. 46 Καὶ εἶπεν Μαριάμ·
from [the] Lord. And said Mary :

Μεγαλύνει ἡ ψυχή μου τὸν κύριον, 47 καὶ
Magnifies the soul of me the Lord, and

ἠγαλλίασεν τὸ πνεῦμά μου ἐπὶ τῷ θεῷ
exulted the spirit of me in - God

τῷ σωτῆρί μου· 48 ὅτι ἐπέβλεψεν ἐπὶ τὴν
the saviour of me; because he looked *on* upon the

ταπείνωσιν τῆς δούλης αὐτοῦ. ἰδοὺ γὰρ
humiliation of the handmaid of him. For behold

ἀπὸ τοῦ νῦν μακαριοῦσίν με πᾶσαι αἱ
from - now ⁴will ⁵deem ⁷blessed ⁶me ¹all ³the

γενεαί· 49 ὅτι ἐποίησέν μοι μεγάλα ὁ
²generations; because did to me great things the

δυνατός. καὶ ἅγιον τὸ ὄνομα αὐτοῦ,
Mighty [one]. And holy the name of him,

50 καὶ τὸ ἔλεος αὐτοῦ εἰς γενεὰς καὶ
and the mercy of him to generations and

γενεὰς τοῖς φοβουμένοις αὐτόν. 51 Ἐποίησεν
generations to the [ones] fearing him. He did

κράτος ἐν βραχίονι αὐτοῦ, διεσκόρπισεν
might with [the] arm of him, he scattered

ὑπερηφάνους διανοίᾳ καρδίας αὐτῶν·
haughty [ones] in [the] understanding of [the] heart of them;

52 καθεῖλεν δυνάστας ἀπὸ θρόνων καὶ ὕψω-
he pulled down potentates from thrones and exalt-

σεν ταπεινούς, 53 πεινῶντας ἐνέπλησεν
ed humble [ones], hungering [ones] he filled

ἀγαθῶν καὶ πλουτοῦντας ἐξαπέστειλεν
of(with) good things and rich [ones] he sent away

κενούς. 54 ἀντελάβετο Ἰσραὴλ παιδὸς αὐτοῦ,
empty. He succoured Israel servant of him,

μνησθῆναι ἐλέους, 55 καθὼς ἐλάλησεν
to remember mercy, as he spoke

πρὸς τοὺς πατέρας ἡμῶν, τῷ Ἀβραὰμ
to the fathers of us, - to Abraham

and to his seed for ever.

56 And Mary abode with her about three months, and returned to her own house.

57 ¶ Now Elisabeth's full time came that she should be delivered; and she brought forth a son.

58 And her neighbours and her cousins heard how the Lord had shewed great mercy upon her; and they rejoiced with her.

59 And it came to pass, that on the eighth day they came to circumcise the child; and they called him Zacharias, after the name of his father.

60 And his mother answered and said, Not so; but he shall be called John.

61 And they said unto her, There is none of thy kindred that is called by this name.

62 And they made signs to his father, how he would have him called.

63 And he asked for a writing table, and wrote, saying, His name is John. And they marvelled all.

64 And his mouth was opened immediately, and his tongue *loosed*, and he spake and praised God.

65 And fear came on all

καὶ τῷ σπέρματι αὐτοῦ εἰς τὸν αἰῶνα.
and to the seed of him unto the age.
=for ever.

56 Ἔμεινεν δὲ Μαριὰμ σὺν αὐτῇ ὡς
And remained Mary with her about

μῆνας τρεῖς, καὶ ὑπέστρεψεν εἰς τὸν
months three, and returned to the

οἶκον αὐτῆς.
house of her.

57 Τῇ δὲ Ἐλισάβετ ἐπλήσθη ὁ χρόνος
- Now ⁴to Elisabeth ³was fulfilled ¹the ²time

τοῦ τεκεῖν αὐτήν, καὶ ἐγέννησεν υἱόν.
- to bear her,ᵇᵈ and she brought forth a son.
=that she should bear,

58 καὶ ἤκουσαν οἱ περίοικοι καὶ οἱ
And heard the neighbours and the

συγγενεῖς αὐτῆς ὅτι ἐμεγάλυνεν κύριος τὸ
relatives of her that magnified [the] Lord the

ἔλεος αὐτοῦ μετ' αὐτῆς, καὶ συνέχαιρον
mercy of him with her, and they rejoiced with

αὐτῇ. 59 Καὶ ἐγένετο ἐν τῇ ἡμέρᾳ τῇ
her. And it came to pass on the day the

ὀγδόῃ ἦλθον περιτεμεῖν τὸ παιδίον, καὶ
eighth they came to circumcise the child, and

ἐκάλουν αὐτὸ ἐπὶ τῷ ὀνόματι τοῦ πατρὸς
were calling it(him) by the name of the father

αὐτοῦ Ζαχαρίαν. 60 καὶ ἀποκριθεῖσα ἡ
of him Zacharias. And answering the

μήτηρ αὐτοῦ εἶπεν· οὐχί, ἀλλὰ κληθήσεται
mother of him said : No, but he shall be called

Ἰωάννης. 61 καὶ εἶπαν πρὸς αὐτὴν ὅτι
John. And they said to her[.] -

οὐδείς ἐστιν ἐκ τῆς συγγενείας σου ὃς
No one there is of the kindred of thee who

καλεῖται τῷ ὀνόματι τούτῳ. 62 ἐνένευον
is called - name by this. they nodded

δὲ τῷ πατρὶ αὐτοῦ τὸ τί ἂν θέλοι
And to the father of him - what he might wish

καλεῖσθαι αὐτό. 63 καὶ αἰτήσας πινακίδιον
²to be called ¹him. And asking for a tablet

ἔγραψεν λέγων· Ἰωάννης ἐστὶν ὄνομα
he wrote saying : John is name

αὐτοῦ. καὶ ἐθαύμασαν πάντες. 64 ἀνεῴχθη δὲ
of him. And they marvelled all. And was opened

τὸ στόμα αὐτοῦ παραχρῆμα καὶ ἡ
the mouth of him instantly and the

γλῶσσα αὐτοῦ, καὶ ἐλάλει εὐλογῶν τὸν
tongue of him, and he spoke blessing the

θεόν. 65 Καὶ ἐγένετο ἐπὶ πάντας φόβος
God. And ²came ³on ⁴all ¹fear

that dwelt round about them : and all these sayings were noised abroad throughout all the hill country of Judæa.

66 And all they that heard *them* laid *them* up in their hearts, saying, What manner of child shall this be! And the hand of the Lord was with him.

67 ¶ And his father Zacharias was filled with the Holy Ghost, and prophesied, saying,

68 Blessed *be* the Lord God of Israel; for he hath visited and redeemed his people,

69 And hath raised up an horn of salvation for us in the house of his servant David;

70 As he spake by the mouth of his holy prophets, which have been since the world began :

71 That we should be saved from our enemies, and from the hand of all that hate us;

72 To perform the mercy *promised* to our fathers, and to remember his holy covenant;

73 The oath which he sware to our father Abraham,

74 That he would grant unto us, that we being delivered out of the hand of our enemies might serve him without fear,

75 In holiness and righteousness before him, all the days of our life.

76 And thou, child, shalt be called the prophet of the Highest : for thou shalt go before the face of

τοὺς περιοικοῦντας αὐτούς, καὶ ἐν ὅλῃ τῇ
the [ones] dwelling round them, and in all the

ὀρεινῇ τῆς Ἰουδαίας διελαλεῖτο πάντα
mountain country - of Judæa ⁴were talked over ¹all

τὰ ῥήματα ταῦτα, 66 καὶ ἔθεντο πάντες
- ²facts ²these, and ⁴put ¹all

οἱ ἀκούσαντες ἐν τῇ καρδίᾳ αὐτῶν,
²the [ones] ³hearing in the heart of them,

λέγοντες· τί ἄρα τὸ παιδίον τοῦτο ἔσται;
saying : What then - child this will be ?

καὶ γὰρ χεὶρ κυρίου ἦν μετ' αὐτοῦ.
for indeed [the] hand of [the] Lord was with him.

67 Καὶ Ζαχαρίας ὁ πατὴρ αὐτοῦ ἐπλήσθη
And Zacharias the father of him was filled

πνεύματος ἁγίου καὶ ἐπροφήτευσεν λέγων·
of(with) Spirit [the] Holy and prophesied saying :

68 Εὐλογητὸς κύριος ὁ θεὸς τοῦ Ἰσραήλ,
Blessed [be] [the] Lord the God - of Israel,

ὅτι ἐπεσκέψατο καὶ ἐποίησεν λύτρωσιν τῷ
because he visited and wrought redemption for the

λαῷ αὐτοῦ, 69 καὶ ἤγειρεν κέρας σωτηρίας
people of him, and raised a horn of salvation

ἡμῖν ἐν οἴκῳ Δαυὶδ παιδὸς αὐτοῦ, 70 καθὼς
for us in [the] house of David servant of him, as

ἐλάλησεν διὰ στόματος τῶν ἁγίων ἀπ'
he spoke through [the] mouth of the ¹holy ⁴from

αἰῶνος προφητῶν αὐτοῦ, 71 σωτηρίαν ἐξ
⁵[the] age ²prophets ³of him, salvation out of

ἐχθρῶν ἡμῶν καὶ ἐκ χειρὸς πάντων τῶν
[the] enemies of us and out of [the] hand of all the [ones]

μισούντων ἡμᾶς, 72 ποιῆσαι ἔλεος μετὰ
hating us, to perform mercy with

τῶν πατέρων ἡμῶν καὶ μνησθῆναι διαθήκης
the fathers of us and to remember [the] covenant

ἁγίας αὐτοῦ, 73 ὅρκον ὃν ὤμοσεν πρὸς Ἀβραὰμ
holy of him, [the] oath which he swore to Abraham

τὸν πατέρα ἡμῶν, τοῦ δοῦναι ἡμῖν
the father of us, - to give[d] us

74 ἀφόβως ἐκ χειρὸς ἐχθρῶν ῥυσθέντας
⁵fearlessly ²out of ³[the] hand ⁴of [our] enemies ¹having been delivered

λατρεύειν αὐτῷ 75 ἐν ὁσιότητι καὶ δικαιοσύνῃ
⁶to serve him in holiness and righteousness

ἐνώπιον αὐτοῦ πάσαις ταῖς ἡμέραις ἡμῶν.
before him all the days[e] of us.

76 Καὶ σὺ δέ, παιδίον, προφήτης ὑψίστου
And thou also, child, a prophet of [the] Most High

κληθήσῃ· προπορεύσῃ γὰρ ἐνώπιον κυρίου
wilt be called; for thou wilt go *before* before [the] Lord

the Lord to prepare his ways;

77 To give knowledge of salvation unto his people by the remission of their sins,

78 Through the tender mercy of our God; whereby the dayspring from on high hath visited us,

79 To give light to them that sit in darkness and *in* the shadow of death, to guide our feet into the way of peace.

80 And the child grew, and waxed strong in spirit, and was in the deserts till the day of his shewing unto Israel.

ἑτοιμάσαι ὁδοὺς αὐτοῦ, 77 τοῦ δοῦναι
to prepare [the] ways of him, – to give[d]
γνῶσιν σωτηρίας τῷ λαῷ αὐτοῦ ἐν
a knowledge of salvation to the people of him by
ἀφέσει ἁμαρτιῶν αὐτῶν, 78 διὰ σπλάγχνα
forgiveness of sins of them, because of [the] bowels
ἐλέους θεοῦ ἡμῶν, ἐν οἷς ἐπισκέψεται
of mercy of God of us, whereby will visit
ἡμᾶς ἀνατολὴ ἐξ ὕψους, 79 ἐπιφᾶναι τοῖς
us a [sun]rising from [the] height, to appear ¹to the [ones]
ἐν σκότει καὶ σκιᾷ θανάτου καθημένοις,
²in ⁴darkness ⁵and ⁶in a shadow ⁷of death ¹sitting,
τοῦ κατευθῦναι τοὺς πόδας ἡμῶν εἰς ὁδὸν
– to guide[d] the feet of us into a way
εἰρήνης.
of peace.

80 Τὸ δὲ παιδίον ηὔξανεν καὶ ἐκραταιοῦτο
And the child grew and became strong
πνεύματι, καὶ ἦν ἐν ταῖς ἐρήμοις ἕως
in spirit, and was in the deserts until
ἡμέρας ἀναδείξεως αὐτοῦ πρὸς τὸν Ἰσραήλ.
[the] days of showing of him to – Israel.

CHAPTER 2

A ND it came to pass in those days, that there went out a decree from Cæsar Augustus, that all the world should be taxed.

2 (*And* this taxing was first made when Cyrenius was governor of Syria.)

3 And all went to be taxed, every one into his own city.

4 And Joseph also went up from Galilee, out of the city of Nazareth, into Judæa, unto the city of David, which is called Bethlehem; (because he was of the house and lineage of David :)

5 To be taxed with Mary his espoused wife, being great with child.

2 Ἐγένετο δὲ ἐν ταῖς ἡμέραις ἐκείναις
Now it came to pass in – days those
ἐξῆλθεν δόγμα παρὰ Καίσαρος Αὐγούστου
went out a decree from Cæsar Augustus
ἀπογράφεσθαι πᾶσαν τὴν οἰκουμένην. 2 αὕτη
to be enrolled all the inhabited earth. This
ἀπογραφὴ πρώτη ἐγένετο ἡγεμονεύοντος τῆς
²enrolment ¹first was governing
= when Cyrenius governed Syria.
Συρίας Κυρηνίου. 3 καὶ ἐπορεύοντο πάντες
Syria Cyrenius.[a] And went all
ἀπογράφεσθαι, ἕκαστος εἰς τὴν ἑαυτοῦ
to be enrolled, each man to the of himself
πόλιν. 4 Ἀνέβη δὲ καὶ Ἰωσὴφ ἀπὸ τῆς
city. So went up also Joseph from –
Γαλιλαίας ἐκ πόλεως Ναζαρὲθ εἰς τὴν
Galilee out of a city Nazareth to –
Ἰουδαίαν εἰς πόλιν Δαυὶδ ἥτις καλεῖται Βηθλέεμ,
Judæa to a city of David which is called Bethlehem,
διὰ τὸ εἶναι αὐτὸν ἐξ οἴκου καὶ
because of the to be him[b] *out* of [the] house and
= because he was
πατριᾶς Δαυίδ, 5 ἀπογράψασθαι σὺν Μαριὰμ
family of David, to be enrolled with Mary
τῇ ἐμνηστευμένῃ αὐτῷ, οὔσῃ ἐγκύῳ.
the [one] *having been* betrothed to him, being pregnant.

6 And so it was, that, while they were there, the days were accomplished that she should be delivered.

7 And she brought forth her firstborn son, and wrapped him in swaddling clothes, and laid him in a manger; because there was no room for them in the inn.

8 ¶ And there were in the same country shepherds abiding in the field, keeping watch over their flock by night.

9 And, lo, the angel of the Lord came upon them, and the glory of the Lord shone round about them: and they were sore afraid.

10 And the angel said unto them, Fear not : for, behold, I bring you good tidings of great joy, which shall be to all people.

11 For unto you is born this day in the city of David a Saviour, which is Christ the Lord.

12 And this *shall be* a sign unto you; Ye shall find the babe wrapped in swaddling clothes, lying in a manger.

13 And suddenly there was with the angel a multitude of the heavenly host praising God, and saying,

14 Glory to God in the highest, and on earth peace, good will toward men.

15 And it came to pass, as the angels were gone

---

6 Ἐγένετο δὲ ἐν τῷ εἶναι αὐτοὺς ἐκεῖ
And it came to pass in the to be them[be] there
=while they were

ἐπλήσθησαν αἱ ἡμέραι τοῦ τεκεῖν αὐτήν,
were fulfilled the days - to bear her,[bd]
=for her to bear,

7 καὶ ἔτεκεν τὸν υἱὸν αὐτῆς τὸν πρωτότοκον,
and she bore the son of her the firstborn,

καὶ ἐσπαργάνωσεν αὐτὸν καὶ ἀνέκλινεν
and she swathed him and laid

αὐτὸν ἐν φάτνῃ, διότι οὐκ ἦν αὐτοῖς
him in a manger, because there was not for them

τόπος ἐν τῷ καταλύματι. 8 Καὶ ποιμένες
place in the inn. And shepherds

ἦσαν ἐν τῇ χώρᾳ τῇ αὐτῇ ἀγραυλοῦντες
there were in the country - same living in the fields

καὶ φυλάσσοντες φυλακὰς τῆς νυκτὸς ἐπὶ
and keeping guard of(in) the night over

τὴν ποίμνην αὐτῶν. 9 καὶ ἄγγελος κυρίου
the flock of them. And an angel of [the] Lord

ἐπέστη αὐτοῖς καὶ δόξα κυρίου περιέλαμψεν
came upon them and [the] glory of [the]Lord shone around

αὐτούς, καὶ ἐφοβήθησαν φόβον μέγαν.
them, and they feared fear a great.
=exceedingly.

10 καὶ εἶπεν αὐτοῖς ὁ ἄγγελος· μὴ
And said to them the angel : not

φοβεῖσθε· ἰδοὺ γὰρ εὐαγγελίζομαι ὑμῖν
Fear ye; for behold I announce to you

χαρὰν μεγάλην, ἥτις ἔσται παντὶ τῷ λαῷ,
joy a great, which will be to all the people,

11 ὅτι ἐτέχθη ὑμῖν σήμερον σωτήρ, ὃς
because was born to you to-day a Saviour, who

ἐστιν χριστὸς κύριος, ἐν πόλει Δαυίδ.
is Christ [the] Lord, in a city of David.

12 καὶ τοῦτο ὑμῖν σημεῖον, εὑρήσετε βρέφος
And this to you a sign, ye will find a babe

ἐσπαργανωμένον καὶ κείμενον ἐν φάτνῃ.
having been swathed and lying in a manger.

13 καὶ ἐξαίφνης ἐγένετο σὺν τῷ ἀγγέλῳ
And suddenly there was with the angel

πλῆθος στρατιᾶς οὐρανίου αἰνούντων τὸν
a multitude army of a heavenly praising -

θεὸν καὶ λεγόντων· 14 δόξα ἐν ὑψίστοις
God and saying : Glory in highest [places]

θεῷ καὶ ἐπὶ γῆς εἰρήνη ἐν ἀνθρώποις
to God and on earth peace among men

εὐδοκίας. 15 Καὶ ἐγένετο ὡς ἀπῆλθον
of goodwill. And it came to pass when went away

away from them into heaven, the shepherds said one to another, Let us now go even unto Bethlehem, and see this thing which is come to pass, which the Lord hath made known unto us.

16 And they came with haste, and found Mary, and Joseph, and the babe lying in a manger.

17 And when they had seen *it*, they made known abroad the saying which was told them concerning this child.

18 And all they that heard *it* wondered at those things which were told them by the shepherds.

19 But Mary kept all these things, and pondered *them* in her heart.

20 And the shepherds returned, glorifying and praising God for all the things that they had heard and seen, as it was told unto them.

21 ¶ And when eight days were accomplished for the circumcising of the child, his name was called JESUS, which was so named of the angel before he was conceived in the womb.

22 And when the days of her purification according to the law of Moses were accomplished, they

ἀπ' αὐτῶν εἰς τὸν οὐρανὸν οἱ ἄγγελοι,
from them to – heaven the angels,

οἱ ποιμένες ἐλάλουν πρὸς ἀλλήλους·
the shepherds said to one another :

διέλθωμεν δὴ ἕως Βηθλέεμ καὶ ἴδωμεν
Let us go then unto Bethlehem and let us see

τὸ ῥῆμα τοῦτο τὸ γεγονὸς ὃ ὁ κύριος
– thing this – having happened which the Lord

ἐγνώρισεν ἡμῖν. 16 καὶ ἦλθαν σπεύσαντες,
made known to us. And they came hastening,

καὶ ἀνεῦραν τήν τε Μαριὰμ καὶ τὸν
and found – both Mary and –

Ἰωσὴφ καὶ τὸ βρέφος κείμενον ἐν τῇ
Joseph and the babe lying in the

φάτνῃ· 17 ἰδόντες δὲ ἐγνώρισαν περὶ τοῦ
manger; and seeing they made known concerning the

ῥήματος τοῦ λαληθέντος αὐτοῖς περὶ τοῦ
word – spoken to them concerning –

παιδίου τούτου. 18 καὶ πάντες οἱ ἀκούσαντες
child this. And all the [ones] hearing

ἐθαύμασαν περὶ τῶν λαληθέντων ὑπὸ τῶν
marvelled concerning the things spoken by the

ποιμένων πρὸς αὐτούς· 19 ἡ δὲ Μαρία
shepherds to them; – but Mary

πάντα συνετήρει τὰ ῥήματα ταῦτα συμβάλλουσα
²all ¹kept – ⁴things ³these pondering

ἐν τῇ καρδίᾳ αὐτῆς. 20 καὶ ὑπέστρεψαν
in the heart of her. And returned

οἱ ποιμένες δοξάζοντες καὶ αἰνοῦντες τὸν
the shepherds glorifying and praising –

θεὸν ἐπὶ πᾶσιν οἷς ἤκουσαν καὶ εἶδον
God at all things which they heard and saw

καθὼς ἐλαλήθη πρὸς αὐτούς.
as was spoken to them.

21 Καὶ ὅτε ἐπλήσθησαν ἡμέραι ὀκτὼ
And when were completed days eight

τοῦ περιτεμεῖν αὐτόν, καὶ ἐκλήθη τὸ
– to circumcise himᵈ, *and* was called the

ὄνομα αὐτοῦ Ἰησοῦς, τὸ κληθὲν ὑπὸ τοῦ
name of him Jesus, the [name] called by the

ἀγγέλου πρὸ τοῦ συλλημφθῆναι αὐτὸν ἐν
angel before the to be conceived himᵇ in
=he was conceived

τῇ κοιλίᾳ.
the womb.

22 Καὶ ὅτε ἐπλήσθησαν αἱ ἡμέραι τοῦ
And when were completed the days of the

καθαρισμοῦ αὐτῶν κατὰ τὸν νόμον
cleansing of them according to the law

brought him to Jerusalem, to present *him* to the Lord;

23 (As it is written in the law of the Lord, Every male that openeth the womb shall be called holy to the Lord;)

24 And to offer a sacrifice according to that which is said in the law of the Lord, A pair of turtledoves, or two young pigeons.

25 And, behold, there was a man in Jerusalem, whose name *was* Simeon; and the same man *was* just and devout, waiting for the consolation of Israel : and the Holy Ghost was upon him.

26 And it was revealed unto him by the Holy Ghost, that he should not see death, before he had seen the Lord's Christ.

27 And he came by the Spirit into the temple : and when the parents brought in the child Jesus, to do for him after the custom of the law,

28 Then took he him up in his arms, and blessed God, and said,

29 Lord, now lettest thou thy servant depart in peace, according to thy word :

30 For mine eyes have seen thy salvation,

Μωϋσέως, ἀνήγαγον αὐτὸν εἰς Ἱεροσόλυμα
of Moses, they took up him to Jerusalem

παραστῆσαι τῷ κυρίῳ, 23 καθὼς γέγραπται
to present to the Lord, as it has been written

ἐν νόμῳ κυρίου ὅτι πᾶν ἄρσεν διανοῖγον
in [the] law of the Lord[,] – Every male opening

μήτραν ἅγιον τῷ κυρίῳ κληθήσεται, 24 καὶ
a womb holy to the Lord shall be called, and

τοῦ δοῦναι θυσίαν κατὰ τὸ εἰρημένον ἐν
– to give[d] a sacrifice according to the thing said in

τῷ νόμῳ κυρίου, ζεῦγος τρυγόνων ἢ δύο
the law of [the] Lord, a pair of turtledoves or two

νοσσοὺς περιστερῶν. 25 Καὶ ἰδοὺ ἄνθρωπος
nestlings of doves. And behold[,] a man

ἦν ἐν Ἱερουσαλὴμ ᾧ ὄνομα Συμεών, καὶ
was in Jerusalem to whom name[c] Simeon, and
= whose name was

ὁ ἄνθρωπος οὗτος δίκαιος καὶ εὐλαβής,
– man this [was] just and devout,

προσδεχόμενος παράκλησιν τοῦ Ἰσραήλ, καὶ
expecting [the] consolation – of Israel, and

πνεῦμα ἦν ἅγιον ἐπ᾽ αὐτόν· 26 καὶ ἦν
¹[the] ³Spirit ⁴was ²Holy upon him; and it was

αὐτῷ κεχρηματισμένον ὑπὸ τοῦ πνεύματος
to him *having been* communicated by the Spirit

τοῦ ἁγίου μὴ ἰδεῖν θάνατον πρὶν ἢ ἂν
– Holy not to see death before

ἴδῃ τὸν χριστὸν κυρίου. 27 καὶ ἦλθεν
he should see the Christ of [the] Lord. And he came

ἐν τῷ πνεύματι εἰς τὸ ἱερόν· καὶ ἐν τῷ
by the Spirit into the temple; and in the
= as the(his) parents brought in

εἰσαγαγεῖν τοὺς γονεῖς τὸ παιδίον Ἰησοῦν
to bring in the parents[be] the child Jesus

τοῦ ποιῆσαι αὐτοὺς κατὰ τὸ εἰθισμένον
– to do them[bd] according to the custom
= for them to do

τοῦ νόμου περὶ αὐτοῦ, 28 καὶ αὐτὸς
of the law concerning him, *and* he

ἐδέξατο αὐτὸ εἰς τὰς ἀγκάλας καὶ
received him in the(his) arms and

εὐλόγησεν τὸν θεὸν καὶ εἶπεν· 29 νῦν
blessed – God and said : Now

ἀπολύεις τὸν δοῦλόν σου, δέσποτα, κατὰ
thou releasest the slave of thee, Master, according to

τὸ ῥῆμά σου ἐν εἰρήνῃ· 30 ὅτι εἶδον οἱ
the word of thee in peace; because saw the

ὀφθαλμοί μου τὸ σωτήριόν σου, 31 ὃ
eyes of me the salvation of thee, which

31 Which thou hast prepared before the face of all people;

32 A light to lighten the Gentiles, and the glory of thy people Israel.

33 And Joseph and his mother marvelled at those things which were spoken of him.

34 And Simeon blessed them, and said unto Mary his mother, Behold, this *child* is set for the fall and rising again of many in Israel; and for a sign which shall be spoken against;

35 (Yea, a sword shall pierce through thy own soul also,) that the thoughts of many hearts may be revealed.

36 And there was one Anna, a prophetess, the daughter of Phanuel, of the tribe of Aser : she was of a great age, and had lived with an husband seven years from her virginity;

37 And she *was* a widow of about fourscore and four years, which departed not from the temple, but served *God* with fastings and prayers night and day.

38 And she coming in that instant gave thanks likewise unto the Lord, and spake of him to all them that looked for redemption in Jerusalem.

ἡτοίμασας κατὰ πρόσωπον πάντων τῶν
thou didst prepare before [the] face of all the

λαῶν, 32 φῶς εἰς ἀποκάλυψιν ἐθνῶν καὶ
peoples, a light for a revelation of [the] nations and

δόξαν λαοῦ σου Ἰσραήλ. 33 καὶ ἦν
a glory of [the] people of thee Israel. And ⁷was(were)

ὁ πατὴρ αὐτοῦ καὶ ἡ μήτηρ θαυμάζοντες
¹the ²father ³of him ⁴and ⁵the ⁶mother ⁸marvelling

ἐπὶ τοῖς λαλουμένοις περὶ αὐτοῦ. 34 καὶ
at the things being said concerning him. And

εὐλόγησεν αὐτοὺς Συμεὼν καὶ εἶπεν πρὸς
blessed them Simeon and said to

Μαριὰμ τὴν μητέρα αὐτοῦ· ἰδοὺ οὗτος
Mary the mother of him : Behold[,] this

κεῖται εἰς πτῶσιν καὶ ἀνάστασιν πολλῶν
is set for fall and rising again of many

ἐν τῷ Ἰσραὴλ καὶ εἰς σημεῖον ἀντιλεγ-
in – Israel and for a sign spoken

όμενον — 35 καὶ σοῦ δὲ αὐτῆς τὴν ψυχὴν
against — and ⁵of thee ⁷also ⁶[thy]self ³the ⁴soul

διελεύσεται ῥομφαία—, ὅπως ἂν ἀποκαλυφθῶσιν
²will go through ¹a sword —, so as – may be revealed

ἐκ πολλῶν καρδιῶν διαλογισμοί. 36 Καὶ
of many hearts [the] thoughts. And

ἦν Ἄννα προφῆτις, θυγάτηρ Φανουήλ, ἐκ
there was Anna a prophetess, a daughter of Phanuel, of

φυλῆς Ἀσήρ· αὕτη προβεβηκυῖα ἐν ἡμέραις
[the] tribe of Asher; this having advanced in days

πολλαῖς, ζήσασα μετὰ ἀνδρὸς ἔτη ἑπτὰ
many, having lived with a husband years seven

ἀπὸ τῆς παρθενίας αὐτῆς, 37 καὶ αὐτὴ
from the virginity of her, and she [was]

χήρα ἕως ἐτῶν ὀγδοήκοντα τεσσάρων, ἣ
a widow until years eighty-four, who

οὐκ ἀφίστατο τοῦ ἱεροῦ νηστείαις καὶ
withdrew not from the temple with fastings and

δεήσεσιν λατρεύουσα νύκτα καὶ ἡμέραν.
petitionings serving night and day.

38 καὶ αὐτῇ τῇ ὥρᾳ ἐπιστᾶσα ἀνθωμολογεῖτο
And at the very hour* coming upon she gave thanks

τῷ θεῷ καὶ ἐλάλει περὶ αὐτοῦ πᾶσιν τοῖς
– to God and spoke about him to all the [ones]

προσδεχομένοις λύτρωσιν Ἰερουσαλήμ. 39 Καὶ
expecting redemption in Jerusalem. And

* Strictly, this construction should mean " the hour itself "; but the context demands " the same hour ". See 10. 7, 21; 12. 12; 13. 1, 31; 20. 19; 23. 12; 24. 13. " Luke seems to be the only N.T. writer who affects the construction " (C. F. D. Moule). See also Acts 16. 18; 22. 13. Of course there is not a great difference between " the hour itself ", " the very hour ", and " the same hour ".

39 And when they had performed all things according to the law of the Lord, they returned into Galilee, to their own city Nazareth.

40 And the child grew, and waxed strong in spirit, filled with wisdom : and the grace of God was upon him.

41 ¶ Now his parents went to Jerusalem every year at the feast of the passover.

42 And when he was twelve years old, they went up to Jerusalem after the custom of the feast.

43 And when they had fulfilled the days, as they returned, the child Jesus tarried behind in Jerusalem; and Joseph and his mother knew not *of it*.

44 But they, supposing him to have been in the company, went a day's journey; and they sought him among *their* kinsfolk and acquaintance.

45 And when they found him not, they turned back again to Jerusalem, seeking him.

46 And it came to pass, that after three days they found him in the temple, sitting in the midst of the doctors, both hearing them, and asking them questions.

47 And all that heard him were astonished at his understanding and answers.

48 And when they saw

ὡς ἐτέλεσαν πάντα τὰ κατὰ τὸν νόμον
when they finished all things – according to the law
κυρίου, ἐπέστρεψαν εἰς τὴν Γαλιλαίαν εἰς
of [the] Lord, they returned to – Galilee to
πόλιν ἑαυτῶν Ναζαρέθ.
a city of them*selves* Nazareth.

40 Τὸ δὲ παιδίον ηὔξανεν καὶ ἐκραταιοῦτο
And the child grew and became strong
πληρούμενον σοφίᾳ, καὶ χάρις θεοῦ ἦν ἐπ'
being filled with wisdom, and [the] grace of God was upon
αὐτό.
him.

41 Καὶ ἐπορεύοντο οἱ γονεῖς αὐτοῦ κατ'
And went the parents of him year
ἔτος εἰς Ἰερουσαλὴμ τῇ ἑορτῇ τοῦ πάσχα.
by year† to Jerusalem at the feast of the Passover.

42 Καὶ ὅτε ἐγένετο ἐτῶν δώδεκα, ἀναβαινόντων
And when he became of years twelve, going up
=as they went up
αὐτῶν κατὰ τὸ ἔθος τῆς ἑορτῆς, **43** καὶ
them[a] according to the custom of the feast, and
τελειωσάντων τὰς ἡμέρας, ἐν τῷ ὑποστρέφειν
fulfilling[a] the days, in the to return
=when they returned
αὐτοὺς ὑπέμεινεν Ἰησοῦς ὁ παῖς ἐν
them[b] 4remained 3Jesus 1the 2boy in
Ἰερουσαλήμ, καὶ οὐκ ἔγνωσαν οἱ γονεῖς
Jerusalem, and 4knew not 1the 2parents
αὐτοῦ. **44** νομίσαντες δὲ αὐτὸν εἶναι ἐν
3of him. But supposing him to be in
τῇ συνοδίᾳ ἦλθον ἡμέρας ὁδὸν καὶ ἀνεζήτουν
the company they went of a day a journey and sought
αὐτὸν ἐν τοῖς συγγενεῦσιν καὶ τοῖς
him among the(ir) relatives and the(ir)
γνωστοῖς, **45** καὶ μὴ εὑρόντες ὑπέστρεψαν
acquaintances, and not finding returned
εἰς Ἰερουσαλὴμ ἀναζητοῦντες αὐτόν. **46** καὶ
to Jerusalem seeking him. And
ἐγένετο μετὰ ἡμέρας τρεῖς εὗρον αὐτὸν
it came to pass after days three they found him
ἐν τῷ ἱερῷ καθεζόμενον ἐν μέσῳ τῶν
in the temple sitting in [the] midst of the
διδασκάλων καὶ ἀκούοντα αὐτῶν καὶ
teachers both hearing them and
ἐπερωτῶντα αὐτούς· **47** ἐξίσταντο δὲ πάντες
questioning them; and were astonished all
οἱ ἀκούοντες αὐτοῦ ἐπὶ τῇ συνέσει καὶ
the [ones] hearing him at the intelligence and
ταῖς ἀποκρίσεσιν αὐτοῦ. **48** καὶ ἰδόντες
the answers of him. And seeing

him, they were amazed : and his mother said unto him, Son, why hast thou thus dealt with us? behold, thy father and I have sought thee sorrowing.

49 And he said unto them, How is it that ye sought me? wist ye not that I must be about my Father's business?

50 And they understood not the saying which he spake unto them.

51 And he went down with them, and came to Nazareth, and was subject unto them : but his mother kept all these sayings in her heart.

52 And Jesus increased in wisdom and stature, and in favour with God and man.

αὐτὸν ἐξεπλάγησαν, καὶ εἶπεν πρὸς αὐτὸν
him   they were astounded,   and   said   to   him

ἡ μήτηρ αὐτοῦ· τέκνον, τί ἐποίησας ἡμῖν
the mother of him :   Child,   why didst thou   to us

οὕτως; ἰδοὺ ὁ πατήρ σου κἀγὼ ὀδυνώμενοι
thus? behold[,] the father of thee and I greatly distressed

ζητοῦμέν σε.   49 καὶ εἶπεν πρὸς αὐτούς·
are seeking thee.   And he said   to   them :

τί ὅτι ἐζητεῖτέ με; οὐκ ᾔδειτε ὅτι ἐν
Why [is it] that ye sought me? did ye not know that in
                                       =I

τοῖς τοῦ πατρός μου δεῖ εἶναί με;
the [affairs] of the Father of me it behoves to be me?
must be about my Father's business?

50 καὶ αὐτοὶ οὐ συνῆκαν τὸ ῥῆμα ὃ
   And   they   did not understand the   word which

ἐλάλησεν αὐτοῖς.   51 καὶ κατέβη μετ᾽
he spoke   to them.   And he went down with

αὐτῶν καὶ ἦλθεν εἰς Ναζαρέθ, καὶ ἦν
them   and came to   Nazareth,   and was

ὑποτασσόμενος αὐτοῖς.   καὶ ἡ μήτηρ
being subject   to them.   And the mother

αὐτοῦ διετήρει πάντα τὰ ῥήματα ἐν τῇ
of him carefully kept all   the   matters   in   the

καρδίᾳ αὐτῆς.   52 Καὶ Ἰησοῦς προέκοπτεν
heart   of her.   And   Jesus   progressed

ἐν τῇ σοφίᾳ καὶ ἡλικίᾳ καὶ χάριτι παρὰ
in   -   wisdom and   age   and favour before

θεῷ καὶ ἀνθρώποις.
God and   men.

CHAPTER 3

NOW in the fifteenth year of the reign of Tiberius Cæsar, Pontius Pilate being governor of Judæa, and Herod being tetrarch of Galilee, and his brother Philip tetrarch of Ituræa and of the region of Trachonitis, and Lysanias the tetrarch of Abilene,

2 Annas and Caiaphas being the high priests, the

3 Ἐν ἔτει δὲ πεντεκαιδεκάτῳ τῆς
  Now in [the] year   fifteenth   of the

ἡγεμονίας Τιβερίου Καίσαρος, ἡγεμονεύοντος
government of Tiberius   Cæsar,   governing
                             =while Pontius Pilate

Ποντίου Πιλάτου τῆς Ἰουδαίας, καὶ
Pontius   Pilate[a]   -   of Judæa,   and
was governing

τετρααρχοῦντος τῆς Γαλιλαίας Ἡρώδου,
ruling as tetrarch   of the   of Galilee   Herod,[a]
=while Herod was ruling as tetrarch of Galilee,

Φιλίππου δὲ τοῦ ἀδελφοῦ αὐτοῦ τετρα-
and Philip   the   brother   of him   ruling

αρχοῦντος τῆς Ἰτουραίας καὶ Τραχωνίτιδος
as tetrarch[a] [1]of the [2]of Ituræa [4]and [5]of Trachonitis

χώρας, καὶ Λυσανίου τῆς Ἀβιληνῆς
[3]country, and Lysanias   -   of Abilene

τετρααρχοῦντος,   2 ἐπὶ ἀρχιερέως Ἄννα
ruling as tetrarch[a],   in the time of [the] high priest Anna

word of God came unto John the son of Zacharias in the wilderness.

3 And he came into all the country about Jordan, preaching the baptism of repentance for the remission of sins;

4 As it is written in the book of the words of Esaias the prophet, saying, The voice of one crying in the wilderness, Prepare ye the way of the Lord, make his paths straight.

5 Every valley shall be filled, and every mountain and hill shall be brought low; and the crooked shall be made straight, and the rough ways *shall be* made smooth;

6 And all flesh shall see the salvation of God.

7 Then said he to the multitude that came forth to be baptized of him, O generation of vipers, who hath warned you to flee from the wrath to come?

8 Bring forth therefore fruits worthy of repentance, and begin not to say within yourselves, We have Abraham to *our* father: for I say unto you, That God is able of these stones to raise up children unto Abraham.

9 And now also the axe is laid unto the root of the trees : every tree therefore which bringeth not forth good fruit is hewn

καὶ Καϊαφᾶ, ἐγένετο ῥῆμα θεοῦ ἐπὶ Ἰωάννην
and Caiaphas,   came   a word of God to   John

τὸν Ζαχαρίου υἱὸν ἐν τῇ ἐρήμῳ. 3 καὶ
the of Zacharias son in the desert.   And

ἦλθεν εἰς πᾶσαν τὴν περίχωρον τοῦ
he came into   all   the neighbourhood of the

Ἰορδάνου κηρύσσων βάπτισμα μετανοίας
Jordan   proclaiming   a baptism   of repentance

εἰς ἄφεσιν ἁμαρτιῶν, 4 ὡς γέγραπται ἐν
for forgiveness of sins,   as it has been written in

βίβλῳ λόγων Ἡσαΐου τοῦ προφήτου·
[the] roll of [the] words of Esaias the   prophet :

φωνὴ βοῶντος ἐν τῇ ἐρήμῳ· ἑτοιμάσατε
Voice of [one] crying in the desert :   Prepare ye

τὴν ὁδὸν κυρίου, εὐθείας ποιεῖτε τὰς
the   way of [the] Lord, straight make   the

τρίβους αὐτοῦ· 5 πᾶσα φάραγξ πληρωθήσεται
paths   of him;   every valley shall be filled up

καὶ πᾶν ὄρος καὶ βουνὸς ταπεινωθήσεται,
and every mountain and hill   shall be laid low,

καὶ ἔσται τὰ σκολιὰ εἰς εὐθείας καὶ αἱ
and shall be the crooked [places] into straight [ones] and the

τραχεῖαι εἰς ὁδοὺς λείας· 6 καὶ ὄψεται
rough [places] into ways   smooth;   and [3]shall see

πᾶσα σὰρξ τὸ σωτήριον τοῦ θεοῦ.
[1]all [2]flesh the   salvation   -   of God.

7 Ἔλεγεν οὖν τοῖς ἐκπορευομένοις ὄχλοις
He said therefore to the [2]going out [1]crowds

βαπτισθῆναι ὑπ’ αὐτοῦ· γεννήματα ἐχιδνῶν,
to be baptized by   him :   Offspring of vipers,

τίς ὑπέδειξεν ὑμῖν φυγεῖν ἀπὸ τῆς
who warned   you to flee from the

μελλούσης ὀργῆς; 8 ποιήσατε οὖν καρποὺς
coming   wrath?   Produce therefore fruits

ἀξίους τῆς μετανοίας· καὶ μὴ ἄρξησθε
worthy   -   of repentance; and   do not begin

λέγειν ἐν ἑαυτοῖς· πατέρα ἔχομεν τὸν
to say among yourselves · Father we have   -

Ἀβραάμ· λέγω γὰρ ὑμῖν ὅτι δύναται ὁ
Abraham;   for I tell you that [2]can   -

θεὸς ἐκ τῶν λίθων τούτων ἐγεῖραι τέκνα
[1]God out of - stones these to raise children

τῷ Ἀβραάμ. 9 ἤδη δὲ καὶ ἡ ἀξίνη πρὸς
 - to Abraham. And [2]already [1]even the axe   at

τὴν ῥίζαν τῶν δένδρων κεῖται· πᾶν οὖν
the root of the trees   is laid ; [2]every [1]therefore

δένδρον μὴ ποιοῦν καρπὸν καλὸν
tree   not producing fruit   good

down, and cast into the fire.

10 And the people asked him, saying, What shall we do then?

11 He answereth and saith unto them, He that hath two coats, let him impart to him that hath none; and he that hath meat, let him do likewise.

12 Then came also publicans to be baptized, and said unto him, Master, what shall we do?

13 And he said unto them, Exact no more than that which is appointed you.

14 And the soldiers likewise demanded of him, saying, And what shall we do? And he said unto them, Do violence to no man, neither accuse *any* falsely; and be content with your wages.

15 ¶ And as the people were in expectation, and all men mused in their hearts of John, whether he were the Christ, or not;

16 John answered, saying unto *them* all, I indeed baptize you with water; but one mightier than I cometh, the latchet of whose shoes I am not worthy to unloose : he shall baptize you with the Holy Ghost and with fire :

17 Whose fan *is* in his hand, and he will throughly purge his floor, and will

ἐκκόπτεται καὶ εἰς πῦρ βάλλεται. 10 Καὶ
is being cut down and into fire is being cast. And

ἐπηρώτων αὐτὸν οἱ ὄχλοι λέγοντες· τί
asked him the crowds saying : What

οὖν ποιήσωμεν; 11 ἀποκριθεὶς δὲ ἔλεγεν
then may we do? And answering he told

αὐτοῖς· ὁ ἔχων δύο χιτῶνας μεταδότω
them : The [one] having two tunics let him impart

τῷ μὴ ἔχοντι, καὶ ὁ ἔχων βρώματα
to the [one] not having, and the [one] having foods

ὁμοίως ποιείτω. 12 ἦλθον δὲ καὶ τελῶναι
likewise let him do. And there came also tax-collectors

βαπτισθῆναι καὶ εἶπαν πρὸς αὐτόν·
to be baptized and they said to him :

διδάσκαλε, τί ποιήσωμεν; 13 ὁ δὲ εἶπεν
Teacher, what may we do? And he said

πρὸς αὐτούς· μηδὲν πλέον παρὰ τὸ
to them : Nothing more besides the [thing]

διατεταγμένον ὑμῖν πράσσετε. 14 ἐπηρώτων δὲ
having been commanded you do ye. And asked

αὐτὸν καὶ στρατευόμενοι λέγοντες· τί
him also men serving in the army saying : What

ποιήσωμεν καὶ ἡμεῖς; καὶ εἶπεν αὐτοῖς·
may do also we? And he told them :

μηδένα διασείσητε μηδὲ συκοφαντήσητε,
No one intimidate nor accuse falsely,

καὶ ἀρκεῖσθε τοῖς ὀψωνίοις ὑμῶν.
and be satisfied with the pay of you.

15 Προσδοκῶντος δὲ τοῦ λαοῦ καὶ
Now expecting the people[a] and
= while the people were expecting and all were debating

διαλογιζομένων πάντων ἐν ταῖς καρδίαις
debating all[a] in the hearts

αὐτῶν περὶ τοῦ Ἰωάννου, μήποτε αὐτὸς
of them concerning – John, perhaps he

εἴη ὁ χριστός, 16 ἀπεκρίνατο λέγων πᾶσιν
might be the Christ, [2]answered [3]saying [4]to all

ὁ Ἰωάννης· ἐγὼ μὲν ὕδατι βαπτίζω ὑμᾶς·
– [1]John : I indeed with water baptize you;

ἔρχεται δὲ ὁ ἰσχυρότερός μου, οὗ οὐκ
but there comes the [one] stronger of me, of whom not
= than I,

εἰμὶ ἱκανὸς λῦσαι τὸν ἱμάντα τῶν ὑποδημά-
I am competent to loosen the thong of the san-

των αὐτοῦ· αὐτὸς ὑμᾶς βαπτίσει ἐν
dals of him; he you will baptize with

πνεύματι ἁγίῳ καὶ πυρί· 17 οὗ τὸ πτύον
Spirit [the] Holy and fire; of whom the fan [is]

ἐν τῇ χειρὶ αὐτοῦ διακαθᾶραι τὴν ἅλωνα
in the hand of him thoroughly to cleanse the threshing-floor

gather the wheat into his garner; but the chaff he will burn with fire unquenchable.

18 And many other things in his exhortation preached he unto the people.

19 ¶ But Herod the tetrarch, being reproved by him for Herodias his brother Philip's wife, and for all the evils which Herod had done,

20 Added yet this above all, that he shut up John in prison.

21 ¶ Now when all the people were baptized, it came to pass, that Jesus also being baptized, and praying, the heaven was opened,

22 And the Holy Ghost descended in a bodily shape like a dove upon him, and a voice came from heaven, which said, Thou art my beloved Son; in thee I am well pleased.

23 ¶ And Jesus himself began to be about thirty years of age, being (as was supposed) the son of Joseph, which was *the son* of Heli,

24 Which was *the son* of Matthat, which was *the son* of Levi, which was *the son* of Melchi, which was *the son* of Janna, which was *the son* of Joseph,

25 Which was *the son* of Mattathias, which was *the son* of Amos, which was *the son* of Naum, which was *the son* of Esli, which was *the son* of Nagge,

26 Which was *the son* of Maath, which was *the son* of Mattathias, which was *the son* of Semei, which was *the son* of Joseph, which was *the son* of Juda,

αὐτοῦ καὶ συναγαγεῖν τὸν σῖτον εἰς τὴν
of him and to gather the wheat into the

ἀποθήκην αὐτοῦ, τὸ δὲ ἄχυρον κατακαύσει
barn of him, but the chaff he will burn up

πυρὶ ἀσβέστῳ. 18 Πολλὰ μὲν οὖν καὶ
with fire unquenchable. Many things indeed therefore and

ἕτερα παρακαλῶν εὐηγγελίζετο τὸν λαόν·
different exhorting he evangelized the people;

19 ὁ δὲ Ἡρῴδης ὁ τετραάρχης, ἐλεγχόμενος
– but Herod the tetrarch, being reproved

ὑπ' αὐτοῦ περὶ Ἡρῳδιάδος τῆς γυναικὸς
by him concerning Herodias the wife

τοῦ ἀδελφοῦ αὐτοῦ καὶ περὶ πάντων ὧν
of the brother of him and concerning [1]all [3]things [4]which

ἐποίησεν πονηρῶν ὁ Ἡρῴδης, 20 προσέθηκεν
[5]did [2]evil – [5]Herod, added

καὶ τοῦτο ἐπὶ πᾶσιν, κατέκλεισεν τὸν
also this above all, he shut up

Ἰωάννην ἐν φυλακῇ.
John in prison.

21 Ἐγένετο δὲ ἐν τῷ βαπτισθῆναι ἅπαντα
Now it came to pass in the to be baptized all
=when all the people were baptized

τὸν λαὸν καὶ Ἰησοῦ βαπτισθέντος καὶ
the people[be] and Jesus being baptized and
=as Jesus had been baptized and was praying

προσευχομένου ἀνεῳχθῆναι τὸν οὐρανὸν 22 καὶ
praying[a] to be opened the heaven and
=the heaven was opened and the Holy Spirit came down

καταβῆναι τὸ πνεῦμα τὸ ἅγιον σωματικῷ
to come down the Spirit – Holy[b] in a bodily

εἴδει ὡς περιστερὰν ἐπ' αὐτόν, καὶ φωνὴν
form as a dove upon him, and a voice

ἐξ οὐρανοῦ γενέσθαι· σὺ εἶ ὁ υἱός μου
out of heaven to come[b]: Thou art the Son of me

ὁ ἀγαπητός, ἐν σοὶ εὐδόκησα. 23 Καὶ
– beloved, in thee I was well pleased. And

αὐτὸς ἦν Ἰησοῦς ἀρχόμενος ὡσεὶ ἐτῶν
[3]himself [2]was [1]Jesus [4]beginning about years

τριάκοντα, ὢν υἱός, ὡς ἐνομίζετο, Ἰωσήφ,
thirty, being son, as was supposed, of Joseph,

τοῦ Ἡλὶ 24 τοῦ Ματθὰτ τοῦ Λευὶ τοῦ
– of Eli – of Matthat – of Levi –

Μελχὶ τοῦ Ἰανναὶ τοῦ Ἰωσὴφ 25 τοῦ
of Melchi – of Jannai – of Joseph –

Ματταθίου τοῦ Ἀμὼς τοῦ Ναοὺμ τοῦ
of Mattathias – of Amos – of Naum –

Ἑσλὶ τοῦ Ναγγαὶ 26 τοῦ Μάαθ τοῦ
of Hesli – of Naggai – of Maath –

27 Which was *the son of* Joanna, which was *the son* of Rhesa, which was *the son* of Zorobabel, which was *the son* of Salathiel, which was *the son* of Neri,
28 Which was *the son of* Melchi, which was *the son* of Addi, which was *the son* of Cosam, which was *the son* of Elmodam, which was *the son* of Er,
29 Which was *the son of* Jose, which was *the son of* Eliezer, which was *the son of* Jorim, which was *the son* of Matthat, which was *the son* of Levi,
30 Which was *the son of* Simeon, which was *the son* of Juda, which was *the son* of Joseph, which was *the son* of Jonan, which was *the son* of Eliakim,
31 Which was *the son of* Melea, which was *the son* of Menan, which was *the son* of Mattatha, which was *the son* of Nathan, which was *the son* of David,
32 Which was *the son of* Jesse, which was *the son of* Obed, which was *the son of* Booz, which was *the son of* Salmon, which was *the son* of Naasson,
33 Which was *the son* of Aminadab, which was *the son* of Aram, which was *the son* of Esrom, which was *the son* of Phares, which was *the son* of Juda,
34 Which was *the son* of Jacob, which was *the son* of Isaac, which was *the son* of Abraham, which was *the son* of Thara, which was *the son* of Nachor,
35 Which was *the son* of Saruch, which was *the son* of Ragau, which was *the son* of Phalec, which was *the son* of Heber,

Ματταθίου	τοῦ	Σεμεῖν	τοῦ	Ἰωσὴχ	τοῦ
of Mattathias	-	of Semein	-	of Josech	-
Ἰωδὰ 27	τοῦ	Ἰωανὰν	τοῦ	Ῥησὰ	τοῦ
of Jodah	-	of Joanan	-	of Rhesa	-
Ζοροβαβὲλ	τοῦ	Σαλαθιὴλ	τοῦ	Νηρὶ 28	τοῦ
of Zorobabel	-	of Salathiel	-	of Neri	-
Μελχὶ	τοῦ	Ἀδδὶ	τοῦ	Κωσὰμ	τοῦ
of Melchi	-	of Addi	-	of Kosam	-
Ἐλμαδὰμ	τοῦ	Ἢρ 29	τοῦ	Ἰησοῦ	τοῦ
of Elmadam	-	of Er	-	of Jesus	-
Ἐλιέζερ	τοῦ	Ἰωρὶμ	τοῦ	Μαθθὰτ	τοῦ
of Eliezer	-	of Jorim	-	of Matthat	-
Λευὶ 30	τοῦ	Συμεὼν	τοῦ	Ἰούδα	τοῦ
of Levi	-	of Simeon	-	of Juda	-
Ἰωσὴφ	τοῦ	Ἰωνὰμ	τοῦ	Ἐλιακὶμ 31	τοῦ
of Joseph	-	of Jonam	-	of Eliakim	-
Μελεὰ	τοῦ	Μεννὰ	τοῦ	Ματταθὰ	τοῦ
of Melea	-	of Menna	-	of Mattatha	-
Ναθὰμ	τοῦ	Δαυὶδ 32	τοῦ	Ἰεσσαὶ	τοῦ
of Natham	-	of David	-	of Jesse	-
Ἰωβὴδ	τοῦ	Βόος	τοῦ	Σάλα	τοῦ	Ναασσὼν
of Jobed	-	of Boos	-	of Sala	-	of Naasson
33 τοῦ	Ἀμιναδὰβ	τοῦ	Ἀδμὶν	τοῦ	Ἀρνὶ
-	of Aminadab	-	of Admin	-	of Arni
τοῦ	Ἐσρὼμ	τοῦ	Φάρες	τοῦ	Ἰούδα
-	of Hesrom	-	of Phares	-	of Juda
34 τοῦ	Ἰακὼβ	τοῦ	Ἰσαὰκ	τοῦ	Ἀβραὰμ
-	of Jacob	-	of Isaac	-	of Abraham
τοῦ	Θάρα	τοῦ	Ναχὼρ 35	τοῦ	Σεροὺχ
-	of Thara	-	of Nachor	-	of Seruch
τοῦ	Ῥαγαὺ	τοῦ	Φάλεκ	τοῦ	Ἔβερ	τοῦ
-	of Rhagau	-	of Phalek	-	of Eber	-
Σάλα 36	τοῦ	Καϊνὰμ	τοῦ	Ἀρφαξὰδ	τοῦ
of Sala	-	of Cainam	-	of Arphaxad	-
Σὴμ	τοῦ	Νῶε	τοῦ	Λάμεχ 37	τοῦ	Μαθουσάλα
of Sem	-	of Noe	-	of Lamech	-	of Mathusala
τοῦ	Ἐνὼχ	τοῦ	Ἰάρετ	τοῦ	Μαλελεὴλ
-	of Henoch	-	of Jaret	-	of Maleleel
τοῦ	Καϊνὰμ 38	τοῦ	Ἐνὼς	τοῦ	Σὴθ	τοῦ
-	of Cainam	-	of Enos	-	of Seth	-
Ἀδὰμ	τοῦ	θεοῦ.			
of Adam	-	of God.			

4 Ἰησοῦς	δὲ	πλήρης	πνεύματος	ἁγίου
And Jesus	full		of [the] [2]Spirit	[1]Holy
ὑπέστρεψεν	ἀπὸ	τοῦ	Ἰορδάνου,	καὶ	ἤγετο
returned	from	the	Jordan,	and	was led

which was *the son* of Sala,

36 Which was *the son* of Cainan, which was *the son* of Arphaxad, which was *the son* of Sem, which was *the son* of Noe, which was *the son* of Lamech,

37 Which was *the son* of Mathusala, which was *the son* of Enoch, which was *the son* of Jared, which was *the son* of Maleleel, which was *the son* of Cainan,

38 Which was *the son* of Enos, which was *the son* of Seth, which was *the son* of Adam, which was *the son* of God.

CHAPTER 4

AND Jesus being full of the Holy Ghost returned from Jordan, and was led by the Spirit into the wilderness,

2 Being forty days tempted of the devil. And in those days he did eat nothing: and when they were ended, he afterward hungered.

3 And the devil said unto him, If thou be the Son of God, command this stone that it be made bread.

4 And Jesus answered him, saying, It is written, That man shall not live by bread alone, but by every word of God.

5 And the devil, taking him up into an high mountain, shewed unto him all the kingdoms of the world in a moment of time.

6 And the devil said unto him, All this power will I give thee, and the glory of them: for that is

ἐν τῷ πνεύματι ἐν τῇ ἐρήμῳ 2 ἡμέρας
by the Spirit in the desert days

τεσσεράκοντα πειραζόμενος ὑπὸ τοῦ διαβόλου.
forty being tempted by the devil.

Καὶ οὐκ ἔφαγεν οὐδὲν ἐν ταῖς ἡμέραις
And he ate not no(any)thing in – days

ἐκείναις, καὶ συντελεσθεισῶν αὐτῶν ἐπεί-
those, and being ended them[a] he
                     =when they were ended

νασεν. 3 εἶπεν δὲ αὐτῷ ὁ διάβολος·
hungered. And said to him the devil:

εἰ υἱὸς εἶ τοῦ θεοῦ, εἰπὲ τῷ λίθῳ
If Son thou art – of God, tell – stone

τούτῳ ἵνα γένηται ἄρτος. 4 καὶ ἀπεκρίθη
this that it become a loaf. And made answer

πρὸς αὐτὸν ὁ Ἰησοῦς· γέγραπται ὅτι
to him – Jesus: It has been written[,] –

οὐκ ἐπ᾽ ἄρτῳ μόνῳ ζήσεται ὁ ἄνθρωπος.
Not on bread only shall live – man.

5 Καὶ ἀναγαγὼν αὐτὸν ἔδειξεν αὐτῷ πάσας
And leading up him he showed him all

τὰς βασιλείας τῆς οἰκουμένης ἐν στιγμῇ
the kingdoms of the inhabited earth in a moment

χρόνου. 6 καὶ εἶπεν αὐτῷ ὁ διάβολος·
of time. And said to him the devil:

σοὶ δώσω τὴν ἐξουσίαν ταύτην ἅπασαν καὶ
To thee I will give authority this all and

τὴν δόξαν αὐτῶν, ὅτι ἐμοὶ παραδέδοται
the glory of them, because to me it has been delivered

καὶ ᾧ ἐὰν θέλω δίδωμι αὐτήν· 7 σὺ οὖν
and to whomever I wish I give it; [a]thou [1]therefore

ἐὰν προσκυνήσῃς ἐνώπιον ἐμοῦ, ἔσται σοῦ
[2]if worship before me, will be of thee

πᾶσα. 8 καὶ ἀποκριθεὶς ὁ Ἰησοῦς εἶπεν
all. And answering – Jesus said

αὐτῷ· γέγραπται· προσκυνήσεις κύριον τὸν
to him: It has been written: Thou shalt worship [the] Lord the

θεόν σου καὶ αὐτῷ μόνῳ λατρεύσεις.
God of thee and him only shalt thou serve.

9 Ἤγαγεν δὲ αὐτὸν εἰς Ἰερουσαλὴμ καὶ
And he led him to Jerusalem and

ἔστησεν ἐπὶ τὸ πτερύγιον τοῦ ἱεροῦ, καὶ
set on the gable of the temple, and

εἶπεν αὐτῷ· εἰ υἱὸς εἶ τοῦ θεοῦ, βάλε
said to him: If Son thou art – of God, throw

σεαυτὸν ἐντεῦθεν κάτω· 10 γέγραπται γὰρ ὅτι
thyself hence down; for it has been written[,] –

τοῖς ἀγγέλοις αὐτοῦ ἐντελεῖται περὶ
The angels of him he will command concerning

delivered unto me; and to whomsoever I will I give it.

7 If thou therefore wilt worship me, all shall be thine.

8 And Jesus answered and said unto him, Get thee behind me, Satan: for it is written, Thou shalt worship the Lord thy God, and him only shalt thou serve.

9 And he brought him to Jerusalem, and set him on a pinnacle of the temple, and said unto him, If thou be the Son of God, cast thyself down from hence:

10 For it is written, He shall give his angels charge over thee, to keep thee:

11 And in *their* hands they shall bear thee up, lest at any time thou dash thy foot against a stone.

12 And Jesus answering said unto him, It is said, Thou shalt not tempt the Lord thy God.

13 And when the devil had ended all the temptation, he departed from him for a season.

14 ¶ And Jesus returned in the power of the Spirit into Galilee: and there went out a fame of him through all the region round about.

15 And he taught in their synagogues, being glorified of all.

16 ¶ And he came to Nazareth, where he had been brought up: and, as his custom was, he went into the synagogue on the sabbath day, and stood up for to read.

σοῦ τοῦ διαφυλάξαι σε, **11** καὶ ὅτι ἐπὶ
thee - ⹂ to preserve[d] thee,   and – on

χειρῶν ἀροῦσίν σε, μήποτε προσκόψῃς
[their] hands they will bear thee,   lest   thou dash

πρὸς λίθον τὸν πόδα σου. **12** καὶ
against a stone the   foot   of thee.   And

ἀποκριθεὶς εἶπεν αὐτῷ ὁ Ἰησοῦς ὅτι
answering   said   to him – Jesus[,]   –

εἴρηται· οὐκ ἐκπειράσεις κύριον τὸν
It has been said : Thou shalt not overtempt [the] Lord   the

θεόν σου. **13** Καὶ συντελέσας πάντα πειρασμὸν
God of thee.   And having finished   every   temptation

ὁ διάβολος ἀπέστη ἀπ’ αὐτοῦ ἄχρι καιροῦ.
the devil   went away from   him   until   a season.

14 Καὶ ὑπέστρεψεν ὁ Ἰησοῦς ἐν τῇ
And   returned   –   Jesus   in   the

δυνάμει τοῦ πνεύματος εἰς τὴν Γαλιλαίαν·
power of the   Spirit   to –   Galilee;

καὶ φήμη ἐξῆλθεν καθ’ ὅλης τῆς περιχώρου
and a rumour went forth throughout all the neighbourhood

περὶ αὐτοῦ. **15** καὶ αὐτὸς ἐδίδασκεν ἐν
concerning him.   And   he   taught   in

ταῖς συναγωγαῖς αὐτῶν, δοξαζόμενος ὑπὸ
the   synagogues   of them,   being glorified   by

πάντων.
all.

16 Καὶ ἦλθεν εἰς Ναζαρά, οὗ ἦν
And he came   to   Nazareth,   where   he was

τεθραμμένος, καὶ εἰσῆλθεν κατὰ τὸ εἰωθὸς
having been   and   entered   accord- the   custom
brought up,   ing to   =his custom

αὐτῷ ἐν τῇ ἡμέρᾳ τῶν σαββάτων εἰς τὴν
to him[c] on the   day   of the   sabbaths   into the

συναγωγήν, καὶ ἀνέστη ἀναγνῶναι. **17** καὶ
synagogue,   and   stood up   to read.   And

ἐπεδόθη αὐτῷ βιβλίον τοῦ προφήτου
was handed   to him   a roll   of the   prophet

Ἠσαΐου, καὶ ἀνοίξας τὸ βιβλίον εὗρεν
Esaias,   and having opened the   roll   he found

[τὸν] τόπον οὗ ἦν γεγραμμένον· **18** πνεῦμα
the   place where it was *having been* written : [The] Spirit

κυρίου ἐπ’ ἐμέ, οὗ εἵνεκεν ἔχρισέν με
of [the] Lord [is] upon me,   wherefore   he anointed   me

εὐαγγελίσασθαι πτωχοῖς, ἀπέσταλκέν με
to evangelize   [the] poor,   he has sent   me

κηρῦξαι αἰχμαλώτοις ἄφεσιν καὶ τυφλοῖς
to proclaim   to captives   release   and to blind [ones]

ἀνάβλεψιν, ἀποστεῖλαι τεθραυσμένους ἐν
sight,   to send away   *having been* crushed [ones] in

17 And there was delivered unto him the book of the prophet Esaias. And when he had opened the book, he found the place where it was written, 18 The Spirit of the Lord is upon me, because he hath anointed me to preach the gospel to the poor; he hath sent me to heal the brokenhearted, to preach deliverance to the captives, and recovering of sight to the blind, to set at liberty them that are bruised,

19 To preach the acceptable year of the Lord.

20 And he closed the book, and he gave it again to the minister, and sat down. And the eyes of all them that were in the synagogue were fastened on him.

21 And he began to say unto them, This day is this scripture fulfilled in your ears.

22 And all bare him witness, and wondered at the gracious words which proceeded out of his mouth. And they said, Is not this Joseph's son?

23 And he said unto them, Ye will surely say unto me this proverb, Physician, heal thyself: whatsoever we have heard done in Capernaum, do also here in thy country.

24 And he said, Verily I say unto you, No prophet is accepted in his own country.

25 But I tell you of a truth, many widows were in Israel in the days of Elias, when the heaven was shut up three years and six months, when great

ἀφέσει, 19 κηρῦξαι ἐνιαυτὸν κυρίου δεκτόν.
release,   to proclaim a year of [the] Lord acceptable.

20 καὶ πτύξας τὸ βιβλίον ἀποδοὺς τῷ
And having closed the roll returning [it] to the

ὑπηρέτῃ ἐκάθισεν· καὶ πάντων οἱ ὀφθαλμοὶ
attendant he sat; and of all the eyes

ἐν τῇ συναγωγῇ ἦσαν ἀτενίζοντες αὐτῷ.
in the synagogue were gazing at him.

21 ἤρξατο δὲ λέγειν πρὸς αὐτοὺς ὅτι
And he began to say to them [,]

σήμερον πεπλήρωται ἡ γραφὴ αὕτη ἐν
To-day has been fulfilled - scripture this in

τοῖς ὠσὶν ὑμῶν. 22 καὶ πάντες ἐμαρτύρουν
the ears of you. And all bore witness

αὐτῷ καὶ ἐθαύμαζον ἐπὶ τοῖς λόγοις τῆς
to him and marvelled at the words -

χάριτος τοῖς ἐκπορευομένοις ἐκ τοῦ στόματος
of grace - proceeding out of the mouth

αὐτοῦ, καὶ ἔλεγον· οὐχὶ υἱός ἐστιν Ἰωσὴφ
of him, and they said : ²not ⁴son ¹Is ⁵of Joseph

οὗτος; 23 καὶ εἶπεν πρὸς αὐτούς· πάντως
³this man? And he said to them : To be sure

ἐρεῖτέ μοι τὴν παραβολὴν ταύτην· ἰατρέ,
ye will say to me - parable this : Physician,

θεράπευσον σεαυτόν· ὅσα ἠκούσαμεν γεν-
heal thyself; what things we heard hap-

όμενα εἰς τὴν Καφαρναούμ, ποίησον καὶ
pening in - Capernaum, do also

ὧδε ἐν τῇ πατρίδι σου. 24 εἶπεν δέ·
here in the native place of thee. And he said :

ἀμὴν λέγω ὑμῖν ὅτι οὐδεὶς προφήτης
Truly I tell you that no prophet

δεκτός ἐστιν ἐν τῇ πατρίδι αὐτοῦ. 25 ἐπ’
acceptable is in the native place of him. ²on(in)

ἀληθείας δὲ λέγω ὑμῖν, πολλαὶ χῆραι ἦσαν
³truth ¹But I tell you. many widows were

ἐν ταῖς ἡμέραις Ἠλίου ἐν τῷ Ἰσραήλ,
in the days of Elias in - Israel.

ὅτε ἐκλείσθη ὁ οὐρανὸς ἐπὶ ἔτη τρία καὶ
when was shut up the heaven over years three and

μῆνας ἕξ, ὡς ἐγένετο λιμὸς μέγας ἐπὶ
months six, when came famine a great over

πᾶσαν τὴν γῆν, 26 καὶ πρὸς οὐδεμίαν
all the land, and to not one

αὐτῶν ἐπέμφθη Ἠλίας εἰ μὴ εἰς Σάρεπτα
of them was sent Elias except to Sarepta

τῆς Σιδωνίας πρὸς γυναῖκα χήραν. 27 καὶ
- of Sidon to a woman a widow. And

famine was throughout all the land;

26 But unto none of them was Elias sent, save unto Sarepta, *a city* of Sidon, unto a woman *that was* a widow.

27 And many lepers were in Israel in the time of Eliseus the prophet; and none of them was cleansed, saving Naaman the Syrian.

28 And all they in the synagogue, when they heard these things, were filled with wrath,

29 And rose up, and thrust him out of the city, and led him unto the brow of the hill whereon their city was built, that they might cast him down headlong.

30 But he passing through the midst of them went his way,

31 And came down to Capernaum, a city of Galilee, and taught them on the sabbath days.

32 And they were astonished at his doctrine: for his word was with power.

33 ¶ And in the synagogue there was a man, which had a spirit of an unclean devil, and cried out with a loud voice,

34 Saying, Let *us* alone; what have we to do with thee, *thou* Jesus of Nazareth? art thou come to destroy us? I know thee who thou art; the Holy One of God.

35 And Jesus rebuked him, saying, Hold thy peace, and come out of him. And when the devil had thrown him in the midst, he came out of him, and hurt him not.

πολλοὶ λεπροὶ ἦσαν ἐν τῷ Ἰσραὴλ ἐπὶ
many   lepers   were   in   –   Israel   during

Ἐλισαίου τοῦ προφήτου, καὶ οὐδεὶς αὐτῶν
Elisæus   the   prophet,   and   not one   of them

ἐκαθαρίσθη εἰ μὴ Ναιμὰν ὁ Σύρος.
was cleansed   except   Naaman   the   Syrian.

28 καὶ ἐπλήσθησαν πάντες θυμοῦ ἐν τῇ
And   [2]were filled   [1]all   of(with) anger   in   the

συναγωγῇ ἀκούοντες ταῦτα, **29** καὶ ἀναστάντες
synagogue   hearing   these things,   and   rising up

ἐξέβαλον αὐτὸν ἔξω τῆς πόλεως, καὶ
they cast *out*   him   outside   the   city,   and

ἤγαγον αὐτὸν ἕως ὀφρύος τοῦ ὄρους ἐφ᾽
led   him   to   a brow   of the   hill   on

οὗ ἡ πόλις ᾠκοδόμητο αὐτῶν, ὥστε
which   the   city   was built   of them,   so as

κατακρημνίσαι αὐτόν· **30** αὐτὸς δὲ διελθὼν
to throw down   him;   but he   passing *through*

διὰ μέσου αὐτῶν ἐπορεύετο.
through [the] midst   of them   went.

31 Καὶ κατῆλθεν εἰς Καφαρναοὺμ πόλιν
And   he went down   to   Capernaum   a city

τῆς Γαλιλαίας. καὶ ἦν διδάσκων αὐτοὺς
of Galilee.   And he was   teaching   them

ἐν τοῖς σάββασιν· **32** καὶ ἐξεπλήσσοντο
on   the   sabbaths;   and   they were astounded

ἐπὶ τῇ διδαχῇ αὐτοῦ, ὅτι ἐν ἐξουσίᾳ
at   the   teaching   of him,   because   with   authority

ἦν ὁ λόγος αὐτοῦ. **33** καὶ ἐν τῇ συναγωγῇ
was   the word   of him.   And   in   the   synagogue

ἦν ἄνθρωπος ἔχων πνεῦμα δαιμονίου
there was   a man   having   a spirit   [2]demon

ἀκαθάρτου, καὶ ἀνέκραξεν φωνῇ μεγάλῃ·
[1]of an unclean,   and   he shouted   voice   with a great :

34 ἔα, τί ἡμῖν καὶ σοί, Ἰησοῦ Ναζαρηνέ;
Ah,   what   to us   and   to thee,   Jesus   Nazarene?

ἦλθες ἀπολέσαι ἡμᾶς; οἶδά σε τίς εἶ,
Camest thou   to destroy   us?   I know   thee   who thou art,

ὁ ἅγιος τοῦ θεοῦ. **35** καὶ ἐπετίμησεν αὐτῷ
the holy one   –   of God.   And   rebuked   him

ὁ Ἰησοῦς λέγων· φιμώθητι καὶ ἔξελθε
–   Jesus   saying :   Be muzzled   and   come out

ἀπ᾽ αὐτοῦ. καὶ ῥῖψαν αὐτὸν τὸ δαιμόνιον
from   him.   And   [3]throwing   [4]him   [1]the   [2]demon

εἰς τὸ μέσον ἐξῆλθεν ἀπ᾽ αὐτοῦ μηδὲν
in   the   midst   came out   from   him   nothing

βλάψαν αὐτόν. **36** καὶ ἐγένετο θάμβος
injuring   him.   And   came   astonishment

36 And they were all amazed, and spake among themselves, saying, What a word *is* this! for with authority and power he commandeth the unclean spirits, and they come out.

37 And the fame of him went out into every place of the country round about.

38 ¶ And he arose out of the synagogue, and entered into Simon's house. And Simon's wife's mother was taken with a great fever; and they besought him for her.

39 And he stood over her, and rebuked the fever; and it left her: and immediately she arose and ministered unto them.

40 ¶ Now when the sun was setting, all they that had any sick with divers diseases brought them unto him; and he laid his hands on every one of them, and healed them.

41 And devils also came out of many, crying out, and saying, Thou art Christ the Son of God. And he rebuking *them* suffered them not to speak: for they knew that he was Christ.

42 And when it was day, he departed and went into a desert place: and the people sought him,

---

ἐπὶ πάντας, καὶ συνελάλουν πρὸς ἀλλήλους
on all, and they spoke to one another

λέγοντες· τίς ὁ λόγος οὗτος, ὅτι ἐν
saying : What [is] – word this, because with

ἐξουσίᾳ καὶ δυνάμει ἐπιτάσσει τοῖς
authority and power he commands the

ἀκαθάρτοις πνεύμασιν καὶ ἐξέρχονται; 37 καὶ
unclean spirits and they come out? And

ἐξεπορεύετο ἦχος περὶ αὐτοῦ εἰς πάντα
went forth a rumour concerning him into every

τόπον τῆς περιχώρου. 38 Ἀναστὰς δὲ
place of the neighbourhood. And rising up

ἀπὸ τῆς συναγωγῆς εἰσῆλθεν εἰς τὴν
from the synagogue he entered into the

οἰκίαν Σίμωνος. πενθερὰ δὲ τοῦ Σίμωνος
house of Simon. And [the] mother-in-law – of Simon

ἦν συνεχομένη πυρετῷ μεγάλῳ, καὶ
was being seized fever with a great, and

ἠρώτησαν αὐτὸν περὶ αὐτῆς. 39 καὶ
they ask him about her. And

ἐπιστὰς ἐπάνω αὐτῆς ἐπετίμησεν τῷ πυρετῷ,
standing over her he rebuked the fever,

καὶ ἀφῆκεν αὐτήν· παραχρῆμα δὲ ἀναστᾶσα
and it left her; and at once rising up

διηκόνει αὐτοῖς. 40 Δύνοντος δὲ τοῦ
she served them. And setting the
= as the sun was setting

ἡλίου ἅπαντες ὅσοι εἶχον ἀσθενοῦντας
sun[a] all as many as had ailing [ones]

νόσοις ποικίλαις ἤγαγον αὐτοὺς πρὸς αὐτόν·
diseases with various brought them to him;

ὁ δὲ ἑνὶ ἑκάστῳ αὐτῶν τὰς χεῖρας
and he [5]one [4]on each [6]of them [2]the(his) [3]hands

ἐπιτιθεὶς ἐθεράπευεν αὐτούς. 41 ἐξήρχετο
[1]putting on healed them. came out

δὲ καὶ δαιμόνια ἀπὸ πολλῶν, κραυγάζοντα
And also demons from many, crying out

καὶ λέγοντα ὅτι σὺ εἶ ὁ υἱὸς τοῦ θεοῦ.
and saying[,] – Thou art the Son – of God.

καὶ ἐπιτιμῶν οὐκ εἴα αὐτὰ λαλεῖν, ὅτι
And rebuking he allowed not them to speak, because

ᾔδεισαν τὸν χριστὸν αὐτὸν εἶναι. 42 Γενομένης
they knew [3]the [4]Christ [1]him [2]to be. coming
= And when

δὲ ἡμέρας ἐξελθὼν ἐπορεύθη εἰς ἔρημον
And day[a] going forth he went to a desert
day came

τόπον· καὶ οἱ ὄχλοι ἐπεζήτουν αὐτόν, καὶ
place; and the crowds sought him, and

and came unto him, and stayed him, that he should not depart from them.

43 And he said unto them, I must preach the kingdom of God to other cities also: for therefore am I sent.

44 And he preached in the synagogues of Galilee.

ἦλθον ἕως αὐτοῦ, καὶ κατεῖχον αὐτὸν
came   up ⁱo   him,   and   detained   him

τοῦ μὴ πορεύεσθαι ἀπ' αὐτῶν. 43 ὁ δὲ
–   not   to goᵈ   from   them.   43   And he
=so that he should not go

εἶπεν πρὸς αὐτοὺς ὅτι καὶ ταῖς ἑτέραις
said   to   them[,]   –   Also to the   other

πόλεσιν εὐαγγελίσασθαί με δεῖ τὴν
cities   ³to preach   ²me   ¹it behoves   the

βασιλείαν τοῦ θεοῦ, ὅτι ἐπὶ τοῦτο ἀπεστάλην.
kingdom   – of God, because on   this   I was sent.

44 καὶ ἦν κηρύσσων εἰς τὰς συναγωγὰς
    And   he was   proclaiming   in   the   synagogues

τῆς Ἰουδαίας.
–   of Judæa.

CHAPTER 5

AND it came to pass, that, as the people pressed upon him to hear the word of God, he stood by the lake of Gennesaret,

2 And saw two ships standing by the lake: but the fishermen were gone out of them, and were washing *their* nets.

3 And he entered into one of the ships, which was Simon's, and prayed him that he would thrust out a little from the land. And he sat down, and taught the people out of the ship.

4 Now when he had left speaking, he said unto Simon, Launch out into the deep, and let down your nets for a draught.

5 And Simon answering said unto him, Master, we have toiled all the night, and have taken nothing: nevertheless at thy word I will let down the net.

5 Ἐγένετο δὲ ἐν τῷ τὸν ὄχλον ἐπικεῖσθαι
   Now it came to pass   in   the   the   crowd   to press upon
       =as the crowd pressed upon him and heard

αὐτῷ καὶ ἀκούειν τὸν λόγον τοῦ θεοῦ,
him   and   to hearᵇᵉ   the   word   –   of God,

καὶ αὐτὸς ἦν ἑστὼς παρὰ τὴν λίμνην
and   he   was   standing   by   the   lake

Γεννησαρέτ, **2** καὶ εἶδεν δύο πλοιάρια
Gennesaret,   and   saw   two   boats

ἑστῶτα παρὰ τὴν λίμνην· οἱ δὲ ἀλεεῖς
standing   by   the   lake;   but the   fishermen

ἀπ' αὐτῶν ἀποβάντες ἔπλυνον τὰ δίκτυα.
from   them   having gone away were washing   the   nets.

3 ἐμβὰς δὲ εἰς ἓν τῶν πλοίων, ὃ ἦν
  And embarking   in   one of the   boats,   which was

Σίμωνος, ἠρώτησεν αὐτὸν ἀπὸ τῆς γῆς
of Simon,   he asked   him   from   the   land

ἐπαναγαγεῖν ὀλίγον· καθίσας δὲ ἐκ τοῦ
to put out   a little;   and sitting   ⁴out of   ⁵the

πλοίου ἐδίδασκεν τοὺς ὄχλους. **4** ὡς δὲ
⁶boat   ¹he taught   ²the   ³crowds.   4   And when

ἐπαύσατο λαλῶν, εἶπεν πρὸς τὸν Σίμωνα·
he ceased   speaking,   he said   to   –   Simon :

ἐπανάγαγε εἰς τὸ βάθος, καὶ χαλάσατε
Put out   into   the   deep,   and   let down

τὰ δίκτυα ὑμῶν εἰς ἄγραν. **5** καὶ
the   nets   of you   for   a draught.   5   And

ἀποκριθεὶς Σίμων εἶπεν· ἐπιστάτα, δι'
answering   Simon   said :   Master,   through

ὅλης νυκτὸς κοπιάσαντες οὐδὲν ἐλάβομεν·
[the] whole night   labouring   nothing   we took;

ἐπὶ δὲ τῷ ῥήματί σου χαλάσω τὰ δίκτυα.
but at   the   word   of thee I will let down   the   nets.

6 And when they had this done, they inclosed a great multitude of fishes: and their net brake.

7 And they beckoned unto *their* partners, which were in the other ship, that they should come and help them. And they came, and filled both the ships, so that they began to sink.

8 When Simon Peter saw *it*, he fell down at Jesus' knees, saying, Depart from me; for I am a sinful man, O Lord.

9 For he was astonished, and all that were with him, at the draught of the fishes which they had taken:

10 And so *was* also James, and John, the sons of Zebedee, which were partners with Simon. And Jesus said unto Simon, Fear not; from henceforth thou shalt catch men.

11 And when they had brought their ships to land, they forsook all, and followed him.

12 ¶ And it came to pass, when he was in a certain city, behold a man full of leprosy: who seeing Jesus fell on *his* face, and besought him, saying, Lord, if thou wilt, thou canst make me clean.

6 καὶ τοῦτο ποιήσαντες συνέκλεισαν πλῆθος
And this doing they enclosed multitude

ἰχθύων πολύ· διερρήσσετο δὲ τὰ δίκτυα
of fishes a much; and were being torn the nets

αὐτῶν. 7 καὶ κατένευσαν τοῖς μετόχοις
of them. And they nodded to the(ir) partners

ἐν τῷ ἑτέρῳ πλοίῳ τοῦ ἐλθόντας
in the other boat – coming
= that they should come

συλλαβέσθαι αὐτοῖς· καὶ ἦλθαν, καὶ ἔπλησαν
to help[d] them; and they came, and filled

ἀμφότερα τὰ πλοῖα ὥστε βυθίζεσθαι αὐτά.
both the boats so as to be sinking them.[b]
= so that they were sinking.

8 ἰδὼν δὲ Σίμων Πέτρος προσέπεσεν τοῖς
And seeing Simon Peter fell at the

γόνασιν Ἰησοῦ λέγων· ἔξελθε ἀπ' ἐμοῦ,
knees of Jesus saying: Depart from me,

ὅτι ἀνὴρ ἁμαρτωλός εἰμι, κύριε. 9 θάμβος
because man a sinful I am, Lord. astonishment

γὰρ περιέσχεν αὐτὸν καὶ πάντας τοὺς
For seized him and all the [ones]

σὺν αὐτῷ ἐπὶ τῇ ἄγρᾳ τῶν ἰχθύων ᾗ
with him at the draught of the fishes which

συνέλαβον, 10 ὁμοίως δὲ καὶ Ἰάκωβον καὶ
they took, and likewise both James and

Ἰωάννην υἱοὺς Ζεβεδαίου, οἳ ἦσαν κοινωνοὶ
John sons of Zebedee, who were sharers

τῷ Σίμωνι. καὶ εἶπεν πρὸς τὸν Σίμωνα
– with Simon. And said to – Simon

ὁ Ἰησοῦς· μὴ φοβοῦ· ἀπὸ τοῦ νῦν
– Jesus: Fear thou not; from – now

ἀνθρώπους ἔσῃ ζωγρῶν. 11 καὶ καταγαγόντες
men thou wilt be taking alive. And bringing down

τὰ πλοῖα ἐπὶ τὴν γῆν, ἀφέντες πάντα
the boats onto the land, leaving all things

ἠκολούθησαν αὐτῷ.
they followed him.

12 Καὶ ἐγένετο ἐν τῷ εἶναι αὐτὸν ἐν
And it came to pass in the to be him[be] in
= as he was

μιᾷ τῶν πόλεων καὶ ἰδοὺ ἀνὴρ πλήρης
one of the cities and behold[,] a man full

λέπρας· ἰδὼν δὲ τὸν Ἰησοῦν, πεσὼν ἐπὶ
of leprosy; and seeing – Jesus, falling on

πρόσωπον ἐδεήθη αὐτοῦ λέγων· κύριε,
[his] face he begged him saying: Lord,

ἐὰν θέλῃς, δύνασαί με καθαρίσαι. 13 καὶ
if thou willest, thou canst me *to* cleanse. And

13 And he put forth *his* hand, and touched him, saying, I will: be thou clean. And immediately the leprosy departed from him.

14 And he charged him to tell no man: but go, and shew thyself to the priest, and offer for thy cleansing, according as Moses commanded, for a testimony unto them.

15 But so much the more went there a fame abroad of him: and great multitudes came together to hear, and to be healed by him of their infirmities.

16 And he withdrew himself into the wilderness, and prayed.

17 ¶ And it came to pass on a certain day, as he was teaching, that there were Pharisees and doctors of the law sitting by, which were come out of every town of Galilee, and Judæa, and Jerusalem: and the power of the Lord was *present* to heal them.

18 ¶ And, behold, men brought in a bed a man which was taken with a palsy: and they sought *means* to bring him in, and to lay *him* before him.

19 And when they could not find by what *way* they might bring him in because of the multitude, they went upon the housetop, and let him down

---

ἐκτείνας   τὴν   χεῖρα   ἥψατο   αὐτοῦ λέγων·
stretching out ˉthe(his) hand   he touched   him   saying :

θέλω,   καθαρίσθητι·   καὶ   εὐθέως   ἡ λέπρα
I am willing, be thou cleansed; and immediately the leprosy

ἀπῆλθεν ἀπ' αὐτοῦ.   14 καὶ αὐτὸς παρήγγειλεν
departed from him.   And   he   charged

αὐτῷ   μηδενὶ   εἰπεῖν,   ἀλλὰ   ἀπελθὼν δεῖξον
him   no one   to tell,   but   going away show

σεαυτὸν   τῷ   ἱερεῖ,   καὶ   προσένεγκε   περὶ
thyself   to the   priest,   and   offer   concerning

τοῦ   καθαρισμοῦ   σου   καθὼς   προσέταξεν
the   cleansing   of thee   as   commanded

Μωϋσῆς, εἰς μαρτύριον αὐτοῖς.   15 διήρχετο
Moses,   for   a testimony   to them.   went

δὲ   μᾶλλον   ὁ   λόγος   περὶ   αὐτοῦ,   καὶ
But   rather   the   word   concerning   him,   and

συνήρχοντο   ὄχλοι   πολλοὶ   ἀκούειν καὶ
²accompanied   ²crowds   ¹many   to hear   and

θεραπεύεσθαι   ἀπὸ   τῶν   ἀσθενειῶν αὐτῶν·
to be healed   from   the   infirmities   of them;

16 αὐτὸς   δὲ   ἦν ὑποχωρῶν ἐν ταῖς ἐρήμοις
but he   was   withdrawing   in   the   deserts

καὶ   προσευχόμενος.
and   praying.

17 Καὶ ἐγένετο ἐν μιᾷ τῶν ἡμερῶν καὶ
    And it came to pass on one of the days *and*

αὐτὸς ἦν διδάσκων, καὶ ἦσαν καθήμενοι
he   was   teaching,   and were   sitting

Φαρισαῖοι   καὶ   νομοδιδάσκαλοι οἳ ἦσαν
Pharisees   and   law-teachers   who   were

ἐληλυθότες ἐκ πάσης κώμης τῆς Γαλιλαίας
having come   out of   every   village   –   of Galilee

καὶ Ἰουδαίας καὶ Ἰερουσαλήμ· καὶ δύναμις
and   Judæa   and   Jerusalem;   and [the] power

κυρίου   ἦν   εἰς   τὸ   ἰᾶσθαι αὐτόν.   18 καὶ
of [the] Lord was   ¹in   –   ²to cure   ³him.   And

ἰδοὺ ἄνδρες φέροντες ἐπὶ κλίνης ἄνθρωπον
behold[,] men   bearing   on   a couch   a man

ὃς ἦν παραλελυμένος, καὶ ἐζήτουν αὐτὸν
who was *having been* paralysed, and they sought   ²him

εἰσενεγκεῖν   καὶ   θεῖναι   [αὐτὸν] ἐνώπιον
¹to carry in   and   to lay   him   before

αὐτοῦ.   19 καὶ μὴ εὑρόντες ποίας εἰσ-
him.   And not finding how† they

ἐνέγκωσιν αὐτὸν διὰ τὸν ὄχλον, ἀναβάντες
might carry in   him because of the   crowd,   going up

ἐπὶ τὸ δῶμα διὰ τῶν κεράμων καθῆκαν
onto the   roof   through the   tiles   they let down

through the tiling with *his* couch into the midst before Jesus.

20 And when he saw their faith, he said unto him, Man, thy sins are forgiven thee.

21 And the scribes and the Pharisees began to reason, saying, Who is this which speaketh blasphemies? Who can forgive sins, but God alone?

22 But when Jesus perceived their thoughts, he answering said unto them, What reason ye in your hearts?

23 Whether is easier, to say, Thy sins be forgiven thee; or to say, Rise up and walk?

24 But that ye may know that the Son of man hath power upon earth to forgive sins, (he said unto the sick of the palsy,) I say unto thee, Arise, and take up thy couch, and go into thine house.

25 And immediately he rose up before them, and took up that whereon he lay, and departed to his own house, glorifying God.

26 And they were all amazed, and they glorified God, and were filled with fear, saying, We have seen strange things to day.

27 ¶ And after these things he went forth, and

αὐτὸν σὺν τῷ κλινιδίῳ εἰς τὸ μέσον
him with the couch into the midst

ἔμπροσθεν τοῦ Ἰησοῦ. 20 καὶ ἰδὼν τὴν
in front of – Jesus. And seeing the

πίστιν αὐτῶν εἶπεν· ἄνθρωπε, ἀφέωνταί
faith of them he said : Man, have been forgiven

σοι αἱ ἁμαρτίαι σου. 21 καὶ ἤρξαντο
thee the sins of thee. And began

διαλογίζεσθαι οἱ γραμματεῖς καὶ οἱ Φαρισαῖοι
to reason the scribes and the Pharisees

λέγοντες· τίς ἐστιν οὗτος ὃς λαλεῖ
saying : Who is this man who speaks

βλασφημίας; τίς δύναται ἁμαρτίας ἀφεῖναι
blasphemies? Who can sins to forgive

εἰ μὴ μόνος ὁ θεός; 22 ἐπιγνοὺς δὲ ὁ
except only – God? But knowing –

Ἰησοῦς τοὺς διαλογισμοὺς αὐτῶν, ἀποκριθεὶς
Jesus the reasonings of them, answering

εἶπεν πρὸς αὐτούς· τί διαλογίζεσθε ἐν
said to them : Why reason ye in

ταῖς καρδίαις ὑμῶν; 23 τί ἐστιν εὐκοπώτερον,
the hearts of you? What is easier,

εἰπεῖν· ἀφέωνταί σοι αἱ ἁμαρτίαι σου, ἢ
to say : Have been forgiven thee the sins of thee, or

εἰπεῖν· ἔγειρε καὶ περιπάτει; 24 ἵνα δὲ
to say : Rise and walk ? but that

εἰδῆτε ὅτι ὁ υἱὸς τοῦ ἀνθρώπου ἐξουσίαν
ye may know that the Son – of man authority

ἔχει ἐπὶ τῆς γῆς ἀφιέναι ἁμαρτίας, —
has on the earth to forgive sins, —

εἶπεν τῷ παραλελυμένῳ· σοὶ λέγω, ἔγειρε
he said to the paralysed [one] : To thee I say, rise

καὶ ἄρας τὸ κλινίδιόν σου πορεύου εἰς
and taking the pallet of thee go to

τὸν οἶκόν σου. 25 καὶ παραχρῆμα ἀναστὰς
the house of thee. And at once rising up

ἐνώπιον αὐτῶν, ἄρας ἐφ᾽ ὃ κατέκειτο,
before them, taking [that] on which he was lying,

ἀπῆλθεν εἰς τὸν οἶκον αὐτοῦ δοξάζων τὸν
he went away to the house of him glorifying –

θεόν. 26 καὶ ἔκστασις ἔλαβεν ἅπαντας, καὶ
God. And bewilderment took all, and

ἐδόξαζον τὸν θεόν, καὶ ἐπλήσθησαν φόβου
they glorified – God, and were filled of(with) fear

λέγοντες ὅτι εἴδομεν παράδοξα σήμερον.
saying[,] We saw wonderful things to-day.

27 Καὶ μετὰ ταῦτα ἐξῆλθεν, καὶ ἐθεάσατο
And after these things he went forth, and saw

saw a publican, named Levi, sitting at the receipt of custom: and he said unto him, Follow me.

28 And he left all, rose up, and followed him.

29 And Levi made him a great feast in his own house: and there was a great company of publicans and of others that sat down with them.

30 But their scribes and Pharisees murmured against his disciples, saying, Why do ye eat and drink with publicans and sinners?

31 And Jesus answering said unto them, They that are whole need not a physician; but they that are sick.

32 I came not to call the righteous, but sinners to repentance.

33 ¶ And they said unto him, Why do the disciples of John fast often, and make prayers, and likewise *the disciples* of the Pharisees; but thine eat and drink?

34 And he said unto them, Can ye make the children of the bride-chamber fast, while the bridegroom is with them?

35 But the days will come, when the bridegroom shall be taken away from them, and then shall they fast in those days.

τελώνην ὀνόματι Λευὶν καθήμενον ἐπὶ τὸ
a tax-collector by name Levi sitting on(in) the

τελώνιον, καὶ εἶπεν αὐτῷ· ἀκολούθει μοι.
custom house, and said to him: Follow me.

28 καὶ καταλιπὼν πάντα ἀναστὰς ἠκολούθει
And abandoning all things rising up he followed

αὐτῷ. **29** Καὶ ἐποίησεν δοχὴν μεγάλην
him. And ²made ⁴feast ³a great

Λευὶς αὐτῷ ἐν τῇ οἰκίᾳ αὐτοῦ· καὶ ἦν
¹Levi for him in the house of him; and there was

ὄχλος πολὺς τελωνῶν καὶ ἄλλων οἳ ἦσαν
crowd a much of tax-collectors and of others who were

μετ' αὐτῶν κατακείμενοι. **30** καὶ ἐγόγγυζον
²with ³them ¹reclining. And grumbled

οἱ Φαρισαῖοι καὶ οἱ γραμματεῖς αὐτῶν
the Pharisees and the scribes of them

πρὸς τοὺς μαθητὰς αὐτοῦ λέγοντες· διὰ
at the disciples of him saying: Why

τί μετὰ τῶν τελωνῶν καὶ ἁμαρτωλῶν
with the tax-collectors and sinners

ἐσθίετε καὶ πίνετε; **31** καὶ ἀποκριθεὶς ὁ
eat ye and drink ye? And answering –

Ἰησοῦς εἶπεν πρὸς αὐτούς· οὐ χρείαν
Jesus said to them: not need

ἔχουσιν οἱ ὑγιαίνοντες ἰατροῦ ἀλλὰ οἱ
have the [ones] being healthy of a physician but the
=those who are ill;

κακῶς ἔχοντες· **32** οὐκ ἐλήλυθα καλέσαι
[ones] ill having; I have not come to call

δικαίους ἀλλὰ ἁμαρτωλοὺς εἰς μετάνοιαν.
righteous persons but sinners to repentance.

33 Οἱ δὲ εἶπαν πρὸς αὐτόν· οἱ μαθηταὶ
And they said to him: The disciples

Ἰωάννου νηστεύουσιν πυκνὰ καὶ δεήσεις
of John fast often and prayers

ποιοῦνται, ὁμοίως καὶ οἱ τῶν Φαρισαίων,
make, likewise also those of the Pharisees,

οἱ δὲ σοὶ ἐσθίουσιν καὶ πίνουσιν. **34** ὁ
but those to theeᵉ eat and drink. –
=but thine

δὲ Ἰησοῦς εἶπεν πρὸς αὐτούς· μὴ δύνασθε
And Jesus said to them: not ¹Can ye

τοὺς υἱοὺς τοῦ νυμφῶνος, ἐν ᾧ ὁ νυμφίος
³the ⁴sons ⁵of the ⁶bride-chamber, ⁸while ⁹the ¹⁰bridegroom

μετ' αὐτῶν ἐστιν, ποιῆσαι νηστεῦσαι;
¹²with ¹³them ¹¹is, ²to make ⁷to fast?

35 ἐλεύσονται δὲ ἡμέραι, καὶ ὅταν ἀπαρθῇ
but will come days, and when is taken away

ἀπ' αὐτῶν ὁ νυμφίος, τότε νηστεύσουσιν
from them the bridegroom, then they will fast

36 ¶ And he spake also a parable unto them; No man putteth a piece of a new garment upon an old; if otherwise, then both the new maketh a rent, and the piece that was *taken* out of the new agreeth not with the old.

37 And no man putteth new wine into old bottles; else the new wine will burst the bottles, and be spilled, and the bottles shall perish.

38 But new wine must be put into new bottles; and both are preserved.

39 No man also having drunk old *wine* straightway desireth new: for he saith, The old is better.

ἐν ἐκείναις ταῖς ἡμέραις. 36 Ἔλεγεν δὲ
in   those   –   days.   And he told

καὶ παραβολὴν πρὸς αὐτοὺς ὅτι οὐδεὶς
also   a parable   to   them[:]   –   No one

ἐπίβλημα ἀπὸ ἱματίου καινοῦ σχίσας
²a patch   ³from   ⁵garment   ⁴a new   ¹tearing

ἐπιβάλλει ἐπὶ ἱμάτιον παλαιόν· εἰ δὲ μή γε,
⁶puts [it]   ⁷on   ⁹a garment   ⁸an old;   otherwise,

καὶ τὸ καινὸν σχίσει καὶ τῷ παλαιῷ
both   the   new   will tear   and   ⁷with the   ⁸old

οὐ συμφωνήσει τὸ ἐπίβλημα τὸ ἀπὸ τοῦ
⁶will not agree   ¹the   ²patch   –   ³from   ⁴the

καινοῦ. 37 καὶ οὐδεὶς βάλλει οἶνον νέον
⁵new.   And   no one   puts   wine   new

εἰς ἀσκοὺς παλαιούς· εἰ δὲ μή γε, ῥήξει
into   wineskins   old;   otherwise,   ⁴will burst

ὁ οἶνος ὁ νέος τοὺς ἀσκούς, καὶ αὐτὸς
¹the   ³wine   –   ²new   ⁵the   ⁶wineskins,   and   it

ἐκχυθήσεται καὶ οἱ ἀσκοὶ ἀπολοῦνται.
will be poured out   and   the   wineskins   will perish.

38 ἀλλὰ οἶνον νέον εἰς ἀσκοὺς καινοὺς
But   wine   new   into   wineskins   new

βλητέον. 39 καὶ οὐδεὶς πιὼν παλαιὸν
one must put.   And   no one having drunk   old

θέλει νέον· λέγει γάρ· ὁ παλαιὸς χρηστός
desires   new;   for he says :   The   old   good

ἐστιν.
is.

CHAPTER 6

AND it came to pass on the second sabbath after the first, that he went through the corn fields; and his disciples plucked the ears of corn, and did eat, rubbing *them* in *their* hands.

2 And certain of the Pharisees said unto them, Why do ye that which is not lawful to do on the sabbath days?

3 And Jesus answering them said, Have ye not read so much as this, what David did, when himself was an hungred, and they which were with him;

6 Ἐγένετο δὲ ἐν σαββάτῳ διαπορεύεσθαι
And it came to pass   on   a sabbath   to go through
                                 = he went through

αὐτὸν διὰ σπορίμων, καὶ ἔτιλλον οἱ
himᵇ   *through*   cornfields,   and   ⁴plucked   ¹the

μαθηταὶ αὐτοῦ καὶ ἤσθιον τοὺς στάχυας
²disciples   ³of him   and   ate   the   ears

ψώχοντες ταῖς χερσίν. 2 τινὲς δὲ τῶν
rubbing   with the(ir)   hands.   And some   of the

Φαρισαίων εἶπαν· τί ποιεῖτε ὃ οὐκ ἔξεστιν
Pharisees   said :   Why   do ye   what   is not lawful

τοῖς σάββασιν; 3 καὶ ἀποκριθεὶς πρὸς
on the   sabbaths?   And   replying   to

αὐτοὺς εἶπεν ὁ Ἰησοῦς· οὐδὲ τοῦτο ἀνέγνωτε
them   said   –   Jesus :   ²not   ³this   ¹read ye

ὃ ἐποίησεν Δαυίδ, ὁπότε ἐπείνασεν αὐτὸς
which did   David,   when   hungered   he

καὶ οἱ μετ᾽ αὐτοῦ ὄντες; 4 ὡς εἰσῆλθεν
and   the [ones] with   him   being?   how   he entered

4 How he went into the house of God, and did take and eat the shewbread, and gave also to them that were with him; which it is not lawful to eat but for the priests alone?

5 And he said unto them, That the Son of man is Lord also of the sabbath.

6 ¶ And it came to pass also on another sabbath, that he entered into the synagogue and taught: and there was a man whose right hand was withered.

7 And the scribes and Pharisees watched him, whether he would heal on the sabbath day; that they might find an accusation against him.

8 But he knew their thoughts, and said to the man which had the withered hand, Rise up, and stand forth in the midst. And he arose and stood forth.

9 Then said Jesus unto them, I will ask you one thing; Is it lawful on the sabbath days to do good, or to do evil? to save life, or to destroy it?

10 And looking round about upon them all, he said unto the man, Stretch forth thy hand. And he did so: and his hand was restored whole as the other.

11 And they were filled with madness; and communed one with another what they might do to Jesus.

εἰς τὸν οἶκον τοῦ θεοῦ καὶ τοὺς ἄρτους
into the house – of God and the loaves

τῆς προθέσεως λαβὼν ἔφαγεν καὶ ἔδωκεν
of the setting forth taking he ate and gave

τοῖς μετ᾽ αὐτοῦ, οὓς οὐκ ἔξεστιν φαγεῖν
to the [ones] with him, which it is not lawful to eat

εἰ μὴ μόνους τοὺς ἱερεῖς; 5 καὶ ἔλεγεν
except only the priests? And he said

αὐτοῖς· κύριός ἐστιν τοῦ σαββάτου ὁ
to them : Lord is of the sabbath the

υἱὸς τοῦ ἀνθρώπου. 6 Ἐγένετο δὲ ἐν
Son – of man. And it came to pass on

ἑτέρῳ σαββάτῳ εἰσελθεῖν αὐτὸν εἰς τὴν
another sabbath to enter him into the
=he entered into the synagogue and

συναγωγὴν καὶ διδάσκειν· καὶ ἦν ἄνθρωπος
synagogue and to teach[b]; and there was a man
taught;

ἐκεῖ καὶ ἡ χεὶρ αὐτοῦ ἡ δεξιὰ ἦν ξηρά·
there and the ²hand ³of him – ¹right was withered;

7 παρετηροῦντο δὲ αὐτὸν οἱ γραμματεῖς
and carefully watched him the scribes

καὶ οἱ Φαρισαῖοι εἰ ἐν τῷ σαββάτῳ
and the Pharisees if on the sabbath

θεραπεύει, ἵνα εὕρωσιν κατηγορεῖν αὐτοῦ.
he heals, that they might find to accuse him.

8 αὐτὸς δὲ ᾔδει τοὺς διαλογισμοὺς αὐτῶν,
But he knew the reasonings of them,

εἶπεν δὲ τῷ ἀνδρὶ τῷ ξηρὰν ἔχοντι τὴν
and said to the man – ²withered ¹having ³the

χεῖρα· ἔγειρε καὶ στῆθι εἰς τὸ μέσον·
⁴hand : Rise and stand in the midst;

καὶ ἀναστὰς ἔστη. 9 εἶπεν δὲ ὁ Ἰησοῦς
and rising up he stood. And said – Jesus

πρὸς αὐτούς· ἐπερωτῶ ὑμᾶς εἰ ἔξεστιν
to them: I ask you if it is lawful

τῷ σαββάτῳ ἀγαθοποιῆσαι ἢ κακοποιῆσαι,
on the sabbath to do good or to do evil,

ψυχὴν σῶσαι ἢ ἀπολέσαι; 10 καὶ περι-
life to save or to destroy? And looking

βλεψάμενος πάντας αὐτοὺς εἶπεν αὐτῷ·
round at all them he said to him :

ἔκτεινον τὴν χεῖρά σου. ὁ δὲ ἐποίησεν,
Stretch out the hand of thee. And he did,

καὶ ἀπεκατεστάθη ἡ χεὶρ αὐτοῦ. 11 αὐτοὶ
and was restored the hand of him. they

δὲ ἐπλήσθησαν ἀνοίας, καὶ διελάλουν πρὸς
But were filled of(with) madness, and talked to

ἀλλήλους τί ἂν ποιήσαιεν τῷ Ἰησοῦ.
one another what they might do – to Jesus.

12¶ And it came to pass in those days, that he went out into a mountain to pray, and continued all night in prayer to God.

13 And when it was day, he called *unto him* his disciples: and of them he chose twelve, whom also he named apostles;

14 Simon, (whom he also named Peter,) and Andrew his brother, James and John, Philip and Bartholomew,

15 Matthew and Thomas, James the *son* of Alphæus, and Simon called Zelotes,

16 And Judas *the brother* of James, and Judas Iscariot, which also was the traitor.

17 And he came down with them, and stood in the plain, and the company of his disciples, and a great multitude of people out of all Judæa and Jerusalem, and from the sea coast of Tyre and Sidon, which came to hear him, and to be healed of their diseases;

18 And they that were vexed with unclean spirits: and they were healed.

19 And the whole multitude sought to touch him: for there went virtue out of him, and healed *them* all.

20¶ And he lifted up

---

12 Ἐγένετο δὲ ἐν ταῖς ἡμέραις ταύταις
Now it came to pass in – days these

ἐξελθεῖν αὐτὸν εἰς τὸ ὄρος προσεύξασθαι,
to go forth himᵇ to the mountain to pray,
=he went forth

καὶ ἦν διανυκτερεύων ἐν τῇ προσευχῇ τοῦ
and was spending the whole in the prayer –
night

θεοῦ. 13 καὶ ὅτε ἐγένετο ἡμέρα, προσεφώνησεν
of God. And when it became day, he called to [him]

τοὺς μαθητὰς αὐτοῦ, καὶ ἐκλεξάμενος ἀπ'
the disciples of him, and choosing from

αὐτῶν δώδεκα, οὓς καὶ ἀποστόλους ὠνόμασεν,
them twelve, whom also apostles he named,

14 Σίμωνα, ὃν καὶ ὠνόμασεν Πέτρον, καὶ
Simon, whom also he named Peter, and

Ἀνδρέαν τὸν ἀδελφὸν αὐτοῦ, καὶ Ἰάκωβον
Andrew the brother of him, and James

καὶ Ἰωάννην, καὶ Φίλιππον καὶ Βαρθο-
and John, and Philip and Bartho-

λομαῖον, 15 καὶ Ματθαῖον καὶ Θωμᾶν,
lomew, and Matthew and Thomas,

[καὶ] Ἰάκωβον Ἁλφαίου καὶ Σίμωνα τὸν
and James [son] of Alphæus and Simon the [one]

καλούμενον ζηλωτήν, καὶ Ἰούδαν Ἰακώβου,
being called a Zealot, and Judas of James,

16 καὶ Ἰούδαν Ἰσκαριώθ, ὃς ἐγένετο προδότης,
and Judas Iscariot, who became betrayer,

17 καὶ καταβὰς μετ' αὐτῶν ἔστη ἐπὶ
and coming down with them he stood on

τόπου πεδινοῦ, καὶ ὄχλος πολὺς μαθητῶν
place a level, and crowd a much of disciples

αὐτοῦ, καὶ πλῆθος πολὺ τοῦ λαοῦ ἀπὸ
of him, and multitude a much of the people from

πάσης τῆς Ἰουδαίας καὶ Ἰερουσαλὴμ καὶ
all – Judæa and Jerusalem and

τῆς παραλίου Τύρου καὶ Σιδῶνος, 18 οἳ
the coast country of Tyre and Sidon, who

ἦλθον ἀκοῦσαι αὐτοῦ καὶ ἰαθῆναι ἀπὸ
came to hear him and to be cured from

τῶν νόσων αὐτῶν, καὶ οἱ ἐνοχλούμενοι
the diseases of them, and the [ones] being tormented

ἀπὸ πνευμάτων ἀκαθάρτων ἐθεραπεύοντο.
from spirits unclean were healed.

19 καὶ πᾶς ὁ ὄχλος ἐζήτουν ἅπτεσθαι
And all the crowd sought to touch

αὐτοῦ, ὅτι δύναμις παρ' αὐτοῦ ἐξήρχετο
him, because power from him went forth

καὶ ἰᾶτο πάντας. 20 Καὶ αὐτὸς ἐπάρας
and cured all. And he lifting up

his eyes on his disciples, and said, Blessed *be ye* poor: for your's is the kingdom of God.

21 Blessed *are ye* that hunger now: for ye shall be filled. Blessed *are ye* that weep now: for ye shall laugh.

22 Blessed are ye, when men shall hate you, and when they shall separate you *from their company*, and shall reproach *you*, and cast out your name as evil, for the Son of man's sake.

23 Rejoice ye in that day, and leap for joy: for, behold, your reward *is* great in heaven: for in the like manner did their fathers unto the prophets.

24 But woe unto you that are rich! for ye have received your consolation.

25 Woe unto you that are full! for ye shall hunger. Woe unto you that laugh now! for ye shall mourn and weep.

26 Woe unto you, when all men shall speak well of you! for so did their fathers to the false prophets.

27 ¶ But I say unto you which hear, Love your enemies, do good to them which hate you,

τοὺς ὀφθαλμοὺς αὐτοῦ εἰς τοὺς μαθητὰς
the   eyes   of him   to   the   disciples
αὐτοῦ ἔλεγεν·
of him   said :
Μακάριοι οἱ πτωχοί, ὅτι ὑμετέρα ἐστὶν
Blessed [are] the poor, because yours   is
ἡ βασιλεία τοῦ θεοῦ. 21 μακάριοι οἱ
the kingdom - of God. Blessed [are] the [ones]
πεινῶντες νῦν, ὅτι χορτασθήσεσθε. μακάριοι
hungering now, because ye will be satisfied. Blessed [are]
οἱ κλαίοντες νῦν, ὅτι γελάσετε. 22 μακάριοί
the [ones] weeping now, because ye will laugh. Blessed
ἐστε ὅταν μισήσωσιν ὑμᾶς οἱ ἄνθρωποι,
are ye when ²hate   ³you   -   ¹men,
καὶ ὅταν ἀφορίσωσιν ὑμᾶς καὶ ὀνειδίσωσιν
and when they separate   you and   reproach
καὶ ἐκβάλωσιν τὸ ὄνομα ὑμῶν ὡς πονηρὸν
and cast out   the name of you as   evil
ἕνεκα τοῦ υἱοῦ τοῦ ἀνθρώπου. 23 χάρητε
for the sake of the Son - of man.   Rejoice
ἐν ἐκείνῃ τῇ ἡμέρᾳ καὶ σκιρτήσατε·
in that   -   day and   leap for joy;
ἰδοὺ γὰρ ὁ μισθὸς ὑμῶν πολὺς ἐν τῷ
for behold[,] the reward of you much in   -
οὐρανῷ· κατὰ τὰ αὐτὰ γὰρ ἐποίουν τοῖς
heaven; for according to the same things ⁴did   ⁵to the
=in the same way
προφήταις οἱ πατέρες αὐτῶν.
⁶prophets ¹the ²fathers   ³of them.
24 Πλὴν οὐαὶ ὑμῖν τοῖς πλουσίοις, ὅτι
But woe to you the rich [ones], because
ἀπέχετε τὴν παράκλησιν ὑμῶν. οὐαὶ ὑμῖν,
ye have the consolation of you. Woe to you,
οἱ ἐμπεπλησμένοι νῦν, ὅτι πεινάσετε.
the [ones] having been filled up now, because ye will hunger.
25 οὐαί, οἱ γελῶντες νῦν, ὅτι πενθήσετε
Woe, the [ones] laughing now, because ye will mourn
καὶ κλαύσετε. 26 οὐαὶ ὅταν καλῶς ὑμᾶς
and lament.   Woe when well [of] you
εἴπωσιν πάντες οἱ ἄνθρωποι· κατὰ τὰ
say   all   -   men;   for according to
=in the same way
αὐτὰ γὰρ ἐποίουν τοῖς ψευδοπροφήταις οἱ
the same things did   to the false prophets   the
πατέρες αὐτῶν. 27 Ἀλλὰ ὑμῖν λέγω
fathers of them.   But   you I tell
τοῖς ἀκούουσιν· ἀγαπᾶτε τοὺς ἐχθροὺς
the [ones] hearing : Love ye the   enemies
ὑμῶν, καλῶς ποιεῖτε τοῖς μισοῦσιν ὑμᾶς,
of you, ²well   ¹do   to the [ones] hating   you,

28 Bless them that curse you, and pray for them which despitefully use you.

29 And unto him that smiteth thee on the *one* cheek offer also the other; and him that taketh away thy cloke forbid not *to take thy* coat also.

30 Give to every man that asketh of thee; and of him that taketh away thy goods ask *them* not again.

31 And as ye would that men should do to you, do ye also to them likewise.

32 For if ye love them which love you, what thank have ye? for sinners also love those that love them.

33 And if ye do good to them which do good to you, what thank have ye? for sinners also do even the same.

34 And if ye lend *to them* of whom ye hope to receive, what thank have ye? for sinners also lend to sinners, to receive as much again.

35 But love ye your enemies, and do good, and lend, hoping for nothing again; and your reward shall be great, and ye shall be the children of the Highest: for he is kind unto the unthankful and *to* the evil.

---

28 εὐλογεῖτε τοὺς καταρωμένους ὑμᾶς,
bless the [ones] cursing you,

προσεύχεσθε περὶ τῶν ἐπηρεαζόντων ὑμᾶς.
pray about the [ones] insulting you.

29 τῷ τύπτοντί σε ἐπὶ τὴν σιαγόνα
To the [one] striking thee on the cheek

πάρεχε καὶ τὴν ἄλλην, καὶ ἀπὸ τοῦ
turn also the other, and from the [one]

αἴροντός σου τὸ ἱμάτιον καὶ τὸν χιτῶνα
taking of thee the garment also the tunic

μὴ κωλύσῃς. 30 παντὶ αἰτοῦντί σε δίδου,
do not prevent. To everyone asking thee give,

καὶ ἀπὸ τοῦ αἴροντος τὰ σὰ μὴ ἀπαίτει.
and from the [one] taking thy things do not ask back.

31 καὶ καθὼς θέλετε ἵνα ποιῶσιν ὑμῖν
And as ye wish that may do to you

οἱ ἄνθρωποι, ποιεῖτε αὐτοῖς ὁμοίως. 32 καὶ
– men, do ye to them likewise. And

εἰ ἀγαπᾶτε τοὺς ἀγαπῶντας ὑμᾶς, ποία
if ye love the [ones] loving you, what

ὑμῖν χάρις ἐστίν; καὶ γὰρ οἱ ἁμαρτωλοὶ
to you thanks is there?ᶜ for even – sinners
=thanks have ye?

τοὺς ἀγαπῶντας αὐτοὺς ἀγαπῶσιν. 33 καὶ
²the [ones] ³loving ⁴them ¹love. even

γὰρ ἐὰν ἀγαθοποιῆτε τοὺς ἀγαθοποιοῦντας
For if ye do good to the [ones] doing good to

ὑμᾶς, ποία ὑμῖν χάρις ἐστίν; καὶ οἱ
you, what to you thanks is there?ᶜ even –
=thanks have ye?

ἁμαρτωλοὶ τὸ αὐτὸ ποιοῦσιν. 34 καὶ ἐὰν
sinners the same thing do. And if

δανείσητε παρ' ὧν ἐλπίζετε λαβεῖν, ποία
ye lend from whom ye hope to receive, what

ὑμῖν χάρις [ἐστίν]; καὶ ἁμαρτωλοὶ
to you thanks is there?ᶜ even sinners
=thanks have ye?

ἁμαρτωλοῖς δανείζουσιν ἵνα ἀπολάβωσιν τὰ
to sinners lend that they may receive back the

ἴσα. 35 πλὴν ἀγαπᾶτε τοὺς ἐχθροὺς ὑμῶν
equal things. But love ye the enemies of you

καὶ ἀγαθοποιεῖτε καὶ δανείζετε μηδὲν
and do good and lend nothing

ἀπελπίζοντες· καὶ ἔσται ὁ μισθὸς ὑμῶν
despairing; and will be the reward of you
=despairing not at all;

πολύς, καὶ ἔσεσθε υἱοὶ ὑψίστου, ὅτι
much, and ye will be sons of [the] Most High, because

αὐτὸς χρηστός ἐστιν ἐπὶ τοὺς ἀχαρίστους
he kind is to the unthankful

36 Be ye therefore merciful, as your Father also is merciful.

37 Judge not, and ye shall not be judged: condemn not, and ye shall not be condemned: forgive, and ye shall be forgiven:

38 Give, and it shall be given unto you; good measure, pressed down, and shaken together, and running over, shall men give into your bosom. For with the same measure that ye mete withal it shall be measured to you again.

39 And he spake a parable unto them, Can the blind lead the blind? shall they not both fall into the ditch?

40 The disciple is not above his master: but every one that is perfect shall be as his master.

41 And why beholdest thou the mote that is in thy brother's eye, but perceivest not the beam that is in thine own eye?

42 Either how canst thou say to thy brother, Brother, let me pull out the mote that is in thine eye, when thou thyself beholdest not the beam that is in thine own eye? Thou hypocrite, cast out first the beam out of thine own eye, and then shalt thou see clearly to pull out the mote that is in thy brother's eye.

καὶ   πονηρούς.
and   evil.

36 Γίνεσθε   οἰκτίρμονες,
Be ye   compassionate,

καθὼς   ὁ   πατὴρ   ὑμῶν   οἰκτίρμων   ἐστίν.
as   the   Father   of you   compassionate   is.

37 καὶ   μὴ   κρίνετε,   καὶ   οὐ   μὴ   κριθῆτε·   καὶ
And   do not judge,   and by no means ye may be   and judged;

μὴ   καταδικάζετε,   καὶ   οὐ   μὴ   καταδικασθῆτε.
do not condemn,   and by no means ye may be condemned.

ἀπολύετε,   καὶ   ἀπολυθήσεσθε·   **38** δίδοτε,   καὶ
Forgive,   and   ye will be forgiven;   give,   and

δοθήσεται   ὑμῖν·   μέτρον   καλὸν   πεπιεσμένον
it will be given to you;   measure   good   *having been* pressed down

σεσαλευμένον   ὑπερεκχυννόμενον   δώσουσιν   εἰς
having been shaken   running over   they will give   into

τὸν   κόλπον   ὑμῶν·   ᾧ   γὰρ   μέτρῳ   μετρεῖτε
the   bosom   of you;   for in what   measure   ye measure

ἀντιμετρηθήσεται   ὑμῖν.   **39** Εἶπεν   δὲ   καὶ
it will be measured in return to you.   And he told   also

παραβολὴν   αὐτοῖς·   μήτι   δύναται   τυφλὸς
a parable   to them :   *Not*   can   a blind man

τυφλὸν   ὁδηγεῖν;   οὐχὶ   ἀμφότεροι   εἰς   βόθυνον
²a blind man   ¹guide?   not   both   into   a ditch

ἐμπεσοῦνται;   **40** οὐκ   ἔστιν   μαθητὴς   ὑπὲρ
will fall *in*?   ³not   ²is   ¹A disciple   above

τὸν   διδάσκαλον·   κατηρτισμένος   δὲ   πᾶς
the   teacher;   but ⁴*having been* perfected   ²everyone

ἔσται   ὡς   ὁ   διδάσκαλος   αὐτοῦ.   **41** Τί   δὲ
³will be   as   the   teacher   of him.   And why

βλέπεις   τὸ   κάρφος   τὸ   ἐν   τῷ   ὀφθαλμῷ
seest thou   the   mote   –   in   the   eye

τοῦ   ἀδελφοῦ   σου,   τὴν   δὲ   δοκὸν   τὴν   ἐν
of the   brother   of thee,   but the   beam   –   in

τῷ   ἰδίῳ   ὀφθαλμῷ   οὐ   κατανοεῖς;   **42** πῶς
thine own   eye   thou considerest not?   how

δύνασαι   λέγειν   τῷ   ἀδελφῷ   σου·   ἀδελφέ,
canst thou   *to* say   to the   brother   of thee :   Brother,

ἄφες   ἐκβάλω   τὸ   κάρφος   τὸ   ἐν   τῷ
allow I may take out   the   mote   –   in   the
=allow me to take out

ὀφθαλμῷ   σου,   αὐτὸς   τὴν   ἐν   τῷ   ὀφθαλμῷ
eye   of thee,   ¹[thy]self   ⁴the   ⁵in   ⁷the   ⁸eye

σου   δοκὸν   οὐ   βλέπων;   ὑποκριτά,   ἔκβαλε
⁶of thee   ⁵beam   ²not   ³seeing?   hypocrite,   take *out*

πρῶτον   τὴν   δοκὸν   ἐκ   τοῦ   ὀφθαλμοῦ   σου,
first   the   beam   out of the   eye   of thee,

καὶ   τότε   διαβλέψεις   τὸ   κάρφος   τὸ   ἐν   τῷ
and   then   thou wilt see clearly   the   mote   –   in   the

43 For a good tree bringeth not forth corrupt fruit; neither doth a corrupt tree bring forth good fruit.
44 For every tree is known by his own fruit. For of thorns men do not gather figs, nor of a bramble bush gather they grapes.
45 A good man out of the good treasure of his heart bringeth forth that which is good; and an evil man out of the evil treasure of his heart bringeth forth that which is evil: for of the abundance of the heart his mouth speaketh.
46 ¶ And why call ye me, Lord, Lord, and do not the things which I say?
47 Whosoever cometh to me, and heareth my sayings, and doeth them, I will shew you to whom he is like:
48 He is like a man which built an house, and digged deep, and laid the foundation on a rock: and when the flood arose, the stream beat vehemently upon that house, and could not shake it: for it was founded upon a rock.
49 But he that heareth, and doeth not, is like a

ὀφθαλμῷ τοῦ ἀδελφοῦ σου ἐκβαλεῖν. 43 Οὐ
eye   of the brother of thee to take out.   ³no

γάρ ἐστιν δένδρον καλὸν ποιοῦν καρπὸν
¹For ²there is ⁵tree ⁴good producing fruit

σαπρόν, οὐδὲ πάλιν δένδρον σαπρὸν ποιοῦν
bad,   nor again tree a bad producing

καρπὸν καλόν. 44 ἕκαστον γὰρ δένδρον
fruit good.   For each   tree

ἐκ τοῦ ἰδίου καρποῦ γινώσκεται· οὐ γὰρ
by the(its) own fruit is known;   for not

ἐξ ἀκανθῶν συλλέγουσιν σῦκα, οὐδὲ ἐκ
of thorns do they gather figs, nor of

βάτου σταφυλὴν τρυγῶσιν. 45 ὁ ἀγαθὸς
a thorn bush a grape do they pick. The good

ἄνθρωπος ἐκ τοῦ ἀγαθοῦ θησαυροῦ τῆς
man   out of the good   treasure of the(his)

καρδίας προφέρει τὸ ἀγαθόν, καὶ ὁ
heart brings forth the good,   and the
              =that which is good,

πονηρὸς ἐκ τοῦ πονηροῦ προφέρει τὸ
evil man out of the evil brings forth the

πονηρόν· ἐκ γὰρ περισσεύματος καρδίας
evil;   for out of [the] abundance of [his] heart
      =that which is evil;

λαλεῖ τὸ στόμα αὐτοῦ. 46 Τί δέ με καλεῖτε·
speaks the mouth of him.   And why me call ye :

κύριε κύριε, καὶ οὐ ποιεῖτε ἃ
Lord[,] Lord, and do not [the things] which

λέγω; 47 Πᾶς ὁ ἐρχόμενος πρός με καὶ
I say? Everyone coming to me and

ἀκούων μου τῶν λόγων καὶ ποιῶν αὐτούς,
hearing of me the words and doing them,

ὑποδείξω ὑμῖν τίνι ἐστὶν ὅμοιος. 48 ὅμοιός
I will show you to whom he is like.   Like

ἐστιν ἀνθρώπῳ οἰκοδομοῦντι οἰκίαν, ὃς
he is to a man building a house, who

ἔσκαψεν καὶ ἐβάθυνεν καὶ ἔθηκεν θεμέλιον
dug   and deepened and laid a foundation

ἐπὶ τὴν πέτραν· πλημμύρης δὲ γενομένης
on the rock;   and a flood occurring ª
               =when a flood occurred

προσέρρηξεν ὁ ποταμὸς τῇ οἰκίᾳ ἐκείνῃ,
³dashed against ¹the ²river - house that,

καὶ οὐκ ἴσχυσεν σαλεῦσαι αὐτὴν διὰ
and was not able to shake it because of

τὸ καλῶς οἰκοδομῆσθαι αὐτήν. 49 ὁ δὲ
the well to be built it.ᵇ   But the
 =because it was well built.   [one]

ἀκούσας καὶ μὴ ποιήσας ὅμοιός ἐστιν
hearing and not doing ²like   ¹is

man that without a
foundation built an house
upon the earth; against
which the stream did beat
vehemently, and imme-
diately it fell; and the
ruin of that house was
great.

ἀνθρώπῳ οἰκοδομήσαντι οἰκίαν ἐπὶ τὴν
a man　　having built　　a house　　on　the
γῆν χωρὶς θεμελίου, ᾗ προσέρρηξεν ὁ
earth　without　a foundation, ²which ⁵dashed ¹against ³the
ποταμός, καὶ εὐθὺς. συνέπεσεν, καὶ ἐγένετο
⁴river,　and immediately it collapsed,　and　　⁵was
τὸ ῥῆγμα τῆς οἰκίας ἐκείνης μέγα.
¹the　²ruin　　－　　⁴house　³of that　⁶great.

CHAPTER 7

NOW when he had
ended all his sayings
in the audience of the
people, he entered into
Capernaum.

2 And a certain cen-
turion's servant, who was
dear unto him, was sick,
and ready to die.

3 And when he heard of
Jesus, he sent unto him
the elders of the Jews,
beseeching him that he
would come and heal his
servant.

4 And when they came
to Jesus, they besought
him instantly, saying, That
he was worthy for whom
he should do this:

5 For he loveth our
nation, and he hath built
us a synagogue.

6 Then Jesus went with
them. And when he was
now not far from the
house, the centurion sent
friends to him, saying
unto him, Lord, trouble
not thyself: for I am not
worthy that thou shouldest
enter under my roof:

7 Wherefore neither
thought I myself worthy
to come unto thee: but

7 Ἐπειδὴ ἐπλήρωσεν πάντα τὰ ῥήματα
When　he completed　all　the　words
αὐτοῦ εἰς τὰς ἀκοὰς τοῦ λαοῦ, εἰσῆλθεν
of him　in　the　ears　of the people,　he entered
εἰς Καφαρναούμ. 2 Ἑκατοντάρχου δέ
into　Capernaum.　　Now ²of ³a ⁴centurion
τινος δοῦλος κακῶς ἔχων ἤμελλεν τελευτᾶν,
⁶certain ¹a slave　⁷ill　⁶having(being) ¹²was about ¹³to die.
ὃς ἦν αὐτῷ ἔντιμος. 3 ἀκούσας δὲ περὶ
⁸who ⁹was ¹¹to him ¹⁰dear.　And hearing　about
τοῦ Ἰησοῦ ἀπέστειλεν πρὸς αὐτὸν πρε-
－　Jesus　he sent　to　him　eld-
σβυτέρους τῶν Ἰουδαίων, ἐρωτῶν αὐτὸν
ers　　of the　Jews,　asking　him
ὅπως ἐλθὼν διασώσῃ τὸν δοῦλον αὐτοῦ.
that　coming he might recover the　slave　of him.
4 οἱ δὲ παραγενόμενοι πρὸς τὸν Ἰησοῦν
And they　coming　to　－　Jesus
παρεκάλουν αὐτὸν σπουδαίως, λέγοντες ὅτι ἄξιός
besought　him　earnestly,　saying[,]　－ Worthy
ἐστιν ᾧ παρέξῃ τοῦτο· 5 ἀγαπᾷ γὰρ
he is for whom thou shouldest grant this;　for he loves
τὸ ἔθνος ἡμῶν καὶ τὴν συναγωγὴν
the　nation　of us　and　the　synagogue
αὐτὸς ᾠκοδόμησεν ἡμῖν. 6 ὁ δὲ Ἰησοῦς
he　　built　for us.　－ And　Jesus
ἐπορεύετο σὺν αὐτοῖς. ἤδη δὲ αὐτοῦ οὐ
went　with　them.　And yet　him　not
　　　　　　　　　　　　　　　＝while he was yet
μακρὰν ἀπέχοντος ἀπὸ τῆς οἰκίας, ἔπεμψεν
far　being awayᵃ from　the　house,　sent
not far away
φίλους ὁ ἑκατοντάρχης λέγων αὐτῷ· κύριε,
friends the　centurion　saying　to him :　Lord,
μὴ σκύλλου· οὐ γὰρ ἱκανός εἰμι ἵνα ὑπὸ
do not trouble;　for not　worthy　am I　that under
τὴν στέγην μου εἰσέλθῃς· 7 διὸ οὐδὲ
the　roof　of me thou shouldest enter;　wherefore　not
ἐμαυτὸν ἠξίωσα πρὸς σὲ ἐλθεῖν· ἀλλὰ εἰπὲ
myself I accounted worthy to　thee to come;　but　say

say in a word, and my servant shall be healed.

8 For I also am a man set under authority, having under me soldiers, and I say unto one, Go, and he goeth; and to another, Come, and he cometh; and to my servant, Do this, and he doeth *it*.

9 When Jesus heard these things, he marvelled at him, and turned him about, and said unto the people that followed him, I say unto you, I have not found so great faith, no, not in Israel.

10 And they that were sent, returning to the house, found the servant whole that had been sick.

11 ¶ And it came to pass the day after, that he went into a city called Nain; and many of his disciples went with him, and much people.

12 Now when he came nigh to the gate of the city, behold, there was a dead man carried out, the only son of his mother, and she was a widow: and much people of the city was with her.

13 And when the Lord saw her, he had compassion on her, and said unto her, Weep not.

14 And he came and touched the bier: and they that bare *him* stood still. And he said, Young man, I say unto thee, Arise.

λόγῳ, καὶ ἰαθήτω ὁ παῖς μου. 8 καὶ
in a word, and let be cured the servant of me. ²also

γὰρ ἐγὼ ἄνθρωπός εἰμι ὑπὸ ἐξουσίαν
¹For ²I ³a man ⁴am ⁷under ⁸authority

τασσόμενος, ἔχων ὑπ᾽ ἐμαυτὸν στρατιώτας,
⁶being set, having under myself soldiers,

καὶ λέγω τούτῳ· πορεύθητι, καὶ πορεύεται,
and I tell this one : Go, and he goes,

καὶ ἄλλῳ· ἔρχου, καὶ ἔρχεται, καὶ τῷ
and another : Come, and he comes, and the

δούλῳ μου· ποίησον τοῦτο, καὶ ποιεῖ.
slave of me : Do this, and he does.

9 ἀκούσας δὲ ταῦτα ὁ Ἰησοῦς ἐθαύμασεν
And hearing these [words] – Jesus marvelled at

αὐτόν, καὶ στραφεὶς τῷ ἀκολουθοῦντι αὐτῷ
him, and turning to the ²following ³him

ὄχλῳ εἶπεν· λέγω ὑμῖν, οὐδὲ ἐν τῷ
¹crowd said : I tell you, not in –

Ἰσραὴλ τοσαύτην πίστιν εὗρον. 10 καὶ
Israel such faith I found. And

ὑποστρέψαντες εἰς τὸν οἶκον οἱ πεμφθέντες
returning to the house the [ones] sent

εὗρον τὸν δοῦλον ὑγιαίνοντα. 11 Καὶ
found the slave well. And

ἐγένετο ἐν τῷ ἑξῆς ἐπορεύθη εἰς πόλιν
it came to pass on the next day he went into a city

καλουμένην Ναΐν, καὶ συνεπορεύοντο αὐτῷ
being called Nain, and went with him

οἱ μαθηταὶ αὐτοῦ καὶ ὄχλος πολύς.
the disciples of him and crowd a much.

12 ὡς δὲ ἤγγισεν τῇ πύλῃ τῆς πόλεως, καὶ
And as he drew near to the gate of the city, and

ἰδοὺ ἐξεκομίζετο τεθνηκὼς μονογενὴς
behold was being carried out having died an only born
[for burial]

υἱὸς τῇ μητρὶ αὐτοῦ, καὶ αὕτη ἦν χήρα,
son to the mother of him, and this was a widow,

καὶ ὄχλος τῆς πόλεως ἱκανὸς ἦν σὺν
and a ²crowd ³of the ⁴city ¹considerable was with

αὐτῇ. 13 καὶ ἰδὼν αὐτὴν ὁ κύριος
her. And seeing her the Lord

ἐσπλαγχνίσθη ἐπ᾽ αὐτῇ καὶ εἶπεν αὐτῇ·
felt compassion over her and said to her :

μὴ κλαῖε. 14 καὶ προσελθὼν ἥψατο τῆς
Do not weep. And approaching he touched the

σοροῦ, οἱ δὲ βαστάζοντες ἔστησαν, καὶ
bier, and the [ones] bearing stood, and

εἶπεν· νεανίσκε, σοί λέγω, ἐγέρθητι. 15 καὶ
he said : Young man, to thee I say, Arise. And

15 And he that was dead sat up, and began to speak. And he delivered him to his mother.

16 And there came a fear on all: and they glorified God, saying, That a great prophet is risen up among us; and, That God hath visited his people.

17 And this rumour of him went forth throughout all Judæa, and throughout all the region round about.

18 ¶ And the disciples of John shewed him of all these things.

19 And John calling *unto him* two of his disciples sent *them* to Jesus, saying, Art thou he that should come? or look we for another?

20 When the men were come unto him, they said, John Baptist hath sent us unto thee, saying, Art thou he that should come? or look we for another?

21 And in that same hour he cured many of *their* infirmities and plagues, and of evil spirits; and unto many *that were* blind he gave sight.

22 Then Jesus answering said unto them, Go your way, and tell John what things ye have seen and heard; how that the blind see, the lame walk, the lepers are cleansed, the deaf hear, the dead are

ἀνεκάθισεν ὁ νεκρὸς καὶ ἤρξατο λαλεῖν,
sat up   the dead man and began to speak,

καὶ ἔδωκεν αὐτὸν τῇ μητρὶ αὐτοῦ.
and he gave him to the mother of him.

16 ἔλαβεν δὲ φόβος πάντας, καὶ ἐδόξαζον
And ²took ¹fear ²all, and they glorified

τὸν θεὸν λέγοντες ὅτι προφήτης μέγας
- God saying[,] - prophet A great

ἠγέρθη ἐν ἡμῖν, καὶ ὅτι ἐπεσκέψατο ὁ
was raised among us, and[,] - ²visited

θεὸς τὸν λαὸν αὐτοῦ. 17 καὶ ἐξῆλθεν ὁ
¹God the people of him. And went forth -

λόγος οὗτος ἐν ὅλῃ τῇ Ἰουδαίᾳ περὶ
word this in all - Judæa ⁵concerning

αὐτοῦ καὶ πάσῃ τῇ περιχώρῳ.
⁶him ¹and ³all ³the ⁴neighbourhood.

18 Καὶ ἀπήγγειλαν Ἰωάννῃ οἱ μαθηταὶ
And reported to John the disciples

αὐτοῦ περὶ πάντων τούτων. καὶ
of him about all these things. And

προσκαλεσάμενος δύο τινὰς τῶν μαθητῶν
calling to [him] ²two ¹a certain of the disciples

αὐτοῦ ὁ Ἰωάννης 19 ἔπεμψεν πρὸς τὸν
of him - John sent to the

κύριον λέγων· σὺ εἶ ὁ ἐρχόμενος, ἢ ἄλλον
Lord saying : Thou art the coming [one], or another

προσδοκῶμεν; 20 παραγενόμενοι δὲ πρὸς
may we expect? And coming to

αὐτὸν οἱ ἄνδρες εἶπαν· Ἰωάννης ὁ βαπτιστὴς
him the men said : John the Baptist

ἀπέστειλεν ἡμᾶς πρὸς σὲ λέγων· σὺ εἶ ὁ
sent us to thee saying : Thou art the

ἐρχόμενος, ἢ ἄλλον προσδοκῶμεν; 21 ἐν
coming [one], or another may we expect? In

ἐκείνῃ τῇ ὥρᾳ ἐθεράπευσεν πολλοὺς ἀπὸ
that - hour he healed many from(of)

νόσων καὶ μαστίγων καὶ πνευμάτων πονηρῶν,
diseases and plagues and spirits evil,

καὶ τυφλοῖς πολλοῖς ἐχαρίσατο βλέπειν.
and blind persons to many he gave to see.

22 καὶ ἀποκριθεὶς εἶπεν αὐτοῖς· πορευθέντες
And answering he said to them : Going

ἀπαγγείλατε Ἰωάννῃ ἃ εἴδετε καὶ
report to John [the things] which ye saw and

ἠκούσατε· τυφλοὶ ἀναβλέπουσιν, χωλοὶ
heard: blind men see again, lame men

περιπατοῦσιν, λεπροὶ καθαρίζονται, καὶ κωφοὶ
walk, lepers are being cleansed, and deaf men

raised, to the poor the
gospel is preached.

23 And blessed is *he*,
whosoever shall not be
offended in me.

24 ¶ And when the mes-
sengers of John were
departed, he began to
speak unto the people
concerning John, What
went ye out into the
wilderness for to see?
A reed shaken with the
wind?

25 But what went ye
out for to see? A man
clothed in soft raiment?
Behold, they which are
gorgeously apparelled, and
live delicately, are in
kings' courts.

26 But what went ye
out for to see? A prophet?
Yea, I say unto you, and
much more than a prophet.

27 This is *he*, of whom
it is written, Behold, I
send my messenger before
thy face, which shall prepare thy way before thee.

28 For I say unto you,
Among those that are
born of women there is
not a greater prophet
than John the Baptist:
but he that is least in the
kingdom of God is greater
than he.

29 And all the people
that heard *him*, and the
publicans, justified God,
being baptized with the
baptism of John.

30 But the Pharisees
and lawyers rejected the
counsel of God against

ἀκούουσιν, νεκροὶ ἐγείρονται, πτωχοὶ
hear, dead men are raised, poor people

εὐαγγελίζονται· 23 καὶ μακάριός ἐστιν ὃς ἐὰν
are evangelized; and blessed is whoever

μὴ σκανδαλισθῇ ἐν ἐμοί. 24 Ἀπελθόντων δὲ
is not offended in me. And going away
=as the

τῶν ἀγγέλων Ἰωάννου ἤρξατο λέγειν πρὸς
the messengers of John[a] he began to say to
messengers of John went away

τοὺς ὄχλους περὶ Ἰωάννου· τί ἐξήλθατε
the crowds concerning John : What went ye forth

εἰς τὴν ἔρημον θεάσασθαι; κάλαμον ὑπὸ
into the desert to see? a reed by

ἀνέμου σαλευόμενον; 25 ἀλλὰ τί ἐξήλθατε
wind being shaken? But what went ye forth

ἰδεῖν; ἄνθρωπον ἐν μαλακοῖς ἱματίοις
to see? a man in soft garments

ἠμφιεσμένον; ἰδοὺ οἱ ἐν ἱματισμῷ ἐνδόξῳ
having been behold[,] the [1]in [2]raiment [3]splendid
clothed? [ones]

καὶ τρυφῇ ὑπάρχοντες ἐν τοῖς βασιλείοις
[4]and [6]in luxury [5]being [3]in - [6]royal palaces

εἰσίν. 26 ἀλλὰ τί ἐξήλθατε ἰδεῖν; προφήτην;
[7]are. But what went ye forth to see? a prophet?

ναὶ λέγω ὑμῖν, καὶ περισσότερον προφήτου.
yes I tell you, and more [than] a prophet.

27 οὗτός ἐστιν περὶ οὗ γέγραπται· ἰδοὺ
This is he concerning whom it has been written : Behold

ἀποστέλλω τὸν ἄγγελόν μου πρὸ προσώπου
I send the messenger of me before [the] face

σου, ὃς κατασκευάσει τὴν ὁδόν σου
of thee, who will prepare the way of thee

ἔμπροσθέν σου. 28 λέγω ὑμῖν, μείζων
before thee. I tell you, [6]greater

ἐν γεννητοῖς γυναικῶν Ἰωάννου οὐδείς
[1]among [2][those] born [3]of women ['than] [3]John [4]no one

ἐστιν· ὁ δὲ μικρότερος ἐν τῇ βασιλείᾳ τοῦ
[5]is; but the less in the kingdom -

θεοῦ μείζων αὐτοῦ ἐστιν. 29 καὶ πᾶς ὁ
of God greater [than] he is. And all the

λαὸς ἀκούσας καὶ οἱ τελῶναι ἐδικαίωσαν
people hearing and the tax-collectors justified

τὸν θεόν, βαπτισθέντες τὸ βάπτισμα
- God, being baptized [with] the baptism

Ἰωάννου· 30 οἱ δὲ Φαρισαῖοι καὶ οἱ
of John; but the Pharisees and the

νομικοὶ τὴν βουλὴν τοῦ θεοῦ ἠθέτησαν εἰς
lawyers [4]the [5]counsel - [6]of God [1]rejected [2]for

themselves, being not baptized of him.

31 ¶ And the Lord said, Whereunto then shall I liken the men of this generation? and to what are they like?

32 They are like unto children sitting in the marketplace, and calling one to another, and saying, We have piped unto you, and ye have not danced; we have mourned to you, and ye have not wept.

33 For John the Baptist came neither eating bread nor drinking wine; and ye say, He hath a devil.

34 The Son of man is come eating and drinking; and ye say, Behold a gluttonous man, and a winebibber, a friend of publicans and sinners!

35 But wisdom is justified of all her children.

36 ¶ And one of the Pharisees desired him that he would eat with him. And he went into the Pharisee's house, and sat down to meat.

37 And, behold, a woman in the city, which was a sinner, when she knew that *Jesus* sat at meat in the Pharisee's house, brought an alabaster box of ointment,

38 And stood at his feet behind *him* weeping, and began to wash his feet with tears, and did wipe *them* with the hairs of her

ἐαυτούς, μὴ βαπτισθέντες ὑπ' αὐτοῦ. 31 Τίνι
³themselves, not being baptized by him. To what

οὖν ὁμοιώσω τοὺς ἀνθρώπους τῆς γενεᾶς
then may I liken the men – generation

ταύτης, καὶ τίνι εἰσὶν ὅμοιοι; 32 ὅμοιοί εἰσιν
of this, and to what are they like? Like are they

παιδίοις τοῖς ἐν ἀγορᾷ καθημένοις καὶ
to children – in a marketplace sitting and

προσφωνοῦσιν ἀλλήλοις ἃ λέγει· ηὐλήσαμεν
calling to one another who says : We piped

ὑμῖν καὶ οὐκ ὠρχήσασθε· ἐθρηνήσαμεν καὶ
to you and ye did not dance; we mourned and

οὐκ ἐκλαύσατε. 33 ἐλήλυθεν γὰρ Ἰωάννης
ye did not weep. For has come John

ὁ βαπτιστὴς μὴ ἐσθίων ἄρτον μήτε πίνων
the Baptist not eating bread nor drinking

οἶνον, καὶ λέγετε· δαιμόνιον ἔχει.
wine, and ye say : A demon he has.

34 ἐλήλυθεν ὁ υἱὸς τοῦ ἀνθρώπου ἐσθίων
Has come the Son – of man eating

καὶ πίνων, καὶ λέγετε· ἰδοὺ ἄνθρωπος
and drinking, and ye say : Behold[,] a man

φάγος καὶ οἰνοπότης, φίλος τελωνῶν καὶ
a glutton and a winebibber, a friend of tax-collectors and

ἁμαρτωλῶν. 35 καὶ ἐδικαιώθη ἡ σοφία
of sinners. And was(is) justified – wisdom

ἀπὸ πάντων τῶν τέκνων αὐτῆς.
from(by) all the children of her.

36 Ἠρώτα δέ τις αὐτὸν τῶν Φαρισαίων
And ⁴asked ¹a certain one ⁵him ²of the ³Pharisees

ἵνα φάγη μετ' αὐτοῦ· καὶ εἰσελθὼν εἰς
that he would eat with him; and entering into

τὸν οἶκον τοῦ Φαρισαίου κατεκλίθη. 37 καὶ
the house of the Pharisee he reclined. And[,]

ἰδοὺ γυνὴ ἥτις ἦν ἐν τῇ πόλει ἁμαρτωλός,
behold[,] a woman who was in the city a sinner,

καὶ ἐπιγνοῦσα ὅτι κατάκειται ἐν τῇ
and knowing that he reclines in the

οἰκίᾳ τοῦ Φαρισαίου, κομίσασα ἀλάβαστρον
house of the Pharisee, bringing an alabaster box

μύρου 38 καὶ στᾶσα ὀπίσω παρὰ τοὺς
of ointment and standing behind at the

πόδας αὐτοῦ κλαίουσα, τοῖς δάκρυσιν
feet of him weeping, with the(her) tears

ἤρξατο βρέχειν τοὺς πόδας αὐτοῦ, καὶ
began to wet the feet of him, and

ταῖς θριξὶν τῆς κεφαλῆς αὐτῆς ἐξέμασσεν,
with the hairs of the head of her wiped off.

head, and kissed his feet, and anointed *them* with the ointment.

39 Now when the Pharisee which had bidden him saw *it*, he spake within himself, saying, This man, if he were a prophet, would have known who and what manner of woman *this is* that toucheth him: for she is a sinner.

40 And Jesus answering said unto him, Simon, I have somewhat to say unto thee. And he saith, Master, say on.

41 There was a certain creditor which had two debtors: the one owed five hundred pence, and the other fifty.

42 And when they had nothing to pay, he frankly forgave them both. Tell me therefore, which of them will love him most?

43 Simon answered and said, I suppose that *he*, to whom he forgave most. And he said unto him, Thou hast rightly judged.

44 And he turned to the woman, and said unto Simon, Seest thou this woman? I entered into thine house, thou gavest me no water for my feet: but she hath washed my feet with tears, and wiped *them* with the hairs of her head.

45 Thou gavest me no kiss: but this woman since the time I came in

καὶ κατεφίλει τοὺς πόδας αὐτοῦ καὶ
and fervently kissed the feet of him and

ἤλειφεν τῷ μύρῳ. 39 ἰδὼν δὲ ὁ Φαρισαῖος
anointed with the ointment. But [5]seeing [1]the [2]Pharisee

ὁ καλέσας αὐτὸν εἶπεν ἐν ἑαυτῷ λέγων·
– [3]having invited [4]him spoke within himself saying :

οὗτος εἰ ἦν [ὁ] προφήτης, ἐγίνωσκεν ἂν
This man if he was the prophet, would have known

τίς καὶ ποταπὴ ἡ γυνὴ ἥτις ἅπτεται
who and what sort the woman who is touching

αὐτοῦ, ὅτι ἁμαρτωλός ἐστιν. 40 καὶ
him, because a sinner she is. And

ἀποκριθεὶς ὁ Ἰησοῦς εἶπεν πρὸς αὐτόν·
answering – Jesus said to him :

Σίμων, ἔχω σοί τι εἰπεῖν. ὁ δέ· διδάσκαλε,
Simon, I have to thee something to say. And he : Teacher,

εἰπέ, φησίν. 41 δύο χρεοφειλέται ἦσαν
say, says. Two debtors were
       =A certain creditor had two debtors:

δανειστῇ τινι· ὁ εἷς ὤφειλεν δηνάρια
creditor to a certain;[c] the one owed denarii

πεντακόσια, ὁ δὲ ἕτερος πεντήκοντα. 42 μὴ
five hundred, and the other fifty. Not
       =As they had no[thing]

ἐχόντων αὐτῶν ἀποδοῦναι ἀμφοτέροις
having them[a] to repay [b]both

ἐχαρίσατο. τίς οὖν αὐτῶν πλεῖον ἀγαπήσει
[1]he freely forgave. Who then of them more will love

αὐτόν; 43 ἀποκριθεὶς Σίμων εἶπεν·
him? Answering Simon said :

ὑπολαμβάνω ὅτι ᾧ τὸ πλεῖον ἐχαρίσατο.
I suppose[.] – to whom the more he freely forgave.

ὁ δὲ εἶπεν αὐτῷ· ὀρθῶς ἔκρινας. 44 καὶ
And he said to him : Rightly thou didst judge. And

στραφεὶς πρὸς τὴν γυναῖκα τῷ Σίμωνι
turning to the woman – to Simon

ἔφη· βλέπεις ταύτην τὴν γυναῖκα; εἰσῆλθόν
he said : Seest thou this – woman? I entered

σου εἰς τὴν οἰκίαν, ὕδωρ μοι ἐπὶ πόδας
of thee into the house, water to me on(for) [my] feet

οὐκ ἔδωκας· αὕτη δὲ τοῖς δάκρυσιν
thou gavest not; but this woman with the(her) tears

ἔβρεξέν μου τοὺς πόδας καὶ ταῖς θριξὶν
wet of me the feet and with the hairs

αὐτῆς ἐξέμαξεν. 45 φίλημά μοι οὐκ ἔδωκας·
of her wiped off. A kiss to me thou gavest not;

αὕτη δὲ ἀφ' ἧς εἰσῆλθον οὐ διέλειπεν
but this woman from [the time] I entered ceased not
       which

hath not ceased to kiss
my feet.

46 My head with oil
thou didst not anoint: but
this woman hath anointed
my feet with ointment.

47 Wherefore I say unto
thee, Her sins, which are
many, are forgiven; for
she loved much: but to
whom little is forgiven,
the same loveth little.

48 And he said unto
her, Thy sins are forgiven.

49 And they that sat at
meat with him began to
say within themselves,
Who is this that forgiveth
sins also?

50 And he said to the
woman, Thy faith hath
saved thee; go in peace.

καταφιλοῦσά μου τοὺς πόδας. 46 ἐλαίῳ
fervently kissing　of me　the　feet.　　With oil

τὴν κεφαλήν μου οὐκ ἤλειψας· αὕτη δὲ
the　head　of me thou didst not anoint; but this woman

μύρῳ ἤλειψεν τοὺς πόδας μου. 47 οὗ
with ointment anointed　the　feet　of me.　47　Of which
　　　　　　　　　　　　　　　　　　　　　　=Wherefore

χάριν λέγω σοι, ἀφέωνται αἱ ἁμαρτίαι
for the sake *of* I tell thee, ⁵have been forgiven ¹the　　⁶sins

αὐτῆς αἱ πολλαί, ὅτι ἠγάπησεν πολύ·
⁶of her　-　²many,　because　she loved　much;

ᾧ δὲ ὀλίγον ἀφίεται, ὀλίγον ἀγαπᾷ.
but to whom little　is forgiven,　little　　he loves.

48 εἶπεν δὲ αὐτῇ· ἀφέωνταί σου αἱ
And he said　to her : Have been forgiven of thee　the

ἁμαρτίαι. 49 καὶ ἤρξαντο οἱ συνανακείμενοι
sins.　　And　began　the [ones] reclining with [him]

λέγειν ἐν ἑαυτοῖς· τίς οὗτός ἐστιν, ὃς καὶ
to say among themselves : Who　this　is,　who even

ἁμαρτίας ἀφίησιν; 50 εἶπεν δὲ πρὸς τὴν
sins　forgives?　50 But he said　to . the

γυναῖκα· ἡ πίστις σου σέσωκέν σε·
woman :　The　faith　of thee　has saved　thee;

πορεύου εἰς εἰρήνην.
go　in　peace.

CHAPTER 8

AND it came to pass
afterward, that he
went throughout every city
and village, preaching and
shewing the glad tidings
of the kingdom of God:
and the twelve *were* with
him,

2 And certain women,
which had been healed of
evil spirits and infirmities,
Mary called Magdalene,
out of whom went seven
devils,

3 And Joanna the wife
of Chuza Herod's steward,
and Susanna, and many
others, which ministered
unto him of their sub-
stance.

8 Καὶ ἐγένετο ἐν τῷ καθεξῆς καὶ αὐτὸς
And it came to pass　afterwards　*and*　he

διώδευεν κατὰ πόλιν καὶ κώμην κηρύσσων
journeyed through every†　city　and　village　proclaiming

καὶ εὐαγγελιζόμενος τὴν βασιλείαν τοῦ
and　preaching　the　kingdom　-

θεοῦ, καὶ οἱ δώδεκα σὺν αὐτῷ, 2 καὶ
of God,　and　the　twelve　with　him,　　and

γυναῖκές τινες αἳ ἦσαν τεθεραπευμέναι ἀπὸ
women　certain who were　having been healed　from

πνευμάτων πονηρῶν καὶ ἀσθενειῶν, Μαρία
spirits　evil　and　infirmities,　Mary

ἡ καλουμένη Μαγδαληνή, ἀφ᾽ ἧς δαιμόνια
-　being called　Magdalene,　from whom　demons

ἑπτὰ ἐξεληλύθει, 3 καὶ Ἰωάννα γυνὴ Χουζᾶ
seven　had gone out,　and　Joanna　wife　of Chuza

ἐπιτρόπου Ἡρῴδου καὶ Σουσάννα καὶ
steward　of Herod　and　Susanna　and

ἕτεραι πολλαί, αἵτινες διηκόνουν αὐτοῖς
others　many,　who　ministered　to them

ἐκ τῶν ὑπαρχόντων αὐταῖς.ᵉ
out of the　possessions　to them.ᵉ

4 ¶ And when much people were gathered together, and were come to him out of every city, he spake by a parable:

5 A sower went out to sow his seed: and as he sowed, some fell by the way side; and it was trodden down, and the fowls of the air devoured it.

6 And some fell upon a rock; and as soon as it was sprung up, it withered away, because it lacked moisture.

7 And some fell among thorns; and the thorns sprang up with it, and choked it.

8 And other fell on good ground, and sprang up, and bare fruit an hundredfold. And when he had said these things, he cried, He that hath ears to hear, let him hear.

9 ¶ And his disciples asked him, saying, What might this parable be?

10 And he said, Unto you it is given to know the mysteries of the kingdom of God: but to others in parables; that seeing they might not see, and hearing they might not understand.

11 Now the parable is this: The seed is the word of God.

---

4 Συνιόντος δὲ ὄχλου πολλοῦ καὶ τῶν
And coming together   crowd   a much   and the [ones]
=when a great crowd came together and people in each city

κατὰ πόλιν ἐπιπορευομένων πρὸς αὐτὸν
in each city†   resorting*   to   him
resorted

εἶπεν διὰ παραβολῆς· **5** ἐξῆλθεν ὁ σπείρων
he said   by   a parable :   Went forth the [one] sowing

τοῦ σπεῖραι τὸν σπόρον αὐτοῦ. καὶ ἐν τῷ
— to sow[d]   the   seed   of him.   And in the

σπείρειν αὐτὸν ὃ μὲν ἔπεσεν παρὰ τὴν
to sow   him[be]   this   fell   by   the
=as he sowed

ὁδὸν καὶ κατεπατήθη, καὶ τὰ πετεινὰ τοῦ
way   and   was trodden down, and   the   birds   of the

οὐρανοῦ κατέφαγεν αὐτό. **6** καὶ ἕτερον
heaven(air)   devoured   it.   And other [seed]

κατέπεσεν ἐπὶ τὴν πέτραν, καὶ φυὲν
fell   on   the   rock,   and   grown

ἐξηράνθη διὰ τὸ μὴ ἔχειν ἰκμάδα.
it was withered because of the   not   to have   moisture.
=because it had no moisture.

7 καὶ ἕτερον ἔπεσεν ἐν μέσῳ τῶν ἀκανθῶν, καὶ
And   other   fell   in [the]   of the   thorns,   and
    midst

συμφυεῖσαι αἱ ἄκανθαι ἀπέπνιξαν αὐτό.
growing up with [it] the   thorns   choked   it.

8 καὶ ἕτερον ἔπεσεν εἰς τὴν γῆν τὴν
And   other   fell   in   the   soil   —

ἀγαθὴν καὶ φυὲν ἐποίησεν καρπὸν
good   and   grown   it produced   fruit

ἑκατονταπλασίονα. ταῦτα λέγων ἐφώνει· ὁ
a hundredfold.   These things saying   he called: The [one]

ἔχων ὦτα ἀκούειν ἀκουέτω. **9** Ἐπηρώτων δὲ
having ears   to hear   let him hear.   And questioned

αὐτὸν οἱ μαθηταὶ αὐτοῦ τίς αὕτη εἴη ἡ
him   the   disciples   of him   what   ¹this ²might be –

παραβολή. **10** ὁ δὲ εἶπεν· ὑμῖν δέδοται
³parable.   And he   said :   To you it has been given

γνῶναι τὰ μυστήρια τῆς βασιλείας τοῦ
to know   the   mysteries   of the   kingdom   —

θεοῦ, τοῖς δὲ λοιποῖς ἐν παραβολαῖς, ἵνα
of God,   but to the   rest   in   parables,   that

βλέποντες μὴ βλέπωσιν καὶ ἀκούοντες μὴ
seeing   they may not see   and   hearing   not

συνιῶσιν. **11** ἔστιν δὲ αὕτη ἡ παραβολή.
they may understand.   ⁴is ¹Now   ²this   —   ³parable.

ὁ σπόρος ἐστὶν ὁ λόγος τοῦ θεοῦ.
The   seed   is   the   word   —   of God.

12 Those by the way side are they that hear; then cometh the devil, and taketh away the word out of their hearts, lest they should believe and be saved.

13 They on the rock *are they,* which, when they hear, receive the word with joy; and these have no root, which for a while believe, and in time of temptation fall away.

14 And that which fell among thorns are they, which, when they have heard, go forth, and are choked with cares and riches and pleasures of *this* life, and bring no fruit to perfection.

15 But that on the good ground are they, which in an honest and good heart, having heard the word, keep *it,* and bring forth fruit with patience.

16 ¶ No man, when he hath lighted a candle, covereth it with a vessel, or putteth *it* under a bed; but setteth *it* on a candlestick, that they which enter in may see the light.

17 For nothing is secret, that shall not be made manifest; neither *any thing* hid, that shall not be known and come abroad.

18 Take heed therefore how ye hear: for whosoever hath, to him shall be given; and whosoever hath not, from him shall

12 οἱ δὲ παρὰ τὴν ὁδόν εἰσιν οἱ ἀκούσαντες,
And the [ones] by the way are the [ones] hearing,

εἶτα ἔρχεται ὁ διάβολος καὶ αἴρει τὸν
then comes the devil and takes the

λόγον ἀπὸ τῆς καρδίας αὐτῶν, ἵνα μὴ
word from the heart of them, lest

πιστεύσαντες σωθῶσιν. 13 οἱ δὲ ἐπὶ τῆς
believing they may be saved. And the [ones] on the

πέτρας οἳ ὅταν ἀκούσωσιν μετὰ χαρᾶς
rock who when they hear with joy

δέχονται τὸν λόγον· καὶ οὗτοι ῥίζαν
receive the word; and these root

οὐκ ἔχουσιν, οἳ πρὸς καιρὸν πιστεύουσιν
have not, who for a time believe

καὶ ἐν καιρῷ πειρασμοῦ ἀφίστανται. 14 τὸ
and in time of trial withdraw. the [one]

δὲ εἰς τὰς ἀκάνθας πεσόν, οὗτοί εἰσιν
And in the thorns falling, these are

οἱ ἀκούσαντες, καὶ ὑπὸ μεριμνῶν καὶ
the [ones] hearing, [1]and [4]by [5]cares [3]and

πλούτου καὶ ἡδονῶν τοῦ βίου πορευόμενοι
[7]riches [8]and [9]pleasures – [10]of life [6]going

συμπνίγονται καὶ οὐ τελεσφοροῦσιν. 15 τὸ
[2]are choked and do not bear [fruit] to maturity. the [one]

δὲ ἐν τῇ καλῇ γῇ, οὗτοί εἰσιν οἵτινες ἐν
And in the good soil, these are [those] who in

καρδίᾳ καλῇ καὶ ἀγαθῇ ἀκούσαντες τὸν
heart a worthy and good hearing the

λόγον κατέχουσιν καὶ καρποφοροῦσιν ἐν
word hold fast and bear fruit in

ὑπομονῇ. 16 Οὐδεὶς δὲ λύχνον ἅψας
patience. Now no one a lamp having lit

καλύπτει αὐτὸν σκεύει ἢ ὑποκάτω κλίνης
hides it with a vessel or underneath a couch

τίθησιν, ἀλλ' ἐπὶ λυχνίας τίθησιν, ἵνα οἱ
puts, but on a lampstand puts, that the

εἰσπορευόμενοι βλέπωσιν τὸ φῶς. 17 οὐ
[ones] coming in may see the light. not

γάρ ἐστιν κρυπτὸν ὃ οὐ φανερὸν
For [anything] is hidden which [3]not [4]manifest

γενήσεται, οὐδὲ ἀπόκρυφον ὃ οὐ μὴ
[1]will [2]become, nor secret which by no means

γνωσθῇ καὶ εἰς φανερὸν ἔλθη. 18 βλέπετε
will be known and to [be] manifest come. See

οὖν πῶς ἀκούετε· ὃς ἂν γὰρ ἔχῃ,
therefore how ye hear; for whoever has,

δοθήσεται αὐτῷ· καὶ ὃς ἂν μὴ ἔχῃ,
it will be given to him; and whoever has not.

be taken even that which
he seemeth to have.

19 ¶ Then came to him
his mother and his brethren, and could not come
at him for the press.

20 And it was told him
by certain which said, Thy
mother and thy brethren
stand without, desiring to
see thee.

21 And he answered
and said unto them, My
mother and my brethren
are these which hear the
word of God, and do it.

22 ¶ Now it came to
pass on a certain day, that
he went into a ship with
his disciples: and he said
unto them, Let us go over
unto the other side of the
lake. And they launched
forth.

23 But as they sailed he
fell asleep: and there
came down a storm of
wind on the lake; and
they were filled *with water,*
and were in jeopardy.

24 And they came to
him, and awoke him,
saying, Master, master, we
perish. Then he arose,
and rebuked the wind and
the raging of the water:
and they ceased, and
there was a calm.

25 And he said unto
them, Where is your faith?
And they being afraid
wondered, saying one to
another, What manner of
man is this! for he com-
mandeth even the winds
and water, and they obey
him.

καὶ ὃ δοκεῖ ἔχειν ἀρθήσεται ἀπ’ αὐτοῦ.
even what he seems to have will be taken from him.

19 Παρεγένετο δὲ πρὸς αὐτὸν ἡ μήτηρ
And came to him the mother

καὶ οἱ ἀδελφοὶ αὐτοῦ, καὶ οὐκ ἠδύναντο
and the brothers of him, and were not able

συντυχεῖν αὐτῷ διὰ τὸν ὄχλον. 20 ἀπηγγέλη δὲ
to come up with him be- the crowd. And it was reported
cause of

αὐτῷ· ἡ μήτηρ σου καὶ οἱ ἀδελφοί σου
to him : The mother of thee and the brothers of thee

ἑστήκασιν ἔξω ἰδεῖν θέλοντές σε. 21 ὁ δὲ
are standing outside ²to see ¹wishing thee. But he

ἀποκριθεὶς εἶπεν πρὸς αὐτούς· μήτηρ μου
answering said to them : Mother of me

καὶ ἀδελφοί μου οὗτοί εἰσιν οἱ τὸν λόγον
and brothers of me ²these ¹are ³the [ones] ⁷the ⁵word

τοῦ θεοῦ ἀκούοντες καὶ ποιοῦντες.
- ⁵of God ⁴hearing ⁵and ⁶doing.

22 Ἐγένετο δὲ ἐν μιᾷ τῶν ἡμερῶν καὶ
And it came to pass on one of the days *and*

αὐτὸς ἐνέβη εἰς πλοῖον καὶ οἱ μαθηταὶ
he embarked in a boat and the disciples

αὐτοῦ, καὶ εἶπεν πρὸς αὐτούς· διέλθωμεν
of him, and he said to them; Let us go over

εἰς τὸ πέραν τῆς λίμνης· καὶ ἀνήχθησαν.
to the other side of the lake; and they put to sea.

23 πλεόντων δὲ αὐτῶν ἀφύπνωσεν. καὶ
And sailing them* he fell asleep. And
= as they sailed

κατέβη λαῖλαψ ἀνέμου εἰς τὴν λίμνην, καὶ
came down a storm of wind to the lake, and

συνεπληροῦντο καὶ ἐκινδύνευον. 24 προσ-
they were filling up and were in danger. ap-

ελθόντες δὲ διήγειραν αὐτὸν λέγοντες·
proaching And they awaken him saying :

ἐπιστάτα ἐπιστάτα, ἀπολλύμεθα. ὁ δὲ
Master[,] Master, we are perishing. But he

διεγερθεὶς ἐπετίμησεν τῷ ἀνέμῳ καὶ τῷ
being awakened rebuked the wind and the

κλύδωνι τοῦ ὕδατος· καὶ ἐπαύσαντο, καὶ ἐγένετο
roughness of the water; and they ceased, and there was

γαλήνη. 25 εἶπεν δὲ αὐτοῖς· ποῦ ἡ πίστις ὑμῶν;
a calm. Then he said to them : Where the faith of you?

φοβηθέντες δὲ ἐθαύμασαν, λέγοντες πρὸς
And fearing they marvelled, saying to

ἀλλήλους· τίς ἄρα οὗτός ἐστιν, ὅτι καὶ
one another : Who then ²this man ¹is, that ²even

τοῖς ἀνέμοις ἐπιτάσσει καὶ τῷ ὕδατι, καὶ
³the ⁴winds ¹he commands and the water, and

26 ¶ And they arrived at the country of the Gadarenes, which is over against Galilee.

27 And when he went forth to land, there met him out of the city a certain man, which had devils long time, and ware no clothes, neither abode in *any* house, but in the tombs.

28 When he saw Jesus, he cried out, and fell down before him, and with a loud voice said, What have I to do with thee, Jesus, *thou* Son of God most high? I beseech thee, torment me not.

29 (For he had commanded the unclean spirit to come out of the man. For oftentimes it had caught him: and he was kept bound with chains and in fetters; and he brake the bands, and was driven of the devil into the wilderness.)

30 And Jesus asked him, saying, What is thy name? And he said, Legion: because many devils were entered into him.

31 And they besought him that he would not command them to go out into the deep.

32 And there was there an herd of many swine feeding on the mountain: and they besought him that he would suffer them

ὑπακούουσιν αὐτῷ; 26 Καὶ κατέπλευσαν εἰς
they obey him? And they sailed down to

τὴν χώραν τῶν Γερασηνῶν, ἥτις ἐστὶν
the country of the Gerasenes, which is

ἀντιπέρα τῆς Γαλιλαίας. 27 ἐξελθόντι δὲ
opposite – Galilee. And going out =as he went out

αὐτῷ ἐπὶ τὴν γῆν ὑπήντησεν ἀνήρ τις
him⁶ onto the land met [him] man a certain

ἐκ τῆς πόλεως ἔχων δαιμόνια, καὶ χρόνῳ
out of the city having demons, and ²time

ἱκανῷ οὐκ ἐνεδύσατο ἱμάτιον, καὶ ἐν οἰκίᾳ
¹for a con- put not on a garment, and in a house
siderable

οὐκ ἔμενεν ἀλλ’ ἐν τοῖς μνήμασιν. 28 ἰδὼν
remained not but among the tombs. seeing

δὲ τὸν Ἰησοῦν ἀνακράξας προσέπεσεν αὐτῷ
And – Jesus crying out he fell prostrate before him

καὶ φωνῇ μεγάλῃ εἶπεν· τί ἐμοὶ καὶ σοί,
and voice in a great(loud) said: What to me and to thee,

Ἰησοῦ υἱὲ τοῦ θεοῦ τοῦ ὑψίστου; δέομαί
Jesus Son – of God – most high? I beg

σου, μή με βασανίσῃς. 29 παρήγγελλεν
of thee, do not me torment. he charged

γὰρ τῷ πνεύματι τῷ ἀκαθάρτῳ ἐξελθεῖν
For the spirit – unclean to come out

ἀπὸ τοῦ ἀνθρώπου. πολλοῖς γὰρ χρόνοις
from the man. For many times

συνηρπάκει αὐτόν, καὶ ἐδεσμεύετο ἁλύσεσιν
it had seized him, and he was bound with chains

καὶ πέδαις φυλασσόμενος, καὶ διαρήσσων
and fetters being guarded, and tearing asunder

τὰ δεσμὰ ἠλαύνετο ἀπὸ τοῦ δαιμονίου εἰς
the bonds he was driven from(by) the demon into

τὰς ἐρήμους. 30 ἐπηρώτησεν δὲ αὐτὸν ὁ
the deserts. And questioned him –

Ἰησοῦς· τί σοι ὄνομά ἐστιν; ὁ δὲ εἶπεν·
Jesus: What to thee name is?ᶜ And he said:

λεγιών, ὅτι εἰσῆλθεν δαιμόνια πολλὰ εἰς
Legion, because ²entered ¹demons ¹many into

αὐτόν. 31 καὶ παρεκάλουν αὐτὸν ἵνα μὴ
him. And they besought him that not

ἐπιτάξῃ αὐτοῖς εἰς τὴν ἄβυσσον ἀπελθεῖν.
he would order them into the abyss to go away.

32 ἦν δὲ ἐκεῖ ἀγέλη χοίρων ἱκανῶν
Now there was there a herd pigs of many

βοσκομένη ἐν τῷ ὄρει· καὶ παρεκάλεσαν
feeding in the mountain; and they besought

αὐτὸν ἵνα ἐπιτρέψῃ αὐτοῖς εἰς ἐκείνους
him that he would allow them into those

to enter into them. And he suffered them.

33 Then went the devils out of the man, and entered into the swine: and the herd ran violently down a steep place into the lake, and were choked.

34 When they that fed *them* saw what was done, they fled, and went and told *it* in the city and in the country.

35 Then they went out to see what was done; and came to Jesus, and found the man, out of whom the devils were departed, sitting at the feet of Jesus, clothed, and in his right mind: and they were afraid.

36 They also which saw *it* told them by what means he that was possessed of the devils was healed.

37 ¶ Then the whole multitude of the country of the Gadarenes round about besought him to depart from them; for they were taken with great fear: and he went up into the ship, and returned back again.

38 Now the man out of whom the devils were departed besought him that he might be with him: but Jesus sent him away, saying,

39 Return to thine own house, and shew how great things God hath done unto thee. And he went his way, and published throughout the

εἰσελθεῖν· καὶ ἐπέτρεψεν αὐτοῖς. 33 ἐξελθόντα
to enter; and he allowed them. ⁴coming out

δὲ τὰ δαιμόνια ἀπὸ τοῦ ἀνθρώπου εἰσῆλθον
¹So ²the ³demons from the man entered

εἰς τοὺς χοίρους, καὶ ὥρμησεν ἡ ἀγέλη
into the pigs, and rushed the herd

κατὰ τοῦ κρημνοῦ εἰς τὴν λίμνην καὶ
down the precipice into the lake and

ἀπεπνίγη. 34 ἰδόντες δὲ οἱ βόσκοντες
was choked. And ³seeing ¹the [ones] ²feeding

τὸ γεγονὸς ἔφυγον καὶ ἀπήγγειλαν εἰς
⁴the thing ⁵having fled and reported in
happened
=what had happened

τὴν πόλιν καὶ εἰς τοὺς ἀγρούς. 35 ἐξῆλθον
the city and in the farms. they went out

δὲ ἰδεῖν τὸ γεγονός, καὶ ἦλθον πρὸς τὸν
And to see the thing having and came to -
happened,
=what had happened,

Ἰησοῦν, καὶ εὗρον καθήμενον τὸν ἄνθρωπον
Jesus, and found sitting the man

ἀφ' οὗ τὰ δαιμόνια ἐξῆλθεν ἱματισμένον
from whom the demons went out *having been* clothed

καὶ σωφρονοῦντα παρὰ τοὺς πόδας τοῦ
and being in his senses by the feet -

Ἰησοῦ, καὶ ἐφοβήθησαν. 36 ἀπήγγειλαν δὲ
of Jesus, and they were afraid. And ³reported

αὐτοῖς οἱ ἰδόντες πῶς ἐσώθη ὁ δαιμο-
⁴to them ¹the [ones] ²seeing ⁵how ⁶was healed ⁶the ⁷demon-

νισθείς. 37 καὶ ἠρώτησεν αὐτὸν ἅπαν τὸ
possessed. And asked him all the

πλῆθος τῆς περιχώρου τῶν Γερασηνῶν
multitude of the neighbourhood of the Gerasenes

ἀπελθεῖν ἀπ' αὐτῶν, ὅτι φόβῳ μεγάλῳ
to go away from them, because fear with a great

συνείχοντο· αὐτὸς δὲ ἐμβὰς εἰς πλοῖον
they were seized; so he embarking in a boat

ὑπέστρεψεν. 38 ἐδεῖτο δὲ αὐτοῦ ὁ ἀνὴρ
returned. And begged of him the man

ἀφ' οὗ ἐξεληλύθει τὰ δαιμόνια εἶναι σὺν
from whom had gone out the demons to be with

αὐτῷ· ἀπέλυσεν δὲ αὐτὸν λέγων· 39 ὑπόστρεφε
him; but he dismissed him saying : Return

εἰς τὸν οἶκόν σου, καὶ διηγοῦ ὅσα σοι
to the house of thee, and relate what ²to thee
things

ἐποίησεν ὁ θεός. καὶ ἀπῆλθεν καθ' ὅλην
¹did - ¹God. And he went away throughout all

whole city how great things Jesus had done unto him.

40 And it came to pass, that, when Jesus was returned, the people *gladly* received him: for they were all waiting for him.

41 ¶ And, behold, there came a man named Jairus, and he was a ruler of the synagogue: and he fell down at Jesus' feet, and besought him that he would come into his house:

42 For he had one only daughter, about twelve years of age, and she lay a dying. But as he went the people thronged him.

43 ¶ And a woman having an issue of blood twelve years, which had spent all her living upon physicians, neither could be healed of any,

44 Came behind *him*, and touched the border of his garment: and immediately her issue of blood stanched.

45 And Jesus said, Who touched me? When all denied, Peter and they that were with him said, Master, the multitude throng thee and press *thee*, and sayest thou, Who touched me?

46 And Jesus said, Somebody hath touched me: for I perceive that virtue is gone out of me.

τὴν πόλιν κηρύσσων ὅσα ἐποίησεν αὐτῷ
the   city   proclaiming   what things   ²did   ²to him

ὁ Ἰησοῦς.
  ¹Jesus.

40 Ἐν δὲ τῷ ὑποστρέφειν τὸν Ἰησοῦν
Now in   the   to return   -   Jesus[be]
=when Jesus returned

ἀπεδέξατο αὐτὸν ὁ ὄχλος· ἦσαν γὰρ
welcomed   him   the   crowd;   for they were

πάντες προσδοκῶντες αὐτόν. **41** καὶ ἰδοὺ
all   expecting   him.   And behold

ἦλθεν ἀνὴρ ᾧ ὄνομα Ἰάϊρος, καὶ οὗτος
came   a man   to whom name   Jairus,[c]   and this man

ἄρχων τῆς συναγωγῆς ὑπῆρχεν· καὶ πεσὼν
a ruler of the   synagogue   was;   and   falling

παρὰ τοὺς πόδας Ἰησοῦ παρεκάλει αὐτὸν
at   the   feet   of Jesus   he besought   him

εἰσελθεῖν εἰς τὸν οἶκον αὐτοῦ, **42** ὅτι
to enter   into   the   house   of him,   because

θυγάτηρ μονογενὴς ἦν αὐτῷ ὡς ἐτῶν
daughter   an only born   was   to him[c]   about of years
=he had an only daughter

δώδεκα καὶ αὕτη ἀπέθνῃσκεν. Ἐν δὲ τῷ
twelve   and   this(she)   was dying.   Now in   the
=as he went

ὑπάγειν αὐτὸν οἱ ὄχλοι συνέπνιγον αὐτόν.
to go   him[be]   the crowds   pressed upon   him.

43 καὶ γυνὴ οὖσα ἐν ῥύσει αἵματος ἀπὸ
And   a woman   being   in   a flow   of blood   from
=having

ἐτῶν δώδεκα, ἥτις οὐκ ἴσχυσεν ἀπ'
years   twelve,   who   was not able   from

οὐδενὸς θεραπευθῆναι, **44** προσελθοῦσα ὄπισθεν
no(any)one   to be healed,   approaching   behind

ἥψατο τοῦ κρασπέδου τοῦ ἱματίου αὐτοῦ,
touched   the   fringe   of the   garment   of him,

καὶ παραχρῆμα ἔστη ἡ ῥύσις τοῦ αἵματος
and   at once   stood   the   flow   of the   blood

αὐτῆς. **45** καὶ εἶπεν ὁ Ἰησοῦς· τίς ὁ
of her.   And   said   -   Jesus :   Who the

ἁψάμενός μου; ἀρνουμένων δὲ πάντων
[one] touching   me?   And denying   all[a]
=when all denied

εἶπεν ὁ Πέτρος· ἐπιστάτα, οἱ ὄχλοι
said   -   Peter :   Master,   the   crowds

συνέχουσίν σε καὶ ἀποθλίβουσιν. **46** ὁ δὲ
press upon   thee   and   jostle.   - But

Ἰησοῦς εἶπεν· ἥψατό μού τις· ἐγὼ γὰρ
Jesus   said :   Touched   me someone;   for I

ἔγνων δύναμιν ἐξεληλυθυῖαν ἀπ' ἐμοῦ.
knew   power   having gone forth   from   me.

47 And when the woman saw that she was not hid, she came trembling, and falling down before him, she declared unto him before all the people for what cause she had touched him, and how she was healed immediately.

48 And he said unto her, Daughter, be of good comfort: thy faith hath made thee whole; go in peace.

49 ¶ While he yet spake, there cometh one from the ruler of the synagogue's *house*, saying to him, Thy daughter is dead; trouble not the Master.

50 But when Jesus heard *it*, he answered him, saying, Fear not: believe only, and she shall be made whole.

51 And when he came into the house, he suffered no man to go in, save Peter, and James, and John, and the father and the mother of the maiden.

52 And all wept, and bewailed her: but he said, Weep not; she is not dead, but sleepeth.

53 And they laughed him to scorn, knowing that she was dead.

54 And he put them all out, and took her by the hand, and called, saying, Maid, arise.

55 And her spirit came again, and she arose straightway: and he commanded to give her meat.

56 And her parents were astonished: but he

47 ἰδοῦσα δὲ ἡ γυνὴ ὅτι οὐκ ἔλαθεν,
And ²seeing ¹the ²woman that she was not hidden,

τρέμουσα ἦλθεν καὶ προσπεσοῦσα αὐτῷ δι'
trembling came and prostrating before him ⁶for

ἣν αἰτίαν ἥψατο αὐτοῦ ἀπήγγειλεν ἐνώπιον
⁷what ⁸cause ⁹she touched ¹⁰him ¹declared ²before

παντὸς τοῦ λαοῦ, καὶ ὡς ἰάθη παραχρῆμα.
³all ⁴the ⁵people, and how she was cured at once.

48 ὁ δὲ εἶπεν αὐτῇ· θυγάτηρ, ἡ πίστις
And he said to her: Daughter, the faith

σου σέσωκέν σε· πορεύου εἰς εἰρήνην.
of thee has healed thee; go in peace.

49 Ἔτι αὐτοῦ λαλοῦντος ἔρχεταί τις παρὰ
Yet him speakingᵃ comes someone from
=While he was yet speaking

τοῦ ἀρχισυναγώγου λέγων ὅτι τέθνηκεν
the synagogue ruler saying[,] — Has died

ἡ θυγάτηρ σου· μηκέτι σκύλλε τὸν
the daughter of thee; no more trouble the

διδάσκαλον. 50 ὁ δὲ Ἰησοῦς ἀκούσας
teacher. — But Jesus hearing

ἀπεκρίθη αὐτῷ· μὴ φοβοῦ· μόνον πίστευσον,
answered him: Fear thou not; only believe,

καὶ σωθήσεται. 51 ἐλθὼν δὲ εἰς τὴν
and she will be healed. And coming into the

οἰκίαν οὐκ ἀφῆκεν εἰσελθεῖν τινα σὺν
house he allowed not to enter anyone with

αὐτῷ εἰ μὴ Πέτρον καὶ Ἰωάννην καὶ
him except Peter and John and

Ἰάκωβον καὶ τὸν πατέρα τῆς παιδὸς καὶ
James and the father of the maid and

τὴν μητέρα. 52 ἔκλαιον δὲ πάντες καὶ
the mother. And were weeping all and

ἐκόπτοντο αὐτήν. ὁ δὲ εἶπεν· μὴ κλαίετε·
bewailing her. But he said: Weep ye not;

οὐκ ἀπέθανεν ἀλλὰ καθεύδει. 53 καὶ
she did not die but sleeps. And

κατεγέλων αὐτοῦ, εἰδότες ὅτι ἀπέθανεν.
they ridiculed him, knowing that she died.

54 αὐτὸς δὲ κρατήσας τῆς χειρὸς αὐτῆς
But he holding the hand of her

ἐφώνησεν λέγων· ἡ παῖς, ἔγειρε. 55 καὶ
called saying: — Maid, arise. And

ἐπέστρεψεν τὸ πνεῦμα αὐτῆς, καὶ ἀνέστη
returned the spirit of her, and she rose up

παραχρῆμα, καὶ διέταξεν αὐτῇ δοθῆναι
at once, and he commanded ³to her ¹to be given

φαγεῖν. 56 καὶ ἐξέστησαν οἱ γονεῖς
to eat. And were amazed the parents

charged them that they
should tell no man what
was done.

αὐτῆς·   ὁ   δὲ   παρήγγειλεν   αὐτοῖς   μηδενὶ
of her;   but he   enjoined   them   ¹no one
εἰπεῖν   τὸ   γεγονός.
¹to tell   the thing having happened.
= what had happened.

CHAPTER 9

THEN he called his
twelve disciples to-
gether, and gave them
power and authority over
all devils, and to cure
diseases.

2 And he sent them to
preach the kingdom of
God, and to heal the sick.

3 And he said unto
them, Take nothing for
your journey, neither
staves, nor scrip, neither
bread, neither money;
neither have two coats
apiece.

4 And whatsoever house
ye enter into, there abide,
and thence depart.

5 And whosoever will
not receive you, when ye
go out of that city, shake
off the very dust from
your feet for a testimony
against them.

6 And they departed,
and went through the
towns, preaching the
gospel, and healing every
where.

7 ¶ Now Herod the
tetrarch heard of all that
was done by him: and he
was perplexed, because
that it was said of some,
that John was risen from
the dead;

8 And of some, that
Elias had appeared; and

9 Συγκαλεσάμενος   δὲ   τοὺς   δώδεκα   ἔδωκεν
And having called together   the   twelve   he gave
αὐτοῖς   δύναμιν   καὶ   ἐξουσίαν   ἐπὶ   πάντα   τὰ
them   power   and   authority   over   all   the
δαιμόνια   καὶ   νόσους   θεραπεύειν·   **2** καὶ
demons   and   diseases   to heal;   and
ἀπέστειλεν   αὐτοὺς   κηρύσσειν   τὴν   βασιλείαν
sent   them   to proclaim   the   kingdom
τοῦ   θεοῦ   καὶ   ἰᾶσθαι,   **3** καὶ   εἶπεν   πρὸς
-   of God   and   to cure,   and   said   to
αὐτούς·   μηδὲν   αἴρετε   εἰς   τὴν   ὁδόν,   μήτε
them :   Nothing   take ye   for   the   way,   neither
ῥάβδον   μήτε   πήραν   μήτε   ἄρτον   μήτε
staff   nor   wallet   nor   bread   nor
ἀργύριον   μήτε   ἀνὰ   δύο   χιτῶνας   ἔχειν.
silver   nor   each   two   tunics   to have.
4 καὶ   εἰς   ἣν   ἂν   οἰκίαν   εἰσέλθητε,   ἐκεῖ
And   into   whatever   house   ye may enter,   there
μένετε   καὶ   ἐκεῖθεν   ἐξέρχεσθε.   **5** καὶ
remain   and   thence   go forth.   And
ὅσοι   ἂν   μὴ   δέχωνται   ὑμᾶς,   ἐξερχόμενοι
as many as   may not receive   you,   going forth
ἀπὸ   τῆς   πόλεως   ἐκείνης   τὸν   κονιορτὸν
from   -   city   that   the   dust
ἀπὸ   τῶν   ποδῶν   ὑμῶν   ἀποτινάσσετε   εἰς
from   the   feet   of you   shake off   for
μαρτύριον   ἐπ᾽   αὐτούς.   **6** ἐξερχόμενοι   δὲ
a testimony   against   them.   And going forth
διήρχοντο   κατὰ   τὰς   κώμας   εὐαγγελιζόμενοι
they went   throughout   the   villages   evangelizing
through
καὶ   θεραπεύοντες   πανταχοῦ.   **7** Ἤκουσεν
and   healing   everywhere.   ²heard
δὲ   Ἡρῴδης   ὁ   τετραάρχης   τὰ   γινόμενα
¹And   ¹Herod   ²the   ³tetrarch   the things   happening
πάντα,   καὶ   διηπόρει   διὰ   τὸ   λέγεσθαι
all,   and   was in perplexity   because of the   to be said
= because it was said
ὑπό   τινων   ὅτι   Ἰωάννης   ἠγέρθη   ἐκ   νεκρῶν,
by   some   that   John   was raised from [the]   dead,
8 ὑπό   τινων   δὲ   ὅτι   Ἠλίας   ἐφάνη,   ἄλλων
and by some   that   Elias   appeared,   ²others

of others, that one of the old prophets was risen again.

9 And Herod said, John have I beheaded: but who is this, of whom I hear such things? And he desired to see him.

10 ¶ And the apostles, when they were returned, told him all that they had done. And he took them, and went aside privately into a desert place belonging to the city called Bethsaida.

11 And the people, when they knew *it*, followed him: and he received them, and spake unto them of the kingdom of God, and healed them that had need of healing.

12 ¶ And when the day began to wear away, then came the twelve, and said unto him, Send the multitude away, that they may go into the towns and country round about, and lodge, and get victuals: for we are here in a desert place.

13 But he said unto them, Give ye them to eat. And they said, We have no more but five loaves and two fishes; except we should go and buy meat for all this people.

14 For they were about five thousand men. And he said to his disciples,

δὲ ὅτι προφήτης τις τῶν ἀρχαίων ἀνέστη.
¹but that   prophet a certain of the   ancients   rose again.

9 εἶπεν   δὲ [ὁ] Ἡρῴδης· Ἰωάννην ἐγὼ
   But said –   Herod :   John   I

ἀπεκεφάλισα· τίς δέ ἐστιν οὗτος περὶ οὗ
beheaded;   but who is   this   about whom

ἀκούω τοιαῦτα; καὶ ἐζήτει ἰδεῖν αὐτόν.
I hear such things? And he sought to see   him.

10 Καὶ   ὑποστρέψαντες   οἱ   ἀπόστολοι
    And   having returned   the   apostles

διηγήσαντο αὐτῷ ὅσα ἐποίησαν.   Καὶ
narrated   to him what things they did.   And

παραλαβὼν αὐτοὺς ὑπεχώρησεν κατ' ἰδίαν
taking   them   he departed   privately

εἰς πόλιν καλουμένην Βηθσαϊδά.   11 οἱ δὲ
to a city   being called   Bethsaida.   But the

ὄχλοι γνόντες ἠκολούθησαν αὐτῷ· καὶ
crowds   knowing   followed   him;   and

ἀποδεξάμενος αὐτοὺς ἐλάλει αὐτοῖς περὶ
welcoming   them   he spoke   to them   about

τῆς βασιλείας τοῦ θεοῦ, καὶ τοὺς χρείαν
the   kingdom   – of God, and the [ones] ³need

ἔχοντας θεραπείας ἰᾶτο.   12 Ἡ δὲ ἡμέρα
¹having   of healing   he cured.   But the   day

ἤρξατο κλίνειν· προσελθόντες δὲ οἱ δώδεκα
began   to decline;   and approaching   the   twelve

εἶπαν αὐτῷ· ἀπόλυσον τὸν ὄχλον, ἵνα
said   to him :   Dismiss   the   crowd,   that

πορευθέντες εἰς τὰς κύκλῳ κώμας καὶ
going   to   ¹the ²around ³villages ²and

ἀγροὺς καταλύσωσιν καὶ εὕρωσιν ἐπισιτισμόν,
⁴farms   they may lodge   and   may find   provisions,

ὅτι ὧδε ἐν ἐρήμῳ τόπῳ ἐσμέν.   13 εἶπεν
because here in a desert   place   we are.   he said

δὲ πρὸς αὐτούς· δότε αὐτοῖς φαγεῖν
And to   them ·   ¹Give   ²them   ⁴to eat

ὑμεῖς.   οἱ δὲ εἶπαν· οὐκ εἰσὶν ἡμῖν
³ye.   But they   said :   There are not   to usᵉ
                                          =We have not

πλεῖον ἢ ἄρτοι πέντε καὶ ἰχθύες δύο, εἰ
more   than loaves   five   and   fishes   two, un-

μήτι πορευθέντες ἡμεῖς ἀγοράσωμεν εἰς
less   going   we   may buy   for

πάντα τὸν λαὸν τοῦτον βρώματα.   14 ἦσαν
all   –   people this   foods.   there were

γὰρ ὡσεὶ ἄνδρες πεντακισχίλιοι.   εἶπεν δὲ
For   about men   five thousand.   And he said

πρὸς τοὺς μαθητὰς αὐτοῦ· κατακλίνατε
to   the   disciples   of him :   ¹Make ²to recline

Make them sit down by fifties in a company.

15 And they did so, and made them all sit down.

16 Then he took the five loaves and the two fishes, and looking up to heaven, he blessed them, and brake, and gave to the disciples to set before the multitude.

17 And they did eat, and were all filled: and there was taken up of fragments that remained to them twelve baskets.

18 ¶ And it came to pass, as he was alone praying, his disciples were with him: and he asked them, saying, Whom say the people that I am?

19 They answering said, John the Baptist; but some say, Elias; and others say, that one of the old prophets is risen again.

20 He said unto them, But whom say ye that I am? Peter answering said, The Christ of God.

21 And he straitly charged them, and commanded them to tell no man that thing;

22 Saying, The Son of man must suffer many things, and be rejected of the elders and chief priests

αὐτοὺς κλισίας ὡσεὶ ἀνὰ πεντήκοντα.
²them [in] groups ¹about ²each ³fifty.

15 καὶ ἐποίησαν οὕτως καὶ κατέκλιναν
And they did so and made to recline

ἅπαντας. 16 λαβὼν δὲ τοὺς πέντε ἄρτους
all. And taking the five loaves

καὶ τοὺς δύο ἰχθύας, ἀναβλέψας εἰς τὸν
and the two fishes, looking up to -

οὐρανὸν εὐλόγησεν αὐτοὺς καὶ κατέκλασεν,
heaven he blessed them and broke,

καὶ ἐδίδου τοῖς μαθηταῖς παραθεῖναι τῷ
and gave to the disciples to set before the

ὄχλῳ. 17 καὶ ἔφαγον καὶ ἐχορτάσθησαν
crowd. And they ate and were satisfied

πάντες· καὶ ἤρθη τὸ περισσεῦσαν αὐτοῖς
all; and were taken the excess to them

κλασμάτων κόφινοι δώδεκα.
of fragments baskets twelve.

18 Καὶ ἐγένετο ἐν τῷ εἶναι αὐτὸν
And it came to pass in the to be him^be
=as he was

προσευχόμενον κατὰ μόνας συνῆσαν αὐτῷ
praying alone were with him

οἱ μαθηταί, καὶ ἐπηρώτησεν αὐτοὺς λέγων·
the disciples, and he questioned them saying :

τίνα με οἱ ὄχλοι λέγουσιν εἶναι; 19 οἱ δὲ
Whom me the crowds say to be? And they
=Whom do the crowds say that I am?

ἀποκριθέντες εἶπαν· Ἰωάννην τὸν βαπτιστήν,
answering said : John the Baptist,

ἄλλοι δὲ Ἠλίαν, ἄλλοι δὲ ὅτι προφήτης
but others Elias, and others that prophet

τις τῶν ἀρχαίων ἀνέστη. 20 εἶπεν δὲ
a certain of the ancients rose again. And he said

αὐτοῖς· ὑμεῖς δὲ τίνα με λέγετε εἶναι;
to them : But ye whom me say to be?
=whom say ye that I am?

Πέτρος δὲ ἀποκριθεὶς εἶπεν· τὸν χριστὸν
And Peter answering said: The Christ

τοῦ θεοῦ. 21 ὁ δὲ ἐπιτιμήσας αὐτοῖς
— of God. But he warning ²them

παρήγγειλεν μηδενὶ λέγειν τοῦτο, 22 εἰπὼν
¹charged ⁴no one ²to tell ⁵this, saying

ὅτι δεῖ τὸν υἱὸν τοῦ ἀνθρώπου πολλὰ
that it behoves the Son — of man many things

παθεῖν καὶ ἀποδοκιμασθῆναι ἀπὸ τῶν
to suffer and to be rejected from(by) the

πρεσβυτέρων καὶ ἀρχιερέων καὶ γραμματέων
elders and chief priests and scribes

and scribes, and be slain, and be raised the third day.

23 ¶ And he said to *them* all, If any *man* will come after me, let him deny himself, and take up his cross daily, and follow me.

24 For whosoever will save his life shall lose it: but whosoever will lose his life for my sake, the same shall save it.

25 For what is a man advantaged, if he gain the whole world, and lose himself, or be cast away?

26 For whosoever shall be ashamed of me and of my words, of him shall the Son of man be ashamed, when he shall come in his own glory, and *in his* Father's, and of the holy angels.

27 But I tell you of a truth, there be some standing here, which shall not taste of death, till they see the kingdom of God.

28 ¶ And it came to pass about an eight days after these sayings, he took Peter and John and James, and went up into a mountain to pray.

29 And as he prayed, the fashion of his countenance was altered, and

καὶ   ἀποκτανθῆναι   καὶ   τῇ   τρίτῃ   ἡμέρᾳ
and   to be killed   and   on the   third   day

ἐγερθῆναι.   23 Ἔλεγεν   δὲ   πρὸς   πάντας·
to be raised.   And he said   to   all :

εἴ   τις   θέλει   ὀπίσω   μου   ἔρχεσθαι,   ἀρνησάσθω
If anyone wishes   after   me   to come,   let him deny

ἑαυτὸν   καὶ   ἀράτω   τὸν   σταυρὸν
himself   and   take   the   cross

αὐτοῦ   καθ'   ἡμέραν,   καὶ   ἀκολουθείτω   μοι.
of him   daily,   and   let him follow   me.

24 ὃς   γὰρ   ἐὰν   θέλῃ   τὴν   ψυχὴν   αὐτοῦ
For whoever   wishes   the   life   of him

σῶσαι,   ἀπολέσει   αὐτήν·   ὃς   δ'   ἂν   ἀπολέσῃ
to save,   he will lose   it;   but whoever   loses

τὴν   ψυχὴν   αὐτοῦ   ἕνεκεν   ἐμοῦ,   οὗτος
the   life   of him for the sake of me,   this [one]

σώσει   αὐτήν.   25 τί   γὰρ   ὠφελεῖται
will save   it.   For what   is profited

ἄνθρωπος   κερδήσας   τὸν   κόσμον   ὅλον   ἑαυτὸν
a man   gaining   the   world   whole   ³himself

δὲ   ἀπολέσας   ἢ   ζημιωθείς;   26 ὃς   γὰρ   ἂν
¹but   ²losing   or   suffering loss?   26 For whoever

ἐπαισχυνθῇ   με   καὶ   τοὺς   ἐμοὺς   λόγους,
is ashamed of   me   and   -   my   words,

τοῦτον   ὁ   υἱὸς   τοῦ   ἀνθρώπου   ἐπαι-
this [one]   the   Son   -   of man   will be

σχυνθήσεται,   ὅταν   ἔλθῃ   ἐν   τῇ   δόξῃ
ashamed of,   when he comes in   the   glory

αὐτοῦ   καὶ   τοῦ   πατρὸς   καὶ   τῶν   ἁγίων
of him   and   of the   Father   and   of the   holy

ἀγγέλων.   27 λέγω   δὲ   ὑμῖν   ἀληθῶς,
angels.   But I tell   you   truly,

εἰσίν   τινες   τῶν   αὐτοῦ   ἑστηκότων   οἳ
there are some of the [ones]   here   standing   who

οὐ   μὴ   γεύσωνται   θανάτου   ἕως   ἂν   ἴδωσιν
by no means   may taste   of death   until   they see

τὴν   βασιλείαν   τοῦ   θεοῦ.
the   kingdom   -   of God.

28 Ἐγένετο   δὲ   μετὰ   τοὺς   λόγους   τούτους
And it came to pass ⁴after   -   ²sayings   ³these

ὡσεὶ   ἡμέραι   ὀκτώ,   καὶ   παραλαβὼν   Πέτρον
¹about   ³days   ²eight,   and   taking   Peter

καὶ   Ἰωάννην   καὶ   Ἰάκωβον   ἀνέβη   εἰς   τὸ
and   John   and   James   he went up into   the

ὄρος   προσεύξασθαι.   29 καὶ   ἐγένετο   ἐν   τῷ
mountain   to pray.   And   ⁹became   in   the
                                                       =¹as ²he ³prayed

προσεύχεσθαι   αὐτὸν   τὸ   εἶδος   τοῦ   προσώπου
to pray   him⁵⁶   ⁴the   ⁵appearance ⁶of the ⁷face

his raiment *was* white *and* glistering.

30 And, behold, there talked with him two men, which were Moses and Elias:

31 Who appeared in glory, and spake of his decease which he should accomplish at Jerusalem.

32 But Peter and they that were with him were heavy with sleep: and when they were awake, they saw his glory, and the two men that stood with him.

33 And it came to pass, as they departed from him, Peter said unto Jesus, Master, it is good for us to be here: and let us make three tabernacles; one for thee, and one for Moses, and one for Elias: not knowing what he said.

34 While he thus spake, there came a cloud, and overshadowed them: and they feared as they entered into the cloud.

35 And there came a voice out of the cloud, saying, This is my beloved Son: hear him.

36 And when the voice was past, Jesus was found alone. And they kept *it* close, and told no man in

αὐτοῦ ἕτερον καὶ ὁ ἱματισμὸς αὐτοῦ
⁸of him ¹⁸different and the raiment of him

λευκὸς ἐξαστράπτων. 30 καὶ ἰδοὺ ἄνδρες
¹white ¹gleaming. And[,] behold[,] men

δύο συνελάλουν αὐτῷ, οἵτινες ἦσαν Μωϋσῆς
two conversed with him, who were Moses

καὶ Ἠλίας, 31 οἳ ὀφθέντες ἐν δόξῃ ἔλεγον
and Elias, who appearing in glory spoke of

τὴν ἔξοδον αὐτοῦ, ἣν ἤμελλεν πληροῦν
the exodus of him, which he was about to accomplish

ἐν Ἰερουσαλήμ. 32 ὁ δὲ Πέτρος καὶ οἱ
in Jerusalem. – But Peter and the [ones]

σὺν αὐτῷ ἦσαν βεβαρημένοι ὕπνῳ· δια-
with him were having been burdened with sleep; ⁸wak-

γρηγορήσαντες δὲ εἶδαν τὴν δόξαν αὐτοῦ
ing thoroughly ¹but they saw the glory of him

καὶ τοὺς δύο ἄνδρας τοὺς συνεστῶτας
and the two men – standing with

αὐτῷ. 33 καὶ ἐγένετο ἐν τῷ διαχωρίζεσθαι
him. And it came to pass in the to part
=when they parted

αὐτοὺς ἀπ' αὐτοῦ εἶπεν ὁ Πέτρος πρὸς
them^(be) from him said – Peter to

τὸν Ἰησοῦν· ἐπιστάτα, καλόν ἐστιν ἡμᾶς
– Jesus: Master, good it is [for] us

ὧδε εἶναι, καὶ ποιήσωμεν σκηνὰς τρεῖς,
here to be, and let us make tents three,

μίαν σοὶ καὶ μίαν Μωϋσεῖ καὶ μίαν
one for thee and one for Moses and one

Ἠλίᾳ, μὴ εἰδὼς ὃ λέγει. 34 ταῦτα δὲ
for Elias, not knowing what he says. And these things

αὐτοῦ λέγοντος ἐγένετο νεφέλη καὶ
him saying^(a) came a cloud and
=while he said these things

ἐπεσκίαζεν αὐτούς· ἐφοβήθησαν δὲ ἐν τῷ
overshadowed them; and they feared in the
=as they entered

εἰσελθεῖν αὐτοὺς εἰς τὴν νεφέλην. 35 καὶ
to enter them^(be) into the cloud. And

φωνὴ ἐγένετο ἐκ τῆς νεφέλης λέγουσα·
a voice came out of the cloud saying:

οὗτός ἐστιν ὁ υἱός μου ὁ ἐκλελεγμένος,
This is the Son of me – having been chosen,

αὐτοῦ ἀκούετε, 36 καὶ ἐν τῷ γενέσθαι
him hear ye, and in the to become
=when the voice came

τὴν φωνὴν εὑρέθη Ἰησοῦς μόνος. καὶ
the voice^(be) was found Jesus alone. And

αὐτοὶ ἐσίγησαν καὶ οὐδενὶ ἀπήγγειλαν ἐν ἐκείναις
they were silent and to no one reported in those

those days any of those
things which they had seen.

37 ¶ And it came to
pass, that on the next day,
when they were come
down from the hill, much
people met him.

38 And, behold, a man
of the company cried out,
saying, Master, I beseech
thee, look upon my son:
for he is mine only child.

39 And, lo, a spirit
taketh him, and he sud-
denly crieth out; and it
teareth him that he foam-
eth again, and bruising
him hardly departeth from
him.

40 And I besought thy
disciples to cast him out;
and they could not.

41 And Jesus answering
said, O faithless and perverse generation, how long
shall I be with you, and
suffer you? Bring thy son
hither.

42 And as he was yet a
coming, the devil threw
him down, and tare him.
And Jesus rebuked the
unclean spirit, and healed
the child, and delivered
him again to his father.

43 ¶ And they were all
amazed at the mighty
power of God. But while
they wondered every one
at all things which Jesus

ταῖς   ἡμέραις   οὐδὲν   ὧν   ἑώρακαν.
-       days   no(any) of [the things] they have
                   thing   which   (had) seen.

37 Ἐγένετο δὲ τῇ ἑξῆς ἡμέρᾳ κατελ-
And it came to pass on the following day   coming
θόντων αὐτῶν ἀπὸ τοῦ ὄρους συνήντησεν
down them* from the mountain   met
=as they came down

αὐτῷ ὄχλος πολύς. 38 καὶ ἰδοὺ ἀνὴρ
him crowd a much.   And[,] behold[,] a man

ἀπὸ τοῦ ὄχλου ἐβόησεν λέγων· διδάσκαλε,
from the crowd called aloud saying : Teacher,

δέομαί σου ἐπιβλέψαι ἐπὶ τὸν υἱόν μου,
I beg of thee to look at at the son of me,

ὅτι μονογενής μοί ἐστιν, 39 καὶ ἰδοὺ
because only born to me he is,   and[,] behold[,]

πνεῦμα λαμβάνει αὐτόν, καὶ ἐξαίφνης
a spirit takes him, and suddenly

κράζει καὶ σπαράσσει αὐτὸν μετὰ ἀφροῦ,
cries out and throws him with foam,

καὶ μόλις ἀποχωρεῖ ἀπ' αὐτοῦ συντρῖβον
and scarcely departs from him bruising

αὐτόν· 40 καὶ ἐδεήθην τῶν μαθητῶν σου
him;   and I begged of the disciples of thee

ἵνα ἐκβάλωσιν αὐτό, καὶ οὐκ ἠδυνήθησαν.
that they would expel it, and they were not able.

41 ἀποκριθεὶς δὲ ὁ Ἰησοῦς εἶπεν· ὦ
And answering - Jesus said : O

γενεὰ ἄπιστος καὶ διεστραμμένη, ἕως πότε
generation unbelieving and having been perverted, until when

ἔσομαι πρὸς ὑμᾶς καὶ ἀνέξομαι ὑμῶν;
shall I be with you and endure you?

προσάγαγε ὧδε τὸν υἱόν σου. 42 ἔτι
Bring here the son of thee.   yet

δὲ προσερχομένου αὐτοῦ ἔρρηξεν αὐτὸν τὸ
But approaching him* tore him the
=But while he was yet approaching

δαιμόνιον καὶ συνεσπάραξεν· ἐπετίμησεν δὲ
demon and threw violently;   but ²rebuked

ὁ Ἰησοῦς τῷ πνεύματι τῷ ἀκαθάρτῳ, καὶ
- ¹Jesus ³the ⁵spirit ⁴unclean, and

ἰάσατο τὸν παῖδα καὶ ἀπέδωκεν αὐτὸν τῷ
cured the boy and restored him to the

πατρὶ αὐτοῦ. 43 ἐξεπλήσσοντο δὲ πάντες
father of him.   And were astounded all

ἐπὶ τῇ μεγαλειότητι τοῦ θεοῦ.
at the majesty - of God.

Πάντων δὲ θαυμαζόντων ἐπὶ πᾶσιν οἷς
And all marvelling* at all things which
=while all marvelled

did, he said unto his disciples,

44 Let these sayings sink down into your ears: for the Son of man shall be delivered into the hands of men.

45 But they understood not this saying, and it was hid from them, that they perceived it not: and they feared to ask him of that saying.

46 ¶ Then there arose a reasoning among them, which of them should be greatest.

47 And Jesus, perceiving the thought of their heart, took a child, and set him by him,

48 And said unto them, Whosoever shall receive this child in my name receiveth me: and whosoever shall receive me receiveth him that sent me: for he that is least among you all, the same shall be great.

49 And John answered and said, Master, we saw one casting out devils in thy name; and we forbad him, because he followeth not with us.

50 And Jesus said unto him, Forbid *him* not: for he that is not against us is for us.

51 ¶ And it came to pass, when the time was come

ἐποίει   εἶπεν   πρὸς   τοὺς   μαθητὰς   αὐτοῦ·
he did   he said   to   the   disciples   of him :

44 θέσθε   ὑμεῖς   εἰς   τὰ   ὦτα   ὑμῶν   τοὺς
Lay   ye   in   the   ears   of you   –

λόγους   τούτους·   ὁ   γὰρ   υἱὸς   τοῦ   ἀνθρώπου
sayings   these;   for the   Son   –   of man

μέλλει   παραδίδοσθαι   εἰς   χεῖρας   ἀνθρώπων.
is about   to be betrayed   into   [the] hands   of men.

45 οἱ   δὲ   ἠγνόουν   τὸ   ῥῆμα   τοῦτο,   καὶ   ἦν
But they   knew not   –   word   this,   and it was

παρακεκαλυμμένον   ἀπ'   αὐτῶν   ἵνα   μὴ
having been veiled   from   them   lest

αἴσθωνται   αὐτό,   καὶ   ἐφοβοῦντο   ἐρωτῆσαι
they should perceive it,   and   they feared   to ask

αὐτὸν   περὶ   τοῦ   ῥήματος   τούτου.   46 Εἰσῆλθεν
him   about –   word   this.   entered

δὲ   διαλογισμὸς   ἐν   αὐτοῖς,   τὸ   τίς   ἂν   εἴη
And   a debate   among   them,   –   who   might be
=a debate arose

μείζων   αὐτῶν.   47 ὁ   δὲ   Ἰησοῦς   εἰδὼς   τὸν
greater(est)   of them.   –   And   Jesus   knowing   the

διαλογισμὸν   τῆς   καρδίας   αὐτῶν,   ἐπιλαβόμενος
debate   of the   heart   of them,   taking

παιδίον   ἔστησεν   αὐτὸ   παρ'   ἑαυτῷ,   48 καὶ
a child   stood   it(him)   beside   himself,   and

εἶπεν   αὐτοῖς·   ὃς   ἐὰν   δέξηται   τοῦτο   τὸ
said   to them :   Whoever   receives   this   –

παιδίον   ἐπὶ   τῷ   ὀνόματί   μου,   ἐμὲ   δέχεται·
child   on(in)   the   name   of me,   me   receives;

καὶ   ὃς   ἂν   ἐμὲ   δέξηται,   δέχεται   τὸν
and   whoever   me   receives,   receives   the [one]

ἀποστείλαντά   με·   ὁ   γὰρ   μικρότερος   ἐν
having sent   me;   for ¹the [one]   ³lesser   ⁴among

πᾶσιν   ὑμῖν   ὑπάρχων,   οὗτός   ἐστιν   μέγας.
⁶all   ⁵you   ²being,   this [one]   is   great.

49 Ἀποκριθεὶς   δὲ   ὁ   Ἰωάννης   εἶπεν·   ἐπιστάτα,
And answering   –   John   said :   Master,

εἴδομέν   τινα   ἐν   τῷ   ὀνόματί   σου   ἐκβάλλοντα
we saw   someone   in   the   name   of thee   expelling

δαιμόνια,   καὶ   ἐκωλύομεν   αὐτόν,   ὅτι
demons,   and   we prevented   him,   because

οὐκ   ἀκολουθεῖ   μεθ'   ἡμῶν.   50 εἶπεν   δὲ   πρὸς
he does not follow   with   us.   And said   to

αὐτὸν   Ἰησοῦς·   μὴ   κωλύετε·   ὃς   γὰρ   οὐκ
him   Jesus: Do not prevent;   for [he] who   not

ἔστιν   καθ'   ὑμῶν,   ὑπὲρ   ὑμῶν   ἐστιν.
is   against   you,   for   you   is.

51 Ἐγένετο   δὲ   ἐν   τῷ   συμπληροῦσθαι
And it came to pass   in   the   to be fulfilled

that he should be received up, he stedfastly set his face to go to Jerusalem,

52 And sent messengers before his face: and they went, and entered into a village of the Samaritans, to make ready for him.

53 And they did not receive him, because his face was as though he would go to Jerusalem.

54 And when his disciples James and John saw *this*, they said, Lord, wilt thou that we command fire to come down from heaven, and consume them, even as Elias did?

55 But he turned, and rebuked them, and said, Ye know not what manner of spirit ye are of.

56 For the Son of man is not come to destroy men's lives, but to save *them*. And they went to another village.

57 ¶ And it came to pass, that, as they went in the way, a certain *man* said unto him, Lord, I will follow thee whithersoever thou goest.

58 And Jesus said unto him, Foxes have holes, and birds of the air *have* nests; but the Son of man hath not where to lay *his* head.

59 And he said unto another, Follow me. But he said, Lord, suffer me first to go and bury my father.

60 Jesus said unto him, Let the dead bury their

τὰς ἡμέρας τῆς ἀναλήμψεως αὐτοῦ καὶ
the   days   of the   assumption   of him[be] *and*
=as the days of his assumption were fulfilled

αὐτὸς τὸ πρόσωπον ἐστήρισεν τοῦ
he   the(his)   face   set   -

πορεύεσθαι εἰς Ἰερουσαλήμ, 52 καὶ ἀπέστειλεν
to go[d]   to   Jerusalem,   and   sent

ἀγγέλους πρὸ προσώπου αὐτοῦ. καὶ
messengers before   face   of him. And

πορευθέντες εἰσῆλθον εἰς κώμην Σαμαριτῶν,
going   they entered into a village of Samaritans,

ὥστε ἑτοιμάσαι αὐτῷ· 53 καὶ οὐκ ἐδέξαντο
so as   to prepare for him; and they did not receive

αὐτόν, ὅτι τὸ πρόσωπον αὐτοῦ ἦν
him,   because the   face   of him   was

πορευόμενον εἰς Ἰερουσαλήμ. 54 ἰδόντες
going   to   Jerusalem.   [e]seeing

δὲ οἱ μαθηταὶ Ἰάκωβος καὶ Ἰωάννης
And [1]the [2]disciples [3]James [4]and [5]John

εἶπαν· κύριε, θέλεις εἴπωμεν πῦρ κατα-
[1]said: Lord, wilt thou we may tell fire   to come-

βῆναι ἀπὸ τοῦ οὐρανοῦ καὶ ἀναλῶσαι
down   from   -   heaven and   to destroy

αὐτούς; 55 στραφεὶς δὲ ἐπετίμησεν αὐτοῖς.
them?   But turning   he rebuked   them.

56 καὶ ἐπορεύθησαν εἰς ἑτέραν κώμην.
And   they went   to   another village.

57 Καὶ πορευομένων αὐτῶν ἐν τῇ ὁδῷ
And   going   them[a] in the way
=as they went

εἶπέν τις πρὸς αὐτόν· ἀκολουθήσω σοι
said one to   him :   I will follow   thee

ὅπου ἐὰν ἀπέρχῃ. 58 καὶ εἶπεν αὐτῷ ὁ
wherever thou goest.   And said to him -

Ἰησοῦς· αἱ ἀλώπεκες φωλεοὺς ἔχουσιν καὶ
Jesus : The foxes   holes   have   and

τὰ πετεινὰ τοῦ οὐρανοῦ κατασκηνώσεις, ὁ
the birds   -   of heaven   nests,   [a]the

δὲ υἱὸς τοῦ ἀνθρώπου οὐκ ἔχει ποῦ τὴν
[1]but Son -   of man   has not where the(his)

κεφαλὴν κλίνῃ. 59 Εἶπεν δὲ πρὸς ἕτερον·
head   he may lay.   And he said   to   another :

ἀκολούθει μοι. ὁ δὲ εἶπεν· ἐπίτρεψόν μοι
Follow   me. But he   said : Allow   me

πρῶτον ἀπελθόντι θάψαι τὸν πατέρα μου.
first   going   to bury the   father of me.

60 εἶπεν δὲ αὐτῷ· ἄφες τοὺς νεκροὺς
But he said to him : Leave the   dead

dead: but go thou and preach the kingdom of God.

61 And another also said, Lord, I will follow thee; but let me first go bid them farewell, which are at home at my house.

62 And Jesus said unto him, No man, having put his hand to the plough, and looking back, is fit for the kingdom of God.

θάψαι τοὺς ἑαυτῶν νεκρούς, σὺ δὲ ἀπελθὼν
to bury   the of themselves dead,   but thou   going
=their own dead,

διάγγελλε τὴν βασιλείαν τοῦ θεοῦ. 61 Εἶπεν
announce   the   kingdom   – of God.   61 said

δὲ καὶ ἕτερος· ἀκολουθήσω σοι, κύριε·
And also   another :   I will follow   thee,   Lord;

πρῶτον δὲ ἐπίτρεψόν μοι ἀποτάξασθαι τοῖς
but first   allow   me   to say farewell   to the [ones]

εἰς τὸν οἶκόν μου. 62 εἶπεν δὲ [πρὸς
in   the   house   of me.   62 But said   to

αὐτὸν] ὁ Ἰησοῦς· οὐδεὶς ἐπιβαλὼν τὴν
him]   –   Jesus :   No one   putting on   the(his)

χεῖρα ἐπ' ἄροτρον καὶ βλέπων εἰς τὰ
hand   on   a plough   and   looking   at the things

ὀπίσω εὔθετός ἐστιν τῇ βασιλείᾳ τοῦ θεοῦ.
behind   fit   is   for the   kingdom   – of God.

CHAPTER 10

AFTER these things the Lord appointed other seventy also, and sent them two and two before his face into every city and place, whither he himself would come.

2 Therefore said he unto them, The harvest truly is great, but the labourers are few: pray ye therefore the Lord of the harvest, that he would send forth labourers into his harvest.

3 Go your ways: behold, I send you forth as lambs among wolves.

4 Carry neither purse, nor scrip, nor shoes: and salute no man by the way.

5 And into whatsoever house ye enter, first say, Peace be to this house.

6 And if the son of peace be there, your peace shall rest upon it: if not,

10 Μετὰ δὲ ταῦτα ἀνέδειξεν ὁ κύριος
Now after   these things   appointed   the   Lord

ἑτέρους ἑβδομήκοντα [δύο], καὶ ἀπέστειλεν
others   seventy-two,   and   sent

αὐτοὺς ἀνὰ δύο πρὸ προσώπου αὐτοῦ εἰς
them   two by two†   before   face   of him   into

πᾶσαν πόλιν καὶ τόπον οὗ ἤμελλεν αὐτὸς
every   city   and   place   where ²was about   ¹he

ἔρχεσθαι. 2 ἔλεγεν δὲ πρὸς αὐτούς· ὁ
to come.   2 And he said   to   them :   the

μὲν θερισμὸς πολύς, οἱ δὲ ἐργάται ὀλίγοι·
Indeed harvest   much,   but the   workmen   few;

δεήθητε οὖν τοῦ κυρίου τοῦ θερισμοῦ
beg ye   therefore of the   Lord   of the   harvest

ὅπως ἐργάτας ἐκβάλῃ εἰς τὸν θερισμὸν
that   workmen   he would thrust forth into the   harvest

αὐτοῦ. 3 ὑπάγετε· ἰδοὺ ἀποστέλλω ὑμᾶς
of him.   3 Go ye;   behold   I send   you

ὡς ἄρνας ἐν μέσῳ λύκων. 4 μὴ βαστάζετε
as   lambs   in [the]   midst of wolves.   4 Do not carry

βαλλάντιον, μὴ πήραν, μὴ ὑποδήματα· καὶ
a purse,   nor   a wallet,   nor   sandals;   and

μηδένα κατὰ τὴν ὁδὸν ἀσπάσησθε. 5 εἰς
no one   by   the   way   greet.   5 ²into

ἣν δ' ἂν εἰσέλθητε οἰκίαν, πρῶτον λέγετε·
¹And ²whatever ³ye enter ⁴house,   first   say :

εἰρήνη τῷ οἴκῳ τούτῳ. 6 καὶ ἐὰν ἐκεῖ
Peace   – house   to this.   6 And   if   there

ᾖ υἱὸς εἰρήνης, ἐπαναπαήσεται ἐπ' αὐτὸν
there is a son   of peace,   shall rest   on   it(?him)

it shall turn to you again.

7 And in the same
house remain, eating and
drinking such things as
they give: for the labourer
is worthy of his hire.
Go not from house to
house.

8 And into whatsoever
city ye enter, and they
receive you, eat such
things as are set before
you:

9 And heal the sick that
are therein, and say unto
them, The kingdom of
God is come nigh unto
you.

10 But into whatsoever
city ye enter, and they
receive you not, go your
ways out into the streets
of the same, and say,

11 Even the very dust
of your city, which
cleaveth on us, we do wipe
off against you: notwith-
standing be ye sure of this,
that the kingdom of God
is come nigh you.

12 But I say unto you,
that it shall be more
tolerable in that day for
Sodom, than for that city.

13 Woe unto thee,
Chorazin! woe unto thee,
Bethsaida! for if the mighty
works had been done in
Tyre and Sidon, which
have been done in you,
they had a great while
ago repented, sitting in
sackcloth and ashes.

ἡ εἰρήνη ὑμῶν· εἰ δὲ μή γε, ἐφ᾽ ὑμᾶς
the peace of you; otherwise, on you

ἀνακάμψει. 7 ἐν αὐτῇ δὲ τῇ οἰκίᾳ μένετε,
it shall return. ³in ⁴same ¹And ²the house⁕ remain,

ἔσθοντες καὶ πίνοντες τὰ παρ᾽ αὐτῶν·
eating and drinking the things with them;

ἄξιος γὰρ ὁ ἐργάτης τοῦ μισθοῦ αὐτοῦ.
for worthy [is] the workman of the pay of him.

μὴ μεταβαίνετε ἐξ οἰκίας εἰς οἰκίαν.
Do not remove from house to house.

8 καὶ εἰς ἣν ἂν πόλιν εἰσέρχησθε καὶ
And into whatever city ye enter and

δέχωνται ὑμᾶς, ἐσθίετε τὰ παρατιθέμενα
they receive you, eat the things being set before

ὑμῖν, 9 καὶ θεραπεύετε τοὺς ἐν αὐτῇ
you, and heal the ²in ³it

ἀσθενεῖς, καὶ λέγετε αὐτοῖς· ἤγγικεν ἐφ᾽
¹sick, and tell them : Has drawn near on(to)

ὑμᾶς ἡ βασιλεία τοῦ θεοῦ. 10 εἰς ἣν δ᾽
you the kingdom - of God. And into what-

ἂν πόλιν εἰσέλθητε καὶ μὴ δέχωνται ὑμᾶς,
ever city ye enter and they do not receive you,

ἐξελθόντες εἰς τὰς πλατείας αὐτῆς εἴπατε·
going forth into the streets of it say :

11 καὶ τὸν κονιορτὸν τὸν κολληθέντα ἡμῖν
Even the dust - adhering to us
=the dust of your city adhering to us, on our feet,

ἐκ τῆς πόλεως ὑμῶν εἰς τοὺς πόδας
of the city of you on the(our) feet

ἀπομασσόμεθα ὑμῖν· πλὴν τοῦτο γινώσκετε,
we shake off to you; nevertheless this know ye,

ὅτι ἤγγικεν ἡ βασιλεία τοῦ θεοῦ. 12 λέγω
that has drawn near the kingdom - of God. I tell

ὑμῖν ὅτι Σοδόμοις ἐν τῇ ἡμέρᾳ ἐκείνῃ
you that for Sodom in - day that

ἀνεκτότερον ἔσται ἢ τῇ πόλει ἐκείνῃ.
more endurable it will be than - city for that.

13 Οὐαί σοι, Χοραζίν, οὐαί σοι, Βηθσαϊδά·
Woe to thee, Chorazin, woe to thee, Bethsaida;

ὅτι εἰ ἐν Τύρῳ καὶ Σιδῶνι ἐγενήθησαν αἱ
because if in Tyre and Sidon happened the

δυνάμεις αἱ γενόμεναι ἐν ὑμῖν, πάλαι ἂν ἐν
powerful deeds - happening in you, long ago - in

σάκκῳ καὶ σποδῷ καθήμενοι μετενόησαν.
sackcloth and ashes sitting they would have repented.

⁕ Luke here, and in 2. 38; 10. 21; 12. 12; 13. 31; 24. 13, as well as in Acts 16. 18; 22. 13, ignores the strict idiomatic construction of αὐτός when in apposition. The words here should mean " in the house itself " but obviously do mean " in the same house ". So elsewhere. See note on Luke 2. 38.

14 But it shall be more tolerable for Tyre and Sidon at the judgment, than for you.

15 And thou, Capernaum, which art exalted to heaven, shalt be thrust down to hell.

16 He that heareth you heareth me; and he that despiseth you despiseth me; and he that despiseth me despiseth him that sent me.

17 ¶ And the seventy returned again with joy, saying, Lord, even the devils are subject unto us through thy name.

18 And he said unto them, I beheld Satan as lightning fall from heaven.

19 Behold, I give unto you power to tread on serpents and scorpions, and over all the power of the enemy: and nothing shall by any means hurt you.

20 Notwithstanding in this rejoice not, that the spirits are subject unto you; but rather rejoice, because your names are written in heaven.

21 ¶ In that hour Jesus rejoiced in spirit, and said, I thank thee, O Father, Lord of heaven and earth, that thou hast hid these things from the wise and prudent, and hast revealed them unto babes: even so,

---

14 πλὴν Τύρῳ καὶ Σιδῶνι ἀνεκτότερον
Nevertheless for Tyre and Sidon more endurable

ἔσται ἐν τῇ κρίσει ἢ ὑμῖν. 15 καὶ σύ,
it will be in the judgment than for you. And thou,

Καφαρναούμ, μὴ ἕως οὐρανοῦ ὑψωθήσῃ;
Capernaum, not to heaven wast thou lifted?

ἕως τοῦ ᾅδου καταβήσῃ. 16 Ὁ ἀκούων
to - hades thou shalt come down. The [one] hearing

ὑμῶν ἐμοῦ ἀκούει, καὶ ὁ ἀθετῶν ὑμᾶς
you me hears, and the [one] rejecting you

ἐμὲ ἀθετεῖ· ὁ δὲ ἐμὲ ἀθετῶν ἀθετεῖ τὸν
me rejects; and the [one] me rejecting rejects the [one]

ἀποστείλαντά με. 17 Ὑπέστρεψαν δὲ οἱ
having sent me. And returned the

ἑβδομήκοντα [δύο] μετὰ χαρᾶς λέγοντες·
seventy-two with joy saying:

κύριε, καὶ τὰ δαιμόνια ὑποτάσσεται ἡμῖν
Lord, even the demons submits to us

ἐν τῷ ὀνόματί σου. 18 εἶπεν δὲ αὐτοῖς·
in the name of thee. And he said to them:

ἐθεώρουν τὸν σατανᾶν ὡς ἀστραπὴν ἐκ
I beheld - Satan as lightning out of

τοῦ οὐρανοῦ πεσόντα. 19 ἰδοὺ δέδωκα
- heaven fall. Behold I have given

ὑμῖν τὴν ἐξουσίαν τοῦ πατεῖν ἐπάνω
you the authority - to tread[d] on

ὄφεων καὶ σκορπίων, καὶ ἐπὶ πᾶσαν τὴν
serpents and scorpions, and on all the

δύναμιν τοῦ ἐχθροῦ, καὶ οὐδὲν ὑμᾶς οὐ μὴ
power of the enemy, and nothing you by no(any) means

ἀδικήσει. 20 πλὴν ἐν τούτῳ μὴ χαίρετε
shall hurt. Nevertheless in this rejoice not

ὅτι τὰ πνεύματα ὑμῖν ὑποτάσσεται, χαίρετε
that the spirits to you submits, [1]rejoice

δὲ ὅτι τὰ ὀνόματα ὑμῶν ἐγγέγραπται ἐν
[1]but that the names of you have been enrolled in

τοῖς οὐρανοῖς. 21 Ἐν αὐτῇ τῇ ὥρᾳ
the heavens. In [2]same [1]the hour

ἠγαλλιάσατο τῷ πνεύματι τῷ ἁγίῳ καὶ
he exulted in(?by) the Spirit - Holy and

εἶπεν· ἐξομολογοῦμαί σοι, πάτερ, κύριε
said: I praise thee, Father, Lord

τοῦ οὐρανοῦ καὶ τῆς γῆς, ὅτι ἀπέκρυψας
- of heaven and - of earth, because thou didst hide

ταῦτα ἀπὸ σοφῶν καὶ συνετῶν, καὶ
these things from wise and intelligent [ones], and

ἀπεκάλυψας αὐτὰ νηπίοις· ναί, ὁ πατήρ,
didst reveal them to infants; yes, - Father,

Father; for so it seemed good in thy sight.

22 All things are delivered to me of my Father; and no man knoweth who the Son is, but the Father; and who the Father is, but the Son, and *he* to whom the Son will reveal *him*.

23 ¶ And he turned him unto *his* disciples, and said privately, Blessed *are* the eyes which see the things that ye see:

24 For I tell you, that many prophets and kings have desired to see those things which ye see, and have not seen *them;* and to hear those things which ye hear, and have not heard *them*.

25 ¶ And, behold, a certain lawyer stood up, and tempted him, saying, Master, what shall I do to inherit eternal life?

26 He said unto him, What is written in the law? how readest thou?

27 And he answering said, Thou shalt love the Lord thy God with all thy heart, and with all thy soul, and with all thy strength, and with all thy mind; and thy neighbour as thyself.

28 And he said unto him, Thou hast answered right: this do, and thou shalt live.

29 But he, willing to justify himself, said unto

ὅτι οὕτως εὐδοκία ἐγένετο ἔμπροσθέν σου.
because thus good pleasure it was before thee.

22 πάντα μοι παρεδόθη ὑπὸ τοῦ πατρός
All things to me were delivered by the Father

μου, καὶ οὐδεὶς γινώσκει τίς ἐστιν ὁ
of me, and no one knows who is the

υἱὸς εἰ μὴ ὁ πατήρ, καὶ τίς ἐστιν ὁ πατὴρ
Son except the Father, and who is the Father

εἰ μὴ ὁ υἱὸς καὶ ᾧ ἐὰν βούληται
except the Son and [he] to whomever wills

ὁ υἱὸς ἀποκαλύψαι. 23 Καὶ στραφεὶς
the Son to reveal [him]. And turning

πρὸς τοὺς μαθητὰς κατ' ἰδίαν εἶπεν·
to the disciples privately he said :

μακάριοι οἱ ὀφθαλμοὶ οἱ βλέποντες ἃ
Blessed the eyes – seeing the things which

βλέπετε. 24 λέγω γὰρ ὑμῖν ὅτι πολλοὶ
ye see. For I tell you that many

προφῆται καὶ βασιλεῖς ἠθέλησαν ἰδεῖν ἃ
prophets and kings desired to see the things which

ὑμεῖς βλέπετε καὶ οὐκ εἶδαν, καὶ ἀκοῦσαι
ye see and did not see, and to hear

ἃ ἀκούετε καὶ οὐκ ἤκουσαν.
the things which ye hear and did not hear.

25 Καὶ ἰδοὺ νομικός τις ἀνέστη
And[,] behold[,] lawyer a certain stood up

ἐκπειράζων αὐτὸν λέγων· διδάσκαλε, τί
tempting him saying : Teacher, what

ποιήσας ζωὴν αἰώνιον κληρονομήσω; 26 ὁ
doing ⁶life ⁴eternal ¹I ¹may ³inherit? he

δὲ εἶπεν πρὸς αὐτόν· ἐν τῷ νόμῳ τί
And said to him : In the law what

γέγραπται; πῶς ἀναγινώσκεις; 27 ὁ δὲ
has been written? how readest thou? And he

ἀποκριθεὶς εἶπεν· ἀγαπήσεις κύριον τὸν
answering said : Thou shalt love [the] Lord the

θεόν σου ἐξ ὅλης τῆς καρδίας σου καὶ
God of thee from all the heart of thee and

ἐν ὅλῃ τῇ ψυχῇ σου καὶ ἐν ὅλῃ τῇ
with all the soul of thee and with all the

ἰσχύϊ σου καὶ ἐν ὅλῃ τῇ διανοίᾳ σου,
strength of thee and with all the mind of thee,

καὶ τὸν πλησίον σου ὡς σεαυτόν. 28 εἶπεν
and the neighbour of thee as thyself. he said

δὲ αὐτῷ· ὀρθῶς ἀπεκρίθης· τοῦτο ποίει
And to him : Rightly thou didst answer; this do

καὶ ζήσῃ. 29 ὁ δὲ θέλων δικαιῶσαι ἑαυτὸν
and thou shalt live. But he wishing to justify himself

Jesus, And who is my neighbour?

30 And Jesus answering said, A certain *man* went down from Jerusalem to Jericho, and fell among thieves, which stripped him of his raiment, and wounded *him*, and departed, leaving *him* half dead.

31 And by chance there came down a certain priest that way: and when he saw him, he passed by on the other side.

32 And likewise a Levite, when he was at the place, came and looked *on him*, and passed by on the other side.

33 But a certain Samaritan, as he journeyed, came where he was: and when he saw him, he had compassion *on him*,

34 And went to *him*, and bound up his wounds, pouring in oil and wine, and set him on his own beast, and brought him to an inn, and took care of him.

35 And on the morrow when he departed, he took out two pence, and gave *them* to the host, and said unto him, Take care of him; and whatsoever thou spendest more, when I come again, I will repay thee.

36 Which now of these three, thinkest thou, was neighbour unto him that fell among the thieves?

37 And he said, He that shewed mercy on him. Then said Jesus unto him,

---

εἶπεν πρὸς τὸν Ἰησοῦν· καὶ τίς ἐστίν
said   to   -   Jesus :   And   who   is

μου πλησίον; 30 ὑπολαβὼν ὁ Ἰησοῦς
of me   neighbour?   Taking [him] up   -   Jesus

εἶπεν· ἄνθρωπός τις κατέβαινεν ἀπὸ
said :   A certain man   was going down   from

Ἰερουσαλὴμ εἰς Ἰεριχώ, καὶ λῃσταῖς
Jerusalem   to   Jericho,   and   ²robbers

περιέπεσεν, οἳ καὶ ἐκδύσαντες αὐτὸν καὶ
¹fell in with,   who both   stripping   him   and

πληγὰς ἐπιθέντες ἀπῆλθον ἀφέντες ἡμιθανῆ.
³blows   ¹laying ²on ⁴[him] went away   leaving [him]   half dead.

31 κατὰ συγκυρίαν δὲ ἱερεύς τις κατέβαινεν
And by a coincidence   a certain priest   was going down

ἐν τῇ ὁδῷ ἐκείνῃ, καὶ ἰδὼν αὐτὸν
in   -   way   that,   and   seeing   him

ἀντιπαρῆλθεν. 32 ὁμοίως δὲ καὶ Λευίτης
passed by opposite.   And likewise   also   a Levite

κατὰ τὸν τόπον ἐλθὼν καὶ ἰδὼν
upon   the   place   coming   and   seeing

ἀντιπαρῆλθεν. 33 Σαμαρίτης δέ τις ὁδεύων
passed by opposite.   And a certain Samaritan   journeying

ἦλθεν κατ' αὐτὸν καὶ ἰδὼν ἐσπλαγχνίσθη,
came   upon   him   and   seeing   was filled with pity,

34 καὶ προσελθὼν κατέδησεν τὰ τραύματα
and   approaching   bound up   the   wounds

αὐτοῦ ἐπιχέων ἔλαιον καὶ οἶνον, ἐπιβιβάσας
of him   pouring on   oil   and   wine,   ¹placing

δὲ αὐτὸν ἐπὶ τὸ ἴδιον κτῆνος ἤγαγεν
¹and   him   on   the(his)   own   beast   brought

αὐτὸν εἰς πανδοχεῖον καὶ ἐπεμελήθη αὐτοῦ.
him   to   an inn   and   cared for   him.

35 καὶ ἐπὶ τὴν αὔριον ἐκβαλὼν δύο
And   on   the   morrow   taking out   two

δηνάρια ἔδωκεν τῷ πανδοχεῖ καὶ εἶπεν·
denarii   he gave   to the   innkeeper   and   said :

ἐπιμελήθητι αὐτοῦ, καὶ ὅ τι ἂν προσδα-
Care thou for   him,   and   whatever   thou spendest

πανήσῃς ἐγὼ ἐν τῷ ἐπανέρχεσθαί με
in addition   I   in   the   to return   me
                          =when I return

ἀποδώσω σοι. 36 τίς τούτων τῶν τριῶν πλησίον
will repay   thee.   Who of these   -   three   ⁴neighbour

δοκεῖ σοι γεγονέναι τοῦ ἐμπεσόντος
¹seems it ³to thee ²to have become   of the [one]   falling *into*

εἰς τοὺς λῃστάς; 37 ὁ δὲ εἶπεν· ὁ ποιήσας
among   the   robbers?   And he   said : The [one]   doing

τὸ ἔλεος μετ' αὐτοῦ. εἶπεν δὲ αὐτῷ ὁ
the   mercy   with   him.   And said   to him

Go, and do thou likewise.

38 ¶ Now it came to pass, as they went, that he entered into a certain village: and a certain woman named Martha received him into her house.

39 And she had a sister called Mary, which also sat at Jesus' feet, and heard his word.

40 But Martha was cumbered about much serving, and came to him, and said, Lord, dost thou not care that my sister hath left me to serve alone? bid her therefore that she help me.

41 And Jesus answered and said unto her, Martha, Martha, thou art careful and troubled about many things:

42 But one thing is needful: and Mary hath chosen that good part, which shall not be taken away from her.

Ἰησοῦς· πορεύου καὶ σὺ ποίει ὁμοίως.
Jesus : Go and thou do likewise.

38 Ἐν δὲ τῷ πορεύεσθαι αὐτοὺς αὐτὸς
And in the to go them^b^• he
=as they went

εἰσῆλθεν εἰς κώμην τινά· γυνὴ δέ τις
entered into a certain village; and a certain woman

ὀνόματι Μάρθα ὑπεδέξατο αὐτὸν εἰς τὴν
by name Martha received him into the

οἰκίαν. 39 καὶ τῇδε ἦν ἀδελφὴ καλουμένη
house. And to this was a sister^c^ being called
=she had a sister

Μαριάμ, ἣ καὶ παρακαθεσθεῖσα πρὸς τοὺς
Mary, who also sitting beside at the

πόδας τοῦ κυρίου ἤκουεν τὸν λόγον αὐτοῦ.
feet of the Lord heard the word of him.

40 ἡ δὲ Μάρθα περιεσπᾶτο περὶ πολλὴν
- But Martha was distracted about much

διακονίαν· ἐπιστᾶσα δὲ εἶπεν· κύριε, οὐ
serving; and coming upon [him] she said : Lord, not

μέλει σοι ὅτι ἡ ἀδελφή μου μόνην με
matters it to thee that the sister of me ²alone ³me

κατέλειπεν διακονεῖν; εἰπὸν οὖν αὐτῇ ἵνα
¹left to serve? tell therefore her that

μοι συναντιλάβηται. 41 ἀποκριθεὶς δὲ εἶπεν
³me ¹she may help. And answering said

αὐτῇ ὁ κύριος· Μάρθα Μάρθα, μεριμνᾷς
to her the Lord : Martha[,] Martha, thou art anxious

καὶ θορυβάζῃ περὶ πολλά, 42 ὀλίγων δέ
and disturbed about many things, but of few things

ἐστιν χρεία ἢ ἑνός· Μαριὰμ γὰρ τὴν
there is need or of one; for Mary the

ἀγαθὴν μερίδα ἐξελέξατο, ἥτις οὐκ
good part chose, which not

ἀφαιρεθήσεται αὐτῆς.
shall be taken from her.

CHAPTER 11

AND it came to pass, that, as he was praying in a certain place, when he ceased, one of his disciples said unto him, Lord, teach us to pray, as John also taught his disciples.

11 Καὶ ἐγένετο ἐν τῷ εἶναι αὐτὸν ἐν
And it came to pass in the to be him^b^• in
=when he was

τόπῳ τινὶ προσευχόμενον, ὡς ἐπαύσατο,
a certain place praying, as he ceased,

εἶπέν τις τῶν μαθητῶν αὐτοῦ πρὸς
said a certain one of the disciples of him to

αὐτόν· κύριε, δίδαξον ἡμᾶς προσεύχεσθαι,
him : Lord, teach us to pray,

καθὼς καὶ Ἰωάννης ἐδίδαξεν τοὺς μαθητὰς
even as also John taught the disciples

2 And he said unto them, When ye pray, say, Our Father which art in heaven, Hallowed be thy name. Thy kingdom come. Thy will be done, as in heaven, so in earth.

3 Give us day by day our daily bread.

4 And forgive us our sins; for we also forgive every one that is indebted to us. And lead us not into temptation; but deliver us from evil.

5 And he said unto them, Which of you shall have a friend, and shall go unto him at midnight, and say unto him, Friend, lend me three loaves;

6 For a friend of mine in his journey is come to me, and I have nothing to set before him?

7 And he from within shall answer and say, Trouble me not: the door is now shut, and my children are with me in bed; I cannot rise and give thee.

8 I say unto you, Though he will not rise and give him, because he is his friend, yet because of his importunity he will rise and give him as many as he needeth.

9 And I say unto you, Ask, and it shall be given you; seek, and ye shall find; knock, and it shall be opened unto you.

10 For every one that asketh receiveth; and he

αὐτοῦ.   2 εἶπεν   δὲ   αὐτοῖς·   ὅταν
of him.   And he said   to them :   When

προσεύχησθε, λέγετε· Πάτερ, ἁγιασθήτω τὸ
ye pray,   say :   Father,   let be hallowed   the

ὄνομά   σου·   ἐλθάτω   ἡ   βασιλεία   σου·
name   of thee;   let come   the   kingdom   of thee;

3 τὸν ἄρτον ἡμῶν τὸν ἐπιούσιον δίδου
the   bread   of us – belonging to the morrow give

ἡμῖν τὸ καθ’ ἡμέραν·   4 καὶ ἄφες ἡμῖν τὰς
us   each day†;   and forgive   us   the

ἁμαρτίας ἡμῶν, καὶ γὰρ αὐτοὶ ἀφίομεν
sins   of us,   for indeed [our]selves we forgive

παντὶ ὀφείλοντι ἡμῖν· καὶ μὴ εἰσενέγκῃς
everyone owing   to us;   and   lead not

ἡμᾶς εἰς πειρασμόν. 5 Καὶ εἶπεν πρὸς
us   into   temptation.   And he said   to

αὐτούς· τίς ἐξ ὑμῶν ἕξει φίλον, καὶ
them : Who of you shall have a friend, and

πορεύσεται πρὸς αὐτὸν μεσονυκτίου καὶ
will come   to   him   at midnight   and

εἴπῃ αὐτῷ· φίλε, χρῆσόν μοι τρεῖς ἄρτους,
say to him : Friend, lend me three loaves,

6 ἐπειδὴ φίλος μου παρεγένετο ἐξ ὁδοῦ
since   a friend of me   arrived off a journey

πρός με καὶ οὐκ ἔχω ὃ παραθήσω αὐτῷ·
to me and I have not what I may set before him;

7 κἀκεῖνος ἔσωθεν ἀποκριθεὶς εἴπῃ· μή
and that one within   answering may say : Not

μοι κόπους πάρεχε· ἤδη ἡ θύρα κέκλεισται,
me troubles cause; now the door has been shut,

καὶ τὰ παιδία μου μετ’ ἐμοῦ εἰς τὴν
and the children of me with me in the

κοίτην εἰσίν· οὐ δύναμαι ἀναστὰς δοῦναί
bed   are;   I cannot   rising up   to give

σοι.   8 λέγω ὑμῖν, εἰ καὶ οὐ δώσει
thee.   I tell you, if even he will not give

αὐτῷ ἀναστὰς διὰ τὸ εἶναι φίλον αὐτοῦ,
him rising up on account of the to be friend of him,
                    =because he is his friend,

διὰ γε τὴν ἀναίδειαν αὐτοῦ ἐγερθεὶς
yet on account of the importunity of him rising

δώσει αὐτῷ ὅσων χρῄζει. 9 Κἀγὼ ὑμῖν
he will give him as many as he needs. And I ¹you

λέγω, αἰτεῖτε, καὶ δοθήσεται ὑμῖν· ζητεῖτε,
¹tell, ask, and it will be given you; seek,

καὶ εὑρήσετε· κρούετε, καὶ ἀνοιγήσεται
and ye will find; knock, and it will be opened

ὑμῖν. 10 πᾶς γὰρ ὁ αἰτῶν λαμβάνει, καὶ
to you.   For everyone asking receives, and

that seeketh findeth; and to him that knocketh it shall be opened.

11 If a son shall ask bread of any of you that is a father, will he give him a stone? or if *he ask* a fish, will he for a fish give him a serpent?

12 Or if he shall ask an egg, will he offer him a scorpion?

13 If ye then, being evil, know how to give good gifts unto your children: how much more shall *your* heavenly Father give the Holy Spirit to them that ask him?

14 ¶ And he was casting out a devil, and it was dumb. And it came to pass, when the devil was gone out, the dumb spake; and the people wondered.

15 But some of them said, He casteth out devils through Beelzebub the chief of the devils.

16 And others, tempting *him*, sought of him a sign from heaven.

17 But he, knowing their thoughts, said unto them, Every kingdom divided against itself is brought to desolation; and a house *divided* against a house falleth.

18 If Satan also be divided against himself, how shall his kingdom stand? because ye say that I cast out devils through Beelzebub.

19 And if I by Beelzebub

ὁ ζητῶν εὑρίσκει, καὶ τῷ κρούοντι
the [one] seeking finds, and to the [one] knocking

ἀνοιγήσεται. 11 τίνα δὲ ἐξ ὑμῶν τὸν
it will be opened. And ¹what ⁶of ⁵you –

πατέρα αἰτήσει ὁ υἱὸς ἰχθύν, μὴ
²father ³[is there] ⁶[of whom] ⁴will ask ⁷the ⁸son ¹⁵a fish, *not*

ἀντὶ ἰχθύος ὄφιν αὐτῷ ἐπιδώσει; 12 ἢ
instead of a fish ³a serpent ²to him ¹will hand? or

καὶ αἰτήσει ᾠόν, ἐπιδώσει αὐτῷ σκορπίον;
even he will ask an egg, will hand to him a scorpion?

13 εἰ οὖν ὑμεῖς πονηροὶ ὑπάρχοντες οἴδατε δόματα
If therefore ye ²evil ¹being know gifts

ἀγαθὰ διδόναι τοῖς τέκνοις ὑμῶν, πόσῳ
good to give to the children of you, how much

μᾶλλον ὁ πατὴρ ὁ ἐξ οὐρανοῦ δώσει
more the Father – of heaven will give

πνεῦμα ἅγιον τοῖς αἰτοῦσιν αὐτόν.
Spirit [the] Holy to the [ones] asking him.

14 Καὶ ἦν ἐκβάλλων δαιμόνιον, καὶ αὐτὸ
And he was expelling a demon, and it

ἦν κωφόν· ἐγένετο δὲ τοῦ δαιμονίου
was dumb; and it came to pass the demon
=as the demon went out

ἐξελθόντος ἐλάλησεν ὁ κωφός· καὶ
going out⁰ spoke the dumb man; and

ἐθαύμασαν οἱ ὄχλοι· 15 τινὲς δὲ ἐξ
marvelled the crowds; but some of

αὐτῶν εἶπαν· ἐν Βεεζεβοὺλ τῷ ἄρχοντι
them said: By Beelzebub the chief

τῶν δαιμονίων ἐκβάλλει τὰ δαιμόνια·
of the demons he expels the demons;

16 ἕτεροι δὲ πειράζοντες σημεῖον ἐξ οὐρανοῦ
and others tempting a sign out of heaven

ἐζήτουν παρ' αὐτοῦ. 17 αὐτὸς δὲ εἰδὼς
sought from him. But he knowing

αὐτῶν τὰ διανοήματα εἶπεν αὐτοῖς· πᾶσα
of them the thoughts said to them: Every

βασιλεία ἐφ' ἑαυτὴν διαμερισθεῖσα ἐρημοῦται,
kingdom against itself divided is made desolate,

καὶ οἶκος ἐπὶ οἶκον πίπτει. 18 εἰ δὲ
and a house against a house falls. And if

καὶ ὁ σατανᾶς ἐφ' ἑαυτὸν διεμερίσθη,
also – Satan against himself was divided,

πῶς σταθήσεται ἡ βασιλεία αὐτοῦ; ὅτι
how will stand the kingdom of him? because

λέγετε ἐν Βεεζεβοὺλ ἐκβάλλειν με τὰ
ye say by Beelzebub to expel meᵇ the
=[that] by Beelzebub I expel

δαιμόνια. 19 εἰ δὲ ἐγὼ ἐν Βεεζεβοὺλ
demons. But if I by Beelzebub

cast out devils, by whom do your sons cast *them* out? therefore shall they be your judges.

20 But if I with the finger of God cast out devils, no doubt the kingdom of God is come upon you.

21 When a strong man armed keepeth his palace, his goods are in peace:

22 But when a stronger than he shall come upon him, and overcome him, he taketh from him all his armour wherein he trusted, and divideth his spoils.

23 He that is not with me is against me: and he that gathereth not with me scattereth.

24 When the unclean spirit is gone out of a man, he walketh through dry places, seeking rest; and finding none, he saith, I will return unto my house whence I came out.

25 And when he cometh, he findeth *it* swept and garnished.

26 Then goeth he, and taketh *to him* seven other spirits more wicked than himself; and they enter in, and dwell there: and the last *state* of that man is worse than the first.

27 ¶ And it came to pass, as he spake these things, a certain woman

---

ἐκβάλλω τὰ δαιμόνια, οἱ υἱοὶ ὑμῶν ἐν
expel the demons, the sons of you by

τίνι ἐκβάλλουσιν; διὰ τοῦτο αὐτοὶ ὑμῶν
what do they expel? therefore they of you

κριταὶ ἔσονται. 20 εἰ δὲ ἐν δακτύλῳ
judges shall be. But if by [the] finger

θεοῦ [ἐγὼ] ἐκβάλλω τὰ δαιμόνια, ἄρα
of God I expel the demons, then

ἔφθασεν ἐφ' ὑμᾶς ἡ βασιλεία τοῦ θεοῦ.
came upon you the kingdom – of God.

21 ὅταν ὁ ἰσχυρὸς καθωπλισμένος φυλάσσῃ
When the strong man *having been* well armed guards

τὴν ἑαυτοῦ αὐλήν, ἐν εἰρήνῃ ἐστὶν τὰ
the of him*self* palace, in peace is(are) the

ὑπάρχοντα αὐτοῦ· 22 ἐπὰν δὲ ἰσχυρότερος
goods of him; but when a stronger

αὐτοῦ ἐπελθὼν νικήσῃ αὐτόν, τὴν πανοπλίαν
[than] him coming upon overcomes him, the armour

αὐτοῦ αἴρει, ἐφ' ᾗ ἐπεποίθει, καὶ τὰ
of him he takes, on which he had relied, and the

σκῦλα αὐτοῦ διαδίδωσιν. 23 Ὁ μὴ ὢν
arms of him distributes. The [one] not being

μετ' ἐμοῦ κατ' ἐμοῦ ἐστιν, καὶ ὁ μὴ
with me against me is, and the [one] not

συνάγων μετ' ἐμοῦ σκορπίζει. 24 Ὅταν
gathering with me scatters. When

τὸ ἀκάθαρτον πνεῦμα ἐξέλθῃ ἀπὸ τοῦ
the unclean spirit goes out from the

ἀνθρώπου, διέρχεται δι' ἀνύδρων τόπων
man, he goes *through* through dry places

ζητοῦν ἀνάπαυσιν, καὶ μὴ εὑρίσκον λέγει·
seeking rest, and not finding says:

ὑποστρέψω εἰς τὸν οἶκόν μου ὅθεν ἐξῆλθον·
I will return to the house of me whence I came out;

25 καὶ ἐλθὸν εὑρίσκει σεσαρωμένον καὶ
and coming he finds [it] *having been* swept and

κεκοσμημένον. 26 τότε πορεύεται καὶ
having been furnished. Then he goes and

παραλαμβάνει ἕτερα πνεύματα πονηρότερα
takes other spirits more wicked

ἑαυτοῦ ἑπτά, καὶ εἰσελθόντα κατοικεῖ
[than] himself seven, and entering he dwells

ἐκεῖ· καὶ γίνεται τὰ ἔσχατα τοῦ ἀνθρώπου
there; and becomes the last things – man

ἐκείνου χείρονα τῶν πρώτων. 27 Ἐγένετο
of that worse [than] the first. it came to pass

δὲ ἐν τῷ λέγειν αὐτὸν ταῦτα ἐπάρασά τις
And in the to say him^be these things ^a lifting up ^1 a certain
=as he said

of the company lifted up her voice, and said unto him, Blessed is the womb that bare thee, and the paps which thou hast sucked.

28 But he said, Yea rather, blessed are they that hear the word of God, and keep it.

29 ¶ And when the people were gathered thick together, he began to say, This is an evil generation: they seek a sign; and there shall no sign be given it, but the sign of Jonas the prophet.

30 For as Jonas was a sign unto the Ninevites, so shall also the Son of man be to this generation.

31 The queen of the south shall rise up in the judgment with the men of this generation, and condemn them: for she came from the utmost parts of the earth to hear the wisdom of Solomon; and, behold, a greater than Solomon is here.

32 The men of Nineve shall rise up in the judgment with this generation, and shall condemn it: for they repented at the preaching of Jonas; and, behold, a greater than Jonas is here.

33 No man, when he hath lighted a candle, putteth it in a secret place, neither under a bushel, but on a candlestick, that they which come in may see the light.

φωνὴν   γυνὴ ἐκ τοῦ ὄχλου εἶπεν αὐτῷ·
¹[her] ²voice ³woman ³of ⁴the ⁵crowd said to him:

μακαρία ἡ κοιλία ἡ βαστάσασά σε καὶ
Blessed the womb – having borne thee and

μαστοὶ οὓς ἐθήλασας. 28 αὐτὸς δὲ εἶπεν·
[the] breasts which thou didst suck. But he said:

μενοῦν μακάριοι οἱ ἀκούοντες τὸν λόγον
Nay rather blessed the [ones] hearing the word

τοῦ θεοῦ καὶ φυλάσσοντες.
– of God and keeping.

29 Τῶν δὲ ὄχλων ἐπαθροιζομένων ἤρξατο
And the crowds pressing upon* he began
=as the crowds pressed upon [him]

λέγειν· ἡ γενεὰ αὕτη γενεὰ πονηρά ἐστιν·
to say: – ²generation ¹This ²generation ⁴an evil ³is;

σημεῖον ζητεῖ, καὶ σημεῖον οὐ δοθήσεται
a sign it seeks, and a sign will not be given

αὐτῇ εἰ μὴ τὸ σημεῖον Ἰωνᾶ. 30 καθὼς
to it except the sign of Jonas. even as

γὰρ ἐγένετο [ὁ] Ἰωνᾶς τοῖς Νινευίταις
For ²became – ¹Jonas ²to the ³Ninevites

σημεῖον, οὕτως ἔσται καὶ ὁ υἱὸς τοῦ
²a sign, so will be also the Son –

ἀνθρώπου τῇ γενεᾷ ταύτῃ. 31 βασίλισσα
of man – generation to this. [The] queen

νότου ἐγερθήσεται ἐν τῇ κρίσει μετὰ τῶν
of [the] south will be raised in the judgment with the

ἀνδρῶν τῆς γενεᾶς ταύτης καὶ κατακρινεῖ
men – generation of this and will condemn

αὐτούς· ὅτι ἦλθεν ἐκ τῶν περάτων τῆς
them; because she came from the extremities of the

γῆς ἀκοῦσαι τὴν σοφίαν Σολομῶνος, καὶ
earth to hear the wisdom of Solomon, and

ἰδοὺ πλεῖον Σολομῶνος ὧδε. 32 ἄνδρες
behold a greater [than] Solomon [is] here. Men

Νινευῖται ἀναστήσονται ἐν τῇ κρίσει μετὰ
Ninevites will rise up in the judgment with

τῆς γενεᾶς ταύτης καὶ κατακρινοῦσιν αὐτήν·
– generation this and will condemn it;

ὅτι μετενόησαν εἰς τὸ κήρυγμα Ἰωνᾶ, καὶ
because they repented at the proclamation of Jonas, and

ἰδοὺ πλεῖον Ἰωνᾶ ὧδε. 33 Οὐδεὶς λύχνον
behold a greater [than] Jonas [is] here. No one ²a lamp

ἅψας εἰς κρύπτην τίθησιν οὐδὲ ὑπὸ τὸν
¹having lit ⁴in ³secret ²places [it] nor under the

μόδιον, ἀλλ' ἐπὶ τὴν λυχνίαν, ἵνα οἱ
bushel, but on the lampstand, that the

εἰσπορευόμενοι τὸ φέγγος βλέπωσιν. 34 ὁ
ones] entering the light may see. The

34 The light of the body is the eye: therefore when thine eye is single, thy whole body also is full of light; but when *thine eye* is evil, thy body also *is* full of darkness.

35 Take heed therefore that the light which is in thee be not darkness.

36 If thy whole body therefore *be* full of light, having no part dark, the whole shall be full of light, as when the bright shining of a candle doth give thee light.

37 ¶ And as he spake, a certain Pharisee besought him to dine with him: and he went in, and sat down to meat.

38 And when the Pharisee saw *it*, he marvelled that he had not first washed before dinner.

39 And the Lord said unto him, Now do ye Pharisees make clean the outside of the cup and the platter; but your inward part is full of ravening and wickedness.

40 *Ye* fools, did not he that made that which is without make that which is within also?

41 But rather give alms of such things as ye have; and, behold, all things are clean unto you.

42 But woe unto you, Pharisees! for ye tithe mint and rue and all manner of herbs, and pass

λύχνος τοῦ σώματός ἐστιν ὁ ὀφθαλμός σου.
lamp   of the   body   is   the   eye   of thee.

ὅταν ὁ ὀφθαλμός σου ἁπλοῦς ᾖ, καὶ
When the   eye   of thee   single   is,   also

ὅλον τὸ σῶμά σου φωτεινόν ἐστιν· ἐπὰν
all   the   body of thee   bright   is;   ²when

δὲ πονηρὸς ᾖ, καὶ τὸ σῶμά σου σκοτεινόν.
¹but   evil   it is, also   the   body of thee   [is] dark.

35 σκόπει οὖν μὴ τὸ φῶς τὸ ἐν σοὶ
   Watch therefore lest   the   light –   in   thee

σκότος ἐστίν. 36 εἰ οὖν τὸ σῶμά σου
darkness   is.   If therefore ¹the   ²body ⁴of thee

ὅλον φωτεινόν, μὴ ἔχον μέρος τι σκοτεινόν,
³whole [is] bright,   not having ³part ¹any   dark,

ἔσται φωτεινὸν ὅλον ὡς ὅταν ὁ λύχνος
²will be   ³bright   ¹all   as   when   the   lamp

τῇ ἀστραπῇ φωτίζῃ σε.
with the(its) shining   enlightens   thee.

37 Ἐν δὲ τῷ λαλῆσαι ἐρωτᾷ αὐτὸν
   Now in   the   to speakᵉ   asks   him
       = as [he] spoke

Φαρισαῖος ὅπως ἀριστήσῃ παρ᾽ αὐτῷ·
a Pharisee   that   he would dine   with   him;

εἰσελθὼν δὲ ἀνέπεσεν. 38 ὁ δὲ Φαρισαῖος
and entering   he reclined.   But the   Pharisee

ἰδὼν ἐθαύμασεν ὅτι οὐ πρῶτον ἐβαπτίσθη
seeing   marvelled   that   not   first   he washed

πρὸ τοῦ ἀρίστου. 39 εἶπεν δὲ ὁ κύριος
before the   dinner.   But said   the   Lord

πρὸς αὐτόν· νῦν ὑμεῖς οἱ Φαρισαῖοι τὸ
to   him :   Now   ye   –   Pharisees   the

ἔξωθεν τοῦ ποτηρίου καὶ τοῦ πίνακος
outside   of the   cup   and   of the   dish

καθαρίζετε, τὸ δὲ ἔσωθεν ὑμῶν γέμει
cleanse,   but the   inside   of you   is full

ἁρπαγῆς καὶ πονηρίας. 40 ἄφρονες, οὐχ
of robbery   and   wickedness.   Foolish men,   not

ὁ ποιήσας τὸ ἔξωθεν καὶ τὸ ἔσωθεν
the [one] making   the   outside   also   the   inside

ἐποίησεν; 41 πλὴν τὰ ἐνόντα δότε
made?   Nevertheless the things being within   give

ἐλεημοσύνην, καὶ ἰδοὺ πάντα καθαρὰ ὑμῖν
alms,   and   behold   all things   clean   to you

ἐστιν. 42 ἀλλὰ οὐαὶ ὑμῖν τοῖς Φαρισαίοις,
is(are).   But   woe to you   –   Pharisees,

ὅτι ἀποδεκατοῦτε τὸ ἡδύοσμον καὶ τὸ
because   ye tithe   the   mint   and   the

πήγανον καὶ πᾶν λάχανον, καὶ παρέρχεσθε
rue   and every   herb,   and   pass by

over judgment and the love of God: these ought ye to have done, and not to leave the other undone.

43 Woe unto you, Pharisees! for ye love the uppermost seats in the synagogues, and greetings in the markets.

44 Woe unto you, scribes and Pharisees, hypocrites! for ye are as graves which appear not, and the men that walk over *them* are not aware *of them.*

45 Then answered one of the lawyers, and said unto him, Master, thus saying thou reproachest us also.

46 And he said, Woe unto you also, *ye* lawyers! for ye lade men with burdens grievous to be borne, and ye yourselves touch not the burdens with one of your fingers.

47 Woe unto you! for ye build the sepulchres of the prophets, and your fathers killed them.

48 Truly ye bear witness that ye allow the deeds of your fathers: for they indeed killed them, and ye build their sepulchres.

49 Therefore also said the wisdom of God, I will send them prophets and apostles, and *some* of them they shall slay and persecute:

50 That the blood of all the prophets, which was

τὴν κρίσιν καὶ τὴν ἀγάπην τοῦ θεοῦ·
the judgment and the love – of God;
ταῦτα δὲ ἔδει ποιῆσαι κἀκεῖνα μὴ
but these things it behoved to do and those not
παρεῖναι. 43 οὐαὶ ὑμῖν τοῖς Φαρισαίοις,
to pass by. Woe to you – Pharisees,
ὅτι ἀγαπᾶτε τὴν πρωτοκαθεδρίαν ἐν ταῖς
because ye love the chief seat in the
συναγωγαῖς καὶ τοὺς ἀσπασμοὺς ἐν ταῖς
synagogues and the greetings in the
ἀγοραῖς. 44 οὐαὶ ὑμῖν, ὅτι ἐστὲ ὡς τὰ
marketplaces. Woe to you, because ye are as the
μνημεῖα τὰ ἄδηλα, καὶ οἱ ἄνθρωποι οἱ
tombs – unseen, and the men –
περιπατοῦντες ἐπάνω οὐκ οἴδασιν.
walking over do not know.
45 Ἀποκριθεὶς δέ τις τῶν νομικῶν λέγει
And answering one of the lawyers says
αὐτῷ· διδάσκαλε, ταῦτα λέγων καὶ ἡμᾶς
to him : Teacher, these things saying also us
ὑβρίζεις. 46 ὁ δὲ εἶπεν· καὶ ὑμῖν τοῖς
thou insultest. And he said : Also to you –
νομικοῖς οὐαί, ὅτι φορτίζετε τοὺς ἀνθρώπους
lawyers woe, because ye burden men
φορτία δυσβάστακτα, καὶ αὐτοὶ ἑνὶ τῶν
[with] burdens difficult to carry, and [your]selves with one of the
δακτύλων ὑμῶν οὐ προσψαύετε τοῖς φορτίοις.
fingers of you ye do not touch the burdens.
47 οὐαὶ ὑμῖν, ὅτι οἰκοδομεῖτε τὰ μνημεῖα
Woe to you, because ye build the tombs
τῶν προφητῶν, οἱ δὲ πατέρες ὑμῶν
of the prophets, and the fathers of you
ἀπέκτειναν αὐτούς. 48 ἄρα μάρτυρές ἐστε
killed them. Therefore witnesses ye are
καὶ συνευδοκεῖτε τοῖς ἔργοις τῶν πατέρων
and ye entirely approve the works of the fathers
ὑμῶν, ὅτι αὐτοὶ μὲν ἀπέκτειναν αὐτούς,
of you, because they on one hand killed them,
ὑμεῖς δὲ οἰκοδομεῖτε. 49 διὰ τοῦτο καὶ
ye on the other hand build. Therefore also
ἡ σοφία τοῦ θεοῦ εἶπεν· ἀποστελῶ εἰς
the Wisdom – of God said : I will send to
αὐτοὺς προφήτας καὶ ἀποστόλους, καὶ ἐξ
them prophets and apostles, and of
αὐτῶν ἀποκτενοῦσιν καὶ διώξουσιν, 50 ἵνα
them they will kill and persecute, that
ἐκζητηθῇ τὸ αἷμα πάντων τῶν προφητῶν
¹¹may be required ¹the ⁸blood ⁹of all ⁴the ⁶prophets

shed from the foundation of the world, may be required of this generation;

51 From the blood of Abel unto the blood of Zacharias, which perished between the altar and the temple: verily I say unto you, It shall be required of this generation.

52 Woe unto you, lawyers! for ye have taken away the key of knowledge: ye entered not in yourselves, and them that were entering in ye hindered.

53 And as he said these things unto them, the scribes and the Pharisees began to urge *him* vehemently, and to provoke him to speak of many things:

54 Laying wait for him, and seeking to catch something out of his mouth, that they might accuse him.

τὸ ἐκκεχυμένον ἀπὸ καταβολῆς κόσμου
– ⁶*having been* shed ⁷from ⁸[the] ⁹foundation ¹⁰of [the] world
ἀπὸ τῆς γενεᾶς ταύτης, 51 ἀπὸ αἵματος
¹¹from – generation this, from [the] blood
Ἄβελ ἕως αἵματος Ζαχαρίου τοῦ
of Abel to [the] blood of Zacharias –
ἀπολομένου μεταξὺ τοῦ θυσιαστηρίου καὶ
destroyed between the altar and
τοῦ οἴκου· ναὶ λέγω ὑμῖν, ἐκζητηθήσεται
the house; yes I tell you, it will be required
ἀπὸ τῆς γενεᾶς ταύτης. 52 οὐαὶ ὑμῖν τοῖς
from – generation this. Woe to you –
νομικοῖς, ὅτι ἤρατε τὴν κλεῖδα τῆς
lawyers, because ye took the key –
γνώσεως· αὐτοὶ οὐκ εἰσήλθατε καὶ τοὺς
of knowledge; [your]selves ye did not enter and the
εἰσερχομένους ἐκωλύσατε. 53 Κἀκεῖθεν ἐξελ-
[ones] entering ye prevented. And thence going
= as he went forth thence
θόντος αὐτοῦ ἤρξαντο οἱ γραμματεῖς καὶ
forth him² began the scribes and
οἱ Φαρισαῖοι δεινῶς ἐνέχειν καὶ ἀποστοματίζειν
the Pharisees ²terribly ¹to be ²angry and to ¹draw ²out
αὐτὸν περὶ πλειόνων, 54 ἐνεδρεύοντες
²him concerning a great number of things, lying in wait for
αὐτὸν θηρεῦσαί τι ἐκ τοῦ στόματος αὐτοῦ.
him to catch something out of the mouth of him.

CHAPTER 12

IN the mean time, when there were gathered together an innumerable multitude of people, insomuch that they trode one upon another, he began to say unto his disciples first of all, Beware ye of the leaven of the Pharisees, which is hypocrisy.

2 For there is nothing covered, that shall not be revealed; neither hid, that shall not be known.

3 Therefore whatsoever ye have spoken in darkness shall be heard in the light; and that which ye have

12 Ἐν οἷς ἐπισυναχθεισῶν τῶν μυριάδων
In which things being assembled the thousands
= Meanwhile as the thousands of the crowd were assembled,
τοῦ ὄχλου, ὥστε καταπατεῖν ἀλλήλους,
of the crowd,ª so as to tread on one another,
ἤρξατο λέγειν πρὸς τοὺς μαθητὰς αὐτοῦ
he began to say to the disciples of him
πρῶτον· προσέχετε ἑαυτοῖς ἀπὸ τῆς ζύμης,
first : Take heed to yourselves from the leaven,
ἥτις ἐστὶν ὑπόκρισις, τῶν Φαρισαίων.
which is hypocrisy, of the Pharisees.
2 οὐδὲν δὲ συγκεκαλυμμένον ἐστὶν ὃ οὐκ
And ²nothing ³having been ¹there is which not
completely covered
ἀποκαλυφθήσεται, καὶ κρυπτὸν ὃ οὐ γνωσθήσεται.
will be uncovered, and hidden which will not be known.
3 ἀνθ᾽ ὧν ὅσα ἐν τῇ σκοτίᾳ εἴπατε ἐν
Therefore what things in the darkness ye said in
τῷ φωτὶ ἀκουσθήσεται, καὶ ὃ πρὸς τὸ
the light will be heard, and what to the

spoken in the ear in closets shall be proclaimed upon the housetops.

4 And I say unto you my friends, Be not afraid of them that kill the body, and after that have no more that they can do.

5 But I will forewarn you whom ye shall fear: Fear him, which after he hath killed hath power to cast into hell; yea, I say unto you, Fear him.

6 Are not five sparrows sold for two farthings, and not one of them is forgotten before God?

7 But even the very hairs of your head are all numbered. Fear not therefore: ye are of more value than many sparrows.

8 Also I say unto you, Whosoever shall confess me before men, him shall the Son of man also confess before the angels of God:

9 But he that denieth me before men shall be denied before the angels of God.

10 And whosoever shall speak a word against the Son of man, it shall be forgiven him: but unto him that blasphemeth against the Holy Ghost it shall not be forgiven.

11 And when they bring

οὓς ἐλαλήσατε ἐν τοῖς ταμιείοις κηρυχθήσεται
ear   ye spoke   in   the private rooms   will be proclaimed

ἐπὶ τῶν δωμάτων. 4 Λέγω δὲ ὑμῖν τοῖς
on   the   roofs.   And I say   to you   the

φίλοις μου, μὴ φοβηθῆτε ἀπὸ τῶν
friends   of me,   do not be afraid   from(of)   the [ones]

ἀποκτεννόντων τὸ σῶμα καὶ μετὰ ταῦτα
killing   the   body   and   after these things

μὴ ἐχόντων περισσότερόν τι ποιῆσαι.
not   having   anything more   to do.

5 ὑποδείξω δὲ ὑμῖν τίνα φοβηθῆτε·
But I will warn   you   whom   ye may fear :

φοβήθητε τὸν μετὰ τὸ ἀποκτεῖναι ἔχοντα
[1]fear [2]the [one] [3]after   the   [4]to kill(killing) [5]having

ἐξουσίαν ἐμβαλεῖν εἰς τὴν γέενναν. ναὶ
[4]authority [7]to cast in   into   gehenna.   Yes[,]

λέγω ὑμῖν, τοῦτον φοβήθητε. 6 οὐχὶ
I say   to you,   this one   fear ye.   Not

πέντε στρουθία πωλοῦνται ἀσσαρίων δύο;
five   sparrows   are sold   of(for) farthings   two?

καὶ ἓν ἐξ αὐτῶν οὐκ ἔστιν ἐπιλελησμένον
and one   of   them   is not   *having been* forgotten

ἐνώπιον τοῦ θεοῦ. 7 ἀλλὰ καὶ αἱ τρίχες
before   –   God.   But   even   the   hairs

τῆς κεφαλῆς ὑμῶν πᾶσαι ἠρίθμηνται.
of the   head   of you   all have been numbered.

μὴ φοβεῖσθε· πολλῶν στρουθίων διαφέρετε.
Fear ye not;   from many   sparrows   ye differ.

8 λέγω δὲ ὑμῖν, πᾶς ὃς ἂν ὁμολογήσῃ
But I tell   you,   everyone   whoever   confesses

ἐν ἐμοὶ ἔμπροσθεν τῶν ἀνθρώπων, καὶ ὁ
–   me   before   –   men,   also the

υἱὸς τοῦ ἀνθρώπου ὁμολογήσει ἐν αὐτῷ
Son   –   of man   will confess   –   him

ἔμπροσθεν τῶν ἀγγέλων τοῦ θεοῦ· 9 ὁ δὲ
before   the   angels   – of God;   and the

ἀρνησάμενός με ἐνώπιον τῶν ἀνθρώπων
[one] denying   me   before   –   men

ἀπαρνηθήσεται ἐνώπιον τῶν ἀγγέλων τοῦ
will be denied   before   the   angels   –

θεοῦ. 10 καὶ πᾶς ὃς ἐρεῖ λόγον εἰς τὸν
of God.   And everyone who shall say a word against   the

υἱὸν τοῦ ἀνθρώπου, ἀφεθήσεται αὐτῷ· τῷ
Son   –   of man,   it will be forgiven him;   [2]the [one]

δὲ εἰς τὸ ἅγιον πνεῦμα βλασφημήσαντι
[1]but against   the   Holy   Spirit   blaspheming

οὐκ ἀφεθήσεται. 11 ὅταν δὲ εἰσφέρωσιν
will not be forgiven.   And when   they bring in

you unto the synagogues, and *unto* magistrates, and powers, take ye no thought how or what thing ye shall answer, or what ye shall say:

12 For the Holy Ghost shall teach you in the same hour what ye ought to say.

13 ¶ And one of the company said unto him, Master, speak to my brother, that he divide the inheritance with me.

14 And he said unto him, Man, who made me a judge or a divider over you?

15 And he said unto them, Take heed, and beware of covetousness: for a man's life consisteth not in the abundance of the things which he possesseth.

16 And he spake a parable unto them, saying, The ground of a certain rich man brought forth plentifully:

17 And he thought within himself, saying, What shall I do, because I have no room where to bestow my fruits?

18 And he said, This will I do: I will pull down my barns, and build greater; and there will I bestow all my fruits and my goods.

19 And I will say to my soul, Soul, thou hast much goods laid up for many years; take thine ease, eat, drink, *and* be merry.

20 But God said unto

ὑμᾶς ἐπὶ τὰς συναγωγὰς καὶ τὰς ἀρχὰς
you before – synagogues and – rulers
καὶ τὰς ἐξουσίας, μὴ μεριμνήσητε πῶς ἢ
and – authorities, do not be anxious how or
τί ἀπολογήσησθε ἢ τί εἴπητε· 12 τὸ γὰρ
what ye may answer or what ye may say; for the
ἅγιον πνεῦμα διδάξει ὑμᾶς ἐν αὐτῇ τῇ
Holy Spirit will teach you in ⁵same ¹the
ὥρᾳ ἃ δεῖ εἰπεῖν. 13 Εἶπεν δέ τις
hour what things it behoves [you] to say. And said someone
ἐκ τοῦ ὄχλου αὐτῷ· διδάσκαλε, εἰπὲ τῷ
out of the crowd to him: Teacher, tell the
ἀδελφῷ μου μερίσασθαι μετ' ἐμοῦ τὴν
brother of me to divide with me the
κληρονομίαν. 14 ὁ δὲ εἶπεν αὐτῷ· ἄνθρωπε,
inheritance. But he said to him: Man,
τίς με κατέστησεν κριτὴν ἢ μεριστὴν ἐφ'
who me appointed a judge or a divider over
ὑμᾶς; 15 εἶπεν δὲ πρὸς αὐτούς· ὁρᾶτε
you? And he said to them: Beware
καὶ φυλάσσεσθε ἀπὸ πάσης πλεονεξίας,
and guard from(against) all covetousness,
ὅτι οὐκ ἐν τῷ περισσεύειν τινὶ ἡ ζωὴ
because ⁵not ⁶in ⁷the ⁸to abound ⁹to anyone ¹the ²life
αὐτοῦ ἐστιν ἐκ τῶν ὑπαρχόντων αὐτῷ.
³of him ⁴is ¹⁰of the things existing to him.ᵉ
=¹¹his ¹²possessions.
16 Εἶπεν δὲ παραβολὴν πρὸς αὐτοὺς λέγων·
And he told a parable to them saying:
ἀνθρώπου τινὸς πλουσίου εὐφόρησεν ἡ
²of a certain ⁵man ⁴rich ⁶bore well ¹The
χώρα. 17 καὶ διελογίζετο ἐν ἑαυτῷ λέγων·
¹land. And he reasoned in himself saying:
τί ποιήσω, ὅτι οὐκ ἔχω ποῦ συνάξω τοὺς
What may I do, because I have not where I may gather the
καρπούς μου; 18 καὶ εἶπεν· τοῦτο ποιήσω·
fruits of me? And he said: This will I do:
καθελῶ μου τὰς ἀποθήκας καὶ μείζονας
I will pull down of me the barns and larger ones
οἰκοδομήσω, καὶ συνάξω ἐκεῖ πάντα τὸν
I will build, and I will gather there all the
σῖτον καὶ τὰ ἀγαθά μου, 19 καὶ ἐρῶ τῇ
wheat and the goods of me, and I will say to the
ψυχῇ μου· ψυχή, ἔχεις πολλὰ ἀγαθὰ
soul of me: Soul, thou hast many goods
κείμενα εἰς ἔτη πολλά· ἀναπαύου, φάγε,
laid [up] for years many; take rest, eat,
πίε, εὐφραίνου. 20 εἶπεν δὲ αὐτῷ ὁ
drink, be glad. But said to him –

him, *Thou* fool, this night thy soul shall be required of thee: then whose shall those things be, which thou hast provided?

21 So *is* he that layeth up treasure for himself, and is not rich toward God.

22 ¶ And he said unto his disciples, Therefore I say unto you, Take no thought for your life, what ye shall eat; neither for the body, what ye shall put on.

23 The life is more than meat, and the body *is more* than raiment.

24 Consider the ravens: for they neither sow nor reap; which neither have storehouse nor barn; and God feedeth them: how much more are ye better than the fowls?

25 And which of you with taking thought can add to his stature one cubit?

26 If ye then be not able to do that thing which is least, why take ye thought for the rest?

27 Consider the lilies how they grow: they toil not, they spin not; and yet I say unto you, that Solomon in all his glory was not arrayed like one of these.

28 If then God so clothe the grass, which is to day in the field, and to morrow is cast into the oven; how much more *will he clothe* you, O ye of little faith?

29 And seek not ye

θεός· ἄφρων, ταύτῃ τῇ νυκτὶ τὴν ψυχήν
God : Foolish man, in this — night the soul

σου ἀπαιτοῦσιν ἀπὸ σοῦ· ἃ δὲ
of thee they demand from thee; then [the] things which

ἡτοίμασας, τίνι ἔσται; 21 οὕτως ὁ
thou preparedst, to whom will they be?ᶜ So the [one]
=whose will they be?

θησαυρίζων αὐτῷ καὶ μὴ εἰς θεὸν πλουτῶν.
treasuring to himself and not toward God being rich.

22 Εἶπεν δὲ πρὸς τοὺς μαθητὰς [αὐτοῦ]· διὰ τοῦτο
And he said to the disciples of him : Therefore

λέγω ὑμῖν· μὴ μεριμνᾶτε, τῇ ψυχῇ τί
I tell you : Do not be anxious for the life what

φάγητε, μηδὲ τῷ σώματι [ὑμῶν] τί
ye may eat, nor for the body of you what

ἐνδύσησθε. 23 ἡ γὰρ ψυχὴ πλεῖόν ἐστιν
ye may put on. For the life more is

τῆς τροφῆς καὶ τὸ σῶμα τοῦ ἐνδύματος.
[than] the food and the body [than] the clothing.

24 κατανοήσατε τοὺς κόρακας, ὅτι οὔτε
Consider ye the ravens, that neither

σπείρουσιν οὔτε θερίζουσιν, οἷς οὐκ ἔστινᶜ
they sow nor reap, to which is not
=which have not

ταμιεῖον οὐδὲ ἀποθήκη, καὶ ὁ θεὸς τρέφει
storehouse nor barn, and — God feeds

αὐτούς· πόσῳ μᾶλλον ὑμεῖς διαφέρετε τῶν
them; by how much rather ye differ from the

πετεινῶν. 25 τίς δὲ ἐξ ὑμῶν μεριμνῶν
birds. And who of you being anxious

δύναται ἐπὶ τὴν ἡλικίαν αὐτοῦ προσθεῖναι
can on the stature of him *to* add

πῆχυν; 26 εἰ οὖν οὐδὲ ἐλάχιστον δύνασθε,
a cubit? If therefore not [the] least ye can,

τί περὶ τῶν λοιπῶν μεριμνᾶτε; 27 κατα-
why concerning the other things are ye anxious? Con-

νοήσατε τὰ κρίνα, πῶς οὔτε νήθει οὔτε
sider ye the lilies, how neither they spin nor

ὑφαίνει· λέγω δὲ ὑμῖν, οὐδὲ Σολομὼν ἐν
weave; but I tell you, not Solomon in

πάσῃ τῇ δόξῃ αὐτοῦ περιεβάλετο ὡς ἓν
all the glory of him was arrayed as one

τούτων. 28 εἰ δὲ ἐν ἀγρῷ τὸν χόρτον
of these. ¹And ²if ⁹in ¹⁰a field ⁴the ⁷grass

ὄντα σήμερον καὶ αὔριον εἰς κλίβανον
⁸being ¹¹to-day ¹²and ¹³tomorrow ¹⁵into ¹⁶an oven

βαλλόμενον ὁ θεὸς οὕτως ἀμφιάζει, πόσῳ
¹⁴being thrown — ³God ⁵so ⁶clothes, by how much

μᾶλλον ὑμᾶς, ὀλιγόπιστοι. 29 καὶ ὑμεῖς
rather you, little-faiths. And ye

what ye shall eat, or what ye shall drink, neither be ye of doubtful mind.

30 For all these things do the nations of the world seek after: and your Father knoweth that ye have need of these things.

31 But rather seek ye the kingdom of God; and all these things shall be added unto you.

32 Fear not, little flock; for it is your Father's good pleasure to give you the kingdom.

33 Sell that ye have, and give alms; provide yourselves bags which wax not old, a treasure in the heavens that faileth not, where no thief approacheth, neither moth corrupteth.

34 For where your treasure is, there will your heart be also.

35 Let your loins be girded about, and *your* lights burning;

36 And ye yourselves like unto men that wait for their lord, when he will return from the wedding; that when he cometh and knocketh, they may open unto him immediately.

37 Blessed *are* those servants, whom the lord when he cometh shall find watching: verily I say unto you, that he shall gird himself, and make them to sit down to meat, and will come forth and serve them.

38 And if he shall come

μὴ ζητεῖτε τί φάγητε καὶ τί πίητε, καὶ
do not seek what ye may eat and what ye may drink, and
μὴ μετεωρίζεσθε· 30 ταῦτα γὰρ πάντα τὰ
do not be in suspense; for these things all the
ἔθνη τοῦ κόσμου ἐπιζητοῦσιν· ὑμῶν δὲ
nations of the world seek after; but of you
ὁ πατὴρ οἶδεν ὅτι χρῄζετε τούτων·
the Father knows that ye have need of them;
31 πλὴν ζητεῖτε τὴν βασιλείαν αὐτοῦ, καὶ
but seek ye the kingdom of him, and
ταῦτα προστεθήσεται ὑμῖν. 32 Μὴ φοβοῦ,
these things will be added to you. Fear not,
τὸ μικρὸν ποίμνιον· ὅτι εὐδόκησεν ὁ
- little flock; because was well pleased the
πατὴρ ὑμῶν δοῦναι ὑμῖν τὴν βασιλείαν.
Father of you to give you the kingdom.
33 Πωλήσατε τὰ ὑπάρχοντα ὑμῶν καὶ
Sell the possessions of you and
δότε ἐλεημοσύνην· ποιήσατε ἑαυτοῖς βαλ-
give alms; make for yourselves
λάντια μὴ παλαιούμενα, θησαυρὸν ἀνέκλειπτον
purses not becoming old, a treasure unfailing
ἐν τοῖς οὐρανοῖς, ὅπου κλέπτης οὐκ
in the heavens, where a thief not
ἐγγίζει οὐδὲ σὴς διαφθείρει· 34 ὅπου γάρ
comes near nor moth corrupts; for where
ἐστιν ὁ θησαυρὸς ὑμῶν, ἐκεῖ καὶ ἡ
is the treasure of you, there also the
καρδία ὑμῶν ἔσται. 35 Ἔστωσαν ὑμῶν αἱ
heart of you will be. Let be of you the
ὀσφύες περιεζωσμέναι καὶ οἱ λύχνοι
loins having been girded and the lamps
καιόμενοι· 36 καὶ ὑμεῖς ὅμοιοι ἀνθρώποις
burning; and ye like men
προσδεχομένοις τὸν κύριον ἑαυτῶν, πότε
awaiting the lord of themselves, when
ἀναλύσῃ ἐκ τῶν γάμων, ἵνα ἐλθόντος
he returns from the wedding festivities, that coming[a]
καὶ κρούσαντος εὐθέως ἀνοίξωσιν αὐτῷ.
and knocking[a] immediately they may open to him.
37 μακάριοι οἱ δοῦλοι ἐκεῖνοι, οὓς ἐλθὼν
Blessed - slaves those, whom coming
ὁ κύριος εὑρήσει γρηγοροῦντας· ἀμὴν λέγω
the lord will find watching; truly I tell
ὑμῖν ὅτι περιζώσεται καὶ ἀνακλινεῖ αὐτοὺς
you that he will gird himself and [1]make [2]to recline [3]them
καὶ παρελθὼν διακονήσει αὐτοῖς. 38 κἂν
and coming up to will serve them. And if

in the second watch, or come in the third watch, and find *them* so, blessed are those servants.

39 And this know, that if the goodman of the house had known what hour the thief would come, he would have watched, and not have suffered his house to be broken through.

40 Be ye therefore ready also: for the Son of man cometh at an hour when ye think not.

41 ¶ Then Peter said unto him, Lord, speakest thou this parable unto us, or even to all?

42 And the Lord said, Who then is that faithful and wise steward, whom *his* lord shall make ruler over his household, to give *them their* portion of meat in due season?

43 Blessed *is* that servant, whom his lord when he cometh shall find so doing.

44 Of a truth I say unto you, that he will make him ruler over all that he hath.

45 But and if that servant say in his heart, My lord delayeth his coming; and shall begin to beat the menservants and maidens, and to eat and drink, and to be drunken;

46 The lord of that servant will come in a day when he looketh not for

---

ἐν τῇ δευτέρᾳ κἂν ἐν τῇ τρίτῃ φυλακῇ
in the second and if in the third watch
ἔλθῃ καὶ εὕρῃ οὕτως, μακάριοί εἰσιν
he comes and finds so, blessed are
ἐκεῖνοι. **39** τοῦτο δὲ γινώσκετε, ὅτι εἰ
those [slaves]. But this know ye, that if
ᾔδει ὁ οἰκοδεσπότης ποίᾳ ὥρᾳ ὁ κλέπτης
knew the house-master in what hour the thief
ἔρχεται, οὐκ ἂν ἀφῆκεν διορυχθῆναι τὸν
comes, he would not have allowed to be dug through the
οἶκον αὐτοῦ. **40** καὶ ὑμεῖς γίνεσθε ἕτοιμοι,
house of him. And ²ye ¹be prepared.
ὅτι ᾗ ὥρᾳ οὐ δοκεῖτε ὁ υἱὸς τοῦ
because in what hour ye think not the Son –
ἀνθρώπου ἔρχεται. **41** Εἶπεν δὲ ὁ Πέτρος·
of man comes. And said – Peter :
κύριε, πρὸς ἡμᾶς τὴν παραβολὴν ταύτην
Lord, to us – parable this
λέγεις ἢ καὶ πρὸς πάντας; **42** καὶ εἶπεν
sayest thou or also to all? And said
ὁ κύριος· τίς ἄρα ἐστὶν ὁ πιστὸς
the Lord : Who then is the faithful
οἰκονόμος ὁ φρόνιμος, ὃν καταστήσει ὁ
steward the prudent, whom will appoint the
κύριος ἐπὶ τῆς θεραπείας αὐτοῦ τοῦ
lord over the household attendants of him –
διδόναι ἐν καιρῷ [τὸ] σιτομέτριον;
to give[d] in season the portion of food?
43 μακάριος ὁ δοῦλος ἐκεῖνος, ὃν ἐλθὼν
Blessed slave that, whom coming
ὁ κύριος αὐτοῦ εὑρήσει ποιοῦντα οὕτως.
the lord of him will find doing so.
44 ἀληθῶς λέγω ὑμῖν ὅτι ἐπὶ πᾶσιν τοῖς
Truly I tell you that over all the
ὑπάρχουσιν αὐτοῦ καταστήσει αὐτόν. **45** ἐὰν
possessions of him he will appoint him. if
δὲ εἴπῃ ὁ δοῦλος ἐκεῖνος ἐν τῇ καρδίᾳ
But says – slave that in the heart
αὐτοῦ· χρονίζει ὁ κύριός μου ἔρχεσθαι,
of him : Delays the lord of me to come,
καὶ ἄρξηται τύπτειν τοὺς παῖδας καὶ τὰς
and begins to strike the menservants and the
παιδίσκας, ἐσθίειν τε καὶ πίνειν καὶ
maidservants, ²to eat ¹both and to drink and
μεθύσκεσθαι, **46** ἥξει ὁ κύριος τοῦ δούλου
to become drunk, will come the lord – slave
ἐκείνου ἐν ἡμέρᾳ ᾗ οὐ προσδοκᾷ καὶ ἐν
of that in a day in which he does not expect and in

him, and at an hour when he is not aware, and will cut him in sunder, and will appoint him his portion with the unbelievers.

47 And that servant, which knew his lord's will, and prepared not *himself*, neither did according to his will, shall be beaten with many *stripes*.

48 But he that knew not, and did commit things worthy of stripes, shall be beaten with few *stripes*. For unto whomsoever much is given, of him shall be much required: and to whom men have committed much, of him they will ask the more.

49 ¶ I am come to send fire on the earth; and what will I, if it be already kindled?

50 But I have a baptism to be baptized with; and how am I straitened till it be accomplished!

51 Suppose ye that I am come to give peace on earth? I tell you, Nay; but rather division:

52 For from henceforth there shall be five in one house divided, three against two, and two against three.

53 The father shall be divided against the son, and the son against the father; the mother against the daughter, and the daughter against the mother; the mother in law against her daughter in law, and the daughter in law against her mother in law.

54 ¶ And he said also to the people, When ye see a cloud rise out of the

ὥρα ᾗ οὐ γινώσκει, καὶ διχοτομήσει
an hour in which he knows not, and will cut asunder

αὐτόν, καὶ τὸ μέρος αὐτοῦ μετὰ τῶν
him, and the portion of him with the

ἀπίστων θήσει. 47 ἐκεῖνος δὲ ὁ δοῦλος
unbelievers will place. But that – slave

ὁ γνοὺς τὸ θέλημα τοῦ κυρίου αὐτοῦ
– having known the will of the lord of him

καὶ μὴ ἑτοιμάσας ἢ ποιήσας πρὸς τὸ θέλημα
and not having prepared or done according to the will

αὐτοῦ δαρήσεται πολλάς· 48 ὁ δὲ
of him will be beaten [with] many [stripes]; but the [one]

μὴ γνούς, ποιήσας δὲ ἄξια πληγῶν,
not having known, but having done things worthy of stripes,

δαρήσεται ὀλίγας. παντὶ δὲ ᾧ
will be beaten [with] few [stripes]. But to everyone to whom

ἐδόθη πολύ, πολὺ ζητηθήσεται παρ' αὐτοῦ, καὶ
was given much, much will be demanded from him, and

ᾧ παρέθεντο πολύ, περισσότερον αἰτήσουσιν
with whom was deposited much, more exceedingly they will ask

αὐτόν. 49 Πῦρ ἦλθον βαλεῖν ἐπὶ τὴν γῆν,
him. Fire I came to cast on the earth,

καὶ τί θέλω εἰ ἤδη ἀνήφθη. 50 βάπτισμα
and what will I if already it was kindled. ²a baptism

δὲ ἔχω βαπτισθῆναι, καὶ πῶς συνέχομαι
¹And ²I have to be baptized [with], and how am I pressed

ἕως ὅτου τελεσθῆ. 51 δοκεῖτε ὅτι εἰρήνην
until it is accomplished. Think ye that peace

παρεγενόμην δοῦναι ἐν τῇ γῇ; οὐχί, λέγω
I came to give in the earth? No, I tell

ὑμῖν, ἀλλ' ἢ διαμερισμόν. 52 ἔσονται γὰρ
you, but rather division. For there will be

ἀπὸ τοῦ νῦν πέντε ἐν ἑνὶ οἴκῳ διαμεμε-
from – now five in one house having been

ρισμένοι, τρεῖς ἐπὶ δυσὶν καὶ δύο ἐπὶ
divided, three against two and two against

τρισὶν 53 διαμερισθήσονται, πατὴρ ἐπὶ υἱῷ
three will be divided, father against son

καὶ υἱὸς ἐπὶ πατρί, μήτηρ ἐπὶ θυγατέρα
and son against father, mother against daughter

καὶ θυγάτηρ ἐπὶ τὴν μητέρα, πενθερὰ
and daughter against the mother, mother-in-law

ἐπὶ τὴν νύμφην αὐτῆς καὶ νύμφη ἐπὶ
against the daughter-in-law of her and daughter-in-law against

τὴν πενθεράν. 54 Ἔλεγεν δὲ καὶ τοῖς
the mother-in-law. And he said also to the

ὄχλοις· ὅταν ἴδητε νεφέλην ἀνατέλλουσαν
crowds : When ye see a cloud rising

west, straightway ye say,
There cometh a shower;
and so it is.

55 And when *ye see* the
south wind blow, ye say,
There will be heat; and it
cometh to pass.

56 *Ye* hypocrites, ye can
discern the face of the sky
and of the earth; but how
is it that ye do not discern
this time?

57 Yea, and why even
of yourselves judge ye not
what is right?

58 ¶ When thou goest
with thine adversary to
the magistrate, *as thou art*
in the way, give diligence
that thou mayest be de-
livered from him; lest he
hale thee to the judge,
and the judge deliver thee
to the officer, and the
officer cast thee into
prison.

59 I tell thee, thou shalt
not depart thence, till
thou hast paid the very
last mite.

ἐπὶ δυσμῶν, εὐθέως λέγετε ὅτι ὄμβρος
over [the] west, immediately ye say that a storm

ἔρχεται, καὶ γίνεται οὕτως· 55 καὶ ὅταν
is coming, and it becomes so; and when

νότον πνέοντα, λέγετε ὅτι καύσων ἔσται,
a south wind blowing, ye say that heat there will be,

καὶ γίνεται. 56 ὑποκριταί, τὸ πρόσωπον
and it becomes. Hypocrites, the face

τῆς γῆς καὶ τοῦ οὐρανοῦ οἴδατε δοκιμάζειν,
of the earth and of the heaven ye know* to discern,

τὸν καιρὸν δὲ τοῦτον πῶς οὐ δοκιμάζετε;
— ²time ¹but ²this how do ye not discern?

57 Τί δὲ καὶ ἀφ' ἑαυτῶν οὐ κρίνετε
And why even from yourselves do ye not judge

τὸ δίκαιον; 58 ὡς γὰρ ὑπάγεις μετὰ τοῦ
the righteous thing? For as thou goest with the

ἀντιδίκου σου ἐπ' ἄρχοντα, ἐν τῇ ὁδῷ
adversary of thee to a ruler, in the way

δὸς ἐργασίαν ἀπηλλάχθαι ἀπ' αὐτοῦ, μήποτε
give(take) pains to be rid from(of) him, lest

κατασύρῃ σε πρὸς τὸν κριτήν, καὶ ὁ
he drag thee to the judge, and the

κριτής σε παραδώσει τῷ πράκτορι, καὶ ὁ
judge thee will deliver to the usher, and the

πράκτωρ σε βαλεῖ εἰς φυλακήν. 59 λέγω
usher thee will cast into prison. I tell

σοι, οὐ μὴ ἐξέλθῃς ἐκεῖθεν ἕως
thee, by no means mayest thou come out thence until

καὶ τὸ ἔσχατον λεπτὸν ἀποδῷς.
even the last lepton thou payest.

CHAPTER 13

THERE were present at
that season some that
told him of the Galilæans,
whose blood Pilate had
mingled with their sacri-
fices.

2 And Jesus answering
said unto them, Suppose
ye that these Galilæans
were sinners above all the
Galilæans, because they
suffered such things?

3 I tell you, Nay: but,

13 Παρῆσαν δέ τινες ἐν αὐτῷ τῷ
And there were present some at ²same ¹the

καιρῷ ἀπαγγέλλοντες αὐτῷ περὶ τῶν
time reporting to him about the

Γαλιλαίων ὧν τὸ αἷμα Πιλᾶτος ἔμιξεν
Galilæans of whom the blood Pilate mixed

μετὰ τῶν θυσιῶν αὐτῶν. 2 καὶ ἀποκριθεὶς
with the sacrifices of them. And answering

εἶπεν αὐτοῖς· δοκεῖτε ὅτι οἱ Γαλιλαῖοι
he said to them : Think ye that — Galilæans

οὗτοι ἁμαρτωλοὶ παρὰ πάντας τοὺς Γαλι-
these sinners above all the Gali-

λαίους ἐγένοντο, ὅτι ταῦτα πεπόνθασιν;
læans were, because these things they have suffered?

3 οὐχί, λέγω ὑμῖν, ἀλλ' ἐὰν μὴ μετανοῆτε,
No, I tell you, but unless ye repent,

* can, as Mat. 16. 3. See note on page xviii.

except ye repent, ye shall all likewise perish.

4 Or those eighteen, upon whom the tower in Siloam fell, and slew them, think ye that they were sinners above all men that dwelt in Jerusalem?

5 I tell you, Nay: but, except ye repent, ye shall all likewise perish.

6 ¶ He spake also this parable; A certain *man* had a fig tree planted in his vineyard; and he came and sought fruit thereon, and found none.

7 Then said he unto the dresser of his vineyard, Behold, these three years I come seeking fruit on this fig tree, and find none: cut it down; why cumbereth it the ground?

8 And he answering said unto him, Lord, let it alone this year also, till I shall dig about it, and dung *it:*

9 And if it bear fruit, *well:* and if not, *then* after that thou shalt cut it down.

10 ¶ And he was teaching in one of the synagogues on the sabbath.

11 And, behold, there was a woman which had a spirit of infirmity eighteen years, and was bowed

πάντες ὁμοίως ἀπολεῖσθε. 4 ἢ ἐκεῖνοι οἱ
all   likewise   ye will perish.   Or   those   –

δεκαοκτὼ ἐφ' οὓς ἔπεσεν ὁ πύργος ἐν
eighteen   on   whom   fell   the   tower   in

τῷ Σιλωὰμ καὶ ἀπέκτεινεν αὐτούς, δοκεῖτε
–   Siloam   and   killed   them,   think ye

ὅτι αὐτοὶ ὀφειλέται ἐγένοντο παρὰ πάντας
that   they   debtors   were   above   all

τοὺς ἀνθρώπους τοὺς κατοικοῦντας Ἰερου-
the   men   –   dwelling in   Jeru-

σαλήμ; 5 οὐχί, λέγω ὑμῖν, ἀλλ' ἐὰν μὴ
salem?   No,   I tell   you,   but   unless

μετανοήσητε, πάντες ὡσαύτως ἀπολεῖσθε.
ye repent,   all   similarly   ye will perish.

6 Ἔλεγεν δὲ ταύτην τὴν παραβολήν. συκῆν
And he told   this   –   parable.   ²A fig-tree

εἶχέν τις πεφυτευμένην ἐν τῷ ἀμπελῶνι
¹had   ¹a certain man   *having been* planted   in   the   vineyard

αὐτοῦ, καὶ ἦλθεν ζητῶν καρπὸν ἐν αὐτῇ
of him,   and   came   seeking   fruit   in   it

καὶ οὐχ εὗρεν. 7 εἶπεν δὲ πρὸς τὸν
ᴀ..d   found not.   And he said   to   the

ἀμπελουργόν· ἰδοὺ τρία ἔτη ἀφ' οὗ
vinedresser :   Behold[,]   three   years   [it is] since

ἔρχομαι ζητῶν καρπὸν ἐν τῇ συκῇ ταύτῃ
I come   seeking   fruit   in   –   fig-tree   this

καὶ οὐχ εὑρίσκω· ἔκκοψον αὐτήν· ἱνατί
and   find not;   cut down   it;   why

καὶ τὴν γῆν καταργεῖ; 8 ὁ δὲ ἀποκριθεὶς
even   the   ground   it spoils?   But he   answering

λέγει αὐτῷ· κύριε, ἄφες αὐτὴν καὶ τοῦτο
says   to him :   Lord,   leave   it   also   this

τὸ ἔτος, ἕως ὅτου σκάψω περὶ αὐτὴν καὶ
–   year,   until   I may dig   round   it   and

βάλω κόπρια, 9 κἂν μὲν ποιήσῃ καρπὸν
may throw dung,   and if indeed   it makes   fruit

εἰς τὸ μέλλον· εἰ δὲ μή γε, ἐκκόψεις
in   the   future;   otherwise,   thou shalt cut down

αὐτήν.
it.

10 Ἦν δὲ διδάσκων ἐν μιᾷ τῶν συναγωγῶν
And he was   teaching   in   one   of the   synagogues

ἐν τοῖς σάββασιν. 11 καὶ ἰδοὺ γυνὴ
on   the   sabbaths.   And[,] beheld[,] a woman

πνεῦμα ἔχουσα ἀσθενείας ἔτη δεκαοκτώ,
²a spirit   ¹having   of infirmity   years   eighteen,

καὶ ἦν συγκύπτουσα καὶ μὴ δυναμένη
and   was   bending double   and   not   being able

together, and could in no wise lift up *herself.*

12 And when Jesus saw her, he called *her to him,* and said unto her, Woman, thou art loosed from thine infirmity.

13 And he laid *his* hands on her: and immediately she was made straight, and glorified God.

14 And the ruler of the synagogue answered with indignation, because that Jesus had healed on the sabbath day, and said unto the people, There are six days in which men ought to work: in them therefore come and be healed, and not on the sabbath day.

15 The Lord then answered him, and said, *Thou* hypocrite, doth not each one of you on the sabbath loose his ox or *his* ass from the stall, and lead *him* away to watering?

16 And ought not this woman, being a daughter of Abraham, whom Satan hath bound, lo, these eighteen years, be loosed from this bond on the sabbath day?

17 And when he had said these things all his adversaries were ashamed: and all the people rejoiced for all the glorious things that were done by him.

18 ¶ Then said he, Unto what is the kingdom of God like? and whereunto shall I resemble it?

ἀνακύψαι εἰς τὸ παντελές. 12 ἰδὼν δὲ
to become erect   entirely.†   And seeing

αὐτὴν ὁ Ἰησοῦς προσεφώνησεν καὶ εἶπεν
her   -   Jesus   called to [him]   and   said

αὐτῇ· γύναι, ἀπολέλυσαι τῆς ἀσθενείας
to her : Woman, thou hast been loosed from the infirmity

σου, 13 καὶ ἐπέθηκεν αὐτῇ τὰς χεῖρας·
of thee, and he put on   her the(his) hands;

καὶ παραχρῆμα ἀνωρθώθη, καὶ ἐδόξαζεν
and   at once   she was straightened, and   glorified

τὸν θεόν. 14 ἀποκριθεὶς δὲ ὁ ἀρχι-
-    God.   But answering   the   syn-

συνάγωγος, ἀγανακτῶν ὅτι τῷ σαββάτῳ
agogue ruler,   being angry   that ²on the ⁴sabbath

ἐθεράπευσεν ὁ Ἰησοῦς, ἔλεγεν τῷ ὄχλῳ
²healed   - ¹Jesus, said   to the crowd[,]

ὅτι ἐξ ἡμέραι εἰσὶν ἐν αἷς δεῖ ἐργάζεσθαι·
- six days there are on which it behoves to work;

ἐν αὐταῖς οὖν ἐρχόμενοι θεραπεύεσθε καὶ
on them therefore coming   be ye healed   and

μὴ τῇ ἡμέρᾳ τοῦ σαββάτου. 15 ἀπεκρίθη δὲ
not on the day   of the sabbath.   But answered

αὐτῷ ὁ κύριος καὶ εἶπεν· ὑποκριταί,
him   the Lord   and said :   Hypocrites,

ἕκαστος ὑμῶν τῷ σαββάτῳ οὐ λύει τὸν
each one of you on the sabbath does he not loosen the

βοῦν αὐτοῦ ἢ τὸν ὄνον ἀπὸ τῆς φάτνης
ox   of him or the ass from the   manger

καὶ ἀπαγαγὼν ποτίζει; 16 ταύτην δὲ
and leading [it] away give drink?   And this woman

θυγατέρα Ἀβραὰμ οὖσαν, ἣν ἔδησεν ὁ
a daughter of Abraham   being, whom bound   -

σατανᾶς ἰδοὺ δέκα καὶ ὀκτὼ ἔτη, οὐκ ἔδει
Satan   behold ten   and eight years, behoved it not

λυθῆναι ἀπὸ τοῦ δεσμοῦ τούτου τῇ
to be loosened from -   bond   this on the

ἡμέρᾳ τοῦ σαββάτου; 17 καὶ ταῦτα λέγοντος
day   of the sabbath?   And these things saying
                                =when he said these things

αὐτοῦ κατῃσχύνοντο πάντες οἱ ἀντικείμενοι
himᵃ   were put to shame   all   the[ones] opposing

αὐτῷ, καὶ πᾶς ὁ ὄχλος ἔχαιρεν ἐπὶ
him,   and all the crowd   rejoiced   over

πᾶσιν τοῖς ἐνδόξοις τοῖς γινομένοις ὑπ'
all   the glorious things the - happening   by

αὐτοῦ. 18 Ἔλεγεν οὖν· τίνι ὁμοία ἐστὶν ἡ
him.   He said therefore: To what like   is   the

βασιλεία τοῦ θεοῦ, καὶ τίνι ὁμοιώσω
kingdom   - of God,   and to what may I liken

19 It is like a grain of mustard seed, which a man took, and cast into his garden; and it grew, and waxed a great tree; and the fowls of the air lodged in the branches of it.

20 ¶ And again he said, Whereunto shall I liken the kingdom of God?

21 It is like leaven, which a woman took and hid in three measures of meal, till the whole was leavened.

22 And he went through the cities and villages, teaching, and journeying toward Jerusalem.

23 ¶ Then said one unto him, Lord, are there few that be saved? And he said unto them,

24 Strive to enter in at the strait gate: for many, I say unto you, will seek to enter in, and shall not be able.

25 When once the master of the house is risen up, and hath shut to the door, and ye begin to stand without, and to knock at the door, saying, Lord, Lord, open unto us; and he shall answer and say unto you, I know you not whence ye are:

26 Then shall ye begin to say, We have eaten and drunk in thy presence, and thou hast taught in our streets.

27 But he shall say, I tell you, I know you not

αὐτήν; **19** ὁμοία ἐστὶν κόκκῳ σινάπεως, ὃν
it? Like it is to a grain of mustard, which

λαβὼν ἄνθρωπος ἔβαλεν εἰς κῆπον ἑαυτοῦ,
²taking ¹a man cast into a garden of him*self*.

καὶ ηὔξησεν καὶ ἐγένετο εἰς δένδρον, καὶ
and it grew and became into a tree, and

τὰ πετεινὰ τοῦ οὐρανοῦ κατεσκήνωσεν
the birds of the heaven(air) lodged

ἐν τοῖς κλάδοις αὐτοῦ. **20** Καὶ πάλιν
in the branches of it. And again

εἶπεν· τίνι ὁμοιώσω τὴν βασιλείαν τοῦ
he said: To what may I liken the kingdom –

θεοῦ; **21** ὁμοία ἐστὶν ζύμῃ, ἣν λαβοῦσα
of God? Like it is to leaven, which ²taking

γυνὴ ἔκρυψεν εἰς ἀλεύρου σάτα τρία,
¹a woman hid in of meal measures three,

ἕως οὗ ἐζυμώθη ὅλον.
until was leavened all.

22 Καὶ διεπορεύετο κατὰ πόλεις καὶ
And he journeyed *through* throughout cities and

κώμας διδάσκων καὶ πορείαν ποιούμενος
villages teaching and journey making

εἰς Ἱεροσόλυμα. **23** Εἶπεν δέ τις αὐτῷ·
to Jerusalem. And said someone to him:

κύριε, εἰ ὀλίγοι οἱ σωζόμενοι; ὁ δὲ εἶπεν
Lord, if few the [ones] being saved? And he said

πρὸς αὐτούς· **24** ἀγωνίζεσθε εἰσελθεῖν διὰ
to them: Struggle to enter through

τῆς στενῆς θύρας, ὅτι πολλοί, λέγω ὑμῖν,
the strait door, because many, I tell you,

ζητήσουσιν εἰσελθεῖν καὶ οὐκ ἰσχύσουσιν.
will seek to enter and will not be able.

25 ἀφ' οὗ ἂν ἐγερθῇ ὁ οἰκοδεσπότης καὶ
From [the time] when is risen the house-master and

ἀποκλείσῃ τὴν θύραν, καὶ ἄρξησθε ἔξω
he shuts the door, and ye begin outside

ἑστάναι καὶ κρούειν τὴν θύραν λέγοντες·
to stand and to knock the door saying:

κύριε, ἄνοιξον ἡμῖν, καὶ ἀποκριθεὶς ἐρεῖ
Lord, open to us, and answering he will say

ὑμῖν· οὐκ οἶδα ὑμᾶς πόθεν ἐστέ. **26** τότε
to you: I know not you whence ye are. Then

ἄρξεσθε λέγειν· ἐφάγομεν ἐνώπιόν σου καὶ
ye will begin to say: We ate before thee and

ἐπίομεν, καὶ ἐν ταῖς πλατείαις ἡμῶν
drank, and in the streets of us

ἐδίδαξας· **27** καὶ ἐρεῖ λέγων ὑμῖν· οὐκ
thou didst teach; and he will say telling you: not

whence ye are; depart from me, all *ye* workers of iniquity.

28 There shall be weeping and gnashing of teeth, when ye shall see Abraham, and Isaac, and Jacob, and all the prophets, in the kingdom of God, and you *yourselves* thrust out.

29 And they shall come from the east, and *from* the west, and from the north, and *from* the south, and shall sit down in the kingdom of God.

30 And, behold, there are last which shall be first, and there are first which shall be last.

31 ¶ The same day there came certain of the Pharisees, saying unto him, Get thee out, and depart hence: for Herod will kill thee.

32 And he said unto them, Go ye, and tell that fox, Behold, I cast out devils, and I do cures to day and to morrow, and the third *day* I shall be perfected.

33 Nevertheless I must walk to day and to morrow, and the *day* following: for it cannot be that a prophet perish out of Jerusalem.

34 O Jerusalem, Jerusalem, which killest the prophets, and stonest them that are sent unto thee; how often would I have

οἶδα πόθεν ἐστέ· ἀπόστητε ἀπ᾽ ἐμοῦ
I know whence ye are; stand away from me

πάντες ἐργάται ἀδικίας. 28 ἐκεῖ ἔσται ὁ
all workers of unrighteousness. There will be the

κλαυθμὸς καὶ ὁ βρυγμὸς τῶν ὀδόντων,
weeping and the gnashing of the teeth,

ὅταν ὄψησθε ᾽Αβραὰμ καὶ ᾽Ισαὰκ καὶ
when ye see Abraham and Isaac and

᾽Ιακὼβ καὶ πάντας τοὺς προφήτας ἐν τῇ
Jacob and all the prophets in the

βασιλείᾳ τοῦ θεοῦ, ὑμᾶς δὲ ἐκβαλλομένους
kingdom – of God, but you being thrust *out*

ἔξω. 29 καὶ ἥξουσιν ἀπὸ ἀνατολῶν καὶ
outside. And they will come from east and

δυσμῶν καὶ ἀπὸ βορρᾶ καὶ νότου, καὶ
west and from north and south, and

ἀνακλιθήσονται ἐν τῇ βασιλείᾳ τοῦ θεοῦ.
will recline in the kingdom – of God.

30 καὶ ἰδοὺ εἰσὶν ἔσχατοι οἳ ἔσονται
And behold there are last [ones] who will be

πρῶτοι, καὶ εἰσὶν πρῶτοι οἳ ἔσονται
first, and there are first [ones] who will be

ἔσχατοι. 31 ᾽Εν αὐτῇ τῇ ὥρᾳ προσῆλθάν
last. In ²same ¹the hour approached

τινες Φαρισαῖοι λέγοντες αὐτῷ· ἔξελθε καὶ
some Pharisees saying to him: Depart and

πορεύου ἐντεῦθεν, ὅτι ῾Ηρῴδης θέλει σε
go hence, because Herod wishes thee

ἀποκτεῖναι. 32 καὶ εἶπεν αὐτοῖς· πορευθέντες
to kill. And he said to them: Going

εἴπατε τῇ ἀλώπεκι ταύτῃ· ἰδοὺ ἐκβάλλω
tell – fox this: Behold I expel

δαιμόνια καὶ ἰάσεις ἀποτελῶ σήμερον καὶ
demons and ²cures ¹accomplish to-day and

αὔριον, καὶ τῇ τρίτῃ τελειοῦμαι. 33 πλὴν
to-morrow, and on the third [day] I am perfected. Nevertheless

δεῖ με σήμερον καὶ αὔριον καὶ τῇ ἐχομένῃ
it be- me to-day and to- and on the following
hoves morrow [day]

πορεύεσθαι, ὅτι οὐκ ἐνδέχεται προφήτην
to journey, because it is not possible a prophet

ἀπολέσθαι ἔξω ᾽Ιερουσαλήμ. 34 ᾽Ιερουσαλὴμ
to perish outside Jerusalem. Jerusalem[.]

᾽Ιερουσαλήμ, ἡ ἀποκτείνουσα τοὺς προφήτας
Jerusalem, the [one] killing the prophets

καὶ λιθοβολοῦσα τοὺς ἀπεσταλμένους πρὸς
and stoning the [ones] *having been* sent to

αὐτήν, ποσάκις ἠθέλησα ἐπισυνάξαι τὰ
her, how often I wished to gather the

gathered thy children to-
gether, as a hen *doth
gather* her brood under *her*
wings, and ye would not!

35 Behold, your house
is left unto you desolate:
and verily I say unto you,
Ye shall not see me, until
the time come when ye
shall say, Blessed *is* he
that cometh in the name
of the Lord.

τέκνα σου ὃν τρόπον ὄρνις τὴν ἑαυτῆς
children of thee   as †   a bird the of herself
νοσσιὰν ὑπὸ τὰς πτέρυγας, καὶ οὐκ
brood   under the(her) wings,   and not
ἠθελήσατε. 35 ἰδοὺ ἀφίεται ὑμῖν ὁ οἶκος
ye wished.   Behold is left to you the house
ὑμῶν. λέγω [δὲ] ὑμῖν, οὐ μὴ ἴδητέ με
of you. And I tell you, by no means ye may see me
ἕως ἥξει ὅτε εἴπητε· εὐλογημένος ὁ
until shall come [the ye say :   Blessed   the
        time] when
ἐρχόμενος ἐν ὀνόματι κυρίου.
[one] coming in [the] name of [the] Lord.

CHAPTER 14

AND it came to pass,
as he went into the
house of one of the chief
Pharisees to eat bread on
the sabbath day, that they
watched him.

2 And, behold, there
was a certain man before
him which had the dropsy.

3 And Jesus answering
spake unto the lawyers
and Pharisees, saying, Is
it lawful to heal on the
sabbath day?

4 And they held their
peace. And he took *him*,
and healed him, and let
him go;

5 And answered them,
saying, Which of you shall
have an ass or an ox fallen
into a pit, and will not
straightway pull him out
on the sabbath day?

6 And they could not
answer him again to these
things.

7 ¶ And he put forth a
parable to those which
were bidden, when he
marked how they chose
out the chief rooms; say-
ing unto them,

8 When thou art bidden
of any *man* to a wedding,

14 Καὶ ἐγένετο ἐν τῷ ἐλθεῖν αὐτὸν εἰς
And it came to pass in the to go him[be] into
                              =as he went
οἶκόν τινος τῶν ἀρχόντων τῶν Φαρισαίων
a house of one of the leaders of the Pharisees
σαββάτῳ φαγεῖν ἄρτον, καὶ αὐτοὶ ἦσαν
on a sabbath to eat bread, *and* they were
παρατηρούμενοι αὐτόν. 2 καὶ ἰδοὺ ἄνθρωπός
carefully watching him.   And[,] behold[,] man
τις ἦν ὑδρωπικὸς ἔμπροσθεν αὐτοῦ. 3 καὶ
a certain was dropsical   before   him.   And
ἀποκριθεὶς ὁ Ἰησοῦς εἶπεν πρὸς τοὺς
answering - Jesus spoke to   the
νομικοὺς καὶ Φαρισαίους λέγων· ἔξεστιν
lawyers   and Pharisees saying : Is it lawful
τῷ σαββάτῳ θεραπεῦσαι ἢ οὔ; 4 οἱ δὲ
on the sabbath to heal   or not? And they
ἡσύχασαν. καὶ ἐπιλαβόμενος ἰάσατο αὐτὸν
were silent. And taking   he cured   him
καὶ ἀπέλυσεν. 5 καὶ πρὸς αὐτοὺς εἶπεν·
and dismissed. And to them he said :
τίνος ὑμῶν υἱὸς ἢ βοῦς εἰς φρέαρ πεσεῖται,
Of whom of you a son or an ox into a pit shall fall,
καὶ οὐκ εὐθέως ἀνασπάσει αὐτὸν ἐν
and not immediately he will pull up it   on
ἡμέρᾳ τοῦ σαββάτου; 6 καὶ οὐκ ἴσχυσαν
a day of the sabbath? And they were not able
ἀνταποκριθῆναι πρὸς ταῦτα. 7 Ἔλεγεν δὲ
to reply   against these things.   And he said
πρὸς τοὺς κεκλημένους παραβολήν, ἐπέχων
to the [ones] *having been* invited a parable, noting
πῶς τὰς πρωτοκλισίας ἐξελέγοντο, λέγων
how ²the ³chief seats ¹they were choosing, saying
πρὸς αὐτούς· 8 ὅταν κληθῇς ὑπό τινος εἰς
to   them :   When thou art invited by anyone to

sit not down in the highest room; lest a more honourable man than thou be bidden of him;

9 And he that bade thee and him come and say to thee, Give this man place; and thou begin with shame to take the lowest room.

10 But when thou art bidden, go and sit down in the lowest room; that when he that bade thee cometh, he may say unto thee, Friend, go up higher: then shalt thou have worship in the presence of them that sit at meat with thee.

11 For whosoever exalteth himself shall be abased; and he that humbleth himself shall be exalted.

12 ¶ Then said he also to him that bade him, When thou makest a dinner or a supper, call not thy friends, nor thy brethren, neither thy kinsmen, nor *thy* rich neighbours; lest they also bid thee again, and a recompence be made thee.

13 But when thou makest a feast, call the poor, the maimed, the lame, the blind:

14 And thou shalt be blessed; for they cannot recompense thee: for thou shalt be recompensed at the resurrection of the just.

15 ¶ And when one of them that sat at meat with him heard these things, he said unto him,

γάμους, μὴ κατακλιθῇς εἰς τὴν πρωτοκλισίαν,
wedding festivities, do not recline in the chief seat,

μήποτε ἐντιμότερός σου ᾖ κεκλημένος ὑπ'
lest a more honourable [than] thou be *having been* invited by

αὐτοῦ, 9 καὶ ἐλθὼν ὁ σὲ καὶ αὐτὸν καλέσας
him, and coming ¹the [one] ³thee ⁴and ⁵him ²inviting

ἐρεῖ σοι· δὸς τούτῳ τόπον, καὶ τότε
will say to thee: Give this man place, and then

ἄρξῃ μετὰ αἰσχύνης τὸν ἔσχατον τόπον
thou wilt begin with shame the last place

κατέχειν. 10 ἀλλ' ὅταν κληθῇς, πορευθεὶς
to take. But when thou art invited, going

ἀνάπεσε εἰς τὸν ἔσχατον τόπον, ἵνα ὅταν ἔλθῃ
recline in the last place, that when ⁴comes

ὁ κεκληκώς σε ἐρεῖ σοι· φίλε,
¹the [one] ²having invited ³thee he will say to thee: Friend,

προσανάβηθι ἀνώτερον· τότε ἔσται σοι δόξα
go up higher; then there will be to thee° glory

ἐνώπιον πάντων τῶν συνανακειμένων σοι.
before all the [ones] reclining with thee.

11 ὅτι πᾶς ὁ ὑψῶν ἑαυτὸν ταπεινωθήσεται,
Because everyone exalting himself will be humbled,

καὶ ὁ ταπεινῶν ἑαυτὸν ὑψωθήσεται.
and the [one] humbling himself will be exalted.

12 Ἔλεγεν δὲ καὶ τῷ κεκληκότι αὐτόν·
And he said also to the [one] having invited him:

ὅταν ποιῇς ἄριστον ἢ δεῖπνον, μὴ φώνει
When thou makest a dinner or a supper, do not call

τοὺς φίλους σου μηδὲ τοὺς ἀδελφούς
the friends of thee nor the brothers

σου μηδὲ τοὺς συγγενεῖς σου μηδὲ
of thee nor the relatives of thee nor

γείτονας πλουσίους, μήποτε καὶ αὐτοὶ
neighbours rich, lest also they

ἀντικαλέσωσίν σε καὶ γένηται ἀνταπόδομά
¹invite ²in ⁴return ³thee and it becomes a recompence

σοι. 13 ἀλλ' ὅταν δοχὴν ποιῇς, κάλει
to thee. But when a party thou makest, invite

πτωχούς, ἀναπήρους, χωλούς, τυφλούς·
poor [persons], maimed, lame, blind:

14 καὶ μακάριος ἔσῃ, ὅτι οὐκ ἔχουσιν
and blessed thou shalt be, because they have not

ἀνταποδοῦναί σοι· ἀνταποδοθήσεται γάρ σοι
to recompense thee; for it will be recompensed to thee

ἐν τῇ ἀναστάσει τῶν δικαίων. 15 Ἀκούσας
in the resurrection of the just. ⁵hearing

δέ τις τῶν συνανακειμένων ταῦτα εἶπεν
¹And ⁴one ⁵of the [ones] ⁶reclining with ²these things said

Blessed *is* he that shall eat bread in the kingdom of God.

16 Then said he unto him, A certain man made a great supper, and bade many:

17 And sent his servant at supper time to say to them that were bidden, Come; for all things are now ready.

18 And they all with one *consent* began to make excuse. The first said unto him, I have bought a piece of ground, and I must needs go and see it: I pray thee have me excused.

19 And another said, I have bought five yoke of oxen, and I go to prove them: I pray thee have me excused.

20 And another said, I have married a wife, and therefore I cannot come.

21 So that servant came, and shewed his lord these things. Then the master of the house being angry said to his servant, Go out quickly into the streets and lanes of the city, and bring in hither the poor, and the maimed, and the halt, and the blind.

22 And the servant said, Lord, it is done as thou hast commanded, and yet there is room.

23 And the lord said unto the servant, Go out

αὐτῷ· μακάριος ὅστις φάγεται ἄρτον ἐν
to him : Blessed [is he] who eats bread in

τῇ βασιλείᾳ τοῦ θεοῦ. 16 ὁ δὲ εἶπεν
the kingdom – of God. And he said

αὐτῷ· ἄνθρωπός τις ἐποίει δεῖπνον μέγα,
to him : A certain man made supper a great,

καὶ ἐκάλεσεν πολλούς, 17 καὶ ἀπέστειλεν
and invited many, and sent

τὸν δοῦλον αὐτοῦ τῇ ὥρᾳ τοῦ δείπνου
the slave of him at the hour of the supper

εἰπεῖν τοῖς κεκλημένοις· ἔρχεσθε, ὅτι ἤδη
to say to the [ones] having been invited : Come, because ²now

ἕτοιμά ἐστιν. 18 καὶ ἤρξαντο ἀπὸ μιᾶς
³prepared ¹it is. And they began from one [mind]

πάντες παραιτεῖσθαι. ὁ πρῶτος εἶπεν
all to beg off. The first said

αὐτῷ· ἀγρὸν ἠγόρασα, καὶ ἔχω ἀνάγκην
to him : ²A farm ¹I bought, and I am obliged†

ἐξελθὼν ἰδεῖν αὐτόν· ἐρωτῶ σε, ἔχε με
going out to see it; I ask thee, have me

παρῃτημένον. 19 καὶ ἕτερος εἶπεν· ζεύγη
begged off. And another said : ³Yoke

βοῶν ἠγόρασα πέντε, καὶ πορεύομαι
⁴of oxen ¹I bought ²five, and I am going

δοκιμάσαι αὐτά· ἐρωτῶ σε, ἔχε με
to prove them; I ask thee, have me

παρῃτημένον. 20 καὶ ἕτερος εἶπεν· γυναῖκα
begged off. And another said : ³A wife

ἔγημα, καὶ διὰ τοῦτο οὐ δύναμαι ἐλθεῖν.
¹I married, and therefore I cannot *to* come.

21 καὶ παραγενόμενος ὁ δοῦλος ἀπήγγειλεν
And coming up the slave reported

τῷ κυρίῳ αὐτοῦ ταῦτα. τότε ὀργισθεὶς ὁ
to the lord of him these things. Then being angry the

οἰκοδεσπότης εἶπεν τῷ δούλῳ αὐτοῦ· ἔξελθε
house-master told the slave of him : Go out

ταχέως εἰς τὰς πλατείας καὶ ῥύμας τῆς
quickly into the streets and lanes of the

πόλεως, καὶ τοὺς πτωχοὺς καὶ ἀναπήρους
city, and the poor and maimed

καὶ τυφλοὺς καὶ χωλοὺς εἰσάγαγε ὧδε.
and blind and lame bring in here.

22 καὶ εἶπεν ὁ δοῦλος· κύριε, γέγονεν ὃ
And said the slave : Lord, has happened what

ἐπέταξας, καὶ ἔτι τόπος ἐστίν. 23 καὶ
thou didst command, and yet room there is. And

εἶπεν ὁ κύριος πρὸς τὸν δοῦλον· ἔξελθε εἰς
said the lord to the slave : Go out into

into the highways and
hedges, and compel *them*
to come in, that my house
may be filled.

24 For I say unto you,
That none of those men
which were bidden shall
taste of my supper.

25 ¶ And there went
great multitudes with him:
and he turned, and said
unto them,

26 If any *man* come to
me, and hate not his
father, and mother, and
wife, and children, and
brethren, and sisters, yea,
and his own life also, he
cannot be my disciple.

27 And whosoever doth
not bear his cross, and
come after me, cannot be
my disciple.

28 For which of you,
intending to build a tower,
sitteth not down first, and
counteth the cost, whether
he have *sufficient* to finish
it?

29 Lest haply, after he
hath laid the foundation,
and is not able to finish *it*,
all that behold *it* begin to
mock him,

30 Saying, This man
began to build, and was
not able to finish.

31 Or what king, going
to make war against an-
other king, sitteth not
down first, and consulteth
whether he be able with

τὰς ὁδοὺς καὶ φραγμοὺς καὶ ἀνάγκασον
the ways and hedges and compel

εἰσελθεῖν, ἵνα γεμισθῇ μου ὁ οἶκος·
to come in, that may be filled of me the house ;

24 λέγω γὰρ ὑμῖν ὅτι οὐδεὶς τῶν ἀνδρῶν
for I tell you that not one – men

ἐκείνων τῶν κεκλημένων γεύσεταί μου
of those – having been invited shall taste of me

τοῦ δείπνου.
the supper.

25 Συνεπορεύοντο δὲ αὐτῷ ὄχλοι πολλοί,
And came together to him crowds many,

καὶ στραφεὶς εἶπεν πρὸς αὐτούς· 26 εἴ τις
and turning he said to them : If anyone

ἔρχεται πρός με καὶ οὐ μισεῖ τὸν πατέρα
comes to me and hates not the father

αὐτοῦ καὶ τὴν μητέρα καὶ τὴν γυναῖκα
of him and the mother and the wife

καὶ τὰ τέκνα καὶ τοὺς ἀδελφοὺς καὶ τὰς
and the children and the brothers and the

ἀδελφάς, ἔτι τε καὶ τὴν ψυχὴν ἑαυτοῦ,
sisters, and besides also the life of himself,

οὐ δύναται εἶναί μου μαθητής. 27 ὅστις
he cannot to be of me a disciple. Who

οὐ βαστάζει τὸν σταυρὸν ἑαυτοῦ καὶ
bears not the cross of himself and

ἔρχεται ὀπίσω μου, οὐ δύναται εἶναί μου
comes after me, he cannot to be of me

μαθητής. 28 Τίς γὰρ ἐξ ὑμῶν θέλων
a disciple. For who of you wishing

πύργον οἰκοδομῆσαι οὐχὶ πρῶτον καθίσας
a tower to build not first sitting

ψηφίζει τὴν δαπάνην, εἰ ἔχει εἰς ἀπαρ-
counts the cost, if he has for com-

τισμόν; 29 ἵνα μὴ ποτε θέντος αὐτοῦ
pletion? Lest when laying him*
= he has laid

θεμέλιον καὶ μὴ ἰσχύοντος ἐκτελέσαι πάντες
a foundation and not being able* to finish all

οἱ θεωροῦντες ἄρξωνται αὐτῷ ἐμπαίζειν
the [ones] seeing begin him to mock

30 λέγοντες ὅτι οὗτος ὁ ἄνθρωπος ἤρξατο
saying[,] – This – man began

οἰκοδομεῖν καὶ οὐκ ἴσχυσεν ἐκτελέσαι.
to build and was not able to finish.

31 Ἢ τίς βασιλεὺς πορευόμενος ἑτέρῳ βασιλεῖ
Or what king ¹going ⁵another ⁶king

συμβαλεῖν εἰς πόλεμον οὐχὶ καθίσας πρῶτον
²to attack ³in ⁴war not sitting first

ten thousand to meet him that cometh against him with twenty thousand?

32 Or else, while the other is yet a great way off, he sendeth an ambassage, and desireth conditions of peace.

33 So likewise, whosoever he be of you that forsaketh not all that he hath, he cannot be my disciple.

34 ¶ Salt *is* good: but if the salt have lost his savour, wherewith shall it be seasoned?

35 It is neither fit for the land, nor yet for the dunghill; *but* men cast it out. He that hath ears to hear, let him hear.

βουλεύσεται   εἰ   δυνατός   ἐστιν   ἐν   δέκα
will deliberate ~   if   able   he is   with   ten

χιλιάσιν   ὑπαντῆσαι   τῷ   μετὰ   εἴκοσι   χιλιάδων
thousands   to meet   ¹the [one] ²with   ⁶twenty   ⁷thousands

ἐρχομένῳ   ἐπ’   αὐτόν;   32 εἰ   δὲ   μή   γε,   ἔτι
²coming   ³upon   ⁴him?   Otherwise,   yet
                                                 =while

αὐτοῦ   πόρρω   ὄντος   πρεσβείαν   ἀποστείλας
him   afar   being²   a delegation   sending
he is yet at a distance

ἐρωτᾷ   τὰ   πρὸς   εἰρήνην.   33 οὕτως   οὖν
he asks the things for   peace.   So therefore

πᾶς   ἐξ   ὑμῶν   ὃς   οὐκ   ἀποτάσσεται   πᾶσιν
everyone of   you   who   does not say farewell   to all

τοῖς   ἑαυτοῦ   ὑπάρχουσιν   οὐ   δύναται   εἶναί
¹the   ³of himself   ²possessions   cannot   *to* be

μου   μαθητής.   34 Καλὸν   οὖν   τὸ   ἅλας·
of me   a disciple.   Good therefore the   salt;

ἐὰν   δὲ   καὶ   τὸ   ἅλας   μωρανθῇ,   ἐν   τίνι
but if   even   the   salt   becomes useless, with   what

ἀρτυθήσεται;   35 οὔτε   εἰς   γῆν   οὔτε   εἰς
will it be seasoned?   neither   for   soil   nor   for

κοπρίαν   εὔθετόν   ἐστιν·   ἔξω   βάλλουσιν
manure   suitable   is it;   outside   they cast

αὐτό.   ὁ   ἔχων   ὦτα   ἀκούειν   ἀκουέτω.
it.   The [one] having   ears   to hear   let him hear.

CHAPTER 15

THEN drew near unto him all the publicans and sinners for to hear him.

2 And the Pharisees and scribes murmured, saying, This man receiveth sinners, and eateth with them.

3 ¶ And he spake this parable unto them, saying,

4 What man of you, having an hundred sheep, if he lose one of them, doth not leave the ninety and nine in the wilderness, and go after that which is lost, until he find it?

15 Ἦσαν   δὲ   αὐτῷ   ἐγγίζοντες   πάντες
Now there were   to him   drawing near   all

οἱ   τελῶναι   καὶ   οἱ   ἁμαρτωλοὶ   ἀκούειν
the   tax-collectors and   the   sinners   to hear

αὐτοῦ.   2 καὶ   διεγόγγυζον   οἵ   τε   Φαρισαῖοι
him.   And greatly murmured both the   Pharisees

καὶ   οἱ   γραμματεῖς   λέγοντες   ὅτι   οὗτος
and the   scribes   saying[,]   –   This man

ἁμαρτωλοὺς   προσδέχεται   καὶ   συνεσθίει   αὐ-
sinners   receives   and   eats with   them.

τοῖς.   3 εἶπεν   δὲ   πρὸς   αὐτοὺς   τὴν   παρα-
         And he spoke   to   them   –   para-

βολὴν   ταύτην   λέγων·   4 τίς   ἄνθρωπος   ἐξ
ble   this   saying :   What   man   of

ὑμῶν   ἔχων   ἑκατὸν   πρόβατα   καὶ   ἀπολέσας
you   having a hundred   sheep   and   losing

ἐξ   αὐτῶν   ἓν   οὐ   καταλείπει   τὰ   ἐνενήκοντα
of   them   one   does not leave   the   ninety-

ἐννέα   ἐν   τῇ   ἐρήμῳ   καὶ   πορεύεται   ἐπὶ
nine   in   the   desert   and   goes   after

τὸ   ἀπολωλὸς   ἕως   εὕρῃ   αὐτό;   5 καὶ
the [one] having been lost   until   he finds   it?   and

5 And when he hath found it, he layeth it on his shoulders, rejoicing.

6 And when he cometh home, he calleth together his friends and neighbours, saying unto them, Rejoice with me; for I have found my sheep which was lost.

7 I say unto you, that likewise joy shall be in heaven over one sinner that repenteth, more than over ninety and nine just persons, which need no repentance.

8 ¶ Either what woman having ten pieces of silver, if she lose one piece, doth not light a candle, and sweep the house, and seek diligently till she find it?

9 And when she hath found it, she calleth her friends and her neighbours together, saying, Rejoice with me; for I have found the piece which I had lost.

10 Likewise, I say unto you, there is joy in the presence of the angels of God over one sinner that repenteth.

11 ¶ And he said, A certain man had two sons:

12 And the younger of them said to his father, Father, give me the portion of goods that falleth to me. And he divided unto them his living.

13 And not many days after the younger son gathered all together, and took his journey into a far country, and there wasted

εὑρὼν ἐπιτίθησιν ἐπὶ τοὺς ὤμους αὐτοῦ
finding places on [it] on the shoulders of him

χαίρων, 6 καὶ ἐλθὼν εἰς τὸν οἶκον
rejoicing, and coming into the house

συγκαλεῖ τοὺς φίλους καὶ τοὺς γείτονας,
he calls together the friends and the neighbours,

λέγων αὐτοῖς· συγχάρητέ μοι, ὅτι εὗρον
saying to them: Rejoice with me, because I found

τὸ πρόβατόν μου τὸ ἀπολωλός. 7 λέγω
the sheep of me - having been lost. I tell

ὑμῖν ὅτι οὕτως χαρὰ ἐν τῷ οὐρανῷ
you that thus joy in - heaven

ἔσται ἐπὶ ἑνὶ ἁμαρτωλῷ μετανοοῦντι ἢ
will be over one sinner repenting than

ἐπὶ ἐνενήκοντα ἐννέα δικαίοις οἵτινες οὐ
over ninety-nine just men who no

χρείαν ἔχουσιν μετανοίας. 8 Ἢ τίς γυνὴ
need have of repentance. Or what woman

δραχμὰς ἔχουσα δέκα, ἐὰν ἀπολέσῃ
³drachmae ¹having ²ten, if she loses

δραχμὴν μίαν, οὐχὶ ἅπτει λύχνον καὶ
drachma one, does not light a lamp and

σαροῖ τὴν οἰκίαν καὶ ζητεῖ ἐπιμελῶς
sweep the house and seek carefully

ἕως οὗ εὕρῃ; 9 καὶ εὑροῦσα συγκαλεῖ
until she finds? and finding she calls together

τὰς φίλας καὶ γείτονας λέγουσα· συγχάρητέ
the friends and neighbours saying: Rejoice with

μοι, ὅτι εὗρον τὴν δραχμὴν ἣν ἀπώλεσα.
me, because I found the drachma which I lost.

10 οὕτως, λέγω ὑμῖν, γίνεται χαρὰ ἐνώπιον
So, I tell you, there is joy before

τῶν ἀγγέλων τοῦ θεοῦ ἐπὶ ἑνὶ ἁμαρτωλῷ
the angels - of God over one sinner

μετανοοῦντι. 11 Εἶπεν δέ· ἄνθρωπός τις
repenting. And he said: A certain man

εἶχεν δύο υἱούς. 12 καὶ εἶπεν ὁ νεώτερος
had two sons. And said the younger

αὐτῶν τῷ πατρί· πάτερ, δός μοι τὸ
of them to the father: Father, give me the

ἐπιβάλλον μέρος τῆς οὐσίας. ὁ δὲ διεῖλες
falling upon share of the property. And he divided
=share of the property falling to [me].

αὐτοῖς τὸν βίον. 13 καὶ μετ’ οὐ πολλὰς
to them the living. And after not many

ἡμέρας συναγαγὼν πάντα ὁ νεώτερος υἱὸς
days having gathered all things the younger son

ἀπεδήμησεν εἰς χώραν μακράν, καὶ ἐκεῖ
departed to country a far, and there

his substance with riotous living.

14 And when he had spent all, there arose a mighty famine in that land; and he began to be in want.

15 And he went and joined himself to a citizen of that country; and he sent him into his fields to feed swine.

16 And he would fain have filled his belly with the husks that the swine did eat: and no man gave unto him.

17 And when he came to himself, he said, How many hired servants of my father's have bread enough and to spare, and I perish with hunger!

18 I will arise and go to my father, and will say unto him, Father, I have sinned against heaven, and before thee,

19 And am no more worthy to be called thy son: make me as one of thy hired servants.

20 And he arose, and came to his father. But when he was yet a great way off, his father saw him, and had compassion, and ran, and fell on his neck, and kissed him.

21 And the son said unto him, Father, I have sinned against heaven, and

διεσκόρπισεν τὴν οὐσίαν αὐτοῦ ζῶν ἀσώτως.
scattered · the   property of him living   prodigally.

14 δαπανήσαντος δὲ αὐτοῦ πάντα ἐγένετο
But having spent   him*   all things   there came
=when he had spent

λιμὸς ἰσχυρὰ κατὰ τὴν χώραν ἐκείνην,
famine   a severe   throughout   –   country   that,

καὶ αὐτὸς ἤρξατο ὑστερεῖσθαι. 15 καὶ
and   he   began   to be in want.   And

πορευθεὶς ἐκολλήθη ἑνὶ τῶν πολιτῶν τῆς
going   he was joined to one of the   citizens   –

χώρας ἐκείνης, καὶ ἔπεμψεν αὐτὸν εἰς
country   of that,   and   he sent   him   into

τοὺς ἀγροὺς αὐτοῦ βόσκειν χοίρους· 16 καὶ
the   fields   of him   to feed   pigs;   and

ἐπεθύμει γεμίσαι τὴν κοιλίαν αὐτοῦ ἐκ
he longed   to fill   the   stomach   of him out of(with)

τῶν κερατίων ὧν ἤσθιον οἱ χοῖροι, καὶ
the   husks   which   ²ate   ¹the   ²pigs,   and

οὐδεὶς ἐδίδου αὐτῷ. 17 εἰς ἑαυτὸν δὲ
no one   gave   to him.   ²to   ⁴himself   ¹But

ἐλθὼν ἔφη· πόσοι μίσθιοι τοῦ πατρός μου
³coming he said: How many hired servants of the   father   of me

περισσεύονται ἄρτων, ἐγὼ δὲ λιμῷ ὧδε
abound   of loaves,   but I   with famine here
=have abundance of bread,

ἀπόλλυμαι. 18 ἀναστὰς πορεύσομαι πρὸς
am perishing.   Rising up   I will go   to

τὸν πατέρα μου καὶ ἐρῶ αὐτῷ· πάτερ,
the   father   of me   and I will say to him :   Father,

ἥμαρτον εἰς τὸν οὐρανὸν καὶ ἐνώπιόν σου,
I sinned against   –   heaven   and   before   thee,

19 οὐκέτι εἰμὶ ἄξιος κληθῆναι υἱός σου·
no longer   am I   worthy   to be called   a son of thee;

ποίησόν με ὡς ἕνα τῶν μισθίων σου.
make   me   as   one   of the hired servants of thee.

20 καὶ ἀναστὰς ἦλθεν πρὸς τὸν πατέρα
And   rising up   he came   to   the   father

ἑαυτοῦ. ἔτι δὲ αὐτοῦ μακρὰν ἀπέχοντος
of himself.   But yet   him   afar   being away*
=while he was yet far away

εἶδεν αὐτὸν ὁ πατὴρ αὐτοῦ καὶ ἐσπλαγχνίσθη,
saw   him the father   of him   and was moved with pity,

καὶ δραμὼν ἐπέπεσεν ἐπὶ τὸν τράχηλον
and   running   fell on   on   the   neck

αὐτοῦ καὶ κατεφίλησεν αὐτόν. 21 εἶπεν δὲ
of him and   fervently kissed   him.   And said

ὁ υἱὸς αὐτῷ· πάτερ, ἥμαρτον εἰς τὸν
the son   to him :   Father,   I sinned   against   –

in thy sight, and am no
more worthy to be called
thy son.

22 But the father said
to his servants, Bring
forth the best robe, and
put it on him; and put a
ring on his hand, and
shoes on his feet:

23 And bring hither the
fatted calf, and kill it;
and let us eat, and be
merry:

24 For this my son was
dead, and is alive again;
he was lost, and is found.
And they began to be
merry.

25 Now his elder son
was in the field: and as
he came and drew nigh to
the house, he heard musick
and dancing.

26 And he called one
of the servants, and asked
what these things meant.

27 And he said unto
him, Thy brother is come;
and thy father hath killed
the fatted calf, because he
hath received him safe and
sound.

28 And he was angry,
and would not go in:
therefore came his father
out, and intreated him.

29 And he answering
said to his father, Lo,
these many years do I
serve thee, neither transgressed I at any time thy
commandment: and yet
thou never gavest me a
kid, that I might make

οὐρανὸν καὶ ἐνώπιόν σου, οὐκέτι εἰμὶ
heaven and before thee, no longer am I
ἄξιος κληθῆναι υἱός σου. 22 εἶπεν δὲ
worthy to be called a son of thee. But said
ὁ πατὴρ πρὸς τοὺς δούλους αὐτοῦ· ταχὺ
the father to the slaves of him : Quickly
ἐξενέγκατε στολὴν τὴν πρώτην καὶ ἐνδύσατε
bring ye out a robe the first and clothe
αὐτόν, καὶ δότε δακτύλιον εἰς τὴν χεῖρα
him, and give(put) a ring to the hand
αὐτοῦ καὶ ὑποδήματα εἰς τοὺς πόδας,
of him and sandals to the feet,
23 καὶ φέρετε τὸν μόσχον τὸν σιτευτόν,
and bring the calf fattened,
θύσατε, καὶ φαγόντες εὐφρανθῶμεν, 24 ὅτι
kill, and eating let us be merry, because
οὗτος ὁ υἱός μου νεκρὸς ἦν καὶ ἀνέζησεν,
this son of me dead was and lived again,
ἦν ἀπολωλὼς καὶ εὑρέθη. καὶ ἤρξαντο
was having been lost and was found. And they began
εὐφραίνεσθαι. 25 ἦν δὲ ὁ υἱὸς αὐτοῦ
to be merry. But was the son of him
ὁ πρεσβύτερος ἐν ἀγρῷ· καὶ ὡς ἐρχόμενος
older in a field; and as coming
ἤγγισεν τῇ οἰκίᾳ, ἤκουσεν συμφωνίας καὶ
he drew near to the house, he heard music and
χορῶν, 26 καὶ προσκαλεσάμενος ἕνα τῶν
dances, and calling to [him] one of the
παίδων ἐπυνθάνετο τί ἂν εἴη ταῦτα.
lads he inquired what might be these things.
27 ὁ δὲ εἶπεν αὐτῷ ὅτι ὁ ἀδελφός σου
And he said to him[.] The brother of thee
ἥκει, καὶ ἔθυσεν ὁ πατήρ σου τὸν μόσχον τὸν
has come, and killed the father of thee the calf
σιτευτόν, ὅτι ὑγιαίνοντα αὐτὸν ἀπέλαβεν.
fattened, because being in health him he received back.
28 ὠργίσθη δὲ καὶ οὐκ ἤθελεν εἰσελθεῖν·
But he was angry and did not wish to enter;
ὁ δὲ πατὴρ αὐτοῦ ἐξελθὼν παρεκάλει
so the father of him coming out besought
αὐτόν. 29 ὁ δὲ ἀποκριθεὶς εἶπεν τῷ
him. But he answering said to the
πατρί· ἰδοὺ τοσαῦτα ἔτη δουλεύω σοι καὶ
father : Behold[,] so many years I serve thee and
οὐδέποτε ἐντολήν σου παρῆλθον, καὶ ἐμοὶ
never a command of thee I transgressed, and to me
οὐδέποτε ἔδωκας ἔριφον ἵνα μετὰ τῶν
never thou gavest a goat that with the

merry with my friends:

30 But as soon as this thy son was come, which hath devoured thy living with harlots, thou hast killed for him the fatted calf.

31 And he said unto him, Son, thou art ever with me, and all that I have is thine.

32 It was meet that we should make merry, and be glad: for this thy brother was dead, and is alive again; and was lost, and is found.

φίλων μου εὐφρανθῶ· 30 ὅτε δὲ ὁ υἱός
friends of me I might be merry;   but when – ²son

σου οὗτος ὁ καταφαγών σου τὸν βίον
²of thee ¹this – having devoured of thee the living

μετὰ πορνῶν ἦλθεν, ἔθυσας αὐτῷ τὸν
with harlots came, thou killedst for him the

σιτευτὸν μόσχον. 31 ὁ δὲ εἶπεν αὐτῷ·
fattened calf. And he said to him :

τέκνον, σὺ πάντοτε μετ' ἐμοῦ εἶ, καὶ
Child, thou always with me art, and

πάντα τὰ ἐμὰ σά ἐστιν· 32 εὐφρανθῆναι
¹all ²things – ³my ⁵thine ⁴is(are); ²to be merry

δὲ καὶ χαρῆναι ἔδει, ὅτι ὁ ἀδελφός
¹And ⁴and ⁵to rejoice ³it be- because – ²brother
                  hoved [us],

σου οὗτος νεκρὸς ἦν καὶ ἔζησεν, καὶ ἀπο-
²of thee ¹this ⁵dead ⁴was and came to life, and having

λωλὼς καὶ εὑρέθη.
been lost also was found.

CHAPTER 16

AND he said also unto his disciples, There was a certain rich man, which had a steward; and the same was accused unto him that he had wasted his goods.

2 And he called him, and said unto him, How is it that I hear this of thee? give an account of thy stewardship; for thou mayest be no longer steward.

3 Then the steward said within himself, What shall I do? for my lord taketh away from me the stewardship: I cannot dig; to beg I am ashamed.

4 I am resolved what to do, that, when I am put out of the stewardship, they may receive me into their houses.

5 So he called every one

16 Ἔλεγεν δὲ καὶ πρὸς τοὺς μαθητάς·
And he said also to the disciples :

ἄνθρωπός τις ἦν πλούσιος ὃς εἶχεν
²A certain ⁴man ¹there was ³rich who had

οἰκονόμον, καὶ οὗτος διεβλήθη αὐτῷ ὡς
a steward, and this was complained of to him as

διασκορπίζων τὰ ὑπάρχοντα αὐτοῦ. 2 καὶ
wasting the possessions of him. And

φωνήσας αὐτὸν εἶπεν αὐτῷ· τί τοῦτο
calling him he said to him : What [is] this

ἀκούω περὶ σοῦ; ἀπόδος τὸν λόγον τῆς
I hear about thee? render the account of the

οἰκονομίας σου· οὐ γὰρ δύνῃ ἔτι οἰκονομεῖν.
stewardship of thee; for thou canst not longer to be steward.

3 εἶπεν δὲ ἐν ἑαυτῷ ὁ οἰκονόμος· τί
And said in himself the steward : What

ποιήσω, ὅτι ὁ κύριός μου ἀφαιρεῖται τὴν
may I do, because the lord of me takes away the

οἰκονομίαν ἀπ' ἐμοῦ; σκάπτειν οὐκ ἰσχύω,
stewardship from me? to dig I am not able,

ἐπαιτεῖν αἰσχύνομαι. 4 ἔγνων τί ποιήσω,
to beg I am ashamed. I knew(know) what I may do,

ἵνα ὅταν μετασταθῶ ἐκ τῆς οἰκονομίας
that when I am removed out of the stewardship

δέξωνταί με εἰς τοὺς οἴκους ἑαυτῶν.
they may receive me into the houses of themselves.

5 καὶ προσκαλεσάμενος ἕνα ἕκαστον τῶν
And calling to [him] ²one ¹each of the

of his lord's debtors *unto him*, and said unto the first, How much owest thou unto my lord?

6 And he said, An hundred measures of oil. And he said unto him, Take thy bill, and sit down quickly, and write fifty.

7 Then said he to another, And how much owest thou? And he said, An hundred measures of wheat. And he said unto him, Take thy bill, and write fourscore.

8 And the lord commended the unjust steward, because he had done wisely: for the children of this world are in their generation wiser than the children of light.

9 And I say unto you, Make to yourselves friends of the mammon of unrighteousness; that, when ye fail, they may receive you into everlasting habitations.

10 He that is faithful in that which is least is faithful also in much: and he that is unjust in the least is unjust also in much.

11 If therefore ye have not been faithful in the unrighteous mammon, who will commit to your trust the true *riches?*

12 And if ye have not been faithful in that which is another man's, who shall give you that which is your own?

13 No servant can serve

χρεοφειλετῶν τοῦ κυρίου ἑαυτοῦ ἔλεγεν τῷ
debtors of the lord of himself he said to the
πρώτῳ· πόσον ὀφείλεις τῷ κυρίῳ μου;
first : How much owest thou to the lord of me?
6 ὁ δὲ εἶπεν· ἑκατὸν βάτους ἐλαίου. ὁ δὲ
And he said : A hundred baths of oil. And he
εἶπεν αὐτῷ· δέξαι σου τὰ γράμματα καὶ
told him : Take of thee the letters(bill) and
καθίσας ταχέως γράψον πεντήκοντα. 7 ἔπειτα
sitting quickly write fifty. Then
ἑτέρῳ εἶπεν· σὺ δὲ πόσον ὀφείλεις; ὁ δὲ
to another he said : ⁴thou ¹And ²how much ³owest? And he
εἶπεν· ἑκατὸν κόρους σίτου. λέγει αὐτῷ·
said : A hundred cors of wheat. He tells him :
δέξαι σου τὰ γράμματα καὶ γράψον
Take of thee the bill and write
ὀγδοήκοντα. 8 καὶ ἐπήνεσεν ὁ κύριος τὸν
eighty. And ³praised ¹the ²lord the
οἰκονόμον τῆς ἀδικίας ὅτι φρονίμως
steward - of unrighteousness because prudently
ἐποίησεν· ὅτι οἱ υἱοὶ τοῦ αἰῶνος τούτου
he acted; because the sons - age of this
φρονιμώτεροι ὑπὲρ τοὺς υἱοὺς τοῦ φωτὸς
more prudent than the sons of the light
εἰς τὴν γενεὰν τὴν ἑαυτῶν εἰσιν. 9 Καὶ
in the generation - of themselves are. And
ἐγὼ ὑμῖν λέγω, ἑαυτοῖς ποιήσατε φίλους
I ²you ¹tell, To yourselves make friends
ἐκ τοῦ μαμωνᾶ τῆς ἀδικίας, ἵνα ὅταν
by the mammon - of unrighteousness, that when
ἐκλίπῃ δέξωνται ὑμᾶς εἰς τὰς αἰωνίους
it fails they may receive you into the eternal
σκηνάς. 10 ὁ πιστὸς ἐν ἐλαχίστῳ καὶ ἐν
tabernacles. The man faithful in least also in
πολλῷ πιστός ἐστιν, καὶ ὁ ἐν ἐλαχίστῳ
much faithful is, and the man in least
ἄδικος καὶ ἐν πολλῷ ἄδικός ἐστιν. 11 εἰ
unrighteous also in much unrighteous is. If
οὖν ἐν τῷ ἀδίκῳ μαμωνᾷ πιστοὶ οὐκ
therefore in the unrighteous mammon faithful not
ἐγένεσθε, τὸ ἀληθινὸν τίς ὑμῖν πιστεύσει;
ye were, the true who to you will entrust ?
12 καὶ εἰ ἐν τῷ ἀλλοτρίῳ πιστοὶ οὐκ
And if in the thing belonging to another faithful not
ἐγένεσθε, τὸ ἡμέτερον τίς δώσει ὑμῖν;
ye were, the ours who will give you?
=that which is ours
13 Οὐδεὶς οἰκέτης δύναται δυσὶ κυρίοις
No household slave can two lords

two masters: for either he will hate the one, and love the other; or else he will hold to the one, and despise the other. Ye cannot serve God and mammon.

14 ¶ And the Pharisees also, who were covetous, heard all these things: and they derided him.

15 And he said unto them, Ye are they which justify yourselves before men; but God knoweth your hearts: for that which is highly esteemed among men is abomination in the sight of God.

16 The law and the prophets were until John: since that time the kingdom of God is preached, and every man presseth into it.

17 And it is easier for heaven and earth to pass, than one tittle of the law to fail.

18 Whosoever putteth away his wife, and marrieth another, committeth adultery: and whosoever marrieth her that is put away from her husband committeth adultery.

19 ¶ There was a certain rich man, which was clothed in purple and fine linen, and fared sumptuously every day:

20 And there was a certain beggar named Lazarus, which was laid at his gate, full of sores,

---

δουλεύειν· ἢ γὰρ τὸν ἕνα μισήσει καὶ τὸν
to serve; for either the one he will hate and the

ἕτερον ἀγαπήσει, ἢ ἑνὸς ἀνθέξεται καὶ
other he will love, or one he will hold fast to and

τοῦ ἑτέρου καταφρονήσει. οὐ δύνασθε
the other he will despise. Ye cannot

θεῷ δουλεύειν καὶ μαμωνᾷ. 14 Ἤκουον
God to serve and mammon. ⁶heard

δὲ ταῦτα πάντα οἱ Φαρισαῖοι φιλάργυροι
¹Now ⁸these things ⁷all ²the ³Pharisees ⁶moneylovers

ὑπάρχοντες, καὶ ἐξεμυκτήριζον αὐτόν. 15 καὶ
⁴being, and they scoffed at him. And

εἶπεν αὐτοῖς· ὑμεῖς ἐστε οἱ δικαιοῦντες
he said to them : Ye are the [ones] justifying

ἑαυτοὺς ἐνώπιον τῶν ἀνθρώπων, ὁ δὲ
yourselves before – men, but

θεὸς γινώσκει τὰς καρδίας ὑμῶν· ὅτι τὸ
God knows the hearts of you; because the thing

ἐν ἀνθρώποις ὑψηλὸν βδέλυγμα ἐνώπιον
²among ³men ¹lofty [is] an abomination before

τοῦ θεοῦ. 16 Ὁ νόμος καὶ οἱ προφῆται
– God. The law and the prophets

μέχρι Ἰωάννου· ἀπὸ τότε ἡ βασιλεία τοῦ
[were] until John; from then the kingdom –

θεοῦ εὐαγγελίζεται καὶ πᾶς εἰς αὐτὴν
of God is being preached and everyone into it

βιάζεται. 17 εὐκοπώτερον δέ ἐστιν τὸν οὐρανὸν
is pressing. But easier it is the heaven

καὶ τὴν γῆν παρελθεῖν ἢ τοῦ νόμου μίαν
and the earth to pass away than of the law one

κεραίαν πεσεῖν. 18 Πᾶς ὁ ἀπολύων τὴν
little horn* to fall. Everyone dismissing the

γυναῖκα αὐτοῦ καὶ γαμῶν ἑτέραν μοιχεύει,
wife of him and marrying another commits adultery,

καὶ ὁ ἀπολελυμένην ἀπὸ
and ¹the [one] ³a woman having been dismissed ⁴from

ἀνδρὸς γαμῶν μοιχεύει. 19 Ἄνθρωπος δέ
²a husband ²marrying ⁶commits adultery. Now a certain

τις ἦν πλούσιος, καὶ ἐνεδιδύσκετο πορφύραν
man was rich, and used to put on a purple robe

καὶ βύσσον εὐφραινόμενος καθ’ ἡμέραν
and fine linen being merry every day†

λαμπρῶς. 20 πτωχὸς δέ τις ὀνόματι
splendidly. And a certain poor man by name

Λάζαρος ἐβέβλητο πρὸς τὸν πυλῶνα αὐτοῦ
Lazarus had been placed at the gate of him

* The little projection which distinguishes some Hebrew letters from those otherwise similar.

21 And desiring to be fed with the crumbs which fell from the rich man's table; moreover the dogs came and licked his sores.

22 And it came to pass, that the beggar died, and was carried by the angels into Abraham's bosom: the rich man also died, and was buried;

23 And in hell he lift up his eyes, being in torments, and seeth Abraham afar off, and Lazarus in his bosom.

24 And he cried and said, Father Abraham, have mercy on me, and send Lazarus, that he may dip the tip of his finger in water, and cool my tongue; for I am tormented in this flame.

25 But Abraham said, Son, remember that thou in thy lifetime receivedst thy good things, and likewise Lazarus evil things: but now he is comforted, and thou art tormented.

26 And beside all this, between us and you there is a great gulf fixed; so that they which would pass from hence to you cannot; neither can they pass to us, that *would come* from thence.

27 Then he said, I pray

εἰλκωμένος **21** καὶ ἐπιθυμῶν χορτασθῆναι
being covered with sores and desiring to be satisfied
ἀπὸ τῶν πιπτόντων ἀπὸ τῆς τραπέζης
from the things falling from the table
τοῦ πλουσίου· ἀλλὰ καὶ οἱ κύνες ἐρχόμενοι
of the rich man; but even the dogs coming
ἐπέλειχον τὰ ἕλκη αὐτοῦ. **22** ἐγένετο δὲ
licked the sores of him. And it came to'pass
ἀποθανεῖν τὸν πτωχὸν καὶ ἀπενεχθῆναι
to die the poor man and to be carried away
=that the poor man died and he was carried away
αὐτὸν ὑπὸ τῶν ἀγγέλων εἰς τὸν κόλπον
him[b] by the angels into the bosom
'Αβραάμ· ἀπέθανεν δὲ καὶ ὁ πλούσιος καὶ
of Abraham; and died also the rich man and
ἐτάφη. **23** καὶ ἐν τῷ ᾅδῃ ἐπάρας τοὺς
was buried. And in – hades lifting up the
ὀφθαλμοὺς αὐτοῦ, ὑπάρχων ἐν βασάνοις,
eyes of him, being in torments,
ὁρᾷ 'Αβραὰμ ἀπὸ μακρόθεν καὶ Λάζαρον
he sees Abraham from afar and Lazarus
ἐν τοῖς κόλποις αὐτοῦ. **24** καὶ αὐτὸς
in the bosoms of him. And he
φωνήσας εἶπεν· πάτερ 'Αβραάμ, ἐλέησόν
calling said : Father Abraham, pity
με καὶ πέμψον Λάζαρον ἵνα βάψῃ τὸ
me and send Lazarus that he may dip the
ἄκρον τοῦ δακτύλου αὐτοῦ ὕδατος καὶ
tip of the finger of him of(in) water and
καταψύξῃ τὴν γλῶσσάν μου, ὅτι ὀδυνῶμαι
may cool the tongue of me, because I am suffering
ἐν τῇ φλογὶ ταύτῃ. **25** εἶπεν δὲ 'Αβραάμ·
in – flame this. But said Abraham :
τέκνον, μνήσθητι ὅτι ἀπέλαβες τὰ ἀγαθά
Child, remember that thou didst receive the good things
σου ἐν τῇ ζωῇ σου, καὶ Λάζαρος ὁμοίως
of thee in the life of thee, and Lazarus likewise
τὰ κακά· νῦν δὲ ὧδε παρακαλεῖται, σὺ δὲ
the bad; but now here he is comforted, but thou
ὀδυνᾶσαι. **26** καὶ ἐν πᾶσι τούτοις μεταξὺ
art suffering. And among all these things between
ἡμῶν καὶ ὑμῶν χάσμα μέγα ἐστήρικται,
us and you chasm a great has been firmly fixed,
ὅπως οἱ θέλοντες διαβῆναι ἔνθεν πρὸς
so that the [ones] wishing to pass hence to
ὑμᾶς μὴ δύνωνται, μηδὲ ἐκεῖθεν πρὸς
you cannot, neither thence to
ἡμᾶς διαπερῶσιν. **27** εἶπεν δέ· ἐρωτῶ
us may they cross over. And he said : I ask

thee therefore, father, that thou wouldest send him to my father's house;

28 For I have five brethren; that he may testify unto them, lest they also come into this place of torment.

29 Abraham saith unto him, They have Moses and the prophets; let them hear them.

30 And he said, Nay, father Abraham: but if one went unto them from the dead, they will repent.

31 And he said unto him, If they hear not Moses and the prophets, neither will they be persuaded, though one rose from the dead.

σε οὖν, πάτερ, ἵνα πέμψῃς αὐτὸν εἰς
thee therefore, father, that thou mayest send him to
τὸν οἶκον τοῦ πατρός μου· 28 ἔχω γὰρ
the house of the father of me; for I have
πέντε ἀδελφούς· ὅπως διαμαρτύρηται αὐτοῖς,
five brothers; so that he may witness to them,
ἵνα μὴ καὶ αὐτοὶ ἔλθωσιν εἰς τὸν τόπον
lest also they come to – place
τοῦτον τῆς βασάνου. 29 λέγει δὲ Ἀβραάμ·
this – of torment. But says Abraham :
ἔχουσι Μωϋσέα καὶ τοὺς προφήτας·
They have Moses and the prophets;
ἀκουσάτωσαν αὐτῶν. 30 ὁ δὲ εἶπεν·
let them hear them. But he said :
οὐχί, πάτερ Ἀβραάμ, ἀλλ' ἐάν τις ἀπὸ
No, father Abraham, but if someone from
νεκρῶν πορευθῇ πρὸς αὐτούς, μετανοήσουσιν.
[the] dead should go to them, they will repent.
31 εἶπεν δὲ αὐτῷ· εἰ Μωϋσέως καὶ τῶν
But he said to him : If Moses and the
προφητῶν οὐκ ἀκούουσιν, οὐδὲ ἐάν τις
prophets they do not hear, neither if someone
ἐκ νεκρῶν ἀναστῇ πεισθήσονται.
out of [the] dead should rise again will they be persuaded.

CHAPTER 17

THEN said he unto the disciples, It is impossible but that offences will come: but woe *unto him*, through whom they come!

2 It were better for him that a millstone were hanged about his neck, and he cast into the sea, than that he should offend one of these little ones.

3 ¶ Take heed to yourselves: If thy brother trespass against thee, rebuke him; and if he repent, forgive him.

4 And if he trespass against thee seven times in a day, and seven times in a day turn again to thee,

17 Εἶπεν δὲ πρὸς τοὺς μαθητὰς αὐτοῦ·
And he said to the disciples of him :
ἀνένδεκτόν ἐστιν τοῦ τὰ σκάνδαλα μὴ ἐλθεῖν,
Impossible it is – the offences not to come,d
οὐαὶ δὲ δι' οὗ ἔρχεται· 2 λυσιτελεῖ
but woe [to him] through whom they come; it profits
αὐτῷ εἰ λίθος μυλικὸς περίκειται περὶ
him if a millstone is put round round
τὸν τράχηλον αὐτοῦ καὶ ἔρριπται εἰς τὴν
the neck of him and he has been thrown into the
θάλασσαν, ἢ ἵνα σκανδαλίσῃ τῶν μικρῶν
sea, than that he should offend – ³little ones
τούτων ἕνα. 3 προσέχετε ἑαυτοῖς. ἐὰν
²of these ¹one. Take heed to yourselves. If
ἁμάρτῃ ὁ ἀδελφός σου, ἐπιτίμησον αὐτῷ,
sins the brother of thee, rebuke him,
καὶ ἐὰν μετανοήσῃ, ἄφες αὐτῷ. 4 καὶ
and if he repents, forgive him. And
ἐὰν ἑπτάκις τῆς ἡμέρας ἁμαρτήσῃ εἰς σὲ
if seven times of(in) the day he sins against thee
καὶ ἑπτάκις ἐπιστρέψῃ πρὸς σὲ λέγων·
and seven times turns to thee saying :

saying, I repent; thou shalt forgive him.

5 ¶ And the apostles said unto the Lord, Increase our faith.

6 And the Lord said, If ye had faith as a grain of mustard seed, ye might say unto this sycamine tree, Be thou plucked up by the root, and be thou planted in the sea; and it should obey you.

7 But which of you, having a servant plowing or feeding cattle, will say unto him by and by, when he is come from the field, Go and sit down to meat?

8 And will not rather say unto him, Make ready wherewith I may sup, and gird thyself, and serve me, till I have eaten and drunken; and afterward thou shalt eat and drink?

9 Doth he thank that servant because he did the things that were commanded him? I trow not.

10 So likewise ye, when ye shall have done all those things which are commanded you, say, We are unprofitable servants: we have done that which was our duty to do.

11 ¶ And it came to pass, as he went to Jerusalem, that he passed through the midst of Samaria and Galilee.

12 And as he entered into a certain village, there met him ten men that were lepers, which stood afar off:

μετανοῶ, ἀφήσεις αὐτῷ. 5 Καὶ εἶπαν οἱ
I repent, thou shalt forgive him.　　And said the

ἀπόστολοι τῷ κυρίῳ· πρόσθες ἡμῖν πίστιν.
apostles to the Lord:　Add　to us　faith.

6 εἶπεν δὲ ὁ κύριος· εἰ ἔχετε πίστιν ὡς
And said the Lord: If ye have faith as

κόκκον σινάπεως, ἐλέγετε ἂν τῇ συκαμίνῳ
a grain of mustard, ye would have said – sycamine-tree

ταύτῃ· ἐκριζώθητι καὶ φυτεύθητι ἐν τῇ
to this: Be thou uprooted and be thou planted in the

θαλάσσῃ· καὶ ὑπήκουσεν ἂν ὑμῖν. 7 Τίς
sea;　and it would have obeyed you.　who

δὲ ἐξ ὑμῶν δοῦλον ἔχων ἀροτριῶντα ἢ
But of you ²a slave ¹having ploughing or

ποιμαίνοντα, ὃς εἰσελθόντι ἐκ τοῦ ἀγροῦ
herding, who on [his] coming inᵉ out of the farm

ἐρεῖ αὐτῷ· εὐθέως παρελθὼν ἀνάπεσε,
will say to him: Immediately coming up recline,

8 ἀλλ' οὐχὶ ἐρεῖ αὐτῷ· ἑτοίμασον τί
but will not say to him: Prepare something

δειπνήσω, καὶ περιζωσάμενος διακόνει μοι
I may dine, and having girded thyself serve me

ἕως φάγω καὶ πίω, καὶ μετὰ ταῦτα
until I eat and drink, and after these things

φάγεσαι καὶ πίεσαι σύ; 9 μὴ ἔχει χάριν
eat and drink thou? Not he has thanks

τῷ δούλῳ ὅτι ἐποίησεν τὰ διαταχθέντα;
to the slave because he did the things commanded?

10 οὕτως καὶ ὑμεῖς, ὅταν ποιήσητε πάντα
So also ye, when ye do all

τὰ διαταχθέντα ὑμῖν, λέγετε ὅτι δοῦλοι
the things commanded you, say[,] – Slaves

ἀχρεῖοί ἐσμεν, ὃ ὠφείλομεν ποιῆσαι
unprofitable we are, what we ought to do

πεποιήκαμεν.
we have done.

11 Καὶ ἐγένετο ἐν τῷ πορεύεσθαι εἰς
And it came to pass in the to goᵉ to
=as [he] went

Ἰερουσαλήμ, καὶ αὐτὸς διήρχετο διὰ μέσον
Jerusalem, and he passed through [the]
　　　　　　　　　　through　　　midst

Σαμαρείας καὶ Γαλιλαίας. 12 καὶ εἰσερχομένου
of Samaria and Galilee. And entering
　　　　　　　　　　　　　　　=as he entered

αὐτοῦ εἴς τινα κώμην ἀπήντησαν δέκα
himᵃ into a certain village met [him] ten

λεπροὶ ἄνδρες, οἳ ἔστησαν πόρρωθεν, 13 καὶ
leprous men, who stood afar off, and

13 And they lifted up
their voices, and said,
Jesus, Master, have mercy
on us.

αὐτοὶ   ἦραν   φωνὴν   λέγοντες·   Ἰησοῦ
they   lifted   voice   saying :   Jesus

14 And when he saw
them, he said unto them,
Go shew yourselves unto
the priests. And it came
to pass, that, as they
went, they were cleansed.

ἐπιστάτα,   ἐλέησον   ἡμᾶς.   14 καὶ   ἰδὼν   εἶπεν
Master,   pity   us.   And seeing   he said

αὐτοῖς·   πορευθέντες   ἐπιδείξατε   ἑαυτοὺς   τοῖς
to them :   Going   show   yourselves   to the

ἱερεῦσιν.   καὶ   ἐγένετο   ἐν   τῷ   ὑπάγειν
priests.   And it came to pass in   the   to go
= as they went

15 And one of them,
when he saw that he was
healed, turned back, and
with a loud voice glorified
God,

αὐτοὺς   ἐκαθαρίσθησαν.   15 εἷς   δὲ   ἐξ
them[be]   they were cleansed.   But one   of

αὐτῶν,   ἰδὼν   ὅτι   ἰάθη,   ὑπέστρεψεν   μετὰ
them,   seeing   that he was cured,   returned   with

16 And fell down on *his*
face at his feet, giving him
thanks: and he was a
Samaritan.

φωνῆς   μεγάλης   δοξάζων   τὸν   θεόν,   16 καὶ
voice   a great   glorifying   –   God,   and

ἔπεσεν   ἐπὶ   πρόσωπον   παρὰ   τοὺς   πόδας
fell   on   [his] face   at   the   feet

17 And Jesus answering
said, Were there not ten
cleansed? but where *are*
the nine?

αὐτοῦ   εὐχαριστῶν   αὐτῷ·   καὶ   αὐτὸς   ἦν
of him   thanking   him;   and   he   was

Σαμαρίτης.   17 ἀποκριθεὶς   δὲ   ὁ   Ἰησοῦς
a Samaritan.   And answering   –   Jesus

18 There are not found
that returned to give glory
to God, save this stranger.

εἶπεν·   οὐχ   οἱ   δέκα   ἐκαθαρίσθησαν;   οἱ   [δὲ]
said :   Not   the   ten   were cleansed?   but the

ἐννέα   ποῦ;   18 οὐχ   εὑρέθησαν   ὑποστρέψαντες
nine   where?   were there not found   returning

19 And he said unto
him, Arise, go thy way:
thy faith hath made thee
whole.

δοῦναι   δόξαν   τῷ   θεῷ   εἰ   μὴ   ὁ   ἀλλογενὴς
to give   glory   –   to God   only   –   stranger

οὗτος;   19 καὶ   εἶπεν   αὐτῷ·   ἀναστὰς   πορεύου·
this ?   And   he said   to him :   Rising up   go;

ἡ   πίστις   σου   σέσωκέν   σε.
the   faith   of thee   has healed   thee.

20 ¶ And when he was
demanded of the Pharisees,
when the kingdom of God
should come, he answered
them and said, The king-
dom of God cometh not
with observation:

20 Ἐπερωτηθεὶς   δὲ   ὑπὸ   τῶν   Φαρισαίων
And being questioned   by   the   Pharisees

πότε   ἔρχεται   ἡ   βασιλεία   τοῦ   θεοῦ,
when   comes   the   kingdom   –   of God,

ἀπεκρίθη   αὐτοῖς   καὶ   εἶπεν·   οὐκ   ἔρχεται
he answered   them   and   said :   Comes not

21 Neither shall they
say, Lo here! or, lo there!
for, behold, the kingdom
of God is within you.

ἡ   βασιλεία   τοῦ   θεοῦ   μετὰ   παρατηρήσεως,
the kingdom   –   of God   with   observation,

21 οὐδὲ   ἐροῦσιν·   ἰδοὺ   ὧδε   ἤ·   ἐκεῖ·   ἰδοὺ
nor   will they say : Behold[,]   here   or: there;   [2]behold

22 ¶ And he said unto
the disciples, The days
will come, when ye shall
desire to see one of the
days of the Son of man,

γὰρ   ἡ   βασιλεία   τοῦ   θεοῦ   ἐντὸς   ὑμῶν
[1]for   the   kingdom   –   of God   within   you

ἐστιν.   22 Εἶπεν   δὲ   πρὸς   τοὺς   μαθητάς·
is.   And he said   to   the   disciples :

ἐλεύσονται   ἡμέραι   ὅτε   ἐπιθυμήσετε   μίαν
Will come   days   when   ye will long   one

τῶν   ἡμερῶν   τοῦ   υἱοῦ   τοῦ   ἀνθρώπου   ἰδεῖν
of the   days   of the Son   –   of man   to see

and ye shall not see *it*.

23 And they shall say to you, See here; or, see there: go not after *them*, nor follow *them*.

24 For as the lightning, that lighteneth out of the one *part* under heaven, shineth unto the other *part* under heaven; so shall also the Son of man be in his day.

25 But first must he suffer many things, and be rejected of this generation.

26 And as it was in the days of Noe, so shall it be also in the days of the Son of man.

27 They did eat, they drank, they married wives, they were given in marriage, until the day that Noe entered into the ark, and the flood came, and destroyed them all.

28 Likewise also as it was in the days of Lot; they did eat, they drank, they bought, they sold, they planted, they builded;

29 But the same day that Lot went out of Sodom it rained fire and brimstone from heaven, and destroyed *them* all.

30 Even thus shall it be in the day when the Son of man is revealed.

31 In that day, he which shall be upon the housetop, and his stuff in the house, let him not come down to take it away: and he that is in the field, let him

καὶ   οὐκ   ὄψεσθε.   23 καὶ   ἐροῦσιν   ὑμῖν·
and   will not see.   And   they will say to you:

ἰδοὺ   ἐκεῖ,   ἰδοὺ   ὧδε·   μὴ   ἀπέλθητε   μηδὲ
Behold   there,   behold   here;   do not go away   nor

διώξητε.   24 ὥσπερ   γὰρ   ἡ   ἀστραπὴ
follow.   For as   the   lightning

ἀστράπτουσα   ἐκ   τῆς   ὑπὸ   τὸν   οὐρανὸν
flashing   out of the [one part]   under   -   heaven

εἰς   τὴν   ὑπ' οὐρανὸν   λάμπει,   οὕτως   ἔσται
to the [other part] under   heaven   shines,   so   will be

ὁ   υἱὸς   τοῦ   ἀνθρώπου   ἐν   τῇ   ἡμέρᾳ   αὐτοῦ.
the   Son   -   of man   in   the   day   of him.

25 πρῶτον   δὲ   δεῖ   αὐτὸν   πολλὰ   παθεῖν   καὶ
But first   it behoves   him   many things   to suffer   and

ἀποδοκιμασθῆναι   ἀπὸ   τῆς   γενεᾶς   ταύτης.
to be rejected   from   -   generation   this.

26 καὶ   καθὼς   ἐγένετο   ἐν   ταῖς   ἡμέραις
And   as   it was   in   the   days

Νῶε,   οὕτως   ἔσται   καὶ   ἐν   ταῖς   ἡμέραις
of Noah,   so   it will be   also   in   the   days

τοῦ   υἱοῦ   τοῦ   ἀνθρώπου·   27 ἤσθιον,   ἔπινον,
of the   Son   -   of man;   they were eating, drinking,

ἐγάμουν,   ἐγαμίζοντο,   ἄχρι   ἧς   ἡμέρας
marrying,   giving in marriage,   until   which   day
                                              =the day when

εἰσῆλθεν   Νῶε   εἰς   τὴν   κιβωτόν,   καὶ
entered   Noah   into   the   ark,   and

ἦλθεν   ὁ   κατακλυσμὸς   καὶ   ἀπώλεσεν   πάντας.
came   the   flood   and   destroyed   all.

28 ὁμοίως   καθὼς   ἐγένετο   ἐν   ταῖς   ἡμέραις
Likewise   as   it was   in   the   days

Λώτ·   ἤσθιον,   ἔπινον,   ἠγόραζον,   ἐπώλουν,
of Lot; they were eating, drinking,   buying,   selling,

ἐφύτευον,   ᾠκοδόμουν·   29 ᾗ   δὲ   ἡμέρᾳ   ἐξῆλθεν
planting,   building;   but on which   day   went forth

Λώτ   ἀπὸ   Σοδόμων,   ἔβρεξεν   πῦρ   καὶ
Lot   from   Sodom,   it rained   fire   and

θεῖον   ἀπ' οὐρανοῦ   καὶ   ἀπώλεσεν   πάντας.
brimstone   from heaven   and   destroyed   all.

30 κατὰ   τὰ   αὐτὰ   ἔσται   ᾗ   ἡμέρᾳ   ὁ   υἱὸς
According to   the same things   it will be   on which   day   the Son
=In the same way   =on the day when

τοῦ   ἀνθρώπου   ἀποκαλύπτεται.   31 ἐν   ἐκείνῃ
-    of man   is revealed.   In   that

τῇ   ἡμέρᾳ   ὃς   ἔσται   ἐπὶ   τοῦ   δώματος   καὶ
-    day   who   will be   on   the   roof   and

τὰ   σκεύη   αὐτοῦ   ἐν   τῇ   οἰκίᾳ,   μὴ   καταβάτω
the   goods   of him   in   the   house,   let him not come down

ἆραι   αὐτά,   καὶ   ὁ   ἐν   ἀγρῷ   ὁμοίως   μὴ
to take them,   and the [one] in   a field   likewise   not

likewise not return back.
32 Remember Lot's wife.
33 Whosoever shall seek to save his life shall lose it; and whosoever shall lose his life shall preserve it.
34 I tell you, in that night there shall be two *men* in one bed; the one shall be taken, and the other shall be left.
35 Two *women* shall be grinding together; the one shall be taken, and the other left.
36 Two *men* shall be in the field; the one shall be taken, and the other left.
37 And they answered and said unto him, Where, Lord? And he said unto them, Wheresoever the body *is*, thither will the eagles be gathered together.

ἐπιστρεψάτω εἰς τὰ ὀπίσω. 32 μνημονεύετε
let him turn back　to the things behind.　　Remember
τῆς γυναικὸς Λώτ. 33 ὃς ἐὰν ζητήσῃ
the　wife　of Lot.　　Whoever　seeks
τὴν ψυχὴν αὐτοῦ περιποιήσασθαι, ἀπολέσει
the　life　of him　to preserve,　he will lose
αὐτήν, καὶ ὃς ἂν ἀπολέσει, ζωογονήσει
it,　and　whoever　will lose,　will preserve
αὐτήν. 34 λέγω ὑμῖν, ταύτῃ τῇ νυκτὶ
it.　　I tell　you,　in this　—　night
ἔσονται δύο ἐπὶ κλίνης μιᾶς, ὁ εἷς
there will be　two men　on　couch　one,　the　one
παραλημφθήσεται καὶ ὁ ἕτερος ἀφεθήσεται·
will be taken　and the　other　will be left;
35 ἔσονται δύο ἀλήθουσαι ἐπὶ τὸ αὐτό, ἡ
there will be two women　grinding　together,†　the
μία παραλημφθήσεται ἡ δὲ ἑτέρα ἀφεθήσεται.‡
one　will be taken　but the other　will be left.
37 καὶ ἀποκριθέντες λέγουσιν αὐτῷ· ποῦ,
　　And　answering　they say　to him : Where,
κύριε; ὁ δὲ εἶπεν αὐτοῖς· ὅπου τὸ σῶμα,
Lord?　And he　said　to them : Where the body,
ἐκεῖ καὶ οἱ ἀετοὶ ἐπισυναχθήσονται.
there　also　the　eagles　will be gathered together.

CHAPTER 18

AND he spake a parable unto them *to this end*, that men ought always to pray, and not to faint;
2 Saying, There was in a city a judge, which feared not God, neither regarded man:
3 And there was a widow in that city; and she came unto him, saying, Avenge me of mine adversary.
4 And he would not for a while: but afterward he said within himself, Though I fear not God, nor regard man;

18 Ἔλεγεν δὲ παραβολὴν αὐτοῖς πρὸς
　　And he told　²a parable　¹them　　to
　　　　　　　　　　　　　　　　　　　　=that
τὸ δεῖν πάντοτε προσεύχεσθαι αὐτοὺς καὶ
the ¹to behove ³always　⁴to pray　　³them　and
they must always pray and not faint,
μὴ ἐγκακεῖν, 2 λέγων· κριτής τις ἦν ἔν
not　to faint,　　saying :　³judge ²a certain ¹There ⁴in
　　　　　　　　　　　　　　　　　　　　　　　was
τινι πόλει τὸν θεὸν μὴ φοβούμενος καὶ
²a certain ²city　—　³God ¹not　　⁵fearing　　and
ἄνθρωπον μὴ ἐντρεπόμενος. 3 χήρα δὲ ἦν
³man　　¹not　²regarding.　And ²a widow¹there was
ἐν τῇ πόλει ἐκείνῃ, καὶ ἤρχετο πρὸς
in　—　city　that,　and　she came　to
αὐτὸν λέγουσα· ἐκδίκησόν με ἀπὸ τοῦ
him　saying :　Vindicate　me　from　the
ἀντιδίκου μου. 4 καὶ οὐκ ἤθελεν ἐπὶ
opponent　of me.　And　he would not　for
χρόνον· μετὰ ταῦτα δὲ εἶπεν ἐν ἑαυτῷ·
a time;　but after these things　he said　in　himself :
εἰ καὶ τὸν θεὸν οὐ φοβοῦμαι οὐδὲ ἄνθρωπον
If indeed　—　God　I fear not　nor　man

‡ Verse 36 omitted by Nestle; *cf.* R.V. marg., etc.

5 Yet because this widow troubleth me, I will avenge her, lest by her continual coming she weary me.

6 And the Lord said, Hear what the unjust judge saith.

7 And shall not God avenge his own elect, which cry day and night unto him, though he bear long with them?

8 I tell you that he will avenge them speedily. Nevertheless when the Son of man cometh, shall he find faith on the earth?

9 ¶ And he spake this parable unto certain which trusted in themselves that they were righteous, and despised others:

10 Two men went up into the temple to pray; the one a Pharisee, and the other a publican.

11 The Pharisee stood and prayed thus with himself, God, I thank thee, that I am not as other men are, extortioners, unjust, adulterers, or even as this publican.

12 I fast twice in the week, I give tithes of all that I possess.

13 And the publican, standing afar off, would not lift up so much as his

ἐντρέπομαι,   5 διά   γε   τὸ   παρέχειν
regard,   at least because of –   to cause
                                 = because this widow causes me trouble

μοι κόπον τὴν χήραν ταύτην ἐκδικήσω αὐτήν,
me trouble –   widow this[b] I will vindicate her,

ἵνα μὴ εἰς τέλος ἐρχομένη ὑπωπιάζῃ με.
lest in [the] end coming she exhausts me.

6 Εἶπεν δὲ ὁ κύριος· ἀκούσατε τί ὁ κριτὴς
And said the Lord: Hear ye what the judge

τῆς ἀδικίας λέγει· 7 ὁ δὲ θεὸς οὐ μὴ
– of unrighteousness says;   – and God by no means

ποιήσῃ τὴν ἐκδίκησιν τῶν ἐκλεκτῶν
will he make the vindication of the chosen [ones]

αὐτοῦ τῶν βοώντων αὐτῷ ἡμέρας καὶ
of him   –   crying to him day and

νυκτός, καὶ μακροθυμεῖ ἐπ' αὐτοῖς; 8 λέγω
night, and be patient over them? I tell

ὑμῖν ὅτι ποιήσει τὴν ἐκδίκησιν αὐτῶν
you that he will make the vindication of them

ἐν τάχει.   πλὴν ὁ υἱὸς τοῦ ἀνθρώπου ἐλθὼν
quickly. Nevertheless the Son – of man coming

ἆρα εὑρήσει τὴν πίστιν ἐπὶ τῆς γῆς;
then will he find the faith on the earth?

9 Εἶπεν δὲ καὶ πρός τινας τοὺς
And he said also to some the [ones]

πεποιθότας ἐφ' ἑαυτοῖς ὅτι εἰσὶν
relying on themselves that they are

δίκαιοι καὶ ἐξουθενοῦντας τοὺς λοιποὺς
righteous and despising the rest

τὴν παραβολὴν ταύτην. 10 Ἄνθρωποι δύο
–   parable this.   Men two

ἀνέβησαν εἰς τὸ ἱερὸν προσεύξασθαι, ὁ εἷς
went up to the temple to pray, the one

Φαρισαῖος καὶ ὁ ἕτερος τελώνης. 11 ὁ
a Pharisee and the other a tax-collector. The

Φαρισαῖος σταθεὶς ταῦτα πρὸς ἑαυτὸν
Pharisee standing these things to himself

προσηύχετο· ὁ θεός, εὐχαριστῶ σοι ὅτι
prayed :   – God, I thank thee that

οὐκ εἰμὶ ὥσπερ οἱ λοιποὶ τῶν ἀνθρώπων,
I am not as the rest – of men,

ἅρπαγες, ἄδικοι, μοιχοί, ἢ καὶ ὡς οὗτος
rapacious, unjust, adulterers, or even as this

ὁ τελώνης· 12 νηστεύω δὶς τοῦ σαββάτου,
– tax-collector; I fast twice of (in) the week,

ἀποδεκατεύω πάντα ὅσα κτῶμαι. 13 ὁ δὲ
I tithe all things how many I get. But the

τελώνης μακρόθεν ἑστὼς οὐκ ἤθελεν οὐδὲ
tax-collector far off standing would not not even

eyes unto heaven, but
smote upon his breast,
saying, God be merciful to
me a sinner.

14 I tell you, this man
went down to his house
justified *rather* than the
other: for every one that
exalteth himself shall be
abased; and he that
humbleth himself shall be
exalted.

15 ¶ And they brought
unto him also infants,
that he would touch them:
but when *his* disciples saw
it, they rebuked them.

16 But Jesus called them
unto him, and said, Suffer
little children to come
unto me, and forbid them
not: for of such is the
kingdom of God.

17 Verily I say unto
you, Whosoever shall not
receive the kingdom of
God as a little child shall
in no wise enter therein.

18 ¶ And a certain ruler
asked him, saying, Good
Master, what shall I do to
inherit eternal life?

19 And Jesus said unto
him, Why callest thou me
good? none *is* good, save
one, *that is*, God.

20 Thou knowest the
commandments, Do not
commit adultery, Do not
kill, Do not steal, Do not
bear false witness, Honour
thy father and thy mother.

21 And he said, All

τοὺς   ὀφθαλμοὺς   ἐπᾶραι   εἰς   τὸν   οὐρανόν,
the(his)   eyes   *to* lift up to   -   heaven,

ἀλλ'   ἔτυπτεν   τὸ   στῆθος   αὐτοῦ   λέγων·   ὁ
but   smote   the   breast   of him   saying :   -

θεός,   ἱλάσθητί   μοι   τῷ   ἁμαρτωλῷ.   **14** λέγω
God,   be propitious to me the   sinner.   I tell

ὑμῖν,   κατέβη   οὗτος   δεδικαιωμένος   εἰς   τὸν
you,   went down this man having been justified to   the

οἶκον   αὐτοῦ   παρ'   ἐκεῖνον·   ὅτι   πᾶς   ὁ
house   of him   [rather] than that one;   because   everyone

ὑψῶν   ἑαυτὸν   ταπεινωθήσεται,   ὁ   δὲ   ταπεινῶν
exalting himself   will be humbled,   and the [one] humbling

ἑαυτὸν   ὑψωθήσεται.
himself   will be exalted.

15 Προσέφερον   δὲ   αὐτῷ   καὶ   τὰ   βρέφη
      And they brought   to him   also   the   babes

ἵνα   αὐτῶν   ἅπτηται·   ἰδόντες   δὲ   οἱ   μαθηταὶ
that   them   he might touch;   but [2]seeing   [1]the   [3]disciples

ἐπετίμων   αὐτοῖς.   **16** ὁ   δὲ   Ἰησοῦς
rebuked   them.   -   But   Jesus

προσεκαλέσατο   αὐτὰ   λέγων·   ἄφετε   τὰ
called to [him]   them[*]   saying :   Allow   the

παιδία   ἔρχεσθαι   πρός   με   καὶ   μὴ   κωλύετε
children   to come   to   me   and   do not prevent

αὐτά·   τῶν   γὰρ   τοιούτων   ἐστὶν   ἡ   βασιλεία
them;   for   of such   is   the   kingdom

τοῦ   θεοῦ.   **17** ἀμὴν   λέγω   ὑμῖν,   ὃς   ἂν
- of God.   Truly   I tell   you,   whoever

μὴ   δέξηται   τὴν   βασιλείαν   τοῦ   θεοῦ   ὡς
does not receive   the   kingdom   -   of God   as

παιδίον,   οὐ   μὴ   εἰσέλθῃ   εἰς   αὐτήν.
a child,   by no means   enters   into   it.

18 Καὶ   ἐπηρώτησέν   τις   αὐτὸν   ἄρχων
      And   [2]questioned   [1]a certain   [4]him   [3]ruler

λέγων·   διδάσκαλε   ἀγαθέ,   τί   ποιήσας   ζωὴν
saying :   Teacher   good,   what   doing   life

αἰώνιον   κληρονομήσω;   **19** εἶπεν   δὲ   αὐτῷ
eternal   may I inherit?   And said   to him

ὁ   Ἰησοῦς·   τί   με   λέγεις   ἀγαθόν;   οὐδεὶς
- Jesus :   Why   me   sayest thou   good?   no one

ἀγαθὸς   εἰ   μὴ   εἷς   [ὁ]   θεός.   **20** τὰς   ἐντολὰς
[is] good   except one[,]   -   God.   The commandments

οἶδας·   μὴ   μοιχεύσῃς,   μὴ   φονεύσῃς,
thou knowest : Do not commit adultery,   Do not kill,

μὴ   κλέψῃς,   μὴ   ψευδομαρτυρήσῃς,   τίμα
Do not steal,   Do not bear false witness,   Honour

τὸν   πατέρα   σου   καὶ   τὴν   μητέρα.   **21** ὁ   δὲ
the   father   of thee   and   the   mother.   And he

* That is, " the babes " (τὰ βρέφη in ver. 15).

these have I kept from my youth up.

22 Now when Jesus heard these things, he said unto him, Yet lackest thou one thing: sell all that thou hast, and distribute unto the poor, and thou shalt have treasure in heaven: and come, follow me.

23 And when he heard this, he was very sorrowful: for he was very rich.

24 And when Jesus saw that he was very sorrowful, he said, How hardly shall they that have riches enter into the kingdom of God!

25 For it is easier for a camel to go through a needle's eye, than for a rich man to enter into the kingdom of God.

26 And they that heard it said, Who then can be saved?

27 And he said, The things which are impossible with men are possible with God.

28 ¶ Then Peter said, Lo, we have left all, and followed thee.

29 And he said unto them, Verily I say unto you, There is no man that hath left house, or parents, or brethren, or wife, or children, for the kingdom of God's sake,

30 Who shall not receive manifold more in this present time, and in the world to come life everlasting.

εἶπεν· ταῦτα πάντα ἐφύλαξα ἐκ νεότητος.
said : All these things I kept from youth.

22 ἀκούσας δὲ ὁ Ἰησοῦς εἶπεν αὐτῷ· ἔτι
But hearing – Jesus said to him : Yet

ἕν σοι λείπει· πάντα ὅσα ἔχεις
one thing to thee is lacking; all things how many thou hast

πώλησον καὶ διάδος πτωχοῖς, καὶ ἕξεις
sell and distribute to poor people, and thou wilt have

θησαυρὸν ἐν [τοῖς] οὐρανοῖς, καὶ δεῦρο
treasure in – heavens, and come

ἀκολούθει μοι. 23 ὁ δὲ ἀκούσας ταῦτα
follow me. But he hearing these things

περίλυπος ἐγενήθη, ἦν γὰρ πλούσιος σφόδρα.
very grieved became, for he was rich exceedingly.

24 ἰδὼν δὲ αὐτὸν ὁ Ἰησοῦς εἶπεν· πῶς
And seeing him – Jesus said : How

δυσκόλως οἱ τὰ χρήματα ἔχοντες εἰς τὴν
hardly ¹the [ones] – ²property ³having into the

βασιλείαν τοῦ θεοῦ εἰσπορεύονται· 25 εὐκο-
kingdom – of God go in; ²easi-

πώτερον γάρ ἐστιν κάμηλον διὰ τρήματος
er ¹for it is [for] a camel through [the] eye

βελόνης εἰσελθεῖν ἢ πλούσιον εἰς τὴν
of a needle to enter than a rich man into the

βασιλείαν τοῦ θεοῦ εἰσελθεῖν. 26 εἶπαν
kingdom – of God to enter. said

δὲ οἱ ἀκούσαντες· καὶ τίς δύναται
And the [ones] hearing : And who can

σωθῆναι; 27 ὁ δὲ εἶπεν· τὰ ἀδύνατα παρὰ
to be saved? And he said : The things impossible with

ἀνθρώποις δυνατὰ παρὰ τῷ θεῷ ἐστιν.
men possible with – God is(are).

28 Εἶπεν δὲ ὁ Πέτρος· ἰδοὺ ἡμεῖς ἀφέντες
And said – Peter : Behold[,] we leaving

τὰ ἴδια ἠκολουθήσαμέν σοι. 29 ὁ δὲ
our own things followed thee. And he

εἶπεν αὐτοῖς· ἀμὴν λέγω ὑμῖν ὅτι οὐδείς
said to them : Truly I tell you that no one

ἐστιν ὃς ἀφῆκεν οἰκίαν ἢ γυναῖκα ἢ
there is who left house or wife or

ἀδελφοὺς ἢ γονεῖς ἢ τέκνα εἵνεκεν τῆς
brothers or parents or children for the sake of the

βασιλείας τοῦ θεοῦ, 30 ὃς οὐχὶ μὴ λάβῃ
kingdom – of God, who by no means receives

πολλαπλασίονα ἐν τῷ καιρῷ τούτῳ καὶ ἐν
many times over in – time this and in

τῷ αἰῶνι τῷ ἐρχομένῳ ζωὴν αἰώνιον.
the age – coming life eternal.

31 ¶ Then he took *unto him* the twelve, and said unto them, Behold, we go up to Jerusalem, and all things that are written by the prophets concerning the Son of man shall be accomplished.

32 For he shall be delivered unto the Gentiles, and shall be mocked, and spitefully entreated, and spitted on:

33 And they shall scourge *him*, and put him to death: and the third day he shall rise again.

34 And they understood none of these things: and this saying was hid from them, neither knew they the things which were spoken.

35 ¶ And it came to pass, that as he was come nigh unto Jericho, a certain blind man sat by the way side begging:

36 And hearing the multitude pass by, he asked what it meant.

37 And they told him, that Jesus of Nazareth passeth by.

38 And he cried, saying, Jesus, *thou* son of David, have mercy on me.

39 And they which went before rebuked him, that he should hold his peace: but he cried so much the more, *Thou* son of David, have mercy on me.

40 And Jesus stood, and commanded him to be brought unto him: and when he was come near, he asked him,

---

31 Παραλαβὼν δὲ τοὺς δώδεκα εἶπεν πρὸς
And taking   the   twelve   he said   to

αὐτούς· ἰδοὺ ἀναβαίνομεν εἰς Ἰερουσαλήμ,
them :   Behold   we are going up   to   Jerusalem,

καὶ τελεσθήσεται πάντα τὰ γεγραμ-
and   will be accomplished   all things   -   having been

μένα διὰ τῶν προφητῶν τῷ υἱῷ τοῦ
written   through   the   prophets   to the   Son   -

ἀνθρώπου· 32 παραδοθήσεται γὰρ τοῖς ἔθνεσιν
of man;   for he will be delivered   to the   nations

καὶ ἐμπαιχθήσεται καὶ ὑβρισθήσεται καὶ
and   will be mocked   and   *will be* insulted   and

ἐμπτυσθήσεται, 33 καὶ μαστιγώσαντες
will be spit at,   and   having scourged

ἀποκτενοῦσιν αὐτόν, καὶ τῇ ἡμέρᾳ τῇ
they will kill   him,   and   on the   day   -

τρίτῃ ἀναστήσεται. 34 καὶ αὐτοὶ οὐδὲν
third   he will rise again.   And   they   none

τούτων συνῆκαν, καὶ ἦν τὸ ῥῆμα τοῦτο
of these things understood,   and ²was - ²utterance ¹this

κεκρυμμένον ἀπ᾽ αὐτῶν, καὶ οὐκ ἐγίνωσκον
⁴having been hidden from   them,   and   they knew not

τὰ λεγόμενα.
the things being said.

35 Ἐγένετο δὲ ἐν τῷ ἐγγίζειν αὐτὸν εἰς
And it came to pass in   the   to draw near   him⁶⁶ to
                          =as he drew near

Ἰεριχὼ τυφλός τις ἐκάθητο παρὰ τὴν ὁδὸν
Jericho a certain blind man   sat   by   the   way

ἐπαιτῶν. 36 ἀκούσας δὲ ὄχλου διαπορευομένου
begging.   And hearing   a crowd   passing through

ἐπυνθάνετο τί εἴη τοῦτο. 37 ἀπήγγειλαν
he inquired   what ²might be ¹this.   And they re-

δὲ αὐτῷ ὅτι Ἰησοῦς ὁ Ναζωραῖος
ported to him[,]   -   Jesus   the   Nazarene

παρέρχεται. 38 καὶ ἐβόησεν λέγων· Ἰησοῦ
is passing by.   And   he cried   saying: Jesus

υἱὲ Δαυίδ, ἐλέησόν με. 39 καὶ οἱ
son of David,   pity   me.   And the [ones]

προάγοντες ἐπετίμων αὐτῷ ἵνα σιγήσῃ.
going before   rebuked   him   that he should be quiet;

αὐτὸς δὲ πολλῷ μᾶλλον ἔκραζεν· υἱὲ
but he   by much   more   cried out :   Son

Δαυίδ, ἐλέησόν με. 40 σταθεὶς δὲ ὁ
of David,   pity   me.   And standing   -

Ἰησοῦς ἐκέλευσεν αὐτὸν ἀχθῆναι πρὸς
Jesus   commanded   him   to be brought   to

αὐτόν. ἐγγίσαντος δὲ αὐτοῦ ἐπηρώτησεν
him.   And drawing near   him*   he questioned
              =as he drew near

41 Saying, What wilt thou that I shall do unto thee? And he said, Lord, that I may receive my sight.

42 And Jesus said unto him, Receive thy sight: thy faith hath saved thee.

43 And immediately he received his sight, and followed him, glorifying God: and all the people, when they saw *it*, gave praise unto God.

αὐτόν· 41 τί σοι θέλεις ποιήσω; ὁ δὲ
him :   What for thee wishest thou I may do? And he

εἶπεν· κύριε, ἵνα ἀναβλέψω. 42 καὶ ὁ Ἰησοῦς
said : Lord, that I may see again. And - Jesus

εἶπεν αὐτῷ· ἀνάβλεψον· ἡ πίστις σου
said to him : See again; the faith of thee

σέσωκέν σε. 43 καὶ παραχρῆμα ἀνέβλεψεν,
has healed thee. And at once he saw again,

καὶ ἠκολούθει αὐτῷ δοξάζων τὸν θεόν.
and followed him glorifying - God.

καὶ πᾶς ὁ λαὸς ἰδὼν ἔδωκεν αἶνον τῷ
And all the people seeing gave praise -

θεῷ.
to God.

CHAPTER 19

AND *Jesus* entered and passed through Jericho.

2 And, behold, *there was* a man named Zacchæus, which was the chief among the publicans, and he was rich.

3 And he sought to see Jesus who he was; and could not for the press, because he was little of stature.

4 And he ran before, and climbed up into a sycomore tree to see him: for he was to pass that *way.*

5 And when Jesus came to the place, he looked up, and saw him, and said unto him, Zacchæus, make haste, and come down; for to day I must abide at thy house.

6 And he made haste, and came down, and received him joyfully.

7 And when they saw *it*, they all murmured, saying, That he was gone to be guest with a man that is a sinner.

19 Καὶ εἰσελθὼν διήρχετο τὴν Ἰεριχώ.
And having entered he passed through - Jericho.

2 Καὶ ἰδοὺ ἀνὴρ ὀνόματι καλούμενος
And behold[,] a man by name *being* called

Ζακχαῖος, καὶ αὐτὸς ἦν ἀρχιτελώνης, καὶ
Zacchæus, and he was a chief tax-collector, and

αὐτὸς πλούσιος· 3 καὶ ἐζήτει ἰδεῖν τὸν
he [was] rich; and he sought to see the

Ἰησοῦν τίς ἐστιν, καὶ οὐκ ἠδύνατο ἀπὸ
Jesus who he is(was), and was not able from

τοῦ ὄχλου, ὅτι τῇ ἡλικίᾳ μικρὸς ἦν.
the crowd, because - ³in stature ²little ¹he was.

4 καὶ προδραμὼν εἰς τὸ ἔμπροσθεν ἀνέβη
And having run forward to the front he went up

ἐπὶ συκομορέαν, ἵνα ἴδῃ αὐτόν, ὅτι
onto a sycamore-tree, that he might see him, because

ἐκείνης ἤμελλεν διέρχεσθαι. 5 καὶ ὡς
³that [way] ¹he was about ²to pass along. And as

ἦλθεν ἐπὶ τὸν τόπον, ἀναβλέψας ὁ Ἰησοῦς
he came upon the place, looking up - Jesus

εἶπεν πρὸς αὐτόν· Ζακχαῖε, σπεύσας
said to him : Zacchæus, making haste

κατάβηθι· σήμερον γὰρ ἐν τῷ οἴκῳ σου
come down; for to-day in the house of thee

δεῖ με μεῖναι. 6 καὶ σπεύσας κατέβη,
it behoves me to remain. And making haste he came down,

καὶ ὑπεδέξατο αὐτὸν χαίρων. 7 καὶ
and welcomed him rejoicing. And

ἰδόντες πάντες διεγόγγυζον λέγοντες ὅτι
seeing all murmured saying[,]

παρὰ ἁμαρτωλῷ ἀνδρὶ εἰσῆλθεν καταλῦσαι.
With a sinful man he entered to lodge.

8 And Zacchæus stood, and said unto the Lord; Behold, Lord, the half of my goods I give to the poor; and if I have taken any thing from any man by false accusation, I restore *him* fourfold.

9 And Jesus said unto him, This day is salvation come to this house, forsomuch as he also is a son of Abraham.

10 For the Son of man is come to seek and to save that which was lost.

11 ¶ And as they heard these things, he added and spake a parable, because he was nigh to Jerusalem, and because they thought that the kingdom of God should immediately appear.

12 He said therefore, A certain nobleman went into a far country to receive for himself a kingdom, and to return.

13 And he called his ten servants, and delivered them ten pounds, and said unto them, Occupy till I come.

14 But his citizens hated him, and sent a message after him, saying, We will not have this *man* to reign over us.

8 σταθεὶς δὲ Ζακχαῖος εἶπεν πρὸς τὸν
And standing Zacchæus said to the

κύριον· ἰδοὺ τὰ ἡμίση μου τῶν ὑπαρχόντων,
Lord: Behold[,] the half of me of the possessions,

κύριε, τοῖς πτωχοῖς δίδωμι, καὶ εἴ τινός
Lord, to the poor I give, and if anyone

τι ἐσυκοφάντησα, ἀποδίδωμι τετραπλοῦν.
anything I accused falsely, I restore fourfold.

9 εἶπεν δὲ πρὸς αὐτὸν ὁ Ἰησοῦς ὅτι
And said to him Jesus[,] —

σήμερον σωτηρία τῷ οἴκῳ τούτῳ ἐγένετο,
To-day salvation — house to this came,

καθότι καὶ αὐτὸς υἱὸς Ἀβραάμ [ἐστιν]·
because even he a son of Abraham is;

10 ἦλθεν γὰρ ὁ υἱὸς τοῦ ἀνθρώπου ζητῆσαι
for came the Son — of man to seek

καὶ σῶσαι τὸ ἀπολωλός.
and to save the thing having been lost.

11 Ἀκουόντων δὲ αὐτῶν ταῦτα προσθεὶς
And hearing them[a] these things adding
=as they heard

εἶπεν παραβολήν, διὰ τὸ ἐγγὺς εἶναι
he told a parable, because of the near to be
=because he was near to Jerusalem and they thought

Ἰερουσαλὴμ αὐτὸν καὶ δοκεῖν αὐτοὺς ὅτι
Jerusalem him and to think them[b] that

παραχρῆμα μέλλει ἡ βασιλεία τοῦ θεοῦ
at once is(was) about the kingdom — of God

ἀναφαίνεσθαι· 12 εἶπεν οὖν· ἄνθρωπός τις
to appear; he said therefore : A certain man

εὐγενὴς ἐπορεύθη εἰς χώραν μακρὰν λαβεῖν
well born went to country a far to receive

ἑαυτῷ βασιλείαν καὶ ὑποστρέψαι. 13 καλέσας
for himself a kingdom and to return. having called

δὲ δέκα δούλους ἑαυτοῦ ἔδωκεν αὐτοῖς
And ten slaves of himself he gave them

δέκα μνᾶς, καὶ εἶπεν πρὸς αὐτούς·
ten minas, and said to them :

πραγματεύσασθε ἐν ᾧ ἔρχομαι. 14 οἱ δὲ
Trade ye while I am coming.[*] But the

πολῖται αὐτοῦ ἐμίσουν αὐτόν, καὶ ἀπέστειλαν
citizens of him hated him, and sent

πρεσβείαν ὀπίσω αὐτοῦ λέγοντες· οὐ θέλομεν
a delegation after him saying : We do not wish

τοῦτον βασιλεῦσαι ἐφ' ἡμᾶς. 15 καὶ
this man to reign over us. And

---

[*] That is, " again." The present of this verb often has a futurist significance; *cf.* John 14. 3.

15 And it came to pass, that when he was returned, having received the kingdom, then he commanded these servants to be called unto him, to whom he had given the money, that he might know how much every man had gained by trading.

16 Then came the first, saying, Lord, thy pound hath gained ten pounds.

17 And he said unto him, Well, thou good servant: because thou hast been faithful in a very little, have thou authority over ten cities.

18 And the second came, saying, Lord, thy pound hath gained five pounds.

19 And he said likewise to him, Be thou also over five cities.

20 And another came, saying, Lord, behold, *here is* thy pound, which I have kept laid up in a napkin:

21 For I feared thee, because thou art an austere man: thou takest up that thou layedst not down, and reapest that thou didst not sow.

22 And he saith unto him, Out of thine own mouth will I judge thee, *thou* wicked servant. Thou knewest that I was an austere man, taking up that I laid not down, and reaping that I did not sow:

23 Wherefore then gavest not thou my money into the bank, that at my coming I might have required mine own with usury?

24 And he said unto them that stood by, Take

ἐγένετο   ἐν τῷ ἐπανελθεῖν αὐτὸν λαβόντα
it came to pass in the   to return   him^be having received
= when he returned

τὴν βασιλείαν καὶ εἶπεν φωνηθῆναι αὐτῷ
the   kingdom   *and* he said   to be called   to him

τοὺς   δούλους   τούτους   οἷς   δεδώκει   τὸ
-        slaves   these   to whom he had given   the

ἀργύριον,   ἵνα   γνοῖ   τίς   τί
money,   that   he might know   ²anyone   ¹what

διεπραγματεύσατο. 16 παρεγένετο δὲ ὁ πρῶτος
gained by trading.   And came   the   first

λέγων· κύριε, ἡ μνᾶ σου δέκα προσηργάσατο
saying : Lord, the mina of thee ²ten   ¹gained

μνᾶς. 17 καὶ εἶπεν αὐτῷ· εὖ γε, ἀγαθὲ δοῦλε,
³minas.   And he said to him : Well, good   slave,

ὅτι   ἐν   ἐλαχίστῳ   πιστὸς   ἐγένου,   ἴσθι
because in a least thing faithful thou wast, be thou

ἐξουσίαν ἔχων ἐπάνω δέκα πόλεων. 18 καὶ
²authority ¹having   over   ten   cities.   And

ἦλθεν   ὁ   δεύτερος   λέγων·   ἡ   μνᾶ   σου,
came   the   second   saying: The mina of thee,

κύριε,   ἐποίησεν   πέντε   μνᾶς. 19 εἶπεν δὲ
lord,   made   five   minas.   And he said

καὶ   τούτῳ·   καὶ   σὺ   ἐπάνω   γίνου   πέντε
also to this one : And ²thou ³over   ¹be   five

πόλεων. 20 καὶ   ὁ   ἕτερος   ἦλθεν   λέγων·
cities.   And   the   other   came   saying :

κύριε,   ἰδοὺ   ἡ   μνᾶ   σου,   ἦν   εἶχον
Lord,   behold[,] the   mina   of thee, which I had

ἀποκειμένην ἐν σουδαρίῳ· 21 ἐφοβούμην γάρ
being put away in   a napkin;   for I feared

σε,   ὅτι   ἄνθρωπος   αὐστηρὸς   εἶ,   αἴρεις   ὃ
thee, because man   an exacting thou art, thou takest what

οὐκ ἔθηκας, καὶ θερίζεις ὃ οὐκ ἔσπειρας.
thou didst not lay, and thou reapest what thou didst not sow.

22 λέγει   αὐτῷ·   ἐκ   τοῦ   στόματός   σου
He says   to him : Out of   the   mouth   of thee

κρινῶ   σε,   πονηρὲ   δοῦλε.   ᾔδεις   ὅτι   ἐγὼ
I will judge thee, wicked slave. Knewest thou that   I

ἄνθρωπος   αὐστηρός   εἰμι,   αἴρων   ὃ   οὐκ
man   an exacting   am,   taking   what   not

ἔθηκα, καὶ θερίζων ὃ οὐκ ἔσπειρα; 23 καὶ
I laid, and reaping what I sowed not ?   And

διὰ   τί   οὐκ   ἔδωκάς   μου   τὸ   ἀργύριον   ἐπὶ
why   didst thou not give of me   the   money   on

τράπεζαν; κἀγὼ ἐλθὼν σὺν τόκῳ ἂν
a table?*   And I   coming   with   interest   –

αὐτὸ   ἔπραξα. 24 καὶ   τοῖς   παρεστῶσιν
it would have exacted.   And to the [ones] standing by

* That is, a moneychanger's or banker's table.

from him the pound, and give *it* to him that hath ten pounds.

25 (And they said unto him, Lord, he hath ten pounds.)

26 For I say unto you, That unto every one which hath shall be given; and from him that hath not, even that he hath shall be taken away from him.

27 But those mine enemies, which would not that I should reign over them, bring hither, and slay *them* before me.

28 And when he had thus spoken, he went before, ascending up to Jerusalem.

29 ¶ And it came to pass, when he was come nigh to Bethphage and Bethany, at the mount called *the mount* of Olives, he sent two of his disciples,

30 Saying, Go ye into the village over against *you;* in the which at your entering ye shall find a colt tied, whereon yet never man sat: loose him, and bring *him hither.*

31 And if any man ask you, Why do ye loose *him?* thus shall ye say unto him, Because the Lord hath need of him.

32 And they that were sent went their way, and found even as he had said unto them.

33 And as they were loosing the colt, the owners thereof said unto them, Why loose ye the colt?

εἶπεν· ἄρατε ἀπ' αὐτοῦ τὴν μνᾶν καὶ
he said : Take from him the mina and
δότε τῷ τὰς δέκα μνᾶς ἔχοντι. 25 καὶ
give ¹to the [one] ³the ⁴ten ⁵minas ²having. And
εἶπαν αὐτῷ· κύριε, ἔχει δέκα μνᾶς.
they said to him : Lord, he has ten minas.
26 λέγω ὑμῖν ὅτι παντὶ τῷ ἔχοντι
I tell you that to everyone having
δοθήσεται, ἀπὸ δὲ τοῦ μὴ ἔχοντος καὶ
it will be given, and from the [one] not having even
ὃ ἔχει ἀρθήσεται. 27 πλὴν τοὺς ἐχθρούς
what he has will be taken. Nevertheless – enemies
μου τούτους τοὺς μὴ θελήσαντάς με
of me these the [ones] not wishing me
βασιλεῦσαι ἐπ' αὐτοὺς ἀγάγετε ὧδε καὶ
to reign over them bring ye here and
κατασφάξατε αὐτοὺς ἔμπροσθέν μου.
slay them before me.
28 Καὶ εἰπὼν ταῦτα ἐπορεύετο ἔμπροσθεν
And having said these things he went in front
ἀναβαίνων εἰς Ἱεροσόλυμα. 29 Καὶ ἐγένετο
going up to Jerusalem. And it came to pass
ὡς ἤγγισεν εἰς Βηθφαγὴ καὶ Βηθανίαν
as he drew near to Bethphage and Bethany
πρὸς τὸ ὄρος τὸ καλούμενον ἐλαιών,
toward the mount – being called of olives,
ἀπέστειλεν δύο τῶν μαθητῶν λέγων·
he sent two of the disciples saying :
30 ὑπάγετε εἰς τὴν κατέναντι κώμην, ἐν ᾗ
Go ye into the opposite village, in which
εἰσπορευόμενοι εὑρήσετε πῶλον δεδεμένον,
entering ye will find a colt *having been* tied,
ἐφ' ὃν οὐδεὶς πώποτε ἀνθρώπων ἐκάθισεν,
on which no one ever yet of men sat,
καὶ λύσαντες αὐτὸν ἀγάγετε. 31 καὶ ἐάν
and loosening it bring. And if
τις ὑμᾶς ἐρωτᾷ· διὰ τί λύετε; οὕτως
anyone you asks : Why loosen ye? thus
ἐρεῖτε· ὅτι ὁ κύριος αὐτοῦ χρείαν ἔχει.
shall ye say : Because the Lord of it need has.
32 ἀπελθόντες δὲ οἱ ἀπεσταλμένοι εὗρον
And going the [ones] *having been* sent found
καθὼς εἶπεν αὐτοῖς. 33 λυόντων δὲ
as he told them. And loosening
                           =as they were
αὐτῶν τὸν πῶλον εἶπαν οἱ κύριοι αὐτοῦ
them* the colt said the owners of it
loosening
πρὸς αὐτούς· τί λύετε τὸν πῶλον; 34 οἱ
to them : Why loosen ye the colt? ²they

34 And they said, The Lord hath need of him.

35 And they brought him to Jesus: and they cast their garments upon the colt, and they set Jesus thereon.

36 And as he went, they spread their clothes in the way.

37 And when he was come nigh, even now at the descent of the mount of Olives, the whole multitude of the disciples began to rejoice and praise God with a loud voice for all the mighty works that they had seen;

38 Saying, Blessed be the King that cometh in the name of the Lord: peace in heaven, and glory in the highest.

39 And some of the Pharisees from among the multitude said unto him, Master, rebuke thy disciples.

40 And he answered and said unto them, I tell you that, if these should hold their peace, the stones would immediately cry out.

41 ¶ And when he was come near, he beheld the city, and wept over it,

42 Saying, If thou hadst known, even thou, at least in this thy day, the things which belong unto thy peace! but now they are hid from thine eyes.

43 For the days shall come upon thee, that thine enemies shall cast a

δὲ εἶπαν· ὅτι ὁ κύριος αὐτοῦ χρείαν ἔχει.
¹And said : Because the Lord of it need has.

35 καὶ ἤγαγον αὐτὸν πρὸς τὸν Ἰησοῦν,
And they led it to - Jesus,

καὶ ἐπιρίψαντες αὐτῶν τὰ ἱμάτια ἐπὶ τὸν
and throwing on of them the garments on the

πῶλον ἐπεβίβασαν τὸν Ἰησοῦν. 36 πορευ-
colt they put on [it] - Jesus. And

ομένου δὲ αὐτοῦ ὑπεστρώννυον τὰ ἱμάτια
going himᵃ they strewed the garments
=as he went

ἑαυτῶν ἐν τῇ ὁδῷ. 37 ἐγγίζοντος δὲ
of themselves in the way. And drawing near
=as he drew near

αὐτοῦ ἤδη πρὸς τῇ καταβάσει τοῦ ὄρους
himᵃ now to the descent of the mount

τῶν ἐλαιῶν ἤρξαντο ἅπαν τὸ πλῆθος τῶν
of the olives began all the multitude of the

μαθητῶν χαίροντες αἰνεῖν τὸν θεὸν φωνῇ
disciples rejoicing to praise - God voice

μεγάλῃ περὶ πασῶν ὧν εἶδον δυνάμεων,
with a about ¹all ³which ⁴they saw ²[the] powerful
great deeds,

38 λέγοντες· εὐλογημένος ὁ ἐρχόμενος, ὁ
saying : Blessed the coming [one], the

βασιλεὺς ἐν ὀνόματι κυρίου· ἐν οὐρανῷ
king in [the] name of [the] Lord; in heaven

εἰρήνη καὶ δόξα ἐν ὑψίστοις. 39 καὶ
peace and glory in highest places. And

τινες τῶν Φαρισαίων ἀπὸ τοῦ ὄχλου
some of the Pharisees from the crowd

εἶπαν πρὸς αὐτόν· διδάσκαλε, ἐπιτίμησον
said to him : Teacher, rebuke

τοῖς μαθηταῖς σου. 40 καὶ ἀποκριθεὶς
the disciples of thee. And answering

εἶπεν· λέγω ὑμῖν, ἐὰν οὗτοι σιωπήσουσιν,
he said : I tell you, if these shall(should) be silent,

οἱ λίθοι κράξουσιν. 41 Καὶ ὡς ἤγγισεν,
the stones will cry out. And as he drew near,

ἰδὼν τὴν πόλιν ἔκλαυσεν ἐπ' αὐτήν,
seeing the city he wept over it,

42 λέγων ὅτι εἰ ἔγνως ἐν τῇ ἡμέρᾳ
saying[,] - If thou knewest in - day

ταύτῃ καὶ σὺ τὰ πρὸς εἰρήνην· νῦν δὲ
this even thou the things for peace; but now

ἐκρύβη ἀπὸ ὀφθαλμῶν σου. 43 ὅτι ἥξουσιν
they were hidden from eyes of thee. Because will come

ἡμέραι ἐπὶ σὲ καὶ παρεμβαλοῦσιν οἱ
days upon thee and ⁴will raise up ¹the

trench about thee, and compass thee round, and keep thee in on every side,

44 And shall lay thee even with the ground, and thy children within thee; and they shall not leave in thee one stone upon another; because thou knewest not the time of thy visitation.

45 And he went into the temple, and began to cast out them that sold therein, and them that bought;

46 Saying unto them, It is written, My house is the house of prayer: but ye have made it a den of thieves.

47 And he taught daily in the temple. But the chief priests and the scribes and the chief of the people sought to destroy him,

48 And could not find what they might do: for all the people were very attentive to hear him.

ἐχθροί σου χάρακά σοι καὶ περικυκλώσουσίν
²enemies ³of thee ⁵a rampart to thee and will surround

σε καὶ συνέξουσίν σε πάντοθεν, **44** καὶ
thee and will press thee on all sides, and

ἐδαφιοῦσίν σε καὶ τὰ τέκνα σου ἐν σοί,
dash to the ground thee and the children of thee in thee,

καὶ οὐκ ἀφήσουσιν λίθον ἐπὶ λίθον ἐν σοί,
and will not leave stone upon stone in thee,

ἀνθ' ὧν οὐκ ἔγνως τὸν καιρὸν τῆς
because† thou knewest not the time of the

ἐπισκοπῆς σου. **45** Καὶ εἰσελθὼν εἰς τὸ
visitation of thee. And entering into the

ἱερὸν ἤρξατο ἐκβάλλειν τοὺς πωλοῦντας,
temple he began to expel the [ones] selling,

46 λέγων αὐτοῖς· γέγραπται· καὶ ἔσται ὁ
telling them : It has been written : And shall be the

οἶκός μου οἶκος προσευχῆς· ὑμεῖς δὲ
house of me a house of prayer; but ye

αὐτὸν ἐποιήσατε σπήλαιον λῃστῶν.
it made a den of robbers.

47 Καὶ ἦν διδάσκων τὸ καθ' ἡμέραν ἐν
And he was teaching daily† in

τῷ ἱερῷ· οἱ δὲ ἀρχιερεῖς καὶ οἱ
the temple; but the chief priests and the

γραμματεῖς ἐζήτουν αὐτὸν ἀπολέσαι καὶ οἱ
scribes ⁸sought ⁶him ⁷to destroy ¹and ²the

πρῶτοι τοῦ λαοῦ, **48** καὶ οὐχ εὕρισκον
³chief men ⁴of the ⁵people, and did not find

τὸ τί ποιήσωσιν· ὁ λαὸς γὰρ ἅπας
– what they might do; ³the ⁴people ¹for ²all

ἐξεκρέματο αὐτοῦ ἀκούων.
hung upon him hearing.

CHAPTER 20

AND it came to pass, *that* on one of those days, as. he taught the people in the temple, and preached the gospel, the chief priests and the scribes came upon *him* with the elders,

2 And spake unto him, saying, Tell us, by what authority doest thou these things? or who is he that gave thee this authority?

20 Καὶ ἐγένετο ἐν μιᾷ τῶν ἡμερῶν
And it came to pass on one of the days

διδάσκοντος αὐτοῦ τὸν λαὸν ἐν τῷ ἱερῷ
teaching himª the people in the temple
= as he was teaching

καὶ εὐαγγελιζομένου ἐπέστησαν οἱ ἀρχιερεῖς
and preaching good newsª came upon [him] the chief priests

καὶ οἱ γραμματεῖς σὺν τοῖς πρεσβυτέροις,
and the scribes with the elders,

2 καὶ εἶπαν λέγοντες πρὸς αὐτόν· εἰπὸν
and spoke saying to him : Tell

ἡμῖν ἐν ποίᾳ ἐξουσίᾳ ταῦτα ποιεῖς, ἢ τίς
us by what authority these things thou doest, or who

ἐστιν ὁ δούς σοι τὴν ἐξουσίαν ταύτην;
is the [one] having given thee – authority this?

3 And he answered and said unto them, I will also ask you one thing; and answer me:

4 The baptism of John, was it from heaven, or of men?

5 And they reasoned with themselves, saying, If we shall say, From heaven; he will say, Why then believed ye him not?

6 But and if we say, Of men; all the people will stone us: for they be persuaded that John was a prophet.

7 And they answered, that they could not tell whence it was.

8 And Jesus said unto them, Neither tell I you by what authority I do these things.

9 Then began he to speak to the people this parable; A certain man planted a vineyard, and let it forth to husbandmen, and went into a far country for a long time.

10 And at the season he sent a servant to the husbandmen, that they should give him of the fruit of the vineyard: but the husbandmen beat him, and sent *him* away empty.

11 And again he sent another servant: and they beat him also, and entreated *him* shamefully, and sent *him* away empty.

12 And again he sent a

3 ἀποκριθεὶς δὲ εἶπεν πρὸς αὐτούς·
And answering he said to them :

ἐρωτήσω ὑμᾶς κἀγὼ λόγον, καὶ εἴπατέ
Will ask you I also a word, and tell ye

μοι· 4 τὸ βάπτισμα Ἰωάννου ἐξ οὐρανοῦ
me : The baptism of John from heaven

ἦν ἢ ἐξ ἀνθρώπων; 5 οἱ δὲ συνελογίσαντο
was it or from men? And they debated

πρὸς ἑαυτοὺς λέγοντες ὅτι ἐὰν εἴπωμεν·
with themselves saying[,] – If we say :

ἐξ οὐρανοῦ, ἐρεῖ· διὰ τί οὐκ ἐπιστεύσατε
From heaven, he will say: Why did ye not believe

αὐτῷ; 6 ἐὰν δὲ εἴπωμεν· ἐξ ἀνθρώπων, ὁ
him? And if we say : From men, the

λαὸς ἅπας καταλιθάσει ἡμᾶς· πεπεισμένος
people all will stone us; for having been per-

γάρ ἐστιν Ἰωάννην προφήτην εἶναι. 7 καὶ
suaded it is* John a prophet to be. And

ἀπεκρίθησαν μὴ εἰδέναι πόθεν. 8 καὶ ὁ
they answered not to know whence. And

Ἰησοῦς εἶπεν αὐτοῖς· οὐδὲ ἐγὼ λέγω
Jesus said to them : Neither I tell

ὑμῖν ἐν ποίᾳ ἐξουσίᾳ ταῦτα ποιῶ. 9 Ἤρξατο
you by what authority these things I do. he began

δὲ πρὸς τὸν λαὸν λέγειν τὴν παραβολὴν
And to the people to tell – parable

ταύτην. ἄνθρωπος ἐφύτευσεν ἀμπελῶνα,
this. A man planted a vineyard,

καὶ ἐξέδοτο αὐτὸν γεωργοῖς, καὶ ἀπεδή-
and let out it to husbandmen, and went

μησεν χρόνους ἱκανούς. 10 καὶ καιρῷ
away periods for considerable. And in time
　　　　　　　=a long time.

ἀπέστειλεν πρὸς τοὺς γεωργοὺς δοῦλον,
he sent to the husbandmen a slave,

ἵνα ἀπὸ τοῦ καρποῦ τοῦ ἀμπελῶνος
that from the fruit of the vineyard

δώσουσιν αὐτῷ· οἱ δὲ γεωργοὶ ἐξαπέστειλαν
they will give him; but the husbandmen ²sent ⁴away out

αὐτὸν δείραντες κενόν. 11 καὶ προσέθετο
³him ¹beating ⁵empty. And he added

ἕτερον πέμψαι δοῦλον· οἱ δὲ κἀκεῖνον
²another ¹to send slave; but they that one also
=he sent another slave in addition;

δείραντες καὶ ἀτιμάσαντες ἐξαπέστειλαν
beating and insulting sent away out

κενόν. 12 καὶ προσέθετο τρίτον πέμψαι·
empty. And he added a third to send;

* That is, the people (a collective singular) have been (=are) persuaded.

third: and they wounded
him also, and cast *him* out.
13 Then said the lord
of the vineyard, What shall
I do? I will send my be-
loved son: it may be they
will reverence *him* when
they see him.
14 But when the hus-
bandmen saw him, they
reasoned among them-
selves, saying, This is the
heir: come, let us kill
him, that the inheritance
may be our's.
15 So they cast him out
of the vineyard, and killed
him. What therefore shall
the lord of the vineyard do
unto them?
16 He shall come and
destroy these husband-
men, and shall give the
vineyard to others. And
when they heard *it*, they
said, God forbid.
17 And he beheld them,
and said, What is this then
that is written, The stone
which the builders rejected,
the same is become the
head of the corner?
18 Whosoever shall fall
upon that stone shall be
broken; but on whom-
soever it shall fall, it will
grind him to powder.
19 And the chief priests
and the scribes the same
hour sought to lay hands
on him; and they feared
the people: for they per-
ceived that he had spoken
this parable against them.
20 ¶ And they watched
him, and sent forth spies,

οἱ δὲ καὶ τοῦτον τραυματίσαντες ἐξέβαλον.
but they also this one   wounding   threw out.

13 εἶπεν δὲ ὁ κύριος τοῦ ἀμπελῶνος· τί
And said   the owner of the   vineyard : What

ποιήσω; πέμψω τὸν υἱόν μου τὸν ἀγαπητόν·
may I do? I will send the son of me –   beloved;

ἴσως τοῦτον ἐντραπήσονται. 14 ἰδόντες δὲ
perhaps this one they will regard.   But seeing

αὐτὸν οἱ γεωργοὶ διελογίζοντο πρὸς
him   the husbandmen   debated   with

ἀλλήλους λέγοντες· οὗτός ἐστιν ὁ κληρονόμος·
one another saying : This   is   the   heir;

ἀποκτείνωμεν αὐτόν, ἵνα ἡμῶν γένηται
let us kill   him,   that of us may become

ἡ κληρονομία. 15 καὶ ἐκβαλόντες αὐτὸν
the inheritance.   And throwing out   him

ἔξω τοῦ ἀμπελῶνος ἀπέκτειναν. τί οὖν
outside the   vineyard   they killed. What therefore

ποιήσει αὐτοῖς ὁ κύριος τοῦ ἀμπελῶνος;
will do to them the owner of the   vineyard?

16 ἐλεύσεται καὶ ἀπολέσει τοὺς γεωργοὺς
he will come and will destroy   –   husbandmen

τούτους, καὶ δώσει τὸν ἀμπελῶνα ἄλλοις.
these,   and will give the   vineyard   to others.

ἀκούσαντες δὲ εἶπαν· μὴ γένοιτο. 17 ὁ δὲ
And hearing   they said : May it not be.   And he

ἐμβλέψας αὐτοῖς εἶπεν· τί οὖν ἐστιν τὸ
looking at   them   said : What therefore is   –

γεγραμμένον τοῦτο· λίθον ὃν ἀπεδοκίμασαν
having been written this : [The] stone which   ²rejected

οἱ οἰκοδομοῦντες, οὗτος ἐγενήθη εἰς κεφαλὴν
¹the [ones] ²building,   this came to be for [the] head

γωνίας; 18 πᾶς ὁ πεσὼν ἐπ’ ἐκεῖνον τὸν
of [the] corner? Everyone falling on   that   –

λίθον συνθλασθήσεται· ἐφ’ ὃν δ’ ἂν πέσῃ,
stone will be broken in pieces; but on whomever   it falls,

λικμήσει αὐτόν. 19 Καὶ ἐζήτησαν οἱ
it will crush to powder him.   And   sought   the

γραμματεῖς καὶ οἱ ἀρχιερεῖς ἐπιβαλεῖν ἐπ’
scribes   and the chief piests   to lay on   on

αὐτὸν τὰς χεῖρας ἐν αὐτῇ τῇ ὥρᾳ, καὶ
him   the(ir) hands in ²same ¹the hour,   and

ἐφοβήθησαν τὸν λαόν· ἔγνωσαν γὰρ ὅτι
feared   the people; for they knew   that

πρὸς αὐτοὺς εἶπεν τὴν παραβολὴν ταύτην.
at   them   he told   –   parable   this.

20 Καὶ παρατηρήσαντες ἀπέστειλαν ἐγκαθέτους
And   watching carefully   they sent   spies

which should feign them-
selves just men, that they
might take hold of his
words, that so they might
deliver him unto the power
and authority of the
governor.

21 And they asked him,
saying, Master, we know
that thou sayest and
teachest rightly, neither
acceptest thou the person
of any, but teachest the
way of God truly:

22 Is it lawful for us to
give tribute unto Cæsar,
or no?

23 But he perceived
their craftiness, and said
unto them, Why tempt ye
me?

24 Shew me a penny.
Whose image and super-
scription hath it? They
answered and said,
Cæsar's.

25 And he said unto
them, Render therefore
unto Cæsar the things
which be Cæsar's, and unto
God the things which be
God's.

26 And they could not
take hold of his words
before the people: and
they marvelled at his
answer, and held their
peace.

27 ¶ Then came to *him*
certain of the Sadducees,
which deny that there is
any resurrection: and they
asked him,

28 Saying, Master,
Moses wrote unto us, If
any man's brother die,
having a wife, and he die
without children, that his
brother should take his

ὑποκρινομένους ἑαυτοὺς δικαίους εἶναι, ἵνα
pretending   themselves righteous   to be,   that
ἐπιλάβωνται αὐτοῦ λόγου, ὥστε παραδοῦναι
they might seize of him a word, so as   to deliver
αὐτὸν τῇ ἀρχῇ καὶ τῇ ἐξουσίᾳ τοῦ
him   to the rule and to the authority of the
ἡγεμόνος. 21 καὶ ἐπηρώτησαν αὐτὸν
governor.   And they questioned   him
λέγοντες· διδάσκαλε, οἴδαμεν ὅτι ὀρθῶς
saying :   Teacher,   we know that ⁴rightly
λέγεις καὶ διδάσκεις καὶ οὐ λαμβάνεις
¹thou speakest ²and ³teachest and   receivest not
                                        =regardest not persons,
πρόσωπον, ἀλλ' ἐπ' ἀληθείας τὴν ὁδὸν τοῦ
a face,   but on [the basis of] truth   the   way –
θεοῦ διδάσκεις· 22 ἔξεστιν ἡμᾶς Καίσαρι
of God teachest;   is it lawful for us to Cæsar
φόρον δοῦναι ἢ οὔ; 23 κατανοήσας δὲ
tribute to give or not?   And perceiving
αὐτῶν τὴν πανουργίαν εἶπεν πρὸς αὐτούς·
of them the cleverness he said to   them :
24 δείξατέ μοι δηνάριον· τίνος ἔχει εἰκόνα
    Show   me a denarius; of whom has it an image
καὶ ἐπιγραφήν; οἱ δὲ εἶπαν· Καίσαρος.
and superscription? And they said :   Of Cæsar.
25 ὁ δὲ εἶπεν πρὸς αὐτούς· τοίνυν ἀπόδοτε
   And he said   to   them :   So   render
τὰ Καίσαρος Καίσαρι καὶ τὰ τοῦ θεοῦ
the things of Cæsar to Cæsar and the things – of God
τῷ θεῷ. 26 καὶ οὐκ ἴσχυσαν ἐπιλαβέσθαι
– to God.   And they were not able   to seize
αὐτοῦ ῥήματος ἐναντίον τοῦ λαοῦ, καὶ
of him a word in the presence of the people, and
θαυμάσαντες ἐπὶ τῇ ἀποκρίσει αὐτοῦ
marvelling   at the   answer   of him
ἐσίγησαν.
they were silent.
27 Προσελθόντες δέ τινες τῶν Σαδ-
   And ⁴approaching   ¹some ²of the ³Sad-
δουκαίων, οἱ ἀντιλέγοντες ἀνάστασιν μὴ
ducees,   the [ones] saying in opposition* a resurrection not
εἶναι, ἐπηρώτησαν αὐτὸν 28 λέγοντες·
to be, they questioned   him   saying :
διδάσκαλε, Μωϋσῆς ἔγραψεν ἡμῖν, ἐάν
Teacher,   Moses   wrote   to us,   If
τινος ἀδελφὸς ἀποθάνῃ ἔχων γυναῖκα, καὶ
of anyone a brother   dies   having a wife,   and
οὗτος ἄτεκνος ᾖ, ἵνα λάβῃ ὁ ἀδελφὸς
this man childless is, that ⁴should take ¹the ²brother

*That is, to the Pharisees and to the generally held opinion.

wife, and raise up seed unto his brother.

29 There were therefore seven brethren: and the first took a wife, and died without children.

30 And the second took her to wife, and he died childless.

31 And the third took her; and in like manner the seven also: and they left no children, and died.

32 Last of all the woman died also.

33 Therefore in the resurrection whose wife of them is she? for seven had her to wife.

34 And Jesus answering said unto them, The children of this world marry, and are given in marriage:

35 But they which shall be accounted worthy to obtain that world, and the resurrection from the dead, neither marry nor are given in marriage:

36 Neither can they die any more: for they are equal unto the angels; and are the children of God, being the children of the resurrection.

37 Now that the dead are raised, even Moses shewed at the bush, when he calleth the Lord the God of Abraham, and the God of Isaac, and the God of Jacob.

38 For he is not a God of the dead, but of the living: for all live unto him.

39 Then certain of the scribes answering said, Master, thou hast well said.

αὐτοῦ τὴν γυναῖκα καὶ ἐξαναστήσῃ σπέρμα
²of him ⁵the ⁶wife and raise up seed

τῷ ἀδελφῷ αὐτοῦ. 29 ἑπτὰ οὖν ἀδελφοὶ
to the brother of him. Seven therefore brothers

ἦσαν· καὶ ὁ πρῶτος λαβὼν γυναῖκα
there were; and the first having taken a wife

ἀπέθανεν ἄτεκνος· 30 καὶ ὁ δεύτερος 31 καὶ
died childless; and the second and

ὁ τρίτος ἔλαβεν αὐτήν, ὡσαύτως δὲ καὶ
the third took her, and similarly also

οἱ ἑπτὰ οὐ κατέλιπον τέκνα καὶ ἀπέθανον.
the seven did not leave children and died.

32 ὕστερον καὶ ἡ γυνὴ ἀπέθανεν. 33 ἡ
Lastly also the woman died. The

γυνὴ οὖν ἐν τῇ ἀναστάσει τίνος αὐτῶν
woman therefore in the resurrection of which of them

γίνεται γυνή; οἱ γὰρ ἑπτὰ ἔσχον αὐτὴν
becomes she wife? for the seven had her

γυναῖκα. 34 καὶ εἶπεν αὐτοῖς ὁ Ἰησοῦς·
[as] wife. And said to them - Jesus:

οἱ υἱοὶ τοῦ αἰῶνος τούτου γαμοῦσιν καὶ
The sons - age of this marry and

γαμίσκονται, 35 οἱ δὲ καταξιωθέντες τοῦ
are given in marriage, but the [ones] counted worthy -

αἰῶνος ἐκείνου τυχεῖν καὶ τῆς ἀναστάσεως
²age ³of that ¹to obtain and of the resurrection

τῆς ἐκ νεκρῶν οὔτε γαμοῦσιν οὔτε
- out of [the] dead neither marry nor

γαμίζονται· 36 οὐδὲ γὰρ ἀποθανεῖν ἔτι
are given in marriage; for not even to die more

δύνανται, ἰσάγγελοι γάρ εἰσιν, καὶ υἱοὶ
can they, for equal to angels they are, and ²sons

εἰσιν θεοῦ τῆς ἀναστάσεως υἱοὶ ὄντες.
¹they are ²of God ⁶of the ⁷resurrection ⁵sons ⁴being.

37 ὅτι δὲ ἐγείρονται οἱ νεκροί, καὶ
But that are raised the dead, even

Μωϋσῆς ἐμήνυσεν ἐπι τῆς βάτου, ὡς
Moses pointed out at the bush, as

λέγει κύριον τὸν θεὸν Ἀβραὰμ καὶ θεὸν
he calls [the] Lord the God of Abraham and God

Ἰσαὰκ καὶ θεὸν Ἰακώβ· 38 θεὸς δὲ οὐκ
of Isaac and God of Jacob; but God not

ἔστιν νεκρῶν ἀλλὰ ζώντων· πάντες γὰρ
he is of dead persons but of living; for all

αὐτῷ ζῶσιν. 39 ἀποκριθέντες δέ τινες
to him live. And answering some

τῶν γραμματέων εἶπαν· διδάσκαλε, καλῶς
of the scribes said: Teacher, well

40 And after that they durst not ask him any *question at all.*

41¶ And he said unto them, How say they that Christ is David's son?

42 And David himself saith in the book of Psalms, The LORD said unto my Lord, Sit thou on my right hand,

43 Till I make thine enemies thy footstool.

44 David therefore calleth him Lord, how is he then his son?

45¶ Then in the audience of all the people he said unto his disciples,

46 Beware of the scribes, which desire to walk in long robes, and love greetings in the markets, and the highest seats in the synagogues, and the chief rooms at feasts;

47 Which devour widows' houses, and for a shew make long prayers: the same shall receive greater damnation.

εἶπας. **40** οὐκέτι γὰρ ἐτόλμων ἐπερωτᾶν
thou sayest.   For no more   dared they   *to* question

αὐτὸν οὐδέν.
him   no(any)thing.

41 Εἶπεν δὲ πρὸς αὐτούς· πῶς λέγουσιν
And he said   to   them :   How   say they

τὸν χριστὸν εἶναι Δαυὶδ υἱόν; **42** αὐτὸς
the   Christ   to be   of David   son?   himself

γὰρ Δαυὶδ λέγει ἐν βίβλω ψαλμῶν·
For   David   says   in   [the] roll   of psalms :

εἶπεν κύριος τῷ κυρίῳ μου· κάθου ἐκ
Said   [the] LORD   to the   Lord   of me :   Sit thou   at

δεξιῶν μου **43** ἕως ἂν θῶ τοὺς ἐχθρούς σου
[the] right of me   until   I put   the   enemies of thee

ὑποπόδιον τῶν ποδῶν σου. **44** Δαυὶδ
a footstool   of the   feet   of thee.   David

οὖν αὐτὸν κύριον καλεῖ, καὶ πῶς αὐτοῦ
therefore him   Lord   calls,   and   how   of him

υἱός ἐστιν;
son   is he?

45 Ἀκούοντος δὲ παντὸς τοῦ λαοῦ εἶπεν
And hearing   all   the   people**ª**   he said
=as all the people heard

τοῖς μαθηταῖς· **46** προσέχετε ἀπὸ τῶν
to the   disciples :   Beware   from(of)   the

γραμματέων τῶν θελόντων περιπατεῖν ἐν
scribes   wishing   to walk about   in

στολαῖς καὶ φιλούντων ἀσπασμοὺς ἐν ταῖς
robes   and   liking   greetings   in   the

ἀγοραῖς καὶ πρωτοκαθεδρίας ἐν ταῖς
marketplaces   and   chief seats   in   the

συναγωγαῖς καὶ πρωτοκλισίας ἐν τοῖς
synagogues   and   chief couches   in   the

δείπνοις, **47** οἳ κατεσθίουσιν τὰς οἰκίας
suppers,   who   devour   the   houses

τῶν χηρῶν καὶ προφάσει μακρὰ προσεύχονται·
of the   widows   and   under pretence   long   pray;

οὗτοι λήμψονται περισσότερον κρίμα.
these   will receive   severer   judgment.

CHAPTER 21

AND he looked up, and saw the rich men casting their gifts into the treasury.

2 And he saw also a certain poor widow casting in thither two mites.

21 Ἀναβλέψας δὲ εἶδεν τοὺς βάλλοντας
And looking up   he saw   ¹the   ²putting

εἰς τὸ γαζοφυλακεῖον τὰ δῶρα αὐτῶν
⁵into   ⁶the   ⁶treasury   ⁷the   ⁸gifts   ⁹of them

πλουσίους. **2** εἶδεν δέ τινα χήραν πενιχρὰν
³rich [ones].   And he saw   a certain   widow   poor

βάλλουσαν ἐκεῖ λεπτὰ δύο, **3** καὶ εἶπεν·
putting   there   lepta   two,   and   he said :

3 And he said, Of a truth I say unto you, that this poor widow hath cast in more than they all:

4 For all these have of their abundance cast in unto the offerings of God: but she of her penury hath cast in all the living that she had.

5 ¶ And as some spake of the temple, how it was adorned with goodly stones and gifts, he said,

6 As for these things which ye behold, the days will come, in the which there shall not be left one stone upon another, that shall not be thrown down.

7 And they asked him, saying, Master, but when shall these things be? and what sign will there be when these things shall come to pass?

8 And he said, Take heed that ye be not deceived: for many shall come in my name, saying, I am Christ; and the time draweth near: go ye not therefore after them.

9 But when ye shall hear of wars and commotions, be not terrified: for these things must first come to pass; but the end is not by and by.

10 Then said he unto them, Nation shall rise against nation, and kingdom against kingdom:

11 And great earthquakes shall be in divers

ἀληθῶς λέγω ὑμῖν ὅτι ἡ χήρα αὕτη ἡ
Truly I tell you that – ²widow ¹this –

πτωχὴ πλεῖον πάντων ἔβαλεν· 4 πάντες
³poor more [than] all put; ²all

γὰρ οὗτοι ἐκ τοῦ περισσεύοντος αὐτοῖς
¹for these out of the abounding to them°
=their abundance

ἔβαλον εἰς τὰ δῶρα, αὕτη δὲ ἐκ τοῦ
put into the gifts, but this woman out of the

ὑστερήματος αὐτῆς πάντα τὸν βίον ὃν
want of her ³all ²the ⁶living ⁵which

εἶχεν ἔβαλεν.
°she had ¹put.

5 Καί τινων λεγόντων περὶ τοῦ ἱεροῦ, ὅτι
And some speaking° about the temple, that
=as some spoke

λίθοις καλοῖς καὶ ἀναθήμασιν κεκόσμηται,
stones with beautiful and gifts it has(had)
been adorned,

εἶπεν· 6 ταῦτα ἃ θεωρεῖτε, ἐλεύσονται
he said: These things which ye behold, will come

ἡμέραι ἐν αἷς οὐκ ἀφεθήσεται λίθος ἐπὶ
days in which there will not be left stone on

λίθῳ ὃς οὐ καταλυθήσεται. 7 ἐπηρώτησαν δὲ
stone which will not be overthrown. And they questioned

αὐτὸν λέγοντες· διδάσκαλε, πότε οὖν
him saying: Teacher, when therefore

ταῦτα ἔσται; καὶ τί τὸ σημεῖον ὅταν
these things will be? And what [will be] the sign when

μέλλῃ ταῦτα γίνεσθαι; 8 ὁ δὲ εἶπεν·
²are about ¹these things ³to happen? And he said:

βλέπετε μὴ πλανηθῆτε· πολλοὶ γὰρ
Beware lest ye be led astray; for many

ἐλεύσονται ἐπὶ τῷ ὀνόματί μου λέγοντες·
will come on(in) the name of me saying:

ἐγώ εἰμι, καί· ὁ καιρὸς ἤγγικεν· μὴ
I am, and: The time has drawn near; not

πορευθῆτε ὀπίσω αὐτῶν. 9 ὅταν δὲ
go ye after them. And when

ἀκούσητε πολέμους καὶ ἀκαταστασίας, μὴ
ye hear [of] wars and commotions, not

πτοηθῆτε· δεῖ γὰρ ταῦτα γενέσθαι
be ye scared; for it behoves these things to happen

πρῶτον, ἀλλ' οὐκ εὐθέως τὸ τέλος. 10 Τότε
first, but not immediately the end. Then

ἔλεγεν αὐτοῖς· ἐγερθήσεται ἔθνος ἐπ' ἔθνος
he said to them: Will be raised nation against nation

καὶ βασιλεία ἐπὶ βασιλείαν, 11 σεισμοί τε
and kingdom against kingdom, and earthquakes

places, and famines, and
pestilences; and fearful
sights and great signs shall
there be from heaven.

12 But before all these,
they shall lay their hands
on you, and persecute
you, delivering *you* up to
the synagogues, and into
prisons, being brought
before kings and rulers
for my name's sake.

13 And it shall turn to
you for a testimony.

14 Settle *it* therefore in
your hearts, not to medi-
tate before what ye shall
answer:

15 For I will give you
a mouth and wisdom,
which all your adversaries
shall not be able to gainsay
nor resist.

16 And ye shall be be-
trayed both by parents,
and brethren, and kins-
folks, and friends; and
some of you shall they
cause to be put to death.

17 And ye shall be
hated of all *men* for my
name's sake.

18 But there shall not
an hair of your head
perish.

19 In your patience
possess ye your souls.

20 And when ye shall
see Jerusalem compassed
with armies, then know
that the desolation thereof
is nigh.

21 Then let them which
are in Judæa flee to the
mountains; and let them
which are in the midst of
it depart out; and let

μεγάλοι καὶ κατὰ τόπους λοιμοὶ καὶ λιμοὶ
great   and from place to place† pestilences and famines

ἔσονται, φόβητρά τε καὶ ἀπ' οὐρανοῦ
there will be,   and terrors   and ²from   ⁴heaven

σημεῖα μεγάλα ἔσται. 12 πρὸ δὲ τούτων
²signs ¹great there will be.   But before these things

πάντων ἐπιβαλοῦσιν ἐφ' ὑμᾶς τὰς χεῖρας
all   they will lay on on you   the hands

αὐτῶν καὶ διώξουσιν, παραδιδόντες εἰς τὰς
of them and will persecute, delivering   to the

συναγωγὰς καὶ φυλακάς, ἀπαγομένους ἐπὶ
synagogues and prisons, being led away on(before)

βασιλεῖς καὶ ἡγεμόνας ἕνεκεν τοῦ ὀνόματός
kings   and governors for the sake of the name

μου· 13 ἀποβήσεται ὑμῖν εἰς μαρτύριον.
of me; it will turn out to you for a testimony.

14 θέτε οὖν ἐν ταῖς καρδίαις ὑμῶν μὴ
   Put therefore in the hearts of you not

προμελετᾶν ἀπολογηθῆναι· 15 ἐγὼ γὰρ
to practise beforehand to defend [yourselves]; for I

δώσω ὑμῖν στόμα καὶ σοφίαν, ᾗ οὐ
will give you a mouth and wisdom, which not

δυνήσονται ἀντιστῆναι ἢ ἀντειπεῖν ἅπαντες οἱ
will be able to withstand or to contradict all the

ἀντικείμενοι ὑμῖν. 16 παραδοθήσεσθε δὲ καὶ
[ones] opposing you.   And ye will be betrayed also

ὑπὸ γονέων καὶ ἀδελφῶν καὶ συγγενῶν
by parents and brothers and relatives

καὶ φίλων, καὶ θανατώσουσιν ἐξ ὑμῶν,
and friends, and they will put to death [some] of you,

17 καὶ ἔσεσθε μισούμενοι ὑπὸ πάντων διὰ
   and ye will be *being* hated by all men because of

τὸ ὄνομά μου. 18 καὶ θρὶξ ἐκ τῆς
the name of me.   And a hair of the

κεφαλῆς ὑμῶν οὐ μὴ ἀπόληται· 19 ἐν τῇ
head   of you by no means will perish; in the

ὑπομονῇ ὑμῶν κτήσεσθε τὰς ψυχὰς ὑμῶν.
endurance of you ye will gain the souls of you.

20 Ὅταν δὲ ἴδητε κυκλουμένην ὑπὸ
   But when ye see ²being surrounded ³by

στρατοπέδων Ἰερουσαλήμ, τότε γνῶτε ὅτι
⁴camps   ¹Jerusalem,   then know ye that

ἤγγικεν ἡ ἐρήμωσις αὐτῆς. 21 τότε οἱ ἐν
has drawn near the desolation of it. Then the [ones] in

τῇ Ἰουδαίᾳ φευγέτωσαν εἰς τὰ ὄρη, καὶ
– Judæa   let them flee to the mountains, and

οἱ ἐν μέσῳ αὐτῆς ἐκχωρείτωσαν, καὶ
the [ones] in [the] midst of it let them depart out, and

not them that are in the countries enter thereinto.

22 For these be the days of vengeance, that all things which are written may be fulfilled.

23 But woe unto them that are with child, and to them that give suck, in those days! for there shall be great distress in the land, and wrath upon this people.

24 And they shall fall by the edge of the sword, and shall be led away captive into all nations: and Jerusalem shall be trodden down of the Gentiles, until the times of the Gentiles be fulfilled.

25 ¶ And there shall be signs in the sun, and in the moon, and in the stars; and upon the earth distress of nations, with perplexity; the sea and the waves roaring;

26 Men's hearts failing them for fear, and for looking after those things which are coming on the earth: for the powers of heaven shall be shaken.

27 And then shall they see the Son of man coming in a cloud with power and great glory.

28 And when these things begin to come to pass, then look up, and lift up your heads; for your redemption draweth nigh.

29 And he spake to them a parable; Behold the fig tree, and all the trees;

30 When they now shoot forth, ye see and

οἱ   ἐν   ταῖς   χώραις   μὴ   εἰσερχέσθωσαν   εἰς
the [ones] in   the   districts   let them not enter   into

αὐτήν,   22   ὅτι   ἡμέραι   ἐκδικήσεως   αὗταί
it,   because   days   of vengeance   these

εἰσιν   τοῦ   πλησθῆναι   πάντα   τὰ   γεγραμμένα.
are   -   to be fulfilled[d]   all the things having been written.

23 οὐαὶ   ταῖς   ἐν   γαστρὶ   ἐχούσαις   καὶ   ταῖς
Woe   to the   pregnant women†   and   to the

θηλαζούσαις   ἐν   ἐκείναις   ταῖς   ἡμέραις·
[ones] giving suck   in   those   -   days;

ἔσται   γὰρ   ἀνάγκη   μεγάλη   ἐπὶ   τῆς   γῆς
for there will be   distress   great   on   the   land

καὶ   ὀργὴ   τῷ   λαῷ   τούτῳ,   24   καὶ   πεσοῦνται
and   wrath   -   people   to this,   and   they will fall

στόματι   μαχαίρης   καὶ   αἰχμαλωτισθή-
by [the] mouth(edge) of [the] sword   and   will be led

σονται   εἰς   τὰ   ἔθνη   πάντα,   καὶ   Ἰερουσαλὴμ
captive   to   the   nations   all,   and   Jerusalem

ἔσται   πατουμένη   ὑπὸ   ἐθνῶν,   ἄχρι   οὗ
will be   *being* trodden down   by   nations,   until

πληρωθῶσιν   καιροὶ   ἐθνῶν.   25   Καὶ   ἔσονται
are accomplished [the] times of [the] nations.   And there will be

σημεῖα   ἐν   ἡλίῳ   καὶ   σελήνῃ   καὶ   ἄστροις,
signs   in   sun   and   moon   and   stars,

καὶ   ἐπὶ   τῆς   γῆς   συνοχὴ   ἐθνῶν   ἐν   ἀπορίᾳ
and   on   the   earth   anxiety   of nations   in   perplexity

ἤχους   θαλάσσης   καὶ   σάλου,   26   ἀποψυχόντων
of [the] sound   of [the] sea   and   surf,   fainting
     =while men faint

ἀνθρώπων   ἀπὸ   φόβου   καὶ   προσδοκίας   τῶν
men[a]   from   fear   and   expectation   of the

ἐπερχομένων   τῇ   οἰκουμένῃ·   αἱ   γὰρ   δυνάμεις
things coming on   the   inhabited earth;   for the   powers

τῶν   οὐρανῶν   σαλευθήσονται.   27   καὶ   τότε
of the   heavens   will be shaken.   And   then

ὄψονται   τὸν   υἱὸν   τοῦ   ἀνθρώπου   ἐρχόμενον
they will see   the   Son   -   of man   coming

ἐν   νεφέλῃ   μετὰ   δυνάμεως   καὶ   δόξης
in   a cloud   with   power   and   glory

πολλῆς.   28   ἀρχομένων   δὲ   τούτων   γίνεσθαι
much(great).   And beginning   these things[a]   to happen
     =when these things begin

ἀνακύψατε   καὶ   ἐπάρατε   τὰς   κεφαλὰς   ὑμῶν,
stand erect   and   lift up   the   heads   of you,

διότι   ἐγγίζει   ἡ   ἀπολύτρωσις   ὑμῶν.   29   Καὶ
because draws near   the   redemption   of you.   And

εἶπεν   παραβολὴν   αὐτοῖς·   ἴδετε   τὴν   συκῆν
he told   ²a parable   ¹them :   Ye see   the   fig-tree

καὶ   πάντα   τὰ   δένδρα·   30   ὅταν   προβάλωσιν
and   all   the   trees;   when   ²they burst into leaf

know of your own selves that summer is now nigh at hand.

31 So likewise ye, when ye see these things come to pass, know ye that the kingdom of God is nigh at hand.

32 Verily I say unto you, This generation shall not pass away, till all be fulfilled.

33 Heaven and earth shall pass away: but my words shall not pass away.

34 ¶ And take heed to yourselves, lest at any time your hearts be overcharged with surfeiting, and drunkenness, and cares of this life, and so that day come upon you unawares.

35 For as a snare shall it come on all them that dwell on the face of the whole earth.

36 Watch ye therefore, and pray always, that ye may be accounted worthy to escape all these things that shall come to pass, and to stand before the Son of man.

37 And in the day time he was teaching in the temple; and at night he went out, and abode in the mount that is called *the mount* of Olives.

38 And all the people came early in the morning to him in the temple, for to hear him.

ἤδη, βλέποντες ἀφ᾽ ἑαυτῶν γινώσκετε ὅτι
now, seeing from(of) yourselves ye know that

ἤδη ἐγγὺς τὸ θέρος ἐστίν· 31 οὕτως καὶ
now near the summer is; so also

ὑμεῖς, ὅταν ἴδητε ταῦτα γινόμενα,
ye, when ye see these things happening,

γινώσκετε ὅτι ἐγγύς ἐστιν ἡ βασιλεία
know that near is the kingdom

τοῦ θεοῦ. 32 ἀμὴν λέγω ὑμῖν ὅτι οὐ μὴ
- of God. Truly I tell you that by no means

παρέλθῃ ἡ γενεὰ αὕτη ἕως ἂν πάντα
will pass away - generation this until all things

γένηται. 33 ὁ οὐρανὸς καὶ ἡ γῆ παρ-
happens. The heaven and the earth will

ελεύσονται, οἱ δὲ λόγοι μου οὐ μὴ παρελεύ-
pass away, but the words of me by no means will pass

σονται. 34 Προσέχετε δὲ ἑαυτοῖς μήποτε
away. And take heed to yourselves lest

βαρηθῶσιν ὑμῶν αἱ καρδίαι ἐν κραιπάλῃ
become burdened of you the hearts with surfeiting

καὶ μέθῃ καὶ μερίμναις βιωτικαῖς, καὶ
and deep drinking and anxieties of life,† and

ἐπιστῇ ἐφ᾽ ὑμᾶς αἰφνίδιος ἡ ἡμέρα ἐκείνη
come on on you suddenly - day that

35 ὡς παγίς· ἐπεισελεύσεται γὰρ ἐπὶ πάντας
as a snare; for it will come in on on all

τοὺς καθημένους ἐπὶ πρόσωπον πάσης τῆς
the [ones] sitting on [the] face of all the

γῆς. 36 ἀγρυπνεῖτε δὲ ἐν παντὶ καιρῷ
earth. But be ye watchful at every time

δεόμενοι ἵνα κατισχύσητε ἐκφυγεῖν ταῦτα
begging that ye may be able to escape these things

πάντα τὰ μέλλοντα γίνεσθαι, καὶ σταθῆναι
all - being about to happen, and to stand

ἔμπροσθεν τοῦ υἱοῦ τοῦ ἀνθρώπου.
before the Son - of man.

37 Ἦν δὲ τὰς ἡμέρας ἐν τῷ ἱερῷ
Now he was [in] the days in the temple

διδάσκων, τὰς δὲ νύκτας ἐξερχόμενος
teaching, and [in] the nights going forth

ηὐλίζετο εἰς τὸ ὄρος τὸ καλούμενον
he lodged in the mountain - *being* called

ἐλαιών. 38 καὶ πᾶς ὁ λαὸς ὤρθριζεν
of olives. And all the people came in the morning

πρὸς αὐτὸν ἐν τῷ ἱερῷ ἀκούειν αὐτοῦ.
to him in the temple to hear him.

CHAPTER 22

NOW the feast of un-leavened bread drew nigh, which is called the Passover.

2 And the chief priests and scribes sought how they might kill him; for they feared the people.

3 ¶ Then entered Satan into Judas surnamed Iscariot, being of the number of the twelve.

4 And he went his way, and communed with the chief priests and captains, how he might betray him unto them.

5 And they were glad, and covenanted to give him money.

6 And he promised, and sought opportunity to betray him unto them in the absence of the multitude.

7 ¶ Then came the day of unleavened bread, when the passover must be killed.

8 And he sent Peter and John, saying, Go and prepare us the passover, that we may eat.

9 And they said unto him, Where wilt thou that we prepare?

10 And he said unto them, Behold, when ye are entered into the city, there shall a man meet you, bearing a pitcher of water; follow him into the house where he entereth in.

11 And ye shall say unto the goodman of the house, The Master saith unto thee, Where is the guestchamber, where I

22 Ἤγγιζεν δὲ ἡ ἑορτὴ τῶν ἀζύμων ἡ
Now drew near the feast of unleavened bread –

λεγομένη πάσχα. 2 καὶ ἐζήτουν οἱ ἀρχιερεῖς
being called Passover. And ⁶sought ¹the ²chief priests

καὶ οἱ γραμματεῖς τὸ πῶς ἀνέλωσιν
³and ⁴the ⁵scribes – how they might destroy

αὐτόν· ἐφοβοῦντο γὰρ τὸν λαόν. 3 Εἰσῆλθεν δὲ
him; for they feared the people. And entered

σατανᾶς εἰς Ἰούδαν τὸν καλούμενον
Satan into Judas – being called

Ἰσκαριώτην, ὄντα ἐκ τοῦ ἀριθμοῦ τῶν
Iscariot, being of the number of the

δώδεκα· 4 καὶ ἀπελθὼν συνελάλησεν τοῖς
twelve; and going he conversed with the

ἀρχιερεῦσιν καὶ στρατηγοῖς τὸ πῶς αὐτοῖς
chief priests and captains – how to them

παραδῷ αὐτόν. 5 καὶ ἐχάρησαν, καὶ
he might betray him. And they rejoiced, and

συνέθεντο αὐτῷ ἀργύριον δοῦναι. 6 καὶ
they agreed ²him ³money ¹to give. And

ἐξωμολόγησεν, καὶ ἐζήτει εὐκαιρίαν τοῦ
he fully consented, and sought opportunity –

παραδοῦναι αὐτὸν ἄτερ ὄχλου αὐτοῖς.
to betray[d] him apart from a crowd to them.

7 Ἦλθεν δὲ ἡ ἡμέρα τῶν ἀζύμων, ἡ
And came the day of unleavened bread, on which

ἔδει θύεσθαι τὸ πάσχα· 8 καὶ ἀπέστειλεν
it behoved to kill the passover [lamb]; and he sent

Πέτρον καὶ Ἰωάννην εἰπών· πορευθέντες
Peter and John saying : Going

ἑτοιμάσατε ἡμῖν τὸ πάσχα, ἵνα φάγωμεν. 9 οἱ
prepare ye for us the passover, that we may eat. they

δὲ εἶπαν αὐτῷ· ποῦ θέλεις ἑτοιμάσωμεν;
And said to him : Where wishest thou [that] we may prepare?

10 ὁ δὲ εἶπεν αὐτοῖς· ἰδοὺ εἰσελθόντων
And he told them : Behold[,] entering
                              =as ye enter

ὑμῶν εἰς τὴν πόλιν συναντήσει ὑμῖν
you[a] into the city will meet you

ἄνθρωπος κεράμιον ὕδατος βαστάζων·
a man a pitcher of water bearing;

ἀκολουθήσατε αὐτῷ εἰς τὴν οἰκίαν εἰς ἣν
follow him into the house into which

εἰσπορεύεται· 11 καὶ ἐρεῖτε τῷ οἰκοδεσπότῃ
he enters; and ye will say to the *house*-master

τῆς οἰκίας· λέγει σοι ὁ διδάσκαλος·
of the house : Says to thee the teacher :

ποῦ ἐστιν τὸ κατάλυμα ὅπου τὸ πάσχα
Where is the guest room where the passover

shall eat the passover with my disciples?

12 And he shall shew you a large upper room furnished: there make ready.

13 And they went, and found as he had said unto them: and they made ready the passover.

14 And when the hour was come, he sat down, and the twelve apostles with him.

15 And he said unto them, With desire I have desired to eat this passover with you before I suffer:

16 For I say unto you, I will not any more eat thereof, until it be fulfilled in the kingdom of God.

17 And he took the cup, and gave thanks, and said, Take this, and divide *it* among yourselves:

18 For I say unto you, I will not drink of the fruit of the vine, until the kingdom of God shall come.

19 ¶ And he took bread, and gave thanks, and brake *it*, and gave unto them, saying, This is my body which is given for you: this do in remembrance of me.

20 Likewise also the cup after supper, saying, This cup *is* the new testament in my blood,

---

μετὰ τῶν μαθητῶν μου φάγω; 12 κἀκεῖνος
with the disciples of me I may eat? And that man

ὑμῖν δείξει ἀνάγαιον μέγα ἐστρωμένον·[*]
you will show upper room a large *having been* spread;

ἐκεῖ ἑτοιμάσατε. 13 ἀπελθόντες δὲ εὗρον
there prepare ye. And going they found

καθὼς εἰρήκει αὐτοῖς, καὶ ἡτοίμασαν τὸ
as he had told them, and they prepared the

πάσχα. 14 Καὶ ὅτε ἐγένετο ἡ ὥρα,
passover. And when came the hour,

ἀνέπεσεν, καὶ οἱ ἀπόστολοι σὺν αὐτῷ.
he reclined, and the apostles with him.

15 καὶ εἶπεν πρὸς αὐτούς· ἐπιθυμίᾳ
And he said to them: With desire

ἐπεθύμησα τοῦτο τὸ πάσχα φαγεῖν μεθ'
I desired this – passover to eat with

ὑμῶν πρὸ τοῦ με παθεῖν· 16 λέγω γὰρ
you before the me to suffer;[b] for I tell
=I suffer;

ὑμῖν ὅτι οὐκέτι οὐ μὴ φάγω αὐτὸ
you that no more by no(any) means I eat it

ἕως ὅτου πληρωθῇ ἐν τῇ βασιλείᾳ τοῦ θεοῦ.
until it is fulfilled in the kingdom – of God.

17 καὶ δεξάμενος ποτήριον εὐχαριστήσας
And taking a cup having given thanks

εἶπεν· λάβετε τοῦτο καὶ διαμερίσατε εἰς
he said: Take this and divide among

ἑαυτούς· 18 λέγω γὰρ ὑμῖν, οὐ μὴ πίω
yourselves; for I tell you, by no means I drink

ἀπὸ τοῦ νῦν ἀπὸ τοῦ γενήματος τῆς
from – now [on] from the produce of the

ἀμπέλου ἕως οὗ ἡ βασιλεία τοῦ θεοῦ
vine until the kingdom – of God

ἔλθῃ. 19 καὶ λαβὼν ἄρτον εὐχαριστήσας
comes. And taking a loaf having given thanks

ἔκλασεν καὶ ἔδωκεν αὐτοῖς λέγων· τοῦτό
he broke and gave to them saying: This

ἐστιν τὸ σῶμά μου [τὸ ὑπὲρ ὑμῶν
is the body of me – for you

διδόμενον· τοῦτο ποιεῖτε εἰς τὴν ἐμὴν
being given; this do ye for – my

ἀνάμνησιν. 20 καὶ τὸ ποτήριον ὡσαύτως
memorial. And the cup similarly

μετὰ τὸ δειπνῆσαι, λέγων· τοῦτο τὸ
after the to sup, saying: This –

ποτήριον ἡ καινὴ διαθήκη ἐν τῷ αἵματι
cup [is] the new covenant in the blood

[*] That is, with carpets, and the dining couches supplied with cushions.

which is shed for you.

21 ¶ But, behold, the hand of him that betrayeth me is with me on the table.

22 And truly the Son of man goeth, as it was determined; but woe unto that man by whom he is betrayed!

23 And they began to enquire among themselves, which of them it was that should do this thing.

24 ¶ And there was also a strife among them, which of them should be accounted the greatest.

25 And he said unto them, The kings of the Gentiles exercise lordship over them; and they that exercise authority upon them are called benefactors.

26 But ye *shall* not *be* so: but he that is greatest among you, let him be as the younger; and he that is chief, as he that doth serve.

27 For whether *is* greater, he that sitteth at meat, or he that serveth? *is* not he that sitteth at meat? but I am among you as he that serveth.

28 Ye are they which have continued with me in my temptations.

29 And I appoint unto you a kingdom, as my Father hath appointed unto me;

30 That ye may eat and drink at my table in my kingdom, and sit on

μου, τὸ ὑπὲρ ὑμῶν ἐκχυννόμενον.] 21 πλὴν
of me, - for you being shed.] However

ἰδοὺ ἡ χεὶρ τοῦ παραδιδόντος με μετ'
behold[,] the hand of the [one] betraying me with

ἐμοῦ ἐπὶ τῆς τραπέζης. 22 ὅτι ὁ υἱὸς μὲν
me on the table. Because [2]the [3]Son [1]indeed

τοῦ ἀνθρώπου κατὰ τὸ ὡρισμένον
- of man according to the [thing] having been
determined

πορεύεται, πλὴν οὐαὶ τῷ ἀνθρώπῳ ἐκείνῳ
goes, nevertheless woe - man to that

δι' οὗ παραδίδοται. 23 καὶ αὐτοὶ ἤρξαντο
through whom he is betrayed. And they began

συζητεῖν πρὸς ἑαυτοὺς τὸ τίς ἄρα εἴη
to debate with themselves - who then it might be

ἐξ αὐτῶν ὁ τοῦτο μέλλων πράσσειν.
of them the [one] [3]this [1]being about [2]to do.

24 Ἐγένετο δὲ καὶ φιλονεικία ἐν αὐτοῖς,
And there was also a rivalry among them,

τὸ τίς αὐτῶν δοκεῖ εἶναι μείζων. 25 ὁ δὲ
- who of them seems to be greater. So he

εἶπεν αὐτοῖς· οἱ βασιλεῖς τῶν ἐθνῶν
said to them : The kings of the nations

κυριεύουσιν αὐτῶν, καὶ οἱ ἐξουσιάζοντες
lord it over them, and the [ones] having authority over

αὐτῶν εὐεργέται καλοῦνται. 26 ὑμεῖς δὲ
them benefactors are called. But ye

οὐχ οὕτως, ἀλλ' ὁ μείζων ἐν ὑμῖν
not so, but the greater among you

γινέσθω ὡς ὁ νεώτερος, καὶ ὁ ἡγούμενος
let him become as the younger, and the [one] governing

ὡς ὁ διακονῶν. 27 τίς γὰρ μείζων, ὁ
as the [one] serving. For who [is] greater, the

ἀνακείμενος ἢ ὁ διακονῶν; οὐχὶ ὁ
[one] reclining or the [one] serving? not the

ἀνακείμενος; ἐγὼ δὲ ἐν μέσῳ ὑμῶν εἰμι
[one] reclining? But I in [the] midst of you am

ὡς ὁ διακονῶν. 28 ὑμεῖς δέ ἐστε οἱ
as the [one] serving. But ye are the [ones]

διαμεμενηκότες μετ' ἐμοῦ ἐν τοῖς πειρα-
having remained throughout with me in the tempta-

σμοῖς μου· 29 κἀγὼ διατίθεμαι ὑμῖν καθὼς
tions of me; and I appoint to you as

διέθετό μοι ὁ πατήρ μου βασιλείαν,
appointed to me the Father of me a kingdom,

30 ἵνα ἔσθητε καὶ πίνητε ἐπὶ τῆς ⁻ραπέζης
that ye may eat and drink at the table

μου ἐν τῇ βασιλείᾳ μου, καὶ καθήσεσθε
of me in the kingdom of me, and ye will sit

thrones judging the twelve tribes of Israel.

31 ¶ And the Lord said, Simon, Simon, behold, Satan hath desired *to have* you, that he may sift *you* as wheat:

32 But I have prayed for thee, that thy faith fail not: and when thou art converted, strengthen thy brethren.

33 And he said unto him, Lord, I am ready to go with thee, both into prison, and to death.

34 And he said, I tell thee, Peter, the cock shall not crow this day, before that thou shalt thrice deny that thou knowest me.

35 ¶ And he said unto them, When I sent you without purse, and scrip, and shoes, lacked ye any thing? And they said, Nothing.

36 Then said he unto them, But now, he that hath a purse, let him take *it*, and likewise *his* scrip: and he that hath no sword, let him sell his garment, and buy one.

37 For I say unto you, that this that is written must yet be accomplished in me, And he was reckoned among the transgressors: for the things concerning me have an end.

38 And they said, Lord, behold, here *are* two swords. And he said unto them, It is enough.

39 ¶ And he came out, and went, as he was wont,

ἐπὶ θρόνων τὰς δώδεκα φυλὰς κρίνοντες
on thrones ²the ²twelve ⁴tribes ¹judging

τοῦ Ἰσραήλ. 31 Σίμων Σίμων, ἰδοὺ ὁ
– of Israel. Simon[,] Simon, behold[,] –

σατανᾶς ἐξῃτήσατο ὑμᾶς τοῦ σινιάσαι ὡς
Satan begged earnestly for you – to sift[d] as

τὸν σῖτον· 32 ἐγὼ δὲ ἐδεήθην περὶ σοῦ
the wheat; but I requested concerning thee

ἵνα μὴ ἐκλίπῃ ἡ πίστις σου· καὶ σύ
that might not fail the faith of thee; and thou

ποτε ἐπιστρέψας στήρισον τοὺς ἀδελφούς
when having turned support the brothers

σου. 33 ὁ δὲ εἶπεν αὐτῷ· κύριε, μετὰ
of thee. And he said to him: Lord, with

σοῦ ἕτοιμός εἰμι καὶ εἰς φυλακὴν καὶ εἰς
thee prepared I am both to prison and to

θάνατον πορεύεσθαι. 34 ὁ δὲ εἶπεν· λέγω
death to go. But he said: I tell

σοι, Πέτρε, οὐ φωνήσει σήμερον ἀλέκτωρ
thee, Peter, will not sound to-day a cock

ἕως τρίς με ἀπαρνήσῃ μὴ εἰδέναι. 35 Καὶ
until thrice me thou wilt deny not to know. And

εἶπεν αὐτοῖς· ὅτε ἀπέστειλα ὑμᾶς ἄτερ
he said to them: When I sent you without

βαλλαντίου καὶ πήρας καὶ ὑποδημάτων, μή
a purse and a wallet and sandals, *not*

τινος ὑστερήσατε; οἱ δὲ εἶπαν· οὐθενός.
of anything were ye short? And they said: Of nothing.

36 εἶπεν δὲ αὐτοῖς· ἀλλὰ νῦν ὁ ἔχων
And he said to them: But now the [one] having

βαλλάντιον ἀράτω, ὁμοίως καὶ πήραν, καὶ
a purse let him take [it], likewise also a wallet, and

ὁ μὴ ἔχων πωλησάτω τὸ ἱμάτιον αὐτοῦ
the [one] not having let him sell the garment of him

καὶ ἀγορασάτω μάχαιραν. 37 λέγω γὰρ
and let him buy a sword. For I tell

ὑμῖν ὅτι τοῦτο τὸ γεγραμμένον δεῖ
you that this – having been written it behoves

τελεσθῆναι ἐν ἐμοί, τό· καὶ μετὰ ἀνόμων
to be finished in me, – And with lawless men

ἐλογίσθη· καὶ γὰρ τὸ περὶ ἐμοῦ τέλος
he was reckoned; for indeed the thing concerning me an end

ἔχει. 38 οἱ δὲ εἶπαν· κύριε, ἰδοὺ μάχαιραι
has. And they said: Lord, behold[,] swords

ὧδε δύο. ὁ δὲ εἶπεν αὐτοῖς· ἱκανόν ἐστιν.
here two. And he said to them: Enough it is.

39 Καὶ ἐξελθὼν ἐπορεύθη κατὰ τὸ ἔθος
And going forth he went according to the(his) habit

to the mount of Olives; and his disciples also followed him.

40 And when he was at the place, he said unto them, Pray that ye enter not into temptation.

41 And he was withdrawn from them about a stone's cast, and kneeled down, and prayed,

42 Saying, Father, if thou be willing, remove this cup from me: nevertheless not my will, but thine, be done.

43 And there appeared an angel unto him from heaven, strengthening him.

44 And being in an agony he prayed more earnestly: and his sweat was as it were great drops of blood falling down to the ground.

45 And when he rose up from prayer, and was come to his disciples, he found them sleeping for sorrow,

46 And said unto them, Why sleep ye? rise and pray, lest ye enter into temptation.

47 ¶ And while he yet spake, behold a multitude, and he that was called Judas, one of the twelve, went before them, and drew near unto Jesus to kiss him.

48 But Jesus said unto him, Judas, betrayest thou the Son of man with a kiss?

49 When they which

εἰς τὸ ὄρος τῶν ἐλαιῶν· ἠκολούθησαν δὲ
to the mountain of the olives; and ⁴followed

αὐτῷ καὶ οἱ μαθηταί. **40** γενόμενος δὲ
³him ²also ¹the ⁵disciples. And coming

ἐπὶ τοῦ τόπου εἶπεν αὐτοῖς· προσεύχεσθε
upon the place he said to them: Pray ye

μὴ εἰσελθεῖν εἰς πειρασμόν. **41** καὶ αὐτὸς
not to enter into temptation. And he

ἀπεσπάσθη ἀπ' αὐτῶν ὡσεὶ λίθου βολήν,
was withdrawn from them about of a stone a throw,

καὶ θεὶς τὰ γόνατα προσηύχετο **42** λέγων·
and placing the knees he prayed saying:

πάτερ, εἰ βούλει παρένεγκε τοῦτο τὸ
Father, if thou wilt take away this —

ποτήριον ἀπ' ἐμοῦ· πλὴν μὴ τὸ θέλημά
cup from me; nevertheless not the will

μου ἀλλὰ τὸ σὸν γινέσθω. **43** [ὤφθη δὲ
of me but — thine let be. And appeared

αὐτῷ ἄγγελος ἀπ' οὐρανοῦ ἐνισχύων αὐτόν.
to him an angel from heaven strengthening him.

44 καὶ γενόμενος ἐν ἀγωνίᾳ ἐκτενέστερον
And becoming in an agony more earnestly

προσηύχετο· καὶ ἐγένετο ὁ ἱδρὼς αὐτοῦ
he prayed; and became the sweat of him

ὡσεὶ θρόμβοι αἵματος καταβαίνοντες ἐπὶ
as drops of blood falling down onto

τὴν γῆν.] **45** καὶ ἀναστὰς ἀπὸ τῆς
the earth. And rising up from the

προσευχῆς, ἐλθὼν πρὸς τοὺς μαθητὰς
prayer, coming to the disciples

εὗρεν κοιμωμένους αὐτοὺς ἀπὸ τῆς λύπης,
he found ²sleeping ¹them from the grief,

46 καὶ εἶπεν αὐτοῖς· τί καθεύδετε;
and said to them: Why sleep ye?

ἀναστάντες προσεύχεσθε, ἵνα μὴ εἰσέλθητε
rising up pray ye, lest ye enter

εἰς πειρασμόν. **47** Ἔτι αὐτοῦ λαλοῦντος
into temptation. Yet him speaking ᵃ
     = While he was yet speaking

ἰδοὺ ὄχλος, καὶ ὁ λεγόμενος Ἰούδας εἷς
behold[,] a crowd, and the [one] being named Judas one

τῶν δώδεκα προήρχετο αὐτούς, καὶ ἤγγισεν
of the twelve came before them, and drew near

τῷ Ἰησοῦ φιλῆσαι αὐτόν. **48** Ἰησοῦς δὲ
— to Jesus to kiss him. But Jesus

εἶπεν αὐτῷ· Ἰούδα, φιλήματι τὸν υἱὸν
said to him: Judas, with a kiss the Son

τοῦ ἀνθρώπου παραδίδως; **49** ἰδόντες δὲ
— of man betrayest thou? And ⁴seeing

were about him saw what
would follow, they said
unto him, Lord, shall we
smite with the sword?

50 ¶ And one of them
smote the servant of the
high priest, and cut off his
right ear.

51 And Jesus answered
and said, Suffer ye thus
far. And he touched his
ear, and healed him.

52 Then Jesus said unto
the chief priests, and
captains of the temple, and
the elders, which were
come to him, Be ye come
out, as against a thief, with
swords and staves?

53 When I was daily
with you in the temple,
ye stretched forth no
hands against me: but
this is your hour, and the
power of darkness.

54 ¶ Then took they
him, and led *him*, and
brought him into the high
priest's house. And Peter
followed afar off.

55 And when they had
kindled a fire in the midst
of the hall, and were set
down together, Peter sat
down among them.

56 But a certain maid
beheld him as he sat by
the fire, and earnestly
looked upon him, and
said, This man was also
with him.

57 And he denied him,
saying, Woman, I know
him not.

οἱ   περὶ αὐτὸν   τὸ   ἐσόμενον εἶπαν· κύριε,
¹the [ones] ²round ³him the thing going to be   said : Lord,

εἰ πατάξομεν ἐν μαχαίρῃ; 50 καὶ ἐπάταξεν
if we shall strike with a sword?   And   ⁴struck

εἷς τις   ἐξ   αὐτῶν τοῦ ἀρχιερέως   τὸν
¹a certain one ⁵of ³them ⁶of the ⁷high priest   ⁸the

δοῦλον καὶ   ἀφεῖλεν τὸ οὖς αὐτοῦ τὸ
⁹slave   and   cut off   ¹the ²ear ⁴of him   –

δεξιόν. 51 ἀποκριθεὶς δὲ ὁ Ἰησοῦς εἶπεν·
³right.   And answering   –   Jesus   said :

ἐᾶτε   ἕως τούτου· καὶ ἁψάμενος τοῦ
Permit ye until this;   and   touching   the

ὠτίου ἰάσατο αὐτόν. 52 Εἶπεν δὲ Ἰησοῦς
ear   he cured   him.   And said   Jesus

πρὸς τοὺς παραγενομένους ἐπ' αὐτὸν
to   ¹the   ⁸coming   ¹⁰upon   ¹¹him

ἀρχιερεῖς καὶ στρατηγοὺς τοῦ ἱεροῦ καὶ
²chief priests ³and ⁴captains   ⁵of the ⁶temple ⁷and

πρεσβυτέρους· ὡς ἐπὶ λῃστὴν ἐξήλθατε
⁸elders :   As against a robber   came ye out

μετὰ μαχαιρῶν καὶ ξύλων; 53 καθ' ἡμέραν
with   swords   and   clubs?   daily

ὄντος μου μεθ' ὑμῶν ἐν τῷ ἱερῷ οὐκ
being   me ᵃ with   you   in the temple not
= while I was

ἐξετείνατε τὰς χεῖρας ἐπ' ἐμέ· ἀλλ' αὕτη
ye stretched out the(your) hands against   me;   but   this

ἐστὶν ὑμῶν ἡ ὥρα καὶ ἡ ἐξουσία τοῦ
is   of you the hour   and the authority of the

σκότους.
darkness.

54 Συλλαβόντες δὲ αὐτὸν ἤγαγον καὶ
And having arrested   him   they led   and

εἰσήγαγον εἰς τὴν οἰκίαν τοῦ ἀρχιερέως·
brought in into   the   house   of the   high priest;

ὁ δὲ Πέτρος ἠκολούθει μακρόθεν. 55 περι-
– and Peter   followed   afar off.   light-

αψάντων δὲ πῦρ ἐν μέσῳ τῆς αὐλῆς καὶ
ing   And a fire in [the] centre of the   court   and
= when they had lit a fire . . . and had sat down together

συγκαθισάντων ἐκάθητο ὁ Πέτρος μέσος
sitting down together ᵃ   sat   –   Peter   among

αὐτῶν. 56 ἰδοῦσα δὲ αὐτὸν παιδίσκη τις
them.   And ²seeing   ³him ¹a certain maidservant

καθήμενον πρὸς τὸ φῶς καὶ ἀτενίσασα
sitting   near   the light   and   gazing at

αὐτῷ εἶπεν· καὶ οὗτος σὺν αὐτῷ ἦν. 57 ὁ
him   said : And this man with   him   was.   he

δὲ ἠρνήσατο λέγων· οὐκ οἶδα αὐτόν,
But   denied   saying :   I know not   him,

58 And after a little while another saw him, and said, Thou art also of them. And Peter said, Man, I am not.

59 And about the space of one hour after another confidently affirmed, saying, Of a truth this *fellow* also was with him: for he is a Galilæan.

60 And Peter said, Man, I know not what thou sayest. And immediately, while he yet spake, the cock crew.

61 And the Lord turned, and looked upon Peter. And Peter remembered the word of the Lord, how he had said unto him, Before the cock crow, thou shalt deny me thrice.

62 And Peter went out, and wept bitterly.

63 ¶ And the men that held Jesus mocked him, and smote *him*.

64 And when they had blindfolded him, they struck him on the face, and asked him, saying, Prophesy, who is it that smote thee?

65 And many other things blasphemously spake they against him.

66 ¶ And as soon as it was day, the elders of the people and the chief priests and the scribes came together, and led him into their council, saying,

67 Art thou the Christ?

γύναι.   **58** καὶ   μετὰ   βραχὺ   ἕτερος   ἰδὼν
woman.   And   after   a short while   another   seeing

αὐτὸν   ἔφη·   καὶ   σὺ   ἐξ   αὐτῶν   εἶ.   ὁ
him   said: And   thou   of   them   art.   –

δὲ   Πέτρος   ἔφη·   ἄνθρωπε,   οὐκ   εἰμί.
But   Peter   said: Man,   I am not.

59 καὶ   διαστάσης   ὡσεὶ   ὥρας   μιᾶς   ἄλλος
And   intervening   about   hour   one[a]   [a]other man
=when about an hour had intervened

τις   διϊσχυρίζετο   λέγων·   ἐπ'   ἀληθείας   καὶ
[a] cer-   emphatically   saying: Of a truth   also
tain   asserted

οὗτος   μετ'   αὐτοῦ   ἦν,   καὶ   γὰρ   Γαλιλαῖός
this man   with   him   was,   for indeed   a Galilæan

ἐστιν.   **60** εἶπεν   δὲ   ὁ   Πέτρος·   ἄνθρωπε,
he is.   But said   –   Peter: Man,

οὐκ   οἶδα   ὃ   λέγεις.   καὶ   παραχρῆμα   ἔτι
I know not   what thou sayest.   And   at once   yet

λαλοῦντος   αὐτοῦ   ἐφώνησεν   ἀλέκτωρ.   **61** καὶ
speaking   him[a]   sounded   a cock.   And
=while he was yet speaking

στραφεὶς   ὁ   κύριος   ἐνέβλεψεν   τῷ   Πέτρῳ,
turning   the   Lord   looked at   –   Peter,

καὶ   ὑπεμνήσθη   ὁ   Πέτρος   τοῦ   λόγου   τοῦ
and   remembered   –   Peter   the   word   of the

κυρίου,   ὡς   εἶπεν   αὐτῷ   ὅτι   πρὶν   ἀλέκτορα
Lord,   as   he told   him   that   before   a cock

φωνῆσαι   σήμερον   ἀπαρνήσῃ   με   τρίς.   **62** καὶ
to sound[b]   to-day   thou wilt deny   me   thrice.   And

ἐξελθὼν   ἔξω   ἔκλαυσεν   πικρῶς.   **63** Καὶ   οἱ
going out   outside   he wept   bitterly.   And the

ἄνδρες   οἱ   συνέχοντες   αὐτὸν   ἐνέπαιζον   αὐτῷ
men   –   having in charge   him*   mocked   him

δέροντες,   **64** καὶ   περικαλύψαντες   αὐτὸν
beating,   and   covering over   him

ἐπηρώτων   λέγοντες·   προφήτευσον,   τίς   ἐστιν
questioned   saying: Prophesy,   who   is

ὁ   παίσας   σε;   **65** καὶ   ἕτερα   πολλὰ
the [one]   playing   thee?   And   other things   many

βλασφημοῦντες   ἔλεγον   εἰς   αὐτόν.
blaspheming   they said   against   him.

66 Καὶ   ὡς   ἐγένετο   ἡμέρα,   συνήχθη   τὸ
And   when   came   day,   was assembled the

πρεσβυτέριον   τοῦ   λαοῦ,   ἀρχιερεῖς   τε   καὶ
body of elders   of the   people,   both chief priests   and

γραμματεῖς,   καὶ   ἀπήγαγον   αὐτὸν   εἰς   τὸ
scribes,   and   led away   him   to   the

συνέδριον   αὐτῶν,   **67** λέγοντες·   εἰ   σὺ   εἶ   ὁ
council   of them,   saying: If   thou   art the

* That is, Jesus (as some texts have it).

tell us. And he said unto them, If I tell you, ye will not believe:

68 And if I also ask *you*, ye will not answer me, nor let *me* go.

69 Hereafter shall the Son of man sit on the right hand of the power of God.

70 Then said they all, Art thou then the Son of God? And he said unto them, Ye say that I am.

71 And they said, What need we any further witness? for we ourselves have heard of his own mouth.

χριστός, εἰπὸν ἡμῖν. εἶπεν δὲ αὐτοῖς·
Christ, tell us. And he said to them:

ἐὰν ὑμῖν εἴπω, οὐ μὴ πιστεύσητε· 68 ἐὰν
If you I tell, by no means will ye believe; ²if

δὲ ἐρωτήσω, οὐ μὴ ἀποκριθῆτε. 69 ἀπὸ
¹and I question, by no means will ye answer. ²from

τοῦ νῦν δὲ ἔσται ὁ υἱὸς τοῦ ἀνθρώπου
- ²now ¹But ⁷will be ⁴the ⁵Son - ⁶of man

καθήμενος ἐκ δεξιῶν τῆς δυνάμεως τοῦ
⁸sitting at [the] right of the power -

θεοῦ. 70 εἶπαν δὲ πάντες· σὺ οὖν εἶ ὁ
of God. And they said all: Thou therefore art the

υἱὸς τοῦ θεοῦ; ὁ δὲ πρὸς αὐτοὺς ἔφη·
Son - of God? And he to them said:

ὑμεῖς λέγετε ὅτι ἐγώ εἰμι. 71 οἱ δὲ
Ye say that I am. And they

εἶπαν· τί ἔτι ἔχομεν μαρτυρίας χρείαν;
said: Why yet have we of witness need?

αὐτοὶ γὰρ ἠκούσαμεν ἀπὸ τοῦ στόματος
for [our]selves we heard from the mouth

αὐτοῦ.
of him.

CHAPTER 23

AND the whole multitude of them arose, and led him unto Pilate.

2 And they began to accuse him, saying, We found this *fellow* perverting the nation, and forbidding to give tribute to Cæsar, saying that he himself is Christ a King.

3 And Pilate asked him, saying, Art thou the King of the Jews? And he answered him and said, Thou sayest *it*.

4 Then said Pilate to the chief priests and *to* the people, I find no fault in this man.

23 Καὶ ἀναστὰν ἅπαν τὸ πλῆθος αὐτῶν
And rising up all the multitude of them

ἤγαγον αὐτὸν ἐπὶ τὸν Πιλᾶτον. 2 ἤρξαντο
led him before - Pilate. they began

δὲ κατηγορεῖν αὐτοῦ λέγοντες· τοῦτον
And to accuse him saying: This man

εὕραμεν διαστρέφοντα τὸ ἔθνος ἡμῶν καὶ
we found perverting the nation of us and

κωλύοντα φόρους Καίσαρι διδόναι, καὶ
forbidding tribute to Cæsar to give, and

λέγοντα ἑαυτὸν χριστὸν βασιλέα εἶναι.
saying himself Christ a king to be.

3 ὁ δὲ Πιλᾶτος ἠρώτησεν αὐτὸν λέγων·
- And Pilate questioned him saying:

σὺ εἶ ὁ βασιλεὺς τῶν Ἰουδαίων; ὁ δὲ
Thou art the king of the Jews? And he

ἀποκριθεὶς αὐτῷ ἔφη· σὺ λέγεις. 4 ὁ δὲ
answering him said: Thou sayest. - And

Πιλᾶτος εἶπεν πρὸς τοὺς ἀρχιερεῖς καὶ
Pilate said to the chief priests and

τοὺς ὄχλους· οὐδὲν εὑρίσκω αἴτιον ἐν
the crowds: ³No ¹I find ²crime in

5 And they were the more fierce, saying, He stirreth up the people, teaching throughout all Jewry, beginning from Galilee to this place.

6 When Pilate heard of Galilee, he asked whether the man were a Galilæan.

7 And as soon as he knew that he belonged unto Herod's jurisdiction, he sent him to Herod, who himself also was at Jerusalem at that time.

8 ¶ And when Herod saw Jesus, he was exceeding glad: for he was desirous to see him of a long *season*, because he had heard many things of him; and he hoped to have seen some miracle done by him.

9 Then he questioned with him in many words; but he answered him nothing.

10 And the chief priests and scribes stood and vehemently accused him.

11 And Herod with his men of war set him at nought, and mocked *him*, and arrayed him in a gorgeous robe, and sent him again to Pilate.

12 ¶ And the same day Pilate and Herod were made friends together: for before they were at enmity between themselves.

13 ¶ And Pilate, when

τῷ ἀνθρώπῳ τούτῳ. 5 οἱ δὲ ἐπίσχυον λέγοντες
- man this. But they insisted saying[,]

ὅτι ἀνασείει τὸν λαόν, διδάσκων καθ᾽
- He excites the people, teaching throughout

ὅλης τῆς Ἰουδαίας, καὶ ἀρξάμενος ἀπὸ
all - Judæa, even beginning from

τῆς Γαλιλαίας ἕως ὧδε. 6 Πιλᾶτος δὲ
- Galilee to here. And Pilate

ἀκούσας ἐπηρώτησεν εἰ ὁ ἄνθρωπος
hearing questioned if the man

Γαλιλαῖός ἐστιν, 7 καὶ ἐπιγνοὺς ὅτι ἐκ
a Galilæan is(was), and perceiving that of

τῆς ἐξουσίας Ἡρώδου ἐστίν, ἀνέπεμψεν
the authority of Herod he is(was), he sent up

αὐτὸν πρὸς Ἡρώδην, ὄντα καὶ αὐτὸν ἐν
him to Herod, being also him(he) in

Ἱεροσολύμοις ἐν ταύταις ταῖς ἡμέραις.
Jerusalem in these - days.

8 ὁ δὲ Ἡρώδης ἰδὼν τὸν Ἰησοῦν ἐχάρη
- And Herod seeing - Jesus rejoiced

λίαν· ἦν γὰρ ἐξ ἱκανῶν χρόνων θέλων
greatly; for he was of a long times wishing

ἰδεῖν αὐτὸν διὰ τὸ ἀκούειν περὶ αὐτοῦ,
to see him because of the to hear[b] about him,
=because he had heard

καὶ ἤλπιζέν τι σημεῖον ἰδεῖν ὑπ᾽ αὐτοῦ
and he hoped some sign to see by him

γινόμενον. 9 ἐπηρώτα δὲ αὐτὸν ἐν λόγοις
brought about. And he questioned him in words

ἱκανοῖς· αὐτὸς δὲ οὐδὲν ἀπεκρίνατο αὐτῷ.
many; but he nothing answered him.

10 εἱστήκεισαν δὲ οἱ ἀρχιερεῖς καὶ οἱ
And stood the chief priests and the

γραμματεῖς εὐτόνως κατηγοροῦντες αὐτοῦ.
scribes vehemently accusing him.

11 ἐξουθενήσας δὲ αὐτὸν ὁ Ἡρώδης σὺν
And despising him - Herod with

τοῖς στρατεύμασιν αὐτοῦ καὶ ἐμπαίξας,
the soldiery of him and mocking,

περιβαλὼν ἐσθῆτα λαμπρὰν ἀνέπεμψεν αὐτὸν
throwing round clothing splendid sent back him

τῷ Πιλάτῳ. 12 ἐγένοντο δὲ φίλοι ὅ τε
- to Pilate. And became friends - both

Ἡρώδης καὶ ὁ Πιλᾶτος ἐν αὐτῇ τῇ
Herod and - Pilate on [2]same [1]the

ἡμέρᾳ μετ᾽ ἀλλήλων· προϋπῆρχον γὰρ ἐν
day with each other; for they were previously in

ἔχθρᾳ ὄντες πρὸς αὐτούς. 13 Πιλᾶτος δὲ
enmity being with themselves. And Pilate

he had called together the chief priests and the rulers and the people,

14 Said unto them, Ye have brought this man unto me, as one that perverteth the people: and, behold, I, having examined *him* before you, have found no fault in this man touching those things whereof ye accuse him:

15 No, nor yet Herod: for I sent you to him; and, lo, nothing worthy of death is done unto him.

16 I will therefore chastise him, and release *him.*

17 (For of necessity he must release one unto them at the feast.)

18 And they cried out all at once, saying, Away with this *man,* and release unto us Barabbas:

19 (Who for a certain sedition made in the city, and for murder, was cast into prison.)

20 Pilate therefore, willing to release Jesus, spake again to them.

21 But they cried, saying, Crucify *him,* crucify him.

22 And he said unto them the third time, Why, what evil hath he done? I have found no cause of death in him: I will therefore chastise him, and let *him* go.

23 And they were instant with loud voices, requiring that he might be crucified. And the voices

---

συγκαλεσάμενος τοὺς ἀρχιερεῖς καὶ τοὺς
calling together   the   chief priests and   the

ἄρχοντας καὶ τὸν λαὸν 14 εἶπεν πρὸς
leaders   and the people   said   to

αὐτούς· προσηνέγκατέ μοι τὸν ἄνθρωπον
them :   Ye brought   to me -   man

τοῦτον ὡς ἀποστρέφοντα τὸν λαόν, καὶ
this   as perverting   the people, and

ἰδοὺ ἐγὼ ἐνώπιον ὑμῶν ἀνακρίνας οὐθὲν
behold I   ²before   ³you   ¹examining ⁵nothing

εὗρον ἐν τῷ ἀνθρώπῳ τούτῳ αἴτιον ὧν
⁴found ⁷in - ⁶man   ⁸this ⁶crime of the
                                              [things]
                                              which

κατηγορεῖτε κατ' αὐτοῦ. 15 ἀλλ' οὐδὲ
ye bring accusation against him.   And neither

Ἡρώδης· ἀνέπεμψεν γὰρ αὐτὸν πρὸς ἡμᾶς·
Herod;   for he sent back him   to   us;

καὶ ἰδοὺ οὐδὲν ἄξιον θανάτου ἐστὶν
and behold nothing worthy of death is

πεπραγμένον αὐτῷ· 16 παιδεύσας οὖν αὐτὸν
having been done by him;   chastising therefore him

ἀπολύσω. ‡ 18 ἀνέκραγον δὲ παμπληθεὶ
I will release.   But they shouted   with the whole
                                           multitude

λέγοντες· αἶρε τοῦτον, ἀπόλυσον δὲ ἡμῖν
saying :   Take this man,   and release   to us

τὸν Βαραββᾶν· 19 ὅστις ἦν διὰ στάσιν
-   Barabbas;   who   was because ²insurrec-
                                        tion
                                        of

τινὰ γενομένην ἐν τῇ πόλει καὶ φόνον
¹some happening   in the city and murder

βληθεὶς ἐν τῇ φυλακῇ. 20 πάλιν δὲ
thrown   in the prison.   But again

ὁ Πιλᾶτος προσεφώνησεν αὐτοῖς, θέλων
- Pilate   called   to them, wishing

ἀπολῦσαι τὸν Ἰησοῦν. 21 οἱ δὲ ἐπεφώνουν
to release -   Jesus.   But they   shouted

λέγοντες· σταύρου σταύρου αὐτόν. 22 ὁ δὲ
saying :   Crucify[,] crucify   him.   But he

τρίτον εἶπεν πρὸς αὐτούς· τί γὰρ κακὸν
a third time said to   them : But what evil

ἐποίησεν οὗτος; οὐδὲν αἴτιον θανάτου
did   this man? nothing cause   of death

εὗρον ἐν αὐτῷ· παιδεύσας οὖν αὐτὸν
I found in him;   chastising therefore him

ἀπολύσω. 23 οἱ δὲ ἐπέκειντο φωναῖς
I will release.   But they   insisted   voices

μεγάλαις αἰτούμενοι αὐτὸν σταυρωθῆναι,
with great asking   him   to be crucified,

‡Ver. 17 omitted by Nestle; *cf.* R.V. marg., etc.

of them and of the chief priests prevailed.

24 And Pilate gave sentence that it should be as they required.

25 And he released unto them him that for sedition and murder was cast into prison, whom they had desired; but he delivered Jesus to their will.

26 ¶ And as they led him away, they laid hold upon one Simon, a Cyrenian, coming out of the country, and on him they laid the cross, that he might bear it after Jesus.

27 And there followed him a great company of people, and of women, which also bewailed and lamented him.

28 But Jesus turning unto them said, Daughters of Jerusalem, weep not for me, but weep for yourselves, and for your children.

29 For, behold, the days are coming, in the which they shall say, Blessed are the barren, and the wombs that never bare, and the paps which never gave suck.

30 Then shall they begin to say to the mountains, Fall on us; and to the hills, Cover us.

31 For if they do these things in a green tree, what shall be done in the dry?

32 ¶ And there were also

καὶ   κατίσχυον   αἱ   φωναὶ   αὐτῶν.   **24** καὶ
and   prevailed   the   voices   of them.   And

Πιλᾶτος   ἐπέκρινεν   γενέσθαι   τὸ   αἴτημα
Pilate   decided   to be [carried out]   the   request

αὐτῶν·   **25** ἀπέλυσεν δὲ   τὸν   διὰ   στάσιν
of them;   and he released   the [one]   because of   insurrection

καὶ   φόνον   βεβλημένον   εἰς   φυλακήν,   ὃν
and   murder   having been thrown   into   prison,   whom

ἠτοῦντο,   τὸν   δὲ   Ἰησοῦν   παρέδωκεν   τῷ
they asked,   –   but   Jesus   he delivered   to the

θελήματι   αὐτῶν.
will   of them.

26 Καὶ   ὡς   ἀπήγαγον   αὐτόν,   ἐπιλαβόμενοι
And   as   they led away   him,   seizing

Σίμωνά   τινα   Κυρηναῖον   ἐρχόμενον   ἀπ'
Simon   a certain   Cyrenian   coming   from

ἀγροῦ   ἐπέθηκαν   αὐτῷ τὸν σταυρὸν φέρειν
[the] country   they placed on   him   the   cross   to carry

ὄπισθεν   τοῦ   Ἰησοῦ.   **27** Ἠκολούθει   δὲ
behind   –   Jesus.   And followed

αὐτῷ   πολὺ   πλῆθος   τοῦ λαοῦ καὶ γυναικῶν
him   a much   multitude   of the people   and   of women

αἱ   ἐκόπτοντο   καὶ   ἐθρήνουν   αὐτόν.   **28** στρα-
who   mourned   and   lamented   him.   turn-

φεὶς   δὲ   πρὸς   αὐτὰς   Ἰησοῦς   εἶπεν·
ing   And   to   them   Jesus   said:

θυγατέρες   Ἰερουσαλήμ,   μὴ   κλαίετε   ἐπ'
Daughters   of Jerusalem,   do not weep   over

ἐμέ·   πλὴν   ἐφ'   ἑαυτὰς   κλαίετε   καὶ   ἐπὶ
me;   but   over   yourselves   weep   and   over

τὰ   τέκνα   ὑμῶν,   **29** ὅτι   ἰδοὺ   ἔρχονται
the   children   of you,   because   behold   come

ἡμέραι   ἐν   αἷς   ἐροῦσιν·   μακάριαι   αἱ
days   in   which   they will say: Blessed   the

στεῖραι,   καὶ   αἱ   κοιλίαι   αἳ   οὐκ   ἐγέννησαν,
barren,   and   the   wombs   which   bare not,

καὶ   μαστοὶ   οἳ   οὐκ   ἔθρεψαν.   **30** τότε
and   breasts   which   gave not suck.   Then

ἄρξονται   λέγειν   τοῖς   ὄρεσιν·   πέσατε   ἐφ'
they will begin to say   to the mountains: Fall   on

ἡμᾶς,   καὶ   τοῖς   βουνοῖς·   καλύψατε   ἡμᾶς·
us,   and   to the   hills: Cover   us;

31 ὅτι   εἰ   ἐν   ὑγρῷ   ξύλῳ   ταῦτα   ποιοῦσιν,
because   if   in   ²full of sap   ¹a tree   these things   they do,

ἐν   τῷ   ξηρῷ   τί   γένηται;   **32** Ἤγοντο   δὲ
in   the   dry   what may happen?   And were led

two other, malefactors, led with him to be put to death.

33 And when they were come to the place, which is called Calvary, there they crucified him, and the malefactors, one on the right hand, and the other on the left.

34 Then said Jesus, Father, forgive them; for they know not what they do. And they parted his raiment, and cast lots.

35 And the people stood beholding. And the rulers also with them derided *him*, saying, He saved others; let him save himself, if he be Christ, the chosen of God.

36 And the soldiers also mocked him, coming to him, and offering him vinegar,

37 And saying, If thou be the king of the Jews, save thyself.

38 And a superscription also was written over him in letters of Greek, and Latin, and Hebrew, THIS IS THE KING OF THE JEWS.

39 ¶ And one of the malefactors which were hanged railed on him, saying, If thou be Christ, save thyself and us.

40 But the other answering rebuked him, saying, Dost not thou fear God, seeing thou art in the same condemnation?

καὶ   ἕτεροι   κακοῦργοι   δύο   σὺν   αὐτῷ
also   others*   criminals   two   with   him

ἀναιρεθῆναι.   **33** Καὶ   ὅτε   ἦλθον   ἐπὶ   τὸν
to be killed.   And   when they came   upon   the

τόπον   τὸν   καλούμενον   Κρανίον,   ἐκεῖ   ἐσταύ-
place   -   being called   Skull,   there   they

ρωσαν   αὐτὸν   καὶ   τοὺς   κακούργους,   ὃν   μὲν
crucified   him   and   the   criminals,   one†

ἐκ   δεξιῶν   ὃν   δὲ   ἐξ   ἀριστερῶν.   **34** [ὁ   δὲ
on [the] right   and one†   on [the] left.   - And

'Ιησοῦς   ἔλεγεν·   πάτερ,   ἄφες   αὐτοῖς·   οὐ
Jesus   said :   Father,   forgive   them;   ²not

γὰρ   οἴδασιν   τί   ποιοῦσιν.]   διαμεριζόμενοι
¹for   ²they know   what   they are doing.   dividing

δὲ   τὰ   ἱμάτια   αὐτοῦ   ἔβαλον   κλήρους.
And the   garments   of him   they cast   lots.

35 καὶ   εἱστήκει   ὁ   λαὸς   θεωρῶν.   ἐξεμυκ-
And   stood   the people   beholding.   scoff-

τήριζον   δὲ   καὶ   οἱ   ἄρχοντες   λέγοντες·
ed   And   also   the   rulers   saying :

ἄλλους   ἔσωσεν,   σωσάτω   ἑαυτόν,   εἰ   οὗτός
Others   he saved,   let him save   himself,   if   this man

ἐστιν   ὁ   χριστὸς   τοῦ   θεοῦ   ὁ   ἐκλεκτός.
is   the   Christ   -   of God the   chosen [one].

36 ἐνέπαιξαν   δὲ   αὐτῷ   καὶ   οἱ   στρατιῶται
And mocked   him   also   the   soldiers

προσερχόμενοι,   ὄξος   προσφέροντες   αὐτῷ
approaching,   vinegar   offering   to him

37 καὶ   λέγοντες·   εἰ   σὺ   εἶ   ὁ   βασιλεὺς
and   saying :   If   thou art   the   king

τῶν   'Ιουδαίων,   σῶσον   σεαυτόν.   **38** ἦν   δὲ
of the   Jews,   save   thyself.   And there was

καὶ   ἐπιγραφὴ   ἐπ'   αὐτῷ·   Ο   ΒΑΣΙΛΕΥΣ
also   a superscription   over   him :   THE   KING

ΤΩΝ   ΙΟΥΔΑΙΩΝ   ΟΥΤΟΣ.   **39** Εἷς   δὲ
OF THE   JEWS   THIS.   And one

τῶν   κρεμασθέντων   κακούργων   ἐβλασφήμει
of the   hanged   criminals   blasphemed

αὐτόν·   οὐχὶ   σὺ   εἶ   ὁ   χριστός;   σῶσον
him :   Not   thou art   the   Christ?   save

σεαυτὸν   καὶ   ἡμᾶς·   **40** ἀποκριθεὶς   δὲ   ὁ
thyself   and   us.   But answering   the

ἕτερος   ἐπιτιμῶν   αὐτῷ   ἔφη·   οὐδὲ   φοβῇ   σὺ
other   rebuking   him   said :   Not   fearest thou

τὸν   θεόν,   ὅτι   ἐν   τῷ   αὐτῷ   κρίματι   εἶ;
-   God,   because in   the   same   judgment thou art?

* Luke uses ἕτεροι here with strict accuracy = "different." Jesus was not himself a criminal. Note punctuation of A.V. Cf. Acts 28. 1.

41 And we indeed justly; for we receive the due reward of our deeds: but this man hath done nothing amiss.

42 And he said unto Jesus, Lord, remember me when thou comest into thy kingdom.

43 And Jesus said unto him, Verily I say unto thee, To day shalt thou be with me in paradise.

44 ¶ And it was about the sixth hour, and there was a darkness over all the earth until the ninth hour.

45 And the sun was darkened, and the veil of the temple was rent in the midst.

46 And when Jesus had cried with a loud voice, he said, Father, into thy hands I commend my spirit: and having said thus, he gave up the ghost.

47 ¶ Now when the centurion saw what was done, he glorified God, saying, Certainly this was a righteous man.

48 And all the people that came together to that sight, beholding the things which were done, smote their breasts, and returned.

49 And all his acquaintance, and the women that followed him from Galilee, stood afar off, beholding these things.

50 ¶ And, behold, *there was* a man named Joseph,

---

41 καὶ ἡμεῖς μὲν δικαίως, ἄξια γὰρ ὧν
And we indeed justly, for things worthy of what

ἐπράξαμεν ἀπολαμβάνομεν· οὗτος δὲ οὐδὲν
we did we receive back; but this man nothing

ἄτοπον ἔπραξεν. 42 καὶ ἔλεγεν· Ἰησοῦ,
amiss did. And he said: Jesus,

μνήσθητί μου ὅταν ἔλθῃς εἰς τὴν βασιλείαν
remember me when thou comest into the kingdom

σου. 43 καὶ εἶπεν αὐτῷ· ἀμήν σοι λέγω,
of thee. And he said to him. Truly thee I tell,

σήμερον μετ' ἐμοῦ ἔσῃ ἐν τῷ παραδείσῳ.
to-day with me thou wilt be in the paradise.

44 Καὶ ἦν ἤδη ὡσεὶ ὥρα ἕκτη καὶ
And it was now about hour sixth and

σκότος ἐγένετο ἐφ' ὅλην τὴν γῆν ἕως
darkness came over all the land until

ὥρας ἐνάτης 45 τοῦ ἡλίου ἐκλιπόντος·[a]
hour ninth the sun failing;
=as the sun failed;

ἐσχίσθη δὲ τὸ καταπέτασμα τοῦ ναοῦ
and was torn the veil of the shrine

μέσον. 46 καὶ φωνήσας φωνῇ μεγάλῃ ὁ
in the middle. And crying voice with a great -

Ἰησοῦς εἶπεν· πάτερ, εἰς χεῖράς σου
Jesus said: Father, into hands of thee

παρατίθεμαι τὸ πνεῦμά μου. τοῦτο δὲ
I commit the spirit of me. And this

εἰπὼν ἐξέπνευσεν. 47 ἰδὼν δὲ ὁ ἑκατον-
saying he expired. And ²seeing ¹the ²cen-

τάρχης τὸ γενόμενον ἐδόξαζεν τὸν θεὸν
turion the thing happening glorified - God

λέγων· ὄντως ὁ ἄνθρωπος οὗτος δίκαιος
saying: Really - man this righteous

ἦν. 48 καὶ πάντες οἱ συμπαραγενόμενοι
was. And all ¹the ²arriving together

ὄχλοι ἐπὶ τὴν θεωρίαν ταύτην, θεωρήσαντες τὰ
²crowds at - sight this, beholding the things

γενόμενα, τύπτοντες τὰ στήθη ὑπέστρεφον.
happening, smiting the(ir) breasts returned.

49 εἰστήκεισαν δὲ πάντες οἱ γνωστοὶ αὐτῷ
And ²stood ¹all ²the [ones] ³known ⁴to him

ἀπὸ μακρόθεν, καὶ γυναῖκες αἱ συνακο-
²afar off, and women the [ones] accom

λουθοῦσαι αὐτῷ ἀπὸ τῆς Γαλιλαίας, ὁρῶσα
panying him from - Galilee, seeing

ταῦτα.
these things.

50 Καὶ ἰδοὺ ἀνὴρ ὀνόματι Ἰωσὴφ
And behold[,] a man by name Joseph

a counsellor; *and he was* | βουλευτὴς ὑπάρχων, ἀνὴρ ἀγαθὸς καὶ
a good man, and a just: | a councillor being, a man good and

51 (The same had not | δίκαιος, — **51** οὗτος οὐκ ἦν συγκατατεθειμένος
consented to the counsel | righteous, — this man was not agreeing with
and deed of them;) *he was*
of Arimathæa, a city of the | τῇ βουλῇ καὶ τῇ πράξει αὐτῶν, — ἀπὸ
Jews: who also himself | the counsel and the action of them, — from
waited for the kingdom of | ᾿Αριμαθαίας πόλεως τῶν ᾿Ιουδαίων, ὃς
God. | Arimathæa a city of the Jews, who

52 This *man* went unto | προσεδέχετο τὴν βασιλείαν τοῦ θεοῦ,
Pilate, and begged the | was awaiting the kingdom - of God,
body of Jesus. | **52** οὗτος προσελθὼν τῷ Πιλάτῳ ἠτήσατο

53 And he took it | this man approaching - to Pilate asked
down, and wrapped it in | τὸ σῶμα τοῦ ᾿Ιησοῦ, **53** καὶ καθελὼν
linen, and laid it in a | the body - of Jesus, and taking down
sepulchre that was hewn
in stone, wherein never | ἐνετύλιξεν αὐτὸ σινδόνι, καὶ ἔθηκεν αὐτὸν
man before was laid. | wrapped it in linen, and placed him

54 And that day was the | ἐν μνήματι λαξευτῷ, οὗ οὐκ ἦν οὐδεὶς
preparation, and the sab- | in tomb a hewn, where was not no(any)one
bath drew on. | οὔπω κείμενος. **54** καὶ ἡμέρα ἦν παρασκευῆς,

55 ¶ And the women | not yet laid. And day it was of preparation,
also, which came with | καὶ σάββατον ἐπέφωσκεν. **55** Κατακολουθήσασαι
him from Galilee, fol- | and a sabbath was coming on. ⁶following after
lowed after, and beheld | δὲ αἱ γυναῖκες, αἵτινες ἦσαν συνεληλυθυῖαι
the sepulchre, and how his | ¹And ²the ³women, who were ¹having come *with*
body was laid. | ἐκ τῆς Γαλιλαίας αὐτῷ, ἐθεάσαντο τὸ

56 And they returned, | ⁵out of - ⁴Galilee ²with him, beheld the
and prepared spices and | μνημεῖον καὶ ὡς ἐτέθη τὸ σῶμα αὐτοῦ,
ointments; and rested the | tomb and how was placed the body of him,
sabbath day according to | **56** ὑποστρέψασαι δὲ ἡτοίμασαν ἀρώματα καὶ
the commandment. | and returning prepared spices and
 | μύρα.
 | ointment.

 | Καὶ τὸ μὲν σάββατον ἡσύχασαν κατὰ
 | And [on] the ²indeed ¹sabbath they rested according to

CHAPTER 24 | τὴν ἐντολήν. **24** τῇ δὲ μιᾷ τῶν σαββάτων
 | the commandment. But on the one of the week

NOW upon the first | ὄρθρου βαθέως ἐπὶ τὸ μνῆμα ἦλθον φέρουσαι
day of the week, very | while still very early† upon the tomb they came carrying
early in the morning, they
came unto the sepulchre, | ἃ ἡτοίμασαν ἀρώματα. **2** εὗρον δὲ τὸν
bringing the spices which | ²which ³they prepared ¹spices. And they found the
they had prepared, and | λίθον ἀποκεκυλισμένον ἀπὸ τοῦ μνημείου,
certain *others* with them. | stone *having been* rolled away from the tomb,

2 And they found the | **3** εἰσελθοῦσαι δὲ οὐχ εὗρον τὸ σῶμα
stone rolled away from | and entering they found not the body
the sepulchre. | τοῦ κυρίου ᾿Ιησοῦ. **4** καὶ ἐγένετο ἐν τῷ

3 And they entered in, | of the Lord Jesus. And it was in the
and found not the body | =as they were perplexed
of the Lord Jesus. | ἀπορεῖσθαι αὐτὰς περὶ τούτου καὶ ἰδοὺ

4 And it came to pass, | to be perplexed them^be about this *and* behold[,]

as they were much per-
plexed thereabout, behold,
two men stood by them in
shining garments:

5 And as they were
afraid, and bowed down
their faces to the earth,
they said unto them, Why
seek ye the living among
the dead?

6 He is not here, but is
risen: remember how he
spake unto you when he
was yet in Galilee,

7 Saying, The Son of
man must be delivered
into the hands of sinful
men, and be crucified,
and the third day rise
again.

8 And they remembered
his words,

9 And returned from
the sepulchre, and told all
these things unto the
eleven, and to all the rest.

10 It was Mary Mag-
dalene, and Joanna, and
Mary *the mother* of James,
and other *women that
were* with them, which
told these things unto the
apostles.

11 And their words
seemed to them as idle
tales, and they believed
them not.

12 Then arose Peter,
and ran unto the
sepulchre; and stooping
down, he beheld the linen
clothes laid by themselves,
and departed, wondering
in himself at that which
was come to pass.

13 ¶ And, behold, two
of them went that same
day to a village called
Emmaus, which was from
Jerusalem *about* threescore
furlongs.

14 And they talked

ἄνδρες   δύο   ἐπέστησαν   αὐταῖς   ἐν   ἐσθῆτι
men   two   stood by   them   in   clothing

ἀστραπτούσῃ·   5 ἐμφόβων   δὲ   γενομένων
shining;   and terrified   becoming
=as they became terrified and bent their faces

αὐτῶν   καὶ   κλινουσῶν   τὰ   πρόσωπα   εἰς   τὴν
them   and   bending   the(ir)   faces*   to   the

γῆν,   εἶπαν   πρὸς   αὐτάς·   τί   ζητεῖτε   τὸν
earth,   they said   to   them :   Why   seek ye   the

ζῶντα   μετὰ   τῶν   νεκρῶν;   6 [οὐκ   ἔστιν
living [one] with   the   dead [ones]?   He is not

ὧδε,   ἀλλὰ   ἠγέρθη.]   μνήσθητε   ὡς   ἐλάλησεν
here,   but   was raised.   Remember   how   he spoke

ὑμῖν   ἔτι   ὢν   ἐν   τῇ   Γαλιλαίᾳ,   7 λέγων
to you   yet   being   in   -   Galilee,   saying[.]

τὸν   υἱὸν   τοῦ   ἀνθρώπου   ὅτι   δεῖ   παραδο-
The   Son   -   of man   - it behoves   to be de-

θῆναι   εἰς   χεῖρας   ἀνθρώπων   ἁμαρτωλῶν   καὶ
livered   into   hands   men   of sinful   and

σταυρωθῆναι   καὶ   τῇ   τρίτῃ   ἡμέρᾳ   ἀναστῆναι.
to be crucified   and on the   third   day   to rise again.

8 καὶ   ἐμνήσθησαν   τῶν   ῥημάτων   αὐτοῦ,
And   they remembered   the   words   of him,

9 καὶ   ὑποστρέψασαι   ἀπὸ   τοῦ   μνημείου
and   returning   from   the   tomb

ἀπήγγειλαν   ταῦτα   πάντα   τοῖς   ἕνδεκα   καὶ
reported   these things   all   to the   eleven   and

πᾶσιν   τοῖς   λοιποῖς.   10 ἦσαν   δὲ   ἡ
to all   the   rest.   Now they were   δὲ   ἡ

Μαγδαληνὴ   Μαρία   καὶ   Ἰωάννα   καὶ   Μαρία
Magdalene   Mary   and   Joanna   and   Mary

ἡ   Ἰακώβου·   καὶ   αἱ   λοιπαὶ*   σὺν   αὐταῖς*
the [mother] of James;   and   the   rest   with   them

ἔλεγον   πρὸς   τοὺς   ἀποστόλους   ταῦτα.   11 καὶ
told   to the   apostles   these things.   And

ἐφάνησαν   ἐνώπιον   αὐτῶν   ὡσεὶ   λῆρος
seemed   before   them   as   folly

τὰ   ῥήματα   ταῦτα,   καὶ   ἠπίστουν   αὐταῖς.* ‡
-   words   these,   and they disbelieved   them.

13 Καὶ   ἰδοὺ   δύο   ἐξ   αὐτῶν   ἐν   αὐτῇ   τῇ
And behold[,] two   of   them   on   same   the

ἡμέρᾳ   ἦσαν   πορευόμενοι   εἰς   κώμην   ἀπέχουσαν
day   were   journeying   to a village   being distant

σταδίους   ἑξήκοντα   ἀπὸ   Ἰερουσαλήμ,   ᾗ
furlongs   sixty   from   Jerusalem,   to which

ὄνομα   Ἐμμαοῦς,   14 καὶ   αὐτοὶ   ὡμίλουν
name   Emmaus,   and   they   talked

* Note the feminines.

‡ Verse 12 omitted by Nestle; *cf.* R.V. marg., etc.

together of all these things
which had happened.

15 And it came to pass,
that, while they com-
muned *together* and
reasoned, Jesus himself
drew near, and went with
them.

16 But their eyes were
holden that they should
not know him.

17 And he said unto
them, What manner of
communications *are* these
that ye have one to
another, as ye walk, and
are sad?

18 And the one of
them, whose name was
Cleopas, answering said
unto him, Art thou only a
stranger in Jerusalem, and
hast not known the things
which are come to pass
there in these days?

19 And he said unto
them, What things? And
they said unto him, Con-
cerning Jesus of Nazareth,
which was a prophet
mighty in deed and word
before God and all the
people:

20 And how the chief
priests and our rulers
delivered him to be con-
demned to death, and have
crucified him.

21 But we trusted that
it had been he which
should have redeemed
Israel: and beside all this,
to day is the third day since
these things were done.

22 Yea, and certain
women also of our com-
pany made us astonished,

πρὸς ἀλλήλους περὶ πάντων τῶν συμβεβηκότων
to   each other about   all   -   ³having occurred

τούτων.   15 καὶ ἐγένετο ἐν τῷ ὁμιλεῖν
¹these things.   And it came to pass in   the   to talk

αὐτοὺς καὶ συζητεῖν, καὶ αὐτὸς Ἰησοῦς
them   and   to discuss^{be},   *and* [him]self   Jesus
=as they talked and discussed,

ἐγγίσας συνεπορεύετο αὐτοῖς· 16 οἱ δὲ
drawing near journeyed with   them;   but the

ὀφθαλμοὶ αὐτῶν ἐκρατοῦντο τοῦ μὴ
eyes   of them   were held   -   not

ἐπιγνῶναι αὐτόν. 17 εἶπεν δὲ πρὸς αὐτούς·
to recognize^d him.   And he said   to   them :

τίνες οἱ λόγοι οὗτοι οὓς ἀντιβάλλετε
What   -   words   these   which   ye exchange

πρὸς ἀλλήλους περιπατοῦντες; καὶ ἐστάθησαν
with   each other   walking?   And   they stood

σκυθρωποί. 18 ἀποκριθεὶς δὲ εἷς ὀνόματι
sad-faced.   And answering   one   by name

Κλεοπᾶς εἶπεν πρὸς αὐτόν· σὺ μόνος
Cleopas   said   to   him :   Thou   only

παροικεῖς Ἰερουσαλὴμ καὶ οὐκ ἔγνως τὰ
a stranger   in Jerusalem   and   knewest not the things

γενόμενα ἐν αὐτῇ ἐν ταῖς ἡμέραις ταύταις;
happening   in it   in   -   days   these ?

19 καὶ εἶπεν αὐτοῖς· ποῖα; οἱ δὲ εἶπαν
And he said to them : What things? And they   said

αὐτῷ· τὰ περὶ Ἰησοῦ τοῦ Ναζαρηνοῦ, ὃς
to him : The things about Jesus   the   Nazarene,   who

ἐγένετο ἀνὴρ προφήτης δυνατὸς ἐν ἔργῳ
was   a *man*   prophet   powerful   in   work

καὶ λόγῳ ἐναντίον τοῦ θεοῦ καὶ παντὸς
and   word   before   -   God   and   all

τοῦ λαοῦ, 20 ὅπως τε παρέδωκαν αὐτὸν οἱ
the people,   how both ⁷delivered   ⁸him ¹the

ἀρχιερεῖς καὶ οἱ ἄρχοντες ἡμῶν εἰς
²chief priests ³and ⁴the ⁵rulers   ⁶of us   to

κρίμα θανάτου καὶ ἐσταύρωσαν αὐτόν.
[the] judgment of death   and   crucified   him.

21 ἡμεῖς δὲ ἠλπίζομεν ὅτι αὐτός ἐστιν
But we   were hoping   that   he   it is(was)

ὁ μέλλων λυτροῦσθαι τὸν Ἰσραήλ· ἀλλά
the [one] being about to redeem   -   Israel;   but

γε καὶ σὺν πᾶσιν τούτοις τρίτην ταύτην
-   also   with   all   these things   third   this
=this is the third day

ἡμέραν ἄγει ἀφ' οὗ ταῦτα ἐγένετο.
day   it leads   since   these things happened.

22 ἀλλὰ καὶ γυναῖκές τινες ἐξ ἡμῶν
But   also   ²women   ¹some   of   us

which were early at the
sepulchre;

23 And when they
found not his body, they
came, saying, that they
had also seen a vision of
angels, which said that he
was alive.

24 And certain of them
which were with us went
to the sepulchre, and
found it even so as the
women had said: but him
they saw not.

25 Then he said unto
them, O fools, and slow
of heart to believe all
that the prophets have
spoken:

26 Ought not Christ to
have suffered these things,
and to enter into his glory?

27 And beginning at
Moses and all the pro-
phets, he expounded unto
them in all the scriptures
the things concerning himself.

28 And they drew nigh
unto the village, whither
they went: and he made
as though he would have
gone further.

29 But they constrained
him, saying, Abide with
us: for it is toward evening, and the day is far
spent. And he went in to
tarry with them.

30 And it came to pass,
as he sat at meat with
them, he took bread, and
blessed it, and brake, and
gave to them.

ἐξέστησαν ἡμᾶς, γενόμεναι ὀρθριναὶ ἐπὶ τὸ
astonished us,   being   early   at   the

μνημεῖον, 23 καὶ μὴ εὑροῦσαι τὸ σῶμα
tomb,   and not finding   the body

αὐτοῦ ἦλθον λέγουσαι καὶ ὀπτασίαν ἀγγέλων
of him came   saying   also a vision of angels

ἑωρακέναι, οἳ λέγουσιν αὐτὸν ζῆν. 24 καὶ
to have seen, who say   him to live.   And
                                  = that he lives.

ἀπῆλθόν τινες τῶν σὺν ἡμῖν ἐπὶ τὸ
⁵went   ¹some ²of the [ones] ³with ⁴us to   the

μνημεῖον, καὶ εὗρον οὕτως καθὼς καὶ αἱ
tomb,   and found so   as   indeed the

γυναῖκες εἶπον, αὐτὸν δὲ οὐκ εἶδον.
women   said,   but him   they saw not.

25 καὶ αὐτὸς εἶπεν πρὸς αὐτούς· ὦ
And   he   said   to   them :   O

ἀνόητοι καὶ βραδεῖς τῇ καρδίᾳ τοῦ πιστεύειν
foolish [ones] and slow   – in heart –   to believeᵈ

ἐπὶ πᾶσιν οἷς ἐλάλησαν οἱ προφῆται·
on(in) all things which spoke   the prophets :

26 οὐχὶ ταῦτα ἔδει παθεῖν τὸν χριστὸν καὶ
²not ⁶these things ¹behoved it ⁵to suffer ³the ⁴Christ and

εἰσελθεῖν εἰς τὴν δόξαν αὐτοῦ; 27 καὶ
to enter   into the glory of him?   And

ἀρξάμενος ἀπὸ Μωϋσέως καὶ ἀπὸ πάντων
beginning from Moses   and from   all

τῶν προφητῶν διηρμήνευσεν αὐτοῖς ἐν
the prophets   he explained   to them in

πάσαις ταῖς γραφαῖς τὰ περὶ ἑαυτοῦ.
all   the scriptures the things concerning himself.

28 Καὶ ἤγγισαν εἰς τὴν κώμην οὗ
And   they drew near to   the   village whither

ἐπορεύοντο, καὶ αὐτὸς προσεποιήσατο
they were journeying, and he   pretended

πορρώτερον πορεύεσθαι. 29 καὶ παρε-
farther   to journey.   And   they

βιάσαντο αὐτὸν λέγοντες· μεῖνον μεθ᾽
urged   him   saying :   Remain with

ἡμῶν, ὅτι πρὸς ἑσπέραν ἐστὶν καὶ κέκλικεν
us, because toward evening it is and has declined

ἤδη ἡ ἡμέρα. καὶ εἰσῆλθεν τοῦ μεῖναι
now the day.   And he went in – to remainᵈ

σὺν αὐτοῖς. 30 καὶ ἐγένετο ἐν τῷ
with them.   And it came to pass in the
                                   = as he reclined

κατακλιθῆναι αὐτὸν μετ᾽ αὐτῶν λαβὼν τὸν
to recline   himᵇᵉ with   them   taking the

ἄρτον εὐλόγησεν καὶ κλάσας ἐπεδίδου
loaf   he blessed   and having broken he handed

31 And their eyes were opened, and they knew him; and he vanished out of their sight.

32 And they said one to another, Did not our heart burn within us, while he talked with us by the way, and while he opened to us the scriptures?

33 And they rose up the same hour, and returned to Jerusalem, and found the eleven gathered together, and them that were with them,

34 Saying, The Lord is risen indeed, and hath appeared to Simon.

35 And they told what things were done in the way, and how he was known of them in breaking of bread.

36 ¶ And as they thus spake, Jesus himself stood in the midst of them, and saith unto them, Peace be unto you.

37 But they were terrified and affrighted, and supposed that they had seen a spirit.

38 And he said unto them, Why are ye troubled? and why do thoughts arise in your hearts?

39 Behold my hands and my feet, that it is I myself: handle me, and see; for a spirit hath not flesh and bones, as ye see me have.

40 And when he had thus spoken, he shewed them his hands and his feet.

41 And while they yet believed not for joy, and wondered, he said unto

αὐτοῖς·   31 αὐτῶν   δὲ   διηνοίχθησαν   οἱ
to them;   and of them   were opened up   the

ὀφθαλμοί,   καὶ   ἐπέγνωσαν   αὐτόν·   καὶ   αὐτὸς
eyes,   and   they recognized   him;   and   he

ἄφαντος   ἐγένετο   ἀπ'   αὐτῶν.   32 καὶ
invisible   became   from   them.   And

εἶπαν   πρὸς   ἀλλήλους·   οὐχὶ   ἡ   καρδία
they said   to   each other :   Not   the   heart

ἡμῶν   καιομένη   ἦν   ἐν   ἡμῖν,   ὡς   ἐλάλει
of us   burning   was   in   us,   as   he spoke

ἡμῖν   ἐν   τῇ   ὁδῷ,   ὡς   διήνοιγεν   ἡμῖν   τὰς
to us   in   the   way,   as   he opened up   to us   the

γραφάς;   33 Καὶ   ἀναστάντες   αὐτῇ   τῇ   ὥρα
scriptures?   And   rising up   [2]same   [1]in the hour

ὑπέστρεψαν   εἰς   Ἰερουσαλήμ,   καὶ   εὗρον
they returned   to   Jerusalem,   and   found

ἠθροισμένους   τοὺς   ἕνδεκα   καὶ   τοὺς   σὺν
having been collected   the   eleven   and the [ones]   with

αὐτοῖς,   34 λέγοντας   ὅτι   ὄντως   ἠγέρθη   ὁ
them,   saying[,]   that   Really   was raised the

κύριος   καὶ   ὤφθη   Σίμωνι.   35 καὶ   αὐτοὶ   ἐξηγοῦντο
Lord   and appeared to Simon.   And   they   related

τὰ   ἐν   τῇ   ὁδῷ   καὶ   ὡς   ἐγνώσθη
the things in   the   way   and   how   he was known

αὐτοῖς   ἐν   τῇ   κλάσει   τοῦ   ἄρτου.   36 Ταῦτα
by them   in   the   breaking   of the   loaf.   these things

δὲ   αὐτῶν   λαλούντων   αὐτὸς   ἔστη   ἐν
And   them   saying [a]   he   stood   in
    =as they said these things

μέσῳ   αὐτῶν.   37 πτοηθέντες   δὲ   καὶ
[the] midst   of them.   But scared   and

ἔμφοβοι   γενόμενοι   ἐδόκουν   πνεῦμα   θεωρεῖν.
terrified   becoming   they thought   a spirit   to behold.

38 καὶ   εἶπεν   αὐτοῖς·   τί   τεταραγμένοι   ἐστέ,
And   he said   to them : Why   having been troubled   are ye,

καὶ   διὰ   τί   διαλογισμοὶ   ἀναβαίνουσιν   ἐν
and   why   thoughts   come up   in

τῇ   καρδίᾳ   ὑμῶν;   39 ἴδετε   τὰς   χεῖράς
the   heart   of you?   See   the   hands

μου   καὶ   τοὺς   πόδας   μου,   ὅτι   ἐγώ   εἰμι
of me   and   the   feet   of me,   that   I   am

αὐτός·   ψηλαφήσατέ   με   καὶ   ἴδετε,   ὅτι
[my]self;   feel   me   and   see,   because

πνεῦμα   σάρκα   καὶ   ὀστέα   οὐκ   ἔχει   καθὼς
a spirit   flesh   and   bones   has not   as

ἐμὲ   θεωρεῖτε   ἔχοντα.   ‡ 41 ἔτι   δὲ   ἀπιστούντων
me   ye behold   having.   And yet   disbelieving
    =while they yet disbelieved

αὐτῶν   ἀπὸ   τῆς   χαρᾶς   καὶ   θαυμαζόντων,
them [a]   from   the   joy   and   marvelling [a],

‡ Verse 40 omitted by Nestle; cf. R.V. marg., etc.

them, Have ye here any meat?

42 And they gave him a piece of a broiled fish, and of an honeycomb.

43 And he took *it*, and did eat before them.

44 And he said unto them, These *are* the words which I spake unto you, while I was yet with you, that all things must be fulfilled, which were written in the law of Moses, and *in* the prophets, and *in* the psalms, concerning me.

45 Then opened he their understanding, that they might understand the scriptures,

46 And said unto them, Thus it is written, and thus it behoved Christ to suffer, and to rise from the dead the third day:

47 And that repentance and remission of sins should be preached in his name among all nations, beginning at Jerusalem.

48 And ye are witnesses of these things.

49 ¶ And, behold, I send the promise of my Father upon you: but tarry ye in the city of Jerusalem, until ye be endued with power from on high.

50 ¶ And he led them out as far as to Bethany, and he lifted up his hands, and blessed them.

51 And it came to pass, while he blessed them, he was parted from them, and carried up into heaven.

εἶπεν αὐτοῖς· ἔχετέ τι βρώσιμον ἐνθάδε;
he said   to them :   Have ye   any   food   here?

42 οἱ δὲ ἐπέδωκαν αὐτῷ ἰχθύος ὀπτοῦ
And they   handed   to him   ²fish ³of a broiled

μέρος· 43 καὶ λαβὼν ἐνώπιον αὐτῶν ἔφαγεν.
¹part;   and   taking   before   them   he ate.

44 Εἶπεν δὲ πρὸς αὐτούς· οὗτοι οἱ λόγοι
And he said   to   them :   These   —   words

μου οὓς ἐλάλησα πρὸς ὑμᾶς ἔτι ὢν σὺν
of me which I spoke   to   you   yet   being   with

ὑμῖν, ὅτι δεῖ πληρωθῆναι πάντα τὰ
you,   that   it behoves   to be fulfilled   all   the things

γεγραμμένα ἐν τῷ νόμῳ Μωϋσέως καὶ
having been written in   the   law   of Moses   and

τοῖς προφήταις καὶ ψαλμοῖς περὶ ἐμοῦ.
the   prophets   and   psalms   concerning me.

45 τότε διήνοιξεν αὐτῶν τὸν νοῦν τοῦ
Then   he opened up   of them   the   mind   —

συνιέναι τὰς γραφάς· 46 καὶ εἶπεν αὐτοῖς
to understand[d] the   scriptures;   and   said   to them[,]

ὅτι οὕτως γέγραπται παθεῖν τὸν χριστὸν
—   Thus — it has been written ²to suffer   ¹the   ²Christ

καὶ ἀναστῆναι ἐκ νεκρῶν τῇ τρίτῃ ἡμέρᾳ,
and   to rise again   out of [the] dead on the third   day,

47 καὶ κηρυχθῆναι ἐπὶ τῷ ὀνόματι αὐτοῦ
and   to be proclaimed   on(in) the   name   of him

μετάνοιαν εἰς ἄφεσιν ἁμαρτιῶν εἰς πάντα
repentance   unto forgiveness   of sins   to   all

τὰ ἔθνη, — ἀρξάμενοι ἀπὸ Ἰερουσαλήμ.
the   nations,   —   beginning   from   Jerusalem.

48 ὑμεῖς μάρτυρες τούτων. 49 καὶ ἰδοὺ
Ye [are] witnesses   of these things.   And   behold

ἐγὼ ἐξαποστέλλω τὴν ἐπαγγελίαν τοῦ
I   send forth   the   promise   of the

πατρός μου ἐφ᾽ ὑμᾶς· ὑμεῖς δὲ καθίσατε
Father of me on   you;   but ye   sit

ἐν τῇ πόλει ἕως οὗ ἐνδύσησθε ἐξ ὕψους
in   the   city   until ¹ye are clothed[with]³out of ⁴height

δύναμιν.
²power.

50 Ἐξήγαγεν δὲ αὐτοὺς ἕως πρὸς
And he led out   them   until   toward

Βηθανίαν, καὶ ἐπάρας τὰς χεῖρας αὐτοῦ
Bethany,   and   lifting up   the   hands   of him

εὐλόγησεν αὐτούς. 51 καὶ ἐγένετο ἐν τῷ
he blessed   them.   And   it came to pass in   the

εὐλογεῖν αὐτὸν αὐτοὺς διέστη ἀπ᾽ αὐτῶν.
to bless   him[be]   them   he withdrew from   them.
=while he blessed

52 And they worshipped him, and returned to Jerusalem with great joy:

53 And were continually in the temple, praising and blessing God. Amen.

52 καὶ   αὐτοὶ   ὑπέστρεψαν   εἰς   'Ιερουσαλὴμ
And   they   returned   to   Jerusalem

μετὰ   χαρᾶς   μεγάλης,   53 καὶ   ἦσαν   διὰ   παντὸς
with   joy   great,   and   were   continually

ἐν   τῷ   ἱερῷ   εὐλογοῦντες   τὸν   θεόν.
in   the temple   blessing   –   God.

CHAPTER 1

IN the beginning was the Word, and the Word was with God, and the Word was God.

2 The same was in the beginning with God.

3 All things were made by him; and without him was not anything made that was made.

4 In him was life; and the life was the light of men.

5 And the light shineth in darkness; and the darkness comprehended it not.

6 ¶ There was a man sent from God, whose name *was* John.

7 The same came for a witness, to bear witness of the Light, that all *men* through him might believe.

8 He was not that Light, but *was sent* to bear witness of that Light.

9 *That* was the true Light, which lighteth every man that cometh into the world.

10 He was in the world, and the world was made by him, and the world knew him not.

11 He came unto his own, and his own received him not.

12 But as many as received him, to them gave he power to become the sons of God, *even* to them

1 Ἐν ἀρχῇ ἦν ὁ λόγος, καὶ ὁ λόγος
In [the] beginning was the Word, and the Word

ἦν πρὸς τὸν θεόν, καὶ θεὸς ἦν ὁ λόγος.*
was with – God, and God was the Word.*

2 οὗτος ἦν ἐν ἀρχῇ πρὸς τὸν θεόν.
This one was in [the] beginning with – God.

3 πάντα δι' αὐτοῦ ἐγένετο, καὶ χωρὶς
All things through him became, and without

αὐτοῦ ἐγένετο οὐδὲ ἕν ὃ γέγονεν. **4** ἐν
him became not one thing which has become. In

αὐτῷ ζωὴ ἦν, καὶ ἡ ζωὴ ἦν τὸ φῶς
him life was, and the life was the light

τῶν ἀνθρώπων· **5** καὶ τὸ φῶς ἐν τῇ
 – of men; and the light in the

σκοτίᾳ φαίνει, καὶ ἡ σκοτία αὐτὸ οὐ
darkness shines, and the darkness it not

κατέλαβεν. **6** Ἐγένετο ἄνθρωπος, ἀπεσταλμένος
overtook.   There was a man, *having been* sent

παρὰ θεοῦ, ὄνομα αὐτῷ Ἰωάννης· **7** οὗτος
from God, name to him[e] John;   this man

ἦλθεν εἰς μαρτυρίαν, ἵνα μαρτυρήσῃ περὶ
came for witness, that he might witness concerning

τοῦ φωτός, ἵνα πάντες πιστεύσωσιν δι'
the light, that all men might believe through

αὐτοῦ. **8** οὐκ ἦν ἐκεῖνος τὸ φῶς, ἀλλ' ἵνα
him.   He was not that – light, but that

μαρτυρήσῃ περὶ τοῦ φωτός. **9** Ἦν τὸ φῶς
he might witness concerning the light.   It was the light

τὸ ἀληθινόν, ὃ φωτίζει πάντα ἄνθρωπον,
 – true, which enlightens every man,

ἐρχόμενον εἰς τὸν κόσμον. **10** ἐν τῷ
coming into the world.   In the

κόσμῳ ἦν, καὶ ὁ κόσμος δι' αὐτοῦ
world he was, and the world through him

ἐγένετο, καὶ ὁ κόσμος αὐτὸν οὐκ ἔγνω.
became, and the world him knew not.

11 εἰς τὰ ἴδια ἦλθεν, καὶ οἱ ἴδιοι αὐτὸν
To his own things he came, and his own people him

οὐ παρέλαβον. **12** ὅσοι δὲ ἔλαβον αὐτόν,
received not.   But as many as received him,

ἔδωκεν αὐτοῖς ἐξουσίαν τέκνα θεοῦ γεν-
he gave to them right children of God to be-

* But note that the subject has the article and the predicate has it not; hence translate—" the Word was God."

that believe on his name:
13 Which were born,
not of blood, nor of the
will of the flesh, nor of the
will of man, but of God.

14 And the Word was
made flesh, and dwelt
among us, (and we beheld
his glory, the glory as of
the only begotten of the
Father,) full of grace and
truth.

15 ¶ John bare witness
of him, and cried, saying,
This was he of whom I
spake, He that cometh
after me is preferred before
me: for he was before me.

16 And of his fulness
have all we received, and
grace for grace.

17 For the law was
given by Moses, *but* grace
and truth came by Jesus
Christ.

18 No man hath seen
God at any time; the only
begotten Son, which is in
the bosom of the Father,
he hath declared *him*.

19 ¶ And this is the
record of John, when the
Jews sent priests and
Levites from Jerusalem to
ask him, Who art thou?

20 And he confessed,
and denied not; but con-
fessed, I am not the Christ.

ἔσθαι, τοῖς πιστεύουσιν εἰς τὸ ὄνομα αὐτοῦ,
come,   to the [ones] believing   in   the   name   of him,

13 οἱ οὐκ ἐξ αἱμάτων οὐδὲ ἐκ θελήματος
who   not   of   bloods   nor   of   [the] will

σαρκὸς οὐδὲ ἐκ θελήματος ἀνδρὸς ἀλλ'
of [the] flesh nor   of   [the] will   of a man   but

ἐκ θεοῦ ἐγεννήθησαν. 14 Καὶ ὁ λόγος
of   God   were born.   And   the   Word

σὰρξ ἐγένετο καὶ ἐσκήνωσεν ἐν ἡμῖν,
flesh   became   and   tabernacled   among   us,

καὶ ἐθεασάμεθα τὴν δόξαν αὐτοῦ, δόξαν
and   we beheld   the   glory   of him,   glory

ὡς μονογενοῦς παρὰ πατρός, πλήρης χάριτος
as of an only begotten from   a father,   full   of grace

καὶ ἀληθείας. 15 Ἰωάννης μαρτυρεῖ περὶ
and   of truth.   John   witnesses   concerning

αὐτοῦ καὶ κέκραγεν λέγων· οὗτος ἦν ὃν
him   and has cried out   saying :   This man was he whom

εἶπον· ὁ ὀπίσω μου ἐρχόμενος ἔμπροσθέν
I said :   The [one]   after   me   coming   before

μου γέγονεν, ὅτι πρῶτός μου ἦν. 16 ὅτι
me   has become, because   first   of me he was.   Because

ἐκ τοῦ πληρώματος αὐτοῦ ἡμεῖς πάντες
of   the   fulness   of him   we   all

ἐλάβομεν, καὶ χάριν ἀντὶ χάριτος· 17 ὅτι
received,   and   grace   instead of   grace;   because

ὁ νόμος διὰ Μωϋσέως ἐδόθη, ἡ χάρις καὶ
the   law   through   Moses   was given,   the   grace   and

ἡ ἀλήθεια διὰ Ἰησοῦ Χριστοῦ ἐγένετο.
the   truth   through   Jesus   Christ   became.

18 Θεὸν οὐδεὶς ἑώρακεν πώποτε· μονογενὴς
   God   no man   has seen   *never*;   [the] only begotten

θεὸς ὁ ὢν εἰς τὸν κόλπον τοῦ πατρός,
God the [one] being   in   the   bosom   of the   Father,

ἐκεῖνος ἐξηγήσατο.
that one   declared [?him].

19 Καὶ αὕτη ἐστὶν ἡ μαρτυρία τοῦ
   And   this   is   the   witness   -

Ἰωάννου, ὅτε ἀπέστειλαν πρὸς αὐτὸν οἱ
of John,   when   ³sent   ⁴to   ⁵him   ¹the

Ἰουδαῖοι ἐξ Ἱεροσολύμων ἱερεῖς καὶ Λευίτας
²Jews   ⁹from   ¹⁰Jerusalem   ⁶priests   ⁷and   ⁸Levites

ἵνα ἐρωτήσωσιν αὐτόν· σὺ τίς εἶ; 20 καὶ
that   they might ask   him :   Thou who art?   And

ὡμολόγησεν καὶ οὐκ ἠρνήσατο, καὶ
he confessed   and   denied not,   and

ὡμολόγησεν ὅτι ἐγὼ οὐκ εἰμὶ ὁ χριστός.
he confessed[,]   -   I   am not   the   Christ.

21 And they asked him, What then? Art thou Elias? And he saith, I am not. Art thou that prophet? And he answered, No.

22 Then said they unto him, Who art thou? that we may give an answer to them that sent us. What sayest thou of thyself?

23 He said, I am the voice of one crying in the wilderness, Make straight the way of the Lord, as said the prophet Esaias.

24 And they which were sent were of the Pharisees.

25 And they asked him, and said unto him, Why baptizest thou then, if thou be not that Christ, nor Elias, neither that prophet?

26 John answered them, saying, I baptize with water: but there standeth one among you, whom ye know not;

27 He it is, who coming after me is preferred before me, whose shoe's latchet I am not worthy to unloose.

28 These things were done in Bethabara beyond Jordan, where John was baptizing.

29 ¶ The next day John seeth Jesus coming unto him, and saith, Behold the Lamb of God, which taketh away the sin of the world.

30 This is he of whom I said, After me cometh a man which is preferred before me: for he was before me.

21 καὶ ἠρώτησαν αὐτόν· τί οὖν; Ἠλίας εἶ
And they asked him: What then? Elias art

σύ; καὶ λέγει· οὐκ εἰμί. ὁ προφήτης εἶ σύ;
thou? And he says: I am not. The prophet art thou?

καὶ ἀπεκρίθη· οὔ. 22 εἶπαν οὖν αὐτῷ·
And he answered: No. They said therefore to him:

τίς εἶ; ἵνα ἀπόκρισιν δῶμεν τοῖς
Who art thou? that an answer we may give to the [ones]

πέμψασιν ἡμᾶς· τί λέγεις περὶ σεαυτοῦ;
having sent us; What sayest thou concerning thyself?

23 ἔφη· ἐγὼ φωνὴ βοῶντος ἐν τῇ ἐρήμῳ·
He said: I [am] a voice of [one] crying in the desert:

εὐθύνατε τὴν ὁδὸν κυρίου, καθὼς εἶπεν
Make straight the way of [the] Lord, as said

Ἠσαΐας ὁ προφήτης. 24 Καὶ ἀπεσταλμένοι
Esaias the prophet. And [the ones] having been sent

ἦσαν ἐκ τῶν Φαρισαίων. 25 καὶ ἠρώτησαν
were of the Pharisees. And they asked

αὐτὸν καὶ εἶπαν αὐτῷ· τι οὖν βαπτίζεις
him and said to him: Why then baptizest thou

εἰ σὺ οὐκ εἶ ὁ χριστὸς οὐδὲ Ἠλίας
if thou art not the Christ nor Elias

οὐδὲ ὁ προφήτης; 26 ἀπεκρίθη αὐτοῖς –
nor the prophet? Answered them –

Ἰωάννης λέγων· ἐγὼ βαπτίζω ἐν ὕδατι·
John saying: I baptize in water;

μέσος ὑμῶν στήκει ὃν ὑμεῖς οὐκ οἴδατε,
among you stands [one] whom ye know not,

27 ὁ ὀπίσω μου ἐρχόμενος, οὗ οὐκ εἰμὶ
the [one] after me coming, of whom am not

ἐγὼ ἄξιος ἵνα λύσω αὐτοῦ τὸν ἱμάντα
I worthy that I should loosen of him the thong

τοῦ ὑποδήματος. 28 Ταῦτα ἐν Βηθανίᾳ
of the sandal. These things in Bethany

ἐγένετο πέραν τοῦ Ἰορδάνου, ὅπου ἦν ὁ
happened beyond the Jordan, where was –

Ἰωάννης βαπτίζων. 29 Τῇ ἐπαύριον βλέπει
John baptizing. On the morrow he sees

τὸν Ἰησοῦν ἐρχόμενον πρὸς αὐτόν, καὶ
– Jesus coming toward him, and

λέγει· ἴδε ὁ ἀμνὸς τοῦ θεοῦ ὁ αἴρων
says: Behold[,] the Lamb – of God – taking

τὴν ἁμαρτίαν τοῦ κόσμου. 30 οὗτός ἐστιν
the sin of the world. This is he

ὑπὲρ οὗ ἐγὼ εἶπον· ὀπίσω μου ἔρχεται
as to whom I said: After me comes

ἀνὴρ ὃς ἔμπροσθέν μου γέγονεν, ὅτι
a man who before me has become, because

31 And I knew him not: but that he should be made manifest to Israel, therefore am I come baptizing with water.

32 And John bare record, saying, I saw the Spirit descending from heaven like a dove, and it abode upon him.

33 And I knew him not: but he that sent me to baptize with water, the same said unto me, Upon whom thou shalt see the Spirit descending, and remaining on him, the same is he which baptizeth with the Holy Ghost.

34 And I saw, and bare record that this is the Son of God.

35 ¶ Again the next day after John stood, and two of his disciples;

36 And looking upon Jesus as he walked, he saith, Behold the Lamb of God!

37 And the two disciples heard him speak, and they followed Jesus.

38 Then Jesus turned, and saw them following, and saith unto them, What seek ye? They said unto him, Rabbi, (which is to say, being interpreted, Master,) where dwellest thou?

39 He saith unto them, Come and see. They came

πρῶτός μου ἦν. 31 κἀγὼ οὐκ ᾔδειν
first of me he was. And I knew not

αὐτόν, ἀλλ' ἵνα φανερωθῇ τῷ Ἰσραήλ,
him, but that he might be manifested – to Israel,

διὰ τοῦτο ἦλθον ἐγὼ ἐν ὕδατι βαπτίζων.
therefore came I in water baptizing.

32 Καὶ ἐμαρτύρησεν Ἰωάννης λέγων ὅτι
And witnessed John saying[.]

τεθέαμαι τὸ πνεῦμα καταβαῖνον ὡς
I have beheld the Spirit coming down as

περιστερὰν ἐξ οὐρανοῦ, καὶ ἔμεινεν ἐπ'
a dove out of heaven, and he remained on

αὐτόν. 33 κἀγὼ οὐκ ᾔδειν αὐτόν, ἀλλ'
him. And I knew not him, but

ὁ πέμψας με βαπτίζειν ἐν ὕδατι, ἐκεῖνός
the [one] having sent me to baptize in water, that [one]

μοι εἶπεν· ἐφ' ὃν ἂν ἴδῃς τὸ πνεῦμα
to me said: On whomever thou seest the Spirit

καταβαῖνον καὶ μένον ἐπ' αὐτόν, οὗτός
coming down and remaining on him, this

ἐστιν ὁ βαπτίζων ἐν πνεύματι ἁγίῳ.
is the [one] baptizing in Spirit Holy.

34 κἀγὼ ἑώρακα, καὶ μεμαρτύρηκα ὅτι
And I have seen, and have witnessed that

οὗτός ἐστιν ὁ υἱὸς τοῦ θεοῦ.
this [one] is the Son – of God.

35 Τῇ ἐπαύριον πάλιν εἱστήκει ὁ Ἰωάννης
On the morrow again stood – John

καὶ ἐκ τῶν μαθητῶν αὐτοῦ δύο, 36 καὶ
and of the disciples of him two, and

ἐμβλέψας τῷ Ἰησοῦ περιπατοῦντι λέγει·
looking at – Jesus walking he says:

ἴδε ὁ ἀμνὸς τοῦ θεοῦ. 37 καὶ ἤκουσαν
Behold[,] the Lamb – of God. And ⁴heard

οἱ δύο μαθηταὶ αὐτοῦ λαλοῦντος καὶ
¹the ²two ³disciples ⁵him ⁶speaking and

ἠκολούθησαν τῷ Ἰησοῦ. 38 στραφεὶς δὲ
they followed – Jesus. And ²turning

ὁ Ἰησοῦς καὶ θεασάμενος αὐτοὺς ἀκολουθοῦντας
– ¹Jesus and beholding them following

λέγει αὐτοῖς· τί ζητεῖτε; οἱ δὲ εἶπαν
says to them: What seek ye? And they said

αὐτῷ· ῥαββί (ὃ λέγεται μεθερμηνευόμενον
to him: Rabbi (which is called being translated

διδάσκαλε), ποῦ μένεις; 39 λέγει αὐτοῖς·
Teacher), where remainest thou? He says to them:

ἔρχεσθε καὶ ὄψεσθε. ἦλθαν οὖν καὶ εἶδαν
Come and ye will see. They went therefore and saw

and saw where he dwelt, and abode with him that day: for it was about the tenth hour.

40 One of the two which heard John *speak*, and followed him, was Andrew, Simon Peter's brother.

41 He first findeth his own brother Simon, and saith unto him, We have found the Messias, which is, being interpreted, the Christ.

42 And he brought him to Jesus. And when Jesus beheld him, he said, Thou art Simon the son of Jona: thou shalt be called Cephas, which is by interpretation, A stone.

43 ¶ The day following Jesus would go forth into Galilee, and findeth Philip, and saith unto him, Follow me.

44 Now Philip was of Bethsaida, the city of Andrew and Peter.

45 Philip findeth Nathanael, and saith unto him, We have found him, of whom Moses in the law, and the prophets, did write, Jesus of Nazareth, the son of Joseph.

46 And Nathanael said unto him, Can there any good thing come out of Nazareth? Philip saith unto him, Come and see.

47 Jesus saw Nathanael

ποῦ μένει, καὶ παρ' αὐτῷ ἔμειναν τὴν
where he remains(ed), and with him remained –

ἡμέραν ἐκείνην· ὥρα ἦν ὡς δεκάτη.
day that; hour was about tenth.

40 Ἦν Ἀνδρέας ὁ ἀδελφὸς Σίμωνος Πέτρου
It was Andrew the brother of Simon Peter

εἷς ἐκ τῶν δύο τῶν ἀκουσάντων παρὰ
one of the two the hearing from

Ἰωάννου καὶ ἀκολουθησάντων αὐτῷ·
John and following him;

41 εὑρίσκει οὗτος πρῶτον τὸν ἀδελφὸν τὸν
³finds ¹this one ²first ⁴the(his) ⁵brother –

ἴδιον Σίμωνα καὶ λέγει αὐτῷ· εὑρήκαμεν
⁶own Simon and tells him : We have found

τὸν Μεσσίαν (ὅ ἐστιν μεθερμηνευόμενον
the Messiah (which is being translated

χριστός). **42** ἤγαγεν αὐτὸν πρὸς τὸν
Christ). He led him to –

Ἰησοῦν. ἐμβλέψας αὐτῷ ὁ Ἰησοῦς εἶπεν·
Jesus. Looking at him – Jesus said :

σὺ εἶ Σίμων ὁ υἱὸς Ἰωάννου, σὺ κληθήσῃ
Thou art Simon the son of John, thou shalt be called

Κηφᾶς (ὃ ἑρμηνεύεται Πέτρος). **43** Τῇ
Cephas (which is translated Peter). On the

ἐπαύριον ἠθέλησεν ἐξελθεῖν εἰς τὴν Γαλιλαίαν,
morrow he wished to go forth into – Galilee,

καὶ εὑρίσκει Φίλιππον. καὶ λέγει αὐτῷ ὁ
and finds Philip. And says to him –

Ἰησοῦς· ἀκολούθει μοι. **44** ἦν δὲ ὁ
Jesus : Follow me. Now was –

Φίλιππος ἀπὸ Βηθσαϊδά, ἐκ τῆς πόλεως
Philip from Bethsaida, of the city

Ἀνδρέου καὶ Πέτρου. **45** εὑρίσκει Φίλιππος
of Andrew and of Peter. ²Finds ¹Philip

τὸν Ναθαναὴλ καὶ λέγει αὐτῷ· ὃν ἔγραψεν
– ³Nathanael and tells him : [He] whom wrote

Μωϋσῆς ἐν τῷ νόμῳ καὶ οἱ προφῆται
Moses in the law and the prophets

εὑρήκαμεν, Ἰησοῦν υἱὸν τοῦ Ἰωσὴφ τὸν
we have found, Jesus son – of Joseph the

ἀπὸ Ναζαρέθ. **46** καὶ εἶπεν αὐτῷ
from Nazareth. And said to him

Ναθαναήλ· ἐκ Ναζαρὲθ δύναταί τι ἀγαθὸν
Nathanael : Out of Nazareth can anything good

εἶναι; λέγει αὐτῷ ὁ Φίλιππος· ἔρχου καὶ
to be? Says to him – Philip : Come and

ἴδε. **47** εἶδεν Ἰησοῦς τὸν Ναθαναὴλ
see. ²Saw ¹Jesus – ³Nathanael

coming to him, and saith of him, Behold an Israelite indeed, in whom is no guile!

48 Nathanael saith unto him, Whence knowest thou me? Jesus answered and said unto him, Before that Philip called thee, when thou wast under the fig tree, I saw thee.

49 Nathanael answered and saith unto him, Rabbi, thou art the Son of God; thou art the King of Israel.

50 Jesus answered and said unto him, Because I said unto thee, I saw thee under the fig tree, believest thou? thou shalt see greater things than these.

51 And he saith unto him, Verily, verily, I say unto you, Hereafter ye shall see heaven open, and the angels of God ascending and descending upon the Son of man.

ἐρχόμενον πρὸς αὐτὸν καὶ λέγει περὶ
coming toward him and says concerning
αὐτοῦ· ἴδε ἀληθῶς Ἰσραηλίτης, ἐν ᾧ
him: Behold[,] truly an Israelite, in whom
δόλος οὐκ ἔστιν. 48 λέγει αὐτῷ Ναθαναήλ·
guile is not. Says to him Nathanael:
πόθεν με γινώσκεις; ἀπεκρίθη Ἰησοῦς καὶ
Whence me knowest thou? Answered Jesus and
εἶπεν αὐτῷ· πρὸ τοῦ σε Φίλιππον φωνῆσαι
said to him: Before *the* thee Philip to call[b]
=Philip called thee
ὄντα ὑπὸ τὴν συκῆν εἶδόν σε. 49 ἀπεκρίθη
being under the fig-tree I saw thee. Answered
αὐτῷ Ναθαναήλ· ῥαββί, σὺ εἶ ὁ υἱὸς τοῦ
him Nathanael: Rabbi, thou art the Son –
θεοῦ, σὺ βασιλεὺς εἶ τοῦ Ἰσραήλ.
of God, thou king art – of Israel.
50 ἀπεκρίθη Ἰησοῦς καὶ εἶπεν αὐτῷ·
Answered Jesus and said to him:
ὅτι εἶπόν σοι ὅτι εἶδόν σε ὑποκάτω τῆς
Because I told thee that I saw thee underneath the
συκῆς, πιστεύεις; μείζω τούτων ὄψῃ.
fig-tree, believest thou? greater [than] these things thou shalt see.
51 καὶ λέγει αὐτῷ· ἀμὴν ἀμὴν λέγω
And he says to him: Truly truly I tell
ὑμῖν, ὄψεσθε τὸν οὐρανὸν ἀνεῳγότα καὶ
you, ye shall see the heaven *having been* opened and
τοὺς ἀγγέλους τοῦ θεοῦ ἀναβαίνοντας καὶ
the angels – of God going up and
καταβαίνοντας ἐπὶ τὸν υἱὸν τοῦ ἀνθρώπου.
coming down on the Son – of man.

CHAPTER 2

A ND the third day there was a marriage in Cana of Galilee; and the mother of Jesus was there:

2 And both Jesus was called, and his disciples, to the marriage.

3 And when they wanted wine, the mother of Jesus saith unto him, They have no wine.

4 Jesus saith unto her, Woman, what have I to do with thee? mine hour is not yet come.

2 Καὶ τῇ ἡμέρᾳ τῇ τρίτῃ γάμος ἐγένετο
And on the day – third a wedding there was
ἐν Κανὰ τῆς Γαλιλαίας, καὶ ἦν ἡ μήτηρ
in Cana – of Galilee, and was the mother
τοῦ Ἰησοῦ ἐκεῖ· 2 ἐκλήθη δὲ καὶ ὁ
– of Jesus there; and was invited both –
Ἰησοῦς καὶ οἱ μαθηταὶ αὐτοῦ εἰς τὸν
Jesus and the disciples of him to the
γάμον. 3 καὶ ὑστερήσαντος οἴνου λέγει ἡ
wedding. And lacking wine[a] says the
=when wine was lacking
μήτηρ τοῦ Ἰησοῦ πρὸς αὐτόν· οἶνον
mother – of Jesus to him: Wine
οὐκ ἔχουσιν. 4 καὶ λέγει αὐτῇ ὁ Ἰησοῦς·
they have not. And says to her – Jesus:
τί ἐμοὶ καὶ σοί, γύναι; οὔπω ἥκει ἡ
What to me and to thee, woman? not yet is come the

5 His mother saith unto the servants, Whatsoever he saith unto you, do *it*.

6 And there were set there six waterpots of stone, after the manner of the purifying of the Jews, containing two or three firkins apiece.

7 Jesus saith unto them, Fill the waterpots with water. And they filled them up to the brim.

8 And he saith unto them, Draw out now, and bear unto the governor of the feast. And they bare *it*.

9 When the ruler of the feast had tasted the water that was made wine, and knew not whence it was: (but the servants which drew the water knew;) the governor of the feast called the bridegroom,

10 And saith unto him, Every man at the beginning doth set forth good wine; and when men have well drunk, then that which is worse: *but* thou hast kept the good wine until now.

11 This beginning of miracles did Jesus in Cana of Galilee, and manifested forth his glory; and his disciples believed on him.

12 ¶ After this he went down to Capernaum, he, and his mother, and his brethren, and his disciples:

ὥρα μου. 5 λέγει ἡ μήτηρ αὐτοῦ τοῖς
hour of me. Says the mother of him to the

διακόνοις· ὅ τι ἂν λέγῃ ὑμῖν, ποιήσατε.
servants: Whatever he tells you, do ye.

6 ἦσαν δὲ ἐκεῖ λίθιναι ὑδρίαι ἓξ κατὰ
Now there were there stone water-pots six according to

τὸν καθαρισμὸν τῶν Ἰουδαίων κείμεναι,
the purifying of the Jews lying,

χωροῦσαι ἀνὰ μετρητὰς δύο ἢ τρεῖς.
containing each† measures two or three.

7 λέγει αὐτοῖς ὁ Ἰησοῦς· γεμίσατε τὰς
Tells them – Jesus: Fill ye the

ὑδρίας ὕδατος. καὶ ἐγέμισαν αὐτὰς ἕως
water-pots of(with) water. And they filled them up to

ἄνω. 8 καὶ λέγει αὐτοῖς· ἀντλήσατε νῦν
[the] top. And he tells them: Draw now

καὶ φέρετε τῷ ἀρχιτρικλίνῳ. οἱ δὲ
and carry to the master of the feast. And they

ἤνεγκαν. 9 ὡς δὲ ἐγεύσατο ὁ ἀρχιτρίκλινος
carried. But when tasted the master of the feast

τὸ ὕδωρ οἶνον γεγενημένον, καὶ οὐκ ᾔδει
the water ²wine ¹having become, and did not know

πόθεν ἐστίν, οἱ δὲ διάκονοι ᾔδεισαν οἱ
whence it is(was), but the servants knew the [ones]

ἠντληκότες τὸ ὕδωρ, φωνεῖ τὸν νυμφίον
having drawn the water, ³calls ⁴the ⁵bridegroom

ὁ ἀρχιτρίκλινος 10 καὶ λέγει αὐτῷ· πᾶς
¹the ²master of the feast and says to him: Every

ἄνθρωπος πρῶτον τὸν καλὸν οἶνον τίθησιν,
man first the good wine sets forth,

καὶ ὅταν μεθυσθῶσιν τὸν ἐλάσσω· σὺ
and when they become drunk the worse; thou

τετήρηκας τὸν καλὸν οἶνον ἕως ἄρτι.
hast kept the good wine until now.

11 Ταύτην ἐποίησεν ἀρχὴν τῶν σημείων ὁ
¹This ⁵did ²beginning ³of the ⁴signs –

Ἰησοῦς ἐν Κανὰ τῆς Γαλιλαίας καὶ
Jesus in Cana of Galilee and

ἐφανέρωσεν τὴν δόξαν αὐτοῦ, καὶ ἐπίστευσαν
manifested the glory of him, and believed

εἰς αὐτὸν οἱ μαθηταὶ αὐτοῦ.
in him the disciples of him.

12 Μετὰ τοῦτο κατέβη εἰς Καφαρναοὺμ
After this went down to Capernaum

αὐτὸς καὶ ἡ μήτηρ αὐτοῦ καὶ
he and the mother of him and

οἱ ἀδελφοὶ καὶ οἱ μαθηταὶ αὐτοῦ, καὶ
the brothers and the disciples of him, and

and they continued there
not many days.

13 ¶ And the Jews' pass-
over was at hand, and
Jesus went up to Jeru-
salem,

14 And found in the
temple those that sold
oxen and sheep and doves,
and the changers of money
sitting:

15 And when he had
made a scourge of small
cords, he drove them all
out of the temple, and the
sheep, and the oxen; and
poured out the changers'
money, and overthrew the
tables;

16 And said unto them
that sold doves, Take these
things hence; make not
my Father's house an
house of merchandise.

17 And his disciples
remembered that it was
written, The zeal of thine
house hath eaten me up.

18 ¶ Then answered the
Jews and said unto him,
What sign shewest thou
unto us, seeing that thou
doest these things?

19 Jesus answered and
said unto them, Destroy
this temple, and in three
days I will raise it up.

20 Then said the Jews,
Forty and six years was
this temple in building,
and wilt thou rear it up in
three days?

21 But he spake of the
temple of his body.

ἐκεῖ ἔμειναν οὐ πολλὰς ἡμέρας.
there remained not many days.

13 Καὶ ἐγγὺς ἦν τὸ πάσχα τῶν Ἰουδαίων,
And near was the Passover of the Jews,
καὶ ἀνέβη εἰς Ἱεροσόλυμα ὁ Ἰησοῦς.
and went up to Jerusalem - Jesus.

14 καὶ εὗρεν ἐν τῷ ἱερῷ τοὺς πωλοῦντας
And he found in the temple the [ones] selling
βόας καὶ πρόβατα καὶ περιστερὰς καὶ τοὺς
oxen and sheep and doves and the
κερματιστὰς καθημένους, 15 καὶ ποιήσας
coindealers sitting, and having made
φραγέλλιον ἐκ σχοινίων πάντας ἐξέβαλεν
a lash out of ropes ²all ¹he expelled
ἐκ τοῦ ἱεροῦ, τά τε πρόβατα καὶ τοὺς
out of the temple, both the sheep and the
βόας, καὶ τῶν κολλυβιστῶν ἐξέχεεν τὰ
oxen, and ⁴of the ⁵moneychangers ¹poured out ³the
κέρματα καὶ τὰς τραπέζας ἀνέτρεψεν,
³coins ⁶and ⁸the ⁹tables ⁷overturned,

16 καὶ τοῖς τὰς περιστερὰς πωλοῦσιν
and ²to the [ones] ⁴the ⁵doves ³selling
εἶπεν· ἄρατε ταῦτα ἐντεῦθεν, μὴ ποιεῖτε
¹said: Take these things hence, do not make
τὸν οἶκον τοῦ πατρός μου οἶκον ἐμπορίου.
the house of the Father of me a house of merchandise.

17 ἐμνήσθησαν οἱ μαθηταὶ αὐτοῦ ὅτι
Remembered the disciples of him that
γεγραμμένον ἐστίν· ὁ ζῆλος τοῦ οἴκου
having been written it is: The zeal of the house
σου καταφάγεταί με. 18 ἀπεκρίθησαν οὖν
of thee will consume me. Answered therefore
οἱ Ἰουδαῖοι καὶ εἶπαν αὐτῷ· τί σημεῖον
the Jews and said to him: What sign
δεικνύεις ἡμῖν, ὅτι ταῦτα ποιεῖς;
showest thou to us, because these things thou doest?

19 ἀπεκρίθη Ἰησοῦς καὶ εἶπεν αὐτοῖς· λύσατε τὸν
Answered Jesus and said to them: Destroy -
ναὸν τοῦτον, καὶ ἐν τρισὶν ἡμέραις ἐγερῶ αὐτόν.
shrine this, and in three days I will raise it.

20 εἶπαν οὖν οἱ Ἰουδαῖοι· τεσσεράκοντα
Said therefore the Jews: In forty
καὶ ἓξ ἔτεσιν οἰκοδομήθη ὁ ναὸς οὗτος,
and six years was built - shrine this,
καὶ σὺ ἐν τρισὶν ἡμέραις ἐγερεῖς αὐτόν;
and thou in three days wilt raise it?

21 ἐκεῖνος δὲ ἔλεγεν περὶ τοῦ ναοῦ τοῦ
But that [one]* spoke about the shrine of the

---

* John repeatedly uses the demonstrative adjective ἐκεῖνος in
the sense of " he," referring to Christ.

22 When therefore he was risen from the dead, his disciples remembered that he had said this unto them; and they believed the scripture, and the word which Jesus had said.

23 ¶ Now when he was in Jerusalem at the passover, in the feast *day*, many believed in his name, when they saw the miracles which he did.

24 But Jesus did not commit himself unto them, because he knew all *men*,

25 And needed not that any should testify of man: for he knew what was in man.

CHAPTER 3

THERE was a man of the Pharisees, named Nicodemus, a ruler of the Jews:

2 The same came to Jesus by night, and said unto him, Rabbi, we know that thou art a teacher come from God: for no man can do these miracles that thou doest, except God be with him.

3 Jesus answered and said unto him, Verily, verily, I say unto thee, Except a man be born again, he cannot see the kingdom of God.

4 Nicodemus saith unto him, How can a man be born when he is old? can

σώματος αὐτοῦ. **22** ὅτε οὖν ἠγέρθη ἐκ
body of him.   When therefore he was raised from
νεκρῶν, ἐμνήσθησαν οἱ μαθηταὶ αὐτοῦ
[the] dead,   remembered   the   disciples   of him
ὅτι τοῦτο ἔλεγεν, καὶ ἐπίστευσαν τῇ
that   this   he said,   and   they believed   the
γραφῇ καὶ τῷ λόγῳ ὃν εἶπεν ὁ Ἰησοῦς.
scripture   and   the   word   which   said   –   Jesus.
23 Ὡς δὲ ἦν ἐν τοῖς Ἱεροσολύμοις ἐν
And when he was in   –   Jerusalem   at
τῷ πάσχα ἐν τῇ ἑορτῇ, πολλοὶ ἐπίστευσαν
the Passover at the   feast,   many   believed
εἰς τὸ ὄνομα αὐτοῦ, θεωροῦντες αὐτοῦ τὰ
in   the   name   of him,   beholding   of him   the
σημεῖα ἃ ἐποίει· **24** αὐτὸς δὲ Ἰησοῦς
signs   which he was doing;   [3]but [3][him]self [2]Jesus
οὐκ ἐπίστευεν αὐτὸν αὐτοῖς διὰ τὸ αὐτὸν
did not commit   himself   to them because of the   him
                                                  =because he knew
γινώσκειν πάντας, **25** καὶ ὅτι οὐ χρείαν εἶχεν
to know[b]   all men,   and because no   need   he had
ἵνα τις μαρτυρήσῃ περὶ τοῦ ἀνθρώπου·
that anyone should witness concerning   –   man;
αὐτὸς γὰρ ἐγίνωσκεν τί ἦν ἐν τῷ ἀνθρώπῳ.
for he   knew   what was in   –   man.
3 Ἦν δὲ ἄνθρωπος ἐκ τῶν Φαρισαίων,
Now there was   a man   of   the   Pharisees,
Νικόδημος ὄνομα αὐτῷ, ἄρχων τῶν
Nicodemus   name   to him[c],   a ruler   of the
                    =his name,
Ἰουδαίων· **2** οὗτος ἦλθεν πρὸς αὐτὸν νυκτὸς
Jews;   this man   came   to   him of(by) night
καὶ εἶπεν αὐτῷ· ῥαββί, οἴδαμεν ὅτι ἀπὸ
and   said   to him :   Rabbi,   we know   that   from
θεοῦ ἐλήλυθας διδάσκαλος· οὐδεὶς γὰρ
God   thou hast come   a teacher;   for no one
δύναται ταῦτα τὰ σημεῖα ποιεῖν ἃ σὺ
can   these   –   signs   *to* do which thou
ποιεῖς, ἐὰν μὴ ᾖ ὁ θεὸς μετ' αὐτοῦ.
doest,   except   [2]is   –   [1]God   with   him.
3 ἀπεκρίθη Ἰησοῦς καὶ εἶπεν αὐτῷ· ἀμὴν
Answered   Jesus   and   said   to him :   Truly
ἀμὴν λέγω σοι, ἐὰν μή τις γεννηθῇ
truly   I tell   thee,   except   anyone   is born
ἄνωθεν, οὐ δύναται ἰδεῖν τὴν βασιλείαν
from above,   he cannot   *to* see   the   kingdom
τοῦ θεοῦ. **4** λέγει πρὸς αὐτὸν ὁ Νικόδημος·
–   of God.   Says   to   him   –   Nicodemus :
πῶς δύναται ἄνθρωπος γεννηθῆναι γέρων ὤν;
How   can   a man   *to* be born   old   being?

he enter the second time into his mother's womb, and be born?

5 Jesus answered, Verily, verily, I say unto thee, Except a man be born of water and of the Spirit, he cannot enter into the kingdom of God.

6 That which is born of the flesh is flesh; and that which is born of the Spirit is spirit.

7 Marvel not that I said unto thee, Ye must be born again.

8 The wind bloweth where it listeth, and thou hearest the sound thereof, but canst not tell whence it cometh, and whither it goeth: so is every one that is born of the Spirit.

9 Nicodemus answered and said unto him, How can these things be?

10 Jesus answered and said unto him, Art thou a master of Israel, and knowest not these things?

11 Verily, verily, I say unto thee, We speak that we do know, and testify that we have seen; and ye receive not our witness.

12 If I have told you earthly things, and ye believe not, how shall ye believe, if I tell you of heavenly things?

13 And no man hath ascended up to heaven,

μὴ δύναται εἰς τὴν κοιλίαν τῆς μητρὸς
not can he into the womb of the mother

αὐτοῦ δεύτερον εἰσελθεῖν καὶ γεννηθῆναι;
of him secondly to enter and to be born?

5 ἀπεκρίθη Ἰησοῦς· ἀμὴν ἀμὴν λέγω σοι,
Answered Jesus : Truly truly I tell thee,

ἐὰν μή τις γεννηθῇ ἐξ ὕδατος καὶ
except anyone is born of water and

πνεύματος, οὐ δύναται εἰσελθεῖν εἰς τὴν
spirit, he cannot to enter into the

βασιλείαν τοῦ θεοῦ. 6 τὸ γεγεννημένον ἐκ
kingdom – of God. The thing having been born of

τῆς σαρκὸς σάρξ ἐστιν, καὶ τὸ γεγεννημένον
the flesh flesh is, and the thing having been

ἐκ τοῦ πνεύματος πνεῦμά ἐστιν. 7 μὴ
of the Spirit spirit is. not

θαυμάσῃς ὅτι εἶπόν σοι· δεῖ ὑμᾶς
Marvel because I told thee : It behoves you

γεννηθῆναι ἄνωθεν. 8 τὸ πνεῦμα ὅπου θέλει
to be born from above. The spirit(?wind) where it wishes

πνεῖ, καὶ τὴν φωνὴν αὐτοῦ ἀκούεις, ἀλλ'
blows, and the sound of it thou hearest, but

οὐκ οἶδας πόθεν ἔρχεται καὶ ποῦ ὑπάγει·
thou knowest not whence it comes and whither it goes;

οὕτως ἐστὶν πᾶς ὁ γεγεννημένος ἐκ τοῦ
so is everyone having been born of the

πνεύματος. 9 ἀπεκρίθη Νικόδημος καὶ
Spirit. Answered Nicodemus and

εἶπεν αὐτῷ· πῶς δύναται ταῦτα γενέσθαι;
said to him : How can these things to come about?

10 ἀπεκρίθη Ἰησοῦς καὶ εἶπεν αὐτῷ· σὺ
Answered Jesus and said to him : Thou

εἶ ὁ διδάσκαλος τοῦ Ἰσραὴλ καὶ ταῦτα
art the teacher – of Israel and these things

οὐ γινώσκεις; 11 ἀμὴν ἀμὴν λέγω σοι ὅτι
knowest not? Truly truly I tell thee[,] –

ὃ οἴδαμεν λαλοῦμεν καὶ ὃ ἑωράκαμεν
What we know we speak and what we have seen

μαρτυροῦμεν, καὶ τὴν μαρτυρίαν ἡμῶν
we witness, and the witness of us

οὐ λαμβάνετε. 12 εἰ τὰ ἐπίγεια εἶπον
ye receive not. If the earthly things I told

ὑμῖν καὶ οὐ πιστεύετε, πῶς ἐὰν εἴπω
you and ye believe not, how if I tell

ὑμῖν τὰ ἐπουράνια πιστεύσετε; 13 καὶ
you the heavenly things will ye believe? And

οὐδεὶς ἀναβέβηκεν εἰς τὸν οὐρανὸν εἰ μὴ
no man has gone up into – heaven except

but he that came down from heaven, *even* the Son of man which is in heaven.

14 And as Moses lifted up the serpent in the wilderness, even so must the Son of man be lifted up:

15 That whosoever believeth in him should not perish, but have eternal life.

16 For God so loved the world, that he gave his only begotten Son, that whosoever believeth in him should not perish, but have everlasting life.

17 For God sent not his Son into the world to condemn the world; but that the world through him might be saved.

18 He that believeth on him is not condemned: but he that believeth not is condemned already, because he hath not believed in the name of the only begotten Son of God.

19 And this is the condemnation, that light is come into the world, and men loved darkness rather than light, because their deeds were evil.

20 For every one that doeth evil hateth the light, neither cometh to the light, lest his deeds should be reproved.

21 But he that doeth truth cometh to the light, that his deeds may be made manifest, that they

---

ὁ ἐκ - τοῦ οὐρανοῦ καταβάς, ὁ υἱὸς
the [one] out of - heaven having come down, the Son
τοῦ ἀνθρώπου. 14 Καὶ καθὼς Μωϋσῆς ὕψωσεν
- of man. And as Moses lifted up
τὸν ὄφιν ἐν τῇ ἐρήμῳ, οὕτως ὑψωθῆναι
the serpent in the desert, so to be lifted up
δεῖ τὸν υἱὸν τοῦ ἀνθρώπου, 15 ἵνα πᾶς ὁ
it behoves the Son of man, that everyone
πιστεύων ἐν αὐτῷ ἔχῃ ζωὴν αἰώνιον.
believing in him may have life eternal.
16 οὕτως γὰρ ἠγάπησεν ὁ θεὸς τὸν
For thus ²loved - ¹God the
κόσμον, ὥστε τὸν υἱὸν τὸν μονογενῆ
world, so as the Son the only begotten
ἔδωκεν, ἵνα πᾶς ὁ πιστεύων εἰς αὐτὸν
he gave, that everyone believing in him
μὴ ἀπόληται ἀλλ' ἔχῃ ζωὴν αἰώνιον.
may not perish but may have life eternal.
17 οὐ γὰρ ἀπέστειλεν ὁ θεὸς τὸν υἱὸν
For ²not ²sent - ¹God the Son
εἰς τὸν κόσμον ἵνα κρίνῃ τὸν κόσμον,
into the world that he might judge the world,
ἀλλ' ἵνα σωθῇ ὁ κόσμος δι' αὐτοῦ.
but that ²might be saved ¹the ²world through him.
18 ὁ πιστεύων εἰς αὐτὸν οὐ κρίνεται·
The [one] believing in him is not judged;
ὁ μὴ πιστεύων ἤδη κέκριται, ὅτι
the [one] not believing already has been judged, because
μὴ πεπίστευκεν εἰς τὸ ὄνομα τοῦ μονογενοῦς
he has not believed in the name of the only begotten
υἱοῦ τοῦ θεοῦ. 19 αὕτη δέ ἐστιν ἡ
Son - of God. And this is the
κρίσις, ὅτι τὸ φῶς ἐλήλυθεν εἰς τὸν
judgment, that the light has come into the
κόσμον καὶ ἠγάπησαν οἱ ἄνθρωποι μᾶλλον
world and ²loved - ¹men ⁵rather
τὸ σκότος ἢ τὸ φῶς· ἦν γὰρ αὐτῶν
³the ⁴darkness ⁶than the light; for was(were) of them
πονηρὰ τὰ ἔργα. 20 πᾶς γὰρ ὁ φαῦλα
evil the works. For everyone evil things
πράσσων μισεῖ τὸ φῶς καὶ οὐκ ἔρχεται
doing hates the light and does not come
πρὸς τὸ φῶς, ἵνα μὴ ἐλεγχθῇ τὰ ἔργα
to the light, lest is(are) reproved the works
αὐτοῦ· 21 ὁ δὲ ποιῶν τὴν ἀλήθειαν ἔρχεται
of him; but the [one] doing the truth comes
πρὸς τὸ φῶς, ἵνα φανερωθῇ αὐτοῦ τὰ
to the light, that may be manifested of him the

are wrought in God.

22 ¶ After these things came Jesus and his disciples into the land of Judæa; and there he tarried with them, and baptized.

23 And John also was baptizing in Ænon near to Salim, because there was much water there: and they came, and were baptized.

24 For John was not yet cast into prison.

25 ¶ Then there arose a question between some of John's disciples and the Jews about purifying.

26 And they came unto John, and said unto him, Rabbi, he that was with thee beyond Jordan, to whom thou barest witness, behold, the same baptizeth, and all men come to him.

27 John answered and said, A man can receive nothing, except it be given him from heaven.

28 Ye yourselves bear me witness, that I said, I am not the Christ, but that I am sent before him.

29 He that hath the bride is the bridegroom: but the friend of the bridegroom, which standeth and heareth him, rejoiceth greatly because of the

ἔργα ὅτι ἐν θεῷ ἐστιν εἰργασμένα.
works that in God they are *having been* wrought.

22 Μετὰ ταῦτα ἦλθεν ὁ Ἰησοῦς καὶ οἱ
After these things came – Jesus and the

μαθηταὶ αὐτοῦ εἰς τὴν Ἰουδαίαν γῆν, καὶ
disciples of him into *the* Judæan *land*, and

ἐκεῖ διέτριβεν μετ᾽ αὐτῶν καὶ ἐβάπτιζεν.
there continued with them and baptized.

23 ἦν δὲ καὶ Ἰωάννης βαπτίζων ἐν
And was also John baptizing in

Αἰνὼν ἐγγὺς τοῦ Σαλίμ, ὅτι ὕδατα
Ainon near – Salim, because waters

πολλὰ ἦν ἐκεῖ, καὶ παρεγίνοντο καὶ
many was(were) there, and they came and

ἐβαπτίζοντο· 24 οὔπω γὰρ ἦν βεβλημένος
were baptized; for ³not yet ²was ¹*having been* cast

εἰς τὴν φυλακὴν Ἰωάννης. 25 Ἐγένετο
³into ⁴the ⁵prison ¹John. There was

οὖν ζήτησις ἐκ τῶν μαθητῶν Ἰωάννου
therefore a questioning of the disciples of John

μετὰ Ἰουδαίου περὶ καθαρισμοῦ. 26 καὶ
with a Jew about purifying. And

ἦλθον πρὸς τὸν Ἰωάννην καὶ εἶπαν αὐτῷ·
they came to – John and said to him:

ῥαββί, ὃς ἦν μετὰ σοῦ πέραν τοῦ
Rabbi, [he] who was with thee beyond the

Ἰορδάνου, ᾧ σὺ μεμαρτύρηκας, ἴδε
Jordan, to whom thou hast borne witness, behold[,]

οὗτος βαπτίζει καὶ πάντες ἔρχονται πρὸς
this man baptizes and all men are coming to

αὐτόν. 27 ἀπεκρίθη Ἰωάννης καὶ εἶπεν·
him. Answered John and said:

οὐ δύναται ἄνθρωπος λαμβάνειν οὐδὲν ἐὰν μὴ
Cannot a man *to* receive no(any)thing unless

ᾖ δεδομένον αὐτῷ ἐκ τοῦ οὐρανοῦ.
it is *having been* given to him out of – heaven.

28 αὐτοὶ ὑμεῖς μοι μαρτυρεῖτε ὅτι εἶπον·
[Your]selves ye to me bear witness that I said:

οὐκ εἰμὶ ἐγὼ ὁ χριστός, ἀλλ᾽ ὅτι
³not ²am ¹I the Christ, but that

ἀπεσταλμένος εἰμὶ ἔμπροσθεν ἐκείνου. 29 ὁ
having been sent I am before that one.* The [one]

ἔχων τὴν νύμφην νυμφίος ἐστίν· ὁ δὲ
having the bride a bridegroom is; but the

φίλος τοῦ νυμφίου, ὁ ἑστηκὼς καὶ ἀκούων
friend of the bridegroom, – standing and hearing

αὐτοῦ, χαρᾷ χαίρει διὰ τὴν φωνὴν τοῦ
him, with joy rejoices because of the voice of the

* See note to 2. 21.

bridegroom's voice: this my joy therefore is fulfilled.

30 He must increase, but I *must* decrease.

31 He that cometh from above is above all: he that is of the earth is earthly, and speaketh of the earth: he that cometh from heaven is above all.

32 And what he hath seen and heard, that he testifieth; and no man receiveth his testimony.

33 He that hath received his testimony hath set to his seal that God is true.

34 For he whom God hath sent speaketh the words of God: for God giveth not the Spirit by measure *unto him.*

35 The Father loveth the Son, and hath given all things into his hand.

36 He that believeth on the Son hath everlasting life: and he that believeth not the Son shall not see life; but the wrath of God abideth on him.

νυμφίου.   αὕτη   οὖν   ἡ   χαρὰ   ἡ   ἐμὴ
bridegroom. ⁺ ²This ¹therefore – ⁴joy – ³my

πεπλήρωται. 30 ἐκεῖνον   δεῖ   αὐξάνειν,   ἐμὲ
has been fulfilled. That one it behoves to increase, ³me

δὲ   ἐλαττοῦσθαι.   31 Ὁ   ἄνωθεν   ἐρχόμενος
¹but   to decrease.   The [one] from above coming

ἐπάνω   πάντων   ἐστίν·   ὁ   ὢν   ἐκ   τῆς   γῆς
over   all   is;   the [one] being of   the   earth

ἐκ   τῆς   γῆς   ἐστιν   καὶ   ἐκ   τῆς   γῆς   λαλεῖ.
of   the   earth   is   and   of   the   earth   speaks.

ὁ   ἐκ   τοῦ   οὐρανοῦ   ἐρχόμενος   ἐπάνω
The [one] of – heaven   coming   over

πάντων   ἐστίν·   32 ὃ   ἑώρακεν   καὶ   ἤκουσεν,
all   is;   what he has seen   and   heard,

τοῦτο   μαρτυρεῖ,   καὶ   τὴν   μαρτυρίαν   αὐτοῦ
this   he witnesses [to],   and   the   witness   of him

οὐδεὶς   λαμβάνει.   33 ὁ   λαβὼν   αὐτοῦ   τὴν
no man   receives.   The [one] receiving of him   the

μαρτυρίαν   ἐσφράγισεν   ὅτι   ὁ   θεὸς   ἀληθής
witness   sealed   that   –   God   true

ἐστιν.   34 ὃν   γὰρ   ἀπέστειλεν   ὁ   θεὸς   τὰ
is.   For [he] whom   ²sent   –   ¹God   the

ῥήματα   τοῦ   θεοῦ   λαλεῖ·   οὐ   γὰρ   ἐκ
words   –   of God   speaks;   for not   by

μέτρου   δίδωσιν   τὸ   πνεῦμα.   35 ὁ   πατὴρ
measure   he gives   the   Spirit.   The   Father

ἀγαπᾷ   τὸν   υἱόν,   καὶ   πάντα   δέδωκεν   ἐν
loves   the   Son,   and   all things   has given   in[to]

τῇ   χειρὶ   αὐτοῦ.   36 ὁ   πιστεύων   εἰς   τὸν
the   hand   of him.   The [one] believing   in   the

υἱὸν   ἔχει   ζωὴν   αἰώνιον·   ὁ   δὲ   ἀπειθῶν
Son   has   life   eternal;   but the [one]   disobeying

τῷ   υἱῷ   οὐκ   ὄψεται   ζωήν,   ἀλλ'   ἡ   ὀργὴ
the   Son   will not see   life,   but   the   wrath

τοῦ   θεοῦ   μένει   ἐπ'   αὐτόν.
–   of God   remains   on   him.

CHAPTER 4

WHEN therefore the Lord knew how the Pharisees had heard that Jesus made and baptized more disciples than John,

2 (Though Jesus himself baptized not, but his disciples,)

3 He left Judæa, and

4 Ὡς   οὖν   ἔγνω   ὁ   κύριος   ὅτι   ἤκουσαν
²When ¹therefore ⁵knew ³the ⁴Lord ⁶that ⁷heard

οἱ   Φαρισαῖοι   ὅτι   Ἰησοῦς   πλείονας   μαθητὰς
⁷the   ⁸Pharisees   that   Jesus   more   disciples

ποιεῖ   καὶ   βαπτίζει   ἢ   Ἰωάννης,   —   2 καίτοι   γε
makes   and   baptizes   than   John,   —   though

Ἰησοῦς   αὐτὸς   οὐκ   ἐβάπτιζεν   ἀλλ'   οἱ
Jesus   [him]self   baptized not   but   the

μαθηταὶ   αὐτοῦ,   —   3 ἀφῆκεν   τὴν   Ἰουδαίαν
disciples   of him,   —   he left   –   Judæa

departed again into Galilee.

4 And he must needs go through Samaria.

5 Then cometh he to a city of Samaria, which is called Sychar, near to the parcel of ground that Jacob gave to his son Joseph.

6 Now Jacob's well was there. Jesus therefore, being wearied with *his* journey, sat thus on the well: *and* it was about the sixth hour.

7 There cometh a woman of Samaria to draw water: Jesus saith unto her, Give me to drink.

8 (For his disciples were gone away unto the city to buy meat.)

9 Then saith the woman of Samaria unto him, How is it that thou, being a Jew, askest drink of me, which am a woman of Samaria? for the Jews have no dealings with the Samaritans.

10 Jesus answered and said unto her, If thou knewest the gift of God, and who it is that saith to thee, Give me to drink; thou wouldest have asked of him, and he would have given thee living water.

11 The woman saith unto him, Sir, thou hast nothing to draw with, and the well is deep: from whence then hast thou that living water?

12 Art thou greater than

καὶ ἀπῆλθεν πάλιν εἰς τὴν Γαλιλαίαν.
and went away again into – Galilee.

4 Ἔδει δὲ αὐτὸν διέρχεσθαι διὰ τῆς
And it behoved him to pass through *through* –

Σαμαρείας. 5 ἔρχεται οὖν εἰς πόλιν τῆς
Samaria. He comes therefore to a city –

Σαμαρείας λεγομένην Σύχαρ, πλησίον τοῦ
of Samaria *being* called Sychar, near the

χωρίου ὃ ἔδωκεν Ἰακὼβ [τῷ] Ἰωσὴφ
piece of land which ²gave ¹Jacob – to Joseph

τῷ υἱῷ αὐτοῦ· 6 ἦν δὲ ἐκεῖ πηγὴ τοῦ
the son of him; and was there a fountain –

Ἰακώβ. ὁ οὖν Ἰησοῦς κεκοπιακὼς ἐκ
of Jacob. – Therefore Jesus having become wearied from

τῆς ὁδοιπορίας ἐκαθέζετο οὕτως ἐπὶ τῇ
the journey sat thus at the

πηγῇ· ὥρα ἦν ὡς ἕκτη. 7 ἔρχεται γυνὴ
fountain; [the] hour was about sixth. Comes a woman

ἐκ τῆς Σαμαρείας ἀντλῆσαι ὕδωρ. λέγει
of – Samaria to draw water. Says

αὐτῇ ὁ Ἰησοῦς· δός μοι πεῖν. 8 οἱ γὰρ
to her – Jesus : Give me to drink. For the

μαθηταὶ αὐτοῦ ἀπεληλύθεισαν εἰς τὴν
disciples of him had gone away into the

πόλιν, ἵνα τροφὰς ἀγοράσωσιν. 9 λέγει
city, that foods they might buy. Says

οὖν αὐτῷ ἡ γυνὴ ἡ Σαμαρῖτις· πῶς
therefore to him the woman – Samaritan : How

σὺ Ἰουδαῖος ὢν παρ᾽ ἐμοῦ πεῖν
thou ²a Jew ¹being ³from ⁵me ⁴to drink

αἰτεῖς γυναικὸς Σαμαρίτιδος οὔσης;
²askest ⁶woman ⁸a Samaritan ⁷being?

[οὐ γὰρ συγχρῶνται Ἰουδαῖοι Σαμαρίταις.]
¹For ⁴not ³associate ²Jews ⁵with Samaritans.

10 ἀπεκρίθη Ἰησοῦς καὶ εἶπεν αὐτῇ· εἰ ᾔδεις
Answered Jesus and said to her : If thou knewest

τὴν δωρεὰν τοῦ θεοῦ, καὶ τίς ἐστιν ὁ
the gift – of God, and who is the [one]

λέγων σοι· δός μοι πεῖν, σὺ ἂν ᾔτησας
saying to thee : Give me to drink, thou wouldest have asked

αὐτὸν καὶ ἔδωκεν ἄν σοι ὕδωρ ζῶν.
him and he would have given thee water living.

11 λέγει αὐτῷ· κύριε, οὔτε ἄντλημα ἔχεις
She says to him : Sir, no pail thou hast

καὶ τὸ φρέαρ ἐστὶν βαθύ· πόθεν οὖν
and the well is deep; whence then

ἔχεις τὸ ὕδωρ τὸ ζῶν; 12 μὴ σὺ μείζων
hast thou the water – living? *not* thou greater

our father Jacob, which gave us the well, and drank thereof himself, and his children, and his cattle?
13 Jesus answered and said unto her, Whosoever drinketh of this water shall thirst again:
14 But w h o s o e v e r drinketh of the water that I shall give him shall never thirst; but the water that I shall give him shall be in him a well of water springing up into everlasting life.
15 The woman saith unto him, Sir, give me this water, that I thirst not, neither come hither to draw.
16 Jesus saith unto her, Go, call thy husband, and come hither.
17 The woman answered and said, I have no husband. Jesus said unto her, Thou hast well said, I have no husband:
18 For thou hast had five husbands; and he whom thou now hast is not thy husband: in that saidst thou truly.
19 The woman saith unto him, Sir, I perceive that thou art a prophet.
20 Our fathers worshipped in this mountain; and ye say, that in Jerusalem is the place where men ought to worship.

εἰ τοῦ πατρὸς ἡμῶν Ἰακώβ, ὃς ἔδωκεν
art [than] the father of us Jacob, who gave
ἡμῖν τὸ φρέαρ, καὶ αὐτὸς ἐξ αὐτοῦ
us the well, and [him]self of it
ἔπιεν καὶ οἱ υἱοὶ αὐτοῦ καὶ τὰ θρέμματα
drank and the sons of him and the cattle
αὐτοῦ; 13 ἀπεκρίθη Ἰησοῦς καὶ εἶπεν αὐτῇ·
of him? Answered Jesus and said to her:
πᾶς ὁ πίνων ἐκ τοῦ ὕδατος τούτου
Everyone drinking of – water this
διψήσει πάλιν· 14 ὃς δ' ἂν πίῃ ἐκ τοῦ
will thirst again; but whoever drinks of the
ὕδατος οὗ ἐγὼ δώσω αὐτῷ, οὐ μὴ
water which I will give him, by no means
διψήσει εἰς τὸν αἰῶνα, ἀλλὰ τὸ ὕδωρ ὃ
will thirst unto the age, but the water which
δώσω αὐτῷ γενήσεται ἐν αὐτῷ πηγὴ
I will give him will become in him a fountain
ὕδατος ἁλλομένου εἰς ζωὴν αἰώνιον. 15 λέγει
of water springing to life eternal. Says
πρὸς αὐτὸν ἡ γυνή· κύριε, δός μοι
to him the woman: Sir, give me
τοῦτο τὸ ὕδωρ, ἵνα μὴ διψῶ μηδὲ
this the water, that I thirst not nor
διέρχωμαι ἐνθάδε ἀντλεῖν. 16 λέγει αὐτῇ·
come through hither to draw. He says to her:
ὕπαγε φώνησον τὸν ἄνδρα σου καὶ ἐλθὲ
Go call the husband of thee and come
ἐνθάδε. 17 ἀπεκρίθη ἡ γυνὴ καὶ εἶπεν·
hither. Answered the woman and said:
οὐκ ἔχω ἄνδρα. λέγει αὐτῇ ὁ Ἰησοῦς·
I have not a husband. Says to her – Jesus:
καλῶς εἶπες ὅτι ἄνδρα οὐκ ἔχω· 18 πέντε
Well sayest thou[,] – A husband I have not; ²five
γὰρ ἄνδρας ἔσχες, καὶ νῦν ὃν ἔχεις
¹for husbands thou hadst, and now [he] whom thou hast
οὐκ ἔστιν σου ἀνήρ· τοῦτο ἀληθὲς εἴρηκας.
is not of thee husband; this truly thou hast said.
19 λέγει αὐτῷ ἡ γυνή· κύριε, θεωρῶ
Says to him the woman: Sir, I perceive
ὅτι προφήτης εἶ σύ. 20 οἱ πατέρες
that a prophet art thou. The fathers
ἡμῶν ἐν τῷ ὄρει τούτῳ προσεκύνησαν·
of us in – mountain this worshipped;
καὶ ὑμεῖς λέγετε ὅτι ἐν Ἱεροσολύμοις
and ye say that in Jerusalem
ἐστὶν ὁ τόπος ὅπου προσκυνεῖν δεῖ.
is the place where to worship it behoves.

21 Jesus saith unto her, Woman, believe me, the hour cometh, when ye shall neither in this mountain, nor yet at Jerusalem, worship the Father.

22 Ye worship ye know not what: we know what we worship: for salvation is of the Jews.

23 But the hour cometh, and now is, when the true worshippers shall worship the Father in spirit and in truth: for the Father seeketh such to worship him.

24 God is a Spirit: and they that worship him must worship him in spirit and in truth.

25 The woman saith unto him, I know that Messias cometh, which is called Christ: when he is come, he will tell us all things.

26 Jesus saith unto her, I that speak unto thee am he.

27 ¶ And upon this came his disciples, and marvelled that he talked with the woman: yet no man said, What seekest thou? or, Why talkest thou with her?

28 The woman then left her waterpot, and went her way into the city, and saith to the men,

21 λέγει αὐτῇ ὁ Ἰησοῦς· πίστευέ μοι,
Says to her – Jesus : Believe me,

γύναι, ὅτι ἔρχεται ὥρα ὅτε οὔτε ἐν
woman, that is coming an hour when neither in

τῷ ὄρει τούτῳ οὔτε ἐν Ἰεροσολύμοις
– mountain this nor in Jerusalem

προσκυνήσετε τῷ πατρί. 22 ὑμεῖς προσκυ-
will ye worship the Father. Ye wor-

νεῖτε ὃ οὐκ οἴδατε, ἡμεῖς προσκυνοῦμεν ὃ
ship what ye know not, we worship what

οἴδαμεν, ὅτι ἡ σωτηρία ἐκ τῶν Ἰουδαίων
we know, because – salvation of the Jews

ἐστίν· 23 ἀλλὰ ἔρχεται ὥρα καὶ νῦν
is; but is coming an hour and now

ἐστιν, ὅτε οἱ ἀληθινοὶ προσκυνηταὶ προσκυνή-
is, when the true worshippers will

σουσιν τῷ πατρὶ ἐν πνεύματι καὶ ἀληθείᾳ·
worship the Father in spirit and truth;

καὶ γὰρ ὁ πατὴρ τοιούτους ζητεῖ τοὺς
for indeed the Father ²such ¹seeks the [ones]

προσκυνοῦντας αὐτόν· 24 πνεῦμα ὁ θεός,
worshipping him; God [is] spirit,*

καὶ τοὺς προσκυνοῦντας ἐν πνεύματι καὶ
and ²the [ones] ³worshipping ⁵in ⁶spirit ⁷and

ἀληθείᾳ δεῖ προσκυνεῖν. 25 λέγει αὐτῷ
⁸truth ¹it behoves ⁴to worship. Says to him

ἡ γυνή· οἶδα ὅτι Μεσσίας ἔρχεται, ὁ
the woman : I know that Messiah is coming, the[one]

λεγόμενος χριστός· ὅταν ἔλθῃ ἐκεῖνος,
being called Christ; when comes that one,

ἀναγγελεῖ ἡμῖν ἅπαντα. 26 λέγει αὐτῇ
he will announce to us all things. Says to her

ὁ Ἰησοῦς· ἐγώ εἰμι, ὁ λαλῶν σοι.
– Jesus : I am, the [one] speaking to thee.

27 Καὶ ἐπὶ τούτῳ ἦλθαν οἱ μαθηταὶ
And on this came the disciples

αὐτοῦ, καὶ ἐθαύμαζον ὅτι μετὰ γυναικὸς
of him, and marvelled that with a woman

ἐλάλει· οὐδεὶς μέντοι εἶπεν· τί ζητεῖς
he was speaking; no one however said : What seekest thou

ἢ τί λαλεῖς μετ' αὐτῆς; 28 ἀφῆκεν οὖν
or why speakest thou with her? ⁴Left ³therefore

τὴν ὑδρίαν αὐτῆς ἡ γυνὴ καὶ ἀπῆλθεν
⁵the ⁶waterpot ⁷of her ¹the ²woman and went away

εἰς τὴν πόλιν, καὶ λέγει τοῖς ἀνθρώποις·
into the city, and says to the men :

* See note on 1. 1.

29 Come, see a man, which told me all things that ever I did: is not this the Christ?

30 Then they went out of the city, and came unto him.

31 ¶ In the mean while his disciples prayed him, saying, Master, eat.

32 But he said unto them, I have meat to eat that ye know not of.

33 Therefore said the disciples one to another, Hath any man brought him *ought* to eat?

34 Jesus saith unto them, My meat is to do the will of him that sent me, and to finish his work.

35 Say not ye, There are yet four months, and *then* cometh harvest? behold, I say unto you, Lift up your eyes, and look on the fields; for they are white already to harvest.

36 And he that reapeth receiveth wages, and gathereth fruit unto life eternal: that both he that soweth and he that reapeth may rejoice together.

37 And herein is that saying true, One soweth, and another reapeth.

38 I sent you to reap that whereon ye bestowed no labour: other men laboured, and ye are entered into their labours.

---

29 δεῦτε ἴδετε ἄνθρωπον ὃς εἶπέν μοι
Come ˜ see a man who told me
πάντα ἃ ἐποίησα· μήτι οὗτός ἐστιν ὁ
all things which I did; *not* this is the
χριστός; **30** ἐξῆλθον ἐκ τῆς πόλεως καὶ
Christ? They went forth out of the city and
ἤρχοντο πρὸς αὐτόν. **31** Ἐν τῷ μεταξὺ
came to him. In the meantime
ἠρώτων αὐτὸν οἱ μαθηταὶ λέγοντες· ραββί,
asked him the disciples saying: Rabbi,
φάγε. **32** ὁ δὲ εἶπεν αὐτοῖς· ἐγὼ βρῶσιν
eat. But he said to them: I food
ἔχω φαγεῖν ἣν ὑμεῖς οὐκ οἴδατε. **33** ἔλεγον
have to eat which ye do not know. Said
οὖν οἱ μαθηταὶ πρὸς ἀλλήλους· μή τις
therefore the disciples to one another: *Not* anyone
ἤνεγκεν αὐτῷ φαγεῖν; **34** λέγει αὐτοῖς ὁ
brought him to eat? Says to them —
Ἰησοῦς· ἐμὸν βρῶμά ἐστιν ἵνα ποιῶ τὸ
Jesus: My food is that I may do the
θέλημα τοῦ πέμψαντός με καὶ τελειώσω
will of the [one] having sent me and may finish
αὐτοῦ τὸ ἔργον. **35** οὐχ ὑμεῖς λέγετε ὅτι
of him the work. ³Not ¹ye ²say that
ἔτι τετράμηνός ἐστιν καὶ ὁ θερισμὸς
yet three months it is and the harvest
ἔρχεται; ἰδοὺ λέγω ὑμῖν, ἐπάρατε τοὺς
comes? Behold I tell you, lift up the
ὀφθαλμοὺς ὑμῶν καὶ θεάσασθε τὰς χώρας,
eyes of you and behold the fields,
ὅτι λευκαί εἰσιν πρὸς θερισμόν. ἤδη
because white they are to harvest. Already
36 ὁ θερίζων μισθὸν λαμβάνει καὶ συνάγει
the [one] reaping wages receives and gathers
καρπὸν εἰς ζωὴν αἰώνιον, ἵνα ὁ σπείρων
fruit to life eternal, that ¹the [one] ²sowing
ὁμοῦ χαίρῃ καὶ ὁ θερίζων. **37** ἐν γὰρ
⁷together ⁶may rejoice ³and ⁴the [one] ⁵reaping. For in
τούτῳ ὁ λόγος ἐστὶν ἀληθινὸς ὅτι ἄλλος
this the word is true that another(one)
ἐστὶν ὁ σπείρων καὶ ἄλλος ὁ θερίζων.
is the [one] sowing and another the [one] reaping.
38 ἐγὼ ἀπέστειλα ὑμᾶς θερίζειν ὃ οὐχ
I sent you to reap what not
ὑμεῖς κεκοπιάκατε· ἄλλοι κεκοπιάκασιν, καὶ
ye have laboured; others have laboured, and
ὑμεῖς εἰς τὸν κόπον αὐ ὧν εἰσεληλύθατε.
ye into the labour of them have entered.

39 ¶ And many of the Samaritans of that city believed on him for the saying of the woman, which testified, He told me all that ever I did.

40 So when the Samaritans were come unto him, they besought him that he would tarry with them: and he abode there two days.

41 And many more believed because of his own word;

42 And said unto the woman, Now we believe, not because of thy saying: for we have heard *him* ourselves, and know that this is indeed the Christ, the Saviour of the world.

43 ¶ Now after two days he departed thence, and went into Galilee.

44 For Jesus himself testified, that a prophet hath no honour in his own country.

45 Then when he was come into Galilee, the Galilæans received him, having seen all the things that he did at Jerusalem at the feast: for they also went unto the feast.

46 So Jesus came again into Cana of Gailee, where he made the water wine. And there was a certain nobleman, whose son was sick at Capernaum.

39 Ἐκ δὲ τῆς πόλεως ἐκείνης πολλοὶ
And out of — city that many
ἐπίστευσαν εἰς αὐτὸν τῶν Σαμαριτῶν διὰ
believed in him of the Samaritans because of
τὸν λόγον τῆς γυναικὸς μαρτυρούσης ὅτι
the word of the woman witnessing[,] that
εἶπέν μοι πάντα ἃ ἐποίησα. 40 ὡς
He told me all things which I did. When
οὖν ἦλθον πρὸς αὐτὸν οἱ Σαμαρῖται,
therefore came to him the Samaritans,
ἠρώτων αὐτὸν μεῖναι παρ' αὐτοῖς· καὶ
they asked him to remain with them; and
ἔμεινεν ἐκεῖ δύο ἡμέρας. 41 καὶ πολλῷ
he remained there two days. And [2]more
πλείους ἐπίστευσαν διὰ τὸν λόγον αὐτοῦ,
[1]many believed because of the word of him,
42 τῇ τε γυναικὶ ἔλεγον ὅτι οὐκέτι διὰ
and to the woman they said[,] — No longer because of
τὴν σὴν λαλιὰν πιστεύομεν· αὐτοὶ γὰρ
— thy talk we believe; for [our]selves
ἀκηκόαμεν, καὶ οἴδαμεν ὅτι οὗτός ἐστιν
we have heard, and we know that this man is
ἀληθῶς ὁ σωτὴρ τοῦ κόσμου.
truly the Saviour of the world.
43 Μετὰ δὲ τὰς δύο ἡμέρας ἐξῆλθεν
And after the two days he went forth
ἐκεῖθεν εἰς τὴν Γαλιλαίαν. 44 αὐτὸς γὰρ
thence into — Galilee. For [2][him]self
Ἰησοῦς ἐμαρτύρησεν ὅτι προφήτης ἐν
[1]Jesus witnessed that a prophet in
τῇ ἰδίᾳ πατρίδι τιμὴν οὐκ ἔχει. 45 ὅτε
the(his) own native place honour has not. When
οὖν ἦλθεν εἰς τὴν Γαλιλαίαν, ἐδέξαντο
therefore he came into — Galilee, received
αὐτὸν οἱ Γαλιλαῖοι, πάντα ἑωρακότες
him the Galilæans, all things having seen
ὅσα ἐποίησεν ἐν Ἱεροσολύμοις ἐν τῇ
which he did in Jerusalem at the
ἑορτῇ· καὶ αὐτοὶ γὰρ ἦλθον εἰς τὴν
feast; [3]also [2]they [1]for went to the
ἑορτήν. 46 Ἦλθεν οὖν πάλιν εἰς τὴν
feast. He came therefore again to —
Κανὰ τῆς Γαλιλαίας, ὅπου ἐποίησεν τὸ
Cana — of Galilee, where he made the
ὕδωρ οἶνον. καὶ ἦν τις βασιλικὸς
water wine. And there was a certain courtier
οὗ ὁ υἱὸς ἠσθένει ἐν Καφαρναούμ· 47 οὗτος
of whom the son ailed in Capernaum; this man

47 When he heard that Jesus was come out of Judæa into Galilee, he went unto him, and besought him that he would come down, and heal his son: for he was at the point of death.

48 Then said Jesus unto him, Except ye see signs and wonders, ye will not believe.

49 The nobleman saith unto him, Sir, come down ere my child die.

50 Jesus saith unto him, Go thy way; thy son liveth. And the man believed the word that Jesus had spoken unto him, and he went his way.

51 And as he was now going down, his servants met him, and told him, saying, Thy son liveth.

52 Then enquired he of them the hour when he began to amend. And they said unto him, Yesterday at the seventh hour the fever left him.

53 So the father knew that it was at the same hour, in the which Jesus said unto him, Thy son liveth: and himself believed, and his whole house.

54 This is again the second miracle that Jesus did, when he was come out of Judæa into Galilee.

ἀκούσας ὅτι Ἰησοῦς ἥκει ἐκ τῆς Ἰουδαίας
hearing that Jesus comes(came) out of – Judæa

εἰς τὴν Γαλιλαίαν, ἀπῆλθεν πρὸς αὐτὸν καὶ
into – Galilee, went to him and

ἠρώτα ἵνα καταβῇ καὶ ἰάσηται αὐτοῦ
asked that he would come down and would cure of him

τὸν υἱόν· ἤμελλεν γὰρ ἀποθνῄσκειν. **48** εἶπεν
the son; for he was about to die. Said

οὖν ὁ Ἰησοῦς πρὸς αὐτόν· ἐὰν μὴ σημεῖα
therefore – Jesus to him: Except signs

καὶ τέρατα ἴδητε, οὐ μὴ πιστεύσητε.
and prodigies ye see, by no means ye believe.

49 λέγει πρὸς αὐτὸν ὁ βασιλικός· κύριε,
Says to him the courtier: Sir,

κατάβηθι πρὶν ἀποθανεῖν τὸ παιδίον μου.
come down before to die the child[b] of me.

50 λέγει αὐτῷ ὁ Ἰησοῦς· πορεύου, ὁ
Tells him – Jesus: Go, the

υἱός σου ζῇ. ἐπίστευσεν ὁ ἄνθρωπος τῷ
son of thee lives. ³Believed ¹the ²man ⁴the

λόγῳ ὃν εἶπεν αὐτῷ ὁ Ἰησοῦς, καὶ
⁵word ⁶which ⁸said ⁹to him – ⁷Jesus, and

ἐπορεύετο. **51** ἤδη δὲ αὐτοῦ καταβαίνοντος
went. And already him going down[a]
=while he was going down

οἱ δοῦλοι ὑπήντησαν αὐτῷ λέγοντες ὅτι
the slaves met him saying that

ὁ παῖς αὐτοῦ ζῇ. **52** ἐπύθετο οὖν τὴν
the boy of him lives. He inquired therefore the

ὥραν παρ᾽ αὐτῶν ἐν ᾗ κομψότερον ἔσχεν·
hour from them in which better he had;
=he got better

εἶπαν οὖν αὐτῷ ὅτι ἐχθὲς ὥραν ἑβδόμην
they said therefore to him[,] – Yesterday [at] hour seventh

ἀφῆκεν αὐτὸν ὁ πυρετός. **53** ἔγνω οὖν
left him the fever. Knew therefore

ὁ πατὴρ ὅτι ἐκείνῃ τῇ ὥρᾳ ἐν ᾗ εἶπεν
the father that in that – hour in which told

αὐτῷ ὁ Ἰησοῦς· ὁ υἱός σου ζῇ· καὶ
him – Jesus: The son of thee lives; and

ἐπίστευσεν αὐτὸς καὶ ἡ οἰκία αὐτοῦ ὅλη.
believed he and the household of him whole.

54 Τοῦτο [δὲ] πάλιν δεύτερον σημεῖον
And this again a second sign

ἐποίησεν ὁ Ἰησοῦς ἐλθὼν ἐκ τῆς Ἰουδαίας
did Jesus having come out of – Judæa

εἰς τὴν Γαλιλαίαν.
into – Galilee.

CHAPTER 5

AFTER this there was a feast of the Jews; and Jesus went up to Jerusalem.

2 Now there is at Jerusalem by the sheep *market* a pool, which is called in the Hebrew tongue Bethesda, having five porches.

3 In these lay a great multitude of impotent folk, of blind, halt, withered, waiting for the moving of the water.

4 For an angel went down at a certain season into the pool, and troubled the water: whosoever then first after the troubling of the water stepped in was made whole of whatsoever disease he had.

5 And a certain man was there, which had an infirmity thirty and eight years.

6 When Jesus saw him lie, and knew that he had been now a long time *in that case*, he saith unto him, Wilt thou be made whole?

7 The impotent man answered him, Sir, I have no man, when the water is troubled, to put me into the pool: but while I am coming, another steppeth down before me.

8 Jesus saith unto him, Rise, take up thy bed, and walk.

9 And immediately the man was made whole, and took up his bed, and walked: and on the same day was the sabbath.

10 ¶ The Jews therefore said unto him that was cured, It is the sabbath day: it is not lawful for thee to carry *thy* bed.

---

5 Μετὰ ταῦτα ἦν ἑορτὴ τῶν Ἰουδαίων,
After these things there was a feast of the Jews,

καὶ ἀνέβη Ἰησοῦς εἰς Ἱεροσόλυμα. **2** ἔστιν
and went up Jesus to Jerusalem. there is

δὲ ἐν τοῖς Ἱεροσολύμοις ἐπὶ τῇ προβατικῇ
Now in - Jerusalem at the sheepgate

κολυμβήθρα, ἡ ἐπιλεγομένη Ἑβραϊστὶ
a pool, the [one] being called in Hebrew

Βηθζαθά, πέντε στοὰς ἔχουσα. **3** ἐν
Bethzatha, five porches having. In

ταύταις κατέκειτο πλῆθος τῶν ἀσθενούντων,
these lay a multitude of the ailing [ones],

τυφλῶν, χωλῶν, ξηρῶν. ‡ **5** ἦν δέ τις
blind, lame, withered. And there was a

ἄνθρωπος ἐκεῖ τριάκοντα καὶ ὀκτὼ ἔτη
certain man there thirty-eight years

ἔχων ἐν τῇ ἀσθενείᾳ αὐτοῦ· **6** τοῦτον
having in the ailment of him; ³this man

ἰδὼν ὁ Ἰησοῦς κατακείμενον, καὶ γνοὺς
⁵seeing - ¹Jesus ⁴lying, and knowing

ὅτι πολὺν ἤδη χρόνον ἔχει, λέγει αὐτῷ·
that ³much ²already ⁴time ¹he has, says to him :

θέλεις ὑγιὴς γενέσθαι; **7** ἀπεκρίθη αὐτῷ
Wishest thou whole to become? Answered him

ὁ ἀσθενῶν· κύριε, ἄνθρωπον οὐκ ἔχω,
the ailing [one] : Sir, a man I have not,

ἵνα ὅταν ταραχθῇ τὸ ὕδωρ βάλῃ με εἰς
that when is troubled the water he may put me into

τὴν κολυμβήθραν· ἐν ᾧ δὲ ἔρχομαι ἐγώ,
the pool; but while am coming I,

ἄλλος πρὸ ἐμοῦ καταβαίνει. **8** λέγει αὐτῷ
another before me goes down. Says to him

ὁ Ἰησοῦς· ἔγειρε ἆρον τὸν κράβατόν
- Jesus : Rise[,] take the mattress

σου καὶ περιπάτει. **9** καὶ εὐθέως ἐγένετο
of thee and walk. And immediately became

ὑγιὴς ὁ ἄνθρωπος, καὶ ἦρεν τὸν κράβατον
whole the man, and took the mattress

αὐτοῦ καὶ περιεπάτει. Ἦν δὲ σάββατον
of him and walked. And it was a sabbath

ἐν ἐκείνῃ τῇ ἡμέρᾳ. **10** ἔλεγον οὖν οἱ
on that - day. Said therefore the

Ἰουδαῖοι τῷ τεθεραπευμένῳ· σάββατόν ἐστιν,
Jews to the [one] having been healed : A sabbath it is,

καὶ οὐκ ἔξεστίν σοι ἆραι τὸν κράβατον.
and it is not lawful for thee to take the mattress.

---

‡ End of ver. 3 and ver. 4 omitted by Nestle; *cf.* R.V. marg., etc.

11 He answered them, He that made me whole, the same said unto me, Take up thy bed, and walk.

12 Then asked they him, What man is that which said unto thee, Take up thy bed, and walk?

13 And he that was healed wist not who it was: for Jesus had conveyed himself away, a multitude being in *that* place.

14 Afterward Jesus findeth him in the temple, and said unto him, Behold, thou art made whole: sin no more, lest a worse thing come unto thee.

15 The man departed, and told the Jews that it was Jesus, which had made him whole.

16 And therefore did the Jews persecute Jesus, and sought to slay him, because he had done these things on the sabbath day.

17 ¶ But Jesus answered them, My Father worketh hitherto, and I work.

18 Therefore the Jews sought the more to kill him, because he not only had broken the sabbath, but said also that God was his Father, making himself equal with God.

19 ¶ Then answered Jesus and said unto them, Verily, verily, I say unto you, The Son can do nothing of himself, but

11 ὃς δὲ ἀπεκρίθη αὐτοῖς· ὁ ποιήσας
But who(he) answered them : The [one] making
με ὑγιῆ, ἐκεῖνός μοι εἶπεν· ἆρον τὸν
me whole, that one me told : Take the
κράβατόν σου καὶ περιπάτει. 12 ἠρώτησαν
mattress of thee and walk. They asked
αὐτόν· τίς ἐστιν ὁ ἄνθρωπος ὁ εἰπών
him : Who is the man – telling
σοι· ἆρον καὶ περιπάτει; 13 ὁ δὲ ἰαθεὶς
thee : Take and walk? But the [one] cured
οὐκ ᾔδει τίς ἐστιν· ὁ γὰρ Ἰησοῦς
did not know who it is(was); – for Jesus
ἐξένευσεν ὄχλου ὄντος ἐν τῷ τόπῳ.
withdrew a crowd being in the place.
=as there was a crowd
14 μετὰ ταῦτα εὑρίσκει αὐτὸν ὁ Ἰησοῦς
After these things finds him – Jesus
ἐν τῷ ἱερῷ καὶ εἶπεν αὐτῷ· ἴδε ὑγιὴς
in the temple and said to him : Behold[,] whole
γέγονας· μηκέτι ἁμάρτανε, ἵνα μὴ χεῖρόν
thou hast become; no longer sin, lest [2]worse
σοί τι γένηται. 15 ἀπῆλθεν ὁ ἄνθρωπος
[4]to thee [1]something [3]happens. Went away the man
καὶ εἶπεν τοῖς Ἰουδαίοις ὅτι Ἰησοῦς
and told the Jews that Jesus
ἐστιν ὁ ποιήσας αὐτὸν ὑγιῆ. 16 καὶ διὰ
it is(was) the [one] having made him whole. And there-
τοῦτο ἐδίωκον οἱ Ἰουδαῖοι τὸν Ἰησοῦν,
fore [3]persecuted [1]the [2]Jews – [4]Jesus,
ὅτι ταῦτα ἐποίει ἐν σαββάτῳ. 17 ὁ δὲ
because these things he did on a sabbath. But he
ἀπεκρίνατο αὐτοῖς· ὁ πατήρ μου ἕως
answered them : The Father of me until
ἄρτι ἐργάζεται, κἀγὼ ἐργάζομαι· 18 διὰ
now works, and I work; because of
τοῦτο οὖν μᾶλλον ἐζήτουν αὐτὸν οἱ
this therefore [4]the more [3]sought [6]him [1]the
Ἰουδαῖοι ἀποκτεῖναι, ὅτι οὐ μόνον ἔλυεν
[2]Jews [5]to kill, because not only he broke
τὸ σάββατον, ἀλλὰ καὶ πατέρα ἴδιον
the sabbath, but also Father [his] own
ἔλεγεν τὸν θεόν, ἴσον ἑαυτὸν ποιῶν τῷ
said – God [to be], equal himself making –
θεῷ. 19 Ἀπεκρίνατο οὖν ὁ Ἰησοῦς καὶ
to God. Answered therefore – Jesus and
ἔλεγεν αὐτοῖς· ἀμὴν ἀμὴν λέγω ὑμῖν,
said to them : Truly truly I say to you,
οὐ δύναται ὁ υἱὸς ποιεῖν ἀφ' ἑαυτοῦ
cannot the Son *to* do from himself

what he seeth the Father do: for what things soever he doeth, these also doeth the Son likewise.

20 For the Father loveth the Son, and sheweth him all things that himself doeth: and he will shew him greater works than these, that ye may marvel.

21 For as the Father raiseth up the dead, and quickeneth *them;* even so the Son quickeneth whom he will.

22 For the Father judgeth no man, but hath committed all judgment unto the Son:

23 That all *men* should honour the Son, even as they honour the Father. He that honoureth not the Son honoureth not the Father which hath sent him.

24 Verily, verily, I say unto you, He that heareth my word, and believeth on him that sent me, hath everlasting life, and shall not come into condemnation; but is passed from death unto life.

25 Verily, verily, I say unto you, The hour is coming, and now is, when the dead shall hear the voice of the Son of God: and they that hear shall live.

26 For as the Father hath life in himself; so hath he given to the Son to have life in himself;

οὐδέν, ἂν μή τι βλέπῃ τὸν πατέρα
no(any)thing, except what he sees the Father
ποιοῦντα· ἃ γὰρ ἂν ἐκεῖνος ποιῇ, ταῦτα
doing; for whatever things that one does, these
καὶ ὁ υἱὸς ὁμοίως ποιεῖ. 20 ὁ γὰρ
also the Son likewise does. For the
πατὴρ φιλεῖ τὸν υἱὸν καὶ πάντα δείκνυσιν
Father loves the Son and all things shows
αὐτῷ ἃ αὐτὸς ποιεῖ, καὶ μείζονα τούτων
him which he does, and ¹greater ³[than] ⁴these
δείξει αὐτῷ ἔργα, ἵνα ὑμεῖς θαυμάζητε.
⁵he will show ⁶him ²works, that ye may marvel.
21 ὥσπερ γὰρ ὁ πατὴρ ἐγείρει τοὺς
For as the Father raises the
νεκροὺς καὶ ζωοποιεῖ, οὕτως καὶ ὁ υἱὸς
dead and quickens, so also the Son
οὓς θέλει ζωοποιεῖ. 22 οὐδὲ γὰρ ὁ
whom he wills quickens. For not the
πατὴρ κρίνει οὐδένα, ἀλλὰ τὴν κρίσιν
Father judges no(any) one, but - judgment
πᾶσαν δέδωκεν τῷ υἱῷ, 23 ἵνα πάντες
all he has given to the Son, that all men
τιμῶσι τὸν υἱὸν καθὼς τιμῶσι τὸν πατέρα.
may honour the Son as they honour the Father.
ὁ μὴ τιμῶν τὸν υἱὸν οὐ τιμᾷ τὸν πατέρα
The [one] not honouring the Son honours not the Father
τὸν πέμψαντα αὐτόν. 24 Ἀμὴν ἀμὴν
- having sent him. Truly truly
λέγω ὑμῖν ὅτι ὁ τὸν λόγον μου ἀκούων
I say to you[,] - The [one] the word of me hearing
καὶ πιστεύων τῷ πέμψαντί με ἔχει
and believing the [one] having sent me has
ζωὴν αἰώνιον, καὶ εἰς κρίσιν οὐκ ἔρχεται
life eternal, and into judgment comes not
ἀλλὰ μεταβέβηκεν ἐκ τοῦ θανάτου εἰς
but has passed over out of - death into
τὴν ζωήν. 25 ἀμὴν ἀμὴν λέγω ὑμῖν ὅτι
- life. Truly truly I say to you[,] -
ἔρχεται ὥρα καὶ νῦν ἐστιν ὅτε οἱ νεκροὶ
Comes an hour and now is when the dead
ἀκούσουσιν τῆς φωνῆς τοῦ υἱοῦ τοῦ
will hear the voice of the Son -
θεοῦ καὶ οἱ ἀκούσαντες ζήσουσιν. 26 ὥσπερ
of God and the[ones] hearing will live. as
γὰρ ὁ πατὴρ ἔχει ζωὴν ἐν ἑαυτῷ, οὕτως
For the Father has life in himself, so
καὶ τῷ υἱῷ ἔδωκεν ζωὴν ἔχειν ἐν ἑαυτῷ.
also to the Son he gave life to have in himself.

27 And hath given him authority to execute judgment also, because he is the Son of man.

28 Marvel not at this: for the hour is coming, in the which all that are in the graves shall hear his voice,

29 And shall come forth; they that have done good, unto the resurrection of life; and they that have done evil, unto the resurrection of damnation.

30 I can of mine own self do nothing: as I hear, I judge: and my judgment is just; because I seek not mine own will, but the will of the Father which hath sent me.

31 If I bear witness of myself, my witness is not true.

32 There is another that beareth witness of me; and I know that the witness which he witnesseth of me is true.

33 Ye sent unto John, and he bare witness unto the truth.

34 But I receive not testimony from man: but these things I say, that ye might be saved.

35 He was a burning and a shining light: and ye were willing for a season to rejoice in his light.

27 καὶ ἐξουσίαν ἔδωκεν αὐτῷ κρίσιν ποιεῖν,
And authority he gave him judgment to do,

ὅτι υἱὸς ἀνθρώπου ἐστίν. 28 μὴ θαυμάζετε
because son of man* he is. Marvel not [at]

τοῦτο, ὅτι ἔρχεται ὥρα ἐν ᾗ πάντες οἱ
this, because comes an hour in which all the [ones]

ἐν τοῖς μνημείοις ἀκούσουσιν τῆς φωνῆς
in the tombs will hear the voice

αὐτοῦ 29 καὶ ἐκπορεύσονται οἱ τὰ ἀγαθὰ
of him and will come forth the [ones] the good things

ποιήσαντες εἰς ἀνάστασιν ζωῆς, οἱ τὰ
having done to a resurrection of life, the [ones] the

φαῦλα πράξαντες εἰς ἀνάστασιν κρίσεως.
evil things having done to a resurrection of judgment.

30 Οὐ δύναμαι ἐγὼ ποιεῖν ἀπ' ἐμαυτοῦ
Cannot I to do from myself

οὐδέν· καθὼς ἀκούω κρίνω, καὶ ἡ κρίσις
no(any)thing; as I hear I judge, and – judgment

ἡ ἐμὴ δικαία ἐστίν, ὅτι οὐ ζητῶ τὸ
– my just is, because I seek not –

θέλημα τὸ ἐμὸν ἀλλὰ τὸ θέλημα τοῦ
will – my but the will of the [one]

πέμψαντός με. 31 Ἐὰν ἐγὼ μαρτυρῶ
having sent me. If I witness

περὶ ἐμαυτοῦ, ἡ μαρτυρία μου οὐκ ἔστιν
concerning myself, the witness of me is not

ἀληθής· 32 ἄλλος ἐστιν ὁ μαρτυρῶν περὶ
true; another there is the [one] witnessing concerning

ἐμοῦ, καὶ οἶδα ὅτι ἀληθής ἐστιν ἡ
me, and I know that true is the

μαρτυρία ἣν μαρτυρεῖ περὶ ἐμοῦ. 33 ὑμεῖς
witness which he witnesses concerning me. Ye

ἀπεστάλκατε πρὸς Ἰωάννην, καὶ μεμαρ-
have sent to John, and he has

τύρηκεν τῇ ἀληθείᾳ· 34 ἐγὼ δὲ οὐ παρὰ
witnessed to the truth; but I not from

ἀνθρώπου τὴν μαρτυρίαν λαμβάνω, ἀλλὰ
man the witness receive, but

ταῦτα λέγω ἵνα ὑμεῖς σωθῆτε. 35 ἐκεῖνος
these things I say that ye may be saved. That man

ἦν ὁ λύχνος ὁ καιόμενος καὶ φαίνων,
was the lamp – burning and shining,

ὑμεῖς δὲ ἠθελήσατε ἀγαλλιαθῆναι πρὸς
and ye were willing to exult for

ὥραν ἐν τῷ φωτὶ αὐτοῦ. 36 Ἐγὼ δὲ
an hour in the light of him. But I

* Note the absence of the definite article here. See also **Rev.** 1. 12 and 14. 14.

36 But I have greater witness than *that* of John: for the works which the Father hath given me to finish, the same works that I do, bear witness of me, that the Father hath sent me.

37 And the Father himself, which hath sent me, hath borne witness of me. Ye have neither heard his voice at any time, nor seen his shape.

38 And ye have not his word abiding in you: for whom he hath sent, him ye believe not.

39 Search the scriptures; for in them ye think ye have eternal life: and they are they which testify of me.

40 And ye will not come to me, that ye might have life.

41 I receive not honour from men.

42 But I know you, that ye have not the love of God in you.

43 I am come in my Father's name, and ye receive me not: if another shall come in his own name, him ye will receive.

44 How can ye believe, which receive honour one of another, and seek not the honour that *cometh* from God only?

45 Do not think that I

ἔχω   τὴν   μαρτυρίαν μείζω   τοῦ   Ἰωάννου·
have   the   witness   greater [than] – of John;

τὰ γὰρ   ἔργα   ἃ δέδωκέν μοι ὁ πατὴρ ἵνα
for the   works which has given me the Father that

τελειώσω αὐτά,   αὐτὰ   τὰ ἔργα   ἃ ποιῶ,
I may finish them, ³[them]selves ¹the ²works which I do,

μαρτυρεῖ περὶ ἐμοῦ ὅτι ὁ πατήρ με
witnesses concerning me that the Father me

ἀπέσταλκεν.   37 καὶ ὁ πέμψας   με πατήρ,
has sent.   And ¹the ³having sent ⁴me ²Father,

ἐκεῖνος μεμαρτύρηκεν περὶ ἐμοῦ.   οὔτε
that [one] has witnessed concerning me. Neither

φωνὴν αὐτοῦ πώποτε ἀκηκόατε οὔτε εἶδος
voice   of him never   ye have heard nor   form

αὐτοῦ ἑωράκατε, 38 καὶ τὸν λόγον αὐτοῦ
of him ye have seen,   and the word   of him

οὐκ ἔχετε ἐν ὑμῖν μένοντα, ὅτι   ὃν
ye have not in you remaining, because [he] whom

ἀπέστειλεν ἐκεῖνος, τούτῳ ὑμεῖς οὐ πιστεύετε.
²sent   ¹that [one], this [one] ye   do not believe.

39 ἐρευνᾶτε τὰς γραφάς, ὅτι ὑμεῖς δοκεῖτε
Ye search   the scriptures, because ye   think

ἐν αὐταῖς ζωὴν αἰώνιον ἔχειν· καὶ ἐκεῖναί
in them   life   eternal to have; and those

εἰσιν αἱ μαρτυροῦσαι περὶ ἐμοῦ·   40 καὶ
are the [ones] witnessing concerning me;   and

οὐ θέλετε ἐλθεῖν πρός με ἵνα ζωὴν
ye wish not to come to   me that life

ἔχητε.   41 Δόξαν παρὰ ἀνθρώπων οὐ
ye may have. Glory from   men   not

λαμβάνω, 42 ἀλλὰ ἔγνωκα ὑμᾶς ὅτι τὴν
I receive,   but I have known you   that the

ἀγάπην τοῦ θεοῦ οὐκ ἔχετε ἐν ἑαυτοῖς.
love   –   of God ye have not in your*selves.*

43 ἐγὼ ἐλήλυθα ἐν τῷ ὀνόματι τοῦ πατρός
I   have come in the name   of the Father

μου, καὶ οὐ λαμβάνετέ με· ἐὰν ἄλλος
of me, and ye receive not   me;   if   another

ἔλθῃ ἐν τῷ ὀνόματι τῷ ἰδίῳ, ἐκεῖνον
comes in –   name the(his) own, that [one]

λήμψεσθε.   44 πῶς δύνασθε ὑμεῖς πιστεῦσαι,
ye will receive. How can   ye   *to* believe,

δόξαν παρὰ ἀλλήλων λαμβάνοντες, καὶ
glory from   one another receiving,   and

τὴν δόξαν τὴν παρὰ τοῦ μόνου θεοῦ
the glory the from   the only   God

οὐ ζητεῖτε; 45 μὴ δοκεῖτε ὅτι ἐγὼ κατηγορήσω
ye seek not?   Do not think that   I   will accuse

will accuse you to the
Father: there is *one* that
accuseth you, *even* Moses,
in whom ye trust.

46 For had ye believed
Moses, ye would have be-
lieved me: for he wrote
of me.

47 But if ye believe not
his writings, how shall ye
believe my words?

ὑμῶν   πρὸς   τὸν   πατέρα·   ἐστιν   ὁ   κατηγορῶν
you   to   the   Father;   there is the [one] accusing

ὑμῶν   Μωϋσῆς,   εἰς   ὃν   ὑμεῖς   ἠλπίκατε.   **46** εἰ
you[,]   Moses,   in   whom   ye   have hoped.   if

γὰρ   ἐπιστεύετε   Μωϋσεῖ,   ἐπιστεύετε   ἂν
For   ye believed   Moses,   ye would have believed

ἐμοί·   περὶ   γὰρ   ἐμοῦ   ἐκεῖνος   ἔγραψεν.
me;   for concerning   me   that [one]   wrote.

47 εἰ   δὲ   τοῖς   ἐκείνου   γράμμασιν   οὐ
But [1]if   [4]the   [5]of that [one]   [5]letters   [2]not

πιστεύετε,   πῶς   τοῖς   ἐμοῖς   ῥήμασιν
[3]ye believe,   how   -   my   words

πιστεύσετε;
will ye believe?

CHAPTER 6

AFTER these things
Jesus went over the
sea of Galilee, which is
the sea of Tiberias.

2 And a great multitude
followed him, because they
saw his miracles which he
did on them that were
diseased.

3 And Jesus went up
into a mountain, and
there he sat with his
disciples.

4 And the passover, a
feast of the Jews, was nigh.

5 When Jesus then lifted
up *his* eyes, and saw a
great company come unto
him, he saith unto Philip,
Whence shall we buy
bread, that these may eat?

6 And this he said to
prove him: for he himself
knew what he would do.

7 Philip answered him,
Two hundred pennyworth
of bread is not sufficient
for them, that every one
of them may take a little.

6 Μετὰ   ταῦτα   ἀπῆλθεν   ὁ   Ἰησοῦς   πέραν
After   these things   went away   -   Jesus   across

τῆς   θαλάσσης   τῆς   Γαλιλαίας   τῆς   Τιβεριάδος.
the   sea   -   of Galilee[,]   -   of Tiberias.

2 ἠκολούθει   δὲ   αὐτῷ   ὄχλος   πολύς,   ὅτι
And followed   him   crowd   a much,   because

ἑώρων   τὰ   σημεῖα   ἃ   ἐποίει   ἐπὶ   τῶν
they saw   the   signs   which   he did   on   the

ἀσθενούντων.   **3** ἀνῆλθεν   δὲ   εἰς   τὸ   ὄρος
ailing [ones].   And went up   to   the   mountain

Ἰησοῦς,   καὶ   ἐκεῖ   ἐκάθητο   μετὰ   τῶν
Jesus,   and   there   sat   with   the

μαθητῶν   αὐτοῦ.   **4** ἦν   δὲ   ἐγγὺς   τὸ   πάσχα,
disciples   of him.   And was   near   the   Passover,

ἡ   ἑορτὴ   τῶν   Ἰουδαίων.   **5** ἐπάρας   οὖν
the   feast   of the   Jews.   Lifting up therefore

τοὺς   ὀφθαλμοὺς   ὁ   Ἰησοῦς   καὶ   θεασάμενος
the(his)   eyes   -   Jesus   and   beholding

ὅτι   πολὺς   ὄχλος   ἔρχεται   πρὸς   αὐτόν,
that   a much   crowd   is(was) coming   toward   him,

λέγει   πρὸς   Φίλιππον·   πόθεν   ἀγοράσωμεν
he says   to   Philip :   Whence   may we buy

ἄρτους   ἵνα   φάγωσιν   οὗτοι;   **6** τοῦτο   δὲ
loaves   that   may eat   these?   And this

ἔλεγεν   πειράζων   αὐτόν·   αὐτὸς   γὰρ   ᾔδει
he said   testing   him;   for he   knew

τί   ἔμελλεν   ποιεῖν.   **7** ἀπεκρίθη   αὐτῷ   ὁ
what   he was about   to do.   Answered   him   -

Φίλιππος·   διακοσίων   δηναρίων   ἄρτοι   οὐκ
Philip :   [3]Of two hundred   [3]denarii   [1]loaves   not

ἀρκοῦσιν   αὐτοῖς,   ἵνα   ἕκαστος   βραχύ   τι
are enough   for them,   that   each   a little

8 One of his disciples, Andrew, Simon Peter's brother, saith unto him,

9 There is a lad here, which hath five barley loaves, and two small fishes: but what are they among so many?

10 And Jesus said, Make the men sit down. Now there was much grass in the place. So the men sat down, in number about five thousand.

11 And Jesus took the loaves; and when he had given thanks, he distributed to the disciples, and the disciples to them that were set down; and likewise of the fishes as much as they would.

12 When they were filled, he said unto his disciples, Gather up the fragments that remain, that nothing be lost.

13 Therefore they gathered *them* together, and filled twelve baskets with the fragments of the five barley loaves, which remained over and above unto them that had eaten.

14 ¶ Then those men, when they had seen the miracle that Jesus did, said, This is of a truth that prophet that should come into the world.

15 When Jesus therefore perceived that they would come and take him by force, to make him a king, he departed again

λάβῃ.	8 λέγει	αὐτῷ	εἷς ἐκ τῶν	μαθητῶν
may take.	Says	to him	one of the	disciples

αὐτοῦ,	᾿Ανδρέας	ὁ ἀδελφὸς	Σίμωνος
of him,	Andrew	the brother	of Simon

Πέτρου·	9 ἔστιν	παιδάριον	ὧδε	ὃς ἔχει
Peter :	There is	a lad	here	who has

πέντε	ἄρτους	κριθίνους	καὶ δύο	ὀψάρια·
five	loaves	barley	and two	fishes;

ἀλλὰ	ταῦτα	τί ἐστιν	εἰς	τοσούτους;
but	³these	¹what	²is(are) among	so many?

10 εἶπεν ὁ ᾿Ιησοῦς·	ποιήσατε	τοὺς	ἀνθρώπους
Said – Jesus :	Make	the	men*

ἀναπεσεῖν.	ἦν δὲ	χόρτος	πολὺς	ἐν τῷ
to recline.	Now there was	grass	much	in the

τόπῳ.	ἀνέπεσαν	οὖν οἱ ἄνδρες	τὸν ἀριθμὸν
place.	Reclined	therefore the men	the number

ὡς	πεντακισχίλιοι.	11 ἔλαβεν	οὖν τοὺς
about	five thousand.	Took	therefore the

ἄρτους	ὁ ᾿Ιησοῦς	καὶ	εὐχαριστήσας
loaves	– Jesus	and	having given thanks

διέδωκεν	τοῖς	ἀνακειμένοις,	ὁμοίως καὶ
distributed	to the [ones]	lying down,	likewise also

ἐκ τῶν	ὀψαρίων	ὅσον ἤθελον.	12 ὡς δὲ
of the	fishes	as much as they wished.	Now when

ἐνεπλήσθησαν,	λέγει	τοῖς μαθηταῖς	αὐτοῦ·
they were filled,	he tells	the disciples	of him:

συναγάγετε	τὰ	περισσεύσαντα	κλάσματα, ἵνα
Gather ye	the	left over	fragments, that

μή τι	ἀπόληται.	13 συνήγαγον	οὖν, καὶ
not anything	is lost.	They gathered	therefore, and

ἐγέμισαν	δώδεκα	κοφίνους	κλασμάτων ἐκ
filled	twelve	baskets	of fragments of

τῶν πέντε	ἄρτων τῶν	κριθίνων	ἃ ἐπερίσσευσαν
the five	loaves –	barley	which were left over

τοῖς	βεβρωκόσιν.	14 Οἱ	οὖν ἄνθρωποι
to the [ones] having eaten.		Therefore the	men*

ἰδόντες	ὃ ἐποίησεν	σημεῖον	ἔλεγον ὅτι
seeing	¹what ³he did	²sign	said[,] –

οὗτός	ἐστιν	ἀληθῶς	ὁ προφήτης ὁ
This	is	truly	the prophet –

ἐρχόμενος	εἰς	τὸν κόσμον.	15 ᾿Ιησοῦς
coming	into	the world.	Jesus

οὖν	γνοὺς ὅτι	μέλλουσιν	ἔρχεσθαι καὶ
therefore	knowing that	they are(were) about	to come and

ἁρπάζειν	αὐτὸν	ἵνα	ποιήσωσιν βασιλέα,
seize	him	that	they might make a king,

* That is, people. Compare ἄνδρες in ver. 10.

into a mountain himself alone.

16 ¶ And when even was *now* come, his disciples went down unto the sea,

17 And entered into a ship, and went over the sea toward Capernaum. And it was now dark, and Jesus was not come to them.

18 And the sea arose by reason of a great wind that blew.

19 So when they had rowed about five and twenty or thirty furlongs, they see Jesus walking on the sea, and drawing nigh unto the ship: and they were afraid.

20 But he saith unto them, It is I; be not afraid.

21 Then they willingly received him into the ship: and immediately the ship was at the land whither they went.

22 ¶ The day following, when the people which stood on the other side of the sea saw that there was none other boat there, save that one whereinto his disciples were entered, and that Jesus went not with his disciples into the boat, but *that* his disciples were gone away alone;

23 (Howbeit there came other boats from Tiberias nigh unto the place where they did eat bread, after that the Lord had given thanks:)

ἀνεχώρησεν πάλιν εἰς τὸ ὄρος αὐτὸς
departed　　again　to　the mountain [him]self

μόνος. **16** Ὡς δὲ ὀψία ἐγένετο, κατέβησαν
alone.　　And when evening came,　went down

οἱ μαθηταὶ αὐτοῦ ἐπὶ τὴν θάλασσαν,
the disciples of him　to　the　sea,

17 καὶ ἐμβάντες εἰς πλοῖον ἤρχοντο πέραν
and embarking in a boat　came　across

τῆς θαλάσσης εἰς Καφαρναούμ. καὶ
the　sea　to　Capernaum.　And

σκοτία ἤδη ἐγεγόνει καὶ οὔπω ἐληλύθει
darkness now had come　and not yet had come

πρὸς αὐτοὺς ὁ Ἰησοῦς, **18** ἥ τε θάλασσα
to them　–　Jesus,　and the　sea

ἀνέμου μεγάλου πνέοντος διηγείρετο.
wind　a great　blowing[a]　was roused.
=as a great wind blew

19 ἐληλακότες οὖν ὡς σταδίους εἴκοσι
Having rowed therefore about furlongs twenty-

πέντε ἢ τριάκοντα θεωροῦσιν τὸν Ἰησοῦν
five or thirty　they behold　–　Jesus

περιπατοῦντα ἐπὶ τῆς θαλάσσης καὶ ἐγγὺς
walking　on　the　sea　and near

τοῦ πλοίου γινόμενον, καὶ ἐφοβήθησαν.
the boat　becoming,　and　they feared.

20 ὁ δὲ λέγει αὐτοῖς· ἐγώ εἰμι· μὴ
But he says to them :　I　am;　not

φοβεῖσθε. **21** ἤθελον οὖν λαβεῖν αὐτὸν εἰς
fear ye.　They wished therefore to take him into

τὸ πλοῖον, καὶ εὐθέως ἐγένετο τὸ πλοῖον
the boat,　and immediately was　the boat

ἐπὶ τῆς γῆς εἰς ἣν ὑπῆγον.
at the land to which they were going.

22 Τῇ ἐπαύριον ὁ ὄχλος ὁ ἑστηκὼς
On the morrow the crowd　–　standing

πέραν τῆς θαλάσσης εἶδον ὅτι πλοιάριον
across the　sea　saw that boat

ἄλλο οὐκ ἦν ἐκεῖ εἰ μὴ ἕν, καὶ ὅτι
other was not there except one, and that

οὐ συνεισῆλθεν τοῖς μαθηταῖς αὐτοῦ ὁ
[2]did not come *in* with [3]the [4]disciples [5]of him

Ἰησοῦς εἰς τὸ πλοῖον ἀλλὰ μόνοι οἱ
[1]Jesus in the boat but alone the

μαθηταὶ αὐτοῦ ἀπῆλθον· **23** ἄλλα ἦλθεν
disciples of him went away;　[1]other [2]came

πλοιάρια ἐκ Τιβεριάδος ἐγγὺς τοῦ τόπου
[2]boats from Tiberias near the place

ὅπου ἔφαγον τὸν ἄρτον εὐχαριστήσαντος
where they ate the bread having given thanks

24 When the people therefore saw that Jesus was not there, neither his disciples, they also took shipping, and came to Capernaum, seeking for Jesus.

25 And when they had found him on the other side of the sea, they said unto him, Rabbi, when camest thou hither?

26 Jesus answered them and said, Verily, verily, I say unto you, Ye seek me, not because ye saw the miracles, but because ye did eat of the loaves, and were filled.

27 Labour not for the meat which perisheth, but for that meat which endureth unto everlasting life, which the Son of man shall give unto you: for him hath God the Father sealed.

28 Then said they unto him, What shall we do, that we might work the works of God?

29 Jesus answered and said unto them, This is the work of God, that ye believe on him whom he hath sent.

30 They said therefore unto him, What sign shewest thou then, that we may see, and believe thee? what dost thou work?

31 Our fathers did eat manna in the desert; as it is written, He gave them

τοῦ κυρίου. 24 ὅτε οὖν εἶδεν ὁ ὄχλος
the Lord.ᵃ   When therefore saw   the   crowd
= when the Lord had given thanks.

ὅτι Ἰησοῦς οὐκ ἔστιν ἐκεῖ οὐδὲ οἱ
that Jesus is(was) not there nor the

μαθηταὶ αὐτοῦ, ἐνέβησαν αὐτοὶ εἰς τὰ
disciples of him, embarked they in the

πλοιάρια καὶ ἦλθον εἰς Καφαρναοὺμ
boats and came to Capernaum

ζητοῦντες τὸν Ἰησοῦν. 25 καὶ εὑρόντες
seeking - Jesus.   And finding

αὐτὸν πέραν τῆς θαλάσσης εἶπον αὐτῷ·
him across the   sea   they said to him:

ραββί, πότε ὧδε γέγονας; 26 ἀπεκρίθη
Rabbi, when here hast thou come? Answered

αὐτοῖς ὁ Ἰησοῦς καὶ εἶπεν· ἀμὴν ἀμὴν
them - Jesus and said: Truly truly

λέγω ὑμῖν, ζητεῖτέ με οὐχ ὅτι εἴδετε
I say to you, ye seek me not because ye saw

σημεῖα, ἀλλ' ὅτι ἐφάγετε ἐκ τῶν ἄρτων
signs, but because ye ate of the loaves

καὶ ἐχορτάσθητε. 27 ἐργάζεσθε μὴ τὴν
and were satisfied.   Work   not [for] the

βρῶσιν τὴν ἀπολλυμένην, ἀλλὰ τὴν βρῶσιν
food - perishing, but [for] the food

τὴν μένουσαν εἰς ζωὴν αἰώνιον, ἣν ὁ
- remaining to life eternal, which the

υἱὸς τοῦ ἀνθρώπου ὑμῖν δώσει· τοῦτον γὰρ
Son - of man you will give; for this [one]

ὁ πατὴρ ἐσφράγισεν ὁ θεός. 28 εἶπον
²the ³Father ⁴sealed - ¹God. They said

οὖν πρὸς αὐτόν· τί ποιῶμεν ἵνα ἐργαζ-
therefore to him : What may we do that we may

ώμεθα τὰ ἔργα τοῦ θεοῦ; 29 ἀπεκρίθη
work the works - of God? Answered

Ἰησοῦς καὶ εἶπεν αὐτοῖς· τοῦτό ἐστιν τὸ
Jesus and said to them : This is the

ἔργον τοῦ θεοῦ, ἵνα πιστεύητε εἰς ὃν
work - of God, that ye believe in [him] whom

ἀπέστειλεν ἐκεῖνος. 30 εἶπον οὖν αὐτῷ·
sent that [one]. They said therefore to him :

τί οὖν ποιεῖς σὺ σημεῖον, ἵνα ἴδωμεν
¹What ²then ³doest ⁴thou ²sign, that we may see

καὶ πιστεύσωμέν σοι; τί ἐργάζῃ; 31 οἱ
and believe thee? what workest thou? The

πατέρες ἡμῶν τὸ μάννα ἔφαγον ἐν τῇ
fathers of us the manna ate in the

ἐρήμῳ, καθώς ἐστιν γεγραμμένον· ἄρτον
desert, as it is *having been* written : Bread

bread from heaven to eat.

32 Then Jesus said unto them, Verily, verily, I say unto you, Moses gave you not that bread from heaven; but my Father giveth you the true bread from heaven.

33 For the bread of God is he which cometh down from heaven, and giveth life unto the world.

34 Then said they unto him, Lord, evermore give us this bread.

35 And Jesus said unto them, I am the bread of life: he that cometh to me shall never hunger; and he that believeth on me shall never thirst.

36 But I said unto you, That ye also have seen me, and believe not.

37 All that the Father giveth me shall come to me; and him that cometh to me I will in no wise cast out.

38 For I came down from heaven, not to do mine own will, but the will of him that sent me.

39 And this is the Father's will which hath sent me, that of all which he hath given me I should lose nothing, but should raise it up again at the last day.

ἐκ τοῦ οὐρανοῦ ἔδωκεν αὐτοῖς φαγεῖν.
out of　–　heaven　he gave　them　to eat.

32 Εἶπεν οὖν αὐτοῖς ὁ Ἰησοῦς· ἀμὴν
Said　therefore to them　–　Jesus :　Truly

ἀμὴν λέγω ὑμῖν, οὐ Μωϋσῆς δέδωκεν
truly　I say　to you,　not　Moses　has given

ὑμῖν τὸν ἄρτον ἐκ τοῦ οὐρανοῦ, ἀλλ' ὁ
you　the　bread out of　–　heaven,　but　the

πατήρ μου δίδωσιν ὑμῖν τὸν ἄρτον ἐκ
Father of me　gives　you　[1]the　[3]bread [4]out of

τοῦ οὐρανοῦ τὸν ἀληθινόν· 33 ὁ γὰρ ἄρτος
–　[5]heaven　the　[2]true;　33 for the　bread

τοῦ θεοῦ ἐστιν ὁ καταβαίνων ἐκ τοῦ
–　of God　is the [one] coming down　out of　–

οὐρανοῦ καὶ ζωὴν διδοὺς τῷ κόσμῳ.
heaven　and　life　giving　to the　world.

34 εἶπον οὖν πρὸς αὐτόν· κύριε, πάντοτε
They said therefore to　him :　Lord,　always

δὸς ἡμῖν τὸν ἄρτον τοῦτον. 35 εἶπεν
give　us　–　bread　this.　35 Said

αὐτοῖς ὁ Ἰησοῦς· ἐγώ εἰμι ὁ ἄρτος τῆς
to them　–　Jesus :　I　am　the　bread　–

ζωῆς· ὁ ἐρχόμενος πρὸς ἐμὲ οὐ μὴ
of life;　the [one]　coming　to　me by no means

πεινάσῃ, καὶ ὁ πιστεύων εἰς ἐμὲ οὐ μὴ
hungers,　and the [one] believing　in　me by no means

διψήσει πώποτε. 36 Ἀλλ' εἶπον ὑμῖν ὅτι
will thirst　never.　36 But　I told　you　that

καὶ ἑωράκατέ [με] καὶ οὐ πιστεύετε.
both　ye have seen　me　and　do not believe.

37 πᾶν ὃ δίδωσίν μοι ὁ πατὴρ πρὸς
All　which gives　to me　the Father　to

ἐμὲ ἥξει, καὶ τὸν ἐρχόμενον πρός με
me will come, and the [one]　coming　to　me

οὐ μὴ ἐκβάλω ἔξω, 38 ὅτι καταβέβηκα
by no means I will cast out outside,　because I have come down

ἀπὸ τοῦ οὐρανοῦ οὐχ ἵνα ποιῶ τὸ θέλημα
from　–　heaven　not　that I may do　the　[2]will

τὸ ἐμὸν ἀλλὰ τὸ θέλημα τοῦ πέμψαντός
–　[1]my　but　the　will　of the [one] having sent

με. 39 τοῦτο δέ ἐστιν τὸ θέλημα τοῦ
me.　And this　is　the　will of the [one]

πέμψαντός με, ἵνα πᾶν ὃ δέδωκέν μοι
having sent　me,　that　all　which he has given　me

μὴ ἀπολέσω ἐξ αὐτοῦ, ἀλλὰ ἀναστήσω
I shall not lose　of　it,　but　shall raise up

αὐτὸ ἐν τῇ ἐσχάτῃ ἡμέρᾳ. 40 τοῦτο
it　in　the　last　day.　40 this

40 And this is the will of him that sent me, that every one which seeth the Son, and believeth on him, may have everlasting life: and I will raise him up at the last day.

41 The Jews then murmured at him, because he said, I am the bread which came down from heaven.

42 And they said, Is not this Jesus, the son of Joseph, whose father and mother we know? how is it then that he saith, I came down from heaven?

43 Jesus therefore answered and said unto them, Murmur not among yourselves.

44 No man can come to me, except the Father which hath sent me draw him: and I will raise him up at the last day.

45 It is written in the prophets, And they shall be all taught of God. Every man therefore that hath heard, and hath learned of the Father, cometh unto me.

46 Not that any man hath seen the Father, save he which is of God, he hath seen the Father.

47 Verily, verily, I say unto you, He that believeth on me hath everlasting life.

48 I am that bread of life.

γάρ ἐστιν τὸ θέλημα τοῦ πατρός μου,
For is the will of the Father of me,

ἵνα πᾶς ὁ θεωρῶν τὸν υἱὸν καὶ πιστεύων
that everyone beholding the Son and believing

εἰς αὐτὸν ἔχῃ ζωὴν αἰώνιον, καὶ ἀναστήσω
in him may have life eternal, and will raise up

αὐτὸν ἐγὼ ἐν τῇ ἐσχάτῃ ἡμέρᾳ. **41** Ἐγόγ-
him I in the last day. Mur-

γυζον οὖν οἱ Ἰουδαῖοι περὶ αὐτοῦ ὅτι
mured therefore the Jews about him because

εἶπεν· ἐγώ εἰμι ὁ ἄρτος ὁ καταβὰς ἐκ
he said: I am the bread – having come down out

τοῦ οὐρανοῦ, **42** καὶ ἔλεγον· οὐχ οὗτός
– of heaven, and they said: Not this man

ἐστιν Ἰησοῦς ὁ υἱὸς Ἰωσήφ, οὗ ἡμεῖς
is Jesus the son of Joseph, of whom we

οἴδαμεν τὸν πατέρα καὶ τὴν μητέρα;
know the father and the mother?

πῶς νῦν λέγει ὅτι ἐκ τοῦ οὐρανοῦ
how now says he[,] – Out of – heaven

καταβέβηκα; **43** ἀπεκρίθη Ἰησοῦς καὶ εἶπεν
I have come down? Answered Jesus and said

αὐτοῖς· μὴ γογγύζετε μετ' ἀλλήλων.
to them: Do not murmur with one another.

44 Οὐδεὶς δύναται ἐλθεῖν πρός με ἐὰν μὴ
No one can to come to me unless

ὁ πατὴρ ὁ πέμψας με ἑλκύσῃ αὐτόν,
the Father the [one] having sent me should draw him,

κἀγὼ ἀναστήσω αὐτὸν ἐν τῇ ἐσχάτῃ
and I will raise up him in the last

ἡμέρᾳ. **45** ἔστιν γεγραμμένον ἐν τοῖς
day. It is having been written in the

προφήταις· καὶ ἔσονται πάντες διδακτοὶ
prophets: And they shall be all taught

θεοῦ· πᾶς ὁ ἀκούσας παρὰ τοῦ πατρὸς
of God; everyone hearing from the Father

καὶ μαθὼν ἔρχεται πρὸς ἐμέ. **46** οὐχ
and learning comes to me. Not

ὅτι τὸν πατέρα ἑώρακέν τις, εἰ μὴ ὁ
that the [4]Father [2]has seen [1]anyone, except the [one]

ὢν παρὰ τοῦ θεοῦ, οὗτος ἑώρακεν τὸν
being with – God, this [one] has seen the

πατέρα. **47** ἀμὴν ἀμὴν λέγω ὑμῖν, ὁ
Father. Truly truly I say to you, the

πιστεύων ἔχει ζωὴν αἰώνιον. **48** Ἐγώ
[one] believing has life eternal. I

εἰμι ὁ ἄρτος τῆς ζωῆς. **49** οἱ πατέρες
am the bread – of life. The fathers

49 Your fathers did eat manna in the wilderness, and are dead.

50 This is the bread which cometh down from heaven, that a man may eat thereof, and not die.

51 I am the living bread which came down from heaven: if any man eat of this bread, he shall live for ever: and the bread that I will give is my flesh, which I will give for the life of the world.

52 The Jews therefore strove among themselves, saying, How can this man give us *his* flesh to eat?

53 Then Jesus said unto them, Verily, verily, I say unto you, Except ye eat the flesh of the Son of man, and drink his blood, ye have no life in you.

54 Whoso eateth my flesh, and drinketh my blood, hath eternal life; and I will raise him up at the last day.

55 For my flesh is meat indeed, and my blood is drink indeed.

56 He that eateth my flesh, and drinketh my blood, dwelleth in me, and I in him.

57 As the living Father hath sent me, and I live by the Father: so he that

---

ὑμῶν ἔφαγον ἐν τῇ ἐρήμῳ τὸ μάννα καὶ
of you   ate   in   the   desert   the   manna   and

ἀπέθανον· 50 οὗτός ἐστιν ὁ ἄρτος ὁ ἐκ
died;   this   is   the   bread   – out of

τοῦ οὐρανοῦ καταβαίνων, ἵνα τις ἐξ
–   heaven   coming down,   that   anyone   of

αὐτοῦ φάγῃ καὶ μὴ ἀποθάνῃ. 51 ἐγώ
it   may eat   and   may not die.   I

εἰμι ὁ ἄρτος ὁ ζῶν ὁ ἐκ τοῦ οὐρανοῦ
am   the   bread   – living   the [one]   out of   –   heaven

καταβάς· ἐάν τις φάγῃ ἐκ τούτου τοῦ
having come down;   if   anyone   eats   of   this   –

ἄρτου, ζήσει εἰς τὸν αἰῶνα· καὶ ὁ ἄρτος
bread,   he will live   to   the   age;   ²indeed ³the ⁴bread

δὲ ὃν ἐγὼ δώσω ἡ σάρξ μού ἐστιν
¹and which   I   will give   the   flesh   of me   is

ὑπὲρ τῆς τοῦ κόσμου ζωῆς. 52 Ἐμάχοντο
for   ¹the ³of the ⁴world   ²life.   Fought

οὖν πρὸς ἀλλήλους οἱ Ἰουδαῖοι λέγοντες·
therefore   with   one another   the   Jews   saying:

πῶς δύναται οὗτος ἡμῖν δοῦναι τὴν
How   can   this man   us   *to* give   the(his)

σάρκα φαγεῖν; 53 εἶπεν οὖν αὐτοῖς ὁ
flesh   to eat?   Said   therefore   to them   –

Ἰησοῦς· ἀμὴν ἀμὴν λέγω ὑμῖν, ἐὰν μὴ
Jesus: Truly   truly   I say   to you,   unless

φάγητε τὴν σάρκα τοῦ υἱοῦ τοῦ ἀνθρώπου
ye eat   the   flesh   of the   Son   –   of man

καὶ πίητε αὐτοῦ τὸ αἷμα, οὐκ ἔχετε
and   drink   of him   the   blood,   ye have not

ζωὴν ἐν ἑαυτοῖς. 54 ὁ τρώγων μου τὴν
life   in   yourselves.   The [one] eating   of me   the

σάρκα καὶ πίνων μου τὸ αἷμα ἔχει ζωὴν
flesh   and   drinking   of me   the   blood   has   life

αἰώνιον, κἀγὼ ἀναστήσω αὐτὸν τῇ ἐσχάτῃ
eternal,   and I   will raise up   him   in the   last

ἡμέρᾳ. 55 ἡ γὰρ σάρξ μου ἀληθής
day.   For the   flesh   of me   ²true

ἐστιν βρῶσις, καὶ τὸ αἷμά μου ἀληθής
¹is   ³food,   and   the   blood of me   ²true

ἐστιν πόσις. 56 ὁ τρώγων μου τὴν
¹is   ³drink.   The [one]   eating   of me   the

σάρκα καὶ πίνων μου τὸ αἷμα ἐν ἐμοὶ
flesh   and   drinking of me   the   blood   in   me

μένει κἀγὼ ἐν αὐτῷ. 57 καθὼς ἀπέστειλέν
remains   and I   in   him.   As   sent

με ΄ ὁ ζῶν πατὴρ κἀγὼ ζῶ διὰ τὸν
me   the   living   Father   and I   live   because of the

eateth me, even he shall live by me.

58 This is that bread which came down from heaven: not as your fathers did eat manna, and are dead: he that eateth of this bread shall live for ever.

59 These things said he in the synagogue, as he taught in Capernaum.

60 Many therefore of his disciples, when they had heard *this*, said, This is an hard saying; who can hear it?

61 When Jesus knew in himself that his disciples murmured at it, he said unto them, Doth this offend you?

62 *What* and if ye shall see the Son of man ascend up where he was before?

63 It is the spirit that quickeneth ; the flesh profiteth nothing: the words that I speak unto you, *they* are spirit, and *they* are life.

64 But there are some of you that believe not. For Jesus knew from the beginning who they were that believed not, and who should betray him.

65 And he said, Therefore said I unto you, that no man can come unto me, except it were given unto him of my Father.

πατέρα,   καὶ   ὁ   τρώγων   με   κἀκεῖνος
Father,   also   the [one]   eating   me   even that one

ζήσει   δι'   ἐμέ.   58 οὗτός   ἐστιν   ὁ   ἄρτος   ὁ
will live because of   me.   This   is   the   bread   –

ἐξ   οὐρανοῦ   καταβάς,   οὐ   καθὼς   ἔφαγον
out of   heaven   having come down,   not   as   ate

οἱ   πατέρες   καὶ   ἀπέθανον·   ὁ   τρώγων
the   fathers   and   died;   the [one]   eating

τοῦτον   τὸν   ἄρτον   ζήσει   εἰς   τὸν   αἰῶνα.
this   –   bread   will live   unto   the   age.

59 Ταῦτα   εἶπεν   ἐν   συναγωγῇ   διδάσκων   ἐν
These things he said   in   a synagogue   teaching   in

Καφαρναούμ.   60 Πολλοὶ   οὖν   ἀκούσαντες
Capernaum.   ²Many   ¹therefore   ⁷hearing

ἐκ   τῶν   μαθητῶν   αὐτοῦ   εἶπαν·   σκληρός
³of   ⁴the   ⁵disciples   ⁶of him   said :   Hard

ἐστιν   ὁ   λόγος   οὗτος·   τίς   δύναται   αὐτοῦ
is   –   word   this;   who   can   it

ἀκούειν;   61 εἰδὼς   δὲ   ὁ   Ἰησοῦς   ἐν   ἑαυτῷ
to hear?   But knowing   –   Jesus   in   himself

ὅτι   γογγύζουσιν   περὶ   τούτου   οἱ   μαθηταὶ
that   ⁴are murmuring   ⁵about   ⁶this   ¹the   ²disciples

αὐτοῦ,   εἶπεν   αὐτοῖς·   τοῦτο   ὑμᾶς   σκανδαλίζει;
³of him,   said   to them :   This   you   offends?

62 ἐὰν   οὖν   θεωρῆτε   τὸν   υἱὸν   τοῦ   ἀνθρώπου
If   then   ye behold   the   Son   –   of man

ἀναβαίνοντα   ὅπου   ἦν   τὸ   πρότερον;   63 τὸ
ascending   where   he was   at first? †   The

πνεῦμά   ἐστιν   τὸ   ζωοποιοῦν,   ἡ   σάρξ   οὐκ
spirit   is   the [thing]   quickening,   the   flesh   not

ὠφελεῖ   οὐδέν·   τὰ   ῥήματα   ἃ   ἐγὼ   λελάληκα
profits   no(any)thing;   the   words   which   I   have spoken

ὑμῖν   πνεῦμά   ἐστιν   καὶ   ζωή   ἐστιν.   64 ἀλλ'
to you   spirit   is(are)   and   life   is(are).   But

εἰσὶν   ἐξ   ὑμῶν   τινες   οἳ   οὐ   πιστεύουσιν.   ἤδει
there are of   you   some   who   do not believe.   knew

γὰρ   ἐξ   ἀρχῆς   ὁ   Ἰησοῦς   τίνες   εἰσὶν
For from [the] beginning   –   Jesus   who   are(were)

οἱ   μὴ   πιστεύοντες   καὶ   τίς   ἐστιν   ὁ
the [ones]   not believing   and   who   is(was)   the

παραδώσων   αὐτόν.   65 καὶ   ἔλεγεν·
[one] betraying   him.   And   he said :

διὰ   τοῦτο   εἴρηκα   ὑμῖν   ὅτι   οὐδεὶς   δύναται
Therefore   I have told   you   that   no one   can

ἐλθεῖν   πρός   με   ἐὰν   μὴ   ᾖ   δεδομένον
to come   to   me   unless   it is *having been* given

αὐτῷ   ἐκ   τοῦ   πατρός.
to him   of   the   Father.

66 ¶ From that *time* many of his disciples went back, and walked no more with him.

67 Then said Jesus unto the twelve, Will ye also go away?

68 Then Simon Peter answered him, Lord, to whom shall we go? thou hast the words of eternal life.

69 And we believe and are sure that thou art that Christ, the Son of the living God.

70 Jesus answered them, Have not I chosen you ⁺welve, and one of you is a devil?

71 He spake of Judas Iscariot *the son* of Simon: for he it was that should betray him, being one of the twelve.

66 Ἐκ τούτου πολλοὶ τῶν μαθητῶν
From this many of the disciples

αὐτοῦ ἀπῆλθον εἰς τὰ ὀπίσω καὶ οὐκέτι
of him went away back† and no longer

μετ᾽ αὐτοῦ περιεπάτουν. 67 εἶπεν οὖν ὁ
with him walked. Said therefore –

Ἰησοῦς τοῖς δώδεκα· μὴ καὶ ὑμεῖς
Jesus to the twelve : *Not* also ye

θέλετε ὑπάγειν; 68 ἀπεκρίθη αὐτῷ Σίμων
wish to go? Answered him Simon

Πέτρος· κύριε, πρὸς τίνα ἀπελευσόμεθα;
Peter : Lord, to whom shall we go away?

ῥήματα ζωῆς αἰωνίου ἔχεις· 69 καὶ ἡμεῖς
words of life eternal thou hast; and we

πεπιστεύκαμεν καὶ ἐγνώκαμεν ὅτι σὺ εἶ
have believed and have known that thou art

ὁ ἅγιος τοῦ θεοῦ. 70 ἀπεκρίθη αὐτοῖς ὁ
the holy one – of God. Answered them –

Ἰησοῦς· οὐκ ἐγὼ ὑμᾶς τοὺς δώδεκα
Jesus : ³Not ²I ⁴you ⁵the ⁶twelve

ἐξελεξάμην; καὶ ἐξ ὑμῶν εἷς διάβολός
¹chose? and of you one a devil

ἐστιν. 71 ἔλεγεν δὲ τὸν Ἰούδαν Σίμωνος
is. Now he spoke [of] – Judas [son] of Simon

Ἰσκαριώτου· οὗτος γὰρ ἔμελλεν παραδιδόναι
Iscariot; for this one was about to betray

αὐτόν, εἷς ἐκ τῶν δώδεκα.
him, one of the twelve.

CHAPTER 7

A FTER these things Jesus walked in Galilee: for he would not walk in Jewry, because the Jews sought to kill him.

2 ¶ Now the Jews' feast of tabernacles was at hand.

3 His brethren therefore said unto him, Depart hence, and go into Judæa, that thy disciples also may see the works that thou doest.

4 For *there is* no man

7 Καὶ μετὰ ταῦτα περιεπάτει ὁ Ἰησοῦς
And after these things walked – Jesus

ἐν τῇ Γαλιλαίᾳ· οὐ γὰρ ἤθελεν ἐν τῇ
in – Galilee; for he did not wish in –

Ἰουδαίᾳ περιπατεῖν, ὅτι ἐζήτουν αὐτὸν οἱ
Judæa to walk, because ²were seeking ³him ¹the

Ἰουδαῖοι ἀποκτεῖναι. 2 ἦν δὲ ἐγγὺς ἡ
³Jews ⁴to kill. Now was near the

ἑορτὴ τῶν Ἰουδαίων ἡ σκηνοπηγία. 3 εἶπον
feast of the Jews the Tabernacles. Said

οὖν πρὸς αὐτὸν οἱ ἀδελφοὶ αὐτοῦ·
therefore to him the brothers of him :

μετάβηθι ἐντεῦθεν καὶ ὕπαγε εἰς τὴν Ἰουδαίαν,
Depart hence and go into – Judæa,

ἵνα καὶ οἱ μαθηταί σου θεωρήσουσιν τὰ
that also the disciples of thee will behold the

ἔργά σου ἃ ποιεῖς· 4 οὐδεὶς γάρ τι ἐν
works of thee which thou doest; for no one anything in

that doeth any thing in secret, and he himself seeketh to be known openly. If thou do these things, shew thyself to the world.

5 For neither did his brethren believe in him.

6 Then Jesus said unto them, My time is not yet come: but your time is alway ready.

7 The world cannot hate you; but me it hateth, because I testify of it, that the works thereof are evil.

8 Go ye up unto this feast: I go not up yet unto this feast; for my time is not yet full come.

9 When he had said these words unto them, he abode *still* in Galilee.

10 ¶ But when his brethren were gone up, then went he also up unto the feast, not openly, but as it were in secret.

11 Then the Jews sought him at the feast, and said, Where is he?

12 And there was much murmuring among the people concerning him: for some said, He is a good man: others said, Nay; but he deceiveth the people.

13 Howbeit no man spake openly of him for fear of the Jews.

κρυπτῷ ποιεῖ καὶ ζητεῖ αὐτὸς ἐν παρρησίᾳ
secret does and seeks [him]self in [the] open

εἶναι. εἰ ταῦτα ποιεῖς, φανέρωσον σεαυτὸν
to be. If these things thou doest, manifest thyself

τῷ κόσμῳ. 5 οὐδὲ γὰρ οἱ ἀδελφοὶ
to the world. For not the brothers

αὐτοῦ ἐπίστευον εἰς αὐτόν. 6 λέγει οὖν
of him believed in him. Says therefore

αὐτοῖς ὁ Ἰησοῦς· ὁ καιρὸς ὁ ἐμὸς
to them – Jesus : The ²time – ¹my

οὔπω πάρεστιν, ὁ δὲ καιρὸς ὁ ὑμέτερος
not yet is arrived, but *the* ²time – ¹your

πάντοτέ ἐστιν ἕτοιμος. 7 οὐ δύναται ὁ
always is ready. Cannot the

κόσμος μισεῖν ὑμᾶς, ἐμὲ δὲ μισεῖ, ὅτι
world *to* hate you, but me it hates, because

ἐγὼ μαρτυρῶ περὶ αὐτοῦ ὅτι τὰ ἔργα
I witness about it that the works

αὐτοῦ πονηρά ἐστιν. 8 ὑμεῖς ἀνάβητε εἰς
of it evil is(are). ²Ye ¹go ³up to

τὴν ἑορτήν· ἐγὼ οὐκ ἀναβαίνω εἰς τὴν
the feast; I am not going up to –

ἑορτὴν ταύτην, ὅτι ὁ ἐμὸς καιρὸς οὔπω
feast this, because *the* my time not yet

πεπλήρωται. 9 ταῦτα δὲ εἰπὼν αὐτοῖς
has been fulfilled. And these things saying to them

ἔμεινεν ἐν τῇ Γαλιλαίᾳ. 10 Ὡς δὲ
he remained in – Galilee. But when

ἀνέβησαν οἱ ἀδελφοὶ αὐτοῦ εἰς τὴν ἑορτήν,
went up the brothers of him to the feast,

τότε καὶ αὐτὸς ἀνέβη, οὐ φανερῶς ἀλλὰ
then also he went up, not manifestly but

ὡς ἐν κρυπτῷ. 11 οἱ οὖν Ἰουδαῖοι
as in secret. Therefore the Jews

ἐζήτουν αὐτὸν ἐν τῇ ἑορτῇ καὶ ἔλεγον·
sought him at the feast and said :

ποῦ ἐστιν ἐκεῖνος; 12 καὶ γογγυσμὸς περὶ
Where is that man? And ³murmuring ⁴about

αὐτοῦ ἦν πολὺς ἐν τοῖς ὄχλοις· οἱ μὲν
⁵him ¹there was ²much in the crowds; some

ἔλεγον ὅτι ἀγαθός ἐστιν· ἄλλοι [δὲ]
said[,] – A good man he is; but others

ἔλεγον· οὔ, ἀλλὰ πλανᾷ τὸν ὄχλον.
said : No, but he deceives the crowd.

13 οὐδεὶς μέντοι παρρησίᾳ ἐλάλει περὶ
No one however openly spoke about

αὐτοῦ διὰ τὸν φόβον τῶν Ἰουδαίων.
him because of the fear of the Jews.

14 ¶ Now about the midst of the feast Jesus went up into the temple, and taught.

15 And the Jews marvelled, saying, How knoweth this man letters, having never learned?

16 Jesus answered them, and said, My doctrine is not mine, but his that sent me.

17 If any man will do his will, he shall know of the doctrine, whether it be of God, or *whether* I speak of myself.

18 He that speaketh of himself seeketh his own glory: but he that seeketh his glory that sent him, the same is true, and no unrighteousness is in him.

19 Did not Moses give you the law, and *yet* none of you keepeth the law? Why go ye about to kill me?

20 The people answered and said, Thou hast a devil: who goeth about to kill thee?

21 Jesus answered and said unto them, I have done one work, and ye all marvel.

22 Moses therefore gave unto you circumcision; (not because it is of Moses, but of the fathers;) and ye on the sabbath day circumcise a man.

14 Ἤδη δὲ τῆς ἑορτῆς μεσούσης ἀνέβη
But now the feast being in [its] middle[a] went up
= in the middle of the feast

Ἰησοῦς εἰς τὸ ἱερὸν καὶ ἐδίδασκεν.
Jesus to the temple and taught.

15 ἐθαύμαζον οὖν οἱ Ἰουδαῖοι λέγοντες·
Marvelled therefore the Jews saying :

πῶς οὗτος γράμματα οἶδεν μὴ μεμαθηκώς;
How this man letters knows not having learned?

16 ἀπεκρίθη οὖν αὐτοῖς Ἰησοῦς καὶ εἶπεν·
Answered therefore them Jesus and said :

ἡ ἐμὴ διδαχὴ οὐκ ἔστιν ἐμὴ ἀλλὰ τοῦ
The my teaching is not mine but of the

πέμψαντός με· 17 ἐάν τις θέλῃ τὸ θέλημα
[one] having sent me; if anyone wishes the will

αὐτοῦ ποιεῖν, γνώσεται περὶ τῆς διδαχῆς,
of him to do, he will know concerning the teaching,

πότερον ἐκ τοῦ θεοῦ ἐστιν ἢ ἐγὼ ἀπ'
whether of - God it is or I from

ἐμαυτοῦ λαλῶ. 18 ὁ ἀφ' ἑαυτοῦ λαλῶν
myself speak. The [one] from himself speaking

τὴν δόξαν τὴν ἰδίαν ζητεῖ· ὁ δὲ ζητῶν
his own glory seeks; but the [one] seeking

τὴν δόξαν τοῦ πέμψαντος αὐτόν, οὗτος
the glory of the [one] having sent him, this man

ἀληθής ἐστιν καὶ ἀδικία ἐν αὐτῷ οὐκ
true is and unrighteousness in him not

ἔστιν. 19 οὐ Μωϋσῆς ἔδωκεν ὑμῖν τὸν
is. Not Moses gave you the

νόμον; καὶ οὐδεὶς ἐξ ὑμῶν ποιεῖ τὸν
law? and no one of you does the

νόμον. τί με ζητεῖτε ἀποκτεῖναι;
law. Why me seek ye to kill?

20 ἀπεκρίθη ὁ ὄχλος· δαιμόνιον ἔχεις·
Answered the crowd : A demon thou hast;

τίς σε ζητεῖ ἀποκτεῖναι; 21 ἀπεκρίθη
who thee seeks to kill? Answered

Ἰησοῦς καὶ εἶπεν αὐτοῖς· ἓν ἔργον ἐποίησα
Jesus and said to them : One work I did

καὶ πάντες θαυμάζετε. 22 διὰ τοῦτο
and all ye marvel. Because of this

Μωϋσῆς δέδωκεν ὑμῖν τὴν περιτομήν, —
Moses has given you - circumcision, —

οὐχ ὅτι ἐκ τοῦ Μωϋσέως ἐστὶν ἀλλ' ἐκ
not that of - Moses it is but of

τῶν πατέρων, — καὶ ἐν σαββάτῳ
the fathers, — and on a sabbath

περιτέμνετε ἄνθρωπον. 23 εἰ περιτομὴν
ye circumcise a man. If [a]circumcision

23 If a man on the sabbath day receive circumcision, that the law of Moses should not be broken; are ye angry at me, because I have made a man every whit whole on the sabbath day?

24 Judge not according to the appearance, but judge righteous judgment.

25 Then said some of them of Jerusalem, Is not this he, whom they seek to kill?

26 But, lo, he speaketh boldly, and they say nothing unto him. Do the rulers know indeed that this is the very Christ?

27 Howbeit we know this man whence he is: but when Christ cometh, no man knoweth whence he is.

28 Then cried Jesus in the temple as he taught, saying, Ye both know me, and ye know whence I am: and I am not come of myself, but he that sent me is true, whom ye know not.

29 But I know him: for I am from him, and he hath sent me.

30 Then they sought to take him: but no man laid hands on him, because his hour was not yet come.

31 And many of the people believed on him, and said, When Christ

λαμβάνει [ὁ] ἄνθρωπος ἐν σαββάτῳ ἵνα
²receives – ¹a man on a sabbath that

μὴ λυθῇ ὁ νόμος Μωϋσέως, ἐμοὶ χολᾶτε
is not broken the law of Moses, with me are ye angry

ὅτι ὅλον ἄνθρωπον ὑγιῆ ἐποίησα ἐν
because a whole man healthy I made on

σαββάτῳ; 24 μὴ κρίνετε κατ' ὄψιν, ἀλλὰ
a sabbath? Judge not according to face, but

τὴν δικαίαν κρίσιν κρίνατε. 25 Ἔλεγον
– righteous judgment judge. Said

οὖν τινες ἐκ τῶν Ἱεροσολυμιτῶν· οὐχ
therefore some of the Jerusalemites : ¹Not

οὗτός ἐστιν ὃν ζητοῦσιν ἀποκτεῖναι; 26 καὶ
²this man ¹is it whom they are seeking to kill? and

ἴδε παρρησίᾳ λαλεῖ, καὶ οὐδὲν αὐτῷ
behold openly he speaks, and nothing to him

λέγουσιν. μήποτε ἀληθῶς. ἔγνωσαν οἱ
they say. Perhaps indeed knew the

ἄρχοντες ὅτι οὗτός ἐστιν ὁ χριστός;*
rulers that this is the Christ?*

27 ἀλλὰ τοῦτον οἴδαμεν πόθεν ἐστίν· ὁ δὲ
But this man we know whence he is; but ²the

χριστὸς ὅταν ἔρχηται, οὐδεὶς γινώσκει
³Christ ¹when comes, no one knows

πόθεν ἐστίν. 28 ἔκραξεν οὖν ἐν τῷ ἱερῷ
whence he is. ³Cried out ⁴therefore ⁴in ⁵the temple

διδάσκων ὁ Ἰησοῦς καὶ λέγων· κἀμὲ
⁷teaching – ¹Jesus ⁸and ⁹saying : Both me

οἴδατε καὶ οἴδατε πόθεν εἰμί· καὶ ἀπ'
ye know and ye know whence I am; and from

ἐμαυτοῦ οὐκ ἐλήλυθα, ἀλλ' ἔστιν ἀληθινὸς
myself I have not come, but he is true

ὁ πέμψας με, ὃν ὑμεῖς οὐκ οἴδατε·
the [one] having sent me, whom ye know not;

29 ἐγὼ οἶδα αὐτόν, ὅτι παρ' αὐτοῦ εἰμι
I know him, because ²from ³him ¹I am

κἀκεῖνός με ἀπέστειλεν. 30 Ἐζήτουν οὖν
⁴and that one ⁵me ⁵sent. They sought therefore

αὐτὸν πιάσαι, καὶ οὐδεὶς ἐπέβαλεν ἐπ'
him to arrest, and no one laid on on

αὐτὸν τὴν χεῖρα, ὅτι οὔπω ἐληλύθει ἡ
him the hand, because not yet had come the

ὥρα αὐτοῦ. 31 Ἐκ τοῦ ὄχλου δὲ πολλοὶ
hour of him. ³of ⁴the ⁵crowd ¹But ²many

ἐπίστευσαν εἰς αὐτόν, καὶ ἔλεγον· ὁ
believed in him, and said : ²The

* As this question is introduced by μήποτε, a negative answer is expected; see page xiii, and note ver. 31 below.

cometh, will he do more miracles than these which this *man* hath done?

32 ¶ The Pharisees heard that the people murmured such things concerning him; and the Pharisees and the chief priests sent officers to take him.

33 Then said Jesus unto them, Yet a little while am I with you, and *then* I go unto him that sent me.

34 Ye shall seek me, and shall not find *me:* and where I am, *thither* ye cannot come.

35 Then said the Jews among themselves, Whither will he go, that we shall not find him? will he go unto the dispersed among the Gentiles, and teach the Gentiles?

36 What *manner of* saying is this that he said, Ye shall seek me, and shall not find *me:* and where I am, *thither* ye cannot come?

37 ¶ In the last day, the great *day* of the feast, Jesus stood and cried, saying, If any man thirst, let him come unto me, and drink.

38 He that believeth on me, as the scripture hath said, out of his belly shall flow rivers of living water.

χριστὸς ὅταν ἔλθῃ, μὴ πλείονα σημεῖα
³Christ ¹when ⁴comes, *not* more signs

ποιήσει ὧν οὗτος ἐποίησεν; 32 ἤκουσαν
will he do [than] which this man did? ³Heard

οἱ Φαρισαῖοι τοῦ ὄχλου γογγύζοντος περὶ
¹the ²Pharisees ⁴the ⁵crowd ⁶murmuring ⁸about

αὐτοῦ ταῦτα, καὶ ἀπέστειλαν οἱ ἀρχιερεῖς
⁹him ⁷these things, and ⁶sent ¹the ²chief priests

καὶ οἱ Φαρισαῖοι ὑπηρέτας ἵνα πιάσωσιν
³and ⁴the ⁵Pharisees ⁷attendants that they might arrest

αὐτόν. 33 εἶπεν οὖν ὁ Ἰησοῦς· ἔτι
him. Said therefore – Jesus : Yet

χρόνον μικρὸν μεθ᾽ ὑμῶν εἰμι καὶ ὑπάγω
time a little with you I am and I go

πρὸς τὸν πέμψαντά με. 34 ζητήσετέ με
to the [one] having sent me. Ye will seek me

καὶ οὐχ εὑρήσετε, καὶ ὅπου εἰμὶ ἐγὼ
and will not find, and where am I

ὑμεῖς οὐ δύνασθε ἐλθεῖν. 35 εἶπον οὖν
ye cannot *to* come. Said therefore

οἱ Ἰουδαῖοι πρὸς ἑαυτούς· ποῦ οὗτος
the Jews to themselves : Where this man

μέλλει πορεύεσθαι, ὅτι ἡμεῖς οὐχ εὑρήσομεν
is about to go, that we will not find

αὐτόν; μὴ εἰς τὴν διασπορὰν τῶν Ἑλλήνων
him? *not* to the dispersion of the Greeks

μέλλει πορεύεσθαι καὶ διδάσκειν τοὺς
is he about to go and to teach the

Ἕλληνας; 36 τίς ἐστιν ὁ λόγος οὗτος
Greeks? What is – word this

ὃν εἶπεν· ζητήσετέ με καὶ οὐχ εὑρήσετε,
which he said : Ye will seek me and will not find,

καὶ ὅπου εἰμὶ ἐγὼ ὑμεῖς οὐ δύνασθε
and where am I ye cannot

ἐλθεῖν;
to come?

37 Ἐν δὲ τῇ ἐσχάτῃ ἡμέρᾳ τῇ μεγάλῃ
Now in the last day the great [day]

τῆς ἑορτῆς εἱστήκει ὁ Ἰησοῦς καὶ ἔκραξεν
of the feast stood – Jesus and cried out

λέγων· ἐάν τις διψᾷ, ἐρχέσθω πρός με
saying : If anyone thirsts, let him come to me

καὶ πινέτω. 38 ὁ πιστεύων εἰς ἐμέ,
and drink. The [one] believing in me,

καθὼς εἶπεν ἡ γραφή, ποταμοὶ ἐκ τῆς
as said the scripture, ¹rivers ⁶out of ⁶the

κοιλίας αὐτοῦ ῥεύσουσιν ὕδατος ζῶντος.
⁷belly ⁵of him ⁴will flow ⁸water ⁹of living.

39 (But this spake he of the Spirit, which they that believe on him should receive: for the Holy Ghost was not yet *given;* because that Jesus was not yet glorified.)

40 Many of the people therefore, when they heard this saying, said, Of a truth this is the Prophet.

41 Others said, This is the Christ. But some said, Shall Christ come out of Galilee?

42 Hath not the scripture said, That Christ cometh of the seed of David, and out of the town of Bethlehem, where David was?

43 So there was a division among the people because of him.

44 And some of them would have taken him, but no man laid hands on him.

45 ¶ Then came the officers to the chief priests and Pharisees; and they said unto them, Why have ye not brought him?

46 The officers answered, Never man spake like this man.

47 Then answered them the Pharisees, Are ye also deceived?

48 Have any of the rulers or of the Pharisees believed on him?

---

39 τοῦτο δὲ εἶπεν περὶ τοῦ πνεύματος
But this he said concerning the Spirit

οὗ ἔμελλον λαμβάνειν οἱ πιστεύσαντες
whom were about to receive the [ones] believing

εἰς αὐτόν· οὔπω γὰρ ἦν πνεῦμα, ὅτι
in him; for not yet was [?the] Spirit, because

Ἰησοῦς οὐδέπω ἐδοξάσθη. **40** Ἐκ τοῦ
Jesus not yet was glorified. [Some] of the

ὄχλου οὖν ἀκούσαντες τῶν λόγων τούτων
crowd therefore hearing — words these

ἔλεγον [ὅτι]· οὗτός ἐστιν ἀληθῶς ὁ
said — : This man is truly the

προφήτης· **41** ἄλλοι ἔλεγον· οὗτός ἐστιν ὁ
prophet; Others said : This man is the

χριστός· οἱ δὲ ἔλεγον· μὴ γὰρ ἐκ τῆς
Christ; But others† said : *Not* then out of -

Γαλιλαίας ὁ χριστὸς ἔρχεται; **42** οὐχ ἡ
Galilee the Christ comes? not the

γραφὴ εἶπεν ὅτι ἐκ τοῦ σπέρματος Δαυίδ,
scripture said that of the seed of David,

καὶ ἀπὸ Βηθλέεμ τῆς κώμης ὅπου ἦν
and from Bethlehem the village where was

Δαυίδ, ἔρχεται ὁ χριστός; **43** σχίσμα
David, comes the Christ? A division

οὖν ἐγένετο ἐν τῷ ὄχλῳ δι᾽ αὐτόν·
therefore became in the crowd because of him;

44 τινὲς δὲ ἤθελον ἐξ αὐτῶν πιάσαι αὐτόν,
and ¹some ⁴wished ²of ³them to arrest him,

ἀλλ᾽ οὐδεὶς ἐπέβαλεν ἐπ᾽ αὐτὸν τὰς χεῖρας.
but no one laid *on* on him the(his) hands.

45 Ἦλθον οὖν οἱ ὑπηρέται πρὸς τοὺς
Came therefore the attendants to the

ἀρχιερεῖς καὶ Φαρισαίους, καὶ εἶπον αὐτοῖς
chief priests and Pharisees, and ²said ³to them

ἐκεῖνοι· διὰ τί οὐκ ἠγάγετε αὐτόν;
¹those: Why did ye not bring him?

46 ἀπεκρίθησαν οἱ ὑπηρέται· οὐδέποτε
Answered the attendants : Never

ἐλάλησεν οὕτως ἄνθρωπος, ὡς οὗτος λαλεῖ
spoke so a man, as ¹this ³speaks

ὁ ἄνθρωπος. **47** ἀπεκρίθησαν οὖν αὐτοῖς
-- ²mən. Answered therefore them

οἱ Φαρισαῖοι· μὴ καὶ ὑμεῖς πεπλάνησθε;
the Pharisees : *Not* also ye have been deceived?

48 μή τις ἐκ τῶν ἀρχόντων ἐπίστευσεν
not anyone of the rulers believed

εἰς αὐτὸν ἢ ἐκ τῶν Φαρισαίων; **49** ἀλλὰ
in him or of the Pharisees? But

49 But this people who knoweth not the law are cursed.

50 Nicodemus saith unto them, (he that came to Jesus by night, being one of them,)

51 Doth our law judge *any* man, before it hear him, and know what he doeth?

52 They answered and said unto him, Art thou also of Galilee? Search, and look: for out of Galilee ariseth no prophet.

53 And every man went unto his own house.

ὁ   ὄχλος   οὗτος   ὁ   μὴ   γινώσκων   τὸν
-   crowd   this   -   not   knowing   the
νόμον   ἐπάρατοί   εἰσιν.   50 λέγει   Νικόδημος
law   cursed   are.   Says   Nicodemus
πρὸς αὐτούς,   ὁ   ἐλθὼν   πρὸς   αὐτὸν   πρότερον,
to   them,   the[one] having come   to   him   firstly,
εἷς   ὢν   ἐξ   αὐτῶν·   51 μὴ   ὁ   νόμος   ἡμῶν
²one   ¹being   of   them :   Not   the   law   of us
κρίνει   τὸν   ἄνθρωπον   ἐὰν   μὴ   ἀκούσῃ
judges   the   man   unless   it hears
πρῶτον   παρ'   αὐτοῦ   καὶ   γνῷ   τί   ποιεῖ;
first   from   him   and   knows   what   he does?
52 ἀπεκρίθησαν   καὶ   εἶπαν   αὐτῷ·   μὴ   καὶ
They answered   and   said   to him :   Not   also
σὺ   ἐκ   τῆς   Γαλιλαίας   εἶ;   ἐρεύνησον   καὶ
thou   of   -   Galilee   art?   search   and
ἴδε   ὅτι   ἐκ   τῆς   Γαλιλαίας   προφήτης   οὐκ
see   that   out of   -   Galilee   a prophet   not
ἐγείρεται.
is raised.

53 Καὶ   ἐπορεύθησαν   ἕκαστος   εἰς   τὸν   οἶκον
And   they went   each one   to   the   house
αὐτοῦ,   8 Ἰησοῦς   δὲ   ἐπορεύθη   εἰς   τὸ
of him,   but Jesus   went   to   the
Ὄρος   τῶν   Ἐλαιῶν.   2 Ὄρθρου   δὲ   πάλιν
Mount   of the   Olives.   And at dawn   again
παρεγένετο   εἰς   τὸ   ἱερόν   [, καὶ   πᾶς   ὁ
he arrived   in   the   temple,   and   all   the
λαὸς   ἤρχετο   πρὸς   αὐτόν,   καὶ   καθίσας
people   came   to   him,   and   sitting
ἐδίδασκεν   αὐτούς].   3 Ἄγουσιν   δὲ   οἱ
he taught   them].   And lead   the
γραμματεῖς   καὶ   οἱ   Φαρισαῖοι   γυναῖκα   ἐπὶ
scribes   and   the   Pharisees   a woman   in
μοιχείᾳ   κατειλημμένην,   καὶ   στήσαντες   αὐτὴν
adultery   *having been* caught,   and   standing   her
ἐν   μέσῳ   4 λέγουσιν   αὐτῷ   Διδάσκαλε,
in [the] midst   they say   to him[,]   Teacher,
αὕτη   ἡ   γυνὴ   κατείληπται   ἐπ'   αὐτοφώρῳ
this   -   woman   has been caught   in   the act
μοιχευομένη·   5 ἐν   δὲ   τῷ   νόμῳ   [ἡμῖν]
committing adultery;   now in   the   law   to us^c
Μωυσῆς   ἐνετείλατο   τὰς   τοιαύτας   λιθάζειν·
Moses   enjoined   -   ²such   ¹to stone;
σὺ   οὖν   τί   λέγεις;   6 [τοῦτο   δὲ   ἔλεγον
thou therefore   what   sayest thou?   But this   they said
πειράζοντες   αὐτόν,   ἵνα   ἔχωσιν   κατηγορεῖν
tempting   him,   that they might have   to accuse

CHAPTER 8

JESUS went unto the mount of Olives.

2 And early in the morning he came again into the temple, and all the people came unto him; and he sat down, and taught them.

3 And the scribes and Pharisees brought unto him a woman taken in adultery; and when they had set her in the midst,

4 They say unto him, Master, this woman was taken in adultery, in the very act.

5 Now Moses in the law commanded us, that such should be stoned: but what sayest thou?

6 This they said, tempting him, that they might have to accuse him. But

Jesus stooped down, and with *his* finger wrote on the ground, *as though he heard them not.*

7 So when they continued asking him, he lifted up himself, and said unto them, He that is without sin among you, let him first cast a stone at her.

8 And again he stooped down, and wrote on the ground.

9 And they which heard *it*, being convicted by *their own* conscience, went out one by one, beginning at the eldest, *even* unto the last: and Jesus was left alone, and the woman standing in the midst.

10 When Jesus had lifted up himself, and saw none but the woman, he said unto her, Woman, where are those thine accusers? hath no man condemned thee?

11 She said, No man, Lord. And Jesus said unto her, Neither do I condemn thee: go, and sin no more.

12 ¶ Then spake Jesus again unto them, saying, I am the light of the world: he that followeth me shall not walk in darkness, but shall have the light of life.

13 The Pharisees therefore said unto him, Thou bearest record of thyself; thy record is not true.

14 Jesus answered and said unto them, Though I bear record of myself, *yet* my record is true: for I know whence I came, and whither I go; but ye can-

αὐτοῦ.] ὁ δὲ Ἰησοῦς κάτω κύψας τῷ
him.   – But Jesus down stooping with the

δακτύλῳ κατέγραφεν εἰς τὴν γῆν. 7 ὡς δὲ
finger   wrote   in the earth. But as

ἐπέμενον ἐρωτῶντες [αὐτόν], ἀνέκυψεν καὶ
they remained questioning him, he stood erect and

εἶπεν [αὐτοῖς] Ὁ ἀναμάρτητος ὑμῶν
said to them[,] The [one] sinless of you

πρῶτος ἐπ' αὐτὴν βαλέτω λίθον. 8 καὶ
first on her let him cast a stone. And

πάλιν κατακύψας ἔγραφεν εἰς τὴν γῆν.
again stooping down he wrote in the earth.

9 οἱ δὲ ἀκούσαντες ἐξήρχοντο εἰς καθ'
And they hearing went out one by

εἷς ἀρξάμενοι ἀπὸ τῶν πρεσβυτέρων, καὶ
one beginning from the older ones, and

κατελείφθη μόνος, καὶ ἡ γυνὴ ἐν μέσῳ
he was left alone, and the woman in [the] midst

οὖσα. 10 ἀνακύψας δὲ ὁ Ἰησοῦς εἶπεν
being. And standing erect – Jesus said

αὐτῇ Γύναι, ποῦ εἰσιν; οὐδείς σε κατέκρινεν;
to her[,] Woman, where are they? no one thee condemned?

11 ἡ δὲ εἶπεν Οὐδείς, κύριε. εἶπεν δὲ
And she said[,] No one, sir. So said

ὁ Ἰησοῦς Οὐδὲ ἐγώ σε κατακρίνω·
– Jesus[,] Neither I thee condemn;

πορεύου, ἀπὸ τοῦ νῦν μηκέτι ἁμάρτανε.
go, from – now no longer sin.

12 Πάλιν οὖν αὐτοῖς ἐλάλησεν ὁ Ἰησοῦς
Again therefore to them spoke – Jesus

λέγων· ἐγώ εἰμι τὸ φῶς τοῦ κόσμου·
saying: I am the light of the world;

ὁ ἀκολουθῶν μοι οὐ μὴ περιπατήσῃ ἐν
the [one] following me by no means will walk in

τῇ σκοτίᾳ, ἀλλ' ἕξει τὸ φῶς τῆς ζωῆς.
the darkness, but will have the light of life.

13 εἶπον οὖν αὐτῷ οἱ Φαρισαῖοι· σὺ περὶ
Said therefore to him the Pharisees; Thou concerning

σεαυτοῦ μαρτυρεῖς· ἡ μαρτυρία σου οὐκ
thyself witnessest; the witness of thee not

ἔστιν ἀληθής. 14 ἀπεκρίθη Ἰησοῦς καὶ
is true. Answered Jesus and

εἶπεν αὐτοῖς· κἂν ἐγὼ μαρτυρῶ περὶ
said to them; Even if I witness concerning

ἐμαυτοῦ, ἀληθής ἐστιν ἡ μαρτυρία μου,
myself, true is the witness of me,

ὅτι οἶδα πόθεν ἦλθον καὶ ποῦ ὑπάγω·
because I know whence I came and where I go;

not tell whence I come, and whither I go.

15 Ye judge after the flesh; I judge no man.

16 And yet if I judge, my judgment is true: for I am not alone, but I and the Father that sent me.

17 It is also written in your law, that the testimony of two men is true.

18 I am one that bear witness of myself, and the Father that sent me beareth witness of me.

19 Then said they unto him, Where is thy Father? Jesus answered, Ye neither know me, nor my Father: if ye had known me, ye should have known my Father also.

20 These words spake Jesus in the treasury, as he taught in the temple: and no man laid hands on him; for his hour was not yet come.

21 Then said Jesus again unto them, I go my way, and ye shall seek me, and shall die in your sins: whither I go, ye cannot come.

22 Then said the Jews, Will he kill himself? because he saith, Whither I go, ye cannot come.

ὑμεῖς δὲ οὐκ οἴδατε πόθεν ἔρχομαι ἢ
but ye　know not　whence　I come　or

ποῦ ὑπάγω. 15 ὑμεῖς κατὰ τὴν σάρκα
where I go.　　Ye according to the flesh

κρίνετε, ἐγὼ οὐ κρίνω οὐδένα. 16 καὶ
judge,　I　judge not no(any)one.　²even

ἐὰν κρίνω δὲ ἐγώ, ἡ κρίσις ἡ ἐμὴ
³if ⁵judge ¹But ⁴I, the ²judgment – ¹my

ἀληθινή ἐστιν, ὅτι μόνος οὐκ εἰμί, ἀλλ'
true is, because alone I am not, but

ἐγὼ καὶ ὁ πέμψας με. 17 καὶ ἐν τῷ
I　and the [one] having sent me.　²even ³in the

νόμῳ δὲ τῷ ὑμετέρῳ γέγραπται ὅτι δύο
⁵law ¹And – ⁴your it has been written that of two

ἀνθρώπων ἡ μαρτυρία ἀληθής ἐστιν.
men　the witness true is.

18 ἐγώ εἰμι ὁ μαρτυρῶν περὶ ἐμαυτοῦ,
I am the [one] witnessing concerning myself,

καὶ μαρτυρεῖ περὶ ἐμοῦ ὁ πέμψας με
and witnesses concerning me ¹the ³having sent ⁴me

πατήρ. 19 ἔλεγον οὖν αὐτῷ· ποῦ ἐστιν ὁ
²Father. They said therefore to him : Where is

πατήρ σου; ἀπεκρίθη Ἰησοῦς· οὔτε ἐμὲ
Father of thee? Answered Jesus : Neither me

οἴδατε οὔτε τὸν πατέρα μου· εἰ ἐμὲ
ye know nor the Father of me; if me

ᾔδειτε, καὶ τὸν πατέρα μου ἂν ᾔδειτε.
ye knew, also the Father of me ye would have known.

20 Ταῦτα τὰ ῥήματα ἐλάλησεν ἐν τῷ
These – words he spoke in the

γαζοφυλακείῳ διδάσκων ἐν τῷ ἱερῷ· καὶ
treasury teaching in the temple; and

οὐδεὶς ἐπίασεν αὐτόν, ὅτι οὔπω ἐληλύθει
no one seized him, because not yet had come

ἡ ὥρα αὐτοῦ.
the hour of him.

21 Εἶπεν οὖν πάλιν αὐτοῖς· ἐγὼ ὑπάγω
He said therefore again to them : I go

καὶ ζητήσετέ με, καὶ ἐν τῇ ἁμαρτίᾳ
and ye will seek me, and in the sin

ὑμῶν ἀποθανεῖσθε· ὅπου ἐγὼ ὑπάγω ὑμεῖς
of you ye will die; where I go ye

οὐ δύνασθε ἐλθεῖν. 22 ἔλεγον οὖν οἱ
cannot to come. Said therefore the

Ἰουδαῖοι· μήτι ἀποκτενεῖ ἑαυτόν, ὅτι
Jews : Not will he kill himself, because

λέγει· ὅπου ἐγὼ ὑπάγω ὑμεῖς οὐ δύνασθε
he says : Where I go ye cannot

JOHN 8

397

23 And he said unto them, Ye are from beneath; I am from above: ye are of this world; I am not of this world.

24 I said therefore unto you, that ye shall die in your sins: for if ye believe not that I am *he*, ye shall die in your sins.

25 Then said they unto him, Who art thou? And Jesus saith unto them, Even *the same* that I said unto you from the beginning.

26 I have many things to say and to judge of you: but he that sent me is true; and I speak to the world those things which I have heard of him.

27 They understood not that he spake to them of the Father.

28 Then said Jesus unto them, When ye have lifted up the Son of man, then shall ye know that I am *he*, and *that* I do nothing of myself; but as my Father hath taught me, I speak these things.

29 And he that sent me is with me: the Father hath not left me alone; for I do always those things that please him.

30 As he spake these words, many believed on him.

31 Then said Jesus to

ἐλθεῖν; 23 καὶ ἔλεγεν αὐτοῖς· ὑμεῖς ἐκ
to come? And he said to them: Ye of
τῶν κάτω ἐστέ, ἐγὼ ἐκ τῶν ἄνω εἰμί·
the things below are, I of the things above am;
ὑμεῖς ἐκ τούτου τοῦ κόσμου ἐστέ, ἐγὼ
ye of this — world are, I
οὐκ εἰμὶ ἐκ τοῦ κόσμου τούτου. 24 εἶπον
am not of — world this. I said
οὖν ὑμῖν ὅτι ἀποθανεῖσθε ἐν ταῖς ἁμαρτίαις
therefore to you that ye will die in the sins
ὑμῶν· ἐὰν γὰρ μὴ πιστεύσητε ὅτι ἐγώ
of you; for if ye believe not that I
εἰμι, ἀποθανεῖσθε ἐν ταῖς ἁμαρτίαις ὑμῶν.
am, ye will die in the sins of you.
25 ἔλεγον οὖν αὐτῷ· σὺ τίς εἶ; εἶπεν
They said therefore to him: ³Thou ¹who ²art? Said
αὐτοῖς ὁ Ἰησοῦς· τὴν ἀρχὴν ὅ τι καὶ
to them — Jesus: ⁵at all † ¹Why ²indeed
λαλῶ ὑμῖν; 26 πολλὰ ἔχω περὶ ὑμῶν
³speak I ⁴to you? Many things I have about you
λαλεῖν καὶ κρίνειν· ἀλλ᾽ ὁ πέμψας με
to speak and to judge; but the [one] having sent me
ἀληθής ἐστιν, κἀγὼ ἃ ἤκουσα παρ᾽
true is, and I what I heard from
αὐτοῦ, ταῦτα λαλῶ εἰς τὸν κόσμον.
him, these things I speak in the world.
27 οὐκ ἔγνωσαν ὅτι τὸν πατέρα αὐτοῖς
They did not know that ²the ³Father ⁴to them
ἔλεγεν. 28 εἶπεν οὖν ὁ Ἰησοῦς· ὅταν
¹he spoke [of]. Said therefore — Jesus: When
ὑψώσητε τὸν υἱὸν τοῦ ἀνθρώπου, τότε
ye lift up the Son — of man, then
γνώσεσθε ὅτι ἐγώ εἰμι, καὶ ἀπ᾽ ἐμαυτοῦ
ye will know that I am, and from myself
ποιῶ οὐδέν, ἀλλὰ καθὼς ἐδίδαξέν με ὁ
I do nothing, but as taught me the
πατήρ, ταῦτα λαλῶ. 29 καὶ ὁ πέμψας
Father, these things I speak. And the [one] having sent
με μετ᾽ ἐμοῦ ἐστιν· οὐκ ἀφῆκέν με
me with me is; he did not leave me
μόνον, ὅτι ἐγὼ τὰ ἀρεστὰ αὐτῷ ποιῶ
alone, because I the things pleasing to him do
πάντοτε.
always.
30 Ταῦτα αὐτοῦ λαλοῦντος πολλοὶ ἐπίσ-
These things him saying^a many be-
= As he said these things
τευσαν εἰς αὐτόν. 31 ἔλεγεν οὖν ὁ Ἰησοῦς
lieved in him. Said therefore — Jesus

those Jews which believed on him, If ye continue in my word, *then* are ye my disciples indeed;

32 And ye shall know the truth, and the truth shall make you free.

33 They answered him, We be Abraham's seed, and were never in bondage to any man: how sayest thou, Ye shall be made free?

34 Jesus answered them, Verily, verily, I say unto you, Whosoever committeth sin is the servant of sin.

35 And the servant abideth not in the house for ever: *but* the Son abideth ever.

36 If the Son therefore shall make you free, ye shall be free indeed.

37 I know that ye are Abraham's seed; but ye seek to kill me, because my word hath no place in you.

38 I speak that which I have seen with my Father: and ye do that which ye have seen with your father.

39 They answered and said unto him, Abraham is our father. Jesus saith unto them, If ye were Abraham's children, ye would do the works of Abraham.

40 But now ye seek to kill me, a man that hath told you the truth, which I

πρὸς τοὺς πεπιστευκότας αὐτῷ Ἰουδαίους·
to ¹the ²having believed ⁴him ³Jews :

ἐὰν ὑμεῖς μείνητε ἐν τῷ λόγῳ τῷ ἐμῷ,
If ye continue in the ²word - ¹my,

ἀληθῶς μαθηταί μού ἐστε, 32 καὶ γνώσεσθε
truly disciples of me ye are, and ye will know

τὴν ἀλήθειαν, καὶ ἡ ἀλήθεια ἐλευθερώσει
the truth, and the truth will free

ὑμᾶς. 33 ἀπεκρίθησαν πρὸς αὐτόν· σπέρμα
you. They answered to him : Seed

Ἀβραάμ ἐσμεν, καὶ οὐδενὶ δεδουλεύκαμεν
of Abraham we are, and to no one have we been enslaved

πώποτε· πῶς σὺ λέγεις ὅτι ἐλεύθεροι
never; how thou sayest that free

γενήσεσθε; 34 ἀπεκρίθη αὐτοῖς ὁ Ἰησοῦς·
ye will become? Answered them - Jesus :

ἀμὴν ἀμὴν λέγω ὑμῖν ὅτι πᾶς ὁ ποιῶν
Truly truly I tell you that everyone doing

τὴν ἁμαρτίαν δοῦλός ἐστιν τῆς ἁμαρτίας.
- sin a slave is - of sin.

35 ὁ δὲ δοῦλος οὐ μένει ἐν τῇ οἰκίᾳ
But the slave does not remain in the house

εἰς τὸν αἰῶνα· ὁ υἱὸς μένει εἰς τὸν
unto the age; the son remains unto the

αἰῶνα. 36 ἐὰν οὖν ὁ υἱὸς ὑμᾶς ἐλευθερώσῃ,
age. If therefore the Son you frees,

ὄντως ἐλεύθεροι ἔσεσθε. 37 Οἶδα ὅτι
really free ye will be. I know that

σπέρμα Ἀβραάμ ἐστε· ἀλλὰ ζητεῖτέ με
seed of Abraham ye are; but ye seek me

ἀποκτεῖναι, ὅτι ὁ λόγος ὁ ἐμὸς οὐ χωρεῖ
to kill, because the ²word ¹my finds no room

ἐν ὑμῖν. 38 ἃ ἐγὼ ἑώρακα παρὰ τῷ
in you. What I have seen with the

πατρὶ λαλῶ· καὶ ὑμεῖς οὖν ἃ ἠκού-
Father I speak; and ye therefore what ye

σατε παρὰ τοῦ πατρὸς ποιεῖτε. 39 ἀπεκρί-
heard from the father ye do. They

θησαν καὶ εἶπαν αὐτῷ· ὁ πατὴρ ἡμῶν Ἀβραάμ
answered and said to him: The father of us Abraham

ἐστιν. λέγει αὐτοῖς ὁ Ἰησοῦς· εἰ τέκνα
is. Says to them - Jesus : If children

τοῦ Ἀβραάμ ἐστε, τὰ ἔργα τοῦ Ἀβραὰμ
- of Abraham ye are, the works - of Abraham

ποιεῖτε· 40 νῦν δὲ ζητεῖτέ με ἀποκτεῖναι,
ye do; but now ye seek me to kill,

ἄνθρωπον ὃς τὴν ἀλήθειαν ὑμῖν λελάληκα,
a man who the truth to you has spoken,

have heard of God: this
did not Abraham.

41 Ye do the deeds of
your father. Then said
they to him, We be not
born of fornication; we
have one Father, even God.

42 Jesus said unto them,
If God were your Father,
ye would love me: for I
proceeded forth and came
from God; neither came
I of myself, but he sent
me.

43 Why do ye not
understand my speech?
even because ye cannot
hear my word.

44 Ye are of your father
the devil, and the lusts of
your father ye will do.
He was a murderer from
the beginning, and abode
not in the truth, because
there is no truth in him.
When he speaketh a lie,
he speaketh of his own:
for he is a liar, and the
father of it.

45 And because I tell
you the truth, ye believe
me not.

46 Which of you con-
vinceth me of sin? And
if I say the truth, why do
ye not believe me?

47 He that is of God
heareth God's words: ye
therefore hear them not,

ἦν ἤκουσα παρὰ τοῦ θεοῦ· τοῦτο Ἀβραὰμ
which I heard from – God; this Abraham

οὐκ ἐποίησεν. 41 ὑμεῖς ποιεῖτε τὰ ἔργα
did not. Ye do the works

τοῦ πατρὸς ὑμῶν. εἶπαν αὐτῷ· ἡμεῖς ἐκ
of the father of you. They said to him : We of

πορνείας οὐκ ἐγεννήθημεν, ἕνα πατέρα
fornication were not born, one father

ἔχομεν τὸν θεόν. 42 εἶπεν αὐτοῖς ὁ
we have[,] – God. Said to them –

Ἰησοῦς· εἰ ὁ θεὸς πατὴρ ὑμῶν ἦν,
Jesus : If – God father of you was,

ἠγαπᾶτε ἂν ἐμέ· ἐγὼ γὰρ ἐκ τοῦ θεοῦ
ye would have loved me; for I of – God

ἐξῆλθον καὶ ἥκω· οὐδὲ γὰρ ἀπ' ἐμαυτοῦ
came forth and have come; for not from myself

ἐλήλυθα, ἀλλ' ἐκεῖνός με ἀπέστειλεν. 43 διὰ τί
I have come, but that one me sent. Why

τὴν λαλιὰν τὴν ἐμὴν οὐ γινώσκετε;
the ²speech – ¹my know ye not?

ὅτι οὐ δύνασθε ἀκούειν τὸν λόγον τὸν
because ye cannot to hear the ²word –

ἐμόν. 44 ὑμεῖς ἐκ τοῦ πατρὸς τοῦ
¹my. Ye of the father of the

διαβόλου ἐστὲ καὶ τὰς ἐπιθυμίας τοῦ
devil are and the desires of the

πατρὸς ὑμῶν θέλετε ποιεῖν. ἐκεῖνος
father of you ye wish to do. That one

ἀνθρωποκτόνος ἦν ἀπ' ἀρχῆς, καὶ ἐν
a murderer was from [the] beginning, and in

τῇ ἀληθείᾳ οὐκ ἔστηκεν, ὅτι οὐκ ἔστιν
the truth stood not, because not is

ἀλήθεια ἐν αὐτῷ. ὅταν λαλῇ τὸ ψεῦδος,
truth in him. When he speaks the lie,

ἐκ τῶν ἰδίων λαλεῖ, ὅτι ψεύστης ἐστὶν
out of his own things he speaks, because a liar he is

καὶ ὁ πατὴρ αὐτοῦ. 45 ἐγὼ δὲ ὅτι τὴν
and the father of it. But ²I ¹because ⁴the

ἀλήθειαν λέγω, οὐ πιστεύετέ μοι. 46 τίς
⁵truth ³say, ye do not believe me. Who

ἐξ ὑμῶν ἐλέγχει με περὶ ἁμαρτίας; εἰ
of you reproves me concerning sin? If

ἀλήθειαν λέγω, διὰ τί ὑμεῖς οὐ πιστεύετέ
truth I say, why ²ye ¹do not believe

μοι; 47 ὁ ὢν ἐκ τοῦ θεοῦ τὰ ῥήματα
me? The [one] being of – God the words

τοῦ θεοῦ ἀκούει· διὰ τοῦτο ὑμεῖς οὐκ
– of God hears; therefore ye not

because ye are not of God.

48 Then answered the Jews, and said unto him, Say we not well that thou art a Samaritan, and hast a devil?

49 Jesus answered, I have not a devil; but I honour my Father, and ye do dishonour me.

50 And I seek not mine own glory: there is one that seeketh and judgeth.

51 Verily, verily, I say unto you, If a man keep my saying, he shall never see death.

52 Then said the Jews unto him, Now we know that thou hast a devil. Abraham is dead, and the prophets; and thou sayest, If a man keep my saying, he shall never taste of death.

53 Art thou greater than our father Abraham, which is dead? and the prophets are dead: whom makest thou thyself?

54 Jesus answered, If I honour myself, my honour is nothing: it is my Father that honoureth me; of whom ye say, that he is your God:

55 Yet ye have not known him; but I know him: and if I should say, I know him not, I shall be

ἀκούετε, ὅτι ἐκ τοῦ θεοῦ οὐκ ἐστέ.
hear, because of – God ye are not.

48 Ἀπεκρίθησαν οἱ Ἰουδαῖοι καὶ εἶπαν
Answered the Jews and said

αὐτῷ· οὐ καλῶς λέγομεν ἡμεῖς ὅτι
to him : ³Not ⁴well ¹say ²we ⁵that

Σαμαρίτης εἶ σὺ καὶ δαιμόνιον ἔχεις;
⁸a Samaritan ⁷art ⁶thou ⁹and ¹¹a demon ¹⁰hast?

49 ἀπεκρίθη Ἰησοῦς· ἐγὼ δαιμόνιον οὐκ
Answered Jesus : I a demon not

ἔχω, ἀλλὰ τιμῶ τὸν πατέρα μου, καὶ
have, but I honour the Father of me, and

ὑμεῖς ἀτιμάζετέ με. 50 ἐγὼ δὲ οὐ ζητῶ
ye dishonour me. But I seek not

τὴν δόξαν μου· ἔστιν ὁ ζητῶν καὶ
the glory of me; there is the [one] seeking and

κρίνων. 51 ἀμὴν ἀμὴν λέγω ὑμῖν, ἐάν
judging. Truly truly I tell you, if

τις τὸν ἐμὸν λόγον τηρήσῃ, θάνατον
anyone – my word keeps, death

οὐ μὴ θεωρήσῃ εἰς τὸν αἰῶνα. 52 εἶπαν
by no means will he behold unto the age. Said

αὐτῷ οἱ Ἰουδαῖοι· νῦν ἐγνώκαμεν ὅτι
to him the Jews : Now we have known that

δαιμόνιον ἔχεις. Ἀβραὰμ ἀπέθανεν καὶ οἱ
a demon thou hast. Abraham died and the

προφῆται, καὶ σὺ λέγεις· ἐάν τις τὸν
prophets, and thou sayest : If anyone the

λόγον μου τηρήσῃ, οὐ μὴ γεύσηται
word of me keeps, by no means will he taste

θανάτου εἰς τὸν αἰῶνα. 53 μὴ σὺ μείζων
of death unto the age. Not thou greater

εἶ τοῦ πατρὸς ἡμῶν Ἀβραάμ, ὅστις
art [than] the father of us Abraham, who

ἀπέθανεν; καὶ οἱ προφῆται ἀπέθανον· τίνα
died? and the prophets died; whom

σεαυτὸν ποιεῖς; 54 ἀπεκρίθη Ἰησοῦς· ἐὰν
thyself makest thou? Answered Jesus : If

ἐγὼ δοξάσω ἐμαυτόν, ἡ δόξα μου οὐδέν
I glorify myself, the glory of me nothing

ἐστιν· ἔστιν ὁ πατήρ μου ὁ δοξάζων με,
is; ⁴is ¹the ²Father ³of me the [one] glorifying me,

ὃν ὑμεῖς λέγετε ὅτι θεὸς ἡμῶν ἐστιν,
whom ye say[,] – God of us he is,

55 καὶ οὐκ ἐγνώκατε αὐτόν, ἐγὼ δὲ
and ye have not known him, but I

οἶδα αὐτόν. κἂν εἴπω ὅτι οὐκ οἶδα
know him. Even if I say that I know not

a liar like unto you: but I know him, and keep his saying.

56 Your father Abraham rejoiced to see my day: and he saw *it*, and was glad.

57 Then said the Jews unto him, Thou art not yet fifty years old, and hast thou seen Abraham?

58 Jesus said unto them, Verily, verily, I say unto you, Before Abraham was, I am.

59 Then took they up stones to cast at him: but Jesus hid himself, and went out of the temple, going through the midst of them, and so passed by.

αὐτόν,   ἔσομαι   ὅμοιος   ὑμῖν   ψεύστης·   ἀλλὰ
him,   I shall be   like   you   a liar;   but

οἶδα   αὐτὸν   καὶ   τὸν   λόγον   αὐτοῦ   τηρῶ.
I know   him   and   the   word   of him   I keep.

56 Ἀβραὰμ   ὁ   πατὴρ   ὑμῶν   ἠγαλλιάσατο
Abraham   the   father   of you   was glad

ἵνα   ἴδῃ   τὴν   ἡμέραν   τὴν   ἐμήν,   καὶ   εἶδεν
that he should see *the* ³day   –   ¹my,   and   he saw

καὶ   ἐχάρη.   57 εἶπαν   οὖν   οἱ   Ἰουδαῖοι
and   rejoiced.   Said   therefore   the   Jews

πρὸς   αὐτόν·   πεντήκοντα   ἔτη   οὔπω   ἔχεις
to   him :   Fifty   years   not yet thou hast

καὶ   Ἀβραὰμ   ἑώρακας;   58 εἶπεν   αὐτοῖς
and   Abraham   hast thou seen?   Said   to them

Ἰησοῦς·   ἀμὴν   ἀμὴν   λέγω   ὑμῖν,   πρὶν
Jesus: Truly   truly   I tell   you,   before

Ἀβραὰμ   γενέσθαι   ἐγὼ   εἰμί.   59 ἦραν
Abraham   to become[b]   I   am.   They took
                   =became

οὖν   λίθους   ἵνα   βάλωσιν   ἐπ'   αὐτόν·
therefore stones   that   they might cast   on   him;

Ἰησοῦς   δὲ   ἐκρύβη   καὶ   ἐξῆλθεν   ἐκ   τοῦ
but Jesus   was hidden   and   went forth   out of the

ἱεροῦ.
temple.

CHAPTER 9

AND as *Jesus* passed by, he saw a man which was blind from *his* birth.

2 And his disciples asked him, saying, Master, who did sin, this man, or his parents, that he was born blind?

3 Jesus answered, Neither hath this man sinned, nor his parents: but that the works of God should be made manifest in him.

4 I must work the works of him that sent me, while it is day: the night cometh, when no man can work.

5 As long as I am in the world, I am the light of the world.

9 Καὶ   παράγων   εἶδεν   ἄνθρωπον   τυφλὸν
And   passing along   he saw   a man   blind

ἐκ   γενετῆς.   2 καὶ   ἠρώτησαν   αὐτὸν   οἱ
from   birth.   And   asked   him   the

μαθηταὶ   αὐτοῦ   λέγοντες·   ῥαββί,   τίς   ἥμαρτεν,
disciples   of him   saying :   Rabbi,   who   sinned,

οὗτος   ἢ   οἱ   γονεῖς   αὐτοῦ,   ἵνα   τυφλὸς
this man   or   the   parents   of him,   that   blind

γεννηθῇ;   3 ἀπεκρίθη   Ἰησοῦς·   οὔτε   οὗτος
he was born?   Answered   Jesus :   Neither this man

ἥμαρτεν   οὔτε   οἱ   γονεῖς   αὐτοῦ,   ἀλλ'   ἵνα
sinned   nor   the   parents   of him,   but   that

φανερωθῇ   τὰ   ἔργα   τοῦ   θεοῦ   ἐν   αὐτῷ.
might be manifested   the   works   –   of God   in   him.

4 ἡμᾶς   δεῖ   ἐργάζεσθαι   τὰ   ἔργα   τοῦ
Us   it behoves   to work   the   works   of the

πέμψαντός   με   ἕως   ἡμέρα   ἐστίν·   ἔρχεται
[one] having sent   me   while   day   it is;   comes

νὺξ   ὅτε   οὐδεὶς   δύναται   ἐργάζεσθαι.   5 ὅταν
night when   no one   can   *to* work.   When

ἐν   τῷ   κόσμῳ   ὦ,   φῶς   εἰμι   τοῦ   κόσμου.
in   the   world   I am,   light   I am   of the   world.

6 When he had thus spoken, he spat on the ground, and made clay of the spittle, and he anointed the eyes of the blind man with the clay,

7 And said unto him, Go, wash in the pool of Siloam, (which is by interpretation, Sent.) He went his way therefore, and washed, and came seeing.

8¶ The neighbours therefore, and they which before had seen him that he was blind, said, Is not this he that sat and begged?

9 Some said, This is he: others *said*, He is like him: but he said, I am *he*.

10 Therefore said they unto him, How were thine eyes opened?

11 He answered and said, A man that is called Jesus made clay, and anointed mine eyes, and said unto me, Go to the pool of Siloam, and wash: and I went and washed, and I received sight.

12 Then said they unto him, Where is he? He said, I know not.

13¶ They brought to the Pharisees him that aforetime was blind.

14 And it was the sabbath day when Jesus made the clay, and opened

6 ταῦτα εἰπὼν ἔπτυσεν χαμαὶ καὶ ἐποίησεν
These things having said he spat on the ground and made

πηλὸν ἐκ τοῦ πτύσματος, καὶ ἐπέθηκεν
clay out of the spittle, and ¹put on

αὐτοῦ τὸν πηλὸν ἐπὶ τοὺς ὀφθαλμούς,
⁷of him ²the ³clay ⁴on ⁵the ⁶eyes,

7 καὶ εἶπεν αὐτῷ· ὕπαγε νίψαι εἰς τὴν
and said to him: Go wash in the

κολυμβήθραν τοῦ Σιλωάμ (ὃ ἑρμηνεύεται
pool – of Siloam (which is translated

ἀπεσταλμένος). ἀπῆλθεν οὖν καὶ ἐνίψατο,
having been sent). He went therefore and washed,

καὶ ἦλθεν βλέπων. 8 Οἱ οὖν γείτονες
and came seeing. Therefore the neighbours

καὶ οἱ θεωροῦντες αὐτὸν τὸ πρότερον, †
and the [ones] beholding him formerly,

ὅτι προσαίτης ἦν, ἔλεγον· οὐχ οὗτός
that a beggar he was, said: ²Not ³this man

ἐστιν ὁ καθήμενος καὶ προσαιτῶν; 9 ἄλλοι
¹is the [one] sitting and begging? Some

ἔλεγον ὅτι οὗτός ἐστιν· ἄλλοι ἔλεγον·
said[,] – This is he; others said:

οὐχί, ἀλλὰ ὅμοιος αὐτῷ ἐστιν. ἐκεῖνος
No, but like *to* him he is. That [one]

ἔλεγεν ὅτι ἐγώ εἰμι. 10 ἔλεγον οὖν
said[,] – I am. They said therefore

αὐτῷ· πῶς [οὖν] ἠνεῴχθησάν σου οἱ
to him: How then were opened of thee the

ὀφθαλμοί; 11 ἀπεκρίθη ἐκεῖνος· ὁ ἄνθρωπος
eyes? Answered that [one]: The man

ὁ λεγόμενος Ἰησοῦς πηλὸν ἐποίησεν καὶ
– *being* named Jesus clay made and

ἐπέχρισέν μου τοὺς ὀφθαλμοὺς καὶ εἶπέν
anointed of me the eyes and told

μοι ὅτι ὕπαγε εἰς τὸν Σιλωὰμ καὶ
me[,] – Go to – Siloam and

νίψαι· ἀπελθὼν οὖν καὶ νιψάμενος ἀνέβλεψα.
wash; going therefore and washing I saw.

12 καὶ εἶπαν αὐτῷ· ποῦ ἐστιν ἐκεῖνος;
And they said to him: Where is that [one]?

λέγει· οὐκ οἶδα. 13 Ἄγουσιν αὐτὸν
He says: I do not know. They lead him

πρὸς τοὺς Φαρισαίους, τόν ποτε τυφλόν.
to the Pharisees, the at one time blind.

14 ἦν δὲ σάββατον ἐν ᾗ ἡμέρᾳ τὸν
Now it was a sabbath on which day ²the

πηλὸν ἐποίησεν ὁ Ἰησοῦς καὶ ἀνέῳξεν
⁴clay ³made – ¹Jesus and opened

his eyes.

15 Then again the Pharisees also asked him how he had received his sight. He said unto them, He put clay upon mine eyes, and I washed, and do see.

16 Therefore said some of the Pharisees, This man is not of God, because he keepeth not the sabbath day. Others said, How can a man that is a sinner do such miracles? And there was a division among them.

17 They say unto the blind man again, What sayest thou of him, that he hath opened thine eyes? He said, He is a prophet.

18 But the Jews did not believe concerning him, that he had been blind, and received his sight, until they called the parents of him that had received his sight.

19 And they asked them, saying, Is this your son, who ye say was born blind? how then doth he now see?

20 His parents answered them and said, We know that this is our son, and that he was born blind:

21 But by what means he now seeth, we know not; or who hath opened

αὐτοῦ τοὺς ὀφθαλμούς. 15 πάλιν οὖν
of him the eyes. Again therefore

ἠρώτων αὐτὸν καὶ οἱ Φαρισαῖοι πῶς
⁴asked ⁵him ²also ¹the ³Pharisees how

ἀνέβλεψεν. ὁ δὲ εἶπεν αὐτοῖς· πηλὸν
he saw. And he said to them: Clay

ἐπέθηκέν μου ἐπὶ τοὺς ὀφθαλμούς, καὶ
he put on ⁴of me ¹on ²the ³eyes, and

ἐνιψάμην, καὶ βλέπω. 16 ἔλεγον οὖν ἐκ
I washed, and I see. Said therefore of

τῶν Φαρισαίων τινές· οὐκ ἔστιν οὗτος
the Pharisees some : ⁴not ³is ¹This

παρὰ θεοῦ ὁ ἄνθρωπος, ὅτι τὸ σάββατον
⁵from ⁴God - ²man, because the sabbath

οὐ τηρεῖ. ἄλλοι [δὲ] ἔλεγον· πῶς δύναται
he keeps not. But others said : How can

ἄνθρωπος ἁμαρτωλὸς τοιαῦτα σημεῖα ποιεῖν;
man a sinful such signs to do?

καὶ σχίσμα ἦν ἐν αὐτοῖς. 17 λέγουσιν
And a division there was among them. They say

οὖν τῷ τυφλῷ πάλιν· τί σὺ λέγεις
therefore to the blind man again : What thou sayest

περὶ αὐτοῦ, ὅτι ἠνέῳξέν σου τοὺς
about him, because he opened of thee the

ὀφθαλμούς; ὁ δὲ εἶπεν ὅτι προφήτης ἐστίν.
eyes? And he said[,] - A prophet he is.

18 οὐκ ἐπίστευσαν οὖν οἱ Ἰουδαῖοι περὶ
Did not believe therefore the Jews about

αὐτοῦ ὅτι ἦν τυφλὸς καὶ ἀνέβλεψεν,
him that he was blind and saw,

ἕως ὅτου ἐφώνησαν τοὺς γονεῖς αὐτοῦ
until they called the parents of him

τοῦ ἀναβλέψαντος 19 καὶ ἠρώτησαν αὐτοὺς
of the [one] having seen and asked them

λέγοντες· οὗτός ἐστιν ὁ υἱὸς ὑμῶν, ὃν
saying : This is the son of you, whom

ὑμεῖς λέγετε ὅτι τυφλὸς ἐγεννήθη; πῶς
ye say that blind he was born? how

οὖν βλέπει ἄρτι; 20 ἀπεκρίθησαν οὖν οἱ
then sees he now? Answered therefore the

γονεῖς αὐτοῦ καὶ εἶπαν· οἴδαμεν ὅτι
parents of him and said : We know that

οὗτός ἐστιν ὁ υἱὸς ἡμῶν καὶ ὅτι τυφλὸς
this is the son of us and that blind

ἐγεννήθη· 21 πῶς δὲ νῦν βλέπει οὐκ
he was born; but how now he sees not

οἴδαμεν, ἢ τίς ἤνοιξεν αὐτοῦ τοὺς ὀφθαλμοὺς
we know, or who opened of him the eyes

his eyes, we know not: he is of age; ask him: he shall speak for himself.

22 These *words* spake his parents, because they feared the Jews: for the Jews had agreed already, that if any man did confess that he was Christ, he should be put out of the synagogue.

23 Therefore said his parents, He is of age; ask him.

24 Then again called they the man that was blind, and said unto him, Give God the praise: we know that this man is a sinner.

25 He answered and said, Whether he be a sinner *or no*, I know not: one thing I know, that, whereas I was blind, now I see.

26 Then said they to him again, What did he to thee? how opened he thine eyes?

27 He answered them, I have told you already, and ye did not hear: wherefore would ye hear *it* again? will ye also be his disciples?

28 Then they reviled him, and said, Thou art his disciple; but we are Moses' disciples.

29 We know that God spake unto Moses: *as for* this *fellow*, we know not from whence he is.

30 The man answered

ἡμεῖς οὐκ οἴδαμεν· αὐτὸν ἐρωτήσατε,
we   know not;   him   ask ye,

ἡλικίαν ἔχει, αὐτὸς περὶ ἑαυτοῦ λαλήσει.
age   he has,   he   about   himself   will speak.

22 ταῦτα εἶπαν οἱ γονεῖς αὐτοῦ ὅτι ἐφο-
These things   said   the   parents   of him   because   they

βοῦντο τοὺς Ἰουδαίους· ἤδη γὰρ συνετέθειντο
feared   the   Jews;   for already   had agreed

οἱ Ἰουδαῖοι ἵνα ἐάν τις αὐτὸν ὁμολογήσῃ
the   Jews   that   if   anyone   him should acknowledge

χριστόν, ἀποσυνάγωγος γένηται.
[to be] Christ,   put away from [the] synagogue   he would be.

23 διὰ τοῦτο οἱ γονεῖς αὐτοῦ εἶπαν ὅτι
Therefore   the   parents   of him   said[,]   –

ἡλικίαν ἔχει, αὐτὸν ἐπερωτήσατε. 24 Ἐφώνησαν
Age   he has,   him   question ye.   They called

οὖν τὸν ἄνθρωπον ἐκ δευτέρου ὃς ἦν
therefore the   man   a second time   who was

τυφλός, καὶ εἶπαν αὐτῷ· δὸς δόξαν τῷ
blind,   and   said   to him :   Give   glory   –

θεῷ· ἡμεῖς οἴδαμεν ὅτι οὗτος ὁ ἄνθρωπος
to God;   we   know   that   this   –   man

ἁμαρτωλός ἐστιν. 25 ἀπεκρίθη οὖν ἐκεῖνος·
sinful   is.   Answered therefore that [one]:

εἰ ἁμαρτωλός ἐστιν οὐκ οἶδα· ἓν οἶδα,
If   sinful   he is   I know not;   one thing I know,

ὅτι τυφλὸς ὢν ἄρτι βλέπω. 26 εἶπαν
that   blind   being   now   I see.   They said

οὖν αὐτῷ· τί ἐποίησέν σοι; πῶς ἤνοιξέν
therefore to him :   What did he   to thee?   how   opened he

σου τοὺς ὀφθαλμούς; 27 ἀπεκρίθη αὐτοῖς·
of thee   the   eyes?   He answered   them :

εἶπον ὑμῖν ἤδη καὶ οὐκ ἠκούσατε· τί
I told   you   already   and   ye heard not;   why

πάλιν θέλετε ἀκούειν; μὴ καὶ ὑμεῖς
again   wish ye   to hear?   *not*   also   ye

θέλετε αὐτοῦ μαθηταὶ γενέσθαι; 28 καὶ
wish   of him   disciples   to become?   And

ἐλοιδόρησαν αὐτὸν καὶ εἶπαν· σὺ μαθητὴς
they reviled   him   and   said :   Thou   a disciple

εἶ ἐκείνου, ἡμεῖς δὲ τοῦ Μωϋσέως ἐσμὲν
art of that man,   but we   –   of Moses   are

μαθηταί· 29 ἡμεῖς οἴδαμεν ὅτι Μωϋσεῖ
disciples;   we   know   that   by Moses

λελάληκεν ὁ θεός, τοῦτον δὲ οὐκ οἴδαμεν
has spoken   –   God,   but this man   we know not

πόθεν ἐστίν. 30 ἀπεκρίθη ὁ ἄνθρωπος
whence he is.   Answered   the   man

and said unto them, Why herein is a marvellous thing, that ye know not from whence he is, and *yet* he hath opened mine eyes.

31 Now we know that God heareth not sinners: but if any man be a worshipper of God, and doeth his will, him he heareth.

32 Since the world began was it not heard that any man opened the eyes of one that was born blind.

33 If this man were not of God, he could do nothing.

34 They answered and said unto him, Thou wast altogether born in sins, and dost thou teach us? And they cast him out.

35 ¶ Jesus heard that they had cast him out; and when he had found him, he said unto him, Dost thou believe on the Son of God?

36 He answered and said, Who is he, Lord, that I might believe on him?

37 And Jesus said unto him, Thou hast both seen him, and it is he that talketh with thee.

38 And he said, Lord, I believe. And he worshipped him.

39 ¶ And Jesus said, For judgment I am come into this world, that they which see not might see; and that they which see might be made blind.

καὶ εἶπεν αὐτοῖς· ἐν τούτῳ γὰρ τὸ
and said to them: In this then the

θαυμαστόν ἐστιν, ὅτι ὑμεῖς οὐκ οἴδατε
marvellous thing is, that ye do not know

πόθεν ἐστίν, καὶ ἤνοιξέν μου τοὺς
whence he is, and he opened of me the

ὀφθαλμούς. 31 οἴδαμεν ὅτι ὁ θεὸς
eyes. We know that – God

ἁμαρτωλῶν οὐκ ἀκούει, ἀλλ᾽ ἐάν τις
sinful men does not hear, but if anyone

θεοσεβὴς ᾖ καὶ τὸ θέλημα αὐτοῦ ποιῇ,
godfearing is and the will of him does,

τούτου ἀκούει. 32 ἐκ τοῦ αἰῶνος οὐκ
this man he hears. From the age not

ἠκούσθη ὅτι ἠνέῳξέν τις ὀφθαλμοὺς τυφλοῦ
it was heard that ²opened ¹anyone eyes of a blind man

γεγεννημένου· 33 εἰ μὴ ἦν οὗτος παρὰ
having been born; if ³not ²was ¹this man from

θεοῦ, οὐκ ἠδύνατο ποιεῖν οὐδέν. 34 ἀπεκρίθησαν
God, he could not *to* do no(any)thing. They answered

καὶ εἶπαν αὐτῷ· ἐν ἁμαρτίαις σὺ ἐγεννήθης
and said to him: In sins thou wast born

ὅλος, καὶ σὺ διδάσκεις ἡμᾶς; καὶ ἐξέβαλον
wholly, and thou teachest us? and they cast *out*

αὐτὸν ἔξω. 35 Ἤκουσεν Ἰησοῦς ὅτι
him outside. Heard Jesus that

ἐξέβαλον αὐτὸν ἔξω, καὶ εὑρὼν αὐτὸν
they cast *out* him outside, and finding him

εἶπεν· σὺ πιστεύεις εἰς τὸν υἱὸν τοῦ
said: Thou believest in the Son –

ἀνθρώπου; 36 ἀπεκρίθη ἐκεῖνος καὶ εἶπεν·
of man? Answered that [one] and said:

καὶ τίς ἐστιν, κύριε, ἵνα πιστεύσω εἰς
And who is he, sir, that I may believe in

αὐτόν; 37 εἶπεν αὐτῷ ὁ Ἰησοῦς· καὶ
him? Said to him – Jesus: Both

ἑώρακας αὐτὸν καὶ ὁ λαλῶν μετὰ σοῦ
thou hast seen him and the [one] speaking with thee

ἐκεῖνός ἐστιν. 38 ὁ δὲ ἔφη· πιστεύω, κύριε·
that [one] is. And he said: I believe, sir;

καὶ προσεκύνησεν αὐτῷ. 39 καὶ εἶπεν ὁ
and he worshipped him. And said –

Ἰησοῦς· εἰς κρίμα ἐγὼ εἰς τὸν κόσμον
Jesus: For judgment I into – world

τοῦτον ἦλθον, ἵνα οἱ μὴ βλέποντες
this came, that the [ones] not seeing

βλέπωσιν καὶ οἱ βλέποντες τυφλοὶ γένωνται.
may see and the [ones] seeing blind may become.

40 And *some* of the Pharisees which were with him heard these words, and said unto him, Are we blind also?

41 Jesus said unto them, If ye were blind, ye should have no sin: but now ye say, We see; therefore your sin remaineth.

40 Ἤκουσαν ἐκ τῶν Φαρισαίων ταῦτα
^{heard ¹[Some] ²of ³the ⁴Pharisees ⁵these things}
οἱ μετ' αὐτοῦ ὄντες, καὶ εἶπαν αὐτῷ·
^{- ⁶with ⁷him ⁵being, and they said to him:}
μὴ καὶ ἡμεῖς τυφλοί ἐσμεν; 41 εἶπεν
^{Not also we blind are? Said}
αὐτοῖς ὁ Ἰησοῦς· εἰ τυφλοὶ ἦτε, οὐκ
^{to them - Jesus: If blind ye were, not}
ἂν εἴχετε ἁμαρτίαν· νῦν δὲ λέγετε ὅτι
^{ye would have had sin; but now ye say[,]}
βλέπομεν· ἡ ἁμαρτία ὑμῶν μένει.
^{We see; the sin of you remains.}

CHAPTER 10

VERILY, verily, I say unto you, He that entereth not by the door into the sheepfold, but climbeth up some other way, the same is a thief and a robber.

2 But he that entereth in by the door is the shepherd of the sheep.

3 To him the porter openeth; and the sheep hear his voice: and he calleth his own sheep by name, and leadeth them out.

4 And when he putteth forth his own sheep, he goeth before them, and the sheep follow him: for they know his voice.

5 And a stranger will they not follow, but will flee from him: for they know not the voice of strangers.

6 This parable spake Jesus unto them: but they understood not what

10 Ἀμὴν ἀμὴν λέγω ὑμῖν, ὁ μὴ
^{Truly truly I say to you, the [one] not}
εἰσερχόμενος διὰ τῆς θύρας εἰς τὴν
^{entering through the door into the}
αὐλὴν τῶν προβάτων ἀλλὰ ἀναβαίνων
^{fold of the sheep but going up}
ἀλλαχόθεν, ἐκεῖνος κλέπτης ἐστὶν καὶ
^{by another way, that [one] a thief is and}
λῃστής· 2 ὁ δὲ εἰσερχόμενος διὰ τῆς
^{a robber; but the [one] entering through the}
θύρας ποιμήν ἐστιν τῶν προβάτων. 3 τούτῳ
^{door shepherd is of the sheep. To this [one]}
ὁ θυρωρὸς ἀνοίγει, καὶ τὰ πρόβατα τῆς
^{the doorkeeper opens, and the sheep the}
φωνῆς αὐτοῦ ἀκούει, καὶ τὰ ἴδια πρόβατα
^{voice of him hears, and the(his) own sheep}
φωνεῖ κατ' ὄνομα καὶ ἐξάγει αὐτά.
^{he calls by name and leads out them.}
4 ὅταν τὰ ἴδια πάντα ἐκβάλῃ, ἔμπροσθεν
^{When the(his) own all he puts forth, in front of}
αὐτῶν πορεύεται, καὶ τὰ πρόβατα αὐτῷ
^{them he goes, and the sheep him}
ἀκολουθεῖ, ὅτι οἴδασιν τὴν φωνὴν αὐτοῦ·
^{follows, because they know the voice of him;}
5 ἀλλοτρίῳ δὲ οὐ μὴ ἀκολουθήσουσιν,
^{but a stranger by no means will they follow,}
ἀλλὰ φεύξονται ἀπ' αὐτοῦ, ὅτι οὐκ
^{but will flee from him, because not}
οἴδασιν τῶν ἀλλοτρίων τὴν φωνήν.
^{they know of the strangers the voice.}
6 Ταύτην τὴν παροιμίαν εἶπεν αὐτοῖς ὁ
^{This - allegory told them -}
Ἰησοῦς· ἐκεῖνοι δὲ οὐκ ἔγνωσαν τίνα
^{Jesus; but those men knew not what things}

things they were which he spake unto them.

7 Then said Jesus unto them again, Verily, verily, I say unto you, I am the door of the sheep.

8 All that ever came before me are thieves and robbers: but the sheep did not hear them.

9 I am the door: by me if any man enter in, he shall be saved, and shall go in and out, and find pasture.

10 The thief cometh not, but for to steal, and to kill, and to destroy: I am come that they might have life, and that they might have *it* more abundantly.

11 I am the good shepherd: the good shepherd giveth his life for the sheep.

12 But he that is an hireling, and not the shepherd, whose own the sheep are not, seeth the wolf coming, and leaveth the sheep, and fleeth: and the wolf catcheth them, and scattereth the sheep.

13 The hireling fleeth, because he is an hireling, and careth not for the sheep.

14 I am the good shepherd, and know my *sheep*, and am known of mine.

15 As the Father knoweth me, even so know I the Father: and I lay down my life for the sheep.

ἦν ἃ ἐλάλει αὐτοῖς. **7** Εἶπεν οὖν πάλιν
they were which he spoke to them. Said therefore again

ὁ Ἰησοῦς· ἀμὴν ἀμὴν λέγω ὑμῖν ὅτι
– Jesus: Truly truly I say to you that

ἐγώ εἰμι ἡ θύρα τῶν προβάτων. **8** πάντες
I am the door of the sheep. All

ὅσοι ἦλθον πρὸ ἐμοῦ κλέπται εἰσὶν καὶ
who came before me thieves are and

λησταί· ἀλλ᾽ οὐκ ἤκουσαν αὐτῶν τὰ
robbers; but did not hear them the

πρόβατα. **9** ἐγώ εἰμι ἡ θύρα· δι᾽ ἐμοῦ
sheep. I am the door; through me

ἐάν τις εἰσέλθῃ, σωθήσεται, καὶ εἰσελεύ-
if anyone enters, he will be saved, and will go

σεται καὶ ἐξελεύσεται καὶ νομὴν εὑρήσει.
in and *will* go out and pasture *will* find.

10 ὁ κλέπτης οὐκ ἔρχεται εἰ μὴ ἵνα
The thief comes not except that

κλέψῃ καὶ θύσῃ καὶ ἀπολέσῃ· ἐγὼ ἦλθον
he may steal and kill and destroy; I came

ἵνα ζωὴν ἔχωσιν καὶ περισσὸν ἔχωσιν.
that life they may have and abundantly *they* may have.

11 Ἐγώ εἰμι ὁ ποιμὴν ὁ καλός. ὁ
I am the shepherd – good. The

ποιμὴν ὁ καλὸς τὴν ψυχὴν αὐτοῦ τίθησιν
shepherd – good the life of him lays down

ὑπὲρ τῶν προβάτων· **12** ὁ μισθωτὸς καὶ
for the sheep; the hireling and

οὐκ ὢν ποιμήν, οὗ οὐκ ἔστιν τὰ πρόβατα
not being a shepherd, of whom is(are) not the sheep

ἴδια, θεωρεῖ τὸν λύκον ἐρχόμενον καὶ
[his] own, beholds the wolf coming and

ἀφίησιν τὰ πρόβατα καὶ φεύγει, — καὶ
leaves the sheep and flees, — and

ὁ λύκος ἁρπάζει αὐτὰ καὶ σκορπίζει· —
the wolf seizes them and scatters; —

13 ὅτι μισθωτός ἐστιν καὶ οὐ μέλει
because a hireling he is and it matters not

αὐτῷ περὶ τῶν προβάτων. **14** ἐγώ εἰμι
to him about the sheep. I am

ὁ ποιμὴν ὁ καλός, καὶ γινώσκω τὰ
the shepherd – good, and I know the

ἐμὰ καὶ γινώσκουσί με τὰ ἐμά, **15** καθὼς
mine and ²know ³me – ¹mine, as

γινώσκει με ὁ πατὴρ κἀγὼ γινώσκω τὸν
³knows ⁴me ¹the ²Father and I know the

πατέρα, καὶ τὴν ψυχήν μου τίθημι ὑπὲρ
Father, and the life of me I lay down for

16 And other sheep I have, which are not of this fold: them also I must bring, and they shall hear my voice; and there shall be one fold, *and* one shepherd.

17 Therefore doth my Father love me, because I lay down my life, that I might take it again.

18 No man taketh it from me, but I lay it down of myself. I have power to lay it down, and I have power to take it again. This commandment have I received of my Father.

19 ¶ There was a division therefore again among the Jews for these sayings.

20 And many of them said, He hath a devil, and is mad; why hear ye him?

21 Others said, These are not the words of him that hath a devil. Can a devil open the eyes of the blind?

22 ¶ And it was at Jerusalem the feast of the dedication, and it was winter.

23 And Jesus walked in the temple in Solomon's porch.

24 Then came the Jews round about him, and said unto him, How long dost thou make us to doubt? If thou be the

τῶν προβάτων. **16** καὶ ἄλλα πρόβατα
the   sheep.   And   other   sheep

ἔχω ἃ οὐκ ἔστιν ἐκ τῆς αὐλῆς ταύτης·
I have which is(are) not of   -   fold   this;

κἀκεῖνα δεῖ με ἀγαγεῖν, καὶ τῆς φωνῆς
those also it behoves me to bring, and the   voice

μου ἀκούσουσιν, καὶ γενήσεται μία ποίμνη,
of me they will hear, and there will become one flock,

εἷς ποιμήν. **17** διὰ τοῦτό με ὁ πατὴρ
one shepherd.   Therefore me the Father

ἀγαπᾷ ὅτι ἐγὼ τίθημι τὴν ψυχήν μου,
loves because I lay down the   life   of me,

ἵνα πάλιν λάβω αὐτήν. **18** οὐδεὶς ἦρεν
that again I may take it.   No one took

αὐτὴν ἀπ᾽ ἐμοῦ, ἀλλ᾽ ἐγὼ τίθημι αὐτὴν
it from me,   but   I lay down it

ἀπ᾽ ἐμαυτοῦ. ἐξουσίαν ἔχω θεῖναι αὐτήν,
from myself. Authority I have to lay down it,

καὶ ἐξουσίαν ἔχω πάλιν λαβεῖν αὐτήν·
and authority I have again to take it;

ταύτην τὴν ἐντολὴν ἔλαβον παρὰ τοῦ
this   - commandment I received from   the

πατρός μου. **19** Σχίσμα πάλιν ἐγένετο ἐν
Father of me.   A division again there was among

τοῖς Ἰουδαίοις διὰ τοὺς λόγους τούτους.
the Jews   because of -   words   these.

20 ἔλεγον δὲ πολλοὶ ἐξ αὐτῶν· δαιμόνιον
  And said many of   them : A demon

ἔχει καὶ μαίνεται· τί αὐτοῦ ἀκούετε;
he has and raves : why him hear ye?

21 ἄλλοι ἔλεγον· ταῦτα τὰ ῥήματα οὐκ
  Others said : These - words not

ἔστιν δαιμονιζομένου· μὴ δαιμόνιον δύναται
is(are) of one demon-possessed; *not* a demon can

τυφλῶν ὀφθαλμοὺς ἀνοῖξαι;
of blind men eyes   *to* open?

22 Ἐγένετο τότε τὰ ἐγκαίνια ἐν τοῖς
  There was then the Dedication in   -

Ἱεροσολύμοις· χειμὼν ἦν· **23** καὶ περιεπάτει
Jerusalem; winter it was; and   walked

ὁ Ἰησοῦς ἐν τῷ ἱερῷ ἐν τῇ στοᾷ τοῦ
- Jesus in the temple in the porch   -

Σολομῶνος. **24** ἐκύκλωσαν οὖν αὐτὸν οἱ
of Solomon.   Surrounded therefore him the

Ἰουδαῖοι καὶ ἔλεγον αὐτῷ· ἕως πότε
Jews   and said to him: Until when

τὴν ψυχὴν ἡμῶν αἴρεις; εἰ σὺ εἶ
the life(soul) of us holdest thou * ? if thou art

* That is, in suspense.

Christ, tell us plainly.

25 Jesus answered them,
I told you, and ye believed
not: the works that I do
in my Father's name,
they bear witness of me.

26 But ye believe not,
because ye are not of my
sheep, as I said unto you.

27 My sheep hear my
voice, and I know them,
and they follow me:

28 And I give unto
them eternal life; and they
shall never perish, neither
shall any *man* pluck them
out of my hand.

29 My Father, which
gave *them* me, is greater
than all; and no *man* is
able to pluck *them* out
of my Father's hand.

30 I and *my* Father are
one.

31 ¶ Then the Jews took
up stones again to stone
him.

32 Jesus answered them,
Many good works have I
shewed you from my
Father; for which of those
works do ye stone me?

33 The Jews answered
him, saying, For a good
work we stone thee not;
but for blasphemy; and
because that thou, being a
man, makest thyself God.

34 Jesus answered them,

ὁ χριστός, εἰπὸν ἡμῖν παρρησίᾳ. 25 ἀπεκρίθη
the Christ, tell us plainly. Answered

αὐτοῖς ὁ Ἰησοῦς· εἶπον ὑμῖν, καὶ
them - Jesus: I told you, and

οὐ πιστεύετε· τὰ ἔργα ἃ ἐγὼ ποιῶ ἐν τῷ
ye do not believe; the works which I do in the

ὀνόματι τοῦ πατρός μου, ταῦτα μαρτυρεῖ
name of the Father of me, these witnesses

περὶ ἐμοῦ· ἀλλὰ ὑμεῖς οὐ πιστεύετε,
concerning me; but ye do not believe,

26 ὅτι οὐκ ἐστὲ ἐκ τῶν προβάτων τῶν
because ye are not of *the* ²sheep -

ἐμῶν. 27 τὰ πρόβατα τὰ ἐμὰ τῆς φωνῆς
¹my. the sheep - My the voice

μου ἀκούουσιν, κἀγὼ γινώσκω αὐτά, καὶ
of me hear, and I know them, and

ἀκολουθοῦσίν μοι, 28 κἀγὼ δίδωμι αὐτοῖς
they follow me, and I give to them

ζωὴν αἰώνιον, καὶ οὐ μὴ ἀπόλωνται εἰς
life eternal, and by no means they perish unto

τὸν αἰῶνα, καὶ οὐχ ἁρπάσει τις αὐτὰ
the age, and ²shall not seize ¹anyone them

ἐκ τῆς χειρός μου. 29 ὁ πατήρ μου ὁ
out of the hand of me. The Father of me who

δέδωκέν μοι πάντων μεῖζόν ἐστιν, καὶ
has given to me [than] all greater is, and

οὐδεὶς δύναται ἁρπάζειν ἐκ τῆς χειρὸς
no one can *to* seize out of the hand

τοῦ πατρός. 30 ἐγὼ καὶ ὁ πατὴρ ἕν
of the Father. I and the Father one

ἐσμεν. 31 Ἐβάστασαν πάλιν λίθους οἱ
we are. Lifted again stones the

Ἰουδαῖοι ἵνα λιθάσωσιν αὐτόν. 32 ἀπ-
Jews that they might stone him. An-

εκρίθη αὐτοῖς ὁ Ἰησοῦς· πολλὰ ἔργα
swered them - Jesus: Many ²works

ἔδειξα ὑμῖν καλὰ ἐκ τοῦ πατρός· διὰ
³I showed ⁴you ¹good of the Father; because of

ποῖον αὐτῶν ἔργον ἐμὲ λιθάζετε;
which ²of them ¹work ⁴me ³stone ye?

33 ἀπεκρίθησαν αὐτῷ οἱ Ἰουδαῖοι· περὶ
Answered him the Jews: Concerning

καλοῦ ἔργου οὐ λιθάζομέν σε ἀλλὰ περὶ
a good work we do not stone thee but concerning

βλασφημίας, καὶ ὅτι σὺ ἄνθρωπος ὢν
blasphemy, and because thou a man being

ποιεῖς σεαυτὸν θεόν. 34 ἀπεκρίθη αὐτοῖς
makest thyself God. Answered them

Is it not written in your law, I said, Ye are gods?

35 If he called them gods, unto whom the word of God came, and the scripture cannot be broken;

36 Say ye of him, whom the Father hath sanctified, and sent into the world, Thou blasphemest; because I said, I am the Son of God?

37 If I do not the works of my Father, believe me not.

38 But if I do, though ye believe not me, believe the works: that ye may know, and believe, that the Father is in me, and I in him.

39 ¶ Therefore they sought again to take him: but he escaped out of their hand,

40 And went away again beyond Jordan into the place where John at first baptized; and there he abode.

41 And many resorted unto him, and said, John did no miracle: but all things that John spake of this man were true.

42 And many believed on him there.

ὁ Ἰησοῦς· οὐκ ἔστιν γεγραμμένον ἐν τῷ
\-   Jesus: Is it not   *having been* written   in   the

νόμῳ ὑμῶν ὅτι ἐγὼ εἶπα· θεοί ἐστε;
law   of you[,]   -   I   said: Gods   ye are?

35 εἰ ἐκείνους εἶπεν θεοὺς πρὸς οὓς ὁ
¹if   ³those   ²he called   ⁴gods   with   whom   the

λόγος τοῦ θεοῦ ἐγένετο, καὶ οὐ δύναται
word   -   of God   was,   and   cannot

λυθῆναι ἡ γραφή, 36 ὃν ὁ πατὴρ
to be broken   the   scripture,   ²[him] whom   ⁴the   ¹Father

ἡγίασεν καὶ ἀπέστειλεν εἰς τὸν κόσμον
⁵sanctified   ⁷and   ⁸sent   ⁹into   ¹⁰the   ¹¹world

ὑμεῖς λέγετε ὅτι βλασφημεῖς, ὅτι εἶπον·
¹ye   ¹tell[,]   -   Thou blasphemest,   because   I said :

υἱὸς τοῦ θεοῦ εἰμι; 37 εἰ οὐ ποιῶ τὰ ἔργα
Son   -   of God   I am?   If   I do not   the   works

τοῦ πατρός μου, μὴ πιστεύετέ μοι· 38 εἰ δὲ
of the   Father   of me,   do not believe   me;   but if

ποιῶ, κἂν ἐμοὶ μὴ πιστεύητε, τοῖς ἔργοις
I do,   even if   me   ye do not believe,   the   works

πιστεύετε, ἵνα γνῶτε καὶ γινώσκητε
believe,   that ye may know*   and   continue to know*

ὅτι ἐν ἐμοὶ ὁ πατὴρ κἀγὼ ἐν τῷ πατρί.
that   in   me   the   Father [is] and I   in   the   Father.

39 Ἐζήτουν οὖν αὐτὸν πάλιν πιάσαι· καὶ
They sought therefore   him   again   to arrest;   and

ἐξῆλθεν ἐκ τῆς χειρὸς αὐτῶν.
he went forth out of   the   hand   of them.

40 Καὶ ἀπῆλθεν πάλιν πέραν τοῦ
And   he went away   again   across   the

Ἰορδάνου εἰς τὸν τόπον ὅπου ἦν Ἰωάννης
Jordan   to   the   place   where was   John

τὸ πρῶτον βαπτίζων, καὶ ἔμενεν ἐκεῖ.
at first   baptizing,   and   remained   there.

41 καὶ πολλοὶ ἦλθον πρὸς αὐτὸν καὶ
And   many   came   to   him   and

ἔλεγον ὅτι Ἰωάννης μὲν σημεῖον ἐποίησεν
said[,]   -   John   indeed   sign   did

οὐδέν, πάντα δὲ ὅσα εἶπεν Ἰωάννης περὶ
none,   but all things   how many   said   John   about

τούτου ἀληθῆ ἦν. 42 καὶ πολλοὶ ἐπίστευσαν
this man   true was(were).   And   many   believed

εἰς αὐτὸν ἐκεῖ.
in   him   there.

CHAPTER 11

Now a certain *man* was sick, *named* Lazarus, of Bethany, the

11 Ἦν δέ τις ἀσθενῶν, Λάζαρος ἀπὸ
Now there was   a certain man ailing,   Lazarus   from

* Different tenses (aorist and present) of the same verb.

town of Mary and her
sister Martha.

2 (It was *that* Mary
which anointed the Lord
with ointment, and wiped
his feet with her hair,
whose brother Lazarus
was sick.)

3 Therefore his sisters
sent unto him, saying,
Lord, behold, he whom
thou lovest is sick.

4 When Jesus heard
that, he said, This sickness is not unto death,
but for the glory of God,
that the Son of God might
be glorified thereby.

5 Now Jesus loved
Martha, and her sister, and
Lazarus.

6 When he had heard
therefore that he was
sick, he abode two days
still in the same place
where he was.

7 Then after that saith
he to *his* disciples, Let us
go into Judæa again.

8 *His* disciples say unto
him, Master, the Jews of
late sought to stone thee;
and goest thou thither
again?

9 Jesus answered, Are
there not twelve hours in
the day? If any man walk
in the day, he stumbleth
not, because he seeth the
light of this world.

10 But if a man walk
in the night, he stumbleth,

Βηθανίας, ἐκ τῆς κώμης Μαρίας καὶ
Bethany, of the village of Mary and

Μάρθας τῆς ἀδελφῆς αὐτῆς. 2 ἦν δὲ
Martha the sister of her. And it was

Μαριὰμ ἡ ἀλείψασα τὸν κύριον μύρῳ
Mary the [one] anointing the Lord with ointment

καὶ ἐκμάξασα τοὺς πόδας αὐτοῦ ταῖς
and wiping off the feet of him with the

θριξὶν αὐτῆς, ἧς ὁ ἀδελφὸς Λάζαρος
hairs of her, of whom the brother Lazarus

ἠσθένει. 3 ἀπέστειλαν οὖν αἱ ἀδελφαὶ
ailed. Sent therefore the sisters

πρὸς αὐτὸν λέγουσαι· κύριε, ἴδε ὃν
to him saying: Lord, behold[,] [he] whom

φιλεῖς ἀσθενεῖ. 4 ἀκούσας δὲ ὁ Ἰησοῦς
thou lovest ails. And hearing – Jesus

εἶπεν· αὕτη ἡ ἀσθένεια οὐκ ἔστιν πρὸς
said: This – ailment is not to

θάνατον ἀλλ' ὑπὲρ τῆς δόξης τοῦ θεοῦ,
death but for the glory – of God,

ἵνα δοξασθῇ ὁ υἱὸς τοῦ θεοῦ δι' αὐτῆς.
that may be glorified the Son – of God through it.

5 ἠγάπα δὲ ὁ Ἰησοῦς τὴν Μάρθαν καὶ
Now ²loved – ¹Jesus – Martha and

τὴν ἀδελφὴν αὐτῆς καὶ τὸν Λάζαρον.
the sister of her and – Lazarus.

6 ὡς οὖν ἤκουσεν ὅτι ἀσθενεῖ, τότε μὲν
When therefore he heard that he ails(ed), then

ἔμεινεν ἐν ᾧ ἦν τόπῳ δύο ἡμέρας·
he remained ¹in ²which ⁴he was ³place two days;

7 ἔπειτα μετὰ τοῦτο λέγει τοῖς μαθηταῖς·
then after this he says to the disciples:

ἄγωμεν εἰς τὴν Ἰουδαίαν πάλιν. 8 λέγουσιν
Let us go into – Judæa again. Say

αὐτῷ οἱ μαθηταί· ῥαββί, νῦν ἐζήτουν
to him the disciples: Rabbi, ⁴now ²were ³seeking

σε λιθάσαι οἱ Ἰουδαῖοι, καὶ πάλιν ὑπάγεις
⁷thee ⁶to stone ¹the ⁵Jews, and again goest thou

ἐκεῖ; 9 ἀπεκρίθη Ἰησοῦς· οὐχὶ δώδεκα
there? Answered Jesus: Not twelve

ὧραί εἰσιν τῆς ἡμέρας; ἐάν τις περιπατῇ
hours are there of the day? if anyone walks

ἐν τῇ ἡμέρᾳ, οὐ προσκόπτει, ὅτι τὸ φῶς
in the day, he does not stumble, because the light

τοῦ κόσμου τούτου βλέπει· 10 ἐὰν δέ
– world of this he sees; but if

τις περιπατῇ ἐν τῇ νυκτί, προσκόπτει,
anyone walks in the night, he stumbles,

because there is no light in him.

11 These things said he: and after that he saith unto them, Our friend Lazarus sleepeth; but I go, that I may awake him out of sleep.

12 Then said his disciples, Lord, if he sleep, he shall do well.

13 Howbeit Jesus spake of his death: but they thought that he had spoken of taking of rest in sleep.

14 Then said Jesus unto them plainly, Lazarus is dead.

15 And I am glad for your sakes that I was not there, to the intent ye may believe; nevertheless let us go unto him.

16 Then said Thomas, which is called Didymus, unto his fellow disciples, Let us also go, that we may die with him.

17 Then when Jesus came, he found that he had *lain* in the grave four days already.

18 Now Bethany was nigh unto Jerusalem, about fifteen furlongs off:

19 And many of the Jews came to Martha and Mary, to comfort them concerning their brother.

20 Then Martha, as soon as she heard that Jesus was coming, went and met him: but Mary sat *still* in the house.

ὅτι τὸ φῶς οὐκ ἔστιν ἐν αὐτῷ. 11 ταῦτα
because the light is not in him. These things

εἶπεν, καὶ μετὰ τοῦτο λέγει αὐτοῖς·
he said, and after this he says to them :

Λάζαρος ὁ φίλος ἡμῶν κεκοίμηται· ἀλλὰ
Lazarus the friend of us has fallen asleep; but

πορεύομαι ἵνα ἐξυπνίσω αὐτόν. 12 εἶπαν
I am going that I may awaken him. Said

οὖν οἱ μαθηταὶ αὐτῷ· κύριε, εἰ κεκοίμηται,
there- the disciples to him: Lord, if he has fallen asleep,
fore

σωθήσεται. 13 εἰρήκει δὲ ὁ Ἰησοῦς περὶ
he will be healed. Now had spoken – Jesus concerning

τοῦ θανάτου αὐτοῦ· ἐκεῖνοι δὲ ἔδοξαν ὅτι
the death of him; but those men thought that

περὶ τῆς κοιμήσεως τοῦ ὕπνου λέγει.
concerning the sleep – of slumber he says.

14 τότε οὖν εἶπεν αὐτοῖς ὁ Ἰησοῦς
Then therefore told them – Jesus

παρρησίᾳ· Λάζαρος ἀπέθανεν, 15 καὶ χαίρω
plainly : Lazarus died, and I rejoice

δι᾽ ὑμᾶς, ἵνα πιστεύσητε, ὅτι οὐκ ἤμην
because of you, that ye may believe, that I was not

ἐκεῖ· ἀλλὰ ἄγωμεν πρὸς αὐτόν. 16 εἶπεν
there; but let us go to him. Said

οὖν Θωμᾶς ὁ λεγόμενος Δίδυμος τοῖς
therefore Thomas – *being* called Twin to the(his)

συμμαθηταῖς· ἄγωμεν καὶ ἡμεῖς ἵνα
fellow-disciples : Let go also we(us) that

ἀποθάνωμεν μετ᾽ αὐτοῦ. 17 Ἐλθὼν οὖν
we may die with him. Coming therefore

ὁ Ἰησοῦς εὗρεν αὐτὸν τέσσαρας ἤδη
– Jesus found him ²four ¹already

ἡμέρας ἔχοντα ἐν τῷ μνημείῳ. 18 ἦν δὲ
³days having(being) in the tomb. Now was

Βηθανία ἐγγὺς τῶν Ἱεροσολύμων ὡς ἀπὸ
Bethany near – Jerusalem about ²away

σταδίων δεκαπέντε. 19 πολλοὶ δὲ ἐκ τῶν
²furlongs ¹fifteen. And many of the

Ἰουδαίων ἐληλύθεισαν πρὸς τὴν Μάρθαν
Jews had come to – Martha

καὶ Μαριάμ, ἵνα παραμυθήσωνται αὐτὰς
and Mary, that they might console them

περὶ τοῦ ἀδελφοῦ. 20 ἡ οὖν Μάρθα ὡς
concerning the(ir) brother. – Therefore Martha when

ἤκουσεν ὅτι Ἰησοῦς ἔρχεται, ὑπήντησεν
she heard that Jesus is(was) coming, met

αὐτῷ· Μαριὰμ δὲ ἐν τῷ οἴκῳ ἐκαθέζετο.
him; but Mary in the house sat.

21 Then said Martha unto Jesus, Lord, if thou hadst been here, my brother had not died.
22 But I know, that even now, whatsoever thou wilt ask of God, God will give it thee.
23 Jesus saith unto her, Thy brother shall rise again.
24 Martha saith unto him, I know that he shall rise again in the resurrection at the last day.
25 Jesus said unto her, I am the resurrection, and the life: he that believeth in me, though he were dead, yet shall he live:
26 And whosoever liveth and believeth in me shall never die. Believest thou this?
27 She saith unto him, Yea, Lord: I believe that thou art the Christ, the Son of God, which should come into the world.
28 And when she had so said, she went her way, and called Mary her sister secretly, saying, The Master is come, and calleth for thee.
29 As soon as she heard that, she arose quickly, and came unto him.
30 Now Jesus was not yet come into the town, but was in that place where Martha met him.
31 The Jews then which were with her in the

21 εἶπεν οὖν ἡ Μάρθα πρὸς Ἰησοῦν·
Said therefore - Martha to Jesus :
κύριε, εἰ ἦς ὧδε, οὐκ ἂν ἀπέθανεν ὁ
Lord, if thou wast here, would not have died the
ἀδελφός μου. 22 καὶ νῦν οἶδα ὅτι ὅσα ἂν
brother of me. And now I know that whatever things
αἰτήσῃ τὸν θεὸν δώσει σοι ὁ θεός.
thou askest - God ²will give ³thee - ¹God.
23 λέγει αὐτῇ ὁ Ἰησοῦς· ἀναστήσεται ὁ
Says to her - Jesus : Will rise again the
ἀδελφός σου. 24 λέγει αὐτῷ ἡ Μάρθα·
brother of thee. Says to him - Martha :
οἶδα ὅτι ἀναστήσεται ἐν τῇ ἀναστάσει
I know that he will rise again in the resurrection
ἐν τῇ ἐσχάτῃ ἡμέρᾳ. 25 εἶπεν αὐτῇ ὁ
in the last day. Said to her -
Ἰησοῦς· ἐγώ εἰμι ἡ ἀνάστασις καὶ ἡ
Jesus : I am the resurrection and the
ζωή· ὁ πιστεύων εἰς ἐμὲ κἂν ἀποθάνῃ
life; the [one] believing in me even if he should die
ζήσεται, 26 καὶ πᾶς ὁ ζῶν καὶ πιστεύων
will live, and everyone living and believing
εἰς ἐμὲ οὐ μὴ ἀποθάνῃ εἰς τὸν αἰῶνα·
in me by no means dies unto the age·
πιστεύεις τοῦτο; 27 λέγει αὐτῷ· ναί, κύριε·
believest thou this? She says to him : Yes, Lord;
ἐγὼ πεπίστευκα ὅτι σὺ εἶ ὁ χριστὸς ὁ
I have believed that thou art the Christ the
υἱὸς τοῦ θεοῦ ὁ εἰς τὸν κόσμον ἐρχόμενος.
Son - of God ¹the ³into ⁴the ⁵world ²[one] coming.
28 καὶ τοῦτο εἰποῦσα ἀπῆλθεν καὶ ἐφώνησεν
And this saying she went away and called
Μαριὰμ τὴν ἀδελφὴν αὐτῆς λάθρα εἰποῦσα·
Mary the sister of her secretly saying :
ὁ διδάσκαλος πάρεστιν καὶ φωνεῖ σε.
The Teacher is here and calls thee.
29 ἐκείνη δὲ ὡς ἤκουσεν, ἐγείρεται ταχὺ
And that [one] when she heard, rose quickly
καὶ ἤρχετο πρὸς αὐτόν· 30 οὔπω δὲ
and came to him; now not yet
ἐληλύθει ὁ Ἰησοῦς εἰς τὴν κώμην, ἀλλ'
had come - Jesus into the village, but
ἦν ἔτι ἐν τῷ τόπῳ ὅπου ὑπήντησεν
was still in the place where met
αὐτῷ ἡ Μάρθα. 31 οἱ οὖν Ἰουδαῖοι
him - Martha. Therefore the Jews
οἱ ὄντες μετ' αὐτῆς ἐν τῇ οἰκίᾳ καὶ
the [ones] being with her in the house and

house, and comforted her, when they saw Mary, that she rose up hastily and went out, followed her, saying, She goeth unto the grave to weep there.

32 Then when Mary was come where Jesus was, and saw him, she fell down at his feet, saying unto him, Lord, if thou hadst been here, my brother had not died.

33 When Jesus therefore saw her weeping, and the Jews also weeping which came with her, he groaned in the spirit, and was troubled,

34 And said, Where have ye laid him? They said unto him, Lord, come and see.

35 Jesus wept.

36 Then said the Jews, Behold how he loved him!

37 And some of them said, Could not this man, which opened the eyes of the blind, have caused that even this man should not have died?

38 Jesus therefore again groaning in himself cometh to the grave. It was a cave, and a stone lay upon it.

39 Jesus said, Take ye away the stone. Martha, the sister of him that was dead, saith unto him,

---

παραμυθούμενοι αὐτήν, ἰδόντες τὴν Μαριὰμ
consoling her, seeing – Mary

ὅτι ταχέως ἀνέστη καὶ ἐξῆλθεν,
that quickly she rose up and went out,

ἠκολούθησαν αὐτῇ, δόξαντες ὅτι ὑπάγει
followed her, thinking[,] – She is going

εἰς τὸ μνημεῖον ἵνα κλαύσῃ ἐκεῖ. 32 ἡ
to the tomb that she may weep there. –

οὖν Μαριὰμ ὡς ἦλθεν ὅπου ἦν Ἰησοῦς,
Therefore Mary when she came where was Jesus,

ἰδοῦσα αὐτὸν ἔπεσεν αὐτοῦ πρὸς τοὺς
seeing him fell of him at the

πόδας, λέγουσα αὐτῷ· κύριε, εἰ ἦς ὧδε,
feet, saying to him : Lord, if thou wast here,

οὐκ ἄν μου ἀπέθανεν ὁ ἀδελφός.
⁴would not ³of me ⁵have died ¹the ²brother.

33 Ἰησοῦς οὖν ὡς εἶδεν αὐτὴν κλαίουσαν
Jesus therefore when he saw her weeping

καὶ τοὺς συνελθόντας αὐτῇ Ἰουδαίους
and ¹the ²coming with ⁴her ³Jews

κλαίοντας, ἐνεβριμήσατο τῷ πνεύματι καὶ
weeping, groaned in the(his) spirit and

ἐτάραξεν ἑαυτόν, 34 καὶ εἶπεν· ποῦ
troubled himself, and said : Where

τεθείκατε αὐτόν; λέγουσιν αὐτῷ· κύριε,
have ye put him? They say to him : Lord,

ἔρχου καὶ ἴδε. 35 ἐδάκρυσεν ὁ Ἰησοῦς.
come and see. Shed tears – Jesus.

36 ἔλεγον οὖν οἱ Ἰουδαῖοι· ἴδε πῶς
Said therefore the Jews : See how

ἐφίλει αὐτόν. 37 τινὲς δὲ ἐξ αὐτῶν
he loved him. But some of them

εἶπαν· οὐκ ἐδύνατο οὗτος ὁ ἀνοίξας
said : Could not this man the [one] opening

τοὺς ὀφθαλμοὺς τοῦ τυφλοῦ ποιῆσαι ἵνα
the eyes of the blind man to cause that

καὶ οὗτος μὴ ἀποθάνῃ; 38 Ἰησοῦς οὖν
even this man should not die ? Jesus therefore

πάλιν ἐμβριμώμενος ἐν ἑαυτῷ ἔρχεται
again groaning in himself comes

εἰς τὸ μνημεῖον· ἦν δὲ σπήλαιον, καὶ
to the tomb; now it was a cave, and

λίθος ἐπέκειτο ἐπ’ αὐτῷ. 39 λέγει ὁ
a stone was lying on on it. Says

Ἰησοῦς· ἄρατε τὸν λίθον. λέγει αὐτῷ
Jesus : Lift ye the stone. Says to him

ἡ ἀδελφὴ τοῦ τετελευτηκότος Μάρθα·
the sister of the [one] having died Martha :

Lord, by this time he stinketh: for he hath been *dead* four days.

40 Jesus saith unto her, Said I not unto thee, that, if thou wouldest believe, thou shouldest see the glory of God?

41 Then they took away the stone *from the place* where the dead was laid. And Jesus lifted up *his* eyes, and said, Father, I thank thee that thou hast heard me.

42 And I knew that thou hearest me always: but because of the people which stand by I said *it*, that they may believe that thou hast sent me.

43 And when he thus had spoken, he cried with a loud voice, Lazarus, come forth.

44 And he that was dead came forth, bound hand and foot with graveclothes: and his face was bound about with a napkin. Jesus saith unto them, Loose him, and let him go.

45 Then many of the Jews which came to Mary, and had seen the things which Jesus did, believed on him.

46 But some of them went their ways to the Pharisees, and told them what things Jesus had done. ¶

47 ¶ Then gathered the chief priests and the Pharisees a council, and said, What do we? for this man doeth many miracles.

κύριε, ἤδη ὄζει· τεταρταῖος γάρ ἐστιν.
Lord, now he smells; for fourth [day] it is.

40 λέγει αὐτῇ ὁ ᾿Ιησοῦς· οὐκ εἶπόν
Says to her - Jesus : Not I told

σοι ὅτι ἐὰν πιστεύσῃς ὄψῃ τὴν δόξαν
thee that if thou believest thou wilt see the glory

τοῦ θεοῦ; 41 ἦραν οὖν τὸν λίθον. ὁ
- of God? They lifted therefore the stone. -

δὲ ᾿Ιησοῦς ἦρεν τοὺς ὀφθαλμοὺς ἄνω
And Jesus lifted the(his) eyes up

καὶ εἶπεν· πάτερ, εὐχαριστῶ σοι ὅτι
and said : Father, I thank thee that

ἤκουσάς μου. 42 ἐγὼ δὲ ᾔδειν ὅτι
thou didst hear me. And I knew that

πάντοτέ μου ἀκούεις· ἀλλὰ διὰ τὸν
always me thou hearest; but because of the

ὄχλον τὸν περιεστῶτα εἶπον, ἵνα
crowd - standing round I said, that

πιστεύσωσιν ὅτι σύ με ἀπέστειλας.
they may believe that thou me didst send.

43 καὶ ταῦτα εἰπὼν φωνῇ μεγάλῃ
And these things saying voice with a great

ἐκραύγασεν· Λάζαρε, δεῦρο ἔξω. 44 ἐξῆλθεν
he cried out : Lazarus, come out. Came out

ὁ τεθνηκὼς δεδεμένος τοὺς πόδας καὶ
the [one] having died *having been* bound the feet and

τὰς χεῖρας κειρίαις, καὶ ἡ ὄψις αὐτοῦ
the hands with bandages, and the face of him

σουδαρίῳ περιεδέδετο. λέγει αὐτοῖς ὁ
with a napkin had been bound round. Says to them -

᾿Ιησοῦς· λύσατε αὐτὸν καὶ ἄφετε αὐτὸν ὑπάγειν.
Jesus : Loosen him and let him *to* go.

45 Πολλοὶ οὖν ἐκ τῶν ᾿Ιουδαίων, οἱ
Many therefore of the Jews, the [ones]

ἐλθόντες πρὸς τὴν Μαριὰμ καὶ θεασάμενοι
having come to - Mary and having beheld

ὃ ἐποίησεν, ἐπίστευσαν εἰς αὐτόν· 46 τινὲς δὲ
what he did, believed in him; but some

ἐξ αὐτῶν ἀπῆλθον πρὸς τοὺς Φαρισαίους
of them went away to the Pharisees

καὶ εἶπαν αὐτοῖς ἃ ἐποίησεν ᾿Ιησοῦς.
and told them what things did Jesus.

47 συνήγαγον οὖν οἱ ἀρχιερεῖς καὶ οἱ
Assembled therefore the chief priests and the

Φαρισαῖοι συνέδριον, καὶ ἔλεγον· τί
Pharisees a council, and said : What

ποιοῦμεν, ὅτι οὗτος ὁ ἄνθρωπος πολλὰ
are we doing, because this - man *many

48 If we let him thus alone, all *men* will believe on him: and the Romans shall come and take away both our place and nation.

49 And one of them, *named* Caiaphas, being the high priest that same year, said unto them, Ye know nothing at all,

50 Nor consider that it is expedient for us, that one man should die for the people, and that the whole nation perish not.

51 And this spake he not of himself: but being high priest that year, he prophesied that Jesus should die for that nation;

52 And not for that nation only, but that also he should gather together in one the children of God that were scattered abroad.

53 Then from that day forth they took counsel together for to put him to death.

54 Jesus therefore walked no more openly among the Jews; but went thence unto a country near to the wilderness, into a city called Ephraim, and there continued with his disciples.

55 ¶ And the Jews' passover was nigh at hand:

ποιεῖ σημεῖα; 48 ἐὰν ἀφῶμεν αὐτὸν οὕτως,
¹does ³signs? If we leave him thus,

πάντες πιστεύσουσιν εἰς αὐτόν, καὶ
all men will believe in him, and

ἐλεύσονται οἱ Ῥωμαῖοι καὶ ἀροῦσιν ἡμῶν
will come the Romans and will take of us

καὶ τὸν τόπον καὶ τὸ ἔθνος. 49 εἷς
both the place and the nation. ²one

δέ τις ἐξ αὐτῶν Καϊάφας, ἀρχιερεὺς
¹But ²a certain of them[,] Caiaphas, high priest

ὢν τοῦ ἐνιαυτοῦ ἐκείνου, εἶπεν αὐτοῖς·
being – year of that, said to them:

ὑμεῖς οὐκ οἴδατε οὐδέν, 50 οὐδὲ λογίζεσθε
Ye know not no(any)thing, nor reckon

ὅτι συμφέρει ὑμῖν ἵνα εἷς ἄνθρωπος
that it is expedient for us that one man

ἀποθάνῃ ὑπὲρ τοῦ λαοῦ καὶ μὴ ὅλον
should die for the people and not all

τὸ ἔθνος ἀπόληται. 51 τοῦτο δὲ ἀφ'
the nation perish. But this from

ἑαυτοῦ οὐκ εἶπεν, ἀλλὰ ἀρχιερεὺς ὢν
himself he said not, but high priest being

τοῦ ἐνιαυτοῦ ἐκείνου ἐπροφήτευσεν ὅτι
– year of that he prophesied that

ἔμελλεν Ἰησοῦς ἀποθνήσκειν ὑπὲρ τοῦ
was about Jesus to die for the

ἔθνους, 52 καὶ οὐχ ὑπὲρ τοῦ ἔθνους
nation, and not for the nation

μόνον, ἀλλ' ἵνα καὶ τὰ τέκνα τοῦ θεοῦ
only, but that also the children – of God

τὰ διεσκορπισμένα συναγάγῃ εἰς ἕν.
– *having been* scattered he might gather into one.

53 ἀπ' ἐκείνης οὖν τῆς ἡμέρας ἐβουλεύσαντο
From ¹that ³therefore – ²day they took counsel

ἵνα ἀποκτείνωσιν αὐτόν. 54 Ὁ οὖν
that they might kill him. – Therefore

Ἰησοῦς οὐκέτι παρρησίᾳ περιεπάτει ἐν
Jesus no longer openly walked among

τοῖς Ἰουδαίοις, ἀλλὰ ἀπῆλθεν ἐκεῖθεν εἰς
the Jews, but went away thence into

τὴν χώραν ἐγγὺς τῆς ἐρήμου, εἰς Ἐφράιμ
the country near the desert, to ³Ephraim

λεγομένην πόλιν, κἀκεῖ ἔμεινεν μετὰ τῶν
²being called ¹a city, and there remained with the

μαθητῶν.
disciples.

55 Ἦν δὲ ἐγγὺς τὸ πάσχα τῶν
Now was near the Passover of the

and many went out of the country up to Jerusalem before the passover, to purify themselves.

56 Then sought they for Jesus, and spake among themselves, as they stood in the temple, What think ye, that he will not come to the feast?

57 Now both the chief priests and the Pharisees had given a commandment, that, if any man knew where he were, he should shew *it*, that they might take him.

CHAPTER 12

THEN Jesus six days before the passover came to Bethany, where Lazarus was which had been dead, whom he raised from the dead.

2 There they made him a supper; and Martha served: but Lazarus was one of them that sat at the table with him.

3 Then took Mary a pound of ointment of spikenard, very costly, and anointed the feet of Jesus, and wiped his feet with her hair: and the house was filled with the odour of the ointment.

4 Then saith one of his disciples, Judas Iscariot, Simon's *son*, which should betray him,

5 Why was not this ointment sold for three hundred pence, and given to the poor?

’Ιουδαίων,   καὶ   ἀνέβησαν   πολλοὶ   εἰς
Jews,   and   went up   many   to

’Ιεροσόλυμα   ἐκ   τῆς   χώρας   πρὸ   τοῦ
Jerusalem   out of   the   country   before   the

πάσχα,   ἵνα   ἁγνίσωσιν   ἑαυτούς.
Passover,   that   they might purify   themselves.

56 ἐζήτουν   οὖν   τὸν   ’Ιησοῦν   καὶ   ἔλεγον
They sought   therefore –   Jesus   and   said

μετ’   ἀλλήλων   ἐν   τῷ   ἱερῷ   ἑστηκότες·
with   one another   in   the   temple   standing :

τί   δοκεῖ   ὑμῖν;   ὅτι   οὐ   μὴ   ἔλθῃ   εἰς
What   seems it   to you?   that   by no means he comes   to

τὴν   ἑορτήν;   **57** δεδώκεισαν   δὲ   οἱ   ἀρχιερεῖς
the   feast?   Now had given   –   the   chief priests

καὶ   οἱ   Φαρισαῖοι   ἐντολὰς   ἵνα   ἐάν   τις
and   the   Pharisees   commands   that   if   anyone

γνῷ   ποῦ   ἐστιν   μηνύσῃ,   ὅπως   πιάσωσιν
knew   where   he is (was) he should inform, so as   they might
                                                                                    arrest

αὐτόν.   **12** Ὁ   οὖν   ’Ιησοῦς   πρὸ   ἐξ   ἡμερῶν
him.   –   Therefore Jesus   ²before ¹six   ³days

τοῦ   πάσχα   ἦλθεν   εἰς   Βηθανίαν,   ὅπου
the   Passover   came   to   Bethany,   where

ἦν   Λάζαρος,   ὃν   ἤγειρεν   ἐκ   νεκρῶν
was   Lazarus,   whom   ²raised   ³out of [the] ⁴dead

’Ιησοῦς.   **2** ἐποίησαν   οὖν   αὐτῷ   δεῖπνον   ἐκεῖ,
¹Jesus.   They made therefore for him   a supper   there,

καὶ   ἡ   Μάρθα   διηκόνει,   ὁ   δὲ   Λάζαρος   εἷς
and   –   Martha   served,   –   but   Lazarus   one

ἦν   ἐκ   τῶν   ἀνακειμένων   σὺν   αὐτῷ·   **3** ἡ
was   of   the [ones]   reclining   with   him;   –

οὖν   Μαριὰμ   λαβοῦσα   λίτραν   μύρου
therefore   Mary   taking   a pound   ²ointment

νάρδου   πιστικῆς   πολυτίμου   ἤλειψεν   τοὺς
⁴of spikenard ¹of pure   ²costly   anointed   the

πόδας   τοῦ   ’Ιησοῦ   καὶ   ἐξέμαξεν   ταῖς
feet   –   of Jesus   and   wiped off   with the

θριξὶν   αὐτῆς   τοὺς   πόδας   αὐτοῦ·   ἡ   δὲ
hairs   of her   the   feet   of him;   and the

οἰκία   ἐπληρώθη   ἐκ   τῆς   ὀσμῆς   τοῦ
house   was filled   of(with)   the   odour   of the

μύρου.   **4** λέγει   δὲ   ’Ιούδας   ὁ   ’Ισκαριώτης
ointment.   And says   –   Judas   the   Iscariot

εἷς   τῶν   μαθητῶν   αὐτοῦ,   ὁ   μέλλων
one   of the   disciples   of him, the [one] being about

αὐτὸν   παραδιδόναι·   **5** διὰ   τί   τοῦτο   τὸ
him   to betray :   Why   this   –

μύρον   οὐκ   ἐπράθη   τριακοσίων   δηναρίων
ointment   not   was sold   of(for) three hundred denarii

6 This he said, not that he cared for the poor; but because he was a thief, and had the bag, and bare what was put therein.

7 Then said Jesus, Let her alone: against the day of my burying hath she kept this.

8 For the poor always ye have with you; but me ye have not always.

9 ¶ Much people of the Jews therefore knew that he was there: and they came not for Jesus' sake only, but that they might see Lazarus also, whom he had raised from the dead.

10 But the chief priests consulted that they might put Lazarus also to death;

11 Because that by reason of him many of the Jews went away, and believed on Jesus.

12 ¶ On the next day much people that were come to the feast, when they heard that Jesus was coming to Jerusalem,

13 Took branches of palm trees, and went forth to meet him, and cried, Hosanna: Blessed *is* the

καὶ   ἐδόθη   πτωχοῖς;   **6** εἶπεν   δὲ   τοῦτο
and   given   to [the] poor?   But he said   this

οὐχ   ὅτι   περὶ   τῶν   πτωχῶν   ἔμελεν   αὐτῷ,
not because about   the   poor   it mattered   to him,

ἀλλ'   ὅτι   κλέπτης   ἦν   καὶ   τὸ   γλωσσόκομον
but because   a thief   he was and   ²the   ³bag

ἔχων   τὰ   βαλλόμενα   ἐβάσταζεν. *
¹having ⁵the things   ⁶being put [in]   ⁴carried. *

7 εἶπεν   οὖν   ὁ   Ἰησοῦς·   ἄφες   αὐτήν,
Said   therefore -   Jesus :   Leave   her,

ἵνα   εἰς   τὴν   ἡμέραν   τοῦ   ἐνταφιασμοῦ
that   to   the   day   of the   burial

μου   τηρήσῃ   αὐτό·   **8** τοὺς   πτωχοὺς   γὰρ
of me she may keep   it;   ²the   ³poor   ¹for

πάντοτε   ἔχετε   μεθ'   ἑαυτῶν,   ἐμὲ   δὲ
always   ye have   with   yourselves, but me

οὐ   πάντοτε   ἔχετε.   **9** Ἔγνω   οὖν   ὁ   ὄχλος
not   always   ye have.   Knew   therefore the   crowd

πολὺς   ἐκ   τῶν   Ἰουδαίων   ὅτι   ἐκεῖ   ἐστιν,
great   of   the   Jews   that   there   he is(was),

καὶ   ἦλθον   οὐ   διὰ   τὸν   Ἰησοῦν   μόνον,
and they came not because of -   Jesus   only,

ἀλλ'   ἵνα   καὶ   τὸν   Λάζαρον   ἴδωσιν   ὃν
but   that   also   -   Lazarus they might see whom

ἤγειρεν   ἐκ   νεκρῶν.   **10** ἐβουλεύσαντο   δὲ
he raised out of [the] dead.   But. took counsel

οἱ   ἀρχιερεῖς   ἵνα   καὶ   τὸν   Λάζαρον
the   chief priests   that   also   -   Lazarus

ἀποκτείνωσιν,   **11** ὅτι   πολλοὶ   δι'   αὐτὸν
they might kill,   because ¹many   ⁴because of ⁵him

ὑπῆγον   τῶν   Ἰουδαίων   καὶ   ἐπίστευον   εἰς
²went   ³of the   ³Jews   and   believed   in

τὸν   Ἰησοῦς.
-    Jesus.

12 Τῇ   ἐπαύριον   ὁ   ὄχλος   πολὺς   ὁ
On the   morrow   the   crowd   much   -

ἐλθὼν   εἰς   τὴν   ἑορτήν,   ἀκούσαντες   ὅτι
coming   to   the   feast,   hearing   that

ἔρχεται   Ἰησοῦς   εἰς   Ἱεροσόλυμα,   **13** ἔλαβον
is(was) coming Jesus   to   Jerusalem,   took

τὰ   βαΐα   τῶν   φοινίκων   καὶ   ἐξῆλθον   εἰς
the branches of the   palm-trees   and   went out   to

ὑπάντησιν   αὐτῷ,   καὶ   ἐκραύγαζον·   ὡσαννά,
a meeting   with him,   and   cried out :   Hosanna,

εὐλογημένος   ὁ   ἐρχόμενος   ἐν   ὀνόματι
being blessed the [one] coming   in [the]   name

---

* This may mean "stole"; *cf.* our euphemism for "steal"—to "lift" a thing.

King of Israel that cometh in the name of the Lord.

14 And Jesus, when he had found a young ass, sat thereon; as it is written,

15 Fear not, daughter of Sion: behold, thy King cometh, sitting on an ass's colt.

16 These things understood not his disciples at the first: but when Jesus was glorified, then remembered they that these things were written of him, and *that* they had done these things unto him.

17 The people therefore that was with him when he called Lazarus out of his grave, and raised him from the dead, bare record.

18 For this cause the people also met him, for that they heard that he had done this miracle.

19 The Pharisees therefore said among themselves, Perceive ye how ye prevail nothing? behold, the world is gone after him.

20 ¶ And there were certain Greeks among them that came up to worship at the feast:

21 The same came therefore to Philip, which was of Bethsaida of Galilee, and desired him, saying, Sir, we would see Jesus.

22 Philip cometh and

κυρίου, καὶ ὁ βασιλεὺς τοῦ Ἰσραήλ.
of [the] Lord, even the king – of Israel.

14 εὑρὼν δὲ ὁ Ἰησοῦς ὀνάριον ἐκάθισεν
And ²having found – ¹Jesus a young ass sat

ἐπ' αὐτό, καθώς ἐστιν γεγραμμένον·
on it, as it is *having been* written :

15 μὴ φοβοῦ, θυγάτηρ Σιών· ἰδοὺ ὁ
Fear not, daughter of Sion : behold[,] the

βασιλεύς σου ἔρχεται, καθήμενος ἐπὶ
king of thee comes, sitting on

πῶλον ὄνου. 16 ταῦτα οὐκ ἔγνωσαν
a foal of an ass. These things knew not

αὐτοῦ οἱ μαθηταὶ τὸ πρῶτον, ἀλλ' ὅτε
of him the disciples at first, but when

ἐδοξάσθη Ἰησοῦς, τότε ἐμνήσθησαν ὅτι
was glorified Jesus, then they remembered that

ταῦτα ἦν ἐπ' αὐτῷ γεγραμμένα καὶ
these things were on him *having been* written and

ταῦτα ἐποίησαν αὐτῷ. 17 ἐμαρτύρει οὖν
these things they did to him. Witnessed therefore

ὁ ὄχλος ὁ ὢν μετ' αὐτοῦ ὅτε τὸν
the crowd – being with him when –

Λάζαρον ἐφώνησεν ἐκ τοῦ μνημείου καὶ
Lazarus he called out of the tomb and

ἤγειρεν αὐτὸν ἐκ νεκρῶν. 18 διὰ τοῦτο
raised him out of [the] dead. Therefore

καὶ ὑπήντησεν αὐτῷ ὁ ὄχλος, ὅτι
also met him the crowd, because

ἤκουσαν τοῦτο αὐτὸν πεποιηκέναι τὸ
¹they heard ⁴this ⁵him ³to have done[b] –

σημεῖον. 19 οἱ οὖν Φαρισαῖοι εἶπαν
⁵sign. Therefore the Pharisees said

πρὸς ἑαυτούς· θεωρεῖτε ὅτι οὐκ ὠφελεῖτε
to themselves : Behold ye that ye profit not

οὐδέν· ἴδε ὁ κόσμος ὀπίσω αὐτοῦ ἀπῆλθεν.
no(any)thing; see[,] the world after him went(is gone).

20 Ἦσαν δὲ Ἕλληνές τινες ἐκ τῶν
Now there were ²Greeks ¹some of the

ἀναβαινόντων ἵνα προσκυνήσωσιν ἐν τῇ
[ones] going up that they might worship at the

ἑορτῇ· 21 οὗτοι οὖν προσῆλθον Φιλίππῳ
feast; these therefore approached *to* Philip

τῷ ἀπὸ Βηθσαϊδὰ τῆς Γαλιλαίας. καὶ
the [one] from Bethsaida – of Galilee, and

ἠρώτων αὐτὸν λέγοντες· κύριε, θέλομεν
asked him saying : Sir, we wish

τὸν Ἰησοῦν ἰδεῖν. 22 ἔρχεται ὁ Φίλιππος
– Jesus to see. Comes – Philip

telleth Andrew: and again Andrew and Philip tell Jesus.

23 ¶ And Jesus answered them, saying, The hour is come, that the Son of man should be glorified.

24 Verily, verily, I say unto you, Except a corn of wheat fall into the ground and die, it abideth alone: but if it die, it bringeth forth much fruit.

25 He that loveth his life shall lose it; and he that hateth his life in this world shall keep it unto life eternal.

26 If any man serve me, let him follow me; and where I am, there shall also my servant be: if any man serve me, him will *my* Father honour.

27 Now is my soul troubled; and what shall I say? Father, save me from this hour: but for this cause came I unto this hour.

28 Father, glorify thy name. Then came there a voice from heaven, *saying*, I have both glorified *it*, and will glorify *it* again.

29 The people therefore, that stood by, and heard *it*, said that it thundered: others said, An angel spake to him.

καὶ λέγει τῷ ᾿Ανδρέᾳ· ἔρχεται ᾿Ανδρέας
and tells - Andrew; comes Andrew

καὶ Φίλιππος καὶ λέγουσιν τῷ ᾿Ιησοῦ.
and Philip and tell - Jesus.

23 ὁ δὲ ᾿Ιησοῦς ἀποκρίνεται αὐτοῖς λέγων·
- And Jesus answers them saying:

ἐλήλυθεν ἡ ὥρα ἵνα δοξασθῇ ὁ υἱὸς τοῦ
Has come the hour that is glorified the Son -

ἀνθρώπου. 24 ἀμὴν ἀμὴν λέγω ὑμῖν,
of man. Truly truly I say to you,

ἐὰν μὴ ὁ κόκκος τοῦ σίτου πεσὼν εἰς
unless the grain - of wheat falling into

τὴν γῆν ἀποθάνῃ, αὐτὸς μόνος μένει·
the ground dies, it alone remains;

ἐὰν δὲ ἀποθάνῃ, πολὺν καρπὸν φέρει.
but if it dies, much fruit it bears.

25 ὁ φιλῶν τὴν ψυχὴν αὐτοῦ ἀπολλύει
The [one] loving the life of him loses

αὐτήν, καὶ ὁ μισῶν τὴν ψυχὴν αὐτοῦ
it, and the [one] hating the life of him

ἐν τῷ κόσμῳ τούτῳ εἰς ζωὴν αἰώνιον
in - world this unto life eternal

φυλάξει αὐτήν. 26 ἐὰν ἐμοί τις διακονῇ,
will keep it. If me anyone serves,

ἐμοὶ ἀκολουθείτω, καὶ ὅπου εἰμὶ ἐγώ,
me let him follow, and where am I,

ἐκεῖ καὶ ὁ διάκονος ὁ ἐμὸς ἔσται·
there also *the* ²servant - ¹my will be;

ἐάν τις ἐμοὶ διακονῇ, τιμήσει αὐτὸν
if anyone me serves, will honour him

ὁ πατήρ. 27 νῦν ἡ ψυχή μου τετάρακται,
the Father. Now the soul of me has been troubled,

καὶ τί εἴπω; πάτερ, σῶσόν με ἐκ
and what may I say? Father, save me out of

τῆς ὥρας ταύτης. ἀλλὰ διὰ τοῦτο ἦλθον
- hour this. But therefore I came

εἰς τὴν ὥραν ταύτην. 28 πάτερ, δόξασόν
to - hour this. Father, glorify

σου τὸ ὄνομα. ἦλθεν οὖν φωνὴ ἐκ
of thee the name. Came therefore a voice out of

τοῦ οὐρανοῦ· καὶ ἐδόξασα καὶ πάλιν
- heaven: Both I glorified and again

δοξάσω. 29 ὁ οὖν ὄχλος ὁ ἑστὼς καὶ
I will glorify. Therefore the crowd - standing and

ἀκούσας ἔλεγεν βροντὴν γεγονέναι· ἄλλοι
hearing said thunder to have happened; others

ἔλεγον· ἄγγελος αὐτῷ λελάληκεν.
said: An angel to him has spoken.

30 Jesus answered and said, This voice came not because of me, but for your sakes.

31 Now is the judgment of this world: now shall the prince of this world be cast out.

32 And I, if I be lifted up from the earth, will draw all *men* unto me.

33 This he said, signifying what death he should die.

34 The people answered him, We have heard out of the law that Christ abideth for ever: and how sayest thou, The Son of man must be lifted up? who is this Son of man?

35 Then Jesus said unto them, Yet a little while is the light with you. Walk while ye have the light, lest darkness come upon you: for he that walketh in darkness knoweth not whither he goeth.

36 While ye have light, believe in the light, that ye may be the children of light. These things spake Jesus, and departed, and did hide himself from them.

37 ¶ But though he had done so many miracles

30 ἀπεκρίθη Ἰησοῦς καὶ εἶπεν· οὐ δι' ἐμὲ
Answered Jesus and said : Not because of me

ἡ φωνὴ αὕτη γέγονεν ἀλλὰ δι' ὑμᾶς.
– voice this has happened but because of you.

31 νῦν κρίσις ἐστὶν τοῦ κόσμου τούτου·
Now judgment is – world of this ;

νῦν ὁ ἄρχων τοῦ κόσμου τούτου
now the ruler – world of this

ἐκβληθήσεται ἔξω· 32 κἀγὼ ἐὰν ὑψωθῶ
shall be cast *out* outside; and I if I am lifted up

ἐκ τῆς γῆς, πάντας ἑλκύσω πρὸς
out of the earth, all men will draw to

ἐμαυτόν. 33 τοῦτο δὲ ἔλεγεν σημαίνων
myself. And this he said signifying

ποίῳ θανάτῳ ἤμελλεν ἀποθνῄσκειν.
by what kind of death he was about to die.

34 ἀπεκρίθη οὖν αὐτῷ ὁ ὄχλος· ἡμεῖς
Answered therefore him the crowd : We

ἠκούσαμεν ἐκ τοῦ νόμου ὅτι ὁ χριστὸς
heard out of the law that the Christ

μένει εἰς τὸν αἰῶνα, καὶ πῶς λέγεις
remains unto the age, and how sayest

σὺ ὅτι δεῖ ὑψωθῆναι τὸν υἱὸν τοῦ
thou that it behoves to be lifted up the Son –

ἀνθρώπου; τίς ἐστιν οὗτος ὁ υἱὸς τοῦ
of man? who is this – Son –

ἀνθρώπου; 35 εἶπεν οὖν αὐτοῖς ὁ Ἰησοῦς·
of man? Said therefore to them – Jesus :

ἔτι μικρὸν χρόνον τὸ φῶς ἐν ὑμῖν
Yet a little time the light among you

ἐστιν. περιπατεῖτε ὡς τὸ φῶς ἔχετε,
is. Walk while the light ye have,

ἵνα μὴ σκοτία ὑμᾶς καταλάβῃ· καὶ
lest darkness you overtakes; and

ὁ περιπατῶν ἐν τῇ σκοτίᾳ οὐκ οἶδεν
the [one] walking in the darkness knows not

ποῦ ὑπάγει. 36 ὡς τὸ φῶς ἔχετε,
where he is going. While the light ye have,

πιστεύετε εἰς τὸ φῶς, ἵνα υἱοὶ φωτὸς
believe in the light, that sons of light

γένησθε.
ye may become.

Ταῦτα ἐλάλησεν Ἰησοῦς, καὶ ἀπελθὼν
These things spoke Jesus, and going away

ἐκρύβη ἀπ' αὐτῶν. 37 Τοσαῦτα δὲ αὐτοῦ
was hidden from them. But so many him

σημεῖα πεποιηκότος ἔμπροσθεν αὐτῶν οὐκ
signs having done[a] before them not

=But while he did so many signs

before them, yet they believed not on him:

38 That the saying of Esaias the prophet might be fulfilled, which he spake, Lord, who hath believed our report? and to whom hath the arm of the Lord been revealed?

39 Therefore they could not believe, because that Esaias said again,

40 He hath blinded their eyes, and hardened their heart; that they should not see with *their* eyes, nor understand with *their* heart, and be converted, and I should heal them.

41 These things said Esaias, when he saw his glory, and spake of him.

42 ¶ Nevertheless among the chief rulers also many believed on him; but because of the Pharisees they did not confess *him*, lest they should be put out of the synagogue:

43 For they loved the praise of men more than the praise of God.

44 ¶ Jesus cried and said, He that believeth on me, believeth not on me, but on him that sent me.

45 And he that seeth me seeth him that sent me.

46 I am come a light into the world, that whosoever believeth on me

ἐπίστευον   εἰς   αὐτόν,   **38** ἵνα   ὁ   λόγος
they believed   in   him,   that   the   word

'Ησαΐου   τοῦ   προφήτου   πληρωθῇ   ὃν
of Esaias   the   prophet   might be fulfilled   which

εἶπεν·   κύριε,   τίς   ἐπίστευσεν   τῇ   ἀκοῇ
he said :   Lord,   who   believed   the   report

ἡμῶν;   καὶ   ὁ   βραχίων   κυρίου   τίνι
of us?   and   the   arm   of [the] Lord   to whom

ἀπεκαλύφθη;   **39** διὰ   τοῦτο   οὐκ   ἠδύναντο
was it revealed?   Therefore   they could not

πιστεύειν,   ὅτι   πάλιν   εἶπεν   'Ησαΐας·
to believe,   because   again   said   Esaias :

40 τετύφλωκεν   αὐτῶν   τοὺς   ὀφθαλμοὺς   καὶ
He has blinded   of them   the   eyes   and

ἐπώρωσεν   αὐτῶν   τὴν   καρδίαν,   ἵνα
hardened   of them   the   heart,   that

μὴ   ἴδωσιν   τοῖς   ὀφθαλμοῖς   καὶ   νοήσωσιν
they might not see   with the   eyes   and   understand

τῇ   καρδίᾳ   καὶ   στραφῶσιν,   καὶ   ἰάσομαι
with the heart   and   might turn,   and   I will cure

αὐτούς.   **41** ταῦτα   εἶπεν   'Ησαΐας   ὅτι
them.   These things   said   Esaias   because

εἶδεν   τὴν   δόξαν   αὐτοῦ,   καὶ   ἐλάλησεν
he saw   the   glory   of him,   and   spoke

περὶ   αὐτοῦ.   **42** ὅμως   μέντοι   καὶ   ἐκ
about   him.   Nevertheless   however   even   of

τῶν   ἀρχόντων   πολλοὶ   ἐπίστευσαν   εἰς   αὐτόν,
the   rulers   many   believed   in   him,

ἀλλὰ   διὰ   τοὺς   Φαρισαίους   οὐχ   ὡμολόγουν,
but because of the   Pharisees   did not confess,

ἵνα   μὴ   ἀποσυνάγωγοι   γένωνται·
lest   put out of [the] synagogue   they should become;

43 ἠγάπησαν   γὰρ   τὴν   δόξαν   τῶν   ἀνθρώπων
for they loved   the   glory   –   of men

μᾶλλον   ἤπερ   τὴν   δόξαν   τοῦ   θεοῦ.
more   than   the   glory   –   of God.

44 'Ιησοῦς   δὲ   ἔκραξεν   καὶ   εἶπεν·   The
But Jesus   cried out   and   said :   The

πιστεύων   εἰς   ἐμὲ   οὐ   πιστεύει   εἰς   ἐμὲ
[one] believing   in   me   believes not   in   me

ἀλλὰ   εἰς   τὸν   πέμψαντά   με,   **45** καὶ   ὁ
but   in   the [one] having sent   me,   and   the

θεωρῶν   ἐμὲ   θεωρεῖ   τὸν   πέμψαντά   με.
[one] beholding me   beholds   the [one] having sent   me.

46 ἐγὼ   φῶς   εἰς   τὸν   κόσμον   ἐλήλυθα,
I   a light   into   the   world   have come,

ἵνα   πᾶς   ὁ   πιστεύων   εἰς   ἐμὲ   ἐν   τῇ
that   everyone   believing   in   me   in   the

should not abide in darkness.

σκοτίᾳ   μὴ   μείνῃ.   47 καὶ   ἐάν   τίς   μου
darkness   may not remain.   And   if   anyone of me

47 And if any man hear my words, and believe not, I judge him not: for I came not to judge the world, but to save the world.

ἀκούσῃ   τῶν   ῥημάτων   καὶ   μὴ   φυλάξῃ,
hears   the   words   and   keeps not,

ἐγὼ   οὐ   κρίνω   αὐτόν·   οὐ   γὰρ   ἦλθον
I   do not judge   him;   for I came not

ἵνα   κρίνω   τὸν   κόσμον,   ἀλλ' ἵνα   σώσω
that I might judge the   world,   but   that I might save

48 He that rejecteth me, and receiveth not my words, hath one that judgeth him: the word that I have spoken, the same shall judge him in the last day.

τὸν   κόσμον.   48 ὁ   ἀθετῶν   ἐμὲ   καὶ   μὴ
the world.   The [one] rejecting   me   and   not

λαμβάνων   τὰ   ῥήματά   μου   ἔχει   τὸν
receiving   the   words   of me   has   the

κρίνοντα   αὐτόν·   ὁ   λόγος   ὃν   ἐλάλησα,
[one] judging   him;   the   word   which   I spoke,

ἐκεῖνος   κρινεῖ   αὐτὸν   ἐν   τῇ   ἐσχάτῃ   ἡμέρᾳ.
that   will judge   him   in   the   last   day.

49 For I have not spoken of myself; but the Father which sent me, he gave me a commandment, what I should say, and what I should speak.

49 ὅτι   ἐγὼ   ἐξ   ἐμαυτοῦ   οὐκ   ἐλάλησα,
Because I   of   myself   did not speak,

ἀλλ'   ὁ   πέμψας   με   πατὴρ   αὐτός   μοι
but   ¹the   ³having sent   ⁴me   ²Father   ⁵he   ⁷me

ἐντολὴν   δέδωκεν   τί   εἴπω   καὶ   τί
⁶commandment   ⁶has given   what   I may say   and   what

50 And I know that his commandment is life everlasting: whatsoever I speak therefore, even as the Father said unto me, so I speak.

λαλήσω.   50 καὶ   οἶδα   ὅτι   ἡ   ἐντολὴ
I may speak.   And   I know   that   the commandment

αὐτοῦ   ζωὴ   αἰώνιός   ἐστιν.   ἃ   οὖν   ἐγὼ
of him   life   eternal   is.   What things therefore I

λαλῶ,   καθὼς   εἴρηκέν   μοι   ὁ   πατήρ,
speak,   as   has said   to me   the   Father,

οὕτως   λαλῶ.
so   I speak.

CHAPTER 13

NOW before the feast of the passover, when Jesus knew that his hour was come that he should depart out of this world unto the Father, having loved his own which were in the world, he loved them unto the end.

13 Πρὸ   δὲ   τῆς   ἑορτῆς   τοῦ   πάσχα
Now before   the   feast   of the   Passover

εἰδὼς   ὁ   Ἰησοῦς   ὅτι   ἦλθεν   αὐτοῦ   ἡ
²knowing –   ¹Jesus   that   came   of him   the

ὥρα   ἵνα   μεταβῇ   ἐκ   τοῦ   κόσμου   τούτου
hour   that he should remove out of –   world   this

πρὸς   τὸν   πατέρα,   ἀγαπήσας   τοὺς   ἰδίους
to   the   Father,   loving   the(his)   own

τοὺς   ἐν   τῷ   κόσμῳ,   εἰς   τέλος   ἠγάπησεν
–   in   the   world,   to [the] end   he loved

2 And supper being ended, the devil having now put into the heart of Judas Iscariot, Simon's son, to betray him;

αὐτούς.   2 καὶ   δείπνου   γινομένου,   τοῦ
them.   And   supper   taking place,ᵃ   the
                                    =during supper,

διαβόλου   ἤδη   βεβληκότος   εἰς   τὴν   καρδίαν
devil   now   having putᵃ   into   the   heart
=as the devil had now put

ἵνα   παραδοῖ   αὐτὸν   Ἰούδας   Σίμωνος
that   ⁶should betray   ⁵him   ¹Judas   ³[son] of Simon

3 Jesus knowing that the Father had given all things into his hands, and that he was come from God, and went to God;

4 He riseth from supper, and laid aside his garments; and took a towel, and girded himself.

5 After that he poureth water into a bason, and began to wash the disciples' feet, and to wipe *them* with the towel wherewith he was girded.

6 Then cometh he to Simon Peter: and Peter saith unto him, Lord, dost thou wash my feet?

7 Jesus answered and said unto him, What I do thou knowest not now; but thou shalt know hereafter.

8 Peter saith unto him, Thou shalt never wash my feet. Jesus answered him, If I wash thee not, thou hast no part with me.

9 Simon Peter saith unto him, Lord, not my feet only, but also *my* hands and *my* head.

10 Jesus saith to him, He that is washed needeth not save to wash *his* feet, but is clean every whit: and ye are clean, but not all.

'Ισκαριώτης, 3 εἰδὼς ὅτι πάντα ἔδωκεν
²Iscariot,   knowing* that all things gave

αὐτῷ ὁ πατὴρ εἰς τὰς χεῖρας, καὶ
him the Father into the(his) hands, and

ὅτι ἀπὸ θεοῦ ἐξῆλθεν καὶ πρὸς τὸν
that from God he came forth and to –

θεὸν ὑπάγει, 4 ἐγείρεται ἐκ τοῦ δείπνου
God goes, he rises out of(from) the supper

καὶ τίθησιν τὰ ἱμάτια, καὶ λαβὼν
and places [aside] the(his) garments, and taking

λέντιον διέζωσεν ἑαυτόν· 5 εἶτα βάλλει
a towel he girded himself; then he puts

ὕδωρ εἰς τὸν νιπτῆρα, καὶ ἤρξατο νίπτειν
water into the basin, and began to wash

τοὺς πόδας τῶν μαθητῶν καὶ ἐκμάσσειν
the feet of the disciples and to wipe off

τῷ λεντίῳ ᾧ ἦν διεζωσμένος.
with the towel with which he was *having been* girded.

6 ἔρχεται οὖν πρὸς Σίμωνα Πέτρον·
He comes therefore to Simon Peter:

λέγει αὐτῷ· κύριε, σύ μου νίπτεις τοὺς
he says to him: Lord, thou of me washest the

πόδας; 7 ἀπεκρίθη Ἰησοῦς καὶ εἶπεν αὐτῷ·
feet? Answered Jesus and said to him:

ὃ ἐγὼ ποιῶ σὺ οὐκ οἶδας ἄρτι,
What I am doing thou knowest not yet,

γνώσῃ δὲ μετὰ ταῦτα. 8 λέγει αὐτῷ
but thou wilt know after these things. Says to him

Πέτρος· οὐ μὴ νίψῃς μου τοὺς πόδας
Peter: By no means shalt thou wash of me the feet

εἰς τὸν αἰῶνα. ἀπεκρίθη Ἰησοῦς αὐτῷ·
unto the age. ²Answered ¹Jesus ³him:

ἐὰν μὴ νίψω σε, οὐκ ἔχεις μέρος μετ'
Unless I wash thee, thou hast no part with

ἐμοῦ. 9 λέγει αὐτῷ Σίμων Πέτρος·
me. Says to him Simon Peter:

κύριε, μὴ τοὺς πόδας μου μόνον ἀλλὰ
Lord, not the feet of me only but

καὶ τὰς χεῖρας καὶ τὴν κεφαλήν. 10 λέγει
also the hands and the head. Says

αὐτῷ Ἰησοῦς· ὁ λελουμένος οὐκ ἔχει
to him Jesus: The [one] having been bathed has not

χρείαν [εἰ μὴ τοὺς πόδας] νίψασθαι,
need except the feet to wash,

ἀλλ' ἔστιν καθαρὸς ὅλος· καὶ ὑμεῖς
but is clean wholly; and ye

καθαροί ἐστε, ἀλλ' οὐχὶ πάντες. 11 ᾔδει
clean are, but not all. he knew

* Repeated from ver. 1; the subject is therefore again "Jesus".

11 For he knew who should betray him; therefore said he, Ye are not all clean.

12 So after he had washed their feet, and had taken his garments, and was set down again, he said unto them, Know ye what I have done to you?

13 Ye call me Master and Lord: and ye say well; for so I am.

14 If I then, your Lord and Master, have washed your feet; ye also ought to wash one another's feet.

15 For I have given you an example, that ye should do as I have done to you.

16 Verily, verily, I say unto you, The servant is not greater than his lord; neither he that is sent greater than he that sent him.

17 If ye know these things, happy are ye if ye do them.

18 ¶ I speak not of you all: I know whom I have chosen: but that the scripture may be fulfilled, He that eateth bread with me hath lifted up his heel against me.

19 Now I tell you before it come, that, when it is come to pass, ye may believe that I am he.

20 Verily, verily, I say

γὰρ τὸν παραδιδόντα αὐτόν· διὰ τοῦτο
For   the [one] betraying   him;   therefore

εἶπεν ὅτι οὐχὶ πάντες καθαροί ἐστε.
he said[,] –   Not   all   clean   ye are.

12 Ὅτε οὖν ἔνιψεν τοὺς πόδας αὐτῶν
When therefore he washed the feet of them

καὶ ἔλαβεν τὰ ἱμάτια αὐτοῦ καὶ ἀνέπεσεν
and took the garments of him and reclined

πάλιν, εἶπεν αὐτοῖς· γινώσκετε τί πε-
again, he said to them : Do ye know what I

ποίηκα ὑμῖν; 13 ὑμεῖς φωνεῖτέ με· ὁ
have done to you? Ye call me : The

διδάσκαλος καὶ ὁ κύριος, καὶ καλῶς
Teacher and the Lord, and well

λέγετε· εἰμὶ γάρ. 14 εἰ οὖν ἐγὼ ἔνιψα
ye say; for I am. If therefore I washed

ὑμῶν τοὺς πόδας ὁ κύριος καὶ ὁ
of you the feet the Lord and the

διδάσκαλος, καὶ ὑμεῖς ὀφείλετε ἀλλήλων
Teacher, also ye ought of one another

νίπτειν τοὺς πόδας· 15 ὑπόδειγμα γὰρ
to wash the feet; for an example

ἔδωκα ὑμῖν ἵνα καθὼς ἐγὼ ἐποίησα
I gave you that as I did

ὑμῖν καὶ ὑμεῖς ποιῆτε. 16 ἀμὴν ἀμὴν
to you also ye may do. Truly truly

λέγω ὑμῖν, οὐκ ἔστιν δοῦλος μείζων
I tell you, is not a slave greater [than]

τοῦ κυρίου αὐτοῦ, οὐδὲ ἀπόστολος μείζων
the lord of him, nor a sent one greater [than]

τοῦ πέμψαντος αὐτόν. 17 εἰ ταῦτα
the [one] sending him. If these things

οἴδατε, μακάριοί ἐστε ἐὰν ποιῆτε αὐτά.
ye know, blessed are ye if ye do them.

18 Οὐ περὶ πάντων ὑμῶν λέγω· ἐγὼ
Not concerning ²all ¹you I speak; I

οἶδα τίνας ἐξελεξάμην· ἀλλ’ ἵνα ἡ
know whom I chose; but that the

γραφὴ πληρωθῇ· ὁ τρώγων μου τὸν
scripture may be fulfilled : The [one] eating of me the

ἄρτον ἐπῆρεν ἐπ’ ἐμὲ τὴν πτέρναν αὐτοῦ.
bread lifted up against me the heel of him.

19 ἀπ’ ἄρτι λέγω ὑμῖν πρὸ τοῦ γενέσθαι,
From now I tell you before the to happen,
=it happens,

ἵνα πιστεύητε ὅταν γένηται ὅτι ἐγώ
that ye may believe when it happens that I

εἰμι. 20 ἀμὴν ἀμὴν λέγω ὑμῖν, ὁ
am. Truly truly I say to you, the

unto you, He that receiveth whomsoever I send receiveth me; and he that receiveth me receiveth him that sent me.

21 When Jesus had thus said, he was troubled in spirit, and testified, and said, Verily, verily, I say unto you, that one of you shall betray me.

22 Then the disciples looked one on another, doubting of whom he spake.

23 Now there was leaning on Jesus' bosom one of his disciples, whom Jesus loved.

24 Simon Peter therefore beckoned to him, that he should ask who it should be of whom he spake.

25 He then lying on Jesus' breast saith unto him, Lord, who is it?

26 Jesus answered, He it is, to whom I shall give a sop, when I have dipped *it*. And when he had dipped the sop, he gave *it* to Judas Iscariot, *the son* of Simon.

27 And after the sop Satan entered into him. Then said Jesus unto him, That thou doest, do quickly.

28 Now no man at the table knew for what intent he spake this unto him.

29 For some *of them*

λαμβάνων ἄν τινα πέμψω ἐμὲ λαμβάνει,
[one] receiving᾿ whomever I may send me receives,

ὁ δὲ ἐμὲ λαμβάνων λαμβάνει τὸν
and the [one] me receiving receives the [one]

πέμψαντά με. 21 ταῦτα εἰπὼν Ἰησοῦς
having sent me. These things saying Jesus

ἐταράχθη τῷ πνεύματι καὶ ἐμαρτύρησεν
was troubled in the(his) spirit and witnessed

καὶ εἶπεν· ἀμὴν ἀμὴν λέγω ὑμῖν ὅτι
and said : Truly truly I tell you that

εἷς ἐξ ὑμῶν παραδώσει με. 22 ἔβλεπον
one of you will betray me. Looked

εἰς ἀλλήλους οἱ μαθηταὶ ἀπορούμενοι περὶ
at one another the disciples being perplexed about

τίνος λέγει. 23 ἦν ἀνακείμενος εἷς ἐκ
whom he speaks. Was reclining one of

τῶν μαθητῶν αὐτοῦ ἐν τῷ κόλπῳ τοῦ
the disciples of him in the bosom -

Ἰησοῦ, ὃν ἠγάπα ὁ Ἰησοῦς· 24 νεύει
of Jesus, whom ᵃloved - ¹Jesus; nods

οὖν τούτῳ Σίμων Πέτρος καὶ λέγει
therefore to this one Simon Peter and says

αὐτῷ· εἰπὲ τίς ἐστιν περὶ οὗ λέγει.
to him : Say who it is about whom he speaks.

25 ἀναπεσὼν ἐκεῖνος οὕτως ἐπὶ τὸ
Falling back that one thus on the

στῆθος τοῦ Ἰησοῦ λέγει αὐτῷ· κύριε,
breast of Jesus he says to him : Lord,

τίς ἐστιν; 26 ἀποκρίνεται οὖν ὁ Ἰησοῦς·
who is it? Answers therefore - Jesus :

ἐκεῖνός ἐστιν ᾧ ἐγὼ βάψω τὸ ψωμίον
That one it is to whom I shall dip the morsel

καὶ δώσω αὐτῷ. βάψας οὖν [τὸ]
and shall give him. Dipping therefore the

ψωμίον λαμβάνει καὶ δίδωσιν Ἰούδα
morsel he takes and gives to Judas

Σίμωνος Ἰσκαριώτου. 27 καὶ μετὰ τὸ
[son] of Simon Iscariot. And after the

ψωμίον τότε εἰσῆλθεν εἰς ἐκεῖνον ὁ
morsel then entered into that one -

σατανᾶς. λέγει οὖν αὐτῷ Ἰησοῦς· ὁ
Satan. Says therefore to him Jesus : What

ποιεῖς ποίησον τάχιον. 28 τοῦτο [δὲ]
thou doest do quickly. But this

οὐδεὶς ἔγνω τῶν ἀνακειμένων πρὸς τί
no one knew of the [ones] reclining for what

εἶπεν αὐτῷ· 29 τινὲς γὰρ ἐδόκουν, ἐπεὶ
he told him; for some thought, since

thought, because Judas had the bag, that Jesus had said unto him, Buy *those things* that we have need of against the feast; or, that he should give something to the poor.

30 He then having received the sop went immediately out: and it was night.

31 ¶ Therefore, when he was gone out, Jesus said, Now is the Son of man glorified, and God is glorified in him.

32 If God be glorified in him, God shall also glorify him in himself, and shall straightway glorify him.

33 Little children, yet a little while I am with you. Ye shall seek me: and as I said unto the Jews, Whither I go, ye cannot come; so now I say to you.

34 A new commandment I give unto you, That ye love one another; as I have loved you, that ye also love one another.

35 By this shall all *men* know that ye are my disciples, if ye have love one to another.

36 ¶ Simon Peter said unto him, Lord, whither goest thou? Jesus answered him, Whither I go, thou canst not follow me now; but thou shalt follow me afterwards.

τὸ γλωσσόκομον εἶχεν Ἰούδας, ὅτι λέγει
²the   ⁴bag   ³had ¹Judas, that tells

αὐτῷ Ἰησοῦς· ἀγόρασον ὧν χρείαν
him   Jesus :   Buy [the] things of which need

ἔχομεν εἰς τὴν ἑορτήν, ἢ τοῖς πτωχοῖς
we have for the   feast,   or to the   poor

ἵνα τι δῷ.   30 λαβὼν οὖν τὸ
that something he should give. Having taken therefore the

ψωμίον ἐκεῖνος ἐξῆλθεν εὐθύς· ἦν δὲ
morsel that one went out immediately; and it was

νύξ.
night.

31 Ὅτε οὖν ἐξῆλθεν, λέγει Ἰησοῦς·
When therefore he went out, says   Jesus :

νῦν ἐδοξάσθη ὁ υἱὸς τοῦ ἀνθρώπου,
Now was(is) glorified the Son -   of man,

καὶ ὁ θεὸς ἐδοξάσθη ἐν αὐτῷ· 32 εἰ
and - God was(is) glorified in him; if

ὁ θεὸς ἐδοξάσθη ἐν αὐτῷ, καὶ ὁ θεὸς
- God was(is) glorified in him, both - God

δοξάσει αὐτὸν ἐν αὐτῷ, καὶ εὐθὺς
will glorify him   in him, and immediately

δοξάσει αὐτόν. 33 τεκνία, ἔτι μικρὸν
will glorify him.   Children, yet a little while

μεθ᾽ ὑμῶν εἰμι· ζητήσετέ με, καὶ καθὼς
with you I am; ye will seek me, and as

εἶπον τοῖς Ἰουδαίοις ὅτι ὅπου ἐγὼ
I said to the   Jews   that where   I

ὑπάγω ὑμεῖς οὐ δύνασθε ἐλθεῖν, καὶ
go   ye cannot   o come, also

ὑμῖν λέγω ἄρτι. 34 Ἐντολὴν καινὴν
to you I say now.   commandment A new

δίδωμι ὑμῖν, ἵνα ἀγαπᾶτε ἀλλήλους,
I give you, that ye love   one another,

καθὼς ἠγάπησα ὑμᾶς ἵνα καὶ ὑμεῖς
as   I loved   you that also   ye

ἀγαπᾶτε ἀλλήλους. 35 ἐν τούτῳ γνώσονται
love   one another.   By this   will know

πάντες ὅτι ἐμοὶ μαθηταί ἐστε, ἐὰν
all men that to meᵉ disciples ye are, if

ἀγάπην ἔχητε ἐν ἀλλήλοις. 36 Λέγει
love   ye have among one another.   Says

αὐτῷ Σίμων Πέτρος· κύριε, ποῦ ὑπάγεις;
to him Simon   Peter :   Lord, where goest thou?

ἀπεκρίθη Ἰησοῦς· ὅπου ὑπάγω οὐ δύνασαί
Answered Jesus : Where I go thou canst not

μοι νῦν ἀκολουθῆσαι, ἀκολουθήσεις δὲ
me now   to follow,   but thou wilt follow

37 Peter said unto him, Lord, why cannot I follow thee now? I will lay down my life for thy sake.

38 Jesus answered him, Wilt thou lay down thy life for my sake? Verily, verily, I say unto thee, The cock shall not crow, till thou hast denied me thrice.

CHAPTER 14

LET not your heart be troubled: ye believe in God, believe also in me.

2 In my Father's house are many mansions: if *it were* not *so*, I would have told you. I go to prepare a place for you.

3 And if I go and prepare a place for you, I will come again, and receive you unto myself; that where I am, *there* ye may be also.

4 And whither I go ye know, and the way ye know.

5 ¶ Thomas saith unto him, Lord, we know not whither thou goest; and how can we know the way?

6 Jesus saith unto him, I am the way, the truth, and the life: no man cometh unto the Father, but by me.

7 If ye had known me, ye should have known my Father also: and from henceforth ye know him, and have seen him.

8 ¶ Philip saith unto

ὕστερον. **37** λέγει αὐτῷ [ὁ] Πέτρος·
later.   Says   to him   – Peter :

κύριε, διὰ τί οὐ δύναμαί σοι ἀκολουθῆσαι
Lord,   why   can I not   thee   to follow

ἄρτι; τὴν ψυχήν μου ὑπὲρ σοῦ θήσω.
yet? the   life   of me   for   thee I will lay down.

38 ἀποκρίνεται Ἰησοῦς· τὴν ψυχήν σου
Answers   Jesus :   The   life   of thee

ὑπὲρ ἐμοῦ θήσεις; ἀμὴν ἀμὴν λέγω
for   me   wilt thou lay down? truly truly   I tell

σοι, οὐ μὴ ἀλέκτωρ φωνήσῃ ἕως οὗ
thee, by no means a cock   crows   until

ἀρνήσῃ με τρίς. **14** Μὴ ταρασσέσθω
thou deniest me thrice.   Let not be troubled

ὑμῶν ἡ καρδία· πιστεύετε εἰς τὸν θεόν, καὶ
of you the heart;   believe in – God, also

εἰς ἐμὲ πιστεύετε. **2** ἐν τῇ οἰκίᾳ τοῦ
in   me   believe.   In   the   house of the

πατρός μου μοναὶ πολλαί εἰσιν· εἰ δὲ μή,
Father of me abodes many there are; otherwise,

εἶπον ἂν ὑμῖν· ὅτι πορεύομαι ἑτοιμάσαι
I would have told you; because I go to prepare

τόπον ὑμῖν· **3** καὶ ἐὰν πορευθῶ καὶ
a place for you;   and   if   I go   and

ἑτοιμάσω τόπον ὑμῖν, πάλιν ἔρχομαι καὶ
prepare a place for you, again   I come   and

παραλήμψομαι ὑμᾶς πρὸς ἐμαυτόν, ἵνα
will receive   you   to   myself,   that

ὅπου εἰμὶ ἐγὼ καὶ ὑμεῖς ἦτε. **4** Καὶ
where am I   also   ye may be.   And

ὅπου ἐγὼ ὑπάγω οἴδατε τὴν ὁδόν.
where I   go ye know the   way.

5 λέγει αὐτῷ Θωμᾶς· κύριε, οὐκ οἴδαμεν
Says to him Thomas : Lord, we know not

ποῦ ὑπάγεις· πῶς οἴδαμεν τὴν ὁδόν;
where thou goest; how do we know the   way?

6 λέγει αὐτῷ Ἰησοῦς· ἐγώ εἰμι ἡ ὁδὸς
Says to him Jesus : I am the way

καὶ ἡ ἀλήθεια καὶ ἡ ζωή· οὐδεὶς ἔρχεται
and the truth and the life; no one comes

πρὸς τὸν πατέρα εἰ μὴ δι' ἐμοῦ. **7** εἰ
to   the   Father   except through me.   If

ἐγνώκειτέ με, καὶ τὸν πατέρα μου
ye had known me, also the Father of me

ἂν ᾔδειτε. ἀπ' ἄρτι γινώσκετε αὐτὸν
ye would have known. From now ye know   him

καὶ ἑωράκατε. **8** Λέγει αὐτῷ Φίλιππος·
and   have seen.   Says   to him   Philip:

him, Lord, shew us the Father, and it sufficeth us.

9 Jesus saith unto him, Have I been so long time with you, and yet hast thou not known me, Philip? he that hath seen me hath seen the Father; and how sayest thou *then*, Shew us the Father?

10 Believest thou not that I am in the Father, and the Father in me? the words that I speak unto you I speak not of myself: but the Father that dwelleth in me, he doeth the works.

11 Believe me that I *am* in the Father, and the Father in me: or else believe me for the very works' sake.

12 Verily, verily, I say unto you, He that believeth on me, the works that I do shall he do also; and greater *works* than these shall he do; because I go unto my Father.

13 And whatsoever ye shall ask in my name, that will I do, that the Father may be glorified in the Son.

14 If ye shall ask anything in my name, I will do *it*.

15 ¶ If ye love me, keep my commandments.

16 And I will pray the Father, and he shall give you another Comforter, that he may abide with you for ever;

κύριε,   δεῖξον   ἡμῖν   τὸν   πατέρα,   καὶ
Lord,   show   us   the   Father,   and

ἀρκεῖ ἡμῖν.   **9** λέγει   αὐτῷ   ὁ   Ἰησοῦς·
it suffices for us.   Says   to him   –   Jesus:

τοσοῦτον   χρόνον   μεθ'   ὑμῶν   εἰμι   καὶ
So long   time   with   you   I am   and

οὐκ   ἔγνωκάς   με,   Φίλιππε;   ὁ   ἑωρακὼς
thou hast not known me,   Philip?   The [one] having seen

ἐμὲ   ἑώρακεν   τὸν   πατέρα·   πῶς   σὺ   λέγεις·
me   has seen   the   Father;   how   thou   sayest:

δεῖξον   ἡμῖν   τὸν   πατέρα;   **10** οὐ   πιστεύεις
Show   us   the   Father?   believest thou not

ὅτι   ἐγὼ   ἐν   τῷ   πατρὶ   καὶ   ὁ   πατὴρ
that   I   in   the   Father   and   the   Father

ἐν   ἐμοί   ἐστιν;   τὰ   ῥήματα   ἃ   ἐγὼ   λέγω
in   me   is?   the   words   which   I   say

ὑμῖν   ἀπ'   ἐμαυτοῦ   οὐ   λαλῶ·   ὁ   δὲ   πατὴρ
to you   from   myself   I speak not;   but the   Father

ἐν   ἐμοὶ   μένων   ποιεῖ   τὰ   ἔργα   αὐτοῦ.
in   me   remaining   does   the   works   of him.

11 πιστεύετέ   μοι   ὅτι   ἐγὼ   ἐν   τῷ   πατρὶ
Believe ye   me   that   I   in   the   Father

καὶ   ὁ   πατὴρ   ἐν   ἐμοί·   εἰ   δὲ   μή,   διὰ
and   the   Father   in   me;   otherwise,   because of

τὰ   ἔργα   αὐτὰ   πιστεύετε.   **12** ἀμὴν   ἀμὴν
the   works [them]selves   believe ye.   Truly   truly

λέγω   ὑμῖν,   ὁ   πιστεύων   εἰς   ἐμὲ   τὰ
I tell   you,   the [one]   believing   in   me   the

ἔργα   ἃ   ἐγὼ   ποιῶ   κἀκεῖνος   ποιήσει,
works   which   I   do   that one also   will do,

καὶ   μείζονα   τούτων   ποιήσει,   ὅτι   ἐγὼ
and   greater [than]   these   he will do,   because   I

πρὸς   τὸν   πατέρα   πορεύομαι·   **13** καὶ   ὅ τι
to   the   Father   am going;   and   what-

ἂν   αἰτήσητε   ἐν   τῷ   ὀνόματί   μου,   τοῦτο
ever   ye ask   in   the   name   of me,   this

ποιήσω,   ἵνα   δοξασθῇ   ὁ   πατὴρ   ἐν   τῷ
I will do,   that may be glorified   the   Father   in   the

υἱῷ.   **14** ἐάν   τι   αἰτήσητέ   με   ἐν   τῷ
Son.   If   anything   ye ask   me   in   the

ὀνόματί   μου,   ἐγὼ   ποιήσω.   **15** Ἐὰν
name   of me,   I   will do.   If

ἀγαπᾶτέ   με,   τὰς   ἐντολὰς   τὰς   ἐμὰς
ye love   me,   *the* ²commandments   –   ¹my

τηρήσετε.   **16** κἀγὼ   ἐρωτήσω   τὸν   πατέρα
ye will keep.   And I   will request   the   Father

καὶ   ἄλλον   παράκλητον   δώσει   ὑμῖν,   ἵνα
and   another   Comforter   he will give   you,   that

17 *Even* the Spirit of
truth; whom the world
cannot receive, because it
seeth him not, neither
knoweth him: but ye
know him; for he dwelleth
with you, and shall be in
you.
18 I will not leave you
comfortless: I will come
to you.
19 Yet a little while,
and the world seeth me
no more; but ye see me:
because I live, ye shall
live also.
20 At that day ye shall
know that I *am* in my
Father, and ye in me, and
I in you.
21 He that hath my
commandments, and keep-
eth them, he it is that
loveth me: and he that
loveth me shall be loved of
my Father, and I will love
him, and will manifest
myself to him.
22 Judas saith unto him,
not Iscariot, Lord, how
is it that thou wilt manifest thyself unto us, and
not unto the world?
23 Jesus answered and
said unto him, If a man
love me, he will keep my
words: and my Father
will love him, and we will

ᾗ   μεθ'   ὑμῶν   εἰς   τὸν   αἰῶνα,   17 τὸ
he may be with   you   unto   the   age,   the
πνεῦμα   τῆς   ἀληθείας,   ὃ   ὁ   κόσμος
Spirit   —   of truth,   which* the   world
οὐ   δύναται   λαβεῖν,   ὅτι   οὐ   θεωρεῖ   αὐτὸ
cannot   to receive, because   it beholds not   it*
οὐδὲ   γινώσκει·   ὑμεῖς   γινώσκετε   αὐτό,
nor   knows;   ye   know   it,*
ὅτι   παρ'   ὑμῖν   μένει   καὶ   ἐν   ὑμῖν   ἔσται.
because with   you   he remains and   in   you   will be.
18 Οὐκ   ἀφήσω   ὑμᾶς   ὀρφανούς,   ἔρχομαι
I will not leave   you   orphans,   I am coming
πρὸς   ὑμᾶς.   19 ἔτι   μικρὸν   καὶ   ὁ   κόσμος
to   you.   Yet   a little   and   the   world
με   οὐκέτι   θεωρεῖ,   ὑμεῖς   δὲ   θεωρεῖτέ
me   no longer   beholds,   but ye   behold
με,   ὅτι   ἐγὼ   ζῶ   καὶ   ὑμεῖς   ζήσετε.
me,   because   I   live   also   ye   will live.
20 ἐν   ἐκείνῃ   τῇ   ἡμέρᾳ   γνώσεσθε   ὑμεῖς
In   that   —   day   will know   ye
ὅτι   ἐγὼ   ἐν   τῷ   πατρί   μου   καὶ   ὑμεῖς
that   I   in   the   Father   of me   and   ye
ἐν   ἐμοὶ   κἀγὼ   ἐν   ὑμῖν.   21 Ὁ   ἔχων
in   me   and I   in   you.   The [one] having
τὰς   ἐντολάς   μου   καὶ   τηρῶν   αὐτάς,
the   commandments   of me   and   keeping   them,
ἐκεῖνός   ἐστιν   ὁ   ἀγαπῶν   με·   ὁ   δὲ   ἀγαπῶν
that   is   the [one] loving   me;   and the [one] loving
με   ἀγαπηθήσεται   ὑπὸ   τοῦ   πατρός   μου,
me   will be loved   by   the   Father   of me,
κἀγὼ   ἀγαπήσω   αὐτὸν   καὶ   ἐμφανίσω   αὐτῷ
and I   will love   him   and   will manifest   to him
ἐμαυτόν.   22 λέγει   αὐτῷ   Ἰούδας,   οὐχ
myself.   Says   to him   Judas,   not
ὁ   Ἰσκαριώτης·   κύριε,   καὶ   τί   γέγονεν
the   Iscariot :   Lord,   and   what has happened
ὅτι   ἡμῖν   μέλλεις   ἐμφανίζειν   σεαυτὸν   καὶ
that   to us thou art about   to manifest   thyself   and
οὐχὶ   τῷ   κόσμῳ;   23 ἀπεκρίθη   Ἰησοῦς
not   to the   world?   Answered   Jesus
καὶ   εἶπεν   αὐτῷ·   ἐάν   τις   ἀγαπᾷ   με,
and   said   to him :   If   anyone   loves   me,
τὸν   λόγον   μου   τηρήσει,   καὶ   ὁ   πατήρ
the   word   of me   he will keep,   and   the   Father
μου   ἀγαπήσει   αὐτόν,   καὶ   πρὸς   αὐτὸν
of me   will love   him,   and   to   him

* The gender of these pronouns agrees, of course, with the antecedent πνεῦμα (neuter); and this has been kept though the personal
Spirit of God is meant. Elsewhere, masculine pronouns are in
fact used.

come unto him, and make our abode with him.

24 He that loveth me not keepeth not my sayings: and the word which ye hear is not mine, but the Father's which sent me.

25 These things have I spoken unto you, being *yet* present with you.

26 But the Comforter, *which is* the Holy Ghost, whom the Father will send in my name, he shall teach you all things, and bring all things to your remembrance, whatsoever I have said unto you.

27 Peace I leave with you, my peace I give unto you: not as the world giveth, give I unto you. Let not your heart be troubled, neither let it be afraid.

28 Ye have heard how I said unto you, I go away, and come *again* unto you. If ye loved me, ye would rejoice, because I said, I go unto the Father: for my Father is greater than I.

29 And now I have told you before it come to pass, that, when it is come to pass, ye might believe.

30 Hereafter I will not talk much with you: for the prince of this world cometh, and hath nothing in me.

31 But that the world may know that I love the Father; and as the Father gave me commandment,

ἐλευσόμεθα καὶ μονὴν παρ' αὐτῷ
we will come and abode with him

ποιησόμεθα. 24 ὁ μὴ ἀγαπῶν με τοὺς
we will make. The [one] not loving me the

λόγους μου οὐ τηρεῖ· καὶ ὁ λόγος ὃν
words of me keeps not; and the word which

ἀκούετε οὐκ ἔστιν ἐμὸς ἀλλὰ τοῦ
ye hear is not mine but [1]of the

πέμψαντός με πατρός. 25 Ταῦτα λελάληκα
[3]having sent [4]me [2]Father. These things I have spoken

ὑμῖν παρ' ὑμῖν μένων· 26 ὁ δὲ παρά-
to you with you remaining; but the Com-

κλητος, τὸ πνεῦμα τὸ ἅγιον ὃ πέμψει ὁ
forter, the Spirit – Holy which will send the

πατὴρ ἐν τῷ ὀνόματί μου, ἐκεῖνος ὑμᾶς
Father in the name of me, that one you

διδάξει πάντα καὶ ὑπομνήσει ὑμᾶς πάντα
will teach all things and remind you [of] all things

ἃ εἶπον ὑμῖν ἐγώ. 27 Εἰρήνην ἀφίημι
which [2]told [3]you [1]I. Peace I leave

ὑμῖν, εἰρήνην τὴν ἐμὴν δίδωμι ὑμῖν·
to you, [2]peace – [1]my I give you;

οὐ καθὼς ὁ κόσμος δίδωσιν ἐγὼ δίδωμι
not as the world gives I give

ὑμῖν. μὴ ταρασσέσθω ὑμῶν ἡ καρδία
you. Let not be troubled of you the heart

μηδὲ δειλιάτω. 28 ἠκούσατε ὅτι ἐγὼ
nor let it be fearful. Ye heard that I

εἶπον ὑμῖν· ὑπάγω καὶ ἔρχομαι πρὸς
told you: I go and come to

ὑμᾶς. εἰ ἠγαπᾶτέ με, ἐχάρητε ἂν ὅτι
you. If ye loved me, ye would have rejoiced that

πορεύομαι πρὸς τὸν πατέρα, ὅτι ὁ πατὴρ
I am going to the Father, because the Father

μείζων μού ἐστιν. 29 καὶ νῦν εἴρηκα
greater [than] me(I) is. And now I have told

ὑμῖν πρὶν γενέσθαι, ἵνα ὅταν γένηται
you before to happen, that when it happens
= it happens,

πιστεύσητε. 30 οὐκέτι πολλὰ λαλήσω μεθ'
ye may believe. No longer many things I will speak with

ὑμῶν, ἔρχεται γὰρ ὁ τοῦ κόσμου ἄρχων·
you, for [5]is coming [1]the [2]of the [4]world [3]ruler;

καὶ ἐν ἐμοὶ οὐκ ἔχει οὐδέν, 31 ἀλλ'
and in me he has not no(any)thing, but

ἵνα γνῷ ὁ κόσμος ὅτι ἀγαπῶ τὸν
that may know the world that I love the

πατέρα, καὶ καθὼς ἐνετείλατό μοι ὁ
Father, and as commanded me the

even so I do. Arise, let us go hence.

πατήρ, οὕτως ποιῶ. 'Εγείρεσθε, ἄγωμεν
Father, 'so I do. Rise, let us go
ἐντεῦθεν.
hence.

CHAPTER 15

I AM the true vine, and my Father is the husbandman.

2 Every branch in me that beareth not fruit he taketh away: and every *branch* that beareth fruit, he purgeth it, that it may bring forth more fruit.

3 Now ye are clean through the word which I have spoken unto you.

4 Abide in me, and I in you. As the branch cannot bear fruit of itself, except it abide in the vine; no more can ye, except ye abide in me.

5 I am the vine, ye *are* the branches: He that abideth in me, and I in him, the same bringeth forth much fruit: for without me ye can do nothing.

6 If a man abide not in me, he is cast forth as a branch, and is withered; and men gather them, and cast *them* into the fire, and they are burned.

7 If ye abide in me, and my words abide in you, ye shall ask what ye will, and it shall be done unto you.

15 'Εγώ εἰμι ἡ ἄμπελος ἡ ἀληθινή,
I am the vine the true,
καὶ ὁ πατήρ μου ὁ γεωργός ἐστιν.
and the Father of me the husbandman is.
2 πᾶν κλῆμα ἐν ἐμοὶ μὴ φέρον καρπόν,
Every branch in me not bearing fruit,
αἴρει αὐτό, καὶ πᾶν τὸ καρπὸν φέρον,
he takes it, and every [branch] the fruit bearing,
καθαίρει αὐτὸ ἵνα καρπὸν πλείονα φέρῃ.
he prunes it that fruit more it may bear.
3 ἤδη ὑμεῖς καθαροί ἐστε διὰ τὸν λόγον
Now ye clean are because of the word
ὃν λελάληκα ὑμῖν· μείνατε ἐν ἐμοί,
which I have spoken to you; remain in me,
κἀγὼ ἐν ὑμῖν. 4 καθὼς τὸ κλῆμα
and I in you. As the branch
οὐ δύναται καρπὸν φέρειν ἀφ' ἑαυτοῦ ἐὰν μὴ
cannot fruit to bear from itself unless
μένῃ ἐν τῇ ἀμπέλῳ, οὕτως οὐδὲ ὑμεῖς
it remains in the vine, so not ye
ἐὰν μὴ ἐν ἐμοὶ μένητε. 5 ἐγώ εἰμι
unless in me ye remain. I am
ἡ ἄμπελος, ὑμεῖς τὰ κλήματα. ὁ μένων
the vine, ye the branches. The [one] remaining
ἐν ἐμοὶ κἀγὼ ἐν αὐτῷ, οὗτος φέρει
in me and I in him, this one bears
καρπὸν πολύν, ὅτι χωρὶς ἐμοῦ οὐ δύνασθε
fruit much, because apart from me ye cannot
ποιεῖν οὐδέν. 6 ἐὰν μή τις μένῃ ἐν
to do no(any)thing. Unless anyone remains in
ἐμοί, ἐβλήθη ἔξω ὡς τὸ κλῆμα καὶ
me, he was(is) cast outside as the branch and
ἐξηράνθη, καὶ συνάγουσιν αὐτὰ καὶ εἰς
was(is) dried, and they gather them and into
τὸ πῦρ βάλλουσιν, καὶ καίεται. 7 ἐὰν
the fire they cast, and they are burned. If
μείνητε ἐν ἐμοὶ καὶ τὰ ῥήματά μου
ye remain in me and the words of me
ἐν ὑμῖν μείνῃ, ὃ ἐὰν θέλητε αἰτήσασθε,
in you remains, whatever ye wish ask,
καὶ γενήσεται ὑμῖν. 8 ἐν τούτῳ ἐδοξάσθη
and it shall happen to you. By this was glorified

8 Herein is my Father glorified, that ye bear much fruit; so shall ye be my disciples.

9 As the Father hath loved me, so have I loved you: continue ye in my love.

10 If ye keep my commandments, ye shall abide in my love; even as I have kept my Father's commandments, and abide in his love.

11 These things have I spoken unto you, that my joy might remain in you, and *that* your joy might be full.

12 This is my commandment, That ye love one another, as I have loved you.

13 Greater love hath no man than this, that a man lay down his life for his friends.

14 Ye are my friends, if ye do whatsoever I command you.

15 Henceforth I call you not servants; for the servant knoweth not what his lord doeth: but I have called you friends; for all things that I have heard of my Father I have made known unto you.

16 Ye have not chosen me, but I have chosen you, and ordained you, that ye should go and bring forth fruit, and *that* your fruit should remain: that what-

ὁ πατήρ μου, ἵνα καρπὸν πολὺν φέρητε
the Father of me, that fruit much ye bear
καὶ γενήσεσθε ἐμοὶ μαθηταί. 9 καθὼς
and ye will be to me° disciples. As
ἠγάπησέν με ὁ πατήρ, κἀγὼ ὑμᾶς
loved me the Father, I also you
ἠγάπησα· μείνατε ἐν τῇ ἀγάπῃ τῇ ἐμῇ.
loved; remain ye in the ²love – ¹my.
10 ἐὰν τὰς ἐντολάς μου τηρήσητε, μενεῖτε
If the commandments of me ye keep, ye will remain
ἐν τῇ ἀγάπῃ μου, καθὼς ἐγὼ τοῦ πατρός
in the love of me, as I of the Father
μου τὰς ἐντολὰς τετήρηκα καὶ μένω
of me the commandments have kept and remain
αὐτοῦ ἐν τῇ ἀγάπῃ. 11 Ταῦτα λελάληκα
of him in the love. These things I have spoken
ὑμῖν ἵνα ἡ χαρὰ ἡ ἐμὴ ἐν ὑμῖν ᾖ
to you that the ²joy – ¹my in you may be
καὶ ἡ χαρὰ ὑμῶν πληρωθῇ. 12 αὕτη
and the joy of you may be filled. This
ἐστὶν ἡ ἐντολὴ ἡ ἐμή, ἵνα ἀγαπᾶτε
is the ²commandment – ¹my, that ye love
ἀλλήλους καθὼς ἠγάπησα ὑμᾶς. 13 μείζονα
one another as I loved you. ¹Greater
ταύτης ἀγάπην οὐδεὶς ἔχει, ἵνα τις
[³than] ⁴this ²love no one has, that anyone
τὴν ψυχὴν αὐτοῦ θῇ ὑπὲρ τῶν φίλων
the life of him should lay down for the friends
αὐτοῦ. 14 ὑμεῖς φίλοι μού ἐστε, ἐὰν
of him. Ye friends of me are, if
ποιῆτε ὃ ἐγὼ ἐντέλλομαι ὑμῖν. 15 οὐκέτι
ye do what I command you. No longer
λέγω ὑμᾶς δούλους, ὅτι ὁ δοῦλος οὐκ οἶδεν
I call you slaves, because the slave knows not
τί ποιεῖ αὐτοῦ ὁ κύριος· ὑμᾶς δὲ
what does of him the lord; but you
εἴρηκα φίλους, ὅτι πάντα ἃ ἤκουσα
I have called friends, because all things which I heard
παρὰ τοῦ πατρός μου ἐγνώρισα ὑμῖν.
from the Father of me I made known to you.
16 οὐχ ὑμεῖς με ἐξελέξασθε, ἀλλ' ἐγὼ
Not ye me chose, but I
ἐξελεξάμην ὑμᾶς, καὶ ἔθηκα ὑμᾶς ἵνα
chose you, and appointed you that
ὑμεῖς ὑπάγητε καὶ καρπὸν φέρητε καὶ
ye should go and fruit should bear and
ὁ καρπὸς ὑμῶν μένῃ, ἵνα ὅ τι ἂν
the fruit of you should remain, that whatever

soever ye shall ask of the Father in my name, he may give it you.

17 These things I command you, that ye love one another.

18 ¶ If the world hate you, ye know that it hated me before *it hated* you.

19 If ye were of the world, the world would love his own: but because ye are not of the world, but I have chosen you out of the world, therefore the world hateth you.

20 Remember the word that I said unto you, The servant is not greater than his lord. If they have persecuted me, they will also persecute you; if they have kept my saying, they will keep your's also.

21 But all these things will they do unto you for my name's sake, because they know not him that sent me.

22 If I had not come and spoken unto them, they had not had sin: but now they have no cloke for their sin.

23 He that hateth me hateth my Father also.

24 If I had not done among them the works which none other man did, they had not had sin: but now have they both seen and hated both me and my Father.

αἰτήσητε τὸν πατέρα ἐν τῷ ὀνόματί
ye may ask ⁻the Father in the name

μου δῷ ὑμῖν. 17 ταῦτα ἐντέλλομαι ὑμῖν,
of me he may give you. These things I command you,

ἵνα ἀγαπᾶτε ἀλλήλους. 18 Εἰ ὁ κόσμος
that ye love one another. If the world

ὑμᾶς μισεῖ, γινώσκετε ὅτι ἐμὲ πρῶτον
you hates, ye know that me before

ὑμῶν μεμίσηκεν. 19 εἰ ἐκ τοῦ κόσμου ἦτε,
you it has hated. If of the world ye were,

ὁ κόσμος ἂν τὸ ἴδιον ἐφίλει· ὅτι δὲ
the world ¹would ²the(its) ⁴own ³have loved; but because

ἐκ τοῦ κόσμου οὐκ ἐστέ, ἀλλ᾽ ἐγὼ
of the world ye are not, but I

ἐξελεξάμην ὑμᾶς ἐκ τοῦ κόσμου, διὰ τοῦτο
chose you out of the world, therefore

μισεῖ ὑμᾶς ὁ κόσμος. 20 μνημονεύετε
hates you the world. Remember ye

τοῦ λόγου οὗ ἐγὼ εἶπον ὑμῖν· οὐκ
the word which I said to you: Not

ἔστιν δοῦλος μείζων τοῦ κυρίου αὐτοῦ.
is a slave greater [than] the lord of him.

εἰ ἐμὲ ἐδίωξαν, καὶ ὑμᾶς διώξουσιν·
If me they persecuted, also you they will persecute;

εἰ τὸν λόγον μου ἐτήρησαν, καὶ τὸν
if the word of me they kept, also –

ὑμέτερον τηρήσουσιν. 21 ἀλλὰ ταῦτα πάντα
yours they will keep. But these things all

ποιήσουσιν εἰς ὑμᾶς διὰ τὸ ὄνομά μου,
they will do to you because of the name of me,

ὅτι οὐκ οἴδασιν τὸν πέμψαντά με.
because they know not the [one] having sent me.

22 εἰ μὴ ἦλθον καὶ ἐλάλησα αὐτοῖς, ἁμαρτίαν
Unless I came and spoke to them, sin

οὐκ εἴχοσαν· νῦν δὲ πρόφασιν οὐκ ἔχουσιν
they had not had; but now cloak they have not

περὶ τῆς ἁμαρτίας αὐτῶν. 23 ὁ ἐμὲ
concerning the sin of them. The [one] me

μισῶν καὶ τὸν πατέρα μου μισεῖ. 24 εἰ
hating also the Father of me hates. If

τὰ ἔργα μὴ ἐποίησα ἐν αὐτοῖς ἃ οὐδεὶς
the works I did not among them which no man

ἄλλος ἐποίησεν, ἁμαρτίαν οὐκ εἴχοσαν
other did, sin they had not had;

νῦν δὲ καὶ ἑωράκασιν καὶ μεμισήκασιν
but now both they have seen and have hated

καὶ ἐμὲ καὶ τὸν πατέρα μου. 25 ἀλλ᾽
both me and the Father of me. But

25 But *this cometh to pass*, that the word might be fulfilled that is written in their law, They hated me without a cause.
26 But when the Comforter is come, whom I will send unto you from the Father, *even* the Spirit of truth, which proceedeth from the Father, he shall testify of me:
27 And ye also shall bear witness, because ye have been with me from the beginning.

ἵνα πληρωθῇ ὁ λόγος ὁ ἐν τῷ νόμῳ
that may be fulfilled the word – in the law
αὐτῶν γεγραμμένος ὅτι ἐμίσησάν με
of them *having been* written[,] – They hated me
δωρεάν. 26 Ὅταν ἔλθῃ ὁ παράκλητος
freely. When comes the Comforter
ὃν ἐγὼ πέμψω ὑμῖν παρὰ τοῦ πατρός,
whom I will send to you from the Father,
τὸ πνεῦμα τῆς ἀληθείας ὃ παρὰ τοῦ
the Spirit – of truth which from the
πατρὸς ἐκπορεύεται, ἐκεῖνος μαρτυρήσει
Father proceeds, that one will witness
περὶ ἐμοῦ· 27 καὶ ὑμεῖς δὲ μαρτυρεῖτε,
concerning me; ³also ²ye ¹and witness,
ὅτι ἀπ' ἀρχῆς μετ' ἐμοῦ ἐστε.
because from [the] beginning with me ye are.

CHAPTER 16

THESE things have I spoken unto you, that ye should not be offended.
2 They shall put you out of the synagogues: yea, the time cometh, that whosoever killeth you will think that he doeth God service.
3 And these things will they do unto you, because they have not known the Father, nor me.
4 But these things have I told you, that when the time shall come, ye may remember that I told you of them. And these things I said not unto you at the beginning, because I was with you.
5 But now I go my way to him that sent me; and none of you asketh me, Whither goest thou?
6 But because I have said these things unto you, sorrow hath filled your heart.
7 Nevertheless I tell you

16 Ταῦτα λελάληκα ὑμῖν ἵνα μὴ
These things I have spoken to you that not
σκανδαλισθῆτε. 2 ἀποσυναγώγους ποιή-
ye be offended. Put away from [the] synagogue they
σουσιν ὑμᾶς· ἀλλ' ἔρχεται ὥρα ἵνα πᾶς ὁ
will make you; but comes an hour that everyone
ἀποκτείνας ὑμᾶς δόξῃ λατρείαν προσφέρειν
killing you thinks service to offer
τῷ θεῷ. 3 καὶ ταῦτα ποιήσουσιν ὅτι
– to God. And these things they will do because
οὐκ ἔγνωσαν τὸν πατέρα οὐδὲ ἐμέ.
they knew not the Father nor me.
4 ἀλλὰ ταῦτα λελάληκα ὑμῖν ἵνα ὅταν
But these things I have spoken to you that when
ἔλθῃ ἡ ὥρα αὐτῶν μνημονεύητε αὐτῶν,
comes the hour of them ye may remember them,
ὅτι ἐγὼ εἶπον ὑμῖν. Ταῦτα δὲ ὑμῖν
that I told you. And these things to you
ἐξ ἀρχῆς οὐκ εἶπον, ὅτι μεθ' ὑμῶν
from [the] beginning I said not, because with you
ἤμην. 5 νῦν δὲ ὑπάγω πρὸς τὸν πέμψαντά
I was. But now I am going to the [one] having sent
με, καὶ οὐδεὶς ἐξ ὑμῶν ἐρωτᾷ με·
me, and not one of you asks me :
ποῦ ὑπάγεις; 6 ἀλλ' ὅτι ταῦτα λελάληκα
Where goest thou? but because these things I have spoken
ὑμῖν, ἡ λύπη πεπλήρωκεν ὑμῶν τὴν
to you, – grief has filled of you the
καρδίαν. 7 ἀλλ' ἐγὼ τὴν ἀλήθειαν λέγω
heart. But I the truth tell

the truth; It is expedient for you that I go away: for if I go not away, the Comforter will not come unto you; but if I depart, I will send him unto you.

8 And when he is come, he will reprove the world of sin, and of righteousness, and of judgment:

9 Of sin, because they believe not on me;

10 Of righteousness, because I go to my Father, and ye see me no more;

11 Of judgment, because the prince of this world is judged.

12 I have yet many things to say unto you, but ye cannot bear them now.

13 Howbeit when he, the Spirit of truth, is come, he will guide you into all truth: for he shall not speak of himself; but whatsoever he shall hear, *that* shall he speak: and he will shew you things to come.

14 He shall glorify me: for he shall receive of mine, and shall shew *it* unto you.

15 All things that the Father hath are mine: therefore said I, that he shall take of mine, and shall shew *it* unto you.

16 A little while, and ye shall not see me: and again, a little while, and ye shall see me, because I go to the Father.

ὑμῖν, συμφέρει ὑμῖν ἵνα ἐγὼ ἀπέλθω.
you, it is expedient for you that I should go away.
ἐὰν γὰρ μὴ ἀπέλθω, ὁ παράκλητος
For if I go not away, the Comforter
οὐ μὴ ἔλθῃ πρὸς ὑμᾶς· ἐὰν δὲ πορευθῶ,
by no means comes to you; but if I go,
πέμψω αὐτὸν πρὸς ὑμᾶς. 8 καὶ ἐλθὼν
I will send him to you. And coming
ἐκεῖνος ἐλέγξει τὸν κόσμον περὶ ἁμαρτίας
that one will reprove the world concerning sin
καὶ περὶ δικαιοσύνης καὶ περὶ κρίσεως·
and concerning righteousness and concerning judgment;
9 περὶ ἁμαρτίας μέν, ὅτι οὐ πιστεύουσιν
concerning sin, - because they believe not
εἰς ἐμέ· 10 περὶ δικαιοσύνης δέ, ὅτι
in me; concerning righteousness, - because
πρὸς τὸν πατέρα ὑπάγω καὶ οὐκέτι
to the Father I am going and no longer
θεωρεῖτέ με· 11 περὶ δὲ κρίσεως, ὅτι
ye behold me; concerning - judgment, because
ὁ ἄρχων τοῦ κόσμου τούτου κέκριται.
the ruler - world of this has been judged.
12 Ἔτι πολλὰ ἔχω ὑμῖν λέγειν, ἀλλ᾽
Yet many things I have you to tell, but
οὐ δύνασθε βαστάζειν ἄρτι· 13 ὅταν δὲ
ye cannot *to* bear now; but when
ἔλθῃ ἐκεῖνος, τὸ πνεῦμα τῆς ἀληθείας,
comes that one, the Spirit - of truth,
ὁδηγήσει ὑμᾶς εἰς τὴν ἀλήθειαν πᾶσαν·
he will guide you into the truth all;
οὐ γὰρ λαλήσει ἀφ᾽ ἑαυτοῦ, ἀλλ᾽ ὅσα
for not will he speak from himself, but what things
ἀκούει λαλήσει, καὶ τὰ ἐρχόμενα
he hears he will speak, and the coming things
ἀναγγελεῖ ὑμῖν. 14 ἐκεῖνος ἐμὲ δοξάσει,
he will announce to you. That one me will glorify,
ὅτι ἐκ τοῦ ἐμοῦ λήμψεται καὶ ἀναγγελεῖ
because of the of me* he will receive and will announce
ὑμῖν. 15 πάντα ὅσα ἔχει ὁ πατὴρ ἐμά
to you. All things which has the Father mine
ἐστιν· διὰ τοῦτο εἶπον ὅτι ἐκ τοῦ ἐμοῦ
is(are); therefore I said that of the of me*
λαμβάνει καὶ ἀναγγελεῖ ὑμῖν. 16 Μικρὸν
he receives and will announce to you. A little while
καὶ οὐκέτι θεωρεῖτέ με, καὶ πάλιν
and no longer ye behold me, and again
μικρὸν καὶ ὄψεσθέ με. 17 εἶπαν οὖν
a little while and ye will see me. Said therefore

* Understand "that which is mine".

17 Then said *some* of his disciples among themselves, What is this that he saith unto us, A little while, and ye shall not see me: and again, a little while, and ye shall see me: and, Because I go to the Father?

18 They said therefore, What is this that he saith, A little while? we cannot tell what he saith.

19 Now Jesus knew that they were desirous to ask him, and said unto them, Do ye enquire among yourselves of that I said, A little while, and ye shall not see me: and again, a little while, and ye shall see me?

20 Verily, verily, I say unto you, That ye shall weep and lament, but the world shall rejoice: and ye shall be sorrowful, but your sorrow shall be turned into joy.

21 A woman when she is in travail hath sorrow, because her hour is come: but as soon as she is delivered of the child, she remembereth no more the anguish, for joy that a man is born into the world.

22 And ye now therefore have sorrow: but I will see you again, and your heart shall rejoice, and your joy no man taketh from you.

23 And in that day ye shall ask me nothing.

ἐκ τῶν μαθητῶν αὐτοῦ πρὸς ἀλλήλους·
[some] of the disciples of him to one another :

τί ἐστιν τοῦτο ὃ λέγει ἡμῖν· μικρὸν
What is this which he tells us : A little while

καὶ οὐ θεωρεῖτέ με, καὶ πάλιν μικρὸν
and ye behold not me, and again a little while

καὶ ὄψεσθέ με; καί· ὅτι ὑπάγω
and ye will see me? and : Because I am going

πρὸς τὸν πατέρα; 18 ἔλεγον οὖν· τοῦτο
to the Father? They said therefore : ³This

τί ἐστιν ὃ λέγει τὸ μικρόν; οὐκ οἴδαμεν
¹what ²is which he says[,] the "little while"? We do not know

τί λαλεῖ. 19 ἔγνω Ἰησοῦς ὅτι ἤθελον
what he speaks. Knew Jesus that they wished

αὐτὸν ἐρωτᾶν, καὶ εἶπεν αὐτοῖς· περὶ
him to question, and said to them : Concerning

τούτου ζητεῖτε μετ᾽ ἀλλήλων ὅτι εἶπον·
this seek ye with one another because I said :

μικρὸν καὶ οὐ θεωρεῖτέ με, καὶ πάλιν
A little while and ye behold not me, and again

μικρὸν καὶ ὄψεσθέ με; 20 ἀμὴν ἀμὴν
a little while and ye will see me? Truly truly

λέγω ὑμῖν ὅτι κλαύσετε καὶ θρηνήσετε
I tell you that will weep and will lament

ὑμεῖς, ὁ δὲ κόσμος χαρήσεται· ὑμεῖς
ye, and the world will rejoice; ye

λυπηθήσεσθε, ἀλλ᾽ ἡ λύπη ὑμῶν εἰς
will be grieved, but the grief of you into

χαρὰν γενήσεται. 21 ἡ γυνὴ ὅταν τίκτῃ
joy will become. The woman when she gives birth

λύπην ἔχει, ὅτι ἦλθεν ἡ ὥρα αὐτῆς·
grief has, because came the hour of her;

ὅταν δὲ γεννήσῃ τὸ παιδίον, οὐκέτι
but when she brings forth the child, no longer

μνημονεύει τῆς θλίψεως διὰ τὴν χαρὰν
she remembers the distress because of the joy

ὅτι ἐγεννήθη ἄνθρωπος εἰς τὸν κόσμον.
that was born a man into the world.

22 καὶ ὑμεῖς οὖν νῦν μὲν λύπην ἔχετε·
And ye therefore now indeed grief have;

πάλιν δὲ ὄψομαι ὑμᾶς, καὶ χαρήσεται
but again I will see you, and ⁴will rejoice

ὑμῶν ἡ καρδία, καὶ τὴν χαρὰν ὑμῶν
³of you ¹the ²heart, and the joy of you

οὐδεὶς αἴρει ἀφ᾽ ὑμῶν. 23 καὶ ἐν ἐκείνῃ τῇ
no one takes from you. And in that -

ἡμέρᾳ ἐμὲ οὐκ ἐρωτήσετε οὐδέν.
day me ye will not question no(any)thing.

Verily, verily, I say unto you, Whatsoever ye shall ask the Father in my name, he will give *it* you.

24 Hitherto have ye asked nothing in my name: ask, and ye shall receive, that your joy may be full.

25 These things have I spoken unto you in proverbs: but the time cometh, when I shall no more speak unto you in proverbs, but I shall shew you plainly of the Father.

26 At that day ye shall ask in my name: and I say not unto you, that I will pray the Father for you:

27 For the Father himself loveth you, because ye have loved me, and have believed that I came out from God.

28 I came forth from the Father, and am come into the world: again, I leave the world, and go to the Father.

29 ¶ His disciples said unto him, Lo, now speakest thou plainly, and speakest no proverb.

30 Now are we sure that thou knowest all things, and needest not that any man should ask thee: by this we believe that thou camest forth from God.

31 Jesus answered them, Do ye now believe?

ἀμὴν ἀμὴν λέγω ὑμῖν, ἄν τι αἰτήσητε
Truly truly I tell you, whatever ye ask
τὸν πατέρα δώσει ὑμῖν ἐν τῷ ὀνόματί
the Father he will give you in the name
μου. **24** ἕως ἄρτι οὐκ ἠτήσατε οὐδὲν
of me. Until now ye asked not no(any)thing
ἐν τῷ ὀνόματί μου· αἰτεῖτε, καὶ λήμψεσθε,
in the name of me; ask, and ye will receive,
ἵνα ἡ χαρὰ ὑμῶν ᾖ πεπληρωμένη.
that the joy of you may be *having been* filled.
25 Ταῦτα ἐν παροιμίαις λελάληκα ὑμῖν·
These things in allegories I have spoken to you;
ἔρχεται ὥρα ὅτε οὐκέτι ἐν παροιμίαις
comes an hour when no longer in allegories
λαλήσω ὑμῖν, ἀλλὰ παρρησίᾳ περὶ τοῦ
I will speak to you, but plainly concerning the
πατρὸς ἀπαγγελῶ ὑμῖν. **26** ἐν ἐκείνῃ τῇ
Father will declare to you. In that –
ἡμέρᾳ ἐν τῷ ὀνόματί μου αἰτήσεσθε,
day in the name of me ye will ask,
καὶ οὐ λέγω ὑμῖν ὅτι ἐγὼ ἐρωτήσω
and I tell not you that I will request
τὸν πατέρα περὶ ὑμῶν· **27** αὐτὸς γὰρ
the Father concerning you; for [him]self
ὁ πατὴρ φιλεῖ ὑμᾶς, ὅτι ὑμεῖς ἐμὲ
the Father loves you, because ye me
πεφιλήκατε καὶ πεπιστεύκατε ὅτι ἐγὼ
have loved and have believed that I
παρὰ τοῦ θεοῦ ἐξῆλθον. **28** ἐξῆλθον
from – God came forth. I came forth
ἐκ τοῦ πατρὸς καὶ ἐλήλυθα εἰς τὸν
out of the Father and have come into the
κόσμον· πάλιν ἀφίημι τὸν κόσμον καὶ
world; again I leave the world and
πορεύομαι πρὸς τὸν πατέρα. **29** Λέγουσιν
go to the Father. Say
οἱ μαθηταὶ αὐτοῦ· ἴδε νῦν ἐν παρρησίᾳ
the disciples of him: Behold[,] now in plainness
λαλεῖς, καὶ παροιμίαν οὐδεμίαν λέγεις.
thou speakest, and ³allegory ¹no thou sayest.
30 νῦν οἴδαμεν ὅτι οἶδας πάντα καὶ
Now we know that thou knowest all things and
οὐ χρείαν ἔχεις ἵνα τίς σε ἐρωτᾷ· ἐν
no need hast that anyone thee should question; by
τούτῳ πιστεύομεν ὅτι ἀπὸ θεοῦ ἐξῆλθες.
this we believe that from God thou camest forth.
31 ἀπεκρίθη αὐτοῖς Ἰησοῦς· ἄρτι πιστεύετε;
Answered them Jesus: Now believe ye?

32 Behold, the hour cometh, yea, is now come, that ye shall be scattered, every man to his own, and shall leave me alone: and yet I am not alone, because the Father is with me.

33 These things I have spoken unto you, that in me ye might have peace. In the world ye shall have tribulation: but be of good cheer; I have overcome the world.

32 ἰδοὺ ἔρχεται ὥρα καὶ ἐλήλυθεν ἵνα
behold[,] comes an hour and has come that
σκορπισθῆτε ἕκαστος εἰς τὰ ἴδια κἀμὲ
ye are scattered each one to the(his) own and me
μόνον ἀφῆτε· καὶ οὐκ εἰμὶ μόνος, ὅτι
alone ye leave; and I am not alone, because
ὁ πατὴρ μετ' ἐμοῦ ἐστιν. 33 ταῦτα
the Father with me is. These things
λελάληκα ὑμῖν ἵνα ἐν ἐμοὶ εἰρήνην
I have spoken to you that in me peace
ἔχητε. ἐν τῷ κόσμῳ θλῖψιν ἔχετε·
ye may have. In the world distress ye have;
ἀλλὰ θαρσεῖτε, ἐγὼ νενίκηκα τὸν κόσμον.
but cheer ye up, I have overcome the world.

CHAPTER 17

THESE words spake Jesus, and lifted up his eyes to heaven, and said, Father, the hour is come; glorify thy Son, that thy Son also may glorify thee:

2 As thou hast given him power over all flesh, that he should give eternal life to as many as thou hast given him.

3 And this is life eternal, that they might know thee the only true God, and Jesus Christ, whom thou hast sent.

4 I have glorified thee on the earth: I have finished the work which thou gavest me to do.

5 And now, O Father, glorify thou me with thine own self with the glory which I had with thee before the world was

6 I have manifested thy name unto the men which thou gavest me out of the

17 Ταῦτα ἐλάλησεν Ἰησοῦς, καὶ ἐπάρας
These things spoke Jesus, and lifting up
τοὺς ὀφθαλμοὺς αὐτοῦ εἰς τὸν οὐρανὸν
the eyes of him to - heaven
εἶπεν· πάτερ, ἐλήλυθεν ἡ ὥρα· δόξασόν
said: Father, has come the hour; glorify
σου τὸν υἱόν, ἵνα ὁ υἱὸς δοξάσῃ σέ,
of thee the Son, that the Son may glorify thee,
2 καθὼς ἔδωκας αὐτῷ ἐξουσίαν πάσης
as thou gavest him authority of(over) all
σαρκός, ἵνα πᾶν ὃ δέδωκας αὐτῷ δώσῃ
flesh, that all which thou hast given him he may give
αὐτοῖς ζωὴν αἰώνιον. 3 αὕτη δέ ἐστιν
to them life eternal. And this is
ἡ αἰώνιος ζωή, ἵνα γινώσκωσιν σὲ τὸν
- eternal life, that they may know thee the
μόνον ἀληθινὸν θεὸν καὶ ὃν ἀπέστειλας
only true God and [he] whom thou didst send
Ἰησοῦν Χριστόν. 4 ἐγώ σε ἐδόξασα
Jesus Christ. I thee glorified
ἐπὶ τῆς γῆς, τὸ ἔργον τελειώσας ὃ
on the earth, the work finishing which
δέδωκάς μοι ἵνα ποιήσω· 5 καὶ νῦν
thou hast given to me that I should do; and now
δόξασόν με σύ, πάτερ, παρὰ σεαυτῷ
glorify me thou, Father, with thyself
τῇ δόξῃ ᾗ εἶχον πρὸ τοῦ τὸν κόσμον
with the glory which I had before the the world
=before the world was
εἶναι παρὰ σοί. 6 Ἐφανέρωσά σου τὸ
to be[b] with thee. I manifested of thee the
ὄνομα τοῖς ἀνθρώποις οὓς ἔδωκάς μοι
name to the men whom thou gavest to me

world: thine they were, and thou gavest them me; and they have kept thy word.

7 Now they have known that all things whatsoever thou hast given me are of thee.

8 For I have given unto them the words which thou gavest me; and they have received *them*, and have known surely that I came out from thee, and they have believed that thou didst send me.

9 I pray for them: I pray not for the world, but for them which thou hast given me; for they are thine.

10 And all mine are thine, and thine are mine; and I am glorified in them.

11 And now I am no more in the world, but these are in the world, and I come to thee. Holy Father, keep through thine own name those whom thou hast given me, that they may be one, as we *are*.

12 While I was with them in the world, I kept them in thy name: those that thou gavest me I have kept, and none of them is lost, but the son of perdition; that the scripture might be fulfilled.

13 And now come I to thee; and these things I speak in the world, that they might have my joy

ἐκ τοῦ κόσμου. σοὶ ἦσαν κἀμοὶ αὐτοὺς
out of the world. To thee° they were and to me them
=Thine

ἔδωκας, καὶ τὸν λόγον σου τετήρηκαν.
thou gavest, and the word of thee they have kept.

7 νῦν ἔγνωκαν ὅτι πάντα ὅσα δέδωκάς
Now they have known that all things as many as thou hast given

μοι παρὰ σοῦ εἰσιν· 8 ὅτι τὰ ῥήματα
to me from thee are; because the words

ἃ ἔδωκάς μοι δέδωκα αὐτοῖς, καὶ αὐτοὶ
which thou gavest to me I have given to them, and they

ἔλαβον, καὶ ἔγνωσαν ἀληθῶς ὅτι παρὰ
received, and knew truly that from

σοῦ ἐξῆλθον, καὶ ἐπίστευσαν ὅτι σύ
thee I came forth, and they believed that thou

με ἀπέστειλας. 9 ἐγὼ περὶ αὐτῶν ἐρωτῶ·
me didst send. I concerning them make request;

οὐ περὶ τοῦ κόσμου ἐρωτῶ, ἀλλὰ περὶ
not concerning the world do I make request, but concerning

ὧν δέδωκάς μοι, ὅτι σοί εἰσιν,
[those] whom thou hast given to me, because to thee° they are,
=thine

10 καὶ τὰ ἐμὰ πάντα σά ἐστιν καὶ
and ³the ²my things ¹all ⁵thine ⁴is(are) and

τὰ σὰ ἐμά, καὶ δεδόξασμαι ἐν αὐτοῖς.
the thy things mine, and I have been glorified in them.

11 καὶ οὐκέτι εἰμὶ ἐν τῷ κόσμῳ, καὶ
And no longer am I in the world, and

αὐτοὶ ἐν τῷ κόσμῳ εἰσίν, κἀγὼ πρὸς
they in the world are, and I to

σὲ ἔρχομαι. πάτερ ἅγιε, τήρησον αὐτοὺς
thee come. Father holy, keep them

ἐν τῷ ὀνόματί σου ᾧ δέδωκάς μοι,
in the name of thee which thou hast given to me,

ἵνα ὦσιν ἓν καθὼς ἡμεῖς. 12 ὅτε ἤμην
that they may be one as we. When I was

μετ᾽ αὐτῶν, ἐγὼ ἐτήρουν αὐτοὺς ἐν
with them, I kept them in

τῷ ὀνόματί σου ᾧ δέδωκάς μοι, καὶ
the name of thee which thou hast given to me, and

ἐφύλαξα, καὶ οὐδεὶς ἐξ αὐτῶν ἀπώλετο
I guarded, and not one of them perished

εἰ μὴ ὁ υἱὸς τῆς ἀπωλείας, ἵνα ἡ
except the son - perdition, that the

γραφὴ πληρωθῇ. 13 νῦν δὲ πρὸς σὲ
scripture might be fulfilled. But now to thee

ἔρχομαι, καὶ ταῦτα λαλῶ ἐν τῷ κόσμῳ
I come, and these things I speak in the world

ἵνα ἔχωσιν τὴν χαρὰν τὴν ἐμὴν
that they may have *the* ²joy - ¹my

fulfilled in themselves.

14 I have given them thy word; and the world hath hated them, because they are not of the world, even as I am not of the world.

15 I pray not that thou shouldest take them out of the world, but that thou shouldest keep them from the evil.

16 They are not of the world, even as I am not of the world.

17 Sanctify them through thy truth: thy word is truth.

18 As thou hast sent me into the world, even so have I also sent them into the world.

19 And for their sakes I sanctify myself, that they also might be sanctified through the truth.

20 Neither pray I for these alone, but for them also which shall believe on me through their word;

21 That they all may be one; as thou, Father, *art* in me, and I in thee, that they also may be one in us; that the world may believe that thou hast sent me.

22 And the glory which thou gavest me I have given them; that they may be one, even as we are one:

23 I in them, and thou in me, that they may be

πεπληρωμένην ἐν ἑαυτοῖς. 14 ἐγὼ δέδωκα
having been fulfilled in themselves. I have given

αὐτοῖς τὸν λόγον σου, καὶ ὁ κόσμος
to them the word of thee, and the world

ἐμίσησεν αὐτούς, ὅτι οὐκ εἰσὶν ἐκ τοῦ
hated them, because they are not of the

κόσμου καθὼς ἐγὼ οὐκ εἰμὶ ἐκ τοῦ
world as I am not of the

κόσμου. 15 οὐκ ἐρωτῶ ἵνα ἄρῃς αὐτοὺς
world. I do not request that thou shouldest take them

ἐκ τοῦ κόσμου, ἀλλ' ἵνα τηρήσῃς αὐτοὺς
out of the world, but that thou shouldest keep them

ἐκ τοῦ πονηροῦ. 16 ἐκ τοῦ κόσμου
out of the evil [?one]. Of the world

οὐκ εἰσὶν καθὼς ἐγὼ οὐκ εἰμὶ ἐκ τοῦ
they are not as I am not of the

κόσμου. 17 ἁγίασον αὐτοὺς ἐν τῇ
world. Sanctify them in(?by) the

ἀληθείᾳ· ὁ λόγος ὁ σὸς ἀλήθειά ἐστιν.
truth; the ²word – ¹thy truth is.

18 καθὼς ἐμὲ ἀπέστειλας εἰς τὸν κόσμον,
As me thou didst send into the world,

κἀγὼ ἀπέστειλα αὐτοὺς εἰς τὸν κόσμον·
I also sent them into the world;

19 καὶ ὑπὲρ αὐτῶν [ἐγὼ] ἁγιάζω ἐμαυτόν,
and on behalf of them I sanctify myself,

ἵνα ὦσιν καὶ αὐτοὶ ἡγιασμένοι ἐν ἀληθείᾳ.
that ²may be ³also ¹they *having been* sanctified in truth.

20 Οὐ περὶ τούτων δὲ ἐρωτῶ μόνον,
²Not ²concerning ⁴these ¹but I make request only,

ἀλλὰ καὶ περὶ τῶν πιστευόντων διὰ
but also concerning the [ones] believing through

τοῦ λόγου αὐτῶν εἰς ἐμέ, 21 ἵνα πάντες
the word of them in me, that all

ἐν ὦσιν, καθὼς σύ, πατήρ, ἐν ἐμοὶ
one may be, as thou, Father, in me

κἀγὼ ἐν σοί, ἵνα καὶ αὐτοὶ ἐν ἡμῖν
and I in thee, that also they in us

ὦσιν, ἵνα ὁ κόσμος πιστεύῃ ὅτι σύ
may be, that the world may believe that thou

με ἀπέστειλας. 22 κἀγὼ τὴν δόξαν ἣν
me didst send. And I the glory which

δέδωκάς μοι δέδωκα αὐτοῖς, ἵνα ὦσιν
thou hast given to me have given to them, that they may be

ἐν καθὼς ἡμεῖς ἕν· 23 ἐγὼ ἐν αὐτοῖς
one as we [are] one; I in them

καὶ σὺ ἐν ἐμοί, ἵνα ὦσιν τετελειωμένοι
and thou in me, that they may be *having been* perfected

made perfect in one; and that the world may know that thou hast sent me, and hast loved them, as thou hast loved me.

24 Father, I will that they also, whom thou hast given me, be with me where I am; that they may behold my glory, which thou hast given me: for thou lovedst me before the foundation of the world.

25 O righteous Father, the world hath not known thee: but I have known thee, and these have known that thou hast sent me.

26 And I have declared unto them thy name, and will declare it: that the love wherewith thou hast loved me may be in them, and I in them.

εἰς   ἕν,   ἵνα   γινώσκῃ   ὁ   κόσμος   ὅτι   σύ
in   one,   that   may know   the   world   that thou

με   ἀπέστειλας   καὶ   ἠγάπησας   αὐτοὺς
me   didst send   and   didst love   them

καθὼς   ἐμὲ   ἠγάπησας.   **24** Πατήρ,   ὃ
as   me   thou didst love.   Father,   what

δέδωκάς   μοι,   θέλω   ἵνα   ὅπου   εἰμὶ   ἐγὼ
thou hast given to me,   I wish   that   where   am   I

κἀκεῖνοι   ὦσιν   μετ'   ἐμοῦ,   ἵνα   θεωρῶσιν
those also   may be   with   me,   that they may behold

τὴν   δόξαν   τὴν   ἐμήν,   ἣν   δέδωκάς   μοι
the   ²glory   –   ¹my,   which thou hast given to me

ὅτι   ἠγάπησάς   με   πρὸ   καταβολῆς   κόσμου.
because thou didst love me   before [the] foundation of [the] world.

25 πατὴρ   δίκαιε,   καὶ   ὁ   κόσμος   σε
Father   righteous,   indeed   the   world   thee

οὐκ   ἔγνω,   ἐγὼ   δέ   σε   ἔγνων,   καὶ   οὗτοι
knew not,   but I   thee   knew,   and   these

ἔγνωσαν   ὅτι   σύ   με   ἀπέστειλας·   **26** καὶ
knew   that   thou   me   didst send;   and

ἐγνώρισα   αὐτοῖς   τὸ   ὄνομά   σου   καὶ
I made known   to them   the   name   of thee   and

γνωρίσω,   ἵνα   ἡ   ἀγάπη   ἣν   ἠγάπησάς
will make known,   that   the   love [with] which   thou lovedst

με   ἐν   αὐτοῖς   ᾖ   κἀγὼ   ἐν   αὐτοῖς.
me   in   them   may be   and I   in   them.

CHAPTER 18

WHEN Jesus had spoken these words, he went forth with his disciples over the brook Cedron, where was a garden, into the which he entered, and his disciples.

2 And Judas also, which betrayed him, knew the place: for Jesus ofttimes resorted thither with his disciples.

3 Judas then, having received a band of men and officers from the chief priests and Pharisees,

18 Ταῦτα   εἰπὼν   Ἰησοῦς   ἐξῆλθεν   σὺν
These things having said   Jesus   went forth   with

τοῖς   μαθηταῖς   αὐτοῦ   πέραν   τοῦ   χειμάρρου
the   disciples   of him   across   the   torrent

τοῦ   Κεδρών,   ὅπου   ἦν   κῆπος,   εἰς   ὃν
–   Kedron,   where there was   a garden,   into which

εἰσῆλθεν   αὐτὸς   καὶ   οἱ   μαθηταὶ   αὐτοῦ.
entered   he   and   the   disciples   of him.

2 ᾔδει   δὲ   καὶ   Ἰούδας   ὁ   παραδιδοὺς
¹Now ⁷knew   ²also   ³Judas   ⁴the [one]   ⁵betraying

αὐτὸν   τὸν   τόπον,   ὅτι   πολλάκις   συνήχθη
⁶him   ⁷the   ⁸place, because   often   assembled

Ἰησοῦς   ἐκεῖ   μετὰ   τῶν   μαθητῶν   αὐτου.
Jesus   there   with   the   disciples   of him.

3 ὁ   οὖν   Ἰούδας   λαβὼν   τὴν   σπεῖραν
–   Therefore   Judas   taking   the   band

καὶ   ἐκ   τῶν   ἀρχιερέων   καὶ   [ἐκ]   τῶν
and   ²from   ³the   ⁴chief priests   ⁵and   ⁶from   ⁷the

Φαρισαίων   ὑπηρέτας   ἔρχεται   ἐκεῖ   μετὰ
⁸Pharisees   ¹attendants   comes   there   with

cometh thither with lanterns and torches and weapons.

4 Jesus therefore, knowing all things that should come upon him, went forth, and said unto them, Whom seek ye?

5 They answered him, Jesus of Nazareth. Jesus saith unto them, I am *he*. And Judas also, which betrayed him, stood with them.

6 As soon then as he had said unto them, I am *he*, they went backward, and fell to the ground.

7 Then asked he them again, Whom seek ye? And they said, Jesus of Nazareth.

8 Jesus answered, I have told you that I am *he*: if therefore ye seek me, let these go their way:

9 That the saying might be fulfilled, which he spake, Of them which thou gavest me have I lost none.

10 Then Simon Peter having a sword drew it, and smote the high priest's servant, and cut off his right ear. The servant's name was Malchus.

11 Then said Jesus unto Peter, Put up thy sword into the sheath: the cup which my Father hath given me, shall I not drink it?

12 Then the band and

φανῶν καὶ λαμπάδων καὶ ὅπλων. 4 Ἰησοῦς
lanterns and lamps and weapons. Jesus

οὖν εἰδὼς πάντα τὰ ἐρχόμενα ἐπ' αὐτὸν
therefore knowing all the things coming on him

ἐξῆλθεν καὶ λέγει αὐτοῖς· τίνα ζητεῖτε;
went forth and says to them: Whom seek ye?

5 ἀπεκρίθησαν αὐτῷ· Ἰησοῦν τὸν
They answered him: Jesus the

Ναζωραῖον. λέγει αὐτοῖς· ἐγώ εἰμι.
Nazarene. He tells them: I am.

εἰστήκει δὲ καὶ Ἰούδας ὁ παραδιδοὺς
Now stood also Judas the [one] betraying

αὐτὸν μετ' αὐτῶν. 6 ὡς οὖν εἶπεν
him with them. When therefore he told

αὐτοῖς· ἐγώ εἰμι, ἀπῆλθαν εἰς τὰ ὀπίσω
them: I am, they went away back †

καὶ ἔπεσαν χαμαί. 7 πάλιν οὖν
and fell on the ground. Again therefore

ἐπηρώτησεν αὐτούς· τίνα ζητεῖτε; οἱ δὲ
he questioned them: Whom seek ye? And they

εἶπαν· Ἰησοῦν τὸν Ναζωραῖον. 8 ἀπεκρίθη
said: Jesus the Nazarene. Answered

Ἰησοῦς· εἶπον ὑμῖν ὅτι ἐγώ εἰμι· εἰ
Jesus: I told you that I am; if

οὖν ἐμὲ ζητεῖτε, ἄφετε τούτους ὑπάγειν·
therefore me ye seek, allow these to go;

9 ἵνα πληρωθῇ ὁ λόγος ὃν εἶπεν, ὅτι
that might be fulfilled the word which he said, –

οὓς δέδωκάς μοι, οὐκ ἀπώλεσα ἐξ
[Those] whom thou hast given to me, I lost not of

αὐτῶν οὐδένα. 10 Σίμων οὖν Πέτρος
them no(any)one. [1]Simon [3]therefore [2]Peter

ἔχων μάχαιραν εἵλκυσεν αὐτὴν καὶ ἔπαισεν
having a sword drew it and smote

τὸν τοῦ ἀρχιερέως δοῦλον καὶ ἀπέκοψεν
[1]the [3]of the [4]high priest [2]slave and cut off

αὐτοῦ τὸ ὠτάριον τὸ δεξιόν· ἦν δὲ
of him the [2]ear [1]right; and was

ὄνομα τῷ δούλῳ Μάλχος. 11 εἶπεν οὖν
name to the slave⁰ Malchus. Said therefore

ὁ Ἰησοῦς τῷ Πέτρῳ· βάλε τὴν μάχαιραν
– Jesus – to Peter: Put the sword

εἰς τὴν θήκην· τὸ ποτήριον ὃ δέδωκέν
into the sheath; the cup which has given

μοι ὁ πατήρ, οὐ μὴ πίω αὐτό;
to me the Father, by no means shall I drink it?

12 Ἡ οὖν σπεῖρα καὶ ὁ χιλίαρχος
Therefore the band and the chiliarch

the captain and officers of the Jews took Jesus, and bound him,

13 And led him away to Annas first; for he was father in law to Caiaphas, which was the high priest that same year.

14 Now Caiaphas was he, which gave counsel to the Jews, that it was expedient that one man should die for the people.

15 ¶ And Simon Peter followed Jesus, and *so did* another disciple : that disciple was known unto the high priest, and went in with Jesus into the palace of the high priest.

16 But Peter stood at the door without. Then went out that other disciple, which was known unto the high priest, and spake unto her that kept the door, and brought in Peter.

17 Then saith the damsel that kept the door unto Peter, Art not thou also *one* of this man's disciples? He saith, I am not.

18 And the servants and officers stood there, who had made a fire of coals; for it was cold: and they warmed themselves: and Peter stood with them, and warmed himself.

19 ¶ The high priest then

καὶ οἱ ὑπηρέται τῶν Ἰουδαίων συνέλαβον
and the attendants of the Jews took

τὸν Ἰησοῦν καὶ ἔδησαν αὐτόν, 13 καὶ
- Jesus and bound him, and

ἤγαγον πρὸς Ἅνναν πρῶτον· ἦν γὰρ
led to Annas first; for he was

πενθερὸς τοῦ Καϊαφᾶ, ὃς ἦν ἀρχιερεὺς
father-in-law of Caiaphas, who was high priest

τοῦ ἐνιαυτοῦ ἐκείνου· 14 ἦν δὲ Καϊαφᾶς
- year of that; now it was Caiaphas

ὁ συμβουλεύσας τοῖς Ἰουδαίοις ὅτι
the [one] having advised the Jews that

συμφέρει ἕνα ἄνθρωπον ἀποθανεῖν ὑπὲρ
it is(was) expedient one man to die on behalf of

τοῦ λαοῦ. 15 Ἠκολούθει δὲ τῷ Ἰησοῦ
the people. And followed - Jesus

Σίμων Πέτρος καὶ ἄλλος μαθητής. ὁ δὲ
Simon Peter and another disciple. - And

μαθητὴς ἐκεῖνος ἦν γνωστὸς τῷ ἀρχιερεῖ,
disciple that was known to the high priest,

καὶ συνεισῆλθεν τῷ Ἰησοῦ εἰς τὴν αὐλὴν
and entered with - Jesus into the court

τοῦ ἀρχιερέως, 16 ὁ δὲ Πέτρος εἱστήκει
of the high priest, - but Peter stood

πρὸς τῇ θύρᾳ ἔξω. ἐξῆλθεν οὖν ὁ
at the door outside. Went out therefore the

μαθητὴς ὁ ἄλλος ὁ γνωστὸς τοῦ ἀρχιερέως
²disciple - ¹other - known of(to) the high priest

καὶ εἶπεν τῇ θυρωρῷ, καὶ εἰσήγαγεν
and told the portress, and brought in

τὸν Πέτρον. 17 λέγει οὖν τῷ Πέτρῳ ἡ
- Peter. Says therefore - to Peter the

παιδίσκη ἡ θυρωρός· μὴ καὶ σὺ ἐκ
maidservant the portress : *Not* also thou of

τῶν μαθητῶν εἶ τοῦ ἀνθρώπου τούτου;
the disciples art - man of this?

λέγει ἐκεῖνος· οὐκ εἰμί. 18 εἱστήκεισαν δὲ
Says that one : I am not. And stood

οἱ δοῦλοι καὶ οἱ ὑπηρέται ἀνθρακιὰν
the slaves and the attendants a fire

πεποιηκότες, ὅτι ψῦχος ἦν, καὶ
having made, because cold it was, and

ἐθερμαίνοντο· ἦν δὲ καὶ ὁ Πέτρος μετ'
were warming themselves; and was also - Peter with

αὐτῶν ἑστὼς καὶ θερμαινόμενος. 19 Ὁ
them standing and warming himself. - ¹The

οὖν ἀρχιερεὺς ἠρώτησεν τὸν Ἰησοῦν
²therefore ²high priest questioned - Jesus

asked Jesus of his disciples, and of his doctrine.

20 Jesus answered him, I spake openly to the world; I ever taught in the synagogue, and in the temple, whither the Jews always resort; and in secret have I said nothing.

21 Why askest thou me? ask them which heard me, what I have said unto them: behold, they know what I said.

22 And when he had thus spoken, one of the officers which stood by struck Jesus with the palm of his hand, saying, Answerest thou the high priest so?

23 Jesus answered him, If I have spoken evil, bear witness of the evil: but if well, why smitest thou me?

24 Now Annas had sent him bound unto Caiaphas the high priest.

25 ¶ And Simon Peter stood and warmed himself. They said therefore unto him, Art not thou also *one* of his disciples? He denied *it*, and said, I am not.

26 One of the servants of the high priest, being *his* kinsman whose ear Peter cut off, saith, Did not I see thee in the garden with him?

περὶ τῶν μαθητῶν αὐτοῦ καὶ περὶ τῆς
about the disciples of him and about the

διδαχῆς αὐτοῦ. 20 ἀπεκρίθη αὐτῷ Ἰησοῦς·
teaching of him. Answered him Jesus:

ἐγὼ παρρησίᾳ λελάληκα τῷ κόσμῳ· ἐγὼ
I with plainness have spoken to the world; I

πάντοτε ἐδίδαξα ἐν συναγωγῇ καὶ ἐν
always taught in a synagogue and in

τῷ ἱερῷ, ὅπου πάντες οἱ Ἰουδαῖοι
the temple, where all the Jews

συνέρχονται, καὶ ἐν κρυπτῷ ἐλάλησα
come together, and in secret I spoke

οὐδέν. 21 τί με ἐρωτᾷς; ἐρώτησον
nothing. Why me questionest thou? question

τοὺς ἀκηκοότας τί ἐλάλησα αὐτοῖς· ἴδε
the [ones] having heard what I spoke to them; behold[,]

οὗτοι οἴδασιν ἃ εἶπον ἐγώ. 22 ταῦτα
these know what things said I. These things

δὲ αὐτοῦ εἰπόντος¹ εἷς παρεστηκὼς τῶν
and him saying² one standing by of the
= And as he said this

ὑπηρετῶν ἔδωκεν ῥάπισμα τῷ Ἰησοῦ
attendants gave a blow – to Jesus

εἰπών· οὕτως ἀποκρίνῃ τῷ ἀρχιερεῖ;
saying: Thus answerest thou the high priest?

23 ἀπεκρίθη αὐτῷ Ἰησοῦς· εἰ κακῶς
Answered him Jesus: If ill

ἐλάλησα, μαρτύρησον περὶ τοῦ κακοῦ·
I spoke, witness concerning the evil;

εἰ δὲ καλῶς, τί με δέρεις; 24 ἀπέστειλεν
but if well, why me beatest thou? ³Sent

οὖν αὐτὸν ὁ Ἅννας δεδεμένον πρὸς
¹therefore ⁴him – ¹Annas *having been* bound to

Καιάφαν τὸν ἀρχιερέα. 25 Ἦν δὲ Σίμων
Caiaphas the high priest. Now was Simon

Πέτρος ἑστὼς καὶ θερμαινόμενος. εἶπον
Peter standing and warming himself. They said

οὖν αὐτῷ· μὴ καὶ σὺ ἐκ τῶν μαθητῶν
therefore to him: Not also thou of the disciples

αὐτοῦ εἶ; ἠρνήσατο ἐκεῖνος καὶ εἶπεν·
of him art? Denied that one and said:

οὐκ εἰμί. 26 λέγει εἷς ἐκ τῶν δούλων τοῦ
I am not. Says one of the slaves of the

ἀρχιερέως, συγγενὴς ὢν οὗ ἀπέκοψεν
high priest, ²a relative ¹being ²[of him] of whom ⁴cut off

Πέτρος τὸ ὠτίον· οὐκ ἐγώ σε εἶδον
⁴Peter ⁶the ⁷ear: ³Not ¹I ⁴thee ¹saw

ἐν τῷ κήπῳ μετ᾽ αὐτοῦ; 27 πάλιν οὖν
in the garden with him? Again therefore

27 Peter then denied again: and immediately the cock crew.

28 ¶ Then led they Jesus from Caiaphas unto the hall of judgment: and it was early; and they themselves went not into the judgment hall, lest they should be defiled; but that they might eat the passover.

29 Pilate then went out unto them, and said, What accusation bring ye against this man?

30 They answered and said unto him, If he were not a malefactor, we would not have delivered him up unto thee.

31 Then said Pilate unto them, Take ye him, and judge him according to your law. The Jews therefore said unto him, It is not lawful for us to put any man to death:

32 That the saying of Jesus might be fulfilled, which he spake, signifying what death he should die.

33 Then Pilate entered into the judgment hall again, and called Jesus, and said unto him, Art thou the King of the Jews?

34 Jesus answered him, Sayest thou this thing of thyself, or did others tell it thee of me?

35 Pilate answered, Am

ἠρνήσατο   Πέτρος,   καὶ   εὐθέως   ἀλέκτωρ
denied   Peter,   and   immediately   a cock
ἐφώνησεν.
sounded(crew).

28 Ἄγουσιν   οὖν   τὸν   Ἰησοῦν   ἀπὸ   τοῦ
They lead   therefore   –   Jesus   from   –
Καϊαφᾶ   εἰς   τὸ   πραιτώριον·   ἦν   δὲ   πρωΐ·
Caiaphas   to   the   praetorium;   and it was   early;
καὶ   αὐτοὶ   οὐκ   εἰσῆλθον   εἰς   τὸ   πραιτώριον,
and   they   entered not   into   the   praetorium,
ἵνα   μὴ   μιανθῶσιν   ἀλλὰ   φάγωσιν   τὸ
lest   they should be defiled   but   might eat   the
πάσχα.   29 ἐξῆλθεν   οὖν   ὁ   Πιλᾶτος   ἔξω
passover.   Went forth therefore   –   Pilate   outside
πρὸς   αὐτοὺς   καὶ   φησίν·   τίνα   κατηγορίαν
to   them   and   says: What   accusation
φέρετε   τοῦ   ἀνθρώπου   τούτου;   30 ἀπεκρίθησαν
bring ye   –   man   of this?   They answered
καὶ   εἶπαν   αὐτῷ·   εἰ   μὴ   ἦν
and   said   to him: Unless   was
οὗτος   κακὸν   ποιῶν,   οὐκ   ἄν   σοι
this man   evil   doing,   ¹would ²not   ⁷to thee
παρεδώκαμεν   αὐτόν.   31 εἶπεν   οὖν   αὐτοῖς
¹we ⁴have ⁵delivered   ⁶him.   Said therefore to them
ὁ   Πιλᾶτος·   λάβετε   αὐτὸν   ὑμεῖς,   καὶ
–   Pilate: Take   him   ye,   and
κατὰ   τὸν   νόμον   ὑμῶν   κρίνατε   αὐτόν.
according to   the   law   of you   judge ye   him.
εἶπον   αὐτῷ   οἱ   Ἰουδαῖοι·   ἡμῖν   οὐκ   ἔξεστιν
Said   to him   the   Jews: For us   it is not lawful
ἀποκτεῖναι   οὐδένα·   32 ἵνα   ὁ   λόγος   τοῦ
to kill   no(any)one;   that   the   word   –
Ἰησοῦ   πληρωθῇ   ὃν   εἶπεν   σημαίνων   ποίῳ
of Jesus might be fulfilled   which he said   signifying   by what
θανάτῳ   ἤμελλεν   ἀποθνήσκειν.   33 Εἰσῆλθεν
death   he was about   to die.   Entered
οὖν   πάλιν   εἰς   τὸ   πραιτώριον   ὁ   Πιλᾶτος
therefore again   into   the   praetorium   –   Pilate
καὶ   ἐφώνησεν   τὸν   Ἰησοῦν   καὶ   εἶπεν
and   called   –   Jesus   and   said
αὐτῷ·   σὺ   εἶ   ὁ   βασιλεὺς   τῶν   Ἰουδαίων;
to him: Thou art   the   king   of the   Jews?
34 ἀπεκρίθη   Ἰησοῦς·   ἀφ’   ἑαυτοῦ   σὺ   τοῦτο
Answered   Jesus: From   [thy]self   ²thou   ³this
λέγεις,   ἢ   ἄλλοι   εἶπόν   σοι   περὶ   ἐμοῦ;
¹sayest,   or   others   told   thee   about   me?
35 ἀπεκρίθη   ὁ   Πιλᾶτος·   μήτι   ἐγὼ
Answered   –   Pilate: not   I

I a Jew? Thine own
nation and the chief priests
have delivered thee unto
me: what hast thou done?
36 Jesus answered, My
kingdom is not of this
world: if my kingdom
were of this world, then
would my servants fight,
that I should not be de-
livered to the Jews: but
now is my kingdom not
from hence.
37 Pilate therefore said
unto him, Art thou a king
then? Jesus answered,
Thou sayest that I am a
king. To this end was I
born, and for this cause
came I into the world, that
I should bear witness unto
the truth. Every one that
is of the truth heareth my
voice.
38 Pilate saith unto him,
What is truth? And when
he had said this, he went
out again unto the Jews,
and saith unto them, I
find in him no fault at all.
39 But ye have a cus-
tom, that I should release
unto you one at the pass-
over: will ye therefore
that I release unto you the
King of the Jews?
40 Then cried they all
again, saying, Not this
man, but Barabbas. Now
Barabbas was a robber.

Ἰουδαῖός   εἰμι;   τὸ   ἔθνος   τὸ   σὸν   καὶ
a Jew   am?   the   ¹nation -   ¹thy   and
οἱ   ἀρχιερεῖς   παρέδωκάν   σε   ἐμοί·   τί
the   chief priests delivered   thee to me;   what
ἐποίησας;   36   ἀπεκρίθη   Ἰησοῦς·   ἡ   βασιλεία
didst thou?   Answered   Jesus: The ²kingdom
ἡ   ἐμὴ   οὐκ   ἔστιν   ἐκ   τοῦ   κόσμου   τούτου·
-    ¹my   is not   of   -   world   this;
εἰ   ἐκ   τοῦ   κόσμου   τούτου   ἦν   ἡ   βασιλεία
if   of   -   world   this   was the ²kingdom
ἡ   ἐμή,   οἱ   ὑπηρέται   ἂν   οἱ   ἐμοὶ   ἠγωνίζοντο,
-    ¹my,   the   ²attendants ³would -   ¹my   ⁴have struggled,
ἵνα   μὴ   παραδοθῶ   τοῖς   Ἰουδαίοις·   νῦν
that I should not be delivered to the Jews;   ²now
δὲ   ἡ   βασιλεία   ἡ   ἐμὴ   οὐκ   ἔστιν   ἐντεῦθεν.
¹but the ²kingdom   -   ¹my   is not   hence.
37   εἶπεν   οὖν   αὐτῷ   ὁ   Πιλᾶτος·   οὐκοῦν
      Said   therefore to him -   Pilate: Not really
βασιλεὺς   εἶ   σύ;   ἀπεκρίθη   [ὁ]   Ἰησοῦς·
a king   art   thou? Answered   -   Jesus:
σὺ   λέγεις   ὅτι   βασιλεύς   εἰμι.   ἐγὼ   εἰς
Thou sayest   that   a king   I am.   I   for
τοῦτο   γεγέννημαι   καὶ   εἰς   τοῦτο   ἐλήλυθα
this   have been born and   for   this   I have come
εἰς   τὸν   κόσμον,   ἵνα   μαρτυρήσω   τῇ
into   the   world,   that   I might witness to the
ἀληθείᾳ·   πᾶς   ὁ   ὢν   ἐκ   τῆς   ἀληθείας
truth;   everyone being of   the   truth
ἀκούει   μου   τῆς   φωνῆς.   38   λέγει   αὐτῷ
hears   of me   the   voice.   Says   to him
ὁ   Πιλᾶτος·   τί   ἐστιν   ἀλήθεια;   Καὶ
-    Pilate: What is   truth?   And
τοῦτο   εἰπὼν   πάλιν   ἐξῆλθεν   πρὸς   τοὺς
this   having said again   he went forth to   the
Ἰουδαίους,   καὶ   λέγει   αὐτοῖς·   ἐγὼ   οὐδεμίαν
Jews,   and   tells   them: ¹I   ³no
εὑρίσκω   ἐν   αὐτῷ   αἰτίαν.   39   ἔστιν   δὲ
²find   in   ⁶him   ⁴crime.   But there is
συνήθεια   ὑμῖν   ἵνα   ἕνα   ἀπολύσω   ὑμῖν
a custom   to youᵉ that   one   I should release to you
ἐν   τῷ   πάσχα·   βούλεσθε   οὖν   ἀπολύσω
at   the   Passover; will ye   therefore [that] I release
ὑμῖν   τὸν   βασιλέα   τῶν   Ἰουδαίων;   40   ἐκραύ-
to you   the   king   of the Jews?   They cried
γασαν   οὖν   πάλιν   λέγοντες·   μὴ   τοῦτον,
out   therefore again   saying: Not   this man,
ἀλλὰ   τὸν   Βαραββᾶν.   ἦν   δὲ   ὁ   Βαραββᾶς
but   -   Barabbas   ¹But ²was -   ¹Barabbas

CHAPTER 19

THEN Pilate therefore took Jesus, and scourged *him*.

2 And the soldiers platted a crown of thorns, and put *it* on his head, and they put on him a purple robe,

3 And said, Hail, King of the Jews! and they smote him with their hands.

4 Pilate therefore went forth again, and saith unto them, Behold, I bring him forth to you, that ye may know that I find no fault in him.

5 Then came Jesus forth, wearing the crown of thorns, and the purple robe. And *Pilate* saith unto them, Behold the man!

6 When the chief priests therefore and officers saw him, they cried out, saying, Crucify *him*, crucify *him*. Pilate saith unto them, Take ye him, and crucify *him:* for I find no fault in him.

7 The Jews answered him, We have a law, and by our law he ought to die, because he made himself the Son of God.

8 ¶ When Pilate therefore heard that saying, he was the more afraid;

λῃστής.   **19** Τότε οὖν ἔλαβεν ὁ Πιλᾶτος
⁴a robber.   Then therefore ²took   -   ¹Pilate

τὸν Ἰησοῦν καὶ ἐμαστίγωσεν.   **2** καὶ οἱ
-    ³Jesus   and   scourged [him].   And the

στρατιῶται πλέξαντες στέφανον ἐξ ἀκανθῶν
soldiers   having plaited   a wreath   out of   thorns

ἐπέθηκαν αὐτοῦ τῇ κεφαλῇ, καὶ ἱμάτιον
put [it] on   of him   the   head,   and   ⁴garment

πορφυροῦν περιέβαλον αὐτόν, **3** καὶ ἤρχοντο
³a purple   ¹threw round   ²him,   and   came

πρὸς αὐτὸν καὶ ἔλεγον· χαῖρε ὁ βασιλεὺς
to   him   and   said :   Hail[,]   -   king

τῶν Ἰουδαίων· καὶ ἐδίδοσαν αὐτῷ
of the   Jews;   and   they gave   him

ῥαπίσματα.   **4** Καὶ ἐξῆλθεν πάλιν ἔξω
blows.   And   went forth   again   outside

ὁ Πιλᾶτος καὶ λέγει αὐτοῖς· ἴδε ἄγω
-   Pilate   and   says   to them :   Behold ¹I bring

ὑμῖν αὐτὸν ἔξω, ἵνα γνῶτε ὅτι οὐδεμίαν
⁴to you   ²him   ³out,   that ye may know   that   no

αἰτίαν εὑρίσκω ἐν αὐτῷ.   **5** ἐξῆλθεν
crime   I find   in   him.   Came forth

οὖν ὁ Ἰησοῦς ἔξω, φορῶν τὸν ἀκάνθινον
therefore -   Jesus   outside,   wearing   the   thorny

στέφανον καὶ τὸ πορφυροῦν ἱμάτιον. καὶ
wreath   and   the   purple   garment.   And

λέγει αὐτοῖς· ἰδοὺ ὁ ἄνθρωπος.   **6** ὅτε
he says   to them : Behold[,] the   man.   When

οὖν εἶδον αὐτὸν οἱ ἀρχιερεῖς καὶ οἱ
therefore saw   him   the   chief priests   and   the

ὑπηρέται, ἐκραύγασαν λέγοντες· σταύρωσον
attendants,   they shouted   saying :   Crucify[,]

σταύρωσον. λέγει αὐτοῖς ὁ Πιλᾶτος·
crucify.   Says   to them   -   Pilate :

λάβετε αὐτὸν ὑμεῖς καὶ σταυρώσατε·
¹Take   ²him   ²ye   and   crucify;

ἐγὼ γὰρ οὐχ εὑρίσκω ἐν αὐτῷ αἰτίαν.
for I   find not   in   him   crime.

7 ἀπεκρίθησαν αὐτῷ οἱ Ἰουδαῖοι· ἡμεῖς
Answered   him   the   Jews :   We

νόμον ἔχομεν, καὶ κατὰ τὸν νόμον
a law   have,   and   according to   the   law

ὀφείλει ἀποθανεῖν, ὅτι υἱὸν θεοῦ ἑαυτὸν
he ought   to die,   because   Son   of God   himself

ἐποίησεν. **8** Ὅτε οὖν ἤκουσεν ὁ Πιλᾶτος
he made.   When therefore   heard   -   Pilate

τοῦτον τὸν λόγον, μᾶλλον ἐφοβήθη, **9** καὶ
this   -   word,   more   he was afraid,   and

9 And went again into the judgment hall, and saith unto Jesus, Whence art thou? But Jesus gave him no answer.

10 Then saith Pilate unto him, Speakest thou not unto me? knowest thou not that I have power to crucify thee, and have power to release thee?

11 Jesus answered, Thou couldest have no power *at all* against me, except it were given thee from above: therefore he that delivered me unto thee hath the greater sin.

12 And from thenceforth Pilate sought to release him: but the Jews cried out, saying, If thou let this man go, thou art not Cæsar's friend: whosoever maketh himself a king speaketh against Cæsar.

13 ¶ When Pilate therefore heard that saying, he brought Jesus forth, and sat down in the judgment seat in a place that is called the Pavement, but in the Hebrew, Gabbatha.

14 And it was the preparation of the passover, and about the sixth hour: and he saith unto the Jews, Behold your King!

15 But they cried out, Away with *him*, away with *him*, crucify him. Pilate saith unto them, Shall I crucify your King? The

εἰσῆλθεν εἰς τὸ πραιτώριον πάλιν καὶ
entered into the prætorium again and

λέγει τῷ Ἰησοῦ· πόθεν εἶ σύ; ὁ δὲ
says – to Jesus : Whence art thou? – But

Ἰησοῦς ἀπόκρισιν οὐκ ἔδωκεν αὐτῷ.
Jesus answer did not give him.

10 λέγει οὖν αὐτῷ ὁ Πιλᾶτος· ἐμοὶ
Says therefore to him – Pilate : To me

οὐ λαλεῖς; οὐκ οἶδας ὅτι ἐξουσίαν ἔχω
speakest thou not? knowest thou not that authority I have

ἀπολῦσαί σε καὶ ἐξουσίαν ἔχω σταυρῶσαί
to release thee and authority I have to crucify

σε; 11 ἀπεκρίθη Ἰησοῦς· οὐκ εἶχες
thee? Answered Jesus : Thou hadst not

ἐξουσίαν κατ᾽ ἐμοῦ οὐδεμίαν εἰ μὴ ἦν
²authority ³against ⁴me ¹no(any) unless it was

δεδομένον σοι ἄνωθεν· διὰ τοῦτο ὁ
having been given thee from above; therefore the [one]

παραδούς μέ σοι μείζονα ἁμαρτίαν ἔχει.
having delivered me to thee a greater sin has.

12 ἐκ τούτου ὁ Πιλᾶτος ἐζήτει ἀπολῦσαι
From this – Pilate sought to release

αὐτόν· οἱ δὲ Ἰουδαῖοι ἐκραύγασαν λέγοντες·
him; but the Jews shouted saying :

ἐὰν τοῦτον ἀπολύσῃς, οὐκ εἶ φίλος τοῦ
If this man thou releasest, thou art not a friend –

Καίσαρος· πᾶς ὁ βασιλέα ἑαυτὸν ποιῶν
of Cæsar; everyone a king himself making

ἀντιλέγει τῷ Καίσαρι. 13 Ὁ οὖν Πιλᾶτος
speaks against – Cæsar. Therefore Pilate

ἀκούσας τῶν λόγων τούτων ἤγαγεν ἔξω
hearing – words these brought outside

τὸν Ἰησοῦν, καὶ ἐκάθισεν ἐπὶ βήματος
– Jesus, and sat on a tribunal

εἰς τόπον λεγόμενον Λιθόστρωτον, Ἑβραϊστὶ δὲ
in a place *being* called Pavement, but in Hebrew

Γαββαθά. 14 ἦν δὲ παρασκευὴ τοῦ
Gabbatha. Now it was preparation of the

πάσχα, ὥρα ἦν ὡς ἕκτη· καὶ λέγει
Passover, hour it was about sixth; and he says

τοῖς Ἰουδαίοις· ἴδε ὁ βασιλεὺς ὑμῶν.
to the Jews; Behold[,] the king of you.

15 ἐκραύγασαν οὖν ἐκεῖνοι· ἆρον ἆρον,
• Shouted therefore those : Take[,] take,

σταύρωσον αὐτόν. λέγει αὐτοῖς ὁ Πιλᾶτος·
crucify him. Says to them – Pilate :

τὸν βασιλέα ὑμῶν σταυρώσω; ἀπεκρίθησαν
The king of you shall I crucify? Answered

chief priests answered, We have no king but Cæsar.

16 Then delivered he him therefore unto them to be crucified. And they took Jesus, and led *him* away.

17 And he bearing his cross went forth into a place called *the place* of a skull, which is called in the Hebrew Golgotha:

18 Where they crucified him, and two other with him, on either side one, and Jesus in the midst.

19 ¶ And Pilate wrote a title, and put *it* on the cross. And the writing was, JESUS OF NAZA-RETH THE KING OF THE JEWS.

20 This title then read many of the Jews: for the place where Jesus was crucified was nigh to the city: and it was written in Hebrew, *and* Greek, *and* Latin.

21 Then said the chief priests of the Jews to Pilate, Write not, The King of the Jews; but that he said, I am King of the Jews.

22 Pilate answered, What I have written I have written.

23 ¶ Then the soldiers, when they had crucified

οἱ   ἀρχιερεῖς·   οὐκ   ἔχομεν   βασιλέα   εἰ
the   chief priests :   We have not   a king   ex-

μὴ   Καίσαρα.   **16** τότε   οὖν   παρέδωκεν
cept   Cæsar.   Then therefore   he delivered

αὐτὸν   αὐτοῖς   ἵνα   σταυρωθῇ.
him   to them   that he should be crucified.

Παρέλαβον   οὖν   τὸν   Ἰησοῦν·   **17** καὶ
They took   therefore   –   Jesus;   and

βαστάζων   ἑαυτῷ   τὸν   σταυρὸν   ἐξῆλθεν
carrying   ³to himself ᶜ   ¹the   ²cross   he went forth

εἰς   τὸν   λεγόμενον   κρανίου   τόπον,   ὃ
to   ¹the   ³*being* called   ⁴of a skull   ⁵place,   which

λέγεται   Ἑβραϊστὶ   Γολγοθά,   **18** ὅπου   αὐτὸν
is called   in Hebrew   Golgotha,   where   him

ἐσταύρωσαν,   καὶ   μετ’   αὐτοῦ   ἄλλους   δύο
they crucified,   and   with   him   others   two

ἐντεῦθεν   καὶ   ἐντεῦθεν,   μέσον   δὲ   τὸν
on this side and on that,   †   and in the middle   –

Ἰησοῦν.   **19** ἔγραψεν   δὲ   καὶ   τίτλον   ὁ
Jesus.   And wrote   also   a title   –

Πιλᾶτος   καὶ   ἔθηκεν   ἐπὶ   τοῦ   σταυροῦ·
Pilate   and   put [it]   on   the   cross;

ἦν   δὲ   γεγραμμένον·   ΙΗΣΟΥΣ   Ο
and it was   *having been* written :   JESUS   THE

ΝΑΖΩΡΑΙΣ   Ο   ΒΑΣΙΛΕΥΣ   ΤΩΝ
NAZARENE   THE   KING   OF THE

ΙΟΥΔΑΙΩΝ.   **20** τοῦτον   οὖν   τὸν   τίτλον
JEWS.   ¹This   ²therefore –   ²title

πολλοὶ   ἀνέγνωσαν   τῶν   Ἰουδαίων,   ὅτι
¹many   ⁴read   ²of the   ³Jews,   because

ἐγγὺς   ἦν   ὁ   τόπος   τῆς   πόλεως   ὅπου
⁷near   ⁶was   ¹the   ²place   ³the   ⁵city   ³where

ἐσταυρώθη   ὁ   Ἰησοῦς·   καὶ   ἦν   γεγραμμένον
⁴was crucified   –   ²Jesus;   and it was   *having been* written

Ἑβραϊστί,   Ῥωμαϊστί,   Ἑλληνιστί.   **21** ἔλεγον
in Hebrew,   in Latin,   in Greek.   Said

οὖν   τῷ   Πιλάτῳ   οἱ   ἀρχιερεῖς   τῶν   Ἰουδαίων·
therefore –   to Pilate   the   chief priests of the   Jews :

μὴ   γράφε·   ὁ   βασιλεὺς   τῶν   Ἰουδαίων,
Write not :   The   king   of the   Jews,

ἀλλ’   ὅτι   ἐκεῖνος   εἶπεν·   βασιλεύς   εἰμι
but   that   that man   said :   King   I am

τῶν   Ἰουδαίων.   **22** ἀπεκρίθη   ὁ   Πιλᾶτος·
of the   Jews.   Answered   –   Pilate :

ὃ   γέγραφα,   γέγραφα.   **23** Οἱ   οὖν
What   I have written,   I have written.   Therefore the

στρατιῶται,   ὅτε   ἐσταύρωσαν   τὸν   Ἰησοῦν,
soldiers.   when   they crucified   –   Jesus,

Jesus, took his garments, and made four parts,. to every soldier a part; and also *his* coat: now the coat was without seam, woven from the top throughout.

24 They said therefore among themselves, Let us not rend it, but cast lots for it, whose it shall be: that the scripture might be fulfilled, which saith, They parted my raiment among them, and for my vesture they did cast lots. These things therefore the soldiers did.

25 ¶ Now there stood by the cross of Jesus his mother, and his mother's sister, Mary the *wife* of Cleophas, and Mary Magdalene.

26 When Jesus therefore saw his mother, and the disciple standing by, whom he loved, he saith unto his mother, Woman, behold thy son!

27 Then saith he to the disciple, Behold thy mother! And from that hour that disciple took her unto his own *home*.

28 ¶ After this, Jesus knowing that all things were now accomplished, that the scripture might be fulfilled, saith, I thirst.

29 Now there was set a vessel full of vinegar: and they filled a spunge with vinegar, and put *it* upon

ἔλαβον τὰ ἱμάτια αὐτοῦ καὶ ἐποίησαν
took   the   garments   of him   and   made

τέσσερα μέρη, ἑκάστῳ στρατιώτῃ μέρος,
four   parts,   to each   soldier   a part,

καὶ τὸν χιτῶνα. ἦν δὲ ὁ χιτὼν ἄρραφος,
and the   tunic.   Now was the   tunic   seamless,

ἐκ τῶν ἄνωθεν ὑφαντὸς δι' ὅλου. 24 εἶπαν
from the   top   woven   throughout. 24 They said

οὖν πρὸς ἀλλήλους· μὴ σχίσωμεν αὐτόν,
therefore to   one another :   Let us not tear   it,

ἀλλὰ λάχωμεν περὶ αὐτοῦ τίνος ἔσται·
but   let us cast lots   about   it   of whom it shall be;

ἵνα ἡ γραφὴ πληρωθῇ· διεμερίσαντο τὰ
that the   scripture   might be fulfilled :   They parted   the

ἱμάτιά μου ἑαυτοῖς καὶ ἐπὶ τὸν ἱματισμόν
garments of me to themselves and   over   the   raiment

μου ἔβαλον κλῆρον. Οἱ μὲν οὖν στρατιῶται
of me   they cast   a lot. [3]The –[*] [3]therefore [4]soldiers

ταῦτα ἐποίησαν. 25 εἱστήκεισαν δὲ παρὰ
[1]these things [2]did. 25 [1]there stood   [2]But   by

τῷ σταυρῷ τοῦ Ἰησοῦ ἡ μήτηρ αὐτοῦ
the   cross   –   of Jesus   the   mother   of him

καὶ ἡ ἀδελφὴ τῆς μητρὸς αὐτοῦ, Μαρία
and   the   sister   of the   mother   of him,   Mary

ἡ τοῦ Κλωπᾶ καὶ Μαρία ἡ Μαγδαληνή.
the [?wife] –   of Clopas and   Mary   the   Magdalene.

26 Ἰησοῦς οὖν ἰδὼν τὴν μητέρα καὶ
26 Jesus   therefore seeing   the(his)   mother   and

τὸν μαθητὴν παρεστῶτα ὃν ἠγάπα, λέγει
the   disciple   standing by   whom he loved,   says

τῇ μητρί· γύναι, ἴδε ὁ υἱός σου.
to the(his) mother :   Woman,   behold[,] the   son   of thee.

27 εἶτα λέγει τῷ μαθητῇ· ἴδε ἡ μήτηρ
27 Then   he says   to the   disciple : Behold[,] the   mother

σου. καὶ ἀπ' ἐκείνης τῆς ὥρας ἔλαβεν
of thee.   And from   that   hour   took

ὁ μαθητὴς αὐτὴν εἰς τὰ ἴδια. 28 Μετὰ
the   disciple   her   to his own [home]. †   28 After

τοῦτο εἰδὼς ὁ Ἰησοῦς ὅτι ἤδη πάντα
this   knowing   –   Jesus   that   now   all things

τετέλεσται, ἵνα τελειωθῇ ἡ γραφή, λέγει·
have been finished,   that   might be fulfilled   the scripture,   says:

διψῶ. 29 σκεῦος ἔκειτο ὄξους μεστόν·
I thirst.   29   A vessel   was set   of vinegar   full;

σπόγγον οὖν μεστὸν τοῦ ὄξους ὑσσώπῳ
[3]a sponge   therefore [4]full   [5]of the [6]vinegar   [8]a hyssop §

---

* μέν is scarcely translatable. But note the δέ in ver. 25 : John contrasts two groups—the soldiers and the women.

§ It has been suggested that ὑσσώπῳ is a graphic error for ὑσσῷ (*pilum*), pike; but *cf.* Mat. 27. 48.

hyssop, and put *it* to his mouth.

30 When Jesus therefore had received the vinegar, he said, It is finished: and he bowed his head, and gave up the ghost.

31 ¶ The Jews therefore, because it was the preparation, that the bodies should not remain upon the cross on the sabbath day, (for that sabbath day was an high day,) besought Pilate that their legs might be broken, and *that* they might be taken away.

32 Then came the soldiers, and brake the legs of the first, and of the other which was crucified with him.

33 But when they came to Jesus, and saw that he was dead already, they brake not his legs:

34 But one of the soldiers with a spear pierced his side, and forthwith came there out blood and water.

35 And he that saw *it* bare record, and his record is true: and he knoweth that he saith true, that ye might believe.

36 For these things were done, that the scripture should be fulfilled, A bone of him shall not be broken.

37 And again another scripture saith, They shall look on him whom they pierced.

περιθέντες προσήνεγκαν αὐτοῦ τῷ στόματι.
²putting ¹round they brought [it] to of him the mouth.

30 ὅτε οὖν ἔλαβεν τὸ ὄξος [ὁ] Ἰησοῦς
When therefore took the vinegar - Jesus

εἶπεν· τετέλεσται, καὶ κλίνας τὴν κεφαλὴν
he said : It has been finished, and inclining the(his) head

παρέδωκεν τὸ πνεῦμα.
delivered up the(his) spirit.

31 Οἱ οὖν Ἰουδαῖοι, ἐπεὶ παρασκευὴ
The ²therefore ¹Jews, since preparation

ἦν, ἵνα μὴ μείνῃ ἐπὶ τοῦ σταυροῦ τὰ
it was, that might not remain on the cross the

σώματα ἐν τῷ σαββάτῳ, ἦν γὰρ μεγάλη
bodies on the sabbath, for was great

ἡ ἡμέρα ἐκείνου τοῦ σαββάτου, ἠρώτησαν
the day of that - sabbath, they asked

τὸν Πιλᾶτον ἵνα κατεαγῶσιν αὐτῶν τὰ
- Pilate that might be broken of them the

σκέλη καὶ ἀρθῶσιν. **32** ἦλθον οὖν οἱ
legs and they might be taken. Came therefore the

στρατιῶται, καὶ τοῦ μὲν πρώτου κατέαξαν
soldiers, and of the -* first broke

τὰ σκέλη καὶ τοῦ ἄλλου τοῦ
the legs and of the other -

συσταυρωθέντος αὐτῷ· **33** ἐπὶ δὲ τὸν
crucified with him; ²on ¹but the

Ἰησοῦν ἐλθόντες, ὡς εἶδον ἤδη αὐτὸν
⁴Jesus ²coming, when they saw already him

τεθνηκότα, οὐ κατέαξαν αὐτοῦ τὰ σκέλη,
to have died, they did not break of him the legs,

34 ἀλλ' εἷς τῶν στρατιωτῶν λόγχῃ αὐτοῦ
but one of the soldiers with a lance of him

τὴν πλευρὰν ἔνυξεν, καὶ ἐξῆλθεν εὐθὺς αἷμα
the side pricked, and there came imme- blood
out diately

καὶ ὕδωρ. **35** καὶ ὁ ἑωρακὼς μεμαρτύρηκεν,
and water. And the [one] having seen has witnessed,

καὶ ἀληθινὴ αὐτοῦ ἐστιν ἡ μαρτυρία,
and true of him is the witness,

καὶ ἐκεῖνος οἶδεν ὅτι ἀληθῆ λέγει, ἵνα
and that one knows that truly he says, that

καὶ ὑμεῖς πιστεύητε. **36** ἐγένετο γὰρ
also ye may believe. For happened

ταῦτα ἵνα ἡ γραφὴ πληρωθῇ· ὀστοῦν
these things that the scripture might be fulfilled : A bone

οὐ συντριβήσεται αὐτοῦ. **37** καὶ πάλιν
shall not be broken of him. And again

ἑτέρα γραφὴ λέγει· ὄψονται εἰς ὃν
another scripture says : They shall look at [him] whom

* See note on 19. 24. Here see ver. 33—two actions contrasted.

38 ¶ And after this Joseph of Arimathæa, being a disciple of Jesus, but secretly for fear of the Jews, besought Pilate that he might take away the body of Jesus: and Pilate gave *him* leave. He came therefore, and took the body of Jesus.

39 And there came also Nicodemus, which at the first came to Jesus by night, and brought a mixture of myrrh and aloes, about an hundred pound *weight*.

40 Then took they the body of Jesus, and wound it in linen clothes with the spices, as the manner of the Jews is to bury.

41 Now in the place where he was crucified there was a garden; and in the garden a new sepulchre, wherein was never man yet laid.

42 There laid they Jesus therefore because of the Jews' preparation *day;* for the sepulchre was nigh at hand.

ἐξεκέντησαν.   **38** Μετὰ δὲ ταῦτα ἠρώτησεν
they pierced.   Now after these things   ¹⁴asked

τὸν Πιλᾶτον Ἰωσὴφ ἀπὸ Ἀριμαθαίας,
\-   ¹⁵Pilate   ¹Joseph   ²from   ³Arimathæa,

ὢν μαθητὴς [τοῦ] Ἰησοῦ κεκρυμμένος
⁴being ⁵a disciple   ⁶of Jesus   ⁸*having been* hidden

δὲ διὰ τὸν φόβον τῶν Ἰουδαίων, ἵνα
⁷but ⁹because ¹⁰the   ¹¹fear ¹²of the   ¹³Jews,   that
       of

ἄρῃ τὸ σῶμα τοῦ Ἰησοῦ· καὶ
he might take the   body   of Jesus;   and

ἐπέτρεψεν ὁ Πιλᾶτος. ἦλθεν οὖν καὶ ἦρεν
allowed   \-   Pilate.   He came there- and   took
                       fore

τὸ σῶμα αὐτοῦ.   **39** ἦλθεν δὲ καὶ Νικόδημος,
the body of him.   And came also   Nicodemus,

ὁ ἐλθὼν πρὸς αὐτὸν νυκτὸς τὸ πρῶτον,
the [one] having come to   him of (by) night   at first,†

φέρων μίγμα σμύρνης καὶ ἀλόης ὡς
bearing a mixture of myrrh   and   aloes   about

λίτρας ἑκατόν.   **40** ἔλαβον οὖν τὸ σῶμα
pounds a hundred.   They took there-   the   body
                    fore

τοῦ Ἰησοῦ καὶ ἔδησαν αὐτὸ ὀθονίοις
\- of Jesus and   bound   it   in sheets

μετὰ τῶν ἀρωμάτων, καθὼς ἔθος ἐστὶν
with   the   spices,   as   custom   is

τοῖς Ἰουδαίοις ἐνταφιάζειν.   **41** ἦν δὲ
with the   Jews   to bury.   Now there was

ἐν τῷ τόπῳ ὅπου ἐσταυρώθη κῆπος,
in the   place   where   he was crucified a garden,

καὶ ἐν τῷ κήπῳ μνημεῖον καινόν, ἐν
and in   the   garden   tomb   a new,   in

ᾧ οὐδέπω οὐδεὶς ἦν τεθειμένος· **42** ἐκεῖ
which never yet no(any) was *having been* put;   there
            one

οὖν διὰ τὴν παρασκευὴν τῶν Ἰουδαίων,
therefore because of the   preparation   of the   Jews,

ὅτι ἐγγὺς ἦν τὸ μνημεῖον, ἔθηκαν τὸν
because near was the   tomb,   they put   \-

Ἰησοῦν.
Jesus.

CHAPTER 20

THE first *day* of the week cometh Mary Magdalene early, when it was yet dark, unto the sepulchre, and seeth the

20 Τῇ δὲ μιᾷ τῶν σαββάτων Μαρία
Now on the one(first) [day] of the   week   Mary

ἡ Μαγδαληνὴ ἔρχεται πρωῒ σκοτίας ἔτι
the Magdalene   comes   early   darkness   yet
                      = while it was yet dark

οὔσης εἰς τὸ μνημεῖον, καὶ βλέπει τὸν
being°   to   the   tomb,   and   sees   the

stone taken away from the
sepulchre.

2 Then she runneth,
and cometh to Simon
Peter, and to the other
disciple, whom Jesus loved,
and saith unto them, They
have taken away the Lord
out of the sepulchre, and
we know not where they
have laid him.

3 Peter therefore went
forth, and that other
disciple, and came to the
sepulchre.

4 So they ran both to-
gether: and the other
disciple did outrun Peter,
and came first to the
sepulchre.

5 And he stooping
down, *and looking in,*
saw the linen clothes
lying; yet went he not in.

6 Then cometh Simon
Peter following him, and
went into the sepulchre,
and seeth the linen clothes
lie,

7 And the napkin, that
was about his head, not
lying with the linen clothes,
but wrapped together in a
place by itself.

8 Then went in also
that other disciple, which
came first to the sepulchre,
and he saw, and believed.

9 For as yet they knew
not the scripture, that he
must rise again from the
dead.

10 Then the disciples
went away again unto
their own home.

λίθον ἠρμένον ἐκ τοῦ μνημείου.
stone having been taken out of the tomb.

2 τρέχει οὖν καὶ ἔρχεται πρὸς Σίμωνα
She runs therefore and comes to Simon

Πέτρον καὶ πρὸς τὸν ἄλλον μαθητὴν ὃν
Peter and to the other disciple whom

ἐφίλει ὁ Ἰησοῦς, καὶ λέγει αὐτοῖς· ἦραν
²loved — ¹Jesus, and says to them: They took

τὸν κύριον ἐκ τοῦ μνημείου, καὶ οὐκ οἴδαμεν
the Lord out of the tomb, and we do not know

ποῦ ἔθηκαν αὐτόν. 3 Ἐξῆλθεν οὖν ὁ
where they put him. Went forth therefore –

Πέτρος καὶ ὁ ἄλλος μαθητής, καὶ ἤρχοντο
Peter and the other disciple, and came

εἰς τὸ μνημεῖον. 4 ἔτρεχον δὲ οἱ δύο
to the tomb. And ran the two

ὁμοῦ· καὶ ὁ ἄλλος μαθητὴς προέδραμεν
together; and the other disciple ran before

τάχιον τοῦ Πέτρου καὶ ἦλθεν πρῶτος
more quickly [than] – Peter and came first

εἰς τὸ μνημεῖον, 5 καὶ παρακύψας βλέπει
to the tomb, and stooping sees

κείμενα τὰ ὀθόνια, οὐ μέντοι εἰσῆλθεν.
lying the sheets, not however he entered.

6 ἔρχεται οὖν καὶ Σίμων Πέτρος ἀκο-
Comes therefore also Simon Peter follow-

λουθῶν αὐτῷ, καὶ εἰσῆλθεν εἰς τὸ
ing him, and entered into the

μνημεῖον· καὶ θεωρεῖ τὰ ὀθόνια κείμενα,
tomb; and he beholds the sheets lying,

7 καὶ τὸ σουδάριον, ὃ ἦν ἐπὶ τῆς
and the kerchief, which was on the

κεφαλῆς αὐτοῦ, οὐ μετὰ τῶν ὀθονίων
head of him, not with the sheets

κείμενον ἀλλὰ χωρὶς ἐντετυλιγμένον εἰς
lying but apart having been wrapped up in

ἕνα τόπον. 8 τότε οὖν εἰσῆλθεν καὶ
one place. Then therefore entered also

ὁ ἄλλος μαθητὴς ὁ ἐλθὼν πρῶτος εἰς
the other disciple – having come first to

τὸ μνημεῖον, καὶ εἶδεν καὶ ἐπίστευσεν·
the tomb, and he saw and believed;

9 οὐδέπω γὰρ ᾔδεισαν τὴν γραφήν, ὅτι
for not yet they knew the scripture, that

δεῖ αὐτὸν ἐκ νεκρῶν ἀναστῆναι.
it behoves him from [the] dead to rise again.

10 ἀπῆλθον οὖν πάλιν πρὸς αὐτοὺς οἱ
Went away therefore again to themselves* the

* That is, to their own home; *cf.* 19. 27.

11 ¶ But Mary stood without at the sepulchre weeping: and as she wept, she stooped down, *and looked* into the sepulchre,

12 And seeth two angels in white sitting, the one at the head, and the other at the feet, where the body of Jesus had lain.

13 And they say unto her, Woman, why weepest thou? She saith unto them, Because they have taken away my Lord, and I know not where they have laid him.

14 And when she had thus said, she turned herself back, and saw Jesus standing, and knew not that it was Jesus.

15 Jesus saith unto her, Woman, why weepest thou? whom seekest thou? She, supposing him to be the gardener, saith unto him, Sir, if thou have borne him hence, tell me where thou hast laid him, and I will take him away.

16 Jesus saith unto her, Mary. She turned herself, and saith unto him, Rabboni; which is to say, Master.

17 Jesus saith unto her, Touch me not; for I am not yet ascended to my Father: but go to my brethren, and say unto them, I ascend unto my Father, and your Father;

μαθηταί.   **11** Μαρία   δὲ   εἱστήκει   πρὸς
disciples.   But Mary   stood   at

τῷ   μνημείῳ   ἔξω   κλαίουσα.   ὡς   οὖν
the   tomb   outside   weeping.   As   therefore

ἔκλαιεν,   παρέκυψεν   εἰς   τὸ   μνημεῖον,
she was weeping,   she stooped   into   the   tomb,

12 καὶ   θεωρεῖ   δύο   ἀγγέλους   ἐν   λευκοῖς
and   beholds   two   angels   in   white

καθεζομένους,   ἕνα   πρὸς   τῇ   κεφαλῇ   καὶ
sitting,   one   at   the   head   and

ἕνα   πρὸς   τοῖς   ποσίν,   ὅπου   ἔκειτο   τὸ
one   at   the   feet,   where   lay   the

σῶμα   τοῦ   Ἰησοῦ.   **13** καὶ   λέγουσιν   αὐτῇ
body   -   of Jesus.   And   say   to her

ἐκεῖνοι·   γύναι,   τί   κλαίεις;   λέγει   αὐτοῖς
those: Woman,   why weepest thou?   She says   to them[,]

ὅτι   ἦραν   τὸν   κύριόν   μου,   καὶ   οὐκ   οἶδα
-   They took   the   Lord   of me,   and   I know not

ποῦ   ἔθηκαν   αὐτόν.   **14** ταῦτα   εἰποῦσα
where   they put   him.   These things   saying

ἐστράφη   εἰς   τὰ   ὀπίσω,   καὶ   θεωρεῖ   τὸν
she turned   back,†   and   beholds   -

Ἰησοῦν   ἑστῶτα,   καὶ   οὐκ   ᾔδει   ὅτι   Ἰησοῦς
Jesus   standing,   and   knew not   that   Jesus

ἐστιν.   **15** λέγει   αὐτῇ   Ἰησοῦς·   γύναι,
it is(was).   Says   to her   Jesus: Woman,

τί   κλαίεις;   τίνα   ζητεῖς;   ἐκείνη   δοκοῦσα
why weepest thou?   whom seekest thou?   That one   thinking

ὅτι   ὁ   κηπουρός   ἐστιν,   λέγει   αὐτῷ·   κύριε,
that   the   gardener   it is(was),   says   to him: Sir,

εἰ   σὺ   ἐβάστασας   αὐτόν,   εἰπέ   μοι   ποῦ
if   thou   didst carry   him,   tell   me   where

ἔθηκας   αὐτόν, κἀγὼ   αὐτὸν   ἀρῶ.   **16** λέγει
thou didst put   him,   and I   him   will take.   Says

αὐτῇ   Ἰησοῦς·   Μαριάμ.   στραφεῖσα   ἐκείνη
to her   Jesus: Mary.   Turning   that one

λέγει   αὐτῷ   Ἑβραϊστί·   ῥαββουνί   (ὃ   λέγεται
says   to him   in Hebrew: Rabboni   (which is said

διδάσκαλε).   **17** λέγει   αὐτῇ   Ἰησοῦς·   μή
Teacher).   Says   to her   Jesus: Not

μου   ἅπτου,   οὔπω   γὰρ   ἀναβέβηκα   πρὸς
me   touch,   for not yet   have I ascended   to

τὸν   πατέρα·   πορεύου   δὲ   πρὸς   τοὺς
the   Father;   but go thou   to   the

ἀδελφούς   μου   καὶ   εἰπὲ   αὐτοῖς·   ἀναβαίνω
brothers   of me   and   tell   them: I ascend

πρὸς   τὸν   πατέρα   μου   καὶ   πατέρα   ὑμῶν
to   the   Father   of me   and   Father   of you

and *to* my God, and your God.

18 Mary Magdalene came and told the disciples that she had seen the Lord, and *that* he had spoken these things unto her.

19¶ Then the same day at evening, being the first *day* of the week, when the doors were shut where the disciples were assembled for fear of the Jews, came Jesus and stood in the midst, and saith unto them, Peace *be* unto you.

20 And when he had so said, he shewed unto them *his* hands and his side. Then were the disciples glad, when they saw the Lord.

21 Then said Jesus to them again, Peace *be* unto you: as *my* Father hath sent me, even so send I you.

22 And when he had said this, he breathed on *them*, and saith unto them, Receive ye the Holy Ghost:

23 Whose soever sins ye remit, they are remitted unto them; *and* whose soever *sins* ye retain, they are retained.

24¶ But Thomas, one of the twelve, called Didymus, was not with them when Jesus came.

25 The other disciples therefore said unto him, We have seen the Lord.

καὶ θεόν μου καὶ θεὸν ὑμῶν. **18** ἔρχεται
and God of me and God of you. Comes

Μαριὰμ ἡ Μαγδαληνὴ ἀγγέλλουσα τοῖς
Mary the Magdalene announcing to the

μαθηταῖς ὅτι ἑώρακα τὸν κύριον, καὶ
disciples[,] – I have seen the Lord, and

ταῦτα εἶπεν αὐτῇ.
these things he said to her.

19 Οὔσης οὖν ὀψίας τῇ ἡμέρᾳ ἐκείνῃ
Being therefore early evening – day on that
=Therefore when it was early evening

τῇ μιᾷ σαββάτων, καὶ τῶν θυρῶν
the one(first) of the week, and the doors

κεκλεισμένων ὅπου ἦσαν οἱ μαθηταὶ διὰ
having been shut where were the disciples because of

τὸν φόβον τῶν Ἰουδαίων, ἦλθεν ὁ Ἰησοῦς
the fear of the Jews, came – Jesus

καὶ ἔστη εἰς τὸ μέσον, καὶ λέγει αὐτοῖς·
and stood in the midst, and says to them :

εἰρήνη ὑμῖν. **20** καὶ τοῦτο εἰπὼν ἔδειξεν
Peace to you. And this saying he showed

καὶ τὰς χεῖρας καὶ τὴν πλευρὰν αὐτοῖς.
both the(his) hands and the(his) side to them.

ἐχάρησαν οὖν οἱ μαθηταὶ ἰδόντες τὸν
Rejoiced therefore the disciples seeing the

κύριον. **21** εἶπεν οὖν αὐτοῖς [ὁ Ἰησοῦς]
Lord. Said therefore to them – Jesus

πάλιν· εἰρήνη ὑμῖν· καθὼς ἀπέσταλκέν
again : Peace to you; as has sent

με ὁ πατήρ, κἀγὼ πέμπω ὑμᾶς. **22** καὶ
me the Father, I also send you. And

τοῦτο εἰπὼν ἐνεφύσησεν καὶ λέγει αὐτοῖς·
this saying he breathed in and says to them :

λάβετε πνεῦμα ἅγιον. **23** ἄν τινων
Receive ye Spirit Holy. Of whomever

ἀφῆτε τὰς ἁμαρτίας, ἀφέωνται αὐτοῖς·
ye forgive the sins, they have been to them;
forgiven

ἄν τινων κρατῆτε, κεκράτηνται.
of whomever ye hold, they have been held.

24 Θωμᾶς δὲ εἷς ἐκ τῶν δώδεκα,
But Thomas one of the twelve,

ὁ λεγόμενος Δίδυμος, οὐκ ἦν μετ' αὐτῶν
– being called Twin, was not with them

ὅτε ἦλθεν Ἰησοῦς. **25** ἔλεγον οὖν αὐτῷ
when came Jesus. Said therefore to him

οἱ ἄλλοι μαθηταί· ἑωράκαμεν τὸν κύριον.
the other disciples : We have seen the Lord.

But he said unto them, Except I shall see in his hands the print of the nails, and put my finger into the print of the nails, and thrust my hand into his side, I will not believe.

26 ¶ And after eight days again his disciples were within, and Thomas with them: *then* came Jesus, the doors being shut, and stood in the midst, and said, Peace *be* unto you.

27 Then saith he to Thomas, Reach hither thy finger, and behold my hands; and reach hither thy hand, and thrust *it* into my side: and be not faithless, but believing.

28 And Thomas answered and said unto him, My Lord and my God.

29 Jesus saith unto him, Thomas, because thou hast seen me, thou hast believed: blessed *are* they that have not seen, and *yet* have believed.

30 ¶ And many other signs truly did Jesus in the presence of his disciples, which are not written in this book:

31 But these are written, that ye might believe that Jesus is the Christ, the

ὁ δὲ εἶπεν αὐτοῖς· ἐὰν μὴ ἴδω ἐν
But he said to them : Unless I see in

ταῖς χερσὶν αὐτοῦ τὸν τύπον τῶν ἥλων
the hands of him the mark of the nails

καὶ βάλω τὸν δάκτυλόν μου εἰς τὸν
and put the finger of me into the

τόπον τῶν ἥλων καὶ βάλω μου τὴν
place of the nails and put of me the

χεῖρα εἰς τὴν πλευρὰν αὐτοῦ, οὐ μὴ
hand into the side of him, by no means

πιστεύσω. 26 Καὶ μεθ’ ἡμέρας ὀκτὼ
will I believe. And after days eight

πάλιν ἦσαν ἔσω οἱ μαθηταὶ αὐτοῦ, καὶ
again were within the disciples of him, and

Θωμᾶς μετ’ αὐτῶν. ἔρχεται ὁ Ἰησοῦς
Thomas with them. Comes - Jesus

τῶν θυρῶν κεκλεισμένων, καὶ ἔστη εἰς
the doors having been shut[a], and stood in

τὸ μέσον καὶ εἶπεν· εἰρήνη ὑμῖν. 27 εἶτα
the midst and said : Peace to you. Then

λέγει τῷ Θωμᾷ· φέρε τὸν δάκτυλόν
he says - to Thomas : Bring the finger

σου ὧδε καὶ ἴδε τὰς χεῖράς μου, καὶ
of thee here and see the hands of me, and

φέρε τὴν χεῖρά σου καὶ βάλε εἰς τὴν
bring the hand of thee and put into the

πλευράν μου, καὶ μὴ γίνου ἄπιστος
side of me, and be not faithless

ἀλλὰ πιστός. 28 ἀπεκρίθη Θωμᾶς καὶ
but faithful. Answered Thomas and

εἶπεν αὐτῷ· ὁ κύριός μου καὶ ὁ θεός
said to him : The Lord of me and the God

μου. 29 λέγει αὐτῷ ὁ Ἰησοῦς· ὅτι
of me. Says to him - Jesus : Because

ἑώρακάς με, πεπίστευκας; μακάριοι οἱ
thou hast seen me, hast thou believed? blessed the [ones]

μὴ ἰδόντες καὶ πιστεύσαντες.
not seeing and§ believing.

30 Πολλὰ μὲν οὖν καὶ ἄλλα σημεῖα
Many -* therefore and other signs

ἐποίησεν ὁ Ἰησοῦς ἐνώπιον τῶν μαθητῶν,
did - Jesus before the disciples,

ἃ οὐκ ἔστιν γεγραμμένα ἐν τῷ βιβλίῳ
which is(are) not *having been* written in - roll

τούτῳ· 31 ταῦτα δὲ γέγραπται ἵνα
this; but these* has(ve) been written that

πιστεύητε ὅτι Ἰησοῦς ἐστιν ὁ χριστὸς ὁ
ye may believe that Jesus is the Christ the

---

* See note on 19. 24 and 32.

§ καί sometimes = and yet; see 5. 40; 8. 55; 9. 30; 16. 32; 17. 11.

Son of God; and that
believing ye might have
life through his name.

υἱὸς τοῦ θεοῦ, καὶ ἵνα πιστεύοντες ζωὴν
Son - of God, and that   believing   life
ἔχητε ἐν τῷ ὀνόματι αὐτοῦ.
ye may have in the   name   of him.

CHAPTER 21

AFTER these things
Jesus shewed himself
again to the disciples at
the sea of Tiberias; and
on this wise shewed he
himself.

2 There were together
Simon Peter, and Thomas
called Didymus, and
Nathanael of Cana in
Galilee, and the *sons* of
Zebedee, and two other
of his disciples.

3 Simon Peter saith un-
to them, I go a fishing.
They say unto him, We
also go with thee. They
went forth, and entered
into a ship immediately;
and that night they caught
nothing.

4 But when the morning
was now come, Jesus stood
on the shore: but the
disciples knew not that
it was Jesus.

5 Then Jesus saith unto
them, Children, have ye
any meat? They answered
him, No.

6 And he said unto
them, Cast the net on the
right side of the ship,
and ye shall find. They
cast therefore, and now
they were not able to draw
it for the multitude of
fishes.

7 Therefore that disciple

21 Μετὰ ταῦτα ἐφανέρωσεν ἑαυτὸν πάλιν
After these things   manifested   himself   again
Ἰησοῦς τοῖς μαθηταῖς ἐπὶ τῆς θαλάσσης
Jesus to the disciples on   the   sea
τῆς Τιβεριάδος· ἐφανέρωσεν δὲ οὕτως.
- of Tiberias; and he manifested [himself] thus.

2 ἦσαν ὁμοῦ Σίμων Πέτρος καὶ Θωμᾶς
There were together Simon Peter and Thomas
ὁ λεγόμενος Δίδυμος καὶ Ναθαναὴλ ὁ
- being called Twin   and   Nathanael   -
ἀπὸ Κανὰ τῆς Γαλιλαίας καὶ οἱ τοῦ
from Cana   - of Galilee and the [sons] -
Ζεβεδαίου καὶ ἄλλοι ἐκ τῶν μαθητῶν
of Zebedee and others of the   disciples
αὐτοῦ δύο. **3** λέγει αὐτοῖς Σίμων Πέτρος·
of him two.   Says to them Simon Peter:
ὑπάγω ἁλιεύειν. λέγουσιν αὐτῷ· ἐρχόμεθα
I am going to fish. They say to him: Are coming
καὶ ἡμεῖς σὺν σοί. ἐξῆλθον καὶ ἐνέβησαν
also we with thee. They went forth and embarked
εἰς τὸ πλοῖον, καὶ ἐν ἐκείνῃ τῇ νυκτὶ
in the boat,   and in that   the night
ἐπίασαν οὐδέν. **4** πρωΐας δὲ ἤδη γινομένης
they caught nothing. Early morning but now becoming*
                    =But when it became early morning
ἔστη Ἰησοῦς εἰς τὸν αἰγιαλόν· οὐ μέντοι
stood Jesus in(on) the   shore;   not however
ᾔδεισαν οἱ μαθηταὶ ὅτι Ἰησοῦς ἐστιν.
knew   the disciples that Jesus it is(was).

5 λέγει οὖν αὐτοῖς Ἰησοῦς· παιδία, μή
Says therefore to them Jesus: Children, *not*
τι προσφάγιον ἔχετε; ἀπεκρίθησαν αὐτῷ·
any fish   have ye? They answered him:
οὔ. **6** ὁ δὲ εἶπεν αὐτοῖς· βάλετε εἰς τὰ
No. So he said to them: Cast in the
δεξιὰ μέρη τοῦ πλοίου τὸ δίκτυον, καὶ
right parts of the boat the   net,   and
εὑρήσετε. ἔβαλον οὖν, καὶ οὐκέτι αὐτὸ
ye will find. They cast therefore, and [1]no longer [4]it
ἑλκύσαι ἴσχυον ἀπὸ τοῦ πλήθους τῶν
[3]to drag [2]were they able from the multitude of the
ἰχθύων. **7** λέγει οὖν ὁ μαθητὴς ἐκεῖνος
fishes.   Says therefore - disciple   that

whom Jesus loved saith unto Peter, It is the Lord. Now when Simon Peter heard that it was the Lord, he girt *his* fisher's coat *unto him,* (for he was naked,) and did cast himself into the sea.

8 And the other disciples came in a little ship; (for they were not far from land, but as it were two hundred cubits,) dragging the net with fishes.

9 As soon then as they were come to land, they saw a fire of coals there, and fish laid thereon, and bread.

10 Jesus saith unto them, Bring of the fish which ye have now caught.

11 Simon Peter went up, and drew the net to land full of great fishes, an hundred and fifty and three: and for all there were so many, yet was not the net broken.

12 Jesus saith unto them, Come *and* dine. And none of the disciples durst ask him, Who art thou? knowing that it was the Lord.

13 Jesus then cometh, and taketh bread, and giveth them, and fish likewise.

14 This is now the third time that Jesus shewed himself to his disciples, after that he was risen from the dead.

ὃν ἠγάπα ὁ Ἰησοῦς τῷ Πέτρῳ· ὁ κύριός
whom [2]loved – [1]Jesus – to Peter: The Lord

ἐστιν. Σίμων οὖν Πέτρος, ἀκούσας ὅτι
it is. [2]Simon [1]therefore [3]Peter, hearing that

ὁ κύριός ἐστιν, τὸν ἐπενδύτην διεζώσατο,
the Lord it is(was), [2][with]the [3]coat [1]girded himself,

ἦν γὰρ γυμνός, καὶ ἔβαλεν ἑαυτὸν εἰς
for he was naked, and threw himself into

τὴν θάλασσαν· 8 οἱ δὲ ἄλλοι μαθηταὶ
the sea; but the other disciples

τῷ πλοιαρίῳ ἦλθον, οὐ γὰρ ἦσαν μακρὰν
in the little boat came, for not they were far

ἀπὸ τῆς γῆς ἀλλὰ ὡς ἀπὸ πηχῶν
from the land but about from cubits

διακοσίων, σύροντες τὸ δίκτυον τῶν ἰχθύων.
two hundred dragging the net of the fishes.

9 ὡς οὖν ἀπέβησαν εἰς τὴν γῆν, βλέπουσιν
When therefore they disembarked onto the land, they see

ἀνθρακιὰν κειμένην καὶ ὀψάριον ἐπικείμενον
a coal fire lying and a fish lying on

καὶ ἄρτον. 10 λέγει αὐτοῖς ὁ Ἰησοῦς·
and bread. Says to them – Jesus:

ἐνέγκατε ἀπὸ τῶν ὀψαρίων ὧν ἐπιάσατε
Bring from the fishes which ye caught

νῦν. 11 ἀνέβη Σίμων Πέτρος καὶ εἵλκυσεν
now. Went up Simon Peter and dragged

τὸ δίκτυον εἰς τὴν γῆν μεστὸν ἰχθύων
the net to the land full fishes

μεγάλων ἑκατὸν πεντήκοντα τριῶν· καὶ
of great a hundred fifty three; and

τοσούτων ὄντων οὐκ ἐσχίσθη τὸ δίκτυον.
so many being[2] was not torn the net.

12 λέγει αὐτοῖς ὁ Ἰησοῦς· δεῦτε ἀριστήσατε.
Says to them – Jesus: Come breakfast ye.

οὐδεὶς ἐτόλμα τῶν μαθητῶν ἐξετάσαι
No one dared of the disciples to question

αὐτόν· σὺ τίς εἶ; εἰδότες ὅτι ὁ κύριός
him: Thou who art? knowing that the Lord

ἐστιν. 13 ἔρχεται Ἰησοῦς καὶ λαμβάνει
it is(was). Comes Jesus and takes

τὸν ἄρτον καὶ δίδωσιν αὐτοῖς, καὶ τὸ
the bread and gives to them, and the

ὀψάριον ὁμοίως. 14 τοῦτο ἤδη τρίτον
fish likewise. This [was] now [the] third [time]
                                    [that]

ἐφανερώθη Ἰησοῦς τοῖς μαθηταῖς ἐγερθεὶς
[2]was manifested [1]Jesus to the disciples raised

ἐκ νεκρῶν.
rom [the] dead.

15¶ So when they had dined, Jesus saith to Simon Peter, Simon, *son* of Jonas, lovest thou me more than these? He saith unto him, Yea, Lord; thou knowest that I love thee. He saith unto him, Feed my lambs.

16 He saith to him again the second time, Simon, *son* of Jonas, lovest thou me? He saith unto him, Yea, Lord; thou knowest that I love thee. He saith unto him, Feed my sheep.

17 He saith unto him the third time, Simon, *son* of Jonas, lovest thou me? Peter was grieved because he said unto him the third time, Lovest thou me? And he said unto him, Lord, thou knowest all things; thou knowest that I love thee. Jesus saith unto him, Feed my sheep.

18 Verily, verily, I say unto thee, When thou wast young, thou girdedst thyself, and walkedst whither thou wouldest: but when thou shalt be old, thou shalt stretch forth thy hands, and another shall gird thee, and carry *thee* whither thou wouldest not.

19 This spake he, signifying by what death he should glorify God. And when he had spoken this, he saith unto him, Follow me.

20 Then Peter, turning about, seeth the disciple whom Jesus loved following; which also leaned

---

15 Ὅτε οὖν ἠρίστησαν, λέγει τῷ
When therefore they breakfasted, says

Σίμωνι Πέτρῳ ὁ Ἰησοῦς· Σίμων Ἰωάννου,
to Simon Peter – Jesus: Simon [son] of John,

ἀγαπᾷς με πλέον τούτων; λέγει αὐτῷ·
lovest thou me more [than] these? He says to him:

ναί, κύριε, σὺ οἶδας ὅτι φιλῶ σε. λέγει
Yes, Lord, thou knowest that I love thee. He says

αὐτῷ· βόσκε τὰ ἀρνία μου. **16** λέγει
to him: Feed the lambs of me. He says

αὐτῷ πάλιν δεύτερον· Σίμων Ἰωάννου,
to him again secondly: Simon [son] of John,

ἀγαπᾷς με; λέγει αὐτῷ· ναί, κύριε,
lovest thou me? He says to him: Yes, Lord,

σὺ οἶδας ὅτι φιλῶ σε. λέγει αὐτῷ·
thou knowest that I love thee. He says to him:

ποίμαινε τὰ προβάτιά μου. **17** λέγει
Shepherd the little sheep of me. He says

αὐτῷ τὸ τρίτον· Σίμων Ἰωάννου, φιλεῖς
to him the third [time]: Simon [son] of John, lovest thou

με; ἐλυπήθη ὁ Πέτρος ὅτι εἶπεν αὐτῷ
me? Was grieved – Peter that he said to him

τὸ τρίτον· φιλεῖς με; καὶ εἶπεν αὐτῷ·
the third [time]: Lovest thou me? and said to him:

κύριε, πάντα σὺ οἶδας, σὺ γινώσκεις
Lord, all things thou knowest, thou knowest

ὅτι φιλῶ σε· λέγει αὐτῷ Ἰησοῦς· βόσκε
that I love thee; says to him Jesus: Feed

τὰ προβάτιά μου. **18** ἀμὴν ἀμὴν λέγω
the little sheep of me. Truly truly I tell

σοι, ὅτε ἦς νεώτερος, ἐζώννυες σεαυτὸν
thee, when thou wast younger, thou girdedst thyself

καὶ περιεπάτεις ὅπου ἤθελες· ὅταν δὲ
and walkedst where thou wishedst; but when

γηράσῃς, ἐκτενεῖς τὰς χεῖράς σου, καὶ
thou growest old, thou wilt stretch out the hands of thee, and

ἄλλος ζώσει σε καὶ οἴσει ὅπου οὐ θέλεις.
another will gird thee and will carry where thou wishest not.

19 τοῦτο δὲ εἶπεν σημαίνων ποίῳ θανάτῳ
And this he said signifying by what death

δοξάσει τὸν θεόν. καὶ τοῦτο εἰπὼν λέγει
he will glorify – God. And this saying he tells

αὐτῷ· ἀκολούθει μοι. **20** ἐπιστραφεὶς ὁ
him: Follow me. Turning –

Πέτρος βλέπει τὸν μαθητὴν ὃν ἠγάπα ὁ
Peter sees the disciple whom ¹loved –

Ἰησοῦς ἀκολουθοῦντα, ὃς καὶ ἀνέπεσεν
¹Jesus following, who also ¹leaned

on his breast at supper, and said, Lord, which is he that betrayeth thee?

21 Peter seeing him saith to Jesus, Lord, and what *shall* this man *do?*

22 Jesus saith unto him, If I will that he tarry till I come, what *is that* to thee? follow thou me.

23 Then went this saying abroad among the brethren, that that disciple should not die: yet Jesus said not unto him, He shall not die; but, If I will that he tarry till I come, what *is that* to thee?

24 This is the disciple which testifieth of these things, and wrote these things: and we know that his testimony is true.

25 And there are also many other things which Jesus did, the which, if they should be written every one, I suppose that even the world itself could not contain the books that should be written. Amen.

ἐν τῷ δείπνῳ ἐπὶ τὸ στῆθος αὐτοῦ καὶ
at   the   supper   on   the   breast   of him   and

εἶπεν· κύριε, τίς ἐστιν ὁ παραδιδούς σε;
said :   Lord,   who   is   the[one] betraying   thee?

21 τοῦτον οὖν ἰδὼν ὁ Πέτρος λέγει τῷ
⁴This one ²therefore ³seeing – ¹Peter   says   –

Ἰησοῦ· κύριε, οὗτος δὲ τί; 22 λέγει
to Jesus :   Lord,   and this one   what?   Says

αὐτῷ ὁ Ἰησοῦς· ἐὰν αὐτὸν θέλω μένειν
to him   –   Jesus :   If   him   I wish to remain

ἕως ἔρχομαι, τί πρὸς σέ; σύ μοι
until   I come,   what   to   thee? ²thou ³me

ἀκολούθει. 23 ἐξῆλθεν οὖν οὗτος ὁ λόγος
¹follow.   Went forth therefore this   –   word

εἰς τοὺς ἀδελφοὺς ὅτι ὁ μαθητὴς ἐκεῖνος
to   the   brothers   that – disciple   that

οὐκ ἀποθνῄσκει· οὐκ εἶπεν δὲ αὐτῷ ὁ
does not die;   but said not   to him   –

Ἰησοῦς ὅτι οὐκ ἀποθνῄσκει, ἀλλ'· ἐὰν
Jesus   that he does not die,   but :   If

αὐτὸν θέλω μένειν ἕως ἔρχομαι, τί πρὸς
him   I wish to remain until   I come,   what   to

σέ;
thee?

24 Οὗτός ἐστιν ὁ μαθητὴς ὁ μαρτυρῶν
This   is   the   disciple   –   witnessing

περὶ τούτων καὶ ὁ γράψας ταῦτα,
concerning these   and   –   having   these
things   written   things,

καὶ οἴδαμεν ὅτι ἀληθὴς αὐτοῦ ἡ μαρτυρία
and we know that   true   of him   the   witness

ἐστίν. 25 Ἔστιν δὲ καὶ ἄλλα πολλὰ ἃ
is.   And there are also   other   many which
things

ἐποίησεν ὁ Ἰησοῦς, ἅτινα ἐὰν γράφηται
did   –   Jesus,   which   if   they were written

καθ' ἕν, οὐδ' αὐτὸν οἶμαι τὸν κόσμον
singly,† ⁵not ⁴[it]self ¹I think ²the ³world

χωρήσειν τὰ γραφόμενα βιβλία.
⁶to contain ⁷the ⁸being written ⁹rolls.

CHAPTER 1

THE former treatise have I made, O Theophilus, of all that Jesus began both to do and teach,

2 Until the day in which he was taken up, after that he through the Holy Ghost had given commandments unto the apostles whom he had chosen:

3 To whom also he shewed himself alive after his passion by many infallible proofs, being seen of them forty days, and speaking of the things pertaining to the kingdom of God:

4 And, being assembled together with *them*, commanded them that they should not depart from Jerusalem, but wait for the promise of the Father, which, *saith he*, ye have heard of me.

5 For John truly baptized with water; but ye shall be baptized with the Holy Ghost not many days hence.

6 When they therefore were come together, they asked of him, saying, Lord, wilt thou at this time restore again the kingdom to Israel?

7 And he said unto them, It is not for you to know the times or the seasons, which the Father hath put in his own power.

8 But ye shall receive power, after that the

---

1 Τὸν μὲν πρῶτον λόγον ἐποιησάμην
The - first account I made

περὶ πάντων, ὦ Θεόφιλε, ὧν ἤρξατο
concerning all things, O Theophilus, which began

ὁ Ἰησοῦς ποιεῖν τε καὶ διδάσκειν,
- Jesus both to do and to teach,

2 ἄχρι ἧς ἡμέρας ἐντειλάμενος τοῖς
until which day [5]having given injunctions [6]to the
=the day on which

ἀποστόλοις διὰ πνεύματος ἁγίου οὓς
[7]apostles [3]through [5]Spirit [4]Holy [8]whom

ἐξελέξατο ἀνελήμφθη· 3 οἷς καὶ παρέστησεν
[9]he chose [1]he was taken up; to whom also he presented

ἑαυτὸν ζῶντα μετὰ τὸ παθεῖν αὐτὸν ἐν
himself living after the to suffer him[b] by
=he suffered

πολλοῖς τεκμηρίοις, δι᾽ ἡμερῶν τεσσεράκοντα
many infallible proofs, through days forty

ὀπτανόμενος αὐτοῖς καὶ λέγων τὰ περὶ
being seen by them and speaking the things concerning

τῆς βασιλείας τοῦ θεοῦ· 4 καὶ συναλιζόμενος
the kingdom - of God; and meeting with [them]

παρήγγειλεν αὐτοῖς ἀπὸ Ἱεροσολύμων μὴ
he charged them from Jerusalem not

χωρίζεσθαι, ἀλλὰ περιμένειν τὴν ἐπαγγελίαν
to depart, but to await the promise

τοῦ πατρὸς ἣν ἠκούσατέ μου· 5 ὅτι
of the Father which ye heard of me: because

Ἰωάννης μὲν ἐβάπτισεν ὕδατι, ὑμεῖς δὲ
John indeed baptized in water, but ye

ἐν πνεύματι βαπτισθήσεσθε ἁγίῳ οὐ μετὰ
in [2]Spirit [4]will be baptized [1]Holy not after

πολλὰς ταύτας ἡμέρας. 6 Οἱ μὲν οὖν
many these days. [2]the [ones] [1]So then

συνελθόντες ἠρώτων αὐτὸν λέγοντες· κύριε,
[3]coming together questioned him saying : Lord,

εἰ ἐν τῷ χρόνῳ τούτῳ ἀποκαθιστάνεις
if at this time restorest thou

τὴν βασιλείαν τῷ Ἰσραήλ; 7 εἶπεν πρὸς
the kingdom - to Israel? He said to

αὐτούς· οὐχ ὑμῶν ἐστιν γνῶναι χρόνους
them : Not of you it is to know times

ἢ καιροὺς οὓς ὁ πατὴρ ἔθετο ἐν τῇ
or seasons which the Father placed in the(his)

ἰδίᾳ ἐξουσίᾳ, 8 ἀλλὰ λήμψεσθε δύναμιν
own authority, but ye will receive power

Holy Ghost is come upon you: and ye shall be witnesses unto me both in Jerusalem, and in all Judæa, and in Samaria, and unto the uttermost part of the earth.

9 And when he had spoken these things, while they beheld, he was taken up; and a cloud received him out of their sight.

10 And while they looked stedfastly toward heaven as he went up, behold, two men stood by them in white apparel;

11 Which also said, Ye men of Galilee, why stand ye gazing up into heaven? this same Jesus, which is taken up from you into heaven, shall so come in like manner as ye have seen him go into heaven.

12 ¶ Then returned they unto Jerusalem from the mount called Olivet, which is from Jerusalem a sabbath day's journey.

13 And when they were come in, they went up into an upper room, where abode both Peter, and James, and John, and Andrew, Philip, and Thomas, Bartholomew, and Matthew, James the son of Alphæus, and Simon

ἐπελθόντος τοῦ ἁγίου πνεύματος ἐφ' ὑμᾶς,
coming *upon* the Holy Spirit[a] upon you,
=when the Holy Spirit comes

καὶ ἔσεσθέ μου μάρτυρες ἔν τε Ἰερουσαλὴμ
and ye will be of me witnesses both in Jerusalem

καὶ ἐν πάσῃ τῇ Ἰουδαίᾳ καὶ Σαμαρείᾳ
and in all the Judæa and Samaria

καὶ ἕως ἐσχάτου τῆς γῆς. 9 καὶ ταῦτα
and unto [the] extremity of the earth. And these things

εἰπὼν βλεπόντων αὐτῶν ἐπήρθη, καὶ
saying looking them[a] he was taken up, and
=as they looked

νεφέλη ὑπέλαβεν αὐτὸν ἀπὸ τῶν ὀφθαλμῶν
a cloud received him from the eyes

αὐτῶν. 10 καὶ ὡς ἀτενίζοντες ἦσαν εἰς
of them. And as gazing they were to

τὸν οὐρανὸν πορευομένου αὐτοῦ, καὶ ἰδοὺ
– heaven going him,[a] – behold[,]
=as he went,

ἄνδρες δύο παρειστήκεισαν αὐτοῖς ἐν ἐσθήσεσι
men two stood by them in garments

λευκαῖς, 11 οἳ καὶ εἶπαν· ἄνδρες Γαλιλαῖοι,
white, who also said : Men Galilæans,

τί ἑστήκατε βλέποντες εἰς τὸν οὐρανόν;
why stand ye looking to – heaven ?

οὗτος ὁ Ἰησοῦς ὁ ἀναλημφθεὶς
This – Jesus the [one] having been taken up

ἀφ' ὑμῶν εἰς τὸν οὐρανὸν οὕτως ἐλεύσεται
from you to – heaven thus will come

ὃν τρόπον ἐθεάσασθε αὐτὸν πορευόμενον
in the way† ye beheld him going

εἰς τὸν οὐρανόν. 12 Τότε ὑπέστρεψαν
to – heaven. Then they returned

εἰς Ἰερουσαλὴμ ἀπὸ ὄρους τοῦ καλου-
to Jerusalem from [the] mount the [one] being

μένου ἐλαιῶνος, ὅ ἐστιν ἐγγὺς Ἰερουσαλὴμ
called of [the] olive grove, which is near Jerusalem

σαββάτου ἔχον ὁδόν. 13 καὶ ὅτε εἰσῆλθον,
of a sabbath having a way. And when they entered,
=a sabbath's journey off.

εἰς τὸ ὑπερῷον ἀνέβησαν οὗ ἦσαν
into the upper room they went up where they were

καταμένοντες, ὅ τε Πέτρος καὶ Ἰωάννης
waiting, – both Peter and John

καὶ Ἰάκωβος καὶ Ἀνδρέας, Φίλιππος καὶ
and James and Andrew, Philip and

Θωμᾶς, Βαρθολομαῖος καὶ Ματθαῖος,
Thomas, Bartholomew and Matthew,

Ἰάκωβος Ἀλφαίου καὶ Σίμων ὁ ζηλωτὴς
James [son] of Alphæus and Simon the zealot

Zelotes, and Judas *the brother* of James.

14 These all continued with one accord in prayer and supplication, with the women, and Mary the mother of Jesus, and with his brethren.

15 ¶ And in those days Peter stood up in the midst of the disciples, and said, (the number of names together were about an hundred and twenty,)

16 Men *and* brethren, this scripture must needs have been fulfilled, which the Holy Ghost by the mouth of David spake before concerning Judas, which was guide to them that took Jesus.

17 For he was numbered with us, and had obtained part of this ministry.

18 Now this man purchased a field with the reward of iniquity; and falling headlong, he burst asunder in the midst, and all his bowels gushed out.

19 And it was known unto all the dwellers at Jerusalem; insomuch as that field is called in their proper tongue, Aceldama, that is to say, The field of blood.

20 For it is written in the book of Psalms, Let his habitation be desolate,

καὶ Ἰούδας Ἰακώβου. **14** οὗτοι πάντες
and Judas [brother] of James. These all

ἦσαν προσκαρτεροῦντες ὁμοθυμαδὸν τῇ
were continuing steadfastly with one mind –

προσευχῇ σὺν γυναιξὶν καὶ Μαριὰμ τῇ
in prayer with [the] women and Mary the

μητρὶ [τοῦ] Ἰησοῦ καὶ σὺν τοῖς ἀδελφοῖς
mother – of Jesus and with the brothers

αὐτοῦ.
of him.

15 Καὶ ἐν ταῖς ἡμέραις ταύταις ἀναστὰς
And in these days standing up

Πέτρος ἐν μέσῳ τῶν ἀδελφῶν εἶπεν·
Peter in [the] midst of the brothers said:

ἦν τε ὄχλος ὀνομάτων ἐπὶ τὸ αὐτὸ
[6]was [1]and [2][the] [3]crowd [4]of names [5]together

ὡσεὶ ἑκατὸν εἴκοσι· **16** ἄνδρες ἀδελφοί,
about a hundred twenty: Men brothers,

ἔδει πληρωθῆναι τὴν γραφὴν ἣν
it behoved to be fulfilled the scripture which

προεῖπεν τὸ πνεῦμα τὸ ἅγιον διὰ στόματος
spoke before the Spirit – Holy through [the] mouth

Δαυὶδ περὶ Ἰούδα τοῦ γενομένου ὁδηγοῦ
of David concerning Judas the [one] having become guide

τοῖς συλλαβοῦσιν Ἰησοῦν, **17** ὅτι κατ–
to the [ones] taking Jesus, because *having*

ἠριθμημένος ἦν ἐν ἡμῖν καὶ ἔλαχεν τὸν
been numbered he was among us and obtained the

κλῆρον τῆς διακονίας ταύτης. **18** οὗτος μὲν οὖν
portion of this ministry. This one therefore

ἐκτήσατο χωρίον ἐκ μισθοῦ τῆς
bought a field out of [the] reward –

ἀδικίας, καὶ πρηνὴς γενόμενος ἐλάκησεν
of unrighteousness, and swollen up having become he burst asunder

μέσος, καὶ ἐξεχύθη πάντα τὰ σπλάγχνα
in the middle, and were poured out all the bowels

αὐτοῦ· **19** καὶ γνωστὸν ἐγένετο πᾶσι τοῖς
of him; and known it became to all the

κατοικοῦσιν Ἱερουσαλήμ, ὥστε κληθῆναι
[ones] inhabiting Jerusalem, so as to be called

τὸ χωρίον ἐκεῖνο τῇ ἰδίᾳ διαλέκτῳ αὐτῶν
that field in their own language

Ἀκελδαμάχ, τοῦτ' ἔστιν χωρίον
Aceldamach, this is Field

αἵματος. **20** γέγραπται γὰρ ἐν βίβλῳ
of blood. For it has been written in [the] roll

ψαλμῶν· γενηθήτω ἡ ἔπαυλις αὐτοῦ ἔρημος
of Psalms: Let become the estate of him deserted

and let no man dwell therein: and his bishoprick let another take.

21 Wherefore of these men which have companied with us all the time that the Lord Jesus went in and out among us,

22 Beginning from the baptism of John, unto that same day that he was taken up from us, must one be ordained to be a witness with us of his resurrection.

23 And they appointed two, Joseph called Barsabas, who was surnamed Justus, and Matthias.

24 And they prayed, and said, Thou, Lord, which knowest the hearts of all *men*, shew whether of these two thou hast chosen,

25 That he may take part of this ministry and apostleship, from which Judas by transgression fell, that he might go to his own place.

26 And they gave forth their lots; and the lot fell upon Matthias; and he was numbered with the eleven apostles.

καὶ   μὴ   ἔστω   ὁ   κατοικῶν   ἐν   αὐτῇ,   καὶ·
and   let not be   the [one]   dwelling   in   it,   and :

τὴν   ἐπισκοπὴν   αὐτοῦ   λαβέτω   ἔτερος.
The   office   of him   let take   another.

21 δεῖ   οὖν   τῶν   συνελθόντων   ἡμῖν   ἀνδρῶν
It behoves* therefore   ¹of the   ³accompanying   ⁴us   ²men

ἐν   παντὶ   χρόνῳ   ᾧ   εἰσῆλθεν   καὶ
in   all   [the] time   in which   went in   and

ἐξῆλθεν   ἐφ’   ἡμᾶς·   ὁ   κύριος   Ἰησοῦς,
went out   among   us   the   Lord   Jesus,

22 ἀρξάμενος   ἀπὸ   τοῦ   βαπτίσματος
beginning   from   the   baptism

Ἰωάννου   ἕως   τῆς   ἡμέρας   ἧς   ἀνελήμφθη
of John   until   the   day   when   he was taken up

ἀφ’   ἡμῶν,   μάρτυρα   τῆς   ἀναστάσεως
from   us,   ⁴a witness*   ⁷of the   ⁸resurrection

αὐτοῦ   σὺν   ἡμῖν   γενέσθαι   ἕνα   τούτων.
⁹of him   ⁵with   ⁶us   ³to become   ¹one*   ²of these.

23 Καὶ   ἔστησαν   δύο,   Ἰωσὴφ   τὸν   καλού-
And   they set   two,   Joseph   the [one]   *being*

μενον   Βαρσαββᾶν,   ὃς   ἐπεκλήθη   Ἰοῦστος,
called   Barsabbas,   who   was surnamed   Justus,

καὶ   Μαθθίαν.   **24** καὶ   προσευξάμενοι   εἶπαν·
and   Matthias.   And   praying   they said :

σὺ   κύριε   καρδιογνῶστα   πάντων,   ἀνάδειξον
Thou Lord   Heart-knower   of all men,   show

ὃν   ἐξελέξω   ἐκ   τούτων   τῶν   δύο   ἕνα
whom thou didst choose of   these   –   two   one

25 λαβεῖν   τὸν   τόπον   τῆς   διακονίας   ταύτης
to take   the   place   of this ministry

καὶ   ἀποστολῆς,   ἀφ’   ἧς   παρέβη   Ἰούδας
and   apostleship,   from which   fell   Judas

πορευθῆναι   εἰς   τὸν   τόπον   τὸν   ἴδιον.
to go   to   the(his)   place   –   own.

26 καὶ   ἔδωκαν   κλήρους   αὐτοῖς,   καὶ   ἔπεσεν
And   they gave   lots   for them,   and   fell

ὁ   κλῆρος ἐπὶ Μαθθίαν,   καὶ   συγκατεψηφίσθη
the   lot   on   Matthias,   and   he was reckoned along *with*

μετὰ   τῶν   ἕνδεκα   ἀποστόλων.
with   the   eleven   apostles.

CHAPTER 2

A ND when the day of Pentecost was fully come, they were all with one accord in one place.

2 Καὶ   ἐν   τῷ   συμπληροῦσθαι   τὴν   ἡμέραν
And   in   the   to be completed   the   day
= when the day of Pentecost was completed

τῆς   πεντηκοστῆς   ἦσαν   πάντες   ὁμοῦ   ἐπὶ
–   of Pentecostᵉ   they were   all   *together*   to-

* The object (according to the Greek construction) of the verb δεῖ is ἕνα, with μάρτυρα as its complement after γενέσθαι.

2 And suddenly there came a sound from heaven as of a rushing mighty wind, and it filled all the house where they were sitting.

3 And there appeared unto them cloven tongues like as of fire, and it sat upon each of them.

4 And they were all filled with the Holy Ghost, and began to speak with other tongues, as the Spirit gave them utterance.

5 And there were dwelling at Jerusalem Jews, devout men, out of every nation under heaven.

6 Now when this was noised abroad, the multitude came together, and were confounded, because that every man heard them speak in his own language.

7 And they were all amazed and marvelled, saying one to another, Behold, are not all these which speak Galilæans?

8 And how hear we every man in our own tongue, wherein we were born?

9 Parthians, and Medes, and Elamites, and the dwellers in Mesopotamia, and in Judæa, and Cappadocia, in Pontus and Asia,

10 Phrygia, and Pamphylia, in Egypt, and in

τὸ αὐτό· **2** καὶ ἐγένετο ἄφνω ἐκ τοῦ
gether;†   and   there was   suddenly   out of   –

οὐρανοῦ ἦχος ὥσπερ φερομένης πνοῆς
heaven   a sound   as   ⁵being borne   ¹of²a ⁴wind

βιαίας καὶ ἐπλήρωσεν ὅλον τὸν οἶκον
³violent   and   it filled   all   the   house

οὗ ἦσαν καθήμενοι, **3** καὶ ὤφθησαν αὐτοῖς
where they were   sitting,   and there appeared   to them

διαμεριζόμεναι γλῶσσαι ὡσεὶ πυρός, καὶ
being distributed   tongues   as   of fire,   and

ἐκάθισεν ἐφ' ἕνα ἕκαστον αὐτῶν, **4** καὶ
it sat   on   ²one   ¹each   of them,   and

ἐπλήσθησαν πάντες πνεύματος ἁγίου, καὶ
they were filled   all   of(with) Spirit   Holy,   and

ἤρξαντο λαλεῖν ἑτέραις γλώσσαις καθὼς
began   to speak   in other   tongues   as

τὸ πνεῦμα ἐδίδου ἀποφθέγγεσθαι αὐτοῖς.
the   Spirit   gave   ²to speak out   ¹them.

5 Ἦσαν δὲ εἰς Ἰερουσαλὴμ κατοικοῦντες
Now there were   in   Jerusalem   dwelling

Ἰουδαῖοι, ἄνδρες εὐλαβεῖς ἀπὸ παντὸς ἔθνους
Jews,   men   devout   from   every   nation

τῶν ὑπὸ τὸν οὐρανόν· **6** γενομένης
of the [ones] under   –   heaven;   happening

δὲ τῆς φωνῆς ταύτης συνῆλθεν τὸ πλῆθος
and   this sound   came together the   multitude
=when this sound happened

καὶ συνεχύθη, ὅτι ἤκουον εἷς ἕκαστος
and were confounded, because   they heard   ⁴one   ³each

τῇ ἰδίᾳ διαλέκτῳ λαλούντων αὐτῶν.
⁵in his own language   ²speaking   ¹them.

7 ἐξίσταντο δὲ καὶ ἐθαύμαζον λέγοντες·
And they were amazed   and   marvelled   saying :

οὐχὶ ἰδοὺ πάντες οὗτοί εἰσιν οἱ λαλοῦντες
³not   ¹behold   ⁴all   ⁵these   ²are   ⁶the [ones] ⁷speaking

Γαλιλαῖοι; **8** καὶ πῶς ἡμεῖς ἀκούομεν
⁸Galilæans?   and   how   ²we   ¹hear

ἕκαστος τῇ ἰδίᾳ διαλέκτῳ ἡμῶν ἐν ᾗ
³each   ⁵in his own language   ⁴of us   in which

ἐγεννήθημεν, **9** Πάρθοι καὶ Μῆδοι καὶ
we were born,   Parthians   and   Medes   and

Ἐλαμῖται, καὶ οἱ κατοικοῦντες τὴν
Elamites,   and the [ones]   inhabiting   –

Μεσοποταμίαν, Ἰουδαίαν τε καὶ Καππα-
Mesopotamia,   both Judæa   and   Cappa-

δοκίαν, Πόντον καὶ τὴν Ἀσίαν, **10** Φρυγίαν
docia,   Pontus   and   –   Asia,   Phrygia

τε καὶ Παμφυλίαν, Αἴγυπτον καὶ τὰ
both   and   Pamphylia,   Egypt   and   the

the parts of Libya about Cyrene, and strangers of Rome, Jews and proselytes,

11 Cretes and Arabians, we do hear them speak in our tongues the wonderful works of God.

12 And they were all amazed, and were in doubt, saying one to another, What meaneth this?

13 Others mocking said, These men are full of new wine.

14 ¶ But Peter, standing up with the eleven, lifted up his voice, and said unto them, Ye men of Judæa, and all ye that dwell at Jerusalem, be this known unto you, and hearken to my words:

15 For these are not drunken, as ye suppose, seeing it is but the third hour of the day.

16 But this is that which was spoken by the prophet Joel;

17 And it shall come to pass in the last days, saith God, I will pour out of my Spirit upon all flesh: and your sons and your daughters shall prophesy, and your young men shall see visions, and your old

μέρη τῆς Λιβύης τῆς κατὰ Κυρήνην,
regions – of Libya – over against Cyrene,

καὶ οἱ ἐπιδημοῦντες Ῥωμαῖοι, 11 Ἰουδαῖοί
and the temporarily residing Romans, ¹Jews

τε καὶ προσήλυτοι, Κρῆτες καὶ Ἄραβες,
¹both and proselytes, Cretans and Arabians,

ἀκούομεν λαλούντων αὐτῶν ταῖς ἡμετέραις
we hear ²speaking ¹them in the our

γλώσσαις τὰ μεγαλεῖα τοῦ θεοῦ;
tongues the great deeds – of God?

12 ἐξίσταντο δὲ πάντες καὶ διηποροῦντο,
And were amazed all and were troubled,

ἄλλος πρὸς ἄλλον λέγοντες· τί θέλει
other to other saying: What wishes

τοῦτο εἶναι; 13 ἕτεροι δὲ διαχλευάζοντες
this to be? But others mocking

ἔλεγον ὅτι γλεύκους μεμεστωμένοι εἰσίν.
said[,] – Of(with) sweet wine having been filled they are.

14 Σταθεὶς δὲ ὁ Πέτρος σὺν τοῖς ἕνδεκα
But standing – Peter with the eleven

ἐπῆρεν τὴν φωνὴν αὐτοῦ καὶ ἀπεφθέγξατο
lifted up the voice of him and spoke out

αὐτοῖς·
to them:

Ἄνδρες Ἰουδαῖοι καὶ οἱ κατοικοῦντες
Men Jews and the [ones] inhabiting

Ἰερουσαλὴμ πάντες, τοῦτο ὑμῖν γνωστὸν
Jerusalem all, this to you known

ἔστω, καὶ ἐνωτίσασθε τὰ ῥήματά μου.
let be, and give ear to the words of me.

15 οὐ γὰρ ὡς ὑμεῖς ὑπολαμβάνετε οὗτοι
For not as ye imagine these men

μεθύουσιν, ἔστιν γὰρ ὥρα τρίτη τῆς
are drunk, for it is hour third of the

ἡμέρας, 16 ἀλλὰ τοῦτό ἐστιν τὸ εἰρημένον
day, but this is the thing having been spoken

διὰ τοῦ προφήτου Ἰωήλ· 17 καὶ ἔσται
through the prophet Joel: And it shall be

ἐν ταῖς ἐσχάταις ἡμέραις, λέγει ὁ θεός,
in the last days, says – God,

ἐκχεῶ ἀπὸ τοῦ πνεύματός μου ἐπὶ
I will pour out from the Spirit of me on

πᾶσαν σάρκα, καὶ προφητεύσουσιν οἱ υἱοὶ
all flesh, and will prophesy the sons

ὑμῶν καὶ αἱ θυγατέρες ὑμῶν, καὶ οἱ
of you and the daughters of you, and the

νεανίσκοι ὑμῶν ὁράσεις ὄψονται, καὶ οἱ
young men of you visions will see, and the

men shall dream dreams:

18 And on my servants and on my handmaidens I will pour out in those days of my Spirit; and they shall prophesy:

19 And I will shew wonders in heaven above, and signs in the earth beneath; blood, and fire, and vapour of smoke:

20 The sun shall be turned into darkness, and the moon into blood, before that great and notable day of the Lord come:

21 And it shall come to pass, *that* whosoever shall call on the name of the Lord shall be saved.

22 Ye men of Israel, hear these words; Jesus of Nazareth, a man approved of God among you by miracles and wonders and signs, which God did by him in the midst of you, as ye yourselves also know:

23 Him, being delivered by the determinate counsel and foreknowledge of God, ye have taken, and by wicked hands have crucified and slain:

24 Whom God hath raised up, having loosed the pains of death: because it was not possible that he should be holden of it.

25 For David speaketh

πρεσβύτεροι ὑμῶν ἐνυπνίοις ἐνυπνιασθήσονται·
old men   of you   dreams   will dream;

18 καὶ γε ἐπὶ τοὺς δούλους μου καὶ ἐπὶ
and –   on the male slaves of me and on

τὰς δούλας μου ἐν ταῖς ἡμέραις ἐκείναις
the female slaves of me in   those days

ἐκχεῶ ἀπὸ τοῦ πνεύματός μου, καὶ
I will pour out from the Spirit   of me, and

προφητεύσουσιν. 19 καὶ δώσω τέρατα ἐν
they will prophesy.   And I will give wonders in

τῷ οὐρανῷ ἄνω καὶ σημεῖα ἐπὶ τῆς
the heaven above and signs   on the

γῆς κάτω, αἷμα καὶ πῦρ καὶ ἀτμίδα
earth below, blood and fire and vapour

καπνοῦ. 20 ὁ ἥλιος μεταστραφήσεται εἰς
of smoke. The sun   will be turned   into

σκότος καὶ ἡ σελήνη εἰς αἷμα, πρὶν
darkness and the moon into blood, before

ἐλθεῖν ἡμέραν κυρίου τὴν μεγάλην καὶ
⁷to come(comes) ⁵day ⁶of [the] Lord ¹the ²great ³and

ἐπιφανῆ. 21 καὶ ἔσται πᾶς ὃς ἐὰν
⁴notable.ᵇ   And it will be everyone whoever

ἐπικαλέσηται τὸ ὄνομα κυρίου σωθήσεται.
invokes   the name of [the] Lord will be saved.

22 Ἄνδρες Ἰσραηλῖται, ἀκούσατε τοὺς
Men   Israelites,   hear ye   –

λόγους τούτους· Ἰησοῦν τὸν Ναζωραῖον,
words   these: Jesus   the Nazarene,

ἄνδρα ἀποδεδειγμένον ἀπὸ τοῦ θεοῦ εἰς
a man having been approved from – God among

ὑμᾶς δυνάμεσι καὶ τέρασι καὶ σημείοις,
you by powerful deeds and wonders and signs,

οἷς ἐποίησεν δι' αὐτοῦ ὁ θεὸς ἐν μέσῳ
which did   through him – God in [the] midst

ὑμῶν, καθὼς αὐτοὶ οἴδατε, 23 τοῦτον
of you, as [your]selves ye know,   this man

τῇ ὡρισμένῃ βουλῇ καὶ προγνώσει τοῦ
³by the ³having been fixed ⁴counsel ⁵and ⁶foreknowledge –

θεοῦ ἔκδοτον διὰ χειρὸς ἀνόμων
⁷of God ¹given up ⁹through ¹⁰[the] hand ¹¹of lawless men

προσπήξαντες ἀνείλατε, 24 ὃν ὁ θεὸς
⁸fastening*   ¹²ye killed, whom – God

ἀνέστησεν λύσας τὰς ὠδῖνας τοῦ θανάτου,
raised up loosening the pangs   of death,

καθότι οὐκ ἦν δυνατὸν κρατεῖσθαι αὐτὸν
because it was not possible ²to be held ¹him

ὑπ' αὐτοῦ. 25 Δαυὶδ γὰρ λέγει εἰς
by it.   For David says [as] to

* That is, to a tree; see ch. 5. 30.

concerning him, I foresaw the Lord always before my face, for he is on my right hand, that I should not be moved:

26 Therefore did my heart rejoice, and my tongue was glad; moreover also my flesh shall rest in hope:

27 Because thou wilt not leave my soul in hell, neither wilt thou suffer thine Holy One to see corruption.

28 Thou hast made known to me the ways of life; thou shalt make me full of joy with thy countenance.

29 Men *and* brethren, let me freely speak unto you of the patriarch David, that he is both dead and buried, and his sepulchre is with us unto this day.

30 Therefore being a prophet, and knowing that God had sworn with an oath to him, that of the fruit of his loins, according to the flesh, he would raise up Christ to sit on his throne;

31 He seeing this before spake of the resurrection of Christ, that his soul was not left in hell, neither his flesh did see corruption.

32 This Jesus hath God raised up, whereof we all are witnesses.

33 Therefore being by the right hand of God

αὐτόν· προορώμην τὸν κύριον ἐνώπιόν
him :   I foresaw   the   Lord   before

μου διὰ παντός, ὅτι ἐκ δεξιῶν μού
me always,   because on right of me

ἐστιν, ἵνα μὴ σαλευθῶ. 26 διὰ τοῦτο
he is, lest I be moved.   Therefore

ηὐφράνθη μου ἡ καρδία καὶ ἠγαλλιάσατο
was glad of me the heart and   exulted

ἡ γλῶσσά μου, ἔτι δὲ καὶ ἡ σάρξ
the tongue of me, and now also the flesh

μου κατασκηνώσει ἐπ' ἐλπίδι, 27 ὅτι οὐκ
of me will dwell on(in) hope, because not

ἐγκαταλείψεις τὴν ψυχήν μου εἰς ᾅδην
thou wilt abandon the soul of me in hades

οὐδὲ δώσεις τὸν ὅσιόν σου ἰδεῖν
nor wilt thou give the holy one of thee to see

διαφθοράν. 28 ἐγνώρισάς μοι ὁδοὺς ζωῆς,
corruption. Thou madest known to me ways of life,

πληρώσεις με εὐφροσύνης μετὰ τοῦ προσώ-
thou wilt fill me of(with) gladness with the pres-

που σου. 29 Ἄνδρες ἀδελφοί, ἐξὸν εἰπεῖν
ence of thee. Men brothers, it is permitted to speak

μετὰ παρρησίας πρὸς ὑμᾶς περὶ τοῦ
with plainness to you concerning the

πατριάρχου Δαυίδ, ὅτι καὶ ἐτελεύτησεν
patriarch David, that both he died

καὶ ἐτάφη, καὶ τὸ μνῆμα αὐτοῦ ἔστιν
and was buried, and the tomb of him is

ἐν ἡμῖν ἄχρι τῆς ἡμέρας ταύτης.
among us until the this day.

30 προφήτης οὖν ὑπάρχων καὶ εἰδὼς ὅτι
A prophet therefore being and knowing that

ὅρκῳ ὤμοσεν αὐτῷ ὁ θεὸς ἐκ καρποῦ
with an oath swore to him - God of [the] fruit

τῆς ὀσφύος αὐτοῦ καθίσαι ἐπὶ τὸν θρόνον
of the loin[s] of him to sit on the throne

αὐτοῦ, 31 προϊδὼν ἐλάλησεν περὶ τῆς
of him, foreseeing he spoke concerning the

ἀναστάσεως τοῦ Χριστοῦ, ὅτι οὔτε
resurrection of the Christ, that neither

ἐγκατελείφθη εἰς ᾅδην οὔτε ἡ σάρξ
he was abandoned in hades nor the flesh

αὐτοῦ εἶδεν διαφθοράν. 32 τοῦτον τὸν
of him saw corruption. This

Ἰησοῦν ἀνέστησεν ὁ θεός, οὗ πάντες
Jesus ²raised up - ¹God, of which all

ἡμεῖς ἐσμεν μάρτυρες· 33 τῇ δεξιᾷ οὖν
we are witnesses; to the right [hand] therefore

exalted, and having received of the Father the promise of the Holy Ghost, he hath shed forth this, which ye now see and hear.

34 For David is not ascended into the heavens: but he saith himself, The LORD said unto my Lord, Sit thou on my right hand,

35 Until I make thy foes thy footstool.

36 Therefore let all the house of Israel know assuredly, that God hath made that same Jesus, whom ye have crucified, both Lord and Christ.

37 ¶ Now when they heard *this*, they were pricked in their heart, and said unto Peter and to the rest of the apostles, Men *and* brethren, what shall we do?

38 Then Peter said unto them, Repent, and be baptized every one of you in the name of Jesus Christ for the remission of sins, and ye shall receive the gift of the Holy Ghost.

39 For the promise is unto you, and to your children, and to all that are afar off, *even* as many as the Lord our God shall call.

40 And with many other words did he testify and

τοῦ θεοῦ ὑψωθεὶς τήν τε ἐπαγγελίαν
\- of God having been exalted *the ¹and ⁷promise

τοῦ πνεύματος τοῦ ἁγίου λαβὼν παρὰ
⁸of the ¹⁰Spirit \- ⁹Holy ²receiving ⁸from

τοῦ πατρὸς ἐξέχεεν τοῦτο ὃ ὑμεῖς καὶ
⁴the ⁵Father he poured out this which ye both

βλέπετε καὶ ἀκούετε. 34 οὐ γὰρ Δαυὶδ
see and hear. For not David

ἀνέβη εἰς τοὺς οὐρανούς, λέγει δὲ αὐτός·
ascended to the heavens, but says he :

εἶπεν κύριος τῷ κυρίῳ μου· κάθου ἐκ
Said [the] LORD to the Lord of me : Sit at

δεξιῶν μου, 35 ἕως ἂν θῶ τοὺς ἐχθρούς
right of me, until I put the enemies

σου ὑποπόδιον τῶν ποδῶν σου. 36 ἀσφαλῶς
of thee a footstool of the feet of thee. Assuredly

οὖν γινωσκέτω πᾶς οἶκος Ἰσραὴλ ὅτι
therefore ⁶let ⁵know ²all³[the] ⁴house ⁵of Israel that

καὶ κύριον αὐτὸν καὶ χριστὸν ἐποίησεν
⁶both ⁶Lord ⁷him ⁶and ⁷Christ ²made

ὁ θεος, τοῦτον τὸν Ἰησοῦν ὃν ὑμεῖς
\- ¹God, this \- Jesus whom ye

ἐσταυρώσατε. 37 Ἀκούσαντες δὲ κατενύγ-
crucified. And hearing they were

ησαν τὴν καρδίαν, εἶπόν τε πρὸς τὸν
stung [in] the heart, and said to \-

Πέτρον καὶ τοὺς λοιποὺς ἀποστόλους·
Peter and the remaining apostles :

τί ποιήσωμεν, ἄνδρες ἀδελφοί; 38 Πέτρος
What may we do, men brothers? Peter

δὲ πρὸς αὐτούς· μετανοήσατε, καὶ
And to them : Repent ye, and

βαπτισθήτω ἕκαστος ὑμῶν ἐπὶ τῷ ὀνόματι
let be baptized each of you on the name

Ἰησοῦ Χριστοῦ εἰς ἄφεσιν τῶν
of Jesus Christ [with a view] to forgiveness of the

ἁμαρτιῶν ὑμῶν, καὶ λήμψεσθε τὴν δωρεὰν
sins of you, and ye will receive the gift

τοῦ ἁγίου πνεύματος. 39 ὑμῖν γάρ ἐστιν
of the Holy Spirit. For to you is

ἡ ἐπαγγελία καὶ τοῖς τέκνοις ὑμῶν καὶ
the promise and to the children of you and

πᾶσιν τοῖς εἰς μακράν, ὅσους ἂν
to all the [ones] far away, as many as

προσκαλέσηται κύριος ὁ θεὸς ἡμῶν.
may call to [him] [the] Lord the God of us.

40 ἑτέροις τε λόγοις πλείοσιν διεμαρτύρατο,
And with other words many he solemnly witnessed,

exhort, saying, Save yourselves from this untoward generation.

41 ¶ Then they that gladly received his word were baptized: and the same day there were added *unto them* about three thousand souls.

42 And they continued stedfastly in the apostles' doctrine and fellowship, and in breaking of bread, and in prayers.

43 And fear came upon every soul: and many wonders and signs were done by the apostles.

44 And all that believed were together, and had all things common;

45 And sold their possessions and goods, and parted them to all *men*, as every man had need.

46 And they, continuing daily with one accord in the temple, and breaking bread from house to house, did eat their meat with gladness and singleness of heart,

47 Praising God, and having favour with all the people. And the Lord added to the church daily such as should be saved.

καὶ   παρεκάλει   αὐτοὺς   λέγων·   σώθητε
and   exhorted   them   saying: Be ye saved

ἀπὸ   τῆς   γενεᾶς   τῆς   σκολιᾶς   ταύτης.   41 οἱ
from   –   ²generation   –   ²perverse   ¹this.   The [ones]

μὲν   οὖν   ἀποδεξάμενοι   τὸν   λόγον   αὐτοῦ
–   therefore   welcoming   the   word   of him

ἐβαπτίσθησαν,   καὶ   προσετέθησαν   ἐν
were baptized,   and   there were added   in

τῇ   ἡμέρᾳ   ἐκείνῃ   ψυχαὶ   ὡσεὶ   τρισχίλιαι·
that day   souls   about   three thousand;

42 ἦσαν   δὲ   προσκαρτεροῦντες   τῇ   διδαχῇ
and they were   continuing steadfastly   in the   teaching

τῶν   ἀποστόλων   καὶ   τῇ   κοινωνίᾳ,   τῇ
of the   apostles   and   in the   fellowship,   in the

κλάσει   τοῦ   ἄρτου   καὶ   ταῖς   προσευχαῖς.
breaking   of the   loaf   and   in the   prayers.

43 Ἐγίνετο   δὲ   πάσῃ   ψυχῇ   φόβος·   πολλὰ   δὲ
And came   to every   soul   fear;   and many

τέρατα   καὶ   σημεῖα   διὰ   τῶν   ἀποστόλων
wonders   and   signs   through   the   apostles

ἐγίνετο.   44 πάντες   δὲ   οἱ   πιστεύσαντες
happened.   And all   the   believing [ones]

ἐπὶ   τὸ   αὐτὸ   εἶχον   ἅπαντα   κοινά,   45 καὶ
together   had   all things   common,   and

τὰ   κτήματα   καὶ   τὰς   ὑπάρξεις   ἐπίπρασκον
the   properties   and the   possessions   they sold

καὶ   διεμέριζον   αὐτὰ   πᾶσιν,   καθότι   ἄν
and   distributed   them   to all,   according as

τις   χρείαν   εἶχεν.   46 καθ'   ἡμέραν   τε
anyone   need   had.   And from day to day†

προσκαρτεροῦντες   ὁμοθυμαδὸν   ἐν   τῷ   ἱερῷ,
continuing steadfastly   with one mind   in   the   temple,

κλῶντές   τε   κατ'   οἶκον   ἄρτον,   μετε-
and ¹breaking   ²from house to house†   ³bread,   they

λάμβανον   τροφῆς   ἐν   ἀγαλλιάσει   καὶ
shared   food   in   gladness   and

ἀφελότητι   καρδίας,   47 αἰνοῦντες   τὸν   θεὸν
simplicity   of heart,   praising   –   God

καὶ   ἔχοντες   χάριν   πρὸς   ὅλον   τὸν   λαόν.
and   having   favour   with   all   the   people.

ὁ   δὲ   κύριος   προσετίθει   τοὺς   σῳζομένους
And the   Lord   added   the [ones]   being saved

καθ'   ἡμέραν   ἐπὶ   τὸ   αὐτό.
from day to day†   together.†

CHAPTER 3

NOW Peter and John went up together into the temple at the hour of prayer, *being* the ninth *hour*.

2 And a certain man lame from his mother's womb was carried, whom they laid daily at the gate of the temple which is called Beautiful, to ask alms of them that entered into the temple;

3 Who seeing Peter and John about to go into the temple asked an alms.

4 And Peter, fastening his eyes upon him with John, said, Look on us.

5 And he gave heed unto them, expecting to receive something of them.

6 Then Peter said, Silver and gold have I none: but such as I have give I thee: In the name of Jesus Christ of Nazareth rise up and walk.

7 And he took him by the right hand, and lifted *him* up: and immediately his feet and ankle bones received strength.

8 And he leaping up stood, and walked, and entered with them into the temple, walking, and leaping, and praising God.

9 And all the people

---

3 Πέτρος δὲ καὶ Ἰωάννης ἀνέβαινον
Now Peter   and   John   were going up

εἰς τὸ ἱερὸν ἐπὶ τὴν ὥραν τῆς προσευχῆς
to the temple at the hour of the prayer

τὴν ἐνάτην. **2** καὶ τις ἀνὴρ χωλὸς ἐκ
the ninth.   And a certain man ²lame ³from

κοιλίας μητρὸς αὐτοῦ ὑπάρχων ἐβαστάζετο,
⁴[the] ⁵of [the] ⁶of him ¹being was being carried,
womb   mother

ὃν ἐτίθουν καθ᾽ ἡμέραν πρὸς τὴν θύραν
whom they used from day to day† at the door
   to put

τοῦ ἱεροῦ τὴν λεγομένην ὡραίαν τοῦ
of the temple the *being* called Beautiful –

αἰτεῖν ἐλεημοσύνην παρὰ τῶν εἰσπορευομέ-
to askᵈ alms from the [ones] enter-

νων εἰς τὸ ἱερόν· **3** ὃς ἰδὼν Πέτρον καὶ
ing into the temple; who seeing Peter and

Ἰωάννην μέλλοντας εἰσιέναι εἰς τὸ ἱερὸν
John   being about to go *in* into the temple

ἠρώτα ἐλεημοσύνην λαβεῖν. **4** ἀτενίσας δὲ
asked alms to receive. And ²gazing

Πέτρος εἰς αὐτὸν σὺν τῷ Ἰωάννῃ εἶπεν·
¹Peter at him with – John said :

βλέψον εἰς ἡμᾶς. **5** ὁ δὲ ἐπεῖχεν αὐτοῖς
Look at us.   And he paid heed to them

προσδοκῶν τι παρ᾽ αὐτῶν λαβεῖν. **6** εἶπεν
expecting something from them to receive. said

δὲ Πέτρος· ἀργύριον καὶ χρυσίον οὐχ
And Peter : Silver and gold not

ὑπάρχει μοι· ὃ δὲ ἔχω, τοῦτό σοι δίδωμι·
is   to meᵉ; but what I have, this to thee I give;
=I have not;

ἐν τῷ ὀνόματι Ἰησοῦ Χριστοῦ τοῦ
in the name of Jesus Christ the

Ναζωραίου περιπάτει. **7** καὶ πιάσας αὐτὸν τῆς
Nazarene walk.   And seizing him of(by)

δεξιᾶς χειρὸς ἤγειρεν αὐτόν· παραχρῆμα
the right hand he raised him; ²at once

δὲ ἐστερεώθησαν αἱ βάσεις αὐτοῦ καὶ τὰ
¹and were made firm the feet of him and the

σφυδρά, **8** καὶ ἐξαλλόμενος ἔστη, καὶ
ankle-bones, and leaping up he stood, and

περιεπάτει, καὶ εἰσῆλθεν σὺν αὐτοῖς εἰς
walked, and entered with them into

τὸ ἱερὸν περιπατῶν καὶ ἁλλόμενος καὶ
the temple walking and leaping and

αἰνῶν τὸν θεόν. **9** καὶ εἶδεν πᾶς ὁ
praising – God.   And ⁴saw ¹all ²the

saw him walking and praising God:

10 And they knew that it was he which sat for alms at the Beautiful gate of the temple: and they were filled with wonder and amazement at that which had happened unto him.

11 ¶ And as the lame man which was healed held Peter and John, all the people ran together unto them in the porch that is called Solomon's, greatly wondering.

12 And when Peter saw it, he answered unto the people, Ye men of Israel, why marvel ye at this? or why look ye so earnestly on us, as though by our own power or holiness we had made this man to walk?

13 The God of Abraham, and of Isaac, and of Jacob, the God of our fathers, hath glorified his Son Jesus; whom ye delivered up, and denied him in the presence of Pilate, when he was determined to let him go.

14 But ye denied the Holy One and the Just, and desired a murderer to be granted unto you;

15 And killed the Prince of life, whom God hath raised from the dead;

λαὸς αὐτὸν περιπατοῦντα καὶ αἰνοῦντα
²people him walking and praising
τὸν θεόν· 10 ἐπεγίνωσκον δὲ αὐτόν, ὅτι
- God; and they recognized him, that
οὗτος ἦν ὁ πρὸς τὴν ἐλεημοσύνην
this was the [one] for - alms
καθήμενος ἐπὶ τῇ ὡραίᾳ πύλῃ τοῦ ἱεροῦ,
sitting at the Beautiful gate of the temple,
καὶ ἐπλήσθησαν θάμβους καὶ ἐκστάσεως
and they were filled of(with) and bewilderment
amazement
ἐπὶ τῷ συμβεβηκότι αὐτῷ. 11 Κρατοῦντος δὲ
at the thing having happened to him. And holding
=as he held
αὐτοῦ τὸν Πέτρον καὶ τὸν Ἰωάννην
him ͣ - Peter and - John
συνέδραμεν πᾶς ὁ λαὸς πρὸς αὐτοὺς
ran together all the people to them
ἐπὶ τῇ στοᾷ τῇ καλουμένῃ Σολομῶντος
at the porch - being called of Solomon
ἔκθαμβοι. 12 ἰδὼν δὲ ὁ Πέτρος ἀπεκρίνατο
greatly amazed. And ²seeing - ¹Peter answered
πρὸς τὸν λαόν· ἄνδρες Ἰσραηλῖται, τί
to the people: Men Israelites, why
θαυμάζετε ἐπὶ τούτῳ, ἢ ἡμῖν τί ἀτενίζετε
marvel ye at this man, or at us why gaze ye
ὡς ἰδίᾳ δυνάμει ἢ εὐσεβείᾳ πεποιηκόσιν
as by [our] own power or piety having made
τοῦ περιπατεῖν αὐτόν; 13 ὁ θεὸς Ἀβραὰμ
- to walk ͩ him? The God of Abraham
καὶ Ἰσαὰκ καὶ Ἰακώβ, ὁ θεὸς τῶν
and Isaac and Jacob, the God of the
πατέρων ἡμῶν, ἐδόξασεν τὸν παῖδα αὐτοῦ
fathers of us, glorified the servant of him
Ἰησοῦν, ὃν ὑμεῖς μὲν παρεδώκατε καὶ
Jesus, whom ye - delivered and
ἠρνήσασθε κατὰ πρόσωπον Πιλάτου,
denied in [the] presence of Pilate,
κρίναντος ἐκείνου ἀπολύειν· 14 ὑμεῖς δὲ
having decided that one ͣ to release [him]; but ye
=when he had decided
τὸν ἅγιον καὶ δίκαιον ἠρνήσασθε, καὶ
the holy and just one denied, and
ᾐτήσασθε ἄνδρα φονέα χαρισθῆναι ὑμῖν,
asked a man a murderer to be granted you,
15 τὸν δὲ ἀρχηγὸν τῆς ζωῆς ἀπεκτείνατε,
and the Author - of life ye killed,
ὃν ὁ θεὸς ἤγειρεν ἐκ νεκρῶν, οὗ ἡμεῖς
whom - God raised from [the] dead, of which we

whereof we are witnesses.

16 And his name through faith in his name hath made this man strong, whom ye see and know: yea, the faith which is by him hath given him this perfect soundness in the presence of you all.

17 And now, brethren, I wot that through ignorance ye did *it*, as *did* also your rulers.

18 But those things, which God before had shewed by the mouth of all his prophets, that Christ should suffer, he hath so fulfilled.

19 Repent ye therefore, and be converted, that your sins may be blotted out, when the times of refreshing shall come from the presence of the Lord;

20 And he shall send Jesus Christ, which before was preached unto you:

21 Whom the heaven must receive until the times of restitution of all things, which God hath spoken by the mouth of all his holy prophets since the world began.

22 For Moses truly said unto the fathers, A prophet shall the Lord your God raise up unto you of your brethren, like unto me; him shall ye hear in all

μάρτυρές ἐσμεν.   **16** καὶ ἐπὶ τῇ πίστει
witnesses are.   And on the faith

τοῦ ὀνόματος αὐτοῦ τοῦτον, ὃν θεωρεῖτε
of(in) name* of him ⁵this man, ⁶whom ⁷ye behold
the

καὶ οἴδατε, ἐστερέωσεν τὸ ὄνομα αὐτοῦ,
⁸and ⁹know, ⁴made firm ¹the ²name ³of him,

καὶ ἡ πίστις ἡ δι' αὐτοῦ ἔδωκεν αὐτῷ
and the faith – through him gave him

τὴν ὁλοκληρίαν ταύτην ἀπέναντι πάντων
this soundness before all

ὑμῶν.   **17** καὶ νῦν, ἀδελφοί, οἶδα ὅτι
you.   And now, brothers, I know that

κατὰ ἄγνοιαν ἐπράξατε, ὥσπερ καὶ οἱ
by way of ignorance ye acted, as also the

ἄρχοντες ὑμῶν·   **18** ὁ δὲ θεὸς ἃ
rulers of you;   – but God the things which

προκατήγγειλεν διὰ στόματος πάντων
he foreannounced through [the] mouth of all

τῶν προφητῶν, παθεῖν τὸν χριστὸν αὐτοῦ,
the prophets, to suffer the Christ of him[b],
=that his Christ was to suffer,

ἐπλήρωσεν οὕτως.   **19** μετανοήσατε οὖν
fulfilled thus.   Repent ye therefore

καὶ ἐπιστρέψατε πρὸς τὸ ἐξαλειφθῆναι
and turn for the to be wiped away
=that your sins may be wiped away,

ὑμῶν τὰς ἁμαρτίας,   **20** ὅπως ἂν ἔλθωσιν
of you the sins,   so as may come

καιροὶ ἀναψύξεως ἀπὸ προσώπου τοῦ
times of refreshing from [the] presence of the

κυρίου καὶ ἀποστείλῃ τὸν προκεχειρισμένον
Lord and he may send ¹the ²having been foreappointed

ὑμῖν χριστὸν Ἰησοῦν,   **21** ὃν δεῖ οὐρανὸν
⁴for you ⁵Christ ⁶Jesus,   whom it behoves heaven

μὲν δέξασθαι ἄχρι χρόνων ἀποκαταστάσεως
– to receive until [the] times of restitution

πάντων ὧν ἐλάλησεν ὁ θεὸς διὰ στόματος
of all things which ⁸spoke – ¹God ²through ⁴[the] mouth

τῶν ἁγίων ἀπ' αἰῶνος αὐτοῦ προφητῶν.
⁵of the ⁶holy ⁸from ¹⁰[the] age ⁹of him ⁷prophets.

22 Μωϋσῆς μὲν εἶπεν ὅτι προφήτην ὑμῖν
Moses indeed said[,] – ⁴A prophet ⁵for you

ἀναστήσει κύριος ὁ θεὸς ἐκ τῶν ἀδελφῶν
³will raise up ¹(the) Lord – ²God of the brothers

ὑμῶν ὡς ἐμέ· αὐτοῦ ἀκούσεσθε κατὰ
of you as me; him shall ye hear according to

---

* Objective genitive; *cf.* "the fear of God" = the fear which has God for its object; and see Gal. 2. 20, etc.

things whatsoever he shall say unto you.

23 And it shall come to pass, *that* every soul, which will not hear that prophet, shall be destroyed from among the people.

24 Yea, and all the prophets from Samuel and those that follow after, as many as have spoken, have likewise foretold of these days.

25 Ye are the children of the prophets, and of the covenant which God made with our fathers, saying unto Abraham, And in thy seed shall all the kindreds of the earth be blessed.

26 Unto you first God, having raised up his Son Jesus, sent him to bless you, in turning away every one of you from his iniquities.

πάντα	ὅσα	ἂν	λαλήσῃ	πρὸς	ὑμᾶς.
all things	whatever		he may speak	to	you.

23 ἔσται δὲ πᾶσα ψυχὴ ἥτις ἐὰν μὴ ἀκούσῃ
And it shall be every   soul   whoever   hears not

τοῦ προφήτου ἐκείνου ἐξολεθρευθήσεται
that prophet   will be utterly destroyed

ἐκ τοῦ λαοῦ. **24** καὶ πάντες δὲ οἱ
out of the   people.   [2]also [3]all [1]And the

προφῆται ἀπὸ Σαμουὴλ καὶ τῶν καθεξῆς
prophets   from   Samuel   and   the [ones] in order

ὅσοι ἐλάλησαν καὶ κατήγγειλαν τὰς ἡμέρας
as many as   spoke   also   announced   -   days

ταύτας. **25** ὑμεῖς ἐστε οἱ υἱοὶ τῶν
these.   Ye   are   the   sons   of the

προφητῶν καὶ τῆς διαθήκης ἧς ὁ θεὸς
prophets   and   of the   covenant   which   -   God

διέθετο πρὸς τοὺς πατέρας ὑμῶν, λέγων
made   with   the   fathers   of us,   saying

πρὸς Ἀβραάμ· καὶ ἐν τῷ σπέρματί
to   Abraham;   And   in   the   seed

σου ἐνευλογηθήσονται πᾶσαι αἱ πατριαὶ
of thee   shall be blessed   all   the   families

τῆς γῆς. **26** ὑμῖν πρῶτον ἀναστήσας ὁ
of the earth.   To you   first   [2]having raised up   -

θεὸς τὸν παῖδα αὐτοῦ ἀπέστειλεν αὐτὸν
[1]God   the   servant   of him   sent   him

εὐλογοῦντα ὑμᾶς ἐν τῷ ἀποστρέφειν
blessing   you   in   the   to turn away
                                =in turning away

ἕκαστον ἀπὸ τῶν πονηριῶν ὑμῶν.
each one   from   the   iniquities   of you.

CHAPTER 4

A ND as they spake unto the people, the priests, and the captain of the temple, and the Sadducees, came upon them,

2 Being grieved that they taught the people, and preached through Jesus the resurrection from the dead.

3 And they laid hands on them, and put *them* in hold unto the next day: for it was now eventide.

4 Howbeit many of

4 Λαλούντων δὲ αὐτῶν πρὸς τὸν λαόν,
And speaking   them[a]   to   the   people,
=while they were speaking

ἐπέστησαν αὐτοῖς οἱ ἱερεῖς καὶ ὁ στρατηγὸς
came upon   them   the   priests   and   the commandant

τοῦ ἱεροῦ καὶ οἱ Σαδδουκαῖοι, **2** διαπονούμενοι
of the temple and   the   Sadducees,   being greatly troubled

διὰ τὸ διδάσκειν αὐτοὺς τὸν λαὸν καὶ
because of   the   to teach   them[b]   the   people   and
=because they taught . . . announced

καταγγέλλειν ἐν τῷ Ἰησοῦ τὴν ἀνάστασιν
to announce[b]   by   -   Jesus   the   resurrection

τὴν ἐκ νεκρῶν, **3** καὶ ἐπέβαλον αὐτοῖς
-    from   [the] dead,   and   laid on   them

τὰς χεῖρας καὶ ἔθεντο εἰς τήρησιν εἰς
the(ir)   hands   and   put   in   guard   till

τὴν αὔριον· ἦν γὰρ ἑσπέρα ἤδη. **4** πολλοὶ
the   morrow;   for it was   evening   now.   many

them which heard the word believed; and the ~~number of the men was~~ about five thousand.

5 ¶ And it came to pass on the morrow, that their rulers, and elders, and scribes,

6 And Annas the high priest, and Caiaphas, and John, and Alexander, and as many as were of the kindred of the high priest, were gathered together at Jerusalem.

7 And when they had set them in the midst, they asked, By what power, or by what name, have ye done this?

8 Then Peter, filled with the Holy Ghost, said unto them, Ye rulers of the people, and elders of Israel,

9 If we this day be examined of the good deed done to the impotent man, by what means he is made whole;

10 Be it known unto you all, and to all the people of Israel, that by the name of Jesus Christ of Nazareth, whom ye crucified, whom God raised from the dead, *even* by him doth this man stand here before you whole.

11 This is the stone which was set at nought of you builders, which is

δὲ τῶν ἀκουσάντων τὸν λόγον ἐπίστευσαν,
But of the [ones] hearing the word believed,

καὶ ἐγενήθη ἀριθμὸς τῶν ἀνδρῶν ὡς
and became [the] number of the men about

χιλιάδες πέντε.
thousands five.

5 Ἐγένετο δὲ ἐπὶ τὴν αὔριον
Now it came to pass on the morrow

συναχθῆναι αὐτῶν τοὺς ἄρχοντας καὶ τοὺς
to be assembled of them the rulers and the

πρεσβυτέρους καὶ τοὺς γραμματεῖς ἐν
elders and the scribes in

Ἰερουσαλήμ, 6 καὶ Ἅννας ὁ ἀρχιερεὺς
Jerusalem, and Annas* the high priest

καὶ Καϊαφᾶς καὶ Ἰωάννης καὶ Ἀλέξανδρος
and Caiaphas and John and Alexander

καὶ ὅσοι ἦσαν ἐκ γένους ἀρχιερατικοῦ,
and as many as were of [the] race high-priestly,

7 καὶ στήσαντες αὐτοὺς ἐν τῷ μέσῳ
and having stood them in the midst

ἐπυνθάνοντο· ἐν ποίᾳ δυνάμει ἢ ἐν ποίῳ
inquired: By what power or in what

ὀνόματι ἐποιήσατε τοῦτο ὑμεῖς; 8 τότε
name did this ye? Then

Πέτρος πλησθεὶς πνεύματος ἁγίου εἶπεν
Peter filled of(with) [the] Spirit Holy said

πρὸς αὐτούς· ἄρχοντες τοῦ λαοῦ καὶ
to them: Rulers of the people and

πρεσβύτεροι, 9 εἰ ἡμεῖς σήμερον ἀνα-
elders, if we to-day are be-

κρινόμεθα ἐπὶ εὐεργεσίᾳ ἀνθρώπου ἀσθενοῦς,
ing examined on a good deed man of an infirm,
= [done to] an infirm man,

ἐν τίνι οὗτος σέσωσται, 10 γνωστὸν ἔστω
by what this man has been healed, known let it be

πᾶσιν ὑμῖν καὶ παντὶ τῷ λαῷ Ἰσραήλ,
to all you and to all the people of Israel,

ὅτι ἐν τῷ ὀνόματι Ἰησοῦ Χριστοῦ τοῦ
that in the name of Jesus Christ the

Ναζωραίου, ὃν ὑμεῖς ἐσταυρώσατε, ὃν ὁ
Nazarene, whom ye crucified, whom –

θεὸς ἤγειρεν ἐκ νεκρῶν, ἐν τούτῳ οὗτος
God raised from [the] dead, in this [name] this man

παρέστηκεν ἐνώπιον ὑμῶν ὑγιής. 11 οὗτός
stands before you whole. This

ἐστιν ὁ λίθος ὁ ἐξουθενηθεὶς ὑφ' ὑμῶν
is the stone – despised by you

* The rough breathing in the Greek is ignored in the transliteration of some familiar proper names.

become the head of the corner.

12 Neither is there salvation in any other: for there is none other name under heaven given among men, whereby we must be saved.

13 ¶ Now when they saw the boldness of Peter and John, and perceived that they were unlearned and ignorant men, they marvelled; and they took knowledge of them, that they had been with Jesus.

14 And beholding the man which was healed standing with them, they could say nothing against it.

15 But when they had commanded them to go aside out of the council, they conferred among themselves,

16 Saying, What shall we do to these men? for that indeed a notable miracle hath been done by them is manifest to all them that dwell in Jerusalem; and we cannot deny it.

17 But that it spread no further among the people, let us straitly threaten them, that they speak henceforth to no man in this name.

18 And they called them, and commanded them not to speak at all nor teach in the name of Jesus.

τῶν οἰκοδόμων, ὁ γενόμενος εἰς κεφαλὴν
the [ones] building, the [one] become to head

γωνίας. 12 καὶ οὐκ ἔστιν ἐν ἄλλῳ οὐδενὶ
of [the] corner. And there is not ¹in ³other ²no(any)

ἡ σωτηρία· οὐδὲ γὰρ ὄνομά ἐστιν ἕτερον
the salvation: for neither ³name ¹is there ²other

ὑπὸ τὸν οὐρανὸν τὸ δεδομένον ἐν
under - heaven - having been given among

ἀνθρώποις ἐν ᾧ δεῖ σωθῆναι ἡμᾶς.
men by which it behoves ²to be saved ¹us.

13 Θεωροῦντες δὲ τὴν τοῦ Πέτρου
And beholding the - of Peter

παρρησίαν καὶ Ἰωάννου, καὶ καταλαβόμενοι
boldness and of John, and perceiving

ὅτι ἄνθρωποι ἀγράμματοί εἰσιν καὶ
that men unlettered they are(were) and

ἰδιῶται, ἐθαύμαζον, ἐπεγίνωσκόν τε αὐτοὺς
laymen, they marvelled, and recognized them

ὅτι σὺν τῷ Ἰησοῦ ἦσαν, 14 τόν τε
that with - Jesus they were(had been), ³the ¹and

ἄνθρωπον βλέποντες σὺν αὐτοῖς ἑστῶτα τὸν
⁴man ²seeing ⁷with ⁸them ⁶standing ⁵

τεθεραπευμένον, οὐδὲν εἶχον ἀντειπεῖν.
⁵having been healed, nothing they had to say against.

15 κελεύσαντες δὲ αὐτοὺς ἔξω τοῦ συνεδρίου
So having commanded them outside the council

ἀπελθεῖν, συνέβαλλον πρὸς ἀλλήλους
to go, they discussed with with one another

16 λέγοντες· τί ποιήσωμεν τοῖς ἀνθρώποις
saying : What may we do - men

τούτοις; ὅτι μὲν γὰρ γνωστὸν σημεῖον
to these? for that indeed a notable sign

γέγονεν δι' αὐτῶν, πᾶσιν τοῖς κατοικοῦσιν
has happened through them, to all the [ones] inhabiting

Ἱερουσαλὴμ φανερόν, καὶ οὐ δυνάμεθα
Jerusalem [is] manifest, and we cannot

ἀρνεῖσθαι· 17 ἀλλ' ἵνα μὴ ἐπὶ πλεῖον
to deny [it]; but ¹lest ²more†

διανεμηθῇ εἰς τὸν λαόν, ἀπειλησώμεθα
²it is spread abroad ⁴to the people, let us threaten

αὐτοῖς μηκέτι λαλεῖν ἐπὶ τῷ ὀνόματι
them no longer to speak on - name

τούτῳ μηδενὶ ἀνθρώπων. 18 καὶ καλέσαντες
this to no(any)one of men. And calling

αὐτοὺς παρήγγειλαν καθόλου μὴ φθέγγεσθαι
them they charged at all not to utter

μηδὲ διδάσκειν ἐπὶ τῷ ὀνόματι τοῦ
nor to teach on the name

19 But Peter and John answered and said unto them, Whether it be right in the sight of God to hearken unto you more than unto God, judge ye.

20 For we cannot but speak the things which we have seen and heard.

21 So when they had further threatened them, they let them go, finding nothing how they might punish them, because of the people: for all *men* glorified God for that which was done.

22 For the man was above forty years old, on whom this miracle of healing was shewed.

23 ¶ And being let go, they went to their own company, and reported all that the chief priests and elders had said unto them.

24 And when they heard *that*, they lifted up their voice to God with one accord, and said, Lord, thou *art* God, which hast made heaven, and earth, and the sea, and all that in them is:

25 Who by the mouth of thy servant David hast said, Why did the heathen rage, and the people imagine vain things?

Ἰησοῦ. **19** ὁ δὲ Πέτρος καὶ Ἰωάννης
of Jesus.   – But   Peter   and   John

ἀποκριθέντες εἶπον πρὸς αὐτούς· εἰ
answering   said   to   them: If

δίκαιόν ἐστιν ἐνώπιον τοῦ θεοῦ, ὑμῶν
right   it is   before   –   God,   you

ἀκούειν μᾶλλον ἢ τοῦ θεοῦ, κρίνατε·
to hear   rather   than   –   God,   decide ye;

20 οὐ δυνάμεθα γὰρ ἡμεῖς ἃ εἴδαμεν
for cannot   we   [the] things which   we saw

καὶ ἠκούσαμεν μὴ λαλεῖν. **21** οἱ δὲ
and   heard   not   *to* speak.   And they

προσαπειλησάμενοι ἀπέλυσαν αὐτούς, μηδὲν
having added threats   released   them,   nothing

εὑρίσκοντες τὸ πῶς κολάσωνται αὐτούς,
finding   –   how   they might punish   them,

διὰ τὸν λαόν, ὅτι πάντες ἐδόξαζον τὸν
because of the people, because all men   glorified   –

θεὸν ἐπὶ τῷ γεγονότι· **22** ἐτῶν γὰρ
God   on   the thing having happened;   for of years

ἦν πλειόνων τεσσεράκοντα ὁ ἄνθρωπος
was   more [than]   forty   the   man

ἐφ' ὃν γεγόνει τὸ σημεῖον τοῦτο τῆς
on whom had happened   this sign   –

ἰάσεως. **23** Ἀπολυθέντες δὲ ἦλθον πρὸς
of cure.   And being released   they went   to

τοὺς ἰδίους καὶ ἀπήγγειλαν ὅσα πρὸς
the(ir) own [people] and   reported   what things to

αὐτοὺς οἱ ἀρχιερεῖς καὶ οἱ πρεσβύτεροι
them   the chief priests   and   the   elders

εἶπαν. **24** οἱ δὲ ἀκούσαντες ὁμοθυμαδὸν
said.   And they   having heard   with one mind

ἦραν φωνὴν πρὸς τὸν θεὸν καὶ εἶπαν·
lifted   voice   to   –   God   and   said :

δέσποτα, σὺ ὁ ποιήσας τὸν οὐρανὸν καὶ
Master,   thou the [one] having made   the   heaven   and

τὴν γῆν καὶ τὴν θάλασσαν καὶ πάντα
the   earth   and   the   sea   and   all things

τὰ ἐν αὐτοῖς, **25** ὁ τοῦ πατρὸς ἡμῶν
–   in   them,   [1]the   [8]the   [9]father   [10]of us
                                  [one]

διὰ πνεύματος ἁγίου στόματος Δαυὶδ
[3]through   [5][the] Spirit   [4]Holy   [6][by] mouth   [7]of David

παιδός σου εἰπών· ἱνατί ἐφρύαξαν ἔθνη
[11]servant [12]of thee   [2]saying :[*] Why   raged   nations

καὶ λαοὶ ἐμελέτησαν κενά; **26** παρέστησαν
and peoples   devised   vain things?   came

---

[*] It is recognized that there is a primitive error in the text in the first half of ver. 25; it is impossible to construe it as it stands. See ch. 1. 16.

26 The kings of the earth ·stood up, and the rulers were gathered together against the Lord, and against his Christ.

27 For of a truth against thy holy child Jesus, whom thou hast anointed, both Herod, and Pontius Pilate, with the Gentiles, and the people of Israel, were gathered together,

28 For to do whatsoever thy hand and thy counsel determined before to be done.

29 And now, Lord, behold their threatenings: and grant unto thy servants, that with all boldness they may speak thy word,

30 By stretching forth thine hand to heal; and that signs and wonders may be done by the name of thy holy child Jesus.

31 And when they had prayed, the place was shaken where they were assembled together; and they were all filled with the Holy Ghost, and they spake the word of God with boldness.

32 ¶ And the multitude of them that believed were of one heart and of one soul: neither said any of them that ought of the things which he possessed was his own; but they had all things common.

οἱ βασιλεῖς τῆς γῆς καὶ οἱ ἄρχοντες
the kings of the earth and the rulers

συνήχθησαν ἐπὶ τὸ αὐτὸ κατὰ τοῦ κυρίου
assembled together against the Lord

καὶ κατὰ τοῦ χριστοῦ αὐτοῦ.
and against the Christ of him.

27 συνήχθησαν γὰρ ἐπ’ ἀληθείας ἐν τῇ
For assembled in truth in -

πόλει ταύτῃ ἐπὶ τὸν ἅγιον παῖδά σου
city this against the holy servant of thee

Ἰησοῦν, ὃν ἔχρισας, Ἡρῴδης τε καὶ
Jesus, whom thou didst anoint, both Herod and

Πόντιος Πιλᾶτος σὺν ἔθνεσιν καὶ λαοῖς
Pontius Pilate with nations and peoples

Ἰσραήλ, 28 ποιῆσαι ὅσα ἡ χείρ σου καὶ
of Israel, to do what the hand of thee and
things

ἡ βουλὴ προώρισεν γενέσθαι. 29 καὶ τὰ
the counsel foreordained to happen. And -

νῦν, κύριε, ἔπιδε ἐπὶ τὰς ἀπειλὰς αὐτῶν,
now, Lord, look on on the threatenings of them,

καὶ δὸς τοῖς δούλοις σου μετὰ παρρησίας
and give to the slaves of thee with ²boldness

πάσης λαλεῖν τὸν λόγον σου, 30 ἐν τῷ
¹all to speak the word of thee, by the

τὴν χεῖρα ἐκτείνειν σε εἰς ἴασιν καὶ
the hand to stretch forth thee[b] for cure and
=by stretching forth thy hand

σημεῖα καὶ τέρατα γίνεσθαι διὰ τοῦ
signs and wonders to happen through the

ὀνόματος τοῦ ἁγίου παιδός σου Ἰησοῦ.
name of the holy servant of thee Jesus.

31 καὶ δεηθέντων αὐτῶν ἐσαλεύθη ὁ τόπος
And requesting them[a] was shaken the place
=as they were making request

ἐν ᾧ ἦσαν συνηγμένοι, καὶ ἐπλήσθησαν
in which they were having been and they were filled
assembled,

ἅπαντες τοῦ ἁγίου πνεύματος, καὶ ἐλάλουν
all of(with) the Holy Spirit, and spoke

τὸν λόγον τοῦ θεοῦ μετὰ παρρησίας.
the word - of God with boldness.

32 Τοῦ δὲ πλήθους τῶν πιστευσάντων
¹Now ⁶of ⁷the ⁸multitude ⁹of the [ones] ¹⁰having believed

ἦν καρδία καὶ ψυχὴ μία, καὶ οὐδὲ
¹¹was ³[the] ⁴heart ⁵and ⁶soul ¹²one, and ¹not

εἷς τι τῶν ὑπαρχόντων αὐτῷ ἔλεγεν
²one ⁴any- ⁵of the ⁶possessions [belonging] ³said
thing ⁷to him⁶

ἴδιον εἶναι, ἀλλ’ ἦν αὐτοῖς πάντα κοινά.
⁹[his] own ⁸to be, but were to them[c] all things common.

33 And with great power gave the apostles witness of the resurrection of the Lord Jesus: and great grace was upon them all.

34 Neither was there any among them that lacked: for as many as were possessors of lands or houses sold them, and brought the prices of the things that were sold,

35 And laid *them* down at the apostles' feet: and distribution was made unto every man according as he had need.

36 And Joses, who by the apostles was surnamed Barnabas, (which is, being interpreted, The son of consolation,) a Levite, *and* of the country of Cyprus,

37 Having land, sold *it*, and brought the money, and laid *it* at the apostles' feet.

33 καὶ δυνάμει μεγάλη ἀπεδίδουν τὸ
And ¹with ³power ²great ⁶gave ⁷the

μαρτύριον οἱ ἀπόστολοι τοῦ κυρίου Ἰησοῦ
³testimony ⁴the ⁵apostles ¹¹of the ¹²Lord ¹³Jesus

τῆς ἀναστάσεως, χάρις τε μεγάλη ἦν
⁹of the ¹⁰resurrection, and ²grace ¹great was

ἐπὶ πάντας αὐτούς. 34 οὐδὲ γὰρ ἐνδεής
upon all them. ¹For ²neither ³needy

τις ἦν ἐν αὐτοῖς· ὅσοι γὰρ κτήτορες
⁴anyone ³was among them; for as many as owners

χωρίων ἢ οἰκιῶν ὑπῆρχον, πωλοῦντες
of lands or of houses were, selling

ἔφερον τὰς τιμὰς τῶν πιπρασκομένων
brought the prices of the things being sold

35 καὶ ἐτίθουν παρὰ τοὺς πόδας τῶν
and placed at the feet of the

ἀποστόλων· διεδίδοτο δὲ ἑκάστῳ καθότι ἄν
apostles; and it was distributed to each according as

τις χρείαν εἶχεν. 36 Ἰωσὴφ δὲ ὁ
anyone need had. And Joseph the [one]

ἐπικληθεὶς Βαρναβᾶς ἀπὸ τῶν ἀποστόλων,
surnamed Barnabas from(by) the apostles,

ὅ ἐστιν μεθερμηνευόμενον υἱὸς παρακλήσεως,
which is being translated Son of consolation,

Λευίτης, Κύπριος τῷ γένει, 37 ὑπάρχοντος
a Levite, a Cypriote – by race, being

αὐτῷ ἀγροῦ, πωλήσας ἤνεγκεν τὸ χρῆμα
to him° a field,ª having sold [it] brought the proceeds
=as he had a field,

καὶ ἔθηκεν πρὸς τοὺς πόδας τῶν ἀποστόλων.
and placed at the feet of the apostles.

CHAPTER 5

BUT a certain man named Ananias, with Sapphira his wife, sold a possession,

2 And kept back *part* of the price, his wife also being privy *to it*, and brought a certain part, and laid *it* at the apostles' feet.

3 But Peter said, Ananias, why hath Satan filled thine heart to lie to

5 Ἀνὴρ δέ τις Ἀνανίας ὀνόματι σὺν
And a certain man Ananias* by name with

Σαπφίρῃ τῇ γυναικὶ αὐτοῦ ἐπώλησεν
Sapphira the wife of him sold

κτῆμα, 2 καὶ ἐνοσφίσατο ἀπὸ τῆς τιμῆς,
a property, and appropriated from the price,

συνειδυίης καὶ τῆς γυναικός, καὶ ἐνέγκας
aware of [it] also the(his) wife,ª and bringing
=his wife also being aware of it,

μέρος τι παρὰ τοὺς πόδας τῶν ἀποστόλων
a certain part at the feet of the apostles

ἔθηκεν. 3 εἶπεν δὲ ὁ Πέτρος· Ἀνανία,
placed [it]. But said – Peter: Ananias,

διὰ τί ἐπλήρωσεν ὁ σατανᾶς τὴν καρδίαν
why filled – Satan the heart

the Holy Ghost, and to
keep back *part* of the
price of the land?
4 Whiles it remained,
was it not thine own?
and after it was sold, was
it not in thine own power?
why hast thou conceived
this thing in thine heart?
thou hast not lied unto
men, but unto God.

5 And Ananias hearing
these words fell down, and
gave up the ghost: and
great fear came on all
them that heard these
things.
6 And the young men
arose, wound him up, and
carried *him* out, and
buried *him*.
7 And it was about the
space of three hours after,
when his wife, not know-
ing what was done, came
in.
8 And Peter answered
unto her, Tell me whether
ye sold the land for so
much? And she said, Yea,
for so much.
9 Then Peter said unto
her, How is it that ye
have agreed together to
tempt the Spirit of the
Lord? behold, the feet
of them which have buried
thy husband *are* at the
door, and shall carry thee
out.
10 Then fell she down
straightway at his feet,
and yielded up the ghost:
and the young men came
in, and found her dead,

σου, ψεύσασθαί σε τὸ πνεῦμα τὸ ἅγιον
of thee, to deceive thee[b] the Spirit - Holy
　　　　=that thou shouldest deceive

καὶ νοσφίσασθαι ἀπὸ τῆς τιμῆς τοῦ
and to appropriate from the price of the

χωρίου; 4 οὐχὶ μένον σοὶ ἔμενεν καὶ
land? Not remaining to thee it remained and

πραθὲν ἐν τῇ σῇ ἐξουσίᾳ ὑπῆρχεν; τί ὅτι
sold in - thy authority it was? Why

ἔθου ἐν τῇ καρδίᾳ σου τὸ πρᾶγμα
was put in the heart of thee - action

τοῦτο; οὐκ ἐψεύσω ἀνθρώποις ἀλλὰ
this? thou didst not lie to men but

τῷ θεῷ. 5 ἀκούων δὲ ὁ 'Ανανίας
- to God. And hearing - Ananias

τοὺς λόγους τούτους πεσὼν ἐξέψυξεν· καὶ
these words falling expired; and

ἐγένετο φόβος μέγας ἐπὶ πάντας τοὺς
came fear great on all the [ones]

ἀκούοντας. 6 ἀναστάντες δὲ οἱ νεώτεροι
hearing. And rising up the young men

συνέστειλαν αὐτὸν καὶ ἐξενέγκαντες ἔθαψαν.
wrapped him and carrying out buried [him].

7 'Εγένετο δὲ ὡς ὡρῶν τριῶν διάστημα
[1]And there was [3]of about [5]hours [4]three [2]an interval

καὶ ἡ γυνὴ αὐτοῦ μὴ εἰδυῖα τὸ γεγονὸς
and the wife of him not knowing the thing having
　　　　　　　　　　　　　　　　　　happened

εἰσῆλθεν. 8 ἀπεκρίθη δὲ πρὸς αὐτὴν
entered. And answered to her

Πέτρος· εἰπέ μοι, εἰ τοσούτου τὸ χωρίον
Peter: Tell me, if of(for) so much the land

ἀπέδοσθε; ἡ δὲ εἶπεν· ναί, τοσούτου.
ye sold? And she said: Yes, of(for) so much.

9 ὁ δὲ Πέτρος πρὸς αὐτήν· τί ὅτι
- And Peter to her: Why

συνεφωνήθη ὑμῖν πειράσαι τὸ πνεῦμα
was it agreed with you to tempt the Spirit

κυρίου; ἰδοὺ οἱ πόδες τῶν θαψάντων τὸν
of [the] behold[,] the feet of the [ones] having the
Lord? buried

ἄνδρα σου ἐπὶ τῇ θύρᾳ καὶ ἐξοίσουσίν
husband of thee at the door and they will
　　　　　　　　　　　　　　　　carry out

σε. 10 ἔπεσεν δὲ παραχρῆμα πρὸς τοὺς
thee. And she fell at once at the

πόδας αὐτοῦ καὶ ἐξέψυξεν· εἰσελθόντες δὲ
feet of him and expired; and entering

οἱ νεανίσκοι εὗρον αὐτὴν νεκράν, καὶ
the young men found her dead, and

and, carrying *her* forth, buried *her* by her husband.

11 And great fear came upon all the church, and upon as many as heard these things.

12 ¶ And by the hands of the apostles were many signs and wonders wrought among the people; (and they were all with one accord in Solomon's porch.

13 And of the rest durst no man join himself to them: but the people magnified them.

14 And believers were the more added to the Lord, multitudes both of men and women.)

15 Insomuch that they brought forth the sick into the streets, and laid *them* on beds and couches, that at the least the shadow of Peter passing by might overshadow some of them.

16 There came also a multitude *out* of the cities round about unto Jerusalem, bringing sick folks, and them which were vexed with unclean spirits: and they were healed every one.

17 ¶ Then the high priest rose up, and all they that were with him, (which is the sect of the Sadducees,) and were filled with indignation,

18 And laid their hands on the apostles, and put

ἐξενέγκαντες ἔθαψαν πρὸς τὸν ἄνδρα
carrying out   buried [her] beside the husband

αὐτῆς. 11 Καὶ ἐγένετο φόβος μέγας
of her.   And   came   fear   great

ἐφ᾽ ὅλην τὴν ἐκκλησίαν καὶ ἐπὶ πάντας
on   all   the   church   and on   all

τοὺς ἀκούοντας ταῦτα.
the [ones] hearing these things.

12 Διὰ δὲ τῶν χειρῶν τῶν ἀποστόλων
And through the hands of the apostles

ἐγίνετο σημεῖα καὶ τέρατα πολλὰ ἐν
⁵happened ²signs ³and ⁴wonders ¹many among

τῷ λαῷ· καὶ ἦσαν ὁμοθυμαδὸν πάντες
the people; and were with one mind all

ἐν τῇ στοᾷ Σολομῶντος· 13 τῶν δὲ
in the porch of Solomon;   and of the

λοιπῶν οὐδεὶς ἐτόλμα κολλᾶσθαι αὐτοῖς,
rest   no one dared to be joined to them,

ἀλλ᾽ ἐμεγάλυνεν αὐτοὺς ὁ λαός· 14 μᾶλλον
but magnified   them the people;   ²more

δὲ προσετίθεντο πιστεύοντες τῷ κυρίῳ,
¹and were added believing [ones] to the Lord,

πλήθη ἀνδρῶν τε καὶ γυναικῶν· 15 ὥστε
multitudes both of men and of women;   so as

καὶ εἰς τὰς πλατείας ἐκφέρειν τοὺς
even into the streets to bring out the
                              =they brought out

ἀσθενεῖς καὶ τιθέναι ἐπὶ κλιναρίων καὶ
ailing   and to place on   pallets   and

κραβάτων, ἵνα ἐρχομένου Πέτρου κἂν ἡ σκιὰ
mattresses, that ⁵coming ⁴of Peter ¹if even ²the ³shadow

ἐπισκιάσῃ τινὶ αὐτῶν. 16 συνήρχετο δὲ
might overshadow some one of them.   And came together

καὶ τὸ πλῆθος τῶν πέριξ πόλεων
also the multitude of the ²round about ¹cities

Ἰερουσαλήμ, φέροντες ἀσθενεῖς καὶ
Jerusalem,   carrying ailing [ones] and

ὀχλουμένους ὑπὸ πνευμάτων ἀκαθάρτων,
being tormented by   spirits   unclean,

οἵτινες ἐθεραπεύοντο ἅπαντες
who   were healed   all.

17 Ἀναστὰς δὲ ὁ ἀρχιερεὺς καὶ πάντες
And rising up the high priest and all

οἱ σὺν αὐτῷ, ἡ οὖσα αἵρεσις τῶν
the[ones] with him, the existing sect of the

Σαδδουκαίων, ἐπλήσθησαν ζήλου 18 καὶ
Sadducees,   were filled of(with) jealousy and

ἐπέβαλον τὰς χεῖρας ἐπὶ τοὺς ἀποστόλους
laid *on* the(ir) hands on the   apostles

them in the common prison.

19 But the angel of the Lord by night opened the prison doors, and brought them forth, and said,

20 Go, stand and speak in the temple to the people all the words of this life.

21 And when they heard *that*, they entered into the temple early in the morning, and taught. But the high priest came, and they that were with him, and called the council together, and all the senate of the children of Israel, and sent to the prison to have them brought.

22 But when the officers came, and found them not in the prison, they returned, and told,

23 Saying, The prison truly found we shut with all safety, and the keepers standing without before the doors: but when we had opened, we found no man within.

24 Now when the high priest and the captain of the temple and the chief priests heard these things, they doubted of them whereunto this would grow.

25 Then came one and told them, saying, Behold, the men whom ye put in

καὶ ἔθεντο αὐτοὺς ἐν τηρήσει δημοσίᾳ.
and put them in custody publicly.

19 Ἄγγελος δὲ κυρίου διὰ νυκτὸς
But an angel of [the] Lord through(during) [the] night

ἤνοιξε τὰς θύρας τῆς φυλακῆς ἐξαγαγών τε
opened the doors of the prison and leading out

αὐτοὺς εἶπεν· 20 πορεύεσθε καὶ σταθέντες
them said : Go ye and standing

λαλεῖτε ἐν τῷ ἱερῷ τῷ λαῷ πάντα
speak in the temple to the people all

τὰ ῥήματα τῆς ζωῆς ταύτης.
the words of this life.

21 ἀκούσαντες δὲ εἰσῆλθον ὑπὸ τὸν ὄρθρον
And having heard they entered about the dawn

εἰς τὸ ἱερὸν καὶ ἐδίδασκον. Παραγενόμενος δὲ
into the temple and taught. And having come

ὁ ἀρχιερεὺς καὶ οἱ σὺν αὐτῷ
the high priest and the [ones] with him

συνεκάλεσαν τὸ συνέδριον καὶ πᾶσαν τὴν
called together the council and all the

γερουσίαν τῶν υἱῶν Ἰσραήλ, καὶ ἀπέστειλαν
senate of the sons of Israel, and sent

εἰς τὸ δεσμωτήριον ἀχθῆναι αὐτούς.
to the jail to be brought them.[b]

22 οἱ δὲ παραγενόμενοι ὑπηρέται οὐχ εὗρον
¹But ²the ⁴having come ³attendants found not

αὐτοὺς ἐν τῇ φυλακῇ· ἀναστρέψαντες δὲ
them in the prison; and having returned

ἀπήγγειλαν 23 λέγοντες ὅτι τὸ δεσμωτήριον
they reported saying[,] – The jail

εὕρομεν κεκλεισμένον ἐν πάσῃ ἀσφαλείᾳ
we found *having been* shut in all security

καὶ τοὺς φύλακας ἑστῶτας ἐπὶ τῶν
and the guards standing at the

θυρῶν, ἀνοίξαντες δὲ ἔσω οὐδένα εὕρομεν.
doors, but having opened ²inside ³no one ¹we found.

24 ὡς δὲ ἤκουσαν τοὺς λόγους τούτους
And as ⁹heard ¹⁰these ¹¹words

ὅ τε στρατηγὸς τοῦ ἱεροῦ καὶ οἱ ἀρχιερεῖς,
²the ¹both ³commandant ⁴of the ⁵temple ⁶and ⁷the ⁸chief priests,

διηπόρουν περὶ αὐτῶν τί ἂν γένοιτο
they were in doubt about them what ²might become

τοῦτο. 25 παραγενόμενος δέ τις ἀπήγγειλεν
¹this thing. And having come someone reported

αὐτοῖς ὅτι ἰδοὺ οἱ ἄνδρες, οὓς
to them[,] – Behold[,] the men, whom

ἔθεσθε ἐν τῇ φυλακῇ, εἰσὶν ἐν τῷ ἱερῷ
ye put in the prison, are in the temple

prison are standing in the temple, and teaching the people.

26 Then went the captain with the officers, and brought them without violence: for they feared the people, lest they should have been stoned.

27 And when they had brought them, they set *them* before the council: and the high priest asked them,

28 Saying, Did not we straitly command you that ye should not teach in this name? and, behold, ye have filled Jerusalem with your doctrine, and intend to bring this man's blood upon us.

29 Then Peter and the *other* apostles answered and said, We ought to obey God rather than men.

30 The God of our fathers raised up Jesus, whom ye slew and hanged on a tree.

31 Him hath God exalted with his right hand *to be* a Prince and a Saviour, for to give repentance to Israel, and forgiveness of sins.

32 And we are his witnesses of these things; and *so is* also the Holy Ghost, whom God hath given to them that obey him.

33 ¶ When they heard

ἑστῶτες   καὶ   διδάσκοντες   τὸν   λαόν.
standing   and   teaching   the   people.

26 Τότε   ἀπελθὼν   ὁ   στρατηγὸς   σὺν   τοῖς
   Then   going   the commandant   with   the

ὑπηρέταις   ἦγεν   αὐτούς,   οὐ   μετὰ   βίας,
attendants   brought   them,   not   with   force,

ἐφοβοῦντο   γὰρ   τὸν   λαόν,   μὴ   λιθασθῶσιν·
for they feared the   people, lest they should be stoned;

27 ἀγαγόντες   δὲ   αὐτοὺς   ἔστησαν   ἐν   τῷ
   and bringing   them   they stood   in   the

συνεδρίῳ.   καὶ   ἐπηρώτησεν   αὐτοὺς   ὁ
council.   And   questioned   them   the

ἀρχιερεὺς   28 λέγων·   παραγγελίᾳ   παρηγ-
high priest   saying :   With charge   we
                             =We strictly

γείλαμεν   ὑμῖν   μὴ   διδάσκειν   ἐπὶ
charged   you   not   to teach   on(in)

τῷ   ὀνόματι   τούτῳ,   καὶ   ἰδοὺ   πεπληρώκατε
     this name,   and   behold   ye have filled

τὴν   Ἰερουσαλὴμ   τῆς   διδαχῆς   ὑμῶν,   καὶ
 -      Jerusalem   of(with) the teaching of you,   and

βούλεσθε   ἐπαγαγεῖν   ἐφ'   ἡμᾶς   τὸ   αἷμα
intend   to bring   on   us   the   blood

τοῦ   ἀνθρώπου   τούτου.   29 ἀποκριθεὶς   δὲ
of this man.   And answering

Πέτρος   καὶ   οἱ   ἀπόστολοι   εἶπαν·   πειθαρχεῖν
Peter   and   the   apostles   said :   [2]to obey

δεῖ   θεῷ   μᾶλλον   ἢ   ἀνθρώποις.   30 ὁ
[1]It behoves God   rather   than   men.   The

θεὸς   τῶν   πατέρων   ἡμῶν   ἤγειρεν   Ἰησοῦν,
God   of the   fathers   of us   raised   Jesus,

ὃν   ὑμεῖς   διεχειρίσασθε   κρεμάσαντες   ἐπὶ
whom   ye   killed   hanging   on

ξύλου·   31 τοῦτον   ὁ   θεὸς   ἀρχηγὸν   καὶ
a tree;   this man   -   God   a Ruler   and

σωτῆρα   ὕψωσεν   τῇ   δεξιᾷ   αὐτοῦ   τοῦ
a Saviour   exalted   to the right [hand] of him   -

δοῦναι   μετάνοιαν   τῷ   Ἰσραὴλ   καὶ   ἄφεσιν
to give[d] repentance   -   to Israel   and forgiveness

ἁμαρτιῶν.   32 καὶ   ἡμεῖς   ἐσμεν   μάρτυρες
of sins.   And   we   are   witnesses

τῶν   ῥημάτων   τούτων,   καὶ   τὸ   πνεῦμα
of these words(things),   and   the   Spirit

τὸ   ἅγιον   ὃ   ἔδωκεν   ὁ   θεὸς   τοῖς
 -    Holy   which   [2]gave   -   [1]God   to the

πειθαρχοῦσιν   αὐτῷ.   33 οἱ   δὲ   ἀκούσαντες
[ones] obeying   him.   And the [ones] hearing

that, they were cut *to the heart*, and took counsel to slay them.

34 Then stood there up one in the council, a Pharisee, named Gamaliel, a doctor of the law, had in reputation among all the people, and commanded to put the apostles forth a little space;

35 And said unto them, Ye men of Israel, take heed to yourselves what ye intend to do as touching these men.

36 For before these days rose up Theudas, boasting himself to be somebody; to whom a number of men, about four hundred, joined themselves: who was slain; and all, as many as obeyed him, were scattered, and brought to nought.

37 After this man rose up Judas of Galilee in the days of the taxing, and drew away much people after him : he also perished; and all, *even* as many as obeyed him, were dispersed.

38 And now I say unto you, Refrain from these men, and let them alone: for if this counsel or this work be of men, it will come to nought:

39 But if it be of God, ye cannot overthrow it;

διεπρίοντο καὶ ἐβούλοντο ἀνελεῖν αὐτούς.
were cut* and intended to kill them.

34 Ἀναστὰς δέ τις ἐν τῷ συνεδρίῳ
¹But ⁴standing up ²a certain ⁵in ⁶the ⁷council

Φαρισαῖος ὀνόματι Γαμαλιήλ, νομοδιδάσκαλος
³Pharisee by name Gamaliel, a teacher of the law

τίμιος παντὶ τῷ λαῷ, ἐκέλευσεν ἔξω
honoured by all the people, commanded ⁴outside

βραχὺ τοὺς ἀνθρώπους ποιῆσαι, 35 εἶπέν
⁵a little ²the ³men ¹to make(put), ²said

τε πρὸς αὐτούς· ἄνδρες Ἰσραηλῖται,
¹and to them : Men Israelites,

προσέχετε ἑαυτοῖς ἐπὶ τοῖς ἀνθρώποις τούτοις
take heed to yourselves ⁴on(to) ⁵these ⁶men

τί μέλλετε πράσσειν. 36 πρὸ γὰρ
¹what ²ye intend ³to do. For before

τούτων τῶν ἡμερῶν ἀνέστη Θευδᾶς, λέγων
these — days stood up Theudas, saying

εἶναί τινα ἑαυτόν, ᾧ προσεκλίθη ἀνδρῶν
to be someone himself, ¹to whom ⁶were attached ³of men

ἀριθμὸς ὡς τετρακοσίων· ὃς ἀνῃρέθη, καὶ
²a number ⁴about ⁵four hundreds; who was killed, and

πάντες ὅσοι ἐπείθοντο αὐτῷ διελύθησαν
all as many as obeyed him were dispersed

καὶ ἐγένοντο εἰς οὐδέν. 37 μετὰ τοῦτον
and came to nothing. After this

ἀνέστη Ἰούδας ὁ Γαλιλαῖος ἐν ταῖς
stood up Judas the Galilæan in the

ἡμέραις τῆς ἀπογραφῆς καὶ ἀπέστησεν
days of the enrolment and drew away

λαὸν ὀπίσω αὐτοῦ· κἀκεῖνος ἀπώλετο,
people after him; and that man perished,

καὶ πάντες ὅσοι ἐπείθοντο αὐτῷ
and all as many as obeyed him

διεσκορπίσθησαν. 38 καὶ τὰ νῦν λέγω
were scattered. And — now I say

ὑμῖν, ἀπόστητε ἀπὸ τῶν ἀνθρώπων τούτων
to you, stand away from these men

καὶ ἄφετε αὐτούς· ὅτι ἐὰν ᾖ ἐξ ἀνθρώπων
and leave them; because if be of men

ἡ βουλὴ αὕτη ἢ τὸ ἔργον τοῦτο,
this counsel or this work,

καταλυθήσεται· 39 εἰ δὲ ἐκ θεοῦ ἐστιν,
it will be destroyed; but if of God it is,

οὐ δυνήσεσθε καταλῦσαι αὐτούς, μήποτε
ye will not be able to destroy them, lest

* That is, to the heart; cf. 7. 54.

lest haply ye be found even to fight against God.

40 And to him they agreed: and when they had called the apostles, and beaten *them*, they commanded that they should not speak in the name of Jesus, and let them go.

41 And they departed from the presence of the council, rejoicing that they were counted worthy to suffer shame for his name.

42 And daily in the temple, and in every house, they ceased not to teach and preach Jesus Christ.

καὶ　θεομάχοι　εὑρεθῆτε.　ἐπείσθησαν　δὲ
even　fighters against God　ye be found.　　And they obeyed

αὐτῷ,　40 καὶ　προσκαλεσάμενοι　τοὺς
him,　　and　　having called to [them]　the

ἀποστόλους　δείραντες　παρήγγειλαν　μὴ
apostles　　beating　　charged　　not

λαλεῖν　ἐπὶ　τῷ　ὀνόματι　τοῦ　'Ιησοῦ　καὶ
to speak　on(in)　the　name　　–　of Jesus　and

ἀπέλυσαν.　41 Οἱ　μὲν　οὖν　ἐπορεύοντο
released [them].　They　–　therefore　went

χαίροντες　ἀπὸ　προσώπου　τοῦ　συνεδρίου,
rejoicing　from [the]　presence　of the　council,

ὅτι　κατηξιώθησαν　ὑπὲρ　τοῦ ὀνόματος
because　they were deemed worthy on behalf of the　name

ἀτιμασθῆναι·　42 πᾶσάν τε　ἡμέραν　ἐν　τῷ
to be dishonoured;　　and every　day　in　the

ἱερῷ　καὶ　κατ'　οἶκον　οὐκ　ἐπαύοντο
temple　and　from house to house†　they ceased not

διδάσκοντες　καὶ　εὐαγγελιζόμενοι　τὸν　χριστὸν
teaching　　and　　preaching　　the　Christ

'Ιησοῦν.
Jesus.

CHAPTER 6

A ND in those days, when the number of the disciples was multiplied, there arose a murmuring of the Grecians against the Hebrews, because their widows were neglected in the daily ministration.

2 Then the twelve called the multitude of the disciples *unto them*, and said, It is not reason that we should leave the word of God, and serve tables.

3 Wherefore, brethren, look ye out among you seven men of honest report, full of the Holy Ghost and wisdom, whom we may appoint over this business.

6 'Εν　δὲ　ταῖς　ἡμέραις　ταύταις
Now in　　the　these days

πληθυνόντων　τῶν　μαθητῶν[a]　ἐγένετο
being multiplied　the　disciples[a]　there was
=as the disciples were multiplied

γογγυσμὸς　τῶν　'Ελληνιστῶν　πρὸς　τοὺς
a murmuring　of the　Hellenists　against　the

'Εβραίους,　ὅτι　παρεθεωροῦντο　ἐν　τῇ
Hebrews,　because　[4]were overlooked　[5]in　[6]the

διακονίᾳ　τῇ　καθημερινῇ　αἱ　χῆραι　αὐτῶν.
[3]service　–　[7]daily　[1]the　[2]widows　[3]of them.

2 προσκαλεσάμενοι　δὲ　οἱ　δώδεκα　τὸ
[4]having called to [them]　[2]And　[2]the　[3]twelve　the

πλῆθος　τῶν　μαθητῶν　εἶπαν·　οὐκ　ἀρεστόν
multitude　of the　disciples　said:　not　pleasing

ἐστιν　ἡμᾶς　καταλείψαντας　τὸν　λόγον　τοῦ
It is　us　leaving　　the　word　–

θεοῦ　διακονεῖν　τραπέζαις.　3 ἐπισκέψασθε
of God　to serve　tables.　　look ye out

δέ,　ἀδελφοί,　ἄνδρας　ἐξ　ὑμῶν　μαρτυρουμένους
But,　brothers,　[2]men　[3]of　[4]you　[5]being witnessed to

ἑπτὰ　πλήρεις　πνεύματος　καὶ　σοφίας,　οὓς
[1]seven　[as] full　of Spirit　and　of wisdom, whom

καταστήσομεν　ἐπὶ　τῆς　χρείας　ταύτης·
we will appoint　over　　this office;

4 But we will give ourselves continually to prayer, and to the ministry of the word.

5 And the saying pleased the whole multitude: and they chose Stephen, a man full of faith and of the Holy Ghost, and Philip, and Prochorus, and Nicanor, and Timon, and Parmenas, and Nicolas a proselyte of Antioch:

6 Whom they set before the apostles: and when they had prayed, they laid *their* hands on them.

7 And the word of God increased; and the number of the disciples multiplied in Jerusalem greatly; and a great company of the priests were obedient to the faith.

8 ¶ And Stephen, full of faith and power, did great wonders and miracles among the people.

9 Then there arose certain of the synagogue, which is called *the synagogue* of the Libertines, and Cyrenians, and Alexandrians, and of them of Cilicia and of Asia, disputing with Stephen.

10 And they were not able to resist the wisdom and the spirit by which he spake.

11 Then they suborned men, which said, We have heard him speak blasphe-

4 ἡμεῖς δὲ τῇ προσευχῇ καὶ τῇ διακονίᾳ
but we   to the prayer   and to the service

τοῦ λόγου προσκαρτερήσομεν. 5 καὶ ἤρεσεν
of the word   will keep.   And ³pleased

ὁ λόγος ἐνώπιον παντὸς τοῦ πλήθους,
¹the ²word before   all   the multitude,

καὶ ἐξελέξαντο Στέφανον, ἄνδρα πλήρη
and they chose   Stephen,   a man   full

πίστεως καὶ πνεύματος ἁγίου, καὶ Φίλιππον
of faith and Spirit   of Holy, and Philip

καὶ Πρόχορον καὶ Νικάνορα καὶ Τίμωνα
and Prochorus and Nicanor   and Timon

καὶ Παρμενᾶν καὶ Νικόλαον προσήλυτον
and Parmenas   and Nicolaus   a proselyte

Ἀντιοχέα, 6 οὓς ἔστησαν ἐνώπιον τῶν
of Antioch,   whom they set   before   the

ἀποστόλων, καὶ προσευξάμενοι ἐπέθηκαν
apostles,   and   having prayed   they placed on

αὐτοῖς τὰς χεῖρας.
them   the(ir) hands.

7 Καὶ ὁ λόγος τοῦ θεοῦ ηὔξανεν, καὶ
And the word   - of God grew,   and

ἐπληθύνετο ὁ ἀριθμὸς τῶν μαθητῶν ἐν
was multiplied the number of the disciples in

Ἰερουσαλὴμ σφόδρα, πολύς τε ὄχλος τῶν
Jerusalem   greatly,   and a much(great) crowd of the

ἱερέων ὑπήκουον τῇ πίστει.
priests   obeyed   the faith.

8 Στέφανος δὲ πλήρης χάριτος καὶ
And Stephen   full   of grace   and

δυνάμεως ἐποίει τέρατα καὶ σημεῖα μεγάλα
of power   did   wonders and   signs   great

ἐν τῷ λαῷ. 9 ἀνέστησαν δέ τινες τῶν
among the people.   But rose up   some of the
                                              [ones]

ἐκ τῆς συναγωγῆς τῆς λεγομένης
of   the synagogue   -   being called

Λιβερτίνων καὶ Κυρηναίων καὶ Ἀλεξ-
of Freedmen and of Cyrenians and   of

ανδρέων καὶ τῶν ἀπὸ Κιλικίας καὶ
Alexandrians and of the [ones] from Cilicia   and

Ἀσίας συζητοῦντες τῷ Στεφάνῳ, 10 καὶ
Asia   discussing   with Stephen,   and

οὐκ ἴσχυον ἀντιστῆναι τῇ σοφίᾳ καὶ
were not able to withstand   the wisdom and

τῷ πνεύματι ᾧ ἐλάλει. 11 τότε ὑπέβαλον
the spirit with which he spoke. Then they suborned

ἄνδρας λέγοντας ὅτι ἀκηκόαμεν αὐτοῦ
men   saying[,]   -   We have heard   him

mous words against
Moses, and *against* God.

12 And they stirred up
the people, and the elders,
and the scribes, and came
upon *him*, and caught him,
and brought *him* to the
council,

13 And set up false
witnesses, which said, This
man ceaseth not to speak
blasphemous words
against this holy place,
and the law:

14 For we have heard
him say, that this Jesus of
Nazareth shall destroy this
place, and shall change the
customs which Moses de-
livered us.

15 And all that sat in
the council, looking stedfastly on him, saw his face
as it had been the face of
an angel.

λαλοῦντος ῥήματα βλάσφημα εἰς Μωϋσῆν
speaking   words   blasphemous   against   Moses

καὶ τὸν θεόν· 12 συνεκίνησάν τε τὸν
and   -   God;   and they stirred up   the

λαὸν καὶ τοὺς πρεσβυτέρους καὶ τοὺς
people   and   the   elders   and   the

γραμματεῖς, καὶ ἐπιστάντες συνήρπασαν
scribes,   and   coming on   they seized

αὐτὸν καὶ ἤγαγον εἰς τὸ συνέδριον,
him   and   led   to   the   council,

13 ἔστησάν τε μάρτυρας ψευδεῖς λέγοντας·
and stood   witnesses   false   saying :

ὁ ἄνθρωπος οὗτος οὐ παύεται λαλῶν
This man   ceases not   speaking

ῥήματα κατὰ τοῦ τόπου τοῦ ἁγίου [τούτου]
words   against   -   ³place   -   ²holy   ¹this

καὶ τοῦ νόμου· 14 ἀκηκόαμεν γὰρ αὐτοῦ
and   the   law;   for we have heard   him

λέγοντος ὅτι Ἰησοῦς ὁ Ναζωραῖος οὗτος
saying   that   ²Jesus   ³the   ⁴Nazarene   ¹this

καταλύσει τὸν τόπον τοῦτον καὶ ἀλλάξει
will destroy   this place   and   will change

τὰ ἔθη ἃ παρέδωκεν ἡμῖν Μωϋσῆς.
the customs which   delivered   to us   Moses.

15 καὶ ἀτενίσαντες εἰς αὐτὸν πάντες οἱ
And   gazing   at   him   all   the

καθεζόμενοι ἐν τῷ συνεδρίῳ εἶδον τὸ
[ones] sitting   in   the   council   saw   the

πρόσωπον αὐτοῦ ὡσεὶ πρόσωπον ἀγγέλου.
face   of him   as   a face   of an angel.

CHAPTER 7

THEN said the high
priest, Are these
things so?

2 And he said, Men,
brethren, and fathers, hearken; The God of glory
appeared unto our father
Abraham, when he was in
Mesopotamia, before he
dwelt in Charran,

3 And said unto him,
Get thee out of thy
country, and from thy
kindred, and come into

7 Εἶπεν δὲ ὁ ἀρχιερεύς· εἰ ταῦτα
And said   the   high priest :   If   these things

οὕτως ἔχει; 2 ὁ δὲ ἔφη·
thus   have(are)?   And he   said:

Ἄνδρες ἀδελφοὶ καὶ πατέρες, ἀκούσατε.
Men   brothers   and   fathers,   hear ye.

Ὁ θεὸς τῆς δόξης ὤφθη τῷ πατρὶ
The   God   of glory   appeared   to the   father

ἡμῶν Ἀβραὰμ ὄντι ἐν τῇ Μεσοποταμίᾳ
of us   Abraham   being   in   -   Mesopotamia

πρὶν ἢ κατοικῆσαι αὐτὸν ἐν Χαρράν,
before   to dwell   him[b]   in   Charran,
         = he dwelt

3 καὶ εἶπεν πρὸς αὐτόν· ἔξελθε ἐκ τῆς
and   said   to   him :   Go forth   out of   the

γῆς σου καὶ τῆς συγγενείας σου, καὶ
land   of thee   and   the   kindred   of thee,   and

the land which I shall shew thee.

4 Then came he out of the land of the Chaldæans, and dwelt in Charran: and from thence, when his father was dead, he removed him into this land, wherein ye now dwell.

5 And he gave him none inheritance in it, no, not *so much as* to set his foot on: yet he promised that he would give it to him for a possession, and to his seed after him, when *as yet* he had no child.

6 And God spake on this wise, That his seed should sojourn in a strange land; and that they should bring them into bondage, and entreat *them* evil four hundred years.

7 And the nation to whom they shall be in bondage will I judge, said God: and after that shall they come forth, and serve me in this place.

8 And he gave him the covenant of circumcision: and so *Abraham* begat Isaac, and circumcised him the eighth day; and Isaac *begat* Jacob; and Jacob *begat* the twelve patriarchs.

9 And the patriarchs, moved with envy, sold

δεῦρο εἰς τὴν γῆν ἥν ἄν σοι δείξω.
come into the land whichever to thee I may show.

4 τότε ἐξελθὼν ἐκ γῆς Χαλδαίων
Then going forth out of [the] land of [the] Chaldæans

κατῴκησεν ἐν Χαρράν. κἀκεῖθεν μετὰ
he dwelt in Charran. And thence after

τὸ ἀποθανεῖν τὸν πατέρα αὐτοῦ[b] μετῴκισεν
the to die the father of him [God] removed
=his father died

αὐτὸν εἰς τὴν γῆν ταύτην εἰς ἥν ὑμεῖς
him into this land in which ye

νῦν κατοικεῖτε, 5 καὶ οὐκ ἔδωκεν αὐτῷ
now dwell, and gave not to him

κληρονομίαν ἐν αὐτῇ οὐδὲ βῆμα ποδός,
an inheritance in it nor a foot's space,

καὶ ἐπηγγείλατο δοῦναι αὐτῷ εἰς
and promised to give him for

κατάσχεσιν αὐτὴν καὶ τῷ σπέρματι αὐτοῦ
a possession it and to the seed of him

μετ᾽ αὐτόν, οὐκ ὄντος αὐτῷ[c] τέκνου.[a]
after him, not being to him a child.
=while he had no child.

6 ἐλάλησεν δὲ οὕτως ὁ θεός, ὅτι ἔσται
And spoke thus – God, that will be

τὸ σπέρμα αὐτοῦ πάροικον ἐν γῇ ἀλλοτρίᾳ,
the seed of him a sojourner in a land belonging to others,

καὶ δουλώσουσιν αὐτὸ καὶ κακώσουσιν
and they will enslave it and will ill-treat

ἔτη τετρακόσια· 7 καὶ τὸ ἔθνος ᾧ ἐὰν
years four hundred; and the nation whichever

δουλεύσουσιν κρινῶ ἐγώ, ὁ θεὸς εἶπεν,
they will serve will judge I, – God said,

καὶ μετὰ ταῦτα ἐξελεύσονται καὶ
and after these things they will come forth and

λατρεύσουσίν μοι ἐν τῷ τόπῳ τούτῳ.
will worship me in this place.

8 καὶ ἔδωκεν αὐτῷ διαθήκην περιτομῆς·
And he gave him a covenant of circumcision;

καὶ οὕτως ἐγέννησεν τὸν Ἰσαὰκ καὶ
and thus he begat – Isaac and

περιέτεμεν αὐτὸν τῇ ἡμέρᾳ τῇ ὀγδόῃ,
circumcised him on the day – eighth,

καὶ Ἰσαὰκ τὸν Ἰακώβ, καὶ Ἰακὼβ
and Isaac [begat] – Jacob, and Jacob [begat]

τοὺς δώδεκα πατριάρχας. 9 Καὶ οἱ
the twelve patriarchs. And the

πατριάρχαι ζηλώσαντες τὸν Ἰωσὴφ
patriarchs becoming jealous – [a]Joseph

Joseph into Egypt: but God was with him,

10 And delivered him out of all his afflictions, and gave him favour and wisdom in the sight of Pharaoh king of Egypt; and he made him governor over Egypt and all his house.

11 Now there came a dearth over all the land of Egypt and Chanaan, and great affliction: and our fathers found no sustenance.

12 But when Jacob heard that there was corn in Egypt, he sent out our fathers first.

13 And at the second *time* Joseph was made known to his brethren; and Joseph's kindred was made known unto Pharaoh.

14 Then sent Joseph, and called his father Jacob to *him*, and all his kindred, threescore and fifteen souls.

15 So Jacob went down into Egypt, and died, he, and our fathers,

16 And were carried over into Sychem, and laid in the sepulchre that Abraham bought for a sum of money of the sons of Emmor *the father* of Sychem.

17 But when the time of the promise drew nigh,

ἀπέδοντο εἰς Αἴγυπτον· καὶ ἦν ὁ θεὸς
¹sold ⁻into Egypt; and was – God

μετ’ αὐτοῦ, 10 καὶ ἐξείλατο αὐτὸν ἐκ
with him, and rescued him out of

πασῶν τῶν θλίψεων αὐτοῦ, καὶ ἔδωκεν
all the afflictions of him, and gave

αὐτῷ χάριν καὶ σοφίαν ἐναντίον Φαραὼ
him favour and wisdom before Pharaoh

βασιλέως Αἰγύπτου, καὶ κατέστησεν αὐτὸν
king of Egypt, and he appointed him

ἡγούμενον ἐπ’ Αἴγυπτον καὶ ὅλον τὸν
governor over Egypt and all the

οἶκον αὐτοῦ. 11 ἦλθεν δὲ λιμὸς ἐφ’
household of him. But came a famine over

ὅλην τὴν Αἴγυπτον καὶ Χανάαν καὶ
all – Egypt and Canaan and

θλῖψις μεγάλη, καὶ οὐχ ηὕρισκον
affliction great, and found not

χορτάσματα οἱ πατέρες ἡμῶν. 12 ἀκούσας
sustenance the fathers of us. ³having heard

δὲ Ἰακὼβ ὄντα σιτία εἰς Αἴγυπτον
¹But ²Jacob ⁵being ⁴corn in Egypt

ἐξαπέστειλεν τοὺς πατέρας ἡμῶν πρῶτον·
sent forth the fathers of us first;

13 καὶ ἐν τῷ δευτέρῳ ἐγνωρίσθη Ἰωσὴφ
and at the second [time] was made known Joseph

τοῖς ἀδελφοῖς αὐτοῦ, καὶ φανερὸν ἐγένετο τῷ
to the brothers of him, and ⁵manifest ⁴became –

Φαραὼ τὸ γένος Ἰωσήφ. 14 ἀποστείλας δὲ
⁶to Pharaoh ¹the ²race ³of Joseph. And sending

Ἰωσὴφ μετεκαλέσατο Ἰακὼβ τὸν πατέρα
Joseph called Jacob the father

αὐτοῦ καὶ πᾶσαν τὴν συγγένειαν ἐν
of him and all the(his) kindred in

ψυχαῖς ἑβδομήκοντα πέντε. 15 καὶ κατέβη
souls seventy-five. And went down

Ἰακὼβ εἰς Αἴγυπτον, καὶ ἐτελεύτησεν
Jacob to Egypt, and died

αὐτὸς καὶ οἱ πατέρες ἡμῶν, 16 καὶ
he and the fathers of us, and

μετετέθησαν εἰς Συχὲμ καὶ ἐτέθησαν ἐν
were transferred to Sychem and were put in

τῷ μνήματι ᾧ ὠνήσατο Ἀβραὰμ τιμῆς
the tomb which ²bought ¹Abraham of(for) a price

ἀργυρίου παρὰ τῶν υἱῶν Ἐμμὼρ ἐν
of silver from the sons of Emmor in

Συχέμ. 17 Καθὼς δὲ ἤγγιζεν ὁ χρόνος
Sychem. And as drew near the time

which God had sworn to Abraham, the people grew and multiplied in Egypt,

18 Till another king arose, which knew not Joseph.

19 The same dealt subtilly with our kindred, and evil entreated our fathers, so that they cast out their young children, to the end they might not live.

20 In which time Moses was born, and was exceeding fair, and nourished up in his father's house three months:

21 And when he was cast out, Pharaoh's daughter took him up, and nourished him for her own son.

22 And Moses was learned in all the wisdom of the Egyptians, and was mighty in words and in deeds.

23 And when he was full forty years old, it came into his heart to visit his brethren the children of Israel.

24 And seeing one of them suffer wrong, he defended him, and avenged him that was oppressed, and smote the Egyptian:

25 For he supposed his brethren would have understood how that God

τῆς ἐπαγγελίας ἧς ὡμολόγησεν ὁ θεὸς
of the promise which ²declared - ¹God

τῷ Ἀβραάμ, ηὔξησεν ὁ λαὸς καὶ
to Abraham, ³grew ¹the ²people and

ἐπληθύνθη ἐν Αἰγύπτῳ, 18 ἄχρι οὗ ἀνέστη
were multiplied in Egypt, until ²rose up

βασιλεὺς ἕτερος ἐπ' Αἴγυπτον, ὃς οὐκ ᾔδει
²king ¹another over Egypt, who did not know

τὸν Ἰωσήφ. 19 οὗτος κατασοφισάμενος
- Joseph. This man dealing craftily with

τὸ γένος ἡμῶν ἐκάκωσεν τοὺς πατέρας
the race of us ill-treated the fathers

τοῦ ποιεῖν τὰ βρέφη ἔκθετα αὐτῶν
- to make[d] ¹the ²babes ⁴exposed ³of them

εἰς τὸ μὴ ζωογονεῖσθαι. 20 Ἐν ᾧ
to the not to be preserved alive. At which
=so that they should not be . . .

καιρῷ ἐγεννήθη Μωϋσῆς, καὶ ἦν ἀστεῖος
time was born Moses, and was fair

τῷ θεῷ· ὃς ἀνετράφη μῆνας τρεῖς ἐν
- to God; who was reared months three in

τῷ οἴκῳ τοῦ πατρός· 21 ἐκτεθέντος δὲ
the house of the(his) father; being exposed and
=and when he was exposed

αὐτοῦ ἀνείλατο αὐτὸν ἡ θυγάτηρ Φαραὼ
him[a] took up him the daughter of Pharaoh

καὶ ἀνεθρέψατο αὐτὸν ἑαυτῇ εἰς υἱόν.
and reared him to herself for a son.
=as her own son.

22 καὶ ἐπαιδεύθη Μωϋσῆς πάσῃ σοφίᾳ
And was trained Moses in all [the] wisdom

Αἰγυπτίων, ἦν δὲ δυνατὸς ἐν λόγοις
of [the] Egyptians, and was powerful in words

καὶ ἔργοις αὐτοῦ. 23 Ὡς δὲ ἐπληροῦτο
and works of him. But when ²was fulfilled

αὐτῷ τεσσερακονταετὴς χρόνος, ἀνέβη ἐπὶ
⁴to him ²of forty years ¹a time, it came up upon

τὴν καρδίαν αὐτοῦ ἐπισκέψασθαι τοὺς
the heart of him to visit the

ἀδελφοὺς αὐτοῦ τοὺς υἱοὺς Ἰσραήλ. 24 καὶ
brothers of him the sons of Israel. And

ἰδών τινα ἀδικούμενον ἠμύνατο, καὶ
seeing one being injured he defended [him], and

ἐποίησεν ἐκδίκησιν τῷ καταπονουμένῳ
he wrought vengeance for the [one] getting the worse

πατάξας τὸν Αἰγύπτιον. 25 ἐνόμιζεν δὲ
striking the Egyptian. Now he supposed

συνιέναι τοὺς ἀδελφοὺς ὅτι ὁ θεὸς διὰ
to understand the(his) brothers[b] that - God through
=that his brothers would understand

by his hand would deliver them: but they understood not.

26 And the next day he shewed himself unto them as they strove, and would have set them at one again, saying, Sirs, ye are brethren; why do ye wrong one to another?

27 But he that did his neighbour wrong thrust him away, saying, Who made thee a ruler and a judge over us?

28 Wilt thou kill me, as thou diddest the Egyptian yesterday?

29 Then fled Moses at this saying, and was a stranger in the land of Madian, where he begat two sons.

30 And when forty years were expired, there appeared to him in the wilderness of mount Sina an angel of the Lord in a flame of fire in a bush.

31 When Moses saw it, he wondered at the sight: and as he drew near to behold it, the voice of the Lord came unto him,

32 Saying, I am the God of thy fathers, the God of Abraham, and the God of Isaac, and the God of Jacob. Then Moses trembled, and durst not behold.

33 Then said the Lord to him, Put off thy shoes from thy feet: for the

χειρὸς αὐτοῦ δίδωσιν σωτηρίαν αὐτοῖς·
hand of him would give salvation to them;

οἱ δὲ οὐ συνῆκαν. 26 τῇ τε ἐπιούσῃ
but they understood not. And on the coming

ἡμέρᾳ ὤφθη αὐτοῖς μαχομένοις, καὶ
day he appeared to them fighting, and

συνήλλασσεν αὐτοὺς εἰς εἰρήνην εἰπών·
attempted to reconcile them in peace saying :

ἄνδρες, ἀδελφοί ἐστε· ἱνατί ἀδικεῖτε
Men, brothers ye are; why injure ye

ἀλλήλους; 27 ὁ δὲ ἀδικῶν τὸν πλησίον
each other? But the [one] injuring the(his) neighbour

ἀπώσατο αὐτὸν εἰπών· τίς σε κατέστησεν
thrust away him saying : Who thee appointed

ἄρχοντα καὶ δικαστὴν ἐφ' ἡμῶν; 28 μὴ
a ruler and a judge over us? not

ἀνελεῖν με σὺ θέλεις ὃν τρόπον ἀνεῖλες
to kill me thou wishest in the same way as† thou killedst

ἐχθὲς τὸν Αἰγύπτιον; 29 ἔφυγεν δὲ
yesterday the Egyptian? So fled

Μωϋσῆς ἐν τῷ λόγῳ τούτῳ, καὶ ἐγένετο
Moses at this word, and became

πάροικος ἐν γῇ Μαδιάμ, οὗ ἐγέννησεν
a sojourner in [the] land Midian, where he begat

υἱοὺς δύο. 30 Καὶ πληρωθέντων ἐτῶν
sons two. And being fulfilled years
=when forty years were fulfilled

τεσσεράκοντα ὤφθη αὐτῷ ἐν τῇ ἐρήμῳ
forty[a] appeared to him in the desert

τοῦ ὄρους Σινὰ ἄγγελος ἐν φλογὶ πυρὸς
of the mount Sinai an angel in a flame of fire

βάτου. 31 ὁ δὲ Μωϋσῆς ἰδὼν ἐθαύμαζεν
of a thorn bush. - And Moses seeing marvelled at

τὸ ὅραμα· προσερχομένου δὲ αὐτοῦ κατα-
the vision; and approaching him[a] to take
=as he approached

νοῆσαι ἐγένετο φωνὴ κυρίου· 32 ἐγὼ ὁ
notice there was a voice of [the] Lord : I the

θεὸς τῶν πατέρων σου, ὁ θεὸς Ἀβραὰμ
God of the fathers of thee, the God of Abraham

καὶ Ἰσαὰκ καὶ Ἰακώβ. ἔντρομος δὲ
and of Isaac and of Jacob. But trembling

γενόμενος Μωϋσῆς οὐκ ἐτόλμα κατανοῆσαι.
becoming Moses dared not to take notice.

33 εἶπεν δὲ αὐτῷ ὁ κύριος· λῦσον τὸ
And said to him the Lord : Loosen the

ὑπόδημα τῶν ποδῶν σου· ὁ γὰρ τόπος
sandal of the feet of thee; for the place

place where thou standest is holy ground.

34 I have seen, I have seen the affliction of my people which is in Egypt, and I have heard their groaning, and am come down to deliver them. And now come, I will send thee into Egypt.

35 This Moses whom they refused, saying, Who made thee a ruler and a judge? the same did God send to be a ruler and a deliverer by the hand of the angel which appeared to him in the bush.

36 He brought them out, after that he had shewed wonders and signs in the land of Egypt, and in the Red sea, and in the wilderness forty years.

37 This is that Moses, which said unto the children of Israel, A prophet shall the Lord your God raise up unto you of your brethren, like unto me; him shall ye hear.

38 This is he, that was in the church in the wilderness with the angel which spake to him in the mount Sina, and with our fathers: who received the lively oracles to give unto us:

39 To whom our fathers would not obey, but thrust him from them, and in their hearts turned back again into Egypt,

ἐφ' ᾧ ἕστηκας γῆ ἁγία ἐστίν. 34 ἰδὼν
on which thou standest ground holy is. Seeing

εἶδον τὴν κάκωσιν τοῦ λαοῦ μου τοῦ
I saw the ill-treatment of the people of me —

ἐν Αἰγύπτῳ, καὶ τοῦ στεναγμοῦ αὐτοῦ
in Egypt, and the groan of it

ἤκουσα, καὶ κατέβην ἐξελέσθαι αὐτούς·
I heard, and I came down to rescue them;

καὶ νῦν δεῦρο ἀποστείλω σε εἰς Αἴγυπτον.
and now come I will send thee to Egypt.

35 Τοῦτον τὸν Μωϋσῆν, ὃν ἠρνήσαντο
This — Moses, whom they denied

εἰπόντες· τίς σε κατέστησεν ἄρχοντα καὶ
saying: Who thee appointed a ruler and

δικαστήν; τοῦτον ὁ θεὸς καὶ ἄρχοντα
a judge? this man — God both a ruler

καὶ λυτρωτὴν ἀπέσταλκεν σὺν χειρὶ
and a redeemer has sent with [the] hand

ἀγγέλου τοῦ ὀφθέντος αὐτῷ ἐν τῇ βάτῳ.
of [the] angel — appearing to him in the bush.

36 οὗτος ἐξήγαγεν αὐτοὺς ποιήσας τέρατα
This man led forth them doing wonders

καὶ σημεῖα ἐν γῇ Αἰγύπτῳ καὶ ἐν
and signs in [the] land Egypt and in

ἐρυθρᾷ θαλάσσῃ καὶ ἐν τῇ ἐρήμῳ ἔτη
[the] Red Sea and in the desert years

τεσσεράκοντα. 37 οὗτός ἐστιν ὁ Μωϋσῆς
forty. This is the Moses

ὁ εἴπας τοῖς υἱοῖς Ἰσραήλ· προφήτην
— saying to the sons of Israel: A prophet

ὑμῖν ἀναστήσει ὁ θεὸς ἐκ τῶν ἀδελφῶν
for you will raise up — God of the brothers

ὑμῶν ὡς ἐμέ. 38 οὗτός ἐστιν ὁ γενόμενος
of you as me. This is the [one] having been

ἐν τῇ ἐκκλησίᾳ ἐν τῇ ἐρήμῳ μετὰ τοῦ
in the church in the desert with the

ἀγγέλου τοῦ λαλοῦντος αὐτῷ ἐν τῷ
angel — speaking to him in the

ὄρει Σινὰ καὶ τῶν πατέρων ἡμῶν, ὃς
mount Sinai and [with] the fathers of us, who

ἐδέξατο λόγια ζῶντα δοῦναι ὑμῖν, 39 ᾧ
received oracles living to give to you, ¹to whom

οὐκ ἠθέλησαν ὑπήκοοι γενέσθαι οἱ πατέρες
⁵wished ⁶not ⁸obedient ⁷to become ²the ³fathers

ἡμῶν, ἀλλὰ ἀπώσαντο καὶ ἐστράφησαν
⁴of us, but thrust away and turned

ἐν ταῖς καρδίαις αὐτῶν εἰς Αἴγυπτον,
in the hearts of them to Egypt,

40 Saying unto Aaron, Make us gods to go before us: for *as for* this Moses, which brought us out of the land of Egypt, we wot not what is become of him.

41 And they made a calf in those days, and offered sacrifice unto the idol, and rejoiced in the works of their own hands.

42 Then God turned, and gave them up to worship the host of heaven; as it is written in the book of the prophets, O ye house of Israel, have ye offered to me slain beasts and sacrifices *by the space of* forty years in the wilderness?

43 Yea, ye took up the tabernacle of Moloch, and the star of your god Remphan, figures which ye made to worship them: and I will carry you away beyond Babylon.

44 Our fathers had the tabernacle of witness in the wilderness, as he had appointed, speaking unto Moses, that he should make it according to the fashion that he had seen.

45 Which also our fathers that came after brought in with Jesus into the possession of the Gentiles, whom God drave

---

40 εἰπόντες τῷ Ἀαρών· ποίησον ἡμῖν
   saying   -   to Aaron :   Make   for us
θεοὺς οἳ προπορεύσονται ἡμῶν· ὁ γὰρ
gods   which   will go before   us;   -   for
Μωϋσῆς οὗτος, ὃς ἐξήγαγεν ἡμᾶς ἐκ
   this Moses,   who   led forth   us   out of
γῆς Αἰγύπτου, οὐκ οἴδαμεν τί ἐγένετο
[the] land   Egypt,   we know not   what   happened
αὐτῷ. 41 καὶ ἐμοσχοποίησαν ἐν
to him.   And   they made [a model of] a calf   in
ταῖς ἡμέραις ἐκείναις καὶ ἀνήγαγον θυσίαν τῷ
   those days   and   brought up   a sacrifice to the
εἰδώλῳ, καὶ εὐφραίνοντο ἐν τοῖς ἔργοις
 idol,   and   made merry   in   the   works
τῶν χειρῶν αὐτῶν. 42 ἔστρεψεν δὲ ὁ
of the   hands   of them.   And [2]turned   -   [1]
θεὸς καὶ παρέδωκεν αὐτοὺς λατρεύειν
[1]God   and   delivered   them   to worship
τῇ στρατιᾷ τοῦ οὐρανοῦ, καθὼς γέγραπται
the   host   -   of heaven,   as   it has been written
ἐν βίβλῳ τῶν προφητῶν· μὴ σφάγια
in   [the] roll   of the   prophets :   Not   victims
καὶ θυσίας προσηνέγκατέ μοι ἔτη
and   sacrifices   ye offered   to me   years
τεσσεράκοντα ἐν τῇ ἐρήμῳ, οἶκος Ἰσραήλ,
   forty   in   the   desert,   [O] house   of Israel,
43 καὶ ἀνελάβετε τὴν σκηνὴν τοῦ Μόλοχ
    and   ye took up   the   tent   -   of Moloch
καὶ τὸ ἄστρον τοῦ θεοῦ Ῥομφά, τοὺς
and   the   star   of the   god   Rompha,   the
τύπους οὓς ἐποιήσατε προσκυνεῖν αὐτοῖς;
models   which   ye made   to worship   them?
καὶ μετοικιῶ ὑμᾶς ἐπέκεινα Βαβυλῶνος.
and   I will deport   you   beyond   Babylon.
44 Ἡ σκηνὴ τοῦ μαρτυρίου ἦν τοῖς
The   tent   -   of witness   was   to the
=Our fathers had the tent of witness
πατράσιν ἡμῶν ἐν τῇ ἐρήμῳ, καθὼς
  fathers   of us[c]   in   the   desert,   as
διετάξατο ὁ λαλῶν τῷ Μωϋσῇ ποιῆσαι
commanded the [one] speaking   -   to Moses   to make
αὐτὴν κατὰ τὸν τύπον ὃν ἑωράκει·
 it   according to   the   model   which   he had seen;
45 ἦν καὶ εἰσήγαγον διαδεξάμενοι οἱ
  which   also   [3]brought in   [4]having received   [1]the
πατέρες ἡμῶν μετὰ Ἰησοῦ ἐν τῇ κατα-
[2]fathers   [3]of us   with   Jesus   in   the   pos-
σχέσει τῶν ἐθνῶν, ὧν ἐξῶσεν ὁ θεὸς
session   of the   nations,   whom   put out   -   God

out before the face of our
fathers, unto the days of
David;
46 Who found favour
before God, and desired
to find a tabernacle for the
God of Jacob.
47 But Solomon built
him an house.
48 Howbeit the most
High dwelleth not in
temples made with hands;
as saith the prophet,
49 Heaven is my throne,
and earth is my footstool:
what house will ye build
me? saith the Lord: or
what is the place of my
rest?
50 Hath not my hand
made all these things?
51 ¶ Ye stiffnecked and
uncircumcised in heart and
ears, ye do always resist
the Holy Ghost: as your
fathers did, so do ye.
52 Which of the
prophets have not your
fathers persecuted? and
they have slain them
which shewed before of the
coming of the Just One;
of whom ye have been now
the betrayers and mur-
derers:
53 Who have received
the law by the disposition
of angels, and have not
kept it.
54 ¶ When they heard
these things, they were cut
to the heart, and they
gnashed on him with their
teeth.
55 But he, being full

ἀπὸ προσώπου τῶν πατέρων ἡμῶν, ἕως
from [the] face of the fathers of us, until

τῶν ἡμερῶν Δαυίδ· 46 ὃς εὗρεν χάριν
the days of David; who found favour

ἐνώπιον τοῦ θεοῦ καὶ ᾐτήσατο εὑρεῖν
before – God and asked to find

σκήνωμα τῷ οἴκῳ Ἰακώβ. 47 Σολομὼν δὲ
a tent for the house of Jacob. But Solomon

οἰκοδόμησεν αὐτῷ οἶκον. 48 ἀλλ'
built for him a house. But

οὐχ ὁ ὕψιστος ἐν χειροποιήτοις κατοικεῖ·
⁴not ¹the ²Most High ⁵in ⁶[places] made by hand ³dwells;

καθὼς ὁ προφήτης λέγει· 49 ὁ οὐρανός
as the prophet says : The heaven

μοι θρόνος, ἡ δὲ γῆ ὑποπόδιον τῶν
to me a throne, and the earth a footstool of the

ποδῶν μου· ποῖον οἶκον οἰκοδομήσετέ μοι,
feet of me; what house will ye build for me,

λέγει κύριος, ἢ τίς τόπος τῆς καταπαύσεώς
says [the] Lord, or what place of the rest

μου; 50 οὐχὶ ἡ χείρ μου ἐποίησεν ταῦτα
of me? not the hand of me made these things

πάντα; 51 Σκληροτράχηλοι καὶ ἀπερίτμητοι
all? Hard-necked and uncircumcised

καρδίαις καὶ τοῖς ὠσίν, ὑμεῖς ἀεὶ τῷ
in hearts and – ears, ye always the

πνεύματι τῷ ἁγίῳ ἀντιπίπτετε, ὡς οἱ
Spirit – Holy oppose, as the

πατέρες ὑμῶν καὶ ὑμεῖς. 52 τίνα τῶν
fathers of you also ye. Which of the

προφητῶν οὐκ ἐδίωξαν οἱ πατέρες ὑμῶν;
prophets persecuted not the fathers of you?

καὶ ἀπέκτειναν τοὺς προκαταγγείλαντας
and they killed the [ones] announcing beforehand

περὶ τῆς ἐλεύσεως τοῦ δικαίου, οὗ
concerning the coming of the righteous one, of whom

νῦν ὑμεῖς προδόται καὶ φονεῖς ἐγένεσθε,
now ye betrayers and murderers became,

53 οἵτινες ἐλάβετε τὸν νόμον εἰς διαταγὰς
who received the law in(by) dispositions

ἀγγέλων, καὶ οὐκ ἐφυλάξατε.
of angels, and did not keep [it].

54 Ἀκούοντες δὲ ταῦτα διεπρίοντο ταῖς
And hearing these things they were cut to the

καρδίαις αὐτῶν καὶ ἔβρυχον τοὺς ὀδόντας
hearts of them and gnashed the teeth

ἐπ' αὐτόν. 55 ὑπάρχων δὲ πλήρης
at him. But being full

of the Holy Ghost, looked
up stedfastly into heaven,
and saw the glory of God,
and Jesus standing on the
right hand of God,

56 And said, Behold, I
see the heavens opened,
and the Son of man
standing on the right hand
of God.

57 Then they cried out
with a loud voice, and
stopped their ears, and
ran upon him with one
accord,

58 And cast *him* out of
the city, and stoned *him:*
and the witnesses laid
down their clothes at a
young man's feet, whose
name was Saul.

59 And they stoned
Stephen, calling upon *God,*
and saying, Lord Jesus,
receive my spirit.

60 And he kneeled
down, and cried with a
loud voice, Lord, lay not
this sin to their charge.
And when he had said
this, he fell asleep.

CHAPTER 8

AND Saul was con-
senting unto his
death. And at that time
there was a great persecution against the church
which was at Jerusalem;
and they were all scattered
abroad throughout the
regions of Judæa and
Samaria, except the
apostles.

2 And devout men
carried Stephen *to his*

πνεύματος ἁγίου ἀτενίσας εἰς τὸν οὐρανὸν
of [the] Spirit ▾ Holy gazing into – heaven
εἶδεν δόξαν θεοῦ καὶ 'Ιησοῦν ἑστῶτα ἐκ
he saw [the] glory of God and Jesus standing at
δεξιῶν τοῦ θεοῦ, 56 καὶ εἶπεν· ἰδοὺ
[the] right [hand] – of God, and said : Behold
θεωρῶ τοὺς οὐρανοὺς διηνοιγμένους καὶ
I see the heavens *having been* opened up and
τὸν υἱὸν τοῦ ἀνθρώπου ἐκ δεξιῶν ἑστῶτα
the Son – of man at [the] right [hand] standing
τοῦ θεοῦ. 57 κράξαντες δὲ φωνῇ μεγάλῃ
– of God. And crying out voice with a great
συνέσχον τὰ ὦτα αὐτῶν, καὶ ὥρμησαν
they closed the ears of them, and rushed
ὁμοθυμαδὸν ἐπ᾽ αὐτόν, 58 καὶ ἐκβαλόντες
with one mind on him, and casting *out*
ἔξω τῆς πόλεως ἐλιθοβόλουν. καὶ οἱ
outside the city they stoned [him]. And the
μάρτυρες ἀπέθεντο τὰ ἱμάτια αὐτῶν παρὰ
witnesses put off the garments of them at
τοὺς πόδας νεανίου καλουμένου Σαύλου.
the feet of a young man *being* called Saul.
59 καὶ ἐλιθοβόλουν τὸν Στέφανον, ἐπικαλ-
And they stoned – Stephen, invok-
ούμενον καὶ λέγοντα· κύριε 'Ιησοῦ, δέξαι
ing [God] and saying : Lord Jesus, receive
τὸ πνεῦμά μου. 60 θεὶς δὲ τὰ γόνατα
the spirit of me. And placing the knees
= kneeling down
ἔκραξεν φωνῇ μεγάλῃ· κύριε, μὴ στήσῃς
he cried voice with a great : Lord, place not
αὐτοῖς ταύτην τὴν ἁμαρτίαν. καὶ τοῦτο
to them this – sin. And ²this
εἰπὼν ἐκοιμήθη. 8 Σαῦλος δὲ ἦν συνευδοκῶν
¹saying he fell asleep. And Saul was consenting
τῇ ἀναιρέσει αὐτοῦ.
to the killing of him.
'Εγένετο δὲ ἐν ἐκείνῃ τῇ ἡμέρᾳ
And there was in that – day
διωγμὸς μέγας ἐπὶ τὴν ἐκκλησίαν τὴν
persecution a great on(against) the church –
ἐν 'Ιεροσολύμοις· πάντες [δὲ] διεσπάρησαν
in Jerusalem; and all were scattered
κατὰ τὰς χώρας τῆς 'Ιουδαίας καὶ
throughout the countries – of Judæa and
Σαμαρείας πλὴν τῶν ἀποστόλων.
Samaria except the apostles.
2 συνεκόμισαν δὲ τὸν Στέφανον ἄνδρες
And ³recovered – ⁴Stephen ²men

burial, and made great lamentation over him.

3 As for Saul, he made havock of the church, entering into every house, and haling men and women committed *them* to prison.

4 Therefore they that were scattered abroad went every where preaching the word.

5 ¶ Then Philip went down to the city of Samaria, and preached Christ unto them.

6 And the people with one accord gave heed unto those things which Philip spake, hearing and seeing the miracles which he did.

7 For unclean spirits, crying with loud voice, came out of many that were possessed *with them*: and many taken with palsies, and that were lame, were healed.

8 And there was great joy in that city.

9 But there was a certain man, called Simon, which beforetime in the same city used sorcery, and bewitched the people of Samaria, giving out that himself was some great one:

10 To whom they all gave heed, from the least to the greatest, saying, This man is the great power of God.

εὐλαβεῖς καὶ ἐποίησαν κοπετὸν μέγαν
¹devout　and　made　lamentation　great

ἐπ' αὐτῷ. 3 Σαῦλος δὲ ἐλυμαίνετο τὴν
over him.　　　But Saul　　ravaged　the

ἐκκλησίαν κατὰ τοὺς οἴκους εἰσπορευόμενος,
church　house by house†　　entering,

σύρων τε ἄνδρας καὶ γυναῖκας παρεδίδου
dragging both　men　and　women　delivered

εἰς φυλακήν.
to　prison.

4 Οἱ μὲν οὖν διασπαρέντες διῆλθον
The [ones] —*　therefore　being scattered passed through

εὐαγγελιζόμενοι τὸν λόγον. 5 Φίλιππος δὲ
preaching　the　word.　　But Philip

κατελθὼν εἰς τὴν πόλιν τῆς
going down　to　the　city　—

Σαμαρείας ἐκήρυσσεν αὐτοῖς τὸν Χριστόν.
of Samaria　proclaimed　to them　the　Christ.

6 προσεῖχον δὲ οἱ ὄχλοι τοῖς
And gave heed　　the　crowds to the things

λεγομένοις ὑπὸ τοῦ Φιλίππου ὁμοθυμαδὸν
being said　by　—　Philip　with one mind

ἐν τῷ ἀκούειν αὐτοὺς καὶ βλέπειν τὰ
in　the　to hear　them　and　to see^be　the
=as they heard and saw

σημεῖα ἃ ἐποίει. 7 πολλοὶ γὰρ τῶν
signs　which he was doing.　For many　of the

ἐχόντων πνεύματα ἀκάθαρτα βοῶντα φωνῇ
[ones] having　spirits　unclean　crying　²voice

μεγάλη ἐξήρχοντο· πολλοὶ δὲ παραλελυμένοι
¹with a great　came out;　and many　*having been* paralysed

καὶ χωλοὶ ἐθεραπεύθησαν· 8 ἐγένετο δὲ
and　lame　were healed;　and there was

πολλὴ χαρὰ ἐν τῇ πόλει ἐκείνη. 9 Ἀνὴρ δέ τις
much　joy in　that city.　And a certain man

ὀνόματι Σίμων προϋπῆρχεν ἐν τῇ
by name　Simon　was previously　in　the

πόλει μαγεύων καὶ ἐξιστάνων τὸ
city　practising sorcery　and　astonishing　the

ἔθνος τῆς Σαμαρείας, λέγων εἶναί τινα
nation　—　of Samaria,　saying　²to be ³someone

ἑαυτὸν μέγαν, 10 ᾧ προσεῖχον πάντες
¹himself　⁴great,　to whom　gave heed　all

ἀπὸ μικροῦ ἕως μεγάλου λέγοντες· οὗτός
from　small　to　great　saying :　This man

ἐστιν ἡ δύναμις τοῦ θεοῦ ἡ καλουμένη
is　the　power　—　of God　—　*being* called

* See note on John 19. 24.

11 And to him they had regard, because that of long time he had bewitched them with sorceries.
12 But when they believed Philip preaching the things concerning the kingdom of God, and the name of Jesus Christ, they were baptized, both men and women.
13 Then Simon himself believed also: and when he was baptized, he continued with Philip, and wondered, beholding the miracles and signs which were done.
14 ¶ Now when the apostles which were at Jerusalem heard that Samaria had received the word of God, they sent unto them Peter and John:
15 Who, when they were come down, prayed for them, that they might receive the Holy Ghost:
16 (For as yet he was fallen upon none of them: only they were baptized in the name of the Lord Jesus.)
17 Then laid they *their* hands on them, and they received the Holy Ghost.
18 And when Simon saw that through laying on of the apostles' hands the Holy Ghost was given, he offered them money,

μεγάλη. **11** προσεῖχον δὲ αὐτῷ διὰ τὸ
great.　　　And they gave heed　to him　because of the

ἱκανῷ χρόνῳ ταῖς μαγείαις ἐξεστακέναι
for a considerable　time　by the　sorceries　to have astonished
= because for a considerable time he had astonished them by his sorceries.

αὐτούς. **12** ὅτε δὲ ἐπίστευσαν τῷ Φιλίππῳ
them.　　But when　they believed　－　Philip

εὐαγγελιζομένῳ περὶ τῆς βασιλείας τοῦ
preaching　about　the　kingdom　－

θεοῦ καὶ τοῦ ὀνόματος Ἰησοῦ Χριστοῦ,
of God　and　the　name　of Jesus　Christ,

ἐβαπτίζοντο ἄνδρες τε καὶ γυναῖκες.
they were baptized　both men　and　women.

13 ὁ δὲ Σίμων καὶ αὐτὸς ἐπίστευσεν,
－　And　Simon　also　[him]self　believed,

καὶ βαπτισθεὶς ἦν προσκαρτερῶν τῷ
and having been baptized was　attaching himself　－

Φιλίππῳ, θεωρῶν τε σημεῖα καὶ δυνάμεις
to Philip,　and beholding　signs　and powerful deeds

μεγάλας γινομένας ἐξίστατο. **14** Ἀκούσαντες
great　happening　he was amazed.　[6]hearing

δὲ οἱ ἐν Ἱεροσολύμοις ἀπόστολοι ὅτι
[1]And [3]the [4]in　[5]Jerusalem　[2]apostles　that

δέδεκται ἡ Σαμάρεια τὸν λόγον τοῦ
[2]has received　－　[1]Samaria　the　word　－

θεοῦ, ἀπέστειλαν πρὸς αὐτοὺς Πέτρον
of God,　they sent　to　them　Peter

καὶ Ἰωάννην, **15** οἵτινες καταβάντες
and　John,　　who　going down

προσηύξαντο περὶ αὐτῶν ὅπως λάβωσιν
prayed　concerning them　so as　they might receive

πνεῦμα ἅγιον· **16** οὐδέπω γὰρ ἦν ἐπ᾽
Spirit　Holy;　for [2]not yet　[1]he was　[6]on

οὐδενὶ αὐτῶν ἐπιπεπτωκός, μόνον δὲ
[5]no(any)one [6]of them　[3]having fallen on,　but only

βεβαπτισμένοι ὑπῆρχον εἰς τὸ ὄνομα τοῦ
having been baptized　they were　in　the　name　of the

κυρίου Ἰησοῦ. **17** τότε ἐπετίθεσαν τὰς
Lord　Jesus.　　Then　they laid on　the(ir)

χεῖρας ἐπ᾽ αὐτούς, καὶ ἐλάμβανον πνεῦμα
hands　on　them,　and　they received　[2]Spirit

ἅγιον. **18** ἰδὼν δὲ ὁ Σίμων ὅτι διὰ
[1]Holy.　　And [2]seeing　－　[1]Simon　that through

τῆς ἐπιθέσεως τῶν χειρῶν τῶν ἀποστόλων
the　laying on　of the　hands　of the　apostles

δίδοται τὸ πνεῦμα, προσήνεγκεν αὐτοῖς
is(was) given the　Spirit,　　he offered　them

19 Saying, Give me also this power, that on whomsoever I lay hands, he may receive the Holy Ghost.

20 But Peter said unto him, Thy money perish with thee, because thou hast thought that the gift of God may be purchased with money.

21 Thou hast neither part nor lot in this matter: for thy heart is not right in the sight of God.

22 Repent therefore of this thy wickedness, and pray God, if perhaps the thought of thine heart may be forgiven thee.

23 For I perceive that thou art in the gall of bitterness, and *in* the bond of iniquity.

24 Then answered Simon, and said, Pray ye to the Lord for me, that none of these things which ye have spoken come upon me.

25 And they, when they had testified and preached the word of the Lord, returned to Jerusalem, and preached the gospel in many villages of the Samaritans.

26 ¶ And the angel of the Lord spake unto Philip, saying, Arise, and

---

χρήματα   λέγων·   **19** δότε   κἀμοὶ   τὴν
money   saying :   Give   me also   –

ἐξουσίαν   ταύτην   ἵνα   ᾧ   ἐὰν   ἐπιθῶ   τὰς
authority   this   that   whomever   I lay on the(my)

χεῖρας   λαμβάνῃ   πνεῦμα   ἅγιον.   **20** Πέτρος δὲ
hands   he may receive   Spirit   Holy.   But Peter

εἶπεν   πρὸς   αὐτόν·   τὸ   ἀργύριόν   σου
said   to   him :   The   silver   of thee

σὺν   σοὶ   εἴη   εἰς   ἀπώλειαν,   ὅτι   τὴν   δωρεὰν
with   thee   may it be into   perdition,   because   the   gift

τοῦ   θεοῦ   ἐνόμισας   διὰ   χρημάτων   κτᾶσθαι.
– of God   thou didst suppose   through   money   to get.

21 οὐκ   ἔστιν   σοι   μερὶς   οὐδὲ   κλῆρος
There is not   to thee°   part   nor   lot
=Thou hast no

ἐν   τῷ   λόγῳ   τούτῳ·   ἡ   γὰρ   καρδία   σου
in   this matter;   for the   heart   of thee

οὐκ   ἔστιν   εὐθεῖα   ἔναντι   τοῦ   θεοῦ.
is not   right   before   –   God.

22 μετανόησον   οὖν   ἀπὸ   τῆς   κακίας   σου
Repent thou   therefore   from   – ²wickedness ³of thee

ταύτης,   καὶ   δεήθητι   τοῦ   κυρίου   εἰ   ἄρα
¹this,   and   petition   the   Lord   if perhaps

ἀφεθήσεταί   σοι   ἡ   ἐπίνοια   τῆς   καρδίας
will be forgiven   thee   the   thought   of the   heart

σου·   **23** εἰς   γὰρ   χολὴν   πικρίας   καὶ
of thee;   for in   gall   of bitterness   and

σύνδεσμον   ἀδικίας   ὁρῶ   σε   ὄντα.
bond   of unrighteousness   I see   thee   being.

24 ἀποκριθεὶς   δὲ   ὁ   Σίμων   εἶπεν·   δεήθητε
And answering   –   Simon   said :   Petition

ὑμεῖς   ὑπὲρ   ἐμοῦ   πρὸς   τὸν   κύριον,   ὅπως
ye   for   me   to   the   Lord,   so as

μηδὲν   ἐπέλθῃ   ἐπ'   ἐμὲ   ὧν   εἰρήκατε.
¹not one ⁴may come on   ⁵on   ³me   ²of the   ⁷ye have
   things which   spoken.

25 Οἱ   μὲν   οὖν   διαμαρτυράμενοι   καὶ   λαλή-
They   – therefore   having solemnly witnessed   and   having

σαντες   τὸν   λόγον   τοῦ   κυρίου   ὑπέστρεφον
spoken   the   word   of the   Lord   returned

εἰς   Ἱεροσόλυμα,   πολλάς   τε   κώμας   τῶν
to   Jerusalem,   and ²many   ³villages   ⁴of the

Σαμαριτῶν   εὐηγγελίζοντο.
⁵Samaritans   ¹evangelized.

26 Ἄγγελος   δὲ   κυρίου   ἐλάλησεν   πρὸς
But an angel   of [the] Lord   spoke   to

Φίλιππον   λέγων·   ἀνάστηθι   καὶ   πορεύου
Philip   saying :   Rise up   and   go

go toward the south unto the way that goeth down from Jerusalem unto Gaza, which is desert.

27 And he arose and went: and, behold, a man of Ethiopia, an eunuch of great authority under Candace queen of the Ethiopians, who had the charge of all her treasure, and had come to Jerusalem for to worship,

28 Was returning, and sitting in his chariot read Esaias the prophet.

29 Then the Spirit said unto Philip, Go near, and join thyself to this chariot.

30 And Philip ran thither to *him*, and heard him read the prophet Esaias, and said, Understandest thou what thou readest?

31 And he said, How can I, except some man should guide me? And he desired Philip that he would come up and sit with him.

32 The place of the scripture which he read was this, He was led as a sheep to the slaughter; and like a lamb dumb before his shearer, so opened he not his mouth:

33 In his humiliation his judgment was taken away: and who shall declare his generation? for

κατὰ μεσημβρίαν ἐπὶ τὴν ὁδὸν τὴν
along -south on the way –

καταβαίνουσαν ἀπὸ Ἰερουσαλὴμ εἰς Γάζαν·
going down from Jerusalem to Gaza;

αὕτη ἐστὶν ἔρημος. 27 καὶ ἀναστὰς
this is desert. And rising up

ἐπορεύθη. καὶ ἰδοὺ ἀνὴρ Αἰθίοψ εὐνοῦχος
he went. And behold[,] a man Ethiopian a eunuch

δυνάστης Κανδάκης βασιλίσσης Αἰθιόπων,
a courtier of Candace queen of [the] Ethiopians,

ὃς ἦν ἐπὶ πάσης τῆς γάζης αὐτῆς,
who was over all the treasure of her,

[ὃς] ἐληλύθει προσκυνήσων εἰς Ἰερουσαλήμ,
who had come worshipping in Jerusalem,

28 ἦν δὲ ὑποστρέφων καὶ καθήμενος ἐπὶ
and was returning and sitting on

τοῦ ἅρματος αὐτοῦ καὶ ἀνεγίνωσκεν τὸν
the chariot of him and was reading the

προφήτην Ἠσαΐαν. 29 εἶπεν δὲ τὸ πνεῦμα
prophet Esaias. And said the Spirit

τῷ Φιλίππῳ· πρόσελθε καὶ κολλήθητι
– to Philip: Approach and keep company with

τῷ ἅρματι τούτῳ. 30 προσδραμὼν δὲ
this chariot. And running up

ὁ Φίλιππος ἤκουσεν αὐτοῦ ἀναγινώσκοντος
– Philip heard him reading

Ἠσαΐαν τὸν προφήτην, καὶ εἶπεν· ἆρά γε
Esaias the prophet, and said: Then

γινώσκεις ἃ ἀναγινώσκεις; 31 ὁ δὲ
knowest thou what things thou art reading? And he

εἶπεν· πῶς γὰρ ἂν δυναίμην ἐὰν μή
said: How indeed should I be able unless

τις ὁδηγήσει με; παρεκάλεσέν τε τὸν
someone shall guide me? And he besought –

Φίλιππον ἀναβάντα καθίσαι σὺν αὐτῷ.
Philip coming up to sit with him.

32 ἡ δὲ περιοχὴ τῆς γραφῆς ἦν ἀνεγίνω-
Now the passage of the scripture which he was

σκεν ἦν αὕτη· ὡς πρόβατον ἐπὶ σφαγὴν
reading was this: As a sheep to slaughter

ἤχθη, καὶ ὡς ἀμνὸς ἐναντίον τοῦ κείροντος
he was led, and as a lamb before the [one] shearing

αὐτὸν ἄφωνος, οὕτως οὐκ ἀνοίγει τὸ
it [is] dumb, so he opens not the

στόμα αὐτοῦ. 33 Ἐν τῇ ταπεινώσει
mouth of him. In the humiliation

ἡ κρίσις αὐτοῦ ἤρθη· τὴν γενεὰν αὐτοῦ
the judgment of him was taken away; the generation of him

his life is taken from the earth.

34 And the eunuch answered Philip, and said, I pray thee, of whom speaketh the prophet this? of himself, or of some other man?

35 Then Philip opened his mouth, and began at the same scripture, and preached unto him Jesus.

36 And as they went on *their* way, they came unto a certain water: and the eunuch said, See, *here is* water; what doth hinder me to be baptized?

37 And Philip said, If thou believest with all thine heart, thou mayest. And he answered and said, I believe that Jesus Christ is the Son of God.

38 And he commanded the chariot to stand still: and they went down both into the water, both Philip and the eunuch; and he baptized him.

39 And when they were come up out of the water, the Spirit of the Lord caught away Philip, that the eunuch saw him no more: and he went on his way rejoicing.

40 But Philip was found at Azotus: and passing through he preached in all the cities, till he came to Cæsarea.

τίς διηγήσεται; ὅτι αἴρεται ἀπὸ τῆς
who will relate? because is taken from the

γῆς ἡ ζωὴ αὐτοῦ. 34 ἀποκριθεὶς δὲ ὁ
earth the life of him. And answering the

εὐνοῦχος τῷ Φιλίππῳ εἶπεν· δέομαί σου,
eunuch - to Philip said: I ask thee,

περὶ τίνος ὁ προφήτης λέγει τοῦτο;
about whom the prophet says this?

περὶ ἑαυτοῦ ἢ περὶ ἑτέρου τινός;
about himself or about other someone?

35 ἀνοίξας δὲ ὁ Φίλιππος τὸ στόμα
And opening - Philip the mouth

αὐτοῦ καὶ ἀρξάμενος ἀπὸ τῆς γραφῆς ταύτης
of him and beginning from this scripture

εὐηγγελίσατο αὐτῷ τὸν Ἰησοῦν.
preached to him - Jesus.

36 ὡς δὲ ἐπορεύοντο κατὰ τὴν ὁδόν,
And as they were going along the way,

ἦλθον ἐπί τι ὕδωρ, καί φησιν ὁ εὐνοῦχος·
they came upon certain water, and says the eunuch·

ἰδοὺ ὕδωρ· τί κωλύει με βαπτισθῆναι;‡
Behold[,] water; what prevents me to be baptized?

38 καὶ ἐκέλευσεν στῆναι τὸ ἅρμα, καὶ
And he commanded to stand the chariot, and

κατέβησαν ἀμφότεροι εἰς τὸ ὕδωρ, ὅ
went down both into the water, -

τε Φίλιππος καὶ ὁ εὐνοῦχος, καὶ ἐβάπτισεν
both Philip and the eunuch, and he baptized

αὐτόν. 39 ὅτε δὲ ἀνέβησαν ἐκ τοῦ ὕδατος,
him. And when they came up out of the water,

πνεῦμα κυρίου ἥρπασεν τὸν Φίλιππον,
[the] Spirit of [the] Lord seized - Philip,

καὶ οὐκ εἶδεν αὐτὸν οὐκέτι ὁ εὐνοῦχος,
and saw not him no(any) more the eunuch,

ἐπορεύετο γὰρ τὴν ὁδὸν αὐτοῦ χαίρων.
for he went the way of him rejoicing.

40 Φίλιππος δὲ εὑρέθη εἰς Ἄζωτον, καὶ
But Philip was found in Azotus, and

διερχόμενος εὐηγγελίζετο τὰς πόλεις πάσας
passing through he evangelized the cities all

ἕως τοῦ ἐλθεῖν αὐτὸν εἰς Καισάρειαν.
until the to come him[b] to Cæsarea.
=he came

‡ Verse 37 omitted by Nestle; *cf.* R.V. marg.

CHAPTER 9

AND Saul, yet breathing out threatenings and slaughter against the disciples of the Lord, went unto the high priest,

2 And desired of him letters to Damascus to the synagogues, that if he found any of this way, whether they were men or women, he might bring them bound unto Jerusalem.

3 And as he journeyed, he came near Damascus: and suddenly there shined round about him a light from heaven:

4 And he fell to the earth, and heard a voice saying unto him, Saul, Saul, why persecutest thou me?

5 And he said, Who art thou, Lord? And the Lord said, I am Jesus whom thou persecutest: it is hard for thee to kick against the pricks.

6 And he trembling and astonished said, Lord, what wilt thou have me to do? And the Lord said unto him, Arise, and go into the city, and it shall be told thee what thou must do.

7 And the men which journeyed with him stood speechless, hearing a voice, but seeing no man.

8 And Saul arose from the earth; and when his eyes were opened, he saw no man: but they led him by the hand, and brought *him* into Damascus.

9 And he was three

---

9 Ὁ δὲ Σαῦλος ἔτι ἐμπνέων ἀπειλῆς
    -    But   Saul   still   breathing   threatening

καὶ φόνου εἰς τοὺς μαθητὰς τοῦ κυρίου,
and   murder   against   the   disciples   of the   Lord,

προσελθὼν τῷ ἀρχιερεῖ **2** ᾐτήσατο παρ'
approaching   *to* the   high priest   asked   from

αὐτοῦ ἐπιστολὰς εἰς Δαμασκὸν πρὸς τὰς
him   letters   to   Damascus   for   the

συναγωγάς, ὅπως ἐάν τινας εὕρῃ τῆς
synagogues,   so as   if   ²any   ¹he found   ⁴of the

ὁδοῦ ὄντας, ἄνδρας τε καὶ γυναῖκας, δεδεμένους
⁵way ³being,   both men   and   women,   ²having been bound

ἀγάγῃ εἰς Ἰερουσαλήμ. **3** Ἐν
¹he might bring [them] to   Jerusalem.   in

δὲ τῷ πορεύεσθαι ἐγένετο αὐτὸν ἐγγίζειν
Now the   to goᵉ   it came to pass   him   to draw nearᵇ
=as he went   =he drew near

τῇ Δαμασκῷ, ἐξαίφνης τε αὐτὸν περιήστ-
  -   to Damascus,   and suddenly   ⁵him   ⁴shone

ραψεν φῶς ἐκ τοῦ οὐρανοῦ, **4** καὶ πεσὼν
round   ¹a light   ²out of   -   ³heaven,   and   falling

ἐπὶ τὴν γῆν ἤκουσεν φωνὴν λέγουσαν
on   the   earth   he heard   a voice   saying

αὐτῷ· Σαοὺλ Σαούλ, τί με διώκεις;
to him: Saul[,]   Saul,   why   me   persecutest thou?

5 εἶπεν δέ· τίς εἶ, κύριε; ὁ δέ· ἐγὼ
And he said: Who art thou, Lord?   And he [said]:   I

εἰμι Ἰησοῦς ὃν σὺ διώκεις· **6** ἀλλὰ
am   Jesus   whom   thou   persecutest·   but

ἀνάστηθι καὶ εἴσελθε εἰς τὴν πόλιν,
rise thou up,   and   enter   into   the   city,

καὶ λαληθήσεταί σοι ὅ τί σε δεῖ ποιεῖν.
and   it shall be told   thee   what   thee it behoves to do.

7 οἱ δὲ ἄνδρες οἱ συνοδεύοντες αὐτῷ
Now the   men   -   journeying with   him

εἱστήκεισαν ἐνεοί, ἀκούοντες μὲν τῆς
stood   speechless,   hearing   indeed   the

φωνῆς, μηδένα δὲ θεωροῦντες. **8** ἠγέρθη δὲ
sound,   but no man   beholding.   And was raised

Σαῦλος ἀπὸ τῆς γῆς, ἀνεῳγμένων δὲ
Saul   from   the   ground,   and having been opened
                =when his eyes were opened

τῶν ὀφθαλμῶν αὐτοῦ οὐδὲν ἔβλεπεν·
the   eyes   of himᵃ   nothing   he saw;

χειραγωγοῦντες δὲ αὐτὸν εἰσήγαγον εἰς
and leading by the hand   him   they brought *in*   into

Δαμασκόν. **9** καὶ ἦν ἡμέρας τρεῖς μὴ
Damascus.   And   he was   days   three   not

days without sight, and neither did eat nor drink.

10 ¶ And there was a certain disciple at Damascus, named Ananias; and to him said the Lord in a vision, Ananias. And he said, Behold, I *am here*, Lord.

11 And the Lord *said* unto him, Arise, and go into the street which is called Straight, and enquire in the house of Judas for *one* called Saul, of Tarsus: for, behold, he prayeth,

12 And hath seen in a vision a man named Ananias coming in, and putting *his* hand on him, that he might receive his sight.

13 Then Ananias answered, Lord, I have heard by many of this man, how much evil he hath done to thy saints at Jerusalem:

14 And here he hath authority from the chief priests to bind all that call on thy name.

15 But the Lord said unto him, Go thy way: for he is a chosen vessel unto me, to bear my name before the Gentiles, and kings, and the children of Israel:

16 For I will shew him how great things he must suffer for my name's sake.

17 And Ananias went his way, and entered into

βλέπων, καὶ οὐκ ἔφαγεν οὐδὲ ἔπιεν.
seeing, and ate not nor drank.

10 *Ἦν δέ τις μαθητὴς ἐν Δαμασκῷ
Now there was a certain disciple in Damascus

ὀνόματι Ἀνανίας, καὶ εἶπεν πρὸς αὐτὸν
by name Ananias, and said to him

ἐν ὁράματι ὁ κύριος· Ἀνανία. ὁ δὲ
in a vision the Lord: Ananias. And he

εἶπεν· ἰδοὺ ἐγώ, κύριε. 11 ὁ δὲ κύριος
said: Behold[,] I, Lord. And the Lord

πρὸς αὐτόν· ἀναστὰς πορεύθητι ἐπὶ τὴν
[said] to him: Rising up go thou to the

ῥύμην τὴν καλουμένην εὐθεῖαν καὶ ζήτησον
street — *being* called Straight and seek

ἐν οἰκίᾳ Ἰούδα Σαῦλον ὀνόματι Ταρσέα·
in [the] house of Judas ²Saul ³by name ¹a Tarsian;

ἰδοὺ γὰρ προσεύχεται, 12 καὶ εἶδεν ἄνδρα
for behold he is praying, and saw ²a man

[ἐν ὁράματι] Ἀνανίαν ὀνόματι εἰσελθόντα
¹in ²a vision Ananias by name coming in

καὶ ἐπιθέντα αὐτῷ χεῖρας, ὅπως ἀναβλέψῃ.
and putting on him hands, so as he may see again.

13 ἀπεκρίθη δὲ Ἀνανίας· κύριε, ἤκουσα
And answered Ananias: Lord, I heard

ἀπὸ πολλῶν περὶ τοῦ ἀνδρὸς τούτου,
from many about this man,

ὅσα κακὰ τοῖς ἁγίοις σου ἐποίησεν
how many evil things to the saints of thee he did

ἐν Ἰερουσαλήμ· 14 καὶ ὧδε ἔχει ἐξουσίαν
in Jerusalem; and here he has authority

παρὰ τῶν ἀρχιερέων δῆσαι πάντας τοὺς
from the chief priests to bind all the

ἐπικαλουμένους τὸ ὄνομά σου. 15 εἶπεν
[ones] invoking the name of thee. said

δὲ πρὸς αὐτὸν ὁ κύριος· πορεύου, ὅτι
But to him the Lord: Go thou, because

σκεῦος ἐκλογῆς ἐστίν μοι οὗτος τοῦ
²a vessel ⁴of choice ³is ⁵to me ¹this man —

βαστάσαι τὸ ὄνομά μου ἐνώπιον [τῶν]
to bear^d the name of me ²before ³the

ἐθνῶν τε καὶ βασιλέων υἱῶν τε Ἰσραήλ·
⁴nations ¹both ⁵and ⁶kings ⁸sons ⁷and ⁹of Israel;

16 ἐγὼ γὰρ ὑποδείξω αὐτῷ ὅσα δεῖ
for I will show him how many things it behoves

αὐτὸν ὑπὲρ τοῦ ὀνόματός μου παθεῖν.
him on behalf of the name of me to suffer.

17 Ἀπῆλθεν δὲ Ἀνανίας καὶ εἰσῆλθεν
And went away Ananias and entered

the house; and putting his hands on him said, Brother Saul, the Lord, *even* Jesus, that appeared unto thee in the way as thou camest, hath sent me, that thou mightest receive thy sight, and be filled with the Holy Ghost.

18 And immediately there fell from his eyes as it had been scales: and he received sight forthwith, and arose, and was baptized.

19 And when he had received meat, he was strengthened. Then was Saul certain days with the disciples which were at Damascus.

20 And straightway he preached Christ in the synagogues, that he is the Son of God.

21 But all that heard *him* were amazed, and said; Is not this he that destroyed them which called on this name in Jerusalem, and came hither for that intent, that he might bring them bound unto the chief priests?

22 But Saul increased the more in strength, and confounded the Jews which dwelt at Damascus, proving that this is very Christ.

23 ¶ And after that many days were fulfilled, the Jews took counsel to kill him:

24 But their laying await was known of Saul. And they watched the

εἰς	τὴν	οἰκίαν,	καὶ	ἐπιθεὶς ἐπ᾽ αὐτὸν
into	the	house,	and	putting on on him

τὰς	χεῖρας	εἶπεν·	Σαοὺλ	ἀδελφέ, ὁ
the(his)	hands	said :	Saul	brother, the

κύριος	ἀπέσταλκέν	με,	Ἰησοῦς	ὁ ὀφθείς σοι
Lord	has sent	me,	Jesus	the [one] appearing to thee

ἐν	τῇ ὁδῷ	ᾗ	ἤρχου,	ὅπως ἀναβλέψῃς
in	the way	which	thou camest,	so as thou mayest see again

καὶ	πλησθῇς	πνεύματος	ἁγίου.	18 καὶ
and	be filled	of(with) Spirit	Holy.	And

εὐθέως	ἀπέπεσαν	αὐτοῦ	ἀπὸ	τῶν ὀφθαλμῶν
immediately	fell away	of him	from	the eyes

ὡς	λεπίδες,	ἀνέβλεψέν	τε,	καὶ ἀναστὰς
as	scales,	and he saw again,		and rising up

ἐβαπτίσθη,	19 καὶ λαβὼν	τροφὴν	ἐνίσχυσεν.
was baptized,	and taking	food	was strengthened.

Ἐγένετο	δὲ μετὰ	τῶν ἐν	Δαμασκῷ
Now he was	with	the in	Damascus

μαθητῶν	ἡμέρας	τινάς,	20 καὶ εὐθέως
disciples	days	some,	and immediately

ἐν ταῖς συναγωγαῖς	ἐκήρυσσεν	τὸν Ἰησοῦν,
in the synagogues	he proclaimed	– Jesus,

ὅτι	οὗτός	ἐστιν	ὁ υἱὸς	τοῦ θεοῦ.
that	this one	is	the Son	– of God.

21 ἐξίσταντο	δὲ πάντες	οἱ ἀκούοντες	καὶ
And were amazed	all	the [ones] hearing	and

ἔλεγον·	οὐχ οὗτός	ἐστιν	ὁ πορθήσας
said :	Not this man	is	the [one] having destroyed

εἰς	Ἰερουσαλὴμ τοὺς	ἐπικαλουμένους
in	Jerusalem the [ones]	invoking

τὸ ὄνομα τοῦτο,	καὶ ὧδε εἰς	τοῦτο ἐληλύθει,
this name,	and here for	this he had come,

ἵνα	δεδεμένους αὐτοὺς ἀγάγῃ	ἐπὶ τοὺς
that	having been bound them he might bring	before the

ἀρχιερεῖς;	22 Σαῦλος	δὲ μᾶλλον ἐνε-
chief priests?	But Saul	more was filled

δυναμοῦτο	καὶ συνέχυννεν	Ἰουδαίους τοὺς κατ-
with power	and confounded	Jews the [ones]

οἰκοῦντας	ἐν Δαμασκῷ,	συμβιβάζων ὅτι οὗτός
dwelling	in Damascus,	proving that this one

ἐστιν ὁ	χριστός.	23 Ὡς δὲ ἐπληροῦντο
is the	Christ.	And when were fulfilled

ἡμέραι	ἱκαναί, 24 συνεβουλεύσαντο
days	considerable(many), consulted together

οἱ Ἰουδαῖοι	ἀνελεῖν	αὐτόν·	ἐγνώσθη δὲ
the Jews	to kill	him;	but was known

τῷ	Σαύλῳ ἡ	ἐπιβουλὴ	αὐτῶν. παρετη-
–	to Saul the	plot	of them. And they

gates day and night to
kill him.

25 Then the disciples
took him by night, and
let *him* down by the wall in
a basket.

26 And when Saul was
come to Jerusalem, he
assayed to join himself
to the disciples: but they
were all afraid of him,
and believed not that he
was a disciple.

27 But Barnabas took
him, and brought *him* to
the apostles, and declared
unto them how he had
seen the Lord in the way,
and that he had spoken
to him, and how he had
preached boldly at Damas-
cus in the name of Jesus.

28 And he was with
them coming in and going
out at Jerusalem.

29 And he spake boldly
in the name of the Lord
Jesus, and disputed against
the Grecians: but they
went about to slay him.

30 *Which* when the
brethren knew, they
brought him down to
Cæsarea, and sent him
forth to Tarsus.

31 Then had the
churches rest throughout
all Judæa and Galilee and
Samaria, and were edified;

ροῦντο δὲ καὶ τὰς πύλας ἡμέρας τε καὶ
carefully watched also the gates both by day and
νυκτὸς ὅπως αὐτὸν ἀνέλωσιν· 25 λαβόντες δὲ
by night so as him they might but ⁴taking
destroy;
οἱ μαθηταὶ αὐτοῦ νυκτὸς διὰ τοῦ
¹the ²disciples ³of him by night through the
τείχους καθῆκαν αὐτὸν χαλάσαντες ἐν
wall let down him lowering in
σπυρίδι. 26 Παραγενόμενος δὲ εἰς
a basket. And arriving at
Ἰερουσαλὴμ ἐπείραζεν κολλᾶσθαι τοῖς
Jerusalem he tried to be joined to the
μαθηταῖς· καὶ πάντες ἐφοβοῦντο αὐτόν,
disciples; and all feared him,
μὴ πιστεύοντες ὅτι ἐστὶν μαθητής.
not believing that he is(was) a disciple.
27 Βαρναβᾶς δὲ ἐπιλαβόμενος αὐτὸν ἤγαγεν
But Barnabas taking hold of him led
πρὸς τοὺς ἀποστόλους, καὶ διηγήσατο
to the apostles, and narrated
αὐτοῖς πῶς ἐν τῇ ὁδῷ εἶδεν τὸν κύριον
to them how in the way he saw the Lord
καὶ ὅτι ἐλάλησεν αὐτῷ, καὶ πῶς ἐν
and that he spoke to him, and how in
Δαμασκῷ ἐπαρρησιάσατο ἐν τῷ ὀνόματι
Damascus he spoke boldly in the name
Ἰησοῦ. 28 καὶ ἦν μετ᾽ αὐτῶν εἰσπορευόμενος
of Jesus. And he was with them going in
καὶ ἐκπορευόμενος εἰς Ἰερουσαλήμ,
and going out in Jerusalem,
παρρησιαζόμενος ἐν τῷ ὀνόματι τοῦ
speaking boldly in the name of the
κυρίου, 29 ἐλάλει τε καὶ συνεζήτει πρὸς
Lord, ²spoke ¹both ³and ⁴discussed with
τοὺς Ἑλληνιστάς· οἱ δὲ ἐπεχείρουν ἀνελεῖν
the Hellenists; and they attempted to kill
αὐτόν. 30 ἐπιγνόντες δὲ οἱ ἀδελφοὶ
him. But ³knowing ¹the ²brothers
κατήγαγον αὐτὸν εἰς Καισάρειαν καὶ
brought down him to Cæsarea and
ἐξαπέστειλαν αὐτὸν εἰς Ταρσόν.
sent forth him to Tarsus.
31 Ἡ μὲν οὖν ἐκκλησία καθ᾽ ὅλης
²The - ¹therefore ³church throughout all
τῆς Ἰουδαίας καὶ Γαλιλαίας καὶ Σαμαρείας
- Judæa and Galilee and Samaria
εἶχεν εἰρήνην οἰκοδομουμένη καὶ πορευομένη
had peace being built and going

and walking in the fear of the Lord, and in the comfort of the Holy Ghost, were multiplied.

32¶ And it came to pass, as Peter passed throughout all *quarters*, he came down also to the saints which dwelt at Lydda.

33 And there he found a certain man named Æneas, which had kept his bed eight years, and was sick of the palsy.

34 And Peter said unto him, Æneas, Jesus Christ maketh thee whole: arise, and make thy bed. And he arose immediately.

35 And all that dwelt at Lydda and Saron saw him, and turned to the Lord.

36¶ Now there was at Joppa a certain disciple named Tabitha, which by interpretation is called Dorcas: this woman was full of good works and almsdeeds which she did.

37 And it came to pass in those days, that she was sick, and died: whom when they had washed, they laid *her* in an upper chamber.

38 And forasmuch as Lydda was nigh to Joppa, and the disciples had heard that Peter was there, they sent unto him two men, desiring *him* that he would not delay to come to them.

τῷ φόβῳ τοῦ κυρίου, καὶ τῇ παρακλήσει
in the fear of the Lord. and in the comfort
τοῦ ἁγίου πνεύματος ἐπληθύνετο.
of the Holy Spirit was multiplied.

32 Ἐγένετο δὲ Πέτρον διερχόμενον διὰ
Now it came to pass Peter passing *through* through
πάντων κατελθεῖν καὶ πρὸς τοὺς ἁγίους
all [quarters] to come down also to the saints
τοὺς κατοικοῦντας Λύδδα. **33** εὗρεν δὲ
– inhabiting Lydda. And he found
ἐκεῖ ἄνθρωπόν τινα ὀνόματι Αἰνέαν ἐξ
there a certain man by name Aeneas of
ἐτῶν ὀκτὼ κατακείμενον ἐπὶ κραβάτου,
years eight lying on a mattress,
ὃς ἦν παραλελυμένος. **34** καὶ εἶπεν αὐτῷ
who was *having been* paralysed. And said to him
ὁ Πέτρος· Αἰνέα, ἰαταί σε Ἰησοῦς Χριστός·
– Peter: Aeneas, cures thee Jesus Christ;
ἀνάστηθι καὶ στρῶσον σεαυτῷ. καὶ
rise up and gird thyself. And
εὐθέως ἀνέστη. **35** καὶ εἶδαν αὐτὸν
immediately he rose up. And saw him
πάντες οἱ κατοικοῦντες Λύδδα καὶ τὸν
all the [ones] inhabiting Lydda and –
Σαρῶνα, οἵτινες ἐπέστρεψαν ἐπὶ τὸν κύριον.
Saron, who turned to the Lord.
Ἐν Ἰόππῃ δέ τις ἦν μαθήτρια ὀνόματι
²in ³Joppa ¹Now ⁵a certain ⁴was ⁶disciple by name
Ταβιθά, **36** ἣ διερμηνευομένη λέγεται
Tabitha, who being translated is called
Δορκάς· αὕτη ἦν πλήρης ἔργων ἀγαθῶν
Dorcas; this woman was full works of good
καὶ ἐλεημοσυνῶν ὧν ἐποίει. **37** ἐγένετο δὲ
and of alms which she did. And it happened
ἐν ταῖς ἡμέραις ἐκείναις ἀσθενήσασαν
in those days ailing
αὐτὴν ἀποθανεῖν· λούσαντες δὲ ἔθηκαν
she to die[b]; and having washed they put [her]
= being ill she died;
ἐν ὑπερῴῳ. **38** ἐγγὺς δὲ οὔσης Λύδδας
in an upper room. Now ³near ²being ¹Lydda[a]
τῇ Ἰόππῃ οἱ μαθηταὶ ἀκούσαντες ὅτι
– to Joppa the disciples having heard that
Πέτρος ἐστὶν ἐν αὐτῇ ἀπέστειλαν δύο
Peter is(was) in it sent two
ἄνδρας πρὸς αὐτὸν παρακαλοῦντες· μὴ
men to him beseeching: ²not
ὀκνήσῃς διελθεῖν ἕως ἡμῶν. **39** ἀναστὰς δὲ
¹hesitate to come to us. And rising up

39 Then Peter arose and went with them. When he was come, they brought him into the upper chamber: and all the widows stood by him weeping, and shewing the coats and garments which Dorcas made, while she was with them.

40 But Peter put them all forth, and kneeled down, and prayed: and turning *him* to the body said, Tabitha, arise. And she opened her eyes: and when she saw Peter, she sat up.

41 And he gave her *his* hand, and lifted her up, and when he had called the saints and widows, presented her alive.

42 And it was known throughout all Joppa; and many believed in the Lord.

43 And it came to pass, that he tarried many days in Joppa with one Simon a tanner.

Πέτρος συνῆλθεν αὐτοῖς· ὃν παραγενόμενον
Peter went with them; whom arriving

ἀνήγαγον εἰς τὸ ὑπερῷον, καὶ παρέστησαν
they led up into the upper room, and stood by

αὐτῷ πᾶσαι αἱ χῆραι κλαίουσαι καὶ
him all the widows weeping and

ἐπιδεικνύμεναι χιτῶνας καὶ ἱμάτια, ὅσα
showing tunics and garments, which

ἐποίει μετ᾽ αὐτῶν οὖσα ἡ Δορκάς.
¹made ⁴with ⁵them ³being - ¹Dorcas.

40 ἐκβαλὼν δὲ ἔξω πάντας ὁ Πέτρος
And ²putting out ⁴outside ³all - ¹Peter

καὶ θεὶς τὰ γόνατα προσηύξατο, καὶ
and placing the knees he prayed, and
   =kneeling down

ἐπιστρέψας πρὸς τὸ σῶμα εἶπεν· Ταβιθά,
turning to the body said: Tabitha,

ἀνάστηθι. ἡ δὲ ἤνοιξεν τοὺς ὀφθαλμοὺς
rise up. And she opened the eyes

αὐτῆς, καὶ ἰδοῦσα τὸν Πέτρον ἀνεκάθισεν.
of her, and seeing - Peter sat up.

41 δοὺς δὲ αὐτῇ χεῖρα ἀνέστησεν αὐτήν·
And giving her a hand he raised up her;

φωνήσας δὲ τοὺς ἁγίους καὶ τὰς χήρας
and calling the saints and the widows

παρέστησεν αὐτὴν ζῶσαν. **42** γνωστὸν δὲ
he presented her living. And known

ἐγένετο καθ᾽ ὅλης τῆς Ἰόππης, καὶ
it became throughout all - Joppa, and

ἐπίστευσαν πολλοὶ ἐπὶ τὸν κύριον.
believed many on the Lord.

43 Ἐγένετο δὲ ἡμέρας ἱκανὰς μεῖναι ἐν
And it came to pass days several to remain in
   =he remained many days

Ἰόππῃ παρά τινι Σίμωνι βυρσεῖ.
Joppa with one Simon a tanner.

CHAPTER 10

THERE was a certain man in Cæsarea called Cornelius, a centurion of the band called the Italian *band*,

2 *A* devout *man*, and one that feared God with all his house, which gave much alms to the people,

10 Ἀνὴρ δέ τις ἐν Καισαρείᾳ ὀνόματι
Now a certain man in Cæsarea by name

Κορνήλιος, ἑκατοντάρχης ἐκ σπείρης τῆς
Cornelius, a centurion of a cohort -

καλουμένης Ἰταλικῆς, **2** εὐσεβὴς καὶ
being called Italian, devout and

φοβούμενος τὸν θεὸν σὺν παντὶ τῷ οἴκῳ
fearing - God with all the household

αὐτοῦ, ποιῶν ἐλεημοσύνας πολλὰς τῷ
of him, doing alms many to the

and prayed to God alway.

3 He saw in a vision evidently about the ninth hour of the day an angel of God coming in to him, and saying unto him, Cornelius.

4 And when he looked on him, he was afraid, and said, What is it, Lord? And he said unto him, Thy prayers and thine alms are come up for a memorial before God.

5 And now send men to Joppa, and call for *one* Simon, whose surname is Peter:

6 He lodgeth with one Simon a tanner, whose house is by the sea side: he shall tell thee what thou oughtest to do.

7 And when the angel which spake unto Cornelius was departed, he called two of his household servants, and a devout soldier of them that waited on him continually;

8 And when he had declared all *these* things unto them, he sent them to Joppa.

9 ¶ On the morrow, as they went on their journey, and drew nigh unto the city, Peter went up upon the housetop to pray about the sixth hour:

10 And he became very hungry, and would have eaten: but while they

λαῷ καὶ δεόμενος τοῦ θεοῦ διὰ παντός,
people and petitioning – God continually,

3 εἶδεν ἐν ὁράματι φανερῶς, ὡσεὶ περὶ
saw in a vision clearly, as it were around

ὥραν ἐνάτην τῆς ἡμέρας, ἄγγελον τοῦ
hour ninth of the day, an angel –

θεοῦ εἰσελθόντα πρὸς αὐτὸν καὶ εἰπόντα
of God entering to him and saying

αὐτῷ· Κορνήλιε. 4 ὁ δὲ ἀτενίσας αὐτῷ
to him: Cornelius. And he gazing at him

καὶ ἔμφοβος γενόμενος εἶπεν· τί ἐστιν,
and terrified becoming said: What is it,

κύριε; εἶπεν δὲ αὐτῷ· αἱ προσευχαί
lord? And he said to him: The prayers

σου καὶ αἱ ἐλεημοσύναι σου ἀνέβησαν
of thee and the alms of thee went up

εἰς μνημόσυνον ἔμπροσθεν τοῦ θεοῦ. 5 καὶ
for a memorial before – God. And

νῦν πέμψον ἄνδρας εἰς Ἰόππην καὶ
now send men to Joppa and

μετάπεμψαι Σίμωνά τινα ὃς ἐπικαλεῖται
[summon ²Simon ¹one who is surnamed

Πέτρος· 6 οὗτος ξενίζεται παρά τινι
Peter; this man is lodged with one

Σίμωνι βυρσεῖ, ᾧ ἐστιν οἰκία παρὰ
Simon a tanner, to whom is a houseᶜ by
= who has a house

θάλασσαν. 7 ὡς δὲ ἀπῆλθεν ὁ ἄγγελος ὁ
[the] sea. And as went away the angel –

λαλῶν αὐτῷ, φωνήσας δύο τῶν οἰκετῶν
speaking to him, calling two of the household
slaves

καὶ στρατιώτην εὐσεβῆ τῶν προσκαρτερούν-
and soldier a devout of the [ones] waiting

των αὐτῷ, 8 καὶ ἐξηγησάμενος ἅπαντα
on him, and explaining all things

αὐτοῖς ἀπέστειλεν αὐτοὺς εἰς τὴν Ἰόππην.
to them sent them to – Joppa.

9 Τῇ δὲ ἐπαύριον ὁδοιπορούντων ἐκείνων
And on the morrow journeying those

καὶ τῇ πόλει ἐγγιζόντων ἀνέβη Πέτρος
and to the city drawing nearᵃ went up Peter
= as they journeyed and drew near to the city

ἐπὶ τὸ δῶμα προσεύξασθαι περὶ ὥραν
onto the roof to pray about hour

ἕκτην. 10 ἐγένετο δὲ πρόσπεινος καὶ
sixth. And he became hungry and

ἤθελεν γεύσασθαι· παρασκευαζόντων δὲ
wished to taste(eat); and preparing
= while they prepared

made ready, he fell into a trance,

11 And saw heaven opened, and a certain vessel descending unto him, as it had been a great sheet knit at the four corners, and let down to the earth:

12 Wherein were all manner of fourfooted beasts of the earth, and wild beasts, and creeping things, and fowls of the air.

13 And there came a voice to him, Rise, Peter; kill, and eat.

14 But Peter said, Not so, Lord; for I have never eaten any thing that is common or unclean.

15 And the voice *spake* unto him again the second time, What God hath cleansed, *that* call not thou common.

16 This was done thrice: and the vessel was received up again into heaven.

17 Now while Peter doubted in himself what this vision which he had seen should mean, behold, the men which were sent from Cornelius had made enquiry for Simon's house, and stood before the gate,

18 And called, and asked whether Simon, which was surnamed Peter, were lodged there.

19 While Peter thought on the vision, the Spirit said unto him, Behold, three men seek thee.

αὐτῶν ἐγένετο ἐπ᾽ αὐτὸν ἔκστασις, 11 καὶ
them[a] there came on him an ecstasy, and

θεωρεῖ τὸν οὐρανὸν ἀνεῳγμένον καὶ
he beholds the heaven having been opened and

καταβαῖνον σκεῦός τι ὡς ὀθόνην μεγάλην,
coming down a certain vessel like sheet a great,

τέσσαρσιν ἀρχαῖς καθιέμενον ἐπὶ τῆς γῆς,
by four corners being let down onto the earth,

12 ἐν ᾧ ὑπῆρχεν πάντα τὰ τετράποδα
in which were all the quadrupeds

καὶ ἑρπετὰ τῆς γῆς καὶ πετεινὰ τοῦ
and reptiles of the earth and birds of the

οὐρανοῦ. 13 καὶ ἐγένετο φωνὴ πρὸς
heaven(air). And there came a voice to

αὐτόν· ἀναστάς, Πέτρε, θῦσον καὶ φάγε.
him: Rise up, Peter, slay and eat.

14 ὁ δὲ Πέτρος εἶπεν· μηδαμῶς, κύριε,
– But Peter said: Not at all, Lord,

ὅτι οὐδέποτε ἔφαγον πᾶν κοινὸν καὶ
because never did I eat every(any)thing common and

ἀκάθαρτον. 15 καὶ φωνὴ πάλιν ἐκ δευτέρου
unclean. And a voice again a second [time]

πρὸς αὐτόν· ἃ ὁ θεὸς ἐκαθάρισεν σὺ
[came] to him: What things – God cleansed [3]thou

μὴ κοίνου. 16 τοῦτο δὲ ἐγένετο ἐπὶ
[2]not [1]treat [4]as [5]unclean. And this occurred on

τρίς, καὶ εὐθὺς ἀνελήμφθη τὸ σκεῦος
three [occasions], and immediately was taken up the vessel

εἰς τὸν οὐρανόν. 17 Ὡς δὲ ἐν ἑαυτῷ
into – heaven. Now as in himself

διηπόρει ὁ Πέτρος τί ἂν εἴη τὸ ὅραμα
was doubting – Peter what might be the vision

ὃ εἶδεν, ἰδοὺ οἱ ἄνδρες οἱ ἀπεσταλμένοι
which he saw, behold[,] the men – having been sent

ὑπὸ τοῦ Κορνηλίου διερωτήσαντες τὴν
by – Cornelius asking for the

οἰκίαν τοῦ Σίμωνος ἐπέστησαν ἐπὶ τὸν
house – of Simon stood at at the

πυλῶνα, 18 καὶ φωνήσαντες ἐπυνθάνοντο
porch, and calling inquired

εἰ Σίμων ὁ ἐπικαλούμενος Πέτρος ἐνθάδε
if Simon – being surnamed Peter here

ξενίζεται. 19 Τοῦ δὲ Πέτρου διενθυμουμένου[a]
is lodged. – And Peter pondering[a]
= while Peter pondered

περὶ τοῦ ὁράματος εἶπεν τὸ πνεῦμα·
about the vision [3]said [1]the [2]Spirit:

ἰδοὺ ἄνδρες δύο ζητοῦντές σε· 20 ἀλλὰ
Behold[,] men two seeking thee; but

20 Arise therefore, and get thee down, and go with them, doubting nothing: for I have sent them.

21 Then Peter went down to the men which were sent unto him from Cornelius; and said, Behold, I am he whom ye seek: what is the cause wherefore ye are come?

22 And they said, Cornelius the centurion, a just man, and one that feareth God, and of good report among all the nation of the Jews, was warned from God by an holy angel to send for thee into his house, and to hear words of thee.

23 Then called he them in, and lodged *them*. And on the morrow Peter went away with them, and certain brethren from Joppa accompanied him.

24 And the morrow after they entered into Cæsarea. And Cornelius waited for them, and had called together his kinsmen and near friends.

25 And as Peter was coming in, Cornelius met him, and fell down at his feet, and worshipped *him*.

26 But Peter took him up, saying, Stand up; I myself also am a man.

27 And as he talked

ἀναστὰς κατάβηθι, καὶ πορεύου σὺν αὐτοῖς
rising up go down, and go with them

μηδὲν διακρινόμενος, ὅτι ἐγὼ ἀπέσταλκα
nothing doubting, because I have sent

αὐτούς. 21 καταβὰς δὲ Πέτρος πρὸς
them. And going down Peter to

τοὺς ἄνδρας εἶπεν· ἰδοὺ ἐγώ εἰμι ὃν
the men said: Behold[,] I am [he] whom

ζητεῖτε· τίς ἡ αἰτία δι᾽ ἣν πάρεστε;
ye seek; what [is] the cause for which ye are here?

22 οἱ δὲ εἶπαν· Κορνήλιος ἑκατοντάρχης,
And they said: Cornelius a centurion,

ἀνὴρ δίκαιος καὶ φοβούμενος τὸν θεόν,
a man just and fearing - God,

μαρτυρούμενός τε ὑπὸ ὅλου τοῦ ἔθνους
and being witnessed to by all the nation

τῶν Ἰουδαίων, ἐχρηματίσθη ὑπὸ ἀγγέλου
of the Jews, was warned by angel

ἁγίου μεταπέμψασθαί σε εἰς τὸν οἶκον
a holy to summon thee to the house

αὐτοῦ καὶ ἀκοῦσαι ῥήματα παρὰ σοῦ.
of him and to hear words from thee.

23 εἰσκαλεσάμενος οὖν αὐτοὺς ἐξένισεν.
Calling in therefore them he lodged.

Τῇ δὲ ἐπαύριον ἀναστὰς ἐξῆλθεν σὺν
And on the morrow rising up he went forth with

αὐτοῖς, καὶ τινες τῶν ἀδελφῶν τῶν
them, and some of the brothers -

ἀπὸ Ἰόππης συνῆλθον αὐτῷ. 24 τῇ δὲ
from Joppa accompanied him. And on the

ἐπαύριον εἰσῆλθεν εἰς τὴν Καισάρειαν·
morrow he entered into - Cæsarea;

ὁ δὲ Κορνήλιος ἦν προσδοκῶν αὐτούς,
- and Cornelius was awaiting them,

συγκαλεσάμενος τοὺς συγγενεῖς αὐτοῦ καὶ
having called together the relatives of him and

τοὺς ἀναγκαίους φίλους. 25 Ὡς δὲ
the intimate friends. Now when

ἐγένετο τοῦ εἰσελθεῖν τὸν Πέτρον,[b]
it came to pass the to enter - Peter,

= Now it came to pass when Peter entered,

συναντήσας αὐτῷ ὁ Κορνήλιος πεσὼν
[2]meeting [3]him - [1]Cornelius falling

ἐπὶ τοὺς πόδας προσεκύνησεν. 26 ὁ δὲ
at the(his) feet worshipped. - But

Πέτρος ἤγειρεν αὐτὸν λέγων· ἀνάστηθι·
Peter raised him saying: Stand up;

καὶ ἐγὼ αὐτὸς ἄνθρωπός εἰμι. 27 καὶ
also I [my]self a man am. And

with him, he went in, and
found many that were
come together.

28 And he said unto
them, Ye know how that
it is an unlawful thing for a
man that is a Jew to keep
company, or come unto
one of another nation; but
God hath shewed me that
I should not call any man
common or unclean.

29 Therefore came I
unto you without gain-
saying, as soon as I was
sent for: I ask therefore
for what intent ye have
sent for me?

30 And Cornelius said,
Four days ago I was fast-
ing until this hour; and
at the ninth hour I prayed
in my house, and, behold,
a man stood before me in
bright clothing,

31 And said, Cornelius,
thy prayer is heard, and
thine alms are had in
remembrance in the sight
of God.

32 Send therefore to
Joppa, and call hither
Simon, whose surname is
Peter; he is lodged in the
house of *one* Simon a
tanner by the sea side:
who, when he cometh,
shall speak unto thee.

33 Immediately there-
fore I sent to thee; and
thou hast well done that
thou art come. Now there-
fore are we all here present
before God, to hear all
things that are commanded
thee of God.

34¶ Then Peter opened

συνομιλῶν αὐτῷ εἰσῆλθεν, καὶ εὑρίσκει
talking with him he entered, and finds

συνεληλυθότας πολλούς, 28 ἔφη τε πρὸς
having come together many, and said to

αὐτούς· ὑμεῖς ἐπίστασθε ὡς ἀθέμιτόν ἐστιν
them: Ye understand how unlawful it is

ἀνδρὶ Ἰουδαίῳ κολλᾶσθαι ἢ προσέρχεσθαι
for *a man* a Jew to adhere or to approach

ἀλλοφύλῳ· κἀμοὶ ὁ θεὸς ἔδειξεν μηδένα
a foreigner; and to me - God showed ²not any

κοινὸν ἢ ἀκάθαρτον λέγειν ἄνθρωπον·
⁴common ⁵or ⁶unclean ¹to call ³man;

29 διὸ καὶ ἀναντιρρήτως ἦλθον μετα-
wherefore indeed ³unquestioningly ²I came ¹being

πεμφθείς. πυνθάνομαι οὖν, τίνι λόγῳ
summoned. I inquire therefore, for what reason

μετεπέμψασθέ με; 30 καὶ ὁ Κορνήλιος
ye summoned me? And - Cornelius

ἔφη· ἀπὸ τετάρτης ἡμέρας μέχρι ταύτης τῆς
said: From fourth day until this -
= Four days ago

ὥρας ἤμην τὴν ἐνάτην προσευχόμενος
hour I was [at] the ninth praying

ἐν τῷ οἴκῳ μου, καὶ ἰδοὺ ἀνὴρ ἔστη
in the house of me, and behold[,] a man stood

ἐνώπιόν μου ἐν ἐσθῆτι λαμπρᾷ, 31 καὶ
before me in clothing bright, and

φησίν· Κορνήλιε, εἰσηκούσθη σου ἡ
says: Cornelius, was heard of thee the

προσευχὴ καὶ αἱ ἐλεημοσύναι σου ἐμνήσθησαν
prayer and the alms of thee were remembered

ἐνώπιον τοῦ θεοῦ. 32 πέμψον οὖν εἰς
before - God. Send thou therefore to

Ἰόππην καὶ μετακάλεσαι Σίμωνα ὃς ἐπι-
Joppa and send for Simon who is

καλεῖται Πέτρος· οὗτος ξενίζεται ἐν οἰκίᾳ
surnamed Peter; this man is lodged in [the] house

Σίμωνος βυρσέως παρὰ θάλασσαν. 33 ἐξαυτῆς
of Simon a tanner by [the] sea. At once

οὖν ἔπεμψα πρὸς σέ, σύ τε καλῶς
therefore I sent to thee, and thou well

ἐποίησας παραγενόμενος. νῦν οὖν πάντες
didst arriving. Now therefore all

ἡμεῖς ἐνώπιον τοῦ θεοῦ πάρεσμεν ἀκοῦσαι
we before - God are present to hear

πάντα τὰ προστεταγμένα σοι ὑπὸ τοῦ
all the things having been commanded thee by the

κυρίου. 34 Ἀνοίξας δὲ Πέτρος τὸ στόμα
Lord. And opening Peter the(his) mouth

his mouth, and said, Of a
truth I perceive that God is
no respecter of persons:

35 But in every nation
he that feareth him, and
worketh righteousness, is
accepted with him.

36 The word which *God*
sent unto the children of
Israel, preaching peace by
Jesus Christ: (he is Lord
of all:)

37 That word, *I say*, ye
know, which was published
throughout all Judæa, and
began from Galilee, after
the baptism which John
preached;

38 How God anointed
Jesus of Nazareth with
the Holy Ghost and with
power: who went about
doing good, and healing
all that were oppressed of
the devil; for God was
with him.

39 And we are witnesses
of all things which he did
both in the land of the
Jews, and in Jerusalem;
whom they slew and
hanged on a tree:

40 Him God raised up
the third day, and shewed
him openly;

41 Not to all the people,
but unto witnesses chosen
before of God, *even* to us,
who did eat and drink with

εἶπεν· ἐπ' ἀληθείας καταλαμβάνομαι ὅτι
said: On(in) truth I perceive that

οὐκ ἔστιν προσωπολήμπτης ὁ θεός, 35 ἀλλ'
³not ²is ⁴a respecter of persons – ¹God, but

ἐν παντὶ ἔθνει ὁ φοβούμενος αὐτὸν καὶ
in every nation the [one] fearing him and

ἐργαζόμενος δικαιοσύνην δεκτὸς αὐτῷ ἐστιν·
working righteousness acceptable to him is;

36 τὸν λόγον ὃν ἀπέστειλεν τοῖς υἱοῖς
the word which he sent to the sons

Ἰσραὴλ εὐαγγελιζόμενος εἰρήνην διὰ Ἰησοῦ
of Israel preaching peace through Jesus

Χριστοῦ· οὗτός ἐστιν πάντων κύριος.
Christ: this one is of all Lord.

37 ὑμεῖς οἴδατε τὸ γενόμενον ῥῆμα καθ'
Ye know the having become thing throughout
=that which took place

ὅλης τῆς Ἰουδαίας, ἀρξάμενος ἀπὸ τῆς
all – Judæa, beginning from

Γαλιλαίας μετὰ τὸ βάπτισμα ὃ ἐκήρυξεν
Galilee after the baptism which ²proclaimed

Ἰωάννης, 38 Ἰησοῦν τὸν ἀπὸ Ναζαρέθ,
¹John, Jesus the one from Nazareth,

ὡς ἔχρισεν αὐτὸν ὁ θεὸς πνεύματι ἁγίῳ
how anointed him – God with Spirit Holy

καὶ δυνάμει, ὃς διῆλθεν εὐεργετῶν καὶ
and power, who went about doing good and

ἰώμενος πάντας τοὺς καταδυναστευομένους
curing all the [ones] being oppressed

ὑπὸ τοῦ διαβόλου, ὅτι ὁ θεὸς ἦν μετ'
by the devil, because – God was with

αὐτοῦ· 39 καὶ ἡμεῖς μάρτυρες πάντων
him; and we [are] witnesses of all things

ὧν ἐποίησεν ἔν τε τῇ χώρᾳ τῶν Ἰουδαίων
which he did both in the country of the Jews

καὶ Ἰερουσαλήμ· ὃν καὶ ἀνεῖλαν
and Jerusalem; whom indeed they killed

κρεμάσαντες ἐπὶ ξύλου. 40 τοῦτον ὁ
hanging on a tree. This one –

θεὸς ἤγειρεν ἐν τῇ τρίτῃ ἡμέρᾳ καὶ
God raised on the third day and

ἔδωκεν αὐτὸν ἐμφανῆ γενέσθαι, 41 οὐ
gave him visible to become, not

παντὶ τῷ λαῷ, ἀλλὰ μάρτυσιν τοῖς
to all the people, but to witnesses –

προκεχειροτονημένοις ὑπὸ τοῦ θεοῦ, ἡμῖν,
having been previously appointed by – God, to us,

οἵτινες συνεφάγομεν καὶ συνεπίομεν αὐτῷ
who ate with and drank with him

him after he rose from the dead.

42 And he commanded us to preach unto the people, and to testify that it is he which was ordained of God *to be* the Judge of quick and dead.

43 To him give all the prophets witness, that through his name whosoever believeth in him shall receive remission of sins.

44 ¶ While Peter yet spake these words, the Holy Ghost fell on all them which heard the word.

45 And they of the circumcision which believed were astonished, as many as came with Peter, because that on the Gentiles also was poured out the gift of the Holy Ghost.

46 For they heard them speak with tongues, and magnify God. Then answered Peter,

47 Can any man forbid water, that these should not be baptized, which have received the Holy Ghost as well as we?

48 And he commanded them to be baptized in the name of the Lord. Then prayed they him to tarry certain days.

μετὰ τὸ ἀναστῆναι αὐτὸν ἐκ νεκρῶν·
after the to rise again him[b] out of [the] dead;
=he rose again

42 καὶ παρήγγειλεν ἡμῖν κηρῦξαι τῷ λαῷ
and he commanded us to proclaim to the people

καὶ διαμαρτύρασθαι ὅτι οὗτός ἐστιν ὁ
and solemnly to witness that this man is the [one]

ὡρισμένος ὑπὸ τοῦ θεοῦ κριτὴς ζώντων
having been by – God judge of living
designated

καὶ νεκρῶν. 43 τούτῳ πάντες οἱ προφῆται
and of dead. To this man all the prophets

μαρτυροῦσιν, ἄφεσιν ἁμαρτιῶν λαβεῖν διὰ
witness, [6]forgiveness [7]of sins [5]to receive [8]through

τοῦ ὀνόματος αὐτοῦ πάντα τὸν πιστεύοντα
[9]the [10]name [11]of him [1]everyone [2]believing

εἰς αὐτόν. 44 Ἔτι λαλοῦντος τοῦ Πέτρου
[3]in [4]him. Yet speaking – Peter[a]
=While Peter was still speaking

τὰ ῥήματα ταῦτα ἐπέπεσεν τὸ πνεῦμα
these words [4]fell *on* [1]the [3]Spirit

τὸ ἅγιον ἐπὶ πάντας τοὺς ἀκούοντας
– [2]Holy on all the [ones] hearing

τὸν λόγον. 45 καὶ ἐξέστησαν οἱ ἐκ
the discourse. And [5]were amazed [1]the [3]of [the]

περιτομῆς πιστοὶ ὅσοι συνῆλθαν τῷ Πέτρῳ,
[4]circumcision [2]faithful as many as accompanied – Peter,

ὅτι καὶ ἐπὶ τὰ ἔθνη ἡ δωρεὰ τοῦ ἁγίου
because also on the nations the gift of the Holy

πνεύματος ἐκκέχυται· 46 ἤκουον γὰρ
Spirit has been poured out; for they heard

αὐτῶν λαλούντων γλώσσαις καὶ μεγαλυνόν-
them speaking in tongues and magnify-

των τὸν θεόν. τότε ἀπεκρίθη Πέτρος·
ing – God. Then answered Peter:

47 μήτι τὸ ὕδωρ δύναται κωλῦσαί τις
Not [4]the [5]water [1]can [2]to forbid [3]anyone

τοῦ μὴ βαπτισθῆναι τούτους, οἵτινες τὸ
– [7]not [8]to be baptized[d] [6]these, who the

πνεῦμα τὸ ἅγιον ἔλαβον ὡς καὶ ἡμεῖς;
Spirit – Holy received as also we?

48 προσέταξεν δὲ αὐτοὺς ἐν τῷ ὀνόματι
And he commanded them in the name

Ἰησοῦ Χριστοῦ βαπτισθῆναι. τότε ἠρώτησαν
of Jesus Christ to be baptized. Then they asked

αὐτὸν ἐπιμεῖναι ἡμέρας τινάς.
him to remain days some.

CHAPTER 11

AND the apostles and brethren that were in Judæa heard that the Gentiles had also received the word of God.

2 And when Peter was come up to Jerusalem, they that were of the circumcision contended with him,

3 Saying, Thou wentest in to men uncircumcised, and didst eat with them.

4 But Peter rehearsed *the matter* from the beginning, and expounded *it* by order unto them, saying,

5 I was in the city of Joppa praying: and in a trance I saw a vision, A certain vessel descend, as it had been a great sheet, let down from heaven by four corners; and it came even to me:

6 Upon the which when I had fastened mine eyes, I considered, and saw fourfooted beasts of the earth, and wild beasts, and creeping things, and fowls of the air.

7 And I heard a voice saying unto me, Arise, Peter; slay and eat.

8 But I said, Not so, Lord: for nothing common or unclean hath at any time entered into my mouth.

9 But the voice answered me again from heaven, What God hath cleansed, *that* call not thou common.

10 And this was done three times: and all were

11 Ἤκουσαν δὲ οἱ ἀπόστολοι καὶ οἱ
Now heard the apostles and the

ἀδελφοὶ οἱ ὄντες κατὰ τὴν Ἰουδαίαν
brothers – being throughout – Judæa

ὅτι καὶ τὰ ἔθνη ἐδέξαντο τὸν λόγον
that also the nations received the word

τοῦ θεοῦ. 2 Ὅτε δὲ ἀνέβη Πέτρος εἰς
– of God. And when went up Peter to

Ἱερουσαλήμ, διεκρίνοντο πρὸς αὐτὸν οἱ
Jerusalem, disputed with him the [ones]

ἐκ περιτομῆς 3 λέγοντες ὅτι εἰσῆλθες
of [the] circumcision saying[,] – Thou enteredst

πρὸς ἄνδρας ἀκροβυστίαν ἔχοντας καὶ
to men uncircumcision having and

συνέφαγες αὐτοῖς. 4 ἀρξάμενος δὲ Πέτρος
didst eat with them. And beginning Peter

ἐξετίθετο αὐτοῖς καθεξῆς λέγων· 5 ἐγὼ
explained to them in order saying: I

ἤμην ἐν πόλει Ἰόππῃ προσευχόμενος, καὶ
was in [the] city Joppa praying, and

εἶδον ἐν ἐκστάσει ὅραμα, καταβαῖνον
I saw in an ecstasy a vision, coming down

σκεῦός τι ὡς ὀθόνην μεγάλην τέσσαρσιν
a certain vessel as sheet a great by four

ἀρχαῖς καθιεμένην ἐκ τοῦ οὐρανοῦ, καὶ
corners having been let down out of heaven, and

ἦλθεν ἄχρι ἐμοῦ· 6 εἰς ἣν ἀτενίσας
it came up to me; into which gazing

κατενόουν, καὶ εἶδον τὰ τετράποδα τῆς
I perceived, and I saw the quadrupeds of the

γῆς καὶ τὰ θηρία καὶ τὰ ἑρπετὰ καὶ τὰ
earth and the wild beasts and the reptiles and the

πετεινὰ τοῦ οὐρανοῦ. 7 ἤκουσα δὲ καὶ
birds of the heaven(air). And I heard also

φωνῆς λεγούσης μοι· ἀναστάς, Πέτρε,
a voice saying to me: Rise up, Peter,

θῦσον καὶ φάγε. 8 εἶπον δέ· μηδαμῶς,
slay and eat. And I said : Not at all,

κύριε, ὅτι κοινὸν ἢ ἀκάθαρτον οὐδέποτε
Lord, because a common or unclean thing never

εἰσῆλθεν εἰς τὸ στόμα μου. 9 ἀπεκρίθη δὲ
entered into the mouth of me. And answered

ἐκ δευτέρου φωνὴ ἐκ τοῦ οὐρανοῦ·
a second [time] a voice out of heaven:

ἃ ὁ θεὸς ἐκαθάρισεν σὺ μὴ κοίνου.
What – God cleansed thou regard not common.
things

10 τοῦτο δὲ ἐγένετο ἐπὶ τρίς, καὶ
And this happened on three [occasions], and

drawn up again into heaven.

11 And, behold, immediately there were three men already come unto the house where I was, sent from Cæsarea unto me.

12 And the Spirit bade me go with them, nothing doubting. Moreover these six brethren accompanied me, and we entered into the man's house:

13 And he shewed us how he had seen an angel in his house, which stood and said unto him, Send men to Joppa, and call for Simon, whose surname is Peter;

14 Who shall tell thee words, whereby thou and all thy house shall be saved.

15 And as I began to speak, the Holy Ghost fell on them, as on us at the beginning.

16 Then remembered I the word of the Lord, how that he said, John indeed baptized with water; but ye shall be baptized with the Holy Ghost.

17 Forasmuch then as God gave them the like gift as *he did* unto us, who believed on the Lord Jesus Christ; what was I, that I could withstand God?

18 When they heard these things, they held their

ἀνεσπάσθη πάλιν ἅπαντα εἰς τὸν οὐρανόν.
was pulled up again all things to – heaven.

11 καὶ ἰδοὺ ἐξαυτῆς τρεῖς ἄνδρες ἐπέστησαν
And behold at once three men stood *at*

ἐπὶ τὴν οἰκίαν ἐν ᾗ ἦμεν, ἀπεσταλμένοι
at the house in which I was, having been sent

ἀπὸ Καισαρείας πρός με. 12 εἶπεν δὲ
from Cæsarea to me. And ³told

τὸ πνεῦμά μοι συνελθεῖν αὐτοῖς μηδὲν
¹the ²Spirit ⁴me to go with them nothing

διακρίναντα. ἦλθον δὲ σὺν ἐμοὶ καὶ
doubting. And came with me also

οἱ ἓξ ἀδελφοὶ οὗτοι, καὶ εἰσήλθομεν εἰς
– six brothers these, and we entered into

τὸν οἶκον τοῦ ἀνδρός. 13 ἀπήγγειλεν δὲ
the house of the man. And he reported

ἡμῖν πῶς εἶδεν τὸν ἄγγελον ἐν τῷ
to us how he saw the angel in the

οἴκῳ αὐτοῦ σταθέντα καὶ εἰπόντα·
house of him standing and saying:

ἀπόστειλον εἰς Ἰόππην καὶ μετάπεμψαι
Send to Joppa and summon

Σίμωνα τὸν ἐπικαλούμενον Πέτρον, 14 ὃς
Simon – *being* surnamed Peter, who

λαλήσει ῥήματα πρὸς σὲ ἐν οἷς σωθήσῃ
will speak words to thee by which mayest be saved

σὺ καὶ πᾶς ὁ οἶκός σου. 15 ἐν δὲ
thou and all the household of thee. And in

τῷ ἄρξασθαί με λαλεῖν ἐπέπεσεν τὸ
the to begin me^be to speak ⁴fell *on* ¹the
=as I began

πνεῦμα τὸ ἅγιον ἐπ᾽ αὐτοὺς ὥσπερ καὶ
³Spirit – ²Holy on them as also

ἐφ᾽ ἡμᾶς ἐν ἀρχῇ. 16 ἐμνήσθην δὲ τοῦ
on us at [the] beginning. And I remembered the

ῥήματος τοῦ κυρίου, ὡς ἔλεγεν· Ἰωάννης
word of the Lord, how he said: John

μὲν ἐβάπτισεν ὕδατι, ὑμεῖς δὲ βαπτισθήσεσθε
indeed baptized with water, but ye will be baptized

ἐν πνεύματι ἁγίῳ. 17 εἰ οὖν τὴν ἴσην
in Spirit Holy. If therefore ⁴the ⁵equal

δωρεὰν ἔδωκεν αὐτοῖς ὁ θεὸς ὡς καὶ
⁶gift ²gave ³them – ¹God as also

ἡμῖν, πιστεύσασιν ἐπὶ τὸν κύριον Ἰησοῦν
to us, having believed on the Lord Jesus

Χριστόν, ἐγὼ τίς ἤμην δυνατὸς κωλῦσαι
Christ, ³I ¹who ²was [to be] able to hinder

τὸν θεόν; 18 ἀκούσαντες δὲ ταῦτα ἡσύχασαν,
– God? And hearing these things they kept silence

peace, and glorified God, saying, Then hath God also to the Gentiles granted repentance unto life.

19 ¶ Now they which were scattered abroad upon the persecution that arose about Stephen travelled as far as Phenice, and Cyprus, and Antioch, preaching the word to none but unto the Jews only.

20 And some of them were men of Cyprus and Cyrene, which, when they were come to Antioch, spake unto the Grecians, preaching the Lord Jesus.

21 And the hand of the Lord was with them: and a great number believed, and turned unto the Lord.

22 ¶ Then tidings of these things came unto the ears of the church which was in Jerusalem: and they sent forth Barnabas, that he should go as far as Antioch.

23 Who, when he came, and had seen the grace of God, was glad, and exhorted them all, that with purpose of heart they would cleave unto the Lord.

24 For he was a good man, and full of the Holy Ghost and of faith: and much people was added unto the Lord.

καὶ ἐδόξασαν τὸν θεὸν λέγοντες· ἄρα καὶ
and glorified – God saying: Then also
τοῖς ἔθνεσιν ὁ θεὸς τὴν μετάνοιαν εἰς
to the nations – God – repentance to
ζωὴν ἔδωκεν.
life gave.

19 Οἱ μὲν οὖν διασπαρέντες ἀπὸ τῆς
The [ones] – therefore being scattered from the
θλίψεως τῆς γενομένης ἐπὶ Στεφάνῳ
affliction – occurring over Stephen
διῆλθον ἕως Φοινίκης καὶ Κύπρου καὶ
passed through to Phœnicia and Cyprus and
'Αντιοχείας, μηδενὶ λαλοῦντες τὸν λόγον
Antioch, to no one speaking the word
εἰ μὴ μόνον 'Ιουδαίοις. **20** 'Ησαν δὲ
except only to Jews. But ⁴were
τινες ἐξ αὐτῶν ἄνδρες Κύπριοι καὶ
¹some ²of ³them *men* Cypriotes and
Κυρηναῖοι, οἵτινες ἐλθόντες εἰς 'Αντιόχειαν
Cyrenians, who coming to Antioch
ἐλάλουν καὶ πρὸς τοὺς ῞Ελληνας,
spoke also to the Greeks,
εὐαγγελιζόμενοι τὸν κύριον 'Ιησοῦν. **21** καὶ ἦν
preaching the Lord Jesus. And was
χεὶρ κυρίου μετ' αὐτῶν, πολύς τε
[the] hand of [the] Lord with them, and a much(great)
ἀριθμὸς ὁ πιστεύσας ἐπέστρεψεν ἐπὶ τὸν
number – believing turned to the
κύριον. **22** 'Ηκούσθη δὲ ὁ λόγος εἰς
Lord. And was heard the account in
τὰ ὦτα τῆς ἐκκλησίας τῆς οὔσης ἐν
the ears of the church – being in
'Ιερουσαλὴμ περὶ αὐτῶν, καὶ ἐξαπέστειλαν
Jerusalem about them, and they sent out
Βαρναβᾶν ἕως 'Αντιοχείας· **23** ὃς παραγεν-
Barnabas to Antioch; who arriv-
όμενος καὶ ἰδὼν τὴν χάριν τὴν τοῦ
ing and seeing the grace – of
θεοῦ ἐχάρη, καὶ παρεκάλει πάντας τῇ
of God rejoiced, and exhorted all –
προθέσει τῆς καρδίας προσμένειν τῷ
with purpose – of heart to remain with the
κυρίῳ, **24** ὅτι ἦν ἀνὴρ ἀγαθὸς καὶ
Lord, because he was man a good and
πλήρης πνεύματος ἁγίου καὶ πίστεως.
full of [the] Spirit Holy and of faith.
καὶ προσετέθη ὄχλος ἱκανὸς τῷ κυρίῳ.
And was added a crowd considerable to the Lord.

25 Then departed Barnabas to Tarsus, for to seek Saul:
26 And when he had found him, he brought him unto Antioch. And it came to pass, that a whole year they assembled themselves with the church, and taught much people. And the disciples were called Christians first in Antioch.
27 ¶ And in these days came prophets from Jerusalem unto Antioch.
28 And there stood up one of them named Agabus, and signified by the spirit that there should be great dearth throughout all the world: which came to pass in the days of Claudius Cæsar.
29 Then the disciples, every man according to his ability, determined to send relief unto the brethren which dwelt in Judæa:
30 Which also they did, and sent it to the elders by the hands of Barnabas and Saul.

25 ἐξῆλθεν δὲ εἰς Ταρσὸν ἀναζητῆσαι
And he went forth　to　Tarsus　to seek
Σαῦλον, 26 καὶ εὑρὼν ἤγαγεν εἰς Ἀντιόχειαν.
Saul,　　and finding brought to　Antioch.
ἐγένετο δὲ αὐτοῖς καὶ ἐνιαυτὸν ὅλον
And it happened　to them　also　year　a whole
συναχθῆναι ἐν τῇ ἐκκλησίᾳ καὶ διδάξαι
to be assembled in　the　church　and　to teach
ὄχλον ἱκανόν, χρηματίσαι τε πρώτως ἐν
a crowd considerable,　and to call　firstly　in
Ἀντιοχείᾳ τοὺς μαθητὰς Χριστιανούς.
Antioch　the　disciples　Christians.
27 Ἐν ταύταις δὲ ταῖς ἡμέραις κατῆλθον
And in these　－　days　came down
ἀπὸ Ἱεροσολύμων προφῆται εἰς Ἀντιόχειαν·
from　Jerusalem　prophets　to　Antioch;
28 ἀναστὰς δὲ εἷς ἐξ αὐτῶν ὀνόματι
and rising up　one　of　them　by name
Ἄγαβος ἐσήμαινεν διὰ τοῦ πνεύματος
Agabus　signified　through　the　Spirit
λιμὸν μεγάλην μέλλειν ἔσεσθαι ἐφ' ὅλην τὴν
famine　a great　to be about　to be　over　all　the
οἰκουμένην· ἥτις ἐγένετο ἐπὶ Κλαυδίου.
inhabited earth;　which　happened　in the time of Claudius.
29 τῶν δὲ μαθητῶν καθὼς εὐπορεῖτό
So ²of the　⁴disciples　¹as　⁶was prosperous
τις, ὥρισαν ἕκαστος αὐτῶν εἰς διακονίαν
³anyone, they determined　each　of them　for ministration
πέμψαι τοῖς κατοικοῦσιν ἐν τῇ Ἰουδαίᾳ
to send　¹to the　³dwelling　⁴in　－　⁵Judæa
ἀδελφοῖς· 30 ὃ καὶ ἐποίησαν ἀποστείλαντες
²brothers;　which indeed　they did　sending
πρὸς τοὺς πρεσβυτέρους διὰ χειρὸς
to　the　elders　through [the] hand
Βαρναβᾶ καὶ Σαύλου.
of Barnabas and　of Saul.

CHAPTER 12

NOW about that time Herod the king stretched forth *his* hands to vex certain of the church.
2 And he killed James the brother of John with the sword.
3 And because he saw it pleased the Jews, he

12 Κατ' ἐκεῖνον δὲ τὸν καιρὸν ἐπέβαλεν
Now at that　－　time　laid on
Ἡρώδης ὁ βασιλεὺς τὰς χεῖρας κακῶσαί
Herod　the　king　the(his) hands　to ill-treat
τινας τῶν ἀπὸ τῆς ἐκκλησίας. 2 ἀνεῖλεν δὲ
some of the[ones] from the　church.　And he killed
Ἰάκωβον τὸν ἀδελφὸν Ἰωάννου μαχαίρῃ.
James　the　brother　of John　with a sword.
3 ἰδὼν δὲ ὅτι ἀρεστόν ἐστιν τοῖς Ἰουδαίοις
And seeing　that　pleasing　it is(was) to the　Jews

proceeded further to take Peter also. (Then were the days of unleavened bread.)

4 And when he had apprehended him, he put *him* in prison, and delivered *him* to four quaternions of soldiers to keep him; intending after Easter to bring him forth to the people.

5 Peter therefore was kept in prison: but prayer was made without ceasing of the church unto God for him.

6 And when Herod would have brought him forth, the same night Peter was sleeping between two soldiers, bound with two chains: and the keepers before the door kept the prison.

7 And, behold, the angel of the Lord came upon *him*, and a light shined in the prison: and he smote Peter on the side, and raised him up, saying, Arise up quickly. And his chains fell off from *his* hands.

8 And the angel said unto him, Gird thyself, and bind on thy sandals. And so he did. And he saith unto him, Cast thy garment about thee, and follow me.

9 And he went out, and followed him; and wist

προσέθετο συλλαβεῖν καὶ Πέτρον, ἦσαν δὲ
he added   to arrest   also   Peter,   and they were

ἡμέραι τῶν ἀζύμων, 4 ὃν καὶ πιάσας
days   –   of unleavened bread, whom also seizing

ἔθετο εἰς φυλακήν, παραδοὺς τέσσαρσιν
he put in prison,   delivering   to four

τετραδίοις στρατιωτῶν φυλάσσειν αὐτόν,
quaternions of soldiers   to guard   him,

βουλόμενος μετὰ τὸ πάσχα ἀναγαγεῖν
intending   after the Passover to bring up

αὐτὸν τῷ λαῷ. 5 ὁ μὲν οὖν Πέτρος
him   to the people. – * therefore Peter

ἐτηρεῖτο ἐν τῇ φυλακῇ· προσευχὴ δὲ ἦν
was kept in the prison; but prayer   was

ἐκτενῶς γινομένη ὑπὸ τῆς ἐκκλησίας πρὸς
earnestly being made by the church   to

τὸν θεὸν περὶ αὐτοῦ. 6 Ὅτε δὲ ἤμελλεν
–   God concerning him.   And when ²was about

προαγαγεῖν αὐτὸν ὁ Ἡρῴδης, τῇ νυκτὶ
³to bring forward ⁴him – ¹Herod, – ²night

ἐκείνῃ ἦν ὁ Πέτρος κοιμώμενος μεταξὺ
¹in that was – Peter   sleeping   between

δύο στρατιωτῶν δεδεμένος ἁλύσεσιν δυσίν,
two soldiers   having been bound with chains two,

φύλακές τε πρὸ τῆς θύρας ἐτήρουν τὴν
and guards   before the door were keeping the

φυλακήν. 7 καὶ ἰδοὺ ἄγγελος κυρίου
prison.   And behold[,] an angel of [the] Lord

ἐπέστη, καὶ φῶς ἔλαμψεν ἐν τῷ οἰκήματι·
came upon, and a light shone in the building;

πατάξας δὲ τὴν πλευρὰν τοῦ Πέτρου
and striking the side   –   of Peter

ἤγειρεν αὐτὸν λέγων· ἀνάστα ἐν τάχει.
he raised him   saying: Rise up in haste.

καὶ ἐξέπεσαν αὐτοῦ αἱ ἁλύσεις ἐκ τῶν
And fell off   of him the chains   off the(his)

χειρῶν. 8 εἶπεν δὲ ὁ ἄγγελος πρὸς
hands.   And said the   angel   to

αὐτόν· ζῶσαι καὶ ὑπόδησαι τὰ σανδάλιά
him: Gird thyself and put on   the sandals

σου. ἐποίησεν δὲ οὕτως. καὶ λέγει
of thee. And he did so.   And he tells

αὐτῷ· περιβαλοῦ τὸ ἱμάτιόν σου καὶ
him: Cast round the garment of thee and

ἀκολούθει μοι. 9 καὶ ἐξελθὼν ἠκολούθει,
follow   me.   And going forth he followed,

* μέν and δέ are in contrast : " on one hand ... "—"on the other ... "

not that it was true which
was done by the angel;
but thought he saw a
vision.

10 When they were past
the first and the second
ward, they came unto the
iron gate that leadeth unto
the city; which opened
to them of his own accord:
and they went out, and
passed on through one
street; and forthwith the
angel departed from him.

11 And when Peter was
come to himself, he said,
Now I know of a surety,
that the Lord hath sent
his angel, and hath de-
livered me out of the
hand of Herod, and *from*
all the expectation of the
people of the Jews.

12 And when he had
considered *the thing*, he
came to the house of
Mary the mother of John,
whose surname was Mark;
where many were gathered
together praying.

13 And as Peter
knocked at the door of
the gate, a damsel came
to hearken, named Rhoda.

14 And when she knew
Peter's voice, she opened
not the gate for gladness,
but ran in, and told how
Peter stood before the
gate.

15 And they said unto
her, Thou art mad. But
she constantly affirmed

καὶ   οὐκ   ᾔδει   ὅτι   ἀληθές ἐστιν   τὸ
and   knew not   that   ³true ²is(was) ¹the thing
γινόμενον   διὰ   τοῦ   ἀγγέλου,   ἐδόκει   δὲ
happening   through the   angel,   but he thought
ὅραμα   βλέπειν.   10 διελθόντες   δὲ   πρώτην
a vision to see.   And going through [the] first
φυλακὴν   καὶ   δευτέραν   ἦλθαν   ἐπὶ   τὴν
prison   and   [the] second they came on   the
πύλην   τὴν   σιδηρᾶν   τὴν   φέρουσαν   εἰς   τὴν
gate   -   iron   -   leading   to   the
πόλιν,   ἥτις   αὐτομάτη   ἠνοίγη   αὐτοῖς,   καὶ
city,   which   of itself   was opened to them,   and
ἐξελθόντες   προῆλθον   ῥύμην   μίαν,   καὶ
going out   they went forward street   one,   and
εὐθέως   ἀπέστη   ὁ   ἄγγελος   ἀπ'   αὐτοῦ.
immediately departed the   angel   from   him.

11 καὶ   ὁ   Πέτρος   ἐν   ἑαυτῷ   γενόμενος
   And   -   Peter   in   himself   having become
εἶπεν·   νῦν   οἶδα   ἀληθῶς   ὅτι   ἐξαπέστειλεν
said: Now   I know   truly   that   sent forth
ὁ   κύριος   τὸν   ἄγγελον   αὐτοῦ   καὶ   ἐξείλατό
the   Lord   the   angel   of him   and   delivered
με   ἐκ   χειρὸς   Ἡρῴδου   καὶ   πάσης   τῆς
me   out of [the] hand of Herod   and   of all   the
προσδοκίας   τοῦ   λαοῦ   τῶν   Ἰουδαίων.
expectation   of the   people   of the   Jews.

12 συνιδών   τε   ἦλθεν   ἐπὶ   τὴν   οἰκίαν   τῆς
   And realizing   he came on   the   house   -
Μαρίας   τῆς   μητρὸς   Ἰωάννου   τοῦ
of Mary   the   mother   of John   -
ἐπικαλουμένου   Μάρκου,   οὗ   ἦσαν   ἱκανοὶ
being surnamed   Mark,   where   were   many
συνηθροισμένοι   καὶ   προσευχόμενοι.   13 κρού-
having been assembled and   praying.   And
σαντος   δὲ   αὐτοῦ   τὴν   θύραν   τοῦ   πυλῶνος
knocking   himᵃ   the   door   of the   porch
=as he knocked
προσῆλθεν   παιδίσκη   ὑπακοῦσαι   ὀνόματι
approached   a maidservant to listen   by name
Ῥόδη,   14 καὶ   ἐπιγνοῦσα   τὴν   φωνὴν   τοῦ
Rhoda,   and   recognizing   the   voice   -
Πέτρου   ἀπὸ   τῆς   χαρᾶς   οὐκ   ἤνοιξεν   τὸν
of Peter   from   -   joy   she did not open the
πυλῶνα,   εἰσδραμοῦσα   δὲ   ἀπήγγειλεν   ἑστάναι
porch,   but running in   announced   ²to stand
τὸν   Πέτρον   πρὸ   τοῦ   πυλῶνος.   15 οἱ   δὲ
-      ¹Peter   before the   porch.   But they
πρὸς   αὐτὴν   εἶπαν·   μαίνῃ.   ἡ   δὲ   διϊσχυρίζετο
to   her   said: Thou ravest. But she emphatically asserted

that it was even so. Then said they, It is his angel.

16 But Peter continued knocking: and when they had opened *the door*, and saw him, they were astonished.

17 But he, beckoning unto them with the hand to hold their peace, declared unto them how the Lord had brought him out of the prison. And he said, Go shew these things unto James, and to the brethren. And he departed, and went into another place.

18 Now as soon as it was day, there was no small stir among the soldiers, what was become of Peter.

19 And when Herod had sought for him, and found him not, he examined the keepers, and commanded that *they* should be put to death. And he went down from Judæa to Cæsarea, and *there* abode.

20 ¶ And Herod was highly displeased with them of Tyre and Sidon: but they came with one accord to him, and, having made Blastus the king's chamberlain their friend, desired peace; because their country was nourished by the king's *country*.

21 And upon a set day Herod, arrayed in royal apparel, sat upon his throne, and made an oration unto them.

οὕτως ἔχειν. οἱ δὲ ἔλεγον· ὁ ἄγγελός
so to have(be). So they said: The angel

ἐστιν αὐτοῦ. 16 ὁ δὲ Πέτρος ἐπέμενεν
it is of him. – But Peter continued

κρούων· ἀνοίξαντες δὲ εἶδαν αὐτὸν καὶ
knocking; and having opened they saw him and

ἐξέστησαν. 17 κατασείσας δὲ αὐτοῖς τῇ
were amazed. And beckoning to them with the

χειρὶ σιγᾶν διηγήσατο αὐτοῖς πῶς ὁ
hand to be quiet he related to them how the

κύριος αὐτὸν ἐξήγαγεν ἐκ τῆς φυλακῆς,
Lord him led *out* out of the prison,

εἶπέν τε· ἀπαγγείλατε Ἰακώβῳ καὶ τοῖς
and said: Report to James and to the

ἀδελφοῖς ταῦτα. καὶ ἐξελθὼν ἐπορεύθη εἰς
brothers these things. And going out he went to

ἕτερον τόπον. 18 Γενομένης δὲ ἡμέρας ἦν
another place. And becoming day[a] there was
　　　　　　　　　　=when it became day

τάραχος οὐκ ὀλίγος ἐν τοῖς στρατιώταις,
disturbance not a little among the soldiers,

τί ἄρα ὁ Πέτρος ἐγένετο. 19 Ἡρώδης δὲ
what then – [of] Peter became. And Herod

ἐπιζητήσας αὐτὸν καὶ μὴ εὑρών,
searching for him and not finding,

ἀνακρίνας τοὺς φύλακας ἐκέλευσεν ἀπ-
examining the guards commanded to

αχθῆναι, καὶ κατελθὼν ἀπὸ τῆς Ἰουδαίας
be led away,* and going down from – Judæa

εἰς Καισάρειαν διέτριβεν. 20 Ἦν δὲ
to Cæsarea stayed. Now he was

θυμομαχῶν Τυρίοις καὶ Σιδωνίοις·
being furiously angry with Tyrians and Sidonians;

ὁμοθυμαδὸν δὲ παρῆσαν πρὸς αὐτόν, καὶ
and with one mind they came to him, and

πείσαντες Βλάστον τὸν ἐπὶ τοῦ κοιτῶνος
having persuaded Blastus the one over the bedchamber

τοῦ βασιλέως ἠτοῦντο εἰρήνην, διὰ τὸ
of the king they asked peace, because the

τρέφεσθαι αὐτῶν τὴν χώραν ἀπὸ τῆς
to be fed of them the country[b] from the
　　　　　　　　　　　=their country was fed

βασιλικῆς. 21 τακτῇ δὲ ἡμέρᾳ ὁ Ἡρώδης
royal. And on an appointed day – Herod

ἐνδυσάμενος ἐσθῆτα βασιλικὴν καθίσας ἐπὶ
having been arrayed with clothing regal sitting on

τοῦ βήματος ἐδημηγόρει πρὸς αὐτούς·
the tribunal made a public speech to them;

* That is, to execution.

22 And the people gave a shout, *saying, It is* the voice of a god, and not of a man.

23 And immediately the angel of the Lord smote him, because he gave not God the glory: and he was eaten of worms, and gave up the ghost.

24 ¶ But the word of God grew and multiplied.

25 And Barnabas and Saul returned from Jerusalem, when they had fulfilled *their* ministry, and took with them John, whose surname was Mark.

22 ὁ δὲ δῆμος ἐπεφώνει· θεοῦ φωνὴ
and the　mob　cried out :　Of a god　a voice
καὶ οὐκ ἀνθρώπου. 23 παραχρῆμα δὲ
and　not　of a man.　　　　　And at once
ἐπάταξεν αὐτὸν ἄγγελος κυρίου ἀνθ’ ὧν
smote　him　an angel　of [the] Lord　because
οὐκ ἔδωκεν τὴν δόξαν τῷ θεῷ, καὶ
he gave not　the　glory　–　to God,　and
γενόμενος σκωληκόβρωτος ἐξέψυξεν.
becoming　eaten by worms　he expired.
24 Ὁ δὲ λόγος τοῦ κυρίου ηὔξανεν
But the　word　of the　Lord　grew
καὶ ἐπληθύνετο. 25 Βαρναβᾶς δὲ καὶ
and　increased.　　　And Barnabas　and
Σαῦλος ὑπέστρεψαν ἐξ Ἰερουσαλήμ,
Saul　returned　out of　Jerusalem,
πληρώσαντες τὴν διακονίαν, συμπαρα-
having completed　the　ministration,　taking
λαβόντες Ἰωάννην τὸν ἐπικληθέντα Μᾶρκον.
with [them]　John　–　surnamed　Mark.

CHAPTER 13

NOW there were in the church that was at Antioch certain prophets and teachers; as Barnabas, and Simeon that was called Niger, and Lucius of Cyrene, and Manaen, which had been brought up with Herod the tetrarch, and Saul.

2 As they ministered to the Lord, and fasted, the Holy Ghost said, Separate me Barnabas and Saul for the work whereunto I have called them.

3 And when they had fasted and prayed, and laid *their* hands on them, they sent *them* away.

4 ¶ So they, being sent

13 Ἦσαν δὲ ἐν Ἀντιοχείᾳ κατὰ τὴν
Now there were　in　Antioch　among　the
οὖσαν ἐκκλησίαν προφῆται καὶ διδάσκαλοι
existing　church　prophets　and　teachers
ὅ τε Βαρναβᾶς καὶ Συμεὼν ὁ καλούμενος
– both　Barnabas　and　Simeon　–　being called
Νίγερ, καὶ Λούκιος ὁ Κυρηναῖος, Μαναήν τε
Niger,　and　Lucius　the　Cyrenian,　and Manaen
Ἡρώδου τοῦ τετραάρχου σύντροφος
²of Herod　³the　⁴tetrarch　¹foster brother
καὶ Σαῦλος. 2 Λειτουργούντων δὲ αὐτῶν
and　Saul.　　　And ministering　　them
　　　　　　　　　= as they ministered
τῷ κυρίῳ καὶ νηστευόντων εἶπεν τὸ
to the　Lord　and　fasting　said　the
πνεῦμα τὸ ἅγιον· ἀφορίσατε δή μοι
Spirit　–　Holy:　²Separate ye　¹so then　²to me
τὸν Βαρναβᾶν καὶ Σαῦλον εἰς τὸ ἔργον
–　Barnabas　and　Saul　for　the　work
ὃ προσκέκλημαι αὐτούς· 3 τότε νηστεύ-
[to] which　I have called　them;　then　having
σαντες καὶ προσευξάμενοι καὶ ἐπιθέντες
fasted　and　*having* prayed　and　¹laying ⁴on
τὰς χεῖρας αὐτοῖς ἀπέλυσαν.
²the(ir)　³hands　⁵them　they dismissed [them].
4 Αὐτοὶ μὲν οὖν ἐκπεμφθέντες ὑπὸ τοῦ
They　–　therefore　sent out　by　the

forth by the Holy Ghost, departed unto Seleucia; and from thence they sailed to Cyprus.

5 And when they were at Salamis, they preached the word of God in the synagogues of the Jews: and they had also John to *their* minister.

6 And when they had gone through the isle unto Paphos, they found a certain sorcerer, a false prophet, a Jew, whose name *was* Bar-jesus:

7 Which was with the deputy of the country, Sergius Paulus, a prudent man; who called for Barnabas and Saul, and desired to hear the word of God.

8 But Elymas the sorcerer (for so is his name by interpretation) withstood them, seeking to turn away the deputy from the faith.

9 Then Saul, (who also *is called* Paul,) filled with the Holy Ghost, set his eyes on him,

10 And said, O full of all subtilty and all mischief, *thou* child of the devil, *thou* enemy of all righteousness, wilt thou not cease to pervert the right ways of the Lord?

11 And now, behold, the hand of the Lord *is* upon thee, and thou shalt be blind, not seeing the sun for a season. And immediately there fell on

ἁγίου	πνεύματος	κατῆλθον	εἰς	Σελεύκειαν,
Holy	Spirit	went down	to	Seleucia,

ἐκεῖθέν	τε	ἀπέπλευσαν	εἰς	Κύπρον,	5 καὶ
and thence		sailed away	to	Cyprus,	and

γενόμενοι	ἐν	Σαλαμῖνι	κατήγγελλον	τὸν
being	in	Salamis	they announced	the

λόγον	τοῦ	θεοῦ	ἐν	ταῖς	συναγωγαῖς	τῶν
word	–	of God	in	the	synagogues	of the

Ἰουδαίων·	εἶχον	δὲ	καὶ	Ἰωάννην	ὑπηρέτην.
Jews;	and they had		also	John [as]	attendant.

6 | Διελθόντες | δὲ | ὅλην | τὴν | νῆσον | ἄχρι |
|---|---|---|---|---|---|
| And passing through | | all | the | island | unto |

Πάφου	εὗρον	ἄνδρα	τινὰ	μάγον	ψευδο-
Paphos	they found	a certain man		a sorcerer	a ²false

προφήτην	Ἰουδαῖον,	ᾧ	ὄνομα	Βαριησοῦς,
²prophet	¹Jewish,	to whom	nameᵉ	Barjesus,
			=whose name was	

7 | ὃς | ἦν | σὺν | τῷ | ἀνθυπάτῳ | Σεργίῳ |
|---|---|---|---|---|---|
| who | was | with | the | proconsul | Sergius |

Παύλῳ,	ἀνδρὶ	συνετῷ.	οὗτος	προσ-
Paulus,	man	an intelligent.	This man	calling

καλεσάμενος	Βαρναβᾶν	καὶ	Σαῦλον	ἐπεζήτησεν
to [him]	Barnabas	and	Saul	sought

ἀκοῦσαι	τὸν	λόγον	τοῦ	θεοῦ·	8 ἀνθίστατο	δὲ
to hear	the	word	–	of God;	but opposed	

αὐτοῖς	Ἐλύμας	ὁ	μάγος,	οὕτως	γὰρ
them	Elymas	the	sorcerer,	for so	

μεθερμηνεύεται	τὸ	ὄνομα	αὐτοῦ,	ζητῶν
is translated	the	name	of him,	seeking

διαστρέψαι	τὸν	ἀνθύπατον	ἀπὸ	τῆς
to divert	the	proconsul	from	the

πίστεως.	9 Σαῦλος	δέ,	ὁ	καὶ	Παῦλος,
faith.	But Saul,		the [one]	also	Paul,

πλησθεὶς	πνεύματος	ἁγίου	ἀτενίσας	εἰς
filled	of(with) Spirit	Holy	gazing	at

αὐτὸν	εἶπεν·	10 ὦ	πλήρης	παντὸς	δόλου
him	said:	O	full	of all	deceit

καὶ	πάσης	ῥᾳδιουργίας,	υἱὲ	διαβόλου,
and	of all	fraud,	son	of [the] devil,

ἐχθρὲ	πάσης	δικαιοσύνης,	οὐ	παύσῃ
enemy	of all	righteousness,	wilt thou not cease	

διαστρέφων	τὰς	ὁδοὺς	τοῦ	κυρίου	τὰς
perverting	the	ways	of the	Lord	–

εὐθείας;	11 καὶ	νῦν	ἰδοὺ	χεὶρ	κυρίου
right?	And	now	behold[,]	[the] hand	of [the] Lord

ἐπὶ	σέ,	καὶ	ἔσῃ	τυφλὸς	μὴ	βλέπων
[is] on	thee,	and thou wilt be	blind		not	seeing

τὸν	ἥλιον	ἄχρι	καιροῦ.	παραχρῆμα	δὲ
the	sun	until	[such] a time.	And at once	

him a mist and a darkness; and he went about seeking some to lead him by the hand.

12 Then the deputy, when he saw what was done, believed, being astonished at the doctrine of the Lord.

13 ¶ Now when Paul and his company loosed from Paphos, they came to Perga in Pamphylia: and John departing from them returned to Jerusalem.

14 ¶ But when they departed from Perga, they came to Antioch in Pisidia, and went into the synagogue on the sabbath day, and sat down.

15 And after the reading of the law and the prophets the rulers of the synagogue sent unto them, saying, Ye men *and* brethren, if ye have any word of exhortation for the people, say on.

16 Then Paul stood up, and beckoning with *his* hand said, Men of Israel, and ye that fear God, give audience.

17 The God of this people of Israel chose our fathers, and exalted the people when they dwelt as strangers in the land of Egypt, and with an

ἔπεσεν ἐπ' αὐτὸν ἀχλὺς καὶ σκότος, καὶ
fell   on   him   a mist   and darkness, and

περιάγων ἐζήτει χειραγωγούς.   12 τότε
going about he sought leaders by the hand.   Then

ἰδὼν ὁ   ἀνθύπατος τὸ   γεγονὸς
²seeing ¹the   ²proconsul   the thing having occurred

ἐπίστευσεν, ἐκπλησσόμενος ἐπὶ τῇ διδαχῇ
believed,   being astounded   at the teaching

τοῦ κυρίου.
of the Lord.

13 Ἀναχθέντες δὲ ἀπὸ τῆς Πάφου οἱ
And setting sail   from –   Paphos the ones

περὶ Παῦλον ἦλθον εἰς Πέργην τῆς
around(with) Paul came to   Perga the

Παμφυλίας· Ἰωάννης δὲ ἀποχωρήσας ἀπ'
of Pamphylia; and John   departing   from

αὐτῶν ὑπέστρεψεν εἰς Ἱεροσόλυμα.
them   returned   to   Jerusalem.

14 Αὐτοὶ δὲ διελθόντες ἀπὸ τῆς Πέργης
And they   going through from –   Perga

παρεγένοντο εἰς Ἀντιόχειαν τὴν Πισιδίαν,
arrived   in   Antioch   the Pisidian,

καὶ ἐλθόντες εἰς τὴν συναγωγὴν τῇ
and going   into the synagogue on the

ἡμέρᾳ τῶν σαββάτων ἐκάθισαν. 15 μετὰ δὲ
day   of the sabbaths sat down.   And after

τὴν ἀνάγνωσιν τοῦ νόμου καὶ τῶν
the reading   of the law   and of the

προφητῶν ἀπέστειλαν οἱ ἀρχισυνάγωγοι
prophets   sent   the synagogue rulers

πρὸς αὐτοὺς λέγοντες· ἄνδρες ἀδελφοί,
to   them   saying: Men   brothers,

εἴ τίς ἐστιν ἐν ὑμῖν λόγος παρακλήσεως
¹if ⁵any ²there is ³among ⁴you ⁶word of exhortation

πρὸς τὸν λαόν, λέγετε. 16 ἀναστὰς δὲ
to   the people, say ye.   And ¹rising up

Παῦλος καὶ κατασείσας τῇ χειρὶ εἶπεν·
⁶Paul   ²and ³beckoning ⁴with the(his) ⁵hand said:

ἄνδρες Ἰσραηλῖται καὶ οἱ φοβούμενοι τὸν
Men   Israelites   and the [ones] fearing –

θεόν, ἀκούσατε. 17 ὁ θεὸς τοῦ λαοῦ
God, hear ye.   The God –   people

τούτου Ἰσραὴλ ἐξελέξατο τοὺς πατέρας
of this Israel   chose   the   fathers

ἡμῶν, καὶ τὸν λαὸν ὕψωσεν ἐν τῇ
of us, and ²the ³people ¹exalted in the

παροικίᾳ ἐν γῇ Αἰγύπτου, καὶ μετὰ
sojourn   in [the] land of Egypt, and with

high arm brought he them out of it.

18 And about the time of forty years suffered he their manners in the wilderness.

19 And when he had destroyed seven nations in the land of Chanaan, he divided their land to them by lot.

20 And after that he gave *unto them* judges about the space of four hundred and fifty years, until Samuel the prophet.

21 And afterward they desired a king: and God gave unto them Saul the son of Cis, a man of the tribe of Benjamin, by the space of forty years.

22 And when he had removed him, he raised up unto them David to be their king; to whom also he gave testimony, and said, I have found David the *son* of Jesse, a man after mine own heart, which shall fulfil all my will.

23 Of this man's seed hath God according to *his* promise raised unto Israel a Saviour, Jesus:

24 When John had first preached before his coming the baptism of repentance to all the people of Israel.

25 And as John fulfilled his course, he said, Whom think ye that I am? I am not *he*. But, behold, there cometh one after me,

---

βραχίονος   ὑψηλοῦ   ἐξήγαγεν   αὐτοὺς   ἐξ
arm   a high   he led forth   them   out of

αὐτῆς,   18 καὶ   ὡς   τεσσερακονταέτη   χρόνον
it,   and   about   forty years   time

ἐτροποφόρησεν   αὐτοὺς   ἐν   τῇ   ἐρήμῳ,   19 καὶ
endured   them   in   the   desert,   and

καθελὼν   ἔθνη   ἑπτὰ   ἐν   γῇ   Χανάαν
having destroyed   nations   seven   in   [the] land   Canaan

κατεκληρονόμησεν   τὴν   γῆν   αὐτῶν   20 ὡς
gave as an inheritance   the   land   of them   about

ἔτεσιν   τετρακοσίοις   καὶ   πεντήκοντα.   καὶ
years   four hundreds   and   fifty.   And

μετὰ   ταῦτα   ἔδωκεν   κριτὰς   ἕως   Σαμουὴλ
after these things   he gave   judges   until   Samuel

προφήτου.   21 κἀκεῖθεν   ᾐτήσαντο   βασιλέα,
a prophet.   And thence   they asked   a king,

καὶ   ἔδωκεν   αὐτοῖς   ὁ   θεὸς   τὸν   Σαοὺλ
and   gave   them   –   God   –   Saul

υἱὸν   Κίς,   ἄνδρα   ἐκ   φυλῆς   Βενιαμίν,
son   of Cis,   a man   of [the] tribe   of Benjamin,

ἔτη   τεσσεράκοντα·   22 καὶ   μεταστήσας
years   forty;   and   removing

αὐτὸν   ἤγειρεν   τὸν   Δαυὶδ   αὐτοῖς   εἰς
him   he raised   –   David   to them   for

βασιλέα,   ᾧ   καὶ   εἶπεν   μαρτυρήσας·
a king,   to whom   also   he said   giving witness:

εὗρον   Δαυὶδ   τὸν   τοῦ   Ἰεσσαί,   ἄνδρα
I found   David   the [son]   –   of Jesse,   a man

κατὰ   τὴν   καρδίαν   μου,   ὃς   ποιήσει   πάντα
according to the   heart   of me,   who   will do   all

τὰ   θελήματά   μου.   23 τούτου   ὁ   θεὸς
the   wishes   of me.   [4]Of this man   –   [5]God

ἀπὸ   τοῦ   σπέρματος   κατ'   ἐπαγγελίαν
[1]from   [2]the   [3]seed   according to   promise

ἤγαγεν   τῷ   Ἰσραὴλ   σωτῆρα   Ἰησοῦν,
brought   –   to Israel   a Saviour   Jesus,

24 προκηρύξαντος   Ἰωάννου   πρὸ   προσώπου
previously proclaiming   John[a]   before   face
= when John had previously proclaimed

τῆς   εἰσόδου   αὐτοῦ   βάπτισμα   μετανοίας
of the   entrance   of him   a baptism   of repentance

παντὶ   τῷ   λαῷ   Ἰσραήλ.   25 ὡς   δὲ
to all   the   people   of Israel.   Now as

ἐπλήρου   Ἰωάννης   τὸν   δρόμον,   ἔλεγεν·
completed   John   the(his)   course,   he said:

τί   ἐμὲ   ὑπονοεῖτε   εἶναι;   οὐκ   εἰμὶ   ἐγώ·
What   me   suppose ye   to be?   [3]Not   [2]am   [1]I;

ἀλλ'   ἰδοὺ   ἔρχεται   μετ'   ἐμὲ   οὗ   οὐκ   εἰμὶ
but   behold   he comes   after   me   of whom   I am not

whose shoes of *his* feet I am not worthy to loose.

26 Men *and* brethren, children of the stock of Abraham, and whosoever among you feareth God, to you is the word of this salvation sent.

27 For they that dwell at Jerusalem, and their rulers, because they knew him not, nor yet the voices of the prophets which are read every sabbath day, they have fulfilled *them* in condemning *him*.

28 And though they found no cause of death *in him*, yet desired they Pilate that he should be slain.

29 And when they had fulfilled all that was written of him, they took *him* down from the tree, and laid *him* in a sepulchre.

30 But God raised him from the dead:

31 And he was seen many days of them which came up with him from Galilee to Jerusalem, who are his witnesses unto the people.

32 And we declare unto you glad tidings, how that the promise which was made unto the fathers,

33 God hath fulfilled the same unto us their children, in that he hath raised up Jesus again; as it is also written in the second psalm, Thou art my Son, this day have I begotten thee.

34 And as concerning

ἄξιος τὸ ὑπόδημα τῶν ποδῶ. λῦσαι.
worthy the sandal of the feet to loosen.

26 Ἄνδρες ἀδελφοί, υἱοὶ γένους Ἀβραὰμ
Men brothers, sons of [the] race of Abraham

καὶ οἱ ἐν ὑμῖν φοβούμενοι τὸν θεόν,
and the [ones] among you fearing – God,

ἡμῖν ὁ λόγος τῆς σωτηρίας ταύτης
to us the word of this salvation

ἐξαπεστάλη. 27 οἱ γὰρ κατοικοῦντες ἐν
was sent forth. For the [ones] dwelling in

Ἰερουσαλὴμ καὶ οἱ ἄρχοντες αὐτῶν τοῦτον
Jerusalem and the rulers of them ²this man

ἀγνοήσαντες καὶ τὰς φωνὰς τῶν προφητῶν τὰς
¹not knowing and the voices of the prophets –

κατὰ πᾶν σάββατον ἀναγινωσκομένας
²throughout(on) ³every ⁴sabbath ¹being read

κρίναντες ἐπλήρωσαν, 28 καὶ μηδεμίαν
judging they fulfilled, and no

αἰτίαν θανάτου εὑρόντες ἠτήσαντο Πιλᾶτον
cause of death finding they asked Pilate

ἀναιρεθῆναι αὐτόν· 29 ὡς δὲ ἐτέλεσαν πάντα
to be destroyed him; and when they finished all

τὰ περὶ αὐτοῦ γεγραμμένα, καθελόντες
the things concerning him having been written, taking down

ἀπὸ τοῦ ξύλου ἔθηκαν εἰς μνημεῖον.
from the tree they laid in a tomb.

30 ὁ δὲ θεὸς ἤγειρεν αὐτὸν ἐκ νεκρῶν·
– But God raised him out of [the] dead;

31 ὃς ὤφθη ἐπὶ ἡμέρας πλείους τοῖς
who appeared over days many to the [ones]

συναναβᾶσιν αὐτῷ ἀπὸ τῆς Γαλιλαίας εἰς
having come up with him from – Galilee to

Ἰερουσαλήμ, οἵτινες [νῦν] εἰσιν μάρτυρες
Jerusalem, who now are witnesses

αὐτοῦ πρὸς τὸν λαόν. 32 καὶ ἡμεῖς
of him to the people. And we

ὑμᾶς εὐαγγελιζόμεθα τὴν πρὸς τοὺς
[to] you preach ¹the ⁴to ⁵the

πατέρας ἐπαγγελίαν γενομένην, 33 ὅτι
⁶fathers ²promise ³having come, that

ταύτην ὁ θεὸς ἐκπεπλήρωκεν τοῖς τέκνοις
this [promise] – God has fulfilled ²to the ³children

ἡμῖν ἀναστήσας Ἰησοῦν, ὡς καὶ ἐν τῷ
¹to us raising up Jesus, as also in the

ψαλμῷ γέγραπται τῷ δευτέρῳ· υἱός μου
²psalm ³it has been written – ¹second : Son of me

εἶ σύ, ἐγὼ σήμερον γεγέννηκά σε. 34 ὅτι δὲ
art thou, I to-day have begotten thee. And that

that he raised him up from the dead, *now* no more to return to corruption, he said on this wise, I will give you the sure mercies of David.

35 Wherefore he saith also in another *psalm*, Thou shalt not suffer thine Holy One to see corruption.

36 For David, after he had served his own generation by the will of God, fell on sleep, and was laid unto his fathers, and saw corruption:

37 But he, whom God raised again, saw no corruption.

38 ¶ Be it known unto you therefore, men *and* brethren, that through this man is preached unto you the forgiveness of sins:

39 And by him all that believe are justified from all things, from which ye could not be justified by the law of Moses.

40 Beware therefore, lest that come upon you, which is spoken of in the prophets;

41 Behold, ye despisers, and wonder, and perish: for I work a work in your days, a work which ye shall in no wise believe, though a man declare it unto you.

42 ¶ And when the Jews were gone out of the synagogue, the Gentiles besought that these words might be preached to them the next sabbath.

ἀνέστησεν αὐτὸν ἐκ νεκρῶν μηκέτι
he raised up him out of [the] dead no more

μέλλοντα ὑποστρέφειν εἰς διαφθοράν, οὕτως
being about to return to corruption, thus

εἴρηκεν ὅτι δώσω ὑμῖν τὰ ὅσια Δαυὶδ τὰ
he has said[,] — I will give you the ²holy things ³of David the

πιστά. 35 διότι καὶ ἐν ἑτέρῳ λέγει·
¹faithful. Wherefore also in another [psalm] he says:

οὐ δώσεις τὸν ὅσιόν σου ἰδεῖν διαφθοράν.
Thou wilt not give the holy one of thee to see corruption.

36 Δαυὶδ μὲν γὰρ ἰδίᾳ γενεᾷ ὑπηρετήσας
For David indeed [his] own generation having served

τῇ τοῦ θεοῦ βουλῇ ἐκοιμήθη καὶ προσετέθη
by the — of God counsel fell asleep and was added

πρὸς τοὺς πατέρας αὐτοῦ καὶ εἶδεν
to the fathers of him and saw

διαφθοράν· 37 ὃν δὲ ὁ θεὸς ἤγειρεν,
corruption; but [he] whom — God raised,

οὐκ εἶδεν διαφθοράν. 38 γνωστὸν οὖν
did not see corruption. Known therefore

ἔστω ὑμῖν, ἄνδρες ἀδελφοί, ὅτι διὰ
let it be to you, men brothers, that through

τούτου ὑμῖν ἄφεσις ἁμαρτιῶν καταγγέλ-
this man to you forgiveness of sins is an-

λεται, καὶ ἀπὸ πάντων ὧν οὐκ ἠδυνήθητε
nounced, and from all things from which ye could not

ἐν νόμῳ Μωϋσέως δικαιωθῆναι, 39 ἐν
by [the] law of Moses to be justified, by

τούτῳ πᾶς ὁ πιστεύων δικαιοῦται. 40 βλέπετε
this man everyone believing is justified. Look ye

οὖν μὴ ἐπέλθῃ τὸ εἰρημένον
therefore lest come on [you] the thing having been said

ἐν τοῖς προφήταις· 41 ἴδετε, οἱ κατα-
in the prophets: See, the des-

φρονηταί, καὶ θαυμάσατε καὶ ἀφανίσθητε,
pisers, and marvel ye and perish,

ὅτι ἔργον ἐργάζομαι ἐγὼ ἐν ταῖς ἡμέραις
because a work work I in the days

ὑμῶν, ἔργον ὃ οὐ μὴ πιστεύσητε ἐάν
of you, a work which by no means ye believe if

τις ἐκδιηγῆται ὑμῖν. 42 Ἐξιόντων δὲ
anyone declares to you. And going out
=as they went out

αὐτῶν παρεκάλουν εἰς τὸ μεταξὺ σάββατον
them[a] they besought in the intervening sabbath(week)

λαληθῆναι αὐτοῖς τὰ ῥήματα ταῦτα.
to be spoken to them these words.

43 Now when the congregation was broken up, many of the Jews and religious proselytes followed Paul and Barnabas: who, speaking to them, persuaded them to continue in the grace of God.

44 ¶ And the next sabbath day came almost the whole city together to hear the word of God.

45 But when the Jews saw the multitudes, they were filled with envy, and spake against those things which were spoken by Paul, contradicting and blaspheming.

46 Then Paul and Barnabas waxed bold, and said, It was necessary that the word of God should first have been spoken to you: but seeing ye put it from you, and judge yourselves unworthy of everlasting life, lo, we turn to the Gentiles.

47 For so hath the Lord commanded us, *saying*, I have set thee to be a light of the Gentiles, that thou shouldest be for salvation unto the ends of the earth.

48 And when the Gentiles heard this, they were glad, and glorified the word of the Lord: and as many as were ordained to eternal life believed.

49 And the word of the Lord was published throughout all the region.

50 But the Jews stirred up the devout and honourable women, and the

---

43 λυθείσης δὲ τῆς συναγωγῆς ἠκολούθησαν
And being broken up the assembly[a] [8]followed
= when the assembly was broken up

πολλοὶ τῶν Ἰουδαίων καὶ τῶν σεβομένων
[1]many [5]of the [3]Jews [4]and [5]of the [6]worshipping

προσηλύτων τῷ Παύλῳ καὶ τῷ Βαρναβᾷ,
[7]proselytes [9]Paul and Barnabas,

οἵτινες προσλαλοῦντες αὐτοῖς ἔπειθον αὐτοὺς
who speaking to them persuaded them

προσμένειν τῇ χάριτι τοῦ θεοῦ. 44 Τῷ δὲ
to continue in the grace - of God. And on the

ἐρχομένῳ σαββάτῳ σχεδὸν πᾶσα ἡ
coming sabbath almost all the

πόλις συνήχθη ἀκοῦσαι τὸν λόγον τοῦ
city was assembled to hear the word -

θεοῦ. 45 ἰδόντες δὲ οἱ Ἰουδαῖοι τοὺς
of God. But [3]seeing [1]the [2]Jews the

ὄχλους ἐπλήσθησαν ζήλου, καὶ ἀντέλεγον
crowds were filled of(with) jealousy, and contradicted

τοῖς ὑπὸ Παύλου λαλουμένοις βλασφημοῦντες.
the things by Paul being spoken blaspheming.

46 παρρησιασάμενοί τε ὁ Παῦλος καὶ ὁ
And speaking boldly - Paul and -

Βαρναβᾶς εἶπαν· ὑμῖν ἦν ἀναγκαῖον πρῶτον
Barnabas said: To you it was necessary firstly

λαληθῆναι τὸν λόγον τοῦ θεοῦ· ἐπειδὴ
to be spoken the word - of God; since

ἀπωθεῖσθε αὐτὸν καὶ οὐκ ἀξίους κρίνετε
ye put away it and not worthy judge

ἑαυτοὺς τῆς αἰωνίου ζωῆς, ἰδοὺ στρεφόμεθα
yourselves of the eternal life, behold we turn

εἰς τὰ ἔθνη. 47 οὕτως γὰρ ἐντέταλται
to the nations. For thus has commanded

ἡμῖν ὁ κύριος· τέθεικά σε εἰς φῶς
us the Lord: I have set thee for a light

ἐθνῶν τοῦ εἶναί σε εἰς σωτηρίαν ἕως
of nations - to be thee[b] for salvation to

ἐσχάτου τῆς γῆς. 48 ἀκούοντα δὲ τὰ ἔθνη
[the] end of the earth. And [3]hearing [1]the [2]nations

ἔχαιρον καὶ ἐδόξαζον τὸν λόγον τοῦ κυρίου, καὶ
rejoiced and glorified the word of the Lord, and

ἐπίστευσαν ὅσοι ἦσαν τεταγμένοι εἰς
[7]believed [1]as many as [2]were [3]having been disposed [4]to

ζωὴν αἰώνιον· 49 διεφέρετο δὲ ὁ λόγος τοῦ
[6]life [5]eternal; and was carried *through* the word of the

κυρίου δι᾽ ὅλης τῆς χώρας. 50 οἱ δὲ
Lord through all the country. But the

Ἰουδαῖοι παρώτρυναν τὰς σεβομένας γυναῖκας
Jews urged on the [2]worshipping [3]women

chief men of the city, and raised persecution against Paul and Barnabas, and expelled them out of their coasts.

51 But they shook off the dust of their feet against them, and came unto Iconium.

52 And the disciples were filled with joy, and with the Holy Ghost.

τὰς εὐσχήμονας καὶ τοὺς πρώτους τῆς
\-　　¹honourable　　and　　the　　chief men　of the
πόλεως, καὶ ἐπήγειραν διωγμὸν ἐπὶ τὸν
city,　　and　　raised up　　persecution　against　　\-
Παῦλον καὶ Βαρναβᾶν, καὶ ἐξέβαλον αὐτοὺς
Paul　　and　　Barnabas,　　and　　expelled　　them
ἀπὸ τῶν ὁρίων αὐτῶν. 51 οἱ δὲ ἐκτιναξάμενοι
from　the　borders　of them.　　But they　shaking off
τὸν κονιορτὸν τῶν ποδῶν ἐπ᾽ αὐτοὺς ἦλθον
the　　dust　　of the(ir)　feet　　on　　them　　came
εἰς Ἰκόνιον, 52 οἵ τε μαθηταὶ ἐπλη-
to　Iconium,　　and the　　disciples　　were
ροῦντο χαρᾶς καὶ πνεύματος ἁγίου.
filled　of(with) joy and　of(with) Spirit　Holy.

CHAPTER 14

AND it came to pass in Iconium, that they went both together into the synagogue of the Jews, and so spake, that a great multitude both of the Jews and also of the Greeks believed.

2 But the unbelieving Jews stirred up the Gentiles, and made their minds evil affected against the brethren.

3 Long time therefore abode they speaking boldly in the Lord, which gave testimony unto the word of his grace, and granted signs and wonders to be done by their hands.

4 But the multitude of the city was divided: and part held with the Jews, and part with the apostles.

5 And when there was an assault made both of the Gentiles, and also of the Jews with their rulers,

14 Ἐγένετο δὲ ἐν Ἰκονίῳ κατὰ τὸ αὐτὸ
Now it happened　in　　Iconium　　²together†
εἰσελθεῖν αὐτοὺς εἰς τὴν συναγωγὴν
¹to enter　　them^b　into　the　　synagogue
=they entered
τῶν Ἰουδαίων καὶ λαλῆσαι οὕτως ὥστε
of the　Jews　　and　to speak^b　so　　as
πιστεῦσαι Ἰουδαίων τε καὶ Ἑλλήνων
to believe　both of Jews　and　　of Greeks
πολὺ πλῆθος. 2 οἱ δὲ ἀπειθήσαντες
a much(great) multitude.　But the　　disobeying
Ἰουδαῖοι ἐπήγειραν καὶ ἐκάκωσαν τὰς
Jews　　excited　　and　　embittered　the
ψυχὰς τῶν ἐθνῶν κατὰ τῶν ἀδελφῶν.
minds　of the　nations　against　the　　brothers.
3 ἱκανὸν μὲν οὖν χρόνον διέτριψαν
A considerable　\-　　²therefore　¹time　they continued
παρρησιαζόμενοι ἐπὶ τῷ κυρίῳ τῷ μαρ-
speaking boldly　　on　the　Lord　　wit-
τυροῦντι ἐπὶ τῷ λόγῳ τῆς χάριτος αὐτοῦ,
nessing　to　the　word　of the　grace　　of him,
διδόντι σημεῖα καὶ τέρατα γίνεσθαι διὰ
giving　signs　and　wonders　to happen　through
τῶν χειρῶν αὐτῶν. 4 ἐσχίσθη δὲ τὸ
the　hands　of them.　But was divided　the
πλῆθος τῆς πόλεως, καὶ οἱ μὲν ἦσαν
multitude　of the　　city,　　and　　some　　were
σὺν τοῖς Ἰουδαίοις, οἱ δὲ σὺν τοῖς
with　the　　Jews,　　but others　with　the
ἀποστόλοις. 5 ὡς δὲ ἐγένετο ὁρμὴ τῶν
apostles.　　And when　there was　a rush　³of the
ἐθνῶν τε καὶ Ἰουδαίων σὺν τοῖς ἄρχουσιν
²nations ¹both ⁴and　of Jews　with　the　　rulers

to use *them* despitefully, and to stone them,

6 They were ware of *it*, and fled unto Lystra and Derbe, cities of Lycaonia, and unto the region that lieth round about:

7 And there they preached the gospel.

8 ¶ And there sat a certain man at Lystra, impotent in his feet, being a cripple from his mother's womb, who never had walked:

9 The same heard Paul speak: who stedfastly beholding him, and perceiving that he had faith to be healed,

10 Said with a loud voice, Stand upright on thy feet. And he leaped and walked.

11 And when the people saw what Paul had done, they lifted up their voices, saying in the speech of Lycaonia, The gods are come down to us in the likeness of men.

12 And they called Barnabas, Jupiter; and Paul, Mercurius, because he was the chief speaker.

13 Then the priest of Jupiter, which was before their city, brought oxen and garlands unto the gates, and would have done sacrifice with the people.

14 *Which* when the apostles, Barnabas and Paul, heard *of*, they rent their clothes, and ran in

αὐτῶν   ὑβρίσαι   καὶ   λιθοβολῆσαι   αὐτούς,
of them   to insult   and   to stone   them,

6 συνιδόντες   κατέφυγον   εἰς   τὰς   πόλεις
perceiving   they escaped   to   the   cities

τῆς   Λυκαονίας   Λύστραν   καὶ   Δέρβην   καὶ
 -      of Lycaonia   Lystra   and   Derbe   and

τὴν   περίχωρον·   7 κἀκεῖ   εὐαγγελιζόμενοι
the   neighbourhood;   and there   evangelizing

ἦσαν.   8 Καὶ   τις   ἀνὴρ   ἀδύνατος   ἐν
they were.   And   a certain man   impotent   in

Λύστροις   τοῖς   ποσὶν   ἐκάθητο,   χωλὸς   ἐκ
Lystra   in the   feet   sat,   lame   from

κοιλίας   μητρὸς   αὐτοῦ   ὃς   οὐδέποτε
[the] womb of [the] mother of him   who   never

περιεπάτησεν.   9 οὗτος   ἤκουεν   τοῦ   Παύλου
walked.   This man   heard   -   Paul

λαλοῦντος·   ὃς   ἀτενίσας   αὐτῷ   καὶ   ἰδὼν
speaking;   who   gazing   at him   and   seeing

ὅτι   ἔχει   πίστιν   τοῦ   σωθῆναι,   10 εἶπεν
that he has(had) faith   -   to be healed,[d]   said

μεγάλῃ   φωνῇ·   ἀνάστηθι   ἐπὶ   τοὺς   πόδας
with a   voice: Stand up   on   the   feet
great(loud)

σου   ὀρθός.   καὶ   ἥλατο   καὶ   περιεπάτει.
of thee   erect.   And   he leaped up and   walked.

11 οἵ   τε   ὄχλοι   ἰδόντες   ὃ   ἐποίησεν   Παῦλος
And the   crowds   seeing   what   did   Paul

ἐπῆραν   τὴν   φωνὴν   αὐτῶν   Λυκαονιστὶ
lifted up   the   voice   of them   in Lycaonian

λέγοντες·   οἱ   θεοὶ   ὁμοιωθέντες   ἀνθρώποις
saying: The   gods   made like   men

κατέβησαν   πρὸς   ἡμᾶς,   12 ἐκάλουν   τε   τὸν
came down   to   us,   and they called   -

Βαρναβᾶν   Δία,   τὸν   δὲ   Παῦλον   Ἑρμῆν,
Barnabas   Zeus,   -   and   Paul   Hermes,

ἐπειδὴ   αὐτὸς   ἦν   ὁ   ἡγούμενος   τοῦ   λόγου.
since   he   was   the   leader   of the   discourse.

13 ὅ   τε   ἱερεὺς   τοῦ   Διὸς   τοῦ   ὄντος   πρὸ
And the   priest   -   of Zeus   -   being   before

τῆς   πόλεως,   ταύρους   καὶ   στέμματα   ἐπὶ
the   city,   bulls   and   garlands   to

τοὺς   πυλῶνας   ἐνέγκας,   σὺν   τοῖς   ὄχλοις
the   gates   bringing,   with   the   crowds

ἤθελεν   θύειν.   14 ἀκούσαντες   δὲ   οἱ
wished   to sacrifice.   But [e]hearing   [1]the

ἀπόστολοι   Βαρναβᾶς   καὶ   Παῦλος,   διαρ-
[2]apostles   [3]Barnabas   [4]and   [5]Paul,   rend-

ρήξαντες   τὰ   ἱμάτια   ἑαυτῶν   ἐξεπήδησαν   εἰς
ing   the   garments of them*selves* rushed out   into

among the people, crying out,

15 And saying, Sirs, why do ye these things? We also are men of like passions with you, and preach unto you that ye should turn from these vanities unto the living God, which made heaven, and earth, and the sea, and all things that are therein:

16 Who in times past suffered all nations to walk in their own ways.

17 Nevertheless he left not himself without witness, in that he did good, and gave us rain from heaven, and fruitful seasons, filling our hearts with food and gladness.

18 And with these sayings scarce restrained they the people, that they had not done sacrifice unto them.

19 ¶ And there came thither *certain* Jews from Antioch and Iconium, who persuaded the people, and, having stoned Paul, drew *him* out of the city, supposing he had been dead.

20 Howbeit, as the disciples stood round about him, he rose up, and came into the city: and the next day he departed with Barnabas to Derbe.

21 And when they had preached the gospel to that

τὸν ὄχλον, κράζοντες **15** καὶ λέγοντες·
the crowd, crying out and saying:

ἄνδρες, τί ταῦτα ποιεῖτε; καὶ ἡμεῖς
Men, why these things do ye? also we

ὁμοιοπαθεῖς ἐσμεν ὑμῖν ἄνθρωποι, εὐαγ-
of like nature are to you men, preach-

γελιζόμενοι ὑμᾶς ἀπὸ τούτων τῶν ματαίων
ing [to] you from these - vanities

ἐπιστρέφειν ἐπὶ θεὸν ζῶντα, ὃς ἐποίησεν
to turn to God a living, who made

τὸν οὐρανὸν καὶ τὴν γῆν καὶ τὴν
the heaven and the earth and the

θάλασσαν καὶ πάντα τὰ ἐν αὐτοῖς· **16** ὃς
sea and all the things in them; who

ἐν ταῖς παρῳχημέναις γενεαῖς εἴασεν πάντα
in the having passed generations allowed all

τὰ ἔθνη πορεύεσθαι ταῖς ὁδοῖς αὐτῶν·
the nations to go in the ways of them;

17 καίτοι οὐκ ἀμάρτυρον αὐτὸν ἀφῆκεν
and yet not unwitnessed himself left

ἀγαθουργῶν, οὐρανόθεν ὑμῖν ὑετοὺς διδοὺς
doing good, from heaven us rain giving

καὶ καιροὺς καρποφόρους, ἐμπιπλῶν τροφῆς
and times fruit-bearing, filling of(with) food

καὶ εὐφροσύνης τὰς καρδίας ὑμῶν. **18** καὶ
and of(with) gladness the hearts of us. And

ταῦτα λέγοντες μόλις κατέπαυσαν τοὺς
these things saying scarcely they restrained the

ὄχλους τοῦ μὴ θύειν αὐτοῖς. **19** Ἐπῆλθαν
crowds - not to sacrifice to them. came upon [the scene]

δὲ ἀπὸ Ἀντιοχείας καὶ Ἰκονίου Ἰουδαῖοι,
And from Antioch and Iconium Jews,

καὶ πείσαντες τοὺς ὄχλους καὶ λιθάσαντες
and persuading the crowds and stoning

τὸν Παῦλον ἔσυρον ἔξω τῆς πόλεως,
- Paul dragged outside the city,

νομίζοντες αὐτὸν τεθνηκέναι. **20** κυκλω-
supposing him to have died. But sur-

σάντων δὲ τῶν μαθητῶν αὐτὸν ἀναστὰς
rounding the disciples him rising up
=as the disciples surrounded

εἰσῆλθεν εἰς τὴν πόλιν. Καὶ τῇ ἐπαύριον
he entered into the city. And on the morrow

ἐξῆλθεν σὺν τῷ Βαρναβᾷ εἰς Δέρβην.
he went forth with - Barnabas to Derbe.

21 εὐαγγελιζόμενοί τε τὴν πόλιν ἐκείνην
And evangelizing that city

city, and had taught many, they returned again to Lystra, and *to* Iconium, and Antioch,

καὶ μαθητεύσαντες ἱκανοὺς ὑπέστρεψαν εἰς
and having made disciples many they returned to

τὴν Λύστραν καὶ εἰς Ἰκόνιον καὶ [εἰς]
– Lystra and to Iconium and to

22 Confirming the souls of the disciples, *and* exhorting them to continue in the faith, and that we must through much tribulation enter into the kingdom of God.

Ἀντιόχειαν, 22 ἐπιστηρίζοντες τὰς ψυχὰς
Antioch, confirming the minds

τῶν μαθητῶν, παρακαλοῦντες ἐμμένειν τῇ
of the disciples, exhorting to continue in the

πίστει, καὶ ὅτι διὰ πολλῶν θλίψεων
faith, and that through many afflictions

δεῖ ἡμᾶς εἰσελθεῖν εἰς τὴν βασιλείαν τοῦ
it behoves us to enter into the kingdom –

23 And when they had ordained them elders in every church, and had prayed with fasting, they commended them to the Lord, on whom they believed.

θεοῦ. 23 χειροτονήσαντες δὲ αὐτοῖς κατ'
of God. And having appointed for them in

ἐκκλησίαν πρεσβυτέρους, προσευξάμενοι
every church elders, praying

μετὰ νηστειῶν παρέθεντο αὐτοὺς τῷ κυρίῳ
with fastings they committed them to the Lord

24 And after they had passed throughout Pisidia, they came to Pamphylia.

εἰς ὃν πεπιστεύκεισαν. 24 καὶ διελθόντες
in whom they had believed. And passing through

25 And when they had preached the word in Perga, they went down into Attalia:

τὴν Πισιδίαν ἦλθον εἰς τὴν Παμφυλίαν,
– Pisidia they came to – Pamphylia,

25 καὶ λαλήσαντες εἰς τὴν Πέργην τὸν
and speaking in – Perga the

26 And thence sailed to Antioch, from whence they had been recommended to the grace of God for the work which they fulfilled.

λόγον κατέβησαν εἰς Ἀττάλειαν, κἀκεῖθεν
word they came down to Attalia, and thence

ἀπέπλευσαν εἰς Ἀντιόχειαν, 26 ὅθεν ἦσαν
sailed away to Antioch, whence they were

27 And when they were come, and had gathered the church together, they rehearsed all that God had done with them, and how he had opened the door of faith unto the Gentiles.

παραδεδομένοι τῇ χάριτι τοῦ θεοῦ εἰς
having been commended to the grace – of God for

τὸ ἔργον ὃ ἐπλήρωσαν. 27 Παραγεν-
the work which they accomplished. And having

όμενοι δὲ καὶ συναγαγόντες τὴν ἐκκλησίαν,
arrived and assembling the church,

ἀνήγγελλον ὅσα ἐποίησεν ὁ θεὸς μετ'
they reported what things did – God with

28 And there they abode long time with the disciples.

αὐτῶν, καὶ ὅτι ἤνοιξεν τοῖς ἔθνεσιν
them, and that he opened to the nations

θύραν πίστεως. 28 διέτριβον δὲ χρόνον
a door of faith. And they continued time

οὐκ ὀλίγον σὺν τοῖς μαθηταῖς.
not a little with the disciples.

CHAPTER 15

AND certain men which came down from Judæa taught the brethren,

15 Καὶ τινες κατελθόντες ἀπὸ τῆς
And some going down from the

Ἰουδαίας ἐδίδασκον τοὺς ἀδελφοὺς ὅτι
Judæa taught the brothers[,] –

and said, Except ye be circumcised after the manner of Moses, ye cannot be saved.

2 When therefore Paul and Barnabas had no small dissension and disputation with them, they determined that Paul and Barnabas, and certain other of them, should go up to Jerusalem unto the apostles and elders about this question.

3 And being brought on their way by the church, they passed through Phenice and Samaria, declaring the conversion of the Gentiles: and they caused great joy unto all the brethren.

4 And when they were come to Jerusalem, they were received of the church, and *of* the apostles and elders, and they declared all things that God had done with them.

5 ¶ But there rose up certain of the sect of the Pharisees which believed, saying, That it was needful to circumcise them, and to command *them* to keep the law of Moses.

6 And the apostles and elders came together for to consider of this matter.

ἐὰν μὴ περιτμηθῆτε τῷ ἔθει τῷ Μωϋσέως,
Unless ye are circumcised by the custom – of Moses,

οὐ δύνασθε σωθῆναι. 2 γενομένης δὲ
ye cannot to be saved. And taking place

στάσεως καὶ ζητήσεως οὐκ ὀλίγης τῷ
discord and questioning not a little[a] –
= when there took place not a little . . .

Παύλῳ καὶ τῷ Βαρναβᾷ πρὸς αὐτούς,
by Paul and – Barnabas with them,

ἔταξαν ἀναβαίνειν Παῦλον καὶ Βαρναβᾶν
they assigned to go up Paul and Barnabas

καὶ τινας ἄλλους ἐξ αὐτῶν πρὸς τοὺς
and some others of them to the

ἀποστόλους καὶ πρεσβυτέρους εἰς Ἰερουσαλὴμ
apostles and elders in Jerusalem

περὶ τοῦ ζητήματος τούτου. 3 Οἱ μὲν
about this question. They –

οὖν προπεμφθέντες ὑπὸ τῆς ἐκκλησίας
therefore being set forward by the church

διήρχοντο τήν τε Φοινίκην καὶ Σαμάρειαν
passed through – both Phœnicia and Samaria

ἐκδιηγούμενοι τὴν ἐπιστροφὴν τῶν ἐθνῶν,
telling in detail the conversion of the nations,

καὶ ἐποίουν χαρὰν μεγάλην πᾶσιν τοῖς
and caused joy great to all the

ἀδελφοῖς. 4 παραγενόμενοι δὲ εἰς Ἰεροσόλυμα
brothers. And having arrived in Jerusalem

παρεδέχθησαν ἀπὸ τῆς ἐκκλησίας καὶ τῶν
they were welcomed from the church and the

ἀποστόλων καὶ τῶν πρεσβυτερων, ἀνήγ-
apostles and the elders, and

γειλάν τε ὅσα ὁ θεὸς ἐποίησεν μετ᾽
reported what things – God did with

αὐτῶν. 5 Ἐξανέστησαν δέ τινες τῶν
them. But stood forth some of the [ones]

ἀπὸ τῆς αἱρέσεως τῶν Φαρισαίων
from the sect of the Pharisees

πεπιστευκότες, λέγοντες ὅτι δεῖ περιτέμνειν
having believed, saying[,] – It behoves to circumcise

αὐτοὺς παραγγέλλειν τε τηρεῖν τὸν νόμον
them and to charge to keep the law

Μωϋσέως.
of Moses.

6 Συνήχθησάν τε οἱ ἀπόστολοι καὶ οἱ
And were assembled the apostles and the

πρεσβύτεροι ἰδεῖν περὶ τοῦ λόγου τούτου.
elders to see about this matter.

7 And when there had been much disputing, Peter rose up, and said unto them, Men *and* brethren, ye know how that a good while ago God made choice among us, that the Gentiles by my mouth should hear the word of the gospel, and believe.

8 And God, which knoweth the hearts, bare them witness, giving them the Holy Ghost, even as *he did* unto us;

9 And put no difference between us and them, purifying their hearts by faith.

10 Now therefore why tempt ye God, to put a yoke upon the neck of the disciples, which neither our fathers nor we were able to bear?

11 But we believe that through the grace of the Lord Jesus Christ we shall be saved, even as they.

12 ¶ Then all the multitude kept silence, and gave audience to Barnabas and Paul, declaring what miracles and wonders God had wrought among the Gentiles by them.

13 ¶ And after they had held their peace, James answered, saying, Men *and* brethren, hearken unto me:

14 Simeon hath declared how God at the first

7 Πολλῆς δὲ ζητήσεως γενομένης ἀναστὰς
And much　questioning having taken place[a] rising up
= When much questioning had . . .

Πέτρος εἶπεν πρὸς αὐτούς· ἄνδρες ἀδελφοί,
Peter said to them: Men brothers,

ὑμεῖς ἐπίστασθε ὅτι ἀφ' ἡμερῶν ἀρχαίων
ye understand that from days olden

ἐν ὑμῖν ἐξελέξατο ὁ θεὸς διὰ τοῦ στόματός
[3]among [4]you [2]chose — [1]God through the mouth

μου ἀκοῦσαι τὰ ἔθνη τὸν λόγον τοῦ
of me [3]to hear [1]the [2]nations the word of the

εὐαγγελίου καὶ πιστεῦσαι. 8 καὶ ὁ
gospel and to believe. 8 And [2]the

καρδιογνώστης θεὸς ἐμαρτύρησεν αὐτοῖς
[3]Heart-knower [1]God witnessed to them

δοὺς τὸ πνεῦμα τὸ ἅγιον καθὼς καὶ
giving the Spirit — Holy as also

ἡμῖν, 9 καὶ οὐθὲν διέκρινεν μεταξὺ ἡμῶν
to us, and nothing distinguished between [2]us

τε καὶ αὐτῶν, τῇ πίστει καθαρίσας τὰς
[1]both and them, by faith cleansing the

καρδίας αὐτῶν. 10 νῦν οὖν τί πειράζετε
hearts of them. Now therefore why test ye

τὸν θεόν, ἐπιθεῖναι ζυγὸν ἐπὶ τὸν
— God, to put *on* a yoke on the

τράχηλον τῶν μαθητῶν, ὃν οὔτε οἱ
neck of the disciples, which neither the

πατέρες ἡμῶν οὔτε ἡμεῖς ἰσχύσαμεν
fathers of us nor we were able

βαστάσαι; 11 ἀλλὰ διὰ τῆς χάριτος τοῦ
to bear? but through the grace of the

κυρίου Ἰησοῦ πιστεύομεν σωθῆναι καθ'
Lord Jesus we believe to be saved in

ὃν τρόπον κἀκεῖνοι. 12 Ἐσίγησεν δὲ
the same way as[†] those also. And was silent

πᾶν τὸ πλῆθος, καὶ ἤκουον Βαρναβᾶ
all the multitude, and heard Barnabas

καὶ Παύλου ἐξηγουμένων ὅσα ἐποίησεν
and Paul relating [1]what [6]did

ὁ θεὸς σημεῖα καὶ τέρατα ἐν τοῖς
— [5]God [2]signs [3]and [4]wonders among the

ἔθνεσιν δι' αὐτῶν. 13 Μετὰ δὲ τὸ σιγῆσαι
nations through them. And after the to keep silence
= they kept silence

αὐτοὺς ἀπεκρίθη Ἰάκωβος λέγων· 14 ἄνδρες
them[b] answered James saying: Men

ἀδελφοί, ἀκούσατέ μου. Συμεὼν ἐξηγήσατο
brothers, hear ye me. Simeon declared

did visit the Gentiles, to take out of them a people for his name.

15 And to this agree the words of the prophets; as it is written,

16 After this I will return, and will build again the tabernacle of David, which is fallen down; and I will build again the ruins thereof, and I will set it up:

17 That the residue of men might seek after the Lord, and all the Gentiles, upon whom my name is called, saith the Lord, who doeth all these things.

18 Known unto God are all his works from the beginning of the world.

19 Wherefore my sentence is, that we trouble not them, which from among the Gentiles are turned to God:

20 But that we write unto them, that they abstain from pollutions of idols, and *from* fornication, and *from* things strangled, and *from* blood.

21 For Moses of old time hath in every city them that preach him, being read in the synagogues every sabbath day.

22 ¶ Then pleased it the apostles and elders, with the whole church, to send chosen men of their own

καθὼς πρῶτον ὁ θεὸς ἐπεσκέψατο λαβεῖν ἐξ
even as   firstly   –   God   visited   to take   out of

ἐθνῶν λαὸν τῷ ὀνόματι αὐτοῦ. 15 καὶ
[the] nations a people for the   name   of him.   And

τούτῳ συμφωνοῦσιν οἱ λόγοι τῶν προφητῶν,
to this   agree   the words   of the   prophets,

καθὼς γέγραπται· 16 μετὰ ταῦτα
even as   it has been written: After   these things

ἀναστρέψω καὶ ἀνοικοδομήσω τὴν σκηνὴν
I will return   and   I will rebuild   the   tent

Δαυὶδ τὴν πεπτωκυῖαν, καὶ τὰ κατεστραμ-
of David   –   having fallen,   and   the things   having been

μένα αὐτῆς ἀνοικοδομήσω καὶ ἀνορθώσω
overturned   of it   I will rebuild   and   I will rear again
=its ruins

αὐτήν, 17 ὅπως ἂν ἐκζητήσωσιν οἱ
it,   so as   –   [4]may seek   [1]the

κατάλοιποι τῶν ἀνθρώπων τὸν κύριον,
[1]rest   –   [3]of men   [5]the   [6]Lord,

καὶ πάντα τὰ ἔθνη ἐφ᾽ οὓς ἐπικέκληται
even   all   the   nations   on   whom   has been invoked

τὸ ὄνομά μου ἐπ᾽ αὐτούς, λέγει [the] κύριος
the   name   of me   *on*   them,   says   [the] Lord

ποιῶν ταῦτα 18 γνωστὰ ἀπ᾽ αἰῶνος.
doing   these things   known   from   [the] age.

19 διὸ ἐγὼ κρίνω μὴ παρενοχλεῖν τοῖς
Wherefore I   decide   not   to trouble   the [ones]

ἀπὸ τῶν ἐθνῶν ἐπιστρέφουσιν ἐπὶ τὸν
from   the   nations   turning   to   –

θεόν, 20 ἀλλὰ ἐπιστεῖλαι αὐτοῖς τοῦ
God,   but   to write word   to them   –

ἀπέχεσθαι τῶν ἀλισγημάτων τῶν εἰδώλων
to abstain from[d] the   pollutions   –   of idols

καὶ τῆς πορνείας καὶ πνικτοῦ καὶ τοῦ
and   –   fornication   and   a thing strangled   and   –

αἵματος. 21 Μωϋσῆς γὰρ ἐκ γενεῶν
blood.   For [1]Moses   [2]from [4]generations

ἀρχαίων κατὰ πόλιν τοὺς κηρύσσοντας
[3]ancient   [6]in every city   [7]the [ones]   [8]proclaiming

αὐτὸν ἔχει ἐν ταῖς συναγωγαῖς κατὰ
[9]him   [5]has   [11]in   [12]the   [13]synagogues   [14]on

πᾶν σάββατον ἀναγινωσκόμενος. 22 Τότε
[15]every   [16]sabbath   [10]being read.   Then

ἔδοξε τοῖς ἀποστόλοις καὶ τοῖς πρεσ-
it seemed [good] to the   apostles   and   to the   el-

βυτέροις σὺν ὅλῃ τῇ ἐκκλησίᾳ ἐκλεξαμένους
ders   with   all   the   church   chosen

company to Antioch with Paul and Barnabas; namely, Judas surnamed Barsabas, and Silas, chief men among the brethren:

23 And they wrote letters by them after this manner; The apostles and elders and brethren send greeting unto the brethren which are of the Gentiles in Antioch and Syria and Cilicia:

24 Forasmuch as we have heard, that certain which went out from us have troubled you with words, subverting your souls, saying, Ye must be circumcised, and keep the law: to whom we gave no such commandment:

25 It seemed good unto us, being assembled with one accord, to send chosen men unto you with our beloved Barnabas and Paul,

26 Men that have hazarded their lives for the name of our Lord Jesus Christ.

27 We have sent therefore Judas and Silas, who shall also tell you the same things by mouth.

28 For it seemed good to the Holy Ghost, and to us, to lay upon you no greater burden than these necessary things;

29 That ye abstain from meats offered to idols, and from blood, and from

---

ἄνδρας ἐξ αὐτῶν πέμψαι εἰς Ἀντιόχειαν
men of them to send to Antioch

σὺν τῷ Παύλῳ καὶ Βαρναβᾷ, Ἰούδαν
with - Paul and Barnabas, Judas

τὸν καλούμενον Βαρσαββᾶν καὶ Σιλᾶν,
- being called Barsabbas and Silas,

ἄνδρας ἡγουμένους ἐν τοῖς ἀδελφοῖς,
men leading among the brothers,

23 γράψαντες διὰ χειρὸς αὐτῶν· Οἱ
writing through [the] hand of them: The

ἀπόστολοι καὶ οἱ πρεσβύτεροι ἀδελφοὶ
apostles and the elder brothers

τοῖς κατὰ ᾿ὴν Ἀντιόχειαν καὶ Συρίαν
¹to the ⁵throughout - ⁶Antioch ⁷and ⁸Syria

καὶ Κιλικίαν ἀδελφοῖς τοῖς ἐξ ἐθνῶν
⁹and ¹⁰Cilicia ²brothers - ³of [the] ⁴nations

χαίρειν. 24 Ἐπειδὴ ἠκούσαμεν ὅτι τινὲς
¹¹greeting. Since we heard that some

ἐξ ἡμῶν ἐτάραξαν ὑμᾶς λόγοις ἀνασκευάζ-
of us troubled you with words unsettl-

οντες τὰς ψυχὰς ὑμῶν, οἷς οὐ διεστειλάμεθα,
ing the minds of you, to whom we did not give commission,

25 ἔδοξεν ἡμῖν γενομένοις ὁμοθυμαδόν,
it seemed [good] to us becoming of one mind,

ἐκλεξαμένους ἄνδρας πέμψαι πρὸς ὑμᾶς
chosen men to send to you

σὺν τοῖς ἀγαπητοῖς ἡμῶν Βαρναβᾷ καὶ
with the beloved of us Barnabas and

Παύλῳ, 26 ἀνθρώποις παραδεδωκόσι τὰς
Paul, men having given up the

ψυχὰς αὐτῶν ὑπὲρ τοῦ ὀνόματος τοῦ
lives of them on behalf of the name of the

κυρίου ἡμῶν Ἰησοῦ Χριστοῦ. 27 ἀπεστάλ-
Lord of us Jesus Christ. We have

καμεν οὖν Ἰούδαν καὶ Σιλᾶν, καὶ αὐτοὺς
sent therefore Judas and Silas, and they

διὰ λόγου ἀπαγγέλλοντας τὰ αὐτά.
through speech announcing the same
(by) things.

28 ἔδοξεν γὰρ τῷ πνεύματι τῷ ἁγίῳ
For it seemed [good] to the Spirit - Holy

καὶ ἡμῖν μηδὲν πλέον ἐπιτίθεσθαι ὑμῖν
and to us ³nothing ⁵more ¹to be put on ²you

βάρος πλὴν τούτων τῶν ἐπάναγκες,
⁴burden than these - necessary things,

29 ἀπέχεσθαι εἰδωλοθύτων καὶ αἵματος καὶ
to abstain from idol sacrifices and blood and

things strangled, and from fornication: from which if ye keep yourselves, ye shall do well.   Fare ye well.

30 So when they were dismissed, they came to Antioch: and when they had gathered the multitude together, they delivered the epistle:

31 *Which* when they had read, they rejoiced for the consolation.

32 And Judas and Silas, being prophets also themselves, exhorted the brethren with many words, and confirmed *them.*

33 And after they had tarried *there* a space, they were let go in peace from the brethren unto the apostles.

34 Notwithstanding it pleased Silas to abide there still.

35 Paul also and Barnabas continued in Antioch, teaching and preaching the word of the Lord, with many others also.

36 ¶ And some days after Paul said unto Barnabas, Let us go again and visit our brethren in every city where we have preached the word of the Lord, *and see* how they do.

37 And Barnabas determined to take with them John, whose surname was Mark.

38 But Paul thought not good to take him with them, who departed from

πνικτῶν   καὶ   πορνείας·   ἐξ   ὧν   διατηροῦντες
things   and   fornication;   from   which   keeping
strangled

ἑαυτοὺς   εὖ   πράξετε.   Ἔρρωσθε.
yourselves   well   ye will do.   Farewell.

30 Οἱ   μὲν   οὖν   ἀπολυθέντες   κατῆλθον   εἰς
They   –   therefore   being dismissed   went down   to

Ἀντιόχειαν,   καὶ   συναγαγόντες   τὸ   πλῆθος
Antioch,   and   assembling   the   multitude

ἐπέδωκαν   τὴν   ἐπιστολήν.   31 ἀναγνόντες   δὲ
handed in   the   letter.   And having read

ἐχάρησαν   ἐπὶ   τῇ   παρακλήσει.   32 Ἰούδας   τε
they rejoiced   at   the   exhortation.   And Judas

καὶ   Σιλᾶς,   καὶ   αὐτοὶ   προφῆται   ὄντες,
and   Silas,   also   [them]selves   prophets   being,

διὰ   λόγου   πολλοῦ   παρεκάλεσαν   τοὺς
through   speech   much   exhorted   the
(by)

ἀδελφοὺς   καὶ   ἐπεστήριξαν·   33 ποιήσαντες   δὲ
brothers   and   confirmed;   and having continued

χρόνον   ἀπελύθησαν   μετ'   εἰρήνης   ἀπὸ
a time   they were dismissed   with   peace   from

τῶν   ἀδελφῶν   πρὸς   τοὺς   ἀποστείλαντας
the   brothers   to   the [ones]   having sent

αὐτούς.   ‡   35 Παῦλος   δὲ   καὶ   Βαρναβᾶς
them.   But Paul   and   Barnabas

διέτριβον   ἐν   Ἀντιοχείᾳ,   διδάσκοντες   καὶ
stayed   in   Antioch,   teaching   and

εὐαγγελιζόμενοι   μετὰ   καὶ   ἑτέρων   πολλῶν
preaching   ¹with   ⁴also   ³others   ²many

τὸν   λόγον   τοῦ   κυρίου.
the   word   of the   Lord.

36 Μετὰ   δέ   τινας   ἡμέρας   εἶπεν   πρὸς
Now after   some   days   ²said   ¹to

Βαρναβᾶν   Παῦλος·   ἐπιστρέψαντες   δὴ
⁴Barnabas   ¹Paul: Returning   then

ἐπισκεψώμεθα   τοὺς   ἀδελφοὺς   κατὰ   πόλιν
let us visit   the   brothers   throughout   ²city

πᾶσαν   ἐν   αἷς   κατηγγείλαμεν   τὸν   λόγον
¹every   in   which   we announced   the   word

τοῦ   κυρίου,   πῶς   ἔχουσιν.   37 Βαρναβᾶς
of the   Lord,   how   they have(are).   Barnabas

δὲ   ἐβούλετο   συμπαραλαβεῖν   καὶ   τὸν
And   wished   to take with [them]   also   –

Ἰωάννην   τὸν   καλούμενον   Μᾶρκον·   38 Παῦλος
John   –   *being* called   Mark;   ²Paul

δὲ   ἠξίου,   τὸν   ἀποστάντα   ἀπ'   αὐτῶν
¹but   ⁸thought fit,   –   ⁷withdrawing   ⁸from   ⁹them

‡ Verse 34 omitted by Nestle; *cf.* R.V. marg.

them from Pamphylia, and went not with them to the work.

39 And the contention was so sharp between them, that they departed asunder one from the other: and so Barnabas took Mark, and sailed unto Cyprus;

40 And Paul chose Silas, and departed, being recommended by the brethren unto the grace of God.

41 And he went through Syria and Cilicia, confirming the churches.

ἀπὸ Παμφυλίας καὶ μὴ συνελθόντα αὐτοῖς
¹⁰from ¹¹Pamphylia ¹²and ¹³not ¹⁴going with ¹⁵them
εἰς τὸ ἔργον, μὴ συμπαραλαμβάνειν τοῦτον.
¹⁶to ¹⁷the ¹⁸work, ⁶not ⁸to take with [them] ⁹this one.
39 ἐγένετο δὲ παροξυσμός, ὥστε ἀποχωρισ-
And there was sharp feeling, so as to separ-
θῆναι αὐτοὺς ἀπ’ ἀλλήλων, τόν τε
ate them from each other, – and
Βαρναβᾶν παραλαβόντα τὸν Μᾶρκον
Barnabas taking – Mark
ἐκπλεῦσαι εἰς Κύπρον. 40 Παῦλος δὲ
to sail away to Cyprus. But Paul
ἐπιλεξάμενος Σιλᾶν ἐξῆλθεν, παραδοθεὶς
having chosen Silas went forth, being commended
τῇ χάριτι τοῦ κυρίου ὑπὸ τῶν
to the grace of the Lord by the
ἀδελφῶν· 41 διήρχετο δὲ τὴν Συρίαν
brothers; and he went through – Syria
καὶ Κιλικίαν ἐπιστηρίζων τὰς ἐκκλησίας.
and Cilicia confirming the churches.

CHAPTER 16

THEN came he to Derbe and Lystra: and, behold, a certain disciple was there, named Timotheus, the son of a certain woman, which was a Jewess, and believed; but his father was a Greek:

2 Which was well reported of by the brethren that were at Lystra and Iconium.

3 Him would Paul have to go forth with him; and took and circumcised him because of the Jews which were in those quarters: for they knew all that his father was a Greek.

4 And as they went through the cities, they delivered them the decrees

16 Κατήντησεν δὲ καὶ εἰς Δέρβην καὶ
And he came down also to Derbe and
εἰς Λύστραν. καὶ ἰδοὺ μαθητής τις ἦν
to Lystra. And behold[,] a certain disciple was
ἐκεῖ ὀνόματι Τιμόθεος, υἱὸς γυναικὸς
there by name Timothy, son ⁸woman
Ἰουδαίας πιστῆς πατρὸς δὲ Ἕλληνος,
¹Jewish ¹of a faithful ⁴but ⁵father ³of a Greek,
2 ὃς ἐμαρτυρεῖτο ὑπὸ τῶν ἐν Λύστροις
who was witnessed to by ¹the ²in ⁴Lystra
καὶ Ἰκονίῳ ἀδελφῶν. 3 τοῦτον ἠθέλησεν
⁵and ⁶Iconium ²brothers. ³This one ²wished
ὁ Παῦλος σὺν αὐτῷ ἐξελθεῖν, καὶ λαβὼν
– ¹Paul with him to go forth, and taking
περιέτεμεν αὐτὸν διὰ τοὺς Ἰουδαίους τοὺς
circumcised him on account the Jews –
    of
ὄντας ἐν τοῖς τόποις ἐκείνοις· ᾔδεισαν
being in those places; ²they knew
γὰρ ἅπαντες ὅτι Ἕλλην ὁ πατὴρ αὐτοῦ
¹for all that a Greek the father of him
ὑπῆρχεν. 4 Ὡς δὲ διεπορεύοντο τὰς
was. Now as they went through the
πόλεις, παρεδίδοσαν αὐτοῖς φυλάσσειν τὰ
cities, they delivered to them* to keep the

* Note the gender: πόλις is feminine.

for to keep, that were ordained of the apostles and elders which were at Jerusalem.

5 And so were the churches established in the faith, and increased in number daily.

6 Now when they had gone throughout Phrygia and the region of Galatia, and were forbidden of the Holy Ghost to preach the word in Asia,

7 After they were come to Mysia, they assayed to go into Bithynia: but the Spirit suffered them not.

8 And they passing by Mysia came down to Troas.

9 ¶ And a vision appeared to Paul in the night; There stood a man of Macedonia, and prayed him, saying, Come over into Macedonia, and help us.

10 And after he had seen the vision, immediately we endeavoured to go into Macedonia, assuredly gathering that the Lord had called us for to preach the gospel unto them.

11 Therefore loosing from Troas, we came with a straight course to Samothracia, and the next *day* to Neapolis;

12 And from thence to

δόγματα τὰ κεκριμένα ὑπὸ τῶν ἀποστόλων
decrees – having been by the apostles
decided [on]

καὶ πρεσβυτέρων τῶν ἐν Ἱεροσολύμοις.
and elders – in Jerusalem.

5 Αἱ μὲν οὖν ἐκκλησίαι ἐστερεοῦντο
¹The ¹therefore ²churches were strengthened

τῇ πίστει καὶ ἐπερίσσευον τῷ ἀριθμῷ
in the faith and increased – in number

καθ᾽ ἡμέραν.
daily.

6 Διῆλθον δὲ τὴν Φρυγίαν καὶ Γαλατικὴν
And they went through the Phrygian and Galatian

χώραν, κωλυθέντες ὑπὸ τοῦ ἁγίου
country, being prevented by the Holy

πνεύματος λαλῆσαι τὸν λόγον ἐν τῇ
Spirit to speak the word in –
=from speaking

Ἀσίᾳ· 7 ἐλθόντες δὲ κατὰ τὴν Μυσίαν
Asia; but coming against – Mysia

ἐπείραζον εἰς τὴν Βιθυνίαν πορευθῆναι,
they attempted into – Bithynia to go,

καὶ οὐκ εἴασεν αὐτοὺς τὸ πνεῦμα Ἰησοῦ·
and ⁶not ⁴allowed ⁵them ¹the ²Spirit ³of Jesus;

8 παρελθόντες δὲ τὴν Μυσίαν κατέβησαν
so passing by – Mysia they came down

εἰς Τρῳάδα. 9 καὶ ὅραμα διὰ νυκτὸς
to Troas. And a vision through [the]
(during) night

τῷ Παύλῳ ὤφθη, ἀνὴρ Μακεδών τις
– to Paul appeared, a *man* Macedonian certain

ἦν ἑστὼς καὶ παρακαλῶν αὐτὸν καὶ
was standing and beseeching him and

λέγων· διαβὰς εἰς Μακεδονίαν βοήθησον
saying: Crossing into Macedonia help

ἡμῖν. 10 ὡς δὲ τὸ ὅραμα εἶδεν, εὐθέως
us. So when the vision he saw, immediately

ἐζητήσαμεν ἐξελθεῖν εἰς Μακεδονίαν,
we sought to go forth to Macedonia,

συμβιβάζοντες ὅτι προσκέκληται ἡμᾶς ὁ
concluding that ²has(had) called ³us –

θεὸς εὐαγγελίσασθαι αὐτούς.
¹God to evangelize them.

11 Ἀναχθέντες δὲ ἀπὸ Τρῳάδος εὐθυδρο-
And setting sail from Troas we ran a

μήσαμεν εἰς Σαμοθρᾴκην, τῇ δὲ ἐπιούσῃ
straight course to Samothracia, and on the next day

εἰς Νέαν πόλιν, 12 κἀκεῖθεν εἰς Φιλίππους,
to Neapolis, and thence to Philippi,

Philippi, which is the chief city of that part of Macedonia, *and* a colony: and we were in that city abiding certain days.

13 And on the sabbath we went out of the city by a river side, where prayer was wont to be made: and we sat down, and spake unto the women which resorted *thither*.

14 ¶ And a certain woman named Lydia, a seller of purple, of the city of Thyatira, which worshipped God, heard *us*: whose heart the Lord opened, that she attended unto the things which were spoken of Paul.

15 And when she ·was baptized, and her household, she besought *us*, saying, If ye have judged me to be faithful to the Lord, come into my house, and abide *there*. And she constrained us.

16 ¶ And it came to pass, as we went to prayer, a certain damsel possessed with a spirit of divination met us, which brought her masters much gain by soothsaying:

17 The same followed Paul and us, and cried, saying, These men are the servants of the most high God, which shew unto us

ἥτις ἐστὶν πρώτη τῆς μερίδος Μακεδονίας
which is ¹[the] ²first ⁴of the ³part· ⁵of. Macedonia

πόλις, κολωνία. Ἦμεν δὲ ἐν· ταύτῃ τῇ
³city, a colony. And we were in this –

πόλει διατρίβοντες ἡμέρας τινάς. 13 τῇ τε
city staying days some. And on the

ἡμέρᾳ τῶν σαββάτων ἐξήλθομεν ἔξω τῆς
day of the sabbaths we went forth outside the

πύλης παρὰ ποταμὸν οὗ ἐνομίζομεν
gate by a river where we supposed

προσευχὴν εἶναι, καὶ καθίσαντες ἐλαλοῦμεν
a place of prayer to be, and sitting we spoke

ταῖς συνελθούσαις γυναιξίν. 14 καί τις
to the ²coming together ¹women. And a certain

γυνὴ ὀνόματι Λυδία, πορφυρόπωλις
woman by name Lydia, a dealer in purple-dyed [garments]

πόλεως Θυατίρων, σεβομένη τὸν θεόν,
of [the] city of Thyatira, worshipping – God,

ἤκουεν, ἧς ὁ κύριος διήνοιξεν τὴν καρδίαν
heard, of whom the Lord opened up the heart

προσέχειν τοῖς λαλουμένοις ὑπὸ Παύλου.
to take heed to the things being spoken by Paul.

15 ὡς δὲ ἐβαπτίσθη καὶ ὁ οἶκος αὐτῆς,
And when she was baptized and. the household of her,

·παρεκάλεσεν λέγουσα· εἰ κεκρίκατέ με
she besought saying: If ye have decided me

πιστὴν τῷ κυρίῳ εἶναι, εἰσελθόντες εἰς
faithful to the Lord to be, entering into

τὸν οἶκόν μου μένετε· καὶ παρεβιάσατο
the house of me remain; and she urged

ἡμᾶς. 16 Ἐγένετο δὲ πορευομένων ἡμῶν
us. And it happened going us°
= as we went

εἰς τὴν προσευχήν, παιδίσκην τινὰ ἔχουσαν
to the place of prayer, a certain maid having

πνεῦμα πύθωνα ὑπαντῆσαι ἡμῖν, ἥτις
a spirit of a python to meet us, who

ἐργασίαν πολλὴν παρεῖχεν τοῖς κυρίοις
³gain ²much ¹brought to the masters

αὐτῆς μαντευομένη. 17 αὕτη κατακολουθοῦσα
of her practising soothsaying. This one following after

τῷ Παύλῳ καὶ ἡμῖν ἔκραζεν λέγουσα·
– Paul and us cried out saying:

οὗτοι οἱ ἄνθρωποι δοῦλοι τοῦ θεοῦ τοῦ
These – men slaves of the God –

ὑψίστου εἰσίν, οἵτινες καταγγέλλουσιν ὑμῖν
most high are, who announce to you

the way of salvation.

18 And this did she many days. But Paul, being grieved, turned and said to the spirit, I command thee in the name of Jesus Christ to come out of her. And he came out the same hour.

19 ¶ And when her masters saw that the hope of their gains was gone, they caught Paul and Silas, and drew *them* into the marketplace unto the rulers,

20 And brought them to the magistrates, saying, These men, being Jews, do exceedingly trouble our city,

21 And teach customs, which are not lawful for us to receive, neither to observe, being Romans.

22 And the multitude rose up together against them: and the magistrates rent off their clothes, and commanded to beat *them*.

23 And when they had laid many stripes upon them, they cast *them* into prison, charging the jailor to keep them safely:

24 Who, having received such a charge, thrust them into the inner prison, and made their feet fast in the stocks.

25 ¶ And at midnight

ὁδὸν σωτηρίας. **18** τοῦτο δὲ ἐποίει ἐπὶ
a way of salvation. And this she did over

πολλὰς ἡμέρας. διαπονηθεὶς δὲ Παῦλος
many days. But becoming greatly troubled Paul

καὶ ἐπιστρέψας τῷ πνεύματι εἶπεν· παραγ-
and turning ¹to the ²spirit ¹he said: charge

γέλλω σοι ἐν ὀνόματι Ἰησοῦ Χριστοῦ
thee in [the] name of Jesus Christ

ἐξελθεῖν ἀπ᾿ αὐτῆς· καὶ ἐξῆλθεν αὐτῇ
to come out from her; and it came out in the

τῇ ὥρᾳ. **19** Ἰδόντες δὲ οἱ κύριοι αὐτῆς
same hour.* And ⁴seeing ¹the ²masters ³of her

ὅτι ἐξῆλθεν ἡ ἐλπὶς τῆς ἐργασίας αὐτῶν,
⁵that ¹¹went out ⁶the ⁷hope ⁸of the ⁹gain ¹⁰of them,

ἐπιλαβόμενοι τὸν Παῦλον καὶ τὸν Σιλᾶν
having seized – Paul and – Silas

εἵλκυσαν εἰς τὴν ἀγορὰν ἐπὶ τοὺς ἄρχοντας,
dragged to the marketplace before the rulers,

20 καὶ προσαγαγόντες αὐτοὺς τοῖς στρατηγοῖς
and ¹bringing ²to ³them the prætors

εἶπαν· οὗτοι οἱ ἄνθρωποι ἐκταράσσουσιν
said: These – men are greatly troubling

ἡμῶν τὴν πόλιν, Ἰουδαῖοι ὑπάρχοντες,
of us the city, ²Jews ¹being,

21 καὶ καταγγέλλουσιν ἔθη ἃ οὐκ ἔξεστιν
and they announce customs which it is not lawful

ἡμῖν παραδέχεσθαι οὐδὲ ποιεῖν Ῥωμαίοις
for us to receive nor to do ²Romans

οὖσιν. **22** καὶ συνεπέστη ὁ ὄχλος κατ᾿
¹being. And rose up together the crowd against

αὐτῶν, καὶ οἱ στρατηγοὶ περιρήξαντες
them, and the prætors tearing off

αὐτῶν τὰ ἱμάτια ἐκέλευον ῥαβδίζειν,
of them the garments commanded to flog,

23 πολλὰς δὲ ἐπιθέντες αὐτοῖς πληγὰς
and ²many ¹laying on ³them ⁴stripes

ἔβαλον εἰς φυλακήν, παραγγείλαντες τῷ
threw into prison, charging the

δεσμοφύλακι ἀσφαλῶς τηρεῖν αὐτούς· **24** ὃς
jailer securely to keep them; who

παραγγελίαν τοιαύτην λαβὼν ἔβαλεν αὐτοὺς
²a charge ³such ¹having received threw them

εἰς τὴν ἐσωτέραν φυλακὴν καὶ τοὺς
into the inner prison and ²the

πόδας ἠσφαλίσατο αὐτῶν εἰς τὸ ξύλον.
³feet ¹secured ⁴of them in the stocks.

25 Κατὰ δὲ τὸ μεσονύκτιον Παῦλος καὶ
And about – midnight Paul and

* See Luke 2. 38.

Paul and Silas prayed, and sang praises unto God: and the prisoners heard them.

26 And suddenly there was a great earthquake, so that the foundations of the prison were shaken: and immediately all the doors were opened, and every one's bands were loosed.

27 And the keeper of the prison awaking out of his sleep, and seeing the prison doors open, he drew out his sword, and would have killed himself, supposing that the prisoners had been fled.

28 But Paul cried with a loud voice, saying, Do thyself no harm: for we are all here.

29 Then he called for a light, and sprang in, and came trembling, and fell down before Paul and Silas,

30 And brought them out, and said, Sirs, what must I do to be saved?

31 And they said, Believe on the Lord Jesus Christ, and thou shalt be saved, and thy house.

32 And they spake unto him the word of the Lord, and to all that were in his house.

33 And he took them the same hour of the night,

Σιλᾶς προσευχόμενοι ὕμνουν τὸν θεόν,
Silas praying ¹praised ³in a hymn – ²God,

ἐπηκροῶντο δὲ αὐτῶν οἱ δέσμιοι· 26 ἄφνω δὲ
and ³listened to ⁴them ¹the ²prisoners; and suddenly

σεισμὸς ἐγένετο μέγας, ὥστε σαλευ-
²earthquake ¹there was ²a great, so as to be

θῆναι τὰ θεμέλια τοῦ δεσμωτηρίου·
shaken the foundations of the jail;

ἠνεῴχθησαν δὲ παραχρῆμα αἱ θύραι πᾶσαι,
and ⁵were opened ¹at once ³the ⁴doors ²all,

καὶ πάντων τὰ δεσμὰ ἀνέθη. 27 ἔξυπνος δὲ
and ³of all ¹the ²bonds were And ⁴awake
loosened.

γενόμενος ὁ δεσμοφύλαξ καὶ ἰδὼν
³having become ¹the ²jailer and seeing

ἀνεῳγμένας τὰς θύρας τῆς φυλακῆς,
having been opened the doors of the prison,

σπασάμενος τὴν μάχαιραν ἤμελλεν ἑαυτὸν
having drawn the sword was about himself

ἀναιρεῖν, νομίζων ἐκπεφευγέναι τοὺς
to kill, supposing to have escaped the

δεσμίους. 28 ἐφώνησεν δὲ Παῦλος μεγάλῃ
prisoners. But called Paul with a
great(loud)

φωνῇ λέγων· μηδὲν πράξῃς σεαυτῷ κακόν,
voice saying: ¹Nothing ³do ²thyself ¹harm,

ἅπαντες γάρ ἐσμεν ἐνθάδε. 29 αἰτήσας
for ²all ¹we are ³here. asking

δὲ φῶτα εἰσεπήδησεν, καὶ ἔντρομος
And lights he rushed in, and trembling

γενόμενος προσέπεσεν τῷ Παύλῳ καὶ
becoming he fell before – Paul and

Σιλᾷ, 30 καὶ προαγαγὼν αὐτοὺς ἔξω ἔφη·
Silas, and ¹leading ³forward ²them outside said:

κύριοι, τί με δεῖ ποιεῖν ἵνα σωθῶ;
Sirs, what ²me ¹behoves it to do that I may
be saved?

31 οἱ δὲ εἶπαν· πίστευσον ἐπὶ τὸν κύριον
And they said: Believe on the Lord

Ἰησοῦν, καὶ σωθήσῃ σὺ καὶ ὁ οἶκός
Jesus, and shalt be saved thou and the household

σου. 32 καὶ ἐλάλησαν αὐτῷ τὸν λόγον
of thee. And they spoke to him the word

τοῦ θεοῦ σὺν πᾶσιν τοῖς ἐν τῇ οἰκίᾳ
– of God with all the [ones] in the house

αὐτοῦ. 33 καὶ παραλαβὼν αὐτοὺς ἐν
of him. And taking them in

ἐκείνῃ τῇ ὥρᾳ τῆς νυκτὸς ἔλουσεν ἀπὸ
that – hour of the night he washed from

and washed *their* stripes; and was baptized, he and all his, straightway.

34 And when he had brought them into his house, he set meat before them, and rejoiced, believing in God with all his house.

35 And when it was day, the magistrates sent the serjeants, saying, Let those men go.

36 And the keeper of the prison told this saying to Paul, The magistrates have sent to let you go: now therefore depart, and go in peace.

37 But Paul said unto them, They have beaten us openly uncondemned, being Romans, and have cast *us* into prison; and now do they thrust us out privily? nay verily; but let them come themselves and fetch us out.

38 And the serjeants told these words unto the magistrates : and they feared, when they heard that they were Romans.

39 And they came and besought them, and brought *them* out, and desired *them* to depart out of the city.

40 And they went out

τῶν πληγῶν, καὶ ἐβαπτίσθη αὐτὸς καὶ
the stripes, and was baptized he and

οἱ αὐτοῦ ἅπαντες παραχρῆμα, 34 ἀναγαγών
the of him all at once, ²bringing up
=all his

τε αὐτοὺς εἰς τὸν οἶκον παρέθηκεν
¹and them to the house he set
before [them]

τράπεζαν, καὶ ἠγαλλιάσατο πανοικεὶ πεπι-
a table, and exulted with all the having
household

στευκὼς τῷ θεῷ. 35 Ἡμέρας δὲ γενομένης
believed – God. And day coming²
=when day came

ἀπέστειλαν οἱ στρατηγοὶ τοὺς ῥαβδούχους
²sent ¹the ²prætors the tipstaffs

λέγοντες· ἀπόλυσον τοὺς ἀνθρώπους
saying: Release – men

ἐκείνους. 36 ἀπήγγειλεν δὲ ὁ δεσμοφύλαξ
those. And announced the jailer

τοὺς λόγους τούτους πρὸς τὸν Παῦλον,
these words to – Paul,

ὅτι ἀπέσταλκαν οἱ στρατηγοὶ ἵνα ἀπολυθῆτε.
– ²have sent ¹The ²prætors that ye may be
released.

νῦν οὖν ἐξελθόντες πορεύεσθε ἐν εἰρήνη.
Now therefore going forth proceed in peace.

37 ὁ δὲ Παῦλος ἔφη πρὸς αὐτούς·
– But Paul said to them:

δείραντες ἡμᾶς δημοσίᾳ ἀκατακρίτους,
Having beaten us publicly uncondemned,

ἀνθρώπους Ῥωμαίους ὑπάρχοντας, ἔβαλαν
men ²Romans ¹being, they threw [us]

εἰς φυλακήν· καὶ νῦν λάθρα ἡμᾶς ἐκβάλ-
into prison; and now secretly us they

λουσιν; οὐ γάρ, ἀλλὰ ἐλθόντες αὐτοὶ
expel? No indeed, but coming [them]selves

ἡμᾶς ἐξαγαγέτωσαν. 38 ἀπήγγειλαν δὲ τοῖς
us let them bring out. And ²reported ⁴to the

στρατηγοῖς οἱ ῥαβδοῦχοι τὰ ῥήματα ταῦτα.
³prætors ¹the ²tipstaffs these words.

ἐφοβήθησαν δὲ ἀκούσαντες ὅτι Ῥωμαῖοί
And they were afraid hearing that Romans

εἰσιν, 39 καὶ ἐλθόντες παρεκάλεσαν
they are(were), and coming besought

αὐτούς, καὶ ἐξαγαγόντες ἠρώτων ἀπελθεῖν
them, and bringing out asked to go away

ἀπὸ τῆς πόλεως. 40 ἐξελθόντες δὲ ἀπὸ
from the city. And going out from

of the prison, and entered into *the house of* Lydia: and when they had seen the brethren, they comforted them, and departed.

τῆς φυλακῆς εἰσῆλθον πρὸς τὴν Λυδίαν,
the prison they entered to [the house of] Lydia,

καὶ ἰδόντες παρεκάλεσαν τοὺς ἀδελφοὺς
and seeing they exhorted the brothers

καὶ ἐξῆλθαν.
and went forth.

CHAPTER 17

NOW when they had passed through Amphipolis and Apollonia, they came to Thessalonica, where was a synagogue of of the Jews:

2 And Paul, as his manner was, went in unto them, and three sabbath days reasoned with them out of the scriptures,

3 Opening and alleging, that Christ must needs have suffered, and risen again from the dead; and that this Jesus, whom I preach unto you, is Christ.

4 And some of them believed, and consorted with Paul and Silas; and of the devout Greeks a great multitude, and of the chief women not a few.

5 ¶ But the Jews which believed not, moved with envy, took unto them certain lewd fellows of the baser sort, and gathered a company, and set all the city on an uproar, and assaulted the house of Jason, and sought to bring them out to the people.

17 Διοδεύσαντες δὲ τὴν Ἀμφίπολιν καὶ
And travelling through - Amphipolis and

τὴν Ἀπολλωνίαν ἦλθον εἰς Θεσσαλονίκην,
- Apollonia they came to Thessalonica,

ὅπου ἦν συναγωγὴ τῶν Ἰουδαίων. **2** κατὰ
where was a synagogue of the Jews. according to

δὲ τὸ εἰωθὸς τῷ Παύλῳ εἰσῆλθεν πρὸς
And the custom - with Paul⁰ he entered to

αὐτούς, καὶ ἐπὶ σάββατα τρία διελέξατο
them, and on sabbaths three lectured

αὐτοῖς ἀπὸ τῶν γραφῶν, **3** διανοίγων
to them from the scriptures, opening up

καὶ παρατιθέμενος ὅτι τὸν χριστὸν ἔδει
and setting before [them] that ¹the ²Christ ³it behoved

παθεῖν καὶ ἀναστῆναι ἐκ νεκρῶν, καὶ
to suffer and to rise again out of [the] dead, and

ὅτι οὗτός ἐστιν ὁ χριστός, ὁ Ἰησοῦς,
that this is(was) the Christ, - Jesus,

ὃν ἐγὼ καταγγέλλω ὑμῖν. **4** καὶ τινες
whom I announce to you. And some

ἐξ αὐτῶν ἐπείσθησαν καὶ προσεκληρώθησαν
of them were persuaded and threw in their lot

τῷ Παύλῳ καὶ τῷ Σιλᾷ, τῶν τε
- with Paul and - Silas, both of the

σεβομένων Ἑλλήνων πλῆθος πολύ, γυναικῶν τε
worshipping Greeks ²multitude ¹a much and of ²women
(great),

τῶν πρώτων οὐκ ὀλίγαι. **5** Ζηλώσαντες δὲ
¹the ²chief not a few. But becoming jealous

οἱ Ἰουδαῖοι καὶ προσλαβόμενοι τῶν
the Jews and taking aside of the

ἀγοραίων ἄνδρας τινὰς πονηροὺς καὶ
loungers in the men some wicked and
marketplace

ὀχλοποιήσαντες ἐθορύβουν τὴν πόλιν, καὶ
having gathered a disturbed the city, and
crowd

ἐπιστάντες τῇ οἰκίᾳ Ἰάσονος ἐζήτουν
coming on the house of Jason sought

αὐτοὺς προαγαγεῖν εἰς τὸν δῆμον· **6** μὴ
them to bring forward to the mob; ²not

6 And when they found them not, they drew Jason and certain brethren unto the rulers of the city, crying, These that have turned the world upside down are come hither also;

7 Whom Jason hath received: and these all do contrary to the decrees of Cæsar, saying that there is another king, *one* Jesus.

8 And they troubled the people and the rulers of the city, when they heard these things.

9 And when they had taken security of Jason, and of the other, they let them go.

10 ¶ And the brethren immediately sent away Paul and Silas by night unto Berea: who coming *thither* went into the synagogue of the Jews.

11 These were more noble than those in Thessalonica, in that they received the word with all readiness of mind, and searched the scriptures daily, whether those things were so.

12 Therefore many of them believed; also of honourable women which were Greeks, and of men, not a few.

13 But when the Jews of Thessalonica had knowledge that the word of God

εὑρόντες δὲ αὐτοὺς ἔσυρον Ἰάσονα καὶ
³finding ¹but them they dragged Jason and

τινας ἀδελφοὺς ἐπὶ τοὺς πολιτάρχας,
some brothers to the politarchs,

βοῶντες ὅτι οἱ τὴν οἰκουμένην ἀναστατώ-
crying[.] – ²the ⁴the ⁵inhabited ³having turned
[ones] earth

σαντες οὗτοι καὶ ἐνθάδε πάρεισιν, 7 οὓς
upside ¹these also here have arrived, whom
down men

ὑποδέδεκται Ἰάσων· καὶ οὗτοι πάντες
²has received ¹Jason; and these all

ἀπέναντι τῶν δογμάτων Καίσαρος
²contrary to ³the ⁴decrees ⁵of Cæsar

πράσσουσιν, βασιλέα ἕτερον λέγοντες εἶναι
¹act, ⁴king ³another ²saying ⁵to be

Ἰησοῦν. 8 ἐτάραξαν δὲ τὸν ὄχλον καὶ
⁵Jesus. And they troubled the crowd and

τοὺς πολιτάρχας ἀκούοντας ταῦτα, 9 καὶ
the politarchs hearing these things, and

λαβόντες τὸ ἱκανὸν παρὰ τοῦ Ἰάσονος
taking the surety from – Jason

καὶ τῶν λοιπῶν ἀπέλυσαν αὐτούς. 10 Οἱ δὲ
and the rest released them. And the

ἀδελφοὶ εὐθέως διὰ νυκτὸς ἐξεπεμψαν
brothers immediately through [the] night sent forth
(during)

τόν τε Παῦλον καὶ τὸν Σιλᾶν εἰς Βέροιαν,
– both Paul and – Silas to Berœa,

οἵτινες παραγενόμενοι εἰς τὴν συναγωγὴν
who having arrived ²into ³the synagogue

τῶν Ἰουδαίων ἀπήεσαν· 11 οὗτοι δὲ ἦσαν
⁴of the ⁵Jews ¹went; and these were

εὐγενέστεροι τῶν ἐν Θεσσαλονίκῃ, οἵτινες
more noble [than] the [ones] in Thessalonica, who

ἐδέξαντο τὸν λόγον μετὰ πάσης προθυμίας,
received the word with all eagerness,

[τὸ] καθ' ἡμέραν ἀνακρίνοντες τὰς γραφὰς
daily examining the scriptures

εἰ ἔχοι ταῦτα οὕτως. 12 πολλοὶ μὲν
if ³have(are) ¹these things ²so. Many –

οὖν ἐξ αὐτῶν ἐπίστευσαν, καὶ τῶν
therefore of them believed, and of the

Ἑλληνίδων γυναικῶν τῶν εὐσχημόνων καὶ
²Greek ⁴women – ¹honourable and

ἀνδρῶν οὐκ ὀλίγοι. 13 Ὡς δὲ ἔγνωσαν
of men not a few. But when ⁵knew

οἱ ἀπὸ τῆς Θεσσαλονίκης Ἰουδαῖοι ὅτι
¹the ³from – ⁴Thessalonica ²Jews that

was preached of Paul at Berea, they came thither also, and stirred up the people.

14 And then immediately the brethren sent away Paul to go as it were to the sea: but Silas and Timotheus abode there still.

15 And they that conducted Paul brought him unto Athens: and receiving a commandment unto Silas and Timotheus for to come to him with all speed, they departed.

16 ¶ Now while Paul waited for them at Athens, his spirit was stirred in him, when he saw the city wholly given to idolatry.

17 Therefore disputed he in the synagogue with the Jews, and with the devout persons, and in the market daily with them that met with him.

18 Then certain philosophers of the Epicureans, and of the Stoicks, encountered him. And some said, What will this babbler say? other some, He seemeth to be a setter forth of strange gods:

καὶ ἐν τῇ Βεροίᾳ κατηγγέλη ὑπὸ τοῦ
also in - Beroea was announced by -

Παύλου ὁ λόγος τοῦ θεοῦ, ἦλθον κἀκεῖ
Paul the word - of God, they came there also

σαλεύοντες καὶ ταράσσοντες τοὺς ὄχλους.
shaking and troubling the crowds.

14 εὐθέως δὲ τότε τὸν Παῦλον ἐξαπέστειλαν
So immediately then -⁴Paul ³sent away

οἱ ἀδελφοὶ πορεύεσθαι ἕως ἐπὶ τὴν
¹the ²brothers to go as far as to the

θάλασσαν· ὑπέμεινάν τε ὅ τε Σιλᾶς καὶ
sea; ¹but ⁶remained - ²both ³Silas ⁴and

ὁ Τιμόθεος ἐκεῖ. 15 οἱ δὲ καθιστάνοντες
- ⁵Timothy ⁷there. And the [ones] conducting

τὸν Παῦλον ἤγαγον ἕως Ἀθηνῶν, καὶ
- Paul brought [him] as far as Athens, and

λαβόντες ἐντολὴν πρὸς τὸν Σιλᾶν καὶ τὸν
receiving a command to - Silas and -

Τιμόθεον ἵνα ὡς τάχιστα ἔλθωσιν πρὸς
Timothy that as quickly they should to
[as possible] come

αὐτὸν ἐξῄεσαν.
him they departed.

16 Ἐν δὲ ταῖς Ἀθήναις ἐκδεχομένου
And in - Athens awaiting
=while Paul awaited them,

αὐτοὺς τοῦ Παύλου, παρωξύνετο τὸ πνεῦμα
them - Paul,ᵃ ⁴was provoked ¹the ²spirit

αὐτοῦ ἐν αὐτῷ θεωροῦντος κατείδωλον
³of him in him beholding ⁴full of images

οὖσαν τὴν πόλιν. 17 διελέγετο μὲν οὖν
³being ¹the ²city. He addressed -* therefore

ἐν τῇ συναγωγῇ τοῖς Ἰουδαίοις καὶ
in the synagogue the Jews and

τοῖς σεβομένοις καὶ ἐν τῇ ἀγορᾷ κατὰ
the [ones] worshipping and in the marketplace -

πᾶσαν ἡμέραν πρὸς τοὺς παρατυγχάνοντας.
every day to the [ones] chancing to be [there].

18 τινὲς δὲ καὶ τῶν Ἐπικουρείων καὶ
But some also of the Epicurean and

Στωϊκῶν φιλοσόφων συνέβαλλον αὐτῷ, καὶ
Stoic philosophers fell in with him, and

τινες ἔλεγον· τί ἂν θέλοι ὁ σπερμολόγος
some said: What may wish -²ignorant plagiarist

οὗτος λέγειν; οἱ δέ· ξένων δαιμονίων
¹this to say? And others [said]: Of foreign demons

δοκεῖ καταγγελεὺς εἶναι· ὅτι τὸν Ἰησοῦν
he seems an announcer to be; because - Jesus

* See note on ch. 12. 5.

because he preached unto them Jesus, and the resurrection.

19 And they took him, and brought him unto Areopagus, saying, May we know what this new doctrine, whereof thou speakest, is?

20 For thou bringest certain strange things to our ears: we would know therefore what these things mean.

21 (For all the Athenians and strangers which were there spent their time in nothing else, but either to tell, or to hear some new thing.)

22 ¶ Then Paul stood in the midst of Mars' hill, and said, Ye men of Athens, I perceive that in all things ye are too superstitious.

23 For as I passed by, and beheld your devotions, I found an altar with this inscription, TO THE UNKNOWN GOD. Whom therefore ye ignorantly worship, him declare I unto you.

24 God that made the world and all things therein, seeing that he is Lord of heaven and earth, dwelleth not in temples made with hands;

25 Neither is worshipped with men's hands, as though he needed any thing, seeing he giveth to all life, and breath, and all things;

26 And hath made of

καὶ τὴν ἀνάστασιν εὐηγγελίζετο. 19 ἐπιλα-
and the resurrection he preached. taking

βόμενοι δὲ αὐτοῦ ἐπὶ τὸν Ἄρειον πάγον
hold And of him to the Areopagus

ἤγαγον, λέγοντες· δυνάμεθα γνῶναι τίς
they led [him], saying: Can we *to* know what

ἡ καινὴ αὕτη ἡ ὑπὸ σοῦ λαλουμένη
¹this ²new – ⁵by ⁶thee ⁴being spoken

διδαχή; 20 ξενίζοντα γάρ τινα εἰσφέρεις
³teaching [is]? for ²startling things ¹some thou bringest *in*

εἰς τὰς ἀκοὰς ἡμῶν· βουλόμεθα οὖν
to the ears of us; we are minded therefore

γνῶναι τίνα θέλει ταῦτα εἶναι. 21 Ἀθηναῖοι
to know what wishes these things to be. ²Athenians

δὲ πάντες καὶ οἱ ἐπιδημοῦντες ξένοι εἰς
Now ¹all ³and ⁴the ⁶dwelling ⁵strangers ⁸for

οὐδὲν ἕτερον ηὐκαίρουν ἢ λέγειν τι ἢ
⁹nothing ¹⁰different ⁷have leisure either to say something or

ἀκούειν τι καινότερον. 22 Σταθεὶς δὲ
to hear something newer. And standing

Παῦλος ἐν μέσῳ τοῦ Ἀρείου πάγου
⁵Paul ¹in ²[the] midst ³of the ⁴Areopagus

ἔφη· ἄνδρες Ἀθηναῖοι, κατὰ πάντα ὡς
said: *Men* Athenians, in everything how

δεισιδαιμονεστέρους ὑμᾶς θεωρῶ. 23 διερχόμενος
very religious ²you ¹I behold. passing along

γὰρ καὶ ἀναθεωρῶν τὰ σεβάσματα ὑμῶν
For and looking up at the objects of worship of you

εὗρον καὶ βωμὸν ἐν ᾧ ἐπεγέγραπτο·
I found also an altar in which had been inscribed:

ΑΓΝΩΣΤΩ ΘΕΩ. ὃ οὖν ἀγνοοῦντες
TO AN UNKNOWN GOD. What therefore being ignorant

εὐσεβεῖτε, τοῦτο ἐγὼ καταγγέλλω ὑμῖν.
ye reverence, this I announce to you.

24 ὁ θεὸς ὁ ποιήσας τὸν κόσμον καὶ
The God the [one] having made the world and

πάντα τὰ ἐν αὐτῷ, οὗτος οὐρανοῦ καὶ
all the things in it, this one ³of heaven ⁴and

γῆς ὑπάρχων κύριος οὐκ ἐν χειροποιήτοις
⁵of earth ¹being ²lord ²not ³in ⁴hand-made

ναοῖς κατοικεῖ, 25 οὐδὲ ὑπὸ χειρῶν
⁵shrines ¹dwells, nor ²by ³hands

ἀνθρωπίνων θεραπεύεται προσδεόμενός
²human ¹is served having need

τινος, αὐτὸς διδοὺς πᾶσι ζωὴν καὶ πνοὴν
of anything, he giving to all life and breath

καὶ τὰ πάντα· 26 ἐποίησέν τε ἐξ ἑνὸς
and – all things; and he made of one

one blood all nations of men for to dwell on all the face of the earth, and hath determined the times before appointed, and the bounds of their habitation;

27 That they should seek the Lord, if haply they might feel after him, and find him, though he be not far from every one of us:

28 For in him we live, and move, and have our being; as certain also of your own poets have said, For we are also his offspring.

29 Forasmuch then as we are the offspring of God, we ought not to think that the Godhead is like unto gold, or silver, or stone, graven by art and man's device.

30 And the times of this ignorance God winked at; but now commandeth all men every where to repent:

31 Because he hath appointed a day, in the which he will judge the world in righteousness by *that* man whom he hath ordained; *whereof* he hath given assurance unto all *men*, in that he hath raised him from the dead.

32 ¶ And when they heard of the resurrection of the dead, some mocked: and others said, We will hear thee again of this *matter*.

πᾶν ἔθνος ἀνθρώπων κατοικεῖν ἐπὶ παντὸς
every nation of men to dwell on all

προσώπου τῆς γῆς, ὁρίσας προστεταγμένους
[the] face of the earth, fixing *having been* appointed

καιροὺς καὶ τὰς ὁροθεσίας τῆς κατοικίας
seasons and the boundaries of the dwelling

αὐτῶν, 27 ζητεῖν τὸν θεόν, εἰ ἄρα γε
of them, to seek – God, if perchance

ψηλαφήσειαν αὐτὸν καὶ εὕροιεν, καί γε
they might feel after him and might find, though

οὐ μακρὰν ἀπὸ ἑνὸς ἑκάστου ἡμῶν
²not ³far ⁴from ⁵one ⁵each ⁶of us

ὑπάρχοντα. 28 ἐν αὐτῷ γὰρ ζῶμεν καὶ
¹being. ²in ³him ¹For we live and

κινούμεθα καὶ ἐσμέν, ὡς καὶ τινες τῶν
move and are, as indeed some of the

καθ' ὑμᾶς ποιητῶν εἰρήκασιν· τοῦ γὰρ
²among ³you ¹poets have said: ⁵of him ¹For

καὶ γένος ἐσμέν. 29 γένος οὖν ὑπάρχοντες
²also ³offspring ⁴we are. Offspring therefore being

τοῦ θεοῦ οὐκ ὀφείλομεν νομίζειν, χρυσῷ
– of God we ought not to suppose, ⁶to gold

ἢ ἀργύρῳ ἢ λίθῳ, χαράγματι τέχνης
⁶or ⁷to silver ⁸or ⁹to stone, ¹⁰to an ¹¹of art
                           engraved work

καὶ ἐνθυμήσεως ἀνθρώπου, τὸ θεῖον εἶναι
¹²and ¹³of meditation ¹⁴of man, ¹the ²divine ³to be
                                   nature

ὅμοιον. 30 τοὺς μὲν οὖν χρόνους τῆς
⁴like. ⁵The ¹so ²then ⁴times –

ἀγνοίας ὑπεριδὼν ὁ θεὸς τὰ νῦν
⁷of ignorance ⁴having ³God – now
         overlooked

ἀπαγγέλλει τοῖς ἀνθρώποις πάντας πανταχοῦ
declares – to men all men everywhere

μετανοεῖν, 31 καθότι ἔστησεν ἡμέραν ἐν
to repent, because he set a day in

ᾗ μέλλει κρίνειν τὴν οἰκουμένην ἐν
which he is about to judge the inhabited earth in

δικαιοσύνῃ, ἐν ἀνδρὶ ᾧ ὥρισεν, πίστιν
righteousness, by a man whom he desig- ²a
                            nated, guarantee

παρασχὼν πᾶσιν ἀναστήσας αὐτὸν ἐκ
¹offering to all having raised up him out of

νεκρῶν. 32 ἀκούσαντες δὲ ἀνάστασιν
[the] dead. And hearing [of] a resurrection

νεκρῶν, οἱ μὲν ἐχλεύαζον, οἱ δὲ εἶπαν·
of dead some scoffed, others said:
persons,

ἀκουσόμεθά σου περὶ τούτου καὶ πάλιν.
We will hear thee concerning this also **again.**

,33 So Paul departed from among them.

34 Howbeit certain men clave unto him, and believed: among the which was Dionysius the Areopagite, and a woman named Damaris, and others with them.

33 οὕτως	ὁ	Παῦλος	ἐξῆλθεν	ἐκ	μέσου
Thus	–	Paul	went forth	from	[the] midst

αὐτῶν.	34 τινὲς	δὲ	ἄνδρες	κολληθέντες
of them.	But some		men	adhering

αὐτῷ	ἐπίστευσαν,	ἐν	οἷς	καὶ	Διονύσιος
to him	believed,	among whom	both		Dionysius

ὁ	Ἀρεοπαγίτης	καὶ	γυνὴ	ὀνόματι	Δαμαρὶς
the	Areopagite	and a woman	by name		Damaris

καὶ	ἕτεροι	σὺν	αὐτοῖς.
and	others	with	them.

CHAPTER 18

AFTER these things Paul departed from Athens, and came to Corinth;

2 And found a certain Jew named Aquila, born in Pontus, lately come from Italy, with his wife Priscilla; (because that Claudius had commanded all Jews to depart from Rome:) and came unto them.

3 And because he was of the same craft, he abode with them, and wrought: for by their occupation they were tentmakers.

4 And he reasoned in the synagogue every sabbath, and persuaded the Jews and the Greeks.

5 And when Silas and Timotheus were come from Macedonia, Paul was pressed in the spirit, and testified to the Jews that Jesus was Christ.

6 And when they opposed themselves, and

18 Μετὰ	ταῦτα	χωρισθεὶς	ἐκ	τῶν
After	these things	departing	out of	–

Ἀθηνῶν	ἦλθεν	εἰς	Κόρινθον.	2 καὶ
Athens	he came	to	Corinth.	And

εὑρών	τινα	Ἰουδαῖον	ὀνόματι	Ἀκύλαν,
finding	a certain	Jew	by name	Aquila,

Ποντικὸν	τῷ	γένει,	προσφάτως	ἐληλυθότα
belonging to	–	by race,	recently	having come
Pontus				

ἀπὸ	τῆς	Ἰταλίας,	καὶ	Πρίσκιλλαν	γυναῖκα
from	–	Italy,	and	Priscilla	wife

αὐτοῦ,	διὰ	τὸ	διατεταχέναι	Κλαύδιον[b]
of him,	because of	the	to have commanded	Claudius[b]
	=because Claudius had commanded			

χωρίζεσθαι	πάντας	τοὺς	Ἰουδαίους	ἀπὸ
ʟo depart	all	the	Jews	from

τῆς	Ῥώμης,	προσῆλθεν	αὐτοῖς,	3 καὶ
–	Rome,	he came to	them,	and

διὰ	τὸ	ὁμότεχνον	εἶναι	ἔμενεν	παρ'
because of	the	of the same trade	to be[b]	he remained	with
	=because [he] was of the same trade				

αὐτοῖς,	καὶ	ἠργάζοντο·	ἦσαν	γὰρ	σκηνοποιοὶ
them,	and	they wrought;	for they were		tentmakers

τῇ	τέχνῃ.	4 διελέγετο	δὲ	ἐν	τῇ	συναγωγῇ
–	by trade.	And he lectured		in	the	synagogue

κατὰ	πᾶν	σάββατον,	ἔπειθέν	τε	Ἰουδαίους
on	every	sabbath,	he persuaded both		Jews

καὶ	Ἕλληνας.	5 Ὡς	δὲ	κατῆλθον	ἀπὸ
and	Greeks.	And when		came down	from

τῆς	Μακεδονίας	ὅ	τε	Σιλᾶς	καὶ	ὁ
–	Macedonia	–	both	Silas	and	–

Τιμόθεος,	συνείχετο	τῷ	λόγῳ	ὁ	Παῦλος,
Timothy,	was pressed	by	the word	–	Paul,

διαμαρτυρόμενος	τοῖς	Ἰουδαίοις	εἶναι	τὸν
solemnly witnessing	to the	Jews	to be	the
		=that Jesus was the Christ.		

χριστὸν	Ἰησοῦν.	6 ἀντιτασσομένων	δὲ	αὐτῶν
Christ	Jesus.	But resisting		them
		=when they resisted and blasphemed		

blasphemed, he shook *his*
raiment, and said unto
them, Your blood *be*
upon your own heads; I
am clean: from hence-
forth I will go unto the
Gentiles.
7 And he departed
thence, and entered into
a certain *man's* house,
named Justus, *one* that
worshipped God, whose
house joined hard to the
synagogue.
8 And Crispus, the chief
ruler of the synagogue, believed on the Lord with
all his house; and many
of the Corinthians hear-
ing believed, and were
baptized.
9 Then spake the Lord
to Paul in the night by a
vision, Be not afraid, but
speak, and hold not thy
peace:
10 For I am with thee,
and no man shall set on
thee to hurt thee: for I
have much people in this
city.
11 And he continued
there a year and six
months, teaching the word
of God among them.
12 ¶ And when Gallio
was the deputy of Achaia,
the Jews made insurrec-
tion with one accord
against Paul, and brought
him to the judgment seat,
13 Saying, This *fellow*

καὶ βλασφημούντων ἐκτιναξάμενος τὰ ἱμάτια
and   blaspheming[a]   shaking off   the(his) garments

εἶπεν πρὸς αὐτούς· τὸ αἷμα ὑμῶν ἐπὶ
he said to   them: The blood of you   on

τὴν κεφαλὴν ὑμῶν· καθαρὸς ἐγὼ ἀπὸ
the   head   of you;   clean   I   from

τοῦ νῦν εἰς τὰ ἔθνη πορεύσομαι. 7 καὶ
 –   now to the nations will go.   And

μεταβὰς ἐκεῖθεν ἦλθεν εἰς οἰκίαν τινὸς
removing   thence   he went into [the] house of one

ὀνόματι Τιτίου Ἰούστου σεβομένου τὸν
by name   Titius   Justus   worshipping   –

θεόν, οὗ ἡ οἰκία ἦν συνομοροῦσα τῇ
God, of whom the house was being next door to the

συναγωγῇ. 8 Κρίσπος δὲ ὁ ἀρχισυνάγωγος
synagogue.   Now Crispus the   synagogue ruler

ἐπίστευσεν τῷ κυρίῳ σὺν ὅλῳ τῷ οἴκῳ
believed   the   Lord with all   the household

αὐτοῦ, καὶ πολλοὶ τῶν Κορινθίων ἀκούοντες
of him, and many of the Corinthians hearing

ἐπίστευον καὶ ἐβαπτίζοντο. 9 Εἶπεν δὲ
believed   and were baptized.   And said

ὁ κύριος ἐν νυκτὶ δι' ὁράματος τῷ
the Lord in [the] night through a vision   –

Παύλῳ· μὴ φοβοῦ, ἀλλὰ λάλει καὶ
to Paul: Do not fear,   but   speak   and

μὴ σιωπήσῃς, 10 διότι ἐγώ εἰμι μετὰ σοῦ
keep not silence,   because I   am   with thee

καὶ οὐδεὶς ἐπιθήσεταί σοι τοῦ κακῶσαί
and no one shall set on thee   –   to illtreat[d]

σε, διότι λαός ἐστί μοι πολὺς ἐν
thee, because people is to me much[e] in
                  = I have a great people

τῇ πόλει ταύτῃ. 11 Ἐκάθισεν δὲ ἐνιαυτὸν
this city.   And he sat   a year

καὶ μῆνας ἓξ διδάσκων ἐν αὐτοῖς τὸν
and months six teaching among them   the

λόγον τοῦ θεοῦ. 12 Γαλλίωνος δὲ
word   –   of God.   And Gallio
                              = when Gallio

ἀνθυπάτου ὄντος τῆς Ἀχαΐας κατεπέστησαν
proconsul   being[a] – of Achaia   [4]set on
was proconsul

ὁμοθυμαδὸν οἱ Ἰουδαῖοι τῷ Παύλῳ καὶ
[3]with one mind [1]the [2]Jews   –   Paul   and

ἤγαγον αὐτὸν ἐπὶ τὸ βῆμα, 13 λέγοντες
brought   him   to the tribunal,   saying[,]

ὅτι παρὰ τὸν νόμον ἀναπείθει · οὗτος
 – [5][differently] from [7]the [8]law [5]urges [1]This man

persuadeth men to worship God contrary to the law.

14 And when Paul was now about to open *his* mouth, Gallio said unto the Jews, If it were a matter of wrong or wicked lewdness, O *ye* Jews, reason would that I should bear with you:

15 But if it be a question of words and names, and *of* your law, look ye *to it*; for I will be no judge of such *matters*.

16 And he drave them from the judgment seat.

17 Then all the Greeks took Sosthenes, the chief ruler of the synagogue, and beat *him* before the judgment seat. And Gallio cared for none of those things.

18 ¶ And Paul *after this* tarried *there* yet a good while, and then took his leave of the brethren, and sailed thence into Syria, and with him Priscilla and Aquila; having shorn *his* head in Cenchrea: for he had a vow.

19 And he came to Ephesus, and left them there: but he himself entered into the synagogue, and reasoned with the Jews.

20 When they desired *him* to tarry longer time with them, he consented not;

τοὺς ἀνθρώπους σέβεσθαι τὸν θεόν.
- ³men ⁴to worship - ⁵God.

14 μέλλοντος δὲ τοῦ Παύλου ἀνοίγειν τὸ
And being about Paul to open the(his)
=when Paul was about

στόμα εἶπεν ὁ Γαλλίων πρὸς τοὺς
mouth said - Gallio to the

Ἰουδαίους· εἰ μὲν ἦν ἀδίκημά τι
Jews: If indeed it was crime some

ἢ ῥᾳδιούργημα πονηρόν, ὦ Ἰουδαῖοι,
or villainy evil, O Jews,

κατὰ λόγον ἂν ἀνεσχόμην ὑμῶν· 15 εἰ δὲ ζητή-
rightly I would endure you; but if ques-

ματά ἐστιν περὶ λόγου καὶ ὀνομάτων καὶ
tions it is concerning a word and names and

νόμου τοῦ καθ' ὑμᾶς, ὄψεσθε αὐτοί·
law the according to you, ye will see [your]selves;
=your law,

κριτὴς ἐγὼ τούτων οὐ βούλομαι εἶναι.
⁴a judge ¹I ⁵of these things ³do not intend ²to be.

16 καὶ ἀπήλασεν αὐτοὺς ἀπὸ τοῦ βήματος.
And he drove away them from the tribunal.

17 ἐπιλαβόμενοι δὲ πάντες Σωσθένην τὸν
But ²seizing ¹all Sosthenes the

ἀρχισυνάγωγον ἔτυπτον ἔμπροσθεν τοῦ
synagogue ruler they struck [him] in front of the

βήματος· καὶ οὐδὲν τούτων τῷ Γαλλίωνι
tribunal; and not one of these things - ²to Gallio

ἔμελεν. 18 Ὁ δὲ Παῦλος ἔτι προσμείνας
¹mattered. - But Paul yet having remained

ἡμέρας ἱκανάς, τοῖς ἀδελφοῖς ἀποταξάμενος
days many, to the brothers bidding farewell

ἐξέπλει εἰς τὴν Συρίαν, καὶ σὺν αὐτῷ
he sailed away to - Syria, and with him

Πρίσκιλλα καὶ Ἀκύλας, κειράμενος ἐν
Priscilla and Aquila, having shorn in

Κεγχρεαῖς τὴν κεφαλήν· εἶχεν γὰρ εὐχήν.
Cenchrea the(his) head; for he had a vow.

19 κατήντησαν δὲ εἰς Ἔφεσον, κἀκείνους
And they came down to Ephesus, and those

κατέλιπεν αὐτοῦ, αὐτὸς δὲ εἰσελθὼν εἰς
he left there, but he entering into

τὴν συναγωγὴν διελέξατο τοῖς Ἰουδαίοις.
the synagogue lectured to the Jews.

20 ἐρωτώντων δὲ αὐτῶν ἐπὶ πλείονα
And asking them over a more(longer)
=as they asked

χρόνον μεῖναι οὐκ ἐπένευσεν, 21 ἀλλὰ
time to remain he consented not, but

21 But bade them farewell, saying, I must by all means keep this feast that cometh in Jerusalem: but I will return again unto you, if God will. And he sailed from Ephesus.

22 And when he had landed at Cæsarea, and gone up, and saluted the church, he went down to Antioch.

23 And after he had spent some time *there*, he departed, and went over *all* the country of Galatia and Phrygia in order, strengthening all the disciples.

24 ¶ And a certain Jew named Apollos, born at Alexandria, an eloquent man, *and* mighty in the scriptures, came to Ephesus.

25 This man was instructed in the way of the Lord; and being fervent in the spirit, he spake and taught diligently the things of the Lord, knowing only the baptism of John.

26 And he began to speak boldly in the synagogue : whom when Aquila and Priscilla had heard, they took him unto *them*, and expounded unto him the way of God more perfectly.

27 And when he was disposed to pass into Achaia, the brethren wrote, exhorting the disciples to receive him: who,

---

ἀποταξάμενος καὶ εἰπών· πάλιν ἀνακάμψω
bidding farewell and saying : Again I will return

πρὸς ὑμᾶς τοῦ θεοῦ θέλοντος, ἀνήχθη
to you - God willing,[a] he set sail
=if God wills,

ἀπὸ τῆς Ἐφέσου, 22 καὶ κατελθὼν εἰς
from the Ephesus, and coming down to

Καισάρειαν, ἀναβὰς καὶ ἀσπασάμενος τὴν
Cæsarea, going up and greeting the

ἐκκλησίαν, κατέβη εἰς Ἀντιόχειαν, 23 καὶ
church, he went down to Antioch, and

ποιήσας χρόνον τινὰ ἐξῆλθεν, διερχόμενος
having spent time some he went forth, passing through

καθεξῆς τὴν Γαλατικὴν χώραν καὶ Φρυγίαν,
in order the Galatian country and Phrygia,

στηρίζων πάντας τοὺς μαθητάς.
confirming all the disciples.

24 Ἰουδαῖος δέ τις Ἀπολλῶς ὀνόματι,
And a certain Jew Apollos by name,

Ἀλεξανδρεὺς τῷ γένει, ἀνὴρ λόγιος,
an Alexandrian - by race, a man eloquent,

κατήντησεν εἰς Ἔφεσον, δυνατὸς ὢν ἐν
came to Ephesus, powerful being in

ταῖς γραφαῖς. 25 οὗτος ἦν κατηχημένος
the scriptures. This man was orally instructed [in]

τὴν ὁδὸν τοῦ κυρίου, καὶ ζέων τῷ
the way of the Lord, and burning -

πνεύματι ἐλάλει καὶ ἐδίδασκεν ἀκριβῶς
in spirit he spoke and taught accurately

τὰ περὶ τοῦ Ἰησοῦ, ἐπιστάμενος
the things concerning - Jesus, understanding

μόνον τὸ βάπτισμα Ἰωάννου· 26 οὗτός τε
only the baptism of John; and this man

ἤρξατο παρρησιάζεσθαι ἐν τῇ συναγωγῇ.
began to speak boldly in the synagogue.

ἀκούσαντες δὲ αὐτοῦ Πρίσκιλλα καὶ
And hearing him Priscilla and

Ἀκύλας προσελάβοντο αὐτὸν καὶ ἀκριβέστε-
Aquila took him and more accurate-

ρον αὐτῷ ἐξέθεντο τὴν ὁδὸν τοῦ θεοῦ.
ly to him explained the way - of God.

27 βουλομένου δὲ αὐτοῦ διελθεῖν εἰς τὴν
And intending him[a] to go through into -
=when he intended

Ἀχαΐαν, προτρεψάμενοι οἱ ἀδελφοὶ ἔγραψαν
Achaia, being encouraged the brothers wrote

τοῖς μαθηταῖς ἀποδέξασθαι αὐτόν· ὃς
to the disciples to welcome him; who

when he was come, helped them much which had believed through grace:

28 For he mightily convinced the Jews, *and that* publickly, shewing by the scriptures that Jesus was Christ.

παραγενόμενος   συνεβάλετο   πολὺ   τοῖς
arriving   contributed   much   to the [ones]

πεπιστευκόσιν   διὰ   τῆς   χάριτος·   28 εὐτόνως
having believed   through   –   grace;   [2]vehemently

γὰρ   τοῖς   Ἰουδαίοις   διακατηλέγχετο   δημοσίᾳ
[1]for [4]the   [5]Jews   [3]he confuted   publicly

ἐπιδεικνὺς   διὰ   τῶν   γραφῶν   εἶναι   τὸν
proving   through   the   scriptures   [2]to be   [3]the

χριστὸν   Ἰησοῦν.
[4]Christ   [1]Jesus.

CHAPTER 19

AND it came to pass, that, while Apollos was at Corinth, Paul having passed through the upper coasts came to Ephesus: and finding certain disciples,

2 He said unto them, Have ye received the Holy Ghost since ye believed? And they said unto him, We have not so much as heard whether there be any Holy Ghost.

3 And he said unto them, Unto what then were ye baptized? And they said, Unto John's baptism.

4 Then said Paul, John verily baptized with the baptism of repentance, saying unto the people, that they should believe on him which should come after him, that is, on Christ Jesus.

5 When they heard *this*, they were baptized in the name of the Lord Jesus.

6 And when Paul had laid *his* hands upon them, the Holy Ghost came on them; and they spake with tongues, and prophesied.

7 And all the men were about twelve.

19 Ἐγένετο   δὲ   ἐν   τῷ   τὸν   Ἀπολλῶ
Now it came to pass   in   the   –   Apollos
                                    =while Apollos was

εἶναι   ἐν   Κορίνθῳ   Παῦλον   διελθόντα   τὰ
to be[be] in   Corinth   Paul   having passed through the

ἀνωτερικὰ   μέρη   ἐλθεῖν   εἰς   Ἔφεσον   καὶ
higher   parts   to come[b] to   Ephesus   and

εὑρεῖν   τινας   μαθητάς,   2 εἶπέν   τε   πρὸς
to find[b] some   disciples,   and said   to

αὐτούς·   εἰ   πνεῦμα   ἅγιον   ἐλάβετε   πιστεύσαν-
them: If   Spirit   Holy   ye received   believ-

τες;   οἱ   δὲ   πρὸς   αὐτόν·   ἀλλ’   οὐδ’   εἰ
ing? And they [said] to   him: But   [2]not   [3]if

πνεῦμα   ἅγιον   ἔστιν   ἠκούσαμεν.   3 εἶπέν   τε·
[5]Spirit [6]Holy [4]there is   [1]we heard.   And he said:

εἰς   τί   οὖν   ἐβαπτίσθητε;   οἱ   δὲ   εἶπαν·
To   what therefore   were ye baptized?   And they   said:

εἰς   τὸ   Ἰωάννου   βάπτισμα.   4 εἶπεν   δὲ
To   the   of John   baptism.   And said

Παῦλος·   Ἰωάννης   ἐβάπτισεν   βάπτισμα   μετα-
Paul: John   baptized [with]   a baptism   of repent-

νοίας,   τῷ   λαῷ   λέγων   εἰς   τὸν   ἐρχόμενον
ance,   [2]to the [3]people [1]saying [2]in [3]the [one]   [4]coming

μετ’   αὐτὸν   ἵνα   πιστεύσωσιν,   τοῦτ’   ἔστιν
[5]after [6]him   [4]that   [1]they should believe,   this   is

εἰς   τὸν   Ἰησοῦν.   5 ἀκούσαντες   δὲ   ἐβαπτίσ-
in   –   Jesus.   And hearing   they were

θησαν   εἰς   τὸ   ὄνομα   τοῦ   κυρίου   Ἰησοῦ.
baptized   in   the   name   of the   Lord   Jesus.

6 καὶ   ἐπιθέντος   αὐτοῖς   τοῦ   Παύλου   χεῖρας
And   laying on   them   –   Paul   hands[a]
=as Paul laid [his] hands on them

ἦλθε   τὸ   πνεῦμα   τὸ   ἅγιον   ἐπ’   αὐτούς,
came   the   Spirit   –   Holy   on   them,

ἐλάλουν   τε   γλώσσαις   καὶ   ἐπροφήτευον.
and they spoke   in tongues   and   prophesied.

7 ἦσαν   δὲ   οἱ   πάντες   ἄνδρες   ὡσεὶ   δώδεκα.
And [4]were [2]the [1]all   [3]men   about   twelve.

8 And he went into the synagogue, and spake boldly for the space of three months, disputing and persuading the things concerning the kingdom of God.

9 But when divers were hardened, and believed not, but spake evil of that way before the multitude, he departed from them, and separated the disciples, disputing daily in the school of one Tyrannus.

10 And this continued by the space of two years; so that all they which dwelt in Asia heard the word of the Lord Jesus, both Jews and Greeks.

11 And God wrought special miracles by the hands of Paul:

12 So that from his body were brought unto the sick handkerchiefs or aprons, and the diseases departed from them, and the evil spirits went out of them.

13 ¶ Then certain of the vagabond Jews, exorcists, took upon them to call over them which had evil spirits the name of the Lord Jesus, saying, We

---

8 Εἰσελθὼν δὲ εἰς τὴν συναγωγὴν
And entering into the synagogue

ἐπαρρησιάζετο ἐπὶ μῆνας τρεῖς διαλεγόμενος
he spoke boldly over months three lecturing

καὶ πείθων περὶ τῆς βασιλείας τοῦ θεοῦ.
and persuading concerning the kingdom - of God.

9 ὡς δέ τινες ἐσκληρύνοντο καὶ ἠπείθουν
But as some were hardened and disobeyed

κακολογοῦντες τὴν ὁδὸν ἐνώπιον τοῦ
speaking ill [of] the way before the

πλήθους, ἀποστὰς ἀπ' αὐτῶν ἀφώρισεν
multitude, withdrawing from them he separated

τοὺς μαθητάς, καθ' ἡμέραν διαλεγόμενος
the disciples, daily lecturing

ἐν τῇ σχολῇ Τυράννου. 10 τοῦτο δὲ
in the school of Tyrannus. And this

ἐγένετο ἐπὶ ἔτη δύο, ὥστε πάντας τοὺς
happened over years two, so as all the
=so that all who inhabited

κατοικοῦντας τὴν Ἀσίαν ἀκοῦσαι τὸν
[ones] inhabiting - Asia to hear[b] the
Asia heard

λόγον τοῦ κυρίου, Ἰουδαίους τε καὶ
word of the Lord, [2]Jews [1]both and

Ἕλληνας. 11 Δυνάμεις τε οὐ τὰς τυχούσας
Greeks. And powerful deeds not the ordinary

ὁ θεὸς ἐποίει διὰ τῶν χειρῶν Παύλου,
- God did through the hands of Paul,

12 ὥστε καὶ ἐπὶ τοὺς ἀσθενοῦντας
so as even onto the [ones] ailing
=so that there were even brought away from his skin hand-

ἀποφέρεσθαι ἀπὸ τοῦ χρωτὸς αὐτοῦ
to be brought away from the skin of him
kerchiefs or aprons onto those who ailed and the diseases were rid

σουδάρια ἢ σιμικίνθια καὶ ἀπαλλάσσεσθαι
handkerchiefs or aprons and to be rid
from them, and the evil spirits went out.

ἀπ' αὐτῶν τὰς νόσους, τά τε πνεύματα
from them the diseases, and the spirits

τὰ πονηρὰ ἐκπορεύεσθαι. 13 Ἐπεχείρησαν δέ
evil to go out. But [7]attempted

τινες καὶ τῶν περιερχομένων Ἰουδαίων
[1]some [2]also [3]of the [4]strolling [5]Jews

ἐξορκιστῶν ὀνομάζειν ἐπὶ τοὺς ἔχοντας
[6]exorcists to name over the [ones] having

τὰ πνεύματα τὰ πονηρὰ τὸ ὄνομα τοῦ
the spirits - evil the name of the

κυρίου Ἰησοῦ λέγοντες· ὁρκίζω ὑμᾶς τὸν
Lord Jesus saying: I exorcise you [by] -

adjure you by Jesus whom Paul preacheth.

14 And there were seven sons of *one* Sceva, a Jew, *and* chief of the priests, which did so.

15 And the evil spirit answered and said, Jesus I know, and Paul I know; but who are ye?

16 And the man in whom the evil spirit was leaped on them, and overcame them, and prevailed against them, so that they fled out of that house naked and wounded.

17 And this was known to all the Jews and Greeks also dwelling at Ephesus; and fear fell on them all, and the name of the Lord Jesus was magnified.

18 And many that believed came, and confessed, and shewed their deeds.

19 Many of them also which used curious arts brought their books together, and burned them before all *men:* and they counted the price of them, and found *it* fifty thousand *pieces* of silver.

20 So mightily grew the word of God and prevailed.

Ἰησοῦν ὃν Παῦλος κηρύσσει. 14 ἦσαν δὲ
Jesus whom Paul proclaims. And there were

τινος Σκευᾶ Ἰουδαίου ἀρχιερέως ἑπτὰ
³of one ⁴Sceva ⁵a Jewish ⁶chief priest ¹seven

υἱοὶ τοῦτο ποιοῦντες. 15 ἀποκριθὲν δὲ
²sons ⁸this ⁷doing. And answering

τὸ πνεῦμα τὸ πονηρὸν εἶπεν αὐτοῖς·
the spirit - evil said to them:

τὸν [μὲν] Ἰησοῦν γινώσκω καὶ τὸν
- ²indeed ¹Jesus I know and -

Παῦλον ἐπίσταμαι· ὑμεῖς δὲ τίνες ἐστέ;
Paul I understand; but ye who are?

16 καὶ ἐφαλόμενος ὁ ἄνθρωπος ἐπ᾽ αὐτούς,
And ⁹leaping on ¹the ²man ¹⁰on ¹¹them,

ἐν ᾧ ἦν τὸ πνεῦμα τὸ πονηρόν,
³in ⁴whom ⁵was ⁶the ⁵spirit - ⁷evil,

κατακυριεύσας ἀμφοτέρων ἴσχυσεν κατ᾽
overmastering both was strong against

αὐτῶν, ὥστε γυμνοὺς καὶ τετραυματισμένους
them, so as naked and *having been* wounded
=so that they escaped out of that house naked and

ἐκφυγεῖν ἐκ τοῦ οἴκου ἐκείνου. 17 τοῦτο
to escape out of that house. this
wounded.

δὲ ἐγένετο γνωστὸν πᾶσιν Ἰουδαίοις τε
And became known to all ²Jews ¹both

καὶ Ἕλλησιν τοῖς κατοικοῦσιν τὴν Ἔφεσον,
and Greeks - inhabiting - Ephesus,

καὶ ἐπέπεσεν φόβος ἐπὶ πάντας αὐτούς,
and ²fell on ¹fear ³on ⁵all ⁴them,

καὶ ἐμεγαλύνετο τὸ ὄνομα τοῦ κυρίου
and was magnified the name of the Lord

Ἰησοῦ· 18 πολλοί τε τῶν πεπιστευκότων
Jesus; and many of the [ones] having believed

ἤρχοντο ἐξομολογούμενοι καὶ ἀναγγέλλοντες
came confessing and telling

τὰς πράξεις αὐτῶν. 19 ἱκανοὶ δὲ τῶν τὰ
the doings of them. And a consider- of the [ones]
able number

περίεργα πραξάντων συνενέγκαντες τὰς βίβλους
curious things doing bringing together the rolls

κατέκαιον ἐνώπιον πάντων· καὶ συνεψήφισαν
burnt before all; and they reckoned up

τὰς τιμὰς αὐτῶν καὶ εὗρον ἀργυρίου μυριάδας
the prices of them and found [pieces] ²thousand
³of silver

πέντε. 20 Οὕτως κατὰ κράτος τοῦ κυρίου
¹five. Thus by might ²of the ¹Lord

ὁ λόγος ηὔξανεν καὶ ἴσχυεν.
¹the ²word increased and was strong.

21 ¶ After these things were ended, Paul purposed in the spirit, when he had passed through Macedonia and Achaia, to go to Jerusalem, saying, After I have been there, I must also see Rome.

22 So he sent into Macedonia two of them that ministered unto him, Timotheus and Erastus; but he himself stayed in Asia for a season.

23 ¶ And the same time there arose no small stir about that way.

24 For a certain *man* named Demetrius, a silversmith, which made silver shrines for Diana, brought no small gain unto the craftsmen;

25 Whom he called together with the workmen of like occupation, and said, Sirs, ye know that by this craft we have our wealth.

26 Moreover ye see and hear, that not alone at Ephesus, but almost throughout all Asia, this Paul hath persuaded and turned away much people, saying that they be no gods, which are made with hands:

27 So that not only

---

21 Ὡς δὲ ἐπληρώθη ταῦτα, ἔθετο ὁ
And when were fulfilled these things, purposed -

Παῦλος ἐν τῷ πνεύματι διελθὼν τὴν
Paul in the(his) spirit passing through -

Μακεδονίαν καὶ Ἀχαΐαν πορεύεσθαι εἰς
Macedonia and Achaia to go to

Ἱεροσόλυμα, εἰπὼν ὅτι μετὰ τὸ γενέσθαι
Jerusalem, saying[,] - After the to become
=After I am

με ἐκεῖ δεῖ με καὶ Ῥώμην ἰδεῖν.
me[b] there it behoves me [2]also [1]Rome [1]to see.

22 ἀποστείλας δὲ εἰς Μακεδονίαν δύο
And sending into Macedonia two

τῶν διακονούντων αὐτῷ, Τιμόθεον καὶ
of the [ones] ministering to him, Timothy and

Ἔραστον, αὐτὸς ἐπέσχεν χρόνον εἰς τὴν
Erastus, he delayed a time in -

Ἀσίαν. **23** Ἐγένετο δὲ κατὰ τὸν καιρὸν
Asia. Now there was about - time

ἐκεῖνον τάραχος οὐκ ὀλίγος περὶ τῆς
that [2]trouble [1]no [3]little concerning the

ὁδοῦ. **24** Δημήτριος γάρ τις ὀνόματι,
way. For [3]Demetrius [1]one by name,

ἀργυροκόπος, ποιῶν ναοὺς ἀργυροῦς
a silversmith, making shrines silver

Ἀρτέμιδος παρείχετο τοῖς τεχνίταις οὐκ
of Artemis provided the artisans no

ὀλίγην ἐργασίαν, **25** οὓς συναθροίσας καὶ
little trade, [2]whom [1]assembling also

τοὺς περὶ τὰ τοιαῦτα ἐργάτας εἶπεν·
[1]the [2]about(in) - [4]such things [3]workmen said:

ἄνδρες, ἐπίστασθε ὅτι ἐκ ταύτης τῆς
Men, ye understand that from this -

ἐργασίας ἡ εὐπορία ἡμῖν ἐστιν, **26** καὶ
trade the gain to us is,[•] and
=we have [our] gain,

θεωρεῖτε καὶ ἀκούετε ὅτι οὐ μόνον
ye behold and hear that [7]not [8]only

Ἐφέσου ἀλλὰ σχεδὸν πάσης τῆς Ἀσίας
[9]of Ephesus [10]but [11]almost [13]of all - [12]Asia

ὁ Παῦλος οὗτος πείσας μετέστησεν ἱκανὸν
- [2]Paul [1]this [3]having [4]perverted [6]a considerable
        persuaded

ὄχλον, λέγων ὅτι οὐκ εἰσὶν θεοὶ οἱ διὰ
[5]crowd, saying that they are not gods [1]the [2]through
                                        [ones]

χειρῶν γινόμενοι. **27** οὐ μόνον δὲ τοῦτο
[4]hands [3]coming into being. [2]not [1]only [1]Now [4]this

this our craft is in danger
to be set at nought; but
also that the temple of
the great goddess Diana
should be despised, and
her magnificence should
be destroyed, whom all
Asia and the world wor-
shippeth.

28 And when they heard
these sayings, they were
full of wrath, and cried
out, saying, Great *is* Diana
of the Ephesians.

29 And the whole city
was filled with confusion:
and having caught Gaius
and Aristarchus, men of
Macedonia, Paul's com-
panions in travel, they
rushed with one accord
into the theatre.

30 And when Paul
would have entered in
unto the people, the dis-
ciples suffered him not.

31 And certain of the
chief of Asia, which were
his friends, sent unto him,
desiring *him* that he would
not adventure himself into
the theatre.

32 Some therefore cried
one thing, and some an-
other: for the assembly
was confused; and the
more part knew not where-
fore they were come to-
gether.

33 And they drew Alex-
ander out of the multitude,
the Jews putting him for-
ward. And Alexander
beckoned with the hand,

κινδυνεύει ἡμῖν τὸ μέρος εἰς ἀπελεγμὸν
[5]is in danger - to us the share[6] [8]into [9]disrepute
       =[6]our share

ἐλθεῖν, ἀλλὰ καὶ τὸ τῆς μεγάλης θεᾶς
[7]to come, but also [1]the [2]of the [4]great [5]goddess

'Αρτέμιδος ἱερὸν εἰς οὐθὲν λογισθῆναι,
[6]Artemis [3]temple [8]for(as) [9]nothing [7]to be reckoned,

μέλλειν τε καὶ καθαιρεῖσθαι τῆς μεγα-
[3]to be about [1]and [2]also [4]to be diminished the great-

λειότητος αὐτῆς, ἣν ὅλη ἡ 'Ασία καὶ
ness of her, whom all - Asia and

ἡ οἰκουμένη σέβεται. 28 ἀκούσαντες δὲ
the inhabited earth worships. And hearing

καὶ γενόμενοι πλήρεις θυμοῦ ἔκραζον
and becoming full of anger they cried out

λέγοντες· μεγάλη ἡ "Αρτεμις 'Εφεσίων.
saying: Great [is] - Artemis of [the] Ephesians.

29 καὶ ἐπλήσθη ἡ πόλις τῆς συγχύσεως,
And was filled the city of(with) the confusion,

ὥρμησάν τε ὁμοθυμαδὸν εἰς τὸ θέατρον,
and they rushed with one mind into the theatre,

συναρπάσαντες Γάϊον καὶ 'Αρίσταρχον
keeping a firm grip on Gaius and Aristarchus[,]

Μακεδόνας, συνεκδήμους Παύλου. 30 Παύλου
Macedonians, travelling companions of Paul. Paul

δὲ βουλομένου εἰσελθεῖν εἰς τὸν δῆμον
And intending[a] to enter into the mob
    =as Paul intended

οὐκ εἴων αὐτὸν οἱ μαθηταί· 31 τινὲς
[5]not [3]allowed [4]him [1]the [2]disciples; some

δὲ καὶ τῶν 'Ασιαρχῶν, ὄντες αὐτῷ
and also of the Asiarchs, being to him

φίλοι, πέμψαντες πρὸς αὐτὸν παρεκάλουν
friends, sending to him besought

μὴ δοῦναι ἑαυτὸν εἰς τὸ θέατρον. 32 ἄλλοι
not to give himself in the theatre. Others

μὲν οὖν ἄλλο τι ἔκραζον· ἦν γὰρ
indeed therefore [3]different [1]something cried out; for [2]was

ἡ ἐκκλησία συγκεχυμένη, καὶ οἱ πλείους
[1]the [2]assembly *having been* confounded, and the majority

οὐκ ᾔδεισαν τίνος ἕνεκα συνεληλύθεισαν.
knew not [3]of what [1]on account they had come
          together.

33 ἐκ δὲ τοῦ ὄχλου συνεβίβασαν 'Αλέξανδρον,
But [some] of the crowd instructed Alexander,

προβαλόντων αὐτὸν τῶν 'Ιουδαίων· ὁ δὲ
putting forward him the Jews[a]; - and
=as the Jews put him forward;

'Αλέξανδρος κατασείσας τὴν χεῖρα ἤθελεν
Alexander waving the(his) hand wished

and would have made his defence unto the people.

34 But when they knew that he was a Jew, all with one voice about the space of two hours cried out, Great *is* Diana of the Ephesians.

35 And when the town-clerk had appeased the people, he said, *Ye* men of Ephesus, what man is there that knoweth not how that the city of the Ephesians is a worshipper of the great goddess Diana, and of the *image* which fell down from Jupiter?

36 Seeing then that these things cannot be spoken against, ye ought to be quiet, and to do nothing rashly.

37 For ye have brought hither these men, which are neither robbers of churches, nor yet blasphemers of your goddess.

38 Wherefore if Demetrius, and the craftsmen which are with him, have a matter against any man, the law is open, and there are deputies: let them implead one another.

39 But if ye enquire any thing concerning other matters, it shall be determined in a lawful assembly.

40 For we are in danger to be called in question for this day's uproar, there being no cause whereby we may give an account of this concourse.

ἀπολογεῖσθαι τῷ δήμῳ. 34 ἐπιγνόντες δὲ
to defend himself   to the   mob.   But knowing

ὅτι Ἰουδαῖός ἐστιν, φωνὴ ἐγένετο μία
that   a Jew   he is(was), ³voice ¹there was ²one

ἐκ πάντων, ὡς ἐπὶ ὥρας δύο κράζοντες·
from all,   about over hours two   crying out:

μεγάλη ἡ Ἄρτεμις Ἐφεσίων. 35 κατα-
Great [is] -   Artemis of [the] Ephesians.   ⁴having

στείλας δὲ ὁ γραμματεὺς τὸν ὄχλον
quietened ¹And ²the ³town clerk   the   crowd

φησίν· ἄνδρες Ἐφέσιοι, τίς γάρ ἐστιν
says: Men   Ephesians, who indeed is there

ἀνθρώπων ὃς οὐ γινώσκει τὴν Ἐφεσίων
of men   who does not know ¹the ²of [the] Ephesians

πόλιν νεωκόρον οὖσαν τῆς μεγάλης
²city   ⁵temple warden ⁴being of the great

Ἀρτέμιδος καὶ τοῦ διοπετοῦς; 36 ἀναντιρ-
Artemis   and of the fallen from   undeni-
                      [image]   the sky?

ρήτων οὖν ὄντων τούτων δέον ἐστὶν
able   therefore being these things² necessary it is
= as these things are undeniable

ὑμᾶς κατεσταλμένους ὑπάρχειν καὶ μηδὲν
you   ²having been quietened ¹to be and ³nothing

προπετὲς πράσσειν. 37 ἠγάγετε γὰρ τοὺς
³rash   ¹to do.   For ye brought   -

ἄνδρας τούτους οὔτε ἱεροσύλους οὔτε
men   these   neither temple robbers   nor

βλασφημοῦντας τὴν θεὸν ἡμῶν. 38 εἰ
blaspheming   the goddess of you.   If

μὲν οὖν Δημήτριος καὶ οἱ σὺν αὐτῷ
indeed therefore Demetrius and ¹the ³with ⁴him

τεχνῖται ἔχουσι πρός τινα λόγον, ἀγοραῖοι
²artisans have against anyone an account, assizes

ἄγονται καὶ ἀνθύπατοί εἰσιν, ἐγκαλείτωσαν
are   and proconsuls there are, let them bring a
being(held)   charge against

ἀλλήλοις. 39 εἰ δέ τι περαιτέρω ἐπιζητεῖτε,
one another. But if ²anything ³further ¹ye seek,

ἐν τῇ ἐννόμῳ ἐκκλησίᾳ ἐπιλυθήσεται.
in the   lawful   assembly   it will be settled.

40 καὶ γὰρ κινδυνεύομεν ἐγκαλεῖσθαι
For indeed   we are in danger to be charged with

στάσεως περὶ τῆς σήμερον, μηδενὸς
insurrection concerning to-day,   nothing

αἰτίου ὑπάρχοντος, περὶ οὗ οὐ δυνησόμεθα
cause   being²,   concerning which we shall not be able
= there being no cause,

ἀποδοῦναι λόγον περὶ τῆς συστροφῆς
to give   account concerning the ²crowding together

41 And when he had thus spoken, he dismissed the assembly.

ταύτης. 41 καὶ ταῦτα εἰπὼν ἀπέλυσεν τὴν
¹this. - And these things saying he dismissed the
ἐκκλησίαν.
assembly.

CHAPTER 20

AND after the uproar was ceased, Paul called unto *him* the disciples, and embraced *them*, and departed for to go into Macedonia.

2 And when he had gone over those parts, and had given them much exhortation, he came into Greece,

3 And *there* abode three months. And when the Jews laid wait for him, as he was about to sail into Syria, he purposed to return through Macedonia.

4 And there accompanied him into Asia Sopater of Berea; and of the Thessalonians, Aristarchus and Secundus; and Gaius of Derbe, and Timotheus; and of Asia, Tychicus and Trophimus.

5 These going before tarried for us at Troas.

6 And we sailed away from Philippi after the days of unleavened bread, and came unto them to Troas in five days; where we abode seven days.

7 ¶ And upon the first

20 Μετὰ δὲ τὸ παύσασθαι τὸν θόρυβον
And after the to cease the uproarᵇ
=after the uproar ceased

μεταπεμψάμενος ὁ Παῦλος τοὺς μαθητὰς
ᵃsummoning - ¹Paul ⁵the ⁶disciples

καὶ παρακαλέσας, ἀσπασάμενος ἐξῆλθεν
³and ⁴exhorting, taking leave he went forth

πορεύεσθαι εἰς Μακεδονίαν. 2 διελθὼν δὲ
to go to Macedonia. And having gone through

τὰ μέρη ἐκεῖνα καὶ παρακαλέσας αὐτοὺς
.those parts and having exhorted them

λόγῳ πολλῷ ἦλθεν εἰς τὴν Ἑλλάδα,
¹with ³speech ²much he came into - Greece,

3 ποιήσας τε μῆνας τρεῖς, γενομένης
and spending months three, there being

ἐπιβουλῆς αὐτῷ ὑπὸ τῶν Ἰουδαίων
a plotᵃ [against] him by the Jews

μέλλοντι ἀνάγεσθαι εἰς τὴν Συρίαν, ἐγένετο
being about to set sail to(for) - Syria, he was
=as he was about

γνώμης τοῦ ὑποστρέφειν διὰ Μακεδονίας.
of a mind - to returnᵈ through Macedonia.

4 συνείπετο δὲ αὐτῷ Σώπατρος Πύρρου
And there accompanied him Sopater [son] of Pyrrhus

Βεροιαῖος, Θεσσαλονικέων δὲ Ἀρίσταρχος
a Beroean, and of Thessalonians Aristarchus

καὶ Σέκουνδος, καὶ Γάϊος Δερβαῖος καὶ
and Secundus, and Gaius a Derbæan and

Τιμόθεος, Ἀσιανοὶ δὲ Τύχικος καὶ
Timothy, and Asians Tychicus and

Τρόφιμος. 5 οὗτοι δὲ προελθόντες ἔμενον
Trophimus. And these men going forward awaited

ἡμᾶς ἐν Τρῳάδι· 6 ἡμεῖς δὲ ἐξεπλεύσαμεν
us in Troas; and we sailed away

μετὰ τὰς ἡμέρας τῶν ἀζύμων ἀπὸ
after the days - of unleavened bread from

Φιλίππων, καὶ ἤλθομεν πρὸς αὐτοὺς εἰς
Philippi, and came to them in

τὴν Τρῳάδα ἄχρι ἡμερῶν πέντε, ὅπου
- Troas until days five, where

διετρίψαμεν ἡμέρας ἑπτά. 7 Ἐν δὲ τῇ
we stayed days seven. And on the

day of the week, when the disciples came together to break bread, Paul preached unto them, ready to depart on the morrow; and continued his speech until midnight.

8 And there were many lights in the upper chamber, where they were gathered together.

9 And there sat in a window a certain young man named Eutychus, being fallen into a deep sleep: and as Paul was long preaching, he sunk down with sleep, and fell down from the third loft, and was taken up dead.

10 And Paul went down, and fell on him, and embracing *him* said, Trouble not yourselves; for his life is in him.

11 When he therefore was come up again, and had broken bread, and eaten, and talked a long while, even till break of day, so he departed.

12 And they brought the young man alive, and were not a little comforted.

13 ¶ And we went before to ship, and sailed unto Assos, there intend-

μιᾷ τῶν σαββάτων συνηγμένων ἡμῶν
one(first) of the sabbaths(week) having been us[a]
[day] assembled
=as we were assembled

κλάσαι ἄρτον ὁ Παῦλος διελέγετο αὐτοῖς,
to break bread – Paul lectured to them,

μέλλων ἐξιέναι τῇ ἐπαύριον, παρέτεινέν τε
being about to depart on the morrow, and continued

τὸν λόγον μέχρι μεσονυκτίου. 8 ἦσαν δὲ
the speech until midnight. Now there were

λαμπάδες ἱκαναὶ ἐν τῷ ὑπερῴῳ οὗ
lamps a considerable in the upper room where
number of

ἦμεν συνηγμένοι. 9 καθεζόμενος δέ τις
we were *having been* assembled. And sitting a certain

νεανίας ὀνόματι Εὔτυχος ἐπὶ τῆς θυρίδος,
young man by name Eutychus on the window sill,

καταφερόμενος ὕπνῳ βαθεῖ, διαλεγομένου
being overborne sleep by a deep, lecturing

τοῦ Παύλου ἐπὶ πλεῖον, κατενεχθεὶς ἀπὸ
– Paul[a] for a longer time, having been from
=while Paul lectured overborne

τοῦ ὕπνου ἔπεσεν ἀπὸ τοῦ τριστέγου
the sleep he fell from the third floor[*]

κάτω καὶ ἤρθη νεκρός. 10 καταβὰς δὲ
down and was taken up dead. But going down

ὁ Παῦλος ἐπέπεσεν αὐτῷ καὶ συμπεριλαβὼν
– Paul fell on him and closely embracing
[him]

εἶπεν· μὴ θορυβεῖσθε· ἡ γὰρ ψυχὴ αὐτοῦ
said: Be ye not terrified; for the life of him

ἐν αὐτῷ ἐστιν. 11 ἀναβὰς δὲ καὶ κλάσας
in him is. And going up and breaking

τὸν ἄρτον καὶ γευσάμενος, ἐφ' ἱκανόν τε
the bread and tasting, and over a considerable
[time]

ὁμιλήσας ἄχρι αὐγῆς, οὕτως ἐξῆλθεν.
conversing until light [of day], thus he went forth.

12 ἤγαγον δὲ τὸν παῖδα ζῶντα, καὶ
And they brought the lad living, and

παρεκλήθησαν οὐ μετρίως. 13 Ἡμεῖς δὲ
were comforted not moderately. And we

προελθόντες ἐπὶ τὸ πλοῖον ἀνήχθημεν
going before onto the ship set sail

ἐπὶ τὴν Ἄσσον, ἐκεῖθεν μέλλοντες ἀνα-
to(for) – Assos, thence intending to

---

* Souter remarks that it is uncertain whether the ground floor was counted or not in the enunciation; " if so, we should have to translate ' the second floor '."

ing to take in Paul: for so had he appointed, minding himself to go afoot.

14 And when he met with us at Assos, we took him in, and came to Mitylene.

15 And we sailed thence, and came the next *day* over against Chios; and the next *day* we arrived at Samos, and tarried at Trogyllium; and the next *day* we came to Miletus.

16 For Paul had determined to sail by Ephesus, because he would not spend the time in Asia: for he hasted, if it were possible for him, to be at Jerusalem the day of Pentecost.

17 ¶ And from Miletus he sent to Ephesus, and called the elders of the church.

18 And when they were come to him, he said unto them, Ye know, from the first day that I came into Asia, after what manner I have been with you at all seasons,

19 Serving the Lord with all humility of mind, and with many tears, and temptations, which befell me by the lying in wait of the Jews:

20 *And* how I kept back nothing that was profitable

λαμβάνειν · τὸν Παῦλον· οὕτως γὰρ
take up   -   Paul;   for thus

διατεταγμένος ἦν, μέλλων αὐτὸς πεζεύειν.
having been arranged it was, ²intending ¹he to go afoot.

14 ὡς δὲ συνέβαλλεν ἡμῖν εἰς τὴν Ἄσσον,
Now when he met with us in - Assos,

ἀναλαβόντες αὐτὸν ἤλθομεν εἰς Μιτυλήνην·
taking up him we came to Mitylene;

15 κἀκεῖθεν ἀποπλεύσαντες τῇ ἐπιούσῃ
and thence sailing away on the next [day]

κατηντήσαμεν ἄντικρυς Χίου, τῇ δὲ ἑτέρᾳ
we arrived off Chios, and on the other(next)

παρεβάλομεν εἰς Σάμον, τῇ δὲ ἐχομένῃ
we crossed over to Samos, and on the next

ἤλθομεν εἰς Μίλητον. **16** κεκρίκει γὰρ ὁ
we came to Miletus. For had decided

Παῦλος παραπλεῦσαι τὴν Ἔφεσον, ὅπως
Paul to sail past - Ephesus, so as

μὴ γένηται αὐτῷ χρονοτριβῆσαι ἐν τῇ
not be to him to spend time in -

Ἀσίᾳ· ἔσπευδεν γάρ, εἰ δυνατὸν εἴη
Asia; for he hasted, if possible it might be

αὐτῷ, τὴν ἡμέραν τῆς πεντηκοστῆς
to him, the day - of Pentecost

γενέσθαι εἰς Ἱεροσόλυμα.
to be in Jerusalem.

17 Ἀπὸ δὲ τῆς Μιλήτου πέμψας εἰς
And from - Miletus sending to

Ἔφεσον μετεκαλέσατο τοὺς πρεσβυτέρους
Ephesus he summoned the elders

τῆς ἐκκλησίας. **18** ὡς δὲ παρεγένοντο
of the church. And when they came

πρὸς αὐτόν, εἶπεν αὐτοῖς· ὑμεῖς ἐπίστασθε,
to him, he said to them: Ye understand,

ἀπὸ πρώτης ἡμέρας ἀφ᾽ ἧς ἐπέβην εἰς
from [the] first day from which I set foot on in

τὴν Ἀσίαν, πῶς μεθ᾽ ὑμῶν τὸν πάντα
- Asia, how with you the whole

χρόνον ἐγενόμην, **19** δουλεύων τῷ κυρίῳ
time I was, serving the Lord

μετὰ πάσης ταπεινοφροσύνης καὶ δακρύων
with all humility and tears

καὶ πειρασμῶν τῶν συμβάντων μοι ἐν
and trials - happening to me by

ταῖς ἐπιβουλαῖς τῶν Ἰουδαίων, **20** ὡς
the plots of the Jews, as

οὐδὲν ὑπεστειλάμην τῶν συμφερόντων τοῦ
²nothing ¹I kept back of the things beneficial

unto you, but have shewed you, and have taught you publickly, and from house to house,

21 Testifying both to the Jews, and also to the Greeks, repentance toward God, and faith toward our Lord Jesus Christ.

22 And now, behold, I go bound in the spirit unto Jerusalem, not knowing the things that shall befall me there:

23 Save that the Holy Ghost witnesseth in every city, saying that bonds and afflictions abide me.

24 But none of these things move me, neither count I my life dear unto myself, so that I might finish my course with joy, and the ministry, which I have received of the Lord Jesus, to testify the gospel of the grace of God.

25 And now, behold, I know that ye all, among whom I have gone preaching the kingdom of God, shall see my face no more.

26 Wherefore I take you to record this day, that I *am* pure from the blood of all *men*.

27 For I have not shunned to declare unto you all the counsel of God.

28 Take heed therefore unto yourselves, and to all the flock, over the which the Holy Ghost

μὴ   ἀναγγεῖλαι   ὑμῖν   καὶ   διδάξαι   ὑμᾶς
not   to declare[d]   to you   and   to teach[d]   you

δημοσίᾳ   καὶ   κατ᾽   οἴκους,   **21**   διαμαρτυρόμενος
publicly   and   from house to house,†   solemnly witnessing

Ἰουδαίοις   τε   καὶ   Ἕλλησιν   τὴν   εἰς   θεὸν
²to Jews   ¹both   and   to Greeks   –   toward   God

μετάνοιαν   καὶ   πίστιν   εἰς   τὸν   κύριον
repentance   and   faith   toward(?in)   the   Lord

ἡμῶν   Ἰησοῦν.   **22**   καὶ   νῦν   ἰδοὺ   δεδεμένος
of us   Jesus.   And   now   behold   having been bound

ἐγὼ   τῷ   πνεύματι   πορεύομαι   εἰς   Ἰερου-
I   by the   Spirit   am going   to   Jeru-

σαλήμ,   τὰ   ἐν   αὐτῇ   συναντήσοντα   ἐμοὶ
salem,   ³the things   ⁶in   ⁷it   ⁴going to meet   ⁵me

μὴ   εἰδώς,   **23**   πλὴν   ὅτι   τὸ   πνεῦμα   τὸ
¹not   ²knowing,   except   that   the   Spirit   –

ἅγιον   κατὰ   πόλιν   διαμαρτύρεταί   μοι   λέγον
Holy   in every city†   solemnly witnesses   to me   saying

ὅτι   δεσμὰ   καὶ   θλίψεις   με   μένουσιν.
that   bonds   and   afflictions   me   await.

24   ἀλλ᾽   οὐδενὸς   λόγου   ποιοῦμαι   τὴν   ψυχὴν
But   ⁴of no*thing*   ⁵account   ¹I make   ²the(my)   ³life

τιμίαν   ἐμαυτῷ   ὡς   τελειώσω   τὸν   δρόμον
precious   to myself   so as   I may finish   the   course

μου   καὶ   τὴν   διακονίαν   ἣν   ἔλαβον   παρὰ
of me   and   the   ministry   which   I received   from

τοῦ   κυρίου   Ἰησοῦ,   διαμαρτύρασθαι   τὸ
the   Lord   Jesus,   to witness solemnly   the

εὐαγγέλιον   τῆς   χάριτος   τοῦ   θεοῦ.   **25**   καὶ
gospel   of the   grace   –   of God.   And

νῦν   ἰδοὺ   ἐγὼ   οἶδα   ὅτι   οὐκέτι   ὄψεσθε
now   behold   I   know   that   ⁴no more   ³will see

τὸ   πρόσωπόν   μου   ὑμεῖς   πάντες   ἐν   οἷς
⁵the   ⁶face   ⁷of me   ¹ye   ²all   among whom

διῆλθον   κηρύσσων   τὴν   βασιλείαν.   **26**   διότι
I went about   proclaiming   the   kingdom.   Wherefore

μαρτύρομαι   ὑμῖν   ἐν   τῇ   σήμερον   ἡμέρᾳ
I witness   to you   on   this day

ὅτι   καθαρός   εἰμι   ἀπὸ   τοῦ   αἵματος   πάντων·
that   clean   I am   from   the   blood   of all men;

27   οὐ   γὰρ   ὑπεστειλάμην   τοῦ   μὴ   ἀναγγεῖλαι
for I kept not back   –   not   to declare[d]

πᾶσαν   τὴν   βουλὴν   τοῦ   θεοῦ   ὑμῖν.
all   the   counsel   –   of God   to you.

28   προσέχετε   ἑαυτοῖς   καὶ   παντὶ   τῷ
Take heed   to yourselves   and   to all   the

ποιμνίῳ,   ἐν   ᾧ   ὑμᾶς   τὸ   πνεῦμα   τὸ
flock,   in   which   ⁵you   ¹the   ³Spirit   –

hath made you overseers, to feed the church of God, which he hath purchased with his own blood.

29 For I know this, that after my departing shall grievous wolves enter in among you, not sparing the flock.

30 Also of your own selves shall men arise, speaking perverse things, to draw away disciples after them.

31 Therefore watch, and remember, that by the space of three years I ceased not to warn every one night and day with tears.

32 And now, brethren, I commend you to God, and to the word of his grace, which is able to build you up, and to give you an inheritance among all them which are sanctified.

33 I have coveted no man's silver, or gold, or apparel.

34 Yea, ye yourselves know, that these hands have ministered unto my necessities, and to them that were with me.

35 I have shewed you all things, how that so labouring ye ought to support the weak, and to remember the words of the Lord Jesus, how he said, It is more blessed

ἅγιον ἔθετο ἐπισκόπους, ποιμαίνειν τὴν
¹Holy   ⁴placed   overseers,   to shepherd   the

ἐκκλησίαν τοῦ θεοῦ, ἣν περιεποιήσατο
church   –   of God,   which   he acquired

διὰ τοῦ αἵματος τοῦ ἰδίου. 29 ἐγὼ
through the   blood   of the(his)   own.*   I

οἶδα ὅτι εἰσελεύσονται μετὰ τὴν ἄφιξίν
know   that   ⁷will come in   ¹after   ²the   ³departure

μου λύκοι βαρεῖς εἰς ὑμᾶς μὴ φειδόμενοι
⁴of me   ⁶wolves   ⁵grievous   ⁸into   you   not   sparing

τοῦ ποιμνίου, 30 καὶ ἐξ ὑμῶν αὐτῶν
the   flock,   and   of   you   [your]selves

ἀναστήσονται ἄνδρες λαλοῦντες διεστραμμένα
will rise up   men   speaking   *having been perverted things*

τοῦ ἀποσπᾶν τοὺς μαθητὰς ὀπίσω ἑαυτῶν.
– to drag awayᵈ   the   disciples   after   themselves.

31 διὸ γρηγορεῖτε, μνημονεύοντες ὅτι
Wherefore   watch ye,   remembering   that

τριετίαν νύκτα καὶ ἡμέραν οὐκ ἐπαυσάμην
for three years night   and   day   I ceased not

μετὰ δακρύων νουθετῶν ἕνα ἕκαστον.
with   tears   admonishing   ²one   ¹each.

32 καὶ τὰ νῦν παρατίθεμαι ὑμᾶς τῷ
And   –   now   I commend   you   to the

κυρίῳ καὶ τῷ λόγῳ τῆς χάριτος αὐτοῦ
Lord   and   to the   word   of the   grace   of him

τῷ δυναμένῳ οἰκοδομῆσαι καὶ δοῦναι τὴν
–   being able   to build   and   to give   the

κληρονομίαν ἐν τοῖς ἡγιασμένοις πᾶσιν.
inheritance   among ²the [ones]   ³having been sanctified   ¹all.

33 ἀργυρίου ἢ χρυσίου ἢ ἱματισμοῦ οὐδενὸς
Silver   or   gold   or   raiment   of no one

ἐπεθύμησα· 34 αὐτοὶ γινώσκετε ὅτι ταῖς
I coveted;   [your]selves   ye know   that   ⁴to the

χρείαις μου καὶ τοῖς οὖσιν μετ' ἐμοῦ
⁵needs   ⁶of me   ⁷and   ⁸to the [ones]   ⁹being   ¹⁰with   ¹¹me

ὑπηρέτησαν αἱ χεῖρες αὗται. 35 πάντα
³ministered   ¹these   ²hands.   All things

ὑπέδειξα ὑμῖν, ὅτι οὕτως κοπιῶντας δεῖ
I showed   you,   that   thus   labouring   it behoves

ἀντιλαμβάνεσθαι τῶν ἀσθενούντων, μνημονεύειν
to succour   the   ailing [ones],   ²to remember

τε τῶν λόγων τοῦ κυρίου Ἰησοῦ, ὅτι
¹and   the   words   of the   Lord   Jesus,   that

αὐτὸς εἶπεν· μακάριόν ἐστιν μᾶλλον διδόναι
he   said: Blessed   it is   rather   to give

---

* This = his own blood *or* the blood of his own [?Son].

to give than to receive.

36¶ And when he had thus spoken, he kneeled down, and prayed with them all.

37 And they all wept sore, and fell on Paul's neck, and kissed him,

38 Sorrowing most of all for the words which he spake, that they should see his face no more. And they accompanied him unto the ship.

ἢ   λαμβάνειν.   36 καὶ   ταῦτα   εἰπών,
than   to receive.   And   ²these things ¹having said,

θεὶς   τὰ   γόνατα   αὐτοῦ   σὺν   πᾶσιν   αὐτοῖς
placing the   knees   of him   with   ²all   ¹them
=kneeling down

προσηύξατο.   37 ἱκανὸς   δὲ   κλαυθμὸς   ἐγένετο
he prayed.   And ²considerable ³weeping ¹there was

πάντων,   καὶ   ἐπιπεσόντες   ἐπὶ   τὸν   τράχηλον
of all,   and   falling on   on   the   neck

τοῦ   Παύλου   κατεφίλουν   αὐτόν,   38 ὀδυνώ-
of Paul   they kissed fervently   him,   suffer-

μενοι   μάλιστα   ἐπὶ   τῷ   λόγῳ   ᾧ   εἰρήκει,
ing   most   over   the   word   which he had said,

ὅτι   οὐκέτι   μέλλουσιν   τὸ   πρόσωπον   αὐτοῦ
that   no more   they are(were)   the   face   of him

θεωρεῖν.   προέπεμπον   δὲ   αὐτὸν   εἰς   τὸ
to behold.   And they escorted   him   to   the

πλοῖον.
ship.

CHAPTER 21

AND it came to pass, that after we were gotten from them, and had launched, we came with a straight course unto Coos, and the day following unto Rhodes, and from thence unto Patara:

2 And finding a ship sailing over unto Phenicia, we went aboard, and set forth.

3 Now when we had discovered Cyprus, we left it on the left hand, and sailed into Syria, and landed at Tyre: for there the ship was to unlade her burden.

4 And finding disciples, we tarried there seven days: who said to Paul through the Spirit, that he should not go up to Jerusalem.

5 And when we had accomplished those days,

21 Ὡς   δὲ   ἐγένετο   ἀναχθῆναι   ἡμᾶς
Now when   it came to pass   to set sail   we

ἀποσπασθέντας   ἀπ'   αὐτῶν,   εὐθυδρομήσαντες
having been withdrawn from   them,   taking a straight course

ἤλθομεν   εἰς   τὴν   Κῶ,   τῇ   δὲ   ἑξῆς   εἰς
we came   to   -   Cos,   and on the next [day]   to

τὴν   Ῥόδον   κἀκεῖθεν   εἰς   Πάταρα·   2 καὶ
-   Rhodes   and thence   to   Patara;   and

εὑρόντες   πλοῖον   διαπερῶν   εἰς   Φοινίκην,
having found   a ship   crossing over   to   Phœnice,

ἐπιβάντες   ἀνήχθημεν.   3 ἀναφάναντες   δὲ
embarking   we set sail.   And sighting

τὴν   Κύπρον   καὶ   καταλιπόντες   αὐτὴν
-   Cyprus   and   leaving   it

εὐώνυμον   ἐπλέομεν   εἰς   Συρίαν,   καὶ   κατήλ-
on the left   we sailed   to   Syria,   and   came

θομεν   εἰς   Τύρον·   ἐκεῖσε   γὰρ   τὸ   πλοῖον
down   to   Tyre;   for there   the   ship

ἦν   ἀποφορτιζόμενον   τὸν   γόμον.   4 ἀνευρ-
was   unloading   the   cargo.   find-

όντες   δὲ   τοὺς   μαθητὰς   ἐπεμείναμεν   αὐτοῦ
ing   And   the   disciples   we remained   there

ἡμέρας   ἑπτά·   οἵτινες   τῷ   Παύλῳ   ἔλεγον
days   seven;   who   -   ¹Paul   ¹told

διὰ   τοῦ   πνεύματος   μὴ   ἐπιβαίνειν   εἰς
through the   Spirit   not   to go up   to

Ἱεροσόλυμα.   5 ὅτε   δὲ   · ἐγένετο   ἐξαρτίσαι
Jerusalem.   But when   it came to pass   to accomplish
=we accomplished

we departed and went our way; and they all brought us on our way, with wives and children, till *we were* out of the city: and we kneeled down on the shore, and prayed.

6 And when we had taken our leave one of another, we took ship; and they returned home again.

7 And when we had finished *our* course from Tyre, we came to Ptolemais, and saluted the brethren, and abode with them one day.

8 And the next *day* we that were of Paul's company departed, and came unto Cæsarea: and we entered into the house of Philip the evangelist, which was *one* of the seven; and abode with him.

9 And the same man had four daughters, virgins, which did prophesy.

10 And as we tarried *there* many days, there came down from Judæa a certain prophet, named Agabus.

11 And when he was come unto us, he took Paul's girdle, and bound his own hands and feet, and said, Thus saith the Holy Ghost, So shall the

---

ἡμᾶς τὰς ἡμέρας, ἐξελθόντες ἐπορευόμεθα
us[b] the days, going forth we journeyed

προπεμπόντων ἡμᾶς πάντων σὺν γυναιξὶ
[2]escorting [3]us [1]all[a] with women

καὶ τέκνοις ἕως ἔξω τῆς πόλεως, καὶ
and children as far as outside the city, and

θέντες τὰ γόνατα ἐπὶ τὸν αἰγιαλὸν
placing the knees on the shore
=kneeling

προσευξάμενοι 6 ἀπησπασάμεθα ἀλλήλους,
praying we gave parting greetings to one another.

καὶ ἐνέβημεν εἰς τὸ πλοῖον, ἐκεῖνοι δὲ
and embarked in the ship, and those

ὑπέστρειψαν εἰς τὰ ἴδια. 7 Ἡμεῖς δὲ
returned to ¹the(ir) ³things ²own. But we
=home.

τὸν πλοῦν διανύσαντες ἀπὸ Τύρου κατηντή-
²the ³voyage ¹finishing from Tyre ar-

σαμεν εἰς Πτολεμαΐδα, καὶ ἀσπασάμενοι
rived at Ptolemais, and greeting

τοὺς ἀδελφοὺς ἐμείναμεν ἡμέραν μίαν
the brothers we remained day one

παρ' αὐτοῖς. 8 τῇ δὲ ἐπαύριον ἐξελθόντες
with them. And on the morrow going forth

ἤλθομεν εἰς Καισάρειαν, καὶ εἰσελθόντες
we came to Cæsarea, and entering

εἰς τὸν οἶκον Φιλίππου τοῦ εὐαγγελιστοῦ
into the house of Philip the evangelist

ὄντος ἐκ τῶν ἑπτά, ἐμείναμεν παρ'
being of the seven, we remained with

αὐτῷ. 9 τούτῳ δὲ ἦσαν θυγατέρες
him. Now to this man were daughters
=this man had four daughters

τέσσαρες παρθένοι προφητεύουσαι. 10 Ἐπιμεν-
four[c] virgins prophesying. remain-

όντων δὲ ἡμέρας πλείους κατῆλθέν τις
ing[a] And days more(many) ⁵came down ¹a certain

ἀπὸ τῆς Ἰουδαίας προφήτης ὀνόματι
⁶from – ⁷Judæa ²prophet ³by name

Ἄγαβος, 11 καὶ ἐλθὼν πρὸς ἡμᾶς καὶ
⁴Agabus, and coming to us and

ἄρας τὴν ζώνην τοῦ Παύλου, δήσας
taking the girdle – of Paul, having bound

ἑαυτοῦ τοὺς πόδας καὶ τὰς χεῖρας εἶπεν·
of himself the feet and the hands said:

τάδε λέγει τὸ πνεῦμα τὸ ἅγιον· τὸν
These things says the Spirit – Holy: ⁷The

ἄνδρα οὗ ἐστιν ἡ ζώνη αὕτη οὕτως
⁸man ⁹of whom ¹⁰is ¹¹this ¹²girdle ¹thus

Jews at Jerusalem bind the man that owneth this girdle, and shall deliver *him* into the hands of the Gentiles.

12 And when we heard these things, both we, and they of that place, besought him not to go up to Jerusalem.

13 Then Paul answered, What mean ye to weep and to break mine heart? for I am ready not to be bound only, but also to die at Jerusalem for the name of the Lord Jesus.

14 And when he would not be persuaded, we ceased, saying, The will of the Lord be done.

15 And after those days we took up our carriages, and went up to Jerusalem.

16 There went with us also *certain* of the disciples of Cæsarea, and brought with them one Mnason of Cyprus, an old disciple, with whom we should lodge.

17 And when we were come to Jerusalem, the brethren received us gladly.

18 And the *day* following Paul went in with us unto James; and all the elders were present.

19 And when he had saluted them, he declared

δήσουσιν ἐν Ἰερουσαλὴμ οἱ Ἰουδαῖοι καὶ
⁴will bind ⁵in ⁶Jerusalem ²the ³Jews and

παραδώσουσιν εἰς χεῖρας ἐθνῶν. 12 ὡς
will deliver into [the] hands of [the] nations. when

δὲ ἠκούσαμεν ταῦτα, παρεκαλοῦμεν ἡμεῖς
And we heard these things, ⁶besought ¹we

τε καὶ οἱ ἐντόπιοι τοῦ μὴ ἀναβαίνειν
¹both ³and ⁴the ⁵residents – ⁸not ⁹to go up^d

αὐτὸν εἰς Ἰερουσαλήμ. 13 τότε ἀπεκρίθη
⁷him to Jerusalem. Then answered

ὁ Παῦλος τί ποιεῖτε κλαίοντες καὶ
– Paul: What are ye doing weeping and

συνθρύπτοντές μου τὴν καρδίαν; ἐγὼ γὰρ
weakening of me the heart? For I

οὐ μόνον δεθῆναι ἀλλὰ καὶ ἀποθανεῖν
not only to be bound but also to die

εἰς Ἰερουσαλὴμ ἑτοίμως ἔχω ὑπὲρ τοῦ
in Jerusalem readily have on behalf of the
= am ready

ὀνόματος τοῦ κυρίου Ἰησοῦ. 14 μὴ
name of the Lord Jesus. Not

πειθομένου δὲ αὐτοῦ ἡσυχάσαμεν εἰπόντες·
being persuaded and him^a we kept silence having said:
= And when he was not persuaded

τοῦ κυρίου τὸ θέλημα γινέσθω.
⁴Of the ⁵Lord ²the ³will ¹let ⁶be [done].

15 Μετὰ δὲ τὰς ἡμέρας ταύτας
And after these days

ἐπισκευασάμενοι ἀνεβαίνομεν εἰς Ἰεροσόλυμα·
having made ready we went up to Jerusalem;

16 συνῆλθον δὲ καὶ τῶν μαθητῶν ἀπὸ
and went *with* also [some] of the disciples from

Καισαρείας σὺν ἡμῖν, ἄγοντες παρ' ᾧ
Cæsarea with us, bringing [one] with whom

ξενισθῶμεν Μνάσωνί τινι Κυπρίῳ,
we might be lodged Mnason a certain Cypriote,

ἀρχαίῳ μαθητῇ. 17 Γενομένων δὲ ἡμῶν εἰς
an ancient disciple. And being us^a in
(early) = when we were

Ἰεροσόλυμα ἀσμένως ἀπεδέξαντο ἡμᾶς οἱ
Jerusalem ³joyfully ²received ⁴us ¹the

ἀδελφοί. 18 τῇ δὲ ἐπιούσῃ εἰσῄει ὁ
²brothers. And on the next day went in –

Παῦλος σὺν ἡμῖν πρὸς Ἰάκωβον, πάντες
Paul with us to James, ²all

τε παρεγένοντο οἱ πρεσβύτεροι. 19 καὶ
¹and ²came ³the ⁴elders. And

ἀσπασάμενος αὐτοὺς ἐξηγεῖτο καθ' ἓν
having greeted them he related according to one
= singly

particularly what things God had wrought among the Gentiles by his ministry.

20 And when they heard *it*, they glorified the Lord, and said unto him, Thou seest, brother, how many thousands of Jews there are which believe; and they are all zealous of the law:

21 And they are informed of thee, that thou teachest all the Jews which are among the Gentiles to forsake Moses, saying that they ought not to circumcise *their* children, neither to walk after the customs.

22 What is it therefore? the multitude must needs come together: for they will hear that thou art come.

23 Do therefore this that we say to thee: We have four men which have a vow on them;

24 Them take, and purify thyself with them, and be at charges with them, that they may shave *their* heads: and all may know that those things, whereof they were informed concerning thee, are nothing; but *that* thou thyself also walkest orderly, and keepest the law.

25 As touching the Gentiles which believe, we have written *and* concluded that they observe no such thing, save only that they keep themselves from *things* offered to idols, and from blood, and from strangled, and from fornication.

ἕκαστον ὧν ἐποίησεν ὁ θεὸς ἐν τοῖς
each of [the things] which did – God among the

ἔθνεσιν διὰ τῆς διακονίας αὐτοῦ. 20 οἱ
nations through the ministry of him. they

δὲ ἀκούσαντες ἐδόξαζον τὸν θεόν, εἶπάν τε
And hearing glorified – God, and said

αὐτῷ· θεωρεῖς, ἀδελφέ, πόσαι μυριάδες
to him: Thou beholdest, brother, how many *ten* thousands

εἰσὶν ἐν τοῖς Ἰουδαίοις τῶν πεπιστευκότων,
there are among the Jews – having believed,

καὶ πάντες ζηλωταὶ τοῦ νόμου ὑπάρχουσιν·
and all zealots of the law are;

21 κατηχήθησαν δὲ περὶ σοῦ ὅτι ἀποστα-
and they were informed about thee that ⁸apo-

σίαν διδάσκεις ἀπὸ Μωϋσέως τοὺς κατὰ
stasy ¹thou teachest ⁹from ¹⁰Moses ³the ⁵throughout

τὰ ἔθνη πάντας Ἰουδαίους, λέγων μὴ
⁶the ⁷nations ²all ⁴Jews, ¹telling ²not

περιτέμνειν αὐτοὺς τὰ τέκνα μηδὲ τοῖς
⁴to circumcise ³them the children nor in the

ἔθεσιν περιπατεῖν. 22 τί οὖν ἐστιν;
customs to walk. What therefore is it?

πάντως ἀκούσονται ὅτι ἐλήλυθας. 23 τοῦτο
At all events they will hear that thou hast come. This

οὖν ποίησον ὅ σοι λέγομεν· εἰσὶν ἡμῖν
therefore do thou which thee we tell: There are to us = We have

ἄνδρες τέσσαρες εὐχὴν ἔχοντες ἐφ᾽ ἑαυτῶν·
men four a vow having on themselves;

24 τούτους παραλαβὼν ἁγνίσθητι σὺν αὐτοῖς,
these taking be thou purified with them,

καὶ δαπάνησον ἐπ᾽ αὐτοῖς ἵνα ξυρήσονται
and spend on them that they will shave

τὴν κεφαλήν, καὶ γνώσονται πάντες ὅτι
the head, and will know all men that

ὧν κατήχηνται περὶ σοῦ οὐδέν
⁵[of the things] ⁴they have been ³about ²thee ¹nothing
of which informed

ἔστιν, ἀλλὰ στοιχεῖς καὶ αὐτὸς φυλάσσων τὸν
¹there is, but thou walkest also [thy]self keeping the

νόμον. 25 περὶ δὲ τῶν πεπιστευκότων
law. And concerning ¹the ²having believed

ἐθνῶν ἡμεῖς ἐπεστείλαμεν κρίναντες φυλάσ-
³nations we joined in writing ¹judging ²to keep

σεσθαι αὐτοὺς τό τε εἰδωλόθυτον καὶ
themselves ³them ⁴[from] ⁶the ⁵both idol sacrifice and

αἷμά καὶ πνικτὸν καὶ πορνείαν. 26 τότε
blood and a thing strangled and fornication. Then

26 Then Paul took the men, and the next day purifying himself with them entered into the temple, to signify the accomplishment of the days of purification, until that an offering should be offered for every one of them.

27 And when the seven days were almost ended, the Jews which were of Asia, when they saw him in the temple, stirred up all the people, and laid hands on him,

28 Crying out, Men of Israel, help: This is the man, that teacheth all *men* every where against the people, and the law, and this place: and further brought Greeks also into the temple, and hath polluted this holy place.

29 (For they had seen before with him in the city Trophimus an Ephesian, whom they supposed that Paul had brought into the temple.)

30 And all the city was moved, and the people ran together: and they took Paul, and drew him out of the temple: and forthwith the doors were shut.

31 And as they went

ὁ Παῦλος παραλαβὼν τοὺς ἄνδρας τῇ
– Paul taking the men on the

ἐχομένῃ ἡμέρᾳ σὺν αὐτοῖς ἁγνισθεὶς εἰσῄει
next day with them having been purified went in

εἰς τὸ ἱερόν, διαγγέλλων τὴν ἐκπλήρωσιν
to the temple, announcing the completion

τῶν ἡμερῶν τοῦ ἁγνισμοῦ, ἕως οὗ
of the days of the purification, until

προσηνέχθη ὑπὲρ ἑνὸς ἑκάστου αὐτῶν ἡ
should be offered on behalf of ²one ¹each of them the

προσφορά.
offering.

27 Ὡς δὲ ἔμελλον αἱ ἑπτὰ ἡμέραι
Now when were about the seven days

συντελεῖσθαι, οἱ ἀπὸ τῆς Ἀσίας Ἰουδαῖοι
to be fulfilled, ¹the ³from – ⁴Asia ²Jews

θεασάμενοι αὐτὸν ἐν τῷ ἱερῷ συνέχεον
seeing him in the temple stirred up

πάντα τὸν ὄχλον, καὶ ἐπέβαλαν ἐπ'
all the crowd, and laid *on* on

αὐτὸν τὰς χεῖρας, **28** κράζοντες· ἄνδρες
him the(ir) hands, crying out: Men

Ἰσραηλῖται, βοηθεῖτε· οὗτός ἐστιν ὁ
Israelites, help: this is the

ἄνθρωπος ὁ κατὰ τοῦ λαοῦ καὶ τοῦ
man ¹the [one] ⁴against ⁵the ⁷people ⁸and ⁹the

νόμου καὶ τοῦ τόπου τούτου πάντας
¹⁰law ¹¹and ¹²this ¹³place ²all men

πανταχῇ διδάσκων, ἔτι τε καὶ Ἕλληνας
⁴everywhere ³teaching, and even also Greeks

εἰσήγαγεν εἰς τὸ ἱερὸν καὶ κεκοίνωκεν
brought *in* into the temple and has profaned

τὸν ἅγιον τόπον τοῦτον. **29** ἦσαν γὰρ
– ²holy ³place ¹this. For they were

προεωρακότες Τρόφιμον τὸν Ἐφέσιον ἐν
having previously seen Trophimus the Ephesian in

τῇ πόλει σὺν αὐτῷ, ὃν ἐνόμιζον ὅτι
the city with him, whom they supposed that

εἰς τὸ ἱερὸν εἰσήγαγεν ὁ Παῦλος. **30** ἐκινήθη
³into ⁴the ⁵temple ²brought *in* – ¹Paul. ⁵was moved

τε ἡ πόλις ὅλη καὶ ἐγένετο συνδρομὴ
¹And ²the ⁴city ³whole and there was a running together

τοῦ λαοῦ, καὶ ἐπιλαβόμενοι τοῦ Παύλου
of the people, and laying hold – of Paul

εἷλκον αὐτὸν ἔξω τοῦ ἱεροῦ, καὶ εὐθέως
they dragged him outside the temple, and immediately

ἐκλείσθησαν αἱ θύραι. **31** Ζητούντων τε
were shut the doors. And [while they were]
seekingᵃ

about to kill him, tidings came unto the chief captain of the band, that all Jerusalem was in an uproar.

32 Who immediately took soldiers and centurions, and ran down unto them: and when they saw the chief captain and the soldiers, they left beating of Paul.

33 Then the chief captain came near, and took him, and commanded *him* to be bound with two chains; and demanded who he was, and what he had done.

34 And some cried one thing, some another, among the multitude: and when he could not know the certainty for the tumult, he commanded him to be carried into the castle.

35 And when he came upon the stairs, so it was, that he was borne of the soldiers for the violence of the people.

36 For the multitude of the people followed after, crying, Away with him.

37 And as Paul was to be led into the castle, he said unto the chief captain, May I speak unto thee? Who said, Canst thou speak Greek?

αὐτὸν	ἀποκτεῖναι	ἀνέβη	φάσις	τῷ
[2]him	[1]to kill	[4]came up	[3]information	to the

χιλιάρχῳ	τῆς	σπείρης	ὅτι	ὅλη	συγχύν-
chiliarch	of the	cohort	that	[1]all	[2]is(was) in

νεται	Ἰερουσαλήμ·	32 ὃς	ἐξαυτῆς	παρα-
confusion	[2]Jerusalem;	who	at once	tak-

λαβὼν	στρατιώτας	καὶ	ἑκατοντάρχας
ing	soldiers	**and**	centurions

κατέδραμεν	ἐπ’	αὐτούς·	οἱ	δὲ	ἰδόντες
ran down	on	them;	and they		seeing

τὸν	χιλίαρχον	καὶ	τοὺς	στρατιώτας
the	chiliarch	and	the	soldiers

ἐπαύσαντο	τύπτοντες	τὸν	Παῦλον.	33 τότε
ceased	beating	–	Paul.	Then

ἐγγίσας	ὁ	χιλίαρχος	ἐπελάβετο	αὐτοῦ
drawing near	the	chiliarch	laid hold	of him

καὶ	ἐκέλευσεν	δεθῆναι	ἁλύσεσι	δυσί,	καὶ
and	commanded	to be bound	chains	with two,	and

ἐπυνθάνετο	τίς	εἴη	καὶ	τί	ἐστιν	πεποιηκώς.
inquired	who	he might be	and	what	he is	having done.

34 ἄλλοι	δὲ	ἄλλο	τι	ἐπεφώνουν	ἐν	τῷ
And [1]others		[7]different	[6]something	[5]called out	[2]among	[3]the

ὄχλῳ·	μὴ	δυναμένου	δὲ	αὐτοῦ	γνῶναι
[4]crowd;	and not being able =as he was not able			him[a]	to know

τὸ	ἀσφαλὲς	διὰ	τὸν	θόρυβον,	ἐκέλευσεν
the	certain thing	because of the		uproar,	he commanded

ἄγεσθαι	αὐτὸν	εἰς	τὴν	παρεμβολήν.	35 ὅτε
to be brought	him	into	the	fort.	when

δὲ	ἐγένετο	ἐπὶ	τοὺς	ἀναβαθμούς,	συνέβη
And	he was	on	the	steps,	it happened

βαστάζεσθαι	αὐτὸν	ὑπὸ	τῶν	στρατιωτῶν
to be carried =he was carried	him[b]	by	he	soldiers

διὰ	τὴν	βίαν	τοῦ	ὄχλου·	36 ἠκολούθει
because of the		violence	of the	crowd;	[6]followed

γὰρ	τὸ	πλῆθος	τοῦ	λαοῦ	κράζοντες·
[1]for	[2]the	[3]multitude	[4]of the	[5]people	crying out:

αἶρε	αὐτόν.	37 Μέλλων	τε	εἰσάγεσθαι
Take away	him.	And being about		to be brought *in*

εἰς	τὴν	παρεμβολὴν	ὁ	Παῦλος	λέγει	τῷ
into	the	fort	–	Paul	says	to the

χιλιάρχῳ·	εἰ	ἔξεστίν	μοι	εἰπεῖν	τι	πρὸς
chiliarch:	If	it is lawful	for me	to say	something	to

σέ;	ὁ	δὲ	ἔφη·	Ἑλληνιστὶ	γινώσκεις;
thee?	And he		said:	in Greek	Knowest thou [to speak]?*

* See note on page xviii.

38 Art not thou that Egyptian, which before these days madest an uproar, and leddest out into the wilderness four thousand men that were murderers?

39 But Paul said, I am a man which am a Jew of Tarsus, a city in Cilicia, a citizen of no mean city: and, I beseech thee, suffer me to speak unto the people.

40 And when he had given him licence, Paul stood on the stairs, and beckoned with the hand unto the people. And when there was made a great silence, he spake unto them in the Hebrew tongue, saying,

38 οὐκ ἄρα σὺ εἶ ὁ Αἰγύπτιος ὁ πρὸ
   [2]Not [4]then [3]thou [1]art the Egyptian the [one] before
τούτων τῶν ἡμερῶν ἀναστατώσας καὶ
   these   -   days   unsettling   and
ἐξαγαγὼν εἰς τὴν ἔρημον τοὺς τετρα-
leading out into the desert the   four
κισχιλίους ἄνδρας τῶν σικαρίων; 39 εἶπεν
thousand   men   of the Sicarii?   said
δὲ ὁ Παῦλος· ἐγὼ ἄνθρωπος μέν εἰμι
And - Paul: I   a man   indeed am
Ἰουδαῖος, Ταρσεύς, τῆς Κιλικίας οὐκ
 a Jew,   a Tarsian, - of Cilicia not
ἀσήμου πόλεως πολίτης· δέομαι δέ σου,
of a mean city   a citizen; and I beg of thee,
ἐπίτρεψόν μοι λαλῆσαι πρὸς τὸν λαόν.
permit   me to speak to   the people.
40 ἐπιτρέψαντος δὲ αὐτοῦ ὁ Παῦλος ἑστὼς
   And permitting him[a] - Paul standing
   =when he gave permission
ἐπὶ τῶν ἀναβαθμῶν κατέσεισεν τῇ χειρὶ
on   the steps   beckoned with the(his) hand
τῷ λαῷ· πολλῆς δὲ σιγῆς γενομένης
to the people; and much silence becoming[a]
   =when there was great silence
προσεφώνησεν τῇ Ἑβραΐδι διαλέκτῳ λέγων·
he addressed in the Hebrew   language   saying:

CHAPTER 22

MEN, brethren, and fathers, hear ye my defence which I make now unto you.

2 (And when they heard that he spake in the Hebrew tongue to them, they kept the more silence: and he saith,)

3 I am verily a man which am a Jew, born in Tarsus, a city in Cilicia, yet brought up in this city at the feet of Gamaliel, and taught according to the perfect manner of the law of the fathers, and was zealous toward God, as ye all are this day.

22 Ἄνδρες ἀδελφοὶ καὶ πατέρες, ἀκούσατέ
    Men   brothers and fathers,   hear ye
μου τῆς πρὸς ὑμᾶς νυνὶ ἀπολογίας.
[3]of me [1]the [2]to [4]you [5]now [2]defence.
— 2 ἀκούσαντες δὲ ὅτι τῇ Ἑβραΐδι
   (And hearing that in the Hebrew
διαλέκτῳ προσεφώνει αὐτοῖς μᾶλλον
language   he addressed them   more
παρέσχον ἡσυχίαν. καὶ φησίν· — 3 ἐγώ εἰμι
they showed quietness. And he says:)   I   am
ἀνὴρ Ἰουδαῖος, γεγεννημένος ἐν Ταρσῷ
a man a Jew, having been born in Tarsus
τῆς Κιλικίας, ἀνατεθραμμένος δὲ ἐν τῇ
 - of Cilicia, and having been brought up in -
πόλει ταύτῃ, παρὰ τοὺς πόδας Γαμαλιὴλ
city this,   at   the   feet of Gamaliel
πεπαιδευμένος κατὰ ἀκρίβειαν τοῦ πατρῴου
having been trained according exactness of the ancestral
   to [the]
νόμου, ζηλωτὴς ὑπάρχων τοῦ θεοῦ καθὼς
law.   a zealot   being   - of God even as

4 And I persecuted this way unto the death, binding and delivering into prisons both men and women.

5 As also the high priest doth bear me witness, and all the estate of the elders: from whom also I received letters unto the brethren, and went to Damascus, to bring them which were there bound unto Jerusalem, for to be punished.

6 And it came to pass, that, as I made my journey, and was come nigh unto Damascus about noon, suddenly there shone from heaven a great light round about me.

7 And I fell unto the ground, and heard a voice saying unto me, Saul, Saul, why persecutest thou me?

8 And I answered, Who art thou, Lord? And he said unto me, I am Jesus of Nazareth, whom thou persecutest.

9 And they that were with me saw indeed the light, and were afraid; but they heard not the voice of him that spake to me.

10 And I said, What shall I do, Lord? And the Lord said unto me, Arise, and go into Damascus; and there it shall be told thee of all things which are appointed for thee to do.

11 And when I could

πάντες ὑμεῖς ἐστε σήμερον· **4** ὃς ταύτην
all   ye   are   to-day;   who   this

τὴν ὁδὸν ἐδίωξα ἄχρι θανάτου, δεσμεύων
–   way   persecuted as far as to   death,   binding

καὶ παραδιδοὺς εἰς φυλακὰς ἄνδρας τε
and   delivering   to   prisons   both men

καὶ γυναῖκας. **5** ὡς καὶ ὁ ἀρχιερεὺς
and   women.   As   even   the   high priest

μαρτυρεῖ μοι καὶ πᾶν τὸ πρεσβυτέριον·
witnesses   to me   and   all   the   senate;

παρ᾽ ὧν καὶ ἐπιστολὰς δεξάμενος πρὸς
from whom also   letters   having received   to

τοὺς ἀδελφοὺς εἰς Δαμασκὸν ἐπορευόμην,
the   brothers   in   Damascus   I journeyed,

ἄξων καὶ τοὺς ἐκεῖσε ὄντας δεδεμένους
leading   also the [ones] [2]there   [1]being *having been* bound

εἰς Ἱερουσαλὴμ ἵνα τιμωρηθῶσιν.
to   Jerusalem   that   they might be punished.

6 Ἐγένετο δέ μοι πορευομένῳ καὶ ἐγγίζοντι
Now it happened to me   journeying   and drawing near

τῇ Δαμασκῷ περὶ μεσημβρίαν ἐξαίφνης ἐκ
– to Damascus   about   midday   suddenly out of

τοῦ οὐρανοῦ περιαστράψαι φῶς ἱκανὸν
–   heaven   [4]to shine *round*   [1]a [3]light [2]considerable

περὶ ἐμέ, **7** ἔπεσά τε εἰς τὸ ἔδαφος
round   me,   and I fell   to   the   ground

καὶ ἤκουσα φωνῆς λεγούσης μοι· Σαούλ
and   heard   a voice   saying   to me: Saul[.]

Σαούλ, τί με διώκεις; **8** ἐγὼ δὲ ἀπεκρίθην·
Saul,   why me persecutest thou?   And I   answered:

τίς εἶ, κύριε; εἶπέν τε πρὸς ἐμέ· ἐγώ
Who art thou, Lord?   And he said   to   me: I

εἰμι Ἰησοῦς ὁ Ναζωραῖος, ὃν σὺ διώκεις.
am   Jesus   the   Nazarene,   whom thou persecutest.

9 οἱ δὲ σὺν ἐμοὶ ὄντες τὸ μὲν φῶς
Now [1]the [ones] [3]with   [4]me   [2]being [7]the [indeed] [5]light

ἐθεάσαντο, τὴν δὲ φωνὴν οὐκ ἤκουσαν
[6]beheld,   but the   voice   they heard not

τοῦ λαλοῦντός μοι. **10** εἶπον δέ· τί
of the [one] speaking   to me.   And I said: What

ποιήσω, κύριε; ὁ δὲ κύριος εἶπεν πρός
may I do,   Lord? And the   Lord   said   to

με· ἀναστὰς πορεύου εἰς Δαμασκόν, κἀκεῖ σοι
me: Rising up   go   into   Damascus, and there to thee

λαληθήσεται περὶ πάντων ὧν τέτακταί
it will be told   concerning all things   which   has(ve) been
                                                           arranged

σοι ποιῆσαι. **11** ὡς δὲ οὐκ ἐνέβλεπον
for thee to do.   And as   I saw not

not see for the glory of that light, being led by the hand of them that were with me, I came into Damascus

12 And one Ananias, a devout man according to the law, having a good report of all the Jews which dwelt *there*,

13 Came unto me, and stood, and said unto me, Brother Saul, receive thy sight. And the same hour I looked up upon him.

14 And he said, The God of our fathers hath chosen thee, that thou shouldest know his will, and see that Just One, and shouldest hear the voice of his mouth.

15 For thou shalt be his witness unto all men of what thou hast seen and heard.

16 And now why tarriest thou? arise, and be baptized, and wash away thy sins, calling on the name of the Lord.

17 And it came to pass, that, when I was come again to Jerusalem, even while I prayed in the temple, I was in a trance;

18 And saw him saying unto me, Make haste, and get thee quickly out of Jerusalem: for they will not receive thy testimony concerning me.

19 And I said, Lord,

ἀπὸ τῆς δόξης τοῦ φωτὸς ἐκείνου,
from the glory   of that light,

χειραγωγούμενος ὑπὸ τῶν συνόντων μοι
being led by the hand by the [ones] being with me

ἦλθον εἰς Δαμασκόν. 12 Ἀνανίας δέ τις,
I went into Damascus.   And a certain Ananias,

ἀνὴρ εὐλαβὴς κατὰ τὸν νόμον, μαρτυρού-
a man devout according to the law,   being witness-

μενος ὑπὸ πάντων τῶν κατοικούντων
[to]   by   all   ¹the   ²dwelling ⁴[there]

Ἰουδαίων, 13 ἐλθὼν πρὸς ἐμὲ καὶ ἐπιστὰς
³Jews,   coming to me and and standing by

εἶπέν μοι· Σαοὺλ ἀδελφέ, ἀνάβλεψον.
said to me: Saul brother,   look up.

κἀγὼ αὐτῇ τῇ ὥρᾳ ἀνέβλεψα εἰς αὐτόν.
And I in that hour*   looked up   at him.

14 ὁ δὲ εἶπεν· ὁ θεὸς τῶν πατέρων
And he said: The God of the fathers

ἡμῶν προεχειρίσατό σε γνῶναι τὸ θέλημα
of us previously appointed thee to know the will

αὐτοῦ καὶ ἰδεῖν τὸν δίκαιον καὶ ἀκοῦσαι
of him and to see the Just One and to hear

φωνὴν ἐκ τοῦ στόματος αὐτοῦ, 15 ὅτι
a voice out of the mouth   of him, because

ἔσῃ μάρτυς αὐτῷ πρὸς πάντας ἀνθρώπους
thou wilt be a witness to himᶜ to all   men

ὧν ἑώρακας καὶ ἤκουσας. 16 καὶ νῦν
of things which thou hast seen and didst hear. And now

τί μέλλεις; ἀναστὰς βάπτισαι καὶ ἀπόλου-
what intendest thou? Rising up be baptized and wash

σαι τὰς ἁμαρτίας σου, ἐπικαλεσάμενος τὸ
away the sins of thee, invoking   the

ὄνομα αὐτοῦ. 17 Ἐγένετο δέ μοι ὑποστρέ-
name of him.   And it happened to me having

ψαντι εἰς Ἰερουσαλὴμ καὶ προσευχομένου
returned to Jerusalem and   praying
                                =as I was praying

μου ἐν τῷ ἱερῷ γενέσθαι με ἐν ἐκστάσει,
meᵃ in the temple to become meᵇ in an ecstasy,
                                   =I became

18 καὶ ἰδεῖν αὐτὸν λέγοντά μοι· σπεῦσον
and to seeᵇ him saying to me; Haste
   =I saw

καὶ ἔξελθε ἐν τάχει ἐξ Ἰερουσαλήμ,
and go forth quickly out of Jerusalem,

διότι οὐ παραδέξονταί σου μαρτυρίαν
because they will not receive of thee witness

περὶ ἐμοῦ. 19 κἀγὼ εἶπον· κύριε, αὐτοὶ
concerning me.   And I said: Lord, they

* See Luke 2. 38.

they know that I imprisoned and beat in every synagogue them that believed on thee:

20 And when the blood of thy martyr Stephen was shed, I also was standing by, and consenting unto his death, and kept the raiment of them that slew him.

21 And he said unto me, Depart: for I will send thee far hence unto the Gentiles.

22 ¶ And they gave him audience unto this word, and *then* lifted up their voices, and said, Away with such a *fellow* from the earth: for it is not fit that he should live.

23 And as they cried out, and cast off *their* clothes, and threw dust into the air,

24 The chief captain commanded him to be brought into the castle, and bade that he should be examined by scourging; that he might know wherefore they cried so against him.

25 And as they bound him with thongs, Paul said unto the centurion that stood by, Is it lawful for you to scourge a man that is a Roman, and uncondemned?

26 When the centurion heard *that*, he went and told the chief captain, saying, Take heed what

ἐπίστανται ὅτι ἐγὼ ἤμην φυλακίζων καὶ
understand that I was imprisoning and

δέρων κατὰ τὰς συναγωγὰς τοὺς πιστεύον-
beating throughout the synagogues the [ones] believ-

τας ἐπὶ σέ· 20 καὶ ὅτε ἐξεχύννετο τὸ αἷμα
ing on thee; and when was being shed the blood

Στεφάνου τοῦ μάρτυρός σου, καὶ αὐτὸς
of Stephen the witness of thee, even [my]self

ἤμην ἐφεστὼς καὶ συνευδοκῶν καὶ
I was standing by and consenting and

φυλάσσων τὰ ἱμάτια τῶν ἀναιρούντων
keeping the garments of the [ones] killing

αὐτόν. 21 καὶ εἶπεν πρός με· πορεύου,
him. And he said to me: Go,

ὅτι ἐγὼ εἰς ἔθνη μακρὰν ἐξαποστελῶ σε.
because I to nations afar will send forth thee.

22 Ἤκουον δὲ αὐτοῦ ἄχρι τούτου τοῦ
And they heard him as far as to this –

λόγου, καὶ ἐπῆραν τὴν φωνὴν αὐτῶν
word, and lifted up the voice of them

λέγοντες· αἶρε ἀπὸ τῆς γῆς τὸν τοιοῦτον·
saying: Take from the earth such a man;

οὐ γὰρ καθῆκεν αὐτὸν ζῆν. 23 κραυγαζόν-
for not it is fitting him to live. And shout-

των τε αὐτῶν καὶ ῥιπτούντων τὰ ἱμάτια
ing them and tearing[a] the(ir) garments
=as they shouted and tore . . .

καὶ κονιορτὸν βαλλόντων εἰς τὸν ἀέρα,
and [2]dust [1]throwing[a] in the air,
=threw dust

24 ἐκέλευσεν ὁ χιλίαρχος εἰσάγεσθαι αὐτὸν
commanded the chiliarch to be brought *in* him

εἰς τὴν παρεμβολήν, εἴπας μάστιξιν
into the fort, bidding [3]with scourges

ἀνετάζεσθαι αὐτόν, ἵνα ἐπιγνῶ δι' ἣν
[2]to be examined [1]him, that he might fully know for what

αἰτίαν οὕτως ἐπεφώνουν αὐτῷ. 25 ὡς δὲ
crime thus they were calling against him. But as

προέτειναν αὐτὸν τοῖς ἱμᾶσιν, εἶπεν πρὸς
they stretched him with the thongs, [1]said [2]to
forward

τὸν ἑστῶτα ἑκατόνταρχον ὁ Παῦλος· εἰ
[4]the [6]standing [by] [5]centurion [1]Paul: [1]If

ἄνθρωπον Ῥωμαῖον καὶ ἀκατάκριτον ἔξεστιν
a man [5]a Roman [6]and [7]uncondemned [2]it is lawful

ὑμῖν μαστίζειν; 26 ἀκούσας δὲ ὁ ἑκατον-
[3]for you [4]to scourge? And [3]hearing [1]the [2]cen-

τάρχης προσελθὼν τῷ χιλιάρχῳ ἀπήγγειλεν
turion approaching *to* the chiliarch reported

thou doest: for this man is a Roman.

27 Then the chief captain came, and said unto him, Tell me, art thou a Roman? He said, Yea.

28 And the chief captain answered, With a great sum obtained I this freedom. And Paul said, But I was *free* born.

29 Then straightway they departed from him which should have examined him: and the chief captain also was afraid, after he knew that he was a Roman, and because he had bound him.

30 On the morrow, because he would have known the certainty wherefore he was accused of the Jews, he loosed him from *his* bands, and commanded the chief priests and all their council to appear, and brought Paul down, and set him before them.

λέγων· τί μέλλεις ποιεῖν; ὁ γὰρ ἄνθρωπος
saying· What art thou about to do? – for ²man

οὗτος 'Ρωμαῖός ἐστιν. 27 προσελθὼν δὲ
¹this ⁴a Roman ³is. And approaching

ὁ χιλίαρχος εἶπεν αὐτῷ· λέγε μοι, σὺ
the chiliarch said to him: Tell me, thou

'Ρωμαῖος εἶ; ὁ δὲ ἔφη· ναί. 28 ἀπεκρίθη
a Roman art? And he said: Yes. answered

δὲ ὁ χιλίαρχος· ἐγὼ πολλοῦ κεφαλαίου
And the chiliarch: ¹I ⁵of(for) ⁶sum [of money] much(great)

τὴν πολιτείαν ταύτην ἐκτησάμην. ὁ δὲ
³this ⁴citizenship ²acquired. – So

Παῦλος ἔφη· ἐγὼ δὲ καὶ γεγέννημαι.
Paul said: But I indeed have been born.

29 εὐθέως οὖν ἀπέστησαν ἀπ' αὐτοῦ οἱ
Immediately therefore ⁵stood away ⁶from ⁷him ¹the [ones]

μέλλοντες αὐτὸν ἀνετάζειν· καὶ ὁ χιλίαρχος
²being about ⁴him ³to examine; ⁴also ¹the ²chiliarch

δὲ ἐφοβήθη ἐπιγνοὺς ὅτι 'Ρωμαῖός ἐστιν
¹and feared fully knowing that a Roman he is(was)

καὶ ὅτι αὐτὸν ἦν δεδεκώς.
and that ³him ¹he was ²having bound.

30 Τῇ δὲ ἐπαύριον βουλόμενος γνῶναι τὸ
And on the morrow being minded to know the

ἀσφαλές, τὸ τί κατηγορεῖται ὑπὸ τῶν
certain thing, – why he was accused by the

'Ιουδαίων, ἔλυσεν αὐτόν, καὶ ἐκέλευσεν
Jews, he released him, and commanded

συνελθεῖν τοὺς ἀρχιερεῖς καὶ πᾶν τὸ
to come together the chief priests and all the

συνέδριον, καὶ καταγαγὼν τὸν Παῦλον
council, and having brought down – Paul

CHAPTER 23

A ND Paul, earnestly beholding the council, said, Men *and* brethren, I have lived in all good conscience before God until this day.

2 And the high priest Ananias commanded them that stood by him to smite him on the mouth.

3 Then said Paul unto

ἔστησεν εἰς αὐτούς. 23 ἀτενίσας δὲ
set [him] among them. And ²gazing

ὁ Παῦλος τῷ συνεδρίῳ εἶπεν· ἄνδρες
– ¹Paul at the council said: Men

ἀδελφοί, ἐγὼ πάσῃ συνειδήσει ἀγαθῇ
brothers, I in all conscience good

πεπολίτευμαι τῷ θεῷ ἄχρι ταύτης τῆς
have lived – to God until this

ἡμέρας. 2 ὁ δὲ ἀρχιερεὺς 'Ανανίας
day. And the high priest Ananias

ἐπέταξεν τοῖς παρεστῶσιν αὐτῷ τύπτειν
gave order to the [ones] standing by him to strike

αὐτοῦ τὸ στόμα. 3 τότε ὁ Παῦλος πρὸς
of him the mouth. Then – Paul to

him, God shall smite thee, *thou* whited wall: for sittest thou to judge me after the law, and commandest me to be smitten contrary to the law?

4 And they that stood by said, Revilest thou God's high priest?

5 Then said Paul, I wist not, brethren, that he was the high priest: for it is written, Thou shalt not speak evil of the ruler of thy people.

6 But when Paul perceived that the one part were Sadducees, and the other Pharisees, he cried out in the council, Men *and* brethren, I am a Pharisee, the son of a Pharisee: of the hope and resurrection of the dead I am called in question.

7 And when he had so said, there arose a dissension between the Pharisees and the Sadducees: and the multitude was divided.

8 For the Sadducees say that there is no resurrection, neither angel, nor spirit: but the Pharisees confess both.

9 And there arose a great cry: and the scribes *that were* of the Pharisees' part arose, and strove, saying, We find no evil in this man: but if a

αὐτὸν εἶπεν· τύπτειν σε μέλλει ὁ θεός,
him said: ³To strike ⁴thee ²is about – ¹God,

τοῖχε κεκονιαμένε· καὶ σὺ κάθῃ κρίνων
wall *having been* whitened; and thou sittest judging

με κατὰ τὸν νόμον, καὶ παρανομῶν
me according to the law, and contravening law

κελεύεις με τύπτεσθαι; 4 οἱ δὲ παρεστῶτες
commandest me to be struck? And the [ones] standing by

εἶπαν· τὸν ἀρχιερέα τοῦ θεοῦ λοιδορεῖς;
said: The high priest – of God revilest thou?

5 ἔφη τε ὁ Παῦλος· οὐκ ᾔδειν, ἀδελφοί,
And said – Paul: I did not know, brothers,

ὅτι ἐστὶν ἀρχιερεύς· γέγραπται γὰρ ὅτι
that he is high priest; for it has been written[,] –

ἄρχοντα τοῦ λαοῦ σου οὐκ ἐρεῖς κακῶς.
A ruler of the people of thee thou shalt not speak evilly.

6 γνοὺς δὲ ὁ Παῦλος ὅτι τὸ ἓν μέρος
And knowing – Paul that the one part

ἐστὶν Σαδδουκαίων τὸ δὲ ἕτερον Φαρισαίων
is(was) of Sadducees but the other of Pharisees

ἔκραζεν ἐν τῷ συνεδρίῳ· ἄνδρες ἀδελφοί,
cried out in the council: Men brothers,

ἐγὼ Φαρισαῖός εἰμι, υἱὸς Φαρισαίων· περὶ
I a Pharisee am, a son of Pharisees; concerning

ἐλπίδος καὶ ἀναστάσεως νεκρῶν κρίνομαι.
hope and resurrection of dead ones I am being judged.

7 τοῦτο δὲ αὐτοῦ λαλοῦντος ἐγένετο
And this him saying* there was
=as he said this

στάσις τῶν Φαρισαίων καὶ Σαδδουκαίων,
a discord of the Pharisees and Sadducees,

καὶ ἐσχίσθη τὸ πλῆθος. 8 Σαδδουκαῖοι
and was divided the multitude. Sadducees

γὰρ λέγουσιν μὴ εἶναι ἀνάστασιν μήτε
For say not to be a resurrection nor

ἄγγελον μήτε πνεῦμα, Φαρισαῖοι δὲ
angel nor spirit, but Pharisees

ὁμολογοῦσιν τὰ ἀμφότερα. 9 ἐγένετο δὲ
confess – both. And there was

κραυγὴ μεγάλη, καὶ ἀναστάντες τινὲς
cry a great, and rising up some

τῶν γραμματέων τοῦ μέρους τῶν Φαρισαίων
of the scribes of the part of the Pharisees

διεμάχοντο λέγοντες· οὐδὲν κακὸν εὑρίσκομεν
strove saying: Nothing evil we find

ἐν τῷ ἀνθρώπῳ τούτῳ· εἰ δὲ πνεῦμα
in this man; and if ¹a spirit

spirit or an angel hath spoken to him, let us not fight against God.

10 And when there arose a great dissension, the chief captain, fearing lest Paul should have been pulled in pieces of them, commanded the soldiers to go down, and to take him by force from among them, and to bring *him* into the castle.

11 And the night following the Lord stood by him, and said, Be of good cheer, Paul: for as thou hast testified of me in Jerusalem, so must thou bear witness also at Rome.

12 And when it was day, certain of the Jews banded together, and bound themselves under a curse, saying that they would neither eat nor drink till they had killed Paul.

13 And they were more than forty which had made this conspiracy.

14 And they came to the chief priests and elders, and said, We have bound ourselves under a great curse, that we will eat nothing until we have slain Paul.

15 Now therefore ye with the council signify to the chief captain that he bring him down unto you to morrow, as though ye would enquire something more perfectly concerning him: and we, or ever he

ἐλάλησεν αὐτῷ ἢ ἄγγελος —. 10 Πολλῆς δὲ
⁴spoke   ⁵to him ³or ²an angel —.   And much

γινομένης στάσεως φοβηθεὶς ὁ χιλίαρχος
arising   discordᵃ ³fearing ¹the ²chiliarch
= when much discord arose

μὴ διασπασθῇ ὁ Παῦλος ὑπ' αὐτῶν,
⁴lest ⁵should be - ⁵Paul by them,
torn asunder

ἐκέλευσεν τὸ στράτευμα καταβὰν ἁρπάσαι
commanded the soldiery coming down to seize

αὐτὸν ἐκ μέσου αὐτῶν ἄγειν τε εἰς
him out of [the] midst of them and to bring [him] into

τὴν παρεμβολήν. 11 Τῇ δὲ ἐπιούσῃ
the   fort.   And in the following

νυκτὶ ἐπιστὰς αὐτῷ ὁ κύριος εἶπεν·
night ²coming *on* ⁴to him ¹the ³Lord said:

θάρσει· ὡς γὰρ διεμαρτύρω τὰ περὶ
Be of good for as thou didst the concerning
courage;   solemnly witness things

ἐμοῦ εἰς Ἰερουσαλήμ, οὕτω σε δεῖ καὶ
me   in Jerusalem,   so thee it behoves also

εἰς Ῥώμην μαρτυρῆσαι. 12 Γενομένης δὲ
in Rome to witness.   And becoming

ἡμέρας ποιήσαντες συστροφὴν οἱ Ἰουδαῖοι
dayᵃ   ³making   ⁴a conspiracy ¹the ²Jews
= when it became day

ἀνεθεμάτισαν ἑαυτούς, λέγοντες μήτε φαγεῖν
cursed   themselves, saying neither to eat

μήτε πεῖν ἕως οὗ ἀποκτείνωσιν τὸν
nor to drink until   they should kill -

Παῦλον. 13 ἦσαν δὲ πλείους τεσσεράκοντα
Paul.   And there were more [than] forty

οἱ ταύτην τὴν συνωμοσίαν ποιησάμενοι·
the [ones] this the plot   making;

14 οἵτινες προσελθόντες τοῖς ἀρχιερεῦσιν
who   approaching   *to* the chief priests

καὶ τοῖς πρεσβυτέροις εἶπαν· ἀναθέματι
and *to* the elders   said: With a curse

ἀνεθεματίσαμεν ἑαυτοὺς μηδενὸς γεύσασθαι
we cursed   ourselves *of* nothing to taste

ἕως οὗ ἀποκτείνωμεν τὸν Παῦλον. 15 νῦν
until   we may kill   -   Paul.   Now

οὖν ὑμεῖς ἐμφανίσατε τῷ χιλιάρχῳ σὺν
therefore ²ye ¹inform the chiliarch with

τῷ συνεδρίῳ ὅπως καταγάγῃ αὐτὸν εἰς
the council so as he may bring down him to

ὑμᾶς ὡς μέλλοντας διαγινώσκειν ἀκριβέστε-
you as intending to ascertain *exactly* more accurate-

ρον τὰ περὶ αὐτοῦ· ἡμεῖς δὲ πρὸ τοῦ
ly the things concerning him; and we before   -

'come near, are ready to kill him.

16 And when Paul's sister's son heard of their lying in wait, he went and entered into the castle, and told Paul.

17 Then Paul called one of the centurions unto *him*, and said, Bring this young man unto the chief captain: for he hath a certain thing to tell him.

18 So he took him, and brought *him* to the chief captain, and said, Paul the prisoner called me unto *him*, and prayed me to bring this young man unto thee, who hath something to say unto thee.

19 Then the chief captain took him by the hand, and went *with him* aside privately, and asked *him*, What is that thou hast to tell me?

20 And he said, The Jews have agreed to desire thee that thou wouldest bring down Paul to morrow into the council, as though they would enquire somewhat of him more perfectly.

21 But do not thou yield unto them: for there lie in wait for him of them more than forty men, which have bound themselves with an oath, that they will neither eat nor

ἐγγίσαι αὐτὸν ἕτοιμοί ἐσμεν τοῦ ἀνελεῖν
to draw near him[b] ready are – to kill[d]
=he draws near

αὐτόν. 16 Ἀκούσας δὲ ὁ υἱὸς τῆς ἀδελφῆς
him. And [5]hearing [1]the [2]son [3]of the [4]sister

Παύλου τὴν ἐνέδραν, παραγενόμενος καὶ
[5]of Paul the treachery, coming and

εἰσελθὼν εἰς τὴν παρεμβολὴν ἀπήγγειλεν
entering into the fort reported

τῷ Παύλῳ. 17 προσκαλεσάμενος δὲ ὁ
– to Paul. And [2]calling to [him] –

Παῦλος ἕνα τῶν ἑκατονταρχῶν ἔφη· τὸν
[1]Paul one of the centurions said: –

νεανίαν τοῦτον ἄπαγε πρὸς τὸν χιλίαρχον,
[3]youth [2]this [1]Bring up to the chiliarch,

ἔχει γὰρ ἀπαγγεῖλαί τι αὐτῷ. 18 ὁ
for [1]he has [3]to report [2]something [4]to him. He

μὲν οὖν παραλαβὼν αὐτὸν ἤγαγεν πρὸς
– therefore taking [2]him [1]brought to

τὸν χιλίαρχον καὶ φησίν· ὁ δέσμιος
the chiliarch and says: The prisoner

Παῦλος προσκαλεσάμενός με ἠρώτησεν
Paul calling to [him] me asked

τοῦτον τὸν νεανίσκον ἀγαγεῖν πρὸς σέ,
[2]this – [3]young man [1]to bring to thee,

ἔχοντά τι λαλῆσαί σοι. 19 ἐπιλαβόμενος
having something to tell thee. [2]laying hold

δὲ τῆς χειρὸς αὐτοῦ ὁ χιλίαρχος καὶ
And [4]of the [5]hand [6]of him [1]the [2]chiliarch and

ἀναχωρήσας κατ' ἰδίαν ἐπυνθάνετο· τί
retiring [2]privately [1]inquired: What

ἐστιν ὃ ἔχεις ἀπαγγεῖλαί μοι; 20 εἶπεν
is it which thou hast to report to me? he said[,]

δὲ ὅτι οἱ Ἰουδαῖοι συνέθεντο τοῦ ἐρωτῆσαί
And – The Jews agreed – to ask[d]

σε ὅπως αὔριον τὸν Παῦλον καταγάγῃς
thee so as to-morrow – [2]Paul [1]thou shouldest bring down

εἰς τὸ συνέδριον ὡς μέλλον τι ἀκριβέστερον
to the council as intending some- more accurately thing

πυνθάνεσθαι περὶ αὐτοῦ. 21 σὺ οὖν μὴ
to inquire concerning him. Thou therefore not

πεισθῇς αὐτοῖς· ἐνεδρεύουσιν γὰρ αὐτὸν
be persuaded by them; for there lie in wait for him

ἐξ αὐτῶν ἄνδρες πλείους τεσσεράκοντα,
of them [1]men [1]more [2][than] forty,

οἵτινες ἀνεθεμάτισαν ἑαυτοὺς μήτε φαγεῖν
who cursed themselves neither to eat

drink till they have killed him: and now are they ready, looking for a promise from thee.

22 So the chief captain *then* let the young man depart, and charged *him*, *See thou* tell no man that thou hast shewed these things to me.

23 And he called unto *him* two centurions, saying, Make ready two hundred soldiers to go to Cæsarea, and horsemen threescore and ten, and spearmen two hundred, at the third hour of the night;

24 And provide *them* beasts, that they may set Paul on, and bring *him* safe unto Felix the governor.

25 And he wrote a letter after this manner:

26 Claudius Lysias unto the most excellent governor Felix *sendeth* greeting.

27 This man was taken of the Jews, and should have been killed of them: then came I with an army, and rescued him, having understood that he was a Roman.

28 And when I would have known the cause wherefore they accused him, I brought him forth into their council:

29 Whom I perceived to be accused of questions of their law, but to have

μήτε πεῖν ἕως οὗ ἀνέλωσιν αὐτόν, καὶ νῦν
nor to drink until they kill him, and now

εἰσιν ἕτοιμοι προσδεχόμενοι τὴν ἀπὸ σοῦ
they are ready awaiting ¹the ²from ⁴thee

ἐπαγγελίαν. 22 ὁ μὲν οὖν χιλίαρχος
²promise. the – Therefore chiliarch

ἀπέλυσε τὸν νεανίσκον, παραγγείλας μηδενὶ
dismissed the young man, charging [him] to no one

ἐκλαλῆσαι ὅτι ταῦτα ἐνεφάνισας πρὸς ἐμέ.
to divulge that these things thou reportedst to me.

23 Καὶ προσκαλεσάμενός τινας δύο τῶν
And calling to [him] a certain two of the

ἑκατονταρχῶν εἶπεν· ἑτοιμάσατε στρατιώτας
centurions he said: Prepare ye soldiers

διακοσίους ὅπως πορευθῶσιν ἕως Καισαρείας,
two hundred so as they may go as far as Cæsarea,

καὶ ἱππεῖς ἑβδομήκοντα καὶ δεξιολάβους
and horsemen seventy and spearmen

διακοσίους, ἀπὸ τρίτης ὥρας τῆς νυκτός,
two hundred, from third hour of the night,

24 κτήνη τε παραστῆσαι, ἵνα ἐπιβιβάσαντες
and beasts to stand by, that putting on

τὸν Παῦλον διασώσωσι πρὸς Φήλικα τὸν
– Paul they may bring to Felix the
[him] safely

ἡγεμόνα, 25 γράψας ἐπιστολὴν ἔχουσαν
governor, writing a letter having

τὸν τύπον τοῦτον· 26 Κλαύδιος Λυσίας τῷ
this pattern: Claudius Lysias to the

κρατίστῳ ἡγεμόνι Φήλικι χαίρειν. 27 Τὸν
most excellent governor Felix greeting. –

ἄνδρα τοῦτον συλλημφθέντα ὑπὸ τῶν
man This having been arrested by the

Ἰουδαίων καὶ μέλλοντα ἀναιρεῖσθαι ὑπ'
Jews and being about to be killed by

αὐτῶν ἐπιστὰς σὺν τῷ στρατεύματι
them coming on with the soldiery
[the scene]

ἐξειλάμην, μαθὼν ὅτι Ῥωμαῖός ἐστιν·
I rescued, having learned that a Roman he is;

28 βουλόμενός τε ἐπιγνῶναι τὴν αἰτίαν
and being minded to know fully the cause

δι' ἣν ἐνεκάλουν αὐτῷ, κατήγαγον εἰς
on ac- which they were him, I brought to
count of accusing [him] down

τὸ συνέδριον αὐτῶν· 29 ὃν εὗρον ἐγκαλούμενον
the council of them; whom I found being accused

περὶ ζητημάτων τοῦ νόμου αὐτῶν, μηδὲν
about questions of the law of them, ²nothing

nothing laid to his charge worthy of death or of bonds.

30 And when it was told me how that the Jews laid wait for the man, I sent straightway to thee, and gave commandment to his accusers also to say before thee what *they had* against him. Farewell.

31 Then the soldiers, as it was commanded them, took Paul, and brought *him* by night to Antipatris.

32 On the morrow they left the horsemen to go with him, and returned to the castle:

33 Who, when they came to Cæsarea, and delivered the epistle to the governor, presented Paul also before him.

34 And when the governor had read *the letter*, he asked of what province he was. And when he understood that *he was* of Cilicia;

35 I will hear thee, said he, when thine accusers are also come. And he commanded him to be kept in Herod's judgment hall.

δὲ   ἄξιον   θανάτου   ἢ   δεσμῶν   ἔχοντα
¹and   ²worthy   ⁶of death   ⁷or   ⁸of bonds   ²having

ἔγκλημα.   30 μηνυθείσης   δέ   μοι   ἐπιβουλῆς
⁴charge.   And being revealed   to me   a plot²
        = when it was revealed to me that there was a plot

εἰς   τὸν   ἄνδρα   ἔσεσθαι,   ἐξαυτῆς   ἔπεμψα
against the   man   to be,   at once   I sent

πρὸς   σέ,   παραγγείλας   καὶ   τοῖς   κατηγόροις
to   thee,   commanding   also   the   accusers

λέγειν   πρὸς   αὐτὸν   ἐπὶ   σοῦ.   31 Οἱ   μὲν
to say   to   him   before   thee.   the   –

οὖν   στρατιῶται   κατὰ   τὸ   διατεταγμένον
Therefore   soldiers   according   the   having been
        to   thing   appointed

αὐτοῖς   ἀναλαβόντες   τὸν   Παῦλον   ἤγαγον
them   taking up   –   Paul   brought

διὰ   νυκτὸς   εἰς   τὴν   Ἀντιπατρίδα·   32 τῇ   δὲ
through [the] night to   –   Antipatris;   and on the
(during)

ἐπαύριον   ἐάσαντες   τοὺς   ἱππεῖς   ἀπέρχεσθαι
morrow   allowing   the   horsemen   to depart

σὺν   αὐτῷ,   ὑπέστρεψαν   εἰς   τὴν   παρεμβολήν·
with   him,   they returned   to   the   fort;

33 οἵτινες   εἰσελθόντες   εἰς   τὴν   Καισάρειαν
who   entering   into   –   Caesarea

καὶ   ἀναδόντες   τὴν   ἐπιστολὴν   τῷ   ἡγεμόνι,
and   handing over   the   letter   to the   governor,

παρέστησαν   καὶ   τὸν   Παῦλον   αὐτῷ.
presented   also   –   Paul   to him.

34 ἀναγνοὺς   δὲ   καὶ   ἐπερωτήσας   ἐκ   ποίας
And having read   and   asking   of   what

ἐπαρχείας   ἐστίν,   καὶ   πυθόμενος   ὅτι   ἀπὸ
province   he is(was),   and   learning[,]   –   From

Κιλικίας,   35 διακούσομαί   σου,   ἔφη,   ὅταν
Cilicia,   I will hear   thee,   he said,   when

καὶ   οἱ   κατήγοροί   σου   παραγένωνται·
also   the   accusers   of thee   arrive;

κελεύσας   ἐν   τῷ   πραιτωρίῳ   τοῦ   Ἡρώδου
commanding   in   the   prætorium   –   of Herod
        = that he be kept in Herod's prætorium.

φυλάσσεσθαι   αὐτόν.
to be kept   him.

CHAPTER 24

AND after five days Ananias the high priest descended with the elders, and *with* a certain orator *named* Tertullus,

24 Μετὰ   δὲ   πέντε   ἡμέρας   κατέβη   ὁ
And after   five   days   came down the

ἀρχιερεὺς   Ἀνανίας   μετὰ   πρεσβυτέρων   τινῶν
high priest   Ananias   with   elders   some

καὶ   ῥήτορος   Τερτύλλου   τινός,   οἵτινες
and   an orator   Tertullus   one,   who

who informed the governor against Paul.

2 And when he was called forth, Tertullus began to accuse *him*, saying, Seeing that by thee we enjoy great quietness, and that very worthy deeds are done unto this nation by thy providence,

3 We accept *it* always, and in all places, most noble Felix, with all thankfulness.

4 Notwithstanding, that I be not further tedious unto thee, I pray thee that thou wouldest hear us of thy clemency a few words.

5 For we have found this man *a* pestilent *fellow*, and a mover of sedition among all the Jews throughout the world, and a ringleader of the sect of the Nazarenes:

6 Who also hath gone about to profane the temple: whom we took, and would have judged according to our law.

7 But the chief captain Lysias came *upon us*, and with great violence took *him* away out of our hands,

8 Commanding his accusers to come unto thee: by examining of whom thyself mayest take knowledge of all these things, whereof we accuse him.

9 And the Jews also assented, saying that these things were so.

10 ¶ Then Paul, after that the governor had beckoned unto him to speak, answered, Forasmuch as I know that thou hast been of many years a judge unto this nation,

ἐνεφάνισαν τῷ ἡγεμόνι κατὰ τοῦ Παύλου.
informed   the governor against -   Paul.

2 κληθέντος δὲ [αὐτοῦ] ἤρξατο κατηγορεῖν
And being called   him[a] [2]began [3]to accuse
= when he was called

ὁ Τέρτυλλος λέγων· πολλῆς εἰρήνης
- [1]Tertullus saying: Much   peace

τυγχάνοντες διὰ σοῦ καὶ διορθωμάτων
obtaining   through thee and   reforms

γινομένων τῷ ἔθνει τούτῳ διὰ τῆς σῆς
coming   to this nation   through - thy

προνοίας, 3 πάντῃ τε καὶ πανταχοῦ
forethought, both in everything and everywhere

ἀποδεχόμεθα, κράτιστε Φῆλιξ, μετὰ πάσης
we welcome, most excellent Felix, with   all

εὐχαριστίας. 4 ἵνα δὲ μὴ ἐπὶ πλεῖόν
thankfulness.   But that [3]not   [4]more

σε ἐγκόπτω, παρακαλῶ ἀκοῦσαί σε ἡμῶν
[3]thee [1]I hinder, I beseech [2]to hear [1]thee   us

συντόμως τῇ σῇ ἐπιεικείᾳ. 5 εὑρόντες γὰρ
briefly   - in thy forbearance.   For having found

τὸν ἄνδρα τοῦτον λοιμὸν καὶ κινοῦντα
this man   pestilent and   moving

στάσεις πᾶσιν τοῖς Ἰουδαίοις τοῖς κατὰ
seditions [among] all the   Jews   - throughout

τὴν οἰκουμένην πρωτοστάτην τε τῆς τῶν
the inhabited [earth] and a ringleader of the [3]of the

Ναζωραίων αἱρέσεως, 6 ὃς καὶ τὸ ἱερὸν
[3]Nazarenes [1]sect,   who also [3]the [4]temple

ἐπείρασεν βεβηλῶσαι, ὃν καὶ ἐκρατήσαμεν,‡
[1]attempted [2]to profane, whom also we laid hold of,‡

8 παρ' οὗ δυνήσῃ αὐτὸς ἀνακρίνας
from whom thou wilt be able [thy]self [2]having examined

περὶ πάντων τούτων ἐπιγνῶναι ὧν ἡμεῖς
[3]concerning [4]all [5]these things [1]to know fully of which   we

κατηγοροῦμεν αὐτοῦ. 9 συνεπέθεντο δὲ
accuse   him.   And [4]joined in

καὶ οἱ Ἰουδαῖοι φάσκοντες ταῦτα οὕτως
[3]also [1]the [2]Jews   alleging   these things thus

ἔχειν. 10 Ἀπεκρίθη τε ὁ Παῦλος,
to have(be).   And answered   -   Paul,

νεύσαντος αὐτῷ τοῦ ἡγεμόνος λέγειν· ἐκ
[3]having [4]to him [1]the [2]governor[a] to speak: [5]of
beckoned   (for)

πολλῶν ἐτῶν ὄντα σε κριτὴν τῷ ἔθνει τούτῳ
[5]many [6]years [3]being [1]thee [7]a judge [8]to [9]this [10]nation
          (to be)

‡ Verse 7 omitted by Nestle; *cf.* R.V. marg.

I do the more cheerfully answer for myself:

11 Because that thou mayest understand, that there are yet but twelve days since I went up to Jerusalem for to worship.

12 And they neither found me in the temple disputing with any man, neither raising up the people, neither in the synagogues, nor in the city:

13 Neither can they prove the things whereof they now accuse me.

14 But this I confess unto thee, that after the way which they call heresy, so worship I the God of my fathers, believing all things which are written in the law and in the prophets:

15 And have hope toward God, which they themselves also allow, that there shall be a resurrection of the dead, both of the just and unjust.

16 And herein do I exercise myself, to have always a conscience void of offence toward God, and *toward* men.

17 Now after many years I came to bring alms to my nation, and offerings.

ἐπιστάμενος   εὐθύμως   τὰ   περὶ
[1]understanding   [12]cheerfully [13][as to] [14]the things [15]concerning

ἐμαυτοῦ   ἀπολογοῦμαι,   11 δυναμένου   σου
[16]myself   [11]I defend myself,   being able   thee[a]
                                        =as thou art able

ἐπιγνῶναι   ὅτι   οὐ   πλείους   εἰσίν   μοι   ἡμέραι
to know fully that [3]not [4]more [1]there [2]to [5][than] [7]days
                                     are   me

δώδεκα   ἀφ'   ἧς   ἀνέβην   προσκυνήσων   εἰς
[6]twelve from which I went up worshipping   in
          =since

Ἰερουσαλήμ.   12 καὶ   οὔτε   ἐν   τῷ   ἱερῷ
Jerusalem.   And neither in the temple

εὗρόν   με   πρός   τινα   διαλεγόμενον   ἢ
they found me [2]with [3]anyone [1]discoursing or

ἐπίστασιν   ποιοῦντα   ὄχλου,   οὔτε   ἐν   ταῖς
[2]collection [1]making of a crowd, neither in the

συναγωγαῖς   οὔτε   κατὰ   τὴν   πόλιν,   13 οὐδὲ
synagogues   nor throughout the city,   nor

παραστῆσαι   δύνανταί   σοι   περὶ   ὧν   νυνὶ
[2]to prove   [1]are they able to thee con- [the] things now
                                     cerning of which

κατηγοροῦσίν   μου.   14 ὁμολογῶ   δὲ   τοῦτό
they accuse   me.   But I confess   this

σοι,   ὅτι   κατὰ   τὴν   ὁδὸν   ἣν   λέγουσιν
to thee, that according to the way which they say(call)

αἵρεσιν   οὕτως   λατρεύω   τῷ   πατρῴῳ   θεῷ,
a sect   thus   I worship the ancestral God,

πιστεύων   πᾶσι   τοῖς   κατὰ   τὸν   νόμον   καὶ
believing   all   the according the law   and
                 things to

τοῖς   ἐν   τοῖς   προφήταις   γεγραμμένοις,
the things in the   prophets   *having been* written,

15 ἐλπίδα   ἔχων   εἰς   τὸν   θεόν,   ἣν   καὶ
    hope   having toward -   God, which [3]also

αὐτοὶ   οὗτοι   προσδέχονται,   ἀνάστασιν   μέλ-
[2][them]selves [1]these expect,   a resurrection to be

λειν   ἔσεσθαι   δικαίων   τε   καὶ   ἀδίκων.
about   to be   both of just and   of unjust.

16 ἐν   τούτῳ   καὶ   αὐτὸς   ἀσκῶ   ἀπρόσκοπον
   By   this   also [2][my]self [1]I exercise [4]a blameless

συνείδησιν   ἔχειν   πρὸς   τὸν   θεὸν   καὶ   τοὺς
[5]conscience [3]to have toward -   God   and   -

ἀνθρώπους   διὰ   παντός.   17 δι'   ἐτῶν   δὲ
men   always.   And after years

πλειόνων   ἐλεημοσύνας   ποιήσων   εἰς   τὸ
many   [2]alms   [1]making(bringing) [3]to [4]the

ἔθνος   μου   παρεγενόμην   καὶ   προσφοράς,
[5]nation [6]of me [9]I arrived   [7]and   [8]offerings,

18 Whereupon certain Jews from Asia found me purified in the temple, neither with multitude, nor with tumult.

19 Who ought to have been here before thee, and object, if they had ought against me.

20 Or else let these same *here* say, if they have found any evil doing in me, while I stood before the council,

21 Except it be for this one voice, that I cried standing among them, Touching the resurrection of the dead I am called in question by you this day.

22 ¶ And when Felix heard these things, having more perfect knowledge of *that* way, he deferred them, and said, When Lysias the chief captain shall come down, I will know the uttermost of your matter.

23 And he commanded a centurion to keep Paul, and to let *him* have liberty, and that he should forbid none of his acquaintance to minister or come unto him.

24 And after certain days, when Felix came with his wife Drusilla, which was a Jewess, he sent for Paul, and heard him concerning the faith in Christ.

25 And as he reasoned of righteousness, temperance, and judgment to

---

18 ἐν αἷς εὗρόν με ἡγνισμένον ἐν τῷ
among which they found me *having been* purified in the

ἱερῷ, οὐ μετὰ ὄχλου οὐδὲ μετὰ θορύβου,
temple, not with a crowd nor with uproar,

19 τινὲς δὲ ἀπὸ τῆς 'Ασίας 'Ιουδαῖοι,
but some ²from – ³Asia ¹Jews,

οὓς ἔδει ἐπὶ σοῦ παρεῖναι καὶ κατηγορεῖν
whom it be- before thee to be present and to accuse
hoved

εἴ τι ἔχοιεν πρὸς ἐμέ. **20** ἢ αὐτοὶ
if anything they have against me. Or ³[them]selves

οὗτοι εἰπάτωσαν τί εὗρον ἀδίκημα στάντος
²these ¹let ⁴say ¹what ²they found ²misdeed standing

μου ἐπὶ τοῦ συνεδρίου, **21** ἢ περὶ μιᾶς
meª before the council, unless concerning ²one
=while I stood

ταύτης φωνῆς ἧς ἐκέκραξα ἐν αὐτοῖς
¹this voice which I have cried out ²among ³them

ἑστὼς ὅτι περὶ ἀναστάσεως νεκρῶν ἐγὼ
¹standing[,] – Concerning a resurrection of dead persons I

κρίνομαι σήμερον ἐφ' ὑμῶν. **22** 'Ανεβάλετο
am being judged to-day before you. ²postponed

δὲ αὐτοὺς ὁ Φῆλιξ, ἀκριβέστερον εἰδὼς
And ³them – ¹Felix, more exactly knowing

τὰ περὶ τῆς ὁδοῦ, εἴπας· ὅταν Λυσίας ὁ
the con- the way, saying: When Lysias the
things cerning

χιλίαρχος καταβῇ, διαγνώσομαι τὰ καθ'
chiliarch comes down, I will determine the things as to

ὑμᾶς· **23** διαταξάμενος τῷ ἑκατοντάρχῃ
you; commanding the centurion

τηρεῖσθαι αὐτὸν ἔχειν τε ἄνεσιν καὶ
to keep him and to have indulgence and

μηδένα κωλύειν τῶν ἰδίων αὐτοῦ ὑπηρετεῖν
²no one ¹to forbid of his own [people] to attend

αὐτῷ. **24** Μετὰ δὲ ἡμέρας τινὰς παραγενό-
him. And after days some ²arriv-

μενος ὁ Φῆλιξ σὺν Δρουσίλλῃ τῇ ἰδίᾳ
ing – ¹Felix with Drusilla the(his) own

γυναικὶ οὔσῃ 'Ιουδαίᾳ μετεπέμψατο τὸν
wife being a Jewess he sent for –

Παῦλον, καὶ ἤκουσεν αὐτοῦ περὶ τῆς
Paul, and heard him about ¹the(?his)

εἰς Χριστὸν 'Ιησοῦν πίστεως. **25** διαλεγομέ-
³in ⁴Christ ⁵Jesus ²faith. ,=And as he discoursed

νου δὲ αὐτοῦ περὶ δικαιοσύνης καὶ
ing And himª concerning righteousness and

come, Felix trembled, and answered, Go thy way for this time; when I have a convenient season, I will call for thee.

26 He hoped also that money should have been given him of Paul, that he might loose him: wherefore he sent for him the oftener, and communed with him.

27 But after two years Porcius Festus came into Felix' room: and Felix, willing to shew the Jews a pleasure, left Paul bound.

ἐγκρατείας	καὶ	τοῦ	κρίματος	τοῦ	μέλλοντος
self-control	and	the	²judgment	–	¹coming

ἔμφοβος	γενόμενος	ὁ	Φῆλιξ	ἀπεκρίθη·
afraid	becoming	–	Felix	answered:

τὸ	νῦν	ἔχον	πορεύου,	καιρὸν	δὲ	μεταλαβὼν
For the present†		go thou,	but ²time		¹taking ³later

μετακαλέσομαί	σε·	26 ἅμα	καὶ	ἐλπίζων
I will send for	thee;	at the same time	also	hoping

ὅτι	χρήματα	δοθήσεται	αὐτῷ	ὑπὸ	τοῦ
that	money	will be given	him	by	–

Παύλου·	διὸ	καὶ	πυκνότερον	αὐτὸν
Paul;	wherefore	also	more frequently	him

μεταπεμπόμενος	ὡμίλει	αὐτῷ.	27 Διετίας	δὲ
sending for	he conversed with	him.		And two years

πληρωθείσης	ἔλαβεν	διάδοχον	ὁ	Φῆλιξ
being completedᵃ	²received	³a successor	–	¹Felix

Πόρκιον	Φῆστον·	θέλων	τε	χάριτα	κατα-
Porcius	Festus;	and wishing		a favour	to

θέσθαι	τοῖς	Ἰουδαίοις	ὁ	Φῆλιξ	κατέλιπε
show	to the	Jews	–	Felix	left

τὸν	Παῦλον	δεδεμένον.
–	Paul	*having been* bound.

CHAPTER 25

NOW when Festus was come into the province, after three days he ascended from Cæsarea to Jerusalem.

2 Then the high priest and the chief of the Jews informed him against Paul, and besought him,

3 And desired favour against him, that he would send for him to Jerusalem, laying wait in the way to kill him.

4 But Festus answered, that Paul should be kept at Cæsarea, and that he himself would depart shortly *thither*.

5 Let them therefore,

25 Φῆστος	οὖν	ἐπιβὰς	τῇ	ἐπαρχείῳ
Festus	therefore	having entered	the	province

μετὰ	τρεῖς	ἡμέρας	ἀνέβη	εἰς	Ἱεροσόλυμα
after	three	days	went up	to	Jerusalem

ἀπὸ	Καισαρείας,	2 ἐνεφάνισάν	τε	αὐτῷ
from	Caesarea,	and ³informed		⁹him

οἱ	ἀρχιερεῖς	καὶ	οἱ	πρῶτοι	τῶν	Ἰουδαίων
¹the	²chief priests	³and	⁴the	⁵chiefs	⁶of the	⁷Jews

κατὰ	τοῦ	Παύλου,	καὶ	παρεκάλουν	αὐτὸν
against	–	Paul,	and	they besought	him

3 αἰτούμενοι	χάριν	κατ'	αὐτοῦ,	ὅπως	μετα-
asking	a favour	against	him,	so as	he might

πέμψηται	αὐτὸν	εἰς	Ἱερουσαλήμ,	ἐνέδραν
summon	him	to	Jerusalem,	a plot

ποιοῦντες	ἀνελεῖν	αὐτὸν	κατὰ	τὴν	ὁδόν.
making	to kill	him	by	the	way.

4 ὁ	μὲν	οὖν	Φῆστος	ἀπεκρίθη	τηρεῖσθαι
–	–	Therefore	Festus	answered	²to be kept

τὸν	Παῦλον	εἰς	Καισάρειαν,	ἑαυτὸν	δὲ
–	¹Paul	in	Caesarea,	and ²himself

μέλλειν	ἐν	τάχει	ἐκπορεύεσθαι·	5 οἱ	οὖν
¹to intend		shortly	to go forth;	²the	¹therefore

said he, which among you are able, go down with *me*, and accuse this man, if there be any wickedness in him.

6 And when he had tarried among them more than ten days, he went down unto Cæsarea; and the next day sitting on the judgment seat commanded Paul to be brought.

7 And when he was come, the Jews which came down from Jerusalem stood round about, and laid many and grievous complaints against Paul, which they could not prove.

8 While he answered for himself, Neither against the law of the Jews, neither against the temple, nor yet against Cæsar, have I offended any thing at all.

9 But Festus, willing to do the Jews a pleasure, answered Paul, and said, Wilt thou go up to Jerusalem, and there be judged of these things before me?

10 Then said Paul, I stand at Cæsar's judgment seat, where I ought to be judged: to the Jews have I done no wrong, as thou very well knowest.

11 For if I be an offender, or have committed any thing worthy of death, I refuse not to die:

ἐν ὑμῖν, φησίν, δυνατοὶ συγκαταβάντες,
'among ²you, ⁶he says, ²able men going down with [me],

εἴ τί ἐστιν ἐν τῷ ἀνδρὶ ἄτοπον,
if anything there is in the man amiss,

κατηγορείτωσαν αὐτοῦ. 6 Διατρίψας δὲ ἐν
let them accuse him. And having stayed among

αὐτοῖς ἡμέρας οὐ πλείους ὀκτὼ ἢ δέκα,
them days not more [than] eight or ten,

καταβὰς εἰς Καισάρειαν, τῇ ἐπαύριον
going down to Cæsarea, on the morrow

καθίσας ἐπὶ τοῦ βήματος ἐκέλευσεν τὸν
sitting on the tribunal he commanded -

Παῦλον ἀχθῆναι. 7 παραγενομένου δὲ
Paul to be brought. And arriving
=when he arrived

αὐτοῦ περιέστησαν αὐτὸν οἱ ἀπὸ Ἱεροσο-
him² ⁵stood round ³him ¹the ⁴from ⁵Jeru-

λύμων καταβεβηκότες Ἰουδαῖοι, πολλὰ καὶ
salem ⁸having come down ⁷Jews, many and

βαρέα αἰτιώματα καταφέροντες, ἃ οὐκ
heavy charges bringing against [him], which not

ἴσχυον ἀποδεῖξαι, 8 τοῦ Παύλου ἀπολογου-
they were able to prove, - Paul defending him-

μένου ὅτι οὔτε εἰς τὸν νόμον τῶν
self[,]² - Neither against the law of the
=while Paul defended himself,

Ἰουδαίων οὔτε εἰς τὸ ἱερὸν οὔτε εἰς
Jews nor against the temple nor against

Καίσαρά τι ἥμαρτον. 9 ὁ Φῆστος δὲ,
Cæsar anything I sinned. - But Festus,

θέλων τοῖς Ἰουδαίοις χάριν καταθέσθαι,
wishing the Jews a favour to show,

ἀποκριθεὶς τῷ Παύλῳ εἶπεν· θέλεις εἰς
answering - Paul said: Dost thou wish ²to

Ἱεροσόλυμα ἀναβὰς ἐκεῖ περὶ τούτων
³Jerusalem ¹going up ⁴there ⁵concerning ⁶these things

κριθῆναι ἐπ᾽ ἐμοῦ; 10 εἶπεν δὲ ὁ Παῦλος·
⁵to be judged ⁶before ⁷me? And said - Paul:

ἑστὼς ἐπὶ τοῦ βήματος Καίσαρός εἰμι,
Standing before the tribunal of Cæsar I am,

οὗ με δεῖ κρίνεσθαι. Ἰουδαίους οὐδὲν
where me it behoves to be judged. Jews nothing

ἠδίκηκα, ὡς καὶ σὺ κάλλιον ἐπιγινώσκεις.
I have wronged, as indeed thou very well knowest.

11 εἰ μὲν οὖν ἀδικῶ καὶ ἄξιον θανάτου
If - therefore I do wrong and worthy of death

πέπραχά τι, οὐ παραιτοῦμαι τὸ ἀποθανεῖν·
I have done anything, I do not refuse *the* to die;

but if there be none of these things whereof these accuse me, no man may deliver me unto them. I appeal unto Cæsar.

12 Then Festus, when he had conferred with the council, answered, Hast thou appealed unto Cæsar? unto Cæsar shalt thou go.

13 ¶ And after certain days king Agrippa and Bernice came unto Cæsarea to salute Festus.

14 And when they had been there many days, Festus declared Paul's cause unto the king, saying, There is a certain man left in bonds by Felix:

15 About whom, when I was at Jerusalem, the chief priests and the elders of the Jews informed *me*, desiring *to have* judgment against him.

16 To whom I answered, It is not the manner of the Romans to deliver any man to die, before that he which is accused have the accusers face to face, and have licence to answer for himself concerning the crime laid against him.

17 Therefore, when they were come hither, without any delay on the

εἰ δὲ οὐδέν ἐστιν ὧν οὗτοι κατηγοροῦσίν
but if not one there is of [the things] which these accuse

μου, οὐδείς με δύναται αὐτοῖς χαρίσασθαι·
me, no one ²me ¹can ⁴to them ²to grant;

Καίσαρα ἐπικαλοῦμαι. 12 τότε ὁ Φῆστος
²Cæsar ¹I appeal to. Then – Festus

συλλαλήσας μετὰ τοῦ συμβουλίου ἀπεκρίθη·
having talked *with* with the council answered:

Καίσαρα ἐπικέκλησαι, ἐπὶ Καίσαρα πορεύσῃ.
²Cæsar ¹thou hast appealed to, before Cæsar thou shalt go.

13 Ἡμερῶν δὲ διαγενομένων τινῶν
And days passing some^a
=when some days had passed

Ἀγρίππας ὁ βασιλεὺς καὶ Βερνίκη
Agrippa the king and Bernice

κατήντησαν εἰς Καισάρειαν ἀσπασάμενοι
arrived at Cæsarea greeting

τὸν Φῆστον. 14 ὡς δὲ πλείους ἡμέρας
– Festus. And as more days

διέτριβον ἐκεῖ, ὁ Φῆστος τῷ βασιλεῖ
they stayed there, – Festus ²to the ³king

ἀνέθετο τὰ κατὰ τὸν Παῦλον λέγων·
¹set forth the matters regarding – Paul saying:

ἀνήρ τίς ἐστιν καταλελειμμένος ὑπὸ
A certain man there is having been left behind by

Φήλικος δέσμιος, 15 περὶ οὗ γενομένου
Felix prisoner, about whom being
=when I was

μου εἰς Ἱεροσόλυμα ἐνεφάνισαν οἱ ἀρχιερεῖς
me^a in Jerusalem ⁸informed ¹the ²chief priests

καὶ οἱ πρεσβύτεροι τῶν Ἰουδαίων,
³and ⁴the ⁵elders ⁶of the ⁷Jews,

αἰτούμενοι κατ' αὐτοῦ καταδίκην· 16 πρὸς
asking against him sentence; to

οὓς ἀπεκρίθην ὅτι οὐκ ἔστιν ἔθος Ῥωμαίοις
whom I answered that it is not a custom with Romans

χαρίζεσθαί τινα ἄνθρωπον πρὶν ἢ ὁ
to grant any man before the

κατηγορούμενος κατὰ πρόσωπον ἔχοι τοὺς
[one] being accused face to face† should have the

κατηγόρους τόπον τε ἀπολογίας λάβοι
accusers ³place* ¹and ⁴of defence ²receive

περὶ τοῦ ἐγκλήματος. 17 συνελθόντων
concerning the charge. Coming together^a

οὖν ἐνθάδε ἀναβολὴν μηδεμίαν ποιησάμενος
therefore thither ²delay ³no ¹making

* That is, opportunity.

morrow I sat on the judgment seat, and commanded the man to be brought forth.

18 Against whom when the accusers stood up, they brought none accusation of such things as I supposed:

19 But had certain questions against him of their own superstition, and of one Jesus, which was dead, whom Paul affirmed to be alive.

20 And because I doubted of such manner of questions, I asked *him* whether he would go to Jerusalem, and there be judged of these matters.

21 But when Paul had appealed to be reserved unto the hearing of Augustus, I commanded him to be kept till I might send him to Cæsar.

22 Then Agrippa said unto Festus, I would also hear the man myself. To morrow, said he, thou shalt hear him.

23 And on the morrow, when Agrippa was come, and Bernice, with great pomp, and was entered into the place of hearing, with the chief captains, and principal men of the city, at Festus' commandment Paul was brought forth.

24 And Festus said, King Agrippa, and all

τῇ ἑξῆς καθίσας ἐπὶ τοῦ βήματος ἐκέλευσα
on the next [day] sitting on the tribunal I commanded

ἀχθῆναι τὸν ἄνδρα· 18 περὶ οὗ σταθέντες
to be brought the man; concerning whom standing

οἱ κατήγοροι οὐδεμίαν αἰτίαν ἔφερον ὧν
the accusers ²no ³charge ¹brought ⁴of ⁵things ⁷which

ἐγὼ ὑπενόουν πονηρῶν, 19 ζητήματα δέ
⁸I ⁹suspected ⁶evil, but ²questions

τινα περὶ τῆς ἰδίας δεισιδαιμονίας εἶχον
²certain ⁴about ⁵the(ir) own ³religion ¹they had

πρὸς αὐτὸν καὶ περὶ τινος Ἰησοῦ
with him and about one Jesus

τεθνηκότος, ὃν ἔφασκεν ὁ Παῦλος ζῆν.
having died, whom ²asserted - ¹Paul to live.

20 ἀπορούμενος δὲ ἐγὼ τὴν περὶ τούτων
And ²being perplexed at ¹I ³the ⁵about ⁶these things

ζήτησιν ἔλεγον εἰ βούλοιτο πορεύεσθαι εἰς
⁴debate said if he wished to go to

Ἱεροσόλυμα κἀκεῖ κρίνεσθαι περὶ τούτων.
Jerusalem and there to be judged about these things.

21 τοῦ δὲ Παύλου ἐπικαλεσαμένου τηρηθῆναι
- But Paul having appealed ᵃ to be kept
=when Paul appealed

αὐτὸν εἰς τὴν τοῦ Σεβαστοῦ διάγνωσιν,
him to the - ²of Augustus ¹decision,

ἐκέλευσα τηρεῖσθαι αὐτὸν ἕως οὗ ἀναπέμψω
I commanded to be kept him until I may send up

αὐτὸν πρὸς Καίσαρα. 22 Ἀγρίππας δὲ
him to Cæsar. And Agrippa

πρὸς τὸν Φῆστον· ἐβουλόμην καὶ αὐτὸς
[said] to - Festus: I was minded also [my]self

τοῦ ἀνθρώπου ἀκοῦσαι. αὔριον, φησίν,
the man to hear. Tomorrow, he says,

ἀκούσῃ αὐτοῦ. 23 Τῇ οὖν ἐπαύριον
thou shalt hear him. ²On the ¹therefore ³morrow

ἐλθόντος τοῦ Ἀγρίππα καὶ τῆς Βερνίκης
coming - Agrippa and the Berniceᵃ
=when Agrippa and Bernice came

μετὰ πολλῆς φαντασίας καὶ εἰσελθόντων
with much display and entering⟩

εἰς τὸ ἀκροατήριον σύν τε χιλιάρχοις
into the place of audience with both chiliarchs

καὶ ἀνδράσιν τοῖς κατ᾽ ἐξοχὴν τῆς πόλεως,
and ²men ¹the ²chief † of the city,

καὶ κελεύσαντος τοῦ Φήστου ἤχθη ὁ
and having commanded - Festusᵃ ²was brought -
=when Festus commanded

Παῦλος. 24 καί φησιν ὁ Φῆστος· Ἀγρίππα
¹Paul. And says - Festus: Agrippa

men which are here present with us, ye see this man, about whom all the multitude of the Jews have dealt with me, both at Jerusalem, and *also* here, crying that he ought not to live any longer.

25 But when I found that he had committed nothing worthy of death, and that he himself hath appealed to Augustus, I have determined to send him.

26 Of whom I have no certain thing to write unto my lord. Wherefore I have brought him forth before you, and specially before thee, O king Agrippa, that, after examination had, I might have somewhat to write.

27 For it seemeth to me unreasonable to send a prisoner, and not withal to signify the crimes *laid* against him.

βασιλεῦ καὶ πάντες οἱ συμπαρόντες ἡμῖν
king   and   all   the [2]present togeth:r with [3]us

ἄνδρες, θεωρεῖτε τοῦτον περὶ οὗ ἅπαν τὸ
[1]men,   ye behold   this man   about whom   all   the

πλῆθος τῶν Ἰουδαίων ἐνέτυχόν μοι ἔν τε
multitude of the   Jews   petitioned   me [2]in [1]both

Ἱεροσολύμοις καὶ ἐνθάδε, βοῶντες μὴ
Jerusalem   and   here,   crying   not

δεῖν αὐτὸν ζῆν μηκέτι. 25 ἐγὼ δὲ κατε-
ought   him   to live *no* longer.   But I   dis-
=that he ought not to live any longer.

λαβόμην μηδὲν ἄξιον αὐτὸν θανάτου
covered [3]nothing [4]worthy [1]him [5]of death

πεπραχέναι, αὐτοῦ δὲ τούτου ἐπικαλεσαμένου
[2]to have done,   but [him]self   this man   appealing to[a]
=when he himself appealed to

τὸν Σεβαστὸν ἔκρινα πέμπειν. 26 περὶ
-   Augustus   I decided   to send.   Concerning

οὗ ἀσφαλές τι γράψαι τῷ κυρίῳ οὐκ
whom [4]certain [3]anything [5]to write [6]to the [7]lord [2]not

ἔχω· διὸ προήγαγον αὐτὸν ἐφ᾽ ὑμῶν καὶ
[1]I have;   where-   I brought   him   before   you   and
    fore   forth

μάλιστα ἐπὶ σοῦ, βασιλεῦ Ἀγρίππα, ὅπως
most of all before thee,   king   Agrippa,   so as
     =when

τῆς ἀνακρίσεως γενομένης σχῶ τί γράψω·
the   examination   being[a]   I may what   I may
there has been an examination   have   write;

27 ἄλογον γάρ μοι δοκεῖ πέμποντα δέσμιον
  for [2]unreasonable [3]to me [1]it seems   sending   a prisoner

μὴ καὶ τὰς κατ᾽ αὐτοῦ αἰτίας σημᾶναι.
not   also [2]the [4]against [5]him [3]charges [1]to signify.

CHAPTER 26

THEN Agrippa said unto Paul, Thou art permitted to speak for thyself. Then Paul stretched forth the hand, and answered for himself:

2 I think myself happy, king Agrippa, because I shall answer for myself this day before thee touching all the things whereof I am accused of the Jews:

3 Especially *because I know* thee to be expert in

26 Ἀγρίππας δὲ πρὸς τὸν Παῦλον ἔφη·
  And Agrippa   to   -   Paul   said:

ἐπιτρέπεταί σοι ὑπὲρ σεαυτοῦ λέγειν.
It is permitted   to thee on behalf of   thyself   to speak.

τότε ὁ Παῦλος ἐκτείνας τὴν χεῖρα
Then   -   Paul   stretching out the(his)   hand

ἀπελογεῖτο· 2 Περὶ πάντων ὧν ἐγκαλοῦμαι
defended himself: Concerning all things of which   I am being
     accused

ὑπὸ Ἰουδαίων, βασιλεῦ Ἀγρίππα, ἥγημαι
by   Jews,   king   Agrippa,   I consider

ἐμαυτὸν μακάριον ἐπὶ σοῦ μέλλων σήμερον
myself   happy [3]before [4]thee [1]being about [5]to-day

ἀπολογεῖσθαι, 3 μάλιστα γνώστην ὄντα σε
[2]to defend myself,   most of all [2]an expert [3]being [1]thee

all customs and questions which are among the Jews: wherefore I beseech thee to hear me patiently.

4 My manner of life from my youth, which was at the first among mine own nation at Jerusalem, know all the Jews;

5 Which knew me from the beginning, if they would testify, that after the most straitest sect of our religion I lived a Pharisee.

6 And now I stand and am judged for the hope of the promise made of God unto our fathers:

7 Unto which *promise* our twelve tribes, instantly serving *God* day and night, hope to come. For which hope's sake, king Agrippa, I am accused of the Jews.

8 Why should it be thought a thing incredible with you, that God should raise the dead?

9 I verily thought with myself, that I ought to do many things contrary to the name of Jesus of Nazareth.

10 Which thing I also did in Jerusalem: and many of the saints did I shut up in prison, having received authority from the chief priests; and when they were put to death, I

πάντων τῶν κατὰ Ἰουδαίους ἐθῶν τε
⁵of all ⁶the ⁸among ⁹Jews ⁷customs ⁴both

καὶ ζητημάτων· διὸ δέομαι μακροθύμως
¹⁰and ¹¹questions; wherefore I beg patiently

ἀκοῦσαί μου. 4 Τὴν μὲν οὖν βίωσίν
to hear me. ³the ¹So ²then ⁴manner of life

μου ἐκ νεότητος τὴν ἀπ' ἀρχῆς γενομένην
of me from youth – ²from ⁴beginning ¹having been ³[the]

ἐν τῷ ἔθνει μου ἔν τε Ἱεροσολύμοις
in the nation of me ¹in ¹and Jerusalem

ἴσασι πάντες Ἰουδαῖοι, 5 προγινώσκοντές
know all Jews, previously knowing

με ἄνωθεν, ἐὰν θέλωσι μαρτυρεῖν, ὅτι
me from the first, if they are willing to testify, that

κατὰ τὴν ἀκριβεστάτην αἵρεσιν τῆς
according to the most exact sect –

ἡμετέρας θρησκείας ἔζησα Φαρισαῖος. 6 καὶ
of our religion I lived a Pharisee. And

νῦν ἐπ' ἐλπίδι τῆς εἰς τοὺς πατέρας
now on(in) hope of the ⁵to ⁶the ⁷fathers

ἡμῶν ἐπαγγελίας γενομένης ὑπὸ τοῦ θεοῦ
⁸of us ¹promise ²having been [made] ³by – ⁴God

ἔστηκα κρινόμενος, 7 εἰς ἣν τὸ δωδεκά-
I stand being judged, to which the twelve

φυλον ἡμῶν ἐν ἐκτενείᾳ νύκτα καὶ
tribes of us with earnestness night and

ἡμέραν λατρεῦον ἐλπίζει καταντῆσαι· περὶ
day worshipping hopes to arrive; concerning

ἧς ἐλπίδος ἐγκαλοῦμαι ὑπὸ Ἰουδαίων,
which hope I am accused by Jews,

βασιλεῦ. 8 τί ἄπιστον κρίνεται παρ'
[O] king. Why incredible is it judged by

ὑμῖν εἰ ὁ θεὸς νεκροὺς ἐγείρει; 9 ἐγὼ
you if – God ⁸dead persons ¹raises? ³I

μὲν οὖν ἔδοξα ἐμαυτῷ πρὸς τὸ ὄνομα
¹indeed ²then ⁴thought ⁵to myself ¹⁰to ¹¹the ¹²name

Ἰησοῦ τοῦ Ναζωραίου δεῖν πολλὰ ἐναντία
¹³of Jesus ¹⁴the ¹⁵Nazarene ⁶ought ⁸many ⁹contrary things

πρᾶξαι· 10 ὃ καὶ ἐποίησα ἐν Ἱεροσολύμοις,
⁷to do; which indeed I did in Jerusalem,

καὶ πολλούς τε τῶν ἁγίων ἐγὼ ἐν
and many – of the saints ¹I ²in

φυλακαῖς κατέκλεισα τὴν παρὰ τῶν
⁴prisons ²shut up ⁵the ⁸from ⁹the

ἀρχιερέων ἐξουσίαν λαβών, ἀναιρουμένων τε
¹⁰chief priests ⁷authority ⁶having received, being killed and
=and when they were killed

gave my voice against *them*.

11 And I punished them oft in every synagogue, and compelled *them* to blaspheme; and being exceedingly mad against them, I persecuted *them* even unto strange cities.

12 Whereupon as I went to Damascus with authority and commission from the chief priests,

13 At midday, O king, I saw in the way a light from heaven, above the brightness of the sun, shining round about me and them which journeyed with me.

14 And when we were all fallen to the earth, I heard a voice speaking unto me, and saying in the Hebrew tongue, Saul, Saul, why persecutest thou me? *it is* hard for thee to kick against the pricks.

15 And I said, Who art thou, Lord? And he said, I am Jesus whom thou persecutest.

16 But rise, and stand upon thy feet: for I have appeared unto thee for this purpose, to make thee a minister and a witness both of these things which thou hast seen, and of those things in the which I will appear unto thee;

17 Delivering thee from the people, and *from* the Gentiles, unto whom now I send thee,

18 To open their eyes, *and* to turn *them* from

αὐτῶν   κατήνεγκα   ψῆφον,   11 καὶ   κατὰ
them[a]   I cast   a vote,   and   throughout

πάσας   τὰς   συναγωγὰς   πολλάκις   τιμωρῶν
all   the   synagogues   often   punishing

αὐτοὺς   ἠνάγκαζον   βλασφημεῖν,   περισσῶς   τε
them   I compelled [them] to blaspheme,   and excessively

ἐμμαινόμενος   αὐτοῖς   ἐδίωκον   ἕως   καὶ   εἰς
raging against   them   I persecuted as far as even   to

τὰς   ἔξω   πόλεις.   12 Ἐν   οἷς   πορευόμενος
the   outside cities.   In   which   journeying

εἰς   τὴν   Δαμασκὸν   μετ'   ἐξουσίας   καὶ
to   -   Damascus   with   authority   and

ἐπιτροπῆς   τῆς   τῶν   ἀρχιερέων,   13 ἡμέρας
power to decide -   of the chief priests,   at [a]day

μέσης   κατὰ   τὴν   ὁδὸν   εἶδον,   βασιλεῦ,
[a]mid   along   the   way   I saw,   [O] king,

οὐρανόθεν   ὑπὲρ   τὴν   λαμπρότητα   τοῦ   ἡλίου
[3]from heaven [2]above [4]the [5]brightness [6]of the [7]sun

περιλάμψαν   με   φῶς   καὶ   τοὺς   σὺν   ἐμοὶ
[8]shining round [9]me [1]a light [10]and [11]the [ones] [13]with [14]me

πορευομένους·   14 πάντων   τε   καταπεσόντων
[12]journeying;   and all   having fallen down
                                 = when we had all fallen

ἡμῶν   εἰς   τὴν   γῆν   ἤκουσα   φωνὴν   λέγουσαν
us[a]   to   the   earth   I heard   a voice   saying

πρός   με   τῇ   Ἑβραῒδι   διαλέκτῳ·   Σαοὺλ
to   me   in   the Hebrew   language: Saul[,]

Σαούλ,   τί   με   διώκεις;   σκληρόν   σοι
Saul,   why   me   persecutest thou? hard   for thee

πρὸς   κέντρα   λακτίζειν.   15 ἐγὼ   δὲ   εἶπα·
against goads   to kick.   And I   said:

τίς   εἶ,   κύριε;   ὁ   δὲ   κύριος   εἶπεν·   ἐγώ
Who art thou, Lord?   And the   Lord   said: I

εἰμι   Ἰησοῦς   ὃν   σὺ   διώκεις.   16 ἀλλὰ
am   Jesus   whom   thou   persecutest.   But

ἀνάστηθι   καὶ   στῆθι   ἐπὶ   τοὺς   πόδας   σου·
rise thou up and   stand   on   the   feet   of thee;

εἰς   τοῦτο   γὰρ   ὤφθην   σοι,   προχειρίσασθαί
[3]for [4]this [purpose] [1]for I appeared to thee,   to appoint

σε   ὑπηρέτην   καὶ   μάρτυρα   ὧν   τε
thee   an attendant and   a witness [2]of the things [1]both
                                                     which

εἰδές   με   ὧν   τε   ὀφθήσομαί   σοι,
[3]thou sawest [4]me [6]of the things [5]and   I will appear to thee,
                                  which

17 ἐξαιρούμενός   σε   ἐκ   τοῦ   λαοῦ   καὶ   ἐκ
delivering   thee   from   the   people   and   from

τῶν   ἐθνῶν,   εἰς   οὓς   ἐγὼ   ἀποστέλλω   σε,
the   nations,   to   whom   I   send   thee,

18 ἀνοῖξαι   ὀφθαλμοὺς   αὐτῶν,   τοῦ   ἐπιστρέψαι
to open   eyes   of them,   -   to turn[b]

darkness to light, and *from* the power of Satan unto God, that they may receive forgiveness of sins, and inheritance among them which are sanctified by faith that is in me.

19 Whereupon, O king Agrippa, I was not disobedient unto the heavenly vision:

20 But shewed first unto them of Damascus, and at Jerusalem, and throughout all the coasts of Judæa, and *then* to the Gentiles, that they should repent and turn to God, and do works meet for repentance.

21 For these causes the Jews caught me in the temple, and went about to kill *me*.

22 Having therefore obtained help of God, I continue unto this day, witnessing both to small and great, saying none other things than those which the prophets and Moses did say should come:

23 That Christ should suffer, *and* that he should be the first that should rise from the dead, and should shew light unto the people, and to the Gentiles.

24 ¶ And as he thus spake for himself, Festus

ἀπὸ σκότους εἰς φῶς καὶ τῆς ἐξουσίας
from　darkness　to　light　and [from] the　authority

τοῦ σατανᾶ ἐπὶ τὸν θεόν, τοῦ λαβεῖν
–　of Satan　to　–　God,　–　to receive
　　　　　　　　　　　　　　　　=that they may receive

αὐτοὺς ἄφεσιν ἁμαρτιῶν καὶ κλῆρον ἐν
them[bd]　forgiveness　of sins　and　a lot　among

τοῖς ἡγιασμένοις πίστει τῇ εἰς ἐμέ.
the [ones] *having been* sanctified　by faith　–　in　me.

19 Ὅθεν, βασιλεῦ Ἀγρίππα, οὐκ ἐγενόμην
Whence,　king　Agrippa,　I was not

ἀπειθὴς τῇ οὐρανίῳ ὀπτασίᾳ, **20** ἀλλὰ
disobedient to the　heavenly　vision,　but

τοῖς ἐν Δαμασκῷ πρῶτόν τε καὶ
to the [ones] in　Damascus　first*ly*　and　also

Ἱεροσολύμοις, πᾶσάν τε τὴν χώραν τῆς
[in] Jerusalem,　and all　the　country　–

Ἰουδαίας καὶ τοῖς ἔθνεσιν ἀπήγγελλον
of Judæa　and　to the　nations　I announced

μετανοεῖν καὶ ἐπιστρέφειν ἐπὶ τὸν θεόν,
to repent　and　to turn　to　–　God,

ἄξια τῆς μετανοίας ἔργα πράσσοντας.
³worthy　⁴of the　⁵repentance　²works　¹doing.

21 ἕνεκα τούτων με Ἰουδαῖοι συλλαβόμενοι
On　these things　³me　¹Jews　²having seized
account of

ἐν τῷ ἱερῷ ἐπειρῶντο διαχειρίσασθαι.
in　the　temple　tried　to kill [me].

22 ἐπικουρίας οὖν τυχὼν τῆς ἀπὸ τοῦ
Succour　therefore　having　–　from　–
　　　　　　　　　obtained

θεοῦ ἄχρι τῆς ἡμέρας ταύτης ἕστηκα
God　until　the　this day　I stand

μαρτυρόμενος μικρῷ τε καὶ μεγάλῳ, οὐδὲν
witnessing　²to small　¹both and　to great,　²nothing

ἐκτὸς λέγων ὧν τε οἱ προφῆται
³apart　¹saying　⁴the things　⁵both　⁶the　⁷prophets
from　　　　　　which

ἐλάλησαν μελλόντων γίνεσθαι καὶ Μωϋσῆς,
¹⁰said　¹¹being about　¹²to happen　⁸and　⁹Moses,

23 εἰ παθητὸς ὁ χριστός, εἰ πρῶτος
if subject to suffering the　Christ,　if　first

ἐξ ἀναστάσεως νεκρῶν φῶς μέλλει
by　a resurrection　of dead　²a light　¹he is
　　　　　　　persons　　　　about

καταγγέλλειν τῷ τε λαῷ καὶ τοῖς ἔθνεσιν.
²to announce　⁵to the　⁴both　people　and　to the　nations.

24 Ταῦτα δὲ αὐτοῦ ἀπολογουμένου ὁ Φῆστος
And these things　him　defending himself[a]　–　Festus
=as he defended himself with these things

said with a loud voice, Paul, thou art beside thyself; much learning doth make thee mad.

25 But he said, I am not mad, most noble Festus; but speak forth the words of truth and soberness.

26 For the king knoweth of these things, before whom also I speak freely: for I am persuaded that none of these things are hidden from him; for this thing was not done in a corner.

27 King Agrippa, believest thou the prophets? I know that thou believest.

28 Then Agrippa said unto Paul, Almost thou persuadest me to be a Christian.

29 And Paul said, I would to God, that not only thou, but also all that hear me this day, were both almost, and altogether such as I am, except these bonds.

30 And when he had thus spoken, the king rose up, and the governor, and Bernice, and they that sat with them:

31 And when they were gone aside, they talked between themselves, saying, This man doeth nothing worthy of death or of bonds.

32 Then said Agrippa

μεγάλῃ τῇ φωνῇ φησιν· μαίνῃ, Παῦλε·
³great ¹with the(his) ²voice says: Thou ravest, Paul:

τὰ πολλά σε γράμματα εἰς μανίαν
¹the ⁴many ⁵thee ³letters ⁶to ⁷madness

περιτρέπει. 25 ὁ δὲ Παῦλος· οὐ μαίνομαι,
⁴turn[s]. – But Paul: I do not rave,

φησίν, κράτιστε Φῆστε, ἀλλὰ ἀληθείας
he says, most excellent Festus, but ³of truth

καὶ σωφροσύνης ῥήματα ἀποφθέγγομαι.
⁴and ⁵of good sense ²words ¹speak forth.

26 ἐπίσταται γὰρ περὶ τούτων ὁ βασιλεύς,
For ²understands ⁴about ⁵these things ¹the ³king,

πρὸς ὃν καὶ παρρησιαζόμενος λαλῶ·
to whom indeed being bold of speech I speak;

λανθάνειν γὰρ αὐτὸν τούτων οὐ πείθομαι
for ⁴to be hidden [from] ⁵him ³of these things not ¹I am persuaded

οὐθέν· οὐ γάρ ἐστιν ἐν γωνίᾳ πεπραγμένον
²nothing; for ³not ²is ⁵in ⁶a corner ⁴having been done

τοῦτο. 27 πιστεύεις, βασιλεῦ Ἀγρίππα,
¹this. Believest thou, king Agrippa,

τοῖς προφήταις; οἶδα ὅτι πιστεύεις. 28 ὁ
the prophets? I know that thou believest. –

δὲ Ἀγρίππας πρὸς τὸν Παῦλον· ἐν
And Agrippa [said] to Paul: In

ὀλίγῳ με πείθεις Χριστιανὸν ποιῆσαι.
a little ²me ¹thou persuadest ⁴a Christian ³to make(act).

29 ὁ δὲ Παῦλος· εὐξαίμην ἂν τῷ θεῷ
– And Paul [said]: I would pray – God

καὶ ἐν ὀλίγῳ καὶ ἐν μεγάλῳ οὐ μόνον
both in a little and in great not only

σὲ ἀλλὰ καὶ πάντας τοὺς ἀκούοντάς
thee but also all the [ones] hearing

μου σήμερον γενέσθαι τοιούτους ὁποῖος
me to-day ²to become ¹such of what kind

καὶ ἐγώ εἰμι, παρεκτὸς τῶν δεσμῶν
indeed I am, except – bonds

τούτων. 30 Ἀνέστη τε ὁ βασιλεὺς καὶ
these. Rose up both the king and

ὁ ἡγεμὼν ἥ τε Βερνίκη καὶ οἱ συγ-
the governor – and Bernice and the [ones] sit-

καθήμενοι αὐτοῖς, 31 καὶ ἀναχωρήσαντες
ting with them, and having left

ἐλάλουν πρὸς ἀλλήλους λέγοντες ὅτι οὐδὲν
spoke to one another saying [.] – ⁴nothing

θανάτου ἢ δεσμῶν ἄξιον πράσσει ὁ
⁶of death ⁷or ⁸of bonds ⁵worthy ³does –

ἄνθρωπος οὗτος. 32 Ἀγρίππας δὲ τῷ
²man ¹This. And Agrippa –

Φήστῳ	ἔφη·	ἀπολελύσθαι	ἐδύνατο
to Festus	said:	²to have been released	²was able(could)

ὁ ἄνθρωπος οὗτος	εἰ μὴ ἐπεκέκλητο	Καίσαρα.
¹This man	if he had not appealed to	Cæsar.

CHAPTER 27

A ND when it was determined that we should sail into Italy, they delivered Paul and certain other prisoners unto *one* named Julius, a centurion of Augustus' band.

2 And entering into a ship of Adramyttium, we launched, meaning to sail by the coasts of Asia; *one* Aristarchus, a Macedonian of Thessalonica, being with us.

3 And the next *day* we touched at Sidon. And Julius courteously entreated Paul, and gave *him* liberty to go unto his friends to refresh himself.

4 And when we had launched from thence, we sailed under Cyprus, because the winds were contrary.

5 And when we had sailed over the sea of Cilicia and Pamphylia, we came to Myra, *a city* of Lycia.

6 And there the centurion found a ship of Alexandria sailing into Italy; and he put us therein.

7 And when we had sailed slowly many days,

27 Ὡς	δὲ	ἐκρίθη	τοῦ ἀποπλεῖν	ἡμᾶς
And when	it was decided	–	to sail	us[b] =that we should sail

εἰς	τὴν	Ἰταλίαν,	παρεδίδουν	τόν τε
to	–	Italy,	they delivered	– both

Παῦλον	καί τινας	ἑτέρους	δεσμώτας
Paul	and some	other	prisoners

ἑκατοντάρχῃ	ὀνόματι	Ἰουλίῳ	σπείρης
to a centurion	by name	Julius	of a cohort

Σεβαστῆς.	2 ἐπιβάντες δὲ	πλοίῳ	Ἀδρα-
Augustan.	And embarking in	a ship	belonging to

μυττηνῷ	μέλλοντι	πλεῖν	εἰς τοὺς	κατὰ
Adramyttium	being about	to sail	¹for	²the ³along[the coast of]

τὴν	Ἀσίαν	τόπους	ἀνήχθημεν,	ὄντος σὺν
–	⁵Asia	³places	we set sail,	being with

ἡμῖν	Ἀριστάρχου	Μακεδόνος	Θεσσαλονικέως·
us	Aristarchus	a Macedonian[a]	of Thessalonica,

3 τῇ τε	ἑτέρᾳ	κατήχθημεν	εἰς Σιδῶνα,
and on the	next [day]	we were brought to land	at Sidon,

φιλανθρώπως	τε	ὁ Ἰούλιος	τῷ	Παύλῳ
and ³kindly	–	¹Julius	–	⁵Paul

χρησάμενος	ἐπέτρεψεν	πρὸς τοὺς	φίλους
²treating [him]	⁴allowed	⁷to	⁸the ⁹friends

πορευθέντι	ἐπιμελείας	τυχεῖν.	4 κἀκεῖθεν
⁶going	¹¹attention	¹⁰to obtain.	And thence

ἀναχθέντες	ὑπεπλεύσαμεν	τὴν Κύπρον	διὰ
putting to sea	we sailed close to	– Cyprus	because of

τὸ τοὺς	ἀνέμους	εἶναι	ἐναντίους,	5 τό τε
– the	winds	to be(being)	contrary,	and ²the

πέλαγος	τὸ κατὰ	τὴν	Κιλικίαν καὶ
³sea	– ⁴against	–	⁵Cilicia ⁶and

Παμφυλίαν	διαπλεύσαντες	κατήλθαμεν	εἰς
⁷Pamphylia	¹sailing over	we came down	to

Μύρα	τῆς	Λυκίας.	6 Κἀκεῖ εὑρὼν	ὁ
Myra	–	of Lycia.	And there ³having found	¹the

ἑκατοντάρχης	πλοῖον	Ἀλεξανδρῖνον	πλέον
²centurion	ship	an Alexandrian	sailing

εἰς	τὴν	Ἰταλίαν	ἐνεβίβασεν ἡμᾶς	εἰς
to	–	Italy	he embarked us	in

αὐτό.	7 ἐν ἱκαναῖς	δὲ ἡμέραις	βραδυπλο-
it.	And in a number of	days	sailing

and scarce were come over against Cnidus, the wind not suffering us, we sailed under Crete, over against Salmone;

8 And, hardly passing it, came unto a place which is called The fair havens; nigh whereunto was the city of Lasea.

9 ¶ Now when much time was spent, and when sailing was now dangerous, because the fast was now already past, Paul admonished them,

10 And said unto them, Sirs, I perceive that this voyage will be with hurt and much damage, not only of the lading and ship, but also of our lives.

11 Nevertheless the centurion believed the master and the owner of the ship, more than those things which were spoken by Paul.

12 And because the haven was not commodious to winter in, the more part advised to depart thence also, if by any means they might attain to Phenice, and there to winter; which is an haven of Crete, and

οὖντες καὶ μόλις γενόμενοι κατὰ τὴν
slowly and hardly coming against –

Κνίδον, μὴ προσεῶντος ἡμᾶς τοῦ ἀνέμου,
Cnidus, not allowing us the wind,[a]
= as the wind did not allow us,

ὑπεπλεύσαμεν τὴν Κρήτην κατὰ Σαλμώνην,
we sailed close to – Crete against Salmone,

8 μόλις τε παραλεγόμενοι αὐτὴν ἤλθομεν
and hardly sailing along it we came

εἰς τόπον τινὰ καλούμενον Καλοὺς λιμένας,
to place a certain being called Fair Havens,

ᾧ ἐγγὺς ἦν πόλις Λασαία. 9 Ἱκανοῦ δὲ
[2]to which [1]near was a city Lasæa. And much
= when

χρόνου διαγενομένου καὶ ὄντος ἤδη
time having passed[a] and being now
much time had passed = as the voyage

ἐπισφαλοῦς τοῦ πλοὸς διὰ τὸ καὶ τὴν
dangerous the voyage[a] on account of – also the
was now dangerous = because also the fast had now

νηστείαν ἤδη παρεληλυθέναι, παρῄνει ὁ
fast now to have gone by, [2]advised –
gone by,

Παῦλος 10 λέγων αὐτοῖς· ἄνδρες, θεωρῶ
[1]Paul saying to them: Men, I see

ὅτι μετὰ ὕβρεως καὶ πολλῆς ζημίας οὐ
that with injury and much loss not

μόνον τοῦ φορτίου καὶ τοῦ πλοίου ἀλλὰ
only of the cargo and of the ship but

καὶ τῶν ψυχῶν ἡμῶν μέλλειν ἔσεσθαι
also of the lives of us [3]to be about [4]to be
= will be

τὸν πλοῦν. 11 ὁ δὲ ἑκατοντάρχης τῷ
[1]the [2]voyage. But the centurion [2]the

κυβερνήτῃ καὶ τῷ ναυκλήρῳ μᾶλλον
[3]steersman [4]and [5]the [6]shipmaster [7]rather

ἐπείθετο ἢ τοῖς ὑπὸ Παύλου λεγομένοις.
[1]was persuaded by [8]than [9]the [11]by [12]Paul [10]things said.

12 ἀνευθέτου δὲ τοῦ λιμένος ὑπάρχοντος
But unsuitable the port being[a]
= as the port was unsuitable

πρὸς παραχειμασίαν οἱ πλείονες ἔθεντο
for wintering the majority placed
= decided

βουλὴν ἀναχθῆναι ἐκεῖθεν, εἴ πως δύναιντο
counsel to set sail thence, if some- they might
how be able

καταντήσαντες εἰς Φοίνικα παραχειμάσαι,
having arrived at Phœnix to pass the winter,

λιμένα τῆς Κρήτης βλέποντα κατὰ λίβα
a port – of Crete looking toward south-
west

lieth toward the south west and north west.

13 And when the south wind blew softly, supposing that they had obtained *their* purpose, loosing *thence*, they sailed close by Crete.

14 But not long after there arose against it a tempestuous wind, called Euroclydon.

15 And when the ship was caught, and could not bear up into the wind, we let *her* drive.

16 And running under a certain island which is called Clauda, we had much work to come by the boat:

17 Which when they had taken up, they used helps, undergirding the ship; and, fearing lest they should fall into the quicksands, strake sail, and so were driven.

18 And we being exceedingly tossed with a tempest, the next *day* they lightened the ship;

19 And the third *day* we cast out with our own hands the tackling of the ship.

20 And when neither sun nor stars in many days appeared, and no small tempest lay on *us*, all hope that we should be saved was then taken away.

καὶ κατὰ χῶρον.   13 Ὑποπνεύσαντος δὲ
and   toward   north-west.   And blowing gently
                                          =when a south wind

νότου δόξαντες τῆς προθέσεως κεκρατηκέναι,
a south wind[a] thinking ²the(ir) ³purpose ¹to have obtained.
blew gently

ἄραντες ἆσσον παρελέγοντο τὴν Κρήτην.
raising ²close in- ¹they coasted by   –   ²Crete.
[anchor]   shore

14 μετ' οὐ πολὺ δὲ ἔβαλεν κατ' αὐτῆς
    And after not much   there beat down   it

ἄνεμος τυφωνικὸς ὁ καλούμενος εὐρακύλων·
wind   a tempestuous   –   *being* called   Euraquilo;

15 συναρπασθέντος δὲ τοῦ πλοίου καὶ μὴ
    and ³being seized   ¹the   ²ship[a]   and   not

δυναμένου ἀντοφθαλμεῖν τῷ ἀνέμῳ ἐπιδόντες
being able[a]   to beat up against   the   wind   giving way

ἐφερόμεθα.   16 νησίον δέ τι ὑποδραμόντες
we were borne.   And ³islet   ²a certain   ¹running under
                                             the lee of

καλούμενον Κλαῦδα ἰσχύσαμεν μόλις
being called   Clauda   we were able   hardly

περικρατεῖς γενέσθαι τῆς σκάφης,   17 ἦν
control   to get   of the   boat,   which

ἄραντες βοηθείαις ἐχρῶντο, ὑποζωννύντες
taking   ²helps   ¹they used,   undergirding

τὸ πλοῖον· φοβούμενοί τε μὴ εἰς τὴν
the   ship;   and fearing   lest   into   –

Σύρτιν ἐκπέσωσιν, χαλάσαντες τὸ σκεῦος,
Syrtis   they might fall off,*   lowering   the   tackle,

οὕτως ἐφέροντο.   18 σφοδρῶς δὲ χειμαζ-
thus   they were borne.   But exceedingly   being in
                                 =as we were exceedingly in . . .

ομένων ἡμῶν τῇ ἑξῆς ἐκβολὴν ἐποιοῦντο,
the grip   us[a]   on the next   a jettisoning   they made,
of a storm   [day]

19 καὶ τῇ τρίτῃ αὐτόχειρες τὴν σκευὴν
    and   on the   third   with their   the   tackle
               [day]   own hands

τοῦ πλοίου ἔρριψαν.   20 μήτε δὲ ἡλίου
of the   ship   they threw [out].   And neither   sun
                                 =when neither . . .

μήτε ἄστρων ἐπιφαινόντων ἐπὶ πλείονας
nor   stars   appearing[a]   over   many
appeared

ἡμέρας, χειμῶνός τε οὐκ ὀλίγου ἐπικειμένου,
days,   and stormy weather   no   little   pressing hard.[a]

λοιπὸν περιῃρεῖτο ἐλπὶς πᾶσα τοῦ σῴζεσθαι
now   was taken away   ²hope   ¹all   –   to be saved
                                   =that we might

---

* This is the classical Greek word for a ship being driven out of her course on to shoals, rocks, etc. (Page).   See also vers 26 and 29.

21 ¶ But after long ab-stinence Paul stood forth in the midst of them, and said, Sirs, ye should have hearkened unto me, and not have loosed from Crete, and to have gained this harm and loss.

22 And now I exhort you to be of good cheer: for there shall be no loss of *any man's* life among you, but of the ship.

23 For there stood by me this night the angel of God, whose I am, and whom I serve,

24 Saying, Fear not, Paul ; thou must be brought before Cæsar: and, lo, God hath given thee all them that sail with thee.

25 Wherefore, sirs, be of good cheer: for I be-lieve God, that it shall be even as it was told me.

26 Howbeit we must be cast upon a certain island.

27 But when the four-teenth night was come, as we were driven up and down in Adria, about mid-night the shipmen deemed that they drew near to some country;

28 And sounded, and found *it* twenty fathoms: and when they had gone a

ἡμᾶς.   **21** Πολλῆς τε ἀσιτίας ὑπαρχούσης
us.ᵇᵈ   And much   abstinence   beingª
be saved.   = when there was long abstinence

τότε σταθεὶς ὁ Παῦλος ἐν μέσῳ αὐτῶν εἶπεν·
then ²standing - ¹Paul in [the] midst of them said:

ἔδει   μέν,   ὦ   ἄνδρες,   πειθαρχήσαντάς
It behoved -   O   men,   obeying
[you],

μοι   μὴ   ἀνάγεσθαι ἀπὸ τῆς Κρήτης
me   not   to set sail   from   -   Crete

κερδῆσαί τε τὴν ὕβριν ταύτην καὶ τὴν
and to come by -   injury   this   and   -

ζημίαν.   **22** καὶ τὰ νῦν παραινῶ ὑμᾶς
loss.   And -   now I advise   you

εὐθυμεῖν· ἀποβολὴ γὰρ ψυχῆς οὐδεμία
to be of good for ³throwing away ⁴of life   ²no
cheer;

ἔσται ἐξ ὑμῶν πλὴν τοῦ πλοίου.
¹there will be of you   but   of the   ship.

23 παρέστη γὰρ μοι ταύτῃ τῇ νυκτὶ
For there stood by me in this   -   night

τοῦ θεοῦ οὗ εἰμι, ᾧ καὶ λατρεύω,
-   ²of God ³of whom ⁴I am, ⁵whom ⁶also ⁷I serve,

ἄγγελος **24** λέγων· μὴ φοβοῦ, Παῦλε·
¹an angel   saying: Fear not,   Paul;

Καίσαρί σε δεῖ παραστῆναι, καὶ ἰδοὺ
⁴Cæsar ²thee ¹it behoves ³to stand before, and behold

κεχάρισταί σοι ὁ θεὸς πάντας τοὺς
²has given ³thee - ¹God   all   the [ones]

πλέοντας μετὰ σοῦ. **25** διὸ εὐθυμεῖτε,
sailing   with   thee.   Wherefore be ye of
good cheer,

ἄνδρες· πιστεύω γὰρ τῷ θεῷ ὅτι οὕτως
men;   for I believe -   God   that   thus

ἔσται καθ' ὃν τρόπον λελάληταί μοι.
it will be in the way in which† it has been spoken to me.

26 εἰς νῆσον δέ τινα δεῖ ἡμᾶς ἐκπεσεῖν.
⁵Onto ⁷island ¹but ⁶a   ²it   ³us   ⁴to fall off.
                        certain behoves

27 Ὡς δὲ τεσσαρεσκαιδεκάτη νὺξ ἐγένετο
Now when   [the] fourteenth   night   came

διαφερομένων ἡμῶν ἐν τῷ Ἀδρίᾳ, κατ'
being carried about usª in the   Adria,   abou
= while we were being carried about

μέσον τῆς νυκτὸς ὑπενόουν οἱ ναῦται
[the] middle of the night   ³supposed ¹the ²sailors

προσάγειν τινὰ αὐτοῖς χώραν. **28** καὶ
⁴to approach ⁶some ⁵to them ⁷country.   And

βολίσαντες εὗρον ὀργυιὰς εἴκοσι, βραχὺ δὲ
sounding they found fathoms   twenty, and ²a little

little further, they sounded again, and found *it* fifteen fathoms.

29 Then fearing lest we should have fallen upon rocks, they cast four anchors out of the stern, and wished for the day.

30 And as the shipmen were about to flee out of the ship, when they had let down the boat into the sea, under colour as though they would have cast anchors out of the foreship,

31 Paul said to the centurion and to the soldiers, Except these abide in the ship, ye cannot be saved.

32 Then the soldiers cut off the ropes of the boat, and let her fall off.

33 And while the day was coming on, Paul besought *them* all to take meat, saying, This day is the fourteenth day that ye have tarried and continued fasting, having taken nothing.

34 Wherefore I pray you to take *some* meat: for this is for your health: for there shall not a hair fall from the head of any of you.

35 And when he had thus spoken, he took

διαστήσαντες	καὶ	πάλιν	βολίσαντες	εὗρον
¹having moved	also	again	sounding	they found

ὀργυιὰς	δεκαπέντε·	29	φοβούμενοί	τε	μή
fathoms	fifteen;		and fearing		lest

που	κατὰ	τραχεῖς	τόπους	ἐκπέσωμεν,
²somewhere	³against	⁴rough	⁵places	¹we might fall off,

ἐκ	πρύμνης	ῥίψαντες	ἀγκύρας	τέσσαρας
out of	[the] stern	throwing	anchors	four

ηὔχοντο	ἡμέραν	γενέσθαι.	30	Τῶν	δὲ
they prayed	day	to become.			And the

ναυτῶν	ζητούντων	φυγεῖν	ἐκ	τοῦ	πλοίου
sailors	seeking²	to flee	out of	the	ship
=when the sailors sought				

καὶ	χαλασάντων	τὴν	σκάφην	εἰς	τὴν
and	lowering²	the	boat	into	the
	=lowered			

θάλασσαν	προφάσει	ὡς	ἐκ	πρῴρης	ἀγκύρας
sea	under pretence	as	⁴out of	⁵[the] prow	²anchors

μελλόντων	ἐκτείνειν,	31	εἶπεν	ὁ	Παῦλος
¹intending	²to cast *out*,		said	–	Paul

τῷ	ἑκατοντάρχῃ	καὶ	τοῖς	στρατιώταις·
to the	centurion	and	to the	soldiers:

ἐὰν	μὴ	οὗτοι	μείνωσιν	ἐν	τῷ	πλοίῳ,
Unless		these	remain	in	the	ship,

ὑμεῖς	σωθῆναι	οὐ	δύνασθε.	32	τότε
ye	²to be saved	¹cannot.			Then

ἀπέκοψαν	οἱ	στρατιῶται	τὰ	σχοινία	τῆς
cut away	the	soldiers	the	ropes	of the

σκάφης	καὶ	εἴασαν	αὐτὴν	ἐκπεσεῖν.
boat	and	let	it	*to fall off.*

33	Ἄχρι	δὲ	οὗ	ἡμέρα	ἤμελλεν	γίνεσθαι,
	And until			day	was about	to come,

παρεκάλει	ὁ	Παῦλος	ἅπαντας	μεταλαβεῖν
besought	–	Paul	all	to partake

τροφῆς	λέγων·	τεσσαρεσκαιδεκάτην	σήμερον
of food	saying:	²[the] fourteenth	¹To-day [is]

ἡμέραν	προσδοκῶντες	ἄσιτοι	διατελεῖτε,
³day	⁵waiting	⁶without food	⁴ye continued,

μηθὲν	προσλαβόμενοι.	34	διὸ	παρακαλῶ
nothing	taking.		Wherefore	I beseech

ὑμᾶς	μεταλαβεῖν	τροφῆς·	τοῦτο	γὰρ	πρὸς
you	to partake	of food;	for this		to

τῆς	ὑμετέρας	σωτηρίας	ὑπάρχει·	οὐδενὸς
–	your	salvation	is;	²of no one

γὰρ	ὑμῶν	θρὶξ	ἀπὸ	τῆς	κεφαλῆς	ἀπολεῖται.
¹for	of you	a hair	from	the	head	shall perish.

35	εἴπας	δὲ	ταῦτα	καὶ	λαβὼν	ἄρτον
	And saying		these things	and	taking	bread

bread, and gave thanks to God in presence of them all: and when he had broken *it*, he began to eat.

36 Then were they all of good cheer, and they also took *some* meat.

37 And we were in all in the ship two hundred threescore and sixteen souls.

38 And when they had eaten enough, they lightened the ship, and cast out the wheat into the sea.

39 And when it was day, they knew not the land: but they discovered a certain creek with a shore, into the which they were minded, if it were possible, to thrust in the ship.

40 And when they had taken up the anchors, they committed *themselves* unto the sea, and loosed the rudder bands, and hoisted up the mainsail to the wind, and made toward shore.

41 And falling into a place where two seas met, they ran the ship aground; and the forepart stuck fast, and remained unmoveable, but the hinder part was broken with the violence of the waves.

42 And the soldiers' counsel was to kill the prisoners, lest any of them should swim out, and escape.

43 But the centurion, willing to save Paul, kept them from *their* purpose;

εὐχαρίστησεν τῷ θεῷ ἐνώπιον πάντων
he gave thanks – to God before all

καὶ κλάσας ἤρξατο ἐσθίειν. 36 εὔθυμοι δὲ
and breaking began to eat. And [4]in good spirits

γενόμενοι πάντες καὶ αὐτοὶ προσελάβοντο
[3]becoming [1]all [2]also they took

τροφῆς. 37 ἤμεθα δὲ αἱ πᾶσαι ψυχαὶ
food. Now we were [2]the [1]all souls

ἐν τῷ πλοίῳ διακόσιαι ἑβδομήκοντα ἕξ.
in the ship two hundreds [and] seventy six.

38 κορεσθέντες δὲ τροφῆς ἐκούφιζον τὸ
And having been satisfied of(with) food they lightened the

πλοῖον ἐκβαλλόμενοι τὸν σῖτον εἰς τὴν
ship ᵗhrowing out the wheat into the

θάλασσαν. 39 Ὅτε δὲ ἡμέρα ἐγένετο,
sea. And when day came,

τὴν γῆν οὐκ ἐπεγίνωσκον, κόλπον δέ
[2]the [3]land [1]they did not recognize, but [2]bay

τινα κατενόουν ἔχοντα αἰγιαλόν, εἰς ὃν
[2]a certain [1]they noticed having a shore, into which

ἐβουλεύοντο εἰ δύναιντο ἐξῶσαι τὸ πλοῖον.
they were minded if they were able to drive the ship.

40 καὶ τὰς ἀγκύρας περιελόντες εἴων
And [2]the [3]anchors [1]having cast off they left [them]

εἰς τὴν θάλασσαν, ἅμα ἀνέντες τὰς
in the sea, at the same time loosening the

ζευκτηρίας τῶν πηδαλίων, καὶ ἐπάραντες
fastenings of the rudders, and raising

τὸν ἀρτέμωνα τῇ πνεούσῃ κατεῖχον εἰς
the foresail to the breeze they held [the ship] to

τὸν αἰγιαλόν. 41 περιπεσόντες δὲ εἰς
the shore. And coming upon to

τόπον διθάλασσον ἐπέκειλαν τὴν ναῦν.
a place between two seas they drove the vessel.

καὶ ἡ μὲν πρῷρα ἐρείσασα ἔμεινεν
and [2]the [1]while prow having run aground remained

ἀσάλευτος, ἡ δὲ πρύμνα ἐλύετο ὑπὸ
immovable, [2]the [1]yet stern was broken by

τῆς βίας.* 42 Τῶν δὲ στρατιωτῶν βουλὴ
the force.* Now [2]of the [3]soldiers [1][the] mind

ἐγένετο ἵνα τοὺς δεσμώτας ἀποκτείνωσιν,
was that [2]the [3]prisoners [1]they should kill,

μή τις ἐκκολυμβήσας διαφύγῃ· 43 ὁ δὲ
lest anyone swimming out should escape; but the

ἑκατοντάρχης βουλόμενος διασῶσαι τὸν
centurion being minded to save –

Παῦλον ἐκώλυσεν αὐτοὺς τοῦ βουλήματος,
Paul forbade them the(ir) intention,

* That is, of the waves, as indeed some MSS have.

and commanded that they which could swim should cast *themselves* first *into the sea*, and get to land:

44 And the rest, some on boards, and some on *broken pieces* of the ship. And so it came to pass, that they escaped all safe to land.

ἐκέλευσέν	τε	τοὺς	δυναμένους	κολυμβᾶν
and commanded		the [ones]	being able	to swim

ἀπορίψαντας	πρώτους	ἐπὶ	τὴν	γῆν
casting [themselves] overboard	first	onto	the	land

ἐξιέναι,	44 καὶ	τοὺς	λοιποὺς	οὓς	μὲν	ἐπὶ
to go out,	and	the	rest	some		on

σανίσιν,	οὓς	δὲ	ἐπί	τινων	τῶν	ἀπὸ	τοῦ
planks,	others	on		some of the things		from	the

πλοίου.	καὶ	οὕτως	ἐγένετο	πάντας
ship.	And	thus	it came to pass	all

διασωθῆναι	ἐπὶ	τὴν	γῆν.
to be saved	on	the	land.

CHAPTER 28

AND when they were escaped, then they knew that the island was called Melita.

2 And the barbarous people shewed us no little kindness: for they kindled a fire, and received us every one, because of the present rain, and because of the cold.

3 And when Paul had gathered a bundle of sticks, and laid *them* on the fire, there came a viper out of the heat, and fastened on his hand.

4 And when the barbarians saw the *venomous* beast hang on his hand, they said among themselves, No doubt this man is a murderer, whom, though he hath escaped the sea, yet vengeance suffereth not to live.

5 And he shook off the beast into the fire, and felt no harm.

28 Καὶ	διασωθέντες	τότε	ἐπέγνωμεν	ὅτι
And	having been saved	then	we found out	that

Μελίτη	ἡ	νῆσος	καλεῖται.	2 οἵ	τε
Melita	the	island	is(was) called.		And the

βάρβαροι	παρεῖχον	οὐ	τὴν	τυχοῦσαν
foreigners	[1]showed	[3]not	[4]the	[5]ordinary

φιλανθρωπίαν	ἡμῖν·	ἅψαντες	γὰρ	πυρὰν
[6]kindness	[2]us;	for having lit		a fire

προσελάβοντο	πάντας	ἡμᾶς	διὰ	τὸν	ὑετὸν
they welcomed	[2]all	[1]us	because of the		rain

τὸν	ἐφεστῶτα	καὶ	διὰ	τὸ	ψῦχος.	3 συστρέ-
-	coming on	and	because of the		cold.	col-

ψαντος	δὲ	τοῦ	Παύλου[a]	φρυγάνων	τι
lecting	And	-	Paul[a] = when Paul collected	[3]of sticks	[1]a

πλῆθος	καὶ	ἐπιθέντος	ἐπὶ	τὴν	πυράν,
[2]quantity	and	putting on[a] = put them	on	the	fire,

ἔχιδνα	ἀπὸ	τῆς	θέρμης	ἐξελθοῦσα	καθῆψεν
a snake	from	the	heat	coming out	fastened on

τῆς	χειρὸς	αὐτοῦ.	4 ὡς	δὲ	εἶδον	οἱ
the	hand	of him.	And when		[3]saw	[1]the

βάρβαροι	κρεμάμενον	τὸ	θηρίον	ἐκ	τῆς
[2]foreigners	[6]hanging	[4]the	[5]beast	from	the

χειρὸς	αὐτοῦ,	πρὸς	ἀλλήλους	ἔλεγον·
hand	of him,	to	one another	they said:

πάντως	φονεύς	ἐστιν	ὁ	ἄνθρωπος	οὗτος,
To be sure	[4]a murderer	[3]is		[1]this man,

ὃν	διασωθέντα	ἐκ	τῆς	θαλάσσης	ἡ	δίκη
whom	having been saved	out of	the	sea	-	justice

ζῆν	οὐκ	εἴασεν.	5 ὁ	μὲν	οὖν	ἀποτινάξας
[2]to live	[1]did not allow.		He	-	then	shaking off

τὸ	θηρίον	εἰς	τὸ	πῦρ	ἔπαθεν	οὐδὲν
the	beast	into	the	fire	suffered	no

6 Howbeit they looked when he should have swollen, or fallen down dead suddenly: but after they had looked a great while, and saw no harm come to him, they changed their minds, and said that he was a god.

7 ¶ In the same quarters were possessions of the chief man of the island, whose name was Publius; who received us, and lodged us three days courteously.

8 And it came to pass, that the father of Publius lay sick of a fever and of a bloody flux: to whom Paul entered in, and prayed, and laid his hands on him, and healed him.

9 So when this was done, others also, which had diseases in the island, came, and were healed:

10 Who also honoured us with many honours; and when we departed, they laded us with such things as were necessary.

11 ¶ And after three months we departed in a ship of Alexandria, which had wintered in the isle, whose sign was Castor and Pollux.

12 And landing at Syracuse, we tarried there three days.

κακόν· 6 οἱ δὲ προσεδόκων αὐτὸν μέλλειν
harm; but they expected him to be about

πίμπρασθαι ἢ καταπίπτειν ἄφνω νεκρόν.
to swell or to fall down suddenly dead.

ἐπὶ πολὺ δὲ αὐτῶν προσδοκώντων καὶ
But over much [time] they expecting and
=while they expected and beheld

θεωρούντων μηδὲν ἄτοπον εἰς αὐτὸν
beholding² nothing amiss ²to ³him

γινόμενον, μεταβαλόμενοι ἔλεγον αὐτὸν εἶναι
¹happening, changing their minds they said him to be

θεόν. 7 Ἐν δὲ τοῖς περὶ τὸν τόπον
a god. Now in the [parts] about – place

ἐκεῖνον ὑπῆρχεν χωρία τῷ πρώτῳ τῆς
that were lands to the chief manᶜ of the
=the chief man . . . had lands

νήσου ὀνόματι Ποπλίῳ, ὃς ἀναδεξάμενος
island by name Publius, who welcoming

ἡμᾶς ἡμέρας τρεῖς φιλοφρόνως ἐξένισεν.
us ⁴days ³three ²friendlily ¹lodged [us].

8 ἐγένετο δὲ τὸν πατέρα τοῦ Ποπλίου
Now it happened the father – of Publius

πυρετοῖς καὶ δυσεντερίῳ συνεχόμενον
³feverish attacks ⁴and ⁵dysentery ²suffering from

κατακεῖσθαι, πρὸς ὃν ὁ Παῦλος εἰσελθὼν
¹to be lying down, to whom – Paul entering

καὶ προσευξάμενος, ἐπιθεὶς τὰς χεῖρας
and praying, ¹putting ⁴on ²the(his) ³hands

αὐτῷ ἰάσατο αὐτόν. 9 τούτου δὲ γενομένου
⁵him cured him. And this happening²
=when this happened

καὶ οἱ λοιποὶ οἱ ἐν τῇ νήσῳ ἔχοντες
²also ¹the ²rest – in the island having

ἀσθενείας προσήρχοντο καὶ ἐθεραπεύοντο,
ailments came up and were healed,

10 οἳ καὶ πολλαῖς τιμαῖς ἐτίμησαν ἡμᾶς
who also with many honours honoured us

καὶ ἀναγομένοις ἐπέθεντο τὰ πρὸς τὰς
and on our putting to sea placed on [us] the things for the(our)

χρείας.
needs.

11 Μετὰ δὲ τρεῖς μῆνας ἀνήχθημεν ἐν
And after three months we embarked in

πλοίῳ παρακεχειμακότι ἐν τῇ νήσῳ,
a ship having passed the winter in the island,

Ἀλεξανδρίνῳ, παρασήμῳ Διοσκούροις. 12 καὶ
an Alexandrian, with a sign Dioscuri. And

καταχθέντες εἰς Συρακούσας ἐπεμείναμεν
being brought to land to(at) Syracuse we remained

13 And from thence we fetched a compass, and came to Rhegium: and after one day the south wind blew, and we came the next day to Puteoli:

14 Where we found brethren, and were desired to tarry with them seven days: and so we went toward Rome.

15 And from thence, when the brethren heard of us, they came to meet us as far as Appii forum, and The three taverns: whom when Paul saw, he thanked God, and took courage.

16 And when we came to Rome, the centurion delivered the prisoners to the captain of the guard: but Paul was suffered to dwell by himself with a soldier that kept him.

17 And it came to pass, that after three days Paul called the chief of the Jews together: and when they were come together, he said unto them, Men and brethren, though I have committed nothing against the people, or customs of our fathers, yet was I delivered prisoner from Jerusalem into the hands of the Romans.

18 Who, when they had examined me, would have

ἡμέρας τρεῖς, 13 ὅθεν περιελθόντες κατην-
days   three,   whence   tacking   we ar-

τήσαμεν εἰς Ῥήγιον. καὶ μετὰ μίαν
rived   at   Rhegium.   And after   one

ἡμέραν ἐπιγενομένου νότου δευτεραῖοι
day   coming on   a south wind[a]   on the
     =as a south wind came on   second day

ἤλθομεν εἰς Ποτιόλους, 14 οὗ εὑρόντες
we came   to   Puteoli,   where having found

ἀδελφοὺς παρεκλήθημεν παρ' αὐτοῖς ἐπιμεῖναι
brothers   we were besought   with   them   to remain

ἡμέρας ἑπτά· καὶ οὕτως εἰς τὴν Ῥώμην
days   seven;   and   thus   to   –   Rome

ἤλθαμεν. 15 κἀκεῖθεν οἱ ἀδελφοὶ ἀκούσαντες
we went.   And thence   the   brothers   having heard

τὰ περὶ ἡμῶν ἦλθαν εἰς ἀπάντησιν ἡμῖν
the   con-   us   came   to   a meeting   with us
things cerning

ἄχρι Ἀππίου φόρου καὶ Τριῶν ταβερνῶν,
as far as   Appii   Forum   and   Three   Taverns,

οὓς ἰδὼν ὁ Παῦλος εὐχαριστήσας τῷ
whom   seeing –   Paul   thanking   –

θεῷ ἔλαβε θάρσος. 16 Ὅτε δὲ εἰσήλθομεν
God   he took   courage.   And when   we entered

εἰς Ῥώμην, ἐπετράπη τῷ Παύλῳ μένειν
into   Rome,   he[*] permitted –   Paul   to remain

καθ' ἑαυτὸν σὺν τῷ φυλάσσοντι αὐτὸν
by   himself   with   [1]the   [3]guarding   [4]him

στρατιώτῃ.
[2]soldier.

17 Ἐγένετο δὲ μετὰ ἡμέρας τρεῖς
   And it came to pass   after   days   three

συγκαλέσασθαι αὐτὸν τοὺς ὄντας τῶν
to call together   him[b]   the [ones]   being   of the
=he called together

Ἰουδαίων πρώτους· συνελθόντων δὲ αὐτῶν
Jews   first(chief);   and coming together   them[a]
     =and when they came together

ἔλεγεν πρὸς αὐτούς· ἐγώ, ἄνδρες ἀδελφοί,
he said   to   them: I,   *men*   brothers,

οὐδὲν ἐναντίον ποιήσας τῷ λαῷ ἢ τοῖς
[2]nothing [3]contrary [1]having done to the   people   or   to the

ἔθεσι τοῖς πατρῴοις, δέσμιος ἐξ Ἱεροσο-
customs –   ancestral,   a prisoner from   Jeru-

λύμων παρεδόθην εἰς τὰς χεῖρας τῶν
salem   I was delivered   into   the   hands   of the

Ῥωμαίων, 18 οἵτινες ἀνακρίναντές με ἐβούλοντο
Romans,   who   having examined   me   were minded

* That is, the officer to whom Paul was handed over by the centurion Julius.

let *me* go, because there was no cause of death in me.

19 But when the Jews spake against *it*, I was constrained to appeal unto Cæsar; not that I had ought to accuse my nation of.

20 For this cause therefore have I called for you, to see *you*, and to speak with *you*: because that for the hope of Israel I am bound with this chain.

21 And they said unto him, We neither received letters out of Judæa concerning thee, neither any of the brethren that came shewed or spake any harm of thee.

22 But we desire to hear of thee what thou thinkest: for as concerning this sect, we know that every where it is spoken against.

23 And when they had appointed him a day, there came many to him into *his* lodging; to whom he expounded and testified the kingdom of God, persuading them concerning Jesus, both out of the law of Moses, and *out of* the prophets, from morning till evening.

24 And some believed the things which were spoken, and some believed not.

25 And when they

ἀπολῦσαι διὰ τὸ μηδεμίαν αἰτίαν θανάτου
to release on account – no cause of death
of

ὑπάρχειν ἐν ἐμοί· 19 ἀντιλεγόντων δὲ
to be in me; but speaking against [this]
= when the Jews spoke

τῶν Ἰουδαίων ἠναγκάσθην ἐπικαλέσασθαι
the Jews² I was compelled to appeal to
against this

Καίσαρα, οὐχ ὡς τοῦ ἔθνους μου ἔχων
Cæsar, not as ⁴the ⁵nation ⁶of me ¹having

τι κατηγορεῖν. 20 διὰ ταύτην οὖν τὴν
²anything ³to accuse. ¹On account of ²this ⁴therefore –

αἰτίαν παρεκάλεσα ὑμᾶς ἰδεῖν καὶ προσ-
³cause I called you to see and to

λαλῆσαι· εἵνεκεν γὰρ τῆς ἐλπίδος τοῦ
speak to; for for the sake of the hope –

Ἰσραὴλ τὴν ἅλυσιν ταύτην περίκειμαι.
of Israel ³this ²chain ¹I have round [me].

21 οἱ δὲ πρὸς αὐτὸν εἶπαν· ἡμεῖς οὔτε
And they to him said: We neither

γράμματα περὶ σοῦ ἐδεξάμεθα ἀπὸ τῆς
²letters ³about ⁴thee ¹received from –

Ἰουδαίας, οὔτε παραγενόμενός τις τῶν
Judæa, nor arriving anyone of the

ἀδελφῶν ἀπήγγειλεν ἢ ἐλάλησέν τι περὶ
brothers told or spoke anything ²about

σοῦ πονηρόν. 22 ἀξιοῦμεν δὲ παρὰ σοῦ
³thee ¹evil. But we think fit from thee

ἀκοῦσαι ἃ φρονεῖς· περὶ μὲν γὰρ τῆς
to hear what thou ²concerning ²indeed ¹for –
things thinkest;

αἱρέσεως ταύτης γνωστὸν ἡμῖν ἐστιν ὅτι
⁵sect ⁴this ⁷known ⁸to us ⁶it is that

πανταχοῦ ἀντιλέγεται. 23 Ταξάμενοι δὲ
everywhere it is spoken against. And arranging

αὐτῷ ἡμέραν ἦλθον πρὸς αὐτὸν εἰς τὴν
with him a day ²came ³to ⁴him ⁵in ⁶the(his)

ξενίαν πλείονες, οἷς ἐξετίθετο διαμαρτυρ-
⁷lodging ¹more, to whom he set forth solemnly

όμενος τὴν βασιλείαν τοῦ θεοῦ, πείθων
witnessing the kingdom – of God, ²persuading

τε αὐτοὺς περὶ τοῦ Ἰησοῦ ἀπό τε τοῦ
¹and them concerning – Jesus from both the

νόμου Μωϋσέως καὶ τῶν προφητῶν, ἀπὸ
law of Moses and the prophets, from

πρωῒ ἕως ἑσπέρας. 24 καὶ οἱ μὲν
morning until evening. And some

ἐπείθοντο τοῖς λεγομένοις, 25 οἱ δὲ
were persuaded by the things being said, others

agreed not among themselves, they departed, after that Paul had spoken one word, Well spake the Holy Ghost by Esaias the prophet unto our fathers,

26 Saying, Go unto this people, and say, Hearing ye shall hear, and shall not understand; and seeing ye shall see, and not perceive:

27 For the heart of this people is waxed gross, and their ears are dull of hearing, and their eyes have they closed; lest they should see with *their* eyes, and hear with *their* ears, and understand with *their* heart, and should be converted, and I should heal them.

28 Be it known therefore unto you, that the salvation of God is sent unto the Gentiles, and *that* they will hear it.

29 And when he had said these words, the Jews departed, and had great reasoning among themselves.

30 ¶ And Paul dwelt two whole years in his own hired house, and received all that came in unto him,

31 Preaching the kingdom of God, and teaching those things which concern the Lord Jesus Christ, with all confidence, no man forbidding him.

ἠπίστουν· ἀσύμφωνοι δὲ ὄντες πρὸς ἀλλή-
disbelieved;   and ²disagreed   ¹being   with   one an-

λους ἀπελύοντο, εἰπόντος τοῦ Παύλου
other   they were dismissed,   having said   –   Paulᵃ
=after Paul had said

ῥῆμα ἕν, ὅτι καλῶς τὸ πνεῦμα τὸ ἅγιον
word one, – Well the Spirit the Holy

ἐλάλησεν διὰ 'Ησαΐου τοῦ προφήτου πρὸς
spoke through Esaias the prophet to

τοὺς πατέρας ὑμῶν 26 λέγων· πορεύθητι
the fathers of you   saying: Go thou

πρὸς τὸν λαὸν τοῦτον καὶ εἰπόν· ἀκοῇ
to   this people   and say: In hearing

ἀκούσετε καὶ οὐ μὴ συνῆτε, καὶ βλέποντες
ye will hear and by no means understand, and looking

βλέψετε καὶ οὐ μὴ ἴδητε· 27 ἐπαχύνθη
ye will look and by no means see;   ²was thickened

γὰρ ἡ καρδία τοῦ λαοῦ τούτου, καὶ
¹for the heart   of this people,   and

τοῖς ὠσὶν βαρέως ἤκουσαν, καὶ τοὺς
with the(ir) ears heavily they heard, and the

ὀφθαλμοὺς αὐτῶν ἐκάμμυσαν· μήποτε ἴδωσιν
eyes   of them they closed; lest at any time they see

τοῖς ὀφθαλμοῖς καὶ τοῖς ὠσὶν ἀκούσωσιν
with the   eyes   and with the ears   hear

καὶ τῇ καρδίᾳ συνῶσιν καὶ ἐπιστρέψωσιν,
and with the heart understand and   turn,

καὶ ἰάσομαι αὐτούς. 28 γνωστὸν οὖν
and I shall cure them.   Known therefore

ἔστω ὑμῖν ὅτι τοῖς ἔθνεσιν ἀπεστάλη
let it be to you that to the nations   was sent

τοῦτο τὸ σωτήριον τοῦ θεοῦ· αὐτοὶ καὶ
this – salvation of God; and they

ἀκούσονται.‡
will hear.

30 'Ενέμεινεν δὲ διετίαν ὅλην ἐν ἰδίῳ
And he remained a whole two years in [his] own

μισθώματι, καὶ ἀπεδέχετο πάντας τοὺς
hired apartment, and welcomed   all   the

εἰσπορευομένους πρὸς αὐτόν, 31 κηρύσσων
[ones] coming in   to him,   proclaiming

τὴν βασιλείαν τοῦ θεοῦ καὶ διδάσκων
the kingdom   – of God and teaching

τὰ περὶ τοῦ κυρίου 'Ιησοῦ Χριστοῦ
the things concerning the Lord Jesus Christ

μετὰ πάσης παρρησίας ἀκωλύτως.
with   all   boldness   unhinderedly.

‡ Verse 29 omitted by Nestle; *cf.* R.V. marg.

CHAPTER 1

PAUL, a servant of Jesus Christ, called *to be* an apostle, separated unto the gospel of God,

2 (Which he had promised afore by his prophets in the holy scriptures,)

3 Concerning his Son Jesus Christ our Lord, which was made of the seed of David according to the flesh;

4 And declared *to be* the Son of God with power, according to the spirit of holiness, by the resurrection from the dead:

5 By whom we have received grace and apostleship, for obedience to the faith among all nations, for his name:

6 Among whom are ye also the called of Jesus Christ:

7 To all that be in Rome, beloved of God, called *to be* saints: Grace to you and peace from God our Father, and the Lord Jesus Christ.

8 First, I thank my God through Jesus Christ for you all, that your faith is spoken of throughout the whole world.

9 For God is my witness, whom I serve with

1 Παῦλος δοῦλος Χριστοῦ Ἰησοῦ, κλητὸς
Paul   a slave   of Christ   Jesus,   called

ἀπόστολος ἀφωρισμένος εἰς εὐαγγέλιον
an apostle   *having been* separated   to   [the] gospel

θεοῦ, **2** ὃ προεπηγγείλατο διὰ τῶν
of God,   which   he promised beforehand   through   the

προφητῶν αὐτοῦ ἐν γραφαῖς ἁγίαις **3** περὶ
prophets   of him   in   writings   holy   concerning

τοῦ υἱοῦ αὐτοῦ τοῦ γενομένου ἐκ
the   Son   of him   –   come   of

σπέρματος Δαυὶδ κατὰ σάρκα, **4** τοῦ
[the] seed   of David   according to   [the] flesh,   –

ὁρισθέντος υἱοῦ θεοῦ ἐν δυνάμει
designated   Son   of God   in   power

κατὰ πνεῦμα ἁγιωσύνης ἐξ ἀναστάσεως
according to   [the] Spirit   of holiness   by   a resurrection

νεκρῶν, Ἰησοῦ Χριστοῦ τοῦ κυρίου ἡμῶν,
of dead persons,   Jesus   Christ   the   Lord   of us.

5 δι' οὗ ἐλάβομεν χάριν καὶ ἀποστολὴν
through   whom   we received   grace   and   apostleship

εἰς ὑπακοὴν πίστεως ἐν πᾶσιν τοῖς
for   obedience   of faith   among   all   the

ἔθνεσιν ὑπὲρ τοῦ ὀνόματος αὐτοῦ, **6** ἐν
nations   on behalf of   the   name   of him,   among

οἷς ἐστε καὶ ὑμεῖς κλητοὶ Ἰησοῦ Χριστοῦ,
whom are   also   ye   called   of Jesus   Christ,

7 πᾶσιν τοῖς οὖσιν ἐν Ῥώμῃ ἀγαπητοῖς
to all   the [ones]   being   in   Rome   beloved

θεοῦ, κλητοῖς ἁγίοις· χάρις ὑμῖν καὶ
of God,   called   holy: Grace   to you   and

εἰρήνη ἀπὸ θεοῦ πατρὸς ἡμῶν καὶ κυρίου
peace   from   God   [the] Father   of us   and   Lord

Ἰησοῦ Χριστοῦ.
Jesus   Christ.

8 Πρῶτον μὲν εὐχαριστῶ τῷ θεῷ μου
Firstly   –   I thank   the   God   of me

διὰ Ἰησοῦ Χριστοῦ περὶ πάντων ὑμῶν,
through   Jesus   Christ   concerning   all   you,

ὅτι ἡ πίστις ὑμῶν καταγγέλλεται ἐν
because the   faith   of you   is being announced   in

ὅλῳ τῷ κόσμῳ. **9** μάρτυς γάρ μού
all   the   world.   For witness   of me

ἐστιν ὁ θεός, ᾧ λατρεύω ἐν τῷ πνεύματί
is   –   God, whom   I serve   in   the   spirit

my spirit in the gospel of his Son, that without ceasing I make mention of you always in my prayers;

10 Making request, if by any means now at length I might have a prosperous journey by the will of God to come unto you.

11 For I long to see you, that I may impart unto you some spiritual gift, to the end ye may be established;

12 That is, that I may be comforted together with you by the mutual faith both of you and me.

13 Now I would not have you ignorant, brethren, that oftentimes I purposed to come unto you, (but was let hitherto,) that I might have some fruit among you also, even as among other Gentiles.

14 I am debtor both to the Greeks, and to the Barbarians; both to the wise, and to the unwise.

15 So, as much as in me is, I am ready to preach the gospel to you that are at Rome also.

16 For I am not ashamed of the gospel of Christ: for it is the power of God unto salvation to every one that believeth; to the Jew first, and also to the Greek.

17 For therein is the righteousness of God revealed from faith to faith:

μου ἐν τῷ εὐαγγελίῳ τοῦ υἱοῦ αὐτοῦ,
of me in the gospel of the Son of him,

ὡς ἀδιαλείπτως μνείαν ὑμῶν ποιοῦμαι
how unceasingly mention of you I make

10 πάντοτε ἐπὶ τῶν προσευχῶν μου,
always on(in) the prayers of me,

δεόμενος εἴ πως ἤδη ποτὲ εὐοδω-
requesting if somehow now at some time I shall have

θήσομαι ἐν τῷ θελήματι τοῦ θεοῦ ἐλθεῖν
a happy journey in the will — of God to come

πρὸς ὑμᾶς. **11** ἐπιποθῶ γὰρ ἰδεῖν ὑμᾶς,
unto you. For I long to see you,

ἵνα τι μεταδῶ χάρισμα ὑμῖν πνευματικὸν
that ²some ¹I may impart ⁴gift ⁵to you ³spiritual

εἰς τὸ στηριχθῆναι ὑμᾶς, **12** τοῦτο δέ
for the to be established you,[b] and this
=that ye may be established,

ἐστιν συμπαρακληθῆναι ἐν ὑμῖν διὰ τῆς
is to be encouraged *with* among you through ¹the

ἐν ἀλλήλοις πίστεως ὑμῶν τε καὶ ἐμοῦ.
²in ⁴one another ³faith ⁵of you ⁶both ⁷and ⁸of me.

13 οὐ θέλω δὲ ὑμᾶς ἀγνοεῖν, ἀδελφοί,
²not ³I wish ¹But you to be ignorant, brothers,

ὅτι πολλάκις προεθέμην ἐλθεῖν πρὸς ὑμᾶς,
that often I purposed to come unto you,

καὶ ἐκωλύθην ἄχρι τοῦ δεῦρο, ἵνα τινὰ
and was hindered until the present, that some

καρπὸν σχῶ καὶ ἐν ὑμῖν καθὼς καὶ
fruit I may have also among you as indeed

ἐν τοῖς λοιποῖς ἔθνεσιν. **14** Ἕλλησίν
among the remaining nations. ²to Greeks

τε καὶ βαρβάροις, σοφοῖς τε καὶ ἀνοήτοις
¹Both ³and ⁴to foreigners, ⁵to wise men ⁶both ⁷and ⁸to foolish

ὀφειλέτης εἰμί· **15** οὕτως τὸ κατ' ἐμὲ
¹⁰a debtor ⁹I am; so as far as in me lies†

πρόθυμον καὶ ὑμῖν τοῖς ἐν Ῥώμῃ
[I am] eager ²also ³to you ⁴*the [ones]* ⁵in ⁶Rome

εὐαγγελίσασθαι. **16** οὐ γὰρ ἐπαισχύνομαι
¹to preach. For I am not ashamed of

τὸ εὐαγγέλιον· δύναμις γὰρ θεοῦ ἐστιν
the gospel; ³power ¹for of God it is

εἰς σωτηρίαν παντὶ τῷ πιστεύοντι, Ἰουδαίῳ
to salvation to everyone believing, ³to Jew

τε πρῶτον καὶ Ἕλληνι. **17** δικαιοσύνη
¹both firstly and to Greek. a righteousness

γὰρ θεοῦ ἐν αὐτῷ ἀποκαλύπτεται ἐκ
For of God in it is revealed from

πίστεως εἰς πίστιν, καθὼς γέγραπται·
faith to faith, as it has been written:

as it is written, The just shall live by faith.

ὁ δὲ δίκαιος ἐκ πίστεως ζήσεται.
Now the · just man · by · faith · will live.

18 For the wrath of God is revealed from heaven against all ungodliness and unrighteousness of men, who hold the truth in unrighteousness;

18 Ἀποκαλύπτεται γὰρ ὀργὴ θεοῦ ἀπ'
For [4]is revealed [1][the] [2]wrath [3]of God from
οὐρανοῦ ἐπὶ πᾶσαν ἀσέβειαν καὶ ἀδικίαν
heaven against all impiety and unrighteousness
ἀνθρώπων τῶν τὴν ἀλήθειαν ἐν ἀδικίᾳ
of men – [2]the [3]truth [4]in [5]unrighteousness

19 Because that which may be known of God is manifest in them; for God hath shewed it unto them.

κατεχόντων, 19 διότι τὸ γνωστὸν τοῦ θεοῦ
[1]holding fast, because the thing known – of God
φανερόν ἐστιν ἐν αὐτοῖς· ὁ θεὸς γὰρ αὐτοῖς
manifest is among them; – for God to them
ἐφανέρωσεν.
manifested [it].

20 For the invisible things of him from the creation of the world are clearly seen, being understood by the things that are made, even his eternal power and Godhead; so that they are without excuse:

20 τὰ γὰρ ἀόρατα αὐτοῦ
For the invisible things of him
ἀπὸ κτίσεως κόσμου τοῖς ποιήμασιν
[1]from [3][the] [4]creation [5]of [the] world [7]by the [8]things made
νοούμενα καθορᾶται, ἥ τε
[6]being understood [1]is(are) clearly seen, [10]the [9]both
ἀΐδιος αὐτοῦ δύναμις καὶ θειότης, εἰς
[11]everlasting [15]of him [12]power [13]and [14]divinity, for

21 Because that, when they knew God, they glorified him not as God, neither were thankful; but became vain in their imaginations, and their foolish heart was darkened.

τὸ εἶναι αὐτοὺς ἀναπολογήτους, 21 διότι
the to be them[b] without excuse, because
=so that they are
γνόντες τὸν θεὸν οὐχ ὡς θεὸν ἐδόξασαν
knowing – God [2]not [3]as [4]God [1]they glorified [him]
ἢ ηὐχαρίστησαν, ἀλλὰ ἐματαιώθησαν ἐν
[5]or [6]thanked [him], but became vain in
τοῖς διαλογισμοῖς αὐτῶν, καὶ ἐσκοτίσθη
the reasonings of them, and [5]was darkened

22 Professing themselves to be wise, they became fools,

ἡ ἀσύνετος αὐτῶν καρδία. 22 φάσκοντες
[1]the [2]undiscerning [4]of them [3]heart. Asserting

23 And changed the glory of the uncorruptible God into an image made like to corruptible man, and to birds, and four-footed beasts, and creeping things.

εἶναι σοφοὶ ἐμωράνθησαν, 23 καὶ ἤλλαξαν
to be wise they became foolish, and changed
τὴν δόξαν τοῦ ἀφθάρτου θεοῦ ἐν ὁμοιώματι
the glory of the incorruptible God in[to] a likeness
εἰκόνος φθαρτοῦ ἀνθρώπου καὶ πετεινῶν
of an image of corruptible man and birds

24 Wherefore God also gave them up to uncleanness through the lusts of their own hearts, to dishonour their own bodies between themselves:

καὶ τετραπόδων καὶ ἑρπετῶν· 24 διὸ
and quadrupeds and reptiles; wherefore
παρέδωκεν αὐτοὺς ὁ θεὸς ἐν ταῖς
[2]gave up [3]them – [1]God in the
ἐπιθυμίαις τῶν καρδιῶν αὐτῶν εἰς ἀκαθαρ-
desires of the hearts of them to unclean-
σίαν τοῦ ἀτιμάζεσθαι τὰ σώματα αὐτῶν
ness – to be dishonoured[d] the bodies of them

25 Who changed the truth of God into a lie,

ἐν αὐτοῖς. 25 Οἵτινες μετήλλαξαν τὴν
among them[selves]. Who changed the
ἀλήθειαν τοῦ θεοῦ ἐν τῷ ψεύδει, καὶ
truth – of God in[to] the lie, and

and worshipped and served the creature more than the Creator, who is blessed for ever. Amen.

26 For this cause God gave them up unto vile affections: for even their women did change the natural use into that which is against nature:

27 And likewise also the men, leaving the natural use of the woman, burned in their lust one toward another; men with men working that which is unseemly, and receiving in themselves that recompence of their error which was meet.

28 And even as they did not like to retain God in *their* knowledge, God gave them over to a reprobate mind, to do those things which are not convenient;

29 Being filled with all unrighteousness, fornication, wickedness, covetousness, maliciousness; full of envy, murder, debate, deceit, malignity; whisperers,

30 Backbiters, haters of God, despiteful, proud, boasters, inventors of evil things, disobedient to parents,

31 Without understanding, covenantbreakers, without natural affection, implacable, unmerciful:

ἐσεβάσθησαν   καὶ   ἐλάτρευσαν   τῇ   κτίσει
worshipped   and   served   the   creature

παρὰ   τὸν   κτίσαντα,   ὅς   ἐστιν   εὐλογητὸς
rather the [one] having created, who   is   blessed
than

εἰς   τοὺς   αἰῶνας·   ἀμήν.   26 διὰ   τοῦτο
unto   the   ages: Amen.   Therefore

παρέδωκεν   αὐτοὺς   ὁ   θεὸς   εἰς   πάθη
²gave up   ³them   –   ¹God   to   passions

ἀτιμίας·   αἵ   τε   γὰρ   θήλειαι   αὐτῶν
of dishonour; ³the ²even ¹for   females   of them

μετήλλαξαν   τὴν   φυσικὴν   χρῆσιν   εἰς   τὴν
changed   the   natural   use   to the [use]

παρὰ   φύσιν,   27 ὁμοίως   τε   καὶ   οἱ   ἄρσενες
against nature,   ²likewise ¹and also   the   males

ἀφέντες   τὴν   φυσικὴν   χρῆσιν   τῆς   θηλείας
leaving   the   natural   use   of the   female

ἐξεκαύθησαν   ἐν   τῇ   ὀρέξει   αὐτῶν   εἰς
burned   in   the   desire   of them   toward

ἀλλήλους,   ἄρσενες   ἐν   ἄρσεσιν   τὴν
one another,   males   among   males   ²the

ἀσχημοσύνην   κατεργαζόμενοι   καὶ   τὴν
³unseemliness   ¹working   and   ⁴the

ἀντιμισθίαν   ἣν   ἔδει   τῆς   πλάνης   αὐτῶν
⁵requital   ⁹which ¹⁰behoved ⁶of the   ⁷error   ⁸of them

ἐν   ἑαυτοῖς   ἀπολαμβάνοντες.   28 Καὶ
²in   ³themselves   ¹receiving back.   And

καθὼς   οὐκ   ἐδοκίμασαν   τὸν   θεὸν   ἔχειν
as   they thought not fit   –   God   to have

ἐν   ἐπιγνώσει,   παρέδωκεν   αὐτοὺς   ὁ   θεὸς
in   knowledge,   ²gave up   ³them   –   ¹God

εἰς   ἀδόκιμον   νοῦν,   ποιεῖν   τὰ   μὴ   καθήκοντα,
to   a reprobate   mind,   to do   the   not *being* proper,
                                    things

29 πεπληρωμένους   πάσῃ   ἀδικίᾳ   πονηρίᾳ
   having been filled   with all unrighteousness   wickedness

πλεονεξίᾳ   κακίᾳ,   μεστοὺς   φθόνου   φόνου
covetousness   evil,   full   of envy *of* murder

ἔριδος   δόλου   κακοηθείας,   ψιθυριστάς,
of strife   of guile   of malignity,   whisperers, *

30 καταλάλους,   θεοστυγεῖς,   ὑβριστάς,   ὑπερ-
   railers,   God-haters,   insolent,   arro-

ηφάνους,   ἀλαζόνας,   ἐφευρετὰς   κακῶν,
gant,   boasters,   inventors   of evil things,

γονεῦσιν   ἀπειθεῖς,   31 ἀσυνέτους,   ἀσυνθέτους,
to parents   disobedient,   undiscerning,   faithless,

ἀστόργους,   ἀνελεήμονας·   32 οἵτινες   τὸ
without   unmerciful;   who   ²the
natural affection,

* " In a bad sense " (Abbott-Smith).

32 Who knowing the judgment of God, that they which commit such things are worthy of death, not only do the same, but have pleasure in them that do them.

δικαίωμα τοῦ θεοῦ ἐπιγνόντες, ὅτι οἱ
³ordinance – ⁴of God ¹knowing, that the

τὰ τοιαῦτα πράσσοντες ἄξιοι θανάτου
the ²such things ¹[ones] practising worthy of death

εἰσίν, οὐ μόνον αὐτὰ ποιοῦσιν, ἀλλὰ
are, not only them do, but

καὶ συνευδοκοῦσιν τοῖς πράσσουσιν.
also consent to the [ones] practising.

CHAPTER 2

THEREFORE thou art inexcusable, O man, whosoever thou art that judgest: for wherein thou judgest another, thou condemnest thyself; for thou that judgest doest the same things.

2 But we are sure that the judgment of God is according to truth against them which commit such things.

3 And thinkest thou this, O man, that judgest them which do such things, and doest the same, that thou shalt escape the judgment of God?

4 Or despisest thou the riches of his goodness and forbearance and long-suffering; not knowing that the goodness of God leadeth thee to repentance?

5 But after thy hardness and impenitent heart treasurest up unto thyself wrath against the day of wrath and revelation of the righteous judgment of God;

6 Who will render to every man according to his deeds:

2 Διὸ ἀναπολόγητος εἶ, ὦ ἄνθρωπε
Wherefore inexcusable thou art, O man

πᾶς ὁ κρίνων· ἐν ᾧ γὰρ κρίνεις τὸν
everyone judging; ²in ³what ¹for thou judgest the

ἕτερον, σεαυτὸν κατακρίνεις· τὰ γὰρ αὐτὰ
other, thyself thou for the same
condemnest; things

πράσσεις ὁ κρίνων. 2 οἴδαμεν δὲ ὅτι τὸ
thou the judging. But we know that the
practisest [one]

κρίμα τοῦ θεοῦ ἐστιν κατὰ ἀλήθειαν ἐπὶ
judg- – of is accord- truth on
ment God ing to

τοὺς τὰ τοιαῦτα πράσσοντας. 3 λογίζῃ
the the ²such things ¹[ones] practising. reckonest thou

δὲ τοῦτο, ὦ ἄνθρωπε ὁ κρίνων τοὺς
And this, O man the judging the
[one] [ones]

τὰ τοιαῦτα πράσσοντας καὶ ποιῶν αὐτά,
the such things practising and doing them,

ὅτι σὺ ἐκφεύξῃ τὸ κρίμα τοῦ θεοῦ;
that thou wilt escape the judgment – of God?

4 ἢ τοῦ πλούτου τῆς χρηστότητος αὐτοῦ
or the riches of the kindness of him

καὶ τῆς ἀνοχῆς καὶ τῆς μακροθυμίας
and the forbearance and the longsuffering

καταφρονεῖς, ἀγνοῶν ὅτι τὸ χρηστὸν τοῦ
despisest thou, not knowing that the kindness –

θεοῦ εἰς μετάνοιάν σε ἄγει; 5 κατὰ δὲ
of God to repentance thee leads? but according to

τὴν σκληρότητά σου καὶ ἀμετανόητον
the hardness of thee and impenitent

καρδίαν θησαυρίζεις σεαυτῷ ὀργὴν ἐν
heart treasurest for thyself wrath in

ἡμέρᾳ ὀργῆς καὶ ἀποκαλύψεως δικαιοκρισίας
a day of wrath and of revelation of a righteous
judgment

τοῦ θεοῦ, 6 ὃς ἀποδώσει ἑκάστῳ κατὰ τὰ
– of God, who will requite to each man accord- the
ing to

7 To them who by patient continuance in well doing seek for glory and honour and immortality, eternal life:

8 But unto them that are contentious, and do not obey the truth, but obey unrighteousness, indignation and wrath,

9 Tribulation and anguish, upon every soul of man that doeth evil, of the Jew first, and also of the Gentile;

10 But glory, honour, and peace, to every man that worketh good, to the Jew first, and also to the Gentile:

11 For there is no respect of persons with God.

12 For as many as have sinned without law shall also perish without law: and as many as have sinned in the law shall be judged by the law;

13 (For not the hearers of the law *are* just before God, but the doers of the law shall be justified.

14 For when the Gentiles, which have not the law, do by nature the things contained in the law, these, having not the law, are a law unto themselves:

15 Which shew the work of the law written in their hearts, their conscience also bearing witness, and

ἔργα αὐτοῦ· 7 τοῖς μὲν καθ' ὑπομονὴν
works of him : to the on [ones] ²by ³endurance
 one hand

ἔργου ἀγαθοῦ δόξαν καὶ τιμὴν καὶ
⁵work ⁴of(in) good ⁶glory ⁷and ⁸honour ⁹and

ἀφθαρσίαν ζητοῦσιν ζωὴν αἰώνιον·
¹⁰incorruption ¹seeking ¹²life ¹¹eternal;

8 τοῖς δὲ ἐξ ἐριθείας καὶ ἀπειθοῦσι τῇ
to the [ones] of self-seeking and disobeying the
on the other

ἀληθείᾳ πειθομένοις δὲ τῇ ἀδικίᾳ, ὀργὴ
truth ²obeying ¹but - unrighteousness, wrath

καὶ θυμός. 9 θλῖψις καὶ στενοχωρία ἐπὶ
and anger. Affliction and anguish on

πᾶσαν ψυχὴν ἀνθρώπου τοῦ κατεργαζομένου
every soul of man working

τὸ κακόν, Ἰουδαίου τε πρῶτον καὶ
the evil, both of Jew firstly and

Ἕλληνος· 10 δόξα δὲ καὶ τιμὴ καὶ
of Greek; but glory and honour and

εἰρήνη παντὶ τῷ ἐργαζομένῳ τὸ ἀγαθόν,
peace to everyone working the good,

Ἰουδαίῳ τε πρῶτον καὶ Ἕλληνι. 11 οὐ
both to Jew firstly and to Greek. not

γὰρ ἐστιν προσωπολημψία παρὰ τῷ θεῷ.
For is respect of persons with - God.

12 Ὅσοι γὰρ ἀνόμως ἥμαρτον, ἀνόμως
For as many as without law sinned, without law

καὶ ἀπολοῦνται· καὶ ὅσοι ἐν νόμῳ
also will perish; and as in law
 many as (under)

ἥμαρτον, διὰ νόμου κριθήσονται· 13 οὐ
sinned, through law will be judged; ²not

γὰρ οἱ ἀκροαταὶ νόμου δίκαιοι παρὰ
¹for the hearers of law [are] just with

[τῷ] θεῷ, ἀλλ' οἱ ποιηταὶ νόμου
 - God, but the doers of law

δικαιωθήσονται. 14 ὅταν γὰρ ἔθνη τὰ
will be justified. For whenever nations -

μὴ νόμον ἔχοντα φύσει τὰ τοῦ νόμου
¹not ³law ²having by nature the things of the law

ποιῶσιν, οὗτοι νόμον μὴ ἔχοντες ἑαυτοῖς
do, these ³law ¹not ²having to themselves

εἰσιν νόμος· 15 οἵτινες ἐνδείκνυνται τὸ
are a law; who show the

ἔργον τοῦ νόμου γραπτὸν ἐν ταῖς καρδίαις
work of the law written in the hearts

αὐτῶν, συμμαρτυρούσης αὐτῶν τῆς συνει-
of them, witnessing with of them the con-
 = while their conscience witnesses with and their

their thoughts the mean while accusing or else excusing one another;)

16 In the day when God shall judge the secrets of men by Jesus Christ according to my gospel.

17 Behold, thou art called a Jew, and restest in the law, and makest thy boast of God,

18 And knowest *his* will, and approvest the things that are more excellent, being instructed out of the law;

19 And art confident that thou thyself art a guide of the blind, a light of them which are in darkness,

20 An instructor of the foolish, a teacher of babes, which hast the form of knowledge and of the truth in the law.

21 Thou therefore which teachest another, teachest thou not thyself? thou that preachest a man should not steal, dost thou steal?

22 Thou that sayest a man should not commit adultery, dost thou commit adultery? thou that abhorrest idols, dost thou commit sacrilege?

23 Thou that makest thy boast of the law, through breaking the law dishonourest thou God?

24 For the name of God is blasphemed among the Gentiles through you, as it is written.

25 For　　　circumcision

δήσεως καὶ μεταξὺ ἀλλήλων τῶν λογισμῶν
science and between one another the thoughts
thoughts among themselves accuse or even excuse,

κατηγορούντων ἢ καὶ ἀπολογουμένων, 16 ἐν
accusing or even excusing,[a] in

ᾗ ἡμέρᾳ κρίνει ὁ θεὸς τὰ κρυπτὰ τῶν
what day judges – God the hidden things –

ἀνθρώπων κατὰ τὸ εὐαγγέλιόν μου διὰ
of men according to the gospel of me through

Χριστοῦ Ἰησοῦ. 17 Εἰ δὲ σὺ Ἰουδαῖος
Christ Jesus. But if thou [2]a Jew

ἐπονομάζῃ καὶ ἐπαναπαύῃ νόμῳ καὶ
[1]art named and restest on law and

καυχᾶσαι ἐν θεῷ 18 καὶ γινώσκεις τὸ
boastest in God and knowest the

θέλημα καὶ δοκιμάζεις τὰ διαφέροντα
will and approvest the things excelling

κατηχούμενος ἐκ τοῦ νόμου, 19 πέποιθάς τε
being instructed out of the law, and having persuaded

σεαυτὸν ὁδηγὸν εἶναι τυφλῶν, φῶς
thyself a guide to be of blind a light
[persons],

τῶν ἐν σκότει, 20 παιδευτὴν ἀφρόνων,
of the in darkness, an instructor of foolish
[ones] [persons],

διδάσκαλον νηπίων, ἔχοντα τὴν μόρφωσιν
a teacher of infants, having the form

τῆς γνώσεως καὶ τῆς ἀληθείας ἐν τῷ
– of knowledge and of the truth in the

νόμῳ· 21 ὁ οὖν διδάσκων ἕτερον σεαυτὸν
law: the there- teaching another thyself
[one] fore

οὐ διδάσκεις; ὁ κηρύσσων μὴ κλέπτειν
teachest thou not? the [one] proclaiming not to steal

κλέπτεις; 22 ὁ λέγων μὴ μοιχεύειν
stealest thou? the [one] saying not to commit adultery

μοιχεύεις; ὁ βδελυσσόμενος τὰ εἴδωλα
dost thou com- the detesting the idols
mit adultery? [one]

ἱεροσυλεῖς; 23 ὃς ἐν νόμῳ καυχᾶσαι, διὰ
dost thou rob who in law boastest, through
temples?

τῆς παραβάσεως τοῦ νόμου τὸν θεὸν
– transgression of the law – [2]God

ἀτιμάζεις; 24 τὸ γὰρ ὄνομα τοῦ θεοῦ
[1]dishonourest thou? for the name – of God

δι' ὑμᾶς βλασφημεῖται ἐν τοῖς ἔθνεσιν,
because you is blasphemed among the nations,
of

καθὼς γέγραπται. 25 περιτομὴ μὲν γὰρ
as it has been written. circumcision indeed For

verily profiteth, if thou keep the law: but if thou be a breaker of the law, thy circumcision is made uncircumcision.

26 Therefore if the uncircumcision keep the righteousness of the law, shall not his uncircumcision be counted for circumcision?

27 And shall not uncircumcision which is by nature, if it fulfil the law, judge thee, who by the letter and circumcision dost transgress the law?

28 For he is not a Jew, which is one outwardly; neither *is that* circumcision, which is outward in the flesh:

29 But he *is* a Jew, which is one inwardly; and circumcision *is that* of the heart, in the spirit, *and* not in the letter; whose praise *is* not of men, but of God.

CHAPTER 3

WHAT advantage then hath the Jew? or what profit *is there* of circumcision?

2 Much every way: chiefly, because that unto them were committed the oracles of God.

3 For what if some did not believe? shall their unbelief make the faith of God without effect?

4 God forbid: yea, let God be true, but every man a liar; as it is written, That thou mightest be justified in thy say-

---

ὠφελεῖ ἐὰν νόμον πράσσης· ἐὰν δὲ
profits   if   law   thou practisest;   but if

παραβάτης νόμου ἧς, ἡ περιτομή σου
a transgressor of law thou art, the circumcision of thee

ἀκροβυστία γέγονεν. 26 ἐὰν οὖν ἡ ἀκρο-
uncircumcision has become.   If therefore the uncir-

βυστία τὰ δικαιώματα τοῦ νόμου φυλάσσῃ,
cumcision the ordinances of the law keeps,

οὐχ ἡ ἀκροβυστία αὐτοῦ εἰς περιτομὴν
not the uncircumcision of him for circumcision

λογισθήσεται; 27 καὶ κρινεῖ ἡ ἐκ φύσεως
will be reckoned?   and [8]will judge [1]the [3]by [4]nature

ἀκροβυστία τὸν νόμον τελοῦσα σὲ τὸν
[2]uncircumcision [6]the [7]law [5]keeping [9]thee [10]the

διὰ γράμματος καὶ περιτομῆς παραβάτην
[13]through [14]letter [15]and [16]circumcision [11]transgressor

νόμου. 28 οὐ γὰρ ὁ ἐν τῷ φανερῷ
[12]of law.   For [2]not [3]the [5]in [6]the [7]open

Ἰουδαῖός ἐστιν, οὐδὲ ἡ ἐν τῷ φανερῷ
[4]Jew [1]he is, nor [1]the [3]in [4]the [5]open

ἐν σαρκὶ περιτομή· 29 ἀλλ' ὁ ἐν τῷ
[6]in [7]flesh [2]circumcision;   but [1]the [3]in [4]the

κρυπτῷ Ἰουδαῖος, καὶ περιτομὴ καρδίας
[5]secret [2]Jew [is], and circumcision [is] of heart

ἐν πνεύματι οὐ γράμματι, οὗ ὁ ἔπαινος
in spirit not letter, of the praise [is]
                                        whom

οὐκ ἐξ ἀνθρώπων ἀλλ' ἐκ τοῦ θεοῦ.
not from men but from - God.

3 Τί οὖν τὸ περισσὸν τοῦ Ἰουδαίου,
What therefore the advantage of the Jew,

ἢ τίς ἡ ὠφέλεια τῆς περιτομῆς; 2 πολὺ
or what the profit - of circumcision? Much

κατὰ πάντα τρόπον. πρῶτον μὲν [γὰρ]
by every way. [2]Firstly [3]indeed [1]for

ὅτι ἐπιστεύθησαν τὰ λόγια τοῦ θεοῦ.
because they were the oracles - of God.
        entrusted [with]

3 τί γάρ; εἰ ἠπίστησάν τινες, μὴ ἡ
For what? If [2]disbelieved [1]some, not the

ἀπιστία αὐτῶν τὴν πίστιν τοῦ θεοῦ
unbelief of them the faith - of God

καταργήσει; 4 μὴ γένοιτο· γινέσθω δὲ
will destroy?   May it not be;   but let be

ὁ θεὸς ἀληθής, πᾶς δὲ ἄνθρωπος ψεύστης,
- God true, and every man a liar,

καθάπερ γέγραπται· ὅπως ἂν δικαιωθῇς
as it has been So as - thou mayest
        written: be justified

ings, and mightest over-
come when thou art
judged.

5 But if our unright-
eousness commend the
righteousness of God,
what shall we say? *Is*
God unrighteous who
taketh vengeance? (I
speak as a man)

6 God forbid: for then
how shall God judge the
world?

7 For if the truth of
God hath more abounded
through my lie unto his
glory; why yet am I also
judged as a sinner?

8 And not *rather*, (as
we be slanderously re-
ported, and as some affirm
that we say,) Let us do
evil, that good may come?
whose damnation is just.

9 What then? are we
better *than they?* No, in
no wise: for we have
before proved both Jews
and Gentiles, that they are
all under sin;

10 As it is written,
There is none righteous,
no, not one:

11 There is none that
understandeth, there is
none that seeketh after
God.

12 They are all gone
out of the way, they are
together become unprofit-
able; there is none that
doeth good, no, not one.

13 Their throat *is* an
open sepulchre; with their

ἐν   τοῖς   λόγοις   σου   καὶ   νικήσεις   ἐν
in   the   sayings   of thee   and   wilt overcome   in

τῷ   κρίνεσθαί   σε.   5 εἰ   δὲ   ἡ   ἀδικία
the   to be judged   thee.[be]   Now if   the   unright-
=when thou art judged.   eousness

ἡμῶν   θεοῦ   δικαιοσύνην   συνίστησιν,   τί
of us   [2]of God   [2]a righteousness   [1]commends,   what

ἐροῦμεν;   μὴ   ἄδικος   ὁ   θεὸς   ὁ   ἐπιφέρων
shall we say?   not   unrighteous   –   God   the [one] inflicting

τὴν   ὀργήν;   κατὰ   ἄνθρωπον   λέγω.   6 μὴ
–   wrath?   according to   man   I say.   not

γένοιτο·   ἐπεὶ   πῶς   κρινεῖ   ὁ   θεὸς   τὸν
May it be;   otherwise   how   will judge   –   God   the

κόσμον;   7 εἰ   δὲ   ἡ   ἀλήθεια   τοῦ   θεοῦ
world?   But if   the   truth   –   of God

ἐν   τῷ   ἐμῷ   ψεύσματι   ἐπερίσσευσεν   εἰς
by   –   my   lie   abounded   to

τὴν   δόξαν   αὐτοῦ,   τί   ἔτι   κἀγὼ   ὡς
the   glory   of him,   why   still   I also   as

ἁμαρτωλὸς   κρίνομαι;   8 καὶ   μὴ   καθὼς
a sinner   am judged?   and   not   as

βλασφημούμεθα   καὶ   καθὼς   φασίν   τινες
we are blasphemed   and   as   [2]say   [1]some

ἡμᾶς   λέγειν   ὅτι   ποιήσωμεν   τὰ   κακὰ
us   to say[,]   –   Let us do   –   evil things
=that we say,

ἵνα   ἔλθῃ   τὰ   ἀγαθά;   ὧν   τὸ   κρίμα
that may come   –   good things?   of whom   the   judgment

ἔνδικόν   ἐστιν.   9 Τί   οὖν;   προεχόμεθα;
just   is.   What therefore?   Do we excel?

οὐ   πάντως·   προῃτιασάμεθα   γὰρ   Ἰουδαίους
not   at all;   for we previously accused   [2]Jews

τε   καὶ   Ἕλληνας   πάντας   ὑφ᾽   ἁμαρτίαν
[1]both and   Greeks   all   under   sin

εἶναι,   10 καθὼς   γέγραπται   ὅτι   οὐκ   ἔστιν
to be,   as   it has been written[,]   –   There is not

δίκαιος   οὐδὲ   εἷς,   οὐκ   ἔστιν   ὁ
a righteous man   not   one,   there is not   the [one]

συνίων,   11 οὐκ   ἔστιν   ὁ   ἐκζητῶν   τὸν   θεόν·
under-   there is not   the   seeking   –   God;
standing,   [one]

12 πάντες   ἐξέκλιναν,   ἅμα   ἠχρεώθησαν·
all   turned away,   together   became unprofitable;

οὐκ   ἔστιν   ὁ   ποιῶν   χρηστότητα,   οὐκ
there is not   the [one]   doing   kindness,   not

ἔστιν   ἕως   ἑνός.   13 τάφος   ἀνεῳγμένος
there is   so much as   one.   A grave *having been* opened

tongues they have used deceit; the poison of asps *is* under their lips:

14 Whose mouth *is* full of cursing and bitterness:

15 Their feet *are* swift to shed blood:

16 Destruction and misery *are* in their ways:

17 And the way of peace have they not known:

18 There is no fear of God before their eyes.

19 Now we know that what things soever the law saith, it saith to them who are under the law: that every mouth may be stopped, and all the world may become guilty before God.

20 Therefore by the deeds of the law there shall no flesh be justified in his sight: for by the law *is* the knowledge of sin.

21 But now the righteousness of God without the law is manifested, being witnessed by the law and the prophets;

22 Even the righteousness of God *which is* by faith of Jesus Christ unto all and upon all them that believe: for there is no difference:

23 For all have sinned, and come short of the glory of God;

24 Being justified freely by his grace through the redemption that is in Christ Jesus:

ὁ λάρυγξ αὐτῶν, ταῖς γλώσσαις αὐτῶν
the throat of them, with the tongues of them

ἐδολιοῦσαν, ἰὸς ἀσπίδων ὑπὸ τὰ χείλη
they acted poison of asps under the lips
deceitfully,

αὐτῶν· 14 ὧν τὸ στόμα ἀρᾶς καὶ πικρίας
of them; of whom the mouth ²of cursing ³and ⁴bitterness

γέμει· 15 ὀξεῖς οἱ πόδες αὐτῶν ἐκχέαι
¹is full; swift the feet of them to shed

αἷμα, 16 σύντριμμα καὶ ταλαιπωρία ἐν
blood, ruin and misery in

ταῖς ὁδοῖς αὐτῶν, 17 καὶ ὁδὸν εἰρήνης
the ways of them, and a way of peace

οὐκ ἔγνωσαν. 18 οὐκ ἔστιν φόβος θεοῦ
they knew not. There is not fear of God

ἀπέναντι τῶν ὀφθαλμῶν αὐτῶν. 19 οἴδαμεν
before the eyes of them. we know

δὲ ὅτι ὅσα ὁ νόμος λέγει τοῖς ἐν τῷ
But that whatever the law says to the in the
things [ones]

νόμῳ λαλεῖ, ἵνα πᾶν στόμα φραγῇ καὶ
law it speaks, in order that every mouth may be stopped and

ὑπόδικος γένηται πᾶς ὁ κόσμος τῷ
⁵under ⁴may become ¹all ²the ³world –
judgment

θεῷ· 20 διότι ἐξ ἔργων νόμου οὐ
to God; because by works of law not

δικαιωθήσεται πᾶσα σὰρξ ἐνώπιον αὐτοῦ·
will be justified all flesh* before him;

διὰ γὰρ νόμου ἐπίγνωσις ἁμαρτίας.
for through law [is] full knowledge of sin.

21 Νυνὶ δὲ χωρὶς νόμου δικαιοσύνη
But now without law a righteousness

θεοῦ πεφανέρωται, μαρτυρουμένη ὑπὸ τοῦ
of God has been manifested, being witnessed by the

νόμου καὶ τῶν προφητῶν, 22 δικαιοσύνη
law and the prophets, ²a righteousness

δὲ θεοῦ διὰ πίστεως [Ἰησοῦ] Χριστοῦ,
¹and of God through faith of(in) Jesus Christ,

εἰς πάντας τοὺς πιστεύοντας· οὐ γάρ
to all the [ones] believing; for not

ἐστιν διαστολή· 23 πάντες γὰρ ἥμαρτον
there is difference; for all sinned

καὶ ὑστεροῦνται τῆς δόξης τοῦ θεοῦ,
and come short • of the glory – of God,

24 δικαιούμενοι δωρεὰν τῇ αὐτοῦ χάριτι
being justified freely by the of him grace

διὰ τῆς ἀπολυτρώσεως τῆς ἐν Χριστῷ
through the redemption – in Christ

* That is, no flesh will be justified . . .

25 Whom God hath set forth *to be* a propitiation through faith in his blood, to declare his righteousness for the remission of sins that are past, through the forbearance of God;

26 To declare, *I say*, at this time his righteousness: that he might be just, and the justifier of him which believeth in Jesus.

27 Where *is* boasting then? It is excluded. By what law? of works? Nay: but by the law of faith.

28 Therefore we conclude that a man is justified by faith without the deeds of the law.

29 *Is he* the God of the Jews only? *is he* not also of the Gentiles? Yes, of the Gentiles also:

30 Seeing *it is* one God, which shall justify the circumcision by faith, and uncircumcision through faith.

31 Do we then make void the law through faith? God forbid: yea, we establish the law.

25 ὃν προέθετο ὁ θεὸς ἱλαστήριον
   whom set forth – God a propitiation

διὰ πίστεως ἐν τῷ αὐτοῦ αἵματι, εἰς
through faith by the of him blood, for

ἔνδειξιν τῆς δικαιοσύνης αὐτοῦ διὰ τὴν
a showing of the righteousness of him because of the
forth

πάρεσιν τῶν προγεγονότων ἁμαρτημάτων
passing by of the ²having previously ¹sins
              occurred

26 ἐν τῇ ἀνοχῇ τοῦ θεοῦ, πρὸς τὴν
in the forbearance – of God, for the

ἔνδειξιν τῆς δικαιοσύνης αὐτοῦ ἐν τῷ
showing of the righteousness of him in the
forth

νῦν καιρῷ, εἰς τὸ εἶναι αὐτὸν δίκαιον
present time, for the to be him[b] just
               =that he should be

καὶ δικαιοῦντα τὸν ἐκ πίστεως Ἰησοῦ.
and justifying the [one] of faith of(in) Jesus.

27 Ποῦ οὖν ἡ καύχησις; ἐξεκλείσθη. διὰ
   Where there- the boasting? It was shut out. Through
   fore

ποίου νόμου; τῶν ἔργων; οὐχί, ἀλλὰ
what law? – of works? no, but

διὰ νόμου πίστεως. 28 λογιζόμεθα γὰρ
through a law of faith. For we reckon

δικαιοῦσθαι πίστει ἄνθρωπον χωρὶς ἔργων
²to be justified ³by faith ¹a man without works

νόμου. 29 ἢ Ἰουδαίων ὁ θεὸς μόνον;
of law. Or of Jews [is he] the God only?

οὐχὶ καὶ ἐθνῶν; ναὶ καὶ ἐθνῶν, 30 εἴπερ
not also of nations? Yes[,] also of nations, since [there is]

εἷς ὁ θεὸς ὃς δικαιώσει περιτομὴν ἐκ
one – God who will justify circumcision by

πίστεως καὶ ἀκροβυστίαν διὰ τῆς πίστεως.
faith and uncircumcision through the faith.

31 νόμον οὖν καταργοῦμεν διὰ τῆς
³Law ²therefore ¹do we destroy through the

πίστεως; μὴ γένοιτο, ἀλλὰ νόμον ἱστάνομεν.
faith? May it not be, but ²law ¹we establish.

CHAPTER 4

WHAT shall we say then that Abraham our father, as pertaining to the flesh, hath found?

2 For if Abraham were justified by works, he hath *whereof* to glory; but not before God.

4 Τί οὖν ἐροῦμεν εὑρηκέναι Ἀβραὰμ
  What therefore shall we say to have found Abraham

τὸν προπάτορα ἡμῶν κατὰ σάρκα; 2 εἰ
the forefather of us according to flesh? if

γὰρ Ἀβραὰμ ἐξ ἔργων ἐδικαιώθη, ἔχει
For Abraham by works was justified, he has

καύχημα· ἀλλ' οὐ πρὸς θεόν. 3 τί γὰρ
a boast; but not with God. For what

3 For what saith the scripture? Abraham believed God, and it was counted unto him for righteousness.

4 Now to him that worketh is the reward not reckoned of grace, but of debt.

5 But to him that worketh not, but believeth on him that justifieth the ungodly, his faith is counted for righteousness.

6 Even as David also describeth the blessedness of the man, unto whom God imputeth righteousness without works,

7 Saying, Blessed are they whose iniquities are forgiven, and whose sins are covered.

8 Blessed is the man to whom the Lord will not impute sin.

9 Cometh this blessedness then upon the circumcision only, or upon the uncircumcision also? for we say that faith was reckoned to Abraham for righteousness.

10 How was it then reckoned? when he was in circumcision, or in uncircumcision? Not in circumcision, but in uncircumcision.

11 And he received the sign of circumcision, a seal of the righteousness of the faith which he had yet being uncircumcised: that he might be the father of

ἡ γραφὴ λέγει; ἐπίστευσεν δὲ ᾿Αβραὰμ
the scripture says? And ²believed ¹Abraham
τῷ θεῷ, καὶ ἐλογίσθη αὐτῷ εἰς
- God, and it was reckoned to him for
δικαιοσύνην. 4 τῷ δὲ ἐργαζομένῳ ὁ
righteousness. Now to the [one] working the
μισθὸς οὐ λογίζεται κατὰ χάριν ἀλλὰ
reward is not reckoned according to grace but
κατὰ ὀφείλημα· τῷ δὲ μὴ ἐργαζομένῳ,
according to debt; but to the [one] not working,
5 πιστεύοντι δὲ ἐπὶ τὸν δικαιοῦντα τὸν
but believing on the [one] justifying the
ἀσεβῆ, λογίζεται ἡ πίστις αὐτοῦ εἰς
impious man, is reckoned the faith of him for
δικαιοσύνην, 6 καθάπερ καὶ Δαυὶδ λέγει
righteousness, even as also David says
τὸν μακαρισμὸν τοῦ ἀνθρώπου ᾧ ὁ
the blessedness of the man to whom -
θεὸς λογίζεται δικαιοσύνην χωρὶς ἔργων·
God reckons righteousness without works :
7 μακάριοι ὧν ἀφέθησαν αἱ ἀνομίαι
Blessed [are they] of whom were forgiven the lawlessnesses
καὶ ὧν ἐπεκαλύφθησαν αἱ ἁμαρτίαι·
and of whom were covered over the sins;
8 μακάριος ἀνὴρ οὗ οὐ μὴ λογίσηται
blessed [is] a man of whom by no means ²may reckon
κύριος ἁμαρτίαν. 9 ὁ μακαρισμὸς οὖν
¹[the] Lord sin. - ²blessedness ³then
οὗτος ἐπὶ τὴν περιτομὴν ἢ καὶ ἐπὶ
¹This on the circumcision or also on
τὴν ἀκροβυστίαν; λέγομεν γάρ· ἐλογίσθη
the uncircumcision? for we say : ³was reckoned
τῷ ᾿Αβραὰμ ἡ πίστις· εἰς δικαιοσύνην.
- ⁴to Abraham ¹The(his) ²faith for righteousness.
10 πῶς οὖν ἐλογίσθη; ἐν περιτομῇ ὄντι
How then was it reckoned? in circumcision being
ἢ ἐν ἀκροβυστίᾳ; οὐκ ἐν περιτομῇ ἀλλ᾿
or in uncircumcision? not in circumcision but
ἐν ἀκροβυστίᾳ· 11 καὶ σημεῖον ἔλαβεν
in uncircumcision; and ²a sign ¹he received
περιτομῆς σφραγῖδα τῆς δικαιοσύνης τῆς
of circumcision a seal of the righteousness of the
πίστεως τῆς ἐν τῇ ἀκροβυστίᾳ, εἰς
faith - [while] in - uncircumcision, for
=so
τὸ εἶναι αὐτὸν πατέρα πάντων τῶν
the to be him[b] a father of all the
that he should be

all them that believe, though they be not circumcised; that righteousness might be imputed unto them also:

12 And the father of circumcision to them who are not of the circumcision only, but who also walk in the steps of that faith of our father Abraham, which *he had* being *yet* uncircumcised.

13 For the promise, that he should be the heir of the world, *was* not to Abraham, or to his seed, through the law, but through the righteousness of faith.

14 For if they which are of the law *be* heirs, faith is made void, and the promise made of none effect:

15 Because the law worketh wrath: for where no law is, *there is* no transgression.

16 Therefore *it is* of faith, that *it might be* by grace; to the end the promise might be sure to all the seed; not to that only which is of the law, but to that also which is of the faith of Abraham; who is the father of us all,

17 (As it is written, I have made thee a father of many nations,) before him whom he believed, *even* God, who quickeneth

πιστευόντων δι' ἀκροβυστίας, εἰς τὸ
[ones] believing through uncircumcision, for the
=that right-

λογισθῆναι αὐτοῖς [τὴν] δικαιοσύνην, 12 καὶ
to be reckoned to them – righteousness,[b] and
eousness should be reckoned to them,

πατέρα περιτομῆς τοῖς οὐκ ἐκ περιτομῆς
a father of circumcision to the not of circumcision
[ones]

μόνον ἀλλὰ καὶ τοῖς στοιχοῦσιν τοῖς
only but also to the [ones] walking in the

ἴχνεσιν τῆς ἐν ἀκροβυστίᾳ πίστεως τοῦ
steps [1]of the [7]in [8]uncircumcision [2]faith [3]of the

πατρὸς ἡμῶν Ἀβραάμ. 13 Οὐ γὰρ διὰ
[4]father [5]of us [6]Abraham. For not through

νόμου ἡ ἐπαγγελία τῷ Ἀβραὰμ ἢ τῷ
law the promise – to Abraham or to the

σπέρματι αὐτοῦ, τὸ κληρονόμον αὐτὸν
seed of him, the heir him
=that he should be heir

εἶναι κόσμου, ἀλλὰ διὰ δικαιοσύνης πίστεως.
to be[b] of [the] world, but through a righteousness of faith.

14 εἰ γὰρ οἱ ἐκ νόμου κληρονόμοι,
For if [1]the [2][are] [4]of [5]law [3]heirs,

κεκένωται ἡ πίστις καὶ κατήργηται
[3]has been emptied – [1]faith and [2]has been destroyed

ἡ ἐπαγγελία· 15 ὁ γὰρ νόμος ὀργὴν
[1]the [2]promise; for the law wrath

κατεργάζεται· οὗ δὲ οὐκ ἔστιν νόμος,
[1]works; and where there is not law,

οὐδὲ παράβασις. 16 Διὰ τοῦτο ἐκ πίστεως,
neither [is there] Therefore [it is] of faith,
transgression.

ἵνα κατὰ χάριν, εἰς τὸ εἶναι βεβαίαν
in [it may be] grace, for the to be firm
order according =so that the promise shall be firm
that to

τὴν ἐπαγγελίαν παντὶ τῷ σπέρματι, οὐ
the promise[b] to all the seed, not

τῷ ἐκ τοῦ νόμου μόνον ἀλλὰ καὶ τῷ
to the of the law only but also to the
[seed] [seed]

ἐκ πίστεως Ἀβραάμ, ὅς ἐστιν πατὴρ
of [the] faith of Abraham, who is father

πάντων ἡμῶν, 17 καθὼς γέγραπται ὅτι
of all us, as it has been written[,] –

πατέρα πολλῶν ἐθνῶν τέθεικά σε,
A father of many nations I have appointed thee,

κατέναντι οὗ ἐπίστευσεν θεοῦ τοῦ ζωο-
before [2]whom [3]he believed [1]God the [one] quick-

the dead, and calleth those things which be not as though they were.

18 Who against hope believed in hope, that he might become the father of many nations, according to that which was spoken, So shall thy seed be.

19 And being not weak in faith, he considered not his own body now dead, when he was about an hundred years old, neither yet the deadness of Sarah's womb:

20 He staggered not at the promise of God through unbelief; but was strong in faith, giving glory to God;

21 And being fully persuaded that, what he had promised, he was able also to perform.

22 And therefore it was imputed to him for righteousness.

23 Now it was not written for his sake alone, that it was imputed to him;

24 But for us also, to whom it shall be imputed, if we believe on him that raised up Jesus our Lord from the dead;

25 Who was delivered for our offences, and was raised again for our justification.

ποιοῦντος τοὺς νεκροὺς καὶ καλοῦντος
ening   the   dead [ones]   and   calling

τὰ μὴ ὄντα ὡς ὄντα· 18 ὃς παρ' ἐλπίδα
the not being as being; who beyond hope
things

ἐπ' ἐλπίδι ἐπίστευσεν, εἰς τὸ γενέσθαι
on hope believed, for the to become
                           =so that he should become

αὐτὸν πατέρα πολλῶν ἐθνῶν κατὰ τὸ
him[b] a father of many nations accord- the
                              ing to thing

εἰρημένον· οὕτως ἔσται τὸ σπέρμα σου·
having been said : So shall be the seed of thee;

19 καὶ μὴ ἀσθενήσας τῇ πίστει κατενόησεν
and not weakening – in faith he considered

τὸ ἑαυτοῦ σῶμα νενεκρωμένον, ἑκατονταέτης
[1]the ³of himself ²body to have died, a hundred years

που ὑπάρχων, καὶ τὴν νέκρωσιν τῆς
about being, and the death of the

μήτρας Σάρρας· 20 εἰς δὲ τὴν ἐπαγγελίαν
womb of Sarah; but ²against ³the ⁴promise

τοῦ θεοῦ οὐ διεκρίθη τῇ ἀπιστίᾳ, ἀλλὰ
– ⁵of God ¹he did not decide – ⁶by unbelief, but

ἐνεδυναμώθη τῇ πίστει, δοὺς δόξαν τῷ
was empowered – by faith, giving glory –

θεῷ 21 καὶ πληροφορηθεὶς ὅτι ὃ ἐπήγγελται
to God and being fully that what he has
             persuaded   promised

δυνατός ἐστιν καὶ ποιῆσαι. 22 διὸ [καὶ]
able he is also to do. Wherefore also

ἐλογίσθη αὐτῷ εἰς δικαιοσύνην. 23 Οὐκ
it was to him for righteousness. not
reckoned

ἐγράφη δὲ δι' αὐτὸν μόνον ὅτι ἐλογίσθη
it was Now because him only that it was
written of   reckoned

αὐτῷ, 24 ἀλλὰ καὶ δι' ἡμᾶς, οἷς μέλλει
to him, but also because us, to whom it is
                of   about

λογίζεσθαι, τοῖς πιστεύουσιν ἐπὶ τὸν
to be reckoned, to the [ones] believing on the [one]

ἐγείραντα Ἰησοῦν τὸν κύριον ἡμῶν ἐκ
having raised Jesus the Lord of us out of

νεκρῶν, 25 ὃς παρεδόθη διὰ τὰ παραπ-
[the] dead, who was delivered because of the of-

τώματα ἡμῶν καὶ ἠγέρθη διὰ τὴν
fences of us and was raised because of the

δικαίωσιν ἡμῶν.
justification of us.

CHAPTER 5

THEREFORE being justified by faith, we have peace with God through our Lord Jesus Christ:

2 By whom also we have access by faith into this grace wherein we stand, and rejoice in hope of the glory of God.

3 And not only so, but we glory in tribulations also: knowing that tribulation worketh patience;

4 And patience, experience; and experience, hope:

5 And hope maketh not ashamed; because the love of God is shed abroad in our hearts by the Holy Ghost which is given unto us.

6 For when we were yet without strength, in due time Christ died for the ungodly.

7 For scarcely for a righteous man will one die: yet peradventure for a good man some would even dare to die.

8 But God commendeth his love toward us, in that, while we were yet sinners, Christ died for us.

9 Much more then, being now justified by his

---

5 Δικαιωθέντες οὖν ἐκ πίστεως εἰρήνην
Having been justified therefore by faith peace

ἔχομεν πρὸς τὸν θεὸν διὰ τοῦ κυρίου
we have with — God through the Lord

ἡμῶν Ἰησοῦ Χριστοῦ, **2** δι' οὗ καὶ τὴν
of us Jesus Christ, through whom also the

προσαγωγὴν ἐσχήκαμεν [τῇ πίστει] εἰς
access we have had — by faith into

τὴν χάριν ταύτην ἐν ᾗ ἑστήκαμεν, καὶ
this grace in which we stand, and

καυχώμεθα ἐπ' ἐλπίδι τῆς δόξης τοῦ
boast on hope of the glory —

θεοῦ. **3** οὐ μόνον δέ, ἀλλὰ καὶ καυχώμεθα
of God. And not only [so], but also we boast

ἐν ταῖς θλίψεσιν, εἰδότες ὅτι ἡ θλῖψις
in — afflictions, knowing that the affliction

ὑπομονὴν κατεργάζεται, **4** ἡ δὲ ὑπομονὴ
patience works, — and patience

δοκιμήν, ἡ δὲ δοκιμὴ ἐλπίδα· **5** ἡ δὲ
proof, — and proof hope; — and

ἐλπὶς οὐ καταισχύνει, ὅτι ἡ ἀγάπη
hope does not put to shame, because the love

τοῦ θεοῦ ἐκκέχυται ἐν ταῖς καρδίαις
— of God has been poured out in the hearts

ἡμῶν διὰ πνεύματος ἁγίου τοῦ δοθέντος
of us through Spirit Holy — given

ἡμῖν· **6** εἴ γε Χριστὸς ὄντων ἡμῶν
to us; indeed [7]Christ [2]being [1]us
= when we were weak

ἀσθενῶν ἔτι κατὰ καιρὸν ὑπὲρ ἀσεβῶν
[4]weak[a] [3]yet [5]accord- [6]time [9]on [10]impious
ing to behalf of ones

ἀπέθανεν. **7** μόλις γὰρ ὑπὲρ δικαίου
[8]died. For hardly on behalf of a just man

τις ἀποθανεῖται· ὑπὲρ γὰρ τοῦ ἀγαθοῦ
anyone will die; for on behalf of the good man

τάχα τις καὶ τολμᾷ ἀποθανεῖν· **8** συνίστησιν
perhaps some- even dares to die; [2]commends
one

δὲ τὴν ἑαυτοῦ ἀγάπην εἰς ἡμᾶς ὁ θεὸς
but [3]the [5]of himself [4]love [6]to [7]us — [1]God

ὅτι ἔτι ἁμαρτωλῶν ὄντων ἡμῶν Χριστὸς
that yet sinners being us[a] Christ
= while we were yet sinners

ὑπὲρ ἡμῶν ἀπέθανεν. **9** πολλῷ οὖν μᾶλλον
on be- us died. By much there- rather
half of fore

δικαιωθέντες νῦν ἐν τῷ αἵματι αὐτοῦ
having been justified now by the blood of him

blood, we shall be saved from wrath through him.

10 For if, when we were enemies, we were reconciled to God by the death of his Son, much more, being reconciled, we shall be saved by his life.

11 And not only so, but we also joy in God through our Lord Jesus Christ, by whom we have now received the atonement.

12 Wherefore, as by one man sin entered into the world, and death by sin; and so death passed upon all men, for that all have sinned:

13 (For until the law sin was in the world: but sin is not imputed when there is no law.

14 Nevertheless death reigned from Adam to Moses, even over them that had not sinned after the similitude of Adam's transgression, who is the figure of him that was to come.

15 But not as the offence, so also is the free gift. For if through the offence of one many be dead, much more the grace of God, and the gift by grace, which is

σωθησόμεθα δι' αὐτοῦ ἀπὸ τῆς ὀργῆς.
we shall be saved through him from the wrath.

10 εἰ γὰρ ἐχθροὶ ὄντες κατηλλάγημεν
For if enemies being we were reconciled
τῷ θεῷ διὰ τοῦ θανάτου τοῦ υἱοῦ αὐτοῦ,
– to God through the death of the Son of him,
πολλῷ μᾶλλον καταλλαγέντες σωθησόμεθα
by much rather having been reconciled we shall be saved
ἐν τῇ ζωῇ αὐτοῦ· **11** οὐ μόνον δὲ, ἀλλὰ
by the life of him; and not only [so], but
καὶ καυχώμενοι ἐν τῷ θεῷ διὰ τοῦ
also boasting in – God through the
κυρίου ἡμῶν Ἰησοῦ [Χριστοῦ], δι' οὗ
Lord of us Jesus [Christ], through whom
νῦν τὴν καταλλαγὴν ἐλάβομεν.
now the reconciliation we received.

12 Διὰ τοῦτο ὥσπερ δι' ἑνὸς ἀνθρώπου
Therefore as through one man
ἡ ἁμαρτία εἰς τὸν κόσμον εἰσῆλθεν,
– sin into the world entered,
καὶ διὰ τῆς ἁμαρτίας ὁ θάνατος, καὶ
and through – sin death, ²also
οὕτως εἰς πάντας ἀνθρώπους ὁ θάνατος
¹so to all men – death
διῆλθεν, ἐφ' ᾧ πάντες ἥμαρτον· **13** ἄχρι
passed, inasmuch as all sinned; until
γὰρ νόμου ἁμαρτία ἦν ἐν κόσμῳ, ἁμαρτία
for law sin was in [the] world, sin
δὲ οὐκ ἐλλογεῖται μὴ ὄντος νόμου·
but is not reckoned not being law²;
=when there is no law;

14 ἀλλὰ ἐβασίλευσεν ὁ θάνατος ἀπὸ Ἀδὰμ
but ¹reigned – ¹death from Adam
μέχρι Μωϋσέως καὶ ἐπὶ τοὺς μὴ
until Moses even over the [ones] not
ἁμαρτήσαντας ἐπὶ τῷ ὁμοιώματι τῆς
sinning on the likeness of the
παραβάσεως Ἀδάμ, ὅς ἐστιν τύπος τοῦ
transgression of Adam, who is a type of the
μέλλοντος. **15** Ἀλλ' οὐχ ὡς τὸ παράπτωμα,
[one] coming. But not as the offence,
οὕτως [καὶ] τὸ χάρισμα· εἰ γὰρ τῷ
so also the free gift; for if ¹by the
τοῦ ἑνὸς παραπτώματι οἱ πολλοὶ
³of the ⁴one [man] ²offence the many
ἀπέθανον, πολλῷ μᾶλλον ἡ χάρις τοῦ θεοῦ
died, by much rather the grace – of God
καὶ ἡ δωρεὰ ἐν χάριτι τῇ τοῦ ἑνὸς
and the gift in grace – of the one

by one man, Jesus Christ, hath abounded unto many.

16 And not as *it was* by one that sinned, *so is* the gift: for the judgment *was* by one to condemnation, but the free gift *is* of many offences unto justification.

17 For if by one man's offence death reigned by one; much more they which receive abundance of grace and of the gift of righteousness shall reign in life by one, Jesus Christ.)

18 Therefore as by the offence of one *judgment came* upon all men to condemnation; even so by the righteousness of one *the free gift came* upon all men unto justification of life.

19 For as by one man's disobedience many were made sinners, so by the obedience of one shall many be made righteous.

20 Moreover the law entered, that the offence might abound. But where sin abounded, grace did much more abound:

21 That as sin hath

ἀνθρώπου Ἰησοῦ Χριστοῦ εἰς τοὺς πολλοὺς
man   ˉ Jesus   Christ   to   the   many

ἐπερίσσευσεν. 16 καὶ οὐχ ὡς δι’ ἑνὸς
abounded.   And   not   as   through   one
                                             [man]

ἁμαρτήσαντος τὸ δώρημα· τὸ μὲν γὰρ
sinning   the   gift;   ³the ²on one hand ¹for

κρίμα ἐξ ἑνὸς εἰς κατάκριμα, τὸ δὲ
judgment [is] of   one   to   condemna-   on the other
           [offence]   tion,   the

χάρισμα ἐκ πολλῶν παραπτωμάτων εἰς
free gift [is]   of   many   offences   to

δικαίωμα. 17 εἰ γὰρ τῷ τοῦ ἑνὸς
justification.   For if   ¹by the ³of the ⁴one [man]

παραπτώματι ὁ θάνατος ἐβασίλευσεν διὰ
²offence   –   death   reigned   through

τοῦ ἑνός, πολλῷ μᾶλλον οἱ τὴν περισσείαν
the   one   by much   rather   ¹the   ³the   ⁴abundance
[man],   [ones]

τῆς χάριτος καὶ τῆς δωρεᾶς τῆς
⁵of the   ⁶grace   ⁷and   ⁸of the   ⁹gift   –

δικαιοσύνης λαμβάνοντες ἐν ζωῇ βασιλεύ-
¹⁰of righteousness   ²receiving   ¹²in   ¹³life   ¹¹will

σουσιν διὰ τοῦ ἑνὸς Ἰησοῦ Χριστοῦ.
reign   through   the   one [man]   Jesus   Christ.

18 Ἄρα οὖν ὡς δι’ ἑνὸς παραπτώματος
So   therefore   as   through   one   offence

εἰς πάντας ἀνθρώπους εἰς κατάκριμα,
to   all   men   to   condemnation,

οὕτως καὶ δι’ ἑνὸς δικαιώματος εἰς
so   also   through   one   righteous act   to

πάντας ἀνθρώπους εἰς δικαίωσιν ζωῆς·
all   men   to   justification   of life;

19 ὥσπερ γὰρ διὰ τῆς παρακοῆς τοῦ
for as   through   the   disobedience   of the

ἑνὸς ἀνθρώπου ἁμαρτωλοὶ κατεστάθησαν
one   man   ⁴sinners   ³were constituted

οἱ πολλοί, οὕτως καὶ διὰ τῆς ὑπακοῆς
¹the   ²many,   so   also   through   the   obedience

τοῦ ἑνὸς δίκαιοι κατασταθήσονται οἱ
of the   one [man]   ⁴righteous   ³will be constituted   ¹the

πολλοί. 20 νόμος δὲ παρεισῆλθεν ἵνα
²many.   But   law   entered   in order
                                                      that

πλεονάσῃ τὸ παράπτωμα· οὗ δὲ ἐπλεόνασεν
might abound the   offence;   but where   abounded

ἡ ἁμαρτία, ὑπερεπερίσσευσεν ἡ χάρις,
–   sin,   more abounded   –   grace,

21 ἵνα ὥσπερ ἐβασίλευσεν ἡ ἁμαρτία ἐν
in order that   as   reigned   –   sin   by

reigned unto death, even so might grace reign through righteousness unto eternal life by Jesus Christ our Lord.

τῷ θανάτῳ, οὕτως καὶ ἡ χάρις βασιλεύσῃ
\- death, so also - grace might reign
διὰ δικαιοσύνης εἰς ζωὴν αἰώνιον διὰ
through righteousness to life eternal through
Ἰησοῦ Χριστοῦ τοῦ κυρίου ἡμῶν.
Jesus Christ the Lord of us.

CHAPTER 6

WHAT shall we say then? Shall we continue in sin, that grace may abound?

2 God forbid. How shall we, that are dead to sin, live any longer therein?

3 Know ye not, that so many of us as were baptized into Jesus Christ were baptized into his death?

4 Therefore we are buried with him by baptism into death: that like as Christ was raised up from the dead by the glory of the Father, even so we also should walk in newness of life.

5 For if we have been planted together in the likeness of his death, we shall be also *in the likeness* of *his* resurrection:

6 Knowing this, that our old man is crucified with *him*, that the body of sin might be destroyed, that henceforth we should not serve sin.

7 For he that is dead is freed from sin.

8 Now if we be dead with Christ, we believe

6 Τί οὖν ἐροῦμεν; ἐπιμένωμεν τῇ
What therefore shall we say? May we continue
ἁμαρτίᾳ, ἵνα ἡ χάρις πλεονάσῃ; 2 μὴ
in sin, in order that - grace may abound? not
γένοιτο. οἵτινες ἀπεθάνομεν τῇ ἁμαρτίᾳ,
May it be. Who we died - to sin,
πῶς ἔτι ζήσομεν ἐν αὐτῇ; 3 ἢ ἀγνοεῖτε
how yet shall we live in it? or are ye ignorant
ὅτι ὅσοι ἐβαπτίσθημεν εἰς Χριστὸν
that as many as we were baptized into Christ
Ἰησοῦν, εἰς τὸν θάνατον αὐτοῦ ἐβαπτίσ-
Jesus, into the death of him we were
θημεν; 4 συνετάφημεν οὖν αὐτῷ διὰ τοῦ
baptized? ¹We were ¹there him through -
fore
βαπτίσματος εἰς τὸν θάνατον, ἵνα ὥσπερ
baptism into - death, in order as
that
ἠγέρθη Χριστὸς ἐκ νεκρῶν διὰ τῆς
was raised Christ from [the] dead through the
δόξης τοῦ πατρός, οὕτως καὶ ἡμεῖς ἐν
glory of the Father, so also we in
καινότητι ζωῆς περιπατήσωμεν. 5 εἰ γὰρ
newness of life might walk. For if
σύμφυτοι γεγόναμεν τῷ ὁμοιώματι τοῦ
united with we have become in the likeness of the
θανάτου αὐτοῦ, ἀλλὰ καὶ τῆς ἀναστάσεως
death of him, but(so) also of the(his) resurrection
ἐσόμεθα· 6 τοῦτο γινώσκοντες, ὅτι ὁ
we shall be; this knowing, that the
παλαιὸς ἡμῶν ἄνθρωπος συνεσταυρώθη, ἵνα
¹old ²of us ²man was crucified in or-
with [him], der that
καταργηθῇ τὸ σῶμα τῆς ἁμαρτίας, τοῦ
might be the body - of sin, -
destroyed
μηκέτι δουλεύειν ἡμᾶς τῇ ἁμαρτίᾳ· 7 ὁ
no longer to serve us ᵇᵈ - sin; ²the
=that we should no longer serve (one)
γὰρ ἀποθανὼν δεδικαίωται ἀπὸ τῆς
¹for having died has been justified from -
ἁμαρτίας. 8 εἰ δὲ ἀπεθάνομεν σὺν Χριστῷ,
sin. But if we died with Christ

that we shall also live with him:

9 Knowing that Christ being raised from the dead dieth no more; death hath no more dominion over him.

10 For in that he died, he died unto sin once: but in that he liveth, he liveth unto God.

11 Likewise reckon ye also yourselves to be dead indeed unto sin, but alive unto God through Jesus Christ our Lord.

12 Let not sin therefore reign in your mortal body, that ye should obey it in the lusts thereof.

13 Neither yield ye your members *as* instruments of unrighteousness unto sin: but yield yourselves unto God, as those that are alive from the dead, and your members *as* instruments of righteousness unto God.

14 For sin shall not have dominion over you: for ye are not under the law, but under grace.

15 What then? shall we sin, because we are not under the law, but under grace? God forbid.

16 Know ye not, that to whom ye yield yourselves servants to obey, his servants ye are to whom ye obey; whether of sin unto death, or of

πιστεύομεν   ὅτι   καὶ   συζήσομεν   αὐτῷ,
we believe   ~   that   also   we shall live with   him,

9 εἰδότες   ὅτι   Χριστὸς   ἐγερθεὶς   ἐκ   νεκρῶν
knowing   that   Christ   having   from   [the] dead
been raised

οὐκέτι   ἀποθνῄσκει,   θάνατος   αὐτοῦ   οὐκέτι
no more   dies,   death   ³of him   ¹no more

κυριεύει.   **10** ὁ   γὰρ   ἀπέθανεν,   τῇ   ἁμαρτίᾳ
²lords it over.   For in that†   he died,   –   to sin

ἀπέθανεν   ἐφάπαξ·   ὁ   δὲ   ζῇ,   ζῇ   τῷ   θεῷ.
he died   once;   but in that† he   he   –   to
lives, lives   God.

11 οὕτως   καὶ   ὑμεῖς   λογίζεσθε   ἑαυτοὺς
So   also   ²ye   ¹reckon   yourselves

εἶναι   νεκροὺς   μὲν   τῇ   ἁμαρτίᾳ   ζῶντας
to be   dead   indeed   –   to sin   ²living

δὲ   τῷ   θεῷ   ἐν   Χριστῷ   Ἰησοῦ.   **12** μὴ
¹but   –   to God   in   Christ   Jesus.   ¯not

οὖν   βασιλευέτω   ἡ   ἁμαρτία   ἐν   τῷ   θνητῷ
¹There-   ²let ⁶reign   –   ⁴sin   ⁵in   ⁷the   ⁸mortal
fore

ὑμῶν   σώματι   εἰς   τὸ   ὑπακούειν   ταῖς
¹⁰of you   ⁹body   for   the   to obey   the
=to obey its lusts,

ἐπιθυμίαις   αὐτοῦ,   **13** μηδὲ   παριστάνετε   τὰ
lusts   of it,   neither   present ye   the

μέλη   ὑμῶν   ὅπλα   ἀδικίας   τῇ   ἁμαρτίᾳ,
members of you   weapons   of unright-   –   to sin,
eousness

ἀλλὰ   παραστήσατε   ἑαυτοὺς   τῷ   θεῷ   ὡσεὶ
but   present ye   yourselves   –   to God   as

ἐκ   νεκρῶν   ζῶντας   καὶ   τὰ   μέλη   ὑμῶν
from [the] dead   living   and   the   members   of you

ὅπλα   δικαιοσύνης   τῷ   θεῷ,   **14** ἁμαρτία
weapons   of righteousness   –   to God,   ²sin

γὰρ   ὑμῶν   οὐ   κυριεύσει·   οὐ   γάρ   ἐστε
¹for   ⁴of you   ³shall not lord it over;   for ye are not

ὑπὸ   νόμον   ἀλλὰ   ὑπὸ   χάριν.   **15** Τί   οὖν;
under   law   but   under   grace.   What therefore?

ἁμαρτήσωμεν,   ὅτι   οὐκ   ἐσμὲν   ὑπὸ   νόμον
may we sin,   because   we are not   under   law

ἀλλὰ   ὑπὸ   χάριν;   μὴ   γένοιτο.   **16** οὐκ
but   under   grace?   May it not be.   not

οἴδατε   ὅτι   ᾧ   παριστάνετε   ἑαυτοὺς   δούλους
Know ye   that   to   ye present   yourselves   slaves
whom

εἰς   ὑπακοήν,   δοῦλοί   ἐστε   ᾧ   ὑπακούετε,
for   obedience,   slaves   ye are   whom   ye obey,

ἤτοι   ἁμαρτίας   εἰς   θάνατον   ἢ   ὑπακοῆς
whether   of sin   to   death   or   of obedience

obedience unto righteous-
ness?

17 But God be thanked,
that ye were the servants
of sin, but ye have obeyed
from the heart that form
of doctrine which was de-
livered you.

18 Being then made free
from sin, ye became the
servants of righteousness.

19 I speak after the
manner of men because of
the infirmity of your flesh:
for as ye have yielded your
members servants to un-
cleanness and to iniquity
unto iniquity; even so
now yield your members
servants to righteousness
unto holiness.

20 For when ye were
the servants of sin, ye
were free from righteous-
ness.

21 What fruit had ye
then in those things whereof ye are now ashamed?
for the end of those things
is death.

22 But now being made
free from sin, and be-
come servants to God, ye
have your fruit unto holiness, and the end ever-
lasting life.

23 For the wages of
sin is death; but the gift
of God is eternal life
through Jesus Christ our
Lord.

εἰς   δικαιοσύνην,   17 χάρις   δὲ   τῷ   θεῷ
to   righteousness?   But thanks   -   to God

ὅτι   ἦτε   δοῦλοι   τῆς   ἁμαρτίας,   ὑπηκούσατε
that   ye were slaves   -   of sin,   ²ye obeyed

δὲ   ἐκ   καρδίας   εἰς   ὃν   παρεδόθητε   τύπον
¹but out of [the] heart   ³to   ⁴which ⁵ye were delivered ¹a form

διδαχῆς,   18 ἐλευθερωθέντες   δὲ   ἀπὸ   τῆς
²of teaching,   and having been freed   from

ἁμαρτίας   ἐδουλώθητε   τῇ   δικαιοσύνῃ.
sin   ye were enslaved   -   to righteousness.

19 ἀνθρώπινον   λέγω   διὰ   τὴν   ἀσθένειαν
Humanly   I say   because of the   weakness

τῆς   σαρκὸς   ὑμῶν.   ὥσπερ   γὰρ   παρεστήσατε
of the   flesh   of you.   For as   ye presented

τὰ   μέλη   ὑμῶν   δοῦλα   τῇ   ἀκαθαρσίᾳ   καὶ
the   members of you   slaves   -   to uncleanness   and

τῇ   ἀνομίᾳ   εἰς   τὴν   ἀνομίαν,   οὕτως   νῦν
-    to iniquity unto   -   iniquity,   so   now

παραστήσατε   τὰ   μέλη   ὑμῶν   δοῦλα   τῇ
present ye   the   members   of you   slaves   -

δικαιοσύνῃ   εἰς   ἁγιασμόν.   20 ὅτε   γὰρ
to righteousness unto   sanctification.   For when

δοῦλοι   ἦτε   τῆς   ἁμαρτίας,   ἐλεύθεροι   ἦτε
slaves   ye were   -   of sin,   free   ye were

τῇ   δικαιοσύνῃ.   21 τίνα   οὖν   καρπὸν   εἴχετε
-    to righteousness.   What ²therefore ¹fruit   had ye

τότε;   ἐφ'   οἷς   νῦν   ἐπαισχύνεσθε·   τὸ   γὰρ
then?   Over   which now   ye are ashamed;   for the
        things

τέλος   ἐκείνων   θάνατος.   22 νυνὶ   δὲ   ἐλευ-
end of those things [is] death.   But now   having

θερωθέντες   ἀπὸ   τῆς   ἁμαρτίας   δουλωθέντες
been freed   from   -   sin   ²having been enslaved

δὲ   τῷ   θεῷ,   ἔχετε   τὸν   καρπὸν   ὑμῶν   εἰς
¹and -   to God, ye have   the   fruit   of you   to

ἁγιασμόν,   τὸ   δὲ   τέλος   ζωὴν   αἰώνιον.
sanctification,   and the   end   life   eternal.

23 τὰ   γὰρ   ὀψώνια   τῆς   ἁμαρτίας   θάνατος,
For the   wages   -   of sin   [is] death,

τὸ   δὲ   χάρισμα   τοῦ   θεοῦ   ζωὴ   αἰώνιος
but the   free gift   -   of God   life   eternal

ἐν   Χριστῷ   Ἰησοῦ   τῷ   κυρίῳ   ἡμῶν.
in   Christ   Jesus   the   Lord   of us.

CHAPTER 7

KNOW ye not, brethren, (for I speak to them that know the law,) how that the law hath dominion over a man as long as he liveth?

2 For the woman which hath an husband is bound by the law to *her* husband so long as he liveth; but if the husband be dead, she is loosed from the law of *her* husband.

3 So then if, while *her* husband liveth, she be married to another man, she shall be called an adulteress: but if her husband be dead, she is free from that law; so that she is no adulteress, though she be married to another man.

4 Wherefore, my brethren, ye also are become dead to the law by the body of Christ; that ye should be married to another, *even* to him who is raised from the dead, that we should bring forth fruit unto God.

5 For when we were in the flesh, the motions of sins, which were by the law, did work in our members to bring forth fruit unto death.

6 But now we are delivered from the law, that being dead wherein we were held; that we should serve in newness of spirit,

7 Ἢ ἀγνοεῖτε, ἀδελφοί, γινώσκουσιν γὰρ
Or   are ye ignorant, brothers,   for to [ones] knowing

νόμον   λαλῶ,   ὅτι   ὁ   νόμος   κυριεύει   τοῦ
law   I speak, that the law   lords it over the

ἀνθρώπου   ἐφ’   ὅσον   χρόνον   ζῇ;   2 ἡ   γὰρ
man   over   such   time [as] he lives? For the

ὕπανδρος   γυνὴ   τῷ   ζῶντι   ἀνδρὶ   δέδεται
¹married   ¹woman to the living husband has
                                              been bound

νόμῳ·   ἐὰν   δὲ   ἀποθάνῃ   ὁ   ἀνήρ,   κατήργηται
by law; but if   dies   the husband, she has been
                                              discharged

ἀπὸ   τοῦ   νόμου   τοῦ   ἀνδρός.   3 ἄρα   οὖν
from   the   law   of the husband.   Therefore

ζῶντος   τοῦ   ἀνδρὸς   μοιχαλὶς   χρηματίσει
living   the   husband[a] an adulteress she will be called
= while the husband lives

ἐὰν   γένηται   ἀνδρὶ   ἑτέρῳ·   ἐὰν   δὲ   ἀποθάνῃ
if   she   ²husband ¹to a   but if   dies
      becomes   different;

ὁ   ἀνήρ,   ἐλευθέρα   ἐστὶν   ἀπὸ   τοῦ   νόμου,
the husband, free   she is from   the   law,

τοῦ   μὴ   εἶναι   αὐτὴν   μοιχαλίδα   γενομένην
 -   not   to be   her[d]   an adulteress having become
=so that she is not

ἀνδρὶ   ἑτέρῳ.   4 ὥστε,   ἀδελφοί   μου,   καὶ
²husband ¹to a   So,   brothers   of me,   also
          different.

ὑμεῖς   ἐθανατώθητε   τῷ   νόμῳ   διὰ   τοῦ
ye   were put to death to the law   through the

σώματος   τοῦ   Χριστοῦ,   εἰς   τὸ   γενέσθαι
body   -   of Christ,   for   the   to become
                                   =that ye might belong

ὑμᾶς   ἑτέρῳ,   τῷ   ἐκ   νεκρῶν   ἐγερθέντι,
you[b]   to a   to the from   dead   having been
        different, one] [the]   raised,

ἵνα   καρποφορήσωμεν   τῷ   θεῷ.   5 ὅτε
in order we may bear fruit   -   to God.   when
that

γὰρ   ἦμεν   ἐν   τῇ   σαρκί,   τὰ   παθήματα
For   we were in   the   flesh,   the   passions

τῶν   ἁμαρτιῶν   τὰ   διὰ   τοῦ   νόμου   ἐνηργεῖτο
 -   of sins   - through the   law   operated

ἐν   τοῖς   μέλεσιν   ἡμῶν   εἰς   τὸ   καρποφορῆσαι
in   the   members   of us   for   the   to bear fruit

τῷ   θανάτῳ·   6 νυνὶ   δὲ   κατηργήθημεν   ἀπὸ
 -   to death;   but now   we were discharged from

τοῦ   νόμου,   ἀποθανόντες   ἐν   ᾧ   κατειχόμεθα,
the   law,   having died [to that] in which we were held fast,

ὥστε   δουλεύειν   [ἡμᾶς]   ἐν   καινότητι
so as   to serve   us[b]   in   newness

and not *in* the oldness of the letter.

7 What shall we say then? *Is* the law sin? God forbid. Nay, I had not known sin, but by the law: for I had not known lust, except the law had said, Thou shall not covet.

8 But sin, taking occasion by the commandment, wrought in me all manner of concupiscence. For without the law sin *was* dead.

9 For I was alive without the law once: but when the commandment came, sin revived, and I died.

10 And the commandment, which *was ordained* to life, I found *to be* unto death.

11 For sin, taking occasion by the commandment, deceived me, and by it slew *me*.

12 Wherefore the law *is* holy, and the commandment holy, and just, and good.

13 Was then that which is good made death unto me? God forbid. But sin, that it might appear sin, working death in me by that which is good; that sin by the commandment might become exceeding sinful.

πνεύματος καὶ οὐ παλαιότητι γράμματος.
of spirit and not [in] oldness of letter.

7 Τί οὖν ἐροῦμεν; ὁ νόμος ἁμαρτία;
What therefore shall we say? the law sin?

μὴ γένοιτο· ἀλλὰ τὴν ἁμαρτίαν οὐκ
May it not be; yet – sin not

ἔγνων εἰ μὴ διὰ νόμου· τήν τε γὰρ
I knew except through law; – ²also ¹for

ἐπιθυμίαν οὐκ ᾔδειν εἰ μὴ ὁ νόμος
lust I knew not except the law

ἔλεγεν· οὐκ ἐπιθυμήσεις· 8 ἀφορμὴν δὲ
said : Thou shalt not lust; but ²occasion

λαβοῦσα ἡ ἁμαρτία διὰ τῆς ἐντολῆς
²taking – ¹sin through the commandment

κατειργάσατο ἐν ἐμοὶ πᾶσαν ἐπιθυμίαν·
wrought in me every lust;

χωρὶς γὰρ νόμου ἁμαρτία νεκρά. 9 ἐγὼ
for without law sin [is] dead. I

δὲ ἔζων χωρὶς νόμου ποτέ· ἐλθούσης δὲ
And was living without law then; but coming = when the

τῆς ἐντολῆς ἡ ἁμαρτία ἀνέζησεν, 10 ἐγὼ
the commandmentª – sin revived, ²I
commandment came

δὲ ἀπέθανον, καὶ εὑρέθη μοι ἡ ἐντολὴ
¹and died, and ⁶was ⁷to me ¹the ²command-
found ment

ἡ εἰς ζωήν, αὕτη εἰς θάνατον· 11 ἡ γὰρ
– ³for ⁴life, ⁵this to death; – for

ἁμαρτία ἀφορμὴν λαβοῦσα διὰ τῆς
sin ²occasion ¹taking through the

ἐντολῆς ἐξηπάτησέν με καὶ δι᾽ αὐτῆς
commandment deceived me and through it

ἀπέκτεινεν. 12 ὥστε ὁ μὲν νόμος ἅγιος,
killed [me]. So the – law [is] holy,

καὶ ἡ ἐντολὴ ἁγία καὶ δικαία καὶ ἀγαθή.
and the command- holy and just and good.
ment

13 Τὸ οὖν ἀγαθὸν ἐμοὶ ἐγένετο θάνατος;
²The ¹therefore good to me became death?

μὴ γένοιτο· ἀλλὰ ἡ ἁμαρτία, ἵνα φανῇ
May it not be; yet – sin, in or- it might
der that appear

ἁμαρτία, διὰ τοῦ ἀγαθοῦ μοι κατεργα-
sin, through the good ³to me ¹work-

ζομένη θάνατον, ἵνα γένηται καθ᾽ ὑπερβολὴν
ing ²death, in or- ⁵might ⁶excessively†
der that become

ἁμαρτωλὸς ἡ ἁμαρτία διὰ τῆς ἐντολῆς.
⁷sinful – ¹sin ²through ³the ⁴commandment.

14 For we know that the law is spiritual: but I am carnal, sold under sin.

15 For that which I do I allow not: for what I would, that do I not; but what I hate, that do I.

16 If then I do that which I would not, I consent unto the law that *it is* good.

17 Now then it is no more I that do it, but sin that dwelleth in me.

18 For I know that in me (that is, in my flesh,) dwelleth no good thing: for to will is present with me; but *how* to perform that which is good I find not.

19 For the good that I would I do not: but the evil which I would not, that I do.

20 Now if I do that I would not, it is no more I that do it, but sin that dwelleth in me.

21 I find then a law, that, when I would do good, evil is present with me.

22 For I delight in the law of God after the inward man:

23 But I see another law in my members, warring against the law of my mind, and bringing me into captivity to the law

14 οἴδαμεν γὰρ ὅτι ὁ νόμος πνευματικός
For we know that the law spiritual

ἐστιν· ἐγὼ δὲ σάρκινός εἰμι, πεπραμένος
is; but I fleshy am, *having been* sold

ὑπὸ τὴν ἁμαρτίαν. **15** ὃ γὰρ κατεργάζομαι
under – sin. For what I work

οὐ γινώσκω· οὐ γὰρ ὃ θέλω τοῦτο
I know not; for not what I wish this

πράσσω, ἀλλ᾽ ὃ μισῶ τοῦτο ποιῶ. **16** εἰ
I practise, but what I hate this I do. if

δὲ ὃ οὐ θέλω τοῦτο ποιῶ, σύμφημι
But what I wish not this I do, I agree with

τῷ νόμῳ ὅτι καλός. **17** νυνὶ δὲ οὐκέτι
the law that [it is] good. But now no longer

ἐγὼ κατεργάζομαι αὐτὸ ἀλλὰ ἡ ἐνοικοῦσα
I work it but [1]the [3]indwelling

ἐν ἐμοὶ ἁμαρτία. **18** οἶδα γὰρ ὅτι οὐκ
[1]in [5]me [2]sin. For I know that not

οἰκεῖ ἐν ἐμοί, τοῦτ᾽ ἔστιν ἐν τῇ σαρκί
dwells in me, this is in the flesh

μου, ἀγαθόν· τὸ γὰρ θέλειν παράκειταί
of me, [that which is] – for to wish is present
             good;

μοι, τὸ δὲ κατεργάζεσθαι τὸ καλὸν
to me, – but [2]to work [3]the [4]good

οὔ· **19** οὐ γὰρ ὃ θέλω ποιῶ ἀγαθόν,
[1]not; for not what [1]I wish [3]I do [1]good,

ἀλλὰ ὃ οὐ θέλω κακὸν τοῦτο πράσσω.
but what [2]I wish not [1]evil this I practise.

20 εἰ δὲ ὃ οὐ θέλω ἐγὼ τοῦτο ποιῶ,
But if what [2]wish not [1]I this I do,

οὐκέτι ἐγὼ κατεργάζομαι αὐτὸ ἀλλὰ ἡ
no longer I work it but [1]the

οἰκοῦσα ἐν ἐμοὶ ἁμαρτία. **21** εὑρίσκω
[3]dwelling [4]in [5]me [2]sin. I find

ἄρα τὸν νόμον τῷ θέλοντι ἐμοὶ ποιεῖν
then the law [2]the [one] [3]wishing [1]to me to do

τὸ καλόν, **22** ὅτι ἐμοὶ τὸ κακὸν παράκειται·
the good, that to me the evil is present;

συνήδομαι γὰρ τῷ νόμῳ τοῦ θεοῦ κατὰ
for I delight in the law – of God according to

τὸν ἔσω ἄνθρωπον, **23** βλέπω δὲ ἕτερον
the inner man, but I see a different

νόμον ἐν τοῖς μέλεσίν μου ἀντιστρατευόμενον
law in the members of me warring against

τῷ νόμῳ τοῦ νοός μου καὶ αἰχμαλωτίζοντά
the law of the mind of me and taking captive

of sin which is in my members.

24 O wretched man that I am! who shall deliver me from the body of this death?

25 I thank God through Jesus Christ our Lord. So then with the mind I myself serve the law of God; but with the flesh the law of sin.

CHAPTER 8

THERE is therefore now no condemnation to them which are in Christ Jesus, who walk not after the flesh, but after the Spirit.

2 For the law of the Spirit of life in Christ Jesus hath made me free from the law of sin and death.

3 For what the law could not do, in that it was weak through the flesh, God sending his own Son in the likeness of sinful flesh, and for sin, condemned sin in the flesh:

4 That the righteousness of the law might be fulfilled in us, who walk not after the flesh, but after the Spirit.

5 For they that are after the flesh do mind the things of the flesh; but they that are after the

---

με   ἐν   τῷ   νόμῳ   τῆς   ἁμαρτίας   τῷ   ὄντι
me   by   the   law   -   of sin   the [one] being

ἐν   τοῖς   μέλεσίν   μου.   24 Ταλαίπωρος
in   the   members   of me.   [1]Wretched

ἐγὼ   ἄνθρωπος·   τίς   με   ῥύσεται   ἐκ   τοῦ
[2]I   [3]man;   who   me   will deliver   from   the

σώματος   τοῦ   θανάτου   τούτου;   25 χάρις
body   of   death   of this death?   25 Thanks

τῷ   θεῷ   διὰ   'Ιησοῦ   Χριστοῦ   τοῦ   κυρίου
-     to God   through   Jesus   Christ   the   Lord

ἡμῶν.   Ἄρα   οὖν   αὐτὸς   ἐγὼ   τῷ   μὲν
of us.   So then   [3][my]self   [1]I   [4]with [5]on one
                                                the hand

νοῒ   δουλεύω   νόμῳ   θεοῦ,   τῇ   δὲ   σαρκὶ
[2]mind   serve   [the] law   of God,   on the other   flesh
                                            with the

νόμῳ   ἁμαρτίας.   8 οὐδὲν   ἄρα   νῦν   κατάκριμα
[the] law   of sin.   8 [4]No   [1]then   [3]now   [5]condemnation
                                    [2][there is]

τοῖς   ἐν   Χριστῷ   'Ιησοῦ.   2 ὁ   γὰρ   νόμος   τοῦ
to the   in   Christ   Jesus.   For   the   law   of the
[ones]

πνεύματος   τῆς   ζωῆς   ἐν   Χριστῷ   'Ιησοῦ
spirit   -   of life   in   Christ   Jesus

ἠλευθέρωσέν   σε   ἀπὸ   τοῦ   νόμου   τῆς
freed   thee   from   the   law   -

ἁμαρτίας   καὶ   τοῦ   θανάτου.   3 τὸ   γὰρ
of sin   and   -   of death.   3 For the

ἀδύνατον   τοῦ   νόμου,   ἐν   ᾧ   ἠσθένει   διὰ
impossible   of the   law,   in   which   it was   through
thing   weak

τῆς   σαρκός,   ὁ   θεὸς   τὸν   ἑαυτοῦ   υἱὸν
the   flesh,   -   [1]God   [3]the   [2]of himself   [4]Son

πέμψας   ἐν   ὁμοιώματι   σαρκὸς   ἁμαρτίας
[5]sending   in   likeness   of flesh   of sin

καὶ   περὶ   ἁμαρτίας   κατέκρινεν   τὴν   ἁμαρτίαν
and   concerning   sin   condemned   -   sin

ἐν   τῇ   σαρκί,   4 ἵνα   τὸ   δικαίωμα   τοῦ
in   the   flesh,   in order   the   ordinance   of the
                        that

νόμου   πληρωθῇ   ἐν   ἡμῖν   τοῖς   μὴ   κατὰ
law   may be   in   us   the   not   accord-
         fulfilled   [ones]   ing to

σάρκα   περιπατοῦσιν   ἀλλὰ   κατὰ   πνεῦμα.
flesh   walking   but   according to   spirit.

5 οἱ   γὰρ   κατὰ   σάρκα   ὄντες   τὰ   τῆς
For the [ones]   accord-   flesh   being   the   of the
                   ing to   things

σαρκὸς   φρονοῦσιν,   οἱ   δὲ   κατὰ   πνεῦμα
flesh   mind,   the   but   accord-   spirit
                        [ones]   ing to

Spirit the things of the Spirit.

6 For to be carnally minded *is* death; but to be spiritually minded *is* life and peace.

7 Because the carnal mind *is* enmity against God: for it is not subject to the law of God, neither indeed can be.

8 So then they that are in the flesh cannot please God.

9 But ye are not in the flesh, but in the Spirit, if so be that the Spirit of God dwell in you. Now if any man have not the Spirit of Christ, he is none of his.

10 And if Christ *be* in you, the body *is* dead because of sin; but the Spirit *is* life because of righteousness.

11 But if the Spirit of him that raised up Jesus from the dead dwell in you, he that raised up Christ from the dead shall also quicken your mortal bodies by his Spirit that dwelleth in you.

12 Therefore, brethren, we are debtors, not to the flesh, to live after the flesh.

13 For if ye live after the flesh, ye shall die: but

τὰ τοῦ πνεύματος. **6** τὸ γὰρ φρόνημα
the of the Spirit. For the mind
things

τῆς σαρκὸς θάνατος, τὸ δὲ φρόνημα
of the flesh [is] death, but the mind

τοῦ πνεύματος ζωὴ καὶ εἰρήνη. **7** διότι
of the Spirit life and peace. Wherefore

τὸ φρόνημα τῆς σαρκὸς ἔχθρα εἰς θεόν·
the mind of the flesh [is] enmity against God;

τῷ γὰρ νόμῳ τοῦ θεοῦ οὐχ ὑποτάσσεται,
for to the law - of God it is not subject,

οὐδὲ γὰρ δύναται· **8** οἱ δὲ ἐν σαρκὶ
neither indeed can it; and the [ones] ²in ³flesh

ὄντες θεῷ ἀρέσαι οὐ δύνανται. **9** ὑμεῖς
¹being ⁵God ⁴to please ⁴cannot. ye

δὲ οὐκ ἐστὲ ἐν σαρκὶ ἀλλὰ ἐν πνεύματι,
But are not in flesh but in Spirit,

εἴπερ πνεῦμα θεοῦ οἰκεῖ ἐν ὑμῖν. εἰ
since [the] Spirit of God dwells in you. if

δέ τις πνεῦμα Χριστοῦ οὐκ ἔχει, οὗτος
But anyone [the] Spirit of Christ has not, this one

οὐκ ἔστιν αὐτοῦ. **10** εἰ δὲ Χριστὸς
is not of him. But if Christ

ἐν ὑμῖν, τὸ μὲν σῶμα νεκρὸν διὰ
[is] in you, ²the ¹on one ³body [is] dead because
hand of

ἁμαρτίαν, τὸ δὲ πνεῦμα ζωὴ διὰ
sin, ²the ¹on the ²spirit [is] because
other life of

δικαιοσύνην. **11** εἰ δὲ τὸ πνεῦμα τοῦ
righteousness. But if the Spirit of the
[one]

ἐγείραντος τὸν Ἰησοῦν ἐκ νεκρῶν οἰκεῖ ἐν
having raised - Jesus from [the] dead dwells in

ὑμῖν, ὁ ἐγείρας ἐκ νεκρῶν Χριστὸν
you, the having from [the] dead Christ
[one] raised

Ἰησοῦν ζωοποιήσει καὶ τὰ θνητὰ σώματα
Jesus will quicken also the mortal bodies

ὑμῶν διὰ τοῦ ἐνοικοῦντος αὐτοῦ πνεύματος
of you through the ³indwelling ²of him ¹Spirit

ἐν ὑμῖν.
⁴in ⁵you.

12 Ἄρα οὖν, ἀδελφοί, ὀφειλέται ἐσμέν,
So then, brothers, debtors we are,

οὐ τῇ σαρκὶ τοῦ κατὰ σάρκα ζῆν. **13** εἰ
not to the flesh - accord- flesh to liveᵈ if
ing to

γὰρ κατὰ σάρκα ζῆτε, μέλλετε ἀποθνήσκειν·
For accord- flesh ye live, ye are to die:
ing to about

if ye through the Spirit do mortify the deeds of the body, ye shall live.

14 For as many as are led by the Spirit of God, they are the sons of God.

15 For ye have not received the spirit of bondage again to fear; but ye have received the Spirit of adoption, whereby we cry, Abba, Father.

16 The Spirit itself beareth witness with our spirit, that we are the children of God:

17 And if children, then heirs; heirs of God, and joint-heirs with Christ; if so be that we suffer with *him*, that we may be also glorified together.

18 For I reckon that the sufferings of this present time *are* not worthy *to be compared* with the glory which shall be revealed in us.

19 For the earnest expectation of the creature waiteth for the manifestation of the sons of God.

20 For the creature was made subject to vanity, not willingly, but by reason of him who hath subjected *the same* in hope,

21 Because the creature itself also shall be delivered from the bondage of corruption into the glorious liberty of the children of God.

22 For we know that the whole creation groan-

εἰ δὲ πνεύματι τὰς πράξεις τοῦ σώματος
but if by [the] Spirit the practices of the body

θανατοῦτε, ζήσεσθε. 14 ὅσοι γὰρ πνεύματι
ye put to death, ye will live. For as many as by [the] Spirit

θεοῦ ἄγονται, οὗτοι υἱοί εἰσιν θεοῦ.
of God are led, these sons are of God.

15 οὐ γὰρ ἐλάβετε πνεῦμα δουλείας πάλιν
For ye received not a spirit of slavery again

εἰς φόβον, ἀλλὰ ἐλάβετε πνεῦμα υἱοθεσίας,
for fear, but ye received a spirit of adoption,

ἐν ᾧ κράζομεν· ἀββὰ ὁ πατήρ. 16 αὐτὸ
by which we cry : Abba - Father. [3]it(him)self

τὸ πνεῦμα συμμαρτυρεῖ τῷ πνεύματι ἡμῶν
[1]The [2]Spirit witnesses with the spirit of us

ὅτι ἐσμὲν τέκνα θεοῦ. 17 εἰ δὲ τέκνα,
that we are children of God. And if children,

καὶ κληρονόμοι· κληρονόμοι μὲν θεοῦ,
also heirs; heirs on one hand of God,

συγκληρονόμοι δὲ Χριστοῦ, εἴπερ συμπάσ-
joint heirs on the of Christ, since we suffer
other

χομεν ἵνα καὶ συνδοξασθῶμεν. 18 Λογίζομαι
with[him] in or- also we may be glorified I reckon
der that with [him].

γὰρ ὅτι οὐκ ἄξια τὰ παθήματα τοῦ
For that [6][are] [7]not [8]worthy [1]the [2]sufferings [3]of the

νῦν καιροῦ πρὸς τὴν μέλλουσαν δόξαν
[4]now [5]time [to with the coming glory
(present) be compared]

ἀποκαλυφθῆναι εἰς ἡμᾶς. 19 ἡ γὰρ
to be revealed to us. For the

ἀποκαραδοκία τῆς κτίσεως τὴν ἀποκάλυψιν
anxious watching of the creation [2]the [3]revelation

τῶν υἱῶν τοῦ θεοῦ ἀπεκδέχεται. 20 τῇ
[4]of the [5]sons - [6]of God [1]is eagerly expecting.

γὰρ ματαιότητι ἡ κτίσις ὑπετάγη, οὐχ
For to vanity the creation was subjected, not

ἑκοῦσα, ἀλλὰ διὰ τὸν ὑποτάξαντα, ἐφ'
willing[ly], but because of the [one] subjecting, in

ἐλπίδι 21 διότι καὶ αὐτὴ ἡ κτίσις
hope because even itself the creation

ἐλευθερωθήσεται ἀπὸ τῆς δουλείας τῆς
will be freed from the slavery -

φθορᾶς εἰς τὴν ἐλευθερίαν τῆς δόξης
of corruption to the freedom of the glory

τῶν τέκνων τοῦ θεοῦ. 22 οἴδαμεν γὰρ
of the children - of God. For we know

ὅτι πᾶσα ἡ κτίσις συστενάζει καὶ
that all [the creation groans together and

eth and travaileth in pain together until now.

23 And not only *they*, but ourselves also, which have the firstfruits of the Spirit, even we ourselves groan within ourselves, waiting for the adoption, *to wit*, the redemption of our body.

24 For we are saved by hope: but hope that is seen is not hope: for what a man seeth, why doth he yet hope for?

25 But if we hope for that we see not, *then* do we with patience wait for *it*.

26 Likewise the Spirit also helpeth our infirmities: for we know not what we should pray for as we ought: but the Spirit itself maketh intercession for us with groanings which cannot be uttered.

27 And he that searcheth the hearts knoweth what *is* the mind of the Spirit, because he maketh intercession for the saints according to *the will of* God.

28 And we know that all things work together for good to them that love God, to them who are the called according to *his* purpose.

29 For whom he did foreknow, he also did predestinate *to be* conformed to the image of his Son, that he might be the firstborn among many brethren.

30 Moreover whom he did predestinate, them he

συνωδίνει ἄχρι τοῦ νῦν· **23** οὐ μόνον δέ,
travails together until – now; and not only [so],

ἀλλὰ καὶ αὐτοὶ τὴν ἀπαρχὴν τοῦ πνεύματος
but also [our]selves ²the ³firstfruit ⁴of the ⁵Spirit

ἔχοντες [ἡμεῖς] καὶ αὐτοὶ ἐν ἑαυτοῖς
¹having we also [our]selves in ourselves

στενάζομεν υἱοθεσίαν ἀπεκδεχόμενοι, τὴν
groan adoption eagerly expecting, the

ἀπολύτρωσιν τοῦ σώματος ἡμῶν. **24** τῇ
redemption of the body of us. –

γὰρ ἐλπίδι ἐσώθημεν· ἐλπὶς δὲ βλεπομένη
For by hope we were saved; but hope being seen

οὐκ ἔστιν ἐλπίς· ὃ γὰρ βλέπει τις,
is not hope; for what sees anyone,

τί καὶ ἐλπίζει; **25** εἰ δὲ ὃ οὐ βλέπομεν
why also he hopes? but if what we do not see

ἐλπίζομεν, δι᾽ ὑπομονῆς ἀπεκδεχόμεθα.
we hope [for], through patience we eagerly expect.

26 ὡσαύτως δὲ καὶ τὸ πνεῦμα συναντιλαμ-
And similarly also the Spirit takes

βάνεται τῇ ἀσθενείᾳ ἡμῶν· τὸ γὰρ τί
share in the weakness of us; – for what

προσευξώμεθα καθὸ δεῖ οὐκ οἴδαμεν, ἀλλὰ
we may pray as it behoves we know not, but

αὐτὸ τὸ πνεῦμα ὑπερεντυγχάνει στεναγμοῖς
it(him)self the Spirit supplicates on [our] behalf with groanings

ἀλαλήτοις· **27** ὁ δὲ ἐρευνῶν τὰς καρδίας
unutterable; and the [one] searching the hearts

οἶδεν τί τὸ φρόνημα τοῦ πνεύματος,
knows what [is] the mind of the Spirit,

ὅτι κατὰ θεὸν ἐντυγχάνει ὑπὲρ ἁγίων.
be- according God he supplicates on behalf saints.
cause to of

28 οἴδαμεν δὲ ὅτι τοῖς ἀγαπῶσιν τὸν
And we know that to the [ones] loving

θεὸν πάντα συνεργεῖ [ὁ θεὸς] εἰς ἀγαθόν,
God ³all things ²works together – ¹God for good.

τοῖς κατὰ πρόθεσιν κλητοῖς οὖσιν. **29** ὅτι
to the ²accord- ⁴purpose ²called ¹being. Because
[ones] ing to

οὓς προέγνω, καὶ προώρισεν συμμόρφους
whom he foreknew, also he foreordained conformed to

τῆς εἰκόνος τοῦ υἱοῦ αὐτοῦ, εἰς τὸ
of the image of the Son of him, for *the*
= that he should be

εἶναι αὐτὸν πρωτότοκον ἐν πολλοῖς
to be him[b] firstborn among many

ἀδελφοῖς· **30** οὓς δὲ προώρισεν, τούτους
brothers; but whom he foreordained, these

also called: and whom he called, them he also justified: and whom he justified, them he also glorified.

31 What shall we then say to these things? If God *be* for us, who *can be* against us?

32 He that spared not his own Son, but delivered him up for us all, how shall he not with him also freely give us all things?

33 Who shall lay any thing to the charge of God's elect? *It is* God that justifieth.

34 Who *is* he that condemneth? *It is* Christ that died, yea rather, that is risen again, who is even at the right hand of God, who also maketh intercession for us.

35 Who shall separate us from the love of Christ? *shall* tribulation, or distress, or persecution, or famine, or nakedness, or peril, or sword?

36 As it is written, For thy sake we are killed all the day long; we are accounted as sheep for the slaughter.

37 Nay, in all these things we are more than conquerors through him that loved us.

38 For I am persuaded, that neither death, nor life, nor angels, nor principalities, nor powers, nor things present, nor things to come,

39 Nor height, nor

καὶ ἐκάλεσεν· καὶ οὓς ἐκάλεσεν, τούτους
also   he called;   and whom   he called,   these

καὶ ἐδικαίωσεν· οὓς δὲ ἐδικαίωσεν, τούτους
also   he justified;   but whom   he justified,   these

καὶ ἐδόξασεν. 31 Τί οὖν ἐροῦμεν πρὸς
also   he glorified.   What therefore shall we say   to

ταῦτα; εἰ ὁ θεὸς ὑπὲρ ἡμῶν, τίς καθ᾽
these things? If – God on behalf of us,   who against

ἡμῶν; ὅς γε τοῦ ἰδίου υἱοῦ οὐκ ἐφείσατο,
us? Who indeed the(his) own   Son   spared not,

32 ἀλλὰ ὑπὲρ ἡμῶν πάντων παρέδωκεν
but   on behalf of us   all   delivered

αὐτόν, πῶς οὐχὶ καὶ σὺν αὐτῷ τὰ πάντα
him,   how   not   also   with   him   – all things

ἡμῖν χαρίσεται; 33 τίς ἐγκαλέσει κατὰ
to us   will he   Who   will bring a   against
       freely give?   charge *against*

ἐκλεκτῶν θεοῦ; θεὸς ὁ δικαιῶν· 34 τίς
chosen ones of God? God [is] the [one] justifying;   who

ὁ κατακρινῶν; Χριστὸς Ἰησοῦς ὁ ἀποθανών,
the condemning? Christ   Jesus [is] the   having died,
[one]   [one]

μᾶλλον δὲ ἐγερθείς, ὅς ἐστιν ἐν δεξιᾷ
but rather   having   who   is   at [the] right
             been raised,   [hand]

τοῦ θεοῦ, ὃς καὶ ἐντυγχάνει ὑπὲρ ἡμῶν.
– of God, who also   supplicates   on behalf of us.

35 τίς ἡμᾶς χωρίσει ἀπὸ τῆς ἀγάπης
Who   us   will separate   from   the   love

τοῦ Χριστοῦ; θλῖψις ἢ στενοχωρία ἢ
– of Christ? affliction   or   distress   or

διωγμὸς ἢ λιμὸς ἢ γυμνότης ἢ κίνδυνος
persecution or famine or nakedness or   peril

ἢ μάχαιρα; 36 καθὼς γέγραπται ὅτι ἕνεκεν
or sword?   As   it has been   – For the
                     written[,]   sake

σοῦ θανατούμεθα ὅλην τὴν ἡμέραν,
of thee we are being put to death all   the   day,

ἐλογίσθημεν ὡς πρόβατα σφαγῆς. 37 ἀλλ᾽
we were reckoned as sheep of(for) slaughter.   But

ἐν τούτοις πᾶσιν ὑπερνικῶμεν διὰ τοῦ
in   these things   all   we overconquer   through   the

ἀγαπήσαντος ἡμᾶς. 38 πέπεισμαι γὰρ
[one] having loved us.   For I have been persuaded

ὅτι οὔτε θάνατος οὔτε ζωὴ οὔτε ἄγγελοι
that not   death   nor   life   nor   angels

οὔτε ἀρχαὶ οὔτε ἐνεστῶτα οὔτε μέλλοντα
nor   rulers   nor   things present   nor   things coming

οὔτε δυνάμεις 39 οὔτε ὕψωμα οὔτε βάθος
nor   powers   nor   height   nor   depth

depth, nor any other creature, shall be able to separate us from the love of God, which is in Christ Jesus our Lord.

οὔτε   τις   κτίσις   ἑτέρα   δυνήσεται   ἡμᾶς
nor   any   creature   other   will be able   us

χωρίσαι   ἀπὸ   τῆς   ἀγάπης   τοῦ   θεοῦ   τῆς
to separate   from   the   love   –   of God   –

ἐν   Χριστῷ   Ἰησοῦ   τῷ   κυρίῳ   ἡμῶν.
in   Christ   Jesus   the   Lord   of us.

CHAPTER 9

I SAY the truth in Christ, I lie not, my conscience also bearing me witness in the Holy Ghost,

2 That I have great heaviness and continual sorrow in my heart.

3 For I could wish that myself were accursed from Christ for my brethren, my kinsmen according to the flesh:

4 Who are Israelites; to whom *pertaineth* the adoption, and the glory, and the covenants, and the giving of the law, and the service *of God*, and the promises;

5 Whose *are* the fathers, and of whom as concerning the flesh Christ *came*, who is over all, God blessed for ever. Amen.

6 Not as though the word of God hath taken none effect. For they *are* not all Israel, which are of Israel:

7 Neither, because they are the seed of Abraham, *are they* all children: but, In Isaac shall thy seed be called.

8 That is, They which are the children of the

9 Ἀλήθειαν   λέγω   ἐν   Χριστῷ,   οὐ
Truth   I say   in   Christ,   not

ψεύδομαι,   συμμαρτυρούσης   μοι   τῆς
I lie,   witnessing with   me   the

συνειδήσεώς   μου   ἐν   πνεύματι   ἁγίῳ,   2 ὅτι
conscienceª   of me   in   [the] Spirit   Holy,   that

λύπη   μοί   ἐστιν   μεγάλη   καὶ   ἀδιάλειπτος
grief   to me   is   great   and   incessant
= I have great grief and . . .

ὀδύνη   τῇ   καρδίᾳ   μου.   3 ηὐχόμην   γὰρ
painᶜ   in the   heart   of me.   For I was praying

ἀνάθεμα   εἶναι   αὐτὸς   ἐγὼ   ἀπὸ   τοῦ   Χριστοῦ
⁴a curse   ⁵to be   ¹[my]self   ¹I   from   –   Christ

ὑπὲρ   τῶν   ἀδελφῶν   μου   τῶν   συγγενῶν
on behalf of the   brothers   of me   the   kinsmen

μου   κατὰ   σάρκα,   4 οἵτινές   εἰσιν   Ἰσραη-
of me   according to flesh,   who   are   Israel-

λῖται,   ὧν   ἡ   υἱοθεσία   καὶ   ἡ   δόξα   καὶ
ites,   of whom the   adoption   and   the   glory   and

αἱ   διαθῆκαι   καὶ   ἡ   νομοθεσία   καὶ   ἡ
the   covenants   and   the   giving of [the] law   and   the

λατρεία   καὶ   αἱ   ἐπαγγελίαι,   5 ὧν   οἱ
service   and   the   promises,   of whom the

πατέρες,   καὶ   ἐξ   ὧν   ὁ   Χριστὸς   τὸ   κατὰ
fathers,   and   from whom   the   Christ   –   according to

σάρκα·   ὁ   ὢν   ἐπὶ   πάντων   θεὸς   εὐλογητὸς
flesh;   the [one] being over   all   God   blessed

εἰς   τοὺς   αἰῶνας,   ἀμήν.   6 Οὐχ   οἷον   δὲ
unto   the   ages,   amen.   Not   of course

ὅτι   ἐκπέπτωκεν   ὁ   λόγος   τοῦ   θεοῦ.   οὐ
that   has failed   the   word   –   of God.   not

γὰρ   πάντες   οἱ   ἐξ   Ἰσραήλ,   οὗτοι   Ἰσραήλ·
For   all   the [ones] of   Israel,   these [are of]   Israel;

7 οὐδ'   ὅτι   εἰσὶν   σπέρμα   Ἀβραάμ,   πάντες
neither because they are   seed   of   [are they]
Abraham,   all

τέκνα,   ἀλλ'·   ἐν   Ἰσαὰκ   κληθήσεταί   σοι
children,   but: In   Isaac   will be called   to thee

σπέρμα.   8 τοῦτ'   ἔστιν,   οὐ   τὰ   τέκνα   τῆς
seed.ᶜ   This   is,   not   the   children of the
= thy seed.

flesh, these *are* not the
children of God: but the
children of the promise
are counted for the seed.

9 For this *is* the word
of promise, At this time
will I come, and Sarah
shall have a son.

10 And not only *this*;
but when Rebecca also
had conceived by one,
even by our father Isaac;

11 (For *the children*
being not yet born, neither
having done any good or
evil, that the purpose of
God according to election
might stand, not of works,
but of him that calleth;)

12 It was said unto her,
The elder shall serve the
younger.

13 As it is written,
Jacob have I loved, but
Esau have I hated.

14 What shall we say
then ? *Is there* unrighteousness with God? God
forbid.

15 For he saith to
Moses, I will have mercy
on whom I will have
mercy, and I will have
compassion on whom I
will have compassion.

16 So then *it is* not of
him that willeth, nor of
him that runneth, but of
God that sheweth mercy.

17 For the scripture
saith unto Pharaoh, Even
for this same purpose
have I raised thee up,
that I might shew my

σαρκὸς ταῦτα τέκνα τοῦ θεοῦ, ἀλλὰ
flesh, these children of God, but

τὰ τέκνα τῆς ἐπαγγελίας λογίζεται εἰς
the children of the promise is(are) reckoned for

σπέρμα. 9 ἐπαγγελίας γὰρ ὁ λόγος οὗτος·
a seed. For ⁵of promise ³the ⁴word ¹this ²[is]:

κατὰ τὸν καιρὸν τοῦτον ἐλεύσομαι καὶ
According to this time I will come and

ἔσται τῇ Σάρρᾳ υἱός. 10 οὐ μόνον δέ,
will be – to Sara a son.ᶜ And not only [so],
=Sarah will have a son.

ἀλλὰ καὶ ʽΡεβεκκὰ ἐξ ἑνὸς κοίτην ἔχουσα,
but also Rebecca ²from ³one ¹conceiving,†

Ἰσαὰκ τοῦ πατρὸς ἡμῶν· 11 μήπω γὰρ
Isaac the father of us; for not yet

γεννηθέντων μηδὲ πραξάντων τι ἀγαθὸν
being bornᵃ nor practisingᵃ anything good

ἢ φαῦλον, ἵνα ἡ κατ' ἐκλογὴν πρόθεσις
or bad, in order ¹the ⁴accord- ⁵choice ²purpose
that ing to

τοῦ θεοῦ μένῃ, 12 οὐκ ἐξ ἔργων ἀλλ'
– ³of God might not of works but
remain,

ἐκ τοῦ καλοῦντος, ἐρρέθη αὐτῇ ὅτι ὁ
of the [one] calling, it was said to her[,] – The

μείζων δουλεύσει τῷ ἐλάσσονι· 13 καθάπερ
greater will serve the lesser; even as

γέγραπται· τὸν Ἰακὼβ ἠγάπησα, τὸν δὲ
it has been – Jacob I loved, – but
written:

Ἠσαῦ ἐμίσησα.
Esau I hated.

14 Τί οὖν ἐροῦμεν; μὴ ἀδικία παρὰ
What therefore shall we say? *not* unrighteousness with

τῷ θεῷ; μὴ γένοιτο. 15 τῷ Μωϋσεῖ
– God? May it not be. ²to Moses

γὰρ λέγει· ἐλεήσω ὃν ἂν ἐλεῶ, καὶ
¹For he says: I will whomever I have and
have mercy on mercy,

οἰκτιρήσω ὃν ἂν οἰκτίρω. 16 ἄρα οὖν
I will pity whomever I pity. So therefore
[it is]

οὐ τοῦ θέλοντος οὐδὲ τοῦ τρέχοντος,
not of the [one] wishing nor of the [one] running,

ἀλλὰ τοῦ ἐλεῶντος θεοῦ. 17 λέγει γὰρ
but of the [one] having mercy God. For says

ἡ γραφὴ τῷ Φαραὼ ὅτι εἰς αὐτὸ τοῦτο
the scripture – to Pharaoh[,] – For this very thing

ἐξήγειρά σε, ὅπως ἐνδείξωμαι ἐν σοὶ
I raised up thee, so as I may show forth in thee

power in thee, and that
my name might be de-
clared throughout all the
earth.

18 Therefore hath he
mercy on whom he will
have mercy, and whom he
will he hardeneth.

19 Thou wilt say then
unto me, Why doth he
yet find fault? For who
hath resisted his will?

20 Nay but, O man,
who art thou that repliest
against God? Shall the
thing formed say to him
that formed *it*, Why hast
thou made me thus?

21 Hath not the potter
power over the clay, of
the same lump to make one
vessel unto honour, and
another unto dishonour?

22 *What* if God, willing
to shew *his* wrath, and to
make his power known,
endured with much long-
suffering the vessels of
wrath fitted to destruc-
tion:

23 And that he might
make known the riches
of his glory on the vessels
of mercy, which he had
afore prepared unto glory,

24 Even us, whom he
hath called, not of the
Jews only, but also of the
Gentiles?

25 As he saith also in
Osee, I will call them my
people, which were not my
people; and her beloved,
which was not beloved.

26 And it shall come to
pass, *that* in the place

τὴν δύναμίν μου, καὶ ὅπως διαγγελῇ τὸ
the power of me, and so as might be pub- the
                                              lished abroad

ὄνομά μου ἐν πάσῃ τῇ γῇ. 18 ἄρα οὖν
name of me in all the earth. So therefore

ὃν θέλει ἐλεεῖ, ὃν δὲ θέλει σκληρύνει.
whom he he has but whom he wishes he hardens.
      wishes mercy,

19 Ἐρεῖς μοι οὖν· τί ἔτι μέμφεται;
Thou wilt say to me therefore: Why still finds he fault?

τῷ γὰρ βουλήματι αὐτοῦ τίς ἀνθέστηκεν;
for ²the ⁴counsel ⁵of him ¹who ⁶resisted?

20 ὦ ἄνθρωπε, μενοῦν γε σὺ τίς εἶ ὁ
O man, nay rather ⁵thou ¹who ⁶art the

ἀνταποκρινόμενος τῷ θεῷ; μὴ ἐρεῖ τὸ
[one] replying against – God? *not* ⁵Will say ¹the

πλάσμα τῷ πλάσαντι· τί με ἐποίησας
¹thing to the having formed: Why ²me ¹madest
formed [one]   thou

οὕτως; 21 ἢ οὐκ ἔχει ἐξουσίαν ὁ κεραμεὺς
thus? or has not ³authority ¹the ²potter

τοῦ πηλοῦ ἐκ τοῦ αὐτοῦ φυράματος
of the clay out of the same lump

ποιῆσαι ὃ μὲν εἰς τιμὴν σκεῦος, ὃ δὲ
to make ¹this ³to ⁴honour ²vessel, that

εἰς ἀτιμίαν; 22 εἰ δὲ θέλων ὁ θεὸς
to dishonour? But if wishing – God

ἐνδείξασθαι τὴν ὀργὴν καὶ γνωρίσαι τὸ
to show forth the(his) wrath and to make known

δυνατὸν αὐτοῦ ἤνεγκεν ἐν πολλῇ μακρο-
ability of him bore in much long-

θυμίᾳ σκεύη ὀργῆς κατηρτισμένα εἰς
suffering vessels of wrath *having been* fitted for

ἀπώλειαν, 23 καὶ ἵνα γνωρίσῃ τὸν πλοῦτον
destruction, and in or- he might the riches
                    der that make known

τῆς δόξης αὐτοῦ ἐπὶ σκεύη ἐλέους, ἃ
of the glory of him on vessels of mercy, which

προητοίμασεν εἰς δόξαν, 24 οὓς καὶ
he previously prepared for glory, whom also

ἐκάλεσεν ἡμᾶς οὐ μόνον ἐξ Ἰουδαίων
he called[,] us not only of Jews

ἀλλὰ καὶ ἐξ ἐθνῶν; 25 ὡς καὶ ἐν τῷ
but also of nations? As also in –

Ὡσηὲ λέγει· καλέσω τὸν οὐ λαόν μου
Osee he says: I will call the ²not ¹people of me

λαόν μου καὶ τὴν οὐκ ἠγαπημένην
a people of me and the not having been loved

ἠγαπημένην· 26 καὶ ἔσται ἐν τῷ τόπῳ
having been loved; and it shall be in the place

where it was said unto them, Ye *are* not my people; there shall they be called the children of the living God.

27 Esaias also crieth concerning Israel, Though the number of the children of Israel be as the sand of the sea, a remnant shall be saved:

28 For he will finish the work, and cut *it* short in righteousness: because a short work will the Lord make upon the earth.

29 And as Esaias said before, Except the Lord of Sabaoth had left us a seed, we had been as Sodoma, and been made like unto Gomorrha.

30 What shall we say then? That the Gentiles, which followed not after righteousness, have attained to righteousness, even the righteousness which is of faith.

31 But Israel, which followed after the law of righteousness, hath not attained to the law of righteousness.

32 Wherefore? Because *they sought it* not by faith, but as it were by the works of the law. For they stumbled at that stumblingstone;

33 As it is written, Behold, I lay in Sion a stumblingstone and rock of offence: and whosoever believeth on him shall not be ashamed.

οὗ ἐρρέθη [αὐτοῖς]· οὐ λαός μου ὑμεῖς,
where it was said to them: not a people of me ye [are],

ἐκεῖ κληθήσονται υἱοὶ θεοῦ ζῶντος.
there they will be called sons [2]God [1]of a living.

27 Ἡσαΐας δὲ κράζει ὑπὲρ τοῦ Ἰσραήλ·
But Esaias cries on behalf of - Israel:

ἐὰν ᾖ ὁ ἀριθμὸς τῶν υἱῶν Ἰσραήλ
If be the number of the sons of Israel

ὡς ἡ ἄμμος τῆς θαλάσσης, τὸ ὑπόλειμμα
as the sand of the sea, the remnant

σωθήσεται· **28** λόγον γὰρ συντελῶν καὶ
will be saved; for [2]an account [1]accomplishing [2]and

συντέμνων ποιήσει κύριος ἐπὶ τῆς γῆς.
[3]cutting short [5]will make [4][the] Lord on the earth.

29 καὶ καθὼς προείρηκεν Ἡσαΐας· εἰ μὴ
And as [2]has previously said [1]Esaias: Except

κύριος σαβαὼθ ἐγκατέλιπεν ἡμῖν σπέρμα,
[the] Lord of hosts left to us a seed,

ὡς Σόδομα ἂν ἐγενήθημεν καὶ ὡς Γόμορρα
as Sodom we would have become and as Gomorra

ἂν ὡμοιώθημεν.
we would have been likened.

30 Τί οὖν ἐροῦμεν; ὅτι ἔθνη τὰ μὴ
What therefore shall we say? that nations - not

διώκοντα δικαιοσύνην κατέλαβεν δικαιοσύνην,
pursuing righteousness apprehended righteousness,

δικαιοσύνην δὲ τὴν ἐκ πίστεως· **31** Ἰσραὴλ
but a righteousness - of faith; [1]Israel

δὲ διώκων νόμον δικαιοσύνης εἰς νόμον
[1]but pursuing a law of righteousness [2]to(at) [3]a law

οὐκ ἔφθασεν. **32** διὰ τί; ὅτι οὐκ ἐκ
[1]did not arrive. Why? Because not of

πίστεως ἀλλ' ὡς ἐξ ἔργων· προσέκοψαν
faith but as of works; they stumbled

τῷ λίθῳ τοῦ προσκόμματος, **33** καθὼς
at the stone - of stumbling, as

γέγραπται· ἰδοὺ τίθημι ἐν Σιὼν λίθον
it has been Behold I place in Sion a stone
written:

προσκόμματος καὶ πέτραν σκανδάλου, καὶ
of stumbling and a rock of offence, and

ὁ πιστεύων ἐπ' αὐτῷ οὐ καταισχυνθήσεται.
the [one] believing on him will not be put to shame.

CHAPTER 10

BRETHREN, my heart's desire and prayer to God for Israel is, that they might be saved.

2 For I bear them record that they have a zeal of God, but not according to knowledge.

3 For they being ignorant of God's righteousness, and going about to establish their own righteousness, have not submitted themselves unto the righteousness of God.

4 For Christ is the end of the law for righteousness to every one that believeth.

5 For Moses describeth the righteousness which is of the law, That the man which doeth those things shall live by them.

6 But the righteousness which is of faith speaketh on this wise, Say not in thine heart, Who shall ascend into heaven? (that is, to bring Christ down from above:)

7 Or, Who shall descend into the deep? (that is, to bring up Christ again from the dead.)

8 But what saith it? The word is nigh thee, even in thy mouth, and in thy heart: that is, the word of faith, which we preach;

9 That if thou shalt confess with thy mouth the Lord Jesus, and shalt believe in thine heart that God hath raised him

---

10 Ἀδελφοί, ἡ μὲν εὐδοκία τῆς ἐμῆς
Brothers, the - good pleasure - of my

καρδίας καὶ ἡ δέησις πρὸς τὸν θεὸν
heart and the request to - God

ὑπὲρ αὐτῶν εἰς σωτηρίαν. **2** μαρτυρῶ
on behalf of them [is] for salvation. I witness

γὰρ αὐτοῖς ὅτι ζῆλον θεοῦ ἔχουσιν, ἀλλ'
For to them that a zeal of God they have, but

οὐ κατ' ἐπίγνωσιν· **3** ἀγνοοῦντες γὰρ τὴν
not according to knowledge; for not knowing the

τοῦ θεοῦ δικαιοσύνην, καὶ τὴν ἰδίαν
- ²of God ¹righteousness, and the(ir) own

ζητοῦντες στῆσαι, τῇ δικαιοσύνῃ τοῦ θεοῦ
seeking to establish, to the righteousness - of God

οὐχ ὑπετάγησαν. **4** τέλος γὰρ νόμου
they did not submit. For end of law

Χριστὸς εἰς δικαιοσύνην παντὶ τῷ
Christ [is] for righteousness to everyone

πιστεύοντι. **5** Μωϋσῆς γὰρ γράφει ὅτι
believing. For Moses writes[,] -

τὴν δικαιοσύνην τὴν ἐκ νόμου ὁ ποιήσας
⁴the ⁵righteousness - ⁶of ⁷law ¹The ²doing

ἄνθρωπος ζήσεται ἐν αὐτῇ. **6** ἡ δὲ
³man will live by it. But the

ἐκ πίστεως δικαιοσύνη οὕτως λέγει· μὴ
²of ³faith ¹righteousness thus says: not

εἴπῃς ἐν τῇ καρδίᾳ σου· τίς ἀναβήσεται
Say in the heart of thee: Who will ascend

εἰς τὸν οὐρανόν; τοῦτ' ἔστιν Χριστὸν
into - heaven? this is Christ

καταγαγεῖν· **7** ἤ· τίς καταβήσεται εἰς
to bring down; or: Who will descend into

τὴν ἄβυσσον; τοῦτ' ἔστιν Χριστὸν ἐκ
the abyss? this is Christ from

νεκρῶν ἀναγαγεῖν. **8** ἀλλὰ τί λέγει;
[the] dead to bring up. But what says it?

ἐγγύς σου τὸ ῥῆμά ἐστιν, ἐν τῷ στόματί
Near thee the word is, in the mouth

σου καὶ ἐν τῇ καρδίᾳ σου· τοῦτ' ἔστιν
of thee and in the heart of thee; this is

τὸ ῥῆμα τῆς πίστεως ὃ κηρύσσομεν.
the word - of faith which we proclaim.

9 ὅτι ἐὰν ὁμολογήσῃς ἐν τῷ στόματί
Because if thou confessest with the mouth

σου κύριον Ἰησοῦν, καὶ πιστεύσῃς ἐν
of thee Lord Jesus, and believest in

τῇ καρδίᾳ σου ὅτι ὁ θεὸς αὐτὸν ἤγειρεν
the heart of thee that - God him raised

from the dead, thou shalt be saved.

10 For with the heart man believeth unto righteousness; and with the mouth confession is made unto salvation.

11 For the scripture saith, Whosoever believeth on him shall not be ashamed.

12 For there is no difference between the Jew and the Greek: for the same Lord over all is rich unto all that call upon him.

13 For whosoever shall call upon the name of the Lord shall be saved.

14 How then shall they call on him in whom they have not believed? and how shall they believe in him of whom they have not heard? and how shall they hear without a preacher?

15 And how shall they preach, except they be sent? as it is written, How beautiful are the feet of them that preach the gospel of peace, and bring glad tidings of good things!

16 But they have not all obeyed the gospel. For Esaias saith, Lord, who hath believed our report?

17 So then faith *cometh* by hearing, and hearing by the word of God.

18 But I say, Have they not heard? Yes verily, their sound went into all

---

ἐκ νεκρῶν, σωθήσῃ·
from [the] dead, thou wilt be saved;

10 καρδίᾳ γὰρ πιστεύεται εἰς δικαιοσύνην,
for with heart [one] believes to righteousness,

στόματι δὲ ὁμολογεῖται εἰς σωτηρίαν.
and with mouth [one] confesses to salvation.

11 λέγει γὰρ ἡ γραφή·
For says the scripture:

πᾶς ὁ πιστεύων ἐπ' αὐτῷ
Everyone believing on him

οὐ καταισχυνθήσεται.
will not be put to shame.

12 οὐ γάρ ἐστιν διαστολὴ Ἰουδαίου τε καὶ Ἕλληνος. ὁ
For there is no difference *of Jew* ¹both ²and ⁴of Greek.* the

γὰρ αὐτὸς κύριος πάντων, πλουτῶν εἰς
For same Lord of all, is rich to

πάντας τοὺς ἐπικαλουμένους αὐτόν·
all the [ones] calling on him;

13 πᾶς γὰρ ὃς ἂν ἐπικαλέσηται τὸ ὄνομα κυρίου
²everyone ¹for whoever calls on the name of [the] Lord

σωθήσεται.
will be saved.

14 Πῶς οὖν ἐπικαλέσωνται εἰς [one]
How therefore may they call on in

ὃν οὐκ ἐπίστευσαν; πῶς δὲ πιστεύσωσιν
whom they believed not? And how may they believe

οὗ οὐκ ἤκουσαν; πῶς δὲ ἀκούσωσιν
of whom they heard not? And how may they hear

χωρὶς κηρύσσοντος;
without [one] heralding?

15 πῶς δὲ κηρύξωσιν ἐὰν μὴ ἀποσταλῶσιν;
And how may they herald if they are not sent?

καθάπερ γέγραπται·
As it has been written:

ὡς ὡραῖοι οἱ πόδες τῶν εὐαγγελιζομένων
How beautiful the feet of the [ones] announcing *good*

ἀγαθά.
good things.

16 ἀλλ' οὐ πάντες ὑπήκουσαν τῷ εὐαγγελίῳ.
But not all obeyed the gospel.

Ἡσαΐας γὰρ λέγει· κύριε,
For Esaias says: Lord,

τίς ἐπίστευσεν τῇ ἀκοῇ ἡμῶν;
who believed the hearing of us?

17 ἄρα ἡ πίστις ἐξ ἀκοῆς, ἡ δὲ ἀκοὴ διὰ
Then — faith [is] from hearing, and the hearing through

ῥήματος Χριστοῦ.
a word of Christ.

18 ἀλλὰ λέγω, μὴ οὐκ ἤκουσαν;
But I say, *not* did they not hear?

μενοῦν γε· εἰς πᾶσαν
Nay rather: To all

τὴν γῆν ἐξῆλθεν ὁ φθόγγος αὐτῶν,
the earth went out the utterance of them,

---

* That is, between these two classes.

the earth, and their words unto the ends of the world.

19 But I say, Did not Israel know? First Moses saith, I will provoke you to jealousy by *them that are* no people, *and* by a foolish nation I will anger you.

20 But Esaias is very bold, and saith, I was found of them that sought me not; I was made manifest unto them that asked not after me.

21 But to Israel he saith, All day long I have stretched forth my hands unto a disobedient and gainsaying people.

καὶ εἰς τὰ πέρατα τῆς οἰκουμένης τὰ
and to the ends of the inhabited earth the

ῥήματα αὐτῶν. 19 ἀλλὰ λέγω, μὴ Ἰσραὴλ
words of them. But I say, not Israel

οὐκ ἔγνω; πρῶτος Μωϋσῆς λέγει· ἐγὼ
did not know? First Moses says : I

παραζηλώσω ὑμᾶς ἐπ’ οὐκ ἔθνει, ἐπ’
will provoke to you on(by) not a nation, on(by)
jealousy

ἔθνει ἀσυνέτῳ παροργιῶ ὑμᾶς. 20 Ἡσαΐας
a nation unintelligent I will anger you. Esaias

δὲ ἀποτολμᾷ καὶ λέγει· εὑρέθην τοῖς
But is quite bold and says : I was found by the
[ones]

ἐμὲ μὴ ζητοῦσιν, ἐμφανὴς ἐγενόμην τοῖς
²me ¹not ²seeking, manifest I became to the
[ones]

ἐμὲ μὴ ἐπερωτῶσιν. 21 πρὸς δὲ τὸν
³me ¹not ²inquiring [for]. But to –

Ἰσραὴλ λέγει· ὅλην τὴν ἡμέραν ἐξεπέτασα
Israel he says: All the day I stretched out

τὰς χεῖράς μου πρὸς λαὸν ἀπειθοῦντα
the hands of me to a people disobeying

καὶ ἀντιλέγοντα.
and contradicting.

CHAPTER 11

I SAY then, Hath God cast away his people? God forbid. For I also am an Israelite, of the seed of Abraham, *of* the tribe of Benjamin.

2 God hath not cast away his people which he foreknew. Wot ye not what the scripture saith of Elias? how he maketh intercession to God against Israel, saying,

3 Lord, they have killed thy prophets, and digged down thine altars; and I am left alone, and they seek my life.

4 But what saith the

11 Λέγω οὖν, μὴ ἀπώσατο ὁ θεὸς
I say therefore, ²did *not* put away – ¹God

τὸν λαὸν αὐτοῦ; μὴ γένοιτο· καὶ γὰρ
the people of him? May it not be; for even

ἐγὼ Ἰσραηλίτης εἰμί, ἐκ σπέρματος
I an Israelite am, of [the] seed

Ἀβραάμ, φυλῆς Βενιαμίν. 2 οὐκ ἀπώσατο
of Abraham, of [the] of Benjamin. did not put away
tribe

ὁ θεὸς τὸν λαὸν αὐτοῦ ὃν προέγνω.
– God the people of him whom he foreknew.

ἢ οὐκ οἴδατε ἐν Ἡλίᾳ τί λέγει ἡ
Or know ye not in Elias what says the

γραφή, ὡς ἐντυγχάνει τῷ θεῷ κατὰ τοῦ
scripture, how he supplicates – God against –

Ἰσραήλ; 3 κύριε, τοὺς προφήτας σου
Israel? Lord, the prophets of thee

ἀπέκτειναν, τὰ θυσιαστήριά σου κατέσκαψαν,
they killed, the altars of thee they dug down,

κἀγὼ ὑπελείφθην μόνος καὶ ζητοῦσιν τὴν
and I was left behind alone and they seek the

ψυχήν μου. 4 ἀλλὰ τί λέγει αὐτῷ ὁ
life of me. But what says to him the

answer of God unto him?
I have reserved to myself
seven thousand men, who
have not bowed the knee
to *the image of* Baal.

5 Even so then at this
present time also there is a
remnant according to the
election of grace.

6 And if by grace, then
is it no more of works:
otherwise grace is no more
grace. But if *it be* of works,
then is it no more grace:
otherwise work is no more
work.

7 What then? Israel
hath not obtained that
which he seeketh for, but
the election hath obtained
it, and the rest were
blinded

8 (According as it is
written, God hath given
them the spirit of slumber,
eyes that they should not
see, and ears that they
should not hear;) unto
this day.

9 And David saith, Let
their table be made a
snare, and a trap, and a
stumblingblock, and a re-
compence unto them:

10 Let their eyes be
darkened, that they may
not see, and bow down
their back alway.

11 I say then, Have
they stumbled that they
should fall? God forbid:
but *rather* through their
fall salvation *is come* unto
the Gentiles, for to pro-
voke them to jealousy.

12 Now if the fall of
them *be* the riches of the
world, and the diminish-
ing of them the riches

χρηματισμός; κατέλιπον ἐμαυτῷ ἑπτακισ-
[divine] response? I reserved to myself seven
χιλίους ἄνδρας, οἵτινες οὐκ ἔκαμψαν γόνυ
thousands men, who bowed not knee
τῇ Βάαλ. 5 οὕτως οὖν καὶ ἐν τῷ νῦν
– to Baal. So therefore also in the present
καιρῷ λεῖμμα κατ’ ἐκλογὴν χάριτος
time a remnant according to a choice of grace
γέγονεν· 6 εἰ δὲ χάριτι, οὐκέτι ἐξ ἔργων,
has become; and if by grace, no more of works,
ἐπεὶ ἡ χάρις οὐκέτι γίνεται χάρις. 7 Τί
since – grace no more becomes grace. What
οὖν; ὃ ἐπιζητεῖ Ἰσραήλ, τοῦτο οὐκ
there- What ²seeks after ¹Israel, this not
fore?
ἐπέτυχεν, ἡ δὲ ἐκλογὴ ἐπέτυχεν· οἱ δὲ
he obtained, but the choice obtained [it]; and the
λοιποὶ ἐπωρώθησαν, 8 καθάπερ γέγραπται·
rest were hardened, as it has been written:
ἔδωκεν αὐτοῖς ὁ θεὸς πνεῦμα κατανύξεως,
Gave to them – God a spirit of torpor,
ὀφθαλμοὺς τοῦ μὴ βλέπειν καὶ ὦτα
eyes – not to see[d] and ears
τοῦ μὴ ἀκούειν, ἕως τῆς σήμερον ἡμέρας·
– not to hear,[d] until the present[†] day.
9 καὶ Δαυὶδ λέγει· γενηθήτω ἡ τράπεζα
And David says: Let become the table
αὐτῶν εἰς παγίδα καὶ εἰς θήραν καὶ
of them for a snare and for a net and
εἰς σκάνδαλον καὶ εἰς ἀνταπόδομα αὐτοῖς,
for an offence and for a recompence to them,
10 σκοτισθήτωσαν οἱ ὀφθαλμοὶ αὐτῶν τοῦ
let be darkened the eyes of them –
μὴ βλέπειν, καὶ τὸν νῶτον αὐτῶν διὰ
not to see,[d] and the back of them al-
παντὸς σύγκαμψον.
ways bending.
11 Λέγω οὖν, μὴ ἔπταισαν ἵνα πέσωσιν;
I say therefore, did they *not* in order they might
stumble that fall?
μὴ γένοιτο· ἀλλὰ τῷ αὐτῶν παραπτώματι
May it not be; but by the ²of them ¹trespass
ἡ σωτηρία τοῖς ἔθνεσιν, εἰς τὸ παραζηλῶσαι
– salvation to the nations, *for the* to provoke to
[came] jealousy
αὐτούς. 12 εἰ δὲ τὸ παράπτωμα αὐτῶν
them. But if the trespass of them
πλοῦτος κόσμου καὶ τὸ ἥττημα αὐτῶν
[is] [the] of [the] and the defect of them
riches world

of the Gentiles; how much more their fulness?

13 For I speak to you Gentiles, inasmuch as I am the apostle of the Gentiles, I magnify mine office:

14 If by any means I may provoke to emulation *them which are* my flesh, and might save some of them.

15 For if the casting away of them *be* the reconciling of the world, what *shall* the receiving *of them be*, but life from the dead?

16 For if the firstfruit *be* holy, the lump *is* also *holy:* and if the root *be* holy, so *are* the branches.

17 And if some of the branches be broken off, and thou, being a wild olive tree, wert graffed in among them, and with them partakest of the root and fatness of the olive tree;

18 Boast not against the branches. But if thou boast, thou bearest not the root, but the root thee.

19 Thou wilt say then, The branches were broken off, that I might be graffed in.

20 Well; because of unbelief they were broken off, and thou standest by faith. Be not highminded, but fear:

21 For if God spared not the natural branches, *take heed* lest he also spare not thee.

πλοῦτος ἐθνῶν, πόσῳ μᾶλλον τὸ πλήρωμα
[is] [the] of [the] by how more the fulness
riches nations, much

αὐτῶν. 13 Ὑμῖν δὲ λέγω τοῖς ἔθνεσιν.
of them. But to you ³I say[,] ¹the ²nations.

ἐφ' ὅσον μὲν οὖν εἰμι ἐγὼ ἐθνῶν ἀπόστο-
Forasmuch in- there- ²am ¹I ⁴of ³an apos-
as deed fore nations

λος, τὴν διακονίαν μου δοξάζω, 14 εἴ πως
tle, the ministry of me I glorify, if somehow

παραζηλώσω μου τὴν σάρκα καὶ σώσω
I may provoke to of me the flesh and may save
jealousy

τινὰς ἐξ αὐτῶν. 15 εἰ γὰρ ἡ ἀποβολὴ
some of them. For if the casting away

αὐτῶν καταλλαγὴ κόσμου, τίς ἡ πρόσλημψις
of them [is] [the] of [the] what the reception
reconciliation world,

εἰ μὴ ζωὴ ἐκ νεκρῶν; 16 εἰ δὲ ἡ
if not life from [the] dead? And if the

ἀπαρχὴ ἁγία, καὶ τὸ φύραμα· καὶ εἰ
firstfruit [is] holy, also the lump; and if

ἡ ῥίζα ἁγία, καὶ οἱ κλάδοι. 17 Εἰ δέ
the root [is] holy, also the branches. But if

τινες τῶν κλάδων ἐξεκλάσθησαν, σὺ δὲ
some of the branches were broken off, and thou

ἀγριέλαιος ὢν ἐνεκεντρίσθης ἐν αὐτοῖς
²a wild olive ¹being wast grafted in among them

καὶ συγκοινωνὸς τῆς ῥίζης τῆς πιότητος
and ²a partaker ³of the ⁴root* ⁵of the ⁶fatness

τῆς ἐλαίας ἐγένου, 18 μὴ κατακαυχῶ
⁷of the ⁸olive-tree ¹didst become, boast not against

τῶν κλάδων· εἰ δὲ κατακαυχᾶσαι, οὐ
of the branches; but if thou boastest, not

σὺ τὴν ῥίζαν βαστάζεις ἀλλὰ ἡ ῥίζα σέ.
thou the root bearest but the root thee.

19 ἐρεῖς οὖν· ἐξεκλάσθησαν κλάδοι ἵνα
Thou wilt therefore: ²Were broken off ¹branches in order
say that

ἐγὼ ἐγκεντρισθῶ. 20 καλῶς· τῇ ἀπιστίᾳ
I might be grafted in. Well: – for unbelief

ἐξεκλάσθησαν, σὺ δὲ τῇ πίστει ἕστηκας.
they were broken off, and thou – by faith standest.

μὴ ὑψηλὰ φρόνει, ἀλλὰ φοβοῦ· 21 εἰ
²Not ³high things ¹mind, but fear; ²if

γὰρ ὁ θεὸς τῶν κατὰ φύσιν κλάδων
¹for – ³God ⁵the ⁷according to ⁸nature ⁶branches

οὐκ ἐφείσατο, οὐδὲ σοῦ φείσεται. 22 ἴδε
¹spared not, neither thee will he spare. See

---

* Some MSS insert καί (and) here; as it is, the two nouns in the genitive must be in apposition; *cf.* Col. 1. 18, 2. 2; John 8. 44.

22 Behold therefore the goodness and severity of God: on them which fell, severity; but toward thee, goodness, if thou continue in *his* goodness: otherwise thou also shalt be cut off.

23 And they also, if they abide not still in unbelief, shall be graffed in: for God is able to graff them in again.

24 For if thou wert cut out of the olive tree which is wild by nature, and wert graffed contrary to nature into a good olive tree: how much more shall these, which be the natural *branches*, be graffed into their own olive tree?

25 For I would not, brethren, that ye should be ignorant of this mystery, lest ye should be wise in your own conceits; that blindness in part is happened to Israel, until the fulness of the Gentiles be come in.

26 And so all Israel shall be saved: as it is written, There shall come out of Sion the Deliverer, and shall turn away ungodliness from Jacob:

27 For this *is* my covenant unto them, when I shall take away their sins.

28 As concerning the gospel, *they are* enemies

οὖν χρηστότητα καὶ ἀποτομίαν θεοῦ· ἐπὶ
therefore [the] kindness and [the] severity of God: ²on

μὲν τοὺς πεσόντας ἀποτομία, ἐπὶ δὲ
¹on one the having fallen severity, ²on ¹on the
hand [ones] other

σὲ χρηστότης θεοῦ, ἐὰν ἐπιμένῃς τῇ
thee [the] kindness of God, if thou continuest in the
(his)

χρηστότητι, ἐπεὶ καὶ σὺ ἐκκοπήσῃ.
kindness, since also thou wilt be cut off.

23 κἀκεῖνοι δέ, ἐὰν μὴ ἐπιμένωσιν τῇ
And those also, if they continue not –

ἀπιστίᾳ, ἐγκεντρισθήσονται· δυνατὸς γάρ
in unbelief, will be grafted in; for ²able

ἐστιν ὁ θεὸς πάλιν ἐγκεντρίσαι αὐτούς.
²is – ¹God ²again ⁴to graft ³in ⁵them.

24 εἰ γὰρ σὺ ἐκ τῆς κατὰ φύσιν ἐξεκόπης
For if thou ²out ³the ⁵according ⁶nature ¹wast cut
of to out

ἀγριελαίου καὶ παρὰ φύσιν ἐνεκεντρίσθης
⁴wild olive and against nature wast grafted *in*

εἰς καλλιέλαιον, πόσῳ μᾶλλον οὗτοι οἱ
into a cultivated by how more these the
olive, much [ones]

κατὰ φύσιν ἐγκεντρισθήσονται τῇ ἰδίᾳ
according to nature will be grafted in the(ir) own

ἐλαίᾳ. 25 Οὐ γὰρ θέλω ὑμᾶς ἀγνοεῖν,
olive-tree. For I wish not you to be ignorant,

ἀδελφοί, τὸ μυστήριον τοῦτο, ἵνα μὴ
brothers, [of] this mystery, lest

ἦτε ἐν ἑαυτοῖς φρόνιμοι, ὅτι πώρωσις
ye be in yourselves wise, that hardness

ἀπὸ μέρους τῷ Ἰσραὴλ γέγονεν ἄχρι οὗ
from(in) part – to Israel has happened until

τὸ πλήρωμα τῶν ἐθνῶν εἰσέλθῃ, 26 καὶ
the fulness of the nations comes in, and

οὕτως πᾶς Ἰσραὴλ σωθήσεται, καθὼς
so all Israel will be saved, as

γέγραπται· ἥξει ἐκ Σιὼν ὁ ῥυόμενος,
it has been ²will ⁴out ⁵Sion ¹The ²delivering,
written: come of [one]

ἀποστρέψει ἀσεβείας ἀπὸ Ἰακώβ. 27 καὶ
he will turn away impiety from Jacob. And

αὕτη αὐτοῖς ἡ παρ᾽ ἐμοῦ διαθήκη, ὅταν
this [is] ⁶with them ¹the ³from ⁴me ²covenant, when

ἀφέλωμαι τὰς ἁμαρτίας αὐτῶν. 28 κατὰ
I take away the sins of them. ²According to

μὲν τὸ εὐαγγέλιον ἐχθροὶ δι᾽ ὑμᾶς,
¹on one the gospel enemies because you,
hand of

for your sakes: but as touching the election, *they are* beloved for the fathers' sakes.

29 For the gifts and calling of God *are* without repentance.

30 For as ye in times past have not believed God, yet have now obtained mercy through their unbelief:

31 Even so have these also now not believed, that through your mercy they also may obtain mercy.

32 For God hath concluded them all in unbelief, that he might have mercy upon all.

33 O the depth of the riches both of the wisdom and knowledge of God! how unsearchable *are* his judgments, and his ways past finding out!

34 For who hath known the mind of the Lord? or who hath been his counsellor?

35 Or who hath first given to him, and it shall be recompensed unto him again?

36 For of him, and through him, and to him, *are* all things: to whom *be* glory for ever. Amen.

κατὰ δὲ τὴν ἐκλογὴν ἀγαπητοὶ διὰ
²accord- ¹on the the choice beloved because
ing to other of

τοὺς πατέρας· 29 ἀμεταμέλητα γὰρ τὰ
the fathers; for unrepented the

χαρίσματα καὶ ἡ κλῆσις τοῦ θεοῦ.
free gifts and the calling – of God.

30 ὥσπερ γὰρ ὑμεῖς ποτε ἠπειθήσατε
For as ye then disobeyed

τῷ θεῷ, νῦν δὲ ἠλεήθητε τῇ τούτων
– God, but now ye obtained mercy ¹by the ³of these

ἀπειθείᾳ, 31 οὕτως καὶ οὗτοι νῦν ἠπείθησαν
²disobedience, so also these now disobeyed

τῷ ὑμετέρῳ ἐλέει ἵνα καὶ αὐτοὶ νῦν
– ²by your ³mercy ¹in order also they now
that

ἐλεηθῶσιν. 32 συνέκλεισεν γὰρ ὁ θεὸς
may obtain mercy. For ²shut up – ¹God

τοὺς πάντας εἰς ἀπείθειαν ἵνα τοὺς
– all in disobedience in order that –

πάντας ἐλεήσῃ.
to all he may show mercy.

33 Ὦ βάθος πλούτου καὶ σοφίας καὶ
O [the] depth of [the] riches and of [the] wisdom and

γνώσεως θεοῦ· ὡς ἀνεξερεύνητα τὰ κρίματα
of [the] of God; how inscrutable the judgments
knowledge

αὐτοῦ καὶ ἀνεξιχνίαστοι αἱ ὁδοὶ αὐτοῦ.
of him and unsearchable the ways of him.

34 τίς γὰρ ἔγνω νοῦν κυρίου; ἢ τίς
For who knew [the] mind of [the] Lord? or who

σύμβουλος αὐτοῦ ἐγένετο; 35 ἢ τίς
counsellor of him became? or who

προέδωκεν αὐτῷ, καὶ ἀνταποδοθήσεται
previously gave to him, and it will be repaid

αὐτῷ; 36 ὅτι ἐξ αὐτοῦ καὶ δι᾽ αὐτοῦ
to him? Because of him and through him

καὶ εἰς αὐτὸν τὰ πάντα· αὐτῷ ἡ δόξα
and to him – all things; to him the glory

εἰς τοὺς αἰῶνας· ἀμήν.
unto the ages: Amen.

CHAPTER 12

I BESEECH you therefore, brethren, by the mercies of God, that ye present your bodies a living sacrifice, holy, ac-

12 Παρακαλῶ οὖν ὑμᾶς, ἀδελφοί, διὰ
I beseech therefore you, brothers, through

τῶν οἰκτιρμῶν τοῦ θεοῦ, παραστῆσαι τὰ
the compassions – of God, to present the

σώματα ὑμῶν θυσίαν ζῶσαν ἁγίαν τῷ
bodies of you sacrifice a living holy –

ceptable unto God, *which is* your reasonable service.

2 And be not conformed to this world: but be ye transformed by the renewing of your mind, that ye may prove what *is* that good, and acceptable, and perfect, will of God.

3 For I say, through the grace given unto me, to every man that is among you, not to think *of himself* more highly than he ought to think; but to think soberly, according as God hath dealt to every man the measure of faith.

4 For as we have many members in one body, and all members have not the same office:

5 So we, *being* many, are one body in Christ, and every one members one of another.

6 Having then gifts differing according to the grace that is given to us, whether prophecy, *let us prophesy* according to the proportion of faith;

7 Or ministry, *let us wait* on *our* ministering: or he that teacheth, on teaching;

8 Or he that exhorteth, on exhortation: he that giveth, *let him do it* with simplicity; he that ruleth,

θεῷ　εὐάρεστον,　τὴν　λογικὴν　λατρείαν
²to God ¹well-pleasing,　the　reasonable　service

ὑμῶν·　2 καὶ　μὴ　συσχηματίζεσθε　τῷ　αἰῶνι
of you;　　and　be ye not conformed　-　age

τούτῳ,　ἀλλὰ　μεταμορφοῦσθε　τῇ　ἀνακαινώσει
to this,　but　be ye transformed　by the　renewing

τοῦ　νοός,　εἰς　τὸ　δοκιμάζειν　ὑμᾶς　τί　τὸ
of the mind,　for　the　to prove　you[b]　what　the
　　　　　　　　　　=so that ye may prove

θέλημα　τοῦ　θεοῦ,　τὸ　ἀγαθὸν　καὶ　εὐάρεστον
will　-　of God,　the　good　and　well-pleasing

καὶ　τέλειον.
and　perfect.

3 Λέγω　γὰρ　διὰ　τῆς　χάριτος　τῆς
For I say　through　the　grace　-

δοθείσης　μοι　παντὶ　τῷ　ὄντι　ἐν　ὑμῖν,
given　to me　to everyone　being　among　you,

μὴ　ὑπερφρονεῖν　παρ'　ὃ　δεῖ　φρονεῖν,
not　to have high　beyond　what　it　to think,
　　thoughts　　　　　behoves

ἀλλὰ　φρονεῖν　εἰς　τὸ　σωφρονεῖν,　ἑκάστῳ
but　to think　to　the to be sober-minded, ⁴to each

ὡς　ὁ　θεὸς　ἐμέρισεν　μέτρον　πίστεως.
¹as　-　²God　³divided　a measure　of faith.

4 καθάπερ　γὰρ　ἐν　ἑνὶ　σώματι　πολλὰ
For as　in　one　body　many

μέλη　ἔχομεν,　τὰ　δὲ　μέλη　πάντα　οὐ　τὴν
members we have, but ²the ³members ¹all ⁵not ⁶the

αὐτὴν　ἔχει　πρᾶξιν,　5 οὕτως　οἱ　πολλοὶ
⁷same　⁴has(ve)　⁸action,　so　the　many

ἓν　σῶμά　ἐσμεν　ἐν　Χριστῷ,　τὸ　δὲ　καθ'
one　body　we are　in　Christ,　-　and　each

εἷς　ἀλλήλων　μέλη.　6 ἔχοντες　δὲ　χαρίσματα
one　²of one ¹members.　And having　gifts
　　another

κατὰ　τὴν　χάριν　τὴν　δοθεῖσαν　ἡμῖν　διάφορα,
²accord- ³the ⁴grace　-　⁵given　⁶to us　¹differing,
ing to

εἴτε　προφητείαν,　κατὰ　τὴν　ἀναλογίαν　τῆς
whether　prophecy,　according to the　proportion　of the

πίστεως·　7 εἴτε　διακονίαν,　ἐν　τῇ　διακονίᾳ·
faith;　　or　ministry,　in　the　ministry;

εἴτε　ὁ　διδάσκων,　ἐν　τῇ　διδασκαλίᾳ·
or　the [one]　teaching,　in　the　teaching;

8 εἴτε　ὁ　παρακαλῶν,　ἐν　τῇ　παρακλήσει·
or　the [one]　exhorting,　in　the　exhortation;

ὁ　μεταδιδοὺς　ἐν　ἁπλότητι,　ὁ　προϊστάμενος
the [one] sharing　in　simplicity,　the [one] taking the lead

with diligence; he that sheweth mercy, with cheerfulness.

9 *Let* love be without dissimulation. Abhor that which is evil; cleave to that which is good.

10 *Be* kindly affectioned one to another with brotherly love; in honour preferring one another;

11 Not slothful in business; fervent in spirit; serving the Lord;

12 Rejoicing in hope; patient in tribulation; continuing instant in prayer;

13 Distributing to the necessity of saints; given to hospitality.

14 Bless them which persecute you: bless, and curse not.

15 Rejoice with them that do rejoice, and weep with them that weep.

16 *Be* of the same mind one toward another. Mind not high things, but condescend to men of low estate. Be not wise in your own conceits.

17 Recompense to no man evil for evil. Provide things honest in the sight of all men.

18 If it be possible, as much as lieth in you, live peaceably with all men.

19 D e a r l y b e l o v e d, avenge not yourselves, but *rather* give place unto wrath: for it is written, Vengeance *is* mine; I will repay, saith the Lord.

ἐν σπουδῇ, ὁ ἐλεῶν ἐν ἱλαρότητι. **9** ἡ
in diligence, the showing in cheerfulness. –
[one] mercy

ἀγάπη ἀνυπόκριτος. ἀποστυγοῦντες τὸ
[Let] love [be] unassumed. Shrinking from the

πονηρόν, κολλώμενοι τῷ ἀγαθῷ· **10** τῇ
evil, cleaving to the good; –

φιλαδελφίᾳ εἰς ἀλλήλους φιλόστοργοι, τῇ
in brotherly love to one another loving warmly, –

τιμῇ ἀλλήλους προηγούμενοι, **11** τῇ σπουδῇ
in one another preferring, – in zeal
honour

μὴ ὀκνηροί, τῷ πνεύματι ζέοντες, τῷ
not slothful, – in spirit burning, the

κυρίῳ δουλεύοντες, **12** τῇ ἐλπίδι χαίροντες,
Lord serving, – in hope rejoicing,

τῇ θλίψει ὑπομένοντες, τῇ προσευχῇ
– in affliction showing endurance, – in prayer

προσκαρτεροῦντες, **13** ταῖς χρείαις τῶν
steadfastly continuing, to the needs of the

ἁγίων κοινωνοῦντες, τὴν φιλοξενίαν
saints imparting, – hospitality

διώκοντες. **14** εὐλογεῖτε τοὺς διώκοντας,
pursuing. Bless ye the [ones] persecuting,

εὐλογεῖτε καὶ μὴ καταρᾶσθε. **15** χαίρειν
bless and do not curse. To rejoice

μετὰ χαιρόντων, κλαίειν μετὰ κλαιόντων.
with rejoicing [ones], to weep with weeping [ones].

16 τὸ αὐτὸ εἰς ἀλλήλους φρονοῦντες· μὴ
The same thing toward one another minding; not

τὰ ὑψηλὰ φρονοῦντες ἀλλὰ τοῖς ταπεινοῖς
²the ³high things ¹minding but to the humble

συναπαγόμενοι. μὴ γίνεσθε φρόνιμοι παρ᾽
condescending. Become not wise with

ἑαυτοῖς. **17** μηδενὶ κακὸν ἀντὶ κακοῦ
yourselves. To no one evil instead of evil

ἀποδιδόντες· προνοούμενοι καλὰ ἐνώπιον
returning; providing for good things before

πάντων ἀνθρώπων· **18** εἰ δυνατόν, τὸ ἐξ
all men; if possible, as far as it

ὑμῶν, μετὰ πάντων ἀνθρώπων εἰρηνεύοντες·
rests with with all men seeking peace;
you,†

19 μὴ ἑαυτοὺς ἐκδικοῦντες, ἀγαπητοί, ἀλλὰ
not ²yourselves ¹avenging, beloved, but

δότε τόπον τῇ ὀργῇ· γέγραπται γάρ·
give place – to wrath; for it has been written:

ἐμοὶ ἐκδίκησις, ἐγὼ ἀνταποδώσω, λέγει
To me vengeance,ᵉ I will repay, says
=Vengeance is mine,

20 Therefore if thine enemy hunger, feed him; if he thirst, give him drink: for in so doing thou shalt heap coals of fire on his head.

21 Be not overcome of evil, but overcome evil with good.

CHAPTER 13

LET every soul be subject unto the higher powers. For there is no power but of God: the powers that be are ordained of God.

2 Whosoever therefore resisteth the power, resisteth the ordinance of God: and they that resist shall receive to themselves damnation.

3 For rulers are not a terror to good works, but to the evil. Wilt thou then not be afraid of the power? do that which is good, and thou shalt have praise of the same:

4 For he is the minister of God to thee for good. But if thou do that which is evil, be afraid; for he beareth not the sword in vain: for he is the minister of God, a revenger to *execute* wrath upon him that doeth evil.

5 Wherefore *ye* must needs be subject, not only for wrath, but also for conscience sake.

κύριος. **20** ἀλλὰ ἐὰν πεινᾷ ὁ ἐχθρός
[the] Lord.　　　But　　if　hungers　the　enemy

σου, ψώμιζε αὐτόν· ἐὰν διψᾷ, πότιζε
of thee,　feed　　him;　　if　he thirsts, give ²drink

αὐτόν· τοῦτο γὰρ ποιῶν ἄνθρακας πυρὸς
¹him;　　for this　　doing　　coals　　of fire

σωρεύσεις ἐπὶ τὴν κεφαλὴν αὐτοῦ. **21** μὴ
thou wilt heap on　the　　head　　of him.　　not

νικῶ ὑπὸ τοῦ κακοῦ, ἀλλὰ νίκα
Be conquered by　the　　evil,　　but　conquer

ἐν τῷ ἀγαθῷ τὸ κακόν. **13** Πᾶσα
²by　⁴the　⁵good　¹the　²evil.　　³Every

ψυχὴ ἐξουσίαις ὑπερεχούσαις ὑποτασσέσθω.
³soul　⁷authorities　⁸to superior　¹let ⁴be ⁶subject.

οὐ γὰρ ἔστιν ἐξουσία εἰ μὴ
For there is no　　　authority　　except

ὑπὸ θεοῦ, αἱ δὲ οὖσαι ὑπὸ θεοῦ
by　God,　and the　existing [ones] by　　God

τεταγμέναι εἰσίν. **2** ὥστε ὁ ἀντιτασσόμενος
having been　are.　　So　the [one] resisting
ordained

τῇ ἐξουσίᾳ τῇ τοῦ θεοῦ διαταγῇ ἀνθέστη-
the authority ²the　－　⁴of God ³ordinance　¹has op-

κεν· οἱ δὲ ἀνθεστηκότες ἑαυτοῖς κρίμα
posed; and the [ones]　having opposed　to themselves judgment

λήμψονται. **3** οἱ γὰρ ἄρχοντες οὐκ εἰσὶν
will receive.　For the　　rulers　　are not

φόβος τῷ ἀγαθῷ ἔργῳ ἀλλὰ τῷ κακῷ.
a fear　to the　good　work　but　to the　evil.

θέλεις δὲ μὴ φοβεῖσθαι τὴν ἐξουσίαν;
And wishest thou　not　to fear　　the　authority?

τὸ ἀγαθὸν ποίει, καὶ ἕξεις ἔπαινον ἐξ
²the　³good　¹do,　and　thou wilt　praise　from
　　　　　　　　　　　　have

αὐτῆς· **4** θεοῦ γὰρ διάκονός ἐστιν σοὶ
it;　　for of God　a minister　he is　to thee

εἰς τὸ ἀγαθόν. ἐὰν δὲ τὸ κακὸν ποιῇς,
for the　good.　But if　the　evil thou doest,

φοβοῦ· οὐ γὰρ εἰκῇ τὴν μάχαιραν φορεῖ·
fear;　for not　in vain　the　sword　he bears;

θεοῦ γὰρ διάκονός ἐστιν ἔκδικος εἰς
for of God　a minister　he is　an avenger　for

ὀργὴν τῷ τὸ κακὸν πράσσοντι. **5** διὸ
wrath　to the [one] ²the　²evil　¹practising.　Wherefore

ἀνάγκη ὑποτάσσεσθαι, οὐ μόνον διὰ τὴν
it is necessary　to be subject,　not　only　because of －

ὀργὴν ἀλλὰ καὶ διὰ τὴν συνείδησιν.
wrath　but　also because of　－　conscience.

6 For for this cause pay ye tribute also: for they are God's ministers, attending continually upon this very thing.

7 Render therefore to all their dues: tribute to whom tribute *is due;* custom to whom custom; fear to whom fear; honour to whom honour.

8 Owe no man any thing, but to love one another: for he that loveth another hath fulfilled the law.

9 For this, Thou shalt not commit adultery, Thou shalt not kill, Thou shalt not steal, Thou shalt not bear false witness, Thou shalt not covet; and if *there be* any other commandment, it is briefly comprehended in this saying, namely, Thou shalt love thy neighbour as thyself.

10 Love worketh no ill to his neighbour: therefore love *is* the fulfilling of the law.

11 And that, knowing the time, that now *it is* high time to awake out of sleep: for now *is* our salvation nearer than when we believed.

12 The night is far spent, the day is at hand: let us therefore cast off the works of darkness, and

6 διὰ　τοῦτο　γὰρ　καὶ　φόρους　τελεῖτε·
For therefore　　　　also　taxes　pay ye;

λειτουργοὶ　γὰρ　θεοῦ　εἰσιν　εἰς　αὐτὸ　τοῦτο
for ministers　　of God　they are　for　this very thing

προσκαρτεροῦντες.　**7** ἀπόδοτε　πᾶσιν　τὰς
attending constantly.　　　Render　to all men　the

ὀφειλάς,　τῷ　τὸν　φόρον　τὸν　φόρον,
dues,　to the [one]　the　tax　the　tax,*

τῷ　τὸ　τέλος　τὸ　τέλος,　τῷ　τὸν　φόβον
to the　the　tribute　the　tribute,　to the　the　fear
[one]　　　　　　　　　[one]

τὸν　φόβον,　τῷ　τὴν　τιμὴν　τὴν　τιμήν.
the　fear,　to the [one]　the　honour　the　honour.

8 Μηδενὶ　μηδὲν　ὀφείλετε,　εἰ　μὴ　τὸ
To no one　no(any)thing　owe ye,　　except　–

ἀλλήλους　ἀγαπᾶν·　ὁ　γὰρ　ἀγαπῶν　τὸν
one another　to love;　for the [one]　loving　the

ἕτερον　νόμον　πεπλήρωκεν.　**9** τὸ　γὰρ
other　law　has fulfilled.　　For

οὐ　μοιχεύσεις,　οὐ　φονεύσεις,　οὐ　κλέψεις,
Thou shalt not　Thou shalt not kill,　Thou shalt not
commit adultery,　　　　　　　　steal,

οὐκ　ἐπιθυμήσεις,　καὶ　εἴ　τις　ἑτέρα　ἐντολή,
Thou shalt not covet,　and　if　any　other　command-
　　　　　　　　　　　[there is]　　　　ment,

ἐν　τῷ　λόγῳ　τούτῳ　ἀνακεφαλαιοῦται,　[ἐν
²in　　³this　⁴word　　　¹it is summed up,　　in

τῷ]·　ἀγαπήσεις　τὸν　πλησίον　σου　ὡς
–:　　Thou shalt love　the　neighbour　of thee　as

σεαυτόν.　**10** ἡ　ἀγάπη　τῷ　πλησίον　κακὸν
thyself.　　　–　　Love　³to the　⁴neighbour　²evil
　　　　　　　　　　　　　　(one's)

οὐκ　ἐργάζεται·　πλήρωμα　οὖν　νόμου　ἡ
¹works not;　　²[is]　⁴fulfilment　¹therefore　³of law

ἀγάπη.　**11** Καὶ　τοῦτο　εἰδότες　τὸν　καιρόν,
²love.　　　　And　　this[,]　knowing　the　time,

ὅτι　ὥρα　ἤδη　ὑμᾶς　ἐξ　ὕπνου　ἐγερθῆναι·
that　hour　now　you　out of　sleep　to be raised;ᵇ
= it is now an hour for you to be raised out of sleep;

νῦν　γὰρ　ἐγγύτερον　ἡμῶν　ἡ　σωτηρία
for now　nearer　[is] of us　the　salvation

ἢ　ὅτε　ἐπιστεύσαμεν.　**12** ἡ　νὺξ　προέκοψεν,
than when　we believed.　　　The　night　advanced,

ἡ　δὲ　ἡμέρα　ἤγγικεν.　ἀποθώμεθα　οὖν
and the　day　has drawn near.　Let us cast off therefore

τὰ　ἔργα　τοῦ　σκότους,　ἐνδυσώμεθα　δὲ
the　works　of the　darkness,　and let us put on

---

* The phrase between the commas is elliptical; understand—
to the [one demanding] the tax [render] the tax. So of the
following phrases.

let us put on the armour of light.

13 Let us walk honestly, as in the day; not in rioting and drunkenness, not in chambering and wantonness, not in strife and envying.

14 But put ye on the Lord Jesus Christ, and make not provision for the flesh, to *fulfil* the lusts *thereof.*

τὰ   ὅπλα   τοῦ   φωτός.   13 ὡς   ἐν   ἡμέρᾳ
the weapons of the light.   As in [the] day

εὐσχημόνως   περιπατήσωμεν,   μὴ   κώμοις   καὶ
becomingly   let us walk,   not in revellings and

μέθαις,   μὴ   κοίταις   καὶ   ἀσελγείαις,   μὴ
in drunken not in beds*   and   excesses,   not
bouts,

ἔριδι   καὶ   ζήλῳ·   14 ἀλλὰ   ἐνδύσασθε   τὸν
in strife and in jealousy;   but   put ye on   the

κύριον   Ἰησοῦν   Χριστόν,   καὶ   τῆς   σαρκὸς
Lord   Jesus   Christ,   and of the   flesh

πρόνοιαν   μὴ   ποιεῖσθε   εἰς   ἐπιθυμίας.
forethought   make not   for [its]   lusts.

CHAPTER 14

HIM that is weak in the faith receive ye, *but* not to doubtful disputations.

2 For one believeth that he may eat all things: another, who is weak, eateth herbs.

3 Let not him that eateth despise him that eateth not; and let not him which eateth not judge him that eateth: for God hath received him.

4 Who art thou that judgest another man's servant? to his own master he standeth or falleth. Yea, he shall be holden up: for God is able to make him stand.

5 One man esteemeth one day above another: another esteemeth every day *alike.* Let every man be fully persuaded in his own mind.

6 He that regardeth the day, regardeth *it* unto the

14 Τὸν   δὲ   ἀσθενοῦντα   τῇ   πίστει
Now the [one]   being weak   in the   faith

προσλαμβάνεσθε,   μὴ   εἰς   διακρίσεις   διαλογισ-
receive ye,   not to judgments   of

μῶν.   2 ὃς   μὲν   πιστεύει   φαγεῖν   πάντα,
thoughts.   One indeed   believes   to eat   all things,
man†

ὁ   δὲ   ἀσθενῶν   λάχανα   ἐσθίει.   3 ὁ   ἐσθίων
but the being weak   herbs   eats.   ³The ⁴eating
[one]   [one]

τὸν   μὴ   ἐσθίοντα   μὴ   ἐξουθενείτω,   ὁ   δὲ
⁶the ⁷not ⁸eating   ²not   ¹let ⁵despise,   and ⁹the
[one]   [one]

μὴ   ἐσθίων   τὸν   ἐσθίοντα   μὴ   κρινέτω,
⁴not ⁵eating ⁷the [one] ⁶eating   ²not ¹let ³judge,

ὁ   θεὸς   γὰρ   αὐτὸν   προσελάβετο.   4 σὺ
–   for God   him   received.   ²Thou

τίς   εἶ   ὁ   κρίνων   ἀλλότριον   οἰκέτην;   τῷ
¹who ²art ⁴the   ³judging   ⁵belonging to ⁶a household to
[one]   another   servant? the(his)

ἰδίῳ   κυρίῳ   στήκει   ἢ   πίπτει·   σταθήσεται
own   lord   he stands or   falls;   ²he will stand

δέ,   δυνατεῖ   γὰρ   ὁ   κύριος   στῆσαι   αὐτόν.
¹but,   for is able   the   Lord   to stand   him.

5 ὃς   μὲν   [γὰρ]   κρίνει   ἡμέραν   παρ'
one man†   indeed   judges   a day   above

ἡμέραν,   ὃς   δὲ   κρίνει   πᾶσαν   ἡμέραν·
a day,   another†   judges   every   day;

ἕκαστος   ἐν   τῷ   ἰδίῳ   νοῒ   πληροφορείσθω.
each man in the(his)   own   mind   let him be fully
persuaded.

6 ὁ   φρονῶν   τὴν   ἡμέραν   κυρίῳ   φρονεῖ.
The   minding   the   day   to [the] he minds
[one]   Lord   [it].

* That is, illicit sexual intercourse.

Lord; and he that regardeth not the day, to the Lord he doth not regard *it*. He that eateth, eateth to the Lord, for he giveth God thanks; and he that eateth not, to the Lord he eateth not, and giveth God thanks.

7 For none of us liveth to himself, and no man dieth to himself.

8 For whether we live, we live unto the Lord; and whether we die, we die unto the Lord : whether we live therefore, or die, we are the Lord's.

9 For to this end Christ both died, and rose, and revived, that he might be Lord both of the dead and living.

10 But why dost thou judge thy brother? or why dost thou set at nought thy brother? for we shall all stand before the judgment seat of Christ.

11 For it is written, *As* I live, saith the Lord, every knee shall bow to me, and every tongue shall confess to God.

12 So then every one of us shall give account of himself to God.

13 Let us not therefore judge one another any more: but judge this rather, that no man put a stumblingblock or an occasion to fall in *his* brother's way.

14 I know, and am persuaded by the Lord Jesus, that *there is* nothing unclean of itself: but to him

καὶ ὁ ἐσθίων κυρίῳ ἐσθίει, εὐχαριστεῖ γὰρ
And the eating to [the] he eats, for he gives thanks
    [one]   Lord

τῷ θεῷ· καὶ ὁ μὴ ἐσθίων κυρίῳ
– to God; and the [one] not eating to [the] Lord

οὐκ ἐσθίει, καὶ εὐχαριστεῖ τῷ θεῷ.
he eats not, and gives thanks – to God.

7 οὐδεὶς γὰρ ἡμῶν ἑαυτῷ ζῇ, καὶ οὐδεὶς
For no one of us to himself lives, and no one

ἑαυτῷ ἀποθνῄσκει· 8 ἐάν τε γὰρ ζῶμεν,
to himself dies; for whether we live,

τῷ κυρίῳ ζῶμεν, ἐάν τε ἀποθνῄσκωμεν,
to the Lord we live, or if we die,

τῷ κυρίῳ ἀποθνῄσκομεν. ἐάν τε οὖν
to the Lord we die. Whether therefore

ζῶμεν ἐάν τε ἀποθνῄσκωμεν, τοῦ κυρίου
we live or if we die, of the Lord

ἐσμέν. 9 εἰς τοῦτο γὰρ Χριστὸς ἀπέθανεν
we are. for this For Christ died

καὶ ἔζησεν, ἵνα καὶ νεκρῶν καὶ ζώντων
and lived [again], in order both of dead and of living
    that   [ones]

κυριεύσῃ. 10 σὺ δὲ τί κρίνεις τὸν ἀδελφόν
he might be Lord. ²thou And ¹why ²judgest the brother

σου; ἢ καὶ σὺ τί ἐξουθενεῖς τὸν ἀδελφόν
of thee? or ²indeed ⁴thou ¹why ²despisest the brother

σου; πάντες γὰρ παραστησόμεθα τῷ
of thee? for all we shall stand before the

βήματι τοῦ θεοῦ. 11 γέγραπται γάρ·
tribunal – of God. For it has been written:

ζῶ ἐγώ, λέγει κύριος, ὅτι ἐμοὶ κάμψει
Live I, says [the] Lord, that to me will bend

πᾶν γόνυ, καὶ πᾶσα γλῶσσα ἐξομολογήσεται
every knee, and every tongue will confess

τῷ θεῷ. 12 ἄρα [οὖν] ἕκαστος ἡμῶν
– to God. So therefore each one of us

περὶ ἑαυτοῦ λόγον δώσει [τῷ θεῷ].
concerning himself account will give – to God.

13 Μηκέτι οὖν ἀλλήλους κρίνωμεν· ἀλλὰ
No longer therefore one another let us judge; but

τοῦτο κρίνατε μᾶλλον, τὸ μὴ τιθέναι
this judge ye rather, – not to put

πρόσκομμα τῷ ἀδελφῷ ἢ σκάνδαλον.
a stumbling-block to the brother or an offence.

14 οἶδα καὶ πέπεισμαι ἐν κυρίῳ Ἰησοῦ
I know and have been by [the] Lord Jesus
    persuaded

ὅτι οὐδὲν κοινὸν δι’ ἑαυτοῦ· εἰ μὴ
that nothing [is] common through itself; except

that esteemeth any thing to be unclean, to him *it is* unclean.

15 But if thy brother be grieved with *thy* meat, now walkest thou not charitably. Destroy not him with thy meat, for whom Christ died.

16 Let not then your good be evil spoken of:

17 For the kingdom of God is not meat and drink; but righteousness, and peace, and joy in the Holy Ghost.

18 For he that in these things serveth Christ *is* acceptable to God, and approved of men.

19 Let us therefore follow after the things which make for peace, and things wherewith one may edify another.

20 For meat destroy not the work of God. All things indeed *are* pure; but *it is* evil for that man who eateth with offence.

21 *It is* good neither to eat flesh, nor to drink wine, nor *any thing*, whereby thy brother stumbleth, or is offended, or is made weak.

22 Hast thou faith? have *it* to thyself before God. Happy *is* he that condemneth not himself in that thing which he alloweth.

τῷ λογιζομένῳ τι κοινὸν εἶναι, ἐκείνῳ
to the reckoning anything common to be, to that man
[one]   [it is]

κοινόν. **15** εἰ γὰρ διὰ βρῶμα ὁ ἀδελφός
common. For if because food the brother
    of

σου λυπεῖται, οὐκέτι κατὰ ἀγάπην
of thee is grieved, no longer according to [l]ove

περιπατεῖς. μὴ τῷ βρώματί σου ἐκεῖνον
thou walkest. [2]Not [3]by the [4]food [5]of thee [6]that man

ἀπόλλυε, ὑπὲρ οὗ Χριστὸς ἀπέθανεν.
[1]destroy, on behalf of whom Christ died.

16 μὴ βλασφημείσθω οὖν ὑμῶν τὸ ἀγαθόν.
Let not be blasphemed therefore of you the good.

17 οὐ γάρ ἐστιν ἡ βασιλεία τοῦ θεοῦ
For not is the kingdom - of God

βρῶσις καὶ πόσις, ἀλλὰ δικαιοσύνη καὶ
eating and drinking, but righteousness and

εἰρήνη καὶ χαρὰ ἐν πνεύματι ἁγίῳ·
peace and joy in [the] Spirit Holy;

18 ὁ γὰρ ἐν τούτῳ δουλεύων τῷ Χριστῷ
for the [one] in this serving - Christ

εὐάρεστος τῷ θεῷ καὶ δόκιμος τοῖς
[is] well-pleasing - to God and approved -

ἀνθρώποις. **19** ἄρα οὖν τὰ τῆς εἰρήνης
by men. So there- the - of peace
    fore things

διώκωμεν καὶ τὰ τῆς οἰκοδομῆς τῆς
let us pursue and the things - of building [up] -

εἰς ἀλλήλους. **20** μὴ ἕνεκεν βρώματος
for one another. Not for the sake of food

κατάλυε τὸ ἔργον τοῦ θεοῦ. πάντα
undo thou the work - of God. All things

μὲν καθαρά, ἀλλὰ κακὸν τῷ ἀνθρώπῳ
indeed [are] clean, but evil to the man

τῷ διὰ προσκόμματος ἐσθίοντι. **21** καλὸν
- [2]through [3]a stumbling-block [1]eating. Good [it is]

τὸ μὴ φαγεῖν κρέα μηδὲ 'πιεῖν οἶνον
- not to eat flesh nor to drink wine

μηδὲ ἐν ᾧ ὁ ἀδελφός σου προσκόπτει.
nor by which the brother of thee stumbles.
[anything]

22 σὺ πίστιν ἣν ἔχεις κατὰ σεαυτὸν
[3]Thou [1]faith [2]which [4]hast [6]by [7]thyself

ἔχε ἐνώπιον τοῦ θεοῦ. μακάριος ὁ
[5]have before - God. Blessed the
    [one]

μὴ κρίνων ἑαυτὸν ἐν ᾧ δοκιμάζει·
not judging himself in what he approves;

23 And he that doubteth is damned if he eat, because *he eateth* not of faith: for whatsoever *is* not of faith is sin.

CHAPTER 15

WE then that are strong ought to bear the infirmities of the weak, and not to please ourselves.

2 Let every one of us please *his* neighbour for *his* good to edification.

3 For even Christ pleased not himself; but, as it is written, The reproaches of them that reproached thee fell on me.

4 For whatsoever things were written aforetime were written for our learning, that we through patience and comfort of the scriptures might have hope.

5 Now the God of patience and consolation grant you to be likeminded one toward another according to Christ Jesus:

6 That ye may with one mind *and* one mouth glorify God, even the Father of our Lord Jesus Christ.

7 Wherefore receive ye one another, as Christ

23 ὁ δὲ διακρινόμενος ἐὰν φάγῃ κατα-
but the [one] doubting if he eats has been

κέκριται, ὅτι οὐκ ἐκ πίστεως· πᾶν
condemned, because not of faith; ²all

δὲ ὁ οὐκ ἐκ πίστεως ἁμαρτία ἐστίν.
¹and which [is] not of faith sin is.

15 Ὀφείλομεν δὲ ἡμεῖς οἱ δυνατοὶ τὰ
⁵Ought ¹so ²we ³the ⁴strong ⁷the

ἀσθενήματα τῶν ἀδυνάτων βαστάζειν, καὶ
⁸weaknesses ⁹of the ¹⁰not strong ⁶to bear, and

μὴ ἑαυτοῖς ἀρέσκειν. 2 ἕκαστος ἡμῶν
not [our]selves to please. Each one of us

τῷ πλησίον ἀρεσκέτω εἰς τὸ ἀγαθὸν
the(his) neighbour let him please for – good

πρὸς οἰκοδομήν· 3 καὶ γὰρ ὁ Χριστὸς
to building [up]; for even – Christ

οὐχ ἑαυτῷ ἤρεσεν· ἀλλὰ καθὼς γέ-
²not ³himself ¹pleased; but as it has

γραπται· οἱ ὀνειδισμοὶ τῶν ὀνειδιζόντων
been written: The reproaches of the [ones] reproaching

σε ἐπέπεσαν ἐπ' ἐμέ. 4 ὅσα γὰρ
thee fell on on me. For whatever things

προεγράφη, εἰς τὴν ἡμετέραν διδασκαλίαν
were previously for – our teaching
written,

ἐγράφη, ἵνα διὰ τῆς ὑπομονῆς καὶ
were in order through – patience and
written, that

διὰ τῆς παρακλήσεως τῶν γραφῶν τὴν
through the comfort of the writings the

ἐλπίδα ἔχωμεν. 5 ὁ δὲ θεὸς τῆς ὑπομονῆς
hope we may have. And the God – of patience

καὶ τῆς παρακλήσεως δῴη ὑμῖν τὸ
and – of comfort give to you ²the

αὐτὸ φρονεῖν ἐν ἀλλήλοις κατὰ Χριστὸν
³same ¹to mind among one another according to Christ
thing

Ἰησοῦν, 6 ἵνα ὁμοθυμαδὸν ἐν ἑνὶ στόματι
Jesus, in order with one accord with one mouth
that

δοξάζητε τὸν θεὸν καὶ πατέρα τοῦ
ye may glorify the God and Father of the

κυρίου ἡμῶν Ἰησοῦ Χριστοῦ.
Lord of us Jesus Christ.

7 Διὸ προσλαμβάνεσθε ἀλλήλους, καθὼς
Wherefore receive ye one another, as

καὶ ὁ Χριστὸς προσελάβετο ἡμᾶς εἰς
also – Christ received us to

also received us to the glory of God. ٬

8 Now I say that Jesus Christ was a minister of the circumcision for the truth of God, to confirm the promises *made* unto the fathers:

9 And that the Gentiles might glorify God for *his* mercy; as it is written, For this cause I will confess to thee among the Gentiles, and sing unto thy name.

10 And again he saith, Rejoice, ye Gentiles, with his people.

11 And again, Praise the Lord, all ye Gentiles; and laud him, all ye people.

12 And again, Esaias saith, There shall be a root of Jesse, and he that shall rise to reign over the Gentiles; in him shall the Gentiles trust.

13 Now the God of hope fill you with all joy and peace in believing, that ye may abound in hope, through the power of the Holy Ghost.

14 And I myself also am persuaded of you, my brethren, that ye also are full of goodness, filled with all knowledge, able

δόξαν τοῦ θεοῦ. 8 λέγω γὰρ Χριστὸν
[the] glory – of God.   For I say   Christ

διάκονον γεγενῆσθαι περιτομῆς ὑπὲρ
a minister   to have become   of [the]   on be-
                        circumcision   half of

ἀληθείας θεοῦ, εἰς τὸ βεβαιῶσαι τὰς
[the] truth   of God,   –   –   to confirm   the

ἐπαγγελίας τῶν πατέρων, 9 τὰ δὲ ἔθνη
promises   of the   fathers,   and [1]the [2]nations

ὑπὲρ ἐλέους δοξάσαι τὸν θεόν, καθὼς
[5]on be- [4]mercy [3]to glorify   –   [4]God,   as
half of

γέγραπται· διὰ τοῦτο ἐξομολογήσομαί σοι
it has been written: Therefore   I will confess   to thee

ἐν ἔθνεσιν καὶ τῷ ὀνόματί σου ψαλῶ.
among nations   and   to the   name   of thee   I will sing
                                        praise.

10 καὶ πάλιν λέγει· εὐφράνθητε, ἔθνη,
And   again   he says: Be glad,   nations,

μετὰ τοῦ λαοῦ αὐτοῦ. 11 καὶ πάλιν·
with   the   people   of him.   And   again:

αἰνεῖτε, πάντα τὰ ἔθνη, τὸν κύριον,
Praise,   all   the   nations,   the   Lord,

καὶ ἐπαινεσάτωσαν αὐτὸν πάντες οἱ λαοί.
and   let praise   him   all   the peoples.

12 καὶ πάλιν Ἡσαΐας λέγει· ἔσται
And   again   Esaias   says: There
                                   shall be

ἡ ῥίζα τοῦ Ἰεσσαί, καὶ ὁ ἀνιστάμενος
the root   –   of Jesse,   and   the [one]   rising up

ἄρχειν ἐθνῶν· ἐπ' αὐτῷ ἔθνη ἐλπιοῦσιν.
to rule   nations;   on   him   nations   will hope.

13 Ὁ δὲ θεὸς τῆς ἐλπίδος πληρώσαι
Now the   God   –   of hope   fill

ὑμᾶς πάσης χαρᾶς καὶ εἰρήνης ἐν τῷ
you   of(with) all   joy   and   peace   in   –

πιστεύειν, εἰς τὸ περισσεύειν ὑμᾶς ἐν
to believe   for   –   to abound   you[b]   in
(believing),

τῇ ἐλπίδι ἐν δυνάμει πνεύματος ἁγίου.
–   hope   by   [the] power   of [the] Spirit   Holy.

14 Πέπεισμαι δέ, ἀδελφοί μου, καὶ
But I have been persuaded,   brothers   of me,   even

αὐτὸς ἐγὼ περὶ ὑμῶν, ὅτι καὶ αὐτοί
[2my]self [1]I   concerning   you,   that   also   [your]-
                                       selves

μεστοί ἐστε ἀγαθωσύνης, πεπληρωμένοι
full   ye are   of goodness,   having been filled

πάσης τῆς γνώσεως, δυνάμενοι καὶ
of(with) all   –   knowledge,   being able   also

also to admonish one another.

15 Nevertheless, brethren, I have written the more boldly unto you in some sort, as putting you in mind, because of the grace that is given to me of God,

16 That I should be the minister of Jesus Christ to the Gentiles, ministering the gospel of God, that the offering up of the Gentiles might be acceptable, being sanctified by the Holy Ghost.

17 I have therefore whereof I may glory through Jesus Christ in those things which pertain to God.

18 For I will not dare to speak of any of those things which Christ hath not wrought by me, to make the Gentiles obedient, by word and deed,

19 Through mighty signs and wonders, by the power of the Spirit of God; so that from Jerusalem, and round about unto Illyricum, I have fully preached the gospel of Christ.

20 Yea, so have I strived to preach the gospel, not where Christ was named, lest I should build upon another man's foundation:

21 But as it is written, To whom he was not

ἀλλήλους νουθετεῖν. **15** τολμηροτέρως δὲ
one another   to admonish.   And more daringly

ἔγραψα ὑμῖν ἀπὸ μέρους, ὡς ἐπαναμιμνή-
I wrote to you in part, as remind-

σκων ὑμᾶς διὰ τὴν χάριν τὴν δοθεῖσάν
ing you by the grace - given

μοι ἀπὸ τοῦ θεοῦ **16** εἰς τὸ εἶναί με[b]
to me from - God for the to be me
                  =that I should be

λειτουργὸν Χριστοῦ Ἰησοῦ εἰς τὰ ἔθνη,
a minister of Christ Jesus to the nations,

ἱερουργοῦντα τὸ εὐαγγέλιον τοῦ θεοῦ,
sacrificing the gospel - of God,

ἵνα γένηται ἡ προσφορὰ τῶν ἐθνῶν
in order [5]may be [1]the [2]offering [3]of the [4]nations
that

εὐπρόσδεκτος, ἡγιασμένη ἐν πνεύματι
acceptable, having been sanctified by [the] Spirit

ἁγίῳ. **17** ἔχω οὖν τὴν καύχησιν ἐν
Holy. I have therefore the boasting in

Χριστῷ Ἰησοῦ τὰ πρὸς τὸν θεόν· **18** οὐ
Christ Jesus the things with* - God; [4]not

γὰρ τολμήσω τι λαλεῖν ὧν οὐ
[1]for [2]I [3]will [5]dare [7]any- [6]to speak of [the] [8]not
                            thing things which

κατειργάσατο Χριστὸς δι' ἐμοῦ εἰς ὑπακοὴν
[3]did [4]work [5]out [1]Christ through me for obedience

ἐθνῶν, λόγῳ καὶ ἔργῳ, **19** ἐν δυνάμει
of [the] in word and work, by power
nations,

σημείων καὶ τεράτων, ἐν δυνάμει πνεύματος·
of signs and wonders, by power of [the] Spirit;

ὥστε με ἀπὸ Ἰερουσαλὴμ καὶ κύκλῳ
so as me from Jerusalem and around
=I should fulfil the gospel . . . from . . . Illyricum.

μέχρι τοῦ Ἰλλυρικοῦ πεπληρωκέναι τὸ
unto - Illyricum to have fulfilled[b] the

εὐαγγέλιον τοῦ Χριστοῦ. **20** οὕτως δὲ
gospel - of Christ. And so

φιλοτιμούμενον εὐαγγελίζεσθαι οὐχ ὅπου
eagerly striving to evangelize not where

ὠνομάσθη Χριστός, ἵνα μὴ ἐπ' ἀλλότριον
[2]was named [1]Christ, in order not on [2]belonging to
              that another

θεμέλιον οἰκοδομῶ, **21** ἀλλὰ καθὼς
[1]a foundation I should build, but as

γέγραπται· ὄψονται οἷς οὐκ ἀνηγγέλη
it has been They shall see to whom it was not announced
written:

* That is, the things that have to do with . . .

spoken of, they shall see: and they that have not heard shall understand.

22 For which cause also I have been much hindered from coming to you.

23 But now having no more place in these parts, and having a great desire these many years to come unto you;

24 Whensoever I take my journey into Spain, I will come to you: for I trust to see you in my journey, and to be brought on my way thitherward by you, if first I be somewhat filled with your *company*.

25 But now I go unto Jerusalem to minister unto the saints.

26 For it hath pleased them of Macedonia and Achaia to make a certain contribution for the poor saints which are at Jerusalem.

27 It hath pleased them verily; and their debtors they are. For if the Gentiles have been made partakers of their spiritual things, their duty is also to minister unto them in carnal things.

28 When therefore I have performed this, and have sealed to them this fruit, I will come by you into Spain.

29 And I am sure that, when I come unto you, I shall come in the fulness of the blessing of the gospel of Christ.

30 Now I beseech you,

περὶ αὐτοῦ, καὶ οἳ οὐκ ἀκηκόασιν
concerning him, and [those] who have not heard

συνήσουσιν. 22 διὸ καὶ ἐνεκοπτόμην τὰ
will understand. Wherefore also I was hindered –

πολλὰ τοῦ ἐλθεῖν πρὸς ὑμᾶς· 23 νυνὶ
many(much) – to come[d] to you; [2]now

δὲ μηκέτι τόπον ἔχων ἐν τοῖς κλίμασι
[1]but no longer [2]place [1]having in – [2]regions

τούτοις, ἐπιποθίαν δὲ ἔχων τοῦ ἐλθεῖν
[1]these, and [2]a desire [1]having – to come[d]

πρὸς ὑμᾶς ἀπὸ ἱκανῶν ἐτῶν, 24 ὡς ἂν
to you from several years, whenever

πορεύωμαι εἰς τὴν Σπανίαν· ἐλπίζω γὰρ
I journey to – Spain; for I hope

διαπορευόμενος θεάσασθαι ὑμᾶς καὶ ὑφ᾽
journeying through to behold you and by

ὑμῶν προπεμφθῆναι ἐκεῖ, ἐὰν ὑμῶν πρῶτον
you to be set forward there, if of(with) you firstly

ἀπὸ μέρους ἐμπλησθῶ, 25 — νυνὶ δὲ
in part I may be filled, — but now

πορεύομαι εἰς Ἰερουσαλὴμ διακονῶν τοῖς
I am going to Jerusalem ministering to the

ἁγίοις. 26 ηὐδόκησαν γὰρ Μακεδονία καὶ
saints. For thought it good Macedonia and

Ἀχαΐα κοινωνίαν τινὰ ποιήσασθαι εἰς
Achaia [3]contribution [2]some [1]to make for

τοὺς πτωχοὺς τῶν ἁγίων τῶν ἐν Ἰερου-
the poor of the saints – in Jeru-

σαλήμ. 27 ηὐδόκησαν γάρ, καὶ ὀφειλέται
salem. For they thought it good, and debtors

εἰσὶν αὐτῶν· εἰ γὰρ τοῖς πνευματικοῖς
they are of them; for if in the spiritual things

αὐτῶν ἐκοινώνησαν τὰ ἔθνη, ὀφείλουσιν
of them [3]shared [1]the [2]nations, they ought

καὶ ἐν τοῖς σαρκικοῖς λειτουργῆσαι αὐτοῖς.
also in the fleshly things to minister to them.

28 τοῦτο οὖν ἐπιτελέσας, καὶ σφραγισάμενος
This therefore having and having sealed
completed,

αὐτοῖς τὸν καρπὸν τοῦτον, 29 ἀπελεύσομαι
to them this fruit, I will go away

δι᾽ ὑμῶν εἰς Σπανίαν· οἶδα δὲ ὅτι
through you to Spain; and I know that

ἐρχόμενος πρὸς ὑμᾶς ἐν πληρώματι
coming to you in [the] fulness

εὐλογίας Χριστοῦ ἐλεύσομαι. 30 Παρακαλῶ
of [the] of Christ I will come. I beseech
blessing

brethren, for the Lord Jesus Christ's sake, and for the love of the Spirit, that ye strive together with me in *your* prayers to God for me;

31 That I may be delivered from them that do not believe in Judæa; and that my service which *I have* for Jerusalem may be accepted of the saints;

32 That I may come unto you with joy by the will of God, and may with you be refreshed.

33 Now the God of peace *be* with you all. Amen.

δὲ ὑμᾶς, [ἀδελφοί], διὰ τοῦ κυρίου
Now you, brothers, through the Lord
ἡμῶν Ἰησοῦ Χριστοῦ καὶ διὰ τῆς ἀγάπης
of us Jesus Christ and through the love
τοῦ πνεύματος, συναγωνίσασθαί μοι ἐν
of the Spirit, to strive with me in
ταῖς προσευχαῖς ὑπὲρ ἐμοῦ πρὸς τὸν
the prayers on behalf of me to
θεόν, 31 ἵνα ῥυσθῶ ἀπὸ τῶν ἀπειθούντων
God, in order I may be from the disobeying
that delivered [ones]
ἐν τῇ Ἰουδαίᾳ καὶ ἡ διακονία μου
in - Judæa and the ministry of me
ἡ εἰς Ἰερουσαλὴμ εὐπρόσδεκτος τοῖς
- to Jerusalem ²acceptable ³to the
ἁγίοις γένηται, 32 ἵνα ἐν χαρᾷ ἐλθὼν
⁴saints ¹may be, in order that in joy coming
πρὸς ὑμᾶς διὰ θελήματος θεοῦ συνανα-
to you through [the] will of God I may
παύσωμαι ὑμῖν. 33 ὁ δὲ θεὸς τῆς
rest with you. And the God -
εἰρήνης μετὰ πάντων ὑμῶν· ἀμήν.
of peace [be] with all you: Amen.

CHAPTER 16

I COMMEND unto you Phebe our sister, which is a servant of the church which is at Cenchrea:

2 That ye receive her in the Lord, as becometh saints, and that ye assist her in whatsoever business she hath need of you: for she hath been a succourer of many, and of myself also.

3 Greet Priscilla and Aquila my helpers in Christ Jesus:

4 Who have for my life laid down their own necks: unto whom not only I

16 Συνίστημι δὲ ὑμῖν Φοίβην τὴν
Now I commend to you Phœbe the
ἀδελφὴν ἡμῶν, οὖσαν [καὶ] διάκονον τῆς
sister of us, being also a minister of the
ἐκκλησίας τῆς ἐν Κεγχρεαῖς, 2 ἵνα
church - in Cenchrea, in order that
αὐτὴν προσδέξησθε ἐν κυρίῳ ἀξίως τῶν
²her ¹ye may receive in [the] Lord worthily of the
ἁγίων, καὶ παραστῆτε αὐτῇ ἐν ᾧ ἂν
saints, and may stand by her in ¹whatever
ὑμῶν χρῄζῃ πράγματι· καὶ γὰρ αὐτὴ
⁴of you ³she may ²thing; for indeed she
have need
προστάτις πολλῶν ἐγενήθη καὶ ἐμοῦ αὐτοῦ.
a protectress of many became and of myself.
3 Ἀσπάσασθε Πρίσκαν καὶ Ἀκύλαν τοὺς
Greet ye Prisca and Aquila the
συνεργούς μου ἐν Χριστῷ Ἰησοῦ, 4 οἵτινες
fellow-workers of me in Christ Jesus, who
ὑπὲρ τῆς ψυχῆς μου τὸν ἑαυτῶν τράχηλον
on be- the life of me ²the ⁴of ³neck
half of themselves
ὑπέθηκαν, οἷς οὐκ ἐγὼ μόνος εὐχαριστῶ
¹risked, to whom not I only give thanks

give thanks, but also all the churches of the Gentiles.

5 Likewise *greet* the church that is in their house. Salute my wellbeloved Epænetus, who is the firstfruits of Achaia unto Christ.

6 Greet Mary, who bestowed much labour on us.

7 Salute Andronicus and Junia, my kinsmen, and my fellowprisoners, who are of note among the apostles, who also were in Christ before me.

8 Greet Amplias my beloved in the Lord.

9 Salute Urbane, our helper in Christ, and Stachys my beloved.

10 Salute Apelles approved in Christ. Salute them which are of Aristobulus' *household*.

11 Salute Herodion my kinsman. Greet them that be of the *household* of Narcissus, which are in the Lord.

12 Salute Tryphena and Tryphosa, who labour in the Lord. Salute the beloved Persis, which laboured much in the Lord.

13 Salute Rufus chosen in the Lord, and his mother and mine.

14 Salute Asyncritus, Phlegon. Hermas, Patro-

ἀλλὰ καὶ πᾶσαι αἱ ἐκκλησίαι τῶν ἐθνῶν,
but also all   the churches   of the nations,

5 καὶ τὴν κατ’ οἶκον αὐτῶν ἐκκλησίαν.
and ¹the ³in ⁴house ⁵of them ²church.

ἀσπάσασθε Ἐπαίνετον τὸν ἀγαπητόν μου,
Greet   Epænetus   the beloved   of me,

ὅς ἐστιν ἀπαρχὴ τῆς Ἀσίας εἰς Χριστόν.
who is   firstfruit – of Asia for Christ.

6 ἀσπάσασθε Μαρίαν, ἥτις πολλὰ ἐκοπίασεν
Greet   Mary,   who many things laboured
                                  (much)

εἰς ὑμᾶς. 7 ἀσπάσασθε Ἀνδρόνικον καὶ
for you.   Greet   Andronicus and

Ἰουνιᾶν τοὺς συγγενεῖς μου καὶ συναιχμα-
Junius the kinsmen   of me and fellow-

λώτους μου, οἵτινές εἰσιν ἐπίσημοι ἐν
captives of me, who are notable among

τοῖς ἀποστόλοις, οἳ καὶ πρὸ ἐμοῦ γέγοναν
the apostles, who indeed before me have been

ἐν Χριστῷ. 8 ἀσπάσασθε Ἀμπλιᾶτον τὸν
in Christ.   Greet   Ampliatus   the

ἀγαπητόν μου ἐν κυρίῳ. 9 ἀσπάσασθε
beloved   of me in [the] Lord.   Greet

Οὐρβανὸν τὸν συνεργὸν ἡμῶν ἐν Χριστῷ
Urbanus   the fellow-worker of us in Christ

καὶ Στάχυν τὸν ἀγαπητόν μου. 10 ἀσπάσ-
and Stachys the beloved   of me.   Greet

ασθε Ἀπελλῆν τὸν δόκιμον ἐν Χριστῷ.
     Apelles   the approved in Christ.

ἀσπάσασθε τοὺς ἐκ τῶν Ἀριστοβούλου.
Greet   the [ones] of the [family] of Aristobulus.

11 ἀσπάσασθε Ἡρωδίωνα τὸν συγγενῆ μου.
   Greet   Herodion   the kinsman of me.

ἀσπάσασθε τοὺς ἐκ τῶν Ναρκίσσου τοὺς
Greet   the [ones] of the [family] of Narcissus –

ὄντας ἐν κυρίῳ. 12 ἀσπάσασθε Τρύφαιναν
being in [the] Lord.   Greet   Tryphæna

καὶ Τρυφῶσαν τὰς κοπιώσας ἐν κυρίῳ.
and Tryphosa the [ones] labouring in [the] Lord.

ἀσπάσασθε Περσίδα τὴν ἀγαπητήν, ἥτις
Greet   Persis   the beloved,   who

πολλὰ ἐκοπίασεν ἐν κυρίῳ. 13 ἀσπάσασθε
many things laboured in [the] Lord.   Greet
(much)

Ῥοῦφον τὸν ἐκλεκτὸν ἐν κυρίῳ καὶ
Rufus   the chosen   in [the] Lord and

τὴν μητέρα αὐτοῦ καὶ ἐμοῦ. 14 ἀσπάσασθε
the mother of him and of me.   Greet

Ἀσύγκριτον, Φλέγοντα, Ἑρμῆν, Πατροβᾶν,
Asyncritus, Phlegon,   Hermes, Patrobas,

bas, Hermes, and the brethren which are with them.

15 Salute Philologus, and Julia, Nereus, and his sister, and Olympas, and all the saints which are with them.

16 Salute one another with an holy kiss. The churches of Christ salute you.

17 Now I beseech you, brethren, mark them which cause divisions and offences contrary to the doctrine which ye have learned; and avoid them.

18 For they that are such serve not our Lord Jesus Christ, but their own belly; and by good words and fair speeches deceive the hearts of the simple.

19 For your obedience is come abroad unto all *men*. I am glad therefore on your behalf: but yet I would have you wise unto that which is good, and simple concerning evil.

20 And the God of peace shall bruise Satan under your feet shortly. The grace of our Lord Jesus Christ *be* with you. Amen.

'Ερμᾶν, καὶ τοὺς σὺν αὐτοῖς ἀδελφούς.
Hermas, and the ²with ³them ¹brothers.

15 ἀσπάσασθε Φιλόλογον καὶ 'Ιουλίαν,
Greet Philologus and Julia,

Νηρέα καὶ τὴν ἀδελφὴν αὐτοῦ, καὶ
Nereus and the sister of him, and

'Ολυμπᾶν, καὶ τοὺς σὺν αὐτοῖς πάντας
Olympas, and ²the ⁴with ⁵them ¹all

ἁγίους. 16 ἀσπάσασθε ἀλλήλους ἐν φιλήματι
³saints. Greet one another with kiss

ἁγίῳ. ἀσπάζονται ὑμᾶς αἱ ἐκκλησίαι
a holy. ⁵greet ⁴you ²the ³churches

πᾶσαι τοῦ Χριστοῦ.
¹All – ⁴of Christ.

17 Παρακαλῶ δὲ ὑμᾶς, ἀδελφοί, σκοπεῖν
Now I beseech you, brothers, to watch

τοὺς τὰς διχοστασίας καὶ τὰ σκάνδαλα
¹the ³the ⁴divisions ⁵and ⁶the ⁷offences
[ones]

παρὰ τὴν διδαχὴν ἣν ὑμεῖς ἐμάθετε
⁸beside ⁹the ¹⁰teaching ¹¹which ¹²ye ¹³learned

ποιοῦντας, καὶ ἐκκλίνετε ἀπ' αὐτῶν· 18 οἱ
²making, and turn away from them; –

γὰρ τοιοῦτοι τῷ κυρίῳ ἡμῶν Χριστῷ
for such men ³the ⁴Lord ⁵of us ²Christ

οὐ δουλεύουσιν ἀλλὰ τῇ ἑαυτῶν κοιλίᾳ,
¹serve not but the of themselves belly,

καὶ διὰ τῆς χρηστολογίας καὶ εὐλογίας
and through – fair speech and flattering speech

ἐξαπατῶσιν τὰς καρδίας τῶν ἀκάκων.
deceive the hearts of the guileless.

19 ἡ γὰρ ὑμῶν ὑπακοὴ εἰς πάντας
²the ¹For ⁴of you ³obedience ⁵to ⁷all men

ἀφίκετο· ἐφ' ὑμῖν οὖν χαίρω, θέλω
⁶came; over you therefore I rejoice, ⁸I wish

δὲ ὑμᾶς σοφοὺς εἶναι εἰς τὸ ἀγαθόν,
¹and you wise to be to the good,

ἀκεραίους δὲ εἰς τὸ κακόν. 20 ὁ δὲ
but simple to the evil. And the

θεὸς τῆς εἰρήνης συντρίψει τὸν σατανᾶν
God – of peace will crush – Satan

ὑπὸ τοὺς πόδας ὑμῶν ἐν τάχει.
under the feet of you soon.

'Η χάρις τοῦ κυρίου ἡμῶν 'Ιησοῦ
The grace of the Lord of us Jesus [be]

μεθ' ὑμῶν.
with you.

21 Timotheus my work-fellow, and Lucius, and Jason, and Sosipater, my kinsmen, salute you.

22 I Tertius, who wrote *this* epistle, salute you in the Lord.

23 Gaius mine host, and of the whole church, saluteth you. Erastus the chamberlain of the city saluteth you, and Quartus a brother.

24 The grace of our Lord Jesus Christ *be* with you all. Amen.

25 Now to him that is of power to stablish you according to my gospel, and the preaching of Jesus Christ, according to the revelation of the mystery, which was kept secret since the world began,

26 But now is made manifest, and by the scriptures of the prophets, according to the commandment of the everlasting God, made known to all nations for the obedience of faith:

27 To God only wise, *be* glory through Jesus Christ for ever. Amen.

21 Ἀσπάζεται ὑμᾶς Τιμόθεος ὁ συνεργός
⁵greets ⁶you ¹Timothy ²the ³fellow-worker

μου, καὶ Λούκιος καὶ Ἰάσων καὶ
⁴of me, and Lucius and Jason and

Σωσίπατρος οἱ συγγενεῖς μου. **22** ἀσπάζ-
Sosipater the kinsmen of me. ⁷greet

ομαι ὑμᾶς ἐγὼ Τέρτιος ὁ γράψας τὴν
⁸you ¹I ²Tertius ³the [one] ⁴writing ⁵the

ἐπιστολὴν ἐν κυρίῳ. **23** ἀσπάζεται ὑμᾶς
⁶epistle in [the] Lord. ⁹greets ¹⁰you

Γάϊος ὁ ξένος μου καὶ ὅλης τῆς
¹Gaius ²the ³host ⁴of me ⁵and ⁶of all ⁷the

ἐκκλησίας. ἀσπάζεται ὑμᾶς Ἔραστος ὁ
⁸church. ⁶greets ⁷you ¹Erastus ²the

οἰκονόμος τῆς πόλεως καὶ Κούαρτος ὁ
³treasurer ⁴of the ⁵city and Quartus the (?his)

ἀδελφός.‡
brother.

25 Τῷ δὲ δυναμένῳ ὑμᾶς στηρίξαι κατὰ
Now to the *being* able ²you ¹to establish accord-
[one] ing to

τὸ εὐαγγέλιόν μου καὶ τὸ κήρυγμα
the gospel of me and the proclamation

Ἰησοῦ Χριστοῦ, κατὰ ἀποκάλυψιν μυστηρίου
of Jesus Christ, according [the] revelation of [the]
to mystery

χρόνοις αἰωνίοις σεσιγημένου, **26** φανερω-
²in times ³eternal ¹having been kept silent, ³mani-

θέντος δὲ νῦν διά τε γραφῶν προφητικῶν
fested ¹but now and through writings prophetic

κατ' ἐπιταγὴν τοῦ αἰωνίου θεοῦ εἰς
accord- [the] of the eternal God ⁵for
ing to command

ὑπακοὴν πίστεως εἰς πάντα τὰ ἔθνη
⁷obedience ⁸of faith ⁹to ²all ⁴the ⁵nations

γνωρισθέντος, **27** μόνῳ σοφῷ θεῷ, διὰ
¹made known, ²only ³wise ¹to God, through

Ἰησοῦ Χριστοῦ, ᾧ ἡ δόξα εἰς τοὺς
Jesus Christ, to whom the glory unto the
(him)ᵉ

αἰῶνας τῶν αἰώνων· ἀμήν.
ages of the ages: Amen.

‡ Verse 24 omitted by Nestle; *cf.* R.V. marg.

CHAPTER 1

PAUL, called *to be* an apostle of Jesus Christ through the will of God, and Sosthenes *our* brother,

2 Unto the church of God which is at Corinth, to them that are sanctified in Christ Jesus, called *to be* saints, with all that in every place call upon the name of Jesus Christ our Lord, both their's and our's:

3 Grace *be* unto you, and peace, from God our Father, and *from* the Lord Jesus Christ.

4 I thank my God always on your behalf, for the grace of God which is given you by Jesus Christ;

5 That in every thing ye are enriched by him, in all utterance, and *in* all knowledge;

6 Even as the testimony of Christ was confirmed in you:

7 So that ye come behind in no gift; waiting for the coming of our Lord Jesus Christ:

8 Who shall also confirm you unto the end, *that ye may be* blameless in the day of our Lord Jesus Christ.

9 God *is* faithful, by whom ye were called unto

---

1 Παῦλος κλητὸς ἀπόστολος Χριστοῦ
Paul   a called   apostle   of Christ

'Ιησοῦ διὰ θελήματος θεοῦ καὶ Σωσθένης
Jesus through [the] will of God and Sosthenes

ὁ ἀδελφὸς **2** τῇ ἐκκλησίᾳ τοῦ θεοῦ
the(?his) brother   to the church   - of God

τῇ οὔσῃ ἐν Κορίνθῳ, ἡγιασμένοις ἐν
- existing in Corinth,   to [ones]   in
         having been sanctified

Χριστῷ 'Ιησοῦ, κλητοῖς ἁγίοις, σὺν πᾶσιν
Christ   Jesus,   called   saints,   with   all

τοῖς ἐπικαλουμένοις τὸ ὄνομα τοῦ κυρίου
the [ones]   calling on   the   name   of the Lord

ἡμῶν 'Ιησοῦ Χριστοῦ ἐν παντὶ τόπῳ,
of us Jesus Christ in every place,

αὐτῶν καὶ ἡμῶν· **3** χάρις ὑμῖν καὶ
of them and of us: Grace to you and

εἰρήνη ἀπὸ θεοῦ πατρὸς ἡμῶν καὶ κυρίου
peace from God Father of us and Lord

'Ιησοῦ Χριστοῦ.
Jesus Christ.

4 Εὐχαριστῶ τῷ θεῷ πάντοτε περὶ
I gave thanks - to God always concerning

ὑμῶν ἐπὶ τῇ χάριτι τοῦ θεοῦ τῇ δοθείσῃ
you on the grace - of God - given

ὑμῖν ἐν Χριστῷ 'Ιησοῦ, **5** ὅτι ἐν παντὶ
to you in Christ Jesus, because in everything

ἐπλουτίσθητε ἐν αὐτῷ, ἐν παντὶ λόγῳ
ye were enriched in him, in all speech

καὶ πάσῃ γνώσει, **6** καθὼς τὸ μαρτύριον
and all knowledge, as the testimony

τοῦ Χριστοῦ ἐβεβαιώθη ἐν ὑμῖν, **7** ὥστε
- of Christ was confirmed in you, so as

ὑμᾶς μὴ ὑστερεῖσθαι ἐν μηδενὶ χαρίσματι,
you not to be wanting[b] in no(any) gift,

ἀπεκδεχομένους τὴν ἀποκάλυψιν τοῦ κυρίου
awaiting the revelation of the Lord

ἡμῶν 'Ιησοῦ Χριστοῦ· **8** ὃς καὶ βεβαιώσει
of us Jesus Christ; who also will confirm

ὑμᾶς ἕως τέλους ἀνεγκλήτους ἐν τῇ
you till [the] end blameless in the

ἡμέρᾳ τοῦ κυρίου ἡμῶν 'Ιησοῦ [Χριστοῦ].
day of the Lord of us Jesus Christ.

9 πιστὸς ὁ θεός, δι' οὗ ἐκλήθητε εἰς
Faithful [is] - God, through whom ye were called to

the fellowship of his Son Jesus Christ our Lord.

10 Now I beseech you, brethren, by the name of our Lord Jesus Christ, that ye all speak the same thing, and *that* there be no divisions among you; but *that* ye be perfectly joined together in the same mind and in the same judgment.

11 For it hath been declared unto me of you, my brethren, by them *which are of the house of* Chloe, that there are contentions among you.

12 Now this I say, that every one of you saith, I am of Paul; and I of Apollos; and I of Cephas; and I of Christ.

13 Is Christ divided? was Paul crucified for you? or were ye baptized in the name of Paul?

14 I thank God that I baptized none of you, but Crispus and Gaius;

15 Lest any should say that I had baptized in mine own name.

16 And I baptized also the household of Stephanas: besides, I know not whether I baptized any other.

17 For Christ sent me not to baptize, but to preach the gospel: not with wisdom of words,

κοινωνίαν τοῦ υἱοῦ αὐτοῦ Ἰησοῦ Χριστοῦ
[the] fellowship of the Son of him Jesus Christ

τοῦ κυρίου ἡμῶν.
the Lord of us.

10 Παρακαλῶ δὲ ὑμᾶς, ἀδελφοί, διὰ
Now I beseech you, brothers, through

τοῦ ὀνόματος τοῦ κυρίου ἡμῶν Ἰησοῦ
the name of the Lord of us Jesus

Χριστοῦ, ἵνα τὸ αὐτὸ λέγητε πάντες,
Christ, in order the same ye say all,
that thing

καὶ μὴ ᾖ ἐν ὑμῖν σχίσματα, ἦτε δὲ
and not be among you divisions, but ye may be

κατηρτισμένοι ἐν τῷ αὐτῷ νοΐ καὶ
having been joined in the same mind and
together

ἐν τῇ αὐτῇ γνώμῃ. 11 ἐδηλώθη γάρ μοι
in the same opinion. For it was shown to me

περὶ ὑμῶν, ἀδελφοί μου, ὑπὸ τῶν
concerning you, brothers of me, by the [ones]

Χλόης, ὅτι ἔριδες ἐν ὑμῖν εἰσιν. 12 λέγω
of Chloe, that strifes among you there are. I say

δὲ τοῦτο, ὅτι ἕκαστος ὑμῶν λέγει· ἐγὼ
Now this, because each of you says: I

μέν εἰμι Παύλου, ἐγὼ δὲ Ἀπολλῶ,
indeed am of Paul, but I of Apollos,

ἐγὼ δὲ Κηφᾶ, ἐγὼ δὲ Χριστοῦ.
but I of Cephas, but I of Christ.

13 μεμέρισται ὁ Χριστός; μὴ Παῦλος
Has been divided – Christ? Not Paul

ἐσταυρώθη ὑπὲρ ὑμῶν, ἢ εἰς τὸ ὄνομα
was crucified on behalf of you, or in the name

Παύλου ἐβαπτίσθητε; 14 εὐχαριστῶ ὅτι
of Paul were ye baptized? I give thanks that

οὐδένα ὑμῶν ἐβάπτισα εἰ μὴ Κρίσπον
not one of you I baptized except Crispus

καὶ Γάϊον· 15 ἵνα μή τις εἴπῃ ὅτι
and Gaius; lest anyone should say that

εἰς τὸ ἐμὸν ὄνομα ἐβαπτίσθητε. 16 ἐβάπτισα δὲ
in – my name ye were baptized. But I baptized

καὶ τὸν Στεφανᾶ οἶκον· λοιπὸν οὐκ οἶδα
also the of Stephanas household; for the rest I know not

εἴ τινα ἄλλον ἐβάπτισα. 17 οὐ
if any other I baptized. ⁵not

γὰρ ἀπέστειλέν με Χριστὸς βαπτίζειν
¹For ²sent ⁴me ³Christ to baptize

ἀλλὰ εὐαγγελίζεσθαι, οὐκ ἐν σοφίᾳ λόγου,
but to evangelize, not in wisdom of speech,

lest the cross of Christ should be made of none effect.

18 For the preaching of the cross is to them that perish foolishness; but unto us which are saved it is the power of God.

19 For it is written, I will destroy the wisdom of the wise, and will bring to nothing the understanding of the prudent.

20 Where is the wise? where is the scribe? where is the disputer of this world? hath not God made foolish the wisdom of this world?

21 For after that in the wisdom of God the world by wisdom knew not God, it pleased God by the foolishness of preaching to save them that believe.

22 For the Jews require a sign, and the Greeks seek after wisdom:

23 But we preach Christ crucified, unto the Jews a stumblingblock, and unto the Greeks foolishness;

24 But unto them which are called, both Jews and Greeks, Christ the power of God, and the wisdom of God.

25 Because the foolishness of God is wiser than men; and the weakness of God is stronger than men.

ἵνα   μὴ   κενωθῇ   ὁ   σταυρὸς   τοῦ   Χριστοῦ.
lest   ⁴be made vain   ¹the   ²cross   -   ³of Christ.

18 Ὁ   λόγος   γὰρ   ὁ   τοῦ   σταυροῦ   τοῖς
For the word   -   of the   cross   ³to the [ones]

μὲν   ἀπολλυμένοις   μωρία   ἐστίν,   τοῖς
¹on one ³perishing   ⁵folly   ⁴is,   ³to the
hand   [ones]

δὲ   σῳζομένοις   ἡμῖν   δύναμις   θεοῦ   ἐστιν.
¹on the ⁴being saved   ²to us   ⁶[the] ⁷power   ⁸of God   ⁵it is.
other

19 γέγραπται   γάρ·   ἀπολῶ   τὴν   σοφίαν
For it has been written: I will destroy   the   wisdom

τῶν   σοφῶν,   καὶ   τὴν   σύνεσιν   τῶν   συνετῶν
of the   wise ones,   and   the   understanding   of the   prudent

ἀθετήσω.   20 ποῦ   σοφός;   ποῦ   γραμματεύς;
I will set   Where   [is the]   where   [is the] scribe?
aside.   wise man?

ποῦ   συζητητὴς   τοῦ   αἰῶνος   τούτου;   οὐχὶ
where   disputant   of this age?   ³Not
[is the]

ἐμώρανεν   ὁ   θεὸς   τὴν   σοφίαν   τοῦ   κόσμου;
¹made ⁵foolish   -   ²God   ⁴the   ⁵wisdom   ⁶of the   ⁷world?

21 ἐπειδὴ   γὰρ   ἐν   τῇ   σοφίᾳ   τοῦ   θεοῦ
for since   in   the   wisdom   -   of God

οὐκ   ἔγνω   ὁ   κόσμος   διὰ   τῆς   σοφίας
⁶knew ⁷not   ¹the   ²world   ³through   ⁴the(its)   ⁵wisdom

τὸν   θεόν,   εὐδόκησεν   ὁ   θεὸς   διὰ   τῆς
-   ⁸God,   ²thought well   -   ¹God   through   the

μωρίας   τοῦ   κηρύγματος   σῶσαι   τοὺς
folly   of the   proclamation   to save   the

πιστεύοντας.   22 ἐπειδὴ   καὶ   Ἰουδαῖοι   σημεῖα
[ones] believing.   Seeing that   both   Jews   ²signs

αἰτοῦσιν   καὶ   Ἕλληνες   σοφίαν   ζητοῦσιν,
¹ask   and   Greeks   ²wisdom   ¹seek,

23 ἡμεῖς   δὲ   κηρύσσομεν   Χριστὸν   ἐσταυρωμένον,
²we   ¹yet   proclaim   Christ   having been crucified,

Ἰουδαίοις   μὲν   σκάνδαλον,   ἔθνεσιν   δὲ
to Jews   on one hand   an offence,   to nations on the
                                        other

μωρίαν,   24 αὐτοῖς   δὲ   τοῖς   κλητοῖς,
folly,   but to them   the   called ones,

Ἰουδαίοις   τε   καὶ   Ἕλλησιν,   Χριστὸν   θεοῦ
²to Jews   ¹both   and   to Greeks,   Christ   of God

δύναμιν   καὶ   θεοῦ   σοφίαν.   25 ὅτι   τὸ
power   and   of God   wisdom.   Because   the

μωρὸν   τοῦ   θεοῦ   σοφώτερον   τῶν   ἀνθρώπων
foolish   -   of God   wiser [than]   -   men
thing

ἐστίν,   καὶ   τὸ   ἀσθενὲς   τοῦ   θεοῦ   ἰσχυρότερον
is,   and   the   weak thing   -   of God   stronger [than]

26 For ye see your call-
ing, brethren, how that
not many wise men after
the flesh, not many mighty,
not many noble, *are called:*
27 But God hath chosen
the foolish things of the
world to confound the
wise; and God hath
chosen the weak things of
the world to confound the
things which are mighty;
28 And base things of
the world, and things
which are despised, hath
God chosen, *yea,* and
things which are not, to
bring to nought things
that are:
29 That no flesh should
glory in his presence.
30 But of him are ye in
Christ Jesus, who of God
is made unto us wisdom,
and righteousness, and
sanctification, and redemption:
31 That, according as
it is written, He that
glorieth, let him glory in
the Lord.

τῶν   ἀνθρώπων.   26 Βλέπετε   γὰρ   τὴν
–   men.   For ye see   the

κλῆσιν   ὑμῶν,   ἀδελφοί,   ὅτι   οὐ   πολλοὶ
calling   of you,   brothers,   that   not   many

σοφοὶ   κατὰ   σάρκα,   οὐ   πολλοὶ   δυνατοί,
wise men   according   flesh,   not   many   powerful,
            to

οὐ   πολλοὶ   εὐγενεῖς·   27 ἀλλὰ   τὰ   μωρὰ
not   many   well born;   but   the   foolish
                                            things

τοῦ   κόσμου   ἐξελέξατο   ὁ   θεὸς   ἵνα   καται-
of the   world   ²chose   –   ¹God   in order he might
                                            that

σχύνῃ   τοὺς   σοφούς,   καὶ   τὰ   ἀσθενῆ   τοῦ
shame   the   wise men,   and   the weak things of the

κόσμου   ἐξελέξατο   ὁ   θεὸς   ἵνα   καταισχύνῃ
world   ²chose   –   ¹God   in order he might shame
                                    that

τὰ   ἰσχυρά,   28 καὶ   τὰ   ἀγενῆ   τοῦ   κόσμου
the strong things,   and   the   base things of the   world

καὶ   τὰ   ἐξουθενημένα   ἐξελέξατο   ὁ   θεός,
and   the things   being despised   ²chose   –   ¹God,

τὰ   μὴ   ὄντα,   ἵνα   τὰ   ὄντα   καταργήσῃ,
the   not   being,   in order   ²the   ³being   ¹he might
things   that   things   abolish,

29 ὅπως   μὴ   καυχήσηται   πᾶσα   σὰρξ
so as   not   might boast   all   flesh*

ἐνώπιον   τοῦ   θεοῦ.   30 ἐξ   αὐτοῦ   δὲ   ὑμεῖς
before   –   God.   And of him   ye

ἐστε   ἐν   Χριστῷ   Ἰησοῦ,   ὃς   ἐγενήθη
are   in   Christ   Jesus,   who   became

σοφία   ἡμῖν   ἀπὸ   θεοῦ,   δικαιοσύνη   τε
wisdom   to us   from   God,   ²righteousness   ¹both

καὶ   ἁγιασμὸς   καὶ   ἀπολύτρωσις,   31 ἵνα   καθὼς
and   sanctification and   redemption,   in order that   as

γέγραπται·   ὁ   καυχώμενος   ἐν   κυρίῳ   καυχάσθω.
it has been   The [one] boasting   ²in   ³[the]   ¹let him boast.
written: Lord

CHAPTER 2

AND I, brethren, when
I came to you, came
not with excellency of
speech or of wisdom, de-
claring unto you the testimony of God.
2 For I determined not
to know any thing among

2 Κἀγὼ   ἐλθὼν   πρὸς   ὑμᾶς,   ἀδελφοί,
And I   coming   to   you,   brothers,

ἦλθον   οὐ   καθ'   ὑπεροχὴν   λόγου   ἢ   σοφίας
came   not   accord-   excellence   of speech   or   of wisdom
            ing to

καταγγέλλων   ὑμῖν   τὸ   μαρτύριον   τοῦ   θεοῦ.
announcing   to you   the   testimony   –   of God.

2 οὐ   γὰρ   ἔκρινά   τι   εἰδέναι   ἐν   ὑμῖν
For I decided not   anything   to know   among   you

* That is, so that no flesh might boast. *Cf.* Mat. 24. 22.

you, save Jesus Christ, and him crucified.

3 And I was with you in weakness, and in fear, and in much trembling.

4 And my speech and my preaching *was* not with enticing words of man's wisdom, but in demonstration of the Spirit and of power:

5 That your faith should not stand in the wisdom of men, but in the power of God.

6 Howbeit we speak wisdom among them that are perfect: yet not the wisdom of this world, nor of the princes of this world, that come to nought:

7 But we speak the wisdom of God in a mystery, *even* the hidden *wisdom*, which God ordained before the world unto our glory:

8 Which none of the princes of this world knew: for had they known *it*, they would not have crucified the Lord of glory.

9 But as it is written, Eye hath not seen, nor ear heard, neither have entered into the heart of man, the things which God hath prepared for them that love him.

10 But God hath revealed *them* unto us by

εἰ μὴ ’Ιησοῦν Χριστὸν καὶ τοῦτον
except Jesus Christ and this one

ἐσταυρωμένον. 3 κἀγὼ ἐν ἀσθενείᾳ καὶ
having been crucified. And I in weakness and

ἐν φόβῳ καὶ ἐν τρόμῳ πολλῷ ἐγενόμην
in fear and in trembling much was

πρὸς ὑμᾶς, 4 καὶ ὁ λόγος μου καὶ τὸ
with you, and the speech of me and the

κήρυγμά μου οὐκ ἐν πειθοῖς σοφίας
proclamation of me not in ¹persuasive ²of wisdom

λόγοις, ἀλλ’ ἐν ἀποδείξει πνεύματος καὶ
²words, but in demonstration of spirit and

δυνάμεως, 5 ἵνα ἡ πίστις ὑμῶν μὴ ᾖ
of power, in order that the faith of you may not be

ἐν σοφίᾳ ἀνθρώπων ἀλλ’ ἐν δυνάμει
in [the] wisdom of men but in [the] power

θεοῦ.
of God.

6 Σοφίαν δὲ λαλοῦμεν ἐν τοῖς τελείοις,
But ²wisdom ¹we speak among the perfect ones,

σοφίαν δὲ οὐ τοῦ αἰῶνος τούτου οὐδὲ
yet wisdom not of this age neither

τῶν ἀρχόντων τοῦ αἰῶνος τούτου τῶν
of the leaders of this age of the [ones]

καταργουμένων· 7 ἀλλὰ λαλοῦμεν θεοῦ
being brought to naught; but we speak ²of God

σοφίαν ἐν μυστηρίῳ, τὴν ἀποκεκρυμμένην,
¹a wisdom in mystery, – having been hidden,

ἣν προώρισεν ὁ θεὸς πρὸ τῶν αἰώνων
which ²foreordained – ¹God before the ages

εἰς δόξαν ἡμῶν· 8 ἣν οὐδεὶς τῶν ἀρχόντων
for glory of us; which not one of the leaders

τοῦ αἰῶνος τούτου ἔγνωκεν· εἰ γὰρ
of this age has known; for if

ἔγνωσαν, 9 οὐκ ἂν τὸν κύριον τῆς δόξης
they knew, not – the Lord – of glory

ἐσταύρωσαν· ἀλλὰ καθὼς γέγραπται· ἃ
they would have but as it has been written: Things
crucified;*   which

ὀφθαλμὸς οὐκ εἶδεν καὶ οὖς οὐκ ἤκουσεν
eye saw not and ear heard not

καὶ ἐπὶ καρδίαν ἀνθρώπου οὐκ ἀνέβη,
and on heart of man came not up,

ὅσα ἡτοίμασεν ὁ θεὸς τοῖς ἀγαπῶσιν
how many ²prepared – ¹God for the [ones] loving

αὐτόν. 10 ἡμῖν γὰρ ἀπεκάλυψεν ὁ θεὸς
him. ¹For ⁴to us ²revealed – ³God

* This rendering is demanded by the preceding ἄν.

his Spirit: for the Spirit searcheth all things, yea, the deep things of God.

11 For what man knoweth the things of a man, save the spirit of man which is in him? even so the things of God knoweth no man, but the Spirit of God.

12 Now we have received, not the spirit of the world, but the spirit which is of God; that we might know the things that are freely given to us of God.

13 Which things also we speak, not in the words which man's wisdom teacheth, but which the Holy Ghost teacheth; comparing spiritual things with spiritual.

14 But the natural man receiveth not the things of the Spirit of God: for they are foolishness unto him: neither can he know them, because they are spiritually discerned.

15 But he that is spiritual judgeth all things, yet he himself is judged of no man.

16 For who hath known the mind of the Lord, that he may instruct him? But we have the mind of Christ.

διὰ τοῦ πνεύματος· τὸ γὰρ πνεῦμα πάντα
through the Spirit; for the Spirit all things
ἐρευνᾷ, καὶ τὰ βάθη τοῦ θεοῦ. 11 τίς
searches, even the deep things - of God. ³who
γὰρ οἶδεν ἀνθρώπων τὰ τοῦ ἀνθρώπου
¹For ⁴knows ²of men the things - of a man
εἰ μὴ τὸ πνεῦμα τοῦ ἀνθρώπου τὸ
except the spirit - of a man -
ἐν αὐτῷ; οὕτως καὶ τὰ τοῦ θεοῦ οὐδεὶς
in him? so also the things - of God no one
ἔγνωκεν εἰ μὴ τὸ πνεῦμα τοῦ θεοῦ.
has known except the Spirit - of God.
12 ἡμεῖς δὲ οὐ τὸ πνεῦμα τοῦ κόσμου
And we not the spirit of the world
ἐλάβομεν ἀλλὰ τὸ πνεῦμα τὸ ἐκ τοῦ θεοῦ,
received but the Spirit - from - God,
ἵνα εἰδῶμεν τὰ ὑπὸ τοῦ θεοῦ
in order we may the things by - God
that know
χαρισθέντα ἡμῖν· 13 ἃ καὶ λαλοῦμεν οὐκ
freely given to us; which things also we speak not
ἐν διδακτοῖς ἀνθρωπίνης σοφίας λόγοις,
in ³taught ²of human ⁴wisdom ¹words,
ἀλλ' ἐν διδακτοῖς πνεύματος, πνευματικοῖς
but in [words] taught of [the] Spirit, ⁵with spiritual things
πνευματικὰ συγκρίνοντες. 14 ψυχικὸς δὲ
³spiritual things ¹comparing. But a natural
ἄνθρωπος οὐ δέχεται τὰ τοῦ πνεύματος
man receives not the things of the Spirit
τοῦ θεοῦ· μωρία γὰρ αὐτῷ ἐστιν, καὶ
- of God; for folly to him they are, and
οὐ δύναται γνῶναι, ὅτι πνευματικῶς
he cannot to know, because ²spiritually
ἀνακρίνεται. 15 ὁ δὲ πνευματικὸς ἀνακρίνει
¹they are ³discerned. But the spiritual man ²discerns
μὲν πάντα, αὐτὸς δὲ ὑπ' οὐδενὸς
¹on one all things, ³he ¹on the ⁴by ⁵no one
hand other
ἀνακρίνεται. 16 τίς γὰρ ἔγνω νοῦν
³is discerned. For who knew [the] mind
κυρίου, ὃς συμβιβάσει αὐτόν; ἡμεῖς δὲ
of [the] who will instruct him? But we
Lord,
νοῦν Χριστοῦ ἔχομεν.
[the] mind of Christ have.

CHAPTER 3

AND I, brethren, could not speak unto you as unto spiritual, but as unto carnal, *even* as unto babes in Christ.

2 I have fed you with milk, and not with meat: for hitherto ye were not able *to bear it*, neither yet now are ye able.

3 For ye are yet carnal: for whereas *there is* among you envying, and strife, and divisions, are ye not carnal, and walk as men?

4 For while one saith, I am of Paul; and another, I *am* of Apollos; are ye not carnal?

5 Who then is Paul, and who *is* Apollos, but ministers by whom ye believed, even as the Lord gave to every man?

6 I have planted, Apollos watered; but God gave the increase.

7 So then neither is he that planteth any thing, neither he that watereth; but God that giveth the increase.

8 Now he that planteth and he that watereth are one: and every man shall receive his own reward according to his own labour.

9 For we are labourers together with God: ye are God's husbandry, *ye are* God's building.

10 According to the grace of God which is

3 Κἀγώ, ἀδελφοί, οὐκ ἠδυνήθην λαλῆσαι
And I,   brothers,   was not able   to speak

ὑμῖν ὡς πνευματικοῖς ἀλλ' ὡς σαρκίνοις,
to you   as   to spiritual men   but   as   to fleshy,

ὡς νηπίοις ἐν Χριστῷ. **2** γάλα ὑμᾶς
as   to infants   in   Christ.   ²Milk   ²you

ἐπότισα, οὐ βρῶμα· οὔπω γὰρ ἐδύνασθε.
¹I gave   not   food;   for ye were not then able.
⁴to drink,

ἀλλ' οὐδὲ [ἔτι] νῦν δύνασθε, **3** ἔτι γὰρ
But   neither   yet   now   are ye able,   for still

σαρκικοί ἐστε. ὅπου γὰρ ἐν ὑμῖν ζῆλος
fleshly   ye are.   For whereas   among   you   [there is]
jealousy

καὶ ἔρις, οὐχὶ σαρκικοί ἐστε καὶ κατὰ
and   strife,   ²not   ³fleshly   ¹are ye   ⁴and   ⁵according to

ἄνθρωπον περιπατεῖτε; **4** ὅταν γὰρ λέγῃ
⁷man   ⁶walk?   For whenever   says

τις· ἐγὼ μέν εἰμι Παύλου, ἕτερος δέ·
anyone: I   –   am   of Paul,   and another:

ἐγὼ Ἀπολλῶ, οὐκ ἄνθρωποί ἐστε; **5** Τί
I   of Apollos,   ²not   ³men   ¹are ye?   What

οὖν ἐστιν Ἀπολλῶς; τί δέ ἐστιν Παῦλος;
there-   is   Apollos?   and what   is   Paul?
fore

διάκονοι δι' ὧν ἐπιστεύσατε, καὶ ἑκάστῳ
Ministers through whom   ye believed,   even ²to each one

ὡς ὁ κύριος ἔδωκεν. **6** ἐγὼ ἐφύτευσα,
¹as   the   Lord   gave.   I   planted,

Ἀπολλῶς ἐπότισεν, ἀλλὰ ὁ θεὸς ηὔξανεν·
Apollos   watered,   but   –   God   made to
grow;

7 ὥστε οὔτε ὁ φυτεύων ἐστίν τι οὔτε
so as   neither the [one] planting   is   anything nor

ὁ ποτίζων, ἀλλ' ὁ αὐξάνων θεός. **8** ὁ
the watering,   but   ²the   ³making to   ¹God.   ²The
[one]   [one]   grow   [one]

φυτεύων δὲ καὶ ὁ ποτίζων ἕν εἰσιν,
¹planting   ¹so   and the [one] watering   one*   are,

ἕκαστος δὲ τὸν ἴδιον μισθὸν λήμψεται
and each one   the(his)   own   reward   will receive

κατὰ τὸν ἴδιον κόπον. **9** θεοῦ γάρ ἐσμεν
accord-   his   own   labour.   For of God   we are
ing to

συνεργοί· θεοῦ γεώργιον, θεοῦ οἰκοδομή
fellow-workers;   ²of God   ³a tillage,   ⁵of God   ⁴a building

ἐστε. **10** Κατὰ τὴν χάριν τοῦ θεοῦ τὴν
¹ye are.   According to   the   grace   –   of God   –

---

* Notice the neuter gender, though "thing" cannot very well be expressed; *cf.* John 10. 30.

given unto me, as a wise masterbuilder, I have laid the foundation, and another buildeth thereon. But let every man take heed how he buildeth thereupon.

11 For other foundation can no man lay than that is laid, which is Jesus Christ.

12 Now if any man build upon this foundation gold, silver, precious stones, wood, hay, stubble;

13 Every man's work shall be made manifest: for the day shall declare it, because it shall be revealed by fire; and the fire shall try every man's work of what sort it is.

14 If any man's work abide which he hath built thereupon, he shall receive a reward.

15 If any man's work shall be burned, he shall suffer loss: but he himself shall be saved; yet so as by fire.

16 Know ye not that ye are the temple of God, and that the Spirit of God dwelleth in you?

17 If any man defile the temple of God, him shall God destroy; for the temple of God is holy, which temple ye are.

18 Let no man deceive himself. If any man among you seemeth to be wise in this world, let him become a fool, that he may be wise.

δοθεῖσάν   μοι   ὡς   σοφὸς   ἀρχιτέκτων
given   to me   as   a wise   master builder
θεμέλιον   ἔθηκα,   ἄλλος   δὲ   ἐποικοδομεῖ.
a foundation I laid,   but another   builds on [it].
ἕκαστος   δὲ   βλεπέτω   πῶς   ἐποικοδομεῖ.
But each one   let him look   how   he builds on [it].
11 θεμέλιον   γὰρ   ἄλλον   οὐδεὶς   δύναται   θεῖναι
For foundation   other   no one   is able   to lay
παρὰ   τὸν   κείμενον,   ὅς   ἐστιν   Ἰησοῦς
beside   the [one]   being laid,   who   is   Jesus
Χριστός.   12 εἰ   δέ   τις   ἐποικοδομεῖ   ἐπὶ
Christ.   Now if   anyone   builds on   on
τὸν   θεμέλιον   χρυσίον,   ἀργύριον,   λίθους
the   foundation   gold,   silver,   stones
τιμίους,   ξύλα,   χόρτον,   καλάμην,   13 ἑκάστου
precious,   woods,   hay,   stubble,   of each one
τὸ   ἔργον   φανερὸν   γενήσεται·   ἡ   γὰρ   ἡμέρα
the   work   manifest   will become;   for the   day
δηλώσει,   ὅτι   ἐν   πυρὶ   ἀποκαλύπτεται,
will declare   because   by   fire   it is revealed,
[it],
καὶ   ἑκάστου   τὸ   ἔργον   ὁποῖόν   ἐστιν
and   ²of each one   ¹the   ²work   ⁸of what sort   ⁹it is
τὸ   πῦρ   αὐτὸ   δοκιμάσει.   14 εἴ   τινος
⁴the   ⁵fire   ⁷it   ⁶will prove.   If of anyone
τὸ   ἔργον   μενεῖ   ὃ   ἐποικοδόμησεν,   μισθὸν
the   work   remains which   he built on,   a reward
λήμψεται·   15 εἴ   τινος   τὸ   ἔργον   κατακαής-
he will receive;   if of anyone   the   work   will be con-
εται,   ζημιωθήσεται,   αὐτὸς   δὲ   σωθήσεται,
sumed,   he will suffer loss,   but he   will be saved,
οὕτως   δὲ   ὡς   διὰ   πυρός.   16 Οὐκ   οἴδατε
yet so   as   through   fire.   Know ye not
ὅτι   ναὸς   θεοῦ   ἐστε   καὶ   τὸ   πνεῦμα   τοῦ
that a shrine   of God are   and   the   Spirit   of
θεοῦ   ἐν   ὑμῖν   οἰκεῖ;   17 εἴ   τις   τὸν   ναὸν
of God   in   you   dwells?   If anyone   the   shrine
τοῦ   θεοῦ   φθείρει,   φθερεῖ   τοῦτον   ὁ   θεός·
- of God   defiles,   ²will defile   ³this man   - ¹God;
ὁ   γὰρ   ναὸς   τοῦ   θεοῦ   ἅγιός   ἐστιν,   οἵτινές
for the   shrine   - of God   holy   is,   who(which)
ἐστε   ὑμεῖς.
are   ye.
18 Μηδεὶς   ἑαυτὸν   ἐξαπατάτω·   εἴ   τις
No one   himself   let deceive;   if   anyone
δοκεῖ   σοφὸς   εἶναι   ἐν   ὑμῖν   ἐν   τῷ   αἰῶνι
thinks   wise   to be   among   you   in   -   age
τούτῳ,   μωρὸς   γενέσθω,   ἵνα   γένηται
this,   foolish   let him   in order   he may
become,   that   become

19 For the wisdom of this world is foolishness with God. For it is written, He taketh the wise in their own craftiness.

20 And again, The Lord knoweth the thoughts of the wise, that they are vain.

21 Therefore let no man glory in men. For all things are your's;

22 Whether Paul, or Apollos, or Cephas, or the world, or life, or death, ór things present, or things to come; all are your's;

23 And ye are Christ's; and Christ is God's.

CHAPTER 4

LET a man so account of us, as of the ministers of Christ, and stewards of the mysteries of God.

2 Moreover it is required in stewards, that a man be found faithful.

3 But with me it is a very small thing that I should be judged of you, or of man's judgment: yea, I judge not mine own self.

4 For I know nothing by myself; yet am I not hereby justified: but he that judgeth me is the Lord.

5 Therefore judge nothing before the time, until the Lord come, who both will bring to light the

σοφός.   **19** ἡ   γὰρ   σοφία   τοῦ   κόσμου
wise.   For the   wisdom   –   world

τούτου   μωρία   παρὰ   τῷ   θεῷ   ἐστιν.
of this   folly   with   –   God   is.

γέγραπται   γάρ·   ὁ   δρασσόμενος   τοὺς   σοφοὺς
For it has been written: The [one] grasping   the   wise

ἐν   τῇ   πανουργίᾳ   αὐτῶν·   **20** καὶ   πάλιν·
in   the   craftiness   of them;   and   again :

κύριος   γινώσκει   τοὺς   διαλογισμοὺς   τῶν
[The] Lord   knows   the   reasonings   of the

σοφῶν,   ὅτι   εἰσὶν   μάταιοι.   **21** ὥστε   μηδεὶς
wise,   that   they are   vain.   So as   no one

καυχάσθω   ἐν   ἀνθρώποις·   πάντα   γὰρ   ὑμῶν
let boast   in   men;   for all things   of you

ἐστιν,   **22** εἴτε   Παῦλος   εἴτε   Ἀπολλῶς
is(are),   whether   Paul   or   Apollos

εἴτε   Κηφᾶς,   εἴτε   κόσμος   εἴτε   ζωὴ   εἴτε
or   Cephas,   or   [the] world   or   life   or

θάνατος,   εἴτε   ἐνεστῶτα   εἴτε   μέλλοντα,
death,   or   things present   or   things coming,

πάντα   ὑμῶν,   **23** ὑμεῖς   δὲ   Χριστοῦ,   Χριστὸς   δὲ
all things of you,   and ye   of Christ,   and Christ

θεοῦ.   **4** Οὕτως   ἡμᾶς   λογιζέσθω   ἄνθρωπος   ὡς
of God.   So   ⁴us   ¹let ²reckon   ³a man   as

ὑπηρέτας   Χριστοῦ   καὶ   οἰκονόμους   μυστηρίων
attendants   of Christ   and   stewards   of mysteries

θεοῦ.   **2** ὧδε   λοιπὸν   ζητεῖται   ἐν   τοῖς
of God.   Here   for the rest   it is sought   among   –

οἰκονόμοις   ἵνα   πιστός   τις   εὑρεθῇ.   **3** ἐμοὶ
stewards   in order ²faithful   ¹anyone   ³be found.   to me
that

δὲ   εἰς   ἐλάχιστόν   ἐστιν   ἵνα   ὑφ'   ὑμῶν
And   for   a very little thing   it is   in order that   by   you

ἀνακριθῶ   ἢ   ὑπὸ   ἀνθρωπίνης   ἡμέρας·   ἀλλ'
I am judged   or   by   a human   day;*   but

οὐδὲ   ἐμαυτὸν   ἀνακρίνω·   **4** οὐδὲν   γὰρ
not   myself   I judge;   for nothing

ἐμαυτῷ   σύνοιδα,   ἀλλ'   οὐκ   ἐν   τούτῳ
against myself   I know,   but   not   by   this

δεδικαίωμαι·   ὁ   δὲ   ἀνακρίνων   με   κύριός
have I been   but the [one]   judging   me   [the] Lord
justified;

ἐστιν.   **5** ὥστε   μὴ   πρὸ   καιροῦ   τι   κρίνετε,
is.   So as   not   before   time   anything   judge ye,

ἕως   ἂν   ἔλθῃ   ὁ   κύριος,   ὃς   καὶ   φωτίσει
until   comes   the   Lord,   who   both   will shed
light on

* ? of judgment.

hidden things of darkness, and will make manifest the counsels of the hearts: and then shall every man have praise of God.

6 And these things, brethren, I have in a figure transferred to myself and *to* Apollos for your sakes; that ye might learn in us not to think *of men* above that which is written, that no one of you be puffed up for one against another.

7 For who maketh thee to differ *from another?* and what hast thou that thou didst not receive? now if thou didst receive *it,* why dost thou glory, as if thou hadst not received *it?*

8 Now ye are full, now ye are rich, ye have reigned as kings without us: and I would to God ye did reign, that we also might reign with you.

9 For I think that God hath set forth us the apostles last, as it were appointed to death: for we are made a spectacle unto the world, and to angels, and to men.

10 We *are* fools for Christ's sake, but ye *are* wise in Christ; we *are* weak, but ye *are* strong; ye *are* honourable, but we *are* despised.

11 Even unto this present hour we both hunger, and thirst, and are naked, and are buffeted, and have no certain dwellingplace;

τὰ κρυπτὰ τοῦ σκότους καὶ φανερώσει
the hidden things of the darkness and will manifest

τὰς βουλὰς τῶν καρδιῶν· καὶ τότε ὁ
the counsels of the hearts; and then the

ἔπαινος γενήσεται ἑκάστῳ ἀπὸ τοῦ θεοῦ.
praise will be to each one⁰ from - God.

6 Ταῦτα δέ, ἀδελφοί, μετεσχημάτισα εἰς
Now these things, brothers, I adapted to

ἐμαυτὸν καὶ Ἀπολλῶν δι᾽ ὑμᾶς, ἵνα
myself and Apollos because you, in order
of that

ἐν ἡμῖν μάθητε τὸ μὴ ὑπὲρ ἃ
among us ye may learn - not [to think] above what
things

γέγραπται, ἵνα μὴ εἷς ὑπὲρ τοῦ ἑνὸς
has(ve) been written, lest ²one ³on behalf of ⁴the ⁵one

φυσιοῦσθε κατὰ τοῦ ἑτέρου. 7 τίς γάρ σε
¹ye are puffed up against the other. For who thee

διακρίνει; τί δὲ ἔχεις ὃ οὐκ ἔλαβες;
distinguishes? and what hast thou which thou didst not receive?

εἰ δὲ καὶ ἔλαβες, τί καυχᾶσαι ὡς μὴ
and if indeed thou didst why boastest thou as not
receive,

λαβών; 8 ἤδη κεκορεσμένοι ἐστέ· ἤδη
receiving? Now *having been* glutted ye are; now

ἐπλουτήσατε· χωρὶς ἡμῶν ἐβασιλεύσατε· καὶ
ye became rich; without us ye reigned; and

ὄφελόν γε ἐβασιλεύσατε, ἵνα
²an advantage ³really ¹[it is] [that] ye reigned, in order that

καὶ ἡμεῖς ὑμῖν συμβασιλεύσωμεν. 9 δοκῶ
also we ²you ¹might reign with. I think

γάρ, ὁ θεὸς ἡμᾶς τοὺς ἀποστόλους
For, - God us the apostles

ἐσχάτους ἀπέδειξεν ὡς ἐπιθανατίους, ὅτι
last showed forth as doomed to death, because

θέατρον ἐγενήθημεν τῷ κόσμῳ καὶ ἀγγέλοις
a spectacle we became to the world both to angels

καὶ ἀνθρώποις. 10 ἡμεῖς μωροὶ διὰ
and to men. We [are] fools because of

Χριστόν, ὑμεῖς δὲ φρόνιμοι ἐν Χριστῷ·
Christ, but ye [are] prudent in Christ;

ἡμεῖς ἀσθενεῖς, ὑμεῖς δὲ ἰσχυροί· ὑμεῖς
we [are] weak, but ye [are] strong; ye [are]

ἔνδοξοι, ἡμεῖς δὲ ἄτιμοι. 11 ἄχρι τῆς
held in honour, but we [are] unhonoured. Until the

ἄρτι ὥρας καὶ πεινῶμεν καὶ διψῶμεν
present hour ²both ¹we ³hunger and thirst

καὶ γυμνιτεύομεν καὶ κολαφιζόμεθα καὶ
and are naked and are buffeted and

12 And labour, working with our own hands: being reviled, we bless; being persecuted, we suffer it:

13 Being defamed, we intreat: we are made as the filth of the world, *and are* the offscouring of all things unto this day.

14 I write not these things to shame you, but as my beloved sons I warn *you*.

15 For though ye have ten thousand instructers in Christ, yet *have ye* not many fathers: for in Christ Jesus I have begotten you through the gospel.

16 Wherefore I beseech you, be ye followers of me.

17 For this cause have I sent unto you Timotheus, who is my beloved son, and faithful in the Lord, who shall bring you into remembrance of my ways which be in Christ, as I teach every where in every church.

18 Now some are puffed up, as though I would not come to you.

19 But I will come to you shortly, if the Lord will, and will know, not the speech of them which are puffed up, but the power.

20 For the kingdom of

ἀστατοῦμεν **12** καὶ κοπιῶμεν ἐργαζόμενοι
are unsettled   and   labour   working

ταῖς ἰδίαις χερσίν· λοιδορούμενοι εὐλο-
with the(our) own   hands;   being reviled   we

γοῦμεν, διωκόμενοι ἀνεχόμεθα, **13** δυσφημού-
bless,   being persecuted   we endure,   being de-

μενοι παρακαλοῦμεν· ὡς περικαθάρματα τοῦ
famed   we beseech;   as   refuse   of the

κόσμου ἐγενήθημεν, πάντων περίψημα ἕως
world   we became,   [2]of all things   [1]offscouring   until

ἄρτι.
now.

14 Οὐκ ἐντρέπων ὑμᾶς γράφω ταῦτα,
Not   shaming   you   I write   these things,

ἀλλ᾽ ὡς τέκνα μου ἀγαπητὰ νουθετῶν.
but   as   children   of me   beloved   admonishing.

15 ἐὰν γὰρ μυρίους παιδαγωγοὺς ἔχητε
For if   ten thousand   trainers   ye have

ἐν Χριστῷ, ἀλλ᾽ οὐ πολλοὺς πατέρας·
in   Christ,   yet   not   many   fathers;

ἐν γὰρ Χριστῷ Ἰησοῦ διὰ τοῦ εὐαγγελίου
for in   Christ   Jesus   through the   gospel

ἐγὼ ὑμᾶς ἐγέννησα. **16** παρακαλῶ οὖν
I   [2]you   [1]begat.   I beseech   therefore

ὑμᾶς, μιμηταί μου γίνεσθε. **17** Διὰ τοῦτο
you,   imitators   of me   become ye.   Because of this

αὐτὸ ἔπεμψα ὑμῖν Τιμόθεον, ὅς ἐστίν
very thing   I sent   to you   Timothy,   who   is

μου τέκνον ἀγαπητὸν καὶ πιστὸν ἐν
of me   a child   beloved   and   faithful   in

κυρίῳ, ὃς ὑμᾶς ἀναμνήσει τὰς ὁδούς
[the] Lord,   who   [2]you   [1]will remind   [of] the   ways

μου τὰς ἐν Χριστῷ [Ἰησοῦ], καθὼς
of me   -   in   Christ   Jesus,   as

πανταχοῦ ἐν πάσῃ ἐκκλησίᾳ διδάσκω.
everywhere   in   every   church   I teach.

18 ὡς μὴ ἐρχομένου δέ μου πρὸς ὑμᾶς
When not   coming   now   me[a]   to   you
=Now when I did not come

ἐφυσιώθησάν τινες· **19** ἐλεύσομαι δὲ ταχέως
[2]were puffed up   [1]some;   but I will come   shortly

πρὸς ὑμᾶς, ἐὰν ὁ κύριος θελήσῃ, καὶ
to   you,   if   the   Lord   wills,   and

γνώσομαι οὐ τὸν λόγον τῶν πεφυσιωμένων
I will know   not   the   speech   of the   having been
                    [ones]   puffed up

ἀλλὰ τὴν δύναμιν· **20** οὐ γὰρ ἐν λόγῳ
but   the   power;   for [4][is]   [5]not   [6]in   [7]speech

God *is* not in word, but in power.

21 What will ye? shall I come unto you with a rod, or in love, and *in* the spirit of meekness?

ἡ βασιλεία τοῦ θεοῦ, ἀλλ' ἐν δυνάμει.
¹the ²kingdom   -   ³of God, but in power.

21 τί θέλετε; ἐν ῥάβδῳ ἔλθω πρὸς ὑμᾶς,
What will ye? with a rod I come to you,

ἢ ἐν ἀγάπῃ πνεύματί τε πραΰτητος;
or in love   and a spirit of meekness?

CHAPTER 5

IT is reported commonly *that there is* fornication among you, and such fornication as is not so much as named among the Gentiles, that one should have his father's wife.

2 And ye are puffed up, and have not rather mourned, that he that hath done this deed might be taken away from among you.

3 For I verily, as absent in body, but present in spirit, have judged already, as though I were present, *concerning* him that hath so done this deed,

4 In the name of our Lord Jesus Christ, when ye are gathered together, and my spirit, with the power of our Lord Jesus Christ,

5 To deliver such an one unto Satan for the destruction of the flesh, that the spirit may be saved in the day of the Lord Jesus.

6 Your glorying *is* not good. Know ye not that a little leaven leaveneth the whole lump?

7 Purge out therefore the old leaven, that ye may be a new lump, as ye

5 Ὅλως ἀκούεται ἐν ὑμῖν πορνεία,
Actually is heard among you fornication,

καὶ τοιαύτη πορνεία ἥτις οὐδὲ ἐν τοῖς
and such fornication which [is] not among the

ἔθνεσιν, ὥστε γυναῖκά τινα τοῦ πατρὸς
nations, so as ³wife ¹one ⁴of the ⁵father

ἔχειν. 2 καὶ ὑμεῖς πεφυσιωμένοι ἐστέ,
²to have.ᵇ And ye *having been* puffed up are,

καὶ οὐχὶ μᾶλλον ἐπενθήσατε, ἵνα ἀρθῇ
and not rather mourned, *in order* ⁵might be
                          that removed

ἐκ μέσου ὑμῶν ὁ τὸ ἔργον τοῦτο πράξας;
⁶from ⁷midst ⁸of you ¹the ²this ⁴deed ⁵having done?
                      ⁷[the] [one]

3 ἐγὼ μὲν γάρ, ἀπὼν τῷ σώματι,
For I indeed, being absent in the body,

παρὼν δὲ τῷ πνεύματι, ἤδη κέκρικα
but being present in the spirit, already have judged

ὡς παρὼν τὸν οὕτως τοῦτο κατεργα-
as being present ¹the [one] ²thus ³this thing ⁵having

σάμενον 4 ἐν τῷ ὀνόματι τοῦ κυρίου
wrought in the name of the Lord

Ἰησοῦ συναχθέντων ὑμῶν καὶ τοῦ ἐμοῦ
Jesus being assembled you and - my
       =when you are assembled . . .

πνεύματος σὺν τῇ δυνάμει τοῦ κυρίου
spiritᵃ with the power of the Lord

ἡμῶν Ἰησοῦ 5 παραδοῦναι τὸν τοιοῦτον
of us Jesus to deliver such a person

τῷ σατανᾷ εἰς ὄλεθρον τῆς σαρκός,
- to Satan for destruction of the flesh,

ἵνα τὸ πνεῦμα σωθῇ ἐν τῇ ἡμέρᾳ τοῦ
in order the spirit may be in the day of the
that   ⁷saved

κυρίου. 6 Οὐ καλὸν τὸ καύχημα ὑμῶν.
Lord. Not good [is] the boast of you.

οὐκ οἴδατε ὅτι μικρὰ ζύμη ὅλον τὸ
Know ye not that a little leaven all the

φύραμα ζυμοῖ; 7 ἐκκαθάρατε τὴν παλαιὰν
lump leavens? Purge out the old

ζύμην, ἵνα ἦτε νέον φύραμα, καθώς
leaven, in order ye a new lump, as
         that may be

are unleavened. For even Christ our passover is sacrificed for us:

8 Therefore let us keep the feast, not with old leaven, neither with the leaven of malice and wickedness; but with the unleavened *bread* of sincerity and truth.

9 I wrote unto you in an epistle not to company with fornicators:

10 Yet not altogether with the fornicators of this world, or with the covetous, or extortioners, or with idolaters; for then must ye needs go out of the world.

11 But now I have written unto you not to keep company, if any man that is called a brother be a fornicator, or covetous, or an idolater, or a railer, or a drunkard, or an extortioner; with such an one no not to eat.

12 For what have I to do to judge them also that are without? do not ye judge them that are within?

13 But them that are without God judgeth. Therefore put away from among yourselves that wicked person.

ἐστε ἄζυμοι.   καὶ   γὰρ   τὸ   πάσχα ἡμῶν
ye are unleavened.   For indeed   the   passover of us

ἐτύθη   Χριστός.   8 ὥστε   ἑορτάζωμεν   μὴ
was   Christ.   So as   let us keep feast   not
sacrificed[,]

ἐν   ζύμῃ   παλαιᾷ   μηδὲ   ἐν   ζύμῃ   κακίας
with leaven   old   nor   with   leaven   of malice

καὶ   πονηρίας,   ἀλλ᾽   ἐν   ἀζύμοις   εἰλικρινείας
and   of evil,   but   with   unleavened   of sincerity
                              [loaves]

καὶ   ἀληθείας.   9 Ἔγραψα   ὑμῖν   ἐν   τῇ
and   of truth.   I wrote   to you   in   the

ἐπιστολῇ   μὴ   συναναμίγνυσθαι   πόρνοις,
epistle   not   to associate   with
             intimately *with*   fornicators,

10 οὐ   πάντως   τοῖς   πόρνοις   τοῦ   κόσμου
not   altogether   with the fornicators   –   world

τούτου   ἢ   τοῖς   πλεονέκταις   καὶ   ἅρπαξιν
of this   or   with the   covetous   and   rapacious

ἢ   εἰδωλολάτραις,   ἐπεὶ   ὠφείλετε   ἄρα   ἐκ
or   idolaters,   since   ye ought   then out of

τοῦ   κόσμου   ἐξελθεῖν.   11 νῦν   δὲ   ἔγραψα
the   world   to go *out.*   But now   I wrote

ὑμῖν   μὴ   συναναμίγνυσθαι   ἐάν   τις   ἀδελφὸς
to you   not to associate intimately with   if   anyone   a brother

ὀνομαζόμενος   ᾖ   πόρνος   ἢ   πλεονέκτης   ἢ
being named   is   a fornicator   or   a covetous man   or

εἰδωλολάτρης   ἢ   λοίδορος   ἢ   μέθυσος   ἢ
an idolater   or   a railer   or   a drunkard   or

ἅρπαξ,   τῷ   τοιούτῳ   μηδὲ   συνεσθίειν.   12 τί
a rapa-   with such a man   not   to eat *with.*   what
cious man,

γάρ   μοι   τοὺς   ἔξω   κρίνειν;   οὐχὶ   τοὺς
For [is it] to me ²the ones ³without ¹to judge?   ³Not ⁴the ones

ἔσω   ὑμεῖς   κρίνετε;   13 τοὺς   δὲ   ἔξω
⁵within   ²ye   ¹judge?   But the ones   without

ὁ   θεὸς   κρινεῖ.   ἐξάρατε   τὸν   πονηρὸν   ἐξ
–   God   will judge.   Remove   the   evil man out of

ὑμῶν   αὐτῶν.
yourselves.

CHAPTER 6

DARE any of you, having a matter against another, go to law before the unjust, and not before the saints?

2 Do ye not know that the saints shall judge the

6 Τολμᾷ   τις   ὑμῶν   πρᾶγμα   ἔχων   πρὸς
Dares   anyone   of you   ²a matter   ¹having against

τὸν   ἕτερον   κρίνεσθαι   ἐπὶ   τῶν   ἀδίκων,
the(an)   other   to be judged   before   the   unjust,

καὶ   οὐχὶ   ἐπὶ   τῶν   ἁγίων;   2 ἢ   οὐκ   οἴδατε
and   not before   the   saints?   or   know ye not

ὅτι   οἱ   ἅγιοι   τὸν   κόσμον   κρινοῦσιν;   καὶ
that   the   saints   the   world   will judge?   and

world? and if the world shall be judged by you, are ye unworthy to judge the smallest matters?

3 Know ye not that we shall judge angels? how much more things that pertain to this life?

4 If then ye have judgments of things pertaining to this life, set them to judge who are least esteemed in the church.

5 I speak to your shame. Is it so, that there is not a wise man among you? no, not one that shall be able to judge between his brethren?

6 But brother goeth to law with brother, and that before the unbelievers.

7 Now therefore there is utterly a fault among you, because ye go to law one with another. Why do ye not rather take wrong? why do ye not rather *suffer yourselves to* be defrauded?

8 Nay, ye do wrong, and defraud, and that *your* brethren.

9 Know ye not that the unrighteous shall not inherit the kingdom of God? Be not deceived: neither fornicators, nor idolaters, nor adulterers, nor effeminate, nor abusers of themselves with mankind,

10 Nor thieves, nor covetous, nor drunkards, nor revilers, nor extortioners, shall inherit the kingdom of God.

11 And such were some

εἰ   ἐν   ὑμῖν   κρίνεται   ὁ   κόσμος,   ἀνάξιοί
if   ⁶by ⁵you   ³is judged ¹the ²world,   ²unworthy

ἐστε   κριτηρίων   ἐλαχίστων;   3 οὐκ   οἴδατε
¹are ye ⁴judgments? ³of very little?   Know ye not

ὅτι   ἀγγέλους   κρινοῦμεν,   μήτι   γε   βιωτικά;
that   angels   we will judge, not to speak of things
                                                    of this life?

4 βιωτικὰ   μὲν   οὖν   κριτήρια   ἐὰν   ἔχητε,
⁶Of this life ⁴indeed ²therefore ⁵judgments ¹if ²ye have,

τοὺς   ἐξουθενημένους   ἐν   τῇ   ἐκκλησίᾳ,
the ones *being* despised   in   the   church,

τούτους   καθίζετε;   5 πρὸς   ἐντροπὴν   ὑμῖν
these   sit ye?   For   shame   to you

λέγω.   οὕτως   οὐκ   ἔνι   ἐν   ὑμῖν   οὐδεὶς
I say. Thus there is no room among you [for] *no* one

σοφός,   ὃς   δυνήσεται   διακρῖναι   ἀνὰ   μέσον
wise man, who will be able to discern   in your midst

τοῦ   ἀδελφοῦ   αὐτοῦ;   6 ἀλλὰ   ἀδελφὸς   μετὰ
the   brother   of him?   But   brother   with

ἀδελφοῦ   κρίνεται,   καὶ   τοῦτο   ἐπὶ   ἀπίστων;
brother   is judged, and   this   before unbelievers?

7 ἤδη   μὲν   οὖν   ὅλως   ἥττημα   ὑμῖν   ἐστιν
  Now indeed there- ²altogether ³a failure ⁴with ¹there is
             fore   you

ὅτι   κρίματα   ἔχετε   μεθ'   ἑαυτῶν.   διὰ   τί
⁵that ⁷lawsuits ⁶ye have with yourselves.   Why

οὐχὶ   μᾶλλον   ἀδικεῖσθε;   διὰ   τί   οὐχὶ
not   rather   be wronged?   Why   not

μᾶλλον   ἀποστερεῖσθε;   8 ἀλλὰ   ὑμεῖς   ἀδικεῖτε
rather   be deprived?   But   ye   do wrong

καὶ   ἀποστερεῖτε,   καὶ   τοῦτο   ἀδελφούς.
and   deprive,   and   this   brothers.

9 ἢ   οὐκ   οἴδατε   ὅτι   ἄδικοι   θεοῦ   βασιλείαν
  Or know ye not   that unrighteous ²of God   ³[the]
                              men   kingdom

οὐ   κληρονομήσουσιν;   μὴ   πλανᾶσθε·   οὔτε
¹will not inherit?   Be not led astray;   not

πόρνοι   οὔτε   εἰδωλολάτραι   οὔτε   μοιχοὶ
fornicators nor   idolaters   nor   adulterers

οὔτε   μαλακοὶ   οὔτε   ἀρσενοκοῖται   10 οὔτε
nor   voluptuous nor   sodomites   nor
      persons

κλέπται   οὔτε   πλεονέκται,   οὐ   μέθυσοι,
thieves   nor   covetous persons, not drunkards,

οὐ   λοίδοροι,   οὐχ   ἅρπαγες   βασιλείαν   θεοῦ
not   revilers,   not   rapacious   ²[the] kingdom ²of
                        persons   God

κληρονομήσουσιν.   11 καὶ   ταῦτά   τινες   ἦτε·
¹will inherit.   And   these ²some   ¹ye
                          things [of you] were;

of you: but ye are washed, but ye are sanctified, but ye are justified in the name of the Lord Jesus, and by the Spirit of our God.

12 All things are lawful unto me, but all things are not expedient: all things are lawful for me, but I will not be brought under the power of any.

13 Meats for the belly, and the belly for meats: but God shall destroy both it and them. Now the body *is* not for fornication, but for the Lord; and the Lord for the body.

14 And God hath both raised up the Lord, and will also raise up us by his own power.

15 Know ye not that your bodies are the members of Christ? shall I then take the members of Christ, and make *them* the members of an harlot? God forbid.

16 What? know ye not that he which is joined to an harlot is one body? for two, saith he, shall be one flesh.

17 But he that is joined unto the Lord is one spirit.

18 Flee fornication. Every sin that a man doeth is without the body; but he that committeth

ἀλλὰ　ἀπελούσασθε,　ἀλλὰ　ἡγιάσθητε,　ἀλλὰ
but　　　ye were washed,　　but　ye were sanctified,　but

ἐδικαιώθητε　ἐν　τῷ　ὀνόματι　τοῦ　κυρίου
ye were justified　in　the　name　of the　Lord

'Ιησοῦ　Χριστοῦ　καὶ　ἐν　τῷ　πνεύματι
Jesus　　Christ　and　by　the　Spirit

τοῦ　θεοῦ　ἡμῶν.
of the　God　of us.

12 Πάντα　μοι　ἔξεστιν,　ἀλλ'　οὐ　πάντα
All things　to me　[are] lawful,　but　not　all things

συμφέρει.　πάντα　μοι　ἔξεστιν,　ἀλλ'　οὐκ
expedient.　All things　to me　[are] lawful,　but　not

ἐγὼ　ἐξουσιασθήσομαι　ὑπό　τινος.　13 τὰ
I　　will be ruled　　　by　anyone.　　　　-

βρώματα　τῇ　κοιλίᾳ,　καὶ　ἡ　κοιλία　τοῖς
Foods　for the　belly,　and　the　belly　-

βρώμασιν·　ὁ　δὲ　θεὸς　καὶ　ταύτην　καὶ
for foods;　-　but　God　both　this　and

ταῦτα　καταργήσει.　τὸ　δὲ　σῶμα　οὐ　τῇ
these　will destroy.　But the　body [is]　not　-

πορνείᾳ　ἀλλὰ　τῷ　κυρίῳ,　καὶ　ὁ　κύριος
for fornication but　for the　Lord,　and　the　Lord

τῷ　σώματι·　14 ὁ　δὲ　θεὸς　καὶ　τὸν　κύριον
for the body;　-　and　God　both　the　Lord

ἤγειρεν　καὶ　ἡμᾶς　ἐξεγερεῖ　διὰ　τῆς
raised　and　us　will raise up　through　the

δυνάμεως　αὐτοῦ.　15 οὐκ　οἴδατε　ὅτι　τὰ
power　of him.　　Know ye not　that　the

σώματα　ὑμῶν　μέλη　Χριστοῦ　ἐστιν;　ἄρας
bodies　of you　members　of Christ　(is)are?　Taking

οὖν　τὰ　μέλη　τοῦ　Χριστοῦ　ποιήσω　πόρνης
there-　the　members　-　of Christ　shall I make　²of a
fore　　　　　　　　　　　　　　　　[them]　　harlot

μέλη;　μὴ　γένοιτο.　16 ἢ　οὐκ　οἴδατε　ὅτι
¹members?　May it not be.　　Or　know ye not　that

ὁ　κολλώμενος　τῇ　πόρνῃ　ἓν　σῶμά　ἐστιν;
the　being joined　-　to a harlot　one　body　is?
[one]

ἔσονται　γάρ,　φησίν,　οἱ　δύο　εἰς　σάρκα
For ⁴will be,　⁵he says,　¹the　²two　³into　⁷flesh

μίαν.　17 ὁ　δὲ　κολλώμενος　τῷ　κυρίῳ
⁶one.　　But the [one]　being joined　to the　Lord

ἐν　πνεῦμά　ἐστιν.　18 φεύγετε　τὴν　πορνείαν.
one　spirit　is.　　Flee ye　-　fornication.

πᾶν　ἁμάρτημα　ὃ　ἐὰν　ποιήσῃ　ἄνθρωπος
Every　sin　whichever　²may do　¹a man

ἐκτὸς　τοῦ　σώματός　ἐστιν·　ὁ　δὲ　πορνεύων
outside　the　body　is;　but the　committing
[one]　fornication

fornication sinneth against his own body.

19 What? know ye not that your body is the temple of the Holy Ghost *which is* in you, which ye have of God, and ye are not your own?

20 For ye are bought with a price: therefore glorify God in your body, and in your spirit, which are God's.

CHAPTER 7

NOW concerning the things whereof ye wrote unto me: *It is* good for a man not to touch a woman.

2 Nevertheless, *to avoid* fornication, let every man have his own wife, and let every woman have her own husband.

3 Let the husband render unto the wife due benevolence: and likewise also the wife unto the husband.

4 The wife hath not power of her own body, but the husband: and likewise also the husband hath not power of his own body, but the wife.

5 Defraud ye not one the other, except *it be* with consent for a time, that ye may give yourselves to fasting and prayer; and come together again, that Satan tempt you not for your incontinency.

6 But I speak this by

εἰς τὸ ἴδιον σῶμα ἁμαρτάνει. 19 ἢ
against the(his) own body sins.   Or

οὐκ οἴδατε ὅτι τὸ σῶμα ὑμῶν ναὸς
know ye not that the body of you ²a shrine

τοῦ ἐν ὑμῖν ἁγίου πνεύματός ἐστιν,
²of the ⁵in ⁷you ⁴Holy ⁵Spirit ¹is,

οὗ ἔχετε ἀπὸ θεοῦ, καὶ οὐκ ἐστὲ ἑαυτῶν;
which ye from God, and ye are not of
   have   yourselves?

20 ἠγοράσθητε γὰρ τιμῆς· δοξάσατε δὴ
For ye were bought of(with) a price; glorify ye then

τὸν θεὸν ἐν τῷ σώματι ὑμῶν.
–   God in the body of you.

7 Περὶ δὲ ὧν ἐγράψατε, καλὸν ἀνθρώπῳ
Now about things ye wrote, [it is] good for a man
     of which

γυναικὸς μὴ ἅπτεσθαι· 2 διὰ δὲ τὰς
²a woman* ¹not ³to touch;   but because of the

πορνείας ἕκαστος τὴν ἑαυτοῦ γυναῖκα
fornications each man ³the ⁴of himself ²wife

ἐχέτω, καὶ ἑκάστη τὸν ἴδιον ἄνδρα
¹let him have, and each woman the(her) own husband

ἐχέτω. 3 τῇ γυναικὶ ὁ ἀνὴρ τὴν ὀφειλὴν
let her have. To the ²wife ¹the ³husband ⁴the ⁵debt

ἀποδιδότω, ὁμοίως δὲ καὶ ἡ γυνὴ τῷ
¹let *him* pay, and likewise also the wife to the

ἀνδρί. 4 ἡ γυνὴ τοῦ ἰδίου σώματος
husband. The wife of the(her) own body

οὐκ ἐξουσιάζει ἀλλὰ ὁ ἀνήρ· ὁμοίως
has not authority but the husband; ¹likewise

δὲ καὶ ὁ ἀνὴρ τοῦ ἰδίου σώματος οὐκ
¹and also the husband of the(his) own body not

ἐξουσιάζει ἀλλὰ ἡ γυνή. 5 μὴ ἀποστερεῖτε
has authority but the wife.   Deprive not ye

ἀλλήλους, εἰ μήτι ἂν ἐκ συμφώνου πρὸς
each other, unless by agreement for

καιρὸν ἵνα σχολάσητε τῇ προσευχῇ καὶ
a time in order ye may have – for prayer and
       that leisure

πάλιν ἐπὶ τὸ αὐτὸ ἦτε, ἵνα μὴ πειράζῃ
²again ¹together ¹ye may be, lest ²tempt

ὑμᾶς ὁ σατανᾶς διὰ τὴν ἀκρασίαν [ὑμῶν].
³you – ¹Satan because the want of of you.
      of   self-control

6 τοῦτο δὲ λέγω κατὰ συγγνώμην, οὐ
Now this I say by allowance, not

---

* As the same Greek word γυνή means "wife" or "(?married) woman" it is not always easy to differentiate in translating. So also the one Greek word ἀνήρ means "man" or "husband".

permission, *and* not of commandment.

7 For I would that all men were even as I myself. But every man hath his proper gift of God, one after this manner, and another after that.

8 I say therefore to the unmarried and widows, It is good for them if they abide even as I.

9 But if they cannot contain, let them marry: for it is better to marry than to burn.

10 And unto the married I command, *yet* not I, but the Lord, Let not the wife depart from *her* husband:

11 But and if she depart, let her remain unmarried, or be reconciled to *her* husband: and let not the husband put away *his* wife.

12 But to the rest speak I, not the Lord: If any brother hath a wife that believeth not, and she be pleased to dwell with him, let him not put her away.

13 And the woman which hath an husband that believeth not, and if he be pleased to dwell with her, let her not leave him.

14 For the unbelieving husband is sanctified by the wife, and the unbelieving wife is sanctified by the husband: else were your children unclean; but now are they holy.

κατ’ ἐπιταγήν. 7 θέλω δὲ πάντας
by command.   And I wish   all

ἀνθρώπους εἶναι ὡς καὶ ἐμαυτόν· ἀλλὰ
men   to be   as   even   myself;   but

ἕκαστος ἴδιον ἔχει χάρισμα ἐκ θεοῦ,
each man ²[his] own ¹has   gift   of   God,

ὁ μὲν οὕτως, ὁ δὲ οὕτως.
one   thus,   another   thus.

8 Λέγω δὲ τοῖς ἀγάμοις καὶ ταῖς χήραις,
   Now I say   to the unmarried men and   to the   widows,

καλὸν αὐτοῖς ἐὰν μείνωσιν ὡς κἀγώ· 9 εἰ δὲ
[it is] good for them   if   they remain   as   I also;   but if

οὐκ ἐγκρατεύονται, γαμησάτωσαν· κρεῖττον
they do not exercise self-control,   let them marry;   better

γάρ ἐστιν γαμεῖν ἢ πυροῦσθαι. 10 τοῖς
for   it is   to marry than to burn.   to the [ones]

δὲ γεγαμηκόσιν παραγγέλλω, οὐκ ἐγὼ
But   having married   I enjoin,   not   I

ἀλλὰ ὁ κύριος, γυναῖκα ἀπὸ ἀνδρὸς μὴ
but   the Lord,   a woman   from [her] husband not

χωρισθῆναι,[b] 11 — ἐὰν δὲ καὶ χωρισθῇ,
to be separated,   but if   indeed   she is separated,

μενέτω ἄγαμος ἢ τῷ ἀνδρὶ καταλλαγήτω,
let her   unmarried or   to   husband   be reconciled, remain   the(her)

— καὶ ἄνδρα γυναῖκα μὴ ἀφιέναι. 12 Τοῖς
  and a husband [his] wife   not to leave.[b]   to the

δὲ λοιποῖς λέγω ἐγώ, οὐχ ὁ κύριος·
And   rest   say   I,   not   the   Lord:

εἴ τις ἀδελφὸς γυναῖκα ἔχει ἄπιστον, καὶ
If any   brother ²a wife ¹has   unbelieving,   and

αὕτη συνευδοκεῖ οἰκεῖν μετ’ αὐτοῦ, μὴ
this one   consents   to dwell   with   him,   not

ἀφιέτω αὐτήν· 13 καὶ γυνὴ ἥτις ἔχει
let him leave   her;   and a woman who   has

ἄνδρα ἄπιστον, καὶ οὗτος συνευδοκεῖ οἰκεῖν
a husband unbelieving, and this one   consents   to dwell

μετ’ αὐτῆς, μὴ ἀφιέτω τὸν ἄνδρα.
with   her,   let her not leave   the(her)   husband.

14 ἡγίασται γὰρ ὁ ἀνὴρ ὁ ἄπιστος ἐν
For ⁴has been sanctified ¹the ³husband - ²unbelieving by

τῇ γυναικί, καὶ ἡγίασται ἡ γυνὴ ἡ
the   wife,   and   ⁴has been   ¹the ²wife -   sanctified

ἄπιστος ἐν τῷ ἀδελφῷ· ἐπεὶ ἄρα τὰ
²unbelieving by   the   brother;   since   then   the

τέκνα ὑμῶν ἀκάθαρτά ἐστιν, νῦν δὲ
children of you   ²unclean   ¹is(are).   but now

15 But if the unbelieving depart, let him depart. A brother or a sister is not under bondage in such cases: but God hath called us to peace.

16 For what knowest thou, O wife, whether thou shalt save thy husband? or how knowest thou, O man, whether thou shalt save thy wife?

17 But as God hath distributed to every man, as the Lord hath called every one, so let him walk. And so ordain I in all churches.

18 Is any man called being circumcised? let him not become uncircumcised. Is any called in uncircumcision? let him not be circumcised.

19 Circumcision is nothing, and uncircumcision is nothing, but the keeping of the commandments of God.

20 Let every man abide in the same calling wherein he was called.

21 Art thou called being a servant? care not for it: but if thou mayest be made free, use it rather.

22 For he that is called in the Lord, being a servant, is the Lord's freeman: likewise also he that is called, being free, is Christ's servant.

23 Ye are bought with

ἄγιά ἐστιν.   15 εἰ δὲ ὁ ἄπιστος χωρίζ-
holy   they are.   But if   the   unbelieving   separates
                                             one

εται,   χωριζέσθω·   οὐ δεδούλωται ὁ
him/herself,   let him/her be   has not been enslaved   the
              separated;

ἀδελφὸς ἢ ἡ ἀδελφὴ ἐν τοῖς τοιούτοις·
brother   or   the   sister   in   such matters;

ἐν δὲ εἰρήνῃ κέκληκεν ὑμᾶς ὁ θεός.
but in   peace   has called   you   -   God.

16 τί γὰρ οἶδας, γύναι, εἰ τὸν ἄνδρα
For what   knowest thou, wife,   if the(thy) husband

σώσεις; ἢ τί οἶδας, ἄνερ, εἰ τὴν
thou wilt   or what   knowest   husband,   if the(thy)
save?   thou,

γυναῖκα σώσεις; 17 Εἰ μὴ ἑκάστῳ ὡς
wife   thou wilt save?   Only   to each   as

μεμέρικεν ὁ κύριος, ἕκαστον ὡς κέκληκεν
has divided   the   Lord,   each   as   has called

ὁ θεός, οὕτως περιπατείτω. καὶ οὕτως
-   God,   so   let him walk.   And   so

ἐν ταῖς ἐκκλησίαις πάσαις διατάσσομαι.
in   the   churches   all   I command.

18 περιτετμημένος τις ἐκλήθη; μὴ
Having been circumcised   anyone   was called?   not

ἐπισπάσθω· ἐν ἀκροβυστίᾳ κέκληταί τις;
let him be un-   in   uncircumcision   has been   anyone?
circumcised;   called

μὴ περιτεμνέσθω. 19 ἡ περιτομὴ οὐδέν
let him not be circumcised.   -   Circumcision   nothing

ἐστιν, καὶ ἡ ἀκροβυστία οὐδέν ἐστιν,
is,   and   -   uncircumcision   nothing   is,

ἀλλὰ τήρησις ἐντολῶν θεοῦ. 20 ἕκαστος
but   [the]   of command-   of   Each one
keeping   ments   God.

ἐν τῇ κλήσει ᾗ ἐκλήθη, ἐν ταύτῃ
in   the   calling in which he was called,   in   this

μενέτω. 21 δοῦλος ἐκλήθης; μή σοι
let him remain.   A slave   wast thou called?   not to thee

μελέτω· ἀλλ' εἰ καὶ δύνασαι ἐλεύθερος
let it matter;   but   if   indeed   thou art able   free

γενέσθαι, μᾶλλον χρῆσαι. 22 ὁ γὰρ ἐν
to become,   rather   use [it].   For the [one]   in

κυρίῳ κληθεὶς δοῦλος ἀπελεύθερος κυρίου
[the]   called   a slave   a freed man   of [the]
Lord   Lord

ἐστίν· ὁμοίως ὁ ἐλεύθερος κληθεὶς δοῦλός
is;   likewise   the   a free man   called   a slave
             [one]

ἐστιν Χριστοῦ. 23 τιμῆς ἠγοράσθητε· μὴ
is   of Christ.   Of(with) a price ye were bought;   not

a price; be not ye the servants of men.

24 Brethren, let every man, wherein he is called, therein abide with God.

25 Now concerning virgins I have no commandment of the Lord: yet I give my judgment, as one that hath obtained mercy of the Lord to be faithful.

26 I suppose therefore that this is good for the present distress, *I say*, that *it is* good for a man so to be.

27 Art thou bound unto a wife? seek not to be loosed. Art thou loosed from a wife? seek not a wife.

28 But and if thou marry, thou hast not sinned; and if a virgin marry, she hath not sinned. Nevertheless such shall have trouble in the flesh: but I spare you.

29 But this I say, brethren, the time *is* short: it remaineth, that both they that have wives be as though they had none;

30 And they that weep, as though they wept not; and they that rejoice, as though they rejoiced not; and they that buy, as though they possessed not;

31 And they that use this world, as not abusing

γίνεσθε δοῦλοι ἀνθρώπων. **24** ἕκαστος ἐν
become ye slaves of men.   Each one in

ᾧ ἐκλήθη, ἀδελφοί, ἐν τούτῳ μενέτω
what he was brothers, in this let him
[state] called,   remain

παρὰ θεῷ.
with God.

25 Περὶ δὲ τῶν παρθένων ἐπιταγὴν
Now about the virgins a command

κυρίου οὐκ ἔχω, γνώμην δὲ δίδωμι ὡς
of [the] Lord I have not, but an opinion I give as

ἠλεημένος ὑπὸ κυρίου πιστὸς εἶναι.
having had mercy by [the] Lord faithful to be.

26 Νομίζω οὖν τοῦτο καλὸν ὑπάρχειν
I suppose therefore this good to be

διὰ τὴν ἐνεστῶσαν ἀνάγκην, ὅτι καλὸν
because the present necessity, that [it is] good
of

ἀνθρώπῳ τὸ οὕτως εἶναι. **27** δέδεσαι
for a man – so to be.   Hast thou
been bound

γυναικί; μὴ ζήτει λύσιν· λέλυσαι ἀπὸ
to a woman? do not seek release; hast thou been from
released

γυναικός; μὴ ζήτει γυναῖκα. **28** ἐὰν
a woman? do not seek a woman.   if

δὲ καὶ γαμήσῃς, οὐχ ἥμαρτες, καὶ ἐὰν
But indeed thou marriest, thou sinnedst not, and if

γήμῃ ἡ παρθένος, οὐχ ἥμαρτεν· θλῖψιν
²marries ¹the ²virgin, she sinned not; ³affliction

δὲ τῇ σαρκὶ ἕξουσιν οἱ τοιοῦτοι, ἐγὼ
but ⁴in the ⁵flesh ²will have – ¹such, ²I

δὲ ὑμῶν φείδομαι. **29** Τοῦτο δέ φημι,
¹and ⁴you ²am sparing.   But this I say,

ἀδελφοί, ὁ καιρὸς συνεσταλμένος ἐστίν·
brothers, the time *having been* shortened is;

τὸ λοιπὸν ἵνα καὶ οἱ ἔχοντες γυναῖκας
for the rest in order both the [ones] having wives
that

ὡς μὴ ἔχοντες ὦσιν, **30** καὶ οἱ κλαίοντες
as not having may be, and the [ones] weeping

ὡς μὴ κλαίοντες, καὶ οἱ χαίροντες ὡς
as not weeping, and the [ones] rejoicing as

μὴ χαίροντες, καὶ οἱ ἀγοράζοντες ὡς
not rejoicing, and the [ones] buying as

μὴ κατέχοντες, **31** καὶ οἱ χρώμενοι τὸν
not holding, and the [ones] using the

κόσμον ὡς μὴ καταχρώμενοι· παράγει
world as not abusing [it]; ⁴is passing
away

it: for the fashion of this world passeth away.

32 But I would have you without carefulness. He that is unmarried careth for the things that belong to the Lord, how he may please the Lord:

33 But he that is married careth for the things that are of the world, how he may please *his* wife.

34 There is difference *also* between a wife and a virgin. The unmarried woman careth for the things of the Lord, that she may be holy both in body and in spirit: but she that is married careth for the things of the world, how she may please *her* husband.

35 And this I speak for your own profit; not that I may cast a snare upon you, but for that which is comely, and that ye may attend upon the Lord without distraction.

36 But if any man think that he behaveth himself uncomely toward his virgin, if she pass the flower of *her* age, and need so require, let him do what he will, he sinneth not: let them marry.

37 Nevertheless he that standeth stedfast in his heart, having no necessity, but hath power over his own will, and hath so de-

γὰρ τὸ σχῆμα τοῦ κόσμου τούτου.
for ¹the ²fashion ³of this world.

32 Θέλω δὲ ὑμᾶς ἀμερίμνους εἶναι. ὁ
But I wish you without care to be. The

ἄγαμος μεριμνᾷ τὰ τοῦ κυρίου, 33 πῶς
unmarried cares for the of the Lord, how
man things

ἀρέσῃ τῷ κυρίῳ· ὁ δὲ γαμήσας μεριμνᾷ
he may the Lord; but the having married cares for
please [one]

τὰ τοῦ κόσμου, πῶς ἀρέσῃ τῇ γυναικί,
the of the world, how he may the(his) wife,
things please

34 καὶ μεμέρισται. καὶ ἡ γυνὴ ἡ ἄγαμος
and has been divided. And the ²woman – ¹unmarried

καὶ ἡ παρθένος μεριμνᾷ τὰ τοῦ κυρίου,
and the virgin cares for the things of the Lord,

ἵνα ᾖ ἁγία καὶ τῷ σώματι καὶ τῷ
in she holy both in the body and in
order may the
that be

πνεύματι· ἡ δὲ γαμήσασα μεριμνᾷ τὰ
spirit; but the [one] having married cares for the
things

τοῦ κόσμου, πῶς ἀρέσῃ τῷ ἀνδρί.
of the world, how she may please the(her) husband.

35 τοῦτο δὲ πρὸς τὸ ὑμῶν αὐτῶν σύμφορον
And ¹this ²for ⁴the ⁵of yourselves ⁶advantage

λέγω, οὐχ ἵνα βρόχον ὑμῖν ἐπιβάλω,
¹I say, not in order ³a restraint ²you ¹I may put on,
that

ἀλλὰ πρὸς τὸ εὔσχημον καὶ εὐπάρεδρον
but for the thing comely and waiting on

τῷ κυρίῳ ἀπερισπάστως. 36 Εἰ δέ τις
the Lord undistractedly. But if anyone

ἀσχημονεῖν ἐπὶ τὴν παρθένον αὐτοῦ
²to behave ³toward ⁴the ⁵virgin ⁶of him
dishonourably

νομίζει, ἐὰν ᾖ ὑπέρακμος, καὶ οὕτως
¹thinks, if he/she is past the bloom and so
of youth,

ὀφείλει γίνεσθαι, ὃ θέλει ποιείτω· οὐχ
ought to be, what he wishes let him do; not

ἁμαρτάνει· γαμείτωσαν. 37 ὃς δὲ ἕστηκεν
he sins; let them marry. But [he] who stands

ἐν τῇ καρδίᾳ αὐτοῦ ἑδραῖος, μὴ
in the heart of him firm, not

ἔχων ἀνάγκην, ἐξουσίαν δὲ ἔχει περὶ
having necessity, but authority has concerning

τοῦ ἰδίου θελήματος, καὶ τοῦτο κέκρικεν
the(his) own will, and this **has decided**

creed in his heart that he will keep his virgin, doeth well.

ἐν   τῇ   ἰδίᾳ   καρδίᾳ,   τηρεῖν   τὴν   ἑαυτοῦ
in the(his) own   heart,   to keep   the   of himself

38 So then he that giveth *her* in marriage doeth well; but he that giveth *her* not in marriage doeth better.

παρθένον,   καλῶς   ποιήσει.   38 ὥστε   καὶ
virgin,   ²well   ¹he will do.   So as   both

ὁ   γαμίζων   τὴν   ἑαυτοῦ   παρθένον   καλῶς
the marrying   the   of himself   virgin   ²well
[one]

ποιεῖ,   καὶ   ὁ   μὴ   γαμίζων   κρεῖσσον   ποιήσει.
¹does, and the not marrying   ²better   ¹will do.
[one]

39 The wife is bound by the law as long as her husband liveth; but if her husband be dead, she is at liberty to be married to whom she will; only in the Lord.

39 Γυνὴ   δέδεται   ἐφ'   ὅσον   χρόνον   ζῇ
A wife has been bound for so long a time as   lives

ὁ   ἀνὴρ   αὐτῆς·   ἐὰν   δὲ   κοιμηθῇ   ὁ   ἀνήρ,
the husband of her;   but if   sleeps   the husband,

ἐλευθέρα   ἐστὶν   ᾧ   θέλει   γαμηθῆναι,   μόνον
²free   ¹she is   ⁴to   ³she   ⁵to be married,   only
    whom   wishes

40 But she is happier if she so abide, after my judgment: and I think also that I have the Spirit of God.

ἐν   κυρίῳ.   40 μακαριωτέρα   δέ   ἐστιν
in [the] Lord.   But happier   she is

ἐὰν   οὕτως   μείνῃ,   κατὰ   τὴν   ἐμὴν   γνώμην·
if   so   she   according   -   my   opinion;
        remains,   to

δοκῶ   δὲ   κἀγὼ   πνεῦμα   θεοῦ   ἔχειν.
and I think   I also   [the] Spirit   of God   *to* have.

CHAPTER 8

NOW as touching things offered unto idols, we know that we all have knowledge. Knowledge puffeth up, but charity edifieth.

8 Περὶ   δὲ   τῶν   εἰδωλοθύτων,   οἴδαμεν
Now about   *the*   idolatrous sacrifices,   we know

ὅτι   πάντες   γνῶσιν   ἔχομεν.   ἡ   γνῶσις
that ²all ⁴knowledge ¹we ³have.   -   Knowledge

φυσιοῖ,   ἡ   δὲ   ἀγάπη   οἰκοδομεῖ·   εἴ   τις
puffs up,   -   but   love   builds up;   if anyone

2 And if any man think that he knoweth any thing, he knoweth nothing yet as he ought to know.

δοκεῖ   ἐγνωκέναι   τι,   2 οὔπω   ἔγνω   καθὼς
thinks to have known anything, not yet he knew   as

3 But if any man love God, the same is known of him.

δεῖ   γνῶναι·   3 εἰ   δέ   τις   ἀγαπᾷ   τὸν
it be- to know;   but if   anyone   loves   -
hoves [him]

θεόν,   οὗτος   ἔγνωσται   ὑπ'   αὐτοῦ.   4 Περὶ
God, this one has been known by   him.   About

4 As concerning therefore the eating of those things that are offered in sacrifice unto idols, we know that an idol *is* nothing in the world, and that *there is* none other God but one.

τῆς   βρώσεως   οὖν   τῶν   εἰδωλοθύτων
the   eating   therefore   - of idolatrous sacrifices

οἴδαμεν   ὅτι   οὐδὲν   εἴδωλον   ἐν   κόσμῳ,
we know   that [there is] no   idol   in [the] world,

καὶ   ὅτι   οὐδεὶς   θεὸς   εἰ   μὴ   εἷς.   5 καὶ
and that [there is] no   God   except   one.   even

5 For though there be that are called gods, whether in heaven or in

γὰρ   εἴπερ   εἰσὶν   λεγόμενοι   θεοὶ   εἴτε   ἐν
For   if   there are   *being* called   gods   either   in

οὐρανῷ   εἴτε   ἐπὶ   γῆς,   ὥσπερ   εἰσὶν   θεοὶ
heaven   or   on   earth,   even as   there are   gods

earth, (as there be gods many, and lords many,)

6 But to us *there is but* one God, the Father, of whom *are* all things, and we in him; and one Lord Jesus Christ, by whom *are* all things, and we by him.

7 Howbeit *there is* not in every man that knowledge: for some with conscience of the idol unto this hour eat *it* as a thing offered unto an idol; and their conscience being weak is defiled.

8 But meat commendeth us not to God: for neither, if we eat, are we the better; neither, if we eat not, are we the worse.

9 But take heed lest by any means this liberty of your's become a stumblingblock to them that are weak.

10 For if any man see thee which hast knowledge sit at meat in the idol's temple, shall not the conscience of him which is weak be emboldened to eat those things which are offered to idols;

11 And through thy knowledge shall the weak brother perish, for whom Christ died?

12 But when ye sin so against the brethren, and wound their weak conscience, ye sin against Christ.

13 Wherefore, if meat make my brother to offend,

πολλοὶ καὶ κύριοι πολλοί, 6 ἀλλ' ἡμῖν
many and lords many, yet to us

εἷς θεὸς ὁ πατήρ, ἐξ οὗ τὰ πάντα καὶ
[there God the Father, of whom – [are] all and
is] one things

ἡμεῖς εἰς αὐτόν, καὶ εἷς κύριος Ἰησοῦς
we in him, and one Lord Jesus

Χριστός, δι' οὗ τὰ πάντα καὶ ἡμεῖς
Christ, through whom – [are] all and we
things

δι' αὐτοῦ. 7 Ἀλλ' οὐκ ἐν πᾶσιν ἡ
through him. But [there is] not in all men the
(this)

γνῶσις· τινὲς δὲ τῇ συνηθείᾳ ἕως ἄρτι
knowledge; and some by the habit until now

τοῦ εἰδώλου ὡς εἰδωλόθυτον ἐσθίουσιν,
³of the ²idol ⁴as ⁵an idolatrous sacrifice ¹eat,

καὶ ἡ συνείδησις αὐτῶν ἀσθενὴς οὖσα
and the conscience of them ²weak ¹being

μολύνεται. 8 βρῶμα δὲ ἡμᾶς οὐ παραστήσει
is defiled. But food ²us ¹will not commend

τῷ θεῷ· οὔτε ἐὰν μὴ φάγωμεν ὑστερούμεθα,
– to God; neither if we eat not are we behind,

οὔτε ἐὰν φάγωμεν περισσεύομεν. 9 βλέπετε
nor if we eat do we excel. look ye

δὲ μή πως ἡ ἐξουσία ὑμῶν αὕτη
But lest somehow the ²authority ³of you ¹this

πρόσκομμα γένηται τοῖς ἀσθενέσιν. 10 ἐὰν
a stumbling-block becomes to the weak ones. if

γάρ τις ἴδῃ σὲ τὸν ἔχοντα γνῶσιν ἐν
For anyone sees thee the [one] having knowledge ²in

εἰδωλείῳ κατακείμενον, οὐχὶ ἡ συνείδησις
³an idol's temple ¹sitting, ²not ¹the ⁴conscience

αὐτοῦ ἀσθενοῦς ὄντος οἰκοδομηθήσεται εἰς
⁵of him ⁷weak ⁶[he]being³ ¹will ⁸be emboldened –

τὸ τὰ εἰδωλόθυτα ἐσθίειν; 11 ἀπόλλυται
– ¹⁰the ¹¹idolatrous sacrifices ⁹to eat? ³is destroyed

γὰρ ὁ ἀσθενῶν ἐν τῇ σῇ γνώσει, ὁ
For ¹the [one] ²being weak by – thy knowledge, the

ἀδελφὸς δι' ὃν Χριστὸς ἀπέθανεν. 12 οὕτως
brother because whom Christ died. so
of

δὲ ἁμαρτάνοντες εἰς τοὺς ἀδελφοὺς καὶ
And sinning against the brothers and

τύπτοντες αὐτῶν τὴν συνείδησιν ἀσθενοῦσαν
wounding of them the conscience being weak

εἰς Χριστὸν ἁμαρτάνετε. 13 διόπερ εἰ
²against ³Christ ¹ye sin. Wherefore if

βρῶμα σκανδαλίζει τὸν ἀδελφόν μου, οὐ
food offends the brother of me, by no

I will eat no flesh while the world standeth, lest I make my brother to offend.

μὴ   φάγω   κρέα   εἰς   τὸν   αἰῶνα,   ἵνα   μὴ
means I eat⁻ flesh   unto   the   age,   lest
τὸν   ἀδελφόν   μου   σκανδαλίσω.
²the   ³brother   ⁴of me   ¹I offend.

CHAPTER 9

AM I not an apostle? am I not free? have I not seen Jesus Christ our Lord? are not ye my work in the Lord?

2 If I be not an apostle unto others, yet doubtless I am to you: for the seal of mine apostleship are ye in the Lord.

3 Mine answer to them that do examine me is this,

4 Have we not power to eat and to drink?

5 Have we not power to lead about a sister, a wife, as well as other apostles, and as the brethren of the Lord, and Cephas?

6 Or I only and Barnabas, have not we power to forbear working?

7 Who goeth a warfare any time at his own charges? who planteth a vineyard, and eateth not of the fruit thereof? or who feedeth a flock, and eateth not of the milk of the flock?

8 Say I these things as a man? or saith not the law the same also?

9 For it is written in the law of Moses, Thou shalt not muzzle the mouth of the ox that treadeth

9 Οὐκ   εἰμὶ   ἐλεύθερος;   οὐκ   εἰμὶ   ἀπόστολος;
Am I not   free?   am I not   an apostle?
οὐχὶ   Ἰησοῦν   τὸν   κύριον   ἡμῶν   ἑόρακα;
not   Jesus   the   Lord   of us   I have seen?
οὐ   τὸ   ἔργον   μου   ὑμεῖς   ἐστε   ἐν   κυρίῳ;
not   the   work   of me   ye   are   in   [the] Lord?
2 εἰ   ἄλλοις   οὐκ   εἰμὶ   ἀπόστολος,   ἀλλά
If   to others   I am not   an apostle,   yet
γε   ὑμῖν   εἰμι·   ἢ   γὰρ   σφραγίς   μου   τῆς
indeed to you I am;   for the   seal   ²of me ¹of the
ἀποστολῆς   ὑμεῖς   ἐστε   ἐν   κυρίῳ.   3 Ἡ
¹apostleship ye   are   in   [the] Lord.
ἐμὴ   ἀπολογία   τοῖς   ἐμὲ   ἀνακρίνουσίν   ἐστιν
My   defence   to the   ²me   ¹examining   is
                   [ones]
αὕτη.   4 μὴ   οὐκ   ἔχομεν   ἐξουσίαν   φαγεῖν
this.   not   Have we not   authority   to eat
καὶ   πεῖν;   5 μὴ   οὐκ   ἔχομεν   ἐξουσίαν
and   to drink?   not   have we not   authority
ἀδελφὴν   γυναῖκα   περιάγειν,   ὡς   καὶ   οἱ
a sister   a wife   to lead about, as   also   the
λοιποὶ   ἀπόστολοι   καὶ   οἱ   ἀδελφοὶ   τοῦ
remaining apostles   and   the   brothers   of the
κυρίου   καὶ   Κηφᾶς;   6 ἢ   μόνος   ἐγὼ   καὶ
Lord   and   Cephas?   or   only   I   and
Βαρναβᾶς   οὐκ   ἔχομεν   ἐξουσίαν   μὴ
Barnabas   have we not   authority   not
ἐργάζεσθαι;   7 Τίς   στρατεύεται   ἰδίοις
to work?   Who   soldiers   at [his] own
ὀψωνίοις   ποτέ;   τίς   φυτεύει   ἀμπελῶνα   καὶ
wages   at any time? who   plants   a vineyard   and
τὸν   καρπὸν   αὐτοῦ   οὐκ   ἐσθίει;   ἢ   τίς
the   fruit   of it   eats not?   or   who
ποιμαίνει   ποίμνην   καὶ   ἐκ   τοῦ   γάλακτος
shepherds   a flock   and   of   the   milk
τῆς   ποίμνης   οὐκ   ἐσθίει;   8 μὴ   κατὰ
of the flock   eats not?   Not according to
ἄνθρωπον   ταῦτα   λαλῶ,   ἢ   καὶ   ὁ   νόμος
man   these things I speak,   or   also   the   law
ταῦτα   οὐ   λέγει;   9 ἐν   γὰρ   τῷ   Μωϋσέως
these things says not?   for in   the   of Moses
νόμῳ   γέγραπται·   οὐ   κημώσεις   βοῦν
law   it has been written: Thou shalt not muzzle   an ox

out the corn. Doth God take care for oxen?

10 Or saith he *it* altogether for our sakes? For our sakes, no doubt, *this* is written: that he that ploweth should plow in hope; and that he that thresheth in hope should be partaker of his hope.

11 If we have sown unto you spiritual things, *is it* a great thing if we shall reap your carnal things?

12 If others be partakers of *this* power over you, *are* not we rather? Nevertheless we have not used this power; but suffer all things, lest we should hinder the gospel of Christ.

13 Do ye not know that they which minister about holy things live *of the things* of the temple? and they which wait at the altar are partakers with the altar?

14 Even so hath the Lord ordained that they which preach the gospel should live of the gospel.

15 But I have used none of these things: neither have I written these things, that it should be so done unto me: for *it were* better for me to die, than that any man should make my glorying void.

16 For though I preach the gospel, I have nothing

ἀλοῶντα. μὴ τῶν βοῶν μέλει τῷ θεῷ;
threshing. not - of oxen matters it - to God?

10 ἢ δι' ἡμᾶς πάντως λέγει; δι' ἡμᾶς
or because of us altogether he says? because of us

γὰρ ἐγράφη, ὅτι ὀφείλει ἐπ' ἐλπίδι
for it was written, because °ought °on(in) °hope

ὁ ἀροτριῶν ἀροτριᾶν, καὶ ὁ ἀλοῶν ἐπ'
¹the ²ploughing ⁴to plough, and the threshing on(in)
[one] [one]

ἐλπίδι τοῦ μετέχειν. 11 εἰ ἡμεῖς ὑμῖν
hope of the to partake. If we to you
=of partaking.

τὰ πνευματικὰ ἐσπείραμεν, μέγα εἰ ἡμεῖς
- spiritual things sowed, [is it] a great thing if we

ὑμῶν τὰ σαρκικὰ θερίσομεν; 12 εἰ ἄλλοι
of you - fleshly things shall reap? If others

τῆς ὑμῶν ἐξουσίας μετέχουσιν, οὐ
²of the ⁴of you ³authority ¹have a share of, not

μᾶλλον ἡμεῖς; ἀλλ' οὐκ ἐχρησάμεθα
rather we? But we did not use

τῇ ἐξουσίᾳ ταύτῃ, ἀλλὰ πάντα στέγομεν
this authority, but ²all things ¹we put up with

ἵνα μή τινα ἐγκοπὴν δῶμεν τῷ εὐαγγελίῳ
lest ²anyone ³an obstacle ¹we should to the gospel
give

τοῦ Χριστοῦ. 13 Οὐκ οἴδατε ὅτι οἱ
- of Christ. Know ye not that the
[ones]

τὰ ἱερὰ ἐργαζόμενοι τὰ ἐκ τοῦ ἱεροῦ
- ²sacred things ¹working [at] ⁴the things ³of ⁵the ⁶temple

ἐσθίουσιν, οἱ τῷ θυσιαστηρίῳ παρεδρεύοντες
²eat, the ²the ³altar ¹attending [on]
[ones]

τῷ θυσιαστηρίῳ συμμερίζονται; 14 οὕτως
⁴the ⁵altar ¹partake with? So

καὶ ὁ κύριος διέταξεν τοῖς τὸ εὐαγγέλιον
also the Lord ordained the [ones] ²the ³gospel

καταγγέλλουσιν ἐκ τοῦ εὐαγγελίου ζῆν.
¹announcing ⁵of ⁶the ⁷gospel ⁴to live.

15 ἐγὼ δὲ οὐ κέχρημαι οὐδενὶ τούτων.
But I have not used not one of these things.

Οὐκ ἔγραψα δὲ ταῦτα ἵνα οὕτως γένηται
And I did not write these in order so it might be
things that

ἐν ἐμοί· καλὸν γάρ μοι μᾶλλον ἀποθανεῖν
in me; for good [it is] to me rather to die

ἢ — τὸ καύχημά μου οὐδεὶς κενώσει.
than — the boast of me no man shall empty.

16 ἐὰν γὰρ εὐαγγελίζωμαι, οὐκ ἔστιν
For if I preach good news, there is not
=I have no boast;

to glory of: for necessity is laid upon me; yea, woe is unto me, if I preach not the gospel!

17 For if I do this thing willingly, I have a reward: but if against my will, a dispensation *of the gospel* is committed unto me.

18 What is my reward then? *Verily* that, when I preach the gospel, I may make the gospel of Christ without charge, that I abuse not my power in the gospel.

19 For though I be free from all *men*, yet have I made myself servant unto all, that I might gain the more.

20 And unto the Jews I became as a Jew, that I might gain the Jews; to them that are under the law, as under the law, that I might gain them that are under the law;

21 To them that are without law, as without law, (being not without law to God, but under the law to Christ,) that I might gain them that are without law.

22 To the weak became I as weak, that I might gain the weak: I am made all things to all *men*, that I might by all means save some.

23 And this I do for the gospel's sake, that I might be partaker thereof with *you.*

μοι καύχημα· ἀνάγκη γάρ μοι ἐπίκειτα
to me boast;° for necessity ²me ¹is laid on;

οὐαὶ γάρ μοί ἐστιν ἐὰν μὴ εὐαγγελίσωμαι
for woe ²to me ¹is if I do not preach good tiding;

17 εἰ γὰρ ἑκὼν τοῦτο πράσσω, μισθὸ;
For if ²willingly ¹this ¹I do, ²a reward

ἔχω· εἰ δὲ ἄκων, οἰκονομίαν πεπίστευμαι
¹I have; but if unwillingly, ²a stewardship ¹I have been
entrusted [with]

18 τίς οὖν μού ἐστιν ὁ μισθός; ἵνα
What therefore ⁴of me ¹is ²the ³reward? in order
that

εὐαγγελιζόμενος ἀδάπανον θήσω τὸ
preaching good tidings ⁴without charge ¹I may place ²the

εὐαγγέλιον, εἰς τὸ μὴ καταχρήσασθαι
³good tidings, so as† not to use to the full

τῇ ἐξουσίᾳ μου ἐν τῷ εὐαγγελίῳ.
the authority of me in the good tidings.

19 Ἐλεύθερος γὰρ ὢν ἐκ πάντων πᾶσιν
For ²free ¹being of all men ³to all men

ἐμαυτὸν ἐδούλωσα, ἵνα τοὺς πλείονας
¹myself ¹I enslaved, in order that the more

κερδήσω· 20 καὶ ἐγενόμην τοῖς Ἰουδαίοις
I might gain; and I became to the Jews

ὡς Ἰουδαῖος, ἵνα Ἰουδαίους κερδήσω·
as a Jew, in order that Jews I might gain;

τοῖς ὑπὸ νόμον ὡς ὑπὸ νόμον, μὴ ὢν
to the under law as under law, not being
ones

αὐτὸς ὑπὸ νόμον, ἵνα τοὺς ὑπὸ νόμον
[my]self under law, in order the under law
that ones

κερδήσω· 21 τοῖς ἀνόμοις ὡς ἄνομος,
I might gain; to the ones without law as without law,

μὴ ὢν ἄνομος θεοῦ ἀλλ' ἔννομος Χριστοῦ,
not being without of God but under of Christ,
[the] law [the] law

ἵνα κερδάνω τοὺς ἀνόμους· 22 ἐγενόμην
in order I may gain the ones without law; I became
that

τοῖς ἀσθενέσιν ἀσθενής, ἵνα τοὺς ἀσθενεῖς
³to the ³weak ¹weak, in order the weak
that

κερδήσω· τοῖς πᾶσιν γέγονα πάντα, ἵνα
I might gain; — to all men I have all in order
become things, that

πάντως τινὰς σώσω. 23 πάντα δὲ ποιῶ
in any case ²some ¹I might save. But all things I do

διὰ τὸ εὐαγγέλιον, ἵνα συγκοινωνὸς αὐτοῦ
because the good tidings, in order ²a joint partaker ³of it
of that

24 Know ye not that they which run in a race run all, but one receiveth the prize? So run, that ye may obtain.

25 And every man that striveth for the mastery is temperate in all things. Now they *do it* to obtain a corruptible crown; but we an incorruptible.

26 I therefore so run, not as uncertainly; so fight I, not as one that beateth the air:

27 But I keep under my body, and bring *it* into subjection: lest that by any means, when I have preached to others, I myself should be a castaway.

γένωμαι.   24 Οὐκ οἴδατε ὅτι οἱ ἐν
¹I may become.   Know ye not   that the [ones] ²in

σταδίῳ τρέχοντες πάντες μὲν τρέχουσιν,
²a racecourse ¹running   all   indeed   run,

εἷς δὲ λαμβάνει τὸ βραβεῖον; οὕτως
but one   receives   the   prize?   So

τρέχετε ἵνα καταλάβητε. 25 πᾶς δὲ ὁ
run   in order that ye may obtain.   And everyone

ἀγωνιζόμενος πάντα ἐγκρατεύεται, ἐκεῖνοι
struggling   [in] all things exercises self-control,   those

μὲν οὖν ἵνα φθαρτὸν στέφανον λάβωσιν,
indeed there- in order ²a corruptible ³crown   ¹they may
fore   that   receive,

ἡμεῖς δὲ ἄφθαρτον. 26 ἐγὼ τοίνυν οὕτως
but we   an incorruptible.   I   accordingly   so

τρέχω ὡς οὐκ ἀδήλως, οὕτως πυκτεύω
run   as   not   unclearly,   so   I box

ὡς οὐκ ἀέρα δέρων· 27 ἀλλὰ ὑπωπιάζω
as   not   ²air   ¹beating;   but   I treat severely

μου τὸ σῶμα καὶ δουλαγωγῶ, μή πως
of me the   body   and lead [it] as a slave,   lest

ἄλλοις κηρύξας αὐτὸς ἀδόκιμος γένωμαι.
to others having pro- ²[my]self ³disapproved   ¹I ³may
claimed   ⁴become.

CHAPTER 10

MOREOVER, brethren, I would not that ye should be ignorant, how that all our fathers were under the cloud, and all passed through the sea;

2 And were all baptized unto Moses in the cloud and in the sea;

3 And did all eat the same spiritual meat;

4 And did all drink the same spiritual drink: for they drank of that spiritual Rock that followed them: and that Rock was Christ.

5 But with many of them God was not well pleased: for they were overthrown in the wilderness.

10 Οὐ θέλω γὰρ ὑμᾶς ἀγνοεῖν, ἀδελφοί,
For I wish not   you · to be ignorant,   brothers,

ὅτι οἱ πατέρες ἡμῶν πάντες ὑπὸ τὴν
that the   fathers   of us   all   under the

νεφέλην ἦσαν καὶ πάντες διὰ τῆς θαλάσσης
cloud   were and   all   through the   sea

διῆλθον, 2 καὶ πάντες εἰς τὸν Μωϋσῆν
passed *through,* and   all   ²to   -   ³Moses

ἐβαπτίσαντο ἐν τῇ νεφέλῃ καὶ ἐν τῇ
¹were baptized   in   the   cloud   and   in   the

θαλάσσῃ, 3 καὶ πάντες τὸ αὐτὸ πνευματικὸν
sea,   and   all   ²the ³same   ⁴spiritual

βρῶμα ἔφαγον, 4 καὶ πάντες τὸ αὐτὸ
⁵food   ¹ate,   and   all   ²the   ³same

πνευματικὸν ἔπιον πόμα· ἔπινον γὰρ ἐκ
⁴spiritual   ¹drank   ⁵drink;   for they drank   of

πνευματικῆς ἀκολουθούσης πέτρας, ἡ πέτρα
a spiritual   ²following   ¹rock,   ²the   ³rock

δὲ ἦν ὁ Χριστός. 5 Ἀλλ᾽ οὐκ ἐν τοῖς
¹and was *the*   Christ.   But   ⁷not ¹in(with) ²the

πλείοσιν αὐτῶν εὐδόκησεν ὁ θεός·
³majority   ⁴of them   ⁶was ⁵well ⁹pleased   -   ⁸God;

κατεστρώθησαν γὰρ ἐν τῇ ἐρήμῳ.
for they were scattered   in   the   desert.

6 Now these things were our examples, to the intent we should not lust after evil things, as they also lusted.

7 Neither be ye idolaters, as *were* some of them; as it is written, The people sat down to eat and drink, and rose up to play.

8 Neither let us commit fornication, as some of them committed, and fell in one day three and twenty thousand.

9 Neither let us tempt Christ, as some of them also tempted, and were destroyed of serpents.

10 Neither murmur ye, as some of them also murmured, and were destroyed of the destroyer.

11 Now all these things happened unto them for ensamples: and they are written for our admonition, upon whom the ends of the world are come.

12 Wherefore let him that thinketh he standeth take heed lest he fall.

13 There hath no temptation taken you but such as is common to man: but God *is* faithful, who will not suffer you to be tempted above that ye are able; but will with the temptation also make a way to escape, that ye may be able to bear *it*.

6 ταῦτα δὲ τύποι ἡμῶν ἐγενήθησαν, εἰς
Now these things types of us were, for

τὸ μὴ εἶναι ἡμᾶς ἐπιθυμητὰς κακῶν,
the not to be us[b] longers after evil things,
=so that we should not be . . .

καθὼς κἀκεῖνοι ἐπεθύμησαν. 7 μηδὲ
as those indeed longed. Neither

εἰδωλολάτραι γίνεσθε, καθώς τινες αὐτῶν·
idolaters be ye, as some of them;

ὥσπερ γέγραπται· ἐκάθισεν ὁ λαὸς φαγεῖν
as it has been written: Sat the people to eat

καὶ πεῖν, καὶ ἀνέστησαν παίζειν. 8 μηδὲ
and to drink, and stood up to play. Neither

πορνεύωμεν, καθώς τινες αὐτῶν ἐπόρνευσαν
let us commit as some of them committed
fornication, fornication

καὶ ἔπεσαν μιᾷ ἡμέρᾳ εἴκοσι τρεῖς
and fell in one day twenty-three

χιλιάδες. 9 μηδὲ ἐκπειράζωμεν τὸν κύριον,
thousands. Neither let us overtempt the Lord,

καθώς τινες αὐτῶν ἐπείρασαν καὶ ὑπὸ
as some of them tempted and by

τῶν ὄφεων ἀπώλλυντο. 10 μηδὲ γογγύζετε,
the serpents were destroyed. Neither murmur ye,

καθάπερ τινὲς αὐτῶν ἐγόγγυσαν, καὶ
even as some of them murmured, and

ἀπώλοντο ὑπὸ τοῦ ὀλεθρευτοῦ. 11 ταῦτα δὲ
were destroyed by the destroyer. Now these things

τυπικῶς συνέβαινεν ἐκείνοις, ἐγράφη δὲ
[a]typically [1]happened [2]to those men, and was(were)
written

πρὸς νουθεσίαν ἡμῶν, εἰς οὓς τὰ
for admonition of us, to whom the

τέλη τῶν αἰώνων κατήντηκεν. 12 Ὥστε
ends of the ages has(ve) arrived. So as

ὁ δοκῶν ἑστάναι βλεπέτω μὴ πέσῃ.
the thinking to stand let him look lest he falls.
[one]

13 πειρασμὸς ὑμᾶς οὐκ εἴληφεν εἰ μὴ
Temptation you has not taken except

ἀνθρώπινος· πιστὸς δὲ ὁ θεός, ὃς οὐκ
[what is] human; but faithful [is] – God, who not

ἐάσει ὑμᾶς πειρασθῆναι ὑπὲρ ὃ δύνασθε,
will allow you to be tempted beyond what you are able
[to bear],

ἀλλὰ ποιήσει σὺν τῷ πειρασμῷ καὶ τὴν
but will make with the temptation also the

ἔκβασιν τοῦ δύνασθαι ὑπενεγκεῖν.
way out – to be able to endure.[d]
=so that ye may be able . . .

14 Wherefore, my dearly beloved, flee from idolatry.

15 I speak as to wise men; judge ye what I say.

16 The cup of blessing which we bless, is it not the communion of the blood of Christ? The bread which we break, is it not the communion of the body of Christ?

17 For we *being* many are one bread, *and* one body: for we are all partakers of that one bread.

18 Behold Israel after the flesh: are not they which eat of the sacrifices partakers of the altar?

19 What say I then? that the idol is any thing, or that which is offered in sacrifice to idols is any thing?

20 But *I* say, that the things which the Gentiles sacrifice, they sacrifice to devils, and not to God: and I would not that ye should have fellowship with devils.

21 Ye cannot drink the cup of the Lord, and the cup of devils: ye cannot be partakers of the Lord's table, and of the table of devils.

22 Do we provoke the Lord to jealousy? are we stronger than he?

23 All things are lawful for me, but all things are not expedient: all things are lawful for me, but all things edify not.

---

14 Διόπερ, ἀγαπητοί μου, φεύγετε ἀπὸ
Wherefore, beloved of me, flee ye from

τῆς εἰδωλολατρίας. 15 ὡς φρονίμοις λέγω·
- idolatry. ²As ²to prudent men ¹I say;

κρίνατε ὑμεῖς ὃ φημι. 16 Τὸ ποτήριον
judge ye what I say. The cup

τῆς εὐλογίας ὃ εὐλογοῦμεν, οὐχὶ κοινωνία
- of blessing which we bless, ²not ²a communion

ἐστὶν τοῦ αἵματος τοῦ Χριστοῦ; τὸν
¹is it of the blood - of Christ? the

ἄρτον ὃν κλῶμεν, οὐχὶ κοινωνία τοῦ
bread which we break, ²not ²a communion ⁴of the

σώματος τοῦ Χριστοῦ ἐστιν; 17 ὅτι εἰς
⁵body - ⁶of Christ ¹is it? Because ⁴one

ἄρτος, ἓν σῶμα οἱ πολλοί ἐσμεν· οἱ γὰρ
⁵bread, ⁶one ⁷body ³the ⁸many ¹we are; - for

πάντες ἐκ τοῦ ἑνὸς ἄρτου μετέχομεν.
all of the one bread we partake.

18 βλέπετε τὸν Ἰσραὴλ κατὰ σάρκα·
See ye - Israel according to [the] flesh;

οὐχ οἱ ἐσθίοντες τὰς θυσίας κοινωνοὶ
²not ²the [ones] ⁴eating ⁵the ⁶sacrifices ⁷sharers

τοῦ θυσιαστηρίου εἰσίν; 19 τί οὖν φημι;
¹of the ⁸altar ¹are? What there- do I say?
fore

ὅτι εἰδωλόθυτόν τί ἐστιν; ἢ ὅτι εἴδωλόν
that an idolatrous ²anything ¹is? or that an idol
sacrifice

τί ἐστιν; 20 ἀλλ’ ὅτι ἃ θύουσιν,
²anything ¹is? but that [the] things they
which sacrifice,

δαιμονίοις καὶ οὐ θεῷ θύουσιν· οὐ θέλω
to demons and not to God they sacrifice; ²not ³I wish

δὲ ὑμᾶς κοινωνοὺς τῶν δαιμονίων γίνεσθαι.
¹and you sharers of the demons to become.

21 οὐ δύνασθε ποτήριον κυρίου πίνειν
Ye cannot ²a cup ³of [the] Lord ¹to drink

καὶ ποτήριον δαιμονίων· οὐ δύνασθε
and a cup of demons; ye cannot

τραπέζης κυρίου μετέχειν καὶ τραπέζης
²of a table ³of [the] Lord ¹to partake and of a table

δαιμονίων. 22 ἢ παραζηλοῦμεν τὸν κύριον;
of demons. Or do we make jealous the Lord?

μὴ ἰσχυρότεροι αὐτοῦ ἐσμεν;
Not ²stronger [than] ³he ¹are we?

23 Πάντα ἔξεστιν, ἀλλ’ οὐ πάντα
All things [are] lawful, but not all things

συμφέρει· πάντα ἔξεστιν, ἀλλ’ οὐ πάντα
¯are] expedient; all things lawful, but not all things
[are]

24 Let no man seek his own, but every man another's *wealth*.

25 Whatsoever is sold in the shambles, *that* eat, asking no question for conscience sake:

26 For the earth *is* the Lord's, and the fulness thereof.

27 If any of them that believe not bid you *to a feast*, and ye be disposed to go; whatsoever is set before you, eat, asking no question for conscience sake.

28 But if any man say unto you, This is offered in sacrifice unto idols, eat not for his sake that shewed it, and for conscience sake: for the earth *is* the Lord's, and the fulness thereof:

29 Conscience, I say, not thine own, but of the other: for why is my liberty judged of another *man's* conscience?

30 For if I by grace be a partaker, why am I evil spoken of for that for which I give thanks?

31 Whether therefore ye eat, or drink, or whatsoever ye do, do all to the glory of God.

32 Give none offence, neither to the Jews, nor to the Gentiles, nor to the church of God:

33 Even as I please all *men* in all *things*, not seeking mine own profit, but the *profit* of many, that they may be saved.

οἰκοδομεῖ. **24** μηδεὶς τὸ ἑαυτοῦ ζητείτω
edifies(fy).   No one the thing of himself let him seek

ἀλλὰ τὸ τοῦ ἑτέρου. **25** Πᾶν τὸ ἐν
but the thing of the other.   Everything   ²in

μακέλλῳ πωλούμενον ἐσθίετε μηδὲν
³a meat market   ¹being sold   eat ye   ²nothing

ἀνακρίνοντες διὰ τὴν συνείδησιν· **26** τοῦ
¹examining because of   conscience;   ²of the

κυρίου γὰρ ἡ γῆ καὶ τὸ πλήρωμα
³Lord   ¹for the earth and the   fulness

αὐτῆς. **27** εἴ τις καλεῖ ὑμᾶς τῶν ἀπίστων
of it.   If anyone invites you of the unbelievers

καὶ θέλετε πορεύεσθαι, πᾶν τὸ παρατι-
and ye wish   to go,   ²everything ³being set

θέμενον ὑμῖν ἐσθίετε μηδὲν ἀνακρίνοντες
before ⁴you   ¹eat ⁶nothing   ⁵examining

διὰ τὴν συνείδησιν. **28** ἐὰν δέ τις ὑμῖν
because – conscience.   But if anyone ²to you
of

εἴπῃ· τοῦτο ἱερόθυτόν ἐστιν, μὴ ἐσθίετε
¹says: This ²slain in sacrifice ¹is,   do not eat

δι' ἐκεῖνον τὸν μηνύσαντα καὶ τὴν
because that   the pointing out and   –
of   man   [one]

συνείδησιν· **29** συνείδησιν δὲ λέγω οὐχὶ
conscience: ³conscience ¹but ²I say not

τὴν ἑαυτοῦ ἀλλὰ τὴν τοῦ ἑτέρου. ἱνατί
the one of himself but the one of the other.*   why

γὰρ ἡ ἐλευθερία μου κρίνεται ὑπὸ ἄλλης
For the freedom of me is judged by ²of another

συνειδήσεως; **30** εἰ ἐγὼ χάριτι μετέχω,
¹conscience?   If   I by grace partake,

τί βλασφημοῦμαι ὑπὲρ οὗ ἐγὼ εὐχαριστῶ;
why   am I evil because what I give thanks
        spoken of   [for]?

31 Εἴτε οὖν ἐσθίετε εἴτε πίνετε εἴτε
Whether therefore ye eat   or ye drink or

τι ποιεῖτε, πάντα εἰς δόξαν θεοῦ ποιεῖτε.
what ye do, all things to [the] glory of God do ye.
[ever]

32 ἀπρόσκοποι καὶ Ἰουδαίοις γίνεσθε καὶ
²Without offence ³both ⁴to Jews   ¹be ye ⁵and

Ἕλλησιν καὶ τῇ ἐκκλησίᾳ τοῦ θεοῦ,
⁶to Greeks and to the church   – of God,

33 καθὼς κἀγὼ πάντα πᾶσιν ἀρέσκω,
as   I also [in] all things all men please,

μὴ ζητῶν τὸ ἐμαυτοῦ σύμφορον ἀλλὰ
not seeking the of myself advantage but

* That is, not the conscience of the person invited, to whom the apostle's words are addressed, but the conscience of the person "pointing out."

CHAPTER 11

BE ye followers of me, even as I also *am* of Christ.

2 Now I praise you, brethren, that ye remember me in all things, and keep the ordinances, as I delivered *them* to you.

3 But I would have you know, that the head of every man is Christ; and the head of the woman *is* the man; and the head of Christ *is* God.

4 Every man praying or prophesying, having *his* head covered, dishonoureth his head.

5 But every woman that prayeth or prophesieth with *her* head uncovered dishonoureth her head: for that is even all one as if she were shaven.

6 For if the woman be not covered, let her also be shorn: but if it be a shame for a woman to be shorn or shaven, let her be covered.

7 For a man indeed ought not to cover *his* head, forasmuch as he is the image and glory of God: but the woman is the glory of the man.

8 For the man is not of the woman; but the woman of the man.

9 Neither was the man

τὸ τῶν πολλῶν, ἵνα σωθῶσιν. 11 μιμηταί
the of the many, in order they may   Imitators
(that)   that   be saved.

μου γίνεσθε, καθὼς κἀγὼ Χριστοῦ.
of me be ye,   as   I also [am] of Christ.

2 Ἐπαινῶ δὲ ὑμᾶς ὅτι πάντα μου
But I praise   you because ²all things ³of me

μέμνησθε καὶ καθὼς παρέδωκα ὑμῖν τὰς
¹ye have   and ⁴as   ⁵I delivered ⁶to you ²the
remembered

παραδόσεις κατέχετε. 3 Θέλω δὲ ὑμᾶς
²traditions ¹ye hold fast. But I wish   you

εἰδέναι ὅτι παντὸς ἀνδρὸς ἡ κεφαλὴ ὁ
to know that ⁵of every ⁶man ³the ⁴head -

Χριστός ἐστιν, κεφαλὴ δὲ γυναικὸς ὁ
¹Christ   ²is,   and [the] head of a woman the

ἀνήρ, κεφαλὴ δὲ τοῦ Χριστοῦ ὁ θεός.
man, and [the] head - of Christ - God.

4 πᾶς ἀνὴρ προσευχόμενος ἢ προφητεύων
Every man   praying   or prophesying

κατὰ κεφαλῆς ἔχων καταισχύνει τὴν
³down over ⁴[his] head ¹having shames   the
                      ²[anything]

κεφαλὴν αὐτοῦ. 5 πᾶσα δὲ γυνὴ προσ-
head   of him. But every woman   pray-

ευχομένη ἢ προφητεύουσα ἀκατακαλύπτῳ
ing   or prophesying   ³unveiled

τῇ κεφαλῇ καταισχύνει τὴν κεφαλὴν αὐτῆς·
¹with ²head shames   the   head   of her;
the(her)

ἕν γάρ ἐστιν καὶ τὸ αὐτὸ τῇ ἐξυρημένῃ.
for ²one ¹it is and the same with the having been
                     thing woman shaved.

6 εἰ γὰρ οὐ κατακαλύπτεται γυνή, καὶ
For if   ²is not veiled ¹a woman, also

κειράσθω· εἰ δὲ αἰσχρὸν γυναικὶ τὸ
let her be shorn; but if shameful for a woman -

κείρασθαι ἢ ξυρᾶσθαι, κατακαλυπτέσθω.
to be shorn or *to be* shaved, let her be veiled.

7 ἀνὴρ μὲν γὰρ οὐκ ὀφείλει κατα-
For a man indeed   ought not   to be

καλύπτεσθαι τὴν κεφαλήν,ᵇ ²[the] image ³and ⁴glory
veiled   the   head,ᵇ

θεοῦ ὑπάρχων· ἡ γυνὴ δὲ δόξα ἀνδρός
⁵of God ¹being; but the woman ²[the] glory ³of a man

ἐστιν. 8 οὐ γάρ ἐστιν ἀνὴρ ἐκ γυναικός,
¹is.   For ²not ²is ¹man of woman,

ἀλλὰ γυνὴ ἐξ ἀνδρός· 9 καὶ γὰρ οὐκ
but woman of man; for indeed ²not

created for the woman; but the woman for the man.

10 For this cause ought the woman to have power on *her* head because of the angels.

11 Nevertheless neither is the man without the woman, neither the woman without the man, in the Lord.

12 For as the woman *is* of the man, even so *is* the man also by the woman; but all things of God.

13 Judge in yourselves: is it comely that a woman pray unto God uncovered?

14 Doth not even nature itself teach you, that, if a man have long hair, it is a shame unto him?

15 But if a woman have long hair, it is a glory to her: for *her* hair is given her for a covering.

16 But if any man seem to be contentious, we have no such custom, neither the churches of God.

17 Now in this that I declare *unto you* I praise *you* not, that ye come together not for the better, but for the worse.

18 For first of all, when ye come together in the church, I hear that there be divisions among you; and I partly believe it.

ἐκτίσθη ἀνὴρ διὰ τὴν γυναῖκα, ἀλλὰ
¹was ⁴created ³man because of the   woman,   but

γυνὴ διὰ τὸν ἄνδρα. 10 διὰ τοῦτο
woman because of the   man.   Therefore

ὀφείλει ἡ γυνὴ ἐξουσίαν ἔχειν ἐπὶ τῆς
ought   the   woman   authority   to have   on   the

κεφαλῆς διὰ τοὺς ἀγγέλους. 11 πλὴν
head   because of the   angels.   Nevertheless

οὔτε γυνὴ χωρὶς ἀνδρὸς οὔτε ἀνὴρ χωρὶς
neither woman   without   man   nor   man   without

γυναικὸς ἐν κυρίῳ· 12 ὥσπερ γὰρ ἡ
woman   in   [the] Lord;   for as   the

γυνὴ ἐκ τοῦ ἀνδρός, οὕτως καὶ ὁ ἀνὴρ
woman of   the   man,   so   also the   man

διὰ τῆς γυναικός· τὰ δὲ πάντα ἐκ τοῦ
through the   woman;   - but all things of

θεοῦ. 13 Ἐν ὑμῖν αὐτοῖς κρίνατε· πρέπον
God.   Among   you   [your]selves   judge: ²fitting

ἐστὶν γυναῖκα ἀκατακάλυπτον τῷ θεῷ
¹is it   ³[for] ⁴a woman   ⁷unveiled   -   ⁵to God

προσεύχεσθαι; 14 οὐδὲ ἡ φύσις αὐτὴ
⁵to pray?   Not   -   nature   [her]self

διδάσκει ὑμᾶς ὅτι ἀνὴρ μὲν ἐὰν κομᾷ,
teaches   you   that   a man   indeed   if   he wears his hair long,

ἀτιμία αὐτῷ ἐστιν, 15 γυνὴ δὲ ἐὰν
²a dishonour ³to him   ¹it is,   but a woman   if

κομᾷ, δόξα αὐτῇ ἐστιν; ὅτι ἡ κόμη
she wears ²a glory ³to her   ¹it is?   because the long hair
her hair long,

ἀντὶ περιβολαίου δέδοται αὐτῇ. 16 Εἰ
instead of   a veil   has been given   to her.   if

δέ τις δοκεῖ φιλόνεικος εἶναι, ἡμεῖς
But anyone   thinks   ²contentious   ¹to be,   we

τοιαύτην συνήθειαν οὐκ ἔχομεν, οὐδὲ αἱ
²such   ³a custom   ¹have not,   neither the

ἐκκλησίαι τοῦ θεοῦ.
churches   -   of God.

17 Τοῦτο δὲ παραγγέλλων οὐκ ἐπαινῶ
But this   charging   I do not praise

ὅτι οὐκ εἰς τὸ κρεῖσσον ἀλλὰ εἰς τὸ
because not   for   the   better   but   for   the

ἧσσον συνέρχεσθε. 18 πρῶτον μὲν γὰρ
worse   ye come together.   For firstly indeed

συνερχομένων ὑμῶν ἐν ἐκκλησίᾳ ἀκούω
coming together   you²   in   church   I hear
=when ye come together

σχίσματα ἐν ὑμῖν ὑπάρχειν, καὶ μέρος
divisions   among   you   to be,   and   ²part

19 For there must be also heresies among you, that they which are approved may be made manifest among you.

20 When ye come together therefore into one place, *this* is not to eat the Lord's supper.

21 For in eating every one taketh before *other* his own supper: and one is hungry, and another is drunken.

22 What? have ye not houses to eat and to drink in? or despise ye the church of God, and shame them that have not? What shall I say to you? shall I praise you in this? I praise *you* not.

23 For I have received of the Lord that which also I delivered unto you, That the Lord Jesus the *same* night in which he was betrayed took bread:

24 And when he had given thanks, he brake *it*, and said, Take, eat: this is my body, which is broken for you: this do in remembrance of me.

25 After the same manner also *he took* the cup, when he had supped, saying, This cup is the new testament in my blood: this do ye, as oft

τι πιστεύω. **19** δεῖ γὰρ καὶ αἱρέσεις
¹some I believe.   For it behoves indeed sects

ἐν ὑμῖν εἶναι, ἵνα [καὶ] οἱ δόκιμοι
among you to be, in order also the approved
    that   ones

φανεροὶ γένωνται ἐν ὑμῖν. **20** Συν-
manifest may become among you.   Coming

ἐρχομένων οὖν ὑμῶν ἐπὶ τὸ αὐτὸ οὐκ
together therefore you²   together not
= When therefore ye come

ἔστιν κυριακὸν δεῖπνον φαγεῖν· **21** ἕκαστος
it is of the Lord* a supper to eat;   ²each one

γὰρ τὸ ἴδιον δεῖπνον προλαμβάνει ἐν
¹for the(his) own supper takes before in

τῷ φαγεῖν, καὶ ὃς μὲν πεινᾷ, ὃς δὲ
- to eat(eating), and one† hungers, another†

μεθύει. **22** μὴ γὰρ οἰκίας οὐκ ἔχετε
is drunken.   *Not* indeed ²houses ¹have ye not

εἰς τὸ ἐσθίειν καὶ πίνειν; ἢ τῆς ἐκκλησίας
- to eat and to drink? or the church

τοῦ θεοῦ καταφρονεῖτε, καὶ καταισχύνετε
- of God despise ye, and shame

τοὺς μὴ ἔχοντας; τί εἴπω ὑμῖν; ἐπαινέσω
the not having? What may I say to you? shall I praise
[ones]

ὑμᾶς; ἐν τούτῳ οὐκ ἐπαινῶ. **23** Ἐγὼ
you? In this I praise not.   I

γὰρ παρέλαβον ἀπὸ τοῦ κυρίου, ὃ καὶ
For received from the Lord, what also

παρέδωκα ὑμῖν, ὅτι ὁ κύριος Ἰησοῦς
I delivered to you, that the Lord Jesus

ἐν τῇ νυκτὶ ᾗ παρεδίδοτο ἔλαβεν ἄρτον
in the night in which he was took bread
    betrayed

24 καὶ εὐχαριστήσας ἔκλασεν καὶ εἶπεν·
and having given thanks broke and said:

τοῦτό μού ἐστιν τὸ σῶμα τὸ ὑπὲρ
This of me is the body - on be-
    half of

ὑμῶν· τοῦτο ποιεῖτε εἰς τὴν ἐμὴν
you; this do ye for - my

ἀνάμνησιν. **25** ὡσαύτως καὶ τὸ ποτήριον
remembrance.   Similarly also the cup

μετὰ τὸ δειπνῆσαι, λέγων· τοῦτο τὸ
after the to sup, saying: This -

ποτήριον ἡ καινὴ διαθήκη ἐστὶν ἐν τῷ
cup ²the ³new ⁴covenant ¹is in -

ἐμῷ αἵματι· τοῦτο ποιεῖτε, ὁσάκις ἐὰν
my blood; this do ye, as often as

---

* Note that κυριακός is an adjective, for which no exact English equivalent is available. Only other occurrence in N.T., Rev. 1. 10.

as ye drink *it*, in remembrance of me.

26 For as often as ye eat this bread, and drink this cup, ye do shew the Lord's death till he come.

27 Wherefore whosoever shall eat this bread, and drink *this* cup of the Lord, unworthily, shall be guilty of the body and blood of the Lord.

28 But let a man examine himself, and so let him eat of *that* bread, and drink of *that* cup.

29 For he that eateth and drinketh unworthily, eateth and drinketh damnation to himself, not discerning the Lord's body.

30 For this cause many *are* weak and sickly among you, and many sleep.

31 For if we would judge ourselves, we should not be judged.

32 But when we are judged, we are chastened of the Lord, that we should not be condemned with the world.

33 Wherefore, my brethren, when ye come together to eat, tarry one for another.

34 And if any man hunger, let him eat at home; that ye come not together unto condemnation. And the rest will I set in order when I come.

πίνητε, εἰς τὴν ἐμὴν ἀνάμνησιν. 26 ὁσάκις
ye drink,   for⁻   -   my   remembrance.   as often
γὰρ ἐὰν ἐσθίητε τὸν ἄρτον τοῦτον καὶ
For   as   ye eat   this bread   and
τὸ ποτήριον πίνητε, τὸν θάνατον τοῦ
²the ²cup ¹drink, the death of the
κυρίου καταγγέλλετε, ἄχρι οὗ ἔλθῃ.
Lord   ye declare,   until   he comes.
27 Ὥστε ὃς ἂν ἐσθίῃ τὸν ἄρτον ἢ
So as whoever eats the bread or
πίνῃ τὸ ποτήριον τοῦ κυρίου ἀναξίως,
drinks the cup of the Lord unworthily,
ἔνοχος ἔσται τοῦ σώματος καὶ τοῦ
guilty will be of the body and of the
αἵματος τοῦ κυρίου. 28 δοκιμαζέτω δὲ
blood of the Lord. But ¹let ³prove
ἄνθρωπος ἑαυτόν, καὶ οὕτως ἐκ τοῦ
²a man ⁴himself, and so of the
ἄρτου ἐσθιέτω καὶ ἐκ τοῦ ποτηρίου
bread let him eat and of the cup
πινέτω· 29 ὁ γὰρ ἐσθίων καὶ πίνων
let him drink; for the [one] eating and drinking
κρίμα ἑαυτῷ ἐσθίει καὶ πίνει μὴ διακρίνων
⁴judgment ⁵to ¹eats ²and ³drinks not discerning
himself
τὸ σῶμα. 30 διὰ τοῦτο ἐν ὑμῖν πολλοὶ
the body. Therefore among you many
ἀσθενεῖς καὶ ἄρρωστοι καὶ κοιμῶνται
[are] weak and feeble and ²sleep
ἱκανοί. 31 εἰ δὲ ἑαυτοὺς διεκρίνομεν,
¹a number. But if ourselves we discerned,
οὐκ ἂν ἐκρινόμεθα· 32 κρινόμενοι δὲ ὑπὸ
we should not be judged; but being judged by
τοῦ κυρίου παιδευόμεθα, ἵνα μὴ σὺν
the Lord we are chastened, lest with
τῷ κόσμῳ κατακριθῶμεν. 33 Ὥστε,
the world we are condemned. So as,
ἀδελφοί μου, συνερχόμενοι εἰς τὸ φαγεῖν
brothers of me, coming together for the to eat
ἀλλήλους ἐκδέχεσθε. 34 εἴ τις πεινᾷ,
one another await ye. If anyone hungers,
ἐν οἴκῳ ἐσθιέτω, ἵνα μὴ εἰς κρίμα
at home let him eat, lest to judgment
συνέρχησθε. τὰ δὲ λοιπὰ ὡς ἂν ἔλθω
ye come together. And the remaining matters whenever I come
διατάξομαι.
I will arrange.

CHAPTER 12

NOW concerning spiritual *gifts*, brethren, I would not have you ignorant.

2 Ye know that ye were Gentiles, carried away unto these dumb idols, even as ye were led.

3 Wherefore I give you to understand, that no man speaking by the Spirit of God calleth Jesus accursed: and *that* no man can say that Jesus is the Lord, but by the Holy Ghost.

4 Now there are diversities of gifts, but the same Spirit.

5 And there are differences of administrations, but the same Lord.

6 And there are diversities of operations, but it is the same God which worketh all in all.

7 But the manifestation of the Spirit is given to every man to profit withal.

8 For to one is given by the Spirit the word of wisdom; to another the word of knowledge by the same Spirit;

9 To another faith by the same Spirit; to another the gifts of healing by the same Spirit;

10 To another the working of miracles; to another prophecy; to another discerning of spirits; to another *divers* kinds of tongues; to another the

12 Περὶ δὲ τῶν πνευματικῶν, ἀδελφοί,
Now about the spiritual matters, brothers,

οὐ θέλω ὑμᾶς ἀγνοεῖν. 2 Οἴδατε ὅτι
I do not wish you to be ignorant. Ye know that

ὅτε ἔθνη ἦτε πρὸς τὰ εἴδωλα τὰ ἄφωνα
when ²nations ¹ye were ⁴to ⁵the ⁷idols - ⁶voiceless

ὡς ἂν ἤγεσθε ἀπαγόμενοι. 3 διὸ γνωρίζω
⁸however ⁹ye were led ⁹[ye were] Where- I make
¹⁰being led away.* fore known

ὑμῖν ὅτι οὐδεὶς ἐν πνεύματι θεοῦ λαλῶν
to you that no one ²by ³[the] Spirit ⁴of God ¹speaking

λέγει· ΑΝΑΘΕΜΑ ΙΗΣΟΥΣ, καὶ οὐδεὶς
says: A CURSE [IS] JESUS, and no one

δύναται εἰπεῖν· ΚΥΡΙΟΣ ΙΗΣΟΥΣ, εἰ μὴ
can to say: LORD JESUS, except

ἐν πνεύματι ἁγίῳ.
by [the] ²Spirit ¹Holy.

4 Διαιρέσεις δὲ χαρισμάτων εἰσίν, τὸ δὲ αὐτὸ
Now differences of gifts there are, but the same

πνεῦμα· 5 καὶ διαιρέσεις διακονιῶν εἰσιν, καὶ
Spirit; and differences of ministries there are, and

ὁ αὐτὸς κύριος· 6 καὶ διαιρέσεις ἐνεργημάτων
the same Lord; and differences of operations

εἰσίν, ὁ δὲ αὐτὸς θεὸς ὁ ἐνεργῶν τὰ
there are, but the same God - operating -

πάντα ἐν πᾶσιν. 7 ἑκάστῳ δὲ δίδοται
all things in all. But to each one is given

ἡ φανέρωσις τοῦ πνεύματος πρὸς τὸ
the manifestation of the Spirit to the

συμφέρον. 8 ᾧ μὲν γὰρ διὰ τοῦ πνεύματος
profit*ing*. For to one through the Spirit

δίδοται λόγος σοφίας, ἄλλῳ δὲ λόγος
is given a word of wisdom, and to another a word

γνώσεως κατὰ τὸ αὐτὸ πνεῦμα, 9 ἑτέρῳ
of accord- the same Spirit, to
knowledge ing to another

πίστις ἐν τῷ αὐτῷ πνεύματι, ἄλλῳ δὲ
faith by the same Spirit, and to another

χαρίσματα ἰαμάτων ἐν τῷ ἑνὶ πνεύματι,
gifts of cures by the one Spirit,

10 ἄλλῳ δὲ ἐνεργήματα δυνάμεων, ἄλλῳ
and to another operations of powers, to another

[δὲ] προφητεία, ἄλλῳ δὲ διακρίσεις πνευ-
and prophecy, and to another discernings of

μάτων, ἑτέρῳ γένη γλωσσῶν, ἄλλῳ δὲ
spirits, to another kinds of tongues, and to another

---

* It is thought that there is a scribal error in this verse; see commentaries on the Greek text. We have been guided by G. G. Findlay, *The Expositor's Greek Testament.*

interpretation of tongues:
11 But all these worketh that one and the selfsame Spirit, dividing to every man severally as he will.

12 For as the body is one, and hath many members, and all the members of that one body, being many, are one body: so also is Christ.

13 For by one Spirit are we all baptized into one body, whether we be Jews or Gentiles, whether we be bond or free; and have been all made to drink into one Spirit.

14 For the body is not one member, but many.

15 If the foot shall say, Because I am not the hand, I am not of the body; is it therefore not of the body?

16 And if the ear shall say, Because I am not the eye, I am not of the body; is it therefore not of the body?

17 If the whole body were an eye, where were the hearing? If the whole were hearing, where were the smelling?

18 But now hath God set the members every one of them in the body, as it hath pleased him.

19 And if they were all one member, where were the body?

20 But now are they

ἑρμηνεία γλωσσῶν· 11 πάντα δὲ ταῦτα
interpretation ⁻ of tongues: and ³all ⁹these things

ἐνεργεῖ τὸ ἓν καὶ τὸ αὐτὸ πνεῦμα,
⁷operates ¹the ²one ³and ⁴the ⁵same ⁶Spirit,

διαιροῦν ἰδίᾳ ἑκάστῳ καθὼς βούλεται.
distributing ²separately† ¹to each one   as   he purposes.

12 Καθάπερ γὰρ τὸ σῶμα ἕν ἐστιν
For as   the body ⁹one ¹is

καὶ μέλη πολλὰ ἔχει, πάντα δὲ τὰ
and ³members ²many ¹has,   but all   the

μέλη τοῦ σώματος πολλὰ ὄντα ἕν ἐστιν
members of the body ²many ¹being ⁴one ³is(are)

σῶμα, οὕτως καὶ ὁ Χριστός· 13 καὶ γὰρ
body,   so   also the Christ;   for indeed

ἐν ἑνὶ πνεύματι ἡμεῖς πάντες εἰς ἓν
⁴by ⁵one ⁶Spirit ¹we ²all ⁷into ⁸one

σῶμα ἐβαπτίσθημεν, εἴτε Ἰουδαῖοι εἴτε
⁹body ³were baptized,   whether   Jews   or

Ἕλληνες, εἴτε δοῦλοι εἴτε ἐλεύθεροι, καὶ
Greeks, whether slaves or free,   and

πάντες ἓν πνεῦμα ἐποτίσθημεν. 14 καὶ
all   one Spirit   we were given to drink.   indeed

γὰρ τὸ σῶμα οὐκ ἔστιν ἓν μέλος ἀλλὰ
For the body is not one member but

πολλά. 15 ἐὰν εἴπῃ ὁ πούς· ὅτι οὐκ
many.   If ²says ¹the ²foot: Because not

εἰμὶ χείρ, οὐκ εἰμὶ ἐκ τοῦ σώματος,
I am a hand,   I am not of the body,

οὐ παρὰ τοῦτο οὐκ ἔστιν ἐκ τοῦ σώματος.
not for this   it is not of the body.

16 καὶ ἐὰν εἴπῃ τὸ οὖς· ὅτι οὐκ εἰμὶ
And if says the ear: Because I am not

ὀφθαλμός, οὐκ εἰμὶ ἐκ τοῦ σώματος,
an eye,   I am not of the body,

οὐ παρὰ τοῦτο οὐκ ἔστιν ἐκ τοῦ σώματος.
not for this   it is not of the body.

17 εἰ ὅλον τὸ σῶμα ὀφθαλμός, ποῦ
If all the body [was] an eye, where

ἡ ἀκοή; εἰ ὅλον ἀκοή, ποῦ ἡ ὄσφρησις;
[would be] if all hearing, where the smelling?
the hearing?

18 νῦν δὲ ὁ θεὸς ἔθετο τὰ μέλη, ἓν
But now   — God set the members, ²one

ἕκαστον αὐτῶν ἐν τῷ σώματι καθὼς
¹each of them in the body as

ἠθέλησεν. 19 εἰ δὲ ἦν τὰ πάντα ἓν
he wished.   And if ²was — ¹all one

μέλος, ποῦ τὸ σῶμα; 20 νῦν δὲ πολλὰ
member, where the body?   But now many

many members, yet but one body.

21 And the eye cannot say unto the hand, I have no need of thee: nor again the head to the feet, I have no need of you.

22 Nay, much more those members of the body, which seem to be more feeble, are necessary:

23 And those *members* of the body, which we think to be less honourable, upon these we bestow more abundant honour; and our uncomely *parts* have more abundant comeliness.

24 For our comely *parts* have no need: but God hath tempered the body together, having given more abundant honour to that *part* which lacked:

25 That there should be no schism in the body; but *that* the members should have the same care one for another.

26 And whether one member suffer, all the members suffer with it; or one member be honoured, all the members rejoice with it.

27 Now ye are the body of Christ, and members in particular.

28 And God hath set some in the church, first apostles, secondarily prophets, thirdly teachers, after that miracles, then gifts of healings, helps,

μὲν μέλη, ἐν δὲ σῶμα. 21 οὐ δύναται
¹indeed ²members, but one body. ³cannot

δὲ ὁ ὀφθαλμὸς εἰπεῖν τῇ χειρί· χρείαν
And ¹the ²eye *to* say to the hand: Need

σου οὐκ ἔχω, ἢ πάλιν ἡ κεφαλὴ τοῖς
of thee I have not, or again the head to the

ποσίν· χρείαν ὑμῶν οὐκ ἔχω· 22 ἀλλὰ
feet: Need of you I have not; but

πολλῷ μᾶλλον τὰ δοκοῦντα μέλη τοῦ
by much more ¹the ²seeming ³members ⁴of the

σώματος ἀσθενέστερα ὑπάρχειν ἀναγκαῖά ἐστιν,
⁵body ⁷weaker ⁸to be ⁹necessary ⁶is(are),

23 καὶ ἃ δοκοῦμεν ἀτιμότερα εἶναι
and ¹[members] ⁵we think ⁷less honourable ⁶to be
⁴which

τοῦ σώματος, τούτοις τιμὴν περισσοτέραν
²of the ³body, to these honour more abundant

περιτίθεμεν, καὶ τὰ ἀσχήμονα ἡμῶν
we put round, and the uncomely [members] of us

εὐσχημοσύνην περισσοτέραν ἔχει, 24 τὰ δὲ
²comeliness ³more abundant ¹has(ve), but th~

εὐσχήμονα ἡμῶν οὐ χρείαν ἔχει. ἀλλὰ ὁ
comely [members] of us ²no ³need ¹has(ve). But –

θεὸς συνεκέρασεν τὸ σῶμα, τῷ ὑστερουμένῳ
God blended together the body, ⁴to the [member] ⁵lacking

περισσοτέραν δοὺς τιμήν, 25 ἵνα μὴ ᾖ
²more abundant ¹giving ³honour, lest there be

σχίσμα ἐν τῷ σώματι, ἀλλὰ τὸ αὐτὸ
division in the body, but ⁴the ⁵same

ὑπὲρ ἀλλήλων μεριμνῶσιν τὰ μέλη.
⁶on be- ⁷one ²should care ¹the ³members.
half of another

26 καὶ εἴτε πάσχει ἐν μέλος, συμπάσχει
And whether ²suffers ¹one ³member, ⁷suffers with [it]

πάντα τὰ μέλη· εἴτε δοξάζεται μέλος,
⁴all ⁵the ⁶members; or ²is glorified ¹a member,

συγχαίρει πάντα τὰ μέλη. 27 ὑμεῖς
⁵rejoices with [it] ³all ⁴the ⁶members. ye

δέ ἐστε σῶμα Χριστοῦ καὶ μέλη ἐκ
And are a body of Christ and members in

μέρους. 28 Καὶ οὓς μὲν ἔθετο ὁ θεὸς
part. And ²some† ²placed – ¹God

ἐν τῇ ἐκκλησίᾳ πρῶτον ἀποστόλους, δεύτε-
in the church firstly apostles, second-

ρον προφήτας, τρίτον διδασκάλους, ἔπειτα
ly prophets, thirdly teachers, then

δυνάμεις, ἔπειτα χαρίσματα ἰαμάτων,
powers, then gifts of cures,

governments, diversities of tongues.

29 *Are* all apostles? *are* all prophets? *are* all teachers? *are* all workers of miracles?

30 Have all the gifts of healing? do all speak with tongues? do all interpret?

31 But covet earnestly the best gifts: and yet shew I unto you a more excellent way.

CHAPTER 13

THOUGH I speak with the tongues of men and of angels, and have not charity, I am become *as* sounding brass, or a tinkling cymbal.

2 And though I have *the gift of* prophecy, and understand all mysteries, and all knowledge; and though I have all faith, so that I could remove mountains, and have not charity, I am nothing.

3 And though I bestow all my goods to feed *the poor*, and though I give my body to be burned, and have not charity, it profiteth me nothing.

4 Charity suffereth long, *and* is kind; charity envieth not; charity vaunteth not itself, is not puffed up,

5 Doth not behave itself unseemly, seeketh not her own, is not easily provoked, thinketh no evil;

6 Rejoiceth not in in-

ἀντιλήμψεις, κυβερνήσεις, γένη γλωσσῶν,
helps, governings, kinds of tongues.

29 μὴ πάντες ἀπόστολοι; μὴ πάντες
Not all [are] apostles? not all

προφῆται; μὴ πάντες διδάσκαλοι; μὴ
prophets; not all teachers? not

πάντες δυνάμεις; 30 μὴ πάντες χαρίσματα
all powers? not all ²gifts

ἔχουσιν ἰαμάτων; μὴ πάντες γλώσσαις
¹have of cures? not all ²with tongues

λαλοῦσιν; μὴ πάντες διερμηνεύουσιν;
¹speak? not all interpret?

31 ζηλοῦτε δὲ τὰ χαρίσματα τὰ μείζονα.
but desire ye eagerly the ²gifts - ¹greater.

Καὶ ἔτι καθ' ὑπερβολὴν ὁδὸν ὑμῖν
And yet ⁴according to ⁵excellence ³a way ¹to you

δείκνυμι. 13 Ἐὰν ταῖς γλώσσαις τῶν ἀνθρώπων
¹I show. If in the tongues - of men

λαλῶ καὶ τῶν ἀγγέλων, ἀγάπην δὲ
I speak and - of angels, but love

μὴ ἔχω, γέγονα χαλκὸς ἠχῶν ἢ
I have not, I have become ²brass ¹sounding or

κύμβαλον ἀλαλάζον. 2 καὶ ἐὰν ἔχω
cymbal a tinkling. And if I have

προφητείαν καὶ εἰδῶ τὰ μυστήρια πάντα
prophecy and know ²the ³mysteries ¹all

καὶ πᾶσαν τὴν γνῶσιν, κἂν ἔχω πᾶσαν
and all - knowledge, and if I have all

τὴν πίστιν ὥστε ὄρη μεθιστάναι, ἀγάπην
- faith so as mountains to remove, ²love

δὲ μὴ ἔχω, οὐθέν εἰμι. 3 κἂν ψωμίσω
¹but I have not, nothing I am. And if I dole out

πάντα τὰ ὑπάρχοντά μου, καὶ ἐὰν παραδῶ
all the goods of me, and if I deliver

τὸ σῶμά μου ἵνα καυθήσομαι, ἀγάπην
the body of me in order that I shall be burned, ²love

δὲ μὴ ἔχω, οὐδὲν ὠφελοῦμαι. 4 Ἡ
¹but I have not, nothing I am profited. -

ἀγάπη μακροθυμεῖ, χρηστεύεται ἡ ἀγάπη,
Love suffers long, is kind - love,

οὐ ζηλοῖ, ἡ ἀγάπη οὐ περπερεύεται,
is not jealous, - love does not vaunt itself,

οὐ φυσιοῦται, 5 οὐκ ἀσχημονεῖ, οὐ ζητεῖ
is not puffed up, does not act unbecomingly, does not seek

τὰ ἑαυτῆς, οὐ παροξύνεται, οὐ λογίζεται
the of things her(it)self, is not provoked, does not reckon

τὸ κακόν, 6 οὐ χαίρει ἐπὶ τῇ ἀδικίᾳ,
the evil, rejoices not over the wrong,

iquity, but rejoiceth in the truth;

7 Beareth all things, believeth all things, hopeth all things, endureth all things.

8 Charity never faileth: but whether *there be* prophecies, they shall fail; whether *there be* tongues, they shall cease; whether *there be* knowledge, it shall vanish away.

9 For we know in part, and we prophesy in part.

10 But when that which is perfect is come, then that which is in part shall be done away.

11 When I was a child, I spake as a child, I understood as a child, I thought as a child: but when I became a man, I put away childish things.

12 For now we see through a glass, darkly; but then face to face: now I know in part; but then shall I know even as also I am known.

13 And now abideth faith, hope, charity, these three; but the greatest of these *is* charity.

CHAPTER 14

FOLLOW after charity, and desire spiritual *gifts*, but rather that ye may prophesy.

2 For he that speaketh in an *unknown* tongue speaketh not unto men, but unto God: for no man understandeth *him;* howbeit in the spirit he speaketh mysteries.

συγχαίρει δὲ τῇ ἀληθείᾳ· **7** πάντα στέγει,
but rejoices with the truth; all things covers,

πάντα πιστεύει, πάντα ἐλπίζει, πάντα
all things believes, all things hopes, all things

ὑπομένει. **8** Ἡ ἀγάπη οὐδέποτε πίπτει·
endures. – Love never falls;

εἴτε δὲ προφητεῖαι, καταργηθήσονται· εἴτε
but whether prophecies, they will be abolished; or

γλῶσσαι, παύσονται· εἴτε γνῶσις, κατ-
tongues, they will cease; or knowledge, it will

αργηθήσεται. **9** ἐκ μέρους γὰρ γινώσκομεν
be abolished. For in part we know

καὶ ἐκ μέρους προφητεύομεν· **10** ὅταν
and in part we prophesy; ²when

δὲ ἔλθῃ τὸ τέλειον, τὸ ἐκ μέρους
¹but ⁵comes ³the ⁴perfect thing, the thing in part

καταργηθήσεται. **11** ὅτε ἤμην νήπιος,
will be abolished. When I was an infant,

ἐλάλουν ὡς νήπιος, ἐφρόνουν ὡς νήπιος,
I spoke as an infant, I thought as an infant,

ἐλογιζόμην ὡς νήπιος· ὅτε γέγονα ἀνήρ,
I reckoned as an infant; when I have become a man,

κατήργηκα τὰ τοῦ νηπίου. **12** βλέπομεν
I have the of the infant. we see
abolished things

γὰρ ἄρτι δι᾽ ἐσόπτρου ἐν αἰνίγματι,
For yet through a mirror in a riddle,

τότε δὲ πρόσωπον πρὸς πρόσωπον· ἄρτι
but then face to face; yet

γινώσκω ἐκ μέρους, τότε δὲ ἐπιγνώσομαι
I know in part, but then I shall fully know

καθὼς καὶ ἐπεγνώσθην. **13** νυνὶ δὲ μένει
as also I was fully known. But now remains

πίστις, ἐλπίς, ἀγάπη, τὰ τρία ταῦτα·
faith, hope, love, these three;

μείζων δὲ τούτων ἡ ἀγάπη.
and [the] greater of these [is] – love.

14 Διώκετε τὴν ἀγάπην, ζηλοῦτε δὲ
Pursue ye – love, but desire eagerly

τὰ πνευματικά, μᾶλλον δὲ ἵνα προφητεύητε.
the spiritual [gifts], and rather in order ye may prophesy.
that

2 ὁ γὰρ λαλῶν γλώσσῃ οὐκ ἀνθρώποις
For the [one] speaking in a tongue ²not to men

λαλεῖ ἀλλὰ θεῷ· οὐδεὶς γὰρ ἀκούει,
¹speaks but to God; for no one hears,

πνεύματι δὲ λαλεῖ μυστήρια· **3** ὁ δὲ
but in spirit he speaks mysteries; but the [one]

3 But he that prophesieth speaketh unto men *to* edification, and exhortation, and comfort.

4 He that speaketh in an *unknown* tongue edifieth himself; but he that prophesieth edifieth the church.

5 I would that ye all spake with tongues, but rather that ye prophesied: for greater *is* he that prophesieth than he that speaketh with tongues, except he interpret, that the church may receive edifying.

6 Now, brethren, if I come unto you speaking with tongues, what shall I profit you, except I shall speak to you either by revelation, or by knowledge, or by prophesying, or by doctrine?

7 And even things without life giving sound, whether pipe or harp, except they give a distinction in the sounds, how shall it be known what is piped or harped?

8 For if the trumpet give an uncertain sound, who shall prepare himself to the battle?

9 So likewise ye, except ye utter by the tongue words easy to be understood, how shall it be known what is spoken? for ye shall speak into the air.

10 There are, it may be, so many kinds of voices

προφητεύων ἀνθρώποις λαλεῖ οἰκοδομὴν καὶ
prophesying   to men   speaks   edification and

παράκλησιν καὶ παραμυθίαν.   4 ὁ λαλῶν
encouragement and consolation. The [one] speaking

γλώσσῃ ἑαυτὸν οἰκοδομεῖ· ὁ δὲ προφητεύων
in a tongue himself edifies; but the [one] prophesying

ἐκκλησίαν οἰκοδομεῖ. 5 θέλω δὲ πάντας
a church   edifies.   Now I wish   all

ὑμᾶς λαλεῖν γλώσσαις, μᾶλλον δὲ ἵνα
you to speak in tongues,   but rather *in order*
                                          that

προφητεύητε· μείζων δὲ ὁ προφητεύων ἢ
ye may prophesy; and greater the [one] prophesying than

ὁ λαλῶν γλώσσαις, ἐκτὸς εἰ μὴ διερμηνεύῃ,
the speaking in tongues, *except* unless he interprets,
[one]

ἵνα ἡ ἐκκλησία οἰκοδομὴν λάβῃ. 6 νῦν δέ,
in or- the church   edification may receive. But now,
der that

ἀδελφοί, ἐὰν ἔλθω πρὸς ὑμᾶς γλώσσαις
brothers,   if I come to   you   in tongues

λαλῶν, τί ὑμᾶς ὠφελήσω, ἐὰν μὴ ὑμῖν
speaking, what *you ¹shall I profit,   except ²to you

λαλήσω ἢ ἐν ἀποκαλύψει ἢ ἐν γνώσει
¹I speak either in a revelation or in knowledge

ἢ ἐν προφητείᾳ ἢ διδαχῇ; 7 ὅμως τὰ
or in   prophecy or in teaching? Yet   -

ἄψυχα φωνὴν διδόντα, εἴτε αὐλὸς εἴτε
lifeless things ²a sound ¹giving, whether pipe   or

κιθάρα, ἐὰν διαστολὴν τοῖς φθόγγοις μὴ
harp,   if ²a distinction ⁴in the ⁵sounds ³not

δῶ, πῶς γνωσθήσεται τὸ αὐλούμενον ἢ
²they how will it be known the being piped or
give,

τὸ κιθαριζόμενον; 8 καὶ γὰρ ἐὰν ἄδηλον
the being harped?   For indeed if ²an
thing   uncertain

σάλπιγξ φωνὴν δῶ, τίς παρασκευάσεται
¹a trumpet ⁴sound ²gives, who will prepare himself

εἰς πόλεμον; 9 οὕτως καὶ ὑμεῖς διὰ
for war?   so   also ²ye ³through

τῆς γλώσσης ἐὰν μὴ εὔσημον λόγον
⁷the ⁸tongue ¹unless ⁴a clear ⁵word

δῶτε, πῶς γνωσθήσεται τὸ λαλούμενον;
⁶give, how will it be known the thing being said?

ἔσεσθε γὰρ εἰς ἀέρα λαλοῦντες. 10 τοσαῦτα
for ¹ye will be ²into ⁴air ³speaking.   ¹So many

εἰ τύχοι γένη φωνῶν εἰσιν ἐν κόσμῳ,
²it may be† ⁴kinds ⁵of sounds ¹there are in [the] world,

in the world, and none of them *is* without signification.

11 Therefore if I know not the meaning of the voice, I shall be unto him that speaketh a barbarian, and he that speaketh *shall be* a barbarian unto me.

12 Even so ye, forasmuch as ye are zealous of spiritual *gifts*, seek that ye may excel to the edifying of the church.

13 Wherefore let him that speaketh in an *unknown* tongue pray that he may interpret.

14 For if I pray in an *unknown* tongue, my spirit prayeth, but my understanding is unfruitful.

15 What is it then? I will pray with the spirit, and I will pray with the understanding also: I will sing with the spirit, and I will sing with the understanding also.

16 Else when thou shalt bless with the spirit, how shall he that occupieth the room of the unlearned say Amen at thy giving of thanks, seeing he understandeth not what thou sayest?

17 For thou verily givest thanks well, but the other is not edified.

18 I thank my God, I speak with tongues more than ye all:

19 Yet in the church I had rather speak five words with my understanding, that *by my voice* I might teach others also,

καὶ οὐδὲν ἄφωνον·
and not one [is] voiceless;
11 ἐὰν οὖν μὴ εἰδῶ
if therefore I know not
τὴν δύναμιν τῆς φωνῆς, ἔσομαι τῷ
the power of the sound, I shall be to the
λαλοῦντι βάρβαρος καὶ ὁ λαλῶν ἐν ἐμοὶ
[one] speaking a foreigner and the speaking in(to) me
[one]
βάρβαρος. 12 οὕτως καὶ ὑμεῖς. ἐπεὶ
a foreigner. So also ye, since
ζηλωταί ἐστε πνευμάτων, πρὸς τὴν
zealots ye are of spirit[ual thing]s, ²to ³the
οἰκοδομὴν τῆς ἐκκλησίας ζητεῖτε ἵνα περισ-
⁴edification ⁵of the ⁶church ¹seek ye in order ye may
that
σεύητε. 13 Διὸ ὁ λαλῶν γλώσσῃ προσευχ-
abound. Wherefore the speaking in a tongue let him
[one]
έσθω ἵνα διερμηνεύῃ. 14 ἐὰν γὰρ προσεύχωμαι
pray *in order* he may For if I pray
that interpret.
γλώσσῃ, τὸ πνεῦμά μου προσεύχεται,
in a tongue, the spirit of me prays,
ὁ δὲ νοῦς μου ἄκαρπός ἐστιν. 15 τί
but the mind of me unfruitful is. What
οὖν ἐστιν; προσεύξομαι τῷ πνεύματι,
therefore is it? I will pray with the spirit,
προσεύξομαι δὲ καὶ τῷ νοΐ· ψαλῶ τῷ
²I will pray ²and ³also with the mind; I will with
the sing the
πνεύματι, ψαλῶ δὲ καὶ τῷ νοΐ. 16 ἐπεὶ
spirit, ³I will sing¹and ²also with the mind. Otherwise
ἐὰν εὐλογῇς [ἐν] πνεύματι, ὁ ἀναπληρῶν
if thou blessest in spirit, the [one] occupying
τὸν τόπον τοῦ ἰδιώτου πῶς ἐρεῖ τὸ
the place of the uninstructed how will he say the
ἀμὴν ἐπὶ τῇ σῇ εὐχαριστίᾳ; ἐπειδὴ τί
"amen" at – thy giving thanks? Since what
λέγεις οὐκ οἶδεν· 17 σὺ μὲν γὰρ καλῶς
thou sayest he knows not; ²thou ³indeed ¹for ⁴well
εὐχαριστεῖς, ἀλλ' ὁ ἕτερος οὐκ οἰκοδομεῖται.
⁵givest thanks, but the other is not edified.
18 εὐχαριστῶ τῷ θεῷ, πάντων ὑμῶν μᾶλ-
I give thanks – to God, ²all ³you ⁴more
λον γλώσσαις λαλῶ· 19 ἀλλὰ ἐν ἐκκλησίᾳ
than ²in tongues ¹I speak; but in a church
θέλω πέντε λόγους τῷ νοΐ μου λαλῆσαι,
¹I wish ²five ⁴words ⁵with the ⁶mind ⁷of me ³to speak,
ἵνα καὶ ἄλλους κατηχήσω, ἢ μυρίους
in or- also others I may instruct, than ten
der that thousands

than ten thousand words in an *unknown* tongue.

20 Brethren, be not children in understanding: howbeit in malice be ye children, but in understanding be men.

21 In the law it is written, With *men of* other tongues and other lips will I speak unto this people; and yet for all that will they not hear me, saith the Lord.

22 Wherefore tongues are for a sign, not to them that believe, but to them that believe not: but prophesying *serveth* not for them that believe not, but for them which believe.

23 If therefore the whole church be come together into one place, and all speak with tongues, and there come in *those that are* unlearned, or unbelievers, will they not say that ye are mad?

24 But if all prophesy, and there come in one that believeth not, or *one* unlearned, he is convinced of all, he is judged of all:

25 And thus are the secrets of his heart made manifest; and so falling down on *his* face he will worship God, and report that God is in you of a truth.

26 How is it then, brethren? when ye come together, every one of you hath a psalm, hath a doctrine, hath a tongue, hath a revelation, hath an interpretation. Let all things be done unto edifying.

λόγους   ἐν   γλώσσῃ.   **20** Ἀδελφοί,   μὴ
words   in   a tongue.   Brothers,   ²not

παιδία   γίνεσθε   ταῖς   φρεσίν,   ἀλλὰ   τῇ
³children   ¹be ye   in the(your) minds,   but   –

κακίᾳ   νηπιάζετε,   ταῖς   δὲ   φρεσὶν   τέλειοι
in malice   be ye infantlike,   and in the(your) minds   mature

γίνεσθε.   **21** ἐν   τῷ   νόμῳ   γέγραπται   ὅτι
be ye.   In   the   law   it has been written that

ἐν   ἑτερογλώσσοις   καὶ   ἐν   χείλεσιν   ἑτέρων
in   other tongues   and   in   lips   of others

λαλήσω   τῷ   λαῷ   τούτῳ,   καὶ   οὐδ'   οὕτως
I will speak   to this people,   and   not   so

εἰσακούσονταί   μου,   λέγει   κύριος.   **22** ὥστε
will they hear   me,   says   [the] Lord.   So as

αἱ   γλῶσσαι   εἰς   σημεῖόν   εἰσιν   οὐ   τοῖς
the   tongues   ²for   ³a sign   ¹are   not   to the

πιστεύουσιν   ἀλλὰ   τοῖς   ἀπίστοις,   ἡ   δὲ
[ones] believing   but   to the   unbelievers,   and *the*

προφητεία   οὐ   τοῖς   ἀπίστοις   ἀλλὰ   τοῖς
prophecy [is]   not   to the   unbelievers   but   to the

πιστεύουσιν.   **23** Ἐὰν   οὖν   συνέλθῃ   ἡ
[ones] believing.   If   therefore   ⁴comes   ¹the
                  together

ἐκκλησία   ὅλη   ἐπὶ   τὸ   αὐτὸ   καὶ   πάντες
²church   ³whole   together   and   all

λαλῶσιν   γλώσσαις,   εἰσέλθωσιν   δὲ   ἰδιῶται
speak   in tongues,   and ⁴enter   ¹uninstructed

ἢ   ἄπιστοι,   οὐκ   ἐροῦσιν   ὅτι   μαίνεσθε;
²or   ³unbelievers,   will they not say   that   ye rave?

24 ἐὰν   δὲ   πάντες   προφητεύωσιν,   εἰσέλθῃ   δέ
but if   all   prophesy,   and ⁵enters

τις   ἄπιστος   ἢ   ἰδιώτης,   ἐλέγχεται   ὑπὸ
¹some   ²unbeliever   ³or   ⁴uninstructed,   he is convicted   by

πάντων,   ἀνακρίνεται   ὑπὸ   πάντων,   **25** τὰ
all,   he is judged   by   all,   the

κρυπτὰ   τῆς   καρδίας   αὐτοῦ   φανερὰ   γίνεται,
hidden   of the   heart   of him   ²manifest   ¹becomes,
things

καὶ   οὕτως   πεσὼν   ἐπὶ   πρόσωπον   προσκυνή-
and   so   falling   on [his] face   he will wor-

σει   τῷ   θεῷ,   ἀπαγγέλλων   ὅτι   ὄντως
ship   –   God,   declaring   that   really

ὁ   θεὸς   ἐν   ὑμῖν   ἐστιν.   **26** Τί   οὖν   ἐστιν,
–   God   ²among   ³you   ¹is.   What therefore is it,

ἀδελφοί;   ὅταν   συνέρχησθε,   ἕκαστος   ψαλμὸν
brothers?   whenever ye come together,   each one   a psalm

ἔχει,   διδαχὴν   ἔχει,   ἀποκάλυψιν   ἔχει,   γλῶσ-
has,   a teaching   he has,   a revelation   he has,   a

σαν   ἔχει,   ἑρμηνείαν   ἔχει·   πάντα   πρὸς
tongue   he has,   an interpretation   he has;   ³all things   ⁴for

27 If any man speak in an *unknown* tongue, *let it be* by two, or at the most *by* three, and *that* by course; and let one interpret.

28 But if there be no interpreter, let him keep silence in the church; and let him speak to himself, and to God.

29 Let the prophets speak two or three, and let the other judge.

30 If *any thing* be revealed to another that sitteth by, let the first hold his peace.

31 For ye may all prophesy one by one, that all may learn, and all may be comforted.

32 And the spirits of the prophets are subject to the prophets.

33 For God is not *the author* of confusion, but of peace, as in all churches of the saints.

34 Let your women keep silence in the churches: for it is not permitted unto them to speak; but *they are commanded* to be under obedience, as also saith the law.

35 And if they will learn any thing, let them ask their husbands at home: for it is a shame for women to speak in the church.

36 What? came the word of God out from you? or came it unto you only?

37 If any man think himself to be a prophet, or spiritual, let him ac-

---

οἰκοδομὴν γινέσθω. 27 εἴτε γλώσσῃ τις
edification ¹let ²be.   If in a tongue anyone

λαλεῖ, κατὰ δύο ἢ τὸ πλεῖστον τρεῖς,
speaks, by two or the most three,

καὶ ἀνὰ μέρος, 28 καὶ εἷς διερμηνευέτω·
and in turn,†   and ²one ¹let ³interpret;

ἐὰν δὲ μὴ ᾖ διερμηνευτής, σιγάτω ἐν
but if there is not an interpreter, let him be silent in

ἐκκλησίᾳ, ἑαυτῷ δὲ λαλείτω καὶ τῷ
church, and to himself let him speak and –

θεῷ. 29 προφῆται δὲ δύο ἢ τρεῖς λαλεί-
to God. And prophets two or three let them

τωσαν, 30 καὶ οἱ ἄλλοι διακρινέτωσαν·
speak, and the others let discern;

ἐὰν δὲ ἄλλῳ ἀποκαλυφθῇ καθημένῳ, ὁ
but if ¹to another ³[something] ²sitting, the
                                      ⁴is revealed

πρῶτος σιγάτω. 31 δύνασθε γὰρ καθ'
first let be silent. For ye can ²sin-

ἕνα πάντες προφητεύειν, ἵνα πάντες
gly† ¹all ²to prophesy, in order that all

μανθάνωσιν καὶ πάντες παρακαλῶνται.
may learn and all may be encouraged.

32 καὶ πνεύματα προφητῶν προφήταις
And [the] spirits of prophets to prophets

ὑποτάσσεται· 33 οὐ γάρ ἐστιν ἀκαταστασίας
is(are) subject; for ²not ³is ⁴of tumult

ὁ θεὸς ἀλλὰ εἰρήνης. Ὡς ἐν πάσαις
– ¹God but of peace. As in all

ταῖς ἐκκλησίαις τῶν ἁγίων, 34 αἱ γυναῖκες
the churches of the saints, ²the ³women

ἐν ταῖς ἐκκλησίαις σιγάτωσαν· οὐ γὰρ
⁵in ⁶the ⁷churches ¹let ⁴be silent; ²not ¹for

ἐπιτρέπεται αὐταῖς λαλεῖν, ἀλλὰ ὑποτασ-
²it is ¹permitted to them to speak, but let them

σέσθωσαν, καθὼς καὶ ὁ νόμος λέγει.
be subject, as also the law says.

35 εἰ δέ τι μαθεῖν θέλουσιν, ἐν οἴκῳ
But if ²anything ³to learn ¹they wish, ²at home

τοὺς ἰδίους ἄνδρας ἐπερωτάτωσαν· αἰσχρὸν
²the(ir) ³own ⁴husbands ¹let them question; ²a shame

γάρ ἐστιν γυναικὶ λαλεῖν ἐν ἐκκλησίᾳ.
¹for ²it is for a woman to speak in a church.

36 ἢ ἀφ' ὑμῶν ὁ λόγος τοῦ θεοῦ ἐξῆλθεν,
Or from you ²the ³word – ⁴of God ¹went forth,

ἢ εἰς ὑμᾶς μόνους κατήντησεν; 37 Εἴ
or to you only did it reach? If

τις δοκεῖ προφήτης εἶναι ἢ πνευματικός,
any- thinks ²a prophet ¹to be or a spiritual man,
one

knowledge that the things that I write unto you are the commandments of the Lord.

38 But if any man be ignorant, let him be ignorant.

39 Wherefore, brethren, covet to prophesy, and forbid not to speak with tongues.

40 Let all things be done decently and in order.

ἐπιγινωσκέτω   ἃ   γράφω   ὑμῖν   ὅτι
let him clearly   [the] things   I write   to you   that
know   which

κυρίου   ἐστὶν   ἐντολή·   38 εἰ   δέ   τις
of [the] Lord they are   a commandment;   but if   anyone

ἀγνοεῖ,   ἀγνοεῖται.   39 Ὥστε,   ἀδελφοί
is ignorant, let him be ignorant.   So as,   brothers

μου,   ζηλοῦτε   τὸ   προφητεύειν,   καὶ   τὸ
of me,   be ye eager   –   to prophesy,   and   –

λαλεῖν   μὴ   κωλύετε   γλώσσαις·   40 πάντα
²to speak   ¹forbid not   in tongues;   ²all things

δὲ   εὐσχημόνως   καὶ   κατὰ   τάξιν   γινέσθω.
and   ⁴becomingly   ⁵and ⁶according to   ⁷order   ¹let ³be done.

CHAPTER 15

MOREOVER, brethren, I declare unto you the gospel which I preached unto you, which also ye have received, and wherein ye stand;

2 By which also ye are saved, if ye keep in memory what I preached unto you, unless ye have believed in vain.

3 For I delivered unto you first of all that which I also received, how that Christ died for our sins according to the scriptures;

4 And that he was buried, and that he rose again the third day according to the scriptures:

5 And that he was seen of Cephas, then of the twelve:

6 After that, he was seen of above five hundred brethren at once; of whom the greater part remain unto this present, but some are fallen asleep.

7 After that, he was seen of James; then of all the apostles.

8 And last of all he

15 Γνωρίζω   δὲ   ὑμῖν,   ἀδελφοί,   τὸ
Now I make known   to you,   brothers,   the

εὐαγγέλιον   ὃ   εὐηγγελισάμην   ὑμῖν,   ὃ   καὶ
good tidings   which   I preached   to you,   which also

παρελάβετε,   ἐν   ᾧ   καὶ   ἑστήκατε,   2 δι’
ye received,   in   which also   ye stand,   through

οὗ   καὶ   σῴζεσθε,   τίνι   λόγῳ   εὐηγγελισάμην
which also   ye are saved,   ³to what ⁴word   ⁵I preached

ὑμῖν   εἰ   κατέχετε,   ἐκτὸς   εἰ   μὴ   εἰκῇ
⁶to you   ¹if   ²ye hold fast,   except   unless   in vain

ἐπιστεύσατε.   3 παρέδωκα   γὰρ   ὑμῖν   ἐν
ye believed.   For I delivered   to you among

πρώτοις,   ὃ   καὶ   παρέλαβον,   ὅτι   Χριστὸς
[the] first things,   what   also   I received,   that   Christ

ἀπέθανεν   ὑπὲρ   τῶν   ἁμαρτιῶν   ἡμῶν   κατὰ
died   on behalf of   the   sins   of us   according to

τὰς   γραφάς,   4 καὶ   ὅτι   ἐτάφη,   καὶ   ὅτι
the   scriptures,   and   that he was buried, and   that

ἐγήγερται   τῇ   ἡμέρᾳ   τῇ   τρίτῃ   κατὰ
he has been raised   on the   ²day   –   ¹third   according to

τὰς   γραφάς,   5 καὶ   ὅτι   ὤφθη   Κηφᾷ,
the   scriptures,   and   that he was seen by Cephas,

εἶτα   τοῖς   δώδεκα·   6 ἔπειτα   ὤφθη   ἐπάνω
then   by the   twelve;   afterward he was seen   ²over

πεντακοσίοις   ἀδελφοῖς   ἐφάπαξ,   ἐξ   ὧν   οἱ
¹by ³five hundreds   brothers   at one time,   of whom   the

πλείονες   μένουσιν   ἕως   ἄρτι,   τινὲς   δὲ
majority   remain   until   now,   though some

ἐκοιμήθησαν·   7 ἔπειτα   ὤφθη   Ἰακώβῳ,   εἶτα
fell asleep;   afterward he was seen by James,   then

τοῖς   ἀποστόλοις   πᾶσιν·   8 ἔσχατον   δὲ
by the   apostles   all;   and lastly

was seen of me also, as of one born out of due time.

9 For I am the least of the apostles, that am not meet to be called an apostle, because I persecuted the church of God.

10 But by the grace of God I am what I am: and his grace which *was bestowed* upon me was not in vain; but I laboured more abundantly than they all: yet not I, but the grace of God which was with me.

11 Therefore whether *it were* I or they, so we preach, and so ye believed.

12 Now if Christ be preached that he rose from the dead, how say some among you that there is no resurrection of the dead?

13 But if there be no resurrection of the dead, then is Christ not risen:

14 And if Christ be not risen, then *is* our preaching vain, and your faith *is* also vain.

15 Yea, and we are found false witnesses of God; because we have testified of God that he raised up Christ: whom he raised not up, if so be that the dead rise not.

16 For if the dead rise not, then is not Christ raised:

17 And if Christ be not raised, your faith *is*

πάντων ὡσπερεὶ τῷ ἐκτρώματι ὤφθη
of all even as if to the(an) abortion he was seen

κἀμοί. 9 Ἐγὼ γάρ εἰμι ὁ ἐλάχιστος
by me also. For I am the least

τῶν ἀποστόλων, ὃς οὐκ εἰμὶ ἱκανὸς
of the apostles, who am not sufficient

καλεῖσθαι ἀπόστολος, διότι ἐδίωξα τὴν
to be called an apostle, because I persecuted the

ἐκκλησίαν τοῦ θεοῦ· 10 χάριτι δὲ θεοῦ
church - of God; but by [the] grace of God

εἰμι ὅ εἰμι, καὶ ἡ χάρις αὐτοῦ ἡ εἰς
I am what I am, and the grace of him - to

ἐμὲ οὐ κενὴ ἐγενήθη, ἀλλὰ περισσότερον
me not empty was, but [2]more abundantly
[than]

αὐτῶν πάντων ἐκοπίασα, οὐκ ἐγὼ δὲ
[3]them [4]all [1]I laboured, [5]not [3]I [1]yet

ἀλλὰ ἡ χάρις τοῦ θεοῦ σὺν ἐμοί. 11 εἴτε
but the grace - of God with me. Whether

οὖν ἐγὼ εἴτε ἐκεῖνοι, οὕτως κηρύσσομεν
therefore I or those, so we proclaim

καὶ οὕτως ἐπιστεύσατε.
and so ye believed.

12 Εἰ δὲ Χριστὸς κηρύσσεται ὅτι ἐκ
But if Christ is proclaimed that from

νεκρῶν ἐγήγερται, πῶς λέγουσιν ἐν ὑμῖν
[the] dead he has been raised, how say [2]among [3]you

τινες ὅτι ἀνάστασις νεκρῶν οὐκ ἔστιν;
[1]some that a resurrection of dead persons there is not?

13 εἰ δὲ ἀνάστασις νεκρῶν οὐκ ἔστιν,
Now if a resurrection of dead persons there is not,

οὐδὲ Χριστὸς ἐγήγερται· 14 εἰ δὲ Χριστὸς
neither Christ has been raised; and if Christ

οὐκ ἐγήγερται, κενὸν ἄρα τὸ κήρυγμα
has not been raised, empty then the proclamation

ἡμῶν, κενὴ καὶ ἡ πίστις ὑμῶν· 15 εὑρισκ-
of us, empty also the faith of you; [2]we are

όμεθα δὲ καὶ ψευδομάρτυρες τοῦ θεοῦ,
found [1]and also false witnesses - of God,

ὅτι ἐμαρτυρήσαμεν κατὰ τοῦ θεοῦ ὅτι
because we witnessed as to - God that

ἤγειρεν τὸν Χριστόν, ὃν οὐκ ἤγειρεν
he raised - Christ, whom he raised not

εἴπερ ἄρα νεκροὶ οὐκ ἐγείρονται. 16 εἰ
if then dead persons are not raised. if

γὰρ νεκροὶ οὐκ ἐγείρονται, οὐδὲ Χριστὸς
For dead persons are not raised, neither Christ

ἐγήγερται· 17 εἰ δὲ Χριστὸς οὐκ ἐγήγερται,
has been raised; and if Christ has not been raised,

vain; ye are yet in your sins.

18 Then they also which are fallen asleep in Christ are perished.

19 If in this life only we have hope in Christ, we are of all men most miserable.

20 But now is Christ risen from the dead, *and* become the firstfruits of them that slept.

21 For since by man *came* death, by man *came* also the resurrection of the dead.

22 For as in Adam all die, even so in Christ shall all be made alive.

23 But every man in his own order: Christ the firstfruits; afterward they that are Christ's at his coming.

24 Then *cometh* the end, when he shall have delivered up the kingdom to God, even the Father; when he shall have put down all rule and all authority and power.

25 For he must reign, till he hath put all enemies under his feet.

26 The last enemy *that* shall be destroyed *is* death.

27 For he hath put all things under his feet. But when he saith all things are put under *him,*

ματαία ἡ πίστις ὑμῶν [ἐστιν], ἔτι ἐστὲ
⁶useless ¹the ²faith ³of you ⁴is, ⁵still ¹ye are
ἐν ταῖς ἁμαρτίαις ὑμῶν. 18 ἄρα καὶ οἱ
in the sins of you. Then also the [ones]
κοιμηθέντες ἐν Χριστῷ ἀπώλοντο. 19 εἰ
having fallen asleep in Christ perished. If
ἐν τῇ ζωῇ ταύτῃ ἐν Χριστῷ ἠλπικότες
in this life ³in ⁴Christ ²having hoped
ἐσμὲν μόνον, ἐλεεινότεροι πάντων ἀνθρώπων
¹we are ⁵only, more pitiful [than] all men
ἐσμέν. 20 Νυνὶ δὲ Χριστὸς ἐγήγερται
we are. But now Christ has been raised
ἐκ νεκρῶν, ἀπαρχὴ τῶν κεκοιμημένων.
from [the] dead, firstfruit of the [ones] having fallen asleep.
21 ἐπειδὴ γὰρ δι' ἀνθρώπου θάνατος, καὶ
For since through a man death [came], also
δι' ἀνθρώπου ἀνάστασις νεκρῶν. 22 ὥσπερ
through a man a resurrection of dead persons as
[came].
γὰρ ἐν τῷ Ἀδὰμ πάντες ἀποθνήσκουσιν,
For in - Adam all die,
οὕτως καὶ ἐν τῷ Χριστῷ πάντες ζωοποιη-
so also in - Christ all will be
θήσονται. 23 Ἕκαστος δὲ ἐν τῷ ἰδίῳ
made alive. But each one in the(his) own
τάγματι· ἀπαρχὴ Χριστός, ἔπειτα οἱ τοῦ
order: [the] Christ, afterward the -
firstfruit [ones]
Χριστοῦ ἐν τῇ παρουσίᾳ αὐτοῦ, 24 εἶτα
of Christ in the presence of him, then
τὸ τέλος, ὅταν παραδιδοῖ τὴν βασιλείαν
the end, whenever he delivers the kingdom
τῷ θεῷ καὶ πατρί, ὅταν καταργήσῃ
- to God even [the] Father, whenever he abolishes
πᾶσαν ἀρχὴν καὶ πᾶσαν ἐξουσίαν καὶ
all rule and all authority and
δύναμιν. 25 δεῖ γὰρ αὐτὸν βασιλεύειν
power. For it behoves him to reign
ἄχρι οὗ θῇ πάντας τοὺς ἐχθροὺς ὑπὸ
until he puts all the(his) enemies under
τοὺς πόδας αὐτοῦ. 26 ἔσχατος ἐχθρὸς
the feet of him. [The] last enemy
καταργεῖται ὁ θάνατος· πάντα γὰρ ὑπέταξεν
is abolished - death; for all things he subjected
ὑπὸ τοὺς πόδας αὐτοῦ. 27 ὅταν δὲ
under the feet of him. But whenever
εἴπῃ ὅτι πάντα ὑποτέτακται, δῆλον ὅτι
he says that all things have been subjected, [it is] clear that

it is manifest that he is excepted, which did put all things under him.

28 And when all things shall be subdued unto him, then shall the Son also himself be subject unto him that put all things under him, that God may be all in all.

29 Else what shall they do which are baptized for the dead, if the dead rise not at all? why are they then baptized for the dead?

30 And why stand we in jeopardy every hour?

31 I protest by your rejoicing which I have in Christ Jesus our Lord, I die daily.

32 If after the manner of men I have fought with beasts at Ephesus, what advantageth it me, if the dead rise not? let us eat and drink; for to morrow we die.

33 Be not deceived: evil communications corrupt good manners.

34 Awake to righteousness, and sin not; for some have not the knowledge of God: I speak this to your shame.

35 But some man will say, How are the dead raised up? and with what body do they come?

36 Thou fool, that which thou sowest is not quickened, except it die:

ἐκτὸς τοῦ ὑποτάξαντος αὐτῷ τὰ πάντα.
[it is] the having subjected to him – all
apart from [one] things.

28 ὅταν δὲ ὑποταγῇ αὐτῷ τὰ πάντα,
But whenever is(are) subjected to him – all things,

τότε καὶ αὐτὸς ὁ υἱὸς ὑποταγήσεται
then also ²[him]self ¹the ²Son will be subjected

τῷ ὑποτάξαντι αὐτῷ τὰ πάντα, ἵνα
to the having to him – all in order
[one] subjected things, that

ᾖ ὁ θεὸς πάντα ἐν πᾶσιν. 29 Ἐπεὶ
²may – ¹God all in all. Other-
be things wise

τί ποιήσουσιν οἱ βαπτιζόμενοι ὑπὲρ τῶν
what will they do the [ones] being baptized on behalf of the

νεκρῶν; εἰ ὅλως νεκροὶ οὐκ ἐγείρονται,
dead? if actually dead persons are not raised,

τί καὶ βαπτίζονται ὑπὲρ αὐτῶν; 30 τί
why indeed are they baptized on behalf of them? why

καὶ ἡμεῖς κινδυνεύομεν πᾶσαν ὥραν;
also ²we ¹are ³in danger every hour?

31 καθ' ἡμέραν ἀποθνήσκω, νὴ τὴν
Daily I die, by –

ὑμετέραν καύχησιν, ἀδελφοί, ἣν ἔχω ἐν
your boasting, brothers, which I have in

Χριστῷ Ἰησοῦ τῷ κυρίῳ ἡμῶν. 32 εἰ
Christ Jesus the Lord of us. If

κατὰ ἄνθρωπον ἐθηριομάχησα ἐν Ἐφέσῳ,
according man I fought with wild in Ephesus,
to beasts

τί μοι τὸ ὄφελος; εἰ νεκροὶ οὐκ ἐγείρονται,
what to me the profit?ᶜ If dead persons are not raised,
=what profit have I?

φάγωμεν καὶ πίωμεν, αὔριον γὰρ ἀποθνή-
let us eat and let us drink, for to-morrow we

σκομεν. 33 μὴ πλανᾶσθε· φθείρουσιν ἤθη
die. Be ye not led astray: ²Corrupt ⁵customs

χρηστὰ ὁμιλίαι κακαί. 34 ἐκνήψατε δικαίως
⁴good ²associations ¹bad. Become ye sober righteously

καὶ μὴ ἁμαρτάνετε· ἀγνωσίαν γὰρ θεοῦ
and do not sin; for ³ignorance ⁴of God

τινες ἔχουσιν· πρὸς ἐντροπὴν ὑμῖν λαλῶ.
¹some ²have· ³for ³shame ²to you ¹I speak.

35 Ἀλλὰ ἐρεῖ τις· πῶς ἐγείρονται οἱ
But ²will say ¹someone: How are raised the

νεκροί; ποίῳ δὲ σώματι ἔρχονται; 36 ἄφρων,
dead? and with what body do they Foolish
sort [of] come? man,

σὺ ὃ σπείρεις, οὐ ζωοποιεῖται ἐὰν μὴ
²thou ¹what sowest, is not made alive unless

37 And that which thou sowest, thou sowest not that body that shall be, but bare grain, it may chance of wheat, or of some other *grain:*

38 But God giveth it a body as it hath pleased him, and to every seed his own body.

39 All flesh *is* not the same flesh: but *there is* one *kind of* flesh of men, another flesh of beasts, another of fishes, *and* another of birds.

40 *There are* also celestial bodies, and bodies terrestrial: but the glory of the celestial *is* one, and the *glory* of the terrestrial *is* another.

41 *There is* one glory of the sun, and another glory of the moon, and another glory of the stars: for *one* star differeth from *another* star in glory.

42 So also *is* the resurrection of the dead. It is sown in corruption; it is raised in incorruption:

43 It is sown in dishonour; it is raised in glory: it is sown in weakness; it is raised in power:

44 It is sown a natural body ; it is raised a spiritual body. There is a natural body, and there is a spiritual body.

45 And so it is written, The first man Adam was made a living soul; the last

ἀποθάνῃ· καὶ ὃ σπείρεις, **37** οὐ τὸ σῶμα
it dies;   and   what thou sowest,   not   the   body

τὸ γενησόμενον σπείρεις, ἀλλὰ γυμνὸν
–   going to become   thou sowest,   but   a naked

κόκκον εἰ τύχοι σίτου ἤ τινος τῶν
grain   it may be†   of wheat   or   some one   of the

λοιπῶν· **38** ὁ δὲ θεὸς δίδωσιν αὐτῷ
rest;   –   but   God   gives   to it

σῶμα καθὼς ἠθέλησεν, καὶ ἑκάστῳ τῶν
a body   as   he wished,   and   to each   of the

σπερμάτων ἴδιον σῶμα. **39** οὐ πᾶσα
seeds   [its]   own   body.   ³[is] not   ¹All

σὰρξ ἡ αὐτὴ σάρξ, ἀλλὰ ἄλλη μὲν
²flesh   the   same   flesh,   but   other(one) indeed

ἀνθρώπων, ἄλλη δὲ σὰρξ κτηνῶν, ἄλλη δὲ
of men,   and another   flesh   of animals, and another

σὰρξ πτηνῶν, ἄλλη δὲ ἰχθύων. **40** καὶ
flesh   of birds,   and another   of fishes.   And [there

σώματα ἐπουράνια, καὶ σώματα ἐπίγεια·
are] bodies   heavenly,   and   bodies   earthly;

ἀλλὰ ἑτέρα μὲν ἡ τῶν ἐπουρανίων δόξα,
but   ⁷other   ⁵[is]   ¹the   ³of the   ⁴heavenly   ²glory,
    (one)   ⁶indeed   [bodies]

ἑτέρα δὲ ἡ τῶν ἐπιγείων. **41** ἄλλη
and other   the [glory] of the   earthly [bodies].   Other(one)

δόξα ἡλίου, καὶ ἄλλη δόξα σελήνης,
glory   of [the] sun,   and   another   glory   of [the] moon,

καὶ ἄλλη δόξα ἀστέρων· ἀστὴρ γὰρ
and   another   glory   of [the] stars ;   for star

ἀστέρος διαφέρει ἐν δόξῃ. **42** οὕτως καὶ
from star   differs   in   glory.   So   also

ἡ ἀνάστασις τῶν νεκρῶν. σπείρεται ἐν
the resurrection   of the   dead.   It is sown   in

φθορᾷ, ἐγείρεται ἐν ἀφθαρσίᾳ· **43** σπείρεται
corruption,   it is raised   in   incorruption;   it is sown

ἐν ἀτιμίᾳ, ἐγείρεται ἐν δόξῃ· σπείρεται
in   dishonour,   it is raised   in   glory;   it is sown

ἐν ἀσθενείᾳ, ἐγείρεται ἐν δυνάμει· **44** σπείρ-
in   weakness,   it is raised   in   power;   it is

εται σῶμα ψυχικόν, ἐγείρεται σῶμα
sown   body   a natural,   it is raised   body

πνευματικόν Εἰ ἔστιν σῶμα ψυχικόν,
a spiritual.   If   there is   body   a natural.

ἔστιν καὶ πνευματικόν. **45** οὕτως καὶ
there is   also   a spiritual [body].   So   also

γέγραπται· ἐγένετο ὁ πρῶτος ἄνθρωπος
it has been written: ⁵became   ¹The   ²first   ³man

Ἀδὰμ εἰς ψυχὴν ζῶσαν· ὁ ἔσχατος
⁴Adam   –   soul   a living;   the   last

Adam *was made* a quickening spirit.
46 Howbeit that *was* not first which is spiritual, but that which is natural; and afterward that which is spiritual.
47 The first man *is* of the earth, earthy: the second man *is* the Lord from heaven.
48 As *is* the earthy, such *are* they also that are earthy: and as *is* the heavenly, such *are* they also that are heavenly.
49 And as we. have borne the image of the earthy, we shall also bear the image of the heavenly.
50 Now this I say, brethren, that flesh and blood cannot inherit the kingdom of God; neither doth corruption inherit incorruption.
51 Behold, I shew you a mystery; We shall not all sleep, but we shall all be changed,
52 In a moment, in the twinkling of an eye, at the last trump: for the trumpet shall sound, and the dead shall be raised incorruptible, and we shall be changed.
53 For this corruptible must put on incorruption, and this mortal *must* put on immortality.
54 So when this corruptible shall have put on incorruption, and this mortal shall have put on immortality, then shall be brought to pass the saying

Ἀδὰμ   εἰς   πνεῦμα   ζωοποιοῦν.   46 ἀλλ'
Adam – spirit a life-giving. But
οὐ   πρῶτον   τὸ   πνευματικὸν   ἀλλὰ   τὸ
not firstly the spiritual [body] but the
ψυχικόν,   ἔπειτα   τὸ   πνευματικόν.   47 ὁ
natural, afterward the spiritual. The
πρῶτος   ἄνθρωπος   ἐκ   γῆς   χοϊκός,   ὁ
first man [was] out of earth earthy, the
δεύτερος   ἄνθρωπος   ἐξ   οὐρανοῦ.   48 οἷος ὁ
second man [is] out of heaven. Such the
χοϊκός,   τοιοῦτοι   καὶ   οἱ   χοϊκοί,   καὶ   οἷος
earthy man, such also the earthy ones, and such
ὁ   ἐπουράνιος,   τοιοῦτοι   καὶ   οἱ   ἐπουράνιοι·
the heavenly man, such also the heavenly ones;
49 καὶ   καθὼς   ἐφορέσαμεν   τὴν   εἰκόνα   τοῦ
and as we bore the image of the
χοϊκοῦ,   φορέσομεν   καὶ   τὴν   εἰκόνα   τοῦ
earthy man, we shall bear also the image of the
ἐπουρανίου.   50 Τοῦτο   δέ   φημι,   ἀδελφοί,
heavenly man. And this I say, brothers,
ὅτι   σὰρξ   καὶ   αἷμα   βασιλείαν   θεοῦ   κληρο-
that flesh and blood [the] kingdom of God to
νομῆσαι   οὐ   δύναται,   οὐδὲ   ἡ   φθορὰ   τὴν
inherit cannot, neither – corruption –
ἀφθαρσίαν   κληρονομεῖ.   51 ἰδοὺ   μυστήριον
incorruption inherits. Behold[,] a mystery
ὑμῖν   λέγω·   πάντες   οὐ   κοιμηθησόμεθα,
to you I tell: all We shall not fall asleep,
πάντες   δὲ   ἀλλαγησόμεθα,   52 ἐν   ἀτόμῳ,
but all we shall be changed, in a moment,
ἐν   ῥιπῇ   ὀφθαλμοῦ,   ἐν   τῇ   ἐσχάτῃ   σάλπιγγι·
in a glance of an eye, at the last trumpet;
σαλπίσει   γάρ,   καὶ   οἱ   νεκροὶ   ἐγερθήσονται
for a trumpet will and the dead will be raised
sound,
ἄφθαρτοι,   καὶ   ἡμεῖς   ἀλλαγησόμεθα.   53 Δεῖ
incorruptible, and we shall be changed. it behoves
γὰρ   τὸ   φθαρτὸν   τοῦτο   ἐνδύσασθαι
For – corruptible this to put on
ἀφθαρσίαν   καὶ   τὸ   θνητὸν   τοῦτο   ἐνδύσασθαι
incorruption and – mortal this to put on
ἀθανασίαν.   54 ὅταν   δὲ   τὸ   φθαρτὸν   τοῦτο
immortality. And whenever this [that is] corruptible
ἐνδύσηται   ἀφθαρσίαν   καὶ   τὸ   θνητὸν   τοῦτο
shall put on incorruption and this [that is] mortal
ἐνδύσηται   ἀθανασίαν,   τότε   γενήσεται   ὁ
shall put on immortality, then will be the
λόγος   ὁ   γεγραμμένος·   κατεπόθη   ὁ   θάνατος
word – having been was – Death
written: swallowed up

that is written, Death is swallowed up in victory.

55 O death, where *is* thy sting? O grave, where *is* thy victory?

56 The sting of death *is* sin; and the strength of sin *is* the law.

57 But thanks *be* to God, which giveth us the victory through our Lord Jesus Christ.

58 Therefore, my beloved brethren, be ye stedfast, unmoveable, always abounding in the work of the Lord, forasmuch as ye know that your labour is not in vain in the Lord.

εἰς νῖκος. 55 ποῦ σου, θάνατε, τὸ νῖκος;
in victory. Where of thee, [O] death, the victory?

ποῦ σου, θάνατε, τὸ κέντρον; 56 τὸ δὲ
where of thee, [O] death, the sting? Now the

κέντρον τοῦ θανάτου ἡ ἁμαρτία, ἡ δὲ
sting – of death – [is] sin, and the

δύναμις τῆς ἁμαρτίας ὁ νόμος· 57 τῷ
power – of sin [is] the law; –

δὲ θεῷ χάρις τῷ διδόντι ἡμῖν τὸ νῖκος
but to God thanks the [one] giving to us the victory

διὰ τοῦ κυρίου ἡμῶν Ἰησοῦ Χριστοῦ.
through the Lord of us Jesus Christ.

58 Ὥστε, ἀδελφοί μου ἀγαπητοί, ἑδραῖοι
So as, brothers of me beloved, firm

γίνεσθε, ἀμετακίνητοι, περισσεύοντες ἐν τῷ
be ye, unmovable, abounding in the

ἔργῳ τοῦ κυρίου πάντοτε, εἰδότες ὅτι
work of the Lord always, knowing that

ὁ κόπος ὑμῶν οὐκ ἔστιν κενὸς ἐν κυρίῳ.
the labour of you is not empty in [the] Lord.

CHAPTER 16

NOW concerning the collection for the saints, as I have given order to the churches of Galatia, even so do ye.

2 Upon the first *day* of the week let every one of you lay by him in store, as *God* hath prospered him, that there be no gatherings when I come.

3 And when I come, whomsoever ye shall approve by *your* letters, them will I send to bring your liberality unto Jerusalem.

4 And if it be meet that I go also, they shall go with me.

5 Now I will come unto you, when I shall pass through Macedonia: for

16 Περὶ δὲ τῆς λογείας τῆς εἰς τοὺς
Now about the collection – for the

ἁγίους, ὥσπερ διέταξα ταῖς ἐκκλησίαις
saints, as I charged the churches

τῆς Γαλατίας, οὕτως καὶ ὑμεῖς ποιήσατε.
– of Galatia, so also ²ye ¹do.

2 κατὰ μίαν σαββάτου ἕκαστος ὑμῶν
Every one of a week each of you
=On the first day of every week

παρ᾽ ἑαυτῷ τιθέτω θησαυρίζων ὅ τι ἐὰν
by himself let him put storing up whatever

εὐοδῶται, ἵνα μὴ ὅταν ἔλθω τότε λογεῖαι
he is prospered, lest whenever I come then ²collections

γίνωνται. 3 ὅταν δὲ παραγένωμαι, οὓς
¹there are. And whenever I arrive, whom-

ἐὰν δοκιμάσητε, δι᾽ ἐπιστολῶν τούτους
ever ye approve, through epistles these

πέμψω ἀπενεγκεῖν τὴν χάριν ὑμῶν εἰς
I will send to carry the grace(gift) of you to

Ἰερουσαλήμ· 4 ἐὰν δὲ ἄξιον ᾖ τοῦ κἀμὲ
Jerusalem; and if ²fitting ¹it is – me also

πορεύεσθαι, σὺν ἐμοὶ πορεύσονται.
to go,ᵈ with me they shall go.

5 Ἐλεύσομαι δὲ πρὸς ὑμᾶς ὅταν Μακε-
And I will come to you whenever ¹Mace-

I do pass through Macedonia.

6 And it may be that I will abide, yea, and winter with you, that ye may bring me on my journey whithersoever I go.

7 For I will not see you now by the way; but I trust to tarry a while with you, if the Lord permit.

8 But I will tarry at Ephesus until Pentecost.

9 For a great door and effectual is opened unto me, and *there are* many adversaries.

10 Now if Timotheus come, see that he may be with you without fear: for he worketh the work of the Lord, as I also *do*.

11 Let no man therefore despise him: but conduct him forth in peace, that he may come unto me: for I look for him with the brethren.

12 As touching *our* brother Apollos, I greatly desired him to come unto you with the brethren: but his will was not at all to come at this time; but he will come when he shall have convenient time.

13 Watch ye, stand fast

δονίαν διέλθω· Μακεδονίαν γὰρ διέρχομαι,
donia ¹I pass for ²Macedonia ¹I am passing
through; through,*

6 πρὸς ὑμᾶς δὲ τυχὸν καταμενῶ ἢ
⁷with ⁸you ¹and ²possibly ³I will remain ⁴or

καὶ παραχειμάσω, ἵνα ὑμεῖς με προπέμ-
⁵even ⁶spend the winter, in order ²ye ¹me may set
that

ψητε οὗ ἐὰν πορεύωμαι. 7 οὐ θέλω γὰρ
forward wherever I may go. For I do not wish

ὑμᾶς ἄρτι ἐν παρόδῳ ἰδεῖν· ἐλπίζω γὰρ
²you ³yet ⁴in ⁵passage ¹to see; for I am hoping

χρόνον τινὰ ἐπιμεῖναι πρὸς ὑμᾶς, ἐὰν
³time ²some ¹to remain with you, if

ὁ κύριος ἐπιτρέψῃ. 8 ἐπιμενῶ δὲ ἐν
the Lord permits. But I will remain in

Ἐφέσῳ ἕως τῆς πεντηκοστῆς· 9 θύρα
Ephesus until - Pentecost; ⁵door

γάρ μοι ἀνέῳγεν μεγάλη καὶ ἐνεργής,
¹for ⁷to me ⁶opened ²a great ³and ⁴effective,

καὶ ἀντικείμενοι πολλοί. 10 Ἐὰν δὲ
and ²opposing ¹many. Now if
[there are]

ἔλθῃ Τιμόθεος, βλέπετε ἵνα ἀφόβως
²comes ¹Timothy, see in order that fearlessly

γένηται πρὸς ὑμᾶς· τὸ γὰρ ἔργον κυρίου
he is with you; for the work of [the] Lord

ἐργάζεται ὡς κἀγώ· 11 μή τις οὖν αὐτὸν
he works as I also; ³not ⁵any- ⁴there- ²him
one fore

ἐξουθενήσῃ. προπέμψατε δὲ αὐτὸν ἐν
¹despise. But set ye forward him in

εἰρήνῃ, ἵνα ἔλθῃ πρός με· ἐκδέχομαι γὰρ
peace, in order he may to me; for I am awaiting
that come

αὐτὸν μετὰ τῶν ἀδελφῶν. 12 Περὶ δὲ
him with the brothers. Now about

Ἀπολλῶ τοῦ ἀδελφοῦ, πολλὰ παρεκάλεσα
²Apollos the ¹brother, ³much ¹I besought

αὐτὸν ἵνα ἔλθῃ πρὸς ὑμᾶς μετὰ τῶν
³him in order he would to you with the
that come

ἀδελφῶν· καὶ πάντως οὐκ ἦν θέλημα
brothers; and altogether it was not [his] will

ἵνα νῦν ἔλθῃ, ἐλεύσεται δὲ ὅταν εὐκαιρήσῃ.
in ²now ¹he but he will come whenever he has
order should opportunity.
that come,

13 Γρηγορεῖτε, στήκετε ἐν τῇ πίστει,
Watch ye, stand in the faith,

---

* "Futuristic present"; *cf.* John 14. 3 and ch. 15. 32.

in the faith, quit you like men, be strong.

14 Let all your things be done with charity.

15 I beseech you, brethren, (ye know the house of Stephanas, that it is the firstfruits of Achaia, and *that* they have addicted themselves to the ministry of the saints,)

16 That ye submit yourselves unto such, and to every one that helpeth with *us*, and laboureth.

17 I am glad of the coming of Stephanas and Fortunatus and Achaicus: for that which was lacking on your part they have supplied.

18 For they have refreshed my spirit and your's: therefore acknowledge ye them that are such.

19 The churches of Asia salute you. Aquila and Priscilla salute you much in the Lord, with the church that is in their house.

20 All the brethren greet you. Greet ye one another with an holy kiss.

21 The salutation of *me* Paul with mine own hand.

22 If any man love not the Lord Jesus Christ, let him be Anathema Maranatha.

23 The grace of our Lord Jesus Christ *be* with you.

24 My love *be* with you all in Christ Jesus. Amen.

ἀνδρίζεσθε, κραταιοῦσθε.   14 πάντα ὑμῶν
play the man,   be strong.   ¹All things ²of you

ἐν ἀγάπῃ γινέσθω.
⁴in ⁵love ¹let be.

15 Παρακαλῶ δὲ ὑμᾶς, ἀδελφοί· οἴδατε
   Now I beseech   you,   brothers: Know ye

τὴν οἰκίαν Στεφανᾶ, ὅτι ἐστὶν ἀπαρχὴ
the household of Stephanas, that   it is   firstfruit

τῆς Ἀχαΐας καὶ εἰς διακονίαν τοῖς
  –   of Achaia   and   to   ministry   to the

ἁγίοις ἔταξαν ἑαυτούς· 16 ἵνα καὶ ὑμεῖς
saints   they   themselves;   in order also   ye
    appointed   that

ὑποτάσσησθε τοῖς τοιούτοις καὶ παντὶ τῷ
may submit   –   to such ones   and   to everyone

συνεργοῦντι καὶ κοπιῶντι. 17 χαίρω δὲ
working with [?me] and   labouring.   Now I rejoice

ἐπὶ τῇ παρουσίᾳ Στεφανᾶ καὶ Φορτουνάτου
at   the   presence   of Stephanas and   of Fortunatus

καὶ Ἀχαϊκοῦ, ὅτι τὸ ὑμέτερον ὑστέρημα
and   of Achaicus,   that   –   ³your   ⁴lack

οὗτοι ἀνεπλήρωσαν· 18 ἀνέπαυσαν γὰρ τὸ
¹these   ²supplied;   for they refreshed   –

ἐμὸν πνεῦμα καὶ τὸ ὑμῶν. ἐπιγινώσκετε
my   spirit   and   – of you(yours).   Recognize ye

οὖν τοὺς τοιούτους.
therefore –   such ones.

19 Ἀσπάζονται ὑμᾶς αἱ ἐκκλησίαι τῆς
   ⁴Greet   ⁵you   ¹the   ²churches   –

Ἀσίας. ἀσπάζεται ὑμᾶς ἐν κυρίῳ πολλὰ
³of Asia.   ⁴Greets   ⁵you   ⁷in   ⁸[the] Lord   ⁶much

Ἀκύλας καὶ Πρίσκα σὺν τῇ κατ' οἶκον
¹Aquila   ²and   ³Prisca   ⁹with   ¹⁰the   ¹¹in [the] house

αὐτῶν ἐκκλησίᾳ. 20 ἀσπάζονται ὑμᾶς οἱ
¹²of them   ¹¹church.   ⁴Greet   ⁵you   ³the

ἀδελφοὶ πάντες. Ἀσπάσασθε ἀλλήλους ἐν
³brothers   ¹all.   Greet ye   one another   with

φιλήματι ἁγίῳ. 21 Ὁ ἀσπασμὸς τῇ
kiss   a holy.   ¹The   ²greeting   –

ἐμῇ χειρὶ Παύλου. 22 εἴ τις οὐ φιλεῖ
⁴with my ⁵hand   ³of Paul.   If anyone   loves not

τὸν κύριον, ἤτω ἀνάθεμα. μαράνα θά.
the   Lord,   let him be   a curse.   Marana   tha.

23 ἡ χάρις τοῦ κυρίου Ἰησοῦ μεθ' ὑμῶν.
The   grace   of the   Lord   Jesus [be] with   you.

24 ἡ ἀγάπη μου μετὰ πάντων ὑμῶν ἐν
The   love   of me [be] with   ²all   ¹you   in

Χριστῷ Ἰησοῦ.
Christ   Jesus.

CHAPTER 1

PAUL, an apostle of Jesus Christ by the will of God, and Timothy *our* brother, unto the church of God which is at Corinth, with all the saints which are in all Achaia:

2 Grace *be* to you and peace from God our Father, and *from* the Lord Jesus Christ.

3 Blessed *be* God, even the Father of our Lord Jesus Christ, the Father of mercies, and the God of all comfort;

4 Who comforteth us in all our tribulation, that we may be able to comfort them which are in any trouble, by the comfort wherewith we ourselves are comforted of God.

5 For as the sufferings of Christ abound in us, so our consolation also aboundeth by Christ.

6 And whether we be afflicted, *it is* for your consolation and salvation, which is effectual in the enduring of the same

1 Παῦλος ἀπόστολος Χριστοῦ Ἰησοῦ
Paul   an apostle   of Christ   Jesus

διὰ   θελήματος θεοῦ   καὶ Τιμόθεος ὁ
through [the] will of God and Timothy the

ἀδελφὸς τῇ ἐκκλησίᾳ τοῦ θεοῦ τῇ οὔσῃ
brother to the church - of God - being

ἐν Κορίνθῳ σὺν τοῖς ἁγίοις πᾶσιν τοῖς
in Corinth with ²the ³saints ¹all -

οὖσιν ἐν ὅλῃ τῇ Ἀχαΐᾳ· **2** χάρις ὑμῖν καὶ
being in all - Achaia: Grace to you and

εἰρήνη ἀπὸ θεοῦ πατρὸς ἡμῶν καὶ κυρίου
peace from God [the] Father of us and [the] Lord

Ἰησοῦ Χριστοῦ.
Jesus Christ.

3 Εὐλογητὸς ὁ θεὸς καὶ πατὴρ τοῦ
Blessed [be] the God and Father of the

κυρίου ἡμῶν Ἰησοῦ Χριστοῦ, ὁ πατὴρ
Lord of us Jesus Christ, the Father

τῶν οἰκτιρμῶν καὶ θεὸς πάσης παρακλήσ-
- of compassions and God of all com-

εως, **4** ὁ παρακαλῶν ἡμᾶς ἐπὶ πάσῃ
fort, the [one] comforting us on(in) all

τῇ θλίψει ἡμῶν, εἰς τὸ δύνασθαι ἡμᾶς
the affliction of us, [with a - to be able us[b]
                          view] to =our being able

παρακαλεῖν τοὺς ἐν πάσῃ θλίψει διὰ
to comfort the ones in every affliction through

τῆς παρακλήσεως ἧς παρακαλούμεθα αὐτοὶ
the comfort of(with) we are comforted [our-]
              which   selves

ὑπὸ τοῦ θεοῦ. **5** ὅτι καθὼς περισσεύει τὰ
by - God. Because as abounds the

παθήματα τοῦ Χριστοῦ εἰς ἡμᾶς, οὕτως
sufferings - of Christ in us, so

διὰ τοῦ Χριστοῦ περισσεύει καὶ ἡ παρά-
through - Christ abounds also the com-

κλησις ἡμῶν. **6** εἴτε δὲ θλιβόμεθα, ὑπὲρ
fort of us. Now whether we are on be-
                            afflicted,   half of

τῆς ὑμῶν παρακλήσεως καὶ σωτηρίας· εἴτε
the ⁴of you ¹comfort ²and ³salvation; or

παρακαλούμεθα, ὑπὲρ τῆς ὑμῶν παρακλή-
we are comforted, on behalf of the ²of you ¹com-

σεως τῆς ἐνεργουμένης ἐν ὑπομονῇ τῶν
fort - operating in endurance of the

sufferings which we also suffer: or whether we be comforted, *it is* for your consolation and salvation.

7 And our hope of you *is* stedfast, knowing, that as ye are partakers of the sufferings, so *shall ye be* also of the consolation.

8 For we would not, brethren, have you ignorant of our trouble which came to us in Asia, that we were pressed out of measure, above strength, insomuch that we despaired even of life:

9 But we had the sentence of death in ourselves, that we should not trust in ourselves, but in God which raiseth the dead:

10 Who delivered us from so great a death, and doth deliver: in whom we trust that he will yet deliver *us;*

11 Ye also helping together by prayer for us, that for the gift *bestowed* upon us by the means of many persons thanks may be given by many on our behalf.

12 For our rejoicing is this, the testimony of our conscience, that in simplicity and godly sincerity,

αὐτῶν παθημάτων ὧν καὶ ἡμεῖς πάσχομεν,
same sufferings which also we suffer,

7 καὶ ἡ ἐλπὶς ἡμῶν βεβαία ὑπὲρ ὑμῶν
and the hope of us [is] firm on behalf of you

εἰδότες ὅτι ὡς κοινωνοί ἐστε τῶν παθημά-
knowing that as partakers ye are of the suffer-

των, οὕτως καὶ τῆς παρακλήσεως. 8 Οὐ
ings, so also of the comfort. not

γὰρ θέλομεν ὑμᾶς ἀγνοεῖν, ἀδελφοί, ὑπὲρ
For we wish you to be ignorant, brothers, as to

τῆς θλίψεως ἡμῶν τῆς γενομένης ἐν
the affliction of us – having been in

τῇ Ἀσίᾳ, ὅτι καθ᾽ ὑπερβολὴν ὑπὲρ
– Asia, that excessively† beyond

δύναμιν ἐβαρήθημεν, ὥστε ἐξαπορηθῆναι
power we were burdened, so as to despair
=so that we despaired even

ἡμᾶς καὶ τοῦ ζῆν· 9 ἀλλὰ αὐτοὶ ἐν
usᵇ even – to live; but [our]selves in
of life;

ἑαυτοῖς τὸ ἀπόκριμα τοῦ θανάτου ἐσχήκα-
ourselves the sentence – of death we have

μεν, ἵνα μὴ πεποιθότες ὦμεν ἐφ᾽ ἑαυτοῖς
had, in order ²not ³having ¹we be on ourselves
that trusted might be

ἀλλ᾽ ἐπὶ τῷ θεῷ τῷ ἐγείροντι τοὺς
but on – God the [one] raising the

νεκρούς· 10 ὃς ἐκ τηλικούτου θανάτου
dead; who out of so great a death

ἐρρύσατο ἡμᾶς καὶ ῥύσεται, εἰς ὃν
delivered us and will deliver, in whom

ἠλπίκαμεν [ὅτι] καὶ ἔτι ῥύσεται, 11 συν-
we have hoped that indeed yet he will deliver, co-

υπουργούντων καὶ ὑμῶν ὑπὲρ ἡμῶν τῇ
operating also youᵃ on behalf of us –
=while ye also coöperate

δεήσει, ἵνα ἐκ πολλῶν προσώπων τὸ
in petition, in order ⁴by ⁵many ⁶persons ⁷[for]
that ⁸the

εἰς ἡμᾶς χάρισμα διὰ πολλῶν εὐχαριστηθῇ
¹⁰to ¹¹us ⁹gift ¹²through ¹³many ¹thanks may
be given

ὑπὲρ ἡμῶν.
²on behalf of ³us.

12 Ἡ γὰρ καύχησις ἡμῶν αὕτη ἐστίν,
For the boasting of us ²this ¹is,

τὸ μαρτύριον τῆς συνειδήσεως ἡμῶν, ὅτι
the testimony of the conscience of us, because

ἐν ἁγιότητι καὶ εἰλικρινείᾳ τοῦ θεοῦ,
in sanctity and sincerity – of God,

not with fleshly wisdom, but by the grace of God, we have had our conversation in the world, and more abundantly to you-ward.

13 For we write none other things unto you, than what ye read or acknowledge; and I trust ye shall acknowledge even to the end;

14 As also ye have acknowledged us in part, that we are your rejoicing, even as ye also *are* our's in the day of the Lord Jesus.

15 And in this confidence I was minded to come unto you before, that ye might have a second benefit;

16 And to pass by you into Macedonia, and to come again out of Macedonia unto you, and of you to be brought on my way toward Judæa.

17 When I therefore was thus minded, did I use lightness? or the things that I purpose, do I purpose according to the flesh, that with me there should be yea yea, and nay nay?

18 But *as* God *is* true, our word toward you was not yea and nay.

19 For the Son of God, Jesus Christ, who was preached among you by

οὐκ ἐν σοφίᾳ σαρκικῇ ἀλλ' ἐν χάριτι
not in wisdom fleshly but in [the] grace

θεοῦ, ἀνεστράφημεν ἐν τῷ κόσμῳ, περισ-
of God, we behaved in the world, ²more

σοτέρως δὲ πρὸς ὑμᾶς. 13 οὐ γὰρ ἄλλα
²especially ¹and with you. ³Not ¹for ⁴other
things

γράφομεν ὑμῖν ἀλλ' ἢ ἃ ἀναγινώσκετε
²we write to you *other* than what ye read

ἢ καὶ ἐπιγινώσκετε, ἐλπίζω δὲ ὅτι
or even perceive, and I hope that

ἕως τέλους ἐπιγνώσεσθε, 14 καθὼς καὶ
to [the] end ye will perceive, as also

ἐπέγνωτε ἡμᾶς ἀπὸ μέρους, ὅτι καύχημα
ye perceived us from(in) part, because ²boast

ὑμῶν ἐσμεν καθάπερ καὶ ὑμεῖς ἡμῶν
³of you ¹we are even as also ye of us

ἐν τῇ ἡμέρᾳ τοῦ κυρίου ἡμῶν Ἰησοῦ.
in the day of the Lord of us Jesus.

15 Καὶ ταύτῃ τῇ πεποιθήσει ἐβουλόμην
And in this – persuasion I determined

πρότερον πρὸς ὑμᾶς ἐλθεῖν ἵνα δευτέραν
formerly to you to come in order a second
that

χάριν σχῆτε, 16 καὶ δι' ὑμῶν διελθεῖν
grace ye might have, and through you to pass *through*

εἰς Μακεδονίαν, καὶ πάλιν ἀπὸ Μακεδονίας
into Macedonia, and again from Macedonia

ἐλθεῖν πρὸς ὑμᾶς καὶ ὑφ' ὑμῶν
to come to you and by you

προπεμφθῆναι εἰς τὴν Ἰουδαίαν. 17 τοῦτο
to be set forward to – Judæa. This

οὖν βουλόμενος μήτι ἄρα τῇ ἐλαφρίᾳ
therefore determining *not* ³then – ²fickleness

ἐχρησάμην; ἢ ἃ βουλεύομαι κατὰ σάρκα
¹did I use? or [the] I determine according [the]
things which to flesh

βουλεύομαι, ἵνα ᾖ παρ' ἐμοὶ τὸ ναὶ
do I determine, in order there with me the Yes
that may be

ναὶ καὶ τὸ οὒ οὔ; 18 πιστὸς δὲ ὁ
yes and the No no? But faithful [is] –

θεὸς ὅτι ὁ λόγος ἡμῶν ὁ πρὸς ὑμᾶς
God that the word of us – to you

οὐκ ἔστιν ναὶ καὶ οὔ. 19 ὁ τοῦ θεοῦ
is not yes and no. ²the – ⁴of God

γὰρ υἱὸς Χριστὸς Ἰησοῦς ὁ ἐν ὑμῖν
¹For ³Son Christ Jesus ¹the ²among ⁴you
[one]

us, *even* by me and Silvanus and Timotheus, was not yea and nay, but in him was yea.

20 For all the promises of God in him *are* yea, and in him Amen, unto the glory of God by us.

21 Now he which stablisheth us with you in Christ, and hath anointed us, *is* God;

22 Who hath also sealed us, and given the earnest of the Spirit in our hearts.

23 Moreover I call God for a record upon my soul, that to spare you I came not as yet unto Corinth.

24 Not for that we have dominion over your faith, but are helpers of your joy: for by faith ye stand.

CHAPTER 2

BUT I determined this with myself, that I would not come again to you in heaviness.

2 For if I make you sorry, who is he then that maketh me glad, but the same which is made sorry by me?

3 And I wrote this same unto you, lest, when I came, I should have sorrow from them of whom I ought to rejoice; having confidence in you all,

δι᾽ ἡμῶν κηρυχθείς, δι᾽ ἐμοῦ καὶ Σιλουανοῦ
through ⁴us ³proclaimed, through me and Silvanus

καὶ Τιμοθέου, οὐκ ἐγένετο ναὶ καὶ οὔ,
and Timothy, was not yes and no,

ἀλλὰ ναὶ ἐν αὐτῷ γέγονεν. 20 ὅσαι γὰρ
but ²Yes ³in ⁴him ¹has been. For as many

ἐπαγγελίαι θεοῦ, ἐν αὐτῷ τὸ ναί· διὸ
[as are] of God, in him [is] the Yes; where-
promises fore

καὶ δι᾽ αὐτοῦ τὸ ἀμὴν τῷ θεῷ πρὸς
also through him the Amen – ²to God ¹unto

δόξαν δι᾽ ἡμῶν. 21 ὁ δὲ βεβαιῶν ἡμᾶς
²glory through us. But the [one] making firm us

σὺν ὑμῖν εἰς Χριστὸν καὶ χρίσας ἡμᾶς
with you in Christ and having anointed us [is]

θεός, 22 ὁ καὶ σφραγισάμενος ἡμᾶς καὶ
God, the [one] both having sealed us and

δοὺς τὸν ἀρραβῶνα τοῦ πνεύματος ἐν
having the earnest of the Spirit in
given

ταῖς καρδίαις ἡμῶν.
the hearts of us.

23 Ἐγὼ δὲ μάρτυρα τὸν θεὸν ἐπικαλοῦμαι
Now ⁶I ⁷[as] witness – ⁸God ¹invoke

ἐπὶ τὴν ἐμὴν ψυχήν, ὅτι φειδόμενος
¹on – ²my ³life, that sparing

ὑμῶν οὐκέτι ἦλθον εἰς Κόρινθον. 24 οὐχ ὅτι
you ²no more ¹I came to Corinth. Not that

κυριεύομεν ὑμῶν τῆς πίστεως, ἀλλὰ συνεργοί
we rule over ²of you ¹the ²faith, but ³fellow-
workers

ἐσμεν τῆς χαρᾶς ὑμῶν· τῇ γὰρ πίστει
¹we are of the joy of you; – for by faith

ἑστήκατε. 2 ἔκρινα δὲ ἐμαυτῷ τοῦτο, τὸ μὴ
ye stand. But I decided in myself this, – not

πάλιν ἐν λύπῃ πρὸς ὑμᾶς ἐλθεῖν. 2 εἰ
again ⁴in ⁵grief ²to ³you ¹to come. if

γὰρ ἐγὼ λυπῶ ὑμᾶς, καὶ τίς ὁ εὐφραίνων
For I grieve you, then who the making glad
[one]

με εἰ μὴ ὁ λυπούμενος ἐξ ἐμοῦ; 3 καὶ
me except the [one] being grieved by me? And

ἔγραψα τοῦτο αὐτὸ ἵνα μὴ ἐλθὼν λύπην
I wrote this very thing lest coming grief

σχῶ ἀφ᾽ ὧν ἔδει με χαίρειν, πεποιθὼς
I should from [those] it me to rejoice, having
have whom behoved confidence

ἐπὶ πάντας ὑμᾶς ὅτι ἡ ἐμὴ χαρὰ πάντων
in ²all ¹you that – my joy ²all

that my joy is *the joy* of you all.

4 For out of much affliction and anguish of heart I wrote unto you with many tears; not that ye should be grieved, but that ye might know the love which I have more abundantly unto you.

5 But if any have caused grief, he hath not grieved me, but in part: that I may not overcharge you all.

6 Sufficient to such a man *is* this punishment, which *was inflicted* of many.

7 So that contrariwise ye *ought* rather to forgive *him*, and comfort *him*, lest perhaps such a one should be swallowed up with overmuch sorrow.

8 Wherefore I beseech you that ye would confirm *your* love toward him.

9 For to this end also did I write, that I might know the proof of you, whether ye be obedient in all things.

10 To whom ye forgive any thing, I *forgive* also: for if I forgave any thing, to whom I forgave *it*, for your sakes *forgave I it* in the person of Christ;

11 Lest Satan should get an advantage of us: for we are not ignorant of his devices.

12 Furthermore, when I came to Troas to *preach* Christ's gospel, and a door was opened unto me of the Lord,

13 I had no rest in my

ὑμῶν ἐστιν. 4 ἐκ γὰρ πολλῆς θλίψεως
²of you ¹is. For out of much affliction

καὶ συνοχῆς καρδίας ἔγραψα ὑμῖν διὰ
and anxiety of heart I wrote to you through

πολλῶν δακρύων, οὐχ ἵνα λυπηθῆτε, ἀλλὰ
many tears, not in order ye should be but
that grieved,

τὴν ἀγάπην ἵνα γνῶτε ἣν ἔχω περισ-
²the ⁴love ¹in order ²ye should ³which I have more
that know

σοτέρως εἰς ὑμᾶς. 5 Εἰ δέ τις λελύπηκεν,
abundantly to you. But if anyone has grieved,

οὐκ ἐμὲ λελύπηκεν, ἀλλὰ ἀπὸ μέρους,
not me he has grieved, but from(in) part,

ἵνα μὴ ἐπιβαρῶ, πάντας ὑμᾶς. 6 ἱκανὸν
lest I am burdensome, ²all ¹you. Enough

τῷ τοιούτῳ ἡ ἐπιτιμία αὕτη ἡ ὑπὸ
for such a one this punishment – by

τῶν πλειόνων, 7 ὥστε τοὐναντίον μᾶλλον
the majority, so as on the contrary rather

ὑμᾶς χαρίσασθαι καὶ παρακαλέσαι, μή πως
you to forgive and to comfort,[b] lest
=ye should rather forgive and comfort,

τῇ περισσοτέρᾳ λύπῃ καταποθῇ ὁ τοιοῦτος.
³by ⁴more abundant ⁵grief ³should be ¹such a one.
the swallowed up

8 διὸ παρακαλῶ ὑμᾶς κυρῶσαι εἰς αὐτὸν
Wherefore I beseech you to confirm to him

ἀγάπην· 9 εἰς τοῦτο γὰρ καὶ ἔγραψα,
[your] love; ²to ³this [end] ¹for indeed I wrote,

ἵνα γνῶ τὴν δοκιμὴν ὑμῶν, εἰ εἰς πάντα
in or- I might the proof of you, if in all things
der that know

ὑπήκοοί ἐστε. 10 ᾧ δέ τι χαρίζεσθε,
obedient ye are. Now *to* whom anything ye forgive,

κἀγώ· καὶ γὰρ ἐγὼ ὃ κεχάρισμαι, εἴ
I also; for indeed ²I ¹what ²have forgiven, if

τι κεχάρισμαι, δι' ὑμᾶς ἐν προσώπῳ
²any- ¹I have [it is] on you in [the] person
thing forgiven, account of

Χριστοῦ, 11 ἵνα μὴ πλεονεκτηθῶμεν ὑπὸ
of Christ, lest we are taken advantage of by

τοῦ σατανᾶ· οὐ γὰρ αὐτοῦ τὰ νοήματα
– Satan; for ²not ⁷of him ⁵the ⁶designs

ἀγνοοῦμεν. 12 Ἐλθὼν δὲ εἰς τὴν Τρῳάδα εἰς
¹we ²are ⁴ignorant [of]. But coming to – Troas in

τὸ εὐαγγέλιον τοῦ Χριστοῦ, καὶ θύρας
the gospel – of Christ, and a door

μοι ἀνεῳγμένης ἐν κυρίῳ, 13 οὐκ ἔσχηκα
to me having been by [the] Lord, I *have* had no
opened[a]

spirit, because I found not Titus my brother: but taking my leave of them, I went from thence into Macedonia.

14 Now thanks be unto God, which always causeth us to triumph in Christ, and maketh manifest the savour of his knowledge by us in every place.

15 For we are unto God a sweet savour of Christ, in them that are saved, and in them that perish:

16 To the one *we are* the savour of death unto death; and to the other the savour of life unto life. And who *is* sufficient for these things?

17 For we are not as many, which corrupt the word of God: but as of sincerity, but as of God, in the sight of God speak we in Christ.

ἄνεσιν   τῷ   πνεύματί   μου   τῷ   μὴ   εὑρεῖν
rest   to the   spirit   of me   in the   not   to find
               =when I did not find ...

με   Τίτον   τὸν   ἀδελφόν   μου,   ἀλλὰ   ἀποτα-
me[be]   Titus   the   brother   of me,   but   saying

ξάμενος   αὐτοῖς   ἐξῆλθον   εἰς   Μακεδονίαν.
farewell   to them   I went forth   into   Macedonia.

14 Τῷ   δὲ   θεῷ   χάρις   τῷ   πάντοτε
  -   But   [2]to God   [1]thanks   the [one]   always

θριαμβεύοντι   ἡμᾶς   ἐν   τῷ   Χριστῷ   καὶ
leading in triumph   us   in   -   Christ   and

τὴν   ὀσμὴν   τῆς   γνώσεως   αὐτοῦ   φανεροῦντι
[4]the   [5]odour   [6]of the   [7]knowledge   [8]of him   [1]manifesting

δι'   ἡμῶν   ἐν   παντὶ   τόπῳ·   15 ὅτι   Χριστοῦ
[2]through [3]us   in   every   place;   because   of Christ

εὐωδία   ἐσμὲν   τῷ   θεῷ   ἐν   τοῖς   σωζομένοις
a sweet   we are   -   to God   in   the [ones] being saved
smell

καὶ   ἐν   τοῖς   ἀπολλυμένοις,   16 οἷς   μὲν
and   in   the [ones]   perishing,   to the [latter]†

ὀσμὴ   ἐκ   θανάτου   εἰς   θάνατον,   οἷς   δὲ
an odour out of   death   unto   death,   to the [former]†

ὀσμὴ   ἐκ   ζωῆς   εἰς   ζωήν.   καὶ   πρὸς
an odour out of   life   unto   life.   And   for

ταῦτα   τίς   ἱκανός;   17 οὐ   γάρ   ἐσμεν
these things   who [is] competent?   For we are not

ὡς   οἱ   πολλοὶ   καπηλεύοντες   τὸν   λόγον
as   the   many   hawking   the   word

τοῦ   θεοῦ,   ἀλλ'   ὡς   ἐξ   εἰλικρινείας,   ἀλλ'
 - of God,   but   as   of   sincerity,   but

ὡς   ἐκ   θεοῦ   κατέναντι   θεοῦ   ἐν   Χριστῷ
as   of   God   before   God   in   Christ

λαλοῦμεν.
we speak.

CHAPTER 3

DO we begin again to commend ourselves? or need we, as some *others*, epistles of commendation to you, or *letters* of commendation from you?

2 Ye are our epistle written in our hearts, known and read of all men:

3 *Forasmuch as ye are* manifestly declared to be the epistle of Christ minis-

---

3 Ἀρχόμεθα   πάλιν   ἑαυτοὺς   συνιστάνειν;
  Do we begin   again   ourselves   to commend?

ἢ   μὴ   χρῄζομεν   ὥς   τινες   συστατικῶν
or   *not*   need we   as   some   commendatory

ἐπιστολῶν   πρὸς   ὑμᾶς   ἢ   ἐξ   ὑμῶν;   2 ἡ
epistles   to   you   or from   you?   The

ἐπιστολὴ   ἡμῶν   ὑμεῖς   ἐστε,   ἐγγεγραμμένη
epistle   of us   ye   are,   *having been* inscribed

ἐν   ταῖς   καρδίαις   ἡμῶν,   γινωσκομένη   καὶ
in   the   hearts   of us,   *being* known   and

ἀναγινωσκομένη   ὑπὸ   πάντων   ἀνθρώπων,
being read   by   all   men,

3 φανερούμενοι   ὅτι   ἐστὲ   ἐπιστολὴ   Χριστοῦ
being manifested   that   ye are   an epistle   of Christ

tered by us, written not with ink, but with the Spirit of the living God; not in tables of stone, but in fleshy tables of the heart.

4 And such trust have we through Christ to Godward:

5 Not that we are sufficient of ourselves to think any thing as of ourselves; but our sufficiency is of God;

6 Who also hath made us able ministers of the new testament; not of the letter, but of the spirit: for the letter killeth, but the spirit giveth life.

7 But if the ministration of death, written and engraven in stones, was glorious, so that the children of Israel could not stedfastly behold the face of Moses for the glory of his countenance; which glory was to be done away:

8 How shall not the ministration of the spirit be rather glorious?

9 For if the ministration of condemnation be glory, much more doth the ministration of righteousness exceed in glory.

10 For even that which was made glorious had no glory in this respect,

διακονηθεῖσα ὑφ᾽ ἡμῶν, ἐγγεγραμμένη οὐ
ministered   by   us,   *having been* inscribed   not

μέλανι ἀλλὰ πνεύματι θεοῦ ζῶντος, οὐκ
by ink   but   by [the] Spirit   of ²God   ¹a living,   not

ἐν πλαξὶν λιθίναις ἀλλ᾽ ἐν πλαξὶν καρδίαις
in   ²tablets   ¹stony   but   in   tablets   [which are]

σαρκίναις.
²hearts
¹fleshy.

4 Πεποίθησιν δὲ τοιαύτην ἔχομεν διὰ
²confidence   ¹And   ²such   we have through

τοῦ Χριστοῦ πρὸς τὴν θεόν. 5 οὐχ
-   Christ   toward   -   God.   Not

ὅτι ἀφ᾽ ἑαυτῶν ἱκανοί ἐσμεν λογίσασθαί
that   ³from   ⁴ourselves ²competent   ¹we are   to reckon

τι ὡς ἐξ ἑαυτῶν, ἀλλ᾽ ἡ ἱκανότης
any-thing   as   of   ourselves,   but   the   competence

ἡμῶν ἐκ τοῦ θεοῦ, 6 ὃς καὶ ἱκάνωσεν
of us [is]   of   -   God,   who   also made competent

ἡμᾶς διακόνους καινῆς διαθήκης, οὐ
us   [as] ministers   of a new   covenant,   not

γράμματος ἀλλὰ πνεύματος· τὸ γὰρ γράμμα
of letter   but   of spirit;   for the   letter

ἀποκτείνει, τὸ δὲ πνεῦμα ζωοποιεῖ. 7 Εἰ
kills,   but the   spirit   makes alive.   if

δὲ ἡ διακονία τοῦ θανάτου ἐν γράμμασιν
Now the   ministry   -   of death   in   letters

ἐντετυπωμένη λίθοις ἐγενήθη ἐν δόξῃ,
having been engraved in stones   was   in   glory,

ὥστε μὴ δύνασθαι ἀτενίσαι τοὺς υἱοὺς
so as   not   to be able   to gaze   the   sons
=so that the sons of Israel were not able to gaze

Ἰσραὴλ εἰς τὸ πρόσωπον Μωϋσέως διὰ
of Israel[b]   at   the   face   of Moses   on account of

τὴν δόξαν τοῦ προσώπου αὐτοῦ τὴν
the   glory   of the   face   of him   -

καταργουμένην, 8 πῶς οὐχὶ μᾶλλον ἡ
being done away,   how   ²not   ³rather   ⁴the

διακονία τοῦ πνεύματος ἔσται ἐν δόξῃ;
⁵ministry   ⁶of the   ⁷Spirit   ¹will ⁸be   in   glory?

9 εἰ γὰρ ἡ διακονία τῆς κατακρίσεως
For if   the   ministry   -   of condemnation

δόξα, πολλῷ μᾶλλον περισσεύει ἡ διακονία
[was]   by much   rather   ⁴abounds   ¹the   ²ministry
glory,

τῆς δικαιοσύνης δόξῃ. 10 καὶ γὰρ οὐ
-   ³of righteousness   in glory.   For indeed   ²not

δεδόξασται τὸ δεδοξασμένον ἐν τούτῳ
⁴has been   ¹the   ²having been   in   this
glorified   [thing]   glorified

by reason of the glory that excelleth.

11 For if that which is done away *was* glorious, much more that which remaineth *is* glorious.

12 Seeing then that we have such hope, we use great plainness of speech:

13 And not as Moses, *which* put a vail over his face, that the children of Israel could not stedfastly look to the end of that which is abolished:

14 But their minds were blinded: for until this day remaineth the same vail untaken away in the reading of the old testament; which *vail* is done away in Christ.

15 But even unto this day, when Moses is read, the vail is upon their heart.

16 Nevertheless when it shall turn to the Lord, the vail shall be taken away.

17 Now the Lord is that Spirit: and where the Spirit of the Lord *is*, there *is* liberty.

18 But we all, with open face beholding as in a glass the glory of the Lord, are changed into the same image from glory to glory, *even* as by the Spirit of the Lord.

τῷ μέρει εἵνεκεν τῆς ὑπερβαλλούσης δόξης.
- respect for the the excelling glory.
      sake of

11 εἰ γὰρ τὸ καταργούμενον διὰ δόξης,
For if the being done away [was] glory,
         [thing] through

πολλῷ μᾶλλον τὸ μένον ἐν δόξῃ.
by much more the [thing] remaining [is] in glory.

12 Ἔχοντες οὖν τοιαύτην ἐλπίδα πολλῇ
Having therefore such hope ²much

παρρησίᾳ χρώμεθα, 13 καὶ οὐ καθάπερ
³boldness ¹we use, and not as

Μωϋσῆς ἐτίθει κάλυμμα ἐπὶ τὸ πρόσωπον
Moses put a veil on the face

αὐτοῦ, πρὸς τὸ μὴ ἀτενίσαι τοὺς υἱοὺς
of him, for the ⁴not ²to gaze ¹the ³sons

Ἰσραὴλ εἰς τὸ τέλος τοῦ καταργουμένου.
³of Israel[b] at the end of the [thing] being done away.

14 ἀλλὰ ἐπωρώθη τὰ νοήματα αὐτῶν.
But were hardened the thoughts of them.

ἄχρι γὰρ τῆς σήμερον ἡμέρας τὸ αὐτὸ
For until the present day the same

κάλυμμα ἐπὶ τῇ ἀναγνώσει τῆς παλαιᾶς
veil ³on(at) ⁴the ⁵reading ⁶of the ⁶old

διαθήκης μένει, μὴ ἀνακαλυπτόμενον ὅτι
⁷covenant ¹remains, not being unveiled* that

ἐν Χριστῷ καταργεῖται. 15 ἀλλ' ἕως
in Christ it is being done away. But until

σήμερον ἡνίκα ἂν ἀναγινώσκηται Μωϋσῆς
to-day whenever ²is being read ¹Moses

κάλυμμα ἐπὶ τὴν καρδίαν αὐτῶν κεῖται·
a veil ²on ³the ⁴heart ⁵of them ¹lies;

16 ἡνίκα δὲ ἐὰν ἐπιστρέψῃ πρὸς κύριον,
but whenever it § turns to [the] Lord,

περιαιρεῖται τὸ κάλυμμα. 17 ὁ δὲ κύριος
²is taken away ¹the ²veil. Now the Lord

τὸ πνεῦμά ἐστιν· οὗ δὲ τὸ πνεῦμα
²the ²Spirit ¹is; and where the Spirit

κυρίου, ἐλευθερία. 18 ἡμεῖς δὲ πάντες
of [the] [there is] freedom. But we all
Lord [is],

ἀνακεκαλυμμένῳ προσώπῳ τὴν δόξαν
²having been unveiled ¹with face ²the ²glory

κυρίου κατοπτριζόμενοι τὴν αὐτὴν εἰκόνα
⁴of [the] ¹beholding in ⁴the ⁷same ⁸image
Lord a mirror

μεταμορφούμεθα ἀπὸ δόξης εἰς δόξαν,
²are being changed [into] from glory to glory,

καθάπερ ἀπὸ κυρίου πνεύματος.
even as from [the] Lord Spirit.

* That is, revealed (Conybeare and Howson). § ? their heart.

CHAPTER 4

THEREFORE seeing we have this ministry, as we have received mercy, we faint not;

2 But have renounced the hidden things of dishonesty, not walking in craftiness, nor handling the word of God deceitfully; but by manifestation of the truth commending ourselves to every man's conscience in the sight of God.

3 But if our gospel be hid, it is hid to them that are lost:

4 In whom the god of this world hath blinded the minds of them which believe not, lest the light of the glorious gospel of Christ, who is the image of God, should shine unto them.

5 For we preach not ourselves, but Christ Jesus the Lord; and ourselves your servants for Jesus' sake.

6 For God, who commanded the light to shine out of darkness, hath shined in our hearts, to *give* the light of the knowledge of the glory of God in the face of Jesus Christ.

7 But we have this treasure in earthen vessels, that the excellency of the

---

4 Διὰ τοῦτο, ἔχοντες τὴν διακονίαν
Therefore, having – ministry

ταύτην, καθὼς ἠλεήθημεν, οὐκ ἐγκακοῦμεν,
this, as we obtained mercy, we faint not,

2 ἀλλὰ ἀπειπάμεθα τὰ κρυπτὰ τῆς αἰσχύνης,
but we have renounced the hidden things – of shame,

μὴ περιπατοῦντες ἐν πανουργίᾳ μηδὲ
not walking in craftiness nor

δολοῦντες τὸν λόγον τοῦ θεοῦ, ἀλλὰ
adulterating the word – of God, but

τῇ φανερώσει τῆς ἀληθείας συνιστάνοντες
by the manifestation of the truth commending

ἑαυτοὺς πρὸς πᾶσαν συνείδησιν ἀνθρώπων
ourselves to every conscience of men

ἐνώπιον τοῦ θεοῦ. **3** εἰ δὲ καὶ ἔστιν
before – God. But if indeed ⁴is

κεκαλυμμένον τὸ εὐαγγέλιον ἡμῶν, ἐν
⁵*having been* hidden ¹the ²gospel ³of us, in

τοῖς ἀπολλυμένοις ἐστὶν κεκαλυμμένον, **4** ἐν
the [ones] perishing it is *having been* hidden, in

οἷς ὁ θεὸς τοῦ αἰῶνος τούτου ἐτύφλωσεν
whom the god of this age blinded

τὰ νοήματα τῶν ἀπίστων εἰς τὸ μὴ
the thoughts of the unbelieving [with a *the* not
[ones] view] to

==so that the enlightenment . . . should not shine forth,

αὐγάσαι τὸν φωτισμὸν τοῦ εὐαγγελίου
to shine forth the enlightenment of the gospel

τῆς δόξης τοῦ Χριστοῦ, ὅς ἐστιν εἰκὼν
of the glory – of Christ, who is [the] image

τοῦ θεοῦ. **5** οὐ γὰρ ἑαυτοὺς κηρύσσομεν
– of God. For ⁸not ⁹ourselves ¹we proclaim

ἀλλὰ Χριστὸν Ἰησοῦν κύριον, ἑαυτοὺς δὲ
but Christ Jesus [as] Lord, and ourselves

δούλους ὑμῶν διὰ Ἰησοῦν. **6** ὅτι ὁ
slaves of you on account of Jesus. Because –

θεὸς ὁ εἰπών· ἐκ σκότους φῶς λάμψει,
God the [one] saying: Out of darkness light shall shine,

ὃς ἔλαμψεν ἐν ταῖς καρδίαις ἡμῶν πρὸς
[is] [he] shone in the hearts of us for
who

φωτισμὸν τῆς γνώσεως τῆς δόξης τοῦ
enlightenment of the knowledge of the glory –

θεοῦ ἐν προσώπῳ Χριστοῦ.
of God in [the] face of Christ.

7 Ἔχομεν δὲ τὸν θησαυρὸν τοῦτον ἐν
And we have this treasure in

ὀστρακίνοις σκεύεσιν, ἵνα ἡ ὑπερβολὴ
earthenware vessels, in order that the excellence

power may be of God, and not of us.

8 *We are* troubled on every side, yet not distressed; *we are* perplexed, but not in despair;

9 Persecuted, but not forsaken; cast down, but not destroyed;

10 Always bearing about in the body the dying of the Lord Jesus, that the life also of Jesus might be made manifest in our body.

11 For we which live are alway delivered unto death for Jesus' sake, that the life also of Jesus might be made manifest in our mortal flesh.

12 So then death worketh in us, but life in you.

13 We having the same spirit of faith, according as it is written, I believed, and therefore have I spoken; we also believe, and therefore speak;

14 Knowing that he which raised up the Lord Jesus shall raise up us also by Jesus, and shall present *us* with you.

15 For all things *are* for your sakes, that the abundant grace might

---

τῆς δυνάμεως ᾖ τοῦ θεοῦ καὶ μὴ ἐξ
of the power may be - of God and not of

ἡμῶν· 8 ἐν παντὶ θλιβόμενοι ἀλλ' οὐ
us; in every [way] *being* afflicted but not

στενοχωρούμενοι, ἀπορούμενοι ἀλλ' οὐκ
being restrained, *being* in difficulties but not

ἐξαπορούμενοι, 9 διωκόμενοι ἀλλ' οὐκ
despairing, *being* persecuted but not

ἐγκαταλειπόμενοι, καταβαλλόμενοι ἀλλ' οὐκ
being deserted, *being* cast down but not

ἀπολλύμενοι, 10 πάντοτε τὴν νέκρωσιν τοῦ
perishing, always ⁵the ⁶dying -

Ἰησοῦ ἐν τῷ σώματι περιφέροντες, ἵνα
⁷of Jesus ²in ³the ⁴body ¹bearing about, in order that

καὶ ἡ ζωὴ τοῦ Ἰησοῦ ἐν τῷ σώματι
also the life - of Jesus in the body

ἡμῶν φανερωθῇ. 11 ἀεὶ γὰρ ἡμεῖς οἱ
of us might be manifested. For always we the

ζῶντες εἰς θάνατον παραδιδόμεθα διὰ
[ones] living to death are being on ac-
                        delivered count of

Ἰησοῦν, ἵνα καὶ ἡ ζωὴ τοῦ Ἰησοῦ
Jesus, in order that also the life - of Jesus

φανερωθῇ ἐν τῇ θνητῇ σαρκὶ ἡμῶν.
might be in the mortal flesh of us.
manifested

12 ὥστε ὁ θάνατος ἐν ἡμῖν ἐνεργεῖται,
So as - death in us operates,

ἡ δὲ ζωὴ ἐν ὑμῖν. 13 ἔχοντες δὲ τὸ
- but life in you. And having the

αὐτὸ πνεῦμα τῆς πίστεως, κατὰ τὸ
same spirit - of faith, according to the
                                        thing

γεγραμμένον· ἐπίστευσα, διὸ ἐλάλησα, καὶ
having been written: I believed, therefore I spoke, both

ἡμεῖς πιστεύομεν, διὸ καὶ λαλοῦμεν, 14 εἰδότες
we believe, and therefore we speak, knowing

ὅτι ὁ ἐγείρας τὸν κύριον Ἰησοῦν καὶ
that the having the Lord Jesus ²also
       [one] raised

ἡμᾶς σὺν Ἰησοῦ ἐγερεῖ καὶ παραστήσει
²us ⁴with ⁵Jesus ¹will raise and will present [us]

σὺν ὑμῖν. 15 τὰ γὰρ πάντα δι' ὑμᾶς,
with you. - For all things [are] on ac- you,
                           count of

ἵνα ἡ χάρις πλεονάσασα διὰ τῶν πλειόνων
in or- - grace increased through the majority
der that

through the thanksgiving of many redound to the glory of God.

16 For which cause we faint not; but though our outward man perish, yet the inward *man* is renewed day by day.

17 For our light affliction, which is but for a moment, worketh for us a far more exceeding *and* eternal weight of glory;

18 While we look not at the things which are seen, but at the things which are not seen: for the things which are seen *are* temporal; but the things which are not seen *are* eternal.

CHAPTER 5

F OR we know that if our earthly house of *this* tabernacle were dissolved, we have a building of God, an house not made with hands, eternal in the heavens.

2 For in this we groan, earnestly desiring to be clothed upon with our house which is from heaven:

3 If so be that being clothed we shall not be found naked.

4 For we that are in *this* tabernacle do groan, being burdened: not for that we would be unclothed, but clothed upon, that mortality might be swallowed up of life.

τὴν εὐχαριστίαν περισσεύσῃ εἰς τὴν δόξαν
²the ³thanksgiving ¹may cause to abound to the glory

τοῦ θεοῦ. 16 Διὸ οὐκ ἐγκακοῦμεν, ἀλλ’
– of God. Wherefore we faint not, but

εἰ καὶ ὁ ἔξω ἡμῶν ἄνθρωπος διαφθείρεται,
if indeed the outward ²of us ¹man is being disabled,

ἀλλ’ ὁ ἔσω ἡμῶν ἀνακαινοῦται ἡμέρᾳ
yet the inward [man] of us is being renewed day

καὶ ἡμέρᾳ. 17 τὸ γὰρ παραυτίκα ἐλαφρὸν
and (by) day. For the present lightness

τῆς θλίψεως καθ’ ὑπερβολὴν εἰς ὑπερβολὴν
of the affliction ³excessively ⁴to ⁵excess

αἰώνιον βάρος δόξης κατεργάζεται ἡμῖν,
⁶an eternal ⁷weight ⁸of glory ¹works ²for us,

18 μὴ σκοπούντων ἡμῶνª τὰ βλεπόμενα
not considering us the things *being* seen
= while we do not consider

ἀλλὰ τὰ μὴ βλεπόμενα· τὰ γὰρ βλεπόμενα
but the not *being* seen; for the things *being* seen
things

πρόσκαιρα, τὰ δὲ μὴ βλεπόμενα αἰώνια.
[are] temporary, but the things not *being* seen [are] eternal.

5 Οἴδαμεν γὰρ ὅτι ἐὰν ἡ ἐπίγειος
For we know that if the earthly

ἡμῶν οἰκία τοῦ σκήνους καταλυθῇ,
⁴of us ¹house ²of the ³tabernacle is destroyed,

οἰκοδομὴν ἐκ θεοῦ ἔχομεν, οἰκίαν ἀχειρο-
a building of God we have, a house not made

ποίητον αἰώνιον ἐν τοῖς οὐρανοῖς. 2 καὶ
by hands eternal in *the* heavens. indeed

γὰρ ἐν τούτῳ* στενάζομεν, τὸ οἰκητήριον
For in this* we groan, ³the ⁴dwelling-place

ἡμῶν τὸ ἐξ οὐρανοῦ ἐπενδύσασθαι ἐπιπο-
⁵of us – ⁶out of ⁷heaven ²to put on ¹greatly

θοῦντες, 3 εἴ γε καὶ ἐνδυσάμενοι οὐ
desiring, if indeed being clothed not

γυμνοὶ εὑρεθησόμεθα. 4 καὶ γὰρ οἱ
naked we shall be found. For indeed ²the
[ones]

ὄντες ἐν τῷ σκήνει στενάζομεν βαρούμενοι,
³being ⁴in ⁵the ⁶tabernacle ¹we groan being burdened,

ἐφ’ ᾧ οὐ θέλομεν ἐκδύσασθαι ἀλλ’
inasmuch as we do not wish to put off but

ἐπενδύσασθαι, ἵνα καταποθῇ τὸ θνητὸν
to put on, in order ³may be ¹the ²mortal
that swallowed up

ὑπὸ τῆς ζωῆς. 5 ὁ δὲ κατεργασάμενος
by *the* life. Now the [one] having wrought

* Neuter, going back to σκῆνος in the preceding verse.

5 Now he that hath wrought us for the self-same thing *is* God, who also hath given unto us the earnest of the Spirit.

6 Therefore *we are* always confident, knowing that, whilst we are at home in the body, we are absent from the Lord:

7 (For we walk by faith, not by sight:)

8 We are confident, *I say,* and willing rather to be absent from the body, and to be present with the Lord.

9 Wherefore we labour, that, whether present or absent, we may be accepted of him.

10 For we must all appear before the judgment seat of Christ; that every one may receive the things *done* in *his* body, according to that he hath done, whether *it be* good or bad.

11 Knowing therefore the terror of the Lord, we persuade men; but we are made manifest unto God; and I trust also are made manifest in your consciences.

12 For we commend not ourselves again unto you, but give you occasion to glory on our behalf, that ye may have some-

---

ἡμᾶς   εἰς   αὐτὸ   τοῦτο   θεός,   ὁ   δοὺς
us   for   this very thing   [is] God,   the [one]   having given

ἡμῖν   τὸν   ἀρραβῶνα   τοῦ   πνεύματος.   6 Θαρ-
to us   the   earnest   of the   Spirit.   Being

ροῦντες   οὖν   πάντοτε   καὶ   εἰδότες   ὅτι
of good cheer   therefore   always   and   knowing   that

ἐνδημοῦντες   ἐν   τῷ   σώματι   ἐκδημοῦμεν
being at home   in   the   body   we are away from home

ἀπὸ   τοῦ   κυρίου·   7 διὰ   πίστεως   γὰρ
from   the   Lord;   [2]through   [3]faith   [1]for

περιπατοῦμεν,   οὐ   διὰ   εἴδους·   8 θαρροῦμεν
we walk,   not through appearance;   we are of good cheer

δὲ   καὶ   εὐδοκοῦμεν   μᾶλλον   ἐκδημῆσαι   ἐκ
then and   think it good   rather   to go away from home   out of

τοῦ   σώματος   καὶ   ἐνδημῆσαι   πρὸς   τὸν
the   body   and   to come home   to   the

κύριον.   9 διὸ   καὶ   φιλοτιμούμεθα,   εἴτε
Lord.   Wherefore also   we are ambitious,   whether

ἐνδημοῦντες   εἴτε   ἐκδημοῦντες,   εὐάρεστοι
being at home   or   being away from home,   wellpleasing

αὐτῷ   εἶναι.   10 τοὺς   γὰρ   πάντας   ἡμᾶς
to him   to be.   -   For   [2]all   [3]us

φανερωθῆναι   δεῖ   ἔμπροσθεν   τοῦ   βήματος
[4]to be manifested   [1]it behoves   before   the   tribunal

τοῦ   Χριστοῦ,   ἵνα   κομίσηται   ἕκαστος   τὰ
-   of Christ,   in order that   [2]may receive   [1]each one   the things

διὰ   τοῦ   σώματος   πρὸς   ἃ   ἔπραξεν,   εἴτε
through the   body   according to   what   he things practised,   either

ἀγαθὸν   εἴτε   φαῦλον.
good   or   worthless.

11 Εἰδότες   οὖν   τὸν   φόβον   τοῦ   κυρίου
Knowing   therefore   the   fear   of the   Lord

ἀνθρώπους   πείθομεν,   θεῷ   δὲ   πεφανερώμεθα·
[2]men   [1]we persuade,   and to God   we have been made manifest;

ἐλπίζω   δὲ   καὶ   ἐν   ταῖς   συνειδήσεσιν
and I hope   also   in   the   consciences

ὑμῶν   πεφανερῶσθαι.   12 οὐ   πάλιν   ἑαυτοὺς
of you   to have been made manifest.   Not   again   [2]ourselves

συνιστάνομεν   ὑμῖν,   ἀλλὰ   ἀφορμὴν   διδόντες
[1]we commend   to you,   but   [2]an occasion   [1]giving

ὑμῖν   καυχήματος   ὑπὲρ   ἡμῶν,   ἵνα   ἔχητε
[3]to you   of a boast   on behalf of   us,   in order that   ye may have [it]

what to *answer* them which glory in appearance, and not in heart.

13 For whether we be beside ourselves, *it is* to God: or whether we be sober, *it is* for your cause.

14 For the love of Christ constraineth us; because we thus judge, that if one died for all, then were all dead:

15 And *that* he died for all, that they which live should not henceforth live unto themselves, but unto him which died for them, and rose again.

16 Wherefore henceforth know we no man after the flesh: yea, though we have known Christ after the flesh, yet now henceforth know we *him* no more.

17 Therefore if any man be in Christ, *he is* a new creature: old things are passed away; behold, all things are become new.

18 And all things *are* of God, who hath reconciled us to himself by Jesus Christ, and hath given to us the ministry of reconciliation;

19 To wit, that God was in Christ, reconciling the world unto himself, not imputing their trespasses unto them; and hath committed unto us the word of reconciliation.

20 Now then we are ambassadors for Christ,

πρὸς τοὺς ἐν προσώπῳ καυχωμένους καὶ
in refer- the ²in ²face ¹boasting and
ence to [ones]

μὴ ἐν καρδίᾳ. **13** εἴτε γὰρ ἐξέστημεν,
not in heart. For whether we are mad,

θεῷ· εἴτε σωφρονοῦμεν. ὑμῖν. **14** ἡ γὰρ
[it is] or we are in our senses, [it is] For the
to God; for you.

ἀγάπη τοῦ Χριστοῦ συνέχει ἡμᾶς, κρίναντας
love of Christ constrains us, judging

τοῦτο, ὅτι εἷς ὑπὲρ πάντων ἀπέθανεν·
this, that one on behalf of all men died;

ἄρα οἱ πάντες ἀπέθανον· **15** καὶ ὑπὲρ
then the all died; and ²on behalf of

πάντων ἀπέθανεν ἵνα οἱ ζῶντες μηκέτι
²all ¹he died in order the living no more
that [ones]

ἑαυτοῖς ζῶσιν ἀλλὰ τῷ ὑπὲρ αὐτῶν
to themselves may live but to the on behalf them
[one] of

ἀποθανόντι καὶ ἐγερθέντι. **16** Ὥστε ἡμεῖς
having died and having been raised. So as ²we

ἀπὸ τοῦ νῦν οὐδένα οἴδαμεν κατὰ σάρκα·
¹from - ²now ⁵no man ⁴know according to flesh;

εἰ καὶ ἐγνώκαμεν κατὰ σάρκα Χριστόν,
if indeed ¹we have known ²according to ⁴flesh ²Christ,

ἀλλὰ νῦν οὐκέτι γινώσκομεν. **17** ὥστε
yet now no more we know [him]. So as

εἴ τις ἐν Χριστῷ, καινὴ κτίσις· τὰ
if anyone [is] in Christ, [he is] a new creation; the

ἀρχαῖα παρῆλθεν, ἰδοὺ γέγονεν καινά.
old things passed away, behold they have become new.

18 τὰ δὲ πάντα ἐκ τοῦ θεοῦ τοῦ καταλ-
- And all things [are] of - God the [one] having

λάξαντος ἡμᾶς ἑαυτῷ διὰ Χριστοῦ καὶ
reconciled us to himself through Christ and

δόντος ἡμῖν τὴν διακονίαν τῆς καταλλαγῆς,
having given to us the ministry - of reconciliation,

19 ὡς ὅτι θεὸς ἦν ἐν Χριστῷ κόσμον
as that God was in Christ ²[the] world

καταλλάσσων ἑαυτῷ, μὴ λογιζόμενος αὐτοῖς
¹reconciling to himself, not reckoning to them

τὰ παραπτώματα αὐτῶν, καὶ θέμενος
the trespasses of them, and placing

ἐν ἡμῖν τὸν λόγον τῆς καταλλαγῆς.
in us the word - of reconciliation.

20 Ὑπὲρ Χριστοῦ οὖν πρεσβεύομεν ὡς
On behalf of Christ therefore we are ambassadors as

as though God did be-
seech *you* by us: we pray
you in Christ's stead, be ye
reconciled to God.

21 For he hath made
him *to be* sin for us, who
knew no sin; that we
might be made the right-
eousness of God in him.

τοῦ θεοῦ παρακαλοῦντος δι᾽ ἡμῶν· δεόμεθα
– God beseeching[a] through us; we beg

ὑπὲρ Χριστοῦ, καταλλάγητε τῷ θεῷ.
on behalf of Christ, Be ye reconciled – to God.

21 τὸν μὴ γνόντα ἁμαρτίαν ὑπὲρ ἡμῶν
[2]The [one] [3]not [4]knowing [5]sin [7]on behalf of [6]us

ἁμαρτίαν ἐποίησεν, ἵνα ἡμεῖς γενώμεθα
[1]sin [1]he made, in order that we might become

δικαιοσύνη θεοῦ ἐν αὐτῷ.
[the] righteousness of God in him.

CHAPTER 6

WE then, *as* workers
together *with him*,
beseech *you* also that ye
receive not the grace of
God in vain.

2 (For he saith, I have
heard thee in a time
accepted, and in the day
of salvation have I suc-
coured thee: behold, now
is the accepted time;
behold, now *is* the day of
salvation.)

3 Giving no offence in
any thing, that the
ministry be not blamed:

4 But in all *things* ap-
proving ourselves as the
ministers of God, in much
patience, in afflictions, in
necessities, in distresses,

5 In stripes, in im-
prisonments, in tumults, in
labours, in watchings, in
fastings;

6 By pureness, by know-
ledge, by longsuffering,
by kindness, by the Holy
Ghost, by love unfeigned,

7 By the word of truth,
by the power of God, by
the armour of righteous-
ness on the right hand
and on the left,

8 By honour and dis-

6 Συνεργοῦντες δὲ καὶ παρακαλοῦμεν μὴ
And working together also we beseech [2]not

εἰς κενὸν τὴν χάριν τοῦ θεοῦ δέξασθαι
[7]to no purpose [4]the [5]grace – [6]of God [3]to receive

ὑμᾶς· 2 λέγει γάρ· καιρῷ δεκτῷ ἐπήκουσά
[1]you; for he says: In a time acceptable I heard

σου καὶ ἐν ἡμέρα σωτηρίας ἐβοήθησά
thee and in a day of salvation I helped

σοι· ἰδοὺ νῦν καιρὸς εὐπρόσδεκτος, ἰδοὺ
thee; behold now a time acceptable, behold

νῦν ἡμέρα σωτηρίας· 3 — μηδεμίαν ἐν
now a day of salvation; [2]no [1]in

μηδενὶ διδόντες προσκοπήν, ἵνα μὴ
[6]no(any)thing [1]giving [3]cause of stumbling, lest

μωμηθῇ ἡ διακονία, 4 ἀλλ᾽ ἐν παντὶ
[5]be blamed [1]the [2]ministry, but in everything

συνιστάνοντες ἑαυτοὺς ὡς θεοῦ διάκονοι,
commending ourselves as [2]of God [1]ministers,

ἐν ὑπομονῇ πολλῇ, ἐν θλίψεσιν, ἐν
in [2]endurance [1]much, in afflictions, in

ἀνάγκαις, ἐν στενοχωρίαις, ἐν πληγαῖς,
necessities, in straits, in stripes,

5 ἐν φυλακαῖς, ἐν ἀκαταστασίαις, ἐν κόποις,
in prisons, in commotions, in labours,

ἐν ἀγρυπνίαις, ἐν νηστείαις, 6 ἐν ἁγνότητι,
in watchings, in fastings, in purity,

ἐν γνώσει, ἐν μακροθυμίᾳ, ἐν χρηστότητι,
in knowledge, in long-suffering, in kindness,

ἐν πνεύματι ἁγίῳ, ἐν ἀγάπῃ ἀνυποκρίτῳ,
in spirit a holy, in love unfeigned,

7 ἐν λόγῳ ἀληθείας, ἐν δυνάμει θεοῦ·
in a word of truth, in power of God;

διὰ τῶν ὅπλων τῆς δικαιοσύνης τῶν
through the weapons – of righteousness of the

δεξιῶν καὶ ἀριστερῶν, 8 διὰ δόξης καὶ
right [hand] and of left, through glory and

honour, by evil report and good report: as deceivers, and *yet* true;

9 As unknown, and *yet* well known; as dying, and, behold, we live; as chastened, and not killed;

10 As sorrowful, yet alway rejoicing; as poor, yet making many rich; as having nothing, and *yet* possessing all things.

11 O *ye* Corinthians, our mouth is open unto you, our heart is enlarged.

12 Ye are not straitened in us, but ye are straitened in your own bowels.

13 Now for a recompence in the same, (I speak as unto *my* children,) be ye also enlarged.

14 Be ye not unequally yoked together with unbelievers: for what fellowship hath righteousness with unrighteousness? and what communion hath light with darkness?

15 And what concord hath Christ with Belial? or what part hath he that believeth with an infidel?

16 And what agreement hath the temple of God with idols? for ye are the temple of the living God; as God hath said, I will dwell in them, and walk

---

ἀτιμίας,　διὰ　δυσφημίας　καὶ　εὐφημίας·
dishonour,　through　ill report　and　good report;

ὡς　πλάνοι　καὶ　ἀληθεῖς,　9 ὡς　ἀγνοούμενοι
as　deceivers　and*　true men,　as　being unknown

καὶ　ἐπιγινωσκόμενοι,　ὡς　ἀποθνήσκοντες　καὶ
and*　being well known,　as　dying　and

ἰδοὺ　ζῶμεν,　ὡς　παιδευόμενοι　καὶ　μὴ
behold　we live,　as　being chastened　and　not

θανατούμενοι,　10 ὡς　λυπούμενοι　ἀεὶ　δὲ
being put to death,　as　being grieved　²always　¹but

χαίροντες,　ὡς　πτωχοὶ　πολλοὺς　δὲ　πλουτίζ-
rejoicing,　as　poor　³many　¹but　²en-

οντες,　ὡς　μηδὲν　ἔχοντες　καὶ　πάντα
riching,　as　²nothing　¹having　²and*　²all things

κατέχοντες.
⁴possessing.

11 Τὸ　στόμα　ἡμῶν　ἀνέῳγεν　πρὸς　ὑμᾶς,
The　mouth　of us　has opened　to　you,

Κορίνθιοι,　ἡ　καρδία　ἡμῶν　πεπλάτυνται·
Corinthians,　the　heart　of us　has been enlarged;

12 οὐ　στενοχωρεῖσθε　ἐν　ἡμῖν,　²ye are restrained
ye are not restrained　in　us,

δὲ　ἐν　τοῖς　σπλάγχνοις　ὑμῶν·　13 τὴν　δὲ
¹but　in　the　bowels　of you;　but [for] the

αὐτὴν　ἀντιμισθίαν,　ὡς　τέκνοις　λέγω,
same　recompence,　as　to children　I say.

πλατύνθητε　καὶ　ὑμεῖς.
be enlarged　also　ye.

14 Μὴ　γίνεσθε　ἑτεροζυγοῦντες　ἀπίστοις·
Do not ye become　unequally yoked [with] unbelievers;

τίς　γὰρ　μετοχὴ　δικαιοσύνῃ　καὶ　ἀνομίᾳ,
for what　share　righteousness^c　and　lawlessness,^c
　　　　　= have righteousness and lawlessness;

ἢ　τίς　κοινωνία　φωτὶ　πρὸς　σκότος;　15 τίς
or　what　fellowship　light^c　with　darkness?　what
　　　　　= has light

δὲ　συμφώνησις　Χριστοῦ　πρὸς　Βελιάρ,
and　agreement　of Christ　with　Beliar,

ἢ　τίς　μερὶς　πιστῷ　μετὰ　ἀπίστου;　16 τίς
or　what　part　a believer^c　with　an unbeliever?　what
　　　　　= has a believer

δὲ　συγκατάθεσις　ναῷ　θεοῦ　μετὰ　εἰδώλων;
and　union　a shrine^c of God　with　idols?
　　　　　= has a shrine

ἡμεῖς　γὰρ　ναὸς　θεοῦ　ἐσμεν　ζῶντος·
For ¹we　³a shrine　⁵God　²are　⁴of a living;

καθὼς　εἶπεν　ὁ　θεὸς　ὅτι　ἐνοικήσω　ἐν
as　said　-　God[,]　-　I will dwell among

---

* Evidently = and yet, as in some other places; *cf.* John 20. 29.

in *them;* and I will be their God, and they shall be my people.

17 Wherefore come out from among them, and be ye separate, saith the Lord, and touch not the unclean *thing;* and I will receive you,

18 And will be a Father unto you, and ye shall be my sons and daughters, saith the Lord Almighty.

CHAPTER 7

HAVING therefore these promises, dearly beloved, let us cleanse ourselves from all filthiness of the flesh and spirit, perfecting holiness in the fear of God.

2 Receive us; we have wronged no man, we have corrupted no man, we have defrauded no man.

3 I speak not *this* to condemn *you:* for I have said before, that ye are in our hearts to die and live with *you.*

4 Great *is* my boldness of speech toward you, great *is* my glorying of you: I am filled with comfort, I am exceeding joyful in all our tribulation.

5 For, when we were come into Macedonia, our flesh had no rest, but we were troubled on every side; without *were* fightings, within *were* fears.

αὐτοῖς καὶ ἐμπεριπατήσω, καὶ ἔσομαι
them and *I* will walk among [them], and I will be

αὐτῶν θεός, καὶ αὐτοὶ ἔσονταί μου λαός.
of them God, and they shall be of me a people.

17 διὸ ἐξέλθατε ἐκ μέσου αὐτῶν καὶ
Wherefore come ye out from [the] midst of them and

ἀφορίσθητε, λέγει κύριος, καὶ ἀκαθάρτου
be ye separated, says [the] Lord, and an unclean thing

μὴ ἅπτεσθε· 18 κἀγὼ εἰσδέξομαι ὑμᾶς, καὶ
do not touch; and I will welcome in you, and

ἔσομαι ὑμῖν εἰς πατέρα, καὶ ὑμεῖς ἔσεσθέ
I will be to you *for* a father, and ye shall be

μοι εἰς υἱοὺς καὶ θυγατέρας, λέγει κύριος
to me *for* sons and daughters, says [the] Lord

παντοκράτωρ. 7 ταύτας οὖν ἔχοντες τὰς ἐπ-
[the] Almighty. ³These ²therefore ¹having – ⁴pro-

αγγελίας, ἀγαπητοί, καθαρίσωμεν ἑαυτοὺς ἀπὸ
mises, beloved, let us cleanse ourselves from

παντὸς μολυσμοῦ σαρκὸς καὶ πνεύματος,
all pollution of flesh and of spirit,

ἐπιτελοῦντες ἁγιωσύνην ἐν φόβῳ θεοῦ.
perfecting holiness in [the] fear of God.

2 Χωρήσατε ἡμᾶς· οὐδένα ἠδικήσαμεν,
Make room for us; no one we wronged,

οὐδένα ἐφθείραμεν, οὐδένα ἐπλεονεκτήσαμεν.
no one we injured, no one we defrauded.

3 πρὸς κατάκρισιν οὐ λέγω· προείρηκα
For condemnation I say not; ¹I have previously said

γὰρ ὅτι ἐν ταῖς καρδίαις ἡμῶν ἐστε
¹for that in the hearts of us ye are

εἰς τὸ συναποθανεῖν καὶ συζῆν. 4 πολλή
for – to die with [you] and to live with [you]. Much

μοι παρρησία πρὸς ὑμᾶς, πολλή μοι
to meᵉ boldness toward you, much to meᵉ
=I have much   =I have much

καύχησις ὑπὲρ ὑμῶν· πεπλήρωμαι τῇ
boasting on behalf of you; I have been filled

παρακλήσει, ὑπερπερισσεύομαι τῇ χαρᾷ ἐπὶ
with comfort, I overflow – with joy on(in)

πάσῃ τῇ θλίψει ἡμῶν. 5 Καὶ γὰρ
all the affliction of us. For indeed

ἐλθόντων ἡμῶν εἰς Μακεδονίαν οὐδεμίαν
coming usᵃ into Macedonia ⁵no
=when we came

ἔσχηκεν ἄνεσιν ἡ σὰρξ ἡμῶν, ἀλλ' ἐν
⁴has had ⁶rest ¹the ²flesh ³of us, but in

παντὶ θλιβόμενοι· ἔξωθεν μάχαι, ἔσωθεν
every way being afflicted; without [were] fightings, within

6 Nevertheless God, that comforteth those that are cast down, comforted us by the coming of Titus;

7 And not by his coming only, but by the consolation wherewith he was comforted in you, when he told us your earnest desire, your mourning, your fervent mind toward me; so that I rejoiced the more.

8 For though I made you sorry with a letter, I do not repent, though I did repent: for I perceive that the same epistle hath made you sorry, though *it were* but for a season.

9 Now I rejoice, not that ye were made sorry, but that ye sorrowed to repentance: for ye were made sorry after a godly manner, that ye might receive damage by us in nothing.

10 For godly sorrow worketh repentance to salvation not to be repented of: but the sorrow of the world worketh death.

11 For behold this selfsame thing, that ye sorrowed after a godly sort, what carefulness it wrought in you, yea, *what* clearing of yourselves, yea, *what* indignation, yea, *what* fear, yea, *what* vehement desire, yea, *what* zeal, yea, *what* revenge! In all *things* ye have approved yourselves to be clear in this matter.

φόβοι. 6 ἀλλ᾽ ὁ παρακαλῶν τοὺς ταπεινοὺς
[were] fears. But ²the [one] ²comforting ⁴the   ⁵humble

παρεκάλεσεν ἡμᾶς ὁ θεὸς ἐν τῇ παρουσίᾳ
³comforted   ¹us — ¹God by the   presence

Τίτου· 7 οὐ μόνον δὲ ἐν τῇ παρουσίᾳ
of Titus;   and not only   by the   presence

αὐτοῦ, ἀλλὰ καὶ ἐν τῇ παρακλήσει ᾗ
of him, but   also by the comfort   with
                                        which

παρεκλήθη ἐφ᾽ ὑμῖν, ἀναγγέλλων ἡμῖν
he was comforted over you,   reporting   to us

τὴν ὑμῶν ἐπιπόθησιν, τὸν ὑμῶν ὀδυρμόν,
¹the ²of you ³eager longing, ¹the ²of you ³mourning,

τὸν ὑμῶν ζῆλον ὑπὲρ ἐμοῦ, ὥστε με
¹the ²of you ³zeal on behalf of me, so as me

μᾶλλον χαρῆναι. 8 Ὅτι εἰ καὶ ἐλύπησα
more to rejoice.ᵇ Because if indeed I grieved
=so that I rejoiced more.

ὑμᾶς ἐν τῇ ἐπιστολῇ, οὐ μεταμέλομαι·
you by the epistle,   I do not regret;

εἰ καὶ μετεμελόμην, βλέπω ὅτι ἡ ἐπιστολὴ
if indeed I regretted, I see that — epistle

ἐκείνη εἰ καὶ πρὸς ὥραν ἐλύπησεν ὑμᾶς,
that if indeed for an hour it grieved you,

9 νῦν χαίρω, οὐχ ὅτι ἐλυπήθητε, ἀλλ᾽
now I rejoice, not that ye were grieved,   but

ὅτι ἐλυπήθητε εἰς μετάνοιαν· ἐλυπήθητε
that ye were grieved to repentance; ²ye were grieved

γὰρ κατὰ θεόν, ἵνα ἐν μηδενὶ ζημιωθῆτε
¹for according God, in order in nothing ye might suffer
       to   that   loss

ἐξ ἡμῶν. 10 ἡ γὰρ κατὰ θεὸν λύπη
by us.   For ¹the ²according to ⁴God ³grief

μετάνοιαν εἰς σωτηρίαν ἀμεταμέλητον
¹repentance ²to ³salvation   ⁴unregrettable

ἐργάζεται· ἡ δὲ τοῦ κόσμου λύπη θάνατον
⁵works; but ¹the ²of the ³world ⁴grief ⁵death

κατεργάζεται. 11 ἰδοὺ γὰρ αὐτὸ τοῦτο
⁶works out.   For behold this very thing[.]

τὸ κατὰ θεὸν λυπηθῆναι πόσην κατειργά-
— ²according to ³God ¹to be grieved[,] ¹what ²it worked

σατο ὑμῖν σπουδήν, ἀλλὰ ἀπολογίαν, ἀλλὰ
out ³in you ⁴earnestness, but [what] defence,   but

ἀγανάκτησιν, ἀλλὰ φόβον, ἀλλὰ ἐπιπόθησιν,
vexation,   but   fear,   but eager desire,

ἀλλὰ ζῆλον, ἀλλὰ ἐκδίκησιν, ἐν παντὶ
but   zeal,   but vengeance.   In everything

συνεστήσατε ἑαυτοὺς ἁγνοὺς εἶναι τῷ
ye commended yourselves pure to be in the

12 Wherefore, though I wrote unto you, *I did it* not for his cause that had done the wrong, nor for his cause that suffered wrong, but that our care for you in the sight of God might appear unto you.

13 Therefore we were comforted in your comfort: yea, and exceedingly the more joyed we for the joy of Titus, because his spirit was refreshed by you all.

14 For if I have boasted any thing to him of you, I am not ashamed; but as we spake all things to you in truth, even so our boasting, which *I made* before Titus, is found a truth.

15 And his inward affection is more abundant toward you, whilst he remembereth the obedience of you all, how with fear and trembling ye received him.

16 I rejoice therefore that I have confidence in you in all *things*.

πράγματι. 12 ἄρα εἰ καὶ ἔγραψα ὑμῖν,
affair. Then if indeed I wrote to you,

οὐχ ἕνεκεν τοῦ ἀδικήσαντος οὐδὲ ἕνεκεν
not for the the [one] having done nor for the
sake of wrong sake of

τοῦ ἀδικηθέντος, ἀλλ᾽ ἕνεκεν τοῦ φανερω-
the having been but for the - to be mani-
[one] wronged, sake of

θῆναι τὴν σπουδὴν ὑμῶν τὴν ὑπὲρ ἡμῶν
fested the earnestness[bd] of you - on behalf of us

πρὸς ὑμᾶς ἐνώπιον τοῦ θεοῦ. 13 διὰ
toward you before - God. There-

τοῦτο παρακεκλήμεθα. Ἐπὶ δὲ τῇ
fore we have been comforted. But as to the

παρακλήσει ἡμῶν περισσοτέρως μᾶλλον
comfort of us abundantly more

ἐχάρημεν ἐπὶ τῇ χαρᾷ Τίτου, ὅτι ἀναπέ-
we rejoiced over the joy of Titus, because has been

παυται τὸ πνεῦμα αὐτοῦ ἀπὸ πάντων
rested the spirit of him from(by) all

ὑμῶν· 14 ὅτι εἴ τι αὐτῷ ὑπὲρ ὑμῶν
you; because if [2]anything [3]to him [4]on behalf of [5]you

κεκαύχημαι, οὐ κατησχύνθην, ἀλλ᾽ ὡς
[1]I have boasted, I was not shamed, but as

πάντα ἐν ἀληθείᾳ ἐλαλήσαμεν ὑμῖν, οὕτως
[3]all things [2]in [4]truth [1]we spoke [5]to you, so

καὶ ἡ καύχησις ἡμῶν ἐπὶ Τίτου ἀλήθεια
also the boasting of us over Titus [2]truth

ἐγενήθη. 15 καὶ τὰ σπλάγχνα αὐτοῦ
[1]became. And the bowels of him

περισσοτέρως εἰς ὑμᾶς ἐστιν ἀναμιμνησκομέ-
[2]abundantly [3]toward [4]you [1]is(are) [he] remember-

νου τὴν πάντων ὑμῶν ὑπακοήν, ὡς μετὰ
ing[a] [1]the [3]of all [4]you [2]obedience, as with

φόβου καὶ τρόμου ἐδέξασθε αὐτόν.
fear and trembling ye received him.

16 χαίρω ὅτι ἐν παντὶ θαρρῶ ἐν ὑμῖν.
I rejoice that in everything I am confident in you.

CHAPTER 8

MOREOVER, brethren, we do you to wit of the grace of God bestowed on the churches of Macedonia;

2 How that in a great trial of affliction the abundance of their joy and their deep poverty

8 Γνωρίζομεν δὲ ὑμῖν, ἀδελφοί, τὴν
Now we make known to you, brothers, the

χάριν τοῦ θεοῦ τὴν δεδομένην ἐν ταῖς
grace - of God - *having been* given among the

ἐκκλησίαις τῆς Μακεδονίας, 2 ὅτι ἐν πολλῇ
churches - of Macedonia, that in much

δοκιμῇ θλίψεως ἡ περισσεία τῆς χαρᾶς
proving of affliction the abundance of the joy

αὐτῶν καὶ ἡ κατὰ βάθους πτωχεία
of them and [1]the [2]according to [4]depth [3]poverty
= their extreme poverty

abounded unto the riches of their liberality.

3 For to *their* power, I bear record, yea, and beyond *their* power *they were* willing of themselves;

4 Praying us with much intreaty that we would receive the gift, and *take upon us* the fellowship of the ministering to the saints.

5 And *this they did,* not as we hoped, but first gave their own selves to the Lord, and unto us by the will of God.

6 Insomuch that we desired Titus, that as he had begun, so he would also finish in you the same grace also.

7 Therefore, as ye abound in every *thing, in* faith, and utterance, and knowledge, and *in* all diligence, and *in* your love to us, *see* that ye abound in this grace also.

8 I speak not by commandment, but by occasion of the forwardness of others, and to prove the sincerity of your love.

9 For ye know the grace of our Lord Jesus Christ, that, though he was rich, yet for your sakes he became poor, that ye through his poverty might be rich.

10 And herein I give *my*

αὐτῶν ἐπερίσσευσεν εἰς τὸ πλοῦτος τῆς
of them abounded to the riches of the

ἁπλότητος αὐτῶν· 3 ὅτι κατὰ δύναμιν,
liberality of them; that according [their]
                          to power,

μαρτυρῶ, καὶ παρὰ δύναμιν, αὐθαίρετοι
I witness, and beyond [their] power, of their own
                                          accord

4 μετὰ πολλῆς παρακλήσεως δεόμενοι ἡμῶν
  with much beseeching requesting of us

τὴν χάριν καὶ τὴν κοινωνίαν τῆς διακονίας
the grace and the fellowship of the ministry

τῆς εἰς τοὺς ἁγίους, 5 καὶ οὐ καθὼς
– to the saints, and not as

ἠλπίσαμεν, ἀλλὰ ἑαυτοὺς ἔδωκαν πρῶτον
we hoped, but themselves gave first*ly*

τῷ κυρίῳ καὶ ἡμῖν διὰ θελήματος θεοῦ,
to the Lord and to us through [the] will of God,

6 εἰς τὸ παρακαλέσαι ἡμᾶς Τίτον, ἵνα
for – to beseech us[b] Titus, in order
=that we should beseech   that

καθὼς προενήρξατο οὕτως καὶ ἐπιτελέσῃ
as previously he began so also he should
                                  complete

εἰς ὑμᾶς καὶ τὴν χάριν ταύτην. 7 ἀλλ'
in you also this grace. But

ὥσπερ ἐν παντὶ περισσεύετε, πίστει καὶ
as in everything ye abound, in faith and

λόγῳ καὶ γνώσει καὶ πάσῃ σπουδῇ
in word and in knowledge and in all diligence

καὶ τῇ ἐξ ἡμῶν ἐν ὑμῖν ἀγάπῃ, ἵνα
and – [2]from [3]us [4]in(to) [5]you [1]in love, [see] that

καὶ ἐν ταύτῃ τῇ χάριτι περισσεύητε.
[6]also [2]in [3]this – [4]grace [1]ye may abound.

8 Οὐ κατ' ἐπιταγὴν λέγω, ἀλλὰ διὰ
[3]Not [2]by way of [4]command [1]I say,* but through

τῆς ἑτέρων σπουδῆς καὶ τὸ τῆς ὑμετέρας
[1]the [2]of others [3]diligence also [2]the – [4]of your

ἀγάπης γνήσιον δοκιμάζων· 9 γινώσκετε
[5]love [3]reality [1]proving; [2]ye know

γὰρ τὴν χάριν τοῦ κυρίου ἡμῶν Ἰησοῦ
[1]for the grace of the Lord of us Jesus

[Χριστοῦ], ὅτι δι' ὑμᾶς ἐπτώχευσεν
Christ, that on account you [3]he impoverished
                    of   [himself]

πλούσιος ὤν, ἵνα ὑμεῖς τῇ ἐκείνου πτωχείᾳ
[3]rich [1]being, in or- ye [1]by [3]of that [2]poverty
             der that   the one

πλουτήσητε. 10 καὶ γνώμην ἐν τούτῳ
might become rich. And [4]an opinion [1]in [3]this

---

* That is, Paul is not issuing a command. *Cf.* I. Cor. 7. 6.

advice: for this is expedient for you, who have begun before, not only to do, but also to be forward a year ago.

11 Now therefore perform the doing of it; that as there was a readiness to will, so there may be a performance also out of that which ye have.

12 For if there be first a willing mind, it is accepted according to that a man hath, and not according to that he hath not.

13 For I mean not that other men be eased, and ye burdened:

14 But by an equality, that now at this time your abundance may be a supply for their want, that their abundance also may be a supply for your want: that there may be equality:

15 As it is written, He that had gathered much had nothing over; and he that had gathered little had no lack.

16 But thanks be to God, which put the same earnest care into the heart of Titus for you.

17 For indeed he accepted the exhortation; but being more forward, of his own accord he went unto you.

18 And we have sent with him the brother,

δίδωμι· τοῦτο γὰρ ὑμῖν συμφέρει, οἵτινες
¹I give: for this   ²for you   ¹is expedient,   who

οὐ μόνον τὸ ποιῆσαι ἀλλὰ καὶ τὸ θέλειν
not only   the   to do   but   also   the   to will

προενήρξασθε ἀπὸ πέρυσι· 11 νυνὶ δὲ καὶ
previously ye began   from   last year;   but now   also
=a year ago;

τὸ ποιῆσαι ἐπιτελέσατε, ὅπως καθάπερ ἡ
²the   ²to do   ¹complete ye,   so as   as   the

προθυμία τοῦ θέλειν, οὕτως καὶ τὸ
eagerness   of the   to will,   so   also   the

ἐπιτελέσαι ἐκ τοῦ ἔχειν. 12 εἰ γὰρ ἡ
to complete   out of   the   to have.   For if   the
=what ye have.

προθυμία πρόκειται, καθὸ ἐὰν ἔχῃ
eagerness   is already there,   according to whatever one has

εὐπρόσδεκτος, οὐ καθὸ οὐκ ἔχει. 13 οὐ
it is acceptable,   not according   [what] one   not
to   has not.

γὰρ ἵνα ἄλλοις ἄνεσις, ὑμῖν θλῖψις,
For   in order   to others   relief,   to you   distress,
that   [there may be]

ἀλλ' ἐξ ἰσότητος 14 ἐν τῷ νῦν καιρῷ
but   by   equality   at   the   present   time

τὸ ὑμῶν περίσσευμα εἰς τὸ ἐκείνων
the   ²of you   ¹abundance [may be] for   the   ²of those

ὑστέρημα, ἵνα καὶ τὸ ἐκείνων περίσσευμα
¹lack,   in order   also   the   ²of those   ¹abundance
that

γένηται εἰς τὸ ὑμῶν ὑστέρημα, ὅπως
may be   for   the   ²of you   ¹lack,   so as

γένηται ἰσότης, 15 καθὼς γέγραπται· ὁ
there may be   equality,   as   it has been   He
written:

τὸ πολὺ οὐκ ἐπλεόνασεν, καὶ ὁ τὸ
the   much   did not abound,   and   he   the

ὀλίγον οὐκ ἠλαττόνησεν. 16 Χάρις δὲ
little   had not less.   But thanks [be]

τῷ θεῷ τῷ διδόντι τὴν αὐτὴν σπουδὴν
-   to God   -   giving   the   same   diligence

ὑπὲρ ὑμῶν ἐν τῇ καρδίᾳ Τίτου, 17 ὅτι
on be-   you   in   the   heart   of Titus,   because
half of

τὴν μὲν παράκλησιν ἐδέξατο, σπουδαιότερος
²the   ¹indeed   ²beseeching   ²he received,   ²more diligent

δὲ ὑπάρχων αὐθαίρετος ἐξῆλθεν πρὸς ὑμᾶς.
¹and   ²being   of his own   he went   to   you.
accord   forth

18 συνεπέμψαμεν δὲ μετ' αὐτοῦ τὸν
And we sent with   with   him   the

whose praise *is* in the gospel throughout all the churches;

19 And not *that* only, but who was also chosen of the churches to travel with us with this grace, which is administered by us to the glory of the same Lord, and *declaration of* your ready mind:

20 Avoiding this, that no man should blame us in this abundance which is administered by us:

21 Providing for honest things, not only in the sight of the Lord, but also in the sight of men.

22 And we have sent with them our brother, whom we have oftentimes proved diligent in many things, but now much more diligent, upon the great confidence which *I have* in you.

23 Whether *any do enquire* of Titus, *he is* my partner and fellowhelper concerning you: or our brethren *be enquired of, they are* the messengers of the churches, *and* the glory of Christ.

24 Wherefore shew ye to them, and before the churches, the proof of your love, and of our boasting on your behalf.

ἀδελφὸν οὗ ὁ ἔπαινος ἐν τῷ εὐαγγελίῳ
brother of whom the praise in the gospel

διὰ πασῶν τῶν ἐκκλησιῶν, 19 οὐ μόνον δὲ
[is] all the churches, and not only [this]
through[out]

ἀλλὰ καὶ χειροτονηθεὶς ὑπὸ τῶν ἐκκλησιῶν
but also ²having been elected ⁴by ⁵the ⁶churches

συνέκδημος ἡμῶν ἐν τῇ χάριτι ταύτῃ
¹a travelling ²of us in this grace
companion

τῇ διακονουμένῃ ὑφ' ἡμῶν πρὸς τὴν
– being ministered by us to ¹the

αὐτοῦ τοῦ κυρίου δόξαν καὶ προθυμίαν
²[him]self ³of the ⁴Lord ²glory and eagerness

ἡμῶν, 20 στελλόμενοι τοῦτο, μή τις ἡμᾶς
of us, avoiding this, lest anyone ²us

μωμήσηται ἐν τῇ ἀδρότητι ταύτῃ τῇ
¹should blame in this bounty –

διακονουμένῃ ὑφ' ἡμῶν· 21 προνοοῦμεν γὰρ
being ministered by us; for we provide

καλὰ οὐ μόνον ἐνώπιον κυρίου ἀλλὰ καὶ
good not only before [the] Lord but also
things

ἐνώπιον ἀνθρώπων. 22 συνεπέμψαμεν δὲ
before men. And we sent with

αὐτοῖς τὸν ἀδελφὸν ἡμῶν, ὃν ἐδοκιμάσαμεν
them the brother of us, whom ¹we proved

ἐν πολλοῖς πολλάκις σπουδαῖον ὄντα, νυνὶ
²in ³many things ⁴many times ³diligent ⁴being, ¹now

δὲ πολὺ σπουδαιότερον πεποιθήσει πολλῇ
¹and much more diligent ¹in ²confidence ²much

τῇ εἰς ὑμᾶς. 23 εἴτε ὑπὲρ Τίτου, κοινωνὸς
– toward you. Whether as to Titus, ²partner

ἐμὸς καὶ εἰς ὑμᾶς συνεργός· εἴτε ἀδελφοὶ
¹my ²and ⁵for ⁴you ⁶fellow-worker; or brothers

ἡμῶν, ἀπόστολοι ἐκκλησιῶν, δόξα Χριστοῦ.
of us, apostles of churches, [the] of Christ.
glory

24 τὴν οὖν ἔνδειξιν τῆς ἀγάπης ὑμῶν
⁷The ¹therefore ⁸demon- ⁹of the ¹⁰love ¹¹of you
stration

καὶ ἡμῶν καυχήσεως ὑπὲρ ὑμῶν εἰς
¹²and ¹⁴of us ¹⁵boasting ¹⁶on behalf of ¹⁶you ¹⁷to

αὐτοὺς ἐνδεικνύμενοι εἰς πρόσωπον τῶν
¹⁸them ²showing forth ³in ⁴[the] presence ⁵of the

ἐκκλησιῶν.
⁶churches.

CHAPTER 9

FOR as touching the ministering to the saints, it is superfluous for me to write to you:

2 For I know the forwardness of your mind, for which I boast of you to them of Macedonia, that Achaia was ready a year ago; and your zeal hath provoked very many.

3 Yet have I sent the brethren, lest our boasting of you should be in vain in this behalf; that, as I said, ye may be ready:

4 Lest haply if they of Macedonia come with me, and find you unprepared, we (that we say not, ye) should be ashamed in this same confident boasting.

5 Therefore I thought it necessary to exhort the brethren, that they would go before unto you, and make up beforehand your bounty, whereof ye had notice before, that the same might be ready, as *a matter of* bounty, and not as *of* covetousness.

6 But this *I say,* He which soweth sparingly shall reap also sparingly; and he which soweth bountifully shall reap also bountifully.

7 Every man according

9 Περὶ   μὲν   γὰρ   τῆς   διακονίας   τῆς
²Concerning ³indeed ¹for   the   ministry   -

εἰς   τοὺς   ἁγίους   περισσόν   μοί   ἐστιν   τὸ
to   the   saints   ²superfluous ³for me ¹it is -

γράφειν   ὑμῖν· **2** οἶδα   γὰρ   τὴν   προθυμίαν
to write to you;   for I know the   eagerness

ὑμῶν   ἣν   ὑπὲρ   ὑμῶν   καυχῶμαι   Μακε-
of you which on behalf of you I boast to Mace-

δόσιν   ὅτι   Ἀχαΐα   παρεσκεύασται   ἀπὸ
donians that Achaia has made preparations from

πέρυσι,   καὶ   τὸ   ὑμῶν   ζῆλος   ἠρέθισεν
last year, and the ²of you ¹zeal stirred up
=a year ago,

τοὺς   πλείονας. **3** ἔπεμψα   δὲ   τοὺς   ἀδελφούς,
the greater number. And I sent the brothers,

ἵνα   μὴ   τὸ   καύχημα   ἡμῶν   τὸ   ὑπὲρ
lest the boast of us - on behalf

ὑμῶν   κενωθῇ   ἐν   τῷ   μέρει   τούτῳ,   ἵνα
of you should be in this respect, in order
emptied that

καθὼς   ἔλεγον   παρεσκευασμένοι   ἦτε, **4** μή
as   I said   *having been* prepared ye were,

πως   ἐὰν   ἔλθωσιν   σὺν   ἐμοὶ   Μακεδόνες
lest if ²come ³with ⁴me ¹Macedonians

καὶ   εὕρωσιν   ὑμᾶς   ἀπαρασκευάστους
and find you unprepared

καταισχυνθῶμεν   ἡμεῖς,   ἵνα   μὴ   λέγωμεν
²should be shamed ¹we, *in order* we say not
that

ὑμεῖς,   ἐν   τῇ   ὑποστάσει   ταύτῃ. **5** ἀναγκαῖον
ye, in this confidence. ³Necessary

οὖν   ἡγησάμην   παρακαλέσαι   τοὺς   ἀδελφοὺς
²there- ¹I thought [it] to beseech the brothers
fore

ἵνα   προέλθωσιν   εἰς   ὑμᾶς   καὶ   προκαταρτί-
in order they go to you and arrange before-
that forward

σωσιν   τὴν   προεπηγγελμένην   εὐλογίαν   ὑμῶν,
hand ¹the ⁴having been promised ²blessing ³of you,

ταύτην   ἑτοίμην   εἶναι   οὕτως   ὡς   εὐλογίαν
this ready tó be thus as a blessing

καὶ   μὴ   ὡς   πλεονεξίαν. **6** Τοῦτο   δέ,
and not as greediness. And this,

ὁ   σπείρων   φειδομένως   φειδομένως   καὶ
the [one] sowing sparingly ³sparingly ²alsc

θερίσει,   καὶ   ὁ   σπείρων   ἐπ’   εὐλογίαις   ἐπ’
¹will reap, and the [one] sowing on(for) blessings ³on(for)

εὐλογίαις   καὶ   θερίσει. **7** ἕκαστος   καθὼς
⁴blessings ²also ¹will reap. Each one as

as he purposeth in his heart, *so let him give;* not grudgingly, or of necessity: for God loveth a cheerful giver.

8 And God *is* able to make all grace abound toward you; that ye, always having all sufficiency in all *things,* may abound to every good work:

9 (As it is written, He hath dispersed abroad; he hath given to the poor; his righteousness remaineth for ever.

10 Now he that ministereth seed to the sower both minister bread for *your* food, and multiply your seed sown, and increase the fruits of your righteousness;)

11 Being enriched in every thing to all bountifulness, which causeth through us thanksgiving to God.

12 For the administration of this service not only supplieth the want of the saints, but is abundant also by many thanksgivings unto God;

13 Whiles by the experiment of this ministration they glorify God for your professed subjection unto the gospel of Christ, and for *your* liberal distribution unto them, and unto all *men;*

14 And by their prayer for you, which long after

προῄρηται τῇ καρδίᾳ, μὴ ἐκ λύπης ἢ
he chose　in the(his) heart,　not　of　grief　or

ἐξ ἀνάγκης· ἱλαρὸν γὰρ δότην ἀγαπᾷ ὁ
of　necessity;　for ²a cheerful　⁴giver　³loves　-

θεός. 8 δυνατεῖ δὲ ὁ θεὸς πᾶσαν χάριν
¹God.　　And ²is able　-　¹God　⁴all　⁵grace

περισσεῦσαι εἰς ὑμᾶς, ἵνα ἐν παντὶ
³to cause to abound toward　you, in order that ⁵in　⁶everything

πάντοτε πᾶσαν αὐτάρκειαν ἔχοντες περισ-
¹always　³all　⁴self-sufficiency　²having　ye may

σεύητε εἰς πᾶν ἔργον ἀγαθόν, 9 καθὼς
abound　to　every　work　good,　　as

γέγραπται· ἐσκόρπισεν, ἔδωκεν τοῖς πένησιν,
it has been written: He scattered,　he gave　to the　poor,

ἡ δικαιοσύνη αὐτοῦ μένει εἰς τὸν αἰῶνα.
the righteousness　of him　remains unto the　age.

10 ὁ δὲ ἐπιχορηγῶν σπέρμα τῷ σπείροντι
Now the [one]　providing　seed for the [one] sowing

καὶ ἄρτον εἰς βρῶσιν χορηγήσει καὶ
¹both　³bread　⁴for　⁵food　²will supply　and

πληθυνεῖ τὸν σπόρον ὑμῶν καὶ αὐξήσει
will multiply　the　seed　of you　and will increase

τὰ γενήματα τῆς δικαιοσύνης ὑμῶν· 11 ἐν
the　fruits　of the　righteousness　of you;　in

παντὶ πλουτιζόμενοι εἰς πᾶσαν ἁπλότητα,
everything　being enriched　to　all　liberality,

ἥτις κατεργάζεται δι' ἡμῶν εὐχαριστίαν
which　works out　through　us　thanksgiving

τῷ θεῷ· 12 ὅτι ἡ διακονία τῆς λειτουργίας
- to God; because the　ministry　-　service

ταύτης οὐ μόνον ἐστὶν προσαναπληροῦσα
of this　not　only　is　making up

τὰ ὑστερήματα τῶν ἁγίων, ἀλλὰ καὶ
the　things lacking　of the　saints,　but [is]　also

περισσεύουσα διὰ πολλῶν εὐχαριστιῶν τῷ
abounding　through　many　thanksgivings　-

θεῷ· 13 διὰ τῆς δοκιμῆς τῆς διακονίας
to God; through the　proof　-　ministry

ταύτης δοξάζοντες τὸν θεὸν ἐπὶ τῇ
of this　glorifying　-　God　on　the

ὑποταγῇ τῆς ὁμολογίας ὑμῶν εἰς τὸ
submission　of the　confession　of you　to　the

εὐαγγέλιον τοῦ Χριστοῦ καὶ ἁπλότητι
gospel　-　of Christ　and [on the] liberality

τῆς κοινωνίας εἰς αὐτοὺς καὶ εἰς πάντας,
of the　fellowship　toward　them　and　toward all men,

14 καὶ αὐτῶν δεήσει ὑπὲρ ὑμῶν ἐπιποθούν-
and　¹them　⁴with　⁵on be-　³you　²longing
　　　　　　request　half of

you for the exceeding grace of God in you.
15 Thanks be unto God for his unspeakable gift.

των   ὑμᾶς   διὰ   τὴν   ὑπερβάλλουσαν   χάριν
after[a] [a]you on account the excelling grace
        of

τοῦ   θεοῦ   ἐφ᾽   ὑμῖν.   15 Χάρις   τῷ   θεῷ
–   of God   upon   you.   Thanks   –   to God

ἐπὶ   τῇ   ἀνεκδιηγήτῳ   αὐτοῦ   δωρεᾷ.
for   the   indescribable   of him   gift.

CHAPTER 10

NOW I Paul myself beseech you by the meekness and gentleness of Christ, who in presence am base among you, but being absent am bold toward you:

2 But I beseech you, that I may not be bold when I am present with that confidence, wherewith I think to be bold against some, which think of us as if we walked according to the flesh.

3 For though we walk in the flesh, we do not war after the flesh:

4 (For the weapons of our warfare are not carnal, but mighty through God to the pulling down of strong holds;)

5 Casting down imaginations, and every high thing that exalteth itself against the knowledge of God, and bringing into captivity every thought to the obedience of Christ;

6 And having in a readiness to revenge all disobedience, when your obedience is fulfilled.

7 Do ye look on things after the outward appearance? If any man trust to himself that he is Christ's, let him of himself

10 Αὐτὸς   δὲ   ἐγὼ   Παῦλος   παρακαλῶ
[my]self   Now   I   Paul   beseech

ὑμᾶς   διὰ   τῆς   πραΰτητος   καὶ   ἐπιεικείας
you   through the   meekness   and   forbearance

τοῦ   Χριστοῦ,   ὃς   κατὰ   πρόσωπον   μὲν
–   of Christ,   who   according to   face   indeed

ταπεινὸς   ἐν   ὑμῖν,   ἀπὼν   δὲ   θαρρῶ   εἰς
[am] humble among you,   but being absent am bold toward

ὑμᾶς·   2 δέομαι   δὲ   τὸ   μὴ   παρὼν   θαρρῆσαι
you: now I request   –   not being present to be bold

τῇ   πεποιθήσει   ᾗ   λογίζομαι   τολμῆσαι   ἐπί
in the   confidence   which I reckon   to be daring toward

τινας   τοὺς   λογιζομένους   ἡμᾶς   ὡς   κατὰ
some   the [ones]   reckoning   us   as   [a]according to

σάρκα   περιπατοῦντας.   3 Ἐν   σαρκὶ   γὰρ
[a]flesh   [1]walking.   in   flesh   For

περιπατοῦντες   οὐ   κατὰ   σάρκα   στρατευόμεθα,
walking   not according to   flesh   we war,

4 τὰ   γὰρ   ὅπλα   τῆς   στρατείας   ἡμῶν
for the   weapons   of the   warfare   of us [are]

οὐ   σαρκικὰ   ἀλλὰ   δυνατὰ   τῷ   θεῷ   πρὸς
not   fleshly   but   powerful   –   to God   to

καθαίρεσιν   ὀχυρωμάτων,   λογισμοὺς   καθαιροῦν-
overthrow   of strongholds,   [a]reasonings   [1]overthrow-

τες   5 καὶ   πᾶν   ὕψωμα   ἐπαιρόμενον   κατὰ
ing   and   every   high thing   rising up   against

τῆς   γνώσεως   τοῦ   θεοῦ,   καὶ   αἰχμαλωτίζοντες
the   knowledge   –   of God,   and   taking captive

πᾶν   νόημα   εἰς   τὴν   ὑπακοὴν   τοῦ   Χριστοῦ,
every   design   to   the   obedience   –   of Christ,

6 καὶ   ἐν   ἑτοίμῳ   ἔχοντες   ἐκδικῆσαι   πᾶσαν
and   in   readiness   having   to avenge   all
    = being ready

παρακοήν,   ὅταν   πληρωθῇ   ὑμῶν   ἡ   ὑπακοή.
disobedience, whenever [a]is fulfilled [a]of you [1]the [a]obedience.

7 Τὰ   κατὰ   πρόσωπον   βλέπετε.   εἴ   τις
[a]The   [a]according   [a]face   [1]ye look [at].   If   any-
things   to   (appearance)   one

πέποιθεν   ἑαυτῷ   Χριστοῦ   εἶναι,   τοῦτο
has persuaded himself   [a]of Christ   [1]to be,   this

think this again, that, as he *is* Christ's, even so *are* we Christ's.

8 For though I should boast somewhat more of our authority, which the Lord hath given us for edification, and not for your destruction, I should not be ashamed:

9 That I may not seem as if I would terrify you by letters.

10 For *his* letters, say they, *are* weighty and powerful; but *his* bodily presence *is* weak, and *his* speech contemptible.

11 Let such an one think this, that, such as we are in word by letters when we are absent, such *will we be* also in deed when we are present.

12 For we dare not make ourselves of the number, or compare ourselves with some that commend themselves: but they measuring themselves by themselves, and comparing themselves among themselves, are not wise.

13 But we will not boast of things without *our* measure, but according to the measure of the rule which God hath distributed to us, a measure to reach even unto you.

14 For we stretch not ourselves beyond *our measure*, as though we reached not unto you: for we are come as far as

λογιζέσθω πάλιν ἐφ' ἑαυτοῦ, ὅτι καθὼς
let him reckon   again   as to   himself,   that   as

αὐτὸς Χριστοῦ, οὕτως καὶ ἡμεῖς. 8 ἐάν
he [is]   of Christ,   so   also [are]   we.   [8]if

τε γὰρ περισσότερόν τι καυχήσωμαι περὶ
[2]even [1]For   [3]more abundantly [5]some-   [4]I should boast concern-
          what   ing

τῆς ἐξουσίας ἡμῶν, ἧς ἔδωκεν ὁ κύριος
the   authority   of us,   which   [2]gave   [1]the   [3]Lord

εἰς οἰκοδομὴν καὶ οὐκ εἰς καθαίρεσιν
for   edification   and   not   for   overthrow

ὑμῶν, οὐκ αἰσχυνθήσομαι, 9 ἵνα μὴ δόξω
of you,   I shall not be shamed,   in order that I may not seem

ὡσὰν ἐκφοβεῖν ὑμᾶς διὰ τῶν ἐπιστολῶν.
as though to frighten   you   through   the   epistles.

10 ὅτι αἱ ἐπιστολαὶ μέν, φησίν, βαρεῖαι
Because the(his)   epistles   indeed,   he says, [are] weighty

καὶ ἰσχυραί, ἡ δὲ παρουσία τοῦ σώματος
and   strong,   but the   presence   of the(his) body [is]

ἀσθενὴς καὶ ὁ λόγος ἐξουθενημένος.
weak   and   the(his)   speech   *being* despised.

11 τοῦτο λογιζέσθω ὁ τοιοῦτος, ὅτι οἷοί
   This   let reckon   such a one,   that such as

ἐσμεν τῷ λόγῳ δι' ἐπιστολῶν ἀπόντες,
we are   -   in word through   epistles   being absent,

τοιοῦτοι καὶ παρόντες τῷ ἔργῳ. 12 Οὐ
such   also   being present   -   in work.   [3]not

γὰρ τολμῶμεν ἐγκρῖναι ἢ συγκρῖναι
[1]For   [2]we dare   *to* class with   or   *to* compare

ἑαυτούς τισιν τῶν ἑαυτοὺς συνιστανόντων·
ourselves   with some   of the [2]themselves   [1]commending;
                  [ones]

ἀλλὰ αὐτοὶ ἐν ἑαυτοῖς ἑαυτοὺς μετροῦντες
but   they [2]among   [4]them-   [3]them-   [1]measuring
              selves   selves

καὶ συγκρίνοντες ἑαυτοὺς ἑαυτοῖς οὐ
and   comparing   themselves with themselves   not

συνιᾶσιν. 13 ἡμεῖς δὲ οὐκ εἰς τὰ ἄμετρα
do understand.   But we   [2]not   [4]immeasurably†

καυχησόμεθα, ἀλλὰ κατὰ τὸ μέτρον τοῦ
  [1]will [3]boast,   but according to the   measure   of the

κανόνος οὗ ἐμέρισεν ἡμῖν ὁ θεὸς μέτρου,
rule   which [3]divided   [2]to us   -   [1]God of(in) measure,

ἐφικέσθαι ἄχρι καὶ ὑμῶν. 14 οὐ γὰρ
to reach   as far as   even   you.   14   For not

ὡς μὴ ἐφικνούμενοι εἰς ὑμᾶς ὑπερεκτείνομεν
as   not   reaching   to   you   do we overstretch

ἑαυτούς, ἄχρι γὰρ καὶ ὑμῶν ἐφθάσαμεν
ourselves,   for as far as   even   you   we came

to you also in *preaching* the gospel of Christ:

15 Not boasting of things without *our* measure, *that is,* of other men's labours; but having hope, when your faith is increased, that we shall be enlarged by you according to our rule abundantly,

16 To preach the gospel in the *regions* beyond you, *and* not to boast in another man's line of things made ready to our hand.

17 But he that glorieth, let him glory in the Lord.

18 For not he that commendeth himself is approved, but whom the Lord commendeth.

ἐν τῷ εὐαγγελίῳ τοῦ Χριστοῦ, 15 οὐκ
in the gospel – of Christ, not
εἰς τὰ ἄμετρα καυχώμενοι ἐν ἀλλοτρίοις
immeasurably† boasting in others'†
κόποις, ἐλπίδα δὲ ἔχοντες αὐξανομένης
labours, but ²hope ¹having growing
                                       =as your faith grows
τῆς πίστεως ὑμῶν ἐν ὑμῖν μεγαλυνθῆναι
the faith of you² ²among ³you ¹to be magnified
κατὰ τὸν κανόνα ἡμῶν εἰς περισσείαν,
according the rule of us in abundance,
to
16 εἰς τὰ ὑπερέκεινα ὑμῶν εὐαγγελίσασθαι,
in the [parts] beyond you to preach good tidings,
οὐκ ἐν ἀλλοτρίῳ κανόνι εἰς τὰ ἕτοιμα
not ²in ³another's† ⁴rule ¹in – ⁵things ready
καυχήσασθαι. 17 Ὁ δὲ καυχώμενος ἐν
¹to boast. But the [one] boasting ²in
κυρίῳ καυχάσθω· 18 οὐ γὰρ ὁ ἑαυτὸν
³[the] Lord ¹let him boast; for not the [one] himself
συνιστάνων, ἐκεῖνός ἐστιν δόκιμος, ἀλλὰ
commending, that one is approved, but
ὃν ὁ κύριος συνίστησιν.
whom the Lord commends.

CHAPTER 11

WOULD to God ye could bear with me a little in *my* folly: and indeed bear with me.

2 For I am jealous over you with godly jealousy: for I have espoused you to one husband, that I may present *you as* a chaste virgin to Christ.

3 But I fear, lest by any means, as the serpent beguiled Eve through his subtilty, so your minds should be corrupted from the simplicity that is in Christ.

4 For if he that cometh preacheth another Jesus, whom we have not preached, or *if* ye receive another spirit, which ye

11 Ὄφελον ἀνείχεσθέ μου μικρόν τι
I would that ye endured me a little [bit]
ἀφροσύνης· ἀλλὰ καὶ ἀνέχεσθέ μου.
of foolishness; but indeed ye do endure me.
2 ζηλῶ γὰρ ὑμᾶς θεοῦ ζήλῳ, ἡρμοσάμην
For I am jealous [of] you ²of God ¹with a ¹I betrothed
jealousy,
γὰρ ὑμᾶς ἑνὶ ἀνδρὶ παρθένον ἁγνὴν
¹for you to one husband ³virgin ²a pure
παραστῆσαι τῷ Χριστῷ· 3 φοβοῦμαι δὲ
¹to present – to Christ; and I fear
μή πως, ὡς ὁ ὄφις ἐξηπάτησεν Εὔαν
lest somehow, as the serpent deceived Eve
ἐν τῇ πανουργίᾳ αὐτοῦ, φθαρῇ τὰ νοήματα
by the cleverness of him, ⁴should ¹the ²thoughts
be seduced
ὑμῶν ἀπὸ τῆς ἁπλότητος [καὶ τῆς
³of you from the simplicity ⁵and the
ἁγνότητος] τῆς εἰς Χριστόν. 4 εἰ μὲν
purity] – in Christ. ²if ³indeed
γὰρ ὁ ἐρχόμενος ἄλλον Ἰησοῦν κηρύσσει
¹For the [one] coming ²another ³Jesus ¹proclaims
ὃν οὐκ ἐκηρύξαμεν, ἢ πνεῦμα ἕτερον
whom we did not proclaim, or ³spirit ²a different

have not received, or another gospel, which ye have not accepted, ye might well bear with *him*.

λαμβάνετε   ὃ   οὐκ   ἐλάβετε,   ἢ   εὐαγγέλιον
¹ye receive   which   ye did not receive,   or   ²gospel

ἕτερον   ὃ   οὐκ   ἐδέξασθε,   καλῶς   ἀνέχεσθε.
¹a different   which ye did not receive,   ²[him] ³well   ¹ye endure.

5 For I suppose I was not a whit behind the very chiefest apostles.

5 λογίζομαι   γὰρ   μηδὲν   ὑστερηκέναι   τῶν
For I reckon   nothing   to have come behind   *of* the

6 But though *I be* rude in speech, yet not in knowledge; but we have been throughly made manifest among you in all things.

ὑπερλίαν   ἀποστόλων.   6 εἰ   δὲ   καὶ   ἰδιώτης
super-   apostles.   But if   indeed   unskilled
[I am]

τῷ   λόγῳ,   ἀλλ'   οὐ   τῇ   γνώσει,   ἀλλ'   ἐν
–   in speech,   yet   not   –   in knowledge,   but   in

παντὶ   φανερώσαντες   ἐν   πᾶσιν   εἰς   ὑμᾶς.
every   having manifested   in   all things   to   you.
[way]   [ourselves]

7 Have I committed an offence in abasing myself that ye might be exalted, because I have preached to you the gospel of God freely?

7 Ἢ   ἁμαρτίαν   ἐποίησα   ἐμαυτὸν   ταπεινῶν
Or   ²sin   ¹did I commit   ⁴myself   ⁵humbling

ἵνα   ὑμεῖς   ὑψωθῆτε,   ὅτι   δωρεὰν   τὸ   τοῦ
in order   ye   might be   because   ⁶freely   ⁵the   –
that   exalted,

8 I robbed other churches, taking wages *of them*, to do you service.

θεοῦ   εὐαγγέλιον   εὐηγγελισάμην   ὑμῖν;
²of God   ³gospel   ¹I preached *good tidings*   to you?

8 ἄλλας   ἐκκλησίας   ἐσύλησα   λαβὼν   ὀψώνιον
Other   churches   I robbed   taking   wages

9 And when I was present with you, and wanted, I was chargeable to no man: for that which was lacking to me the brethren which came from Macedonia supplied: and in all *things* I have kept myself from being burdensome unto you, and *so* will I keep *myself*.

πρὸς   τὴν   ὑμῶν   διακονίαν,   9 καὶ   παρὼν
for   ¹the   ²of you   ²ministry,   and being present

πρὸς   ὑμᾶς   καὶ   ὑστερηθεὶς   οὐ   κατενάρκησα
with   you   and   lacking   I was *not* an encumbrance

οὐθενός·   τὸ   γὰρ   ὑστέρημά   μου   προσανε-
of no man;   for the   lack   of me   ⁶made

πλήρωσαν   οἱ   ἀδελφοὶ   ἐλθόντες   ἀπὸ   Μακε-
up   ¹the   ²brothers   ³coming   ⁴from   ⁵Mace-

10 As the truth of Christ is in me, no man shall stop me of this boasting in the regions of Achaia.

δονίας·   καὶ   ἐν   παντὶ   ἀβαρῆ   ἐμαυτὸν
donia;   and   in every [way]   ²unburdensome   ³myself

ὑμῖν   ἐτήρησα   καὶ   τηρήσω.   10 ἔστιν
⁴to you   ¹I kept   and   I will keep.   ²is

11 Wherefore? because I love you not? God knoweth.

ἀλήθεια   Χριστοῦ   ἐν   ἐμοί,   ὅτι   ἡ   καύχησις
¹[The] truth   ²of Christ   in   me,   that   –   boasting

12 But what I do, that I will do, that I may cut off occasion from them which desire occasion; that

αὕτη   οὐ   φραγήσεται   εἰς   ἐμὲ   ἐν   τοῖς
this   shall not be stopped   in   me   in   the

κλίμασιν   τῆς   Ἀχαΐας.   11 διὰ   τί;   ὅτι
regions   –   of Achaia.   Why?   because

οὐκ   ἀγαπῶ   ὑμᾶς;   ὁ   θεὸς   οἶδεν.   12 Ὃ
I love not   you?   –   God   knows.   what

δὲ   ποιῶ,   καὶ   ποιήσω,   ἵνα   ἐκκόψω   τὴν
But   I do,   also   I will do,   in order   I may cut   the
that   off

ἀφορμὴν   τῶν   θελόντων   ἀφορμήν,   ἵνα   ἐν
occasion   of the   desiring   an occasion,   in or-   where-
[ones]   der that

wherein they glory, they may be found even as we.

13 For such *are* false apostles, deceitful workers, transforming t h e m s e l v e s into the apostles of Christ.

14 And no marvel; for Satan himself is transformed into an angel of light.

15 Therefore *it is* no great thing if his ministers also be transformed as the ministers of righteousness; whose end shall be according to their works.

16 I say again, Let no man think me a fool; if otherwise, yet as a fool receive me, that I may boast myself a little.

17 That which I speak, I speak *it* not after the Lord, but as it were foolishly, in this confidence of boasting.

18 Seeing that many glory after the flesh, I will glory also.

19 For ye suffer fools gladly, seeing ye *yourselves* are wise.

20 For ye suffer, if a man bring you into bondage, if a man devour *you,* if a man take *of you,* if a man exalt himself, if a man smite you on the face.

21 I speak as concerning reproach, as though we had been weak. Howbeit whereinsoever any is bold, (I speak foolishly,) I am bold also.

ᾧ   καυχῶνται   εὑρεθῶσιν καθὼς καὶ ἡμεῖς.
in   they boast   they may be found   as   also we.

13 οἱ γὰρ τοιοῦτοι ψευδαπόστολοι, ἐργάται
-   For   such [are]   false apostles,   ²workmen

δόλιοι, μετασχηματιζόμενοι εἰς ἀποστόλους
¹deceitful,   transforming themselves   into   apostles

Χριστοῦ. 14 καὶ οὐ θαῦμα· αὐτὸς γὰρ
of Christ.   And no wonder; ²[him]self ¹for

ὁ σατανᾶς μετασχηματίζεται εἰς ἄγγελον
-   ³Satan   transforms himself   into   an angel

φωτός. 15 οὐ μέγα οὖν εἰ καὶ οἱ
of light.   No great thing therefore if   also   the

διάκονοι αὐτοῦ μετασχηματίζονται ὡς
ministers   of him   transform themselves   as

διάκονοι δικαιοσύνης· ὧν τὸ τέλος ἔσται
ministers   of righteousness; of whom the   end   will be

κατὰ τὰ ἔργα αὐτῶν.
according to the works   of them.

16 Πάλιν λέγω, μή τίς με δόξῃ ἄφρονα
Again   I say, ³not ²anyone ⁴me ¹think ⁵foolish

εἶναι· εἰ δὲ μή γε, κἂν ὡς ἄφρονα
⁶to be;   otherwise,   even if as   foolish

δέξασθέ με, ἵνα κἀγὼ μικρόν τι καυχήσ-
receive ye me, in order I also   a little [bit]   may
        that

ωμαι. 17 ὃ λαλῶ, οὐ κατὰ κύριον λαλῶ,
boast.   What I speak, not according to [the] Lord I speak,
        to

ἀλλ' ὡς ἐν ἀφροσύνῃ, ἐν ταύτῃ τῇ
but   as in   folly,   in   this -

ὑποστάσει τῆς καυχήσεως. 18 ἐπεὶ πολλοὶ
confidence   - of boasting.   Since   many

καυχῶνται κατὰ [τὴν] σάρκα, κἀγὼ
boast   according to the   flesh,   I also

καυχήσομαι. 19 ἡδέως γὰρ ἀνέχεσθε τῶν
will boast.   For gladly   ye endure   -

ἀφρόνων φρόνιμοι ὄντες· 20 ἀνέχεσθε γὰρ
fools   ²prudent ¹being;   for ye endure

εἴ τις ὑμᾶς καταδουλοῖ, εἴ τις κατεσθίει,
if anyone ²you ¹enslaves,   if anyone devours [you],

εἴ τις λαμβάνει, εἴ τις ἐπαίρεται, εἴ
if anyone receives [you],* if anyone lifts himself up, if

τις εἰς πρόσωπον ὑμᾶς δέρει. 21 κατὰ
anyone ²in ⁴[the] face ³you ¹beats(hits). According to

ἀτιμίαν λέγω, ὡς ὅτι ἡμεῖς ἠσθενήκαμεν·
dishonour I say, as   that we   have been weak;

ἐν ᾧ δ' ἄν τις τολμᾷ, ἐν ἀφροσύνῃ
but in whatever [respect] anyone dares,   in   folly

          * ? takes [you in].

22 Are they Hebrews? so *am* I. Are they Israelites? so *am* I. Are they the seed of Abraham? so *am* I.

23 Are they ministers of Christ? (I speak as a fool) I *am* more; in labours more abundant, in stripes above measure, in prisons more frequent, in deaths oft.

24 Of the Jews five times received I forty *stripes* save one.

25 Thrice was I beaten with rods, once was I stoned, thrice I suffered shipwreck, a night and a day I have been in the deep;

26 *In* journeyings often, *in* perils of waters, *in* perils of robbers, *in* perils by *mine own* countrymen, *in* perils by the heathen, *in* perils in the city, *in* perils in the wilderness, *in* perils in the sea, *in* perils among false brethren;

27 In weariness and painfulness, in watchings often, in hunger and thirst, in fastings often, in cold and nakedness.

28 Beside those things that are without, that which cometh upon me daily, the care of all the churches.

29 Who is weak, and I am not weak? who is offended, and I burn not?

30 If I must needs glory, I will glory of the things which concern mine infirmities.

λέγω,	τολμῶ	κἀγώ.	22 Ἑβραῖοί	εἰσιν;
I say,	³dare	¹I ²also.	Hebrews	are they?

κἀγώ.	Ἰσραηλῖταί εἰσιν;	κἀγώ.	σπέρμα
I also.	Israelites are they?	I also.	Seed

Ἀβραάμ εἰσιν;	κἀγώ.	23 διάκονοι	Χριστοῦ
of Abraham are they?	I also.	Ministers	of Christ

εἰσιν;	παραφρονῶν	λαλῶ,	ὑπὲρ ἐγώ·	ἐν
are they?	being out of my mind	I speak,	²beyond ¹I: (more)	in

κόποις	περισσοτέρως,	ἐν φυλακαῖς	περισ-
labours	more abundantly,	in prisons	more

σοτέρως,	ἐν πληγαῖς	ὑπερβαλλόντως,	ἐν
abundantly,	in stripes	excessively,	in

θανάτοις	πολλάκις.	24 ὑπὸ	Ἰουδαίων
deaths	many times.	By	Jews

πεντάκις	τεσσεράκοντα	παρὰ μίαν	ἔλαβον,
five times	forty [stripes]	less one	I received,

25 τρὶς	ἐρραβδίσθην,	ἅπαξ ἐλιθάσθην,	τρὶς
thrice I was beaten with rods,	once	I was stoned,	thrice

ἐναυάγησα,	26 νυχθήμερον	ἐν τῷ	βυθῷ
I was shipwrecked,	a night and a day	in the	deep

πεποίηκα·	ὁδοιπορίαις	πολλάκις,	κινδύνοις
I have done(been);	in travels	many times,	in perils

ποταμῶν,	κινδύνοις λῃστῶν,	κινδύνοις	ἐκ
of rivers,	in perils of robbers,	in perils	of

γένους,	κινδύνοις ἐξ ἐθνῶν,	κινδύνοις	ἐν
[my] kind,	in perils of nations,	in perils	in

πόλει,	κινδύνοις ἐν ἐρημίᾳ,	κινδύνοις	ἐν
a city,	in perils in a desert,	in perils	in(at)

θαλάσσῃ,	κινδύνοις ἐν ψευδαδέλφοις,	27 κόπῳ
sea,	in perils among false brothers,	in labour

καὶ μόχθῳ,	ἐν ἀγρυπνίαις	πολλάκις,	ἐν
and hardship,	in watchings	many times,	in

λιμῷ καὶ	δίψει,	ἐν νηστείαις	πολλάκις,
famine and	thirst,	in fastings	many times,

ἐν ψύχει καὶ	γυμνότητι·	28 χωρὶς	τῶν
in cold and	nakedness;	apart from	the things

παρεκτὸς	ἡ ἐπίστασίς	μοι ἡ καθ'	ἡμέραν,
without[,]	the conspiring against	me –	daily,

ἡ μέριμνα	πασῶν τῶν	ἐκκλησιῶν.	29 τίς
the care	of all the	churches.	Who

ἀσθενεῖ,	καὶ οὐκ ἀσθενῶ;	τίς σκανδαλίζεται,
is weak,	and I am not weak?	who is offended,

καὶ οὐκ	ἐγὼ	πυροῦμαι;	30 εἰ καυχᾶσθαι
and	²not ¹I	²burn?	If to boast

δεῖ,	τὰ	τῆς	ἀσθενείας	μου καυχήσομαι.
it behoves [me],	things	of the	weakness	of me I will boast.

31 The God and Father of our Lord Jesus Christ, which is blessed for evermore, knoweth that I lie not.

32 In Damascus the governor under Aretas the king kept the city of the Damascenes with a garrison, desirous to apprehend me:

33 And through a window in a basket was I let down by the wall, and escaped his hands.

CHAPTER 12

IT is not expedient for me doubtless to glory. I will come to visions and revelations of the Lord.

2 I knew a man in Christ above fourteen years ago, (whether in the body, I cannot tell; or whether out of the body, I cannot tell: God knoweth;) such an one caught up to the third heaven.

3 And I knew such a man, (whether in the body, or out of the body, I cannot tell: God knoweth;)

4 How that he was caught up into paradise, and heard unspeakable words, which it is not lawful for a man to utter.

5 Of such an one will I glory: yet of myself I will not glory, but in mine infirmities.

6 For though I would desire to glory, I shall not be a fool; for I will say the truth: but *now* I

---

31 ὁ θεὸς καὶ πατὴρ τοῦ κυρίου Ἰησοῦ
The God and Father of the Lord Jesus

οἶδεν, ὁ ὢν εὐλογητὸς εἰς τοὺς αἰῶνας,
knows, the [one] being blessed unto the ages,

ὅτι οὐ ψεύδομαι. 32 ἐν Δαμασκῷ ὁ
that I am not lying. In Damascus the

ἐθνάρχης Ἀρέτα τοῦ βασιλέως ἐφρούρει
ethnarch of Aretas *of* the king guarded

τὴν πόλιν Δαμασκηνῶν πιάσαι με, 33 καὶ
the city of [the] Damascenes to seize me, and

διὰ θυρίδος ἐν σαργάνῃ ἐχαλάσθην διὰ
through a window in a basket I was lowered through

τοῦ τείχους καὶ ἐξέφυγον τὰς χεῖρας αὐτοῦ.
the wall and escaped the hands of him.

12 Καυχᾶσθαι δεῖ, οὐ συμφέρον μέν,
To boast it behoves not expedient indeed,
[me],

ἐλεύσομαι δὲ εἰς ὀπτασίας καὶ ἀποκαλύψεις
so I will come to visions and revelations

κυρίου. 2 οἶδα ἄνθρωπον ἐν Χριστῷ
of [the] Lord. I know a man in Christ

πρὸ ἐτῶν δεκατεσσάρων, — εἴτε ἐν
before years fourteen, (whether in

σώματι οὐκ οἶδα, εἴτε ἐκτὸς τοῦ σώματος
[the] body I know not, or outside the body

οὐκ οἶδα, ὁ θεὸς οἶδεν, — ἁρπαγέντα
I know not, - God knows,) ¹caught

τὸν τοιοῦτον ἕως τρίτου οὐρανοῦ. 3 καὶ
- ¹such a one to [the] third heaven. And

οἶδα τὸν τοιοῦτον ἄνθρωπον — εἴτε
I know - such a man (whether

ἐν σώματι εἴτε χωρὶς τοῦ σώματος
in [the] body or apart from the body

[οὐκ οἶδα], ὁ θεὸς οἶδεν, — 4 ὅτι
I know not, - God knows,) that

ἡρπάγη εἰς τὸν παράδεισον καὶ ἤκουσεν
he was caught into the paradise and heard

ἄρρητα ῥήματα, ἃ οὐκ ἐξὸν ἀνθρώπῳ
unspeakable words, which it is not for a man
permissible

λαλῆσαι. 5 ὑπὲρ τοῦ τοιούτου καυχήσομαι,
to speak. On behalf of - such a one I will boast,

ὑπὲρ δὲ ἐμαυτοῦ οὐ καυχήσομαι εἰ
but on behalf of myself I will not boast ex-

μὴ ἐν ταῖς ἀσθενείαις. 6 ἐὰν γὰρ θελήσω
cept in the(my) weaknesses. For if I shall wish

καυχήσασθαι, οὐκ ἔσομαι ἄφρων, ἀλήθειαν
to boast, I shall not be foolish, ²truth

forbear, lest any man should think of me above that which he seeth me *to be*, or *that* he heareth of me.

7 And lest I should be exalted above measure through the abundance of the revelations, there was given to me a thorn in the flesh, the messenger of Satan to buffet me, lest I should be exalted above measure.

8 For this thing I besought the Lord thrice, that it might depart from me.

9 And he said unto me, My grace is sufficient for thee: for my strength is made perfect in weakness. Most gladly therefore will I rather glory in my infirmities, that the power of Christ may rest upon me.

10 Therefore I take pleasure in infirmities, in reproaches, in necessities, in persecutions, in distresses for Christ's sake: for when I am weak, then am I strong.

11 I am become a fool in glorying; ye have compelled me: for I ought to have been commended of you: for in nothing am I behind the very chiefest apostles, though I be nothing.

12 Truly the signs of an apostle were wrought among you in all patience, in signs, and wonders, and mighty deeds.

13 For what is it where-

γὰρ ἐρῶ· φείδομαι δέ, μή τις εἰς ἐμὲ
¹for ²I will speak; but I spare, lest anyone to me

λογίσηται ὑπὲρ ὃ βλέπει με ἢ ἀκούει
reckons beyond what he sees me or hears

ἐξ ἐμοῦ 7 καὶ τῇ ὑπερβολῇ τῶν ἀποκα-
of me and by the excess of the revela-

λύψεων. διὸ ἵνα μὴ ὑπεραίρωμαι, ἐδόθη
tions. Where- lest I should be there was
fore exceedingly uplifted, given

μοι σκόλοψ τῇ σαρκί, ἄγγελος σατανᾶ,
to me a thorn in the flesh, a messenger of Satan,

ἵνα με κολαφίζῃ, ἵνα μὴ ὑπεραίρωμαι.
in order ²me ¹he might buffet, lest I should be
that exceedingly uplifted.

8 ὑπὲρ τούτου τρὶς τὸν κύριον παρεκάλεσα,
As to this thrice the Lord I besought,

ἵνα ἀποστῇ ἀπ' ἐμοῦ. 9 καὶ εἴρηκέν
in or- it might from me. And he *has* said
der that depart

μοι· ἀρκεῖ σοι ἡ χάρις μου· ἡ γὰρ
to me: ⁴Suffices ⁵thee ¹the ²grace ³of me; for the(my)

δύναμις ἐν ἀσθενείᾳ τελεῖται. Ἥδιστα
power in weakness is perfected. Most gladly

οὖν μᾶλλον καυχήσομαι ἐν ταῖς ἀσθενείαις,
therefore rather I will boast in the(my) weaknesses,

ἵνα ἐπισκηνώσῃ ἐπ' ἐμὲ ἡ δύναμις τοῦ
in order ⁴might over ⁵me ¹the ²power -
that overshadow

Χριστοῦ. 10 διὸ εὐδοκῶ ἐν ἀσθενείαις,
³of Christ. Wherefore I am well in weaknesses,
pleased

ἐν ὕβρεσιν, ἐν ἀνάγκαις, ἐν διωγμοῖς
in insults, in necessities, in persecutions

καὶ στενοχωρίαις, ὑπὲρ Χριστοῦ· ²whenever
and difficulties, on behalf of Christ;

γὰρ ἀσθενῶ, τότε δυνατός εἰμι.
¹for I am weak, then ²powerful ¹I am.

11 Γέγονα ἄφρων· ὑμεῖς με ἠναγκάσατε.
I have become foolish; ye me compelled.

ἐγὼ γὰρ ὤφειλον ὑφ' ὑμῶν συνίστασθαι.
For I ought by you to be commended.

οὐδὲν γὰρ ὑστέρησα τῶν ὑπερλίαν
For nothing I lacked of the super-

ἀποστόλων, εἰ καὶ οὐδέν εἰμι. 12 τὰ
apostles, ²if ¹even ⁴nothing ³I am. ²The

μὲν σημεῖα τοῦ ἀποστόλου κατειργάσθη
¹indeed signs of the apostle were wrought

ἐν ὑμῖν ἐν πάσῃ ὑπομονῇ, σημείοις τε
among you in all endurance, ²by signs ¹both

καὶ τέρασιν καὶ δυνάμεσιν. 13 τί γὰρ
and by wonders and by powerful deeds. For what

in ye were inferior to other churches, except *it be* that I myself was not burdensome to you? forgive me this wrong.

14 Behold, the third time I am ready to come to you; and I will not be burdensome to you: for I seek not your's, but you: for the children ought not to lay up for the parents, but the parents for the children.

15 And I will very gladly spend and be spent for you; though the more abundantly I love you, the less I be loved.

16 But be it so, I did not burden you: nevertheless, being crafty, I caught you with guile.

17 Did I make a gain of you by any of them whom I sent unto you?

18 I desired Titus, and with *him* I sent a brother. Did Titus make a gain of you? walked we not in the same spirit? *walked we* not in the same steps?

19 Again, think ye that we excuse ourselves unto you? we speak before God in Christ: but *we do* all things, dearly beloved, for your edifying.

ἐστιν ὃ ἡσσώθητε ὑπὲρ τὰς λοιπὰς
is it which ye were less than the remaining

ἐκκλησίας, εἰ μὴ ὅτι αὐτὸς ἐγὼ οὐ
churches, except that ²[my]self ¹I ³not

κατενάρκησα ὑμῶν; χαρίσασθέ μοι τὴν
⁵encumbered ⁴of you? Forgive ye me –

ἀδικίαν ταύτην. 14 Ἰδοὺ τρίτον τοῦτο
wrong this. Behold ²[the] ¹this
                             third [time] [is]

ἑτοίμως ἔχω ἐλθεῖν πρὸς ὑμᾶς, καὶ
I am ready† to come to you, and

οὐ καταναρκήσω· οὐ γὰρ ζητῶ τὰ ὑμῶν
I will not encumber [you]; ²not ¹for ³I seek the of
                                         things you

ἀλλὰ ὑμᾶς. οὐ γὰρ ὀφείλει τὰ τέκνα
but you. ²not ¹for ³ought ¹the ²children

τοῖς γονεῦσιν θησαυρίζειν, ἀλλὰ οἱ γονεῖς
for the parents to lay up treasure, but the parents

τοῖς τέκνοις. 15 ἐγὼ δὲ ἥδιστα δαπανήσω
for the children. But I most gladly will spend

καὶ ἐκδαπανηθήσομαι ὑπὲρ τῶν ψυχῶν
and will be spent out on behalf of the souls

ὑμῶν. εἰ περισσοτέρως ὑμᾶς ἀγαπῶ,
of you. If more abundantly ²you ¹I love,

ἧσσον ἀγαπῶμαι; 16 Ἔστω δέ, ἐγὼ οὐ
[the] less am I loved? But let it be, I not

κατεβάρησα ὑμᾶς· ἀλλὰ ὑπάρχων πανοῦργος
burdened you; but being crafty

δόλῳ ὑμᾶς ἔλαβον. 17 μή τινα ὧν
³with guile ²you ¹I took. Not anyone of
                                        whom

ἀπέσταλκα πρὸς ὑμᾶς, 18 δι' αὐτοῦ
I have sent to you, through him

ἐπλεονέκτησα ὑμᾶς; παρεκάλεσα Τίτον καὶ
did I defraud you? I besought Titus and

συναπέστειλα τὸν ἀδελφόν· μήτι ἐπλεο-
sent with [him] the brother; not ²de-

νέκτησεν ὑμᾶς Τίτος; οὐ τῷ αὐτῷ
frauded ³you ¹Titus? ²not ³by the ⁴same

πνεύματι περιεπατήσαμεν; οὐ τοῖς αὐτοῖς
⁵spirit ¹walked we? not in the same

ἴχνεσιν;
steps?

19 Πάλαι δοκεῖτε ὅτι ὑμῖν ἀπολογούμεθα.
   Already ye think that to you we are making a
                                   defence.

κατέναντι θεοῦ ἐν Χριστῷ λαλοῦμεν· τὰ
Before God in Christ we speak; –

δὲ πάντα, ἀγαπητοί, ὑπὲρ τῆς ὑμῶν
but all things, beloved, [are] on behalf of ¹the ²of you

20 For I fear, lest, when I come, I shall not find you such as I would, and that I shall be found unto you such as ye would not: lest there be debates, envyings, wraths, strifes, backbitings, whisperings, swellings, tumults:

21 And lest, when I come again, my God will humble me among you, and that I shall bewail many which have sinned already, and have not repented of the uncleanness and fornication and lasciviousness which they have committed.

CHAPTER 13

THIS is the third time I am coming to you. In the mouth of two or three witnesses shall every word be established.

2 I told you before, and foretell you, as if I were present, the second time; and being absent now I write to them which heretofore have sinned, and to all other, that, if I come again, I will not spare:

3 Since ye seek a proof of Christ speaking in me, which to you-ward is not weak, but is mighty in you.

4 For though he was crucified through weakness, yet he liveth by the power of God. For we also are weak in him, but we shall live with him

οἰκοδομῆς. **20** φοβοῦμαι γὰρ μή πως ἐλθὼν
²edification.   For I fear   lest   coming

οὐχ οἵους θέλω εὕρω ὑμᾶς, κἀγὼ εὑρεθῶ
²not ⁴such as ⁵I wish ³I may find ²you,   and I   am found

ὑμῖν οἷον οὐ θέλετε, μή πως ἔρις,
by you such as   ye wish not,   lest   strife,

ζῆλος, θυμοί, ἐριθεῖαι, καταλαλιαί, ψιθυρισ-
jealousy, angers, rivalries,   detractions,   whisper-

μοί, φυσιώσεις, ἀκαταστασίαι· **21** μὴ πάλιν
ings, puffings up, disturbances;   lest   again

ἐλθόντος μου ταπεινώσῃ με ὁ θεός μου
coming   meᵃ ⁴may humble ⁵me ¹the ²God ³of me
=when I come

πρὸς ὑμᾶς, καὶ πενθήσω πολλοὺς τῶν
with   you, and I shall mourn many   of the
                                        [ones]

προημαρτηκότων καὶ μὴ μετανοησάντων
having previously sinned and not   repenting

ἐπὶ τῇ ἀκαθαρσίᾳ καὶ πορνείᾳ καὶ
over the   uncleanness and fornication and

ἀσελγείᾳ ᾗ ἔπραξαν. **13** Τρίτον τοῦτο
lewdness which they practised.   ²[The] third ¹this
                                   [time]   [is]

ἔρχομαι πρὸς ὑμᾶς· ἐπὶ στόματος
I am coming to   you;   at   [the] mouth

δύο μαρτύρων καὶ τριῶν σταθήσεται
of two witnesses and of three shall be established

πᾶν ῥῆμα. **2** προείρηκα καὶ προλέγω,
every word.   I have previously and   I say
                   said   beforehand,

ὡς παρὼν τὸ δεύτερον καὶ ἀπὼν
as being present the   second [time] and being absent

νῦν, τοῖς προημαρτηκόσιν καὶ τοῖς
now, to the [ones] having previously sinned and ¹to ²the

λοιποῖς πᾶσιν, ὅτι ἐὰν ἔλθω εἰς τὸ
⁴remaining ³all,   that if   I come in   the
[ones]

πάλιν οὐ φείσομαι, **3** ἐπεὶ δοκιμὴν ζητεῖτε
again I will not spare,   since   ²a proof ¹ye seek

τοῦ ἐν ἐμοὶ λαλοῦντος Χριστοῦ, ὃς εἰς
 -   ⁵in ⁶me ⁴speaking   ³of Christ, who toward

ὑμᾶς οὐκ ἀσθενεῖ ἀλλὰ δυνατεῖ ἐν ὑμῖν.
you   is not weak   but   is powerful in you.

4 καὶ γὰρ ἐσταυρώθη ἐξ ἀσθενείας, ἀλλὰ
For indeed he was crucified out of weakness,   but

ζῇ ἐκ δυνάμεως θεοῦ. καὶ γὰρ ἡμεῖς
he lives by [the] power of God. For indeed   we

ἀσθενοῦμεν ἐν αὐτῷ, ἀλλὰ ζήσομεν σὺν
are weak   in him,   but we shall live with

by the power of God toward you.

5 Examine yourselves, whether ye be in the faith; prove your own selves. Know ye not your own selves, how that Jesus Christ is in you, except ye be reprobates?

6 But I trust that ye shall know that we are not reprobates.

7 Now I pray to God that ye do no evil; not that we should appear approved, but that ye should do that which is honest, though we be as reprobates.

8 For we can do nothing against the truth, but for the truth.

9 For we are glad, when we are weak, and ye are strong: and this also we wish, *even* your perfection.

10 Therefore I write these things being absent, lest being present I should use sharpness, according to the power which the Lord hath given me to edification, and not to destruction.

11 Finally, brethren, farewell. Be perfect, be of good comfort, be of one mind, live in peace; and the God of love and peace shall be with you.

12 Greet one another with an holy kiss.

αὐτῷ　ἐκ　δυνάμεως　θεοῦ　εἰς　ὑμᾶς.
him　by　[the] power　of God　toward　you.

5 Ἑαυτοὺς　πειράζετε　εἰ　ἐστὲ　ἐν　τῇ
²Yourselves　¹test　if　ye are　in　the

πίστει,　ἑαυτοὺς　δοκιμάζετε·　ἢ　οὐκ
faith,　²yourselves　¹prove;　or　not

ἐπιγινώσκετε　ἑαυτοὺς　ὅτι　Ἰησοῦς　Χριστὸς
perceive ye　yourselves　that　Jesus　Christ [is]

ἐν　ὑμῖν,　εἰ　μήτι　ἀδόκιμοί　ἐστε.　6 ἐλπίζω
in　you,　unless　²counterfeits　¹ye are.　I hope

δὲ　ὅτι　γνώσεσθε　ὅτι　ἡμεῖς　οὐκ　ἐσμὲν
But that　ye will know　that　we　are not

ἀδόκιμοι.　7 εὐχόμεθα　δὲ　πρὸς　τὸν　θεὸν
counterfeits.　Now we pray　to　-　God

μὴ　ποιῆσαι　ὑμᾶς　κακὸν　μηδέν,　οὐχ
not　to do　youᵇ　evil　*none*,　not
=that ye do no . . .

ἵνα　ἡμεῖς　δόκιμοι　φανῶμεν,　ἀλλ’　ἵνα
in order　we　²approved　¹may appear,　but　in order
that　　　　　　　　　　　　　　　　　that

ὑμεῖς　τὸ　καλὸν　ποιῆτε,　ἡμεῖς　δὲ　ὡς
ye　²the　²good　¹may do,　and we　²as

ἀδόκιμοι　ὦμεν.　8 οὐ　γὰρ　δυνάμεθά
²counterfeits　¹may be.　For we cannot [do]

τι　κατὰ　τῆς　ἀληθείας,　ἀλλὰ　ὑπὲρ　τῆς
any-　against　the　truth,　but　on behalf of the
thing

ἀληθείας.　9 χαίρομεν　γὰρ　ὅταν　ἡμεῖς
truth.　For we rejoice　when*ever*　we

ἀσθενῶμεν,　ὑμεῖς　δὲ　δυνατοὶ　ἦτε·　τοῦτο
are weak,　and ye　powerful　are;　this

καὶ　εὐχόμεθα,　τὴν　ὑμῶν　κατάρτισιν.　10 Διὰ
also　we pray,　the　²of you　¹restoration.　There-

τοῦτο　ταῦτα　ἀπὼν　γράφω,　ἵνα　παρὼν
fore　²these things　³being　¹I write,　in order　being
absent　　　　　　　　that　　　present

μὴ　ἀποτόμως　χρήσωμαι　κατὰ　τὴν　ἐξουσίαν
²not　³sharply　¹I may deal　according to the　authority

ἣν　ὁ　κύριος　ἔδωκέν　μοι　εἰς　οἰκοδομὴν
which the　Lord　gave　me　for　edification

καὶ　οὐκ　εἰς　καθαίρεσιν.
and　not　for　overthrow.

11 Λοιπόν,　ἀδελφοί,　χαίρετε,　καταρτίζεσθε,
For the rest,†　brothers,　rejoice,　restore yourselves,

παρακαλεῖσθε,　τὸ　αὐτὸ　φρονεῖτε,　εἰρηνεύετε,
admonish yourselves,　the same thing　think,　be at peace.

καὶ　ὁ　θεὸς　τῆς　ἀγάπης　καὶ　εἰρήνης
and　the　God　-　of love　and　of peace

ἔσται　μεθ’　ὑμῶν.　12 Ἀσπάσασθε　ἀλλήλους
will be　with　you.　Greet ye　one another

13 All the saints salute you.

14 The grace of the Lord Jesus Christ, and the love of God, and the communion of the Holy Ghost, *be* with you all. Amen.

ἐν ἁγίῳ φιλήματι. Ἀσπάζονται ὑμᾶς οἱ
with a holy kiss. [4]greet [5]you [3]the

ἅγιοι πάντες.
[3]saints [1]All.

13 Ἡ χάρις τοῦ κυρίου Ἰησοῦ Χριστοῦ
The grace of the Lord Jesus Christ

καὶ ἡ ἀγάπη τοῦ θεοῦ καὶ ἡ κοινωνία
and the love – of God and the fellowship

τοῦ ἁγίου πνεύματος μετὰ πάντων ὑμῶν.
of the Holy Spirit [be] with [2]all [1]you.

GALATIANS 1

ΠΡΟΣ ΓΑΛΑΤΑΣ
To Galatians

CHAPTER 1

PAUL, an apostle, (not of men, neither by man, but by Jesus Christ, and God the Father, who raised him from the dead;)

2 And all the brethren which are with me, unto the churches of Galatia:

3 Grace *be* to you and peace from God the Father, and *from* our Lord Jesus Christ,

4 Who gave himself for our sins, that he might deliver us from this present evil world, according to the will of God and our Father:

5 To whom *be* glory for ever and ever. Amen.

1 Παῦλος ἀπόστολος, οὐκ ἀπ' ἀνθρώπων
Paul an apostle, not from men

οὐδὲ δι' ἀνθρώπου ἀλλὰ διὰ Ἰησοῦ
nor through man but through Jesus

Χριστοῦ καὶ θεοῦ πατρὸς τοῦ ἐγείραντος
Christ and God [the] Father the [one] having raised

αὐτὸν ἐκ νεκρῶν, 2 καὶ οἱ σὺν ἐμοὶ
him out of [the] dead, and [2]with [4]me

πάντες ἀδελφοί, ταῖς ἐκκλησίαις τῆς
[1]all [3]brothers, to the churches –

Γαλατίας· 3 χάρις ὑμῖν καὶ εἰρήνη ἀπὸ
of Galatia: Grace to you and peace from

θεοῦ πατρὸς ἡμῶν καὶ κυρίου Ἰησοῦ
God Father of us and Lord Jesus

Χριστοῦ, 4 τοῦ δόντος ἑαυτὸν ὑπὲρ τῶν
Christ, the [one] having given himself on behalf of the

ἁμαρτιῶν ἡμῶν, ὅπως ἐξέληται ἡμᾶς ἐκ
sins of us, so as he might deliver us out of

τοῦ αἰῶνος τοῦ ἐνεστῶτος πονηροῦ κατὰ
the [2]age – [1]present [2]evil according to

τὸ θέλημα τοῦ θεοῦ καὶ πατρὸς ἡμῶν,
the will of the God and Father of us,

5 ᾧ ἡ δόξα εἰς τοὺς αἰῶνας τῶν
to whom the glory unto the ages of the
[be]

αἰώνων· ἀμήν.
ages: Amen.

6 I marvel that ye are so soon removed from him that called you into the grace of Christ unto another gospel:

7 Which is not another; but there be some that trouble you, and would pervert the gospel of Christ.

8 But though we, or an angel from heaven, preach any other gospel unto you than that which we have preached unto you, let him be accursed.

9 As we said before, so say I now again, If any *man* preach any other gospel unto you than that ye have received, let him be accursed.

10 For do I now persuade men, or God? or do I seek to please men? for if I yet pleased men, I should not be the servant of Christ.

11 But I certify you, brethren, that the gospel which was preached of me is not after man.

12 For I neither received it of man, neither was I taught *it*, but by the revelation of Jesus Christ.

13 For ye have heard of my conversation in time past in the Jews' religion, how that beyond measure

---

6 Θαυμάζω ὅτι οὕτως ταχέως μετατίθεσθε
  I wonder   that   thus   quickly   ye are removing

ἀπὸ τοῦ καλέσαντος ὑμᾶς ἐν χάριτι
from the [one] having called you by [the] grace

Χριστοῦ εἰς ἕτερον εὐαγγέλιον, 7 ὃ οὐκ
of Christ to another   gospel,   which not

ἔστιν ἄλλο· εἰ μή τινές εἰσιν οἱ ταράσ-
is another; only ²some ¹there are -   troubl-

σοντες ὑμᾶς καὶ θέλοντες μεταστρέψαι
ing   you and wishing   to pervert

τὸ εὐαγγέλιον τοῦ Χριστοῦ. 8 ἀλλὰ
the gospel   -   of Christ.   But

καὶ ἐὰν ἡμεῖς ἢ ἄγγελος ἐξ οὐρανοῦ
even if we or an angel out of heaven

εὐαγγελίσηται [ὑμῖν] παρ’ ὃ εὐηγγελισάμεθα
should preach to you beside what we preached
a gospel

ὑμῖν, ἀνάθεμα ἔστω. 9 ὡς προειρήκαμεν,
to you, ²a curse ¹let him be.   As we have previously said,

καὶ ἄρτι πάλιν λέγω, εἴ τις ὑμᾶς εὐαγ-
also now again I say, if anyone ²you ¹preaches

γελίζεται παρ’ ὃ παρελάβετε, ἀνάθεμα
²a gospel beside what ye received,   ²a curse

ἔστω.
¹let him be.

10 Ἄρτι γὰρ ἀνθρώπους πείθω ἢ τὸν
   For now   men   do I persuade or -

θεόν; ἢ ζητῶ ἀνθρώποις ἀρέσκειν; εἰ
God? or do I seek men   to please? If

ἔτι ἀνθρώποις ἤρεσκον, Χριστοῦ δοῦλος
still men   I pleased, ²of Christ ²a slave

οὐκ ἂν ἤμην. 11 γνωρίζω γὰρ ὑμῖν,
¹I would not have been.   For I make known to you,

ἀδελφοί, τὸ εὐαγγέλιον τὸ εὐαγγελισθὲν
brothers, the gospel   -   preached

ὑπ’ ἐμοῦ ὅτι οὐκ ἔστιν κατὰ ἄνθρωπον
by me that it is not according to man;

12 οὐδὲ γὰρ ἐγὼ παρὰ ἀνθρώπου παρέλαβον
for ⁴not ¹I ⁵from ⁶man   ²received

αὐτὸ οὔτε ἐδιδάχθην, ἀλλὰ δι’ ἀποκαλύψεως
³it nor was I taught but through a revelation
[by man],

Ἰησοῦ Χριστοῦ. 13 Ἠκούσατε γὰρ τὴν
of Jesus Christ.   For ye heard -

ἐμὴν ἀναστροφήν ποτε ἐν τῷ Ἰουδαϊσμῷ,
my conduct then in - Judaism,

ὅτι καθ’ ὑπερβολὴν ἐδίωκον τὴν ἐκκλησίαν
that excessively†   I persecuted the church

I persecuted the church of God, and wasted it:

14 And profited in the Jews' religion above many my equals in mine own nation, being more exceedingly zealous of the traditions of my fathers.

15 But when it pleased God, who separated me from my mother's womb, and called me by his grace,

16 To reveal his Son in me, that I might preach him among the heathen; immediately I conferred not with flesh and blood:

17 Neither went I up to Jerusalem to them which were apostles before me; but I went into Arabia, and returned again unto Damascus.

18 Then after three years I went up to Jerusalem to see Peter, and abode with him fifteen days.

19 But other of the apostles saw I none, save James the Lord's brother.

20 Now the things which I write unto you, behold, before God, I lie not.

21 Afterwards I came into the regions of Syria and Cilicia;

22 And was unknown by face unto the churches

τοῦ θεοῦ καὶ ἐπόρθουν αὐτήν, 14 καὶ
- of God and wasted it, and

προέκοπτον ἐν τῷ Ἰουδαϊσμῷ ὑπὲρ πολλοὺς
progressed in - Judaism beyond many

συνηλικιώτας ἐν τῷ γένει μου, περισ-
contemporaries in the race of me, ²abun-

σοτέρως ζηλωτὴς ὑπάρχων τῶν πατρικῶν
dantly ³a zealot ¹being ⁴of the ⁵ancestral

μου παραδόσεων. 15 Ὅτε δὲ εὐδόκησεν
⁷of me ⁶traditions. But when ¹⁴was pleased

ὁ ἀφορίσας με ἐκ κοιλίας μητρός μου
¹the ²having ³me ⁴from ⁵[the] womb ⁶of mother ⁷of me
[one] separated

καὶ καλέσας διὰ τῆς χάριτος αὐτοῦ
⁸and ⁹having called ¹⁰through ¹¹the ¹²grace ¹³of him

16 ἀποκαλύψαι τὸν υἱὸν αὐτοῦ ἐν ἐμοί,
to reveal the Son of him in me,

ἵνα εὐαγγελίζωμαι αὐτὸν ἐν τοῖς ἔθνεσιν,
in order I might preach him among the nations,
that

εὐθέως οὐ προσανεθέμην σαρκὶ καὶ αἵματι,
immediately I conferred not with flesh and blood,

17 οὐδὲ ἀνῆλθον εἰς Ἱεροσόλυμα πρὸς
neither did I go up to Jerusalem to

τοὺς πρὸ ἐμοῦ ἀποστόλους, ἀλλὰ ἀπῆλθον
¹the ³before ⁴me ²apostles, but I went away

εἰς Ἀραβίαν, καὶ πάλιν ὑπέστρεψα εἰς
into Arabia, and again returned to

Δαμασκόν. 18 Ἔπειτα μετὰ τρία ἔτη
Damascus. Then after three years

ἀνῆλθον εἰς Ἱεροσόλυμα ἱστορῆσαι Κηφᾶν,
I went up to Jerusalem to visit Cephas,

καὶ ἐπέμεινα πρὸς αὐτὸν ἡμέρας δεκαπέντε·
and remained with him days fifteen;

19 ἕτερον δὲ τῶν ἀποστόλων οὐκ εἶδον,
but other of the apostles I saw not,

εἰ μὴ Ἰάκωβον τὸν ἀδελφὸν τοῦ κυρίου.
except James the brother of the Lord.

20 ἃ δὲ γράφω ὑμῖν, ἰδοὺ ἐνώπιον τοῦ
Now what I write to you, behold before -
things

θεοῦ ὅτι οὐ ψεύδομαι. 21 ἔπειτα ἦλθον
God - I lie not. Then I went

εἰς τὰ κλίματα τῆς Συρίας καὶ τῆς
into the regions - of Syria and ~

Κιλικίας. 22 ἤμην δὲ ἀγνοούμενος τῷ
of Cilicia. And I was being unknown -

προσώπῳ ταῖς ἐκκλησίαις τῆς Ἰουδαίας
by face to the churches - of Judæa

of Judæa which were in Christ:

23 But they had heard only, That he which persecuted us in times past now preacheth the faith which once he destroyed.

24 And they glorified God in me.

CHAPTER 2

THEN fourteen years after I went up again to Jerusalem with Barnabas, and took Titus with *me* also.

2 And I went up by revelation, and communicated unto them that gospel which I preach among the Gentiles, but privately to them which were of reputation, lest by any means I should run, or had run, in vain.

3 But neither Titus, who was with me, being a Greek, was compelled to be circumcised:

4 And that because of false brethren unawares brought in, who came in privily to spy out our liberty which we have in Christ Jesus, that they might bring us into bondage:

5 To whom we gave place by subjection, no, not for an hour; that the truth of the gospel might continue with you.

6 But of these who seemed to be somewhat, (whatsoever they were, it maketh no matter to me: God accepteth no man's person:) for they who seemed *to be somewhat* in conference added nothing to me:

ταῖς ἐν Χριστῷ. 23 μόνον δὲ ἀκούοντες
　　　 in 　Christ. 　　But only 　　hearing

ἦσαν ὅτι ὁ διώκων ἡμᾶς ποτε νῦν
they were that the [one] ²persecuting ³us ¹then now

εὐαγγελίζεται τὴν πίστιν ἥν ποτε ἐπόρθει,
preaches 　the 　faith 　which then 　he was
　　　　　　　　　　　　　　　　　destroying,

24 καὶ ἐδόξαζον ἐν ἐμοὶ τὸν θεόν.
　and 　they glorified ²in ³me 　- 　¹God.

2 Ἔπειτα διὰ δεκατεσσάρων ἐτῶν πάλιν
　Then 　through 　fourteen 　　years 　again

ἀνέβην εἰς Ἱεροσόλυμα μετὰ Βαρναβᾶ,
I went up 　to 　Jerusalem 　with 　Barnabas,

συμπαραλαβὼν καὶ Τίτον· 2 ἀνέβην δὲ
taking with [me] 　also 　Titus; 　and I went up

κατὰ ἀποκάλυψιν· καὶ ἀνεθέμην αὐτοῖς
according to a revelation; 　and 　I put before 　them

τὸ εὐαγγέλιον ὃ κηρύσσω ἐν τοῖς ἔθνεσιν,
the 　gospel 　which I proclaim among the 　nations,

κατ' ἰδίαν δὲ τοῖς δοκοῦσιν, μή πως
²privately 　¹but to the [ones] 　seeming,* 　　lest

εἰς κενὸν τρέχω ἢ ἔδραμον. 3 ἀλλ'
in 　vain 　I run 　or 　I ran. 　　But

οὐδὲ Τίτος ὁ σὺν ἐμοί, Ἕλλην ὢν,
not 　Titus 　the [one] with 　me, 　a Greek 　being,

ἠναγκάσθη περιτμηθῆναι· 4 διὰ δὲ τοὺς
was compelled 　to be circumcised; 　but on account of ¹the

παρεισάκτους ψευδαδέλφους, οἵτινες παρεισ-
²brought in secretly ³false brothers, 　　who 　　stole

ἦλθον κατασκοπῆσαι τὴν ἐλευθερίαν ἡμῶν
in 　　to spy on 　the 　freedom 　of us

ἣν ἔχομεν ἐν Χριστῷ Ἰησοῦ, ἵνα ἡμᾶς
which we have in 　Christ 　Jesus, in order that ²us

καταδουλώσουσιν· 5 οἷς οὐδὲ πρὸς ὥραν
¹they will(might) enslave; 　to whom not 　for 　an hour

εἴξαμεν τῇ ὑποταγῇ, ἵνα ἡ ἀλήθεια
yielded we 　- 　in subjection, in order that the 　truth

τοῦ εὐαγγελίου διαμείνῃ πρὸς ὑμᾶς. 6 ἀπὸ
of the 　gospel 　might continue with 　you. 　from

δὲ τῶν δοκούντων εἶναί τι, — ὁποῖοί
But the [ones] 　seeming 　to be something, —(of what kind

ποτε ἦσαν οὐδέν μοι διαφέρει· πρόσωπον
²then ¹they were ⁴nothing ⁵to me ³matters: 　⁶[the] face

[ὁ] θεὸς ἀνθρώπου οὐ λαμβάνει — ἐμοὶ
- 　⁶God 　⁹of a man 　⁷receives not,) 　　²to me

γὰρ οἱ δοκοῦντες οὐδὲν προσανέθεντο,
¹for 　the [ones] seeming* 　nothing 　　added,

---

* Cf. the full expressions in vers. 6 (earlier) and 9.

7 But contrariwise, when they saw that the gospel of the uncircumcision was committed unto me, as *the gospel* of the circumcision *was* unto Peter;

8 (For he that wrought effectually in Peter to the apostleship of the circumcision, the same was mighty in me toward the Gentiles:)

9 And when James, Cephas, and John, who seemed to be pillars, perceived the grace that was given unto me, they gave to me and Barnabas the right hands of fellowship; that we *should go* unto the heathen, and they unto the circumcision.

10 Only *they would* that we should remember the poor; the same which I also was forward to do.

11 But when Peter was come to Antioch, I withstood him to the face, because he was to be blamed.

12 For before that certain came from James, he did eat with the Gentiles: but when they were come, he withdrew and separated himself, fearing them which were of the circumcision.

13 And the other Jews dissembled likewise with him; insomuch that Barnabas also was carried away with their dissimulation.

14 But when I saw that they walked not uprightly according to the truth of the gospel, I said unto

7 ἀλλὰ τοὐναντίον ἰδόντες ὅτι πεπίστευμαι
but on the contrary seeing that I have been entrusted [with]

τὸ εὐαγγέλιον τῆς ἀκροβυστίας καθὼς
the gospel of the uncircumcision as

Πέτρος τῆς περιτομῆς, 8 ὁ γὰρ ἐνεργήσας
Peter [that] of the circumcision, for the [one] operating

Πέτρῳ εἰς ἀποστολὴν τῆς περιτομῆς
in Peter to an apostleship of the circumcision

ἐνήργησεν καὶ ἐμοὶ εἰς τὰ ἔθνη, 9 καὶ
operated also in me to the nations, and

γνόντες τὴν χάριν τὴν δοθεῖσάν μοι,
knowing the grace - given to me,

Ἰάκωβος καὶ Κηφᾶς καὶ Ἰωάννης, οἱ
James and Cephas and John, the

δοκοῦντες στῦλοι εἶναι, δεξιὰς ἔδωκαν
[ones] seeing ²pillars ¹to be, ⁵right [hands] ¹gave

ἐμοὶ καὶ Βαρναβᾷ κοινωνίας, ἵνα ἡμεῖς
²to me ³and ⁴to Barnabas ⁶of fellowship, in order we
                                         that [should

εἰς τὰ ἔθνη, αὐτοὶ δὲ εἰς τὴν περιτομήν·
go] to the nations, but they to the circumcision;

10 μόνον τῶν πτωχῶν ἵνα μνημονεύωμεν,
only ³the ⁴poor *in order* ¹that ²we might remember,

ὁ καὶ ἐσπούδασα αὐτὸ τοῦτο ποιῆσαι.
which indeed ²I was eager ¹this very thing to do.

11 Ὅτε δὲ ἦλθεν Κηφᾶς εἰς Ἀντιόχειαν,
But when ²came ¹Cephas to Antioch,

κατὰ πρόσωπον αὐτῷ ἀντέστην, ὅτι
against [his] face *to* him I opposed, because

κατεγνωσμένος ἦν. 12 πρὸ τοῦ γὰρ
²having been condemned ¹he was. Before the for
                              = For before some came . . .

ἐλθεῖν τινας ἀπὸ Ἰακώβου μετὰ τῶν
to come some[b] from James ²with ¹the

ἐθνῶν συνήσθιεν· ὅτε δὲ ἦλθον, ὑπέστελλεν
⁴nations ¹he ate *with*; but when they came, he withdrew

καὶ ἀφώριζεν ἑαυτόν, φοβούμενος τοὺς
and separated himself, fearing the [ones]

ἐκ περιτομῆς· 13 καὶ συνυπεκρίθησαν αὐτῷ
of [the] circumcision; and dissembled along with him

[καὶ] οἱ λοιποὶ Ἰουδαῖοι, ὥστε καὶ
also the remaining Jews, so as even

Βαρναβᾶς συναπήχθη αὐτῶν τῇ ὑποκρίσει.
Barnabas was led away with ³of them ¹the ²dissembling.

14 ἀλλ’ ὅτε εἶδον ὅτι οὐκ ὀρθοποδοῦσιν
But when I saw that they walk[ed] not straight

πρὸς τὴν ἀλήθειαν τοῦ εὐαγγελίου, εἶπον
with the truth of the gospel, I said

Peter before *them* all, If thou, being a Jew, livest after the manner of Gentiles, and not as do the Jews, why compellest thou the Gentiles to live as do the Jews?

15 We *who are* Jews by nature, and not sinners of the Gentiles,

16 Knowing that a man is not justified by the works of the law, but by the faith of Jesus Christ, even we have believed in Jesus Christ, that we might be justified by the faith of Christ, and not by the works of the law: for by the works of the law shall no flesh be justified.

17 But if, while we seek to be justified by Christ, we ourselves also are found sinners, *is* therefore Christ the minister of sin? God forbid.

18 For if I build again the things which I destroyed, I make myself a transgressor.

19 For I through the law am dead to the law, that I might live unto God.

20 I am crucified with Christ: nevertheless I live; yet not I, but Christ liveth in me: and the life which I now live in the flesh I live by the faith of the Son of God, who loved me, and gave himself for me.

τῷ Κηφᾷ ἔμπροσθεν πάντων· εἰ σὺ
– to Cephas in front of all: If thou
Ἰουδαῖος ὑπάρχων ἐθνικῶς καὶ οὐκ
²a Jew ¹being as a Gentile and not
Ἰουδαϊκῶς ζῆς, πῶς τὰ ἔθνη ἀναγκάζεις
as a Jew livest, how ²the ³nations ¹compellest thou
ἰουδαΐζειν; 15 Ἡμεῖς φύσει Ἰουδαῖοι καὶ
to judaize? We by nature Jews and
οὐκ ἐξ ἐθνῶν ἁμαρτωλοί, 16 εἰδότες δὲ
not ²of ³nations ¹sinners, and knowing
ὅτι οὐ δικαιοῦται ἄνθρωπος ἐξ ἔργων
that ²is not justified ¹a man by works
νόμου ἐὰν μὴ διὰ πίστεως Χριστοῦ
of law except(but) through faith of(in) Christ
Ἰησοῦ, καὶ ἡμεῖς εἰς Χριστὸν Ἰησοῦν
Jesus,* even we ²in ³Christ ⁴Jesus
ἐπιστεύσαμεν, ἵνα δικαιωθῶμεν ἐκ πίστεως
¹believed, in order that we might be by faith
justified
Χριστοῦ καὶ οὐκ ἐξ ἔργων νόμου, ὅτι
of(in) Christ* and not by works of law, because
ἐξ ἔργων νόμου οὐ δικαιωθήσεται πᾶσα
by works of law not will be justified all
=no flesh will be justified.
σάρξ. 17 εἰ δὲ ζητοῦντες δικαιωθῆναι
flesh. But if seeking to be justified
ἐν Χριστῷ εὑρέθημεν καὶ αὐτοὶ ἁμαρτωλοί,
in Christ we were found also [our]selves sinners,
ἆρα Χριστὸς ἁμαρτίας διάκονος; μὴ
then [is] Christ ²of sin ¹a minister? not
γένοιτο. 18 εἰ γὰρ ἃ κατέλυσα ταῦτα
May it be. For if what things I destroyed these things
πάλιν οἰκοδομῶ, παραβάτην ἐμαυτὸν συνισ-
again I build, ³a transgressor ²myself ¹I con-
τάνω. 19 ἐγὼ γὰρ διὰ νόμου νόμῳ
stitute. For I through law ²to law
ἀπέθανον ἵνα θεῷ ζήσω. Χριστῷ συνεσ-
¹died in order to God I might live. With Christ I have
that
ταύρωμαι· 20 ζῶ δὲ οὐκέτι ἐγώ, ζῇ δὲ
been co-crucified; and ²live ³no more ¹I, but ²lives
ἐν ἐμοὶ Χριστός· ὁ δὲ νῦν ζῶ ἐν σαρκί,
³in ⁴me ¹Christ; and what now I live in [the] flesh,
ἐν πίστει ζῶ τῇ τοῦ υἱοῦ τοῦ θεοῦ
²by ³faith ¹I live – of(in) the Son – of God
τοῦ ἀγαπήσαντός με καὶ παραδόντος ἑαυτὸν
– loving me and giving up himself

* Objective genitive, as is shown by the intervening sentence see also 3. 22, 26). *Cf.* " fear of God ".

21 I do not frustrate the grace of God: for if righteousness *come* by the law, then Christ is dead in vain.

ὑπὲρ ἐμοῦ. 21 Οὐκ ἀθετῶ τὴν χάριν
on behalf of me. I do not set aside the grace

τοῦ θεοῦ· εἰ γὰρ διὰ νόμου δικαιοσύνη,
– of God; for if through law righteousness
[comes],

ἄρα Χριστὸς δωρεὰν ἀπέθανεν.
then Christ without cause died.

CHAPTER 3

O FOOLISH Galatians, who hath bewitched you, that ye should not obey the truth, before whose eyes Jesus Christ hath been evidently set forth, crucified among you?

2 This only would I learn of you, Received ye the Spirit by the works of the law, or by the hearing of faith?

3 Are ye so foolish? having begun in the Spirit, are ye now made perfect by the flesh?

4 Have ye suffered so many things in vain? if *it be* yet in vain.

5 He therefore that ministereth to you the Spirit, and worketh miracles among you, *doeth he it* by the works of the law, or by the hearing of faith?

6 Even as Abraham believed God, and it was accounted to him for righteousness.

7 Know ye therefore that they which are of faith, the same are the children of Abraham.

8 And the scripture, foreseeing that God would justify the heathen through faith, preached before the gospel unto Abraham, *saying,* In thee shall all nations be blessed.

9 So then they which be

3 Ὦ ἀνόητοι Γαλάται, τίς ὑμᾶς
O foolish Galatians, who you

ἐβάσκανεν, οἷς κατ' ὀφθαλμοὺς Ἰησοῦς
bewitched, to before eyes Jesus
whom [the]

Χριστὸς προεγράφη ἐσταυρωμένος; 2 τοῦτο
Christ was portrayed having been crucified? This

μόνον θέλω μαθεῖν ἀφ' ὑμῶν, ἐξ ἔργων
only I wish to learn from you, by works

νόμου τὸ πνεῦμα ἐλάβετε ἢ ἐξ ἀκοῆς
of law the Spirit received ye or by hearing

πίστεως; 3 οὕτως ἀνόητοί ἐστε; ἐναρξάμενοι
of faith? thus foolish are ye? having begun

πνεύματι νῦν σαρκὶ ἐπιτελεῖσθε; 4 τοσαῦτα
in [the] Spirit now in [the] flesh are ye being so many things
perfected?

ἐπάθετε εἰκῆ; 5 εἴ γε καὶ εἰκῆ. ὁ
suffered ye in vain? if indeed in vain. The [one]

οὖν ἐπιχορηγῶν ὑμῖν τὸ πνεῦμα καὶ
therefore supplying to you the Spirit and

ἐνεργῶν δυνάμεις ἐν ὑμῖν ἐξ ἔργων
working powerful deeds among you [is it] by works

νόμου ἢ ἐξ ἀκοῆς πίστεως; 6 Καθὼς
of law or by hearing of faith? As

Ἀβραὰμ ἐπίστευσεν τῷ θεῷ, καὶ ἐλογίσθη
Abraham believed – God, and it was reckoned

αὐτῷ εἰς δικαιοσύνην. 7 γινώσκετε ἄρα
to him for righteousness. Know ye then

ὅτι οἱ ἐκ πίστεως, οὗτοι υἱοί εἰσιν
that the [ones] of faith, ¹these ²sons ³are

Ἀβραάμ. 8 προϊδοῦσα δὲ ἡ γραφὴ ὅτι
⁴of Abraham. And ²foreseeing ¹the ²scripture ³that

ἐκ πίστεως δικαιοῖ τὰ ἔθνη ὁ θεός,
⁹by ¹⁰faith ⁶would justify ⁷the ⁸nations – ⁵God,

προευηγγελίσατο τῷ Ἀβραὰμ ὅτι ἐνευλογη-
preached good tidings – to Abraham that ⁶will be
before

θήσονται ἐν σοὶ πάντα τὰ ἔθνη. 9 ὥστε
blessed ¹in ²thee ³all ⁴the ⁵nations. So as

οἱ ἐκ πίστεως εὐλογοῦνται σὺν τῷ πιστῷ
the [ones] of faith are blessed with the believing

of faith are blessed with faithful Abraham.

10 For as many as are of the works of the law are under the curse: for it is written, Cursed is every one that continueth not in all things which are written in the book of the law to do them.

11 But that no man is justified by the law in the sight of God, it is evident: for, The just shall live by faith.

12 And the law is not of faith: but, The man that doeth them shall live in them.

13 Christ hath redeemed us from the curse of the law, being made a curse for us: for it is written, Cursed is every one that hangeth on a tree:

14 That the blessing of Abraham might come on the Gentiles through Jesus Christ; that we might receive the promise of the Spirit through faith.

15 Brethren, I speak after the manner of men; Though it be but a man's covenant, yet if it be confirmed, no man disannulleth, or addeth thereto.

16 Now to Abraham and his seed were the promises made. He saith not, And to seeds, as of many; but as of one, And to thy seed, which is Christ.

17 And this I say, that

Ἀβραάμ.   10 Ὅσοι γὰρ ἐξ ἔργων νόμου
Abraham.   For as many as ²of ³works ⁴of law

εἰσίν, ὑπὸ κατάραν εἰσίν· γέγραπται γὰρ
¹are, ⁶under ⁷a curse ⁵are; for it has been written[,]

ὅτι ἐπικατάρατος πᾶς ὃς οὐκ ἐμμένει
-   Accursed   everyone who   continues not

πᾶσιν τοῖς γεγραμμένοις ἐν τῷ βιβλίῳ
in all   the things having been written   in   the   roll

τοῦ νόμου τοῦ ποιῆσαι αὐτά.   11 ὅτι
of the   law   -   to doᵈ   them.   that

δὲ ἐν νόμῳ οὐδεὶς δικαιοῦται παρὰ τῷ
Now by   law   no man   is justified   before   -

θεῷ δῆλον, ὅτι ὁ δίκαιος ἐκ πίστεως
God [is] clear, because the just man   by   faith

ζήσεται· 12 ὁ δὲ νόμος οὐκ ἔστιν ἐκ
will live;   and the   law   is not   of

πίστεως, ἀλλ' ὁ ποιήσας αὐτὰ ζήσεται
faith,   but the [one] doing   them   will live

ἐν αὐτοῖς. 13 Χριστὸς ἡμᾶς ἐξηγόρασεν
by them.   Christ   ²us   ¹redeemed

ἐκ τῆς κατάρας τοῦ νόμου γενόμενος
out of the   curse   of the   law   becoming

ὑπὲρ ἡμῶν κατάρα, ὅτι γέγραπται·
²on behalf of ³us   ¹a curse,   because   it has been written:

ἐπικατάρατος πᾶς ὁ κρεμάμενος ἐπὶ
Accursed   everyone   hanging   on

ξύλου, 14 ἵνα εἰς τὰ ἔθνη ἡ εὐλογία
a tree,   in order that ⁵to ⁶the ⁷nations ¹the ²blessing

τοῦ Ἀβραὰμ γένηται ἐν Ἰησοῦ Χριστῷ,
-   ³of Abraham ⁴might be   in   Jesus   Christ,

ἵνα τὴν ἐπαγγελίαν τοῦ πνεύματος λάβωμεν
in order ²the   ³promise   ⁴of the ⁵Spirit ¹we might
that   receive

διὰ τῆς πίστεως. 15 Ἀδελφοί, κατὰ
through the   faith.   Brothers,   according to

ἄνθρωπον λέγω. ὅμως ἀνθρώπου κεκυρω-
man   I say. Nevertheless ⁶of man ⁷having been

μένην διαθήκην οὐδεὶς ἀθετεῖ ἢ ἐπιδια-
ratified ²a covenant ¹no one ³sets aside ²or ³makes

τάσσεται. 16 τῷ δὲ Ἀβραὰμ ἐρρέθησαν
additions [to].   -   Now to Abraham   were said

αἱ ἐπαγγελίαι καὶ τῷ σπέρματι αὐτοῦ.
the   promises   and to the   seed   of him.

οὐ λέγει· καὶ τοῖς σπέρμασιν, ὡς ἐπὶ
It says not: And to the   seeds,   as concerning

πολλῶν, ἀλλ' ὡς ἐφ' ἑνός· καὶ τῷ
many,   but   as concerning one: And to the

σπέρματί σου, ὅς ἐστιν Χριστός. 17 τοῦτο δὲ
seed   of thee, who is   Christ.   And this

the covenant, that was confirmed before of God in Christ, the law, which was four hundred and thirty years after, cannot disannul, that it should make the promise of none effect.

18 For if the inheritance *be* of the law, *it is* no more of promise: but God gave *it* to Abraham by promise.

19 Wherefore then *serveth* the law? It was added because of transgressions, till the seed should come to whom the promise was made; *and it was* ordained by angels in the hand of a mediator.

20 Now a mediator is not *a mediator* of one, but God is one.

21 *Is* the law then against the promises of God? God forbid: for if there had been a law given which could have given life, verily righteousness should have been by the law.

22 But the scripture hath concluded all under sin, that the promise by faith of Jesus Christ might be given to them that believe.

23 But before faith came, we were kept under the law, shut up unto the faith which should afterwards be revealed.

24 Wherefore the law was our schoolmaster *to bring us* unto Christ, that

λέγω· διαθήκην προκεκυρωμένην ὑπὸ
I say: [10]A covenant   [11]having been previously ratified   [12]by

τοῦ θεοῦ ὁ μετὰ τετρακόσια καὶ τριάκοντα
–   [13]God   [1]the   [4]after   [5]four hundred   [6]and   [7]thirty

ἔτη γεγονὼς νόμος οὐκ ἀκυροῖ, εἰς τὸ
[8]years   [9]having come   [2]law   [9]does not annul,   so as†
    into being

καταργῆσαι τὴν ἐπαγγελίαν. 18 εἰ γὰρ
to abolish   the   promise.   18 For if

ἐκ νόμου ἡ κληρονομία, οὐκέτι ἐξ
[4]of   [5]law   [1]the   [2]inheritance [3][is],   no more [is it]   of

ἐπαγγελίας· τῷ δὲ Ἀβραὰμ δι᾽ ἐπαγγελίας
promise;   – but   [4]to Abraham   [5]through   [6]promise

κεχάρισται ὁ θεός. 19 Τί οὖν ὁ νόμος;
[2]has given [3][it]   – [1]God.   19 Why therefore the   law?

τῶν παραβάσεων χάριν προσετέθη, ἄχρις
[3]the   [4]transgressions [2]by reason of   [1]it was added,   until

ἂν ἔλθῃ τὸ σπέρμα ᾧ ἐπήγγελται,
[3]should come   [1]the   [2]seed   to whom   it has been promised,

διαταγεὶς δι᾽ ἀγγέλων, ἐν χειρὶ μεσίτου.
being ordained through   angels,   by [the]   hand of a mediator.

20 ὁ δὲ μεσίτης ἑνὸς οὐκ ἔστιν, ὁ
  Now the   mediator   [2]of one   [1]is not,   –

δὲ θεὸς εἷς ἐστιν. 21 ὁ οὖν νόμος κατὰ
but God   [2]one   [1]is.   [Is] the [2]therefore [1]law   against

τῶν ἐπαγγελιῶν [τοῦ θεοῦ]; μὴ γένοιτο.
the   promises   of God?   May it not be.

εἰ γὰρ ἐδόθη νόμος ὁ δυνάμενος ζωοποι-
For if   [2]was given [1]a law   – being able   to make

ῆσαι, ὄντως ἐκ νόμου ἂν ἦν ἡ δικαιοσύνη·
alive,   really   [2]by   [4]law   [1]would –   [1]righteousness;
    have been

22 ἀλλὰ συνέκλεισεν ἡ γραφὴ τὰ πάντα
but   [2]shut up   [1]the   [2]scripture   all mankind†

ὑπὸ ἁμαρτίαν ἵνα ἡ ἐπαγγελία ἐκ πίστεως
under   sin   in or- the   promise   by   faith
    der that

Ἰησοῦ Χριστοῦ δοθῇ τοῖς πιστεύουσιν.
of(in) Jesus   Christ   might be given to the [ones] believing.

23 Πρὸ τοῦ δὲ ἐλθεῖν τὴν πίστιν ὑπὸ
  before   *the*   But   to come   *the*   faith[b]   under
  =But before faith came

νόμον ἐφρουρούμεθα συγκλειόμενοι εἰς τὴν
law   we were guarded   being shut up   to   the

μέλλουσαν πίστιν ἀποκαλυφθῆναι. 24 ὥστε
[2]being about   [1]faith   to be revealed.   24 So as

ὁ νόμος παιδαγωγὸς ἡμῶν γέγονεν εἰς
the   law   [2]a trainer   [3]of us   [1]has become [up] to

we might be justified by faith.

25 But after that faith is come, we are no longer under a schoolmaster.

26 For ye are all the children of God by faith in Christ Jesus.

27 For as many of you as have been baptized into Christ have put on Christ.

28 There is neither Jew nor Greek, there is neither bond nor free, there is neither male nor female: for ye are all one in Christ Jesus.

29 And if ye *be* Christ's, then are ye Abraham's seed, and heirs according to the promise.

CHAPTER 4

NOW I say, *That* the heir, as long as he is a child, differeth nothing from a servant, though he be lord of all;

2 But is under tutors and governors until the time appointed of the father.

3 Even so we, when we were children, were in bondage under the elements of the world:

4 But when the fulness of the time was come, God sent forth his Son, made of a woman, made under the law,

5 To redeem them that were under the law, that we might receive the adoption of sons.

6 And because ye are

Χριστόν, ἵνα ἐκ πίστεως δικαιωθῶμεν·
Christ, in order that by faith we might be justified;

25 ἐλθούσης δὲ τῆς πίστεως οὐκέτι ὑπὸ
but ³having come ¹the ²faith³ ²no more ⁴under

παιδαγωγόν ἐσμεν. 26 Πάντες γὰρ υἱοὶ
⁷a trainer ⁴we are. For all sons

θεοῦ ἐστε διὰ τῆς πίστεως ἐν Χριστῷ
of God ye are through the faith in Christ

Ἰησοῦ· 27 ὅσοι γὰρ εἰς Χριστὸν ἐβαπτίσ-
Jesus; for as many as ²into ³Christ ¹ye were

θητε, Χριστὸν ἐνεδύσασθε. 28 οὐκ ἔνι
baptized, ²Christ ¹ye put on. There cannot be

Ἰουδαῖος οὐδὲ Ἕλλην, οὐκ ἔνι δοῦλος
Jew nor Greek, there cannot be slave

οὐδὲ ἐλεύθερος, οὐκ ἔνι ἄρσεν καὶ θῆλυ·
nor freeman, there cannot be male and female;

πάντες γὰρ ὑμεῖς εἷς ἐστε ἐν Χριστῷ
for ²all ¹ye ⁴one ²are in Christ

Ἰησοῦ. 29 εἰ δὲ ὑμεῖς Χριστοῦ, ἄρα
Jesus. But if ye [are] of Christ, then

τοῦ Ἀβραὰμ σπέρμα ἐστέ, κατ᾽ ἐπαγγελίαν
– ³of Abraham ²a seed ¹are ye, according to promise

κληρονόμοι. 4 Λέγω δέ, ἐφ᾽ ὅσον χρόνον ὁ
heirs. But I say, over so long a time as the

κληρονόμος νήπιός ἐστιν, οὐδὲν διαφέρει
heir ²an infant ¹is, ³nothing ¹he differs
²[from]

δούλου κύριος πάντων ὤν, 2 ἀλλὰ ὑπὸ
⁴a slave ⁶lord ⁷of all ⁵being, but ¹under

ἐπιτρόπους ἐστὶν καὶ οἰκονόμους ἄχρι τῆς
²guardians ¹is and stewards until the

προθεσμίας τοῦ πατρός. 3 οὕτως καὶ
term previously of the father. So also
appointed

ἡμεῖς, ὅτε ἦμεν νήπιοι, ὑπὸ τὰ στοιχεῖα
we, when we were infants, under the elements

τοῦ κόσμου ἤμεθα δεδουλωμένοι· 4 ὅτε
of the world we were *having been* enslaved; when

δὲ ἦλθεν τὸ πλήρωμα τοῦ χρόνου,
but came the fulness of the time,

ἐξαπέστειλεν ὁ θεὸς τὸν υἱὸν αὐτοῦ,
sent forth – God the Son of him,

γενόμενον ἐκ γυναικός, γενόμενον ὑπὸ
becoming of a woman, becoming under

νόμον, 5 ἵνα τοὺς ὑπὸ νόμον ἐξαγοράσῃ,
law, in order that ²the ones ³under ⁴law ¹he might redeem,

ἵνα τὴν υἱοθεσίαν ἀπολάβωμεν. 6 Ὅτι δέ
in order ²the ³adoption of sons ¹we might receive. And because
that

sons, God hath sent forth the Spirit of his Son into your hearts, crying, Abba, Father.

ἐστε   υἱοί,   ἐξαπέστειλεν   ὁ   θεὸς   τὸ
ye are   sons,   ²sent forth   -   ¹God   the

πνεῦμα   τοῦ   υἱοῦ   αὐτοῦ   εἰς   τὰς   καρδίας
Spirit   of the   Son   of him   into   the   hearts

7 Wherefore thou art no more a servant, but a son; and if a son, then an heir of God through Christ.

ἡμῶν,   κρᾶζον·   ἀββὰ   ὁ   πατήρ.   7 ὥστε
of us,   crying: Abba   -   Father.   So as

οὐκέτι   εἶ   δοῦλος   ἀλλὰ   υἱός·   εἰ   δὲ   υἱός,
no more art thou a slave   but   a son;   and if   a son,

καὶ   κληρονόμος   διὰ   θεοῦ.
also   an heir   through   God.

8 Howbeit then, when ye knew not God, ye did service unto them which by nature are no gods.

8 Ἀλλὰ   τότε   μὲν   οὐκ   εἰδότες   θεὸν
But   then   indeed   not   knowing   God

ἐδουλεύσατε   τοῖς   φύσει   μὴ   οὖσιν   θεοῖς·
ye served as slaves   ¹the   ³by nature   ⁴not   ⁵being   ²gods;

9 But now, after that ye have known God, or rather are known of God, how turn ye again to the weak and beggarly elements, whereunto ye desire again to be in bondage?

9 νῦν   δὲ   γνόντες   θεόν,   μᾶλλον   δὲ
but now   knowing   God,   but rather

γνωσθέντες   ὑπὸ   θεοῦ,   πῶς   ἐπιστρέφετε
being known   by   God,   how   turn ye

πάλιν   ἐπὶ   τὰ   ἀσθενῆ   καὶ   πτωχὰ   στοιχεῖα,
again   to the   weak   and   poor   elements,

οἷς   πάλιν   ἄνωθεν   δουλεῦσαι   θέλετε;
to which   again   ²anew   ³to serve   ¹ye wish?

10 Ye observe days, and months, and times, and years.

10 ἡμέρας   παρατηρεῖσθε   καὶ   μῆνας   καὶ
²days   ¹Ye observe   and   months   and

καιροὺς   καὶ   ἐνιαυτούς.   11 φοβοῦμαι   ὑμᾶς
seasons   and   years.   I fear [for]   you

11 I am afraid of you, lest I have bestowed upon you labour in vain.

μή   πως   εἰκῇ   κεκοπίακα   εἰς   ὑμᾶς.
lest   in vain   I have laboured   among   you.

12 Brethren, I beseech you, be as I am; for I am as ye are: ye have not injured me at all.

12 Γίνεσθε   ὡς   ἐγώ,   ὅτι   κἀγὼ   ὡς
Be ye   as   I [am],   because   I also [am]   as

ὑμεῖς,   ἀδελφοί,   δέομαι   ὑμῶν.   οὐδέν   με
ye [are],   brothers,   I beg   of you.   Nothing   me

13 Ye know how through infirmity of the flesh I preached the gospel unto you at the first.

ἠδικήσατε·   13 οἴδατε   δὲ   ὅτι   δι'   ἀσθένειαν
ye wronged;   and ye know   that an account of   weakness

τῆς   σαρκὸς   εὐηγγελισάμην   ὑμῖν   τὸ
of the   flesh   I preached good tidings   to you   -

14 And my temptation which was in my flesh ye despised not, nor rejected; but received me as an angel of God, even as Christ Jesus.

πρότερον,   14 καὶ   τὸν   πειρασμὸν   ὑμῶν
formerly,   and   the   trial   of you

ἐν   τῇ   σαρκί   μου   οὐκ   ἐξουθενήσατε   οὐδὲ
in   the   flesh   of me   ye despised not   nor

ἐξεπτύσατε,   ἀλλὰ   ὡς   ἄγγελον   θεοῦ   ἐδέξασθέ
disdained ye,   but   as   a messenger of God   ye received

15 Where is then the blessedness ye spake of? for I bear you record, that, if it had been possible, ye would have plucked out

με,   ὡς   Χριστὸν   Ἰησοῦν.   15 ποῦ   οὖν
me,   as   Christ   Jesus.   Where therefore

ὁ   μακαρισμὸς   ὑμῶν;   μαρτυρῶ   γὰρ   ὑμῖν
the   felicitation   of you?*   for I witness   to you

ὅτι   εἰ   δυνατὸν   τοὺς   ὀφθαλμοὺς   ὑμῶν
that   if   possible   ²the   ³eyes   ⁴of you

* That is, "your felicitation [of me]".

your own eyes, and have given them to me.

16 Am I therefore become your enemy, because I tell you the truth?

17 They zealously affect you, *but* not well; yea, they would exclude you, that ye might affect them.

18 But *it is* good to be zealously affected always in *a* good *thing*, and not only when I am present with you.

19 My little children, of whom I travail in birth again until Christ be formed in you,

20 I desire to be present with you now, and to change my voice; for I stand in doubt of you.

21 Tell me, ye that desire to be under the law, do ye not hear the law?

22 For it is written, that Abraham had two sons, the one by a bondmaid, the other by a freewoman.

23 But he *who was* of the bondwoman was born after the flesh; but he of the freewoman *was* by promise.

24 Which things are an allegory: for these are the two covenants; the one from the mount Sinai, which gendereth to bondage, which is Agar.

25 For this Agar is mount Sinai in Arabia, and answereth to Jerusalem which now is, and is in bondage with her children.

ἐξορύξαντες ἐδώκατέ μοι. 16 ὥστε ἐχθρὸς
¹gouging out ye gave [them] to me. So that ²an enemy

ὑμῶν γέγονα ἀληθεύων ὑμῖν; 17 ζηλοῦσιν
³of you ¹have I become speaking truth to you? They are zealous of

ὑμᾶς οὐ καλῶς, ἀλλὰ ἐκκλεῖσαι ὑμᾶς
you not well, but ²to exclude ³you

θέλουσιν, 18 ἵνα αὐτοὺς ζηλοῦτε. καλὸν δὲ
¹wish, in order them ye may be But [it is] good
that zealous of.

ζηλοῦσθαι ἐν καλῷ πάντοτε, καὶ μὴ
to be zealous in a good thing always, and not

μόνον ἐν τῷ παρεῖναί με πρὸς ὑμᾶς,
only in the to be present me^be with you,
=when I am present

19 τέκνα μου, οὓς πάλιν ὠδίνω μέχρις οὗ
children of me,[for] whom again I travail until
in birth

μορφωθῇ Χριστὸς ἐν ὑμῖν· 20 ἤθελον δὲ
²is formed ¹Christ in you; and I wished

παρεῖναι πρὸς ὑμᾶς ἄρτι καὶ ἀλλάξαι
to be present with you just now and to change

τὴν φωνήν μου, ὅτι ἀποροῦμαι ἐν ὑμῖν.
the voice of me, because I am perplexed in(about) you.

21 Λέγετέ μοι, οἱ ὑπὸ νόμον θέλοντες
Tell me, the [ones] ³under ⁴law ¹wishing

εἶναι, τὸν νόμον οὐκ ἀκούετε; 22 γέγραπται
²to be, ²the ³law ¹hear ye not? ²it has been written

γὰρ ὅτι Ἀβραὰμ δύο υἱοὺς ἔσχεν, ἕνα
¹for that Abraham two sons had, one

ἐκ τῆς παιδίσκης καὶ ἕνα ἐκ τῆς ἐλευ-
of the maidservant and one of the free

θέρας. 23 ἀλλ᾽ ὁ [μὲν] ἐκ τῆς παιδίσκης
woman. But the [one] indeed of the maidservant

κατὰ σάρκα γεγέννηται, ὁ δὲ ἐκ τῆς
according to flesh has been born, and the [one] of the

ἐλευθέρας διὰ τῆς ἐπαγγελίας. 24 ἅτινά
free woman through the promise. Which things

ἐστιν ἀλληγορούμενα· αὗται γὰρ εἰσιν
is(are) being allegorized; for these are

δύο διαθῆκαι, μία μὲν ἀπὸ ὄρους Σινά,
two covenants, one indeed from mount Sina,

εἰς δουλείαν γεννῶσα, ἥτις ἐστὶν Ἁγάρ.
to slavery bringing forth, which is Hagar.

25 τὸ δὲ Ἁγὰρ Σινὰ ὄρος ἐστὶν ἐν
⁴The ²now ⁵Hagar ⁴Sina ⁵mount ³is in

τῇ Ἀραβίᾳ· συστοιχεῖ δὲ τῇ νῦν
- Arabia; and corresponds to the now

Ἰερουσαλήμ, δουλεύει γὰρ μετὰ τῶν
Jerusalem, for she serves as a slave with the

26 But Jerusalem which is above is free, which is the mother of us all.

27 For it is written, Rejoice, *thou* barren that bearest not; break forth and cry, thou that travailest not: for the desolate hath many more children than she which hath an husband.

28 Now we, brethren, as Isaac was, are the children of promise.

29 But as then he that was born after the flesh persecuted him *that was born* after the Spirit, even so *it is* now.

30 Nevertheless what saith the scripture? Cast out the bondwoman and her son: for the son of the bondwoman shall not be heir with the son of the freewoman.

31 So then, brethren, we are not children of the bondwoman, but of the free.

τέκνων αὐτῆς. 26 ἡ δὲ ἄνω Ἰερουσαλὴμ
children of her.   But the above   Jerusalem

ἐλευθέρα ἐστίν, ἥτις ἐστὶν μήτηρ ἡμῶν·
free   is,   who   is   mother of us;

27 γέγραπται γάρ· εὐφράνθητι, στεῖρα ἡ
for it has been written: Be thou glad, barren[,] the
                                              [one]

οὐ τίκτουσα, ῥῆξον καὶ βόησον, ἡ οὐκ
not bearing, break forth and shout, the [one] not

ὠδίνουσα· ὅτι πολλὰ τὰ τέκνα τῆς ἐρήμου
travailing; because many [are] the children of the desolate

μᾶλλον ἢ τῆς ἐχούσης τὸν ἄνδρα. 28 ὑμεῖς
rather than of the having   the husband.   ye
         [one]

δέ, ἀδελφοί, κατὰ Ἰσαὰκ ἐπαγγελίας τέκνα
But, brothers, ²according to ¹Isaac ³of promise ⁴children

ἐστέ. 29 ἀλλ' ὥσπερ τότε ὁ κατὰ σάρκα
¹are. But even as then the [one] according to flesh

γεννηθεὶς ἐδίωκεν τὸν κατὰ πνεῦμα, οὕτως
born   persecuted the [one] according spirit,   so
                     [born] to

καὶ νῦν. 30 ἀλλὰ τί λέγει ἡ γραφή;
also now. But what says the scripture?

ἔκβαλε τὴν παιδίσκην καὶ τὸν υἱὸν αὐτῆς·
Cast out the maidservant and the son   of her;

οὐ γὰρ μὴ κληρονομήσει ὁ υἱὸς τῆς
for by no means ²shall inherit ¹the ²son ³of the

παιδίσκης μετὰ τοῦ υἱοῦ τῆς ἐλευθέρας.
⁴maidservant with the son of the free woman.

31 διό, ἀδελφοί, οὐκ ἐσμὲν παιδίσκης
Wherefore, brothers, we are not ²of a maidservant

τέκνα ἀλλὰ τῆς ἐλευθέρας.
¹children but of the free woman.

CHAPTER 5

STAND fast therefore in the liberty wherewith Christ hath made us free, and be not entangled again with the yoke of bondage.

2 Behold, I Paul say unto you, that if ye be circumcised, Christ shall profit you nothing.

3 For I testify again to every man that is circum-

5 Τῇ ἐλευθερίᾳ ἡμᾶς Χριστὸς ἠλευθέρωσεν·
For the freedom ²us ¹Christ ²freed;

στήκετε οὖν καὶ μὴ πάλιν ζυγῷ δουλείας
stand firm therefore and not again with a yoke of slavery

ἐνέχεσθε.
be entangled.

2 Ἴδε ἐγὼ Παῦλος λέγω ὑμῖν ὅτι
Behold[,] I Paul tell you that

ἐὰν περιτέμνησθε Χριστὸς ὑμᾶς οὐδὲν
if ye are circumcised Christ ²you ²nothing

ὠφελήσει. 3 μαρτύρομαι δὲ πάλιν παντὶ
¹will profit. And I testify again to every

ἀνθρώπῳ περιτεμνομένῳ ὅτι ὀφειλέτης ἐστὶν
man   being circumcised that ²a debtor ¹he is

cised, that he is a debtor to do the whole law.

4 Christ is become of no effect unto you, whosoever of you are justified by the law; ye are fallen from grace.

5 For we through the Spirit wait for the hope of righteousness by faith.

6 For in Jesus Christ neither circumcision availeth any thing, nor uncircumcision; but faith which worketh by love.

7 Ye did run well; who did hinder you that ye should not obey the truth?

8 This persuasion *cometh* not of him that calleth you.

9 A little leaven leaveneth the whole lump.

10 I have confidence in you through the Lord, that ye will be none otherwise minded: but he that troubleth you shall bear his judgment, whosoever he be.

11 And I, brethren, if I yet preach circumcision, why do I yet suffer persecution? then is the offence of the cross ceased.

12 I would they were even cut off which trouble you.

13 For, brethren, ye have been called unto liberty; only *use* not liberty for an occasion to the flesh, but by love serve one another.

14 For all the law is fulfilled in one word, *even* in this; Thou shalt love thy neighbour as thyself.

ὅλον τὸν νόμον ποιῆσαι. 4 κατηργήθητε
all the law to do. Ye were discharged

ἀπὸ Χριστοῦ οἵτινες ἐν νόμῳ δικαιοῦσθε,
from Christ who by law are justified,

τῆς χάριτος ἐξεπέσατε. 5 ἡμεῖς γὰρ
the grace ye fell from. For we

πνεύματι ἐκ πίστεως ἐλπίδα δικαιοσύνης
in spirit by faith [the] hope of righteousness

ἀπεκδεχόμεθα. 6 ἐν γὰρ Χριστῷ Ἰησοῦ
eagerly expect. For in Christ Jesus

οὔτε περιτομή τι ἰσχύει οὔτε ἀκροβυστία,
neither circumcision ²anything ¹avails nor uncircumcision,

ἀλλὰ πίστις δι᾽ ἀγάπης ἐνεργουμένη.
but faith ²through ³love ¹operating.

7 Ἐτρέχετε καλῶς· τίς ὑμᾶς ἐνέκοψεν
Ye were running well: who ²you ¹hindered

ἀληθείᾳ μὴ πείθεσθαι; 8 ἡ πεισμονὴ οὐκ
⁵by truth ³not ⁴to be persuaded? the(this) persuasion not

ἐκ τοῦ καλοῦντος ὑμᾶς. 9 μικρὰ ζύμη
of the [one] calling you. A little leaven

ὅλον τὸ φύραμα ζυμοῖ. 10 ἐγὼ πέποιθα
all the lump leavens. I trust

εἰς ὑμᾶς ἐν κυρίῳ ὅτι οὐδὲν ἄλλο φρο-
as to† you in [the] Lord that ²nothing ³other ¹ye

νήσετε· ὁ δὲ ταράσσων ὑμᾶς βαστάσει
will think; but the [one] troubling you shall bear

τὸ κρίμα, ὅστις ἐὰν ᾖ. 11 Ἐγὼ δέ,
the judgment, whoever he may be. ¹But ²I,

ἀδελφοί, εἰ περιτομὴν ἔτι κηρύσσω, τί
²brothers, ³if ¹circumcision ⁵still ⁶proclaim, why

ἔτι διώκομαι; ἄρα κατήργηται τὸ
still am I being persecuted? then has been annulled the

σκάνδαλον τοῦ σταυροῦ. 12 Ὄφελον καὶ
offence of the cross. I would that indeed

ἀποκόψονται οἱ ἀναστατοῦντες ὑμᾶς.
⁴will(might) cut ¹the [ones] ²unsettling ³you.
themselves off

13 Ὑμεῖς γὰρ ἐπ᾽ ἐλευθερίᾳ ἐκλήθητε,
For ye for freedom were called,

ἀδελφοί· μόνον μὴ τὴν ἐλευθερίαν εἰς
brothers; only [use] not the freedom for

ἀφορμὴν τῇ σαρκί, ἀλλὰ διὰ τῆς ἀγάπης
advantage to the flesh, but through – love

δουλεύετε ἀλλήλοις. 14 ὁ γὰρ πᾶς νόμος
serve ye as slaves one another. For the whole law

ἐν ἑνὶ λόγῳ πεπλήρωται, ἐν τῷ· ἀγα-
in one word has been summed up, in the [word]: Thou

πήσεις τὸν πλησίον σου ὡς σεαυτόν.
shalt love the neighbour of thee as thyself.

15 But if ye bite and devour one another, take heed that ye be not consumed one of another.

16 *This* I say then, Walk in the Spirit, and ye shall not fulfil the lust of the flesh.

17 For the flesh lusteth against the Spirit, and the Spirit against the flesh: and these are contrary the one to the other: so that ye cannot do the things that ye would.

18 But if ye be led of the Spirit, ye are not under the law.

19 Now the works of the flesh are manifest, which are *these;* Adultery, fornication, uncleanness, lasciviousness,

20 Idolatry, witchcraft, hatred, variance, emulations, wrath, strife, seditions, heresies,

21 Envyings, murders, drunkenness, revellings, and such like: of the which I tell you before, as I have also told *you* in time past, that they which do such things shall not inherit the kingdom of God.

22 But the fruit of the Spirit is love, joy, peace, longsuffering, gentleness, goodness, faith,

23 Meekness, temperance: against such there is no law.

24 And they that are Christ's have crucified the flesh with the affections and lusts.

25 If we live in the Spirit, let us also walk in the Spirit.

---

15 εἰ δὲ ἀλλήλους δάκνετε καὶ κατεσθίετε,
But if ⁴one another ¹ye bite ²and ³ye devour,

βλέπετε μὴ ὑπ᾽ ἀλλήλων ἀναλωθῆτε.
see lest by one another ye are destroyed.

16 Λέγω δέ, πνεύματι περιπατεῖτε καὶ
Now I say, in spirit walk ye and

ἐπιθυμίαν σαρκὸς οὐ μὴ τελέσητε. **17** ἡ
[the] lust of [the] flesh by no means ye will perform. the

γὰρ σὰρξ ἐπιθυμεῖ κατὰ τοῦ πνεύματος,
For flesh lusts against the spirit,

τὸ δὲ πνεῦμα κατὰ τῆς σαρκός, ταῦτα
and the spirit against the flesh, ²these

γὰρ ἀλλήλοις ἀντίκειται, ἵνα μὴ ἃ ἐὰν
¹for ⁴each other ²opposes, lest whatever things

θέλητε ταῦτα ποιῆτε. **18** εἰ δὲ πνεύματι
ye wish these ye do. But if by [the] Spirit

ἄγεσθε, οὐκ ἐστὲ ὑπὸ νόμον. **19** φανερὰ δέ
ye are led, ye are not under law. Now ⁶manifest

ἐστιν τὰ ἔργα τῆς σαρκός, ἅτινά ἐστιν
⁵is(are) ¹the ²works ³of the ⁴flesh, which is(are)

πορνεία, ἀκαθαρσία, ἀσέλγεια, **20** εἰδωλο-
fornication, uncleanness, lewdness, idola-

λατρία, φαρμακεία, ἔχθραι, ἔρις, ζῆλος,
try, sorcery, enmities, strife, jealousy,

θυμοί, ἐριθεῖαι, διχοστασίαι, αἱρέσεις,
angers, rivalries, divisions, sects,

21 φθόνοι, μέθαι, κῶμοι, καὶ τὰ ὅμοια
envyings, drunken- revellings, and – like
nesses, things

τούτοις, ἃ προλέγω ὑμῖν καθὼς προεῖπον,
to these, which I tell ²beforehand ¹you as I previously said,

ὅτι οἱ τὰ τοιαῦτα πράσσοντες βασιλείαν
that the [ones] – ²such things ¹practising ⁴[the] kingdom

θεοῦ οὐ κληρονομήσουσιν. **22** ὁ δὲ καρπὸς
³of God ⁵will not inherit. But the fruit

τοῦ πνεύματός ἐστιν ἀγάπη, χαρά, εἰρήνη,
of the Spirit is love, joy, peace,

μακροθυμία, χρηστότης, ἀγαθωσύνη, πίστις,
longsuffering, kindness, goodness, faithfulness,

23 πραΰτης, ἐγκράτεια· κατὰ τῶν τοιούτων
meekness, self-control; against – such things

οὐκ ἔστιν νόμος. **24** οἱ δὲ τοῦ Χριστοῦ
there is no law. Now the ones – of Christ

Ἰησοῦ τὴν σάρκα ἐσταύρωσαν σὺν τοῖς
Jesus ²the ³flesh ¹crucified with the(its)

παθήμασιν καὶ ταῖς ἐπιθυμίαις. **25** Εἰ
passions and the(its) lusts. If

ζῶμεν πνεύματι, πνεύματι καὶ στοιχῶμεν.
we live in [the] Spirit, in [the] Spirit also let us walk.

26 Let us not be desirous of vain glory, provoking one another, envying one another.

CHAPTER 6

BRETHREN, if a man be overtaken in a fault, ye which are spiritual, restore such an one in the spirit of meekness; considering thyself, lest thou also be tempted.

2 Bear ye one another's burdens, and so fulfil the law of Christ.

3 For if a man think himself to be something, when he is nothing, he deceiveth himself.

4 But let every man prove his own work, and then shall he have rejoicing in himself alone, and not in another.

5 For every man shall bear his own burden.

6 Let him that is taught in the word communicate unto him that teacheth in all good things.

7 Be not deceived; God is not mocked: for whatsoever a man soweth, that shall he also reap.

8 For he that soweth to his flesh shall of the flesh reap corruption; but he that soweth to the Spirit shall of the Spirit reap life everlasting.

9 And let us not be weary in well doing: for

26 μὴ γινώμεθα κενόδοξοι, ἀλλήλους
Let us not become vainglorious, one another

προκαλούμενοι, ἀλλήλοις φθονοῦντες.
provoking, one another envying.

6 Ἀδελφοί, ἐὰν καὶ προλημφθῇ ἄνθρω-
Brothers, if indeed ²is overtaken ¹a

πος ἔν τινι παραπτώματι, ὑμεῖς οἱ
man in some trespass, ye the

πνευματικοὶ καταρτίζετε τὸν τοιοῦτον ἐν
spiritual [ones] restore – such a one in

πνεύματι πραΰτητος, σκοπῶν σεαυτόν, μὴ
a spirit of meekness, considering thyself, lest

καὶ σὺ πειρασθῇς· 2 Ἀλλήλων τὰ βάρη
also thou art tempted. Of one another the loads

βαστάζετε, καὶ οὕτως ἀναπληρώσετε τὸν
bear ye, and so ye will fulfil the

νόμον τοῦ Χριστοῦ. 3 εἰ γὰρ δοκεῖ
law – of Christ. For if ²thinks

τις εἶναί τι μηδὲν ὤν, φρεναπατᾷ ἑαυτόν.
¹anyone ²to be ³some- ⁴no- ⁵being, he deceives himself.
thing, thing

4 τὸ δὲ ἔργον ἑαυτοῦ δοκιμαζέτω ἕκαστος,
But the work of himself ¹let ²prove ²each man,

καὶ τότε εἰς ἑαυτὸν μόνον τὸ καύχημα
and then in himself alone the boast

ἕξει καὶ οὐκ εἰς τὸν ἕτερον· 5 ἕκαστος
he will and not in the other man; ²each man
have

γὰρ τὸ ἴδιον φορτίον βαστάσει. 6 Κοινωνείτω δὲ
¹for the(his) own burden will bear. And ³let him share

ὁ κατηχούμενος τὸν λόγον τῷ κατη-
¹the ²being instructed [in] ³the ⁴word ⁵with the [one] in-
[one]

χοῦντι ἐν πᾶσιν ἀγαθοῖς. 7 Μὴ πλανᾶσθε,
structing in all good things. Be ye not led astray,

θεὸς οὐ μυκτηρίζεται. ὃ γὰρ ἐὰν σπείρῃ
God is not mocked. For whatever ²may sow

ἄνθρωπος, τοῦτο καὶ θερίσει· 8 ὅτι ὁ
¹a man, this also he will reap; because the

σπείρων εἰς τὴν σάρκα ἑαυτοῦ ἐκ τῆς
[one] sowing to the flesh of himself of the

σαρκὸς θερίσει φθοράν, ὁ δὲ σπείρων
flesh will reap corruption, but the [one] sowing

εἰς τὸ πνεῦμα ἐκ τοῦ πνεύματος θερίσει
to the spirit of the Spirit will reap

ζωὴν αἰώνιον. τὸ δὲ καλὸν ποιοῦντες
life eternal. And ²the ³good ¹doing

μὴ ἐγκακῶμεν· 9 καιρῷ γὰρ ἰδίῳ
let us not lose heart; for in its own time

in due season we shall reap, if we faint not.

10 As we have therefore opportunity, let us do good unto all *men*, especially unto them who are of the household of faith.

11 Ye see how large a letter I have written unto you with mine own hand.

12 As many as desire to make a fair shew in the flesh, they constrain you to be circumcised; only lest they should suffer persecution for the cross of Christ.

13 For neither they themselves who are circumcised keep the law; but desire to have you circumcised, that they may glory in your flesh.

14 But God forbid that I should glory, save in the cross of our Lord Jesus Christ, by whom the world is crucified unto me, and I unto the world.

15 For in Christ Jesus neither circumcision availeth any thing, nor uncircumcision, but a new creature.

16 And as many as walk according to this rule, peace *be* on them, and mercy, and upon the Israel of God.

17 From henceforth let no man trouble me: for I bear in my body the marks of the Lord Jesus.

θερίσομεν   μὴ   ἐκλυόμενοι.   **10** Ἄρα   οὖν
we shall reap   not   failing.   Then therefore

ὡς   καιρὸν   ἔχομεν,   ἐργαζώμεθα   τὸ   ἀγαθὸν
as   ²time   ¹we have,   let us do   the   good

πρὸς   πάντας,   μάλιστα   δὲ   πρὸς   τοὺς
to   all men,   and most of all   to   the

οἰκείους   τῆς   πίστεως.
members of   of the   faith.
the family

11 Ἴδετε   πηλίκοις   ὑμῖν   γράμμασιν
Ye see   in how large   ²to you   ¹letters

ἔγραψα   τῇ   ἐμῇ   χειρί.   **12** Ὅσοι   θέλουσιν
¹I wrote   -   with my   hand.   As many as   wish

εὐπροσωπῆσαι   ἐν   σαρκί,   οὗτοι   ἀναγκάζουσιν
to look well   in [the] flesh,   these   compel

ὑμᾶς   περιτέμνεσθαι,   μόνον   ἵνα   τῷ
you   to be circumcised,   only   in order that   ²for the

σταυρῷ   τοῦ   Χριστοῦ   [Ἰησοῦ]   μὴ
⁴cross   -   ³of Christ   ³Jesus   ¹not

διώκωνται.   **13** οὐδὲ   γὰρ   οἱ   περιτεμνόμενοι
²they are persecuted.   For ⁵not   ¹the [ones]   ³being circumcised

αὐτοὶ   νόμον   φυλάσσουσιν,   ἀλλὰ   θέλουσιν
²themselves   ⁴law   ³keep,   but   they wish

ὑμᾶς   περιτέμνεσθαι   ἵνα   ἐν   τῇ   ὑμετέρᾳ
you   to be circumcised   in order that   ²in   -   ³your

σαρκὶ   καυχήσωνται.   **14** ἐμοὶ   δὲ   μὴ   γένοιτο
⁴flesh   ¹they may boast.   But to me   may it not be

καυχᾶσθαι   εἰ   μὴ   ἐν   τῷ   σταυρῷ   τοῦ
to boast   except   in   the   cross   of the

κυρίου   ἡμῶν   Ἰησοῦ   Χριστοῦ,   δι'   οὗ
Lord   of us   Jesus   Christ,   through whom

ἐμοὶ   κόσμος   ἐσταύρωται   κἀγὼ   κόσμῳ.
to me   [the] world   has been crucified   and I to [the] world.

15 οὔτε   γὰρ   περιτομή   τί   ἐστιν   οὔτε
For neither   circumcision   ²anything   ¹is   nor

ἀκροβυστία,   ἀλλὰ   καινὴ   κτίσις.   **16** καὶ
uncircumcision,   but   a new   creation.   And

ὅσοι   τῷ   κανόνι   τούτῳ   στοιχήσουσιν,
as many as   by this rule   will walk,

εἰρήνη   ἐπ'   αὐτοὺς   καὶ   ἔλεος,   καὶ   ἐπὶ   τὸν
peace   on   them   and   mercy,   and   on   the

Ἰσραὴλ   τοῦ   θεοῦ.
Israel   -   of God.

17 Τοῦ   λοιποῦ   κόπους   μοι   μηδεὶς
For the rest   ⁵troubles   ⁴me   ²no one

παρεχέτω·   ἐγὼ   γὰρ   τὰ   στίγματα   τοῦ
¹let ³cause;   for ¹I   ³the   ⁴brands   -

Ἰησοῦ   ἐν   τῷ   σώματί   μου   βαστάζω.
⁵of Jesus   ⁶in   ⁷the   ⁸body   ⁹of me   ²bear.

18 Brethren, the grace of our Lord Jesus Christ *be* with your spirit. Amen.

18 Ἡ χάρις τοῦ κυρίου ἡμῶν Ἰησοῦ
The grace of the Lord of us Jesus

Χριστοῦ μετὰ τοῦ πνεύματος ὑμῶν,
Christ with the spirit of you,

ἀδελφοί· ἀμήν.
brothers : Amen.

EPHESIANS 1

ΠΡΟΣ ΕΦΕΣΙΟΥΣ
To Ephesians

CHAPTER 1

PAUL, an apostle of Jesus Christ by the will of God, to the saints which are at Ephesus, and to the faithful in Christ Jesus:

2 Grace *be* to you, and peace, from God our Father, and *from* the Lord Jesus Christ.

3 Blessed *be* the God and Father of our Lord Jesus Christ, who hath blessed us with all spiritual blessings in heavenly *places* in Christ:

4 According as he hath chosen us in him before the foundation of the world, that we should be holy and without blame before him in love:

5 Having predestinated us unto the adoption of children by Jesus Christ to himself, according to the good pleasure of his will,

6 To the praise of the

1 Παῦλος ἀπόστολος Χριστοῦ Ἰησοῦ διὰ
Paul an apostle of Christ Jesus through

θελήματος θεοῦ τοῖς ἁγίοις τοῖς οὖσιν
[the] will of God to the saints – being

[ἐν Ἐφέσῳ] καὶ πιστοῖς ἐν Χριστῷ
in Ephesus and faithful in Christ

Ἰησοῦ· **2** χάρις ὑμῖν καὶ εἰρήνη ἀπὸ
Jesus: Grace to you and peace from

θεοῦ πατρὸς ἡμῶν καὶ κυρίου Ἰησοῦ
God Father of us and Lord Jesus

Χριστοῦ.
Christ.

3 Εὐλογητὸς ὁ θεὸς καὶ πατὴρ τοῦ
Blessed the God and Father of the

κυρίου ἡμῶν Ἰησοῦ Χριστοῦ, ὁ εὐλογήσας
Lord of us Jesus Christ, the having
[one] blessed

ἡμᾶς ἐν πάσῃ εὐλογίᾳ πνευματικῇ ἐν
us with every blessing spiritual in

τοῖς ἐπουρανίοις ἐν Χριστῷ, **4** καθὼς
the heavenlies in Christ, as

ἐξελέξατο ἡμᾶς ἐν αὐτῷ πρὸ καταβολῆς
he chose us in him before [the] foundation

κόσμου, εἶναι ἡμᾶς ἁγίους καὶ ἀμώμους
of [the] world, to be us holy and unblemished[b]
=that we should be ...

κατενώπιον αὐτοῦ, ἐν ἀγάπῃ **5** προορίσας
before him, in love predestinating

ἡμᾶς εἰς υἱοθεσίαν διὰ Ἰησοῦ Χριστοῦ
us to adoption of sons through Jesus Christ

εἰς αὐτόν, κατὰ τὴν εὐδοκίαν τοῦ
to him[self], according to the good pleasure of the

θελήματος αὐτοῦ, **6** εἰς ἔπαινον δόξης
will of him, to [the] praise of [the] glory

glory of his grace, wherein he hath made us accepted in the beloved.

7 In whom we have redemption through his blood, the forgiveness of sins, according to the riches of his grace;

8 Wherein he hath abounded toward us in all wisdom and prudence;

9 Having made known unto us the mystery of his will, according to his good pleasure which he hath purposed in himself:

10 That in the dispensation of the fulness of times he might gather together in one all things in Christ, both which are in heaven, and which are on earth; *even* in him:

11 In whom also we have obtained an inheritance, being predestinated according to the purpose of him who worketh all things after the counsel of his own will:

12 That we should be to the praise of his glory, who first trusted in Christ.

13 In whom ye also *trusted*, after that ye heard the word of truth, the gospel of your salvation: in whom also after that ye believed, ye were sealed with that holy Spirit of promise,

τῆς   χάριτος   αὐτοῦ,   ἧς   ἐχαρίτωσεν   ἡμᾶς
of the   grace   of him,   of(with)   he favoured   us
                            which

ἐν   τῷ   ἠγαπημένῳ,   7 ἐν   ᾧ   ἔχομεν   τὴν
in   the [one] *having been* loved,   in   whom   we have   the

ἀπολύτρωσιν   διὰ   τοῦ   αἵματος   αὐτοῦ,   τὴν
redemption   through   the   blood   of him,   the

ἄφεσιν   τῶν   παραπτωμάτων,   κατὰ   τὸ
forgiveness   –   of trespasses,   according to   the

πλοῦτος   τῆς   χάριτος   αὐτοῦ,   8 ἧς   ἐπερίσ-
riches   of the   grace   of him,   which   he made to

σευσεν   εἰς   ἡμᾶς   ἐν   πάσῃ   σοφίᾳ   καὶ
abound   to   us   in   all   wisdom   and

φρονήσει   9 γνωρίσας   ἡμῖν   τὸ   μυστήριον
intelligence   making known   to us   the   mystery

τοῦ   θελήματος   αὐτοῦ,   κατὰ   τὴν   εὐδοκίαν
of the   will   of him,   according to the   good pleasure

αὐτοῦ,   ἣν   προέθετο   ἐν   αὐτῷ   10 εἰς
of him,   which   he purposed   in   him[self]   for

οἰκονομίαν   τοῦ   πληρώματος   τῶν   καιρῶν,
a stewardship   of the   fulness   of the   times,

ἀνακεφαλαιώσασθαι   τὰ   πάντα   ἐν   τῷ
to head up   –   all things   in   –

Χριστῷ,   τὰ   ἐπὶ   τοῖς   οὐρανοῖς   καὶ   τὰ
Christ,   the things on(in)   *the*   heavens   and   the   things

ἐπὶ   τῆς   γῆς·   ἐν   αὐτῷ,   11 ἐν   ᾧ   καὶ
on   the   earth;   in   him,   in   whom   also

ἐκληρώθημεν   προορισθέντες   κατὰ   πρόθεσιν
we were chosen as   being predestinated according to [the] purpose
[his] inheritance

τοῦ   τὰ   πάντα   ἐνεργοῦντος   κατὰ   τὴν
of the   –   ²all things   ¹operating   according to   the
[one]

βουλὴν   τοῦ   θελήματος   αὐτοῦ,   12 εἰς   τὸ
counsel   of the   will   of him,   for   *the*

εἶναι   ἡμᾶς   εἰς   ἔπαινον   δόξης   αὐτοῦ
to be   us[b]   to   [the] praise   of [the] glory   of him
=that we should be

τοὺς   προηλπικότας   ἐν   τῷ   Χριστῷ·   13 ἐν
the   having previously   in   –   Christ;   in
[ones]   hoped

ᾧ   καὶ   ὑμεῖς,   ἀκούσαντες   τὸν   λόγον
whom also   ye,   hearing   the   word

τῆς   ἀληθείας,   τὸ   εὐαγγέλιον   τῆς   σωτηρίας
–   of truth,   the   gospel   of the   salvation

ὑμῶν,   ἐν   ᾧ   καὶ   πιστεύσαντες   ἐσφραγίσθητε
of you,   in   whom also   believing   ye were sealed

τῷ   πνεύματι   τῆς   ἐπαγγελίας   τῷ   ἁγίῳ,
with ¹the   ³Spirit   –   ⁴of promise   –   ²holy,

14 Which is the earnest of our inheritance until the redemption of the purchased possession, unto the praise of his glory.

15 Wherefore I also, after I heard of your faith in the Lord Jesus, and love unto all the saints,

16 Cease not to give thanks for you, making mention of you in my prayers;

17 That the God of our Lord Jesus Christ, the Father of glory, may give unto you the spirit of wisdom and revelation in the knowledge of him:

18 The eyes of your understanding being enlightened; that ye may know what is the hope of his calling, and what the riches of the glory of his inheritance in the saints,

19 And what *is* the exceeding greatness of his power to us-ward who believe, according to the working of his mighty power,

20 Which he wrought in Christ, when he raised him from the dead, and set *him* at his own right hand in the heavenly *places*,

21 Far above all principality, and power, and might, and dominion, and

14 ὅς ἐστιν ἀρραβὼν τῆς κληρονομίας
who is an earnest of the inheritance
ἡμῶν, εἰς ἀπολύτρωσιν τῆς περιποιήσεως,
of us, till [the] redemption of the possession.
εἰς ἔπαινον τῆς δόξης αὐτοῦ.
to [the] praise of the glory of him.

15 Διὰ τοῦτο κἀγώ, ἀκούσας τὴν καθ'
Therefore I also, hearing the ªamong
ὑμᾶς πίστιν ἐν τῷ κυρίῳ Ἰησοῦ καὶ
ªyou ¹faith in the Lord Jesus and
τὴν ἀγάπην τὴν εἰς πάντας τοὺς ἁγίους,
the love – to all the saints,

16 οὐ παύομαι εὐχαριστῶν ὑπὲρ ὑμῶν
do not cease giving thanks on behalf of you
μνείαν ποιούμενος ἐπὶ τῶν προσευχῶν
mention making on(in) the prayers
μου, 17 ἵνα ὁ θεὸς τοῦ κυρίου ἡμῶν
of me, in order that the God of the Lord of us
Ἰησοῦ Χριστοῦ, ὁ πατὴρ τῆς δόξης,
Jesus Christ, the Father – of glory,
δῴη ὑμῖν πνεῦμα σοφίας καὶ ἀποκαλύψεως
may give to you a spirit of wisdom and of revelation
ἐν ἐπιγνώσει αὐτοῦ, 18 πεφωτισμένους τοὺς
in a full knowledge of him, having been enlightened the
ὀφθαλμοὺς τῆς καρδίας [ὑμῶν,] εἰς τὸ
eyes of the heart of you, for the
εἰδέναι ὑμᾶς τίς ἐστιν ἡ ἐλπὶς τῆς
to know youᵇ what is the hope of the
=that ye should know
κλήσεως αὐτοῦ, τίς ὁ πλοῦτος τῆς δόξης
calling of him, what the riches of the glory
τῆς κληρονομίας αὐτοῦ ἐν τοῖς ἁγίοις,
of the inheritance of him in the saints.

19 καὶ τί τὸ ὑπερβάλλον μέγεθος τῆς
and what the excelling greatness of the
δυνάμεως αὐτοῦ εἰς ἡμᾶς τοὺς πιστεύοντας
power of him toward us the [ones] believing
κατὰ τὴν ἐνέργειαν τοῦ κράτους τῆς
according to the operation of the might of the
ἰσχύος αὐτοῦ, 20 ἣν ἐνήργηκεν ἐν τῷ
strength of him, which he has operated in –
Χριστῷ ἐγείρας αὐτὸν ἐκ νεκρῶν, καὶ
Christ raising him from [the] dead, and
καθίσας ἐν δεξιᾷ αὐτοῦ ἐν τοῖς ἐπου-
seating [him] at [the] right [hand] of him in the heaven-
ρανίοις 21 ὑπεράνω πάσης ἀρχῆς καὶ
lies far above all rule and
ἐξουσίας καὶ δυνάμεως καὶ κυριότητος
authority and power and lordship

every name that is named, not only in this world, but also in that which is to come:

22 And hath put all *things* under his feet, and gave him *to be* the head over all *things* to the church,

23 Which is his body, the fulness of him that filleth all in all.

καὶ   παντὸς   ὀνόματος   ὀνομαζομένου   οὐ
and   every   name   being named   not

μόνον   ἐν   τῷ   αἰῶνι   τούτῳ   ἀλλὰ   καὶ
only   in   this age   but   also

ἐν   τῷ   μέλλοντι·   22 καὶ   πάντα   ὑπέταξεν
in   the   coming;   and   all things   subjected

ὑπὸ   τοὺς   πόδας   αὐτοῦ,   καὶ   αὐτὸν   ἔδωκεν
under   the   feet   of him,   and   ²him   ¹gave

κεφαλὴν   ὑπὲρ   πάντα   τῇ   ἐκκλησίᾳ,   23 ἥτις
[to be] head   over   all things   to the   church,   which

ἐστὶν   τὸ   σῶμα   αὐτοῦ,   τὸ   πλήρωμα
is   the   body   of him,   the   fulness

τοῦ   τὰ   πάντα   ἐν   πᾶσιν   πληρουμένου.
of the   –   ²all things   ³with   ⁴all things   ¹filling.
[one]

CHAPTER 2

AND you *hath he quickened*, who were dead in trespasses and sins;

2 Wherein in time past ye walked according to the course of this world, according to the prince of the power of the air, the spirit that now worketh in the children of disobedience:

3 Among whom also we all had our conversation in times past in the lusts of our flesh, fulfilling the desires of the flesh and of the mind; and were by nature the children of wrath, even as others.

4 But God, who is rich in mercy, for his great love wherewith he loved us,

5 Even when we were dead in sins, hath quickened us together with Christ, (by grace ye are saved;)

2 Καὶ   ὑμᾶς   ὄντας   νεκροὺς   τοῖς   παραπτώ-
And   you   being   dead   in the   tres-

μασιν   καὶ   ταῖς   ἁμαρτίαις   ὑμῶν,   2 ἐν
passes   and   in the   sins   of you,   in

αἷς   ποτε   περιεπατήσατε   κατὰ   τὸν   αἰῶνα
which   then   ye walked   according to the   age

τοῦ   κόσμου   τούτου,   κατὰ   τὸν   ἄρχοντα
of this world,   according to the   ruler

τῆς   ἐξουσίας   τοῦ   ἀέρος,   τοῦ   πνεύματος
of the   authority   of the   air,   of the   spirit

τοῦ   νῦν   ἐνεργοῦντος   ἐν   τοῖς   υἱοῖς   τῆς
–   now   operating   in   the   sons   –

ἀπειθείας·   3 ἐν   οἷς   καὶ   ἡμεῖς   πάντες
of disobedience;   among whom   also   we   all

ἀνεστράφημέν   ποτε   ἐν   ταῖς   ἐπιθυμίαις
conducted ourselves   then   in   the   lusts

τῆς   σαρκὸς   ἡμῶν,   ποιοῦντες   τὰ   θελήματα
of the   flesh   of us,   doing   the   wishes

τῆς   σαρκὸς   καὶ   τῶν   διανοιῶν,   καὶ
of the   flesh   and   of the   understandings,   and

ἤμεθα   τέκνα   φύσει   ὀργῆς   ὡς   καὶ   οἱ
were   ²children   ¹by nature   of wrath   as   also   the

λοιποί·   4 ὁ   δὲ   θεὸς   πλούσιος   ὢν   ἐν
rest;   –   but   God   ²rich   ¹being   in

ἐλέει,   διὰ   τὴν   πολλὴν   ἀγάπην   αὐτοῦ
mercy,   because of   the   much   love   of his

ἣν   ἠγάπησεν   ἡμᾶς,   5 καὶ   ὄντας   ἡμᾶς
[with]   he loved   us,   even   being   us
which   =when we were

νεκροὺς   τοῖς   παραπτώμασιν   συνεζωοποίησεν
dead   –   in trespasses   quickened [us] with

τῷ   Χριστῷ,   —   χάριτί   ἐστε   σεσωσμένοι,
–   Christ,   (by grace   ye are *having been* saved,)

6 And hath raised *us* up together, and made *us* sit together in heavenly *places* in Christ Jesus:

7 That in the ages to come he might shew the exceeding riches of his grace in *his* kindness toward us through Christ Jesus.

8 For by grace are ye saved through faith; and that not of yourselves: *it is* the gift of God:

9 Not of works, lest any man should boast.

10 For we are his workmanship, created in Christ Jesus unto good works, which God hath before ordained that we should walk in them.

11 Wherefore remember, that ye *being* in time past Gentiles in the flesh, who are called Uncircumcision by that which is called the Circumcision in the flesh made by hands;

12 That at that time ye were without Christ, being aliens from the commonwealth of Israel, and strangers from the covenants of promise, having no hope, and without God in the world:

13 But now in Christ Jesus ye who sometimes were far off are made nigh by the blood of Christ.

14 For he is our peace,

---

6 καὶ συνήγειρεν καὶ συνεκάθισεν ἐν
and raised [us] with and seated [us] with in

τοῖς ἐπουρανίοις ἐν Χριστῷ Ἰησοῦ, 7 ἵνα
the heavenlies in Christ Jesus, in order that

ἐνδείξηται ἐν τοῖς αἰῶσιν τοῖς ἐπερχομένοις
he might show in the ages – coming on
forth

τὸ ὑπερβάλλον πλοῦτος τῆς χάριτος αὐτοῦ
the excelling riches of the grace of him

ἐν χρηστότητι ἐφ᾽ ἡμᾶς ἐν Χριστῷ
in kindness toward us in Christ

Ἰησοῦ. 8 τῇ γὰρ χάριτί ἐστε σεσωσμένοι
Jesus. – For by grace ye are *having been* saved

διὰ πίστεως· καὶ τοῦτο οὐκ ἐξ ὑμῶν,
through faith; and this not of you,

θεοῦ τὸ δῶρον· 9 οὐκ ἐξ ἔργων, ἵνα μή
of [is] the gift; not of works, lest
God

τις καυχήσηται. 10 αὐτοῦ γάρ ἐσμεν
anyone should boast. For of him we are

ποίημα, κτισθέντες ἐν Χριστῷ Ἰησοῦ
a product, created in Christ Jesus

ἐπὶ ἔργοις ἀγαθοῖς, οἷς προητοίμασεν
unto works good, which [2]previously prepared

ὁ θεὸς ἵνα ἐν αὐτοῖς περιπατήσωμεν.
– [1]God in order that in them we might walk.

11 Διὸ μνημονεύετε ὅτι ποτὲ ὑμεῖς τὰ
Wherefore remember ye that when ye the

ἔθνη ἐν σαρκί, οἱ λεγόμενοι ἀκροβυστία
nations in [the] flesh, the [ones] *being* called uncircumcision

ὑπὸ τῆς λεγομένης περιτομῆς ἐν σαρκὶ
by the *being* called circumcision in [the] flesh

χειροποιήτου, 12 ὅτι ἦτε τῷ καιρῷ ἐκείνῳ
made by hand, that ye were at that time

χωρὶς Χριστοῦ, ἀπηλλοτριωμένοι τῆς
without Christ, having been alienated from the

πολιτείας τοῦ Ἰσραὴλ καὶ ξένοι τῶν
commonwealth – of Israel and strangers of(from)
the

διαθηκῶν τῆς ἐπαγγελίας, ἐλπίδα μὴ
covenants – of promise, hope not

ἔχοντες καὶ ἄθεοι ἐν τῷ κόσμῳ. 13 νυνὶ
having and godless in the world. now

δὲ ἐν Χριστῷ Ἰησοῦ ὑμεῖς οἳ ποτε
But in Christ Jesus ye the [ones] then

ὄντες μακρὰν ἐγενήθητε ἐγγὺς ἐν τῷ
being afar became near by the

αἵματι τοῦ Χριστοῦ. 14 Αὐτὸς γάρ
blood – of Christ. For he

who hath made both one, and hath broken down the middle wall of partition *between us;*

15 Having abolished in his flesh the enmity, *even* the law of commandments *contained* in ordinances; for to make in himself of twain one new man, *so* making peace;

16 And that he might reconcile both unto God in one body by the cross, having slain the enmity thereby:

17 And came and preached peace to you which were afar off, and to them that were nigh.

18 For through him we both have access by one Spirit unto the Father.

19 Now therefore ye are no more strangers and foreigners, but fellowcitizens with the saints, and of the household of God;

20 And are built upon the foundation of the apostles and prophets, Jesus Christ himself being the chief corner *stone;*

21 In whom all the building fitly framed together groweth unto an holy temple in the Lord:

22 In whom ye also are builded together for an habitation of God through the Spirit.

ἐστιν ἡ εἰρήνη ἡμῶν, ὁ ποιήσας τὰ
is the peace of us, the [one] having made -

ἀμφότερα ἓν καὶ τὸ μεσότοιχον τοῦ
both one and ³the ⁵middle wall -

φραγμοῦ λύσας, τὴν ἔχθραν, ἐν τῇ σαρκὶ
⁴of partition ¹having the enmity, ²in ³the ⁴flesh
broken,

αὐτοῦ 15 τὸν νόμον τῶν ἐντολῶν ἐν
⁵of him ⁶the ⁷law ⁸of the ⁹commandments ¹⁰in

δόγμασιν καταργήσας, ἵνα τοὺς δύο κτίσῃ
¹¹decrees ¹having abolished, in order ⁴the ⁵two ³he might
that create

ἐν αὐτῷ εἰς ἕνα καινὸν ἄνθρωπον ποιῶν
⁶in ⁷him[self] ⁸into ⁹one ¹⁰new ¹¹man ¹making

εἰρήνην, 16 καὶ ἀποκαταλλάξῃ τοὺς
²peace, and might reconcile

ἀμφοτέρους ἐν ἑνὶ σώματι τῷ θεῷ διὰ
both in one body - to God through

τοῦ σταυροῦ, ἀποκτείνας τὴν ἔχθραν ἐν
the cross, killing the enmity in

αὐτῷ· 17 καὶ ἐλθὼν εὐηγγελίσατο εἰρήνην
him[self]; and coming preached peace

ὑμῖν τοῖς μακρὰν καὶ εἰρήνην τοῖς ἐγγύς·
to you the ones afar and peace to the ones near;

18 ὅτι δι' αὐτοῦ ἔχομεν τὴν προσαγωγὴν
because through him ¹we ²have - ⁴access

οἱ ἀμφότεροι ἐν ἑνὶ πνεύματι πρὸς τὸν
- ³both by one Spirit unto the

πατέρα. 19 ἄρα οὖν οὐκέτι ἐστὲ ξένοι
Father. Then therefore no more are ye strangers

καὶ πάροικοι, ἀλλὰ ἐστὲ συμπολῖται τῶν
and sojourners, but ye are fellow-citizens of the

ἁγίων καὶ οἰκεῖοι τοῦ θεοῦ, 20 ἐποικοδομη-
saints and members of - of God, having been
the family

θέντες ἐπὶ τῷ θεμελίῳ τῶν ἀποστόλων
built *on* on the foundation of the apostles

καὶ προφητῶν, ὄντος ἀκρογωνιαίου αὐτοῦ
and prophets, ⁴being ⁵cornerstone ³[him]self

Χριστοῦ Ἰησοῦ, 21 ἐν ᾧ πᾶσα οἰκοδομὴ
¹Christ ²Jesus,² in whom all [the] building

συναρμολογουμένη αὔξει εἰς ναὸν ἅγιον
being fitted together grows into shrine a holy

ἐν κυρίῳ, 22 ἐν ᾧ καὶ ὑμεῖς συνοικοδομεῖσθε
in [the] Lord, in whom also ye are being built together

εἰς κατοικητήριον τοῦ θεοῦ ἐν πνεύματι.
into a dwelling-place - of God in spirit.

764   EPHESIANS 3

CHAPTER 3

FOR this cause I Paul, the prisoner of Jesus Christ for you Gentiles,

2 If ye have heard of the dispensation of the grace of God which is given me to you-ward:

3 How that by revelation he made known unto me the mystery; (as I wrote afore in few words,

4 Whereby, when ye read, ye may understand my knowledge in the mystery of Christ)

5 Which in other ages was not made known unto the sons of men, as it is now revealed unto his holy apostles and prophets by the Spirit;

6 That the Gentiles should be fellowheirs, and of the same body, and partakers of his promise in Christ by the gospel:

7 Whereof I was made a minister, according to the gift of the grace of God given unto me by the effectual working of his power.

8 Unto me, who am less than the least of all saints, is this grace given, that I should preach among the Gentiles the unsearchable riches of Christ;

9 And to make all *men* see what *is* the fellowship of the mystery, which from

3 Τούτου χάριν ἐγὼ Παῦλος ὁ δέσμιος
²*of* this   ¹By reason of   I   Paul   the   prisoner

τοῦ Χριστοῦ Ἰησοῦ ὑπὲρ ὑμῶν τῶν
 -    of Christ   Jesus   on behalf of   you   the

ἐθνῶν 2 — εἴ γε ἠκούσατε τὴν οἰκονομίαν
nations   —   if indeed   ye heard   the   stewardship

τῆς χάριτος τοῦ θεοῦ τῆς δοθείσης μοι
of the   grace   -   of God   -   given   to me

εἰς ὑμᾶς, 3 ὅτι κατὰ ἀποκάλυψιν ἐγνωρίσθη
for   you,   that by way of   revelation   was made known

μοι τὸ μυστήριον, καθὼς προέγραψα ἐν
to me   the   mystery,   as   I previously wrote   in

ὀλίγῳ, 4 πρὸς ὃ δύνασθε ἀναγινώσκοντες
brief,   as to   which   ²ye can   ²reading

νοῆσαι τὴν σύνεσίν μου ἐν τῷ μυστηρίῳ
to realize   the understanding of me   in   the   mystery

τοῦ Χριστοῦ, 5 ὃ ἑτέραις γενεαῖς οὐκ
 -    of Christ,   which   in other   generations   not

ἐγνωρίσθη τοῖς υἱοῖς τῶν ἀνθρώπων ὡς
was made known to the   sons   --   of men   as

νῦν ἀπεκαλύφθη τοῖς ἁγίοις ἀποστόλοις
now   it was revealed   to the   holy   apostles

αὐτοῦ καὶ προφήταις ἐν πνεύματι, 6 εἶναι
of him   and   prophets   in   spirit,   ²to be

τὰ ἔθνη συγκληρονόμα καὶ σύσσωμα καὶ
¹the ²nations   joint-heirs   and   a joint-body   and

συμμέτοχα τῆς ἐπαγγελίας ἐν Χριστῷ
joint-sharers   of the   promise   in   Christ

Ἰησοῦ διὰ τοῦ εὐαγγελίου, 7 οὗ ἐγενήθην
Jesus   through   the   gospel,   of which   I became

διάκονος κατὰ τὴν δωρεὰν τῆς χάριτος
a minister   according to the   gift   of the   grace

τοῦ θεοῦ τῆς δοθείσης μοι κατὰ τὴν
 -    of God   -   given   to me according to   the

ἐνέργειαν τῆς δυνάμεως αὐτοῦ. 8 ἐμοὶ
operation   of the   power   of him.   To me

τῷ ἐλαχιστοτέρῳ πάντων ἁγίων ἐδόθη
the   leaster*   of all   saints   was given

ἡ χάρις αὕτη, τοῖς ἔθνεσιν εὐαγγελίσασθαι
this grace,   to the   nations   to preach

τὸ ἀνεξιχνίαστον πλοῦτος τοῦ Χριστοῦ,
the   unsearchable   riches   -   of Christ,

9 καὶ φωτίσαι τίς ἡ οἰκονομία τοῦ
   and   to bring to light   what [is] the   stewardship   of the

μυστηρίου τοῦ ἀποκεκρυμμένου ἀπὸ τῶν
mystery   -   *having been* hidden   from   the

---

* This is quite literal!—the apostle coins a word.

the beginning of the world hath been hid in God, who created all things by Jesus Christ:

αἰώνων ἐν τῷ θεῷ τῷ τὰ πάντα κτίσαντι,
ages   in   the God ¹the - ²all things ²having
                          [one]   created,

10 To the intent that now unto the principalities and powers in heavenly *places* might be known by the church the manifold wisdom of God,

10 ἵνα   γνωρισθῇ   νῦν   ταῖς   ἀρχαῖς   καὶ
in order might be made now to the   rulers   and
that   known

ταῖς   ἐξουσίαις   ἐν   τοῖς   ἐπουρανίοις   διὰ
to the   authorities in   the   heavenlies   through

τῆς   ἐκκλησίας   ἡ   πολυποίκιλος   σοφία   τοῦ
the   church   the   manifold   wisdom   -

11 According to the eternal purpose which he purposed in Christ Jesus our Lord:

θεοῦ,   11 κατὰ   πρόθεσιν   τῶν   αἰώνων   ἣν
of God, according to [the] purpose of the   ages   which

ἐποίησεν ἐν τῷ   Χριστῷ   Ἰησοῦ   τῷ   κυρίῳ
he made in -   Christ   Jesus   the   Lord

12 In whom we have boldness and access with confidence by the faith of him.

ἡμῶν,   12 ἐν   ᾧ   ἔχομεν   τὴν   παρρησίαν
of us,   in   whom   we have   -   boldness

καὶ   προσαγωγὴν   ἐν   πεποιθήσει   διὰ   τῆς
and   access   in   confidence   through   *the*

13 Wherefore I desire that ye faint not at my tribulations for you, which is your glory.

πίστεως   αὐτοῦ.   13 διὸ   αἰτοῦμαι   μὴ
faith   of(in) him.*   Wherefore I ask [you]   not

ἐγκακεῖν   ἐν   ταῖς   θλίψεσίν   μου   ὑπὲρ
to faint   in   the   afflictions   of me   on behalf

14 For this cause I bow my knees unto the Father of our Lord Jesus Christ,

ὑμῶν,   ἥτις   ἐστὶν   δόξα   ὑμῶν.   14 Τούτου
of you,   which   is   glory   of you.   ²*of* this

χάριν   κάμπτω   τὰ   γόνατά   μου   πρὸς
¹By reason of I bend   the   knees   of me   unto

15 Of whom the whole family in heaven and earth is named,

τὸν   πατέρα,   15 ἐξ   οὗ   πᾶσα   πατριὰ
the   Father,   of   whom   every   fatherhood

ἐν   οὐρανοῖς   καὶ   ἐπὶ   γῆς   ὀνομάζεται,
in   heavens   and   on   earth   is named,

16 That he would grant you, according to the riches of his glory, to be strengthened with might by his Spirit in the inner man;

16 ἵνα   δῷ   ὑμῖν   κατὰ   τὸ   πλοῦτος   τῆς
in order he may you according to the   riches   of the
that   give

δόξης   αὐτοῦ   δυνάμει   κραταιωθῆναι   διὰ
glory   of him   by power   to become mighty   through

τοῦ   πνεύματος   αὐτοῦ   εἰς   τὸν   ἔσω   ἄνθρω-
the   Spirit   of him   in   the   inward   man,

17 That Christ may dwell in your hearts by faith; that ye, being rooted and grounded in love,

πον,   17 κατοικῆσαι   τὸν   Χριστὸν   διὰ   τῆς
to dwell   -   Christᵇ   through   -
=that Christ may dwell

πίστεως   ἐν   ταῖς   καρδίαις   ὑμῶν,   ἐν
faith   in   the   hearts   of you,   in

ἀγάπῃ   ἐρριζωμένοι   καὶ   τεθεμελιωμένοι,
love   *having been* rooted   and   *having been* founded,

18 May be able to comprehend with all saints what *is* the breadth, and

18 ἵνα   ἐξισχύσητε   καταλαβέσθαι   σὺν   πᾶσιν
in order ye may have strength to apprehend   with   all
that

τοῖς   ἁγίοις   τί   τὸ   πλάτος   καὶ   μῆκος
the   saints   what [is] the   breadth   and   length

* See Gal. 2. 16.

length, and depth, and height;

19 And to know the love of Christ, which passeth knowledge, that ye might be filled with all the fulness of God.

20 Now unto him that is able to do exceeding abundantly above all that we ask or think, according to the power that worketh in us,

21 Unto him be glory in the church by Christ Jesus throughout all ages, world without end. Amen.

καὶ ὕψος καὶ βάθος, **19** γνῶναί τε τὴν
and height and depth, and to know [the](the)

ὑπερβάλλουσαν τῆς γνώσεως ἀγάπην τοῦ
excelling – knowledge love –

Χριστοῦ, ἵνα πληρωθῆτε εἰς πᾶν τὸ
of Christ, *in order* that ye may be filled to all the

πλήρωμα τοῦ θεοῦ.
fulness of God.

20 Τῷ δὲ δυναμένῳ ὑπὲρ πάντα ποιῆσαι
Now to the [one] being able beyond all things to do

ὑπερεκπερισσοῦ ὧν αἰτούμεθα ἢ νοοῦμεν
superabundantly *of* which we ask or *we* think

κατὰ τὴν δύναμιν τὴν ἐνεργουμένην ἐν
according to the power – operating in

ἡμῖν, **21** αὐτῷ ἡ δόξα ἐν τῇ ἐκκλησίᾳ
us, to him [be] the glory in the church

καὶ ἐν Χριστῷ Ἰησοῦ εἰς πάσας τὰς
and in Christ Jesus unto all the

γενεὰς τοῦ αἰῶνος τῶν αἰώνων· ἀμήν.
generations of the age of the ages: Amen.

CHAPTER 4

I THEREFORE, the prisoner of the Lord, beseech you that ye walk worthy of the vocation wherewith ye are called,

2 With all lowliness and meekness, with longsuffering, forbearing one another in love;

3 Endeavouring to keep the unity of the Spirit in the bond of peace.

4 *There is* one body, and one Spirit, even as ye are called in one hope of your calling;

5 One Lord, one faith, one baptism,

6 One God and Father of all, who *is* above all, and through all, and in you all.

7 But unto every one of us is given grace ac-

4 Παρακαλῶ οὖν ὑμᾶς ἐγὼ ὁ δέσμιος
beseech therefore you I the prisoner

ἐν κυρίῳ ἀξίως περιπατῆσαι τῆς κλήσεως
in [the] Lord worthily to walk of the calling

ἧς ἐκλήθητε, **2** μετὰ πάσης ταπεινοφροσύνης
of(with) ye were with all humility
which called,

καὶ πραΰτητος, μετὰ μακροθυμίας,
and meekness, with longsuffering,

ἀνεχόμενοι ἀλλήλων ἐν ἀγάπῃ, **3** σπου-
forbearing one another in love, being

δάζοντες τηρεῖν τὴν ἑνότητα τοῦ πνεύματος
eager to keep the unity of the Spirit

ἐν τῷ συνδέσμῳ τῆς εἰρήνης· ἓν σῶμα
in the bond – of peace; [there is] one body

καὶ ἓν πνεῦμα, **4** καθὼς καὶ ἐκλήθητε
and one Spirit, as also ye were called

ἐν μιᾷ ἐλπίδι τῆς κλήσεως ὑμῶν· **5** εἷς
in one hope of the calling of you; one

κύριος, μία πίστις, ἓν βάπτισμα· **6** εἷς
Lord, one faith, one baptism; one

θεὸς καὶ πατὴρ πάντων, ὁ ἐπὶ πάντων
God and Father of all, the [one] over all

καὶ διὰ πάντων καὶ ἐν πᾶσιν. **7** Ἑνὶ
and through all and in all. to one

δὲ ἑκάστῳ ἡμῶν ἐδόθη ἡ χάρις κατὰ
But each of us was given – grace according to

cording to the measure of the gift of Christ.

8 Wherefore he saith, When he ascended up on high, he led captivity captive, and gave gifts unto men.

9 (Now that he ascended, what is it but that he also descended first into the lower parts of the earth?

10 He that descended is the same also that ascended up far above all heavens, that he might fill all things.)

11 And he gave some, apostles; and some, prophets; and some, evangelists; and some, pastors and teachers;

12 For the perfecting of the saints, for the work of the ministry, for the edifying of the body of Christ:

13 Till we all come in the unity of the faith, and of the knowledge of the Son of God, unto a perfect man, unto the measure of the stature of the fulness of Christ:

14 That we *henceforth* be no more children, tossed to and fro, and carried about with every wind of doctrine, by the sleight of men, *and* cunning craftiness, whereby they lie in wait to deceive;

15 But speaking the truth in love, may grow up into him in all things,

---

τὸ   μέτρον   τῆς   δωρεᾶς   τοῦ   Χριστοῦ.
the   measure   of the   gift   -   of Christ.

8 διὸ   λέγει·   ἀναβὰς   εἰς   ὕψος   ᾐχμαλώτευσεν
Where-   he says: Having   to   height   he led captive
fore   ascended

αἰχμαλωσίαν,   ἔδωκεν   δόματα   τοῖς   ἀνθρώποις.
captivity,   he gave   gifts   -   to men.

9 τὸ   δὲ   ἀνέβη   τί   ἐστιν   εἰ   μὴ   ὅτι   καὶ
Now the   "he   what   is it   except   that   also
     ascended"

κατέβη   εἰς   τὰ   κατώτερα   μέρη   τῆς   γῆς;
he descended into   the   lower   parts   of the   earth?

10 ὁ   καταβὰς   αὐτός   ἐστιν   καὶ   ὁ   ἀναβὰς
The   descending   himself   is   also   the   ascending
[one]   [one]

ὑπεράνω   πάντων   τῶν   οὐρανῶν,   ἵνα
far above   all   the   heavens,   in order that

πληρώσῃ   τὰ   πάντα.   **11** καὶ   αὐτὸς   ἔδωκεν
he might fill   -   all things.   And   he   gave

τοὺς   μὲν   ἀποστόλους,   τοὺς   δὲ   προφήτας,
some†   apostles,   some†   prophets,

τοὺς   δὲ   εὐαγγελιστάς,   τοὺς   δὲ   ποιμένας
some†   evangelists,   some†   shepherds

καὶ   διδασκάλους,   **12** πρὸς   τὸν   καταρτισμὸν
and   teachers,   for   the   perfecting

τῶν   ἁγίων   εἰς   ἔργον   διακονίας,   εἰς
of the   saints   to [the] work   of ministry,   to

οἰκοδομὴν   τοῦ   σώματος   τοῦ   Χριστοῦ,
building   of the   body   -   of Christ,

13 μέχρι   καταντήσωμεν   οἱ   πάντες   εἰς
until   ¹we ²arrive   -   ²all   at

τὴν   ἑνότητα   τῆς   πίστεως   καὶ   τῆς   ἐπιγνώ-
the   unity   of the   faith   and   of the   full know-

σεως   τοῦ   υἱοῦ   τοῦ   θεοῦ,   εἰς   ἄνδρα   τέλειον,
ledge   of the Son   -   of God,   at   ²man   ¹a complete,

εἰς   μέτρον   ἡλικίας   τοῦ   πληρώματος   τοῦ
at   [the] measure   of [the]   of the   fulness   -
                stature

Χριστοῦ,   **14** ἵνα   μηκέτι   ὦμεν   νήπιοι,
of Christ,   in order that   no more   we may be   infants,

κλυδωνιζόμενοι   καὶ   περιφερόμενοι   παντὶ   ἀνέμῳ
being blown   and *being* carried round   by every   wind

τῆς   διδασκαλίας   ἐν   τῇ   κυβείᾳ   τῶν   ἀνθρώ-
-   of teaching   in   the   sleight   -   of

πων,   ἐν   πανουργίᾳ   πρὸς   τὴν   μεθοδείαν
men,   in   cleverness   unto   the   craftiness

τῆς   πλάνης,   **15** ἀληθεύοντες   δὲ   ἐν   ἀγάπῃ
-   of error,   but speaking truth   in   love

αὐξήσωμεν   εἰς   αὐτὸν   τὰ   πάντα,   ὅς   ἐστιν
we may grow   into   him   in all respects,†   who   is

which is the head, *even* Christ:

16 From whom the whole body fitly joined together and compacted by that which every joint supplieth, according to the effectual working in the measure of every part, maketh increase of the body unto the edifying of itself in love.

17 This I say therefore, and testify in the Lord, that ye henceforth walk not as other Gentiles walk, in the vanity of their mind,

18 Having the understanding darkened, being alienated from the life of God through the ignorance that is in them, because of the blindness of their heart:

19 Who being past feeling have given themselves over unto lasciviousness, to work all uncleanness with greediness.

20 But ye have not so learned Christ;

21 If so be that ye have heard him, and have been taught by him, as the truth is in Jesus:

22 That ye put off concerning the former conversation the old man, which is corrupt according to the deceitful lusts;

23 And be renewed in the spirit of your mind;

ἡ κεφαλή, Χριστός, **16** ἐξ οὗ πᾶν τὸ
the head, Christ, of whom all the

σῶμα συναρμολογούμενον καὶ συμβιβαζόμενον
body being fitted together and *being* brought together

διὰ πάσης ἁφῆς τῆς ἐπιχορηγίας κατ'
through every band - of supply according to

ἐνέργειαν ἐν μέτρῳ ἑνὸς ἑκάστου μέρους
[the] operation in measure of ²one ¹each part

τὴν αὔξησιν τοῦ σώματος ποιεῖται εἰς
²the ³growth ⁴of the ⁵body ¹makes for

οἰκοδομὴν ἑαυτοῦ ἐν ἀγάπῃ.
building of itself in love.

17 Τοῦτο οὖν λέγω καὶ μαρτύρομαι ἐν
This therefore I say and witness in

κυρίῳ, μηκέτι ὑμᾶς περιπατεῖν καθὼς
[the] Lord, no more you to walk as

καὶ τὰ ἔθνη περιπατεῖ ἐν ματαιότητι
also the nations walks in vanity

τοῦ νοὸς αὐτῶν, **18** ἐσκοτωμένοι τῇ
of the mind of them, ²having been darkened ³in the (their)

διανοίᾳ ὄντες, ἀπηλλοτριωμένοι τῆς ζωῆς
⁴intellect ¹being, having been alienated [from] the life

τοῦ θεοῦ, διὰ τὴν ἄγνοιαν τὴν οὖσαν
- of God, through the ignorance the being

ἐν αὐτοῖς, διὰ τὴν πώρωσιν τῆς καρδίας
in them, on account of the hardness of the heart

αὐτῶν, **19** οἵτινες ἀπηλγηκότες ἑαυτοὺς
of them, who having ceased to care ²themselves

παρέδωκαν τῇ ἀσελγείᾳ εἰς ἐργασίαν
¹gave up - to lewdness for work

ἀκαθαρσίας πάσης ἐν πλεονεξίᾳ. **20** ὑμεῖς
²uncleanness ¹of all in greediness. ye

δὲ οὐχ οὕτως ἐμάθετε τὸν Χριστόν,
But not so learned - Christ,

21 εἴ γε αὐτὸν ἠκούσατε καὶ ἐν αὐτῷ
if indeed ²him ¹ye heard and ²by ¹him

ἐδιδάχθητε καθώς ἐστιν ἀλήθεια ἐν τῷ
¹were taught as ²is ¹truth in -

Ἰησοῦ, **22** ἀποθέσθαι ὑμᾶς κατὰ τὴν
Jesus, to put off youᵇ as regards the(your)
=that ye put off

προτέραν ἀναστροφὴν τὸν παλαιὸν ἄνθρωπον
former conduct the old man

τὸν φθειρόμενον κατὰ τὰς ἐπιθυμίας τῆς
- being corrupted according to the lusts

ἀπάτης, **23** ἀνανεοῦσθαι δὲ τῷ πνεύματι
of deceit, and to be renewed in the spirit

24 And that ye put on the new man, which after God is created in righteousness and true holiness.

25 Wherefore putting away lying, speak every man truth with his neighbour: for we are members one of another.

26 Be ye angry, and sin not: let not the sun go down upon your wrath:

27 Neither give place to the devil.

28 Let him that stole steal no more: but rather let him labour, working with *his* hands the thing which is good, that he may have to give to him that needeth.

29 Let no corrupt communication proceed out of your mouth, but that which is good to the use of edifying, that it may minister grace unto the hearers.

30 And grieve not the holy Spirit of God, whereby ye are sealed unto the day of redemption.

31 Let all bitterness, and wrath, and anger, and clamour, and evil speaking, be put away from you, with all malice:

32 And be ye kind one to another, tenderhearted,

τοῦ   νοὸς   ὑμῶν   24 καὶ   ἐνδύσασθαι   τὸν
of the   mind   of you   and   *to* put on   the

καινὸν   ἄνθρωπον   τὸν   κατὰ   θεὸν   κτισθέντα
new   man   –   ²according to ³God   ¹created

ἐν   δικαιοσύνῃ   καὶ   ὁσιότητι   τῆς   ἀληθείας.
in   righteousness   and   holiness   –   of truth.

25 Διὸ   ἀποθέμενοι   τὸ   ψεῦδος   λαλεῖτε
Wherefore   putting off   the   lie   speak ye

ἀλήθειαν   ἕκαστος   μετὰ   τοῦ   πλησίον   αὐτοῦ,
truth   each man   with   the   neighbour   of him,

ὅτι   ἐσμὲν   ἀλλήλων   μέλη.   26 ὀργίζεσθε
because we are of one another members.   Be ye wrathful

καὶ   μὴ   ἁμαρτάνετε·   ὁ   ἥλιος   μὴ
and   do not sin;   ²the   ⁴sun   ⁵not

ἐπιδυέτω   ἐπὶ   παροργισμῷ   ὑμῶν,   27 μηδὲ
¹let ⁵set *on*   on   provocation   of you,   nor

δίδοτε   τόπον   τῷ   διαβόλῳ.   28 ὁ   κλέπτων
give ye   place   to the   devil.   The [one] stealing

μηκέτι   κλεπτέτω,   μᾶλλον   δὲ   κοπιάτω
no more   let him steal,   but rather   let him labour

ἐργαζόμενος   ταῖς   ἰδίαις   χερσὶν   τὸ   ἀγαθόν,
working   with the(his) own   hands   the   good thing,

ἵνα   ἔχῃ   μεταδιδόναι   τῷ   χρείαν   ἔχοντι.
in order he may   to share [with]   the [one]   ²need   ¹having
that   have

29 πᾶς   λόγος   σαπρὸς   ἐκ   τοῦ   στόματος
Every   ²word   ¹corrupt   out of   the   mouth

ὑμῶν   μὴ   ἐκπορευέσθω,   ἀλλὰ   εἴ   τις
of you   let not proceed*,   but   if   any

ἀγαθὸς   πρὸς   οἰκοδομὴν   τῆς   χρείας,   ἵνα
[is] good   to   improvement   of the   need,   in order
that

δῷ   χάριν   τοῖς   ἀκούουσιν.   30 καὶ   μὴ   λυπεῖτε
it may   grace   to the [ones] hearing.   And   do not grieve
give

τὸ   πνεῦμα   τὸ   ἅγιον   τοῦ   θεοῦ,   ἐν   ᾧ
the   Spirit   –   Holy   –   of God,   by whom

ἐσφραγίσθητε   εἰς   ἡμέραν   ἀπολυτρώσεως.
ye were sealed   for   a day   of redemption.

31 πᾶσα   πικρία   καὶ   θυμὸς   καὶ
All   bitterness   and   anger   and

ὀργὴ   καὶ   κραυγὴ   καὶ   βλασφημία   ἀρθήτω
wrath   and   clamour   and   blasphemy   let it be
removed

ἀφ᾽   ὑμῶν   σὺν   πάσῃ   κακίᾳ.   32 γίνεσθε
from   you   with   all   evil.   be ye

δὲ   εἰς   ἀλλήλους   χρηστοί,   εὔσπλαγχνοι,
And   to   one another   kind,   tenderhearted,

---

* That is, " let no corrupt word proceed . . . "

forgiving one another, even as God for Christ's sake hath forgiven you.

CHAPTER 5

BE ye therefore followers of God, as dear children;

2 And walk in love, as Christ also hath loved us, and hath given himself for us an offering and a sacrifice to God for a sweetsmelling savour.

3 But fornication, and all uncleanness, or covetousness, let it not be once named among you, as becometh saints:

4 Neither filthiness, nor foolish talking, nor jesting, which are not convenient: but rather giving of thanks.

5 For this ye know, that no whoremonger, nor unclean person, nor covetous man, who is an idolater, hath any inheritance in the kingdom of Christ and of God.

6 Let no man deceive you with vain words: for because of these things cometh the wrath of God upon the children of disobedience.

7 Be not ye therefore partakers with them.

8 For ye were sometimes darkness, but now *are ye* light in the Lord: walk as children of light:

9 (For the fruit of the Spirit *is* in all goodness and righteousness and truth;)

10 Proving what is acceptable unto the Lord.

χαριζόμενοι ἑαυτοῖς καθὼς καὶ ὁ θεὸς
forgiving　yourselves　as　also　-　God

ἐν Χριστῷ ἐχαρίσατο ὑμῖν. 5 Γίνεσθε
in　Christ　forgave　you.　　Be ye

οὖν μιμηταὶ τοῦ θεοῦ, ὡς τέκνα
therefore imitators　-　of God,　as　children

ἀγαπητά, 2 καὶ περιπατεῖτε ἐν ἀγάπῃ,
beloved,　　and　walk ye　in　love,

καθὼς καὶ ὁ Χριστὸς ἠγάπησεν ὑμᾶς
as　also　-　Christ　loved　you

καὶ παρέδωκεν ἑαυτὸν ὑπὲρ ἡμῶν
and　gave up　himself　on behalf of　us

προσφορὰν καὶ θυσίαν τῷ θεῷ εἰς ὀσμὴν
an offering　and　a sacrifice　-　to God　for　an odour

εὐωδίας. 3 Πορνεία δὲ καὶ ἀκαθαρσία
of sweet smell.　But fornication　and　¹uncleanness

πᾶσα ἢ πλεονεξία μηδὲ ὀνομαζέσθω ἐν
¹all　or　greediness　not　let it be named　among

ὑμῖν, καθὼς πρέπει ἁγίοις, 4 καὶ αἰσχρότης
you,　as　is fitting　for saints,　and　baseness

καὶ μωρολογία ἢ εὐτραπελία, ἃ οὐκ
and　foolish talking　or　raillery,　which things not

ἀνῆκεν, ἀλλὰ μᾶλλον εὐχαριστία. 5 τοῦτο
are becoming, but　rather　thanksgiving.　this

γὰρ ἴστε γινώσκοντες, ὅτι πᾶς πόρνος
For　be ye　knowing,　that　every　fornicator

ἢ ἀκάθαρτος ἢ πλεονέκτης, ὅ ἐστιν
or　unclean man　or　greedy,　who　is

εἰδωλολάτρης, οὐκ ἔχει κληρονομίαν ἐν τῇ
an idolater,　not　has　inheritance　in　the

βασιλείᾳ τοῦ Χριστοῦ καὶ θεοῦ. 6 Μηδεὶς
kingdom　-　of Christ　and　of God.　²No man

ὑμᾶς ἀπατάτω κενοῖς λόγοις· διὰ ταῦτα
²you　¹let ³deceive　with empty　words;　because of　these things

γὰρ ἔρχεται ἡ ὀργὴ τοῦ θεοῦ ἐπὶ τοὺς
for　is coming　the wrath　-　of God　on　the

υἱοὺς τῆς ἀπειθείας. 7 μὴ οὖν γίνεσθε
sons　-　of disobedience.　Not therefore　be ye

συμμέτοχοι αὐτῶν· 8 ἦτε γὰρ ποτε σκότος,
partakers　of them;　for ye were　then　darkness,

νῦν δὲ φῶς ἐν κυρίῳ· ὡς τέκνα φωτὸς
but now　light　in [the] Lord;　as　children　of light

περιπατεῖτε, 9 — ὁ γὰρ καρπὸς τοῦ
walk ye,　　(for the　fruit　of the

φωτὸς ἐν πάσῃ ἀγαθωσύνῃ καὶ δικαιοσύνῃ
light [is] in　all　goodness　and　righteousness

καὶ ἀληθείᾳ, — 10 δοκιμάζοντες τί ἐστιν
and　truth,)　proving　what　is

11 And have no fellowship with the unfruitful works of darkness, but rather reprove *them.*

12 For it is a shame even to speak of those things which are done of them in secret.

13 But all things that are reproved are made manifest by the light: for whatsoever doth make manifest is light.

14 Wherefore he saith, Awake thou that sleepest, and arise from the dead, and Christ shall give thee light.

15 See then that ye walk circumspectly, not as fools, but as wise,

16 Redeeming the time, because the days are evil.

17 Wherefore be ye not unwise, but understanding what the will of the Lord *is.*

18 And be not drunk with wine, wherein is excess; but be filled with the Spirit;

19 Speaking to yourselves in psalms and hymns and spiritual songs, singing and making melody in your heart to the Lord;

20 Giving thanks always for all things unto God and the Father in the name of our Lord Jesus Christ;

21 Submitting yourselves one to another in the fear of God.

22 Wives, submit yourselves unto your own husbands, as unto the Lord.

εὐάρεστον τῷ κυρίῳ, 11 καὶ μὴ συγκοι-
well-pleasing to the Lord, and do not have fellow-

νωνεῖτε τοῖς ἔργοις τοῖς ἀκάρποις τοῦ
ship with the ²works – ¹unfruitful –

σκότους, μᾶλλον δὲ καὶ ἐλέγχετε, 12 τὰ
of darkness, but rather even reprove [them], ⁵the

γὰρ κρυφῇ γινόμενα ὑπ' αὐτῶν αἰσχρόν
for ⁶hidden things ⁷being done ⁸by ⁹them ²shameful

ἐστιν καὶ λέγειν· 13 τὰ δὲ πάντα ἐλεγχόμενα
¹it is ³even ⁴to speak [of]; – but all things being reproved

ὑπὸ τοῦ φωτὸς φανεροῦται· 14 πᾶν γὰρ
by the light is(are) manifested; for everything

τὸ φανερούμενον φῶς ἐστιν. διὸ λέγει·
– being manifested ²light ¹is. Wherefore he says:

ἔγειρε, ὁ καθεύδων, καὶ ἀνάστα ἐκ τῶν
Rise, the sleeping [one], and stand up out of the

νεκρῶν, καὶ ἐπιφαύσει σοι ὁ Χριστός.
dead [ones], and will shine on thee – Christ.

15 Βλέπετε οὖν ἀκριβῶς πῶς περιπατεῖτε,
See ye therefore carefully how ye walk,

μὴ ὡς ἄσοφοι ἀλλ' ὡς σοφοί, 16 ἐξαγοραζ-
not as unwise but as wise, redeem-

όμενοι τὸν καιρόν, ὅτι αἱ ἡμέραι πονηραί
ing the time, because the days evil

εἰσιν. 17 διὰ τοῦτο μὴ γίνεσθε ἄφρονες,
are. Therefore be ye not foolish,

ἀλλὰ συνίετε τί τὸ θέλημα τοῦ κυρίου.
but understand what the will of the Lord [is].

18 καὶ μὴ μεθύσκεσθε οἴνῳ, ἐν ᾧ ἐστιν
And be ye not drunk with wine, in which is

ἀσωτία, ἀλλὰ πληροῦσθε ἐν πνεύματι,
wantonness, but be filled by [the] Spirit,

19 λαλοῦντες ἑαυτοῖς ψαλμοῖς καὶ ὕμνοις
speaking to yourselves in psalms and hymns

καὶ ᾠδαῖς πνευματικαῖς, ᾄδοντες καὶ
and songs spiritual, singing and

ψάλλοντες τῇ καρδίᾳ ὑμῶν τῷ κυρίῳ,
psalming with the heart of you to the Lord,

20 εὐχαριστοῦντες πάντοτε ὑπὲρ πάντων
giving thanks always for all things

ἐν ὀνόματι τοῦ κυρίου ἡμῶν Ἰησοῦ
in [the] name of the Lord of us Jesus

Χριστοῦ τῷ θεῷ καὶ πατρί, 21 ὑποτασσ-
Christ – to God even [the] Father, being

όμενοι ἀλλήλοις ἐν φόβῳ Χριστοῦ. 22 Αἱ
subject to one another in [the] fear of Christ. The

γυναῖκες τοῖς ἰδίοις ἀνδράσιν ὡς τῷ
wives to the(ir) own husbands as to the

23 For the husband is the head of the wife, even as Christ is the head of the church: and he is the saviour of the body.

24 Therefore as the church is subject unto Christ, so let the wives be to their own husbands in every thing.

25 Husbands, love your wives, even as Christ also loved the church, and gave himself for it;

26 That he might sanctify and cleanse it with the washing of water by the word,

27 That he might present it to himself a glorious church, not having spot, or wrinkle, or any such thing; but that it should be holy and without blemish.

28 So ought men to love their wives as their own bodies. He that loveth his wife loveth himself.

29 For no man ever yet hated his own flesh; but nourisheth and cherisheth it, even as the Lord the church:

30 For we are members of his body, of his flesh, and of his bones.

31 For this cause shall a man leave his father and mother, and shall be

κυρίῳ, 23 ὅτι ἀνήρ ἐστιν κεφαλὴ τῆς
Lord, because a man is head of the

γυναικὸς ὡς καὶ ὁ Χριστὸς κεφαλὴ
woman as also – Christ [is] head

τῆς ἐκκλησίας, αὐτὸς σωτὴρ τοῦ σώματος.
of the church, [him]self Saviour of the body.

24 ἀλλὰ ὡς ἡ ἐκκλησία ὑποτάσσεται τῷ
But as the church is subject to the

Χριστῷ, οὕτως καὶ αἱ γυναῖκες τοῖς
to Christ, so also the wives to the(ir)

ἀνδράσιν ἐν παντί. 25 Οἱ ἄνδρες, ἀγαπᾶτε
husbands in everything. The husbands, love ye

τὰς γυναῖκας, καθὼς καὶ ὁ Χριστὸς
the(your) wives, as also – Christ

ἠγάπησεν τὴν ἐκκλησίαν καὶ ἑαυτὸν
loved the church and himself

παρέδωκεν ὑπὲρ αὐτῆς, 26 ἵνα αὐτὴν
gave up on behalf of it, in order that it

ἁγιάσῃ καθαρίσας τῷ λουτρῷ τοῦ
he might sanctify cleansing by the washing of the

ὕδατος ἐν ῥήματι, 27 ἵνα παραστήσῃ αὐτὸς
water by word, in order [2]might present [1]he
that

ἑαυτῷ ἔνδοξον τὴν ἐκκλησίαν, μὴ ἔχουσαν
[5]to himself [6]glorious [3]the [4]church, not having

σπίλον ἢ ῥυτίδα ἤ τι τῶν τοιούτων,
spot or wrinkle or any of the such things,

ἀλλ᾽ ἵνα ᾖ ἁγία καὶ ἄμωμος. 28 οὕτως
but in order it might holy and unblemished. So
that be

ὀφείλουσιν [καὶ] οἱ ἄνδρες ἀγαπᾶν τὰς
ought also the husbands to love the

ἑαυτῶν γυναῖκας ὡς τὰ ἑαυτῶν σώματα.
of themselves wives as the of themselves bodies.

ὁ ἀγαπῶν τὴν ἑαυτοῦ γυναῖκα ἑαυτὸν
The [one] loving the of himself wife himself

ἀγαπᾷ· 29 οὐδεὶς γάρ ποτε τὴν ἑαυτοῦ
loves; for no man ever the of himself

σάρκα ἐμίσησεν, ἀλλὰ ἐκτρέφει καὶ θάλπει
flesh hated, but nourishes and cherishes

αὐτήν, καθὼς καὶ ὁ Χριστὸς τὴν ἐκ-
it, as also – Christ the

κλησίαν, 30 ὅτι μέλη ἐσμὲν τοῦ σώματος
church, because members we are of the body

αὐτοῦ. 31 ἀντὶ τούτου καταλείψει ἄνθρωπος
of him. For this [2]shall leave [1]a man

[τὸν] πατέρα καὶ [τὴν] μητέρα καὶ
the(his) father and the(his) mother and

joined unto his wife, and they two shall be one flesh.

32 This is a great mystery: but I speak concerning Christ and the church.

33 Nevertheless let every one of you in particular so love his wife even as himself; and the wife *see* that she reverence *her* husband.

CHAPTER 6

CHILDREN, obey your parents in the Lord: for this is right.

2 Honour thy father and mother; which is the first commandment with promise;

3 That it may be well with thee, and thou mayest live long on the earth.

4 And, ye fathers, provoke not your children to wrath: but bring them up in the nurture and admonition of the Lord.

5 Servants, be obedient to them that are *your* masters according to the flesh, with fear and trembling, in singleness of your heart, as unto Christ;

6 Not with eyeservice, as menpleasers; but as the servants of Christ, doing the will of God from the heart;

7 With good will doing service, as to the Lord, and not to men:

8 Knowing that what-

προσκολληθήσεται προς την γυναικα αυτου,
shall cleave　　　to　the　wife　of him,

και εσονται οι δυο εις σαρκα μιαν.
and ³shall be ¹the ²two ⁴for ⁵flesh ⁵one.

32 το μυστήριον τουτο μέγα εστίν, εγω
This mystery　　　　great　is,　　³I

δε λέγω εις Χριστον και [εις] την
¹but　say　as to　Christ　and　as to　the

εκκλησίαν. 33 πλην και υμεις οι
church.　　　Nevertheless also　ye　the

καθ᾽ ενα εκαστος την εαυτου γυναικα
one by one†　each　¹the　³of himself　²wife

ουτως αγαπάτω ως εαυτόν, η δε
so　let him love　as　himself,　and the

γυνη ινα φοβηται τον ανδρα. 6 Τα
wife *in order* that she fears　the(her) husband.　The

τέκνα, υπακούετε τοις γονευσιν υμων
children,　obey ye　the　parents　of you

εν κυρίω· τουτο γαρ εστιν δικαίον.
in [the] Lord;　for this　is　right.

2 τίμα τον πατέρα σου και την μητέρα,
Honour　the　father　of thee and　the　mother,

ητις εστιν εντολη πρώτη εν επαγγελία,
which　is　³commandment ¹[the] ²first with　a promise,

3 ινα ευ σοι γένηται και εση μακρο-
in order well with thee it may be and thou may-　long-
that　　　　　　　　　　　　　　　　　est be

χρόνιος επι της γης. 4 Και οι πατέρες,
timed(lived) on　the　earth.　And the　fathers,

μη παροργίζετε τα τέκνα υμων, αλλα
do not ye provoke to wrath the　children　of you,　but

εκτρέφετε αυτα εν παιδεία και νουθεσία
nurture　them　in [the] discipline and　admonition

κυρίου. 5 Οι δουλοι, υπακούετε τοις
of [the] Lord.　The　slaves,　obey ye　¹the(your)

κατα σάρκα κυρίοις μετα φόβου και
²according to ⁴flesh ³lords　with　fear　and

τρόμου εν απλότητι της καρδίας υμων
trembling　in　singleness　of the　heart　of you

ως τω Χριστω, 6 μη κατ᾽ οφθαλμοδουλίαν
as　－　to Christ,　not by way of　eye-service

ως ανθρωπάρεσκοι, αλλ᾽ ως δουλοι Χριστου
as　men-pleasers,　but　as　slaves　of Christ

ποιουντες το θέλημα του θεου εκ ψυχης,
doing　the　will　－　of God from [the] soul,

7 μετ᾽ ευνοίας δουλεύοντες ως τω κυρίω
with　goodwill　serving as slaves　as　to the　Lord

και ουκ ανθρώποις, 8 ειδότες οτι εκαστος
and　not　to men,　　knowing　that　each man

soever good thing any man doeth, the same shall he receive of the Lord, whether *he be* bond or free.

9 And, ye masters, do the same things unto them, forbearing threatening: knowing that your Master also is in heaven; neither is there respect of persons with him.

10 Finally, my brethren, be strong in the Lord, and in the power of his might.

11 Put on the whole armour of God, that ye may be able to stand against the wiles of the devil.

12 For we wrestle not against flesh and blood, but against principalities, against powers, against the rulers of the darkness of this world, against spiritual wickedness in high *places*.

13 Wherefore take unto you the whole armour of God, that ye may be able to withstand in the evil day, and having done all, to stand.

14 Stand therefore, having your loins girt about with truth, and having on the breastplate of righteousness;

15 And your feet shod

ἐάν τι ποιήσῃ ἀγαθόν, τοῦτο κομίσεται
whatever ⁸he does ¹good thing, this he will get

παρὰ κυρίου, εἴτε δοῦλος εἴτε ἐλεύθερος.
from [the] Lord, whether a slave or a freeman.

9 Καὶ οἱ κύριοι, τὰ αὐτὰ ποιεῖτε πρὸς
And the lords, the same things do ye toward

αὐτούς, ἀνιέντες τὴν ἀπειλήν, εἰδότες ὅτι
them, forbearing *the* threatening, knowing that

καὶ αὐτῶν καὶ ὑμῶν ὁ κύριός ἐστιν
both of them and of you the Lord is

ἐν οὐρανοῖς, καὶ προσωπολημψία οὐκ
in heavens, and respect of persons not

ἔστιν παρ' αὐτῷ.
is with him.

10 Τοῦ λοιποῦ, ἐνδυναμοῦσθε ἐν κυρίῳ
For the rest,† be ye empowered in [the] Lord

καὶ ἐν τῷ κράτει τῆς ἰσχύος αὐτοῦ.
and in the might of the strength of him.

11 ἐνδύσασθε τὴν πανοπλίαν τοῦ θεοῦ
Put ye on the whole armour – of God

πρὸς τὸ δύνασθαι ὑμᾶς στῆναι πρὸς
for the to be able youᵇ to stand against
=so that ye are able . . .

τὰς μεθοδείας τοῦ διαβόλου· 12 ὅτι οὐκ
the craftinesses of the devil; because not

ἔστιν ἡμῖν ἡ πάλη πρὸς αἷμα καὶ σάρκα,
is to us the conflictᵉ against blood and flesh,
=our conflict is not

ἀλλὰ πρὸς τὰς ἀρχάς, πρὸς τὰς ἐξουσίας,
but against the rulers, against the authorities,

πρὸς τοὺς κοσμοκράτορας τοῦ σκότους
against the world rulers – darkness

τούτου, πρὸς τὰ πνευματικὰ τῆς πονηρίας
of this, against the spiritual [hosts] – of evil

ἐν τοῖς ἐπουρανίοις. 13 διὰ τοῦτο
in the heavenlies. Therefore

ἀναλάβετε τὴν πανοπλίαν τοῦ θεοῦ, ἵνα
take ye up the whole armour – of God, in order
that

δυνηθῆτε ἀντιστῆναι ἐν τῇ ἡμέρᾳ τῇ
ye may be able to resist in the day –

πονηρᾷ καὶ ἅπαντα κατεργασάμενοι στῆναι.
evil and all things having wrought to stand.

14 στῆτε οὖν περιζωσάμενοι τὴν ὀσφὺν
Stand ye therefore girding round the loin[s]

ὑμῶν ἐν ἀληθείᾳ, καὶ ἐνδυσάμενοι τὸν
of you with truth, and putting on the

θώρακα τῆς δικαιοσύνης, 15 καὶ ὑπο-
breastplate – of righteousness, and shoe-

with the preparation of the gospel of peace;

16 Above all, taking the shield of faith, wherewith ye shall be able to quench all the fiery darts of the wicked.

17 And take the helmet of salvation, and the sword of the Spirit, which is the word of God:

18 Praying always with all prayer and supplication in the Spirit, and watching thereunto with all perseverance and supplication for all saints;

19 And for me, that utterance may be given unto me, that I may open my mouth boldly, to make known the mystery of the gospel,

20 For which I am an ambassador in bonds: that therein I may speak boldly, as I ought to speak.

21 But that ye also may know my affairs, and how I do, Tychicus, a beloved brother and faithful minister in the Lord, shall make known to you all things:

22 Whom I have sent

δησάμενοι τοὺς πόδας ἐν ἑτοιμασίᾳ τοῦ
ing   the   feet with readiness of the

εὐαγγελίου τῆς εἰρήνης, 16 ἐν πᾶσιν
gospel   -   of peace,   in   all

ἀναλαβόντες τὸν θυρεὸν τῆς πίστεως, ἐν
taking up   the shield of faith,   by

ᾧ δυνήσεσθε πάντα τὰ βέλη τοῦ πονηροῦ
which ye will be able ²all ³the ⁴darts ⁵of the ⁶evil one

τὰ πεπυρωμένα σβέσαι· 17 καὶ τὴν
- ⁵having been equipped ¹to quench; and the
   with fire

περικεφαλαίαν τοῦ σωτηρίου δέξασθε, καὶ
helmet   -   of salvation take ye, and

τὴν μάχαιραν τοῦ πνεύματος, ὃ ἐστιν
the sword   of the Spirit,   which* is

ῥῆμα θεοῦ, 18 διὰ πάσης προσευχῆς καὶ
[the] word of God, by means of all prayer   and

δεήσεως, προσευχόμενοι ἐν παντὶ καιρῷ
petition, praying   at every   time

ἐν πνεύματι, καὶ εἰς αὐτὸ ἀγρυπνοῦντες
in spirit,   and ²to ³it   ¹watching

ἐν πάσῃ προσκαρτερήσει καὶ δεήσει περὶ
in all   perseverance   and petition con-
                                        cerning

πάντων τῶν ἁγίων, 19 καὶ ὑπὲρ ἐμοῦ,
all   the saints,   and on behalf of me,

ἵνα μοι δοθῇ λόγος ἐν ἀνοίξει τοῦ
in order to me may be given speech in opening of the
that

στόματός μου, ἐν παρρησίᾳ γνωρίσαι τὸ
mouth   of me, in boldness to make known the

μυστήριον τοῦ εὐαγγελίου, 20 ὑπὲρ οὗ
mystery   of the gospel,   on behalf of which

πρεσβεύω ἐν ἁλύσει, ἵνα ἐν αὐτῷ παρ-
I am an   in a chain, in order in it   I may
ambassador   that

ρησιάσωμαι ὡς δεῖ με λαλῆσαι.
speak boldly as it behoves me to speak.

21 Ἵνα δὲ εἰδῆτε καὶ ὑμεῖς τὰ κατ᾽
Now in order that ²may know ²also ¹ye the things about

ἐμέ, τί πράσσω, πάντα γνωρίσει ὑμῖν
me, what I am doing, all things ¹⁰will make ¹¹to you
                                   known

Τύχικος ὁ ἀγαπητὸς ἀδελφὸς καὶ πιστὸς
¹Tychicus ³the ²beloved ⁴brother ⁵and ⁶faithful

διάκονος ἐν κυρίῳ, 22 ὃν ἔπεμψα πρὸς
⁷minister ⁸in ⁹[the] Lord, whom I sent to

* Neuter, agreeing with πνεῦμα, not feminine to agree with μάχαιρα.

unto you for the same purpose, that ye might know our affairs, and *that* he might comfort your hearts.

23 Peace *be* to the brethren, and love with faith, from God the Father and the Lord Jesus Christ.

24 Grace *be* with all them that love our Lord Jesus Christ in sincerity. Amen.

ὑμᾶς   εἰς   αὐτὸ   τοῦτο,   ἵνα   γνῶτε   τὰ
you   for   this very thing, in order ye may   the
                                 that   know   things

περὶ   ἡμῶν   καὶ   παρακαλέσῃ   τὰς   καρδίας
concerning us   and   may comfort   the   hearts

ὑμῶν.
of you.

23 Εἰρήνη   τοῖς   ἀδελφοῖς   καὶ   ἀγάπη
   Peace   to the   brothers   and   love

μετὰ   πίστεως   ἀπὸ   θεοῦ   πατρὸς   καὶ
with   faith   from   God   [the] Father and

κυρίου   Ἰησοῦ   Χριστοῦ.   24 ἡ   χάρις   μετὰ
[the] Lord Jesus   Christ.   - Grace [be] with

πάντων   τῶν   ἀγαπώντων   τὸν   κύριον   ἡμῶν
all   the [ones] loving   the   Lord   of us

Ἰησοῦν   Χριστὸν   ἐν   ἀφθαρσίᾳ.
Jesus   Christ   in   incorruptibility.

PHILIPPIANS 1   ΠΡΟΣ ΦΙΛΙΠΠΗΣΙΟΥΣ
                                      To Philippians

CHAPTER 1

PAUL and Timotheus, the servants of Jesus Christ, to all the saints in Christ Jesus which are at Philippi, with the bishops and deacons:

2 Grace *be* unto you, and peace, from God our Father, and *from* the Lord Jesus Christ.

3 I thank my God upon every remembrance of you,

4 Always in every prayer of mine for you all making request with joy,

5 For your fellowship

1 Παῦλος   καὶ   Τιμόθεος   δοῦλοι   Χριστοῦ
  Paul   and   Timothy   slaves   of Christ

Ἰησοῦ   πᾶσιν   τοῖς   ἁγίοις   ἐν   Χριστῷ
Jesus   to all   the   saints   in   Christ

Ἰησοῦ   τοῖς   οὖσιν   ἐν   Φιλίπποις   σὺν
Jesus   -   being   in   Philippi   with

ἐπισκόποις   καὶ   διακόνοις·   2 χάρις   ὑμῖν
bishops   and   ministers: Grace   to you

καὶ   εἰρήνη   ἀπὸ   θεοῦ   πατρὸς   ἡμῶν   καὶ
and   peace   from   God   Father   of us   and

κυρίου   Ἰησοῦ   Χριστοῦ.
[the] Lord Jesus   Christ.

3 Εὐχαριστῶ   τῷ   θεῷ   μου   ἐπὶ   πάσῃ
  I thank   the   God   of me   at   all

τῇ   μνείᾳ   ὑμῶν,   4 πάντοτε   ἐν   πάσῃ
the   remembrance of you, always   in   every

δεήσει   μου   ὑπὲρ   πάντων   ὑμῶν   μετὰ
petition   of me on behalf of all   you   with

χαρᾶς   τὴν   δέησιν   ποιούμενος,   5 ἐπὶ   τῇ
joy   the   petition   making,   over   the

κοινωνίᾳ   ὑμῶν   εἰς   τὸ   εὐαγγέλιον   ἀπὸ
fellowship   of you   in   the   gospel   from

in the gospel from the first day until now;

6 Being confident of this very thing, that he which hath begun a good work in you will perform *it* until the day of Jesus Christ:

7 Even as it is meet for me to think this of you all, because I have you in my heart; inasmuch as both in my bonds, and in the defence and confirmation of the gospel, ye all are partakers of my grace.

8 For God is my record, how greatly I long after you all in the bowels of Jesus Christ.

9 And this I pray, that your love may abound yet more and more in knowledge and *in* all judgment;

10 That ye may approve things that are excellent; that ye may be sincere and without offence till the day of Christ;

11 Being filled with the fruits of righteousness, which are by Jesus Christ, unto the glory and praise of God.

12 But I would ye should understand, brethren, that the things *which happened* unto me have fallen out rather unto the furtherance of the gospel;

τῆς   πρώτης   ἡμέρας   ἄχρι   τοῦ   νῦν,
the   first   day   until   *the*   now,

6 πεποιθὼς   αὐτὸ   τοῦτο,   ὅτι   ὁ   ἐναρξάμενος
being confident   this very thing,   that   the   having begun
     [of]   [one]

ἐν   ὑμῖν   ἔργον   ἀγαθὸν   ἐπιτελέσει   ἄχρι
in   you   work   a good   will complete [it]   until

ἡμέρας   Χριστοῦ   Ἰησοῦ·   7 καθώς   ἐστιν
[the] day   of Christ   Jesus;   as   it is

δίκαιον   ἐμοὶ   τοῦτο   φρονεῖν   ὑπὲρ   πάντων
right   for me   this   to think   *on behalf of*   all

ὑμῶν,   διὰ   τὸ   ἔχειν   με   ἐν   τῇ   καρδίᾳ
you,   because of the   to have   me[b]   in   the   heart
    = because I have you in the(my) heart,

ὑμᾶς,   ἔν   τε   τοῖς   δεσμοῖς   μου   καὶ   ἐν
you,   both in   the   bonds   of me   and   in

τῇ   ἀπολογίᾳ   καὶ   βεβαιώσει   τοῦ   εὐαγγελίου
the   defence   and   confirmation   of the   gospel

συγκοινωνούς   μου   τῆς   χάριτος   πάντας
⁵partakers   ⁷of me   ⁶of the   ⁸grace   ²all

ὑμᾶς   ὄντας.   8 μάρτυς   γάρ   μου   ὁ   θεός,
¹you   ³being.   ⁴witness   ¹For   ⁵of me   -   ²God
                                     ³[is],

ὡς   ἐπιποθῶ   πάντας   ὑμᾶς   ἐν   σπλάγχνοις
how   I long after   all   you   in   [the] bowels

Χριστοῦ   Ἰησοῦ.   9 Καὶ   τοῦτο   προσεύχομαι,
of Christ   Jesus.   And   this   I pray,

ἵνα   ἡ   ἀγάπη   ὑμῶν   ἔτι   μᾶλλον   καὶ
in order   the   love   of you   yet   more   and
that

μᾶλλον   περισσεύῃ   ἐν   ἐπιγνώσει   καὶ   πάσῃ
more   may abound   in   full knowledge   and   all

αἰσθήσει,   10 εἰς   τὸ   δοκιμάζειν   ὑμᾶς   τὰ
perception,   for   the   to prove   you[b]   the
          = that ye may prove   things

διαφέροντα,   ἵνα   ἦτε   εἰλικρινεῖς   καὶ
differing,   in order   ye may   sincere   and
          that   be

ἀπρόσκοποι   εἰς   ἡμέραν   Χριστοῦ,   11 πεπληρω-
unoffending   in   [the] day   of Christ,   having been

μένοι   καρπὸν   δικαιοσύνης   τὸν   διὰ   Ἰησοῦ
filled [with]   [the] fruit   of righteousness   -   through   Jesus

Χριστοῦ,   εἰς   δόξαν   καὶ   ἔπαινον   θεοῦ.
Christ,   to [the]   glory   and   praise   of God.

12 Γινώσκειν   δὲ   ὑμᾶς   βούλομαι,   ἀδελφοί,
Now ³to know   ²you   ¹I wish,   brothers,

ὅτι   τὰ   κατ᾽   ἐμὲ   μᾶλλον   εἰς   προκοπὴν
that   the   about   me*   ²rather   ³to   ⁴[the] advance
      things
      = my affairs

* *Cf.* ver. 27; ch. 2. 19, 20, 23; Eph. 6. 21, 22; Col. 4. 7, 8.

13 So that my bonds in Christ are manifest in all the palace, and in all other *places;*

14 And many of the brethren in the Lord, waxing confident by my bonds, are much more bold to speak the word without fear.

15 Some indeed preach Christ even of envy and strife; and some also of good will:

16 The one preach Christ of contention, not sincerely, supposing to add affliction to my bonds:

17 But the other of love, knowing that I am set for the defence of the gospel.

18 What then? notwithstanding, every way, whether in pretence, or in truth, Christ is preached; and I therein do rejoice, yea, and will rejoice.

19 For I know that this shall turn to my salvation through your prayer, and the supply of the Spirit of Jesus Christ,

20 According to my earnest expectation and *my* hope, that in nothing I shall be ashamed, but *that* with all boldness, as always, *so* now also Christ shall be magnified in my

τοῦ   εὐαγγελίου   ἐλήλυθεν,   13 ὥστε   τοὺς
⁵of the   ⁶gospel   ¹has(ve) come,   so as   the

δεσμούς   μου   φανεροὺς   ἐν   Χριστῷ   γενέσθαι
bonds   of me   ²manifest   ³in   ⁴Christ   ¹to become

ἐν   ὅλῳ   τῷ   πραιτωρίῳ   καὶ   τοῖς   λοιποῖς
in ,   all   the   prætorium   and   to ²the   ²rest

πᾶσιν,   14 καὶ   τοὺς   πλείονας   τῶν   ἀδελφῶν
¹all,   and   the   majority   of the   brothers

ἐν   κυρίῳ   πεποιθότας   τοῖς   δεσμοῖς   μου
in   [the] Lord   being confident   in the   bonds   of me

περισσοτέρως   τολμᾶν   ἀφόβως   τὸν   λόγον
²more exceedingly   ¹to dare   ³fearlessly   ⁵the   ⁶word

τοῦ   θεοῦ   λαλεῖν.   15 τινὲς   μὲν   καὶ   διὰ
-   ⁷of God   ⁴to speak.   Some   indeed   even   because of

φθόνον   καὶ   ἔριν,   τινὲς   δὲ   καὶ   δι'   εὐδοκίαν
envy   and   strife,   but some   also because of   good-will

τὸν   Χριστὸν   κηρύσσουσιν·   16 οἱ   μὲν   ἐξ
-   Christ   proclaim;   these†   from

ἀγάπης,   εἰδότες   ὅτι   εἰς   ἀπολογίαν   τοῦ
love,   knowing   that   for   defence   of the

εὐαγγελίου   κεῖμαι,   17 οἱ   δὲ   ἐξ   ἐριθείας
gospel   I am set,   those†   from   rivalry

τὸν   Χριστὸν   καταγγέλλουσιν,   οὐχ   ἀγνῶς,
-   ²Christ   ¹announce,   not   purely,

οἰόμενοι   θλῖψιν   ἐγείρειν   τοῖς   δεσμοῖς   μου.
thinking   ²affliction   ¹to raise   to the   bonds   of me.

18 Τί   γάρ;   πλὴν   ὅτι   παντὶ   τρόπῳ,
What   then?   nevertheless   that   in every   way,

εἴτε   προφάσει   εἴτε   ἀληθείᾳ,   Χριστὸς
whether   in pretence   or   in truth,   Christ

καταγγέλλεται,   καὶ   ἐν   τούτῳ   χαίρω·   ἀλλὰ
is announced,   and   in   this   I rejoice;   yet

καὶ   χαρήσομαι·   19 οἶδα   γὰρ   ὅτι   τοῦτό
also   I will rejoice;   for I know   that   this

μοι   ἀποβήσεται   εἰς   σωτηρίαν   διὰ   τῆς
to me   will result   in   salvation   through   the

ὑμῶν   δεήσεως   καὶ   ἐπιχορηγίας   τοῦ
²of you   ¹petition   and   supply   of the

πνεύματος   Ἰησοῦ   Χριστοῦ,   20 κατὰ   τὴν
spirit   of Jesus   Christ,   according to   the

ἀποκαραδοκίαν   καὶ   ἐλπίδα   μου   ὅτι   ἐν
eager expectation   and   hope   of me   that   in

οὐδενὶ   αἰσχυνθήσομαι,   ἀλλ'   ἐν   πάσῃ   παρ-
nothing   I shall be shamed,   but   with   all   bold-

ρησίᾳ   ὡς   πάντοτε   καὶ   νῦν   μεγαλυνθήσεται
ness   as   always   also   now   shall be magnified

body, whether *it be* by life, or by death.

21 For to me to live *is* Christ, and to die *is* gain.

22 But if I live in the flesh, this *is* the fruit of my labour: yet what I shall choose I wot not.

23 For I am in a strait betwixt two, having a desire to depart, and to be with Christ; which is far better:

24 Nevertheless to abide in the flesh *is* more needful for you.

25 And having this confidence, I know that I shall abide and continue with you all for your furtherance and joy of faith;

26 That your rejoicing may be more abundant in Jesus Christ for me by my coming to you again.

27 Only let your conversation be as it becometh the gospel of Christ: that whether I come and see you, or else be absent, I may hear of your affairs, that ye stand fast in one spirit, with one mind striving together for the faith of the gospel;

28 And in nothing terri-

Χριστὸς ἐν τῷ σώματί μου, εἴτε διὰ
Christ in the body of me, whether through

ζωῆς εἴτε διὰ θανάτου. 21 ἐμοὶ γὰρ
life or through death. For to me

τὸ ζῆν Χριστὸς καὶ τὸ ἀποθανεῖν κέρδος.
- to live [is] Christ and - to die [is] gain.

22 εἰ δὲ τὸ ζῆν ἐν σαρκί, τοῦτό μοι
But if - to live in [the] flesh, this to me

καρπὸς ἔργου, καὶ τί αἱρήσομαι οὐ
[is] fruit of [?my] work, and what I shall choose not

γνωρίζω. 23 συνέχομαι δὲ ἐκ τῶν δύο,
I perceive. But I am constrained by the two,

τὴν ἐπιθυμίαν ἔχων εἰς τὸ ἀναλῦσαι καὶ
²the ³desire ¹having *for the* to depart and

σὺν Χριστῷ εἶναι, πολλῷ γὰρ μᾶλλον
¹with ²Christ ¹to be, for by much [this is] rather

κρεῖσσον· 24 τὸ δὲ ἐπιμένειν τῇ σαρκὶ
better; - but to remain in the flesh [is]

ἀναγκαιότερον δι' ὑμᾶς. 25 καὶ τοῦτο
more necessary on account of you. And this

πεποιθὼς οἶδα, ὅτι μενῶ καὶ παραμενῶ
being I know, that I shall and continue
confident remain

πᾶσιν ὑμῖν εἰς τὴν ὑμῶν προκοπὴν καὶ
with all you for the ⁶of you ¹advance ²and

χαρὰν τῆς πίστεως, 26 ἵνα τὸ καύχημα
³joy ⁴of the ⁵faith, in order the boast
that

ὑμῶν περισσεύῃ ἐν Χριστῷ Ἰησοῦ ἐν
of you may abound in Christ Jesus in

ἐμοὶ διὰ τῆς ἐμῆς παρουσίας πάλιν
me through - my presence again

πρὸς ὑμᾶς.
with you.

27 Μόνον ἀξίως τοῦ εὐαγγελίου τοῦ
Only ²worthily ³of the ⁴gospel -

Χριστοῦ πολιτεύεσθε, ἵνα εἴτε ἐλθὼν καὶ
⁵of Christ ¹conduct in order whether coming and
yourselves, that

ἰδὼν ὑμᾶς εἴτε ἀπὼν ἀκούω τὰ περὶ
seeing you or being I hear the con-
absent things cerning

ὑμῶν, ὅτι στήκετε ἐν ἑνὶ πνεύματι,
you, that ye stand in one spirit,

μιᾷ ψυχῇ συναθλοῦντες τῇ πίστει τοῦ
with one soul striving together in the faith of the

εὐαγγελίου, 28 καὶ μὴ πτυρόμενοι ἐν
gospel, and not being terrified in

fied by your adversaries: which is to them an evident token of perdition, but to you of salvation, and that of God.

29 For unto you it is given in the behalf of Christ, not only to believe on him, but also to suffer for his sake;

30 Having the same conflict which ye saw in me, and now hear *to be* in me.

CHAPTER 2

IF *there be* therefore any consolation in Christ, if any comfort of love, if any fellowship of the Spirit, if any bowels and mercies,

2 Fulfil ye my joy, that ye be likeminded, having the same love, *being* of one accord, of one mind.

3 *Let* nothing *be done* through strife or vainglory; but in lowliness of mind let each esteem other better than themselves.

4 Look not every man on his own things, but every man also on the things of others.

5 Let this mind be in you, which was also in Christ Jesus:

6 Who, being in the form of God, thought it not robbery to be equal with God:

7 But made himself of

μηδενὶ ὑπὸ τῶν ἀντικειμένων, ἥτις ἐστὶν
no(any) by the [ones] opposing, which is
thing

αὐτοῖς ἔνδειξις ἀπωλείας, ὑμῶν δὲ
to them a proof of destruction, but of you

σωτηρίας, καὶ τοῦτο ἀπὸ θεοῦ· 29 ὅτι
of salvation, and this from God; because

ὑμῖν ἐχαρίσθη τὸ ὑπὲρ Χριστοῦ, οὐ
to you it was given – on behalf of Christ, not

μόνον τὸ εἰς αὐτὸν πιστεύειν ἀλλὰ καὶ
only – in him to believe but also

τὸ ὑπὲρ αὐτοῦ πάσχειν, 30 τὸν αὐτὸν
– on behalf of him to suffer, the same

ἀγῶνα ἔχοντες οἷον εἴδετε ἐν ἐμοὶ
struggle having which ye saw in me

καὶ νῦν ἀκούετε ἐν ἐμοί. 2 Εἴ τις
and now hear in me. ¹If [there ²any
is]

οὖν παράκλησις ἐν Χριστῷ, εἴ τι
¹therefore comfort in Christ, if any

παραμύθιον ἀγάπης, εἴ τις κοινωνία
consolation of love, if any fellowship

πνεύματος, εἴ τις σπλάγχνα καὶ οἰκτιρμοί,
of spirit, if any compassions and pities,

2 πληρώσατέ μου τὴν χαρὰν ἵνα τὸ
fulfil ye of me the joy *in order* that the

αὐτὸ φρονῆτε, τὴν αὐτὴν ἀγάπην ἔχοντες,
same thing ye think, the same love having,

σύμψυχοι, τὸ ἓν φρονοῦντες, 3 μηδὲν κατ'
one in soul, the one thinking, [doing] by
thing nothing way of

ἐριθείαν μηδὲ κατὰ κενοδοξίαν, ἀλλὰ τῇ
rivalry nor by way of vainglory, but –

ταπεινοφροσύνῃ ἀλλήλους ἡγούμενοι ὑπερ-
in humility ²one another ¹deeming sur-

έχοντας ἑαυτῶν, 4 μὴ τὰ ἑαυτῶν ἕκαστοι
passing themselves, not ³the ⁴of them- ¹each ones
things selves

σκοποῦντες, ἀλλὰ καὶ τὰ ἑτέρων ἕκαστοι.
²looking at, but ²also ³the ⁴of ¹each ones.
things others

5 τοῦτο φρονεῖτε ἐν ὑμῖν ὃ καὶ ἐν
This think ye among you which also [was] in

Χριστῷ Ἰησοῦ, 6 ὃς ἐν μορφῇ θεοῦ
Christ Jesus, who in [the] form of God

ὑπάρχων οὐχ ἁρπαγμὸν ἡγήσατο τὸ εἶναι
subsisting ²not ²robbery ¹deemed [it] *the* to be

ἴσα θεῷ, 7 ἀλλὰ ἑαυτὸν ἐκένωσεν μορφὴν
equal with God, but himself emptied ²[the] form
things

no reputation, and took upon him the form of a servant, and was made in the likeness of men:

8 And being found in fashion as a man, he humbled himself, and became obedient unto death, even the death of the cross.

9 Wherefore God also hath highly exalted him, and given him a name which is above every name:

10 That at the name of Jesus every knee should bow, of *things* in heaven, and *things* in earth, and *things* under the earth;

11 And *that* every tongue should confess that Jesus Christ *is* Lord, to the glory of God the Father.

12 Wherefore, my beloved, as ye have always obeyed, not as in my presence only, but now much more in my absence, work out your own salvation with fear and trembling.

13 For it is God which worketh in you both to will and to do of *his* good pleasure.

14 Do all things without murmurings and disputings:

15 That ye may be blameless and harmless, the sons of God, without rebuke, in the midst of a crooked and perverse nation, among whom ye shine as lights in the world;

δούλου λαβών, ἐν ὁμοιώματι ἀνθρώπων
³of a slave ¹taking, ²in ³likeness ⁴of men

γενόμενος· καὶ σχήματι εὑρεθεὶς ὡς
¹becoming; and ²in fashion ¹being found as

ἄνθρωπος 8 ἐταπείνωσεν ἑαυτὸν γενόμενος
a man he humbled himself becoming

ὑπήκοος μέχρι θανάτου, θανάτου δὲ σταυροῦ.
obedient until death, and death of a cross.

9 διὸ καὶ ὁ θεὸς αὐτὸν ὑπερύψωσεν
Wherefore also – God ²him ¹highly exalted

καὶ ἐχαρίσατο αὐτῷ τὸ ὄνομα τὸ ὑπὲρ
and gave to him the name – above

πᾶν ὄνομα, 10 ἵνα ἐν τῷ ὀνόματι Ἰησοῦ
every name, in order in the name of Jesus
that

πᾶν γόνυ κάμψῃ ἐπουρανίων καὶ ἐπιγείων
every knee should of heavenly and earthly
bend [beings] [beings]

καὶ καταχθονίων, 11 καὶ πᾶσα γλῶσσα
and [beings] under the earth, and every tongue

ἐξομολογήσηται ὅτι κύριος Ἰησοῦς
should acknowledge that ³Lord ¹Jesus

Χριστὸς εἰς δόξαν θεοῦ πατρός.
²Christ [is] to [the] glory of God [the] Father.

12 Ὥστε, ἀγαπητοί μου, καθὼς πάντοτε
So as, beloved of me, as always

ὑπηκούσατε, μὴ ὡς ἐν τῇ παρουσίᾳ
ye obeyed, not as in the presence

μου μόνον ἀλλὰ νῦν πολλῷ μᾶλλον ἐν
of me only but now by more rather in

τῇ ἀπουσίᾳ μου, μετὰ φόβου καὶ τρόμου
the absence of me, with fear and trembling

τὴν ἑαυτῶν σωτηρίαν κατεργάζεσθε· 13 θεὸς
¹the ³of yourselves ²salvation work out; ¹God

γάρ ἐστιν ὁ ἐνεργῶν ἐν ὑμῖν καὶ τὸ
¹for is the [one] operating in you both *the*

θέλειν καὶ τὸ ἐνεργεῖν ὑπὲρ τῆς εὐδοκίας.
to will and *the* to operate on behalf of the(his) goodwill.

14 πάντα ποιεῖτε χωρὶς γογγυσμῶν καὶ
All things do ye without murmurings and

διαλογισμῶν, 15 ἵνα γένησθε ἄμεμπτοι καὶ
disputings, in order that ye may be blameless and

ἀκέραιοι, τέκνα θεοῦ ἄμωμα μέσον
harmless, children of God faultless in the
midst

γενεᾶς σκολιᾶς καὶ διεστραμμένης, ἐν
a generation crooked and *having been* perverted, among

οἷς φαίνεσθε ὡς φωστῆρες ἐν κόσμῳ,
whom ye shine as luminaries in [the] world,

16 Holding forth the word of life; that I may rejoice in the day of Christ, that I have not run in vain, neither laboured in vain.

17 Yea, and if I be offered upon the sacrifice and service of your faith, I joy, and rejoice with you all.

18 For the same cause also do ye joy, and rejoice with me.

19 But I trust in the Lord Jesus to send Timotheus shortly unto you, that I also may be of good comfort, when I know your state.

20 For I have no man likeminded, who will naturally care for your state.

21 For all seek their own, not the things which are Jesus Christ's.

22 But ye know the proof of him, that, as a son with the father, he hath served with me in the gospel.

23 Him therefore I hope to send presently, so soon as I shall see how it will go with me.

24 But I trust in the Lord that I also myself shall come shortly.

25 Yet I supposed it necessary to send to you Epaphroditus, my brother, and companion in labour, and fellowsoldier, but your

16 λόγον ζωῆς ἐπέχοντες, εἰς καύχημα
a word of life holding up, for a boast
ἐμοὶ εἰς ἡμέραν Χριστοῦ, ὅτι οὐκ εἰς
to me[c] in [the] day of Christ, that not in
κενὸν ἔδραμον οὐδὲ εἰς κενὸν ἐκοπίασα.
vain I ran nor in vain laboured.

17 Ἀλλὰ εἰ καὶ σπένδομαι ἐπὶ τῇ θυσίᾳ
But if indeed I am poured out on the sacrifice
καὶ λειτουργίᾳ τῆς πίστεως ὑμῶν, χαίρω
and service of the faith of you, I rejoice
καὶ συγχαίρω πᾶσιν ὑμῖν· 18 τὸ δὲ αὐτὸ
and rejoice with ²all ¹you; and the same
καὶ ὑμεῖς χαίρετε καὶ συγχαίρετέ μοι.
also ye rejoice and rejoice with me.

19 Ἐλπίζω δὲ ἐν κυρίῳ Ἰησοῦ Τιμόθεον
But I hope in [the] Lord Jesus ¹Timothy
ταχέως πέμψαι ὑμῖν, ἵνα κἀγὼ εὐψυχῶ
⁴shortly ¹to send ²to you, in order I also may be of
that good cheer
γνοὺς τὰ περὶ ὑμῶν. 20 οὐδένα γὰρ
knowing the con- you. For no one
things cerning
ἔχω ἰσόψυχον, ὅστις γνησίως τὰ περὶ
I have likeminded, who genuinely ³the ²con-
things cerning
ὑμῶν μεριμνήσει· 21 οἱ πάντες γὰρ τὰ
⁴you ¹will care for; the for all ²the
things
ἑαυτῶν ζητοῦσιν, οὐ τὰ Χριστοῦ Ἰησοῦ.
³of them- ¹seek, not the of Christ Jesus.
selves things
22 τὴν δὲ δοκιμὴν αὐτοῦ γινώσκετε, ὅτι
But the character of him ye know, that
ὡς πατρὶ τέκνον σὺν ἐμοὶ ἐδούλευσεν
as ²a father ¹a child²[serves] ⁵with ⁴me ⁴he served
εἰς τὸ εὐαγγέλιον. 23 τοῦτον μὲν οὖν
in the gospel. This one – therefore
ἐλπίζω πέμψαι ὡς ἂν ἀφίδω τὰ περὶ
I hope to send ²whenever ³I see ⁴the ⁵con-
things cerning
ἐμὲ ἐξαυτῆς· 24 πέποιθα δὲ ἐν κυρίῳ
⁶me ¹immediately; but I trust in [the] Lord
ὅτι καὶ αὐτὸς ταχέως ἐλεύσομαι. 25 Ἀναγ-
that ²also ³[my]self ⁴shortly ¹I will come. ²neces-
καῖον δὲ ἡγησάμην Ἐπαφρόδιτον τὸν
sary But ¹I deemed [it] ⁶Epaphroditus ⁷the
ἀδελφὸν καὶ συνεργὸν καὶ συστρατιώτην
⁸brother ⁹and ¹⁰fellow-worker ¹¹and ¹²fellow-soldier
μου, ὑμῶν δὲ ἀπόστολον καὶ λειτουργὸν
¹³of me, ¹⁴and ¹⁶of you ¹⁵apostle ¹⁷and ¹⁸minister

messenger, and he that ministered to my wants.

26 For he longed after you all, and was full of heaviness, because that ye had heard that he had been sick.

27 For indeed he was sick nigh unto death: but God had mercy on him; and not on him only, but on me also, lest I should have sorrow upon sorrow.

28 I sent him therefore the more carefully, that, when ye see him again, ye may rejoice, and that I may be the less sorrowful.

29 Receive him therefore in the Lord with all gladness; and hold such in reputation:

30 Because for the work of Christ he was nigh unto death, not regarding his life, to supply your lack of service toward me.

τῆς χρείας μου, πέμψαι πρὸς ὑμᾶς,
[19]of the [10]need [11]of me, [9]to send [4]to [5]you,

26 ἐπειδὴ ἐπιποθῶν ἦν πάντας ὑμᾶς, καὶ
since [2]longing after [1]he was [4]all [5]you, and

ἀδημονῶν, διότι ἠκούσατε ὅτι ἠσθένησεν.
[was] being because ye heard that he ailed.
troubled,

27 καὶ γὰρ ἠσθένησεν παραπλήσιον θανάτῳ·
For indeed he ailed coming near to death;

ἀλλὰ ὁ θεὸς ἠλέησεν αὐτόν, οὐκ αὐτὸν
but – God had mercy on him, [2]not [3]him

δὲ μόνον ἀλλὰ καὶ ἐμέ, ἵνα μὴ λύπην
[1]and only but also me, lest grief

ἐπὶ λύπην σχῶ. 28 σπουδαιοτέρως οὖν
on grief I should have. More eagerly therefore

ἔπεμψα αὐτόν, ἵνα ἰδόντες αὐτὸν πάλιν
I sent him, in order that seeing him again

χαρῆτε κἀγὼ ἀλυπότερος ὦ. 29 προσδέχεσθε
ye may and [1]I [2]less grieved [3]may be. Receive ye
rejoice

οὖν αὐτὸν ἐν κυρίῳ μετὰ πάσης χαρᾶς,
therefore him in [the] Lord with all joy,

καὶ τοὺς τοιούτους ἐντίμους ἔχετε, 30 ὅτι
and [2]such ones [3]honoured [1]hold ye, because

διὰ τὸ ἔργον Χριστοῦ μέχρι θανάτου
on ac- the work of Christ [2]as far as [3]death
count of

ἤγγισεν παραβολευσάμενος τῇ ψυχῇ, ἵνα
[1]he drew exposing the(his) life, in or-
near der that

ἀναπληρώσῃ τὸ ὑμῶν ὑστέρημα τῆς πρός
he might fill up [1]the [2]of you [3]lack – [4]toward

με λειτουργίας.
[5]me [4]of service.

CHAPTER 3

FINALLY, my brethren, rejoice in the Lord. To write the same things to you, to me indeed is not grievous, but for you it is safe.

2 Beware of dogs, beware of evil workers, beware of the concision.

3 Τὸ λοιπόν, ἀδελφοί μου, χαίρετε ἐν
For the rest, brothers of me, rejoice ye in

κυρίῳ. τὰ αὐτὰ γράφειν ὑμῖν ἐμοὶ μὲν
[the] Lord. [2]The [3]same things [1]to write to you for me indeed

οὐκ ὀκνηρόν, ὑμῖν δὲ ἀσφαλές.
[is] not irksome, but for you safe.

2 Βλέπετε τοὺς κύνας, βλέπετε τοὺς
Look [to] the dogs, look [to] the

κακοὺς ἐργάτας, βλέπετε τὴν κατατομήν.*
evil workmen, look [to] the concision.*

* The apostle uses a " studiously contemptuous paronomasia " (Ellicott). He does not use περιτομή, the proper word for " circumcision ", " as this, though now abrogated in Christ, had still its spiritual aspects."

3 For we are the circumcision, which worship God in the spirit, and rejoice in Christ Jesus, and have no confidence in the flesh.

4 Though I might also have confidence in the flesh. If any other man thinketh that he hath whereof he might trust in the flesh, I more:

5 Circumcised the eighth day, of the stock of Israel, *of* the tribe of Benjamin, an Hebrew of the Hebrews; as touching the law, a Pharisee;

6 Concerning zeal, persecuting the church; touching the righteousness which is in the law, blameless.

7 But what things were gain to me, those I counted loss for Christ.

8 Yea doubtless, and I count all things *but* loss for the excellency of the knowledge of Christ Jesus my Lord: for whom I have suffered the loss of all things, and do count them *but* dung, that I may win Christ,

9 And be found in him, not having mine own righteousness, which is of the law, but that which is through the faith of Christ, the righteousness which is of God by faith:

---

3 ἡμεῖς γάρ ἐσμεν ἡ περιτομή, οἱ
For we are the circumcision, the
[ones]

πνεύματι θεοῦ λατρεύοντες καὶ καυχώμενοι
[2]by [the] Spirit [3]of God [1]worshipping and boasting

ἐν Χριστῷ Ἰησοῦ καὶ οὐκ ἐν σαρκὶ
in Christ Jesus and [2]not [3]in [the] [4]flesh

πεποιθότες, **4** καίπερ ἐγὼ ἔχων πεποίθησιν
[1]trusting, even though I having trust

καὶ ἐν σαρκί. Εἴ τις δοκεῖ ἄλλος
also in [the] flesh. If any [2]thinks [1]other man

πεποιθέναι ἐν σαρκί, ἐγὼ μᾶλλον·
to trust in [the] flesh, I more:

5 περιτομῇ ὀκταήμερος, ἐκ γένους Ἰσραήλ,
in circumcision eighth day, of [the] race of Israel,

φυλῆς Βενιαμίν, Ἑβραῖος ἐξ Ἑβραίων,
[the] tribe of Benjamin, a Hebrew of Hebrew [parents],

κατὰ νόμον Φαρισαῖος, **6** κατὰ ζῆλος
according [the] law a Pharisee, by way of zeal
to

διώκων τὴν ἐκκλησίαν, κατὰ δικαιοσύνην
persecuting the church, according [the]
to righteousness

τὴν ἐν νόμῳ γενόμενος ἄμεμπτος. **7** ἀλλὰ
– in [the] law being blameless. But

ἅτινα ἦν μοι κέρδη, ταῦτα ἥγημαι διὰ
what were to me gain, these I have [2]on ac-
things deemed count of

τὸν Χριστὸν ζημίαν. **8** ἀλλὰ μενοῦν γε
– [2]Christ [1]loss. But nay rather

καὶ ἡγοῦμαι πάντα ζημίαν εἶναι διὰ
[2]also [1]I deem [3]all things [5]loss [4]to be on account of

τὸ ὑπερέχον τῆς γνώσεως Χριστοῦ Ἰησοῦ
the excellency of the knowledge of Christ Jesus

τοῦ κυρίου μου, δι’ ὃν τὰ πάντα
the Lord of me, on ac- whom – all things
count of

ἐζημιώθην, καὶ ἡγοῦμαι σκύβαλα ἵνα
I suffered loss, and deem [them] refuse in order
that

Χριστὸν κερδήσω **9** καὶ εὑρεθῶ ἐν αὐτῷ,
Christ I might gain and be found in him,

μὴ ἔχων ἐμὴν δικαιοσύνην τὴν ἐκ νόμου,
not having my righteousness the [one] of law,

ἀλλὰ τὴν διὰ πίστεως Χριστοῦ, τὴν
but the [one] through faith of(in) Christ,[*] [1]the

ἐκ θεοῦ δικαιοσύνην ἐπὶ τῇ πίστει,
[2]of [4]God [3]righteousness [based] on – faith,

---

[*] See Gal. 2. 20.

10 That I may know him, and the power of his resurrection, and the fellowship of his sufferings, being made conformable unto his death;

11 If by any means I might attain unto the resurrection of the dead.

12 Not as though I had already attained, either were already perfect: but I follow after, if that I may apprehend that for which also I am apprehended of Christ Jesus.

13 Brethren, I count not myself to have apprehended: but *this* one thing *I do*, forgetting those things which are behind, and reaching forth unto those things which are before,

14 I press toward the mark for the prize of the high calling of God in Christ Jesus.

15 Let us therefore, as many as be perfect, be thus minded: and if in any thing ye be otherwise minded, God shall reveal even this unto you.

16 Nevertheless, whereto we have already attained, let us walk by the same rule, let us mind the same thing.

17 Brethren, be followers together of me, and mark them which walk so as ye have us for an ensample.

18 (For many walk, of whom I have told you often, and now tell you even weeping, *that they are* the enemies of the cross of Christ:

---

10 τοῦ γνῶναι αὐτὸν καὶ τὴν δύναμιν
- to know[d] him, and the power

τῆς ἀναστάσεως αὐτοῦ καὶ κοινωνίαν
of the resurrection of him and [the] fellowship

παθημάτων αὐτοῦ, συμμορφιζόμενος τῷ
of sufferings of him, being conformed to the

θανάτῳ αὐτοῦ, 11 εἴ πως καταντήσω εἰς
death of him, if [some]how I may attain *to* to

τὴν ἐξανάστασιν τὴν ἐκ νεκρῶν. 12 Οὐχ
the out-resurrection - from [the] dead. Not

ὅτι ἤδη ἔλαβον ἢ ἤδη τετελείωμαι,
that already I received or already have been perfected,

διώκω δὲ εἰ καὶ καταλάβω, ἐφ’ ᾧ
but I follow if indeed I may lay hold, inasmuch as

καὶ κατελήμφθην ὑπὸ Χριστοῦ Ἰησοῦ.
also I was laid hold of by Christ Jesus.

13 ἀδελφοί, ἐγὼ ἐμαυτὸν οὔπω λογίζομαι
Brothers, [3]I [4]myself [1]not yet [2]reckon

κατειληφέναι· ἐν δέ, τὰ μὲν ὀπίσω
to have but one thing [3]the [2]on one [4]behind
laid hold; [I do], things hand

ἐπιλανθανόμενος τοῖς δὲ ἔμπροσθεν ἐπεκ-
[1]forgetting [3]the [1]on the [4]before [2]stretching
things other

τεινόμενος, 14 κατὰ σκοπὸν διώκω εἰς
forward to, according to a mark I follow for

τὸ βραβεῖον τῆς ἄνω κλήσεως τοῦ θεοῦ
the prize of the above calling - of God

ἐν Χριστῷ Ἰησοῦ. 15 Ὅσοι οὖν τέλειοι,
in Christ Jesus. [2]As many [1]there- [are]
as fore perfect,

τοῦτο φρονῶμεν· καὶ εἴ τι ἑτέρως
[2]this [1]let us think; and if anything otherwise

φρονεῖτε, καὶ τοῦτο ὁ θεὸς ὑμῖν ἀποκα-
ye think, even this - God to you will

λύψει· 16 πλὴν εἰς ὃ ἐφθάσαμεν, τῷ
reveal; nevertheless to what we arrived, by the

αὐτῷ στοιχεῖν. 17 Συμμιμηταί μου
same to walk. Fellow-imitators of me

γίνεσθε, ἀδελφοί, καὶ σκοπεῖτε τοὺς οὕτω
be ye, brothers, and mark the [ones] thus

περιπατοῦντας καθὼς ἔχετε τύπον ἡμᾶς.
walking as ye have [2]an example [1]us.

18 πολλοὶ γὰρ περιπατοῦσιν οὓς πολλάκις
For many walk [of] whom often

ἔλεγον ὑμῖν, νῦν δὲ καὶ κλαίων λέγω,
I said to you, and now also weeping I say,

τοὺς ἐχθροὺς τοῦ σταυροῦ τοῦ Χριστοῦ,
the enemies of the cross - of Christ,

19 Whose end *is* de-struction, whose God *is* *their* belly, and *whose* glory *is* in their shame, who mind earthly things.)

20 For our conversation is in heaven; from whence also we look for the Saviour, the Lord Jesus Christ:

21 Who shall change our vile body, that it may be fashioned like unto his glorious body, according to the working whereby he is able even to subdue all things unto himself.

CHAPTER 4

THEREFORE, my brethren, dearly be-loved and longed for, my joy and crown, so stand fast in the Lord, *my* dearly beloved.

2 I beseech Euodias, and beseech Syntyche, that they be of the same mind in the Lord.

3 And I intreat thee also, true yokefellow, help those women which la-boured with me in the gospel, with Clement also, and *with* other my fellow-labourers, whose names *are* in the book of life.

4 Rejoice in the Lord alway: *and* again I say, Rejoice.

5 Let your moderation be known unto all men. The Lord *is* at hand.

6 Be careful for no-thing; but in every thing by prayer and supplication

---

19 ὧν τὸ τέλος ἀπώλεια, ὧν ὁ θεὸς
of whom the end [is] destruction, of whom the god [is]

ἡ κοιλία καὶ ἡ δόξα ἐν τῇ αἰσχύνῃ
the belly and the glory in the shame

αὐτῶν, οἱ τὰ ἐπίγεια φρονοῦντες. **20** ἡμῶν
of them, the the earthly things thinking. of us
[ones]

γὰρ τὸ πολίτευμα ἐν οὐρανοῖς ὑπάρχει,
For the citizenship in heavens is,

ἐξ οὗ καὶ σωτῆρα ἀπεκδεχόμεθα κύριον
from where also ³a Saviour ¹we await Lord

Ἰησοῦν Χριστόν, **21** ὃς μετασχηματίσει τὸ
Jesus Christ, who will change the

σῶμα τῆς ταπεινώσεως ἡμῶν σύμμορφον
body of the humiliation of us [making it] conformed

τῷ σώματι τῆς δόξης αὐτοῦ, κατὰ τὴν
to the body of the glory of him, according to the

ἐνέργειαν τοῦ δύνασθαι αὐτὸν καὶ ὑποτάξαι
operation of the to be able him[b] even to subject
=of his ability

αὐτῷ τὰ πάντα. **4** Ὥστε, ἀδελφοί μου
to him[self] – all things. So as, brothers of me

ἀγαπητοὶ καὶ ἐπιπόθητοι, χαρὰ καὶ
beloved and longed for, joy and

στέφανός μου, οὕτως στήκετε ἐν κυρίῳ, ἀγαπητοί.
crown of me, so stand in [the] Lord, beloved.

2 Εὐοδίαν παρακαλῶ καὶ Συντύχην
³Euodia ¹I beseech and ¹Syntyche

παρακαλῶ τὸ αὐτὸ φρονεῖν ἐν κυρίῳ.
¹I beseech ⁴the ⁵same thing ³to think in [the] Lord.

3 ναὶ ἐρωτῶ καὶ σέ, γνήσιε σύζυγε,
Yes[,] I ask also thee, genuine yoke-fellow,

συλλαμβάνου αὐταῖς, αἵτινες ἐν τῷ εὐαγ-
help them, who ³in ⁴the ⁵gos-

γελίῳ συνήθλησάν μοι μετὰ καὶ Κλήμεντος
pel ¹struggled with ²me with both Clement

καὶ τῶν λοιπῶν συνεργῶν μου, ὧν
and the remaining fellow-workers of me, of
whom

τὰ ὀνόματα ἐν βίβλῳ ζωῆς. **4** Χαίρετε
the names [are] in [the] book of life. Rejoice ye

ἐν κυρίῳ πάντοτε· πάλιν ἐρῶ, χαίρετε.
in [the] Lord always; again I will say, rejoice.

5 τὸ ἐπιεικὲς ὑμῶν γνωσθήτω πᾶσιν
The forbearance of you let it be known to all

ἀνθρώποις. ὁ κύριος ἐγγύς. **6** μηδὲν
men. The Lord [is] near. ²Nothing

μεριμνᾶτε, ἀλλ' ἐν παντὶ τῇ προσευχῇ
¹be ye anxious but in everything – by prayer
about,

with thanksgiving let your
requests be made known
unto God.

7 And the peace of God,
which passeth all under-
standing, shall keep your
hearts and minds through
Christ Jesus.

8 Finally, brethren,
whatsoever things are true,
whatsoever things *are*
honest, whatsoever things
are just, whatsoever things
are pure, whatsoever things
are lovely, whatsoever
things *are* of good report;
if *there be* any virtue, and
if *there be* any praise,
think on these things.

9 Those things, which
ye have both learned, and
received, and heard, and
seen in me, do: and the
God of peace shall be
with you.

10 But I rejoiced in the
Lord greatly, that now at
the last your care of me
hath flourished again;
wherein ye were also careful, but ye lacked oppor-
tunity.

11 Not that I speak in
respect of want: for I
have learned, in whatso-
ever state I am, *therewith*
to be content.

12 I know both how to
be abased, and I know
how to abound: every
where and in all things I
am instructed both to be
full and to be hungry,

καὶ   τῇ   δεήσει   μετὰ   εὐχαριστίας   τὰ
and   -   *by* petition   with   thanksgivings   the

αἰτήματα   ὑμῶν   γνωριζέσθω   πρὸς   τὸν
requests   of you   let be made known   to   -

θεόν.   7 καὶ   ἡ   εἰρήνη   τοῦ   θεοῦ   ἡ
God.   And   the   peace   -   of God   -

ὑπερέχουσα   πάντα   νοῦν   φρουρήσει   τὰς
surpassing   all   understanding   will guard   the

καρδίας   ὑμῶν   καὶ   τὰ   νοήματα   ὑμῶν
hearts   of you   and   the   thoughts   of you

ἐν   Χριστῷ   Ἰησοῦ.   8 Τὸ   λοιπόν,   ἀδελφοί,
in   Christ   Jesus.   For the rest,   brothers,

ὅσα   ἐστὶν   ἀληθῆ,   ὅσα   σεμνά,   ὅσα   δίκαια,
whatever are   true,   whatever grave,   whatever   just,
things   things   things

ὅσα   ἁγνά,   ὅσα   προσφιλῆ,   ὅσα   εὔφημα,
whatever pure,   whatever   lovable,   whatever well-spoken
things   things   things   of,

εἴ   τις   ἀρετὴ   καὶ   εἴ   τις   ἔπαινος,   9 ταῦτα
if   any   virtue   and   if   any   praise,   these things

λογίζεσθε·   ἃ   καὶ   ἐμάθετε   καὶ   παρελάβετε
consider ye;   which ²both   ¹ye ³learned   and   *ye* received
things

καὶ   ἠκούσατε   καὶ   εἴδετε   ἐν   ἐμοί,   ταῦτα
and   *ye* heard   and   *ye* saw   in   me,   these

πράσσετε·   καὶ   ὁ   θεὸς   τῆς   εἰρήνης   ἔσται
practise;   and   the   God   -   of peace   will be

μεθ'   ὑμῶν.
with   you.

10 Ἐχάρην   δὲ   ἐν   κυρίῳ   μεγάλως   ὅτι
Now I rejoiced   in   [the] Lord   greatly   that

ἤδη   ποτὲ   ἀνεθάλετε   τὸ   ὑπὲρ   ἐμοῦ   φρονεῖν·
al-   at one   ye revived   the   on behalf   me   to think;
ready   time   of
= now at length   = your thought for me;

ἐφ'   ᾧ   καὶ   ἐφρονεῖτε,   ἠκαιρεῖσθε   δέ.
as to   which   indeed   ye thought,   but ye had no opportunity.

11 οὐχ   ὅτι   καθ'   ὑστέρησιν   λέγω·   ἐγὼ
Not   that   ²by way of   ³lack   ¹I say;   ²I

γὰρ   ἔμαθον   ἐν   οἷς   εἰμι   αὐτάρκης   εἶναι.
¹for   learned   in   what   I am   ²self-   ¹to be.
conditions   sufficient

12 οἶδα   καὶ   ταπεινοῦσθαι,   οἶδα   καὶ   περισ-
I know   both   to be humbled,   and I know   to

σεύειν·   ἐν   παντὶ   καὶ   ἐν   πᾶσιν   μεμύημαι,
abound;   in everything   and   in   all things   I have been
initiated,

καὶ   χορτάζεσθαι   καὶ   πεινᾶν,   καὶ   περισ-
both   to be filled   and   to hunger,   both   to

788 PHILIPPIANS 4

both to abound and to
suffer need.
13 I can do all things
through Christ which
strengtheneth me.
14 Notwithstanding ye
have well done, that ye
did communicate with my
affliction.
15 Now ye Philippians
know also, that in the
beginning of the gospel,
when I departed from
Macedonia, no church
communicated with me as
concerning giving and re-
ceiving, but ye only.
16 For even in Thessa-
lonica ye sent once and
again unto my necessity.
17 Not because I desire
a gift: but I desire fruit
that may abound to your
account.
18 But I have all, and
abound: I am full, having
received of Epaphroditus
the things *which were sent*
from you, an odour of a
sweet smell, a sacrifice
acceptable, wellpleasing to
God.
19 But my God shall
supply all your need ac-
cording to his riches in
glory by Christ Jesus.
20 Now unto God and
our Father *be* glory for
ever and ever. Amen.
21 Salute every saint in
Christ Jesus. The breth-
ren which are with me
greet you.
22 All the saints salute

σεύειν καὶ ὑστερεῖσθαι. 13 πάντα ἰσχύω
abound and to lack. ³All things ¹I can do

ἐν τῷ ἐνδυναμοῦντί με. 14 πλὴν καλῶς
in the [one] empowering me. Nevertheless ²well

ἐποιήσατε συγκοινωνήσαντές μου τῇ θλίψει.
¹ye did having partnership in ²of me ¹the ²affliction.

15 οἴδατε δὲ καὶ ὑμεῖς, Φιλιππήσιοι, ὅτι
And ²know ³also ¹ye, Philippians, that

ἐν ἀρχῇ τοῦ εὐαγγελίου, ὅτε ἐξῆλθον
in [the] of the gospel, when I went out
beginning

ἀπὸ Μακεδονίας, οὐδεμία μοι ἐκκλησία
from Macedonia, not one ²me ¹church

ἐκοινώνησεν εἰς λόγον δόσεως καὶ λήμψεως
²shared with in matter of giving and receiving

εἰ μὴ ὑμεῖς μόνοι, 16 ὅτι καὶ ἐν
except ye only, because indeed in

Θεσσαλονίκῃ καὶ ἅπαξ καὶ δὶς εἰς τὴν
Thessalonica both once and twice to the
=to my need

χρείαν μοι ἐπέμψατε. 17 οὐχ ὅτι ἐπιζητῶ
need to meᵉ ye sent. Not that I seek

τὸ δόμα, ἀλλὰ ἐπιζητῶ τὸν καρπὸν
the gift, but I seek the fruit

τὸν πλεονάζοντα εἰς λόγον ὑμῶν. 18 ἀπέχω
- increasing to account of you. I have

δὲ πάντα καὶ περισσεύω· πεπλήρωμαι
But all things and abound; I have been filled

δεξάμενος παρὰ Ἐπαφροδίτου τὰ παρ'
receiving from Epaphroditus the things from

ὑμῶν, ὀσμὴν εὐωδίας, θυσίαν δεκτήν,
you, an odour of sweet smell, a sacrifice acceptable,

εὐάρεστον τῷ θεῷ. 19 ὁ δὲ θεός μου
well-pleasing - to God. And the God of me

πληρώσει πᾶσαν χρείαν ὑμῶν κατὰ τὸ
will fill every need of you according to the

πλοῦτος αὐτοῦ ἐν δόξῃ ἐν Χριστῷ Ἰησοῦ.
riches of him in glory in Christ Jesus.

20 τῷ δὲ θεῷ καὶ πατρὶ ἡμῶν ἡ δόξα
to the Now God and Father of us [be] the glory

εἰς τοὺς αἰῶνας τῶν αἰώνων· ἀμήν.
unto the ages of the ages: Amen.

21 Ἀσπάσασθε πάντα ἅγιον ἐν Χριστῷ
Greet ye every saint in Christ

Ἰησοῦ. ἀσπάζονται ὑμᾶς οἱ σὺν ἐμοὶ
Jesus. ³greet ⁴you ¹The ²with ⁴me

ἀδελφοί. 22 ἀσπάζονται ὑμᾶς πάντες οἱ
²brothers. ⁴greet ⁵you ¹All ²the

you, chiefly they that are
of Cæsar's household.

23 The grace of our
Lord Jesus Christ *be* with
you all. Amen.

ἄγιοι, μάλιστα δὲ οἱ ἐκ τῆς Καίσαρος
²saints,   but most of all   the ones of   ¹the   ²of Cæsar

οἰκίας.
¹household.

23 Ἡ χάρις τοῦ κυρίου Ἰησοῦ Χριστοῦ
The   grace   of the   Lord   Jesus   Christ

μετὰ τοῦ πνεύματος ὑμῶν.
[be] with   the   spirit   of you.

COLOSSIANS 1

ΠΡΟΣ ΚΟΛΟΣΣΑΕΙΣ
To Colossians

CHAPTER 1

PAUL, an apostle of
Jesus Christ by the
will of God, and Timo-
theus *our* brother,

2 To the saints and
faithful brethren in Christ
which are at Colosse:
Grace *be* unto you, and
peace, from God our
Father and the Lord
Jesus Christ.

3 We give thanks to
God and the Father of our
Lord Jesus Christ, praying
always for you,

4 Since we heard of
your faith in Christ Jesus,
and of the love *which ye
have* to all the saints,

5 For the hope which is
laid up for you in heaven,
whereof ye heard before in
the word of the truth of
the gospel;

6 Which is come unto
you, as *it is* in all the
world; and bringeth forth
fruit, as *it doth* also in you,

1 Παῦλος ἀπόστολος Χριστοῦ Ἰησοῦ διὰ
Paul   an apostle   of Christ   Jesus through

θελήματος θεοῦ καὶ Τιμόθεος ὁ ἀδελφὸς
[the] will   of God   and   Timothy   the   brother

2 τοῖς ἐν Κολοσσαῖς ἁγίοις καὶ πιστοῖς
to the   in   Colossae   saints   and   faithful

ἀδελφοῖς ἐν Χριστῷ· χάρις ὑμῖν καὶ
brothers   in   Christ: Grace   to you   and

εἰρήνη ἀπὸ θεοῦ πατρὸς ἡμῶν.
peace   from   God   Father   of us.

3 Εὐχαριστοῦμεν τῷ θεῷ πατρὶ τοῦ
We give thanks   –   to God   Father   of the

κυρίου ἡμῶν Ἰησοῦ [Χριστοῦ] πάντοτε
Lord   of us   Jesus   Christ   always

περὶ ὑμῶν προσευχόμενοι, 4 ἀκούσαντες
²concerning ³you   ¹praying,   having heard

τὴν πίστιν ὑμῶν ἐν Χριστῷ Ἰησοῦ
the   faith   of you   in   Christ   Jesus

καὶ τὴν ἀγάπην ἣν ἔχετε εἰς πάντας
and   the   love   which ye have   toward   all

τοὺς ἁγίους 5 διὰ τὴν ἐλπίδα τὴν
the   saints   because of   the   hope   the

ἀποκειμένην ὑμῖν ἐν τοῖς οὐρανοῖς, ἣν
being laid up   for you   in   *the*   heavens,   which

προηκούσατε ἐν τῷ λόγῳ τῆς ἀληθείας
ye previously   in   the   word   of the   truth
heard

τοῦ εὐαγγελίου 6 τοῦ παρόντος εἰς ὑμᾶς,
of the   gospel   –   coming   to   you,

καθὼς καὶ ἐν παντὶ τῷ κόσμῳ ἐστὶν
as   also   in   all   the   world   it is

καρποφορούμενον καὶ αὐξανόμενον καθὼς
bearing fruit   and   growing   as

since the day ye heard *of it*, and knew the grace of God in truth:

7 As ye also learned of Epaphras our dear fellowservant, who is for you a faithful minister of Christ;

8 Who also declared unto us your love in the Spirit.

9 For this cause we also, since the day we heard *it*, do not cease to pray for you, and to desire that ye might be filled with the knowledge of his will in all wisdom and spiritual understanding;

10 That ye might walk worthy of the Lord unto all pleasing, being fruitful in every good work, and increasing in the knowledge of God;

11 Strengthened with all might, according to his glorious power, unto all patience and longsuffering with joyfulness;

12 Giving thanks unto the Father, which hath made us meet to be partakers of the inheritance of the saints in light:

13 Who hath delivered us from the power of

καὶ ἐν ὑμῖν, ἀφ' ἧς ἡμέρας ἠκούσατε
also in you, from which day ye heard
= the day on which

καὶ ἐπέγνωτε τὴν χάριν τοῦ θεοῦ ἐν
and fully knew the grace - of God in

ἀληθείᾳ· 7 καθὼς ἐμάθετε ἀπὸ Ἐπαφρᾶ
truth; as ye learned from Epaphras

τοῦ ἀγαπητοῦ συνδούλου ἡμῶν, ὅς ἐστιν
the beloved fellow-slave of us, who is

πιστὸς ὑπὲρ ὑμῶν διάκονος τοῦ Χριστοῦ,
¹a ⁴on behalf ⁵you ²minister - ³of Christ,
faithful of

8 ὁ καὶ δηλώσας ἡμῖν τὴν ὑμῶν ἀγάπην
the also having shown to us ¹the ²of you ³love
[one]

ἐν πνεύματι.
in spirit.

9 Διὰ τοῦτο καὶ ἡμεῖς, ἀφ' ἧς ἡμέρας
Therefore also we, from which day
= the day on which

ἠκούσαμεν, οὐ παυόμεθα ὑπὲρ ὑμῶν
we heard, do not cease on behalf of you

προσευχόμενοι καὶ αἰτούμενοι ἵνα πληρω-
praying and asking in order ye may be
that

θῆτε τὴν ἐπίγνωσιν τοῦ θελήματος αὐτοῦ
filled the full knowledge of the will of him
[with]

ἐν πάσῃ σοφίᾳ καὶ συνέσει πνευματικῇ,
in all wisdom and understanding spiritual,

10 περιπατῆσαι ἀξίως τοῦ κυρίου εἰς
to walk worthily of the Lord to

πᾶσαν ἀρεσκείαν, ἐν παντὶ ἔργῳ ἀγαθῷ
all pleasing, in every work good

καρποφοροῦντες καὶ αὐξανόμενοι τῇ
bearing fruit and growing

ἐπιγνώσει τοῦ θεοῦ, 11 ἐν πάσῃ δυνάμει
full knowledge - of God, with all power

δυναμούμενοι κατὰ τὸ κράτος τῆς δόξης
being empowered according to the might of the glory

αὐτοῦ εἰς πᾶσαν ὑπομονὴν καὶ μακρο-
of him to all endurance and long-

θυμίαν, μετὰ χαρᾶς 12 εὐχαριστοῦντες τῷ
suffering, with joy giving thanks to the

πατρὶ τῷ ἱκανώσαντι ὑμᾶς εἰς τὴν μερίδα
Father - having made ²fit ¹you for the part

τοῦ κλήρου τῶν ἁγίων ἐν τῷ φωτί·
of the lot of the saints in *the* light;

13 ὃς ἐρρύσατο ἡμᾶς ἐκ τῆς ἐξουσίας
who delivered us out of the authority

darkness, and hath translated *us* into the kingdom of his dear Son:

14 In whom we have redemption through his blood, *even* the forgiveness of sins:

15 Who is the image of the invisible God, the firstborn of every creature:

16 For by him were all things created, that are in heaven, and that are in earth, visible and invisible, whether *they be* thrones, or dominions, or principalities, or powers: all things were created by him, and for him:

17 And he is before all things, and by him all things consist.

18 And he is the head of the body, the church: who is the beginning, the firstborn from the dead; that in all *things* he might have the preeminence.

19 For it pleased the *Father* that in him should all fulness dwell;

20 And, having made peace through the blood of his cross, by him to reconcile all things unto himself; by him, *I say*, whether *they be* things in earth, or things in heaven.

21 And you, that were sometime alienated and

τοῦ	σκότους	καὶ	μετέστησεν	εἰς	τὴν
of *the*	darkness	and	transferred	into	the

βασιλείαν	τοῦ	υἱοῦ	τῆς	ἀγάπης	αὐτοῦ,
kingdom	of the	Son	of the	love	of him,

14 ἐν ᾧ ἔχομεν τὴν ἀπολύτρωσιν, τὴν
in whom we have *the* redemption, the

ἄφεσιν τῶν ἁμαρτιῶν· **15** ὅς ἐστιν εἰκὼν
forgiveness of the sins; who is an image
(our)

τοῦ θεοῦ τοῦ ἀοράτου, πρωτότοκος πάσης
of the God – invisible, firstborn of all

κτίσεως, **16** ὅτι ἐν αὐτῷ ἐκτίσθη τὰ
creation, because in him were created –

πάντα ἐν τοῖς οὐρανοῖς καὶ ἐπὶ τῆς
all things in *the* heavens and on the

γῆς, τὰ ὁρατὰ καὶ τὰ ἀόρατα, εἴτε
earth, the visible and the invisible, whether

θρόνοι εἴτε κυριότητες εἴτε ἀρχαὶ εἴτε
thrones or lordships or rulers or

ἐξουσίαι· τὰ πάντα δι' αὐτοῦ καὶ εἰς
authorities; – all things through him and for

αὐτὸν ἔκτισται· **17** καὶ αὐτός ἐστιν πρὸ
him have been created; and he is before

πάντων καὶ τὰ πάντα ἐν αὐτῷ συνέστηκεν,
all things and – all things in him consisted,

18 καὶ αὐτός ἐστιν ἡ κεφαλὴ τοῦ σώματος,
and he is the head of the body,

τῆς ἐκκλησίας· ὅς ἐστιν ἀρχή, πρωτότοκος
of the church; who is [the] firstborn
beginning,

ἐκ τῶν νεκρῶν, ἵνα γένηται ἐν πᾶσιν
from the dead, in order ⁴may be ²in ³all
that things

αὐτὸς πρωτεύων, **19** ὅτι ἐν αὐτῷ εὐδόκησεν
¹he ⁵holding the because in him ⁴was well
first place, pleased

πᾶν τὸ πλήρωμα κατοικῆσαι **20** καὶ δι'
¹all ²the ³fulness to dwell and through

αὐτοῦ ἀποκαταλλάξαι τὰ πάντα εἰς αὐτόν,
him to reconcile – all things to him[?self],

εἰρηνοποιήσας διὰ τοῦ αἵματος τοῦ σταυροῦ
making peace through the blood of the cross

αὐτοῦ, δι' αὐτοῦ εἴτε τὰ ἐπὶ τῆς γῆς
of him, through him whether the on the earth
things

εἴτε τὰ ἐν τοῖς οὐρανοῖς. **21** Καὶ ὑμᾶς
or the things in *the* heavens. And you

ποτε ὄντας ἀπηλλοτριωμένους καὶ ἐχθροὺς
then being *having been* alienated and enemies

enemies in *your* mind by wicked works, yet now hath he reconciled

22 In the body of his flesh through death, to present you holy and unblameable and unreproveable in his sight:

23 If ye continue in the faith grounded and settled, and *be* not moved away from the hope of the gospel, which ye have heard, *and* which was preached to every creature which is under heaven; whereof I Paul am made a minister;

24 Who now rejoice in my sufferings for you, and fill up that which is behind of the afflictions of Christ in my flesh for his body's sake, which is the church:

25 Whereof I am made a minister, according to the dispensation of God which is given to me for you, to fulfil the word of God;

26 *Even* the mystery which hath been hid from ages and from generations, but now is made manifest to his saints:

27 To whom God would make known what *is* the riches of the glory of this

---

τῇ διανοίᾳ ἐν τοῖς ἔργοις τοῖς πονηροῖς,
in *the* mind by the(your) works - evil,

22 νυνὶ δὲ ἀποκατήλλαξεν ἐν τῷ σώματι
but now he reconciled in the body

τῆς σαρκὸς αὐτοῦ διὰ τοῦ θανάτου,
of the flesh of him through the(his) death,

παραστῆσαι ὑμᾶς ἁγίους καὶ ἀμώμους
to present you holy and blameless

καὶ ἀνεγκλήτους κατενώπιον αὐτοῦ, 23 εἴ
and irreproachable before him, if

γε ἐπιμένετε τῇ πίστει τεθεμελιωμένοι
indeed ye continue in the faith having been founded

καὶ ἑδραῖοι καὶ μὴ μετακινούμενοι ἀπὸ
and steadfast and not being moved away from

τῆς ἐλπίδος τοῦ εὐαγγελίου οὗ ἠκούσατε,
the hope of the gospel which ye heard,

τοῦ κηρυχθέντος ἐν πάσῃ κτίσει τῇ
- proclaimed in all creation -

ὑπὸ τὸν οὐρανόν, οὗ ἐγενόμην ἐγὼ
under *the* heaven, of which [2]became [1]I

Παῦλος διάκονος.
[1]Paul a minister.

24 Νῦν χαίρω ἐν τοῖς παθήμασιν ὑπὲρ
Now I rejoice in the(my) sufferings on behalf of

ὑμῶν, καὶ ἀνταναπληρῶ τὰ ὑστερήματα
you, and fill up the things lacking

τῶν θλίψεων τοῦ Χριστοῦ ἐν τῇ σαρκί
of the afflictions - of Christ in the flesh

μου ὑπὲρ τοῦ σώματος αὐτοῦ, ὅ ἐστιν
of me on behalf of the body of him, which is

ἡ ἐκκλησία, 25 ἧς ἐγενόμην ἐγὼ διάκονος
the church, of which became I a minister

κατὰ τὴν οἰκονομίαν τοῦ θεοῦ τὴν
according- the stewardship - of God -
ing to

δοθεῖσάν μοι εἰς ὑμᾶς πληρῶσαι τὸν
given to me for you to fulfil the

λόγον τοῦ θεοῦ, 26 τὸ μυστήριον τὸ
word - of God, the mystery -

ἀποκεκρυμμένον ἀπὸ τῶν αἰώνων καὶ
having been hidden from the ages and

ἀπὸ τῶν γενεῶν — νῦν δὲ ἐφανερώθη
from the generations — but now was manifested

τοῖς ἁγίοις αὐτοῦ, 27 οἷς ἠθέλησεν ὁ
to the saints of him, to whom [2]wished -

θεὸς γνωρίσαι τί τὸ πλοῦτος τῆς δόξης
[1]God to make known what [is] the riches of the glory

mystery among the Gentiles; which is Christ in you, the hope of glory:

28 Whom we preach, warning every man, and teaching every man in all wisdom; that we may present every man perfect in Christ Jesus:

29 Whereunto I also labour, striving according to his working, which worketh in me mightily.

τοῦ μυστηρίου τούτου ἐν τοῖς ἔθνεσιν,
of the mystery of this among the nations,

ὅς ἐστιν Χριστὸς ἐν ὑμῖν, ἡ ἐλπὶς τῆς
who is Christ in you, the hope of the

δόξης· 28 ὃν ἡμεῖς καταγγέλλομεν νου-
glory; whom we announce warn-

θετοῦντες πάντα ἄνθρωπον καὶ διδάσκοντες
ing every man and teaching

πάντα ἄνθρωπον ἐν πάσῃ σοφίᾳ,
every man in all wisdom,

ἵνα παραστήσωμεν πάντα ἄνθρωπον
in order we may present every man
der that

τέλειον ἐν Χριστῷ· 29 εἰς ὃ καὶ κοπιῶ
mature in Christ; for which also I labour

ἀγωνιζόμενος κατὰ τὴν ἐνέργειαν αὐτοῦ
struggling accord- the operation of him
ing to

τὴν ἐνεργουμένην ἐν ἐμοὶ ἐν δυνάμει.
- operating in me in power.

CHAPTER 2

FOR I would that ye knew what great conflict I have for you, and for them at Laodicea, and for as many as have not seen my face in the flesh;

2 That their hearts might be comforted, being knit together in love, and unto all riches of the full assurance of understanding, to the acknowledgement of the mystery of God, and of the Father, and of Christ;

3 In whom are hid all the treasures of wisdom and knowledge.

4 And this I say, lest any man should beguile you with enticing words.

5 For though I be absent in the flesh, yet am I with you in the spirit, joying and behold-

2 Θέλω γὰρ ὑμᾶς εἰδέναι ἡλίκον ἀγῶνα
For I wish you to know how great a struggle

ἔχω ὑπὲρ ὑμῶν καὶ τῶν ἐν Λαοδικείᾳ
I have on behalf of you and the [ones] in Laodicea

καὶ ὅσοι οὐχ ἑόρακαν τὸ πρόσωπόν μου
and as many as have not seen the face of me

ἐν σαρκί, 2 ἵνα παρακληθῶσιν αἱ καρδίαι
in flesh, in order ⁴may be ¹the ²hearts
that comforted

αὐτῶν, συμβιβασθέντες ἐν ἀγάπῃ καὶ εἰς
³of them, being joined together in love and for

πᾶν πλοῦτος τῆς πληροφορίας τῆς
all riches of the full assurance

συνέσεως, εἰς ἐπίγνωσιν τοῦ μυστηρίου
of under- for full knowledge of the mystery
standing,

τοῦ θεοῦ, Χριστοῦ, 3 ἐν ᾧ εἰσιν πάντες
- of God, of Christ, in whom ¹are ³all

οἱ θησαυροὶ τῆς σοφίας καὶ γνώσεως
⁴the ⁵treasures - ⁶of wisdom ⁷and ⁸of knowledge

ἀπόκρυφοι. 4 Τοῦτο λέγω ἵνα μηδεὶς
²hidden. This I say in order no one
that

ὑμᾶς παραλογίζηται ἐν πιθανολογίᾳ. 5 εἰ
²you ¹may beguile with persuasive speech. if

γὰρ καὶ τῇ σαρκὶ ἄπειμι, ἀλλὰ τῷ
For indeed in the flesh I am absent, yet in the

πνεύματι σὺν ὑμῖν εἰμι, χαίρων καὶ
spirit ²with ³you ¹I am, rejoicing and

ing your order, and the stedfastness of your faith in Christ.

6 As ye have therefore received Christ Jesus the Lord, *so* walk ye in him:

7 Rooted and built up in him, and stablished in the faith, as ye have been taught, abounding therein with thanksgiving.

8 Beware lest any man spoil you through philosophy and vain deceit, after the tradition of men, after the rudiments of the world, and not after Christ.

9 For in him dwelleth all the fulness of the Godhead bodily.

10 And ye are complete in him, which is the head of all principality and power:

11 In whom also ye are circumcised with the circumcision made without hands, in putting off the body of the sins of the flesh by the circumcision of Christ:

12 Buried with him in baptism, wherein also ye are risen with *him* through the faith of the operation of God, who hath raised him from the dead.

13 And you, being dead

βλέπων ὑμῶν τὴν τάξιν καὶ τὸ στερέωμα
seeing ²of you ¹the ²order and the firmness

τῆς εἰς Χριστὸν πίστεως ὑμῶν.
of the ³in ⁴Christ ¹faith ²of you.

6 Ὡς οὖν παρελάβετε τὸν Χριστὸν
As therefore ye received - Christ

Ἰησοῦν τὸν κύριον, ἐν αὐτῷ περιπατεῖτε,
Jesus the Lord, in him walk ye,

7 ἐρριζωμένοι καὶ ἐποικοδομούμενοι ἐν αὐτῷ
having been rooted and being built up in him

καὶ βεβαιούμενοι τῇ πίστει καθὼς ἐδιδάχ-
and being confirmed in the faith as ye were

θητε, περισσεύοντες ἐν εὐχαριστίᾳ.
taught, abounding in thanksgiving.

8 Βλέπετε μή τις ὑμᾶς ἔσται ὁ συλαγωγῶν
Look ye lest ²anyone ⁴you ¹there - ³robbing
shall be

διὰ τῆς φιλοσοφίας καὶ κενῆς ἀπάτης
through - philosophy and empty deceit

κατὰ τὴν παράδοσιν τῶν ἀνθρώπων, κατὰ
accord- the tradition - of men, according to ing to

τὰ στοιχεῖα τοῦ κόσμου καὶ οὐ κατὰ
the elements of the world and not according to

Χριστόν· 9 ὅτι ἐν αὐτῷ κατοικεῖ πᾶν
Christ; because in him dwells all

τὸ πλήρωμα τῆς θεότητος σωματικῶς,
the fulness of the Godhead bodily,

10 καὶ ἐστὲ ἐν αὐτῷ πεπληρωμένοι, ὅς
and ye are in him *having been* filled, who

ἐστιν ἡ κεφαλὴ πάσης ἀρχῆς καὶ ἐξουσίας,
is the head of all rule and authority,

11 ἐν ᾧ καὶ περιετμήθητε περιτομῇ
in whom also ye were with a
circumcised circumcision

ἀχειροποιήτῳ ἐν τῇ ἀπεκδύσει τοῦ σώματος
not handwrought by the putting off of the body

τῆς σαρκός, ἐν τῇ περιτομῇ τοῦ Χριστοῦ,
of the flesh, by the circumcision - of Christ,

12 συνταφέντες αὐτῷ ἐν τῷ βαπτίσματι,
co-buried with him in the baptism,

ἐν ᾧ καὶ συνηγέρθητε διὰ τῆς πίστεως
in whom also ye were co-raised through the faith

τῆς ἐνεργείας τοῦ θεοῦ τοῦ ἐγείραντος
of (in) the operation - of God - raising

αὐτὸν ἐκ νεκρῶν· 13 καὶ ὑμᾶς νεκροὺς
him from [the] dead; and you dead

in your sins and the uncircumcision of your flesh, hath he quickened together with him, having forgiven you all trespasses;

14 Blotting out the handwriting of ordinances that was against us, which was contrary to us, and took it out of the way, nailing it to his cross;

15 And having spoiled principalities and powers, he made a shew of them openly, triumphing over them in it.

16 Let no man therefore judge you in meat, or in drink, or in respect of an holyday, or of the new moon, or of the sabbath *days*:

17 Which are a shadow of things to come; but the body *is* of Christ.

18 Let no man beguile you of your reward in a voluntary humility and worshipping of angels, intruding into those things which he hath not seen, vainly puffed up by his fleshly mind,

19 And not holding the Head, from which all the body by joints and bands having nourishment ministered, and knit together, increaseth with the increase of God.

ὄντας τοῖς παραπτώμασιν καὶ τῇ ἀκρο-
being   in the   trespasses   and in the   uncir-

βυστίᾳ τῆς σαρκὸς ὑμῶν, συνεζωοποίησεν
cumcision of the   flesh   of you,   he co-quickened

ὑμᾶς σὺν αὐτῷ, χαρισάμενος ἡμῖν πάντα
you   with   him,   forgiving   you   all

τὰ παραπτώματα· 14 ἐξαλείψας τὸ καθ'
the   trespasses;   wiping out   [1]the   [2]against

ἡμῶν χειρόγραφον τοῖς δόγμασιν ὃ ἦν
[4]us   [3]handwriting   –   in ordinances which was

ὑπεναντίον ἡμῖν, καὶ αὐτὸ ἦρκεν ἐκ
contrary   to us,   and   [2]it   [1]has taken out of

τοῦ μέσου, προσηλώσας αὐτὸ τῷ σταυρῷ·
the midst(way),   nailing   it   to the   cross;

15 ἀπεκδυσάμενος τὰς ἀρχὰς καὶ τὰς
putting off   the   rulers   and   the

ἐξουσίας ἐδειγμάτισεν ἐν παρρησίᾳ,
authorities   he exposed [them]   with   openness,

θριαμβεύσας αὐτοὺς ἐν αὐτῷ.
triumphing [over]   them   in   it.

16 Μὴ οὖν τις ὑμᾶς κρινέτω ἐν βρώσει
[2]Not [3]there-[4]any-[5]you [1]let [6]judge in eating
fore one

καὶ ἐν πόσει ἢ ἐν μέρει ἑορτῆς ἢ
and   in   drinking   or   in   respect   of a feast   or

νεομηνίας ἢ σαββάτων, 17 ἅ ἐστιν σκιὰ
of a new moon or   of sabbaths,   which is(are)   a
things   shadow

τῶν μελλόντων, τὸ δὲ σῶμα τοῦ Χριστοῦ.
of things coming,   but the   body [is]   –   of Christ.

18 μηδεὶς ὑμᾶς καταβραβευέτω θέλων ἐν
[2]No one   [4]you   [1]let [3]give judgment   wishing   in
against   [to do so]

ταπεινοφροσύνῃ καὶ θρησκείᾳ τῶν ἀγγέλων,
humility*   and   worship   of the   angels,

ἃ ἑόρακεν ἐμβατεύων, εἰκῇ φυσιούμενος
[2]things [3]he has [1]intruding into, in vain   being puffed up
which   seen

ὑπὸ τοῦ νοὸς τῆς σαρκὸς αὐτοῦ, 19 καὶ
by   the   mind   of the   flesh   of him,   and

οὐ κρατῶν τὴν κεφαλήν, ἐξ οὗ πᾶν
not   holding   the   head,   from whom   all

τὸ σῶμα διὰ τῶν ἀφῶν καὶ συνδέσμων
the   body [4]by means [5]the   [6]joints   [7]and   [8]bands
of   (its)

ἐπιχορηγούμενον καὶ συμβιβαζόμενον αὔξει
[1]being supplied   [2]and   [3]*being* joined together   will grow

τὴν αὔξησιν τοῦ θεοῦ.
[with] the   growth   –   of God.

* Ellicott supplies " false ". *Cf.* ver. 23.

20 Wherefore if ye be dead with Christ from the rudiments of the world, why, as though living in the world, are ye subject to ordinances,

21 (Touch not; taste not; handle not;

22 Which all are to perish with the using;) after the commandments and doctrines of men?

23 Which things have indeed a shew of wisdom in will worship, and humility, and neglecting of the body; not in any honour to the satisfying of the flesh.

20 Εἰ ἀπεθάνετε σὺν Χριστῷ ἀπὸ τῶν στοι-
　　If　ye died　with　Christ　from　the　ele-

χείων τοῦ κόσμου, τί ὡς ζῶντες ἐν κόσμῳ
ments of the　world, why　as　living　in [the] world

δογματίζεσθε· **21** μὴ ἅψῃ μηδὲ γεύσῃ μηδὲ
are ye subject to　　　Do not touch　nor　taste　nor
[its] decrees:

θίγῃς, **22** ἅ ἐστιν πάντα εἰς φθορὰν
handle,　　which　is(are)　all　for　corruption
　　　　　　things

τῇ ἀποχρήσει, κατὰ τὰ ἐντάλματα καὶ
in the　using,　according to the　injunctions　and

διδασκαλίας τῶν ἀνθρώπων; **23** ἅτινά ἐστιν
teachings　　－　of men?　　¹which ³is(are)
　　　　　　　　　　　　things

λόγον μὲν ἔχοντα σοφίας ἐν ἐθελοθρησκίᾳ
⁵a repute ²indeed ⁴having of wisdom in　self-imposed
　　　　　　　　　　　　　　　　　worship

καὶ ταπεινοφροσύνῃ καὶ ἀφειδίᾳ σώματος, οὐκ
and　humility　and severity of [the] body, not

ἐν τιμῇ τινι πρὸς πλησμονὴν τῆς σαρκός.
in ²honour ¹any　for　satisfaction of the　flesh.

CHAPTER 3

IF ye then be risen with Christ, seek those things which are above, where Christ sitteth on the right hand of God.

2 Set your affection on things above, not on things on the earth.

3 For ye are dead, and your life is hid with Christ in God.

4 When Christ, *who is* our life, shall appear, then shall ye also appear with him in glory.

5 Mortify therefore your members which are upon the earth; fornication, uncleanness, inordinate affection, evil concupiscence, and covetousness, which is idolatry:

6 For which things' sake

3 Εἰ οὖν συνηγέρθητε τῷ Χριστῷ, τὰ
　　If therefore ye were co-raised　－　with Christ,　the
　　　　　　　　　　　　　　　　　　　things

ἄνω ζητεῖτε, οὗ ὁ Χριστός ἐστιν ἐν
above　seek,　where　－　Christ　¹is　²at

δεξιᾷ τοῦ θεοῦ καθήμενος· **2** τὰ ἄνω
⁴[the] right　－　⁵of God　²sitting;　the above
[hand]　　　　　　　　　　　　　　things

φρονεῖτε, μὴ τὰ ἐπὶ τῆς γῆς. **3** ἀπεθάνετε
mind ye,　not the　on　the earth.　　ye died
　　　　　　things

γάρ, καὶ ἡ ζωὴ ὑμῶν κέκρυπται σὺν
For,　and　the　life　of you　has been hidden　with

τῷ Χριστῷ ἐν τῷ θεῷ· **4** ὅταν ὁ Χριστὸς
－　Christ　in　－　God; whenever　－　Christ

φανερωθῇ, ἡ ζωὴ ἡμῶν, τότε καὶ ὑμεῖς
is manifested,　the　life　of us,　then also　ye

σὺν αὐτῷ φανερωθήσεσθε ἐν δόξῃ.
with　him　will be manifested　in　glory.

5 Νεκρώσατε οὖν τὰ μέλη τὰ ἐπὶ
　　Put ye to death therefore the members　－　on
　　　　　　　　　　　　　(your)

τῆς γῆς, πορνείαν, ἀκαθαρσίαν, πάθος,
the　earth,　fornication,　uncleanness,　passion,

ἐπιθυμίαν κακήν, καὶ τὴν πλεονεξίαν ἥτις
desire　bad,　and　the　covetousness　which

ἐστὶν εἰδωλολατρία, **6** δι' ἃ ἔρχεται ἡ
is　idolatry,　　because which is coming the
　　　　　　　　　　of　things

the wrath of God cometh on the children of disobedience:

7 In the which ye also walked some time, when ye lived in them.

8 But now ye also put off all these; anger, wrath, malice, blasphemy, filthy communication out of your mouth.

9 Lie not one to another, seeing that ye have put off the old man with his deeds;

10 And have put on the new *man*, which is renewed in knowledge after the image of him that created him:

11 Where there is neither Greek nor Jew, circumcision nor uncircumcision, Barbarian, Scythian, bond *nor* free: but Christ *is* all, and in all.

12 Put on therefore, as the elect of God, holy and beloved, bowels of mercies, kindness, humbleness of mind, meekness, longsuffering;

13 Forbearing one another, and forgiving one another, if any man have a quarrel against any: even as Christ forgave you, so also *do* ye.

14 And above all these things *put on* charity, which is the bond of perfectness.

15 And let the peace of God rule in your hearts,

ὀργὴ τοῦ θεοῦ· 7 ἐν οἷς καὶ ὑμεῖς
wrath   –   of God;   in   which indeed   ye

περιεπατήσατέ ποτε, ὅτε ἐζῆτε ἐν τούτοις·
walked   then,   when   ye lived   in these things;

8 νυνὶ δὲ ἀπόθεσθε καὶ ὑμεῖς τὰ πάντα,
but now ¹put ³away ⁴also ²ye – all things,

ὀργήν, θυμόν, κακίαν, βλασφημίαν, αἰσχρο-
wrath, anger, malice, blasphemy, a-

λογίαν ἐκ τοῦ στόματος ὑμῶν· 9 μὴ
buse out of the mouth of you; not

ψεύδεσθε εἰς ἀλλήλους, ἀπεκδυσάμενοι τὸν
lie ye to one another, having put off the

παλαιὸν ἄνθρωπον σὺν ταῖς πράξεσιν
old man with the practices

αὐτοῦ, 10 καὶ ἐνδυσάμενοι τὸν νέον τὸν
of him, and having put on the new man –

ἀνακαινούμενον εἰς ἐπίγνωσιν κατ᾽ εἰκόνα
being renewed in full knowledge according [the]
  to image

τοῦ κτίσαντος αὐτόν, 11 ὅπου οὐκ ἔνι
of the [one] creating him, where ⁴have no place

Ἕλλην καὶ Ἰουδαῖος, περιτομὴ καὶ
¹Greek ²and ³Jew, circumcision and

ἀκροβυστία, βάρβαρος, Σκύθης, δοῦλος,
uncircumcision, barbarian, Scythian, slave,

ἐλεύθερος, ἀλλὰ πάντα καὶ ἐν πᾶσιν
freeman, but ³all things ⁴and ⁵in ⁶all

Χριστός. 12 Ἐνδύσασθε οὖν, ὡς ἐκλεκτοὶ
¹Christ ²[is]. Put ye on therefore, as chosen ones

τοῦ θεοῦ ἅγιοι καὶ ἠγαπημένοι, σπλάγχνα
– of God holy and having been loved, bowels

οἰκτιρμοῦ, χρηστότητα, ταπεινοφροσύνην,
of compassion, kindness, humility,

πραΰτητα, μακροθυμίαν, 13 ἀνεχόμενοι ἀλ-
meekness, long-suffering, forbearing one

λήλων καὶ χαριζόμενοι ἑαυτοῖς, ἐάν τις
another and forgiving yourselves, if anyone

πρός τινα ἔχῃ μομφήν· καθὼς καὶ ὁ
³against ⁴anyone ¹has ²a complaint; as indeed the

κύριος ἐχαρίσατο ὑμῖν οὕτως καὶ ὑμεῖς·
Lord forgave you so also ye;

14 ἐπὶ πᾶσιν δὲ τούτοις τὴν ἀγάπην,
²over ³all ¹and these things – love,

ὅ ἐστιν σύνδεσμος τῆς τελειότητος. 15 καὶ
which is [the] bond – of completeness. And

ἡ εἰρήνη τοῦ Χριστοῦ βραβευέτω ἐν ταῖς
²the ³peace – ⁴of Christ ¹let ⁵rule in the

to the which also ye are called in one body; and be ye thankful.

16 Let the word of Christ dwell in you richly in all wisdom; teaching and admonishing one another in psalms and hymns and spiritual songs, singing with grace in your hearts to the Lord.

17 And whatsoever ye do in word or deed, *do* all in the name of the Lord Jesus, giving thanks to God and the Father by him.

18 Wives, submit yourselves unto your own husbands, as it is fit in the Lord.

19 Husbands, love *your* wives, and be not bitter against them.

20 Children, obey *your* parents in all things: for this is well pleasing unto the Lord.

21 Fathers, provoke not your children *to anger,* lest they be discouraged.

22 Servants, obey in all things *your* masters according to the flesh; not with eyeservice, as menpleasers; but in singleness of heart, fearing God:

23 And whatsoever ye

καρδίαις ὑμῶν, εἰς ἣν καὶ ἐκλήθητε
hearts of you, to which indeed ye were called

ἐν ἑνὶ σώματι· καὶ εὐχάριστοι γίνεσθε.
in one body; and thankful be ye.

16 ὁ λόγος τοῦ Χριστοῦ ἐνοικείτω ἐν
²The ³word – ⁴of Christ ¹let ⁵indwell in

ὑμῖν πλουσίως, ἐν πάσῃ σοφίᾳ διδάσκοντες
you richly, in all wisdom teaching

καὶ νουθετοῦντες ἑαυτούς, ψαλμοῖς ὕμνοις
and admonishing yourselves, in psalms[,] hymns[,]

ᾠδαῖς πνευματικαῖς ἐν τῇ χάριτι ᾄδοντες
[and] ²songs ¹spiritual with – grace singing

ἐν ταῖς καρδίαις ὑμῶν τῷ θεῷ· 17 καὶ
in the hearts of you – to God; and

πᾶν ὅ τι ἐὰν ποιῆτε ἐν λόγῳ ἢ ἐν
every-thing whatever ye do in word or in

ἔργῳ, πάντα ἐν ὀνόματι κυρίου Ἰησοῦ,
work, all things [do] in [the] name of [the] Lord Jesus,

εὐχαριστοῦντες τῷ θεῷ πατρὶ δι' αὐτοῦ.
giving thanks – to God [the] through him.
Father

18 Αἱ γυναῖκες, ὑποτάσσεσθε τοῖς
The wives, be ye subject to the(your)

ἀνδράσιν, ὡς ἀνῆκεν ἐν κυρίῳ. 19 Οἱ
husbands, as is befitting in [the] Lord. The

ἄνδρες, ἀγαπᾶτε τὰς γυναῖκας καὶ μὴ
husbands, love ye the(your) wives and not

πικραίνεσθε πρὸς αὐτάς. 20 Τὰ τέκνα,
be bitter toward them. The children,

ὑπακούετε τοῖς γονεῦσιν κατὰ πάντα,
obey ye the(your) parents in all respects,

τοῦτο γὰρ εὐάρεστόν ἐστιν ἐν κυρίῳ.
for this well-pleasing is in [the] Lord.

21 Οἱ πατέρες, μὴ ἐρεθίζετε τὰ τέκνα
The fathers, do not ye provoke the children

ὑμῶν, ἵνα μὴ ἀθυμῶσιν. 22 Οἱ δοῦλοι,
of you, lest they be disheartened. The slaves,

ὑπακούετε κατὰ πάντα τοῖς κατὰ σάρκα
obey ye in all respects ¹the ²accord- ⁴[the]
(your) ing to flesh

κυρίοις, μὴ ἐν ὀφθαλμοδουλίαις ὡς
²lords, not with eyeservice as

ἀνθρωπάρεσκοι, ἀλλ' ἐν ἁπλότητι καρδίας
men-pleasers, but in singleness of heart

φοβούμενοι τὸν κύριον. 23 ὃ ἐὰν ποιῆτε,
fearing the Lord. Whatever ye do,

do, do *it* heartily, as to the Lord, and not unto men;

24 Knowing that of the Lord ye shall receive the reward of the inheritance: for ye serve the Lord Christ.

25 But he that doeth wrong shall receive for the wrong which he hath done: and there is no respect of persons.

CHAPTER 4

MASTERS, give unto *your* servants that which is just and equal; knowing that ye also have a Master in heaven.

2 Continue in prayer, and watch in the same with thanksgiving;

3 Withal praying also for us, that God would open unto us a door of utterance, to speak the mystery of Christ, for which I am also in bonds:

4 That I may make it manifest, as I ought to speak.

5 Walk in wisdom toward them that are without, redeeming the time.

6 Let your speech *be* alway with grace, seasoned with salt, that ye may know how ye ought to answer every man.

7 All my state shall Tychicus declare unto you,

ἐκ ψυχῆς ἐργάζεσθε ὡς τῷ κυρίῳ καὶ
from [the] soul work ye as to the Lord and

οὐκ ἀνθρώποις, 24 εἰδότες ὅτι ἀπὸ κυρίου
not to men, knowing that from [the] Lord

ἀπολήμψεσθε τὴν ἀνταπόδοσιν τῆς κλη-
ye will receive the reward of the in-

ρονομίας. τῷ κυρίῳ Χριστῷ δουλεύετε·
heritance. The Lord Christ ye serve;

25 ὁ γὰρ ἀδικῶν κομίσεται ὃ ἠδίκησεν,
for the [one] doing wrong will receive what he did wrong,

καὶ οὐκ ἔστιν προσωπολημψία. 4 Οἱ κύριοι,
and there is no respect of persons. The lords,

τὸ δίκαιον καὶ τὴν ἰσότητα τοῖς δούλοις
³the ²just thing ⁴and ⁵the ⁶equality ⁷to the(your) ⁸slaves

παρέχεσθε, εἰδότες ὅτι καὶ ὑμεῖς ἔχετε
¹supply ye, knowing that also ye have

κύριον ἐν οὐρανῷ.
a Lord in heaven.

2 Τῇ προσευχῇ προσκαρτερεῖτε, γρηγο-
In *the* prayer continue ye, watch-

ροῦντες ἐν αὐτῇ ἐν εὐχαριστίᾳ, 3 προσευ-
ing in it with thanksgiving, pray-

χόμενοι ἅμα καὶ περὶ ἡμῶν, ἵνα ὁ
ing together also concerning us, *in order that* –

θεὸς ἀνοίξῃ ἡμῖν θύραν τοῦ λόγου,
God may open to us a door of the word,

λαλῆσαι τὸ μυστήριον τοῦ Χριστοῦ, δι'
to speak the mystery – of Christ, because of

ὃ καὶ δέδεμαι, 4 ἵνα φανερώσω αὐτὸ
which indeed I have been bound, in order that I may manifest it

ὡς δεῖ με λαλῆσαι. 5 Ἐν σοφίᾳ
as it behoves me to speak. In wisdom

περιπατεῖτε πρὸς τοὺς ἔξω, τὸν καιρὸν
walk ye toward the ones outside, ²the ³time

ἐξαγοραζόμενοι. 6 ὁ λόγος ὑμῶν πάντοτε
¹redeeming. The speech of you always
[let it be]

ἐν χάριτι, ἅλατι ἠρτυμένος, εἰδέναι πῶς
in grace, with salt *having been* to know how
seasoned,

δεῖ ὑμᾶς ἑνὶ ἑκάστῳ ἀποκρίνεσθαι.
it be- you ³one ²each ¹to answer.
hoves

7 Τὰ κατ' ἐμὲ πάντα γνωρίσει ὑμῖν Τύχικος
²The ³about ⁴me ¹all ⁶will make ⁷to you ⁵Tychicus
things known

who is a beloved brother, and a faithful minister and fellowservant in the Lord:

8 Whom I have sent unto you for the same purpose, that he might know your estate, and comfort your hearts;

9 With Onesimus, a faithful and beloved brother, who is one of you. They shall make known unto you all things which are done here.

10 Aristarchus my fellowprisoner saluteth you, and Marcus, sister's son to Barnabas, (touching whom ye received commandments: if he come unto you, receive him;)

11 And Jesus, which is called Justus, who are of the circumcision. These only are my fellowworkers unto the kingdom of God, which have been a comfort unto me.

12 Epaphras, who is one of you, a servant of Christ, saluteth you, always labouring fervently for you in prayers, that ye may stand perfect and complete in all the will of God.

13 For I bear him record, that he hath a great zeal for you, and them that are in Laodicea, and them in Hierapolis.

ὁ ἀγαπητὸς ἀδελφὸς καὶ πιστὸς διάκονος
the beloved brother and faithful minister

καὶ σύνδουλος ἐν κυρίῳ, 8 ὃν ἔπεμψα
and fellow-slave in [the] Lord, whom I sent

πρὸς ὑμᾶς εἰς αὐτὸ τοῦτο, ἵνα γνῶτε
to you for this very thing, in order ye might
that know

τὰ περὶ ἡμῶν καὶ παρακαλέσῃ τὰς
the concern-us and he might comfort the
things ing

καρδίας ὑμῶν, 9 σὺν Ὀνησίμῳ τῷ πιστῷ
hearts of you, with Onesimus the faithful

καὶ ἀγαπητῷ ἀδελφῷ, ὅς ἐστιν ἐξ ὑμῶν·
and beloved brother, who is of you;

πάντα ὑμῖν γνωρίσουσιν τὰ ὧδε.
¹all ⁵to you ⁴they will ²the ³here.
make known things

10 Ἀσπάζεται ὑμᾶς Ἀρίσταρχος ὁ
¹greets ⁶you ¹Aristarchus ²the

συναιχμάλωτός μου, καὶ Μᾶρκος ὁ ἀνεψιὸς
³fellow-captive ⁴of me, and Mark the cousin

Βαρναβᾶ, (περὶ οὗ ἐλάβετε ἐντολάς, ἐὰν
of Barnabas, (concerning whom ye received commandments, if

ἔλθῃ πρὸς ὑμᾶς, δέξασθε αὐτόν,) 11 καὶ
he comes to you, receive ye him,) and

Ἰησοῦς ὁ λεγόμενος Ἰοῦστος, οἱ ὄντες
Jesus the [one] being named Justus, the [ones] being

ἐκ περιτομῆς οὗτοι μόνοι συνεργοὶ εἰς
of [the] circumcision these only fellow-workers for

τὴν βασιλείαν τοῦ θεοῦ, οἵτινες ἐγενή-
the kingdom - of God, who be-

θησάν μοι παρηγορία. 12 ἀσπάζεται ὑμᾶς
came to me a comfort. ²greets ³you

Ἐπαφρᾶς ὁ ἐξ ὑμῶν, δοῦλος Χριστοῦ
¹Epaphras the [one] of you, a slave of Christ

Ἰησοῦ, πάντοτε ἀγωνιζόμενος ὑπὲρ ὑμῶν
Jesus, always struggling on behalf of you

ἐν ταῖς προσευχαῖς, ἵνα σταθῆτε τέλειοι
in the prayers, in order ye may complete
that stand

καὶ πεπληροφορημένοι ἐν παντὶ θελήματι
and having been fully assured in all [the] will

τοῦ Θεοῦ. 13 μαρτυρῶ γὰρ αὐτῷ ὅτι
- of God. For I bear witness to him that

ἔχει πολὺν πόνον ὑπὲρ ὑμῶν καὶ τῶν
he has much distress on behalf of you and the ones

ἐν Λαοδικείᾳ καὶ τῶν ἐν Ἱεραπόλει.
in Laodicea and the ones in Hierapolis.

14 Luke, the beloved physician, and Demas, greet you.

15 Salute the brethren which are in Laodicea, and Nymphas, and the church which is in his house.

16 And when this epistle is read among you, cause that it be read also in the church of the Laodiceans; and that ye likewise read the *epistle* from Laodicea.

17 And say to Archippus, Take heed to the ministry which thou hast received in the Lord, that thou fulfil it.

18 The salutation by the hand of me Paul. Remember my bonds. Grace *be* with you. Amen.

14 ἀσπάζεται ὑμᾶς Λουκᾶς ὁ ἰατρὸς ὁ
      7greets   8you   1Luke   2the 4physician –
ἀγαπητὸς καὶ Δημᾶς.   15 Ἀσπάσασθε
    3beloved   5and   6Demas.   Greet ye
τοὺς ἐν Λαοδικείᾳ ἀδελφοὺς καὶ Νύμφαν
1the   2in   4Laodicea   2brothers   and   Nymphas
καὶ τὴν κατ’ οἶκον αὐτῆς ἐκκλησίαν.
and   1the   3at 4[the] house   5of her   2church.
16 καὶ ὅταν ἀναγνωσθῇ παρ’ ὑμῖν ἡ
    And whenever   is read   before   you the(this)
ἐπιστολή, ποιήσατε ἵνα καὶ ἐν τῇ
    epistle,   cause   in order that 2also   3in   4the
Λαοδικέων ἐκκλησίᾳ ἀναγνωσθῇ, καὶ τὴν
5of [the]   5church   1it is read,   and   5the
Laodiceans   [one]
ἐκ Λαοδικείας ἵνα καὶ ὑμεῖς ἀναγνῶτε.
6of   7Laodicea   1in order 2also   3ye   4read.
               that
17 καὶ εἴπατε Ἀρχίππῳ· βλέπε τὴν
    And   tell   Archippus :   Look [to]   the
διακονίαν ἣν παρέλαβες ἐν κυρίῳ, ἵνα
    ministry   which   thou receivedst in [the] Lord,   in order that
αὐτὴν πληροῖς.
    2it   1thou mayest fulfil.
18 Ὁ ἀσπασμὸς τῇ ἐμῇ χειρὶ Παύλου.
    The   greeting   –   by my   hand[,]   of Paul.
μνημονεύετέ μου τῶν δεσμῶν. ἡ χάρις
    Remember ye   of me   the   bonds.   – Grace [be]
μεθ’ ὑμῶν.
    with   you.

I. THESSALONIANS 1

CHAPTER 1

PAUL, and Silvanus, and Timotheus, unto the church of the Thessalonians *which is* in God the Father and *in* the Lord Jesus Christ: Grace *be* unto you, and peace, from God our Father, and the Lord Jesus Christ.

2 We give thanks to

ΠΡΟΣ ΘΕΣΣΑΛΟΝΙΚΕΙΣ Α

To Thessalonians 1

1 Παῦλος καὶ Σιλουανὸς καὶ Τιμόθεος
    Paul   and   Silvanus   and   Timothy
τῇ ἐκκλησίᾳ Θεσσαλονικέων ἐν θεῷ πατρὶ
to the   church   of [the] Thessalonians   in   God [the] Father
καὶ κυρίῳ Ἰησοῦ Χριστῷ· χάρις ὑμῖν
and   [the] Lord   Jesus   Christ: Grace [be] to you
καὶ εἰρήνη.
and   peace.
2 Εὐχαριστοῦμεν τῷ θεῷ πάντοτε περὶ
    We give thanks   –   to God   always   con-
                               cerning

God always for you all, making mention of you in our prayers;

3 Remembering without ceasing your work of faith, and labour of love, and patience of hope in our Lord Jesus Christ, in the sight of God and our Father;

4 Knowing, brethren beloved, your election of God.

5 For our gospel came not unto you in word only, but also in power, and in the Holy Ghost, and in much assurance; as ye know what manner of men we were among you for your sake.

6 And ye became followers of us, and of the Lord, having received the word in much affliction, with joy of the Holy Ghost:

7 So that ye were ensamples to all that believe in Macedonia and Achaia.

8 For from you sounded out the word of the Lord not only in Macedonia and Achaia, but also in every place your faith to Godward is spread abroad; so that we need not to speak any thing.

9 For they themselves

πάντων ὑμῶν, μνείαν ποιούμενοι ἐπὶ τῶν
²all ¹you, mention making on(in) the

προσευχῶν ἡμῶν, ἀδιαλείπτως 3 μνημο-
prayers of us, unceasingly remember-

νεύοντες ὑμῶν τοῦ ἔργου τῆς πίστεως
ing of you the work – of faith

καὶ τοῦ κόπου τῆς ἀγάπης καὶ τῆς
and the labour – of love and the

ὑπομονῆς τῆς ἐλπίδος τοῦ κυρίου ἡμῶν
endurance – of hope of(in) the Lord of us

Ἰησοῦ Χριστοῦ ἔμπροσθεν τοῦ θεοῦ καὶ
Jesus Christ before the God and

πατρὸς ἡμῶν, 4 εἰδότες, ἀδελφοὶ ἠγαπημένοι
Father of us, knowing, brothers having been loved

ὑπὸ [τοῦ] θεοῦ, τὴν ἐκλογὴν ὑμῶν,
by – God, the choice of you,

5 ὅτι τὸ εὐαγγέλιον ἡμῶν οὐκ ἐγενήθη
because the gospel of us became not

εἰς ὑμᾶς ἐν λόγῳ μόνον, ἀλλὰ καὶ ἐν
to you in word only, but also in

δυνάμει καὶ ἐν πνεύματι ἁγίῳ καὶ
power and in Spirit Holy and

πληροφορίᾳ πολλῇ, καθὼς οἴδατε οἷοι
²assurance ¹much, as ye know what sort

ἐγενήθημεν ἐν ὑμῖν δι᾽ ὑμᾶς. 6 καὶ
we were among you because of you. And

ὑμεῖς μιμηταὶ ἡμῶν ἐγενήθητε καὶ τοῦ
¹ye ³imitators ⁴of us ²became and of the

κυρίου, δεξάμενοι τὸν λόγον ἐν θλίψει
Lord, welcoming the word in ²affliction

πολλῇ μετὰ χαρᾶς πνεύματος ἁγίου, 7 ὥστε
¹much with joy of ³Spirit ¹[the] Holy, so as

γενέσθαι ὑμᾶς τύπον πᾶσιν τοῖς πιστεύουσιν
to become youᵇ a pattern to all the [ones] believing
=so that ye became

ἐν τῇ Μακεδονίᾳ καὶ ἐν τῇ Ἀχαΐᾳ.
in – Macedonia and in – Achaia.

8 ἀφ᾽ ὑμῶν γὰρ ἐξήχηται ὁ λόγος τοῦ
²from ³you ¹For sounded the word of the

κυρίου οὐ μόνον ἐν τῇ Μακεδονίᾳ καὶ
Lord not only in – Macedonia and

Ἀχαΐᾳ, ἀλλ᾽ ἐν παντὶ τόπῳ ἡ πίστις
Achaia, but in every place the faith

ὑμῶν ἡ πρὸς τὸν θεὸν ἐξελήλυθεν, ὥστε
of you – toward – God has gone out, so as

μὴ χρείαν ἔχειν ἡμᾶς λαλεῖν τι· 9 αὐτοὶ
not need to have usᵇ to speak anything; ²[them]-
=so that we have no need selves

shew of us what manner of entering in we had unto you, and how ye turned to God from idols to serve the living and true God;

10 And to wait for his Son from heaven, whom he raised from the dead, *even* Jesus, which delivered us from the wrath to come.

γὰρ   περὶ   ἡμῶν   ἀπαγγέλλουσιν   ὁποίαν
¹for   ⁴concerning   ⁵us   ³they relate   what sort of

εἴσοδον   ἔσχομεν   πρὸς   ὑμᾶς,   καὶ   πῶς
entrance   we had   to   you,   and   how

ἐπεστρέψατε   πρὸς   τὸν   θεὸν   ἀπὸ   τῶν
ye turned   to   -   God   from   *the*

εἰδώλων   δουλεύειν   θεῷ   ζῶντι   καὶ   ἀληθινῷ,
idols   to serve   a God   living   and   true,

10 καὶ   ἀναμένειν   τὸν   υἱὸν   αὐτοῦ   ἐκ
and   to await   the   Son   of him   from

τῶν   οὐρανῶν,   ὃν   ἤγειρεν   ἐκ   τῶν   νεκρῶν,
the   heavens,   whom   he raised   from   the   dead,

Ἰησοῦν   τὸν   ῥυόμενον   ἡμᾶς   ἐκ   τῆς   ὀργῆς
Jesus   the [one]   delivering   us   from   the   wrath

τῆς   ἐρχομένης.
coming.

CHAPTER 2

FOR yourselves, brethren, know our entrance in unto you, that it was not in vain:

2 But even after that we had suffered before, and were shamefully entreated, as ye know, at Philippi, we were bold in our God to speak unto you the gospel of God with much contention.

3 For our exhortation *was* not of deceit, nor of uncleanness, nor in guile:

4 But as we were allowed of God to be put in trust with the gospel, even so we speak; not as pleasing men, but God, which trieth our hearts.

5 For neither at any time used we flattering words, as ye know, nor

2 Αὐτοὶ   γὰρ   οἴδατε,   ἀδελφοί,   τὴν
For [your]selves   ye know,   brothers,   the

εἴσοδον   ἡμῶν   τὴν   πρὸς   ὑμᾶς,   ὅτι   οὐ
entrance   of us   -   to   you,   that   not

κενὴ   γέγονεν,   2 ἀλλὰ   προπαθόντες   καὶ
in vain   it has been,   but   having previously   and
                                 suffered

ὑβρισθέντες   καθὼς   οἴδατε   ἐν   Φιλίπποις
having been   as   ye know   in   Philippi
insulted

ἐπαρρησιασάμεθα   ἐν   τῷ   θεῷ   ἡμῶν   λαλῆσαι
we were bold   in   the   God   of us   to speak

πρὸς   ὑμᾶς   τὸ   εὐαγγέλιον   τοῦ   θεοῦ   ἐν
to   you   the   gospel   -   of God   in

πολλῷ   ἀγῶνι.   3 ἡ   γὰρ   παράκλησις
much   struggle.   For the   exhortation

ἡμῶν   οὐκ   ἐκ   πλάνης   οὐδὲ   ἐξ   ἀκαθαρσίας
of us   not   of   error   nor   of   uncleanness

οὐδὲ   ἐν   δόλῳ,   4 ἀλλὰ   καθὼς   δεδοκιμάσμεθα
nor   in   guile,   but   as   we have been
                                     approved

ὑπὸ   τοῦ   θεοῦ   πιστευθῆναι   τὸ   εὐαγγέλιον
by   -   God   to be entrusted [with]   the   gospel

οὕτως   λαλοῦμεν,   οὐχ   ὡς   ἀνθρώποις   ἀρέ-
so   we speak,   not   as   ¹men   ¹pleas-

σκοντες,   ἀλλὰ   θεῷ   τῷ   δοκιμάζοντι   τὰς
ing,   but   God   the [one]   proving   the

καρδίας   ἡμῶν.   5 οὔτε   γὰρ   ποτε   ἐν
hearts   of us.   For neither   then   with

λόγῳ   κολακείας   ἐγενήθημεν,   καθὼς   οἴδατε,
word   of flattery   were we,   as   ye know,

a cloke of covetousness; God *is* witness:

6 Nor of men sought we glory, neither of you, nor *yet* of others, when we might have been burdensome, as the apostles of Christ.

7 But we were gentle among you, even as a nurse cherisheth her children:

8 So being affectionately desirous of you, we were willing to have imparted unto you, not the gospel of God only, but also our own souls, because ye were dear unto us.

9 For ye remember, brethren, our labour and travail: for labouring night and day, because we would not be chargeable unto any of you, we preached unto you the gospel of God.

10 Ye *are* witnesses, and God *also*, how holily and justly and unblameably we behaved ourselves among you that believe:

11 As ye know how we exhorted and comforted and charged every one of you, as a father *doth* his children,

12 That ye would walk worthy of God, who hath

οὔτε ἐν προφάσει πλεονεξίας, θεὸς μάρτυς,
nor with pretext of covetousness, God [is] witness,

6 οὔτε ζητοῦντες ἐξ ἀνθρώπων δόξαν,
nor seeking from men glory,

οὔτε ἀφ' ὑμῶν οὔτε ἀπ' ἄλλων, 7 δυνάμε-
neither from you nor from others, being

νοι ἐν βάρει εἶναι ὡς Χριστοῦ ἀπόστολοι·
able [1]with [2]weight* [1]to be as [2]of Christ [1]apostles;

ἀλλὰ ἐγενήθημεν ἤπιοι ἐν μέσῳ ὑμῶν,
but we were gentle in [the] midst of you,

ὡς ἐὰν τροφὸς θάλπῃ τὰ ἑαυτῆς τέκνα·
as if a nurse should [1]the [2]of herself [3]children;
       cherish

8 οὕτως ὁμειρόμενοι ὑμῶν ηὐδοκοῦμεν
so longing for you we were well
       pleased

μεταδοῦναι ὑμῖν οὐ μόνον τὸ εὐαγγέλιον
to impart to you not only the gospel

τοῦ θεοῦ ἀλλὰ καὶ τὰς ἑαυτῶν ψυχάς,
– of God but also [1]the [2]of ourselves [1]souls,

διότι ἀγαπητοὶ ἡμῖν ἐγενήθητε. 9 μνημο-
because [2]beloved [3]to us [1]ye became. ye re-

νεύετε γάρ, ἀδελφοί, τὸν κόπον ἡμῶν
member For, brothers, the labour of us

καὶ τὸν μόχθον· νυκτὸς καὶ ἡμέρας
and the toil; night and day

ἐργαζόμενοι πρὸς τὸ μὴ ἐπιβαρῆσαί τινα
working for *the* not to put a burden any-
       on   one

ὑμῶν ἐκηρύξαμεν εἰς ὑμᾶς τὸ εὐαγγέλιον
of you we proclaimed to you the gospel

τοῦ θεοῦ. 10 ὑμεῖς μάρτυρες καὶ ὁ
– of God. Ye [are] witnesses and –

θεός, ὡς ὁσίως καὶ δικαίως καὶ ἀμέμπτως
God, how holily and righteously and blamelessly

ὑμῖν τοῖς πιστεύουσιν ἐγενήθημεν, 11 καθά-
[1]to you [2]the [ones] [3]believing [1]we were, even

περ οἴδατε ὡς ἕνα ἕκαστον ὑμῶν ὡς
as ye know how [2]one [1]each of you as

πατὴρ τέκνα ἑαυτοῦ 12 παρακαλοῦντες ὑμᾶς
a father children of himself exhorting you

καὶ παραμυθούμενοι καὶ μαρτυρόμενοι εἰς
and consoling and witnessing for

τὸ περιπατεῖν ὑμᾶς ἀξίως τοῦ θεοῦ
the to walk you[b] worthily – of God
=that ye should walk

* ? dignity, authority.

called you unto his kingdom and glory.

13 For this cause also thank we God without ceasing, because, when ye received the word of God which ye heard of us, ye received *it* not *as* the word of men, but as it is in truth, the word of God, which effectually worketh also in you that believe.

14 For ye, brethren, became followers of the churches of God which in Judæa are in Christ Jesus: for ye also have suffered like things of your own countrymen, even as they *have* of the Jews:

15 Who both killed the Lord Jesus, and their own prophets, and have persecuted us; and they please not God, and are contrary to all men:

16 Forbidding us to speak to the Gentiles that they might be saved, to fill up their sins alway: for the wrath is come upon them to the uttermost.

17 But we, brethren, being taken from you for

τοῦ   καλοῦντος   ὑμᾶς   εἰς   τὴν   ἑαυτοῦ
the [one] calling you to ¹the ²of himself

βασιλείαν   καὶ   δόξαν.
³kingdom ³and ⁴glory.

13 Καὶ   διὰ   τοῦτο   καὶ   ἡμεῖς   εὐχαρισ-
And therefore also we give

τοῦμεν   τῷ   θεῷ   ἀδιαλείπτως,   ὅτι   παρα-
thanks – to God unceasingly, that having

λαβόντες   λόγον   ἀκοῆς   παρ'   ἡμῶν   τοῦ
received ¹[the] word ²of hearing ⁴from ⁵us –

θεοῦ   ἐδέξασθε   οὐ   λόγον   ἀνθρώπων   ἀλλὰ
³of God ye welcomed not [as] a of men but
[it] word

καθὼς   ἀληθῶς   ἐστιν   λόγον   θεοῦ,   ὃς
as truly it is a word of God, which

καὶ   ἐνεργεῖται   ἐν   ὑμῖν   τοῖς   πιστεύουσιν.
also operates in you the [ones] believing.

14 ὑμεῖς   γὰρ   μιμηταὶ   ἐγενήθητε,   ἀδελφοί,
For ye ²imitators ¹became, brothers,

τῶν   ἐκκλησιῶν   τοῦ   θεοῦ   τῶν   οὐσῶν   ἐν
of the churches – of God the being in

τῇ   Ἰουδαίᾳ   ἐν   Χριστῷ   Ἰησοῦ,   ὅτι   τὰ
– Judæa in Christ Jesus, because ⁴the

αὐτὰ   ἐπάθετε   καὶ   ὑμεῖς   ὑπὸ   τῶν   ἰδίων
⁵same ³suffered ²also ¹ye by the(your) own
things

συμφυλετῶν,   καθὼς   καὶ   αὐτοὶ   ὑπὸ   τῶν
fellow-tribesmen, as also they by the

Ἰουδαίων,   15 τῶν   καὶ   τὸν   κύριον
Jews, the [ones] ¹both ³the ⁴Lord

ἀποκτεινάντων   Ἰησοῦν   καὶ   τοὺς   προφήτας,
²killing ⁵Jesus and the prophets,

καὶ   ἡμᾶς   ἐκδιωξάντων,   καὶ   θεῷ   μὴ
and ²us ¹chasing ³out, and ³God ¹not

ἀρεσκόντων,   καὶ   πᾶσιν   ἀνθρώποις   ἐναντίων,
²pleasing, and to all men contrary,

16 κωλυόντων   ἡμᾶς   τοῖς   ἔθνεσιν   λαλῆσαι
hindering us ²to the ³nations ¹to speak
=from speaking . . .

ἵνα   σωθῶσιν,   εἰς   τὸ   ἀναπληρῶσαι   αὐτῶν
in order they may for the to fill up ³of them
that be saved,

τὰς   ἁμαρτίας   πάντοτε.   ἔφθασεν   δὲ   ἐπ'
¹the ²sins always. But ³came ⁴on

αὐτοὺς   ἡ   ὀργὴ   εἰς   τέλος.
⁵them ¹the ²wrath to [the] end.

17 Ἡμεῖς   δέ,   ἀδελφοί,   ἀπορφανισθέντες
But we brothers, being bereaved

a short time in presence, not in heart, endeavoured the more abundantly to see your face with great desire.

18 Wherefore we would have come unto you, even I Paul, once and again; but Satan hindered us.

19 For what *is* our hope, or joy, or crown of rejoicing? *Are* not even ye in the presence of our Lord Jesus Christ at his coming?

20 For ye are our glory and joy.

ἀφ'	ὑμῶν	πρὸς	καιρὸν	ὥρας	προσώπῳ
from	you	for	time	of an hour	in face (presence)

οὐ	καρδίᾳ,	περισσοτέρως	ἐσπουδάσαμεν	τὸ
not	in heart,	more abundantly	were eager	²the

πρόσωπον	ὑμῶν	ἰδεῖν	ἐν	πολλῇ	ἐπιθυμίᾳ.
²face	⁴of you	¹to see	with	much	desire.

18 διότι ἠθελήσαμεν ἐλθεῖν πρὸς ὑμᾶς,
Wherefore we wished to come to you,

ἐγὼ μὲν Παῦλος καὶ ἅπαξ καὶ δίς,
I ²indeed ¹Paul both once and twice (again),

καὶ ἐνέκοψεν ἡμᾶς ὁ σατανᾶς. **19** τίς
and ²hindered ³us – ¹Satan. what

γὰρ ἡμῶν ἐλπὶς ἢ χαρὰ ἢ στέφανος
For [is] ²of us ¹hope or joy or crown

καυχήσεως — ἢ οὐχὶ καὶ ὑμεῖς —
of boasting — or not even ye —

ἔμπροσθεν τοῦ κυρίου ἡμῶν Ἰησοῦ
before the Lord of us Jesus

ἐν τῇ αὐτοῦ παρουσίᾳ; **20** ὑμεῖς γὰρ
in(at) the ²of him ¹presence? for ye

ἐστε ἡ δόξα ἡμῶν καὶ ἡ χαρά.
are ¹the ²glory ⁶of us ³and ⁴the ⁵joy.

CHAPTER 3

WHEREFORE when we could no longer forbear, we thought it good to be left at Athens alone;

2 And sent Timotheus, our brother, and minister of God, and our fellow-labourer in the gospel of Christ, to establish you, and to comfort you concerning your faith:

3 That no man should be moved by these afflictions: for yourselves know that we are appointed thereunto.

4 For verily, when we were with you, we told you before that we should suffer tribulation; even as it came to pass, and ye know.

5 For this cause, when

3 Διὸ μηκέτι στέγοντες ηὐδοκήσαμεν
Wherefore no longer bearing up we were well pleased

καταλειφθῆναι ἐν Ἀθήναις μόνοι, **2** καὶ
to be left in Athens alone, and

ἐπέμψαμεν Τιμόθεον, τὸν ἀδελφὸν ἡμῶν
we sent Timothy, the brother of us

καὶ συνεργὸν τοῦ θεοῦ ἐν τῷ εὐαγγελίῳ
and fellow-worker – of God in the gospel

τοῦ Χριστοῦ, εἰς τὸ στηρίξαι ὑμᾶς καὶ
– of Christ, for the to establish you and

παρακαλέσαι ὑπὲρ τῆς πίστεως ὑμῶν **3** τὸ
to exhort on behalf of the faith of you –

μηδένα σαίνεσθαι ἐν ταῖς θλίψεσιν ταύταις.
no one to be drawn by these afflictions. asideᵇ

αὐτοὶ γὰρ οἴδατε ὅτι εἰς τοῦτο κείμεθα·
For [your]selves ye know that to this we are appointed;

4 καὶ γὰρ ὅτε πρὸς ὑμᾶς ἦμεν,
for even when with you we were,

προελέγομεν ὑμῖν ὅτι μέλλομεν θλίβεσθαι,
we said before to you that we are about to be afflicted,

καθὼς καὶ ἐγένετο καὶ οἴδατε. **5** διὰ
as indeed it happened and ye know. There-

I could no longer forbear, I sent to know your faith, lest by some means the tempter have tempted you, and our labour be in vain.

6 But now when Timotheus came from you unto us, and brought us good tidings of your faith and charity, and that ye have good remembrance of us always, desiring greatly to see us, as we also *to see* you:

7 Therefore, brethren, we were comforted over you in all our affliction and distress by your faith:

8 For now we live, if ye stand fast in the Lord.

9 For what thanks can we render to God again for you, for all the joy wherewith we joy for your sakes before our God;

10 Night and day praying exceedingly that we might see your face, and might perfect that which is lacking in your faith?

11 Now God himself and our Father, and our Lord Jesus Christ, direct our way unto you.

τοῦτο κἀγὼ μηκέτι στέγων ἔπεμψα εἰς
fore I also no longer bearing up sent for

τὸ γνῶναι τὴν πίστιν ὑμῶν, μή πως
the to know the faith of you, lest [some]how

ἐπείρασεν ὑμᾶς ὁ πειράζων καὶ εἰς
³tempted ⁴you ¹the [one] ²tempting and in
= the tempter

κενὸν γένηται ὁ κόπος ἡμῶν. 6 Ἄρτι
vain became the labour of us. now

δὲ ἐλθόντος Τιμοθέου πρὸς ἡμᾶς ἀφ'
But coming Timothyᵃ to us from
= when Timothy came

ὑμῶν καὶ εὐαγγελισαμένου ἡμῖν τὴν πίστιν
you and announcing good newsᵃ to us [of] the faith

καὶ τὴν ἀγάπην ὑμῶν, καὶ ὅτι ἔχετε
and the love of you, and that ye have

μνείαν ἡμῶν ἀγαθὴν πάντοτε, ἐπιποθοῦντες
²remem-brance ³of us ¹good always, longing

ἡμᾶς ἰδεῖν καθάπερ καὶ ἡμεῖς ὑμᾶς,
²us ¹to see even as also we you,

7 διὰ τοῦτο παρεκλήθημεν, ἀδελφοί, ἐφ'
therefore we were comforted, brothers, over

ὑμῖν ἐπὶ πάσῃ τῇ ἀνάγκῃ καὶ θλίψει
you on all the distress and affliction

ἡμῶν διὰ τῆς ὑμῶν πίστεως, 8 ὅτι
of us through the ²of you ¹faith, because

νῦν ζῶμεν ἐὰν ὑμεῖς στήκετε ἐν κυρίῳ.
now we live if ye stand in [the] Lord.

9 τίνα γὰρ εὐχαριστίαν δυνάμεθα τῷ θεῷ
For what thanks are we able – to God

ἀνταποδοῦναι περὶ ὑμῶν ἐπὶ πάσῃ τῇ
to return concerning you over all the

χαρᾷ ᾗ χαίρομεν δι' ὑμᾶς ἔμπροσθεν
joy [with] which we rejoice because of you before

τοῦ θεοῦ ἡμῶν, 10 νυκτὸς καὶ ἡμέρας
the God of us, night and day

ὑπερεκπερισσοῦ δεόμενοι εἰς τὸ ἰδεῖν ὑμῶν
exceedingly petitioning *for the* to see of you

τὸ πρόσωπον καὶ καταρτίσαι τὰ ὑστερήματα
the face and to adjust the shortcomings

τῆς πίστεως ὑμῶν; 11 Αὐτὸς δὲ ὁ θεὸς
of the faith of you? Now [him]self the God

καὶ πατὴρ ἡμῶν καὶ ὁ κύριος ἡμῶν
and Father of us and the Lord of us

Ἰησοῦς κατευθύναι τὴν ὁδὸν ἡμῶν πρὸς
Jesus may he direct the way of us to

12 And the Lord make you to increase and abound in love one toward another, and toward all *men*, even as we *do* toward you:

13 To the end he may stablish your hearts unblameable in holiness before God, even our Father, at the coming of our Lord Jesus Christ with all his saints.

ὑμᾶς·   12 ὑμᾶς   δὲ   ὁ   κύριος   πλεονάσαι
you;   and ⁴you   ¹the   ⁵Lord   ²make ⁶to abound

καὶ   περισσεύσαι   τῇ   ἀγάπῃ   εἰς   ἀλλήλους
and   to exceed   –   in love   to   one another

καὶ   εἰς   πάντας,   καθάπερ   καὶ   ἡμεῖς
and   to   all men,   even as   also   we

εἰς   ὑμᾶς,   13 εἰς   τὸ   στηρίξαι   ὑμῶν   τὰς
to   you,   for   the   to establish   of you   the

καρδίας   ἀμέμπτους   ἐν   ἁγιωσύνῃ   ἔμπροσθεν
hearts   blameless   in   holiness   before

τοῦ   θεοῦ   καὶ   πατρὸς   ἡμῶν   ἐν   τῇ   παρουσίᾳ
the   God   and   Father   of us   in(at) the   presence

τοῦ   κυρίου   ἡμῶν   Ἰησοῦ   μετὰ   πάντων
of the   Lord   of us   Jesus   with   all

τῶν   ἁγίων   αὐτοῦ.
the   saints   of him.

CHAPTER 4

FURTHERMORE then we beseech you, brethren, and exhort *you* by the Lord Jesus, that as ye have received of us how ye ought to walk and to please God, *so* ye would abound more and more.

2 For ye know what commandments we gave you by the Lord Jesus.

3 For this is the will of God, *even* your sanctification, that ye should abstain from fornication:

4 That every one of you should know how to possess his vessel in sanctification and honour;

5 Not in the lust of concupiscence, even as the Gentiles which know not God:

6 That no *man* go beyond and defraud his

4 Λοιπὸν   οὖν,   ἀδελφοί,   ἐρωτῶμεν   ὑμᾶς
For the rest therefore,   brothers,   we ask   you

καὶ   παρακαλοῦμεν   ἐν   κυρίῳ   Ἰησοῦ,   ἵνα
and   we beseech   in   [the] Lord   Jesus,   in order
                                                            that

καθὼς   παρελάβετε   παρ'   ἡμῶν   τὸ   πῶς
as   ye received   from   us   the   how

δεῖ   ὑμᾶς   περιπατεῖν   καὶ   ἀρέσκειν   θεῷ,
it   you   to walk   and   to please   God,
behoves

καθὼς   καὶ   περιπατεῖτε,   ἵνα   περισσεύητε
as   indeed   ye do walk,   in order that   ye abound

μᾶλλον.   2 οἴδατε   γὰρ   τίνας   παραγγελίας
more.   For ye know   what   injunctions

ἐδώκαμεν   ὑμῖν   διὰ   τοῦ   κυρίου   Ἰησοῦ.
we gave   you   through   the   Lord   Jesus.

3 Τοῦτο   γάρ   ἐστιν   θέλημα   τοῦ   θεοῦ,
For this   is   [the] will   –   of God,

ὁ   ἁγιασμὸς   ὑμῶν,   ἀπέχεσθαι   ὑμᾶς   ἀπὸ
the   sanctification   of you,   to abstain   you[b]   from

τῆς   πορνείας,   4 εἰδέναι   ἕκαστον   ὑμῶν
–   fornication,   ³to know*   ¹each one[b]   ²of you

τὸ   ἑαυτοῦ   σκεῦος   κτᾶσθαι   ἐν   ἁγιασμῷ
⁵the   ⁷of himself   ⁶vessel   ⁴to possess   in   sanctification

καὶ   τιμῇ,   5 μὴ   ἐν   πάθει   ἐπιθυμίας
and   honour,   not   in   passion   of lust

καθάπερ   καὶ   τὰ   ἔθνη   τὰ   μὴ   εἰδότα
even as   indeed   the   nations   –   not   knowing

τὸν   θεόν,   6 τὸ   μὴ   ὑπερβαίνειν   καὶ
–   God,   –   not   to go beyond   and

* That is, " to be able "; see note on page xviii.

brother in *any* matter: because that the Lord *is* the avenger of all such, as we also have forewarned you and testified.

7 For God hath not called us unto uncleanness, but unto holiness.

8 He therefore that despiseth, despiseth not man, but God, who hath also given unto us his holy Spirit.

9 But as touching brotherly love ye need not that I write unto you: for ye yourselves are taught of God to love one another.

10 And indeed ye do it toward all the brethren which are in all Macedonia: but we beseech you, brethren, that ye increase more and more;

11 And that ye study to be quiet, and to do your own business, and to work with your own hands, as we commanded you;

12 That ye may walk honestly toward them that are without, and *that* ye may have lack of nothing.

13 But I would not have you to be ignorant,

πλεονεκτεῖν ἐν τῷ πράγματι τὸν ἀδελφὸν
to defraud in the matter the brother

αὐτοῦ, διότι ἔκδικος κύριος περὶ πάντων
of him, be-   ²[the] ¹[the] Lord con-   all
cause avenger [is] cerning

τούτων, καθὼς καὶ προείπαμεν ὑμῖν καὶ
these, as in-   we previously you and
deed told

διεμαρτυράμεθα. 7 οὐ γὰρ ἐκάλεσεν ἡμᾶς
solemnly witnessed. For ⁴not ²called ³us

ὁ θεὸς ἐπὶ ἀκαθαρσίᾳ ἀλλ' ἐν ἁγιασμῷ.
– ¹God to uncleanness but in sanctification.

8 τοιγαροῦν ὁ ἀθετῶν οὐκ ἄνθρωπον
Wherefore the [one] rejecting ²not ³man

ἀθετεῖ ἀλλὰ τὸν θεὸν τὸν καὶ διδόντα
¹rejects but – God the in-   giving
[one] deed

τὸ πνεῦμα αὐτοῦ τὸ ἅγιον εἰς ὑμᾶς.
the ²Spirit ³of him – ¹Holy to you.

9 Περὶ δὲ τῆς φιλαδελφίας οὐ χρείαν
Now concerning – brotherly love not need

ἔχετε γράφειν ὑμῖν· αὐτοὶ γὰρ ὑμεῖς
ye have to write to you; for ²[your]selves ¹ye
[for me]

θεοδίδακτοί ἐστε εἰς τὸ ἀγαπᾶν ἀλλήλους·
⁴taught by God ³are for the to love one another;

10 καὶ γὰρ ποιεῖτε αὐτὸ εἰς πάντας
for indeed ye do it toward all

τοὺς ἀδελφοὺς [τοὺς] ἐν ὅλῃ τῇ Μακεδο-
the brothers – in all – Macedo-

νίᾳ. Παρακαλοῦμεν δὲ ὑμᾶς, ἀδελφοί,
nia. But we exhort you, brothers,

περισσεύειν μᾶλλον, 11 καὶ φιλοτιμεῖσθαι
to abound more, and to strive eagerly

ἡσυχάζειν καὶ πράσσειν τὰ ἴδια καὶ
to be quiet and to practise the own and
(your) things

ἐργάζεσθαι ταῖς χερσὶν ὑμῶν, καθὼς ὑμῖν
to work with the hands of you, as ²you

παρηγγείλαμεν, 12 ἵνα περιπατῆτε εὐσχη-
¹we enjoined, in or-   ye may walk becom-
der that

μόνως πρὸς τοὺς ἔξω καὶ μηδενὸς
ingly toward the [ones] outside and ³of nothing

χρείαν ἔχητε.
²need ¹ye may have.

13 Οὐ θέλομεν δὲ ὑμᾶς ἀγνοεῖν, ἀδελφοί,
Now we do not wish you to be brothers,
ignorant,

brethren, concerning them which are asleep, that ye sorrow not, even as others which have no hope.

14 For if we believe that Jesus died and rose again, even so them also which sleep in Jesus will God bring with him.

15 For this we say unto you by the word of the Lord, that we which are alive and remain unto the coming of the Lord shall not prevent them which are asleep.

16 For the Lord himself shall descend from heaven with a shout, with the voice of the archangel, and with the trump of God: and the dead in Christ shall rise first:

17 Then we which are alive and remain shall be caught up together with them in the clouds, to meet the Lord in the air: and so shall we ever be with the Lord.

18 Wherefore comfort one another with these words.

περὶ   τῶν   κοιμωμένων,   ἵνα   μὴ   λυπῆσθε
con-   the -   sleeping,   lest   ye grieve
cerning [ones]

καθὼς   καὶ   οἱ   λοιποὶ   οἱ   μὴ   ἔχοντες
as   indeed   the   rest   -   not   having

ἐλπίδα.   **14** εἰ   γὰρ   πιστεύομεν   ὅτι   Ἰησοῦς
hope.   For if   we believe   that   Jesus

ἀπέθανεν   καὶ   ἀνέστη,   οὕτως   καὶ   ὁ   θεὸς
died   and   rose again,   so   also -   ⁵God

τοὺς   κοιμηθέντας   διὰ   τοῦ   Ἰησοῦ   ἄξει
¹the   ²having slept   ³through   -   ⁴Jesus   will
[ones]   bring

σὺν   αὐτῷ.   **15** Τοῦτο   γὰρ   ὑμῖν   λέγομεν
with   him.   For this   to you   we say

ἐν   λόγῳ   κυρίου,   ὅτι   ἡμεῖς   οἱ   ζῶντες
by   a word   of [the]   that   we   the   living
    Lord,   [ones]

οἱ   περιλειπόμενοι   εἰς   τὴν   παρουσίαν   τοῦ
-    remaining   to   the   presence   of the

κυρίου   οὐ   μὴ   φθάσωμεν   τοὺς   κοιμηθέντας·
Lord   by no   may precede   the   having slept;
    means   [ones]

16 ὅτι   αὐτὸς   ὁ   κύριος   ἐν   κελεύσματι,
be-   ³[him]-   ¹the   ²Lord   with   a word of
cause   self   command,

ἐν   φωνῇ   ἀρχαγγέλου   καὶ   ἐν   σάλπιγγι
with   a voice   of an archangel   and   with   a trumpet

θεοῦ,   καταβήσεται   ἀπ'   οὐρανοῦ,   καὶ   οἱ
of God,   will descend   from   heaven,   and   the

νεκροὶ   ἐν   Χριστῷ   ἀναστήσονται   πρῶτον,
dead   in   Christ   will rise again   firstly,

17 ἔπειτα   ἡμεῖς   οἱ   ζῶντες   οἱ   περιλειπόμενοι
then   we   the   living   -   remaining
    [ones]

ἅμα   σὺν   αὐτοῖς   ἁρπαγησόμεθα   ἐν   νεφέλαις
to-   with   them   shall be seized   in   clouds
gether

εἰς   ἀπάντησιν   τοῦ   κυρίου   εἰς   ἀέρα·
to   a meeting   of the   Lord   in   air;

καὶ   οὕτως   πάντοτε   σὺν   κυρίῳ   ἐσόμεθα.
and   so   always   with   [the] Lord   we shall be.

18 Ὥστε   παρακαλεῖτε   ἀλλήλους   ἐν   τοῖς   λόγοις
Therefore   comfort ye   one   with -   words
    another

τούτοις.
these.

CHAPTER 5

BUT of the times and the seasons, brethren, ye have no need that I write unto you.

2 For yourselves know perfectly that the day of the Lord so cometh as a thief in the night.

3 For when they shall say, Peace and safety; then sudden destruction cometh upon them, as travail upon a woman with child; and they shall not escape.

4 But ye, brethren, are not in darkness, that that day should overtake you as a thief.

5 Ye are all the children of light, and the children of the day: we are not of the night, nor of darkness.

6 Therefore let us not sleep, as *do* others; but let us watch and be sober.

7 For they that sleep sleep in the night; and they that be drunken are drunken in the night.

8 But let us, who are of the day, be sober, putting on the breastplate of faith and love; and for an helmet, the hope of salvation.

9 For God hath not appointed us to wrath, but to obtain salvation by our Lord Jesus Christ,

10 Who died for us, that, whether we wake

5 Περὶ δὲ τῶν χρόνων καὶ τῶν καιρῶν,
But concerning the times and the seasons,

ἀδελφοί, οὐ χρείαν ἔχετε ὑμῖν γράφεσθαι·
brothers, ²not ³need ¹ye have ⁵to you ⁴to be written;

2 αὐτοὶ γὰρ ἀκριβῶς οἴδατε ὅτι ἡμέρα
for ²[your]selves ²accurately ¹ye know that [the] day

κυρίου ὡς κλέπτης ἐν νυκτὶ οὕτως
of [the] Lord as a thief at night so

ἔρχεται. 3 ὅταν λέγωσιν· εἰρήνη καὶ
it comes. Whenever they say : Peace and

ἀσφάλεια, τότε αἰφνίδιος αὐτοῖς ἐφίσταται
safety, then ¹sudden ⁴them ⁵comes on

ὄλεθρος ὥσπερ ἡ ὠδὶν τῇ ἐν γαστρὶ
²destruction as the birth pang to the pregnant

ἐχούσῃ, καὶ οὐ μὴ ἐκφύγωσιν. 4 ὑμεῖς
woman,† and by no may they ye
               means escape.

δέ, ἀδελφοί, οὐκ ἐστὲ ἐν σκότει, ἵνα
But, brothers, are not in dark- in or-
                ness, der that

ἡ ἡμέρα ὑμᾶς ὡς κλέπτης καταλάβῃ·
the day you as a thief should overtake;

5 πάντες γὰρ ὑμεῖς υἱοὶ φωτός ἐστε
for all ye ²sons ³of light ¹are

καὶ υἱοὶ ἡμέρας. Οὐκ ἐσμὲν νυκτὸς
and sons of [the] day. We are not of [the]
                        night

οὐδὲ σκότους· 6 ἄρα οὖν μὴ καθεύδωμεν
nor of darkness; therefore let us not sleep

ὡς οἱ λοιποί, ἀλλὰ γρηγορῶμεν καὶ
as the rest, but let us watch and

νήφωμεν. 7 οἱ γὰρ καθεύδοντες νυκτὸς
be sober. For the [ones] sleeping by night

καθεύδουσιν, καὶ οἱ μεθυσκόμενοι νυκτὸς
sleep, and the [ones] being drunk by night

μεθύουσιν· 8 ἡμεῖς δὲ ἡμέρας ὄντες
are drunk; but we of [the] day being

νήφωμεν, ἐνδυσάμενοι θώρακα πίστεως καὶ
let us be sober, putting on a breastplate of faith and

ἀγάπης καὶ περικεφαλαίαν ἐλπίδα σωτηρίας·
of love and a helmet hope of salvation;

9 ὅτι οὐκ ἔθετο ἡμᾶς ὁ θεὸς εἰς ὀργὴν
because ²did not appoint ³us — ¹God to wrath

ἀλλὰ εἰς περιποίησιν σωτηρίας διὰ τοῦ
but to obtainment of salvation through the

κυρίου ἡμῶν Ἰησοῦ Χριστοῦ, 10 τοῦ
Lord of us Jesus Christ, the

ἀποθανόντος περὶ ἡμῶν, ἵνα εἴτε γρηγορ-
[one] having died concern- us, in or- whether we
            ing   der that

or sleep, we should live together with him.

11 Wherefore comfort yourselves together, and edify one another, even as also ye do.

12 And we beseech you, brethren, to know them which labour among you, and are over you in the Lord, and admonish you;

13 And to esteem them very highly in love for their work's sake. *And* be at peace among yourselves.

14 Now we exhort you, brethren, warn them that are unruly, comfort the feebleminded, support the weak, be patient toward all *men.*

15 See that none render evil for evil unto any *man;* but ever follow that which is good, both among yourselves, and to all *men.*

16 Rejoice evermore.

17 Pray without ceasing.

18 In every thing give thanks: for this is the will of God in Christ Jesus concerning you.

19 Quench not the Spirit.

20 Despise not prophesyings.

21 Prove all things; hold fast that which is good.

22 Abstain from all appearance of evil.

ὦμεν   εἴτε   καθεύδωμεν   ἅμα   σὺν   αὐτῷ
watch   or   we sleep   ²together   ³with   ⁴him

ζήσωμεν.   **11** Διὸ   παρακαλεῖτε   ἀλλήλους
¹we may live.   Therefore   comfort ye   one another

καὶ   οἰκοδομεῖτε   εἷς   τὸν   ἕνα,   καθὼς   καὶ
and   edify ye   one   the one(other),   as   indeed

ποιεῖτε.
ye do.

12 Ἐρωτῶμεν   δὲ   ὑμᾶς,   ἀδελφοί,   εἰδέναι
Now we ask   you,   brothers,   to know

τοὺς   κοπιῶντας   ἐν   ὑμῖν   καὶ   προϊσταμένους
the [ones] labouring   among   you   and   taking the lead

ὑμῶν   ἐν   κυρίῳ   καὶ   νουθετοῦντας   ὑμᾶς,
of you   in   [the] Lord   and   admonishing   you,

13 καὶ   ἡγεῖσθαι   αὐτοὺς   ὑπερεκπερισσῶς
and   consider   them   most exceedingly

ἐν   ἀγάπῃ   διὰ   τὸ   ἔργον   αὐτῶν.   εἰρηνεύετε
in   love   because of   the   work   of them.   Be at peace

ἐν   ἑαυτοῖς.   **14** Παρακαλοῦμεν   δὲ   ὑμᾶς,
among yourselves.   And we exhort   you,

ἀδελφοί,   νουθετεῖτε   τοὺς   ἀτάκτους,   παρα-
brothers,   admonish   the   idle,   con-

μυθεῖσθε   τοὺς   ὀλιγοψύχους,   ἀντέχεσθε   τῶν
sole   the   faint-hearted,   hold on to   the [ones]

ἀσθενῶν,   μακροθυμεῖτε   πρὸς   πάντας.
being weak,   be longsuffering   with   all men.

15 ὁρᾶτε   μή   τις   κακὸν   ἀντὶ   κακοῦ   τινι
See   lest anyone   ³evil   ⁴instead of   ⁵evil   ²to anyone

ἀποδῷ,   ἀλλὰ   πάντοτε   τὸ   ἀγαθὸν   διώκετε
¹returns,   but   always   ²the   ³good   ¹follow ye

εἰς   ἀλλήλους   καὶ   εἰς   πάντας.   **16** Πάντοτε
in regard to   one another   and   in regard to   all men.   Always

χαίρετε,   **17** ἀδιαλείπτως   προσεύχεσθε,   **18** ἐν
rejoice ye,   unceasingly   pray,   in

παντὶ   εὐχαριστεῖτε·   τοῦτο   γὰρ   θέλημα
everything   give thanks;   for this [is]   [the] will

θεοῦ   ἐν   Χριστῷ   Ἰησοῦ   εἰς   ὑμᾶς.   **19** τὸ
of God   in   Christ   Jesus   in regard to you.   The

πνεῦμα   μὴ   σβέννυτε,   **20** προφητείας   μὴ
Spirit   do not quench,   prophecies   not

ἐξουθενεῖτε·   **21** πάντα   δὲ   δοκιμάζετε,   τὸ
despise;   and ²all things   ¹prove,   the

καλὸν   κατέχετε·   **22** ἀπὸ   παντὸς   εἴδους
good   hold fast;   from   every   form

23 And the very God of peace sanctify you wholly; and *I pray God* your whole spirit and soul and body be preserved blameless unto the coming of our Lord Jesus Christ.

24 Faithful *is* he that calleth you, who also will do *it*.

25 Brethren, pray for us.

26 Greet all the brethren with an holy kiss.

27 I charge you by the Lord that this epistle be read unto all the holy brethren.

28 The grace of our Lord Jesus Christ *be* with you. Amen.

πονηροῦ ἀπέχεσθε.   23 Αὐτὸς δὲ ὁ θεὸς
of evil   abstain.   And ⁴[him]self ¹the ²God

τῆς εἰρήνης ἀγιάσαι ὑμᾶς ὁλοτελεῖς, καὶ
–   ³of peace may he sanctify you   complete,   and

ὁλόκληρον ὑμῶν τὸ πνεῦμα καὶ ἡ ψυχὴ
entire   of you the   spirit   and the   soul

καὶ τὸ σῶμα ἀμέμπτως ἐν τῇ παρουσίᾳ
and the body blamelessly in(at) the   presence

τοῦ κυρίου ἡμῶν Ἰησοῦ Χριστοῦ τηρηθείη.
of the Lord   of us   Jesus   Christ   may be kept.

24 πιστὸς ὁ καλῶν ὑμᾶς, ὃς καὶ ποιήσει.
Faithful [is] the [one] calling you, who indeed will do [it].

25 Ἀδελφοί, προσεύχεσθε [καὶ] περὶ
Brothers,   pray ye   also concerning

ἡμῶν.
us.

26 Ἀσπάσασθε τοὺς ἀδελφοὺς πάντας
Greet ye   ²the   ³brothers   ¹all

ἐν φιλήματι ἁγίῳ. 27 Ἐνορκίζω ὑμᾶς τὸν
with kiss   a holy.   I adjure   you [by] the

κύριον ἀναγνωσθῆναι τὴν ἐπιστολὴν πᾶσιν
Lord   ²to be read   ¹the(this)   ²epistle   to all

τοῖς ἀδελφοῖς.
the   brothers.

28 Ἡ χάρις τοῦ κυρίου ἡμῶν Ἰησοῦ
The grace of the Lord   of us   Jesus

Χριστοῦ μεθ᾽ ὑμῶν.
Christ [be] with   you.

II. THESSALONIANS 1

CHAPTER 1

PAUL, and Silvanus, and Timotheus, unto the church of the Thessalonians in God our Father and the Lord Jesus Christ:

2 Grace unto you, and peace, from God our Father and the Lord Jesus Christ.

3 We are bound to

ΠΡΟΣ ΘΕΣΣΑΛΟΝΙΚΕΙΣ Β
To Thessalonians 2

1 Παῦλος καὶ Σιλουανὸς καὶ Τιμόθεος
Paul   and   Silvanus   and   Timothy

τῇ ἐκκλησίᾳ Θεσσαλονικέων ἐν θεῷ πατρὶ
to the church of [the] Thessalonians in God Father

ἡμῶν καὶ κυρίῳ Ἰησοῦ Χριστῷ· 2 χάρις
of us   and [the] Lord Jesus   Christ: Grace [be]

ὑμῖν καὶ εἰρήνη ἀπὸ θεοῦ πατρὸς καὶ
to you and   peace   from God [the] Father and

κυρίου Ἰησοῦ Χριστοῦ.
[the] Lord Jesus   Christ.

3 Εὐχαριστεῖν ὀφείλομεν τῷ θεῷ πάντοτε
To give thanks   we ought   –   to God   always

thank God always for you, brethren, as it is meet, because that your faith groweth exceedingly, and the charity of every one of you all toward each other aboundeth;

4 So that we ourselves glory in you in the churches of God for your patience and faith in all your persecutions and tribulations that ye endure:

5 Which is a manifest token of the righteous judgment of God, that ye may be counted worthy of the kingdom of God, for which ye also suffer:

6 Seeing it is a righteous thing with God to recompense tribulation to them that trouble you;

7 And to you who are troubled rest with us, when the Lord Jesus shall be revealed from heaven with his mighty angels,

8 In flaming fire taking vengeance on them that know not God, and that obey not the gospel of our Lord Jesus Christ:

9 Who shall be punished with everlasting destruc-

περὶ ὑμῶν, ἀδελφοί, καθὼς ἄξιόν ἐστιν,
con- you, brothers, as ²meet ¹it is,
cerning

ὅτι ὑπεραυξάνει ἡ πίστις ὑμῶν καὶ
because ⁴grows ¹the ²faith ³of you and
exceedingly

πλεονάζει ἡ ἀγάπη ἑνὸς ἑκάστου πάντων
³increases ¹the ²love ⁴one ³of each ⁵all

ὑμῶν εἰς ἀλλήλους, 4 ὥστε αὐτοὺς ἡμᾶς
⁶of you ⁷to ⁸one another. so as [our]selves us
=so that we ourselves boast

ἐν ὑμῖν ἐγκαυχᾶσθαι ἐν ταῖς ἐκκλησίαις
in you to boastᵇ in the churches
in you

τοῦ θεοῦ ὑπὲρ τῆς ὑπομονῆς ὑμῶν καὶ
— of God for the ¹endurance ⁴of you ³and

πίστεως ἐν πᾶσιν τοῖς διωγμοῖς ὑμῶν
²faith in all the persecutions of you

καὶ ταῖς θλίψεσιν αἷς ἀνέχεσθε, 5 ἔνδειγμα
and the afflictions which ye endure, a plain token

τῆς δικαίας κρίσεως τοῦ θεοῦ, εἰς τὸ
of the just judgment — of God, for the

καταξιωθῆναι ὑμᾶς τῆς βασιλείας τοῦ
to be accounted youᵇ of the kingdom —
worthy
=so that ye may be accounted worthy

θεοῦ, ὑπὲρ ἧς καὶ πάσχετε, 6 εἴπερ
of God, on behalf which indeed ye suffer, since
of

δίκαιον παρὰ θεῷ ἀνταποδοῦναι τοῖς
[it is] a just with God to repay ¹to the
thing [ones]

θλίβουσιν ὑμᾶς θλῖψιν 7 καὶ ὑμῖν τοῖς
²afflicting ³you ¹affliction and ⁴to you ⁵the
[ones]

θλιβομένοις ἄνεσιν μεθ᾽ ἡμῶν, ἐν τῇ
⁶being afflicted ¹rest ²with ³us, at the

ἀποκαλύψει τοῦ κυρίου Ἰησοῦ ἀπ᾽
revelation of the Lord Jesus from

οὐρανοῦ μετ᾽ ἀγγέλων δυνάμεως αὐτοῦ
heaven with angels of power of him

8 ἐν πυρὶ φλογός, διδόντος ἐκδίκησιν τοῖς
in fire of flame, giving full vengeance to the
[ones]

μὴ εἰδόσιν θεὸν καὶ τοῖς μὴ ὑπακούουσιν
not knowing God and to the not obeying
[ones]

τῷ εὐαγγελίῳ τοῦ κυρίου ἡμῶν Ἰησοῦ,
the gospel of the Lord of us Jesus,

9 οἵτινες δίκην τίσουσιν ὄλεθρον αἰώνιον
who ²[the] penalty ¹will pay ⁴destruction ³eternal

tion from the presence of the Lord, and from the glory of his power;

10 When he shall come to be glorified in his saints, and to be admired in all them that believe (because our testimony among you was believed) in that day.

11 Wherefore also we pray always for you, that our God would count you worthy of *this* calling, and fulfil all the good pleasure of *his* goodness, and the work of faith with power:

12 That the name of our Lord Jesus Christ may be glorified in you, and ye in him, according to the grace of our God and the Lord Jesus Christ.

ἀπὸ προσώπου τοῦ κυρίου καὶ ἀπὸ
from [the] face of the Lord and from

τῆς δόξης τῆς ἰσχύος αὐτοῦ, 10 ὅταν
the glory of the strength of him, whenever

ἔλθῃ ἐνδοξασθῆναι ἐν τοῖς ἁγίοις αὐτοῦ
he comes to be glorified in the saints of him

καὶ θαυμασθῆναι ἐν πᾶσιν τοῖς πιστεύσασιν,
and to be admired in all the [ones] having believed,

ὅτι ἐπιστεύθη τὸ μαρτύριον ἡμῶν ἐφ'
be- ²was believed ¹the ²testimony ³of us ⁴to
cause

ὑμᾶς, ἐν τῇ ἡμέρᾳ ἐκείνῃ. 11 Εἰς ὃ
⁵you, in that day. For which

καὶ προσευχόμεθα πάντοτε περὶ ὑμῶν,
indeed we pray always concerning you,

ἵνα ὑμᾶς ἀξιώσῃ τῆς κλήσεως ὁ θεὸς
in or- ⁴you ⁴may ⁵deem ⁸of the ⁹calling ¹the ²God
der that ⁷worthy

ἡμῶν καὶ πληρώσῃ πᾶσαν εὐδοκίαν
³of us and may fulfil every good pleasure

ἀγαθωσύνης καὶ ἔργον πίστεως ἐν δυνάμει,
of goodness and work of faith in power,

12 ὅπως ἐνδοξασθῇ τὸ ὄνομα τοῦ κυρίου
so as ⁷may be glorified ¹the ²name ³of the ⁴Lord

ἡμῶν Ἰησοῦ ἐν ὑμῖν, καὶ ὑμεῖς ἐν
⁵of us ⁶Jesus in you, and ye in

αὐτῷ, κατὰ τὴν χάριν τοῦ θεοῦ ἡμῶν
him, according to the grace of the ¹God ²of us

καὶ κυρίου Ἰησοῦ Χριστοῦ.
²and ³Lord Jesus Christ.

CHAPTER 2

NOW we beseech you, brethren, by the coming of our Lord Jesus Christ, and *by* our gathering together unto him,

2 That ye be not soon shaken in mind, or be troubled, neither by spirit, nor by word, nor by letter as from us, as that the day of Christ is at hand.

3 Let no man deceive

2 Ἐρωτῶμεν δὲ ὑμᾶς, ἀδελφοί, ὑπὲρ
Now we request you, brothers, by

τῆς παρουσίας τοῦ κυρίου [ἡμῶν] Ἰησοῦ
the presence of the Lord of us Jesus

Χριστοῦ καὶ ἡμῶν ἐπισυναγωγῆς ἐπ' αὐτόν,
Christ and ²of us ¹gathering together to him,

2 εἰς τὸ μὴ ταχέως σαλευθῆναι ὑμᾶς
- - not quickly to be shaken youᵇ

ἀπὸ τοῦ νοὸς μηδὲ θροεῖσθαι, μήτε
from the(your) mind nor to be disturbed, neither

διὰ πνεύματος μήτε διὰ λόγου μήτε
through a spirit nor through speech nor

δι' ἐπιστολῆς ὡς δι' ἡμῶν, ὡς ὅτι
through an epistle as through us, as that

ἐνέστηκεν ἡ ἡμέρα τοῦ κυρίου. 3 μὴ
²is come ¹the ²day ³of the ⁴Lord. Not

you by any means: for *that day shall not come*, except there come a falling away first, and that man of sin be revealed, the son of perdition;

4 Who opposeth and exalteth himself above all that is called God, or that is worshipped; so that he as God sitteth in the temple of God, shewing himself that he is God.

5 Remember ye not, that, when I was yet with you, I told you these things?

6 And now ye know what withholdeth that he might be revealed in his time.

7 For the mystery of iniquity doth already work: only he who now letteth *will let*, until he be taken out of the way.

8 And then shall that Wicked be revealed, whom the Lord shall consume with the spirit of his mouth, and shall destroy with the brightness of his coming:

9 *Even him*, whose coming is after the working of Satan with all power and signs and lying wonders,

10 And with all deceivableness of unrighteousness in them that perish; because they re-

τις ὑμᾶς ἐξαπατήσῃ κατὰ μηδένα τρόπον·
anyone ²you ¹may deceive by(in) no(any) way;

ὅτι ἐὰν μὴ ἔλθῃ ἡ ἀποστασία πρῶτον
because unless ²comes ¹the ²apostasy ¹firstly

καὶ ἀποκαλυφθῇ ὁ ἄνθρωπος τῆς ἀνομίας,
and ⁴is revealed ¹the ²man – ³of lawlessness,

ὁ υἱὸς τῆς ἀπωλείας, 4 ὁ ἀντικείμενος
the son – of perdition, the [one] setting against

καὶ ὑπεραιρόμενος ἐπὶ πάντα λεγόμενον
and exalting himself over everything *being* called

θεὸν ἢ σέβασμα, ὥστε αὐτὸν εἰς τὸν
God or object of worship, so as him in the

ναὸν τοῦ θεοῦ καθίσαι, ἀποδεικνύντα ἑαυ-
shrine – of God to sit,ᵇ showing him-

τὸν ὅτι ἐστὶν θεός. 5 Οὐ μνημονεύετε
self that he is a god. Do ye not remember

ὅτι ἔτι ὢν πρὸς ὑμᾶς ταῦτα ἔλεγον
that yet being with you ²these things ¹I used to tell

ὑμῖν; 6 καὶ νῦν τὸ κατέχον οἴδατε,
²you? and now the restraining ye know, [thing]

εἰς τὸ ἀποκαλυφθῆναι αὐτὸν ἐν τῷ
for *the* ²to be revealed ¹himᵇ in the

αὐτοῦ καιρῷ. 7 τὸ γὰρ μυστήριον ἤδη
²of him ¹time. For the mystery ²already

ἐνεργεῖται τῆς ἀνομίας· μόνον ὁ κατέχων
³operates – ¹of lawlessness; only the [one] restraining [there is]

ἄρτι ἕως ἐκ μέσου γένηται. 8 καὶ τότε
just now until ²out of ³[the] midst ¹it comes. And then

ἀποκαλυφθήσεται ὁ ἄνομος, ὃν ὁ κύριος
will be revealed the lawless one, whom the Lord

['Ιησοῦς] ἀνελεῖ τῷ πνεύματι τοῦ στό-
Jesus will destroy by the spirit of the mouth

ματος αὐτοῦ καὶ καταργήσει τῇ ἐπιφανείᾳ
of him and bring to nothing by the outshining

τῆς παρουσίας αὐτοῦ, 9 οὗ ἐστιν ἡ
of the presence of him, of whom ³is ¹the

παρουσία κατ' ἐνέργειαν τοῦ σατανᾶ ἐν
²presence according to [the] operation – of Satan with

πάσῃ δυνάμει καὶ σημείοις καὶ τέρασιν
all power and signs and wonders

ψεύδους 10 καὶ ἐν πάσῃ ἀπάτῃ ἀδικίας
of a lie and with all deceit of unrighteousness

τοῖς ἀπολλυμένοις, ἀνθ' ὧν τὴν ἀγάπην
in the [ones] perishing, because the love

ceived not the love of the truth, that they might be saved.

11 And for this cause God shall send them strong delusion, that they should believe a lie:

12 That they all might be damned who believed not the truth, but had pleasure in unrighteousness.

13 But we are bound to give thanks alway to God for you, brethren beloved of the Lord, because God hath from the beginning chosen you to salvation through sanctification of the Spirit and belief of the truth:

14 Whereunto he called you by our gospel, to the obtaining of the glory of our Lord Jesus Christ.

15 Therefore, brethren, stand fast, and hold the traditions which ye have been taught, whether by word, or our epistle.

16 Now our Lord Jesus Christ himself, and God, even our Father, which hath loved us, and hath given us everlasting consolation and good hope through grace,

17 Comfort your hearts, and stablish you in every good word and work.

τῆς ἀληθείας οὐκ ἐδέξαντο εἰς τὸ σωθῆναι
of the   truth   they received not   for the [2]to be saved

αὐτούς. 11 καὶ διὰ τοῦτο πέμπει αὐτοῖς
[1]them.[b]   And therefore   [2]sends   [3]to them

ὁ θεὸς ἐνέργειαν πλάνης εἰς τὸ πιστεῦσαι
- [1]God an operation of error for the [2]to believe

αὐτοὺς τῷ ψεύδει, 12 ἵνα κριθῶσιν πάντες
[1]them[b] the lie,   in or-   [10]may be [1]all
                            der that judged

οἱ μὴ πιστεύσαντες τῇ ἀληθείᾳ ἀλλὰ
[2]the [3]not [4]having believed [5]the [6]truth [7]but
[ones]

εὐδοκήσαντες τῇ ἀδικίᾳ.
[8]having had pleasure - [9]in unrighteousness.

13 Ἡμεῖς δὲ ὀφείλομεν εὐχαριστεῖν τῷ
    But we   ought   to thank

θεῷ πάντοτε περὶ ὑμῶν, ἀδελφοὶ ἠγαπη-
God always concerning you, brothers having been

μένοι ὑπὸ κυρίου, ὅτι εἵλατο ὑμᾶς ὁ
loved by [the] Lord, because [2]chose [3]you -

θεὸς ἀπαρχὴν εἰς σωτηρίαν ἐν ἁγιασμῷ
[1]God firstfruit to salvation   by sanctification

πνεύματος καὶ πίστει ἀληθείας, 14 εἰς
of spirit   and faith of(in) [the] truth,   to

ὃ καὶ ἐκάλεσεν ὑμᾶς διὰ τοῦ εὐαγγελίου
which also he called   you   through the   gospel

ἡμῶν, εἰς περιποίησιν δόξης τοῦ κυρίου
of us,   to   obtainment of [the] glory of the Lord

ἡμῶν Ἰησοῦ Χριστοῦ. 15 Ἄρα οὖν,
of us Jesus Christ.   So   then,

ἀδελφοί, στήκετε, καὶ κρατεῖτε τὰς
brothers,   stand,   and   hold   the

παραδόσεις ἃς ἐδιδάχθητε εἴτε διὰ λόγου
traditions which ye were taught either through speech

εἴτε δι᾽ ἐπιστολῆς ἡμῶν. 16 Αὐτὸς δὲ
or through an epistle of us.   And [6][him]self

ὁ κύριος ἡμῶν Ἰησοῦς Χριστὸς καὶ
[1]the [2]Lord [3]of us [4]Jesus   [5]Christ   and

ὁ θεὸς ὁ πατὴρ ἡμῶν, ὁ ἀγαπήσας
the God the Father   of us, the [one] having loved

ἡμᾶς καὶ δοὺς παράκλησιν αἰωνίαν καὶ
us   and having given [2]comfort   [1]eternal [3]and

ἐλπίδα ἀγαθὴν ἐν χάριτι, 17 παρακαλέσαι
[5]hope [4]a good by grace,   may he comfort

ὑμῶν τὰς καρδίας καὶ στηρίξαι ἐν παντὶ
of you the hearts   and   may he   in every
                            confirm

ἔργῳ καὶ λόγῳ ἀγαθῷ.
[2]work [3]and [4]word [1]good.

CHAPTER 3

FINALLY, brethren, pray for us, that the word of the Lord may have *free* course, and be glorified, even as *it is* with you:

2 And that we may be delivered from unreasonable and wicked men: for all *men* have not faith.

3 But the Lord is faithful, who shall stablish you, and keep *you* from evil.

4 And we have confidence in the Lord touching you, that ye both do and will do the things which we command you.

5 And the Lord direct your hearts into the love of God, and into the patient waiting for Christ.

6 Now we command you, brethren, in the name of our Lord Jesus Christ, that ye withdraw yourselves from every brother that walketh disorderly, and not after the tradition which he received of us.

7 For yourselves know how ye ought to follow us: for we behaved not ourselves disorderly among you;

8 Neither did we eat any man's bread for nought; but wrought with labour and travail night

3 Τὸ λοιπὸν προσεύχεσθε, ἀδελφοί, περὶ
For the rest   pray ye,   brothers,   concerning

ἡμῶν, ἵνα ὁ λόγος τοῦ κυρίου τρέχῃ
us,   in order that   the   word   of the   Lord   may run

καὶ δοξάζηται καθὼς καὶ πρὸς ὑμᾶς,
and   be glorified   as   indeed   with   you,

2 καὶ ἵνα ῥυσθῶμεν ἀπὸ τῶν ἀτόπων
and   in order that   we may be delivered   from   –   perverse

καὶ πονηρῶν ἀνθρώπων· οὐ γὰρ πάντων
and   evil   men;   for [is] not   of all men

ἡ πίστις. **3** Πιστὸς δέ ἐστιν ὁ κύριος,
the faith.   But faithful   is   the   Lord,

ὃς στηρίξει ὑμᾶς καὶ φυλάξει ἀπὸ τοῦ
who will confirm   you   and   will guard   from   the

πονηροῦ. **4** πεποίθαμεν δὲ ἐν κυρίῳ
evil [?one].   And we are persuaded   in   [the] Lord

ἐφ' ὑμᾶς, ὅτι ἃ παραγγέλλομεν [καὶ]
as to   you,   that what things   we charge   both

ποιεῖτε καὶ ποιήσετε. **5** Ὁ δὲ κύριος
ye do   and   will do.   And the   Lord

κατευθύναι ὑμῶν τὰς καρδίας εἰς τὴν
may direct   of you   the   hearts   into   the

ἀγάπην τοῦ θεοῦ καὶ εἰς τὴν ὑπομονὴν
love   –   of God   and   into   the   patience

τοῦ Χριστοῦ.
–   of Christ.

6 Παραγγέλλομεν δὲ ὑμῖν, ἀδελφοί, ἐν
Now we charge   you,   brothers,   in

ὀνόματι τοῦ κυρίου Ἰησοῦ Χριστοῦ,
[the] name   of the   Lord   Jesus   Christ,

στέλλεσθαι ὑμᾶς ἀπὸ παντὸς ἀδελφοῦ
to draw back   you   from   every   brother

ἀτάκτως περιπατοῦντος καὶ μὴ κατὰ τὴν
idly   walking   and   not   according to   the

παράδοσιν ἣν παρελάβετε παρ' ἡμῶν.
tradition   which   ye received   from   us.

7 αὐτοὶ γὰρ οἴδατε πῶς δεῖ μιμεῖσθαι
For [your]selves   ye know   how   it behoves   to imitate

ἡμᾶς, ὅτι οὐκ ἠτακτήσαμεν ἐν ὑμῖν,
us,   because   we were not idle   among   you,

8 οὐδὲ δωρεὰν ἄρτον ἐφάγομεν παρά τινος,
nor   [as] a gift   bread   ate   from   anyone,

ἀλλ' ἐν κόπῳ καὶ μόχθῳ νυκτὸς καὶ
but   by   labour   and   struggle   by night   and

and day, that we might not be chargeable to any of you:

9 Not because we have not power, but to make ourselves an ensample unto you to follow us.

10 For even when we were with you, this we commanded you, that if any would not work, neither should he eat.

11 For we hear that there are some which walk among you disorderly, working not at all, but are busybodies.

12 Now them that are such we command and exhort by our Lord Jesus Christ, that with quietness they work, and eat their own bread.

13 But ye, brethren, be not weary in well doing.

14 And if any man obey not our word by this epistle, note that man, and have no company with him, that he may be ashamed.

15 Yet count *him* not as an enemy, but admonish *him* as a brother.

16 Now the Lord of peace himself give you peace always by all means. The Lord *be* with you all.

ἡμέρας ἐργαζόμενοι πρὸς τὸ μὴ ἐπιβαρῆσαί
by day   working   for *the* not to emburden

τινα ὑμῶν· 9 οὐχ ὅτι οὐκ ἔχομεν
anyone of you;   not that   we have not

ἐξουσίαν, ἀλλ' ἵνα ἑαυτοὺς τύπον δῶμεν
authority, but in or- ²our-   ³an ¹we might
             der that selves example give

ὑμῖν εἰς τὸ μιμεῖσθαι ἡμᾶς. 10 καὶ
to you for *the* to imitate   us.   even

γὰρ ὅτε ἦμεν πρὸς ὑμᾶς, τοῦτο παρηγ-
For when we were with you, this   we

γέλλομεν ὑμῖν, ὅτι εἴ τις οὐ θέλει
charged you, that if anyone does not wish

ἐργάζεσθαι, μηδὲ ἐσθιέτω. 11 ἀκούομεν
to work,   neither let him eat. we hear [of]

γάρ τινας περιπατοῦντας ἐν ὑμῖν ἀτάκτως,
For some   walking   among you   idly,

μηδὲν ἐργαζομένους ἀλλὰ περιεργαζομένους·
nothing working   but working round;

12 τοῖς δὲ τοιούτοις παραγγέλλομεν καὶ
   – and *to* such   we charge   and

παρακαλοῦμεν ἐν κυρίῳ Ἰησοῦ Χριστῷ
exhort   in [the] Lord Jesus Christ

ἵνα μετὰ ἡσυχίας ἐργαζόμενοι τὸν
in or- ²with ³quietness ¹working   ⁵the
der that

ἑαυτῶν ἄρτον ἐσθίωσιν. 13 Ὑμεῖς δέ,
⁷of them- ⁶bread ⁴they may eat. And ye,
selves

ἀδελφοί, μὴ ἐγκακήσητε καλοποιοῦντες
brothers, do not lose heart doing good.

14 εἰ δέ τις οὐχ ὑπακούει τῷ λόγῳ
And if anyone obeys not   the   word

ἡμῶν διὰ τῆς ἐπιστολῆς, τοῦτον σημειοῦσθε,
of us through the epistle,   this man mark,

μὴ συναναμίγνυσθαι αὐτῷ, ἵνα ἐντραπῇ·
not to mix with*   him, in or- he may be put
                          der that to shame;

15 καὶ μὴ ὡς ἐχθρὸν ἡγεῖσθε, ἀλλὰ
and yet not as an enemy deem ye [him], but

·ουθετεῖτε ὡς ἀδελφόν. 16 Αὐτὸς δὲ
admonish as a brother.   And ⁴[him]self

ὁ κύριος τῆς εἰρήνης δῴη ὑμῖν τὴν
¹the ³Lord – ²of peace may he to you the
                        give   (?his)

εἰρήνην διὰ παντὸς ἐν παντὶ τρόπῳ.
peace   always   in every   way.

ὁ κύριος μετὰ πάντων ὑμῶν.
The Lord [be] with ²all ¹you.

* Imperatival infinitive, as elsewhere (Phil. 3. 16, etc.).

17 The salutation of Paul with mine own hand, which is the token in every epistle: so I write.
18 The grace of our Lord Jesus Christ *be* with you all. Amen.

17 Ὁ ἀσπασμὸς τῇ ἐμῇ χειρὶ Παύλου,
The   greeting   –   by my hand[,]   of Paul,
ὅ   ἐστιν   σημεῖον   ἐν   πάσῃ   ἐπιστολῇ·
which is   a sign   in   every   epistle:
οὕτως   γράφω.   18 ἡ   χάρις   τοῦ   κυρίου
thus   I write.   The   grace   of the   Lord
ἡμῶν   Ἰησοῦ   Χριστοῦ   μετὰ   πάντων   ὑμῶν.
of us   Jesus   Christ [be]   with   [a]all   [1]you.

I. TIMOTHY
1

CHAPTER 1

PAUL, an apostle of Jesus Christ by the commandment of God our Saviour, and Lord Jesus Christ, *which is* our hope;
2 Unto Timothy, *my* own son in the faith: Grace, mercy, *and* peace, from God our Father and Jesus Christ our Lord.
3 As I besought thee to abide still at Ephesus, when I went into Macedonia, that thou mightest charge some that they teach no other doctrine,
4 Neither give heed to fables and endless genealogies, which minister questions, rather than godly edifying which is in faith: *so do.*
5 Now the end of the commandment is charity out of a pure heart, and *of* a good conscience, and *of* faith unfeigned:
6 From which some

ΠΡΟΣ ΤΙΜΟΘΕΟΝ Α
To Timothy 1

1 Παῦλος   ἀπόστολος   Χριστοῦ   Ἰησοῦ   κατ'
Paul   an apostle   of Christ   Jesus   according to
ἐπιταγὴν   θεοῦ   σωτῆρος   ἡμῶν   καὶ   Χριστοῦ
a command of God   Saviour   of us   and   of Christ
Ἰησοῦ   τῆς   ἐλπίδος   ἡμῶν   2 Τιμοθέῳ
Jesus   the   hope   of us   to Timothy
γνησίῳ   τέκνῳ   ἐν   πίστει·   χάρις,   ἔλεος,
a true   child   in   [the] faith: Grace,   mercy,
εἰρήνη   ἀπὸ   θεοῦ   πατρὸς   καὶ   Χριστοῦ
peace   from   God   [the] Father   and   Christ
Ἰησοῦ   τοῦ   κυρίου   ἡμῶν.
Jesus   the   Lord   of us.

3 Καθὼς   παρεκάλεσά   σε   προσμεῖναι   ἐν
As   I besought   thee   to remain   in
Ἐφέσῳ,   πορευόμενος   εἰς   Μακεδονίαν,   ἵνα
Ephesus,   [I] going   into   Macedonia,   in order that
παραγγείλῃς   τισὶν   μὴ   ἑτεροδιδασκαλεῖν
thou mightest   certain   not   to teach differently
charge   persons
4 μηδὲ   προσέχειν   μύθοις   καὶ   γενεαλογίαις
nor   to pay attention   to tales   and   to [2]genealogies
ἀπεράντοις,   αἵτινες   ἐκζητήσεις   παρέχουσιν
[1]unending,   which   [2]questionings   [1]provide
μᾶλλον   ἢ   οἰκονομίαν   θεοῦ   τὴν   ἐν   πίστει·
rather   than   a stewardship   of God   –   in   faith:
5 τὸ   δὲ   τέλος   τῆς   παραγγελίας   ἐστὶν
now the   end   of the   charge   is
ἀγάπη   ἐκ   καθαρᾶς   καρδίας   καὶ   συνειδήσεως
love   out of   a clean   heart   and   conscience
ἀγαθῆς   καὶ   πίστεως   ἀνυποκρίτου,   6 ὧν
a good   and   faith   unfeigned,   from which
things

having swerved have turned aside unto vain jangling;

7 Desiring to be teachers of the law; understanding neither what they say, nor whereof they affirm.

8 But we know that the law *is* good, if a man use it lawfully;

9 Knowing this, that the law is not made for a righteous man, but for the lawless and disobedient, for the ungodly and for sinners, for unholy and profane, for murderers of fathers and murderers of mothers, for manslayers,

10 For whoremongers, for them that defile themselves with mankind, for menstealers, for liars, for perjured persons, and if there be any other thing that is contrary to sound doctrine;

11 According to the glorious gospel of the blessed God, which was committed to my trust.

12 And I thank Christ Jesus our Lord, who hath enabled me, for that he counted me faithful, putting me into the ministry;

13 Who was before a blasphemer, and a persecutor, and injurious: but I obtained mercy, because I did *it* ignorantly in unbelief.

14 And the grace of our Lord was exceeding abundant with faith and love which is in Christ Jesus.

15 This *is* a faithful

τινες	ἀστοχήσαντες	ἐξετράπησαν	εἰς
some	missing aim	turned aside	to

ματαιολογίαν,	**7** θέλοντες	εἶναι	νομοδιδάσ-
vain talking,	wishing	to be	law-

καλοι,	μὴ	νοοῦντες	μήτε	ἃ	λέγουσιν
teachers,	not	understanding	either	what things	they say

μήτε	περὶ	τίνων	διαβεβαιοῦνται.	**8** οἴδαμεν
nor	concerning	what things	they emphatically assert.	we know

δὲ	ὅτι	καλὸς	ὁ	νόμος,	ἐάν	τις	αὐτῷ
Now	that	[3][is] [4]good	[1]the	[2]law,	if	anyone	[5]it

νομίμως	χρῆται,	**9** εἰδὼς	τοῦτο,	ὅτι
[3]lawfully	[1]uses,	knowing	this,	that

δικαίῳ	νόμος	οὐ	κεῖται,	ἀνόμοις	δὲ
[2]for a just man	[1]law	[3]is not laid down,	but for lawless men	

καὶ	ἀνυποτάκτοις,	ἀσεβέσι	καὶ	ἁμαρτωλοῖς,
and	for unruly,	for impious	and	for sinners,

ἀνοσίοις	καὶ	βεβήλοις,	πατρολῴαις	καὶ
for unholy	and	for profane,	for parricides	and

μητρολῴαις,	ἀνδροφόνοις,	**10** πόρνοις,	ἀρ-
for matricides,	for menkillers,	for fornicators,	for

σενοκοίταις,	ἀνδραποδισταῖς,	ψεύσταις,	ἐπιόρ-
paederasts,	for menstealers,	for liars,	for per-

κοις,	καὶ	εἴ	τι	ἕτερον	τῇ	ὑγιαινούσῃ
jurers,	and	if	any	other thing	[2]to the	[3]*being* healthful

διδασκαλίᾳ	ἀντίκειται,	**11** κατὰ	τὸ	εὐαγ-
[4]teaching	[1]opposes,	according to	the	gos-

γέλιον	τῆς	δόξης	τοῦ	μακαρίου	θεοῦ,
pel	of the	glory	of the	blessed	God,

ὃ	ἐπιστεύθην	ἐγώ.	**12** Χάριν	ἔχω	τῷ
which	[2]was entrusted [with]	[1]I.	Thanks	I have	to the

ἐνδυναμώσαντί	με	Χριστῷ	Ἰησοῦ	τῷ	κυρίῳ
[one] empowering	me	Christ	Jesus	the	Lord

ἡμῶν,	ὅτι	πιστόν	με	ἡγήσατο	θέμενος
of us,	because	[3]faithful	[2]me	[1]he deemed	putting [me]

εἰς	διακονίαν,	**13** τὸ	πρότερον	ὄντα
into	[the] ministry,		formerly	being

βλάσφημον	καὶ	διώκτην	καὶ	ὑβριστήν·
a blasphemer	and	a persecutor	and	insolent;

ἀλλὰ	ἠλεήθην,	ὅτι	ἀγνοῶν	ἐποίησα	ἐν
but	I obtained mercy,	because	being ignorant	I acted	in

ἀπιστίᾳ,	**14** ὑπερεπλεόνασεν	δὲ	ἡ	χάρις
unbelief,	and superabounded		the	grace

τοῦ	κυρίου	ἡμῶν	μετὰ	πίστεως	καὶ
of the	Lord	of us	with	faith	and

ἀγάπης	τῆς	ἐν	Χριστῷ	Ἰησοῦ.	**15** πιστὸς
love	–	in	Christ	Jesus.	Faithful [is]

saying, and worthy of all acceptation, that Christ Jesus came into the world to save sinners; of whom I am chief.

16 Howbeit for this cause I obtained mercy, that in me first Jesus Christ might shew forth all longsuffering, for a pattern to them which should hereafter believe on him to life everlasting.

17 Now unto the King eternal, immortal, invisible, the only wise God, be honour and glory for ever and ever. Amen.

18 This charge I commit unto thee, son Timothy, according to the prophecies which went before on thee, that thou by them mightest war a good warfare;

19 Holding faith, and a good conscience; which some having put away concerning faith have made shipwreck:

20 Of whom is Hymenæus and Alexander; whom I have delivered unto Satan, that they may learn not to blaspheme.

ὁ λόγος καὶ πάσης ἀποδοχῆς ἄξιος,
the word and ²of all ²acceptance ¹worthy,

ὅτι Χριστὸς Ἰησοῦς ἦλθεν εἰς τὸν κόσμον
that Christ Jesus came into the world

ἁμαρτωλοὺς σῶσαι· ὧν πρῶτός εἰμι ἐγώ·
sinners to save; of whom first(chief) am I;

16 ἀλλὰ διὰ τοῦτο ἠλεήθην, ἵνα ἐν
but because of this I obtained mercy, in order that in

ἐμοὶ πρώτῳ ἐνδείξηται Ἰησοῦς Χριστὸς
me first might show forth Jesus Christ

τὴν ἅπασαν μακροθυμίαν, πρὸς ὑποτύπωσιν
– all longsuffering, for a pattern

τῶν μελλόντων πιστεύειν ἐπ' αὐτῷ εἰς
of the [ones] coming to believe on him to

ζωὴν αἰώνιον. 17 Τῷ δὲ βασιλεῖ τῶν
life eternal. Now to the King of the

αἰώνων, ἀφθάρτῳ ἀοράτῳ μόνῳ θεῷ, τιμὴ
ages, incorruptible invisible only God, [be] honour

καὶ δόξα εἰς τοὺς αἰῶνας τῶν αἰώνων·
and glory unto the ages of the ages:

ἀμήν. 18 Ταύτην τὴν παραγγελίαν παρα-
Amen. This – charge I com-

τίθεμαί σοι, τέκνον Τιμόθεε, κατὰ τὰς
mit to thee, child Timothy, according to the

προαγούσας ἐπὶ σὲ προφητείας, ἵνα
preceding ²respecting ²thee ¹prophecies, in order that

στρατεύῃ ἐν αὐταῖς τὴν καλὴν στρατείαν,
thou mightest war by them the good warfare,

19 ἔχων πίστιν καὶ ἀγαθὴν συνείδησιν,
having faith and a good conscience,

ἥν τινες ἀπωσάμενοι περὶ τὴν πίστιν
which some thrusting away ²concerning ²the ⁴faith

ἐναυάγησαν· 20 ὧν ἐστιν Ὑμέναιος καὶ
¹made shipwreck; of whom is Hymenæus and

Ἀλέξανδρος, οὓς παρέδωκα τῷ σατανᾷ,
Alexander, whom I delivered – to Satan,

ἵνα παιδευθῶσιν μὴ βλασφημεῖν.
in order that they may be taught not to blaspheme.

CHAPTER 2

I EXHORT therefore, that, first of all, supplications, prayers, inter-

2 Παρακαλῶ οὖν πρῶτον πάντων
I exhort therefore firstly of all

ποιεῖσθαι δεήσεις, προσευχάς, ἐντεύξεις,
to be made petitions, prayers, intercessions,

cessions, *and* giving of thanks, be made for all men;

2 For kings, and *for* all that are in authority; that we may lead a quiet and peaceable life in all godliness and honesty.

3 For this *is* good and acceptable in the sight of God our Saviour;

4 Who will have all men to be saved, and to come unto the knowledge of the truth.

5 For *there is* one God, and one mediator between God and men, the man Christ Jesus;

6 Who gave himself a ransom for all, to be testified in due time.

7 Whereunto I am ordained a preacher, and an apostle, (I speak the truth in Christ, *and* lie not;) a teacher of the Gentiles in faith and verity.

8 I will therefore that men pray every where, lifting up holy hands, without wrath and doubting.

9 In like manner also, that women adorn themselves in modest apparel, with shamefacedness and sobriety; not with broided hair, or gold, or pearls, or costly array;

10 But (which becometh

εὐχαριστίας, 2 ὑπὲρ πάντων ἀνθρώπων,
thanksgivings, on behalf of all men,

ὑπὲρ βασιλέων καὶ πάντων τῶν ἐν
on behalf of kings and all the [ones] ²in

ὑπεροχῇ ὄντων, ἵνα ἤρεμον καὶ ἡσύχιον
²eminence ¹being, in or-der that ²a tranquil ³and ⁴quiet

βίον διάγωμεν ἐν πάσῃ εὐσεβείᾳ καὶ
⁵life ¹we may lead in all piety and

σεμνότητι. 3 τοῦτο καλὸν καὶ ἀπόδεκτον
gravity. This [is] good and acceptable

ἐνώπιον τοῦ σωτῆρος ἡμῶν θεοῦ, 4 ὃς
before the Saviour of us God, who

πάντας ἀνθρώπους θέλει σωθῆναι καὶ εἰς
²all ³men ¹wishes to be saved and ²to

ἐπίγνωσιν ἀληθείας ἐλθεῖν. 5 εἷς γὰρ
²a full knowledge ⁴of truth ¹to come. For ²one

θεός, εἷς καὶ μεσίτης θεοῦ καὶ ἀνθρώπων,
¹[there one also mediator of God and of men,
is] ³God,

ἄνθρωπος Χριστὸς Ἰησοῦς, 6 ὁ δοὺς
a man Christ Jesus, the [one] having given

ἑαυτὸν ἀντίλυτρον ὑπὲρ πάντων, τὸ
himself a ransom on behalf of all, the

μαρτύριον καιροῖς ἰδίοις· 7 εἰς ὃ ἐτέθην
testimony in its own times; for which ¹was appointed

ἐγὼ κῆρυξ καὶ ἀπόστολος, ἀλήθειαν λέγω,
¹I a herald and an apostle, ²truth ¹I say,

οὐ ψεύδομαι, διδάσκαλος ἐθνῶν ἐν πίστει
I do not lie, a teacher of nations in faith

καὶ ἀληθείᾳ. 8 Βούλομαι οὖν προσεύχεσθαι
and truth. I desire therefore ²to pray

τοὺς ἄνδρας ἐν παντὶ τόπῳ ἐπαίροντας
¹the ²men in every place lifting up

ὁσίους χεῖρας χωρὶς ὀργῆς καὶ διαλογισμοῦ.
holy hands without wrath and doubting.

9 Ὡσαύτως γυναῖκας ἐν καταστολῇ κοσμίῳ,
Similarly women in clothing orderly,

μετὰ αἰδοῦς καὶ σωφροσύνης κοσμεῖν
³with ⁴modesty ²and ⁵sobriety ¹to adorn

ἑαυτάς, μὴ ἐν πλέγμασιν καὶ χρυσίῳ
²themselves, not with plaiting and gold

ἢ μαργαρίταις ἢ ἱματισμῷ πολυτελεῖ,
or pearls or raiment costly,

10 ἀλλ' ὃ πρέπει γυναιξὶν ἐπαγγελλομέναις
but what suits women professing

women professing godliness) with good works.

11 Let the woman learn in silence with all subjection.

12 But I suffer not a woman to teach, nor to usurp authority over the man, but to be in silence.

13 For Adam was first formed, then Eve.

14 And Adam was not deceived, but the woman being deceived was in the transgression.

15 Notwithstanding she shall be saved in childbearing, if they continue in faith and charity and holiness with sobriety.

θεοσέβειαν,   δι᾽   ἔργων   ἀγαθῶν.   **11** γυνὴ
reverence,   by   ²works   ¹good.   A woman
   means of

ἐν   ἡσυχίᾳ   μανθανέτω   ἐν   πάσῃ   ὑποταγῇ·
in   silence   let learn   in   all   subjection;

12 διδάσκειν   δὲ   γυναικὶ   οὐκ   ἐπιτρέπω,
   but ³to teach   ²a woman   ¹I do not permit,

οὐδὲ   αὐθεντεῖν   ἀνδρός,   ἀλλ᾽   εἶναι   ἐν
nor   to exercise   of(over) a man,   but   to be   in
   authority

ἡσυχίᾳ.   **13** Ἀδὰμ   γὰρ   πρῶτος   ἐπλάσθη,
silence.   For Adam   first   was formed,

εἶτα   Εὔα.   **14** καὶ   Ἀδὰμ   οὐκ   ἠπατήθη,
then   Eve.   And   Adam   was not deceived,

ἡ   δὲ   γυνὴ   ἐξαπατηθεῖσα   ἐν   παραβάσει
but the   woman   being deceived   ²in   ³transgression

γέγονεν·   **15** σωθήσεται   δὲ   διὰ   τῆς
¹has become;   but she will be saved   through   the(her)

τεκνογονίας,   ἐὰν   μείνωσιν   ἐν   πίστει   καὶ
childbearing,   if   they remain   in   faith   and

ἀγάπῃ   καὶ   ἁγιασμῷ   μετὰ   σωφροσύνης.
love   and   sanctification   with   sobriety.

CHAPTER 3

THIS *is* a true saying, If a man desire the office of a bishop, he desireth a good work.

2 A bishop then must be blameless, the husband of one wife, vigilant, sober, of good behaviour, given to hospitality, apt to teach;

3 Not given to wine, no striker, not greedy of filthy lucre; but patient, not a brawler, not covetous;

4 One that ruleth well his own house, having his children in subjection with all gravity;

5 (For if a man know not how to rule his own house, how shall he take care of the church of God?)

3 Πιστὸς   ὁ   λόγος·   εἴ   τις   ἐπισκοπῆς
   Faithful [is]   the   word: If   anyone   ²oversight

ὀρέγεται,   καλοῦ   ἔργου   ἐπιθυμεῖ.   **2** δεῖ
¹aspires to,   ²a good   ³work   ¹he desires.   It behoves

οὖν   τὸν   ἐπίσκοπον   ἀνεπίλημπτον   εἶναι,
therefore   the   bishop   without reproach   to be,

μιᾶς   γυναικὸς   ἄνδρα,   νηφάλιον,   σώφρονα,
of one   wife   husband,   temperate,   sensible,

κόσμιον,   φιλόξενον,   διδακτικόν,   **3** μὴ
orderly,   hospitable,   apt at teaching,   not

πάροινον,   μὴ   πλήκτην,   ἀλλὰ   ἐπιεικῆ,
an excessive   not   a striker,   but   forbearing,
drinker,

ἄμαχον,   ἀφιλάργυρον,   **4** τοῦ   ἰδίου   οἴκου
uncontentious,   not avaricious,   ³the(his)   ⁴own   ⁵household

καλῶς   προϊστάμενον,   τέκνα   ἔχοντα   ἐν
²well   ¹ruling,   children   having   in

ὑποταγῇ   μετὰ   πάσης   σεμνότητος,   **5** (εἰ
subjection   with   all   gravity,   ¹(if

δέ   τις   τοῦ   ἰδίου   οἴκου   προστῆναι   οὐκ
¹but²anyone   ⁷the(his)   ⁸own   ⁹household   ⁶to rule   ⁵not*

οἶδεν,   πῶς   ἐκκλησίας   θεοῦ   ἐπιμελήσεται;)
⁴knows,   how   ²a church   ³of God   ¹will he care for?)

* That is, " cannot "; see note on page xviii.

6 Not a novice, lest being lifted up with pride he fall into the condemnation of the devil.

7 Moreover he must have a good report of them which are without; lest he fall into reproach and the snare of the devil.

8 Likewise *must* the deacons *be* grave, not doubletongued, not given to much wine, not greedy of filthy lucre;

9 Holding the mystery of the faith in a pure conscience.

10 And let these also first be proved; then let them use the office of a deacon, being *found* blameless.

11 Even so *must their* wives *be* grave, not slanderers, sober, faithful in all things.

12 Let the deacons be the husbands of one wife, ruling their children and their own houses well.

13 For they that have used the office of a deacon well purchase to themselves a good degree, and great boldness in the faith which is in Christ Jesus.

14 These things write I unto thee, hoping to come unto thee shortly;

15 But if I tarry long, that thou mayest know how thou oughtest to behave thyself in the house of God, which is the church of the living God,

---

6 μὴ νεόφυτον, ἵνα μὴ τυφωθεὶς εἰς
not a neophyte(recent lest being puffed up ²into
convert),

κρίμα ἐμπέσῃ τοῦ διαβόλου. 7 δεῖ δὲ
³judgment ¹he fall *in* of the devil. And it behoves

καὶ μαρτυρίαν καλὴν ἔχειν ἀπὸ τῶν
also ³witness ²a good ¹to have from the [ones]

ἔξωθεν, 7 ἵνα μὴ εἰς ὀνειδισμὸν ἐμπέσῃ
outside, lest ²into ³reproach ¹he fall *in*

καὶ παγίδα τοῦ διαβόλου. 8 Διακόνους
and a snare of the devil. [It behoves] deacons

ὡσαύτως σεμνούς, μὴ διλόγους, μὴ οἴνῳ
similarly [to be] grave, not double-tongued, not ³wine

πολλῷ προσέχοντας, μὴ αἰσχροκερδεῖς,
²to much ¹being addicted, not fond of base gain,

9 ἔχοντας τὸ μυστήριον τῆς πίστεως ἐν
having the mystery of the faith with

καθαρᾷ συνειδήσει. 10 καὶ οὗτοι δὲ
a clean conscience. ⁴Also ³these ¹and

δοκιμαζέσθωσαν πρῶτον, εἶτα διακονείτωσαν
²let ⁵be proved firstly, then let them minister

ἀνέγκλητοι ὄντες. 11 γυναῖκας ὡσαύτως
²irreproachable ¹being. [It behoves]* wives similarly

σεμνάς, μὴ διαβόλους, νηφαλίους, πιστὰς
[to be] grave, not slanderers, sober, faithful

ἐν πᾶσιν. 12 διάκονοι ἔστωσαν μιᾶς
in all things. ²Deacons ¹let ³be ⁵of one

γυναικὸς ἄνδρες, τέκνων καλῶς προϊστάμενοι
⁶wife ⁴husbands, ²children ⁶well ¹ruling

καὶ τῶν ἰδίων οἴκων. 13 οἱ γὰρ καλῶς
³and ⁴the(ir) own ⁵households. For the [ones] ²well

διακονήσαντες βαθμὸν ἑαυτοῖς καλὸν
¹having ministered ⁶position ⁴for themselves ⁵a good

περιποιοῦνται καὶ πολλὴν παρρησίαν ἐν
³acquire and much boldness in

πίστει τῇ ἐν Χριστῷ Ἰησοῦ. 14 Ταῦτά
faith the [one] in Christ Jesus. These things

σοι γράφω ἐλπίζων ἐλθεῖν πρὸς σὲ
to thee I write hoping to come to thee

τάχιον· 15 ἐὰν δὲ βραδύνω, ἵνα εἰδῇς
shortly; but if I delay, in order thou
that mayest
know

πῶς δεῖ ἐν οἴκῳ θεοῦ ἀναστρέφεσθαι,
how it behoves in [the] of God to behave,
household

ἥτις ἐστὶν ἐκκλησία θεοῦ ζῶντος, στῦλος
which is [the] church ²God ¹of [the] living, pillar

---

* See verses 7 and 8.

the pillar and ground of the truth.

16 And without controversy great is the mystery of godliness: God was manifest in the flesh, justified in the Spirit, seen of angels, preached unto the Gentiles, believed on in the world, received up into glory

καὶ ἑδραίωμα τῆς ἀληθείας. **16** καὶ
and   bulwark   of the   truth.   And

ὁμολογουμένως μέγα ἐστὶν τὸ τῆς εὐσεβείας
confessedly   great   is   the   –   [2]of piety

μυστήριον· ὃς ἐφανερώθη ἐν σαρκί,
[1]mystery: Who   was manifested   in   flesh,

ἐδικαιώθη ἐν πνεύματι, ὤφθη ἀγγέλοις,
was justified   in   spirit,   was seen   by angels,

ἐκηρύχθη ἐν ἔθνεσιν, ἐπιστεύθη ἐν κόσμῳ,
was pro-   among   nations,   was believed   in [the] world,
claimed

ἀνελήμφθη ἐν δόξῃ.
was taken up   in   glory.

CHAPTER 4

NOW the Spirit speaketh expressly, that in the latter times some shall depart from the faith, giving heed to seducing spirits, and doctrines of devils;

2 Speaking lies in hypocrisy; having their conscience seared with a hot iron;

3 Forbidding to marry, *and commanding* to abstain from meats, which God hath created to be received with thanksgiving of them which believe and know the truth.

4 For every creature of God *is* good, and nothing to be refused, if it be received with thanksgiving:

5 For it is sanctified by the word of God and prayer.

6 If thou put the brethren in remembrance of these things, thou shalt be a good minister of Jesus Christ, nourished up in

4 Τὸ δὲ πνεῦμα ῥητῶς λέγει ὅτι
Now the   Spirit   [2]says   that

ἐν ὑστέροις καιροῖς ἀποστήσονταί τινες
in   later   times   [2]will depart from   [1]some

τῆς πίστεως, προσέχοντες πνεύμασιν
the   faith,   attending to   [2]spirits

πλάνοις καὶ διδασκαλίαις δαιμονίων, **2** ἐν
[1]misleading   and   teachings   of demons,   [2]in

ὑποκρίσει ψευδολόγων, κεκαυστηριασμένων
[3]hypocrisy   [1]of men who speak lies,   having been branded on

τὴν ἰδίαν συνείδησιν, **3** κωλυόντων γαμεῖν,
the(ir) own   conscience,   forbidding   to marry,

ἀπέχεσθαι βρωμάτων, ἃ ὁ θεὸς ἔκτισεν
[bidding] to   foods,   which   –   God   created
abstain from

εἰς μετάλημψιν μετὰ εὐχαριστίας τοῖς
for   partaking   with   thanksgiving   by the

πιστοῖς καὶ ἐπεγνωκόσι τὴν ἀλήθειαν.
believers   and [those] having fully   the   truth.
                known

4 ὅτι πᾶν κτίσμα θεοῦ καλόν, καὶ
Because   every   creature   of God [is]   good,   and

οὐδὲν ἀπόβλητον μετὰ εὐχαριστίας λαμβαν-
nothing   to be put away   [2]with   [3]thanksgiving   [1]being
[is]

όμενον· **5** ἁγιάζεται γὰρ διὰ λόγου θεοῦ
received;   for it is *being* sanctified   through   a word   of God

καὶ ἐντεύξεως. **6** Ταῦτα ὑποτιθέμενος
and   petition.   [2]These things   [1]suggesting

τοῖς ἀδελφοῖς καλὸς ἔσῃ διάκονος Χριστοῦ
[2]to the   [4]brothers   [6]a good   [5]thou   [7]minister   of Christ
                 wilt be

Ἰησοῦ, ἐντρεφόμενος τοῖς λόγοις τῆς
Jesus,   being nourished   by the   words   of the

the words of faith and of good doctrine, whereunto thou hast attained.

7 But refuse profane and old wives' fables, and exercise thyself *rather* unto godliness.

8 For bodily exercise profiteth little: but godliness is profitable unto all things, having promise of the life that now is, and of that which is to come.

9 This *is* a faithful saying and worthy of all acceptation.

10 For therefore we both labour and suffer reproach, because we trust in the living God, who is the Saviour of all men, specially of those that believe.

11 These things command and teach.

12 Let no man despise thy youth; but be thou an example of the believers, in word, in conversation, in charity, in spirit, in faith, in purity.

13 Till I come, give attendance to reading, to exhortation, to doctrine.

14 Neglect not the gift that is in thee, which was given thee by prophecy, with the laying on of the hands of the presbytery.

πίστεως   καὶ   τῆς   καλῆς   διδασκαλίας   ᾗ
faith   and   of the   good   teaching   which

παρηκολούθηκας·   7 τοὺς   δὲ   βεβήλους   καὶ
thou hast followed;   but the   profane   and

γραώδεις   μύθους   παραιτοῦ.   γύμναζε   δὲ
old-womanish   tales   refuse.   And exercise

σεαυτὸν   πρὸς   εὐσέβειαν.   8 ἡ   γὰρ   σωματικὴ
thyself   to   piety.   – For   bodily

γυμνασία   πρὸς   ὀλίγον   ἐστὶν   ὠφέλιμος·
exercise   [2]for   [4]a little   [1]is   [3]profitable;

ἡ   δὲ   εὐσέβεια   πρὸς   πάντα   ὠφέλιμός
–   but   piety   [3]for   [4]all things   [2]profitable

ἐστιν,   ἐπαγγελίαν   ἔχουσα   ζωῆς   τῆς   νῦν
[1]is,   promise   having   [3]life   [1]of the [2]now
                                                    (present)

καὶ   τῆς   μελλούσης.   9 πιστὸς   ὁ   λόγος
and   of the   coming.   Faithful [is]   the   word

καὶ   πάσης   ἀποδοχῆς   ἄξιος·   10 εἰς   τοῦτο
and   [3]of all   [2]acceptance   [1]worthy;   [2]to   [1]this

γὰρ   κοπιῶμεν   καὶ   ἀγωνιζόμεθα,   ὅτι
[1]for   we labour   and   struggle,   because

ἠλπίκαμεν   ἐπὶ   θεῷ   ζῶντι,   ὅς   ἐστιν
we have set   on   [3]God   [1]a living,   who   is
[our] hope

σωτὴρ   πάντων   ἀνθρώπων,   μάλιστα   πιστῶν.
[the]   of all   men,   especially of believers.
Saviour

11 Παράγγελλε   ταῦτα   καὶ   δίδασκε.
   Charge thou   these things   and   teach.

12 μηδείς   σου   τῆς   νεότητος   καταφρονείτω,
   [1]No one   [2]of thee   [3]the   [4]youth   [1]let despise,

ἀλλὰ   τύπος   γίνου   τῶν   πιστῶν   ἐν   λόγῳ,
but   [2]a pattern   [1]become   of the   believers   in   speech,
                thou

ἐν   ἀναστροφῇ,   ἐν   ἀγάπῃ,   ἐν   πίστει,
in   behaviour,   in   love,   in   faith,

ἐν   ἁγνείᾳ.   13 ἕως   ἔρχομαι   πρόσεχε
in   purity.   Until   I come   attend

τῇ   ἀναγνώσει,   τῇ   παρακλήσει,   τῇ   διδασ-
to the   reading,[*]   to the   exhortation,   to the   teach-

καλίᾳ.   14 μὴ   ἀμέλει   τοῦ   ἐν   σοὶ
ing.   Do not be neglectful   [1]of the   [3]in   [4]thee

χαρίσματος,   ὃ   ἐδόθη   σοι   διὰ   προφητείας
[2]gift,   which   was   to thee   by   prophecy
                  given   means of

μετὰ   ἐπιθέσεως   τῶν   χειρῶν   τοῦ   πρε-
with   laying on   of the   hands   of the   body

---

[*] That is, the reading aloud in public worship of the Scriptures (as nearly always in the N.T.).

15 Meditate upon these things; give thyself wholly to them; that thy profiting may appear to all.

16 Take heed unto thyself, and unto the doctrine; continue in them: for in doing this thou shalt both save thyself, and them that hear thee.

σβυτερίου. **15** ταῦτα μελέτα, ἐν τούτοις
of elders.   ²These things ¹attend to,   ²in ³these things

ἴσθι, ἵνα σου ἡ προκοπὴ φανερὰ ᾖ
¹be   in order   of thee   the   advance   clear   may
thou,   that   be

πᾶσιν. **16** ἔπεχε σεαυτῷ καὶ τῇ διδασκαλίᾳ,
to all men.   Take heed to thyself   and   to the   teaching,

ἐπίμενε αὐτοῖς· τοῦτο γὰρ ποιῶν καὶ
continue   in them;   for this   doing   both

σεαυτὸν σώσεις καὶ τοὺς ἀκούοντάς σου.
thyself   thou wilt save   and   the [ones] hearing   thee.

CHAPTER 5

REBUKE not an elder, but intreat *him* as a father; *and* the younger men as brethren;

2 The elder women as mothers; the younger as sisters, with all purity.

3 Honour widows that are widows indeed.

4 But if any widow have children or nephews, let them learn first to shew piety at home, and to requite their parents: for that is good and acceptable before God.

5 Now she that is a widow indeed, and desolate, trusteth in God, and continueth in supplications and prayers night and day.

6 But she that liveth in pleasure is dead while she liveth.

7 And these things give in charge, that they may be blameless.

8 But if any provide not for his own, and specially

5 Πρεσβυτέρῳ μὴ ἐπιπλήξῃς, ἀλλὰ
An older man   do not rebuke,   but

παρακάλει ὡς πατέρα, νεωτέρους ὡς
exhort   as   a father,   younger men   as

ἀδελφούς, **2** πρεσβυτέρας ὡς μητέρας,
brothers,   older women   as   mothers,

νεωτέρας ὡς ἀδελφὰς ἐν πάσῃ ἁγνείᾳ.
younger women as   sisters   with   all   purity.

3 Χήρας τίμα τὰς ὄντως χήρας. **4** εἰ δέ
²Widows ¹honour   ³the   ⁴real*ly*   ⁵widows.   But if

τις χήρα τέκνα ἢ ἔκγονα ἔχει, μαν-
any   widow   ²children   ³or ⁴grandchildren ¹has,   let

θανέτωσαν πρῶτον τὸν ἴδιον οἶκον εὐσεβεῖν
them learn   firstly   ²the(ir) ¹own ⁴household ¹to show
                                           piety to

καὶ ἀμοιβὰς ἀποδιδόναι τοῖς προγόνοις·
and   ²requitals   ¹to return   to the(ir)   forebears;

τοῦτο γάρ ἐστιν ἀπόδεκτον ἐνώπιον τοῦ
for this   is   acceptable   before   --

θεοῦ. **5** ἡ δὲ ὄντως χήρα καὶ μεμονωμένη
God.   But the   real*ly*   widow   and   *having been* left
                                           alone

ἤλπικεν ἐπὶ θεὸν καὶ προσμένει ταῖς
has set   on   God   and   continues   in the
[her] hope

δεήσεσιν καὶ ταῖς προσευχαῖς νυκτὸς καὶ
petitions   and   the   prayers   night   and

ἡμέρας· **6** ἡ δὲ σπαταλῶσα ζῶσα τέθνηκεν.
day;   but the   living wantonly   ²living   ¹has died.
           [one]

7 καὶ ταῦτα παράγγελλε, ἵνα ἀνεπίλημπτοι
And   these   charge thou,   in order ²without reproach
       things   that

ὦσιν. **8** εἰ δέ τις τῶν ἰδίων καὶ μάλιστα
¹they   But if anyone ²the(his) ³own   ⁴and   ⁵especially
may be.   [people]

for those of his own house, he hath denied the faith, and is worse than an infidel.

9 Let not a widow be taken into the number under threescore years old, having been the wife of one man,

10 Well reported of for good works; if she have brought up children, if she have lodged strangers, if she have washed the saints' feet, if she have relieved the afflicted, if she have diligently followed every good work.

11 But the younger widows refuse: for when they have begun to wax wanton against Christ, they will marry;

12 Having damnation, because they have cast off their first faith.

13 And withal they learn to be idle, wandering about from house to house; and not only idle, but tattlers also and busybodies, speaking things which they ought not.

14 I will therefore that the younger women marry, bear children, guide the house, give none occasion to the adversary to speak reproachfully.

15 For some are already turned aside after Satan.

16 If any man or woman that believeth have widows, let them relieve them, and let not the church be charged; that

οἰκείων   οὐ   προνοεῖ,   τὴν   πίστιν   ἤρνηται
[his] ¹provides not [for], ²the ³faith ¹he has denied
⁶family

καὶ   ἔστιν   ἀπίστου   χείρων.   9 χήρα
and   is   ²an unbeliever ¹worse [than].   A widow

καταλεγέσθω   μὴ   ἔλαττον   ἐτῶν   ἐξήκοντα
let be enrolled ²not ³less [than] ⁵of years ⁴sixty

γεγονυῖα,   ἑνὸς   ἀνδρὸς   γυνή,   10 ἐν   ἔργοις
¹having   of one   man   wife,   ²by ⁴works
become,

καλοῖς   μαρτυρουμένη,   εἰ   ἐτεκνοτρόφησεν,
³good   ¹being witnessed, if she brought up children,

εἰ   ἐξενοδόχησεν,   εἰ   ἁγίων   πόδας   ἔνιψεν,
if   she entertained if ³of saints ²feet   ¹she washed,
      strangers,

εἰ   θλιβομένοις   ἐπήρκεσεν,   εἰ   παντὶ   ἔργῳ
if   ²being afflicted ¹she relieved, if ²every ⁴work
     [ones],

ἀγαθῷ   ἐπηκολούθησεν.   11 νεωτέρας   δὲ
³good   ¹she followed after.   But younger

χήρας   παραιτοῦ· ὅταν   γὰρ   καταστρηνιάσωσιν
widows   refuse;   for whenever they grow wanton against

τοῦ   Χριστοῦ,   γαμεῖν   θέλουσιν,   12 ἔχουσαι
 -    Christ,   ²to marry ¹they wish,   having

κρίμα   ὅτι   τὴν   πρώτην   πίστιν   ἠθέτησαν·
judgment because ²the(ir) ³first ⁴faith ¹they set aside;

13 ἅμα   δὲ   καὶ   ἀργαὶ   μανθάνουσιν
and at the same time also   ²idle   ¹they learn [to be]

περιερχόμεναι   τὰς   οἰκίας,   οὐ   μόνον   δὲ
going round   the   houses, ²not ³only ¹and

ἀργαὶ   ἀλλὰ   καὶ   φλύαροι   καὶ   περίεργοι,
idle   but   also   gossips   and   busybodies,

λαλοῦσαι   τὰ   μὴ   δέοντα.   14 βούλομαι
speaking the things not proper.   I will

οὖν   νεωτέρας   γαμεῖν,   τεκνογονεῖν,
there- younger women to marry, to bear children,
fore

οἰκοδεσποτεῖν,   μηδεμίαν   ἀφορμὴν   διδόναι
to be mistress of   ²no   ³occasion   ¹to give
a house,

τῷ   ἀντικειμένῳ   λοιδορίας   χάριν·   15 ἤδη
to the [one] opposing ²reproach ¹on account of; ²already

γάρ   τινες   ἐξετράπησαν   ὀπίσω   τοῦ   σατανᾶ.
¹for some   turned aside   behind   -   Satan.

16 εἴ   τις   πιστὴ   ἔχει   χήρας,   ἐπαρκείτω
   If   any believing has   widows, let her relieve
            woman

αὐταῖς,   καὶ   μὴ   βαρείσθω   ἡ   ἐκκλησία,
them,   and   not let be burdened the church,

it may relieve them that are widows indeed.

17 Let the elders that rule well be counted worthy of double honour, especially they who labour in the word and doctrine.

18 For the scripture saith, Thou shalt not muzzle the ox that treadeth out the corn. And, The labourer *is* worthy of his reward.

19 Against an elder receive not an accusation, but before two or three witnesses.

20 Them that sin rebuke before all, that others also may fear.

21 I charge *thee* before God, and the Lord Jesus Christ, and the elect angels, that thou observe these things without preferring one before another, doing nothing by partiality.

22 Lay hands suddenly on no man, neither be partaker of other men's sins: keep thyself pure.

23 Drink no longer water, but use a litt!e wine for thy stomach's sake and thine often infirmities.

24 Some men's sins are open beforehand, going before to judgment; and some *men* they follow after.

25 Likewise also the

ἵνα	ταῖς	ὄντως	χήραις	ἐπαρκέσῃ. **17** *Oἱ*
in or-der that	²the	³real*ly*	⁴widows	¹it may relieve. ²The

καλῶς προεστῶτες πρεσβύτεροι διπλῆς
⁵well ⁴ruling ³elders ⁶of double

τιμῆς ἀξιούσθωσαν, μάλιστα οἱ κοπιῶντες
¹⁰honour ¹let ⁶be ⁷deemed especially the labouring
⁸worthy, [ones]

ἐν λόγῳ καὶ διδασκαλίᾳ. **18** λέγει γὰρ
in speech and teaching. For says

ἡ γραφή· βοῦν ἀλοῶντα οὐ φιμώσεις,
the scripture: An ox threshing thou shalt not muzzle,

καὶ· ἄξιος ὁ ἐργάτης τοῦ μισθοῦ αὐτοῦ.
and: Worthy [is] the workman of the pay of him.

19 κατὰ πρεσβυτέρου κατηγορίαν μὴ παρα-
Against an elder accusation do not re-

δέχου, ἐκτὸς εἰ μὴ ἐπὶ δύο ἢ τριῶν
ceive, except unless on [the two or three
word of]

μαρτύρων. **20** Τοὺς ἁμαρτάνοντας ἐνώπιον
witnesses. The [ones] sinning ²before

πάντων ἔλεγχε, ἵνα καὶ οἱ λοιποὶ φόβον
³all ¹reprove in ³also ¹the ²rest ⁵fear
thou, order that

ἔχωσιν. **21** Διαμαρτύρομαι ἐνώπιον τοῦ
⁴may have. I solemnly witness before –

θεοῦ καὶ Χριστοῦ Ἰησοῦ καὶ τῶν
God and Christ Jesus and the

ἐκλεκτῶν ἀγγέλων ἵνα ταῦτα φυλάξῃς
chosen angels in order these things thou guard
that

χωρὶς προκρίματος, μηδὲν ποιῶν κατὰ
without prejudgment, ²nothing ¹doing by way of

πρόσκλισιν. **22** χεῖρας ταχέως μηδενὶ
inclination. ²Hands ⁵quickly ⁴no man

ἐπιτίθει, μηδὲ κοινώνει ἁμαρτίαις ἀλ-
¹lay ³on, nor share ²sins ¹in

λοτρίαις· σεαυτὸν ἁγνὸν τήρει. **23** Μηκέτι
others'†; ²thyself ³pure ¹keep. No longer

ὑδροπότει, ἀλλὰ οἴνῳ ὀλίγῳ χρῶ διὰ
drink water, but ³wine ²a little ¹use on account of

τὸν στόμαχον καὶ τὰς πυκνάς σου
the(thy) stomach and the frequent ²of thee

ἀσθενείας. **24** Τινῶν ἀνθρώπων αἱ ἁμαρτίαι
¹weaknesses. ³of some ⁴men ¹The ²sins

πρόδηλοί εἰσιν προάγουσαι εἰς κρίσιν,
⁶clear ⁵are going before to judgment,
beforehand

τισὶν δὲ καὶ ἐπακολουθοῦσιν· **25** ὡσαύτως
but some indeed they follow on; similarly

good works *of some* are manifest beforehand; and they that are otherwise cannot be hid.

καὶ   τὰ   ἔργα   τὰ   καλὰ   πρόδηλα,   καὶ
also   the   ²works   –   ¹good   [are] clear   and
beforehand,

τὰ   ἄλλως   ἔχοντα   κρυβῆναι   οὐ   δύνανται.
the   ²otherwise   ¹having   ⁴to be hidden   ³cannot.
[ones]   (being)

CHAPTER 6

LET as many servants as are under the yoke count their own masters worthy of all honour, that the name of God and *his* doctrine be not blasphemed.

6 Ὅσοι   εἰσὶν   ὑπὸ   ζυγὸν   δοῦλοι,   τοὺς
As many as   are   under   a yoke   slaves,   ²the(ir)
[being]

ἰδίους   δεσπότας   πάσης   τιμῆς   ἀξίους   ἡγείσ-
³own   ⁴masters   ⁶of all   ⁷honour   ⁵worthy   ¹let them

θωσαν,   ἵνα   μὴ   τὸ   ὄνομα   τοῦ   θεοῦ   καὶ
deem,   lest   the   name   –   of God   and

ἡ   διδασκαλία   βλασφημῆται.   2 οἱ   δὲ
the   teaching   be blasphemed.   And ¹the [ones]

2 And they that have believing masters, let them not despise *them*, because they are brethren; but rather do *them* service, because they are faithful and beloved, partakers of the benefit. These things teach and exhort.

πιστοὺς   ἔχοντες   δεσπότας   μὴ   καταφρο-
³believing   ²having   ⁴masters   not   let them

νείτωσαν,   ὅτι   ἀδελφοί   εἰσιν,   ἀλλὰ   μᾶλλον
despise [them], because   brothers   they are,   but   rather

δουλευέτωσαν,   ὅτι   πιστοί   εἰσιν   καὶ
let them serve as slaves, because   ⁶believing   ⁵are   ⁷and

ἀγαπητοὶ   οἱ   τῆς   εὐεργεσίας   ἀντιλαμ-
⁸beloved   ¹the [ones]   ³of the   ⁴good service   ²receiving in

βανόμενοι.
return.

3 If any man teach otherwise, and consent not to wholesome words, *even* the words of our Lord Jesus Christ, and to the doctrine which is according to godliness;

Ταῦτα   δίδασκε   καὶ   παρακάλει.   3 εἴ
These things   teach thou   and   exhort.   If

τις   ἑτεροδιδασκαλεῖ   καὶ   μὴ   προσέρχεται
anyone   teaches differently   and   consents not

ὑγιαίνουσιν   λόγοις   τοῖς   τοῦ   κυρίου   ἡμῶν
to *being* healthy   words   the   of the   Lord   of us
[words]

Ἰησοῦ   Χριστοῦ,   καὶ   τῇ   κατ'   εὐσέβειαν
Jesus   Christ,   and   ¹to the   ³accord-   ⁴piety
ing to

4 He is proud, knowing nothing, but doting about questions and strifes of words, whereof cometh envy, strife, railings, evil surmisings,

διδασκαλίᾳ,   4 τετύφωται,   μηδὲν   ἐπιστά-
²teaching,   he has been puffed up,   ²nothing   ¹under-

μενος,   ἀλλὰ   νοσῶν   περὶ   ζητήσεις   καὶ
standing,   but   being diseased   about   questionings   and

λογομαχίας,   ἐξ   ὧν   γίνεται   φθόνος,   ἔρις,
battles of words,   out of which   comes   envy,   strife,

5 Perverse disputings of men of corrupt minds, and destitute of the truth, supposing that gain is godliness: from such withdraw thyself.

βλασφημίαι,   ὑπόνοιαι   πονηραί,   5 διαπαρα-
blasphemies,   ²suspicions   ¹evil,   perpetual

τριβαὶ   διεφθαρμένων   ἀνθρώπων   τὸν   νοῦν
wranglings ²having been corrupted   ¹of men   the   mind
=of men with corrupted mind

καὶ   ἀπεστερημένων   τῆς   ἀληθείας,   νομιζ-
and   *having been* deprived   of the   truth,   sup-

όντων   πορισμὸν   εἶναι   τὴν   εὐσέβειαν.*
posing   ³gain   ²to be   *the*   ¹piety.*

* For order of words see note on John 1. 1.

6 But godliness with contentment is great gain.

7 For we brought nothing into *this* world, *and it is* certain we can carry nothing out.

8 And having food and raiment let us be therewith content.

9 But they that will be rich fall into temptation and a snare, and *into* many foolish and hurtful lusts, which drown men in destruction and perdition.

10 For the love of money is the root of all evil: which while some coveted after, they have erred from the faith, and pierced themselves through with many sorrows.

11 But thou, O man of God, flee these things; and follow after righteousness, godliness, faith, love, patience, meekness.

12 Fight the good fight of faith, lay hold on eternal life, whereunto thou art also called, and hast professed a good profession before many witnesses.

13 I give thee charge in the sight of God, who quickeneth all things, and *before* Christ Jesus,

---

6 ἔστιν δὲ πορισμὸς μέγας ἡ εὐσέβεια
But ⁴is ⁶gain ⁵great *the* ¹piety
μετὰ αὐταρκείας· **7** οὐδὲν γὰρ εἰσηνέγκαμεν
²with ³self-sufficiency;* for nothing we have brought *in*
εἰς τὸν κόσμον, ὅτι οὐδὲ ἐξενεγκεῖν
into the world, because neither ²to carry out
τι δυνάμεθα· **8** ἔχοντες δὲ διατροφὰς καὶ
³any- ¹can we; but having foods and
thing
σκεπάσματα, τούτοις ἀρκεσθησόμεθα. **9** οἱ
clothings, with these things we will be satisfied. the
δὲ βουλόμενοι πλουτεῖν ἐμπίπτουσιν εἰς
But [ones] resolving to be rich fall *in* into
πειρασμὸν καὶ παγίδα καὶ ἐπιθυμίας πολλὰς
temptation and a snare and ⁵lusts ¹many
ἀνοήτους καὶ βλαβεράς, αἵτινες βυθίζουσιν
²foolish ³and ⁴injurious, which ¹cause ³to sink
τοὺς ἀνθρώπους εἰς ὄλεθρον καὶ ἀπώλειαν.
– ²men into ruin and destruction.
10 ῥίζα γὰρ πάντων τῶν κακῶν ἐστιν
For ⁴a root ⁵of all – ⁶evils ³is
ἡ φιλαργυρία, ἧς τινες ὀρεγόμενοι
¹the ²love of money,* of which some hankering after
ἀπεπλανήθησαν ἀπὸ τῆς πίστεως καὶ
wandered away from the faith and
ἑαυτοὺς περιέπειραν ὀδύναις πολλαῖς. **11** Σὺ
themselves pierced round ²pains ¹by many. thou
δέ, ὦ ἄνθρωπε θεοῦ, ταῦτα φεῦγε· δίωκε
But, O man of God, these things flee; ²pursue
δὲ δικαιοσύνην, εὐσέβειαν, πίστιν, ἀγάπην,
¹and righteousness, piety, faith, love,
ὑπομονήν, πραϋπαθίαν. **12** ἀγωνίζου τὸν
endurance, meekness. Struggle the
καλὸν ἀγῶνα τῆς πίστεως, ἐπιλαβοῦ τῆς
good struggle of the faith, lay hold on *the*
αἰωνίου ζωῆς, εἰς ἣν ἐκλήθης καὶ ὡμολό-
eternal life, to which thou wast and didst con-
called
γησας τὴν καλὴν ὁμολογίαν ἐνώπιον
fess the good confession before
πολλῶν μαρτύρων. **13** παραγγέλλω ἐνώπιον
many witnesses. I charge before
τοῦ θεοῦ τοῦ ζωογονοῦντος τὰ πάντα
– God the [one] quickening – all things
καὶ Χριστοῦ Ἰησοῦ τοῦ μαρτυρήσαντος
and Christ Jesus the [one] having witnessed

---

* For order of words see note on John 1. 1.

who before Pontius Pilate witnessed a good confession;

14 That thou keep *this* commandment without spot, unrebukeable, until the appearing of our Lord Jesus Christ:

15 Which in his times he shall shew, *who is* the blessed and only Potentate, the King of kings, and Lord of lords;

16 Who only hath immortality, dwelling in the light which no man can approach unto; whom no man hath seen, nor can see: to whom *be* honour and power everlasting. Amen.

17 Charge them that are rich in this world, that they be not highminded, nor trust in uncertain riches, but in the living God, who giveth us richly all things to enjoy;

18 That they do good, that they be rich in good works, ready to distribute, willing to communicate:

19 Laying up in store for themselves a good foundation against the time to come, that they may lay hold on eternal life.

20 O Timothy, keep that which is committed to thy trust, avoiding pro-

---

ἐπὶ Ποντίου Πιλάτου τὴν καλὴν ὁμολογίαν,
in the Pontius Pilate the good confession,
time of

14 τηρῆσαί σε τὴν ἐντολὴν ἄσπιλον
²to keep ¹thee* the(this) commandment unspotted

ἀνεπίλημπτον μέχρι τῆς ἐπιφανείας τοῦ
without reproach until the appearance of the

κυρίου ἡμῶν ᾽Ιησοῦ Χριστοῦ, 15 ἣν
Lord of us Jesus Christ, which§

καιροῖς ἰδίοις δείξει ὁ μακάριος καὶ
⁷in its/his own times ⁶will show ¹the ²blessed ³and

μόνος δυνάστης, ὁ βασιλεὺς τῶν βασιλευ-
⁴only ⁵Potentate, the King of the [ones] reign-

όντων καὶ κύριος τῶν κυριευόντων, 16 ὁ
ing and Lord of the [ones] ruling, the

μόνος ἔχων ἀθανασίαν, φῶς οἰκῶν
only [one] having immortality, ¹light ¹inhabiting

ἀπρόσιτον, ὃν εἶδεν οὐδεὶς ἀνθρώπων οὐδὲ
unapproach- whom ²saw ¹no one ²of men nor
able,

ἰδεῖν δύναται· ᾧ τιμὴ καὶ κράτος αἰώνιον·
²to see ¹can; to [be] and might eternal:
whom honour

ἀμήν. 17 Τοῖς πλουσίοις ἐν τῷ νῦν
Amen. ²the ³rich ⁴in ⁵the ⁶now
(present)

αἰῶνι παράγγελλε μὴ ὑψηλοφρονεῖν, μηδὲ
⁷age ¹Charge thou not to be highminded, nor

ἠλπικέναι ἐπὶ πλούτου ἀδηλότητι, ἀλλ᾽
to have set on ²of riches ¹[the] uncertainty, but
[their] hope

ἐπὶ θεῷ τῷ παρέχοντι ἡμῖν πάντα
on God the [one] offering to us all things

πλουσίως εἰς ἀπόλαυσιν, 18 ἀγαθοεργεῖν,
richly for enjoyment, to work good,

πλουτεῖν ἐν ἔργοις καλοῖς, εὐμεταδότους
to be rich in ²works ¹good, ²ready to impart

εἶναι, κοινωνικούς, 19 ἀποθησαυρίζοντας
¹to be, generous, treasuring away

ἑαυτοῖς θεμέλιον καλὸν εἰς τὸ μέλλον,
for ²foundation ¹a good for the future,
themselves

ἵνα ἐπιλάβωνται τῆς ὄντως ζωῆς. 20 ᾽Ω
in or- they may lay the real*ly* life. O
der that hold on

Τιμόθεε, τὴν παραθήκην φύλαξον, ἐκτρεπ-
Timothy, ²the ³deposit ¹guard, turning

---

* " thee " is the direct object of the verb " charge " in ver. 13:
"I charge . . . thee to keep ،. .."

§ The antecedent to this relative pronoun is " appearance ",
not " Jesus Christ ".

fane *and* vain babblings, and oppositions of science falsely so called:

21 Which some professing have erred concerning the faith. Grace *be* with thee. Amen.

ὅμενος   τὰς   βεβήλους   κενοφωνίας   καὶ
aside from   *the*   profane   empty utterances   and

ἀντιθέσεις   τῆς   ψευδωνύμου   γνώσεως,   **21** ἥν
opposing   of *the*   falsely named   knowledge,   which
tenets

τινες   ἐπαγγελλόμενοι   περὶ   τὴν   πίστιν
some   promising   concerning   the   faith

ἠστόχησαν.
missed aim.

Ἡ   χάρις   μεθ᾽   ὑμῶν.
–   Grace [be]   with   you.

II. TIMOTHY 1

ΠΡΟΣ ΤΙΜΟΘΕΟΝ Β
To Timothy 2

CHAPTER 1

PAUL, an apostle of Jesus Christ by the will of God, according to the promise of life which is in Christ Jesus,

2 To Timothy, *my* dearly beloved son: Grace, mercy, *and* peace, from God the Father and Christ Jesus our Lord.

3 I thank God, whom I serve from *my* forefathers with pure conscience, that without ceasing I have remembrance of thee in my prayers night and day;

4 Greatly desiring to see thee, being mindful of thy tears, that I may be filled with joy;

5 When I call to remembrance the unfeigned faith

1 Παῦλος   ἀπόστολος   Χριστοῦ   Ἰησοῦ   διὰ
Paul   an apostle   of Christ   Jesus through

θελήματος   θεοῦ   κατ᾽   ἐπαγγελίαν   ζωῆς
[the] will   of God   by way of   a promise   of life

τῆς   ἐν   Χριστῷ   Ἰησοῦ   **2** Τιμοθέῳ   ἀγαπητῷ
–   in   Christ   Jesus   to Timothy   beloved

τέκνῳ·   χάρις,   ἔλεος,   εἰρήνη   ἀπὸ   θεοῦ
child: Grace,   mercy,   peace   from   God

πατρὸς   καὶ   Χριστοῦ   Ἰησοῦ   τοῦ   κυρίου
[our] Father   and   Christ   Jesus   the   Lord

ἡμῶν.
of us.

3 Χάριν   ἔχω   τῷ   θεῷ,   ᾧ   λατρεύω
Thanks   I have   –   to God,   whom   I worship

ἀπὸ   προγόνων   ἐν   καθαρᾷ   συνειδήσει,   ὡς
from   [my] forebears   in   a clean   conscience,   as

ἀδιάλειπτον   ἔχω   τὴν   περὶ   σοῦ   μνείαν
unceasingly   I have   ¹the   ³concerning   ⁴thee   ²remembrance

ἐν   ταῖς   δεήσεσίν   μου   νυκτὸς   καὶ   ἡμέρας,
in   the   petitions   of me   night   and   day,

4 ἐπιποθῶν   σε   ἰδεῖν,   μεμνημένος   σου
longing   ³thee   ¹to see,   having been   ²of thee
reminded

τῶν   δακρύων,   ἵνα   χαρᾶς   πληρωθῶ,
¹of the   ²tears,   in order   of(with) joy   I may be filled,
that

5 ὑπόμνησιν   λαβὼν   τῆς   ἐν   σοὶ   ἀνυποκρίτου
²recollection   ¹taking   ⁵of the   ⁶in   ⁷thee   ⁸unfeigned

that is in thee, which dwelt first in thy grandmother Lois, and thy mother Eunice; and I am persuaded that in thee also.

6 Wherefore I put thee in remembrance that thou stir up the gift of God, which is in thee by the putting on of my hands.

7 For God hath not given us the spirit of fear; but of power, and of love, and of a sound mind.

8 Be not thou therefore ashamed of the testimony of our Lord, nor of me his prisoner: but be thou partaker of the afflictions of the gospel according to the power of God;

9 Who hath saved us, and called us with an holy calling, not according to our works, but according to his own purpose and grace, which was given us in Christ Jesus before the world began,

10 But is now made manifest by the appearing of our Saviour Jesus Christ, who hath abolished death, and hath brought life and immortality to light through the gospel:

11 Whereunto I am appointed a preacher, and an

πίστεως, ἥτις ἐνῴκησεν πρῶτον ἐν τῇ
⁵faith, which indwelt firstly in the

μάμμῃ σου Λωΐδι καὶ τῇ μητρί σου
grand- of thee Lois and [in] the mother of thee
mother

Εὐνίκη, πέπεισμαι δὲ ὅτι καὶ ἐν σοί.
Eunice, and I have been that [it dwells] in thee.
persuaded also

6 Δι᾽ ἣν αἰτίαν ἀναμιμνήσκω σε ἀνα-
For which cause I remind thee to fan

ζωπυρεῖν τὸ χάρισμα τοῦ θεοῦ, ὅ ἐστιν
the flame [of] the gift – of God, which is

ἐν σοὶ διὰ τῆς ἐπιθέσεως τῶν χειρῶν
in thee through the laying on of the hands

μου. 7 οὐ γὰρ ἔδωκεν ἡμῖν ὁ θεὸς
of me. ³not For ²gave ⁴to us – ¹God

πνεῦμα δειλίας, ἀλλὰ δυνάμεως καὶ ἀγάπης
a spirit of cowardice, but of power and of love

καὶ σωφρονισμοῦ. 8 μὴ οὖν ἐπαισχυνθῇς
and of self-control. ³not ¹Therefore ²be ⁴thou
ashamed [of]

τὸ μαρτύριον τοῦ κυρίου ἡμῶν μηδὲ
the testimony of the Lord of us nor

ἐμὲ τὸν δέσμιον αὐτοῦ, ἀλλὰ συγ-
[of] me the prisoner of him, but suffer

κακοπάθησον τῷ εὐαγγελίῳ κατὰ δύναμιν
ill with the gospel according to [the] power

θεοῦ, 9 τοῦ σώσαντος ἡμᾶς καὶ καλέσαντος
of God, of the having saved us and having called
[one]

κλήσει ἁγίᾳ, οὐ κατὰ τὰ ἔργα ἡμῶν
²calling ¹with a holy, not according to the works of us

ἀλλὰ κατὰ ἰδίαν πρόθεσιν καὶ χάριν,
but according to [his] own purpose and grace,

τὴν δοθεῖσαν ἡμῖν ἐν Χριστῷ Ἰησοῦ
– given to us in Christ Jesus

πρὸ χρόνων αἰωνίων, 10 φανερωθεῖσαν δὲ
before times eternal, but manifested

νῦν διὰ τῆς ἐπιφανείας τοῦ σωτῆρος
now through the appearance of the Saviour

ἡμῶν Χριστοῦ Ἰησοῦ, καταργήσαντος μὲν
of us Christ Jesus, ²abrogating ¹on one
hand

τὸν θάνατον φωτίσαντος δὲ ζωὴν καὶ
– death ²bringing to ¹on the life and
light other

ἀφθαρσίαν διὰ τοῦ εὐαγγελίου, 11 εἰς ὃ
incorruption through the gospel, for which

ἐτέθην ἐγὼ κῆρυξ καὶ ἀπόστολος καὶ
²was ¹I a herald and an apostle and
appointed

apostle, and a teacher of the Gentiles.

12 For the which cause I also suffer these things: nevertheless I am not ashamed: for I know whom I have believed, and am persuaded that he is able to keep that which I have committed unto him against that day.

13 Hold fast the form of sound words, which thou hast heard of me, in faith and love which is in Christ Jesus.

14 That good thing which was committed unto thee keep by the Holy Ghost which dwelleth in us.

15 This thou knowest, that all they which are in Asia be turned away from me; of whom are Phygellus and Hermogenes.

16 The Lord give mercy unto the house of Onesiphorus; for he oft refreshed me, and was not ashamed of my chain:

17 But, when he was in Rome, he sought me out very diligently, and found me.

18 The Lord grant unto him that he may find mercy of the Lord in that day: and in how many things he ministered unto me at Ephesus, thou knowest very well.

διδάσκαλος· **12** δι’ ἣν αἰτίαν καὶ ταῦτα
a teacher;   for which cause also these things

πάσχω, ἀλλ’ οὐκ ἐπαισχύνομαι, οἶδα γὰρ
I suffer,   but   I am not ashamed,   for I know

ᾧ πεπίστευκα, καὶ πέπεισμαι ὅτι δυνατός
whom I have   and   I have been   that   [2]able
believed,   persuaded

ἐστιν τὴν παραθήκην μου φυλάξαι εἰς
[1]he is [4]the [5]deposit [6]of me [3]to guard   to

ἐκείνην τὴν ἡμέραν. **13** ὑποτύπωσιν ἔχε
that   –   day.   [2]a pattern [1]Have
                                thou

ὑγιαινόντων λόγων ὧν παρ’ ἐμοῦ ἤκουσας
of being healthy words which [2]from [3]me   [1]thou
                                 heardest

ἐν πίστει καὶ ἀγάπῃ τῇ ἐν Χριστῷ
in faith   and   love   –   in   Christ

Ἰησοῦ· **14** τὴν καλὴν παραθήκην φύλαξον
Jesus;   the   good   deposit   guard

διὰ πνεύματος ἁγίου τοῦ ἐνοικοῦντος ἐν
through Spirit [the] Holy   –   indwelling   in

ἡμῖν. **15** Οἶδας τοῦτο, ὅτι ἀπεστράφησάν
us.   Thou knowest this,   that   turned away from

με πάντες οἱ ἐν τῇ Ἀσίᾳ, ὧν ἐστιν
me   all   the ones in   –   Asia, of whom   is

Φύγελος καὶ Ἑρμογένης. **16** δῴη ἔλεος
Phygelus and Hermogenes.   [1]May [4]give [5]mercy

ὁ κύριος τῷ Ὀνησιφόρου οἴκῳ, ὅτι
[2]the [3]Lord [4]to the [5]of Onesiphorus [7]house- because
                                 hold,

πολλάκις με ἀνέψυξεν καὶ τὴν ἅλυσίν
often   me   he refreshed   and   the   chain

μου οὐκ ἐπαισχύνθη, **17** ἀλλὰ γενόμενος
of me was not ashamed [of],   but   coming to be

ἐν Ῥώμῃ σπουδαίως ἐζήτησέν με καὶ
in   Rome   [2]diligently [1]he [3]sought [4]me [4]and

εὗρεν· — **18** δῴη αὐτῷ ὁ κύριος εὑρεῖν
[5]found;   (¹May ⁴give ⁵to him ²the ³Lord   to find

ἔλεος παρὰ κυρίου ἐν ἐκείνῃ τῇ ἡμέρᾳ·
mercy from [the] Lord in   that   –   day;)

— καὶ ὅσα ἐν Ἐφέσῳ διηκόνησεν,
and what things in   Ephesus   he served,

βέλτιον σὺ γινώσκεις.
very well thou knowest.

CHAPTER 2

THOU therefore, my son, be strong in the grace that is in Christ Jesus

2 Σὺ οὖν, τέκνον μου, ἐνδυναμοῦ ἐν
Thou therefore, child of me, be empowered by

τῇ χάριτι τῇ ἐν Χριστῷ Ἰησοῦ, **2** καὶ
the   grace   –   in   Christ   Jesus,   and

2 And the things that thou hast heard of me among many witnesses, the same commit thou to faithful men, who shall be able to teach others also.

3 Thou therefore endure hardness, as a good soldier of Jesus Christ.

4 No man that warreth entangleth himself with the affairs of *this* life; that he may please him who hath chosen him to be a soldier.

5 And if a man also strive for masteries, *yet* is he not crowned, except he strive lawfully.

6 The husbandman that laboureth must be first partaker of the fruits.

7 Consider what I say; and the Lord give thee understanding in all things.

8 Remember that Jesus Christ of the seed of David was raised from the dead according to my gospel:

9 Wherein I suffer trouble, as an evil doer, *even* unto bonds; but the word of God is not bound.

10 Therefore I endure all things for the elect's sakes, that they may also obtain the salvation which is in Christ Jesus with eternal glory.

11 *It is* a faithful saying: For if we be dead

ἃ ἤκουσας παρ' ἐμοῦ διὰ πολλῶν
what thou from me through many
things heardest

μαρτύρων, ταῦτα παράθου πιστοῖς ἀνθρώ-
witnesses, these commit to faithful men,

ποις, οἵτινες ἱκανοὶ ἔσονται καὶ ἑτέρους
who ²competent ¹will be ³also ⁴others

διδάξαι. 3 Συγκακοπάθησον ὡς καλὸς
⁵to teach. Suffer ill with* as a good

στρατιώτης Χριστοῦ Ἰησοῦ. 4 οὐδεὶς
soldier of Christ Jesus. No one

στρατευόμενος ἐμπλέκεται ταῖς τοῦ βίου
soldiering is involved ¹with the - ²of life

πραγματείαις, ἵνα τῷ στρατολογήσαντι
²affairs, in order ²the ³having enlisted
that [one] [him]

ἀρέσῃ. 5 ἐὰν δὲ καὶ ἀθλῇ τις, οὐ
¹he may And if also ²wrestles ¹any- not
please. one,

στεφανοῦται ἐὰν μὴ νομίμως ἀθλήσῃ.
he is crowned unless ²lawfully ¹he wrestles.

6 τὸν κοπιῶντα γεωργὸν δεῖ πρῶτον τῶν
²the ⁴labouring ⁵husbandman ¹It be- ⁶firstly ⁷of the
hoves

καρπῶν μεταλαμβάνειν. 7 νόει ὃ λέγω·
⁸fruits ³to partake. Consider what I say;

δώσει γάρ σοι ὁ κύριος σύνεσιν ἐν
for ³will give ²thee ¹the ²Lord understanding in

πᾶσιν. 8 μνημόνευε Ἰησοῦν Χριστὸν
all things. Remember Jesus Christ

ἐγηγερμένον ἐκ νεκρῶν, ἐκ σπέρματος
having been raised from [the] dead, of [the] seed

Δαυίδ, κατὰ τὸ εὐαγγέλιόν μου· 9 ἐν
of David, according to the gospel of me; in

ᾧ κακοπαθῶ μέχρι δεσμῶν ὡς κακοῦργος,
which I suffer ill unto bonds as an evildoer,

ἀλλὰ ὁ λόγος τοῦ θεοῦ οὐ δέδεται.
but the word - of God has not been bound.

10 διὰ τοῦτο πάντα ὑπομένω διὰ τοὺς
Therefore all things I endure on ac- the
count of

ἐκλεκτούς, ἵνα καὶ αὐτοὶ σωτηρίας τύχωσιν
chosen ones, in or- ²also ¹they ⁴salvation ³may obtain
der that

τῆς ἐν Χριστῷ Ἰησοῦ μετὰ δόξης
- in Christ Jesus with glory

αἰωνίου. 11 πιστὸς ὁ λόγος· εἰ γὰρ
eternal. Faithful [is] the word: for if

* See 1. 8.

with *him*, we shall also live with *him:*

12 If we suffer, we shall also reign with *him:* if we deny *him*, he also will deny us:

13 If we believe not, *yet* he abideth faithful: he cannot deny himself.

14 Of these things put *them* in remembrance, charging *them* before the Lord that they strive not about words to no profit, *but* to the subverting of the hearers.

15 Study to shew thyself approved unto God, a workman that needeth not to be ashamed, rightly dividing the word of truth.

16 But shun profane *and* vain babblings: for they will increase unto more ungodliness.

17 And their word will eat as doth a canker: of whom is Hymenæus and Philetus;

18 Who concerning the truth have erred, saying that the resurrection is past already; and overthrow the faith of some.

19 Nevertheless the foundation of God standeth sure, having this seal, The Lord knoweth them that are his. And, Let every one that nameth the name of Christ depart from iniquity.

συναπεθάνομεν, καὶ συζήσομεν· **12** εἰ
we died with [him], also we shall live with [him]; if

ὑπομένομεν, καὶ συμβασιλεύσομεν· εἰ
we endure, also we shall reign with [him]; if

ἀρνησόμεθα, κἀκεῖνος ἀρνήσεται ἡμᾶς· **13** εἰ
we *shall* deny, that one also will deny us; if

ἀπιστοῦμεν, ἐκεῖνος πιστὸς μένει, ἀρνή-
we disbelieve, that one ²faithful ¹remains, ³to

σασθαι γὰρ ἑαυτὸν οὐ δύναται. **14** Ταῦτα
deny ¹for ⁴himself ²he cannot. These things

ὑπομίμνησκε, διαμαρτυρόμενος ἐνώπιον τοῦ
remind thou solemnly witnessing before –
[them] [of],

θεοῦ μὴ λογομαχεῖν, ἐπ᾽ οὐδὲν χρήσιμον,
God not to fight with words, ²for ³nothing ¹useful,

ἐπὶ καταστροφῇ τῶν ἀκουόντων. **15** σπού-
for overthrowing of the [ones] hearing. ¹Be

δασον σεαυτὸν δόκιμον παραστῆσαι τῷ
eager ²thyself ⁴approved ³to present to

θεῷ, ἐργάτην ἀνεπαίσχυντον, ὀρθοτομοῦντα
to God, a workman unashamed, cutting straight

τὸν λόγον τῆς ἀληθείας. **16** τὰς δὲ
the word – of truth. – But

βεβήλους κενοφωνίας περιΐστασο· ²ἐπὶ πλεῖον
profane empty shun; ²to ⁴more
utterances

γὰρ προκόψουσιν ἀσεβείας, **17** καὶ ὁ λόγος
¹for ³they will advance of impiety, and the word

αὐτῶν ὡς γάγγραινα νομὴν ἕξει· ὧν
of them as a canker feeding will have; of
whom

ἐστιν Ὑμέναιος καὶ Φίλητος, **18** οἵτινες
is(are) Hymenæus and Philetus, who

περὶ τὴν ἀλήθειαν ἠστόχησαν, λέγοντες
con- the truth missed aim, saying
cerning

ἀνάστασιν ἤδη γεγονέναι, καὶ ἀνατρέπουσιν
[the] already to have and overturn
resurrection become,

τήν τινων πίστιν. **19** ὁ μέντοι στερεὸς
the ²of some ¹faith. ²the ¹However firm

θεμέλιος τοῦ θεοῦ ἕστηκεν, ἔχων τὴν
foundation – of God stands, having –

σφραγῖδα ταύτην· ἔγνω κύριος τοὺς ὄντας
seal this: ²knew ¹[The] the being
Lord [ones]

αὐτοῦ, καὶ· ἀποστήτω ἀπὸ ἀδικίας πᾶς
of him, and: Let stand away from iniquity every-

ὁ ὀνομάζων τὸ ὄνομα κυρίου. **20** ἐν
one naming the name of [the] Lord. ²in

20 But in a great house there are not only vessels of gold and of silver, but also of wood and of earth; and some to honour, and some to dishonour.

21 If a man therefore purge himself from these, he shall be a vessel unto honour, sanctified, and meet for the master's use, *and* prepared unto every good work.

22 Flee also youthful lusts: but follow righteousness, faith, charity, peace, with them that call on the Lord out of a pure heart.

23 But foolish and unlearned questions avoid, knowing that they do gender strifes.

24 And the servant of the Lord must not strive; but be gentle unto all *men*, apt to teach, patient,

25 In meekness instructing those that oppose themselves; if God peradventure will give them repentance to the acknowledging of the truth;

26 And *that* they may recover themselves out of the snare of the devil, who are taken captive by him at his will.

μεγάλη δὲ οἰκίᾳ οὐκ ἔστιν μόνον σκεύη
²a great ¹Now ⁴house there is(are) not only vessels

χρυσᾶ καὶ ἀργυρᾶ, ἀλλὰ καὶ ξύλινα
golden and silvern, but also wooden

καὶ ὀστράκινα, καὶ ἃ μὲν εἰς τιμὴν ἃ δὲ
and earthen, and some to honour others

εἰς ἀτιμίαν· 21 ἐὰν οὖν τις ἐκκαθάρῃ
to dishonour; if therefore anyone cleanses

ἑαυτὸν ἀπὸ τούτων, ἔσται σκεῦος εἰς
himself from these [latter], he will be a vessel to

τιμήν, ἡγιασμένον, εὔχρηστον τῷ δεσπότῃ,
honour, *having been* suitable for the master,
sanctified,

εἰς πᾶν ἔργον ἀγαθὸν ἡτοιμασμένον.
to every work good *having been* prepared.

22 τὰς δὲ νεωτερικὰς ἐπιθυμίας φεῦγε,
Now *the* ²youthful ¹lusts ¹flee,

δίωκε δὲ δικαιοσύνην, πίστιν, ἀγάπην,
but pursue righteousness, faith, love,

εἰρήνην μετὰ τῶν ἐπικαλουμένων τὸν
peace with the [ones] calling on the

κύριον ἐκ καθαρᾶς καρδίας. 23 τὰς δὲ
Lord out of a clean heart. – But

μωρὰς καὶ ἀπαιδεύτους ζητήσεις παραιτοῦ,
foolish and uninstructed questionings refuse,

εἰδὼς ὅτι γεννῶσιν μάχας· 24 δοῦλον δὲ
knowing that they beget fights; and ²a slave

κυρίου οὐ δεῖ μάχεσθαι ἀλλὰ ἤπιον
³of [the] ¹it behoves not to fight but gentle
Lord

εἶναι πρὸς πάντας, διδακτικόν, ἀνεξίκακον,
to be toward all men, apt to teach, forbearing,

25 ἐν πραΰτητι παιδεύοντα τοὺς ἀντιδιατι-
in meekness instructing the [ones] oppos-

θεμένους, μήποτε δώῃ αὐτοῖς ὁ θεὸς
ing, [if] perhaps ²may ³them – ¹God
give

μετάνοιαν εἰς ἐπίγνωσιν ἀληθείας, 26 καὶ
repentance for a full knowledge of truth, and

ἀνανήψωσιν ἐκ τῆς τοῦ διαβόλου παγίδος,
they may return out of ¹the ³of the ⁴devil ²snare,
to soberness

ἐζωγρημένοι ὑπ᾽ αὐτοῦ εἰς τὸ ἐκείνου θέλημα.
having been by him[,] to ¹the ³of that ²will.
caught one*

---

* That is, of God (the remoter antecedent).

CHAPTER 3

THIS know also that, in the last days perilous times shall come.

2 For men shall be lovers of their own selves, covetous, boasters, proud, blasphemers, disobedient to parents, unthankful, unholy,

3 Without natural affection, trucebreakers, false accusers, incontinent, fierce, despisers of those that are good,

4 Traitors, heady, highminded, lovers of pleasures more than lovers of God;

5 Having a form of godliness, but denying the power thereof: from such turn away.

6 For of this sort are they which creep into houses, and lead captive silly women laden with sins, led away with divers lusts,

7 Ever learning, and never able to come to the knowledge of the truth.

8 Now as Jannes and Jambres withstood Moses, so do these also resist the truth: men of corrupt minds, reprobate concerning the faith.

9 But they shall proceed no further: for their

---

3 Τοῦτο δὲ γίνωσκε, ὅτι ἐν ἐσχάταις
And this   know thou,   that   in   [the] last

ἡμέραις ἐνστήσονται καιροὶ χαλεποί·
days   ²will be at hand   ²times   ¹grievous;

2 ἔσονται γὰρ οἱ ἄνθρωποι φίλαυτοι,
for ²will be   -   ¹men   self-lovers,

φιλάργυροι, ἀλαζόνες, ὑπερήφανοι, βλάσφημοι,
money-lovers,   boasters,   arrogant,   blasphemers,

γονεῦσιν ἀπειθεῖς, ἀχάριστοι, ἀνόσιοι,
²to parents   ¹disobedient,   unthankful,   unholy,

3 ἄστοργοι, ἄσπονδοι, διάβολοι, ἀκρατεῖς,
without natural   implacable,   slanderers,   incontinent,
affection,

ἀνήμεροι, ἀφιλάγαθοι, **4** προδόται, προπετεῖς,
untamed,   haters of good   betrayers,   reckless,
      [things/men],

τετυφωμένοι, φιλήδονοι μᾶλλον ἢ φιλόθεοι,
having been   pleasure-lovers   rather   than   God-lovers,
puffed up,

5 ἔχοντες μόρφωσιν εὐσεβείας τὴν δὲ
having   a form   of piety   but the

δύναμιν αὐτῆς ἠρνημένοι· καὶ τούτους
power   of it   having denied: and   ²these

ἀποτρέπου. **6** ἐκ τούτων γὰρ εἰσιν οἱ
²turn away ¹from.   ²of   ²these   ¹For   are   the

ἐνδύνοντες εἰς τὰς οἰκίας καὶ αἰχμαλωτίζ-
[ones] creeping into   -   houses   and   captur-

οντες γυναικάρια σεσωρευμένα ἁμαρτίαις,
ing   silly women   having been heaped*   with sins,

ἀγόμενα ἐπιθυμίαις ποικίλαις, **7** πάντοτε
being led*   lusts   by various,   always

μανθάνοντα καὶ μηδέποτε εἰς ἐπίγνωσιν
learning*   and   never   ²to ⁴a full knowledge

ἀληθείας ἐλθεῖν δυνάμενα. **8** ὃν τρόπον
⁴of truth   ²to come   ¹being able.*   by what way

δὲ Ἰάννης καὶ Ἰαμβρῆς ἀντέστησαν
Now   Jannes   and   Jambres   opposed

Μωϋσεῖ, οὕτως καὶ οὗτοι ἀνθίστανται τῇ
Moses,   so   also   these   oppose   the

ἀληθείᾳ, ἄνθρωποι κατεφθαρμένοι τὸν νοῦν,
truth,   men   having been corrupted   the   mind,
      =with corrupted mind,

ἀδόκιμοι περὶ τὴν πίστιν. **9** ἀλλ' οὐ
reprobate   as to   the   faith.   But   not

προκόψουσιν ἐπὶ πλεῖον· ἢ γὰρ ἄνοια
they will advance   to   more;   for the   folly
=farther;

---

* Agreeing with "silly women" (neut. pl.).

folly shall be manifest unto all *men*, as their's also was.

10 But thou hast fully known my doctrine, manner of life, purpose, faith, longsuffering, charity, patience,

11 Persecutions, afflictions, which came unto me at Antioch, at Iconium, at Lystra; what persecutions I endured: but out of *them* all the Lord delivered me.

12 Yea, and all that will live godly in Christ Jesus shall suffer persecution.

13 But evil men and seducers shall wax worse and worse, deceiving, and being deceived.

14 But continue thou in the things which thou hast learned and hast been assured of, knowing of whom thou hast learned *them;*

15 And that from a child thou hast known the holy scriptures, which are able to make thee wise unto salvation through faith which is in Christ Jesus.

16 All scripture *is* given by inspiration of God, and *is* profitable for doctrine, for reproof, for correction, for instruction in righteousness:

17 That the man of God may be perfect,

αὐτῶν ἔκδηλος ἔσται πᾶσιν, ὡς καὶ
of them very clear will be to all men, as also
ἡ ἐκείνων ἐγένετο. 10 Σὺ δὲ παρηκολού-
the of those became. But thou hast closely
[folly]
θησάς μου τῇ διδασκαλίᾳ, τῇ ἀγωγῇ,
followed of me the teaching, the conduct,
τῇ προθέσει, τῇ πίστει, τῇ μακροθυμίᾳ,
the purpose, the faith, the longsuffering,
τῇ ἀγάπῃ, τῇ ὑπομονῇ, 11 τοῖς διωγμοῖς,
the love, the endurance, the persecutions,
τοῖς παθήμασιν, οἷά μοι ἐγένετο ἐν
the sufferings, which ²to me ¹happened in
Ἀντιοχείᾳ, ἐν Ἰκονίῳ, ἐν Λύστροις· οἵους
Antioch, in Iconium, in Lystra: what
διωγμοὺς ὑπήνεγκα, καὶ ἐκ πάντων με
persecutions I bore, and out of all ⁴me
ἐρρύσατο ὁ κύριος. 12 καὶ πάντες δὲ
³delivered ¹the ²Lord. ³indeed ²all ¹And
οἱ θέλοντες ζῆν εὐσεβῶς ἐν Χριστῷ
the [ones] wishing to live piously in Christ
Ἰησοῦ διωχθήσονται. 13 πονηροὶ δὲ ἄν-
Jesus will be persecuted. But evil men
θρωποι καὶ γόητες προκόψουσιν ἐπὶ τὸ
and impostors will advance to the
χεῖρον, πλανῶντες καὶ πλανώμενοι. 14 σὺ
worse, deceiving and being deceived. ²thou
δὲ μένε ἐν οἷς ἔμαθες καὶ ἐπιστώθης,
But ¹continue in what thou didst and wast assured of,
         things learn
εἰδὼς παρὰ τίνων ἔμαθες, 15 καὶ ὅτι
knowing from whom* thou didst learn, and that
ἀπὸ βρέφους ἱερὰ γράμματα οἶδας, τὰ
from a babe ²sacred ³letters ¹thou know- the
                                   est, [ones]
δυνάμενά σε σοφίσαι εἰς σωτηρίαν διὰ
being able thee to make wise to salvation through
πίστεως τῆς ἐν Χριστῷ Ἰησοῦ. 16 πᾶσα
faith – in Christ Jesus. Every
γραφὴ θεόπνευστος καὶ ὠφέλιμος πρὸς
scripture [is] God-breathed and profitable for
διδασκαλίαν, πρὸς ἐλεγμόν, πρὸς ἐπανόρ-
teaching, for reproof, for cor-
θωσιν, πρὸς παιδείαν τὴν ἐν δικαιοσύνῃ,
rection, for instruction – in righteousness,
17 ἵνα ἄρτιος ᾖ ὁ τοῦ θεοῦ ἄνθρωπος,
in order ⁵fitted ⁴may ²the – ³of God ¹man,
that   be

* Plural.

throughly furnished unto all good works.

CHAPTER 4

I CHARGE *thee* therefore before God, and the Lord Jesus Christ, who shall judge the quick and the dead at his appearing and his kingdom;

2 Preach the word; be instant in season, out of season; reprove, rebuke, exhort with all longsuffering and doctrine.

3 For the time will come when they will not endure sound doctrine; but after their own lusts shall they heap to themselves teachers, having itching ears;

4 And they shall turn away *their* ears from the truth, and shall be turned unto fables.

5 But watch thou in all things, endure afflictions, do the work of an evangelist, make full proof of thy ministry.

6 For I am now ready to be offered, and the time of my departure is at hand.

7 I have fought a good fight, I have finished *my* course, I have kept the faith:

8 Henceforth there is laid up for me a crown of righteousness, which the Lord, the righteous judge,

πρὸς πᾶν ἔργον ἀγαθὸν ἐξηρτισμένος.
for every work good *having been* furnished.

4 Διαμαρτύρομαι ἐνώπιον τοῦ θεοῦ καὶ
I solemnly witness before – God and

Χριστοῦ Ἰησοῦ, τοῦ μέλλοντος κρίνειν
Christ Jesus, the [one] being about to judge

ζῶντας καὶ νεκρούς, καὶ τὴν ἐπιφάνειαν
living [ones] and dead, both [by] the appearance

αὐτοῦ καὶ τὴν βασιλείαν αὐτοῦ· **2** κήρυξον
of him and [by] the kingdom of him: proclaim

τὸν λόγον, ἐπίστηθι εὐκαίρως ἀκαίρως,
the word, be attentive seasonably[,] unseasonably,

ἔλεγξον, ἐπιτίμησον, παρακάλεσον, ἐν πάσῃ
reprove, admonish, exhort, with all

μακροθυμίᾳ καὶ διδαχῇ. **3** ἔσται γὰρ
longsuffering and teaching. For there will be

καιρὸς ὅτε τῆς ὑγιαινούσης διδασκαλίας
a time when ²the ³*being* healthy ⁴teaching

οὐκ ἀνέξονται, ἀλλὰ κατὰ τὰς ἰδίας
¹they will not bear with, but according to the(ir) own

ἐπιθυμίας ἑαυτοῖς ἐπισωρεύσουσιν διδασ-
lusts ³to themselves ¹they will heap up ²teach-

κάλους κνηθόμενοι τὴν ἀκοήν, **4** καὶ ἀπὸ
ers tickling the ear, and ⁵from

μὲν τῆς ἀληθείας τὴν ἀκοὴν ἀποστρέψουσιν,
²on ⁶the ⁷truth ⁸the ⁴ear ¹will turn away,
one hand

ἐπὶ δὲ τοὺς μύθους ἐκτραπήσονται. **5** σὺ
³to ¹on the the ⁴tales ²will be turned aside. ²thou
      other

δὲ νῆφε ἐν πᾶσιν, κακοπάθησον, ἔργον
But ¹be in all things, suffer evil, ³[the] work
    sober

ποίησον εὐαγγελιστοῦ, τὴν διακονίαν σου
¹do of an evangelist, ²the ³ministry ⁴of thee

πληροφόρησον. **6** Ἐγὼ γὰρ ἤδη σπένδομαι,
¹fulfil. For I already am being
                            poured out,

καὶ ὁ καιρὸς τῆς ἀναλύσεώς μου ἐφέστη-
and the time of the departure of me has

κεν. **7** τὸν καλὸν ἀγῶνα ἠγώνισμαι,
arrived. The good struggle I have struggled,

τὸν δρόμον τετέλεκα, τὴν πίστιν τετήρηκα·
the course I have finished, the faith I have kept:

8 λοιπὸν ἀπόκειταί μοι ὁ τῆς δικαιοσύνης
for the rest there is laid up for me ¹the – ³of righteousness

στέφανος, ὃν ἀποδώσει μοι ὁ κύριος
²crown, which ⁶will render ⁷to me ¹the ²Lord

ἐν ἐκείνῃ τῇ ἡμέρᾳ, ὁ δίκαιος κριτής,
⁸in ⁹that – ¹⁰day, ³the ⁴righteous ⁵judge,

shall give me at that day: and not to me only, but unto all them also that love his appearing.

9 Do thy diligence to come shortly unto me:

10 For Demas hath forsaken me, having loved this present world, and is departed unto Thessalonica; Crescens to Galatia, Titus unto Dalmatia.

11 Only Luke is with me. Take Mark, and bring him with thee: for he is profitable to me for the ministry.

12 And Tychicus have I sent to Ephesus.

13 The cloke that I left at Troas with Carpus, when thou comest, bring *with thee,* and the books, *but* especially the parchments.

14 Alexander the coppersmith did me much evil: the Lord reward him according to his works:

15 Of whom be thou ware also; for he hath greatly withstood our words.

16 At my first answer no man stood with me, but all *men* forsook me: *I pray God* that it may not be laid to their charge.

17 Notwithstanding the Lord stood with me, and strengthened me; that by me the preaching might be fully known, and *that* all the Gentiles might hear: and I was de-

οὐ μόνον δὲ ἐμοὶ ἀλλὰ καὶ πᾶσι τοῖς
not only and to me but also to all the [ones]

ἠγαπηκόσι τὴν ἐπιφάνειαν αὐτοῦ.
having loved the appearance of him.

9 Σπούδασον ἐλθεῖν πρός με ταχέως·
Hasten to come to me shortly;

10 Δημᾶς γάρ με ἐγκατέλιπεν ἀγαπήσας
Demas For me forsook loving

τὸν νῦν αἰῶνα, καὶ ἐπορεύθη εἰς Θεσσαλο-
the now age, and went to Thessalo-
(present)

νίκην, Κρήσκης εἰς Γαλατίαν, Τίτος εἰς
nica, Crescens to Galatia, Titus to

Δαλματίαν· 11 Λουκᾶς ἐστιν μόνος μετ᾽
Dalmatia; Luke is alone with

ἐμοῦ. Μᾶρκον ἀναλαβὼν ἄγε μετὰ σεαυτοῦ·
me. Mark taking bring with thyself;

ἔστιν γάρ μοι εὔχρηστος εἰς διακονίαν.
he is for to me useful for ministry.

12 Τύχικον δὲ ἀπέστειλα εἰς Ἔφεσον.
And Tychicus I sent to Ephesus.

13 τὸν φαιλόνην, ὃν ἀπέλιπον ἐν Τρωάδι
The cloak, which I left in Troas

παρὰ Κάρπῳ, ἐρχόμενος φέρε, καὶ τὰ
with Carpus, coming bring thou, and the

βιβλία, μάλιστα τὰς μεμβράνας. 14 Ἀλέξ-
scrolls, especially the parchments. Alex-

ανδρος ὁ χαλκεὺς πολλά μοι κακὰ
ander the coppersmith many to me evils

ἐνεδείξατο· ἀποδώσει αὐτῷ ὁ κύριος κατὰ
showed; will render to him the Lord according to

τὰ ἔργα αὐτοῦ· 15 ὃν καὶ σὺ φυλάσσου·
the works of him; whom also thou guard
[against];

λίαν γὰρ ἀντέστη τοῖς ἡμετέροις λόγοις.
for greatly he opposed – our words.

16 Ἐν τῇ πρώτῃ μου ἀπολογίᾳ οὐδείς
At the first of me defence no one

μοι παρεγένετο, ἀλλὰ πάντες με ἐγκατέ-
me was beside, but all men me for-

λιπον· μὴ αὐτοῖς λογισθείη· 17 ὁ δὲ
sook; not to them may it be reckoned; but the

κύριός μοι παρέστη καὶ ἐνεδυνάμωσέν με,
Lord me stood with and empowered me,

ἵνα δι᾽ ἐμοῦ τὸ κήρυγμα πληροφορηθῇ
in or- through me the proclamation might be
der that accomplished

καὶ ἀκούσωσιν πάντα τὰ ἔθνη, καὶ
and might hear all the nations, and

livered out of the mouth of the lion.

18 And the Lord shall deliver me from every evil work, and will preserve *me* unto his heavenly kingdom: to whom *be* glory for ever and ever. Amen.

19 Salute Prisca and Aquila, and the household of Onesiphorus.

20 Erastus abode at Corinth: but Trophimus have I left at Miletum sick.

21 Do thy diligence to come before winter. Eubulus greeteth thee, and Pudens, and Linus, and Claudia, and all the brethren.

22 The Lord Jesus Christ *be* with thy spirit. Grace *be* with you. Amen.

ἐρρύσθην ἐκ στόματος λέοντος. 18 ῥύσεταί
I was   out of [the] mouth of [the] lion.   ²will deliver
delivered

με ὁ κύριος ἀπὸ παντὸς ἔργου πονηροῦ
⁴me ¹The ²Lord from every work wicked

καὶ σώσει εἰς τὴν βασιλείαν αὐτοῦ τὴν
and will save to the ²kingdom ³of him –

ἐπουράνιον· ᾧ ἡ δόξα εἰς τοὺς αἰῶνας
¹heavenly: to [be] glory unto the ages
        whom the

τῶν αἰώνων, ἀμήν.
of the ages, Amen.

19 Ἄσπασαι Πρίσκαν καὶ Ἀκύλαν καὶ
   Greet Prisca and Aquila and

τὸν Ὀνησιφόρου οἶκον. 20 Ἔραστος
the ²of Onesiphorus ¹household.   Erastus

ἔμεινεν ἐν Κορίνθῳ, Τρόφιμον δὲ ἀπέλιπον
remained in Corinth, but Trophimus I left

ἐν Μιλήτῳ ἀσθενοῦντα. 21 Σπούδασον
in Miletus ailing.   Hasten

πρὸ χειμῶνος ἐλθεῖν. Ἀσπάζεταί σε
before winter to come. Greets thee

Εὔβουλος καὶ Πούδης καὶ Λίνος καὶ
Eubulus and Pudens and Linus and

Κλαυδία καὶ οἱ ἀδελφοὶ πάντες.
Claudia and ²the ²brothers ¹all.

22 Ὁ κύριος μετὰ τοῦ πνεύματός σου.
   The Lord [be] with the spirit of thee.

ἡ χάρις μεθ’ ὑμῶν.
– Grace [be] with you.

TITUS 1

ΠΡΟΣ ΤΙΤΟΝ
To Titus

CHAPTER 1

PAUL, a servant of God, and an apostle of Jesus Christ, according to the faith of God's elect, and the acknowledging of the truth which is after godliness;

2 In hope of eternal life, which God, that

1 Παῦλος δοῦλος θεοῦ, ἀπόστολος δὲ
  Paul a slave of God, and an apostle

Ἰησοῦ Χριστοῦ κατὰ πίστιν ἐκλεκτῶν
of Jesus Christ according to [the] faith of chosen ones

θεοῦ καὶ ἐπίγνωσιν ἀληθείας τῆς κατ’
of God and full know- of [the] – accord-
         ledge truth   ing to

εὐσέβειαν 2 ἐπ’ ἐλπίδι ζωῆς αἰωνίου,
piety   on(in) hope life of eternal,

ἣν ἐπηγγείλατο ὁ ἀψευδὴς θεὸς πρὸ
which ⁴promised ¹the ²unlying ³God before

cannot lie, promised before the world began;

3 But hath in due times manifested his word through preaching, which is committed unto me according to the commandment of God our Saviour;

4 To Titus, *mine* own son after the common faith: Grace, mercy, *and* peace, from God the Father and the Lord Jesus Christ our Saviour.

5 For this cause left I thee in Crete, that thou shouldest set in order the things that are wanting, and ordain elders in every city, as I had appointed thee:

6 If any be blameless, the husband of one wife, having faithful children not accused of riot or unruly.

7 For a bishop must be blameless, as the steward of God; not selfwilled, not soon angry, not given to wine, no striker, not given to filthy lucre;

8 But a lover of hospitality, a lover of good men, sober, just, holy, temperate;

9 Holding fast the faithful word as he hath been taught, that he may be able by sound doctrine both to exhort and to convince the gainsayers.

10 For there are many

χρόνων αἰωνίων, 3 ἐφανέρωσεν δὲ καιροῖς
times   eternal,   but [2]manifested   [3]times

ἰδίοις τὸν λόγον αὐτοῦ ἐν κηρύγματι
[1]in [its] own the   word   of him   in   a proclamation

ὃ ἐπιστεύθην ἐγὼ κατ' ἐπιταγὴν τοῦ
which [2]was entrust- [1]I   accord- [the]   of the
ed [with]   ing to   command

σωτῆρος ἡμῶν θεοῦ, 4 Τίτῳ γνησίῳ τέκνῳ
Saviour   of us   God,   to Titus a true   child

κατὰ κοινὴν πίστιν· χάρις καὶ εἰρήνη
accord- a common   faith: Grace and   peace
ing to

ἀπὸ θεοῦ πατρὸς καὶ Χριστοῦ Ἰησοῦ
from   God   [the] Father and   Christ   Jesus

τοῦ σωτῆρος ἡμῶν.
the   Saviour   of us.

5 Τούτου χάριν ἀπέλιπόν σε ἐν Κρήτῃ,
For this reason†   I left   thee   in   Crete,

ἵνα τὰ λείποντα ἐπιδιορθώσῃ, καὶ
in or- the   wanting   thou shouldest   and
der that   set in order,

καταστήσῃς κατὰ πόλιν πρεσβυτέρους, ὡς ἐγώ
shouldest appoint in each city   elders,   as   I

σοι διεταξάμην, 6 εἴ τίς ἐστιν ἀνέγκλητος,
[2]thee [1]charged,   if anyone is   unreprovable,

μιᾶς γυναικὸς ἀνήρ, τέκνα ἔχων πιστά,
[2]of one [1]wife   [1]husband, [3]children [1]having [2]believing,

μὴ ἐν κατηγορίᾳ ἀσωτίας ἢ ἀνυπότακτα.*
not in   accusation   of profligacy or   unruly.*

7 δεῖ γὰρ τὸν ἐπίσκοπον ἀνέγκλητον εἶναι
For it behoves the   bishop   [2]unreprovable [1]to be

ὡς θεοῦ οἰκονόμον, μὴ αὐθάδη, μὴ
as   of God   a steward,   not self-pleasing, not

ὀργίλον, μὴ πάροινον, μὴ πλήκτην, μὴ
passionate, not given to wine, not   a striker,   not

αἰσχροκερδῆ, 8 ἀλλὰ φιλόξενον, φιλάγαθον,
greedy of   but   hospitable, a lover of good
base gain,   [men/things],

σώφρονα, δίκαιον, ὅσιον, ἐγκρατῆ, 9 ἀντεχ-
sensible,   just,   holy, self-controlled, holding

όμενον τοῦ κατὰ τὴν διδαχὴν πιστοῦ
to   [1]the [4]according to [5]the   [6]teaching [2]faithful

λόγου, ἵνα δυνατὸς ᾖ καὶ παρακαλεῖν
[3]word, in order [2]able [1]he may both   to exhort
       that   be

ἐν τῇ διδασκαλίᾳ τῇ ὑγιαινούσῃ καὶ
by   the [2]teaching – [1]being healthy and

τοὺς ἀντιλέγοντας ἐλέγχειν. 10 Εἰσὶν γὰρ
[2]the [ones] [3]contradicting [1]to convince.   For there are

* In agreement with " children " (neut. pl.).

unruly and vain talkers and deceivers, specially they of the circumcision:

11 Whose mouths must be stopped, who subvert whole houses, teaching things which they ought not, for filthy lucre's sake.

12 One of themselves, *even* a prophet of their own, said, The Cretians *are* alway liars, evil beasts, slow bellies.

13 This witness is true. Wherefore rebuke them sharply, that they may be sound in the faith;

14 Not giving heed to Jewish fables, and commandments of men, that turn from the truth.

15 Unto the pure all things *are* pure: but unto them that are defiled and unbelieving *is* nothing pure; but even their mind and conscience is defiled.

16 They profess that they know God; but in works they deny *him*, being abominable, and disobedient, and unto every good work reprobate.

πολλοὶ ἀνυπότακτοι, ματαιολόγοι καὶ
many   unruly men,   vain talkers   and

φρεναπάται, μάλιστα οἱ ἐκ τῆς περιτομῆς,
deceivers,   specially the ones of the circumcision,

11 οὓς δεῖ ἐπιστομίζειν, οἵτινες ὅλους
whom it   to stop the   who   ³whole
      behoves mouth,

οἴκους ἀνατρέπουσιν διδάσκοντες ἃ μὴ
³households ¹overturn   teaching   things ²not
                                          which

δεῖ αἰσχροῦ κέρδους χάριν. 12 εἶπέν
¹it be- ⁴base   ⁵gain   ²for the   ⁷Said
hoves   sake of.

τις ἐξ αὐτῶν ἴδιος αὐτῶν προφήτης·
¹a cer- ²of ³them ⁴an own ⁵of them ⁶prophet:
tain one

Κρῆτες ἀεὶ ψεῦσται, κακὰ θηρία, γαστέρες
Cretans always liars,   evil beasts, ²gluttons
[are]

ἀργαί. 13 ἡ μαρτυρία αὕτη ἐστὶν ἀληθής.
¹idle.   This witness   is   : true.

δι' ἣν αἰτίαν ἔλεγχε αὐτοὺς ἀποτόμως,
For which cause reprove them   severely,

ἵνα ὑγιαίνωσιν ἐν τῇ πίστει, 14 μὴ
in or- they may   in the faith,   not
der that be healthy

προσέχοντες Ἰουδαϊκοῖς μύθοις καὶ
giving heed to Jewish   tales   and

ἐντολαῖς ἀνθρώπων ἀποστρεφομένων τὴν
commandments of men   perverting   the

ἀλήθειαν. 15 πάντα καθαρὰ τοῖς καθαροῖς·
truth.   All things [are] clean to the clean;

τοῖς δὲ μεμιαμμένοις καὶ ἀπίστοις οὐδὲν
but to   *having been*   and unfaithful nothing
the [ones] defiled

καθαρόν, ἀλλὰ μεμίανται αὐτῶν καὶ ὁ
[is] clean, but ³has(ve) been defiled ⁷of them ¹both ²the

νοῦς καὶ ἡ συνείδησις. 16 θεὸν ὁμολο-
³mind ⁴and ⁵the ⁶conscience.   ³God ¹they pro-

γοῦσιν εἰδέναι, τοῖς δὲ ἔργοις ἀρνοῦνται,
fess   ²to know, but by the(ir) works they deny [him],

βδελυκτοὶ ὄντες καὶ ἀπειθεῖς καὶ πρὸς
²abominable ¹being and disobedient and   to

πᾶν ἔργον ἀγαθὸν ἀδόκιμοι.
every ²work ¹good   reprobate.

CHAPTER 2

BUT speak thou the things which become sound doctrine:

2 Σὺ δὲ λάλει ἃ πρέπει τῇ ὑγιαινούσῃ
But ²thou ¹speak things becomes the *being*
              which   healthy

διδασκαλίᾳ. 2 Πρεσβύτας νηφαλίους εἶναι,
teaching.   Aged men   ²sober   ¹to be,

2 That the aged men be sober, grave, temperate, sound in faith, in charity, in patience.

3 The aged women likewise, that *they be* in behaviour as becometh holiness, not false accusers, not given to much wine, teachers of good things;

4 That they may teach the young women to be sober, to love their husbands, to love their children,

5 *To be* discreet, chaste, keepers at home, good, obedient to their own husbands, that the word of God be not blasphemed.

6 Young men likewise exhort to be sober minded.

7 In all things shewing thyself a pattern of good works: in doctrine *shewing* uncorruptness, gravity, sincerity,

8 Sound speech, that cannot be condemned: that he that is of the contrary part may be ashamed, having no evil thing to say of you.

9 *Exhort* servants to be obedient unto their own masters, *and* to please *them* well in all *things;* not answering again;

10 Not purloining, but shewing all good fidelity; that they may adorn the doctrine of God our Saviour in all things.

11 For the grace of God that bringeth salvation hath appeared to all men,

σεμνούς, σώφρονας, ὑγιαίνοντας τῇ πίστει,
grave,   sensible,   *being* healthy   in the   faith,

τῇ ἀγάπῃ, τῇ ὑπομονῇ· 3 πρεσβύτιδας
–   in love,   –   in endurance;   aged women

ὡσαύτως ἐν καταστήματι ἱεροπρεπεῖς, μὴ
similarly   in   demeanour   reverent,   not

διαβόλους, μηδὲ οἴνῳ πολλῷ δεδουλωμένας,
slanderers,   nor   ²wine ²by much   ¹having been enslaved,

καλοδιδασκάλους, 4 ἵνα σωφρονίζωσιν τὰς
teachers of what is good,   in order that   they may train   the

νέας φιλάνδρους εἶναι, φιλοτέκνους,
young women   ²lovers of [their] husbands   ¹to be,   child-lovers,

5 σώφρονας, ἁγνάς, οἰκουργούς, ἀγαθάς,
sensible,   pure,   home-workers,   good,

ὑποτασσομένας τοῖς ἰδίοις ἀνδράσιν,
being subject   to the(ir)   own   husbands,

ἵνα μὴ ὁ λόγος τοῦ θεοῦ βλασφημῆται.
lest   the word   – of God   be blasphemed.

6 Τοὺς νεωτέρους ὡσαύτως παρακάλει
The   younger men   similarly   exhort

σωφρονεῖν 7 περὶ πάντα, σεαυτὸν παρ-
to be sensible   about   all things,   ²thyself   ¹show-

εχόμενος τύπον καλῶν ἔργων, ἐν τῇ
ing   a pattern   of good   works,   in   the

διδασκαλίᾳ ἀφθορίαν, σεμνότητα, 8 λόγον
teaching   uncorruptness,   gravity,   ²speech

ὑγιῆ ἀκατάγνωστον, ἵνα ὁ ἐξ ἐναντίας
¹healthy ²irreprehensible,   in order that   man   the of [the]   contrary [side]

ἐντραπῇ μηδὲν ἔχων λέγειν περὶ ἡμῶν
may be put to shame   ²nothing ¹having   ⁴to say   ⁵about   ⁶us

φαῦλον. 9 Δούλους ἰδίοις δεσπόταις
³bad.   Slaves   to [their] own   masters

ὑποτάσσεσθαι ἐν πᾶσιν, εὐαρέστους εἶναι,
to be subject   in   all things,   well-pleasing   to be,

μὴ ἀντιλέγοντας, 10 μὴ νοσφιζομένους, ἀλλὰ
not   contradicting,   not   peculating,   but

πᾶσαν πίστιν ἐνδεικνυμένους ἀγαθήν, ἵνα
²all   ⁴faith   ¹showing   ³good,   in order that

τὴν διδασκαλίαν τὴν τοῦ σωτῆρος ἡμῶν
²the   ³teaching   –   ⁴of the   ⁵Saviour   ⁶of us

θεοῦ κοσμῶσιν ἐν πᾶσιν. 11 Ἐπεφάνη
⁷God   ¹they may adorn   in   all things.   ⁸appeared

γὰρ ἡ χάρις τοῦ θεοῦ σωτήριος πᾶσιν
For   ¹the   ²grace   –   ³of God   ⁴saving   to all

12 Teaching us that, denying ungodliness and worldly lusts, we should live soberly, righteously, and godly, in this present world;

13 Looking for that blessed hope, and the glorious appearing of the great God and our Saviour Jesus Christ;

14 Who gave himself for us, that he might redeem us from all iniquity, and purify unto himself a peculiar people, zealous of good works.

15 These things speak, and exhort, and rebuke with all authority. Let no man despise thee.

CHAPTER 3

PUT them in mind to be subject to principalities and powers, to obey magistrates, to be ready to every good work,

2 To speak evil of no man, to be no brawlers, but gentle, shewing all meekness unto all men.

3 For we ourselves also were sometimes foolish, disobedient, deceived, serving divers lusts and pleasures, living in malice and envy, hateful, and hating one another.

4 But after that the kindness and love of God our Saviour toward man appeared,

ἀνθρώποις,   12 παιδεύουσα   ἡμᾶς,   ἵνα
men,   instructing   us,   in order
                                                                            that

ἀρνησάμενοι τὴν ἀσέβειαν καὶ τὰς κοσμικὰς
denying   -   impiety   and   -   worldly

ἐπιθυμίας σωφρόνως καὶ δικαίως καὶ
lusts   ²sensibly   ³and   ⁴righteously ⁵and

εὐσεβῶς ζήσωμεν ἐν τῷ νῦν αἰῶνι,
⁶piously ¹we might live in the now(present) age,

13 προσδεχόμενοι τὴν μακαρίαν ἐλπίδα καὶ
expecting   the   blessed   hope   and

ἐπιφάνειαν τῆς δόξης τοῦ μεγάλου θεοῦ
appearance of the glory of the great God

καὶ σωτῆρος ἡμῶν Χριστοῦ Ἰησοῦ, 14 ὃς
and Saviour of us Christ   Jesus,   who

ἔδωκεν ἑαυτὸν ὑπὲρ ἡμῶν ἵνα λυτρώσηται
gave   himself on behalf us in or- he might
                              of   der that ransom

ἡμᾶς ἀπὸ πάσης ἀνομίας καὶ καθαρίσῃ
us   from   all   iniquity and might cleanse

ἑαυτῷ λαὸν περιούσιον, ζηλωτὴν καλῶν ἔργων.
for   a people [his] own zealous of good works.
himself   possession,

15 Ταῦτα λάλει καὶ παρακάλει καὶ ἔλεγχε
These things speak thou and   exhort   and   reprove

μετὰ πάσης ἐπιταγῆς· μηδείς σου περιφρονείτω.
with   all   command; ²no one ⁴of thee ¹let ³despise.

3 Ὑπομίμνησκε αὐτοὺς ἀρχαῖς ἐξουσίαις
Remind thou   them   ¹to rulers ²[and] ³authorities

ὑποτάσσεσθαι, πειθαρχεῖν, πρὸς πᾶν ἔργον
¹to be subject,   to be obedient,   ²to ⁴every ⁶work

ἀγαθὸν ἑτοίμους εἶναι, 2 μηδένα βλασ-
⁵good   ²ready   ¹to be,   no one   to

φημεῖν, ἀμάχους εἶναι, ἐπιεικεῖς, πᾶσαν
rail at,   uncontentious to be, forbearing,   ²all

ἐνδεικνυμένους πραΰτητα πρὸς πάντας
¹showing forth   meekness   to   all

ἀνθρώπους. 3 Ἦμεν γάρ ποτε καὶ ἡμεῖς
men.   For ³were ⁴then ²also ¹we

ἀνόητοι, ἀπειθεῖς, πλανώμενοι, δουλεύοντες
senseless, disobedient, being deceived, serving [as slaves]

ἐπιθυμίαις καὶ ἡδοναῖς ποικίλαις, ἐν κακίᾳ
²lusts   ³and ⁴pleasures ¹various,   ²in ³evil

καὶ φθόνῳ διάγοντες, στυγητοί, μισοῦντες
⁴and ⁵envy ¹living,   hateful,   hating

ἀλλήλους. 4 ὅτε δὲ ἡ χρηστότης καὶ
one another.   But when the   kindness   and

ἡ φιλανθρωπία ἐπεφάνη τοῦ σωτῆρος ἡμῶν
the love to man   ⁵appeared ¹of the ³Saviour ²of us

5 Not by works of righteousness which we have done, but according to his mercy he saved us, by the washing of regeneration, and renewing of the Holy Ghost;

6 Which he shed on us abundantly through Jesus Christ our Saviour;

7 That being justified by his grace, we should be made heirs according to the hope of eternal life.

8 This is a faithful saying, and these things I will that thou affirm constantly, that they which have believed in God might be careful to maintain good works. These things are good and profitable unto men.

9 But avoid foolish questions, and genealogies, and contentions, and strivings about the law; for they are unprofitable and vain.

10 A man that is an heretick after the first and second admonition reject;

11 Knowing that he that is such is subverted, and sinneth, being condemned of himself.

12 When I shall send Artemas unto thee, or Tychicus, be diligent to

---

θεοῦ, 5 οὐκ ἐξ ἔργων τῶν ἐν δικαιοσύνῃ
⁴God,   not by works – ⁴in ⁵righteousness

ἃ ἐποιήσαμεν ἡμεῖς, ἀλλὰ κατὰ τὸ
¹which ²did ³we, but according to the

αὐτοῦ ἔλεος ἔσωσεν ἡμᾶς διὰ λουτροῦ
of him mercy he saved us through [the] washing

παλιγγενεσίας καὶ ἀνακαινώσεως πνεύματος
of regeneration and renewal ³Spirit

ἁγίου, 6 οὗ ἐξέχεεν ἐφ' ἡμᾶς πλουσίως
¹of [the] which he shed on us richly
Holy,

διὰ Ἰησοῦ Χριστοῦ τοῦ σωτῆρος ἡμῶν,
through Jesus Christ the Saviour of us,

7 ἵνα δικαιωθέντες τῇ ἐκείνου χάριτι
in or- being justified ¹by the ²of that one ³grace
der that

κληρονόμοι γενηθῶμεν κατ' ἐλπίδα ζωῆς
heirs we might become accord- a hope of life
                        ing to

αἰωνίου. 8 Πιστὸς ὁ λόγος, καὶ περὶ
eternal. Faithful [is] the word, and as to

τούτων βούλομαί σε διαβεβαιοῦσθαι, ἵνα
these I wish thee to affirm in or-
things   confidently, der that

φροντίζωσιν καλῶν ἔργων προΐστασθαι οἱ
⁴may take ⁶of good ⁷works ⁵to maintain ¹the
thought   [ones]

πεπιστευκότες θεῷ. ταῦτά ἐστιν καλὰ
²having believed ³God. These things is(are) good

καὶ ὠφέλιμα τοῖς ἀνθρώποις· 9 μωρὰς
and profitable – to men; ²foolish

δὲ ζητήσεις καὶ γενεαλογίας καὶ ἔριν
¹but questionings and genealogies and strife

καὶ μάχας νομικὰς περιΐστασο· εἰσὶν γὰρ
and ²fights ¹legal shun thou; for they are

ἀνωφελεῖς καὶ μάταιοι. 10 αἱρετικὸν
unprofitable and vain. A factious

ἄνθρωπον μετὰ μίαν καὶ δευτέραν
man after one and a second

νουθεσίαν παραιτοῦ, 11 εἰδὼς ὅτι ἐξέστραπ-
admonition avoid, knowing that ²has been per-

ται ὁ τοιοῦτος καὶ ἁμαρτάνει ὢν αὐτο-
verted ¹such a man and sins being self-

κατάκριτος.
condemned.

12 Ὅταν πέμψω Ἀρτεμᾶν πρὸς σὲ
Whenever I send Artemas to thee

ἢ Τύχικον, σπούδασον ἐλθεῖν πρός με
or Tychicus, hasten to come to me

come unto me to Nicopolis: for I have determined there to winter.

13 Bring Zenas the lawyer and Apollos on their journey diligently, that nothing be wanting unto them.

14 And let our's also learn to maintain good works for necessary uses, that they be not unfruitful.

15 All that are with me salute thee. Greet them that love us in the faith. Grace *be* with you all. Amen.

εἰς Νικόπολιν· ἐκεῖ γὰρ κέκρικα παραχειμά-
in Nicopolis;   for there I have decided to spend [the]

σαι. 13 Ζηνᾶν τὸν νομικὸν καὶ Ἀπολλῶν
winter.   Zenas   the   lawyer   and   Apollos

σπουδαίως πρόπεμψον, ἵνα μηδὲν αὐτοῖς
urgently   send forward, in or- nothing   to them
                        der that

λείπῃ. 14 μανθανέτωσαν δὲ καὶ οἱ ἡμέτεροι
may be lacking. And ¹let ⁴learn ³also – ²our [people]

καλῶν ἔργων προΐστασθαι εἰς τὰς ἀναγ-
⁵of good ⁷works ⁶to maintain for – neces-

καίας χρείας, ἵνα μὴ ὦσιν ἄκαρποι.
sary   wants, lest they be unfruitful.

15 Ἀσπάζονταί σε οἱ μετ' ἐμοῦ πάντες.
    ²greet   ⁶thee ²the ³with   ⁴me   ¹All.
                  [ones]

ἄσπασαι τοὺς φιλοῦντας ἡμᾶς ἐν πίστει.
Greet thou the [ones] loving   us in [the] faith.

Ἡ χάρις μετὰ πάντων ὑμῶν.
– Grace [be] with ²all ¹you.

PHILEMON

ΠΡΟΣ ΦΙΛΗΜΟΝΑ
To Philemon

PAUL, a prisoner of Jesus Christ, and Timothy *our* brother, unto Philemon our dearly beloved, and fellow labourer,

2 And to *our* beloved Apphia, and Archippus our fellowsoldier, and to the church in thy house:

3 Grace to you, and peace, from God our Father and the Lord Jesus Christ.

4 I thank my God, making mention of thee always in my prayers,

5 Hearing of thy love

1 Παῦλος δέσμιος Χριστοῦ Ἰησοῦ καὶ
  Paul a prisoner of Christ Jesus and

Τιμόθεος ὁ ἀδελφὸς Φιλήμονι τῷ ἀγαπητῷ
Timothy the brother to Philemon the beloved

καὶ συνεργῷ ἡμῶν 2 καὶ Ἀπφίᾳ τῇ
and a fellow-worker of us   and to Apphia the

ἀδελφῇ καὶ Ἀρχίππῳ τῷ συστρατιώτῃ
sister and to Archippus the   fellow-soldier

ἡμῶν καὶ τῇ κατ' οἶκόν σου ἐκκλησίᾳ·
of us and ¹to the ³at ⁴house ⁵of thee ²church:

3 χάρις ὑμῖν καὶ εἰρήνη ἀπὸ θεοῦ πατρὸς
  Grace to you and peace from God Father

ἡμῶν καὶ κυρίου Ἰησοῦ Χριστοῦ.
of us and Lord Jesus Christ.

4 Εὐχαριστῶ τῷ θεῷ μου πάντοτε μνείαν
  I give thanks to the God of me always ²mention

σου ποιούμενος ἐπὶ τῶν προσευχῶν μου,
³of thee ¹making at   the   prayers of me,

5 ἀκούων σου τὴν ἀγάπην καὶ τὴν
  hearing of thee the   love and the

and faith, which thou hast toward the Lord Jesus, and toward all saints;

6 That the communication of thy faith may become effectual by the acknowledging of every good thing which is in you in Christ Jesus.

7 For we have great joy and consolation in thy love, because the bowels of the saints are refreshed by thee, brother.

8 Wherefore, though I might be much bold in Christ to enjoin thee that which is convenient,

9 Yet for love's sake I rather beseech *thee*, being such an one as Paul the aged, and now also a prisoner of Jesus Christ.

10 I beseech thee for my son Onesimus, whom I have begotten in my bonds:

11 Which in time past was to thee unprofitable, but now profitable to thee and to me:

12 Whom I have sent again: thou therefore receive him, that is, mine own bowels:

13 Whom I would have retained with me, that in thy stead he might have ministered unto me in the bonds of the gospel:

14 But without thy mind

πίστιν ἣν ἔχεις πρὸς τὸν κύριον Ἰησοῦν
faith which thou hast toward the Lord Jesus

καὶ εἰς πάντας τοὺς ἁγίους, 6 ὅπως
and to all the saints, so as

ἡ κοινωνία τῆς πίστεώς σου ἐνεργὴς
the fellowship of the faith of thee ²operative

γένηται ἐν ἐπιγνώσει παντὸς ἀγαθοῦ τοῦ
¹may become in a full knowledge of every good thing –

ἐν ἡμῖν εἰς Χριστόν. 7 χαρὰν γὰρ
in us for Christ. ⁴joy ¹For

πολλὴν ἔσχον καὶ παράκλησιν ἐπὶ τῇ
²much ³I had and consolation over the

ἀγάπῃ σου, ὅτι τὰ σπλάγχνα τῶν ἁγίων
love of thee, because the bowels of the saints

ἀναπέπαυται διὰ σοῦ, ἀδελφέ. 8 Διό,
has(ve) been refreshed through thee, brother. Wherefore,

πολλὴν ἐν Χριστῷ παρρησίαν ἔχων ἐπιτάσ-
²much ⁴in ⁵Christ ³boldness ¹having to

σειν σοι τὸ ἀνῆκον, 9 διὰ τὴν ἀγάπην
charge thee the befitting thing, because of – love

μᾶλλον παρακαλῶ· τοιοῦτος ὢν ὡς Παῦλος
rather I beseech; such a one being as Paul

πρεσβύτης, νυνὶ δὲ καὶ δέσμιος Χριστοῦ
an old man, and now also a prisoner of Christ

Ἰησοῦ, 10 παρακαλῶ σε περὶ τοῦ ἐμοῦ
Jesus, I beseech thee concerning – my

τέκνου, ὃν ἐγέννησα ἐν τοῖς δεσμοῖς,
child, whom I begat in the(my) bonds,

Ὀνήσιμον, 11 τόν ποτέ σοι ἄχρηστον
Onesimus, the [one] then ²to thee ¹useless
(formerly)

νυνὶ δὲ καὶ σοὶ καὶ ἐμοὶ εὔχρηστον,
but now ³both ²to thee ⁴and ⁵to me ¹useful,

12 ὃν ἀνέπεμψά σοι, αὐτόν, τοῦτ' ἔστιν
whom I sent back to thee, him, this is

τὰ ἐμὰ σπλάγχνα· 13 ὃν ἐγὼ ἐβουλόμην
– my bowels; whom I resolved

πρὸς ἐμαυτὸν κατέχειν, ἵνα ὑπὲρ σοῦ
with myself to retain, in order that on behalf of thee

μοι διακονῇ ἐν τοῖς δεσμοῖς τοῦ εὐαγ-
to me he might minister in the bonds of the gos-

γελίου, 14 χωρὶς δὲ τῆς σῆς γνώμης
pel, but without – thy opinion

would I do nothing; that thy benefit should not be as it were of necessity, but willingly.

15 For perhaps he therefore departed for a season, that thou shouldest receive him for ever;

16 Not now as a servant, but above a servant, a brother beloved, specially to me, but how much more unto thee, both in the flesh, and in the Lord?

17 If thou count me therefore a partner, receive him as myself.

18 If he hath wronged thee, or oweth *thee* ought, put that on mine account;

19 I Paul have written *it* with mine own hand, I will repay *it*: albeit I do not say to thee how thou owest unto me even thine own self besides.

20 Yea, brother, let me have joy of thee in the Lord: refresh my bowels in the Lord.

21 Having confidence in thy obedience I wrote unto thee, knowing that thou wilt also do more than I say.

22 But withal prepare me also a lodging: for I trust that through your prayers I shall be given unto you.

23 There salute thee

οὐδὲν ἠθέλησα ποιῆσαι, ἵνα μὴ ὡς κατὰ
²nothing ¹I was ²to do, lest ³as ⁴by way
willing of

ἀνάγκην τὸ ἀγαθόν σου ᾖ ἀλλὰ κατὰ
⁷necessity ¹the ²good ³of ⁴might but by way
thee be of

ἑκούσιον. 15 τάχα γὰρ διὰ τοῦτο ἐχωρίσθη
[being] For perhaps therefore he departed
voluntary.

πρὸς ὥραν, ἵνα αἰώνιον αὐτὸν ἀπέχῃς,
for an hour, in order ²eternally ²him ¹thou mightest
that receive,

16 οὐκέτι ὡς δοῦλον ἀλλὰ ὑπὲρ δοῦλον,
no longer as a slave but beyond a slave,

ἀδελφὸν ἀγαπητόν, μάλιστα ἐμοί, πόσῳ
a brother beloved, specially to me, ²by how
much

δὲ μᾶλλον σοὶ καὶ ἐν σαρκὶ καὶ ἐν
¹and more to thee both in [the] flesh and in

κυρίῳ. 17 εἰ οὖν με ἔχεις κοινωνόν,
[the] Lord. If therefore me thou hast [as] a partner,

προσλαβοῦ αὐτὸν ὡς ἐμέ. 18 εἰ δέ
receive him as me. And if

τι ἠδίκησέν σε ἢ ὀφείλει, τοῦτο ἐμοὶ
any- he wronged thee or owes, ²this ²to me
thing

ἐλλόγα· 19 ἐγὼ Παῦλος ἔγραψα τῇ ἐμῇ
¹reckon: I Paul wrote – with my

χειρί, ἐγὼ ἀποτίσω· ἵνα μὴ λέγω σοι
hand, I will repay; lest I say to thee

ὅτι καὶ σεαυτόν μοι προσοφείλεις. 20 ναί,
that indeed ²thyself ³to me ¹thou owest besides. Yes,

ἀδελφέ, ἐγώ σου ὀναίμην ἐν κυρίῳ·
brother, ²I ³of thee ¹may ³have ⁴help in [the] Lord;

ἀνάπαυσόν μου τὰ σπλάγχνα ἐν Χριστῷ.
refresh of me the bowels in Christ.

21 Πεποιθὼς τῇ ὑπακοῇ σου ἔγραψά
Having trusted to the obedience of thee I wrote

σοι, εἰδὼς ὅτι καὶ ὑπὲρ ἃ λέγω ποιήσεις.
to knowing that indeed beyond what I say thou wilt
thee, things do.

22 ἅμα δὲ καὶ ἑτοίμαζέ μοι ξενίαν·
And at the also prepare for me lodging;
same time

ἐλπίζω γὰρ ὅτι διὰ τῶν προσευχῶν
for I hope that through the prayers

ὑμῶν χαρισθήσομαι ὑμῖν.
of you I shall be given to you.

23 Ἀσπάζεταί σε Ἐπαφρᾶς ὁ συναιχμά-
²greets ²thee ¹Epaphras ²the ³fellow-

Epaphras, my fellow-prisoner in Christ Jesus;

24 Marcus, Aristarchus, Demas, Lucas, my fellow-labourers.

25 The grace of our Lord Jesus Christ *be* with your spirit. Amen.

λωτός μου ἐν Χριστῷ Ἰησοῦ, **24** Μᾶρκος,
captive ⁴of me ⁵in ⁶Christ ⁷Jesus, [also] Mark,

Ἀρίσταρχος, Δημᾶς, Λουκᾶς, οἱ συνεργοί
Aristarchus, Demas, Luke, the fellow-workers

μου.
of me.

25 Ἡ χάρις τοῦ κυρίου Ἰησοῦ Χριστοῦ
The grace of the Lord Jesus Christ

μετὰ τοῦ πνεύματος ὑμῶν.
[be] with the spirit of you.

HEBREWS 1

ΠΡΟΣ ΕΒΡΑΙΟΥΣ
To Hebrews

CHAPTER 1

GOD, who at sundry times and in divers manners spake in time past unto the fathers by the prophets,

2 Hath in these last days spoken unto us by *his* Son, whom he hath appointed heir of all things, by whom also he made the worlds;

3 Who being the brightness of *his* glory, and the express image of his person, and upholding all things by the word of his power, when he had by himself purged our sins, sat down on the right hand of the Majesty on high;

4 Being made so much better than the angels, as he hath by inheritance obtained a more excellent name than they.

1 Πολυμερῶς καὶ πολυτρόπως πάλαι ὁ
⁵In many portions ⁶and ⁷in many ways ⁸of old –

θεὸς λαλήσας τοῖς πατράσιν ἐν τοῖς
¹God ³having spoken ²to the ⁴fathers by the

προφήταις **2** ἐπ’ ἐσχάτου τῶν ἡμερῶν
prophets in [the] last – days

τούτων ἐλάλησεν ἡμῖν ἐν υἱῷ, ὃν ἔθηκεν
of these spoke to us in a Son, whom he ap-pointed

κληρονόμον πάντων, δι’ οὗ καὶ ἐποίησεν
heir of all through whom indeed he made
things,

τοὺς αἰῶνας· **3** ὃς ὢν ἀπαύγασμα τῆς
the ages; who being [the] radiance of the
(his)

δόξης καὶ χαρακτὴρ τῆς ὑποστάσεως αὐτοῦ,
glory and [the] of the reality of him,
representation

φέρων τε τὰ πάντα τῷ ῥήματι τῆς
and bearing – all things by the word of the

δυνάμεως αὐτοῦ, καθαρισμὸν τῶν ἁμαρτιῶν
power of him, ²cleansing – ³of sins

ποιησάμενος ἐκάθισεν ἐν δεξιᾷ τῆς
¹having made sat on [the] right [hand] of the

μεγαλωσύνης ἐν ὑψηλοῖς, **4** τοσούτῳ
greatness in high places, ²by so much

κρείττων γενόμενος τῶν ἀγγέλων ὅσῳ
²better ¹becoming ⁴[than] the angels as

διαφορώτερον παρ’ αὐτοὺς κεκληρονόμηκεν
³a more excellent ⁴than ⁵them ¹he has inherited

5 For unto which of the angels said he at any time, Thou art my Son, this day have I begotten thee? And again, I will be to him a Father, and he shall be to me a Son?

6 And again, when he bringeth in the firstbegotten into the world, he saith, And let all the angels of God worship him.

7 And of the angels he saith, Who maketh his angels spirits, and his ministers a flame of fire.

8 But unto the Son *he saith*, Thy throne, O God, *is* for ever and ever: a sceptre of righteousness *is* the sceptre of thy kingdom.

9 Thou hast loved righteousness, and hated iniquity; therefore God, *even* thy God, hath anointed thee with the oil of gladness above thy fellows.

10 And, Thou, Lord, in the beginning hast laid the foundation of the earth; and the heavens are the works of thine hands:

11 They shall perish; but thou remainest; and they all shall wax old as doth a garment;

12 And as a vesture shalt thou fold them up,

ὄνομα.   **5** Τίνι γὰρ εἶπέν ποτε τῶν
[3]name.   For to which [3]said he [4]ever [1]of the

ἀγγέλων· υἱός μου εἶ σύ, ἐγὼ σήμερον
[3]angels: Son of me art thou,   I   to-day

γεγέννηκά σε; καὶ πάλιν· ἐγὼ ἔσομαι
have begotten thee? and again: I   will be

αὐτῷ εἰς πατέρα, καὶ αὐτὸς ἔσται μοι
to him for a father,   and   he   shall be to me

εἰς υἱόν;   **6** ὅταν δὲ πάλιν εἰσαγάγῃ
for a son?   and whenever   again   he brings *in*

τὸν πρωτότοκον εἰς τὴν οἰκουμένην, λέγει·
the firstborn   into the inhabited [earth], he says:

καὶ προσκυνησάτωσαν αὐτῷ πάντες ἄγγελοι
And   let worship   him   all   angels

θεοῦ.   **7** καὶ πρὸς μὲν τοὺς ἀγγέλους
of God.   And with re-   –   the   angels
       gard to

λέγει· ὁ ποιῶν τοὺς ἀγγέλους αὐτοῦ
he says: The making the   angels   of him
     [one]

πνεύματα, καὶ τοὺς λειτουργοὺς αὐτοῦ
spirits,   and   the   ministers   of him

πυρὸς φλόγα·   **8** πρὸς δὲ τὸν υἱόν· ὁ
[3]of fire [1]a flame;   but with regard to the   Son: The

θρόνος σου ὁ θεὸς εἰς τὸν αἰῶνα τοῦ
throne of thee[,] – God[,]*[is] unto the   age   of the

αἰῶνος, καὶ ἡ ῥάβδος τῆς εὐθύτητος
age,   and   the   rod   – of uprightness [is]

ῥάβδος τῆς βασιλείας αὐτοῦ.   **9** ἠγάπησας
[the] rod of the   kingdom   of him.   Thou lovedst

δικαιοσύνην καὶ ἐμίσησας ἀνομίαν· διὰ
righteousness and   hatedst   lawlessness; there-

τοῦτο ἔχρισέν σε, ὁ θεός, ὁ θεός σου
fore [4]anointed [3]thee, – [1]God,* [2]the [1]God [5]of thee

ἔλαιον ἀγαλλιάσεως παρὰ τοὺς μετόχους
[with] oil   of gladness   above   the   partners

σου.   **10** καὶ· σὺ κατ' ἀρχάς, κύριε,
of thee.   And: Thou at [the] beginnings, Lord,

τὴν γῆν ἐθεμελίωσας, καὶ ἔργα τῶν
[3]the [2]earth [1]didst found,   and   [4]works [5]of the

χειρῶν σού εἰσιν οἱ οὐρανοί·   **11** αὐτοὶ
[6]hands [7]of thee [2]are [1]the [3]heavens;   they

ἀπολοῦνται, σὺ δὲ διαμένεις· καὶ πάντες
will perish,   but thou   remainest;   and   all

ὡς ἱμάτιον παλαιωθήσονται, **12** καὶ ὡσεὶ
as a garment   will become old,   and   as

περιβόλαιον ἑλίξεις αὐτούς, ὡς ἱμάτιον
a mantle   thou wilt roll up them,   as   a garment

* Articular vocative; see ver. 10.

and they shall be changed: but thou art the same, and thy years shall not fail.

13 But to which of the angels said he at any time, Sit on my right hand, until I make thine enemies thy footstool?

14 Are they not all ministering spirits, sent forth to minister for them who shall be heirs of salvation?

CHAPTER 2

THEREFORE we ought to give the more earnest heed to the things which we have heard, lest at any time we should let *them* slip.

2 For if the word spoken by angels was stedfast, and every transgression and disobedience received a just recompence of reward;

3 How shall we escape, if we neglect so great salvation; which at the first began to be spoken by the Lord, and was confirmed unto us by them that heard *him;*

4 God also bearing *them* witness, both with signs and wonders, and with divers miracles, and gifts of the Holy Ghost, according to his own will?

5 For unto the angels hath he not put in subjection the world to come, whereof we speak.

καὶ ἀλλαγήσονται· σὺ δὲ ὁ αὐτὸς εἶ
also they will be changed; but thou the same art

καὶ τὰ ἔτη σου οὐκ ἐκλείψουσιν. 13 πρὸς
and the years of thee will not fail. [2]to

τίνα δὲ τῶν ἀγγέλων εἴρηκέν ποτε·
[3]which [1]But of the angels has he said at any time:

κάθου ἐκ δεξιῶν μου ἕως ἂν θῶ τοὺς
Sit at [the] right of me until I put the

ἐχθρούς σου ὑποπόδιον τῶν ποδῶν σου;
enemies of thee a footstool of the feet of thee?

14 οὐχὶ πάντες εἰσὶν λειτουργικὰ πνεύματα
[2]not [3]all [1]are they [4]ministering [5]spirits

εἰς διακονίαν ἀποστελλόμενα διὰ τοὺς
[7]for [8]service [6]being sent forth because of the [ones]

μέλλοντας κληρονομεῖν σωτηρίαν; 2 Διὰ
being about to inherit salvation? There-

τοῦτο δεῖ περισσοτέρως προσέχειν ἡμᾶς
fore [1]it behoves [4]more abundantly [3]to give heed [2]us

τοῖς ἀκουσθεῖσιν, μήποτε παραρυῶμεν.
to the things heard, lest we drift away.

2 εἰ γὰρ ὁ δι’ ἀγγέλων λαληθεὶς λόγος
For if [1]the [4]through [3]angels [5]spoken [2]word

ἐγένετο βέβαιος, καὶ πᾶσα παράβασις
was firm, and every transgression

καὶ παρακοὴ ἔλαβεν ἔνδικον μισθαποδοσίαν,
and disobedience received a just recompence,

3 πῶς ἡμεῖς ἐκφευξόμεθα τηλικαύτης
how [2]we [1]shall [2]escape [6]so great

ἀμελήσαντες σωτηρίας; ἥτις ἀρχὴν λαβοῦσα
[4]neglecting [6]a salvation? which [2]a beginning [1]having received

λαλεῖσθαι διὰ τοῦ κυρίου, ὑπὸ τῶν
to be spoken through the Lord, by the

ἀκουσάντων εἰς ἡμᾶς ἐβεβαιώθη, 4 συνεπι-
[ones] hearing to us was confirmed, [2]bearing

μαρτυροῦντος τοῦ θεοῦ σημείοις τε καὶ
witness with – [1]God[a] [4]by signs [3]both and

τέρασιν καὶ ποικίλαις δυνάμεσιν καὶ
by wonders and by various powerful deeds and

πνεύματος ἁγίου μερισμοῖς κατὰ τὴν αὐτοῦ
[2]Spirit [3]of [the] [1]by distribu- according to the [3]of him
Holy tions

θέλησιν.
[1]will.

5 Οὐ γὰρ ἀγγέλοις ὑπέταξεν τὴν
For not to angels subjected he the

οἰκουμένην τὴν μέλλουσαν, περὶ ἧς
[2]inhabited [earth] – [1]coming, about which

6 But one in a certain place testified, saying, What is man, that thou art mindful of him? or the son of man, that thou visitest him?

7 Thou madest him a little lower than the angels; thou crownedst him with glory and honour, and didst set him over the works of thy hands:

8 Thou hast put all things in subjection under his feet. For in that he put all in subjection under him, he left nothing *that is* not put under him. But now we see not yet all things put under him.

9 But we see Jesus, who was made a little lower than the angels for the suffering of death, crowned with glory and honour; that he by the grace of God should taste death for every man.

10 For it became him, for whom *are* all things, and by whom *are* all things, in bringing many sons unto glory, to make the captain of their salvation perfect through sufferings.

11 For both he that sanctifieth and they who are sanctified *are* all of one: for which cause he

λαλοῦμεν.   **6** διεμαρτύρατο δέ πού τις
we speak.   But ²solemnly witnessed ³some- ¹one
                                              where

λέγων· τί ἐστιν ἄνθρωπος ὅτι μιμνήσκῃ
saying: What is man that thou rememberest

αὐτοῦ; ἢ υἱὸς ἀνθρώπου ὅτι ἐπισκέπτῃ
him? or a son of man that thou observest

αὐτόν; **7** ἠλάττωσας αὐτὸν βραχύ τι παρ'
him? Thou madest ²less ¹him ²a little than

ἀγγέλους, δόξῃ καὶ τιμῇ ἐστεφάνωσας
angels, with glory and *with* honour thou crownedst

αὐτόν, **8** πάντα ὑπέταξας ὑποκάτω τῶν
him, all things thou subjectedst underneath the

ποδῶν αὐτοῦ. ἐν τῷ γὰρ ὑποτάξαι
feet of him. ¹in *the* For ²to subject[ing]

[αὐτῷ] τὰ πάντα οὐδὲν ἀφῆκεν αὐτῷ
⁴to him – ³all things ⁶nothing ⁵he left ⁸to him

ἀνυπότακτον. Νῦν δὲ οὔπω ὁρῶμεν
⁷unsubjected. But now not yet we see

αὐτῷ τὰ πάντα ὑποτεταγμένα· **9** τὸν δὲ
³to him – ¹all things ²having been ³the ¹but
                                       subjected;   [one]

βραχύ τι παρ' ἀγγέλους ἠλαττωμένον
⁵a little ⁶than ⁷angels ⁴having been
                                     made less

βλέπομεν Ἰησοῦν διὰ τὸ πάθημα τοῦ
²we see ³Jesus because of the suffering –

θανάτου δόξῃ καὶ τιμῇ ἐστεφανωμένον,
of death with glory and *with* honour having been
                                     crowned,

ὅπως χάριτι θεοῦ ὑπὲρ παντὸς γεύσηται
so as by [the] of God ³on ⁴every man ¹he might
       grace   behalf of   taste

θανάτου. **10** ἔπρεπεν γὰρ αὐτῷ, δι'
of ²death.   For it was fitting for him, because
                                         of

ὃν τὰ πάντα καὶ δι' οὗ τὰ πάντα,
whom – all things and through whom – all things,

πολλοὺς υἱοὺς εἰς δόξαν ἀγαγόντα τὸν
¹⁰many ¹¹sons ¹²to ¹³glory ⁵leading ⁴the

ἀρχηγὸν τῆς σωτηρίας αὐτῶν διὰ
⁵author ⁶of the ⁷salvation ⁸of them ⁹through

παθημάτων τελειῶσαι. **11** ὅ τε γὰρ
³sufferings ¹to perfect.   ³the [one] ²both ¹For

ἁγιάζων καὶ οἱ ἁγιαζόμενοι ἐξ ἑνὸς
sanctifying and the [ones] being sanctified [are] ³of ²one

πάντες· δι' ἣν αἰτίαν οὐκ ἐπαισχύνεται
¹all;   for which cause he is not ashamed

is not ashamed to call them brethren,

12 Saying, I will declare thy name unto my brethren, in the midst of the church will I sing praise unto thee.

13 And again, I will put my trust in him. And again, Behold I and the children which God hath given me.

14 Forasmuch then as the children are partakers of flesh and blood, he also himself likewise took part of the same; that through death he might destroy him that had the power of death, that is, the devil;

15 And deliver them who through fear of death were all their lifetime subject to bondage.

16 For verily he took not on *him the nature of angels*; but he took on *him* the seed of Abraham.

17 Wherefore in all things it behoved him to be made like unto *his* brethren, that he might be a merciful and faithful high priest in things *pertaining* to God, to make reconciliation for the sins of the people.

18 For in that he himself hath suffered being tempted, he is able to succour them that are tempted.

ἀδελφοὺς αὐτοὺς καλεῖν, 12 λέγων· ἀπαγ-
³brothers ²them ¹to call, saying: I will

γελῶ τὸ ὄνομά σου τοῖς ἀδελφοῖς μου,
announce the name of thee to the brothers of me,

ἐν μέσῳ ἐκκλησίας ὑμνήσω σε· 13 καὶ
in [the] midst of [the] church I will hymn thee; and

πάλιν· ἐγὼ ἔσομαι πεποιθὼς ἐπ' αὐτῷ·
again: I will be having trusted on(in) him;

καὶ πάλιν· ἰδοὺ ἐγὼ καὶ τὰ παιδία
and again: Behold[,] I and the children

ἅ μοι ἔδωκεν ὁ θεός. 14 Ἐπεὶ οὖν
whom ²to me ²gave – ¹God. Since therefore

τὰ παιδία κεκοινώνηκεν αἵματος καὶ
the children has(ve) partaken of blood and

σαρκός, καὶ αὐτὸς παραπλησίως μετέσχεν
of flesh, ²also ³[him]self ⁴in like manner ¹he shared

τῶν αὐτῶν, ἵνα διὰ τοῦ θανάτου
the same things, in order through the(?his) death
that

καταργήσῃ τὸν τὸ κράτος ἔχοντα τοῦ
he might destroy ¹the [one] ³the ⁴might ²having –

θανάτου, τοῦτ' ἔστιν τὸν διάβολον, 15 καὶ
of death, this is the devil, and

ἀπαλλάξῃ τούτους, ὅσοι φόβῳ θανάτου
release these, as many as by fear of death

διὰ παντὸς τοῦ ζῆν ἔνοχοι ἦσαν δουλείας.
through all the(ir) live ²involved ¹were slavery.
[time] in

16 οὐ γὰρ δήπου ἀγγέλων ἐπιλαμβάνεται,
⁴not ¹For ²of course ⁵of angels ³he takes hold,

ἀλλὰ σπέρματος Ἀβραὰμ ἐπιλαμβάνεται.
but of [the] seed of Abraham he takes hold.

17 ὅθεν ὤφειλεν κατὰ πάντα τοῖς ἀδελφοῖς
Whence he owed by all means† ²to the ³brothers
(ought) (his)

ὁμοιωθῆναι, ἵνα ἐλεήμων γένηται καὶ
¹to become like, in order ²a merciful ¹he might become and
that

πιστὸς ἀρχιερεὺς τὰ πρὸς τὸν θεόν,
faithful high priest [in] the in regard – God,
things to

εἰς τὸ ἱλάσκεσθαι τὰς ἁμαρτίας τοῦ
for the to make propitia- the sins of the
tion for

λαοῦ. 18 ἐν ᾧ γὰρ πέπονθεν αὐτὸς
people. ²in ³what ¹For ⁵has suffered ⁴he
[way]

πειρασθείς, δύναται τοῖς πειραζομένοις
being tempted, he is able ²the [ones] ³being tempted

βοηθῆσαι.
¹to help.

CHAPTER 3

WHEREFORE, holy brethren, partakers of the heavenly calling, consider the Apostle and High Priest of our profession, Christ Jesus;

2 Who was faithful to him that appointed him, as also Moses *was faithful* in all his house.

3 For this *man* was counted worthy of more glory than Moses, inasmuch as he who hath builded the house hath more honour than the house.

4 For every house is builded by some *man;* but he that built all things *is* God.

5 And Moses verily *was* faithful in all his house, as a servant, for a testimony of those things which were to be spoken after;

6 But Christ as a son over his own house; whose house are we, if we hold fast the confidence and the rejoicing of the hope firm unto the end.

7 Wherefore (as the Holy Ghost saith, To day if ye will hear his voice,

8 Harden not your hearts, as in the provocation, in the day of temptation in the wilderness:

9 When your fathers

3 Ὅθεν, ἀδελφοὶ ἅγιοι, κλήσεως
Whence, brothers holy, [2]calling
ἐπουρανίου μέτοχοι, κατανοήσατε τὸν
[3]of a heavenly [1]sharers, consider the
ἀπόστολον καὶ ἀρχιερέα τῆς ὁμολογίας
apostle and high priest of the confession
ἡμῶν Ἰησοῦν, 2 πιστὸν ὄντα τῷ ποιήσαντι
of us[,] Jesus, faithful being to the [one] making
αὐτόν, ὡς καὶ Μωϋσῆς ἐν [ὅλῳ] τῷ
him, as also Moses in all the
οἴκῳ αὐτοῦ. 3 πλείονος γὰρ οὗτος δόξης
household of him. For [3]of more [1]this one [4]glory
παρὰ Μωϋσῆν ἠξίωται καθ᾽ ὅσον πλείονα
[5]than [6]Moses [2]has been by so much as [5]more
counted worthy
τιμὴν ἔχει τοῦ οἴκου ὁ κατασκευάσας
[6]honour [4]has [8]the [9]house [1]the [2]having prepared
[7][than] [one]
αὐτόν. 4 πᾶς γὰρ οἶκος κατασκευάζεται
[3]it. For every house is prepared
ὑπό τινος, ὁ δὲ πάντα κατασκευάσας
by someone, but [1]the [one] [3]all things [2]having prepared
θεός. 5 καὶ Μωϋσῆς μὲν πιστὸς ἐν
[is] God. And Moses on one hand faithful in
[was]
ὅλῳ τῷ οἴκῳ αὐτοῦ ὡς θεράπων εἰς
all the household of him as a servant for
μαρτύριον τῶν λαληθησομένων, 6 Χριστὸς
a testimony of the things being spoken Christ
[in the future],
δὲ ὡς υἱὸς ἐπὶ τὸν οἶκον αὐτοῦ· οὗ
on the as a Son over the household of him; of
other whom
οἶκός ἐσμεν ἡμεῖς, ἐὰν τὴν παρρησίαν
a household are we, if [2]the [3]confidence
καὶ τὸ καύχημα τῆς ἐλπίδος [μέχρι
[4]and [5]the [6]boast [7]of the [8]hope [10]until
τέλους βεβαίαν] κατάσχωμεν. 7 Διό,
[11][the] end [9]firm [1]we hold fast. Wherefore,
καθὼς λέγει τὸ πνεῦμα τὸ ἅγιον· σήμερον
as says the Spirit – Holy: To-day
ἐὰν τῆς φωνῆς αὐτοῦ ἀκούσητε, 8 μὴ
if the voice of him ye hear, not
σκληρύνητε τὰς καρδίας ὑμῶν ὡς ἐν
harden ye the hearts of you as in
τῷ παραπικρασμῷ κατὰ τὴν ἡμέραν τοῦ
the provocation in the day of the
πειρασμοῦ ἐν τῇ ἐρήμῳ, 9 οὗ ἐπείρασαν
temptation in the desert, when [4]tempted

tempted me, proved me, and saw my works forty years.

10 Wherefore I was grieved with that generation, and said, They do alway err in *their* heart; and they have not known my ways.

11 So I sware in my wrath, They shall not enter into my rest.)

12 Take heed, brethren, lest there be in any of you an evil heart of unbelief, in departing from the living God.

13 But exhort one another daily, while it is called To day; lest any of you be hardened through the deceitfulness of sin.

14 For we are made partakers of Christ, if we hold the beginning of our confidence stedfast unto the end;

15 While it is said, To day if ye will hear his voice, harden not your hearts, as in the provocation.

16 For some, when they had heard, did provoke: howbeit not all that came out of Egypt by Moses.

17 But with whom was he grieved forty years?

οἱ πατέρες ὑμῶν ἐν δοκιμασίᾳ καὶ εἶδον
[1]the [2]fathers [3]of you in proving and saw

τὰ ἔργα μου 10 τεσσεράκοντα ἔτη· διὸ
the works of me forty years; wherefore

προσώχθισα τῇ γενεᾷ ταύτῃ καὶ εἶπον·
I was angry with this generation and I said:

ἀεὶ πλανῶνται τῇ καρδίᾳ· αὐτοὶ δὲ
Always they err in the heart; and they

οὐκ ἔγνωσαν τὰς ὁδούς μου, 11 ὡς
knew not the ways of me, as

ὤμοσα ἐν τῇ ὀργῇ μου· εἰ εἰσελεύσονται
I swore in the wrath of me: If they shall enter

εἰς τὴν κατάπαυσίν μου. 12 Βλέπετε,
into the rest of me. Look ye,

ἀδελφοί, μήποτε ἔσται ἔν τινι ὑμῶν
brothers, lest there shall be in anyone of you

καρδία πονηρὰ ἀπιστίας ἐν τῷ ἀποστῆναι
[2]heart [1]an evil of unbelief in the to depart[ing]

ἀπὸ θεοῦ ζῶντος, 13 ἀλλὰ παρακαλεῖτε
from God a living, but exhort

ἑαυτοὺς καθ᾽ ἑκάστην ἡμέραν, ἄχρις οὗ
yourselves — each day, while

τὸ σήμερον καλεῖται, ἵνα μὴ σκληρυνθῇ
the to-day it is being called, lest [4]be hardened

τις ἐξ ὑμῶν ἀπάτῃ τῆς ἁμαρτίας· 14 μέτ-
[1]any- [2]of [3]you by [the] — of sin; [3]shar-
one deceit

οχοι γὰρ τοῦ Χριστοῦ γεγόναμεν, ἐάνπερ
ers [1]for [4]of [5]Christ [2]we have if indeed
the become,

τὴν ἀρχὴν τῆς ὑποστάσεως μέχρι τέλους
[2]the [3]beginning [4]of the [5]assurance [6]until [6][the] end

βεβαίαν κατάσχωμεν. 15 ἐν τῷ λέγεσθαι·
[5]firm [1]we hold fast. In the to be said*:
=While it is said:

σήμερον ἐὰν τῆς φωνῆς αὐτοῦ ἀκούσητε,
To-day if the voice of him ye hear,

μὴ σκληρύνητε τὰς καρδίας ὑμῶν ὡς
do not harden the hearts of you as

ἐν τῷ παραπικρασμῷ. 16 τίνες γὰρ
in the provocation. For some

ἀκούσαντες παρεπίκραναν; ἀλλ᾽ οὐ πάντες
hearing provoked? yet not all

οἱ ἐξελθόντες ἐξ Αἰγύπτου διὰ
the [ones] coming *out* out of Egypt through

Μωϋσέως; 17 τίσιν δὲ προσώχθισεν τεσ-
Moses? but with whom was he angry for-

was it not with them that had sinned, whose carcases fell in the wilderness?

18 And to whom sware he that they should not enter into his rest, but to them that believed not?

19 So we see that they could not enter in because of unbelief.

CHAPTER 4

LET us therefore fear, lest, a promise being left us of entering into his rest, any of you should seem to come short of it.

2 For unto us was the gospel preached, as well as unto them: but the word preached did not profit them, not being mixed with faith in them that heard it.

3 For we which have believed do enter into rest, as he said, As I have sworn in my wrath, if they shall enter into my rest: although the works were finished from the foundation of the world.

4 For he spake in a certain place of the seventh day on this wise, And God did rest the seventh day from all his works.

5 And in this place again, If they shall enter into my rest.

σεράκοντα ἔτη; οὐχὶ τοῖς ἁμαρτήσασιν,
ty   years?   [was it]   with the [ones] sinning,
             not

ὧν τὰ κῶλα ἔπεσεν ἐν τῇ ἐρήμῳ;
of the corpses fell in the desert?
whom

18 τίσιν δὲ ὤμοσεν μὴ εἰσελεύσεσθαι εἰς
and to whom swore he not to enter into

τὴν κατάπαυσιν αὐτοῦ εἰ μὴ τοῖς
the rest of him except to the

ἀπειθήσασιν; **19** καὶ βλέπομεν ὅτι οὐκ
[ones] disobeying? and we see that not

ἠδυνήθησαν εἰσελθεῖν δι' ἀπιστίαν.
they were able to enter because of disbelief.

4 Φοβηθῶμεν οὖν μήποτε καταλειπομένης
Let us fear therefore lest ²being left

ἐπαγγελίας εἰσελθεῖν εἰς τὴν κατάπαυσιν
¹a promise° to enter into the rest

αὐτοῦ δοκῇ τις ἐξ ὑμῶν ὑστερηκέναι.
of him ⁴seems ¹anyone ²of ³you to have come short.

2 καὶ γάρ ἐσμεν εὐηγγελισμένοι καθάπερ
For indeed we are having had good news even as
                     preached [to us]

κἀκεῖνοι· ἀλλ' οὐκ ὠφέλησεν ὁ λόγος
those also; but ⁴did not profit ¹the ²word

τῆς ἀκοῆς ἐκείνους μὴ συγκεκερασμένος
– ³of hearing those not having been mixed
                        together

τῇ πίστει τοῖς ἀκούσασιν. **3** Εἰσερχόμεθα
– with faith in the [ones] hearing. we enter

γὰρ εἰς [τὴν] κατάπαυσιν οἱ πιστεύσαντες,
For into the rest the [ones] believing,

καθὼς εἴρηκεν· ὡς ὤμοσα ἐν τῇ ὀργῇ
as he has said: As I swore in the wrath

μου· εἰ εἰσελεύσονται εἰς τὴν κατάπαυσίν
of me: If they shall enter into the rest

μου, καίτοι τῶν ἔργων ἀπὸ καταβολῆς
of me, though the works ²from ³[the] foundation

κόσμου γενηθέντων. **4** εἴρηκεν γάρ που
⁴of [the] ¹having come into For he has said some-
world being.°   where

περὶ τῆς ἑβδόμης οὕτως· καὶ κατέπαυσεν
con- the seventh [day] thus: And ²rested
cerning

ὁ θεὸς ἐν τῇ ἡμέρᾳ τῇ ἑβδόμῃ ἀπὸ
– ¹God in the ²day – ¹seventh from

πάντων τῶν ἔργων αὐτοῦ· **5** καὶ ἐν
all the works of him; and in

τούτῳ πάλιν· εἰ εἰσελεύσονται εἰς τὴν
this [place] again: If they shall enter into the

6 Seeing therefore it remaineth that some must enter therein, and they to whom it was first preached entered not in because of unbelief:

7 Again, he limiteth a certain day, saying in David, To day, after so long a time; as it is said, To day if ye will hear his voice, harden not your hearts.

8 For if Jesus had given them rest, then would he not afterward have spoken of another day.

9 There remaineth therefore a rest to the people of God.

10 For he that is entered into his rest, he also hath ceased from his own works, as God *did* from his.

11 Let us labour therefore to enter into that rest, lest any man fall after the same example of unbelief.

12 For the word of God *is* quick, and powerful, and sharper than any two-edged sword, piercing even to the dividing asunder of soul and spirit, and of the

κατάπαυσίν μου. 6 ἐπεὶ οὖν ἀπολείπεται
rest of me.   Since therefore it remains

τινὰς εἰσελθεῖν εἰς αὐτήν, καὶ οἱ πρότερον
[for] to enter into it, and the formerly
some   [ones]

εὐαγγελισθέντες οὐκ εἰσῆλθον δι᾽ ἀπείθειαν,
having good news did not enter because disobedience,
preached [to them]   of

7 πάλιν τινὰ ὁρίζει ἡμέραν, σήμερον, ἐν
again ²a certain ¹he de- day, to-day, ²in
              fines

Δαυὶδ λέγων μετὰ τοσοῦτον χρόνον, καθὼς
³David ¹saying after such a time, as

προείρηται· σήμερον ἐὰν τῆς φωνῆς αὐτοῦ
he has To-day if the voice of him
previously said:

ἀκούσητε, μὴ σκληρύνητε τὰς καρδίας
ye hear, do not harden the hearts

ὑμῶν. 8 εἰ γὰρ αὐτοὺς Ἰησοῦς κατέπαυσεν,
of you. For if ³them ¹Jesus(Joshua) ²rested,

οὐκ ἂν περὶ ἄλλης ἐλάλει μετὰ ταῦτα
³not – ⁵concerning ⁶another ¹he ²would ⁸after ⁹these
                   ⁴have spoken   things

ἡμέρας. 9 ἄρα ἀπολείπεται σαββατισμὸς
⁷day.   Then ²remains ¹a sabbath rest

τῷ λαῷ τοῦ θεοῦ. 10 ὁ γὰρ εἰσελθὼν
to the people – of God. For the [one] having
                           entered

εἰς τὴν κατάπαυσιν αὐτοῦ καὶ αὐτὸς
into the rest of him also [him]self

κατέπαυσεν ἀπὸ τῶν ἔργων αὐτοῦ,
rested from the works of him,

ὥσπερ ἀπὸ τῶν ἰδίων ὁ θεός. 11 Σπου-
as from the(his) own - God [did]. Let us

δάσωμεν οὖν εἰσελθεῖν εἰς ἐκείνην τὴν
be eager therefore to enter into that –

κατάπαυσιν, ἵνα μὴ ἐν τῷ αὐτῷ τις
rest, lest ³in ⁴the ⁵same ¹any-
                             one

ὑποδείγματι πέσῃ τῆς ἀπειθείας. 12 Ζῶν
⁶example ²falls – of dis- [⁴is] ⁵living
                     obedience.

γὰρ ὁ λόγος τοῦ θεοῦ καὶ ἐνεργὴς
For ¹the ²word – ³of God and operative

καὶ τομώτερος ὑπὲρ πᾶσαν μάχαιραν
and sharper beyond every ³sword

δίστομον καὶ διϊκνούμενος ἄχρι μερισμοῦ
¹two-mouthed and passing through as far as division
(edged)

ψυχῆς καὶ πνεύματος, ἁρμῶν τε καὶ
of soul and of spirit, ²of joints ¹both and

joints and marrow, and *is* a discerner of the thoughts and intents of the heart.

13 Neither is there any creature that is not manifest in his sight: but all things *are* naked and opened unto the eyes of him with whom we have to do.

14 Seeing then that we have a great high priest, that is passed into the heavens, Jesus the Son of God, let us hold fast *our* profession.

15 For we have not an high priest which cannot be touched with the feeling of our infirmities; but was in all points tempted like as *we are*, yet without sin.

16 Let us therefore come boldly unto the throne of grace, that we may obtain mercy, and find grace to help in time of need.

μυελῶν, καὶ κριτικὸς ἐνθυμήσεων καὶ
of marrows, and able to judge of thoughts and
ἐννοιῶν καρδίας· 13 καὶ οὐκ ἔστιν κτίσις
intentions of a heart; and there is no creature
ἀφανὴς ἐνώπιον αὐτοῦ, πάντα δὲ γυμνὰ
unmanifest before him, but all things [are] naked
καὶ τετραχηλισμένα τοῖς ὀφθαλμοῖς αὐτοῦ,
and *having been* laid open to the eyes of him,
πρὸς ὃν ἡμῖν ὁ λόγος.
with whom to us [is] the word(account).°
　　　　　　　　　　=is our account.

14 Ἔχοντες οὖν ἀρχιερέα μέγαν διεληλυ-
Having there- high priest a great having gone
fore
θότα τοὺς οὐρανούς, Ἰησοῦν τὸν υἱὸν
through the heavens, Jesus the Son
τοῦ θεοῦ, κρατῶμεν τῆς ὁμολογίας. 15 οὐ
- of God, let us hold the confession. ²not
γὰρ ἔχομεν ἀρχιερέα μὴ δυνάμενον
¹For ²we have a high priest not being able
συμπαθῆσαι ταῖς ἀσθενείαις ἡμῶν, πεπει-
to suffer with the weaknesses of us, ²having
ρασμένον δὲ κατὰ πάντα καθ' ὁμοιότητα
been tempted ¹but in all respects† accord- [our] likeness
ing to
χωρὶς ἁμαρτίας. 16 προσερχώμεθα οὖν
apart from sin. Let us approach therefore
μετὰ παρρησίας τῷ θρόνῳ τῆς χάριτος,
with confidence *to* the throne - of grace,
ἵνα λάβωμεν ἔλεος καὶ χάριν εὕρωμεν
in or- we may mercy and ²grace *we* ¹may
der that receive find
εἰς εὔκαιρον βοήθειαν.
for timely help.

CHAPTER 5

FOR every high priest taken from among men is ordained for men in things *pertaining* to God, that he may offer both gifts and sacrifices for sins:

2 Who can have compassion on the ignorant, and on them that are out of the way; for that he himself also is compassed with infirmity.

5 Πᾶς γὰρ ἀρχιερεὺς ἐξ ἀνθρώπων
For every high priest ²out of ³men
λαμβανόμενος ὑπὲρ ἀνθρώπων καθίσταται
¹being taken on behalf of men is appointed [in]
τὰ πρὸς τὸν θεόν, ἵνα προσφέρῃ δῶρά
the in re- - God, in order he may offer ²gifts
things gard to that
τε καὶ θυσίας ὑπὲρ ἁμαρτιῶν, 2 μετριο-
¹both and sacrifices on behalf of sins, ²to feel in
παθεῖν δυνάμενος τοῖς ἀγνοοῦσιν καὶ
due measure ¹being able for the [ones] not knowing and
πλανωμένοις, ἐπεὶ καὶ αὐτὸς περίκειται
being led astray, since also he is set round
[with]

3 And by reason hereof he ought, as for the people, so also for himself, to offer for sins.

4 And no man taketh this honour unto himself, but he that is called of God, as *was* Aaron.

5 So also Christ glorified not himself to be made an high priest; but he that said unto him, Thou art my Son, to day have I begotten thee.

6 As he saith also in another *place*, Thou *art* a priest for ever after the order of Melchisedec.

7 Who in the days of his flesh, when he had offered up prayers and supplications with strong crying and tears unto him that was able to save him from death, and was heard in that he feared;

8 Though he were a Son, yet learned he obedience by the things which he suffered;

9 And being made perfect, he became the author of eternal salvation unto all them that obey him;

10 Called of God an high priest after the order of Melchisedec.

ἀσθένειαν, 3 καὶ δι᾽ αὐτὴν ὀφείλει, καθὼς
weakness, and because it he ought, as
of

περὶ τοῦ λαοῦ, οὕτως καὶ περὶ ἑαυτοῦ
concern- the people, so also concerning himself
ing

προσφέρειν περὶ ἁμαρτιῶν. 4 καὶ οὐχ
to offer concerning sins. And ⁸not

ἑαυτῷ τις λαμβάνει τὴν τιμήν, ἀλλὰ
⁴to him- ¹anyone ²takes the honour, but
self

καλούμενος ὑπὸ τοῦ θεοῦ, καθώσπερ καὶ
being called by – God, even as indeed

Ἀαρών. 5 Οὕτως καὶ ὁ Χριστὸς οὐχ
Aaron. So also – Christ ¹not

ἑαυτὸν ἐδόξασεν γενηθῆναι ἀρχιερέα, ἀλλ᾽
²himself ¹glorified to become a high priest, but

ὁ λαλήσας πρὸς αὐτόν· υἱός μου εἶ
the [one] speaking to him: Son of me art

σύ, ἐγὼ σήμερον γεγέννηκά σε· 6 καθὼς
thou, I to-day have begotten thee; as

καὶ ἐν ἑτέρῳ λέγει· σὺ ἱερεὺς εἰς τὸν
also in another he says: Thou a priest unto the
[psalm] [art]

αἰῶνα κατὰ τὴν τάξιν Μελχισέδεκ. 7 ὃς
age according the order of Melchisedec. Who
to

ἐν ταῖς ἡμέραις τῆς σαρκὸς αὐτοῦ δεήσεις
in the days of the flesh of him ²petitions

τε καὶ ἱκετηρίας πρὸς τὸν δυνάμενον
³both ⁴and ⁵entreaties ¹¹to ¹²the [one] ¹³being able

σῴζειν αὐτὸν ἐκ θανάτου μετὰ κραυγῆς
¹⁴to save ¹⁵him ¹⁶out of ¹⁷death ⁹with ⁸crying

ἰσχυρᾶς καὶ δακρύων προσενέγκας καὶ
⁷strong ⁸and ¹⁰tears ¹offering and

εἰσακουσθεὶς ἀπὸ τῆς εὐλαβείας, 8 καίπερ
being heard from(for) the(his) devoutness, though

ὢν υἱός, ἔμαθεν ἀφ᾽ ὧν ἔπαθεν τὴν
being a Son, he ²from ⁸[the] ⁴he suffered –
learned things which

ὑπακοήν, 9 καὶ τελειωθεὶς ἐγένετο πᾶσιν
¹obedience, and being perfected he became to all

τοῖς ὑπακούουσιν αὐτῷ αἴτιος σωτηρίας
the [ones] obeying him [the] cause ²salvation

αἰωνίου, 10 προσαγορευθεὶς ὑπὸ τοῦ θεοῦ
¹of eternal, being designated by – God

ἀρχιερεὺς κατὰ τὴν τάξιν Μελχισέδεκ.
a high priest accord- the order of Melchisedec.
ing to

11 Of whom we have many things to say, and hard to be uttered, seeing ye are dull of hearing.

12 For when for the time ye ought to be teachers, ye have need that one teach you again which *be* the first principles of the oracles of God; and are become such as have need of milk, and not of strong meat.

13 For every one that useth milk *is* unskilful in the word of righteousness: for he is a babe.

14 But strong meat belongeth to them that are of full age, *even* those who by reason of use have their senses exercised to discern both good and evil.

CHAPTER 6

THEREFORE leaving the principles of the doctrine of Christ, let us go on unto perfection; not laying again the foundation of repentance from dead works, and of faith toward God,

2 Of the doctrine of baptisms, and of laying on of hands, and of resurrection of the dead, and of eternal judgment.

3 And this will we do, if God permit.

4 For *it is* impossible

---

11 Περὶ οὗ πολὺς ἡμῖν ὁ λόγος καὶ
Concern- whom much to us the [1]word[e] [a]and
ing = we have much to say and hard ...

δυσερμήνευτος λέγειν, ἐπεὶ νωθροὶ γεγόνατε
[4]hard to interpret [3]to say, since dull ye have
become

ταῖς ἀκοαῖς. **12** καὶ γὰρ ὀφείλοντες
in the hearings. For indeed owing[*]

εἶναι διδάσκαλοι διὰ τὸν χρόνον, πάλιν
to be teachers because of the time, [2]again

χρείαν ἔχετε τοῦ διδάσκειν ὑμᾶς τινα
[3]need [1]ye have [1]to teach[d] [5]you [4]someone

τὰ στοιχεῖα τῆς ἀρχῆς τῶν λογίων
the rudiments of the beginning of the oracles

τοῦ θεοῦ, καὶ γεγόνατε χρείαν ἔχοντες
— of God, and ye have become [2]need [1]having

γάλακτος, οὐ στερεᾶς τροφῆς. **13** πᾶς
of milk, not of solid food. every

γὰρ ὁ μετέχων γάλακτος ἄπειρος λόγου
For one partaking of milk [is] without of [the]
experience word

δικαιοσύνης, νήπιος γάρ ἐστιν· **14** τελείων δέ
of righteousness, for [2]an infant [1]he is; but [4]of mature
men

ἐστιν ἡ στερεὰ τροφή, τῶν διὰ τὴν
[3]is the [1]solid [2]food, of the because the(ir)
[ones] of

ἕξιν τὰ αἰσθητήρια γεγυμνασμένα ἐχόντων
con- [3]the(ir) [2]faculties having been [4]exercised [1]having
dition

πρὸς διάκρισιν καλοῦ τε καὶ κακοῦ.
for distinction [2]of good [1]both and of bad.

6 Διὸ ἀφέντες τὸν τῆς ἀρχῆς τοῦ Χριστοῦ
Wherefore leaving [1]the [3]of the [4]beginning — [5]of Christ

λόγον ἐπὶ τὴν τελειότητα φερώμεθα, μὴ
[2]word [7]on to — [8]maturity [6]let us be borne, not

πάλιν θεμέλιον καταβαλλόμενοι μετανοίας
again [2]a foundation [1]laying down of repentance

ἀπὸ νεκρῶν ἔργων, καὶ πίστεως ἐπὶ
from dead works, and of faith toward

θεόν, **2** βαπτισμῶν διδαχῆς, ἐπιθέσεώς τε
God, [2]of baptisms [1]of teaching, and of laying on

χειρῶν, ἀναστάσεως νεκρῶν, καὶ κρίματος
of hands, of resurrection of dead persons, and [1]judgment

αἰωνίου. **3** καὶ τοῦτο ποιήσομεν, ἐάνπερ
[1]of eternal. And this will we do, if indeed

ἐπιτρέπῃ ὁ θεός. **4** Ἀδύνατον γὰρ τοὺς
[2]permits — [1]God. For [it is] impossible the
[for] [ones]

[*] That is, "ye ought ..."

for those who were once enlightened, and have tasted of the heavenly gift, and were made partakers of the Holy Ghost,

5 And have tasted the good word of God, and the powers of the world to come,

6 If they shall fall away, to renew them again unto repentance; seeing they crucify to themselves the Son of God afresh, and put *him* to an open shame.

7 For the earth which drinketh in the rain that cometh oft upon it, and bringeth forth herbs meet for them by whom it is dressed, receiveth blessing from God:

8 But that which beareth thorns and briers *is* rejected, and *is* nigh unto cursing; whose end *is* to be burned.

9 But, beloved, we are persuaded better things of you, and things that accompany salvation, though we thus speak.

10 For God *is* not unrighteous to forget your work and labour of love, which ye have shewed toward his name, in that ye have ministered to the saints, and do minister.

11 And we desire that every one of you do shew the same diligence to the full assurance of hope unto the end:

ἅπαξ φωτισθέντας γευσαμένους τε τῆς
once   being enlightened   and tasting   of the

δωρεᾶς τῆς ἐπουρανίου καὶ μετόχους
²gift   –   ¹heavenly   and   sharers

γενηθέντας πνεύματος ἁγίου 5 καὶ καλὸν
becoming   Spirit   of [the] Holy   and ²[the] good

γευσαμένους θεοῦ ῥῆμα δυνάμεις τε
¹tasting   ⁴of God   ³word   and powerful deeds

μέλλοντος αἰῶνος, 6 καὶ παραπεσόντας, πάλιν
of a coming   age,   and   falling away,   again

ἀνακαινίζειν εἰς μετάνοιαν, ἀνασταυροῦντας
to renew   to   repentance,   crucifying again

ἑαυτοῖς τὸν υἱὸν τοῦ θεοῦ καὶ παρα-
for them-   the   Son   –   of God   and   putting
selves

δειγματίζοντας. 7 γῆ γὰρ ἡ πιοῦσα
[him] to open shame.   For earth   –   drinking

τὸν ⁻ἐπ᾿ αὐτῆς ἐρχόμενον πολλάκις ὑετὸν
¹the   ²upon   ⁵it   ⁴coming   ³often   ²rain

καὶ τίκτουσα βοτάνην εὔθετον ἐκείνοις
and   bearing   fodder   suitable   for those

δι᾿ οὓς καὶ γεωργεῖται, μεταλαμβάνει
on ac-   whom   indeed   it is farmed,   receives
count of

εὐλογίας ἀπὸ τοῦ θεοῦ· 8 ἐκφέρουσα δὲ
blessing   from   –   God;   but bringing forth

ἀκάνθας καὶ τριβόλους ἀδόκιμος καὶ
thorns   and   thistles [it is]   disapproved   and

κατάρας ἐγγύς, ἧς τὸ τέλος εἰς καῦσιν.
²a curse   ¹near,   of which the   end [is] for   burning.

9 Πεπείσμεθα δὲ περὶ ὑμῶν, ἀγαπητοί,
But we have been   concerning   you,   beloved,
persuaded

τὰ κρείσσονα καὶ ἐχόμενα σωτηρίας, εἰ
the   better things   and   having   salvation,   if

καὶ οὕτως λαλοῦμεν. 10 οὐ γὰρ ἄδικος
indeed   ²so   ¹we speak.   For ²not   ³unjust

ὁ θεὸς ἐπιλαθέσθαι τοῦ ἔργου ὑμῶν
–   ¹God [is] to be forgetful   of the   work   of you

καὶ τῆς ἀγάπης ἧς ἐνεδείξασθε εἰς τὸ
and   of the   love   which   ye showed   to   the

ὄνομα αὐτοῦ, διακονήσαντες τοῖς ἁγίοις
name   of him,   having ministered   to the   saints

καὶ διακονοῦντες. 11 ἐπιθυμοῦμεν δὲ
and   ministering.   But we desire

ἕκαστον ὑμῶν τὴν αὐτὴν ἐνδείκνυσθαι
each one   of you   ²the   ³same   ¹to show

σπουδὴν πρὸς τὴν πληροφορίαν τῆς ἐλπίδος
eagerness   to   the   full assurance   of *the* hope

12 That ye be not sloth-
ful, but followers of them
who through faith and
patience inherit the promises.
13 For when God made
promise to Abraham, be-
cause he could swear by no
greater, he sware by him-
self,
14 Saying, Surely bless-
ing I will bless thee, and
multiplying I will multiply
thee.
15 And so, after he had
patiently endured, he ob-
tained the promise.
16 For men verily swear
by the greater: and an
oath for confirmation is
to them an end of all strife.
17 Wherein God, will-
ing more abundantly to
shew unto the heirs of
promise the immutability
of his counsel, confirmed
it by an oath:
18 That by two im-
mutable things, in which
it was impossible for God
to lie, we might have a
strong consolation, who
have fled for refuge to
lay hold upon the hope
set before us:
19 Which hope we have
as an anchor of the soul,
both sure and stedfast,
and which entereth into
that within the veil;
20 Whither the fore-
runner is for us entered,

ἄχρι τέλους, 12 ἵνα μὴ νωθροὶ γένησθε,
unto [the] end,   lest   dull ye become,

μιμηταὶ δὲ τῶν διὰ πίστεως καὶ μακρο-
but imitators of the through faith and long-
                              [ones]

θυμίας κληρονομούντων τὰς ἐπαγγελίας.
suffering inheriting   the   promises.

13 Τῷ γὰρ Ἀβραὰμ ἐπαγγειλάμενος ὁ
 -   For ²to Abraham ²making promise   -

θεός, ἐπεὶ κατ' οὐδενὸς εἶχεν μείζονος
¹God, since ²by ³no one ¹he had ⁴greater

ὀμόσαι, ὤμοσεν καθ' ἑαυτοῦ, 14 λέγων·
to swear, swore by himself,   saying:

εἰ μὴν εὐλογῶν εὐλογήσω σε καὶ πληθύνων
If surely blessing I will bless thee and multiplying

πληθυνῶ σε· 15 καὶ οὕτως μακροθυμήσας
I will multiply thee; and so   being longsuffering

ἐπέτυχεν τῆς ἐπαγγελίας. 16 ἄνθρωποι γὰρ
he obtained the   promise.   For men

κατὰ τοῦ μείζονος ὀμνύουσιν, καὶ πάσης
by the greater   swear,   and ⁶of all

αὐτοῖς ἀντιλογίας πέρας εἰς βεβαίωσιν ὁ
²[is] ⁴to ⁷contradiction ⁵an end ⁸for ⁹confirmation ¹the
 them

ὅρκος· 17 ἐν ᾧ περισσότερον βουλόμενος
²oath; wherein ³more abundantly ²resolving

ὁ θεὸς ἐπιδεῖξαι τοῖς κληρονόμοις τῆς
 - ¹God to show   to the   heirs   of the

ἐπαγγελίας τὸ ἀμετάθετον τῆς βουλῆς
promise   the unchangeableness of the resolve

αὐτοῦ ἐμεσίτευσεν ὅρκῳ, 18 ἵνα διὰ
of him interposed by an   in or- through
                     oath, der that

δύο πραγμάτων ἀμεταθέτων, ἐν οἷς ἀδύνατον
two ²things ¹unchangeable, in which impossible
                             [it was]

ψεύσασθαι θεόν, ἰσχυρὰν παράκλησιν ἔχωμεν
²to lie ¹God,ᵇ ²a strong ³consolation ¹we may
                                        have[,]

οἱ καταφυγόντες κρατῆσαι τῆς προκειμένης
the [ones] having fled to lay hold of the ²set before [us]

ἐλπίδος· 19 ἣν ὡς ἄγκυραν ἔχομεν τῆς
¹hope; which as an anchor we have of the

ψυχῆς ἀσφαλῆ τε καὶ βεβαίαν καὶ
soul ²safe ¹both and firm   and

εἰσερχομένην εἰς τὸ ἐσώτερον τοῦ κατα-
entering into the inner [side] of the veil,

πετάσματος, 20 ὅπου πρόδρομος ὑπὲρ ἡμῶν
where   a forerunner on   us
                            behalf of

even Jesus, made an high priest for ever after the order of Melchisedec.

εἰσῆλθεν   ᾽Ιησοῦς,   κατὰ   τὴν   τάξιν   Μελχισέ-
entered[,]   Jesus,   ⁶according   ⁷the   ⁸order   ⁹of Melchise-
                           to

δεκ   ἀρχιερεὺς   γενόμενος   εἰς   τὸν   αἰῶνα.
dec   ⁵a high priest   ¹becoming   ²unto   ³the   ⁴age.

CHAPTER 7

FOR this Melchisedec, king of Salem, priest of the most high God, who met Abraham returning from the slaughter of the kings, and blessed him;

2 To whom also Abraham gave a tenth part of all; first being by interpretation King of righteousness, and after that also King of Salem, which is, King of peace;

3 Without father, without mother, without descent, having neither beginning of days, nor end of life; but made like unto the Son of God; abideth a priest continually.

4 Now consider how great this man *was*, unto whom even the patriarch Abraham gave the tenth of the spoils.

5 And verily they that are of the sons of Levi, who receive the office of the priesthood, have a commandment to take tithes of the people according to the law, that is, of their brethren, though they come out of the loins of Abraham:

7 Οὗτος   γὰρ   ὁ   Μελχισέδεκ,   βασιλεὺς
For this   –   Melchisedec,   king

Σαλήμ,   ἱερεὺς   τοῦ   θεοῦ   τοῦ   ὑψίστου,
of Salem,   priest   –   ⁹God   ¹of the   ²most high,

ὁ   συναντήσας   ᾽Αβραὰμ   ὑποστρέφοντι   ἀπὸ
the [one] meeting   Abraham   returning   from

τῆς   κοπῆς   τῶν   βασιλέων   καὶ   εὐλογήσας
the   slaughter   of the   kings   and   blessing

αὐτόν,   2 ᾧ   καὶ   δεκάτην   ἀπὸ   πάντων
him,   to whom indeed   ³a tenth   ⁴from   ⁵all

ἐμέρισεν   ᾽Αβραάμ,   πρῶτον   μὲν   ἑρμηνευ-
²divided   ¹Abraham,   firstly   on one   being inter-
                           hand

όμενος   βασιλεὺς   δικαιοσύνης,   ἔπειτα   δὲ   καὶ
preted   King   of righteousness,   then   on the   also
                           other

βασιλεὺς   Σαλήμ,   ὅ   ἐστιν   βασιλεὺς   εἰρήνης,
King   of Salem,   which is   King   of peace,

3 ἀπάτωρ,   ἀμήτωρ,   ἀγενεαλόγητος,   μήτε
without father,   without mother,   without pedigree,   ⁹neither

ἀρχὴν   ἡμερῶν   μήτε   ζωῆς   τέλος   ἔχων,
³beginning   ⁴of days   ⁵nor   ⁷of life   ⁶end   ¹having,

ἀφωμοιωμένος   δὲ   τῷ   υἱῷ   τοῦ   θεοῦ,   μένει
but *having been* made   *to* the   Son   –   of God, remains
like

ἱερεὺς   εἰς   τὸ   διηνεκές.   4 Θεωρεῖτε   δὲ
a priest   in   *the*   perpetuity.   Now behold ye

πηλίκος   οὗτος,   ᾧ   δεκάτην   ᾽Αβραὰμ
how great   this man   to   ³a tenth   ²Abraham
                [was],   whom

ἔδωκεν   ἐκ   τῶν   ἀκροθινίων   ὁ   πατριάρχης.
⁴gave   ⁶of   ⁷the   ⁵spoils   ¹the   ²patriarch.

5 καὶ   οἱ   μὲν   ἐκ   τῶν   υἱῶν   Λευὶ   τὴν
And   ²the   ¹on one   ³of   ⁴the   ⁵sons   ⁶of Levi   ⁸the
      [ones]   hand

ἱερατείαν   λαμβάνοντες   ἐντολὴν   ἔχουσιν
⁹priesthood   ⁷receiving   ¹¹a commandment   ¹⁰have

ἀποδεκατοῦν   τὸν   λαὸν   κατὰ   τὸν   νόμον,
to take tithes   the   people   accord-   the   law,
from   ing to

τοῦτ᾽   ἔστιν   τοὺς   ἀδελφοὺς   αὐτῶν,   καίπερ
this   is   the   brothers   of them,   though

ἐξεληλυθότας   ἐκ   τῆς   ὀσφύος   ᾽Αβραάμ·
having come forth   out of   the   loin[s]   of Abraham;

6 But he whose descent is not counted from them received tithes of Abraham, and blessed him that had the promises.

7 And without all contradiction the less is blessed of the better.

8 And here men that die receive tithes; but there he *receiveth them*, of whom it is witnessed that he liveth.

9 And as I may so say, Levi also, who receiveth tithes, payed tithes in Abraham.

10 For he was yet in the loins of his father, when Melchisedec met him.

11 If therefore perfection were by the Levitical priesthood, (for under it the people received the law,) what further need *was there* that another priest should rise after the order of Melchisedec, and not be called after the order of Aaron?

12 For the priesthood being changed, there is made of necessity a change also of the law.

13 For he of whom these things are spoken pertaineth to another tribe, of which no man gave attendance at the altar.

6 ὁ δὲ μὴ γενεαλογούμενος ἐξ αὐτῶν
²the ¹on the not counting [his] pedigree from them
[one] other

δεδεκάτωκεν ᾿Αβραάμ, καὶ τὸν ἔχοντα
has tithed Abraham, and ²the [one] ³having

τὰς ἐπαγγελίας εὐλόγηκεν. 7 χωρὶς δὲ
⁴the ⁵promises ¹has blessed. And without

πάσης ἀντιλογίας τὸ ἔλαττον ὑπὸ τοῦ
all(any) contradiction the less ³by ²the

κρείττονος εὐλογεῖται. 8 καὶ ὧδε μὲν
⁴better ¹is blessed. And here on one
hand

δεκάτας ἀποθνήσκοντες ἄνθρωποι λαμβά-
⁴tithes ¹dying ²men ³re-

νουσιν, ἐκεῖ δὲ μαρτυρούμενος ὅτι ζῆ.
ceive, there on the being witnessed that he
other lives.

9 καὶ ὡς ἔπος εἰπεῖν, δι᾿ ᾿Αβραάμ
And as a word to say, through Abraham
=so to speak,

καὶ Λευὶς ὁ δεκάτας λαμβάνων δεδε-
indeed Levi ¹the [one] ²tithes ²receiving has

κάτωται· 10 ἔτι γὰρ ἐν τῇ ὀσφύι τοῦ
been tithed; for ²yet ³in ⁴the ⁵loin[s] ⁶of
the(his)

πατρὸς ἦν ὅτε συνήντησεν αὐτῷ Μελχισέ-
⁷father ¹he was ⁸when ¹⁰met ¹¹him ⁹Melchise-

δεκ. 11 Εἰ μὲν οὖν τελείωσις διὰ τῆς
dec. If – therefore perfection ³through ²the

Λευιτικῆς ἱερωσύνης ἦν, ὁ λαὸς γὰρ
⁴Levitical ⁵priestly office ¹was, ⁴the ⁵people ¹for

ἐπ᾿ αὐτῆς νενομοθέτηται, τίς ἔτι χρεία
²under* ³it has been furnished why yet need
with law,

κατὰ τὴν τάξιν Μελχισέδεκ ἕτερον
[was there ⁵the ⁶order ⁷of Melchisedec ¹another
for] ⁴accord-
ing to

ἀνίστασθαι ἱερέα καὶ οὐ κατὰ τὴν τάξιν
³to arise ²priest and not ³accord- ³the ⁴order
ing to

᾿Ααρὼν λέγεσθαι; 12 μετατιθεμένης γὰρ
⁵of Aaron ¹to be said(named)? for ³being changed

τῆς ἱερωσύνης ἐξ ἀνάγκης καὶ νόμου
¹the ²priestly office⁴ ⁶of ⁷necessity ⁶also ⁵of law

μετάθεσις γίνεται. 13 ἐφ᾿ ὃν γὰρ λέγεται
⁸a change ⁴there ²[he] ³with ⁴whom ¹For ¹is(are) said
occurs. respect to

ταῦτα, φυλῆς ἑτέρας μετέσχηκεν, ἀφ᾿
⁵these things, ²tribe ³of another ¹has partaken, from

ἧς οὐδεὶς προσέσχηκεν τῷ θυσιαστηρίῳ·
which no one has devoted himself to the altar;

* See note on ch. 9. 15.

14 For *it is* evident that our Lord sprang out of Juda; of which tribe Moses spake nothing concerning priesthood.

15 And it is yet far more evident: for that after the similitude of Melchisedec there ariseth another priest,

16 Who is made, not after the law of a carnal commandment, but after the power of an endless life.

17 For he testifieth, Thou *art* a priest for ever after the order of Melchisedec.

18 For there is verily a disannulling of the commandment going before for the weakness and unprofitableness thereof.

19 For the law made nothing perfect, but the bringing in of a better hope *did;* by the which we draw nigh unto God.

20 And inasmuch as not without an oath he *was made priest:*

21 (For those priests were made without an oath; but this with an oath by him that said unto him, The Lord sware and will not repent, Thou *art* a priest for ever after the order of Melchisedec:)

22 By so much was

14 πρόδηλον γὰρ ὅτι ἐξ Ἰούδα ἀνατέταλκεν
for it is perfectly clear   that out of   Juda   has risen

ὁ κύριος ἡμῶν, εἰς ἣν φυλὴν περὶ ἱερέων
the Lord   of us,   as to which   tribe   concerning priests

οὐδὲν Μωϋσῆς ἐλάλησεν. 15 καὶ περισ-
²nothing ¹Moses   ²spoke.   And   more

σότερον ἔτι κατάδηλόν ἐστιν, εἰ κατὰ
abundantly still   quite clear   is it,   if   accord-
                                          ing to

τὴν ὁμοιότητα Μελχισέδεκ ἀνίσταται ἱερεὺς
the   likeness   of Melchisedec   arises   priest

ἕτερος, 16 ὃς οὐ κατὰ νόμον ἐντολῆς
another,   who   not   accord- [the] law ²command-
                        ing to   ment

σαρκίνης γέγονεν ἀλλὰ κατὰ δύναμιν ζωῆς
¹of a fleshy has become but   accord- [the] power life
                                ing to

ἀκαταλύτου. 17 μαρτυρεῖται γὰρ ὅτι σὺ
of an indissoluble.   For it is witnessed   that Thou

ἱερεὺς εἰς τὸν αἰῶνα κατὰ τὴν τάξιν
a priest unto the age according to the order

Μελχισέδεκ. 18 ἀθέτησις μὲν γὰρ γίνεται
of Melchisedec.   ⁴an annul- ²on one ¹For   ⁵there
                    ment   hand   comes about

προαγούσης ἐντολῆς διὰ τὸ αὐτῆς ἀσθενὲς
of [the]   command- because ¹the ⁵of it ²weak[ness]
preceding   ment   of

καὶ ἀνωφελές, 19 οὐδὲν γὰρ ἐτελείωσεν
³and ⁴unprofitable[ness],   for ⁴nothing   ³perfected

ὁ νόμος, ἐπεισαγωγὴ δὲ κρείττονος ἐλπίδος,
¹the ²law,   ²a bringing in ¹on the of a better hope,
                              other

δι᾽ ἧς ἐγγίζομεν τῷ θεῷ. 20 καὶ καθ᾽
through we draw near   –   to God.   And in pro-
which

ὅσον οὐ χωρὶς ὁρκωμοσίας, — οἱ μὲν
portion not without oath-taking,   ³the ²on one
as   (they) hand

γὰρ χωρὶς ὁρκωμοσίας εἰσὶν ἱερεῖς
¹for ⁷without ⁸oath-taking ⁴are ⁶priests

γεγονότες, 21 ὁ δὲ μετὰ ὁρκωμοσίας διὰ
⁵having   the on the with oath-taking through
become,   (he) other

τοῦ λέγοντος πρὸς αὐτόν· ὤμοσεν κύριος,
the [one] saying to him: swore [The] Lord,

καὶ οὐ μεταμεληθήσεται· σὺ ἱερεὺς εἰς
and will not change [his] mind: Thou [art] a priest unto

τὸν αἰῶνα· — 22 κατὰ τοσοῦτο καὶ
the age;)   by   so much indeed

Jesus made a surety of a better testament.

23 And they truly were many priests, because they were not suffered to continue by reason of death:

24 But this *man*, because he continueth ever, hath an unchangeable priesthood.

25 Wherefore he is able also to save them to the uttermost that come unto God by him, seeing he ever liveth to make intercession for them.

26 For such an high priest became us, *who is* holy, harmless, undefiled, separate from sinners, and made higher than the heavens;

27 Who needeth not daily, as those high priests, to offer up sacrifice, first for his own sins, and then for the people's: for this he did once, when he offered up himself.

28 For the law maketh men high priests which have infirmity; but the word of the oath, which was since the law. *maketh* the Son, who is consecrated for evermore.

κρείττονος   διαθήκης   γέγονεν   ἔγγυος   Ἰησοῦς.
[4]of a better   [5]covenant   [2]has become   [3]surety   [1]Jesus.

23 καὶ   οἱ   μὲν   πλείονές   εἰσιν   γεγονότες
And   the   on one   [3]many   [1]are   [2]having become
    (they) hand

ἱερεῖς   διὰ   τὸ   θανάτῳ   κωλύεσθαι   παραμέ-
[4]priests because   *the*   [2]by death   [1]to be prevented   [3]to con-
of   = being prevented by death from continuing;

νειν·   24 ὁ   δὲ   διὰ   τὸ   μένειν   αὐτὸν   εἰς
tinue;   the   on   the because *the*   to remain   him[b]   unto
    (he)   other   of
    = because he remains

τὸν   αἰῶνα   ἀπαράβατον   ἔχει   τὴν   ἱερωσύνην·
the   age   [4]intransmissible   [1]has   [2]the   [3]priestly office;

25 ὅθεν   καὶ   σώζειν   εἰς   τὸ   παντελὲς
whence   indeed   [2]to save   [3]to   [4]the   [5]entire
    = entirely

δύναται   τοὺς   προσερχομένους   δι'   αὐτοῦ
[1]he is able   the [ones]   [1]approaching   [3]through   [4]him

τῷ   θεῷ,   πάντοτε   ζῶν   εἰς   τὸ   ἐντυγχάνειν
–   [2]to God,   always   living   *for the*   to intercede

ὑπὲρ   αὐτῶν.   26 τοιοῦτος   γὰρ   ἡμῖν   καὶ
on be-   them.   For [1]such   [5]to us [3]indeed
half of

ἔπρεπεν   ἀρχιερεύς,   ὅσιος,   ἄκακος,   ἀμίαντος,
[4]was   [2]a high priest,   holy,   harmless,   undefiled,
suitable

κεχωρισμένος   ἀπὸ   τῶν   ἁμαρτωλῶν,   καὶ
having been   from   –   sinners,   and
separated

ὑψηλότερος   τῶν   οὐρανῶν   γενόμενος·   27 ὃς
higher [than]   the   heavens   becoming;   who

οὐκ   ἔχει   καθ'   ἡμέραν   ἀνάγκην,   ὥσπερ
has not   [2]daily   [1]necessity,   as

οἱ   ἀρχιερεῖς,   πρότερον   ὑπὲρ   τῶν   ἰδίων
the   high priests,   firstly   on behalf of the(his)   own

ἁμαρτιῶν   θυσίας   ἀναφέρειν,   ἔπειτα   τῶν
sins   sacrifices   to offer up,   then   the [sins]

τοῦ   λαοῦ·   τοῦτο   γὰρ   ἐποίησεν   ἐφάπαξ
of the   people;   for this   he did   once for all

ἑαυτὸν   ἀνενέγκας.   28 ὁ   νόμος   γὰρ
himself   offering up.   the   For the law

ἀνθρώπους   καθίστησιν   ἀρχιερεῖς   ἔχοντας
[2]men   [1]appoints   [5]high priests   [3]having

ἀσθένειαν,   ὁ   λόγος   δὲ   τῆς   ὀρκωμοσίας
[4]weakness,   but the word   of the   oath-taking

τῆς   μετὰ   τὸν   νόμον   υἱὸν   εἰς   τὸν   αἰῶνα
–   after   the   law   a Son   [1]unto   [3]the   [4]age
    [appoints]

τετελειωμένον.
[1]having been perfected.

CHAPTER 8

NOW of the things which we have spoken *this is* the sum: We have such an high priest, who is set on the right hand of the throne of the Majesty in the heavens;

2 A minister of the sanctuary, and of the true tabernacle, which the Lord pitched, and not man.

3 For every high priest is ordained to offer gifts and sacrifices: wherefore *it is* of necessity that this man have somewhat also to offer.

4 For if he were on earth, he should not be a priest, seeing that there are priests that offer gifts according to the law:

5 Who serve unto the example and shadow of heavenly things, as Moses was admonished of God when he was about to make the tabernacle: for, See, saith he, *that* thou make all things according to the pattern shewed to thee in the mount.

6 But now hath he obtained a more excellent ministry, by how much also he is the mediator of a better covenant, which was established upon better promises.

7 For if that first *covenant* had been faultless, then should no place

8 Κεφάλαιον δὲ ἐπὶ τοῖς λεγομένοις,
Now a summary over(of) the things being said,

τοιοῦτον ἔχομεν ἀρχιερέα, ὃς ἐκάθισεν
²such ¹we have a high priest, who sat

ἐν δεξιᾷ τοῦ θρόνου τῆς μεγαλωσύνης
at [the] right of the throne of the greatness

ἐν τοῖς οὐρανοῖς, 2 τῶν ἁγίων λειτουργὸς
in the heavens, ²of the ³holy things ¹a minister

καὶ τῆς σκηνῆς τῆς ἀληθινῆς, ἣν ἔπηξεν
and of the ²tabernacle – ¹true, which ³erected

ὁ κύριος, οὐκ ἄνθρωπος. 3 Πᾶς γὰρ
¹the ²Lord, not man. For every

ἀρχιερεὺς εἰς τὸ προσφέρειν δῶρά τε
high priest for the ²to offer ⁴gifts ³both

καὶ θυσίας καθίσταται· ὅθεν ἀναγκαῖον
⁵and ⁶sacrifices ¹is appointed; whence [it is] necessary

ἔχειν τι καὶ τοῦτον ὃ προσενέγκῃ. 4 εἰ
³to have ⁴some- ²also ¹this which he may offer. If
thing [priest]

μὲν οὖν ἦν ἐπὶ γῆς, οὐδ᾽ ἂν ἦν ἱερεύς,
– there- he on earth, he would not be a priest,
fore were

ὄντων τῶν προσφερόντων κατὰ νόμον
[there] the [ones] offering³ ³according to ⁴law
being

τὰ δῶρα· 5 οἵτινες ὑποδείγματι καὶ σκιᾷ
¹the ²gifts; who ²an example ³and ⁴a
shadow

λατρεύουσιν τῶν ἐπουρανίων, καθὼς
²serve of the heavenly things, as

κεχρημάτισται Μωϋσῆς μέλλων ἐπιτελεῖν
¹has been warned ¹Moses being about to complete

τὴν σκηνήν· ὅρα γάρ φησιν, ποιήσεις
the tabernacle; for See[,] he says, thou shalt
make

πάντα κατὰ τὸν τύπον τὸν δειχθέντα
all according to the pattern – shown
things

σοι ἐν τῷ ὄρει· 6 νῦν δὲ διαφορωτέρας
to thee in the mount; but now ²a more excellent

τέτυχεν λειτουργίας, ὅσῳ καὶ κρείττονός
¹he has ministry, by so indeed ⁴of a better
obtained much

ἐστιν διαθήκης μεσίτης, ἥτις ἐπὶ κρείττοσιν
¹[as] ⁵covenant ³mediator, which ²on ³better
²he is

ἐπαγγελίαις νενομοθέτηται. 7 εἰ γὰρ ἡ
⁴promises ¹has been enacted. For if –

πρώτη ἐκείνη ἦν ἄμεμπτος, οὐκ ἂν
²first [covenant] ¹that was faultless, ²would not

have been sought for the second.

8 For finding fault with them, he saith, Behold, the days come, saith the Lord, when I will make a new covenant with the house of Israel and with the house of Judah:

9 Not according to the covenant that I made with their fathers in the day when I took them by the hand to lead them out of the land of Egypt; because they continued not in my covenant, and I regarded them not, saith the Lord.

10 For this is the covenant that I will make with the house of Israel after those days, saith the Lord; I will put my laws into their mind, and write them in their hearts: and I will be to them a God, and they shall be to me a people:

11 And they shall not teach every man his neighbour, and every man his brother, saying, Know the Lord: for all shall know me, from the least to the greatest.

12 For I will be merciful to their unrighteousness, and their sins and their

---

δευτέρας   ἐζητεῖτο   τόπος.   8 μεμφόμενος
⁶of(for) a   ³have been   ¹place.   finding fault [with]
second   sought

γὰρ   αὐτοὺς   λέγει·   ἰδοὺ ἡμέραι   ἔρχονται,
For   them   he says: Behold[,] days   are coming,

λέγει   κύριος,   καὶ   συντελέσω   ἐπὶ   τὸν
says [the] Lord,   and   I will effect   over   the

οἶκον Ἰσραὴλ   καὶ   ἐπὶ   τὸν οἶκον Ἰούδα
household of Israel   and   over   the household of Juda

διαθήκην   καινήν,   9 οὐ   κατὰ   τὴν   διαθήκην
covenant   a new,   not   accord-   the   covenant
ing to

ἣν   ἐποίησα   τοῖς   πατράσιν   αὐτῶν   ἐν
which   I made   with the   fathers   of them   in

ἡμέρᾳ   ἐπιλαβομένου   μου   τῆς   χειρὸς   αὐτῶν
[the] day   taking   meᵃ   the   hand   of them
=when I took

ἐξαγαγεῖν   αὐτοὺς   ἐκ   γῆς   Αἰγύπτου,   ὅτι
to lead forth   them   out   [the]   of Egypt,   because
of
land

αὐτοὶ   οὐκ   ἐνέμειναν   ἐν   τῇ   διαθήκῃ   μου,
they   continued not   in   in   the   covenant   of me,

κἀγὼ   ἠμέλησα   αὐτῶν,   λέγει κύριος.   10 ὅτι
and I   disregarded   them,   says [the] Lord.   Because

αὕτη   ἡ   διαθήκη   ἣν   διαθήσομαι   τῷ   οἴκῳ
this [is] the   covenant   which   I will   with   house-
covenant   the   hold

Ἰσραὴλ   μετὰ   τὰς   ἡμέρας   ἐκείνας,   λέγει
of Israel   after   those days,   says

κύριος,   διδοὺς   νόμους   μου   εἰς   τὴν   διάνοιαν
[the] Lord,   giving   laws   of me   into   the   mind

αὐτῶν,   καὶ   ἐπὶ   καρδίας   αὐτῶν   ἐπιγράψω
of them,   and   on   hearts   of them   I will inscribe

αὐτούς,   καὶ   ἔσομαι   αὐτοῖς   εἰς   θεὸν
them,   and   I will be   to them   for   God

καὶ   αὐτοὶ   ἔσονταί   μοι   εἰς   λαόν.   11 καὶ
and   they   shall be   to me   for   a people.   And

οὐ   μὴ   διδάξωσιν   ἕκαστος   τὸν   πολίτην
by no means   may they teach   each man   the   citizen

αὐτοῦ   καὶ   ἕκαστος   τὸν   ἀδελφὸν   αὐτοῦ,
of him   and   each man   the   brother   of him,

λέγων·   γνῶθι   τὸν   κύριον,   ὅτι   πάντες
saying: Know thou   the   Lord,   because   all

εἰδήσουσίν   με   ἀπὸ   μικροῦ   ἕως   μεγάλου
will know   me   from   little   to   great

αὐτῶν.   12 ὅτι   ἵλεως   ἔσομαι   ταῖς   ἀδικίαις
of them.   Because   merciful   I will be   to the unrighteous-
nesses

αὐτῶν,   καὶ   τῶν   ἁμαρτιῶν   αὐτῶν   οὐ   μὴ
of them,   and   the   sins   of them   by no means

iniquities will I remember no more.

13 In that he saith, A new *covenant*, he hath made the first old. Now that which decayeth and waxeth old *is* ready to vanish away.

μνησθῶ ἔτι. **13** ἐν τῷ λέγειν καινὴν
I may remember more. In the to say° 'new'
=When he says

πεπαλαίωκεν τὴν πρώτην· τὸ δὲ παλαι-
he has made old the first; and the thing being

ούμενον καὶ γηράσκον ἐγγὺς ἀφανισμοῦ.
made° old and growing aged [is] near vanishing.

CHAPTER 9

THEN verily the first *covenant* had also ordinances of divine service, and a worldly sanctuary.

2 For there was a tabernacle made; the first, wherein *was* the candlestick, and the table, and the shewbread; which is called the sanctuary.

3 And after the second veil, the tabernacle which is called the Holiest of all;

4 Which had the golden censer, and the ark of the covenant overlaid round about with gold, wherein *was* the golden pot that had manna, and Aaron's rod that budded, and the tables of the covenant;

5 And over it the cherubims of glory shadowing the mercyseat; of which we cannot now speak particularly.

6 Now when these things were thus ordained, the priests went always into the first tabernacle,

9 Εἶχε μὲν οὖν καὶ ἡ πρώτη δικαι-
⁵had ¹So then ⁶both ²the ³first ordin-
⁴[covenant]

ώματα λατρείας τό τε ἅγιον κοσμικόν.
ances of service ²the ¹and ⁴holy place ³worldly.

2 σκηνὴ γὰρ κατεσκευάσθη ἡ πρώτη,
For a tabernacle was prepared[,] the first,

ἐν ᾗ ἥ τε λυχνία καὶ ἡ τράπεζα καὶ
in which ²the ¹both lampstand and the table and
[were]

ἡ πρόθεσις τῶν ἄρτων, ἥτις λέγεται
the setting forth of the loaves, which is called

Ἅγια· **3** μετὰ δὲ τὸ δεύτερον καταπέτασμα
Holy; and after the second veil

σκηνὴ ἡ λεγομένη Ἅγια Ἁγίων, **4** χρυσοῦν
a taber- the *being* called Holy of Holies, ²a golden
nacle [one]

ἔχουσα θυμιατήριον καὶ τὴν κιβωτὸν τῆς
¹having altar and the · ark of the

διαθήκης περικεκαλυμμένην πάντοθεν χρυσίῳ,
covenant *having been* covered round on all sides with gold,

ἐν ᾗ στάμνος χρυσῆ ἔχουσα τὸ μάννα
in which pot a golden having the manna
[were]

καὶ ἡ ῥάβδος Ἀαρὼν ἡ βλαστήσασα
and the rod of Aaron – budded

καὶ αἱ πλάκες τῆς διαθήκης, **5** ὑπεράνω
and the tablets of the covenant, ²above

δὲ αὐτῆς Χερουβὶν δόξης κατασκιάζοντα
¹and it cherubim of glory overshadowing

τὸ ἱλαστήριον· περὶ ὧν οὐκ ἔστιν νῦν
the mercy-seat; concern- which there is not now
ing things [?time]

λέγειν κατὰ μέρος. **6** τούτων δὲ οὕτως
to speak in detail. These things now thus
=Now when these things had

κατεσκευασμένων εἰς μὲν τὴν πρώτην
having been prepared° ⁵into ¹on one ⁷the ⁸first
been thus prepared hand

σκηνὴν διὰ παντὸς εἰσίασιν οἱ ἱερεῖς
⁹tabernacle ⁴at all times ²go *in* ³the ¹priests

accomplishing the service of God.

7 But into the second *went* the high priest alone once every year, not without blood, which he offered for himself, and *for* the errors of the people:

8 The Holy Ghost this signifying, that the way into the holiest of all was not yet made manifest, while as the first tabernacle was yet standing:

9 Which *was* a figure for the time then present, in which were offered both gifts and sacrifices, that could not make him that did the service perfect, as pertaining to the conscience;

10 *Which stood* only in meats and drinks, and divers washings, and carnal ordinances, imposed *on them* until the time of reformation.

11 But Christ being come an high priest of good things to come, by a greater and more perfect tabernacle, not made with hands, that is to say, not of this building;

12 Neither by the blood of goats and calves, but by his own blood he entered in once into the holy place, having obtained eternal redemption *for us.*

τὰς λατρείας ἐπιτελοῦντες, 7 εἰς δὲ τὴν
[11]the [12]services [10]accomplishing, [2]into [1]on the [3]the
　　　　　　　　　　　　　　　　　　　　　　other

δευτέραν ἅπαξ τοῦ ἐνιαυτοῦ μόνος ὁ
[4]second [5]once [9]of(in) the [10]year [goes] [6]the
　　　　　　　　　　　　　　　　　[7]alone

ἀρχιερεύς, οὐ χωρὶς αἵματος ὃ προσφέρει
[6]high priest, not without blood which he offers

ὑπὲρ ἑαυτοῦ καὶ τῶν τοῦ λαοῦ ἀγνοημά-
on be- himself and [1]the [3]of the [4]people [2]ignor-
half of

των, 8 τοῦτο δηλοῦντος τοῦ πνεύματος
ances, [5]this [4]showing [1]the [3]Spirit

τοῦ ἁγίου, μήπω πεφανερῶσθαι τὴν τῶν
– [2]Holy,ᵃ [5]not yet [6]to have been [1]the [3]of the
　　　　　　　　　　　manifested

ἁγίων ὁδὸν ἔτι τῆς πρώτης σκηνῆς
[4]holies [2]way [10]still [7]the [8]first [9]tabernacle

ἐχούσηςᵃ στάσιν, 9 ἥτις παραβολὴ εἰς τὸν
[11]havingᵃ [12]standing, which [was] a parable for the

καιρὸν τὸν ἐνεστηκότα, καθ᾽ ἣν δῶρά
time – present, accord- which [2]gifts
　　　　　　　　　　　ing to

τε καὶ θυσίαι προσφέρονται μὴ δυνάμεναι
[1]both and sacrifices are being offered not being able

κατὰ συνείδησιν τελειῶσαι τὸν λατρεύοντα,
in respect conscience to perfect the [one] serving,
of

10 μόνον ἐπὶ βρώμασιν καὶ πόμασιν καὶ
only on foods and drinks and

διαφόροις βαπτισμοῖς, δικαιώματα σαρκὸς
various washings, ordinances of flesh

μέχρι καιροῦ διορθώσεως ἐπικείμενα.
[2]until [3]a time [4]of amendment [1]*being* imposed.

11 Χριστὸς δὲ παραγενόμενος ἀρχιερεὺς
But Christ having appeared a high priest

τῶν γενομένων ἀγαθῶν, διὰ τῆς μείζονος
[1]of the [3]having come [2]good things, through the greater
　　　about

καὶ τελειοτέρας σκηνῆς οὐ χειροποιήτου,
and more perfect tabernacle not made by hand,

τοῦτ᾽ ἔστιν οὐ ταύτης τῆς κτίσεως,
this is not of this – creation,

12 οὐδὲ δι᾽ αἵματος τράγων καὶ μόσχων,
nor through blood of goats and of calves,

διὰ δὲ τοῦ ἰδίου αἵματος εἰσῆλθεν ἐφάπαξ
but the own blood entered once for
through (his) all

εἰς τὰ ἅγια, αἰωνίαν λύτρωσιν εὑράμενος.
into the holies, eternal redemption having found.

13 For if the blood of bulls and of goats, and the ashes of an heifer sprinkling the unclean, sanctifieth to the purifying of the flesh:

14 How much more shall the blood of Christ, who through the eternal Spirit offered himself without spot to God, purge your conscience from dead works to serve the living God?

15 And for this cause he is the mediator of the new testament, that by means of death, for the redemption of the transgressions *that were* under the first testament, they which are called might receive the promise of eternal inheritance.

16 For where a testament *is*, there must also of necessity be the death of the testator.

17 For a testament *is* of force after men are dead: otherwise it is of no strength at all while the testator liveth.

18 Whereupon neither the first *testament* was dedicated without blood.

19 For when Moses had spoken every precept to all the people according to the law, he took the blood of calves and of

13 εἰ γὰρ τὸ αἷμα τράγων καὶ ταύρων
   For if   the   blood   of goats   and   *of* bulls

καὶ σποδὸς δαμάλεως ῥαντίζουσα τοὺς
and   ashes   of a heifer   sprinkling   the [ones]

κεκοινωμένους ἁγιάζει πρὸς τὴν τῆς
having been polluted   sanctifies   to   [1]the   [3]of the

σαρκὸς καθαρότητα, 14 πόσῳ μᾶλλον τὸ
[4]flesh   [2]cleanness,   by how much   more   the

αἷμα τοῦ Χριστοῦ, ὃς διὰ πνεύματος
blood   –   of Christ,   who through   [2]Spirit

αἰωνίου ἑαυτὸν προσήνεγκεν ἄμωμον τῷ
[1][the] eternal   [4]himself   [3]offered   unblemished   –

θεῷ, καθαριεῖ τὴν συνείδησιν ἡμῶν ἀπὸ
to God,   will cleanse   the   conscience   of us   from

νεκρῶν ἔργων εἰς τὸ λατρεύειν θεῷ
dead   works   *for*   *the*   to serve   [2]God

ζῶντι. 15 καὶ διὰ τοῦτο διαθήκης καινῆς
[1][the] living.   And   therefore   [4]covenant   [5]of a new

μεσίτης ἐστίν, ὅπως θανάτου γενομένου[a]
[2]mediator   [1]he is,   so as   death   having occurred[a]

εἰς ἀπολύτρωσιν τῶν ἐπὶ τῇ πρώτῃ
for   redemption   [1]of the   [2]under *   [4]the   [5]first

διαθήκῃ παραβάσεων τὴν ἐπαγγελίαν
[6]covenant   [7]transgressions   [10]the   [11]promise

λάβωσιν οἱ κεκλημένοι τῆς αἰωνίου
[9]may receive   [7]the   [8]having been   [12]of the   [13]eternal
           [ones]   called

κληρονομίας. 16 Ὅπου γὰρ διαθήκη,
[14]inheritance.   For where   [there is] a
                                covenant,

θάνατον ἀνάγκη φέρεσθαι τοῦ διαθεμένου·
[3][the] death   [1][there is]   [2]to be offered   [4]of the   [5]making
           necessity   [one]   covenant;

17 διαθήκη γὰρ ἐπὶ νεκροῖς βεβαία, ἐπεὶ
   for a covenant   over dead [? bodies] [is] firm,   since

μήποτε ἰσχύει ὅτε ζῇ ὁ διαθέμενος.
never   has it   when   [3]lives   [1]the   [2]making
        strength   [one]   covenant.

18 ὅθεν οὐδὲ ἡ πρώτη χωρὶς αἵματος
   Whence   neither   the first [covenant] [2]without   [3]blood

ἐγκεκαίνισται. 19 λαληθείσης γὰρ πάσης
[1]has been dedicated.   For [3]having been spoken   [1]every

ἐντολῆς κατὰ τὸν νόμον ὑπὸ Μωϋσέως
[2]command-   [9]accord-   [10]the   [11]law   [4]by   [5]Moses
ment[a]   ing to

παντὶ τῷ λαῷ, λαβὼν τὸ αἷμα τῶν
[6]to all   [7]the   [8]people,   taking   the   blood   of the

---

* It may seem strange to translate a preposition which means "on" or "over" by "under"; but ἐπί has the meaning of "during the time of" (see Mark 2. 26; I. Tim. 6. 13).

goats, with water, and scarlet wool, and hyssop, and sprinkled both the book, and all the people,

20 Saying, This *is* the blood of the testament which God hath enjoined unto you.

21 M o r e o v e r he sprinkled with blood both the tabernacle, and all the vessels of the ministry.

22 And almost all things are by the law purged with blood; and without shedding of blood is no remission.

23 *It was* therefore necessary that the patterns of things in the heavens should be purified with these; but the heavenly things themselves with better sacrifices than these.

24 For Christ is not entered into the holy places made with hands, *which are* the figures of the true; but into heaven itself, now to appear in the presence of God for us:

25 Nor yet that he should offer himself often, as the high priest entereth into the holy place every year with blood of others;

26 For then must he often have suffered since the foundation of the

μόσχων καὶ τῶν τράγων μετὰ ὕδατος
calves ãnd of the goats with water

καὶ ἐρίου κοκκίνου καὶ ὑσσώπου, αὐτό
and ²wool ¹scarlet and hyssop, ⁵it[self]

τε τὸ βιβλίον καὶ πάντα τὸν λαὸν
²both ³the ⁴scroll ⁶and ⁷all ⁸the ⁹people

ἐρράντισεν, 20 λέγων· τοῦτο τὸ αἷμα τῆς
¹he sprinkled, saying: This [is] the blood of the

διαθήκης ἧς ἐνετείλατο πρὸς ὑμᾶς ὁ
covenant which ²enjoined ³to ⁴you -

θεός. 21 καὶ τὴν σκηνὴν δὲ καὶ πάντα
¹God. ²both ³the ⁴tabernacle ¹And and all

τὰ σκεύη τῆς λειτουργίας τῷ αἵματι
the vessels of the service with the blood

ὁμοίως ἐρράντισεν. 22 καὶ σχεδὸν ἐν
likewise he sprinkled. And ⁴almost ⁷by

αἵματι πάντα καθαρίζεται κατὰ τὸν νόμον,
⁸blood ⁵all things ⁶is(are) cleansed ¹according to ²the ³law,

καὶ χωρὶς αἱματεκχυσίας οὐ γίνεται
and without bloodshedding there becomes no

ἄφεσις. 23 ἀνάγκη οὖν τὰ μὲν ὑπο-
remission. [There was] therefore ²[for] ¹on one ⁴ex-
necessity ³the hand

δείγματα τῶν ἐν τοῖς οὐρανοῖς τούτοις
amples of the in *the* heavens ²by these
things

καθαρίζεσθαι, αὐτὰ δὲ τὰ ἐπουράνια
¹to be cleansed, ⁵[them]- ¹on the ²[for] ⁴heavenly
selves other ³the things

κρείττοσιν θυσίαις παρὰ ταύτας. 24 οὐ
by better sacrifices than these. not

γὰρ εἰς χειροποίητα εἰσῆλθεν ἅγια Χριστός,
For into ²made by hand ⁴entered ¹holies ³Christ,

ἀντίτυπα τῶν ἀληθινῶν, ἀλλ' εἰς αὐτὸν
figures of the true things, but into ³[it]self

τὸν οὐρανόν, νῦν ἐμφανισθῆναι τῷ προσώπῳ
¹the ²heaven, now to appear in the presence

τοῦ θεοῦ ὑπὲρ ἡμῶν· 25 οὐδ' ἵνα πολ-
- of God on behalf of us; nor *in order* that often

λάκις προσφέρῃ ἑαυτόν, ὥσπερ ὁ ἀρχιερεὺς
he should offer himself, even as the high priest

εἰσέρχεται εἰς τὰ ἅγια κατ' ἐνιαυτὸν
enters into the holies year by year†

ἐν αἵματι ἀλλοτρίῳ, 26 ἐπεὶ ἔδει αὐτὸν
with blood belonging to others, since it behoved him

πολλάκις παθεῖν ἀπὸ καταβολῆς κόσμου·
often to suffer from [the] foundation of [the]
world;

world: but now once in the end of the world hath he appeared to put away sin by the sacrifice of himself.

27 And as it is appointed unto men once to die, but after this the judgment:

28 So Christ was once offered to bear the sins of many; and unto them that look for him shall he appear the second time without sin unto salvation.

νυνὶ δὲ ἅπαξ ἐπὶ συντελείᾳ τῶν αἰώνων
but now once at [the] completion of the ages

εἰς ἀθέτησιν τῆς ἁμαρτίας διὰ τῆς θυσίας
for annulment – of sin through the sacrifice

αὐτοῦ πεφανέρωται. 27 καὶ καθ' ὅσον
of him he has been manifested. And as

ἀπόκειται τοῖς ἀνθρώποις ἅπαξ ἀποθανεῖν,
it is reserved – to men once to die,

μετὰ δὲ τοῦτο κρίσις, 28 οὕτως καὶ
and after this judgment, so also

ὁ Χριστός, ἅπαξ προσενεχθεὶς εἰς τὸ
– Christ, once having been offered for the

πολλῶν ἀνενεγκεῖν ἁμαρτίας, ἐκ δευτέρου
³of many ¹to bear ²sins, ²a second [time]

χωρὶς ἁμαρτίας ὀφθήσεται τοῖς αὐτὸν
³without ⁴sin ¹will appear ⁵to the [ones] ⁷him

ἀπεκδεχομένοις εἰς σωτηρίαν.
⁶expecting for salvation.

CHAPTER 10

FOR the law having a shadow of good things to come, *and* not the very image of the things, can never with those sacrifices which they offered year by year continually make the comers thereunto perfect.

2 For then would they not have ceased to be offered? because that the worshippers once purged should have had no more conscience of sins.

3 But in those *sacrifices there is* a remembrance again *made* of sins every year.

4 For *it is* not possible that the blood of bulls and of goats should take away sins.

5 Wherefore when he cometh into the world, he saith, Sacrifice and offering thou wouldest not, but a body hast thou prepared me:

10 Σκιὰν γὰρ ἔχων ὁ νόμος τῶν
For ⁴a shadow ³having ¹the ²law of the

μελλόντων ἀγαθῶν, οὐκ αὐτὴν τὴν εἰκόνα
coming good things, not ³[it]self ¹the ²image

τῶν πραγμάτων, κατ' ἐνιαυτὸν ταῖς αὐταῖς
of the matters, ⁸every ⁹year† ³by the ⁴same

θυσίαις ἃς προσφέρουσιν εἰς τὸ διηνεκὲς
⁵sacrifices ⁶which ⁷they offer ¹⁰continually

οὐδέποτε δύναται τοὺς προσερχομένους
²never ¹can ¹²the [ones] ¹³approaching

τελειῶσαι· 2 ἐπεὶ οὐκ ἂν ἐπαύσαντο
¹¹to perfect; since would not they have ceased

προσφερόμεναι, διὰ τὸ μηδεμίαν ἔχειν
being offered, because of *the* ⁷no ⁵to have

ἔτι συνείδησιν ἁμαρτιῶν τοὺς λατρεύοντας
⁸still ⁶conscience ⁹of sins ¹the [ones] ²serving

ἅπαξ κεκαθαρισμένους; 3 ἀλλ' ἐν αὐταῖς
³once ⁴having been cleansed? But in them [there

ἀνάμνησις ἁμαρτιῶν κατ' ἐνιαυτόν·
is] a remembrance of sins yearly†;

4 ἀδύνατον γὰρ αἷμα ταύρων καὶ τράγων
for [it is] impossible blood of bulls and of goats

ἀφαιρεῖν ἁμαρτίας. 5 Διὸ εἰσερχόμενος εἰς
to take away sins. Wherefore entering into

τὸν κόσμον λέγει· θυσίαν καὶ προσφορὰν
the world he says: Sacrifice and offering

οὐκ ἠθέλησας, σῶμα δὲ κατηρτίσω μοι·
thou didst not wish, but a body thou didst prepare for me;

6 In burnt offerings and *sacrifices* for sin thou hast had no pleasure.

7 Then said I, Lo, I come (in the volume of the book it is written of me,) to do thy will, O God.

8 Above when he said, Sacrifice and offering and burnt offerings and *offering* for sin thou wouldest not, neither hadst pleasure *therein;* which are offered by the law;

9 Then said he, Lo, I come to do thy will, O God. He taketh away the first, that he may establish the second.

10 By the which will we are sanctified through the offering of the body of Jesus Christ once *for all.*

11 And every priest standeth daily ministering and offering oftentimes the same sacrifices, which can never take away sins:

12 But this man, after he had offered one sacrifice for sins for ever, sat down on the right hand of God;

13 From henceforth ex-

6 ὁλοκαυτώματα	καὶ	περὶ	ἁμαρτίας	οὐκ
burnt offerings	and	concerning [sacrifices]	sins	not

εὐδόκησας.	7 τότε	εἶπον·	ἰδοὺ	ἥκω,
thou wast well pleased [with].	Then	I said:	Behold	I have come,

ἐν	κεφαλίδι	βιβλίου	γέγραπται	περὶ ἐμοῦ,
in	a heading	of a scroll	it has been written	concerning me,

τοῦ	ποιῆσαι	ὁ θεὸς	τὸ	θέλημά σου.
–	to do[,]d	– God[,]*	the	will of thee.

8 ἀνώτερον	λέγων	ὅτι	θυσίας	καὶ προσ-
Above	saying	that	sacrifices	and offer-

φορὰς	καὶ	ὁλοκαυτώματα	καὶ περὶ	ἁμαρτίας
ings	and	burnt offerings	and [sacrifices] concerning	sins

οὐκ	ἠθέλησας	οὐδὲ	εὐδόκησας,	αἵτινες
thou didst not wish		nor	*thou* wast well pleased [with],	which

κατὰ	νόμον	προσφέρονται,	9 τότε	εἴρηκεν·
according to	law	are offered,	then	he *has* said:

ἰδοὺ	ἥκω	τοῦ	ποιῆσαι	τὸ	θέλημά σου.
Behold	I have come	–	to dod	the	will of thee.

ἀναιρεῖ	τὸ	πρῶτον	ἵνα	τὸ	δεύτερον
He takes away	the	first	in order that	the	second

στήσῃ·	10 ἐν	ᾧ	θελήματι	ἡγιασμένοι	ἐσμὲν
he may set up;		by which	will	²having been sanctified	¹we are

διὰ	τῆς	προσφορᾶς	τοῦ	σώματος	Ἰησοῦ
through	the	offering	of the	body	of Jesus

Χριστοῦ	ἐφάπαξ.	11 Καὶ	πᾶς μὲν	ἱερεὺς
Christ	once for all.	And	²every ¹on one hand	³priest

ἕστηκεν	καθ'	ἡμέραν	λειτουργῶν	καὶ	τὰς
stands		daily†	ministering	and	³the

αὐτὰς	πολλάκις	προσφέρων	θυσίας,	αἵτινες
⁴same	¹often	²offering	⁵sacrifices,	which

οὐδέποτε	δύνανται	περιελεῖν	ἁμαρτίας·	12 οὗτος
never	can	*to* take away	sins;	²this [priest]

δὲ	μίαν	ὑπὲρ	ἁμαρτιῶν	προσενέγκας
¹on the other	⁴one	⁶on behalf of	⁷sins	³having offered

θυσίαν	εἰς	τὸ	διηνεκὲς	ἐκάθισεν	ἐν	δεξιᾷ
⁵sacrifice	⁹in	–	¹⁰perpetuity	⁸sat	at [the] right [hand]

τοῦ	θεοῦ,	13 τὸ	λοιπὸν	ἐκδεχόμενος	ἕως
–	of God,	henceforth		expecting	till

* The "articular vocative"; *cf.* 1. 8, 9.

pecting till his enemies be made his footstool.

14 For by one offering he hath perfected for ever them that are sanctified.

15 *Whereof* the Holy Ghost also is a witness to us: for after that he had said before,

16 This *is* the covenant that I will make with them after those days, saith the Lord, I will put my laws into their hearts, and in their minds will I write them;

17 And their sins and iniquities will I remember no more.

18 Now where remission of these *is, there is* no more offering for sin.

19 Having therefore, brethren, boldness to enter into the holiest by the blood of Jesus,

20 By a new and living way, which he hath consecrated for us, through the veil, that is to say, his flesh;

21 And *having* an high priest over the house of God;

22 Let us draw near with a true heart in full assurance of faith, having our hearts sprinkled from an evil conscience, and our

τεθῶσιν οἱ ἐχθροὶ αὐτοῦ ὑποπόδιον τῶν
⁴are put ¹the ²enemies ³of him a footstool of the

ποδῶν αὐτοῦ. **14** μιᾷ γὰρ προσφορᾷ
feet of him. For by one offering

τετελείωκεν εἰς τὸ διηνεκὲς τοὺς ἁγιαζ-
he has perfected in – perpetuity the [ones] being

ομένους. **15** Μαρτυρεῖ δὲ ἡμῖν καὶ
sanctified. And ⁵witnesses ⁶to us ⁴indeed

τὸ πνεῦμα τὸ ἅγιον· μετὰ γὰρ τὸ
¹the ²Spirit – ³Holy; for after the

εἰρηκέναι· **16** αὕτη ἡ διαθήκη ἣν δια-
to have said: This [is] the covenant which I will
=having said:

θήσομαι πρὸς αὐτοὺς μετὰ τὰς ἡμέρας
covenant to them after – days

ἐκείνας, λέγει κύριος· διδοὺς νόμους μου
those, says [the] Lord: Giving laws of me

ἐπὶ καρδίας αὐτῶν, καὶ ἐπὶ τὴν διάνοιαν
on hearts of them, also on the mind

αὐτῶν ἐπιγράψω αὐτούς, **17** καὶ τῶν
of them I will inscribe them, and the

ἁμαρτιῶν αὐτῶν καὶ τῶν ἀνομιῶν αὐτῶν
sins of them and the iniquities of them

οὐ μὴ μνησθήσομαι ἔτι. **18** ὅπου δὲ
by no means I will remember still. Now where

ἄφεσις τούτων, οὐκέτι προσφορὰ περὶ
forgiveness of these [is], no longer offering concerning
[there is]

ἁμαρτίας.
sins.

19 Ἔχοντες οὖν, ἀδελφοί, παρρησίαν εἰς
Having therefore, brothers, confidence for

τὴν εἴσοδον τῶν ἁγίων ἐν τῷ αἵματι
the entering of the holies by the blood

Ἰησοῦ, **20** ἣν ἐνεκαίνισεν ἡμῖν ὁδὸν
of Jesus, which he dedicated for us[,] a way

πρόσφατον καὶ ζῶσαν διὰ τοῦ κατα-
fresh and living through the veil,

πετάσματος, τοῦτ' ἔστιν τῆς σαρκὸς αὐτοῦ,
this is the flesh of him,

21 καὶ ἱερέα μέγαν ἐπὶ τὸν οἶκον τοῦ
and priest a great over the household –

θεοῦ, **22** προσερχώμεθα μετὰ ἀληθινῆς
of God, let us approach with a true

καρδίας ἐν πληροφορίᾳ πίστεως, ῥεραν-
heart in full assurance of faith, having been

τισμένοι τὰς καρδίας ἀπὸ συνειδήσεως
sprinkled [as to] the hearts from ²conscience

bodies washed with pure water.

23 Let us hold fast the profession of *our* faith without wavering; (for he *is* faithful that promised;)

24 And let us consider one another to provoke unto love and to good works:

25 Not forsaking the assembling of ourselves together, as the manner of some *is;* but exhorting *one another:* and so much the more, as ye see the day approaching.

26 For if we sin wilfully after that we have received the knowledge of the truth, there remaineth no more sacrifice for sins,

27 But a certain fearful looking for of judgment and fiery indignation, which shall devour the adversaries.

28 He that despised Moses' law died without mercy under two or three witnesses:

29 Of how much sorer punishment, suppose ye, shall he be thought worthy, who hath trodden under foot the Son of God, and hath counted the blood of the covenant, wherewith he was sanctified, an unholy thing, and hath done despite unto the Spirit of grace?

πονηρᾶς   καὶ   λελουσμένοι   τὸ   σῶμα   ὕδατι
[1]an evil   and   having been bathed   [as to]   body   [2]water
                                        the

καθαρῷ·   23 κατέχωμεν   τὴν   ὁμολογίαν   τῆς
[1]in clean;   let us hold fast   the   confession   of the
                                                    (our)

ἐλπίδος   ἀκλινῆ,   πιστὸς   γὰρ   ὁ   ἐπαγ-
hope   unyieldingly,   for faithful [is]   the [one] pro-

γειλάμενος,   24 καὶ   κατανοῶμεν   ἀλλήλους
mising,   and   let us consider   one another

εἰς   παροξυσμὸν   ἀγάπης   καὶ   καλῶν   ἔργων,
to   incitement   of love   and   of good   works,

25 μὴ   ἐγκαταλείποντες   τὴν   ἐπισυναγωγὴν
not   forsaking   the   coming together

ἑαυτῶν,   καθὼς   ἔθος   τισίν,   ἀλλὰ   παρα-
of [our]selves,   as   custom   with some [is], but   ex-

καλοῦντες,   καὶ   τοσούτῳ   μᾶλλον   ὅσῳ
horting,   and   by so much   more   as

βλέπετε   ἐγγίζουσαν   τὴν   ἡμέραν.   26 Ἑκουσίως
ye see   [2]drawing near   [1]the   [2]day.   wilfully

γὰρ   ἁμαρτανόντων   ἡμῶν   μετὰ   τὸ   λαβεῖν
For   sinning   us[a]   after   the   to receive
        =when we sin wilfully   =receiving

τὴν   ἐπίγνωσιν   τῆς   ἀληθείας,   οὐκέτι   περὶ
the   full knowledge   of the   truth,   [5]no more   [2]con-
                                                cerning

ἁμαρτιῶν   ἀπολείπεται   θυσία,   27 φοβερὰ
[3]sins   [4]remains   [1]a sacrifice,   [3]fearful

δέ   τις   ἐκδοχὴ   κρίσεως   καὶ   πυρὸς   ζῆλος
[1]but   [2]some   expectation of judgment   and   [2]of fire   [1]zeal

ἐσθίειν   μέλλοντος   τοὺς   ὑπεναντίους.
[4]to consume   [5]being about   the   adversaries.

28 ἀθετήσας   τις   νόμον   Μωϋσέως   χωρὶς
[2]Disregarding   [1]anyone   [3]law   [4]of Moses   [5]without

οἰκτιρμῶν   ἐπὶ   δυσὶν   ἢ   τρισὶν   μάρτυσιν
[7]compassions   [8]on [the   [9]two   [10]or   [11]three   [11]witnesses
                word of]

ἀποθνήσκει·   29 πόσῳ   δοκεῖτε   χείρονος
[6]dies;   by how much   think ye   [2]of worse

ἀξιωθήσεται   τιμωρίας   ὁ   τὸν   υἱὸν   τοῦ
[1]will be thought   [3]punishment   [4]the   [5]the   [7]Son   –
worthy   [one]

θεοῦ   καταπατήσας   καὶ   τὸ   αἷμα   τῆς
[6]of God   [5]having trampled   and   [2]the   [4]blood   [5]of the
            [on]

διαθήκης   κοινὸν   ἡγησάμενος,   ἐν   ᾧ   ἡγιάσθη,
[6]covenant   [2]common   [1]having   by which   he was
                deemed,   sanctified,

καὶ   τὸ   πνεῦμα   τῆς   χάριτος   ἐνυβρίσας.
and   [2]the   [3]Spirit   –   [4]of grace   [1]having insulted.

30 For we know him that hath said, Vengeance *belongeth* unto me, I will recompense, saith the Lord. And again, The Lord shall judge his people.

31 *It is* a fearful thing to fall into the hands of the living God.

32 But call to remembrance the former days, in which, after ye were illuminated, ye endured a great fight of afflictions;

33 Partly, whilst ye were made a gazingstock both by reproaches and afflictions; and partly, whilst ye became companions of them that were so used.

34 For ye had compassion of me in my bonds, and took joyfully the spoiling of your goods, knowing in yourselves that ye have in heaven a better and an enduring substance.

35 Cast not away therefore your confidence, which hath great recompence of reward.

36 For ye have need of patience, that, after ye have done the will of God, ye might receive the promise.

37 For yet a little while, and he that shall come will come, and will not tarry.

38 Now the just shall live by faith: but if *any*

---

30 οἴδαμεν   γὰρ   τὸν   εἰπόντα·   ἐμοὶ
For we know   the [one]   having said: To me
= Vengeance

ἐκδίκησις,   ἐγὼ   ἀνταποδώσω   καὶ   πάλιν·
vengeance,°   I   will repay;   and   again:
is mine,

κρινεῖ   κύριος   τὸν   λαὸν   αὐτοῦ.   31 φοβερὸν
³will judge [¹The]   the   people   of him.   A fearful
Lord   thing [it is]

τὸ   ἐμπεσεῖν   εἰς   χεῖρας   θεοῦ   ζῶντος.
the   to fall *in*   into   [the] hands   ²God   ¹of a living.

32 Ἀναμιμνήσκεσθε   δὲ   τὰς   πρότερον   ἡμέρας,
But remember ye   the   ²formerly   ¹days,

ἐν   αἷς   φωτισθέντες   πολλὴν   ἄθλησιν
in   which   being enlightened   ²a much(great)   ³struggle

ὑπεμείνατε   παθημάτων,   33 τοῦτο   μὲν
¹ye endured   ⁴of sufferings,   this on one hand

ὀνειδισμοῖς   τε   καὶ   θλίψεσιν   θεατριζόμενοι,
³to reproaches   ²both   ⁴and   ⁵to afflictions   ¹being exposed,

τοῦτο   δὲ   κοινωνοὶ   τῶν   οὕτως   ἀναστρεφ-
this   on the   ²sharers   ³of the   ⁴thus   ⁴liv-
         other   [ones]

ομένων   γενηθέντες.   34 καὶ   γὰρ   τοῖς
ing   ¹having become.   For indeed   in *the*

δεσμίοις   συνεπαθήσατε,   καὶ   τὴν   ἁρπαγὴν
bonds   ye suffered together,   and   ⁴the   ⁵seizure

τῶν   ὑπαρχόντων   ὑμῶν   μετὰ   χαρᾶς
⁶of the   ⁷possessions   ⁸of you   ²with   ³joy

προσεδέξασθε,   γινώσκοντες   ἔχειν   ἑαυτοὺς
¹ye accepted,   knowing   ²to have   ¹[your]selves

κρείσσονα   ὕπαρξιν   καὶ   μένουσαν.   35 Μὴ
³a better   ⁴possession   ⁵and   ⁶remaining.   not

ἀποβάλητε   οὖν   τὴν   παρρησίαν   ὑμῶν,   ἥτις
Cast ye away   therefore   the   confidence   of you,   which

ἔχει   μεγάλην   μισθαποδοσίαν.   36 ὑπομονῆς
has   a great   recompence.   ²of endurance

γὰρ   ἔχετε   χρείαν   ἵνα   τὸ   θέλημα   τοῦ
For   ¹ye have   ³need   in order   ⁵the   ⁶will   –
                        that

θεοῦ   ποιήσαντες   κομίσησθε   τὴν   ἐπαγγελίαν.
⁴of God   ¹having   ye may obtain   the   promise.
         done

37 ἔτι   γὰρ   μικρὸν   ὅσον   ὅσον,   ὁ   ἐρχόμενος
For yet   ³little   ¹a very,*   the   coming [one]

ἥξει   καὶ   οὐ   χρονίσει·   38 ὁ   δὲ   δίκαιός
will come   and   will not   delay;   but the   just man

μου   ἐκ   πίστεως   ζήσεται,   καὶ   ἐὰν   ὑπο-
of me   by   faith   will live,   and   if   he

---

* Cf. our "so so".

man draw back, my soul shall have no pleasure in him.

39 But we are not of them who draw back unto perdition ; but of them that believe to the saving of the soul.

στείληται,   οὐκ   εὐδοκεῖ   ἡ   ψυχή   μου
withdraws,   -   ⁴is not well pleased   ¹the   ²soul   ³of me

ἐν αὐτῷ. 39 ἡμεῖς δὲ οὐκ ἐσμὲν ὑποστολῆς
in   him.   39   But we   are not   of withdrawal

εἰς   ἀπώλειαν,   ἀλλὰ   πίστεως   εἰς   περιποίησιν
to   destruction,   but   of faith   to   possession

ψυχῆς.
of soul.

CHAPTER 11

NOW faith is the substance of things hoped for, the evidence of things not seen.

2 For by it the elders obtained a good report.

3 Through faith we understand that the worlds were framed by the word of God, so that things which are seen were not made of things which do appear.

4 By faith Abel offered unto God a more excellent sacrifice than Cain, by which he obtained witness that he was righteous, God testifying of his gifts: and by it he being dead yet speaketh.

5 By faith Enoch was translated that he should not see death; and was not found, because God had translated him: for before his translation he had this testimony, that he pleased God.

6 But without faith *it is* impossible to please *him:* for he that cometh to God

11 Ἔστιν   δὲ   πίστις   ἐλπιζομένων   ὑπό-
   Now ²is   ¹faith   ⁴of things being hoped   ⁵[the]

στασις,   πραγμάτων   ἔλεγχος   οὐ   βλεπομένων.
reality,   ²of things   ¹[the] proof   not   being seen.

2 ἐν   ταύτῃ   γὰρ   ἐμαρτυρήθησαν   οἱ
   by   this   For   ²obtained witness   ¹the

πρεσβύτεροι. 3 Πίστει νοοῦμεν κατηρτίσθαι
²elders.   By faith   we understand   ⁵to have been
                                     adjusted

τοὺς   αἰῶνας   ῥήματι   θεοῦ,   εἰς   τὸ   μὴ
¹the   ²ages   by a word   of God,   so as†   ³not

ἐκ   φαινομένων   τὸ   βλεπόμενον   γεγονέναι.
⁵out   ⁶things   ¹the   ²being seen   ⁴to have
of   appearing   thing   become.

4 Πίστει   πλείονα   θυσίαν   Ἄβελ   παρὰ
   By faith   ⁴a greater(? better)   ⁵sacrifice   ¹Abel   ²than

Κάϊν   προσήνεγκεν   τῷ   θεῷ,   δι'   ἧς
⁷Cain   ⁶offered   -   ³to God, through which

ἐμαρτυρήθη εἶναι δίκαιος, μαρτυροῦντος ἐπὶ
he obtained   to be   just,   ²witnessing   ³over
witness

τοῖς   δώροις   αὐτοῦ   τοῦ   θεοῦ,   καὶ   δι'
⁴the   ⁵gifts   ⁶of him   -   ¹God,¹   and through

αὐτῆς   ἀποθανὼν   ἔτι   λαλεῖ.   5 Πίστει
it   having died   still   he speaks.   By faith

Ἐνὼχ   μετετέθη   τοῦ   μὴ   ἰδεῖν   θάνατον,
Enoch   was removed   -   not   to seeᵈ   death,

καὶ   οὐχ   ηὑρίσκετο   διότι   μετέθηκεν   αὐτὸν
and   was not found   because   ²removed   ³him

ὁ   θεός.   6 πρὸ   γὰρ   τῆς   μεταθέσεως
-    ¹God.   For before   the(his)   removal

μεμαρτύρηται εὐαρεστηκέναι τῷ θεῷ· χωρὶς
he has obtained   to have been well-   to God; ²without
witness   pleasing

δὲ   πίστεως   ἀδύνατον   εὐαρεστῆσαι·   πιστεῦσαι
¹but faith [it is] impossible to be well-pleasing [to God]; ⁴to believe

γὰρ   δεῖ   τὸν   προσερχόμενον   [τῷ]   θεῷ,
¹for   ²it   ³the [one]   ⁴approaching   -   ⁵to God,
   behoves

must believe that he is, and *that* he is a rewarder of them that diligently seek him.

7 By faith Noah, being warned of God of things not seen as yet, moved with fear, prepared an ark to the saving of his house; by the which he condemned the world, and became heir of the righteousness which is by faith.

8 By faith Abraham, when he was called to go out into a place which he should after receive for an inheritance, obeyed; and he went out, not knowing whither he went.

9 By faith he sojourned in the land of promise, as *in* a strange country, dwelling in tabernacles with Isaac and Jacob, the heirs with him of the same promise:

10 For he looked for a city which hath foundations, whose builder and maker *is* God.

11 Through faith also Sara herself received strength to conceive seed, and was delivered of a child when she was past age, because she judged him faithful who had promised.

12 Therefore sprang there even of one, and him as good as dead, *so many* as the stars of the

ὅτι   ἔστιν   καὶ   τοῖς   ἐκζητοῦσιν   αὐτὸν
that   he is   and ²to the [ones] ⁴seeking ⁶out   ⁵him

μισθαποδότης   γίνεται.   7 Πίστει   χρηματισ-
²a rewarder   ¹becomes.   By faith   ²having been
                                            warned [by

θεὶς   Νῶε   περὶ   τῶν   μηδέπω   βλεπομένων,
God*]   ¹Noah concerning the things not yet   being seen,

εὐλαβηθεὶς   κατεσκεύασεν   κιβωτὸν   εἰς
being devout   prepared   an ark   for

σωτηρίαν   τοῦ   οἴκου   αὐτοῦ,   δι᾽   ἧς
[the] salvation of the   household   of him,   through which

κατέκρινεν   τὸν   κόσμον,   καὶ   τῆς   κατὰ
he condemned   the   world,   and   ²of the ³accord-
                                                  ing to

πίστιν   δικαιοσύνης   ἐγένετο   κληρονόμος.
⁵faith   ⁴righteousness   ¹became   ²heir.

8 Πίστει   καλούμενος   Ἀβραὰμ   ὑπήκουσεν
By faith   ²being called   ¹Abraham   ¹¹obeyed

ἐξελθεῖν   εἰς   τόπον   ὃν   ἤμελλεν   λαμβάνειν
³to go forth ⁴to   ⁵a place ⁶which ⁷he was about ⁸to receive

εἰς   κληρονομίαν,   καὶ   ἐξῆλθεν   μὴ   ἐπιστάμε-
⁹for   ¹⁰an inheritance,   and   went forth   not   understand-

νος   ποῦ   ἔρχεται.   9 Πίστει   παρῴκησεν
ing   where   he goes(went).   By faith   he sojourned

εἰς   γῆν   τῆς   ἐπαγγελίας   ὡς   ἀλλοτρίαν,
in   a land   –   of promise   as   a foreigner,

ἐν   σκηναῖς   κατοικήσας,   μετὰ   Ἰσαὰκ   καὶ
in   tents   dwelling,   with   Isaac   and

Ἰακὼβ   τῶν   συγκληρονόμων   τῆς   ἐπαγ-
Jacob   the   co-heirs   of the   ²pro-

γελίας   τῆς   αὐτῆς·   10 ἐξεδέχετο   γὰρ   τὴν
mise   –   ¹same;   for he expected   the

τοὺς   θεμελίους   ἔχουσαν   πόλιν,   ἧς   τεχνίτης
²the   ⁴foundations   ²having   ¹city, of which   ³artificer

καὶ   δημιουργὸς   ὁ   θεός.   11 Πίστει   καὶ
⁴and   ⁵maker   –   ¹God ²[is].   By faith   also

αὐτὴ   Σάρρα   δύναμιν   εἰς   καταβολὴν
²[her]self   ¹Sara   ⁴power   ⁵for   ⁶conception

σπέρματος   ἔλαβεν   καὶ   παρὰ   καιρὸν   ἡλικίας,
⁷of seed   ³received   even   beyond   time   of age,

ἐπεὶ   πιστὸν   ἡγήσατο   τὸν   ἐπαγγειλάμενον.
since   ²faithful   ¹she deemed the [one]   having promised.

12 διὸ   καὶ   ἀφ᾽   ἑνὸς   ἐγενήθησαν,   καὶ
Wherefore indeed   from   one   there became,   and

ταῦτα   νενεκρωμένου,   καθὼς   τὰ   ἄστρα
that too†   [he] having died,ª   as   the   stars

---

* This must be understood, as the word always (or at least generally) has reference to a divine communication.

sky in multitude, and as the sand which is by the sea shore innumerable.

13 These all died in faith, not having received the promises, but having seen them afar off, and were persuaded of *them*, and embraced *them*, and confessed that they were strangers and pilgrims on the earth.

14 For they that say such things declare plainly that they seek a country.

15 And truly, if they had been mindful of that *country* from whence they came out, they might have had opportunity to have returned.

16 But now they desire a better *country*, that is, an heavenly: wherefore God is not ashamed to be called their God: for he hath prepared for them a city.

17 By faith Abraham, when he was tried, offered up Isaac: and he that had received the promises offered up his only begotten *son*,

18 Of whom it was said, That in Isaac shall thy seed be called:

19 Accounting that God *was* able to raise *him* up, even from the dead; from whence also he received him in a figure.

20 By faith Isaac blessed

τοῦ οὐρανοῦ τῷ πλήθει καὶ ὡς ἡ ἄμμος
of *the* heaven – in multitude and as the ³sand

ἡ παρὰ τὸ χεῖλος τῆς θαλάσσης ἡ
– ³by ⁴the ⁵lip ⁶of the ⁷sea –

ἀναρίθμητος. 13 Κατὰ πίστιν ἀπέθανον
¹innumerable. ⁴By way of ⁵faith ³died

οὗτοι πάντες, μὴ κομισάμενοι τὰς ἐπαγ-
¹these ²all, not having obtained the pro-

γελίας, ἀλλὰ πόρρωθεν αὐτὰς ἰδόντες καὶ
mises, but ⁵from afar ⁴them ¹seeing ²and

ἀσπασάμενοι, καὶ ὁμολογήσαντες ὅτι ξένοι
³greeting, and confessing that ²strangers

καὶ παρεπίδημοί εἰσιν ἐπὶ τῆς γῆς.
²and ⁴sojourners ¹they are on the earth
(? land).

14 οἱ γὰρ τοιαῦτα λέγοντες ἐμφανίζουσιν
For the [ones] ²such things ¹saying make manifest

ὅτι πατρίδα ἐπιζητοῦσιν. 15 καὶ εἰ μὲν
that ²a fatherland ¹they seek. And if on one hand

ἐκείνης ἐμνημόνευον ἀφ᾽ ἧς ἐξέβησαν,
²that ¹they remembered from which they came out,

εἶχον ἂν καιρὸν ἀνακάμψαι· 16 νῦν
they might have had time(opportunity) to return; now

δὲ κρείττονος ὀρέγονται, τοῦτ᾽ ἔστιν
on the ²a better ¹they aspire to, this is
other

ἐπουρανίου. διὸ οὐκ ἐπαισχύνεται αὐτοὺς
a heavenly. Wherefore ²is not ashamed [of] ³them

ὁ θεὸς θεὸς ἐπικαλεῖσθαι αὐτῶν· ἡτοίμασεν
– ¹God ⁵God ⁴to be called ⁶of them; ³he prepared

γὰρ αὐτοῖς πόλιν. 17 Πίστει προσενήνοχεν
¹for for them a city. By faith ¹has offered up

Ἀβραὰμ τὸν Ἰσαὰκ πειραζόμενος, καὶ
¹Abraham – ⁴Isaac ²being tested, and

τὸν μονογενῆ προσέφερεν ὁ τὰς ἐπαγγελίας
⁶the ⁷only begotten ⁵was ¹the ²the ⁴promises
(his) offering up [one]

ἀναδεξάμενος, 18 πρὸς ὃν ἐλαλήθη ὅτι
³having undertaken, as to whom it was spoken[,] –

ἐν Ἰσαὰκ κληθήσεταί σοι σπέρμα,
In Isaac shall be called to thee a seed,°
=thy seed,

19 λογισάμενος ὅτι καὶ ἐκ νεκρῶν ἐγείρειν
reckoning that ⁴even ⁶from ⁷dead ⁵to raise

δυνατὸς ὁ θεός· ὅθεν αὐτὸν καὶ ἐν
²[was] ³able – ¹God; whence ⁵him ¹indeed ²in

παραβολῇ ἐκομίσατο. 20 Πίστει καὶ περὶ
³a parable ⁴he obtained. By faith also ⁶con-
cerning

Jacob and Esau concerning things to come.

21 By faith Jacob, when he was a dying, blessed both the sons of Joseph; and worshipped, *leaning* upon the top of his staff.

22 By faith Joseph, when he died, made mention of the departing of the children of Israel; and gave commandment concerning his bones.

23 By faith Moses, when he was born, was hid three months of his parents, because they saw *he was* a proper child; and they were not afraid of the king's commandment.

24 By faith Moses, when he was come to years, refused to be called the son of Pharaoh's daughter;

25 Choosing rather to suffer affliction with the people of God, than to enjoy the pleasures of sin for a season;

26 Esteeming the reproach of Christ greater riches than the treasures in Egypt: for he had respect unto the recompence of the reward.

27 By faith he forsook Egypt, not fearing the wrath of the king: for he endured, as seeing him who is invisible.

28 Through faith he kept the passover, and the sprinkling of blood,

μελλόντων εὐλόγησεν ’Ισαὰκ τὸν ’Ιακὼβ
[7]coming things [8]blessed [1]Isaac – [2]Jacob

καὶ τὸν ’Ησαῦ. 21 Πίστει ’Ιακὼβ
[6]and – [5]Esau. By faith Jacob

ἀποθνήσκων ἕκαστον τῶν υἱῶν ’Ιωσὴφ
dying [2]each [3]of the [4]sons [5]of Joseph

εὐλόγησεν, καὶ προσεκύνησεν ἐπὶ τὸ ἄκρον
[1]blessed, and worshipped on the tip

τῆς ῥάβδου αὐτοῦ. 22 Πίστει ’Ιωσὴφ
of the rod of him. By faith Joseph

τελευτῶν περὶ τῆς ἐξόδου τῶν υἱῶν
dying [2]concerning [3]the [4]exodus [5]of the [6]sons

’Ισραὴλ ἐμνημόνευσεν καὶ περὶ τῶν
[7]of Israel [1]remembered and [2]concerning [3]the

ὀστέων αὐτοῦ ἐνετείλατο. 23 Πίστει
[4]bones [5]of him [1]gave orders. By faith

Μωϋσῆς γεννηθεὶς ἐκρύβη τρίμηνον ὑπὸ
Moses having been born was hidden three months by

τῶν πατέρων αὐτοῦ, διότι εἶδον ἀστεῖον
the parents of him, because they saw [2][to be] fine

τὸ παιδίον, καὶ οὐκ ἐφοβήθησαν τὸ
[1]the [2]child, and they did not fear the

διάταγμα τοῦ βασιλέως. 24 Πίστει Μωϋσῆς
decree of the king. By faith Moses

μέγας γενόμενος ἠρνήσατο λέγεσθαι υἱὸς
[2]great [1]having become denied to be said(called) son

θυγατρὸς Φαραώ, 25 μᾶλλον ἑλόμενος
of [the] daughter of Pharaoh, rather choosing

συγκακουχεῖσθαι τῷ λαῷ τοῦ θεοῦ ἢ
to be ill treated with the people – of God than

πρόσκαιρον ἔχειν ἁμαρτίας ἀπόλαυσιν,
for a time to have [2]of sin [1]enjoyment,

26 μείζονα πλοῦτον ἡγησάμενος τῶν
[5]greater [6]riches [1]deeming [7][than] [8]the

Αἰγύπτου θησαυρῶν τὸν ὀνειδισμὸν τοῦ
[10]of Egypt [9]treasures [3]the [2]reproach –

Χριστοῦ· ἀπέβλεπεν γὰρ εἰς τὴν μισθ-
[4]of Christ; for he was looking away to the recom-

αποδοσίαν. 27 Πίστει κατέλιπεν Αἴγυπτον,
pence. By faith he left Egypt,

μὴ φοβηθεὶς τὸν θυμὸν τοῦ βασιλέως·
not fearing the anger of the king;

τὸν γὰρ ἀόρατον ὡς ὁρῶν ἐκαρτέρησεν.
for [2]the [4]unseen [one] [3]as [5]seeing [1]he endured.

28 Πίστει πεποίηκεν τὸ πάσχα καὶ τὴν
By faith he *has* made the passover and the

πρόσχυσιν τοῦ αἵματος, ἵνα μὴ ὁ
affusion of the blood, lest the

lest he that destroyed the
firstborn should touch
them.

29 By faith they passed
through the Red sea as
by dry *land:* which the
Egyptians assaying to do
were drowned.

30 By faith the walls of
Jericho fell down, after
they were compassed
about seven days.

31 By faith the harlot
Rahab perished not with
them that believed not,
when she had received the
spies with peace.

32 And what shall I
more say? for the time
would fail me to tell of
Gedeon, and *of* Barak,
and *of* Samson, and *of*
Jephthae; *of* David also,
and Samuel, and *of* the
prophets:

33 Who through faith
subdued kingdoms,
wrought righteousness, obtained promises, stopped
the mouths of lions,

34 Quenched the vio-
lence of fire, escaped the
edge of the sword, out
of weakness were made
strong, waxed valiant in
fight, turned to flight the
armies of the aliens.

35 Women received
their dead raised to life
again: and others were
tortured, not accepting deliverance; that they might
obtain a better resur-
rection:

36 And others had trial

ὀλεθρεύων τὰ πρωτότοκα θίγῃ αὐτῶν.
[one] destroying ²the ²firstborn*s* ¹should ⁴of them.
touch

29 Πίστει διέβησαν τὴν ἐρυθρὰν θάλασσαν
By faith they went the Red Sea
through

ὡς διὰ ξηρᾶς γῆς, ἧς πεῖραν λαβόντες
as through dry land, which ⁴trial ²taking

οἱ Αἰγύπτιοι κατεπόθησαν. 30 Πίστει
¹the ²Egyptians were swallowed up. By faith

τὰ τείχη Ἰεριχὼ ἔπεσαν κυκλωθέντα ἐπὶ
the walls of Jericho fell having been during
encircled

ἑπτὰ ἡμέρας. 31 Πίστει Ῥαὰβ ἡ πόρνη
seven days. By faith Rahab the prostitute

οὐ συναπώλετο τοῖς ἀπειθήσασιν, δεξαμένη
did not perish with the [ones] disobeying, having received

τοὺς κατασκόπους μετ' εἰρήνης. 32 Καὶ
the spies with peace. And

τί ἔτι λέγω; ἐπιλείψει με γὰρ διηγούμενον
what more may ⁴will fail ⁵me ¹for ⁶recounting
I say?

ὁ χρόνος περὶ Γεδεών, Βαράκ, Σαμψών,
²the ³time concerning Gedeon, Barak, Sampson,

Ἰεφθάε, Δαυὶδ τε καὶ Σαμουὴλ καὶ
Jephthae, ³David ¹both and Samuel and

τῶν προφητῶν, 33 οἳ διὰ πίστεως
the prophets, who through faith

κατηγωνίσαντο βασιλείας, ἠργάσαντο δι-
overcame kingdoms, wrought right-

καιοσύνην, ἐπέτυχον ἐπαγγελιῶν, ἔφραξαν
eousness, obtained promises, stopped

στόματα λεόντων, 34 ἔσβεσαν δύναμιν
mouths of lions, quenched [the] power

πυρός, ἔφυγον στόματα μαχαίρης, ἐδυναμώ-
of fire, escaped mouths(edges) of [the] sword, were em-

θησαν ἀπὸ ἀσθενείας, ἐγενήθησαν ἰσχυροὶ
powered from weakness, became strong

ἐν πολέμῳ, παρεμβολὰς ἔκλιναν ἀλλοτρίων.
in war, ¹armies ²made to yield ³of foreigners.

35 ἔλαβον γυναῖκες ἐξ ἀναστάσεως τοὺς
¹received ¹women ⁶by ⁷resurrection ⁸the

νεκροὺς αὐτῶν· ἄλλοι δὲ ἐτυμπανίσθησαν,
⁴dead ⁵of them; but others were beaten to death,

οὐ προσδεξάμενοι τὴν ἀπολύτρωσιν, ἵνα
not accepting – deliverance, in order that

κρείττονος ἀναστάσεως τύχωσιν· 36 ἕτεροι
²a better ³resurrection ¹they might others
obtain;

of *cruel* mockings and scourgings, yea, moreover of bonds and imprisonment:

37 They were stoned, they were sawn asunder, were tempted, were slain with the sword : they wandered about in sheepskins and goatskins; being destitute, afflicted, tormented;

38 (Of whom the world was not worthy:) they wandered in deserts, and *in* mountains, and *in* dens and caves of the earth.

39 And these all, having obtained a good report through faith, received not the promise:

40 God having provided some better thing for us, that they without us should not be made perfect.

δὲ ἐμπαιγμῶν καὶ μαστίγων πεῖραν ἔλαβον,
and ³of mockings ⁴and ⁵of scourgings ²trial ¹took,

ἔτι δὲ δεσμῶν καὶ φυλακῆς· 37 ἐλιθάσ-
and more of bonds and of prison; they were

θησαν, ἐπειράσθησαν, ἐπρίσθησαν, ἐν φόνῳ
stoned, they were tried, they were ²by ³murder
                                    sawn asunder,

μαχαίρης ἀπέθανον, περιῆλθον ἐν μηλωταῖς,
⁴of sword ¹they died, they went about in sheepskins,

ἐν αἰγείοις δέρμασιν, ὑστερούμενοι,
in goatskins, being in want,

θλιβόμενοι, κακουχούμενοι, 38 ὧν οὐκ ἦν
being afflicted, *being* ill treated, of whom was not

ἄξιος ὁ κόσμος, ἐπὶ ἐρημίαις πλανώμενοι
worthy the world, ²over ³deserts ¹wandering

καὶ ὄρεσιν καὶ σπηλαίοις καὶ ταῖς ὀπαῖς
and mountains and caves and the holes

τῆς γῆς. 39 Καὶ οὗτοι πάντες μαρτυρη-
of the earth. And these all having obtained

θέντες διὰ τῆς πίστεως οὐκ ἐκομίσαντο
witness through the(ir) faith obtained not

τὴν ἐπαγγελίαν, 40 τοῦ θεοῦ περὶ ἡμῶν
the promise, – God ⁴concerning ⁵us

κρεῖττόν τι προβλεψαμένου, ἵνα μὴ χωρὶς
³better ²some- ¹having foreseen,² in or- not without
       thing   der that

ἡμῶν τελειωθῶσιν.
us they should be perfected.

CHAPTER 12

WHEREFORE seeing we also are compassed about with so great a cloud of witnesses, let us lay aside every weight, and the sin which doth so easily beset *us*, and let us run with patience the race that is set before us,

2 Looking unto Jesus the author and finisher of *our* faith; who for the joy that was set before him endured the cross, despising the shame, and is set down at the right hand of the throne of God.

12 Τοιγαροῦν καὶ ἡμεῖς, τοσοῦτον ἔχοντες
So therefore ²also ¹we, ²such ¹having

περικείμενον ἡμῖν νέφος μαρτύρων, ὄγκον
⁵lying around ⁴us ³a cloud ⁴of witnesses, ²encum-
                                          brance

ἀποθέμενοι πάντα καὶ τὴν εὐπερίστατον
¹putting away ²every ⁴and ⁵the ⁷most besetting

ἁμαρτίαν, δι᾽ ὑπομονῆς τρέχωμεν τὸν
⁶sin, through endurance let us run ¹the

προκείμενον ἡμῖν ἀγῶνα, 2 ἀφορῶντες εἰς
³set before ⁴us ²contest(race), looking away to

τὸν τῆς πίστεως ἀρχηγὸν καὶ τελειωτὴν
¹the ⁵of the ⁶faith ²author ³and ⁴finisher

Ἰησοῦν, ὃς ἀντὶ τῆς προκειμένης αὐτῷ
Jesus, who against ¹the ²set before ⁶him

χαρᾶς ὑπέμεινεν σταυρὸν αἰσχύνης κατα-
²joy endured a cross ²shame ¹de-

φρονήσας, ἐν δεξιᾷ τε τοῦ θρόνου τοῦ
spising, ³at ⁴[the] ¹and ⁵of the ⁶throne –.
         right [hand]

3 For consider him that endured such contradiction of sinners against himself, let ye be wearied and faint in your minds.

4 Ye have not yet resisted unto blood, striving against sin.

5 And ye have forgotten the exhortation which speaketh unto you as unto children, My son, despise not thou the chastening of the Lord, nor faint when thou art rebuked of him:

6 For whom the Lord loveth he chasteneth, and scourgeth every son whom he receiveth.

7 If ye endure chastening, God dealeth with you as with sons; for what son is he whom the father chasteneth not?

8 But if ye be without chastisement, whereof all are partakers, then are ye bastards, and not sons.

9 Furthermore we have had fathers of our flesh which corrected *us*, and we gave *them* reverence: shall we not much rather be in subjection unto the Father of spirits, and live?

10 For they verily for a few days chastened *us* after their own pleasure; but he for *our* profit, that

---

θεοῦ κεκάθικεν. 3 ἀναλογίσασθε γὰρ τὸν
⁷of ²has taken   For consider ye   ¹the
God [his] seat.   [one]

τοιαύτην ὑπομεμενηκότα ὑπὸ τῶν ἁμαρτω-
³such   ²having endured   ⁵by -   ⁶of sin-

λῶν εἰς ἑαυτὸν ἀντιλογίαν, ἵνα μὴ κάμητε
ners ⁷against ⁸himself ⁴contradiction, lest ye grow
                                              weary

ταῖς ψυχαῖς ὑμῶν ἐκλυόμενοι. 4 Οὔπω
²in the ³souls ⁴of you ¹fainting.   Not yet

μέχρις αἵματος ἀντικατέστητε πρὸς τὴν
²until ³blood   ¹ye resisted   ⁵against -

ἁμαρτίαν ἀνταγωνιζόμενοι, 5 καὶ ἐκλέλησθε
⁶sin   ⁴struggling *against*,   and   ye have
                                         forgotten

τῆς παρακλήσεως, ἥτις ὑμῖν ὡς υἱοῖς
the exhortation, which ²with you ²as ³with sons

διαλέγεται· υἱέ μου, μὴ ὀλιγώρει παιδείας
¹discourses: Son of me, do not make [the]
                               light of discipline

κυρίου, μηδὲ ἐκλύου ὑπ᾽ αὐτοῦ ἐλεγχόμενος·
of [the] nor faint ²by ³him ¹being reproved;
Lord,

6 ὃν γὰρ ἀγαπᾷ κύριος παιδεύει, μαστιγοῖ
for whom ²loves ¹[the] Lord he disciplines, ²scourges

δὲ πάντα υἱὸν ὃν παραδέχεται. 7 εἰς
¹and every son whom he receives.   For

παιδείαν ὑπομένετε· ὡς υἱοῖς ὑμῖν
discipline endure ye; ⁴as ⁵with sons ³with you

προσφέρεται ὁ θεός· τίς γὰρ υἱὸς ὃν
²is dealing - ¹God; for what son whom
                              [is there]

οὐ παιδεύει πατήρ; 8 εἰ δὲ χωρίς ἐστε
²disciplines not ¹a father? But if ²without ¹ye are

παιδείας, ἧς μέτοχοι γεγόνασιν πάντες,
discipline, of which ³sharers ²have become ¹all,

ἄρα νόθοι καὶ οὐχ υἱοί ἐστε. 9 εἶτα
then bastards and not sons ye are. Furthermore

τοὺς μὲν τῆς σαρκὸς ἡμῶν πατέρας
the - ²of the ⁴flesh ⁵of us ²fathers

εἴχομεν παιδευτὰς καὶ ἐνετρεπόμεθα· οὐ
¹we had ⁶correctors and we respected [them]: ³not

πολὺ μᾶλλον ὑποταγησόμεθα τῷ πατρὶ
⁴much ⁷more ¹shall ²we ⁶be ⁵subject to the Father

τῶν πνευμάτων καὶ ζήσομεν; 10 οἱ μὲν
- of spirits and we shall live? ³they³indeed

γὰρ πρὸς ὀλίγας ἡμέρας κατὰ τὸ δοκοῦν
¹for for a few days accord- ⁊ὸ thing seeming
                      ing to   [good]

αὐτοῖς ἐπαίδευον, ὁ δὲ ἐπὶ τὸ συμφέρον
to them disciplined [us], but he for the(our) profit

we might be partakers of his holiness.

11 Now no chastening for the present seemeth to be joyous, but grievous: nevertheless afterward it yieldeth the peaceable fruit of righteousness unto them which are exercised thereby.

12 Wherefore lift up the hands which hang down, and the feeble knees;

13 And make straight paths for your feet, lest that which is lame be turned out of the way; but let it rather be healed.

14 Follow peace with all *men*, and holiness, without which no man shall see the Lord:

15 Looking diligently lest any man fail of the grace of God; lest any root of bitterness springing up trouble *you*, and thereby many be defiled;

16 Lest there *be* any fornicator, or profane person, as Esau, who for one morsel of meat sold his birthright.

17 For ye know how that afterward, when he would have inherited the blessing, he was rejected: for he found no place of repentance, though he sought it carefully with tears.

18 For ye are not come

εἰς τὸ μεταλαβεῖν τῆς ἁγιότητος αὐτοῦ.
for the to partake of the sanctity of him.

11 πᾶσα μὲν παιδεία πρὸς μὲν τὸ παρὸν
²All ¹on ³discipline ⁴for ⁷in- ⁵the ⁶present
 one hand deed

οὐ δοκεῖ χαρᾶς εἶναι ἀλλὰ λύπης, ὕστερον
seems not ²of joy ¹to be but of grief, ²later

δὲ καρπὸν εἰρηνικὸν τοῖς δι' αὐτῆς
¹on the ⁵fruit ⁴peaceable ⁷to the ⁹through ¹⁰it
 other [ones]

γεγυμνασμένοις ἀποδίδωσιν δικαιοσύνης.
⁸having been exercised ³it gives back ⁶of righteousness.

12 Διὸ τὰς παρειμένας χεῖρας καὶ τὰ
Where- ²the ³having been ⁴hands ⁵and ⁶the
fore wearied

παραλελυμένα γόνατα ἀνορθώσατε, 13 καὶ
⁷having been paralysed ⁸knees ¹straighten ye, and

τροχιὰς ὀρθὰς ποιεῖτε τοῖς ποσὶν ὑμῶν,
tracks straight make for the feet of you,

ἵνα μὴ τὸ χωλὸν ἐκτραπῇ, ἰαθῇ δὲ
lest the lame be turned ³may ¹but
 aside, be cured

μᾶλλον. 14 Εἰρήνην διώκετε μετὰ πάντων,
²rather. Peace follow with all men,

καὶ τὸν ἁγιασμόν, οὗ χωρὶς οὐδεὶς
and – sanctification, ²which ¹without no one

ὄψεται τὸν κύριον, 15 ἐπισκοποῦντες μή
will see the Lord, observing not(lest)

τις ὑστερῶν ἀπὸ τῆς χάριτος τοῦ θεοῦ,
anyone fail*ing* from the grace – of God,

μή τις ῥίζα πικρίας ἄνω φύουσα ἐνοχλῇ
not any root of bitterness ²up ¹growing disturb
(lest)

καὶ διὰ ταύτης μιανθῶσιν οἱ πολλοί,
and through this ²be defiled *the* ¹many,

16 μή τις πόρνος ἢ βέβηλος ὡς Ἠσαῦ,
not(lest) any fornicator or profane man as Esau,

ὃς ἀντὶ βρώσεως μιᾶς ἀπέδοτο τὰ
who against ²eating ¹one gave up the

πρωτοτόκια ἑαυτοῦ. 17 ἴστε γὰρ ὅτι
rights of of himself. For ye know that
the firstborn

καὶ μετέπειτα θέλων κληρονομῆσαι τὴν
indeed afterwards wishing to inherit the

εὐλογίαν ἀπεδοκιμάσθη, μετανοίας γὰρ
blessing he was rejected, for ⁴of repentance

τόπον οὐχ εὗρεν, καίπερ μετὰ δακρύων
²place ²not ¹he found, though with tears

ἐκζητήσας αὐτήν. 18 Οὐ γὰρ προσεληλύθατε
seeking out it. For ²not ¹ye ²have ⁴approached

unto the mount that might be touched, and that burned with fire, nor unto blackness, and darkness, and tempest,

19 And the sound of a trumpet, and the voice of words; which *voice* they that heard intreated that the word should not be spoken to them any more:

20 (For they could not endure that which was commanded, And if so much as a beast touch the mountain, it shall be stoned, or thrust through with a dart:

21 And so terrible was the sight, *that* Moses said, I exceedingly fear and quake:)

22 But ye are come unto mount Sion, and unto the city of the living God, the heavenly Jerusalem, and to an innumerable company of angels,

23 To the general assembly and church of the firstborn, which are written in heaven, and to God the Judge of all, and to the spirits of just men made perfect,

24 And to Jesus the mediator of the new covenant, and to the blood of sprinkling, that speaketh better things than *that of* Abel.

25 See that ye refuse not him that speaketh. For if they escaped not who refused him that spake on earth, much more *shall not* we *escape*, if we turn away from him that *speaketh* from heaven:

ψηλαφωμένῳ   καὶ   κεκαυμένῳ   πυρὶ   καὶ
to [a mountain]   and   having been   with   and
being felt   ignited   fire

γνόφῳ   καὶ   ζόφῳ   καὶ   θυέλλῃ   19 καὶ
to darkness   and   *to* deep gloom   and   *to* whirlwind   and

σάλπιγγος   ἤχῳ   καὶ   φωνῇ   ῥημάτων,   ἧς
²of trumpet   ¹*to* a sound   and   *to* a voice   of words,   which

οἱ   ἀκούσαντες   παρῃτήσαντο   μὴ   προστεθῆναι
the [ones] hearing   entreated   not   to be added

αὐτοῖς   λόγον·   20 οὐκ   ἔφερον   γὰρ   τὸ
to them   a word;   ³not   ²they bore   ¹for   the
thing

διαστελλόμενον·   κἂν   θηρίον   θίγῃ   τοῦ   ὄρους,
being charged: If even   a beast   touches   the mountain,

λιθοβοληθήσεται·   21 καὶ,   οὕτω   φοβερὸν   ἦν
it shall be stoned;   and,   so   fearful   was

τὸ   φανταζόμενον,   Μωϋσῆς   εἶπεν·   ἔκφοβός
the thing   appearing,   Moses   said: ¹Terrified

εἰμι   καὶ   ἔντρομος·   22 ἀλλὰ   προσεληλύθατε
¹I am   and   trembling;   but   ye have approached

Σιὼν   ὄρει   καὶ   πόλει   θεοῦ   ζῶντος,
²Zion   ¹*to* mount   and   *to* a city   ²God   ¹of [the] living,

Ἰερουσαλὴμ   ἐπουρανίῳ,   καὶ   μυριάσιν
²Jerusalem   ¹*to* a heavenly,   and   *to* myriads

ἀγγέλων,   23 πανηγύρει   καὶ   ἐκκλησίᾳ
of angels,   *to* an assembly   and   a church

πρωτοτόκων   ἀπογεγραμμένων   ἐν   οὐρανοῖς,
of firstborn [ones]   having been enrolled   in   heavens,

καὶ   κριτῇ   θεῷ   πάντων,   καὶ   πνεύμασι
and   ²judge   ¹*to* God   of all men,   and   *to* spirits

δικαίων   τετελειωμένων,   24 καὶ   διαθήκης
of just men   having been made   and   ⁴covenant
perfect,

νέας   μεσίτῃ   Ἰησοῦ,   καὶ   αἵματι   ῥαντισμοῦ
²of a   ²mediator   ¹*to* Jesus,   and   *to* blood   of sprinkling
new

κρεῖττον   λαλοῦντι   παρὰ   τὸν   Ἄβελ.
²a better thing   ¹speaking   than   –   Abel.

25 Βλέπετε   μὴ   παραιτήσησθε   τὸν   λαλοῦντα·
Look ye [that]   ²not   ¹ye refuse   the [one] speaking;

εἰ   γὰρ   ἐκεῖνοι   οὐκ   ἐξέφυγον   ἐπὶ   γῆς
for if   those   escaped not   ⁴on   ⁵earth

παραιτησάμενοι   τὸν   χρηματίζοντα,   πολὺ
¹refusing   ²the [one]   ³warning,   much

μᾶλλον   ἡμεῖς   οἱ   τὸν   ἀπ'   οὐρανῶν
more   we*   ¹the   ²the [one]   ⁵from   ⁶heavens
[ones]   ⁴[warning]

* That is, "much more [shall] we [not escape]"; or, putting it in another way, "much less shall we escape."

26 Whose voice then shook the earth: but now he hath promised, saying, Yet once more I shake not the earth only, but also heaven.

27 And this *word*, Yet once more, signifieth the removing of those things that are shaken, as of things that are made, that those things which cannot be shaken may remain.

28 Wherefore we receiving a kingdom which cannot be moved, let us have grace, whereby we may serve God acceptably with reverence and godly fear:

29 For our God *is* a consuming fire.

ἀποστρεφόμενοι·   26 οὗ   ἡ   φωνὴ   τὴν γῆν
²turning from;   of whom the   voice   ³the ⁴earth
ἐσάλευσεν τότε,   νῦν δὲ ἐπήγγελται λέγων·
²shook   ¹then,   but now he has promised   saying:
ἔτι   ἅπαξ   ἐγὼ   σείσω   οὐ   μόνον   τὴν
Yet   once   I   will shake   not   only   the
γῆν   ἀλλὰ   καὶ   τὸν   οὐρανόν.   27 τὸ   δὲ
earth but   also   *the*   heaven.   Now the
                                                [phrase]
ἔτι   ἅπαξ   δηλοῖ   τὴν   τῶν   σαλευομένων
'Yet   once'   declares   ¹the ³of the things ⁴being shaken
μετάθεσιν   ὡς   πεποιημένων,   ἵνα   μείνῃ   τὰ
²removal   as   of things having   in or-   ⁴may   ¹the
                        been made,   der that remain things
μὴ   σαλευόμενα.   28 Διὸ   βασιλείαν   ἀσάλευτος
²not ³being shaken.   Wherefore ³kingdom ²an unshakable
παραλαμβάνοντες   ἔχωμεν   χάριν,   δι'   ἧς
     ¹receiving   let us have   grace, through which
λατρεύωμεν   εὐαρέστως   τῷ   θεῷ,   μετὰ
we may serve   ²well-pleasingly   the   ¹God,   with
εὐλαβείας   καὶ   δέους·   29 καὶ   γὰρ   ὁ   θεὸς
devoutness   and   awe;   for indeed   the   God
ἡμῶν   πῦρ   καταναλίσκον.
of us [is] fire   a consuming.

CHAPTER 13

LET brotherly love continue.

2 Be not forgetful to entertain strangers: for thereby some have entertained angels unawares.

3 Remember them that are in bonds, as bound with them ; *and* them which suffer adversity, as being yourselves also in the body.

4 Marriage *is* honourable in all, and the bed undefiled : but whoremongers and adulterers God will judge.

5 *Let your* conversation *be* without covetousness; *and be* content with such things as ye have: for he

13 Ἡ   φιλαδελφία   μενέτω.   2 τῆς
      ²brotherly love   ¹Let it ³remain.   -
φιλοξενίας   μὴ   ἐπιλανθάνεσθε·   διὰ   ταύτης
of hospitality   Be ye not forgetful;   ²through   ³this
γὰρ   ἔλαθόν   τινες   ξενίσαντες   ἀγγέλους.
¹for   ⁵unconsciously† ⁴some   ⁶entertaining(ed)   ⁷angels.
3 μιμνῄσκεσθε   τῶν   δεσμίων   ὡς   συνδεδεμένοι,
Be ye mindful   of the   prisoners   as   *having been* bound
                                              with [them],
τῶν   κακουχουμένων   ὡς   καὶ   αὐτοὶ   ὄντες
of the   *being* ill treated   as   also [your]selves   being
[ones]
ἐν   σώματι.   4 Τίμιος   ὁ   γάμος   ἐν   πᾶσιν
in [the] body.   ⁴honourable -   ²marriage   in   all
                      ¹[Let]   ³[be]
καὶ   ἡ   κοίτη   ἀμίαντος·   πόρνους   γὰρ
and   the   bed   undefiled;   for fornicators
καὶ   μοιχοὺς   κρινεῖ   ὁ   θεός.   5 Ἀφιλάργυρος
and   adulterers ²will judge   -   ¹God.   ⁵without love of
                                                    money
ὁ   τρόπος,   ἀρκούμενοι   τοῖς   παροῦσιν·
¹[Let] ³way of   being satisfied   the things   present;
²the   life ⁴[be],   with
(your)

hath said, I will never leave thee, nor forsake thee.

6 So that we may boldly say, The Lord *is* my helper, and I will not fear what man shall do unto me.

7 Remember them which have the rule over you, who have spoken unto you the word of God: whose faith follow, considering the end of *their* conversation.

8 Jesus Christ the same yesterday, and to day, and for ever.

9 Be not carried about with divers and strange doctrines. For *it is* a good thing that the heart be established with grace; not with meats, which have not profited them that have been occupied therein.

10 We have an altar, whereof they have no right to eat which serve the tabernacle.

11 For the bodies of those beasts, whose blood is brought into the sanctuary by the high priest for sin, are burned without the camp.

12 Wherefore Jesus also, that he might sanctify the people with his own blood, suffered without the gate.

13 Let us go forth

αὐτὸς γὰρ εἴρηκεν· οὐ μή σε ἀνῶ οὐδ'
for he has said: By no means thee will I nor
                                     leave

οὐ μή σε ἐγκαταλίπω· 6 ὥστε θαρροῦντας
by no(any) thee I forsake; so as being of good
means   cheer

ἡμᾶς λέγειν· κύριος ἐμοὶ βοηθός, οὐ
us to say[b]: [The] Lord to me[c] [is] a helper, not

φοβηθήσομαι· τί ποιήσει μοι ἄνθρωπος;
I will fear; what [1]will [3]do [4]to me [2]man ?

7 Μνημονεύετε τῶν ἡγουμένων ὑμῶν,
   Remember the [ones] leading of you,

οἵτινες ἐλάλησαν ὑμῖν τὸν λόγον τοῦ
who spoke to you the word –

θεοῦ, ὧν ἀναθεωροῦντες τὴν ἔκβασιν τῆς
of God, [6]of [1]looking at [2]the [3]result [4]of
     whom   the

ἀναστροφῆς μιμεῖσθε τὴν πίστιν. 8 Ἰησοῦς
[5]conduct imitate ye the(ir) faith. Jesus

Χριστὸς ἐχθὲς καὶ σήμερον ὁ αὐτὸς
Christ [4]yesterday [5]and [6]to-day [1][is] [2]the [3]same

καὶ εἰς τοὺς αἰῶνας. 9 Διδαχαῖς ποικίλαις
and unto the ages. [1]teachings [2]by various

καὶ ξέναις μὴ παραφέρεσθε· καλὸν γὰρ
[3]and [4]strange [1]Do not be carried away; for [it is] good

χάριτι βεβαιοῦσθαι τὴν καρδίαν, οὐ
[4]by grace [3]to be confirmed [1]the [2]heart,[b] not

βρώμασιν, ἐν οἷς οὐκ ὠφελήθησαν οἱ
by foods, by which [3]were not profited [1]the

περιπατοῦντες. 10 ἔχομεν θυσιαστήριον ἐξ
[2][ones] walking. We have an altar of

οὗ φαγεῖν οὐκ ἔχουσιν ἐξουσίαν οἱ τῇ
which [7]to eat [5]have not [4]authority [1]the [3]the
                                              [ones]

σκηνῇ λατρεύοντες. 11 ὧν γὰρ εἰσφέρεται
[4]tabernacle [2]serving. For [3]of what [1]is brought in

ζῴων τὸ αἷμα περὶ ἁμαρτίας εἰς τὰ
[4]animals [1]the [2]blood [3]concerning [5]sins into the

ἅγια διὰ τοῦ ἀρχιερέως, τούτων τὰ
holies through the high priest, of these the

σώματα κατακαίεται ἔξω τῆς παρεμβολῆς.
bodies is(are) burned outside the camp.

12 διὸ καὶ Ἰησοῦς, ἵνα ἁγιάσῃ διὰ
Where- in- Jesus, in order he might [3]through
fore deed   that sanctify

τοῦ ἰδίου αἵματος τὸν λαόν, ἔξω τῆς
[4]the(his) [5]own [6]blood [1]the [2]people, outside the

πύλης ἔπαθεν. 13 τοίνυν ἐξερχώμεθα πρὸς
gate suffered. So let us go forth to

therefore unto him without the camp, bearing his reproach.

14 For here have we no continuing city, but we seek one to come.

15 By him therefore let us offer the sacrifice of praise to God continually, that is, the fruit of *our* lips giving thanks to his name.

16 But to do good and to communicate forget not: for with such sacrifices God is well pleased.

17 Obey them that have the rule over you, and submit yourselves: for they watch for your souls, as they that must give account, that they may do it with joy, and not with grief: for that *is* unprofitable for you.

18 Pray for us: for we trust we have a good conscience, in all things willing to live honestly.

19 But I beseech *you* the rather to do this, that I may be restored to you the sooner.

20 Now the God of peace, that brought again from the dead our Lord Jesus, that great shepherd

αὐτὸν ἔξω τῆς παρεμβολῆς τὸν ὀνειδισμὸν
him outside the camp the reproach

αὐτοῦ φέροντες· **14** οὐ γὰρ ἔχομεν ὧδε
of him bearing; for ²not ¹we have here

μένουσαν πόλιν, ἀλλὰ τὴν μέλλουσαν
a continuing city, but the [one] coming

ἐπιζητοῦμεν. **15** Δι' αὐτοῦ οὖν ἀναφέρωμεν
we seek. Through him therefore let us offer up

θυσίαν αἰνέσεως διὰ παντὸς τῷ θεῷ,
a sacrifice of praise always – to God,

τοῦτ' ἔστιν καρπὸν χειλέων ὁμολογούντων
this is fruit of lips confessing

τῷ ὀνόματι αὐτοῦ. **16** τῆς δὲ εὐποιΐας
to the name of him. But of the doing good

καὶ κοινωνίας μὴ ἐπιλανθάνεσθε· τοιαύταις
and sharing be ye not forgetful; ²with such

γὰρ θυσίαις εὐαρεστεῖται ὁ θεός. **17** Πεί-
¹for sacrifices ²is well pleased – ¹God. Obey

θεσθε τοῖς ἡγουμένοις ὑμῶν καὶ ὑπείκετε·
ye the [ones] leading of you and submit to
[them];

αὐτοὶ γὰρ ἀγρυπνοῦσιν ὑπὲρ τῶν ψυχῶν
for they watch on behalf of the souls

ὑμῶν ὡς λόγον ἀποδώσοντες· ἵνα μετὰ
of you as ²account ¹rendering*; in or- with
der that

χαρᾶς τοῦτο ποιῶσιν καὶ μὴ στενάζ-
joy ²this ¹they may do and not groan-

οντες· ἀλυσιτελὲς γὰρ ὑμῖν τοῦτο.
ing; for profitless to you this
[would be].

18 Προσεύχεσθε περὶ ἡμῶν· πειθόμεθα
Pray ye concerning us; ²we are persuaded

γὰρ ὅτι καλὴν συνείδησιν ἔχομεν, ἐν
¹for that a good conscience we have, ⁴in

πᾶσιν καλῶς θέλοντες ἀναστρέφεσθαι.
⁵all [respects] ³well ¹wishing ²to behave.

19 περισσοτέρως δὲ παρακαλῶ τοῦτο
And more abundantly I beseech [you] this

ποιῆσαι, ἵνα τάχιον ἀποκατασταθῶ ὑμῖν.
to do, in or- sooner I may be restored to you.
der that

20 Ὁ δὲ θεὸς τῆς εἰρήνης, ὁ ἀναγαγὼν
Now the God – of peace, the having led up
[one]

ἐκ νεκρῶν τὸν ποιμένα τῶν προβάτων
out [the] dead the ²shepherd ³of the ⁴sheep
of

* In the future.

of the sheep, through the
blood of the everlasting
covenant,
21 Make you perfect in
every good work to do
his will, working in you
that which is wellpleasing
in his sight, through Jesus
Christ; to whom *be* glory
for ever and ever. Amen.
22 And I beseech you,
brethren, suffer the word
of exhortation: for I
have written a letter unto
you in few words.
23 Know ye that *our*
brother Timothy is set at
liberty; with whom, if he
come shortly, I will see
you.
24 Salute all them that
have the rule over you,
and all the saints. They of
Italy salute you.
25 Grace *be* with you
all. Amen.

τὸν   μέγαν   ἐν   αἵματι   διαθήκης   αἰωνίου,
the   ¹great   in (? with) blood   ²covenant   ¹of an eternal,

τὸν   κύριον   ἡμῶν   'Ιησοῦν,   21 καταρτίσαι
the   Lord   of us   Jesus,   *may he* adjust

ὑμᾶς   ἐν   παντὶ   ἀγαθῷ   εἰς   τὸ   ποιῆσαι
you   in   every   good thing   *for*   *the*   to do

τὸ   θέλημα   αὐτοῦ,   ποιῶν   ἐν   ἡμῖν   τὸ
the   will   of him,   doing   in   us   the
[thing]

εὐάρεστον   ἐνώπιον   αὐτοῦ   διὰ   'Ιησοῦ
wellpleasing   before   him   through   Jesus

Χριστοῦ,   ᾧ   ἡ   δόξα   εἰς   τοὺς   αἰῶνας
Christ,   to [be]   glory   unto   the   ages
whom the

τῶν   αἰώνων·   ἀμήν.   22 Παρακαλῶ   δὲ
of the   ages: Amen.   And I beseech

ὑμᾶς,   ἀδελφοί,   ἀνέχεσθε   τοῦ   λόγου   τῆς
you,   brothers,   endure   the   word   of the

παρακλήσεως·   καὶ   γὰρ   διὰ   βραχέων
of beseeching;   for indeed   through   few [words]

ἐπέστειλα   ὑμῖν.   23 Γινώσκετε   τὸν   ἀδελφὸν
I wrote   to you.   Know ye   the   brother

ἡμῶν   Τιμόθεον   ἀπολελυμένον,   μεθ'   οὗ
of us   Timothy   having been released,   with whom

ἐὰν   τάχιον   ἔρχηται   ὄψομαι   ὑμᾶς.
if   sooner   I come   I will see   you.

24 'Ασπάσασθε   πάντας   τοὺς   ἡγουμένους
Greet ye   all   the [ones] leading

ὑμῶν   καὶ   πάντας   τοὺς   ἁγίους.   'Ασπάζονται
of you   and   all   the   saints.   ⁴greet

ὑμᾶς   οἱ   ἀπὸ   τῆς   'Ιταλίας.
²you   ¹The [ones]   ²from   -   ³Italy.

25 'Η   χάρις   μετὰ   πάντων   ὑμῶν.
-   Grace [be]   with   all   you.

JAMES 1

ΙΑΚΩΒΟΥ ΕΠΙΣΤΟΛΗ
²Of James ¹Epistle

CHAPTER 1

JAMES, a servant of
God and of the Lord
Jesus Christ, to the twelve
tribes which are scattered
abroad, greeting.

1 'Ιάκωβος   θεοῦ   καὶ   κυρίου   'Ιησοῦ
James   ²of God   ³and   ⁴of [the] Lord   ⁵Jesus

Χριστοῦ   δοῦλος   ταῖς   δώδεκα   φυλαῖς   ταῖς
⁶Christ   ¹a slave   to the   twelve   tribes   -

ἐν   τῇ   διασπορᾷ   χαίρειν.
in   the   dispersion   greeting.*

* See note on Phil. 3.16 in Introduction.

2 My brethren, count it all joy when ye fall into divers temptations;

3 Knowing *this*, that the trying of your faith worketh patience.

4 But let patience have *her* perfect work, that ye may be perfect and entire, wanting nothing.

5 If any of you lack wisdom, let him ask of God, that giveth to all *men* liberally, and upbraideth not; and it shall be given him.

6 But let him ask in faith, nothing wavering. For he that wavereth is like a wave of the sea driven with the wind and tossed.

7 For let not that man think that he shall receive any thing of the Lord.

8 A double minded man *is* unstable in all his ways.

9 Let the brother of low degree rejoice in that he is exalted:

10 But the rich, in that he is made low: because as the flower of the grass he shall pass away.

11 For the sun is no sooner risen with a burning heat, but it withereth the grass, and the flower thereof falleth, and the grace of the fashion of it

---

2 Πᾶσαν χαρὰν ἡγήσασθε, ἀδελφοί μου,
All joy deem [it], brothers of me,

ὅταν πειρασμοῖς περιπέσητε ποικίλοις,
whenever ³trials ¹ye fall ²into various,

3 γινώσκοντες ὅτι τὸ δοκίμιον ὑμῶν τῆς
knowing that the approved part ³of you ¹of the
=that which is approved in your faith

πίστεως κατεργάζεται ὑπομονήν. 4 ἡ δὲ
²faith works endurance. — And

ὑπομονὴ ἔργον τέλειον ἐχέτω, ἵνα ἦτε
endurance ³work ²perfect ¹let it in or- ye may
have, der that be

τέλειοι καὶ ὁλόκληροι, ἐν μηδενὶ λειπόμενοι.
perfect and entire, in nothing wanting.

5 Εἰ δέ τις ὑμῶν λείπεται σοφίας, αἰτείτω
if But any- of you wants wisdom, let him
one ask ·

παρὰ τοῦ διδόντος θεοῦ πᾶσιν ἁπλῶς
from ²the ³giving ¹God to all unre-
[one] men servedly

καὶ μὴ ὀνειδίζοντος, καὶ δοθήσεται αὐτῷ.
and not reproaching, and it will be given to him.

6 αἰτείτω δὲ ἐν πίστει, μηδὲν διακριν-
But let him ask in faith, nothing doubt-

όμενος· ὁ γὰρ διακρινόμενος ἔοικεν κλύδωνι
ing; for the [one] doubting is like a wave

θαλάσσης ἀνεμιζομένῳ καὶ ῥιπιζομένῳ.
of [the] sea being driven by wind and being tossed.

7 μὴ γὰρ οἰέσθω ὁ ἄνθρωπος ἐκεῖνος
For let not ³suppose ¹that ²man

ὅτι λήμψεταί τι παρὰ τοῦ κυρίου, 8 ἀνὴρ
that he will any- from the Lord, a man
receive thing

δίψυχος, ἀκατάστατος ἐν πάσαις ταῖς
two-souled, unsettled in all the

ὁδοῖς αὐτοῦ. 9 Καυχάσθω δὲ ὁ ἀδελφὸς
ways of him. But let ⁴boast ¹the ³brother

ὁ ταπεινὸς ἐν τῷ ὕψει αὐτοῦ, 10 ὁ δὲ
— ²humble in the height of him, and the

πλούσιος ἐν τῇ ταπεινώσει αὐτοῦ, ὅτι
rich one in the humiliation of him, because

ὡς ἄνθος χόρτου παρελεύσεται. 11 ἀνέτειλεν
as a flower of grass he will pass away. ⁴rose

γὰρ ὁ ἥλιος σὺν τῷ καύσωνι καὶ ἐξήρανεν
¹For ²the ³sun with the hot wind and dried

τὸν χόρτον, καὶ τὸ ἄνθος αὐτοῦ ἐξέπεσεν
the grass, and the flower of it fell out

καὶ ἡ εὐπρέπεια τοῦ προσώπου αὐτοῦ
and the comeliness of the appearance of it

perisheth: so also shall the rich man fade away in his ways.

12 Blessed *is* the man that endureth temptation: for when he is tried, he shall receive the crown of life, which the Lord hath promised to them that love him.

13 Let no man say when he is tempted, I am tempted of God: for God cannot be tempted with evil, neither tempteth he any man:

14 But every man is tempted, when he is drawn away of his own lust, and enticed.

15 Then when lust hath conceived, it bringeth forth sin: and sin, when it is finished, bringeth forth death.

16 Do not err, my beloved brethren.

17 Every good gift and every perfect gift is from above, and cometh down from the Father of lights, with whom is no variableness, neither shadow of turning.

18 Of his own will begat he us with the word of truth, that we should be a kind of firstfruits of his creatures.

19 Wherefore, my beloved brethren, let every

ἀπώλετο· οὕτως καὶ ὁ πλούσιος ἐν ταῖς
perished; thus also the rich man in the

πορείαις αὐτοῦ μαρανθήσεται. 12 Μακάριος
goings of him will fade away. Blessed

ἀνὴρ ὃς ὑπομένει πειρασμόν, ὅτι δόκιμος
[the] who endures trial, because ²approved
man

γενόμενος λήμψεται τὸν στέφανον τῆς
¹having become he will receive the crown -

ζωῆς, ὃν ἐπηγγείλατο τοῖς ἀγαπῶσιν αὐτόν.
of life, which he promised to the [ones] loving him.

13 Μηδεὶς πειραζόμενος λεγέτω ὅτι ἀπὸ
²no man ³being tempted ¹Let ⁴say[,] - From

θεοῦ πειράζομαι· ὁ γὰρ θεὸς ἀπείραστός
God I am tempted; - for God ²untempted

ἐστιν κακῶν, πειράζει δὲ αὐτὸς οὐδένα.
¹is of(with) and ²tempts ¹he no man.
evil things,

14 ἕκαστος δὲ πειράζεται ὑπὸ τῆς ἰδίας
But each man is tempted by the(his) own

ἐπιθυμίας ἐξελκόμενος καὶ δελεαζόμενος·
lusts being drawn out and *being* enticed;

15 εἶτα ἡ ἐπιθυμία συλλαβοῦσα τίκτει
then - lust having conceived bears

ἁμαρτίαν, ἡ δὲ ἁμαρτία ἀποτελεσθεῖσα
sin, - and sin having been
fully formed

ἀποκύει θάνατον. 16 Μὴ πλανᾶσθε, ἀδελφοί
brings forth death. Do not err, ²brothers

μου ἀγαπητοί.
²of me ¹beloved.

17 Πᾶσα δόσις ἀγαθὴ καὶ πᾶν δώρημα
Every ²giving ¹good and every ²gift

τέλειον ἄνωθέν ἐστιν καταβαῖνον ἀπὸ τοῦ
¹perfect ⁴from above ³is coming down from the

πατρὸς τῶν φώτων, παρ' ᾧ οὐκ ἔνι
Father of the lights, with whom ⁵has no place

παραλλαγὴ ἢ τροπῆς ἀποσκίασμα. 18 βου-
¹change ²or ⁴of turning ³shadow. Having

ληθεὶς ἀπεκύησεν ἡμᾶς λόγῳ ἀληθείας,
purposed he brought forth us by a word of truth,

εἰς τὸ εἶναι ἡμᾶς ἀπαρχήν τινα τῶν
for the to be us[b] ²firstfruit ¹a certain ²of
=that we should be the

αὐτοῦ κτισμάτων.
⁵of him ⁴creatures.

19 Ἴστε, ἀδελφοί μου ἀγαπητοί. ἔστω
Know ye, ²brothers ³of me ¹beloved. ²let be

man be swift to hear, slow
to speak, slow to wrath:
20 For the wrath of
man worketh not the righteousness of God.
21 Wherefore lay apart
all filthiness and super-
fluity of naughtiness, and
receive with meekness the
engrafted word, which is
able to save your souls.
22 But be ye doers of
the word, and not hearers
only, deceiving your own
selves.
23 For if any be a
hearer of the word, and
not a doer, he is like unto a man beholding his
natural face in a glass:
24 For he beholdeth
himself, and goeth his way,
and straightway forgetteth
what manner of man he
was.
25 But whoso looketh
into the perfect law of
liberty, and continueth
therein, he being not a forgetful hearer, but a doer
of the work, this man shall
be blessed in his deed.
26 If any man among
you seem to be religious,
and bridleth not his
tongue, but deceiveth his
own heart, this man's
religion *is* vain.
27 Pure religion and
undefiled before God and

δὲ   πᾶς   ἄνθρωπος   ταχὺς   εἰς   τὸ   ἀκοῦσαι,
¹But every   man   swift   *for* *the* to hear,
βραδὺς   εἰς   τὸ   λαλῆσαι,   βραδὺς   εἰς   ὀργήν·
slow   *for* *the* to speak,   slow   to   wrath;
20 ὀργὴ   γὰρ   ἀνδρὸς   δικαιοσύνην   θεοῦ
for [the] wrath of a man ²[the] righteousness ³of God
οὐκ   ἐργάζεται.   21 διὸ   ἀποθέμενοι   πᾶσαν
¹works not.   Wherefore putting away   all
ῥυπαρίαν   καὶ   περισσείαν   κακίας   ἐν   πραΰ-
filthiness   and   superfluity   of evil in   meek-
τητι   δέξασθε   τὸν   ἔμφυτον   λόγον   τὸν
ness   receive ye   the   implanted   word   –
δυνάμενον   σῶσαι   τὰς   ψυχὰς   ὑμῶν.   22 γίν-
being able   to save   the   souls   of you.   be-
εσθε   δὲ   ποιηταὶ   λόγου,   καὶ   μὴ   ἀκροαταὶ
come ye And   doers of [the] word, and   not   hearers
μόνον   παραλογιζόμενοι   ἑαυτούς.   23 ὅτι
only   misleading   yourselves.   Because
εἴ   τις   ἀκροατὴς   λόγου   ἐστὶν   καὶ   οὐ
if   anyone ²a hearer ³of [the] word ¹is   and   not
ποιητής,   οὗτος   ἔοικεν   ἀνδρὶ   κατανοοῦντι
a doer,   this one   is like   a man   perceiving
τὸ   πρόσωπον   τῆς   γενέσεως   αὐτοῦ   ἐν
the   face   of the   birth   of him   in
ἐσόπτρῳ·   24 κατενόησεν   γὰρ   ἑαυτὸν   καὶ
a mirror·   for he perceived   himself   and
ἀπελήλυθεν,   καὶ   εὐθέως   ἐπελάθετο   ὁποῖος
has gone away,   and   straightway   forgot   what sort
ἦν.   25 ὁ   δὲ   παρακύψας   εἰς   νόμον
he was.   But the [one] having looked *into* into   ³law
τέλειον   τὸν   τῆς   ἐλευθερίας   καὶ   παραμείνας,
²perfect   ¹the   –   of freedom   and   remaining,
οὐκ   ἀκροατὴς   ἐπιλησμονῆς   γενόμενος   ἀλλὰ
not   ²a hearer   ³of forgetfulness* ¹becoming   but
ποιητὴς   ἔργου,   οὗτος   μακάριος   ἐν   τῇ
a doer   of [the] work, this one   ²blessed   ³in   ⁴the
ποιήσει   αὐτοῦ   ἔσται.   26 Εἴ   τις   δοκεῖ
⁵doing   ⁶of him   ¹will be.   If   anyone   thinks
θρησκὸς   εἶναι,   μὴ   χαλιναγωγῶν   γλῶσσαν
²religious   ¹to be,   not   bridling   tongue
ἑαυτοῦ   ἀλλὰ   ἀπατῶν   καρδίαν   ἑαυτοῦ,
of himself   but   deceiving   heart   of himself,
τούτου   μάταιος   ἡ   θρησκεία.   27 θρησκεία
of this one   vain   the   religion.   Religion
καθαρὰ   καὶ   ἀμίαντος   παρὰ   τῷ   θεῷ
clean   and   undefiled   before   the   God

* Genitive of quality: " a forgetful hearer."

the Father is this, To visit the fatherless and widows in their affliction, *and* to keep himself unspotted from the world.

καὶ πατρὶ αὕτη ἐστίν, ἐπισκέπτεσθαι
and Father ²this ¹is, to visit

ὀρφανοὺς καὶ χήρας ἐν τῇ θλίψει αὐτῶν,
orphans and widows in the affliction of them,

ἄσπιλον ἑαυτὸν τηρεῖν ἀπὸ τοῦ κόσμου.
unspotted himself to keep from the world.

CHAPTER 2

MY brethren, have not the faith of our Lord Jesus Christ, *the Lord* of glory, with respect of persons.

2 For if there come unto your assembly a man with a gold ring, in goodly apparel, and there come in also a poor man in vile raiment;

3 And ye have respect to him that weareth the gay clothing, and say unto him, Sit thou here in a good place; and say to the poor, Stand thou there, or sit here under my footstool:

4 Are ye not then partial in yourselves, and are become judges of evil thoughts?

5 Hearken, my beloved brethren, Hath not God chosen the poor of this world rich in faith, and heirs of the kingdom which he hath promised to them that love him?

6 But ye have despised the poor. Do not rich men oppress you, and draw you before the judgment seats?

7 Do not they blas-

2 Ἀδελφοί μου, μὴ ἐν προσωπολημψίαις
Brothers of me, not in respects of persons

ἔχετε τὴν πίστιν τοῦ κυρίου ἡμῶν Ἰησοῦ
have ye the faith of the Lord of us Jesus

Χριστοῦ τῆς δόξης. 2 ἐὰν γὰρ εἰσέλθῃ
Christ[,] *of* the glory.* For if [there] enters

εἰς συναγωγὴν ὑμῶν ἀνὴρ χρυσοδακτύλιος
into a synagogue of you a man gold-fingered

ἐν ἐσθῆτι λαμπρᾷ, εἰσέλθῃ δὲ καὶ πτωχὸς
in ²clothing ¹splendid, and [there] enters also a poor man

ἐν ῥυπαρᾷ ἐσθῆτι, 3 ἐπιβλέψητε δὲ ἐπὶ
in shabby clothing, and ye look *on* on

τὸν φοροῦντα τὴν ἐσθῆτα τὴν λαμπρὰν
the [one] wearing the clothing – splendid

καὶ εἴπητε· σὺ κάθου ὧδε καλῶς, καὶ
and say: ²thou ¹Sit here well, and

τῷ πτωχῷ εἴπητε· σὺ στῆθι ἐκεῖ ἢ
to the poor man ye say: ²thou ¹Stand there or

κάθου ὑπὸ τὸ ὑποπόδιόν μου, 4 οὐ
sit under the footstool of me, not

διεκρίθητε ἐν ἑαυτοῖς καὶ ἐγένεσθε κριταὶ
did ye dis- among yourselves and became judges
criminate

διαλογισμῶν πονηρῶν; 5 Ἀκούσατε, ἀδελφοί
²thoughts ¹of evil ?§ Hear ye, brothers

μου ἀγαπητοί. οὐχ ὁ θεὸς ἐξελέξατο
of me beloved. ²not – ³God ¹Chose

τοὺς πτωχοὺς τῷ κόσμῳ πλουσίους ἐν
the poor in the world rich in

πίστει καὶ κληρονόμους τῆς βασιλείας
faith and heirs of the kingdom

ἧς ἐπηγγείλατο τοῖς ἀγαπῶσιν αὐτόν;
which he promised to the [ones] loving him?

6 ὑμεῖς δὲ ἠτιμάσατε τὸν πτωχόν. οὐχ
But ye dishonoured the poor man. [Do] not

οἱ πλούσιοι καταδυναστεύουσιν ὑμῶν, καὶ
the rich men oppress you, and

αὐτοὶ ἕλκουσιν ὑμᾶς εἰς κριτήρια; 7 οὐκ
they drag you to tribunals? [Do] not

* That is, taking "the glory" as in apposition to "Jesus Christ"; see Luke 2. 32*b*.

§ Genitive of quality: "evil-thinking judges."

pheme that worthy name by the which ye are called?

8 If ye fulfil the royal law according to the scripture, Thou shalt love thy neighbour as thyself, ye do well:

9 But if ye have respect to persons, ye commit sin, and are convinced of the law as transgressors.

10 For whosoever shall keep the whole law, and yet offend in one *point*, he is guilty of all.

11 For he that said, Do not commit adultery, said also, Do not kill. Now if thou commit no adultery, yet if thou kill, thou art become a transgressor of the law.

12 So speak ye, and so do, as they that shall be judged by the law of liberty.

13 For he shall have judgment without mercy, that hath shewed no mercy; and mercy rejoiceth against judgment.

14 What *doth it* profit, my brethren, though a man say he hath faith, and have not works? can faith save him?

15 If a brother or sister be naked, and destitute of daily food,

16 And one of you say unto them, Depart in

αὐτοὶ βλασφημοῦσιν τὸ καλὸν ὄνομα τὸ
they blaspheme the good name -

ἐπικληθὲν ἐφ᾽ ὑμᾶς; 8 εἰ μέντοι νόμον
called *on* on you? If indeed ³law

τελεῖτε βασιλικὸν κατὰ τὴν γραφήν·
¹ye fulfil ²a royal according to the scripture:

ἀγαπήσεις τὸν πλησίον σου ὡς σεαυτόν,
Thou shalt love the neighbour of thee as thyself,

καλῶς ποιεῖτε· 9 εἰ δὲ προσωπολημπτεῖτε,
²well ¹ye do; but if ye respect persons,

ἁμαρτίαν ἐργάζεσθε, ἐλεγχόμενοι ὑπὸ τοῦ
²sin ¹ye work, being reproved by the

νόμου ὡς παραβάται. 10 ὅστις γὰρ
law as transgressors. For ¹[he] who

ὅλον τὸν νόμον τηρήσῃ, πταίσῃ δὲ ἐν
³all ⁴the ⁵law ²keeps, yet stumbles in

ἑνί, γέγονεν πάντων ἔνοχος. 11 ὁ γὰρ
one he has ²of all ¹guilty. For the
thing, become [one]

εἰπών· μὴ μοιχεύσῃς, εἶπεν καὶ· μὴ
saying: Do not commit adultery, said also: not

φονεύσῃς· εἰ δὲ οὐ μοιχεύεις, φονεύεις
Do murder; now if thou dost not ²murderest
commit adultery,

δέ, γέγονας παραβάτης νόμου. 12 οὕτως
¹but, thou hast a transgressor of [the] So
become law.

λαλεῖτε καὶ οὕτως ποιεῖτε ὡς διὰ νόμου
speak ye and so do ye as ³through ⁴a law

ἐλευθερίας μέλλοντες κρίνεσθαι. 13 ἡ γὰρ
⁵of freedom ¹being about ²to be judged. For the

κρίσις ἀνέλεος τῷ μὴ ποιήσαντι ἔλεος·
judg- [will unmerci- to the not do(show)ing mercy;
ment be] ful [one]

κατακαυχᾶται ἔλεος κρίσεως. 14 Τί τὸ
²exults over ¹mercy *of* judgment. What [is] the

ὄφελος, ἀδελφοί μου, ἐὰν πίστιν λέγῃ
profit, brothers of me, if ⁴faith ²says

τις ἔχειν ἔργα δὲ μὴ ἔχῃ; μὴ δύναται
¹any- ³to have ⁵works ⁶but ⁷not ⁶has? *not* can
one

ἡ πίστις σῶσαι αὐτόν; 15 ἐὰν ἀδελφὸς
the faith *to* save him? If a brother

ἢ ἀδελφὴ γυμνοὶ ὑπάρχωσιν καὶ λειπόμενοι
or a sister ²naked ¹are and lacking

τῆς ἐφημέρου τροφῆς, 16 εἴπῃ δέ τις
of the daily food, and ⁴says ¹anyone

αὐτοῖς ἐξ ὑμῶν· ὑπάγετε ἐν εἰρήνῃ,
³to them ²of ²you: Go ye in peace,

peace, be *ye* warmed and filled; notwithstanding ye give them not those things which are needful to the body; what *doth it* profit?

17 Even so faith, if it hath not works, is dead, being alone.

18 Yea, a man may say, Thou hast faith, and I have works: shew me thy faith without thy works, and I will shew thee my faith by my works.

19 Thou believest that there is one God; thou doest well: the devils also believe, and tremble.

20 But wilt thou know, O vain man, that faith without works is dead?

21 Was not Abraham our father justified by works, when he had offered Isaac his son upon the altar?

22 Seest thou how faith wrought with his works, and by works was faith made perfect?

23 And the scripture was fulfilled which saith, Abraham believed God, and it was imputed unto him for righteousness: and he was called the Friend of God.

24 Ye see then how that by works a man is justified, and not by faith only.

25 Likewise also was

θερμαίνεσθε καὶ χορτάζεσθε, μὴ δῶτε
be warmed and filled, ⁴not ²ye give

δὲ αὐτοῖς τὰ ἐπιτήδεια τοῦ σώματος,
¹but ³them the necessaries of the body,

τί τὸ ὄφελος; 17 οὕτως καὶ ἡ πίστις,
what [is] the profit? So indeed - faith,

ἐὰν μὴ ἔχῃ ἔργα, νεκρά ἐστιν καθ'
if it has not works, ²dead ¹is by

ἑαυτήν. 18 ἀλλ' ἐρεῖ τις· σὺ πίστιν
itself. But ²will say ¹someone: Thou ²faith

ἔχεις, κἀγὼ ἔργα ἔχω· δεῖξόν μοι τὴν
¹hast, and I ²works ¹have; show me the

πίστιν σου χωρὶς τῶν ἔργων, κἀγώ
faith of thee without the works, and I

σοι δείξω ἐκ τῶν ἔργων μου τὴν πίστιν.
thee will show ⁴by ⁵the ⁶works ³of me ¹the ²faith.

19 σὺ πιστεύεις ὅτι εἷς ἐστιν ὁ θεός;
Thou believest that ²one ²is - ¹God?

καλῶς ποιεῖς· καὶ τὰ δαιμόνια πιστεύουσιν
²well ¹thou doest; also the demons believe

καὶ φρίσσουσιν. 20 θέλεις δὲ γνῶναι,
and shudder. But art thou willing to know,

ὦ ἄνθρωπε κενέ, ὅτι ἡ πίστις χωρὶς
O ²man ¹vain, that - faith without

τῶν ἔργων ἀργή ἐστιν; 21 Ἀβραὰμ ὁ
- works barren is? Abraham the

πατὴρ ἡμῶν οὐκ ἐξ ἔργων ἐδικαιώθη,
father of us not by works was justified,

ἀνενέγκας Ἰσαὰκ τὸν υἱὸν αὐτοῦ ἐπὶ
offering up Isaac the son of him on

τὸ θυσιαστήριον; 22 βλέπεις ὅτι ἡ πίστις
the altar? Thou seest that - faith

συνήργει τοῖς ἔργοις αὐτοῦ, καὶ ἐκ
worked with the works of him, and by

τῶν ἔργων ἡ πίστις ἐτελειώθη, 23 καὶ
the works the faith was perfected, and

ἐπληρώθη ἡ γραφὴ ἡ λέγουσα· ἐπίστευσεν
was fulfilled the scripture - saying: believed

δὲ Ἀβραὰμ τῷ θεῷ, καὶ ἐλογίσθη αὐτῷ
And Abraham - God, and it was reckoned to him

εἰς δικαιοσύνην, καὶ φίλος θεοῦ ἐκλήθη.
for righteousness, and ²friend ³of God ¹he was called.

24 ὁρᾶτε ὅτι ἐξ ἔργων δικαιοῦται ἄνθρωπος
Ye see that by works ²is justified ¹a man

καὶ οὐκ ἐκ πίστεως μόνον. 25 ὁμοίως
and not by faith only. likewise

not Rahab the harlot justified by works, when she had received the messengers, and had sent *them* out another way?

26 For as the body without the spirit is dead, so faith without works is dead also.

δὲ καὶ 'Ραὰβ ἡ πόρνη οὐκ ἐξ ἔργων
And also Rahab the prostitute not by works

ἐδικαιώθη, ὑποδεξαμένη τοὺς ἀγγέλους καὶ
was justified, entertaining the messengers and

ἑτέρᾳ ὁδῷ ἐκβαλοῦσα; 26 ὥσπερ γὰρ τὸ
by a way sending [them] For as the
different forth?

σῶμα χωρὶς πνεύματος νεκρόν ἐστιν, οὕτως
body without spirit ²dead ¹is, so

καὶ ἡ πίστις χωρὶς ἔργων νεκρά ἐστιν.
also - faith without works ²dead ¹is.

CHAPTER 3

MY brethren, be not many masters, knowing that we shall receive the greater condemnation.

2 For in many things we offend all. If any man offend not in word, the same *is* a perfect man, *and* able also to bridle the whole body.

3 Behold, we put bits in the horses' mouths, that they may obey us; and we turn about their whole body.

4 Behold also the ships, which though *they be* so great, and *are* driven of fierce winds, yet are they turned about with a very small helm, whithersoever the governor listeth.

5 Even so the tongue is a little member, and boasteth great things. Behold, how great a matter a little fire kindleth!

6 And the tongue *is* a fire, a world of iniquity: so is the tongue among our members, that it de-

3 Μὴ πολλοὶ διδάσκαλοι γίνεσθε, ἀδελφοί
²not ³many ⁴teachers ¹Become ye, brothers

μου, εἰδότες ὅτι μεῖζον κρίμα λημψόμεθα.
of me, knowing that greater judgment we shall receive.

2 πολλὰ γὰρ πταίομεν ἅπαντες· εἴ τις
For [in] many [respects] we stumble all; if anyone

ἐν λόγῳ οὐ πταίει, οὗτος τέλειος ἀνήρ,
²in ³word ¹stumbles not, this [is] a perfect man,

δυνατὸς χαλιναγωγῆσαι καὶ ὅλον τὸ σῶμα.
able ²to bridle ¹indeed all the body.

3 εἰ δὲ τῶν ἵππων τοὺς χαλινοὺς εἰς
Now if - ⁶of horses - ²bridles ³into

τὰ στόματα βάλλομεν εἰς τὸ πείθεσθαι
⁴the ⁵mouths ¹we put for the to obey
=to make them obey us,

αὐτοὺς ἡμῖν, καὶ ὅλον τὸ σῶμα αὐτῶν
them to us, and ²all ³the ⁴body ⁵of them

μετάγομεν. 4 ἰδοὺ καὶ τὰ πλοῖα, τηλικαῦτα
¹we direct. Behold also the ships, ²so great

ὄντα καὶ ὑπὸ ἀνέμων σκληρῶν ἐλαυνόμενα,
¹being ³and ⁵by ⁷winds ⁶hard(strong) ⁴being driven,

μετάγεται ὑπὸ ἐλαχίστου πηδαλίου ὅπου
is(are) directed by a very little helm where

ἡ ὁρμὴ τοῦ εὐθύνοντος βούλεται· 5 οὕτως
the impulse of the [one] steering resolves; so

καὶ ἡ γλῶσσα μικρὸν μέλος ἐστὶν καὶ
also the tongue ²a little ³member ¹is and

μεγάλα αὐχεῖ. ἰδοὺ ἡλίκον πῦρ ἡλίκον
great things boasts. Behold how little a fire ²how great

ὕλην ἀνάπτει· 6 καὶ ἡ γλῶσσα πῦρ,
³wood ¹kindles; and the tongue [is] a fire,

ὁ κόσμος τῆς ἀδικίας, ἡ γλῶσσα καθίστα-
the world - of iniquity, the tongue is

ται ἐν τοῖς μέλεσιν ἡμῶν, ἡ σπιλοῦσα
set among the members of us, - spotting

fileth the whole body, and setteth on fire the course of nature; and it is set on fire of hell.

7 For every kind of beasts, and of birds, and of serpents, and of things in the sea, is tamed, and hath been tamed of mankind:

8 But the tongue can no man tame; *it is* an unruly evil, full of deadly poison.

9 Therewith bless we God, even the Father; and therewith curse we men, which are made after the similitude of God.

10 Out of the same mouth proceedeth blessing and cursing. My brethren, these things ought not so to be.

11 Doth a fountain send forth at the same place sweet *water* and bitter?

12 Can the fig tree, my brethren, bear olive berries? either a vine, figs? so *can* no fountain both yield salt water and fresh.

13 Who *is* a wise man and endued with knowledge among you? let him shew out of a good conversation his works with meekness of wisdom.

14 But if ye have bitter envying and strife in your

ὅλον τὸ σῶμα καὶ φλογίζουσα τὸν
all the body and inflaming the

τροχὸν τῆς γενέσεως καὶ φλογιζομένη
course - of nature and being inflamed

ὑπὸ τῆς γεέννης. 7 πᾶσα γὰρ φύσις
by - gehenna. For every nature

θηρίων τε καὶ πετεινῶν, ἑρπετῶν τε
²of beasts ¹both and of birds, ²of reptiles ¹both

καὶ ἐναλίων δαμάζεται καὶ δεδάμασται
and of marine is tamed and has been tamed
creatures

τῇ φύσει τῇ ἀνθρωπίνῃ, 8 τὴν δὲ
by the ²nature - ¹human, but the

γλῶσσαν οὐδεὶς δαμάσαι δύναται ἀνθρώπων·
tongue ¹no one ⁴to tame ³is able ²of men;

ἀκατάστατον κακόν, μεστὴ ἰοῦ θανατηφόρου.
an unruly evil, full ²poison ¹of death-dealing.

9 ἐν αὐτῇ εὐλογοῦμεν τὸν κύριον καὶ
By this we bless the Lord and

πατέρα, καὶ ἐν αὐτῇ καταρώμεθα τοὺς
Father, and by this we curse -

ἀνθρώπους τοὺς καθ' ὁμοίωσιν θεοῦ
men - ²according to ³likeness ⁴of God

γεγονότας· 10 ἐκ τοῦ αὐτοῦ στόματος ἐξέρχεται
¹having become; out of the same mouth comes forth

εὐλογία καὶ κατάρα. οὐ χρή, ἀδελφοί
blessing and cursing. It is not fitting, brothers

μου, ταῦτα οὕτως γίνεσθαι. 11 μήτι
of me, these things so to be. Not

ἡ πηγὴ ἐκ τῆς αὐτῆς ὀπῆς βρύει τὸ
the fountain out of the same hole sends forth the

γλυκὺ καὶ τὸ πικρόν; 12 μὴ δύναται,
sweet and the bitter ? Not can,

ἀδελφοί μου, συκῆ ἐλαίας ποιῆσαι ἤ
brothers of me, a fig-tree ²olives ¹to produce or

ἄμπελος σῦκα; οὔτε ἁλυκὸν γλυκὺ
a vine figs ? neither ¹salt ⁴sweet

ποιῆσαι ὕδωρ. 13 Τίς σοφὸς καὶ ἐπιστήμων
²to make ²water. Who [is] wise and knowing

ἐν ὑμῖν; δειξάτω ἐκ τῆς καλῆς ἀναστροφῆς
among you ? let him show by the(his) good conduct

τὰ ἔργα αὐτοῦ ἐν πραΰτητι σοφίας.*
the works of him in meekness of wisdom.*

14 εἰ δὲ ζῆλον πικρὸν ἔχετε καὶ ἐριθείαν
But if ³jealousy ²bitter ¹ye have and rivalry

ἐν τῇ καρδίᾳ ὑμῶν, μὴ κατακαυχᾶσθε
in the heart of you, do not exult over

---

* Genitive of quality : " a wise meekness."

hearts, glory not, and lie not against the truth.

15 This wisdom descendeth not from above, but *is* earthly, sensual, devilish.

16 For where envying and strife *is*, there *is* confusion and every evil work.

17 But the wisdom that is from above is first pure, then peaceable, gentle, *and* easy to be intreated, full of mercy and good fruits, without partiality, and without hypocrisy.

18 And the fruit of righteousness is sown in peace of them that make peace.

καὶ ψεύδεσθε κατὰ τῆς ἀληθείας. **15** οὐκ
and   lie   against the truth.   ⁴not

ἔστιν αὕτη ἡ σοφία ἄνωθεν κατερχομένη,
³is ¹This – ²wisdom ⁶from above ⁵coming down,

ἀλλὰ ἐπίγειος, ψυχική, δαιμονιώδης· **16** ὅπου
but [is] earthly, natural, demon-like;   ²where

γὰρ ζῆλος καὶ ἐριθεία, ἐκεῖ ἀκαταστασία
¹for jealousy and rivalry [are], there [is] tumult

καὶ πᾶν φαῦλον πρᾶγμα. **17** ἡ δὲ ἄνωθεν
and every worthless practice.   But ¹the ²from
                                              above

σοφία πρῶτον μὲν ἀγνή ἐστιν, ἔπειτα
²wisdom ⁵firstly – ⁶pure ⁴is,   then

εἰρηνική, ἐπιεικής, εὐπειθής, μεστὴ ἐλέους
peaceable, forbearing, compliant, full of mercy

καὶ καρπῶν ἀγαθῶν, ἀδιάκριτος, ἀνυπό-
and ²fruits ¹of good, without uncertainty, un-

κριτος. **18** καρπὸς δὲ δικαιοσύνης ἐν
feigned.   And [the] fruit of righteousness ²in

εἰρήνῃ σπείρεται τοῖς ποιοῦσιν εἰρήνην.
²peace ¹is sown for the [ones] making peace.

CHAPTER 4

F ROM whence *come* wars and fightings among you? *come they* not hence, *even* of your lusts that war in your members?

2 Ye lust, and have not: ye kill, and desire to have, and cannot obtain: ye fight and war, yet ye have not, because ye ask not.

3 Ye ask, and receive not, because ye ask amiss, that ye may consume *it* upon your lusts.

4 Ye adulterers and adulteresses, know ye not that the friendship of the world is enmity with God?

4 Πόθεν πόλεμοι καὶ πόθεν μάχαι ἐν
Whence wars and whence fights among

ὑμῖν; οὐκ ἐντεῦθεν, ἐκ τῶν ἡδονῶν
you? not thence, out of the pleasures

ὑμῶν τῶν στρατευομένων ἐν τοῖς μέλεσιν
of you – soldiering in the members

ὑμῶν; **2** ἐπιθυμεῖτε, καὶ οὐκ ἔχετε·
of you? Ye desire, and have not;

φονεύετε καὶ ζηλοῦτε, καὶ οὐ δύνασθε
ye murder and are jealous, and are not able

ἐπιτυχεῖν· μάχεσθε καὶ πολεμεῖτε. οὐκ
to obtain; ye fight and ye war. not

ἔχετε διὰ τὸ μὴ αἰτεῖσθαι ὑμᾶς· **3** αἰτεῖτε
Ye have be- *the* not to ask youᵇ;   ye ask
cause of
=because ye ask not;

καὶ οὐ λαμβάνετε, διότι κακῶς αἰτεῖσθε,
and receive not, because ²ill ¹ye ask,

ἵνα ἐν ταῖς ἡδοναῖς ὑμῶν δαπανήσητε.
in or- in the pleasures of you ye may spend.
der that

4 μοιχαλίδες, οὐκ οἴδατε ὅτι ἡ φιλία
    Adulteresses, know ye not that the friendship

τοῦ κόσμου ἔχθρα τοῦ θεοῦ ἐστιν; ὃς
of the world ²enmity – ³of God ¹is? Who-

whosoever therefore will be a friend of the world is the enemy of God.

5 Do ye think that the scripture saith in vain, The spirit that dwelleth in us lusteth to envy?

6 But he giveth more grace. Wherefore he saith, God resisteth the proud, but giveth grace unto the humble.

7 Submit yourselves therefore to God. Resist the devil, and he will flee from you.

8 Draw nigh to God, and he will draw nigh to you. Cleanse *your* hands, *ye* sinners; and purify *your* hearts, *ye* double minded.

9 Be afflicted, and mourn, and weep: let your laughter be turned to mourning, and *your* joy to heaviness.

10 Humble yourselves in the sight of the Lord, and he shall lift you up.

11 Speak not evil one of another, brethren. He that speaketh evil of *his* brother, and judgeth his brother, speaketh evil of the law, and judgeth the law: but if thou judge the law, thou art not a doer of the law, but a judge.

12 There is one lawgiver, who is able to save

ἐὰν οὖν βουληθῇ φίλος εἶναι τοῦ κόσμου,
ever therefore ¹resolves ³a friend ²to be of the world,

ἐχθρὸς τοῦ θεοῦ καθίσταται. 5 ἢ δοκεῖτε
²an enemy – ³of God ¹is constituted. Or think ye

ὅτι κενῶς ἡ γραφὴ λέγει· πρὸς φθόνον
that vainly the scripture says: ³to ⁴envy

ἐπιποθεῖ τὸ πνεῦμα ὃ κατῴκισεν ἐν
⁷yearns ¹The ²Spirit ³which ⁴dwelt ⁵in

ἡμῖν; 6 μείζονα δὲ δίδωσιν χάριν· διὸ
⁶you? But ²greater ¹he gives ³grace; wherefore

λέγει· ὁ θεὸς ὑπερηφάνοις ἀντιτάσσεται,
it* says: – God ²arrogant men ¹resists,

ταπεινοῖς δὲ δίδωσιν χάριν. 7 ὑποτάγητε
but to humble men he gives grace. Be ye subject

οὖν τῷ θεῷ· ἀντίστητε δὲ τῷ διαβόλῳ,
there- – to God; but oppose the devil,
fore

καὶ φεύξεται ἀφ᾽ ὑμῶν· 8 ἐγγίσατε τῷ
and he will flee from you; draw near

θεῷ, καὶ ἐγγίσει ὑμῖν. καθαρίσατε
to God, and he will draw near to you. Cleanse ye

χεῖρας, ἁμαρτωλοί, καὶ ἁγνίσατε καρδίας,
hands, sinners, and purify hearts,

δίψυχοι. 9 ταλαιπωρήσατε καὶ πενθήσατε
two-souled Be ye distressed and mourn
(double-minded).

καὶ κλαύσατε· ὁ γέλως ὑμῶν εἰς πένθος
and weep; the laughter of you to mourning

μετατραπήτω καὶ ἡ χαρὰ εἰς κατήφειαν.
let it be turned and the joy to dejection.

10 ταπεινώθητε ἐνώπιον κυρίου, καὶ ὑψώσει
Be ye humbled before [the] Lord, and he will exalt

ὑμᾶς. 11 Μὴ καταλαλεῖτε ἀλλήλων, ἀδελφοί.
you. Speak not against one another, brothers.

ὁ καταλαλῶν ἀδελφοῦ ἢ κρίνων τὸν
The speaking a brother or judging the
[one] against

ἀδελφὸν αὐτοῦ καταλαλεῖ νόμου καὶ κρίνει
brother of him speaks against law and judges

νόμον· εἰ δὲ νόμον κρίνεις, οὐκ εἶ
law; and if law thou judgest, thou art not

ποιητὴς νόμου ἀλλὰ κριτής. 12 εἷς ἐστιν
a doer of law but a judge. One is

νομοθέτης καὶ κριτής, ὁ δυνάμενος
lawgiver and judge, the [one] being able

* That is, " the scripture " (as ver. 5).

and to destroy: who art thou that judgest another?

13 Go to now, ye that say, To day or to morrow we will go into such a city, and continue there a year, and buy and sell, and get gain:

14 Whereas ye know not what *shall be* on the morrow. For what *is* your life? It is even a vapour, that appeareth for a little time, and then vanisheth away.

15 For that ye *ought* to say, If the Lord will, we shall live, and do this, or that.

16 But now ye rejoice in your boastings: all such rejoicing is evil.

17 Therefore to him that knoweth to do good, and doeth *it* not, to him it is sin.

σῶσαι καὶ ἀπολέσαι· σὺ δὲ τίς εἶ, ὁ
to save and to destroy; ⁴thou ¹and ²who ³art, the

κρίνων τὸν πλησίον;
[one] judging the(thy) neighbour?

13 "Αγε νῦν οἱ λέγοντες· σήμερον ἢ
Come now the [ones] saying: To-day or

αὔριον πορευσόμεθα εἰς τήνδε τὴν πόλιν
to-morrow we will go into this – city

καὶ ποιήσομεν ἐκεῖ ἐνιαυτὸν καὶ ἐμπορευ-
and we will do there a year and *we will*

σόμεθα καὶ κερδήσομεν· 14 οἵτινες οὐκ
trade and *we will* make a profit; who not

ἐπίστασθε τῆς αὔριον ποία ἡ ζωὴ ὑμῶν.
ye know ⁵of the ⁶morrow ¹what ²the ³life ⁴of you
[will be].

ἀτμὶς γάρ ἐστε ἡ πρὸς ὀλίγον φαινομένη,
For ³a vapour ¹ye are – 'for ²a little while ³appearing,

ἔπειτα καὶ ἀφανιζομένη· 15 ἀντὶ τοῦ
thereafter indeed disappearing; instead of *the*

λέγειν ὑμᾶς· ἐὰν ὁ κύριος θελήσῃ, καὶ
to say you[b]: If the Lord wills, both
=your saying:

ζήσομεν καὶ ποιήσομεν τοῦτο ἢ ἐκεῖνο.
we will live and *we will* do this or that.

16 νῦν δὲ καυχᾶσθε ἐν ταῖς ἀλαζονείαις
But now ye boast in the vauntings

ὑμῶν· πᾶσα καύχησις τοιαύτη πονηρά
of you; all ³boasting ¹such ⁴evil

ἐστιν. 17 εἰδότι οὖν καλὸν ποιεῖν καὶ
²is. ²to [one] ¹There- ⁴good ³to do and
knowing* fore

μὴ ποιοῦντι, ἁμαρτία αὐτῷ ἐστιν.
not doing, ³sin ¹to him ²it is.

CHAPTER 5

GO to now, *ye* rich men, weep and howl for your miseries that shall come upon *you*.

2 Your riches are corrupted, and your garments are motheaten.

3 Your gold and silver is cankered; and the rust of them shall be a witness against you, and shall eat

5 "Αγε νῦν οἱ πλούσιοι, κλαύσατε
Come now *the* rich men, weep ye

ὀλολύζοντες ἐπὶ ταῖς ταλαιπωρίαις ὑμῶν
crying aloud over the hardships of you

ταῖς ἐπερχομέναις. 2 ὁ πλοῦτος ὑμῶν
– coming upon. The riches of you

σέσηπεν, καὶ τὰ ἱμάτια ὑμῶν σητόβρωτα
have become and the garments of you moth-eaten
corrupted,

γέγονεν, 3 ὁ χρυσὸς ὑμῶν καὶ ὁ ἄργυρος
have become, the gold of you and the silver

κατίωται, καὶ ὁ ἰὸς αὐτῶν εἰς μαρτύριον
has become and the poison of them for a testimony
rusted over,

ὑμῖν ἔσται καὶ φάγεται τὰς σάρκας
to(against) will and will eat the flesh*es*
you be

* See note on page xviii.

your flesh as it were fire.
Ye have heaped treasure
together for the last days.
4 Behold, the hire of
the labourers who have
reaped down your fields,
which is of you kept back
by fraud, crieth: and the
cries of them which have
reaped are entered into
the ears of the Lord of
sabaoth.
5 Ye have lived in
pleasure on the earth, and
been wanton; ye have
nourished your hearts, as
in a day of slaughter.
6 Ye have condemned
and killed the just; *and*
he doth not resist you.
7 Be patient therefore,
brethren, unto the coming
of the Lord. Behold, the
husbandman waiteth for
the precious fruit of the
earth, and hath long
patience for it, until he
receive the early and
latter rain.
8 Be ye also patient;
stablish your hearts: for
the coming of the Lord
draweth nigh.
9 Grudge not one
against another, brethren,
lest ye be condemned:
behold, the judge standeth
before the door.
10 Take, my brethren,
the prophets, who have
spoken in the name of the
Lord, for an example of
suffering affliction, and
of patience.
11 Behold, we count
them happy which endure.

ὑμῶν ὡς πῦρ. ἐθησαυρίσατε ἐν ἐσχάταις
of you   as   fire.   Ye treasured   in   [the] last

ἡμέραις. 4 ἰδοὺ ὁ μισθὸς τῶν ἐργατῶν
days.   Behold[,] the   wages   of the   workmen

τῶν ἀμησάντων τὰς χώρας ὑμῶν ὁ
—   having reaped   the   lands   of you   —

ἀφυστερημένος ἀφ' ὑμῶν κράζει, καὶ αἱ
being kept back   from(by)   you   cries,   and   the

βοαὶ τῶν θερισάντων εἰς τὰ ὦτα κυρίου
cries   of the   having reaped   ²into ³the ⁴ears ⁵of [the]
[ones]   Lord

σαβαὼθ εἰσελήλυθαν. 5 ἐτρυφήσατε ἐπὶ
⁶of hosts   ¹have entered.   Ye lived daintily   on

τῆς γῆς καὶ ἐσπαταλήσατε, ἐθρέψατε τὰς
the   earth   and   lived riotously,   ye nourished   the

καρδίας ὑμῶν ἐν ἡμέρᾳ σφαγῆς. 6 κατε-
hearts   of you   in   a day   of slaughter.   Ye

δικάσατε, ἐφονεύσατε τὸν δίκαιον· οὐκ
condemned,   ye murdered   the   righteous man;   not

ἀντιτάσσεται ὑμῖν.
he resists   you.

7 Μακροθυμήσατε οὖν, ἀδελφοί, ἕως τῆς
Be ye longsuffering   therefore,   brothers,   until   the

παρουσίας τοῦ κυρίου. ἰδοὺ ὁ γεωργὸς
presence   of the   Lord.   Behold[,] the   farmer

ἐκδέχεται τὸν τίμιον καρπὸν τῆς γῆς,
awaits   the   precious   fruit   of the   earth,

μακροθυμῶν ἐπ' αὐτῷ ἕως λάβῃ πρόϊμον
being   over   it   until   he receives   early
longsuffering

καὶ ὄψιμον. 8 μακροθυμήσατε καὶ ὑμεῖς,
and   latter [rain].   Be ²longsuffering   ²also   ¹ye,

στηρίξατε τὰς καρδίας ὑμῶν, ὅτι ἡ
establish   the   hearts   of you,   because   the

παρουσία τοῦ κυρίου ἤγγικεν. 9 μὴ
presence   of the   Lord   has drawn near.   not

στενάζετε, ἀδελφοί, κατ' ἀλλήλων ἵνα μὴ
Murmur ye,   brothers,   against   one another   lest

κριθῆτε· ἰδοὺ ὁ κριτὴς πρὸ τῶν θυρῶν
ye be   behold[,] the   judge   ²before ³the ⁴doors
judged;

ἕστηκεν. 10 ὑπόδειγμα λάβετε, ἀδελφοί,
¹stands.   ⁵an example   ¹Take ye,   ²brothers,

τῆς κακοπαθίας καὶ τῆς μακροθυμίας
—   ⁶of suffering ill   ⁷and   —   ⁸of longsuffering

τοὺς προφήτας, οἳ ἐλάλησαν ἐν τῷ
³the   ⁴prophets,   who   spoke   in   the

ὀνόματι κυρίου. 11 ἰδοὺ μακαρίζομεν τοὺς
name   of [the] Lord.   Behold   we count blessed   the

Ye have heard of the patience of Job, and have seen the end of the Lord; that the Lord is very pitiful, and of tender mercy.

12 But above all things, my brethren, swear not, neither by heaven, neither by the earth, neither by any other oath: but let your yea be yea; and your nay, nay; lest ye fall into condemnation.

13 Is any among you afflicted? let him pray. Is any merry? let him sing psalms.

14 Is any sick among you? let him call for the elders of the church: and let them pray over him, anointing him with oil in the name of the Lord:

15 And the prayer of faith shall save the sick, and the Lord shall raise him up; and if he have committed sins, they shall be forgiven him.

16 Confess your faults one to another, and pray one for another, that ye may be healed. The effectual fervent prayer of a righteous man availeth much.

17 Elias was a man subject to like passions as we are, and he prayed earnestly that it might

ὑπομείναντας· τὴν ὑπομονὴν Ἰὼβ ἠκούσατε,
[ones] enduring; ²the ³endurance ⁴of Job ¹ye heard [of],

καὶ τὸ τέλος κυρίου εἴδετε, ὅτι πολύ-
and ²the ³end ⁴of [the] Lord ¹ye saw, that ⁴very

σπλαγχνός ἐστιν ὁ κύριος καὶ οἰκτίρμων.
compassionate ³is ¹the ²Lord and pitiful.

12 Πρὸ πάντων δέ, ἀδελφοί μου, μὴ
²before ³all things ¹But, brothers of me, not

ὀμνύετε, μήτε τὸν οὐρανὸν μήτε τὴν
swear ye, neither by the heaven nor by the

γῆν μήτε ἄλλον τινὰ ὅρκον· ἤτω δὲ
earth nor ²other ¹any oath; but let be

ὑμῶν τὸ ναὶ ναί, καὶ τὸ οὒ οὔ, ἵνα μὴ
of you the Yes yes, and the No no, lest

ὑπὸ κρίσιν πέσητε. 13 Κακοπαθεῖ τις
²under ³judgment ¹ye fall. Suffers ill anyone

ἐν ὑμῖν; προσευχέσθω· εὐθυμεῖ τις;
among you? let him pray; is cheerful anyone?

ψαλλέτω. 14 ἀσθενεῖ τις ἐν ὑμῖν;
let him sing a psalm. Is weak anyone among you?

προσκαλεσάσθω τοὺς πρεσβυτέρους τῆς
let him summon the elders of the

ἐκκλησίας, καὶ προσευξάσθωσαν ἐπ' αὐτὸν
church, and let them pray over him

ἀλείψαντες ἐλαίῳ ἐν τῷ ὀνόματι τοῦ
having anointed with oil in the name of the [him]

κυρίου. 15 καὶ ἡ εὐχὴ τῆς πίστεως
Lord. And the prayer - of faith

σώσει τὸν κάμνοντα, καὶ ἐγερεῖ αὐτὸν
will heal the [one] being sick, and ²will raise ⁴him

ὁ κύριος· κἂν ἁμαρτίας ᾖ πεποιηκώς,
¹the ²Lord; and if ²sins ¹he ³having done, may be

ἀφεθήσεται αὐτῷ. 16 ἐξομολογεῖσθε οὖν
it will be forgiven him. Confess ye therefore

ἀλλήλοις τὰς ἁμαρτίας, καὶ προσεύχεσθε
to one the (your) sins, and pray ye another

ὑπὲρ ἀλλήλων, ὅπως ἰαθῆτε. πολὺ
on behalf of one another, so as ye may be cured. ⁵much(very)

ἰσχύει δέησις δικαίου ἐνεργουμένη.
⁴is ⁶strong ¹a petition ²of a ³being made effective. righteous man

17 Ἠλίας ἄνθρωπος ἦν ὁμοιοπαθὴς ἡμῖν,
Elias ²a man ¹was of like feeling to us,

καὶ προσευχῇ προσηύξατο τοῦ μὴ βρέξαι,
and ²in prayer ¹he prayed - not to rain,ᵈ =that it should not rain,

not rain: and it rained not
on the earth by the space
of three years and six
months.

18 And he prayed again,
and the heaven gave rain,
and the earth brought
forth her fruit.

19 Brethren, if any of
you do err from the truth,
and one convert him;

20 Let him know, that
he which converteth the
sinner from the error of
his way shall save a soul
from death, and shall hide
a multitude of sins.

καὶ   οὐκ   ἔβρεξεν   ἐπὶ   τῆς   γῆς   ἐνιαυτοὺς
and   it rained not   on   the   earth   ²years

τρεῖς   καὶ   μῆνας   ἕξ·   **18** καὶ   πάλιν   προσ-
¹three   and   ²months   ¹six;   and   again   he

ηύξατο,   καὶ   ὁ   οὐρανὸς   ὑετὸν   ἔδωκεν   καὶ
prayed,   and   the   heaven   ²rain   ¹gave   and

ἡ   γῆ   ἐβλάστησεν   τὸν   καρπὸν   αὐτῆς.
the earth   brought forth   the   fruit   of it.

19 Ἀδελφοί   μου,   ἐάν   τις   ἐν   ὑμῖν   πλανηθῇ
Brothers   of me,   if   anyone among you   errs

ἀπὸ   τῆς   ἀληθείας   καὶ   ἐπιστρέψῃ   τις
from   the   truth   and   ²turns   ¹anyone

αὐτόν,   **20** γινώσκετε   ὅτι   ὁ   ἐπιστρέψας
him,   know ye   that   the [one]   turning

ἁμαρτωλὸν   ἐκ   πλάνης   ὁδοῦ   αὐτοῦ   σώσει
a sinner   out of [the] error   of way   of him   will save

ψυχὴν   αὐτοῦ   ἐκ   θανάτου   καὶ   καλύψει
soul   of him   out of   death   and   will hide

πλῆθος   ἁμαρτιῶν.
a multitude   of sins.

I. PETER 1

CHAPTER 1

PETER, an apostle of
Jesus Christ, to the
strangers scattered
throughout Pontus,
Galatia, Cappadocia, Asia,
and Bithynia,

2 Elect according to the
foreknowledge of God the
Father, through sanctification of the Spirit, unto
obedience and sprinkling
of the blood of Jesus
Christ: Grace unto you,
and peace, be multiplied.

3 Blessed be the God
and Father of our Lord
Jesus Christ, which ac-
cording to his abundant

ΠΕΤΡΟΥ Α
Of Peter 1

1 Πέτρος   ἀπόστολος   Ἰησοῦ   Χριστοῦ
Peter   an apostle   of Jesus   Christ

ἐκλεκτοῖς   παρεπιδήμοις   διασπορᾶς   Πόντου,
to [the] chosen   sojourners   of [the] dispersion   of Pontus,

Γαλατίας,   Καππαδοκίας,   Ἀσίας   καὶ
of Galatia,   of Cappadocia,   of Asia   and

Βιθυνίας,   **2** κατὰ   πρόγνωσιν   θεοῦ   πατρός,
of Bithynia,   according to   [the] foreknowledge   of God   Father,

ἐν   ἁγιασμῷ   πνεύματος,   εἰς   ὑπακοὴν   καὶ
in   sanctification   of spirit,   to   obedience   and

ῥαντισμὸν   αἵματος   Ἰησοῦ   Χριστοῦ·   χάρις
sprinkling   of [the] blood   of Jesus   Christ: Grace

ὑμῖν   καὶ   εἰρήνη   πληθυνθείη.
to you   and   peace   may it be multiplied.

3 Εὐλογητὸς   ὁ   θεὸς   καὶ   πατὴρ   τοῦ
Blessed [be]   the   God   and   Father   of the

κυρίου   ἡμῶν   Ἰησοῦ   Χριστοῦ,   ὁ   κατὰ   τὸ
Lord   of us   Jesus   Christ,   the [one]   according to   the

mercy hath begotten us again unto a lively hope by the resurrection of Jesus Christ from the dead,

4 To an inheritance incorruptible, and undefiled, and that fadeth not away, reserved in heaven for you,

5 Who are kept by the power of God through faith unto salvation ready to be revealed in the last time.

6 Wherein ye greatly rejoice, though now for a season, if need be, ye are in heaviness through manifold temptations:

7 That the trial of your faith, being much more precious than of gold that perisheth, though it be tried with fire, might be found unto praise and honour and glory at the appearing of Jesus Christ:

8 Whom having not seen, ye love; in whom, though now ye see him not, yet believing, ye rejoice with joy unspeakable and full of glory:

9 Receiving the end of your faith, even the salvation of your souls.

10 Of which salvation the prophets have enquired and searched diligently, who prophesied of the grace that should come unto you:

11 Searching what, or what manner of time the Spirit of Christ which was

πολὺ   αὐτοῦ   ἔλεος   ἀναγεννήσας   ἡμᾶς   εἰς
much   of him   mercy   having regenerated   us   to
(great)

ἐλπίδα   ζῶσαν   δι'   ἀναστάσεως   Ἰησοῦ
²hope   ¹a living   through   [the] resurrection   of Jesus

Χριστοῦ   ἐκ   νεκρῶν,   4 εἰς   κληρονομίαν
Christ   from   [the] dead,   to   an inheritance

ἄφθαρτον   καὶ   ἀμίαντον   καὶ   ἀμάραντον,
incorruptible   and   undefiled   and   unfading,

τετηρημένην   ἐν   οὐρανοῖς   εἰς   ὑμᾶς   5 τοὺς
having been kept   in   heavens   for   you   the [ones]

ἐν   δυνάμει   θεοῦ   φρουρουμένους   διὰ   πίστεως
²by   ³[the] power   ⁴of God   ¹being guarded   through   faith

εἰς   σωτηρίαν   ἑτοίμην   ἀποκαλυφθῆναι   ἐν
to   a salvation   ready   to be revealed   at

καιρῷ   ἐσχάτῳ.   6 ἐν   ᾧ   ἀγαλλιᾶσθε,
²time   ¹[the] last.   In   which   ye exult,

ὀλίγον   ἄρτι   εἰ   δέον   λυπηθέντες   ἐν
a little [while]   yet   if   necessary   grieving   by

ποικίλοις   πειρασμοῖς,   7 ἵνα   τὸ   δοκίμιον
manifold   trials,   in order that   the   proving

ὑμῶν   τῆς   πίστεως   πολυτιμότερον   χρυσίου
³of you   ¹of the   ²faith[,]   much more precious [than]   ²gold

τοῦ   ἀπολλυμένου,   διὰ   πυρὸς   δὲ   δοκιμαζ-
-    ¹of perishing,   ³through   ⁴fire   ¹yet   ²being

ομένου,   εὑρεθῇ   εἰς   ἔπαινον   καὶ   δόξαν
proved,   may be found   to   praise   and   glory

καὶ   τιμὴν   ἐν   ἀποκαλύψει   Ἰησοῦ   Χριστοῦ·
and   honour   at   [the] revelation   of Jesus   Christ;

8 ὃν   οὐκ   ἰδόντες   ἀγαπᾶτε,   εἰς   ὃν   ἄρτι
whom   not   having seen   ye love,   in   whom   yet

μὴ   ὁρῶντες   πιστεύοντες   δὲ   ἀγαλλιᾶσθε
not   seeing   ²believing   ¹but   ye exult

χαρᾷ   ἀνεκλαλήτῳ   καὶ   δεδοξασμένῃ,
with joy   unspeakable   and   having been glorified,

9 κομιζόμενοι   τὸ   τέλος   τῆς   πίστεως
obtaining   the   end   of the(your)   faith

σωτηρίαν   ψυχῶν.   10 περὶ   ἧς   σωτηρίας
[the] salvation   of [your] souls.   Concerning   which   salvation

ἐξεζήτησαν   καὶ   ἐξηρεύνησαν   προφῆται   οἱ
⁹sought out   ¹⁰and   ¹¹searched out   ¹prophets   ²the

περὶ   τῆς   εἰς   ὑμᾶς   χάριτος   προφητεύσαντες,
⁴con-   ⁵the   ⁷for   ⁸you   ⁶grace   ³[ones] prophesying,
cerning

11 ἐρευνῶντες   εἰς   τίνα   ἢ   ποῖον   καιρὸν
searching   for   what   or what sort of   time

ἐδήλου   τὸ   ἐν   αὐτοῖς   πνεῦμα   Χριστοῦ
⁶made clear   ¹the   ⁴in   ⁵them   ²Spirit   ³of Christ

in them did signify, when it testified beforehand the sufferings of Christ, and the glory that should follow.

12 Unto whom it was revealed, that not unto themselves, but unto us they did minister the things, which are now reported unto you by them that have preached the gospel unto you with the Holy Ghost sent down from heaven; which things the angels desire to look into.

13 Wherefore gird up the loins of your mind, be sober, and hope to the end for the grace that is to be brought unto you at the revelation of Jesus Christ;

14 As obedient children, not fashioning yourselves according to the former lusts in your ignorance:

15 But as he which hath called you is holy, so be ye holy in all manner of conversation;

16 Because it is written, Be ye holy; for I am holy.

17 And if ye call on the Father, who without respect of persons judgeth according to every man's work, pass the time of your sojourning *here* in fear:

18 Forasmuch as ye know that ye were not redeemed with corruptible

προμαρτυρόμενον τὰ εἰς Χριστὸν παθήματα
[7]forewitnessing [8]the [10]for [11]Christ [9]sufferings

καὶ τὰς μετὰ ταῦτα δόξας. 12 οἷς
[12]and [13]the [15]after [16]these [14]glories. To whom

ἀπεκαλύφθη ὅτι οὐχ ἑαυτοῖς ὑμῖν δὲ
it was revealed that not to themselves [2]to you [1]but

διηκόνουν αὐτά, ἃ νῦν ἀνηγγέλη ὑμῖν
they ministered the same things, which now were announced to you

διὰ τῶν εὐαγγελισαμένων ὑμᾶς ἐν
through the [ones] having evangelized you by

πνεύματι ἁγίῳ ἀποσταλέντι ἀπ' οὐρανοῦ,
[2]Spirit [1][the] Holy sent forth from heaven,

εἰς ἃ ἐπιθυμοῦσιν ἄγγελοι παρακύψαι.
into [1]which things [3]long [2]angels [4]to look into.

13 Διὸ ἀναζωσάμενοι τὰς ὀσφύας τῆς
Wherefore girding up the loins of the

διανοίας ὑμῶν, νήφοντες, τελείως ἐλπίσατε
mind of you, being sober, perfectly hope

ἐπὶ τὴν φερομένην ὑμῖν χάριν ἐν
on [1]the [3]being brought [4]to you [2]grace at

ἀποκαλύψει Ἰησοῦ Χριστοῦ. 14 ὡς τέκνα
[the] revelation of Jesus Christ. As children

ὑπακοῆς, μὴ συσχηματιζόμενοι ταῖς πρότε-
of obedience,* not fashioning yourselves to the [6]form-

ρον ἐν τῇ ἀγνοίᾳ ὑμῶν ἐπιθυμίαις, 15 ἀλλὰ
erly [2]in [3]the [4]ignorance [5]of you [1]longings, but

κατὰ τὸν καλέσαντα ὑμᾶς ἅγιον καὶ
according to [1]the [3]having called [4]you [2]holy [one] [5]also

αὐτοὶ ἅγιοι ἐν πάσῃ ἀναστροφῇ γενήθητε,
[6][your]-selves [8]holy [9]in [10]all [11]conduct [5]become ye,

16 διότι γέγραπται· [ὅτι] ἅγιοι ἔσεσθε,
because it has been written: – Holy ye shall be,

ὅτι ἐγὼ ἅγιος. 17 καὶ εἰ πατέρα
because I [am] holy. And if [2]Father

ἐπικαλεῖσθε τὸν ἀπροσωπολήμπτως κρίνοντα
[1]ye invoke [as] [3]the [one] [5]without respect to persons [4]judging

κατὰ τὸ ἑκάστου ἔργον, ἐν φόβῳ τὸν
according to the [2]of each man [1]work, [2]in [3]fear [4]the

τῆς παροικίας ὑμῶν χρόνον ἀναστράφητε,
[6]of the [7]sojourning [8]of you [5]time [1]pass,

18 εἰδότες ὅτι οὐ φθαρτοῖς, ἀργυρίῳ ἢ
knowing that not with corruptible things, silver or

---

* Genitive of quality: " obedient children."

things, *as* silver and gold, from your vain conversation *received* by tradition from your fathers;

19 But with the precious blood of Christ, as of a lamb without blemish and without spot:

20 Who verily was foreordained before the foundation of the world, but was manifest in these last times for you,

21 Who by him do believe in God, that raised him up from the dead, and gave him glory; that your faith and hope might be in God.

22 Seeing ye have purified your souls in obeying the truth through the Spirit unto unfeigned love of the brethren, *see that ye* love one another with a pure heart fervently:

23 Being born again, not of corruptible seed, but of incorruptible, by the word of God, which liveth and abideth for ever.

24 For all flesh *is* as grass, and all the glory of man as the flower of grass. The grass withereth, and the flower thereof falleth away:

25 But the word of the Lord endureth for ever. And this is the word which by the gospel is preached unto you.

CHAPTER 2

WHEREFORE laying aside all malice, and all guile, and hypocrisies, and envies, and all evil speakings,

χρυσίῳ, ἐλυτρώθητε ἐκ τῆς ματαίας ὑμῶν
gold, ye were redeemed from the vain ²of you

ἀναστροφῆς πατροπαραδότου, 19 ἀλλὰ τιμίῳ
¹conduct delivered from but with
[your] fathers,

αἵματι ὡς ἀμνοῦ ἀμώμου καὶ ἀσπίλου
blood[,] as of a lamb unblemished and unspotted[,]

Χριστοῦ, 20 προεγνωσμένου μὲν πρὸ κατα-
of Christ, having been foreknown on one from [the]
hand

βολῆς κόσμου, φανερωθέντος δὲ ἐπ᾽ ἐσχάτου
founda- of [the] manifested on the in [the] last
tion world, other

τῶν χρόνων δι᾽ ὑμᾶς 21 τοὺς δι᾽ αὐτοῦ
of the times because of you the ones through him

πιστοὺς εἰς θεὸν τὸν ἐγείραντα αὐτὸν
believing in God the [one] having raised him

ἐκ νεκρῶν καὶ δόξαν αὐτῷ δόντα, ὥστε
from [the] dead and ²glory ³to him ¹having given, so as

τὴν πίστιν ὑμῶν καὶ ἐλπίδα εἶναι εἰς
the ¹faith ⁴of you ²and ³hope to be in

θεόν. 22 Τὰς ψυχὰς ὑμῶν ἡγνικότες
God. ²The ³souls ⁴of you ¹having purified

ἐν τῇ ὑπακοῇ τῆς ἀληθείας εἰς φιλαδελφίαν
by – obedience of(to) the truth to ²brotherly love

ἀνυπόκριτον, ἐκ καρδίας ἀλλήλους ἀγαπήσατε
¹unfeigned, ⁴from ⁵[the] heart ²one another ¹love ye

ἐκτενῶς, 23 ἀναγεγεννημένοι οὐκ ἐκ σπορᾶς
³earnestly, having been regenerated not by ²seed

φθαρτῆς ἀλλὰ ἀφθάρτου, διὰ λόγου ζῶντος
¹corruptible but incorruptible, through ⁴word ¹[the] living

θεοῦ καὶ μένοντος. 24 διότι πᾶσα σὰρξ
⁵of God ²and ³remaining. Because all flesh [is]

ὡς χόρτος, καὶ πᾶσα δόξα αὐτῆς ὡς
as grass, and all [the] glory of it as

ἄνθος χόρτου· ἐξηράνθη ὁ χόρτος, καὶ
a flower of grass; was dried the grass, and

τὸ ἄνθος ἐξέπεσεν· 25 τὸ δὲ ῥῆμα κυρίου
the flower fell out; but the word of [the] Lord

μένει εἰς τὸν αἰῶνα. τοῦτο δέ ἐστιν
remains unto the age. And this is

τὸ ῥῆμα τὸ εὐαγγελισθὲν εἰς ὑμᾶς.
the word – preached [as good news] to you.

2 Ἀποθέμενοι οὖν πᾶσαν κακίαν καὶ
Putting away therefore all malice and

πάντα δόλον καὶ ὑποκρίσεις καὶ φθόνους
all guile and hypocrisies and envies

καὶ πάσας καταλαλιάς, 2 ὡς ἀρτιγέννητα
and all detractions, as newborn

2 As newborn babes, desire the sincere milk of the word, that ye may grow thereby:

3 If so be ye have tasted that the Lord *is* gracious.

4 To whom coming, *as unto* a living stone, disallowed indeed of men, but chosen of God, *and* precious,

5 Ye also, as lively stones, are built up a spiritual house, an holy priesthood, to offer up spiritual sacrifices, acceptable to God by Jesus Christ.

6 Wherefore also it is contained in the scripture, Behold, I lay in Sion a chief corner stone, elect, precious: and he that believeth on him shall not be confounded.

7 Unto you therefore which believe *he is* precious: but unto them which be disobedient, the stone which the builders disallowed, the same is made the head of the corner,

8 And a stone of stumbling, and a rock of offence, *even to them* which stumble at the word, being disobedient: whereunto also they were appointed.

9 But ye *are* a chosen generation, a royal priesthood, an holy nation, a peculiar people; that ye should shew forth the

βρέφη τὸ λογικὸν ἄδολον γάλα ἐπιποθήσατε,
babes ²the ³spiritual ⁴pure ⁵milk ¹desire ye,

ἵνα ἐν αὐτῷ αὐξηθῆτε εἰς σωτηρίαν,
in or- by it ye may grow to salvation,
der that

3 εἰ ἐγεύσασθε ὅτι χρηστὸς ὁ κύριος.
if ye tasted that ²good ¹the ²Lord [is].

4 πρὸς ὃν προσερχόμενοι, λίθον ζῶντα,
to whom approaching, ²stone ¹a living,

ὑπὸ ἀνθρώπων μὲν ἀποδεδοκιμασμένον παρὰ
by men on one *having been* rejected ³by
hand

δὲ θεῷ ἐκλεκτὸν ἔντιμον, 5 καὶ
¹on the ⁴God ²chosen[,] precious, ²also
other

αὐτοὶ ὡς λίθοι ζῶντες οἰκοδομεῖσθε οἶκος
¹[your]- ²as ⁵stones ⁴living are being built ²house
selves

πνευματικὸς εἰς ἱεράτευμα ἅγιον, ἀνενέγκαι
¹a spiritual for ²priesthood ¹a holy, to offer

πνευματικὰς θυσίας εὐπροσδέκτους θεῷ διὰ
spiritual sacrifices acceptable to through
God

Ἰησοῦ Χριστοῦ· 6 διότι περιέχει ἐν γραφῇ·
Jesus Christ; because it is in scripture:
contained

ἰδοὺ τίθημι ἐν Σιὼν λίθον ἐκλεκτὸν
Behold I lay in Sion ²stone ¹a chosen

ἀκρογωνιαῖον ἔντιμον, καὶ ὁ πιστεύων
³corner foundation ²precious, and the [one] believing

ἐπ' αὐτῷ οὐ μὴ καταισχυνθῇ. 7 ὑμῖν
on it(him) by no means will be shamed. To you
=Yours

οὖν ἡ τιμὴ τοῖς πιστεύουσιν· ἀπιστοῦσιν
there- ³[is] ⁵honour ¹the [ones] ²believing°; ²to unbelieving
fore ⁴the [ones]
therefore who believe is the honour;

δὲ λίθος ὃν ἀπεδοκίμασαν οἱ οἰκοδομοῦντες,
¹but a stone which ²rejected ¹the [ones] ³building,

οὗτος ἐγενήθη εἰς κεφαλὴν γωνίας 8 καὶ
this came to be for head of [the] corner and

λίθος προσκόμματος καὶ πέτρα σκανδάλου·
a stone of stumbling and a rock of offence;

οἳ προσκόπτουσιν τῷ λόγῳ ἀπειθοῦντες,
who stumble at the word disobeying,

9 εἰς ὃ καὶ ἐτέθησαν· ὑμεῖς δὲ γένος
to which indeed they were but ye [are] ²race
appointed;

ἐκλεκτόν, βασίλειον ἱεράτευμα, ἔθνος ἅγιον,
¹a chosen, a royal priesthood, nation a holy,

λαὸς εἰς περιποίησιν, ὅπως τὰς ἀρετὰς
a people for possession, so as ²the ³virtues

praises of him who hath called you out of darkness into his marvellous light:

10 Which in time past *were* not a people, but *are* now the people of God: which had not obtained mercy, but now have obtained mercy.

11 Dearly beloved, I beseech *you* as strangers and pilgrims, abstain from fleshly lusts, which war against the soul;

12 Having your conversation honest among the Gentiles: that, whereas they speak against you as evildoers, they may by *your* good works, which they shall behold, glorify God in the day of visitation.

13 Submit yourselves to every ordinance of man for the Lord's sake: whether it be to the king, as supreme;

14 Or unto governors, as unto them that are sent by him for the punishment of evildoers, and for the praise of them that do well.

15 For so is the will of God, that with well doing ye may put to silence the ignorance of foolish men:

16 As free, and not using *your* liberty for a cloke of maliciousness, but as the servants of God.

17 Honour all *men.*

ἐξαγγείλητε τοῦ ἐκ σκότους ὑμᾶς καλέ-
¹ye may tell out ⁴of the ⁷out ⁸darkness ⁶you ⁵having
[one]   of

σαντος εἰς τὸ θαυμαστὸν αὐτοῦ φῶς·
called into the marvellous ²of him ¹light;

10 οἳ ποτε οὐ λαός, νῦν δὲ λαὸς θεοῦ,
who then not a but [are] a of
[were] people, now people God,

οἱ οὐκ ἠλεημένοι, νῦν δὲ ἐλεηθέντες.
the not having been pitied, but now pitied.
[ones]

11 Ἀγαπητοί, παρακαλῶ ὡς παροίκους
Beloved, I exhort [you] as sojourners

καὶ παρεπιδήμους ἀπέχεσθαι τῶν σαρκικῶν
and aliens to abstain from - fleshly

ἐπιθυμιῶν, αἵτινες στρατεύονται κατὰ τῆς
lusts, which war against the

ψυχῆς· 12 τὴν ἀναστροφὴν ὑμῶν ἐν τοῖς
soul; ²the ³conduct ⁴of you ⁵among ⁶the

ἔθνεσιν ἔχοντες καλήν, ἵνα ἐν ᾧ κατα-
⁷nations ¹having ⁸good, in order while they
that

λαλοῦσιν ὑμῶν ὡς κακοποιῶν, ἐκ τῶν
speak against you as evildoers, by the
(your)

καλῶν ἔργων ἐποπτεύοντες δοξάσωσιν τὸν
good works observing they may glorify -

θεὸν ἐν ἡμέρᾳ ἐπισκοπῆς.
God in a day of visitation.

13 Ὑποτάγητε πάσῃ ἀνθρωπίνῃ κτίσει
Submit to every human ordinance

διὰ τὸν κύριον· εἴτε βασιλεῖ ὡς ὑπερέχοντι,
be- the Lord: whether to a king as being supreme,
cause of

14 εἴτε ἡγεμόσιν ὡς δι' αὐτοῦ πεμπομένοις
or to governors as through him being sent

εἰς ἐκδίκησιν κακοποιῶν ἔπαινον δὲ
for vengeance of(on) evildoers ²praise ¹but

ἀγαθοποιῶν· 15 ὅτι οὕτως ἐστὶν τὸ
of welldoers; because so is the

θέλημα τοῦ θεοῦ, ἀγαθοποιοῦντας φιμοῦν
will - of God, doing good to silence

τὴν τῶν ἀφρόνων ἀνθρώπων ἀγνωσίαν·
¹the - ³of foolish ⁴men ²ignorance;

16 ὡς ἐλεύθεροι, καὶ μὴ ὡς ἐπικάλυμμα
as free, and not ³as ⁴a cloak

ἔχοντες τῆς κακίας τὴν ἐλευθερίαν, ἀλλ'
¹having *the* ⁵of evil *the* ²freedom, but

ὡς θεοῦ δοῦλοι. 17 πάντας τιμήσατε,
as of God slaves. ²All men ¹honour ye,

Love the brotherhood. Fear God. Honour the king.

18 Servants, *be* subject to *your* masters with all fear; not only to the good and gentle, but also to the froward.

19 For this *is* thankworthy, if a man for conscience toward God endure grief, suffering wrongfully.

20 For what glory *is it*, if, when ye be buffeted for your faults, ye shall take it patiently? but if, when ye do well, and suffer *for it*, ye take it patiently, this *is* acceptable with God.

21 For even hereunto were ye called: because Christ also suffered for us, leaving us an example, that ye should follow his steps:

22 Who did no sin, neither was guile found in his mouth:

23 Who, when he was reviled, reviled not again; when he suffered, he threatened not; but committed *himself* to him that judgeth righteously:

24 Who his own self bare our sins in his own body on the tree, that we, being dead to sins, should live unto righteousness: by whose stripes ye were healed.

τὴν ἀδελφότητα ἀγαπᾶτε, τὸν θεὸν
²the ³brotherhood ¹love, – ²God

φοβεῖσθε, τὸν βασιλέα τιμᾶτε. 18 Οἱ
¹fear, ²the ³king ¹honour. –

οἰκέται, ὑποτασσόμενοι ἐν παντὶ φόβῳ
House submitting yourselves in all fear
servants,

τοῖς δεσπόταις, οὐ μόνον τοῖς ἀγαθοῖς
to the(your) masters, not only to the good

καὶ ἐπιεικέσιν ἀλλὰ καὶ τοῖς σκολιοῖς.
and forbearing but also to the perverse.

19 τοῦτο γὰρ χάρις εἰ διὰ συνείδησιν
For this [is] a favour if because of conscience

θεοῦ ὑποφέρει τις λύπας πάσχων ἀδίκως.
of God ²bears ¹anyone griefs suffering unjustly.

20 ποῖον γὰρ κλέος εἰ ἁμαρτάνοντες καὶ
For what glory [is it] if sinning and

κολαφιζόμενοι ὑπομενεῖτε; ἀλλ᾽ εἰ ἀγαθο-
being buffeted ye endure? but if doing

ποιοῦντες καὶ πάσχοντες ὑπομενεῖτε, τοῦτο
good and suffering ye endure, this [is]

χάρις παρὰ θεῷ. 21 εἰς τοῦτο γὰρ
a favour with God. ²to ³this ¹For

ἐκλήθητε, ὅτι καὶ Χριστὸς ἔπαθεν ὑπὲρ
ye were because indeed Christ suffered on be-
called, half of

ὑμῶν, ὑμῖν ὑπολιμπάνων ὑπογραμμὸν ἵνα
you, ²to you ¹leaving behind an example in order that

ἐπακολουθήσητε τοῖς ἴχνεσιν αὐτοῦ· 22 ὃς
ye should follow the steps of him; who

ἁμαρτίαν οὐκ ἐποίησεν οὐδὲ εὑρέθη δόλος
³sin ²not ¹did nor was ²found ¹guile

ἐν τῷ στόματι αὐτοῦ· 23 ὃς λοιδορούμενος
in the mouth of him; who being reviled

οὐκ ἀντελοιδόρει, πάσχων οὐκ ἠπείλει,
reviled not in return, suffering he threatened not,

παρεδίδου δὲ τῷ κρίνοντι δικαίως· 24 ὃς
but delivered to the judging righteously; who
[himself] [one]

τὰς ἁμαρτίας ἡμῶν αὐτὸς ἀνήνεγκεν ἐν
³the ⁴sins ⁵of us ⁶[him]self ²carried up in

τῷ σώματι αὐτοῦ ἐπὶ τὸ ξύλον, ἵνα
the body of him onto the tree, in order that

ταῖς ἁμαρτίαις ἀπογενόμενοι τῇ δικαιοσύνῃ
– ²to sins ¹dying – ⁴to righteousness

ζήσωμεν· οὗ τῷ μώλωπι ἰάθητε.
³we might live; ³of ¹by ²bruise ye were cured.
whom the

25 For ye were as sheep going astray; but are now returned unto the Shepherd and Bishop of your souls.

25 ἦτε γὰρ ὡς πρόβατα πλανώμενοι,
²ye were ¹For ⁴as ⁵sheep ³wandering,
ἀλλὰ ἐπεστράφητε νῦν ἐπὶ τὸν ποιμένα
but ye turned now to the shepherd
καὶ ἐπίσκοπον τῶν ψυχῶν ὑμῶν.
and bishop of the souls of you.

CHAPTER 3

LIKEWISE, ye wives, *be* in subjection to your own husbands; that, if any obey not the word, they also may without the word be won by the conversation of the wives;

2 While they behold your chaste conversation *coupled* with fear.

3 Whose adorning let it not be that outward *adorning* of plaiting the hair, and of wearing of gold, or of putting on of apparel;

4 But *let it be* the hidden man of the heart, in that which is not corruptible, *even the ornament* of a meek and quiet spirit, which is in the sight of God of great price.

5 For after this manner in the old time the holy women also, who trusted in God, adorned themselves, being in subjection unto their own husbands:

6 Even as Sara obeyed Abraham, calling him lord: whose daughters ye are, as long as ye do well, and are not afraid with any amazement.

7 Likewise, ye husbands, dwell with *them* according to knowledge, giving honour unto the wife, as unto the weaker

3 Ὁμοίως γυναῖκες, ὑποτασσόμεναι τοῖς
Likewise wives, submitting yourselves to the
(your)
ἰδίοις ἀνδράσιν, ἵνα καὶ εἴ τινες ἀπειθοῦσιν
own husbands, in or-even if any disobey
der that
τῷ λόγῳ, διὰ τῆς τῶν γυναικῶν ἀναστροφῆς
the word, through ¹the ³of ⁴wives ²conduct
the(ir)
ἄνευ λόγου κερδηθήσονται, 2 ἐποπτεύσαντες
without a word they will(may) be gained, observing
τὴν ἐν φόβῳ ἁγνὴν ἀναστροφὴν ὑμῶν.
¹the ⁵in ⁶fear ²pure ³conduct ⁴of you.
3 ὧν ἔστω οὐχ ὁ ἔξωθεν ἐμπλοκῆς
Of whom let it be not ¹the ²outward ⁴of plaiting
τριχῶν καὶ περιθέσεως χρυσίων ἢ ἐνδύσεως
⁵of hairs ⁶and ⁷of putting ⁸of gold ⁹or ¹⁰of clothing
round(on) [ornaments]
ἱματίων κόσμος, 4 ἀλλ' ὁ κρυπτὸς τῆς
¹¹of(with) ³adorning, but ¹the ²hidden ⁴of the
garments
καρδίας ἄνθρωπος ἐν τῷ ἀφθάρτῳ τοῦ
⁵heart ³man in(?by) the incorruptible of the
[adorning]
πραέος καὶ ἡσυχίου πνεύματος, ὅ ἐστιν
meek and quiet spirit, which is
ἐνώπιον τοῦ θεοῦ πολυτελές. 5 οὕτως
before - God of great value. so
γὰρ ποτε καὶ αἱ ἅγιαι γυναῖκες αἱ
For then indeed the holy women -
ἐλπίζουσαι εἰς θεὸν ἐκόσμουν ἑαυτάς,
hoping in God adorned themselves,
ὑποτασσόμεναι τοῖς ἰδίοις ἀνδράσιν, 6 ὡς
submitting themselves to the(ir) own husbands, as
Σάρρα ὑπήκουσεν τῷ Ἀβραάμ, κύριον
Sara obeyed Abraham, ³lord
αὐτὸν καλοῦσα· ἧς ἐγενήθητε τέκνα
²him ¹calling; of whom ye became children
ἀγαθοποιοῦσαι καὶ μὴ φοβούμεναι μηδεμίαν
doing good and not fearing no(any)
πτόησιν. 7 Οἱ ἄνδρες ὁμοίως, συνοικοῦντες
terror. - Husbands likewise, dwelling together
κατὰ γνῶσιν ὡς ἀσθενεστέρῳ σκεύει τῷ
accord-knowledge as with a weaker vessel the
ing to

vessel, and as being heirs together of the grace of life; that your prayers be not hindered.

8 Finally, *be ye* all of one mind, having compassion one of another, love as brethren, *be* pitiful, *be* courteous:

9 Not rendering evil for evil, or railing for railing: but contrariwise blessing; knowing that ye are thereunto called, that ye should inherit a blessing.

10 For he that will love life, and see good days, let him refrain his tongue from evil, and his lips that they speak no guile:

11 Let him eschew evil, and do good; let him seek peace, and ensue it.

12 For the eyes of the Lord *are* over the righteous, and his ears *are open* unto their prayers: but the face of the Lord *is* against them that do evil.

13 And who *is* he that will harm you, if ye be followers of that which is good?

14 But and if ye suffer for righteousness' sake, happy *are ye:* and be not afraid of their terror, neither be troubled;

15 But sanctify the Lord

γυναικείῳ,   ἀπονέμοντες   τιμὴν   ὡς   καὶ
female,   assigning   honour   as   indeed

συγκληρονόμοις   χάριτος   ζωῆς,   εἰς   τὸ   μὴ
co-heirs   of [the] grace   of life,   *for*   *the*   not

ἐγκόπτεσθαι   τὰς   προσευχὰς   ὑμῶν.   8 Τὸ   δὲ
to be hindered   the   prayers   of you.[b]   Now the

τέλος   πάντες   ὁμόφρονες,   συμπαθεῖς,
end[,]   [be ye] all   of one mind,   sympathetic,

φιλάδελφοι,   εὔσπλαγχνοι,   ταπεινόφρονες,
loving [the] brothers,   compassionate,   humble-minded,

9 μὴ   ἀποδιδόντες   κακὸν   ἀντὶ   κακοῦ   ἢ
not   giving back   evil   instead of   evil   or

λοιδορίαν   ἀντὶ   λοιδορίας,   τοὐναντίον   δὲ
reviling   instead of   reviling,   but on the contrary

εὐλογοῦντες,   ὅτι   εἰς   τοῦτο   ἐκλήθητε   ἵνα
blessing,   because   to   this   ye were called   in order that

εὐλογίαν   κληρονομήσητε.   10 ὁ   γὰρ   θέλων
blessing   ye might inherit.   For the [one] wishing

ζωὴν   ἀγαπᾶν   καὶ   ἰδεῖν   ἡμέρας   ἀγαθάς,
[2]life   [1]to love   and   to see   [2]days   [1]good,

παυσάτω   τὴν   γλῶσσαν   ἀπὸ   κακοῦ   καὶ
let him restrain   the(his)   tongue   from   evil   and

χείλη   τοῦ   μὴ   λαλῆσαι   δόλον,   11 ἐκκλινάτω
[his] lips   –   not   to speak[d]   guile,   [2]let him turn aside

δὲ   ἀπὸ   κακοῦ   καὶ   ποιησάτω   ἀγαθόν,
[1]and   from   evil   and   let him do   good,

ζητησάτω   εἰρήνην   καὶ   διωξάτω   αὐτήν·
let him seek   peace   and   pursue   it;

12 ὅτι   ὀφθαλμοὶ   κυρίου   ἐπὶ   δικαίους   καὶ
because   [the] eyes   of [the] Lord   [are] on   [the] righteous   and

ὦτα   αὐτοῦ   εἰς   δέησιν   αὐτῶν,   πρόσωπον
[the] ears   of him   [open] to   [the] petition   of them,   [2][the] face

δὲ   κυρίου   ἐπὶ   ποιοῦντας   κακά.
[1]but   of [the] Lord   [is] against   [ones] doing   evil things.

13 Καὶ   τίς   ὁ   κακώσων   ὑμᾶς   ἐὰν   τοῦ
And   who   the [is] [one]   harming   you   if   [3]of the

ἀγαθοῦ   ζηλωταὶ   γένησθε;   14 ἀλλ'   εἰ   καὶ
[4]good   [2]zealots   [1]ye become ?   but   if   indeed

πάσχοιτε   διὰ   δικαιοσύνην,   μακάριοι.   τὸν
ye suffer   because of   righteousness,   blessed [are ye].   [3]the

δὲ   φόβον   αὐτῶν   μὴ   φοβηθῆτε   μηδὲ
[1]But   [4]fear   [5]of them   [2]fear ye not   nor

ταραχθῆτε,   15 κύριον   δὲ   τὸν   Χριστὸν
be ye troubled,   [1]but [4][as] [5]Lord   –   [3]Christ

God in your hearts: and be ready always to *give* an answer to every man that asketh you a reason of the hope that is in you with meekness and fear:

16 Having a good conscience; that, whereas they speak evil of you, as of evildoers, they may be ashamed that falsely accuse your good conversation in Christ.

17 For *it is* better, if the will of God be so, that ye suffer for well doing, than for evil doing.

18 For Christ also hath once suffered for sins, the just for the unjust, that he might bring us to God, being put to death in the flesh, but quickened by the Spirit:

19 By which also he went and preached unto the spirits in prison;

20 Which sometime were disobedient, when once the longsuffering of God waited in the days of Noah, while the ark was a preparing, wherein few, that is, eight souls were saved by water.

21 The like figure whereunto *even* baptism doth also now save us (not the putting away of the filth of the flesh, but the answer of a good con-

ἁγιάσατε ἐν ταῖς καρδίαις ὑμῶν, ἕτοιμοι
²sanctify   in   the   hearts   of you,   ready

ἀεὶ πρὸς ἀπολογίαν παντὶ τῷ αἰτοῦντι
always for   defence   to every one   asking

ὑμᾶς λόγον περὶ τῆς ἐν ὑμῖν ἐλπίδος,
you   a word concerning ¹the ³in ⁴you   ²hope,

16 ἀλλὰ μετὰ πραΰτητος καὶ φόβου,
but   with   meekness   and   fear,

συνείδησιν ἔχοντες ἀγαθήν, ἵνα ἐν ᾧ
³conscience ¹having ²a good, in order that while

καταλαλεῖσθε καταισχυνθῶσιν οἱ ἐπηρεάζον-
ye are spoken against ³may be shamed [by] ¹the [ones] ²abusing

τες ὑμῶν τὴν ἀγαθὴν ἐν Χριστῷ
[you] ⁷of you ⁴the ⁵good ⁸in ⁹Christ

ἀναστροφήν. 17 κρεῖττον γὰρ ἀγαθοποι-
⁶conduct.   For [it is] better   doing

οῦντας, εἰ θέλοι τὸ θέλημα τοῦ θεοῦ,
good,   if ⁴wills ¹the ²will — ³of God,

πάσχειν ἢ κακοποιοῦντας. 18 ὅτι καὶ
to suffer than   doing evil.   Because indeed

Χριστὸς ἅπαξ περὶ ἁμαρτιῶν ἀπέθανεν,
Christ   once ²concerning ³sins   ¹died,

δίκαιος ὑπὲρ ἀδίκων, ἵνα ὑμᾶς προσαγάγῃ
a righteous on be- unrighteous in or- ²you ¹he might
man   half of   ones,   der that   bring

τῷ θεῷ, θανατωθεὶς μὲν σαρκὶ ζωοποιηθεὶς
— to   being put to on one in [the] quickened
God,   death   hand   flesh[,]

δὲ πνεύματι· 19 ἐν ᾧ καὶ τοῖς ἐν
on the in [the]   in which indeed ³to the ⁴in
other   spirit;

φυλακῇ πνεύμασιν πορευθεὶς ἐκήρυξεν,
⁵prison   ³spirits   ¹going   he proclaimed,

20 ἀπειθήσασίν ποτε ὅτε ἀπεξεδέχετο ἡ
to disobeying ones   then when ⁴waited ¹the

τοῦ θεοῦ μακροθυμία ἐν ἡμέραις Νῶε
— ³of God ²longsuffering in [the] days of Noe

κατασκευαζομένης κιβωτοῦ, εἰς ἣν ὀλίγοι,
²being prepared   ¹an ark,ᵃ   in which a few,

τοῦτ᾽ ἔστιν ὀκτὼ ψυχαί, διεσώθησαν δι᾽
this   is   eight   souls,   were   through
quite saved

ὕδατος. 21 ὃ καὶ ὑμᾶς ἀντίτυπον νῦν
water.   ¹Which ³also ⁶us ²figure ⁴now

σώζει βάπτισμα, οὐ σαρκὸς ἀπόθεσις
⁵saves [even] baptism, not ³of [the] ¹a putting
flesh   away

ῥύπου ἀλλὰ συνειδήσεως ἀγαθῆς ἐπερώτημα
²of [the] but ³conscience ²of a good ¹an answer
filth

science toward God,) by
the resurrection of Jesus
Christ:

22 Who is gone into
heaven, and is on the right
hand of God; angels and
authorities and powers
being made subject unto
him.

CHAPTER 4

FORASMUCH then as
Christ hath suffered
for us in the flesh, arm
yourselves likewise with
the same mind: for he
that hath suffered in the
flesh hath ceased from sin;

2 That he no longer
should live the rest of *his*
time in the flesh to the lusts
of men, but to the will of
God.

3 For the time past of
our life may suffice us to
have wrought the will of
the Gentiles, when we
walked in lasciviousness,
lusts, excess of wine, revellings, banquetings, and
abominable idolatries:

4 Wherein they think it
strange that ye run not
with *them* to the same
excess of riot, speaking
evil of *you:*

5 Who shall give ac-
count to him that is ready
to judge the quick and
the dead.

6 For for this cause
was the gospel preached
also to them that are
dead, that they might be
judged according to men
in the flesh, but live
according to God in the
spirit.

εἰς θεόν, δι' ἀναστάσεως Ἰησοῦ Χριστοῦ,
toward God, through [the] resurrection of Jesus Christ,

22 ὅς ἐστιν ἐν δεξιᾷ θεοῦ, πορευθεὶς
who is at [the] right of God, having gone
[hand]

εἰς οὐρανόν, ὑποταγέντων αὐτῷ ἀγγέλων
into heaven, ⁶being subjected ⁷to him ¹angels

καὶ ἐξουσιῶν καὶ δυνάμεων.
²and ³authorities ⁴and ⁵powersᵃ.

4 Χριστοῦ οὖν παθόντος σαρκὶ καὶ ὑμεῖς
²Christ ¹there- sufferedᵃ in [the] ³also ¹ye
fore flesh

τὴν αὐτὴν ἔννοιαν ὁπλίσασθε, ὅτι ὁ
⁴the ⁵same ⁶mind ³arm your- because the
selves [with], [one]

παθὼν σαρκὶ πέπαυται ἁμαρτίας, 2 εἰς
having in [the] flesh has ceased from sin, for
suffered

τὸ μηκέτι ἀνθρώπων ἐπιθυμίαις ἀλλὰ
the ¹no longer ⁹of men ⁸in [the] lusts ¹⁰but

θελήματι θεοῦ τὸν ἐπίλοιπον ἐν σαρκὶ
¹¹in [the] will ¹²of God ³the ⁴remaining ⁵in ⁷[the] flesh

βιῶσαι χρόνον. 3 ἀρκετὸς γὰρ ὁ παρεληλυ-
⁶to live ⁵time. For ⁵sufficient ¹the ²having passed

θὼς χρόνος τὸ βούλημα τῶν ἐθνῶν
away ²time ⁴[is] ⁷the ⁸purpose ⁹of the ¹⁰nations

κατειργάσθαι, πεπορευμένους ἐν ἀσελγείαις,
⁶to have worked out, having gone [on] in licentiousnesses,

ἐπιθυμίαις, οἰνοφλυγίαις, κώμοις, πότοις
lusts, debaucheries, carousals, drinking
bouts

καὶ ἀθεμίτοις εἰδωλολατρίαις. 4 ἐν ᾧ
and unlawful idolatries. While

ξενίζονται μὴ συντρεχόντων ὑμῶν εἰς
they are surprised ²not ³running with ¹youᵃ to

τὴν αὐτὴν τῆς ἀσωτίας ἀνάχυσιν, βλασ-
the same - ²of profligacy ¹excess, blas-

φημοῦντες· 5 οἳ ἀποδώσουσιν λόγον τῷ
pheming; who will render account to the
[one]

ἑτοίμως ἔχοντι κρῖναι ζῶντας καὶ νεκρούς.
readily having to judge living and dead.
=who is ready

6 εἰς τοῦτο γὰρ καὶ νεκροῖς εὐηγγελίσθη,
²for ³this ¹For indeed ²to ¹good news
dead men was preached,

ἵνα κριθῶσι μὲν κατὰ ἀνθρώπους
in order ³they might ¹on one according to men
that be judged hand

σαρκί, ζῶσι δὲ κατὰ θεὸν πνεύματι.
in [the] ²might ¹on the according God in [the] spirit.
flesh, live other to

7 But the end of all things is at hand: be ye therefore sober, and watch unto prayer.

8 And above all things have fervent charity among yourselves: for charity shall cover the multitude of sins.

9 Use hospitality one to another without grudging.

10 As every man hath received the gift, *even so* minister the same one to another, as good stewards of the manifold grace of God.

11 If any man speak, *let him speak* as the oracles of God; if any man minister, *let him do it* as of the ability which God giveth: that God in all things may be glorified through Jesus Christ, to whom be praise and dominion for ever and ever. Amen.

12 Beloved, think it not strange concerning the fiery trial which is to try you, as though some strange thing happened unto you:

13 But rejoice, inasmuch as ye are partakers of Christ's sufferings; that, when his glory shall be revealed, ye may be glad also with exceeding joy.

14 If ye be reproached for the name of Christ, happy *are ye;* for the spirit of glory and of God

7 Πάντων δὲ τὸ τέλος ἤγγικεν.
Now of all things the end has drawn near.

σωφρονήσατε οὖν καὶ νήψατε εἰς
Be ye soberminded therefore and be ye sober unto

προσευχάς· 8 πρὸ πάντων τὴν εἰς ἑαυτοὺς
prayers; before all things – ⁴to ⁵yourselves

ἀγάπην ἐκτενῆ ἔχοντες, ὅτι ἀγάπη
³love ²fervent ¹having, because love

καλύπτει πλῆθος ἁμαρτιῶν· 9 φιλόξενοι εἰς
covers a multitude of sins; [be] hospitable to

ἀλλήλους ἄνευ γογγυσμοῦ· 10 ἕκαστος καθὼς
one another without murmuring; each one as

ἔλαβεν χάρισμα, εἰς ἑαυτοὺς αὐτὸ διακον-
he received a gift, ³to ⁴yourselves ²it ¹minister-

οῦντες ὡς καλοὶ οἰκονόμοι ποικίλης χάριτος
ing as good stewards of [the] manifold grace

θεοῦ· 11 εἴ τις λαλεῖ, ὡς λόγια θεοῦ·
of God; if anyone speaks, as [the] of God;
                                  oracles

εἴ τις διακονεῖ, ὡς ἐξ ἰσχύος ἧς χορηγεῖ
if anyone ministers, as by strength which ⁵supplies

ὁ θεός· ἵνα ἐν πᾶσιν δοξάζηται ὁ θεὸς
– ¹God; in or- in all things ²may be glorified – ¹God
                der that

διὰ Ἰησοῦ Χριστοῦ, ᾧ ἐστιν ἡ δόξα
through Jesus Christ, to whom isᶜ the glory
                          =whose is

καὶ τὸ κράτος εἰς τοὺς αἰῶνας τῶν
and the might unto the ages of the

αἰώνων· ἀμήν.
ages : Amen.

12 Ἀγαπητοί, μὴ ξενίζεσθε τῇ ἐν ὑμῖν
Beloved, be not surprised [at] ¹the ⁴among ⁵you

πυρώσει πρὸς πειρασμὸν ὑμῖν γινομένῃ,
²fiery trial ³for ⁷trial ⁸to you ⁹happening,

ὡς ξένου ὑμῖν συμβαίνοντος, 13 ἀλλὰ
as a surprising ²to you ¹occurringᵃ, but
       thing

καθὸ κοινωνεῖτε τοῖς τοῦ Χριστοῦ
²as ³ye share ⁴the – ⁵of Christ

παθήμασιν χαίρετε, ἵνα καὶ ἐν τῇ ἀπο-
⁶sufferings ¹rejoice, in order also at the reve-
                      that

καλύψει τῆς δόξης αὐτοῦ χαρῆτε ἀγαλ-
lation of the glory of him ye may exult-
                            rejoice

λιώμενοι. 14 εἰ ὀνειδίζεσθε ἐν ὀνόματι
ing. If ye are reproached in [the] name

Χριστοῦ, μακάριοι, ὅτι τὸ τῆς δόξης
of Christ, blessed [are ye], because ¹the – ²of glory

resteth upon you: on their part he is evil spoken of, but on your part he is glorified.

15 But let none of you suffer as a murderer, or *as* a thief, or *as* an evildoer, or as a busybody in other men's matters.

16 Yet if *any man suffer* as a Christian, let him not be ashamed; but let him glorify God on this behalf.

17 For the time *is come* that judgment must begin at the house of God: and if *it* first *begin* at us, what shall the end *be* of them that obey not the gospel of God?

18 And if the righteous scarcely be saved, where shall the ungodly and the sinner appear?

19 Wherefore let them that suffer according to the will of God commit the keeping of their souls *to him* in well doing, as unto a faithful Creator.

καὶ   τὸ   τοῦ   θεοῦ   πνεῦμα   ἐφ᾽   ὑμᾶς
⁴and   ⁵*the*(?that) –   ⁶of God ⁷spirit   ⁸on   ⁹you

ἀναπαύεται.   15 μὴ   γάρ   τις   ὑμῶν   πασχέτω
⁷rests.   ³Not ¹for ⁴anyone ⁵of you ²let ⁶suffer

ὡς   φονεὺς   ἢ   κλέπτης   ἢ   κακοποιὸς   ἢ
as a murderer or a thief or an evildoer or

ὡς   ἀλλοτριεπίσκοπος·   16 εἰ   δὲ   ὡς
as   a pryer into other men's affairs;   but if   as

Χριστιανός,   μὴ   αἰσχυνέσθω,   δοξαζέτω   δὲ
a Christian, let him not be shamed,   but let him glorify

τὸν   θεὸν   ἐν   τῷ   ὀνόματι   τούτῳ.   17 ὅτι
–   God   by   this name.   Because

[ὁ]   καιρὸς   τοῦ   ἄρξασθαι   τὸ   κρίμα   ἀπὸ
the   time   –   to begin^d   the   judgment   from
[?has come]

τοῦ   οἴκου   τοῦ   θεοῦ·   εἰ   δὲ   πρῶτον   ἀφ᾽
the household – of God; and if firstly from

ἡμῶν,   τί   τὸ   τέλος   τῶν   ἀπειθούντων
us, what [will be] the end of the [ones] disobeying

τῷ   τοῦ   θεοῦ   εὐαγγελίῳ;   18 καὶ   εἰ   ὁ
the – ²of God   ¹gospel?   and   if   the

δίκαιος   μόλις   σώζεται,   ὁ   [δὲ]   ἀσεβὴς
righteous man scarcely is saved, ²the – ⁴impious

καὶ   ἁμαρτωλὸς   ποῦ   φανεῖται;   19 ὥστε
⁵and   ⁶sinner   ¹where   ²will ⁷appear?   so as

καὶ   οἱ   πάσχοντες   κατὰ   τὸ   θέλημα   τοῦ
indeed the   suffering   accord- the   will   –
[ones]   ing to

θεοῦ   πιστῷ   κτίστῃ   παρατιθέσθωσαν   τὰς
of God ⁵to a ⁶Creator   ¹let them commit   ²the
       faithful

ψυχὰς   αὐτῶν   ἐν   ἀγαθοποιΐᾳ.
³souls   ⁴of them   in   welldoing.

CHAPTER 5

THE elders which are among you I exhort, who am also an elder, and a witness of the sufferings of Christ, and also a partaker of the glory that shall be revealed:

2 Feed the flock of God which is among you, taking the oversight *thereof*, not by constraint, but

5 Πρεσβυτέρους   οὖν   ἐν   ὑμῖν   παρακαλῶ
Elders   there- among you   I exhort
         fore

ὁ   συμπρεσβύτερος   καὶ   μάρτυς   τῶν   τοῦ
the   co-elder   and   witness   ¹of the   –

Χριστοῦ   παθημάτων,   ὁ   καὶ   τῆς   μελλούσης
²of Christ ³sufferings, ¹the ³also ⁴of the ⁵being about

ἀποκαλύπτεσθαι   δόξης   κοινωνός·   2 ποιμάνατε
⁷to be revealed   ⁶glory   ²sharer :   shepherd

τὸ   ἐν   ὑμῖν   ποίμνιον   τοῦ   θεοῦ,   μὴ
¹the ⁴among ⁵you   ³flock   ²of God,   not

ἀναγκαστῶς   ἀλλὰ   ἑκουσίως   κατὰ   θεόν,
by way of   but   willingly   accord-   God,
compulsion   ing to

willingly; not for filthy lucre, but of a ready mind;

3 Neither as being lords over God's heritage, but being ensamples to the flock.

4 And when the chief Shepherd shall appear, ye shall receive a crown of glory that fadeth not away.

5 Likewise, ye younger, submit yourselves unto the elder. Yea, all of you be subject one to another, and be clothed with humility: for God resisteth the proud, and giveth grace to the humble.

6 Humble yourselves therefore under the mighty hand of God, that he may exalt you in due time:

7 Casting all your care upon him; for he careth for you.

8 Be sober, be vigilant; because your adversary the devil, as a roaring lion, walketh about, seeking whom he may devour:

9 Whom resist stedfast in the faith, knowing that the same afflictions are accomplished in your brethren that are in the world.

10 But the God of all grace, who hath called us unto his eternal glory by Christ Jesus, after that ye have suffered a while, make you perfect, stablish, strengthen, settle you.

μηδὲ αἰσχροκερδῶς ἀλλὰ προθύμως, 3 μηδ'
nor   from eagerness for   but   eagerly,   nor
      base gain

ὡς κατακυριεύοντες τῶν κλήρων ἀλλὰ
as exercising lordship over the lots*   but

τύποι γινόμενοι τοῦ ποιμνίου· 4 καὶ
²examples ¹becoming of the flock;   and

φανερωθέντος τοῦ ἀρχιποίμενος κομιεῖσθε
appearing   the   chief shepherd* ye will receive
=when the chief shepherd appears

τὸν ἀμαράντινον τῆς δόξης στέφανον.
the   unfading   -   ²of glory ¹crown.

5 Ὁμοίως, νεώτεροι, ὑποτάγητε πρεσβυτέ-
Likewise, younger men, submit yourselves to older

ροις· πάντες δὲ ἀλλήλοις τὴν ταπεινοφρο-
men;   and all ²to one another -   ²humil-

σύνην ἐγκομβώσασθε, ὅτι ὁ θεὸς ὑπερηφάνοις
ity   ¹gird ye on, because - God ²arrogant men

ἀντιτάσσεται, ταπεινοῖς δὲ δίδωσιν χάριν.
¹resists,   but to humble men he gives   grace.

6 Ταπεινώθητε οὖν ὑπὸ τὴν κραταιὰν
Be ye humbled therefore under the   mighty

χεῖρα τοῦ θεοῦ, ἵνα ὑμᾶς ὑψώσῃ ἐν
hand   - of God, in order ²you ¹he may exalt in
                   that

καιρῷ, 7 πᾶσαν τὴν μέριμναν ὑμῶν
time,   ²all ³the ⁴anxiety ⁵of you

ἐπιρίψαντες ἐπ' αὐτόν, ὅτι αὐτῷ μέλει
¹casting   on   him, because ²to him ¹it matters

περὶ ὑμῶν. 8 Νήψατε, γρηγορήσατε. ὁ
concerning you. Be ye sober, watch ye.   The

ἀντίδικος ὑμῶν διάβολος ὡς λέων ὠρυόμενος
adversary of you [the] devil as a lion roaring

περιπατεῖ ζητῶν τινα καταπιεῖν· 9 ᾧ
walks about seeking whom to devour;   whom

ἀντίστητε στερεοὶ τῇ πίστει, εἰδότες τὰ
oppose   firm   in the faith, knowing the

αὐτὰ τῶν παθημάτων τῇ ἐν τῷ κόσμῳ
same of the sufferings ³in ⁵in ⁴the ⁷world
things   the

ὑμῶν ἀδελφότητι ἐπιτελεῖσθαι. 10 Ὁ δὲ
⁴of you ³brotherhood ¹to be accomplished. ²the ¹Now

θεὸς πάσης χάριτος, ὁ καλέσας ὑμᾶς
God   of all grace, the [one] having called you

εἰς τὴν αἰώνιον αὐτοῦ δόξαν ἐν Χριστῷ,
to   the ¹eternal ²of him ³glory in Christ,

ὀλίγον παθόντας αὐτὸς καταρτίσει, στηρίξει,
¹[you] ²having [him]self will adjust, confirm,
³a little suffered

* That is, the various spheres assigned to the elders.

11 To him *be* glory and dominion for ever and ever. Amen.

12 By Silvanus, a faithful brother unto you, as I suppose, I have written briefly, exhorting, and testifying that this is the true grace of God wherein ye stand.

13 The *church that is* at Babylon, elected together with *you*, saluteth you; and *so doth* Marcus my son.

14 Greet ye one another with a kiss of charity. Peace *be* with you all that are in Christ Jesus. Amen.

σθενώσει, θεμελιώσει.
strengthen,   found.

11 αὐτῷ τὸ κράτος
To him [is]e the   might
=His is*

εἰς τοὺς αἰῶνας τῶν αἰώνων· ἀμήν.
unto the   ages   of the   ages: Amen.

12 Διὰ Σιλουανοῦ ὑμῖν τοῦ πιστοῦ
Through   Silvanus   to you   the   faithful

ἀδελφοῦ, ὡς λογίζομαι, δι᾽ ὀλίγων ἔγραψα,
brother,   as   I reckon,   by   a few   I wrote,
                      means of [words]

παρακαλῶν καὶ ἐπιμαρτυρῶν ταύτην εἶναι
exhorting   and   witnessing   this   to be

ἀληθῆ χάριν τοῦ θεοῦ, εἰς ἣν στῆτε.
[the] true   grace   –   of God,   in   which   ye stand.

13 Ἀσπάζεται ὑμᾶς ἡ ἐν Βαβυλῶνι
¹⁰greets   ¹¹you   ¹The   ³in   ⁴Babylon

συνεκλεκτὴ καὶ Μᾶρκος ὁ υἱός μου.
²co-chosen   ⁵and   ⁶Mark   ⁷the   ⁸son   ⁹of me.
[? church]

14 ἀσπάσασθε ἀλλήλους ἐν φιλήματι ἀγάπης.
Greet ye   one another   with   a kiss   of love.

Εἰρήνη ὑμῖν πᾶσιν τοῖς ἐν Χριστῷ.
Peace   to you   all   the ones   in   Christ.

II. PETER 1

CHAPTER 1

SIMON PETER, a servant and an apostle of Jesus Christ, to them that have obtained like precious faith with us through the righteousness of God and our Saviour Jesus Christ:

2 Grace and peace be multiplied unto you through the knowledge of God, and of Jesus our Lord,

3 According as his divine power hath given

ΠΕΤΡΟΥ Β
Of Peter 2

1 Συμεὼν Πέτρος δοῦλος καὶ ἀπόστολος
Symeon   Peter   a slave   and   an apostle

Ἰησοῦ Χριστοῦ τοῖς ἰσότιμον ἡμῖν
of Jesus   Christ   ¹to the   ²equally   ⁵with
           [ones]   precious   us

λαχοῦσιν πίστιν ἐν δικαιοσύνῃ τοῦ θεοῦ
³having   ⁴faith   in   righteousness   of the   God
obtained   [the]

ἡμῶν καὶ σωτῆρος Ἰησοῦ Χριστοῦ·
of us   and   Saviour   Jesus   Christ :

2 χάρις ὑμῖν καὶ εἰρήνη πληθυνθείη ἐν
Grace   to you   and   peace   *may it* be multiplied by

ἐπιγνώσει τοῦ θεοῦ καὶ Ἰησοῦ τοῦ
a full knowledge   –   of God   and   of Jesus   the

κυρίου ἡμῶν.
Lord   of us.

3 Ὡς τὰ πάντα ἡμῖν τῆς θείας δυνάμεως
As   –   all things   to us   the   divine   power
=his divine power has given us all things . . .

* *Cf.* 4. 11 (a statement of fact, not a wish).

unto us all things that *pertain* unto life and godliness, through the knowledge of him that hath called us to glory and virtue:

4 Whereby are given unto us exceeding great and precious promises: that by these ye might be partakers of the divine nature, having escaped the corruption that is in the world through lust.

5 And beside this, giving all diligence, add to your faith virtue; and to virtue knowledge;

6 And to knowledge temperance; and to temperance patience; and to patience godliness;

7 And to godliness brotherly kindness; and to brotherly kindness charity.

8 For if these things be in you, and abound, they make *you that ye shall* neither *be* barren nor unfruitful in the knowledge of our Lord Jesus Christ.

9 But he that lacketh these things is blind, and cannot see afar off, and hath forgotten that he was purged from his old sins.

10 Wherefore the rather, brethren, give diligence to

αὐτοῦ τὰ πρὸς ζωὴν καὶ εὐσέβειαν δεδωρημένης
of him — [belong- life and piety having given[a]
             ing] to

διὰ τῆς ἐπιγνώσεως τοῦ καλέσαντος ἡμᾶς
through the full knowledge of the [one] having called us

ἰδίᾳ δόξῃ καὶ ἀρετῇ, 4 δι' ὧν τὰ τίμια
to [his] glory and virtue, through which *the* [3]precious
own   things

καὶ μέγιστα ἡμῖν ἐπαγγέλματα δεδώρηται,
[4]and [5]very great [2]to us [6]promises [1]he has given.

ἵνα διὰ τούτων γένησθε θείας κοινωνοὶ
in or- through these ye might [2]of a divine [1]sharers
der that   become

φύσεως, ἀποφυγόντες τῆς ἐν τῷ κόσμῳ
[3]nature, escaping from [1]the [2]in [4]the [5]world

ἐν ἐπιθυμίᾳ φθορᾶς. 5 καὶ αὐτὸ τοῦτο
[6]by [7]lust [2]corruption. [2]also [3]for this very thing
                             (reason)

δὲ σπουδὴν πᾶσαν παρεισενέγκαντες
[1]But [4]diligence [3]all [4]bringing in

ἐπιχορηγήσατε ἐν τῇ πίστει ὑμῶν τὴν
supply in the faith of you

ἀρετήν, ἐν δὲ τῇ ἀρετῇ τὴν γνῶσιν,
virtue, and in — virtue — knowledge,

6 ἐν δὲ τῇ γνώσει τὴν ἐγκράτειαν,
and in — knowledge — self-control,

ἐν δὲ τῇ ἐγκρατείᾳ τὴν ὑπομονήν, ἐν
and in — self-control — endurance, [2]in

δὲ τῇ ὑπομονῇ τὴν εὐσέβειαν, 7 ἐν δὲ
[1]and — endurance — piety, and in

τῇ εὐσεβείᾳ τὴν φιλαδελφίαν, ἐν δὲ
— piety — brotherly friendship, and in

τῇ φιλαδελφίᾳ τὴν ἀγάπην. 8 ταῦτα
— brotherly friendship — love. these things

γὰρ ὑμῖν ὑπάρχοντα καὶ πλεονάζοντα
For [2]in you [1]being and abounding

οὐκ ἀργοὺς οὐδὲ ἀκάρπους καθίστησιν
[3]not [4]barren [5]nor [6]unfruitful [1]makes [2][you]

εἰς τὴν τοῦ κυρίου ἡμῶν Ἰησοῦ Χριστοῦ
in [1]the [3]of the [4]Lord [5]of us [6]Jesus [7]Christ

ἐπίγνωσιν· 9 ᾧ γὰρ μὴ πάρεστιν ταῦτα,
[2]full knowledge; for [he] [3]not [2]is(are) [1]these
          in whom   [4]present things.

τυφλός ἐστιν μυωπάζων, λήθην λαβὼν
[2]blind [1]is being short-sighted, forgetfulness taking
                            = being forgetful

τοῦ καθαρισμοῦ τῶν πάλαι αὐτοῦ ἁμαρτιῶν.
of the cleansing of the [3]in time [2]of him [1]sins.
                    past

10 διὸ μᾶλλον, ἀδελφοί, σπουδάσατε
Wherefore rather, brothers, be ye diligent

make your calling and election sure: for if ye do these things, ye shall never fall:

11 For so an entrance shall be ministered unto you abundantly into the everlasting kingdom of our Lord and Saviour Jesus Christ.

12 Wherefore I will not be negligent to put you always in remembrance of these things, though ye know *them*, and be established in the present truth.

13 Yea, I think it meet, as long as I am in this tabernacle, to stir you up by putting *you* in remembrance;

14 Knowing that shortly I must put off *this* my tabernacle, even as our Lord Jesus Christ hath shewed me.

15 Moreover I will endeavour that ye may be able after my decease to have these things always in remembrance.

16 For we have not followed cunningly devised fables, when we made known unto you the power and coming of our Lord Jesus Christ, but were eyewitnesses of his majesty.

17 For he received from God the Father honour and glory, when there came such a voice to him

βεβαίαν ὑμῶν τὴν κλῆσιν καὶ ἐκλογὴν
²firm ⁷of you ³the ⁴calling ⁵and ⁶choice

ποιεῖσθαι· ταῦτα γὰρ ποιοῦντες οὐ μὴ
¹to make; for these things doing by no means

πταίσητέ ποτε. 11 οὕτως γὰρ πλουσίως
ye will fail ever. For so ³richly

ἐπιχορηγηθήσεται ὑμῖν ἡ εἴσοδος εἰς τὴν
¹will be supplied ²to you the entrance into the

αἰώνιον βασιλείαν τοῦ κυρίου ἡμῶν καὶ
eternal kingdom of the Lord of us and

σωτῆρος Ἰησοῦ Χριστοῦ.
Saviour Jesus Christ.

12 Διὸ μελλήσω ἀεὶ ὑμᾶς ὑπομιμνῄσκειν
Wherefore I *will* intend always you to remind

περὶ τούτων, καίπερ εἰδότας καὶ
concerning these things, though knowing and

ἐστηριγμένους ἐν τῇ παρούσῃ ἀληθείᾳ.
having been confirmed in the present truth.

13 δίκαιον δὲ ἡγοῦμαι, ἐφ' ὅσον εἰμὶ
And ²right ¹I deem [it], so long as† I am

ἐν τούτῳ τῷ σκηνώματι, διεγείρειν ὑμᾶς
in this – tabernacle, to rouse you

ἐν ὑπομνήσει, 14 εἰδὼς ὅτι ταχινή ἐστιν
by a reminder, knowing that soon is

ἡ ἀπόθεσις τοῦ σκηνώματός μου, καθὼς
the putting off of the tabernacle of me, as

καὶ ὁ κύριος ἡμῶν Ἰησοῦς Χριστὸς
indeed the Lord of us Jesus Christ

ἐδήλωσέν μοι· 15 σπουδάσω δὲ καὶ
made clear to me; and I will be diligent also

ἑκάστοτε ἔχειν ὑμᾶς μετὰ τὴν ἐμὴν
⁵always ⁷to have ²you ⁴after – ³my

ἔξοδον τὴν τούτων μνήμην ποιεῖσθαι.
⁶exodus ⁸the ¹⁰of these things ⁹memory ¹to cause.

16 οὐ γὰρ σεσοφισμένοις μύθοις ἐξακολου-
For not ³having been ²fables ¹follow-
cleverly devised

θήσαντες ἐγνωρίσαμεν ὑμῖν τὴν τοῦ κυρίου
ing we made known to you ¹the ⁵of the ⁶Lord

ἡμῶν Ἰησοῦ Χριστοῦ δύναμιν καὶ
⁷of us ⁸Jesus ⁹Christ ²power ³and

παρουσίαν, ἀλλ' ἐπόπται γενηθέντες τῆς
⁴presence, but ²eyewitnesses ¹having become ³of the

ἐκείνου μεγαλειότητος. 17 λαβὼν γὰρ
⁵of that one ⁴majesty. For receiving

παρὰ θεοῦ πατρὸς τιμὴν καὶ δόξαν
from God [the] Father honour and glory

φωνῆς ἐνεχθείσης αὐτῷ τοιᾶσδε ὑπὸ τῆς
²a voice ³being borne² ⁴to him ¹such by the

from the excellent glory,
This is my beloved Son,
in whom I am well pleased.

18 And this voice which
came from heaven we
heard, when we were with
him in the holy mount.

19 We have also a more
sure word of prophecy;
whereunto ye do well that
ye take heed, as unto a
light that shineth in a
dark place, until the day
dawn, and the day star
arise in your hearts:

20 Knowing this first,
that no prophecy of the
scripture is of any private
interpretation.

21 For the prophecy
came not in old time by
the will of man: but holy
men of God spake *as they
were* moved by the Holy
Ghost.

μεγαλοπρεποῦς δόξης· ὁ υἱός μου ὁ
magnificent glory : The Son of me the

ἀγαπητός μου οὗτός ἐστιν, εἰς ὃν ἐγὼ
beloved of me this is, in whom I

εὐδόκησα, — 18 καὶ ταύτην τὴν φωνὴν
was wellpleased,— and this - voice

ἡμεῖς ἠκούσαμεν ἐξ οὐρανοῦ ἐνεχθεῖσαν
we heard ²out of ³heaven ¹being borne

σὺν αὐτῷ ὄντες ἐν τῷ ἁγίῳ ὄρει. 19 καὶ
⁵with ⁶him ⁴being in the holy mountain. And

ἔχομεν βεβαιότερον τὸν προφητικὸν λόγον,
we have more firm the prophetic word,

ᾧ καλῶς ποιεῖτε προσέχοντες ὡς λύχνῳ
to ²well ¹ye do taking heed as to a lamp
which

φαίνοντι ἐν αὐχμηρῷ τόπῳ, ἕως οὗ
shining in a murky place, until

ἡμέρα διαυγάσῃ καὶ φωσφόρος ἀνατείλῃ
day dawns and [the] daystar rises

ἐν ταῖς καρδίαις ὑμῶν· 20 τοῦτο πρῶτον
in the hearts of you; ²this ³firstly

γινώσκοντες, ὅτι πᾶσα προφητεία γραφῆς
¹knowing, that every prophecy of scripture
=no . . . is . . .

ἰδίας ἐπιλύσεως οὐ γίνεται· 21 οὐ γὰρ
of [its] own solution not becomes; for not

θελήματι ἀνθρώπου ἠνέχθη προφητεία
by will of man ²was borne ¹prophecy

ποτέ, ἀλλὰ ὑπὸ πνεύματος ἁγίου φερόμενοι
at any but ⁶by ⁸Spirit ⁷[the] ⁵being borne
time, Holy

ἐλάλησαν ἀπὸ θεοῦ ἄνθρωποι.
²spoke ³from ⁴God ¹men.

CHAPTER 2

BUT there were false
prophets also among
the people, even as there
shall be false teachers
among you, who privily
shall bring in damnable
heresies, even denying the
Lord that bought them,
and bring upon themselves
swift destruction.

2 And many shall

2 Ἐγένοντο δὲ καὶ ψευδοπροφῆται ἐν
But there were also false prophets among

τῷ λαῷ, ὡς καὶ ἐν ὑμῖν ἔσονται
the people, as indeed among you there will be

ψευδοδιδάσκαλοι, οἵτινες παρεισάξουσιν
false teachers, who will secretly bring in

αἱρέσεις ἀπωλείας, καὶ τὸν ἀγοράσαντα
opinions of destruction,* and ²the ⁴having bought

αὐτοὺς δεσπότην ἀρνούμενοι, ἐπάγοντες
⁵them ³Master ¹denying, bringing on

ἑαυτοῖς ταχινὴν ἀπώλειαν· 2 καὶ πολλοὶ
themselves swift destruction; and many

* Genitive of quality : " destructive opinions."

follow their pernicious ways; by reason of whom the way of truth shall be evil spoken of.

3 And through covetousness shall they with feigned words make merchandise of you: whose judgment now of a long time lingereth not, and their damnation slumbereth not.

4 For if God spared not the angels that sinned, but cast *them* down to hell, and delivered *them* into chains of darkness, to be reserved unto judgment;

5 And spared not the old world, but saved Noah the eighth *person*, a preacher of righteousness, bringing in the flood upon the world of the ungodly;

6 And turning the cities of Sodom and Gomorrha into ashes condemned *them* with an overthrow, making *them* an ensample unto those that after should live ungodly;

7 And delivered just Lot, vexed with the filthy conversation of the wicked:

8 (For that righteous man dwelling among them, in seeing and hearing, vexed *his* righteous soul from day to day with *their* unlawful deeds;)

9 The Lord knoweth how to deliver the godly out of temptations, and

ἐξακολουθήσουσιν αὐτῶν ταῖς ἀσελγείαις,
will follow ³of them ¹the ²licentiousness*es*,

δι' οὓς ἡ ὁδὸς τῆς ἀληθείας βλασφημη-
be- whom the way of *the* truth will be
cause of

θήσεται· 3 καὶ ἐν πλεονεξίᾳ πλαστοῖς
blasphemed; and by covetousness with fabricated

λόγοις ὑμᾶς ἐμπορεύσονται· οἷς τὸ κρίμα
words ²you ¹they will make for the judg-
merchandise of; whom ment

ἔκπαλαι οὐκ ἀργεῖ, καὶ ἡ ἀπώλεια
of old lingers not, and the destruction

αὐτῶν οὐ νυστάζει. 4 εἰ γὰρ ὁ θεὸς
of them slumbers not. For if — God

ἀγγέλων ἁμαρτησάντων οὐκ ἐφείσατο, ἀλλὰ
²angels ³sinning ¹spared not, but

σιροῖς ζόφου ταρταρώσας παρέδωκεν
²in pits ³of gloom ¹consigning to Tartarus ⁴delivered [them]

εἰς κρίσιν τηρουμένους, 5 καὶ ἀρχαίου
⁵to ⁷judgment ⁶being kept, and ²[the] ancient

κόσμου οὐκ ἐφείσατο, ἀλλὰ ὄγδοον Νῶε
³world ¹spared not, but ²[the] ³Noe
eighth man

δικαιοσύνης κήρυκα ἐφύλαξεν, κατακλυσμὸν
⁵of righteousness ⁴a herald ¹guarded, ²a flood

κόσμῳ ἀσεβῶν ἐπάξας, 6 καὶ πόλεις
⁴a world ⁵of impious men ³bringing ³on, and ³[the] cities

Σοδόμων καὶ Γομόρρας τεφρώσας
⁴of Sodom ⁵and ⁶Gomorra ¹covering [them]
with ashes

καταστροφῇ κατέκρινεν, ὑπόδειγμα μελ-
⁷by an overthrow ²condemned, ²an example ³of men

λόντων ἀσεβεῖν τεθεικώς, 7 καὶ δίκαιον
intending ⁴to live ¹having set(made), and ²righteous
impiously

Λὼτ καταπονούμενον ὑπὸ τῆς τῶν ἀθέσμων
³Lot ⁴being oppressed ⁵by ⁶the ¹⁰of the ¹¹lawless

ἐν ἀσελγείᾳ ἀναστροφῆς ἐρρύσατο· 8 βλέμ-
⁸in ⁹licentiousness ⁷conduct ¹delivered; ²in

ματι γὰρ καὶ ἀκοῇ ὁ δίκαιος ἐγκατοικῶν
seeing ¹for and in hear- the righteous dwelling
ing (that) man

ἐν αὐτοῖς ἡμέραν ἐξ ἡμέρας ψυχὴν
among them day after† day ²[his] ⁴soul

δικαίαν ἀνόμοις ἔργοις ἐβασάνιζεν·
³righteous ⁵with [their] lawless ⁶works ¹tormented;

9 οἶδεν κύριος εὐσεβεῖς ἐκ πειρασμοῦ
²knows* ¹[the] Lord ⁴pious men ⁵out of ⁶trial

* That is, " the Lord can deliver "; see note on page xviii.

to reserve the unjust unto the day of judgment to be punished:

10 But chiefly them that walk after the flesh in the lust of uncleanness, and despise government. Presumptuous *are they*, self-willed, they are not afraid to speak evil of dignities.

11 Whereas angels, which are greater in power and might, bring not railing accusation against them before the Lord.

12 But these, as natural brute beasts, made to be taken and destroyed, speak evil of the things that they understand not; and shall utterly perish in their own corruption;

13 And shall receive the reward of unrighteousness, *as* they that count it pleasure to riot in the day time. Spots *they are* and blemishes, sporting themselves with their own deceivings while they feast with you;

14 Having eyes full of adultery, and that cannot cease from sin; beguiling unstable souls: an heart they have exercised with covetous practices; cursed children:

15 Which have forsaken the right way, and are gone astray, following the way of Balaam *the son* of Bosor, who loved the wages of unrighteousness;

ῥύεσθαι, ἀδίκους δὲ εἰς ἡμέραν κρίσεως
³to deliver, ³unjust men ¹but ⁶for ⁵a day ⁷of judgment

κολαζομένους τηρεῖν, 10 μάλιστα δὲ τοὺς
⁴being punished ²to keep, and most of all ¹the

ὀπίσω σαρκὸς ἐν ἐπιθυμίᾳ μιασμοῦ
⁵after ⁴flesh ⁵in ⁶lust ⁷of defilement*

πορευομένους καὶ κυριότητος καταφρονοῦντας.
²[ones] going ⁸and ¹⁰dominion ⁹despising.

τολμηταὶ αὐθάδεις, δόξας οὐ τρέμουσιν
²darers ¹Self-satisfied, glories they do not tremble [at]

βλασφημοῦντες, 11 ὅπου ἄγγελοι ἰσχύϊ καὶ
blaspheming, where angels ³in strength ⁴and

δυνάμει μείζονες ὄντες οὐ φέρουσιν κατ'
⁵in power ²greater ¹being do not bring against

αὐτῶν παρὰ κυρίῳ βλάσφημον κρίσιν.
them before [the] Lord railing judgment.

12 οὗτοι δέ, ὡς ἄλογα ζῷα γεγεννημένα
But these, ¹as ⁴without ²animals ⁵having been
men, reason born

φυσικὰ εἰς ἅλωσιν καὶ φθοράν, ἐν οἷς
²natural for capture and corruption, ²in ³things which

ἀγνοοῦσιν βλασφημοῦντες, ἐν τῇ φθορᾷ
⁴they are ¹railing, in the corruption
ignorant [of]

αὐτῶν καὶ φθαρήσονται, 13 ἀδικούμενοι
of them indeed they will be corrupted, suffering wrong

μισθὸν ἀδικίας· ἡδονὴν ἡγούμενοι τὴν
[as] wages of wrong; ⁵[to be] pleasure ¹deeming –

ἐν ἡμέρᾳ τρυφήν, σπίλοι καὶ μῶμοι
³in ⁴[the] day ²luxury, spots and blemishes

ἐντρυφῶντες ἐν ταῖς ἀπάταις αὐτῶν
revelling in the deceits of them

συνευωχούμενοι ὑμῖν, 14 ὀφθαλμοὺς ἔχοντες
feasting along with you, ²eyes ¹having

μεστοὺς μοιχαλίδος καὶ ἀκαταπαύστους
full of an adulteress and not ceasing from

ἁμαρτίας, δελεάζοντες ψυχὰς ἀστηρίκτους,
sin, alluring ²souls ¹unsteady,

καρδίαν γεγυμνασμένην πλεονεξίας ἔχοντες,
²a heart ³having been exercised ⁴of(in) covetousness ¹having,

κατάρας τέκνα· 15 καταλείποντες εὐθεῖαν
²of curse ¹children; forsaking a straight

ὁδὸν ἐπλανήθησαν, ἐξακολουθήσαντες τῇ
way they erred, following the

ὁδῷ τοῦ Βαλαὰμ τοῦ Βεώρ, ὃς μισθὸν
way – of Balaam the [son] of who ²[the]
Beor, wages

---

* Genitive of quality: " defiling lust."

16 But was rebuked for his iniquity: the dumb ass speaking with man's voice forbad the madness of the prophet.

17 These are wells without water, clouds that are carried with a tempest; to whom the mist of darkness is reserved for ever.

18 For when they speak great swelling *words* of vanity, they allure through the lusts of the flesh, *through much* wantonness, those that were clean escaped from them who live in error.

19 While they promise them liberty, they themselves are the servants of corruption: for of whom a man is overcome, of the same is he brought in bondage.

20 For if after they have escaped the pollutions of the world through the knowledge of the Lord and Saviour Jesus Christ, they are again entangled therein, and overcome, the latter end is worse with them than the beginning.

21 For it had been better for them not to have known the way of righteousness, than, after they have known *it*, to turn from the holy commandment delivered unto them.

22 But it is happened unto them according to the true proverb, The dog

---

ἀδικίας ἠγάπησεν, 16 ἔλεγξιν δὲ ἔσχεν
²of wrong ¹loved,   and ²reproof ¹had

ἰδίας παρανομίας· ὑποζύγιον ἄφωνον ἐν
of [his] own transgression;   ²ass   ¹a dumb ⁴with

ἀνθρώπου φωνῇ φθεγξάμενον ἐκώλυσεν
⁶of a man ⁵voice   ³speaking   restrained

τὴν τοῦ προφήτου παραφρονίαν. 17 οὗτοί
¹the ³of the ⁴prophet   ²madness.   These men

εἰσιν πηγαὶ ἄνυδροι καὶ ὁμίχλαι ὑπὸ
are ²springs ¹waterless and   mists   ²by

λαίλαπος ἐλαυνόμεναι, οἷς ὁ ζόφος τοῦ
³storm ¹being driven, for whom the gloom of *the*

σκότους τετήρηται. 18 ὑπέρογκα γὰρ
darkness has been kept. For ²immoderate [words]

ματαιότητος φθεγγόμενοι δελεάζουσιν ἐν
³of vanity ¹speaking   they allure   by

ἐπιθυμίαις σαρκὸς ἀσελγείαις τοὺς ὀλίγως
[the] lusts of [the] flesh in excesses the [ones] almost

ἀποφεύγοντας τοὺς ἐν πλάνῃ ἀναστρε-
escaping   ¹the [ones] ³in ⁴error   ²liv-

φομένους, 19 ἐλευθερίαν αὐτοῖς ἐπαγγελ-
ing,   ³freedom   ²to them ¹promis-

λόμενοι, αὐτοὶ δοῦλοι ὑπάρχοντες τῆς
ing, [them]selves ²slaves   ¹being   –

φθορᾶς· ᾧ γάρ τις ἥττηται, τούτῳ
of corrup- for by whom anyone has been to this
tion;   defeated,   man

δεδούλωται. 20 εἰ γὰρ ἀποφυγόντες τὰ
he has been enslaved. For if   having escaped the

μιάσματα τοῦ κόσμου ἐν ἐπιγνώσει τοῦ
defilements of the world by a full knowledge of the

κυρίου καὶ σωτῆρος Ἰησοῦ Χριστοῦ,
Lord and Saviour Jesus Christ,

τούτοις δὲ πάλιν ἐμπλακέντες ἡττῶνται,
yet by these again   having been   have been
                 entangled   defeated,

γέγονεν αὐτοῖς τὰ ἔσχατα χείρονα τῶν
³have become ⁴to them ¹the ²last things worse [than] the

πρώτων. 21 κρεῖττον γὰρ ἦν αὐτοῖς
first.   For better   it was for them

μὴ ἐπεγνωκέναι τὴν ὁδὸν τῆς δικαιοσύνης,
not to have fully known the   way   – of righteousness,

ἢ ἐπιγνοῦσιν ὑποστρέψαι ἐκ τῆς παρα-
than fully knowing to turn from ¹the ⁴de-

δοθείσης αὐτοῖς ἁγίας ἐντολῆς. 22 συμβέ-
livered ⁵to them ²holy ³commandment.   ¹has

βηκεν αὐτοῖς τὸ τῆς ἀληθοῦς παροιμίας·
happened ⁶to them ¹The ²of the ³true ⁴proverb:
           thing

is turned to his own vomit again; and the sow that was washed to her wallowing in the mire.

κύων ἐπιστρέψας ἐπὶ τὸ ἴδιον ἐξέραμα,
[The] dog turning upon the(its) own vomit,
καὶ· ὓς λουσαμένη εἰς κυλισμὸν βορβόρου.
and: [The] washed to wallowing of mud.
      sow

CHAPTER 3

THIS second epistle, beloved, I now write unto you; in *both* which I stir up your pure minds by way of remembrance:

2 That ye may be mindful of the words which were spoken before by the holy prophets, and of the commandment of us the apostles of the Lord and Saviour:

3 Knowing this first, that there shall come in the last days scoffers, walking after their own lusts,

4 And saying, Where is the promise of his coming? for since the fathers fell asleep, all things continue as *they were* from the beginning of the creation.

5 For this they willingly are ignorant of, that by the word of God the heavens were of old, and the earth standing out of the water and in the water:

6 Whereby the world that then was, being over-

3 Ταύτην ἤδη, ἀγαπητοί, δευτέραν ὑμῖν
  ¹This   ⁶now,   ⁵beloved,   ²second ⁷to you
γράφω ἐπιστολήν, ἐν αἷς διεγείρω ὑμῶν
³I write ⁴epistle, in [both] which I rouse ⁴of you
ἐν ὑπομνήσει τὴν εἰλικρινῆ διάνοιαν,
⁵by ⁶reminder ¹the ²sincere ³mind,
2 μνησθῆναι τῶν προειρημένων ῥημάτων
 to remember the ²having been ¹words
                previously spoken
ὑπὸ τῶν ἁγίων προφητῶν καὶ τῆς τῶν
by the holy prophets and ¹the ³of the
ἀποστόλων ὑμῶν ἐντολῆς τοῦ κυρίου καὶ
⁴apostles ⁵of you ²commandment of the Lord and
σωτῆρος, 3 τοῦτο πρῶτον γινώσκοντες, ὅτι
Saviour, ²this ³first*ly* ¹knowing, that
ἐλεύσονται ἐπ' ἐσχάτων τῶν ἡμερῶν ἐν
there will come during [the] last of the days ²in
ἐμπαιγμονῇ ἐμπαῖκται κατὰ τὰς ἰδίας
⁴mocking ¹mockers ⁵according to ⁶the(ir) ⁷own
ἐπιθυμίας αὐτῶν πορευόμενοι 4 καὶ λέγοντες·
³lusts *of them* ²going and saying :
ποῦ ἐστιν ἡ ἐπαγγελία τῆς παρουσίας
Where is the promise of the presence
αὐτοῦ; ἀφ' ἧς γὰρ οἱ πατέρες ἐκοι-
of him? ²from ³which [day] ¹for the fathers fell
    =for from the day when . . .
μήθησαν, πάντα οὕτως διαμένει ἀπ'
asleep, all things so remains from
ἀρχῆς κτίσεως. 5 λανθάνει γὰρ αὐτοὺς
[the] of creation. For ²is concealed ³them
beginning   [from]
τοῦτο θέλοντας ὅτι οὐρανοὶ ἦσαν ἔκπαλαι
¹this wishing* that heavens were of old
καὶ γῆ ἐξ ὕδατος καὶ δι' ὕδατος
and earth by water and through water
συνεστῶσα τῷ τοῦ θεοῦ λόγῳ, 6 δι'
¹having been ²by — ⁴of God ³word, through
held together the
ὧν ὁ τότε κόσμος ὕδατι κατακλυσθεὶς
which the then§ world ²by water ¹being inundated
things

* That is, they wish it to be so.
§ This is allowable English : *cf.* " the then Prime Minister."

flowed with water, perished:

7 But the heavens and the earth, which are now, by the same word are kept in store, reserved unto fire against the day of judgment and perdition of ungodly men.

8 But, beloved, be not ignorant of this one thing, that one day *is* with the Lord as a thousand years, and a thousand years as one day.

9 The Lord is not slack concerning his promise, as some men count slackness; but is longsuffering to us-ward, not willing that any should perish, but that all should come to repentance.

10 But the day of the Lord will come as a thief in the night; in the which the heavens shall pass away with a great noise, and the elements shall melt with fervent heat, the earth also and the works that are therein shall be burned up.

11 *Seeing* then *that* all these things shall be dissolved, what manner *of persons* ought ye to be in *all* holy conversation and godliness,

12 Looking for and hasting unto the coming of the day of God, wherein the heavens being on fire shall be dissolved, and the elements shall melt with fervent heat?

ἀπώλετο· 7 οἱ δὲ νῦν οὐρανοὶ καὶ ἡ
perished; but the now heavens and the

γῆ τῷ αὐτῷ λόγῳ τεθησαυρισμένοι εἰσὶν
earth by the same word ²having been stored up ¹are

πυρὶ τηρούμενοι εἰς ἡμέραν κρίσεως καὶ
²for fire ¹being kept in a day of judgment and

ἀπωλείας τῶν ἀσεβῶν ἀνθρώπων. 8 Ἕν
destruction of *the* impious men. ²one

δὲ τοῦτο μὴ λανθανέτω ὑμᾶς, ἀγαπητοί,
But ¹this let not be concealed you, beloved,
³thing [from]

ὅτι μία ἡμέρα παρὰ κυρίῳ ὡς χίλια
that one day with [the] Lord [is] as a thousand

ἔτη καὶ χίλια ἔτη ὡς ἡμέρα μία. 9 οὐ
years and a thousand years as ²day ¹one. ³not

βραδύνει κύριος τῆς ἐπαγγελίας, ὥς τινες
¹is ⁴slow ¹[The] of the promise, as some
Lord (his)

βραδύτητα ἡγοῦνται, ἀλλὰ μακροθυμεῖ εἰς
²slowness ¹deem, but is longsuffering toward

ὑμᾶς, μὴ βουλόμενός τινας ἀπολέσθαι
you, not purposing any to perish

ἀλλὰ πάντας εἰς μετάνοιαν χωρῆσαι.
but all men ²to ²repentance ¹to come.

10 Ἥξει δὲ ἡμέρα κυρίου ὡς κλέπτης,
But will come [the] day of [the] Lord as a thief,

ἐν ᾗ οἱ οὐρανοὶ ῥοιζηδὸν παρελεύσονται,
in which the heavens ²with rushing ¹will pass away,
sound

στοιχεῖα δὲ καυσούμενα λυθήσεται, καὶ
and [the] elements burning will be dissolved, and

γῆ καὶ τὰ ἐν αὐτῇ ἔργα εὑρεθήσεται.
[the] and ¹the ³in ⁴it ²works will be
earth discovered.

11 Τούτων οὕτως πάντων λυομένων
²these things ³thus ¹All ⁴being dissolved*

ποταπούς δεῖ ὑπάρχειν [ὑμᾶς] ἐν ἁγίαις
what sort it be- ²to be ¹you in holy
of men hoves

ἀναστροφαῖς καὶ εὐσεβείαις, 12 προσδοκῶντας
conduct* and piety,* awaiting

καὶ σπεύδοντας τὴν παρουσίαν τῆς τοῦ
and hastening the presence ¹of the –

θεοῦ ἡμέρας, δι’ ἣν οὐρανοὶ πυρούμενοι
²of God ¹day, on ac- which [the] being set on fire
count of heavens

λυθήσονται καὶ στοιχεῖα καυσούμενα
will be dissolved and [the] elements burning

---

* The Greek plurals cannot be literally reproduced in English.

13 Nevertheless we, according to his promise, look for new heavens and a new earth, wherein dwelleth righteousness.

14 Wherefore, beloved, seeing that ye look for such things, be diligent that ye may be found of him in peace, without spot, and blameless.

15 And account *that* the longsuffering of our Lord *is* salvation; even as our beloved brother Paul also according to the wisdom given unto him hath written unto you;

16 As also in all *his* epistles, speaking in them of these things; in which are some things hard to be understood, which they that are unlearned and unstable wrest, as *they do* also the other scriptures, unto their own destruction.

17 Ye therefore, beloved, seeing ye know *these things* before, beware lest ye also, being led away with the error of the wicked, fall from your own stedfastness.

18 But grow in grace, and *in* the knowledge of our Lord and Saviour Jesus Christ. To him *be* glory both now and for ever. Amen.

τήκεται. *melts.* **13** καινοὺς δὲ οὐρανοὺς καὶ *But new heavens and* γῆν καινὴν κατὰ τὸ ἐπάγγελμα αὐτοῦ ²earth ¹a new according- the promise of him to προσδοκῶμεν, ἐν οἷς δικαιοσύνη κατοικεῖ. *we await, in which righteousness dwells.*

14 Διό, ἀγαπητοί, ταῦτα προσδοκῶντες *Wherefore, beloved, ²these things ¹awaiting* σπουδάσατε ἄσπιλοι καὶ ἀμώμητοι αὐτῷ *be diligent ⁶spotless ⁶and ⁷unblemished ⁸by him* εὑρεθῆναι ἐν εἰρήνῃ, **15** καὶ τὴν τοῦ ¹to be found ³in ⁴peace, and ²the ⁴of the κυρίου ἡμῶν μακροθυμίαν σωτηρίαν ἡγεῖσθε, ⁵Lord ⁶of us ³longsuffering ⁷salvation ¹deem, καθὼς καὶ ὁ ἀγαπητὸς ἡμῶν ἀδελφὸς *as indeed the beloved ²of us ¹brother* Παῦλος κατὰ τὴν δοθεῖσαν αὐτῷ σοφίαν *Paul accord- ¹the ²given ⁴to him ²wisdom* ing to ἔγραψεν ὑμῖν, **16** ὡς καὶ ἐν πάσαις *wrote to you, as also in all [his]* ἐπιστολαῖς λαλῶν ἐν αὐταῖς περὶ τούτων, *epistles speaking in them concerning these things,* ἐν αἷς ἐστιν δυσνόητά τινα, ἃ οἱ *in which is(are) ³hard to ¹some which the* understand things, ἀμαθεῖς καὶ ἀστήρικτοι στρεβλοῦσιν ὡς *unlearned and unsteady twist as* καὶ τὰς λοιπὰς γραφὰς πρὸς τὴν ἰδίαν *also the remaining scriptures to the(ir) own* αὐτῶν ἀπώλειαν. **17** Ὑμεῖς οὖν, ἀγαπητοί, *of them destruction. Ye therefore, beloved,* προγινώσκοντες φυλάσσεσθε ἵνα μὴ τῇ *knowing before guard lest ²by the* τῶν ἀθέσμων πλάνῃ συναπαχθέντες ἐκπέ- ⁴of the ⁵lawless ³error ¹being led away *with* ye fall σητε τοῦ ἰδίου στηριγμοῦ, **18** αὐξάνετε *from the(your) own stability, ²grow ye* δὲ ἐν χάριτι καὶ γνώσει τοῦ κυρίου ¹but in grace and knowledge of the Lord ἡμῶν καὶ σωτῆρος Ἰησοῦ Χριστοῦ. *of us and Saviour Jesus Christ.* αὐτῷ ἡ δόξα καὶ νῦν καὶ εἰς *To him⁰ [is] the glory both now and unto* =His is* =for ever. ἡμέραν αἰῶνος. *a day of age.§*

* See note on I. Pet. 5. 11.   § ? "An age-lasting (*i.e.* eternal) day."

CHAPTER 1

THAT which was from the beginning, which we have heard, which we have seen with our eyes, which we have looked upon, and our hands have handled, of the Word of life;

2 (For the life was manifested, and we have seen it, and bear witness, and shew unto you that eternal life, which was with the Father, and was manifested unto us;)

3 That which we have seen and heard declare we unto you, that ye also may have fellowship with us: and truly our fellowship is with the Father, and with his Son Jesus Christ.

4 And these things write we unto you, that your joy may be full.

5 This then is the message which we have heard of him, and declare unto you, that God is light, and in him is no darkness at all.

6 If we say that we have fellowship with him, and walk in darkness, we

1 Ὃ ἦν ἀπ' ἀρχῆς, ὃ ἀκηκόαμεν,
What was from [the] what we have heard,
beginning,

ὃ ἑωράκαμεν τοῖς ὀφθαλμοῖς ἡμῶν, ὃ
what we have seen with the eyes of us, what

ἐθεασάμεθα καὶ αἱ χεῖρες ἡμῶν ἐψηλάφησαν,
we beheld and the hands of us touched,

περὶ τοῦ λόγου τῆς ζωῆς, — 2 καὶ
concern- the word - of life, — and
ing

ἡ ζωὴ ἐφανερώθη, καὶ ἑωράκαμεν καὶ
the life was manifested, and we have seen and

μαρτυροῦμεν καὶ ἀπαγγέλλομεν ὑμῖν τὴν
we bear witness and we announce to you the

ζωὴν τὴν αἰώνιον, ἥτις ἦν πρὸς τὸν
life - eternal, which was with the

πατέρα καὶ ἐφανερώθη ἡμῖν, — 3 ὃ
Father and was manifested to us, — what

ἑωράκαμεν καὶ ἀκηκόαμεν, ἀπαγγέλλομεν
we have seen and we have heard, we announce

καὶ ὑμῖν, ἵνα καὶ ὑμεῖς κοινωνίαν ἔχητε
also to you, in order ²also ¹ye ⁴fellowship ³may
that have

μεθ' ἡμῶν. καὶ ἡ κοινωνία δὲ ἡ ἡμετέρα
with us. ²indeed the ⁴fellowship ¹And - ³our

μετὰ τοῦ πατρὸς καὶ μετὰ τοῦ υἱοῦ
[is] with the Father and with the Son

αὐτοῦ Ἰησοῦ Χριστοῦ. 4 καὶ ταῦτα
of him Jesus Christ. And these things

γράφομεν ἡμεῖς ἵνα ἡ χαρὰ ἡμῶν ᾖ
write we in order the joy of us may
that be

πεπληρωμένη.
having been fulfilled.

5 Καὶ ἔστιν αὕτη ἡ ἀγγελία ἣν
And ²is ¹this the message which

ἀκηκόαμεν ἀπ' αὐτοῦ καὶ ἀναγγέλλομεν
we have heard from him and we announce

ὑμῖν, ὅτι ὁ θεὸς φῶς ἐστιν καὶ σκοτία
to you, that - God ²light ¹is and ⁵darkness

ἐν αὐτῷ οὐκ ἔστιν οὐδεμία. 6 Ἐὰν
¹in ²him ⁴not ³is none. If

εἴπωμεν ὅτι κοινωνίαν ἔχομεν μετ' αὐτοῦ
we say that ²fellowship ¹we have with him

καὶ ἐν τῷ σκότει περιπατῶμεν, ψευδόμεθα
and ²in ³the ⁴darkness ¹we walk, we lie

lie, and do not the truth:

7 But if we walk in the light, as he is in the light, we have fellowship one with another, and the blood of Jesus Christ his Son cleanseth us from all sin.

8 If we say that we have no sin, we deceive ourselves, and the truth is not in us.

9 If we confess our sins, he is faithful and just to forgive us *our* sins, and to cleanse us from all unrighteousness.

10 If we say that we have not sinned, we make him a liar, and his word is not in us.

CHAPTER 2

MY little children, these things write I unto you, that ye sin not. And if any man sin, we have an advocate with the Father, Jesus Christ the righteous:

2 And he is the propitiation for our sins: and not for our's only, but also for *the sins of* the whole world.

3 And hereby we do know that we know him, if we keep his commandments.

καὶ οὐ ποιοῦμεν τὴν ἀλήθειαν· 7 ἐὰν
and are not doing the truth; ²if

δὲ ἐν τῷ φωτὶ περιπατῶμεν ὡς αὐτός
¹but ⁴in ⁵the ⁶light ³we walk as he

ἐστιν ἐν τῷ φωτί, κοινωνίαν ἔχομεν
is in the light, ²fellowship ¹we have

μετ' ἀλλήλων καὶ τὸ αἷμα Ἰησοῦ τοῦ
with each other and the blood of Jesus the

υἱοῦ αὐτοῦ καθαρίζει ἡμᾶς ἀπὸ πάσης
Son of him cleanses us from all

ἁμαρτίας. 8 ἐὰν εἴπωμεν ὅτι ἁμαρτίαν
sin. If we say that sin

οὐκ ἔχομεν, ἑαυτοὺς πλανῶμεν καὶ ἡ
we have not, ²ourselves ¹we deceive and the

ἀλήθεια οὐκ ἔστιν ἐν ἡμῖν. 9 ἐὰν
truth is not in us. If

ὁμολογῶμεν τὰς ἁμαρτίας ἡμῶν, πιστός
we confess the sins of us, faithful

ἐστιν καὶ δίκαιος, ἵνα ἀφῇ ἡμῖν τὰς
he is and righteous, in order he may us the
that forgive

ἁμαρτίας καὶ καθαρίσῃ ἡμᾶς ἀπὸ πάσης
sins and *he* may cleanse us from all

ἀδικίας. 10 ἐὰν εἴπωμεν ὅτι οὐχ
iniquity. If we say that not

ἡμαρτήκαμεν, ψεύστην ποιοῦμεν αὐτὸν
we have sinned, a liar we make him

καὶ ὁ λόγος αὐτοῦ οὐκ ἔστιν ἐν ἡμῖν.
and the word of him is not in us.

2 Τεκνία μου, ταῦτα γράφω ὑμῖν ἵνα
Little children of me, these things I write to you in order
that

μὴ ἁμάρτητε. καὶ ἐάν τις ἁμάρτῃ,
ye sin not. And if anyone sins,

παράκλητον ἔχομεν πρὸς τὸν πατέρα,
an advocate we have with the Father,

Ἰησοῦν Χριστὸν δίκαιον· 2 καὶ αὐτὸς
Jesus Christ [the] righteous; and he

ἱλασμός ἐστιν περὶ τῶν ἁμαρτιῶν ἡμῶν,
²a propitiation ¹is concerning the sins of us,

οὐ περὶ τῶν ἡμετέρων δὲ μόνον ἀλλὰ
²not ³concerning – ⁴ours ¹but only but

καὶ περὶ ὅλου τοῦ κόσμου. 3 καὶ ἐν
also concerning all the world. And by

τούτῳ γινώσκομεν ὅτι ἐγνώκαμεν αὐτόν,
this we know that we have known him,

ἐὰν τὰς ἐντολὰς αὐτοῦ τηρῶμεν. 4 ὁ
if ²the ³command- ⁴of him ¹we keep. The
ments [one]

4 He that saith, I know him, and keepeth not his commandments, is a liar, and the truth is not in him.

5 But whoso keepeth his word, in him verily is the love of God perfected: hereby know we that we are in him.

6 He that saith he abideth in him ought himself also so to walk, even as he walked.

7 Brethren, I write no new commandment unto you, but an old commandment which ye had from the beginning. The old commandment is the word which ye have heard from the beginning.

8 Again, a new commandment I write unto you, which thing is true in him and in you: because the darkness is past, and the true light now shineth.

9 He that saith he is in the light, and hateth his brother, is in darkness even until now.

10 He that loveth his brother abideth in the light, and there is none occasion of stumbling in him.

11 But he that hateth his brother is in darkness,

λέγων ὅτι ἔγνωκα αὐτόν, καὶ τὰς ἐντολὰς
saying[,]   - ˉI have known   him,   and   ²the ⁴commandments

αὐτοῦ μὴ τηρῶν, ψεύστης ἐστίν, καὶ
⁵of him   ¹not   ³keeping,   ²a liar   ¹is,   and

ἐν τούτῳ ἡ ἀλήθεια οὐκ ἔστιν· 5 ὃς δ’
in   this man   the   truth   is not;   but who-

ἂν τηρῇ αὐτοῦ τὸν λόγον, ἀληθῶς ἐν
ever   keeps   ²of him   ¹the   ²word,   truly   in

τούτῳ ἡ ἀγάπη τοῦ θεοῦ τετελείωται.
this man   the   love   -   of God   has been perfected.

ἐν τούτῳ γινώσκομεν ὅτι ἐν αὐτῷ ἐσμεν.
By   this   we know   that   ²in   ³him   ¹we are.

6 ὁ λέγων ἐν αὐτῷ μένειν ὀφείλει καθὼς
The [one] saying   in   him   to remain   ought   as

ἐκεῖνος περιεπάτησεν καὶ αὐτὸς οὕτως
that [one]*   walked   also   [him]self   so

περιπατεῖν.
to walk.

7 Ἀγαπητοί, οὐκ ἐντολὴν καινὴν γράφω
Beloved,   ²not ⁴commandment ³a new   ¹I write

ὑμῖν, ἀλλ’ ἐντολὴν παλαιὰν ἣν εἴχετε
to you,   but   ²commandment   ¹an old   which   ye had

ἀπ’ ἀρχῆς· ἡ ἐντολὴ ἡ παλαιά ἐστιν
from   [the]   the   ²command-   -   ¹old   is
    beginning;   ment

ὁ λόγος ὃν ἠκούσατε. 8 πάλιν ἐντολὴν
the   word   which   ye heard.   Again   ²command-
                             ment

καινὴν γράφω ὑμῖν, ὅ ἐστιν ἀληθὲς
¹a new   I write   to you,   what   is   true

ἐν αὐτῷ καὶ ἐν ὑμῖν, ὅτι ἡ σκοτία
in   him   and   in   you,   because   the   darkness

παράγεται καὶ τὸ φῶς τὸ ἀληθινὸν
is passing   and   the   ²light   -   ¹true

ἤδη φαίνει. 9 ὁ λέγων ἐν τῷ φωτὶ
already   shines.   The [one] saying   in   the   light

εἶναι καὶ τὸν ἀδελφὸν αὐτοῦ μισῶν
to be   and   the   brother   of him   hating

ἐν τῇ σκοτίᾳ ἐστὶν ἕως ἄρτι. 10 ὁ
in   the   darkness   is   until   now.   The

ἀγαπῶν τὸν ἀδελφὸν αὐτοῦ ἐν τῷ φωτὶ
[one] loving   the   brother   of him   in   the   light

μένει, καὶ σκάνδαλον ἐν αὐτῷ οὐκ ἔστιν·
remains,   and   offence   in   him   is not;

11 ὁ δὲ μισῶν τὸν ἀδελφὸν αὐτοῦ ἐν
but the [one] hating   the   brother   of him   in

---

* In a number of places John uses this demonstrative adjective as a substitute for " Christ " : " the remoter antecedent." See also John 2. 21.

and walketh in darkness,
and knoweth not whither
he goeth, because that
darkness hath blinded his
eyes.

12 I write unto you,
little children, because
your sins are forgiven you
for his name's sake.

13 I write unto you,
fathers, because ye have
known him *that is* from
the beginning. I write
unto you, young men, be-
cause ye have overcome
the wicked one. I write
unto you, little children,
because ye have known
the Father.

14 I have written unto
you, fathers, because ye
have known him *that is*
from the beginning. I
have written unto you,
young men, because ye
are strong, and the word
of God abideth in you,
and ye have overcome the
wicked one.

15 Love not the world,
neither the things *that are*
in the world. If any man
love the world, the love
of the Father is not in him.

16 For all that *is* in the
world, the lust of the flesh,
and the lust of the eyes,
and the pride of life, is
not of the Father, but is
of the world.

τῇ σκοτίᾳ ἐστὶν καὶ ἐν τῇ σκοτίᾳ
the darkness is and in the darkness

περιπατεῖ, καὶ οὐκ οἶδεν ποῦ ὑπάγει,
walks, and knows not where he is going,

ὅτι ἡ σκοτία ἐτύφλωσεν τοὺς ὀφθαλμοὺς
be- the darkness blinded the eyes
cause

αὐτοῦ. 12 Γράφω ὑμῖν, τεκνία, ὅτι
of him. I write to you, little because
children,

ἀφέωνται ὑμῖν αἱ ἁμαρτίαι διὰ τὸ ὄνομα
have been *to* you the sins on ac- the name
forgiven (your) count of

αὐτοῦ. 13 γράφω ὑμῖν, πατέρες, ὅτι
of him. I write to you, fathers, because

ἐγνώκατε τὸν ἀπ' ἀρχῆς. γράφω ὑμῖν,
ye have the from [the] I write to
known [one] beginning. you,

νεανίσκοι, ὅτι νενικήκατε τὸν πονηρόν.
young men, because ye have overcome the evil one.

14 ἔγραψα ὑμῖν, παιδία, ὅτι ἐγνώκατε
I wrote to you, young because ye have
children, known

τὸν πατέρα. ἔγραψα ὑμῖν, πατέρες,
the Father. I wrote to you, fathers,

ὅτι ἐγνώκατε τὸν ἀπ' ἀρχῆς. ἔγραψα
be- ye have the from [the] I wrote
cause known [one] beginning.

ὑμῖν, νεανίσκοι, ὅτι ἰσχυροί ἐστε καὶ
to you, young men, because strong ye are and

ὁ λόγος τοῦ θεοῦ ἐν ὑμῖν μένει καὶ
the word – of God in you remains and

νενικήκατε τὸν πονηρόν. 15 Μὴ ἀγαπᾶτε
ye have overcome the evil one. Love ye not

τὸν κόσμον μηδὲ τὰ ἐν τῷ κόσμῳ.
the world nor the things in the world.

ἐάν τις ἀγαπᾷ τὸν κόσμον, οὐκ ἔστιν
If anyone loves the world, ⁶not ⁵is

ἡ ἀγάπη τοῦ πατρὸς ἐν αὐτῷ· 16 ὅτι
¹the ²love ³of the ⁴Father in him; because

πᾶν τὸ ἐν τῷ κόσμῳ, ἡ ἐπιθυμία τῆς
all that in the world, the lust of the
which† [is]

σαρκὸς καὶ ἡ ἐπιθυμία τῶν ὀφθαλμῶν
flesh and the lust of the eyes

καὶ ἡ ἀλαζονεία τοῦ βίου, οὐκ ἔστιν
and the vainglory – of life, is not

ἐκ τοῦ πατρός, ἀλλὰ ἐκ τοῦ κόσμου
of the Father, but of the world

17 And the world passeth away, and the lust thereof: but he that doeth the will of God abideth for ever.

18 Little children, it is the last time: and as ye have heard that antichrist shall come, even now are there many antichrists; whereby we know that it is the last time.

19 They went out from us, but they were not of us; for if they had been of us, they would *no doubt* have continued with us: but *they went out*, that they might be made manifest that they were not all of us.

20 But ye have an unction from the Holy One, and ye know all things.

21 I have not written unto you because ye know not the truth, but because ye know it, and that no lie is of the truth.

22 Who is a liar but he that denieth that Jesus is the Christ? He is antichrist, that denieth the Father and the Son.

23 Whosoever denieth the Son, the same hath not the Father: [*but*] *he that acknowledgeth the Son hath the Father also.*

24 Let that therefore abide in you, which ye have heard from the be-

ἐστίν. **17** καὶ ὁ κόσμος παράγεται καὶ
is.   And the world is passing away and

ἡ ἐπιθυμία αὐτοῦ· ὁ δὲ ποιῶν τὸ θέλημα
the lust of it; but the [one] doing the will

τοῦ θεοῦ μένει εἰς τὸν αἰῶνα.
– of God remains unto the age.

18 Παιδία, ἐσχάτη ὥρα ἐστίν, καὶ
Young children, a last hour it is, and

καθὼς ἠκούσατε ὅτι ἀντίχριστος ἔρχεται,
as ye heard that antichrist is coming,

καὶ νῦν ἀντίχριστοι πολλοὶ γεγόνασιν·
even now ²antichrists ¹many have arisen;

ὅθεν γινώσκομεν ὅτι ἐσχάτη ὥρα ἐστίν.
whence we know that a last hour it is.

19 ἐξ ἡμῶν ἐξῆλθαν, ἀλλ' οὐκ ἦσαν
From us they went out, but they were not

ἐξ ἡμῶν· εἰ γὰρ ἐξ ἡμῶν ἦσαν, μεμενή-
of us; for if of us they were, they would

κεισαν ἂν μεθ' ἡμῶν· ἀλλ' ἵνα φανερω-
have remained with us; but in order it might be
                                            that

θῶσιν ὅτι οὐκ εἰσὶν πάντες ἐξ ἡμῶν.
manifested that they are not all of us.

20 καὶ ὑμεῖς χρῖσμα ἔχετε ἀπὸ τοῦ
And ye an anointing have from the

ἁγίου, καὶ οἴδατε πάντες. **21** οὐκ ἔγραψα
Holy One, and ¹ye ³know ²all.   I wrote not

ὑμῖν ὅτι οὐκ οἴδατε τὴν ἀλήθειαν, ἀλλ'
to you because ye know not the truth, but

ὅτι οἴδατε αὐτήν, καὶ ὅτι πᾶν ψεῦδος
because ye know it, and because every lie
                                     =no lie is . . .

ἐκ τῆς ἀληθείας οὐκ ἔστιν. **22** Τίς
of the truth is not.   Who

ἐστιν ὁ ψεύστης εἰ μὴ ὁ ἀρνούμενος
is the liar except the [one] denying

ὅτι Ἰησοῦς οὐκ ἔστιν ὁ χριστός; οὗτός
that Jesus *not* is the Christ? this

ἐστιν ὁ ἀντίχριστος, ὁ ἀρνούμενος τὸν
is the antichrist, the [one] denying the

πατέρα καὶ τὸν υἱόν. **23** πᾶς ὁ ἀρνούμενος
Father and the Son.   Everyone denying

τὸν υἱὸν οὐδὲ τὸν πατέρα ἔχει· ὁ
the Son ²neither ³the ⁴Father ¹has; the

ὁμολογῶν τὸν υἱὸν καὶ τὸν πατέρα ἔχει.
[one] confessing the Son ²also ³the ⁴Father ¹has.

24 ὑμεῖς ὃ ἠκούσατε ἀπ' ἀρχῆς, ἐν
²Ye ¹what heard from [the] beginning, in

ginning. If that which ye
have heard from the be-
ginning shall remain in
you, ye also shall con-
tinue in the Son, and in
the Father.

25 And this is the
promise that he hath
promised us, *even* eternal
life.

26 These *things* have I
written unto you con-
cerning them that seduce
you.

27 But the anointing
which ye have received of
him abideth in you, and
ye need not that any man
teach you: but as the
same anointing teacheth
you of all things, and is
truth, and is no lie, and
even as it hath taught
you, ye shall abide in him.

28 And now, little child-
ren, abide in him; that,
when he shall appear, we
may have confidence, and
not be ashamed before
him at his coming.

29 If ye know that he is
righteous, ye know that
every one that doeth righteousness is born of him.

CHAPTER 3

BEHOLD, what man-
ner of love the Father
hath bestowed upon us,
that we should be called
the sons of God: therefore

ὑμῖν μενέτω. ἐὰν ἐν ὑμῖν μείνῃ ὃ ἀπ’
you let it remain. If ⁶in ⁷you ⁸remains ¹what ²from

ἀρχῆς ἠκούσατε, καὶ ὑμεῖς ἐν τῷ υἱῷ
⁴[the] ²ye heard, ³both ¹ye ⁴in ⁵the ⁶Son
beginning

καὶ [ἐν] τῷ πατρὶ μενεῖτε.   25 καὶ
⁷and ⁸in ⁹the ¹⁰Father ⁹will remain.   And

αὕτη ἐστὶν ἡ ἐπαγγελία ἣν αὐτὸς ἐπηγ-
this is the promise which he pro-

γείλατο ἡμῖν, τὴν ζωὴν τὴν αἰώνιον.
mised us, the life – eternal.

26 Ταῦτα ἔγραψα ὑμῖν περὶ τῶν πλανών-
These I wrote to you concern- the leading
things ing [ones]

των ὑμᾶς.   27 καὶ ὑμεῖς τὸ χρῖσμα
²astray ¹you.   And ⁴ye ¹the ²anointing

ὃ ἐλάβετε ἀπ’ αὐτοῦ μένει ἐν ὑμῖν,
³which received from him remains in you,

καὶ οὐ χρείαν ἔχετε ἵνα τις διδάσκῃ
and ²no ³need ¹ye have *in order* anyone should
that teach

ὑμᾶς· ἀλλ’ ὡς τὸ αὐτοῦ χρῖσμα διδάσκει
you; but as the ²of him ¹anointing teaches

ὑμᾶς περὶ πάντων, καὶ ἀληθές ἐστιν
you concerning all things, and ²true ¹is

καὶ οὐκ ἔστιν ψεῦδος, καὶ καθὼς ἐδίδαξεν
and is not a lie, and as he/it taught

ὑμᾶς, μένετε ἐν αὐτῷ.
you, remain ye in him.

28 Καὶ νῦν, τεκνία, μένετε ἐν αὐτῷ,
And now, little children, remain ye in him,

ἵνα ἐὰν φανερωθῇ σχῶμεν παρρησίαν καὶ
in or- if he is manifested we may confidence and
der that have

μὴ αἰσχυνθῶμεν ἀπ’ αὐτοῦ ἐν τῇ παρουσίᾳ
not be shamed from him in the presence

αὐτοῦ.   29 ἐὰν εἰδῆτε ὅτι δίκαιός ἐστιν,
of him. If ye know that ²righteous ¹he is,

γινώσκετε ὅτι καὶ πᾶς ὁ ποιῶν τὴν
know ye that also every one doing –

δικαιοσύνην ἐξ αὐτοῦ γεγέννηται.
righteousness ²of ³him ¹has been born.

3 Ἴδετε ποταπὴν ἀγάπην δέδωκεν ἡμῖν
See ye what manner of love ³has given ⁴to us

ὁ πατὴρ ἵνα τέκνα θεοῦ κληθῶμεν,
¹the ²Father in order ²children ³of God ¹we may be
that called,

καὶ ἐσμέν. διὰ τοῦτο ὁ κόσμος οὐ
and we are. Therefore the world ²not

the world knoweth us not, because it knew him not.

2 Beloved, now are we the sons of God, and it doth not yet appear what we shall be: but we know that, when he shall appear, we shall be like him; for we shall see him as he is.

3 And every man that hath this hope in him purifieth himself, even as he is pure.

4 Whosoever committeth sin transgresseth also the law: for sin is the transgression of the law.

5 And ye know that he was manifested to take away our sins; and in him is no sin.

6 Whosoever abideth in him sinneth not: whosoever sinneth hath not seen him, neither known him.

7 Little children, let no man deceive you: he that doeth righteousness is righteous, even as he is righteous.

8 He that committeth sin is of the devil; for the devil sinneth from the beginning. For this purpose the Son of God was manifested, that he might destroy the works of the devil.

9 Whosoever is born of

γινώσκει ἡμᾶς, ὅτι οὐκ ἔγνω αὐτόν.
[1]knows ~ [2]us, because it knew not him.

2 ἀγαπητοί, νῦν τέκνα θεοῦ ἐσμεν, καὶ
Beloved, [2]now [3]children [4]of God [1]we are, and

οὔπω ἐφανερώθη τί ἐσόμεθα. οἴδαμεν
not yet was it manifested what we shall be. We know

ὅτι ἐὰν φανερωθῇ ὅμοιοι αὐτῷ ἐσόμεθα,
that if he(?it) is manifested like him we shall be,

ὅτι ὀψόμεθα αὐτὸν καθώς ἐστιν. 3 καὶ
because we shall see him as he is. And

πᾶς ὁ ἔχων τὴν ἐλπίδα ταύτην ἐπ᾽
everyone having this hope on

αὐτῷ ἁγνίζει ἑαυτὸν καθὼς ἐκεῖνος ἁγνός
him purifies himself as that one* [2]pure

ἐστιν. 4 πᾶς ὁ ποιῶν τὴν ἁμαρτίαν
[1]is. Everyone doing – sin

καὶ τὴν ἀνομίαν ποιεῖ, καὶ ἡ ἁμαρτία
[2]also – [3]lawlessness [1]does, and – sin

ἐστὶν ἡ ἀνομία. 5 καὶ οἴδατε ὅτι ἐκεῖνος
is lawlessness. And ye know that that one*

ἐφανερώθη ἵνα τὰς ἁμαρτίας ἄρῃ, καὶ
was manifested in order that – sins he might bear, and

ἁμαρτία ἐν αὐτῷ οὐκ ἔστιν. 6 πᾶς ὁ
sin [2]in [3]him [1]is not. Everyone

ἐν αὐτῷ μένων οὐχ ἁμαρτάνει· πᾶς ὁ
[2]in [3]him [1]remaining sins not; everyone

ἁμαρτάνων οὐχ ἑώρακεν αὐτὸν οὐδὲ
sinning has not seen him nor

ἔγνωκεν αὐτόν. 7 Τεκνία, μηδεὶς πλανάτω
has known him. Little children, [2]no man [1]let [3]lead astray

ὑμᾶς· ὁ ποιῶν τὴν δικαιοσύνην δίκαιός
[4]you; the [one] doing – righteousness [2]righteous

ἐστιν, καθὼς ἐκεῖνος δίκαιός ἐστιν· 8 ὁ
[1]is, as that one* [2]righteous [1]is; the

ποιῶν τὴν ἁμαρτίαν ἐκ τοῦ διαβόλου
[one] doing – sin [2]of [3]the [4]devil

ἐστίν, ὅτι ἀπ᾽ ἀρχῆς ὁ διάβολος ἁμαρτάνει.
[1]is, because [4]from [5][the] [1]the [3]devil [2]sins.
beginning

εἰς τοῦτο ἐφανερώθη ὁ υἱὸς τοῦ θεοῦ,
For this was manifested the Son – of God,

ἵνα λύσῃ τὰ ἔργα τοῦ διαβόλου.
in or- he might the works of the devil.
der that undo

9 Πᾶς ὁ γεγεννημένος ἐκ τοῦ θεοῦ
Everyone having been begotten of – God

* See ch. 2. 6.

God doth not commit sin; for his seed remaineth in him: and he cannot sin, because he is born of God.

10 In this the children of God are manifest, and the children of the devil: whosoever doeth not righteousness is not of God, neither he that loveth not his brother.

11 For this is the message that ye heard from the beginning, that we should love one another.

12 Not as Cain, *who* was of that wicked one, and slew his brother. And wherefore slew he him? Because his own works were evil, and his brother's righteous.

13 Marvel not, my brethren, if the world hate you.

14 We know that we have passed from death unto life, because we love the brethren. He that loveth not *his* brother abideth in death.

15 Whosoever hateth his brother is a murderer: and ye know that no murderer hath eternal life abiding in him.

ἁμαρτίαν οὐ ποιεῖ; ὅτι σπέρμα αὐτοῦ
²sin ²not ¹does, because seed of him

ἐν αὐτῷ μένει· καὶ οὐ δύναται ἁμαρτάνειν,
in him remains; and he cannot to sin,

ὅτι ἐκ τοῦ θεοῦ γεγέννηται. 10 ἐν
because of – God he has been begotten. By

τούτῳ φανερά ἐστιν τὰ τέκνα τοῦ θεοῦ
this ²manifest ¹is(are) the children – of God

καὶ τὰ τέκνα τοῦ διαβόλου· πᾶς ὁ
and the children of the devil; everyone

μὴ ποιῶν δικαιοσύνην οὐκ ἔστιν ἐκ
not doing righteousness is not of

τοῦ θεοῦ, καὶ ὁ μὴ ἀγαπῶν τὸν ἀδελφὸν
– God, and the not loving the brother
              [one]

αὐτοῦ. 11 ὅτι αὕτη ἐστὶν ἡ ἀγγελία
of him. Because this is the message

ἣν ἠκούσατε ἀπ᾽ ἀρχῆς, ἵνα ἀγαπῶμεν
which ye heard from [the] in order we should love
              beginning, that

ἀλλήλους· 12 οὐ καθὼς Κάϊν ἐκ τοῦ
one another; not as Cain ²of ³the

πονηροῦ ἦν καὶ ἔσφαξεν τὸν ἀδελφὸν
⁴evil one ¹was and slew the brother

αὐτοῦ· καὶ χάριν τίνος ἔσφαξεν αὐτόν;
of him; and for the what slew he him ?
        sake of

ὅτι τὰ ἔργα αὐτοῦ πονηρὰ ἦν, τὰ δὲ
be- the works of him ²evil ¹was(were), but the
cause   [works]

τοῦ ἀδελφοῦ αὐτοῦ δίκαια. 13 μὴ
of the brother of him righteous. not

θαυμάζετε, ἀδελφοί, εἰ μισεῖ ὑμᾶς ὁ
Marvel ye, brothers, if ³hates ⁴you ¹the

κόσμος. 14 ἡμεῖς οἴδαμεν ὅτι μεταβεβή-
²world. We know that we have re-

καμεν ἐκ τοῦ θανάτου εἰς τὴν ζωήν,
moved out of *the* death into *the* life,

ὅτι ἀγαπῶμεν τοὺς ἀδελφούς· ὁ μὴ
because we love the brothers; the [one] not

ἀγαπῶν μένει ἐν τῷ θανάτῳ. 15 πᾶς
loving remains in – death. Every-

ὁ μισῶν τὸν ἀδελφὸν αὐτοῦ ἀνθρωποκτόνος
one hating the brother of him ²a murderer

ἐστίν, καὶ οἴδατε ὅτι πᾶς ἀνθρωποκτόνος
¹is, and ye know that every murderer
                    =no murderer has . . .

οὐκ ἔχει ζωὴν αἰώνιον ἐν αὐτῷ μένουσαν.
has not life eternal in him remaining.

16 Hereby perceive we the love *of God*, because he laid down his life for us: and we ought to lay down *our* lives for the brethren.

17 But whoso hath this world's good, and seeth his brother have need, and shutteth up his bowels *of compassion* from him, how dwelleth the love of God in him?

18 My little children, let us not love in word, neither in tongue; but in deed and in truth.

19 And hereby we know that we are of the truth, and shall assure our hearts before him.

20 For if our heart condemn us, God is greater than our heart, and knoweth all things.

21 Beloved, if our heart condemn us not, *then* have we confidence toward God.

22 And whatsoever we ask, we receive of him, because we keep his commandments, and do those things that are pleasing in his sight.

23 And this is his commandment, That we should believe on the

16 ἐν τούτῳ ἐγνώκαμεν τὴν ἀγάπην, ὅτι
By this⁻ we have known – love, because

ἐκεῖνος ὑπὲρ ἡμῶν τὴν ψυχὴν αὐτοῦ
that one* on behalf of us the life of him

ἔθηκεν· καὶ ἡμεῖς ὀφείλομεν ὑπὲρ τῶν
laid down; and we ought on behalf of the

ἀδελφῶν τὰς ψυχὰς θεῖναι. 17 ὃς δ'
brothers the(our) lives to lay down. Who-

ἂν ἔχῃ τὸν βίον τοῦ κόσμου καὶ θεωρῇ
ever has the means of the world and beholds
of life

τὸν ἀδελφὸν αὐτοῦ χρείαν ἔχοντα καὶ
the brother of him ²need ¹having and

κλείσῃ τὰ σπλάγχνα αὐτοῦ ἀπ' αὐτοῦ,
shuts the bowels of him from him,

πῶς ἡ ἀγάπη τοῦ θεοῦ μένει ἐν αὐτῷ;
how ²the ³love – ⁴of God ¹remains in him?

18 Τεκνία, μὴ ἀγαπῶμεν λόγῳ μηδὲ τῇ
Little children, let us not love in word nor in *the*

γλώσσῃ, ἀλλὰ ἐν ἔργῳ καὶ ἀληθείᾳ.
tongue, but in work and truth.

19 ἐν τούτῳ γνωσόμεθα ὅτι ἐκ τῆς ἀληθείας
By this we shall know that ²of ³the ⁴truth

ἐσμέν, καὶ ἔμπροσθεν αὐτοῦ πείσομεν
¹we are, and before him shall persuade

τὴν καρδίαν ἡμῶν 20 ὅτι ἐὰν καταγινώσκῃ
the heart of us that if ⁴blames [us]

ἡμῶν ἡ καρδία, ὅτι μείζων ἐστὶν ὁ
³of us ¹the ²heart, that greater is –

θεὸς τῆς καρδίας ἡμῶν καὶ γινώσκει
God [than] the heart of us and knows

πάντα. 21 Ἀγαπητοί, ἐὰν ἡ καρδία
all things. Beloved, if the(our) heart

μὴ καταγινώσκῃ, παρρησίαν ἔχομεν πρὸς
does not blame [us], confidence we have with

τὸν θεόν, 22 καὶ ὃ ἐὰν αἰτῶμεν λαμβάν-
– God, and whatever we ask we re-

ομεν ἀπ' αὐτοῦ, ὅτι τὰς ἐντολὰς αὐτοῦ
ceive from him, because ²the ³command- ⁴of him
ments

τηροῦμεν καὶ τὰ ἀρεστὰ ἐνώπιον αὐτοῦ
¹we keep and ²the ³pleasing ⁴before ⁵him
things

ποιοῦμεν. 23 καὶ αὕτη ἐστὶν ἡ ἐντολὴ
¹*we do*. And this is the commandment

αὐτοῦ, ἵνα πιστεύσωμεν τῷ ὀνόματι τοῦ
of him, *in order* we should believe the name of the
that

* See ch. 2. 6, 3. 3, 5, 7.

name of his Son Jesus Christ, and love one another, as he gave us commandment.

24 And he that keepeth his commandments dwelleth in him, and he in him. And hereby we know that he abideth in us, by the Spirit which he hath given us.

υἱοῦ αὐτοῦ Ἰησοῦ Χριστοῦ καὶ ἀγαπῶμεν
Son of him Jesus Christ and love
ἀλλήλους καθὼς ἔδωκεν ἐντολὴν ἡμῖν.
one another as he gave commandment to us.
24 καὶ ὁ τηρῶν τὰς ἐντολὰς αὐτοῦ ἐν
And the keeping the command- of him in
[one] ments
αὐτῷ μένει καὶ αὐτὸς ἐν αὐτῷ· καὶ
him remains and he in him; and
ἐν τούτῳ γινώσκομεν ὅτι μένει ἐν ἡμῖν,
by this we know that he remains in us,
ἐκ τοῦ πνεύματος οὗ ἡμῖν ἔδωκεν.
by the Spirit whom to us he gave.

CHAPTER 4

BELOVED, believe not every spirit, but try the spirits whether they are of God: because many false prophets are gone out into the world.

2 Hereby know ye the Spirit of God: Every spirit that confesseth that Jesus Christ is come in the flesh is of God:

3 And every spirit that confesseth not that Jesus Christ is come in the flesh is not of God: and this is that *spirit* of antichrist, whereof ye have heard that it should come; and even now already is it in the world.

4 Ye are of God, little children, and have overcome them : because greater is he that is in you, than he that is in the world.

5 They are of the world:

4 Ἀγαπητοί, μὴ παντὶ πνεύματι
Beloved, ²not ³every ⁴spirit
πιστεύετε, ἀλλὰ δοκιμάζετε τὰ πνεύματα
¹believe ye, but prove the spirits
εἰ ἐκ τοῦ θεοῦ ἐστιν, ὅτι πολλοὶ
if of – God they are, because many
ψευδοπροφῆται ἐξεληλύθασιν εἰς τὸν
false prophets have gone forth into the
κόσμον. 2 ἐν τούτῳ γινώσκετε τὸ πνεῦμα
world. By this know ye the Spirit
τοῦ θεοῦ· πᾶν πνεῦμα ὃ ὁμολογεῖ Ἰησοῦν
– of God: every spirit which confesses Jesus
Χριστὸν ἐν σαρκὶ ἐληλυθότα ἐκ τοῦ
Christ ²in ³[the] flesh ¹having come ⁵of –
θεοῦ ἐστιν, 3 καὶ πᾶν πνεῦμα ὃ μὴ
⁶God ⁴is, and every spirit which not
ὁμολογεῖ τὸν Ἰησοῦν ἐκ τοῦ θεοῦ οὐκ
confesses – Jesus ²of – ⁴God ²not
ἔστιν· καὶ τοῦτό ἐστιν τὸ τοῦ ἀντιχρίστου,
¹is; and this is the of antichrist,
[spirit] the
ὃ ἀκηκόατε ὅτι ἔρχεται, καὶ νῦν ἐν
which ye have that it is coming, and ²now ⁴in
heard
τῷ κόσμῳ ἐστὶν ἤδη. 4 ὑμεῖς ἐκ τοῦ
⁵the ⁶world ¹is ³already. Ye of –
θεοῦ ἐστε, τεκνία, καὶ νενικήκατε αὐτούς,
God are, little and have overcome them,
children,
ὅτι μείζων ἐστὶν ὁ ἐν ὑμῖν ἢ ὁ ἐν
because greater is the in you than the in
[one] [one]
τῷ κόσμῳ. 5 αὐτοὶ ἐκ τοῦ κόσμου
the world. ¹They ³of ⁴the ⁵world

therefore speak they of the world, and the world heareth them.

6 We are of God: he that knoweth God heareth us; he that is not of God heareth not us. Hereby know we the spirit of truth, and the spirit of error.

7 Beloved, let us love one another: for love is of God; and every one that loveth is born of God, and knoweth God.

8 He that loveth not knoweth not God; for God is love.

9 In this was manifested the love of God toward us, because that God sent his only begotten Son into the world, that we might live through him.

10 Herein is love, not that we loved God, but that he loved us, and sent his Son *to be* the propitiation for our sins.

11 Beloved, if God so loved us, we ought also to love one another.

12 No man hath seen God at any time. If we love one another, God

εἰσίν· διὰ τοῦτο ἐκ τοῦ κόσμου λαλοῦσιν
²are; therefore ²of ³the ⁴world ¹they speak
καὶ ὁ κόσμος αὐτῶν ἀκούει. 6 ἡμεῖς
and the world them hears. ¹We
ἐκ τοῦ θεοῦ ἐσμεν· ὁ γινώσκων τὸν
²of - ⁴God ²are; the [one] knowing -
θεὸν ἀκούει ἡμῶν, ὃς οὐκ ἔστιν ἐκ
God hears us, [he] who is not of
τοῦ θεοῦ οὐκ ἀκούει ἡμῶν. ἐκ τούτου
- God hears not us. From this
γινώσκομεν τὸ πνεῦμα τῆς ἀληθείας καὶ
we know the spirit - of truth and
τὸ πνεῦμα τῆς πλάνης.
the spirit - of error.

7 Ἀγαπητοί, ἀγαπῶμεν ἀλλήλους, ὅτι
Beloved, let us love one another, because
ἡ ἀγάπη ἐκ τοῦ θεοῦ ἐστιν, καὶ πᾶς ὁ
- love ²of - ³God ¹is, and everyone
ἀγαπῶν ἐκ τοῦ θεοῦ γεγέννηται καὶ
loving ²of - ³God ¹has been begotten and
γινώσκει τὸν θεόν. 8 ὁ μὴ ἀγαπῶν
knows - God. The [one] not loving
οὐκ ἔγνω τὸν θεόν, ὅτι ὁ θεὸς ἀγάπη
knew not - God, because - God ²love
ἐστίν. 9 ἐν τούτῳ ἐφανερώθη ἡ ἀγάπη
¹is. By this was manifested the love
τοῦ θεοῦ ἐν ἡμῖν, ὅτι τὸν υἱὸν αὐτοῦ
- of God in(to) us, because ³the ⁵Son ⁶of him
τὸν μονογενῆ ἀπέσταλκεν ὁ θεὸς εἰς
- ⁴only begotten ²has sent - ¹God into
τὸν κόσμον ἵνα ζήσωμεν δι' αὐτοῦ.
the world in order we might live through him.
that

10 ἐν τούτῳ ἐστὶν ἡ ἀγάπη, οὐχ ὅτι
In this is - love, not that
ἡμεῖς ἠγαπήκαμεν τὸν θεόν, ἀλλ' ὅτι
we have loved - God, but that
αὐτὸς ἠγάπησεν ἡμᾶς καὶ ἀπέστειλεν τὸν
he loved us and sent the
υἱὸν αὐτοῦ ἱλασμὸν περὶ τῶν ἁμαρτιῶν
Son of him a propitiation concerning the sins
ἡμῶν. 11 ἀγαπητοί, εἰ οὕτως ὁ θεὸς
of us. Beloved, if so - God
ἠγάπησεν ἡμᾶς, καὶ ἡμεῖς ὀφείλομεν
loved us, ²also ¹we ³ought
ἀλλήλους ἀγαπᾶν. 12 θεὸν οὐδεὶς πώποτε
⁵one another ⁴to love. ⁴God ¹no man ²ever
τεθέαται· ἐὰν ἀγαπῶμεν ἀλλήλους, ὁ θεὸς
³has beheld; if we love one another, - God

dwelleth in us, and his love is perfected in us.

13 Hereby know we that we dwell in him, and he in us, because he hath given us of his Spirit.

14 And we have seen and do testify that the Father sent the Son *to be* the Saviour of the world.

15 Whosoever shall confess that Jesus is the Son of God, God dwelleth in him, and he in God.

16 And we have known and believed the love that God hath to us. God is love; and he that dwelleth in love dwelleth in God, and God in him.

17 Herein is our love made perfect, that we may have boldness in the day of judgment: because as he is, so are we in this world.

18 There is no fear in love; but perfect love casteth out fear: because fear hath torment. He that feareth is not made perfect in love.

19 We love him, because he first loved us.

ἐν   ἡμῖν   μένει   καὶ   ἡ   ἀγάπη   αὐτοῦ
in   us   remains   and   the   love   of him

τετελειωμένη   ἐν   ἡμῖν   ἐστιν.   13 Ἐν
[2]*having been* perfected [3]in   [4]us   [1]is.   By

τούτῳ   γινώσκομεν   ὅτι   ἐν   αὐτῷ   μένομεν
this   we know   that   in   him   we remain

καὶ   αὐτὸς   ἐν   ἡμῖν,   ὅτι   ἐκ   τοῦ   πνεύματος
and   he   in   us,   because [3]of   [4]the   [5]Spirit

αὐτοῦ   δέδωκεν   ἡμῖν.   14 καὶ   ἡμεῖς
[6]of him   [1]he has given   [2]us.   And   we

τεθεάμεθα   καὶ   μαρτυροῦμεν   ὅτι   ὁ   πατὴρ
have beheld   and   bear witness   that   the   Father

ἀπέσταλκεν   τὸν   υἱὸν   σωτῆρα   τοῦ   κόσμου.
has sent   the   Son [as] Saviour   of the   world.

15 ὃς   ἐὰν   ὁμολογήσῃ   ὅτι   Ἰησοῦς   ἐστιν
   Whoever   confesses   that   Jesus   is

ὁ   υἱὸς   τοῦ   θεοῦ,   ὁ   θεὸς   ἐν   αὐτῷ   μένει
the Son   -   of God,   -   God   in   him   remains

καὶ   αὐτὸς   ἐν   τῷ   θεῷ.   16 καὶ   ἡμεῖς
and   he   in   -   God.   And   we

ἐγνώκαμεν   καὶ   πεπιστεύκαμεν   τὴν   ἀγάπην
have known   and   have believed   the   love

ἣν   ἔχει   ὁ   θεὸς   ἐν   ἡμῖν.   Ὁ   θεὸς   ἀγάπη
which [2]has   [1]God in(to) us.   -   God   [2]love

ἐστίν,   καὶ   ὁ   μένων   ἐν   τῇ   ἀγάπῃ   ἐν
[1]is,   and   the remaining   in   -   love   [2]in
           [one]

τῷ   θεῷ   μένει   καὶ   ὁ   θεὸς   ἐν   αὐτῷ
-    [3]God   [1]remains   and   -   God   [2]in   [3]him

μένει.   17 Ἐν   τούτῳ   τετελείωται   ἡ   ἀγάπη
[1]remains.   By   this   [2]has been perfected -   [1]love

μεθ'   ἡμῶν,   ἵνα   παρρησίαν   ἔχωμεν   ἐν
with   us,   in order that   [2]confidence   [1]we may have   in

τῇ   ἡμέρᾳ   τῆς   κρίσεως,   ὅτι   καθὼς   ἐκεῖνός
the   day   -   of judgment, because   as   that one*

ἐστιν   καὶ   ἡμεῖς   ἐσμεν   ἐν   τῷ   κόσμῳ
is   [3]also   [1]we   [2]are   in   -   world

τούτῳ.   18 φόβος   οὐκ   ἔστιν   ἐν   τῇ   ἀγάπῃ,
this.   Fear   is not   in   -   love,

ἀλλ'   ἡ   τελεία   ἀγάπη   ἔξω   βάλλει   τὸν
but   -   perfect   love   [2]out   [1]casts   *the*

φόβον,   ὅτι   ὁ   φόβος   κόλασιν   ἔχει,   ὁ   δὲ
fear,   because   -   fear   [2]punishment   [1]has,   and the

φοβούμενος   οὐ   τετελείωται   ἐν   τῇ   ἀγάπῃ.
[one] fearing   has not been perfected   in   -   love.

19 ἡμεῖς   ἀγαπῶμεν,   ὅτι   αὐτὸς   πρῶτος
   We   love,   because   he   first

* See ch. 2. 6, 3. 3, 5, 7, 16.

20 If a man say, I love God, and hateth his brother, he is a liar: for he that loveth not his brother whom he hath seen, how can he love God whom he hath not seen?

21 And this commandment have we from him, That he who loveth God love his brother also.

ἠγάπησεν ἡμᾶς. **20** ἐάν τις εἴπῃ ὅτι
loved   us.   If anyone says[.]   –

ἀγαπῶ τὸν θεόν, καὶ τὸν ἀδελφὸν αὐτοῦ
I love –   God, and ²the ³brother ⁴of him

μισῇ, ψεύστης ἐστίν· ὁ γὰρ μὴ ἀγαπῶν
¹hates, ²a liar ¹he is; for the [one] not loving

τὸν ἀδελφὸν αὐτοῦ ὃν ἑώρακεν, τὸν
the brother of him whom he has seen, the

θεὸν ὃν οὐχ ἑώρακεν οὐ δύναται ἀγαπᾶν.
²God ⁴whom ⁵he has not seen ¹he cannot ²to love.

21 καὶ ταύτην τὴν ἐντολὴν ἔχομεν ἀπ'
And this   the   –   commandment we have from

αὐτοῦ, ἵνα ὁ ἀγαπῶν τὸν θεὸν ἀγαπᾷ
him, in order the loving   –   God loves
      that [one]

καὶ τὸν ἀδελφὸν αὐτοῦ.
also the brother of him.

CHAPTER 5

WHOSOEVER believeth that Jesus is the Christ is born of God: and every one that loveth him that begat loveth him also that is begotten of him.

2 By this we know that we love the children of God, when we love God, and keep his commandments.

3 For this is the love of God, that we keep his commandments: and his commandments are not grievous.

4 For whatsoever is born of God overcometh the world: and this is the victory that overcometh the world, *even* our faith.

5 Who is he that over-

5 Πᾶς ὁ πιστεύων ὅτι Ἰησοῦς ἐστιν
Everyone believing that Jesus is

ὁ χριστὸς ἐκ τοῦ θεοῦ γεγέννηται, καὶ
the Christ ²of – ²God ¹has been begotten, and

πᾶς ὁ ἀγαπῶν τὸν γεννήσαντα ἀγαπᾷ
everyone loving the [one] begetting loves

τὸν γεγεννημένον ἐξ αὐτοῦ. **2** ἐν τούτῳ
the having been begotten of him. By this
[one]

γινώσκομεν ὅτι ἀγαπῶμεν τὰ τέκνα τοῦ
we know   that we love   the children –

θεοῦ, ὅταν τὸν θεὸν ἀγαπῶμεν καὶ τὰς
of God, whenever – ²God ¹we love and ²the

ἐντολὰς αὐτοῦ ποιῶμεν. **3** αὕτη γάρ
³command- ⁴of him ¹we do. For this
ments

ἐστιν ἡ ἀγάπη τοῦ θεοῦ, ἵνα τὰς ἐντολὰς
is the love – of in order ²the ³command-
         God, that ments

αὐτοῦ τηρῶμεν· καὶ αἱ ἐντολαὶ αὐτοῦ
⁴of him ¹we keep; and the commandments of him

βαρεῖαι οὐκ εἰσίν, **4** ὅτι πᾶν τὸ γεγεν-
heavy are not,   because everything having

νημένον ἐκ τοῦ θεοῦ νικᾷ τὸν κόσμον·
been begotten of – God overcomes the world;

καὶ αὕτη ἐστὶν ἡ νίκη ἡ νικήσασα τὸν
and this is the victory – overcoming the

κόσμον, ἡ πίστις ἡμῶν. **5** Τίς ἐστιν
world, the faith of us. ²Who ¹is

cometh the world, but he that believeth that Jesus is the Son of God?

6 This is he that came by water and blood, *even* Jesus Christ; not by water only, but by water and blood. And it is the Spirit that beareth witness, because the Spirit is truth.

7 For there are three that bear record in heaven, the Father, the Word, and the Holy Ghost: and these three are one.

8 And there are three that bear witness in earth, the spirit, and the water, and the blood: and these three agree in one.

9 If we receive the witness of men, the witness of God is greater: for this is the witness of God which he hath testified of his Son.

10 He that believeth on the Son of God hath the witness in himself: he that believeth not God hath made him a liar; because he believeth not the record that God gave of his Son.

11 And this is the record, that God hath given to us eternal life, and this life is in his Son.

[δὲ] ὁ νικῶν τὸν κόσμον εἰ μὴ ὁ
[and] the overcoming the world except the
[one]

πιστεύων ὅτι ᾿Ιησοῦς ἐστιν ὁ υἱὸς τοῦ
[one] believing that Jesus is the Son -

θεοῦ; 6 οὗτός ἐστιν ὁ ἐλθὼν δι᾿ ὕδατος
of God? This is the coming through water
[one]

καὶ αἵματος, ᾿Ιησοῦς Χριστός· οὐκ ἐν
and blood, Jesus Christ; not by

τῷ ὕδατι μόνον, ἀλλ᾿ ἐν τῷ ὕδατι καὶ
the water only, but by the water and

ἐν τῷ αἵματι· καὶ τὸ πνεῦμά ἐστιν τὸ
by the blood; and the Spirit is the

μαρτυροῦν, ὅτι τὸ πνεῦμά ἐστιν ἡ ἀλήθεια.
[one] bearing be- the Spirit is the truth.
witness, cause

7 ὅτι τρεῖς εἰσιν οἱ μαρτυροῦντες, 8 τὸ
Because three there are the bearing witness, the
[ones]

πνεῦμα καὶ τὸ ὕδωρ καὶ τὸ αἷμα, καὶ
Spirit and the water and the blood, and

οἱ τρεῖς εἰς τὸ ἓν εἰσιν. 9 εἰ τὴν
the three ²in *the* ³one ¹are. If ²the

μαρτυρίαν τῶν ἀνθρώπων λαμβάνομεν, ἡ
³witness - ⁴of men ¹we receive, the

μαρτυρία τοῦ θεοῦ μείζων ἐστίν, ὅτι
witness - of God ²greater ¹is, because

αὕτη ἐστὶν ἡ μαρτυρία τοῦ θεοῦ, ὅτι
this is the witness - of God, because

μεμαρτύρηκεν περὶ τοῦ υἱοῦ αὐτοῦ. 10 ὁ
he has borne concern- the Son of him. The
witness ing

πιστεύων εἰς τὸν υἱὸν τοῦ θεοῦ ἔχει
[one] believing in the Son - of God has

τὴν μαρτυρίαν ἐν αὐτῷ. ὁ μὴ πιστεύων
the witness in him. The not believing
[one]

τῷ θεῷ ψεύστην πεποίηκεν αὐτόν, ὅτι
- God ³a liar ¹has made ²him, because

οὐ πεπίστευκεν εἰς τὴν μαρτυρίαν ἣν
he has not believed in the witness which

μεμαρτύρηκεν ὁ θεὸς περὶ τοῦ υἱοῦ
³has borne witness - ¹God concerning the Son

αὐτοῦ. 11 καὶ αὕτη ἐστὶν ἡ μαρτυρία,
of him. And this is the witness,

ὅτι ζωὴν αἰώνιον ἔδωκεν ὁ θεὸς ἡμῖν,
that ⁵life ⁴eternal ²gave - ¹God ³to us,

καὶ αὕτη ἡ ζωὴ ἐν τῷ υἱῷ αὐτοῦ
and this - life ²in ³the ⁴Son ⁵of him

12 He that hath the Son hath life; *and* he that hath not the Son of God hath not life.

13 These things have I written unto you that believe on the name of the Son of God; that ye may know that ye have eternal life, and that ye may believe on the name of the Son of God.

14 And this is the confidence that we have in him, that, if we ask any thing according to his will, he heareth us:

15 And if we know that he hear us, whatsoever we ask, we know that we have the petitions that we desired of him.

16 If any man see his brother sin a sin *which is* not unto death, he shall ask, and he shall give him life for them that sin not unto death. There is a sin únto death: I do not say that he shall pray for it.

17 All unrighteousness is sin: and there is a sin not unto death.

18 We know that whosoever is born of God sinneth not; but he that is begotten of God keepeth himself, and that wicked one toucheth him not.

19 *And* we know that

ἐστιν. **12** ὁ ἔχων τὸν υἱὸν ἔχει τὴν
¹is.   The [one] having the Son has *the*

ζωήν· ὁ μὴ ἔχων τὸν υἱὸν τοῦ θεοῦ
life; the not having the Son - of God
      [one]

τὴν ζωὴν οὐκ ἔχει.
the life has not.

13 Ταῦτα ἔγραψα ὑμῖν ἵνα εἰδῆτε ὅτι
These I wrote to you in order ye may that
things   that know

ζωὴν ἔχετε αἰώνιον, τοῖς πιστεύουσιν
³life ¹ye have ²eternal, to the [ones] believing

εἰς τὸ ὄνομα τοῦ υἱοῦ τοῦ θεοῦ. **14** Καὶ
in the name of the Son - of God.   And

αὕτη ἐστὶν ἡ παρρησία ἣν ἔχομεν πρὸς
this is the confidence which we have toward

αὐτόν, ὅτι ἐάν τι αἰτώμεθα κατὰ τὸ
him, that if ³anything ¹we ask according to the

θέλημα αὐτοῦ ἀκούει ἡμῶν. **15** καὶ
will of him he hears us.   And

ἐὰν οἴδαμεν ὅτι ἀκούει ἡμῶν ὃ ἐὰν
if we know that he hears us whatever

αἰτώμεθα, οἴδαμεν ὅτι ἔχομεν τὰ αἰτήματα
we ask, we know that we have the requests

ἃ ἠτήκαμεν ἀπ' αὐτοῦ. **16** Ἐάν τις
which we have from him.   If anyone
asked

ἴδῃ τὸν ἀδελφὸν αὐτοῦ ἁμαρτάνοντα
sees the brother of him sinning

ἁμαρτίαν μὴ πρὸς θάνατον, αἰτήσει, καὶ
a sin not unto death, he shall ask, and

δώσει αὐτῷ ζωήν, τοῖς ἁμαρτάνουσιν
he will give to him life, to the [ones] sinning

μὴ πρὸς θάνατον. ἔστιν ἁμαρτία πρὸς
not unto death. There is a sin unto

θάνατον· οὐ περὶ ἐκείνης λέγω ἵνα
death; not concerning that do I say *in order*
that

ἐρωτήσῃ. **17** πᾶσα ἀδικία ἁμαρτία ἐστίν,
he should inquire. All iniquity ²sin ¹is,

καὶ ἔστιν ἁμαρτία οὐ πρὸς θάνατον.
and there is a sin not unto death.

18 Οἴδαμεν ὅτι πᾶς ὁ γεγεννημένος ἐκ
We know that everyone having been begotten of

τοῦ θεοῦ οὐχ ἁμαρτάνει, ἀλλ' ὁ γεννηθεὶς
 - God sins not, but the [one] begotten

ἐκ τοῦ θεοῦ τηρεῖ αὐτόν, καὶ ὁ πονηρὸς
of - God keeps him, and the evil one

οὐχ ἅπτεται αὐτοῦ. **19** οἴδαμεν ὅτι ἐκ
does not touch him.   We know that of

we are of God, and the whole world lieth in wickedness.

20 And we know that the Son of God is come, and hath given us an understanding, that we may know him that is true, and we are in him that is true, *even* in his Son Jesus Christ. This is the true God, and eternal life.

21 Little children, keep yourselves from idols. Amen.

τοῦ θεοῦ ἐσμεν, καὶ ὁ κόσμος ὅλος ἐν
– God we are, and the ²world ¹whole in
τῷ πονηρῷ κεῖται. 20 οἴδαμεν δὲ ὅτι
the evil one lies. ²we know ¹And that
ὁ υἱὸς τοῦ θεοῦ ἥκει, καὶ δέδωκεν
the Son – of God is come, and has given
ἡμῖν διάνοιαν ἵνα γινώσκωμεν τὸν
to us an understanding in order we might know the
that
ἀληθινόν· καὶ ἐσμὲν ἐν τῷ ἀληθινῷ,
true [one]; and we are in the true [one],
ἐν τῷ υἱῷ αὐτοῦ Ἰησοῦ Χριστῷ. οὗτός
in the Son of him Jesus Christ. This
ἐστιν ὁ ἀληθινὸς θεὸς καὶ ζωὴ αἰώνιος.
is the true God and life eternal.
|21 Τεκνία, φυλάξατε ἑαυτὰ ἀπὸ τῶν
Little children, guard yourselves from *the*
εἰδώλων.
idols.

II. JOHN

ΙΩΑΝΝΟΥ Β
Of John 2

THE elder unto the elect lady and her children, whom I love in the truth; and not I only, but also all they that have known the truth;

2 For the truth's sake, which dwelleth in us, and shall be with us for ever.

3 Grace be with you, mercy, *and* peace, from God the Father, and from the Lord Jesus Christ, the Son of the Father, in truth and love.

1 Ὁ πρεσβύτερος ἐκλεκτῇ κυρίᾳ καὶ
The elder to [the] chosen lady and
τοῖς τέκνοις αὐτῆς, οὓς ἐγὼ ἀγαπῶ ἐν
to the children of her, whom I love in
ἀληθείᾳ, καὶ οὐκ ἐγὼ μόνος ἀλλὰ καὶ
truth, and not I alone but also
πάντες οἱ ἐγνωκότες τὴν ἀλήθειαν, 2 διὰ
all the having known the truth, because of
[ones]
τὴν ἀλήθειαν τὴν μένουσαν ἐν ἡμῖν,
the truth – remaining among us,
καὶ μεθ' ἡμῶν ἔσται εἰς τὸν αἰῶνα.
and with us will be unto the age.
3 ἔσται μεθ' ἡμῶν χάρις ἔλεος εἰρήνη
⁴will be ⁵with ⁶us ¹Grace[,] ²mercy[,] ³peace
παρὰ θεοῦ πατρός, καὶ παρὰ Ἰησοῦ
from God [the] Father, and from Jesus
Χριστοῦ τοῦ υἱοῦ τοῦ πατρός, ἐν ἀληθείᾳ
Christ the Son of the Father, in truth
καὶ ἀγάπῃ.
and love.

4 I rejoiced greatly that I found of thy children walking in truth, as we have received a commandment from the Father.

5 And now I beseech thee, lady, not as though I wrote a new commandment unto thee, but that which we had from the beginning, that we love one another.

6 And this is love, that we walk after his commandments. This is the commandment, That, as ye have heard from the beginning, ye should walk in it.

7 For many deceivers are entered into the world, who confess not that Jesus Christ is come in the flesh. This is a deceiver and an antichrist.

8 Look to yourselves, that we lose not those things which we have wrought, but that we receive a full reward.

9 Whosoever transgresseth, and abideth not in the doctrine of Christ, hath not God. He that abideth in the doctrine of Christ, he hath both the Father and the Son.

10 If there come any unto you, and bring not

4 Ἐχάρην λίαν ὅτι εὕρηκα ἐκ τῶν
I rejoiced greatly because I have of the
found [some]

τέκνων σου περιπατοῦντας ἐν ἀληθείᾳ,
children of thee walking in truth,

καθὼς ἐντολὴν ἐλάβομεν παρὰ τοῦ πατρός.
as command- we received from the Father.
ment

5 καὶ νῦν ἐρωτῶ σε, κυρία, οὐχ ὡς
And now I request thee, lady, not as

ἐντολὴν γράφων σοι καινήν, ἀλλὰ ἣν
³command- ¹writing ⁴to thee ²a new, but which
ment

εἴχομεν ἀπ' ἀρχῆς, ἵνα ἀγαπῶμεν
we had from [the] in order we should
beginning, that love

ἀλλήλους. **6** καὶ αὕτη ἐστὶν ἡ ἀγάπη,
one another. And this is – love,

ἵνα περιπατῶμεν κατὰ τὰς ἐντολὰς
in order we should walk accord- the command-
that ing to ments

αὐτοῦ· αὕτη ἡ ἐντολή ἐστιν, καθὼς
of him; this ²the ³commandment ¹is, as

ἠκούσατε ἀπ' ἀρχῆς, ἵνα ἐν αὐτῇ
ye heard from [the] in order ²in ³it
beginning, that

περιπατῆτε. **7** ὅτι πολλοὶ πλάνοι ἐξῆλθον
¹ye should walk. Because many deceivers went forth

εἰς τὸν κόσμον, οἱ μὴ ὁμολογοῦντες
into the world, the not confessing
[ones]

Ἰησοῦν Χριστὸν ἐρχόμενον ἐν σαρκί·
Jesus Christ coming in [the] flesh;

οὗτός ἐστιν ὁ πλάνος καὶ ὁ ἀντίχριστος.
this is the deceiver and the antichrist.

8 βλέπετε ἑαυτούς, ἵνα μὴ ἀπολέσητε
See yourselves, lest ye lose

ἃ ἠργασάμεθα, ἀλλὰ μισθὸν πλήρη
[the] we wrought, but ²reward ²a full
things which

ἀπολάβητε. **9** πᾶς ὁ προάγων καὶ μὴ
¹ye may receive. Everyone going forward and not

μένων ἐν τῇ διδαχῇ τοῦ Χριστοῦ θεὸν
remaining in the teaching – of Christ ²God

οὐκ ἔχει· ὁ μένων ἐν τῇ διδαχῇ, οὗτος
²not ¹has; the remaining in the teaching, this one
[one]

καὶ τὸν πατέρα καὶ τὸν υἱὸν ἔχει.
²both ³the ⁴Father ⁵and ⁶the ⁷Son ¹has.

10 εἴ τις ἔρχεται πρὸς ὑμᾶς καὶ ταύτην
If anyone comes to you and this

this doctrine, receive him not into *your* house, neither bid him God speed:

11 For he that biddeth him God speed is partaker of his evil deeds.

12 Having many things to write unto you, I would not *write* with paper and ink: but I trust to come unto you, and speak face to face, that our joy may be full.

13 The children of thy elect sister greet thee. Amen.

τὴν διδαχὴν οὐ φέρει, μὴ λαμβάνετε
– teaching brings not, do not ye receive

αὐτὸν εἰς οἰκίαν, καὶ χαίρειν αὐτῷ μὴ
him into [your] and ⁴to rejoice ³him ²not
house,

λέγετε· 11 ὁ λέγων γὰρ αὐτῷ χαίρειν
¹tell ye*; ²the ³telling ¹for him to rejoice
[one]

κοινωνεῖ τοῖς ἔργοις αὐτοῦ τοῖς πονηροῖς.
shares in the ²works ³of him – ¹evil.

12 Πολλὰ ἔχων ὑμῖν γράφειν οὐκ
²Many things ¹having ⁴to you ³to write ⁵not

ἐβουλήθην διὰ χάρτου καὶ μέλανος, ἀλλὰ
⁶I purpose by means paper and ink, but
of

ἐλπίζω γενέσθαι πρὸς ὑμᾶς καὶ στόμα
I am hoping to be with you and ²mouth

πρὸς στόμα λαλῆσαι, ἵνα ἡ χαρὰ ἡμῶν
³to ⁴mouth ¹to speak, in or- the joy of us
der that

πεπληρωμένη ᾖ. 13 Ἀσπάζεταί σε τὰ
having been may be. ⁷greets ⁸thee ¹The
fulfilled

τέκνα τῆς ἀδελφῆς σου τῆς ἐκλεκτῆς.
²children ³of the ⁵sister ⁴of thee – ⁶chosen.

III. JOHN

ΙΩΑΝΝΟΥ Γ
Of John 3

THE elder unto the wellbeloved Gaius, whom I love in the truth.

2 Beloved, I wish above all things that thou mayest prosper and be in health, even as thy soul prospereth.

3 For I rejoiced greatly, when the brethren came and testified of the truth

1 Ὁ πρεσβύτερος Γαΐῳ τῷ ἀγαπητῷ,
The elder to Gaius the beloved,

ὃν ἐγὼ ἀγαπῶ ἐν ἀληθείᾳ.
whom I love in truth.

2 Ἀγαπητέ, περὶ πάντων εὔχομαί σε
Beloved, concerning all things I pray thee
=that

εὐοδοῦσθαι καὶ ὑγιαίνειν, καθὼς εὐοδοῦταί
to prosper and to be in health, as ⁴prospers
thou mayest prosper . . .

σου ἡ ψυχή. 3 ἐχάρην γὰρ λίαν ἐρχομένων
²of ¹the ³soul. For I rejoiced greatly coming
thee =when [some]

ἀδελφῶν καὶ μαρτυρούντων σου τῇ
brothers and bearing witness⁸ of thee in the
brothers came and bore witness

* That is, "do not greet him."

that is in thee, even as thou walkest in the truth.

4 I have no greater joy than to hear that my children walk in truth.

5 Beloved, thou doest faithfully whatsoever thou doest to the brethren, and to strangers;

6 Which have borne witness of thy charity before the-church: whom if thou bring forward on their journey after a godly sort, thou shalt do well:

7 Because that for his name's sake they went forth, taking nothing of the Gentiles.

8 We therefore ought to receive such, that we might be fellowhelpers to the truth.

9 I wrote unto the church: but Diotrephes, who loveth to have the preeminence among them, receiveth us not.

10 Wherefore, if I come, I will remember his deeds which he doeth, prating against us with malicious words: and not content therewith, neither doth he himself receive the brethren, and forbiddeth them that would, and casteth *them* out of the church.

11 Beloved, follow not that which is evil, but that

ἀληθείᾳ,   καθὼς   σὺ   ἐν   ἀληθείᾳ   περιπατεῖς.
truth,   as   thou   in   truth   walkest.

4 μειζοτέραν   τούτων   οὐκ   ἔχω   χαράν,   ἵνα
²greater ⁴[than] ³these   ¹I have no   ⁵joy,   *in or-*
            things   *der* that

ἀκούω   τὰ   ἐμὰ   τέκνα   ἐν   τῇ   ἀληθείᾳ
I hear   -   my   children   ²in   ³the   ⁴truth

περιπατοῦντα.   5 Ἀγαπητέ,   πιστὸν   ποιεῖς
¹walking.   Beloved,   faithfully   thou
                                          doest

ὃ   ἐὰν   ἐργάσῃ   εἰς   τοὺς   ἀδελφοὺς   καὶ
whatever   thou workest   for   the   brothers   and

τοῦτο   ξένους,   6 οἳ   ἐμαρτύρησάν   σου   τῇ
this   strangers,   who   bore witness   of thee   -

ἀγάπῃ   ἐνώπιον   ἐκκλησίας,   οὓς   καλῶς
in love   before   [the] church,   whom   well

ποιήσεις   προπέμψας   ἀξίως   τοῦ   θεοῦ·
thou wilt do   sending forward   worthily   -   of God;

7 ὑπὲρ   γὰρ   τοῦ   ὀνόματος   ἐξῆλθαν   μηδὲν
for on behalf of   the   name   they went forth   ²nothing

λαμβάνοντες   ἀπὸ   τῶν   ἐθνικῶν.   8 ἡμεῖς
¹taking   from   the   Gentiles.   We

οὖν   ὀφείλομεν   ὑπολαμβάνειν   τοὺς   τοιούτους,
there-   ought   to entertain   -   such men,
fore

ἵνα   συνεργοὶ   γινώμεθα   τῇ   ἀληθείᾳ.
in or-   ²co-workers   ¹we may become   in the   truth.
der that

9 Ἔγραψά   τι   τῇ   ἐκκλησίᾳ·   ἀλλ'   ὁ
I wrote   some-   to the   church;   but   the
           thing   [one]

φιλοπρωτεύων   αὐτῶν   Διοτρέφης   οὐκ
loving to be first   of them   Diotrephes   not

ἐπιδέχεται   ἡμᾶς.   10 διὰ   τοῦτο,   ἐὰν
receives   us.   Therefore,   if

ἔλθω,   ὑπομνήσω   αὐτοῦ   τὰ   ἔργα   ἃ   ποιεῖ
I come,   I will remember   ²of him   ¹the   ³works   which he does

λόγοις   πονηροῖς   φλυαρῶν   ἡμᾶς,   καὶ   μὴ
⁴words   ³with evil   ¹prating against   ²us,   and   not

ἀρκούμενος   ἐπὶ   τούτοις   οὔτε   αὐτὸς
being satisfied   on(with)   these   ²neither   ¹he

ἐπιδέχεται   τοὺς   ἀδελφοὺς   καὶ   τοὺς
²receives   the   brothers   and   the

βουλομένους   κωλύει   καὶ   ἐκ   τῆς   ἐκκλησίας
[ones] purposing   he prevents   and   ²out of   ³the   ⁴church

ἐκβάλλει.
¹puts *out.*

11 Ἀγαπητέ,   μὴ   μιμοῦ   τὸ   κακὸν   ἀλλὰ
Beloved,   imitate not   the   bad   but

which is good. He that doeth good is of God: but he that doeth evil hath not seen God.

12 Demetrius hath good report of all *men*, and of the truth itself: yea, and we *also* bear record; and ye know that our record is true.

13 I had many things to write, but I will not with ink and pen write unto thee:

14 But I trust I shall shortly see thee, and we shall speak face to face. Peace *be* to thee. *Our* friends salute thee. Greet the friends by name.

τὸ ἀγαθόν. ὁ ἀγαθοποιῶν ἐκ τοῦ θεοῦ
the good. The doing good ²of – ²God
[one]

ἐστιν· ὁ κακοποιῶν οὐχ ἑώρακεν τὸν
¹is; the [one] doing ill has not seen –

θεόν. 12 Δημητρίῳ μεμαρτύρηται ὑπὸ
God. To Demetrius witness has been borne by

πάντων καὶ ὑπὸ αὐτῆς τῆς ἀληθείας·
all and by ³[it]self ¹the ²truth;

καὶ ἡμεῖς δὲ μαρτυροῦμεν, καὶ οἶδας
³also ²we ¹and bear witness, and thou
knowest

ὅτι ἡ μαρτυρία ἡμῶν ἀληθής ἐστιν.
that the witness of us ²true ¹is.

13 Πολλὰ εἶχον γράψαι σοι, ἀλλ' οὐ
Many things ¹I had to write to thee, but not

θέλω διὰ μέλανος καὶ καλάμου σοι
I wish ³by means of ⁴ink ⁵and ⁶pen ²to thee

γράφειν· 14 ἐλπίζω δὲ εὐθέως σε ἰδεῖν,
¹to write; but I am hoping ³immediately ²thee ¹to see,

καὶ στόμα πρὸς στόμα λαλήσομεν.
and ²mouth ³to ⁴mouth ¹we will speak.

15 Εἰρήνη σοι. ἀσπάζονταί σε οἱ φίλοι.
Peace to thee. ³greet ⁴thee ¹The ²friends.

ἀσπάζου τοὺς φίλους κατ' ὄνομα.
Greet thou the friends by name.

JUDE

ΙΟΥΔΑ
Of Jude

JUDE, the servant of Jesus Christ, and brother of James, to them that are sanctified by God the Father, and preserved in Jesus Christ, *and* called:

2 Mercy unto you, and peace, and love, be multiplied.

3 Beloved, when I gave

1 Ἰούδας Ἰησοῦ Χριστοῦ δοῦλος, ἀδελφὸς
Jude of Jesus Christ a slave, ²brother

δὲ Ἰακώβου, τοῖς ἐν θεῷ πατρὶ
¹and of James, ¹to the ⁴by ⁵God ⁶[the]
[ones] Father

ἠγαπημένοις καὶ Ἰησοῦ Χριστῷ
²having been loved ⁷and ⁸for Jesus ¹⁰Christ

τετηρημένοις κλητοῖς. 2 ἔλεος ὑμῖν καὶ
⁸having been kept ²called. Mercy to you and

εἰρήνη καὶ ἀγάπη πληθυνθείη.
peace and love may it be multiplied.

3 Ἀγαπητοί, πᾶσαν σπουδὴν ποιούμενος
Beloved, ²all ³haste ¹making

all diligence to write unto you of the common salvation, it was needful for me to write unto you, and exhort *you* that ye should earnestly contend for the faith which was once delivered unto the saints.

4 For there are certain men crept in unawares, who were before of old ordained to this condemnation, ungodly men, turning the grace of our God into lasciviousness, and denying the only Lord God, and our Lord Jesus Christ.

5 I will therefore put you in remembrance, though ye once knew this, how that the Lord, having saved the people out of the land of Egypt, afterward destroyed them that believed not.

6 And the angels which kept not their first estate, but left their own habitation, he hath reserved in everlasting chains under darkness unto the judgment of the great day.

7 Even as Sodom and Gomorrha, and the cities about them in like manner, giving themselves over to fornication, and going after strange flesh, are set forth for an example, suffering the vengeance of eternal fire.

8 Likewise also these

γράφειν ὑμῖν περὶ τῆς κοινῆς ἡμῶν
to write to you concerning the common [2]of us

σωτηρίας, ἀνάγκην ἔσχον γράψαι ὑμῖν
[1]salvation, necessity I had to write to you

παρακαλῶν ἐπαγωνίζεσθαι τῇ ἅπαξ
exhorting to contend for [1]the [2]once

παραδοθείσῃ τοῖς ἁγίοις πίστει. 4 παρεισε-
[4]delivered [5]to the [6]saints [3]faith. [2]crept

δύησαν γάρ τινες ἄνθρωποι, οἱ πάλαι
in For [1]certain [2]men, the [ones] of old

προγεγραμμένοι εἰς τοῦτο τὸ κρίμα,
having been previously written for this – judgment,

ἀσεβεῖς, τὴν τοῦ θεοῦ ἡμῶν χάριτα
impious men, [2]the [4]of the [5]God [6]of us [3]grace

μετατιθέντες εἰς ἀσέλγειαν καὶ τὸν μόνον
[1]making [7]a pretext for wantonness and [8]the [9]only

δεσπότην καὶ κύριον ἡμῶν Ἰησοῦν Χριστὸν
[4]Master [5]and [6]Lord [7]of us [8]Jesus [9]Christ

ἀρνούμενοι. 5 Ὑπομνῆσαι δὲ ὑμᾶς βούλομαι,
[1]denying. But [2]to remind [3]you [1]I purpose,

εἰδότας ἅπαξ πάντα, ὅτι κύριος λαὸν
[2]knowing [1]once all things, that [the] Lord [2][the] people

ἐκ γῆς Αἰγύπτου σώσας τὸ δεύτερον
[3]out of [4][the] land [5]of Egypt [1]having saved in the second place

τοὺς μὴ πιστεύσαντας ἀπώλεσεν, 6 ἀγγέλους
[3]the [ones] [2]not [4]believing [1]destroyed, [2]angels

τε τοὺς μὴ τηρήσαντας τὴν ἑαυτῶν
[1]and – not having kept the [3]of themselves

ἀρχὴν ἀλλὰ ἀπολιπόντας τὸ ἴδιον
[1]rule but having deserted the(ir) own

οἰκητήριον εἰς κρίσιν μεγάλης ἡμέρας
habitation [6]for [7][the] judgment [8]of [the] great [9]day

δεσμοῖς ἀϊδίοις ὑπὸ ζόφον τετήρηκεν·
[3]bonds [2]in everlasting [4]under [5]gloom [1]he has kept;

7 ὡς Σόδομα καὶ Γόμορρα καὶ αἱ περὶ
as Sodom and Gomorra and [1]the [2]round

αὐτὰς πόλεις, τὸν ὅμοιον τρόπον τούτοις
[4]them [3]cities, in the like manner to these

ἐκπορνεύσασαι καὶ ἀπελθοῦσαι ὀπίσω σαρκὸς
committing fornication and going away after [2]flesh,

ἑτέρας, πρόκεινται δεῖγμα πυρὸς αἰωνίου
[1]different, are set forth an example [4]fire [3]of eternal

δίκην ὑπέχουσαι. 8 Ὁμοίως μέντοι καὶ
[2]vengeance [1]undergoing. Likewise indeed also

filthy dreamers defile the flesh, despise dominion, and speak evil of dignities.

9 Yet Michael the archangel, when contending with the devil he disputed about the body of Moses, durst not bring against him a railing accusation, but said, The Lord rebuke thee.

10 But these speak evil of those things which they know not: but what they know naturally, as brute beasts, in those things they corrupt themselves.

11 Woe unto them! for they have gone in the way of Cain, and ran greedily after the error of Balaam for reward, and perished in the gainsaying of Core.

12 These are spots in your feasts of charity, when they feast with you, feeding themselves without fear: clouds *they are* without water, carried about of winds; trees whose fruit withereth, without fruit, twice dead, plucked up by the roots;

13 Raging waves of the sea, foaming out their own shame; wandering stars, to whom is reserved the blackness of darkness for ever.

οὗτοι ἐνυπνιαζόμενοι σάρκα μὲν μιαίνουσιν,
these dreaming [ones] ³flesh ¹on one ²defile,
hand

κυριότητα δὲ ἀθετοῦσιν, δόξας δὲ
³lordship ¹on the other ²despise, and ²glories

βλασφημοῦσιν. 9 Ὁ δὲ Μιχαὴλ ὁ ἀρχάγ-
¹rail at. – But Michael the arch-

γελος, ὅτε τῷ διαβόλῳ διακρινόμενος
angel, when ²with the ³devil ¹contending

διελέγετο περὶ τοῦ Μωϋσέως σώματος,
he argued about ¹the ³of Moses ²body,

οὐκ ἐτόλμησεν κρίσιν ἐπενεγκεῖν βλασφημίας,
durst not ²a judgment ¹to bring on of railing,

ἀλλὰ εἶπεν· ἐπιτιμήσαι σοι κύριος. 10 οὗτοι
but said: ²rebuke ³thee ¹[The] Lord. these men

δὲ ὅσα μὲν οὐκ οἴδασιν βλασφημοῦσιν,
But what on one they know not they rail at,
things hand

ὅσα δὲ φυσικῶς ὡς τὰ ἄλογα ζῷα
what on the ²naturally ³as ⁴the ⁶without ⁵animals
things other reason

ἐπίστανται, ἐν τούτοις φθείρονται. 11 οὐαὶ
¹they understand, by these they are corrupted. Woe

αὐτοῖς, ὅτι τῇ ὁδῷ τοῦ Κάϊν ἐπορεύθησαν,
to them, because in the way – of Cain they went,

καὶ τῇ πλάνῃ τοῦ Βαλαὰμ μισθοῦ
and ²to the ³error – ⁴of Balaam ⁶of(for)
reward

ἐξεχύθησαν, καὶ τῇ ἀντιλογίᾳ τοῦ Κόρε
¹gave themselves and ²in the ³dispute – ⁴of
up, Korah

ἀπώλοντο. 12 Οὗτοί εἰσιν οἱ ἐν ταῖς
¹perished. These men are ¹the ²in ⁴the

ἀγάπαις ὑμῶν σπιλάδες συνευωχούμενοι
⁵love feasts ⁶of you ³rocks feasting together

ἀφόβως, ἑαυτοὺς ποιμαίνοντες, νεφέλαι
without fear, ²themselves ¹feeding, ³clouds

ἄνυδροι ὑπὸ ἀνέμων παραφερόμεναι, δένδρα
¹waterless ⁴by ⁵winds ³being carried away, ²trees

φθινοπωρινὰ ἄκαρπα δὶς ἀποθανόντα
¹autumn without fruit twice dying

ἐκριζωθέντα, 13 κύματα ἄγρια θαλάσσης
having been uprooted, ²waves ¹fierce ³of [the] sea

ἐπαφρίζοντα τὰς ἑαυτῶν αἰσχύνας, ἀστέρες
⁴foaming up ⁵the ⁷of themselves ⁶shames, ²stars

πλανῆται, οἷς ὁ ζόφος τοῦ σκότους
¹wandering, for whom the gloom – of darkness

εἰς αἰῶνα τετήρηται. 14 Ἐπροφήτευσεν
unto [the] age has been kept. ⁷prophesied

14 And Enoch also, the seventh from Adam, prophesied of these, saying, Behold, the Lord cometh with ten thousands of his saints,

15 To execute judgment upon all, and to convince all that are ungodly among them of all their ungodly deeds which they have ungodly committed, and of all their hard *speeches* which ungodly sinners have spoken against him.

16 These are murmurers, complainers, walking after their own lusts; and their mouth speaketh great swelling *words*, having men's persons in admiration because of advantage.

17 But, beloved, remember ye the words which were spoken before of the apostles of our Lord Jesus Christ;

18 How that they told you there should be mockers in the last time, who should walk after their own ungodly lusts.

19 These be they who separate themselves, sensual, having not the Spirit.

20 But ye, beloved, building up yourselves on your most holy faith, praying in the Holy Ghost,

21 Keep yourselves in the love of God, looking

δὲ καὶ τούτοις ἕβδομος ἀπὸ Ἀδὰμ
[1]And [2]also [3]to these men [4][the] seventh [5]from [6]Adam

Ἐνὼχ λέγων· ἰδοὺ ἦλθεν κύριος ἐν
[2]Enoch saying : Behold came [the] Lord with

ἁγίαις μυριάσιν αὐτοῦ, 15 ποιῆσαι κρίσιν
saints ten thousands of him, to do judgment

κατὰ πάντων καὶ ἐλέγξαι πάντας τοὺς
against all men and to rebuke all the

ἀσεβεῖς περὶ πάντων τῶν ἔργων ἀσεβείας
impious concerning all the works of impiety

αὐτῶν ὧν ἠσέβησαν καὶ περὶ πάντων
of them which they impiously did and concerning all

τῶν σκληρῶν ὧν ἐλάλησαν κατ' αὐτοῦ
the hard things which [3]spoke [4]against [5]him

ἁμαρτωλοὶ ἀσεβεῖς. 16 Οὗτοί εἰσιν γογ-
[2]sinners [1]impious. These men are [1]mur-

γυσταὶ μεμψίμοιροι, κατὰ τὰς ἐπιθυμίας
murers [1]querulous, [2]according to [3]the [4]lusts

αὐτῶν πορευόμενοι, καὶ τὸ στόμα αὐτῶν
[5]of them [1]going, and the mouth of them

λαλεῖ ὑπέρογκα, θαυμάζοντες πρόσωπα
speaks arrogant things, admiring faces

ὠφελείας χάριν.
[2]advantage [1]for the sake of.

17 Ὑμεῖς δέ, ἀγαπητοί, μνήσθητε τῶν
But ye, beloved, be mindful of the

ῥημάτων τῶν προειρημένων ὑπὸ τῶν
words – previously spoken by the

ἀποστόλων τοῦ κυρίου ἡμῶν Ἰησοῦ
apostles of the Lord of us Jesus

Χριστοῦ, 18 ὅτι ἔλεγον ὑμῖν· ἐπ' ἐσχάτου
Christ, because they told you: At [the] last

τοῦ χρόνου ἔσονται ἐμπαῖκται κατὰ τὰς
of the time will be mockers [2]according to [3]the

ἑαυτῶν ἐπιθυμίας πορευόμενοι τῶν ἀσεβειῶν.
[5]of them-selves [4]lusts [1]going – [6]of impious things.

19 Οὗτοί εἰσιν οἱ ἀποδιορίζοντες, ψυχικοί,
These men are the [ones] making separations, natural,

πνεῦμα μὴ ἔχοντες. 20 ὑμεῖς δέ, ἀγαπητοί,
[3]spirit [1]not [2]having. But ye, beloved,

ἐποικοδομοῦντες ἑαυτοὺς τῇ ἁγιωτάτῃ ὑμῶν
building up yourselves in the most holy [2]of you

πίστει, ἐν πνεύματι ἁγίῳ προσευχόμενοι,
[1]faith, [2]in [4]Spirit [3][the] Holy [1]praying,

21 ἑαυτοὺς ἐν ἀγάπῃ θεοῦ τηρήσατε,
[2]yourselves [3]in [4][the] love [5]of God [1]keep,

for the mercy of our Lord Jesus Christ unto eternal life.

22 And of some have compassion, making a difference:

23 And others save with fear, pulling *them* out of the fire; hating even the garment spotted by the flesh.

24 Now unto him that is able to keep you from falling, and to present *you* faultless before the presence of his glory with exceeding joy,

25 To the only wise God our Saviour, *be* glory and majesty, dominion and power, both now and ever. Amen.

προσδεχόμενοι τὸ ἔλεος τοῦ κυρίου ἡμῶν
awaiting the mercy of the Lord of us

'Ιησοῦ Χριστοῦ εἰς ζωὴν αἰώνιον. 22 καὶ
Jesus Christ to life eternal. And

οὓς μὲν ἐλεᾶτε διακρινομένους 23 σῴζετε
some ²pity ye ¹[who are] wavering ²save

ἐκ πυρὸς ἁρπάζοντες, οὓς δὲ ἐλεᾶτε
³out of ⁴fire ¹seizing, others pity

ἐν φόβῳ, μισοῦντες καὶ τὸν ἀπὸ τῆς
with fear, hating even ¹the ⁴from ⁵the

σαρκὸς ἐσπιλωμένον χιτῶνα.
⁶flesh ³having been spotted ²tunic.

24 Τῷ δὲ δυναμένῳ φυλάξαι ὑμᾶς
Now to the [one] *being* able to guard you

ἀπταίστους καὶ στῆσαι κατενώπιον τῆς
without and to set [you] before the
stumbling

δόξης αὐτοῦ ἀμώμους ἐν ἀγαλλιάσει,
glory of him unblemished with exultation,

25 μόνῳ θεῷ σωτῆρι ἡμῶν διὰ 'Ιησοῦ
to [the] only God Saviour of us through Jesus

Χριστοῦ τοῦ κυρίου ἡμῶν δόξα μεγαλωσύνη
Christ the Lord of us [be] glory[,] greatness[,]

κράτος καὶ ἐξουσία πρὸ παντὸς τοῦ
might[,] and authority before all the

αἰῶνος καὶ νῦν καὶ εἰς πάντας τοὺς
age and now and unto all the

αἰῶνας· ἀμήν.
ages: Amen.

ΑΠΟΚΑΛΥΨΙΣ ΙΩΑΝΝΟΥ
A Revelation of John

CHAPTER 1

THE Revelation of Jesus Christ, which God gave unto him, to shew unto his servants things which must shortly come to pass; and he sent and signified *it* by his angel unto his servant John:

2 Who bare record of the word of God, and of the testimony of Jesus Christ, and of all things that he saw.

3 Blessed *is* he that readeth, and they that hear the words of this prophecy, and keep those things which are written therein: for the time *is* at hand.

4 JOHN to the seven churches which are in Asia: Grace *be* unto you, and peace, from him which is, and which was, and which is to come; and from the seven Spirits which are before his throne;

5 And from Jesus Christ, *who is* the faithful witness, *and* the first begotten of the dead, and the prince of the kings of the earth. Unto him that loved us, and washed us from our sins in his own blood,

1 Ἀποκάλυψις Ἰησοῦ Χριστοῦ, ἦν
  A revelation   of Jesus   Christ,   which

ἔδωκεν αὐτῷ ὁ θεός, δεῖξαι τοῖς δούλοις
²gave   ³to him   –   ¹God,   to show   to the   slaves

αὐτοῦ ἃ δεῖ γενέσθαι ἐν τάχει, καὶ
of him   things   it be-   to occur   with   speed,   and
       which   hoves

ἐσήμανεν ἀποστείλας διὰ τοῦ ἀγγέλου
he signified   sending   through   the   angel

αὐτοῦ τῷ δούλῳ αὐτοῦ Ἰωάννῃ, 2 ὃς
of him   to the   slave   of him   John,   who

ἐμαρτύρησεν τὸν λόγον τοῦ θεοῦ καὶ
bore witness [of]   the   word   –   of God   and

τὴν μαρτυρίαν Ἰησοῦ Χριστοῦ, ὅσα εἶδεν.
the   witness   of Jesus   Christ,   as many as he saw.
                               things as

3 Μακάριος ὁ ἀναγινώσκων καὶ οἱ
  Blessed [is]   the [one]   reading   and   the

ἀκούοντες τοὺς λόγους τῆς προφητείας
[ones] hearing   the   words   of the   prophecy

καὶ τηροῦντες τὰ ἐν αὐτῇ γεγραμμένα·
and   keeping   the things ²in   ³it ¹having been written;

ὁ γὰρ καιρὸς ἐγγύς.
²the ¹for   time [is]   near.

4 Ἰωάννης ταῖς ἑπτὰ ἐκκλησίαις ταῖς
  John   to the   seven   churches   –

ἐν τῇ Ἀσίᾳ· χάρις ὑμῖν καὶ εἰρήνη
in   –   Asia: Grace   to you   and   peace

ἀπὸ ὁ ὢν καὶ ὁ ἦν καὶ ὁ ἐρχόμενος,
from   the being   and   the was   and   the [one] coming,
     [one]   [one who]
     =the one who is

καὶ ἀπὸ τῶν ἑπτὰ πνευμάτων ἃ ἐνώπιον
and   from   the   seven   spirits   which   before
                                  [are]

τοῦ θρόνου αὐτοῦ, 5 καὶ ἀπὸ Ἰησοῦ
the   throne   of him,   and   from   Jesus

Χριστοῦ, ὁ μάρτυς ὁ πιστός, ὁ πρωτότοκος
Christ,   the ²witness   – ¹faithful,   the   firstborn

τῶν νεκρῶν καὶ ὁ ἄρχων τῶν βασιλέων
of the   dead   and   the   ruler   of the   kings

τῆς γῆς. Τῷ ἀγαπῶντι ἡμᾶς καὶ λύσαντι
of the earth.   To   loving   us   and   having
          the [one]   loosed

ἡμᾶς ἐκ τῶν ἁμαρτιῶν ἡμῶν ἐν τῷ
us   out of   the   sins   of us   by   the

6 And hath made us kings and priests unto God and his Father; to him be glory and dominion for ever and ever. Amen.

7 Behold, he cometh with clouds; and every eye shall see him, and they also which pierced him: and all kindreds of the earth shall wail because of him. Even so, Amen.

8 I am Alpha and Omega, the beginning and the ending, saith the Lord, which is, and which was, and which is to come, the Almighty.

9 I John, who also am your brother, and companion in tribulation, and in the kingdom and patience of Jesus Christ, was in the isle that is called Patmos, for the word of God, and for the testimony of Jesus Christ.

10 I was in the Spirit on the Lord's day, and heard behind me a great voice, as of a trumpet,

11 Saying, I am Alpha and Omega, the first and the last: and, What thou seest, write in a book, and sent it unto the seven churches which are in

αἵματι αὐτοῦ, **6** καὶ ἐποίησεν ἡμᾶς
blood of him, and made us

βασιλείαν, ἱερεῖς τῷ θεῷ καὶ πατρὶ
a kingdom, priests to the God and Father

αὐτοῦ, αὐτῷ ἡ δόξα καὶ τὸ κράτος
of him, to him[e] [is] the glory and the might
= his is

εἰς τοὺς αἰῶνας τῶν αἰώνων· ἀμήν.
unto the ages of the ages: Amen.

7 Ἰδοὺ ἔρχεται μετὰ τῶν νεφελῶν,
Behold he comes with the clouds,

καὶ ὄψεται αὐτὸν πᾶς ὀφθαλμὸς καὶ
and [4]will see [3]him [1]every [2]eye and

οἵτινες αὐτὸν ἐξεκέντησαν, καὶ κόψονται
[those] who [2]him [1]pierced, and [5]will wail

ἐπ' αὐτὸν πᾶσαι αἱ φυλαὶ τῆς γῆς.
[7]over [6]him [1]all [3]the [2]tribes [4]of the [5]land.

ναί, ἀμήν.
Yes, amen.

8 Ἐγώ εἰμι τὸ ἄλφα καὶ τὸ ὦ, λέγει
I am the alpha and the omega, says

κύριος ὁ θεός, ὁ ὢν καὶ ὁ ἦν
[the] – God, the [one] being and the was
Lord = the one who is [one who]

καὶ ὁ ἐρχόμενος, ὁ παντοκράτωρ.
and the [one] coming, the Almighty.

9 Ἐγώ Ἰωάννης, ὁ ἀδελφὸς ὑμῶν καὶ
I John, the brother of you and

συγκοινωνὸς ἐν τῇ θλίψει καὶ βασιλείᾳ
co-sharer in the affliction and kingdom

καὶ ὑπομονῇ ἐν Ἰησοῦ, ἐγενόμην ἐν
and endurance in Jesus, came to be in

τῇ νήσῳ τῇ καλουμένῃ Πάτμῳ διὰ
the island – being called Patmos on account of

τὸν λόγον τοῦ θεοῦ καὶ τὴν μαρτυρίαν
the word – of God and the witness

Ἰησοῦ. **10** ἐγενόμην ἐν πνεύματι ἐν
of Jesus. I came to be in [the] spirit on

τῇ κυριακῇ ἡμέρᾳ, καὶ ἤκουσα ὀπίσω
the imperial* day, and heard behind

μου φωνὴν μεγάλην ὡς σάλπιγγος
me [2]voice [1]a great(loud) as of a trumpet

11 λεγούσης· ὃ βλέπεις γράψον εἰς βιβλίον
saying: What thou seest write in a scroll

καὶ πέμψον ταῖς ἑπτὰ ἐκκλησίαις, εἰς
and send to the seven churches, to

* See I. Cor. 11. 20.

Asia; unto Ephesus, and unto Smyrna, and unto Pergamos, and unto Thyatira, and unto Sardis, and unto Philadelphia, and unto Laodicea.

12 And I turned to see the voice that spake with me. And being turned, I saw seven golden candlesticks;

13 And in the midst of the seven candlesticks *one* like unto the Son of man, clothed with a garment down to the foot, and girt about the paps with a golden girdle.

14 His head and *his* hairs *were* white like wool, as white as snow; and his eyes *were* as a flame of fire;

15 And his feet like unto fine brass, as if they burned in a furnace; and his voice as the sound of many waters.

16 And he had in his right hand seven stars: and out of his mouth went a sharp twoedged sword: and his countenance *was* as the sun shineth in his strength.

17 And when I saw him, I fell at his feet as dead. And he laid his right hand upon me, saying unto me, Fear not; I am the first and the last:

Ἔφεσον καὶ εἰς Σμύρναν καὶ εἰς Πέργαμον
Ephesus and to Smyrna and to Pergamum
καὶ εἰς Θυάτιρα καὶ εἰς Σάρδεις καὶ
and to Thyatira and to Sardis and
εἰς Φιλαδέλφειαν καὶ εἰς Λαοδίκειαν.
to Philadelphia and to Laodicea.

12 Καὶ ἐπέστρεψα βλέπειν τὴν φωνὴν
And I turned to see the voice
ἥτις ἐλάλει μετ' ἐμοῦ· καὶ ἐπιστρέψας
which spoke with me; and having turned
εἶδον ἑπτὰ λυχνίας χρυσᾶς, 13 καὶ ἐν
I saw seven ¹lampstands ¹golden, and in
μέσῳ τῶν λυχνιῶν ὅμοιον υἱὸν ἀνθρώπου,
[the] of the lampstands [one] like a son of man,*
midst
ἐνδεδυμένον ποδήρη καὶ περιεζωσμένον
having been clothed to the feet and *having been* girdled round
πρὸς τοῖς μαστοῖς ζώνην χρυσᾶν· 14 ἡ
at the breasts ¹girdle ¹[with] a golden; ¹the
δὲ κεφαλὴ αὐτοῦ καὶ αἱ τρίχες λευκαὶ
¹and head of him and the hairs white
ὡς ἔριον λευκὸν ὡς χιών, καὶ οἱ ὀφθαλμοὶ
as wool white as snow, and the eyes
αὐτοῦ ὡς φλὸξ πυρός, 15 καὶ οἱ πόδες
of him as a flame of fire, and the feet
αὐτοῦ ὅμοιοι χαλκολιβάνῳ ὡς ἐν καμίνῳ
of him like *to* burnished brass as ²in ¹a furnace
πεπυρωμένης, καὶ ἡ φωνὴ αὐτοῦ ὡς
¹having been fired, and the voice of him as
φωνὴ ὑδάτων πολλῶν, 16 καὶ ἔχων ἐν
a sound waters of many, and having in
τῇ δεξιᾷ χειρὶ αὐτοῦ ἀστέρας ἑπτά,
the right hand of him ²stars ¹seven,
καὶ ἐκ τοῦ στόματος αὐτοῦ ῥομφαία
and out of the mouth of him ⁴sword
δίστομος ὀξεῖα ἐκπορευομένη, καὶ ἡ ὄψις
³two- ²a sharp ¹proceeding, and the face
mouthed(edged)
αὐτοῦ ὡς ὁ ἥλιος φαίνει ἐν τῇ δυνάμει
of him as the sun shines in the power
αὐτοῦ. 17 Καὶ ὅτε εἶδον αὐτόν, ἔπεσα
of it. And when I saw him, I fell
πρὸς τοὺς πόδας αὐτοῦ ὡς νεκρός· καὶ
at the feet of him as dead; and
ἔθηκεν τὴν δεξιὰν αὐτοῦ ἐπ' ἐμὲ λέγων·
he placed the right [hand] of him on me saying:
μὴ φοβοῦ· ἐγώ εἰμι ὁ πρῶτος καὶ
Fear not: I am the first and

* Anarthrous; see also ch. 14. 14 and John 5. 27, and *cf*. Heb. 2. 6.

18 *I am* he that liveth, and was dead; and, behold, I am alive for evermore, Amen; and have the keys of hell and of death.

19 Write the things which thou hast seen, and the things which are, and the things which shall be hereafter;

20 The mystery of the seven stars which thou sawest in my right hand, and the seven golden candlesticks. The seven stars are the angels of the seven churches: and the seven candlesticks which thou sawest are the seven churches.

ὁ ἔσχατος 18 καὶ ὁ ζῶν, καὶ ἐγενόμην
the   last   and   the living [one], and   I became

νεκρὸς καὶ ἰδοὺ ζῶν εἰμι εἰς τοὺς
dead   and   behold ²living ¹I am   unto   the

αἰῶνας τῶν αἰώνων, καὶ ἔχω τὰς κλεῖς
ages   of the   ages,   and   I have the   keys

τοῦ θανάτου καὶ τοῦ ᾅδου.   19 γράψον
-   of death   and   -   of hades.   Write thou

οὖν ἃ εἶδες καὶ ἃ εἰσὶν καὶ ἃ
there- [the] thou and [the] are   and [the]
fore   things sawest   things   things
       which   which   which

μέλλει γενέσθαι μετὰ ταῦτα.   20 τὸ
(is)are *about* to occur   after these things.   The

μυστήριον τῶν ἑπτὰ ἀστέρων οὓς εἶδες
mystery   of the   seven   stars   which thou
                                            sawest

ἐπὶ τῆς δεξιᾶς μου, καὶ τὰς ἑπτὰ
on   the right [hand] of me, and   the   seven

λυχνίας τὰς χρυσᾶς· οἱ ἑπτὰ ἀστέρες
²lampstands ¹golden: the   seven   stars

ἄγγελοι* τῶν ἑπτὰ ἐκκλησιῶν εἰσιν, καὶ
messengers* of the seven   churches   are,   and

αἱ λυχνίαι αἱ ἑπτὰ ἑπτὰ ἐκκλησίαι εἰσίν.
the ²lampstands - ¹seven ⁴seven ⁵churches ³are.

CHAPTER 2

UNTO the angel of the church of Ephesus write; These things saith he that holdeth the seven stars in his right hand, who walketh in the midst of the seven golden candlesticks;

2 I know thy works, and thy labour, and thy patience, and how thou canst not bear them which are evil: and thou hast tried them which say they are apostles, and are not, and hast found them liars:

2 Τῷ ἀγγέλῳ τῆς ἐν Ἐφέσῳ ἐκκλησίας
To the   messenger ¹of the ³in ⁴Ephesus ²church

γράψον·
write thou:

Τάδε λέγει ὁ κρατῶν τοὺς ἑπτὰ
These things says the [one] holding   the   seven

ἀστέρας ἐν τῇ δεξιᾷ αὐτοῦ, ὁ περιπατῶν
stars   in   the right [hand] of him, the [one] walking

ἐν μέσῳ τῶν ἑπτὰ λυχνιῶν τῶν
in [the] midst of the seven   ²lampstands   -

χρυσῶν· 2 οἶδα τὰ ἔργα σου καὶ τὸν
¹golden: I know the works of thee and   the

κόπον καὶ τὴν ὑπομονήν σου, καὶ ὅτι
labour and   the endurance   of thee, and that

οὐ δύνῃ βαστάσαι κακούς, καὶ ἐπείρασας
thou canst not *to* bear bad men,   and   didst try

τοὺς λέγοντας ἑαυτοὺς ἀποστόλους καὶ
the [ones] say(call)ing themselves   apostles   and

οὐκ εἰσίν, καὶ εὗρες αὐτοὺς ψευδεῖς·
are not,   and   didst find them   liars;

* This, of course, is the prime meaning of the word: whether these beings were " messengers " from the churches, or supernatural beings, " angels " as usually understood, is a matter of exegesis.

3 And hast borne, and hast patience, and for my name's sake hast laboured, and hast not fainted.

4 Nevertheless I have *somewhat* against thee, because thou hast left thy first love.

5 Remember therefore from whence thou art fallen, and repent, and do the first works; or else I will come unto thee quickly, and will remove thy candlestick out of his place, except thou repent.

6 But this thou hast, that thou hatest the deeds of the Nicolaitanes, which I also hate.

7 He that hath an ear, let him hear what the Spirit saith unto the churches; To him that overcometh will I give to eat of the tree of life, which is in the midst of the paradise of God.

8 And unto the angel of the church in Smyrna write; These things saith the first and the last, which was dead, and is alive;

9 I know thy works, and tribulation, and poverty, (but thou art rich) and *I know* the blasphemy of them which say they are Jews, and are not, but *are* the synagogue of Satan.

3 καὶ ὑπομονὴν ἔχεις, καὶ ἐβάστασας
and ²endurance ¹thou hast, and didst bear
διὰ τὸ ὄνομά μου, καὶ οὐ κεκοπίακας.
be- the name of me, and hast not grown weary.
cause of
4 ἀλλὰ ἔχω κατὰ σοῦ ὅτι τὴν ἀγάπην
But I have against thee that ²the ⁴love
σου τὴν πρώτην ἀφῆκας. 5 μνημόνευε
⁵of thee – ³first ¹thou didst leave. Remember
οὖν πόθεν πέπτωκας, καὶ μετανόησον
therefore whence thou hast fallen, and repent
καὶ τὰ πρῶτα ἔργα ποίησον· εἰ δὲ
and ²the ³first ⁴works ¹do; and if
μή, ἔρχομαί σοι καὶ κινήσω τὴν λυχνίαν
not, I am coming to thee and will move the lampstand
σου ἐκ τοῦ τόπου αὐτῆς, ἐὰν μὴ
of thee out of the place of it, unless
μετανοήσῃς. 6 ἀλλὰ τοῦτο ἔχεις, ὅτι
thou repentest. But this thou hast, that
μισεῖς τὰ ἔργα τῶν Νικολαϊτῶν, ἃ
thou hatest the works of the Nicolaitans, which
κἀγὼ μισῶ. 7 Ὁ ἔχων οὖς ἀκουσάτω
I also hate. The [one] having an ear let him hear
τί τὸ πνεῦμα λέγει ταῖς ἐκκλησίαις.
what the Spirit says to the churches.
Τῷ νικῶντι δώσω αὐτῷ φαγεῖν ἐκ
To overcoming I will give *to him* to eat of
the [one]
τοῦ ξύλου τῆς ζωῆς, ὃ ἐστιν ἐν τῷ
the tree – of life, which is in the
παραδείσῳ τοῦ θεοῦ.
paradise – of God.
8 Καὶ τῷ ἀγγέλῳ τῆς ἐν Σμύρνῃ
And to the messenger ¹of the ²in ⁴Smyrna
ἐκκλησίας γράψον·
²church write thou:
Τάδε λέγει ὁ πρῶτος καὶ ὁ ἔσχατος,
These things says the first and the last,
ὃς ἐγένετο νεκρὸς καὶ ἔζησεν· 9 οἶδά
who became dead and lived [again]: I know
σου τὴν θλῖψιν καὶ τὴν πτωχείαν, ἀλλὰ
⁶of thee ¹the ²affliction ³and ⁴the ⁵poverty, but
πλούσιος εἶ, καὶ τὴν βλασφημίαν ἐκ
rich thou art, and the railing of
τῶν λεγόντων Ἰουδαίους εἶναι ἑαυτούς,
the [ones] say(call)ing ³Jews ²to be ¹themselves,
καὶ οὐκ εἰσὶν ἀλλὰ συναγωγὴ τοῦ σατανᾶ.
and they are not but a synagogue – of Satan.

10 Fear none of those things which thou shalt suffer: behold, the devil shall cast *some* of you into prison, that ye may be tried; and ye shall have tribulation ten days: be thou faithful unto death, and I will give thee a crown of life.

11 He that hath an ear, let him hear what the Spirit saith unto the churches; He that overcometh shall not be hurt of the second death.

12 And to the angel of the church in Pergamos write; These things saith he which hath the sharp sword with two edges;

13 I know thy works, and where thou dwellest, *even* where Satan's seat *is:* and thou holdest fast my name, and hast not denied my faith, even in those days wherein Antipas *was* my faithful martyr, who was slain among you, where Satan dwelleth.

14 But I have a few things against thee, because thou hast there them that hold the doctrine of Balaam, who taught Balac to cast a stumblingblock before the children

10 μὴ φοβοῦ ἃ μέλλεις πάσχειν. ἰδοὺ
Do not fear [the] thou art to suffer. Behold[,]
things which about

μέλλει βάλλειν ὁ διάβολος ἐξ ὑμῶν
³is about ⁴to cast ¹the ²devil [some] of you

εἰς φυλακὴν ἵνα πειρασθῆτε, καὶ ἕξετε
into prison in order that ye may be tried, and ye will have

θλῖψιν ἡμερῶν δέκα. γίνου πιστὸς ἄχρι
affliction ²days ¹ten. Be thou faithful until

θανάτου, καὶ δώσω σοι τὸν στέφανον
death, and I will give thee the crown

τῆς ζωῆς. 11 Ὁ ἔχων οὖς ἀκουσάτω
- of life. The [one] having an ear let him hear

τί τὸ πνεῦμα λέγει ταῖς ἐκκλησίαις.
what the Spirit says to the churches.

Ὁ νικῶν οὐ μὴ ἀδικηθῇ ἐκ τοῦ θανάτου
The over- by no will be by the ²death
[one] coming means hurt

τοῦ δευτέρου.
- ¹second.

12 Καὶ τῷ ἀγγέλῳ τῆς ἐν Περγάμῳ
And to the messenger ¹of the ³in ⁴Pergamum

ἐκκλησίας γράψον·
²church write thou:

Τάδε λέγει ὁ ἔχων τὴν ῥομφαίαν τὴν
These things says the having the ²sword -
[one]

δίστομον τὴν ὀξεῖαν· 13 οἶδα ποῦ κατοικεῖς·
¹two-mouthed - ²sharp: I know where thou
(edged) dwellest;

ὅπου ὁ θρόνος τοῦ σατανᾶ· καὶ κρατεῖς
where the throne - of Satan [is]; and thou holdest

τὸ ὄνομά μου, καὶ οὐκ ἠρνήσω τὴν
the name of me, and didst not deny the

πίστιν μου καὶ ἐν ταῖς ἡμέραις Ἀντιπᾶς
faith of me even in the days of Antipas

ὁ μάρτυς μου ὁ πιστός μου, ὃς
¹the ³witness ⁴of me *the* ²faithful *of me*, who

ἀπεκτάνθη παρ' ὑμῖν, ὅπου ὁ σατανᾶς
was killed among you, where - Satan

κατοικεῖ. 14 ἀλλ' ἔχω κατὰ σοῦ ὀλίγα,
dwells. But I have against thee a few
things,

ὅτι ἔχεις ἐκεῖ κρατοῦντας τὴν διδαχὴν
be- thou there [ones] holding the teaching
cause hast

Βαλαάμ, ὃς ἐδίδασκεν τῷ Βαλὰκ βαλεῖν
of Balaam, who taught - Balak to cast

σκάνδαλον ἐνώπιον τῶν υἱῶν Ἰσραήλ,
a stumbling-block before the sons of Israel,

of Israel, to eat things
sacrificed unto idols, and
to commit fornication.

15 So hast thou also
them that hold the doc-
trine of the Nicolaitanes,
which thing I hate.

16 Repent; or else I will
come unto thee quickly,
and will fight against
them with the sword of my
mouth.

17 He that hath an ear,
let him hear what the
Spirit saith unto the
churches; To him that
overcometh will I give to
eat of the hidden manna,
and will give him a white
stone, and in the stone a
new name written, which
no man knoweth saving
he that receiveth *it*.

18 And unto the angel
of the church in Thyatira
write; These things saith
the Son of God, who
hath his eyes like unto a
flame of fire, and his feet
are like fine brass;

19 I know thy works,
and charity, and service,
and faith, and thy patience,
and thy works; and the
last *to be* more than the
first.

20 Notwithstanding I
have a few things against
thee, because thou suf-
ferest that woman Jezebel,
which calleth herself a
prophetess, to teach and

φαγεῖν εἰδωλόθυτα καὶ πορνεῦσαι. 15 οὕτως
to eat   idol sacrifices   and to commit fornication.   So

ἔχεις καὶ σὺ κρατοῦντας τὴν διδαχὴν
²hast ³also ¹thou [ones] holding the teaching

τῶν Νικολαϊτῶν ὁμοίως. 16 μετανόησον
of the Nicolaitans likewise.   Repent thou

οὖν· εἰ δὲ μή, ἔρχομαί σοι ταχὺ καὶ
therefore; otherwise, I am coming to thee quickly and

πολεμήσω μετ' αὐτῶν ἐν τῇ ῥομφαίᾳ
will fight with them with the sword

τοῦ στόματός μου. 17 Ὁ ἔχων οὖς
of the mouth of me.   The [one] having an ear

ἀκουσάτω τί τὸ πνεῦμα λέγει ταῖς
let him hear what the Spirit says to the

ἐκκλησίαις. Τῷ νικῶντι δώσω αὐτῷ
churches.   To the [one] overcoming I will give to him

τοῦ μάννα τοῦ κεκρυμμένου, καὶ δώσω
of the ²manna – ¹having been hidden, and I will give

αὐτῷ ψῆφον λευκήν, καὶ ἐπὶ τὴν ψῆφον
him ²stone ¹a white, and on the stone

ὄνομα καινὸν γεγραμμένον, ὃ οὐδεὶς οἶδεν
²name ¹a new having been written, which no man knows

εἰ μὴ ὁ λαμβάνων.
except the [one] receiving [it].

18 Καὶ τῷ ἀγγέλῳ τῆς ἐν Θυατίροις
And to the messenger ¹of the ³in ⁴Thyatira

ἐκκλησίας γράψον·
²church   write thou:

Τάδε λέγει ὁ υἱὸς τοῦ θεοῦ, ὁ ἔχων
These things says the Son – of God, the having
                                              [one]

τοὺς ὀφθαλμοὺς [αὐτοῦ] ὡς φλόγα πυρός,
the eyes of him as a flame of fire,

καὶ οἱ πόδες αὐτοῦ ὅμοιοι χαλκολιβάνῳ·
and the feet of him like *to* burnished brass:

19 οἶδά σου τὰ ἔργα καὶ τὴν ἀγάπην
I know of thee the works and the love

καὶ τὴν πίστιν καὶ τὴν διακονίαν καὶ
and the faith and the ministry and

τὴν ὑπομονήν σου, καὶ τὰ ἔργα σου
the endurance *of thee*, and the ²works ³of thee

τὰ ἔσχατα πλείονα τῶν πρώτων. 20 ἀλλὰ
the ¹last more [than] the first.   But

ἔχω κατὰ σοῦ ὅτι ἀφεῖς τὴν γυναῖκα
I have against thee that thou permittest the woman

Ἰεζάβελ, ἡ λέγουσα ἑαυτὴν προφῆτιν,
Jezabel, the [one] say(call)ing herself a prophetess,

καὶ διδάσκει καὶ πλανᾷ τοὺς ἐμοὺς
and she teaches and deceives – my

to seduce my servants to commit fornication, and to eat things sacrificed unto idols.

21 And I gave her space to repent of her fornication; and she repented not.

22 Behold, I will cast her into a bed, and them that commit adultery with her into great tribulation, except they repent of their deeds.

23 And I will kill her children with death; and all the churches shall know that I am he which searcheth the reins and hearts: and I will give unto every one of you according to your works.

24 But unto you I say, and unto the rest in Thyatira, as many as have not this doctrine, and which have not known the depths of Satan, as they speak; I will put upon you none other burden.

25 But that which ye have *already* hold fast till I come.

26 And he that overcometh, and keepeth my works unto the end, to him will I give power over the nations:

27 And he shall rule them with a rod of iron; as the vessels of a potter shall they be broken to shivers: even as I received of my Father.

28 And I will give him the morning star.

δούλους πορνεῦσαι καὶ φαγεῖν εἰδωλόθυτα·
slaves to commit fornication and to eat idol sacrifices;

21 καὶ ἔδωκα αὐτῇ χρόνον ἵνα μετανοήσῃ,
and I gave her time in order she might repent,

καὶ οὐ θέλει μετανοῆσαι ἐκ τῆς πορνείας
and she wishes not to repent of the fornication

αὐτῆς. 22 ἰδοὺ βάλλω αὐτὴν εἰς κλίνην,
of her. Behold[,] I am casting her into a bed,

καὶ τοὺς μοιχεύοντας μετ' αὐτῆς εἰς
and the [ones] committing adultery with her into

θλῖψιν μεγάλην, ἐὰν μὴ μετανοήσουσιν
¹affliction ¹great, unless they shall repent

ἐκ τῶν ἔργων αὐτῆς· 23 καὶ τὰ τέκνα
of the works of her; and the children

αὐτῆς ἀποκτενῶ ἐν θανάτῳ· καὶ γνώσονται
of her I will kill with death; and ⁴will know

πᾶσαι αἱ ἐκκλησίαι ὅτι ἐγώ εἰμι ὁ
¹all ²the ³churches that I am the [one]

ἐρευνῶν νεφροὺς καὶ καρδίας, καὶ δώσω
searching kidneys and hearts, and I will give

ὑμῖν ἑκάστῳ κατὰ τὰ ἔργα ὑμῶν.
to you each one according to the works of you.

24 ὑμῖν δὲ λέγω τοῖς λοιποῖς τοῖς ἐν
But to you I say to the rest in

Θυατίροις, ὅσοι οὐκ ἔχουσιν τὴν διδαχὴν
Thyatira, as many as have not - teaching

ταύτην, οἵτινες οὐκ ἔγνωσαν τὰ βαθέα
this, who knew not the deep things

τοῦ σατανᾶ, ὡς λέγουσιν· οὐ βάλλω
- of Satan, as they say: I am not casting

ἐφ' ὑμᾶς ἄλλο βάρος· 25 πλὴν ὃ ἔχετε
on you another burden; nevertheless what ye have

κρατήσατε ἄχρι οὗ ἂν ἥξω. 26 Καὶ
hold until I shall come. And

ὁ νικῶν καὶ ὁ τηρῶν ἄχρι τέλους τὰ
the over- and the keeping until [the] the
[one] coming [one] end

ἔργα μου, δώσω αὐτῷ ἐξουσίαν ἐπὶ
works of me, I will give him authority over

τῶν ἐθνῶν, 27 καὶ ποιμανεῖ αὐτοὺς ἐν
the nations, and he will shepherd them with

ῥάβδῳ σιδηρᾷ, ὡς τὰ σκεύη τὰ κεραμικὰ
²staff ¹an iron, as *the* ²vessels - ¹clay

συντρίβεται, 28 ὡς κἀγὼ εἴληφα παρὰ
is(are) broken, as I also have received from

τοῦ πατρός μου, καὶ δώσω αὐτῷ τὸν
the Father of me, and I will give him the

29 He that hath an ear, let him hear what the Spirit saith unto the churches.

ἀστέρα τὸν πρωϊνόν.
²star – ¹morning.

29 Ὁ ἔχων οὖς
The [one] having an ear

ἀκουσάτω τί τὸ πνεῦμα λέγει ταῖς
let him hear what the Spirit says to the

ἐκκλησίαις
churches.

CHAPTER 3

AND unto the angel of the church in Sardis write; These things saith he that hath the seven Spirits of God, and the seven stars; I know thy works, that thou hast a name that thou livest, and art dead.

2 Be watchful, and strengthen the things which rem in, that are ready to die: for I have not found thy works perfect before God.

3 Remember therefore how thou hast received and heard, and hold fast, and repent. If therefore thou shalt not watch, I will come on thee as a thief, and thou shalt not know what hour I will come upon thee.

4 Thou hast a few names even in Sardis which have not defiled their garments; and they shall walk with me in white: for they are worthy.

5 He that overcometh, the same shall be clothed in white raiment; and I will not blot out his name

3 Καὶ τῷ ἀγγέλῳ τῆς ἐν Σάρδεσιν
And to the messenger ¹of the ³in ⁴Sardis

ἐκκλησίας γράψον·
²church write thou:

Τάδε λέγει ὁ ἔχων τὰ ἑπτὰ πνεύματα
These things says the having the seven Spirits
                    [one]

τοῦ θεοῦ καὶ τοὺς ἑπτὰ ἀστέρας· οἶδά
 – of God and the seven stars: I know

σου τὰ ἔργα, ὅτι ὄνομα ἔχεις ὅτι ζῆς,
³of ¹the ²works, that a name thou that thou
thee   hast   livest,

καὶ νεκρὸς εἶ. 2 γίνου γρηγορῶν, καὶ
and [yet] ²dead ¹thou art. Be thou watching, and

στήρισον τὰ λοιπὰ ἃ ἔμελλον ἀποθανεῖν·
establish the remain- which were to die;
          things ing   about

οὐ γὰρ εὕρηκά σου ἔργα πεπληρωμένα
for I have not found of thee works having been fulfilled

ἐνώπιον τοῦ θεοῦ μου· 3 μνημόνευε οὖν
before the God of me; remember therefore

πῶς εἴληφας καὶ ἤκουσας, καὶ τήρει
how thou hast received and didst hear, and keep

καὶ μετανόησον. ἐὰν οὖν μὴ γρηγορήσῃς,
and repent. If therefore thou dost not watch,

ἥξω ὡς κλέπτης, καὶ οὐ μὴ γνῷς ποίαν
I will as a thief, and by no thou at what
come   means knowest

ὥραν ἥξω ἐπὶ σέ. 4 ἀλλὰ ἔχεις ὀλίγα
hour I will come on thee. But thou hast a few

ὀνόματα ἐν Σάρδεσιν ἃ οὐκ ἐμόλυναν τὰ
names in Sardis which did not defile the

ἱμάτια αὐτῶν, καὶ περιπατήσουσιν μετ'
garments of them, and they shall walk with

ἐμοῦ ἐν λευκοῖς, ὅτι ἄξιοί εἰσιν. 5 Ὁ
me in white because ²worthy ¹they are. The
    [garments],   [one]

νικῶν οὕτως περιβαλεῖται ἐν ἱματίοις
overcoming ²thus ¹shall be clothed in ²garments

λευκοῖς, καὶ οὐ μὴ ἐξαλείψω τὸ ὄνομα
¹white, and by no means will I blot out the name

out of the book of life, but I will confess his name before my Father, and before his angels.

6 He that hath an ear, let him hear what the Spirit saith unto the churches.

7 And to the angel of the church in Philadelphia write; These things saith he that is holy, he that is true, he that hath the key of David, he that openeth, and no man shutteth; and shutteth, and no man openeth;

8 I know thy works: behold, I have set before thee an open door, and no man can shut it: for thou hast a little strength, and hast kept my word, and hast not denied my name.

9 Behold, I will make them of the synagogue of Satan, which say they are Jews, and are not, but do lie; behold, I will make them to come and worship before thy feet, and to know that I have loved thee.

10 Because thou hast kept the word of my

αὐτοῦ ἐκ τῆς βίβλου τῆς ζωῆς, καὶ
of him   out of   the   scroll   –   of life,   and

ὁμολογήσω τὸ ὄνομα αὐτοῦ ἐνώπιον τοῦ
I will confess   the   name   of him   before   the

πατρός μου καὶ ἐνώπιον τῶν ἀγγέλων
Father   of me   and   before   the   angels

αὐτοῦ. 6 Ὁ ἔχων οὖς ἀκουσάτω τί τὸ
of him.   The [one] having an ear let him hear what the

πνεῦμα λέγει ταῖς ἐκκλησίαις.
Spirit   says   to the   churches.

7 Καὶ τῷ ἀγγέλῳ τῆς ἐν Φιλαδελφείᾳ
And to the messenger ¹of the ²in ⁴Philadelphia

ἐκκλησίας γράψον·
²church   write thou:

Τάδε λέγει ὁ ἅγιος, ὁ ἀληθινός, ὁ
These says   the   holy   the   true   the
things   [one],   [one],   [one]

ἔχων τὴν κλεῖν Δαυίδ, ὁ ἀνοίγων καὶ
having   the   key   of David, the [one] opening   and

οὐδεὶς κλείσει, καὶ κλείων καὶ οὐδεὶς
no one   shall shut,   and   shutting   and   no one

ἀνοίγει· 8 οἶδά σου τὰ ἔργα· ἰδοὺ
opens: I know of thee the   works; behold[,]

δέδωκα ἐνώπιόν σου θύραν ἠνεῳγμένην,
I have given   before   thee   a door having been opened,

ἣν οὐδεὶς δύναται κλεῖσαι αὐτήν· ὅτι
which no one   can   to shut   it;   because

μικρὰν ἔχεις δύναμιν, καὶ ἐτήρησάς μου
²a little ¹thou hast   power,   and   didst keep   of me

τὸν λόγον καὶ οὐκ ἠρνήσω τὸ ὄνομά
the   word   and   didst not deny   the   name

μου. 9 ἰδοὺ διδῶ ἐκ τῆς συναγωγῆς
of me.   Behold[,] I may [some] the   synagogue
            (will) give   of

τοῦ σατανᾶ, τῶν λεγόντων ἑαυτοὺς
–   of Satan,   the [ones] say(call)ing   themselves

Ἰουδαίους εἶναι, καὶ οὐκ εἰσὶν ἀλλὰ
Jews   to be,   and   they are not   but

ψεύδονται· ἰδοὺ ποιήσω αὐτοὺς ἵνα
they lie;   behold[,] I will make   them   in order
                        that

ἥξουσιν καὶ προσκυνήσουσιν ἐνώπιον τῶν
they shall   and they shall worship   before   the
come

ποδῶν σου, καὶ γνῶσιν ὅτι ἐγὼ ἠγάπησά
feet   of thee, and   shall know   that   I   loved
               they

σε. 10 ὅτι ἐτήρησας τὸν λόγον τῆς
thee.   Because thou didst keep   the   word   of the

patience, I also will keep thee from the hour of temptation, which shall come upon all the world, to try them that dwell upon the earth.

11 Behold, I come quickly: hold that fast which thou hast, that no man take thy crown.

12 Him that overcometh will I make a pillar in the temple of my God, and he shall go no more out: and I will write upon him the name of my God, and the name of the city of my God, *which is* new Jerusalem, which cometh down out of heaven from my God: and *I will write upon him* my new name.

13 He that hath an ear, let him hear what the Spirit saith unto the churches.

14 And unto the angel of the church of the Laodiceans write; These things saith the Amen, the faithful and true witness, the beginning of the creation of God;

15 I know thy works, that thou art neither cold nor hot: I would thou wert cold or hot.

16 So then because thou art lukewarm, and neither

ὑπομονῆς μου, κἀγώ σε τηρήσω ἐκ
endurance of me, I also ⁵thee ¹will keep out of

τῆς ὥρας τοῦ πειρασμοῦ τῆς μελλούσης
the hour – of trial – *being* about

ἔρχεσθαι ἐπὶ τῆς οἰκουμένης ὅλης, πειράσαι
to come on ³the ²inhabited [earth] ¹all, to try

τοὺς κατοικοῦντας ἐπὶ τῆς γῆς. 11 ἔρχομαι
the [ones] dwelling on the earth. I am coming

ταχύ· κράτει ὃ ἔχεις, ἵνα μηδεὶς λάβῃ
quickly; hold what thou in order no one takes
hast, that

τὸν στέφανόν σου. 12 Ὁ νικῶν, ποιήσω
the crown of thee. The [one] overcoming, I will make

αὐτὸν στῦλον ἐν τῷ ναῷ τοῦ θεοῦ
him a pillar in the shrine of the God

μου, καὶ ἔξω οὐ μὴ ἐξέλθῃ ἔτι, καὶ
of me, and out by no he will [any] and
means go forth longer,

γράψω ἐπ' αὐτὸν τὸ ὄνομα τοῦ θεοῦ
I will write on him the name of the God

μου καὶ τὸ ὄνομα τῆς πόλεως τοῦ
of me and the name of the city of the

θεοῦ μου, τῆς καινῆς Ἰερουσαλὴμ ἡ
God of me, *of* the new Jerusalem –

καταβαίνουσα ἐκ τοῦ οὐρανοῦ ἀπὸ τοῦ
descending out of – heaven from the

θεοῦ μου, καὶ τὸ ὄνομά μου τὸ καινόν.
God of me, and ¹the ²name ⁴of me – ³new.

13 Ὁ ἔχων οὖς ἀκουσάτω τί τὸ πνεῦμα
The [one] having an ear let him hear what the Spirit

λέγει ταῖς ἐκκλησίαις.
says to the churches.

14 Καὶ τῷ ἀγγέλῳ τῆς ἐν Λαοδικείᾳ
And to the messenger ¹of the ²in ⁴Laodicea

ἐκκλησίας γράψον·
³church write thou:

Τάδε λέγει ὁ ἀμήν, ὁ μάρτυς ὁ
These things says the Amen, the ⁴witness –

πιστὸς καὶ ἀληθινός, ἡ ἀρχὴ τῆς κτίσεως
¹faithful ²and ³true, the chief of the creation

τοῦ θεοῦ· 15 οἶδά σου τὰ ἔργα, ὅτι
– of God: I know of thee the works, that

οὔτε ψυχρὸς εἶ οὔτε ζεστός. ὄφελον
neither cold art thou nor hot. I would that†

ψυχρὸς ἦς ἢ ζεστός. 16 οὕτως ὅτι
cold thou wast or hot. So because

χλιαρὸς εἶ, καὶ οὔτε ζεστὸς οὔτε ψυχρός,
lukewarm thou art, and neither hot nor cold,

cold nor hot, I will spue thee out of my mouth.

17 Because thou sayest, I am rich, and increased with goods, and have need of nothing; and knowest not that thou art wretched, and miserable, and poor, and blind, and naked:

18 I counsel thee to buy of me gold tried in the fire, that thou mayest be rich; and white raiment, that thou mayest be clothed, and *that* the shame of thy nakedness do not appear; and anoint thine eyes with eyesalve, that thou mayest see.

19 As many as I love, I rebuke and chasten: be zealous therefore, and repent.

20 Behold, I stand at the door, and knock: if any man hear my voice, and open the door, I will come in to him, and will sup with him, and he with me.

21 To him that overcometh will I grant to sit with me in my throne, even as I also overcame, and am set down with my Father in his throne.

μέλλω   σε   ἐμέσαι   ἐκ   τοῦ   στόματός   μου.
I am   ²thee   ¹to vomit   out of   the   mouth   of me.
about*

17 ὅτι   λέγεις   ὅτι   πλούσιός   εἰμι   καὶ
Because thou sayest[,]   –   ²rich   ¹I am   and

πεπλούτηκα   καὶ   οὐδὲν   χρείαν   ἔχω,   καὶ
I have become rich   and   ²no   ³need   ¹I have,   and

οὐκ   οἶδας   ὅτι   σὺ   εἶ   ὁ   ταλαίπωρος
knowest not   that   thou   art the [one]   wretched

καὶ   ἐλεεινὸς   καὶ   πτωχὸς   καὶ   τυφλὸς
and   pitiable   and   poor   and   blind

καὶ   γυμνός,   18 συμβουλεύω   σοι   ἀγοράσαι
and   naked,   I counsel   thee   to buy

παρ'   ἐμοῦ   χρυσίον   πεπυρωμένον   ἐκ   πυρὸς
from   me   gold   *having been* refined   by   fire
by fire

ἵνα   πλουτήσῃς,   καὶ   ἱμάτια   λευκὰ   ἵνα
in or-   thou mayest   and   ²garments   ¹white   in order
der that   be rich,   that

περιβάλῃ   καὶ   μὴ   φανερωθῇ   ἡ   αἰσχύνη
thou mayest   and   ⁴may not be   ¹the   ²shame
be clothed   manifested

τῆς   γυμνότητός   σου,   καὶ   κολλύριον
³of the   ⁴nakedness   ⁵of thee,   and   eyesalve

ἐγχρῖσαι   τοὺς   ὀφθαλμούς   σου   ἵνα   βλέπῃς.
to anoint   the   eyes   of   in order   thou
thee   that mayest see.

19 ἐγὼ   ὅσους   ἐὰν   φιλῶ   ἐλέγχω   καὶ
²I   ¹as many as   love   I rebuke   and

παιδεύω·   ζήλευε   οὖν   καὶ   μετανόησον.
I chasten;   be hot   therefore   and   repent thou.

20 Ἰδοὺ   ἔστηκα   ἐπὶ   τὴν   θύραν   καὶ
Behold[,]   I stand   at   the   door   and

κρούω·   ἐάν   τις   ἀκούσῃ   τῆς   φωνῆς   μου
I knock;   if   anyone   hears   the   voice   of me

καὶ   ἀνοίξῃ   τὴν   θύραν,   εἰσελεύσομαι   πρὸς
and   opens   the   door,   I will enter   to

αὐτὸν   καὶ   δειπνήσω   μετ'   αὐτοῦ   καὶ
him   and   I will dine   with   him   and

αὐτὸς   μετ'   ἐμοῦ.   21 Ὁ   νικῶν,   δώσω
he   with   me.   The   overcoming,   I will
[one]   give

αὐτῷ   καθίσαι   μετ'   ἐμοῦ   ἐν   τῷ   θρόνῳ
him   to sit   with   me   in   the   throne

μου,   ὡς   κἀγὼ   ἐνίκησα   καὶ   ἐκάθισα
of me,   as   I also   overcame   and   sat

μετὰ   τοῦ   πατρός   μου   ἐν   τῷ   θρόνῳ
with   the   Father   of me   in   the   throne

---

* As so often (see also ch. 1. 19, 2. 10), this verb does not necessarily connote imminence, but only simple futurity.

22 He that hath an ear, let him hear what the Spirit saith unto the churches.

αὐτοῦ. **22** Ὁ ἔχων οὖς ἀκουσάτω τί
of him.   The [one] having an ear let him hear what
τὸ πνεῦμα λέγει ταῖς ἐκκλησίαις.
the Spirit says to the churches.

CHAPTER 4

AFTER this I looked, and, behold, a door was opened in heaven: and the first voice which I heard was as it were of a trumpet talking with me; which said, Come up hither, and I will shew thee things which must be hereafter.

2 And immediately I was in the spirit: and, behold, a throne was set in heaven, and one sat on the throne.

3 And he that sat was to look upon like a jasper and a sardine stone: and there was a rainbow round about the throne, in sight like unto an emerald.

4 And round about the throne were four and twenty seats: and upon the seats I saw four and twenty elders sitting, clothed in white raiment; and they had on their heads crowns of gold.

5 And out of the throne proceeded lightnings and thunderings and voices: and there were seven lamps of fire burning before the throne, which are the seven Spirits of God.

4 Μετὰ ταῦτα εἶδον, καὶ ἰδοὺ θύρα
After these things I saw, and behold[,] a door
ἠνεῳγμένη ἐν τῷ οὐρανῷ, καὶ ἡ φωνὴ
having been in - heaven, and the ²voice
opened
ἡ πρώτη ἦν ἤκουσα ὡς σάλπιγγος
- ¹first which I heard as of a trumpet
λαλούσης μετ᾽ ἐμοῦ, λέγων· ἀνάβα ὧδε,
speaking with me, saying: Come up here,
καὶ δείξω σοι ἃ δεῖ γενέσθαι μετὰ
and I will thee things it be- to occur after
show which hoves
ταῦτα. εὐθέως ἐγενόμην ἐν πνεύματι·
these things. Immediately I became in spirit;
2 καὶ ἰδοὺ θρόνος ἔκειτο ἐν τῷ οὐρανῷ,
and behold[,] a throne was set in - heaven,
καὶ ἐπὶ τὸν θρόνον καθήμενος, **3** καὶ
and on the throne a sitting [one], and
ὁ καθήμενος ὅμοιος ὁράσει λίθῳ ἰάσπιδι
the [one] sitting [was] like in appearance ⁴stone ¹to a jasper
καὶ σαρδίῳ, καὶ ἶρις κυκλόθεν τοῦ
²and ³a sardius, and a rain- round the
[there was] bow
θρόνου ὅμοιος ὁράσει σμαραγδίνῳ. **4** καὶ
throne like in appearance to an emerald. And
κυκλόθεν τοῦ θρόνου θρόνους εἴκοσι
round the throne [I saw] ²thrones ¹twenty-
τέσσαρας, καὶ ἐπὶ τοὺς θρόνους εἴκοσι
four, and on the thrones twenty-
τέσσαρας πρεσβυτέρους καθημένους περι-
four elders sitting having been
βεβλημένους ἐν ἱματίοις λευκοῖς, καὶ ἐπὶ
clothed in garments white, and on
τὰς κεφαλὰς αὐτῶν στεφάνους χρυσοῦς
the heads of them ²crowns ¹golden.
5 καὶ ἐκ τοῦ θρόνου ἐκπορεύονται ἀστραπαὶ
And out of the throne come forth lightnings
καὶ φωναὶ καὶ βρονταί· καὶ ἑπτὰ λαμπάδες
and voices* and thunders; and seven lamps
πυρὸς καιόμεναι ἐνώπιον τοῦ θρόνου, ἃ
of fire [are] burning before the throne, which
εἰσιν τὰ ἑπτὰ πνεύματα τοῦ θεοῦ· **6** καὶ
are the seven Spirits - of God; and

* Or "sounds"; and so elsewhere.

6 And before the throne *there was* a sea of glass like unto crystal: and in the midst of the throne, and round about the throne, *were* four beasts full of eyes before and behind.

7 And the first beast *was* like a lion, and the second beast like a calf, and the third beast had a face as a man, and the fourth beast *was* like a flying eagle.

8 And the four beasts had each of them six wings about *him;* and *they were* full of eyes within: and they rest not day and night, saying, Holy, holy, holy, Lord God Almighty, which was, and is, and is to come.

9 And when those beasts give glory and honour and thanks to him that sat on the throne, who liveth for ever and ever,

10 The four and twenty elders fall down before him that sat on the throne,

ἐνώπιον τοῦ θρόνου ὡς θάλασσα ὑαλίνη
before the throne as ²sea ¹a glassy

ὁμοία κρυστάλλῳ· καὶ ἐν μέσῳ τοῦ
like to crystal; and in [the] midst of the

θρόνου καὶ κύκλῳ τοῦ θρόνου τέσσερα
throne and round the throne four

ζῷα γέμοντα ὀφθαλμῶν ἔμπροσθεν καὶ
living filling(full) of eyes before and
creatures

ὄπισθεν. 7 καὶ τὸ ζῷον τὸ πρῶτον
behind. And the ²living – ¹first
creature

ὅμοιον λέοντι, καὶ τὸ δεύτερον ζῷον
[was] to a lion, and the second living
like creature

ὅμοιον μόσχῳ, καὶ τὸ τρίτον ζῷον ἔχων
like to a calf, and the third living having
creature

τὸ πρόσωπον ὡς ἀνθρώπου, καὶ τὸ
the(its) face as of a man, and the

τέταρτον ζῷον ὅμοιον ἀετῷ πετομένῳ.
fourth living creature like eagle to a flying.

8 καὶ τὰ τέσσερα ζῷα, ἓν καθ’ ἕν
And the four living one by one
creatures,

αὐτῶν ἔχων ἀνὰ πτέρυγας ἕξ, κυκλόθεν
of them having each ²wings ¹six, around

καὶ ἔσωθεν γέμουσιν ὀφθαλμῶν· καὶ
and within are full of eyes; and

ἀνάπαυσιν οὐκ ἔχουσιν ἡμέρας καὶ νυκτὸς
respite they have not day and night

λέγοντες· ἅγιος ἅγιος ἅγιος κύριος ὁ
saying: Holy[,] holy[,] holy[,] Lord –

θεὸς ὁ παντοκράτωρ, ὁ ἦν καὶ ὁ ὢν
God the Almighty, the was and the being
[one who] [one]
= the one who is

καὶ ὁ ἐρχόμενος. 9 Καὶ ὅταν δώσουσιν
and the coming [one]. And whenever ³shall give

τὰ ζῷα δόξαν καὶ τιμὴν καὶ εὐχαριστίαν
¹the ²living glory and honour and thanks
creatures

τῷ καθημένῳ ἐπὶ τῷ θρόνῳ τῷ ζῶντι
to the sitting on the throne[,] to the living
[one] [one]

εἰς τοὺς αἰῶνας τῶν αἰώνων, 10 πεσοῦνται
unto the ages of the ages, ⁴will fall

οἱ εἴκοσι τέσσαρες πρεσβύτεροι ἐνώπιον
¹the ²twenty-four ³elders before

τοῦ καθημένου ἐπὶ τοῦ θρόνου, καὶ
the [one] sitting on the throne, and

and worship him that liveth for ever and ever, and cast their crowns before the throne, saying,

11 Thou art worthy, O Lord, to receive glory and honour and power: for thou hast created all things, and for thy pleasure they are and were created.

προσκυνήσουσιν τῷ ζῶντι εἰς τοὺς αἰῶνας
they will worship the [one] living unto the ages

τῶν αἰώνων, καὶ βαλοῦσιν τοὺς στεφάνους
of the ages, and will cast the crowns

αὐτῶν ἐνώπιον τοῦ θρόνου, λέγοντες·
of them before the throne, saying:

11 ἄξιος εἶ, ὁ κύριος καὶ ὁ θεὸς ἡμῶν,
Worthy art thou, the Lord and the God of us,

λαβεῖν τὴν δόξαν καὶ τὴν τιμὴν καὶ
to receive the glory and the honour and

τὴν δύναμιν, ὅτι σὺ ἔκτισας τὰ πάντα,
the power, because thou createdst – all things,*

καὶ διὰ τὸ θέλημά σου ἦσαν καὶ
and on ac- the will of thee they were and
count of

ἐκτίσθησαν.
they were created.

CHAPTER 5

AND I saw in the right hand of him that sat on the throne a book written within and on the backside, sealed with seven seals.

2 And I saw a strong angel proclaiming with a loud voice, Who is worthy to open the book, and to loose the seals thereof?

3 And no man in heaven, nor in earth, neither under the earth, was able to open the book, neither to look thereon.

4 And I wept much, because no man was found worthy to open and to read the book, neither to look thereon.

5 And one of the elders saith unto me, Weep not:

5 Καὶ εἶδον ἐπὶ τὴν δεξιὰν τοῦ
And I saw on the right of the
[hand] [one]

καθημένου ἐπὶ τοῦ θρόνου βιβλίον
sitting on the throne a scroll

γεγραμμένον ἔσωθεν καὶ ὄπισθεν,
having been written within and on the reverse side,

κατεσφραγισμένον σφραγῖσιν ἑπτά. 2 καὶ
having been sealed with ²seals ¹seven. And

εἶδον ἄγγελον ἰσχυρὸν κηρύσσοντα ἐν
I saw angel a strong proclaiming in

φωνῇ μεγάλῃ· τίς ἄξιος ἀνοῖξαι τὸ
²voice ¹a great(loud): Who [is] worthy to open the

βιβλίον καὶ λῦσαι τὰς σφραγῖδας αὐτοῦ;
scroll and to loosen the seals of it?

3 καὶ οὐδεὶς ἐδύνατο ἐν τῷ οὐρανῷ
And no one was able in – heaven

οὐδὲ ἐπὶ τῆς γῆς οὐδὲ ὑποκάτω τῆς
nor on the earth nor underneath the

γῆς ἀνοῖξαι τὸ βιβλίον οὔτε βλέπειν
earth to open the scroll nor to see(look at)

αὐτό. 4 καὶ ἔκλαιον πολύ, ὅτι οὐδεὶς
it. And I wept much, because no one

ἄξιος εὑρέθη ἀνοῖξαι τὸ βιβλίον οὔτε
worthy was found to open the scroll nor

βλέπειν αὐτό. 5 καὶ εἷς ἐκ τῶν πρεσ-
to look at it. And one of the el-

βυτέρων λέγει μοι· μὴ κλαῖε· ἰδοὺ
ders says to me: Weep not; behold[,]

. * τὰ πάντα = the universe.

behold, the Lion of the tribe of Juda, the Root of David, hath prevailed to open the book, and to loose the seven seals thereof.

6 And I beheld, and, lo, in the midst of the throne and of the four beasts, and in the midst of the elders, stood a Lamb as it had been slain, having seven horns and seven eyes, which are the seven Spirits of God sent forth into all the earth.

7 And he came and took the book out of the right hand of him that sat upon the throne.

8 And when he had taken the book, the four beasts and four *and* twenty elders fell down before the Lamb, having every one of them harps, and golden vials full of odours, which are the prayers of saints.

9 And they sung a new song, saying, Thou art worthy to take the book, and to open the seals thereof: for thou wast slain, and hast redeemed us to God by thy blood out of every kindred, and tongue, and people, and nation;

10 And hast made us unto our God kings and

ἐνίκησεν ὁ λέων ὁ ἐκ τῆς φυλῆς Ἰούδα,
[10]overcame [1]the [2]Lion – [3]of [4]the [5]tribe [6]Juda,

ἡ ῥίζα Δαυίδ, ἀνοῖξαι τὸ βιβλίον καὶ
[7]the [8]root [9]of David, to open the scroll and

τὰς ἑπτὰ σφραγῖδας αὐτοῦ. 6 Καὶ εἶδον
the seven seals of it. And I saw

ἐν μέσῳ τοῦ θρόνου καὶ τῶν τεσσάρων
in [the] midst of the throne and of the four

ζῴων καὶ ἐν μέσῳ τῶν πρεσβυτέρων
living and in [the] of the elders
creatures   midst

ἀρνίον ἑστηκὸς ὡς ἐσφαγμένον, ἔχων
a Lamb standing as having been slain, having

κέρατα ἑπτὰ καὶ ὀφθαλμοὺς ἑπτά, οἳ
[2]horns [1]seven and [2]eyes [1]seven, which

εἰσιν τὰ ἑπτὰ πνεύματα τοῦ θεοῦ
are the seven Spirits – of God

ἀπεσταλμένοι εἰς πᾶσαν τὴν γῆν. 7 καὶ
having been sent forth into all the earth. And

ἦλθεν καὶ εἴληφεν ἐκ τῆς δεξιᾶς τοῦ
he came and has taken out of the right [hand] of the

καθημένου ἐπὶ τοῦ θρόνου. 8 Καὶ ὅτε
[one] sitting on the throne. And when

ἔλαβεν τὸ βιβλίον, τὰ τέσσερα ζῷα
he took the scroll, the four living
creatures

καὶ οἱ εἴκοσι τέσσαρες πρεσβύτεροι ἔπεσαν
and the twenty-four elders fell

ἐνώπιον τοῦ ἀρνίου, ἔχοντες ἕκαστος
before the Lamb, having each one

κιθάραν καὶ φιάλας χρυσᾶς γεμούσας
a harp and [2]bowls [1]golden *being* full

θυμιαμάτων, αἵ εἰσιν αἱ προσευχαὶ τῶν
of incenses, which are the prayers of the

ἁγίων. 9 καὶ ᾄδουσιν ᾠδὴν καινὴν
saints. And they sing [1]song [1]a new

λέγοντες· ἄξιος εἶ λαβεῖν τὸ βιβλίον
saying: Worthy art thou to receive the scroll

καὶ ἀνοῖξαι τὰς σφραγῖδας αὐτοῦ, ὅτι
and to open the seals of it, because

ἐσφάγης καὶ ἠγόρασας τῷ θεῷ ἐν τῷ
thou wast slain and didst purchase – to God by the

αἵματί σου ἐκ πάσης φυλῆς καὶ γλώσσης
blood of thee out of every tribe and tongue

καὶ λαοῦ καὶ ἔθνους, 10 καὶ ἐποίησας
and people and nation, and didst make

αὐτοὺς τῷ θεῷ ἡμῶν βασιλείαν καὶ
them to the God of us a kingdom and

priests: and we shall reign on the earth.

11 And I beheld, and I heard the voice of many angels round about the throne and the beasts and the elders: and the number of them was ten thousand times ten thousand, and thousands of thousands;

12 Saying with a loud voice, Worthy is the Lamb that was slain to receive power, and riches, and wisdom, and strength, and honour, and glory, and blessing.

13 And every creature which is in heaven, and on the earth, and under the earth, and such as are in the sea, and all that are in them, heard I saying, Blessing, and honour, and glory, and power, *be* unto him that sitteth upon the throne, and unto the Lamb for ever and ever.

14 And the four beasts said, Amen. And the four *and* twenty elders fell down and worshipped him that liveth for ever and ever.

ἱερεῖς,   καὶ   βασιλεύσουσιν   ἐπὶ   τῆς   γῆς.
priests,   and   they will reign   on(? over) the   earth.

11 καὶ   εἶδον,   καὶ   ἤκουσα   φωνὴν   ἀγγέλων
And   I saw,   and   I heard   a sound   ²angels

πολλῶν   κύκλῳ   τοῦ   θρόνου   καὶ   τῶν
¹of many   round   the   throne   and   the

ζῴων   καὶ   τῶν   πρεσβυτέρων,   καὶ   ἦν
living creatures   and   the   elders,   and   ⁴was

ὁ   ἀριθμὸς   αὐτῶν   μυριάδες   μυριάδων   καὶ
¹the   ²number   ³of them   myriads   of myriads   and

χιλιάδες   χιλιάδων,   12 λέγοντες   φωνῇ
thousands   of thousands,   saying   ²voice

μεγάλῃ·   ἄξιός   ἐστιν   τὸ   ἀρνίον   τὸ
¹with a great (loud):   Worthy   is   the   Lamb   –

ἐσφαγμένον   λαβεῖν   τὴν   δύναμιν   καὶ   πλοῦτον
having been slain   to receive   the   power   and   riches

καὶ   σοφίαν   καὶ   ἰσχὺν   καὶ   τιμὴν   καὶ
and   wisdom   and   strength   and   honour   and

δόξαν   καὶ   εὐλογίαν.   13 καὶ   πᾶν   κτίσμα
glory   and   blessing.   And   every   creature

ὃ   ἐν   τῷ   οὐρανῷ   καὶ   ἐπὶ   τῆς   γῆς   καὶ
which ²in   –   ³heaven   ⁴and   ⁵on   ⁶the   ⁷earth   ⁸and

ὑποκάτω   τῆς   γῆς   καὶ   ἐπὶ   τῆς   θαλάσσης
⁹underneath   ¹⁰the   ¹¹earth   ¹²and   ¹³on   ¹⁴the   ¹⁵sea

[ἐστίν],   καὶ   τὰ   ἐν   αὐτοῖς   πάντα,   ἤκουσα
¹is,   and   the   ²in   ³them   ¹all things,   I heard

λέγοντας·   τῷ   καθημένῳ   ἐπὶ   τῷ   θρόνῳ
saying: To the [one] sitting   on   the   throne

καὶ   τῷ   ἀρνίῳ   ἡ   εὐλογία   καὶ   ἡ   τιμὴ
and   to the   Lamb   the   blessing   and   the   honour

καὶ   ἡ   δόξα   καὶ   τὸ   κράτος   εἰς   τοὺς
and   the   glory   and   the   might   unto   the

αἰῶνας   τῶν   αἰώνων.   14 καὶ   τὰ   τέσσερα
ages   of the   ages.   And   the   four

ζῷα   ἔλεγον·   ἀμήν,   καὶ   οἱ   πρεσβύτεροι
living creatures   said: Amen,   and   the   elders

ἔπεσαν   καὶ   προσεκύνησαν.
fell   and   worshipped.

CHAPTER 6

AND I saw when the Lamb opened one of the seals, and I heard, as it were the noise of thunder,

6 Καὶ   εἶδον   ὅτε   ἤνοιξεν   τὸ   ἀρνίον
And   I saw   when   ²opened   ¹the   ²Lamb

μίαν   ἐκ   τῶν   ἑπτὰ   σφραγίδων,   καὶ   ἤκουσα
one   of   the   seven   seals,   and   I heard

ἑνὸς   ἐκ   τῶν   τεσσάρων   ζῴων   λέγοντος
one   of   the   four   living creatures   saying

one of the four beasts saying, Come and see.

2 And I saw, and behold a white horse: and he that sat on him had a bow; and a crown was given unto him: and he went forth conquering, and to conquer.

3 And when he had opened the second seal, I heard the second beast say, Come and see.

4 And there went out another horse *that was* red: and *power* was given to him that sat thereon to take peace from the earth, and that they should kill one another: and there was given unto him a great sword.

5 And when he had opened the third seal, I heard the third beast say, Come and see. And I beheld, and lo a black horse; and he that sat on him had a pair of balances in his hand.

6 And I heard a voice in the midst of the four beasts say, A measure of wheat for a penny, and three measures of barley for a penny; and *see* thou hurt not the oil and the wine.

7 And when he had opened the fourth seal,

ὡς φωνῇ βροντῆς· ἔρχου. 2 καὶ εἶδον,
as with a sound of thunder: Come. And I saw,

καὶ ἰδοὺ ἵππος λευκός, καὶ ὁ καθήμενος
and behold[,] ²horse ¹a white, and the [one] sitting

ἐπ' αὐτὸν ἔχων τόξον, καὶ ἐδόθη αὐτῷ
on it having a bow, and ²was given ³to him

στέφανος, καὶ ἐξῆλθεν νικῶν καὶ ἵνα
¹a crown, and he went forth overcoming and in order that

νικήσῃ. 3 Καὶ ὅτε ἤνοιξεν τὴν σφραγῖδα
he might And when he opened the ²seal
overcome.

τὴν δευτέραν, ἤκουσα τοῦ δευτέρου ζῴου
- ¹second, I heard the second living
creature

λέγοντος· ἔρχου. 4 καὶ ἐξῆλθεν ἄλλος
saying: Come. And ⁴went forth ¹another

ἵππος πυρρός, καὶ τῷ καθημένῳ ἐπ'
²horse[,] ³red, and to the [one] sitting on

αὐτὸν ἐδόθη αὐτῷ λαβεῖν τὴν εἰρήνην
it was given *to him* to take - peace

ἐκ τῆς γῆς καὶ ἵνα ἀλλήλους σφάξουσιν,
out the earth and *in order* ²one ¹they
of that another shall slay,

καὶ ἐδόθη αὐτῷ μάχαιρα μεγάλη. 5 Καὶ
and ²was given ⁴to him ³sword ¹a great. And

ὅτε ἤνοιξεν τὴν σφραγῖδα τὴν τρίτην,
when he opened the ²seal - ¹third,

ἤκουσα τοῦ τρίτου ζῴου λέγοντος· ἔρχου.
I heard the third living saying: Come.
creature

καὶ εἶδον, καὶ ἰδοὺ ἵππος μέλας, καὶ
And I saw, and behold[,] ²horse ¹a black, and

ὁ καθήμενος ἐπ' αὐτὸν ἔχων ζυγὸν
the [one] sitting on it having a balance

ἐν τῇ χειρὶ αὐτοῦ. 6 καὶ ἤκουσα ὡς
in the hand of him. And I heard as

φωνὴν ἐν μέσῳ τῶν τεσσάρων ζῴων
a voice in [the] of the four living
midst creatures

λέγουσαν· χοῖνιξ σίτου δηναρίου, καὶ τρεῖς
saying: A of of(for) and three
chœnix wheat a denarius,

χοίνικες κριθῶν δηναρίου· καὶ τὸ ἔλαιον
chœnixes of barley of(for) and ²the ³oil
a denarius;

καὶ τὸν οἶνον μὴ ἀδικήσῃς. 7 Καὶ
⁴and ⁵the ⁶wine ¹do not harm. And

ὅτε ἤνοιξεν τὴν σφραγῖδα τὴν τετάρτην,
when he opened the ²seal - ¹fourth,

I heard the voice of the fourth beast say, Come and see.

8 And I looked, and behold a pale horse: and his name that sat on him was Death, and Hell followed with him. And power was given unto them over the fourth part of the earth, to kill with sword, and with hunger, and with death, and with the beasts of the earth.

9 And when he had opened the fifth seal, I saw under the altar the souls of them that were slain for the word of God, and for the testimony which they held:

10 And they cried with a loud voice, saying, How long, O Lord, holy and true, dost thou not judge and avenge our blood on them that dwell on the earth?

11 And white robes were given unto every one of them; and it was said unto them, that they should rest yet for a little season, until their fellow-servants also and their brethren, that should be killed as they were, should be fulfilled.

12 And I beheld when

ἤκουσα φωνὴν τοῦ τετάρτου ζῴου λέγοντος·
I heard [the] voice of the fourth living creature saying:

ἔρχου. 8 καὶ εἶδον, καὶ ἰδοὺ ἵππος
Come.　　　And I saw, and behold[,] [the] horse

χλωρός, καὶ ὁ καθήμενος ἐπάνω αὐτοῦ,
[a] pale green, and the [one] sitting upon it,

ὄνομα αὐτῷ [ὁ] θάνατος, καὶ ὁ ᾅδης
name to him[c] – death, and – hades

ἠκολούθει μετ᾽ αὐτοῦ, καὶ ἐδόθη αὐτοῖς
followed with him, and [2]was [3]to them
　　　　　　　　　　　　　　given

ἐξουσία ἐπὶ τὸ τέταρτον τῆς γῆς,
[1]authority over the fourth [part] of the earth,

ἀποκτεῖναι ἐν ῥομφαίᾳ καὶ ἐν λιμῷ
to kill with sword and with famine

καὶ ἐν θανάτῳ καὶ ὑπὸ τῶν θηρίων
and with death and by the wild beasts

τῆς γῆς. 9 Καὶ ὅτε ἤνοιξεν τὴν πέμπτην
of the earth. And when he opened the fifth

σφραγῖδα, εἶδον ὑποκάτω τοῦ θυσιαστηρίου
seal, I saw underneath the altar

τὰς ψυχὰς τῶν ἐσφαγμένων διὰ τὸν
the souls of the having been on account the
　　　　　　 [ones] slain of

λόγον τοῦ θεοῦ καὶ διὰ τὴν μαρτυρίαν
word – of God and on the witness
　　　　　　　 account of

ἣν εἶχον. 10 καὶ ἔκραξαν φωνῇ μεγάλῃ
which they had. And they cried [3]voice [1]with a
　　　　　　　　　　　　　　　 great(loud)

λέγοντες· ἕως πότε, ὁ δεσπότης ὁ ἅγιος
saying: Until when, the Master – holy

καὶ ἀληθινός, οὐ κρίνεις καὶ ἐκδικεῖς
and true, judgest thou not and avengest

τὸ αἷμα ἡμῶν ἐκ τῶν κατοικούντων
the blood of us of the [ones] dwelling

ἐπὶ τῆς γῆς; 11 καὶ ἐδόθη αὐτοῖς ἑκάστῳ
on the earth? And [2]was [4]to them [5]each one
　　　　　　　　 given

στολὴ λευκή, καὶ ἐρρέθη αὐτοῖς ἵνα
[2]robe [1]a white, and it was said to them in order
　　　　　　　　　　　　　　　　　 that

ἀναπαύσωνται ἔτι χρόνον μικρόν, ἕως
they should rest yet [2]time [1]a little, until

πληρωθῶσιν καὶ οἱ σύνδουλοι αὐτῶν καὶ
should be fulfilled also the fellow-slaves of them and

οἱ ἀδελφοὶ αὐτῶν οἱ μέλλοντες ἀποκτέν-
the brothers of them the [ones] being about to be

νεσθαι ὡς καὶ αὐτοί. 12 Καὶ εἶδον
killed as also they. And I saw

he had opened the sixth seal, and, lo, there was a great earthquake; and the sun became black as sackcloth of hair, and the moon became as blood;

13 And the stars of heaven fell unto the earth, even as a fig tree casteth her untimely figs, when she is shaken of a mighty wind.

14 And the heaven departed as a scroll when it is rolled together; and every mountain and island were moved out of their places.

15 And the kings of the earth, and the great men, and the rich men, and the chief captains, and the mighty men, and every bondman, and every free man, hid themselves in the dens and in the rocks of the mountains;

16 And said to the mountains and rocks, Fall on us, and hide us from the face of him that sitteth on the throne, and from the wrath of the Lamb:

17 For the great day of his wrath is come; and who shall be able to stand?

ὅτε   ἤνοιξεν   τὴν   σφραγῖδα   τὴν   ἔκτην,
when   he opened   the   ²seal   –   ¹sixth,

καὶ   σεισμὸς   μέγας   ἐγένετο,   καὶ   ὁ   ἥλιος
and   ²earthquake   ¹a great   occurred,   and   the   sun

ἐγένετο   μέλας   ὡς   σάκκος   τρίχινος,   καὶ
became   black   as   sackcloth   made of hair,   and

ἡ   σελήνη   ὅλη   ἐγένετο   ὡς   αἷμα,   13 καὶ
the   ²moon   ¹whole   became   as   blood,   and

οἱ   ἀστέρες   τοῦ   οὐρανοῦ   ἔπεσαν   εἰς   τὴν
the   stars   –   of heaven   fell   to   the

γῆν,   ὡς   συκῆ   βάλλει   τοὺς   ὀλύνθους
earth,   as   a fig-tree   casts   the   unripe figs

αὐτῆς   ὑπὸ   ἀνέμου   μεγάλου   σειομένη,
of it   ³by   ⁴wind   ²a great(strong)   ¹being shaken,

14 καὶ   ὁ   οὐρανὸς   ἀπεχωρίσθη   ὡς   βιβλίον
and   the   heaven   departed   as   a scroll

ἑλισσόμενον,   καὶ   πᾶν   ὄρος   καὶ   νῆσος
being rolled up,   and   every   mountain   and   island

ἐκ   τῶν   τόπων   αὐτῶν   ἐκινήθησαν.   15 καὶ
out   of the   places   of them   were moved.   And

οἱ   βασιλεῖς   τῆς   γῆς   καὶ   οἱ   μεγιστᾶνες
the   kings   of the   earth   and   the   great men

καὶ   οἱ   χιλίαρχοι   καὶ   οἱ   πλούσιοι   καὶ
and   the   chiliarchs   and   the   rich men   and

οἱ   ἰσχυροὶ   καὶ   πᾶς   δοῦλος   καὶ   ἐλεύθερος
the   strong men   and   every   slave   and   free man

ἔκρυψαν   ἑαυτοὺς   εἰς   τὰ   σπήλαια   καὶ
hid   themselves   in   the   caves   and

εἰς   τὰς   πέτρας   τῶν   ὀρέων,   16 καὶ
in   the   rocks   of the   mountains,   and

λέγουσιν   τοῖς   ὄρεσιν   καὶ   ταῖς   πέτραις·
they say   to the   mountains   and   to the   rocks:

πέσετε   ἐφ'   ἡμᾶς   καὶ   κρύψατε   ἡμᾶς
Fall ye   on   us   and   hide   us

ἀπὸ   προσώπου   τοῦ   καθημένου   ἐπὶ   τοῦ
from   [the] face   of the [one]   sitting   on   the

θρόνου   καὶ   ἀπὸ   τῆς   ὀργῆς   τοῦ   ἀρνίου,
throne   and   from   the   wrath   of the   Lamb,

17 ὅτι   ἦλθεν   ἡ   ἡμέρα   ἡ   μεγάλη   τῆς
because   ²came   ¹the   ³day   –   ²great   ⁴of the

ὀργῆς   αὐτῶν,   καὶ   τίς   δύναται   σταθῆναι;
⁵wrath   ⁶of them,   and   who   can   to stand?

CHAPTER 7

AND after these things I saw four angels standing on the four

7 Μετὰ   τοῦτο   εἶδον   τέσσαρας   ἀγγέλους
After   this   I saw   four   angels

ἑστῶτας   ἐπὶ   τὰς   τέσσαρας   γωνίας   τῆς
standing   on   the   four   corners   of the

corners of the earth, holding the four winds of the earth, that the wind should not blow on the earth, nor on the sea, nor on any tree.

2 And I saw another angel ascending from the east, having the seal of the living God: and he cried with a loud voice to the four angels, to whom it was given to hurt the earth and the sea,

3 Saying, Hurt not the earth, neither the sea, nor the trees, till we have sealed the servants of our God in their foreheads.

4 And I heard the number of them which were sealed: *and there were* sealed an hundred *and* forty *and* four thousand of all the tribes of the children of Israel.

5 Of the tribe of Juda *were* sealed twelve thousand. Of the tribe of Reuben *were* sealed twelve thousand. Of the tribe of Gad *were* sealed twelve thousand.

6 Of the tribe of Aser *were* sealed twelve thousand. Of the tribe of Nephthalim *were* sealed twelve thousand. Of the tribe of Manasses *were* sealed twelve thousand.

7 Of the tribe of Simeon *were* sealed twelve thousand. Of the tribe of Levi *were* sealed twelve

γῆς,   κρατοῦντας   τοὺς   τέσσαρας   ἀνέμους
earth,   holding   the   four   winds

τῆς   γῆς,   ἵνα   μὴ   πνέῃ   ἄνεμος   ἐπὶ   τῆς
of the   earth,   in order   ³not   ²should   ¹wind   on   the
     that   ⁴blow

γῆς   μήτε   ἐπὶ   τῆς   θαλάσσης   μήτε   ἐπὶ
earth   nor   on   the   sea   nor   on

πᾶν   δένδρον.   2 καὶ   εἶδον   ἄλλον   ἄγγελον
every(any) tree.   And   I saw   another   angel

ἀναβαίνοντα   ἀπὸ   ἀνατολῆς   ἡλίου,   ἔχοντα
coming up   from   [the] rising   of [the] sun,   having

σφραγῖδα   θεοῦ   ζῶντος,   καὶ   ἔκραξεν   φωνῇ
a seal   God   of [the] living,   and   he cried   ²voice

μεγάλῃ   τοῖς   τέσσαρσιν   ἀγγέλοις   οἷς
¹with a   to the   four   angels   to whom
great(loud)

ἐδόθη   αὐτοῖς   ἀδικῆσαι   τὴν   γῆν   καὶ
it was given   *to them*   to harm   the   earth   and

τὴν   θάλασσαν,   3 λέγων·   μὴ   ἀδικήσητε
the   sea,   saying: Do not harm

τὴν   γῆν   μήτε   τὴν   θάλασσαν   μήτε   τὰ
the   earth   nor   the   sea   nor   the

δένδρα,   ἄχρι   σφραγίσωμεν   τοὺς   δούλους
trees,   until   we *may* seal   the   slaves

τοῦ   θεοῦ   ἡμῶν   ἐπὶ   τῶν   μετώπων   αὐτῶν.
of the   God   of us   on   the   foreheads   , of them.

4 Καὶ   ἤκουσα   τὸν   ἀριθμὸν   τῶν   ἐσφραγισ-
   And   I heard   the   number   of the [ones] *having been*

μένων,   ἑκατὸν   τεσσεράκοντα   τέσσαρες
sealed,   a hundred [and]   forty-four

χιλιάδες   ἐσφραγισμένοι   ἐκ   πάσης   φυλῆς
thousands   *having been* sealed   out of   every   tribe

υἱῶν   Ἰσραήλ·   5 ἐκ   φυλῆς   Ἰούδα   δώδεκα
of sons   of Israel: of [the] tribe   Juda   twelve

χιλιάδες   ἐσφραγισμένοι,   ἐκ   φυλῆς   Ῥουβὴν
thousands   *having been* sealed,   of [the] tribe   Reuben

δώδεκα   χιλιάδες,   ἐκ   φυλῆς   Γὰδ   δώδεκα
twelve   thousands,   of [the] tribe   Gad   twelve

χιλιάδες,   6 ἐκ   φυλῆς   Ἀσὴρ   δώδεκα
thousands,   of [the] tribe   Aser   twelve

χιλιάδες,   ἐκ   φυλῆς   Νεφθαλὶμ   δώδεκα
thousands,   of [the] tribe   Nephthalim   twelve

χιλιάδες,   ἐκ   φυλῆς   Μανασσῆ   δώδεκα
thousands,   of [the] tribe   Manasse   twelve

χιλιάδες,   7 ἐκ   φυλῆς   Συμεὼν   δώδεκα
thousands,   of [the] tribe   Symeon   twelve

χιλιάδες,   ἐκ   φυλῆς   Λευὶ   δώδεκα   χιλιάδες,
thousands,   of [the] tribe   Levi   twelve   thousands,

thousand. Of the tribe of Issachar *were* sealed twelve thousand.

8 Of the tribe of Zabulon *were* sealed twelve thousand. Of the tribe of Joseph *were* sealed twelve thousand. Of the tribe of Benjamin *were* sealed twelve thousand.

9 After this I beheld, and, lo, a great multitude, which no man could number, of all nations, and kindreds, and people, and tongues, stood before the throne, and before the Lamb, clothed with white robes, and palms in their hands;

10 And cried with a loud voice, saying, Salvation to our God which sitteth upon the throne, and unto the Lamb.

11 And all the angels stood round about the throne, and *about* the elders and the four beasts, and fell before the throne on their faces, and worshipped God,

12 Saying, Amen: Blessing, and glory, and wisdom, and thanksgiving, and honour, and power, and might, *be* unto our God for ever and ever. Amen.

13 And one of the

ἐκ φυλῆς Ἰσσαχὰρ δώδεκα χιλιάδες,
of [the] tribe Issachar twelve thousands,

8 ἐκ φυλῆς Ζαβουλὼν δώδεκα χιλιάδες,
of [the] tribe Zabulon twelve thousands,

ἐκ φυλῆς Ἰωσὴφ δώδεκα χιλιάδες, ἐκ
of [the] tribe Joseph twelve thousands, of

φυλῆς Βενιαμίν δώδεκα χιλιάδες ἐσφραγισ-
[the] tribe Benjamin twelve thousands *having been*

μένοι. 9 Μετὰ ταῦτα εἶδον, καὶ ἰδοὺ ὄχλος
sealed. After these things I saw, and behold[,] ²crowd

πολύς, ὃν ἀριθμῆσαι αὐτὸν οὐδεὶς ἐδύνατο,
¹a much which ³to number *it* ¹no one ²was able,
(great),

ἐκ παντὸς ἔθνους καὶ φυλῶν καὶ λαῶν
out of every nation and tribes and peoples

καὶ γλωσσῶν, ἑστῶτες ἐνώπιον τοῦ θρόνου
and tongues, standing before the throne

καὶ ἐνώπιον τοῦ ἀρνίου, περιβεβλημένους
and before the Lamb, *having been* clothed [with]

στολὰς λευκάς, καὶ φοίνικες ἐν ταῖς
²robes ¹white, and palms in the

χερσὶν αὐτῶν· 10 καὶ κράζουσιν φωνῇ
hands of them; and they cry ²voice

μεγάλη λέγοντες· ἡ σωτηρία τῷ θεῷ
¹with a great(loud) saying: – Salvation to the God°

ἡμῶν τῷ καθημένῳ ἐπὶ τῷ θρόνῳ καὶ
of us – sitting on the throne and

τῷ ἀρνίῳ. 11 καὶ πάντες οἱ ἄγγελοι
to the Lamb.° And all the angels

εἱστήκεισαν κύκλῳ τοῦ θρόνου καὶ τῶν
stood round the throne and the

πρεσβυτέρων καὶ τῶν τεσσάρων ζῴων,
elders and the four living creatures,

καὶ ἔπεσαν ἐνώπιον τοῦ θρόνου ἐπὶ
and fell before the throne on

τὰ πρόσωπα αὐτῶν καὶ προσεκύνησαν
the faces of them and worshipped

τῷ θεῷ, 12 λέγοντες· ἀμήν, ἡ εὐλογία
– God, saying: Amen, – blessing

καὶ ἡ δόξα καὶ ἡ σοφία καὶ ἡ εὐχαριστία
and – glory and – wisdom and – thanks

καὶ ἡ τιμὴ καὶ ἡ δύναμις καὶ ἡ ἰσχὺς
and – honour and – power and – strength

τῷ θεῷ ἡμῶν εἰς τοὺς αἰῶνας τῶν
to the God° of us unto the ages of the

αἰώνων· ἀμήν. 13 Καὶ ἀπεκρίθη εἷς
ages: Amen. And ³answered ¹one

elders answered, saying unto me, What are these which are arrayed in white robes? and whence came they?

14 And I said unto him, Sir, thou knowest. And he said to me, These are they which came out of great tribulation, and have washed their robes, and made them white in the blood of the Lamb.

15 Therefore are they before the throne of God, and serve him day and night in his temple: and he that sitteth on the throne shall dwell among them.

16 They shall hunger no more, neither thirst any more; neither shall the sun light on them, nor any heat.

17 For the Lamb which is in the midst of the throne shall feed them, and shall lead them unto living fountains of waters: and God shall wipe away all tears from their eyes.

ἐκ τῶν πρεσβυτέρων λέγων μοι· οὗτοι
²of　³the　　⁴elders　　saying　to me:　These

οἱ περιβεβλημένοι τὰς στολὰς τὰς
the　having been clothed　the　²robes　　−
[ones]　[with]

λευκὰς τίνες εἰσὶν καὶ πόθεν ἦλθον;
¹white　who　are they　and　whence came they?

14 καὶ εἴρηκα αὐτῷ· κύριέ μου, σὺ
And　I have said　to him:　Lord　of me,　thou

οἶδας. καὶ εἶπέν μοι· οὗτοί εἰσιν οἱ
knowest.　And　he told　me:　These　are　the

ἐρχόμενοι ἐκ τῆς θλίψεως τῆς μεγάλης
[ones] coming out of the　²affliction　−　¹great

καὶ ἔπλυναν τὰς στολὰς αὐτῶν καὶ
and　washed　the　robes　of them　and

ἐλεύκαναν αὐτὰς ἐν τῷ αἵματι τοῦ
whitened　them　in　the　blood　of the

ἀρνίου. 15 διὰ τοῦτό εἰσιν ἐνώπιον τοῦ
Lamb.　　Therefore　are they　before　the

θρόνου τοῦ θεοῦ, καὶ λατρεύουσιν αὐτῷ
throne　−　of God,　and　serve　him

ἡμέρας καὶ νυκτὸς ἐν τῷ ναῷ αὐτοῦ,
day　and　night　in　the　shrine　of him,

καὶ ὁ καθήμενος ἐπὶ τοῦ θρόνου σκηνώσει
and the [one] sitting　on　the　throne　will spread
[his] tent

ἐπ' αὐτούς. 16 οὐ πεινάσουσιν ἔτι οὐδὲ
over　them.　They will not hunger　longer　nor

διψήσουσιν ἔτι, οὐδὲ μὴ πέσῃ ἐπ' αὐτοὺς
will they thirst　longer, neither　not　fall　on　them

ὁ ἥλιος οὐδὲ πᾶν καῦμα, 17 ὅτι τὸ
the　sun　nor　every(any)　heat,　because the

ἀρνίον τὸ ἀνὰ μέσον τοῦ θρόνου ποιμανεῖ
Lamb　−　in the midst　of the　throne　will shepherd

αὐτοὺς καὶ ὁδηγήσει αὐτοὺς ἐπὶ ζωῆς
them　and　will lead　them　upon　³of life

πηγὰς ὑδάτων· καὶ ἐξαλείψει ὁ θεὸς
¹fountains　²of waters;　and　²will wipe off　−　¹God

πᾶν δάκρυον ἐκ τῶν ὀφθαλμῶν αὐτῶν.
every　tear　out of the　eyes　of them.

CHAPTER 8

AND when he had opened the seventh seal, there was silence in heaven about the space of half an hour.

2 And I saw the seven

8 Καὶ ὅταν ἤνοιξεν τὴν σφραγῖδα τὴν
And　whenever he opened　the　²seal　−

ἑβδόμην, ἐγένετο σιγὴ ἐν τῷ οὐρανῷ
¹seventh,　occurred　a silence in　−　heaven

ὡς ἡμίωρον. 2 Καὶ εἶδον τοὺς ἑπτὰ
about　a half-hour.　And　I saw　the　seven

angels which stood before God; and to them were given seven trumpets.

3 And another angel came and stood at the altar, having a golden censer; and there was given unto him much incense, that he should offer *it* with the prayers of all saints upon the golden altar which was before the throne.

4 And the smoke of the incense, *which came* with the prayers of the saints, ascended up before God out of the angel's hand.

5 And the angel took the censer, and filled it with fire of the altar, and cast *it* into the earth: and there were voices, and thunderings, and lightnings, and an earthquake.

6 And the seven angels which had the seven trumpets prepared themselves to sound.

7 The first angel sounded, and there followed hail and fire mingled with blood, and they were cast upon the earth: and the third part of trees

ἀγγέλους οἱ ἐνώπιον τοῦ θεοῦ ἑστήκασιν,
angels　who　before　–　God　stood,

καὶ ἐδόθησαν αὐτοῖς ἑπτὰ σάλπιγγες.
and there were given　to them　seven　trumpets.

3 Καὶ ἄλλος ἄγγελος ἦλθεν καὶ ἐστάθη
And another　angel　came　and　stood

ἐπὶ τοῦ θυσιαστηρίου ἔχων λιβανωτὸν
on　the　altar　having　²censer

χρυσοῦν, καὶ ἐδόθη αὐτῷ θυμιάματα πολλά,
¹a golden,　and there was　to him　incenses　many
　　　　　　　given　　　　　　　　　(much),

ἵνα δώσει ταῖς προσευχαῖς τῶν ἁγίων
in order he will　with the　prayers　of ²the　³saints
that　give [it]

πάντων ἐπὶ τὸ θυσιαστήριον τὸ χρυσοῦν
¹all　on　the　²altar　–　¹golden

τὸ ἐνώπιον τοῦ θρόνου. 4 καὶ ἀνέβη
–　before　the　throne.　And　went up

ὁ καπνὸς τῶν θυμιαμάτων ταῖς προσευχαῖς
the smoke of the　incenses　with the　prayers

τῶν ἁγίων ἐκ χειρὸς τοῦ ἀγγέλου ἐνώπιον
of the　saints out of [the] hand of the　angel　before

τοῦ θεοῦ. 5 καὶ εἴληφεν ὁ ἄγγελος
–　God.　And　³has taken ¹the　²angel

τὸν λιβανωτόν, καὶ ἐγέμισεν αὐτὸν ἐκ
the　censer,　and　filled　it　from

τοῦ πυρὸς τοῦ θυσιαστηρίου καὶ ἔβαλεν
the　fire　of the　altar　and　cast

εἰς τὴν γῆν· καὶ ἐγένοντο βρονταὶ καὶ
into　the　earth;　and there occurred thunders　and

φωναὶ καὶ ἀστραπαὶ καὶ σεισμός.
sounds　and　lightnings　and an earthquake.

6 Καὶ οἱ ἑπτὰ ἄγγελοι οἱ ἔχοντες
And　the　seven　angels　–　having

τὰς ἑπτὰ σάλπιγγας ἡτοίμασαν αὐτοὺς
the　seven　trumpets　prepared　themselves

ἵνα σαλπίσωσιν. 7 Καὶ ὁ πρῶτος
in order　they might　And　the　first
that　trumpet.

ἐσάλπισεν· καὶ ἐγένετο χάλαζα καὶ πῦρ
trumpeted;　and there occurred　hail　and　fire

μεμιγμένα ἐν αἵματι καὶ ἐβλήθη εἰς
having been　in　blood　and　it was cast　to
mixed　(with)

τὴν γῆν· καὶ τὸ τρίτον τῆς γῆς
the　earth;　and　the　third [part] of the　earth

κατεκάη, καὶ τὸ τρίτον τῶν δένδρων
was burnt　and　the　third [part] of the　trees
down(up),

was burnt up, and all green grass was burnt up.

8 And the second angel sounded, and as it were a great mountain burning with fire was cast into the sea: and the third part of the sea became blood;

9 And the third part of the creatures which were in the sea, and had life, died; and the third part of the ships were destroyed.

10 And the third angel sounded, and there fell a great star from heaven, burning as it were a lamp, and it fell upon the third part of the rivers, and upon the fountains of waters;

11 And the name of the star is called Wormwood: and the third part of the waters became wormwood; and many men died of the waters, because they were made bitter.

12 And the fourth angel sounded, and the third part of the sun was smitten, and the third part of the moon, and the third part of the stars; so as the third part of them was darkened, and the day shone not for a third part of it, and the night likewise.

κατεκάη, καὶ πᾶς χόρτος χλωρὸς κατεκάη.
was burnt and all ¹grass ¹green was burnt
down(up), down(up).

8 Καὶ ὁ δεύτερος ἄγγελος ἐσάλπισεν·
And the second angel trumpeted;

καὶ ὡς ὄρος μέγα πυρὶ καιόμενον ἐβλήθη
and as ³mountain ¹a great ⁴with fire ²burning was cast

εἰς τὴν θάλασσαν· καὶ ἐγένετο τὸ τρίτον
into the sea; and ⁶became ¹the ²third
[part]

τῆς θαλάσσης αἷμα, 9 καὶ ἀπέθανεν τὸ
³of the ⁴sea ⁵blood, and ¹⁰died ¹the

τρίτον τῶν κτισμάτων τῶν ἐν τῇ θαλάσσῃ,
²third ³of the ⁴creatures – ⁵in ⁶the ⁷sea,
[part]

τὰ ἔχοντα ψυχάς, καὶ τὸ τρίτον τῶν
– ⁸having ⁹souls, and the third [part] of the

πλοίων διεφθάρησαν. 10 Καὶ ὁ τρίτος
ships were destroyed. And the third

ἄγγελος ἐσάλπισεν· καὶ ἔπεσεν ἐκ τοῦ
angel trumpeted; and fell out of –

οὐρανοῦ ἀστὴρ μέγας καιόμενος ὡς
heaven star a great burning as

λαμπάς, καὶ ἔπεσεν ἐπὶ τὸ τρίτον τῶν
a lamp, and it fell onto the third [part] of the

ποταμῶν καὶ ἐπὶ τὰς πηγὰς τῶν ὑδάτων.
rivers and onto the fountains of the waters.

11 καὶ τὸ ὄνομα τοῦ ἀστέρος λέγεται
And the name of the star is said(called)

ὁ Ἄψινθος. καὶ ἐγένετο τὸ τρίτον τῶν
– Wormwood. And ⁵became ¹the ²third ³of
[part] the

ὑδάτων εἰς ἄψινθον, καὶ πολλοὶ τῶν
⁴waters into wormwood, and many of the

ἀνθρώπων ἀπέθανον ἐκ τῶν ὑδάτων ὅτι
men died from the waters because

ἐπικράνθησαν. 12 Καὶ ὁ τέταρτος ἄγγελος
they were made bitter. And the fourth angel

ἐσάλπισεν· καὶ ἐπλήγη τὸ τρίτον τοῦ
trumpeted; and ⁶was struck ¹the ²third [part] ³of the

ἡλίου καὶ τὸ τρίτον τῆς σελήνης καὶ
⁴sun and the third [part] of the moon and

τὸ τρίτον τῶν ἀστέρων, ἵνα σκοτισθῇ
the third of the stars, in order ⁴might be
[part] that darkened

τὸ τρίτον αὐτῶν καὶ ἡ ἡμέρα μὴ φάνῃ
¹the ²third [part] ³of them and the day might not appear

τὸ τρίτον αὐτῆς, καὶ ἡ νὺξ ὁμοίως.
the third [part] of it, and the night likewise.

13 And I beheld, and heard an angel flying through the midst of heaven, saying with a loud voice, Woe, woe, woe, to the inhabiters of the earth by reason of the other voices of the trumpet of the three angels, which are yet to sound!

13 Καὶ εἶδον, καὶ ἤκουσα ἑνὸς ἀετοῦ
And   I saw,   and   I heard   one   eagle

πετομένου ἐν μεσουρανήματι λέγοντος φωνῇ
flying   in   mid-heaven   saying   ²voice

μεγάλῃ· οὐαὶ οὐαὶ οὐαὶ τοὺς κατοικοῦν-
¹with a   Woe[,]   woe[,]   woe   to the [ones]   dwell-
great(loud):

τας ἐπὶ τῆς γῆς ἐκ τῶν λοιπῶν φωνῶν
ing   on   the   earth   from   the   remaining   voices

τῆς σάλπιγγος τῶν τριῶν ἀγγέλων τῶν
of the   trumpet   of the   three   angels   –

μελλόντων σαλπίζειν.
being about   to trumpet.

CHAPTER 9

AND the fifth angel sounded, and I saw a star fall from heaven unto the earth: and to him was given the key of the bottomless pit.

2 And he opened the bottomless pit; and there arose a smoke out of the pit, as the smoke of a great furnace; and the sun and the air were darkened by reason of the smoke of the pit.

3 And there came out of the smoke locusts upon the earth: and unto them was given power, as the scorpions of the earth have power.

4 And it was commanded them that they should not hurt the grass of the earth, neither any green thing, neither any tree; but only those men which have not the seal of God in their foreheads.

9 Καὶ ὁ πέμπτος ἄγγελος ἐσάλπισεν·
And   the   fifth   angel   trumpeted;

καὶ εἶδον ἀστέρα ἐκ τοῦ οὐρανοῦ πεπτω-
and   I saw   a star   out of   –   heaven   having

κότα εἰς τὴν γῆν, καὶ ἐδόθη αὐτῷ
fallen   onto   the   earth,   and   was given   to it

ἡ κλεὶς τοῦ φρέατος τῆς ἀβύσσου. 2 καὶ
the   key   of the   shaft   of the   abyss.   And

ἤνοιξεν τὸ φρέαρ τῆς ἀβύσσου· καὶ
he opened   the   shaft   of the   abyss;   and

ἀνέβη καπνὸς ἐκ τοῦ φρέατος ὡς
went up   a smoke   out of   the   shaft   as

καπνὸς καμίνου μεγάλης, καὶ ἐσκοτώθη
smoke   ²furnace   ¹of a great,   and   ⁸was darkened

ὁ ἥλιος καὶ ὁ ἀὴρ ἐκ τοῦ καπνοῦ
¹the   ²sun   ³and   ⁴the   ⁵air   by   the   smoke

τοῦ φρέατος. 3 καὶ ἐκ τοῦ καπνοῦ
of the   shaft.   And out of   the   smoke

ἐξῆλθον ἀκρίδες εἰς τὴν γῆν, καὶ ἐδόθη
came forth   locusts   to   the   earth,   and ³was given

αὐτοῖς ἐξουσία ὡς ἔχουσιν ἐξουσίαν οἱ
²to them   ¹authority   as   ⁵have   ⁶authority   ¹the

σκορπίοι τῆς γῆς. 4 καὶ ἐρρέθη αὐτοῖς
²scorpions   ³of the   ⁴earth.   And   it was said   to them

ἵνα μὴ ἀδικήσουσιν τὸν χόρτον τῆς
in order   they shall not harm   the   grass   of the
that

γῆς οὐδὲ πᾶν χλωρὸν οὐδὲ πᾶν δένδρον,
earth   nor   every   greenstuff   nor   every   tree,
(any)   (any)

εἰ μὴ τοὺς ἀνθρώπους οἵτινες οὐκ ἔχουσιν
except   the   men   who   have not

τὴν σφραγῖδα τοῦ θεοῦ ἐπὶ τῶν μετώπων.
the   seal   –   of God   on   the(ir)   foreheads.

5 And to them it was given that they should not kill them, but that they should be tormented five months: and their torment *was* as the torment of a scorpion, when he striketh a man.

6 And in those days shall men seek death, and shall not find it: and shall desire to die, and death shall flee from them.

7 And the shapes of the locusts *were* like unto horses prepared unto battle; and on their heads *were* as it were crowns like gold, and their faces *were* as the faces of men.

8 And they had hair as the hair of women, and their teeth were as *the teeth* of lions.

9 And they had breastplates, as it were breastplates of iron; and the sound of their wings *was* as the sound of chariots of many horses running to battle.

10 And they had tails like unto scorpions, and there were stings in their tails: and their power *was* to hurt men five months.

11 And they had a king over them, *which is* the angel of the bottom-

5 καὶ   ἐδόθη   αὐτοῖς   ἵνα   μὴ   ἀποκτείνωσιν
And   it was   to them   *in order*   they should not kill
        given   *that*

αὐτούς,   ἀλλ'   ἵνα   βασανισθήσονται   μῆνας
them,   but   *in order*   they shall be tormented   ⁵months
                 that

πέντε·   καὶ   ὁ   βασανισμὸς   αὐτῶν   ὡς
⁴five;   and   the   torment   of them   [is] as

βασανισμὸς   σκορπίου,   ὅταν   παίσῃ   ἄνθρωπον.
[the] torment   of a scorpion,   whenever it stings   a man.

6 καὶ   ἐν   ταῖς   ἡμέραις   ἐκείναις   ζητήσουσιν
And   in   those days   ²will seek

οἱ   ἄνθρωποι   τὸν   θάνατον   καὶ   οὐ   μὴ
–   ¹men   –   death   and   by no means

εὑρήσουσιν   αὐτόν,   καὶ   ἐπιθυμήσουσιν
will they find   it,   and   they will long

ἀποθανεῖν   καὶ   φεύγει   ὁ   θάνατος   ἀπ'
to die   and   ²flees   –   ¹death   from

αὐτῶν.   7 καὶ   τὰ   ὁμοιώματα   τῶν   ἀκρίδων
them.   And   the   likeness*es*   of the   locusts

ὅμοιοι   ἵπποις   ἡτοιμασμένοις   εἰς   πόλεμον,
like   to horses   *having been* prepared   for   war,

καὶ   ἐπὶ   τὰς   κεφαλὰς   αὐτῶν   ὡς   στέφανοι
and   on   the   heads   of them   as   crowns

ὅμοιοι   χρυσῷ,   καὶ   τὰ   πρόσωπα   αὐτῶν
like   to gold,   and   the   faces   of them

ὡς   πρόσωπα   ἀνθρώπων,   8 καὶ   εἶχον
as   faces   of men,   and   they had

τρίχας   ὡς   τρίχας   γυναικῶν,   καὶ   οἱ
hairs   as   hairs   of women,   and   the

ὀδόντες   αὐτῶν   ὡς   λεόντων   ἦσαν,   9 καὶ
teeth   of them   ²as   ³of lions   ¹were,   and

εἶχον   θώρακας   ὡς   θώρακας   σιδηροῦς,
they had   breastplates   as   ²breastplates   ¹iron,

καὶ   ἡ   φωνὴ   τῶν   πτερύγων   αὐτῶν   ὡς
and   the   sound   of the   wings   of them   as

φωνὴ   ἁρμάτων   ἵππων   πολλῶν   τρεχόντων
sound   ²chariots   ³of horses   ¹of many   running

εἰς   πόλεμον.   10 καὶ   ἔχουσιν   οὐρὰς   ὁμοίας
to   war.   And   they have   tails   like

σκορπίοις   καὶ   κέντρα,   καὶ   ἐν   ταῖς   οὐραῖς
to scorpions   and   stings,   and   ⁶with   ⁷the   ⁸tails

αὐτῶν   ἡ   ἐξουσία   αὐτῶν   ἀδικῆσαι   τοὺς
⁵of them   ¹the   ²authority   ³of them   ⁴[is] to harm   –

ἀνθρώπους   μῆνας   πέντε.   11 ἔχουσιν   ἐπ'
⁹men   ¹¹months   ¹⁰five.   They have   over

αὐτῶν   βασιλέα   τὸν   ἄγγελον   τῆς   ἀβύσσου,
them   a king   the   angel   of the   abyss,

less pit, whose name in the Hebrew tongue *is* Abaddon, but in the Greek tongue hath *his* name Apollyon.

12 One woe is past; *and*, behold, there come two woes more hereafter.

13 And the sixth angel sounded, and I heard a voice from the four horns of the golden altar which is before God,

14 Saying to the sixth angel which had the trumpet, Loose the four angels which are bound in the great river Euphrates.

15 And the four angels were loosed, which were prepared for an hour, and a day, and a month, and a year, for to slay the third part of men.

16 And the number of the army of the horsemen *were* two hundred thousand thousand: and I heard the number of them.

17 And thus I saw the horses in the vision, and them that sat on them, having breastplates of fire, and of jacinth, and brimstone: and the heads of the horses *were* as the heads of lions; and out of their mouths issued fire and smoke and brimstone.

ὄνομα αὐτῷ Ἑβραϊστὶ Ἀβαδδών, καὶ
name to him° in Hebrew Abaddon, and

ἐν τῇ Ἑλληνικῇ ὄνομα ἔχει Ἀπολλύων.
in the Greek ²[the] name ¹he has Apollyon.

12 Ἡ οὐαὶ ἡ μία ἀπῆλθεν· ἰδοὺ ἔρχεται
The ²woe - ¹one(first) passed away; behold ⁴comes

ἔτι δύο οὐαὶ μετὰ ταῦτα.
¹yet ²two ³woes after these things.

13 Καὶ ὁ ἕκτος ἄγγελος ἐσάλπισεν·
And the sixth angel trumpeted;

καὶ ἤκουσα φωνὴν μίαν ἐκ τῶν τεσσάρων
and I heard ²voice ¹one out of the four

κεράτων τοῦ θυσιαστηρίου τοῦ χρυσοῦ
horns of the ²altar - ¹golden

τοῦ ἐνώπιον τοῦ θεοῦ, 14 λέγοντα τῷ
- before - God, saying to the

ἕκτῳ ἀγγέλῳ, ὁ ἔχων τὴν σάλπιγγα·
sixth angel, - having the trumpet:

λῦσον τοὺς τέσσαρας ἀγγέλους τοὺς
Loose the four angels -

δεδεμένους ἐπὶ τῷ ποταμῷ τῷ μεγάλῳ
having been bound at the ²river - ¹great

Εὐφράτῃ. 15 καὶ ἐλύθησαν οἱ τέσσαρες
Euphrates. And were loosed the four

ἄγγελοι οἱ ἡτοιμασμένοι εἰς τὴν ὥραν
angels - *having been* prepared for the hour

καὶ ἡμέραν καὶ μῆνα καὶ ἐνιαυτόν,
and day and month and year,

ἵνα ἀποκτείνωσιν τὸ τρίτον τῶν ἀνθρώπων.
in or- they should kill the third - of men.
der that [part]

16 καὶ ὁ ἀριθμὸς τῶν στρατευμάτων τοῦ
And the number of the bodies of soldiers of the

ἱππικοῦ δισμυριάδες μυριάδων· ἤκουσα τὸν
cavalry [was] two myriads of myriads; I heard the

ἀριθμὸν αὐτῶν. 17 καὶ οὕτως εἶδον
number of them. And thus I saw

τοὺς ἵππους ἐν τῇ ὁράσει καὶ τοὺς
the horses in the vision and the

καθημένους ἐπ᾽ αὐτῶν, ἔχοντας θώρακας
[ones] sitting on them, having breastplates

πυρίνους καὶ ὑακινθίνους καὶ θειώδεις·
fire-coloured and dusky red and sulphurous;

καὶ αἱ κεφαλαὶ τῶν ἵππων ὡς κεφαλαὶ
and the heads of the horses as heads

λεόντων, καὶ ἐκ τῶν στομάτων αὐτῶν
of lions, and out of the mouths of them

ἐκπορεύεται πῦρ καὶ καπνὸς καὶ θεῖον.
proceeds fire and smoke and sulphur.

18 By these three was the third part of men killed, by the fire, and by the smoke, and by the brimstone, which issued out of their mouths.

19 For their power is in their mouth, and in their tails: for their tails *were* like unto serpents, and had heads, and with them they do hurt.

20 And the rest of the men which were not killed by these plagues yet repented not of the works of their hands, that they should not worship devils, and idols of gold, and silver, and brass, and stone, and of wood: which neither can see, nor hear, nor walk:

21 Neither repented they of their murders, nor of their sorceries, nor of their fornication, nor of their thefts.

18 ἀπὸ τῶν τριῶν πληγῶν τούτων ἀπεκτάν-
From   the   ²three   ³plagues   ¹these   were

θησαν   τὸ   τρίτον   τῶν   ἀνθρώπων,   ἐκ
killed   the   third [part]   –   of men,   by

τοῦ   πυρὸς   καὶ   τοῦ   καπνοῦ   καὶ   τοῦ
the   fire   and   the   smoke   and   the

θείου   τοῦ   ἐκπορευομένου   ἐκ   τῶν   στομάτων
sulphur   –   proceeding   out of   the   mouths

αὐτῶν.   19 ἡ   γὰρ   ἐξουσία   τῶν   ἵππων
of them.   For the   authority   of the   horses

ἐν   τῷ   στόματι   αὐτῶν   ἐστιν   καὶ   ἐν
¹in   ³the   ⁴mouth   ⁵of them   ¹is   and   in

ταῖς   οὐραῖς   αὐτῶν·   αἱ   γὰρ   οὐραὶ   αὐτῶν
the   tails   of them;   for the   tails   of them

ὅμοιαι   ὄφεσιν,   ἔχουσαι   κεφαλάς,   καὶ   ἐν
[are] like   to serpents,   having   heads,   and with

αὐταῖς   ἀδικοῦσιν.   20 καὶ   οἱ   λοιποὶ   τῶν
them   they do harm.   And   the   rest   –

ἀνθρώπων,   οἳ   οὐκ   ἀπεκτάνθησαν   ἐν   ταῖς
of men,   who   were not killed   by   the

πληγαῖς   ταύταις,   οὐδὲ   μετενόησαν   ἐκ
plagues   these,   not even   repented   of

τῶν   ἔργων   τῶν   χειρῶν   αὐτῶν,   ἵνα   μὴ
the   works   of the   hands   of them,   in order not that

προσκυνήσουσιν   τὰ   δαιμόνια   καὶ   τὰ   εἴδωλα
they will worship   –   demons   and   –   idols

τὰ   χρυσᾶ   καὶ   τὰ   ἀργυρᾶ   καὶ   τὰ   χαλκᾶ
–   golden   and   –   silver   and   –   bronze

καὶ   τὰ   λίθινα   καὶ   τὰ   ξύλινα,   ἃ   οὔτε
and   –   stone   and   –   wooden,   which   ²neither

βλέπειν   δύνανται   οὔτε   ἀκούειν   οὔτε
³to see   ¹can   nor   to hear   nor

περιπατεῖν,   21 καὶ   οὐ   μετενόησαν   ἐκ   τῶν
to walk,   and   they repented not   of   the

φόνων   αὐτῶν   οὔτε   ἐκ   τῶν   φαρμακειῶν
murders   of them   nor   of   the   sorceries

αὐτῶν   οὔτε   ἐκ   τῆς   πορνείας   αὐτῶν
of them   nor   of   the   fornication   of them

οὔτε   ἐκ   τῶν   κλεμμάτων   αὐτῶν.
nor   of   the   thefts   of them.

CHAPTER 10

AND I saw another mighty angel come down from heaven, clothed with a cloud: and a rainbow *was* upon his head,

10 Καὶ   εἶδον   ἄλλον   ἄγγελον   ἰσχυρὸν
And   I saw   another   ²angel   ¹strong

καταβαίνοντα   ἐκ   τοῦ   οὐρανοῦ,   περιβεβλημέ-
coming down   out of   –   heaven,   *having been* clothed

νον   νεφέλην,   καὶ   ἡ   ἶρις   ἐπὶ   τὴν   κεφαλὴν
[with] a cloud,   and   the rainbow   on   the   head

and his face *was* as it were the sun, and his feet as pillars of fire:

2 And he had in his hand a little book open: and he set his right foot upon the sea, and *his* left *foot* on the earth,

3 And cried with a loud voice, as *when* a lion roareth: and when he had cried, seven thunders uttered their voices.

4 And when the seven thunders had uttered their voices, I was about to write: and I heard a voice from heaven saying unto me, Seal up those things which the seven thunders uttered, and write them not.

5 And the angel which I saw stand upon the sea and upon the earth lifted up his hand to heaven,

6 And sware by him that liveth for ever and ever, who created heaven, and the things that therein are, and the earth, and the things that therein are, and the sea, and the things which are therein, that there should be time no longer:

7 But in the days of the voice of the seventh angel, when he shall begin to

αὐτοῦ,   καὶ   τὸ   πρόσωπον   αὐτοῦ   ὡς   ὁ
of him,   and   the   face   of him   as   the

ἥλιος,   καὶ   οἱ   πόδες   αὐτοῦ   ὡς   στῦλοι
sun,   and   the   feet   of him   as   pillars

πυρός,   2 καὶ   ἔχων   ἐν   τῇ   χειρὶ   αὐτοῦ
of fire,   and   having   in   the   hand   of him

βιβλαρίδιον   ἠνεῳγμένον.   καὶ   ἔθηκεν   τὸν
a little scroll   *having been* opened.   And   he placed   [1]the

πόδα   αὐτοῦ   τὸν   δεξιὸν   ἐπὶ   τῆς   θαλάσσης,
[3]foot   [4]of him   –   [2]right   on   the   sea,

τὸν   δὲ   εὐώνυμον   ἐπὶ   τῆς   γῆς,   3 καὶ
and the   left   on   the   land,   and

ἔκραξεν   φωνῇ   μεγάλῃ   ὥσπερ   λέων   μυκᾶται.
cried   [2]voice   [1]with a   as   a lion   roars.
     great(loud)

καὶ   ὅτε   ἔκραξεν,   ἐλάλησαν   αἱ   ἑπτὰ
And   when   he cried,   [4]spoke(uttered)   [1]the   [3]seven

βρονταὶ   τὰς   ἑαυτῶν   φωνάς.   4 Καὶ   ὅτε
[2]thunders   [5]the   [6]of them*selves*   [7]voices.   And   when

ἐλάλησαν   αἱ   ἑπτὰ   βρονταί,   ἤμελλον
spoke   the   seven   thunders,   I was about

γράφειν·   καὶ   ἤκουσα   φωνὴν   ἐκ   τοῦ
to write;   and   I heard   a voice   out of   –

οὐρανοῦ   λέγουσαν·   σφράγισον   ἃ   ἐλάλησαν
heaven   saying: Seal thou   [the]   [4]spoke
     things which

αἱ   ἑπτὰ   βρονταί,   καὶ   μὴ   αὐτὰ   γράψῃς.
[1]the   [2]seven   [3]thunders,   and   [5]not   [6]them   *thou mayest*
     [7]write.

5 Καὶ   ὁ   ἄγγελος,   ὃν   εἶδον   ἑστῶτα
And   the   angel,   whom   I saw   standing

ἐπὶ   τῆς   θαλάσσης   καὶ   ἐπὶ   τῆς   γῆς,
on   the   sea   and   on   the   land,

ἦρεν   τὴν   χεῖρα   αὐτοῦ   τὴν   δεξιὰν   εἰς
lifted   [1]the   [3]hand   [4]of him   –   [2]right   to

τὸν   οὐρανόν,   6 καὶ   ὤμοσεν   ἐν   τῷ   ζῶντι
–   heaven,   and   swore   by the [one] living

εἰς   τοὺς   αἰῶνας   τῶν   αἰώνων,   ὃς   ἔκτισεν
unto   the   ages   of the   ages,   who   created

τὸν   οὐρανὸν   καὶ   τὰ   ἐν   αὐτῷ   καὶ   τὴν
the   heaven   and the things in   it   and   the

γῆν   καὶ   τὰ   ἐν   αὐτῇ   καὶ   τὴν   θάλασσαν
earth   and   the   in   it   and   the   sea
     things

καὶ   τὰ   ἐν   αὐτῇ,   ὅτι   χρόνος   οὐκέτι
and the things in   it,   that   time   [2]no longer

ἔσται,   7 ἀλλ᾽   ἐν   ταῖς   ἡμέραις   τῆς
[1]shall be,   but   in   the   days   of the

φωνῆς   τοῦ   ἑβδόμου   ἀγγέλου,   ὅταν   μέλλῃ
voice   of the   seventh   angel,   whenever he is about

sound, the mystery of God should be finished, as he hath declared to his servants the prophets.

8 And the voice which I heard from heaven spake unto me again, and said, Go *and* take the little book which is open in the hand of the angel which standeth upon the sea and upon the earth.

9 And I went unto the angel, and said unto him, Give me the little book. And he said unto me, Take *it*, and eat it up; and it shall make thy belly bitter, but it shall be in thy mouth sweet as honey.

10 And I took the little book out of the angel's hand, and ate it up; and it was in my mouth sweet as honey: and as soon as I had eaten it, my belly was bitter.

11 And he said unto me, Thou must prophesy again before many peoples, and nations, and tongues, and kings.

CHAPTER 11

A ND there was given me a reed like unto a rod: and the angel stood, saying, Rise, and measure the temple of God, and the altar, and them that worship therein.

2 But the court which is

σαλπίζειν, καὶ ἐτελέσθη τὸ μυστήριον
to trumpet, even was finished the mystery

τοῦ θεοῦ, ὡς εὐηγγέλισεν τοὺς ἑαυτοῦ
- of God, as he preached [to] the [2]of him*self*

δούλους τοὺς προφήτας. **8** Καὶ ἡ φωνὴ
[1]slaves the prophets. And the voice

ἣν ἤκουσα ἐκ τοῦ οὐρανοῦ, πάλιν
which I heard out of - heaven, again

λαλοῦσαν μετ' ἐμοῦ καὶ λέγουσαν· ὕπαγε
speaking with me and saying: Go thou

λάβε τὸ βιβλίον τὸ ἠνεῳγμένον ἐν τῇ
take the scroll - *having been* opened in the

χειρὶ τοῦ ἀγγέλου τοῦ ἑστῶτος ἐπὶ
hand of the angel - standing on

τῆς θαλάσσης καὶ ἐπὶ τῆς γῆς. **9** καὶ
the sea and on the land. And

ἀπῆλθα πρὸς τὸν ἄγγελον, λέγων αὐτῷ
I went away toward the angel, telling him

δοῦναί μοι τὸ βιβλαρίδιον. καὶ λέγει
to give me the little scroll. And he says

μοι· λάβε καὶ κατάφαγε αὐτό, καὶ
to me: Take and devour it, and

πικρανεῖ σου τὴν κοιλίαν, ἀλλ' ἐν τῷ
it will embitter [3]of thee [1]the [2]stomach, but in the

στόματί σου ἔσται γλυκὺ ὡς μέλι.
mouth of thee it will be sweet as honey.

10 καὶ ἔλαβον τὸ βιβλαρίδιον ἐκ τῆς
And I took the little scroll out of the

χειρὸς τοῦ ἀγγέλου καὶ κατέφαγον αὐτό,
hand of the angel and devoured it,

καὶ ἦν ἐν τῷ στόματί μου ὡς μέλι
and it was in the mouth of me as [2]honey

γλυκύ· καὶ ὅτε ἔφαγον αὐτό, ἐπικράνθη
[1]sweet; and when I ate it, [4]was made bitter

ἡ κοιλία μου. **11** καὶ λέγουσίν μοι·
[1]the [2]stomach [3]of me. And they say to me:

δεῖ σε πάλιν προφητεῦσαι ἐπὶ λαοῖς
It behoves thee again to prophesy before peoples

καὶ ἔθνεσιν καὶ γλώσσαις καὶ βασιλεῦσιν
and nations and tongues and [2]kings

πολλοῖς. **11** Καὶ ἐδόθη μοι κάλαμος ὅμοιος
[1]many. And was given to me a reed like

ῥάβδῳ, λέγων· ἔγειρε καὶ μέτρησον τὸν ναὸν
to a staff, saying: Rise and measure the shrine

τοῦ θεοῦ καὶ τὸ θυσιαστήριον καὶ τοὺς
- of God and the altar and the

προσκυνοῦντας ἐν αὐτῷ. **2** καὶ τὴν
[ones] worshipping in it. And the

without the temple leave out, and measure it not; for it is given unto the Gentiles; and the holy city shall they tread under foot forty *and* two months.

3 And I will give *power* unto my two witnesses, and they shall prophesy a thousand two hundred *and* threescore days, clothed in sackcloth.

4 These are the two olive trees, and the two candlesticks standing before the God of the earth.

5 And if any man will hurt them, fire proceedeth out of their mouth, and devoureth their enemies: and if any man will hurt them, he must in this manner be killed.

6 These have power to shut heaven, that it rain not in the days of their prophecy: and have power over waters to turn them to blood, and to smite the earth with all plagues, as often as they will.

7 And when they shall have finished their testimony, the beast that ascendeth out of the bottomless pit shall make war

αὐλὴν   τὴν   ἔξωθεν   τοῦ   ναοῦ   ἔκβαλε
¹court   –   ¹outside   of the   shrine   cast *out*

ἔξωθεν   καὶ   μὴ   αὐτὴν   μετρήσῃς,   ὅτι
outside   and   ²not   ²it   thou mayest   because
                                 ¹measure,

ἐδόθη   τοῖς   ἔθνεσιν,   καὶ   τὴν   πόλιν   τὴν
it was given to the   nations,   and   the   ²city   –

ἀγίαν   πατήσουσιν   μῆνας   τεσσεράκοντα
¹holy   they will trample   ³months   ¹forty-

[καὶ]   δύο.   3 καὶ   δώσω   τοῖς   δυσὶν
and   ²two.   And   I will give   to the   two

μάρτυσίν   μου,   καὶ   προφητεύσουσιν   ἡμέρας
witnesses   of me,   and   they will prophesy   ⁵days

χιλίας   διακοσίας   ἑξήκοντα   περιβεβλημένοι
¹a thousand   ²two hundred   ³[and] ⁴sixty   having been clothed

σάκκους.   4 οὗτοί   εἰσιν   αἱ   δύο   ἐλαῖαι
[in] sackclothes.   These   are   the   two   olive-trees

καὶ   αἱ   δύο   λυχνίαι   αἱ   ἐνώπιον   τοῦ
and   the   two   lampstands   –   ²before   ³the

κυρίου   τῆς   γῆς   ἑστῶτες.   5 καὶ   εἴ   τις
⁴Lord   ⁵of the   ⁶earth   ¹standing.   And   if anyone

αὐτοὺς   θέλει   ἀδικῆσαι,   πῦρ   ἐκπορεύεται
³them   ¹wishes   ²to harm,   fire   proceeds

ἐκ   τοῦ   στόματος   αὐτῶν   καὶ   κατεσθίει
out of the   mouth   of them   and   devours

τοὺς   ἐχθροὺς   αὐτῶν·   καὶ   εἴ   τις   θελήσῃ
the   enemies   of them;   and   if anyone should wish

αὐτοὺς   ἀδικῆσαι,   οὕτως   δεῖ   αὐτὸν
³them   ¹to harm,   thus   it behoves   him

ἀποκτανθῆναι.   6 οὗτοι   ἔχουσιν   τὴν   ἐξουσίαν
to be killed.   These   have   the   authority

κλεῖσαι   τὸν   οὐρανόν,   ἵνα   μὴ   ὑετὸς
to shut   –   heaven,   in order that ²not   ¹rain

βρέχῃ   τὰς   ἡμέρας   τῆς   προφητείας   αὐτῶν,
³may   the   days   of the   prophecy   of them,
⁴rain(fall)

καὶ   ἐξουσίαν   ἔχουσιν   ἐπὶ   τῶν   ὑδάτων
and   authority   they have   over   the   waters

στρέφειν   αὐτὰ   εἰς   αἷμα   καὶ   πατάξαι
to turn   them   into   blood   and   to strike

τὴν   γῆν   ἐν   πάσῃ   πληγῇ   ὁσάκις   ἐὰν
the   earth   with   every [kind of] plague   as often as

θελήσωσιν.   7 Καὶ   ὅταν   τελέσωσιν   τὴν
they may wish.   And   whenever   they finish   the

μαρτυρίαν   αὐτῶν,   τὸ   θηρίον   τὸ   ἀναβαῖνον
witness   of them,   the   beast   –   coming up

ἐκ   τῆς   ἀβύσσου   ποιήσει   μετ'   αὐτῶν
out of the   abyss   ¹will make   ²with   ⁴them

against them, and shall overcome them, and kill them.

8 And their dead bodies *shall lie* in the street of the great city, which spiritually is called Sodom and Egypt, where also our Lord was crucified.

9 And they of the people and kindreds and tongues and nations shall see their dead bodies three days and an half, and shall not suffer their dead bodies to be put in graves.

10 And they that dwell upon the earth shall rejoice over them, and make merry, and shall send gifts one to another; because these two prophets tormented them that dwelt on the earth.

11 And after three days and an half the Spirit of life from God entered into them, and they stood upon their feet; and great fear fell upon them which saw them.

12 And they heard a great voice from heaven saying unto them, Come up hither. And they ascended up to heaven in a cloud; and their enemies beheld them.

13 And the same hour

πόλεμον καὶ νικήσει αὐτοὺς καὶ ἀποκτενεῖ
²war   and will overcome them   and   will kill

αὐτούς.   8 καὶ   τὸ   πτῶμα αὐτῶν ἐπὶ
them.   And the corpse of them on

τῆς πλατείας τῆς πόλεως τῆς μεγάλης,
the open street of the ²city   - ¹great,

ἥτις καλεῖται πνευματικῶς Σόδομα καὶ
which is called spiritually Sodom and

Αἴγυπτος, ὅπου καὶ ὁ κύριος αὐτῶν
Egypt,   where indeed the Lord of them

ἐσταυρώθη.   9 καὶ βλέπουσιν ἐκ τῶν
was crucified.   And ¹⁰see   ¹[some] of ²the

λαῶν   καὶ   φυλῶν καὶ γλωσσῶν καὶ
³peoples ⁴and ⁵tribes ⁶and ⁷tongues ⁸and

ἐθνῶν   τὸ   πτῶμα αὐτῶν ἡμέρας τρεῖς
⁹nations the corpse of them ⁴days ¹three

καὶ   ἥμισυ, καὶ τὰ   πτώματα αὐτῶν
²and ³a half, and ²the ³corpses ⁴of them

οὐκ ἀφίουσιν τεθῆναι εἰς μνῆμα.   10 καὶ
¹they do not allow to be placed in a tomb.   And

οἱ κατοικοῦντες ἐπὶ τῆς γῆς χαίρουσιν
the [ones] dwelling on the earth rejoice

ἐπ᾽ αὐτοῖς καὶ εὐφραίνονται, καὶ δῶρα
over them and are glad,   and ²gifts

πέμψουσιν ἀλλήλοις, ὅτι οὗτοι οἱ δύο
¹they will send to one another, because these - two

προφῆται ἐβασάνισαν τοὺς κατοικοῦντας
prophets   tormented   the [ones]   dwelling

ἐπὶ τῆς γῆς. 11 Καὶ μετὰ [τὰς] τρεῖς
on the earth.   And after the   ¹three

ἡμέρας καὶ ἥμισυ πνεῦμα ζωῆς ἐκ τοῦ
⁴days   ²and ³a half a spirit of life out of -

θεοῦ εἰσῆλθεν ἐν αὐτοῖς, καὶ ἔστησαν
God entered in[to] them, and they stood

ἐπὶ τοὺς πόδας αὐτῶν, καὶ φόβος μέγας
on the   feet of them, and ²fear ¹great

ἐπέπεσεν ἐπὶ τοὺς θεωροῦντας αὐτούς.
fell on   on the [ones] beholding   them.

12 καὶ ἤκουσαν φωνῆς μεγάλης ἐκ τοῦ
And they heard ²voice ¹a great(loud) out of -

οὐρανοῦ λεγούσης αὐτοῖς· ἀνάβατε ὧδε·
heaven   saying   to them: Come ye up here;

καὶ ἀνέβησαν εἰς τὸν οὐρανὸν ἐν τῇ
and they went up to   -   heaven in the

νεφέλῃ, καὶ ἐθεώρησαν αὐτοὺς οἱ ἐχθροὶ
cloud, and ⁴beheld   ⁵them ¹the ²enemies

αὐτῶν. 13 Καὶ ἐν ἐκείνῃ τῇ ὥρᾳ ἐγένετο
²of them. And in that   - hour ²occurred

was there a great earthquake, and the tenth part of the city fell, and in the earthquake were slain of men seven thousand: and the remnant were affrighted, and gave glory to the God of heaven.

14 The second woe is past; *and*, behold, the third woe cometh quickly.

15 And the seventh angel sounded; and there were great voices in heaven, saying, The kingdoms of this world are become *the kingdoms* of our Lord, and of his Christ; and he shall reign for ever and ever.

16 And the four and twenty elders, which sat before God on their seats, fell upon their faces, and worshipped God,

17 Saying, We give thee thanks, O Lord God Almighty, which art, and wast, and art to come; because thou hast taken to thee thy great power, and hast reigned.

18 And the nations were angry, and thy wrath is come, and the time of the dead, that they should be judged, and that thou shouldest give reward unto

σεισμὸς μέγας, καὶ τὸ δέκατον τῆς
⁸earthquake ¹a great, and the tenth [part] of the

πόλεως ἔπεσεν, καὶ ἀπεκτάνθησαν ἐν τῷ
city fell, and ⁵were killed ⁶in ⁷the

σεισμῷ ὀνόματα ἀνθρώπων χιλιάδες ἑπτά,
⁸earthquake ³names ⁴of men ²thousands ¹seven,

καὶ οἱ λοιποὶ ἔμφοβοι ἐγένοντο καὶ
and the rest ²terrified ¹became and

ἔδωκαν δόξαν τῷ θεῷ τοῦ οὐρανοῦ.
gave glory to the God - of heaven.

14 Ἡ οὐαὶ ἡ δευτέρα ἀπῆλθεν· ἰδοὺ
The ²woe - ¹second passed away; behold[,]

ἡ οὐαὶ ἡ τρίτη ἔρχεται ταχύ.
the ²woe - ¹third is coming quickly.

15 Καὶ ὁ ἕβδομος ἄγγελος ἐσάλπισεν·
And the seventh angel trumpeted;

καὶ ἐγένοντο φωναὶ μεγάλαι ἐν τῷ
and there were voices great(loud) in -

οὐρανῷ, λέγοντες· ἐγένετο ἡ βασιλεία
heaven, saying: ⁵became ¹The ²kingdom

τοῦ κόσμου τοῦ κυρίου ἡμῶν καὶ τοῦ
³of the ⁴world of the Lord of us and of the

⁶[the kingdom]

χριστοῦ αὐτοῦ, καὶ βασιλεύσει εἰς τοὺς
Christ of him, and he shall reign unto the

αἰῶνας τῶν αἰώνων. **16** καὶ οἱ εἴκοσι
ages of the ages. And the twenty-

τέσσαρες πρεσβύτεροι, οἱ ἐνώπιον τοῦ
four elders, - ²before -

θεοῦ καθήμενοι ἐπὶ τοὺς θρόνους αὐτῶν,
³God ¹sitting on the thrones of them,

ἔπεσαν ἐπὶ τὰ πρόσωπα αὐτῶν καὶ
fell on the faces of them and

προσεκύνησαν τῷ θεῷ, **17** λέγοντες·
worshipped - God, saying:

εὐχαριστοῦμέν σοι, κύριε ὁ θεὸς ὁ
We thank thee, [O] Lord - God the

παντοκράτωρ, ὁ ὢν καὶ ὁ ἦν, ὅτι
Almighty, the [one] being and the was, because
=the one who is [one who]

εἴληφας τὴν δύναμίν σου τὴν μεγάλην
thou hast taken ¹the ³power ⁴of thee - ²great

καὶ ἐβασίλευσας· **18** καὶ τὰ ἔθνη ὠργίσ-
and didst reign; and the nations were

θησαν, καὶ ἦλθεν ἡ ὀργή σου καὶ ὁ
wrathful, and ⁴came ¹the ²wrath ³of thee and the

καιρὸς τῶν νεκρῶν κριθῆναι καὶ δοῦναι
time of the dead to be judged and to give

thy servants the prophets, and to the saints, and them that fear thy name, small and great; and shouldest destroy them which destroy the earth.

19 And the temple of God was opened in heaven, and there was seen in his temple the ark of his testament: and there were lightnings, and voices, and thunderings, and an earthquake, and great hail.

τὸν μισθὸν τοῖς δούλοις σου τοῖς προφήταις
the reward to the slaves of thee to the prophets

καὶ τοῖς ἁγίοις καὶ τοῖς φοβουμένοις
and to the saints and to the [ones] fearing

τὸ ὄνομά σου, τοῖς μικροῖς καὶ τοῖς
the name of thee, to the small and to the

μεγάλοις, καὶ διαφθεῖραι τοὺς διαφθείροντας
great, and to destroy the [ones] destroying

τὴν γῆν. 19 καὶ ἠνοίγη ὁ ναὸς τοῦ
the earth. And was opened the shrine –

θεοῦ ὁ ἐν τῷ οὐρανῷ, καὶ ὤφθη ἡ
of God – in – heaven, and was seen the

κιβωτὸς τῆς διαθήκης αὐτοῦ ἐν τῷ
ark of the covenant of him in the

ναῷ αὐτοῦ, καὶ ἐγένοντο ἀστραπαὶ καὶ
shrine of him, and occurred lightnings and

φωναὶ καὶ βρονταὶ καὶ σεισμὸς καὶ
voices and thunders and an earthquake and

χάλαζα μεγάλη.
[3]hail [1]a great.

CHAPTER 12

AND there appeared a great wonder in heaven; a woman clothed with the sun, and the moon under her feet, and upon her head a crown of twelve stars:

2 And she being with child cried, travailing in birth, and pained to be delivered.

3 And there appeared another wonder in heaven; and behold a great red dragon, having seven heads and ten horns, and seven crowns upon his heads.

4 And his tail drew the third part of the stars of heaven, and did cast them to the earth: and the

12 Καὶ σημεῖον μέγα ὤφθη ἐν τῷ
And [3]sign [1]a great was seen in –

οὐρανῷ, γυνὴ περιβεβλημένη τὸν ἥλιον,
heaven, a woman *having been* clothed [with] the sun,

καὶ ἡ σελήνη ὑποκάτω τῶν ποδῶν αὐτῆς,
and the moon underneath the feet of her,

καὶ ἐπὶ τῆς κεφαλῆς αὐτῆς στέφανος
and on the head of her a crown

ἀστέρων δώδεκα, 2 καὶ ἐν γαστρὶ ἔχουσα,
[2]stars [1]of twelve, and in womb having,
＝being pregnant,

καὶ κράζει ὠδίνουσα καὶ βασανιζομένη
and she cries suffering birth-pains and being distressed

τεκεῖν. 3 καὶ ὤφθη ἄλλο σημεῖον
to bear. And was seen another sign

ἐν τῷ οὐρανῷ, καὶ ἰδοὺ δράκων μέγας
in – heaven, and behold[,] [3]dragon [1]a great

πυρρός, ἔχων κεφαλὰς ἑπτὰ καὶ κέρατα
[2]red, having [2]heads [1]seven and [2]horns

δέκα καὶ ἐπὶ τὰς κεφαλὰς αὐτοῦ ἑπτὰ
[1]ten and on the heads of him seven

διαδήματα, 4 καὶ ἡ οὐρὰ αὐτοῦ σύρει
diadems, and the tail of him draws

τὸ τρίτον τῶν ἀστέρων τοῦ οὐρανοῦ,
the third [part] of the stars – of heaven,

καὶ ἔβαλεν αὐτοὺς εἰς τὴν γῆν. Καὶ
and cast them to the earth. And

dragon stood before the woman which was ready to be delivered, for to devour her child as soon as it was born.

5 And she brought forth a man child, who was to rule all nations with a rod of iron: and her child was caught up unto God, and to his throne.

6 And the woman fled into the wilderness, where she hath a place prepared of God, that they should feed her there a thousand two hundred and threescore days.

7 And there was war in heaven: Michael and his angels fought against the dragon; and the dragon fought and his angels,

8 And prevailed not; neither was their place found any more in heaven.

9 And the great dragon was cast out, that old serpent, called the Devil, and Satan, which deceiveth the whole world: he was cast out into the earth, and his angels were cast out with him.

10 And I heard a loud voice saying in heaven,

ὁ	δράκων	ἔστηκεν	ἐνώπιον	τῆς	γυναικὸς
the	dragon	stood	before	the	woman

τῆς	μελλούσης	τεκεῖν,	ἵνα	ὅταν	τέκῃ
-	being about	to bear,	in order that	whenever	she bears

τὸ	τέκνον	αὐτῆς	καταφάγῃ.	5 καὶ
²the	³child	⁴of her	¹he might devour.	And

ἔτεκεν	υἱὸν	ἄρσεν,	ὃς	μέλλει	ποιμαίνειν
she bore	a son[,]	a male,	who	is about	to shepherd

πάντα	τὰ	ἔθνη	ἐν	ῥάβδῳ	σιδηρᾷ·	καὶ
all	the	nations	with	²staff	¹an iron;	and

ἡρπάσθη	τὸ	τέκνον	αὐτῆς	πρὸς	τὸν
⁴was seized	¹the	²child	³of her	to	-

θεὸν	καὶ	πρὸς	τὸν	θρόνον	αὐτοῦ.	6 καὶ
God	and	to	the	throne	of him.	And

ἡ	γυνὴ	ἔφυγεν	εἰς	τὴν	ἔρημον,	ὅπου
the	woman	fled	into	the	desert,	where

ἔχει	ἐκεῖ	τόπον	ἡτοιμασμένον	ἀπὸ
she has	there	a place	having been prepared	from

τοῦ	θεοῦ,	ἵνα	ἐκεῖ	τρέφωσιν	αὐτὴν
-	God,	in order that	there	they might nourish	her

ἡμέρας	χιλίας	διακοσίας	ἑξήκοντα.
²days	¹a thousand	²two hundred	³[and] ⁴sixty.

7 Καὶ	ἐγένετο	πόλεμος	ἐν	τῷ	οὐρανῷ,
And	occurred	war	in	-	heaven,

ὁ	Μιχαὴλ	καὶ	οἱ	ἄγγελοι	αὐτοῦ	τοῦ
-	Michael	and	the	angels	of him	-

πολεμῆσαι	μετὰ	τοῦ	δράκοντος.	καὶ	ὁ
to make war⁴	with	the	dragon.	And	the

δράκων	ἐπολέμησεν	καὶ	οἱ	ἄγγελοι	αὐτοῦ,
dragon	warred	and	the	angels	of him,

8 καὶ	οὐκ	ἴσχυσεν,	οὐδὲ	τόπος	εὑρέθη
and	prevailed not,		not even	place	was found

αὐτῶν	ἔτι	ἐν	τῷ	οὐρανῷ.	9 καὶ	ἐβλήθη
of them	still	in	-	heaven.	And	was cast

ὁ	δράκων	ὁ	μέγας,	ὁ	ὄφις	ὁ	ἀρχαῖος,
¹the	²dragon	-	³great,	⁴the	⁵serpent	-	⁶old,

ὁ	καλούμενος	Διάβολος	καὶ	ὁ	Σατανᾶς,
-	being called	Devil	and	the	Satan,

ὁ	πλανῶν	τὴν	οἰκουμένην	ὅλην,	ἐβλήθη
the [one]	deceiving	the	²inhabited [earth]	¹whole,	was cast

εἰς	τὴν	γῆν,	καὶ	οἱ	ἄγγελοι	αὐτοῦ	μετ'
to	the	earth,	and	the	angels	of him	with

αὐτοῦ	ἐβλήθησαν.	10 καὶ	ἤκουσα	φωνὴν
him	were cast.	And	I heard	¹voice

μεγάλην	ἐν	τῷ	οὐρανῷ	λέγουσαν·	ἄρτι
¹a great(loud)	in	-	heaven	saying:	Now

Now is come salvation, and strength, and the kingdom of our God, and the power of his Christ: for the accuser of our brethren is cast down, which accused them before our God day and night.

11 And they overcame him by the blood of the Lamb, and by the word of their testimony; and they loved not their lives unto the death.

12 Therefore rejoice, ye heavens, and ye that dwell in them. Woe to the inhabiters of the earth and of the sea! for the devil is come down unto you, having great wrath, because he knoweth that he hath but a short time.

13 And when the dragon saw that he was cast unto the earth, he persecuted the woman which brought forth the man *child*.

14 And to the woman were given two wings of a great eagle, that she might fly into the wilderness, into her place, where she is nourished for a time, and times, and half a time, from the face of the serpent.

15 And the serpent cast out of his mouth water

ἐγένετο ἡ σωτηρία καὶ ἡ δύναμις καὶ
became the salvation and the power and

ἡ βασιλεία τοῦ θεοῦ ἡμῶν καὶ ἡ ἐξουσία
the kingdom of the God of us and the authority

τοῦ χριστοῦ αὐτοῦ, ὅτι ⁶ἐβλήθη ὁ κατήγωρ
of the Christ of him, because ⁶was cast ¹the ²accuser

τῶν ἀδελφῶν ἡμῶν, ὁ κατηγορῶν αὐτοὺς
³of the ⁴brothers ⁵of us, the [one] accusing them

ἐνώπιον τοῦ θεοῦ ἡμῶν ἡμέρας καὶ
before the God of us day and

νυκτός. 11 καὶ αὐτοὶ ἐνίκησαν αὐτὸν
night. And they overcame him

διὰ τὸ αἷμα τοῦ ἀρνίου καὶ διὰ τὸν
be-cause of the blood of the Lamb and because of the

λόγον τῆς μαρτυρίας αὐτῶν, καὶ οὐκ
word of the witness of them, and not

ἠγάπησαν τὴν ψυχὴν αὐτῶν ἄχρι θανάτου.
they loved the life of them until death.

12 διὰ τοῦτο εὐφραίνεσθε, οὐρανοὶ καὶ
Therefore be ye glad, heavens and

οἱ ἐν αὐτοῖς σκηνοῦντες· οὐαὶ τὴν
the ²in ³them ¹tabernacling; woe [to] the
[ones]

γῆν καὶ τὴν θάλασσαν, ὅτι κατέβη ὁ
earth and the sea, because ²came down ¹the

διάβολος πρὸς ὑμᾶς ἔχων θυμὸν μέγαν,
²devil to you having ³anger ¹great,

εἰδὼς ὅτι ὀλίγον καιρὸν ἔχει. 13 Καὶ
knowing that ²few(short) ³time ¹he has. And

ὅτε εἶδεν ὁ δράκων ὅτι ἐβλήθη εἰς
when ²saw ¹the ²dragon that he was cast to

τὴν γῆν, ἐδίωξεν τὴν γυναῖκα ἥτις
the earth, he pursued the woman who

ἔτεκεν τὸν ἄρσενα. 14 καὶ ἐδόθησαν
bore the male. And were given

τῇ γυναικὶ αἱ δύο πτέρυγες τοῦ ἀετοῦ
to the woman the two wings of the ²eagle

τοῦ μεγάλου, ἵνα πέτηται εἰς τὴν ἔρημον
– ¹great, in order she might to the desert
that fly

εἰς τὸν τόπον αὐτῆς, ὅπου τρέφεται
to the place of her, where she is nourished

ἐκεῖ καιρὸν καὶ καιροὺς καὶ ἥμισυ καιροῦ
there a time and times and half of a time

ἀπὸ προσώπου τοῦ ὄφεως. 15 καὶ ἔβαλεν
from [the] face of the serpent. And ²cast

ὁ ὄφις ἐκ τοῦ στόματος αὐτοῦ ὀπίσω
¹the ²serpent out of the mouth of him **behind**

as a flood after the woman, that he might cause her to be carried away of the flood.

16 And the earth helped the woman, and the earth opened her mouth, and swallowed up the flood which the dragon cast out of his mouth.

17 And the dragon was wroth with the woman, and went to make war with the remnant of her seed, which keep the commandments of God, and have the testimony of Jesus Christ.

The transposition of verse (18) from chapter 13 is necessitated by the reading "he stood", instead of "I stood" as in the A.V. (13. 1).

τῆς γυναικὸς ὕδωρ ὡς ποταμόν, ἵνα
the woman water as a river, in order that

αὐτὴν ποταμοφόρητον ποιήσῃ. 16 καὶ
¹her ²carried off by [the] river ¹he might make. And

ἐβοήθησεν ἡ γῆ τῇ γυναικί, καὶ ἤνοιξεν
²helped ¹the ²earth the woman, and ²opened

ἡ γῆ τὸ στόμα αὐτῆς καὶ κατέπιεν
¹the ²earth the mouth of it and swallowed

τὸν ποταμὸν ὃν ἔβαλεν ὁ δράκων ἐκ
the river which ²cast ¹the ²dragon out of

τοῦ στόματος αὐτοῦ. 17 καὶ ὠργίσθη
the mouth of him. And ²was enraged

ὁ δράκων ἐπὶ τῇ γυναικί, καὶ ἀπῆλθεν
¹the ²dragon over the woman, and went away

ποιῆσαι πόλεμον μετὰ τῶν λοιπῶν τοῦ
to make war with the rest of the

σπέρματος αὐτῆς, τῶν τηρούντων τὰς
seed of her, the [ones] keeping the

ἐντολὰς τοῦ θεοῦ καὶ ἐχόντων τὴν
commandments – of God and having the

μαρτυρίαν Ἰησοῦ· (18) καὶ ἐστάθη ἐπὶ τὴν
witness of Jesus; and he stood on the

ἄμμον τῆς θαλάσσης.
sand of the sea.

CHAPTER 13

AND I stood upon the sand of the sea, and saw a beast rise up out of the sea, having seven heads and ten horns, and upon his horns ten crowns, and upon his heads the name of blasphemy.

2 And the beast which I saw was like unto a leopard, and his feet were as the feet of a bear, and his mouth as the mouth of a lion: and the dragon

13 Καὶ εἶδον ἐκ τῆς θαλάσσης θηρίον
And I saw ²out of ⁴the ⁵sea ¹a beast

ἀναβαῖνον, ἔχον κέρατα δέκα καὶ κεφαλὰς
²coming up, having ²horns ¹ten and ²heads

ἑπτά, καὶ ἐπὶ τῶν κεράτων αὐτοῦ δέκα
¹seven, and on the horns of it* ten

διαδήματα, καὶ ἐπὶ τὰς κεφαλὰς αὐτοῦ
diadems, and on the heads of it

ὀνόματα βλασφημίας. 2 καὶ τὸ θηρίον
names of blasphemy. And the beast

ὃ εἶδον ἦν ὅμοιον παρδάλει, καὶ οἱ
which I saw was like to a leopard, and the

πόδες αὐτοῦ ὡς ἄρκου, καὶ τὸ στόμα
feet of it as of a bear, and the mouth

αὐτοῦ ὡς στόμα λέοντος. καὶ ἔδωκεν
of it as [the] mouth of a lion. And ²gave

* αὐτοῦ, of course, may be neuter or masculine—"of it" or "of him". δράκων being masculine (=Satan), we have kept to the masculine. But θηρίον is neuter. Yet if it stands for a person, as ἀρνίον certainly does, it too should be treated, as to the pronoun, as a masculine. However, not to enter the province of interpretation, we have rendered αὐτοῦ by "of it", though it will be seen that αὐτόν (him) is used in ver. 8, τίς (who?) in ver. 4, and ὅς (who) in ver. 14. See also ch. 17. 11.

gave him his power, and his seat, and great authority.

3 And I saw one of his heads as it were wounded to death; and his deadly wound was healed: and all the world wondered after the beast.

4 And they worshipped the dragon which gave power unto the beast: and they worshipped the beast, saying, Who *is* like unto the beast? who is able to make war with him?

5 And there was given unto him a mouth speaking great things and blasphemies; and power was given unto him to continue forty *and* two months.

6 And he opened his mouth in blasphemy against God, to blaspheme his name, and his tabernacle, and them that dwell in heaven.

7 And it was given unto him to make war with the saints, and to overcome them: and power was given him over all kindreds, and tongues, and nations.

8 And all that dwell upon the earth shall worship him, whose names are not written in the book

αὐτῷ ὁ δράκων τὴν δύναμιν αὐτοῦ καὶ
⁴to it ¹the ²dragon the power of it and
τὸν θρόνον αὐτοῦ καὶ ἐξουσίαν μεγάλην.
the throne of it and ²authority ¹great.
3 καὶ μίαν ἐκ τῶν κεφαλῶν αὐτοῦ ὡς
And one of the heads of it as
ἐσφαγμένην εἰς θάνατον, καὶ ἡ πληγὴ
having been slain to death, and the stroke
τοῦ θανάτου αὐτοῦ ἐθεραπεύθη. καὶ
of the death of it was healed. And
ἐθαυμάσθη ὅλη ἡ γῆ ὀπίσω τοῦ θηρίου,
⁴wondered ¹all ²the ³earth after the beast,
4 καὶ προσεκύνησαν τῷ δράκοντι, ὅτι
and they worshipped the dragon, because
ἔδωκεν τὴν ἐξουσίαν τῷ θηρίῳ, καὶ
he gave the authority to the beast, and
προσεκύνησαν τῷ θηρίῳ λέγοντες· τίς
they worshipped the beast saying: Who
ὅμοιος τῷ θηρίῳ, καὶ τίς δύναται
[is] like *to the* beast, and who can
πολεμῆσαι μετ' αὐτοῦ; 5 καὶ ἐδόθη αὐτῷ
to make war with it? And was given to it
στόμα λαλοῦν μεγάλα καὶ βλασφημίας,
a mouth speaking great things and blasphemies,
καὶ ἐδόθη αὐτῷ ἐξουσία ποιῆσαι μῆνας
and was given to it authority to act ²months
τεσσεράκοντα [καὶ] δύο. 6 καὶ ἤνοιξεν
¹forty-two. And it opened
τὸ στόμα αὐτοῦ εἰς βλασφημίας πρὸς
the mouth of it in blasphemies against
τὸν θεόν, βλασφημῆσαι τὸ ὄνομα αὐτοῦ
– God, to blaspheme the name of him
καὶ τὴν σκηνὴν αὐτοῦ, τοὺς ἐν τῷ
and the tabernacle of him, ¹the [ones] ²in –
οὐρανῷ σκηνοῦντας. 7 καὶ ἐδόθη αὐτῷ
⁴heaven ³tabernacling. And it was given to it
ποιῆσαι πόλεμον μετὰ τῶν ἁγίων καὶ
to make war with the saints and
νικῆσαι αὐτούς, καὶ ἐδόθη αὐτῷ ἐξουσία
to overcome them, and ²was given ³to it ¹authority
ἐπὶ πᾶσαν φυλὴν καὶ λαὸν καὶ γλῶσσαν
over every tribe and people and tongue
καὶ ἔθνος. 8 καὶ προσκυνήσουσιν αὐτὸν
and nation. And ⁷will worship ⁸him
πάντες οἱ κατοικοῦντες ἐπὶ τῆς γῆς,
¹all ²the [ones] ³dwelling ⁴on ⁵the ⁶earth,
οὗ οὐ γέγραπται τὸ ὄνομα αὐτοῦ ἐν
⁵of ⁴has not been written ¹the ²name *of him* in
whom

of life of the **Lamb** slain from the foundation of the world.

9 If any man have an ear, let him hear.

10 He that leadeth into captivity shall go into captivity: he that killeth with the sword must be killed with the sword. Here is the patience and the faith of the saints.

11 And I beheld another beast coming up out of the earth; and he had two horns like a lamb, and he spake as a dragon.

12 And he exerciseth all the power of the first beast before him, and causeth the earth and them which dwell therein to worship the first beast, whose deadly wound was healed.

13 And he doeth great wonders, so that he maketh fire come down from heaven on the earth in the sight of men,

14 And deceiveth them that dwell on the earth by *the means of* those miracles which he had power to do in the sight of the beast; saying to them that dwell on the

τῷ	βιβλίῳ	τῆς	ζωῆς	τοῦ	ἀρνίου τοῦ
the	scroll	–	of life	of the	Lamb –

ἐσφαγμένου	ἀπὸ	καταβολῆς	κόσμου.
having been slain	from	[the] foundation	of [the] world.

9 Εἴ	τις	ἔχει	οὖς	ἀκουσάτω.	10 εἴ
If	anyone	has	an ear	let him hear.	If

τις	εἰς	αἰχμαλωσίαν,	εἰς	αἰχμαλωσίαν
anyone [is] for	captivity,	to	captivity

ὑπάγει·	εἴ	τις	ἐν	μαχαίρῃ ἀποκτενεῖ,
he goes;	if	anyone	by	a sword will kill,

δεῖ	αὐτὸν	ἐν	μαχαίρῃ ἀποκτανθῆναι.
it behoves him	by	a sword to be killed.

Ὧδέ	ἐστιν	ἡ	ὑπομονὴ	καὶ	ἡ πίστις
Here	is	the	endurance	and	the faith

τῶν	ἁγίων.
of the	saints.

11 Καὶ	εἶδον	ἄλλο	θηρίον	ἀναβαῖνον
And	I saw	another	beast	coming up

ἐκ	τῆς	γῆς,	καὶ	εἶχεν	κέρατα δύο
out of	the	earth,	and	it had	²horns ¹two

ὅμοια	ἀρνίῳ,	καὶ	ἐλάλει	ὡς	δράκων.
like	to a lamb,	and	spoke	as	a dragon.

12 καὶ	τὴν	ἐξουσίαν	τοῦ	πρώτου	θηρίου
And	²the	⁴authority	³of the	⁶first	⁵beast

πᾶσαν	ποιεῖ	ἐνώπιον	αὐτοῦ.	καὶ ποιεῖ
³all	¹it does(exercises)	before	it.	And it makes

τὴν	γῆν	καὶ	τοὺς	ἐν	αὐτῇ κατοικοῦντας
the	earth	and	¹the [ones]	²in	⁴it ³dwelling

ἵνα	προσκυνήσουσιν	τὸ	θηρίον	τὸ	πρῶτον,
in or-der that	they shall worship	the	²beast	–	¹first,

οὗ	ἐθεραπεύθη	ἡ	πληγὴ	τοῦ θανάτου
of which ⁴was healed	¹the	²stroke	–	³of death

αὐτοῦ.	13 καὶ	ποιεῖ	σημεῖα	μεγάλα,
of it.	And	it does	²signs	¹great,

ἵνα	καὶ	πῦρ	ποιῇ	ἐκ	τοῦ	οὐρανοῦ
in or-der that	³even	⁴fire	¹it ²makes	⁶out of	–	⁷heaven

καταβαίνειν	εἰς	τὴν	γῆν	ἐνώπιον	τῶν
⁵to come down	onto	the	earth	before	–

ἀνθρώπων.	14 καὶ	πλανᾷ	τοὺς	κατοι-
men.	And	it deceives	the [ones]	dwell-

κοῦντας	ἐπὶ	τῆς	γῆς	διὰ	τὰ σημεῖα
ing	on	the	earth	because of	the signs

ἃ	ἐδόθη	αὐτῷ	ποιῆσαι	ἐνώπιον τοῦ
which it was given	to it	to do	before	the

θηρίου,	λέγων	τοῖς	κατοικοῦσιν	ἐπὶ τῆς
beast,	telling	*to* the	[ones] dwelling	on the

earth, that they should make an image to the beast, which had the wound by a sword, and did live.

15 And he had power to give life unto the image of the beast, that the image of the beast should both speak, and cause that as many as would not worship the image of the beast should be killed.

16 And he causeth all, both small and great, rich and poor, free and bond, to receive a mark in their right hand, or in their foreheads:

17 And that no man might buy or sell, save he that had the mark, or the name of the beast, or the number of his name.

18 Here is wisdom. Let him that hath understanding count the number of the beast: for it is the number of a man; and his number is Six hundred threescore and six.

γῆς   ποιῆσαι   εἰκόνα   τῷ   θηρίῳ,   ὃς   ἔχει
earth   to make   an image   to the   beast,   who   has

τὴν   πληγὴν   τῆς   μαχαίρης   καὶ   ἔζησεν.
the   stroke   of the   sword   and lived [again].

15 καὶ   ἐδόθη   αὐτῷ   δοῦναι   πνεῦμα   τῇ
And   it was given   to it   to give   spirit   to the

εἰκόνι   τοῦ   θηρίου,   ἵνα   καὶ   λαλήσῃ   ἡ
image   of the   beast,   in order   [6]even   [5]might   [4]the
                                      that

εἰκὼν   τοῦ   θηρίου,   καὶ   ποιήσῃ   [ἵνα]
[1]image   [2]of the   [4]beast,   and   might make   in order
                                                              that

ὅσοι   ἐὰν   μὴ   προσκυνήσωσιν   τῇ   εἰκόνι
as many as   might not worship   the   image

τοῦ   θηρίου   ἀποκτανθῶσιν.   16 καὶ   ποιεῖ
of the   beast   should be killed.   And   it makes

πάντας,   τοὺς   μικροὺς   καὶ   τοὺς   μεγάλους,
all men,   the   small   and   the   great,

καὶ   τοὺς   πλουσίους   καὶ   τοὺς   πτωχούς,
both   the   rich   and   the   poor,

καὶ   τοὺς   ἐλευθέρους   καὶ   τοὺς   δούλους,
both   the   free men   and   the   slaves,

ἵνα   δῶσιν   αὐτοῖς   χάραγμα   ἐπὶ   τῆς
in order   they   to them   a mark   on   the
that   should give

χειρὸς   αὐτῶν   τῆς   δεξιᾶς   ἢ   ἐπὶ   τὸ
[3]hand   [2]of them   -   [1]right   or   on   the

μέτωπον   αὐτῶν,   17 [καὶ]   ἵνα   μή   τις
forehead   of them,   and   lest   anyone

δύνηται   ἀγοράσαι   ἢ   πωλῆσαι   εἰ   μὴ
could   to buy   or   to sell   except

ὁ   ἔχων   τὸ   χάραγμα   τὸ   ὄνομα   τοῦ
the   having   the   mark[,]   the   name   of the
[one]

θηρίου   ἢ   τὸν   ἀριθμὸν   τοῦ   ὀνόματος
beast   or   the   number   of the   name

αὐτοῦ.   18 Ὧδε   ἡ   σοφία   ἐστίν.   ὁ   ἔχων
of it.   Here   -   [2]wisdom   [1]is.   The   having
                                                        [one]

νοῦν   ψηφισάτω   τὸν   ἀριθμὸν   τοῦ   θηρίου·
reason   let him count   the   number   of the   beast;

ἀριθμὸς   γὰρ   ἀνθρώπου   ἐστίν.   καὶ   ὁ
for   [2][the]   [3]number   [4]of a man   [1]it is.   And   the

ἀριθμὸς   αὐτοῦ   ἑξακόσιοι   ἑξήκοντα   ἕξ.
number   of it   [is] six hundreds   [and] sixty-six.

CHAPTER 14

AND I looked, and, lo, a Lamb stood on the mount Sion, and with him

14 Καὶ   εἶδον,   καὶ   ἰδοὺ   τὸ   ἀρνίον
And   I saw,   and   behold[,]   the   Lamb

ἑστὸς   ἐπὶ   τὸ   ὄρος   Σιών,   καὶ   μετ'   αὐτοῦ
standing   on   the   mount   Sion,   and   with   him

an hundred forty *and* four **thousand, having his** Father's name written in their foreheads.

2 And I heard a voice from heaven, as the voice of many waters, and as the voice of a great thunder: and I heard the voice of harpers harping with their harps:

3 And they sung as it were a new song before the throne, and before the four beasts, and the elders: and no man could learn that song but the hundred *and* forty *and* four thousand, which were redeemed from the earth.

4 These are they which were not defiled with women; for they are virgins. These are they which follow the Lamb whithersoever he goeth. These were redeemed from among men, *being* the firstfruits unto God and to the Lamb.

5 And in their mouth was found no guile: for they are without fault before the throne of God.

6 And I saw another angel fly in the midst of heaven, having the everlasting gospel to preach unto them that dwell on

ἑκατὸν   τεσσεράκοντα   τέσσαρες   χιλιάδες
a hundred   [and]   forty-four   thousands

ἔχουσαι   τὸ   ὄνομα   αὐτοῦ   καὶ   τὸ   ὄνομα
having   the   name   of him   and   the   name

τοῦ   πατρὸς   αὐτοῦ   γεγραμμένον   ἐπὶ   τῶν
of the Father   of him   *having been* written on   the

μετώπων   αὐτῶν.   2 καὶ   ἤκουσα   φωνὴν
foreheads of them.   And   I heard   a sound

ἐκ   τοῦ   οὐρανοῦ   ὡς   φωνὴν   ὑδάτων   πολλῶν
out of -   heaven   as   a sound   ²waters   ¹of many

καὶ   ὡς   φωνὴν   βροντῆς   μεγάλης,   καὶ
and   as   a sound   ²thunder   ¹of great(loud), and

ἡ   φωνὴ   ἦν   ἤκουσα   ὡς   κιθαρῳδῶν
the sound   which I heard   [was] as   of harpers

κιθαριζόντων   ἐν   ταῖς   κιθάραις   αὐτῶν.
harping   with the   harps   of them.

3 καὶ   ᾄδουσιν   ᾠδὴν   καινὴν   ἐνώπιον   τοῦ
And   they sing ²song   ¹a new   before   the

θρόνου   καὶ   ἐνώπιον   τῶν   τεσσάρων   ζῴων
throne   and   before   the   four   living
                                                creatures

καὶ   τῶν   πρεσβυτέρων·   καὶ   οὐδεὶς   ἐδύνατο
and   the   elders;   and   no man   could

μαθεῖν   τὴν   ᾠδὴν   εἰ   μὴ   αἱ   ἑκατὸν
to learn   the   song   except   the   hundred

τεσσεράκοντα   τέσσαρες   χιλιάδες,   οἱ
[and] forty-four   thousands,   the

ἠγορασμένοι   ἀπὸ   τῆς   γῆς.   4 οὗτοί   εἰσιν
[ones] *having* from   the   earth.   These   are
been purchased

οἳ   μετὰ   γυναικῶν   οὐκ   ἐμολύνθησαν·
[those] ²with   ²women   ¹were not defiled;
who

παρθένοι   γάρ   εἰσιν.   οὗτοι   οἱ   ἀκολουθοῦντες
for ²celibates ¹they are.   These   the [ones] following
                                             [are]

τῷ   ἀρνίῳ   ὅπου   ἂν   ὑπάγῃ.   οὗτοι   ἠγοράσ-
the   Lamb   wherever he may go.   These   were

θησαν   ἀπὸ   τῶν   ἀνθρώπων   ἀπαρχὴ   τῷ
purchased from   -   men   firstfruit   -

θεῷ   καὶ   τῷ   ἀρνίῳ,   5 καὶ   ἐν   τῷ   στόματι
to God and to the   Lamb,   and   in   the   mouth

αὐτῶν   οὐχ   εὑρέθη   ψεῦδος·   ἄμωμοί   εἰσιν.
of them   was not found   a lie;   ²unblemished ¹they are.

6 Καὶ   εἶδον   ἄλλον   ἄγγελον   πετόμενον
And   I saw   another   angel   flying

ἐν   μεσουρανήματι,   ἔχοντα   εὐαγγέλιον
in   mid-heaven,   having   ²gospel

αἰώνιον   εὐαγγελίσαι   ἐπὶ   τοὺς   καθημένους
¹an eternal to preach   over   the [ones] sitting

the earth, and to every nation, and kindred, and tongue, and people,

7 Saying with a loud voice, Fear God, and give glory to him; for the hour of his judgment is come: and worship him that made heaven, and earth, and the sea, and the fountains of waters.

8 And there followed another angel, saying, Babylon is fallen, is fallen, that great city, because she made all nations drink of the wine of the wrath of her fornication.

9 And the third angel followed them, saying with a loud voice, If any man worship the beast and his image, and receive *his* mark in his forehead, or in his hand,

10 The same shall drink of the wine of the wrath of God, which is poured out without mixture into the cup of his indignation; and he shall be tormented with fire and brimstone in the presence of the holy angels, and in the presence of the Lamb:

11 And the smoke of their torment ascendeth up for ever and ever: and they have no rest day nor night, who worship the

ἐπὶ τῆς γῆς καὶ ἐπὶ πᾶν ἔθνος καὶ
on the earth and over every nation and

φυλὴν καὶ γλῶσσαν καὶ λαόν, 7 λέγων
tribe and tongue and people, saying

ἐν φωνῇ μεγάλῃ· φοβήθητε τὸν θεὸν
in [2]voice [1]a great(loud): Fear ye - God

καὶ δότε αὐτῷ δόξαν, ὅτι ἦλθεν ἡ ὥρα
and give [2]to him [1]glory, because came the hour

τῆς κρίσεως αὐτοῦ, καὶ προσκυνήσατε
of the judgment of him, and worship

τῷ ποιήσαντι τὸν οὐρανὸν καὶ τὴν γῆν
the [one] having made the heaven and the earth

καὶ θάλασσαν καὶ πηγὰς ὑδάτων. 8 Καὶ
and sea and fountains of waters. And

ἄλλος ἄγγελος δεύτερος ἠκολούθησεν λέγων·
another angel a second followed saying:

ἔπεσεν ἔπεσεν Βαβυλὼν ἡ μεγάλη, ἣ
Fell[,] fell Babylon the great, which

ἐκ τοῦ οἴνου τοῦ θυμοῦ τῆς πορνείας
of the wine of the anger of the fornication

αὐτῆς πεπότικεν πάντα τὰ ἔθνη. 9 Καὶ
of her has made to drink all the nations. And

ἄλλος ἄγγελος τρίτος ἠκολούθησεν αὐτοῖς
another angel a third followed them

λέγων ἐν φωνῇ μεγάλῃ· εἴ τις προσκυνεῖ
saying in [2]voice [1]a great(loud): If anyone worships

τὸ θηρίον καὶ τὴν εἰκόνα αὐτοῦ, καὶ
the beast and the image of it, and

λαμβάνει χάραγμα ἐπὶ τοῦ μετώπου αὐτοῦ
receives a mark on the forehead of him

ἢ ἐπὶ τὴν χεῖρα αὐτοῦ, 10 καὶ αὐτὸς
or on the hand of him, even he

πίεται ἐκ τοῦ οἴνου τοῦ θυμοῦ τοῦ
shall drink of the wine of the anger -

θεοῦ τοῦ κεκερασμένου ἀκράτου ἐν τῷ
of God - having been mixed undiluted in the

ποτηρίῳ τῆς ὀργῆς αὐτοῦ, καὶ βασανισθήσε-
cup of the wrath of him, and will be torment-

ται ἐν πυρὶ καὶ θείῳ ἐνώπιον ἀγγέλων
ed by fire and sulphur before [2]angels

ἁγίων καὶ ἐνώπιον τοῦ ἀρνίου. 11 καὶ
[1]holy and before the Lamb. And

ὁ καπνὸς τοῦ βασανισμοῦ αὐτῶν εἰς
the smoke of the torment of them unto

αἰῶνας αἰώνων ἀναβαίνει, καὶ οὐκ ἔχουσιν
ages of ages goes up, and they have not

ἀνάπαυσιν ἡμέρας καὶ νυκτὸς οἱ προσκυ-
rest day and night the [ones] wor-

beast and his image, and whosoever receiveth the mark of his name.

12 Here is the patience of the saints: here *are* they that keep the commandments of God, and the faith of Jesus.

13 And I heard a voice from heaven saying unto me, Write, Blessed *are* the dead which die in the Lord from henceforth: Yea, saith the Spirit, that they may rest from their labours; and their works do follow them.

14 And I looked, and behold a white cloud, and upon the cloud *one* sat like unto the Son of man, having on his head a golden crown, and in his hand a sharp sickle.

15 And another angel came out of the temple, crying with a loud voice to him that sat on the cloud, Thrust in thy sickle, and reap: for the time is come for thee to reap; for the harvest of the earth is ripe.

16 And he that sat on the cloud thrust in his

νοῦντες   τὸ   θηρίον   καὶ   τὴν   εἰκόνα   αὐτοῦ,
shipping   the   beast   and   the   image   of it,

καὶ   εἴ   τις   λαμβάνει   τὸ   χάραγμα   τοῦ
and   if   anyone   receives   the   mark   of the

ὀνόματος   αὐτοῦ.   12 ˝Ωδε   ἡ   ὑπομονὴ
name   of it.   [1]Here   [3]the   [4]endurance

τῶν   ἁγίων   ἐστίν,   οἱ   τηροῦντες   τὰς
[2]of the   [5]saints   [2]is,   the [ones]   keeping   the

ἐντολὰς   τοῦ   θεοῦ   καὶ   τὴν   πίστιν   Ἰησοῦ.
command-   -   of God   and   the   faith   of Jesus.
ments

13 Καὶ   ἤκουσα   φωνῆς   ἐκ   τοῦ   οὐρανοῦ
And   I heard   a voice   out of   -   heaven

λεγούσης·   γράψον·   μακάριοι   οἱ   νεκροὶ
saying: Write thou: Blessed [are]   the   dead

οἱ   ἐν   κυρίῳ   ἀποθνήσκοντες   ἀπ'   ἄρτι.
[1]the   [2]in   [3][the] Lord   [4]dying   from   now.
[ones]

ναί,   λέγει   τὸ   πνεῦμα,   ἵνα   ἀναπαήσονται
Yes,   says   the   Spirit,   in order   they shall rest
that

ἐκ   τῶν   κόπων   αὐτῶν·   τὰ   γὰρ   ἔργα
from   the   labours   of them;   for the   work-

αὐτῶν   ἀκολουθεῖ   μετ'   αὐτῶν.
of them   follows   with   them.

14 Καὶ   εἶδον,   καὶ   ἰδοὺ   νεφέλη   λευκή,
And   I saw,   and   behold[,]   [2]cloud   [1]a white,

καὶ   ἐπὶ   τὴν   νεφέλην   καθήμενον   ὅμοιον
and   on   the   cloud   [one] sitting   like

υἱὸν   ἀνθρώπου,   ἔχων   ἐπὶ   τῆς   κεφαλῆς
a son   of man,*   having   on   the   head

αὐτοῦ   στέφανον   χρυσοῦν   καὶ   ἐν   τῇ   χειρὶ
of him   crown   a golden   and   in   the   hand

αὐτοῦ   δρέπανον   ὀξύ.   15 καὶ   ἄλλος   ἄγγελος
of him   sickle   a sharp.   And   another   angel

ἐξῆλθεν   ἐκ   τοῦ   ναοῦ,   κράζων   ἐν   φωνῇ
went forth   out of   the   shrine,   crying   in   [2]voice

μεγάλῃ   τῷ   καθημένῳ   ἐπὶ   τῆς   νεφέλης·
[1]a great   to the   sitting   on   the   cloud:
(loud)   [one]

πέμψον   τὸ   δρέπανόν   σου   καὶ   θέρισον,
Send(Thrust)   the   sickle   of thee   and   reap thou,

ὅτι   ἦλθεν   ἡ   ὥρα   θερίσαι,   ὅτι   ἐξηράνθη
because came   the   hour   to reap,   because   was dried

ὁ   θερισμὸς   τῆς   γῆς.   16 καὶ   ἔβαλεν
the   harvest   of the   earth.   And   [6]thrust

ὁ   καθήμενος   ἐπὶ   τῆς   νεφέλης   τὸ   δρέπανον
[1]the   [2]sitting   [3]on   [4]the   [5]cloud   the   sickle
[one]

* See also ch. 1. 13 and John 5. 27.

sickle on the earth; and the earth was reaped.

17 And another angel came out of the temple which is in heaven, he also having a sharp sickle.

18 And another angel came out from the altar, which had power over fire: and cried with a loud cry to him that had the sharp sickle, saying, Thrust in thy sharp sickle, and gather the clusters of the vine of the earth; for her grapes are fully ripe.

19 And the angel thrust in his sickle into the earth, and gathered the vine of the earth, and cast *it* into the great winepress of the wrath of God.

20 And the winepress was trodden without the city, and blood came out of the winepress, even unto the horse bridles, by the space of a thousand *and* six hundred furlongs.

αὐτοῦ ἐπὶ τὴν γῆν, καὶ ἐθερίσθη ἡ
of him over the earth, and ²was reaped ¹the

γῆ. 17 Καὶ ἄλλος ἄγγελος ἐξῆλθεν ἐκ
²earth. And another angel went forth out of

τοῦ ναοῦ τοῦ ἐν τῷ οὐρανῷ, ἔχων καὶ
the shrine - in heaven, ²having ¹also

αὐτὸς δρέπανον ὀξύ. 18 καὶ ἄλλος ἄγγελος
¹he ³sickle ⁴a sharp. And another angel

ἐξῆλθεν ἐκ τοῦ θυσιαστηρίου, [ὁ] ἔχων
went forth out of the altar, the [one] having

ἐξουσίαν ἐπὶ τοῦ πυρός, καὶ ἐφώνησεν
authority over the fire, and he spoke

φωνῇ μεγάλῃ τῷ ἔχοντι τὸ δρέπανον
²voice ¹in a great to the having the ²sickle
    (loud) [one]

τὸ ὀξὺ λέγων· πέμψον σου τὸ δρέπανον
- ¹sharp saying: Send(Thrust) ⁴of thee ¹the ²sickle

τὸ ὀξὺ καὶ τρύγησον τοὺς βότρυας τῆς
- ³sharp and gather the clusters of the

ἀμπέλου τῆς γῆς, ὅτι ἤκμασαν αἱ
vine of the earth, because ²ripened ¹the

σταφυλαὶ αὐτῆς. 19 καὶ ἔβαλεν ὁ ἄγγελος
²grapes ³of it. And ³thrust ¹the ²angel

τὸ δρέπανον αὐτοῦ εἰς τὴν γῆν, καὶ
the sickle of him into the earth, and

ἐτρύγησεν τὴν ἄμπελον τῆς γῆς καὶ
gathered the vine of the earth and

ἔβαλεν εἰς τὴν ληνὸν τοῦ θυμοῦ τοῦ
cast into the ²winepress ³of the ⁴anger

θεοῦ τὸν μέγαν. 20 καὶ ἐπατήθη ἡ
⁵of God - ¹great. And ²was trodden ¹the

ληνὸς ἔξωθεν τῆς πόλεως, καὶ ἐξῆλθεν
winepress outside the city, and ²went *out*

αἷμα ἐκ τῆς ληνοῦ ἄχρι τῶν χαλινῶν
¹blood out of the winepress as far as the bridles

τῶν ἵππων, ἀπὸ σταδίων χιλίων ἑξακοσίων.
of the horses, from ³furlongs ¹a thousand ²six hundred.

CHAPTER 15

AND I saw another sign in heaven, great and marvellous, seven angels having the seven last plagues; for in them is filled up the wrath of God.

2 And I saw as it were a sea of glass mingled with

15 Καὶ εἶδον ἄλλο σημεῖον ἐν τῷ
And I saw another sign in -

οὐρανῷ μέγα καὶ θαυμαστόν, ἀγγέλους
heaven[,] great and wonderful, ²angels

ἑπτὰ ἔχοντας πληγὰς ἑπτὰ τὰς ἐσχάτας,
¹seven having ²plagues seven the last,

ὅτι ἐν αὐταῖς ἐτελέσθη ὁ θυμὸς τοῦ
because in them ⁴was finished ¹the ²anger -

θεοῦ. 2 Καὶ εἶδον ὡς θάλασσαν ὑαλίνην
³of God. And I saw as ²sea ¹a glassy

fire: and them that had gotten the victory over the beast, and over his image, and over his mark, *and* over the number of his name, stand on the sea of glass, having the harps of God.

3 And they sing the song of Moses the servant of God, and the song of the Lamb, saying, Great and marvellous *are* thy works, Lord God Almighty; just and true *are* thy ways, thou King of saints.

4 Who shall not fear thee, O Lord, and glorify thy name? for *thou* only *art* holy: for all nations shall come and worship before thee; for thy judgments are made manifest.

5 And after that I looked, and, behold, the temple of the tabernacle of the testimony in heaven was opened:

6 And the seven angels came out of the temple, having the seven plagues, clothed in pure and white linen, and having their breasts girded with golden girdles.

7 And one of the four beasts gave unto the seven angels seven golden vials

μεμιγμένην πυρί, καὶ τοὺς νικῶντας
having been mixed with fire, and the [ones] overcoming

ἐκ τοῦ θηρίου καὶ ἐκ τῆς εἰκόνος αὐτοῦ
of the beast and of the image of it

καὶ ἐκ τοῦ ἀριθμοῦ τοῦ ὀνόματος αὐτοῦ
and of the number of the name of it

ἑστῶτας ἐπὶ τὴν θάλασσαν τὴν ὑαλίνην,
standing on the ²sea – ¹glassy,

ἔχοντας κιθάρας τοῦ θεοῦ. 3 καὶ ᾄδουσιν
having harps – of God. And they sing

τὴν ᾠδὴν Μωϋσέως τοῦ δούλου τοῦ
the song of Moses the slave –

θεοῦ καὶ τὴν ᾠδὴν τοῦ ἀρνίου, λέγοντες·
of God and the song of the Lamb, saying:

μεγάλα καὶ θαυμαστὰ τὰ ἔργα σου,
Great and wonderful the works of thee,

κύριε ὁ θεὸς ὁ παντοκράτωρ· δίκαιαι
[O] Lord – God the Almighty; righteous

καὶ ἀληθιναὶ αἱ ὁδοί σου, ὁ βασιλεὺς
and true the ways of thee, the king

τῶν ἐθνῶν· 4 τίς οὐ μὴ φοβηθῇ, κύριε,
of the nations; who will not fear, [O] Lord,

καὶ δοξάσει τὸ ὄνομά σου; ὅτι μόνος
and *will* glorify the name of thee? because [thou] only

ὅσιος, ὅτι πάντα τὰ ἔθνη ἥξουσιν καὶ
[art] holy, because all the nations will come and

προσκυνήσουσιν ἐνώπιόν σου, ὅτι τὰ
will worship before thee, because the

δικαιώματά σου ἐφανερώθησαν. 5 Καὶ
ordinances of thee were made manifest. And

μετὰ ταῦτα εἶδον, καὶ ἠνοίγη ὁ ναὸς
after these things I saw, and was opened the shrine

τῆς σκηνῆς τοῦ μαρτυρίου ἐν τῷ οὐρανῷ,
of the tabernacle of the testimony in – heaven,

6 καὶ ἐξῆλθον οἱ ἑπτὰ ἄγγελοι οἱ ἔχοντες
and ⁶came forth ¹the ²seven ³angels ⁴having

τὰς ἑπτὰ πληγὰς ἐκ τοῦ ναοῦ, ἐνδεδυμένοι
⁵the ⁶seven ⁷plagues out of the shrine, *having been* clothed [in]

λίνον καθαρὸν λαμπρὸν καὶ περιεζωσμένοι
²linen ¹clean ²bright and *having been* girdled

περὶ τὰ στήθη ζώνας χρυσᾶς. 7 καὶ
round the breasts [with] ²girdles ¹golden. And

ἓν ἐκ τῶν τεσσάρων ζῴων ἔδωκεν τοῖς
one of the four living creatures gave to the

ἑπτὰ ἀγγέλοις ἑπτὰ φιάλας χρυσᾶς
seven angels seven ²bowls ¹golden

full of the wrath of God, who liveth for ever and ever.

8 And the temple was filled with smoke from the glory of God, and from his power; and no man was able to enter into the temple, till the seven plagues of the seven angels were fulfilled.

CHAPTER 16

AND I heard a great voice out of the temple saying to the seven angels, Go your ways, and pour out the vials of the wrath of God upon the earth.

2 And the first went, and poured out his vial upon the earth; and there fell a noisome and grievous sore upon the men which had the mark of the beast, and upon them which worshipped his image.

3 And the second angel poured out his vial upon the sea; and it became as the blood of a dead man: and every living soul died in the sea.

4 And the third angel poured out his vial upon the rivers and fountains of waters; and they became blood.

5 And I heard the angel of the waters say, Thou art righteous, O Lord,

---

γεμούσας τοῦ θυμοῦ τοῦ θεοῦ τοῦ ζῶντος
being filled of(with) anger – of – living
    the   God

εἰς τοὺς αἰῶνας τῶν αἰώνων. **8** καὶ
unto the ages of the ages.   And

ἐγεμίσθη ὁ ναὸς καπνοῦ ἐκ τῆς δόξης
was filled the shrine of(with) smoke of the glory

τοῦ θεοῦ καὶ ἐκ τῆς δυνάμεως αὐτοῦ,
– of God and of the power of him,

καὶ οὐδεὶς ἐδύνατο εἰσελθεῖν εἰς τὸν
and no one could *to* enter into the

ναὸν ἄχρι τελεσθῶσιν αἱ ἑπτὰ πληγαὶ
shrine until should be finished the seven plagues

τῶν ἑπτὰ ἀγγέλων. **16** Καὶ ἤκουσα
of the seven angels.   And I heard

μεγάλης φωνῆς ἐκ τοῦ ναοῦ λεγούσης τοῖς
a great(loud) voice out of the shrine saying to the

ἑπτὰ ἀγγέλοις· ὑπάγετε καὶ ἐκχέετε τὰς ἑπτὰ
seven angels: Go ye and pour out the seven

φιάλας τοῦ θυμοῦ τοῦ θεοῦ εἰς τὴν γῆν.
bowls of the anger – of God onto the earth.

2 Καὶ ἀπῆλθεν ὁ πρῶτος καὶ ἐξέχεεν τὴν
And ²went away ¹the ⁵first and poured out the

φιάλην αὐτοῦ εἰς τὴν γῆν· καὶ ἐγένετο
bowl of him onto the earth; and ⁵came

ἕλκος κακὸν καὶ πονηρὸν ἐπὶ τοὺς ἀνθρώπους
⁴sore ¹a bad ²and ³evil on the men

τοὺς ἔχοντας τὸ χάραγμα τοῦ θηρίου καὶ
– having the mark of the beast and

τοὺς προσκυνοῦντας τῇ εἰκόνι αὐτοῦ. **3** Καὶ
– worshipping the image of it.   And

ὁ δεύτερος ἐξέχεεν τὴν φιάλην αὐτοῦ
the second poured out the bowl of him

εἰς τὴν θάλασσαν· καὶ ἐγένετο αἷμα
onto the sea; and it became blood

ὡς νεκροῦ, καὶ πᾶσα ψυχὴ ζωῆς ἀπέθανεν,
as of a dead and every soul of life died,
    man,

τὰ ἐν τῇ θαλάσσῃ. **4** Καὶ ὁ τρίτος
the in the sea.   And the third
things

ἐξέχεεν τὴν φιάλην αὐτοῦ εἰς τοὺς
poured out the bowl of him onto the

ποταμοὺς καὶ τὰς πηγὰς τῶν ὑδάτων·
rivers and the fountains of the waters;

καὶ ἐγένετο αἷμα. **5** Καὶ ἤκουσα τοῦ
and it became blood.   And I heard the

ἀγγέλου τῶν ὑδάτων λέγοντος· δίκαιος
angel of the waters saying: Righteous

which art, and wast, and shalt be, because thou hast judged thus.

6 For they have shed the blood of saints and prophets, and thou hast given them blood to drink; for they are worthy.

7 And I heard another out of the altar say, Even so, Lord God Almighty, true and righteous *are* thy judgments.

8 And the fourth angel poured out his vial upon the sun; and power was given unto him to scorch men with fire.

9 And men were scorched with great heat, and blasphemed the name of God, which hath power over these plagues: and they repented not to give him glory.

10 And the fifth angel poured out his vial upon the seat of the beast; and his kingdom was full of darkness; and they gnawed their tongues for pain,

11 And blasphemed the God of heaven because of their pains and their sores, and repented not of their deeds.

12 And the sixth angel poured out his vial upon the great river Euphrates;

εἶ, ὁ ὢν καὶ ὁ ἦν, ὁ ὅσιος, ὅτι
art the being and the was, the holy because
thou, [one]   [one who]   [one],
= the one who is

ταῦτα ἔκρινας, 6 ὅτι αἷμα ἁγίων
²these ¹thou judgedst, because ²[the] blood ³of saints
things

καὶ προφητῶν ἐξέχεαν, καὶ αἷμα αὐτοῖς
⁴and ⁵of prophets ¹they shed, and blood to them

δέδωκας πεῖν· ἄξιοί εἰσιν. 7 Καὶ ἤκουσα
thou hast to drink; ²worthy ¹they are. And I heard
given

τοῦ θυσιαστηρίου λέγοντος· ναί, κύριε
the altar saying: Yes, [O] Lord

ὁ θεὸς ὁ παντοκράτωρ, ἀληθιναὶ καὶ
- God the Almighty, true and

δίκαιαι αἱ κρίσεις σου. 8 Καὶ ὁ τέταρτος
righteous the judgments of thee. And the fourth

ἐξέχεεν τὴν φιάλην αὐτοῦ ἐπὶ τὸν ἥλιον·
poured out the bowl of him onto the sun;

καὶ ἐδόθη αὐτῷ καυματίσαι τοὺς
and it was given to him to burn -

ἀνθρώπους ἐν πυρί. 9 καὶ ἐκαυματίσθησαν
men with fire. And ²were burnt [with]

οἱ ἄνθρωποι καῦμα μέγα, καὶ ἐβλασ-
- ¹men ⁴heat ³great, and they blas-

φήμησαν τὸ ὄνομα τοῦ θεοῦ τοῦ ἔχοντος
phemed the name - of God the [one] having

τὴν ἐξουσίαν ἐπὶ τὰς πληγὰς ταύτας,
the authority over these plagues,

καὶ οὐ μετενόησαν δοῦναι αὐτῷ δόξαν.
and they repented not to give ²to him ¹glory.

10 Καὶ ὁ πέμπτος ἐξέχεεν τὴν φιάλην
And the fifth poured out the bowl

αὐτοῦ ἐπὶ τὸν θρόνον τοῦ θηρίου· καὶ
of him onto the throne of the beast; and

ἐγένετο ἡ βασιλεία αὐτοῦ ἐσκοτωμένη,
⁴became ¹the ²kingdom ³of it *having been* darkened,

καὶ ἐμασῶντο τὰς γλώσσας αὐτῶν ἐκ
and they(men) gnawed the tongues of them from

τοῦ πόνου, 11 καὶ ἐβλασφήμησαν τὸν θεὸν
the pain, and *they* blasphemed the God

τοῦ οὐρανοῦ ἐκ τῶν πόνων αὐτῶν καὶ
- of heaven from the pains of them and

ἐκ τῶν ἑλκῶν αὐτῶν, καὶ οὐ μετενόησαν
from the sores of them, and they repented not

ἐκ τῶν ἔργων αὐτῶν. 12 Καὶ ὁ ἕκτος
of the works of them. And the sixth

ἐξέχεεν τὴν φιάλην αὐτοῦ ἐπὶ τὸν ποταμὸν
poured out the bowl of him onto the ²river

and the water thereof was dried up, that the way of the kings of the east might be prepared.

13 And I saw three unclean spirits like frogs *come* out of the mouth of the dragon, and out of the mouth of the beast, and out of the mouth of the false prophet.

14 For they are the spirits of devils, working miracles, *which* go forth unto the kings of the earth and of the whole world, to gather them to the battle of that great day of God Almighty.

15 Behold, I come as a thief. Blessed *is* he that watcheth, and keepeth his garments, lest he walk naked, and they see his shame.

16 And he gathered them together into a place called in the Hebrew tongue Armageddon.

17 And the seventh angel poured out his vial into the air; and there came a great voice out of the temple of heaven, from the throne, saying, It is done.

18 And there were voices, and thunders, and lightnings; and there was a great earthquake, such as was not since men

τὸν   μέγαν   Εὐφράτην·   καὶ   ἐξηράνθη   τὸ
-     ¹great   Euphrates;   and   ⁴was dried   ¹the

ὕδωρ   αὐτοῦ,   ἵνα   ἑτοιμασθῇ   ἡ   ὁδὸς   τῶν
²water   ³of it,   in order   ⁵might be   ¹the   ²way   ³of the
                    that   prepared

βασιλέων   τῶν   ἀπὸ   ἀνατολῆς   ἡλίου.   13 Καὶ
⁴kings   -   ⁵from   ⁶[the] rising   ⁷of [the] sun.   And

εἶδον   ἐκ   τοῦ   στόματος   τοῦ   δράκοντος
I saw   out of   the   mouth   of the   dragon

καὶ   ἐκ   τοῦ   στόματος   τοῦ   θηρίου   καὶ
and   out of   the   mouth   of the   beast   and

ἐκ   τοῦ   στόματος   τοῦ   ψευδοπροφήτου
out of   the   mouth   of the   false prophet

πνεύματα   τρία   ἀκάθαρτα   ὡς   βάτραχοι·
³spirits   ¹three   ²unclean [coming] as   frogs;

14 εἰσὶν   γὰρ   πνεύματα   δαιμονίων   ποιοῦντα
for they are   spirits   of demons   doing

σημεῖα,   ἃ   ἐκπορεύεται   ἐπὶ   τοὺς   βασιλεῖς
signs,   which   goes forth   unto   the   kings

τῆς   οἰκουμένης   ὅλης,   συναγαγεῖν   αὐτοὺς
of the   ²inhabited [earth]   ¹whole,   to assemble   them

εἰς   τὸν   πόλεμον   τῆς   ἡμέρας   τῆς   μεγάλης
to   the   war   of the   ²day   -   ¹great

τοῦ   θεοῦ   τοῦ   παντοκράτορος.   15 Ἰδοὺ
-     of God   of the   Almighty.   Behold

ἔρχομαι   ὡς   κλέπτης·   μακάριος   ὁ   γρηγορῶν
I am coming as   a thief: blessed [is]   the [one] watching

καὶ   τηρῶν   τὰ   ἱμάτια   αὐτοῦ,   ἵνα   μὴ
and   keeping   the   garments   of him,   lest

γυμνὸς   περιπατῇ   καὶ   βλέπωσιν   τὴν
naked   he walk   and   they(men) see   the

ἀσχημοσύνην   αὐτοῦ.   16 Καὶ   συνήγαγεν
shame   of him.   And [t]he[y] assembled

αὐτοὺς   εἰς   τὸν   τόπον   τὸν   καλούμενον
them   in   the   place   -   *being* called

Ἑβραϊστὶ   Ἁρμαγεδών.   17 Καὶ   ὁ   ἕβδομος
in Hebrew   Harmagedon.   And   the   seventh

ἐξέχεεν   τὴν   φιάλην   αὐτοῦ   ἐπὶ   τὸν   ἀέρα·
poured out   the   bowl   of him   on   the   air;

καὶ   ἐξῆλθεν   φωνὴ   μεγάλη   ἐκ   τοῦ   ναοῦ
and   ²came *out*   ³voice   ¹a great(loud)   out of   the   shrine

ἀπὸ   τοῦ   θρόνου   λέγουσα·   γέγονεν.   18 καὶ
from   the   throne   saying: It has occurred.   And

ἐγένοντο   ἀστραπαὶ   καὶ   φωναὶ   καὶ   βρονταί,
there were   lightnings   and   voices   and   thunders,

καὶ   σεισμὸς   ἐγένετο   μέγας,   οἷος   οὐκ
and   ²earthquake   ³occurred   ¹a great,   such as   not

were upon the earth, so mighty an earthquake, *and* so great.

19 And the great city was divided into three parts, and the cities of the nations fell: and great Babylon came in remembrance before God, to give unto her the cup of the wine of the fierceness of his wrath.

20 And every island fled away, and the mountains were not found.

21 And there fell upon men a great hail out of heaven, *every stone* about the weight of a talent: and men blasphemed God because of the plague of the hail; for the plague thereof was exceeding great.

ἐγένετο   ἀφ'   οὗ   ἄνθρωπος   ἐγένετο   ἐπὶ
did occur   from when†   man   was   on

τῆς   γῆς,   τηλικοῦτος   σεισμὸς   οὕτω   μέγας.
the   earth,   such   an earthquake   so   great.

19 καὶ   ἐγένετο   ἡ   πόλις   ἡ   μεγάλη   εἰς
And   ⁴became   ¹the   ²city   –   ³great   into

τρία   μέρη,   καὶ   αἱ   πόλεις   τῶν   ἐθνῶν
three   parts,   and   the   cities   of the   nations

ἔπεσαν.   καὶ   Βαβυλὼν   ἡ   μεγάλη   ἐμνήσθη
fell.   And   Babylon   the   great   was
                                                        remembered

ἐνώπιον   τοῦ   θεοῦ   δοῦναι   αὐτῇ   τὸ   ποτήριον
before   –   God   to give   to her/it*   the   cup

τοῦ   οἴνου   τοῦ   θυμοῦ   τῆς   ὀργῆς   αὐτοῦ.
of the   wine   of the   anger   of the   wrath   of him.

20 καὶ   πᾶσα   νῆσος   ἔφυγεν,   καὶ   ὄρη
And   every   island   fled,   and mountains

οὐχ   εὑρέθησαν.   **21** καὶ   χάλαζα   μεγάλη
were not found.   And   ²hail   ¹a great

ὡς   ταλαντιαία   καταβαίνει   ἐκ   τοῦ   οὐρανοῦ
as   a talent in size   comes down   out of   –   heaven

ἐπὶ   τοὺς   ἀνθρώπους·   καὶ   ἐβλασφήμησαν
on   –   men;   and   ²blasphemed

οἱ   ἄνθρωποι   τὸν   θεὸν   ἐκ   τῆς   πληγῆς
–   ¹men   –   God   from   the   plague

τῆς   χαλάζης,   ὅτι   μεγάλη   ἐστὶν   ἡ   πληγὴ
of the   hail,   because   ⁶great   ⁴is   ¹the   ²plague

αὐτῆς   σφόδρα.
³of it   ⁵exceeding.

<hr/>

CHAPTER 17

AND there came one of the seven angels which had the seven vials, and talked with me, saying unto me, Come hither; I will shew unto thee the judgment of the great whore that sitteth upon many waters:

2 With whom the kings of the earth have committed fornication, and the inhabitants of the earth have been made drunk with the wine of her fornication.

17 Καὶ   ἦλθεν   εἷς   ἐκ   τῶν   ἑπτὰ   ἀγγέλων
And   came   one   of   the   seven   angels

τῶν   ἐχόντων   τὰς   ἑπτὰ   φιάλας,   καὶ
–   having   the   seven   bowls,   and

ἐλάλησεν   μετ'   ἐμοῦ   λέγων·   δεῦρο,   δείξω
spoke   with   me   saying: Come, I will show

σοι   τὸ   κρίμα   τῆς   πόρνης   τῆς   μεγάλης
thee   the   judgment   of the   ²harlot   –   ¹great

τῆς   καθημένης   ἐπὶ   ὑδάτων   πολλῶν,   **2** μεθ'
–   sitting   on   ²waters   ¹many,   with

ἧς   ἐπόρνευσαν   οἱ   βασιλεῖς   τῆς   γῆς,
whom   ⁵practised   ¹the   ²kings   ³of the   ⁴earth,
            fornication

καὶ   ἐμεθύσθησαν   οἱ   κατοικοῦντες   τὴν   γῆν
and   ⁵became drunk   ¹the   ²dwelling [on]   ³the   ⁴earth
                                    [ones]

ἐκ   τοῦ   οἴνου   τῆς   πορνείας   αὐτῆς.   **3** καὶ
from   the   wine   of the   fornication   of her.   And

* Even in English a city is often personified as feminine.

3 So he carried me away in the spirit into the wilderness: and I saw a woman sit upon a scarlet coloured beast, full of names of blasphemy, having seven heads and ten horns.

4 And the woman was arrayed in purple and scarlet colour, and decked with gold and precious stones and pearls, having a golden cup in her hand full of abominations and filthiness of her fornication:

5 And upon her forehead *was* a name written, MYSTERY, BABYLON THE GREAT, THE MOTHER OF HARLOTS AND ABOMINATIONS OF THE EARTH.

6 And I saw the woman drunken with the blood of the saints, and with the blood of the martyrs of Jesus: and when I saw her, I wondered with great admiration.

7 And the angel said unto me, Wherefore didst thou marvel? I will tell thee the mystery of the woman, and of the beast that carrieth her, which hath the seven heads and ten horns.

8 The beast that thou sawest was, and is not;

ἀπήνεγκέν με εἰς ἔρημον ἐν πνεύματι.
he carried away me into a desert in spirit.

καὶ εἶδον γυναῖκα καθημένην ἐπὶ θηρίον
And I saw a woman sitting on ²beast

κόκκινον, γέμοντα ὀνόματα βλασφημίας,
¹a scarlet, *being* filled [with] names of blasphemy,

ἔχοντα κεφαλὰς ἑπτὰ καὶ κέρατα δέκα.
having ²heads ¹seven and ²horns ¹ten.

4 καὶ ἡ γυνὴ ἦν περιβεβλημένη πορφυροῦν
And the woman was *having been* clothed [in] purple

καὶ κόκκινον, καὶ κεχρυσωμένη χρυσίῳ
and scarlet, and *having been* gilded with gold

καὶ λίθῳ τιμίῳ καὶ μαργαρίταις, ἔχουσα
and ²stone ¹precious and pearls, having

ποτήριον χρυσοῦν ἐν τῇ χειρὶ αὐτῆς
¹cup ¹a golden in the hand of her

γέμον βδελυγμάτων καὶ τὰ ἀκάθαρτα
being filled of(with) and the unclean things
abominations

τῆς πορνείας αὐτῆς, 5 καὶ ἐπὶ τὸ
of the fornication of her, and on the

μέτωπον αὐτῆς ὄνομα γεγραμμένον,
forehead of her a name *having been* written,

μυστήριον, ΒΑΒΥΛΩΝ Η ΜΕΓΑΛΗ,
a mystery, BABYLON THE GREAT,

Η ΜΗΤΗΡ ΤΩΝ ΠΟΡΝΩΝ ΚΑΙ
The Mother of the Harlots and

ΤΩΝ ΒΔΕΛΥΓΜΑΤΩΝ ΤΗΣ ΓΗΣ.
of the Abominations of the Earth.

6 καὶ εἶδον τὴν γυναῖκα μεθύουσαν ἐκ
And I saw the woman *being* drunk from

τοῦ αἵματος τῶν ἁγίων καὶ ἐκ τοῦ
the blood of the saints and from the

αἵματος τῶν μαρτύρων Ἰησοῦ. Καὶ
blood of the witnesses of Jesus. And

ἐθαύμασα ἰδὼν αὐτὴν θαῦμα μέγα. 7 καὶ
²I wondered ¹seeing ³her ⁴[with] ⁶wonder ⁵a great. And

εἶπέν μοι ὁ ἄγγελος· διὰ τί ἐθαύμασας;
²said ⁴to me ¹the ²angel: Why didst thou wonder?

ἐγὼ ἐρῶ σοι τὸ μυστήριον τῆς γυναικὸς
I will tell thee the mystery of the woman

καὶ τοῦ θηρίου τοῦ βαστάζοντος αὐτὴν
and of the beast – carrying her

τοῦ ἔχοντος τὰς ἑπτὰ κεφαλὰς καὶ τὰ
– having the seven heads and the

δέκα κέρατα. 8 Τὸ θηρίον ὃ εἶδες ἦν
ten horns. The beast which thou wa⋅
sawest

and shall ascend out of the bottomless pit, and go into perdition: and they that dwell on the earth shall wonder, whose names were not written in the book of life from the foundation of the world, when they behold the beast that was, and is not, and yet is.

9 And here *is* the mind which hath wisdom. The seven heads are seven mountains, on which the woman sitteth.

10 And there are seven kings: five are fallen, and one is, *and* the other is not yet come; and when he cometh, he must continue a short space.

11 And the beast that was, and is not, even he is the eighth, and is of the seven, and goeth into perdition.

12 And the ten horns which thou sawest are ten kings, which have received no kingdom as yet; but receive power as kings one hour with the beast.

13 These have one mind, and shall give their power and strength unto the beast.

14 These shall make war with the Lamb, and the

καὶ οὐκ ἔστιν, καὶ μέλλει ἀναβαίνειν
and   is not,   and   is about   to come up

ἐκ τῆς ἀβύσσου καὶ εἰς ἀπώλειαν ὑπάγει·
out of the   abyss   and   ²to   ³destruction   ¹goes;

καὶ θαυμασθήσονται οἱ κατοικοῦντες ἐπὶ
and   ⁴will wonder   ¹the [ones]   ²dwelling   ³on

τῆς γῆς, ὧν οὐ γέγραπται τὸ ὄνομα
⁴the   ⁵earth, of whom ³has not been written ¹the   ²name

ἐπὶ τὸ βιβλίον τῆς ζωῆς ἀπὸ καταβολῆς
on   the   scroll   –   of life   from [the] foundation

κόσμου, βλεπόντων τὸ θηρίον ὅτι ἦν
of [the] world,   seeing   the   beast   that it was

καὶ οὐκ ἔστιν καὶ παρέσται. 9 ὧδε
and   is not   and   is present.   9 Here [is]

ὁ νοῦς ὁ ἔχων σοφίαν. αἱ ἑπτὰ
the mind   –   having   wisdom.   The   seven

κεφαλαὶ ἑπτὰ ὄρη εἰσίν, ὅπου ἡ γυνὴ
heads   ²seven ³mountains ¹are,   where   the woman

κάθηται ἐπ' αὐτῶν, καὶ βασιλεῖς ἑπτά
sits   on   them,   and   ²kings   ¹seven

εἰσιν· 10 οἱ πέντε ἔπεσαν, ὁ εἷς ἔστιν,
¹are: the   five   fell,   the one   is,

ὁ ἄλλος οὔπω ἦλθεν, καὶ ὅταν ἔλθῃ
the other   not yet   came,   and whenever he comes

ὀλίγον αὐτὸν δεῖ μεῖναι. 11 καὶ τὸ
⁴a little   ³him   ¹it behoves   ²to   And   the
[while]   remain.

θηρίον ὃ ἦν καὶ οὐκ ἔστιν, καὶ αὐτὸς
beast   which was   and   is not,   even   he

ὄγδοός ἐστιν, καὶ ἐκ τῶν ἑπτά ἐστιν,
²an eighth   ¹is,   and   ³of   ³the   ⁴seven   ¹is,

καὶ εἰς ἀπώλειαν ὑπάγει. 12 καὶ τὰ
and   to   destruction   goes.   And   the

δέκα κέρατα ἃ εἶδες δέκα βασιλεῖς
ten   horns   which thou   ²ten   ³kings
     sawest

εἰσιν, οἵτινες βασιλείαν οὔπω ἔλαβον,
¹are,   who   a kingdom   not yet   received,

ἀλλὰ ἐξουσίαν ὡς βασιλεῖς μίαν ὥραν
but   ²authority   ³as   ⁴kings   ⁵one   ⁶hour

λαμβάνουσιν μετὰ τοῦ θηρίου. 13 οὗτοι
¹receive   with   the   beast.   These

μίαν γνώμην ἔχουσιν, καὶ τὴν δύναμιν
one   mind   have,   and   the   power

καὶ ἐξουσίαν αὐτῶν τῷ θηρίῳ διδόασιν.
and   authority   of them   to the beast   they give.

14 οὗτοι μετὰ τοῦ ἀρνίου πολεμήσουσιν
These   ²with   ³the   ⁴Lamb   ¹will make war

Lamb shall overcome them: for he is Lord of lords, and King of kings: and they that are with him *are* called, and chosen, and faithful.

15 And he saith unto me, The waters which thou sawest, where the whore sitteth, are peoples, and multitudes, and nations, and tongues.

16 And the ten horns which thou sawest upon the beast, these shall hate the whore, and shall make her desolate and naked, and shall eat her flesh, and burn her with fire.

17 For God hath put in their hearts to fulfil his will, and to agree, and give their kingdom unto the beast, until the words of God shall be fulfilled.

18 And the woman which thou sawest is that great city, which reigneth over the kings of the earth.

καὶ τὸ ἀρνίον νικήσει αὐτούς, ὅτι κύριος
and the Lamb will overcome them, because ²Lord

κυρίων ἐστὶν καὶ βασιλεὺς βασιλέων, καὶ
²of lords ¹he is and King of kings, and

οἱ μετ᾽ αὐτοῦ κλητοὶ καὶ ἐκλεκτοὶ καὶ
the with him [are] called and chosen and
[ones]

πιστοί. **15** Καὶ λέγει μοι· τὰ ὕδατα
faithful. And he says to me: The waters

ἃ εἶδες, οὗ ἡ πόρνη κάθηται, λαοὶ
which thou where the harlot sits, peoples
sawest,

καὶ ὄχλοι εἰσὶν καὶ ἔθνη καὶ γλῶσσαι.
and crowds are and nations and tongues.

16 καὶ τὰ δέκα κέρατα ἃ εἶδες καὶ
And the ten horns which thou sawest and

τὸ θηρίον, οὗτοι μισήσουσιν τὴν πόρνην,
the beast, these will hate the harlot,

καὶ ἠρημωμένην ποιήσουσιν αὐτὴν καὶ
and ³having been desolated ¹will make ²her and

γυμνήν, καὶ τὰς σάρκας αὐτῆς φάγονται,
naked, and ²the ³fleshes ⁴of her ¹will eat,

καὶ αὐτὴν κατακαύσουσιν [ἐν] πυρί· **17** ὁ
and ²her ¹will consume with fire;

γὰρ θεὸς ἔδωκεν εἰς τὰς καρδίας αὐτῶν
for God gave into the hearts of them

ποιῆσαι τὴν γνώμην αὐτοῦ, καὶ ποιῆσαι
to do the mind of him, and to make

μίαν γνώμην καὶ δοῦναι τὴν βασιλείαν
one mind and to give the kingdom

αὐτῶν τῷ θηρίῳ, ἄχρι τελεσθήσονται οἱ
of them to the beast, until ⁴shall be accomplished ¹the

λόγοι τοῦ θεοῦ. **18** καὶ ἡ γυνὴ ἣν
²words – ³of God. And the woman whom

εἶδες ἔστιν ἡ πόλις ἡ μεγάλη ἡ ἔχουσα
thou is the ²city – ¹great – having
sawest

βασιλείαν ἐπὶ τῶν βασιλέων τῆς γῆς.
a kingdom over the kings of the earth.

CHAPTER 18

A ND after these things I saw another angel come down from heaven, having great power; and the earth was lightened with his glory.

2 And he cried mightily

18 Μετὰ ταῦτα εἶδον ἄλλον ἄγγελον
After these things I saw another angel

καταβαίνοντα ἐκ τοῦ οὐρανοῦ, ἔχοντα
coming down out of – heaven, having

ἐξουσίαν μεγάλην, καὶ ἡ γῆ ἐφωτίσθη
²authority ¹great, and the earth was enlightened

ἐκ τῆς δόξης αὐτοῦ. **2** καὶ ἔκραξεν
from the glory of him. And he cried

with a strong voice, saying, Babylon the great is fallen, is fallen, and is become the habitation of devils, and the hold of every foul spirit, and a cage of every unclean and hateful bird.

3 For all nations have drunk of the wine of the wrath of her fornication, and the kings of the earth have committed fornication with her, and the merchants of the earth are waxed rich through the abundance of her delicacies.

4 And I heard another voice from heaven, saying, Come out of her, my people, that ye be not partakers of her sins, and that ye receive not of her plagues.

5 For her sins have reached unto heaven, and God hath remembered her iniquities.

6 Reward her even as she rewarded you, and double unto her double according to her works: in the cup which she hath filled fill to her double.

7 How much she hath glorified herself, and lived deliciously, so much torment and sorrow give her:

ἐν	ἰσχυρᾷ	φωνῇ	λέγων·	ἔπεσεν	ἔπεσεν
in	a strong	voice	saying:	Fell[,]	fell

Βαβυλὼν	ἡ	μεγάλη,	καὶ ἐγένετο	κατοικητή-
Babylon	the	great,	and became	a dwelling-

ριον	δαιμονίων	καὶ	φυλακὴ	παντὸς
place	of demons	and	a prison	of every

πνεύματος	ἀκαθάρτου	καὶ	φυλακὴ	παντὸς
²spirit	¹unclean	and	a prison	of every

ὀρνέου	ἀκαθάρτου	καὶ	μεμισημένου,	3 ὅτι
⁴bird	¹unclean	²and	³having been hated,	because

ἐκ	τοῦ	οἴνου	τοῦ	θυμοῦ	τῆς πορνείας
⁵of	⁶the	⁷wine	⁸of the	⁹anger	¹⁰of the ¹¹fornication

αὐτῆς	πέπωκαν	πάντα	τὰ	ἔθνη, καὶ
¹²of her	⁴have drunk	¹all	²the	³nations, and

οἱ βασιλεῖς	τῆς γῆς	μετ᾽	αὐτῆς	ἐπόρνευσαν,
the kings	of the earth	with	her	practised fornication,

καὶ οἱ ἔμποροι	τῆς γῆς	ἐκ	τῆς	δυνάμεως
and the merchants	of the earth	³from	⁵the	⁴power

τοῦ	στρήνους	αὐτῆς	ἐπλούτησαν. 4 Καὶ
⁶of the	⁷luxury	²of her	¹became rich. And

ἤκουσα	ἄλλην	φωνὴν	ἐκ τοῦ	οὐρανοῦ
I heard	another	voice	out of —	heaven

λέγουσαν·	ἐξέλθατε	ὁ λαός μου	ἐξ αὐτῆς,
saying:	Come ye out[,]	the people of me[,]	out of her,

ἵνα	μὴ	συγκοινωνήσητε	ταῖς ἁμαρτίαις
lest		ye share	in the sins

αὐτῆς,	καὶ	ἐκ τῶν	πληγῶν	αὐτῆς ἵνα
of her,	and	³of ⁴the	⁵plagues	⁶of her ¹lest

μὴ	λάβητε·	5 ὅτι ἐκολλήθησαν	αὐτῆς αἱ
²ye receive;		because ⁴joined together	²of her ¹the

ἁμαρτίαι	ἄχρι τοῦ	οὐρανοῦ,	καὶ ἐμνημό-
³sins	up to —	heaven,	and ¹remem-

νευσεν	ὁ θεὸς	τὰ ἀδικήματα	αὐτῆς.
bered	— ¹God	the misdeeds	of her.

6 ἀπόδοτε	αὐτῇ	ὡς καὶ	αὐτὴ ἀπέδωκεν,
Give ye back	to her	as indeed	she gave back,

καὶ διπλώσατε	τὰ	διπλᾶ κατὰ	τὰ ἔργα
and double ye	the	double according to the	works

αὐτῆς·	ἐν τῷ	ποτηρίῳ	ᾧ ἐκέρασεν
of her;	in the	cup	in which she mixed

κεράσατε	αὐτῇ	διπλοῦν·	7 ὅσα ἐδόξασεν
mix ye	to her	double;	by what she glorified things

αὐτὴν	καὶ	ἐστρηνίασεν,	τοσοῦτον δότε
her[self]	and	luxuriated,	by so much give ye

αὐτῇ	βασανισμὸν	καὶ	πένθος. ὅτι ἐν
to her	torment	and	sorrow. Because in

for she saith in her heart, I sit a queen, and am no widow, and shall see no sorrow.

τῇ καρδίᾳ αὐτῆς λέγει ὅτι κάθημαι
the heart of her she says[,] – I sit

βασίλισσα καὶ χήρα οὐκ εἰμὶ καὶ πένθος
a queen and a widow I am not and sorrow

οὐ μὴ ἴδω· 8 διὰ τοῦτο ἐν μιᾷ ἡμέρᾳ
by no means I see; therefore in one day

8 Therefore shall her plagues come in one day, death, and mourning, and famine; and she shall be utterly burned with fire: for strong is the Lord God who judgeth her.

ἥξουσιν αἱ πληγαὶ αὐτῆς, θάνατος καὶ
will come the plagues of her, death and

πένθος καὶ λιμός, καὶ ἐν πυρὶ κατακαυ-
sorrow and famine, and with fire she will be

θήσεται· ὅτι ἰσχυρὸς κύριος ὁ θεὸς ὁ
consumed; because strong [is] [the] Lord – God the

κρίνας αὐτήν. 9 καὶ κλαύσουσιν καὶ
[one] judging her. And [one] will weep and

9 And the kings of the earth, who have committed fornication and lived deliciously with her, shall bewail her, and lament for her, when they shall see the smoke of her burning,

κόψονται ἐπ' αὐτὴν οἱ βασιλεῖς τῆς
wail over her the kings of the

γῆς οἱ μετ' αὐτῆς πορνεύσαντες καὶ
earth the with her having practised and
[ones] fornication

στρηνιάσαντες, ὅταν βλέπωσιν τὸν καπνὸν
having luxuriated, whenever they see the smoke

τῆς πυρώσεως αὐτῆς, 10 ἀπὸ μακρόθεν
of the burning of her, from afar

10 Standing afar off for the fear of her torment, saying, Alas, alas that great city Babylon, that mighty city! for in one hour is thy judgment come.

ἑστηκότες διὰ τὸν φόβον τοῦ βασανισμοῦ
standing because of the fear of the torment

αὐτῆς, λέγοντες· οὐαὶ οὐαί, ἡ πόλις
of her, saying: Woe[,] woe, the city

ἡ μεγάλη, Βαβυλὼν ἡ πόλις ἡ ἰσχυρά,
– great, Babylon the city – strong,

ὅτι μιᾷ ὥρᾳ ἦλθεν ἡ κρίσις σου. 11 καὶ
because in one hour came the judgment of thee. And

11 And the merchants of the earth shall weep and mourn over her; for no man buyeth their merchandise any more:

οἱ ἔμποροι τῆς γῆς κλαίουσιν καὶ
the merchants of the earth weep and

πενθοῦσιν ἐπ' αὐτήν, ὅτι τὸν γόμον
sorrow over her, because the cargo

αὐτῶν οὐδεὶς ἀγοράζει οὐκέτι, 12 γόμον
of them no one buys any more, cargo

12 The merchandise of gold, and silver, and precious stones, and of pearls, and fine linen, and purple, and silk, and scarlet, and all thyine wood, and all manner vessels of ivory, and all manner vessels of most precious

χρυσοῦ καὶ ἀργύρου καὶ λίθου τιμίου
of gold and of silver and stone of valuable

καὶ μαργαριτῶν καὶ βυσσίνου καὶ πορφύρας
and of pearls and of fine linen and of purple

καὶ σηρικοῦ καὶ κοκκίνου, καὶ πᾶν
and of silk and of scarlet, and all

ξύλον θύϊνον καὶ πᾶν σκεῦος ἐλεφάντινον
wood thyine and every vessel ivory

καὶ πᾶν σκεῦος ἐκ ξύλου τιμιωτάτου
and every vessel of wood very valuable

wood, and of brass, and iron, and marble,

13 And cinnamon, and odours, and ointments, and wine, and oil, and fine flour, and wheat, and beasts, and sheep, and horses, and chariots, and slaves, and souls of men.

14 And the fruits that thy soul lusted after are departed from thee, and all things which were dainty and goodly are departed from thee, and thou shalt find them no more at all.

15 The merchants of these things, which were made rich by her, shall stand afar off for the fear of her torment, weeping and wailing,

16 And saying, Alas, alas that great city, that was clothed in fine linen, and purple, and scarlet, and decked with gold, and precious stones, and pearls!

17 For in one hour so great riches is come to nought. And every shipmaster, and all the company in ships, and sailors, and as many as trade by sea, stood afar off,

---

καὶ χαλκοῦ καὶ σιδήρου καὶ μαρμάρου,
and of bronze and of iron and of marble,

13 καὶ κιννάμωμον καὶ ἄμωμον καὶ
and cinnamon and spice and

θυμιάματα καὶ μύρον καὶ λίβανον καὶ
incenses and ointment and frankincense and

οἶνον καὶ ἔλαιον καὶ σεμίδαλιν καὶ σῖτον
wine and oil and fine meal and corn

καὶ κτήνη καὶ πρόβατα, καὶ ἵππων
and beasts of burden and sheep, and of horses

καὶ ῥεδῶν καὶ σωμάτων, καὶ ψυχὰς
and of carriages and of bodies, and souls

ἀνθρώπων. 14 καὶ ἡ ὀπώρα σου τῆς
of men. And the fruit ²of thee ¹of the

ἐπιθυμίας τῆς ψυχῆς ἀπῆλθεν ἀπὸ σοῦ,
¹lust ³of the ⁴soul went away from thee,

καὶ πάντα τὰ λιπαρὰ καὶ τὰ λαμπρὰ
and all the sumptuous and the bright
things things

ἀπώλετο ἀπὸ σοῦ, καὶ οὐκέτι οὐ μὴ
perished from thee, and no more by no(any)
means

αὐτὰ εὑρήσουσιν. 15 οἱ ἔμποροι τούτων,
²them ¹shall they find. The merchants of these
things,

οἱ πλουτήσαντες ἀπ᾽ αὐτῆς, ἀπὸ μακρόθεν
the having been rich from her, ²from ¹afar
[ones]

στήσονται διὰ τὸν φόβον τοῦ βασανισμοῦ
¹will stand because of the fear of the torment

αὐτῆς κλαίοντες καὶ πενθοῦντες, 16 λέγοντες·
of her weeping and sorrowing, saying:

οὐαὶ οὐαί, ἡ πόλις ἡ μεγάλη, ἡ περι-
Woe[,] woe, the ²city – ¹great, – having

βεβλημένη βύσσινον καὶ πορφυροῦν καὶ
been clothed [with] fine linen and purple and

κόκκινον, καὶ κεχρυσωμένη ἐν χρυσίῳ
scarlet, and having been gilded with gold

καὶ λίθῳ τιμίῳ καὶ μαργαρίτῃ, 17 ὅτι
and ²stone ¹valuable and pearl, because

μιᾷ ὥρᾳ ἠρημώθη ὁ τοσοῦτος πλοῦτος.
in one hour ³was made ¹such great ²wealth.
desolate

καὶ πᾶς κυβερνήτης καὶ πᾶς ὁ ἐπὶ
And every steersman and ¹every ²one ³to

τόπον πλέων καὶ ναῦται καὶ ὅσοι τὴν
²a place ³sailing and sailors and as many as ¹the

θάλασσαν ἐργάζονται, ἀπὸ μακρόθεν ἔστησαν
³sea ¹work, ²from ³afar ¹stood

18 And cried when they saw the smoke of her burning, saying, What *city is* like unto this great city!

19 And they cast dust on their heads, and cried, weeping and wailing, saying, Alas, alas that great city, wherein were made rich all that had ships in the sea by reason of her costliness! for in one hour is she made desolate.

20 Rejoice over her, *thou* heaven, and *ye* holy apostles and prophets; for God hath avenged you on her.

21 And a mighty angel took up a stone like a great millstone, and cast *it* into the sea, saying, Thus with violence shall that great city Babylon be thrown down, and shall be found no more at all.

22 And the voice of harpers, and musicians, and of pipers, and trumpeters, shall be heard no more at all in thee; and no craftsman, of whatsoever craft *he be*, shall be found any more in thee; and the sound of a millstone shall be heard no more at all in thee;

23 And the light of a candle shall shine no more at all in thee; and the

18 καὶ ἔκραζον βλέποντες τὸν καπνὸν
and cried out seeing the smoke

τῆς πυρώσεως αὐτῆς λέγοντες· τίς ὁμοία
of the burning of her saying: Who(What) [is] like

τῇ πόλει τῇ μεγάλῃ; 19 καὶ ἔβαλον
to the ²city – ¹great? And they cast

χοῦν ἐπὶ τὰς κεφαλὰς αὐτῶν καὶ ἔκραζον
dust on the heads of them and cried out

κλαίοντες καὶ πενθοῦντες, λέγοντες· οὐαὶ
weeping and sorrowing, saying: Woe[,]

οὐαί, ἡ πόλις ἡ μεγάλη, ἐν ᾗ ἐπλούτησαν
woe, the ²city – ¹great, by which ³were rich

πάντες οἱ ἔχοντες τὰ πλοῖα ἐν τῇ
¹all ²the [ones] ³having ⁴the ⁵ships ⁶in ⁷the

θαλάσσῃ ἐκ τῆς τιμιότητος αὐτῆς, ὅτι
⁸sea from the worth of her, because

μιᾷ ὥρᾳ ἠρημώθη. 20 Εὐφραίνου ἐπ᾽
in one hour she was made desolate. Be thou glad over

αὐτῇ, οὐρανὲ καὶ οἱ ἅγιοι καὶ οἱ ἀπό-
her, heaven and *the* saints and *the* apost-

στολοι καὶ οἱ προφῆται, ὅτι ἔκρινεν ὁ
les and *the* prophets, because ²judged –

θεὸς τὸ κρίμα ὑμῶν ἐξ αὐτῆς. 21 Καὶ
¹God the judgment of you by her. And

ἦρεν εἷς ἄγγελος ἰσχυρὸς λίθον ὡς
⁴lifted ¹one ³angel ²strong a stone as

μύλινον μέγαν, καὶ ἔβαλεν εἰς τὴν θά-
²millstone ¹a great, and threw into the sea

λασσαν λέγων· οὕτως ὁρμήματι βληθήσεται
saying: Thus with a rush ⁵shall be thrown

Βαβυλὼν ἡ μεγάλη πόλις, καὶ οὐ μὴ
¹Babylon ²the ³great ⁴city, and by no means

εὑρεθῇ ἔτι. 22 καὶ φωνὴ κιθαρῳδῶν
[shall] be found longer. And sound of harpers

καὶ μουσικῶν καὶ αὐλητῶν καὶ σαλπιστῶν
and of musicians and of flutists and of trumpeters

οὐ μὴ ἀκουσθῇ ἐν σοὶ ἔτι, καὶ πᾶς
by no means [shall] be heard in thee longer, and every

τεχνίτης πάσης τέχνης οὐ μὴ εὑρεθῇ
craftsman of every craft by no means [shall] be found

ἐν σοὶ ἔτι, καὶ φωνὴ μύλου οὐ μὴ
in thee longer, and sound of a mill by no means

ἀκουσθῇ ἐν σοὶ ἔτι, 23 καὶ φῶς
[shall] be heard in thee longer, and light

λύχνου οὐ μὴ φάνῃ ἐν σοὶ ἔτι, καὶ
of a by no means [shall] in thee longer, and
lamp shine

voice of the bridegroom
and of the bride shall be
heard no more at all in
thee: for thy merchants
were the great men of the
earth; for by thy sorceries
were all nations deceived.

24 And in her was
found the blood of pro-
phets, and of saints, and
of all that were slain upon the earth.

φωνὴ   νυμφίου   καὶ   νύμφης   οὐ   μὴ
voice   of bridegroom   and   of bride   by no means

ἀκουσθῇ   ἐν   σοὶ   ἔτι·   ὅτι   [οἱ]   ἔμποροί
[shall] be heard in   thee   longer; because   the   merchants

σου   ἦσαν   οἱ   μεγιστᾶνες   τῆς   γῆς,   ὅτι
of thee   were   the   great ones   of the   earth, because

ἐν   τῇ   φαρμακείᾳ   σου   ἐπλανήθησαν   πάντα
by   the   sorcery   of thee   ⁴were deceived   ¹all

τὰ   ἔθνη,   24 καὶ   ἐν   αὐτῇ   αἷμα   προφητῶν
²the   ³nations,   and   in   her   ³blood   ²of prophets

καὶ   ἁγίων   εὑρέθη   καὶ   πάντων   τῶν
⁴and   ⁵of saints   ¹was found   and   of all   the [ones]

ἐσφαγμένων   ἐπὶ   τῆς   γῆς.
having been slain   on   the   earth.

CHAPTER 19

A ND after these things
I heard a great voice
of much people in heaven,
saying, Alleluia; Salva-
tion, and glory, and hon-
our, and power, unto the
Lord our God:

2 For true and righteous
are his judgments: for he
hath judged the great
whore, which did corrupt
the earth with her fornication, and hath avenged the
blood of his servants at
her hand.

3 And again they said,
Alleluia. And her smoke
rose up for ever and ever.

4 And the four and
twenty elders and the four
beasts fell down and wor-
shipped God that sat on
the throne, saying, Amen;
Alleluia.

19 Μετὰ   ταῦτα   ἤκουσα   ὡς   φωνὴν
After   these things   I heard   as   ²voice

μεγάλην   ὄχλου   πολλοῦ   ἐν   τῷ   οὐρανῷ
¹a great   ⁴crowd   ³of a much   in   –   heaven
(loud)   (great)

λεγόντων·   ἀλληλουϊά·   ἡ   σωτηρία   καὶ   ἡ
saying: Halleluia: The   salvation   and   the

δόξα   καὶ   ἡ   δύναμις   τοῦ   θεοῦ   ἡμῶν,
glory   and   the   power   of the   God   of us,

2 ὅτι   ἀληθιναὶ   καὶ   δίκαιαι   αἱ   κρίσεις
because   true   and   righteous   the   judgments

αὐτοῦ·   ὅτι   ἔκρινεν   τὴν   πόρνην   τὴν
of him;   because   he judged   the   ²harlot

μεγάλην   ἥτις   ἔφθειρεν   τὴν   γῆν   ἐν   τῇ
¹great   who   defiled   the   earth   with   the

πορνείᾳ   αὐτῆς,   καὶ   ἐξεδίκησεν   τὸ   αἷμα
fornication   of her,   and   *he* avenged   the   blood

τῶν   δούλων   αὐτοῦ   ἐκ   χειρὸς   αὐτῆς.
of the   slaves   of him   out of   [the] hand   of her.

3 καὶ   δεύτερον   εἴρηκαν·   ἀλληλουϊά·   καὶ
And   secondly   they *have* said: Halleluia;   and

ὁ   καπνὸς   αὐτῆς   ἀναβαίνει   εἰς   τοὺς
the   smoke   of her   goes up   unto   the

αἰῶνας   τῶν   αἰώνων.   **4** καὶ   ἔπεσαν   οἱ
ages   of the   ages.   And   ²fell   ¹the

πρεσβύτεροι   οἱ   εἴκοσι   τέσσαρες   καὶ   τὰ
³elders   –   ²twenty-four   ⁴and   ⁵the

τέσσερα   ζῷα,   καὶ   προσεκύνησαν   τῷ   θεῷ
⁶four   ⁷living   and   worshipped   –   God
    creatures,

τῷ   καθημένῳ   ἐπὶ   τῷ   θρόνῳ   λέγοντες·
–   sitting   on   the   throne   saying:

5 And a voice came out of the throne, saying, Praise our God, all ye his servants, and ye that fear him, both small and great.

6 And I heard as it were the voice of a great multitude, and as the voice of many waters, and as the voice of mighty thunderings, saying, Alleluia: for the Lord God omnipotent reigneth.

7 Let us be glad and rejoice, and give honour to him: for the marriage of the Lamb is come, and his wife hath made herself ready.

8 And to her was granted that she should be arrayed in fine linen, clean and white: for the fine linen is the righteousness of saints.

9 And he saith unto me, Write, Blessed *are* they which are called unto the marriage supper of the Lamb. And he saith unto me, These are the true sayings of God.

10 And I fell at his feet to worship him. And he said unto me, See *thou do it* not: I am thy fellowservant, and of thy breth-

ἀμὴν	ἀλληλουϊά.	5 καὶ	φωνὴ	ἀπὸ	τοῦ
Amen[,]	halleluia.	And	a voice	⁹from	⁸the

θρόνου	ἐξῆλθεν	λέγουσα·	αἰνεῖτε	τῷ	θεῷ
⁴throne	¹came out	saying:	Praise ye	the	God

ἡμῶν,	πάντες	οἱ	δοῦλοι	αὐτοῦ,	οἱ
of us,	all	the	slaves	of him,	the

φοβούμενοι	αὐτόν,	οἱ	μικροὶ	καὶ	οἱ
[ones] fearing	him,	the	small	and	the

μεγάλοι.	6 Καὶ	ἤκουσα	ὡς	φωνὴν	ὄχλου
great.	And	I heard	as	a sound	²crowd

πολλοῦ	καὶ	ὡς	φωνὴν	ὑδάτων	πολλῶν
¹of a much(great)	and	as	a sound	²waters	¹of many

καὶ	ὡς	φωνὴν	βροντῶν	ἰσχυρῶν,	λεγόντων·
and	as	a sound	²thunders	¹of strong (loud),	saying:

ἀλληλουϊά,	ὅτι	ἐβασίλευσεν	κύριος	ὁ	θεὸς
Halleluia,	because	⁷reigned	¹[the] Lord	²the	³God

ἡμῶν	ὁ	παντοκράτωρ.	7 χαίρωμεν	καὶ
⁴of us	⁵the	⁶Almighty.	Let us rejoice	and

ἀγαλλιῶμεν,	καὶ	δώσομεν	τὴν	δόξαν	αὐτῷ,
let us exult,	and	we will give	the	glory	to him,

ὅτι	ἦλθεν	ὁ	γάμος	τοῦ	ἀρνίου,	καὶ
because	³came	¹the	²marriage	³of the	⁴Lamb,	and

ἡ	γυνὴ	αὐτοῦ	ἡτοίμασεν	ἑαυτήν,	8 καὶ
the	wife	of him	prepared	herself,	and

ἐδόθη	αὐτῇ	ἵνα	περιβάληται	βύσσινον
it was given	to her	*in order* that	she might be clothed [with]	⁹fine linen

λαμπρὸν	καθαρόν·	τὸ	γὰρ	βύσσινον	τὰ
¹bright	²clean;	for the		fine linen	¹the

δικαιώματα	τῶν	ἁγίων	ἐστίν.	9 Καὶ
²righteous deeds	⁴of the	³saints	¹is.	And

λέγει	μοι·	γράψον·	μακάριοι	οἱ	εἰς	τὸ
he tells	me:	Write thou;	blessed	¹the [ones]	³to	⁴the

δεῖπνον	τοῦ	γάμου	τοῦ	ἀρνίου	κεκλημένοι.
⁵supper	⁶of the	⁷marriage	⁸of the	⁹Lamb	²having been called.

καὶ	λέγει	μοι·	οὗτοι	οἱ	λόγοι	ἀληθινοὶ
And	he says	to me:	¹These	-	²words	³true

τοῦ	θεοῦ	εἰσιν.	10 καὶ	ἔπεσα	ἔμπροσθεν
-	⁵of God	⁴are.	And	I fell	before

τῶν	ποδῶν	αὐτοῦ	προσκυνῆσαι	αὐτῷ.
the	feet	of him	to worship	him.

καὶ	λέγει	μοι·	ὅρα	μή·	σύνδουλός	σού
And	he says	to me:	See thou [do it]	not;	²a fellow-slave	³of thee

εἰμι	καὶ	τῶν	ἀδελφῶν	σου	τῶν	ἐχόντων
¹I am	and	of the	brothers	of thee	-	having

ren that have the testimony of Jesus: worship God: for the testimony of Jesus is the spirit of prophecy.

11 And I saw heaven opened, and behold a white horse; and he that sat upon him *was* called Faithful and True, and in righteousness he doth judge and make war.

12 His eyes *were* as a flame of fire, and on his head *were* many crowns; and he had a name written, that no man knew, but he himself.

13 And he *was* clothed with a vesture dipped in blood: and his name is called The Word of God.

14 And the armies *which were* in heaven followed him upon white horses, clothed in fine linen, white and clean.

15 And out of his mouth goeth a sharp sword, that with it he should smite the nations: and he shall rule them with a rod of iron: and he treadeth the winepress of the fierceness and wrath of Almighty God.

16 And he hath on *his* vesture and on his thigh

τὴν μαρτυρίαν Ἰησοῦ· τῷ θεῷ προσκύνησον.
the　witness　of Jesus;　–　²God　¹worship thou.

ἡ γὰρ μαρτυρία Ἰησοῦ ἐστιν τὸ πνεῦμα
For the　witness　of Jesus　is　the　spirit

τῆς προφητείας.
–　of prophecy.

11 Καὶ εἶδον τὸν οὐρανὸν ἠνεῳγμένον,
And　I saw　–　heaven　*having been* opened,

καὶ ἰδοὺ ἵππος λευκός, καὶ ὁ καθήμενος
and　behold[,]　²horse　¹a white,　and the [one]　sitting

ἐπ' αὐτὸν πιστὸς καλούμενος καὶ ἀληθινός,
on　it　²faithful　¹*being* called　and　true,

καὶ ἐν δικαιοσύνῃ κρίνει καὶ πολεμεῖ.
and　in　righteousness　he judges　and　makes war.

12 οἱ δὲ ὀφθαλμοὶ αὐτοῦ φλὸξ πυρός,
And the　eyes　of him [are as] a flame　of fire,

καὶ ἐπὶ τὴν κεφαλὴν αὐτοῦ διαδήματα
and　on　the　head　of him　²diadems

πολλά, ἔχων ὄνομα γεγραμμένον ὃ οὐδεὶς
¹many,　having　a name　*having been* written　which　no one

οἶδεν εἰ μὴ αὐτός, 13 καὶ περιβεβλημένος
knows　except　[him]self,　and　*having been* clothed [with]

ἱμάτιον βεβαμμένον αἵματι, καὶ κέκληται
a garment　*having been* dipped　in blood,　and　²*has been* called

τὸ ὄνομα αὐτοῦ ὁ λόγος τοῦ θεοῦ.
¹the　²name　³of him　The　Word　–　of God.

14 καὶ τὰ στρατεύματα τὰ ἐν τῷ οὐρανῷ
And the　armies　–　in　–　heaven

ἠκολούθει αὐτῷ ἐφ' ἵπποις λευκοῖς, ἐνδεδυμένοι
followed　him　on　²horses　¹white,　*having been* dressed [in]

βύσσινον λευκὸν καθαρόν. 15 καὶ ἐκ
²fine linen　¹white　³clean.　And out of

τοῦ στόματος αὐτοῦ ἐκπορεύεται ῥομφαία
the　mouth　of him　proceeds　²sword

ὀξεῖα, ἵνα ἐν αὐτῇ πατάξῃ τὰ ἔθνη·
¹a sharp,　in order that　with　it　he may smite　the　nations;

καὶ αὐτὸς ποιμανεῖ αὐτοὺς ἐν ῥάβδῳ
and　he　will shepherd　them　with　²staff

σιδηρᾷ· καὶ αὐτὸς πατεῖ τὴν ληνὸν
¹an iron;　and　he　treads　the　winepress

τοῦ οἴνου τοῦ θυμοῦ τῆς ὀργῆς τοῦ
of the　wine　of the　anger[,]　of the　wrath　–

θεοῦ τοῦ παντοκράτορος. 16 καὶ ἔχει
of God　of the　Almighty.　And　he has

ἐπὶ τὸ ἱμάτιον καὶ ἐπὶ τὸν μηρὸν
on　the　garment　and　on　the　thigh

a name written, KING OF KINGS, AND LORD OF LORDS.

17 And I saw an angel standing in the sun; and he cried with a loud voice, saying to all the fowls that fly in the midst of heaven, Come and gather yourselves together unto the supper of the great God;

18 That ye may eat the flesh of kings, and the flesh of captains, and the flesh of mighty men, and the flesh of horses, and of them that sit on them, and the flesh of all *men*, *both* free and bond, both small and great.

19 And I saw the beast, and the kings of the earth, and their armies, gathered together to make war against him that sat on the horse, and against his army.

20 And the beast was taken, and with him the false prophet that wrought miracles before him, with which he deceived them that had received the mark of the beast, and them that worshipped his image. These both were cast alive

αὐτοῦ ὄνομα γεγραμμένον· ΒΑΣΙΛΕΥΣ
of him a name *having been* written: KING

ΒΑΣΙΛΕΩΝ ΚΑΙ ΚΥΡΙΟΣ ΚΥΡΙΩΝ.
OF KINGS AND LORD OF LORDS.

17 Καὶ εἶδον ἕνα ἄγγελον ἑστῶτα ἐν
And I saw one angel standing in

τῷ ἡλίῳ, καὶ ἔκραξεν ἐν φωνῇ μεγάλῃ
the sun, and he cried out in ²voice ¹a great
(loud)

λέγων πᾶσιν τοῖς ὀρνέοις τοῖς πετομένοις
saying to all the birds — flying

ἐν μεσουρανήματι· δεῦτε συνάχθητε εἰς
in mid-heaven: Come ye[,] assemble ye to

τὸ δεῖπνον τὸ μέγα τοῦ θεοῦ, 18 ἵνα
the ²supper — ¹great — of God, in order that

φάγητε σάρκας βασιλέων καὶ σάρκας
ye may eat flesh*es* of kings and flesh*es*

χιλιάρχων καὶ σάρκας ἰσχυρῶν καὶ σάρκας
of chiliarchs and flesh*es* of strong men and flesh*es*

ἵππων καὶ τῶν καθημένων ἐπ' αὐτῶν,
of horses and of the [ones] sitting on them,

καὶ σάρκας πάντων ἐλευθέρων τε καὶ
and flesh*es* of all ²free men ¹both and

δούλων καὶ μικρῶν καὶ μεγάλων. 19 Καὶ
slaves both small and great. And

εἶδον τὸ θηρίον καὶ τοὺς βασιλεῖς τῆς
I saw the beast and the kings of the

γῆς καὶ τὰ στρατεύματα αὐτῶν συνηγμένα
earth and the armies of them *having been assembled*

ποιῆσαι τὸν πόλεμον μετὰ τοῦ καθημένου
to make the war with the [one] sitting

ἐπὶ τοῦ ἵππου καὶ μετὰ τοῦ στρατεύματος
on the horse and with the army

αὐτοῦ. 20 καὶ ἐπιάσθη τὸ θηρίον καὶ
of him. And ³was seized ¹the ²beast and

μετ' αὐτοῦ ὁ ψευδοπροφήτης ὁ ποιήσας
with it the false prophet the [one] having done

τὰ σημεῖα ἐνώπιον αὐτοῦ, ἐν οἷς ἐπλάνη-
the signs before it, by which he de-

σεν τοὺς λαβόντας τὸ χάραγμα τοῦ
ceived the [ones] having received the mark of the

θηρίου καὶ τοὺς προσκυνοῦντας τῇ εἰκόνι
beast and the [ones] worshipping the image

αὐτοῦ· ζῶντες ἐβλήθησαν οἱ δύο εἰς
of it; ⁴living ³were cast ¹the ²two into

into a lake of fire burning
with brimstone.

21 And the remnant
were slain with the sword
of him that sat upon the
horse, which *sword* pro-
ceeded out of his mouth,
and all the fowls were
filled with their flesh.

τὴν   λίμνην   τοῦ   πυρὸς   τῆς   καιομένης
the   lake   -   of fire   -   burning*

ἐν   θείῳ.   21 καὶ   οἱ   λοιποὶ   ἀπεκτάνθησαν
with sulphur.   And   the   rest   were killed

ἐν   τῇ   ῥομφαίᾳ   τοῦ   καθημένου   ἐπὶ   τοῦ
with the   sword   of the [one] sitting   on   the

ἵππου   τῇ   ἐξελθούσῃ   ἐκ   τοῦ   στόματος
horse   -   proceeding§   out of   the   mouth

αὐτοῦ,   καὶ   πάντα   τὰ   ὄρνεα   ἐχορτάσθησαν
of him,   and   all   the   birds   were filled

ἐκ   τῶν   σαρκῶν   αὐτῶν.
by   the   flesh*es*   of them.

CHAPTER 20

AND I saw an angel
come down from
heaven, having the key
of the bottomless pit and
a great chain in his hand.

2 And he laid hold on
the dragon, that old ser-
pent, which is the Devil,
and Satan, and bound him
a thousand years,

3 And cast him into the
bottomless pit, and shut
him up, and set a seal
upon him, that he should
deceive the nations no
more, till the thousand
years should be fulfilled:
and after that he must be
loosed a little season.

4 And I saw thrones,
and they sat upon them,
and judgment was given
unto them: and *I saw* the
souls of them that were
beheaded for the witness of
Jesus, and for the word of

20 Καὶ   εἶδον   ἄγγελον   καταβαίνοντα   ἐκ
And   I saw   an angel   coming down   out of

τοῦ   οὐρανοῦ,   ἔχοντα   τὴν   κλεῖν   τῆς
-    heaven,   having   the   key   of the

ἀβύσσου   καὶ   ἅλυσιν   μεγάλην   ἐπὶ   τὴν   χεῖρα
abyss   and   ²chain   ¹a great   on   the   hand

αὐτοῦ.   2 καὶ   ἐκράτησεν   τὸν   δράκοντα,
of him.   And   he laid hold [of]   the   dragon,

ὁ   ὄφις   ὁ   ἀρχαῖος,   ὅς   ἐστιν   Διάβολος
the ²serpent   -   ¹old,   who   is   Devil

καὶ   ὁ   Σατανᾶς,   καὶ   ἔδησεν   αὐτὸν   χίλια
and   -   Satan,   and   bound   him   a thousand

ἔτη,   3 καὶ   ἔβαλεν   αὐτὸν   εἰς   τὴν   ἄβυσσον,
years,   and   cast   him   into   the   abyss,

καὶ   ἔκλεισεν   καὶ   ἐσφράγισεν   ἐπάνω   αὐτοῦ,
and   shut   and   sealed   over   him,

ἵνα   μὴ   πλανήσῃ   ἔτι   τὰ   ἔθνη,   ἄχρι
in or-   he should not deceive   longer   the   nations,   until
der that

τελεσθῇ   τὰ   χίλια   ἔτη·   μετὰ   ταῦτα
⁴are finished   ¹the   ²thousand   ³years;   after   these things

δεῖ   λυθῆναι   αὐτὸν   μικρὸν   χρόνον.
it be-   ²to be   ¹him   a little   time.
hoves   loosed

4 Καὶ   εἶδον   θρόνους,   καὶ   ἐκάθισαν   ἐπ'
And   I saw   thrones,   and   they sat   on

αὐτούς,   καὶ   κρίμα   ἐδόθη   αὐτοῖς,   καὶ
them,   and   judgment   was given   to them,   and

τὰς   ψυχὰς   τῶν   πεπελεκισμένων   διὰ   τὴν
the   souls   of the   having been   because   the
[ones]   beheaded   of

μαρτυρίαν   Ἰησοῦ   καὶ   διὰ   τὸν   λόγον
witness   of Jesus   and   because of   the   word

---

* Feminine, agreeing with λίμνη, not with the neuter πῦρ.

§ Agreeing, of course, with ῥομφαίᾳ.

God, and which had not worshipped the beast, neither his image, neither had received *his* mark upon their foreheads, or in their hands; and they lived and reigned with Christ a thousand years.

5 But the rest of the dead lived not again until the thousand years were finished. This *is* the first resurrection.

6 Blessed and holy *is* he that hath part in the first resurrection: on such the second death hath no power, but they shall be priests of God and of Christ, and shall reign with him a thousand years.

7 And when the thousand years are expired, Satan shall be loosed out of his prison,

8 And shall go out to deceive the nations which are in the four quarters of the earth, Gog and Magog, to gather them together to battle: the number of whom *is* as the sand of the sea.

9 And they went up on the breadth of the earth, and compassed the camp of the saints about, and the beloved city: and

τοῦ θεοῦ, καὶ οἵτινες οὐ προσεκύνησαν
– of God, and who did not worship

τὸ θηρίον οὐδὲ τὴν εἰκόνα αὐτοῦ καὶ
the beast nor the image of it and

οὐκ ἔλαβον τὸ χάραγμα ἐπὶ τὸ μέτωπον
did not receive the mark on the forehead

καὶ ἐπὶ τὴν χεῖρα αὐτῶν· καὶ ἔζησαν
and on the hand of them; and they lived
[again]

καὶ ἐβασίλευσαν μετὰ τοῦ Χριστοῦ χίλια
and reigned with – Christ a thousand

ἔτη. 5 οἱ λοιποὶ τῶν νεκρῶν οὐκ ἔζησαν
years. The rest of the dead did not live [again]

ἄχρι τελεσθῇ τὰ χίλια ἔτη. Αὕτη ἡ
until were finished the thousand years. This [is] the

ἀνάστασις ἡ πρώτη. 6 μακάριος καὶ
²resurrection – ¹first. Blessed and

ἅγιος ὁ ἔχων μέρος ἐν τῇ ἀναστάσει
holy [is] the [one] having part in the ²resurrection

τῇ πρώτῃ· ἐπὶ τούτων ὁ δεύτερος θάνατος
– ¹first; over these the second death

οὐκ ἔχει ἐξουσίαν, ἀλλ᾽ ἔσονται ἱερεῖς
has not authority, but they will be priests

τοῦ θεοῦ καὶ τοῦ Χριστοῦ, καὶ βασιλεύ-
– of God and – of Christ, and will

σουσιν μετ᾽ αὐτοῦ [τὰ] χίλια ἔτη.
reign with him the thousand years.

7 Καὶ ὅταν τελεσθῇ τὰ χίλια ἔτη,
And whenever are finished the thousand years,

λυθήσεται ὁ σατανᾶς ἐκ τῆς φυλακῆς
²will be loosed – ¹Satan out of the prison

αὐτοῦ, 8 καὶ ἐξελεύσεται πλανῆσαι τὰ
of him, and will go forth to deceive the

ἔθνη τὰ ἐν ταῖς τέσσαρσιν γωνίαις τῆς
nations – in the four corners of the

γῆς, τὸν Γὼγ καὶ Μαγώγ, συναγαγεῖν
earth, – Gog and Magog, to assemble

αὐτοὺς εἰς τὸν πόλεμον, ὧν ὁ ἀριθμὸς
them to the war, of whom the number

αὐτῶν ὡς ἡ ἄμμος τῆς θαλάσσης. 9 καὶ
of them as the sand of the sea. And
[is]

ἀνέβησαν ἐπὶ τὸ πλάτος τῆς γῆς, καὶ
they went up over the breadth of the land, and

ἐκύκλευσαν τὴν παρεμβολὴν τῶν ἁγίων
encircled the camp of the saints

καὶ τὴν πόλιν τὴν ἠγαπημένην· καὶ
and the ²city – having been ¹loved; and

fire came down from God out of heaven, and devoured them.

10 And the devil that deceived them was cast into the lake of fire and brimstone, where the beast and the false prophet *are*, and shall be tormented day and night for ever and ever.

11 And I saw a great white throne, and him that sat on it, from whose face the earth and the heaven fled away; and there was found no place for them.

12 And I saw the dead, small and great, stand before God; and the books were opened: and another book was opened, which is *the book* of life: and the dead were judged out of those things which were written in the books, according to their works.

13 And the sea gave up the dead which were in it; and death and hell delivered up the dead which were in them: and they were judged every man according to their works.

14 And death and hell were cast into the lake of

κατέβη πῦρ ἐκ τοῦ οὐρανοῦ καὶ κατέφαγεν
²came ¹fire out – heaven and devoured
down of

αὐτούς· 10 καὶ ὁ διάβολος ὁ πλανῶν αὐτοὺς
them; and the Devil – deceiving them

ἐβλήθη εἰς τὴν λίμνην τοῦ πυρὸς καὶ
was cast into the lake – of fire and

θείου, ὅπου καὶ τὸ θηρίον καὶ ὁ
sulphur, where [were] also the beast and the

ψευδοπροφήτης, καὶ βασανισθήσονται ἡμέρας
false prophet, and they will be tormented day

καὶ νυκτὸς εἰς τοὺς αἰῶνας τῶν αἰώνων.
and night unto the ages of the ages.

11 Καὶ εἶδον θρόνον μέγαν λευκὸν καὶ
And I saw ³throne ²a great ¹white and

τὸν καθήμενον ἐπ' αὐτὸν οὗ ἀπὸ τοῦ
the sitting on it ⁶of ⁷from ⁸the
[one] whom

προσώπου ἔφυγεν ἡ γῆ καὶ ὁ οὐρανός,
²face ⁶fled ¹the ²earth ³and ⁴the ⁵heaven,

καὶ τόπος οὐχ εὑρέθη αὐτοῖς. 12 καὶ
and a place was not found for them. And

εἶδον τοὺς νεκρούς, τοὺς μεγάλους καὶ
I saw the dead, the great and

τοὺς μικρούς, ἑστῶτας ἐνώπιον τοῦ θρόνου,
the small, standing before the throne,

καὶ βιβλία ἠνοίχθησαν· καὶ ἄλλο βιβλίον
and scrolls were opened; and another scroll

ἠνοίχθη, ὅ ἐστιν τῆς ζωῆς· καὶ ἐκρίθησαν
was which is [the – of life; and ³were judged
opened, scroll]

οἱ νεκροὶ ἐκ τῶν γεγραμμένων ἐν τοῖς
¹the ²dead by the *having been* in the
things written

βιβλίοις κατὰ τὰ ἔργα αὐτῶν. 13 καὶ
scrolls accord- the works of them. And
ing to

ἔδωκεν ἡ θάλασσα τοὺς νεκροὺς τοὺς
²gave ¹the ²sea the dead –

ἐν αὐτῇ, καὶ ὁ θάνατος καὶ ὁ ᾅδης
in it, and – death and – hades

ἔδωκαν τοὺς νεκροὺς τοὺς ἐν αὐτοῖς,
gave the dead – in them,

καὶ ἐκρίθησαν ἕκαστος κατὰ τὰ ἔργα
and they were judged each one according to the works

αὐτῶν. 14 καὶ ὁ θάνατος καὶ ὁ ᾅδης
of them. And – death and – hades

ἐβλήθησαν εἰς τὴν λίμνην τοῦ πυρός.
were cast into the lake – of fire.

fire. This is the second death.

15 And whosoever was not found written in the book of life was cast into the lake of fire.

οὗτος ὁ θάνατος ὁ δεύτερός ἐστιν, ἡ
This ²the ⁴death – ³second ¹is, the
λίμνη τοῦ πυρός. 15 καὶ εἴ τις οὐχ
lake – of fire. And if anyone not
εὑρέθη ἐν τῇ βίβλῳ τῆς ζωῆς γεγραμ-
was found ²in ³the ⁴scroll – ⁵of life ¹having been
μένος, ἐβλήθη εἰς τὴν λίμνην τοῦ πυρός.
written, he was cast into the lake – of fire.

CHAPTER 21

AND I saw a new heaven and a new earth: for the first heaven and the first earth were passed away ; and there was no more sea.

2 And I John saw the holy city, new Jerusalem, coming down from God out of heaven, prepared as a bride adorned for her husband.

3 And I heard a great voice out of heaven saying, Behold, the tabernacle of God is with men, and he will dwell with them, and they shall be his people, and God himself shall be with them, and be their God.

4 And God shall wipe away all tears from their eyes; and there shall be no more death, neither sorrow, nor crying, neither shall there be any more pain: for the former things are passed away.

5 And he that sat upon the throne said, Behold, I make all things new. And he said unto me,

21 Καὶ εἶδον οὐρανὸν καινὸν καὶ γῆν
And I saw ²heaven ¹a new and ²earth
καινήν· ὁ γὰρ πρῶτος οὐρανὸς καὶ ἡ
¹a new; for the first heaven and the
πρώτη γῆ ἀπῆλθαν, καὶ ἡ θάλασσα
first earth passed away, and the sea
οὐκ ἔστιν ἔτι. 2 καὶ τὴν πόλιν τὴν
is not longer. And ²the ⁴city –
ἁγίαν Ἰερουσαλὴμ καινὴν εἶδον κατα-
³holy ⁴Jerusalem ⁵new ¹I saw coming
βαίνουσαν ἐκ τοῦ οὐρανοῦ ἀπὸ τοῦ θεοῦ,
down out of – heaven from – God,
ἡτοιμασμένην ὡς νύμφην κεκοσμημένην
having been prepared as a bride having been adorned
τῷ ἀνδρὶ αὐτῆς. 3 καὶ ἤκουσα φωνῆς
for the husband of her. And I heard ²voice
μεγάλης ἐκ τοῦ θρόνου λεγούσης· ἰδοὺ
¹a great(loud) out of the throne saying: Behold[,]
ἡ σκηνὴ τοῦ θεοῦ μετὰ τῶν ἀνθρώπων,
the tabernacle – of God [is] with – men,
καὶ σκηνώσει μετ' αὐτῶν, καὶ αὐτοὶ
and he will tabernacle with them, and they
λαοὶ αὐτοῦ ἔσονται, καὶ αὐτὸς ὁ θεὸς
²peoples ³of him ¹will be, and ²[him]self – ¹God
μετ' αὐτῶν ἔσται, 4 καὶ ἐξαλείψει πᾶν
with them will be, and will wipe off every
δάκρυον ἐκ τῶν ὀφθαλμῶν αὐτῶν, καὶ
tear out of the eyes of them, and
ὁ θάνατος οὐκ ἔσται ἔτι, οὔτε πένθος
– death will not be longer, nor sorrow
οὔτε κραυγὴ οὔτε πόνος οὐκ ἔσται ἔτι·
nor clamour nor pain will not be longer;
ὅτι τὰ πρῶτα ἀπῆλθαν. 5 καὶ εἶπεν
because the first things passed away. And ²said
ὁ καθήμενος ἐπὶ τῷ θρόνῳ· ἰδοὺ καινὰ
¹the [one] ²sitting ³on ⁴the ⁵throne: Behold ²new
ποιῶ πάντα. καὶ λέγει· γράψον, ὅτι
¹I make ²all things. And he says: Write thou, because

Write: for these words are true and faithful.

6 And he said unto me, It is done. I am Alpha and Omega, the beginning and the end. I will give unto him that is athirst of the fountain of the water of life freely.

7 He that overcometh shall inherit all things; and I will be his God, and he shall be my son.

8 But the fearful, and unbelieving, and the abominable, and murderers, and whoremongers, and sorcerers, and idolaters, and all liars, shall have their part in the lake which burneth with fire and brimstone: which is the second death.

9 And there came unto me one of the seven angels which had the seven vials full of the seven last plagues, and talked with me, saying, Come hither, I will shew thee the bride, the Lamb's wife.

10 And he carried me away in the spirit to a great and high mountain, and shewed me that great city, the holy Jerusalem, descending out of heaven from God,

11 Having the glory

οὗτοι οἱ λόγοι πιστοὶ καὶ ἀληθινοί εἰσιν.
these – words faithful and true are.

6 καὶ εἶπέν μοι· γέγοναν. ἐγὼ τὸ ἄλφα
And he said to me: It has occurred.* I [am] the alpha

καὶ τὸ ὦ, ἡ ἀρχὴ καὶ τὸ τέλος. ἐγὼ
and the omega, the beginning and the end. ¹I

τῷ διψῶντι δώσω ἐκ τῆς πηγῆς
¹to the [one] ²thirsting ⁴will give out of the fountain

τοῦ ὕδατος τῆς ζωῆς δωρεάν. 7 ὁ νικῶν
of the water – of life freely. The over-[one] coming

κληρονομήσει ταῦτα, καὶ ἔσομαι αὐτῷ
shall inherit these things, and I will be to him

θεὸς καὶ αὐτὸς ἔσται μοι υἱός. 8 τοῖς δὲ
God and he shall be to me a son. But for the

δειλοῖς καὶ ἀπίστοις καὶ ἐβδελυγμένοις
cowardly and unbelieving and having become foul

καὶ φονεῦσιν καὶ πόρνοις καὶ φαρμακοῖς
and murderers and fornicators and sorcerers

καὶ εἰδωλολάτραις καὶ πᾶσιν τοῖς ψευδέσιν
and idolaters and all the false [ones]

τὸ μέρος αὐτῶν ἐν τῇ λίμνῃ τῇ καιομένῃ
the part of them in the lake – burning

πυρὶ καὶ θείῳ, ὅ ἐστιν ὁ θάνατος ὁ
with fire and with which is the ²death
        sulphur,

δεύτερος.
¹second [, shall be].

9 Καὶ ἦλθεν εἷς ἐκ τῶν ἑπτὰ ἀγγέλων
And came one of the seven angels

τῶν ἐχόντων τὰς ἑπτὰ φιάλας, τῶν
– having the seven bowls, –

γεμόντων τῶν ἑπτὰ πληγῶν τῶν ἐσχάτων,
being filled of(with) seven ²plagues – ¹last,
      the

καὶ ἐλάλησεν μετ᾽ ἐμοῦ λέγων· δεῦρο,
and spoke with me saying: Come,

δείξω σοι τὴν νύμφην τὴν γυναῖκα
I will show thee the bride[,] the wife

τοῦ ἀρνίου. 10 καὶ ἀπήνεγκέν με ἐν
of the Lamb. And he bore away me in

πνεύματι ἐπὶ ὄρος μέγα καὶ ὑψηλόν,
spirit onto ⁴mountain ¹a great ²and ³high,

καὶ ἔδειξέν μοι τὴν πόλιν τὴν ἁγίαν
and showed me the ²city – ¹holy

Ἰερουσαλὴμ καταβαίνουσαν ἐκ τοῦ οὐρανοῦ
Jerusalem coming down out of – heaven

ἀπὸ τοῦ θεοῦ, 11 ἔχουσαν τὴν δόξαν
from – God, having the glory

* Collective neuter plural; cf. ch. 16. 17.

of God: and her light
was like unto a stone most
precious, even like a jasper
stone, clear as crystal;

12 And had a wall great
and high, *and* had twelve
gates, and at the gates
twelve angels, and names
written thereon, which are
the names of the twelve
tribes of the children of
Israel:

13 On the east three
gates; on the north three
gates; on the south three
gates; and on the west
three gates.

14 And the wall of
the city had twelve foun-
dations, and in them the
names of the twelve
apostles of the Lamb.

15 And he that talked
with me had a golden
reed to measure the city,
and the gates thereof, and
the wall thereof.

16 And the city lieth
foursquare, and the length
is as large as the breadth:
and he measured the city
with the reed, t w e l v e
thousand furlongs. The
length and the breadth
and the height of it are
equal.

17 And he measured the
wall thereof, an hundred
and forty *and* four cubits,
according to the measure

τοῦ θεοῦ· ὁ φωστὴρ αὐτῆς ὅμοιος λίθῳ
- of God; the light of it [was] like *to* a stone

τιμιωτάτῳ, ὡς λίθῳ ἰάσπιδι κρυσταλλίζοντι·
very valuable, as ²stone ¹to a jasper *being* clear as crystal;

12 ἔχουσα τεῖχος μέγα καὶ ὑψηλόν,
having ⁴wall ¹a great ²and ³high,

ἔχουσα πυλῶνας δώδεκα, καὶ ἐπὶ τοῖς
having ²gates ¹twelve, and at the

πυλῶσιν ἀγγέλους δώδεκα, καὶ ὀνόματα
gates ²angels ¹twelve, and names

ἐπιγεγραμμένα, ἃ ἐστιν τῶν δώδεκα
having been inscribed, which is(are) of the twelve

φυλῶν υἱῶν Ἰσραήλ. 13 ἀπὸ ἀνατολῆς
tribes of sons of Israel. From east

πυλῶνες τρεῖς, καὶ ἀπὸ βορρᾶ πυλῶνες
²gates ¹three, and from north ²gates

τρεῖς, καὶ ἀπὸ νότου πυλῶνες τρεῖς,
¹three, and from south ²gates ¹three,

καὶ ἀπὸ δυσμῶν πυλῶνες τρεῖς. 14 καὶ
and from west ²gates ¹three. And

τὸ τεῖχος τῆς πόλεως ἔχων θεμελίους
the wall of the city having ²foundations

δώδεκα, καὶ ἐπ᾽ αὐτῶν δώδεκα ὀνόματα
¹twelve, and on them twelve names

τῶν δώδεκα ἀποστόλων τοῦ ἀρνίου. 15 Καὶ
of the twelve apostles of the Lamb. And

ὁ λαλῶν μετ᾽ ἐμοῦ εἶχεν μέτρον κάλαμον
the speak- with me had ²measure ²reed
[one] ing

χρυσοῦν, ἵνα μετρήσῃ τὴν πόλιν καὶ
¹a golden, in order he might the city and
that measure

τοὺς πυλῶνας αὐτῆς καὶ τὸ τεῖχος αὐτῆς.
the gates of it and the wall of it.

16 καὶ ἡ πόλις τετράγωνος κεῖται, καὶ
And the city ²square ¹lies, and

τὸ μῆκος αὐτῆς ὅσον τὸ πλάτος. καὶ
the length of it [is] as much as the breadth. And

ἐμέτρησεν τὴν πόλιν τῷ καλάμῳ ἐπὶ
he measured the city with the reed at

σταδίων δώδεκα χιλιάδων· τὸ μῆκος καὶ
³furlongs ¹twelve ²thousands; the length and

τὸ πλάτος καὶ τὸ ὕψος αὐτῆς ἴσα ἐστίν.
the breadth and the height of it ²equal! ¹is(are).

17 καὶ ἐμέτρησεν τὸ τεῖχος αὐτῆς ἑκατὸν
And he measured the wall of it *of* a hundred

τεσσεράκοντα τεσσάρων πηχῶν, μέτρον
[and] forty-four cubits, a measure

of a man, that is, of the angel.

18 And the building of the wall of it was *of* jasper: and the city *was* pure gold, like unto clear glass.

19 And the foundations of the wall of the city *were* garnished with all manner of precious stones. The first foundation *was* jasper; the second, sapphire ; the third, a chalcedony; the fourth, an emerald;

20 The fifth, sardonyx; the sixth, sardius; the seventh, chrysolyte; the eighth, beryl; the ninth, a topaz; the tenth, a chrysoprasus; the eleventh, a jacinth; the twelfth, an amethyst.

21 And the twelve gates *were* twelve pearls; every several gate was of one pearl: and the street of the city *was* pure gold, as it were transparent glass.

22 And I saw no temple therein: for the Lord God Almighty and the Lamb are the temple of it.

23 And the city had no need of the sun, neither of the moon, to shine in it: for the glory of God did lighten it, and the Lamb *is* the light thereof.

24 And the nations of

ἀνθρώπου, ὅ ἐστιν ἀγγέλου. **18** καὶ
of a man, which is of an angel. And

ἡ ἐνδώμησις τοῦ τείχους αὐτῆς ἴασπις,
the coping of the wall of it [was] jasper,

καὶ ἡ πόλις χρυσίον καθαρὸν ὅμοιον
and the city [was] ²gold ¹clean(pure) like

ὑάλῳ καθαρῷ. **19** οἱ θεμέλιοι τοῦ τείχους
²glass ¹to clean(pure). The foundations of the wall

τῆς πόλεως παντὶ λίθῳ τιμίῳ κεκοσμημένοι·
of the city ²with ⁴stone ³precious ¹having been
           every   adorned;

ὁ θεμέλιος ὁ πρῶτος ἴασπις, ὁ δεύτερος
the foundation – first jasper, the second

σάπφιρος, ὁ τρίτος χαλκηδών, ὁ τέταρτος
sapphire, the third chalcedony, the fourth

σμάραγδος, **20** ὁ πέμπτος σαρδόνυξ, ὁ
emerald, the fifth sardonyx, the

ἕκτος σάρδιον, ὁ ἕβδομος χρυσόλιθος,
sixth sardius, the seventh chrysolite,

ὁ ὄγδοος βήρυλλος, ὁ ἔνατος τοπάζιον,
the eighth beryl, the ninth topaz,

ὁ δέκατος χρυσόπρασος, ὁ ἑνδέκατος
the tenth chrysoprasus, the eleventh

ὑάκινθος, ὁ δωδέκατος ἀμέθυστος. **21** καὶ
hyacinth, the twelfth amethyst. And

οἱ δώδεκα πυλῶνες δώδεκα μαργαρῖται·
the twelve gates [were] twelve pearls;

ἀνὰ εἷς ἕκαστος τῶν πυλώνων ἦν ἐξ
respec- ²one ¹each of the gates was of
tively†

ἑνὸς μαργαρίτου. καὶ ἡ πλατεῖα τῆς
one pearl. And the street of the

πόλεως χρυσίον καθαρὸν ὡς ὕαλος διαυγής.
city [was] ²gold ¹clean(pure) as ²glass ¹transparent.

22 Καὶ ναὸν οὐκ εἶδον ἐν αὐτῇ· ὁ γὰρ
And a shrine I saw not in it; for the

κύριος ὁ θεὸς ὁ παντοκράτωρ ναὸς αὐτῆς
Lord – God the Almighty shrine of it

ἐστιν, καὶ τὸ ἀρνίον. **23** καὶ ἡ πόλις
is, and the Lamb. And the city

οὐ χρείαν ἔχει τοῦ ἡλίου οὐδὲ τῆς
not need has of the sun nor of the

σελήνης, ἵνα φαίνωσιν αὐτῇ· ἡ γὰρ
moon, in order they might in it; for the
        that   shine

δόξα τοῦ θεοῦ ἐφώτισεν αὐτήν, καὶ
glory – ⁻of God enlightened it, and

ὁ λύχνος αὐτῆς τὸ ἀρνίον. **24** καὶ
the lamp of it [is] the Lamb. And

them which are saved shall walk in the light of it: and the kings of the earth do bring their glory and honour into it.

25 And the gates of it shall not be shut at all by day: for there shall be no night there.

26 And they shall bring the glory and honour of the nations into it.

27 And there shall in no wise enter into it any thing that defileth, neither *whatsoever* worketh abomination, or *maketh* a lie: but they which are written in the Lamb's book of life.

περιπατήσουσιν τὰ ἔθνη διὰ τοῦ φωτὸς
³shall walk about ¹the ²nations through the light

αὐτῆς, καὶ οἱ βασιλεῖς τῆς γῆς φέρουσιν
of it, and the kings of the earth bring

τὴν δόξαν αὐτῶν εἰς αὐτήν· 25 καὶ οἱ
the glory of them into it; and the

πυλῶνες αὐτῆς οὐ μὴ κλεισθῶσιν ἡμέρας,
gates of it by no means may be shut by day,

νὺξ γὰρ οὐκ ἔσται ἐκεῖ· 26 καὶ οἴσουσιν
for night shall not be there; and they will bring

τὴν δόξαν καὶ τὴν τιμὴν τῶν ἐθνῶν
the glory and the honour of the nations

εἰς αὐτήν. 27 καὶ οὐ μὴ εἰσέλθῃ εἰς
into it. And by no means may enter into

αὐτὴν πᾶν κοινὸν καὶ [ὁ] ποιῶν
it every(any) profane thing and the [one] making

βδέλυγμα καὶ ψεῦδος, εἰ μὴ οἱ γεγραμ-
an and a lie, except the having been
abomination [ones]

μένοι ἐν τῷ βιβλίῳ τῆς ζωῆς τοῦ ἀρνίου.
written in the scroll - of life of the Lamb.

CHAPTER 22

AND he shewed me a pure river of water of life, clear as crystal, proceeding out of the throne of God and of the Lamb.

2 In the midst of the street of it, and on either side of the river, *was there* the tree of life, which bare twelve *manner* of fruits, *and* yielded her fruit every month: and the leaves of the tree *were* for the healing of the nations.

3 And there shall be no more curse: but the throne of God and of the Lamb shall be in it; and his servants shall serve him:

22 Καὶ ἔδειξέν μοι ποταμὸν ὕδατος
And he showed me a river of water

ζωῆς λαμπρὸν ὡς κρύσταλλον, ἐκπορευόμε-
of life bright as crystal, proceed-

νον ἐκ τοῦ θρόνου τοῦ θεοῦ καὶ τοῦ
ing out of the throne - of God and of the

ἀρνίου. 2 ἐν μέσῳ τῆς πλατείας αὐτῆς
Lamb. In [the] midst of the street of it

καὶ τοῦ ποταμοῦ ἐντεῦθεν καὶ ἐκεῖθεν
and of the river hence and thence

ξύλον ζωῆς ποιοῦν καρποὺς δώδεκα,
a tree of life producing fruits twelve,

κατὰ μῆνα ἕκαστον ἀποδιδοῦν τὸν καρπὸν
accord- ²month ¹each rendering the fruit
ing to

αὐτοῦ, καὶ τὰ φύλλα τοῦ ξύλου εἰς
of it, and the leaves of the tree [will be] for

θεραπείαν τῶν ἐθνῶν. 3 καὶ πᾶν κατάθεμα
healing of the nations. And every curse
=no curse will be any

οὐκ ἔσται ἔτι. καὶ ὁ θρόνος τοῦ θεοῦ
will not be longer. And the throne - of God
longer.

καὶ τοῦ ἀρνίου ἐν αὐτῇ ἔσται, καὶ οἱ
and of the Lamb ²in ³it ¹will be, and the

δοῦλοι αὐτοῦ λατρεύσουσιν αὐτῷ, 4 καὶ
slaves of him will do service to him, and

4 And they shall see his face; and his name *shall be* in their foreheads.

5 And there shall be no night there; and they need no candle, neither light of the sun; for the Lord God giveth them light: and they shall reign for ever and ever.

6 And he said unto me, These sayings *are* faithful and true: and the Lord God of the holy prophets sent his angel to shew unto his servants the things which must shortly be done.

7 Behold, I come quickly: blessed *is* he that keepeth the sayings of the prophecy of this book.

8 And I John saw these things, and heard *them.* And when I had heard and seen, I fell down to worship before the feet of the angel which shewed me these things.

9 Then saith he unto me, See *thou do it* not: for I am thy fellowservant, and of thy brethren the prophets, and of them which keep the sayings of this book: worship God.

10 And he saith unto me, Seal not the sayings of the prophecy of this

ὄψονται τὸ πρόσωπον αὐτοῦ, καὶ τὸ
they will see the face of him, and the
ὄνομα αὐτοῦ ἐπὶ τῶν μετώπων αὐτῶν.
name of him [will be] on the foreheads of them.

5 καὶ νὺξ οὐκ ἔσται ἔτι, καὶ οὐκ
And night will not be longer, and not
ἔχουσιν χρείαν φωτὸς λύχνου καὶ φωτὸς
they have need of light of lamp and of light
ἡλίου, ὅτι κύριος ὁ θεὸς φωτίσει ἐπ'
of sun, because [the] Lord — God will shed light on
αὐτούς, καὶ βασιλεύσουσιν εἰς τοὺς
them, and they will reign unto the
αἰῶνας τῶν αἰώνων.
ages of the ages.

6 Καὶ εἶπέν μοι· οὗτοι οἱ λόγοι πιστοὶ
And he said to me: These — words [are] faithful
καὶ ἀληθινοί, καὶ ὁ κύριος ὁ θεὸς τῶν
and true, and the Lord the God of the
πνευμάτων τῶν προφητῶν ἀπέστειλεν τὸν
spirits of the prophets sent the
ἄγγελον αὐτοῦ δεῖξαι τοῖς δούλοις αὐτοῦ
angel of him to show to the slaves of him
ἃ δεῖ γενέσθαι ἐν τάχει. 7 καὶ ἰδοὺ
things it be- to occur quickly. And behold
which hoves
ἔρχομαι ταχύ. μακάριος ὁ τηρῶν τοὺς
I am coming quickly. Blessed [is] the [one] keeping the
λόγους τῆς προφητείας τοῦ βιβλίου τούτου.
words of the prophecy of this scroll.

8 Κἀγὼ Ἰωάννης ὁ ἀκούων καὶ βλέπων
And I John [am] the [one] hearing and seeing
ταῦτα. καὶ ὅτε ἤκουσα καὶ ἔβλεψα,
these things. And when I heard and I saw,
ἔπεσα προσκυνῆσαι ἔμπροσθεν τῶν ποδῶν
I fell to worship before the feet
τοῦ ἀγγέλου τοῦ δεικνύοντός μοι ταῦτα.
of the angel — showing me these things.

9 καὶ λέγει μοι· ὅρα μή· σύνδουλός
And he tells me: See thou [do] not; ²a fellow-slave
σού εἰμι καὶ τῶν ἀδελφῶν σου τῶν
¹of thee ¹I am and of the brothers of thee the
προφητῶν καὶ τῶν τηρούντων τοὺς λόγους
prophets and of the [ones] keeping the words
τοῦ βιβλίου τούτου· τῷ θεῷ προσκύνησον.
of this scroll: — ²God ¹worship thou.

10 Καὶ λέγει μοι· μὴ σφραγίσῃς τοὺς
And he tells me: Seal not the
λόγους τῆς προφητείας τοῦ βιβλίου τούτου·
words of the prophecy of this scroll;

book: for the time is at hand.

11 He that is unjust, let him be unjust still: and he which is filthy, let him be filthy still: and he that is righteous, let him be righteous still: and he that is holy, let him be holy still.

12 And, behold, I come quickly; and my reward is with me, to give every man according as his work shall be.

13 I am Alpha and Omega, the beginning and the end, the first and the last.

14 Blessed are they that do his commandments, that they may have right to the tree of life, and may enter in through the gates into the city.

15 For without are dogs, and sorcerers, and whoremongers, and murderers, and idolaters, and whosoever loveth and maketh a lie.

16 I Jesus have sent mine angel to testify unto you these things in the churches. I am the root and the offspring of David, and the bright and morning star.

17 And the Spirit and the bride say, Come.

ὁ καιρὸς γὰρ ἐγγύς ἐστιν
²the ³time ¹for ⁵near ⁴is.

11 ὁ ἀδικῶν
The acting [one] unjustly

ἀδικησάτω ἔτι, καὶ ὁ ῥυπαρὸς ῥυπανθήτω
let him act still, and the filthy [one] let him act
unjustly filthily

ἔτι, καὶ ὁ δίκαιος δικαιοσύνην ποιησάτω
still, and the righteous [one] ²righteousness ¹let him do

ἔτι, καὶ ὁ ἅγιος ἁγιασθήτω ἔτι.
still, and the holy [one] let him be hallowed still.

12 Ἰδοὺ ἔρχομαι ταχύ, καὶ ὁ μισθός
Behold I am coming quickly, and the reward

μου μετ᾽ ἐμοῦ, ἀποδοῦναι ἑκάστῳ ὡς
of me [is] with me, to render to each man as

τὸ ἔργον ἐστὶν αὐτοῦ. 13 ἐγὼ τὸ ἄλφα
the work ²is ¹of him. I [am] the alpha

καὶ τὸ ὦ, ὁ πρῶτος καὶ ὁ ἔσχατος,
and the omega, the first and the last,

ἡ ἀρχὴ καὶ τὸ τέλος. 14 μακάριοι οἱ
the begin- and the end. Blessed the
ning [are] [ones]

πλύνοντες τὰς στολὰς αὐτῶν, ἵνα ἔσται
washing the robes of them, in or- ⁴will be
der that

ἡ ἐξουσία αὐτῶν ἐπὶ τὸ ξύλον τῆς
¹the ²authority ³of them over the tree –

ζωῆς καὶ τοῖς πυλῶσιν εἰσέλθωσιν εἰς
of life and ²by the ³gates ¹they may enter into

τὴν πόλιν. 15 ἔξω οἱ κύνες καὶ οἱ φαρμακοὶ
the city. Outside the dogs and the sorcerers
[are]

καὶ οἱ πόρνοι καὶ οἱ φονεῖς καὶ οἱ
and the fornicators and the murderers and the

εἰδωλολάτραι καὶ πᾶς φιλῶν καὶ ποιῶν
idolaters and everyone loving and making

ψεῦδος.
a lie.

16 Ἐγὼ Ἰησοῦς ἔπεμψα τὸν ἄγγελόν
I Jesus sent the angel

μου μαρτυρῆσαι ὑμῖν ταῦτα ἐπὶ ταῖς
of me to witness to you these things over(in) the

ἐκκλησίαις. ἐγώ εἰμι ἡ ῥίζα καὶ τὸ
churches. I am the root and the

γένος Δαυίδ, ὁ ἀστὴρ ὁ λαμπρὸς ὁ
offspring of David, the ²star – ¹bright –

πρωϊνός.
²morning.

17 Καὶ τὸ πνεῦμα καὶ ἡ νύμφη λέγουσιν·
And the Spirit and the bride say:

And let him that heareth say, Come. And let him that is athirst come. And whosoever will, let him take the water of life freely.

18 For I testify unto every man that heareth the words of the prophecy of this book, If any man shall add unto these things, God shall add unto him the plagues that are written in this book:

19 And if any man shall take away from the words of the book of this prophecy, God shall take away his part out of the book of life, and out of the holy city, and *from* the things which are written in this book.

20 He which testifieth these things saith, Surely I come quickly. Amen. Even so, come, Lord Jesus.

21 The grace of our Lord Jesus Christ *be* with you all. Amen.

ἔρχου.   καὶ   ὁ   ἀκούων   εἰπάτω·   ἔρχου.
Come.   And the [one] hearing   let him say: Come.

καὶ   ὁ   διψῶν   ἐρχέσθω,   ὁ   θέλων   λαβέτω
And   the thirsting   let him   the wishing   let him
     [one]   come,   [one]   take

ὕδωρ   ζωῆς   δωρεάν.
[the]   of life   freely.
water

18 Μαρτυρῶ   ἐγὼ   παντὶ   τῷ   ἀκούοντι
²witness   ¹I   to everyone   hearing

τοὺς   λόγους   τῆς   προφητείας   τοῦ   βιβλίου
the   words   of the   prophecy   ¹scroll

τούτου·   ἐάν   τις   ἐπιθῇ   ἐπ᾽   αὐτά,   ἐπιθήσει
¹of this: If anyone   adds   upon(to) them,*   ²will add

ὁ   θεὸς   ἐπ᾽   αὐτὸν   τὰς   πληγὰς   τὰς
-    ¹God   upon   him   the   plagues   -

γεγραμμένας   ἐν   τῷ   βιβλίῳ   τούτῳ·   19 καὶ
having been written   in   this scroll;   and

ἐάν   τις   ἀφέλῃ   ἀπὸ   τῶν   λόγων   τοῦ
if   anyone   takes away   from   the   words   of the

βιβλίου   τῆς   προφητείας   ταύτης,   ἀφελεῖ
scroll   of this prophecy,   ²will take
          away

ὁ   θεὸς   τὸ   μέρος   αὐτοῦ   ἀπὸ   τοῦ   ξύλου
-    ¹God   the   part   of him   from   the   tree

τῆς   ζωῆς   καὶ   ἐκ   τῆς   πόλεως   τῆς   ἁγίας,
-    of life   and   out of the   ²city   -   ¹holy,

τῶν   γεγραμμένων   ἐν   τῷ   βιβλίῳ   τούτῳ.
of the   having been   in   this scroll.
things   written

20 Λέγει   ὁ   μαρτυρῶν   ταῦτα·   ναί,   ἔρχομαι
Says the   witnessing   these   Yes,   I am
     [one]   things: coming

ταχύ.   Ἀμήν,   ἔρχου   κύριε   Ἰησοῦ.
quickly.   Amen,   come[,]   Lord   Jesus.

21 Ἡ   χάρις   τοῦ   κυρίου   Ἰησοῦ   μετὰ
The   grace   of the   Lord   Jesus [be]   with

πάντων.
all.

* Neuter plural; see last clause of ver. 19.

DATE DUE